■ CENSORSHIP LANDMARKS

Edward De Grazia

CENSORSHIP LANDMARKS

R. R. BOWKER COMPANY ■ **NEW YORK & LONDON, 1969**

Published by R. R. Bowker Company (A XEROX COMPANY)
1180 Ave. of the Americas, New York, N.Y. 10036

Standard Book Number: 8352-0207-0
Library of Congress Catalog Card Number: 71-79424
Manufactured in the United States of America

■ Contents

1930–1949 CASES

1950–1959 CASES

1960–1968 CASES

■ Cases

■ Introduction

by Edward de Grazia

A FEW WEEKS AGO, as the galleys for this book were being readied, the United States Court of Appeals for the Second Circuit ruled that the exhibition of the Swedish motion picture *I Am Curious—Yellow*, seized by the United States Customs Bureau more than a year ago—"cannot be inhibited." The judgments of the customs officials and of the trial judge and jury below, finding the film obscene, were reversed. Because the Solicitor General of the United States decided it was not in the government's interest to seek review of the case by the Supreme Court, this important film can finally be shown throughout the country.

This case (*United States* v. *A Motion Picture Film Entitled "I Am Curious—Yellow"*) is part of the movement toward freedom of expression taking place in the United States. I was in charge of the defense of *I Am Curious—Yellow* at trial, and I argued for its constitutional protection in the Court of Appeals. The case is illustrative of some of the problems which are posed by obscenity censorship as it is practiced still, in the United States.

In a story written prior to the trial, about the film and the customs bureau practices which had resulted in its seizure, Geoffrey Wolff, literary critic of *The Washington Post*, said:

"*I Am Curious—Yellow is extremely complicated, a movie about its own making, about itself. The director, Vilgot Sjoman, appears as an actor-director. Lena Nyman, its leading actress, appears both as herself and in the role of a radical apostle of non-violence and social equality. Parts of the film consist of documentary footage of interviews with Martin Luther King, poetry reading by Yevtesheko, and Swedish opinion polls about the welfare state.*

"*Interspersed throughout are scenes of extraordinarily explicit sexual activity. Lena and Borje Ahlstedt, the leading actor, are shown naked, often front on. They make love perched on a balustrade in front of the Swedish Royal Palace, on a lawn, in a tree. Everything that happens is shown: there are no delicate fade-outs, there is no disguising behind sheets.*

A majority of the appellate court (Judges Hays and Friendly) ruled that the customs bureau could not constitutionally prevent this motion picture from entering the country because "it is quite certain that *I Am Curious—Yellow* does present ideas and does strive to present these ideas artistically. It falls within the ambit of intellectual effort that the first amendment was designed to protect." The court adhered to this saving constitutional proposition, which finds its beginnings in the 1956 case of *Roth* v. *United States*, although it also believed that "the sexual content of the film is presented with greater explicitness than has been seen in any other film produced for general viewing." Dissenting Chief Judge Lombard vainly argued that since movies are more powerful than books and magazines, they should be held to stricter sexual standards, and that courts ought not upset the judgments of juries on questions of whether such material oversteps constitutional bounds.

Prior to my undertaking to represent the American distributor of this film, I was asked by him to see it. He wanted to know whether I felt about *I Am Curious—Yellow* the way I'd felt about William Burroughs' *Naked Lunch*—was it important enough to fight for with conviction, not merely as a matter of course?* I felt, after seeing the film twice, more or less as Norman Mailer said he felt about it when I questioned him as a witness in the trial: "I think it is a profoundly moral movie." And, as the Reverend Howard Moody testified he felt: "it has a very significant religious dimension."

It may seem ironic to find defenders of an allegedly obscene film declaring it to be moral and religious, for as the cases in this book demonstrate, upholders of censorship have frequently sought to justify their activity on the ground that the material involved was calculated to corrupt someone's morals. On the one hand, this merely shows that "morals" is a word we all can bandy about; on the other, it suggests we are coming to learn that the meaning of "obscene" lies mainly in the mind of the person who is asked "is this book or movie obscene?"—whether he is a judge, a juror, a policeman, a prosecutor, a defense lawyer, or a government bureaucrat.

About thirteen years ago, Mr. William O'Brien, a middle-level bureaucrat in the United States Post Office

---

* Lawyer Ephraim London, an eminent defender of allegedly obscene films, evidently found some of the sexual episodes disappointing; according to *Newsweek*, London thought it a "very interesting movie until the love-making starts." On the other hand, dissenting Chief Judge Lombard had found the film "a continuous and unrelieved boredom except for the sexual scenes. . . ."

Department was asked that question with reference to a rare-edition copy of Aristophanes' undying anti-war play *Lysistrata*. The answer he gave and the reasons he had for giving it did not much differ from the answer and reasons given by Mr. Irving Fishman, the middle-level bureaucrat in the U.S. Customs Bureau who was asked the question with reference to *I Am Curious— Yellow*, a film which, incidentally, contains a powerful anti-war theme. O'Brien did not see the value in *Lysistrata*; Fishman could not see the ideas in *I Am Curious —Yellow*. It has, in fact, proven to be impossible for American government censors to be sensitive to the non-sexual values and ideas inherent in books and films which deal with sex—including new and evolving moral values and ideas. Huntington Cairns, who served as literary and artistic censor for the Customs Bureau for many years was exceptional, but he even failed to clear *Tropic of Cancer*.

As Geoffrey Wolff noticed:

> *Officially, Irving Fishman, with a Bachelor's Degree in Business Administration, tries to keep you and me from reading dirty books and seeing dirty movies brought into New York from abroad. A movie he doesn't want us to see is called* I Am Curious—Yellow. *The film arrived from Sweden December 30 (1967). Fishman saw it January 4 and seized it to prevent its distribution by Grove Press, Inc. In legal terminology the movie was "arrested" but unlike people who are arrested it can't go free on bail until after the moral policeman's judgement is tested in court . . . Irving Fishman swings a big stick. He seized the movie in accordance with Section 1305, Title 19, of the United States Code, which deals with the importation of pornographic or seditous material. Fishman looks at movies and if he thinks they are obscene we don't see them unless the court decides he is wrong.*
>
> *"He was asked how he determines whether a work is prurient: 'As to how I go about making that judgement this is just—it seems to me it would be based on the reaction I had to seeing the film. . . . I think my answer would have to depend on my own judgment, my own experience; I couldn't define it.'*

When *Lysistrata* was seized from the mails thirteen years ago, the responsible bureaucrat, Mr. William O'Brien, told me he had rules of thumb to distinguish art from obscenity; for example, he pointed out: "Breasts, yes, but nipples, no! Buttocks, yes, but cracks, no!" Lysistrata had them all, and got condemned.

Thirteen months after the suppression of Vilgot Sjoman's *I Am Curious—Yellow*, the film was still locked in a government bureau drawer and Mr. Fishman's personal reaction was declared to be in error. During that year the American war on Vietnam went on. Not once during that year, as not once since the war began, had a feature-length motion picture film appeared on U.S. theatre screens, to criticize that war or the American involvement in it. When Grove Press sought to import Vilgot Sjoman's cinematic attack on the middle-class attitudes and values supportive of such wars, the U.S. Customs Service, acting through Mr. Fishman, prevented public American screenings for over a year.

Have the U.S. customs laws and Irving Fishman's views on sex prolonged our government's war on Vietnam? It is a question that should not have to be asked, for the sake of Mr. Fishman's conscience, as well as for the sake of the nation's commitment to free speech, and the open encounter of ideas. The federal constitution plainly was designed so that such questions would not be asked. They get asked because systems of censorship have for almost 100 years operated within Executive Branch agencies and, notwithstanding the Constitution, the judiciary has not yet brought their activities to an end. The two main agencies are the Bureau of Customs and the Post Office Department. I first learned how the latter worked in 1955.

In that year, I found out that postal employees censored people's mail, and refused to deliver printed materials, including works of literature and art, which they considered obscene. The news was given me by the head of the American Civil Liberties Union's newly opened Washington Office, Irving Ferman, who asked if I would volunteer my services on behalf of a Los Angeles book dealer who had ordered the rare-edition *Lysistrata* which had been seized. I was as upset to find out our mailmen could prevent the distribution of *Lysistrata* as I would have been to learn they could keep someone from reading *The Communist Manifesto*.

Within a month following *Lysistrata*'s seizure, I filed suit and a 24,000-word brief meant to persuade a federal judge to enjoin operation of, and declare unconstitutional the so-called Comstock Act of 1873 under which *Lysistrata* and many other books had been seized. I pointed out that: "What is obscene to the Postmaster General is, in fact, the laughter of genius to twenty-four centuries of Western civilization." Postmaster Summerfield, in private life an automobile dealer, responded by slipping the book back to me (in a plain brown wrapper), precipitously ending my case. His response, of course, aborted the opportunity which *Lysistrata* had presented for our federal courts to perceive that a nation committed to freedom of speech and press need not tolerate censorship of literature or art, regardless of "obscenity." Not until 1959 in *Manual Enterprises* v. *Day*, did the Supreme Court obtain a case which squarely challenged the power of the Post Office to remove sexual expression its employees found obscene from the mails. Then, instead of being presented with a classic work of art, the court found itself having to weigh the constitutional rights of, in its words, "dismally unpleasant, uncouth, and tawdry magazines," with little claim to importance.

I have helped publishers and distributors resist governmental censorship of *Lysistrata* and *Stud Broad*, *Eros* Magazine and *Naked Lunch*; *Flaming Creatures* and *Revenge at Daybreak*, magazines condemned because a photographed stripper wore a G-string which looked like a mini-American flag, as well as some seized because a photographed sun-worshipper weighed in the neighborhood of 250 pounds, had elephantine breasts "that hung from her shoulder to her waist. . . ."

They are exceedingly large (said the court). The thighs are very obese. She is standing in snow, wearing galoshes. But the part which is most offensive, obscene, filthy and indecent is the pubic area shown. . . . The hair extends outwardly virtually to the hip bone. . . . The hairline instead of being straight is actually scalloped or in a half-moon shape, which makes the woman grotesque, vile, filthy, the representation is dirty, and the Court will hold that the picture is obscene as a matter of fact . . . (Sunshine Book Co. v. Summerfield, 128 F. Supp. 564, 570–73. (DDC 1955).

I helped liberate Henry Miller's "Tania" and William Burrough's "Mark, Mary and John." I took care not to discourage the publication of unexpurgated versions of deSade's *Justine* and *Juliette*, and the incomparable *Story of O*. Lena of *I Am Curious—Yellow* is a young Swedish girl with a healthy appetite for getting involved with radical sex and politics. Her liberation by the judiciary, from the hands of government censors, should strengthen the conviction that it *is* possible to get rid of all restrictions on the arts.

The cases that make up this book include nearly every type of censorship restraint: post office seizure and blockage; customs confiscation; civil injunction; criminal prosecution; police and prosecutor arrest and seizure; police and citizen group blacklist; and motion picture screening board. They involve books, magazines, motion picture films, dramas, stripteases, phonograph records, telephone calls, pornographic pictures, ordinary people, comic geniuses. They depict the whole range of means invented in this country for inflicting previous restraints and subsequent punishments upon our expression, and for combatting them. The material is intended thereby to have maximum value for interested judges, lawyers, scholars, law enforcement officers, and laymen.

Readers wanting detailed descriptions of Post Office Department and Bureau of Customs censorship operations can find them in Z. Chafee's *Government and Mass Communications* (Shoe String, 1947) and in J. C. N. Paul and M. L. Schwartz', *Federal Censorship* (Free Press, 1961). See also the case *United States* v. *One Carton of Motion Picture Film* ("491"). Previous to the Paul and Schwartz study and following my encounter with *Lysistrata* and the Post Office, I made a study of postal censorship which resulted in an article on post office censorship, "Obscenity and the Mail," published as part of the important Symposium assembled by Melvin Shimm for *Law and Contemporary Problems*, called "Obscenity and the Arts" (20 Law and Contemp. Prob. 531, 608).

The cases in this book reveal how the powers and ambitions of Post Office and Bureau of Customs censors, of prosecuting attorneys and chiefs of police, of motion picture and other censorship boards, throughout the land, have been dramatically curtailed, during the past ten years especially. Today, in the United States, there appears to be a greater measure of freedom for literary, artistic, and cinematic sexual expression than ever before in the American past. The evidence lies in the books and magazines we can obtain from our city newsstands, the films we can see at our neighborhood movie houses, and the plays we can attend at our "off" and "off-off"-Broadway and university theatres.

The cases that make up the main body of this book can be viewed as the legal stepping-stones used by the country in its slow move from conditions of widespread censorship to something approaching full freedom, with respect to books, magazines, stage presentations, motion pictures, and oral expressions having to do with sex. The facts, however, that, within the last few years, the Supreme Court failed to review New York's tragic prosecutions of the comic Lenny Bruce; failed to invalidate the criminal sentences imposed on publishers Ralph Ginsburg and Sam Mishkin; and failed to free Jean Genet's film *Un Chant d'Amour* (*Landau v. Fording*) and Jack Smith's film *Flaming Creatures*, are reminders that freedom, even for artistic works, is still not complete. They also justify continuing efforts on the part of lawyers, scholars, and judges to comprehend and clarify obscenity laws, and for artists, writers, publishers and distributors to combat them.

Although court contests to restrain or free sexual literature and art have been waged since the beginning of the nineteenth century (the earliest reported case of importance, *Commonwealth* v. *Sharpless* (1815) involved a painting), it was not until after the Second World War that American courts began seriously to consider how sexual expressions, like political or religious expressions, might be entitled to the Constitutional guarantees of freedom of speech and press (see *Commonwealth* v. *Gordon* (1949). Restraints upon expression regarding political matters such as sedition had been recognized by the courts to raise constitutional issues as early as the first prosecutions under the 1798 Alien and Sedition Laws, passed just ten years after the adoption of the First Amendment (see, for example, the Trials of Lyon, Haswell, Cooper and Callender in F. Whartons, *State Trials of the United States During the Administrations of Washington and Adams*, B. Franklin, 1849). Although the "clear and present danger" test was used as a constitutional test of free expression as early as the Espionage Act cases arising during World War I, (see *Abrams* v. *United States*, 250 U.S. 616, 1919 and *Milwaukee Pub. Co.* v. *United States*, 255 U.S. 407, 1921) no court appears to have applied that doctrine to the suppression of sexual expression until 1949 (*Commonwealth* v. *Gordon*).

It was 1948 before the U.S. Supreme Court gave sign that it might find constitutional issues raised by the suppression of "obscene" literature. In this case (*Doubleday & Co.* v. *New York*, 335 U.S. 848) involving Edmund Wilson's *Memoirs of Hecate County*, the publisher's conviction was upheld (without opinion) when the Court divided equally on the constitutional question.

Among the small group of lawyers and legal writers who should be credited with bringing the constitutional free speech issues imbedded in obscenity censorship cases to the forefront of the judicial mind, and for pointing the way for the U.S. Supreme Court to find that governmental restraints on allegedly obscene expression necessarily raised grave constitutional questions are Dean William B. Lockhart and Professor Robert C. McClure of the University of Minnesota Law School. Their articles, "Literature, The Law of Obscenity, and The Constitution," 38 Minn. L. Rev. 296 (1954) and "Censorship of Obscenity: The Developing Constitutional Standards," 45 Minn. L. Rev. 5 (1960), are prime examples of the role which legal scholars can play in advancing the development of the law, and remain among the richest sources available for lawyers and laymen interested in this field.

Although American courts failed until the late 40's to see the free speech issues involved in governmental suppression of sexual expression (whether scientific, literary or artistic), legal commentators had been wondering about the constitutional question during the previous two decades. Examples are Chafee's book *Freedom of Speech* (Harcourt, 1920), Theodore Schroeder's book *Obscene Literature and Constitutional Law* (Priv. Ptd., the Author, 1911) Deutsch's article "Freedom of The Press and of The Mails," 36 Mich. L. Rev. 703 (1938), and Alpert's article "Censorship of Obscene Literature," 52 Harv. L. Rev. 40 (1938). Z. Chafee's *Government and Mass Communications*, which was published in 1947, contained an extended, wise and detailed analysis of the main features of obscenity censorship, and how it was being carried out by local authorities in connection with the sale of books, by motion picture and radio censors, and in the Customs and Post Office services; the constitutional free speech and press arguments, however, were left largely implicit.

It was during the Second World War that lawyers first began seriously to press the courts with constitutional arguments in obscenity cases. Only then did the revolution in sexual expression begin. At first, the pioneering lawyers were rebuffed by incredulous judges. In 1945, lawyers for the publisher of the novel *Strange Fruit* by Lillian Smith, urged the "clear and present danger" test upon the Massachusetts Supreme Court. They were turned down with the proposition that "if that constitutional doctrine applied, it was satisfied by the danger of corruption of the public mind" and by the fact that actual publication and sale rendered the danger "imminent" (*Commonwealth* v. *Isenstadt*). When the free speech argument was pressed in 1953 by ACLU-affiliated lawyers who sought to make Henry Miller's *Tropic of Cancer* and *Tropic of Capricorn* available to Americans not lucky enough to get to Brentano's in Paris and buy a copy, the federal courts simply denied it (*Besig* v. *United States*). In Massachusetts in 1950, lawyers defending Caldwell's *God's Little Acre* also advanced the free speech grounds. They were rebuffed by the Supreme Bench ruling that the constitutional issue "requires no discussion" (*Commonwealth* v. *Book Named* "God's Little Acre"). These decisions must today be considered repudiated.

The first *constitutional* breakthroughs for sex literature in American courts—the liberation of James Joyce's *Ulysses*, in 1934, for example, was not achieved on free speech grounds but on the weaker ground of literary merit; see *United States* v. *One Book Called* "Ulysses"—occurred in *State* v. *Lerner* (1948), involving nudist magazines and striptease photographs; in *Commonwealth* v. *Gordon* (1949), involving Farrell's *Studs Lonigan* trilogy, Faulkner's *Sanctuary* and *Wild Palms*, and Caldwell's *God's Little Acre*; in *Bantam Books* v. *Melko* (1953) involving a prosecutor's banning of the *Chinese Room*; and in *New American Library of World Literature* v. *Allen* (1953), involving a list of proscribed books issued by police. The most important of these was *Gordon* in which Judge Curtis Bok held, following a careful and detailed analysis of the constitutional arguments, that the suppression of literature alleged to be obscene could only be tolerated upon a showing that there existed "a clear and present danger that the book will cause criminal behavior." Although this was to become one of the two principle constitutional approaches taken by ACLU and other lawyers in subsequent efforts to rid the country of obscenity censorship, it has not yet gained any significant acceptance among members of the U.S. Supreme Court. Perhaps the closest step taken toward that proposition by the Court was in *Kingsley International Picture* v. *Regents* (1958), where the Court held that if, as the New York courts said, the film *Lady Chatterley's Lover* advocated adultery under certain circumstances, the state could not on that account ban the film, for: "advocacy of conduct proscribed by law is not . . . a justification for denying free speech where the advocacy falls short of incitement and there is nothing to indicate that the advocacy would be immediately acted upon." The main reason the "clear and present danger" doctrine has not been applied to literary and cinematic obscenity cases is that fictional works generally are not interpreted to "advocate" anything.

In 1957, for the first time, the Constitutional issues posed by governmental restraints on "obscene" expression were given serious treatment by the U.S. Supreme Court. The cases are: *Butler* v. *Michigan*, involving the book *The Devil Rides Again*, in which the Court held unconstitutional a Michigan statute making criminal sales, even to adults, of material which might tend to incite minors to "depraved acts," or "corrupt their morals"; *Kinsley Books, Inc.* v. *Brown*, involving a civil injunction proceeding against a group of books entitled *Nights of Horror*, upheld by the Court because judicial procedural safeguards contained in the statute were thought sufficient to guard against prior restraints; and *Roth* v. *United States*, involving the conviction, in federal court, of the publisher and distributor of literature which included a quarterly called *American Aphrodite*, and a magazine called *Good Times, A Review of the World of Pleasure*, for violation of the postal laws. This is the landmark case by whose "dim beacon" publishers, authors, editors, policemen, prosecutors, and judges are still straining to see the limits of the constitutional law protecting sexual expression. Because of the interest and importance residing in *Roth* and the cases decided since then, I propose to trace, in some detail, the more important points and arguments involved.

In *Roth*, Mr. Justice Brennan laid down the principle that "obscenity" was not within the area of constitutionally protected speech because "obscenity" was "utterly without redeeming social importance." What did Brennan intend by "obscenity?": Material "which deals with sex in a manner appealing to prurient interest." What sort of interest was a "prurient" one? Brennan took refuge in *Webster's New International Dictionary* (Unabridged, 2nd ed., 1949) which defined the term, in pertinent part, as: ". . . itching, longing; uneasy with desire or longing; of persons having itching, morbid, or lascivious longings; of desire, curiosity, or propensity, lewd. . . ." This definition always reminds me of the method once prescribed for finding devils in a person: you looked for a mark in some secret place of the body, sore and unhealed, "sometimes like a Blewspot, or a Red-spot, like a flea-biting" (*Lawes Against Witchcraft And Conjuring*).

But Mr. Justice Brennan who, with this case and others soon to follow, became the Court's principal interpreter of the "metaphysics of obscenity" also wrote in *Roth* that: "sex and obscenity are not synonymous;" and that "the portrayal of sex, e.g., in art, literature and scientific works, (noting *United States* v. *Dennett*) is not itself sufficient reason to deny material the constitutional protection of freedom of speech and press." "Sex, a great and mysterious motive force in human life, has indisputably been a subject of absorbing interest to mankind through the ages; it is one of the vital problems of human interest and public concern." All such problems, Brennan continued were embraced by this nation's commitment to "freedom of discussion." Laws directed against "obscenity" thus were obliged to "safeguard the protection of freedom of speech and press for material which does not treat sex in a manner appealing to prurient interest." "Sex—yes! Obscenity—no!" seems to be about what *Roth* stood for.

It was seven years later before the Supreme Court handed down decisions which specified, or attempted to specify, how material dealing with sex might be produced or distributed in condemnable ways appealing to prurient interest: these were the *Ginzburg* and *Mishkin* cases, which I will shortly describe. During the interim, the Court busied itself with (1) handing down a number of unexplained *ad hoc* decisions holding that material which had been condemned as obscene by censors or courts below, could not, in *its* independent judgement, be treated as obscene, (2) eliminating and threatening to eliminate certain forms of police, prosecutor, and administrative board systems of censorship because they involved unconstitutional "prior restraints" on material which might or might not be obscene, and (3) making one important revision in the *Roth* test for obscenity.

Beginning in 1958, the Supreme Court reversed four state and federal cases which had been suppressed as "obscenity": the film *Games of Love* (*Times Film Corp.* v. *City of Chicago*, 355 U.S. 35); a group of imported foreign nudist and artist-model magazines (*Mounce* v. *United States*, 355 U.S. 180); *One—The Homosexual Magazine* (*One, Inc.* v. *Olesen*, 355 U.S.

371); and the magazines *Sunshine & Health* and *Sun* (*Sunshine Book Co.* v. *Summerfield*, 355 U.S. 372). In each case, in reversing, the Court merely cited its decision in *Roth* v. *United States*, signifying, presumably, that although each of these materials dealt with sex, none did so in a manner which appealed to prurient interest, and could constitutionally be held obscene.

In 1962, the Court considered the case of *Manual Enterprises* v. *Day*, in which the Post Office had refused to deliver certain magazines featuring photographs of nude males designed to appeal to homosexual interests—"Manual," "Trim" and "Grecian Guild Pictorial." In an opinion by Mr. Justice Harlan, the Court reversed lower federal court actions declined to give injunctive relief against the Postmaster General's ban on the magazines' mailing. Harlan's opinion modified the *Roth* test for determining "obscenity." He observed that although the magazines might properly be found to have been aimed at the prurient interests of their intended audience, "We find lacking in these magazines an element which, no less than 'prurient interest' is essential to a valid determination of obscenity . . . and to which neither the Post Office nor the Court of Appeals addressed itself at all: These magazines cannot be deemed so offensive on their face as to affront current community standards of decency—a quality which we shall hereafter refer to as 'patent offensiveness' or 'indecency' " (*Manual Enterprises* v. *Day*). This case also allowed the Court to rule for the first time that the "community" embodied in the test for obscenity, certainly when a federal scheme of censorship was involved, was not local or parochial, but "national"— taking in "all parts of the United States whose population reflects many different ethnic and cultural backgrounds." Two years later, in the case of *Jacobellis* v. *Ohio*, the "national community" requirement was extended by Mr. Justice Brennan to instances of state censorship.

In an important concurring opinion in the Manual Enterprises case, Mr. Justice Brennan, joined by Chief Justice Warren and by Mr. Justice Douglas, took up basic questions concerning Post Office powers of the type I had tried to raise when *Lysistrata* was seized. He observed that "this is the first occasion on which the Court has given plenary review to a Post Office order holding matter 'non-mailable' because obscene." The issues which Brennan wanted the Court to face up to as being more important than the question of whether the magazines were legally obscene, were: (a) whether Congress can constitutionally close the mails even to obscenity by any means other than criminal prosecution; (b) if it can, whether Congress can constitutionally authorize any forum other than a court to

determine obscenity; and (c) whether, in any event, Congress actually had conferred upon the Post Office any such power to exclude matter it deemed obscene. In the course of a detailed review of the historical antecedents of both the postal and customs obscenity censorship legislation, Brennan raised serious doubts whether either of the first two questions could be affirmatively answered, and concluded the third could not. Dissenting Justice Tom Clark disagreed with everyone else, remarking:

While those in the majority like ancient Gaul are split into three parts, the ultimate holding of the Court today, despite the clear congressional mandate found in 1461 requires the United States Post Office to be the world's largest disseminator of smut and Grand Informer of the names and places where obscene material may be obtained.

Under the leadership of Mr. Justice Brennan, the Court shortly undertook to invalidate a number of state and municipal obscenity censorship systems, relentlessly exposing their procedural infirmities. Although a majority of the Court apparently could not agree on how to improve further *Roth's* Janus-faced test, a majority could be brought together to strengthen constitutional protections for sexual expression by demonstrating, in concrete cases, as Brennan was to say: "that a State is not free to adopt whatever procedures it pleases for dealing with obscenity. . . . without regard to the possible consequences for constitutionally protected speech" (*Marcus* v. *Search Warrants*).

A Los Angeles city ordinance making it unlawful "for any person to have in his possession any obscene or indecent writing, (or) book . . . (in) any place of business where . . . books . . . are sold or kept for sale," was applied to convict a bookseller for having in his store a book later held obscene by a court. The ordinance did not require the prosecutor to prove "scienter," or knowledge, by the bookseller of the contents of the book; it was struck down by the Court as an unconstitutional abridgement of freedom of expression, because, in Brennan's words:

(by) dispensing with any requirement of knowledge of the contents of the book . . . and (if) the ordinance fulfills its purpose, (the bookseller) will tend to restrict the books he sells to those he has inspected; and thus the State will have imposed a restriction upon the distribution of constitutionally protected as well as obscene literature.

Thus,

The bookseller's burden would become the public's burden, for by restricting him the public's access to reading matter would be restricted. . . . The bookseller's self-censorship, compelled by the State, would be a censorship affecting the whole public, hardly less virulent for being privately administered Smith v. California (1959).

Missouri enacted a statute which authorized a judge or magistrate to issue a warrant to search for and seize obscene material upon the basis of "conclusory assertions of a single police officer, without any scrutiny by the judge of any materials considered by the complainant to be obscene." Warrants of this type were executed by police officers to search the premises of a distributor and to seize all 11,000 copies of 280 publications—magazines, books, and photographs—which the officers considered obscene. One week later, judicial proceedings commenced. Two months thereafter, some 100 of the publications were, and 180 were not, found obscene by the court.

Brennan compared this process to sixteenth-century "Star-Chamber" procedures, and condemned it for being "without any safeguards to protect legitimate expression." The 1957 *Kingsley Books* case, mentioned earlier, was distinguished because, there, no restraint was issued against the publications (*Nights of Horror*) until the material was before a court able to exercise an independent check upon the judgement of the complaining law-enforcement officer, and also because, there, the distributor had an opportunity to circulate the publications claimed to be obscene despite the interim restraint. Thus, he could raise the defense of non-obscenity in a criminal prosecution without having to obtain other copies of the publications illicitly. Moreover, there, the statute required a *judicial* determination within two days of trial, which in turn was required to be within one day of the joinder of issue on the petition to restrain the publications. Concluded Brennan: "The State's power to suppress obscenity is limited by the constitutional protections for free expression." And, "our holding in *Roth* does not recognize any state power to restrict the dissemination of books which are not obscene" *Marcus* v. *Search Warrants of Property*.

Rhode Island passed a law which authorized the creation of a "Commission to Encourage Morality in Youth," whose statutory duties included not only education of the public concerning "obscenity" but the recommendation of prosecutions for violation of Rhode Island's "Obscene and Objectionable Publications" law. The Commission advised distributors of the titles of books it considered obscene and reminded them it had a duty to recommend prosecution of purveyors of obscenity. As a result, distributors stopped distributing books listed by the Commission. Among the books whose circulation was in this manner suppressed were Bantam's best-selling *Peyton Place*, by Grace Metalious, and a book called *The Bramble Bush* by Charles Mer-

gendahl. Bantam sued to invalidate the Commission's activities.

Mr. Justice Brennan's majority opinion deserves extensive quotation:

The Fourteenth Amendment requires that regulation by the states of obscenity conform to procedures that will ensure against the curtailment of constitutionally protected expression, which is often separated from obscenity by a dim and uncertain line.

The Commission's operation is a form of effective State regulation superimposed upon the State's criminal regulation of obscenity and making such regulation largely unnecessary. In thus obviating the need to employ criminal sanctions, the State has at the same time eliminated the safeguards of the criminal process. The commission's practice is in striking contrast, in that it provides no safeguards whatever against the suppression of nonobscene, and therefore constitutionally protected, matter.

What Rhode Island has done, in fact, has been to subject the distribution of publications to a system of prior administrative restraints, since the Commission is not a judicial body and its decisions to list particular publications as objectionable do not follow judicial determinations that such publications may lawfully be banned. . . . There is no provision whatever for judicial superintendence before notices issue or even for judicial review of the Commission's determinations of objectionableness. The Publisher or distributor is not even entitled to notice and hearing before his publications are listed by the Commission as objectionable. . . . Moreover, the Commission's statutory mandate is vague and uninformative, and the Commission has done nothing to make it more precise. Publications are listed as 'objectionable' without further elucidation. . . . The procedures of the Commission are radically deficient. . . . We hold that the system of informal censorship disclosed by this record violates the Fourteenth Amendment. Bantam Books, Inc. v. Sullivan (1963).

A Kansas law authorized the seizure of books, upon the filing of an information alleging they were obscene, prior to an adversary determination of their obscenity. The Attorney General of Kansas filed an information claiming fifty-nine novels published by the same company were obscene, and lodged six of these with the court. Following an *ex parte* examination of the six, the judge issued a warrant authorizing the seizure of all the books named in the information. Seventeen hundred fifteen copies of thirty-one titles listed in the information, and found upon the search made in execution of the warrant, were seized. At a final hearing seven weeks later, the trial court held all the seized books were obscene, and ordered their destruction.

On review, the Supreme Court, by Mr. Justice Brennan, listened to the arguments of California lawyer Stanley Fleishmann and ruled the Kansas statute, as applied, was an unconstitutional abridgement of freedom of expression—because the warrant authorized seizure of all titles of the named books, and a hearing on the question of obscenity was not afforded even with respect to the six novels actually examined by the judge, before the warrant issued. "A seizure of all copies of the named titles is indeed more repressive than an injunction preventing further sale of the books." "(I)f seizure of books precedes an adversary determination of their obscenity, there is danger of abridgement of the right of the public in a free society to unobstructed circulation of nonobscene works." Brennan also denounced the Attorney General's argument that obscene books could be treated in the same manner as gambling paraphernalia, intoxicating liquor, or other contraband, for purposes of lawful search and seizure, for "the separation of legitimate from illegitimate speech calls for . . . sensitive tools . . ." A *Quantity of Books* v. *Kansas* (1963).

The culmination of this important series of decisions outlawing state systems for suppressing allegedly obscene matter was reached in the motion picture area, in the case of *Freedman* v. *Maryland* (1965). In this case, involving the film *Revenge at Daybreak*, Melvin Wulf and I submitted an *amicus curaie* brief on behalf of the ACLU which urged the Court to invalidate the operation of Maryland's State Board of Censors over motion pictures; the film's distributor sought the same result. The case seemed to us to present important constitutional possibilities because not since *Burstyn* v. *Wilson*, in 1952, had the Supreme Court made a move to free this medium of expression from the numerous state and municipal administrative systems of restraints under which it had labored since after the First World War. In *Burstyn*, a unanimous Court invalidated that part of the state of New York's motion picture censorship law which provided for the banning of "sacrilegious" films, and which had been applied to ban from exhibition an Italian film called *The Miracle*. But the Court's opinion, there, by Mr. Justice Clark, expressly reserved the question whether a state might constitutionally censor motion pictures "under a clearly drawn statute designed and applied to prevent the showing of obscene films." The *Burstyn* case was a landmark in the move toward freedom of expression for motion pictures not so much because it invalidated the censorship of "sacrilegious" films, but because it overturned the proposition laid down by an earlier Bench in 1914 in *Mutual Film Corp.* v. *Industrial Commission*, that "the exhibition of motion pictures is a business pure and simple, originating and conducted for profit, like other spectacles, not to be regarded, nor intended to be regarded, we think, as part of the press of the country or as organs of public opinion."

Thirty-eight years later, the Supreme Court followed New York lawyer Ephraim London's arguments on behalf of Burstyn and recanted with these words: "It cannot be doubted that motion pictures are a significant medium for the communication of ideas. They may affect public attitudes and behavior in a variety of ways, ranging from direct espousal of a political or social doctrine to the subtle shaping of thought which characterizes all artistic expression."

Referring to *Winters* v. *New York*, the Court went on to say that "the importance of motion pictures is not lessened by the fact that they are designed to entertain as well as to inform." The argument that motion pictures fell outside the First Amendment's free speech protections because their production, distribution, and exhibition is a large-scale business conducted for private profit was dismissed by the Court, saying: "That books, newspapers, and magazines are published and sold for profit does not prevent them from being a form of expression whose liberty is safeguarded by the First Amendment. We fail to see why operation for profit should have any different effect in the case of motion pictures" *Burstyn* v. *Wilson*.

Prior to *Freedman* v. *Maryland*, three other decisions by the Supreme Court, involving motion pictures, had touched on constitutional points of importance. The earliest was the 1959 ruling, already mentioned, that New York could not constitutionally ban the film *Lady Chatterley's Lover*, on the ground that it advocated adultery *Kingsley International Pictures* v. *Regents* (1959). Next was a case involving the film *Don Juan* in which a majority of the Court refused to adopt the absolute rule urged on it by lawyers Felix Bilgrey and Abner Mikva that Constitutional protection for expression had to include "complete and absolute freedom to exhibit at least once, any and every kind of motion picture . . . even . . . the basest type of pornography." Instead the Court held that Chicago's motion picture censorship system was not "on its face" an unconstitutional abridgement of freedom of expression in its requirement that all motion pictures be submitted in advance of public exhibition to a censorship board *Times Film Corp.* v. *Chicago*.

A vigorous dissent filed in this case by Chief Justice Warren, joined by Justices Brennan, Black and Douglas, signalled that at another time, in somewhat different circumstance, a majority of the Court might be collected to hold rather broadly that state systems for censoring allegedly obscene films abridged freedom of expression.

In an opinion which contained a theory resembling that subsequently developed by Mr. Justice Brennan for the majorities in the *Marcus*, *Bantam Books*, and *Quantity of Books* v. *Kansas* cases, the dissenting judges argued that: "The Chicago (censorship) scheme has no procedural safeguards; there is no trial of the issue (of obscenity) before the blanket injunction against exhibition becomes effective." Moreover, there was "no provision for prompt judicial determination" and the censors worked "free from all procedural safeguards afforded litigants in a court of law." Finally, and conclusively for the dissenters, the Chicago system was defective because, unlike the situation involved in *Kingsley Books*, there was no chance whatever for the material to "pass into the hands of the public."

In the *Times Film Corp.* case, the dissenters had taken pains to describe the shocking extent to which motion picture censorship had developed in this country. We took up this point in our *amicus brief* in the 1965 *Freedman* v. *Maryland* case, and sketched out for the Court in an appendix the systems of motion picture censorship still operative in four states (Maryland, New York, Kansas and Virginia) and in thirteen municipalities (Chicago, Atlanta, Detroit, Fort Worth, Abilene, Houston, Portland, Providence, Birmingham, Memphis, Columbus, Little Rock, and Seattle). Some of these systems, like that of Maryland, required that copies of all the films be submitted to the censors in advance of exhibition. Others required notice of a film's scheduled exhibition to be filed with the censors prior to exhibition. The remainder provided that censors would view films not in advance of, but during their public exhibition.

The main thrust of our brief was that the Court should invalidate the Maryland censorship system because of its failure to provide "a judicial superintendence of the system's action so close as to be either immediate or part and parcel of the system itself," and because there was "no adequate notice" and no "full opportunity for an adversary hearing prior to imposition of any effective restraint."

The *Freedman* Court, once again led by Mr. Justice Brennan, took care to distinguish *Times Film Corp.* by adopting Felix Bilgrey's argument for Freedman that the Maryland system could be held invalid because "it presents a danger of unduly suppressing protected expression," not because (as had been argued unsuccessfully in *Times Film Corp.*) "it may prevent even the first showing of a film whose exhibition may legitimately be the subject of an obscenity prosecution." Brennan proceeded to condemn the Maryland system because there was "no statutory provision for judicial participation in the procedure which bars films nor even assurance of prompt judicial review," and because the exhibitor, rather than the censor was given "the burden of instituting judicial proceedings and persuading the courts that the film is protected expression" *Freedman* v. *Maryland* (1965).

The year before *Freedman*, and two years after the Court in *Manual Enterprises*, had added the "national community" and "patently offensive" requirements to *Roth*'s "prurient interest" test for determining obscenity, the Court acted to strengthen its warning in *Roth* that obscenity was excluded from constitutional protection only because it was "utterly without redeeming social importance." The case was *Jacobellis* v. *Ohio* (1964). Said Brennan, in reversing Ohio's conviction of the distributor of a film called *The Lovers*, defended by Ephraim London:

Material dealing with sex in a manner that advocates ideas (citing the Kinsley International Film *case) or that has literary or scientific or artistic value or any other form of social importance, may not be branded as obscenity and denied the constitutional protection.*

Furthermore, the opinion went on:

Nor may the constitutional status of the material be made to turn on a weighing of its social importance against its prurient appeal, for a work cannot be proscribed unless it is utterly *without social importance (citing the case of* Zeitlin v. Arnebergh).

Brennan also took the opportunity to harden the gloss placed on *Roth* by Harlan in *Manual Enterprises*:

The Roth standard requires in the first instance a finding that the material "goes substantially beyond customary limits of candor in description or representation of such matters." . . . In the absence of such a deviation from society's standards of decency, we do not see how any official inquiry into the alleged prurient appeal of a work of expression can be squared with the guarantees of the First and Fourteenth Amendments.

With *Jacobellis*, then, the Roth formula for identifying obscenity came to involve a three-pronged test. In order to be condemned as obscene material the piece in question had to be found: (a) to have its dominant appeal to the prurient interests of persons; (b) to be patently offensive to contemporary national community standards; and (c) to be utterly without any kind of social importance.

The *Zeitlin* v. *Arnebergh* (1963) case relied upon by Brennan in *Jacobellis* was a California case related to a case considered and decided by the Supreme Court together with *Jacobellis*, *Grove* v. *Gerstein*, I was seeking, on behalf of the publisher of *Tropic of Cancer*, a reversal of a Florida ban on the distribution of Henry Miller's notorious novel, the American publication of which had shattered the nation's literary standards of sexual decency, precipitating more than fifty censorship cases. In the *Gerstein* case, I attempted to do with *Tropic of Cancer* what I had wanted to do with *Lysistrata*—press upon the Supreme Court the need to declare free from obscenity restrictions—regardless of any possible prurient appeal or offensiveness —all literature and art, that is, all printed matter having *any* claim to literary or artistic value. The petition we filed also urged that the Court had a constitutional duty to free such material *uniformly* across the nation. We pointed out that, as the California Supreme Court had observed in *Zeitlin* ". . . in some places *Tropic of Cancer* is 'obscene' and in others it is not; presently its legal status is largely tied into the geography of its sale or publication." I argued that national, rather than local "community standards" of decency had to be applied, even in local prosecutions or restraining actions, that it was a national blanket of constitutional protection which the First Amendment guaranteed to literary and artistic expression. I urged upon the high Court the California Supreme Court's position which, in turn, had been derived from University of Chicago Professor Harry Kalven's brilliant essay in the 1960 *Supreme Court Review* ("The Metaphysics of the Law of Obscenity"). In effect it meant that laws designed to suppress obscenity should apply only to "the worthless." The California court in *Zeitlin* had said:

> [I]f material is commercial obscenity or saleable pornography it is obscenity in the sense that it is utterly without redeeming social importance; it is hard-core pornography; as such it lies without the protective embrace of the First Amendment.
>
> Redeeming refers not to a balancing of the pruriency against the social importance of the material, but to the presence of matters of social importance in the content which will recover for the material its position as constitutionally protected utterance.

Since *Tropic of Cancer* had unquestionable "literary value" it possessed redeeming social importance and was entitled to the full protection of the constitutional guarantees—regardless of its offensiveness or any appeal it could have to prurient interests. In the *Gerstein* petition to the Supreme Court, I plead: "The permissible juridical suppression of obscenity must begin and end with the worthless."

A majority of the Supreme Court responded by granting our petition and reversing the Florida courts' ban on *Tropic of Cancer* (*Grove* v. *Gerstein*) at the same time as they reversed the Ohio court's ban on *The Lovers* in *Jacobellis*, citing that case. Together, the cases made it clear that the Court was not prepared to let constitutional protection for films or books having any demonstrable literary or artistic value be undermined by administrative or judicial notions of "prurient appeal" or "patent offensiveness," nor, to let a book's or film's freedom "vary with state lines." The value inherent in a work cannot, after all, be affected by

changes in legal jurisdictions. In extending to State censorship the proposition already established as to federal censorship, in *Manual Enterprises*, Brennan said: "(t)he constitutional status of an allegedly obscene work must be determined on the basis of a national standard. It is, after all, a national Constitution we are expounding."

During the following term, in a case involving the book sometimes known as *Fanny Hill*, Charles Rembar, the lawyer who had freed the book *Lady Chatterley's Lover* from Post Office censorship (see *Grove Press* v. *Christenberry*) and the *Evergreen Review* from the Nassau County District Attorney (*Evergreen Review, Inc.* v. *Kahn*), was able to persuade the high court further to strengthen the proposition that only material empty of value could be brought within the scope of obscenity laws. *Fanny Hill*, which had been banned in Massachusetts in 1821 (*Commonwealth* v. *Holmes*) had this time been brought under suppression by the state's Attorney General. Laying claim mainly to a sort of historical literary value, the book offered Brennan the opportunity to clarify the implications of Roth's social value rule, as extended in *Jacobellis*, as follows:

> A book cannot be proscribed unless it is found to be utterly *without redeeming social value*. This is so even though the book is found to possess the requisite prurient appeal and to be patently offensive. Each of the three federal criteria is to be applied independently; the social value of the book can neither be weighed against nor canceled by its prurient appeal or patent offensiveness ("Memoirs of a Woman of Pleasure" v. Attorney General).

In support of this, Brennan cited *Zeitlin* v. *Arnebergh* and *Jacobellis* v. *Ohio*, as well as *People v. Bruce*, and *Trans-Lux Distributing Corp.* v. *Maryland Board of Censors.*

At the time that the decision on *Memoirs* was handed down, we had been waiting for months for the Supreme Court of Massachusetts to decide whether the literary or social importance of William Burrough's *Naked Lunch* did not, as I had argued, preclude the book being treated as obscene. Within weeks after *Memoirs* the Court decided that, in view of its reputation among critics, *Naked Lunch* could not be found obscene—unless and until it were shown to be "commercially exploited for the sake of prurient appeal, to the exclusion of all other values" *Attorney General* v. *Book Called "Naked Lunch."* The possibility of such a qualification being placed upon the "social importance" doctrine, had been suggested by the U.S. Supreme Court in a decision already referred to, *Ginzburg* v. *United States*, considered and handed down at the same time as *Memoirs*. In that case, the publisher of a hard-cover magazine called *Eros* and a book called *The Housewife's Handbook on Selective Promiscuity*, failed to persuade the Court to reverse his conviction for violating the postal laws in ways not very different from those which had resulted in the conviction of Mr. Roth, in the case bearing his name. The Court, through an opinion by Mr. Justice Brennan, which resembled the more conservative opinions of Chief Justice Warren, backed off from the social importance doctrine, urging that even the distribution of material having "some slight social importance might support an obscenity conviction if it were promoted by the publisher or distributor in ways which "pandered" to the prurient interests of persons—if, that is, the purveyor's sole emphasis is on the sexually provocative aspects of his publications, a court could accept his evaluation at its face value," and constitutionally convict. This, at least, is how the much-criticized *Ginzburg* decision was depicted by Brennan, in his *Memoirs* opinion, and how it was interpreted by the Massachusetts Supreme Court in the *Naked Lunch* case.

Language contained in a more recent decision of the Supreme Court, *Redrup* v. *New York* (May 8, 1967), is interesting for the signs it contains of the direction which the law of obscenity censorship may take in the future, at least until the day when the American judiciary decides to abandon its anxieties about obscenity and declare, as Denmark did two years ago, that no literature or art may be suppressed, in consideration of its sexual images or ideas, or the manner in which they are communicated. The cases involved: a New York prosecution of a newsstand dealer for selling *Lust Pool* and *Shame Agent*, two paperback books; a Kentucky prosecution against the owner of a bookstore for selling the magazines *High Heels* and *Spree*; and a civil action by a prosecuting attorney in Arkansas to suppress the circulation of *Gent, Swank, Bachelor, Modern Man, Cavalcade, Gentleman, Ace,* and *Sir.* The Supreme Court reversed the lower court judgements, which had upheld the convictions and the restraining order involved, saying that "whichever of our constitutional views is brought to bear upon the cases before us, it is clear that the judgements cannot stand."

The "constitutional views" referred to in *Redrup* are reported here verbatim, for they seem to sum up the positions of the present members of the Bench, and thus the present law of obscenity as presently construed by the Supreme Court:

Two members of the Court have consistently adhered to the view that a State is utterly without power to suppress, control, or punish the distribution of any writings or pictures upon the ground of their "obscenity." (Douglas and Black) A third has held to the opinion that a State's power

in this area is narrowly limited to a distinct and clearly identifiable class of material. (Stewart) Others have subscribed to a not dissimilar standard, holding that a State may not constitutionally inhibit the distribution of literary material as obscene unless "(a) the dominant theme of the material taken as a whole appeals to a prurient interest in sex; (b) the material is patently offensive because it affronts contemporary community standards relating to the description or representation of sexual matters; and (c) the material is utterly without redeeming social value." (Brennan, Warren, Fortas) Another Justice has not viewed the "social value" element as an independent factor in the judgement of obscenity. (White). (parenthetical indications supplied)

Justices Clark and Harlan had dissented, their views departing in one respect or another from those described above.

The Court justified the reversals in a way which suggested that in the future it would be hostile to all state and federal obscenity censorship actions which did not rest on (a) laws "reflecting a specific and limited state concern for juveniles," or (b) upon a claim that the obscenity amounted to an "assault upon individual privacy by publication in a manner so obstrusive as to make it impossible for an unwilling individual to avoid exposure to it," or (c) evidence of "the sort of 'pandering' which the Court found condemnable in *Ginzburg* v. *United States*."

Will the Supreme Court one day abandon entirely its support of obscenity censorship? Looking to the next ten or fifteen years, it seems probable that the Court will decide gradually but entirely to eliminate all *administrative* forms of prior restraint on books, films and magazines, including police and prosecutor actions taken in advance of trial or hearing, any remaining State motion picture censorship system which prevents or delays exhibition, and the still active federal forms of post office and customs censorship which result in seizures and blockages of printed matter and films. These systems are anathema to a free and democratic society for they put enormous power over the nation's means of receiving and communicating images and ideas in the hands of officials who are, on the one hand, inept at distinguishing literary, artistic, scientific and other social values, and who have been, on the other, representative of the more reactionary of the values which compete among social and religious segments of the country.

I believe criminal prosecutions, state and federal, will eventually be held supportable only with respect to material commonly considered to be utterly worthless, i.e., "hard-core pornography" as defined by Mr. Justice Stewart in his dissent to the *Ginzburg* case:

Such materials include photographs, both still and motion picture, with no pretense of artistic value, graphically depicting acts of sexual intercourse, including various acts of sodomy and sadism, and sometimes involving several participants in scenes of orgy-like character. They also include strips of drawings in comic-book format grossly depicting similar activities in exaggerated fashion. There are, in addition, pamphlets and booklets, sometimes with photographic illustrations, verbally describing such activities in a bizarre manner with no attempt whatsoever to afford portrayals of character or situation and with no pretense to literary value.

Yet, exceptions will be made for this material, also, because for some persons, and in some circumstances, even it can have artistic or instructive importance while for many persons, doubtless most, it is unedifying but harmless—which is why the Supreme Court recently held that a State law which makes it a crime to "possess" pornography (for example, in one's home) is unconstitutional (*Stanley* v. *Georgia*, decided April 7, 1969), why the Library of Congress is the depository for all Customs Bureau-seized pornography, why the Kinsey Institute for Sex Research collects hard-core pornography from within the country and abroad, why the Pompeian wall-frescoes have never been destroyed, why it is acceptable for groups of males (and, more recently, for males and females) to view "stag" films together, and why important contemporary artists and great masters have written or painted their own versions of "sexual intercourse, including various acts of sodomy and sadism, and sometimes involving several participants in scenes of orgy-like character." On this, see the hundreds of representations contained in Kronhausen, *Erotic Art* (New York: Grove Press, 1968).

As exceptions to the hard-core or worthless pornography test accrue, the "social value" test* of the *Roth/Manual Enterprises/Memoirs* formula for identifying obscenity will find itself challenged by: the "pandering" test, introduced in *Ginzburg* and *Mishkin*, first proposed by the American Law Institute; the newer "variable obscenity" test, introduced in the 1968 case of *Ginsberg* v. *New York*, originally advanced by Professors Lockhart and McClure; and the still obscure "assault" or "coercion" test, introduced by Mr. Justice Stewart in a footnote to his opinion in the *Ginsberg* case, elevated to the text of the *per curium* opinion handed down by the entire bench in the *Redrup* case, and referred to by Stewart and by Mr. Justice Fortas in the 1968 case of *Ginsberg* v. *New York*, shortly to be examined. This lost approach originally was advanced by a small group of publishers, editors and writers, in a brief which I prepared.

The "pandering" test is attractive to those who publicly or privately wish to see purveyors of obscenity identified, and their work exposed, now and for the indefinite future. It is preferred by those who believe in the "evils" of obscenity in the way their ancestors once believed in the "devils" of witchcraft. It may become the prosecution's answer to the defense's "social value" test, for it can negate the latter's function as an ultimate decidium of obscenity, as, in fact, it did in *Ginzburg*. Legally, it has to do with motive more than intent, and thus imports into the law of obscenity, and the criminal law which surrounds it, a highly subjective element. And although it might have the virtue of freeing *non*-commercial and *private* transactions and uses involving pornography (*see* the case of *Stanley* v. *Georgia*, it cannot. It cannot endure because it is absurd: as Mr. Justice Douglas tried to explain in his dissent in *Ginzburg*, our commercial culture favors "pandering;" it is a nasty word for a certain style of promotional advertising, which encompasses both the seductive smile given us by the long-limbed girl perched invitingly on the latest model car, in full-page advertisements in *Life* magazine, and Mr. Ginzburg's knowing grin, inviting us to subscribe to his magazine *Liaison*, and *The Housewife's Handbook on Selective Promiscuity*. It also should not endure because it resurrects the by now discredited technique of *weighing* adduced artistic and social values against alleged "prurient" and "offensive" elements—a technique which invariably casts material embodying sexual expression into the limbo of a particular judge's or jury's personal sense of shame.

The "variable obscenity" approach is, at first blush, more promising. It resembles the approach advanced by Chief Justice Warren unsuccessfully in *Roth* and mentioned again in his dissent in *Jacobellis*; it was used by Judge Learned Hand in *Rebhuhn* v. *United States*; most recently, it was employed by the Supreme Court of the United States to uphold a new New York obscenity law exclusively aimed at protecting juveniles (*Ginsberg* v. *New York*). This approach goes far toward an admission that obscenity is not a characteristic inherent in certain material, arguing that it is "a chameleonic quality of material that changes with time, place and circumstances" (Lockhart and McClure, "Censorship of Obscenity: The Developing Constitutional Standards," 45 Minn. L. Rev. 3, 68 (1960). And so hard-core pornography would be protected by it, in some circumstances, for certain persons or groups. Evidently, however, this quality of obscenity can also change with the disseminator's motivation, meaning the variable approach is a double-edged sword in danger of being turned into the pandering test.

---

* I do not agree, for reasons which are made clear in the text, with the prediction registered by attorney Charles Rembar—that the "social value" test spells "the end of obscenity"—in his recent book of that name.

The gist of the variable approach is that "material may be obscene when directed to one class of persons but not when directed to another." This means that "a technical or legal treatise on pornography may well be inoffensive under most circumstances but, at the same time, obscene in the extreme when sold or displayed to children" (*Jacobellis* at 201). Thus, a State can enforce a statute aimed at punishing vendors of material not obscene as to adults, but obscene as to juveniles, if the intended and probable audience is made up of juveniles (*Ginsberg* v. *New York*).

A serious problem with this approach is that, in many applications, it will labor under the liabilities of the *Roth* formula: courts and juries will still be obliged to engage in the somewhat disingenuous practice of measuring out the prurient appeal, patent offensiveness and social importance of material—now, however, for theoretically separate and distinct audiences. What the Supreme Court doesn't know about the psychology of adults will only be surpassed by what it can't know about the psychology of juveniles, as well as of other sub-groupings within *Roth's* concept of the "average person."

The proponents of "variable obscenity" are not unaware of its limitations, although they do seem unaware of their root cause. Thus, Lockhart and McClure took the "variable" approach by asserting that "any material directed primarily to an audience of the sexually immature for the purpose of *feeding their craving* for erotic fantasy would be considered obscene, whatever its intrinsic nature when directed at a mature adult audience" (*ibid.* at 80). A more direct rendering of the somewhat dubious psychology underlying this approach occurred in *Ginzburg* v. *United States*, when Mr. Justice Brennan argued that *Eros* had been made "available to exploitation by those who would make a business of pandering to the *widespread weakness for titillation* by pornography."

The thing about those who advocate the "variable obscenity" approach is that they are not entirely free from the moral and psychological biases which have dominated judicial thinking about obscenity for more than one hundred years. They do not perceive the possibility, for example, that children and sexually immature (or, for that matter, mature) adults may read and see "pornographic" books and films not to feed a disgusting "craving" or to indulge a "widespread weakness," but in order to enjoy sexual arousal even in the absence (voluntary or involuntary) of an appropriate sexual partner, or to learn more about sexual conduct, habits and possibilities. We may unload upon natural human interests unnatural deposits of shame and morbidity if we keep from persons materials offering such possibilities and such learning—candid and explicit literary, artistic and photographic representations of sex and sexual relations.

The "assault" or "coercion" approach to obscenity strives to avoid the morass of superstition and guesswork which has characterized much of the judicial psychology and sociology of obscenity, developed to date, and find its base in the approach to obscenity represented by common sense and some earlier cases. In *Roth*, the Supreme Court said obscenity was not protected by the guarantees of freedom of press, but to do so the Court relied on casual dicta contained in earlier cases in which it had been "assumed" that obscenity was "not protected by the freedoms of speech and press." When these cases are examined (see Lockhart and McClure) "Literature, the Law of Obscenity, and the Constitution" (38 Minn. L. Rev. 295, 352–357), it may be seen that the judges involved had simply viewed the obscenity problem as akin to the problems presented by public exhibitions of graffiti, indecent exposures of the person, and profane, insulting or "fighting" words. A common characteristic of these situations is an intentional or reckless assault on the sensibilities of unwilling or captive persons.

In a brief which I prepared in 1960, on behalf of the ACLU, for the Maryland *Tropic of Cancer* case, *Yudkin* v. *Maryland* (the first direct legal action on behalf of this controversial book taken by the national organization), the proposition was advanced that governmental restraints could validly be imposed only upon obscene expression which was assaultive.* The case involved the conviction of a bookseller, Samuel Yudkin, who, in the face of threats from the Maryland District Attorney, insisted on the right of persons to read the books of their choice. In seeking reversal of Mr. Yudkin's conviction (obtained on a different ground), we argued that a State might proscribe and punish such unsolicited assaults on a person's sexual sensibilities as might be expected to result from graffiti in public places, indecent exhibitions of the person, and obscene utterances in public conveyances. The State might also, we suggested (borrowing, as it were, some of the problems to come in the *Ginzburg* case) validly prohibit "the *uninvited* circulation of printed matter *empty* of artistic, instructive or any other social import, *designed* to pander to prurient interest"—at least where the

---

* In the process of attempting to develop an intelligent, radical theory for challenging the obscenity laws, acceptable to the ACLU, I considered but rejected the alternative view, being deliberated at that time in libertarian circles, which would invalidate any prohibition of sexual expression which did not present a "clear and present danger" that an act, validly made criminal by the state, would be committed. This approach, based, of course, on the doctrine made famous by Brandeis and Holmes, had been developed and used by Judge Curtis Bok to free *Studs Lonigan* and other books in *Commonwealth* v. *Gordon*. It was put forward in other cases, but failed to gather additional juridical or intellectual adherents.

disseminator acted "knowingly or willfully." It was only in such cases, our brief stressed, "where the freedom to express ideas is not an issue, yet where unsolicited or willful disturbances of sexual sensibilities may be, that contemporary community standards and the prurient interest may be constitutionally respected and applied by the judge or jury."

When the *Ginzburg* and *Mishkin* cases came before the Supreme Court, an occasion arose to venture the "assault" or "captive" approach once again. In an attempt to help the Court improve upon the *Roth* test, a handful of literary intellectuals agreed that I should prepare and seek to file a brief *amici curiae* in the "toughest" of the cases then pending before the Supreme Court, that involving Mr. Mishkin. The group included Robert Silvers of the *New York Review of Books*, Jason Epstein of Random House, Barney Rosset of Grove Press, Richard Poirier of *Partisan Review*, Norman Podhoretz of *Commentary*, Warren Hinckle of *Ramparts*, Walter Minton of G. P. Putnam's Sons, and writer-philosophers Eric Larrabee, Paul Goodman and Marshall Cohen. We agreed to take the position that Mr. Mishkin's books ought not to be suppressed and he himself ought not to be punished—because of the constitutional guarantees of free expression. We were prepared to assume, and so stated, that Mr. Mishkin's books had no "recognizable literary or artistic value," were "deliberately designed to appeal to the 'prurient interests' of some persons," were also "offensive to putative community standards of decency," and conveyed ideas, "if any," which were without redeeming social importance." In sum, the brief we filed argued that *Roth* should be put to rest, but Mishkin should be saved.

Although each person in the group felt it would be wisest if no restraint whatsoever were placed against allegedly obscene expression, it was agreed to offer a formula which might be substituted for *Roth's*, and present a minimum danger to the values underlying constitutional freedom of expression. In the brief's preliminary statement, which one obscenity lawyer (perhaps not uncharitably) characterized as smacking of a lecture, the group argued:

*At least since the days of Anthony Comstock, those in this country who would limit expression have been able to enlist on their side the police power of local, state and federal government agencies. Insofar as exercises of that power have been upheld by the state and federal courts of the nation, the judiciary too has been involved in the repression of images and ideas expressed in printed and graphic forms. We feel it is a Constitutional error of major proportions for this Court to continue to tolerate censorship activity—civil or criminal, federal, state or local. We believe the Court should once and for all outlaw all govern-*mental policing of the images and ideas disseminated among adults in book and any other printed form.*

Prosecutions for obscenity have always been a major device for the censorship of literature and art in this country. Reputable as well as disreputable publishers, booksellers, writers and artists have been subjected to threats, arrest, prosecution, conviction, fine and imprisonment for their involvement in the production or dissemination of books and other printed material which violate putative norms. No one involved in the creation or distribution of American literature and art has been unaffected by censorship. So long as any censorship of books is permitted by Roth, no one can be sure that if today the police power gets invoked against the publisher of The Dance with the Dominant Whip it will not tomorrow be used against the paperback distributor of The American Dream.

Moreover, freedom, in our democracy, should be uniform as well as full, and the administration of justice needs to be even-handed. Though amici may dislike, even despise, the content of some or many works which are being challenged as "obscene," those who produce them and those who read them were given as much Constitutional right to do so as those who produce and read works which are not challenged.

When we came to the point of specifying precisely what, if anything, the State might properly ban, we said:

It may be true, as a few of this Court's earlier cases and some noted legal comentators have suggested, that ours like most societies may enlist a police power to enforce, in certain situations, the most elemental forms of decency. Thus, blunt scenes of sexual love-making on the day-time television screen, graffiti on highway billboards, indecent utterances in public conveyances, might be outlawed without much danger to, or undue restraint upon those who may object to obscenity and whose right to reject such material should be protected. At the same time, persons having no objection to obscenity must retain a right to be protected from coercion of the other side. There is no coercion involved in reading a book, however vile, or in the attending of a motion picture film, however prurient. Our government, in this area, stays within its Constitutional bounds when it protects persons from public nuisance and shocks from which they can have no immediate escape or recourse.

These propositions had been arrived at, by the sponsors of the *Mishkin* brief, through a method which pretty well assured individual and mutual commitment. As I recall, Silvers, Podhoretz, Goodman and I did most of the thinking and the work. Clients normally leave to their lawyers the development of the points and arguments to be contained in briefs filed on their behalf. Here, because the brief was being volunteered by "friends of the court" (*amici curiae*), and because we were hoping to help reform the law of obscenity through a pragmatic, radical, informed, and personal approach—the brief was made the subject of a general meeting and then, drafted, was circulated among the group's members several times, for suggestions and revisions.

The product, that brief, seems to me sufficiently original and interesting to be appended, in its entirety, to this introduction.

As far as could be told from the opinion of the majority of the Court which voted to uphold Mishkin's conviction, our approach got almost nowhere; the majority, clearly, was in no mood to spare Ginzburg and was thoroughly disgusted by Mishkin and his works. Our brief seems, however, to have contributed to the reasoning underlying Mr. Justice Stewart's crisp dissents in *Mishkin* and *Ginzburg*, for in those he insisted that restraints upon obscenity ought to be limited to "hard-core pornography," strictly defined, or to situations involving publications amounting to an "assault."

Regarding Mishkin's books, Stewart commented: "However tawdry those books may be, they are not hard-core pornography, and their publication is, therefore, protected by the First and Fourteenth Amendments."

Regarding Ginzburg's situation, Stewart said: "Censorship reflects society's lack of confidence in itself. It is a hallmark of an authoritarian regime. . . . A book worthless to me may convey something of value to my neighbor. In the free society to which our Constitution has committed us, it is for each to advise himself."

Then, Stewart noted a proposition which paralleled the argument in our brief: "Different constitutional questions would arise in a case involving an assault upon individual privacy by publication in manner so blatant or obtrusive as to make it difficult or impossible for an unwilling individual to avoid exposure to it."

One year later, the "assault" or "coercion" approach mentioned by Stewart found its way into the text of the Supreme Court's unanimous opinion in *Redrup* v. *New York* (1967), quoted earlier. There, in reversing state cases involving the suppression of obscene materials, the full bench observed that in none was there "any suggestion of an assault upon individual privacy by publication in a manner so obtrusive as to make it impossible for an unwilling individual to avoid exposure to it."

The terminology we had sponsored cropped up again in an important 1968 case, earlier referred to, *Ginsberg* v. *New York*, involving the sale to a juvenile of two "girlie" magazines. Here, the Supreme Court upheld "on its face" a statute enacted specifically to protect juveniles from material obscene to them, which is aimed at them. Mr. Justice Stewart justified his concurrence with the majority in this way:

I think a state may permissibly determine that, at least in some precisely delineated areas, a child—like someone in a captive audience—is not possessed of that full capacity for individual choice which is the presupposition of First Amendment guarantees.

Equally significant, perhaps, was the reasoning of the dissent registered in the same case by Mr. Justice Fortas, who had swung the vote against *Eros'* Ginzburg in that (Fortas' first) obscenity case:

The State's police power may, within very broad limits, protect the parents and their children from public aggression of panderers and pushers. This is defensible on the theory that they cannot protect themselves from such assaults. But it does not follow that the State may convict a passive luncheonette operator of a crime because a sixteen-year-old boy maliciously and designedly picks up and pays for two girlie magazines which are presumably not obscene.

In the brief filed in the *Mishkin* case, the facts did not require otherwise and so we skirted the "juvenile" issue which divided Justices Stewart and Fortas, in the New York *Ginsberg* case. Both Justices, however, appear to subscribe to the "assault" or "coercion" or "captive" approach; their differences seem to have arisen because Stewart accepted, on its face and *in the abstract*, a statute designed to protect youngsters from obtrusive, unconsented-to publications, whereas Fortas focused *on the facts*, appearing from the record below, that the child had behaved more like an adult, and had solicited and invited the publications.

The idea that children, unlike adults, cannot be expected to exercise choice, or consent, in accordance with their interests, is not one which should automatically be embraced. Experience suggests that children, like adults, can screen out unwanted or painful sexual images and ideas, and that children, like adults, are very different from one another in their approaches and responses to sex. Moreover, there is reason, today especially, to question whether children are merely or always children, and whether in awarding children protected status we do not deprive many of them of rights and opportunities which they are capable of exercising and enjoying. We have witnessed during the past few years children defined by law as "too immature" to vote for, or against, candidates who promise to promote or end the Vietnam war, but *not* too immature, under law, to be sent to kill or be killed, in this same war. These children are also sometimes defined by adults as "too immature" to remain in college and not be drafted, when they resist with their bodies and their minds their and this country's involvement in that war.

A legal prohibition against malicious assaults by adults on the sexual sensibilities of children would seem sufficient to satisfy the interests of the State in protecting children from obscenity, where they can't protect themselves. Hopefully, such a legal formula could never be used to support a system of censorship over the films, literature and art which should be made available to children, as well as adults, in our society. It might even rescue from the oblivion of a censor's mind and bureau drawer some book or a film which, read or seen, will hasten the day when American adults and children are discouraged by their laws from making war, not love.

January 20, 1969
Washington, D.C.

■ CENSORSHIP LANDMARKS

1600-1900
Cases

■ Le Roy

v.

Sr. Charles Sidley.

Sr. Ch. S. fuit indict al common ley pur several misdemeanors encounter le peace del Roy & que fueront al grand scandal de Christianity, et le cause fuit quia il monstre son nude corps in un balcony in Covent Garden al grand multitude de people & la fist tiel choses & parle tiel parolls &c. (monstrant ascun particulars de son misbehavior) & cel indictment fuit overtment lie a luy en Court & fuit dit a luy per les justices que coment la ne fuit a cel temps ascun Star-Chamber uncore ils voil fair luy de scaver que cest Court est custos morum de touts les subjects le Roy, et est ore haut temps de punnier tiels profane actions fait encounter tout modesty queux sont cy frequent sicome

nient solement Christianity. Mes auxy morality ad estre derelinquy, et apres que il ad eē continue in Court p recogñ del terme de Trin. al fine del terme de St. Mich. Le Court luy demand daver son triall pur cel al Barr, mes il aiant advise submit luy mesme al Court & confesse l'indictment. Pur que le Court consider quel judgment a doner, et pur ceo q̃ il fuit gent' home de trope aunc̄ family (ore del pays de Kent) & son estate incumber (nient intendaut son ruine mes pur luy reforme) ils fine luy forsque 2000 marks & que serra imprison pur un weeke sans baile & del bone port pur 3 ans.

■ The Queen

againſt

Read.

Per curiam. A crime that ſhakes religion,[1] as profanenefs on THE STAGE, &c. is indictable;[2] but writing an obſcene book, as that intitled, "The Fifteen Plagues of a Maidenhead," is not indictable, but puniſhable only in the fpiritual court.[3]

---

[1] See I. Hawk. P.C. ch. 5.

[2] By 10. *Geo.* 2. c. 28. no drama or other entertainment of the ſtage can be acted, until a true copy thereof has, under a penalty of fifty pounds, been previouſly ſent to the lord chamberlain, who may *prohibit* the performance; and ſuch penalty may be recovered in a fummary way, &c.

[3] This cafe is denied to be law, Rex *v.* Curl, 2. Stra. 789. 1. *Bar.* K.B. 29. See also Rex *v.* Sedley, I. Keb. 620. I. Sid. 168. 10. St. Tr. Aff. 93. Rex *v.* Woolfton, 2. Stra. 8 pp. Rex *v.* Wilkes; II. St. Tr. 324.

■ Dominus Rex

vers.

Curl.

Information exhibited by the Attorney General against the defendant Edmond Curl, for that he existens homo iniquus et sceleratus ac nequiter machinans et intendens bonos mores subditorum hujus regni corrumpere, et eos ad nequitiam inducere, quendam turpem iniquum et obscænum libellum intitulat' Venus in the Cloister, or The Nun in Her Smock, impio et nequiter impressit et publicavit, ac imprimi et publicari causavit (setting out the several lewd passages,) in malum exemplum &c. And of this the defendant was found guilty. And in Trinity term last it was moved in arrest of judgment by Mr. Marsh, that however the defendant may be punishable for this in the Spiritual Court as an offence contra bonos mores, yet it can't be a libel for which he is punishable in the Temporal Court. Libellus is a diminutive of the word liber, and 'tis libellus from it's being a book, and not from the matter of its contents. In the case de libellis famosis my Lord Coke says, [789] that it must be against the publick, or some private person, to be a libel; and I don't remember ever to have heard this opinion contradicted. Whatever tends to corrupt the morals of the people, ought to be censured in the Spiritual Court, to which properly all such causes belong: what their proceedings are I am a stranger to; but for me 'tis sufficient to say, I don't find any case wherein they were ever prohibited in such a cause: in the reign of King Charles the Second there was a filthy run of obscene writings, for which we meet with no prosecution in the Temporal Courts; and since these were things not fit to go unpunished, it is to be supposed that my lords the bishops animadverted upon them in their courts. In the case of *The Queen* v. *Read*,[1] 6 Ann. in B.R. there was an information for a libel in writing an obscene book called The Fifteen Pleagues of a Maidenhead, and after conviction it was moved in arrest of judgment, that this was not punishable in the Temporal Courts; and the opinion of Chief Justice Holt was so strong with the objection, that the prosecutor never thought fit to stir it again.

Mr. Attorney General contra, I do not observe it is pretended there is any other way of punishing the defendant; for if the Spiritual Court had done it, instances might be given; and it is no argument to say we meet with no prohibitions; such a way of arguing would construe them into all sorts of jurisdictions.

What I insist upon is, that this is an offence at common law, as it tends to corrupt the morals of the King's subjects, and is against the peace of the King. Peace includes good order and government, and that peace may be broken in many instances without an actual force. 1. If it be an act against the constitution or civil Government; 2. If it be against religion: and, 3. If against morality.

1. Under the first head fall all the cases of seditious words or writings. 2 Roll. Abr. 78, pl. 2. 1 Vent. 324. 3 Keb. 841, and the case of *The Queen* v. *Bedford*, Mich. 12 Ann. whose treatise of hereditary right was held to be a libel, though it contained no reflection upon any part of the then Government.

2. It is a libel if it reflects upon religion, that great basis of civil Government and society; and it may be both a spiritual and temporal offence. Cro. Jac. 421. 2 Roll. Abr. 78, pl. 2. 1 Vent. 293. 3 Keb. 607, 621. In Tremayne's Entries 226, there is a sentence to have a paper fixed over the defendant's head, intimating that he had uttered blasphemous words tend-[790]-ing to the subversion of Government. There is one Hall now in custody on a conviction as for a libel intitled A Sober Reply to the Merry Arguments about the Trinity, and Pasch. 10 Ann. *Regina* v. *Clendon*, there was a special verdict on a libel about the Trinity, and it was not made a doubt of in that case.

3. As to morality. Destroying that is destroying the peace of the Government, for government is no more than publick order, which is morality. My Lord Chief Justice Hale used to say, Christianity is part of the law, and why not morality too? I do not insist that every immoral act is indictable, such as telling a lie, or the like; but if it is destructive of morality in general, if it does, or may, affect all the King's subjects, it then is an offence of a publick nature. And upon this distinction it is, that particular acts of fornication are not punishable in the Temporal Courts, and bawdy-houses are. In *Sir Charles Sedley's case* it was said, that this Court is the custos morum of the King's subjects. 1 Sid. 168. And upon this foundation there have been many prosecutions against the players for obscene plays, though they have had interest enough to get the proceedings stayed before judgment. Tremayne's Ent. 209, 213, 214, 215. 3 vol. State Trials, *Lord Grey's case*.

Mich. 10 W. 3, *Rex* v. *Hill*, the defendant was indicted for printing some obscene poems of my Lord Rochester's, tending to the corruption of youth; upon which he went

abroad, and was outlawed; which he would not have done if his counsel had thought it no libel.

The Spiritual Courts punish only personal spiritual defamation by words; if it is reduced to writing, it is a temporal offence. Salk. 552. Mo. 627, and it is punishable as a libel. My Lord Coke in the case de libellis famosis had nothing in view but scandalous defamatory libels. Libellus is not always to be taken as a technical word; in this case it may stand as an obscene little book. And as to the case of *Read*, there was no judgment, but it went off upon the Chief Justice's saying, Why don't you go to the Spiritual Court; which was giving a false reason for that sudden opinion, now it appears there is no instance of the Spiritual Court's intermeddling, where it is reduced to writing or in print.

Chief Justice, I think this is a case of very great consequence, though if it was not for the case of *The Queen* v. *Read*, I should make no great difficulty of it. Certainly the Spiritual Court has nothing to do with it, if in writing: and if it reflects on religion, virtue, or morality, if it tends to disturb the civil order of society, I think it is a temporal offence. I do not think libellus is always to be taken as a technical word. Would not trover lie de quodam libello intitulat' the New Testament, and does not the Spiritual Court proceed upon a libel?

[791] FORTESCUE J. I own this is a great offence, but I know of no law by which we can punish it. Common law is common usage, and where there is no law there can be no transgression. At common law drunkenness, or cursing and swearing, were not punishable; and yet I do not find the Spiritual Court took notice of them. This is but a general solicitation of chastity, and not indictable. *Lady Purbeck's case* was for procuring men and women to meet at her house, and held not indictable, unless there had been particular facts to make it a bawdy-house. To make it indictable there should be a breach of the peace, or something tending to it, of which there is nothing in this case. A libel is a technical word at common law, and I must own the case of *The Queen* v. *Read* sticks with me, for there was a rule to arrest the judgment nisi. And in *Sir Charles Sedley's case* there was a force in throwing out bottles upon the people's heads.

REYNOLDS J. It is much to be lamented if this is not punishable: I agree there may be many instances, where acts of immorality are of spiritual cognizance only; but then those are particular acts, where the prosecution is pro salute animæ of the offender, and not where they are of a general immoral tendency: which I take to be a reasonable distinction. *Read's case* is indeed a case in point. But I confess I should not have been of that opinion. Libellus does not ex vi termini import defamation, but is to be governed by the epithet which is added to it. This is surely worse than *Sir Charles Sedley's case*, who only exposed himself to the people then present, who might choose whether they would look upon him or not; whereas this book goes all over the kingdom. Drunkenness and swearing were punishable in the Spiritual Court before the Acts which made them temporal offences, and in which the jurisdiction of the Spiritual Court is saved.

PROBYN J. inclined this to be punishable at common law, as an offence against the peace, in tending to weaken the bonds of civil society, virtue, and morality. But it being a case of great consequence, it was ordered to stand over for a further argument.

---

[1] Fort. 98.

And this term Page J. being come into the King's Bench in the room of Justice Fortescue, it was to have been spoke to by Mr. Solicitor General and myself. But Curl not having attended me in time, I acquainted the Court I was not prepared: and my want of being ready proceeding from his own neglect, they re-[792]-fused to indulge him to the next term. And in two or three days, they gave it as their unanimous opinion, that this was a temporal offence. They said it was plain the force used in *Sedley's case* was but a small ingredient in the judgment of the Court, who fined

him 2000l. And if the force was all they went upon, there was no occasion to talk of the Court's being censor morum of the King's subjects. They said if *Read's case* was to be adjudged, they should rule it otherwise: and therefore in this case they gave judgment for the King. And the defendant was afterwards set in the pillory, as he well deserved.[2]

_____
[2] An information was granted against Mr. Wilkes for a similar offence, and this objection was not taken. 4 Burr. 2527.

■ The Queen, on the Prosecution of Henry Scott, *Appellant,*

v.

Benjamin Hicklin and Another,
Justices of Wolverhampton, *Respondents.*

At the quarter sessions for the borough of Wolverhampton on the 27th of May, 1867, Henry Scott appealed against an order made by two justices of the borough under 20 & 21 Vict. c. 83,[1] whereby the justices ordered

_____
[1] 20 & 21 Vict. c. 83, "An act for more effectually preventing the sale of obscene books, pictures, prints, and other articles," after reciting "that it is expedient to give additional powers for the suppression of the trade in obscene books, prints, drawings, and other obscene articles."

Section 1. It shall be lawful for any metropolitan police magistrate or other stipendiary magistrate, or for any two justices, upon complaint made before them upon oath that the complainant has reason to believe, that any obscene books, &c. are kept in any house, &c., for the purposes of sale or distribution, exhibition for the purposes of gain, lending upon hire, or being otherwise published for purposes of gain, which complainant shall also state upon oath that one or more articles of the like character have been sold, distributed, exhibited, lent, or otherwise published as aforesaid, at or in connection with such place, so as to satisfy such magistrate or justice that the belief of the said complainant is well founded, and upon such justice being also satisfied that any of such articles so kept for any of the purposes aforesaid are of such a character and description that the publication of them would be a misdemeanor, and proper to be prosecuted as such, to give authority by special warrant to any constable or police officer into such house, shop, room or other place, with such assistance as may be necessary, to enter in the daytime, and, if necessary, to use force, by breaking open doors or otherwise, and to search for and seize all such books, papers, writings, prints, pictures, drawings, or other representations as aforesaid found in such house, shop, room, or other place, and to carry all the articles so seized before the magistrate or justices issuing the said warrant, or some of her magistrate or justices exercising the same jurisdiction; and such magistrate or justices shall thereupon issue a summons calling upon the occupier of the house or other place, which may have been so entered by virtue of the said warrant, to appear within seven days before such police stipendiary magistrate or any two justices in petty sessions for the district, to show cause why the articles so seized should not be destroyed; and if such occupier or some other person claiming to be the owner of the said articles shall not appear within the time aforesaid, or shall appear, and such magistrate or justices shall be satisfied that such articles, or any of them, are of the character stated in the warrant, and that such,

certain books which had been seized in the dwelling-house of the appellant, within their jurisdiction, to be destroyed, as being obscene books within the meaning of the statute.

The appellant is a metal broker, residing in the town of Wolverhampton, and a person of respectable position and character. He is a member of a body styled "The Protestant Electoral Union," whose objects are, inter alia, "to protest against those teachings and practices which are un-English, immoral, and blasphemous, to maintain the Protestantism of the Bible and the liberty of England," and "to promote the return to Parliament of men who will assist them in these objects, and particularly will expose and defeat the deep-laid machinations of the Jesuits, and resist grants of money for Romish purposes." In order to promote the objects and principles of this society, the appellant purchased from time to time, at the central office of the society in London, copies of a pamphlet, entitled "The Confessional Unmasked; shewing the depravity of the Romish priesthood, the iniquity of the Confessional, and the questions put to females in confession;" of which pamphlets he sold between two and three thousand copies at the price he gave for them, viz., 1s. each, to any person who applied for them.

A complaint was thereupon made before two justices of the borough, by a police officer acting under the direction of the Watch Committee of the borough, and the justices

_____
or any of them, have been kept for any of the purposes aforesaid, it shall be lawful for the justices, and they are hereby required, to order the articles so seized, except such of them as they may consider necessary to be preserved as evidence in some further proceeding, to be destroyed at the expiration of the time hereinafter allowed for lodging an appeal, unless notice of appeal as hereinafter mentioned [s. 4] be given, and such articles shall be in the mean time impounded; and if such magistrate or justices shall be satisfied that the articles seized are not of the character stated in the warrant, or have not been kept for any of the purposes aforesaid, he or they shall forthwith direct them to be restored to the occupier of the house or other place in which they were seized."

By s. 4, an appeal is given to the next quarter sessions to any one aggrieved by the determination of justices.

issued their warrant under the above statute, by virtue of which warrant 252 of the pamphlets were seized on the premises of the appellant, and ordered by the justices to be destroyed.

The pamphlet[1] consists of extracts taken from the works of certain theologians who have written at various times on the doctrines and discipline of the Church of Rome, and particularly on the practice of auricular confession. On one side of the page are printed passages in the original Latin, correctly extracted from the works of those writers, and opposite to each extract is placed a free translation of such extract into English. The pamphlet also contains a preface and notes and comments, condemnatory of the tracts and principles laid down by the authors from whose works the extracts are taken. About one half of the pamphlet relates to casuistical and controversial questions which are not obscene, but the remainder of the pamphlet is obscene in fact as relating to impure and filthy acts, words, and ideas. The appellant did not keep or sell the pamphlets for purposes of gain, nor to prejudice good morals, though the indiscriminate sale and circulation of them is calculated to have that effect; but he kept and sold the pamphlets, as a member of the Protestant Electoral Union, to promote the objects of that society, and to expose what he deems to be errors of the Church of Rome, and particularly the immorality of the Confessional.

The recorder was of opinion that, under these circumstances, the sale and distribution of the pamphlets would not be a misdemeanor, nor, consequently, be proper to be prosecuted as such, and that the possession of them by the appellant was not unlawful within the meaning of the statute. He therefore quashed the order of the justices, and directed the pamphlets seized to be returned to the appellant, subject to the opinion of the Court of Queen's Bench.

If the Court should be of opinion, upon the facts stated, that the sale and distribution of the pamphlets by the appellant would be a misdemeanor, and proper to be prosecuted as such, the order of the justices for destroying the pamphlets so seized was to be enforced; if not, the order was to be quashed.

Kydd, for the appellant. The decision of the recorder was right, the intention of the appellant being innocent, the publication of this pamphlet was not an indictable misdemeanor; and therefore the justices had no jurisdiction to order the copies to be destroyed. The book is controversial.

[COCKBURN, C.J. The recorder has found that the work, at least the latter half of it, is obscene, and there can be no doubt of it; and the question is, that being so, are the magistrates deprived of jurisdiction to destroy this obscene work, because the real object of the appellant in distributing it was not to do harm, but good?]

The criminal intention must be shewn before the justices have jurisdiction; but here that intent is expressly negatived. Thus in *Woodfall's Case*,[1] Lord Mansfield told the jury, "That, where an act, in itself indifferent, if done with a particular intent becomes criminal, then the intent must be proved and found; but when the act is in itself unlawful, . . the proof of justification or excuse lies on the defendant; and in failure thereof, the law implies a criminal intent." But the question of intent is for the jury, per Lord Ellenborough in *Rex v. Lambert*;[2] although the law was formerly otherwise: *Rex v. Shebbeare*;[3] see also, however, per Holt, C.J., in *Tutchin's Case*.[4] In *Fowler v. Padget*[5] it was held that a debtor leaving his house did not commit an act of bankruptcy, though creditors were delayed, unless there was an intention to delay, and Lord Kenyon observed, "It is a principle of natural justice and of our law, that *actus non facit reum nisi mens sit rea*. The intent and the act must both concur to constitute the crime." In *Reg. v. Sleep*[6] in which an indictment was laid under 9 & 10 Wm. 3, c. 41, s. 2, for having been in possession of naval stores, and the jury negatived that the prisoner knew that the stores were marked with the broad arrow, Cockburn, C.J., said, "It is a principle of our law that to constitute an offence there must be a guilty mind, and that principle must be imported into the statute, although the Act itself does not in terms make a guilty mind necessary to the commission of the offence." *Reg. v. Dodsworth*,[7] and *Reg. v. Allday*,[8] are to the same effect. In *Buckmaster v. Reynolds*,[9] Erle, C.J., says, "A man cannot be said to be guilty of a delict unless to some extent his mind goes with the act. Here it seems that the respondent acted on the belief that he had a right to enter the room, and that he had no intention to do a wrongful act." The mere use of obscene words, or the occurrence of obscene passages, does not make the work obscene. Thus Milton, in his celebrated defence of himself,[1] justifies by examples the use of language adequate to the occasion, though it may be obscene. On this principle it is that the defence of unlicensed printing has always been based. The opposite principle is that of the Church of Rome. Thus in Hallam's Literature of Europe, part ii., c. 8, s. 70, it is said, "Rome struck a fatal blow at literature in the index expurgatorius of prohibited books. . . . The first list of books prohibited by the church was set forth by Paul IV. in 1559. His index includes all bibles in modern languages, enumerating forty-eight editions, chiefly printed in countries still within the obedience of the church." If mere obscenity, without reference to the object, is indictable, Collier's View of the Immorality of the English Stage, written with the best motives and published with the best results, would have been indictable. The same may be said

---

[1] A copy accompanied and was made part of the case. The authors from which the obscene parts of the pamphlet were taken were Peter Dens, Liguori, Delahogue de Pænitentiâ, Bailly, and Cabassutius—chiefly the first two. In the preface, after alluding to the different authors quoted, and shewing that they were held of great authority in the Roman Catholic Church, the compiler proceeds: "Such, then, is the theology, and such the morals which, by granting 30,000*l.* a-year to Maynooth, we assist in propagating." . . . . "In the later part of the pamphlet I have given a few extracts without abridgment, to shew into what minute and disgusting details these *holy men* have entered. This alone has been my object, and not the filling of the work with obscenity."

---

[1] 20 St. Tr. at p. 919; 5 Burr. at pp. 2666–7.
[2] 2 Camp. at p. 404.
[3] 3 T.R. 430, n.
[4] 14 St. Tr. at p. 1125.
[5] 7 T.R. 509, 514.
[6] Leigh and Cave, 44, 54; 30 L.J. (M.C.) 170, 173.
[7] 2 Mood. & Rob. 72.
[8] 8 C. & P. 136.
[9] 13 C.B. (N.S.) 62, 68.
[1] Probably Authoris pro se defensio contra Alexandrum Morum.

of David Clarkson's works, just now republished in Edinburgh, with a preface by Dr. Miller. What can be more obscene than many pictures publicly exhibited, as the Venus in the Dulwich gallery?

[LUSH, J. It does not follow that because such a picture is exhibited in a public gallery, that photographs of it might be sold in the streets with impunity.]

What can be more obscene than Bayle's Dictionary, or many of the works of the standard authors in English poetry, from Chaucer to Byron?—Dryden's translation, for instance, of the sixth satire of Juvenal? Or Savage's St. Valentine's Day? And yet of Savage, the great moralist Dr. Johnson,[2] says, alluding to the attempt to prosecute him in the King's Bench for his "Progress of a Divine," as being an obscene libel: "It was urged in his defence, that obscenity was criminal when it was intended to promote the practice of vice; but that Mr. Savage had only introduced obscene ideas with the view of exposing them to detestation, and of amending the age by showing the deformity of wickedness. This plea was admitted, and Sir Philip Yorke, who then presided in that court, dismissed the information, with encomiums upon the purity and excellence of Mr. Savage's writings." So here, the object of the compiler, as expressed in his preface and his comments throughout the pamphlet, is to expose the obscenity and grossness of the Romish practice of the confessional. In *Murray v. Benbow*[1] shortly noticed with other cases in Phillips on Copyright, pp. 23–25, Lord Eldon, C., refused an injunction to restrain the sale of a pirated edition of Lord Byron's Cain, on the ground that it was a profane libel. Lord Eldon's judgment is given in the prefatory notes to Cain in the collected editions of Byron's works by Moore. And the learned judge expressly puts the distinction of the author's motive. Thus, alluding to Paradise Lost and Regained, he says: "It appears to me that the great object of the author was to promote the cause of Christianity. There are undoubtedly a great many passages in it, of which, if that were not the object, it would be very improper by law to vindicate the publication; but, taking it altogether, it is clear that the object and effect was not to bring disrepute, but to promote the reverence, of our religion."

[BLACKBURN, J. "Object and effect;" concede the object here to be good, what was the effect?]

Starkie, in his Law of Slander and Libel, vol. ii., p. 147, 2nd edit., treating of blasphemy as a crime, says: "A malicious and mischievous intention, or what is equivalent to such an intention, in law, as well as morals, a state of apathy and indifference to the interests of society, is the broad boundary between right and wrong. If it can be collected from the circumstances of the publication, from a display of offensive levity, from contumelious and abusive expressions applied to sacred persons or subjects, that the design of the author was to occasion that mischief to which the matter which he publishes immediately tends, to destroy or even to weaken man's sense of religious or moral obligations, to insult those who believe by casting contumelious abuse and ridicule upon their doctrines, or to being the established religion and form of worship into disgrace and contempt, the offence against society is complete."

[BLACKBURN, J. The argument to meet the present case must go the length, that the object being good, or at all events innocent, would justify the publication of anything however indecent, however obscene, and however mischievous.]

LUSH, J. And by any means such as giving away obscene extracts like these as tracts.

COCKBURN, C.J. A medical treatise, with illustrations necessary for the information of those for whose education or information the work is intended, may, in a certain sense, be obscene, and yet not the subject for indictment; but it can never be that these prints may be exhibited for any one, boys and girls, to see as they pass. The immunity must depend upon the circumstances of the publication.]

The animus must always be looked at. Thus in *Moxon's Case*,[1] which was a prosecution of the publisher of Shelley's works for blasphemy, Lord Denman, C.J., in summing up, is reported to have said: "The purpose of the passage cited from 'Queen Mab' was, he thought, to cast reproach and insult upon what in Christian minds were the peculiar objects of veneration. It was not, however, sufficient that mere passages of such an offensive character should exist in a work, in order to render the publication of it an act of criminality. It must appear that no condemnation of such passages appeared in the context." Such condemnation does appear in page after page of this pamphlet. Alderson, B., distinctly recognized the right of every one to attack the errors of any sect of religion. In *Gathercole's Case*,[2] that learned Judge told the jury, "A person may, without being liable to prosecution for it, attack Judaism, Mohammedanism, or even any sect of the Christian religion (except the established religion of the country). . . . The defendant here has a right to entertain his opinions, to express them, and to discuss the subject of the Roman Catholic religion and its institutions." Lord Mansfield expressed himself to the same effect in a speech in the House of Lords, which is cited by Lord Campbell in his life of Lord Mansfield.[3]

The 20 & 21 Vict. c. 83, s. 1, does not make the mere possession or sale of an obscene work sufficient, and the question is therefore quo animo was the publication; and

---

[2] Lives of the English Poets.

[1] Jac. 474, n.

[1] 2 Mod. St. Tr. by Townsend, at p. 388.

[2] 2 Lewin's C.C. at p. 254.

[3] "There never was a single instance, from the Saxon times down to our own, in which a man was punished for erroneous opinions concerning rites or modes of worship, but upon some positive law. The common law of England, which is only common reason or usage, knows of no prosecution for mere opinions. For atheism, blasphemy, and reviling the Christian religion there have been instances of persons prosecuted and punished upon the common law; but bare nonconformity is no sin by the common law."—Lives of the Chief Justices, vol. ii. pp. 512–14. Life of Lord Mansfield.—The case is that of *Harrison v. Evans* (3 Br. Parl. C. 465), and was an action of debt for penalties commenced in the Sheriff's Court against Evans for not serving the office of sheriff, which he refused, on account of being a dissenter, and not having received the sacrament according to the rites of the church of England within a year before his election. The extracts from Lord Mansfield's speech in the House of Lords, that are quoted by Lord Campbell, are from the speech as given by Dr. Philip Furneaux (not Faraceaux as printed in Campbell's Lives) in an appendix to the second edition of "Letters to Mr. Justice Blackstone concerning his Exposition of the Act of Toleration." London, Cadell, 1771; see pp. 277–8.

the mere committing of the act is not sufficient, as in 3 & 4 Wm. 4, c. 15, s. 2, or 5 & 6 Vict. c. 93, s. 3. Here the publication of this pamphlet, though obscene, was with an honest intention of exposing the Roman Confessional, an object honestly carried out by correct quotations of the original Latin, correctly translated. The recorder has found that this was the intention, and he therefore rightly decided that the publication was not a misdemeanor.

A. S. Hill, Q.C., for the respondents. The preamble of the statute, taken with the enacting part, shows what the intention of the legislature was, and the question is whether the pamphlet was of such a character as to make the publication of it a misdemeanor.

[COCKBURN, C. J. The section says, "for the purposes of gain."]

The word "gain" does not occur in the clause, "for the purpose of sale or distribution." If the work be of an obscene character, it may be questioned whether intention has anything to do with the matter. But, if intention is necessary, it must be inferred that the appellant intended the natural consequences of his act, which the recorder finds are to prejudice good morals, and the motive of such a publication cannot justify it. Thus, an indictment lies for carrying a child with an infectious disease in the public streets, though there was no intention to do injury to the passengers: *Rex v. Vantandillo*.[1] In *Rex v. Topham*,[2] Lord Kenyon says: "It was argued, that even supposing there was sufficient evidence of publication, there was no evidence of a criminal intent in the defendant. To this I can answer in the words of Lord Mansfield in *Rex v. Woodfall*,[1] that 'where the act is in itself unlawful (as in this case), the proof of justification or excuse lies on the defendant; and in failure thereof, the law implies a criminal intent;'" and this passage is again cited with approbation by Lord Ellenborough in *Rex v. Phillips*.[2]

[BLACKBURN, J. Lord Ellenborough propounded the same principle in *Rex v. Dixon*.][3]

The ruling of Alderson B., in *Gathercole's Case*,[4] part of which was cited for the appellant, is also in point. "This indictment charges the defendant with intending to injure the character of the prosecutors; and every man, if he be a rational man, must be considered to intend that which must necessarily follow from what he does." In Starkie, on Slander and Libel, vol. ii. p. 158, 2nd ed., it is said, "Ever since the decision in *Curl's Case*,[5] it seems to have been settled, that any publication tending to the destruction of the morals of society is punishable by indictment. . . . Although many vicious and immoral acts are not indictable, yet, if they tend to the destruction of morality in general, if they do or may affect the mass of society, they become offences of a public nature." *Reg. v. Read*[6] was to the contrary; it was there held that an indictment would not lie for publishing an obscene libel, unless it libelled some one; and the note added by Fortescue is remarkable, and much in point. "N.B. There was the case of the *King v. Curl* in B.R., which was an indictment for printing and

publishing a libel called *The Nun in her Smock*, which contained several bawdy expressions, but did contain no libel against any person whatsoever; the Court gave judgment against the defendant, but contrary to my opinion; and I quoted this case. And, indeed, I thought it rather to be published on purpose to expose the Romish priests, the father confessors, and the popish religion."

[The Court then adjourned; on the Judges' return into court.]

COCKBURN, C.J. We have considered this matter, and we are of opinion that the judgment of the learned recorder must be reversed, and the decision of the magistrates affirmed. This was a proceeding under 20 & 21 Vict. c. 83, s. 1, whereby it is provided that, in respect of obscene books, &c., kept to be sold or distributed, magistrates may order the seizure and condemnation of such works, in case they are of opinion that the publication of them would have been the subject-matter of an indictment at law, and that such a prosecution ought to have been instituted. Now, it is found here as a fact that the work which is the subject-matter of the present proceeding was, to a considerable extent, an obscene publication, and, by reason of the obscene matter in it, calculated to produce a pernicious effect in depraving and debauching the minds of the persons into whose hands it might come. The magistrates must have been of opinion that the work was indictable, and that the publication of it was a fit and proper subject for indictment. We must take the latter finding of the magistrates to have been adopted by the learned recorder when he reversed their decision, because it is not upon that ground that he reversed it; he leaves that ground untouched, but he reversed the magistrates' decision upon the ground that, although this work was an obscene publication, and although its tendency upon the public mind was that suggested upon the part of the information, yet that the immediate intention of the appellant was not so to affect the public mind, but to expose the practices and errors of the confessional system in the Roman Catholic Church. Now, we must take it, upon the finding of the recorder, that such was the motive of the appellant in distributing this publication; that his intention was honestly and bonâ fide to expose the errors and practices of the Roman Catholic Church in the matter of confession; and upon that ground of motive the recorder thought an indictment could not have been sustained, inasmuch as to the maintenance of the indictment it would have been necessary that the intention should be alleged and proved, namely, that of corrupting the public mind by the obscene matter in question. In that respect I differ from the recorder. I think that if there be an infraction of the law the intention to break the law must be inferred, and the criminal character of the publication is not affected or qualified by there being some ulterior object in view (which is the immediate and primary object of the parties) of a different and of an honest character. It is quite clear that the publishing of an obscene book is an offence against the law of the land. It is perfectly true, as has been pointed out by Mr. Kydd, that there are a great many publications of high repute in the literary productions of this country the tendency of which is immodest, and, if you please, immoral, and possibly there might have been subject-matter for indictment in many of the works which have been referred to. But it is not to be said, because there are

---

[1] 4 M. & S. 73.
[2] 4 T.R. at p. 127.
[1] 5 Burr. at p. 2667.
[2] 6 East, at p. 473.
[3] 3 M. & S. 11, 15.
[4] 2 Lewin's C.C. at p. 255.
[5] 2 Strange, 788.
[6] Fort. 98, 100.

in many standard and established works objectionable passages, that therefore the law is not as alleged on the part of this prosecution, namely, that obscene works are the subject-matter of indictment; and I think the test of obscenity is this, whether the tendency of the matter charged as obscenity is to deprave and corrupt those whose minds are open to such immoral influences, and into whose hands a publication of this sort may fall. Now, with regard to this work, it is quite certain that it would suggest to the minds of the young of either sex, or even to persons of more advanced years, thoughts of a most impure and libidinous character. The very reason why this work is put forward to expose the practices of the Roman Catholic confessional is the tendency of questions, involving practices and propensities of a certain description, to do mischief to the minds of those to whom such questions are addressed, by suggesting thoughts and desires which otherwise would not have occurred to their minds. If that be the case as between the priest and the person confessing, it manifestly must equally be so when the whole is put into the shape of a series of paragraphs, one following upon another, each involving some impure practices, some of them of the most filthy and disgusting and unnatural description it is possible to imagine. I take it therefore, that, apart from the ulterior object which the publisher of this work had in view, the work itself is, in every sense of the term, an obscene publication, and that, consequently, as the law of England does not allow of any obscene publication, such publication is indictable. We have it, therefore, that the publication itself is a breach of the law. But, then, it is said for the appellant, "Yes, but his purpose was not to deprave the public mind; his purpose was to expose the errors of the Roman Catholic religion especially in the matter of the confessional." Be it so. The question then presents itself in this simple form: May you commit an offence against the law in order that thereby you may effect some ulterior object which you have in view, which may be an honest and even a laudable one? My answer is, emphatically, no. The law says, you shall not publish an obscene work. An obscene work is here published, and a work the obscenity of which is so clear and decided, that it is impossible to suppose that the man who published it must not have known and seen that the effect upon the minds of many of those into whose hands it would come would be of a mischievous and demoralizing character. Is he justified in doing that which clearly would be wrong, legally as well as morally, because he thinks that some greater good may be accomplished? In order to prevent the spread and progress of Catholicism in this country, or possibly to extirpate it in another, and to prevent the state from affording any assistance to the Roman Catholic Church in Ireland, is he justified in doing that which has necessarily the immediate tendency of demoralizing the public mind wherever this publication is circulated? It seems to me that to adopt the affirmative of that proposition would be to uphold something which, in my sense of what is right and wrong, would be very reprehensible. It appears to me the only good that is to be accomplished is of the most uncertain character. This work, I am told, is sold at the corners of streets, and in all directions, and of course it falls into the hands of persons of all classes, young and old, and the minds of those hitherto pure are exposed to the danger of contamination and pollution from the impurity it contains. And for what? To prevent them, it is

said, from becoming Roman Catholics, when the probability is, that nine hundred and ninety-nine out of every thousand into whose hands this work would fall would never be exposed to the chance of being converted to the Roman Catholic religion. It seems to me that the effect of this work is mischievous and against the law, and is not to be justified because the immediate object of the publication is not to deprave the public mind, but, it may be, to destroy and extirpate Roman Catholicism. I think the old sound and honest maxim, that you shall not do evil that good may come, is applicable in law as well as in morals; and here we have a certain and positive evil produced for the purpose of effecting an uncertain, remote, and very doubtful good. I think, therefore, the case for the order is made out, and although I quite concur in thinking that the motive of the parties who published this work, however mistaken, was an honest one, yet I cannot suppose but what they had that intention which constitutes the criminality of the act, at any rate that they knew perfectly well that this work must have the tendency which, in point of law, makes it an obscene publication, namely, the tendency to corrupt the minds and morals of those into whose hands it might come. The mischief of it, I think, cannot be exaggerated. But it is not upon that I take my stand in the judgment I pronounce. I am of opinion, as the learned recorder has found, that this is an obscene publication. I hold that, where a man publishes a work manifestly obscene, he must be taken to have had the intention which is implied from that act; and that, as soon as you have an illegal act thus established, quoad the intention and quoad the act, it does not lie in the mouth of the man who does it to say, "Well, I was breaking the law, but I was breaking it for some wholesome and salutary purpose." The law does not allow that; you must abide by the law, and if you would accomplish your object, you must do it in a legal manner, or let it alone; you must not do it in a manner which is illegal. I think, therefore, that the recorder's judgment must be reversed, and the order must stand.

BLACKBURN, J. I am of the same opinion. The question arises under the 20 & 21 Vict. c. 83, an act for "the more effectually preventing the sale of obscene books," and so forth; and the provision in the first section is this:—[The learned judge read the section.] Now, what the magistrate or justices are to be satisfied of is that the belief of the complainant is well founded, and also "that any of such articles so published for any of the purposes aforesaid, are of such a character and description," that is to say of such an obscene character and description, that the publication of them would be a misdemeanor, and that the publication in the manner alleged would be proper to be prosecuted; and having satisfied themselves in respect of those things, the magistrates may proceed to order the seizure of the works. And then the justices in petty sessions are also in effect to be satisfied of the same three things; first, that the articles complained of have been kept for any of the purposes aforesaid, and that they are of the character stated in the warrant, that is, that they are of such a character that it would be a misdemeanor to publish them; and that it would not only be a misdemeanor to publish them, but that it would be proper to be prosecuted as such; and then, and then only, are they to order them to be destroyed. I think with respect to the last clause, that the object of the legislature was to guard against the vexatious prosecution of publishers of old and recognized standard works, in which there may be some obscene or mischievous matter. In the case of *Reg. v. Moxon*,[1] and in many of the instances cited by Mr. Kydd, a book had been published which, in its nature, was such as to be called obscene or mischievous, and it might be held to be a misdemeanor to publish it; and on that account an indictable offence. In *Moxon's Case*,[1] the publication of Shelley's "Queen Mab" was found by the jury to be an indictable offence; I hope I may not be understood to agree with what the jury found, that the publication of "Queen Mab" was sufficient to make it an indictable offence. I believe, as everybody knows, that it was a prosecution instituted merely for the purpose of vexation and annoyance. So whether the publication of the whole works of Dryden is or is not a misdemeanor, it would not be a case in which a prosecution would be proper; and I think the legislature put in that provision in order to prevent proceedings in such cases. It appears that the work in question was published, and the magistrates in petty sessions were satisfied that it was a proper subject for indictment, and their finding as to that accords with the view we entertain. Then there was an appeal to the recorder in quarter sessions to reverse their decision, which appeal was successful. The learned recorder, in stating the grounds on which he reversed their decision, says, "About one half of the pamphlet relates to casuistical and controversial questions which are not obscene, but the latter half of the pamphlet is obscene in fact, as containing passages which relate to impure and filthy acts, words and ideas. The appellant did not keep or sell the pamphlets for purposes of gain, nor to prejudice good morals, though the indiscriminate sale and circulation of them is calculated to have that effect; but he kept and sold the pamphlet as a member of the Protestant Electoral Union, to promote the objects of that society, and to expose what he deemed to be errors in the church of Rome, and particularly the immorality of the confessional." The recorder then says he was of opinion that the sale and distribution of the pamphlet would not be a misdemeanor, nor consequently be proper to be prosecuted as such, and upon that ground he quashed the magistrates' order, leaving to this Court the question whether he was right or not. Upon that I understand the recorder to find the facts as follows: He finds that one half of the book was in fact obscene, and he finds that the effect of it would be such, that the sale and circulation of it was calculated to prejudice good morals. He does not find that he differs from the justices at all in matter of fact as to that, but he finds that the publication would not be indictable at all as a misdemeanor, and consequently that it would not be proper to prosecute it as a misdemeanor; and his reason for thinking it was not indictable as a misdemeanor is this, that the object of the person publishing was not to injure public morality, but with a view to expose the errors of the Church of Rome, and particularly the immorality, as he thought it, of the confessional; and, consequently upon those grounds, the recorder held it was not indictable. Then comes the question whether, upon those grounds, the publication was not indictable, and I come to the conclusion that the recorder was wrong, and that it would be indictable. I take the rule of law to be, as stated by

Lord Ellenborough in *Rex v. Dixon*,[1] in the shortest and clearest manner: "It is a universal principle that when a man is charged with doing an act" (that is a wrongful act, without any legal justification) "of which the probable consequence may be highly injurious, the intention is an inference of law resulting from the doing the act." And although the appellant may have had another object in view, he must be taken to have intended that which is the natural consequence of the act. If he does an act which is illegal, it does not make it legal that he did it with some other object. That is not a legal excuse, unless the object was such as under the circumstances rendered the particular act lawful. That is illustrated by the same case of *Rex v. Dixon*.[2] The question in that particular case was, whether or not an indictment would lie against a man who unlawfully and wrongfully gave to children unwholesome bread, but without intent to do them harm. The defendant was a contractor to supply bread to a military asylum, and he supplied the children with bread which was unwholesome and deleterious, and although it was not shewn or suggested that he intended to make the children suffer, yet Lord Ellenborough held that it was quite sufficient that he had done an unlawful act in giving them bread which was deleterious, and that an indictment could be sustained, as he must be taken to intend the natural consequences of his act. So in the case in which a person carried a child which was suffering from a contagious disease, along the public road to the danger of the health of all those who happened to be in that road, it was held to be a misdemeanor, without its being alleged that the defendant intended that anybody should catch the disease: *Rex v. Vantandillo*.[1] Lord Ellenborough said that if there had been any necessity, as supposed, for the defendant's conduct, this would have been matter of defence. If, on the other hand, the small-pox hospital were on fire, and a person in endeavouring to save the infected inmates from the flames, took some of them into the crowd, although some of the crowd would be liable to catch the small-pox, yet, in that case, he would not be guilty of a wrongful act, and he does not do it with a wrong intention, and he would have a good defence, as Lord Ellenborough said, under not guilty. To apply that to the present case, the recorder has found that one half of this book is obscene, and nobody who looks at the pamphlet can for a moment doubt that really one half of it is obscene, and that the indiscriminate circulation of it in the way in which it appears to have been circulated, must be calculated necessarily to prejudice the morals of the people. The object was to produce the effect of exposing and attacking the Roman Catholic religion, or practices rather, and particularly the Roman Catholic confessional, and it was not intended to injure public morals; but that in itself would be no excuse whatever for the illegal act. The occasion of the publication of libellous matter is never irrelevant, and is for the jury, and the jury have to consider, taking into view the occasion on which matter is written which might injure another, is it a fair and proper comment, or is it not more injurious than the circumstances warranted? But on the other hand it has never been held that the occasion being lawful can justify any libel, however gross. I do not say

---

[1] 2 Mod. S. Tr. 356.

[1] 3 M. & S. at p. 15.
[2] 3 M. & S. 11.
[1] 4 M. & S. 73.

there is anything illegal in taking the view that the Roman Catholics are not right. Any Protestant may say that without saying anything illegal. Any Roman Catholic may say, if he pleases, that Protestants are altogether wrong, and that Roman Catholics are right. There is nothing illegal in that. But I think it never can be said that in order to enforce your views, you may do something contrary to public morality; that you are at liberty to publish obscene publications, and distribute them amongst every one— schoolboys and every one else—when the inevitable effect must be to injure public morality, on the ground that you have an innocent object in view, that is to say, that of attacking the Roman Catholic religion, which you have a right to do. It seems to me that never could be made a defence to an act of this sort, which is in fact a public nuisance. If the thing is an obscene publication, then, notwithstanding that the wish was, not to injure public morality, but merely to attack the Roman Catholic religion and practices, still I think it would be an indictable offence. The question, no doubt, would be a question for the jury; but I do not think you could so construe this statute as to say, that whenever there is a wrongful act of this sort committed, you must take into consideration the intention and object of the party in committing it, and if these are laudable, that that would deprive the justices of jurisdiction. The justices must themselves be satisfied that the publication, such as the publication before them, would be a misdemeanor on account of its obscenity, and that it would be proper to indict. The recorder has found that the pamphlet is obscene, and he supports the justices in every finding, except in what he has reversed it upon. He finds the object of the appellant in publishing the work was not to prejudice good morals, and consequently he thinks it would not be indictable at all. But I do not understand him for a moment to say, that if he had not thought there was a legal object in view, it would not have been a misdemeanor at all, and that therefore it would have been vexatious or improper to indict it; nor do I think that anybody who looks at this book would for a moment have a doubt upon the matter. That being so, on the question of whether or not on the facts that the recorder has found it would be a misdemeanor and indictable as such, I come to the conclusion that it is a misdemeanor, and that an indictment would lie; and I say the justices were right, and consequently the recorder's decision is reversed, and the order of justices is confirmed.

Mellor, J. I confess I have with some difficulty, and with some hesitation, arrived very much at the conclusion at which my Lord and my learned Brothers have arrived. My difficulty was mainly, whether or not this publication was, under the finding of the recorder, within the act having reference to obscene publications. I am not certainly in a condition to dissent from the view which my Lord and my Brothers have taken as to the recorder's finding, and if that view be correct then I agree with what has been said by my Lord and my Brother Blackburn. The nature of the subject itself, if it may be discussed at all (and I think it undoubtedly may), is such that it cannot be discussed without to a certain extent producing authorities for the assertion that the confessional would be a mischievous thing to be introduced into this kingdom; and therefore it appears to me very much a question of degree, and if the matter were left to the jury it would depend very much on the opinion which the jury might form of that degree in such a publication as the present. Now, I take it for granted that the magistrates themselves were perfectly satisfied that this work went far beyond anything which was necessary or legitimate for the purpose of attacking the confessional. I take it that the finding of the recorder is (as I suppose was the finding of the justices below) that though one half of the book consists of casuistical and controversial questions, and so on, and which may be discussed very well without detriment to public morals, yet that the other half consists of quotations which are detrimental to public morals. On looking at this book myself, I cannot question the finding either of the recorder or of the justices. It does appear to me that there is a great deal here which there cannot be any necessity for in any legitimate argument on the confessional and the like, and agreeing in that view, I certainly am not in a condition to dissent from my Lord and my Brother Blackburn, and I know my Brother Lush agrees entirely with their opinion. Therefore, with the expression of hesitation I have mentioned, I agree in the result at which they have arrived.

Lush, J. I agree entirely in the result at which the rest of the Court have arrived, and I adopt the arguments and the reasonings of my Lord Chief Justice and my Brother Blackburn.

Order of justices affirmed.

Attorney for appellant: *C. Bassett.*
Attorney for respondents: *Needham.*

■ Steele, *Appellant;*
Brannan, *Respondent.*

Case stated by a police magistrate under 20 & 21 Vict. c. 43.
1. The appellant is the occupier and manager of a shop, being 14, Tavistock Street, Covent Garden, within the metropolitan police district, for a body called or known as the Protestant Electoral Union, whose objects, as set forth in their prospectus, are inter alia "to protest against the teachings of the Romish and Puseyite systems, which are un-English, immoral, and blasphemous; to maintain the Protestantism of the Bible and the liberty of England;"

and "to promote the return to Parliament of men who will assist them in these objects; and particularly will expose and defeat the deep-laid machinations of the Jesuits, and resist grants of money for Romish purposes."

2. On the 26th day of January, 1871, the respondent, who was an inspector of the metropolitan police, under authority given to him by special warrant duly issued under 20 & 21 Vict. c. 83, seized, at the shop, 14, Tavistock Street, aforesaid, about 181 copies of "A Report of the Trial of George Mackey, at the Winchester Quarter Sessions, 18th and 19th October, 1870, from Short-hand Notes of Dr. Soutter, Lecturer on Short-hand in King's College, London; containing the Full Text of the 'Morality of Romish Devotion, or the Confessional Unmasked,' shewing the Depravity of the Romish Priesthood and the Iniquity of the Confessional. For the use of Heads of Families and Persons of Mature Years." The above was the title on the cover and on the first page.

3. Some of these reports were sold in covers on the outside of which no reference was made to the trial, but which contained the following title and description of the book:

"The Morality of Romish Devotion, or the Confessional Unmasked; shewing the Depravity of the Romish Priesthood and the Iniquity of the Confessional.

"The extracts contained in this pamphlet are simply specimens of the moral theology of Rome, taught in the Royal College of Maynooth at a cost of 30,000*l.* per annum to this heavily-taxed Protestant nation. Through the unfaithfulness of both Christians and politicians, lawlessness has become legalized amongst us, and the most atrocious and obscene maxims and practices have been imposed upon the people as moral theology and the requirements of religion. On behalf of morality and religion we adjudge the confessional as here 'unmasked' to be a foul blasphemy, and worthy to be execrated of mankind, and we appeal to the Word of God and the common sense of the people for a confirmation of our verdict.—ED.

"'The time may come when it will become our bounden though painful duty to rouse the indignation of Englishmen at the expense of their modesty by translating and circulating some of the contents of that charnel-house the confessional.'—DR. MCNEILE.

"Protestant Evangelical Mission and Electoral Union, 14, Tavistock Street, Covent Garden, London. Price One Shilling. To be had at all Booksellers.'"

4. On the 2nd day of February last the appellant duly appeared at the Bow Street police court, before Sir Thomas Henry, the chief magistrate of the police courts of the metropolis, in answer to a summons duly issued under the said statute, to shew cause why the said books so seized should not be destroyed.

5. The Protestant Electoral Union had been in the habit of selling and distributing copies of the "Confessional Unmasked" previous to April, 1868, when the decision was given in the case of *Reg. v. Hicklin.*[1] In consequence of that decision the first edition of the book was withdrawn and a new one published, as stated in the following extract from the introduction (p. iii.) to the new edition: "Consequently the society withdraws the condemned edition, and does not intend publishing it; but the publication of a new edition in an altered form—that is,

---

[1] Law Rep. 3 Q.B. 360.

with certain alterations, certain omissions, and certain additions—would not come under the condemnation passed upon the former edition. Such an edition, then, is here presented to the public. In this edition are omitted some of the most filthy and abominable passages occurring in the former edition; also in this edition some passages are added for the sake of illustrating the pernicious influence exercised by the priests in the confessional over the minds and consciences of the laity, even apart from the demoralising and polluting influence exercised by them when employing the obscene language authorized and enforced by the Church. See also page 3 of the 'Apology.'"

7. For selling this new edition one George Mackey was tried at the Winchester Quarter Sessions, the 19th of October, 1870, when the jury, being unable to agree, were discharged without giving any verdict.

8. The appellant kept for sale and distribution, and sold and distributed from time to time at the said shop, copies of various books and pamphlets, and amongst them, the first edition of the "Confessional Unmasked;" and after the decision of the Court of Queen's Bench, the new edition of the book, and after the committal for trial of the said George Mackey, the "Report of the Trial of George Mackey" was published and sold.

The "Confessional Unmasked," consists of extracts from Roman Catholic theologians and divines. On one side of the page are printed passages in the original Latin, extracted from the authors therein named, and on the other side a free translation of the same. Other portions of the pamphlet consist of introductory matter, and of observations by the editor.

9. The "Report of the Trial of George Mackey" was a substantially correct report of the trial of that person, but the "Confessional Unmasked" was not read aloud in open court, and this explains the following paragraph at the bottom of page 2 of the report: "The sale of the "Confessional Unmasked" having been proved, reads as follows:" then follows the full text of the new edition of the "Confessional Unmasked."

10. The retail price of the "Report of the Trial, &c.," was one shilling. It was exposed for sale in the shop window, and sold to any person who applied for it, sometimes in one of the covers before mentioned, and sometimes in the other.

11. A copy of the "Report of the Trial, &c.," which was seized and ordered to be destroyed, and which is annexed hereto, is to form part of the case.

12. It was contended before me on behalf of the appellants, that upon the facts stated, the book seized, viz. the "Report of the Trial, &c.," was a fair report of a trial in a court of competent jurisdiction, and as such privileged.

13. I was of opinion that the "Report of the Trial of George Mackey, &c.," as sold and published, was not privileged.

14. I was further of opinion that the "Report of the Trial, &c.," a copy of which is annexed, was an obscene book, and of such a character and description that the publication of it was a misdemeanour, and proper to be prosecuted as such, and that the copies seized were kept in the shop for the purpose of sale.

15. I therefore ordered all the copies of such book so seized as aforesaid to be destroyed at the expiration of the time mentioned in the statute.

16. The appellant being dissatisfied with my determina-

tion as being erroneous in point of law only, gave me notice in writing to state and sign a case for the opinion of this Honourable Court, under 20 & 21 Vict. c. 43.

17. The question for the opinion of this Court is, whether, upon the facts above stated, I was wrong in point of law in ordering the books to be destroyed.[1]

April 29. *Kydd,* for the appellant. This book was not an obscene book within 20 & 21 Vict. c. 83. In order to bring it within that statute, the publication of it must be a misdemeanour at common law. In order to make such publication a misdemeanour, it must be with a criminal intent. Here the intent was not to pollute the public mind, but to expose an immoral system. The nature of the book is controversial, and the subject with which it deals one of the highest public importance. All the portions of the book which are objected to are extracts from the works of Roman Catholic divines and casuists, which are quoted merely for the purpose of condemning the system of the confessional. What effectual remedy is there in the hands of persons wishing to suppress a system which they conceive to be pernicious, except to expose the tendency of such a system by reference to the writings in which it is expounded?[2]

It is further contended that this work was privileged, as being a fair report of the proceedings at a trial. *Rex v. Carlile*[1] is not in point. The decision of the Court there proceeded upon the fact that the report was not a bonâ fide report. It was headed "Mock Trial," and the object of the publication was clearly to bring the proceedings of the court into disrepute. He also cited on this point *Rex v. Eaton,*[2] *Popham v. Pickburn;*[3] *Hoare v. Silverlock;*[4] *Turner v. Sullivan.*[5]

Sir J. D. Coleridge, A.G. (*Archibald* and *Poland* with him), for the respondent. The decision in *Reg. v. Hicklin*[6] clearly governs the present case. Works such as those from which these extracts are taken may, upon proper occasion calling for their discussion, be made the subject of controversy in a fitting manner. It is clear that parties are not

---

[1] The "Report of the Trial of George Mackey, &c.," set out in full the new edition of the "Confessional Unmasked." The new edition, although differing in some respects from the first edition, the character of which will be found discussed in the report of *Reg.* v. *Hicklin* (Law Rep. 3 Q.B. 360), was substantially of a similar character. It appeared from the "Report of the Trial, &c.," that the "Confessional Unmasked" was not read in full at the trial, but was put in and taken as read, and that counsel in the conduct of the case referred to the various paragraphs of it by their numbers, and read some portions as illustrating the character and object of the work.

[2] In the course of the argument a number of authorities and passages in various works were referred to; but it is not thought necessary to set out the argument on this point at greater length, inasmuch as, although it was contended that there was sufficient difference between the two editions of the "Confessional Unmasked" to take the case out of the decision in *Reg.* v. *Hicklin* (Law Rep. 3 Q.B. 360), substantially the arguments and the authorities cited were the same as those given in the report of that case.

[1] 3 B. & A. 167.
[2] 31 State Trials, 927.
[3] 7 H. & N. 891; 31 L.J. (Ex.) 133.
[4] 9 C.B. 20; 19 L.J. (C.P.) 215.
[5] 6 L.T. (N.S.) 130.
[6] Law Rep. 3 Q.B. 360.

entitled to collect extracts of this nature from books of casuistry and theology of a quasi-scientific character, and publish them in the form of a pamphlet for indiscriminate sale at a cheap rate.

With respect to the question of privilege, *Rex v. Carlile*[1] is directly in point.

Kydd, in reply.

April 30. The following judgments were delivered:—

BOVILL, C.J. This case comes before us by way of appeal from the decision of a magistrate upon a case stated under 20 & 21 Vict. c. 43; and the only question which now arises is whether, upon the facts stated, that decision was right as a matter of law. Upon looking over the book, it appears to me that no inconsiderable portion of its contents is of a most shockingly filthy description. During the argument counsel could do no more than call attention to the pages in which the objectionable passages occur, without referring to them more particularly. The book is one which would manifestly tend to deprave and corrupt the morals, more especially of the young and inexperienced. That being so, it appears to me necessarily to follow that the publication of the book would be a misdemeanour, and the book is consequently obscene within the meaning of the statute, 20 & 21 Vict. c. 83.

It was, however, strongly contended by the counsel for the appellant, that the book treated of a matter which might properly be made the subject of discussion and controversy, and that the object of those who put it forward being not only innocent but praiseworthy, inasmuch as they intended thereby to advance the interests of religion and of the public, the publication of the book was not a misdemeanour, and consequently the book was not obscene within the statute 20 & 21 Vict. c. 83. There is no doubt that all matters of importance to society may be made the subject of full and free discussion, but while the liberty of such discussion is preserved, it must not be allowed to run into obscenity and to be conducted in a matter which tends to the corruption of public morals. The probable effect of the publication of this book being prejudicial to public morality and decency, the appellant must be taken to have intended the natural consequences of such publication, even though the book were published with the objects referred to by his counsel. This point was fully considered in the case of *Reg. v. Hicklin,*[1] in which the principal authorities on the subject were cited and commented upon. There the sessions, on appeal, had reversed the decision of the magistrates, on the ground that the immediate intention of the appellants was not to corrupt the public mind, but to expose the errors of the confessional system. It was assumed, for the purposes of the judgment in that case, that the appellants had really and bonâ fide acted with the intention that they alleged; but the Court were of opinion that the publication of an obscene work was unlawful, and that the publishers of it must be taken to have intended the corruption of morals which would be the natural consequence of such publication.

I will assume, for the present purpose, that the new edition of the "Confessional Unmasked" differs somewhat from the first edition, which was the subject of the deci-

---

[1] Law Rep. 3 Q.B. 360.

sion in *Reg.* v. *Hicklin*;[1] but even this edition only professes to omit some of the most filthy and abominable passages in the former edition. It appears to me that quite sufficient remains to make the present case quite undistinguishable from that case. It is no defence that all the obscene part of this new edition consists of passages from the works of Roman Catholic authorities. That does not justify their publication in their present form, nor does it follow that such works might not themselves be equally liable to condemnation. It appears to me, therefore, that the present case falls within the decision in *Reg.* v. *Hicklin*,[1] with which decision I most fully concur.

A further question raised by this case is, whether this book is privileged as a fair report of proceedings in a court of competent jurisdiction. It is clear, that in general the publication of fair reports of proceedings in courts of justice, like free discussion of matters of public importance, being considered for the public benefit, is privileged; but it is equally clear that discussions offensive to public decency and of a depraving tendency are not privileged. The law on the subject is well expressed in Starkie on Slander and Libel, 3rd. ed. p. 215, where it is said, "Where the very object of the inquiry is to protect the interests of religion, morality, decency, and good order, by repressing infamous, blasphemous, and obscene or seditious publications, it would not only be impolitic, but weak and absurd, to allow the same matters to be afterwards published with impunity as a parcel of the judicial proceeding." The rule there laid down agrees with the law as stated in *Rex* v. *Carlile*,[2] by Bayley, J., as follows: "We are bound, for the purposes of justice, to hear evidence in the course of judicial proceedings, the publication of which at any distant period of time, or at any time afterwards, may have the effect of an utter subversion of the morals and religion of the people. The first time I had occasion to consider this subject was in the case of some trials for adultery. It very often happens that, for the purposes of justice, our ears may be shocked with extremely offensive and indelicate evidence. But though we are bound in a court of justice to hear it, other persons are not at liberty afterwards to circulate it at the risk of those effects which, in the minds of the young and unwary, such evidence may be calculated to produce. I am satisfied that, whenever that point has been under the consideration of this Court, it has always been viewed, and must invariably be viewed, in the same way." The same rule was laid down in *Rex* v. *Creevey*,[1] and there are other authorities to the same effect; but it is unnecessary for me to do more than to express my concurrence with the judgment of Bayley, J., from which I have quoted.

With respect to the circumstances of the present case, I may add that there is a further ground for the exclusion of the privilege. The book now before us publishes in detail offensive passages which were not read aloud at the trial. The outer cover of some of the copies does not even allude to the trial, while it does call attention to the offensive matters contained within. It appears to me pretty clear that the book, as a whole, was not intended to be merely a fair report of a trial, but a means of reproducing the offensive publication under the guise of a report of the prosecution of Mackey for such publication. On these grounds I

[1] Law Rep. 3 Q.B. 360.
[2] 3 B. & A. 167.
[1] 1 M. & S. 273.

think it was clearly not privileged, and that our judgment must be for the respondent.

KEATING, J. I am of the same opinion. The book called the "Confessional Unmasked," purports to be a selection from the works of Roman Catholic divines, containing directions for priests in the conduct of the confessional. These extracts, if correct, do appear to me to contain obscenity of a nature from which any mind of ordinary decency must revolt. The appellant contends, through his counsel, that he was entitled to discuss this subject. I agree that such a subject might be one of importance and one which it might be right to discuss as such. But the appellant's counsel went on to contend that it was impossible to discuss it with effect without setting out the extracts to which objection is taken. It was contended that if this was so, and the object was not to pollute the public mind, but to conduct an effective controversy as to a matter of public importance, the publication of these extracts was no misdemeanour at common law. It may be assumed, for the purposes of argument, that the object of the parties was a meritorious one as alleged, but I agree with my Lord Chief Justice that they are not entitled, in order to accomplish such an object, to set forth matter which in itself has a tendency to corrupt the morals of the public. To adopt the argument for the appellant would be, in truth, to adopt the doctrine assailed in argument by the appellant's counsel and to allow evil to be done that good might follow. It would be strange indeed that in order to prevent the pollution of the public morals the law should allow pollution to be circulated. It was asked, in argument, what remedy there was against works similar to those from which the extracts given in the pamphlet are taken. No such work is now before us judicially, and I pronounce no opinion therefore with respect to any such. It is enough to say that it does not follow that because it is a misdemeanour to publish the present pamphlet that it would not also be a misdemeanour to publish such works as those referred to. In any case, they can afford no argument to justify the present publication. The question then arises whether this book is privileged as a report of proceedings in a court of justice. It is only necessary on this subject to refer to the extract cited by my Lord from Starkie on Libel. The freedom of the press with relation to the proceedings of courts of justice is, doubtless, of the highest importance, and the law does its utmost to protect such freedom, but the law would be self-contradictory if it made the publication of an indecent work an indictable offence and yet sanctioned the republication of such a work under cover of its being part of the proceedings in a court of justice.

For these reasons I think our judgment must be for the respondent, and, I may add, that with respect to the question whether the publication of this book was a misdemeanour, apart from the question of privilege, it appears to me that this case is clearly within the decision in *Reg.* v. *Hicklin*[1] to which, apart from the opinion at which I have arrived from the reason of the thing, I feel bound to defer.

GROVE, J. I am of the same opinion. With respect to the question whether the publication of this book would, apart from any question of privilege, be a misdemeanour, I

[1] Law Rep. 3 Q.B. 360.

think the case is clearly within the decision in *Reg.* v. *Hicklin*.[1] We ought not, it seems to me, except upon the strongest grounds, to dissent from that decision. I can see no reason why we should not adopt it. I would only make one remark with relation to it. I do not take the case as involving the proposition against which Mr. Kydd, in his argument, I think rightly, contended, viz. that the intention which really actuated a person is always to be conclusively deduced from the character of the act itself. The effect of the judgment below as a whole seems to me to be that when, from the act committed, an immediate intention of a particular character would be implied the party doing the act is not exempted by reason of some other paramount intention of a different description, which actually operated upon his mind. The only question, therefore, would appear to be, what is the intention which may be fairly implied from the act of offering for indiscriminate sale a work dealing with subjects of a filthy nature.

Then it is urged that this was a substantially correct report of a trial. If it were permissible to publish a report of a trial, in which the question was whether certain matter was obscene, and the publication of it a misdemeanour, and to reproduce the whole of such disgusting matter under the cover of such report, the result would be that the person publishing an obscene work would only have to be brought before a court of justice for such publication, in order to entitle him to republish the same matter with perfect impunity. His trial would frustrate the very purpose which it had in view, viz. the putting a stop to the publication of such matter. This consideration appears to me to reduce the appellant's contention to an absurdity. I should, therefore, have no difficulty in coming to the conclusion that this book is not privileged without the aid of authority, but, if any were necessary, *Rex* v. *Carlile*[1] is a distinct authority on the subject. It has been urged that the only effectual remedy at the disposal of parties who bonâ fide wish to expose and counteract the effects of works such as those from which the extracts contained in this pamphlet are taken, is to republish them. There is a simple remedy alluded to by my Brother Keating. The question whether the publication of such works is admissible may be made the subject of a prosecution. I express no opinion as to the character of any of the works alluded to in argument; but I make this remark to shew that the parties objecting to such publications are not without a remedy. Upon such a prosecution the matter would be discussed only before the Court and the jury. It cannot be permissible that persons wishing to expose doctrines of an immoral and pernicious tendency, should give an indiscriminate publicity to details of the nature which the pamphlet now in question contains.

Judgment for the respondent.

Attorney for appellant: *Ellerton.*
Attorney for respondent: *Solicitor to the Treasury.*

---

[1] 3 B. & A. 167.

■ Charles Bradlaugh and Annie Besant
v.
The Queen.

Error upon a judgment of the Queen's Bench Division.[1]

The record alleged that at the Central Criminal Court an indictment was presented against the plaintiffs in error, the first count of which was in the following terms:—

"Central Criminal Court, to wit: The jurors for Our Lady the Queen, upon their oath present, that Charles Bradlaugh and Annie Besant unlawfully and wickedly devising, contriving, and intending as much as in them lay to vitiate and corrupt the morals as well of youth as of divers other liege subjects of our said Lady the Queen, and to incite and encourage the said liege subjects to indecent, obscene, unnatural, and immoral practices, and bring them to a state of wickedness, lewdness, and debauchery, heretofore, to wit, on the 24th day of March, in the year of Our Lord, 1877, in the City of London, and within the jurisdiction of the said Central Criminal Court, unlawfully, wickedly, knowingly, wilfully, and designedly, did print, publish, sell, and utter a certain indecent, lewd, filthy, and obscene libel, to wit, a certain indecent, lewd, filthy, bawdy, and obscene book called 'Fruits of Philosophy,' thereby con-taminating, vitiating, and corrupting the morals as well of youth as of other liege subjects of our said Lady the Queen, and bringing the said liege subjects to a state of wickedness, lewdness, debauchery, and immorality, in contempt of our said Lady the Queen and her laws, to the evil and pernicious example of all others in the like case offending, and against the peace of our said Lady the Queen, her crown, and dignity."

The second and only other count was precisely similar, except that the date of the alleged offence was the 29th of March, 1877. The record then set forth the removal of the indictment into the Queen's Bench Division, by a writ specifying Middlesex as the county and jurisdiction in which the indictment was to be tried, the plea of not guilty by the plaintiffs in error, the joinder of issue thereon by F. Cockburn, as the Queen's coroner and attorney, and the award of jury process. The record afterwards alleged, amongst other matters unnecessary to be mentioned, that on the 18th of June, 1877, before Cockburn, C.J., a jury was impanelled and sworn, and a verdict of guilty was found against both the plaintiffs in error. The record afterwards proceeded as follows: "And because the Court of Our Lady the Queen now here, to wit, the Queen's Bench

---

[1] 2 Q.B.D. 569.

Division of the High Court of Justice, is not as yet advised about giving their judgment of and upon the premises whereof the said Charles Bradlaugh and Annie Besant are so convicted as aforesaid, day is therefore given as well to the said F. Cockburn, Esq., who for our said Lady the Queen in this behalf prosecuteth, as to the said Charles Bradlaugh and Annie Besant, until the 28th day of June, in the 41st year of the reign of Our Lady the Queen, before our said Lady the Queen, at Westminster, that is to say, before the Queen's Bench Division of the High Court of Justice, to hear their judgment thereupon."

The record then alleged that on the 28th of June it was adjudged and ordered by the Queen's Bench Division, upon each of the counts of the indictment, that the plaintiffs in error should be severally imprisoned for six calendar months, and should severally pay a fine of 200*l*., and should severally give security for good behaviour for two years.

Error having been brought, the following were alleged as the grounds thereof:—

(I.) That the indictment shews no offence known to the law, and does not warrant the conviction and sentence.

(II.) That the libel in question was professedly a work on medical science and political economy, and that in the indictment in which the said work is alleged to be "an indecent, lewd, filthy, and obscene libel," such portions of the work as were libellous as aforesaid ought to have been set out.

(III.) That the indictment does not shew any specific offence, and that the particular words supposed to be criminal ought to have been expressly specified and set forth in the indictment.

The Queen's coroner and attorney joined in error.

Jan. 29, 30, 31. The plaintiff in error, *Bradlaugh*, in person. The omission to set out the book in the indictment renders it bad; whenever words formed the ground of complaint in an action of law, they must have been set out in the declaration: *Zenobio* v. *Axtell*,[1] *Cook* v. *Cox*,[2] *Wright* v. *Clements*;[3] and this rule also applies to criminal cases: Archbold's Crim. Pl. and Evid. bk. i. pt. 1. ch. 1, s. 3 (ed. 18), p. 58. In *Rex* v. *Sparling*,[4] where the defendant was convicted of profane cursing and swearing under 6 & 7 Wm. 3, c. 11, the conviction was held bad because the curses and oaths were not set out, and *Rex* v. *Popplewell*[5] is to the like effect. In *Hunter's Case*[6] an indictment for forgery was held bad under the then existing law, because the words alleged to be forged were insufficiently described. In *Rex* v. *Mason*[7] it was held to be a fatal objection that the indictment did not disclose the nature of the false pretences, and this case has not been overruled by *Reg.* v. *Goldsmith*,[8] in which the indictment was for unlawfully receiving goods knowing them to have been obtained by a false pretence. In a libel, the words complained of constitute the crime, and it is a rule of criminal pleading, that "whatever circumstances are necessary to constitute the

crime imputed must be set out:" *Rex* v. *Horne*;[9] and the jury are entitled to judge for themselves whether the interpretation put upon the words in the indictment is the meaning intended to be conveyed in the libel: *Rex* v. *Fitzharris*;[10] and any variance between the meaning alleged and the meaning proved will be fatal: Russell on Crimes, vol. iii. bk. 5, ch. 3, s. 13, 5th ed. p. 219, citing *Tabart* v. *Tipper*,[11] and *Rex* v. *Bear*.[12] Before the Queen's Bench Division,[1] for the Crown reliance was placed upon *Dr. Sacheverell's Case*;[2] but that case is really a very strong authority against this prosecution, for the judges present were unanimously of opinion that by the laws of England and constant practice in all prosecutions by indictment or information for crimes and misdemeanours by writing or speaking, the particular words supposed to be criminal must be expressly specified in the indictment or information.[3] This proposition is really identical with the contention of the plaintiffs in error. It is true that the House of Lords decided[4] that in a prosecution by impeachment it was unnecessary to set out the words complained of in the articles of impeachment; but then it may well be that proceedings in Parliament are governed by different rules from proceedings in courts of criminal law. In *Rex* v. *Layer*[5] the judges overruled an objection that in an indictment for high treason the words complained of must be set out; but the real explanation of that decision is that in high treason words are not the gist of the offence, but merely evidence or proof of it: Archbold's Crim. Pl. and Evid. bk. i. pt. 1, ch. 1, s. 3 (ed. 18), p. 58. In *Rex* v. *Curll*,[6] which appears to be the first case where an obscene libel was punished in the temporal courts, the passages complained of were set out. The necessity of setting out the libellous matter correctly is pointed out in Folkard on Slander and Libel, ch. 42, p. 699. Before the Queen's Bench Division the counsel for the Crown relied upon *The Commonwealth* v. *Sharpless*,[7] and *The Commonwealth* v. *Holmes*;[8] but the rule in the American courts is that if the obscene libel is omitted it must be averred that it is too gross to be inserted in the indictment: *The Commonwealth* v. *Tarbox*;[9] and no averment of that kind here occurs. Moreover, those authorities may be dismissed with the remark that they are the decisions of the tribunals of a foreign country, and that the validity of the present indictment depends upon the common law of England. A total omission of a necessary averment is not cured at common law by the verdict: *Hearne* v. *Stowell*;[1] and as the indictment was not intended to relate to an offence either created or regulated by statute, the prosecution can-

---

[1] 6 T.R. 162.
[2] 3 M. & S. 110.
[3] 3 B. & Ald. 503.
[4] 1 Str. 498.
[5] 2 Str. 686.
[6] 2 Lea. C.C. 624.
[7] 2 T.R. 581.
[8] Law Rep. 2 C.C. 74.

[9] 20 How. St. Tr. 792; per De Grey, C.J., delivering the unanimous opinion of the judges in the House of Lords.
[10] 8 How. St. Tr. 356.
[11] 1 Camp. 352.
[12] 2 Salk. 417.
[1] 2 Q.B.D. 571.
[2] 15 How. St. Tr. 1.
[3] 15 How. St. Tr. 466, 467.
[4] 15 How. St. Tr. 467, 473.
[5] 6 Har. St. Tr. 328, 329, 330, 331; 16 How. St. Tr. 315, 316, 317, 318.
[6] 2 Str. 788; 17 How. St. Tr. 154.
[7] 2 Ser. & Raw. (Pennsylvania), 91.
[8] 17 Massachusetts, 336.
[9] 1 Cush. (Massachusetts), 66.
[1] 12 Ad. & E. 719.

not rely upon the latter clause of 7 Geo. 4, c. 64, s. 21. The defect is not of a merely formal nature, and therefore the objection holds good, although this is not an appeal from a decision upon demurrer or upon a motion to quash the indictment before the jury were sworn: 14 & 15 Vict. c. 100, s. 25; *Sill* v. *Reg.*[2]

Annie Besant, plaintiff in error, in person. According to the English precedents the indictment is bad for uncertainty; and the decisions in the American courts were pronounced by foreign tribunals and cannot countervail the current of authorities in England. The indictment alleges simply that the book is obscene: this is a hardship upon the plaintiffs in error, for they could not tell whether the whole of the book or only portions of it would be relied upon as obscene: if the words complained of were set out in the indictment, they would have known what charge they were called upon to meet.

Sir H. S. Giffard, S.G., for the Crown. The indictment discloses an offence at common law, and the objection is only that the facts constituting the crime are imperfectly averred: this defect is cured by the verdict. *Rex* v. *Mason*[3] can hardly be deemed to be good law after *Reg.* v. *Goldsmith;*[4] but if it can be supported it is distinguishable, for the indictment charged the defendant with obtaining money by "false pretences:" now false pretences relating to future events are not indictable, and the indictment was therefore uncertain; but the publication of an obscene book is always indictable, whatever the motive of the person publishing it may be.[5] In *Heymann* v. *Reg.*[6] it was held that a defective averment in an indictment for conspiracy was cured by the verdict of guilty. In *Rex* v. *Bishop of Llandaff*[7] it was held that an omission to allege a presentation was cured by the verdict, and as is pointed out in Serjeant Williams' note to *Stennel* v. *Hogg,*[1] the decision proceeded upon the ground of the common law. Upon a similar principle a declaration, which simply charged the defendant with maliciously prosecuting the plaintiff for perjury, was held good after verdict: *Pippet* v. *Hearn.*[2] The recent decision in this Court of *Reg.* v. *Aspinall*[3] strongly supports the principle laid down in *Heymann* v. *Reg.*[4] An indictment for keeping a disorderly house may be framed in general terms, and no valid reason exists why greater strictness should be required as to an indictment for an obscene libel. The defect being only formal, it is now too late to raise any objection to it: 14 & 15 Vict. c. 100, s. 25; and it may be admitted for the Crown that the indictment would be held bad upon demurrer.

[BRAMWELL, L.J. If the defect were only formal, it might have been amended by the Court; but how could the Court direct the officer to amend the indictment, and thereby make it charge that the grand jury had presented as obscene those portions of the book, which the presiding judge considered to be obscene?]

Even in high treason the words complained of need not be stated: *Rex* v. *Stayley;*[5] *Rex* v. *Layer.*[6] In *Dugdale* v. *Reg.,*[7] the objection was not taken that the obscene words and prints must be set out in the indictment, and this case forms strong negative evidence that the present indictment contains all that is necessary. In many offences it is not necessary that the indictment should state the offence with particularity; thus, in *Rex* v. *Gill,*[8] an indictment charging the defendants with conspiring by false pretences to obtain money was held good. The defect being an imperfect averment only, the cases as to the effect of a total omission, such as *Reg.* v. *Gray,*[9] do not apply: the difference between an imperfect averment and a total omission is pointed out in *Reg.* v. *Aspinall.*[10]

F. Mead, for the Crown. It is unnecessary in an indictment for an obscene libel to set out the words complained of, and no objection can be taken to their omission even upon demurrer, or by motion to quash. The authorities relied upon by the plaintiffs in error relate to defamatory libels; and the publication of a blasphemous, seditious, or defamatory libel is an offence standing upon a different footing from the publication of an obscene libel: thus, by 5 & 6 Vict. c. 38, courts of quarter sessions are forbidden to try blasphemous, seditious, or defamatory libels, but they are not prohibited from trying obscene libels. In *Dugdale* v. *Reg.,*[1] decided after the passing of that statute, the indictment contained counts for obscene libels, and the prisoner was found guilty thereon at the Middlesex sessions. *Rex* v. *Curll*[2] merely established that the publication of an obscene book is indictable as an offence contra bonos mores, and punishable in the temporal courts; it was not decided that it is an offence of the same nature and subject to the same rules as a defamatory, blasphemous, or seditious libel. The offence charged upon this indictment is like that contained in the indictment in *Rex* v. *Sedley,*[3] and it is not a libel in the true sense of the word: it is more like the offence of common nuisance. It is, therefore, unnecessary that the words should be set out; and although there may be no decisions in the English courts to that effect, yet the precedents in 2 Chitty's Criminal Law, ch. 3, pp. 43, 45, shew that the words may be omitted: it is true that this indictment, unlike those precedents, does not contain an averment that the matters contained in the book are too gross to be set out; but that defect is cured by the verdict; and at all events, the omission of that averment is supplied by the description of the book as "an indecent, lewd, filthy, and obscene libel." The cases in the American courts clearly support the argument for the Crown: thus, in *The Commonwealth* v. *Sharpless,*[4] it was held to be unnecessary to set out an indecent picture

---

[2] 1 E. & B. 553; 22 L.J. (M.C.) 41.
[3] 2 T.R. 581.
[4] Law Rep. 2 C.C. 74.
[5] See *Reg.* v. *Hicklin*, Law Rep. 3 Q.B. 360; and *Steele* v. *Brannan*, Law Rep. 7 C.P. 261.
[6] Law Rep. 8 Q.B. 102.
[7] 2 Str. 1006.
[1] 1 Notes to Saunders by Williams, 260, at p. 267.
[2] 5 B. & Ald. 634.
[3] 2 Q.B.D. 48.
[4] Law Rep. 8 Q.B. 102.

[5] 6 How. St. Tr. 1501.
[6] 16 How. St. Tr. 315, 316, 317, 318.
[7] 1 E. & B. 435.
[8] 2 B. & Ald. 204.
[9] L. & C. 365; 33 L.J. (M.C.) 78.
[10] 2 Q.B.D. 48, at p. 58.
[1] See the report in Dearsley, 64, where the indictment is set out in full.
[2] 2 Str. 788.
[3] 1 Sid. 168; 1 Keb. 620; 17 How. St. Tr. 155.
[4] 2 Serg. & Rawl. (Pennsylvania), 91.

in an indictment, and *The Commonwealth* v. *Holmes*,[5] and *The People* v. *Girardin*,[6] and *The Commonwealth* v. *Tarbox*,[7] shew that the words of an obscene libel may be omitted if they are so foul as to defile the records of the Court.

Plaintiff in error, *Bradlaugh*, in reply. The defect consists in an entire omission of a necessary averment. *Heymann* v. *Reg.*[1] is not in point; for the offence there charged was a conspiracy to defeat the operation of a statute; here the offence is regulated solely by the common law. In *Rex* v. *Wilkes*[2] the passages complained of in the Essay on Woman appear to have been set out in the information. *Rex* v. *Sedley*[3] stands upon a totally different footing from the present case. It is submitted that all prosecutions for libel are subject to the same rules, whether the words are defamatory, blasphemous, seditious, or obscene. The general words of the indictment would apply to any book which is in any degree obscene.[4]

Plaintiff in error, *Annie Besant*, in reply. In order to establish that the words ought to have been set out in the present indictment, it is necessary only to cite the following cases: as to a seditious libel, *Rex* v. *Paine*;[5] as to a blasphemous libel, *Rex* v. *Williams*;[6] and to an obscene libel, *Rex* v. *Curll*.[7]

Cur. adv. vult.

Feb. 12. BRAMWELL, L.J. This case comes before us upon a question of substantial importance, but nevertheless of a purely technical nature, and the decision which we have to pronounce is quite apart from the merits, and quite apart from the consideration whether any wrong has or has not been done to the plaintiffs in error.

The question has arisen under the following circumstances:—An indictment was preferred against the plaintiffs in error charging them with publishing an obscene libel, "to wit, a certain indecent, lewd, filthy, and obscene book called 'Fruits of Philosophy;' " upon this indictment they were found guilty. They afterwards moved the Queen's Bench Division in arrest of judgment, and the rule which they asked for was refused; and the question before us is whether the judges of that Court were right in refusing that rule, or whether they ought to have granted it. The objection taken was that the indictment stated, but

---

[5] 17 Massachusetts, 336.
[6] 1 Mann. (Michigan), 90.
[7] 1 Cush. (Massachusetts) 66.
[1] Law Rep. 8 Q.B. 102.
[2] 4 Burr. 2527; 19 How. St. Tr. 1075.
[3] 1 Sid. 168; 1 Keb. 620; 17 How. St. Tr. 155.
[4] The plaintiff in error, *Bradlaugh*, also argued that the judgment in the Queen's Bench Division was erroneous on the ground that the trial having taken place on the 18th of June was held upon a day which, under the practice existing before the Judicature Acts, would have fallen in the sittings after Trinity Term, and that the continuance should have been to a day in what would have been the following Michaelmas Term, and not to the 28th of June. The Court intimated that the argument was unsustainable, the Judicature Act, 1873, s. 26, having abolished terms except for the purpose of computing time. They, however, gave no judgment upon this objection, as the decision of the main question rendered it unnecessary to consider it. See 11 Geo. 4 & 1 Wm. 4, c. 70, s. 9.
[5] 22 How. St. Tr. 357.
[6] 26 How. St. Tr. 653.
[7] 2 Str. 788; 17 How. St. Tr. 153.

did not shew, that an offence had been committed; or, as it may be put in somewhat different language, the objection was that the indictment simply averred that an offence had been committed, and did not shew how it had been committed. For the Crown it was almost admitted by the Solicitor General that if the objection had been taken by demurrer, it would have been good; but it was urged that it was cured by the verdict, on the ground that the jury could not have found the plaintiffs in error guilty, unless an obscene libel had been proved at the trial to have been published by them.

It is undoubtedly a rule that an indictment for any offence must shew that the offence has been committed, and must shew how it has been committed; and if these particulars are omitted judgment will be arrested. No doubt that is the general rule; and I do not intend to allude to alterations made by statute as to criminal pleading, because no statute is applicable to this case; therefore in the observations which I shall make as to the form of indictments, I shall speak as if the common law were unaltered. It is not enough to indict a person for that he committed murder, or murdered A. B.; at common law it must be shewn what he did; so that if the acts charged are proved to have been perpetrated, it would be shewn that he committed murder; in other words, it is not enough to allege that he committed the crime, it must be shewn how he committed it. Similarly in an indictment for burglary, it is not enough to allege that the accused committed a burglary, or to allege that he committed a burglary at the house of A.; it must be charged that he burglariously entered between certain hours, with other circumstances shewing how the crime was committed, and those facts must be stated which constitute the crime said to have been committed. For this rule three reasons were assigned, two of which I do not think very important, at all events, at the present time; but the third is of a more substantial character. One of these reasons was, that the person indicted for the commission of a crime might know what charge he had to meet; if he were charged with murder or burglary generally, he would not know what particular act was alleged against him, and what he had to meet. Another reason was that, if convicted or acquitted on an indictment of that kind, the accused could not plead or prove, with the same facility as otherwise he might, a plea of autrefois convict or autrefois acquit. At the present day, I think those two reasons may be disregarded, because an accused person is very rarely ignorant of the charge which he is called upon to meet, and no real difficulty exists as to pleading or proving a former conviction or acquittal. But even as to these reasons I must admit that a very plausible observation was made by the female plaintiff in error, namely that the book, as a whole, was charged as an offence against her, and she could not possibly tell what passages would be selected as those on which the charge was to be supported. The third reason, in my opinion, is to this day substantial, and cannot be disregarded. It was that a defendant is entitled to take the opinion of the Court before which he is indicted by demurrer, or by motion in arrest of judgment, or the opinion of a Court of Error by writ of error, on the sufficiency of the statements in the indictment. It is true that a defendant has the decision of the judge presiding at the trial as to the validity of the indictment, yet it is not unreasonable that he should be at liberty in some way to question the decision of that judge.

But whether these three reasons were good or bad, they clearly existed with reference to the form of indictment, which accordingly, as I have already intimated, must shew not only that the accused committed the offence, but must also state the facts which constituted it.

In some instances, words are the subject-matter of an indictment; and it follows from this principle, which I have mentioned, that wherever the offence consists of words written or spoken, those words must be stated in the indictment; if they are not, it will be defective upon demurrer, in arrest of judgment or upon writ of error. For instance, upon an indictment for perjury, it was necessary that the facts constituting the perjury should be set forth, and that necessity existed until 23 Geo. 2, c. 11. The authorities will be found in 2 Chitty's Crim. Law, ch. 9, p. 307, 2nd ed. That statute recited the extreme difficulty of getting convictions for perjury by reason of difficulties attending the prosecutions for them, and effected an alteration whereby the offence was allowed to be stated in a more general way. In like manner, upon an indictment for forgery it was necessary to set out the words of the forged instrument, as appears from 3 Chitty's Crim. Law, ch. 15, p. 1040, 2nd ed. In like manner, there can be no doubt that in an indictment for defamatory libel it was necessary to set out the words complained of, so that the Court might judge whether they were or could amount to a libel. Now, in support of this doctrine, I will refer to *Cook v. Cox.*[1] The action was for slander, and after a general verdict for the plaintiff a motion was made in arrest of judgment, on an objection to the last count, which did not set out the words complained of. Lord Ellenborough, C.J., in delivering the judgment of the Court, said:[2] "The objection is, that in a count for slander by words the words themselves should be set out, in order that the defendant may know the certainty of the charge, and may be able to shape his defence, either on the general issue, or by plea of justification accordingly, and that this defect is not cured by verdict." Now, that is what his Lordship states to be the objection. Then he says:[3] "The allegation then amounts to this; that the defendant by words, or by words coupled with acts, slandered the plaintiff in his trade, and therefore it is bad, and not cured by verdict, as a charge in the alternative. But supposing it to be taken as a charge of oral slander only, the weight of authorities is against the setting out words by their effect only. This count is equivalent to an allegation that the defendant used certain words to the effect of imputing insolvency to the plaintiff." Lord Ellenborough then goes on to cite the authorities, beginning with *Newton v. Stubbs*,[1] which he says, "is an express authority that a count for using words to the effect following, &c., is bad after verdict," and he cites a variety of other cases, amongst them, *Dr. Sacheverell's Case*,[2] and he says:[3] "There seems to be no reason for any difference in this respect between civil and criminal cases; the action arises *ex delicto*." And, most certainly, if there was a difference, it would be that less strictness is required in civil than in criminal cases. Then he proceeds, after

mentioning another case: "Unless the very words are set out, by which the charge is conveyed, it is almost, if not entirely, impossible to plead a recovery in one action in bar of a subsequent action for the same cause. Identity may be predicated with certainty of words, but not of the effect of them as produced upon the mind of a hearer. It has been said that this is not like the case of a defective title, but is more analogous to that of a title defectively set out. If, however, the authorities cited are law, and they are supported by more ancient ones, it is of the substance of a charge for slander by words that the words themselves should be set out with sufficient innuendoes, and a sufficient explanation, if required, to make them intelligible; it is of the substance of a charge of slander of any sort that it should not be laid in the alternative. Upon the whole, we think that this count is so defective in substance, that no intendment can be made to supply its defects from what can be presumed to have passed at the trial; and consequently that the judgment must be arrested." Now, that was the opinion of the Court of King's Bench, in an action for slander. I may mention that that case is referred to and recognise in *Solomon v. Lawson*,[4] in which it was held that where a declaration for a libel set out a publication which referred to a previous publication, but, unless by reference to the language of the previous publication, contained no libel, such previous publication must be considered as incorporated in the publication complained of, and must appear in the declaration to be set out verbatim, and not merely in substance. It is true that these two cases relate to actions at law, and the first is an action for slander. But, as was said by Mr. Justice Blackburn, in *Heymann v. Reg.*,[1] at common law there is no difference between civil and criminal pleading except that, as I have before intimated, according to the spirit in which our law is administered, if there were a difference, more strictness would be required in criminal than in civil pleading. On these authorities it is manifest that where words constitute the offence, they must be stated in the indictment; and the authorities distinctly shew that where a defamatory libel is complained of, as was almost admitted by the Solicitor General, it must be stated in the indictment. It seems to me that whatever reason there is for setting out the words of a defamatory libel, is equally applicable to other writings that are called libels; though possibly, as Mr. Mead argued, they are called libels in a different sense from that in which defamatory writing is called a libel. Lord Justice Brett has collected authorities upon the matter. I do not know that there is any case in which judgment has been arrested on an indictment or information for a seditious, a blasphemous, or an obscene libel for want of setting out the words. But no precedent can be found in which they have not been set out, except in certain American cases, to which I shall presently refer; and except in two precedents in 2 Chitty's Crim. Law, pp. 43, 45, with which also I will deal, when I come to the American cases; and then there has been no judgment in an English Court of justice that they need not be set out, and no decision that the indictment will not be bad in arrest of judgment; and I repeat that whatever reason can be given for setting out the very words in defamatory libels, is equally true in blasphemous,

---

[1] 3 M. & S. 110.
[2] Page 113.
[3] Page 114.
[1] 2 Show. 435.
[2] 5 Har. St. Tr. 828; S.C. 15 How. St. Tr. 466, 467.
[3] Page 116.

[4] 8 Q.B. 823, at p. 839.
[1] Law Rep. 8 Q.B. 102, at p. 105.

obscene, or seditious libels. First, I will cite *Rex* v. *Curll*,[2] where it was held that an obscene book is punishable as a libel in the temporal courts, and I will mention *Rex* v. *Sparling*,[3] in which it was held that a conviction for cursing and swearing was bad, because it did not set out the words which had been used.

That being the general principle, we must deal with the argument that obscene libels need not be, and indeed ought not to be, set forth on the record; the reason given being that the records of the court should not be defiled by any indecency of that kind. Speaking with the greatest respect to those who have thought otherwise, I think the objection fanciful and imaginary. The records of a court of justice are not read with a view to entertainment or amusement; and if the objection has any weight, why does it not apply to other libels, and to other offences? I suppose the majority of mankind would think much worse of a blasphemous libel than even of an obscene libel, and would consider it much more objectionable that the terms of the former should be perpetuated than those of the latter. I suppose excellent reasons could be given why seditious language, possibly alluding disrespectfully to the Sovereign, should not be perpetuated on the court rolls. But there is another kind of libels, which, to my mind, if it were possible, ought to be effaced from the rolls, and yet it is admitted that they must be set out on the record—I mean libels defaming the character of a private person. Let us see which is the worst in its consequences. Suppose a man indicted for a libel charging an infamous crime against another. It must be set out upon the record, for it is a defamatory libel. Then the defendant may never plead, or may not be arrested, or he may die, and thus the charge may never be tried, and yet that statement is to remain on the record for all time, and no answer will be given to it. In some respects it would be well that such an imputation as that should be effaced from the records of the court—an imputation so grievous to the individual and all connected with him. However, the argument as to this point on the part of the Crown was supported by authority. The only semblance of authority in English law was the precedents which I have mentioned. We are in the habit of looking at precedents as containing the law; but that is when there is a series of them, so that we may be sure that they would not be in existence or perpetuated unless they had received the sanction of the courts; these are in truth but one precedent, and therefore I do not think I need pay much attention to them. In support of this contention for the Crown, some American cases were cited. Decisions in the Courts of the United States are not binding authorities; and although they may be expressly in point, yet if they are contrary to our law, they must be disregarded. Whatever respect we may be disposed to pay to the judge who pronounced the decision, the only manner in which an American case can be used as a guide is to consider it as the expression of the opinion of an able person acquainted with the general spirit of our law; and therefore we may look at it in much the same way, as we may consider the decisions of the judges of French, Italian, or other courts who have pronounced opinions upon mercantile law, which to a certain extent is common to ourselves. But I do not think that the American cases cited before us assist the

case for the prosecution. It seems to have been assumed in the Queen's Bench Division that *The Commonwealth* v. *Holmes*[1] shewed that generally an obscene libel need not be set forth in terms; but the plaintiff in error, Bradlaugh, has produced before us *The Commonwealth* v. *Tarbox*,[2] which was not cited in the Court below. In that case the indictment was held to be good without setting forth the obscene words, because there was an allegation that the libel was so obscene that it could not be, with decency and propriety, put upon the record. The rule in the American courts appears to be that when there is no allegation excusing the statement of the words on the record, on the ground of what may be called their infamy, they must be set out. In *The People* v. *Girardin*[3] a vigorous and forcible judgment was pronounced in favour of the view now put forward on behalf of the Crown; but even in that case some description of the nature of the obscenity complained of was inserted in the indictment. Here the indictment does not allege that the words are too obscene to be inserted; and therefore in any point of view the American cases assist the argument for the plaintiffs in error. It was suggested that the insertion of the words complained of is sufficiently excused, because it is averred that the plaintiffs in error published "a certain indecent, lewd, filthy, and obscene libel." That was very well met with this argument: Would not those words be the proper prefatory description of every obscene libel? and that in order to bring this indictment within the authority of the American cases it would have been necessary to aver that the libel was so utterly indecent, filthy, lewd, and obscene that it ought not to appear on the records of the court. For the prosecution reliance was placed also on *Dugdale* v. *The Queen*,[1] but the decision in that case does not affect the rule of law laid down in previous authorities.

We are not asked to say that the law is altered, because no power can alter it but the legislature; and it is not pretended that the legislature has altered it. What in effect we are called upon to do is, to say that the law has been mistaken and misunderstood, and that it is not necessary to set forth words when they constitute a crime. Reliance has been placed upon certain cases as to the law relating to false pretences, in which it has been held that after verdict judgment could be arrested, although the false pretence had not been stated. Now I do not think it necessary to go critically into those cases. I do not suggest for a moment that they were not rightly decided, but I wish to make this observation about them, namely, that they are cases in which the courts have held, rightly or wrongly, that the defect was not a failure to state the ingredients of the offence, but they were cases in which those ingredients had been imperfectly stated. This distinction is explained in the judgment of Blackburn, J., in *Heymann* v. *The Queen*,[2] where he says: "The objection to the count therefore is that it does not state that the agreement or confederacy was in contemplation or expectation of an adjudication; and if the question had arisen upon demurrer, I am not quite prepared to say that that might not have been a good objection. But it is a general rule of pleading

---

[2] 2 Str. 788.
[3] 1 Str. 497.

[1] 17 Massachusetts, 336.
[2] 1 Cush. (Massachusetts), 66.
[3] 1 Mann. (Michigan), 90.
[1] 1 E. & B. 435; 22 L.J. (M.C.) 50; Dears. 64.
[2] Law Rep. 8 Q.B. 102, at p. 105.

at common law—and I think it necessary to say where there is a question of pleading at common law there is no distinction between the pleadings in civil cases and criminal cases— where an averment, which is necessary for the support of the pleading, is imperfectly stated, and the verdict on an issue involving that averment is found, if it appears to the Court after verdict that the verdict could not have been found on this issue without proof of this averment, there, after verdict, the defective averment, which might have been bad on demurrer, is cured by the verdict." That rule was held to apply in *Reg.* v. *Gold-smith.*[3] The prisoner was indicted for receiving goods, knowing them to have been obtained by means of false and fraudulent pretences, which were not set out; she was convicted, and the Court for Crown Cases Reserved held the conviction must be affirmed. I concurred in thinking that the judgment ought not to be arrested, and my reason for so thinking was, that it was impossible that if the false pretence used by the principal offender had been proved at the trial to be a future promise, or a matter of opinion, the judge would have let that case go to the jury. A false pretence primâ facie imports not a promise, but a misrepresentation as to something existing. These are the only observations which I shall make about this case; but whether it was rightly or wrongly decided, it is impossible that the judges who decided that case could have intended to lay down a different law from that, which had been established by previous authorities. It is the duty of judges to administer the law as they find it, and to leave the legislature to amend whatever defects there may be. Therefore, even if this case may appear to be difficult to reconcile in principle with previous cases, it does not overrule the current of authorities, which shew that the offence, and the facts constituting the offence, must be stated; that where those facts consist in words, the words must be set forth; and that if they be not, the indictment is bad, either on demurrer, or in arrest of judgment, or upon a writ of error.

Before concluding I ought to consider the reasons given by the judges of the Queen's Bench Division for the opinion they expressed, and I need scarcely say that I entertain the greatest respect for their decision. I think the Lord Chief Justice gives three reasons. First, he thinks it would be inconvenient to set out in an indictment the whole of a book alleged to be obscene, if in its entirety it is made the subject of a prosecution, and he alludes to the inconvenience of setting out in extenso the whole of a publication which may consist of two or three volumes.[1] With great submission to the Lord Chief Justice, I think it very unlikely that a work contained in many volumes will ever be published, the obscenity of which cannot be made apparent without the whole being set out in the indictment. But if the question of convenience were to determine whether the libel is to be set out, it would be necessary to adopt some rule, and that rule would probably be that the words of a libel need not be set out when it is very long. But then it would be very difficult to determine what length would render it unnecessary to set out the libel; would two volumes be too many, would one volume, 100 pages, or what other amount? It may be a great inconvenience that a long libel should be put upon the record; but

whatever the inconvenience may be, it seems to me that upon an indictment for private defamation, blasphemy, obscenity, or sedition, where the objection is to the whole, and not to a part, the whole must be set out.

The next reason assigned by the Lord Chief Justice was that the objection ought to have been taken by demurrer.[1] It might be more convenient for the administration of justice to enact that if a man will not take an objection to an indictment by demurrer, he shall not be at liberty to take it by motion in arrest of judgment, or by error. I think that many reasons can be urged in favour of limiting the power to take advantage of technical defects, but that is a matter to be considered by the legislature, and the answer which I have to give to the second reason assigned by the Lord Chief Justice is that the law of the land, as it at present stands, allows technical objections to an indictment to be taken upon arrest of judgment or by writ of error.

Then the Lord Chief Justice proceeds to mention the third objection, namely,[2] that "although the subject-matter of this indictment falls within the law of libel, it to a certain extent arises out of the general law as being commune nocumentum, a matter complaint as to which arises from its being subversive of public morals, and therefore a public nuisance." It may be admitted that an offence of the kind alleged in the indictment before us is commune nocumentum, and that it may still be so described; but the answer to the third reason assigned by the Lord Chief Justice is, that whether the offence is commune nocumentum or not, the plaintiffs in error are charged with having committed it, and therefore the law requires that it should be fully stated in the indictment. I find no exception to the general rule, that where the offence is alleged to be commune nocumentum, the ingredients of it, the facts which constitute it, need not be stated in the indictment. I cannot feel the force of the difficulties propounded by the Lord Chief Justice.

Then my Brother Mellor bases his decision upon the ground that an objection of this kind could be taken by demurrer to the indictment, and says that the point may still be taken upon error.[1] The Lord Chief Justice also says:[1] "We shall, however, shelter ourselves under the decisions of the American courts, leaving the ultimate decision of this matter—an important one, no doubt—to the Court of Error." I am glad to find those two statements of opinion, because when one has the misfortune to differ from the views of learned judges, it is a very great comfort to know that those views were not entertained strongly. I cannot help thinking that the opinions expressed by the Lord Chief Justice and my Brother Mellor shew that they thought that this was a matter which was fairly open to argument, and which might be reviewed in the Court of Error. It results, therefore, to my mind, that the authorities to which I have referred are unimpeached and are binding upon us, and no sufficient reason has been given why we should not act upon them.

Now this indictment is not merely doubtful, but wholly defective; not only are the words not set forth, but no description of any kind is given. The offence alleged is that the plaintiffs in error "did print, publish, sell, and utter a certain indecent, lewd, filthy, and obscene libel, to wit, a

---

[3] Law Rep. 2 C.C. 74.
[1] 2 Q.B.D. 572, 573.

[1] 2 Q.B.D. 573, 574.
[2] 2 Q.B.D. 574.
[1] 2 Q.B.D. 574.

certain indecent, lewd, bawdy, and obscene book called the 'Fruits of Philosophy.' " The words following "to wit" serve only as a mere identification of the alleged libel, and therefore the indictment may be read as though it had merely charged that the plaintiffs in error had uttered a certain indecent, lewd, filthy, bawdy, and obscene libel. Under these circumstances certainly I am of opinion that the judgment ought to have been arrested, and we ought now to pronounce judgment to that effect, and reverse the judgment of the Queen's Bench Division. I repeat that I wish it to be understood that we express no opinion whether this is a filthy and obscene, or an innocent book. We have not the materials before us for coming to a decision upon that point. We are deciding a dry point of law, which has nothing to do with the actual merits of the case.

BRETT, L.J. It seems to me that we are not called upon to differ from any strongly formed opinion of the Lord Chief Justice and Mr. Justice Mellor; I think that their judgments shew that they did not form a strong opinion as to the point which we shall have to determine in this case. Some of the authorities which we have had to consider were not brought before the Queen's Bench Division; and with regard to the argument for the Crown there, it must be observed that, except *Reg.* v. *Dugdale*,[1] the only decisions cited as to indictments were American cases, and I think it will appear that *Reg.* v. *Dugdale*[1] is not in point for the present proceedings. It is evident from the terms of his judgment that Mr. Justice Mellor came to the conclusion that the words complained of ought to be set out, and that their omission would have made this indictment bad on demurrer; and one ground of the judgment of the Lord Chief Justice was likewise that the objection ought to have been taken by demurrer. The only real point, therefore, upon which we differ from the learned judges, is, that the omission in this case was so great a defect that it is not cured by the verdict.

It seems to me that the questions raised in this case are, first, what is it necessary to set out in such an indictment as this; secondly, what kind of omissions can or cannot be cured by verdict; and thirdly, whether in this indictment the omission was so great a defect that it could not be cured by the verdict.

The first question really comes to this, whether in an indictment of this kind it is necessary to set out the words relied upon as constituting the offence. I cannot express what I believe to be the rule with regard to indictments more accurately in my view than was done in *Reg.* v. *Aspinall*.[2] In that case almost every sentence of the judgment delivered by me on behalf of Lord Justice Mellish and myself was, I may venture to say, the result of many cases; as to each sentence a laborious examination of cases was made, and it was intended to express what we considered to be the result of those cases, and I cannot find better words now in which to express the result. With regard to indictments, it is there said[3] that "every pleading, civil or criminal, must contain allegations of the existence of all the facts necessary to support the charge or defence set up by such pleading. An indictment must,

therefore, contain allegations of every fact necessary to constitute the criminal charge preferred by it. As in order to make acts criminal, they must always be done with a criminal mind, the existence of that criminality of mind must always be alleged. If, in order to support the charge, it is necessary to shew that certain acts have been committed, it is necessary to allege that those acts were in fact committed. If it is necessary to shew that those acts, when they were committed, were done with a particular intent, it is necessary to aver that intention. If it is necessary, in order to support the charge, that the existence of a certain fact should be negatived, that negative must be alleged." Where the crime alleged in an indictment consists of words written or spoken, it seems to me that the words are the facts which constitute the crime, and that for this reason the words must be set out.

Now, the word "libel," as popularly used, seems to mean only defamatory words; but words written, if obscene, blasphemous, or seditious, are technically called libels, and the publication of them is by the law of England an indictable offence. The publication of obscene words comes also under another class of offences, namely, the class of offences against morality. I am aware that in a valuable book lately published, Stephen's Digest of the Criminal Law, ch. xviii. art. 172, p. 104, obscene words written are not put under the class of libels, but they are put under the class of offences against morality. But they have long been treated as falling within the legal meaning of the term "libel." Therefore libels may be divided into seditious, blasphemous, obscene, and defamatory. There are other offences which consist in words, either witten or spoken, such as perjury, false pretences, forgery, letters demanding money with threats, and the administration of unlawful oaths, and I think it will be found that indictments for committing any of these offences are all within the principle which I have stated, namely, that inasmuch as the crime consists in the words, the words must be stated; and I think I shall shew that in every one of those cases there is authority for saying that the words must be set out, unless the necessity for setting out the words is excused by statute; and it seems to me that each of the statutes which have been passed to excuse the necessity of setting out the words, is an authority that without the statute, by the common law, the words must have been set out, and of course wherever it has been decided that the omission to set out the words is a fatal objection, even after verdict, the decision shews still more strongly than the statutes which I have mentioned, the necessity for setting out the words, and that the objection must be fatal on demurrer. As we have to deal with a decision of such high authority as that of the Queen's Bench Division I have thought it right to look carefully into the authorities, and those authorities I feel bound to cite, in order to justify the conclusion at which I have arrived.

One of the earliest cases relates to the offence of cursing and swearing and uttering of profane oaths, which of course consists in words: it is *Rex* v. *Sparling*.[1] This conviction was for profane cursing and swearing under 6 & 7 Wm. 3, c. 11, and it set forth that the defendant did "profanely swear 54 oaths, and did profanely curse 160 curses," but none of them were set out. There having been a conviction there must have been a trial, and a decision of

---

[1] 1 E. & B. 435; 22 L.J. (M.C.) 50; Dears. 64.
[2] 2 Q.B.D. 48.
[3] 2 Q.B.D. at p. 56.

[1] 1 Str. 497.

the court of petty sessions, but it was held that the conviction was nought, because the oaths and curses were not set forth. The Court of King's Bench, including Lord Holt, gave as a reason—"For what is a profane oath or curse is a matter of law, and ought not to be left to the judgment of the witness; he may think false evidence is so; suppose it was for seditious or blasphemous words, must not the words themselves be set out, be they ever so bad, that the Court may judge whether they are seditious or blasphemous." *Rex v. Popplewell*,[2] and *Rex v. Chaveney*[3] are cases of a similar kind, and relate to the same subject-matter. They are all after conviction, and they seem to me to be authorities for saying that whenever words are complained of they must be set out, and that the omission of the words is fatal after verdict or decision.

I will now refer to the law as to letters demanding money. In *Lloyd's Case*,[4] an indictment, following the words of the Black Act, 9 Geo. 1, c. 22, charged the prisoner with feloniously sending a letter, without any name subscribed and signed thereto, demanding money. After conviction it was moved in arrest of judgment that the indictment was bad on two grounds, one of which was that neither the letter nor even the substance of it was set forth in the indictment. It was held bad in arrest of judgment, and the reason was that in every indictment a complete offence must be shewn, and the report states that the precedents which had been looked through generally set forth the letter.

With regard to false pretences, it is only necessary to refer to *Rex v. Mason*.[1] That case is always quoted. I know it was said by Mr. Justice Mellor, in *Heymann v. Reg.*,[2] that it had been virtually overruled, and in *Reg. v. Goldsmith*,[3] Lord Justice Bramwell expressed his concurrence with the remark of Mr. Justice Mellor. But I have failed to find any case before *Heymann v. Reg.*,[4] which treats *Rex v. Mason*[1] as overruled; on the contrary it has been again and again approved of and cited as a binding authority. The indictment was that the defendant had obtained from "one Robert Scofield divers sums of money, that is to say, the sum of two guineas, of the value of two pounds and two shillings of lawful money of Great Britain, of the proper moneys of the said Robert Scofield, by false pretences, with an intent then and there to cheat and defraud the said Robert Scofield of the same." The defendant pleaded not guilty, and on his trial at the quarter sessions at Worcester he was convicted, and sentenced to transportation; but the judgment was reversed by the Court of King's Bench upon a writ of error. The first objection was that the offence imputed was not specified with sufficient particularity. "Several objections," said Mr. Justice Buller (at p. 586), "have been made on the part of the defendant, but the material one on which I found my judgment is, that the indictment does not state what the false pretences were. . . . I am of opinion the first objection is fatal, and that the judgment must be reversed:" and Mr. Justice Grose says he is of opinion, "that the objection that the pretences are not specified is decisive, and for the

reasons mentioned by the defendants' counsel; that the defendant may know what he is to defend, and the Court may see what punishment they are to inflict." I think that those are reasons why the words should be set out, but to my mind the fundamental reason is, that the words are the ground of complaint. *Rex v. Perrott*[1] is to the same effect. It was an indictment for obtaining money by false pretences, and the judgment was arrested for the reason that, although the false pretences were set out, there was not an averment stating that they were false; but Lord Ellenborough says (p. 385): "Every indictment ought to be so framed as to convey to the party charged a certain knowledge of the crime imputed to him. The legislature have so held, and have recorded their opinion to that effect in the cases of perjury." And then he mentions the statute as to perjury, 23 Geo. 2, c. 11, which allows the substance of the charge to be set forth. He also cites *Rex v. Mason*,[2] and approves of it.

The cases with regard to perjury I do not propose to cite, because 23 Geo. 2, c. 11[3] is a strong authority pronounced by the legislature itself, that by the common law, upon an indictment for perjury, the words must be set out.

As to the law of forgery I will mention *Hunter's Case*.[4] The prisoner was charged with the forgery of a navy bill, and the objection taken was that, although the indictment alleged the forgery of a receipt for money, there was not a sufficient averment to shew how the fabricated words amounted to a receipt. I quote the case for the opinion of the judges, delivered by Grose, J.,[5] "The material objection to this indictment was, that it did not contain any averment amounting to a capital offence, for although it avers that the prisoner forged a certain receipt for money, yet there is nothing stated in any of the counts to shew that the instrument set out, which does not on the face of it import to be a receipt, is in fact a receipt." *Rex v. Mason*[2] is then cited, and the learned judge afterwards adds, "In indictments for forging a bill, bond, note, will, or other instrument, an exact copy of the instrument respectively charged to have been forged must be stated."[6]

Now the next head which I will mention is the administering unlawful oaths. This offence clearly consists in using the forbidden words. There are two statutes with regard to it, the 37 Geo. 3, c. 123, which in s. 4 excuses the setting out of the words, and provides that it shall be sufficient to set out only the substance and effect, and the 52 Geo. 3, c. 104, which in s. 5 contains a similar provision. The legislature excuses the setting out of the words, and, therefore, as it seems to me, admits that the words must have been set out if it had not been for the provisions in these statutes.

The next case which I shall cite is a decision with regard to a seditious libel, and it is *Rex v. Horne*.[1] There the words relied upon were set out, and the information was held good. It was in many respects a remarkable case.

---

[2] 2 Str. 686.
[3] 2 Ld. Raym. 1368.
[4] 2 East's Pleas of the Crown, ch. 23, par. 5, p. 1122.
[1] 2 T.R. 581.
[2] Law Rep. 8 Q.B. 102, at p. 103.
[3] Law Rep. 2 C.C. 74, at p. 79.
[4] Law Rep. 8 Q.B. 102.

[1] 2 M. & S. 379.
[2] 2 T.R. 581.
[3] Repealed by 30 & 31 Vict. c. 59, having been practically superseded by 14 & 15 Vict. c. 100, s. 20.
[4] 2 Leach, C.C. 624.
[5] Page 631.
[6] See as to the now existing law, 14 & 15 Vict. c. 100, ss. 5, 6, 7, and 24 & 25 Vict. c. 98, ss. 42, 43.
[1] 2 Cowp. 672.

I will now go to cases as to defamatory words, and the first which I will cite is *Newton* v. *Stubbs*.[2] It was an action for words spoken of the plaintiff, and it was alleged that on one occasion the defendant spoke the words "ad effectum sequentem." It was objected that this was uncertain, and the Court held that this mode of pleading was wrong.

I will next refer to *Zenobio* v. *Axtell*,[3] which was cited in the course of the argument. It was an action for publishing a defamatory libel in the French language, in a newspaper called the *Courrier de Londres*. The declaration alleged that the libel was "according to the purport and effect following in the English language," and then it set out the translation. It stated that what had been said was in the French language, and then assumed to state its purport and effect in English, and it did not say, "which being translated into English has the following meaning." Upon that ground Lord Kenyon, C.J., said: "That this objection must prevail, is evident from the uniform current of precedents, in all of which the original is set forth. The plaintiff should have set out the original words, and then have translated them."

Now in *Wright* v. *Clements*[4] the declaration stated that the defendants did publish a certain libel, "containing amongst other things, certain false, scandalous, malicious, defamatory, and libellous matters, of and concerning the plaintiff, in substance as follows, that is to say," and then it set out the words with innuendoes. The words were introduced by the allegation "in substance as follows." There was a motion in arrest of judgment, and it was argued, that although the words were not set out according to their tenor, yet, inasmuch as they were alleged to be set out according to their substance, it was sufficient after verdict. Lord Tenterden said, p. 506, "Judgment must be arrested. In actions for libel, the law requires the very words of the libel to be set out in the declaration, in order that the Court may judge whether they constitute a ground of action; and unless a plaintiff professes so to set them out, he does not comply with the rules of pleading. The ordinary mode of doing this is to state that the defendant published of and concerning the plaintiff the libellous matters to the tenor and effect following."

Then Holroyd, J., says, p. 508, "Now where a charge either civil or criminal is brought against a defendant arising out of the publication of a written instrument, as is the case in forgery or libel, the invariable rule is, that the instrument itself must be set out in the declaration or indictment, and the reason of that is that the defendant may have an opportunity, if he pleases, of admitting all the facts charged and of having the judgment of the Court, whether the facts stated amounted to a cause of action, or a crime."

Lord Justice Bramwell has cited the case of *Cook* v. *Cox*,[1] and that case lays down the same principle. Now, these decisions were pronounced in 1814 and 1820, after Fox's Act, 32 Geo. 3, c. 60, passed in 1792. Therefore any argument based upon Fox's Act cannot prevail. It is true that before that statute the judges held that upon the trial of an indictment or information for libel, all that the jury

had to find was, whether the defendant had published the writing, and whether the innuendoes were true, and that it was for the Court to say whether the writing was a libel or not. Fox's Act declared that view of the law to be wrong. Whether the legislature were right in principle, or whether the judges were right, is not for us to discuss; and we must accept the declaration of the legislature as an authoritative statement of the law. But it seems to me that Fox's Act leaves untouched the validity of an objection to the omission of words from an indictment or information when they form the substance of the offence charged. In principle the only difference made by that statute is, that if the written instrument can be a libel, then it is for the jury to say whether it is a libel;[1] but there remains a preliminary question which it is for the Court or judge to decide, namely, whether the writing can be a libel, whether in truth there is any evidence upon which a jury can say it is a libel, and that question is still open, and is a question for the Court;[2] and therefore the reason which is given by Holroyd, J., in *Wright* v. *Clements*[3] still prevails, that the words ought to be set out, in order that the defendants may demur and may raise the objection that the words cannot by any reasonable construction amount to a libel. Moreover, by the 4th section of Fox's Act, 32 Geo. 3, c. 60, the power to move in arrest of judgment is expressly preserved for the benefit of a defendant who is found guilty, and I think that the legislature intended to allow a defendant, either before verdict by demurrer, or after verdict by motion in arrest of judgment, to object that the words complained of either do not amount to a libel or are wholly omitted from the information or indictment, as the circumstances of the case may allow.

Now I come to what seems to me to be a remarkable case. It is not a decision of a Court upon the present question, but it seems to me to be a great authority; I mean *Rex* v. *Wilkes*.[4] In that case an information was exhibited in the Court of King's Bench for the publication of an obscene and impious libel. That obscene and impious libel was in the book styled an 'Essay on Woman.' The facts now material are (p. 2528) that Mr. Wilkes having pleaded not guilty, and the records having been made up and sealed, "the counsel for the Crown thought it expedient to amend them by striking out the word 'purport' and in its place inserting the word 'tenor.' The proposed amendments were in all those parts of the information where the charge was that the libel printed and published by Mr. Wilkes contained matters 'to the purport and effect following, to wit:' which the counsel for the Crown thought it advisable to alter into words importing that such libel contained matters 'to the tenor and effect following, to wit.' " It is clear that the words were set out; yet, because they were introduced by the words "to the purport and effect following" instead of "to the tenor and effect following," the Attorney-General, Sir Fletcher Norton, considered it unsafe to go on even after plea pleaded and issue joined, and thought it advisable to amend the record. That seems to me a very important authority.

The second question which I have proposed is what kind of omissions can or cannot be cured by verdict, and all the

---

[2] 2 Show. 435.
[3] 6 T.R. 162.
[4] 3 B. & Ald. 503.
[1] 3 M. & S. 110.

[1] See *Fray* v. *Fray*, 34 L.J. (C.P.) 45.
[2] See *Mulligan* v. *Cole*, Law Rep. 10 Q.B. 549.
[3] 3 B. & Ald. 503, at p. 509.
[4] 4 Burr. 2527.

cases which I have cited seem to me to form a strong current of authorities to shew that in every kind of crime which consists in words, if the words complained of are not set out in the indictment or information, the objection is fatal in arrest of judgment.

Now we come to the cases which are said to be to the contrary, and I will deal very shortly with them. The first is a case upon which the Crown has relied: *Dugdale* v. *Reg.*[1] The only counts of the indictment in that case material to be now mentioned are the first and second; the first count charged the defendant with obtaining and procuring obscene prints, with intent to publish them, and the second count charged him with preserving and keeping them with the like intent. The second was held not to disclose an offence for another reason, that is, that the mere having them in his possession was not indictable. The first count was held to be good, because it alleged a step towards committing a misdemeanour. In my opinion, if a man, knowing prints to be obscene, procures them for the purpose of publishing them, his offence is complete, although he has never looked at them, and therefore the actual nature of the prints was not a part of the charge, and it was unnecessary to describe them. But further, I would strike out of the category of the cases which we are considering all cases with regard to obscene prints and obscene pictures. The publication of obscene prints and obscene pictures may be in one sense libellous, but they are not words, and therefore they do not seem to me to fall within the rules as to criminal pleadings which we are considering here to-day; the publication of them is an offence like that committed by Sir Charles Sedley,[2] who was convicted, not of libel, but of indecent exposure.

Now I come to *Reg.* v. *Goldsmith:*[1] I see but little difficulty in dealing with that case, if it were not for the expressions used by some of the judges. The prisoner was indicted, not for obtaining money by false pretences, but for unlawfully receiving goods knowing them to have been obtained by false pretences. The objection was that the false pretences were not set out. It seems to me that the crime charged in that case is complete, although the prisoner does not know what the false pretences were, and in this view the words actually used in making the false pretences formed no material part of the charge. If a man receives goods, being told and believing that they have been obtained by false pretences, he is just as guilty of the crime, as if he knew what the false pretences were; upon a similar principle if a man receives goods, knowing them to be stolen, he may not know from whom they were stolen, where they were stolen, or when they were stolen; but all that is wanted, in order to constitute the offence, is that he should know the fact that they have been stolen. In *Reg.* v. *Goldsmith*[1] it was sufficient to allege and to prove that the prisoner knew that the goods had been obtained by false pretences. It seems, therefore, to me that it was not necessary for the decision of that case to rely upon Serjeant Williams' note to *Stennel* v. *Hogg*,[2] where it is laid down that a defect, imperfection, or omission in pleading is cured by the verdict by the common law.

Now comes the case of *Heymann* v. *Reg.*[3] That was a case of conspiracy to defraud, and in order to constitute that crime it is only necessary to shew that persons have agreed together to defraud; and as was pointed out in *Heymann* v. *Reg.*,[4] and also *Reg.* v. *Aspinall,*[5] the crime of conspiracy is complete so soon as the agreement to commit the unlawful act is come to; and the conspiracy may be complete, although the guilty parties have not yet agreed upon what means they should use; in a case like *Reg.* v. *Aspinall,*[6] where the agreement was to defraud such persons, as might buy shares, by false pretences with regard to those shares, the conspiracy is complete the moment the parties thereto agree to deceive such purchasers, although they have not as yet agreed on the false pretences. The crime of conspiracy does not consist in words, but in the agreement; and it follows that the crime is complete, although the false pretences never were used, and although the false pretences might never have been agreed upon. In the case of *Reg.* v. *Aspinall,*[1] amongst the objections put forward it was urged that the false pretences were not set out; this objection was overruled upon the authority of the decided cases,[2] but there were other matters which were not perfectly stated, and the imperfection in the statement of the indictment was much relied on, and it was necessary for this Court to consider whether the defect was capable of being cured by verdict. The rule as to what can be cured is pointed out in *Reg.* v. *Aspinall:*[3] "It (the rule) is thus stated in *Heymann* v. *Reg.:*[4] 'Where an averment which is necessary for the support of the pleadings is imperfectly stated, and the verdict on an issue involving that averment is found, if it appears to the Court after verdict that the verdict could not have been found on this issue without proof of this averment, then, after verdict, the defective averment which might have been bad on demurrer is cured by the verdict.' Upon this it should be observed that the averment spoken of is 'an averment imperfectly stated,' i.e. an averment which is stated, but which is imperfectly stated. The rule is not applicable to the case of the total omission of an essential averment. If there be such a total omission, the verdict is no cure. And when it is said that the verdict could not have been found without proof of the averment, the meaning is, the verdict could not have been found without finding this imperfect averment to have been proved in a sense adverse to the accused." And it seems to me obvious that must be the rule, upon referring to Serjeant Williams' note to *Stennel* v. *Hogg*,[5] where it is said that the defect is cured by the verdict, if the issue joined be such as necessarily required on the trial proof of the facts "defectively stated." What are the issues in a criminal case? The plea of not guilty is general, and denies every averment necessary to constitute the offence, in other words, every averment which is a necessary part of the indictment, and does not deny what is totally omitted

---

[1] 1 E. & B. 435; Dears. 64.
[2] 17 How. St. Tr. 155.
[1] Law Rep. 2 C.C. 74.
[2] 1 Notes to Saund. by Williams, at p. 261.

[3] Law Rep. 8 Q.B. 102.
[4] Law Rep. 8 Q.B. 102, at p. 105.
[5] 2 Q.B.D. 48, at p. 58.
[6] 2 Q.B.D. 48.
[1] 2 Q.B.D. 48.
[2] At p. 60.
[3] 2 Q.B.D. 48, at p. 55.
[4] Law Rep. 8 Q.B. 102, at p. 105.
[5] 1 Notes to Saund. by Williams, at p. 261.

therefrom. That which is totally omitted from the indictment is no part of the dispute when issue is taken upon the plea of not guilty, and the jury must find for the Crown, if everything stated on the face of the indictment is proved to be true. Therefore, it is true to say that every averment contained in an indictment, although inaccurately stated, is involved in the issue, and that the inaccurate statement of it is cured by the verdict, because after a conviction that inaccurate averment must be taken to have been proved adversely to the prisoner; and it is immaterial that the indictment would be bad before verdict by reason of that inaccurate statement. Therefore, I take the rule to be that an inaccurate averment is cured by verdict, but that an averment which is totally absent cannot be supplied even after verdict.

Now the third and remaining question is whether there is such a total absence in the present case of material words, that the defect has not been cured by the verdict. The introductory part of each count alleges that the book complained of falls under the category of an obscene libel; but that introductory part does not justify the total omission of the words, which are relied upon as constituting the crime. Now, what is charged as to those words? It is said the defendants did "print, publish, sell, and utter, a certain indecent, lewd, filthy, and obscene libel, to wit, a certain indecent, lewd, filthy, bawdy, and obscene book called the 'Fruits of Philosophy.' It is obvious that the title of the book, 'Fruits of Philosophy,' was not enough to be relied on. Words cannot be more innocent—they never were or could be relied upon as the obscene libel charged. That which was to be relied upon was something written in the book which was so called, and there is no description of anything contained in that book. What is contained in that book, is not even attempted to be described according to its tenor and effect. There is a total omission of the contents, and yet it was the contents, or some part of the contents, which was to be relied on by the Crown. The words complained of are necessary to the averment in the indictment, and the total omission of them cannot be cured by the verdict.

With regard to the American cases, I must say that, to my mind, they are either contrary to the law of England or in favour of the plaintiffs in error. A rule of practice seems to exist in the United States of America, that when an indictment contains an averment that the words are so obscene that if set out they would pollute the records of the Court, it is unnecessary to set them forth; but that where there is not this averment, the words must be set out, and if there is an omission both of the words and of the averment, the indictment is bad in arrest of judgment. Therefore the American cases, if they are to be regarded as authorities, are against the prosecution, and in favour of the plaintiffs in error in this case; because, besides the omission of the words, there is also the omission of that averment which is a necessary substitute for them. I confess, however, that I know of no authority saying that any similar rule exists in English law. I have read Lord Holt's view, as expressed in *Rex* v. *Sparling*,[1] that the words of a blasphemous libel must be set out, however shocking they may be, and it seems to me, to say the least of it, a more robust rule to set out the obscene words upon the face of the indictment than to attempt to preserve the

purity of the records, when the ears of every one in Court must be polluted by the words being read out before the judge and jury. I cannot follow the reasoning as to the advisability of the records of the Court being kept pure. It seems to me that it is a reason which does not bear examination, at all events, the principle that obscene words may be omitted if they are so obscene that they would pollute the records of the Court, is not the law of England, and if it were it does not apply to this case, as the indictment does not contain an averment that the words are too obscene to be inserted. Therefore, to my mind, this indictment is bad, and the plaintiffs in error are entitled to judgment. They are entitled to judgment, as all persons charged with crime in England are, for want of sufficient accuracy in the instrument by which they are charged.

This decision leaves the verdict really untouched. I confess I have felt humiliation in having to discuss such a question as this in the presence of one of the plaintiffs in error. We know not the particular ground on which the verdict passed; but it does seem to me sad that such a charge should have been brought against a woman. Although on a point of law the judgment in this case must be reversed, yet if the book complained of is published again, and the plaintiffs in error are convicted upon a properly framed indictment, the reiteration of the offence must be met by greater punishment.

COTTON, L.J. The question which we have to consider is, whether, on the indictment as framed, there is sufficient to support the judgment against the plaintiffs in error. Although it is a mere question of criminal pleading, it is nevertheless of considerable importance, because especially in criminal matters no departure should be allowed from those rules, which have been laid down for the purpose of guiding the Courts in the administration of justice. In the present case the offence charged is that of publishing an obscene libel. That offence consists of publishing obscene written words. Has any rule been laid down for framing an indictment for it? I cannot do better than take the rule quoted with approval by Lord Ellenborough in *Cook* v. *Cox*.[1] That rule, which was stated by ten judges, is as follows: "By the law of England, and constant practice, in all prosecutions by indictment or information for crimes or misdemeanours by writing or speaking, the particular words supposed to be criminal ought to be expressly specified in the indictment or information."[2]

This rule established so long ago as the reign of Queen Anne, has been ever since recognised, and to shew how uniform the practice has been, it is only necessary to refer to the numerous authorities and cases alluded to by Lord Justice Brett, amongst which I may especially mention *Wright* v. *Clements*.[3] Is there any authority to countervail this rule on behalf of the prosecution? Practically no decision has been quoted which enables it to be argued that this rule does not now prevail. The only English case which was referred to as not following the rule was *Dugdale* v. *Reg.*;[4] but I wish to remark that in that case there was no decision that the actual words need not be set out; the point was not raised, and that case cannot in any

---

[1] 1 Str. 497.

[1] 3 M. & S. 110, at p. 116.
[2] 5 Har. St. Tr. 828.
[3] 3 B. & Ald. 503.
[4] 1 E. & B. 435; Dears. 64.

way be looked upon as a decision meeting the long current of authority establishing and following the rule. When a rule is so well established as this, it is almost unnecessary to consider what the reason of it is; but here certainly one reason is apparent, namely, that when words constitute the alleged crime, if the words complained of are not set out, the defendant is precluded from raising, either by demurrer or by proceedings in the Court of Error, the question whether or not the circumstances charged are in fact, according to the law of England, criminal; and it is of the utmost importance in dealing with cases of this kind, that it should not be considered whether or not in the particular case any injustice has been done to the accused persons, or whether or not they have suffered any substantial disadvantage. In my opinion we ought to adhere strictly to the principles and the rules which have been laid down, without nicely speculating as to whether any advantage or disadvantage exists in the particular case.

On what ground is it contended that this indictment is sufficient? I will first take the point which was principally relied upon in the Queen's Bench Division. I do not understand that either of the learned judges who decided the case in the Court below thought that, according to the English decisions, there was an exception to the general rule in this kind of libel. It is true the Lord Chief Justice does refer to the inconvenience of setting out libels of this sort, or books of this sort, on the indictment; but he does refer to, and expressly says, that he relies upon the decisions of the American courts, and I must therefore consider whether or not those decisions do justify the judgment in the Queen's Bench Division upon this indictment. We are in no way bound by the American decisions, their effect is simply that they may enable us to see how principles recognised by the law of England ought to be applied, by shewing us how learned judges in other countries have acted on those principles; but if in fact the judgments of the American courts are founded upon principles which we do not recognise, then of course those decisions are perfectly useless, and can be neither guides nor authorities. In the American cases referred to the judges certainly recognised the rule to which I have referred, and which I have quoted from *Cook v. Cox;*[1] they recognised it as a general rule; but as against that general rule they rely upon another, namely, that it is necessary to keep the records of the Court pure; but it was only upon an allegation that the book or libel in question was so gross that no records ought to be defiled by it, that they held the indictment to be sufficient without setting out the actual words relied upon. It might be sufficient to say that these cases have no bearing on the present, because there is no such allegation in the present case, and if the present indictment is held to be sufficient, every indictment for any offence in the nature of an obscene libel must also be sufficient, although it does not follow that general rule to which I have referred. But the matter does not rest here. Does the law of England recognise, so as to make it available for the prosecution, that rule upon which the judges in American courts rely? It is perfectly true that the English courts do require their records to be

kept pure in this sense, that they will not allow their records to be the means of propagating defamation or obscenity under the pretence of its being part of a judicial proceeding. They will require anything impure or scandalous to be removed from their records when it is irrelevant to the matter to be tried, but if the matters on the records of the Court or in an affidavit are really relevant to the matter to be tried, they are not scandalous, and no principle recognised by the English courts requires any statement to be removed from their records, if relevant to the issue to be tried, simply because it is impure. Does the principle that the records must be kept pure justify the absence of what would otherwise be a necessary averment in the indictment, on the ground that it is gross and impure? In my opinion it does not, and for this reason, the duty of the Court is to administer justice, either as between party and party, or as between the Crown and those who are accused; and for the purpose of doing so it ought not to consider its records as defiled by the introduction upon them of any matter, which is necessary in order to enable the Court to do justice according to the rules laid down for its guidance; a defendant has a right to say that he shall have fair notice, in order that he may not be prejudiced in defending himself against proceedings, whether civil or criminal, and therefore, in my opinion, the principle upon which those American cases are decided does not avail in this case. Those cases can be no guide or assistance to us. If it is desirable that in cases of this sort there should be an exception to the rule as to the statement of words, it is not the duty of the Court to make an exception; it must be for parliament to interfere, as it has done in other cases mentioned by Lord Justice Brett.

I think that disposes of the ground principally relied on in the Queen's Bench Division, but there is another ground to which I must refer, that is, that the defect has been cured by the verdict. The rule is very simple, and it applies equally to civil and criminal cases; it is, that the verdict only cures defective statements. In the present case the objection is not that there is a defective statement, but an absolute and total want in stating that which constitutes the criminal act, namely, the words complained of, and the judgment of Lord Ellenborough in *Cook v. Cox*[1] shews that the omission of words, when they form the substance of the offence, cannot be cured by verdict, when he says, "It is of the substance of a charge for slander by words that the words themselves should be set out." Here we have not the substance set out, we have not a mere defective averment; we have an absolute omission to aver that which was relied upon as lewd and indecent. My opinion is that the defect is not a matter cured by the verdict, and it is perfectly open to the plaintiffs in error to rely on this as a fatal defect in the indictment even after verdict.

In my view, therefore, this indictment is not framed in accordance with settled rules, and neither on authority or principle can the omission of the words complained of be excused, and this judgment cannot stand.

Judgment reversed.

Solicitor for the prosecution: *T. J. Nelson.*

---

[1] 3 M. & S. 110.

---

[1] 3 M. & S. 110.

■ Reg.
v.
Thomson.

The defendent was indicted as follows:—

"Central Criminal Court: The jurors for our Lady the Queen, upon their oath present that Isabel Florence Thomson on the 17th of April, A.D. 1900, at the parish of . . . in the county of London, and within the jurisdiction of the Central Criminal Court, in a certain open and public shop, situate and being 6, Booksellers'-row, in the said county, she, the said Isabel Florence Thomson, then being a person of wicked and depraved disposition, and unlawfully and wickedly devising, contriving, and intending as much as in her lay to vitiate and corrupt the morals of the people of this kingdom unlawfully, wickedly, and wilfully did publish, sell, and utter a certain lewd, wicked, bawdy, and obscene libel in the form of a book entitled *The Heptameron of Margaret Queen of Navarre*, in which said libel are contained amongst other things divers wicked, lewd, impure, and obscene passages, that is to say, in one part thereof, at pages . . . of the said book according to the tenor and effect following videlicet (the extract, consisting practically of a complete story, was here set out). And in another part thereof at pages . . . of the said book according to the tenor and effect following videlicet (the extract was set out. In similar manner other extracts were set out). In contempt of our said Lady the Queen, and her laws, in violation of common decency, morality, and good order, to the manifest corruption of the morals, manners, and conversation of the people of this kingdom and the increase of lewdness, to the evil and pernicious example of all others in the like case offending and against the peace, &c."

Copies of this indictment were printed and were handed to the jury when the extracts contained therein were read in court.

The defendant pleaded "Not Guilty."

R. D. Muir (*W. H. Leycester* with him) for the prosecution, in the course of opening the case to the jury, said there were three questions for the jury—(1) Did the defendant sell the book? (2) Was the book obscene? (3) Did the defendant publish the book with a view to corrupt the public morals? When the police searched the premises, 6, Booksellers'-row, these premises being a book shop, other books were found, and he proposed to read the titles of some of these other books to the jury.

Biron, for the defence, objected that the prosecution was not entitled to go into other matters outside the book the subject-matter of the indictment. The case must stand or fall on the contents of the book itself, and the contents of other books cannot be relevant.

THE COMMON SERJEANT.—Whilst the question of the intention with which the book was sold is part of the indictment, it is impossible to say that the holding out and offering other books may not bear on that intent. If the defendant sold other books whose titles go to suggest that they are indecent it is some evidence to show that she sold

this book with the intention alleged in the indictment, and not accidentally. I cannot exclude the evidence.

Muir continued his opening, and read the titles of some of the books found on the premises. As to whether the book was obscene, he referred to the test suggested by *Cockburn,* L.C.J., in *Reg.* v. *Hicklin,* L.R. 3 Q.B. 371. It was suggested that this book was a classic; he suggested that though it was a classic in the French language it was not a classic in the English language, and that if the necessary effect of the translation was to corrupt citizens, good motive would not save the publisher. He referred again to *Reg.* v. *Hicklin* (*ubi supra*) and to *Stephen's Digest of the Criminal Law,* p. 134. The extracts from the book set out in the indictment were then read to the jury.

Police-inspector Arrow was the only witness called for the prosecution, no witnesses were called for the defence.

Biron, for the defence, submitted to the jury that this book was a classic both in French and in English, and he read to the jury extracts with reference to the book from the *Encyclopœdia Britannica,* the *Edinburgh Review,* and other works. He submitted that it was not a book against which proceedings ought to have been instituted, he referred especially to the judgment of *Blackburn,* J., in *Reg.* v. *Hicklin* (*ubi supra*).

The COMMON SERJEANT, in the course of summing up the case to the jury, said:—The questions for you are— (1) did the defendant publish the book in question, *i.e.,* did she put it out to other people under such circumstances as to be responsible for it contents? (2) Is it a book of a lewd and lascivious character manifestly calculated to corrupt the public morals? We do not require the help of critics, or of antiquarian research, to help us to decide the above questions. That the defendant is responsible for putting forth the book, and under such circumstances as to be responsible for its contents, is not now disputed. The question that remains is whether it was put out in such a way as to be lewd, lascivious, and to manifestly tend to corrupt the public morals. There is an old saying that dirt is only matter in the wrong place; you have here to deal with the time and circumstances under which the book was put forth. It is material to remember that the police officer said that this shop contained books of every sort and kind in considerable numbers. There are in writings of respectable people sometimes passages of an objectionable nature which no doubt it would be wrong to destroy because to students and to people who have to deal with questions of manners and so on, such passages are valuable; it is right that students should know the manners of the people they are studying, however gross. In the Middle Ages things were discussed, which, if put forward now for the reading of the general public would never be tolerated. In towns buried from the corrupt times of the Roman Empire, now disinterred or in course of being disinterred, there are discovered pictures of the most lewd and filthy character. Nobody would think of destroying those pictures, but to sell photographs of them in the streets of London would be an indictable offence. Coming to the book here in question, it is for you to decide, looking at it as a whole and taking into consideration the extracts that have been read, and the manner in which it was sold, whether it was sold with a view to corrupt the public morals. If it had been in a library to which students had access, no one would deny that the book was properly there and properly kept for a proper use. Here the defendant is not charged with having published the book in a library, on the one hand, nor, on the other, to boys or those to whom its publication would clearly be improper. You are the sole judges whether the book is a fit book to put into people's hands in these days at the end of the nineteenth century. I

am going to hand you the book and you will say whether the book as sold is of such a tendency as I have mentioned. The book is marked "unexpurgated," and we have not to trouble ourselves about other editions which other publishers may have put forward. You will look at the book, and the catalogue with which it was sold, and you will see what proportion the stories set out in the indictment bear to the whole and you will judge whether, sold as it was for 1s 11d. and being what it is, containing the passages set out, is it such a book put forward in such a way as to clearly tend to the corruption of morals.

Verdict: Not Guilty.

Solicitors for the prosecution: Wontner and Sons.
Solicitors for the defence: Dubois and Williams.

The King
v.
Barraclough.

CASE stated by Jelf J. for the opinion of the Court for Consideration of Crown Cases Reserved.

"William Barraclough was arraigned before me at the Leeds Assizes on the 3rd August, 1905, and called upon to plead to the following indictment: [here, the indictment was set out, together with the objections thereto offered by defense counsel].

The trial then proceeded, and it was proved that the defendant, who was an assistant overseer, and held other public offices at Farnley, had published to the men mentioned in the first and third counts of the indictment, who were courting, or intending to court, the girl mentioned in the indictment, to whom he had been for some years engaged to be married, and to herself, copies of the said alleged "Diary of the Rejected One," as well as the following printed postcards, addressed to her and them and others:—

"The Barraclough-Woodhead Diary. The most up-to-date Arabian Nights Entertainment extant, at the Reception by John Bull & Co.," and that this was done by him in pursuance of a threat that if she did not marry him he would make her a whore.

Counsel for the defendant watched the case to the end, but did not cross-examine any of the witnesses, or raise any defence on the merits.

I left the case to the jury to say whether the defendant had published an obscene libel, explaining to them the meaning thereof.

The jury found the defendant guilty, and I sentenced him to a year's imprisonment, but respited the sentence till after the decision of this case, admitting him to bail in the meanwhile.

I desire the opinion of the Court whether I was right in refusing to quash the first and third counts of the indictment on any of the grounds above mentioned.

If so, the conviction is to stand, if not, it is to be quashed.

A. R. JELF."

Tindal Atkinson, K.C. (*C. F. Palmer* with him), for the prisoner. The conviction cannot be sustained. The indictment was drawn as an indictment for defamatory libel, and it cannot be turned into an indictment for obscene libel when it fails as an indictment for defamatory libel. The offences of defamatory libel and obscene libel are entirely different. Defamatory libel is an offence against an individual, and is only incidentally criminal as it may produce a breach of the peace. The very essence of an obscene libel is that it is an offence against the public as tending to corrupt public morals. Obscene libel is a common law offence with no statutory punishment, whereas defamatory libel has a statutory punishment. The two offences cannot be charged in the same count, and if they are, the count is bad for duplicity. It is clear, however, that the intention of the draftsman of the indictment was to charge a defamatory libel in counts one and three, and the word "obscene" is only descriptive of the matter contained in the alleged libel. The words relating to a defamatory libel cannot therefore be rejected as surplusage, as they are in fact the gist of the count.

Assuming, however, that the count charges, and was intended to charge, an obscene libel, it is insufficient. It is an essential part of the offence of publishing an obscene libel that it should have a tendency to corrupt, and should have been published with the intention of corrupting, the public morals, and the indictment must contain an averment to this effect: Archbold's Criminal Pleading, 23rd ed. p. 1190. In *Reg.* v. *Hicklin*[1] Cockburn C.J. says: "The

---
[1] (1868) L.R. 3 Q.B. 360, at p. 371.

test of obscenity is this, whether the tendency of the matter charged as obscenity is to deprave and corrupt those whose minds are open to such immoral influences." The mere allegation that the matter published is obscene is insufficient without an averment of its tendency to corrupt public morals.

[WALTON J. In Stephen's Digest of the Criminal Law, 6th ed. p. 134, it is submitted, "A person is justified in . . . publishing obscene books, papers, writings, &c. . . . if their . . . publication is for the public good, as being necessary or advantageous to religion or morality, &c."]

No doubt the intention of the publication and the tendency of the matter published may be inferred from the character of the work, and the form and circumstances of the publication, but it is insufficient to allege the matter to be obscene without any further averment. The word "obscene" is not of itself descriptive of the tendency to corrupt public morality.

If, however, counts one and three do amount to a sufficient charge of the publication of an obscene libel, the indictment is bad for non-compliance with s. 7 of the Law of Libel Amendment Act, 1888. That section was enacted in consequence of the decision in *Bradlaugh* v. *Reg.*[1] and provided that it should not be necessary to set out the obscene passages in an indictment, "but it shall be sufficient to deposit the book, newspaper, or other documents containing the alleged libel, with the indictment or other judicial proceeding, together with particulars shewing precisely by reference to pages, columns and lines in what part of the book, newspaper, or other document the alleged libel is to be found." Here the alleged libel was a mere exhibit to the depositions, and was not deposited with the indictment and particulars. Although the incriminated document was in the custody of the clerk of assize it did not form part of the indictment, and a copy of it should have been deposited with the indictment.

[The point as to the Vexatious Indictments Act was not pressed.]

Waugh, K. C. (*Compston* with him), for the prosecution.

[LORD ALVERSTONE C.J. We only desire to hear you as to the sufficiency of the indictment.]

It is a criminal offence to publish unlawfully obscene matter. The gist of the offence is the unlawfulness of the publication. If the matter published is obscene there is an inference of law that its tendency is to corrupt public morals, and there is no necessity to aver it in the indictment. The point is really decided by *Reg.* v. *Hicklin,*[2] where Cockburn C.J. said:[3] "I hold that where a man publishes a work manifestly obscene, he must be taken to have had the intention which is implied from that act."

LORD ALVERSTONE C.J. In this case my brother Jelf was put in a very difficult position by the form of the indictment. There is no doubt that an indictment for obscene libel should be so drawn as to include the ordinary averment as to the libel being to the prejudice of public morals. The form of indictment for an obscene libel given in Archbold's Criminal Pleading contains the allegation that the defendant, "devising, contriving and intending

the morals as well of youth as of divers other liege subjects of our lord the King to debauch and corrupt and to raise and create in their minds inordinate and lustful desires," published the libel "to the manifest corruption of the morals as well of youth as of other liege subjects of our said lord the King," and although it is not necessary to follow those precise words, I think there is no doubt that the indictment should contain an allegation that the intention of the libel was to corrupt public morals. But what we have to consider is whether the judge was right in saying that having regard to the objections taken on behalf of the prisoner there was sufficient averment left in the counts one and three to justify those counts in being treated as charging an obscene libel and therefore to support this conviction. Counts two and four of the indictment were withdrawn from the consideration of the jury, but my brother Jelf held that there was sufficient in counts one and three to amount to a charge of obscene libel. He did not as a fact quash any part of either of those counts, but he thought the unnecessary words might be treated as surplusage and that the counts contained sufficient allegation of a charge of publishing an obscene libel to justify the conviction. The indictment alleges that the defendant "unlawfully and maliciously" published a libel in the form of a typewritten document, "which said document . . . contains divers . . . obscene . . . matters and things" concerning Edith Woodhead.

As I have said, I think that in order to prevent any point of this kind from being taken it is better that the old practice should be followed, and that the indictment should contain an averment that the libel was published with the intention of corrupting the public morals. But we have here to consider this indictment, and reading it together with the typewritten document to which it refers, I do not think that these counts could be withdrawn from the jury as though the only charge contained in them was that of a defamatory libel. The indictment contains a distinct allegation of the unlawful publication of an obscene libel, and that is, in my opinion, sufficient to support the conviction. This is not a case in which it is necessary for the indictment to negative possible defences, such, for example, as the defence that the document was published for the public benefit. The document itself was in the possession of the Court, and in my opinion the judge would have been wrong if he had not allowed the case to go to the jury. Assuming that the words of that typewritten document had been set out in the indictment, then, taking with that the allegation that the publication was unlawful, how could he possibly have withdrawn the case from the jury merely because there was no averment that the publication of such details was likely to corrupt the morals of the public? I think Cockburn C.J., in *Reg.* v. *Hicklin,*[1] clearly supports the view I am taking when he says:[2] "The test of obscenity is this, whether the tendency of the matter charged as obscenity is to deprave and corrupt those whose minds are open to such immoral influences."

In my opinion my brother Jelf was right. Only one offence is alleged, that of unlawful publication, and there was the allegation that the matter published was obscene, and that seems to me sufficient in this case to support the conviction.

---

[1] 3 Q.B.D. 607.
[2] L.R. 3 Q.B. 360.
[3] L.R. 3 Q.B. p. 373.

[1] L.R. 3 Q.B. 360.
[2] L.R. 3 Q.B. p. 371.

On the other point also I have no doubt whatever. The object of s. 7 of the Law of Libel Amendment Act, 1888, was to make it unnecessary to set out in the indictment the words complained of, and the section says, "it shall be sufficient to deposit the book, newspaper, or other documents containing the alleged libel with the indictment or other judicial proceeding." Looking at the ordinary practice where there is a charge of obscene libel, the incriminated document is put before the magistrates and is annexed to the depositions (as was done here), and forms part of them. It then is in the legal custody of the magistrates' clerk and is sent by him to the clerk of assize, in whose custody it remains, and is at the disposal of the judge, the grand jury and counsel. I asked Mr. Tindal Atkinson what other deposit of the document there could be, and he was unable to say. Here the bill of indictment (for it is not an indictment until a true bill is found by the grand jury) is deposited with the clerk of assize, in whose custody the incriminated typewritten document already is, and annexed to the bill of indictment are particulars shewing what parts of that document already in the custody of the clerk of the assize are relied upon as being obscene libels. The statute says nothing as to the manner in which the deposit is to be made. The Legislature knew that the book or document would be in the custody of the law, and I think that the words in s. 7, "with the indictment or other judicial proceeding," were inserted because it was known that when the indictment was presented the book or document would be in the custody of the clerk of assize.

No doubt there must in the indictment be a clear and distinct reference to the deposited document, but that is so here, and it is clear that every line of this typewritten document was an obscene libel. I think, therefore, that there has been a compliance with the requirements of s. 7 and that the conviction must be affirmed.

WILLS J. I am of the same opinion and have nothing to add.

DARLING J. I am of the same opinion. It seems to me that if a thing which is properly called obscene is alleged to be unlawfully published, it follows that all the usual allegations in an indictment for obscene libel are included. Even in such an indictment as this, intent is, I think, part of the indictment. It is no doubt *sous-entendu* and not set out with the wearisome reiteration to which we are accustomed in indictments, but it is still part of the charge or the publication would not have been unlawful.

No doubt it would be better to allege the intent to corrupt the public morality in the words usually found in such indictments, because it amounts to a notice to the defendant of the charge against him, and because also of the case of *Reg. v. Thomson*.[1] In that case there was an indictment for publishing an obscene libel, and evidence was tendered by the prosecution to shew that other books of an indecent and obscene character were found on the defendant's premises. This evidence was objected to, and the Common Serjeant (Mr. Bosanquet), for whose opinion I entertain a very high respect, said: "Whilst the question of the intention with which the book was sold is part of the indictment, it is impossible to say that the holding out and offering other books may not bear on that intent. If the defendant sold other books whose titles go to suggest that they are indecent, it is some evidence to shew that she sold this book with the intention alleged in the indictment, and not accidentally. I cannot exclude the evidence."

It seems, therefore, desirable that the intent should be expressly averred in the indictment, as, if it is not, in such a case as *Reg. v. Thomson*,[1] and similar evidence were tendered, it might well be that it would be excluded by the judge, which would be regrettable.

However, in this case I think the indictment is sufficient to support the conviction.

WALTON J. I have felt some doubt as to the sufficiency of this indictment, but on the whole I have come to the conclusion that since it charges that the publication was unlawful and that the matter published was obscene, it is sufficient. The defendant on a plea of not guilty could negative either of those allegations and could shew either that the publication was justifiable or that the matter published was not improper. I agree, therefore, that the conviction must be upheld.

JELF J. I agree with the rest of the Court.

Conviction affirmed.

Solicitors for prisoner: *Scott-Lawson & Palmer, for Arthur Willey, Leeds.*
Solicitors for prosecution: *Peckover & Scriven, Leeds.*

A. P. P. K.

---

[1] (1900) 64 J.P. 456.
[1] 64 J.P. 456.

1800-1900
Cases

The Commonwealth
against
Sharpless and others.

The following indictment was found in the Mayor's Court of the city of *Philadelphia*, and removed to this Court by *certiorari*.

"MARCH SESSIONS, 1815.

"City of *Philadelphia*, ss.

"The Grand Inquest of the Commonwealth of *Pennsyl-* "*vania*, inquiring for the city of *Philadelphia*, upon their "oaths and affirmations respectively do present, that *Jesse* "*Sharpless*, late of the same city yeoman, *John Haines*, late "of the same city yeoman, *George Haines*, late of the "same city yeoman, *John Steel*, late of the same city yeo- "man, *Ephraim Martin*, late of the same city yeoman, and "———*Mayo*, also late of the same city yeoman, being evil "disposed persons, and designing, contriving, and intending "the morals, as well of youth as of divers other citizens of "this commonwealth, to debauch and corrupt, and to "raise and create in their minds inordinate and lustful "desires, on the first day of *March*, in the year one "thousand eight hundred and fifteen, at the city aforesaid, "and within the jurisdiction of this Court, in a *certain* "*house* there situate, unlawfully, wickedly, and scandalously "*did exhibit, and show for money, to persons, to the* "*inquest aforesaid unknown, a certain lewd, wicked,* "*scandalous, infamous, and obscene painting, representing* "*a man in an obscene, impudent, and indecent posture with* "*a woman*, to the manifest corruption and subversion of "youth, and other citizens of this commonwealth, to the "evil example of all others in like case offending, and "against the peace and dignity of the commonwealth of "*Pennsylvania*."

The defendants suffered a verdict to pass against them, and then made a motion in arrest of judgment, for which three reasons were assigned.

First, That the matter laid in the indictment is not an indictable offence.

1. It does not charge any thing to have been committed or omitted contrary to the common law, or any statute or act of assembly.
2. It purports to be an indictment at common law for the commission of an immoral act, yet it does not allege, or in any way shew, that the act was done publicly.

Second, That the acts of the defendants, and the charge made against them, are not sufficiently alleged, nor is there in the indictment a sufficient description of the substance, nature, and manner of the offence meant to be charged, if it be an offence.

Third, That the indictment does not lay the defendants' house to be a nuisance, nor the acts of the defendants to have been to the common nuisance of all the citizens, &c.

Browne, for the defendants. *First exception.* However reprehensible the conduct of the defendants may have been in a moral point of view, and however richly they may have merited the censures of society, they have done nothing to expose themselves to the penalties of the law. In *England*, they might be proper objects for animadversion of the spiritual courts, who would punish them with ecclesiastical censures, *pro salute animarum*; but they could not be reached by the temporal courts of that country. In this state there are no ecclesiastical courts, but that is no reason for stretching the powers of our common law courts, in order to give them cognisance of matters which do not properly belong to them. To render any act undictable, it must appear to be against some statute, or against the common law. Every slight misdemeanour is not indictable. 14 *Vin. Ab.* 369. *Indictment, H.* That there is any statute or act of assembly punishing the offence, with which the defendants are charged, is not pretended. The indictment must, therefore, be sustained, if at all, at common law. In the *King v. Curl*,[a] it was admitted by the attorney general, that every immoral act, is not punishable by indictment. *Blackstone* indeed affirms, (4 *Bl. Com.* 64,) that *open* and *notorious lewdness*, which is an offence against religion and morality, is cognisable by the temporal courts. Admitting the rule there laid down to be correct to the full extent, the present case does not come within its limits. But in fact it is laid down much too broadly; the cases cited do not support it. There are many offences which were not indictable at common law, such as drunkenness, cursing and swearing, fornication, &c.; offences not only immoral in themselves, but of an injurious public tendency. The case of *Rex v. Wheelhorse*,[b] one of those referred to by *Blackstone*, was an indictment against the defendant for being a *night walker*, and also for *frequenting a bawdy house*, but the Court held, that part of the indictment which related to frequenting a bawdy house, void. In Sir *Charles Sedley's* case,[c] which seems to constitute the chief foundation of the commentator's opinion, there were not only acts of the grossest indecency, exhibited in the most impudent and public manner, in one of the most public places in *London*, (*Covent Garden*,) but these acts of indecency were accompanied by acts of violence towards the persons who were passing under the balcony in which Sir *Charles* stood, upon whom he threw down bottles filled with offensive liquor. In the subsequent cases in which Sir *Charles Sedley's* case is mentioned, particularly in *Rex v. Curl*,[d] and in the *Queen v. Reed*,[e] this circumstance is adverted to, and appears to have been considered by some of the judges at least, an important feature. So that independently of the exposure of his person, the assault upon the people was sufficient to support the indictment. But Sir *Charles Sedley's* case forms no prece-

---

[a] 2 *Str.* 788.
[b] *Popham*, 208.
[c] 1 *Sid.* 168. *Latch.* 173.
[d] 2 *Str.* 788.
[e] *Fortesq.* 98.

dent; because all the reports agree, that he submitted *without trial* or *argument*. In the *Queen* v. *Reed*,[a] in which the defendant was indicted for printing and publishing an indecent and lascivious libel, Lord Chief Justice HOLT declared, it was matter for the spiritual courts to punish, not the temporal, and a verdict having passed against the defendant, judgment was arrested by the whole Court. So too in *Rex* v. *Gallard*,[b] an indictment against a woman for running in the common way naked to the waist, was quashed; and in *Rex* v. *McDonald*,[c] the court refused to sustain an indictment against the defendant, for converting his house into an hospital for the delivery of loose, disorderly, unmarried women. Nor is a solicitation of chastity punishable in the criminal courts, as appears from the case of the *Queen* v. *Pearson*.[d] Unless, therefore, the legislature think proper to interpose, improprieties, such as the defendants are charged with, must go unpunished except by the frowns of society.

2. If the acts of the defendants constitute an offence at law, they should have been charged to have been done *publicly*. Publicity is the essence of the crime. For private injuries the remedy is by private action. An indictment is an instrument for the punishment of offences of a public nature, and against the public peace only. Those crimes and misdemeanours, therefore, which are of *public evil example*, and against the common law, or some statute, are indictable. *Hawk. b. 2. ch. 25. s. 4. 14 Vin. 395. Indt. 2. pl. 11. note. 3 Bac. Ab. 549. Indictment E.* Hence those appropriate expressions in an indictment, "to the evil "example of others in like case offending." That the Courts have invariably preserved this distinction, between those cases which affect individuals only, and those which affect the public, will appear from a great number of cases which might be adduced; a few of which only it is now necessary to refer to, as the books furnish no authorities to contradict the position. An indictment for cheating in the quantity of beer which had been contracted for, was held to be bad in *Rex* v. *Combrune*,[a] and *Rex* v. *Wheatley*,[b] because, this was a deceit, a private injury, and therefore fit matter for a private action by the individual injured; but not for a public prosecution, because the public were not affected by it. These two cases are sufficient to this point. If publicity be essential to the offence, it must be averred in the indictment; for nothing is more clear, than that all the features which constitute an offence must be set out. On a motion to arrest the judgment, the Court can exercise no discretion, as they might on a motion to quash the indictment before verdict.[c] If the crime is not sufficiently stated it is the duty of the Court to arrest the judgment. Certain appropriate expressions are required by law in the description of an offence, which cannot possibly be dispensed with. So necessary are these legal expressions, that "no "*periphrasis* or *circumlocution* whatever will supply their "place." *Hawk. b. 2. ch. 25. s. 55.* And Lord MANSFIELD, (2 *Burr.* 1127,) says, "in a criminal charge there is *no lati*-"*tude of intention*, to include any thing more than is "charged. *The charge must be explicit enough to support*

itself." The indictment now under consideration plainly does not support itself; it is deficient in the essential vital principle of the charge; it does not aver that to have been *publicly* done, which is an offence only, if it be an offence at all, when done publicly. Nor is this an objection of mere form. The proof must correspond with the charge. If the exhibition of these pictures had been alleged to have been public, evidence of a secret exhibition would be inadmissible. This was ruled in *The Commonwealth* v. *Catlin*,[d] where it was held, that an indictment for *open* and gross lewdness, could not be supported by proof of a *private* act of lewdness, which an individual saw without the knowledge of the parties.

Second exception. The indictment should set forth every thing material in the description of the *substance, nature,* and *manner* of the offence charged, for no intendment can be admitted to supply a defect of this kind. *Hawk. b. 2. ch. 25. s. 60.*

There are many reasons which call for this certainty.

1. That it may judicially appear that the facts alleged at the trial, are the same as those upon which the bill was found: otherwise the prosecutor might vary the case to the perversion of justice.

2. That a man may know distinctly and *judicially*, with what he is charged, and shape his defence accordingly.

3. That the Court may distinctly and judicially know, what is the offence charged, to enable them to determine, not only the evidence proper to support the charge, but the punishment to be inflicted.

4. That the defendant may, if charged a second time with the same offence, plead his former acquittal or conviction in bar.

The necessity of great strictness in the description of an offence is proved by the following cases. In *Rex* v. *Munoz*,[a] the defendant was indicted for cheating with *false tokens*, but as these tokens were not specified in the indictment, judgment was arrested. The case of the *King* v. *Mason*[b] is of exactly the same character. *Mason* had been convicted of obtaining money upon *false pretences*; and the judgment was reversed upon error, because it was not stated *what* these false pretences were. So an indictment against the steward of a leet for permitting *divers brewers* to brew and sell contrary to the assize, was held to be bad, because it did not state *what people* he suffered. *14 Vin. Abt. 383. Indictment, L.* Many authorities are collected in the same book to the same effect. *Id. 383, 384, 385, 386.* The same principles govern the decisions of our own Courts. The case of *The People* v. *Sands*,[c] was an indictment for a nuisance at common law, "in keeping 50 barrels "of gunpowder in a *certain* house, near the dwelling houses "of *divers* good citizens, and near *a certain public street.*" The judgment was arrested, because the indictment did not aver that the powder was *negligently* and *improvidently* kept. This was the essence of the offence, and therefore, it was decided, it ought to have been stated. To apply these principles to the case before the court: the indictment states, that the picture was exhibited in a "*certain house.*" If the exhibition had been alleged to have been *public*, the place would not have been material; but as there was no allegation of that sort, the house should have

[a] *Fortesq.* 98.
[b] *Keeling,* 163.
[c] 3 *Burr.* 1645.
[d] 1 *Salk.* 382.
[a] 1 *Wils.* 301.
[b] 2 *Burr.* 1125.
[c] 2 *Burr.* 1125. 12 *Mod.* 413.

[d] 1 *Mass. Rep.* 3.
[a] 2 *Str.* 1127.
[b] 2 *T.R.* 581.
[c] 1 *Johns. Rep.* 78.

been particularly described. It ought to have appeared from the indictment, whether it was a public or a private house; whether it was the house of the defendants, or any of them, and which of them. For the same reason it is not sufficient to say, that the picture was shewn "*to persons to the inquest unknown.*" The *number* of persons to whom it was shewn ought to have been stated, that the Court might judge, whether or not it was shewn *publicly.* Again, the description of the picture is much too loose and vague; it conveys no definite idea to the mind. "Lewd, wicked, scandalous, infamous, "and obscene," are words descriptive of desires and qualities, belonging to animated beings, and are incorrectly applied to an inanimate object. The only part of the indictment which contains any thing like a description of the picture, is that which speaks of it as "representing a man in an "obscene, impudent, and indecent posture with a woman." But this is not enough; the posture ought to have been so described as to enable the Court to judge, whether or not it was obscene. Opinions on matters of this sort differ. What to one may appear indecent, may to another appear perfectly chaste and proper. In every public exhibition there are pictures which are viewed with pleasure and approbation, by many respectable and pure minded persons, as noble productions of art, while others more fastidious, consider them improper to be presented to the public eye. Is the offensive picture identified by the description given? *Sharpless* had many pictures in his collection; how is it possible to tell at which of them the indictment points? The evidence to support this indictment might apply with equal force to a picture altogether different from that upon which the grand jury passed. The defendant, therefore, could not tell how to prepare his defence, nor could he plead this indictment to another properly drawn for the same offence. In the *King* v. *Montague,*[a] which was an indictment for enticing a man's wife to elope from her husband and live in adultery, the enticing letters were set out at large. In *Coke's Inst.* 315. *ch.* 9. it is said, that "an "indictment that A killed B, *se defendendo,* is not good; "the special matter must be set down, that the Court may "judge if the killing was upon inevitable necessity." No over-nice delicacy should prevent appropriate language from being used in an indictment. "In prosecution" says Lord HOLT,[a] "people ought to be plain, and not call *bawdy* "houses, *disorderly* houses, &c." But the case of *Knowles* v. *The State of Connecticut,*[b] is directly in point. It was an information for exhibiting at the corner of a public square an *indecent* picture, *describing it particularly;* and also for exhibiting in a public inn the monster represented by the picture, "which said monster was *highly indecent,* and "*improper to be seen or exposed as a shew.*" But the Court decided, that the information should have stated the *circumstances* in which the *indecency* or *immorality* of the monster consisted, that they might judge, whether the exhibition amounted to a crime.

Third exception. If the defendants are indictable at all it is for a *nuisance;* the indictment should therefore conclude, to the common nuisance of all the citizens, &c. On this subject the precedents are uniform. *Stubbs, C.C.C.* 478 to 503. 5 *Bac. Ab.* 151. *Nuisance, B. Hawk. b.* 2. *ch.* 75. *s.* 3. 1 *Saund. Rep.* 135. 14 *Vin. Ab. Indictment, Q.*

[a] *Trem. P.C.* 209.
[a] *Comb.* 303.
[b] 1 *Day's Rep.* 103.

These authorities agree with the distinction taken in the *Queen* v. *Pearson,*[c] between particular acts of bawdry, which are not indictable, and keeping a bawdy house, which is laid as a *nuisance* and is punishable as such.

E. Ingersoll, and *Ingersoll,* (attorney general,) for the commonwealth. The defendants have been convicted, upon their own confession, of conduct indicative of great moral depravity; they are therefore entitled to no favour. This Court is *custos morum* of the public. It is therefore necessarily invested with power to punish, not only open violations of decency and morality, but also whatever tends secretly to undermine the principles of society. After an intimation which fell from the Chief Justice, it may be taken for granted, that a *public* exhibition of an indecent object is indictable. But the law is not circumscribed within such narrow limits. It may be safely affirmed, that whatever tends to the destruction of morality in general, may be punished criminally. Crimes are public offences, not because they are *perpetrated publicly,* but because their effect is to injure the public. Burglary, though done in secret, is a public offence; and secretly destroying fences is indictable. The exhibition of this picture may be considered as the publication of a libel, upon the authority of the case of the *King* v. *Wilkes,*[a] which was an information for publishing an obscene and impious libel, called "An Essay "on Woman," and the *King* v. *Curl,*[b] where an obscene book was held to be a libel. It is true, it must appear, that the picture was exposed to public view, but it is not necessary, that any particular form of words should be used, in order to make this appear. It is sufficient if it appear from the whole language of the indictment. The indictment avers, that the picture was shewn to "*persons to the inquest* "*unknown.*" The use of the plural number proves, that it was shewn to two persons at least; and if it be considered as a libel, its having been shewn to *one* was a sufficient publication. 4 *Bl. Com.* 150. In 10 *State Trials,* 98. *Appx.* the case of Sir *Charles Sedley* is referred to in a note, but it is not said, that the acts done by him were indictable, because they were *publicly* done. The *King* v. *Montague et al.*[c] was an indictment for enticing a man's wife to elope from her husband, and live with one of the defendants in adultery, but there was no allegation, that the acts charged were *publicly* done. So in the case of the *King* v. *Dingley*[d] and again in the *King* v. *Lord Gray.*[e] In none of these cases is the word *publicly* used. Here the picture is laid to have been exhibited for *money,* which necessarily implies that the exhibition was *public.*

It is not denied, that the indictment must shew some *place* in which the offence was committed. "It must ap- "pear," says *Hawkins, b.* 2. *ch.* 25. *s.* 83, 84, "to have been "within the judisdiction of the Court in which the indict- "ment was taken, and must also be alleged in such a "manner as is perfectly free from all repugnance and "inconsistency." This is all that is required, and this is done. The exhibition is stated to have taken place in a certain house, in the city of *Philadelphia,* and within the jurisdiction of the Court. This is a sufficient description of

[c] 4 *Burr.* 2527.
[a] 4 *Burr.* 2527.
[b] 2 *Str.* 788.
[c] *Trem. P. of C.* 209.
[d] *Trem. P. of C.* 213.
[e] *Id.* 215.

the place "perfectly free from all repugnance and incon-"sistency."

The *offence* is described with reasonable certainty. The jury would have had no difficulty in applying the evidence to the picture indicated in the indictment, and that is enough; the records of the Court are not to be polluted by obscene and indecent language. There are many cases in which no greater certainty can be attained than in this. For example, an indictment for an assault and battery upon A; but there may have been two or more breaches of the peace. Again, an indictment may charge the stealing of a bay horse the property of A B, yet A B may be the owner of several bay horses. In *Dougherty's Cr. Cir. Com.* 315, will be found a precedent, which has been pursued by the present indictment as far as the facts would admit of.

It is true, that there the sale of the obscene print, which was the object of the indictment, was alleged to have taken place in a *public* shop, but in this case the house of the defendants could not have been described as a *public* house, because that would have implied, that it was a tavern, which it was not. It is also true, that in the precedent referred to, the name of the offensive print is given, which could not have been done in this case, as *Sharpless's* picture had no name. In every other respect the indictments correspond. In *Starkie on Criminal Pleading*, vol. i. 63. 83. 176. and vol. ii. 463. 464. 469. 471. all the law on this subject is collected.

In reply, it was said, that to call this a prosecution for a *libel* was placing it in a very novel and unexpected point of view: That the offence charged wanted at least one essential feature of a libel; it did not reflect upon any particular person, without which, according to *Hawkins*, b. 1. ch. 73. s. 1. nothing can be esteemed a libel: That in the *King v. Lord Gray*, which had been much relied upon by the counsel for the prosecution, judgment was never entered against the defendant, a *nolle prosequi* having been entered by the attorney general: (see *State Trials*.) That in the case of the *King v. Wilkes*, the question, whether an information or indictment could be sustained for publishing an obscene libel was never made, argued, or decided; the information was tried while Mr. *Wilkes* was in *France*, and his counsel and agents made no objection thereto: That the passage from *Hawkins*, b. 2. ch. 25. s. 83. applied only to those cases in which the *place* was *immaterial*, but that here the place was a material part of the offence: And that the precedent from *Dougherty's Cr. Cir. Com.* differed essentially from the present indictment, the offensive print there spoken of being not only described and named, but further identified by being stated to have been contained in a pamphlet, which is also particularly described.

TILGHMAN C.J. This is an indictment against *Jesse Sharpless* and others, for exhibiting an indecent picture to divers persons for money. The defendants consented, that a verdict should go against them, and afterwards moved in arrest of judgment for several reasons.

1. "That the matter laid in the indictment is not an "indictable offence." It was denied, in the first place, that even a *public* exhibition of an indecent picture was indictable; but supposing it to be so, it was insisted, that this indictment contained no charge of a *public* exhibition. In *England*, there are some acts of immorality, such as adultery, of which the ecclesiastical courts have taken cognisance from very ancient times, and in such cases, al-

though they tended to the corruption of the public morals, the temporal courts have not assumed jurisdiction. This occasioned some uncertainty in the law; some difficulty in discriminating between the offences punishable in the temporal and ecclesiastical courts. Although there was no ground for this distinction in a country like ours, where there was no ecclesiastical jurisdiction, yet the common law principle was supposed to be in force, and to get rid of it, punishments were inflicted by act of assembly. There is no act punishing the offence charged against the defendants, and therefore the case must be decided upon the principles of the common law. That actions of *public indecency*, were always indictable, as tending to corrupt the public morals, I can have no doubt; because, even in the profligate reign of *Charles* II. Sir *Charles Sedley* was punished by imprisonment and a heavy fine, for standing naked in a balcony, in a public part of the city of *London*. It is true, that, besides this shameful exhibition, it is mentioned in some of the reports of that case, that he threw down bottles, containing offensive liquor, among the people; but we have the highest authority for saying, that the most criminal part of his conduct, and that which principally drew upon him the vengeance of the law, was the *exposure of his person*. For this I refer to the opinion of the judges in the *Queen v. Curl*, (2 *Str.* 792.) Lord MANSFIELD, in the *King v. Sir Francis Blake Delaval*, &c. 3 *Burr.* 1438, and of *Blackstone* in the 4th volume of his Commentaries, page 64. Neither is there any doubt, that the publication of *an indecent book* is indictable, although it was once doubted by the Court of King's Bench, in the *Queen v. Reed*, (in the sixth year of Queen *Anne*.) But the authority of that case was destroyed, upon great consideration, in the *King v. Curl*, (1 *George* II.) 2 *Str.* 788. The law was in *Curl's* case established upon true principles. What tended to corrupt society, was held to be a breach of the peace and punishable by indictment. The Courts are guardians of the public morals, and therefore have jurisdiction in such cases. Hence it follows, that an offence may be punishable, if in its nature and by its example, it tends to the corruption of morals; although it be not committed in public. In the *King v. Delaval*, &c. there was a *conspiracy*, and for that reason alone, the Court had jurisdiction; yet Lord MANSFIELD expressed his opinion, that they would have had jurisdiction, from the *nature of the offence*, which was the seduction of a young woman, under the age of twenty-one, and placing her in the situation of a kept mistress, under the pretence of binding her as an apprentice to her keeper; and he cited the opinion of Lord HARDWICKE, who ordered an information to be filed against a man who had made a formal assignment of his wife to another person. In support of this we find an indictment in *Trem. Pl.* 213, (The *King v. Dingley*) for seducing a married woman to elope from her husband. Now to apply these principles to the present case. The defendants are charged with *exhibiting and shewing to sundry persons for money, a lewd, scandalous, and obscene painting*. A picture tends to excite lust as strongly as a writing; and the *shewing* of a picture, is as much a *publication*, as the *selling* of a book. *Curl* was convicted of selling a book. It is true, the indictment charged the act to have been in a *public shop*, but that can make no difference. The mischief was no greater than if he had taken the purchaser into a *private room*, and sold him the book there. The law is not to be evaded by an artifice of that kind. If the privacy of the room was a protection, all the youth of the city might be corrupted by taking them one by one into a chamber, and there inflaming their passions by the exhibition of lascivious pictures. In the eye of the law, this would be a *publication*, and a most pernicious one. Then, although it is not said in the indictment, in express terms, that the defendants published the painting, yet the averment is substantially the same, that is to say, that they exhibited it to sundry persons for money; for that in law is a *publication*.

2. The second reason in arrest of judgment is, that the picture is not sufficiently described in the indictment. It is described as *a lewd and obscene painting, representing a man in an obscene, impudent, and indecent posture with a woman*. We do not know, that the picture had any name, and therefore it might be impossible to designate it by name. What then is expected? Must the indictment describe minutely, the attitude and posture of the figures? I am for paying some respect to the chastity of our records. These are cirmumstances which may be well omitted. Whether the picture was really indecent, the jury might judge from the *evidence*, or if necessary from *inspection*. The witnesses could identify it. I am of opinion, that the description is sufficient.

3. The third and last reason is, that the indictment does not lay the defendants' *house* to be a *nuisance*, nor the act of the defendants to be to the *common nuisance* of all the citizens, &c. The answer is plain. It is not an indictment for a *nuisance*, but for an action of evil example, tending to the corruption of the youth, and other citizens of the commonwealth, and against the peace, &c. In describing an offence of this kind, the technical word *nuisance* would have been improper. My opinion is, that the indictment is good, and therefore the judgment should not be arrested.

YEATES J. I perfectly concur in the sentiments expressed by Sir *Philip Yorke*, in the case of the *King v. Curl*, (2 *Stra.* 790,) that although every immoral act, such as lying, &c. is not indictable, yet where the offence charged, is destructive of morality in general; where it does or may affect every member of the community, it is punishable at common law. The destruction of morality renders the power of the government invalid, for government is no more than public order. It weakens the bands by which society is kept together. The corruption of the public mind in general, and debauching the manners of youth in particular by lewd and obscene pictures exhibited to view, must necessarily be attended with the most injurious consequences, and in such instances Courts of Justice are, or ought to be, the schools of morals. So far from the law of *England* being changed on this point by modern decisions, we find in the case of the *King v. Wilkes* in 1770, (4 *Burr.* 2527,) who was convicted on an information for an obscene and impious libel, called an *Essay on Woman*, the present objection was not taken by his counsel. The wicked intention of the defendants; the exhibition of the obscene painting for money to persons unknown; and the effects of such scandalous conduct, are facts found by the jury, and I cannot bring my mind to doubt for a single moment, that the offence charged, falls within cognisance of a court of criminal jurisdiction.

The defendants' counsel have objected, that should the acts charged against them, constitute an offence at common law, they are not laid with sufficient legal certainty; and that it may so happen, that different evidence may be given to the grand and traverse jurors for the same offence. To this it has been properly answered, that the same difficulty may occur in many indictments, as for assaults and batteries, where there have been several breaches of the peace at different times, by the party charged, and only one indictment has been preferred against him. As to the defendant being twice punished for the same offence, I see no danger whatever. If one obscene, scandalous picture alone has been exhibited to view (whether on canvas, paper, or parchment, cannot be material) a conviction or acquittal on the present indictment may be pleaded in bar to a future prosecution. If more than one such picture has been exhibited they may prove the truth of their plea, of *autrefoits convict*, or *acquit*, by shewing the evidence of the specific charge made against them on their trial. The same seeming difficulty may arise in a charge of felony laid in stealing a bay horse of A B, (which surely would be sufficiently certain, without laying the particular natural marks of the horse), and yet if A B had more than one bay horse which had been stolen, the same objection might have been made as is now taken.

This indictment has evidently been framed from the precedent in *Dougherty's Cro. Circ. Comp.* 315, for exposing to sale an obscene print, which it minutely follows, except so far as the clerical character is attacked, and laying the act to have been done in *an open public shop* of the defendant in exposing it *to J N*, &c. The precedent relied on, states the exposure of the objectionable print to a single individual in an open and public shop: but here the infamous and obscene painting was exhibited and shewn for money, in a *certain house* to *persons* unknown to the inquest. The question then in this part of the case is narrowed to a single point;—Whether the exhibition of a lewd, wicked, scandalous, infamous, and obscene painting, representing, &c. to certain individuals in a private house for money, is dispunishable by the sound principles of common law? On this question I cannot hesitate. It is settled, that the publication of a libel to any *one* person renders the act complete. (4 *Bla. Com.* 150.) No man is permitted to corrupt the morals of the people. Secret poison cannot be thus disseminated. A slight knowledge of human nature teaches us, "that while secresy is affected in "a case like the present, public curiosity is more strongly "excited thereby, and that those persons who may "ignorantly suppose they have had the good fortune of "seeing bawdy pictures, will not content themselves with "keeping the secret in their own bosoms!" Unless we shall consider the conduct of the defendant justifiable, and lawful in the present instance, the indictment is supportable, if it alleges the offence as it really and in truth was committed.

As to the nature and manner in which the painting is represented to have been made, I hold it to be sufficient to state, that it represented a man in an obscene, impudent, and indecent posture with a woman, either clothed or unclothed, without wounding our eyes or ears, with a particular description of their attitude or posture. Why should it be so described? If the jurors are satisfied on the proof, that the persons represented were painted in an impudent and indecent posture, will not this give the Court all the information they can require? Some immodest paintings, it is true, may carry grosser features of indecency than others, and in fact, may produce disgust in the minds even of the most debauched; yet if the painting here, tended to the manifest corruption of youth and other citizens, and was of public evil example to others, I think it sufficiently described. As to the exception, that the indictment does not say, that the defendants have been guilty of a common nuisance, it suffices to remark, that the offence is not alleged as a nuisance, but as a libel on the morals and government of the state, in the same manner as was done in the case of *Wilkes* for his Essay on Woman.

Upon the whole, I am of opinion, that the motion in arrest of judgment be overruled, and that judgment be rendered on the verdict.

BRACKENRIDGE J. concurred, but was absent through indisposition when the opinions were delivered.

Motion in arrest of judgment overruled, and judgment on the verdict.

■ Commonwealth
v.
Peter Holmes.

THE defendant was indicted at the Circuit Court of Common Pleas sitting in this county, for publishing a lewd and obscene print, contained in a certain book entitled "Memoirs of a Woman of Pleasure," and also for publishing the same book. The indictment contained three counts, charging the publishing and delivering of the print to three several persons, and three counts alleging the publishing and delivering of the book to the same three persons. The second count alleged that the defendant, "being a scandalous and evil disposed person, and contriving, devising and intending, the morals as well of youth as of other good citizens of said Commonwealth to debauch and corrupt, and to raise and create in their minds inordinate and lustful desires, with force and arms, at &c. on &c. knowingly, unlawfully, wickedly, maliciously and scandalously, did utter, publish and deliver to A. B. a certain lewd, wicked, scandalous, infamous and obscene printed book, entitled &c. which said printed book is so lewd, wicked and obscene, that the same would be offensive to the court here, and improper to be placed upon the records thereof: wherefore the jurors aforesaid do not set forth the same in this indictment: to the manifest corruption and subversion of the youth and other good citizens of said Commonwealth in their manners and conversation; in contempt of law; to the evil and pernicious example of others in like case offending, and against the peace" &c. The fifth count charged the publishing and delivering to *C. D.* the print contained in the same book, describing the print, and averring the same evil intent and tendency.

The defendant, being convicted in the common pleas, appealed to this court, where being again convicted, he moved in arrest of judgment;—1st. Because the Circuit Court of Common Pleas, at which the indictment was found, had no jurisdiction by law of the offences charged in said indictment.—2d. That in certain counts of the indictment, no part of the book, which is alleged to be a libel, is set forth therein.—3d. That in certain other counts the print is not so particularly described, as it ought to have been, so that the jury might judge whether the same was obscene &c.—4th. Because in all the counts, upon which the defendant was found guilty, it is only alleged that he uttered, published and delivered the said libel to a particular individual: whereas it ought to have been alleged that he uttered, and published the same generally.—5th. Because the facts, as stated in the several counts in the

indictment, upon which the verdict was rendered, do not, as therein stated, constitute an offence against the Commonwealth.—6th. Because the several counts are, and each of them is, informal, uncertain, and insufficient in law to enable the court to pass sentence upon the verdict.

Mills for the defendant supported the three first causes shewn for arresting the judgment; and was replied to by *Davis*, solicitor general, and *Newton*, county solicitor.

PARKER C.J. delivered the opinion of the court.—The second and fifth counts in this indictment are certainly good: for it can never be required that an obscene book and picture should be displayed upon the records of the court: which must be done, if the description in these counts is insufficient. This would be to require that the public itself should give permanency and notoriety to indecency, in order to punish it. These counts being good, it is unnecessary to give an opinion upon the others: since if there be good and bad counts in the same indictment, and a general verdict of guilty returned, the verdict must be applied to the good ones.

The only objection, which has seemed to require much consideration, is that which is founded upon a supposed want of jurisdiction of this offence in the Court of Common Pleas: at which court the indictment was found. A short history of our judicial tribunals will shew clearly, that this objection must also fail.

It is conceded that, by the statute of 1803, *c.* 155, the courts of common pleas, in whatever shapes they have existed since the passage of that act, have enjoyed all the criminal jurisdiction before lawfully exercised by the court of general sessions of the peace. The enquiry then is, what jurisdiction this last mentioned court had in criminal matters, before that statute was enacted.

The jurisdiction of the court of sessions, under the present constitution, was established by the statute of 1782, *c.* 14. By this statute the justices of that court "are empowered to hear and determine all matters relative to the conservation of the peace, and the punishment of such offences as are cognizable by them at common law, or by the acts and laws of the legislature: and to give judgment, order or sentence thereon, as the law directs, and to award execution accordingly."

The existing power of this court, whether at the common law or by legislative act, before the adoption of the constitution, must be sought for, in order to ascertain its present jurisdiction.

By the common law, the court of sessions of the peace in *England*, had jurisdiction of all misdemeanours; and indeed of all felonies, the punishment of which was not capital. [See 4 *Black. Comm.* 270. *Also Note 2 by Christian.*] This court however could not try any offence newly created by statute, unless jurisdiction was expressly given to it. The offence of libel is an offence at common law, of which the court of sessions originally had jurisdiction, without doubt.

But we are rather to look at the common law of our own country, which, at the time of the adoption of the constitution, may as well have existed in the form of statutes and ordinances of the colonial and provincial legislatures, as in any other way. By the provincial act of 11 *Will.* 3. *c.* 1, a court of general sessions of the peace was constituted within each county, who were "empowered to hear and determine all matters relating to the conservation of the peace, and punishment of offenders, and whatsoever is by them cognizable according to law; and to give judgment and award execution therein." Even this early provision rests upon some pre-existing power, resulting from the common law or antecedent legislative acts. By the third section of this act, a provision is made for the summoning of jurors to attend this court. An earlier provincial act, [7 *Will.* 3, *c.* 4.] provides for the attendance upon said court of a grand inquest, whose duty it is made to enquire and duly present the breach of all such good and wholesome laws, as are or shall be established within the province, and all such misdemeanours as are proper to their enquiry and the jurisdiction of the court.

One step further back brings us to colonial judicial establishments, in which will be found the principles and fundamental qualities of the several judicial tribunals since created. As all legislative, so all judicial power seems to have been exercised by the whole body of the people, for a year or two after the arrival of the first colonists. When a representative legislature succeeded to this simple democ-

racy, it exercised judicial power, both criminal and civil. But in the year 1639 this crude system was superseded by the court of assistants, to which was given jurisdiction by appeal in civil actions, and original in all criminal suits which extended to life, member or banishment. And at the same time county courts were established, with jurisdiction civil and criminal, not extending to life, member or banishment; which was reserved to the court of assistants.

This county court was the parent of the courts of common pleas, and of the general sessions of the peace; enjoying the powers of both, as now exercised. And its criminal jurisdiction was analogous to that practically exercised by the court of quarter sessions in *England;* to which the colonial legislature undoubtedly had reference, in determining its jurisdiction. In the year 1699, the provincial legislature divided the criminal and civil jurisdiction between the court of common pleas and the court of sessions; both of which were at that time established by law, and have continued ever since, with various modifications, until the whole criminal jurisdiction of the court of sessions was, in 1804, transferred to the court of common pleas. Thus the county court was abolished.

It then appears, by tracing back our juridical history, that the court of common pleas has criminal jurisdiction, in every thing which does not relate to life, member or banishment: except such crimes as have been since constituted by law, or the punishment of which, by statute, is to be administered by the Supreme Judicial Court. And this is the case with respect to all punishments by hard labour; and in many instances, where fine and imprisonment are the punishment, jurisdiction is given only to the court last mentioned.

The offence, of which the defendant stands convicted, is a misdemeanour, the punishment of which does not extend to life, member or banishment: nor is it an offence created by statute; so that it is clearly cognizable by the court of common pleas, as organized when the indictment was presented.

Commonwealth
v.
S. M. Landis.

PEIRCE, J.—The reasons for a new trial in this case are numerous, but they may all be disposed of under a few heads. They relate:

First. To the exclusion of evidence tending to show the scientific correctness of the book complained of, and the fitness of such a publication for general information.

Second. To an expression of opinion by the judge as to the character of the book.

Third. To errors in charging the jury as to what constituted an obscene libel, and as to what extent a publication is protected as necessary for general information and conducive to the public welfare.

1. Physicians were called as experts to show the scientific correctness of the book and the necessity of such knowledge for general information.

I ruled at the trial that the book might be true and scientifically correct in its statements and descriptions, and yet be obscene; that its obscenity did not depend upon its truthfulness or falsity, but upon its tendency to inflame the passions and debauch society. The character of the book was a question purely for the jury, in which they could not be aided by the testimony of experts. Obscenity is determined by the common sense and feelings of mankind, and not by the skill of the learned. It was therefore a question for the jury, to be determined by their examination of the publication, and not by the opinions of others respecting it. That which offends modesty, and is indecent and lewd, and tends to the creation of lascivious desires, is obscene. Of this the jury were as competent to judge as the most accomplished experts in medical science, whose familiarity with the subjects treated of in the book might, perhaps, render them less susceptible to the emotions which would be excited in the general public by reading such a book.

2. Relative to the expression of opinion by the judge as to the character of the book, it was held by the Supreme Court in *Kilpatrick* vs. *The Commonwealth*, 7 Casey, 198, that a judge may rightfully express his opinion respecting the evidence and it may sometimes be his duty to do it, yet not so as to withdraw it from the consideration and decision of the jury.

My own experience as a judge has taught me that it is sometimes not only expedient but necessary to the proper administration of the law and justice that a judge should express his opinion on the evidence submitted to the jury. His greater familiarity with the rules of evidence, the weight of the testimony, and its application to the subject-matter of investigation, requires that he should do so; but he should always accompany it with the instruction that the facts of the case are for their determination, under the evidence submitted to them.

In this case this instruction was repeated to the jury more than once. They were told that they were not to take my opinion of the book, but were to determine its character from their own examination of it. Again, they were instructed that it was for them to determine the character of the book. If in their judgment the book was fit and proper for publication, and such as should go into their families and be handed to their sons and daughters, and placed in boarding-schools for the beneficial information of the young and others, then it was their duty to acquit the defendant.

They were further instructed that if they had a doubt as to the obscenity of the book, it was their duty to acquit the defendant.

This instruction left the whole question of the character of the publication to the jury. There was no controversy as to the publication of the book by the defendant, as its publication was substantially, if not in terms, admitted by him.

3. The next alleged errors relate to the charge of the Court as to what constitutes an obscene libel, and to what extent a publication is protected as necessary for general information and conducive to the public welfare.

The jury were instructed that it did not matter whether the things published in the book were true, and in conformity with nature and the laws of our being or not. If they were unfit to be published, and tended to inflame improper and lewd passions, it was an obscene libel. That to justify a publication of the character of this book they must be satisfied that the publication was made for a legitimate and useful purpose, and that it was not made from any motive of mere gain or with a corrupt desire to debauch society. That even scientific and medical publications containing illustrations exhibiting the human form, if wantonly exposed in the open markets, with a wanton and wicked desire to create a demand for them, and not to promote the good of society by placing them in proper hands for useful purposes, would, if tending to excite lewd desires, be held to be obscene libels.

That before a medical class, for the purpose of instruction, it might be necessary and proper, and consonant with decency and modesty, to expose the human body for exhibition of disease, or for the purpose of operation, but that if the same human body were exposed in front of one of our medical colleges to the public indiscriminately, even for the purpose of operation, such an exhibition would be held to be indecent and obscene.

The jury were further instructed that publications of this character are protected when made with a view to benefit society, and in a manner not to injure the public, but that a mistaken view of the defendant as to the character and tendency of the book, if it was in itself obscene and unfit for publication, would not excuse his violation of the law.

After having listened to the elaborate and earnest argument of the learned counsel for the defendant, I do not perceive that there was error either in the admission or exclusion of evidence, or in the charge to the jury, and I think that the verdict is sustained by both the law and the evidence. The motion for a new trial is therefore overruled.

■ The People of the State of New York, *Respondent,*
v.
August Muller, *Appellant.*

(Argued June 9, 1884; decided October 7, 1884.)

APPEAL from judgment of the General Term of the Supreme Court in the first judicial department, entered upon an order made March 28, 1882, which affirmed a judgment of the Court of Oyer and Terminer for the city and county of New York, entered upon a verdict convicting defendant of a misdemeanor in selling certain alleged obscene and indecent photographs.

The material facts are stated in the opinion.

John D. Townsend for appellant. The court erred in refusing to allow defendant to prove by experts that there exists a distinguishing line as understood by artists between pure art and obscene and indecent art. (*R. & S. R. R. Co.* v. *Budlong*, 10 How. Pr. 290; *Lamoure* v. *Caryl*, 4 Denio, 370; *Greenfield* v. *People, etc.*, 85 N.Y. 83; *Platner* v. *Platner*, 78 id. 90.)

John Vincent for respondent. Whether the statute was violated was a question of fact to be determined by the jury upon inspection of the pictures, and an examination of them will demonstrate that fact. (*Reg.* v. *Hicklin*, L.R., 3 Q.B. 360.)

ANDREWS, J. The first count in the indictment charges the defendant with selling indecent and obscene photographs, representing nude females in lewd, obscene, indecent, scandalous and lascivious attitudes and postures, and the second count charges him with having in his possession divers, lewd, scandalous, obscene and indecent photographs of the same character, with intent to sell the same. Section 317 of the Penal Code declares among other things that a person who sells, lends, gives away, or offers to give away, or shows, or has in his possession with intent to sell, or give away, or to show, or advertises, or otherwise offers for loan, gift, sale, or distribution, an obscene or indecent book, writing, paper, picture, drawing or photograph, is guilty of a misdemeanor. The evidence on the trial in support of the indictment related to nine photographs produced before the jury, which were proved to have been sold by the defendant in the ordinary course of his employment as a clerk in a store for the sale of books, pictures and photographs, in the city of New York. The record contains no special description of the photographs, except that it appears that they represented nude females, and were photographic copies of paintings which had been exhibited in the Salon in Paris, and one of them at the centennial exhibition in Philadelphia, and that among them were pictures designated "La Asphyxie," "After the Bath," and "La Baigneuse."

The jury by their verdict of guilty necessarily found that the photographs were obscene and indecent. The exhibits were produced on the argument of the appeal at the General Term, and the court in its opinion expressed its concurrence with the finding of the jury, saying that they might very well have found that the photographs were both indecent and obscene. They were not produced in this court, and we are unable to pass upon the question of their obscenity or indecency from an inspection of the pictures themselves. If the defendant's counsel desired to insist in this court that the photographs were not in fact indecent or obscene, and that this appeared from the photographs themselves, and that the finding of the jury was therefore without evidence to support it, it was his duty to have furnished them as a part of the record, or to have insisted upon their production by the district attorney. Upon the case as presented we must assume that the pictures were of the character described in the indictment.

But exceptions were taken by the defendant on the trial which render it necessary to consider to some extent the scope of the statute, the method of trying the issue of obscenity and indecency, and the relevancy of proof of an innocent intent on the part of a defendant charged with a violation of the statute. It is to be observed that the statute does not undertake to define obscene or indecent pictures or publications. But the words used in the statute are themselves descriptive. They are words in common use, and every person of ordinary intelligence understands their meaning, and readily and in most cases accurately applies them to any object or thing brought to his attention which involves a judgment as to the quality indicated. It does not require an expert in art or literature to determine whether a picture is obscene or whether printed words are offensive to decency and good morals. These are matters which fall within the range of ordinary intelligence, and a jury does not require to be informed by an expert before pronouncing upon them. It is evident that mere nudity in painting or sculpture is not obscenity. Some of the great works in painting and sculpture as all know represent nude human forms. It is a false delicacy and mere prudery which would condemn and banish from sight all such objects as obscene, simply on account of their nudity. If the test of obscenity or indecency in a picture or statue is its capability of suggesting impure thoughts, then indeed all such representations might be considered as indecent or obscene. The presence of a woman of the purest character and of the most modest behavior and bearing may suggest to a prurient imagination images of lust, and excite impure desires, and so may a picture or statue not in fact indecent or obscene.

The test of an obscene book was stated in *Regina* v. *Hicklin* (L.R., 3 Q.B. 369), to be, whether the tendency of the matter charged as obscenity is to deprave or corrupt those whose minds are open to such immoral influences, and who might come into contact with it. We think it would also be a proper test of obscenity in a painting or statue, whether the motive of the painting or statue, so to speak, as indicated by it, is pure or impure, whether it is naturally calculated to excite in a spectator impure imaginations, and whether the other incidents and qualities, however attractive, were merely accessory to this as the primary or main purposes of the representation.

The defendant on the trial called as witnesses an artist who had practiced painting for many years, and also a person who had been engaged in the study of art. They were asked by defendant's counsel whether there was a distinguishing line, as understood by artists, between pure art and obscene and indecent art. The question was objected to by the prosecutor and excluded by the court. The issue to be tried was whether the particular photographs in question were obscene or indecent. The defendant was entitled to prove in his defense any facts legitimately bearing upon this issue. The fact that the original pictures of which the photographs were copies had been exhibited in the Salon in Paris was admitted by the prosecution, and it was proved that one of them had been publicly exhibited in Philadelphia. But this did not, as matter of law, exclude a finding by the jury that the photographs were obscene and indecent. It is not impossible certainly that the public exhibition of indecent pictures may have been permitted in Paris or Philadelphia, and the fact that a picture had been publicly exhibited would not necessarily determine its character as decent or indecent. Indeed there is but little scope for proof bearing upon the issue of decency or obscenity, beyond the evidence furnished by the picture itself. The question which was excluded, if intended to bring out the fact that pictures might be either decent or indecent, and that the canons of pure art would accept those of one class and reject those of the other, was properly overruled as an attempt to prove a self-evident proposition. If the question was intended to be followed by proof that, according to the standard of judgment adopted and recognized by artists, the photographs in question were not obscene or indecent, it was properly rejected for the reason that the issue was not whether in the opinion of witnesses, or of a class of people, the photographs were indecent or obscene, but whether they were so in fact, and upon this issue witnesses could neither be permitted to give their own opinions, or to state the aggregate opinion of a particular class or part of the community. To permit such evidence would put the witness in the place of the jury, and the latter would have no function to discharge. The testimony of experts is not admissible upon matters of judgment within the knowledge and experience of ordinary jurymen

(1 Greenl. Ev., § 440). The question whether a picture or writing is obscene is one of the plainest that can be presented to a jury, and under the guidance of a discreet judge there is little danger of their reaching a wrong conclusion. The opinions of witnesses would not aid the jury in reaching a conclusion, and their admission would contravene the general rule that facts and not opinions are to be given in evidence.

The defendant's counsel at the conclusion of the evidence made several requests to charge, which were denied by the trial judge. The leading purpose of those requests was to induce the court to lay down the rule that the intent of a defendant in selling a picture claimed to be indecent and obscene is an important element in determining his guilt. The statute makes the selling of an obscene and indecent picture a misdemeanor. There is no exception by reason of any special intent in making the sale. The object of the statute was to suppress the traffic in obscene publications, and to protect the community against the contamination and pollution arising from their exhibition and distribution. It would we conceive be no answer to an indictment under the statute for the sale of an obscene picture, that it was sold to a person not liable to be injured by it, or that it was a picture, in respect to execution, of distinguished merit. In *Regina* v. *Hicklin* (*supra*), the question was whether a certain book was obscene and liable to seizure for that reason under an English statute. It appeared that it was published to expose the alleged immoralities of private confession in the Roman Catholic Church. But the court having found that passages purporting to be extracts from the writings of Roman Catholics were obscene in fact, it was held that the intent of the publication, however innocent, was no answer to the proceeding.

We do not doubt that whether a publication is obscene or not may in some cases depend on circumstances. For example, a medical book for the instruction of medical men may contain illustrations suitable and proper as a part of the work, but which, if detached and published alone for circulation, might be deemed indecent within the statute. In the present case there was no evidence to which the requests to charge were applicable. The pictures in question were kept for general sale, except that they were not sold to boys under twenty-one years of age. The requests, as applied to the case, were a series of abstract propositions having no relation to the issue, and were on that ground, independently of any other consideration, properly denied. We find no error in the record. The case seems to have been fairly tried and was submitted to the jury in a careful charge, and with the verdict of the jury this court cannot interfere. The statute is an important one, and while it should have a reasonable and not a strained construction, at the same time it ought to have such a practical interpretation by the court and jury, as will subserve the important purpose of its enactment.

The judgment should be affirmed.

All concur.

Judgment affirmed.

■ In re Worthington Co.

(Supreme Court, Special Term, New York County. June 22, 1894.)

Application by the receiver of the Worthington Company for instructions as to disposition of certain books, assets of said company. Receiver allowed to sell the books.

James M. Fisk, for receiver.

Anthony Comstock, opposed.

O'BRIEN, J. After consultation with some of my brethren, we have concluded that the following views should be expressed concerning the merits of this motion: This is an application made by the receiver of the Worthington Company for instructions concerning the final disposition of certain books which were found among the assets of that company, and which are now in his custody, and respecting which it is alleged by certain parties that they are unfit for general circulation, and come under the designation of "immoral literature," and as such should be excluded from sale. That these books constitute valuable assets of this receivership cannot be doubted, and the question before the court for decision on this motion is whether or not they are of such a character as should be condemned and their sale prohibited. The books in question consist of Payne's edition of the Arabian Nights, Fielding's novel, Tom Jones, the works of Rabelais, Ovid's Art of Love, the Decameron of Boccaccio, the Heptameron of Queen Margaret of Navarre, the Confessions of J. J. Rousseau, Tales from the Arabic, and Alladin. Most of the volumes that have been submitted to the inspection of the court are of choice editions, both as to the letter-press and the bindings, and are such, both as to their commercial value and subject-matter, as to prevent their being generally sold or purchased, except by those who would desire them for their literary merit, or for their worth as specimens of fine book-making. It is very difficult to see upon what theory these world-renowned classics can be regarded as specimens of that pornographic literature which it is the office of the Society for the Suppression of Vice to suppress, or how they can come under any stronger condemnation than that high standard literature which consists of the works of Shakespeare, of Chaucer, of Laurence Sterne, and of other great English writers, without making reference to many parts of the Old Testament Scriptures, which are to be found in almost every household in the land. The very artistic character, the high qualities of style, the absence of those glaring and crude pictures, scenes, and descriptions which affect the common and vulgar mind, make a place for books of the character in question, entirely apart from such gross and obscene writings as it is the duty of the public authorities to suppress. It would be quite as unjustifiable to condemn the writings of Shakespeare and Chaucer and Laurence Sterne, the early English novelists, the playwrights of the Restoration, and the dramatic literature which has so much enriched the English language, as to place an interdict upon these volumes, which have received the admiration of literary men for so many years. What has become standard literature of the English language—has been wrought into the very structure of our splendid English literature—is not to be pronounced at this late day unfit for publication or circulation, and stamped with judicial disapprobation, as hurtful to the community. The works under consideration are the product of the greatest literary genius. Payne's Arabian Nights is a wonderful exhibition of Oriental scholarship, and the other volumes have so long held a supreme rank in literature that it would be absurd to call them now foul and unclean. A seeker after the sensual and degrading parts of a narrative may find in all these works, as in those of other great authors, something to satisfy his pruriency. But to condemn a standard literary work, because of a few of its episodes, would compel the exclusion from circulation of a very large proportion of the works of fiction of the most famous writers of the English language. There is no such evil to be feared from the sale of these rare and costly books as the imagination of many even well-disposed people might apprehend. They rank with the higher literature, and would not be bought nor appreciated by the class of people from whom unclean publications ought to be withheld. They are not corrupting in their influence upon the young, for they are not likely to reach them. I am satisfied that it would be a wanton destruction of property to prohibit the sale by the receiver of these works,—for if their sale ought to be prohibited the books should be burned,—but I find no reason in law, morals, or expediency why they should not be sold for the benefit of the creditors of the receivership. The receiver is therefore allowed to sell these volumes.

■ The State
v.
Cone.

[No. 2,087. Filed November 24, 1896.]

W. A. *Ketcham*, Attorney-General, M. R. *McClaskey* and V. W. *VanFleet*, for State.

J. S. Dodge and O. Z. *Hubbell*, for appellee.

Davis, J. This is a prosecution under section 2081, Burns' R.S. 1894 (1995, R.S. 1881), for public indecency. The court below sustained the appellee's motion to quash the affidavit in the cause and discharge the defendant from custody, and the State then excepted. The State of Indiana brings this appeal to reverse said ruling.

The part of section 2081, under which this prosecution was brought, reads as follows: "Whoever, being over fourteen years of age, * * * uses or utters any obscene or licentious language or words in the presence or hearing of any female * * * is guilty of public indecency," etc. The affidavit charges that "in the county of Elkhart, and State of Indiana, on the 7th day of October, 1895, Bert Cone was then and there a male person of over fourteen years of age, and that said Cone did then and there, in the presence of a female, Katie Marker, use and utter obscene and licentious language and words, such words being as follows: 'After my balls are over,' meaning by the word balls his testicles, and further crying out, 'is there anything in it,' meaning thereby to inquire if said Katie Marker was not a woman of bad character for chastity."

The language charged as having been used by appellee is not such as to convey a meaning in its nature obscene or licentious unless aided by extrinsic averments. It is charged, by way of inducement or colloquium, that the words were uttered by him in an obscene or licentious sense, but it is not charged that anyone in his presence, or hearing so understood the words. The crime consists in uttering obscene or licentious language in the presence or hearing of a female. Where language that is obscene or licentious *per se*, is uttered in the presence or hearing of a female the crime is complete, but where the language is not obscene or licentious *per se*, the use of it is not a crime unless it is shown by extrinsic averments that it was used in the presence or hearing of a female in an obscene or licentious sense, and that she so understood the words. The words charged in the affidavit might be used in such connection with other words or with acts to which an obscene or licentious meaning might attach, but nothing is averred showing how or in what connection the words were uttered, or that they had any local or provincial meaning.

Assuming, therefore, that the words set out in the affidavit can be made actionable by the use of extrinsic language, the extrinsic language used in this instance is not, in our opinion, sufficient to charge the crime. *State* v. *Coffing*, 3 Ind. App. 304.

The appeal is not sustained.

Judgment affirmed.

■ Swearingen
v.
United States.

ERROR TO THE DISTRICT COURT OF THE UNITED STATES FOR THE DISTRICT OF KANSAS.

No. 567. Submitted October 21, 1895.—Decided March 9, 1896.

The newspaper article, in the note on the opposite page, while its language is coarse, vulgar, and, as applied to an individual, libellous, was not of such a lewd, lascivious and obscene tendency, calculated to corrupt and debauch the minds and morals of those into whose hands it might fall, as to make it an offence to deposit it in the post office of the United States, to be conveyed by mail and delivered to the person to whom it was addressed.

In the District Court of the United States for the District of Kansas, November term, 1895, Dan K. Swearingen was indicted, under the provisions of section 3893 of the Revised Statutes, for depositing in the post office of the United States, at Burlington, Kansas, to be conveyed by mail and delivered to certain named persons a certain publication or newspaper, entitled "The Burlington Courier," dated September 21, 1894, and containing a certain article charged to be of an obscene, lewd, and lascivious character, and non-mailable matter.[1]

The indictment contained three counts, differing only in the names of the persons to whom copies of the newspapers were addressed. In each count the article was charged to be of an obscene, lewd and lascivious nature. The defendant moved to quash the indictment because the same did not state or charge a public offence, and because there were several offences improperly joined in each count. This motion was overruled. The defendant pleaded not guilty; a trial was had; and a verdict of guilty was rendered. Thereupon the defendant filed a motion in arrest of judgment and for a new trial. These motions were overruled, and the defendant was sentenced to be imprisoned at hard labor in the penitentiary for the period of one year, to pay a fine of $50, and to pay the costs of prosecution. Thereupon a writ of error was sued out to this court.

Mr. J. D. McCleverty for plaintiff in error.

Mr. Assistant Attorney General Whitney for defendants in error.

Mr. Justice Shiras, after stating the case, delivered the opinion of the court.

The record discloses that the defendant below was, in the month of September, 1894, the editor and publisher of a newspaper called "The Burlington Courier," and was indicted for having mailed several copies of the paper, containing the article referred to in the previous statement, addressed to different persons.

The bill of exceptions shows that, at the trial, the government offered the article in question in evidence, and that the defendant objected for the reasons that no public offence was stated in the indictment, that there was a misjoinder of offences, and that the words of said newspaper article did not constitute unmailable matter. These objections were overruled, and an exception was allowed. The article was then read to the jury, and evidence was offered and received tending to show that on September 21, 1894, copies of the newspaper containing the said article were mailed by employés of the defendant, ad-

---

[1] That article is added by the reporter to the statement of the case, only omitting the names and substituting dashes. "About the meanest and most universally hated and detested thing in human shape that ever cursed this community is the red headed mental and physical bastard that flings filth under another man's name down on Neosho street. He has slandered and maligned every Populist in the State, from the governor down to the humblest voter. This black hearted coward is known to every decent man, woman, and child in the community as a liar, perjurer, and slanderer, who would sell a mother's honor with less hesitancy and for much less silver than Judas betrayed the Saviour, and who would pimp and fatten on a sister's shame with as much unction as a buzzard gluts in carrion. He is a contemptible scoundrel and political blackleg of the lowest cut. He is pretending to serve Democracy and is at the same time in the pay of the Republican party. He has been known as the companion of negro strumpets and has revelled in lowest debauches. He has criminally libelled and slandered such men as ____ ____, ____ ____, ____ ____, ____ ____, ____, and dozens of others whom we might name, who are recognized by all parties as among the oldest and most respected citizens of the county. His soul, if he has a soul, is blacker than the blackest shades of hell. He is the embodiment of treachery, cowardice, and dishonor, and hasn't the physical nor moral courage to deny it. He stands to-day hated, despised, and detested as all that is low, mean, debased, and despicable. We propose to have done with the knave. We have already devoted too much valuable space to him. Time and again has he been proven a wilful, malicious, and cowardly liar, and instead of subsiding he has redoubled his lies. He lies faster than ten men could refute; and for what? A little Republican slushmoney! He is lower, meaner, filthier, rottener than the rottenest strumpet that prowls the streets by night. Again we say, we are done with him. The sooner Populists and Populist newspapers snub him, quit him cold, ignore him entirely, the sooner will he cease to be thought of only as a pimp that any man can buy for $1 or less. He is too little and rotten to merit the notice of men. We have been wrong in noticing the poltroon at all, and henceforth are done."

dressed severally to Riggs, Cowgill and Lane, who were regular subscribers to the paper, and whose names were on the mail list. The defendant, on the ground of its insufficiency, moved to strike out the evidence as to the mailing of any paper to Lane or Cowgill. This motion was overruled, as was likewise a motion to compel the district attorney to elect upon which count of the indictment he would rely. The defendant offered no evidence, and the court charged the jury that the newspaper article in evidence, which the defendant admitted he published, was obscene and unmailable matter, and that the only thing for the jury to pass upon was whether the evidence satisfied them, beyond a reasonable doubt, that the defendant deposited, or caused to be deposited, in the post office at Burlington, Kansas, newspapers containing said article. To the rulings of the court overruling the motions and to the charge exceptions were taken and allowed.

As we think that the court erred in charging the jury that the newspaper article in question was obscene and unmailable matter, it will not be necessary for us to consider the merits of those assignments which allege error in the admission of evidence.

This prosecution was brought under section 3893 of the Revised Statutes, which declares that "every obscene, lewd or lascivious book, pamphlet, picture, paper, writing or other publication of an indecent character . . . are hereby declared to be non-mailable matter, and shall not be conveyed in the mails, nor delivered from any post office, nor by any letter carrier; and any person who shall knowingly deposit or cause to be deposited, for mailing or delivery, anything declared by this section to be non-mailable matter, and any person who shall knowingly take the same or cause the same to be taken from the mails for the purpose of circulating or disposing of or aiding in the circulation or disposition of the same, shall be deemed guilty of a misdemeanor, and shall, for each and every offence, be fined not less than one hundred dollars nor more than five thousand dollars, or be imprisoned at hard labor not less than one year nor more than ten years, or both, at the discretion of the court."

The indictment contained three counts, in each of which the offence charged was the mailing of a copy of a newspaper containing the article referred to in the previous statement, and which was alleged to be "an obscene, lewd and lascivious article."

As already stated, the court charged the jury that the newspaper article was obscene and unmailable matter, and that the only question for the jury to pass upon was whether the defendant deposited the same in the post office at Burlington, Kansas.

The language of the statute is that "every obscene, lewd *or* lascivious book or paper" is unmailable, from which it might be inferred that each of those epithets pointed out a distinct offence. But the indictment alleges that the newspaper article in question was obscene, lewd *and* lascivious. If each adjective in the statute described a distinct offence, then these counts would be bad for duplicity, and the defendant's motion in arrest of judgment for that reason ought to have been sustained. We, however, prefer to regard the words "obscene, lewd or lascivious," used in the statute, as describing one and the same offence. That was evidently the view of the pleader and of the court below, and we think this is an admissible construction.

Regarding the indictment as charging, in each count, a single distinctive offence, to wit, the mailing of an obscene, lewd and lascivious paper, we think the court below erred in charging the jury that the evidence, so far as the character of the paper was concerned, sustained the charge, and that the only duty of the jury was to find whether the defendant knowingly deposited or caused to be deposited in the post office newspapers containing the article so described.

Assuming that it was within the province of the judge to determine whether the publication in question was obscene, lewd and lascivious, within the meaning of the statute, we do not agree with the court below in thinking that the language and tenor of this newspaper article brought it within such meaning. The offence aimed at, in that portion of the statute we are now considering, was the use of the mails to circulate or deliver matter to corrupt the morals of the people. The words "obscene," "lewd" and "lascivious," as used in the statute, signify that form of immorality which has relation to sexual impurity, and have the same meaning as is given them at common law in prosecutions for obscene libel. As the statute is highly penal, it should not be held to embrace language unless it is fairly within its letter and spirit.

Referring to this newspaper article, as found in the record, it is undeniable that its language is exceedingly coarse and vulgar, and, as applied to an individual person, plainly libellous. But we cannot perceive in it anything of a lewd, lascivious and obscene tendency, calculated to corrupt and debauch the mind and morals of those into whose hands it might fall.

The judgment of the court below is reversed and the cause remanded with instructions to set aside the verdict and award a new trial.

Justices Harlan, Gray, Brown, and White dissented.

1900-1929
Cases

■ Holcombe
v.
State. (No. 1,280.)

(Court of Appeals of Georgia. Oct. 26, 1908.)

Error from City Court of Cartersville; A. M. Foute, Judge.

Walter Holcombe was convicted of a violation of Pen. Code 1895, §396, making a person who shall use obscene and vulgar language in the presence of a female guilty of a misdemeanor, and he brings error. Affirmed.

The defendant and other ministers had been carrying on a series of revival services in what is known as "the Tabernacle" in Cartersville. On the concluding day, which was Sunday, a large number of people were in attendance. Services were held at 11 o'clock in the morning, and it was announced that early in the afternoon (either at 2:30 o'clock) a preacher named Oliver would deliver a lecture "to men only." The day was rainy. Many of the people had come from the country, and even from surrounding counties, and a large number of women either remained in the building or sought shelter there from the rain, so that when the time arrived for the lecture "to men only" the audience was mixed. It is conceded that more than 2,500 persons were present. The defendant himself estimated the audience as between 2,500 and 3,000 in number. The defendant, when the time arrived for the lecture to begin, asked the ladies to retire. On account of the rain they were slow in leaving, and a considerable number, variously estimated, remained. It seems that in the audience there was a large woman with her back to the rostrum. The defendant, upon being requested by the other preacher to get the ladies out, advanced to the front of the platform, and in the presence of the congregation said, as the state charged and the witnesses for the prosecution testified, "You woman with the big fat rump pointed towards me, get out of the way." The language, according to the defendant's statement, was: "Gentlemen, there is a big old woman, weighing about 400 pounds, with her rump turned this way. If she would turn around and let me speak to her head, I might explain to her the object of this meeting, and we might go on." He was indicted and convicted for violating section 396 of the Penal Code of 1895, which provides that "any person who shall without provocation * * * use obscene and vulgar or profane language in the presence of a female * * * shall be guilty of a misdemeanor." Exceptions are taken to the overruling of a demurrer to the indictment, and also the overruling of a motion for a new trial. Further facts necessary to the understanding of the points presented and decided will be stated in the course of the opinion.

Jno. T. Norris, for plaintiff in error. Thos. C. Milner, Sol., for the State.

POWELL, J. (after stating the facts as above). The indictment charged that the defendant did without provocation use in the presence of females, whose names are to the grand jurors unknown, the following profane, vulgar, and obscene language: "You woman with the big fat rump pointed towards us, get out of the way." The defendant demurred because the language was not profane; also because it was not obscene and vulgar. The language was not profane, and therefore the use of that word in the indictment was pure surplusage. "Defective allegations do not impair an indictment, if, on their being rejected, what remains fully covers the law." Bishop, New. Crim. Proc. § 480. The word "profane," as used, is merely epithetic of the general nature of the offense, and does not fall within the rule that, where the facts of the transaction are alleged with needless particularity, the unnecessary allegations cannot be rejected as surplusage. *Disharoon* v. *State*, 95 Ga. 356, 22 S.E. 698.

2. The language charged was in our judgment clearly obscene and vulgar, within the purview of section 396 of the Penal Code of 1895. As was said in *Dillard* v. *State*, 41 Ga. 280: "This statute does not stand upon the footing of statutes against public indecency. Its object is not to keep pure the public morals. It is to be found in that chapter of the Code which punishes private wrongs, and forms a part of the same clause which makes it a penal offense to use opprobrious and abusive language to another. It is intended to protect females from insult; to furnish to the friends of a female whose modesty has been unlawfully shocked, or whose feelings have been wounded, by the use in her presence of obscene and vulgar language, some other remedy than that which nature dictates, to wit, club law. And the statute is to be construed and understood in the light of its object." We cannot adopt the suggestion of counsel that it is aimed alone at language suggestive of sexual intercourse, or tending to excite lewdness or to debauch the public morals. The word "obscene" means "offensive to the senses; repulsive; disgusting; foul; filthy; offensive to modesty or decency; impure; unchaste; indecent; lewd." Century Dictionary. We think that the phrase "obscene and vulgar language," as used in the statute, includes any foul words which would reasonably offend the sense of modesty and decency of the woman or women, or any of them, in whose presence the words were spoken, under all the circumstances of the case. It would be absurd to tolerate the suggestion that to speak of a woman's rump in a loose or jocular connection would not be offensive to the modesty and decency of the ordinary

woman. As a matter of common knowledge, we know that such language would shock any decent and modest woman.

In other statutes having different objects from the one before us the word "obscene" may not be entitled to so broad a signification. In the federal statute (Rev. St. § 3893 [U.S. Comp. St. 1901, p. 2658]), by reason of its association in immediate context with the words "lewd or lascivious," it partakes of their meaning, and is therefore itself limited to less than its ordinary significance. Hence the many decisions of the federal courts on this statute, which counsel for the plaintiff in error cites, give us no light on the question at bar. *Ours is a statute adapted to the temperament of the people of this state. It is to be understood in the light of our well-known sensibilities on certain subjects. Modesty, that "kind of quick and delicate feeling in the soul, the exquisite sensibility that warns a woman to shun the first appearance of everything hurtful," is, according to the mind of the average citizen of Georgia, as needful and legitimate a subject-matter of protection from invasions as those more familiar subjects of protection through the criminal statutes—life, liberty, and property.* [italics ed.]

Of course, language tending to incite illicit sexual intercourse is obscene and vulgar; and in most of the reported cases in this state (where the words were not profane, so as to fall within the other portion of the statute) the prosecutions were for using words suggestive of sexual intercourse; but it does not follow that no other language is obscene and vulgar. Indeed, in Brady's Case, 48 Ga. 311, the language is characterized as being "quite obscene and vulgar enough to shock the moral sensibilities of all sensible people." The language in that case was not reported, but an inspection of the copy of the original indictment contained in the record in the Supreme Court discloses that it was in no wise suggestive of lewdness or sexual intercourse. The objectionable language there was a threat to kick the same portion of a woman's anatomy as that which is the subject-matter of the present inquiry. Any one doubting that the language of the present indictment is within the meaning of the words "obscene and vulgar" as commonly and ordinarily understood may easily solve that doubt by quoting the language to his different male acquaintances as he meets them in the varying stations of life, and asking them if they would consider it obscene and vulgar to use that language in the presence of ladies.

3. In his charge to the jury the court did not submit the question as to whether the language was obscene and vulgar, but in effect instructed that if the language, substantially as alleged, was used by the defendant in the presence of the females, without provocation, the defendant would be guilty. Under the circumstances this was not error. "Words get their point and meaning almost entirely from the time, place, circumstances, and intent with which they are used" (Dillard's Case, supra); and therefore usually it is issuable, and consequently a question of fact for the jury, as to whether the particular language is actually obscene and vulgar. Certain suggestions are commonly known to be indecent. Certain words are per se obscene and vulgar, if used under any but peculiar and exceptional circumstances. Dillard's Case, supra; *Pierce* v. *State*, 53 Ga. 369; *Kelly* v. *State*, 126 Ga. 548, 55 S.E. 482. Any gross reference to the private parts of a woman, or to any of the surrounding portions of her person, is by common consent of mankind indecent and shocking to

feminine modesty. Such a reference might, however, be made in the presence of a female, and not be per se criminal—for instance, in a brothel. But where the language is gross and prima facie indecent, and such that common consent condemns it as unfit by reason of its obscenity to be used in the presence of women—that is, if it is so universally recognized to be obscene and vulgar that the court can assume its prima facie obscenity and vulgarity through judicial cognizance as a matter of common knowledge—and the conceded time, place, circumstances, and intent are such as to show no reason making or tending to make its use on the particular occasion less obscene and vulgar than it normally would be, there is no issue as to the obscene and vulgar quality to be submitted to the jury.

There is no conflict between this principle and those cases holding that whether particular language is opprobrious and likely to cause a breach of the peace is for the jury, because what effect particular language will have upon a person under particular or even ordinary circumstances is almost always, if not always, an issuable question, and in the nature of things cannot well become a matter of common knowledge, so as to be judicially assumed. In the present case, the reference, whether we take the state's version or the statement of the defendant himself, was gross. The language was prima facie obscene and vulgar. In form and in substance the allusion was indecent. The time, the place, and the circumstances, instead of making or tending to make its use on the particular occasion less likely to offend the modesty of any woman who might hear it than normally it would be, tended distinctly to the contrary. It was not the ribaldry of some low-grade comedian in some second-class theater. It was the indecent jest of a minister of the gospel, made in a house devoted to the service of God, in the presence of some 3,000 worshippers, aimed at a female member of the congregation whose excess of adipose upon an unmentionable part of her person happened to excite his attention. His own statement concedes every element of this characterization, except that the words of his jest were indecent, and as to that we have decided against him. We do not say that even a minister in the pulpit is precluded at all times and under all circumstances from making reference to things which are not usual subjects of conversation in polite society, if he couches his language in an inoffensive context (though even as to these things decency commands that he should be extremely cautious in the choice of his language), and we recognize that real modesty, and not prudery, and not pruriency, is the object of the law's protection; but we do say unequivocally that an indecent jest, couched in language ordinarily considered obscene and vulgar, is never permissible from the sacred desk, and that if it be made in the presence of females it is a criminal act. Our women certainly have a right to come to our places of religious worship without fear of shock or insult by reason of indecent language used by the minister in charge.

The exception to the court's refusal of a written request to charge the jury that it was incumbent on the state to show that the language was used without provocation is not well founded. We find that the judge clearly covered this in his general charge in several places. He did not elaborate the question of provocation. It was not necessary that he should do so. Both sides had been fully heard as to all the circumstances, and no semblance of provocation appeared. Provocation, as used in this statute, means sufficient provocation. *Ray* v. *State*, 113 Ga. 1066, 39 S.E. 408; *Ratteree* v. *State*, 78 Ga. 335; *Dyer* v. *State*, 99 Ga. 22, 25 S.E. 609, 59 Am. St. Rep. 228; *Brady* v. *State*, 48 Ga. 311. It seems that, when the state makes a prima facie case, the burden shifts to the defendant to show provocation. *Pierce* v. *State*, 53 Ga. 365.

4. When the evidence on both sides of the case had been fully heard, about the only question as to which there was any material issue under the proof was whether the language was used in the presence of females. It was not denied that women were present in the building, but the defendant insisted that they were not within the hearing distance of his remark. The phrase "in the presence of a female," as used in this statute, means "within range of the female's hearing." *Brady* v. *State*, supra; *Sailors* v. *State*, 108 Ga. 35, 33 S.E. 813, 75 Am. St. Rep. 17; *Henderson* v. *State*, 63 Ala. 193; *Laney* v. *State*, 105 Ala. 105, 17 South. 107. On this question the court charged that, if any females were present on the occasion in question, the presumption would be that their hearing was ordinarily good, and that they could have heard and did hear any language spoken loud enough to have been heard by any person of ordinary hearing capacity. The plaintiff in error excepts to this instruction on the ground that there is no such presumption. We find no error in this charge. There is a general presumption that the ordinary human faculties are possessed by every individual. *Davis* v. *R. Co.*, 60 Ga. 333. In *Gardner* v. *State*, 81 Ga. 144, 7 S.E. 144, the following charge was approved: "The law presumes sanity, both as to mental and bodily functions."

7. Another ground of error is that while Judge Fite was testifying the court permitted him to state that he and others told the defendant that his language was obscene and vulgar. When we examine the whole context, we find nothing erroneous in this ruling. The defendant had stated on the trial that his remark was not addressed to the woman in question; that he had used the language innocently and as a mere side remark for the hearing only of the men near him; that he used the word "rump" because he was thinking of the word "hump" and the word "rump" rhymed with it. To rebut this explanation Judge Fite was called as a witness. He testified that on the next day after the language was used the defendant was called before a committee of the trustees of the tabernacle and told that offense had been taken on account of his statement and that he ought to make an apology, to which the defendant stated that he declined to apologize, as he thought that he had a right to say what he did. Judge Fite then said to him that the language as he considered it was vulgar and obscene. The defendant replied that he did not think so, and said in this connection: "That's the way I have got of moving them, and I move them." By this, and the further details of the conversation as narrated in this testimony, it was made to appear that the defendant did not deny that he used the language or that he intended for the woman to hear it, but sought to justify his conduct on the ground that it was his usual way of moving recalcitrant female members of his congregation. It will be seen, therefore, that as a part of the res gestæ of the conversation the statement objected to was admissible. * * *

9. The foregoing rulings will cover other points presented in the record and not expressly decided. The evidence fully supported the verdict, the defendant was clearly guilty, and the trial was free from material error.

Judgment affirmed.

RUSSELL, J., dissents from the ruling made in the third division of the opinion.

■ The St. Hubert Guild, *Appellant,*
v.
Peter J. Quinn, *Respondent.*

(Supreme Court, Appellate Term, June, 1909.)

Louis Sachs, for appellant.
H. M. Gescheidt, for respondent.

SEABURY, J. This action is brought to recover $200, the amount alleged to be due under a written contract under which the plaintiff sold and delivered to the defendant forty-two volumes of the works of Voltaire. The defendant admits the making of the contract and the delivery of the books, but alleges that, at the time of the signing of the contract, it was agreed that the books were to be accepted only on approval of himself and family and that these books "contain reading of a licentious, lascivious and lewd character and not fit to be used or read in the defendant's family." No evidence was offered to show that the contract was made on condition that the books should only be accepted by the defendant provided that they met with his approval. The evidence in reference to this alleged agreement does not go further than to show that the plaintiff's agent in selling the books stated to the defendant that "they were very fine reading matter, fit for everybody to read." At best, this statement was mere matter of opinion and cannot be construed to be a representation of fact. The court below held that the contract was founded upon an illegal consideration in that the books referred to were immoral and rendered judgment for the defendant. Only two of the forty-two volumes sold were offered in evidence and these were "The Philosophical Dictionary" and "The Maid of Orleans." These two books were held to be of such a character as to condemn the whole set. From the two books offered in evidence, the court cannot draw any inference as to the other volumes which were sold.

The contention of the appellant that, because the contract for the sale of the books was in writing, oral evidence could not be offered to show that it was founded upon an illegal consideration is untenable. Parol evidence is always competent to show that the consideration for a written contract is illegal. If a different rule prevailed, parties to illegal contracts could make them enforceable "by the simple device of putting them in writing, using such words as would conceal or omit the illegal objects intended by them to be accomplished." 2 Page Cont., § 1212.

The judgment which the learned court below delivered is not the first judicial determination which has condemned "The Philosophical Dictionary." The last time it was judicially condemned, so far as I know, was in France in 1766, when, together with a youth who was suspected of an act of malicious mischief and in whose possession a copy of the book was found, it was publicly burned in the streets of Paris. The other work complained of, "The Maid of Orleans," had a history less tragic, although sufficiently exciting to have given even the careless Voltaire many moments of anxiety for his own safety on account of it.

The "Philosophical Dictionary" is a collection of articles dealing with romance, history, science and religion, many of which were originally contributed to the great Encyclopédie of which Diderot, D'Alembert and Voltaire were the inspiration. It is not only a reservoir of sarcasm and wit, but it has exerted a profound influence in favor of a humane and rational administration of the law. For the other work offered in evidence, "The Maid of Orleans," so much cannot be said. Offensive as some of the verses of this book undoubtedly are to the taste of our day, yet I do not think we can declare a contract for its sale illegal on this account. Its vices are those of its age. Frederick the Great admired it and paid it the doubtful compliment of imitation, and Condorcet regarded it only as an attack upon hypocrisy and superstition. Less prejudiced critics than these condemn it with severity, and even admirers of Voltaire regret that there are passages in it which have dimmed the fame of its author. In passing judgment upon it, perhaps it is not too much to ask that it should be considered in the spirit which the author of "The Treatise On Tolerance" did so much to make general.

The judgment of the court below is based upon a few passages in each of these works, and these passages have been held to be of such a character as to invalidate the contract upon which the action has been brought. These few passages furnish no criterion by which the legality of the consideration of the contract can be determined. That some of these passages, judged by the standard of our day, mar rather than enhance the value of these books can be admitted without condemning the contract for the sale of the books as illegal. The same criticism has been directed against many of the classics of antiquity and against the works of some of our greatest writers from Chaucer to Walt Whitman, without being regarded as sufficient to invalidate contracts for the sale or publication of their works.

The Penal Code of this State makes it a crime to sell or publish immoral or obscene literature (Penal Code, § 317), and contracts for the sale or publication of immoral literature have been held to be illegal. 15 Am. & Eng. Ency. of Law (2d ed.) 595; *Stockdale* v. *Onwhyn*, 5 B. & C. 173; 11 Eng. Com. Law, 417; *Fores* v. *Johnes*, 4 Esp. 97.

The early attitude of the courts upon this subject discloses an illiberality of opinion which is not reflected in the recent cases. Perhaps no one was more responsible for this early position than Lord Eldon, who refused to protect by injunction Southey's "Wat Tyler" until the innocent character of the work was proved. *Southey* v. *Sherwood*, 2 Meriv. 437. He assumed a like position in reference to Byron's Cain (6 Petersdorff Abr. 558, 559), and expressed a doubt (which he hoped was reasonable) as to the innocent character of Milton's "Paradise Lost." When Dr. Johnson heard of some earlier opinions to the same effect, he is reported to have said: "They make me think of your judges, not with that respect which I should wish to do." Judging from the fact that a jury held the publication of Shelley's "Queen Mab" to be an indictable offense (Moxon's Case, 2 Mod. St. Tr. 356), it seems that jurors were no more liberal than judges in these matters. In commenting upon some of Lord Eldon's judgments on the subject of literary property, Lord Campbell remarked that "it must have been a strange occupation for a judge who for many years had meddled with nothing more imaginative than an Act of Parliament to determine in what sense the speculations of Adam, Eve, Cain, and Lucifer are to be understood." 10 Campbell's Lives of the Lord Chancellors, 257.

It is no part of the duty of courts to exercise a censorship over literary productions. I think it is clear that no contract for the sale of a book can be declared illegal because of the character of the book, unless its sale or publication violates the criminal law. This position was distinctly asserted in *Trachè* v. *Dèrome*, 6 Montreal Law Rep., Super. Ct. 178. In that case the defendants sought to defeat a claim upon a contract for the sale of copies of the works of Victor Hugo. It appeared from the evidence that "Notre Dame de Paris," "Les Miserables" and "Le Pape" had been placed upon the *index librorum prohibitorum*, and the defendant claimed that these works were immoral. In rendering judgment for the plaintiff, Mr. Justice Davidson said: "As to English jurisprudence, it may be safely said that, for all practical purposes, the civil law is determined by and co-extensive with the criminal law. The question in a given case is not simply whether the publication be immoral, but whether it is sufficiently so to enable the criminal law to punish it as such." Under no reasonable construction can our law be held to declare the sale or publication of the works of Voltaire a crime. In Matter of Worthington Co., 24 L.R.A. 110, decided at the Special Term of the New York Supreme Court, Mr. Justice O'Brien directed a receiver appointed by the court to sell the following works: Payne's edition of "The Arabian Nights," "Fielding's Novels," "The Works of Rabelais," "Ovid's Art of Love," "The Decameron of Boccaccio," "The Heptameron of Queen Margaret of Navarre," "The Confessions of J. J. Rousseau," "Tales from the Arabic" and "Alladin." This order was made upon the application of the receiver of a publishing house and was opposed by the "Society for the Suppression of Vice" upon the same grounds as those which are urged in the case at bar. In authorizing the sale, the court said: "It is very difficult to see upon what theory these world-renowned classics can be regarded as specimens of that pornographic literature which it is the office of the Society for the Suppression of Vice to suppress; or how they can come under any stronger condemnation than that high standard literature which consists of the works of Shakespeare, of Chaucer, of Laurence Sterne, and of other great

English writers, without making reference to many parts of the Old Testament Scriptures, which are to be found in almost every household in the land." In view of this decision, the good sense of which is manifest, it would indeed be straining the rule of law to hold that the works of Voltaire come within its condemnation. If the works referred to in the opinion in the Worthington Company case could be sold at a judicial sale by a receiver under the direction of the court, certainly the court could not declare that an agreement to sell the works of Voltaire was founded upon an illegal consideration. The rule against the sale of immoral publications cannot be invoked against those works which have been generally recognized as literary classics. As was well said by Mr. Justice O'Brien in the Worthington Co. case, *supra:* "What has become standard literature of the English language,—has been wrought into the very structure of our splendid English literature— is not to be pronounced at this late day unfit for publication or circulation and stamped with judicial disapprobation as hurtful to the community." Contemporaneous literature must, of course, be judged by current opinion; and the test to be applied does not require the testimony of experts, but is one falling within the range of ordinary intelligence. *People* v. *Muller*, 96 N.Y. 408. It is not at all inconceivable, and has frequently been the case, that the works which receive the condemnation of one generation are the objects of veneration and praise in another. Courts will take the same knowledge as the community at large of matters of literature (16 Cyc. 854), and we cannot fail to recognize that the genius of Voltaire has enriched many fields of knowledge. The object of the law which prohibits the sale or publication of immoral literature is to prevent the circulation of literature which is hurtful to the community. To apply this rule so as to prohibit the sale or publication of the works of Voltaire would not give effect to its purpose. Differ as men may as to the views of Voltaire on many questions, none can deny the great influence of his work in promoting justice and humanity and the reign of reason in public affairs. In speaking of the service rendered by Voltaire to this cause in the "Philosophical Dictionary" and some of his other works, Mr. Lecky has finely said of him that "When attacking intolerance, he employed indeed, every weapon, but he employed them all with the concentrated energy of a profound conviction. His success was equal to his zeal. The spirit of intolerance sank blasted beneath his genius. Wherever his influence passed the arm of the inquisitor was palsied, the chain of the captive riven, the prison door flung open. Beneath his withering irony persecution appeared not only criminal but loathsome, and since his time it has ever shrunk from observation, and masked its features under other names. He died, leaving a reputation that is indeed far from spotless, but having done more to destroy the greatest of human curses than any other of the sons of men." Rationalism in Europe, vol. 2, p. 71.

The contract sued upon was a valid contract and no defense to the action upon it was proved.

The judgment is reversed and a new trial ordered, with costs to the appellant to abide the event.

GILDERSLEEVE and GEIGERICH, JJ., concur.

Judgment reversed and new trial ordered, with costs to appellant to abide event.

■ Redd *et al.*
v.
State. (No. 2,393.)

(Court of Appeals of Georgia. April 6, 1910.)

F. M. Longley, for plaintiffs in error. *Henry Reeves*, Sol., *Hatton Lovejoy*, and *E. A. Jones*, for the State.

POWELL, J. The defendants were indicted under the Penal Code of 1895, section 390, which provides, among other things, that "any person who shall be guilty of open lewdness, or any notorious act of public indecency, tending to debauch the morals," shall be punished as for a misdemeanor. The charge is that the defendants were guilty of a notorious act of public indecency tending to debauch the morals, in that they in a public place, adjacent to a highway and in the presence of a lady and several children, caused a bull and a cow to copulate. The proof was that these two men, having been intrusted with a cow that was in heat, for the purpose of taking her to the bull, which was confined in a pasture adjacent to the public road, put the cow in the pasture, and tied her to the fence next to the road and called the bull to her there. The copulation between the animals thus took place publicly, though there was a branch and a thicket about 100 feet away in which the act could have been done privately. About 30 feet away, and just across the road, were a woman and several children. The defendants denied seeing these persons, but the proof was against them as to that. There was ample evidence to sustain the proposition that the defendants willfully, or at least in reckless disregard to the sensibilities of the woman and the children, put the bull to the cow in their presence. The road seems to have been a much frequented highway, for several persons passed in vehicles while the act complained of was in progress.

The contention presented by counsel for plaintiffs in error is that no offense is charged or shown—that the phrase, "public indecency," as used in this section of the Penal Code, relates only to indecent exposure of the human person. The court has been so fortunate as to have both sides of the question ably argued before it, and we must admit that the decision of the question is not un-attended with doubt. There are in this state no offenses in force by reason of the common law. In a sense, all our crimes and misdemeanors are statutory. Yet we have by statute given recognition to many offenses which were known to the common law and which have not been defined otherwise than by the use of the general terms anciently used to describe them; and, in such cases, we look to the common law for more specific definition. Public indecency was a common-law offense, included under the more general head of "indictable nuisances." What research we have been able to make as to the old English cases on the subject tends to corroborate the assertion of the distinguished counsel who, by a fortuitous combination of circumstances, appeared for the plaintiffs in error, that no case can be found at common law where a person was convicted for exhibiting or exposing any of the lower animals in the act of sexual intercourse or in any other way tending to shock the sensibilities of the spectators. Indeed, as to prosecutions for public indecency (omitting cases of the use of obscene language in the presence of females and of the exhibition of obscene and offensive prints, pictures, statuary, etc.—omitted because they are distinct offenses, not here involved), all the old cases, and nearly all the modern ones, so far as the facts have been reported, appear to be cases in which were involved exposures of the human body. It may therefore be conceded that the reported cases, considered as physical precedents, do seem to support the view presented by the plaintiffs in error.

It is true, too, that it is contrary to the genius of our law, as well as repugnant to the popular notions of juridic justice, that punishable offenses should be left undefined. Intuitively, the courts find themselves seeking for and declaring, by construction, limitations in the way of definition, where the Legislature has spoken loosely. In the case of *McJunkins v. State*, 10 Ind. 140, 145, it was said: "The term 'public indecency' has no fixed legal meaning—is vague and indefinite, and cannot in itself imply a definite offense. And hence the courts, by a kind of judicial legislation, in England and the United States, have usually limited the operation of the term to public displays of the naked person, the publication, sale, or exhibition of obscene books and prints, or the exhibition of a monster— acts which have a direct bearing on public morals and affect the body of society. Thus, it will be perceived that, so far as there is a legal meaning attached to the term, it is different from, and more limited than, the commonly accepted meaning given by Webster [in his dictionary] to the word 'indecency.'" This dictum has been widely quoted with approval by the courts and text-writers; and it may be noted that it found its way into general lexicography, for the Century Dictionary cites it in connection with the definition of the word "indecency." Yet, despite the wide currency that has been given the dictum in the McJunkins Case, despite the paucity of physical precedents to the contrary, it must be noticed by every one who has had the occasion to pursue the question that neither the courts nor the text-writers have been willing to commit themselves fully to the proposition that the limitations and definition attempted in that case are wholly accurate or that the enumeration of acts there stated is exhaustive. For instance, we frequently find in cases and textbooks the statement that whatever openly outrages decency and is injurious to public morals is a misdemeanor at common law

and is indictable as such. See Russell, Crimes (9th Amer. Ed.) 449; Id. (7th Eng. Ed., 1st Can. Ed.) 1875; Bishop, New Crim. Law, § 1125 (2); 29 Cyc. 1315; *State v. Rose*, 32 Mo. 560; *State v. Walter*, 2 Marv. (Del.) 444, 43 Atl. 253; *Com. v. Holmes*, 17 Mass. 336; *State v. Appling*, 25 Mo. 315, 69 Am. Dec. 469; *Com. v. Sharpless*, 2 Serg. & R. (Pa.) 91, 7 Am. Dec. 632; *Grisham v. State*, 2 Yerg. (Tenn.) 589; *Knowles v. State*, 3 Day (Conn.) 103, 108; *Rex v. Crunden*, 2 Camp. 89; 4 Blackstone's Com. 64.

The reticence of the courts to violate the chastity of their reports with narratives of indecent acts may account for the fact that we are able to find so few reported cases of public indecency not involving exposure of the person. For example, in *Brigman v. State*, 123 Ga. 505, 51 S.E. 504, a conviction for public indecency was sustained; but the printed report contains no account of the specific act by which the defendant violated the statute. An inspection of the original record shows that it involved no exposure of the person. For the purpose of insulting a young lady who had refused his offer of escort, the defendant in that case emitted an indecent noise in her presence, while she was on the highway in company with another young man. Indeed, in the old and frequently referred to case of Sir Charles Sedley, which was tried during the reign of Charles II (see 1 Siderf. 168), the offense of public indecency alleged against the prisoner was not only that he stood naked on a balcony in a public part of London, but also that he threw down certain "offensive liquor" among the people passing along the highway. In *Nolin v. Mayor*, etc., of Town of Franklin, 4 Yerg. (12 Tenn.) 163, the Supreme Court of Tennessee, on the authority of the common law, held that "the showing of a studhorse in a town is a nuisance." However, we are not prepared to hold that our statute intended to adopt the common law to this extreme.

After careful reflection upon the matter, we have reached the conclusion that our statute, based as it is upon the common law, is broad enough to cover all notorious public and indecent conduct, tending to debauch the public morals, even though it be unattended by any exposure of the human body. If this is not so, then our law, broadly as it has been drawn, is not adequate to protect the public in this state from many acts shockingly obscene and tending to lower the moral standards, for, while we have statutes against the use of obscene and vulgar language, against the exhibition of prints, pictures, and other artificial representations of obscene things, we have no statute other than the one now under review against indecent shows and public exhibitions of things not pictorial in their nature. Can it be said that it would not be a notorious act of public indecency if in a theater or other similar place, one should exhibit trained animals, say monkeys dressed as men and women, and cause them to go through the act of sexual intercourse in the presence of the audience? Can it be doubted that this would tend to debauch the public morals? Yet it would involve no exposure of the human body. Cases even worse than this—cases so extreme that even the duty of speaking plainly, imposed upon us by the nature of the question here involved, will not excuse the indelicacy of mentioning them—and yet involving no exposure of the person, may be imagined. The language of the law, taken in its natural and ordinary sense, is broad enough to reach such cases, and we do not feel warranted in so limiting its meaning as to leave such cases out of its province. Hard as it is to define what "notorious public indecency" means, we feel reasonably sure that it means in law, as well as in common vernacular, more than what the expression "indecent exposure of the person" includes. However, we should keep in mind that the word "indecency," as used in the statute, has not so broad a meaning as it has in popular speech. An act may be unconventional, may be such as to give offense to the finer sensibilities, may relate to acts which would bring a blush (real or feigned) to the cheeks of the prudish, and yet not be indecent. To determine whether an act is indecent within the purview of the statute, the time, the place, the circumstances, and the motives of the actors must be considered. An act may be done under some circumstances without the imputation of indecency, when a similar act done in the presence of women or children would be highly indecent. Many useful, important, and even absolutely necessary acts are to be lawfully accomplished only in private. What is decent and what is indecent is largely a matter of general public opinion, and, hard as it is to define the words "public indecency," most of us who have ordinary sensibilities know what it means. By common consent of the people there are certain things which all know and understand are not to be done publicly, or at least in mixed company. A fair test to determine whether an act is notoriously indecent within the purview of this law is to consider whether the general run of the citizenry of the state would readily recognize it as such (all the attendant facts and circumstances and the motives of the actor being considered), and also whether it tends to debauch the morals. We believe in this case that these defendants, even though they were possessed of less than normal moral sensibilities, knew that it was indecent for them to put the bull to the cow in plain view of the highway and in the presence of this lady and her children, some of them little girls, when the necessary performance could have been accomplished privately with but little trouble and inconvenience.

As was said by Chief Justice Perkins in the case of *Ardery v. State*, 56 Ind. 328, 329, 330: "Immediately after the fall of Adam, there seems to have sprung up in his mind an idea that there was such a thing as decency and such a thing as indecency; that there was a distinction between them; and since that time the ideas of decency and indecency have been instinctive in, and, indeed, parts of, humanity." As tending to preserve chastity, society has erected as one of its inviolable decencies that sexual intercourse, lawful or unlawful, and all things directly suggestive of it, shall be kept private, and has established that it is a shameful and an indecent thing for a person of one sex, especially of the male sex, intentionally, publicly, and unnecessarily to bring before the gaze or hearing of a person of the opposite sex the act of sexual intercourse, or things closely associated with it. Anything which tends to break down this standard of decency tends to promote unchastity, and thereby to debauch the public morals. *If one man may without violating the law deliberately cause his beasts to copulate on the highway and in the very presence of one woman rightfully there, another may lawfully bring his beasts for the same purpose to the school grounds where children are assembled or to the churchyard, while the congregation is there.* Can such things be allowed without offending the common instincts of decency in the strictest sense of the word, or without tending to impair the present standard of morals as now recognized as proper between the sexes?

It is true, as suggested by distinguished counsel for the plaintiffs in error, that, according to the construction here announced, the patriarch Jacob standing at the public watering place and holding the striped rods before Laban's bulls, rams, and he-goats when they leaped, in order that the young might be marked with stripes, would have been guilty of public indecency. Perhaps so. But, as able counsel for the state has replied, it will not do to measure modern morals according to the standards of ancient and Biblical times. King Solomon with his thousand wives would not be tolerated in Georgia; and King David, he the man after God's own heart, could hardly justify his whole life according to the provisions of the Penal Code of this state. Our standards of morals have advanced since then, and our standards of decency have advanced accordingly. The times—the prevailing state of public morality at the particular period—more largely than any other one thing, determine what the decencies and indecencies of that particular day and generation shall be. Many things regarded (by law as well as by secular opinion) a hundred years ago as being indecent are not so regarded now; and, on the other hand, the present age has developed decencies and indecencies unknown to or unobserved by our forefathers.

We conclude that according to the prevailing social standards in this state, and according to the notions of decency and indecency now commonly recognized among our people, the act of the defendants was a notorious act of public indecency, tending to debauch the morals. This, of course, is based on the assumption that the defendants had the intention of obtruding the spectacle upon the gaze of those present, or that they acted so wantonly or recklessly in the matter as to raise the legal imputation of such an intention. The act of the animals was not the thing that was indecent. The indecent thing was the conduct of the defendants in intentionally or wantonly displaying this act to the woman and the children. A moment's thought will develop this distinction. A lady of refined sensibilities, who, though in mixed company, should casually come upon animals in the sexual act, might feel a sense of shame, her refined tastes might be offended; yet it would be to attribute a mock modesty to her to say that her sense of decency was outraged. Yet, if some man were to catch the animals so engaged, and bring them before her and say, either by spoken language or by conduct capable of conveying an equivalent meaning, "Look at this," her sense of decency would be offended—not by the act of the animals, but by the act of the man.

Judgment affirmed.

■ United States
v.
Kennerley.

(District Court, S. D. New York. December 1, 1913.)

John Neville Boyle, of New York City, for the United States.

John L. Lockwood, of New York City, for defendant.

HAND, District Judge.

Whatever be the rule in England, in this country the jury must determine under instructions whether the book is obscene. The court's only power is to decide whether the book is so clearly innocent that the jury should not pass upon it at all. *U.S. v. Clarke* (D.C.) 38 Fed. 500; *U.S. v. Smith* (D.C.) 45 Fed. 478. The same question arises as would arise upon motion to direct a verdict at the close of the case. *Swearingen* v. *U.S.*, 161 U.S. 446, 16 Sup. Ct. 562, 40 L. Ed. 765, did not decide that the court is finally to interpret the words, but that matter was left open, because the instructions in any case misinterpreted the statute. The question here is, therefore, whether the jury might find the book obscene under proper instructions. Lord Cockburn laid down a test in *Reg. v. Hicklin*, L.R. 3 Q.B. 36, in these words:

"Whether the tendency of the matter charged as obscenity is to deprave and corrupt those whose minds are open to such immoral influences and into whose hands a publication of this sort may fall."

That test has been accepted by the lower federal courts until it would be no longer proper for me to disregard it. *U.S. v. Bennett*, 16 Blatch. 338, Fed. Cas. No. 14,571; *U.S. v. Clarke* (D.C.) 38 Fed. 500; *U.S. v. Harmon* (D.C.) 45 Fed. 414; *U.S. v. Smith* (D.C.) 45 Fed. 478. Under this rule, such parts of this book as pages 169 and 170 might be found obscene, because they certainly might tend to corrupt the morals of those into whose hands it might come and whose minds were open to such immoral influences. Indeed, it would be just those who would be most likely to concern themselves with those parts alone, forgetting their setting and their relevancy to the book as a whole.

While, therefore, the demurrer must be overruled, *I hope it is not improper for me to say that the rule as laid down, however consonant it may be with mid-Victorian morals, does not seem to me to answer to the understanding and morality of the present time, as conveyed by the words, "obscene, lewd, or lascivious." I question whether in the end men will regard that as obscene which is honestly relevant to the adequate expression of innocent ideas, and whether they will not believe that truth and beauty are too precious to society at large to be mutilated in the interests of those most likely to pervert them to base uses. Indeed, it seems hardly likely that we are even to-day so lukewarm in our interest in letters or serious discussion as to be content to reduce our treatment of sex to the standard of a child's library in the supposed interest of a salacious few, or that shame will for long prevent us from adequate portrayal of some of the most serious and beautiful sides of human nature. That such latitude gives opportunity for its abuse is true enough; there will be, as there are, plenty who will misuse the privilege as a cover for lewdness and a stalking horse from which to strike at purity, but that is true to-day and only involves us in the same question of fact which we hope that we have the power to answer.* [Italics ed.].

Yet, if the time is not yet when men think innocent all that which is honestly germane to a pure subject, however little it may mince its words, still I scarcely think that they would forbid all which might corrupt the most corruptible, or that society is prepared to accept for its own limitations those which may perhaps be necessary to the weakest of its members. If there be no abstract definition, such as I have suggested, should not the word "obscene" be allowed to indicate the present critical point in the compromise between candor and shame at which the community may have arrived here and now? If letters must, like other kinds of conduct, be subject to the social sense of what is right, it would seem that a jury should in each case establish the standard much as they do in cases of negligence. *To put thought in leash to the average conscience of the time is perhaps tolerable, but to fetter it by the necessities of the lowest and least capable seems a fatal policy.* [Italics ed.].

Nor is it an objection, I think, that such an interpretation gives to the words of the statute a varying meaning from time to time. Such words as these do not embalm the precise morals of an age or place; while they presuppose that some things will always be shocking to the public taste, the vague subject-matter is left to the gradual development of general notions about what is decent. A jury is especially the organ with which to feel the content comprised within such words at any given time, but to do so they must be free to follow the colloquial connotations which they have drawn up instinctively from life and common speech.

Demurrer overruled.

Mutual Film Corporation
v.
Industrial Commission of Ohio.

APPEAL FROM THE DISTRICT COURT OF THE UNITED STATES FOR THE NORTHERN DISTRICT OF OHIO.

No. 456. Argued January 6, 7, 1915.—Decided February 23, 1915.

APPEAL from an order denying appellant, herein designated complainant, an interlocutory injunction sought to restrain the enforcement of an act of the General Assembly of Ohio passed April 16, 1913 (103 Ohio Laws, 399), creating under the authority and superintendence of the Industrial Commission of the State a board of censors of motion picture films. The motion was presented to three judges, upon the bill, supporting affidavits and some oral testimony.

The bill is quite voluminous. It makes the following attacks upon the Ohio statute: (1) The statute is in violation of §§ 5, 16 and 19 of article 1 of the constitution of the State in that it deprives complainant of a remedy by due process of law by placing it in the power of the board of censors to determine from standards fixed by itself what films conform to the statute, and thereby deprives complainant of a judicial determination of a violation of the law. (2) The statute is in violation of articles 1 and 14 of the amendments to the Constitution of the United States, and of § 11 of article 1 of the constitution of Ohio in that it restrains complainant and other persons from freely writing and publishing their sentiments. (3) It attempts to give the board of censors legislative power, which is vested only in the General Assembly of the State, subject to a referendum vote of the people, in that it gives to the board the power to determine the application of the statute without fixing any standard by which the board shall be guided in its determination, and places it in the power of the board, acting with similar boards in other States, to reject, upon any whim or caprice, any film which may be presented, and power to determine the legal status of the foreign board or boards, in conjunction with which it is empowered to act.

The business of the complainant and the description, use, object and effect of motion pictures and other films contained in the bill, stated narratively, are as follows: Complainant is engaged in the business of purchasing, selling and leasing films, the films being produced in other States than Ohio, and in European and other foreign countries. The film consists of a series of instantaneous photographs or positive prints of action upon the stage or in the open. By being projected upon a screen with great rapidity there appears to the eye an illusion of motion. They depict dramatizations of standard novels, exhibiting many subjects of scientific interest, the properties of matter, the growth of the various forms of animal and plant life, and explorations and travels; also events of historical and current interest—the same events which are described in words and by photographs in newspapers,

weekly periodicals, magazines and other publications, of which photographs are promptly secured a few days after the events which they depict happen; thus regularly furnishing and publishing news through the medium of motion pictures under the name of "Mutual Weekly." Nothing is depicted of a harmful or immoral character.

The complainant is selling and has sold during the past year for exhibition in Ohio an average of fifty-six positive prints of films per week to film exchanges doing business in that State, the average value thereof being the sum of $100, aggregating $6,000 per week or $300,000 per annum.

In addition to selling films in Ohio complainant has a film exchange in Detroit, Michigan, from which it rents or leases large quantities to exhibitors in the latter State and in Ohio. The business of that exchange and those in Ohio is to purchase films from complainant and other manufacturers of films and rent them to exhibitors for short periods at stated weekly rentals. The amount of rentals depends upon the number of reels rented, the frequency of the changes of subject, and the age or novelty of the reels rented. The frequency of exhibition is described. It is the custom of the business, observed by all manufacturers, that a subject shall be released or published in all theaters on the same day, which is known as release day, and the age or novelty of the film depends upon the proximity of the day of exhibition to such release day. Films so shown have never been shown in public, and the public to whom they appeal is therefore unlimited. Such public becomes more and more limited by each additional exhibition of the reel.

The amount of business in renting or leasing from the Detroit exchange for exhibition in Ohio aggregates the sum of $1,000 per week.

Complainant has on hand at its Detroit exchange at least 2,500 reels of films which it intends to and will exhibit in Ohio and which it will be impossible to exhibit unless the same shall have been approved by the board of censors. Others exchanges have films, duplicate prints of a large part of complainant's films, for the purpose of selling and leasing to parties residing in Ohio, and the statute of the State will require their examination and the payment of a fee therefor. The amounts of complainant's purchases are stated, and that complainant will be compelled to bear the expense of having them censored because its customers will not purchase or hire uncensored films.

The business of selling and leasing films from its offices outside of the State of Ohio to purchasers and exhibitors within the State is interstate commerce, which will be seriously burdened by the exaction of the fee for censorship, which is not properly an inspection tax and the proceeds of which will be largely in excess of the cost of enforcing the statute, and will in no event be paid to the Treasury of the United States.

The board has demanded of complainant that it submit its films to censorship and threatens, unless complainant complies with the demand, to arrest any and all persons who seek to place on exhibition any film not so censored or approved by the censor congress on and after November 4, 1913, the date to which the act was extended. It is physically impossible to comply with such demand and physically impossible for the board to censor the films with such rapidity as to enable complainant to proceed with its business, and the delay consequent upon such examination would cause great and irreparable injury to such business and would involve a multiplicity of suits.

There were affidavits filed in support of the bill and some testimony taken orally. One of the affidavits showed the manner of shipping and distributing the films and was as follows:

"The films are shipped by the manufacturers to the film exchanges enclosed in circular metal boxes, each of which metal boxes is in turn enclosed in a fibre or wooden container. The film is in most cases wrapped around a spool or core in a circle within the metal case. Sometimes the film is received by the film exchange wound on a reel, which consists of a cylindrical core with circular flanges to prevent the film from slipping off the core, and when so wound on the reel is also received in metal boxes, as above described. When the film is not received on a reel, it is, upon receipt, taken from the metal box, wound on a reel and then replaced in the metal box. So wound and so enclosed in metal boxes, the films are shipped by the film exchanges to their customers. The customers take the film as it is wound on the reel from the metal box and exhibit the pictures in their projecting machines, which are so arranged as to permit of the unwinding of the film from the reel on which it is shipped. During exhibition, the reel of film is unwound from one reel and rewound in reverse order on a second reel. After exhibition, it must be again unwound from the second reel from its reverse position and replaced on the original reel in its proper position. After the exhibitions for the day are over, the film is replaced in the metal box and returned to the film exchange, and this process is followed from day to day during the life of the film.

"All shipments of films from manufacturers to film exchanges, from film exchanges to exhibitors, and from exhibitors back to film exchanges, are made in accordance with regulations of the Interstate Commerce Commission, one of which provides as follows:

" 'Moving picture films must be placed in metal cases, packed in strong and tight wooden boxes or fibrewood pails.' "

Another of the affidavits divided the business as follows:

"The motion-picture business is conducted in three branches; that is to say, by manufacturers, distributors, and exhibitors, the distributors being known as film exchanges. . . . Film is manufactured and produced in lengths of about one thousand feet, which are placed on reels, and the market price per reel of film of a thousand feet in length is at the rate of ten cents per foot, or one hundred

dollars. Manufacturers do not sell their film direct to exhibitors, but sell to film exchanges, and the film exchanges do not resell the film to exhibitors, but rent it out to them."

After stating the popularity of motion pictures and the demand of the public for new ones and the great expense their purchase would be to exhibitors, the affidavit proceeds as follows:

"For that reason film exchanges came into existence, and film exchanges such as the Mutual Film Corporation are like clearing houses or circulating libraries, in that they purchase the film and rent it out to different exhibitors. One reel of film being made to-day serves in many theatres from day to day until it is worn out. The film exchange, in renting out the films, supervises their circulation."

An affidavit was filed made by the "general secretary of the national board of censorship of motion pictures, whose office is at No. 50 Madison Avenue, New York City." The "national board," it is averred, "is an organization maintained by voluntary contributions, whose object is to improve the moral quality of motion pictures." Attached to the affidavit was a list of subjects submitted to the board which are "classified according to the nature of said subjects into scenic, geographic, historical, classic, educational and propagandistic."

Mr. William B. Sanders and *Mr. Walter N. Seligsberg*, with whom *Mr. Harold T. Clark* was on the brief, for appellants:

The Federal courts have jurisdiction to decide all the constitutional questions, whether Federal or state, presented by the records. *Ohio R. & W. R. R.* v. *Dittey*, 232 U.S. 578; *Siler* v. *Louis. & Nash. R. R.*, 213 U.S. 175, 191.

Appellants are entitled to invoke the protection of the constitutional guaranties of freedom of publication and liberty of the press as fully as any person with whom they do business could do. *Savage* v. *Jones*, 225 U.S. 501, at pp. 519–521; *Collins* v. *New Hampshire*, 171 U.S. 30; *Caldwell* v. *North Carolina*, 187 U.S. 622; *Crenshaw* v. *Arkansas*, 227 U.S. 389, 397; *Kahn* v. *Cincinnati Times Star*, 10 Oh. Dec. 599, aff'd 52 Oh. St. 662.

Appellants' motion pictures are publications and entitled as such to the protection afforded by the freedom of publication guaranty contained in § 11, Art. I of the Ohio constitution. *Kalem* v. *Harper Bros.*, 222 U.S. 55, 60; *Harper Bros.* v. *Kalem*, 169 Fed. Rep. 61; *Daly* v. *Webster*, 56 Fed. Rep. 483; *Dailey* v. *San Francisco Superior Court*, 112 California, 94; *United States* v. *Williams*, 3 Fed. Rep. 484; *United States* v. *Loftis*, 12 Fed. Rep. 671; *LeRoy* v. *Jamison*, 15 Fed. Cas. 373.

Appellants' motion pictures constitute part of "the press" of Ohio within the comprehensive meaning of that term. They play an increasingly important part in the spreading of knowledge and the molding of public opinion upon every kind of political, educational, religious, economic and social question. The regular publication of new films under the name of "Mutual Weekly" is clearly a press enterprise.

See § 11, Art I, Ohio constitution, providing that "Every citizen may freely speak, write and publish his sentiments on all subjects, being responsible for the abuse of the right; and no law shall be passed to restrain or abridge the liberty of speech, or of the press.

The Censorship Law violates § 11 in that it imposes a previous restraint upon freedom of publication, which applies to all publications whether made through the medium of speech, writing, acting on the stage, motion pictures, or through any other mode of expression now known or which may hereafter be discovered or invented, and upon the liberty of the press. *Dopp* v. *Doll*, 9 O. Dec. Rep. 428; *Judson* v. *Zurhorst*, 10 O.C.C. (N.S.) 289; S.C., aff'd, 78 O.S. 446; Cooley's Const. Law, 3d ed., Ch. XIV, § V, especially 309; Story on the Constitution, 5th ed., § 1182; Black's Const. Law, 3d ed., 658; Paterson on Liberty of Press, pp. 10 and 41; Cooley's Blackstone, 4th ed., p. 1326; *Patterson* v. *Colorado*, 205 U.S. 454, 462; *Dailey* v. *Superior Court*, 112 California, 94; *Ex parte Neil*, 32 Texas Criminal Court, 275; *Cowan* v. *Fairbrother* (N.C.), 32 L.R.A. 829, 836; *Ulster Square Dealer* v. *Fowler*, 111 N.Y. Supp. 16; *Life Association* v. *Boogher*, 3 Mo. App. 173; *Clothing Co.* v. *Watson*, 168 Missouri, 153; *Atchison &c. Ry.* v. *Brown*, 80 Kansas, 312; Rawle on Constitution, 2d ed., pp. 123, 124; *Levert* v. *Daily States Pub. Co.*, 123 Louisiana, 594; *Sweeney* v. *Baker*, 13 W. Va. 182; *Williams Printing Co.* v. *Saunders*, 113 Virginia, 156; *Williams* v. *Black*, 24 S. Dak. 501.

The constitutional guaranties are not limited to forms of publication known at the time the Constitution was adopted. *Hurtado* v. *California*, 110 U.S. 516, 530; *Boyd* v. *United States*, 116 U.S. 746, 752; *Holden* v. *Hardy*, 169 U.S. 366, 385; In re *Debs*, 158 U.S. 164, 591.

The censorship law is not sustainable as a plan for the regulating of theatres by a system of granting or withholding licenses, because appellants' films are exhibited in churches, libraries, factories, store windows, before open air gatherings, etc. Moreover, even as to theaters, the surrender of the constitutional guaranty of freedom of publication could not be required as a condition precedent to the granting of a license. *Dist. of Col.* v. *Saville*, 8 D.C. App. 581; *People* v. *Steele*, 231 Illinois, 340; *Chicago* v. *Weber*, 246 Illinois, 304; *Indianapolis* v. *Miller*, 168 Indiana, 285; *William Fox Co.* v. *McClellan*, 62 Misc. 100; *Ex parte Quarg*, 84 Pac. Rep. 766; *Empire City Trotting Club* v. *State Racing Commission*, 190 N.Y. 31.

The censorship law cannot be sustained as a proper exercise of the police power, because it directly contravenes the constitutional guaranties of freedom of publication and liberty of the press. *Board of Health* v. *Greenville*, 86 Oh. St. 1, 21; *Lawton* v. *Steele*, 152 U.S. 133, 137; *Mugler* v. *Kansas*, 123 U.S. 623, 661; *Sperry ex rel.* v. *Sperry & Hutchinson*, 94 Nebraska, 785.

The Ohio Motion Picture Censorship violates the provisions of § 11, Art. I of the constitution of Ohio, in that it attempts to delegate legislative power. *Harmon* v. *State*, 66 O.S. 249; *Toledo* v. *Winters*, 21 O. Dec. 171; *Ex parte Sam Lewis*, 14 O.N.P. (N.S.) 609; *Noel* v. *People*, 187 Illinois, 591; *Kerr* v. *Ross*, 5 App. D.C. 441; *State* v. *Burdge* (Wis.), 37 L.R.A. 157, 161; *Mathews* v. *Murphy*, 63 S.W. Rep. 785.

Mr. Robert M. Morgan, with whom *Mr. Timothy S. Hogan*, Attorney General of the State of Ohio, *Mr. James I. Boulger* and *Mr. Clarence D. Laylin* were on the brief, for appellees.

See brief on behalf of State of Kansas in No. 597, *post*, p. 253.

By leave of court, *Mr. Waldo G. Morse* and *Mr. Jacob Schechter* filed a brief as *amici curiæ* in behalf of the Universal Film Manufacturing Company.

Mr. JUSTICE McKENNA, after stating the case as above, delivered the opinion of the court.

Complainant directs its argument to three propositions: (1) The statute in controversy imposes an unlawful burden on interstate commerce; (2) it violates the freedom of speech and publication guaranteed by § 11, art. 1, of the constitution of the State of Ohio;[1] and (3) it attempts to delegate legislative power to censors and to other boards to determine whether the statute offends in the particulars designated.

It is necessary to consider only §§ 3, 4 and 5. Section 3 makes it the duty of the board to examine and censor motion picture films to be publicly exhibited and displayed in the State of Ohio. The films are required to be exhibited to the board before they are delivered to the exhibitor for exhibition, for which a fee is charged.

Section 4. "Only such films as are in the judgment and discretion of the board of censors of a moral, educational or amusing and harmless character shall be passed and approved by such board." The films are required to be stamped or designated in a proper manner.

Section 5. The board may work in conjunction with censor boards of other States as a censor congress, and the action of such congress in approving or rejecting films shall be considered as the action of the state board, and all films passed, approved, stamped and numbered by such congress, when the fees therefor are paid shall be considered approved by the board.

By § 7 a penalty is imposed for each exhibition of films without the approval of the board, and by § 8 any person dissatisfied with the order of the board is given the same rights and remedies for hearing and reviewing, amendment or vacation of the order "as is provided in the case of persons dissatisfied with the orders of the industrial commission."

The censorship, therefore, is only of films intended for exhibition in Ohio, and we can immediately put to one side the contention that it imposes a burden on interstate commerce. It is true that according to the allegations of the bill some of the films of complainant are shipped from Detroit, Michigan, but they are distributed to exhibitors, purchasers, renters and lessors in Ohio, for exhibition in Ohio, and this determines the application of the statute. In other words, it is only films which are "to be publicly exhibited and displayed in the State of Ohio" which are required to be examined and censored. It would be straining the doctrine of original packages to say that the films retain that form and composition even when unrolling and exhibiting to audiences, or, being ready for renting for the purpose of exhibition within the State, could not be disclosed to the state officers. If this be so, whatever the

---

[1] "Section 11. Every citizen may freely speak, write, and publish his sentiments on all subjects, being responsible for the abuse of the right; and no law shall be passed to restrain or abridge the liberty of speech, or of the press. In all criminal prosecutions for libel, the truth may be given in evidence to the jury, and if it shall appear to the jury that the matter charged as libelous is true, and was published with good motives, and for justifiable ends, the party shall be acquitted."

power of the State to prevent the exhibition of films not approved—and for the purpose of this contention we must assume the power is otherwise plenary—films brought from another State, and only because so brought, would be exempt from the power, and films made in the State would be subject to it. There must be some time when the films are subject to the law of the State, and necessarily when they are in the hands of the exchanges ready to be rented to exhibitors or have passed to the latter, they are in consumption, and mingled as much as from their nature they can be with other property of the State.

It is true that the statute requires them to be submitted to the board before they are delivered to the exhibitor, but we have seen that the films are shipped to "exchanges" and by them rented to exhibitors, and the "exchanges" are described as "nothing more or less than circulating libraries or clearing houses." And one film "serves in many theatres from day to day until it is worn out."

The next contention is that the statute violates the freedom of speech and publication guaranteed by the Ohio constitution. In its discussion counsel have gone into a very elaborate description of moving picture exhibitions and their many useful purposes as graphic expressions of opinion and sentiments, as exponents of policies, as teachers of science and history, as useful, interesting, amusing, educational and moral. And a list of the "campaigns," as counsel call them, which may be carried on is given. We may concede the praise. It is not questioned by the Ohio statute and under its comprehensive description, "campaigns" of an infinite variety may be conducted. Films of a "moral, educational or amusing and harmless character shall be passed and approved" are the words of the statute. No exhibition, therefore, or "campaign" of complainant will be prevented if its pictures have those qualities. Therefore, however missionary of opinion films are or may become, however educational or entertaining, there is no impediment to their value or effect in the Ohio statute. But they may be used for evil, and against that possibility the statute was enacted. Their power of amusement and, it may be, education, the audiences they assemble, not of women alone nor of men alone, but together, not of adults only, but of children, make them the more insidious in corruption by a pretense of worthy purpose or if they should degenerate from worthy purpose. Indeed, we may go beyond that possibility. They take their attraction from the general interest, eager and wholesome it may be, in their subjects, but a prurient interest may be excited and appealed to. Besides, there are some things which should not have pictorial representation in public places and to all audiences. And not only the State of Ohio but other States have considered it to be in the interest of the public morals and welfare to supervise moving picture exhibitions. We would have to shut our eyes to the facts of the world to regard the precaution unreasonable or the legislation to effect it a mere wanton interference with personal liberty.

We do not understand that a possibility of an evil employment of films is denied, but a freedom from the censorship of the law and a precedent right of exhibition are asserted, subsequent responsibility only, it is contended, being incurred for abuse. In other words, as we have seen, the constitution of Ohio is invoked and an exhibition of films is assimilated to the freedom of speech, writing and publication assured by that instrument and for the abuse of which only is there responsibility, and, it is insisted, that

as no law may be passed "to restrain the liberty of speech or of the press," no law may be passed to subject moving pictures to censorship before their exhibition.

We need not pause to dilate upon the freedom of opinion and its expression, and whether by speech, writing or printing. They are too certain to need discussion—of such conceded value as to need no supporting praise. Nor can there be any doubt of their breadth nor that their underlying safeguard is, to use the words of another, "that opinion is free and that conduct alone is amenable to the law."

Are moving pictures within the principle, as it is contended they are? They, indeed, may be mediums of thought, but so are many things. So is the theatre, the circus, and all other shows and spectacles, and their performances may be thus brought by the like reasoning under the same immunity from repression or supervision as the public press,—made the same agencies of civil liberty.

Counsel have not shrunk from this extension of their contention and cite a case in this court where the title of drama was accorded to pantomime;[1] and such and other spectacles are said by counsel to be publications of ideas, satisfying the definition of the dictionaries,—that is, and we quote counsel, a means of making or announcing publicly something that otherwise might have remained private or unknown,—and this being peculiarly the purpose and effect of moving pictures they come directly, it is contended, under the protection of the Ohio constitution.

The first impulse of the mind is to reject the contention. We immediately feel that the argument is wrong or strained which extends the guaranties of free opinion and speech to the multitudinous shows which are advertised on the bill-boards of our cities and towns and which regards them as emblems of public safety, to use the words of Lord Camden, quoted by counsel, and which seeks to bring motion pictures and other spectacles into practical and legal similitude to a free press and liberty of opinion.

The judicial sense supporting the common sense of the country is against the contention. As pointed out by the District Court, the police power is familiarly exercised in granting or withholding licenses for theatrical performances as a means of their regulation. The court cited the following cases: *Marmet* v. *State*, 45 Ohio, 63, 72, 73; *Baker* v. *Cincinnati*, 11 Ohio St. 534; *Commonwealth* v. *McGann*, 213 Massachusetts, 213, 215; *People* v. *Steele*, 231 Illinois, 340, 344, 345.

The exercise of the power upon moving picture exhibitions has been sustained. *Greenberg* v. *Western Turf Ass'n*, 148 California, 126; *Laurelle* v. *Bush*, 17 Cal. App. 409; *State* v. *Loden*, 117 Maryland, 373; *Block* v. *Chicago*, 239 Illinois, 251; *Higgins* v. *Lacroix*, 119 Minnesota, 145. See also *State* v. *Morris*, 76 Atl. Rep. 479; *People* v. *Gaynor*, 137 N.Y.S. 196, 199; *McKenzie* v. *McClellan*, 116 N.Y.S. 645, 646.

It seems not to have occurred to anybody in the cited cases that freedom of opinion was repressed in the exertion of the power which was illustrated. The rights of property were only considered as involved. *It cannot be put out of view that the exhibition of moving pictures is a business pure and simple, originated and conducted for profit, like other spectacles, not to be regarded, nor intended to be regarded by the Ohio constitution, we think, as part of the*

---

[1] *Kalem* v. *Harper Bros.*, 222 U.S. 55.

press of the country or as organs of public opinion. They are mere representations of events, of ideas and sentiments published and known, vivid, useful and entertaining no doubt, but, as we have said, capable of evil, having power for it, the greater because of their attractiveness and manner of exhibition. [Italics ed.]. It was this capability and power, and it may be in experience of them, that induced the State of Ohio, in addition to prescribing penalties for immoral exhibitions, as it does in its Criminal Code, to require censorship before exhibition, as it does by the act under review. We cannot regard this as beyond the power of government.

It does not militate against the strength of these considerations that motion pictures may be used to amuse and instruct in other places than theatres—in churches, for instance, and in Sunday schools and public schools. Nor are we called upon to say on this record whether such exceptions would be within the provisions of the statute nor to anticipate that it will be so declared by the state courts or so enforced by the state officers.

The next contention of complainant is that the Ohio statute is a delegation of legislative power and void for that if not for the other reasons charged against it, which we have discussed. While administration and legislation are quite distinct powers, the line which separates exactly their exercise is not easy to define in words. It is best recognized in illustrations. Undoubtedly the legislature must declare the policy of the law and fix the legal principles which are to control in given cases; but an administrative body may be invested with the power to ascertain the facts and conditions to which the policy and principles apply. If this could not be done there would be infinite confusion in the laws, and in an effort to detail and to particularize, they would miss sufficiency both in provision and execution.

The objection to the statute is that it furnishes no standard of what is education, moral, amusing or harmless, and hence leaves decision to arbitrary judgment, whim and caprice; or, aside from those extremes, leaving it to the different views which might be entertained of the effect of the pictures, permitting the "personal equation" to enter, resulting "in unjust discrimination against some propagandist film," while others might be approved without question. But the statute by its provisions guards against such variant judgments, and its terms, like other general terms, get precision from the sense and experience of men and become certain and useful guides in reasoning and conduct. The exact specification of the instances of their application would be as impossible as the attempt would be futile. Upon such sense and experience, therefore, the law properly relies. This has many analogies and direct examples in cases, and we may cite *Gundling v. Chicago,*

177 U.S. 183; *Red "C" Oil Manufacturing Co. v. North Carolina,* 222 U.S. 380; *Bridge Co. v. United States,* 216 U.S. 177; *Buttfield v. Stranahan,* 192 U.S. 470. See also *Waters-Pierce Oil Co. v. Texas,* 212 U.S. 86. If this were not so, the many administrative agencies created by the state and National governments would be denuded of their utility and government in some of its most important exercises become impossible.

To sustain the attack upon the statute as a delegation of legislative power, complainant cites *Harmon v. State,* 66 Ohio St. 249. In that case a statute of the State committing to a certain officer the duty of issuing a license to one desiring to act as an engineer if "found trustworthy and competent," was declared invalid because, as the court said, no standard was furnished by the General Assembly as to qualification, and no specification as to wherein the applicant should be trustworthy and competent, but all was "left to the opinion, finding and caprice of the examiner." The case can be distinguished. Besides, later cases have recognized the difficulty of exact separation of the powers of government, and announced the principle that legislative power is completely exercised where the law "is perfect, final and decisive in all of its parts, and the discretion given only relates to its execution." Cases are cited in illustration. And the principle finds further illustration in the decisions of the courts of lesser authority but which exhibit the juridical sense of the State as to the delegation of powers.

Section 5 of the statute, which provides for a censor congress of the censor board and the boards of other States, is referred to in emphasis of complainant's objection that the statute delegates legislative power. But, as complainant says, such congress is "at present nonexistent and nebulous," and we are, therefore, not called upon to anticipate its action or pass upon the validity of § 5.

We may close this topic with a quotation of the very apt comment of the District Court upon the statute. After remarking that the language of the statute "might have been extended by descriptive and illustrative words," but doubting that it would have been the more intelligible and that probably by being more restrictive might be more easily thwarted, the court said: "In view of the range of subjects which complainants claim to have already compassed, not to speak of the natural development that will ensue, it would be next to impossible to devise language that would be at once comprehensive and automatic."

In conclusion we may observe that the Ohio statute gives a review by the courts of the State of the decision of the board of censors.

Decree affirmed.

■ Mutual Film Company

v.

Industrial Commission of Ohio.

APPEAL FROM THE DISTRICT COURT
OF THE UNITED STATES FOR THE NORTHERN DISTRICT OF OHIO.

No. 457. Argued January 6, 7, 1915.—Decided February 23, 1915.
Decided on authority of
Mutual Film Corporation v. *Industrial Comm. of Ohio, ante,* p. 230.

THE facts are stated in the opinion.
Argued simultaneously with No. 456 by the same counsel on the same briefs.

MR. JUSTICE MCKENNA delivered the opinion of the court.

This case was submitted with No. 456, just decided. In the latter case the complainant in the court below and appellant here was a corporation of Virginia. The appellant in the pending case is a corporation of Ohio, and counsel say "although there are some differences in the way in which their business is conducted, yet the questions involved are the same, the records in both cases are nearly identical, and the court below treated them together, rendering the one opinion to cover both." And counsel have submitted them on the same argument.

On the authority, therefore, of the opinion in No. 456, the decree is

Affirmed.

■ State

v.

Stevens.

(Supreme Court of North Dakota. March 30, 1916.)

John Carmody and *C. E. Leslie,* both of Hillsboro, for appellant. *Chas. A. Lyche,* of Hatton, State's Atty., for the State.

Goss, J. A demurrer was overruled interposed to the following criminal information, omitting formal heading, viz.:

"*Heretofore, to wit, on the 18th day of July, 1915, at the county of Traill in said state of North Dakota, one C. H. Stevens did commit the crime of willfully and unlawfully committing an act which openly outraged public decency and was injurious to public morals, committed as follows, to wit:*

"*That at said time and place the said defendant, C. H. Stevens, did willfully and unlawfully, entice and procure one Florence Stenmo, then and there a married woman the wife of one Martin Stenmo, and with him then and there living as husband and wife, to go with him, the said defendant, into a certain so-called pool hall, situated upon lot 22 in block 30, of the original townsite of Hatton, Traill county, North Dakota, as per the official plat thereof on file and of record in the office of the register of deeds of said county, at or about the hour of 4 o'clock in the afternoon of said day, which was Sunday, and on which day said pool hall was closed to the public, by virtue of the law in such case made and provided, and there remained with her alone until after the hour of 11 o'clock in the afternoon of said day, he, the said defendant, being then and there himself a married man, and so remained with said Florence Stenmo behind locked and barred doors and blinded windows, in the presence of a large crowd of people until said hour, thus openly outraging public decency and injuring public morals. This contrary to the form of the statute in such case made and provided, and against the peace and dignity of the state of North Dakoka.*

"*Dated at Hillsboro, N.D., this 28th day of July, A.D. 1915.*"

[1] The question presented on the demurrer is whether the facts stated constitute the crime charged. The de-

murrer should have been sustained. Whether the information charges a crime under the statute depends not upon acts charged, but upon inferences not charged, but possible to be drawn from certain facts stated. It is entirely possible for said facts stated to have occurred, and yet defendant be not guilty of the crime inferred by the jury. The facts charged are that a married man and a married woman, not husband and wife, remained within said closed building with blinded windows from 4 until 11 o'clock that Sunday afternoon. This statement lacks as much of certainty in charging the commission of this crime as it would in thus attempting to charge instead the commission of the crime of adultery, or of the crime of unlawful cohabitation, or of fornication, or of sodomy, or of maintaining a house of prostitution, or possibly any other sexual crime. Unaided by uncertain inference no crime is charged. That the kind of inferences to be drawn could make the acts charged, so supplemented, any one of several crimes according to the uncertain inference, is in itself sufficient to condemn as vulnerable to demurrer the information, which constitutes a shotgun charge at some one of several crimes possibly charged according to the inferences used to supplement the few facts actually alleged. Defendant could have stated that he committed all the acts charged, and yet plead not guilty, a condition rather anomalous in criminal pleading and procedure as would forcefully appear had the charge been larceny and had the defendant admitted every fact charged in the information, but still pleaded not guilty. And an examination of the proof discloses that this defendant was convicted accordingly, not upon what was charged in the information to have occurred, but instead upon facts or inferences of fact not therein charged, but which the jury inferred and the court likewise must have assumed happened as either the result of or the reason for these two persons remaining behind closed doors during that time. The court evidently realized that there was something necessary to convict this defendant besides mere proof of the facts charged in the information; otherwise the following instruction would not have been given:

"There is foreshadowed in that charge (after reading the information) a clear violation of sex relation such as ought not to exist between a man married and a woman married. Referring to this charge particularly it does not necessarily charge that adultery was committed, but it does charge an improper sex relation, and that is the question for you to answer when you go to your jury room—did the defendant take this woman there for that purpose? He has gone upon the witness stand and given you an explanation of why he was there. His explanation is that which would be consistent with an honest purpose, and if you believe that his explanation is sufficient," defendant should be acquitted; but if "the state has shown you by evidence beyond a reasonable doubt that his purpose was an unlawful purpose, and if you believe by evidence beyond a reasonable doubt that the purpose was a wrong purpose, then he would be guilty as charged." "Ever since the statutes of the state of North Dakota has declared for the purity of the home, not going back any further, relations of the kind charged here are not proper and are calculated to injure public morals; and if such you find the fact to be in this case, you should find the defendant guilty if the evidence mounts up to that high position to which I have called your attention. Upon the other hand, if this explanation

you believe puts him within the category of doing what he did there honestly and not for the purpose of doing wrong, then, even though it may have caused a crowd, you should find him not guilty."

The trouble is with the information. It does not charge acts or inferences or intent, upon which any part of this instruction could be based. Yet without a finding of fact, inference or intent as declared necessary in the instructions no crime is found to have been committed, but instead that would be left to conjecture as to whether any one of several was actually the one committed or if any crime was committed. Defendant is prosecuted under section 10250, C.L. 1913. It reads:

"Every person who willfully and wrongfully commits any act which grossly injures the person or property of another, or which grossly disturbs the public peace or health, or which openly outrages public decency and is injurious to public morals, although no punishment is expressly provided therefor by this Code, is guilty of a misdemeanor."

The defendant is prosecuted for a nondescript crime— that of openly outraging public decency and injuring public morals. The statute is intended to cover acts not specifically criminal by other provisions of the Code. The service of a stallion upon the public streets would be an example as within the plain purview of the statute. But in a prosecution therefor the acts constituting the crime must be charged and those acts as charged must answer to the statutory definition so that proof of the acts establish the commission of a crime. It is entirely possible for the state to prove every act specified in this information, and yet there be no sex relation involved. Another crime entirely might have been committed, as kidnapping for instance. Even assuming that in the words of the instruction that in the information "there is foreshadowed a clear violation of sex relation such as ought not to exist between a man married and a woman married," that inference is that another crime, that of adultery, was committed. And the proof offered in this case would be sufficient to sustain a conviction for adultery, as the jury must have found under the instruction, that this information "foreshadowed a clear violation of sex relation"; that these persons resorted to this place for adulterous intercourse, and of course availed of the ample opportunity of accomplishing that for which they consorted for hours. Had defendant been prosecuted for that crime, instead of upon an information attempting to charge a different crime, but not charging any crime except by possible inferences, the act of sex violation would have been specifically charged. There would have been no necessity of inference as to what was charged. And had this information defined the facts as broadly as the inferences given the jury and which they found, the information would probably have been duplicitous as charging adultery as well as the one attempted to be charged.

[2] Again section 10693, C.L. 1913, requires that:

"The act or omission charged as the offense" be *"clearly and distinctly set forth in ordinary and concise language, without repetition, and in such manner as to enable a person, of common understanding to know what is intended."*

What act is this defendant charged with? The answer is being alone with a married woman, not his wife, from 4 until 11 o'clock in the afternoon of a certain day in a building closed to the public, with locked and barred doors and blinded windows. Nowhere in the information is there any charge of sex violation. That remains wholly to inference and conjecture, and so remained until the information was supplemented by the charge of the court that nevertheless a sex violation was inferentially hidden therein. It is highly probable from the proof that there was a sex violation by these parties that day. But if so, another crime was committed than the one for which this defendant was prosecuted. And if the defendant is tried for a sex violation, most certainly he should be charged with it in the information itself. Otherwise he is, as here, charged with one act and tried for and convicted of additional acts. That the trial court was obliged by its instructions to thus supplement the charge contained in the information is sufficient proof that those facts set forth in the information do not constitute in themselves a crime. Had the jury by a special verdict found every fact charged in the information to have been committed by the defendant, no judgment could be pronounced thereon without supplementing them with the inference with which the court in its instruction supplemented the information. In other words, he is not tried for only being and remaining there, but in the language of the court's instructions, also for "what he did there" as conclusively appears from the following instruction:

"Upon the other hand, if this explanation you believe puts him within the category of doing what he did there honestly and not for any purpose of doing wrong, then even though it may have caused a crowd, you should find him not guilty."

Plainly the gist of the crime as found by the jury was not only the charge laid in the information, but something not therein charged, viz., "What he did there" behind locked doors.

[3] Then too the information is fatally defective from another standpoint under the authority of *Gunn* v. *Territory*, 19 Okl. 240, 91 Pac. 861. The defendant did not openly outrage public decency within the meaning in which the words are used in the statute. Oklahoma has our identical statute, word for word. A physician was prosecuted under this statute for what he attempted with his office girl in his office, and the following from that decision has application here:

"Does the indictment charge a public offense? The indictment charges the defendant with openly outraging public decency and committing an act injurious to public morals. The facts pleaded in the indictment do not sustain the charge. If the defendant did the acts charged he did not openly outrage public decency and commit an act injurious to public morals. The statute is directed against acts which are committed openly and affect the public. As to whether an act is committed openly is generally a mixed question of law and fact, but it cannot be seriously contended that a doctor's private office is such a place as to give an act committed therein the character of an open act, especially when no one was present except the one against whom the act was committed. * * * By referring to cases which discuss the meaning of the words 'openly' and 'public' as, for instance, 'open adultery' and 'public nuisance' and 'public morals,' etc., one will see that the acts charged against the defendant do not fall within the purview of the statute.

And what was there true was equally apparent here. It is difficult to understand how the defendant willfully openly outraged public decency by sneaking behind closed doors and blinded windows and there secretly perpetrating the crime that the jury have inferred he committed; i.e., adultery, and have it constitute the crime charged in the information, simply because outsiders observing the two enter the closed building gathered a mob and guarded the building and occupants secreted therein from public view throughout the afternoon and evening. Certainly defendant and his paramour did not intend their acts done in secret should thus attract the rabble. That was the farthest from their intention, accepting at face the inference that they went there for adulterous purposes. Nor is it possible that this could be done openly "in the presence of a large crowd of people" and occur "behind locked and barred doors and blinded windows" as charged in the information.

The defendant has in effect been tried for and convicted of adultery without being charged with it. [Italics ed.]. Under the court's instructions, presumably followed, it was necessary that the jury find defendant and this woman sustained "an improper sex relation"; and while the instructions told the jury that it was not necessary to convict that adultery was committed, yet the jury must find an improper sex relation existed or acquit. It is difficult to understand what the trial court meant other than that the fact of adultery was necessary to be found upon which to base a verdict of guilty, and this too in addition to the acts charged in the information. And the same proof was introduced as would have been admissible in a prosecution for adultery on the same record, as, for instance, it was practically established that this man and woman had, prior to this time, been upstairs together in bed in an adjoining building. This supposedly for the purpose of showing their adulterous disposition. If, as held in the Oklahoma case under an identical statute, this prosecution is possible only where the acts committed do not constitute a crime otherwise known to the penal Code, the proof of the commission of adultery establishes that the crime was one other than that charged in the information, and that the prosecution should have been for adultery instead of upon "a blanket statute like the section quoted above." This negatives the right to prosecute for this nondescript crime. It is the theory of the criminal law that any violators thereof shall be prosecuted for the crime they commit and which they know they are committing when doing the acts or permitting the omissions which constitute the crime. While oftentimes the same act may constitute more than one crime, yet such is not applicable under the statute in question, as it is designed to cover only those acts not otherwise criminal, but which "openly outrage public decency and injure public morals."

No constitutional question raised is necessary to be passed upon though the statute is assailed in the briefs. The facts contained in the information are insufficient to charge the commission of a crime. And the information on its face shows the acts were not done openly in the sense in which the important modifying term of the statute is used or intended. The demurrer should have been sustained.

If this defendant can be convicted on inferences that are only "foreshadowed" in the information, then a conviction of felony on inferences only thus foreshadowed and not specifically charged should be equally proper where the evidence may establish the party guilty of crime, whether of the crime attempted to be charged or a different one. Such would be precedent dangerous to liberty and contrary to constitutional guaranties as well. Every defendant is constitutionally entitled to be informed of what he is to be tried for by a written accusation of facts consisting of his acts or omissions, which must be sufficient in themselves to disclose the commission of a crime. No matter how heinous or revolting the case, nothing less satisfies those requirements of statute imperatively necessary to safeguard the individual and his rights and liberties can be tolerated or sustained. The invasion of defendant's rights was substantial, not technical. The conviction is ordered set aside.

■ Commonwealth
v.
Allison.

(Supreme Judicial Court of Massachusetts. Suffolk. May 25, 1917.)

Jos. C. Pelletier, Dist. Atty., of Boston, for the Commonwealth. *Geo. E. Roewer*, Jr., of Boston, for defendant.

RUGG, C.J. [1] This indictment in its first six counts charges the defendant with violation of R.L. c. 212 § 20, as amended by St. 1913, c. 259, by distributing pamphlets, the titles of, which are given and which are described as containing "obscene, indecent and impure language, manifestly tending to corrupt the morals of youth, the same being too lewd and obscene to be more particularly set forth." Upon order by the court, the district attorney filed particulars, including the pamphlets, of each offense charged.

These counts follow the words of the statute. The omission to recite at length the actual words of the publications, accompanied by the allegation that they are too indecent to be spread upon the records, conforms to the established practice which has prevailed in this commonwealth at least for almost a century. *Commonwealth v. Holmes*, 17 Mass. 336; *Commonwealth v. Tarbox*, 1 Cush. 66; *Commonwealth v. Wright*, 139 Mass. 382, 1 N.E. 411; *Commonwealth v. Buckley*, 200 Mass. 346, 86 N.E. 910, 22 L.R.A. (N.S.) 225, 128 Am. St. Rep. 425. Although the contrary was once the rule in England (*Bradlaugh v. The Queen*, 3 Q.B. 607), that has now been changed by statute and conforms to the law prevailing here. See St. 51 and 52 Vict. c. 64, § 7, and *King v. Barraclough*, [1906] 1 K.B. 201. Any further specifications in the indictment would be an offense against common decency.

The indictment held insufficient in *Commonwealth v. McCance*, 164 Mass. 162, 41 N.E. 133, 29 L.R.A. 61, designated only by title a book of over seven hundred pages, which was alleged to contain "among other things certain obscene, indecent and impure language" without further specification. The pamphlets in the case at bar were very brief, whose general character might be thought to be not inaptly indicated by their titles. Plainly that decision affords no support to the contentions of this defendant.

Under the recent statutes regulating criminal pleading, the defendant is entitled as of right to a bill of particulars setting out with sufficient minuteness the essential details of the crime charged. R.L. c. 218, § 39. The reference to the titles of the pamphlets in the present indictment was an adequately definite description of them, even before the enactment of R.L. c. 218, § 22, which permits the use of a designation respecting a written or printed instrument in proper instances.

The simplification of the criminal pleading act, with its provision for a bill of particulars, has been upheld as constitutional by numerous decisions. *Commonwealth v. Jordan*, 207 Mass. 259, 266, 93 N.E. 809, and cases there collected.

[2] What has been said upon this point applies equally to counts 8, 9 and 10, which allege a violation of R.L. c. 212, § 26, by advertising certain enumerated drugs, medicines, instruments and articles for the prevention of conception, and to counts 12 and 13, which charge a violation of R.L. c. 212, § 16, as amended by St. 1905, c. 316, by knowingly circulating, distributing and publishing a pamphlet, described by its title, containing words conveying notice, hint or reference to places where designated means for the prevention of conception might be obtained. In each instance the offense was charged in the words of the statute. This was enough. *Commonwealth v. Connelly*, 163 Mass. 539, 40 N.E. 862; *Commonwealth v. Rogers*, 181 Mass. 184, 190, 63 N.E. 421. The motion to quash on the ground that the counts did not contain a reasonably specific description of the language used and of the offense charged was overruled rightly.

[3] The several counts as to the publication of obscene language, in the light of the particulars furnished to the defendant, are quite sufficient. Whether language is indecent and impure is in large part a practical question. One test of obscenity has been said to be whether its tendency is "to deprave and corrupt those whose minds are open to such immoral influences." *Queen v. Hicklin*, L.R. 3 Q.B. 360, 371. The details which are set forth in these pamphlets plainly would have warranted a jury in finding that

they promote wantonness, notwithstanding the contention of the defendant that they are statements of scientific facts. This point is amply covered by *Commonwealth* v. *Buckley*, 200 Mass. 346, 86 N.E. 910, 22 L.R.A. (N.S.) 225, 128 Am. St. Rep. 425.

[4] The counts as to advertising are sufficient. They are not open to objection in that they do not purport to charge that the advertising is done by or in behalf of the person who has the goods to sell. It is a well recognized form of advertising to undertake to cultivate the desire for the purchase or use of certain articles without indicating that any particular person has them for sale. In this connection the word "advertises" is the calling of public attention to any of the prohibited articles by any means whatsoever. It includes every agency of every form and kind directly or indirectly tending to promote their use or purchase.

[5] The counts which charge the publication and distribution of a pamphlet giving hint or information as to the persons from whom or places at which the prohibited articles might be procured are not open to objection even though no specific person or place is named. It is matter of common knowledge that much advertising is conducted by giving a description of definite goods and with the addition that they may be purchased of all dealers, or of dealers of designated kinds.

[6, 7] *The statutes under which the several counts in this indictment are drawn contravene no provision of the Constitution.* [Italics ed.]. Manifestly they are designed to promote the public morals and in a broad sense the public health and safety. *Their plain purpose is to protect purity, to preserve chastity, to encourage continence and self restraint, to defend the sanctity of the home, and thus to engender in the state and nation a virile and virtuous race of men and women. The subject-matter is well within one of the most obvious and necessary branches of the police power of the state. The means adopted are sanctioned by long continued usage. The distribution of obscene printing was indictable at common law.* [Italics ed.]. *Commonwealth* v. *Holmes*, 17 Mass. 336; *Commonwealth* v. *Sharpless*, 2 S. 7 R. 91, 102; *King* v. *Curl*, 2 Strange, 788.

It has been argued that these pamphlets were designed to propagate what is termed "birth control." Whatever may be said about that subject, it is too manifest for discussion that prohibition of the acts described in the statutes upon which this indictment is founded is within the power of the general court.

Exceptions overruled.

■ People
v.
Brainard *et al.*

(Supreme Court, Appellate Division, First Department. July 9, 1920.)

Francis M. Scott, of New York City, for appellant Brainard.
John Larkin, of New York City, for appellant Harper & Bros.
Edward Swann, Dist. Atty., of New York City (Robert S. Johnstone and Felix C. Benvenga, both of New York City, on the brief), for the People.

SMITH, J. The defendant corporation appealed upon the ground that the possession of the book with intent to sell and show the same did not offend against the provisions of the law. The individual defendant appeals upon the same ground, and also upon the ground that he was not a party to the offense charged.

[1, 2] Considering first the appeal of the defendant Brainard, it is sought to sustain his conviction under section 164 of the Penal Law (Consol. Laws, c. 40). The defendant Brainard was the president of Harper & Bros., which corporation confessedly had possession of the book and offered the same for sale. The evidence shows that when the book was presented for publication the same was referred to a literary conference regularly composed of certain officers and employés of the corporation. The president of the corporation was not a member of that conference. The book was considered and passed upon by

the literary conference, and if it were deemed a proper book for sale, and the sale of it promised financial success, the book was accepted and offered for sale. This book received the unanimous approval of this literary conference, but from the evidence it appears that the defendant Brainard had no knowledge of the fact that it had been submitted, or that it had been approved and had been absent from the country part of the time since its offer for sale and sale, had never read the book, and was in no way such a party to its sale or offer for sale as that he could be deemed to have aided or abetted in the sale or offer to sell. In case there was a disagreement in the literary conference, it appears that the matter was submitted to the president of the corporation, and the president had the power to veto its acceptance and sale, if he had knowledge of any reason existing therefor. *The essence of his crime if he committed any, was his failing to so supervise the affairs of the corporation that he should have knowledge of every book offered for sale by the corporation and failure to prevent such sale.* [Italics ed.]. In support of the conviction, the people rely upon section 164 of the Penal Law, which provides that—

"*Every editor or proprietor of a book, newspaper or serial and every manager of a partnership or incorporated association by which a book, newspaper or serial is issued, is chargeable with the publication of any matter contained in such book, newspaper or serial. But in every prosecution therefor, the defendant may show in his defense that the matter complained of was published without his knowledge or fault and against his wishes, by another who had no authority from him to make the publication and whose act was disavowed by him so soon as known."*

It will be noted in the first place that the information did not charge that this book was published by the said corporation, but only that the defendant "had possession of with intent to sell and show the same." Section 164 would seem to create criminal liability in the manager of a publishing firm which "publishes" a book within the contemplation of the section, and it is provided in that section that the defendant may show in his defense that the matter complained of "was published" without his knowledge or fault and against his wishes, by another who had no authority from him to make the publication, and whose act was disavowed by him so soon as known. The section seems to be aimed at those guilty of the publication of the book or article contemplated thereby, and it clearly does not include those who merely have possession of the book with intent to sell and show the same. Again, this section is included in article 14 of the Penal Law, entitled "Anarchy." Every other section in that article has reference to the crime of criminal anarchy, and by well-known rules of interpretation this section must be read in connection with the title thereof, and cannot be deemed to state a general law of liability for all crimes of every description.

[3, 4] That the defendant Brainard, whether as president or manager of the defendant corporation is not liable for the criminal acts of the corporation committed without his knowledge or privity, would seem to be held in *People v. Clark*, 8 N.Y. Cr. R. 179, 14 N.Y. Supp. 642, and in *People* ex rel. *Carvalho v. Warden of City Prison*, 144 App. Div. 24, 128 N.Y. Supp. 837, affirmed 212 N.Y. 612, 106 N.E. 1039. In *Wahlheimer v. Hardenbergh*, 217 N.Y. 264, 111 N.E. 826, the Court of Appeals held that the general manager of an incorporated association was not liable civilly for damages for the publication of a libel, which publication was made without his knowledge or acquiescence. In *People v. Taylor*, 192 N.Y. 398, 85 N.E. 759, the superintendent of a corporation was held not to be liable criminally for the employment by a foreman of a child under 16 years of age, contrary to the statute. It was assumed that the owner was liable, but that the superintendent was not liable, unless he had knowledge of or acquiesced in the employment. In *People v. Sheffield Farms S. D. Co.*, 225 N.Y. 25, 121 N.E. 474, "the corporation" was held liable criminally for the employment by a subordinate of a child under the lawful age. This contention cannot be sustained, unless we are prepared to hold that the manager of a corporation is criminally liable for every criminal act committed by any subordinate officer of the corporation in connection with his duties in behalf of the corporation. I do not understand that any authority has asserted any such broad proposition, and such a proposition of law should only be held upon a statute clearly expressing such an intent. Moreover, an examination of the other sections of article 106, entitled "Indecency," in which section 1141 is found, would indicate the contrary intent. By section 1140a, the section immediately preced-

ing the section here construed, it is provided that any person who "as owner, manager, director or agent," or in any other capacity, prepares, advertises, gives, presents, or participates in any obscene, indecent, or immoral play which would tend to the corruption of the morals of youth or otherwise, and any person aiding or abetting such act, and any owner, lessee, or manager of any garden, building, or room who leases or lets the same for any such purposes of such production or who assents to the use of the same for any such purpose shall be guilty of a misdemeanor. By section 1146 it is made a crime to keep a disorderly house and it is therein provided that whosoever "as owner, agent or lessor" shall agree to lease or rent or contract for letting any building or part thereof, knowing or with good reason to know that it is intended for such use, "or knowingly permits" the same to be so used, shall be guilty of a misdemeanor. By section 1141, however, no reference is made to any manager, agent, or director, but the charge is imputed only to the person who has in his possession with intent to show any obscene, lewd, lascivious book, etc. It would seem that, if it had been the intent of the section to make a manager of a corporation liable for acts done by his subordinates without his knowledge, in view of these other provisions in the same article treating of indecency, this section would have so provided in explicit terms. The appeal, therefore, of the defendant Brainard must prevail, and his conviction must be reversed and the indictment as to him dismissed.

[5] The remaining question is as to the liability of the corporation for the publication of the book complained of. Section 1141 of the Penal Law makes it criminal for a person to have in his possession with intent to sell, lend, or give away, or to show, "any obscene, lewd, lascivious, filthy, indecent or disgusting book," and such is the information upon which these defendants have been convicted. This section is similar to section 317 of the Penal Code. That section was construed by the Court of Appeals in *People v. Eastman*, 188 N.Y. 478, 81 N.E. 459, 11 Ann. Cas. 302, in which it is said:

"From the context of the statute it is apparent that it is directed against lewd, lascivious, and salacious or obscene publications, the tendency of which is to excite lustful and lecherous desire."

[6] I venture that no one can read this book and truthfully say that it contains a single word or picture which tends to excite lustful or lecherous desire. It contains the autobiography of a prostitute, but without the recital of any facts which come within the condemnation of the section as thus interpreted. I can see no useful purpose in the publication of the book. I cannot agree that it has any moral lesson to teach. Its publication might well be prohibited as a recital of life in the underworld, as is prohibited books containing recitals of crimes. Whether prostitution is a crime in the communities wherein the incidents related in the book are stated to have taken place does not appear, and in any event this information upon which this conviction was had does not purport to be under subdivision 2 of section 1141, but under subdivision 1, and specifically under that part thereof which charges that the defendant had "in its possession, with intent to sell and show the same," an indecent book. It is true that whether the book offends against this statute is ordinarily a ques-

tion of fact for the jury in the first place to determine. It is equally true that, upon the review of a conviction for having offended against this provision, it is the duty of this court to examine the publication and see whether the conviction can be sustained under the facts proven.

Upon an examination of the book I am satisfied that neither defendant has been guilty of the offense charged in the information, and for this reason the judgment and conviction of the defendant corporation, as well as the defendant Brainard, should be reversed, and the information dismissed. Settle orders on notice.

CLARKE, P.J., and PAGE, J., concur.
GREENBAUM, J., concurs in result.

CLARKE, P.J. (concurring). It is settled law that whether a book, publication, print, or picture is "obscene, lewd, lascivious, filthy, indecent, or disgusting" is primarily a question of fact to be determined by the triers of fact. Penal Law, § 1141. *Dreiser* v. *John Lane Co.*, 183 App. Div. 773, 171 N.Y. Supp. 605. This court has the same power to review that determination as it has to review any other, and to reverse the same as against the evidence or the weight thereof. Code Cr. Proc. § 527; Inf. Crim. Cts. Act of City of New York (Laws 1910, c. 659), § 40. Within its interpretation by the Court of Appeals in *People* v. *Eastman*, 188 N.Y. 478, 81 N.E. 459, 11 Ann. Cas. 302, the book under consideration does not violate the statute, the finding of obscenity is against the evidence, and the judgments should be reversed.

PAGE, J., concurs.

DOWLING, J. (dissenting). I concur in the reversal of the judgment of conviction of the defendant Brainard, upon the ground that he was not responsible for the publication of the book in question, knew nothing of its acceptance, had no connection with its issue, did not pass judgment upon its suitability, and had no knowledge whatever of its character. He had not even heard of the work, until this prosecution was instituted. No duty devolved upon him as president of the defendant corporation, Harper & Bros., the neglect or violation of which led to the publication of the book. I do not see how liability, therefore, can be in any way charged to him.

I dissent from the reversal of the judgment of conviction of the defendant Harper & Bros. The book in question has been submitted to the triers of the fact, the trial justices, who have found that it comes within the prohibition of the statute. I agree with the conclusion reached by them. Penal Law, § 1141, under which the defendant was convicted, is contained in article 106, entitled "Indecency," and, so far as applicable, reads:

"*A person who sells, lends, gives away or shows, or offers to sell, lend, give away, or show, or has in his possession with intent to sell, lend or give away, or to show, or advertises in any manner, or who otherwise offers for loan, gift, sale or distribution, any obscene, lewd, lascivious, filthy, indecent or disgusting book, magazine, pamphlet, newspaper, story paper, writing, paper, picture, drawing, photograph, figure or image, or any written or printed matter of*

*an indecent character, * * * is guilty of a misdemeanor,*" etc.

The statute "is directed against lewd, lascivious, and salacious or obscene publications, the tendency of which is to excite lustful and lecherous desire." *People* v. *Eastman*, 188 N.Y. 478, 480, 81 N.E. 459, 460 (11 Ann. Cas. 302). Its object is "to protect the public morals, especially of that class of the community whose character is not so completely formed as to be proof against the lewd effects of the pictures, photographs, and publications prohibited." *People* v. *Muller*, 32 Hun, 209, 212, 213, affirmed 96 N.Y. 408, 48 Am. Rep. 635.

The test as to what is an obscene publication is:

"*Whether the tendency of the matter charged as obscenity is to deprave or corrupt those whose minds are open to such immoral influences, and who might come into contact with it.*" People v. Muller, 96 N.Y. 408, 411, 48 Am. Rep. 635; Reg. v. Hicklin, L.R. 3 Q.B. 360, 11 Cox, C.C. 19.
"*What is the judgment of the aggregate sense of the community reached by it? What is its probable, reasonable effect on the sense of decency, purity, and chastity of society, extending to the family, made up of men and women, young boys and girls—the family, which is the common nursery of mankind, the foundation rock upon which the state reposes?*" United States v. Harmon, (D.C.) 45 Fed. 414, reversed on other grounds (C.C.) 50 Fed. 921.

As was said by Cockburn, C.J., in 11 Cox, C.C. 191, the test of obscenity is whether the tendency of the matter charged as obscenity is to deprave and corrupt those whose minds are open to such immoral influences and into whose hands the publication may fall.

This book purports to be the autobiography of a common prostitute. It is filled with the revolting details of the author's live in various houses of ill fame in different sections of this country. It sets forth at length the physical and financial difficulties attendant upon her chosen means of livelihood, as well as her periods of successful operations. Her continued periods of drunkenness, her diseased conditions, her cynical disregard for decency, are all narrated. The book reveals no purpose to act as a warning to others against embarking on a similar career. It is simply an effort to exploit prurient curiosity. If houses of prostitution and resorts of vice are condemned by law, and every possible effort made to suppress them for the good of the community, I see no reason why the vicious and filthy incidents of the lives of the inmates of such illicit resorts should be allowed to be spread before the public, young and old, in the printed page. That the subject-matter of this book is vulgar and degrading does not necessarily destroy its corrupting effect on the minds and morals of those who may read it. It is not necessary that a publication should be of a high order of literary merit, or depict pleasant episodes, to make it obscene.

This book is suggestive throughout. It offends decency and good morals. In my opinion it completely meets the description of the books forbidden by the statute, and I think the conviction of the defendant Harper & Bros. was right, and should be affirmed.

■ Raymond D. Halsey, *Respondent,*
v.
The New York Society for the Suppression of Vice, *Appellant.*

ANDREWS, J. On November 17, 1917, in the city of New York, the plaintiff sold to an agent of the defendant, one Sumner, an English translation of "Mademoiselle de Maupin." Mr. Sumner submitted the book to City Magistrate House who, however, took no action. He then on November 22d presented a marked copy to Magistrate Simms with a letter calling attention to certain pages which he thought deserved examination. On the 28th he also presented a verified complaint to this magistrate charging that the book was obscene and indecent, referring not only to the marked pages but to the entire work. Thereupon an order was issued stating that it appeared "from the within depositions and statements that the crime therein mentioned has been committed" and holding the plaintiff to answer. The plaintiff was arrested at the direction of Sumner and arraigned. He waived examination, was held for the action of the Court of Special Sessions, tried and acquitted. The record of that trial is not before us, but it was conceded that the copy of "Mademoiselle de Maupin" had been sold by the plaintiff and the acquittal was for the reason, apparently, that the book was not obscene or indecent. This action to recover damages for malicious prosecution was then begun. At the close of the evidence the case was submitted to the jury which found a verdict for the plaintiff. The Appellate Division has affirmed the judgment entered thereon.

The entire book was offered in evidence. We are asked to say from its bare perusal that probable cause existed for the belief on the part of Sumner that the plaintiff was guilty by its sale of a violation of section 1141 of the Penal Law.

In an action for malicious prosecution one of the elements of the plaintiff's case is lack of probable cause. Whether or not this fact has been established may be for the jury to determine. Or it may become a question of law for the court. It is for the jury either when the circumstances upon which the answer depends are disputed or where conflicting inferences may fairly be drawn from them. (*Burns v. Wilkinson,* 228 N.Y. 113; *Galley v. Brennan,* 216 N.Y. 118.)

Theophile Gautier is conceded to be among the greatest French writers of the nineteenth century. When some of his earlier works were submitted to Sainte-Beuve, that distinguished critic was astonished by the variety and richness of his expression. Henry James refers to him as a man of genius (North American Review, April, 1873). Arthur Symons (Studies in Prose and Verse), George Saintsbury (A Short History of French Literature), James

Breck Perkins (Atlantic Monthly, March, 1887) all speak of him with admiration. They tell of his command of style, his poetical imagery, his artistic conceptions, his indescribable charm, his high and probably permanent place in French literature. They say that in many respects he resembles Thackeray.

This was the man who in 1836 published "Mademoiselle de Maupin." It is a book of over four hundred pages. The moment it was issued it excited the criticism of many, but not all of the great Frenchmen of the day. It has since become a part of French literature. No review of French writers of the last one hundred years fails to comment upon it. With the author's felicitous style, it contains passages of purity and beauty. It seems to be largely a protest against what the author, we believe mistakenly, regards as the prudery of newspaper criticism. It contains many paragraphs, however, which taken by themselves are undoubtedly vulgar and indecent.

No work may be judged from a selection of such paragraphs alone. Printed by themselves they might, as a matter of law, come within the prohibition of the statute. So might a similar selection from Aristophanes or Chaucer or Boccaccio or even from the Bible. The book, however, must be considered broadly as a whole. [Italics ed.]. So considered, critical opinion is divided. Some critics, while admitting that the novel has been much admired, call it both "pornographic and dull." (The Nation, Nov. 2, 1893.) Mr. Perkins writes that "there is much in Mademoiselle de Maupin that is unpleasant, and is saved only by beauty of expression from being vulgar. Though Gautier's style reached in this novel its full perfection, it is far from his best work and it is unfortunate that it is probably the one best known." An article in the June, 1868, issue of the Atlantic Monthly says that this is Gautier's representative romance. James calls it his one disagreeable performance but "in certain lights the book is almost ludicrously innocent, and we are at a loss what to think of those critics who either hailed or denounced it as a serious profession of faith." Finally in "A Century of French Fiction," Benjamin W. Wells, professor of modern languages in the University of the South, says: "Mademoiselle de Maupin is an exquisite work of art, but it spurns the conventions of received morality with a contempt that was to close the Academy to Gautier forever. With a springboard of fact in the seventeenth century to start from, he conceives a wealthy and energetic girl of twenty, freed from domestic restraints and resolved to acquire, by mingling as man among men, more knowledge of the other sex than the conventions of social intercourse would admit. He transfers the adventures from the real world to a sort of forest of Arden, where the Rosalind of Shakespere might meet a Watteau shepherdess and a melancholy Jacques. Thus he helps us over the instinctive repulsion that we feel for the situation, and gives a purely artistic interest to the self-revelation that comes to his heroine and to Albert from their prolonged association. Various forms of love reaching out for an unattainable ideal occupy the body of the book, and when once the actors learn to know themselves and each other Gautier parts them forever. In its ethics the book is opposed to the professed morality of nearly all, and doubtless to the real morality of most, but as Sainte-Beuve said of it: 'Every physician of the soul, every moralist, should have it on some back shelf of his library,' and those who, like Mithridates, no longer react to such poisons will find in Mlle. de Maupin much food for the purest literary enjoyment."

We have quoted estimates of the book as showing the manner in which it affects different minds. The conflict among the members of this court itself points a finger at the dangers of a censorship entrusted to men of one profession, of like education and similar surroundings. Far better than we, is a jury drawn from those of varied experiences, engaged in various occupations, in close touch with the currents of public feeling, fitted to say whether the defendant had reasonable ground to believe that a book such as this was obscene or indecent. Here is the work of a great author, written in admirable style, which has become a part of classical literature. We may take judicial notice that it has been widely sold, separately and as a part of every collection of the works of Gautier. It has excited admiration as well as opposition. We know that a book merely obscene soon dies. Many a Roman poet wrote a Metamorphoses. Ovid survives. So this book also has lived for a hundred years.

On the other hand, it does contain indecent paragraphs. We are dealing too with a translation where the charm of style may be attenuated. It is possible that the morality of New York city to-day may be on a higher plane than that of Paris in 1836—that there is less vice, less crime. We hope so. We admit freely that a book may be thoroughly indecent, no matter how great the author or how fascinating the style. It is also true that well-known writers have committed crimes, yet it is difficult to trace the connection between this fact and the question we are called upon to decide. Doctor Dodd was hanged for forgery, yet his sermons were not indecent. Oscar Wilde was convicted of personal wrongdoing and confined in Reading gaol. It does not follow that all his plays are obscene. It is also true that the work before us bears the name of no publisher. That the house which issued it was ashamed of its act is an inference not perhaps justified by any evidence before us.

Regarding all these circumstances, so far as they are at all material, we believe it is for the jury, not for us, to draw the conclusion that must be drawn. Was the book as a whole of a character to justify the reasonable belief that its sale was a violation of the Penal Law? The jury has said that it was not. We cannot say as a matter of law that they might not reach this decision. We hold that the question of probable cause was properly submitted to them.

We have examined various other questions called to our attention. The jury was told that malice was to be presumed if there was no probable cause for the prosecution.

This is not an accurate statement of the law. Under such circumstances malice may be presumed. It is not an inference which the jury is required to draw. (*Stewart* v. *Sonneborn*, 98 U.S. 187, 193.) The attention of the trial judge, however, was not called to this error by any exception. Nor do other exceptions as to the exclusion of evidence and as to the refusal of various requests to charge justify a reversal of the judgment appealed from.

The judgment must, therefore, be affirmed, with costs.

CRANE, J. (dissenting). Section 1141 of the Penal Law provides that a person who sells any obscene, lewd, lascivious, indecent or disgusting book is guilty of a misdemeanor.

On the 28th day of November, 1917, the defendant filed an information in the Magistrates Court of the city of New York charging the plaintiff with the violation of this section in having sold a book entitled "Mademoiselle de Maupin" by Theophile Gautier. The accused, having waived examination before the magistrate, was held for the Special Sessions where he was thereafter tried and found not guilty. He thereupon commenced this action charging this defendant with having maliciously prosecuted him, in that it caused his arrest without any probable cause to believe him guilty of having sold an indecent book; in other words, charging the defendant with having no reasonable grounds to believe "Mademoiselle de Maupin" an indecent publication.

There have been two trials of this action. On the first trial the judge charged the jury as a matter of law that there was no probable cause to believe this book indecent.

On appeal this was reversed on the ground that probable cause in this case was a question of fact for the jury and not for the court. (*Halsey* v. *N.Y. Society for the Suppression of Vice*, 191 App. Div. 245.)

The question of probable cause, when there is no conflict in the evidence, no disputed facts, nor any doubt upon the evidence or inferences to be drawn from it, is one of law for the court, and not of fact for the jury. (*Heyne* v. *Blair*, 62 N.Y. 19; *Hazzard* v. *Flury*, 120 N.Y. 223; *Wass* v. *Stephens*, 128 N.Y. 123.)

In *Carl* v. *Ayers* (53 N.Y. 14, 17) the court, speaking through ANDREWS, J., said: "A person making a criminal accusation may act upon appearances, and if the apparent facts are such that a discreet and prudent person would be led to the belief that a crime had been committed by the person charged, he will be justified, although it turns out that he was deceived and that the party accused was innocent. Public policy requires that a person shall be protected, who in good faith and upon reasonable grounds causes an arrest upon a criminal charge, and the law will not subject him to liability therefor. But a groundless suspicion, unwarranted by the conduct of the accused, or by facts known to the accuser, when the accusation is made, will not exempt the latter from liability to an innocent person for damages for causing his arrest."

When facts and circumstances are undisputed, probable cause is a question of law for the court which it is error to submit to the jury. (*Brown* v. *Selfridge*, 224 U.S. 189, 193; *Anderson* v. *How*, 116 N.Y. 336; *Burt* v. *Smith*, 181 N.Y. 1; *Rawson* v. *Leggett*, 184 N.Y. 504.)

In *Besson* v. *Southard* (10 N.Y. 236, 240) we find the law stated as follows: "If the facts which are adduced as proof of a want of probable cause are controverted, if conflicting testimony is to be weighed, or if the credibility of witnesses is to be passed upon, the question of probable cause should go to the jury, with proper instructions as to the law. But where there is no dispute about facts, it is the duty of the court, on the trial, to apply the law to them."

As an instance where the court found on the facts that there was probable cause and dismissed the malicious prosecution complaint see *Murray* v. *Long* (1 Wend. 140). So also, in *Burlingame* v. *Burlingame* (8 Cowen's Rep. 141) where concededly there was a mistake in making the arrest. See *Driggs* v. *Burton* (44 Vt. 124); *Gilbertson* v. *Fuller* (40 Minn. 413); *Bell* v. *Atlantic C.R.R. Co.* (58 N.J. Law, 227); *Stone* v. *Crocker* (24 Pick. 81); *Bell* v. *Keeplers* (37 Kans. 64).

In *Blachford* v. *Dod* (2 B. & Ad. 179) the facts were these. An attorney was indicted for sending a threatening letter. Being acquitted he brought suit for malicious prosecution and was nonsuited. The court said: "Here the question of probable cause depends on a document coming from the plaintiff himself, viz., the letter sent and written by him to the defendant; and the only question is, whether we are justified in point of law in giving to that letter the construction that it contained a threat of charging the defendants with endeavoring to obtain goods under false pretenses. * * * I concur, therefore, in thinking that the letter, independently of the summons, showed a reasonable and probable cause." (See page 187.)

The construction of the letter and its meaning and whether from its contents there was probable cause was held to be a question of law for the court.

"It was for the judge to construe the written instrument."

If it were always for a jury to determine what reasonable men would do on undisputed facts, there would never be a question of law for the court—the rule would be meaningless.

It was for the trial court and it is now for us to say whether or not, as a matter of law, the defendant had probable cause to believe the plaintiff guilty of selling an obscene book.

At the very outset a marked distinction must be drawn. It cannot be too strongly emphasized that we are not determining whether "Mademoiselle de Maupin" be an indecent book. All we are called upon to determine is whether or not, recognizing the latitude afforded all works of literature and of art, and that tastes may differ, a reasonable, cautious and prudent man would be justified in believing that this publication was obscene and lewd, not in certain passages, but in its main purpose and construction.

When the plaintiff was charged with having violated section 1141 of the Penal Law, that is, charged with a misdemeanor, it necessarily became a question of fact for the triers of fact, Special Sessions or jury, to determine his guilt—to determine whether the book sold was indecent and immoral. (*People* v. *Eastman*, 188 N.Y. 478, 481.)

In a criminal case the questions of fact are always for the jury. In *People* v. *Muller* (96 N.Y. 408, 411) Judge ANDREWS said: "The test of an obscene book was stated in *Regina* v. *Hicklin* (L.R. 3 Q.B. 360), to be, whether the tendency of the matter charged as obscenity is to deprave or corrupt those whose minds are open to such immoral influences, and who might come into contact with it."

The Special Sessions, as the triers of fact, have found the plaintiff not guilty, that is, have found that "Mademoiselle de Maupin" was not such an indecent book as had the tendency spoken of in the *Muller* case. When it came, however, to the trial of this action another question was presented, and that was whether the defendant here and the complainant in the criminal case had reason to believe that the book had this tendency, that is—whether reasonable men would have been justified in believing the book lascivious—corrupting to morals, even though in the mind of a jury they were mistaken.

This reasoning clearly shows that the jury, or triers of fact, in a criminal case have a different question to pass upon than those disposing of the malicious prosecution case. In the latter case when the facts are all conceded, and no different inferences are to be drawn from them, probable cause is a question of law for the court. In this case we have the book. The inferences to be drawn from it are all one way. Vice and lewdness are treated as virtues.

The book was submitted to the magistrate a week before the issuance of the warrant for the plaintiff's arrest. The plaintiff appeared, waived examination, and was held for trial before the Special Sessions. (*Schultz* v. *Greenwood Cemetery*, 190 N.Y. 276.)

What is probable cause? We have quoted above what this court said about it in *Carl* v. *Ayers* (*supra*) and we cannot add to it. It is such a state of facts presented to the complainant as would incline or move reasonable minded men of the present day and of this generation to believe the accused guilty of the crime charged. Would reasonable, careful, prudent men acting with caution, and environed with the conditions of life as they exist to-day, and not in some past age, be justified in believing "Mademoiselle de Maupin" a filthy and indecent book and published for no useful purpose, but simply from a desire to cater to the lowest and most sensual part of human nature?

In order to justify my conclusion that the defendant had probable cause to believe this book such an one as mentioned in section 1141 of the Penal Law, it is not necessary to spread upon our pages all the indecent and lascivious part of this work. (*People* v. *Eastman*, *supra*, p. 481.) Some facts, however, may be mentioned to give point and direction to this inquiry. In the first place the Society for the Suppression of Vice was confronted with the fact that the publisher, whoever he was, does not put his name to the book.

The book consists of certain letters purported to be written by a young man of twenty-two as a sort of a satire on virtue and in praise of the sensual passions, adultery and fornication. It counsels vice. He tells his friend of his love for certain women, describes them, and relates the scenes leading up to immoral practices and to intercourse. To have a mistress in the eyes of this young man is the first qualification of a gentleman, and adultery to him appears to be the most innocent thing in the world. He writes: "I deem it quite a simple matter that a young girl should prostitute herself."

No doubt many books of fine literature known as standard works have passages in them which may shock the moral sensibilities of some people of this day, but they appear as expressions of the times and not to my knowledge as in praise of vice and derision of virtue. Most works, wherever prostitution appears, condemn or confess it as a vice or admit its evil effects and influences. The purport of this book seems to be to impress upon the readers that vice and voluptuousness are natural to society, are not wrongs but proper practices to be indulged in by the young. (*Tyomies Pub. Co. v. United States*, 211 Fed. Rep. 385.)

Theophile Gautier published Mlle. de Maupin in 1835. The people of his time condemned it, and by reason of its lasciviousness and bad taste he was forever barred from the French Academy. He acquired a reputation as a writer, but it was not because of this book. The New International Encyclopedia has this to say about Gautier and his Mlle. de Maupin: "Theophile Gautier 1811–1872. Gautier's next book, Mlle. de Maupin (1835), a curious attempt at self-analysis, was a frank expression of Hedonism. Its art is fascinating, but it treats the fundamental postulates of morality with a contempt that closed the Academy to him for life."

In the Encyclopedia Britannica we read the following:

"His first novel of any size, and in many respects his most remarkable work, was Mlle. de Maupin. Unfortunately this book while it establishes his literary reputation on an imperishable basis, was *unfitted* by its subject, and in parts by its treatment, *for general perusal*, and created even in France, a prejudice against its author which he was very far from really deserving." (Article by George Saintsbury.) (Italics mine.)

In the Encyclopedia Americana may be read: "Gautier's whole philosophy is a philosophy of paradox, his ideal of life hardly more than a picturesque viciousness. His besetting sin was a desire to say something clever and wicked to shock the Philistines (see Mlle. de Maupin). The Academy was forever closed to him."

When the people of France and Gautier's time condemned his book as being vicious and unfit for general perusal, are we going to say that the defendant in this case did not have probable cause to believe the same thing, when the translation was published in America by a publisher who was ashamed to put his name to it?

Many things have moved in the past century, and with the teachings of church, synagogue and college, we, at least, have the right to expect that the general tone of morality in America in 1922 is equal to that of France in 1835.

It may be true that Gautier's style is fascinating and his imagination rich, but neither style, imagination or learning can create a privileged class, or permit obscenity because it is dressed up in a fashion difficult to imitate or acquire.

American literature has been fairly clean. That the policy of this state is to keep it so is indicated by section 1141 of the Penal Law. The legislature has declared in this section that no obscene, lewd, lascivious or disgusting book shall be sold. Language could not be plainer.

If the things said by Gautier in this book of Mlle. de Maupin were stated openly and frankly in the language of the street, there would be no doubt in the minds of anybody, I take it, that the work would be lewd, vicious and indecent. The fact that the disgusting details are served up in a polished style with exquisite settings and perfumed words makes it all the more dangerous and insidious and none the less obscene and lascivious.

Gautier may have a reputation as a writer, but his reputation does not create a license for the American market.

Oscar Wilde had a great reputation for style, but went to jail just the same. Literary ability is no excuse for degeneracy.

Sufficient to say that a reading of this book convinces me that as a matter of law the Society for the Suppression of Vice had probable cause to believe the defendant, plaintiff, guilty of violating section 1141 of the Penal Law in selling this book and that the complaint in this case should have been dismissed.

Hiscock, Ch. J., Cardozo, Pound and McLaughlin, JJ., concur with Andrews, J.; Crane, J., reads dissenting opinion in which Hogan, J., concurs.

Judgment affirmed.

■ People
v.
Baylinson.

(Supreme Court, Appellate Division, First Department. November 28, 1924.)

Argued before Clarke, P.J., and Dowling, Smith, Merrell, and McAvoy, JJ.

Otterbourg, Steindler & Houston, of New York City (Charles A. Houston, of New York City, of counsel), for appellant.

Joab H. Banton, Dist. Atty., of New York City (Felix C. Benvenga, Asst. Dist. Atty., of New York City, of counsel; Edwin B. McGuire, Deputy Asst. Dist. Atty., of New York City, on the brief), for the People.

Merrell, J. Section 43 of the Penal Law provides that—

"*A person who willfully and wrongfully commits any act which seriously injures the person or property of another, or which seriously disturbs or endangers the public peace or health, or which openly outrages public decency, for which no other punishment is expressly prescribed by this chapter, is guilty of a misdemeanor. * * *"*

The judgment of conviction from which the defendant has appealed recites his conviction for "the misdemeanor of unlawfully violating section 43 of the Penal Law committed in the city and county of New York on February 21, 1923 (willfully and unlawfully outraging public decency)." The crime charged in the information was that the defendant did "cause and permit to be exhibited to the public in a certain hotel called the Waldorf-Astoria, there situate, a certain picture and painting in the following form, to wit:

"The presence of Christ at the marriage feast in Cana, in Galilee, after having performed His first miracle of changing the water in the water pots into wine at the request of the Blessed Virgin Mary, said picture or painting having inserted in modern street clothes pictures intended to be the persons of ex-Congressman Volstead, William H. Anderson and William Jennings Bryan, the said Volstead holding his right hand upon the shoulder of Christ, William Jennings Bryan spilling the wine out of one of the pots filled with the same, while Anderson is seen standing in the doorway near by behind Volstead and Bryan, the same being a picture or painting obviously offensive to the general public decency and to the religious sensibilities of divers good citizens, in that it purported to portray Christ as a violator of the National Prohibition Law and the Prohibition Law of the state New York against the form of the statute in such case made and provided and against the peace of the people of the state of New York."

The picture was shown at an annual exhibition of the Society of Independent Artists, a domestic corporation, of which society the defendant was the paid secretary. The society holds annual exhibitions of paintings, sculpture, and other works of art of its members. The evidence shows that in the month of October in each year notices are sent out, to former exhibitors and those who are thought to be interested in the approaching annual exhibition, that such an exhibition will be held and inviting the persons notified to become members of the association. Annual dues are exacted from the members, the amount thereof being dependent upon the expense of conducting the exhibition in each year. The testimony of the president of the society was that once a man paid his membership dues he was entitled to have the privilege to show one or two pictures, according to the size of the pictures, at the annual exhibition; that the society did not act as a jury; and that payment of the membership dues entitled the artist to have his picture or pictures hung. The defendant had no voice or discretion as to whether any picture brought in by a member of the society should be hung. Membership in the society was sufficient to entitle any one to hang his picture at the annual exhibition, and no one had authority to deprive him of such right. The picture alleged to have been offensive was painted by an artist by the name of J. Francois Kaufman, who was a member of the society and hung the picture by virtue of such membership. The evidence did not show that the defendant took any part in the hanging of the picture, which was one of over 800 hung at the annual exhibition of the society held at the Waldorf-Astoria Hotel in February, 1923. The exhibition that year lasted for three weeks. A paid admission was charged to all except members of the society and some others who had received complimentary tickets of admission. A regular cashier and ticket seller was provided, whose duty it was, in behalf of the society, to sell tickets to its exhibition. During the three weeks' course of the exhibition in February, 1923, about 10,000 people were admitted thereto, and during the course of the exhibition there was no incident of disorder or a breach of the public peace, nor was there

any evidence that the display of the picture outraged public decency.

[1] The picture itself protrays a scene at the wedding feast at Cana, in Galilee, where the Saviour performed His first miracle by transforming the contents of the water pots into wine for the wedding feast. The picture portrays the Saviour, with the mother of Jesus in an attitude of adoration, with other participants of the feast about the table. There is also shown the likenesses of ex-Congressman Volstead, William Jennings Bryan, and William H. Anderson in present-day garb. Volstead stands with his right hand upon the Saviour's shoulder, his left directing attention to the vessels of wine, one of which lies broken upon the floor, the contents of another is being spilled out by William Jennings Bryan, while the remaining four stand full of wine at the Saviour's feet. Anderson, the erstwhile superintendent of the Anti-Saloon League, stands in the open doorway with his eyes upon the Saviour.

According to the testimony of the police officer, the painting hung at the exhibition bore the title, "Father, Forgive Them, for They Know Not What They Do." Notwithstanding such title, the conception of the artist evidently was to arouse a prejudice in the minds of the public by portraying the physical destruction, by those zealous in the enforcement of existing laws prohibiting the manufacture and sale of intoxicating liquors, of that which the Saviour, through the performance of His miracle, had created. While the work of the artist might have the tendency to create a prejudice in the public mind against the acts of those who were bound to destroy that which the Saviour approved, the arousing of such a sentiment falls far short of outraging public decency, of which the defendant stands convicted. We are unable to see anything about the picture which through any strain of imagination could even tend to outrage public decency. Undoubtedly the picture may be said to be sacrilegious, in that present-day mortals are portrayed as venturing to oppose their judgment as to what is right against that of Christ; but the defendant is not convicted of a sacrilege or blasphemy, nor is either made a crime under any law of this state. The conception of the artist may be said to be in bad taste, but such bad taste in no wise tends to outrage public decency. The word "decency" has a well-defined meaning. Though this picture may be open to criticism, we do not think it can be said to be indecent within the usually accepted meaning of that word. The statute contemplates an act which seriously disturbs or endangers the public peace or which openly outrages public decency. Surely the hanging of the picture, even though the defendant were sufficiently connected therewith to make him chargeable, did not disturb or endanger the public peace. *Ten thousand people attended the exhibition, and no single one of them, so far as the evidence disclosed, objected to the picture or manifested any disposition towards a breach of the peace. The same may be said as to the picture outraging public decency. The evidence is to the effect that no objection was raised to the picture save by the police officer who viewed the same, laid the information, and procured the summons for the defendant's arrest.* [Italics ed.]. The defendant was not convicted of the crime of endangering the peace, but, as stated in the judgment, of "willfully and unlawfully outraging public decency."

[2] Even though the picture could be said to have been indecent within the contemplation of the statute, the people failed to connect the defendant with the commis-

sion of the crime. If any offense was committed, it was by the artist who painted and hung the picture, rather than the defendant, who was merely the secretary of the association, and who took no part in either the selection or the hanging of the picture, and who did not even know of its existence until his attention was called to it by the police officer who discovered the alleged offensive picture.

The picture was hung under a contract between the artist and the association, and the defendant was powerless to prevent the display of the picture or to cause its removal. Under such circumstances, we do not think the defendant can be said to have been a person who willfully and wrongfully committed an act which either seriously disturbed or endangered the public peace or which openly outraged public decency within the purview of the Penal Law. We can ascribe to the defendant no act of willfulness or wrongdoing in the display of the picture. Willfulness implies an intent on the part of the wrongdoer. There is not the slightest evidence in the case that the defendant acted willfully or with wrongful intent. The absence of proof of any willful intent on the part of the defendant absolves him from guilt. *People* v. *Foster*, 204 App. Div. 295, 198 N.Y.S. 7, affirmed 236 N.Y. 610, 142 N.E. 304; *People* v. *Marrin*, 205 N.Y. 275, 98 N.E. 474, 43 L.R.A. (N.S.) 754; *People* v. *Martinitis*, 168 App. Div. 446, 153 N.Y.S. 791. *People* v. *Martinitis*, supra, was decided by the Second Appellate Division and concerned an alleged violation of section 43 of the Penal Law. In that case the Appellate Division said:

*"This is the familiar provision which makes a misdemeanor any willful * * * act which seriously injures the * * * property of another, or which * * * disturbs * * * the public peace or health, or * * * outrages public decency, for which no other punishment is expressly prescribed. This defendant negligently drove on the wrong side of the highway, which resulted in injury to person and property. But this section of the Penal Law requires that the injuring act shall be willful. There must exist an intention designedly and purposely to cause injury. Not every intentional act is willful. It must be with wrongful pur-*

pose, or with a design to injure another, or one committed out of mere wantonness or lawlessness." Citing Wass v. Stephens, *128 N.Y. 123, 28 N.E. 21*

The Court of Appeals, in Wass v. Stephens, supra, said:

"But the word 'willfully' in the statute means something more than a voluntary act, and more also than an intentional act which in fact is wrongful. It includes the idea of an act intentionally done with a wrongful purpose, or with a design to injure another, or one committed out of mere wantonness or lawlessness."

But where a particular intent is an ingredient of the crime, the mere doing of the prohibited act does not constitute the crime unless accompanied with unlawful intent.

[3, 4] The people seek to uphold the conviction of the defendant upon the ground that the picture exhibited at the exhibition tended to outrage public decency or might outrage public decency. There was an entire absence of proof that public decency was outraged as contemplated by the statute. The statute does not prohibit acts tending or likely to outrage public decency, but it expressly relates to acts which do disturb or endanger the public peace or which do openly outrage public decency. The distinction is quite apparent. Here we are dealing with acts and not possibilities. We cannot conceive that the exhibition of a picture in a collection of 800 works of art in private rooms of a hotel to which the public is admitted only on the payment of an admission fee, and where there is not the slightest indication of a public disturbance or that public decency is outraged, can be said to be a violation of said section of the Penal Law. In order to convict the defendant, the Special Sessions must have held, notwithstanding the absence of any evidence of complaint or disturbance, that the picture itself was indecent, and therefore must outrage public decency. There was neither proof that it did so nor that it was intended so to do.

The judgment of conviction should be reversed, the information dismissed, and the fine paid by the defendant remitted to him.

Order filed. All concur.

■ Martin

v.

State. (No. 18955.)

Court of Appeals of Georgia, Division No. 1. July 13, 1928.

R. D. *Feagin* and W. E. *Bartlett*, both of Macon, for plaintiff in error.

Roy W. *Moore*, Sol., of Macon, for the State.

LUKE, J. N. R. Martin was convicted in the city court of Macon on an accusation charging that he "did then and there unlawfully indulge in and do a notorious act of public indecency tending to debauch the morals, by taking pictures of Mrs. N. R. Martin, Madge Lewis, and another whose name is unknown, females' naked limbs and private parts, on or near a public street and highway, known as Ocmulgee street and Second street, in the city of Macon, and at a place where the said act of indecency could have been seen by more than one person," etc. The defendant demurred to the accusation, upon the following grounds: (1) No crime was charged. (2) No specific female was named as the one of whose limbs and private parts pictures were taken. (3) It was not alleged with sufficient particularity where the alleged crime was committed. (4) It was not charged that the defendant persuaded or compelled the alleged female to pose for the pictures. (5) "There is no law of Georgia making it an offense merely to make a picture of the naked limbs and private parts of a female, without more, unless said pictures were developed and exhibited, and this is not alleged." (6) "The word 'posing' is too indefinite and vague to charge any crime," and "posing" pictures is contradictory to the charge of making pictures. The court overruled the demurrer, and, by agreement, the case was tried before the judge without a jury.

In substance, the evidence was as follows: On the day alleged in the accusation an officer of the city of Macon was called to go to the corner of Ocmulgee and Second streets. When he arrived there, he saw Mrs. N. R. Martin and the other accused persons lying on a bank on the side of Ocmulgee street, where they could have been seen by more than one person. Mrs. Martin had her dress up and was exposing her private parts, and the others had their dresses up, exposing their limbs, and the defendant was standing over them with a kodak, taking a picture of the females. The officer arrested the defendant and took the kodak from him and took the undeveloped films out of the kodak, and another role of films from the pocket of the defendant. The officer had the films developed, and one of them was the identical picture which he saw the defendant take of the females. All the developed pictures were introduced in evidence, and they show that the defendant had taken other exposures of the females than the ones the officer actually saw snapped, and that they were taken at the same place, and were reproductions of the private parts of Mrs. Martin and the naked limbs of the other females. The motion for a new trial contained the usual general grounds, and the special ground that the admission of such pictures in evidence, over objection, was a violation of the constitutional provision that, "no person shall be compelled to give testimony tending in any manner to criminate himself."

[1–3] 1. All participating in misdemeanors are guilty as principals; and the allegation that the defendant was taking pictures of the naked limbs and private parts of Mrs. N. R. Martin, Madge Lewis, and another, on a named public street and highway in the city of Macon, at a place where the act could be seen by more than one person, is certainly a sufficient charge that he was participating in the act of public indecency. The word "posing" does not appear in the accusation, and the demurrer in that regard is "speaking." The accusation was sufficiently definite as to the names of the females and the place where the crime was committed, and the demurrer was properly overruled.

[4, 5] 2. Conceding, but not deciding, that the court erred in admitting in evidence the pictures of which complaint is made in the motion for a new trial, this would not require a reversal of the judgment. The defendant did not make a statement denying the charge, and *the undisputed evidence shows that the defendant was taking a picture of the private parts of his wife on the side of a public street where it could be seen by more than one person; and this act alone constituted a notorious act of public indecency, even if the pictures had never been introduced in evidence and even if they had never been developed.* [Italics ed.]. The officer swore that he "saw Mrs. Martin holding up her dress" and the defendant "in the act of snapping the picture," and that "they could be seen by more than one person." "What is decent and what is indecent are determined by the sensibilities and moral standards of a people, as evolved from generation to generation along with their civilization." "When, by general consensus of the people and practical unanimity of public opinion, an act tending to debauch the morals is understood to be offensive to the common instincts of decency if done under particular circumstances, *that act* when so done is, in contemplation of law, a notorious act of indecency." (Italics ours.) *Redd* v. *State*, 7 Ga. App. 576 (2, 4), 67 S.E. 709.

[6] It might reasonably be presumed that the defendant had no earthly reason for making the films if he did not intend to have them developed, and the only reason he did not have them developed was because of the intervention of the officer. Had he developed the films or had them developed, it might have aggravated his crime, if possible; but, without regard to the admission of the pictures in evidence and the development of the films, the act theretofore committed by the woman and the defendant, both participating, was shockingly obscene, and notorious public and indecent conduct. The court did not err in overruling the motion for a new trial.

Judgment affirmed.

BROYLES, C.J. and BLOODWORTH, J., concur.

■ People
v.
Friede *et al.*

City Magistrate's Court of New York City, Borough of Manhattan, Seventh District.

February 21, 1929.

Joab H. Banton, Dist, Atty., of New York City (Felix C. Benvenga and Saul Price, both of New York City, of counsel), for the People.

Greenbaum, Wolff & Ernst, of New York City (Morris L. Ernst, Newman Levy, and Alexander Lindey, all of New York City, of counsel), for defendants.

BUSHEL, City Magistrate. The defendants are charged with having violated section 1141 of the Penal Law by their possession and sale of a book entitled "The Well of Loneliness." Evidence proving possession and sale of the book by the defendants had been introduced and is not controverted by them. The defendants maintain, however, that such possession and sale did not offend against the provisions of the law, and have moved to dismiss the complaint.

Section 1141 of the Penal Law provides: "A person who sells, * * * or has in his possession with intent to sell, * * * any obscene, lewd, lascivious, filthy, indecent or disgusting book, * * * is guilty of a misdemeanor." The defendants contend that as a matter of law "The Well of Loneliness" is not obscene, lewd, lascivious, filthy, or disgusting within the meaning of the statute; that, if any jury held otherwise, it would be incumbent upon the court to set aside the verdict; and accordingly that the complaint should be dismissed.

[1] This court in a prosecution of this character is not the trier of the fact. Its judicial province is limited to a determination of the question as to whether as matter of law it can be said that the book which forms the basis of the charge in question is not violative of the statute. The evidence before me, however, is the same as that which would be presented to the tribunal vested with the power of deciding the facts as well as the law.

The book here involved is a novel dealing with the childhood and early womanhood of a female invert. In broad outline the story shows how these unnatural tendencies manifested themselves from early childhood; the queer attraction of the child to the maid in the household, her affairs with one Angela Crossby, a normally sexed, but unhappily married, woman, causing further dissension between the latter and her husband, her jealousy of another man who later debauched this married woman, and her despair, in being supplanted by him in Angela's affections, are vividly portrayed. The book culminates with an extended elaboration upon her intimate relations with a normal young girl, who becomes a helpless subject of her perverted influence and passion, and pictures the struggle for this girl's affections between this invert and a man from whose normal advances she herself had previously recoiled, because of her own perverted nature. Her sex experiences are set forth in some detail and also her visits to various resorts frequented by male and female inverts.

The author has treated these incidents not without some restraint; nor is it disputed that the book has literary merit. To quote the people's brief: "It is a well-written, carefully constructed piece of fiction," and "contains no unclean words." Yet the narrative does not veer from its central theme, and the emotional and literary setting in which they are found give the incidents described therein great force and poignancy. The unnatural and depraved relationships portrayed are sought to be idealized and extolled. The characters in the book who indulge in these vices are described in attractive terms, and it is maintained throughout that they be accepted on the same plane as persons normally constituted, and that their perverse and inverted love is as worthy as the affection between normal beings and should be considered just as sacred by society.

The book can have no moral value, since it seeks to justify the right of a pervert to prey upon normal members of a community, and to uphold such relationship as noble and lofty. Although it pleads for tolerance on the part of society of those possessed of and inflicted with perverted traits and tendencies, it does not argue for repression or moderation of insidious impulses. An idea of the moral tone which the book assumes may be gained from the attitude taken by its principal character towards her mother, pictured as a hard, cruel, and pitiless woman, because of the abhorrence she displays to unnatural lust, and to whom, because of that reaction, the former says: "But what I will never forgive is your daring to try and make me ashamed of my love. I'm not ashamed of it; there's no shame in me."

The theme of the novel is not only antisocial and offensive to public morals and decency, but the method in which it is developed, in its highly emotional way attracting and focusing attention upon perverted ideas and unnatural vices, and seeking to justify and idealize them, is strongly calculated to corrupt and debase those members of the community who would be susceptible to its immoral influence. [Italics ed.].

Although the book in evidence is prefaced by a laudatory commentary by Havelock Ellis, yet it is he who, in his scientific treatise on the subject, states: "We are bound to protect the helpless members of society against the invert."

Havelock Ellis, Studies in the Psychology of Sex, vol. 2, p. 356. The court is charged with that precise duty here. The test of an obscene book laid down in *Regina* v. *Hicklin*, L.R. 3 Q.B. 360, 369, and quoted in *People* v. *Muller*, 96 N.Y. 408, 411, 48 Am. Rep. 635, is "whether the tendency of the matter charged as obscenity is to deprave or corrupt those whose minds are open to such immoral influences, and who might come into contact with it." Although not sole and exclusive, this test is one which has been frequently applied: *People* v. *Doris*, 14 App. Div. 117, 43 N.Y.S. 571; *People* v. *Seltzer*, 122 Misc. Rep. 329, 203 N.Y.S. 809; *People* v. *Zambounis*, 225 App. Div. 751, 232 N.Y.S. 846. See, also, dissenting opinions of Crane, J., in *Halsey* v. *New York Soc. for Suppression of Vice*, 234 N.Y. 1, 7, 136 N.E. 219, and of Dowling, J., in *People* v. *Brainard*, 192 App. Div. 816, 822, 183 N.Y.S. 452. It may be accepted as a basis for judicial decision here.

Its application and soundness are assailed by learned counsel for the defendants, who argue that it seeks to gauge the mental and moral capacity of the community by that of its dullest-witted and most fallible members. This contention overlooks the fact that those who are subject to perverted influences, and in whom that abnormality may be called into activity, and who might be aroused to lustful and lecherous practices are not limited to the young and immature, the moron, the mentally weak, or the intellectually impoverished, but may be found among those of mature age and of high intellectual development and professional attainment.

[2, 3] Men may differ in their conceptions as to the propriety of placing any restrictions upon a literary work or absolute freedom of expression and interchange of ideas. This conflict between liberty and restraint is not new to the law. Paradoxes of Legal Science, Hon. Benjamin N. Cardozo. However, the Legislature has spoken on that subject in the enactment of the statute in question. Even if the courts were not (as a matter of fact they are) in accord with the public policy it declares, they would not be free to disregard it, because it may be founded upon conceptions of morality with which they disagree. Moreover, the Legislature has not sought to set up a literary censorship, or attempted to confine thought and discussion in a straight-jacket of inflexible legal definition, but has imposed upon the courts the duty of protecting the weaker members of society from corrupt, depraving, and lecherous influences, although exerted through the guise and medium of literature, drama, or art. The public policy so declared was reaffirmed by the Legislature by its recent amendment to the Penal Law (section 1140a), making it a misdemeanor to prepare, advertise, or present any drama, play, etc., dealing with the subject of sex degeneracy or sex perversion. Laws 1927, c. 690.

Defendants' counsel urge that the book is to be judged by the mores of the day. The community, through this recent legislation, has evinced a public policy even more hostile to the presentation and circulation of matter treating of sexual depravity. The argument, therefore, that the mores have so changed as to fully justify the distribution of

a book exalting sex perversion is without force. The amendment to the Penal Law just referred to followed closely upon the decision of the Appellate Division of this department in *Liveright* v. *Waldorf Theatres Corporation*, 220 App. Div. 182, 221 N.Y.S. 194, which involved a dramatization of the same theme as this novel. In the language there employed by McAvoy, J., "It cannot be said dogmatically that the morals of youth, or even of adults, would not be affected by presenting a theme of the character here exhibited," and that it might not "give to some minds a lecherous swing causing a corruption of the moral tone of the susceptible members" of the community.

The defendants' brief refers the court to eminent men of letters, critics, artists, and publishers who have praised "The Well of Loneliness." Were the issue before the court the book's value from a literary standpoint, the opinions of those mentioned might, of course, carry great weight. However, the book's literary merits are not challenged, and the court may not conjecture as to the loss that its condemnation may entail to our general literature, when it is plainly subversive of public morals and public decency, which the statute is designed to safeguard. Moreover, it has been held that the opinions of experts are inadmissible. *People* v. *Muller*, supra; *People* v. *Seltzer*, supra. And as Mr. Justice Wagner (*People* v. *Seltzer*, supra) said, in disposing of a similar situation: "Charm of language, subtilty of thought, faultless style, even distinction of authorship, may all have their lure for the literary critic, yet these qualities may all be present and the book be unfit for dissemination to the reading public. Frequently these attractive literary qualities are the very vehicles by which the destination of illegality is reached."

The learned justice, in the same opinion, then summarizes as follows "the general, though not exclusive, rules as aids to interpretation: The penal provision prohibits the publication of lewd, lascivious, salacious or obscene writings the tendency of which is to excite lustful and lecherous desires; likewise it prohibits the publication of those writings whose tendency is to deprave or corrupt minds open to immoral influences and who might come in contact with it. It is also offensive to the section if the matters charged as obscene are so filthy and disgusting as to be revolting to those who may have occasion to read them."

[4] I am convinced that "The Well of Loneliness" tends to debauch public morals, that its subject-matter is offensive to public decency, and that it is calculated to deprave and corrupt minds open to its immoral influences and who might come in contact with it, and applying the rules and recognized standards of interpretation as laid down by our courts, I refuse to hold as matter of law that the book in question is not violative of the statute. Accordingly, and under the stipulation entered into in this case, that the testimony taken upon the summons shall be the testimony taken upon the complaint, if one is ordered, I hereby order a complaint against these defendants.

The motion to dismiss the complaint is denied, and the defendants are held for the action of the Court of Special Sessions.

1930-1949
Cases

■ United States
v.
Dennett. No. 238.

Circuit Court of Appeals, Second Circuit. March 3, 1930.

The statute under which the defendant was convicted reads as follows: "Every obscene, lewd, or lascivious, and every filthy book, pamphlet, picture, paper, letter, writing, print, or other publication of an indecent character, and every article or thing designed, adapted, or intended for preventing conception or producing abortion, or for any indecent or immoral use; * * * is hereby declared to be nonmailable matter and shall not be conveyed in the mails or delivered from any post office or by any letter carrier. Whoever shall knowingly deposit, or cause to be deposited, for mailing or delivery, anything declared by this section to be nonmailable, or shall knowingly take, or cause the same to be taken, from the mails for the purpose of circulating or disposing thereof, or of aiding in the circulation or disposition thereof, shall be fined not more than $5,000, or imprisoned not more than five years, or both."

The defendant is the mother of two boys. When they had reached the respective ages of eleven and fourteen, she concluded that she ought to teach them about the sex side of life. After examining about sixty publications on the subject and forming the opinion that they were inadequate and unsatisfactory, she wrote the pamphlet entitled "Sex Side of Life," for the mailing of which she was afterwards indicted.

The defendant allowed some of her friends, both parents and young people, to read the manuscript which she had written for her own children, and it finally came to the notice of the owner of the Medical Review of Reviews, who asked if he might read it and afterwards published it. About a year afterwards she published the article herself at twenty-five cents a copy when sold singly, and at lower prices when ordered in quantities. Twenty-five thousand of the pamphlets seem to have been distributed in this way.

At the trial, the defendant sought to prove the cost of publication in order to show that there could have been no motive of gain on her part. She also offered to prove that she had received orders from the Union Theological Seminary, Young Men's Christian Association, the Young Women's Christian Association, the Public Health Departments of the various states and from no less than four hundred welfare and religious organizations, as well as from clergymen, college professors, and doctors, and that the pamphlet was in use in the public schools at Bronxville, N.Y. The foregoing offers were rejected on the ground that the defendant's motive in distributing the pamphlet was irrelevant, and that the only issues were whether she caused the pamphlet to be mailed and whether it was obscene.

The pamphlet begins with a so-called "Introduction for Elders" which sets forth the general views of the writer and is as follows:

"In reading several dozen books on sex matters for the young with a view to selecting the best for my own children, I found none that I was willing to put into their hands, without first guarding them against what I considered very misleading and harmful impressions, which they would otherwise be sure to acquire in reading them. That is the excuse for this article.

"It is far more specific than most sex information written for young people. I believe we owe it to children to be specific if we talk about the subject at all.

"From a careful observation of youthful curiosity and a very vivid recollection of my own childhood, I have tried to explain frankly the points about which there is the greatest inquiry. These points are not frankly or clearly explained in most sex literature. They are avoided, partly from embarrassment, but more, apparently, because those who have undertaken to instruct the children are not really clear in their own minds as to the proper status of the sex relation.

"I found that from the physiological point of view, the question was handled with limitations and reservations. From the point of natural science it was often handled with sentimentality, the child being led from a semi-esthetic study of the reproduction of flowers and animals to the acceptance of a similar idea for human beings. From the moral point of view it was handled least satisfactorily of all, the child being given a jumble of conflicting ideas, with no means of correlating them—fear of venereal disease, one's duty to suppress 'animal passion,' the sacredness of marriage, and so forth. And from the emotional point of view, the subject was not handled at all.

"This one omission seems to me to be the key to the whole situation, and it is the basis of the radical departure I have made from the precedents in most sex literature for children.

"Concerning all four points of view just mentioned, there are certain departures from the traditional method that have seemed to me worth making.

"On the physiological side I have given, as far as possible, the proper terminology for the sex organs and functions. Children have had to read the expurgated literature which has been specially prepared for them in poetic or colloquial terms, and then are needlessly mystified when they hear things called by their real names.

"On the side of natural science, I have emphasized our unlikeness to the plants and animals rather than our likeness, for while the points we have in common with the lower orders make an interesting section in our general education, it is knowing about the vital points in which we differ that helps us to solve the sexual problems of maturity; and the child needs that knowledge precisely as he needs knowledge of everything which will fortify him for wise decisions when he is grown.

"On the moral side, I have tried to avoid confusion and dogmatism in the following ways: by eliminating fear of venereal disease as an appeal for strictly limited sex relations, stating candidly that venereal disease is becoming curable; by barring out all mention of 'brute' or 'animal' passion, terms frequently used in pleas for chastity and self control, as such talk is an aspersion on the brute and has done children much harm in giving them the impression that there is an essential baseness in the sex relation; by inviting the inference that marriage is 'sacred' by virtue of its being a reflection of human ideality rather than because it is a legalized institution.

"Unquestionably the stress which most writers have laid upon the beauty of nature's plans for perpetuating the plant and animal species, and the effort to have the child carry over into human life some sense of that beauty has come from a most commendable instinct to protect the child from the natural shock of the revelation of so much that is unesthetic and revolting in human sex life. The nearness of the sex organs to the excretory organs, the pain and messiness of childbirth are elements which certainly need some compensating antidote to prevent their making too disagreeable and disproportionate an impress on the child's mind.

"The results are doubtless good as far as they go, but they do not go nearly far enough. What else is there to call upon to help out? Why, the one thing which has been persistently neglected by practically all the sex writers,— the emotional side of sex experience. Parents and teachers have been afraid of it and distrustful of it. In not a single one of all the books for young people that I have thus far read has there been the frank unashamed declaration that the climax of sex emotion is an unsurpassed joy, something which rightly belongs to every normal human being, a joy to be proudly and serenely experienced. Instead there has been all too evident an inference that sex emotion is a thing to be ashamed of, that yielding to it is indulgence which must be curbed as much as possible, that all thought and understanding of it must be rigorously postponed, at any rate till after marriage.

"We give to young folks, in their general education, as much as they can grasp of science and ethics and art, and yet in their sex education, which rightly has to do with all of these, we have said, 'Give them only the bare physiological facts, lest they be prematurely stimulated.' Others of us, realizing that the bare physiological facts are shocking to many a sensitive child, and must somehow be softened with something pleasant, have said, 'Give them the facts, yes, but see to it that they are so related to the wonders of evolution and the beauties of the natural world that the shock is minimized.' But none of us has yet dared to say, 'Yes, give them the facts, give them the nature study, too, but also give them some conception of sex life as a vivifying joy, as a vital art, as a thing to be studied and developed with reverence for its big meaning, with understanding of its far-reaching reactions, psychologically and spiritually, with temperant restraint, good taste and the highest idealism.' We have contented ourselves by assuming that marriage makes sex relations respectable. We

have not yet said that it is only beautiful sex relations that can make marriage lovely.

"Young people are just as capable of being guided and inspired in their thought about sex emotion as in their taste and ideals in literature and ethics, and just as they imperatively need to have their general taste and ideals cultivated as a preparation for mature life, so do they need to have some understanding of the marvelous place which sex emotion has in life.

"Only such an understanding can be counted on to give them the self control that is born of knowledge, not fear, the reverence that will prevent premature or trivial connections, the good taste and finesse that will make their sex life when they reach maturity a vitalizing success."

After the foregoing introduction comes the part devoted to sex instruction entitled, "An Explanation for Young People." It proceeds to explain sex life in detail both physiologically and emotionally. It describes the sex organs and their operation and the way children are begotten and born. It negatives the idea that the sex impulse is in itself a base passion, and treats it as normal and its satisfaction as a great and justifiable joy when accompanied by love between two human beings. It warns against perversion, venereal disease, and prostitution, and argues for continence and healthy mindedness and against promiscuous sex relations.

The pamphlet in discussing the emotional side of the human sex relation, says:

"It means that a man and a woman feel that they *belong* to each other in a way that they belong to no one else; it makes them wonderfully happy to be together; they find they want to live together, work together, play together, and to have children together, that is, to marry each other; and their dream is to be happy together all their lives. * * * The idea of sex relations between people who do not love each other, who do not feel any sense of belonging to each other, will always be revolting to highly developed sensitive people."

"People's lives grow finer and their characters better, if they have sex relations only with those they love. And those who make the wretched mistake of yielding to the sex impulse alone when there is no love to go with it, usually live to despise themselves for their weakness and their bad taste. They are always ashamed of doing it, and they try to keep it secret from their families and those they respect. You can be sure that whatever people are ashamed to do is something that can never bring them real happiness. It is true that one's sex relations are the most personal and private matters in the world, and they belong just to us and to no one else, but while we may be shy and reserved about them, *we are not ashamed*.

"When two people really love each other, they don't care who knows it. They are proud of their happiness. But no man is ever proud of his connection with a prostitute and no prostitute is ever proud of her business.

"Sex relations belong to love, and love is never a *business*. Love is the nicest thing in the world, but it can't be bought. And the sex side of it is the biggest and most important side of it, so it is the one side of us that we must be absolutely sure to keep in good order and perfect health, if we are going to be happy ourselves or make any one else happy."

The government proved that the pamphlet was mailed to Mrs. C. A. Miles, Grottoes, Va.

Upon the foregoing record, of which we have given a summary, the trial judge charged the jury that the motive of the defendant in mailing the pamphlet was immaterial, that it was for them to determine whether it was obscene, lewd, or lascivious within the meaning of the statute, and that the test was "whether its language has a tendency to deprave and corrupt the morals of those whose minds are open to such things and into whose hands it may fall; arousing and implanting in such minds lewd and obscene thought or desires."

The court also charged that, "even if the matter sought to be shown in the pamphlet complained of were true, that fact would be immaterial, if the statements of such facts were calculated to deprave the morals of the readers by inciting sexual desires and libidinous thoughts."

The jury returned a verdict of guilty upon which the defendant was sentenced to pay a fine of $300, and from the judgment of conviction she has taken this appeal.

Greenbaum, Wolff & Ernst, of New York City (Morris L. Ernst, Newman Levy, and Alexander Lindey, all of New York City, of counsel), for appellant.

Howard W. Ameli, U.S. Atty., of Brooklyn, N.Y. (Herbert H. Kellogg, James E. Wilkinson, and Emanuel Bublick, Asst. U.S. Attys., all of Brooklyn, N.Y., of counsel), for the United States.

Before SWAN, AUGUSTUS N. HAND, and CHASE, Circuit Judges.

AUGUSTUS N. HAND, Circuit Judge (after stating the facts as above).

[1, 2] It is doubtless true that the personal motive of the defendant in distributing her pamphlet could have no bearing on the question whether she violated the law. Her own belief that a really obscene pamphlet would pay the price for its obscenity by means of intrinsic merits would leave her as much as ever under the ban of the statute. *Regina* v. *Hicklin*, L.R. 3 Q.B. 360; *United States* v. *Bennett*, Fed. Case No. 14,571; *Rosen* v. *United States*, 161 U.S. at page 41, 16 S. Ct. 434, 480, 40 L. Ed. 606.

[3] It was perhaps proper to exclude the evidence offered by the defendant as to the persons to whom the pamphlet was sold, for the reason that such evidence, if relevant at all, was part of the government's proof. In other words, a publication might be distributed among doctors or nurses or adults in cases where the distribution among small children could not be justified. The fact that the latter might obtain it accidently or surreptitiously, as they might see some medical books which would not be desirable for them to read, would hardly be sufficient to bar a publication otherwise proper. Here the pamphlet appears to have been mailed to a married woman. The tract may fairly be said to be calculated to aid parents in the instruction of their children in sex matters. As the record stands, it is a reasonable inference that the pamphlet was to be given to children at the discretion of adults and to be distributed through agencies that had the real welfare of the adolescent in view. There is no reason to suppose that it was to be broadcast among children who would have no capacity to understand its general significance. Even the court in *Regina* v. *Hicklin*, L.R. 3 Q.B. at p. 367, which laid down a more strict rule than the New York Court of Appeals was inclined to adopt in *People* v. *Eastman*, 188 N.Y. 478, 81 N.E. 459, 11 Ann. Cas. 302, said that "the circumstances

of the publication" may determine whether the statute has been violated.

[4] But the important consideration in this case is not the correctness of the rulings of the trial judge as to the admissibility of evidence, but the meaning and scope of those words of the statute which prohibit the mailing of an "*obscene, lewd or lascivious * * * pamphlet.*" It was for the trial court to determine whether the pamphlet could reasonably be thought to be of such a character before submitting any question of the violation of the statute to the jury. *Knowles* v. *United States* (C.C.A.) 170 F. 409; *Magon* v. *United States* (C.C.A.) 248 F. 201. And the test most frequently laid down seems to have been whether it would tend to deprave the morals of those into whose hands the publication might fall by suggesting lewd thoughts and exciting sensual desires. *Dunlop* v. *United States*, 165 U.S. at page 501, 17 S. Ct. 375, 41 L. Ed. 799; *Rosen* v. *United States*, 161 U.S. 29, 16 S. Ct. 434, 480, 40 L. Ed. 606.

It may be assumed that any article dealing with the sex side of life and explaining the functions of the sex organs is capable in some circumstances of arousing lust. The sex impulses are present in every one, and without doubt cause much of the weal and woe of human kind. But it can hardly be said that, because of the risk of arousing sex impulses, there should be no instruction of the young in sex matters, and that the risk of imparting instruction outweighs the disadvantages of leaving them to grope about in mystery and morbid curiosity and of requiring them to secure such information, as they may be able to obtain, from ill-informed and often foul-minded companions, rather than from intelligent and high-minded sources. It may be argued that suggestion plays a large part in such matters, and that on the whole the less sex questions are dwelt upon the better. But it by no means follows that such a desideratum is attained by leaving adolescents in a state of inevitable curiosity, satisfied only by the casual gossip of ignorant playmates.

The old theory that information about sex matters should be left to chance has greatly changed, and, while there is still a difference of opinion as to just the kind of instruction which ought to be given, it is commonly thought in these days that much was lacking in the old mystery and reticence. This is evident from the current literature on the subject, particularly such pamphlets as "Sex Education," issued by the Treasury Department United States Public Health Service in 1927.

[5, 6] The statute we have to construe was never thought to bar from the mails everything which *might* stimulate sex impulses. If so, much chaste poetry and fiction, as well as many useful medical works would be under the ban. Like everything else, this law must be construed reasonably with a view to the general objects aimed at. While there can be no doubt about its constitutionality, it must not be assumed to have been designed to interfere with serious instruction regarding sex matters unless the terms in which the information is conveyed are clearly indecent.

We have been referred to no decision where a truthful exposition of the sex side of life, evidently calculated for instruction and for the explanation of relevant facts, has been held to be obscene. In *Dysart* v. *United States*, 272 U.S. 655, 47 S. Ct. 234, 71 L. Ed. 461, it was decided that the advertisement of a lying-in retreat to enable unmarried women to conceal their missteps, even though written in a coarse and vulgar style, did not fall within prohibition of the statute, and was not "obscene" within the meaning of the law.

[7] The defendant's discussion of the phenomena of sex is written with sincerity of feeling and with an idealization of the marriage relation and sex emotions. We think it tends to rationalize and dignify such emotions rather than to arouse lust. While it may be thought by some that portions of the tract go into unnecessary details that would better have been omitted, it may be fairly answered that the curiosity of many adolescents would not be satisfied without full explanation, and that no more than that is really given. It also may reasonably be thought that accurate information, rather than mystery and curiosity, is better in the long run and is less likely to occasion lascivious thoughts than ignorance and anxiety. Perhaps

instruction other than that which the defendant suggests would be better. That is a matter as to which there is bound to be a wide difference of opinion, but, irrespective of this, *we hold that an accurate exposition of the relevant facts of the sex side of life in decent language and in manifestly serious and disinterested spirit cannot ordinarily be regarded as obscene.* [Italics ed.]. Any incidental tendency to arouse sex impulses which such a pamphlet may perhaps have is apart from and subordinate to its main effect. The tendency can only exist in so far as it is inherent in any sex instruction, and it would seem to be outweighed by the elimination of ignorance, curiosity, and morbid fear. The direct aim and the net result is to promote understanding and self-control.

No case was made for submission to the jury, and the judgment must therefore be reversed.

■ People
v.
Pesky.

Supreme Court, Appellate Division, First Department. June 23, 1930.

K. Henry Rosenberg, of New York City, for appellant.

Thomas C. T. Crain, Dist. Atty., of New York City (John C. McDermott, Deputy Asst. Dist. Atty., of New York City, of counsel), for respondent.

MARTIN, J.

The information herein charged that on October 7, 1929, the defendant, in the county of New York, unlawfully possessed a book called "Hands Around" with intent to sell and show the same, and which was a lewd, lascivious, indecent, obscene, and disgusting book.

The defendant pleaded not guilty to the crime charged, and thereafter on November 18, 1929, was arraigned for trial before the Court of Special Sessions. At the conclusion of the trial a motion was made to acquit and the court reserved decision. Subsequently and on December 9, 1929, the court decided that the book "Hands Around" was an indecent book and that its sale constituted a violation of section 1141 Penal Law, one judge dissenting.

On January 17, 1930, the appellant was arraigned for judgment and the court suspended sentence. For the purpose of appeal, the suspension of sentence is deemed to be a judgment. Section 517, Code Cr. Proc. As stated above, a motion was made at the close of the case to acquit and set aside the determination of the court convicting appellant, and an exception was taken to the denial of that motion. These exceptions raise the question of law presented herein.

On this appeal it is conceded that the facts in the case are uncontradicted. The defendant, Philip Pesky, testified that he was employed at Schulte's Book Store; that he did not know how this particular book came to be on sale in

the store, and he swore that he never read the book and did not know its contents.

The appellant contends that the book "Hands Around" is not an indecent or obscene book, hence its possession and sale did not violate the law. He further contends that the book was written by a well-known scholar; that it contains ten dialogues with life of to-day; that they are literary and psychological studies; that they are free from vulgar details, with no effort to "exploit prurient curiosity"; and that the book has no tendency "to excite lustful and lecherous desire." In effect, the appellant contends that there is no recital of any facts which come within the condemnation of the statute.

It is unnecessary to recite the details of each episode in the cycle set forth in this book. The first commences with a prostitute and the last ends with a prostitute. The first begins with the prostitute soliciting a soldier; the second deals with a soldier and a parlor maid; the third, with the parlor maid and a young man whose parents are absent in the country; the fourth, with this young man and a young wife; the fifth, with the young wife and her husband; the sixth, with the young husband and a sweet young miss; the seventh, with this young miss and a poet; the eighth, with the poet and an actress; the ninth, with the actress and a count; and, tenth, with the count back to the girl of the streets. The statements found in the book are sufficient to condemn it.

On the very first page we are told that this book is "*intended for private circulation only.*" Turning to the introduction, which is the strongest condemnation that this book could have, we find the following:

"Humanity seems gayest when dancing on the brink of a volcano. The culture of a period preceding a social cataclysm is marked by a spirit of light wit and sophisticated elegance which finds expression in a literature of a distinct type. * * * But the *exquisite handling of the licentious* was elaborated into a perfect technique in Eighteenth Century France. * * *

"During the closing years of the Nineteenth Century, *a similar spirit has hovered over Vienna,* when it was the last and staunchest stronghold of aristocracy in the modern world. *Its literature reflected the charm of a fastidious amatory etiquette * * * ."*

Speaking of this "amatory etiquette" it is stated that:

"'Reigen' (ring), here translated as 'Hands Around,' is a series of ten comedies—miniatures in dialogue between man and woman in various ages and walks of life. But, transgressing the merely literary, they are psychological studies of the interplay of sex and keen analysis of the sophisticated modern soul, done with freedom and finesse. There are no grim questions of right and wrong in these subtle revelations of the merely human. In fact, one might call them *studies in the etiquette of the liason and all its nuances."*

We are then told that this cycle which the book depicts would concededly have been a vicious cycle in the hands of any lesser artist than Schnitzler. We are not told why Schnitzler is able to surpass all other writers in the exquisite handling of the licentious. That gift, however, is claimed for him by the writer of the introduction.

The above statements taken from the book show that those connected with its publication clearly appreciated that there was nothing to it except a description of the licentious. There was no attempt to point to any lesson that might be of value to any one that would read it. It was just a clear attempt to portray filthy ideas, for the book is without a single redeeming feature. As usual it is prefaced by the remark that it will not be appreciated by the Puritan fanatic with his jaundiced inhibitions or the moral idealogist with his heart of leather. This is the usual cry of the libertine who is attempting to justify his own life or writings. Any one who differs with his method of living or writing is Puritanical. With such people clean thinking or clean living is Puritanical.

It is unnecessary to set forth the object of this book, except as it is set forth in the introduction. We believe nothing more is needed than the quotation from the introduction which admits that it is "fleshy," but so treated by Schnitzler as to avoid that condemnation: "A vicious cycle, some may say, and such it surely would have been in the hands of a lesser artist than Schnitzler, for he would only have made the book hideously fleshy, instead of a marvelous psychological study in the ecstacies and disillusions of love and the whole tragedy of human wishes, unsatisfied even in their apparent gratification. * * * All stratagems of sex are uncovered * * * through the finer eyes of a connoisseur of things human."

While we appreciate the fact that different people have different standards with reference to such writings and that these standards are often peculiar and difficult to understand, nevertheless people generally and the courts have arrived at what they consider a fair standard by which to judge such books and protect those who need protection.

In *United States* v. *Bennett*, 16 Blatchf. 338, 1 Fed. Cas. No. 14,571, Judges Blatchford, Benedict, and Choate laid down a test on obscenity as used in the statute there under consideration. The court said at page 362, of 16 Blatchf., Fed. Cas. No. 14,571: "It is, whether the ten-

dency of the matter is to deprave and corrupt the morals of those whose minds are open to such influences, and into whose hands a publication of this sort may fall."

The word "lewd" was there defined as "having a tendency to excite lustful thoughts," and it was said that passages in a book are "indecent within the meaning of this act, when they tend to obscenity—that is to say, matter having that form of indecency which is calculated to promote the general corruption of morals. * * * It is not a question whether it would corrupt the morals * * * of every person. * * * It is within the law if it would suggest impure and libidinous thoughts in the young and the inexperienced."

Judge Daniels, in *People* v. *Muller*, 32 Hun, 209, at page 212, affirmed 96 N.Y. 408, 48 Am. Rep. 635, said: "The question in all these cases must be, what is the impression produced upon the mind by perusing or observing the writing or picture referred to in the indictment, and one person is as competent to determine that as another."

In *Commonwealth* v. *Buckley*, 200 Mass. 346, the court said, at page 354, 86 N.E. 910, 911, 22 L.R.A. (N.S.) 225, 128 Am. St. Rep. 425: "Descriptions of seductive actions and of highly wrought sexual passion, even when sanctified by what the author has called 'love,' are very likely to be seen in another light tending towards the obscene and impure. And an author who has disclosed so much of the details of the way to the adulterous bed and who has kept the curtains raised in the way that the author of this book has kept them, can find no fault if the jury say that not the spiritual but the animal, not the pure but the impure, is what the general reader will find as the most conspicuous thought suggested to him as he reads."

These matters must be judged by normal people and not by the abnormal. Conditions would be deplorable if abnormal people were permitted to regulate such matters. [Italics ed.]. Of course, there are some people who seem to be unable to find anything obscene in anything written. *It is very clear that the author of the book now before us for consideration was not thinking of the spiritual, but devoted the whole book to the animal instincts of the human race. His efforts were not a lesson in morality, nor an attempt to uplift the mind of the reader, but an attempt to depict, in a manner that might possibly be called clever, adulterous relations, vulgar and disgusting in the extreme.* [Italics ed.].

While some people may think this quite smart, a book of this kind, which has nothing to recommend it, and dealing wholly with such details, is properly held to be disgusting, indecent, and obscene.

It is admitted that this book deals with a distinct type of literature, a type evidently intended for certain private consumption. One sentence is sufficient to illustrate this fact: "Poet: Then it's your leading man—Benno—. Actress: Nonsense. He doesn't care for women at all—didn't you know that? He carries on with the * * *" This last quotation stamps the author as a man whose thoughts thus expressed cannot escape being characterized as indecent.

There does not appear to be any claim that it is of any value as a literary production or as an intellectual treat. No better appraisal of its value is needed than that given by the introduction. The facts show that the whole book deals with the sensual. It has no other object or purpose.

The judgment of conviction should be affirmed.

MERRELL and O'MALLEY, JJ., concur; McAvoY and SHERMAN, JJ., dissent.

McAvoY, J. (dissenting).

The information charged that on October 7, 1929, in the county of New York, the defendant unlawfully possessed a book called "Hands Around" with intent to sell and show the same, and which was a lewd, lascivious, indecent, obscene, and disgusting book.

Section 1141 of the Penal Law reads, in part, as follows: "A person who sells * * * any obscene, lewd, lascivious, filthy, indecent or disgusting book * * * is guilty of a misdemeanor. * * *"

The facts in the case are uncontradicted.

The book of the play condemned at Special Sessions by a divided court is called in its original version in German "Reigen," and we may take judicial notice that it had an almost world-wide acceptance among litterateurs as of literary merit. The episodes related by the characters less deftly touched would be of a vulgar tone because of the subject and could be, if written in bawdy phrases, classed as too realistic for common reading. But nowhere is there any word in the translation which has a lewd or lascivious connotation. The appeal to passion or lechery is wholly lacking. While the trial court is the judge of the facts, it may not hold as obscene that which in common speech is not within that category.

The proof shows, too, that this publication has been on sale in the book departments of department stores, bookshops, and other merchandising stores in which part of the retail business is the sale of books. It has also been advertised in the daily prints in the city. As a play in German, the work has been produced in many large European continental cities, and has been extant for at least ten years there.

We reversed a conviction for the publication of a book known as "Madeleine," which was the autobiography of a prostitute, and seems in its content more nearly approaching lewd and lascivious descriptions than anything found here. *People* v. *Brainard*, 192 App. Div. 816, 183 N.Y.S. 452.

A receiver was directed by a former justice of this court to sell Fielding's novel, "Tom Jones," the "Works of Rabelais," and Ovid's "Art of Love," and other works of an amatory nature, whose terms and descriptions are much more likely to stimulate sexual impulses than anything in the book now here. In re Worthington Co., 62 N.Y. St. Rep. 116, 30 N.Y.S. 361, 24 L.R.A. 110.

Recently in the federal court, in *United States* v. *Dennett* (C.C.A.) 39 F. (2d) 564, 569, it was pointed out that a similar statute enacted by the Congress, designed to bar from the mails obscene publications, was never thought to bar everything which *might* stimulate sex impulses. It was said that much chaste poetry and fiction, as well as many useful medical works, would be under the ban if such were the rule. Such a statute must be construed reasonably, with a view to attaining the general objects at which the public policy of the state is aimed, to wit, a prohibition of that which is obscene, lascivious, or lewd.

We think it is no part of the duty of courts to exercise a censorship over literary productions.

We conclude that the judgment of conviction should be reversed, and the information dismissed.

SHERMAN, J., concurs.

■ **United States**
v.
One Obscene Book Entitled "Married Love."
Claim of G. P. Putnam's Sons.

District Court, S. D. New York. April 6, 1931.

George Z. Medalie, U.S. Atty., of New York City (Morton Baum, Asst. U.S. Atty., of New York City, of counsel), for the United States.

Greenbaum, Wolff & Ernst, of New York City (Morris L. Ernst and Alexander Lindey, both of New York City, of counsel), for claimant.

WOOLSEY, District Judge.
I dismiss the libel in this case.

[1] I. The first point with which I shall deal is as to the contention that the section of the Tariff Act under which this libel was brought, title 19 U.S.C., § 1305 (19 USCA § 1305), is unconstitutional as impinging on the right of the freedom of the press. I think there is nothing in this contention. The section does not involve the suppression of a book before it is published, but the exclusion of an already published book which is sought to be brought into the United States.

After a book is published, its lot in the world is like that of anything else. It must conform to the law and, if it does not, must be subject to the penalties involved in its failure to do so. Laws which are thus disciplinary of publications, whether involving exclusion from the mails or from this country, do not interfere with freedom of the press. [Italics ed.].

[2] II. Passing to the second point, I think that the matter here involved is res adjudicata by reason of the decision hereinafter mentioned.

This is a proceeding in rem against a book entitled "Married Love," written by Dr. Marie C. Stopes and sent from England by the London branch of G. P. Putnam's Sons to their New York office.

The libel was filed under the provisions of Title 19, U.S.C., § 1305 (19 USCA § 1305), which provides, so far as is here relevant, as follows:

"§ 1305. *Immoral Articles—Importation Prohibited.* (a) *Prohibition of importation.* All persons are prohibited from importing into the United States from any foreign country * * * any obscene book, pamphlet, paper, writing, advertisement, circular, print, pictures, drawing, or other representation, figure, or image on or of paper or other material, or any cast, instrument, or other article which is obscene or immoral, or any drug or medicine or any article whatever for the prevention of conception or for causing unlawful abortion. * * * No such articles, whether imported separately or contained in packages with other goods entitled to entry, shall be admitted to entry; and all such articles * * * shall be subject to seizure and forfeiture as hereinafter provided: * * * *Provided further*, that the Secretary of the Treasury may, in his discretion, admit the so-called classics or books of recognized and established literary or scientific merit, but may, in his discretion, admit such classics or books only when imported for noncommercial purposes."

Then it goes on:

"Upon the appearance of any such book or matter at any customs office, the same shall be seized and held by the collector to await the judgment of the district court as hereinafter provided. * * * Upon the seizure of such book or matter the collector shall transmit information thereof to the district attorney of the district in which is situated the office at which such seizure has taken place, who shall institute proceedings in the district court for the forfeiture, confiscation, and destruction of the book or matter seized. Upon the adjudication that such book or matter thus seized is of the character the entry of which is by this section prohibited, it shall be ordered destroyed and shall be destroyed. Upon adjudication that such book or matter thus seized is not of the character the entry of which is by this section prohibited, it shall not be excluded from entry under the provisions of this section.

"In any such proceeding any party in interest may upon demand have the facts at issue determined by a jury and any party may have an appeal or the right of review as in the case of ordinary actions or suits."

The book before me now has had stricken from it all matters dealing with contraceptive instruction and, hence, does not come now within the prohibition of the statute against imports for such purposes, even if a book dealing with such matters falls within the provisions of this section—which I think it probably does not—and the case falls to be dealt with entirely on the question of whether the book is obscene or immoral.

Another copy of this same book, without the excision of the passages dealing with contraceptive matters, was before Judge Kirkpatrick, United States District Judge for the Eastern District of Pennsylvania, on a forfeiture libel under the Tariff Act of 1922, and he ruled that the book was not obscene or immoral, and directed a verdict for the claimant.[1]

---

[1] No opinion was filed.

Although the government took an exception to this ruling at the time of the trial, it did not mature this exception by an appeal, and the case therefore stands as a final decision of a coordinate court in a proceeding in rem involving the same book that we have here. The answer in this case is amended and pleads res adjudicata on the ground of the proceedings had before Judge Kirkpatrick which involved exactly the same question as that now before me.

The only difference between the Philadelphia case and this case is that another copy of the same book has been here seized and libeled.

[3] I think that the proper view of the meaning of the word "book" in title 19, U.S.C., § 1305 (19 USCA § 1305), is not merely a few sheets of paper bound together in cloth or otherwise, but that a book means an assembly or concourse of ideas expressed in words, the subject-matter which is embodied in the book, which is sought to be excluded, and not merely the physical object called a book which can be held in one's hands.

Assuming it is proper so to view the meaning of the word "book" in the statute under consideration, Judge Kirkpatrick's decision at Philadelphia in a proceeding in rem against this book is a bar to another similar proceeding such as this in this district.

I hold that Judge Kirkpatrick's decision established the book "Married Love" as having an admissible status at any point around the customs' barriers of the United States. In this connection, see *Gelston* v. *Hoyt*, 3 Wheat. 246, 312 to page 316, 4 L. Ed. 381; Waples on Proceedings in Rem, §§ 87, 110, 111, 112, and cases therein cited.

It is perfectly obvious, I think, that, if a vessel had been libeled on a certain count for forfeiture at Philadelphia, and there acquitted of liability to forfeiture, on her coming around to New York she could not properly be libeled again on the same count. That is the real situation in the present case. Cf. *United States* v. *2180 Cases of Champagne*, 9 F. (2d) 710, 712, 713 (C.C.A. 2).

[4, 5] III. However, in case the Circuit Court of Appeals, to which I presume this case will eventually be taken, should disagree with my construction of the word "book," and should consider that it was a copy of the book that was subject to exclusion, and not merely the book regarded as an embodiment of ideas, or should disagree with my application of the admiralty law to a situation of this kind, I will now deal with the case on the merits.

In Murray's Oxford English Dictionary the word "obscene" is defined as follows:

"Obscene—1. Offensive to the senses, or to taste or refinement; disgusting, repulsive, filthy, foul, abominable, loathsome. Now somewhat arch.

"2. Offensive to modesty or decency; expressing or suggesting unchaste or lustful ideas; impure, indecent, lewd."

In the same Dictionary the word "immoral" is defined as follows:

"Immoral—The opposite of moral; not moral.

"1. Not consistent with, or not conforming to, moral law or requirement; opposed to or violating morality; morally evil or impure; unprincipled, vicious, dissolute. (Of persons, things, actions, etc.)

"2. Not having a moral nature or character; non-moral."

The book "Married Love" does not, in my opinion, fall

within these definitions of the words "obscene" or "immoral" in any respect.

Dr. Stopes treats quite as decently and with as much restraint of the sex relations as did Mrs. Mary Ware Dennett in "The Sex Side of Life, An Explanation for Young People," which was held not to be obscene by the Circuit Court of Appeals for this circuit in *United States v. Dennett*, 39 F.(2d) 564.

The present book may fairly be said to do for adults what Mrs. Dennett's book does for adolescents.

The Dennett Case, as I read it, teaches that this court must determine, as a matter of law in the first instance, whether the book alleged to be obscene falls in any sense within the definition of that word. If it does, liability to forfeiture becomes a question for the jury under proper instructions. If it does not, the question is one entirely for the court.

"Married Love" is a considered attempt to explain to married people how their mutual sex life may be made happier.

To one who had read Havelock Ellis, as I have, the subject-matter of Dr. Stope's book is not wholly new, but it emphasizes the woman's side of sex questions. It makes also some apparently justified criticisms of the inopportune exercise by the man in the marriage relation of what are often referred to as his conjugal or marital rights, and it

pleads with seriousness, and not without some eloquence, for a better understanding by husbands of the physical and emotional side of the sex life of their wives.

I do not find anything exceptionable anywhere in the book, and I cannot imagine a normal mind to which this book would seem to be obscene or immoral within the proper definition of these words or whose sex impulses would be stirred by reading it.

Whether or not the book is scientific in some of its theses is unimportant. It is informative and instructive, and I think that any married folk who read it cannot fail to be benefited by its counsels of perfection and its frank discussion of the frequent difficulties which necessarily arise in the more intimate aspects of married life, for as Professor William G. Sumner used aptly to say in his lectures on the Science of Society at Yale, marriage, in its essence, is a status of antagonistic co-operation.

In such a status, necessarily, centripetal and centrifugal forces are continuously at work, and the measure of its success obviously depends on the extent to which the centripetal forces are predominant.

The book before me here has as its whole thesis the strengthening of the centripetal forces in marriage, and instead of being inhospitably received, it should, I think, be welcomed within our borders.

■ United States
v.
One Book, Entitled "Contraception," by Marie C. Stopes.

District Court, S. D. New York. July 16, 1931.

George Z. Medalie, U.S. Atty., of New York City (Morton Baum, of New York City, of counsel; and Walter R. Eaton, of New York City, solicitor to the Collector of the Port of New York, as amicus curiæ), in support of the motion for a decree of forfeiture.

Greenbaum, Wolff & Ernst, of New York City (Alexander Lindey, of New York City, of counsel), in support of motion for a decree dismissing the libel.

WOOLSEY, District Judge.

The motion to dismiss the libel herein is granted.

The motion for a decree of forfeiture is, consequently, denied.

I. This is a libel in rem brought under title 19, U.S.C., § 1305 (19 USCA § 1305), for the forfeiture of the book "Contraception," written by Dr. Marie C. Stopes, on the ground that it falls within the exclusion of that statute.

II. At the time of the argument the counsel for the respective parties submitted to me a stipulation providing that the book "Contraception" should be deemed annexed as an exhibit to the libel, that the words "by United States mails" should be stricken from article 2 of the libel, that

trial by jury, provided for in title 19, U.S.C., § 1305, on forfeiture proceedings thereunder be waived, and that the issues involved herein should be raised and presented before me on a motion by the claimant to dismiss the libel, and by the libelant for a decree of forfeiture thereon.

The provisions of the statute involved, title 19, U.S.C., § 1305, in so far as they are here relevant, are as follows:

"§ 1305. *Immoral Articles—Importation Prohibited.* (a) *Prohibition of importation.* All persons are prohibited from importing into the United States from any foreign country * * * any obscene book, pamphlet, paper, writing, advertisement, circular, print, picture, drawing, or other representation, figure, or image on or of paper or other material, or any cast, instrument, or other article which is obscene or immoral, or any drug or medicine or any article whatever for the prevention of conception or for causing unlawful abortion. * * * No such articles, whether imported separately or contained in packages with other goods entitled to entry, shall be admitted to entry; and all such articles * * * shall be subject to seizure and forfeiture as hereinafter provided: * * * Provided further, that the Secretary of the Treasury may, in his discretion, admit the so-called classics or books of recognized and established literary or scientific merit, but may, in his discretion, admit such classics or books only when imported for non-commercial purposes."

The act further provides for forfeiture proceedings as follows:

"Upon the appearance of any such book or matter at any customs office, the same shall be seized and held by the collector to await the judgment of the district court as hereinafter provided. * * * Upon the seizure of such book or matter the collector shall transmit information thereof to the district attorney of the district in which is situated the office at which such seizure has taken place, who shall institute proceedings in the district court for the forfeiture, confiscation, and destruction of the book or matter seized. Upon the adjudication that such book or matter thus seized is of the character the entry of which is by this section prohibited, it shall be ordered destroyed and shall be destroyed. Upon adjudication that such book or matter thus seized is not of the character the entry of which is by this section prohibited, it shall not be excluded from entry under the provisions of this section.

"In any such proceeding any party in interest may upon demand have the facts at issue determined by a jury and any party may have an appeal or the right of review as in the case of ordinary actions or suits."

[1] III. The contention here made by the claimant that the act just quoted is unconstitutional on the ground that it interferes with the freedom of the press is sufficiently answered by my opinion in the case of *United States* v. *One Obscene Book*, entitled "Married Love," 48 F.(2d) 821, 822.

[2] IV. There is not involved here, however, as the claimant urges, and as there was in the case of the book "Married Love," any possible question of res adjudicata, for the book "Contraception," so far as I am aware, is now for the first time libeled in a federal court to test the question of its admissibility under the section of the statutes above quoted. * * *

I have read "Contraception," and I find that it does not fall, in any respect, within these definitions of the words "obscene" or "immoral."

"Contraception" is written primarily for the medical profession. It is stated, in an introduction written by an eminent English doctor, to be the first book dealing fully with its subject-matter—the theory, history, and practice of birth control. It is a scientific book written with obvious seriousness and with great decency, and it gives information to the medical profession regarding the operation of birth control clinics and the instruction necessary to be given at such clinics to women who resort thereto. It tells of the devices used, now and in the past, to prevent conception, and expresses opinions as to those which are preferable from the point of view of efficiency and of the health of the user.

Such a book, although it may run counter to the views of many persons who disagree entirely with the theory underlying birth control, certainly does not fall within the test of obscenity or immorality laid down by me in the case of United States v. One Obscene Book, Entitled "Married Love," 48 F.(2d) 821, *at page 824, for the reading of it would not stir the sex impulses of any person with a normal mind.* [Italics ed.].

Actually the emotions aroused by the book are merely feelings of sympathy and pity, evoked by the many cases instanced in it of the sufferings of married women due to ignorance of its teachings. This, I believe, will be the inevitable effect of reading it on all persons of sensibility unless by their prejudices the information it contains is tabooed.

VI. It follows that as "Contraception" is not an obscene or immoral book, and, obviously, is not a drug, medicine, or an article for the prevention of conception within the meaning of title 19, U.S.C., § 1305, it may be imported into the United States and the libel brought in this case to test that question must be dismissed.

Settle decree on two days' notice.

■ People
v.
Wendling *et al.*

■ Same
v.
Ellmore *et al.*

Court of Appeals of New York. March 3, 1932.

Harry H. Oshrin, of New York City, for appellants.
Charles P. Sullivan, Acting Dist. Atty., of Long Island City (Mordecai Konowitz, of New York City, of counsel), for the People.

POUND, J.

The prosecution herein arises out of the dramatization of the ancient folk song "Frankie and Johnnie," which told the tale of the adventures of Johnnie, a country boy, in a St. Louis resort for drinking, gambling and prostitution in the middle of the last century.[1]

[1, 2] *The language of the play is coarse, vulgar and profane; the plot cheap and tawdry. As a dramatic composition it serves to degrade the stage where vice is thought by some to lose* "*half its evil by losing all its grossness.*" "*That it is 'indecent' from every consideration of propriety is entirely clear*" (People v. Eastman, 188 N.Y. 478, 480, 81 N.E. 459, 460, 11 Ann. Cas. 302), *but the court is not a censor of plays and does not attempt to regulate manners.* [Italics ed.]. One may call a spade a spade without offending decency, although modesty may be shocked thereby. *People* v. *Muller,* 96 N.Y. 408, 411, 48 Am. Rep. 635. The question is not whether the scene is laid in a low dive where refined people are not found or whether the language is that of the barroom rather than the parlor. The question is whether the tendency of the play is to excite lustful and lecherous desire. *People* v. *Eastman,* supra; *People* v. *Muller,* supra.

Prostitutes are not so rarely represented on the stage as to arouse the sexual propensities of the spectators whenever they appear. G. B. Shaw's play, "Mrs. Warren's Profession," deals, in the language of the polite dramatist, with what has been styled "the oldest profession in the world." The heroine of "Rain" was a seductive harlot. Scenes of "The Shanghai Gesture" are laid in a house of bad character. "Lysistrata" is frank in the discussion of sex relations, but does not excite desire as might the lascivious display of female charms. The Bible talks bluntly of harlots and whores, but it does not incite to immorality. (Rev. 17, 18.)

[3] The play is said to "tend to corrupt the morals of youth." Here again the question is not whether it would tend to coarsen or vulgarize the youth who might witness it, but whether it would tend to lower their standards of right and wrong, specifically as to the sexual relation. *Unless the mere representation on the stage of prostitutes and their patrons would tend to have the effect of stimulating sexual impulses, the performance should not be barred.* [Italics ed.]. *United States* v. *Dennett* (C.C.A.) 39 F.(2d) 564, 76 A.L.R. 1092; *United States* v. *One Obscene Book* Entitled "Married Love" (D.C.) 48 F.(2d) 821; *United States* v. *One Book,* Entitled "Contraception" by Marie C. Stopes (D.C.) 51 F.(2d) 525.

Compare the seductive "studies in the etiquette of the liaison and all its nuances" with their accompanying appeal to sexual passion contained in Schnitzler's "Reigen,"

where it was held by a divided court that the finders of fact might pronounce the book obscene by applying local standards of propriety thereto (*People* v. *Pesky,* 230 App. Div. 200, 202, 243 N.Y.S. 193, affirmed 254 N.Y. 373, 173 N.E. 227), with this uncultured depiction of a phase in the frontier life of the middle west. A coarse realism is its dramatic offense. Perhaps in an age of innocence the facts of life should be withheld from the young, but a theater goer could not give his approval to the modern stage as "spokesman of the thought and sentiment" of Broadway (*Halsey* v. *New York Society for Suppression of Vice,* 234 N.Y. 1, 136 N.E. 219) and at the same time silence this rough hewn and profane representation of scenes which repel rather than seduce.

[4] The production of such a play may be repulsive to puritanical ideas of propriety, as would "Camille," and may be offensive to the more liberal minded as lacking in taste and refinement, as would the morally unobjectionable "Abie's Irish Rose." The play may be gross and its characters wanting in moral sense. It may depict women who carry on a vicious trade and their male associates. It cannot be said to suggest, except "to a prurient imagination," unchaste or lustful ideas. It does not counsel or invite to vice or voluptuousness. It does not deride virtue. Unless we say that it is obscene to use the language of the street rather than that of the scholar, the play is not obscene under the Penal Law (section 1140-a [Consòl. Laws, c. 40]), although it might be so styled by the censorious.

We have repeatedly said that fine language does not excuse the expression of filthy thoughts. *Halsey* v. *New York Society for Suppression of Vice,* supra. Neither do coarse scenes and vulgar language in themselves create such thoughts. *Dysart* v. *United States,* 272 U.S. 655, 47 S. Ct. 234, 71 L. Ed. 461.

[5] We do not purpose to sanction indecency on the stage by this decision or to let down the bars against immoral shows or to hold that the depiction of scenes of bawdry on the stage is to be tolerated. We hold merely that the fact that Frankie and Johnnie and their companions were not nice people does not in itself make the play obscene. A history of prostitution or of sexual life is not per se indecent, although such a book might easily be so written as to offend decency.

The judgment in each action should be reversed, and the informations dismissed.

CARDOZO, C.J., and LEHMAN and KELLOGG, JJ., concur.

CRANE, O'BRIEN, and HUBBS, JJ., dissent.

Judgments reversed, etc.

---

[1] Dr. Sigmund Spaeth, "Read 'em and Weep—The Songs you Forgot to Remember," 34.

People

v.

Viking Press, Inc., *et al.*

City Magistrate's Court of New York City, Fourth District, Borough of Manhattan.

May 23, 1933.

Harold Frankel, Deputy Asst. Dist. Atty., of New York City, for plaintiff.

Hays, Hershfield, Kaufman & Schwabacher, of New York City (Wolfgang S. Schwabacher and James M. Grossman, both of New York City, of counsel), for defendants.

GREENSPAN, City Magistrate.

This prosecution is instituted by the New York Society for the suppression of vice, through Mr. John S. Sumner, its secretary and attorney, against the Viking Press, Inc., the publishers of a certain book by one Erskine Caldwell entitled God's Little Acre, and against Helen Schiller, a clerk in the employ of the publishers, who sold the book to an agent of the society.

[1, 2] It is claimed that the sale of the book is a violation of section 1141 of the Penal Law and that the book is, within the meaning of that statute, "obscene, lewd, lascivious, filthy, indecent or disgusting." In order to sustain the prosecution, the court must find that the tendency of the book as a whole, and indeed its main purpose, is to excite lustful desire and what has been rather fancifully called "impure imaginations." *People* v. *Muller*, 96 N.Y. 408, 48 Am. Rep. 635. The statute is aimed at pornography, and a pornographic book must be taken to be one where all other incidents and qualities are mere accessories to the primary purpose of stimulating immoral thoughts.

The courts have strictly limited the applicability of the statute to works of pornography and they have consistently declined to apply it to books of genuine literary value. If the statute were construed more broadly than in the manner just indicated, its effect would be to prevent altogether the realistic portrayal in literature of a large and important field of life. The Court of Appeals has consistently frowned upon such an interpretation of the statute. *People* v. *Wendling*, 258 N.Y. 451, 180 N.E. 169, 81 A.L.R. 799; *Halsey* v. *New York Society for Suppression of Vice*, 234 N.Y. 1, 136 N.E. 219. See, also, the opinion of the Appellate Division, First Department, in *People* v. *Brainard*, 192 App. Div. 816, 183 N.Y.S. 452, regarding the book called Madeleine, an anonymous autobiography of a prostitute.

It is claimed, on behalf of the defendants, that the book in the instant case, Caldwell's God's Little Acre, has high literary merit. In support of this claim, counsel for the defendants have collected and presented to this court a large number of testimonials from people eminent in the literary life of this city and country, as well as from others distinguished in social work, education, and other fields. Some of these testimonials were written especially for presentation to this court. Others are culled from literary reviews and newspapers. Among the latter, which are necessarily to be given more weight than those written especially for the purpose of defeating this prosecution, the court finds praise of the merits of the book by the following: Franklin P. Adams in the New York Herald Tribune of January 28, 1933; William Soskin in the New York Evening Post of April 29, 1933; Horace Gregory in the New York Herald Tribune Book Review of February 5, 1933; an unnamed reviewer in the London Times Literary Supplement of March 23, 1933; James T. Farrell in the New York Sun of February 7, 1933; Louis Kronenberger in the New York Times of February 5, 1933; a reviewer in the New York Evening Post of February 7, 1933, who refers to the book as "a passionately honest book"; Gilbert Seldes in the New York Journal of February 11, 1933, who describes the book as "engaging and impressive at once"; Jonathan Daniels in the Saturday Review of Literature, as quoted in the Raleigh, N.C., News Observer of March 5, 1933; and Joseph Henry Jackson in the San Francisco Chronicle of February 17, 1933. The court regards this as a fair cross-section of American literary opinion, by a group of men competent to judge with reasonable accuracy the value of contemporary American books.

The brief presented to this court by Mr. Sumner makes the following references to these reviews: "We have seen this attempted before and the question arises as to whether a criminal prosecution is to be determined by interested parties having access to the newspapers and no interest in public welfare or by the Courts existing for that purpose and representing the whole people and not only the literati." Mr. Sumner also refers to the following quotation from *People* v. *Pesky*, 230 App. Div. 200, 203, 243 N.Y.S. 193, 197: *"These matters must be judged by normal people and not by the abnormal. Conditions would be deplorable if abnormal people were permitted to regulate such matters."* Mr. Sumner then says: *"Substitute the word 'literati' for 'abnormal people' and we have an exact explanation of the letters, reviews, and other favorable comments presented in behalf of this book and its author."* [Italics ed.].

Letters have been presented to this court praising the value of the book in question, from Mark Eisner, president of the board of higher education of the city of New York; Lewis Gannett of the New York Herald Tribune; John Mason Brown, dramatic critic of the New York Evening Post; Sidonie M. Gruenberg of the Child Study Association of America; Solomon Lowenstein, executive and director of the Federation for the Support of Jewish Philanthropic Societies; Marc Connelly; Horace M. Kallen, honorary vice president of the American Jewish Congress; Carl Van Doren, a distinguished literary critic; Herbert Bayard Swope, former editor of the New York World; J. Donald Adams, editor of the New York Times Book Review; Prof. Raymond Weaver, of the English Department of Columbia University; Malcolm Cowley, one of the editors of the New Republic; Henry S. Canby, the veteran editor of the Saturday Review of Literature; Nathan Ottinger; Elmer Rice, playwright; John Cowper Powys; and finally Sinclair Lewis.

This court cannot subscribe to Mr. Sumner's opinion of the capacity for fair judgment of these leaders of American literary and educational thought. The court declines to believe that so large and representative a group of people would rally to the support of a book which they did not genuinely believe to be of importance and literary merit. The court is of the opinion, moreover, that this group of people, collectively, has a better capacity to judge of the value of a literary production than one who is more apt to search for obscene passages in a book than to regard the book as a whole.

This court has carefully read the book in question. It is an attempt at the portrayal, in a realistic fashion, of life as lived by an illiterate Southern white farm family. A daughter of this family is married to a worker in a Southern mill town. There is interaction between the run-down farm life and the mill town life. Both on the farm and in the mill town the people are primitive and impoverished. They are deprived of the opportunity for development, and their activities are largely sexual. They are of a simple nature, and savage passion is found close to the surface.

[3] This court is not sufficiently familiar with conditions in the portion of the county described to say, at first hand, that the description is accurate. Nothing in this opinion is to be construed as an expression by the court as to whether or not the book is an accurate piece of reporting. As fiction, however, it contains internal evidence that it was written with a sincere attempt to present with truth and honesty a segment of life in the Southern United States. The author has set out to paint a realistic picture. Such pictures necessarily contain certain details. Because these details relate to what is popularly called the sex side of life, portrayed with brutal frankness, the court may not

say that the picture should not have been created at all. The language, too, is undoubtedly coarse and vulgar. The court may not require the author to put refined language into the mouths of primitive people.

[4, 5] The book as a whole is very clearly not a work of pornography. It is not necessary for the court to decide whether it is an important work of literature. Its subject-matter constitutes a legitimate field for literary effort and the treatment is also legitimate. The court must consider the book as a whole even though some paragraphs standing by themselves might be objectionable. "No work may be judged from a selection of such paragraphs alone. Printed by themselves they might, as a matter of law, come within the prohibition of the statute. So might a similar selection from Aristophanes or Chaucer or Boccaccio or even from the Bible. The book, however, must be considered broadly as a whole." *Halsey* v. *New York Society for Suppression of Vice*, 234 N.Y. 1, at page 4, 136 N.E. 219, 220. The test is whether "not in certain passages, but in its main purpose and construction" (*Halsey* v. *New York Society for Suppression of Vice*, 234 N.Y. 1, at page 10, 136 N.E. 219, 222), the book is obscene and lewd, and, therefore, violative of the statute.

[6, 7] The court holds that it is not. This is not a book where vice and lewdness are treated as virtues or which would tend to incite lustful desires in the normal mind. There is no way of anticipating its effect upon a disordered or diseased mind, and if the courts were to exclude books from sale merely because they might incite lust in disordered minds, our entire literature would very likely be reduced to a relatively small number of uninteresting and barren books. The greater part of the classics would certainly be excluded. In conclusion, God's Little Acre has no tendency to inspire its readers to behave like its characters, therefore, it has no tendency to excite "lustful desire." Those who see the ugliness and not the beauty in a piece of work are unable to see the forest for the trees. I personally feel that the very suppression of books arouses curiosity and leads readers to endeavor to find licentiousness where none was intended. In this book, I believe the author has chosen to write what he believes to be the truth about a certain group in American life. To my way of thinking, truth should always be accepted as a justification for literature.

No complaint will be entertained against the defendants and the summons herein will be dismissed.

United States
v.
One Book Called "Ulysses."

District Court, S.D. New York. Dec. 6, 1933.

The United States Attorney (Samuel C. Coleman and Nicholas Atlas, both of New York City, of counsel), for the United States.
Greenbaum, Wolff & Ernst, of New York City (Morris

L. Ernst and Alexander Lindey, both of New York City, of counsel), for Random House, Inc.

Woolsey, District Judge.

The motion for a decree dismissing the libel herein is granted, and, consequently, of course, the government's motion for a decree of forfeiture and destruction is denied.

Accordingly a decree dismissing the libel without costs may be entered herein.

I. The practice followed in this case is in accordance with the suggestion made by me in the case of *United States v. One Book*, Entitled "Contraception" (D.C.) 51 F.(2d) 525, and is as follows:

After issue was joined by the filing of the claimant's answer to the libel for forfeiture against "Ulysses," a stipulation was made between the United States Attorney's office and the attorneys for the claimant providing:

1. That the book "Ulysses" should be deemed to have been annexed to and to have become part of the libel just as if it had been incorporated in its entirety therein.

2. That the parties waived their right to a trial by jury.

3. That each party agreed to move for decree in its favor.

4. That on such cross-motions the court might decide all the questions of law and fact involved and render a general finding thereon.

5. That on the decision of such motions the decree of the court might be entered as if it were a decree after trial.

It seems to me that a procedure of this kind is highly appropriate in libels such as this for the confiscation of books. It is an especially advantageous procedure in the instant case because, on account of the length of "Ulysses" and the difficulty of reading it, a jury trial would have been an extremely unsatisfactory, if not an almost impossible method of dealing with it.

II. I have read "Ulysses" once in its entirety and I have read those passages of which the government particularly complains several times. In fact, for many weeks, my spare time has been devoted to the consideration of the decision which my duty would require me to make in this matter.

"Ulysses" is not an easy book to read or to understand. But there has been much written about it, and in order properly to approach the consideration of it it is advisable to read a number of other books which have now become its satellites. The study of "Ulysses" is, therefore, a heavy task.

[1] III. The reputation of "Ulysses" in the literary world, however, warranted my taking such time as was necessary to enable me to satisfy myself as to the intent with which the book was written, for, of course, in any case where a book is claimed to be obscene it must first be determined, whether the intent with which it was written was what is called, according to the usual phrase, pornographic, that is, written for the purpose of exploiting obscenity.

If the conclusion is that the book is pornographic, that is the end of the inquiry and forfeiture must follow.

But in "Ulysses," in spite of its unusual frankness, I do not detect anywhere the leer of the sensualist. I hold, therefore, that it is not pornographic.

IV. In writing "Ulysses," Joyce sought to make a serious experiment in a new, if not wholly novel, literary genre. He takes persons of the lower middle class living in Dublin in 1904 and seeks, not only to describe what they did on a certain day early in June of that year as they went about the city bent on their usual occupations, but also to tell what many of them thought about the while.

Joyce had attempted—it seems to me, with astonishing success—to show how the screen of consciousness with its ever-shifting kaleidoscopic impressions carries, as it were on a plastic palimpsest, not only what is in the focus of each man's observation of the actual things about him, but also in a penumbral zone residua of past impressions, some recent and some drawn up by association from the domain of the subconscious. He shows how each of these impressions affects the life and behavior of the character which he is describing.

What he seeks to get is not unlike the result of a double or, if that is possible, a multiple exposure on a cinema film, which would give a clear foreground with a background visible but somewhat blurred and out of focus in varying degrees.

To convey by words an effect which obviously lends itself more appropriately to a graphic technique, accounts, it seems to me, for much of the obscurity which meets a reader of "Ulysses." And it also explains another aspect of the book, which I have further to consider, namely, Joyce's sincerity and his honest effort to show exactly how the minds of his characters operate.

If Joyce did not attempt to be honest in developing the technique which he has adopted in "Ulysses," the result would be psychologically misleading and thus unfaithful to his chosen technique. Such an attitude would be artistically inexcusable.

It is because Joyce has been loyal to his technique and has not funked its necessary implications, but has honestly attempted to tell fully what his characters think about, that he has been the subject of so many attacks and that his purpose has been so often misunderstood and misrepresented. For his attempt sincerely and honestly to realize his objective has required him incidentally to use certain words which are generally considered dirty words and has led at times to what many think is a too poignant preoccupation with sex in the thoughts of his characters.

The words which are criticized as dirty are old Saxon words known to almost all men and, I venture, to many women, and are such words as would be naturally and habitually used, I believe, by the types of folk whose life, physical and mental, Joyce is seeking to describe. In respect of the recurrent emergence of the theme of sex in the minds of his characters, it must always be remembered that his locale was Celtic and his season spring.

Whether or not one enjoys such a technique as Joyce uses is a matter of taste on which disagreement or argument is futile, but to subject that technique to the standards of some other technique seems to me to be little short of absurd.

Accordingly, I hold that "Ulysses" is a sincere and honest book, and I think that the criticisms of it are entirely disposed of by its rationale.

V. Furthermore, "Ulysses" is an amazing tour de force when one considers the success which has been in the main achieved with such a difficult objective as Joyce set for himself. As I have stated, "Ulysses" is not an easy book to read. It is brilliant and dull, intelligible and obscure, by turns. In many places it seems to me to be disgusting, but although it contains, as I have mentioned above, many words usually considered dirty, I have not found anything that I consider to be dirt for dirt's sake. Each word of the book contributes like a bit of mosaic to the detail of the picture which Joyce is seeking to construct for his readers.

If one does not wish to associate with such folk as Joyce describes, that is one's own choice. In order to avoid indirect contact with them one may not wish to read "Ulysses"; that is quite understandable. But when such a great artist in words, as Joyce undoubtedly is, seeks to draw a true picture of the lower middle class in a European city, ought it to be impossible for the American public legally to see that picture?

To answer this question it is not sufficient merely to find, as I have found above, that Joyce did not write "Ulysses" with what is commonly called pornographic intent, I must endeavor to apply a more objective standard to his book in order to determine its effect in the result, irrespective of the intent with which it was written.

VI. The statute under which the libel is filed only denounces, in so far as we are here concerned, the importation into the United States from any foreign country of "any obscene book." Section 305 of the Tariff Act of 1930, title 19 United States Code, § 1305 (19 USCA § 1305). It does not marshal against books the spectrum of condemnatory adjectives found, commonly, in laws dealing with matters of this kind. I am, therefore, only required to determine whether "Ulysses" is obscene within the legal definition of that word.

[2] The meaning of the word "obscene" as legally defined by the courts is: Tending to stir the sex impulses or to lead to sexually impure and lustful thoughts. *Dunlop* v. *United States*, 165 U.S. 486, 501, 17 S. Ct. 375, 41 L. Ed. 799; *United States* v. *One Obscene Book* Entitled "Married Love" (D.C.) 48 F.(2d) 821, 824; *United States* v. *One Book*, entitled "Contraception" (D.C.) 51 F.(2d) 525, 528; and compare *Dysart* v. *United States*, 272 N.Y. 655, 657, 47 S. Ct. 234, 71 L. Ed. 461; *Swearingen* v. *United States*, 161 U.S. 446, 450, 16 S. Ct. 562, 40 L. Ed. 765; *United States* v. *Dennett*, 39 F.(2d) 564, 568, 76 A.L.R. 1092 (C.C.A. 2); *People* v. *Wendling*, 258 N.Y. 451, 453, 180 N.E. 169, 81 A.L.R. 799.

[3] Whether a particular book would tend to excite such impulses and thoughts must be tested by the court's opinion as to its effect on a person with average sex instincts—what the French would call *l'homme moyen sensuel*—who plays, in this branch of legal inquiry, the same role of hypothetical reagent as does the "reasonable man" in the law of torts and "the man learned in the art" on questions of invention in patent law.

The risk involved in the use of such a reagent arises from the inherent tendency of the trier of facts, however fair he may intend to be, to make his reagent too much subservient to his own idiosyncrasies. Here, I have attempted to avoid this, if possible, and to make my reagent herein more objective than he might otherwise be, by adopting the following course:

After I had made my decision in regard to the aspect of "Ulysses," now under consideration, I checked my impressions with two friends of mine who in my opinion answered to the above-stated requirement for my reagent.

These literary assessors—as I might properly describe them—were called on separately, and neither knew that I was consulting the other. They are men whose opinion on literature and on life I value most highly. They had both read "Ulysses," and, of course, were wholly unconnected with this cause.

Without letting either of my assessors know what my decision was, I gave to each of them the legal definition of obscene and asked each whether in his opinion "Ulysses" was obscene within that definition.

I was interested to find that they both agreed with my opinion: That reading "Ulysses" in its entirety, as a book must be read on such a test as this, did not tend to excite sexual impulses or lustful thoughts, but that its net effect on them was only that of a somewhat tragic and very powerful commentary on the inner lives of men and women.

[4] It is only with the normal person that the law is concerned. Such a test as I have described, therefore, is the only proper test of obscenity in the case of a book like "Ulysses" which is a sincere and serious attempt to devise a new literary method for the observation and description of mankind.

I am quite aware that owing to some of its scenes "Ulysses" is a rather strong draught to ask some sensitive, though normal, persons to take. But my considered opinion, after long reflection, is that, whilst in many places the effect of "Ulysses" on the reader undoubtedly is somewhat emetic, nowhere does it tend to be an aphrodisiac.

"Ulysses" may, therefore, be admitted into the United States.

■ United States

v.

One Book Entitled Ulysses by James Joyce (Random House, Inc., Claimant). No. 459.

Circuit Court of Appeals, Second Circuit. Aug. 7, 1934.

Martin Conboy, U.S. Atty., of New York City (Martin Conboy, of New York City, Francis H. Horan, of Washington, D.C., and John F. Davidson, Asst. U.S. Attys., of New York City, of counsel), for libelant-appellant.

Greenbaum, Wolff & Ernst, of New York City (Morris L. Ernst and Alexander Lindey, both of New York City, of counsel), for claimant-appellee.

Before MANTON, L. HAND, and AUGUSTUS N. HAND, Circuit Judges.

AUGUSTUS N. HAND, Circuit Judge.

This appeal raises sharply the question of the proper interpretation of section 305 (a) of the Tariff Act of 1930 (19 USCA § 1305 (a)). That section provides that "all persons are prohibited from importing into the United States from any foreign country * * * any obscene book, pamphlet, paper, writing, advertisement, circular, print, picture, drawing, or other representation, figure, or image on or of paper or other material, * * *" and directs that, upon the appearance of any such book or matter at any customs office, the collector shall seize it and inform the district attorney, who shall institute proceedings for forfeiture. In accordance with the statute, the collector seized Ulysses, a book written by James Joyce, and the United States filed a libel for forfeiture. The claimant, Random House, Inc., the publisher of the American edition, intervened in the cause and filed its answer denying that the book was obscene and was subject to confiscation and praying that it be admitted into the United States. The case came on for trial before Woolsey, J., who found that the book, taken as a whole, "did not tend to excite sexual impulses or lustful thoughts but that its net effect * * * was only that of a somewhat tragic and very powerful commentary on the inner lives of men and women." He accordingly granted a decree adjudging that the book was "not of the character the entry of which is prohibited under the provision of section 305 of the Tariff Act of 1930 * * * and * * * dismissing the libel," from which this appeal has been taken.

James Joyce, the author of Ulysses, may be regarded as a pioneer among those writers who have adopted the "stream of consciousness" method of presenting fiction, which has attracted considerable attention in academic and literary circles. In this field Ulysses is rated as a book of considerable power by persons whose opinions are entitled to weight. Indeed it has become a sort of contemporary classic, dealing with a new subject-matter. It attempts to depict the thoughts and lay bare the souls of a number of people, some of them intellectuals and some social outcasts and nothing more, with a literalism that leaves nothing unsaid. Certain of its passages are of beauty and undoubted distinction, while others are of a vulgarity that is extreme and the book as a whole has a realism characteristic of the present age. It is supposed to portray the thoughts of the principal characters during a period of about eighteen hours.

We may discount the laudation of Ulysses by some of its admirers and reject the view that it will permanently stand among the great works of literature, but it is fair to say that it is a sincere portrayal with skillful artistry of the "streams of consciousness" of its characters. Though the depiction happily is not of the "stream of consciousness" of all men and perhaps of only those of a morbid type, it seems to be sincere, truthful, relevant to the subject, and executed with real art. Joyce, in the words of Paradise Lost, has dealt with "things unattempted yet in prose or rime" —with things that very likely might better have remained "unattempted"—but his book shows originality and is a work of symmetry and excellent craftsmanship of a sort. The question before us is whether such a book of artistic merit and scientific insight should be regarded as "obscene" within section 305 (a) of the Tariff Act.

That numerous long passages in Ulysses contain matter that is obscene under any fair definition of the word cannot be gainsaid; yet they are relevant to the purpose of depicting the thoughts of the characters and are introduced to give meaning to the whole, rather than to promote lust or portray filth for its own sake. [Italics ed.].

The net effect even of portions most open to attack, such as the closing monologue of the wife of Leopold Bloom, is pitiful and tragic, rather than lustful. The book depicts the souls of men and women that are by turns bewildered and keenly apprehensive, sordid and aspiring, ugly and beautiful, hateful and loving. In the end one feels, more than anything else, pity and sorrow for the confusion, misery, and degradation of humanity. Page after page of the book is, or seems to be, incomprehensible. But many passages show the trained hand of an artist, who can at one moment adapt to perfection the style of an ancient chronicler, and at another become a veritable personification of Thomas Carlyle. In numerous places there are found originality, beauty, and distinction. The book as a whole is not pornographic, and, while in not a few spots it is coarse, blasphemous, and obscene, it does not, in our opinion, tend to promote lust. The erotic passages are submerged in the book as a whole and have little resultant effect. If these are to make the book subject to confiscation, by the same test Venus and Adonis, Hamlet, Romeo and Juliet, and the story told in the Eighth Book of the Odyssey by the bard Demodocus of how Ares and Aphrodite were entrapped in a net spread by the outraged Hephaestus amid the laughter of the immortal gods, as well as many other classics, would have to be suppressed. Indeed, it may be questioned whether the obscene passages in Romeo and Juliet were as necessary to the development of the play as those in the monologue of Mrs. Bloom are to the depiction of the latter's tortured soul.

It is unnecessary to add illustrations to show that, in the administration of statutes aimed at the suppression of immoral books, standard works of literature have not been barred merely because they contained *some* obscene passages, and that confiscation for such a reason would destroy much that is precious in order to benefit a few. [1-4] It is settled, at least so far as this court is concerned, that works of physiology, medicine, science, and sex instruction are not within the statute, though to some extent and among some persons they may tend to promote lustful thoughts. *United States* v. *Dennett*, 39 F.(2d) 564, 76 A.L.R. 1092. We think the same immunity should apply to literature as to science, where the presentation, when viewed objectively, is sincere, and the erotic matter is not introduced to promote lust and does not furnish the dominant note of the publication. The question in each case is whether a publication taken as a whole has a libidinous effect. The book before us has such portentous length, is written with such evident truthfulness in its depiction of certain types of humanity, and is so little erotic in its result, that it does not fall within the forbidden class.

In *Halsey* v. *New York Society for Suppression of Vice*, 234 N.Y. 1, 136 N.E. 219, 220, the New York Court of Appeals dealt with Mademoiselle de Maupin, by Theophile

Gautier, for the sale of which the plaintiff had been prosecuted under a New York statute forbidding the sale of obscene books, upon the complaint of the defendant. After acquittal, the plaintiff sued for malicious prosecution, and a jury rendered a verdict in his favor. The Court of Appeals refused to disturb the judgment because the book had become a recognized French classic and its merits on the whole outweighed its objectionable qualities, though, as Judge Andrews said, it contained many paragraphs which, "taken by themselves," were "undoubtedly vulgar and indecent." In referring to the obscene passages, he remarked that: "No work may be judged from a selection of such paragraphs alone. Printed by themselves they might, as a matter of law, come within the prohibition of the statute. So might a similar selection from Aristophanes or Chaucer or Boccaccio, or even from the Bible. The book, however, must be considered broadly, as a whole." We think Judge Andrews was clearly right, and that the effect of the book as a whole is the test.

In the New York Supreme Court, Judge Morgan J. O'Brien declined to prohibit a receiver from selling Arabian Nights, Rabelais, Ovid's Art of Love, the Decameron of Boccaccio, the Heptameron of Queen Margaret of Navarre, or the Confessions of Rousseau. He remarked that a rule which would exclude them would bar "a very large proportion of the works of fiction of the most famous writers of the English language." In re Worthington Co. (Sup.) 30 N.Y.S. 361, 362, 24 L.R.A. 110. The main difference between many standard works and Ulysses is its far more abundant use of coarse and colloquial words and presentation of dirty scenes, rather than in any excess of prurient suggestion. We do not think that Ulysses, taken as a whole, tends to promote lust, and its criticised passages do this no more than scores of standard books that are constantly bought and sold. Indeed a book of physiology in the hands of adolescents may be more objectionable on this ground than almost anything else.

But it is argued that *United States* v. *Bennett*, Fed. Cas. No. 14,571, stands in the way of what has been said, and it certainly does. There a court, consisting of Blatchford, C.J., and Benedict and Choate, D.JJ., held that the offending paragraphs in a book could be taken from their context and the book judged by them alone, and that the test of obscenity was whether the tendency of these passages in themselves was "to deprave the minds of those open to such influences and into whose hands a publication of this character might come." The opinion was founded upon a dictum of Cockburn, C.J., in *Regina* v. *Hicklin*, L.R. 3 Q.B. 360, where half of a book was to attack alleged practices of the confession was obscene and contained, as Mellor, J., said, "a great deal * * * which there cannot be any necessity for in any legitimate argument on the confessional. * * *" It is said that in *Rosen* v. *United States*, 161 U.S. 29, 16 S. Ct. 434, 480, 40 L. Ed. 606, the Supreme Court cited and sanctioned *Regina* v. *Hicklin*, and *United States* v. *Bennett*. The subject-matter of *Rosen* v. *United States* was, however, a pictorial representation of "females, in different attitudes of indecency." The figures were partially covered "with lamp black, that could be easily erased with a piece of bread." Page 31 of 161 U.S., 16 S. Ct. 434. The pictures were evidently obscene, and plainly came within the statute prohibiting their transportation. The citation of *Regina* v. *Hicklin* and *United States* v. *Bennett*, was in support of a ruling that allegations in the indictment as to an obscene publication need

only be made with sufficient particularity to inform the accused of the nature of the charge against him. No approval of other features of the two decisions was expressed, nor were such features referred to. *Dunlop* v. *United States*, 165 U.S. 486, 489, 17 S. Ct. 375, 41 L. Ed. 799, also seems to be relied on by the government, but the publication there was admittedly obscene and the decision in no way sanctioned the rulings in *United States* v. *Bennett* which we first mentioned. The rigorous doctrines laid down in that case are inconsistent with our own decision in *United States* v. *Dennett* (C.C.A.) 39 F.(2d) 564, 76 A.L.R. 1092, as well as with *Konda* v. *United States* (C.C.A.) 166 F. 91, 92, 22 L.R.A. (N.S.) 304; *Clark* v. *United States* (C.C.A.) 211 F. 916, 922; *Halsey* v. *N.Y. Society for Suppression of Vice*, 234 N.Y. 1, 4, 136 N.E. 219; and *St. Hubert Guild* v. *Quinn*, 64 Misc. 336, 339, 118 N.Y.S. 582, and, in our opinion, do not represent the law. They would exclude much of the great works of literature and involve an impracticability that cannot be imputed to Congress and would in the case of many books containing obscene passages inevitably require the court that uttered them to restrict their applicability. [5] It is true that the motive of an author to promote good morals is not the test of whether a book is obscene, and it may also be true that the applicability of the statute does not depend on the persons to whom a publication is likely to be distributed. The importation of obscene books is prohibited generally, and no provision is made permitting such importation because of the character of those to whom they are sold. While any construction of the statute that will fit all cases is difficult, we believe that the proper test of whether a given book is obscene is its dominant effect. In applying this test, relevancy of the objectionable parts to the theme, the established reputation of the work in the estimation of approved critics, if the book is modern, and the verdict of the past, if it is ancient, are persuasive pieces of evidence; for works of art are not likely to sustain a high position with no better warrant for their existence than their obscene content.

It may be that Ulysses will not last as a substantial contribution to literature, and it is certainly easy to believe that, in spite of the opinion of Joyce's laudators, the immortals will still reign, but the same thing may be said of current works of art and music and of many other serious efforts of the mind. Art certainly cannot advance under compulsion to traditional forms, and nothing in such a field is more stifling to progress than limitation of the right to experiment with a new technique. The foolish judgments of Lord Eldon about one hundred years ago, proscribing the works of Byron and Southey, and the finding by the jury under a charge by Lord Denman that the publication of Shelley's "Queen Mab" was an indictable offense are a warning to all who have to determine the limits of the field within which authors may exercise themselves. We think that Ulysses is a book of originality and sincerity of treatment and that it has not the effect of promoting lust. Accordingly it does not fall within the statute, even though it justly may offend many.

Decree affirmed.

MANTON, Circuit Judge.

I dissent. This libel, filed against the book Ulysses prays for a decree of forfeiture, and it is based upon the claim that the book's entry into the United States is prohibited by section 305 (a) of the Tariff Act of 1930 (19 USCA 1305 (a). On motion of appellee, the court below entered an order dismissing the libel, and the collector of customs was ordered to release the book. The motion was considered on the pleadings and a stipulation entered into by the parties.

The sole question presented is whether or not the book is obscene within section 305 (a) which provides:

"All persons are prohibited from importing into the United States from any foreign country * * * any obscene book, pamphlet, paper, writing, advertisement, circular, print, picture, drawing, or other representation, figure, or image on or of paper or other material. * * *

"Upon the appearance of any such book or matter at any customs office, the same shall be seized and held by the collector to await the judgment of the district court as hereinafter provided. * * * Upon the seizure of such book or matter the collector shall transmit information thereof to the district attorney of the district in which is situated the office at which such seizure has taken place, who shall institute proceedings in the district court for the forfeiture, confiscation, and destruction of the book or matter seized. * * *

"In any such proceeding any party in interest may upon demand have the facts at issue determined by a jury and any party may have an appeal or the right of review as in the case of ordinary actions or suits."

The parties agreed as to the facts in the stipulation. There is no conflicting evidence; the decision to be made is dependent entirely upon the reading matter found on the objectionable pages of the book (pages 173, 213, 214, 359, 361, 423, 424, 434, 467, 488, 498, 500, 509, 522, 526, 528, 551, 719, 724–727, 731, 738, 739, 745, 746, 754–756, 761, 762, 765, Random House Edition). The book itself was the only evidence offered.

In a suit of this kind upon stipulation, the ultimate finding based solely on stipulated facts is reviewable on appeal to determine whether the facts support the finding. *Lumbermen's Trust Co.* v. *Town of Ryegate*, 61 F.(2d) 14 (C.C.A. 9); *Order of United Commercial Travelers of America* v. *Shane*, 64 F.(2d) 55 (C.C.A. 8). Moreover, the procedure in this suit in rem conforms to that obtaining in suits in admiralty (*Coffey* v. *United States*, 117 U.S. 233, 6 S. Ct. 717, 29 L. Ed. 890) where the appellate courts may review the facts. The Africa Maru, 54 F.(2d) 265 (C.C.A. 2); The Perry Setzer, 299 F. 586 (C.C.A. 2).

Who can doubt the obscenity of this book after a reading of the pages referred to, which are too indecent to add as a footnote to this opinion? Its characterization as obscene should be quite unanimous by all who read it.

In the year 1868 in *Regina* v. *Hicklin* L.R., 3 Q.B. 359, at page 369, Cockburn C.J., stated that "the test of obscenity is this, whether the tendency of the matter charged as obscenity is to deprave and corrupt those whose minds are open to such immoral influences, and into whose hands a publication of this sort may fall."

In 1879, in *United States* v. *Bennett*, Fed. Cas. No. 14,571 Judge Blatchford, later a justice of the Supreme Court, in this circuit, sitting with Judges Choate and Benedict, approved the rule of the Hicklin Case and held a charge to a jury proper which embodied the test of that case. The Bennett Case clearly holds the test of obscenity, within the meaning of the statute, is "whether the ten-

dency of the matter is to deprave and corrupt the morals of those whose minds are open to such influences, and into whose hands a publication of this sort may fall." The court held that the object of the use of the obscene words was not a subject for consideration.

Judge Blatchford's decision met with approval in *Rosen* v. *United States*, 151 U.S. 29, 16 S. Ct. 434, 438, 480, 40 L. Ed. 606. The court had under consideration an indictment charging the accused with depositing obscene literature in the mails. There instructions to the jury requested that conviction could not be had although the defendant may have had knowledge or notice of the contents of the letter "unless he knew or believed that such paper could be properly or justly characterized as obscene, lewd, and lascivious." The court said the statute was not to be so interpreted. "The inquiry under the statute is whether the paper charged to have been obscene, lewd, and lascivious was in fact of that character; and if it was of that character, and was deposited in the mail by one who knew or had notice at the time of its contents, the offense is complete, although the defendant himself did not regard the paper as one that the statute forbade to be carried in the mails. Congress did not intend that the question as to the character of the paper should depend upon the opinion or belief of the person who, with knowledge or notice of its contents, assumed the responsibility of putting it in the mails of the United States. The evils that congress sought to remedy would continue and increase in volume if the belief of the accused as to what was obscene, lewd, and lascivious were recognized as the test for determining whether the statute has been violated. Every one who uses the mails of the United States for carrying papers or publications must take notice of what, in this enlightened age, is meant by decency, purity, and chastity in social life, and what must be deemed obscene, lewd, and lascivious."

Further the Supreme Court approved the test of the Hicklin Case. On page 43 of 151 U.S., 16 S. Ct. 434, 439, the court states: "That was what the court did when it charged the jury that 'the test of obscenity is whether the tendency of the matter is to deprave and corrupt the morals of those whose minds are open to such influence, and into whose hands a publication of this sort may fall.' 'Would it,' the court said, 'suggest or convey lewd thoughts and lascivious thoughts to the young and inexperienced?' In view of the character of the paper, as an inspection of it will instantly disclose, the test prescribed for the jury was quite as liberal as the defendant had any right to demand."

Again the Supreme Court in *Dunlop* v. *United States*, 165 U.S. 486, 17 S. Ct. 375, 380, 41 L. Ed. 799, reviewed a charge in a criminal case upon the subject of obscene publications as follows: "Now, what is (are) obscene, lascivious, lewd, or indecent publications is largely a question of your own conscience and your own opinion; but it must come—before it can be said of such literature or publication—it must come up to this point: that it must be calculated with the ordinary reader to deprave him, deprave his morals, or lead to impure purposes. * * * It is your duty to ascertain, in the first place, if they are calculated to deprave the morals; if they are calculated to lower that standard which we regard as essential to civilization; if they are calculated to excite those feelings which, in their proper field, are all right, but which, transcending the limits of that proper field, play most of the mischief in the world."

In approving the charge, the court said: "The alleged obscene and indecent matter consisted of advertisements by women, soliciting or offering inducements for the visits of men, usually 'refined gentlemen,' to their rooms, sometimes under the disguise of 'Baths' and 'massage,' and oftener for the mere purpose of acquaintance. It was in this connection that the court charged the jury that, if the publications were such as were calculated to deprave the morals, they were within the statute. There could have been no possible misapprehension on their part as to what was meant. There was no question as to depraving the morals in any other direction than that of impure sexual relations. The words were used by the court in their ordinary signification, and were made more definite by the context and by the character of the publications which have been put in evidence. The court left to the jury to say whether it was within the statute, and whether persons of ordinary intelligence would have any difficulty of divining the intention of the advertiser."

Thus the court sustained a charge having a test as to whether or no the publications depraved the morals of the ordinary reader or tended to lower the standards of civilization. The tendency of the matter to deprave and corrupt the morals of those whose minds are open to such influence and into whose hands the publication of this sort may fall, has become the test thoroughly entrenched in the federal courts. *United States* v. *Bebout* (D.C.) 28 F. 522; *United States* v. *Wightman* (D.C.) 29 F. 636; *United States* v. *Clarke* (D.C.) 38 F. 732; *United States* v. *Smith* (D.C.) 45 F. 476; *Burton* v. *United States*, 142 F. 57 (C.C.A. 8); *United States* v. *Dennett*, 39 F.(2d) 564, 76 A.L.R. 1092 (C.C.A. 2). What is the probable effect on the sense of decency of society, extending to the family made up of men, women, young boys, and girls, was said to be the test in *United States* v. *Harmon* (D.C.) 45 F. 414, 417.

Ulysses is a work of fiction. It may not be compared with books involving medical subjects or description of certain physical or biological facts. It is written for alleged amusement of the reader only. The characters described in the thoughts of the author may in some instances be true, but, be it truthful or otherwise, a book that is obscene is not rendered less so by the statement of truthful fact. *Burton* v. *United States*, supra. It cannot be said that the test above has been rejected by *United States* v. *Dennett* (C.C.A.) 39 F.(2d) 564, 76 A.L.R. 1092, nor can that case be taken to mean that the book is to be judged as a whole. If anything, the case clearly recognizes that the book may be obscene because portions thereof are so, for pains are taken to justify and show not to be obscene portions to which objection is made. The gist of the holding is that a book is not to be declared obscene if it is "an accurate exposition of the relevant facts of the sex side of life in decent language and in manifestly serious and disinterested spirit." A work of obvious benefit to the community was never intended to be within the purview of the statute. No matter what may be said on the side of letters, the effect on the community can and must be the sole determining factor. "Laws of this character are made for society in the aggregate, and not in particular. So, while there may be individuals and societies of men and women of peculiar notions or idiosyncrasies, whose moral sense would neither be depraved nor offended, * * * yet the exceptional sensibility, or want of sensibility, of such

cannot be allowed as a standard." *United States* v. *Harmon*, supra.

In *United States* v. *Kennerley* (D.C.) 209 F. 119, the Bennett Case was followed despite the dictum objecting to a test which protected the "salacious" few. By the very argument used, to destroy a test which protects those most easily influenced, we can discard a test which would protect only the interests of the other comparatively small groups of society. If we disregard the protection of the morals of the susceptible, are we to consider merely the benefits and pleasures derived from letters by those who pose as the more highly developed and intelligent? To do so would show an utter disregard for the standards of decency of the community as a whole and an utter disregard for the effect of a book upon the average less sophisticated member of society, not to mention the adolescent. The court cannot indulge any instinct it may have to foster letters. The statute is designed to protect society at large, of that there can be no dispute; notwithstanding the deprivation of benefits to a few, a work must be condemned if it has a depraving influence.

And are we to refuse to enforce the statute Congress has enacted because of the argument that "obscenity is only the superstition of the day—the modern counterpart of ancient witchcraft"? Are we to be persuaded by the statement, set forth in the brief, made by the judge below in an interview with the press, "Education, not law, must solve problems of taste and choice (of books)," when the statute is clear and our duty plain?

The prevailing opinion states that classics would be excluded if the application of the statute here argued for prevailed. But the statute, Tariff Act 1930, § 305 (a), 19 USCA § 1305 (a), provides as to classics that they may be introduced into the commerce of the United States provided "that the Secretary of the Treasury * * * in his discretion, admit the so-called classics or books of recognized and established literary or scientific merit, but may, in his discretion, admit such classics or books only when imported for noncommercial purposes." The right to admission under this proviso was not sought nor is it justified by reason thereof in the prevailing opinion.

Congress passed this statute against obscenity for the protection of the great mass of our people; the unusual literator can, or thinks he can, protect himself. The people do not exist for the sake of literature, to give the author fame, the publisher wealth, and the book a market. On the contrary, literature exists for the sake of the people, to refresh the weary, to console the sad, to hearten the dull and downcast, to increase man's interest in the world, his joy of living, and his sympathy in all sorts and conditions of men. Art for art's sake is heartless and soon grows artless; art for the public market is not art at all, but commerce; art for the people's service is a noble, vital, and permanent element of human life.

The public is content with the standard of salability; the prigs with the standard of preciosity. The people need and deserve a moral standard; it should be a point of honor with men of letters to maintain it. Masterpieces have never been produced by men given to obscenity or lustful thoughts—men who have no Master. Reverence for good work is the foundation of literary character. A refusal to imitate obscenity or to load a book with it is an author's professional chastity.

Good work in literature has its permanent mark; it is like all good work, noble and lasting. It requires a human aim—to cheer, console, purify, or ennoble the life of people. Without this aim, literature has never sent an arrow close to the mark. It is by good work only that men of letters can justify their right to a place in the world.

Under the authoritative decisions and considering the substance involved in this appeal, it is my opinion that the decree should be reversed.

■ State

v.

Arnold.

Supreme Court of Wisconsin. Feb. 5, 1935.

Bowman, Hofer & Minor, of Milwaukee, for appellant.

James E. Finnegan, Atty. Gen., *J. E. Messerschmidt*, Asst. Atty. Gen., and *William A. Zabel*, Dist. Atty., *Herman A. Mosher*, Deputy Dist. Atty., and *Arthur J. Schmid*, Asst. Dist. Atty., all of Milwaukee, for the State.

WICKHEM, Justice.

Defendant is the lessee of an oil station in the city of Milwaukee. As a part of the service equipment, defendant maintains two washrooms, one for women and the other for men. Two detectives of the Milwaukee police department entered the station on December 19, 1933, and asked permission to use the men's washroom. One of the officers found attached to the wall of the washroom a slot machine. He inserted 10 cents in this slot machine and received a cartridge containing a rubber article, commonly used for contraceptive purposes. This is the basis of the prosecution. On this machine was a sign, "Sold only for the prevention of disease," and "Minors are prohibited to operate this machine." The purchase was made for purposes of evidence, and not for the purpose of illegal use. The machine is not constructed for the sole purpose of vending articles of the character purchased by the officers, but will automatically vend any merchandise so packed as to conform to its size requirements. The defendant had permitted this machine to be placed on his premises and received a commission on the amount taken in by the machine. He had nothing to do with the placing of the cartridges or other contents in the slot machine.

Section 351.235, Stats., provides as follows:

"351.235 *Advertising or display of indecent articles, sale in certain cases prohibited.* (1) As used in this chapter, the term 'indecent articles' means any drug, medicine, mixture, preparation, instrument, article or device of whatsoever nature used or intended or represented to be used to procure a miscarriage or prevent pregnancy.

"(2) No person, firm or corporation shall publish, distribute or circulate any circular, card, advertisement or notice of any kind offering or advertising any indecent article for sale, nor shall exhibit or display any indecent article to the public.

"(3) No person, firm or corporation shall manufacture, purchase, or rent, or have in his or its possession or under his or its control, any slot machine, or other mechanism or means so designed and constructed as to contain and hold indecent articles and to release the same upon the deposit therein of a coin or other thing of value.

"(4) No person, firm or corporation shall sell or dispose of or attempt or offer to sell or dispose of any indecent articles to or for any unmarried person; and no sale in any case of any indecent articles shall be made except by a pharmacist registered under the provisions of chapter 151 or a physician or surgeon duly licensed under the laws of this state.

"(5) Any person, firm or corporation violating any provision of this section shall be deemed guilty of a misdemeanor and upon conviction thereof shall be punished by a fine of not less than one hundred nor more than five hundred dollars or by imprisonment in the county jail for not to exceed six months, or by both such fine and imprisonment. In addition thereto, any license, permit or registration certificate issued under any law or ordinance to any such persons, firm or corporation, shall be canceled or revoked."

This section, which was chapter 420, Laws of 1933, was originally introduced as a bill prohibiting birth control and providing a penalty. Its original purpose failed to secure the sanction of the Legislature, and the section in its present form, which appears to represent a compromise of conflicting views, was enacted.

Defendant's first contention is that the act is so vague and indefinite as to render it unconstitutional under the Fifth Amendment to the United States Constitution. The rule, as stated in *Connally* v. *General Construction Company*, 269 U.S. 385, 46 S. Ct. 126, 127, 70 L. Ed. 322, is as follows: "And a statute which either forbids or requires the doing of an act in terms so vague that men of common intelligence must necessarily guess at its meaning and differ as to its application violates the first essential of due process of law."

[2] Applied to this case, we conclude that the Legislature did not have in mind an omnibus condemnation or regulation of every article capable of producing an abortion or preventing pregnancy; that it was the intent of the Legislature to deal with articles whose sole purpose, or whose intended purpose or represented function was to produce these results; and that, in general, it was the intention of the Legislature wholly to prohibit the sale of

such articles to unmarried persons or by any one except a physician or pharmacist. In aid of the latter provision, it was determined to prevent the sale of these articles by mechanical means. In order to make this effective, the prohibition goes to the manufacture, purchase, rent, or possession of machines solely designed to vend such articles, or by reason of their construction, capable of vending them, and actually containing these articles ready for vending. It will at once be contended that since the definition of an indecent article depends in part upon the purpose of the sale, or the represented function of the article, and that since the device vended by this machine purports to be sold solely for the prevention of disease, the article does not fall within the definition of indecent articles and this conviction cannot be sustained. The particular article involved is as effective for contraceptive purposes as for disease prevention, and this is also true of drugs, the operation of which is antiseptic rather than mechanical. The difficulty with appellant's position in this respect is the insistence that the protestations contained upon this slot machine that this is "sold only for the prevention of disease" and that "minors are prohibited to operate this machine," are conclusive as to the intent. We think they are not. *We think the sale of this particular device in a public toilet by a mechanical vending machine is a sufficient warrant for the inference that the purpose of its sale was contraception and not merely the prevention of disease.* [Italics ed.].

[3] The further contention that this act is unconstitutional because it discriminates between married and unmarried persons raises a question of classification. We find

no necessity for examining this question, since the rights of this defendant are in no way affected by the discrimination, if it exists, and since no one can plead the unconstitutionality of a law other than a person affected thereby. In re Will of Heinemann, 201 Wis. 484, 230 N.W. 698.

[4] Defendant's final contention is that the court erred in denying defendant's motion to make the complaint more definite and certain. It is contended that the particular charge here involved is not sufficiently set forth by couching the complaint in the words of the statute. It is claimed that defendant had a right to know whether his crime consisted in the possession of a slot machine solely designed for an unlawful purpose, or one capable of lawful use which defendant used for unlawful pruposes. It is further claimed that defendant had a right to be informed as to the character of the articles claimed to constitute "indecent articles."

We see no occasion for discussing the merits of the order denying the motion to make more definite and certain. Section 269.43, Stats., requires that this court disregard any error or defect in the pleadings or proceedings which does not affect the substantial rights of the defendant. An examination of the record indicates that there was no misunderstanding upon the part of defendant as to the nature of the offense with which he was charged. There were no issues of fact in the case, and not only no evidence but no probability that the complaint, assuming it to have been somewhat vague and uncertain, in any manner prejudiced defendant in meeting the issues.

Orders and judgment affirmed.

■ People on Complaint of Sumner
v.
Miller.

City Magistrate's Court of New York City, Fourth District, Borough of Manhattan.

May 8, 1935.

John S. Sumner, of New York City, in pro. per.
Greenbaum, Wolff & Ernst, of New York City (Morris L. Ernst and Alexander Lindey, both of New York City, of counsel), for defendant.

GOLDSTEIN, City Magistrate.
The sole question is whether Gustave Flaubert's book "November" is or is not obscene or indecent within the meaning of section 1141 of the Penal Law.

[1] *The criterion of decency is fixed by time, place, geography, and all the elements that make for a constantly changing world. A practice regarded as decent in one period may be indecent in another.* [Italics ed.]. The practice of "bundling" approved in Puritan days would be frowned upon today.

Although section 1141 of the Penal Law has been on our statute books since 1884, the test that the book is

required to meet is the measure of public opinion in the city of New York in the year 1935.

Judge Learned Hand, in *U.S.* v. *Kennerley* (D.C.) 209 F. 119, 121, aptly said: "If there be no abstract definition, such as I have suggested, should not the word 'obscene' be allowed to indicate the present critical point in the compromise between candor and shame at which the community may have arrived here and now? * * * Nor is it an objection, I think, that such an interpretation gives to the words of the statute a varying meaning from time to time. Such words as these do not embalm the precise morals of an age or place; while they presuppose that some things will always be shocking to the public taste, the vague subject-matter is left to the gradual development of general notions about what is decent."

In *St. Hubert Guild* v. *Quinn*, 64 Misc. 336, 341, 118 N.Y.S. 582, 586, Mr. Justice Seabury said for a unanimous

Appellate Term: "Contemporaneous literature must, of course, be judged by current opinion."

Twenty-five years ago women were arrested and convicted for appearing on the beach attired in sleeveless bathing suits, or without stockings.

The language of the law under which they were convicted is identical with the language of the statute today. The ordinance required the wearing of bathing suits that would not "indecently" expose the body. While the language of the ordinance has remained unchanged, the public point of view has undergone distinct change.

In 1906, the play "Sappho" was suppressed because the leading lady was carried up a flight of stairs in the arms of a man. In 1907, Mary Garden was prevented from appearing in the opera "Salome." I could multiply such examples endlessly. Whether we like it or not, the fact is that the public concept of decency has changed. What was regarded as indecent in the days of the Floradora Sextette, is decent in the days of the Fan and Bubble Dances.

It is not my function as a judge to express agreement or disagreement with the present accepted standards.

To change standards of morals is the task of school and church; the task of the judge is to record the tides of public opinion, not to emulate King Canute in an effort to turn back the tide. My duty is to act as observer and recorder, not as regulator.

As Mr. Justice Cardozo has observed in "Paradoxes of Legal Science" (at p. 37): "Law accepts as the pattern of its justice the morality of the community whose conduct it assumes to regulate. * * * The law will not hold the crowd to the morality of saints and seers."

[2] I have read the book carefully, viewing it in the 1935 mirror of public opinion, it reflects no violation of section 1141 of the Penal Law. In every community, public opinion of the day should control the judicial application of "decency" statutes. If the court fails to adopt this standard, then the law becomes, as Prof. Wormser has said (Columbia Law Review, Dec. 1923), "not a true mirror of life as it should be, but a bewildering distortion, alike perplexing and misleading, of which the ordinary man or woman becomes properly distrustful."

[3] The obscenity statute was not intended to suppress bona fide literary effort, but rather to prohibit the exploitation of smut; dirt in the raw. *People* v. *Wendling*, 258 N.Y. 451 at page 453, 180 N.E. 169, 81 A.L.R. 799; *U.S.* v. *One Book* Called "Ulysses" (D.C.) 5 F. Supp. 182, 183, affirmed *U.S.* v. *One Book* Entitled Ulysses by James Joyce (C.C.A.) 72 F.(2d) 705.

For the reasons above stated, I hold as a matter of law that there is not sufficient cause to hold the defendant for trial.

Complaint dismissed; defendant discharged.

■ People on Complaint of Savery
v.
Gotham Book Mart, Inc.

City Magistrate's Court of New York, Seventh District, Borough of Manhattan.

Jan. 24, 1936.

John S. Sumner, of New York City, for New York Society for Suppression of Vice, prosecuting for the People.

Weil, Gotshal & Manges, of New York City (Horace S. Manges, of New York City, of counsel), for defendant.

NATHAN D. PERLMAN, City Magistrate.

The defendant is charged with having violated section 1141 of the Penal Law by its possession and sale of a book entitled, "If It Die," by André Gide.

Section 1141 of the Penal Law reads, in part, as follows: "A person who sells * * * any obscene, lewd, lascivious, filthy, indecent or disgusting book * * * is guilty of a misdemeanor."

Complainant does not contend that the entire book, which is an autobiography of the French novelist André Gide, is obscene within the meaning of our statute. The attack is chiefly upon part II, comprising approximately 76 pages, which, mathematically computed, is approximately one-fifth of the entire book. Further analysis and computation establishes, however, that the complaint is directed only against certain paragraphs contained in 22 of these 76 pages.

Complainant relies mainly upon *U.S.* v. *Bennett*, Fed. Cas. No. 14,571, decided in 1879. There the Circuit Court held that the offending paragraphs in a book could be taken from their context and the book judged by them alone, and that the test of obscenity was whether the tendency of these passages in themselves was "to deprave the minds of those open to such influences and into whose hands a publication of this character might come." Fifty-five years later, the Circuit Court of Appeals held that *U.S.* v. *Bennett* does not represent the law. *United States* v. *One Book* Entitled Ulysses, 72 F.(2d) 705.

Our Court of Appeals has also written: "No work may be judged from a selection of such paragraphs alone. Printed by themselves they might, as a matter of law, come within the prohibition of the statute. So might a similar selection from Aristophanes or Chaucer or Boccacio or even from the Bible. The book, however, must be considered broadly as a whole." Andrews, J., in *Halsey* v. *New York Soc. for Suppression of Vice*, 234 N.Y. 1, 4, 136 N.E. 219, 220. It is unnecessary to add further illustrations to show that, in the administration of statutes aimed at the suppression of immoral books, works of literature have not been barred merely because they contain some obscene passages.

The determination of the issue involved may not, therefore, be found in the slide rule. This is the tool of the engineer. Books are not so dissected. A book does not lend itself to either mathematical or comparative analysis.

Moral standards of thought are not of a static or plastic nature. What seems immoral to one generation will not seem so to another. The heroine of the American novel is no longer the pink-aproned girl making cookies in the kitchen. Hamlet shocked all the Cromwellian Puritans, and shocks nobody to-day. A literary critic of the book involved in this case writes: "Perhaps it is well that the publication * * * in English has been delayed until now. For one thing, the public is no longer so horrified by disclosures of homosexuality that it need regard the book—as it might have regarded it ten years ago—as something sensational." The New York Times, November 10, 1935.

The idea of what constitutes morality differs, not only in different ages, but in different countries. The International Conference on the Suppression of the Circulation and Traffic in Obscene Publications readily admitted that the term "obscenity" has different meanings in different countries. Many years ago, a superintendent of schools in Brooklyn was stirred by the recitation in our public schools of Longfellow's poem, "Building of the Ship." His objection was based upon the fact that the ship was pictured as leaping "into the ocean's arms." In Re Worthington Co. (Sup.) 30 N.Y.S. 361, 24 L.R.A. 110, 62 N.Y. St. Rep. 116, one of the books allowed to be sold as a "classic" was the unexpurgated edition of Decameron. In Ohio a fine was imposed by a federal judge upon a defendant for mailing the same work (New York Times, June 22, 1922).

Opinions are bound to vary. This fact we must recognize. This difference is reflected in the decisions of our own courts. From what is the public to be protected? Who are to be protected? What test shall be applied? Shall we consider the opinion of literary critics? Are "de-luxe" editions exempt from the provisions of our law? The answers to these questions are not in accord. Judges like all human beings vary in their views.

The question, we are told, is whether the tendency of the books is to excite lustful and lecherous desire. *People* v. *Eastman*, 188 N.Y. 478, 81 N.E. 459, 11 Ann. Cas. 302; *People* v. *Muller*, 96 N.Y. 408, 48 Am. Rep. 635. The Appellate Division for this department applied this test in *People* v. *Brainard*, 192 App. Div. 816, 183 N.Y.S. 452, and reversed a conviction for the publication of a book known as "Madeleine," which was the autobiography of a prostitute. This test was called too narrow in a later case, *People* v. *Seltzer*, 122 Misc. 329, 333, 203 N.Y.S. 809. Mr. Justice Wagner in this case adopted the test applied in *Regina* v. *Hicklin* (1868), L.R. 3 Queens Bench, 360, namely: "Is the tendency of the matter charged as obscene to deprave or corrupt those whose minds are open to such immoral influences and who might come in contact with it?" Recently, the Appellate Division for this department stated these matters must be judged by normal people and not by the abnormal. "Conditions would be deplorable if abnormal people were permitted to regulate those matters." *People* v. *Pesky*, 230 App. Div. 200, 204, 243 N.Y.S. 193, 197, affirmed by the Court of Appeals in 254 N.Y. 373, 173 N.E. 227.

In *People* v. *Muller*, supra, the court refused to allow

expert testimony to influence a jury in determining the tenuous line between art and pornography. Later, in *St. Hubert Guild* v. *Quinn*, 64 Misc. 336, 118 N.Y.S. 582, the court itself indulges in an examination of critical opinions, holding that a contract for the sale of Voltaire's works, including the "Philosophical Dictionary" and the "Maid of Orleans" was not unenforceable because of alleged illegality under section 1141 of the Penal Law. In *Halsey* v. *New York Society for Suppression of Vice*, supra, the conflicting opinions arrayed critical authority on either side. In a fairly recent case, a court considered a large number of testimonials from people eminent in the literary life of this city and county, holding that this group of people collectively, has a better capacity to judge of the value of a literary production than one who is more apt to search for obscene passages in a book than to regard the book as a whole. *People* v. *Viking Press*, 147 Misc. 813, 264 N.Y.S. 534.

In Re Worthington Co., supra, allowing the sale of Payne's edition of the "Arabian Nights," Fielding's "Tom Jones," Rabelais' works, Ovid's "Art of Love," "The Decameron," "The Heptameron," etc., the court was influenced in its decision by the fact that they were rare and costly books and would not be bought or appreciated by the class of people from whom unclean publications ought to be withheld.

Recently, a court sought an escape from this apparent confusion and inconsistency and held that the statute is limited to works of pornography. *People* v. *Viking Press*, supra. This offers no real solution. It is the substitution of one term for another. "Pornographic" is defined in Funk & Wagnalls' "New Standard Dictionary" as "of or pertaining to obscene literature; obscene; licentious." The twilight zone between obscenity and pornography, is, therefore, beyond human vision.

With so many books being written yearly by well-known authors, others not too well known, and by would-be authors, a judge-made list of what people should or should not read might not be unwelcome to some persons. However, I, for one, repudiate such an obligation. Book lists, if they are to be prepared, I leave to other and more competent persons. Books, like friends, must be chosen by the readers themselves. We must pick and choose our friends in the book world just as we do in the real world, not looking for perfection in books any more than we do in people. The material must be coextensive with reality, and comprise the ugly as well as the beautiful. It is no part of the duty of courts to exercise a censorship over literary productions or to regulate manners or morals. There are undoubtedly many books intentionally exploiting smut which the public and literature might well do without. Such books the statute condemns, and duty requires that they be suppressed. Filth must remain filth in all ages. *People* v. *Berg*, 241 App. Div. 543, 272 N.Y.S. 586.

In *People* v. *Berg*, supra, the court was unanimous in holding a certain book obscene within the meaning of our statute. Because of the unanimity of opinion, an analysis of the opinion might be useful. The findings of the court may be divided as follows: (1) The book lacks literary merit; (2) it teaches no lesson and points no moral; (3) it describes no period of history and the people or characters of that time and their conduct and habits of life, such, for instance, as the "Elizabethan Age," and no folklore or tales of primitive people in isolated regions; (4) the story is not possibly true or representative of any individual or of any limited class; (5) it is obscene, lewd, lascivious, and disgusting, and nothing more, and was so intended to be for purely mercenary purposes.

[1, 2] This decision, the decision in *U.S. v. One Book Entitled Ulysses*, supra, and the decision in *Halsey* v. *New York Society for Suppression of Vice*, supra, suggest, I believe, suitable tests. Is the book dirt for dirt's sake? *U.S. v. One Book Entitled Ulysses* (D.C.) 5 F. Supp. 182, 184, affirmed (C.C.A.) 72 F.(2d) 705. Stated broadly, the problem is reduced to determination of the following issue: Whether or not, recognizing the latitude afforded all works of literature and of art, and that tastes may differ, a reasonable, cautious, and prudent man environed with the conditions of life as they exist today, and not in some past age, would be justified in believing that the book was obscene and lewd, not in certain passages, but in its main purpose and construction and published for no useful purpose, but simply from a desire to cater to the lowest and most sensual part of human nature? In applying these tests, relevancy of the objectionable parts to the theme, the established reputation of the work in the estimation of approved critics, if the book is modern, and the verdict of the past, if it is ancient, are persuasive pieces of evidence. *U.S.* v. *One Book Entitled Ulysses* (C.C.A.) 72 F.(2d) 705, 708.

[3] Counsel for the defendant urge as factors to be considered by me that the book in question sells for $5 and is part of a very limited edition. Such evidence is immaterial. I cannot say that a 50 cent book is obscene but, that a $5 book or a "de-luxe" edition is respectable. Such a view gives rise to two contrary implications: First, that the rich and extravagant have a monopoly of good manners and morals, which is not true; or, second, that the rich and extravagant had either already been corrupted or were not worth saving, which is also not true.

I have read the book in question carefully. It is, as I have already stated, an autobiography. The author is described in "The Columbia Encyclopedia (1935)" as "one of the most distinguished of contemporary novelists and a leader of French liberal thought." The London Royal Society of Literature, desiring a French member to replace Anatole France, unanimously elected Gide ("André Gide, His Life and Work," by Leon Pierre-Quint). Two of the other words of Gide are "The Counterfeiters" and "Strait is the Gate." Of the former, one reviewer wrote: "The book is one to read and reread; it reveals a hundred new beauties each time, a deeper ironic humor, a more searching tenderness, a more beautiful finesse and tact." New York Evening Post, October 15, 1927. Of the latter book another critic stated: " 'Strait is the Gate,' is deservedly the book which made André Gide famous; it is one of the great classics of French fiction since the death of Flaubert." New Republic, July 23, 1924. Critical opinion on the book in question is divided. In the Saturday Review of Literature, January 4, 1936, Mr. Christopher Morley writes: "Except to special students of its rather intricate author, it is of a devastating and somnambulizing dullness. Those familiar with the author's previous work will value it as the autobiography of a French philosopher of puritan origin, revealing with tormented candor the intellectual and biological griefs of his youth."

Lewis Gannett, writing in the New York Herald Tri-

bune of October 23, 1935, pronounces Gide's autobiography to be "one of those documents of morbidity, which, like the 'Confessions of Rousseau,' is likely to live and perplex and comfort men for generations."

A reviewer in the New Republic of January 22, 1936, makes this observation concerning the portion of the book upon which an attack has been made: "In reality, the amateurs of the scabrous will be disappointed, for Gide is never purer than in 'impurity.' What in another context might have been an obscene anecdote is, in Gide's simple narrative, a subordinate, though necessary, phase in an essentially spiritual adventure."

Autobiographies are written, I suppose, for many reasons: Self-study, request of friends, for the subject's children or descendants, for amusement, no one else likely to do it or to do it so well, for no reason whatsoever. Gide writes his for a penance. "Put the case I am writing it for a penance." Page 4.

Autobiography is a legitimate and an important field of literature. The autobiography of a well-known author or even of an obscure person is sometimes as interesting, illuminating, and as revealing as the autobiography of a famous statesman.

"The value of any biography depends on its being true," said Samuel Johnson. Gide says: "But the whole object of my story is to be truthful." Page 4. In another significant passage, he writes (page 28): "But this is no romance I am writing and I have determined not to flatter myself in these memoirs, either by adding anything agreeable or hiding anything painful." The book contains a few paragraphs dealing with isolated instances of inversion, which, taken by themselves, are undoubtedly vulgar and indecent. The author himself states they are ugly. They are, however, subordinate to, although forming an essential part of, the main theme. The greater portion of the book, however, is devoted to a straightforward and sincere narrative of his early years. The book essentially is an interpretive autobiography. It explains why he acted and not so much how he acted. Gide does not extoll his temporary departure from virtue; he does not deride virtue. In a sense, the book is a piece of special pleading for pardon, in the nature of counsel's speech for clemency.

André Gide is considered a great author; he is therefore entitled to be heard; for the whole value of personal testimony lies in the quality of the witness.

There may be an evil side to many great lives; the vices of a vital nature must not be left out in any estimate of that nature's development. If we eliminate the pages complained of, we would have a distorted and untruthful picture of our subject. If Gide, in unveiling the darker corners of his life, is moved by sincerity, by the deep-rooted desire to appear as he really is, an entire creature, then it is as an entire creature we must study him, omitting nothing. If, and this is not the case, Gide had made vice his major topic, dwelt in with enjoyment for dirt's sake alone, then he would forthwith pass out of our hands into those of the pathologist. We do not go to the sanitarium in quest of friendship.

[4] The book is not obscene, lewd, lascivious, or indecent within the meaning of our statute.

For the reasons above stated, I hold that there is not sufficient cause to hold the defendant for trial. Complaint dismissed; defendant discharged.

■ United States
v.
Levine.
No. 252.

Circuit Court of Appeals, Second Circuit. April 6, 1936.

Harry A. Lieb, of New York City (Morris L. Ernst, Newman Levy, Alexander Lindey, and Eugene M. Kline, all of New York City, of counsel), for appellant.

Lamar Hardy, U.S. Atty., of New York City (Joseph P. Martin, Asst. U.S. Atty., and Thomas B. Flynn, Sp. Asst. U.S. Atty., both of New York City, of counsel), for the United States.

Before MANTON, L. HAND, and AUGUSTUS N. HAND, Circuit Judges.

L. HAND, Circuit Judge.

The defendant was indicted in one count for posting an obscene circular, and in eight subsequent counts for posting obscene circulars advertising obscene books. The jury brought in a verdict of guilty only on the eighth count and the others were dismissed; the circular laid in that count was alleged to have advertised five books, of which only three are before us; they are entitled, "Secret Museum of Anthropology," "Crossways of Sex" and "Black Lust." The first is a reproduction of a collection of photographs, for the most part of nude female savages of different parts of the world; the legitimacy of its pretensions as serious anthropology is, to say the most, extremely tenuous, and, while in the hands of adults it could not be considered obscene, it might be undesirable in those of children or youths. The second book professes to be a scientific treatise on sexual pathology; again its good-faith is more than questionable; for example, the author, a supposititious scientist, remains anonymous. It could have no value to psychiatrists or others genuinely interested in the subject, and in the hands of children it might be injurious. The third is a work of fiction of considerable merit, but patently erotic, describing the adventures of an English girl captured by the Dervishes at the fall of Khartoum and kept in a harem until the Battle of Omdurman, when she is killed. It purports to be a study in sadism and masochism, and would arouse libidinous feelings in almost any reader. There was nothing to distinguish the addressee in the eighth count or to indicate why the jury should have selected him alone. He was only allowed to identify the circular, and objection being sustained to his testimony that he had delivered it over to his father when he got it, as he had been directed. As the record stands he may have been of any age. In the case of several other counts it did appear that the addressees were minors, but the judge declared that the buyer's age was immaterial and took the issue from the jury.

The defendant took a number of exceptions during the trial with most of which we need not concern ourselves, because they will not reappear upon the next trial, which must be had because we cannot accept the charge. The judge first said that the statute (Cr. Code, § 211, 18 U.S.C.A. § 334) was directed against stimulating sensuality, and that this was not to be measured by its effect, either upon "the highly educated" or upon the "highly prudish," but "on the usual, average human mind." This was well enough, so far as it went, but later he in substance took it back. There was a class, he said, "found in every community, the young and immature, the ignorant and those who are sensually inclined"; the statute was meant to protect these and the jury should regard the effect of the books on their minds, rather than on those of "people of a high order of intelligence and those who have reached mature years." If the books contained a "single passage" such as would "excite lustful or sensual desires" in the minds of those "into whose hands they might come," the statute condemned them. This the defendant challenged and the judge said he would modify it, but he did not; the attempted modification was in substance a repetition of what he had said before. The standard so put before the jury was indeed within the doctrine laid down in *Regina* v. *Hicklin,* L.R. 3 Q.B. 360, and *United States* v. *Bennett,* Fed. Cas. No. 14,571, 16 Blatchf. 338, though the Supreme Court has never approved it. *Rosen* v. *U.S.,* 161 U.S. 29, 42, 16 S. Ct. 434, 480, 40 L. Ed. 606, has at times been supposed to do so, and the charge then before the court did indeed follow *Regina* v. *Hicklin,* so that the accused might have raised the point now at bar. But he did not; his only complaint, which the court overruled, was that the judge should not have left it to the jury at all to say whether the publication was obscene, but should have decided the question himself. It is true that *United States* v. *Bennett,* supra, has been followed at nisi prius, but without considering the point specifically, merely repeating the phrase that the decisive question was the effect upon any persons into whose hands the book might fall. *United States* v. *Bebout* (D.C.) 28 F. 522; *United States* v. *Clarke* (D.C.) 38 F. 732; *United States* v. *Smith* (D.C.) 45 F. 476. *United States* v. *Wightman* (D.C.) 29 F. 636, approved this obiter. At times even in these decisions, e.g., *United States* v. *Clarke* and *United States* v. *Smith,* there were intimations that the standard might depend upon those to whom the publication was addressed, and in *Burton* v. *U.S.,* 142 F. 57, 63, the Circuit Court of Appeals for the Eighth Circuit plainly had a relative standard in mind: "It was not a communication from a doctor to his patient, nor a work designed for the use of medical practitioners only." Moreover, the doctrine did not escape criticism [*United States* v. *Ken-*

nerley (D.C.) 209 F. 119], before we, following the New York Court of Appeals in *Halsey* v. *New York Society*, 234 N.Y. 1, 12, 136 N.E. 219, overruled it in two recent decisions, *United States* v. *Dennett*, 39 F.(2d) 564, 76 A.L.R. 1092, *U.S.* v. *One Book* Entitled *Ulysses*, 72 F.(2d) 705.

This earlier doctrine necessarily presupposed that the evil against which the statute is directed so much outweighs all interests of art, letters or science, that they must yield to the mere possibility that some prurient person may get a sensual gratification from reading or seeing what to most people is innocent and may be delightful or enlightening. No civilized community not fanatically puritanical would tolerate such an imposition, and we do not believe that the courts that have declared it, would ever have applied it consistently. As so often happens, the problem is to find a passable compromise between opposing interests, whose relative importance, like that of all social or personal values, is incommensurable. We impose such a duty upon a jury (*Rosen* v. *U.S.*, supra, 161 U.S. 29, 42, 16 S. Ct. 434, 480, 40 L. Ed. 606), because the standard they fix is likely to be an acceptable mesne, and because in such matters a mesne most nearly satisfies the moral demands of the community. There can never be constitutive principles for such judgments, or indeed more than cautions to avoid the personal aberrations of the jurors. We mentioned some of these in *United States* v. *One Book* Entitled *Ulysses*, supra, 72 F.(2d) 705; the work must be taken as a whole, its merits weighed against its defects (*Konda* v. *U.S.* [C.C.A. 7] 166 F. 91, 22 L.R.A. [N.S.] 304); if it is old, its accepted place in the arts must be regarded; if new, the opinions of competent critics in published reviews or the like may be considered; what counts is its effect, not upon any particular class, but upon all those whom it is likely to reach. Thus "obscenity" is a function of many variables, and the verdict of the jury is not the conclusion of a syllogism of which they are to find only the minor premiss, but really a small bit of legislation ad hoc, like the standard of care.

The case was not tried on this theory; on the contrary the judge supposed that a book or picture was obscene or innocent by an absolute standard independent of its readers; moreover he thought that a single passage might condemn it, regardless of its merits as a whole. He was in error as to both points, and the only question is whether the mistakes were serious enough to upset the conviction. Judge Manton and I think that they were; Judge Augustus N. Hand believes that "Crossways of Sex" was so plainly obscene that the errors may be disregarded. Our reversal does not mean that on another trial the proper standard can under no circumstances refer to adolescents. It may appear that the prospective buyer in the eighth count was a youth and that the accused had reason to suppose that he was. The evil against which the statute is directed, would then be the possible injury to such a youthful reader. It is when the crime consists of importing the work, or offering it for general sale, that the test cannot be found in the interests of those to whom it is sent, though abnormally susceptible, lest in their protection the interests may be sacrificed of others who might profit from the work; and that some compromise must be made. But even when the crime consists of a single sale, and so may be judged by possible injury to the buyer, the book must be taken as a whole. In this case the jury may find "Crossways of Sex" and "Black Lust" obscene when sent to any reader; "Secret Museum of Anthropology" can be so regarded only if sent to youths. The standard must be the likelihood that the work will so much arouse the salacity of the reader to whom it is sent as to outweigh any literary, scientific or other merits it may have in that reader's hands; of this the jury is the arbiter.

The judge refused to allow in evidence a list of purchasers of the books, among whom were a number of well-known persons. He was right. Such a list taken alone told nothing of the standing of the works in the minds of the community; even respectable persons may have a taste for salacity. Obviously it would be impossible without hopelessly confusing the issues to undertake any analysis of such a list by finding out why each buyer bought. On the other hand it is reasonable to allow in evidence published reviews of qualified critics—quite another thing incidentally from expert witnesses at the trial—for such evidence does not lead far afield and is rationally helpful, though in the end it is the jury who must declare what the standard shall be. So far as that may be a menace to the free development of the arts, it is a risk which Congress has seen fit to impose, and which we cannot gainsay, even if we would.

Judgment reversed; new trial ordered.

MANTON, Circuit Judge, concurs in the result.

■ Ultem Publications, Inc.,
v.
Arrow Publications, Inc., *et al.*

Supreme Court, Special Term, New York County. March 18, 1938.

Louis H. Solomon, of New York City, for plaintiff.
Weil, Gotshal & Manges, of New York City (H. S. Manges and G. Kaslow, both of New York City, of counsel), for defendants.

COTILLO, Justice.

When this case was tried, the court was of the opinion that the only question involved was the alleged unfair competition of the defendant in publishing a magazine in simulation of that of the plaintiff both as to the name used and the set-up of the magazine itself. Both litigants are publishers of magazines bearing a name the outstanding feature of which is the word "stocking." Neither one caters to the stocking trade and neither one is recognized or considered by the trade to be a trade paper. Upon reading the minutes of the trial and after an examination of the exhibits consisting of the magazines themselves, an entirely new atmosphere was thrown around the case. A prudent caution required that this examination of the exhibits be made in my own room, and the examination compelled me to place the exhibits under lock and key in order to prevent them from falling into the hands of my young daughter. Why was this necessary? Only a detailed description of the two magazines themselves can supply the reason. Upon the trial copies of the plaintiff's magazine, "Silk Stocking Stories," for the months of January, February, March, April, May, June, and July were marked in evidence. Each one of these issues bears on its cover the picture of a young and attractive woman in a state of deshabille, and permissible only in the sanctum of woman's boudoir. Each picture features nakedness, particularly as to her lower limbs and the naked breasts. The table of contents partly published on the cover concern stories each of which relate only to sex matters and bear names of double meaning, such as the "Key to Cora," "Girl in Danger," "Promise Not to Love Me," and "Come and Get Me." The type of fiction is that which has no literary merit and could only appeal to the type of person described in *New Metropolitan Fiction, Inc., v. Dell Pub. Co.*, 57 App. D.C. 244, 19 F.2d 718. Each of the stories are written around and concern sex. The pictures in the body of the magazine are confined to pictures of girls clad with nothing but underwear and stockings, and make a featured display of their arms and breasts, and thus there is an inordinate emphasis of these parts of the body.

But an examination of the magazines is necessary in view of the decision the court is here making. The January issue of the Silk Stocking Magazine reveals a cover upon which there is the picture of a girl, the main feature of which consists of her posing with her legs showing her bare skin between her hips and her stockings, her clothing is of the scantiest, and her breasts are exposed and emphasized. The cover also contains the names of three alleged pieces of fiction under the following names: "Promise—Not to Love Me," "The Key to Cora," and "Girl in Danger." The inside pages contain twenty-four pictures of girls in various stages of deshabille and posing in suggestive and lewd positions. The stories are suggestive of illicit love affairs and some contain outright suggestions of sexual affairs between unmarried persons. One in particular is the story called the "Louse." In this story the female character complains to her friend about the insult received at the hands of a man who after giving her a bedroom in his apartment did not attempt to enter the room, and to quote her own words: "You must be an awful fool, Isabelle. But if you'd been in that room instead of me you'd know exactly how I feel. I locked the door of course, but that— that louse, he never even tried the handle." The last part of this sentence was printed in capital letters. In the story "The Key to Cora," the theme is about a young girl passing the night in her bedroom with an unmarried male, after a bet had been made as to her virtue. In "Promise Not to Love Me," the author uses as the basis of his story

"the whirlwind, glorious temptations of youth had their way" through the excess use of alcohol. "Girl in Danger" is a description of petting parties. Under the title "Sheer Nonsense," the magazine prints jokes and sayings each having a double-edge meaning and salacious ideas, such as, "We heard of an old maid who sued a hotel for mental cruelty. They gave her a room between two honeymooning couples." One of the two advertisements contained in this issue is that advertising sex harmony and eugenics, with such statements as to "know the amazing truth about sex and love," "attract the opposite sex," and "The Forbidden Secrets of Sex are Daringly Revealed." Also set forth in this advertisement is "What Every Man Should Know," with the following subtitles, "The Sexual Embrace," "Secrets of the Honey-Moon," "Mistakes of Early Marriage," "Venereal Diseases," "How to Regain Virility," "Sexual Starvation," "Glands and Sex Instincts," "The Truth About Abuse," also, "What Every Woman Should Know," with the subtitles, "Joys of Perfect Mating," "What to Allow a Lover to Do," "Intimate Feminine Hygiene," "Birth Control Chart," "How to Attract and Hold Men," "Sexual Slavery of Women," and "Sex Organs." The other issues contain the same kind of filth and have the same set-up as to stories and pictures. In the April issue of the magazine the publishers set forth their policy as follows: "Statement of Policy"—"The Editors know what happens to a girl who wears cotton stockings— Nothing."

The make-up of the defendant's magazine differs from that of the plaintiff practically only in the matter of title. The front cover and the pictures in the magazine itself contain the same type of undressed women in suggestive poses. The stories have the same general theme of sex and sex relations. They contain the same type of double-meaning jokes and wisecracks. The pictures in both magazines are for the purpose of merely appealing to neurotic and moronic minds minus even the doubtful virtue of being exotic. The defendant's issue carries the same advertisement for "Eugenics and Sex Harmony" as that of the plaintiff's magazine, including the topics mentioned above. The defendant differs in one respect from the plaintiff inasmuch as it carried a serial, each issue of the magazines containing the stories of adventures sought by a wealthy young man in his endeavors to find out what makes "Girls tick." His adventures consist of drinking to excess and indulging in moments of passion participated in by women, all of whom are either criminals or sex crazy.

The November issue, a typical example of defendant's magazine, carries an advertisement of what is commonly termed exotic literature. The advertisement is entitled "$12 worth of thrills for 98¢" and offers such gems of degenerate literature as "Broadway Racketeers." This book is described in the advertisement as describing the "lusts of the racket mob." Among the other books described are "Replenishing Jessica," a book concerned only with the multitudinous sex adventures of the heroine, "The Time of Her Life," a description of the adventures of a girl who inherited the mad love of pleasure from her mother, the "Grass Widow." Another disgusting book advertised in this issue is "Playthings of Desire," a story of passion. The very titles of the stories published in the defendant's magazine are suggestive and moronic, such as "Fresh Guy," "What Makes Girls Tick," "Sexes & Sevens," "Karen Becomes Exotic," and "Country Slicker."

If justification is sought for the court's relatively great detailed description of the photographs described in the magazines of both litigants, it lies in the obvious answer that pictorial effects, especially such as those in the exhibits before me, can create much greater and more lasting harm on the impressionistic than may be truthfully charged against the most lurid, morbid, or exaggerated descriptions of sex crime which the public has at times charged against our more popular newspapers.

The people of the State of New York, recognizing the difference between art, science, and smut, have enacted proper legislation to prevent the sale and distribution of magazines such as those offered by the parties to this litigation. The purpose of this legislation is to prevent the publication, distribution, and sale of lascivious or obscene prints and publications, the tendency of which is to excite lustful desire. This purpose has been ably sustained by our courts and, although the great majority of judicial decisions is confined to criminal prosecution, the court is of the opinion that when such publications are called to the attention of a court of equity the court should not shut its eyes to the facts.

[1] That legislation affording public protection is found in section 1141 of the Penal Law. The purpose of that very section, as aptly stated in People on complaint of *Sumner* v. *Miller*, 155 Misc. 446, 279 N.Y.S. 583, was to suppress, not bona fide literary effort, but the exploitation of smut. In *People v. Berg*, 241 App. Div. 543, 545, 272 N.Y.S. 586, 587, 588, the Appellate Division of the Second Department affirmed a conviction for having in his (defendant's) possession an obscene and lewd book. In its opinion it held that to "be deemed obscene" it must show "sexual impurity" and result in "the exciting of lustful and lecherous thoughts and desires" or "tend" to stir sex impulses or "lead to sexually impure thoughts." The opinion further stated, in refusing to name the book in question, "In addition it lacks literary merit. It teaches no lesson and points no moral. It describes no period of history and the people or characters of that time and their conduct and habits of life. * * * In our opinion it is obscene, lewd, lascivious and disgusting, and nothing more; and was so intended to be for purely mercenary purposes." The magazines involved in this case fit definitely the book described in this opinion. They have no literary or artistic merit, either in their stories or pictures. As they are not trade magazines, they can have no purpose in their display of stockings and lingerie, except to appeal to that class of people described in *People v. Muller*, 96 N.Y. 408, 411, 48 Am. Rep. 635, as "those whose minds are open to such immoral influences, and who might come into contact with it."

Presiding Justice Martin, of our Appellate Division, in writing the majority opinion in *People v. Pesky*, 230 App. Div. 200, at page 204, 243 N.Y.S. 193, 197, affirmed 254 N.Y. 373, 173 N.E. 227, has to my mind properly and distinctly set forth, the test by which these matters must be determined. He wrote: "These matters must be judged by normal people and not by the abnormal. Conditions would be deplorable if abnormal people were permitted to regulate such matters. Of course there are some people who seem to be unable to find anything obscene in anything written. It is very clear that the author of the book now before us for consideration was not thinking of the spiritual, but devoted the whole book to the animal instincts of the human race. His efforts were not a lesson in morality, nor an attempt to uplift the mind of the reader, but an attempt to depict, in a manner that might possibly be called clever, adulterous relations, vulgar and disgusting in the extreme."

The stories and photographs in the magazines of both plaintiff and defendant justify all that has been said in the quotation above from *People v. Pesky*.

We face a current drive today against sex perverts, all forms of vice engendered by loose morals, and even positive degeneracy. Some portions of the public press print with almost gruesome detail sex practices involved in crimes for which the accused frequently are convicted after trial, and for which crimes the condemned often expiate with their lives. These descriptions of sex crimes under the guise of "news" find avid readers among our youth, are even fed serially to their plastic minds, often being printed minus all condemnatory emphasis, so that the youth and unsophisticated might well secure the feeling that such abuses are more widespread than they actually are.

Indeed, it would not be amiss to say that magazines of this character are actually more pernicious, definitely more harmful, than any newspaper which dares flagrantly to publish in untoward fashion current stories of sex crimes.

[2] In the case at bar, we do not have a criminal charge, but that is not the criterion. Courts of equity have and maintain moral standards based on social needs and demands both. The youth of this city require more than mere negative protection, if incubuslike, the vices described above are not to spread.

I wish our youth to learn safety in avoidance, but not by paying the bitter price of experience. Only by protracted exposure to that kind of literature where conspicuously absent are all forms of salaciousness and lewdness, and which are beyond any taint or suspicion of immorality, can this social objective be obtained. This is the price which any community must pay to protect its youth and which a policy of eternal vigilance requires, demands, and must exact. Only by such positive measures can we protect the minds of our growing boys and girls from this pestilence and noisome filth. These are not too strong words.

If, on the other hand, it appears that the publishing of these salacious stories and daring photographs are designed to stir up jaded sex appetites of those of advanced years, then again, such antisocial consequences warrant no aid from a court of equity, whether the case involved be one litigant against another, as here, or whether it be a case involving mutual incrimination. Surely to such persons as these others, advanced in years, court sermons are but vain whisperings lightly brushed aside.

[3] Here we have the pot calling the kettle black, and equity will furnish no aid in the furtherance of purposes unsound socially as well as tainted by depressed moral levels.

One is no prude who fails to find in the magazines here submitted any compliance with the social standards required in our literature of today. A reading of the details relating to the stories and photographs set forth in the early part of this opinion compels the only possible decision which can be made here.

[4] Granted that there be simulation both as to name and as to the extent that the key word "stocking" current with both magazines is used; that a legitimate doubt is raised as to which identity is involved, the fact remains

that the same degree of licentiousness is involved in the stories and photographs of both litigants. The significant thing here is that the salient objectives which these approximate similarities are designed to promote lack distinguishing earmarks.

Granted also that the same run of advertising, size of paper, kind of jokes used—that these all display such likeness as to establish the trespass here alleged, still no proof has been submitted that the conscience of this court of equity has been moved so as to require that it be employed on behalf of one as against the other.

This court cannot be unmindful that its decrees enjoining one, by negative implication, give a clean bill of health to the other left free. Such left-handed justice would not do true equity under all the circumstances here.

In fact, it is indubitably established in my mind that, regardless of which position either of these litigants occupied in this litigation, only a calloused equity, hindered and fettered by subservience to legal rule (which it is not), could extend its arm and grant the aid sought.

In the case at bar, the litigants both protest their literary and moral sufficiency. It is sought in this litigation to secure and have made available the high privileges found within the broad reach of the arm of equity. By the same token each must be prepared to stand to forfeit penalties, if any, such as that same court may see fit to impose.

The court has no power to stop the publication of magazines of this type in a civil proceeding, but neither will it lend itself to granting to one the sole right to publish such filth. Nor will it grant either magazine a cloak of respectability by issuing an injunction. [Italics ed.]. These magazines can have no useful place in the world of literature, and the very selection of the names is indicative of the fact that the publishers' sole desire is a financial return for the dumping of obscene and filthy publications at a cheap price where the young, immature, and impressionable people can buy.

Others besides this court cannot but be impressed by recent figures quoted in the public press showing that for the seven years from 1929 to 1935, inclusive, sex offense cases averaged 897. In 1936, the increase over this average rose 40 per cent.; in 1937 it is jumped to 110 per cent. In sex offenses other than rape, in 1936 alone, the increase over this seven-year period was 84 per cent.; and in 1937, figures taken from the New York Times cite a 307 per cent. rise.

Obviously, no specific part of such increase can be, nor is it, attributed to the existence of these magazines. Yet the trend behind the above figures might well reflect a rise synchronizing with the increased subscription of magazines such as these are. To reverse this trend means to minimize the influence of both these magazines.

In the interest of common decency and under the powers of the equity side of court, the prayer for an injunction will be denied.

Settle proposed findings of fact.

■ United States
v.
Rebhuhn *et al.* No. 210.

Circuit Court of Appeals, Second Circuit. Feb. 13, 1940.

Frank Aranow, of New York City (Arthur Garfield Hays, Paul Blanshard, Martin A. Roeder, S. Richard Silbert, and Oscar Stabiner, all of New York City, of counsel), for appellants.

John T. Cahill, U.S. Atty. (Richard Delafield and Boris Kostelanetz, Asst. U.S. Attys., both of New York City, of counsel), for appellee.

Before L. HAND, AUGUSTUS N. HAND, and CHASE, Circuit Judges.

L. HAND, Circuit Judge.

[1, 2] The three defendants appeal from a judgment of conviction under § 334, Title 18, U.S. Code, 18 U.S.C.A. § 334, for sending obscene printed matter through the mails, and for a conspiracy to do so. The offending matter consisted of circulars which advertised books for sale, and both the books and the circulars were charged to have been obscene. The defendants raise a number of objections of which we will dispose in the order in which they appear in their brief. The first is that the statute is unconstitutional because it lays down no definite standard of criminal liability. The Supreme Court overruled this in *Rosen* v. *United States*, 161 U.S. 29, 16 St. Ct. 434, 480, 40 L. Ed. 606, and many indictments have since been found, and many persons tried and convicted. These very defendants challenged the indictment at bar in an action brought under § 380a of Title 28, U. S. Code, 28 U.S.C.A. § 380a, and were unsuccessful. If the question is to be reopened the Supreme Court must open it. *Tyomies Publishing Company* v. *United States*, 6 Cir., 211 F. 385.

The next question, and the only serious one in the case, is whether the books and circulars were obscene. This cannot be properly understood without some statement of the enterprise as a whole in which the defendants were engaged. One of them, Ben Rebhuhn, had done business under the name of "Falstaff Press" before any of the mailings here in question. Later the business was incorporated under the same name, and the corporation sent out many thousands of circulars at random; that is to say, the addressees were not selected with any eye to whether they might have a legitimate interest in the books advertised, and whether, on the contrary, it was not likely, or even reasonably certain, that those who bought would do so to gratify their lewdness. Of the fifteen counts in the indictment thirteen were for mailing circulars to individuals, and these made up a group of two girls of fifteen and nineteen, a woman of twenty-one, another who was a trained nurse, a fifth, employed by the Treasury Department, and a sixth who was a chiropractor; in addition there were two lawyers, an assistant United States attorney, a doctor, a business man, a boy at school, and, mirabile dictu, the financial agent of a society for the suppression of vice. The defendants assert that the circulars were not obscene, if taken alone, even if they described the books in such a way that the reader would suppose them to be sexually exciting; and we shall assume arguendo that they made a case only under that part of the section which forbids sending information of where obscene writings can be obtained. It was the books that offended, if offence there was.

[3–5] These purported to be translations of works, written by authors who were either proved, or may be assumed, to have been men of scientific standing, as anthropologists, psychiatrists, and the like. Most of the books could lawfully have passed through the mails, if directed to those who would be likely to use them for the purposes for which they were written, though that was not true of one or two; for example, of that entitled, "Sex Life in England," which was a collection of short and condensed erotic bits, culled from various sources, and plainly put together as pornography. The defendants employed one, Malkin, to make the translations, which he did under various names; and, although there was no evidence as to how complete or accurate his work was, we will assume that it was honest, and that the works themselves had a place, though a limited one, in anthropology and in psychotherapy. They might also have been lawfully sold to laymen who wished seriously to study the sexual practices of savage or barbarous peoples, or sexual aberrations; in other words, most of them were not obscene per se. In several decisions we have held that the statute does not in all circumstances forbid the dissemination of such publications, and that in the trial of an indictment the prosecution must prove that the accused has abused a conditional privilege, which the law gives him. *United States v. Dennett*, 2 Cir., 39 F. 2d 564, 76 A.L.R. 1092; *United States v. One Book* Entitled, Ulysses by James Joyce, 2 Cir., 72 F. 2d 705; *United States v. Levine*, 2 Cir., 83 F. 2d 156. However, in the case at bar, the prosecution succeeded upon that issue, when it showed that the defendants had indiscriminately flooded the mails with advertisements, plainly designed merely to catch the prurient, though under the guise of distributing works of scientific or literary merit. We do not mean that the distributor of such works is charged with a duty to insure that they shall reach only proper hands, nor need we say what care he must use, for these defendants exceeded any possible limits; the circulars were no more than appeals to the salaciously disposed, and no sensible jury could have failed to pierce the fragile screen, set up to cover that purpose.

[6, 7] Since we are assuming arguendo that most of the circulars were not, however, themselves obscene, the question arises whether it was error to couple them with the books in the indictment. The indictment was not duplicitous. (*Burton* v. United States, 8 Cir., 142 F. 57) nor was

there a material variance. The only possible harm, even on the assumption we are making, was that the jury might have based guilt upon the circulars and not upon the books; and if the case was properly presented to them, that danger did not exist. It is true, however, that the judge did not distinguish between the two, and that in theory the jury might have based conviction on the circulars alone, though that chance was extremely remote, for the purport of the enterprise as a whole was unmistakable, as we have said. Be that as it may, the defendants did not ask the judge to tell the jury that the circulars were not obscene; and the fact that during the argument on the motion to dismiss the indictment the point had been bruited, was not enough. If they were dissatisfied with the way in which the judge presented the case, they were bound to tell him so that he might mend his instructions. This they did not do.

[8] Next they challenge the sufficiency of the proof to connect them with mailing the circulars, or to charge them with knowledge of the contents of the books. The evidence against them on these points was overwhelming. Ben Rebhuhn had done business as the "Falstaff Press," as we have already said, and after the company was incorporated, he signed one of the renewals of its lease. When one of the Post Office inspectors talked with him, as he did several times, and brought to his attention a number of complaints made by those who had received the circulars, he admitted that he was the owner of the business, and discussed the books advertised with familiarity, even saying that he was the author of some of them. Moreover, he had taken out the copyrights on nearly all. Ann Rebhuhn was the president of the corporation, and told the inspector that she was part owner of the business; she too was familiar with the books, and did not suggest that she had been ignorant of their contents, though she must have understood that the whole enterprise was under suspicion, and was being investigated for that reason. Ben Raeburn's name was upon many of the circulars and he told the inspector that he was office manager, and the proof-reader of the circulars, an admission which alone was enough to charge him with knowledge of the contents of the books, which the circulars disclosed beyond any question. Nothing more was necessary to prove that all three defendants were the moving spirits in the enterprise. The books put in evidence were, with one exception, certified as identical with copies filed in the Congressional Library upon securing the copyrights. The possibility that the books advertised, though they corresponded with these not only in title, but in contents—as described in the circulars—were in fact other publications, does not deserve discussion.

[9] Next it is objected that the judge refused to allow in evidence a copy of Havelock Ellis's "Psychology of Sex," in which it appeared that he had spoken with commendation of the works of several of the authors of the books in question. This evidence was offered in supposed conformity with what we said in *United States v. One Book* Entitled Ulysses by James Joyce, supra, 72 F. 2d at page 708; and *United States v. Levine*, supra, 83 F. 2d at page 157; i.e., that the opinions of experts were competent to show the standing of the challenged publications. The refusal was error, because the foundation for receiving the book had been laid by proving Ellis' standing as an authority on the subject; it was not necessary that he should himself have been a witness. But the evidence, though competent, was neither necessary, nor even important. As we have

already said, the books were not obscene per se; they had a proper use, but the defendants woefully misused them, and it was that misuse which constituted the gravamen of the crime. Thus it meant little to prove the standing of their authors, and the error ought not to be ground for reversal.

[10] Next the defendants complain of the judge's definition of obscenity in his charge to the jury. It is true that this was contradictory; at the outset he adopted the old and abandoned standard of *Regina* v. *Hicklin*, L.R. 3 Q.B. 360, which he immediately followed by that of *United States* v. *Levine*, supra, and *United States* v. *Dennett*, supra; apparently unconscious that there was any difference between the two. The defendants never objected to the first definition. At the conclusion of the colloquial charge they merely excepted to "any definitions made * * * of the term obscene"; and that was clearly not enough; and later, when the judge himself brought up the first definition and asked what objection the defendants had to it, they merely replied that "the statute stated nothing about any tendency." It is not clear what they meant by this last, but certainly they were not insisting on the doctrine of *United States* v. *Dennett*, supra, or *United States* v. *Levine*, as opposed to what the judge offered. So far as can be inferred, at no time did they wish the jury to be told of any conditional privilege, perhaps for the obvious reason that it would not have helped them, since they had shamefully abused it.

[11–13] They next object that the jury did not adequately examine the evidence, for which they rely upon the short time—less than three hours—that they were out.

Aside from the fact that this was a question for the judge alone in deciding whether to grant a new trial, the point is without merit anyway. It needed less than the time they actually took for reasonably sagacious men and women to see exactly what the defendants had been doing, and how transparent was the pretence that they were not simply pandering to the lascivious cravings of their customers; it would have impugned their intelligence had they hesitated longer. Again, when the judge refused to poll them as to whether they had read all the documents, he was clearly right. It was unimportant whether they had; and in any case polling them could have had no other purpose than to impeach their verdict by showing how they had reached it. *McDonald* v. *Pless*, 238 U.S. 264, 35 S. Ct. 783, 59 L. Ed. 1300.

[14] The last supposed error is that the indictment was invalid because it did not set forth the circulars in full; or did not, in the alternative, allege that they were too obscene to be extended upon the records of the court. That, if it was a defect at all, did not extend to the books themselves as to which the allegation was made. We are assuming that the contents of the circulars was important only as it described the books fully enough to advertise them for sale; moreover, copies of all of them were delivered to the defendants before trial in a bill of particulars. It would be absurd to reverse the conviction for such a formal defect; § 391, Title 28, U.S. Code, 28 U.S.C.A. § 391.

The convictions are affirmed.

■ Parmelee

v.

United States. No. 7332.

United States Court of Appeals for the District of Columbia. Decided May 14, 1940.

Rehearing Denied May 12, 1940.

Edmund D. Campbell, of Washington, D.C., for appellant.

David A. Pine, U.S. Atty., and *H. L. Underwood and John L. Laskey*, Asst. U.S. Attys., all of Washington, D.C., for appellee.

Before GRONER, Chief Justice, and MILLER and VINSON, Associate Justices.

MILLER, Associate Justice.

The Collector of Customs at the Port of Washington, in the District of Columbia, seized six books, entitled "Nudism in Modern Life," which had been imported by Maurice Parmelee via the mails, from England. The United States Attorney filed a libel in the court below seeking the confiscation and destruction of the books. The court determined that they were properly subject to libel and should be destroyed. The applicable statute,[1] so far as pertinent, reads as follows: "All persons are prohibited from importing into the United States from any foreign country * * * any obscene book, pamphlet, paper, writing, advertisement, circular, print, picture, drawing, or other representation, figure, or image on or of paper or other material * * *." The lower court found as follows:

"4. Upon examination of the book the Court finds nothing in the written text thereof which could be considered obscene or immoral. The case of the Government is predicated upon photographic illustrations which appear at various places in the book.

"5. The illustrations which are asserted to be obscene apparently have no relevancy to the written text at the

---

1 Section 305(a), Title III of the Tariff Act of June 17, 1930, 46 Stat. 688, 19 U.S.C.A. § 1305(a).

place in which each of said photographic illustrations is set in the book. The said photographs or illustrations, upon examination, are obscene and within the condemnation of the statute under the authority of which seizure was made and the libel filed."

On argument, it was conceded by the government that the text of the books and most of the photographs are unobjectionable. All that remains in dispute, therefore, is whether the books are objectionable, within the meaning of the statute, because of the presence therein of three or four photographs in which appear full front views of nude female figures, and two photographs in which nude male and female figures appear together. The photographs complained of are uncolored and apparently unretouched and are approximately 2¼ × 3¼ inches in size. The human figures which appear therein are approximately 1½ inches in height.

[1, 2] Our decision of the case requires no expression of opinion, judicial or otherwise, concerning the merits or demerits of nudity as it may be practiced or professed. The only question before us is whether the book "Nudism in Modern Life" is obscene, in the light of the applicable standard intended to be established by the statute. But obscenity is not a technical term of the law and is not susceptible of exact definition.[2] Although the word has been variously defined,[3] the test applied in many of the

earlier cases was that laid down by Lord Chief Justice Cockburn in *Regina* v. *Hicklin*,[4] as follows: "* * * whether the tendency of the matter charged as obscenity is to deprave and corrupt those whose minds are open to such immoral influences, and into whose hands a publication of this sort may fall."[5] And the rule was applied to those portions of the book charged to be obscene rather than to the book as a whole.[6] But more recently this standard has been repudiated, and for it has been substituted the test that a book must be considered as a whole, in its effect, not upon any particular class, but upon all those whom it is likely to reach.[7] Thus considered, obscenity is, as Judge Learned Hand has said, "a function of many variables, and the verdict of the jury is not the conclusion of a syllogism of which they are to find only the minor premiss, but really a small bit of legislation ad hoc, like the standard of care."[8] But in every case it is a question of law for the court to determine, in the first instance, whether the challenged publication can have the tendency attributed to it by the government, and it is only when that determination has been made in the affirmative that the jury is called upon to decide whether it has such a tendency in fact.[8a] In our opinion, the book "Nudism in Modern Life" cannot reasonably be said to fall within the prohibition of the statute.

Probably the fundamental reason why the word obscene is not susceptible of exact definition is that such intangible moral concepts as it purports to connote, vary in meaning from one period to another.[9] It is customary to see, now,

---

[2] *Timmons* v. *United States*, 6 Cir., 85 F. 204, 205. See generally, Alpert, Judicial Censorship of Obscene Literature, 52 Harv. L. Rev. 40.

[3] Thus: Offensive to chastity of mind or to modesty; expressing or presenting to the mind or view something that delicacy, purity, and decency forbid to be exposed (Webster, New International Dictionary); offensive to modesty, decency, or chastity; impure; unchaste; indecent; lewd (Century Dictionary; Black's Law Dictionary; *Timmons* v. *United States*, 6 Cir., 85 F. 204, 205); offensive to the senses; repulsive; disgusting; foul; filthy (*Holcombe* v. *State*, 5 Ga. App. 47, 50, 62 S.E. 647, 648; *Williams* v. *State*, 130 Miss. 827, 843, 94 So. 882, 884); calculated to corrupt, deprave and debauch the morals of the people (See *United States* v. *Males*, D.C. Ind., 51 F. 41, 42; *Commonwealth* v. *Landis*, 8 Phila. 453; 2 Wharton, Criminal Law, 12th Ed. 1932, § 1942. See, also, Schroeder, "Obscene" Literature and Constitutional Law [1911] 33 et seq.) and promote violation of the law (*Missouri* v. *Pfenninger*, 76 Mo. App. 313, 317); of such character as to deprave and corrupt those whose minds are open to such immoral influences (*Regina* v. *Hicklin*, [1868] L.R. 3 Q.B. 360, 369, 371; *United States* v. *Moore*, W.D. Mo., 129 F. 159, 161); calculated to lower that standard which we regard as essential to civilization, or calculated, with the ordinary person, to deprave his morals or lead to impure purposes (*Dunlop* v. *United States*, 165 U.S. 486, 17 S. Ct. 375, 41 L. Ed. 799); licentious and libidinous and tending to excite feelings of an impure or unchaste character (*Duncan* v. *United States*, 9 Cir., 48 F. 2d 128, 131–133, certiorari denied, 283 U.S. 863, 51 S. Ct. 656, 75 L. Ed. 1468); having relation to sexual impurity (*Swearingen* v. *United States*, 161 U.S. 446, 451, 16 S. Ct. 562, 40 L. Ed. 765; *Dysart* v. *United States*, 272 U.S. 655, 657, 47 S. Ct 234, 71 L. Ed. 461; *Rosen* v. *United States*, 161 U.S. 29, 16 S. Ct. 434, 480, 40 L. Ed. 606. See *United States* v. *Limehouse*, 285 U.S. 424, 52 S. Ct. 412, 76 L. Ed. 843); tending to stir the sex impulses or to lead to sexually impure and lustful thoughts (*United States* v. *One Book Called "Ulysses,"* S.D.N.Y., 5 F. Supp. 182, 184, affirmed, 2 Cir., 72 F. 2d 705; *United States* v. *One Obscene Book Entitled "Married Love,"* S.D.N.Y., 48 F. 2d 821; *United States* v. *One Book* Entitled "Contraception," S.D.N.Y., 51 F. 2d 525); tending to corrupt the morals of youth or to lower the standards of right and wrong, specifically as to the sexual relation (*People* v. *Berg*, 241 App. Div. 543, 272 N.Y.S. 586).

[4] [1868] L.R. 3 Q.B. 360, 369.

[5] *MacFadden* v. *United States*, 3 Cir., 165 F. 51, writ of error denied, 213 U.S. 288, 29 S. Ct. 490, 53 L. Ed. 801; *Knowles* v. *United States*, 8 Cir., 170 F. 409; *United States* v. *Bennett*, Fed. Cas. No. 14,571, 16 Blatch. 338; *United States* v. *Clarke*, E.D. Mo., 38 F. 500; *United States* v. *Harmon*, D. Kan., 45 F. 414, reversed on other grounds, 50 F. 921; *United States* v. *Smith*, E.D. Wis., 45 F. 476; *United States* v. *Wightman*, W.D. Pa., 29 F. 636; *United States* v. *Bebout*, N.D. Ohio, 28 F. 522. See generally, Alpert, Judicial Censorship of Obscene Literature, 52 Harv. L. Rev. 40, 53.

[6] *United States* v. *Kennerley*, S.D.N.Y., 209 F. 119, 120.

[7] *United States* v. *Levine*, 2 Cir., 83 F. 2d 156, 157; *United States* v. *One Book* Entitled "Ulysses," 2 Cir., 72 F. 2d 705; *United States* v. *Dennett*, 2 Cir., 39 F. 2d 564, 76 A.L.R. 1092.

[8] *United States* v. *Levine*, 2 Cir., 83 F. 2d 156, 157. See *United States* v. *Kennerley*, S.D.N.Y., 209 F. 119, 121: "If letters must, like other kinds of conduct, be subject to the social sense of what is right, it would seem that a jury should in each case establish the standard much as they do in cases of negligence."

[8a] *Magon* v. *United States*, 9 Cir., 248 F. 201, 203; *United States* v. *One Obscene Book* Entitled "Married Love," S.D.N.Y., 48 F. 2d 821; *United States* v. *Dennett*, 2 Cir., 39 F. 2d 564, 568, 76 A.L.R. 1092.

[9] Cardozo, Paradoxes of Legal Science (1927) 37: "Law accepts as the pattern of its justice the morality of the community whose conduct it assumes to regulate." *People* v. *Miller*, 155 Misc. 446, 279 N.Y.S. 583, 584: "The criterion of decency is fixed by time, place, geography, and all the elements that make for a constantly changing world. A practice regarded as decent in one period may be indecent in another." *Redd* v. *State*, 7 Ga. App. 575, 581, 582, 67 S.E. 709, 711, 712: "* * * it will not do to measure modern morals according to the standards of ancient and Biblical times. King Solomon with his thousand wives would not be tolerated in Georgia; and King David, he the man after God's own heart, could hardly justify his whole

in the daily newspapers and in the magazines, pictures of modeled male and female underwear which might have been shocking to readers of an earlier era. An age accustomed to the elaborate bathing costumes of forty years ago might have considered obscene the present-day beach costume of halters and trunks. But it is also true that the present age might regard those of 1900 as even more obscene.[10]

[3, 4] With such considerations in mind, perhaps the most useful definition of obscene is that suggested in the case of *United States* v. *Kennerley*,[11] i.e., that it indicates "the present critical point in the compromise between candor and shame at which the community may have arrived here and now." But when we attempt to locate that critical point in the situation of the present case, we find nothing in the record to guide us except the book itself. The question is a difficult one, as to which the expert opinions of psychologists and sociologists would seem to be helpful if not necessary. Assumptions to the contrary which appear in some of the earlier cases,[12] reveal the profound ignorance of psychology and sociology[13] which prevailed generally, when those opinions were written. More recently, in the cases and textbooks, the desirability and pertinence of such evidence has been suggested.[14] Lacking such assistance in the present case, we can compensate for it in some measure by noticing, judicially, evidence which is thus available to us.

[5] It cannot be assumed that nudity is obscene per se and under all circumstances. Even the application of the

life according to the provisions of the Penal Code of this state. Our standards of morals have advanced since then, and our standards of decency have advanced accordingly. The times—the prevailing state of public morality at the particular period—more largely than any other one thing, determine what the decencies and indecencies of that particular day and generation shall be. Many things regarded (by law as well as by secular opinion) a hundred years ago as being indecent are not so regarded now; and, on the other hand, the present age has developed decencies and indecencies unknown to or unobserved by our forefathers."

[10] *People* v. *Miller*, 155 Misc. 446, 279 N.Y.S. 583, 584: "The practice of 'bundling' approved in Puritan days would be frowned upon today. * * * Twenty-five years ago women were arrested and convicted for appearing on the beach attired in sleeveless bathing suits, or without stockings. * * * In 1906, the play 'Sappho' was suppressed because the leading lady was carried up a flight of stairs in the arms of a man. In 1907, Mary Garden was prevented from appearing in the opera 'Salome.' * * * What was regarded as indecent in the days of the Floradora Sextette, is decent in the days of the Fan and Bubble Dances."

[11] S.D.N.Y., 209 F. 119, 121, See *Towne* v. *Eisner*, 245 U.S. 418, 425, 38 S. Ct. 158, 159, 62 L. Ed. 372, L.R.A. 1918D, 254: "A word is not a crystal, transparent and unchanged, it is the skin of a living thought and may vary greatly in color and content according to the circumstances and the time in which it is used."

[12] *People* v. *Muller*, 96 N.Y. 408, 412, 48 Am. Rep. 635.

[13] See generally, Herbert Spencer, The Study of Sociology (1903) 1–11.

[14] *United States* v. *One Book* Entitled "*Ulysses*," 2 Cir., 72 F. 2d 705, 706; *Halsey* v. *New York Soc. For Suppression of Vice*, 234 N.Y. 1, 6, 136 N.E. 219, 220; *United States* v. *Levine*, 2 Cir., 83 F. 2d 156, 157; 2 Wigmore, Evidence, 2d Ed. 1923, § 935: "Modern psychology is steadily progressing towards definite generalizations in that field, and towards practical skill in applying precise tests. Whenever such principles and tests can be shown to be accepted in the field of science, expert testimony should and will be freely admitted to demonstrate and apply them." See 1 id. § 662.

narrowest rule would not justify such an assumption. And, from the teachings of psychology[15] and sociology,[16] we

[15] Schroeder, "Obscene" Literature and Constitutional Law (1911) 306, quoting from Havelock Ellis, Psychology of Sex: Modesty, 39, and Erotic Symbolism, p. 15: "Nakedness is always chaster in its effects than partial clothing. A study of pictures or statuary will alone serve to demonstrate this. As a well-known artist, Du Maurier, has remarked (in Trilby), it is "a fact well known to all painters and sculptors who have used the nude model (except a few shady pretenders, whose purity, not being of the right sort, has gone rank from too much watching) that nothing is so chaste as nudity. Venus herself, as she drops her garments and steps on the model-throne, leaves behind her on the floor every weapon in her armory by which she can pierce to the grosser passions of men." Burton, in the Anatomy of Melancholy (Part III, Sec. ii, subsec. iii), deals at length with the "allurements of love," and concludes that the "greatest provocations of lust are from our apparel." '"

[16] Sumner, Folkways (1906) 426: "* * * at the limit, that is at today's fashions, coquetry can be employed again, and a sense stimulus can be exerted again, by simply making variations on the existing fashions at the limit. It is impossible to eliminate the sense stimulus, or to establish a system of societal usage in which indecency shall be impossible. The dresses of Moslem women, nuns, and Quakeresses were invented in order to get rid of any possible question of decency. The attempt fails entirely. A Moslem woman with her veil, a Spanish woman with her mantilla or fan, a Quakeress with her neckerchief, can be as indecent as a barbarian woman with her petticoat of dried grass. * * * It would be difficult to mention anything in Oriental mores which we regard with such horror as Orientals feel for low-necked dresses and round dances. Orientals use dress to conceal the contour of the form. The waist of a woman is made to disappear by a girdle. To an Oriental a corset, which increases the waist line and the plasticity of the figure, is the extreme of indecency—far worse than nudity. It seems like an application of the art of the courtesan to appeal to sensuality." 428: "An elderly lady says that when the present queen of England brought in, at her marriage, the fashion of brushing up the hair so as to uncover the ears, which had long been covered, it seemed indecent." 430, 431: "In the Italian novel Niccolo dei Lapi it is said in honor of the heroine that she never saw herself nude. It was a custom observed by many to wear a garment which covered the whole body even when alone in the bath. Erasmus gives the reason for this. The angels would be shocked at nakedness. He made it a rule for men. One should never, he says, bare the body more than necessary, even when alone. The angels are everywhere and they like to see decency as the adjunct of modesty." 431: "It results from the study of the cases that nakedness is never shameful when it is unconscious (Genesis iii, 7)." 434, 435: "It is very improper for a Chinese woman who has compressed feet to show them. Thomson gives a picture which shows the feet of a woman, but it was very difficult, he says, to persuade the woman to pose in that way. Chinese people would consider the picture obscene. No European would find the slightest suggestion of that kind in it. An Arab woman, in Egypt, cares more to cover her face than any other part of her body, and she is more careful to cover the top or back of her head than her face. It appears that if any part of the body is put under a concealment taboo for any reason whatever, a consequence is that the opinion grows up that it never ought to be exposed. Then interest may attach to it more than to exposed parts, and erotic suggestion may be connected with it." 436: "The natives of New Britain are naked, but modest and chaste. 'Nudity rather checks than stimulates.' The same is observed in English New Guinea. The men wear a bandage which does not conceal, but they attach to this all the importance which we attach to complete dress, and they speak of others who do not wear it as 'naked wild men.' " 437: "On the Uganda railroad, near Lake Victoria, coal-black people are to be seen, of whom both sexes are entirely naked, except ornaments. They are 'the

know that the contrary view is held by social scientists.[17]

Nudity in art has long been recognized as the reverse of obscene.[18] Art galleries and art catalogues contain many nudes, ancient and modern. Even such a conservative source book as Encyclopaedia Britannica, contains nudes, full front view, male and female, and nude males and females pictured together and in physical contact.[19]

The use of nude figures and photographs in medical treatises and textbooks is also commonly practiced today. It was conceded on argument that this, also, constitutes an exception to the earlier prohibition. But this was not always true. In the earlier periods of medical history, censorship of scientific investigation was so restrictive that anatomical drawings alleged to represent the human body were made from studies of animals or upon a basis of pure hypothesis.[20] Later, as indicated by such cases as *Regina* v. *Hicklin* (1868),[21] and *People* v. *Muller* (1884),[22] the old censorship was relaxed to permit the use of such figures and photographs, provided the textbooks and treatises in which they appeared were restricted to use among practitioners and students.[23] No reasonable person at the pres-

---

[17] most moral people in Uganda.' The Nile negroes and Masai are naked. In the midst of them live the Baganda who wear much clothing. The women are covered from the waist to the ankles; the men from the neck to the ankles, except porters and men working in the fields. * * * This character and their dress are accounted for by their long subjection to tyranny. They are 'profoundly immoral,' have indecent dances, and are dying out on account of the 'exhaustion of men and women by premature debauchery.'" 440: "The Japanese do not consider nudity indecent. A Japanese woman pays no heed to the absence of clothing on workmen. European women in Japan are shocked at it, but themselves wear dinner and evening dress which greatly shock Orientals." 446: "There is no 'Natural' and universal instinct, by collision with which some things are recognized as obscene. We shall find that the things which we regard as obscene either were not, in other times and places, so regarded, any more than we so regard bared face and hands, or else that, from ancient usage, the exhibition was covered by a convention in protection of what is archaic or holy, or dramatic, or comical. In primitive times goblinism and magic covered especially the things which later became obscene. * * * As has been shown above, however, so soon as objects were attached to the body for any purpose whatever, the conventional view that bodies so distinguished were alone right and beautiful was started, and all the rest of the convention of ornament and dress followed."
II Pareto, The Mind and Society (1935) § 1374, n. 1: "The Adamites imitated the nakedness of Adam in Paradise before the Fall. * * * They went naked to their meetings and listened to their sermons and took their sacraments naked, thinking of their church, in fact, as Paradise itself."
I Lea, History of the Inquisition (1888) 147, 148: "It was during the preaching of this crusade [against the Albigenses] that villages and towns in Germany were filled with women who, unable to expend their religious ardor in taking the cross, stripped themselves naked and ran silently through the roads and streets."

[17] See generally, Schroeder, "Obscene" Literature and Constitutional Law (1911) c. XIII. Ethnographic Study of Modesty and Obscenity.

[18] *People* v. *Muller*, 96 N.Y. 408, 411, 48 Am. Rep. 635: "It is evident that mere nudity in painting or sculpture is not obscenity. Some of the great works in painting and sculpture as all know represent nude human forms. It is a false delicacy and mere prudery which would condemn and banish from sight all such objects as obscene, simply on account of their nudity. If the test of obscenity or indecency in a picture or statue is its capability of suggesting impure thoughts, then indeed all such representations might be considered as indecent or obscene. The presence of a woman of the purest character and of the most modest behavior and bearing may suggest to a prurient imagination images of lust, and excite impure desires, and so may a picture or statue not in fact indecent or obscene."

[19] Thus, in the article on Painting, in 17 Encyc. Brit., 14th Ed. 1932, 36–64D, there is a front view nude female (Plate VIII, 2) and a front view of nude males and females together (Plate XXIV, 7). In the article on Sculpture in 20 Encyc. Brit. (14th Ed. 1932) 198–217, there are front views of nude females (Plate V, 4 and 6; Plate VI, 8; Plate XVIII, 2 and 4). There are also front views of nude males (Plate IV, 8; Plate XIX, 8), and of nude males and females in physical contact (Plate IV, 2; Plate V, 8; Plate VI, 2; Plate XVIII, 3). In the article on Sculpture Technique, in 20 Encyc. Brit. (14th Ed. 1932) 217–231, there are front views of nude females (Plate VII, 1; Plate IX, 4); front views of nude males (Plate I, 1; Plate II, 6 and 8; Plate V,

7; Plate IX, 2); and a nude male and nude female in physical contact (Plate VIII, 3). These pictures in the Encyclopaedia Britannica are all larger than are the pictures which appear in Parmelee's book, and several of them—contra Parmelee—frankly emphasize sexual subjects.

[20] Clendening, Behind the Doctor (1933) 57, 58: "For nearly fifteen hundred years men had been teaching anatomy out of Galen [131–201 A.D.]. * * * A dog [in 1500] was the usual object to be dissected before the class. As the dissection progressed, the professor would read what Galen said on the subject. Sometimes Professor Sylvius would find something in the course of dissection of the dog which did not agree with Galen. If so, he gave his class to understand the dog was wrong. Sometimes he was unable to find a muscle or tendon or nerve or vein which he had meant to show. * * * The anatomical text of Guido de Vigevano, published in 1345, while it shows dissections, notes that the Church prohibits them."
Garrison, History of Medicine (1913) 149, 168: "Thoroughly as the great artists of the Renaissance may have studied external anatomy, yet dissecting for teaching purposes was still hampered by the theologic idea of the sanctity of the human body and its resurrection. Moreover, as very little anatomic material could be obtained among a sparse and slowly growing population, people were naturally averse to the possible dissection of friends or relatives. The anatomy of the schools was still the anatomy of Galen.

* * *

"*Dissections*, however, became more frequent [after 1500] and were regarded, in each case, as a particular and expensive social function, for which a special papal indulgence was necessary. The cadaver was first made 'respectable' by the reading of an official decree, and was then stamped with the seal of the university. Having been taken into the anatomic hall, it was next beheaded in deference to the then universal prejudice against opening the cranial cavity. The dissection was followed by such festivities as band music or even theatrical performances. All this led in time to the building of the so-called anatomic theaters, notably those at Padua (1549), Montpellier (1551), and Basel (1588). In England the need for anatomic study led to the passing of the law of 1540 (32 Henry VIII, c. 42), authorizing the barbers and surgeons to use four bodies of executed criminals each year for 'anathomyes,' a provision which, however enlarged, remained substantially in force until the passing of the Anatomy Act of 1832."

[21] L.R. 3 Q.B. 360, 367.

[22] 96 N.Y. 408, 413, 48 Am. Rep. 635.

[23] In *Commonwealth* v. *Landis*, 8 Phila. 453, it was held that publications of a scientific or medical character containing illustrations exhibiting the human form, while decent and moral if used in a classroom, would be obscene if wantonly exposed in the open markets. In *United States* v. *Smith*, E.D. Wis., 45 F. 476, a medical treatise, treating in wholesome language of the sex organs, which was distributed promiscuously, was held to be obscene. In *United States* v. *Chesman*, E.D. Mo., 19 F. 497, an illustrated pamphlet, purporting to be on the subject of treatment of spermatorhoea and impotency and consisting partially of extracts from standard medical works, was held to be, when

ent time would suggest even that limitation upon the circulation and use of medical texts, treatises and journals. In many homes such books can be found today; in fact standard dictionaries, generally, contain anatomical illustrations. It is apparent, therefore, that civilization has advanced far enough, at last, to permit picturization of the human body for scientific and educational purposes. That fact is decisive of the present case. The picturization here challenged has been used in the libeled book to accompany an honest, sincere, scientific and educational study and exposition of a sociological phenomenon and is, in our opinion, clearly permitted by present-day concepts of propriety.[24] There is, perhaps, as great or greater need for freedom of scientific research and exposition in this field as in any other.[25] And, at this point, it may be well to repeat

that the question is not whether nudity in practice is justifiable or desirable. All would agree that cancer, leprosy, and syphilis are highly undesirable; still, it is recognized, generally, by normal, intelligent persons, that there is need for scientific study, exposition and picturization of their manifestations.[26]

[6] The statute involved in the present case was interpreted in *United States* v. *One Book* Entitled *Ulysses,*[27] and the decision in that case is equally applicable here. "It is settled," says the court in the *Ulysses* case, "that works of physiology, medicine, science, and sex instruction are not within the statute, though to some extent and among some persons they may tend to promote lustful thoughts." *It should be equally true of works of sociology, as of physiology, medicine and other sciences—to say nothing of general literature and the arts—that* "where the presentation, when viewed objectively, is sincere, and the erotic matter is not introduced to promote lust and does not furnish the dominant note of the publication," the same immunity should apply.[28] [Italics ed.]. Cases relied upon

---

circulated generally, immoral and obscene. In *Burton* v. *United States*, 8 Cir., 142 F. 57, a scientific book was held to be obscene, notwithstanding the contention, assumed to be true, that its contents had been approved by physicians and consisted of accurate and scientific information on the topics discussed; that ignorance upon these topics was quite general and that this ignorance frequently resulted in disease, physical infirmity, unhappiness and misery, which the information given in the book was designed to prevent; that as a whole the book was calculated to be of value to the medical practitioner and to men and women in the marriage relation; and even that some portion of the text was from standard medical works. In *United States* v. *Harmon*, D. Kan., 45 F. 414, reversed on other grounds, 50 F. 921, an article concerning the sexual relation was held obscene notwithstanding it was written solely for the purpose of improving sexual habits, and correcting sexual abuses. But see *Hanson* v. *United States*, 7 Cir., 157 F. 749; *United States* v. *One Book* Entitled "Contraception," S.D.N.Y., 51 F.2d 525; *United States* v. *One Book* Entitled "Ulysses," 2 Cir., 72 F. 705.

[24] In the following cases, the material was held to be nonsensual: *United States* v. *One Obscene Book* Entitled "Married Love", S.D.N.Y., 48 F. 2d 821 (a book written in an effort to explain to married people how their mutual sex life could be made happier); *United States* v. *One Book* Entitled "Contraception", S.D.N.Y., 51 F. 2d 525 (a treatment of the theory, history, and practice of birth control); *United States* v. *Dennett*, 2 Cir., 39 F. 2d 564, 76 A.L.R. 1092 (pamphlet written for sex instruction of adolescents). Cf. *Dysart* v. *United States*, 272 U.S. 655, 47 S. Ct. 234, 71 L. Ed. 461 (holding non–obscene a post card advertising a retreat for unmarried pregnant women which was mailed to women of refinement).

[25] Herbert Spencer, The Study of Sociology (1903) c. I: Our Need of It 5, 6: "But while the prevalence of crude political opinions among those whose conceptions about simple matters are so crude, might be anticipated, it is surprising that the class disciplined by scientific culture should bring to the interpretation of social phenomena, methods but little in advance of those used by others. Now that the transformation and equivalence of forces is seen by men of science to hold not only throughout all inorganic actions, but throughout all organic actions; now that even mental changes are recognized as the correlatives of cerebral changes, which also conform to this principle; and now, that there must be admitted the corollary, that all actions going on in a society are measured by certain antecedent energies, which disappear in effecting them, while they themselves become actual or potential energies from which subsequent questions arise; it is strange that there should not have arisen the consciousness that these highest phenomena are to be studied as lower phenomena have been studied—not, of course, after the same physical methods but in conformity with the same principles."

Sumner and Keller, III The Science of Society (1927) 2246, 2247: "The chief trouble with 'sociology' is that it is not qualifying as a science by subordinating its types of therapeutics

to that which corresponds, within its range, to anatomy and physiology. * * * The art of living reacts upon the apprehension of and the adjustment to immutable conditions; and a knowledge of the conditions is always a prior necessity. * * * Under some Darwin of the future, such studies can result in the apprehension of societal laws; then the race can make a far-sighted and accurately planned campaign against its problems instead of a series of desultory and disconnected engagements. What is now needed is some such collection of scientific materials as Darwin found at hand, a collection assembled by many patient and obscure workers intent, not upon self-glorification, but the discovery of truth."

[26] See *United States* v. *One Book* Entitled "Contraception," S.D.N.Y., 51 F. 2d 525; *United States* v. *One Book* Called "Ulysses", S.D.N.Y., 5 F. Supp. 182, 185: "It is only with the normal person that the law is concerned."

[27] 2 Cir., 72 F. 2d 705, 707. See also, *United States* v. *One Obscene Book* Entitled "Married Love," S.D.N.Y., 48 F. 2d 821; *United States* v. *One Book* Entitled "Contraception," S.D.N.Y., 51 F. 2d 525.

[28] *United States* v. *One Book* Entitled "Ulysses," 2 Cir., 72 F. 2d 705, 707. See *United States* v. *Dennett*, 2 Cir., 39 F. 2d 564, 76 A.L.R. 1092; *United States* v. *One Book* Entitled "Contraception," S.D.N.Y., 51 F. 2d 525; *United States* v. *One Obscene Book* Entitled "Married Love," S.D.N.Y., 48 F. 2d 821; *United States* v. *Levine*, 2 Cir., 83 F. 2d 156. See *United States* v. *Kennerley*, S.D.N.Y., 209 F. 119, 120, in which Judge Learned Hand, in criticizing the doctrine of the Hicklin case, said: "I question whether in the end men will regard that as obscene which is honestly relevant to the adequate expression of innocent ideas, and whether they will not believe that truth and beauty are too precious to society at large to be multilated in the interests of those most likely to pervert them to base uses. Indeed, it seems hardly likely that we are even to-day so lukewarm in our interest in letters or serious discussion as to be content to reduce our treatment of sex to the standard of a child's library in the supposed interest of a salacious few, or that shame will for long prevent us from adequate portrayal of some of the most serious and beautiful sides of human nature. * * * Yet, if the time is not yet when men think innocent all that which is honestly germane to a pure subject, however little it may mince its words, still I scarcely think that they would forbid all which might corrupt the most corruptible, or that society is prepared to accept for its own limitations those which may perhaps be necessary to the weakest of its members."

See also, *Halsey* v. *New York Soc. for Suppression of Vice*, 234 N.Y. 1, 136 N.E. 219; *People* v. *Wendling*, 258 N.Y. 451. 180 N.E. 169, 81 A.L.R. 799.

by the government, in which publication and distribution were "wholly for the purpose of profitably pandering to the lewd and lascivious" have no relevancy to the present case.[29]

[7, 8] As it is conceded that the entire text of "Nudism in Modern Life" is inoffensive, and that only a few of the twenty-three illustrations are questionable, it is obvious that the latter do not furnish the dominant note of the publication. The determining question is, in each case, whether a publication, taken as a whole, has a libidinous effect.[30] In the present case, as in the Ulysses case, the book as a whole is certainly not obscene; here, as there, the book has "such evident truthfulness in its depiction of certain types of humanity, and is so little erotic in its result, that it does not fall within the forbidden class."[31] The author has been known for many years as a well qualified writer in the field of sociology. His textbooks have been long known and used in the colleges and universities of this country. The photographs used in the book here involved have definite relevancy to the written text, even though there are no specific references therein by plate number; and it cannot fairly be said that they were introduced to promote lust or to produce libidinous thoughts. The author expresses his point of view in the preface to the book as follows: "The illustrations depict better than words can describe the natural and normal life, and the beautiful and healthful methods and activities of a gymnosophic society. They portray them as actually applied in several European countries by many thousands of men, women and children of all classes, occupations and conditions, while the text discusses its scientific, hygienic, cultural, aesthetic, ethical and humanitarian significance."

[9, 10] In fact, it is only because social scientists are still working under conditions of enforced self-deception, similar to those which prevailed in the early days of the medical profession, that the propriety of the present book is questioned. Until phenomena such as those discussed in "Nudism in Modern Life" can be studied on a realistic basis, it is reasonable to expect as great professional inadequacy in the solution of social problems as was true of attempts to solve problems affecting the health of the physical body, prior to the present-day development of medical science. There are still some unexplored areas of medical science, but there are many unexplored areas of social science. If anything, there is needed today greater patience and greater tolerance concerning research in sociology than in medicine; looking to the day when social scientists can advise not only courts, but the people generally; just as physicians, chemists and other physical scientists do today.[32] *"Democracy today needs the social scientists, both inside and outside the universities. It needs to free them to think with all possible penetration, wherever that thinking may lead.* [Italics ed.]. New ideas

about human relations and institutional adjustment should be fully, honestly and hospitably analyzed. Society should be most deeply concerned not with ridiculing failures or condemning those whose findings it does not approve, but with aiding that small minority of pioneers whose work in the social studies is reaching up to new levels of scientific achievement. Such persons are to be found in universities, in government and in private life. No greater contribution to the disinterested comprehension of today's issues could be made than by affording these able men and women full opportunity to make their work genuinely effective."[33] It cannot reasonably be contended that the purpose of the pertinent statute is to prevent scientific research and education. To uphold the decision of the lower court would contribute to just that result. So to interpret it would be to abandon the field, in large measure, to the charlatan and the fakir.[34] "The foolish judgments of Lord Eldon about one hundred years ago, proscribing the works of Byron and Southey, and the finding by the jury under a charge by Lord Denman that the publication of Shelley's 'Queen Mab' was an indictable offense are a warning to all who have to determine the limits of the field within which authors may exercise themselves."[35]

Reversed.

Vinson, Associate Justice, dissenting.

The libel of the instant book required the District Court to decide whether it fell within the purview of § 305 of the Tariff Act of 1930.[1] The court, sitting without a jury as a judge of both law and fact, found that it did. The only question presented by this appeal is whether the court followed correctly the mandate of Congress.

---

[29] See *Lynch* v. *United States*, 7 Cir., 285 F. 162, 163.

[30] United States v. Levine, 2 Cir., 83 F. 2d 156, 157; Alpert, Judicial Censorship of Obscene Literature, 52 Harv. L. Rev. 40, 54, 67.

[31] *United States* v. *One Book* Entitled "Ulysses," 2 Cir., 72 F. 2d 705, 707. See *United States* v. *Levine*, 2 Cir., 83 F. 2d 156, 158: "The standard must be the likelihood that the work will so much arouse the salacity of the reader to whom it is sent as to outweigh any literary, scientific or other merits it may have in that reader's hand; * * *."

[32] See 4 Wigmore, Evidence, 2d Ed. 1923, §§ 1923, 1975.

[33] Raymond B. Fosdick, A Review for 1939, The Rockefeller Foundation (1940) 41, 42.

[34] See *United States* v. *Levine*, 2 Cir., 83 F. 2d 156, 157: "This earlier doctrine [of the Hicklin and related cases] necessarily presupposed that the evil against which the statute is directed so much outweighs all interests of art, letters or science, that they must yield to the mere possibility that some prurient person may get a sensual gratification from reading or seeing what to most people is innocent and may be delightful or enlightening. No civilized community not fanatically puritanical would tolerate such an imposition, and we do not believe that the courts that have declared it, would ever have applied it consistently. As so often happens, the problem is to find a passable compromise between opposing interests, whose relative importance, like that of all social or personal values, is incommensurable."

[35] *United States* v. *One Book* Entitled "Ulysses," 2 Cir., 72 F. 2d 705, 708. In Vol. X of Lord Campbell's Lives of the Lord Chancellors, 5th Ed. 1868, 257, the author speaks of a decision by Lord Eldon concerning a poem by Lord Byron and says: "* * * it must have been a strange occupation for a judge who for many years had meddled with nothing more imaginative than an Act of Parliament, to determine in what sense the speculations of Adam, Eve, Cain, and Lucifer are to be understood, and whether the tendency of the whole poem be favourable or injurious to religion." In a footnote, the author quotes, for comparative purposes, a statement by Sir Walter Scott who, he states, was "ever an observer of decency, and a friend to religion and morality," as follows: "I accept, with feelings of great obligation, the flattering proposal of Lord Byron to prefix my name to the very grand and tremendous drama of Cain. I may be partial to it, and you will allow I have cause; but I do not know that his muse has ever taken so lofty a flight amid her former soarings. He has certainly matched Milton on his own ground."

[1] 46 Stat. 688, 19 U.S.C.A. § 1305.

The relevant provisions of § 305 are as follows:

"All persons are prohibited from importing into the United States from any foreign country * * * any obscene book, * * * picture * * *: Provided further, That the Secretary of the Treasury may, in his discretion, admit the so-called classics or books of recognized and established literary or scientific merit, but may, in his discretion, admit such classics or books only when imported for noncommercial purposes.

"* * * Upon the adjudication that such book or matter thus seized is of the character the entry of which is by this section prohibited, it shall be ordered destroyed and shall be destroyed. * * *

"In any such proceeding any party in interest upon demand may have the facts at issue determined by a jury and any party may have an appeal or the right of review as in the case of ordinary actions or suits."

The book in the instant case was not admitted under special dispensation of the Secretary. Hence, if obscene within the meaning of the statute, it clearly is subject to destruction.

In reviewing the District Court judgment we must first ascertain what connotation is to be given the term obscene as it appears in the statute prohibiting the importation of obscene books. It seems clear, contrary to implications in the majority opinion, that the purity of the author's motive and incidental claim the book may have to literary, scientific or educational value is not decisive.[2] Under an English statute prohibiting the sale of obscene literature, Cockburn, C.J., stated in *Regina* v. *Hicklin*, 3 Q.B. 360, 371 that: "the test of obscenity is this: Whether the tendency of the matter charged as obscenity is to deprave and corrupt those whose minds are open to such immoral influences, and into whose hands a publication of this sort may fall." In this country we have several so-called federal obscenity statutes. In addition to the Tariff Act provision here invoked, Congress has provided criminal sanctions against importation, transportation by common carrier, or through the mails, of any "obscene, lewd, or lascivious"

book.[3] With certain modifications the obscenity test of *Regina* v. *Hicklin* has been adopted by the Federal Courts in interpreting all of these statutes.[4] As modified by these decisions the test might be stated as follows: A book is obscene when in the aggregate sense of the community[5] the tendency of the objectionable matter, considered with the book as a whole,[6] is to arouse lustful thought.[7] That such a test of obscenity is required when the term is associated in a criminal statute with lewdness and lasciviousness does not, of course, mean that it is sufficiently broad for the term as it appears in the Tariff Act. Indeed, such a definition seems unduly restrictive of the normal meaning of the term and there is some judicial support for a broader, more inclusive definition.[8] Assuming, however,

---

[2] The author's motive is of no consequence. *United States* v. *One Book* Entitled "Ulysses," 2 Cir., 72 F. 2d 705, 780; *United States* v. *Dennett*, 2 Cir., 89 F. 2d 564, 76 A.L.R. 1092. Likewise it seems clear under the statute that incidental claim to literary, scientific or educational merit will not save a book otherwise obscene. The statutory prohibition is absolute—forbidding importation of "any" obscene book. Moreover, there is a proviso that "the Secretary of the Treasury may, in his discretion, admit the so-called classics or books of recognized and established literary or scientific merit, but may, in his discretion, admit such classics or books only when imported for noncommercial purposes". Under elementary canons of statutory construction, it seems clear that, apart from this exception not here involved, the prohibition of the statute against the importation of "any obscene book" is not subject to relaxation by reason of the latter's claim to literary, scientific or educational merit. Cf. *United States* v. *Chesman*, C.C., E.D. Mo., 19 F. 497; *United States* v. *Smith*, D.C., E.D. Wis., 45 F. 476. This does not mean, of course, that the character of a publication does not enter into a determination of *whether it is obscene*. It is believed that *United States* v. "*Ulysses*," supra, recognizes the general rule, merely emphasizing this last proposition. But cf. *United States* v. *Levine*, 2 Cir., 83 F. 2d 156, 158. It may be observed that permitting importation of this particular book can do little to advance the cause of science and education—it appears from the record that a domestic edition of the same book is being freely sold.

[3] 35 Stat. 1138, amended 41 Stat. 1060, 18 U.S.C.A. § 396 (importing and transporting obscene books); 36 Stat. 1339, 18 U.S.C.A. § 334 (mailing obscene matter).

[4] See Note 76 A.L.R. 1099.

[5] It is believed that the cases establish that the "standard of the community" has been substituted for the "standard of the weak and susceptible", at least where there is no evidence of sales to the latter. See *United States* v. *Harmon*, D.C. Kan., 45 F. 414, 417; *United States* v. *Kennerley*, D.C.N.Y., 209 F. 119, 121; *United States* v. *Dennett*, 2 Cir., 39 F. 2d 564, 76 A.L.R. 1092; *United States* v. *One Book* Called "*Ulysses*," D.C., 5 F. Supp. 182, 184; Id., 2 Cir., 72 F. 2d 705; *United States* v. *Levine*, 2 Cir., 83 F. 2d 156, 158.

[6] *Clark* v. *United States*, 8 Cir., 211 F. 916. See also cases cited supra note 5.

[7] "The word 'obscene' ordinarily means something that is offensive to chastity, something that is foul or filthy, and for that reason is offensive to pure-minded persons. That is the meaning of the word in the concrete. But when used, as in the statute under which this indictment is framed, to describe the character of a book, pamphlet, or paper, it means a book, pamphlet, or paper containing immodest and indecent matter, the reading whereof would have a tendency to deprave and corrupt the minds of those into whose hands the publication might fall whose minds are open to such immoral influences." *United States* v. *Clarke*, D.C., E.D. Mo., 38 F. 732, 733. It seems settled that the term obscene as used in the statutes proscribing obscene books refers to lust rather than to immodesty or indelicacy. See cases cited in Note 76 A.L.R. 1099. See also Anonymous, 1 Fed. Cas. 1024, No. 470; *United States* v. *Three Cases of Toys*, 28 Fed. Cas. 112, No. 16,499. It is stated in some of the cases that the term is to be given the same meaning it had in common law actions for obscene libel. *Swearingen* v. *United States*, 161 U.S. 446, 451, 16 S. Ct. 562, 40 L. Ed. 765; *Knowles* v. *United States*, 8 Cir., 170 F. 409, 412; *United States* v. *Males*, D.C., 51 F. 41, 42.

[8] *United States* v. *One Obscene Book* Entitled "Married Love", D.C., S.D.N.Y., 48 F. 2d 821, 823, Woolsey, J.:

"In Murray's Oxford English Dictionary the word 'obscene' is defined as follows:

"'Obscene—1. Offensive to the senses, or to taste or refinement; disgusting, repulsive, filthy, foul, abominable, loathsome. Now somewhat arch.

"'2. Offensive to modesty or decency; expressing or suggesting unchaste or lustful ideas; impure, indecent, lewd.' * * *

"The book 'Married Love' does not, in my opinion, fall within these definitions of the words 'obscene' * * * in any respect."

For other definitions of the term obscene see note 3 of the majority opinion. See also *United States* v. *Harmon*, D.C., 45 F. 414, 417; *Holcombe* v. *State*, 5 Ga. App. 47, 50, 62 S.E. 647 (in the federal mails statute the term "obscene" is deprived of its usual broad meaning by reason of its association with the other terms "lewd or lascivious"). It is significant to note that the statute prohibiting use of the mails for obscene books, as originally enacted, read as does the present provision in the Tariff Act,

that the stated definition is applicable, can we say that the District Court erred in holding this book obscene within the meaning of the statute?

Preliminarily it may be well to recall some of the fundamental principles respecting the function of an appellate court. First of all, it is settled that in ordinary actions an appeal is limited to matters of law.[9] In § 305 of the Tariff Act it is provided that "In any such proceeding [libel of an allegedly obscene book] any party in interest upon demand may have the facts at issue determined by a jury and any party may have an appeal or the right of review *as in the case of ordinary actions* or suits."[10] (Italics supplied) These proceedings partake, therefore, of the nature of ordinary actions at law. In such actions the verdict of the jury on questions of fact is final and conclusive.[11] Where a jury is waived the finding of the court on factual issues is given the same conclusive weight.[12] There is in respect to every factual question, however, a preliminary legal question—could reasonable men differ on the factual issue in the light of the proof.[13] If so, the question is one for the fact trier. It is settled that whether a book is obscene presents a question of fact, if reasonable men could differ on that question.[14] From this it follows that, where there has been a jury verdict (or a finding by the court where a jury is waived) that a book is obscene, an appellate court cannot disturb that determination unless

it is prepared to say that no reasonable man could have found as did the jury (or court).

We come then to the question, can it be said that no reasonable man could find the book in question obscene within the meaning of the statute? In this connection it is important to recall that under the decisions a book is obscene if in the aggregate sense of the community the tendency of the questionable matter, considered with the book as a whole, is to arouse lustful thought. That is to say—the book must be judged by reference to the "standard of the community."

"Laws of this character are made for society in the aggregate, and not in particular. So, while there may be individuals and societies of men and women of peculiar notions or idiosyncrasies, whose moral sense would neither be depraved nor offended by the publication now under consideration, yet the exceptional sensibility, or want of sensibility, of such cannot be allowed as a standard by which its obscenity or indecency is to be tested. Rather is the test, what is the judgment of the aggregate sense of the community reached by it? What is its probable, reasonable effect on the sense of decency, purity, and chastity of society, extending to the family, made up of men and women, young boys and girls,—* * * Who is to deem, who is to judge, whether a given publication impinges upon the general sense of decency? * * * The answer to this is, that asserted violations of this statute, * * * must be left to the final arbiter under our system of government,—the courts. The jury, the legally constituted triers of the fact under the constitution, is to pass upon the question of fact. Under our institutions of government the panel of 12 are assumed to be the best and truest exponents of the public judgment of the common sense. Their selection and constitution proceed upon the theory that they most nearly represent the average intelligence, the common experience and sense, of the vicinage; and these qualifications they are presumed to carry with them into the jury-box, and apply this average judgment to the law and the facts. Sitting as the court does in this case, in the stead of the jury, it may not apply to the facts its own method of analysis or process of reasoning as a judge, but should try to reflect in its findings the common experience, observation, and judgment of the jury of average intelligence."[15]

The majority opinion recognizes that the book in question must be judged by the "community standard" but it suggests in ascertaining "* * * the present critical point in the compromise between candor and shame at which the community may have arrived here and now"[16] that "the expert opinions of psychologists and sociologists would seem to be helpful if not necessary." While such opinions might be helpful, none appear in the record. Furthermore, it must be remembered that social scientists do not always reflect, or even intend to reflect, the sentiment of the community. Their opinions would seem relevant only if directed to the question of what the present community conscience is, in reference to a book of this character. It would seem clear that a sociologist's opinion on the standards of foreign communities (set forth at some length in note 16 of the majority opinion) would be

---

"no obscene book." Act of July 8, 1872, 17 Stat. 302. Later the mails statute was amended to read "no obscene, lewd or lascivious" book. Act of March 3, 1873, 17 Stat. 599. See *United States v. Loftis*, D.C. Or., 12 F. 671, 672. It seems clear that the provision of the Tariff Act against the importation of "any obscene book" might be given a broader application than the mails statute.

[9] Rev. Stat. § 1011, 28 U.S.C.A. § 879, as amended by 45 Stat. 54, 28 U.S.C.A. §§ 861a, 861b. *Bengoechea Macias v. De La Torre & Ramirez*, 1 Cir., 84 F. 2d 894, 895; *Salt Bayou Drainage Dist. v. Futrall*, 8 Cir., 72 F. 2d 940, 942; *Security Nat. Bank v. Old Nat. Bank*, 8 Cir., 241 F. 1, 6; *United States ex rel. Smith v. Stewart*, 55 App. D.C. 134, 135, 2 F. 2d 936; *Barbour v. Moore*, 10 App. D.C. 30, 50.

[10] 46 Stat. 688, 19 U.S.C.A. § 1305.

[11] *Columbia Aid Ass'n v. Sprague*, 50 App. D.C. 307, 271 F. 381; *O'Dea v. Clark*, 46 App. D.C. 274.

[12] In ordinary actions this court has stated that, where trial by jury has been waived, the finding of the District Court on questions of fact cannot be reviewed. *Neely Electric Construction & Supply Co. v. Browning*, 25 App. D.C. 84, 87; *Shelley v. Wescott*, 23 App. D.C. 135, 140. It is axiomatic that the findings of the court where a jury is waived are given the weight attached to a verdict. See 28 U.S.C.A. § 773. Whether there is substantial evidence to support the finding presents, of course, a legal question. Even in equity practice the rule is settled in this jurisdiction that the findings of the trial court on matters of fact cannot be disturbed unless clearly wrong. *Russell v. Wallace*, 58 App. D.C. 357, 30 F. 2d 981 (reasonable time a question of fact); *Hazen v. Hawley*, 66 App. D.C. 266, 271, 88 F. 2d 217.

[13] *Gunning v. Cooley*, 281 U.S. 90, 94, 50 S. Ct. 231, 74 L. Ed. 720; *Chicago G.W. Ry. Co. v. Price*, 8 Cir., 97 F. 423, 427.

[14] *United States v. One Obscene Book* Entitled "Married Love," D.C., S.D.N.Y., 48 F. 2d 821, 824; *United States v. Dennett*, 2 Cir., 39 F. 2d 564, 76 A.L.R. 1092; *United States v. Levine*, 2 Cir., 83 F. 2d 156; *United States v. Smith*, D.C., E.D. Wis., 45 F. 476, 477; *Knowles v. United States*, 8 Cir., 170 F. 409, 410; *United States v. Kennerley*, D.C., S.D.N.Y., 209 F. 119, 120. Cf. *Dreiser v. John Lane Co.*, 183 App. Div. 773, 171 N.Y.S. 605.

[15] *United States v. Harmon*, D.C., 45 F. 414, 417.

[16] *United States v. Kennerley*, D.C., 209 F. 119, 121.

almost entirely irrelevant to determination of what the standard of the community is in this country.

The District Court was of the view that the book with the pictures in question was obscene within the meaning of the statute, i.e., that it offended the present community standard. From their opinion it seems clear that the majority of this court would agree that just a few years ago a book of this character containing the pictures in question would unquestionably have been regarded as obscene. Undoubtedly, thought changes in respect to what is obscene. The "judgments of Lord Eldon about one hundred years ago, proscribing the works of Byron and Southey" do not damn him as foolish so much as they support the thesis of the majority opinion that the content of the term "obscene" is geared to the clock. The majority have evidently concluded that the country-wide sense of decency has altered in the past few years to the extent that in the present day only a Rip Van Winkle could regard the book in question as obscene. That I cannot believe. Accepting the premise that "time marches on," I am nevertheless unable to agree that we have here and now "progressed" to the point where a publication of this character is, beyond the possibility of reasonable difference of opinion, acceptable to the community. This publication, it must be repeated, is to be judged in the light of the present day

standard, not that of the world of tomorrow It is significant in this respect to note that when the governing provision was last re-enacted in 1930, Congress inserted for the first time a proviso indicating that it did not regard the "so-called classics or books of recognized and established literary or scientific merit" as ipso facto without the prohibition against the importation of obscene books.[17]

I think it important to emphasize that decision of this case calls, not for the individual judge's personal opinion, but, for a gauging of the present community sentiment.[18] It seems obvious to me that a court should rarely attempt that task as a matter of law. Certainly, it seems difficult to conclude that no reasonable man could say that this book offends the community standard and, with a District Court finding that the book with its pictures is obscene, I am unable to understand how my brethren can stand on that proposition. I not only think reasonable men might differ on that question which in itself requires an affirmance, I approve the result reached by the District Court that the matter in question is within the prohibition of the statute. I must therefore dissent.

---

[17] See note 2 supra.
[18] See note 5 supra.

■ The People of the State of New York on the Complaint of Harry Kahan, *Complainant,*
v.
Abraham S. Jaffe, *Defendant.*[1]

City Magistrates' Court of New York, Borough of Manhattan, Yorkville Court, March 20, 1942.

Frank S. Hogan, District Attorney (David Du Vivier of counsel), for the People.
Schacter, Paris, Goldman & Ellison (Samuel Schacter of counsel), for the defendant.

MAHONEY, C.M. The defendant is charged with violation of section 1141 of the Penal Law of the State of New York in that, among other things, he did unlawfully issue advertising matter concerning, and did sell certain obscene, lewd, lascivious and indecent phonograph records.

It was stipulated that the defendant did deliver to the People's witness three pieces of printed advertising matter respecting phonograph records for sale by the defendant (exhibits in the case), and did sell to the said witness two phonograph discs with the recordings of four songs, for which the said witness paid.

Motion to dismiss the complaint is made by the defendant at the close of the People's case. The contentions of the defendant are: (a) that the information is insufficient

as a matter of law to charge a crime: (b) that even if the facts alleged were within the prohibition of section 1141, the law was in fact not violated.

In support of these contentions he urges that the lack of precedent for the information is a cogent argument against criminality; that the statute must be strictly construed with section 1141 of the Penal Law as wholly preoccupied with and directed to the proscription of the indecent presented by way of visual image and not with speech; that the standard by which this case must be judged is "according to our time;" that the language used in the discs does not have a double meaning, and if the advertisement so indicates, then it is false and misleading.

The advertising matter delivered to the witness describes the phonograph discs purchased by him as "real life—lustful, earthy;" as "very naughty songs with full G string dance orchestras."

The additional advertising material in evidence respecting other phonograph records bear such statements as "he sings these naughty, naughty songs with a wink, a grin, and a laugh in each note;" "these song records are wicked, witty, naughty but nice." Included in this printed matter

---

[1] There has since been a conviction and as a result several arrests have been made and cases are pending.

are pictures of scantily attired women in various poses, a bed scene, a description of the various phonograph records and their names. Another expression used is "their naughty, sophisticated, spicy records with plenty of oomph."

The words and expressions in the songs in the phonograph discs in evidence are replete with every-day expressions which are highly suggestive of not only sexual intercourse, but of a most repulsive form of degeneracy. Unquestionably the words and expressions have a double meaning but are so commonly used in connection with sex relations and acts of degeneracy, as experience teaches from various types of cases which come to our courts, that I cannot close my mind to the meaning intended, particularly when considered in connection with the advertising matter. The phonograph discs are intended for an indecent and immoral use or purpose.

Section 1141 of the Penal Law provides in part: "A person who sells, * * * distributes or shows, or offers to sell, * * * distribute, or show * * * any article or instrument of indecent, or immoral use, or purporting to be for indecent or immoral use or purpose * * * is guilty of a misdemeanor."

Section 21 of the Penal Law states: "The rule that a penal statute is to be strictly construed does not apply to this chapter or any of the provisions thereof [adopting the Penal Law], but all such provisions must be construed according to the fair import of their terms, to promote justice and effect the objects of the law."

The primary purpose of section 1141 is to suppress the exploitation of smut. (*People* v. *Wendling*, 258 N.Y. 451 [1932]; *People* [*Complaint of Sumner*] v. *Miller*, 155 Misc. 446 [1935]; *Ultem Publications, Inc.*, v. *Arrow Publications, Inc.*, 166 id. 645 [1938].)

Among the definitions in Funk & Wagnall's New Standard Dictionary of the word "instrument" is: 2. "A mechanical contrivance for the production of musical sounds."

"The Penal Law is not to be strictly construed. * * * Provisions thereof should be interpreted according to the fair import of their terms, so that justice may be promoted and the objects of the law effected." It is the court's duty to give words of the Penal Law their usually accepted meaning, so that a wrongdoer shall be punished. (*People* v. *Reilly*, 255 App. Div. 109 [1938]; affd., 280 N.Y. 509.)

Thus, to limit the meaning of the word "instrument" to the indecent presented by way of visual image, and not with speech or sounds or words from a phonograph disc or any instrument or object which produces sounds or words, would constitute an unreasonable construction of the words and purpose of section 1141 of the Penal Law. Phonograph records do come within the purview of the section.

It is argued that the case must be judged according to our time and, so judged, there is no violation; and that it is a matter of judicial notice (*Halsey* v. *New York Society*, 234 N.Y. 1) that every large music shop in the United States, not to speak of the city of New York, sells the discs involved in this case. No statistics to this effect are offered. It is argued, too, that the advertising matter hereinabove referred to is false and misleading if it leads one to believe that the language in the recorded songs has a double meaning. And from the brief, "It is admittedly neither delicacy nor nicety * * * it is comedy but not lechery." Undoubtedly the purpose of the defendant is to have this charge determined, not by the law or the code of morality or decency, but by what he would want them to be for himself and purveyors of writings, instruments or articles exploiting smut, filth, sexual relations and acts of degeneracy.

The code of morality or decency, upon which laws are based, is as old as the world itself and does not change with the seasons or the years. Although history, and the Testaments, show that at times nations, cities and groups of individuals abandoned the code and revelled in debauchery, degeneracy and crime generally, the code survived and lives with decent, law-abiding peoples to-day, everywhere, as it did in the time of Moses. It would sanction the destruction of all law to give to individuals, or groups of individuals, the privilege of having their violations of the law adjudged by standards made by themselves and labeled "our time." [Italics ed.].

The motion to dismiss the complaint is denied.

■ People
v.
Dial Press

City Magistrates' Court of New York City, Staten Island Court, Borough of Richmond.

May 29, 1944.

John S. Sumner, Secretary, Society for Suppression of Vice, of New York City, for the People.
Weil, Gotshal & Manges, by Horace S. Manges, all of New York City, for the defense.

CHARLES G. KEUTGEN, City Magistrate.

The complaint in this case charges the defendant corporation, the Dial Press, Incorporated, with publishing and having in its possession with intent to sell an obscene book entitled "The First Lady Chatterly" by D. H. Lawrence.

The defendant demanded a hearing in this court. At the hearing, it was proved by sufficient evidence that the defendant had a considerable number of copies of the book in its possession with intent to sell and the defendant admitted that it published this book. A copy of the book was received in evidence.

The statute which the defendant is accused of violating, Section 1141 of the Penal Law, is of complex verbiage. So much of it as is necessary for the decision in this case is as follows:

"1. A person who * * * has in his possession with intent to sell * * * any obscene, lewd, lascivious, filthy, indecent or disgusting book * * * or who * * * publishes * * * any such book * * *

"Is guilty of a misdemeanor."

In the application of this statute, the People contend that I may not resort to the statement of the rule given by the U.S. Circuit Court of Appeals in the Second Circuit for the reason that the case which that court was dealing with came under the Customs Law, Tariff Act 1930, § 305 (a), 19 U.S.C.A. § 1305 (a), which forbade the importation of an obscene book without using the other words quoted.

[1] I have plodded through the definitions in two dictionaries of the several words used and I have come to the conclusion that each of these words is synonymous with the others and that the real intent and meaning of each of these words and all of them is that the ban is against the publication of a book which contravenes the moral law and which tends to subvert respect for decency and morality. I am therefore guided by the rule as stated in *United States* v. *One Book* Entitled Ulysses by James Joyce, 2 Cir., 72 F. 2d 705, and I feel authorized to accept that rule, more particularly because the courts of the State of New York, in making decisions, have acted upon that rule, although they have not said the rule in so many words. I refer particularly to: *People* v. *Pesky*, 230 App. Div. 200, 243 N.Y.S. 193, affirmed 254 N.Y. 373, 173 N.E. 227; *People* v. *Berg*, 241 App. Div. 543, 272 N.Y.S. 586, affirmed 269 N.Y. 514, 199 N.E. 513.

[2] The rule that I gather from these cases is that the whole book must be read and that upon the reading of the entire book, the question to be answered is whether or not the effect of the whole volume is obscene, that is, contrary to the moral law and tending to subvert respect for decency and morality.

The defendant has contended that the literary merit of the particular volume may be considered. For several reasons, it seems to me that the literary merit or demerit of the volume cannot be the criterion. Judges are not trained to be, nor are they, competent literary critics. If judgment in such a case as this will depend upon the determination of the author's skill as a writer, the judicial officer responsible for the enforcement of the statute would have to surrender his own judgment and base his opinion on the opinions of experts who have no responsibility in the premises. More than this, it is easy to imagine a book, let us say, by another Oscar Wilde, clever, scintillating, even brilliant in its writing and utterly foul and disgusting in its central theme and dominating effect.

Considering the book which is here before the court, as a whole, it purports to tell a story. The scene is laid in the English Midlands within an hour by auto of Sheffield. The period is 1920 to 1921 and the time in which the story runs is less than a year, from the late fall of 1920 to the pheasant season of 1921.

The author's own summary of the situation of his heroine, Lady Constance Chatterly, cannot be improved upon in respect to brevity and therefore is quoted—this is taken from page three of the volume:

"She married Clifford Chatterly in 1917 when he was home on leave. They had a month of honeymoon, and he went back to France. In 1918, he was very badly wounded, brought home a wreck. She was 23 years old.

"After two years, he was restored to comparative health. But the lower part of his body was paralyzed forever."

And further on page six:

"He could never be a husband to her. She lived with him like a married nun, a sister of Christ. It was more than that, too. For of course, they had had a month of real marriage. And Clifford knew that in her nature was a heavy, craving physical desire. He knew."

There follows what cannot be called a love story without distorting that term. The author proceeds to recount a series of acts of sexual intercourse which take place between the heroine and her husband's gamekeeper, one Oliver Parkin, which result in the lady's becoming pregnant. The story ends at the point where she is three months pregnant and is making up her mind to leave her husband and flee to the physical delights of life with Parkin. Hung lightly over this story, like the diaphanous veil over the naked body of a dancer, there are certain dialogues between Constance and Parkin regarding the difference in social caste between them. These are of minor importance. They call attention only to the one thing which restrains the heroine from going to live with Parkin earlier, the thought that she will have to give up the luxury of her husband's home. No moral considerations whatever enter into her thinking and she repeatedly proclaims that she is proud of what she is doing.

[3] *The author's central theme and the dominant effect of the whole book is that it is dangerous to the physical and mental health of a young woman to remain continent* (pp. 12, 22, 23, 24, 26, 27, 32, 33, 35, 36) *and that the most important thing in her life, more important than any rule of law or morals, is the gratification of her sexual desire* (pp. 191 to 193, and the last paragraph, page 320). [Italics ed.].

The book is clearly obscene and the defendant will be held for the Court of Special Sessions.

■ Walker, Postmaster General of the United States
v.
Popenoe, et al. No. 8875.

UNITED STATES COURT OF APPEALS DISTRICT OF COLUMBIA.

Argued March 21, 1945. Decided May 28, 1945.

Mr. *Frederick Chait*, of Washington, D.C., Attorney, Department of Justice, pro hac vice, by special leave of Court, with whom Assistant Attorney General *Francis M. Shea* and Messrs. *Edward M. Curran*, United States Attorney, of Washington, D.C., and *Arnold Levy*, Special Assistant to the Attorney General, were on the brief, for appellant. Mr. *Daniel B. Maher*, Assistant United States Attorney, of Washington, D.C., also entered an appearance for appellant.

Mrs. *Virginia Collins Duncombe*, of Washington, D.C. with whom Mr. *Charles A. Horsky*, of Washington, D.C., was on the brief, for appellees.

Before GRONER, Chief Justice, and EDGERTON and ARNOLD, Associate Justices.

EDGERTON, Associate Justice.

Appellees are the author and the publisher of a pamphlet called Preparing for Marriage, which appellant, the Postmaster General, has excluded from the mails. The District Court granted appellees a summary judgment enjoining appellant from refusing to carry the pamphlet.

The pamphlet contains detailed information and advice regarding the physical and emotional aspects of marriage. Appellees have devoted serious study to the subject. The language of their pamphlet is plain but decent. Its obvious purpose is to educate, and so to benefit, persons who are about to marry. Its premises are that marriage should be made as happy, and as permanent, as possible; that too many marriages are unhappy and too many end in divorce; that some sorts of sexual behavior are more conducive than others to happiness and permanence in marriage; that there is a body of knowledge on this subject which is not instinctive and should be made available to those who need it; and that pamphlets can aid in the diffusion of this knowledge.

Appellant relies on a statute which directs him to exclude from the mails publications which are "obscene, lewd, or lascivious."[1] This statute was enacted 72 years ago, during the presidency of General Grant. It assumes that the stimulation of the senses by writing or print is an evil. It does not assume that this is the worst of evils and must be prevented wherever possible at all costs.

[1, 2] Despite the purely educational purpose and the uniformly decent language of appellees' pamphlet it may be that some of its phrases, by reason merely of their subject matter, may stimulate the senses of some persons. But much more than this is necessary to bring a work within the statute; otherwise no work on anatomy, and no dictionary, could be sent through the mails, and much of our most respected literature would be barred. (1) The effect of a publication on the ordinary reader is what counts.[2] The statute does not intend that we shall "reduce our treatment of sex to the standard of a child's library in the supposed interest of a salacious few."[3] (2) The statute does not bar from the mails an obscene phrase or an obscene sentence. It bars an obscene "book, pamphlet * * * or other publication * * *" If a publication as a whole is not stimulating to the senses of the ordinary reader, it is not within the statute.[4] (3) It would make nonsense of the statute to hold that it covers works of value and repute merely because their incidental effects may include some slight stimulation of the senses of the ordinary reader. The *dominant* effect of an entire publication determines its character. "The standard must be the likelihood that the work will so much arouse the salacity of the reader to whom it is sent as to outweigh any literary, scientific or other merits it may have in that reader's hands."[5]

[3] For all three of the foregoing reasons, "works of physiology, medicine, science, and sex instruction are not within the statute * * * ."[6] No serious work of this character, expressed in decent language, is obscene, lewd, or lascivious.[7] The point is emphasized by the fact that the same statute expressly bars from the mails works "giving information, directly or indirectly * * * how or by what means conception may be prevented or abortion pro-

---

[1] Act of March 3, 1873, 17 Stat. 599, Rev. Stat. 1873, § 3893, 35 Stat. 1129, March 4, 1909, 36 Stat. 1339, March 4, 1911, 18 U.S.C.A. § 334, Criminal Code, § 211, as amended.

[2] *Parmelee v. United States*, 72 App. D.C. 203, 113 F. 2d 729; *United States v. One Book* Called "Ulysses," D.C., S.D.N.Y., 5 F. Supp. 182, affirmed, 2 Cir., 72 F. 2d 705, &708.

[3] *United States v. Kennerley*, D.C., S.D.N.Y., 209 F. 119, 121.

[4] *United States v. One Book* Entitled "Ulysses," 2 Cir., 72 F. 2d 705; *Parmelee v. United States*, 72 App. D.C. 203, 211, 113 F. 2d 729.

[5] *United States v. Levine*, 2 Cir., 83 F. 2d 156, 158.

[6] *United States v. One Book* Entitled "Ulysses," 2 Cir., 72 F. 2d 705, 707.

[7] *Parmelee v. United States*, 72 App. D.C. 203, 210, 113 F. 2d 729; *Consumers Union of United States, Inc. v. Walker*, 79 U.S. App. D.C. 229, 145 F. 2d 33; *United States v. Dennett*, 2 Cir., 39 F. 2d 564, 76 A.L.R. 1092; *United States v. One Obscene Book* Entitled "Married Love," D.C., S.D.N.Y., 48 F. 2d 821.

duced." If explicit sex information had been obscene, lewd, or lascivious within the meaning of the statute, particular mention of contraceptive information would not have been necessary.

The statement in appellant's brief that appellees' pamphlet "deals with contraception and gives information as to sources of additional material on the subject" is quite misleading. The pamphlet mentions contraception, but it does not describe or even remotely suggest any contraceptive method. It contains what it calls a "supplementary reading list" of sixteen items. One of these is "Himes, Norman E. Practical Birth Control Methods. N.Y., 1938." The pamphlet gives no further information about this item and does not tell where or how the reader can get it. If, as appellant seems to contend, the listing of it justified exclusion of appellees' pamphlet from the mails, the Index Expurgatorius would have to be excluded from the mails if it should list a similar item. The statute does not go so far. A general statement that works on birth control exist does not give information "how or by what means conception may be prevented," and neither does a statement that a particular work on birth control exists. Information is not even "indirectly" given unless it is at least made easier to get. One need not know the name of a book or an author in order to go to a store or library and ask for a book on birth control. One's probable chance of getting a book, which may be great or small according to circumstances, is not material here. Whether it is great or small, it will not be materially increased if one asks for a particular book; and this is all that appellees' pamphlet enables one to do.

[4] Appellant's order barring the pamphlet from the mails was issued without notice or hearing. The trial court held, and we agree, that the order was for that reason a denial of due process. Our views on this point are expressed in Judge Arnold's opinion in which, as in the present opinion, we all concur. But if the judgment were affirmed solely on this ground, the merits would have to be decided in a future hearing and a future law-suit. To obviate that necessity we are deciding the merits now. The pamphlet is not covered by the statute. Since a contrary finding could not be supported,[8] it is immaterial that the trial court made no finding. The result is that the judgment is affirmed on each of two distinct and independent grounds. If both these grounds were absent, we should have to consider whether Congress may constitutionally confine discussion of sex as it could not confine discussion of other subjects within the limits which it conceives to be good for the community.

Arnold, Associate Justice (concurring).

[5, 6] The statute under which the Postmaster General acted in this case makes the mailing of obscene matter a serious crime. It also provides that obscene material shall not be conveyed in the mails. The Postmaster General construed this statute as giving him power to exclude from the mails, without a hearing, any publication which in his judgment was obscene. The court below correctly decided that the order barring appellees' pamphlet from the mails without a hearing was a violation of due process.

The power to exclude a publication from the mails

without a hearing in practical effect permits the Postmaster General to cause irreparable injury to any publisher without the minimum safeguard of an opportunity to present his case. There are, of course, other means of distribution besides the mails, but they are not effective ones in the case of ordinary publications. To deprive a publisher of the use of the mails is like preventing a seller of goods from using the principal highway which connects him with his market. In making the determination whether any publication is obscene the Postmaster General necessarily passes on a question involving the fundamental liberty of a citizen. This is a judicial and not an executive function. It must be exercised according to the ideas of due process implicit in the Fifth Amendment. As we said in the case of *Pike* v. *Walker*:[1]

"Whatever may have been the voluntary nature of the postal system in the period of its establishment, it is now the main artery through which the business, social, and personal affairs of the people are conducted and upon which depends in a greater degree than upon any other activity of government the promotion of the general welfare. Not only this, but the postal system is a monopoly which the government enforces through penal statutes forbidding the carrying of letters by other means. It would be going a long way, therefore, to say that in the management of the Post Office the people have no definite rights reserved by the First and Fifth Amendments of the Constitution, and if they have, it would follow that in administering the laws established to protect the mail and the regulations thereunder the duty of the Postmaster General would be,—to use the language of Justice Brandeis in the Burleson case, supra, [255 U.S. 407, 41 S. Ct. 352, 65 L. Ed. 704]—that:

"'In making the determination he must, like a court or a jury, form a judgment whether certain conditions prescribed by Congress exist, on controverted facts or by applying the law. The function is a strictly judicial one, although exercised in administering an executive office. And it is not a function which either involves or permits the exercise of discretionary power'—which is to say, that his authority is governed by the Acts of Congress which confer it, and by the law of the land."

The statement of Mr. Justice Brandeis quoted above occurs in a dissent. But on this particular point his conclusion is reinforced by the majority opinion[2] which upheld the order of the Postmaster General on the ground, among others, that a hearing had been accorded in that case which satisfied the requirements of due process.

The Burleson case dealt with matter which was unmailable because of the Espionage Act. But there is no reason of public policy which would require a different rule in case of obscenity. There are no absolute and enduring standards of what is obscene. The border line between obscenity and decency changes with the times, with public taste in literature and with public attitudes on sex instruction. The determination of whether a publication violates such changing standards is certainly one which should not be undertaken without a hearing.

We are not impressed with the argument that a rule

---

[8] Cf. *Parmelee* v. *United States,* 72 App. D.C. 203, 113 F. 2d 729; *American School of Magnetic Healing* v. *McAnnulty,* 187 U.S. 94, 109, 23 S. Ct. 33, 47 L. Ed. 90.

[1] 1941, 73 App. D.C. 289, 291, 121 F. 2d 37, 39.
[2] *United States* ex rel. *Milwaukee Social Democratic Pub. Co.* v. *Burleson,* 1921, 255 U.S. 407, 41 S. Ct. 352, 65 L. Ed. 704.

requiring a hearing before mailing privileges are suspended would permit, while the hearing was going on, the distribution of publications intentionally obscene in plain defiance of every reasonable standard. In such a case the effective remedy is the immediate arrest of the offender for the crime penalized by this statute. Such action would prevent any form of distribution of the obscene material by mail or otherwise. If the offender were released on bail the conditions of that bail should be a sufficient protection against repetition of the offense before trial. But often

mailing privileges are revoked in cases where the prosecuting officers are not sure enough to risk criminal prosecution. That was the situation here. Appellees have been prevented for a long period of time from mailing a publication which we now find contains nothing offensive to current standards of public decency. A full hearing is the minimum protection required by due process to prevent that kind of injury.

Affirmed.

■ Commonwealth

v.

Isenstadt.

Supreme Judicial Court of Massachusetts. Middlesex. Sept. 17, 1945.

Before FIELD, C.J., and LUMMUS, QUA, RONAN, and WILKINS, JJ.

G. E. *Thompson*, Dist. Atty., and A. *Di Cicco, Jr.*, Asst. Dist. Atty., both of Boston, for the Commonwealth.

A. O. *Dawson*, of New York City, and A. A. *Albert* and J. N. *Welch*, both of Boston, for defendant.

H. *Williams*, amicus curiae.

QUA, Justice.

The defendant has been found guilty by a judge of the Superior Court sitting without jury upon two complaints charging him respectively with selling and with having in his possession for the purpose of sale, exhibition, loan, or circulation a book published under the title "Strange Fruit," which is "obscene, indecent, or impure, or manifestly tends to corrupt the morals of youth." G.L. (Ter. Ed.) c. 272, § 28, as amended by St. 1934, c. 231, and St. 1943, c. 239. The section (except the part describing the penalty) is reproduced in the footnote.[1]

[1] "Whoever imports, prints, publishes, sells or distributes a book, pamphlet, ballad, printed paper, phonographic record or other thing which is obscene, indecent or impure, or manifestly tends to corrupt the morals of youth, or an obscene, indecent or impure print, picture, figure, image or description, manifestly tending to corrupt the morals of youth, or introduces into a family, school or place of education, or buys, procures, receives or has in his possession any such book, pamphlet, ballad, printed paper, phonographic record, obscene, indecent or impure print, picture, figure, image or other thing, either for the purpose of sale, exhibition, loan or circulation or with intent to introduce the same into a family, school or place of education, shall * * * be punished * * *." The germ of this statute is to be found in Prov. St. 1711–12, c. 6 § 19, 1 Prov. Laws 682. It assumes a form approximating its present form in Rev. Sts. c. 130, § 10. Changes introduced by St. 1862, c. 168, § 1; St. 1880, c. 97; Pub. Sts. c. 207, § 15; St. 1890, c. 70; St. 1894, c. 433; R.L. c. 212, § 20; St. 1904, c. 120, § 1; St. 1913, c. 259; St. 1934, c. 231; and St. 1943, c. 239, require no comment in this case. Reference will be made later to St. 1930, c. 162, and to St. 1945, c. 278. The statute last mentioned adds an entirely new procedure.

[1] The complaints are in disjunctive form, but this point was not taken. The defendant could therefore be convicted if he committed any one of the several offenses set forth in so far as such offenses are susceptible of differentiation. G.L. (Ter. Ed.) c. 278, § 17; *Commonwealth* v. *McKnight*, 283 Mass. 35, 38, 39, 186 N.E. 42; *Commonwealth* v. *McMenimon*, 295 Mass. 467, 470, 471, 4 N.E. 2d 246.

[2] We do not pretend ignorance of the controversy which has been carried on in this Commonwealth, sometimes with vehemence, over so called "literary censorship."[2] With this background in mind it may not be out of place to recall that it is not our function to assume a "liberal" attitude or a "conservative" attitude. As in other cases of statutory construction and application, it is our plain but not necessarily easy duty to read the words of the statute in the sense in which they were intended, to accept and enforce the public policy of the Commonwealth as disclosed by its policymaking body, whatever our own personal opinions may be, and to avoid judicial legislation in the guise of new constructions to meet real or supposed new popular viewpoints, preserving always to the Legislature alone its proper prerogative of adjusting the statutes to changed conditions.

We are fully aware of the uselessness of all interpretations of the crucial words of this statute which merely define each of those words by means of the others or of still other words of practically the same signification. We do not now attempt by any single formula to furnish a test for all types of publications, including scientific and medical treatises, religious and educational works, newspapers and periodicals, and classical and recent literature, as well as phonograph records, prints, pictures, paintings, images, statuary and sculpture, artistic or otherwise, all of which are within the literal words of the statute and might conceivably fall within its prohibitions. In this case we are

[2] See "Massachusetts Censorship," by S. S. Grant and S. E. Angoff, 10 Boston Univ. L. Rev. 147; "Judicial Censorship of Obscene Literature," by L. M. Alpert, 52 Harv. L. Rev. 40.

dealing with a recent work of fiction—a novel. We shall, in general, confine our observations to the case in hand, without necessarily binding ourselves to apply all that is here said to entirely different forms of writing or to representations by picture or image.

We deal first with a number of pertinent propositions advanced in the able briefs filed in behalf of the defendant. We agree with some of them.

[3, 4] (1) We agree that since the amendment of the section as it appeared in the General Laws by St. 1930, c. 162, the book is to be treated as a whole in determining whether it violates the statute.[3] It is not to be condemned merely because it may contain somewhere between its covers some expressions which, taken by themselves alone, might be obnoxious to the statute. *Halsey* v. *New York Soc. for Suppression of Vice*, 234 N.Y. 1, 4, 136 N.E. 219; *United States* v. *One Book* Entitled "*Ulysses*", 2 Cir., 72 F. 2d 705, 707. *United States* v. *Levine*, 2 Cir., 83 F. 2d 156. But this does not mean that every page of the book must be of the character described in the statute before the statute can apply to the book. It could never have been intended that obscene matter should escape proscription simply by joining to itself some innocent matter. A reasonable construction can be attained only by saying that the book is within the statute if it contains prohibited matter in such quantity or of such nature as to flavor the whole and impart to the whole any of the qualities mentioned in the statute, so that the book as a whole can fairly be described by any of the adjectives or descriptive expressions contained in the statute. The problem is to be solved, not by counting pages, but rather by considering the impressions likely to be created. For example, a book might be found to come within the prohibition of the statute although only a comparatively few passages contained matter objectionable according to the principles herein explained if that matter were such as to offer a strong salacious appeal and to cause the book to be bought and read on account of it.

[5–7] (2) We agree with the weight of authority that under each of the prohibitions contained in the statute the test of unlawfulness is to be found in the effect of the book upon its probable readers and not in any classification of its subject matter or of its words as being in themselves innocent or obscene.[4] A book is "obscene, indecent or

impure" within the statutory prohibition if it has a substantial tendency to deprave or corrupt its readers by inciting lascivious thoughts or arousing lustful desire. It also violates the statute if it "manifestly tends to corrupt the morals of youth." The latter prohibition is expressly limited to the kind of effect specified—the corruption of morals. Under this branch of the statute it is not enough that a book may tend to coarsen or vulgarize youth if it does not manifestly tend to corrupt the morals of youth. *People* v. *Wendling*, 258 N.Y. 451, 453, 180 N.E. 169, 81 A.L.R. 799.

[8–10] Although in their broadest meaning the statutory words "Obscene, indecent or impure" might signify offensive to refinement, propriety and good taste, we are convinced that the Legislature did not intend by those words to set up any standard merely of taste, even if under the Constitution it could do so. Taste depends upon convention, and sometimes upon irrational taboo. It varies "with the period, the place, and the training, environment and characteristics of persons." *Reddington* v. *Reddington*, 317 Mass. 760, 765, 59 N.E. 2d 775, 778. A penal statute requiring conformity to some current standard of propriety defined only by the statutory words quoted above would make the standard an uncertain one, shifting with every new judge or jury. It would be like a statute penalizing a citizen for failing to act in every situation in a gentlemanly manner. Such a statute would be unworkable if not unconstitutional, for in effect it would "[license] the jury to create its own standard in each case," ex post facto. *Herndon* v. *Lowry*, 301 U.S. 242, 263, 57 S. Ct. 732, 741, 81 L. Ed. 1066. Such a test must be rejected. The prohibitions of the statute are concerned with sex and sexual desire. The statute does not forbid realistically coarse scenes or vulgar words merely because they are coarse or vulgar, although such scenes or words may be considered so far as they bear upon the test already stated of the effect of the book upon its readers.

[11, 12] (3) Since effect is the test, it follows that a book is to be judged in the light of the customs and habits of thought of the time and place of the alleged offence. Although the fundamentals of human nature change but slowly, if indeed they change at all, customs and habits of thought do vary with time and place. That which may give rise to impure thought and action in a highly conventional society may pass almost unnoticed in a society habituated to greater freedom. *United States* v. *Kennerley*, D.C., 209 F. 119, 121; *Parmelee* v. *United States*, 72 App. D.C. 203, 113 F. 2d 729, 731, 732. To recognize this is not to change the law. It is merely to acknowledge the facts upon which the application of the law has always depended. And of the operation of this principle it would seem that a jury of the time and place, representing a cross section of the people, both old and young, should commonly be a suitable arbiter. *United States* v. *Clarke*, D.C., 38 F. 500; *United States* v. *Kennerley*, D.C., 209 F. 119, 121.

[13–16] (4) So, too, we think it proper to take into account what we may call the probable "audience" of the book, just as the effect of a lecture might depend in large degree upon the character of those to whom it is addressed. At one extreme may be placed a highly technical medical work, sold at a great price and advertised only among physicians. At the other extreme may be placed a rather

---

[3] Before this amendment the section read, "Whoever * * * sells * * * a book * * * *containing obscene, indecent or impure language,* or manifestly tending to corrupt the morals of youth * * *." After the amendment is read, "whoever * * * sells * * * a book * * * *which is obscene, indecent or impure,* or manifestly tends to corrupt the morals of youth * * *." (Italics ours.) See *Commonwealth* v. *Friede*, 271 Mass. 318, 321, 322, 171 N.E. 472, 69 A.L.R. 640.

[4] *The Queen* v. *Hicklin*, L.R. 3 Q.B. 360, 371; *Commonwealth* v. *Allison*, 227 Mass. 57, 61, 116 N.E. 265; *Commonwealth* v. *Friede*, 271 Mass. 318, 321, 171 N.E. 472, 69 A.L.R. 640; *Rosen* v. *United States*, 161 U.S. 29, 43, 16 S. Ct. 434, 480, 40 L. Ed. 606; *Dunlop* v. *United States*, 165 U.S. 486, 500, 17 S. Ct. 375, 41 L. Ed. 799; *Dysart* v. *United States*, 272 U.S. 655, 47 S. Ct. 234, 71 L. Ed. 461; *United States* v. *Bennett*, Fed. Cas. No. 14,571; 16 Blatchf. 338, 364–366; *United States* v. *Males*, D.C., 51 F. 41; *Knowles* v. *United States*, 8 Cir., 170 F. 409, 412; *United States* v. *Kennerley*, D.C., 209 F. 119; *Griffin* v. *United States*, 1 Cir., 248 F. 6, 8, 9; *Krause* v. *United States*, 4 Cir., 29 F. 2d 248, 250; *United States* v. *Dennett*, 2 Cir., 39 F. 2d 564, 568, 76 A.L.R. 1092; *Duncan* v. *United States*, 9 Cir., 48 F. 2d 128, 132; *People* v. *Brainard*, 192 App. Div. 816, 820,

821, 183 N.Y.S. 452. See also *People* v. *Wendling*, 258 N.Y. 451, 180 N.E. 169, 81 A.L.R. 799.

well known type of the grossest pornography obviously prepared for persons of low standards and generally intended for juvenile consumption and distributed where it is most likely to reach juvenile eyes. Most questioned books will fall between these extremes. Moreover, the statute was designed for the protection of the public as a whole. Putting aside for the moment the reference in the statute itself to that which manifestly tends to corrupt the morals of youth, a book placed in general circulation is not to be condemned merely because it might have an unfortunate effect upon some few members of the community who might be peculiarly susceptible. The statute is to be construed reasonably. The fundamental right of the public to read is not to be trimmed down to the point where a few prurient persons can find nothing upon which their hypersensitive imaginations may dwell. *United States* v. *Kennerley*, D.C., 209 F. 119, 120. The thing to be considered is whether the book will be appreciably injurious to society in the respects previously stated because of its effect upon those who read it, without segregating either the most susceptible or the least susceptible, remembering that many persons who form part of the reading public and who cannot be called abnormal are highly susceptible to influences of the kind in question and that most persons are susceptible to some degree, and without forgetting youth as an important part of the mass, if the book is likely to be read by youth. *United States* v. *Harmon*, D.C., 45 F. 414, 417; *United States* v. *Levine*, 2 Cir., 83 F. 2d 156; *Parmelee* v. *United States*, 72 App. D.C. 203, 113 F. 2d 729, 731. The jury must ask themselves whether the book will in some appreciable measure do the harm the legislature intended to prevent. This is not a matter of mathematics. The answer cannot be found by saying, for example, that only about one third of probable readers would be adversely affected and then classifying that one third as "abnormal" and concluding that as the book does not adversely affect "normal" persons it is not within the statute. A book that adversely affects a substantial proportion of its readers may well be found to lower appreciably the average moral tone of the mass in the respects hereinbefore described and to fall within the intended prohibition.[5] It seems to us that the statute cannot be construed as meaning less than this without impairing its capacity to give the protection to society which the legislature intended it should give.

[17] (5) We cannot accept the proposition which seems to have been accorded hospitality in a few of the more recent cases in another jurisdiction and which perhaps has been suggested rather than argued in the present case, to wit, that even a work of fiction, taken as a whole, cannot be obscene, indecent or impure if it is written with a sincere and lawful purpose and possesses artistic merit, and if sincerity and artistry are more prominent features of

the book than obscenity.[6] In dealing with such a practical matter as the enforcement of the statute here involved there is no room for the pleasing fancy that sincerity and art necessarily dispel obscenity. The purpose of the statute is to protect the public from that which is harmful. The public must be taken as it is. The mass of the public may have no very serious interest in that which has motivated the author, and it can seldom be said that the great majority of the people will be so rapt in admiration of the artistry of a work as to overlook its salacious appeal. Sincerity and literary art are not the antitheses of obscenity, indecency, and impurity in such manner that one set of qualities can be set off against the other and judgment rendered according to an imaginary balance supposed to be left over on one side or the other. The same book may be characterized by all of these qualities. Indeed, obscenity may sometimes be made even more alluring and suggestive by the zeal which comes from sincerity and by the added force of artistic presentation. We are not sure that it would be impossible to produce even a serious treatise on gynecology in such a manner as to make it obscene. Certainly a novel can be so written, even though the thoughtful reader can also find in it a serious message. Sincerity and art can flourish without pornography and seldom, if ever, will obscenity be needed to carry the lesson. See *United States* v. *Kennerley*, D.C., 209 F. 119, 120, 121; *United States* v. *Dennett*, 2 Cir., 19 F. 564, 569, 76 A.L.R. 1092. The statute contains no exception of works of sincerity and art, or of works in which those elements predominate, if the proscribed elements are also present in such manner and degree as to remain characteristic of the book as a whole. If it is thought that modern conditions require that such an exception be made, the Legislature and not this court should make it. This subject was the principal point of the decision in *Commonwealth* v. *Buckley*, 200 Mass. 346, 86 N.E. 910, 22 L.R.A., N.S., 225, 128 Am. St. Rep. 425, where apt illustration is used. We adhere to the reasoning of that case. See further, *Commonwealth* v. *Friede*, 271 Mass. 318, 322, 323, 171 N.E. 472, 69 A.L.R. 640; *Halsey* v. *New York Soc. for Suppression of Vice*, 234 N.Y. 1, 6, 136 N.E. 219; and *People* v. *Pesky*, 230 App. Div. 200, 243 N.Y.S. 193, citing *Commonwealth* v. *Buckley*, supra.

In taking this position, to which we believe ourselves compelled by the words of the statute, the necessity of enforcing it to accomplish its purposes, and our own previous construction of it, we do not go so far as to say that sincerity of purpose and literary merit are to be entirely ignored. These elements may be considered in so far as they bear upon the question whether the book, considered as a whole, is or is not obscene, indecent, or impure. It is possible that, even in the mind of the general reader, overpowering sincerity and beauty may sometimes entirely obscure or efface the evil effect of occasional questionable passages, especially with respect to the classics of literature that have gained recognized place as part of the great heritage of humanity. The question will commonly be one of fact in each case, and if, looking at the book as a whole, the bad is found to persist in substantial degree alongside the good, as the law now stands, the book will fall within the statute.

---

[5] It is for this reason, if not for others, that we think it was not error to deny the defendant's fifteenth request for ruling, which reads, "As a matter of law the defendant cannot be found to be guilty of violating the provisions of General Laws (Ter. Ed.) chap. 272, sec. 28 as amended, unless it is found that the manifest tendency of the book is to corrupt the morals of the normal youth or adult as compared to the abnormal." This request seeks to classify rigidly all persons with respect to susceptibility as "normal" or "abnormal" and overlooks the possible harmful effect upon a substantial proportion of readers who may be less than a majority and therefore overlooks the possible harm to the mass.

[6] See *United States* v. *One Book* Entitled "*Ulysses*," 2 Cir., 72 F. 2d 705, 707, 708; *United States* v. *Levine*, 2 Cir., 83 F. 2d 156, 158; *Parmelee* v. *United States*, 72 App. D.C. 203, 113 F. 2d 729, 736.

A brief description of the book "Strange Fruit" now seems necessary. The scene is laid in a small town in Georgia. A white boy, Tracy Dean, who lacks the forcefulness to get ahead in the world, and an educated but compliant colored girl, Nonnie Anderson, fall genuinely in love, but because of race inhibitions and pressures they cannot marry. Nonnie supplies to Tracy the sympathy and the nourishment of his self-esteem which his other associations deny him. Illicit intercourse occurs, resulting in pregnancy. Tragedy follows in the form of the murder of Tracy committed by Nonnie's outraged brother and the lynching of an innocent colored man for that crime. Distributed through this book (consisting of two hundred fifty pages in the edition submitted with the record) are four scenes of sexual intercourse, including one supposed to have been imagined. The immediate approaches to these acts and the descriptions of the acts themselves vary in length from a few lines to several pages. They differ in the degree of their suggestiveness. Two of them might be thought highly emotional, with strongly erotic connotations. In addition to these there is a fifth scene in an old abandoned cabin in which there are amatory attitudes, kissing, a loosened blouse, exposed breasts, and circumstances suggesting but perhaps not necessarily requiring an act of intercourse. In still another scene Tracy in a confused drunken frenzy "saw somebody" (himself) tear off Nonnie's clothes "until there was nothing between his hands and her body," "press her down against the floor," "press her body hard— saw him try and fail, try and fail, try and fail," but he "couldn't." In addition to the scenes just mentioned there are distributed fairly evenly throughout the book approximately fifty instances where the author introduces into the story such episodes as indecent assaults upon little girls, an instance of, and a soliloquy upon, masturbation by boys, and references to acts of excretion, to "bobbing" or "pointed" breasts, to "nice little rumps, hard * * * light, bouncy * * *", to a group of little girls "giggling mightily" upon discovering a boy behind a bush and looking at his "bared genitals." We need not recite more of these. The instances mentioned will indicate the general character of the others. Some of these minor incidents might be dismissed as of little or no consequence if there were fewer of them, but when they occur on an average on every fifth page from beginning to end of the book it would seem that a jury or a judge performing the function of a jury might find that they had a strong tendency to maintain a salacious interest in the reader's mind and to whet his appetite for the next major episode.

[18] The principal question in the case is whether, consistently with the principles hereinbefore stated, we can say as matter of law that an honest jury, or an honest trial judge taking the place of a jury with the consent of the defendant, as in this case, would not be acting as reasonable men in concluding beyond a reasonable doubt that this book, taken as a whole, possesses the qualities of obscenity, indecency, or impurity. The test is not what we ourselves think of the book, but what in our best judgment a trier of the facts might think of it without going beyond the bounds of honesty and reason. This distinction, difficult for laymen to grasp, is familiar enough to all lawyers. It is constantly applied by appellate courts and must be preserved if jury trial is to be preserved.

[19] It is urged that this book was written with a serious purpose; that its theme is a legitimate one; that it

possesses great literary merit; and that it has met with a generally favorable reception by reviewers and the reading public. We agree that it is a serious work. It brings out in bold relief the depth and the complexity of the race problem in the South, although, so far as we can see, it offers no remedy. We agree that the theme of a love which because of social conditions and conventions cannot be sanctioned by marriage and which leads to illicit relations is a permissible theme. That such a theme can be handled with power and realism without obscenity seems sufficiently demonstrated in George Eliot's "Adam Bede," which we believe is universally recognized as an English classic. We assume that the book before us is a work of literary merit. We are also prepared to assume for the purposes of this opinion that it has been favorably received by reviewers generally and widely sold to the public, although we do not find it necessary to decide whether the opinions of reviewers and the extent of sale are such well known facts that we ought to take judicial notice of them, if the result of the case depended upon our doing so. We hold, however, that the matters mentioned in this paragraph are not decisive of the issue before us.

[20] Regarding the book as a whole, it is our opinion that a jury of honest and reasonable men could find beyond a reasonable doubt that it contains much that, even in this post-Victorian era, would tend to promote lascivious thoughts and to arouse lustful desire in the minds of substantial numbers of that public into whose hands this book, obviously intended for general sale, is likely to fall; that the matter which could be found objectionable is not necessary to convey any sincere message the book may contain and is of such character and so pervades the work as to give to the whole a sensual and licentious quality calculated to produce the harm which the statute was intended to prevent; and that that quality could be found to persist notwithstanding any literary or artistic merit. We are therefore of opinion that the book could be found to be obscene, indecent, and impure within the meaning of the statute. We think that not only the legislators of 1835 who inserted the substance of the present wording in the statute but also the legislators of later years down to 1943 who amended the statute without greatly altering its substance would be surprised to learn that this court had held that a jury or a judge trying the facts could not even consider whether a book which answers the description already given of "Strange Fruit" falls within the statute.

For the same reasons we are of opinion that an honest and reasonable judge or jury could find beyond a reasonable doubt that this book "manifestly tends to corrupt the morals of youth." The statute does not make fitness for juvenile reading the test for all literature regardless of its object and of the manner of its distribution. Yet it cannot be supposed that the Legislature intended to give youth less protection than that given to the community as a whole by the general proscription of that which is "obscene, indecent or impure." Rather it would seem that something in the nature of additional protection of youth was intended by proscribing anything that manifestly tends to corrupt the morals of youth, even though it may not be obscene, indecent, or impure in the more general sense. *At any rate, we think that almost any novel that is obscene, indecent or impure in the general sense also "manifestly tends to corrupt the morals of youth," if it is likely to fall into the hands of youth. The judge could find that the book in question would be read by many youths. Many adolescents are avid readers of novels.* [Italics ed.].

[21–23] It is contended that the conviction of the defendant violates the Fourteenth Amendment to the Constitution of the United States. See *Near v. State of Minnesota*, 283 U.S. 697, 707, 51 S. Ct. 625, 75 L. Ed. 1357; *De Jonge v. State of Oregon*, 299 U.S. 353, 364, 57 S. Ct. 255, 81 L. Ed. 278. If, however, we are right in holding that an honest and reasonable jury could have found the defendant guilty, it seems to us that no substantial constitutional question remains. The State must have power to protect its citizens, and especially its youth, against obscenity in its various forms, including that which is written or printed. Statutes to this end have long existed. The distribution of obscene printed matter was a crime at common law. *Commonwealth v. Holmes*, 17 Mass. 336. Our own statute was held constitutional in *Commonwealth v. Allison*, 227 Mass. 57, 62, 116 N.E. 265, 266, where this court said, "The subject-matter is well within one of the most obvious and necessary branches of the police power of the state." *State v. McKee*, 73 Conn., 18, 45 A. 409, 49 L.R.A. 542, 84 Am. St. Rep. 124. In *Near v. Minnesota*, 283 U.S. 697, at page 716, 51 S. Ct. 625, at page 631, 75 L. Ed. 1357, Chief Justice Hughes, after asserting the right of Government in time of war to prevent the publication of the sailing dates of transports or of the number and location of troops, added this, "On similar grounds, the primary requirements of decency may be enforced against obscene publications." See *Gitlow v. People of State of New York*, 268 U.S. 652, 667, 45 S. Ct. 625, 69 L. Ed. 1138; *Fox v. State of Washington*, 236 U.S. 273, 35 S. Ct. 383, 59 L. Ed. 573. And in *Chaplinsky v. State of New Hampshire*, 315 U.S. 568, at pages 571, 572, 62 S. Ct. 766, at page 769, 86 L. Ed. 1031, the court said that the use of certain well defined and narrowly limited classes of speech, including "the lewd and obscene" may be prevented and punished. If the so called "clear and present danger" doctrine enunciated in such cases as *Schenck v. United States*, 249 U.S. 47, 52, 39 S. Ct. 247, 249, 63 L. Ed. 470; *Herndon v. Lowry*, 301 U.S. 242, 57 S. Ct. 732, 81 L. Ed. 1066; *Bridges v. State of California*, 314 U.S. 252, 62 S. Ct. 190, 86 L. Ed. 192, and *Thomas v. Collins*, 323 U.S. 516, 65 S. Ct. 315, applies to cases like the present, it would seem that danger of corruption of the public mind is a sufficient danger, and that actual publication and sale render that danger sufficiently imminent to satisfy the doctrine.

The defendant complains of the exclusion of testimony offered by him through three witnesses—a writer and teacher of literature, a child psychiatrist, and a professor of theology who was the editor of "Zion's Herald" and who had also been pastor of a church, had taught in a junior college and had been director of a boy's camp—tending to show as matter of expert opinion that the book was sincerely written; that it would elevate rather than corrupt morals; that it would not create lustful or lecherous desires in any one; that it is "perfectly consistent with the regular flow of literature now publicly sold in the Commonwealth * * *"; and that books containing material more likely to corrupt the morals of youth are sold daily without prosecution.

[24, 25] We cannot regard this exclusion as error. The principal matter about which expert opinion was sought was nothing more than the reaction of normal human beings to a kind of stimulation which is well within the experience of all mankind. Since the inquiry relates to the probable effect upon the general public who may read the book, there is reason to believe that a jury, being composed of men drawn from the various segments of that public, would be as good a judge of the effect as experts in literature or psychiatry, whose points of view and mental reactions in such matters are likely to be entirely different from those of the general public. If expert testimony is to be admitted in this instance it is difficult to see why it would not likewise be competent in a vast number of civil and criminal cases where issues of fact depend upon the emotions and reactions of normal persons in the conditions to which they are exposed. If such evidence becomes competent it will follow that an immense number of cases now submitted without hesitation to the good sense of juries and of trial judges performing the functions of juries cannot be adequately tried without an expensive array of experts on both sides. Experience in those fields in which expert testimony is now admittedly necessary does not lead us to look with favor upon such a sweeping extension. Without prejudging the indefinite future, we are not convinced that the time has come for it. In this we agree with *People v. Muller*, 96 N.Y. 408, 48 Am. Rep. 635, and *St. Hubert Guild v. Quinn*, 64 Misc. 336, 341, 342, 118 N.Y.S. 582. See *Commonwealth v. Buckley*, 200 Mass. 346, 352, 86 N.E. 910, 22 L.R.A., N.S., 225, 128 Am. St. Rep. 425; *United States v. Harmon*, D.C., 45 F. 414, 418. Compare *Parmelee v. United States*, 72 App. D.C. 203, 113 F. 2d 729, 732. In so far as the excluded evidence was expected to show that other books of the same kind, or worse, were being sold without prosecution it was obviously incompetent. *Commonwealth v. Buckley*, 200 Mass. 346, 349, 350, 351, 354, 86 N.E. 910, 22 L.R.A., N.S., 225, 128 Am. St. Rep. 425 (request 26). See *Commonwealth v. Friede*, 271 Mass. 318, 322, 171 N.E. 472, 69 A.L.R. 640.

[26–28] What has already been said covers all of the defendant's requests for rulings that were refused, excepting numbers fourteen and sixteen. Request fourteen was rightly refused on the ground stated by the judge that it makes the effect upon youth the sole test of applicability of the statute. Request sixteen asked the judge "as a matter of law" to "take into consideration the attitude of the community in accepting or rejecting the book. * * *." Since there was no evidence bearing upon the "attitude of the community," this seems to be a request that the judge take judicial notice of that "attitude." We do not feel called upon to prolong this opinion by entering upon a discussion as to whether "attitude of the community" in any of its possible aspects might have any bearing upon any of the issues before the judge. Some courts seem to have favored the taking of judicial notice of literary reviews and criticisms. *Halsey v. New York Soc. for Suppression of Vice*, 234 N.Y. 1, 136 N.E. 219; *United States v. One Book* Entitled "Ulysses", 2 Cir., 72 F. 2d 705, 708. In one case it was said that published reviews of qualified critics might reasonably be allowed "in evidence," which was said to be "quite another thing * * * from expert witnesses at the trial." *United States v. Levine*, 2 Cir., 83 F. 2d 156, 158. Whether these decisions are consistent with our own rules, we need not determine. Neither need we determine whether the views of literary critics show the "attitude of the community" or merely that of a very specialized part of the community, or whether they bear upon anything more than the literary value of the work. For purposes of the present case we are satisfied that the defendant could not compel the judge to commit himself to a ruling upon such vague and sweeping generalities as "attitude of the community" and "accepting or rejecting the book." These seem to us to be composite conclusions which, if they could have been determined at all, could have been determined only by weighing subsidiary facts, some of which might perhaps be susceptible of judicial notice and others of which might well require proof by competent evidence. We cannot say that at the time of the trial the generalization, "attitude of the community in accepting or rejecting" this new book, had become in any aspect an established fact so notorious and indisputable that the judge could be compelled against his own judgment to ascertain it without evidence. Wigmore on Evidence, 3d Ed., §§ 2568, 2568a.

In closing this opinion it is proper to call attention to St. 1945, c. 278, which is to take effect October 1, 1945, and which makes substantial changes in the law and adds a new procedure directed against the book itself by which a judicial determination can be had whether or not a book is obscene, indecent, or impure. This statute should go far to remedy complaints that the present law has operated unjustly in that sales people or clerks in stores may be convicted for selling a book when the seller does not know and perhaps as a practical matter cannot know whether or not he is violating the law.

Exceptions overruled.

LUMMUS, Justice (dissenting).

The opinion seems to me to construe the statute rightly. My dissent is only from the conclusion that the evidence warranted a finding of guilty.

It must be conceded that the book in question is blemished by coarse words and scenes, none of which appear irrelevant to the plot. Yet in them I can find no erotic allurement such as the opinion makes necessary for a conviction. On the contrary, their coarseness is repellent.

The book is a serious study of the relations of different races in a small southern town. It is a grim tragedy, not relieved even by humor. Virtue is not derided, neither is vice made attractive. In the book, the wages of sin is literally death. The reader is left depressed, unable to solve a tragic problem.

The opinion rests its support of the conviction upon the statutory words "manifestly tends to corrupt the morals of youth," as well as upon the other prohibition of the statute. It asserts that "Many adolescents are avid readers of novels." The record contains no evidence to warrant that assertion, or to show that any adolescent ever read the book or would read it under normal conditions. Neither is there, in my judgment, any common knowledge upon which in the absence of evidence a court might conclude that under normal conditions the book would be read by any substantial number of adolescents. Of course, conditions that exist after prosecution for obscenity has been brought or publicly threatened, are abnormal and furnish no test of what the opinion calls the "probable audience" of the book. The market for any novel can be artificially stimulated and widened through curiosity aroused by actual or threatened prosecution in this Commonwealth, frequently to the satisfaction and profit of the publisher elsewhere.

Such knowledge as I have leads me to believe that without such artificial stimulation novels of the class into which the book in question falls are read by few girls and by practically no boys. The great mass of readers are mature women. Plainly the book was not written for juveniles. They would find it dull reading. Under normal conditions I think the book could do no substantial harm to the morals of youth, for few juveniles would ever see it, much less read it. And if by chance some should wade through it, I think it could not reasonably be found to have any erotic allurement, even for youth.

■ People
v.
Winters.

Court of Appeals of New York.

July 19, 1945.

Arthur N. Seiff, of New York City, for appellant.

Emanuel Redfield and *Osmond K. Fraenkel*, both of New York City, for New York City Committee of American Civil Liberties Union, amicus curiæ, in support of appellant's position.

Sidney R. Fleisher, of New York City, for Authors' League of America, Inc., amicus curiæ, in support of appellant's position.

Frank S. Hogan, Dist. Atty., of New York City (Alan J. Elliot and Whitman Knapp, both of New York City, of counsel), for respondent.

LOUGHRAN, Judge.

After trial in the Court of Special Sessions of the City of New York, the defendant was convicted upon charges that he had possessed certain printed materials with intent to sell them, contrary to Penal Law, article 106, section 1141, subdivision 2, Consol. Laws, c. 40. The Appellate Division affirmed and the justice who wrote its opinion gave the defendant leave to present the case to us.

The relevant words of section 1141 are these: "A person * * * who * * * 2. Prints, utters, publishes, sells, lends, gives away, distributes or shows, or has in his possession with intent to sell, lend, give away, distribute or show, or otherwise offers for sale, loan, gift or distribution, any book, pamphlet, magazine, newspaper or other printed paper devoted to the publication, and principally made up of criminal news, police reports, or accounts of criminal deeds, or pictures, or stories of deeds of bloodshed, lust or crime * * * is guilty of a misdemeanor * * *." Numerous copies of magazines composed entirely of such pictures and stories were found on the occasion in question in the bookshop of the defendant.

[1, 2] Defense counsel takes the above text at its full literal meaning. "The statute [he says] makes no distinction between truth, fiction, or statistics. All come within its condemnation equally, provided they consist of 'criminal news' or 'police reports' or 'accounts of criminal deeds.'" From his viewpoint the statute "condemns any publication devoted to and principally made up of criminal news or police reports or accounts of criminal deeds, regardless of the manner of treatment." This conception—which would outlaw all commentaries on crime from detective tales to scientific treatises—may, we think, be dismissed at once on the short ground that its manifest injustice and absurdity were never intended by the Legislature. See *Crooks* v. *Harrelson*, 282 U.S. 55, 51 S. Ct. 49, 75 L. Ed. 156. On the other hand, we are to heed the rule which tells us to read a statutory text in accordance with the general subject matter of which it is a part. See Matter of Rouss, 221 N.Y. 81, 91, 116 N.E. 782, 786; Matter of *Kaplan* v. *Peyser*, 273 N.Y. 147, 7 N.E. 2d 21.

[3] In this instance, the general subject matter constitutes Penal Law, article 106, the caption of which is "Indecency." The above text forms subdivision 2 of section 1141 of article 106. The caption of section 1141 is "Obscene prints and articles." Indecency and obscenity are not and never have been technical terms of the law and hence we are without any full or rigorous definition of the uses made thereof in the administration of justice. To be sure, our statutes dealing with indecent or obscene publications have generally been held to speak of that form of immorality which has relation to sexual impurity. *People* v. *Muller*, 96 N.Y. 408, 48 Am. Rep. 635; *Swearingen* v. *United States*, 161 U.S. 446, 16 S. Ct. 562, 40 L. Ed. 765. Such indeed is the way this court has read subdivision 1 of section 1141 of the Penal Law. People of Eastman, 188 N.Y. 478, 81 N.E. 459, 11 Ann. Cas. 302. But to limit the above words of subdivision 2 of section 1141 to that restricted meaning would be to reduce that subdivision to an unnecessary partial reduplication of subdivision 1. Since our respect for the Legislature is enough to keep us away from that interpretation, we move along to the question of the validity of the broader scope of subdivision 2. From this point on, that subdivision will be called the statute.

[4] Indecency or obscenity is an offense against the public order. 9 Halsbury's Laws of England, 1st Ed., pp. 530, 538; Harris & Wilshire's Criminal Law, 17th Ed., p. 216; 1 Bishop's Criminal Law, 9th Ed., §§ 500, 504. Collections of pictures or stories of criminal deeds of bloodshed or lust unquestionably can be so massed as to become vehicles for inciting violent and depraved crimes against the person and in that case such publications are indecent or obscene in an admissible sense, though not necessarily in the sense of being calculated or intended to excite sexual passion. This idea, as it seems to us, was the principal reason for the enactment of the statute. Cf. *Magon* v. *United States*, 9 Cir., 248 F. 201, certiorari denied 249 U.S. 618, 39 S. Ct. 391, 63 L. Ed. 804; Matter of *Foy Productions Limited* v. *Graves*, 278 N.Y. 498, 15 N.E. 2d 435.

[5] There is, as we are also persuaded, ample warrant in the evidence for the finding that the magazines which were taken from the defendant's premises were obnoxious to the statute. The two thousand copies he kept there were tied up in small bundles that were suitable for delivery to distributors. There is proof of an admission by the defendant of his readiness to sell single copies indiscriminately. The contents are nothing but stories and pictures of criminal deeds of bloodshed and lust. The Appellate Division said: "The stories are embellished with pictures of fiendish and gruesome crimes, and are besprinkled with lurid photographs of victims and perpetrators. Featured articles bear such titles as 'Bargains in Bodies,' 'Girl Slave to a Love Cult,' and 'Girls' Reformatory.'" 268 App. Div. 30, 31, 48 N.Y.S. 2d 230, 231. It is not suggested that any of the contributors was distinguished by his place in the literary world or by the quality of his style. Cf. *Halsey* v. *New York Society for Suppression of Vice*, 234 N.Y. 1, 136 N.E. 219. In short, we have here before us accumulations of details of heinous wrongdoing which plainly carried an appeal to that portion of the public who (as many recent records remind us) are disposed to take to vice for its own sake. Whether the statute extends to accounts of criminal deeds not characterized by bloodshed or lust is a question that does not here arise. See *United States* v. *Limehouse*, 285 U.S. 424, 52 S. Ct. 412, 76 L. Ed. 843; *Jeffrey Mfg. Co.* v. *Blagg*, 235 U.S. 571, 576, 35 S. Ct. 167, 59 L. Ed. 364; *People* v. *Sanger*, 222 N.Y. 192, 118 N.E. 637.

[6, 7] We pass now to the defendant's contention that the statute is unconstitutional because the criterion of criminal liability thereunder is "a personal taste standard, uncertain, indefinite and ex post facto in its practical operation." In the nature of things there can be no more precise test of written indecency or obscenity than the continuing and changeable experience of the community as to what types of books are likely to bring about the corruption of public morals or other analogous injury to the public order. Consequently, a question as to whether a particular publication is indecent or obscene in that sense is a question of the times which must be determined as matter of fact, unless the appearances are thought to be necessarily harmless from the standpoint of public order or morality. See *People* v. *Pesky*, 254 N.Y. 373, 173 N.E. 227; *People* v. *Wendling*, 258 N.Y. 451, 180 N.E. 169, 81 A.L.R. 799; *People* v. *Streep*, 264 N.Y. 666, 191 N.E. 616; *People* v. *Berg*, 269 N.Y. 514, 199 N.E. 513; *People* v. *Fellerman*, 269 N.Y. 629, 200 N.E. 30; *People* v. *Brewer*, 272 N.Y. 442, 3 N.E. 2d 860; Matter of *Foy Productions Limited* v. *Graves*, 278 N.Y. 498, 15 N.E. 2d 435; *People* v. *Osher*, 285 N.Y. 793, 35 N.E. 2d 191. Never has this perception been more forcefully expressed than in this sentence by Cardozo, J.: "Law accepts as the pattern of its justice the morality of the community whose

conduct it assumes to regulate." Paradoxes of Legal Science, 37. The constitutional validity of that standard has long been established. *Rosen* v. *United States*, 161 U.S. 29, 16 S. Ct. 434, 40 L. Ed. 606. See *United States* v. *Rebhuhn*, 2 Cir., 109 F. 2d 512, 514; *Magon* v. *United States*, 2 Cir., 248 F. 201, certiorari denied 249 U.S. 618, 39 S. Ct. 391, 63 L. Ed. 804.

[8] Under the statute, as the defendant sees it, "publication of any crime book or magazine would be hazardous." For reasons that have already been stated, we believe this assertion to be an exaggeration; but the point is of little account in any event, since "the law is full of instances where a man's fate depends on his estimating rightly, that is, as the jury subsequently estimates it, some matter of degree." *Nash* v. *United States*, 229 U.S. 373, 377, 33 S. Ct. 780, 781, 57 L. Ed. 1232. A recent illustration comes readily to hand: An occupier of land who by his use of it does an unreasonable injury to his neighbor's property can be held to answer therefor, though he may have been guilty of no more than an error of judgment. *Dixon* v. *New York Trap Rock Corporation*, 293 N.Y. 509, 58 N.E. 2d 517. So when reasonable men may fairly classify a publication as necessarily or naturally indecent or obscene, a mistaken view by the publisher as to its character or tendency is immaterial.

[9] In anticipation perhaps of what we have already said, the defendant lastly argues for a fresh conception of freedom of the press under which the heretofore accepted requirements of decency would no longer be operative against obscene publications. We see no immediate necessity for announcing so radical a departure from the collective reasoning of our ancestors, a position whereof we think ourselves to be assured by the following words of the highest court in the land: "Allowing the broadest scope to the language and purpose of the Fourteenth Amendment, it is well understood that the right of free speech is not absolute at all times and under all circumstances. There are certain well-defined and narrowly limited classes of speech, the prevention and punishment of which have never been thought to raise any Constitutional problem. These include the lewd and obscene, the profane, the libelous, and the insulting or 'fighting' words—those which by their very utterance inflict injury or tend to incite an immediate breach of the peace. It has been well observed that such utterances are no essential part of any exposition of ideas, and are of such slight social value as a step to truth that any benefit that may be derived from them is clearly outweighed by the social interest in order and morality." *Chaplinsky* v. *State of New Hampshire*, 315 U.S. 568, 571, 572, 62 S. Ct. 766, 769, 86 L. Ed. 1031. See the cases there cited and 2 Cooley on Constitutional Limitations [8th ed.], pp. 886, 1328.

The judgment should be affirmed.

Lehman, Chief Judge (dissenting).

I dissent on the ground that the statute, as construed by the court, is so vague and indefinite as to permit punishment of the fair use of freedom of speech. *Stromberg* v. *People of State of California*, 283 U.S. 359, 51 S. Ct. 532, 75 L. Ed. 1117, 73 A.L.R. 1484. Though statutes directed against "obscenity" and "indecency" are not too vague when limited by judicial definition, they may be too vague when not so limited. See *McJunkins* v. *State*, 10 Ind. 140; *Jennings* v. *State*, 16 Ind. 335. It is the function of the Legislature to define the kind of conduct which is harmful from the standpoint of public order or morality and should be prohibited. Then the question whether the conduct of a defendant falls within that definition may be one of fact. The morality of the community does not, however, become the standard of permissible conduct until the Legislature has embodied its conception of that morality in a regulatory statute.

The judgment should be reversed.

Lewis, Conway, Desmond, Thacher, and Dye, JJ., concur with Loughran, J.

Lehman, C.J., dissents in opinion.

Judgment affirmed.

■ Winters

v.

New York

APPEAL FROM THE COURT OF SPECIAL SESSIONS OF NEW YORK CITY.

No. 3. Argued March 27, 1946.—Reargued November 19, 1946.— Reargued November 10, 1947.—Decided March 29, 1948.

Arthur N. Seiff argued the cause and filed the briefs for appellant. With him on the original argument and the first reargument was *Emanuel Redfield*.

Whitman Knapp argued the cause for appellee. With him on the briefs was *Frank S. Hogan*.

Briefs of *amici curiae* urging reversal were filed by

Sidney R. Fleisher for the Authors' League of America, Inc.; and *Emanuel Redfield, Osmond K. Fraenkel* and *Morris L. Ernst* for the American Civil Liberties Union.

MR. JUSTICE REED delivered the opinion of the Court.

Appellant is a New York City bookdealer, convicted, on information,[1] of a misdemeanor for having in his possession with intent to sell certain magazines charged to violate subsection 2 of § 1141 of the New York Penal Law. It reads as follows:

1. A *person . . . who,*
"§ 1141. Obscene prints and articles
2. *Prints, utters, publishes, sells, lends, gives away, distributes or shows, or has in his possession with intent to sell, lend, give away, distribute or show, or otherwise offers for sale, loan, gift or distribution, any book, pamphlet, magazine, newspaper or other printed paper devoted to the publication, and principally made up of criminal news, police reports, or accounts of criminal deeds, or pictures, or stories of deeds of bloodshed, lust or crime; . . .*

Is guilty of a misdemeanor, . . ."

Upon appeal from the Court of Special Sessions, the trial court, the conviction was upheld by the Appellate Division of the New York Supreme Court, 268 App. Div. 30, 48 N.Y.S. 2d 230, whose judgment was later upheld by the New York Court of Appeals. 294 N.Y. 545, 63 N.E. 2d 98.

The validity of the statute was drawn in question in the state courts as repugnant to the Fourteenth Amendment to the Constitution of the United States in that it denied the accused the right of freedom of speech and press, protected against state interference by the Fourteenth Amendment. *Gitlow* v. *New York*, 268 U.S. 652, 666; *Pennekamp* v. *Florida*, 328 U.S. 331, 335. The principle of a free press covers distribution as well as publication. *Lovell* v. *City of Griffin*, 303 U.S. 444, 452. As the validity of the section was upheld in a final judgment by the highest court of the state against this constitutional challenge, this Court has jurisdiction under Judicial Code § 237 (a). This appeal was argued at the October 1945 Term of this Court and set down for reargument before a full bench at the October 1946 Term. It was then reargued and again set down for further reargument at the present term.

The appellant contends that the subsection violates the

right of free speech and press because it is vague and indefinite. It is settled that a statute so vague and indefinite, in form and as interpreted, as to permit within the scope of its language the punishment of incidents fairly within the protection of the guarantee of free speech is void, on its face, as contrary to the Fourteenth Amendment. *Stromberg* v. *California*, 283 U.S. 359, 369; *Herndon* v. *Lowry*, 301 U.S. 242, 258. A failure of a statute limiting freedom of expression to give fair notice of what acts will be punished and such a statute's inclusion of prohibitions against expressions, protected by the principles of the First Amendment, violates an accused's rights under procedural due process and freedom of speech or press. Where the alleged vagueness of a state statute had been cured by an opinion of the state court, confining a statute punishing the circulation of publications "having a tendency to encourage or incite the commission of any crime" to "encouraging an actual breach of law," this Court affirmed a conviction under the stated limitation of meaning. The accused publication was read as advocating the commission of the crime of indecent exposure. *Fox* v. *Washington*, 236 U.S. 273, 277.

We recognize the importance of the exercise of a state's police power to minimize all incentives to crime, particularly in the field of sanguinary or salacious publications with their stimulation of juvenile delinquency. Although we are dealing with an aspect of a free press in its relation to public morals, the principles of unrestricted distribution of publications admonish us of the particular importance of a maintenance of standards of certainty in the field of criminal prosecution for violation of statutory prohibitions against distribution. We do not accede to appellee's suggestion that the constitutional protection for a free press applies only to the exposition of ideas. The line between the informing and the entertaining is too elusive for the protection of that basic right. Everyone is familiar with instances of propaganda through fiction. What is one man's amusement, teaches another's doctrine. Though we can see nothing of any possible value to society in these magazines, they are as much entitled to the protection of free speech as the best of literature. Cf. *Hannegan* v. *Esquire*, 327 U.S. 146, 153, 158. They are equally subject to control if they are lewd, indecent, obscene or profane. *Ex parte Jackson*, 96 U.S. 727, 736; *Chaplinsky* v. *New Hampshire*, 315 U.S. 568.

The section of the Penal Law, § 1141 (2), under which the information was filed is a part of the "indecency" article of that law. It comes under the caption "Obscene prints and articles." Other sections make punishable various acts of indecency. For example, § 1141 (1), a section not here in issue but under the same caption, punishes the distribution of obscene, lewd, lascivious, filthy, indecent or disgusting magazines.[2] Section 1141 (2) originally was

---

[1] The courts of the information upon which appellant was convicted charged, as the state court opinions show, violation of subsection 2 of § 1141. An example follows:

"Fourth Count"

"And I, the District Attorney aforesaid, by this information, further accuse the said defendant of the Crime of Unlawfully Possessing Obscene Prints, committed as follows:

"The said defendant, on the day and in the year aforesaid, at the city and in the county aforesaid, with intent to sell, lend, give away and show, unlawfully did offer for sale and distribution, and have in his possession with intent to sell, lend, give away and show, a certain obscene, lewd, lascivious, filthy, indecent and disgusting magazine entitled 'Headquarters Detective, True Cases from the Police Blotter, June 1940,' the same being devoted to the publication and principally made up of criminal news, police reports, and accounts of criminal deeds, and pictures and stories of deeds of bloodshed, lust and crime.'"

[2] "§ 1141. . . . 1. A person who sells, lends, gives away, distributes or shows, or offers to sell, lend, give away, distribute, or show, or has in his possession with intent to sell, lend, distribute or give away, or to show, or advertises in any manner, or who otherwise offers for loan, gift, sale or distribution, any obscene, lewd, lascivious, filthy, indecent or disgusting book, magazine, pamphlet, newspaper, story paper, writing, paper, picture, drawing, photograph, figure or image, or any written or printed matter of an indecent character; . . .

. . . . .

"Is guilty of a misdemeanor, ..."

aimed at the protection of minors from the distribution of publications devoted principally to criminal news and stories of bloodshed, lust or crime.[3] It was later broadened to include all the population and other phases of production and possession.

Although many other states have similar statutes, they, like the early statutes restricting paupers from changing residence, have lain dormant for decades. *Edwards* v. *California*, 314 U.S. 160, 176. Only two other state courts, whose reports are printed, appear to have construed language in their laws similar to that here involved. In *Strohm* v. *Illinois*, 160 Ill. 582, 43 N.E. 622, a statute to suppress exhibiting to any minor child publications of this character was considered. The conviction was upheld. The case, however, apparently did not involve any problem of free speech or press or denial of due process for uncertainty under the Fourteenth Amendment.

In *State* v. *McKee*, 73 Conn. 18, 46 A. 409, the court considered a conviction under a statute which made criminal the sale of magazines "devoted to the publication, or principally made up of criminal news, police reports, or pictures and stories of deeds of bloodshed, lust, or crime." The gist of the offense was thought to be a "selection of immoralities so treated as to excite attention and interest sufficient to command circulation for a paper devoted mainly to the collection of such matters." Page 27. It was said, apropos of the state's constitutional provision as to free speech, that the act did not violate any constitutional provision relating to the freedom of the press. It was held, p. 31, that the principal evil at which the statute was directed was "the circulation of this massed immorality." As the charge stated that the offense might be committed "whenever the objectionable matter is a leading feature of the paper or when special attention is devoted to the publication of the prohibited items," the court felt that it failed to state the full meaning of the statute and reversed. As in the *Strohm* case, denial of due process for uncertainty was not raised.

On its face, the subsection here involved violates the rule of the *Stromberg* and *Herndon* cases, *supra*, that statutes which include prohibitions of acts fairly within the protection of a free press are void. It covers detective stories, treatises on crime, reports of battle carnage, *et cetera*. In recognition of this obvious defect, the New York Court of Appeals limited the scope by construction. Its only interpretation of the meaning of the pertinent subsection is that given in this case. After pointing out that New York statutes against indecent or obscene publications have generally been construed to refer to sexual impurity, it interpreted the section here in question to forbid these publications as "indecent or obscene" in a different manner. The Court held that collections of criminal deeds of bloodshed or lust "can be so massed as to become vehicles for inciting violent and depraved crimes against the person and in that case such publications are indecent or obscene in an admissible sense, . . ." 294 N.Y. at 550. "This idea," its opinion goes on to say, "was the principal reason for the enactment of the statute." The Court left open the question of whether "the statute extends to accounts of criminal deeds not characterized by bloodshed or lust" because the magazines in question "are nothing but stories

[3] Ch. 380, New York Laws, 1884; ch. 692, New York Laws, 1887; ch. 925, New York Laws, 1941.

and pictures of criminal deeds of bloodshed and lust." As the statute in terms extended to other crimes, it may be supposed that the reservation was on account of doubts as to the validity of so wide a prohibition. The court declared: "In short, we have here before us accumulations of details of heinous wrongdoing which plainly carried an appeal to that portion of the public who (as many recent records remind us) are disposed to take to vice for its own sake." Further, the Court of Appeals, 294 N.Y. at 549, limited the statute so as not to "outlaw all commentaries on crime from detective tales to scientific treatises" on the ground that the legislature did not intend such literalness of construction. It thought that the magazines the possession of which caused the filing of the information were indecent in the sense just explained. The Court had no occasion to and did not weigh the character of the magazine exhibits by the more frequently used scales of § 1141 (1), printed in note 2. It did not interpret § 1141 (2) to punish distribution of indecent or obscene publications, in the usual sense, but that the present magazines were indecent and obscene because they "massed" stories of bloodshed and lust to incite crimes. Thus interpreting § 1141 (2) to include the expanded concept of indecency and obscenity stated in its opinion, the Court of Appeals met appellant's contention of invalidity from indefiniteness and uncertainty of the subsection by saying, 294 N.Y. at 551,

"In the nature of things there can be no more precise test of written indecency or obscenity than the continuing and changeable experience of the community as to what types of books are likely to bring about the corruption of public morals or other analogous injury to the public order. Consequently, a question as to whether a particular publication is indecent or obscene in that sense is a question of the times which must be determined as matter of fact, unless the appearances are thought to be necessarily harmless from the standpoint of public order or morality."

The opinion went on to explain that publication of any crime magazine would be no more hazardous under this interpretation than any question of degree and concluded, p. 552,

"So when reasonable men may fairly classify a publication as necessarily or naturally indecent or obscene, a mistaken view by the publisher as to its character or tendency is immaterial."

The Court of Appeals by this authoritative interpretation made the subsection applicable to publications that, besides meeting the other particulars of the statute, so massed their collection of pictures and stories of bloodshed and of lust "as to become vehicles for inciting violent and depraved crimes against the person." Thus, the statute forbids the massing of stories of bloodshed and lust in such a way as to incite to crime against the person. This construction fixes the meaning of the statute for this case. The interpretation by the Court of Appeals puts these words in the statute as definitely as if it had been so amended by the legislature. *Hebert* v. *Louisiana*, 272 U.S. 312, 317; *Skiriotes* v. *Florida*, 313 U.S. 69, 79. We assume that the defendant, at the time he acted, was chargeable with knowledge of the scope of subsequent interpretation.

Compare *Lanzetta* v. *New Jersey*, 306 U.S. 451. As lewdness in publications is punishable under § 1141 (1) and the usual run of stories of bloodshed, such as detective stories, are excluded, it is the massing as an incitation to crime that becomes the important element.

Acts of gross and open indecency or obscenity, injurious to public morals, are indictable at common law, as violative of the public policy that requires from the offender retribution for acts that flaunt accepted standards of conduct. 1 Bishop, Criminal Law (9th ed.), § 500; Wharton, Criminal Law (12th ed.), § 16. When a legislative body concludes that the mores of the community call for an extension of the impermissible limits, an enactment aimed at the evil is plainly within its power, if it does not transgress the boundaries fixed by the Constitution for freedom of expression. The standards of certainty in statutes punishing for offenses is higher than in those depending primarily upon civil sanction for enforcement. The crime "must be defined with appropriate definiteness." *Cantwell* v. *Connecticut*, 310 U.S. 296; *Pierce* v. *United States*, 314 U.S. 306, 311. There must be ascertainable standards of guilt. Men of common intelligence cannot be required to guess at the meaning of the enactment.[4] The vagueness may be from uncertainty in regard to persons within the scope of the act, *Lanzetta* v. *New Jersey*, 306 U.S. 451, or in regard to the applicable tests to ascertain guilt.[5]

Other states than New York have been confronted with similar problems involving statutory vagueness in connection with free speech. In *State* v. *Diamond*, 27 New Mexico 477, 202 P. 988, a statute punishing "any act of any kind whatsoever which has for its purpose or aim the destruction of organized government, federal, state or municipal, or to do or cause to be done any act which is antagonistic to or in opposition to such organized government, or incite or attempt to incite revolution or opposition to such organized government" was construed. The court said, p. 479: "Under its terms no distinction is made between the man who advocates a change in the form of our government by constitutional means, or advocates the abandonment of organized government by peaceful methods, and the man who advocates the overthrow of our government by armed revolution, or other form of force and violence." Later in the opinion the statute was held void for uncertainty, p. 485:

"Where the statute uses words of no determinative meaning, or the language is so general and indefinite as to embrace not only acts commonly recognized as reprehensible, but also others which it is unreasonable to presume

were intended to be made criminal, it will be declared void for uncertainty."

Again in *State* v. *Klapprott*, 127 N.J.L. 395, 22 A. 2d 877, a statute was held invalid on an attack against its constitutionality under state and federal constitutional provisions that protect an individual's freedom of expression. The statute read as follows, p. 396:

"Any person who shall, in the presence of two or more persons, in any language, make or utter any speech, statement or declaration, which in any way incites, counsels, promotes, or advocates hatred, abuse, violence or hostility against any group or groups of persons residing or being in this state by reason of race, color, religion or manner of worship, shall be guilty of a misdeameanor."

The court said, pp. 401–2:

"It is our view that the statute, supra, by punitive sanction, tends to restrict what one may say lest by one's utterances there be incited or advocated hatred, hostility or violence against a group 'by reason of race, color, religion or manner of worship.' But additionally and looking now to strict statutory construction, is the statute definite, clear and precise so as to be free from the constitutional infirmity of the vague and indefinite? That the terms 'hatred,' 'abuse,' 'hostility,' are abstract and indefinite admits of no contradiction. When do they arise? Is it to be left to a jury to conclude beyond reasonable doubt when the emotion of hatred or hostility is aroused in the mind of the listener as a result of what a speaker has said? Nothing in our criminal law can be invoked to justify so wide a discretion. The criminal code must be definite and informative so that there may be no doubt in the mind of the citizenry that the interdicted act or conduct is illicit."

This Court goes far to uphold state statutes that deal with offenses, difficult to define, when they are not entwined with limitations on free expression.[6] We have the same attitude toward federal statutes.[7] Only a definite conviction by a majority of this Court that the conviction violates the Fourteenth Amendment justifies reversal of the court primarily charged with responsibility to protect persons from conviction under a vague state statute.

The impossibility of defining the precise line between permissible uncertainty in statutes caused by describing crimes by words well understood through long use in the criminal law—obscene, lewd, lascivious, filthy, indecent or disgusting—and the unconstitutional vagueness that leaves a person uncertain as to the kind of prohibited conduct—massing stories to incite crime—has resulted in three arguments of this case in this Court. The legislative bodies in draftsmanship obviously have the same difficulty as do the judicial in interpretation. Nevertheless despite the difficulties, courts must do their best to determine whether or not the vagueness is of such a character "that men of common intelligence must necessarily guess at its meaning." *Connally* v. *General Constr. Co.*, 269 U.S. 385, 391.

---

[4] *Connally* v. *General Construction Co.*, 269 U.S. 385, 391–92: "But it will be enough for present purposes to say generally that the decisions of the court upholding statutes as sufficiently certain, rested upon the conclusion that they employed words or phrases having a technical or other special meaning, well enough known to enable those within their reach to correctly apply them, . . . or a well-settled common law meaning, notwithstanding an element of degree in the definition as to which estimates might differ, . . . or, as broadly stated by Mr. Chief Justice White in *United States* v. *Cohen Grocery Co.*, 255 U.S. 81, 92, 'that, for reasons found to result either from the text of the statutes involved or the subjects with which they dealt, a standard of some sort was afforded.'"

[5] *United States* v. *Cohen Grocery Co.*, 255 U.S. 81, 89–93; *Champlin Refining Co.* v. *Corporation Commission*, 286 U.S. 210, 242; *Smith* v. *Cahoon*, 283 U.S. 553, 564.

[6] *Omaechevarria* v. *Idaho*, 246 U.S. 343; *Waters-Pierce Oil Co.* v. *Texas*, 212 U.S. 86.

[7] *United States* v. *Petrillo*, 332 U.S. 1; *Gorin* v. *United States*, 312 U.S. 19.

The entire text of the statute or the subjects dealt with may furnish an adequate standard.[8] The present case as to a vague statute abridging free speech involves the circulation of only vulgar magazines. The next may call for decision as to free expression of political views in the light of a statute intended to punish subversive activities.

The subsection of the New York Penal Law, as now interpreted by the Court of Appeals, prohibits distribution of a magazine principally made up of criminal news or stories of deeds of bloodshed or lust, so massed as to become vehicles for inciting violent and depraved crimes against the person. But even considering the gloss put upon the literal meaning by the Court of Appeals' restriction of the statute to collections of stories "so massed as to become vehicles for inciting violent and depraved crimes against the person . . . not necessarily . . . sexual passion," we find the specification of publications, prohibited from distribution, too uncertain and indefinite to justify the conviction of this petitioner. Even though all detective tales and treatises on criminology are not forbidden, and though publications made up of criminal deeds not characterized by bloodshed or lust are omitted from the interpretation of the Court of Appeals, we think fair use of collections of pictures and stories would be interdicted because of the utter impossibility of the actor or the trier to know where this new standard of guilt would draw the line between the allowable and the forbidden publications. No intent or purpose is required—no indecency or obscenity in any sense heretofore known to the law. "So massed as to incite to crime" can become meaningful only by concrete instances. This one example is not enough. The clause purposes to punish the printing and circulation of publications that courts or juries may think influence generally persons to commit crimes of violence against the person. No conspiracy to commit a crime is required. See *Musser* v. *Utah*, 333 U.S. 95. It is not an effective notice of new crime. The clause has no technical or common law meaning. Nor can light as to the meaning be gained from the section as a whole or the Article of the Penal Law under which it appears. As said in the *Cohen Grocery Company* case, *supra*, p. 89:

"It leaves open, therefore, the widest conceivable inquiry, the scope of which no one can foresee and the result of which no one can foreshadow or adequately guard against."

The statute as construed by the Court of Appeals does not limit punishment to the indecent and obscene, as formerly understood. When stories of deeds of bloodshed, such as many in the accused magazines, are massed so as to incite to violent crimes, the statute is violated. It does not seem to us that an honest distributor of publications could know when he might be held to have ignored such a prohibition. Collections of tales of war horrors, otherwise unexceptionable, might well be found to be "massed" so as to become "vehicles for inciting violent and depraved crimes." Where a statute is so vague as to make criminal an innocent act, a conviction under it cannot be sustained. *Herndon* v. *Lowry*, 301 U.S. 242, 259.

To say that a state may not punish by such a vague statute carries no implication that it may not punish

circulation of objectionable printed matter, assuming that it is not protected by the principles of the First Amendment, by the use of apt words to describe the prohibited publications. Section 1141, subsection 1, quoted in note 2, is an example. Neither the states nor Congress are prevented by the requirement of specificity from carrying out their duty of eliminating evils to which, in their judgment, such publications give rise.

Reversed.

Mr. Justice Frankfurter, joined by Mr. Justice Jackson and Mr. Justice Burton, dissenting.

By today's decision the Court strikes down an enactment that has been part of the laws of New York for more than sixty years,[1] and New York is but one of twenty States having such legislation. Four more States have statutes of like tenor which are brought into question by this decision, but variations of nicety preclude one from saying that these four enactments necessarily fall within the condemnation of this decision. Most of this legislation is also more than sixty years old. The latest of the statutes which cannot be differentiated from New York's law, that of the State of Washington, dates from 1909. It deserves also to be noted that the legislation was judicially applied and sustained nearly fifty years ago. See *State* v. *McKee*, 73 Conn. 18, 46 A. 409. Nor is this an instance where the pressure of proximity or propaganda led to the enactment of the same measure in a concentrated region of States. The impressiveness of the number of States which have

[8] *Hygrade Provision Co.* v. *Sherman*, 266 U.S. 497, 501; *Mutual Film Corp.* v. *Ohio Industrial Commission*, 236 U.S. 230, 245–46; *Screws* v. *United States*, 325 U.S. 91, 94–100.

[1] The original statute, N.Y.L. 1884, c. 380, has twice since been amended in minor details. N.Y.L. 1887, c. 692; N.Y.L. 1941, c. 925. In its present form, it reads as follows:

"§ 1141. Obscene prints and articles

"1. A person . . . who,

"2. Prints, utters, publishes, sells, lends, gives away, distributes or shows, or has in his possession with intent to sell, lend, give away, distribute or show, or otherwise offers for sale, loan, gift or distribution, any book, pamphlet, magazine, newspaper or other printed paper devoted to the publication, and principally made up of criminal news, police reports, or accounts of criminal deeds, or pictures, or stories of deeds of bloodshed, lust or crime; . . .

"Is guilty of a misdemeanor . . . ."

That this legislation was neither a casual enactment nor a passing whim is shown by the whole course of its history. The original statute was passed as the result of a campaign by the New York Society for the Suppression of Vice and the New York Society for the Prevention of Cruelty to Children. See 8th Ann. Rep., N.Y. Soc. for the Suppression of Vice (1882) p. 7; 9th *id.* (1883) p. 9; 10th *id.* (1884) p. 8; 11th *id.* (1885) pp. 7–8. The former organization, at least, had sought legislation covering many more types of literature and conduct. See 8th *id.* (1882) pp. 6–9; 9th *id.* (1883) pp. 9–12. On the other hand, in 1887, the limitation of the statute to sales, etc., to children was removed. N.Y.L. 1887, c. 692. More recently, it has been found desirable to add to the remedies available to the State to combat this type of literature. A 1941 statute conferred jurisdiction upon the Supreme Court, at the instance of the chief executive of the community, to enjoin the sale or distribution of such literature. N.Y.L. 1941, c. 925, § 2, N.Y. Code Crim. Proc. § 22-a. (The additional constitutional problems that might be raised by such injunctions, cf. *Near* v. *Minnesota*, 283 U.S. 697, are of course not before us.)

this law on their statute books is reinforced by their distribution throughout the country and the time range of the adoption of the measure.[2] Cf. Hughes, C.J., in *West Coast Hotel Co.* v. *Parrish,* 300 U.S. 379, 399.

These are the statutes that fall by this decision:[3]

1. Gen. Stat. Conn. (1930) c. 329, § 6245, derived from L. 1885, c. 47, § 2.*
2. Ill. Ann. Stat. (Smith-Hurd) c. 38, § 106, derived from Act of June 3, 1889, p. 114, § 1 (minors).
3. Iowa Code (1946) § 725.8, derived from 21 Acts, Gen. Assembly, c. 177, § 4 (1886) (minors).
4. Gen. Stats. Kan. (1935) § 21–1102, derived from L. 1886, c. 101, § 1.
5. Ky. Rev. Stat. (1946) § 436.110, derived from L. 1891–93, c. 182, § 217 (1893) (similar).
6. Rev. Stat. Maine (1944) c. 121, § 27, derived from Acts and Resolves 1885, c. 348, § 1 (minors).
7. Ann. Code Md. (1939) Art. 27, § 496, derived from L. 1894, c. 271, § 2.
8. Ann. Laws Mass. (1933) c. 272, § 30, derived from Acts and Resolves 1885, c. 305 (minors).
9. Mich. Stat. Ann. (1938) § 28.576, derived from L. 1885, No. 138.
10. Minn. Stat. (1945) § 617.72, derived from L. 1885, c. 268, § 1 (minors).
11. Mo. Rev. Stat. (1939) § 4656, derived from Act of April 2, 1885, p. 146, § 1 (minors).
12. Rev. Code Mont. (1935) § 11134, derived from Act of March 4, 1891, p. 255, § 1 (minors).
13. Rev. Stat. Neb. (1943) § 28–924, derived from L. 1887, c. 113, § 4 (minors).
14. N.Y. Consol. L. (1938) Penal Law, Art. 106, § 1141 (2), derived from L. 1884, c. 380.
15. N.D. Rev. Code (1943) § 12–2109, derived from L. 1895, c. 84, § 1 (similar).
16. Ohio Code Ann. (Throckmorton, 1940) § 13035, derived from 82 Sess. L. 184 (1885) (similar).
17. Ore. Comp. L. Ann. (1940) § 23–924, derived from Act of Feb. 25, 1885, p. 126 (similar).
18. Pa. Stat. Ann. (1945) Tit. 18, § 4524, derived from L. 1887, P.L. 38, § 2.
19. Rev. Stat. Wash. (Remington, 1932) § 2459 (2), derived from L. 1909, c. 249, § 207 (2).
20. Wis. Stat. (1945) § 351.38 (4), derived from L. 1901, c. 256.

The following statutes are somewhat similar, but may not necessarily be rendered unconstitutional by the Court's decision in the instant case:

1. Colo. Stat. Ann. (1935) c. 48, § 217, derived from Act of April 9, 1885, p. 172, § 1.

2. Ind. Stat. Ann. (1934) § 2607, derived from L. 1895, c. 109.
3. S.D. Code (1939) § 13.1722 (4), derived from L. 1913, c. 241, § 4.
4. Tex. Stat. (Vernon, 1936), Penal Code, Art. 527, derived from L. 1897, c. 116.

This body of laws represents but one of the many attempts by legislatures to solve what is perhaps the most persistent, intractable, elusive, and demanding of all problems of society—the problem of crime, and, more particularly, of its prevention. By this decision the Court invalidates such legislation of almost half the States of the Union. The destructiveness of the decision is even more far-reaching. This is not one of those situations where power is denied to the States because it belongs to the Nation. These enactments are invalidated on the ground that they fall within the prohibitions of the "vague contours" of the Due Process Clause. The decision thus operates equally as a limitation upon Congressional authority to deal with crime, and, more especially, with juvenile delinquency. These far-reaching consequences result from the Court's belief that what New York, among a score of States, has prohibited, is so empty of meaning that no one desirous of obeying the law could fairly be aware that he was doing that which was prohibited.

Fundamental fairness of course requires that people be given notice of what to avoid. If the purpose of a statute is undisclosed, if the legislature's will has not been revealed, it offends reason that punishment should be meted out for conduct which at the time of its commission was not forbidden to the understanding of those who wished to observe the law. This requirement of fair notice that there is a boundary of prohibited conduct not to be overstepped is included in the conception of "due process of law." The legal jargon for such failure to give forewarning is to say that the statute is void for "indefiniteness."

But "indefiniteness" is not a quantitative concept. It is not even a technical concept of definite components. It is itself an indefinite concept. There is no such thing as "indefiniteness" in the abstract, by which the sufficiency of the requirement expressed by the term may be ascertained. The requirement is fair notice that conduct may entail punishment. But whether notice is or is not "fair" depends upon the subject matter to which it relates. Unlike the abstract stuff of mathematics, or the quantitatively ascertainable elements of much of natural science, legislation is greatly concerned with the multiform psychological complexities of individual and social conduct. Accordingly, the demands upon legislation, and its responses, are variable and multiform. That which may appear to be too vague and even meaningless as to one subject matter may be as definite as another subject-matter of legislation permits, if the legislative power to deal with such a subject is not to be altogether denied. The statute books of every State are full of instances of what may look like unspecific definitions of crime, of the drawing of wide circles of prohibited conduct.

In these matters legislatures are confronted with a dilemma. If a law is framed with narrow particularity, too easy opportunities are afforded to nullify the purposes of the legislation. If the legislation is drafted in terms so vague that no ascertainable line is drawn in advance between innocent and condemned conduct, the purpose of

---

[2] We have no statistics or other reliable knowledge as to the incidence of violations of these laws, nor as to the extent of their enforcement. Suffice it to say that the highest courts of three of the most industrialized States—Connecticut, Illinois, and New York—have had this legislation before them.

[3] This assumes a similar construction for essentially the same laws.

* Since this opinion was filed, Conn. L. 1935, c. 216, repealing this provision, has been called to my attention.

the legislation cannot be enforced because no purpose is defined. It is not merely in the enactment of tax measures that the task of reconciling these extremes—of avoiding throttling particularity or unfair generality—is one of the most delicate and difficult confronting legislators. The reconciliation of these two contradictories is necessarily an empiric enterprise largely depending on the nature of the particular legislative problem.

What risks do the innocent run of being caught in a net not designed for them? How important is the policy of the legislation, so that those who really like to pursue innocent conduct are not likely to be caught unaware? How easy is it to be explicitly particular? How necessary is it to leave a somewhat penumbral margin but sufficiently revealed by what is condemned to those who do not want to sail close to the shore of questionable conduct? These and like questions confront legislative draftsmen. Answers to these questions are not to be found in any legislative manual nor in the work of great legislative draftsmen. They are not to be found in the opinions of this Court. These are questions of judgment, peculiarly within the responsibility and the competence of legislatures. The discharge of that responsibility should not be set at naught by abstract notions about "indefiniteness."

The action of this Court today in invalidating legislation having the support of almost half the States of the Union rests essentially on abstract notions about "indefiniteness." The Court's opinion could have been written by one who had never read the issues of "Headquarters Detective" which are the basis of the prosecution before us, who had never deemed their contents as relevant to the form in which the New York legislation was cast, had never considered the bearing of such "literature" on juvenile delinquency, in the allowable judgment of the legislature. Such abstractions disregard the considerations that may well have moved and justified the State in not being more explicit than these State enactments are. Only such abstract notions would reject the judgment of the States that they have outlawed what they have a right to outlaw, in the effort to curb crimes of lust and violence, and that they have not done it so recklessly as to occasion real hazard that other publications will thereby be inhibited, or also be subjected to prosecution.

This brings our immediate problem into focus. No one would deny, I assume, that New York may punish crimes of lust and violence. Presumably also, it may take appropriate measures to lower the crime rate. But he must be a bold man indeed who is confident that he knows what causes crime. Those whose lives are devoted to an understanding of the problem are certain only that they are uncertain regarding the role of the various alleged "causes" of crime. Bibliographies of criminology reveal a depressing volume of writings on theories of causation. See, *e.g.*, Kuhlman, A Guide to Material on Crime and Criminal Justice (1929) Item Nos. 292 to 1211; Culver, Bibliography of Crime and Criminal Justice (1927–1931) Item Nos. 877–1475, and (1932–1937) Item Nos. 799–1560. Is it to be seriously questioned, however, that the State of New York, or the Congress of the United States, may make incitement to crime itself an offense? He too would indeed be a bold man who denied that incitement may be caused by the written word no less than by the spoken. If "the Fourteenth Amendment does not enact Mr. Herbert Spencer's Social Statics," (Holmes, J., dissenting in *Loch-*

ner v. *New York*, 198 U.S. 45, 75), neither does it enact the psychological dogmas of the Spencerian era. The painful experience which resulted from confusing economic dogmas with constitutional edicts ought not to be repeated by finding constitutional barriers to a State's policy regarding crime, because it may run counter to our inexpert psychological assumptions or offend our presuppositions regarding incitements to crime in relation to the curtailment of utterance. This Court is not ready, I assume, to pronounce on causative factors of mental disturbance and their relation to crime. Without formally professing to do so, it may actually do so by invalidating legislation dealing with these problems as too "indefinite."

Not to make the magazines with which this case is concerned part of the Court's opinion is to play "Hamlet" without Hamlet. But the Court sufficiently summarizes one aspect of what the State of New York here condemned when it says "we can see nothing of any possible value to society in these magazines." From which it jumps to the conclusion that, nevertheless, "they are as much entitled to the protection of free speech as the best of literature." Wholly neutral futilities, of course, come under the protection of free speech as fully as do Keats' poems or Donne's sermons. But to say that these magazines have "nothing of any possible value to society" is only half the truth. This merely denies them goodness. It disregards their mischief. As a result of appropriate judicial determination, these magazines were found to come within the prohibition of the law against inciting "violent and depraved crimes against the person," and the defendant was convicted because he exposed for sale such materials. The essence of the Court's decision is that it gives publications which have "nothing of any possible value to society" constitutional protection but denies to the States the power to prevent the grave evils to which, in their rational judgment, such publications give rise. The legislatures of New York and the other States were concerned with these evils and not with neutral abstractions of harmlessness. Nor was the New York Court of Appeals merely resting, as it might have done, on a deep-seated conviction as to the existence of an evil and as to the appropriate means for checking it. That court drew on its experience, as revealed by "many recent records" of criminal convictions before it, for its understanding of the practical concrete reasons that led the legislatures of a score of States to pass the enactments now here struck down.

The New York Court of Appeals thus spoke out of extensive knowledge regarding incitements to crimes of violence. In such matters, local experience, as this Court has said again and again, should carry the greatest weight against our denying a State authority to adjust its legislation to local needs. But New York is not peculiar in concluding that "collections of pictures or stories of criminal deeds of bloodshed or lust unquestionably can be so massed as to become vehicles for inciting violent and depraved crimes against the person." 294 N.Y. at 550. A recent murder case before the High Court of Australia sheds light on the considerations which may well have induced legislation such as that now before us, and on the basis of which the New York Court of Appeals sustained its validity. The murder was committed by a lad who had just turned seventeen years of age, and the victim was the driver of a taxicab. I quote the following from the opinion of Mr. Justice Dixon: "In his evidence on the *voir dire*

Graham [a friend of the defendant and apparently a very reliable witness] said that he knew Boyd Sinclair [the murderer] and his moods very well and that he just left him; that Boyd had on a number of occasions outlined plans for embarking on a life of crime, plans based mainly on magazine thrillers which he was reading at the time. They included the obtaining of a motor car and an automatic gun." *Sinclair v. The King*, 73 Comm. L.R. 316, 330.

"Magazine thrillers" hardly characterizes what New York has outlawed. New York does not lay hold of publications merely because they are "devoted to and principally made up of criminal news or police reports or accounts of criminal deeds, regardless of the manner of treatment." So the Court of Appeals has authoritatively informed us. 294 N.Y. at 549. The aim of the publication must be incitation to "violent and depraved crimes against the person" by so massing "pictures and stories of criminal deeds of bloodshed or lust" as to encourage like deeds in others. It would be sheer dogmatism in a field not within the professional competence of judges to deny to the New York legislature the right to believe that the intent of the type of publications which it has proscribed is to cater to morbid and immature minds—whether chronologically or permanently immature. It would be sheer dogmatism to deny that in some instances, as in the case of young Boyd Sinclair, deeply embedded, unconscious impulses may be discharged into destructive and often fatal action.

If legislation like that of New York "has been enacted upon a belief of evils that is not arbitrary we cannot measure their extent against the estimate of the legislature." *Tanner v. Little*, 240 U.S. 369, 385. The Court fails to give enough force to the influence of the evils with which the New York legislature was concerned "upon conduct and habit, not enough to their insidious potentialities." *Rast v. Van Deman & Lewis Co.*, 240 U.S. 342, 364. The other day we indicated that, in order to support its constitutionality, legislation need not employ the old practice of preambles, nor be accompanied by a memorandum of explanation setting forth the reasons for the enactment. See *Woods v. Cloyd W. Miller Co.*, 333 U.S. 138, 144. Accordingly, the New York statute, when challenged for want of due process on the score of "indefiniteness," must be considered by us as though the legislature had thus spelled out its convictions and beliefs for its enactment:

Whereas, we believe that the destructive and adventurous potentialities of boys and adolescents, and of adults of weak character or those leading a drab existence are often stimulated by collections of pictures and stories of criminal deeds of bloodshed or lust so massed as to incite to violent and depraved crimes against the person; and

Whereas, we believe that such juveniles and other susceptible characters do in fact commit such crimes at least partly because incited to do so by such publications, the purpose of which is to exploit such susceptible characters; and

Whereas, such belief, even though not capable of statistical demonstration, is supported by our experience as well as by the opinions of some specialists qualified to express opinions regarding criminal psychology and not disproved by others; and

Whereas, in any event there is nothing of possible value to society in such publications, so that there is no gain to the State, whether in edification or enlightenment or amusement or good of any kind; and

Whereas, the possibility of harm by restricting free utterance through harmless publications is too remote and too negligible a consequence of dealing with the evil publications with which we are here concerned;

Be it therefore enacted that—

Unless we can say that such beliefs are intrinsically not reasonably entertainable by a legislature, or that the record disproves them, or that facts of which we must take judicial notice preclude the legislature from entertaining such views, we must assume that the legislature was dealing with a real problem touching the commission of crime and not with fanciful evils, and that the measure was adapted to the serious evils to which it was addressed. The validity of such legislative beliefs or their importance ought not to be rejected out of hand.

Surely this Court is not prepared to say that New York cannot prohibit traffic in publications exploiting "criminal deeds of bloodshed or lust" so "as to become vehicles for inciting violent and depraved crimes against the person." Laws have here been sustained outlawing utterance far less confined. A Washington statute, directed against printed matter tending to encourage and advocate disrespect for law, was judged and found not wanting on these broad lines:

"We understand the state court by implication at least to have read the statute as confined to encouraging an actual breach of law. Therefore the argument that this act is both an unjustifiable restriction of liberty and too vague for a criminal law must fail. It does not appear and is not likely that the statute will be construed to prevent publications merely because they tend to produce unfavorable opinions of a particular statute or of law in general. In this present case the disrespect for law that was encouraged was disregard of it—an overt breach and technically criminal act. It would be in accord with the usages of English to interpret disrespect as manifested disrespect, as active disregard going beyond the line drawn by the law. That is all that has happened as yet, and we see no reason to believe that the statute will be stretched beyond that point.

"If the statute should be construed as going no farther than it is necessary to go in order to bring the defendant within it, there is no trouble with it for want of definiteness." *Fox v. Washington*, 236 U.S. 273, 277.

In short, this Court respected the policy of a State by recognizing the practical application which the State court gave to the statute in the case before it. This Court rejected constitutional invalidity based on a remote possibility that the language of the statute, abstractly considered, might be applied with unbridled looseness.

Since Congress and the States may take measures against "violent and depraved crimes," can it be claimed that "due process of law" bars measures against incitement to such crimes? But if they have power to deal with incitement, Congress and the States must be allowed the effective means for translating their policy into law. No doubt such a law presents difficulties in draftsmanship where publications are the instruments of incitement. The problem is to avoid condemnation so unbounded that neither the text of the statute nor its subject matter affords "a standard of some sort" (*United States* v. *Cohen Grocery Co.*, 255 U.S. 81, 92). Legislation must put people on notice as to the kind of conduct from which to refrain. Legislation must also avoid so tight a phrasing as to leave the area for evasion ampler than that which is condemned. How to escape, on the one hand, having a law rendered futile because no standard is afforded by which conduct is to be judged, and, on the other, a law so particularized as to defeat itself through the opportunities it affords for evasion, involves an exercise of judgment which is at the heart of the legislative process. It calls for the accommodation of delicate factors. But this accommodation is for the legislature to make and for us to respect, when it concerns a subject so clearly within the scope of the police power as the control of crime. Here we are asked to declare void the law which expresses the balance so struck by the legislature, on the ground that the legislature has not expressed its policy clearly enough. That is what it gets down to.

What were the alternatives open to the New York legislature? It could of course conclude that publications such as those before us could not "become vehicles for inciting violent and depraved crimes." But surely New York was entitled to believe otherwise. It is not for this Court to impose its belief, even if entertained, that no "massing of print and pictures" could be found to be effective means for inciting crime in minds open to such stimulation. What gives judges competence to say that while print and pictures may be constitutionally outlawed because judges deem them "obscene," print and pictures which in the judgment of half the States of the Union operate as incitements to crime enjoy a constitutional prerogative? When on occasion this Court has presumed to act as an authoritative faculty of chemistry, the result has not been fortunate. See *Burns Baking Co.* v. *Bryan*, 264 U.S. 504, where this Court ventured a view of its own as to what is reasonable "tolerance" in breadmaking. Considering the extent to which the whole domain of psychological inquiry has only recently been transformed and how largely the transformation is still in a pioneer stage, I should suppose that the Court would feel even less confidence in its views on psychological issues. At all events, it ought not to prefer its psychological views—for, at bottom, judgment on psychological matters underlies the legal issue in this case—to those implicit in an impressive body of enactments and explicitly given by the New York Court of Appeals, out of the abundance of its experience, as the reason for sustaining the legislation which the Court is nullifying.

But we are told that New York has not expressed a policy, that what looks like a law is not a law because it is so vague as to be meaningless. Suppose then that the New York legislature now wishes to meet the objection of the Court. What standard of definiteness does the Court furnish the New York legislature in finding indefiniteness in the present law? Should the New York legislature enumerate by name the publications which in its judgment are "inciting violent and depraved crimes"? Should the New York legislature spell out in detail the ingredients of stories or pictures which accomplish such "inciting"? What is there in the condemned law that leaves men in the dark as to what is meant by publications that exploit "criminal deeds of bloodshed or lust" thereby "inciting

violent and depraved crimes"? What real risk do the Conan Doyles, the Edgar Allen Poes, the William Rougheads, the ordinary tribe of detective story writers, their publishers, or their booksellers run?

Insofar as there is uncertainty, the uncertainty derives not from the terms of condemnation, but from the application of a standard of conduct to the varying circumstances of different cases. The Due Process Clause does not preclude such fallibilities of judgment in the administration of justice by men. Our penal codes are loaded with prohibitions of conduct depending on ascertainment through fallible judges and juries of a man's intent or motive—on ascertainment, that is, from without of a man's inner thoughts, feelings and purposes. Of course a man runs the risk of having a jury of his peers misjudge him. Mr. Justice Holmes has given the conclusive answer to the suggestion that the Due Process Clause protects against such a hazard: "the law is full of instances where a man's fate depends on his estimating rightly, that is, as the jury subsequently estimates it, some matter of degree. If his judgment is wrong, not only may he incur a fine or a short imprisonment, as here; he may incur the penalty of death." *Nash* v. *United States*, 229 U.S. 373, 377. To which it is countered that such uncertainty not in the standard but in its application is not objectionable in legislation having a long history, but is inadmissible as to more recent laws. Is this not another way of saying that when new circumstances or new insights lead to new legislation the Due Process Clause denies to legislatures the power to frame legislation with such regard for the subject matter as legislatures had in the past? When neither the Constitution nor legislation has formulated legal principles for courts, and they must pronounce them, they find it impossible to impose upon themselves such a duty of definiteness as this decision exacts from legislatures.

The Court has been led into error, if I may respectfully suggest, by confusing want of certainty as to the outcome of different prosecutions for similar conduct, with want of definiteness in what the law prohibits. But diversity in result for similar conduct in different trials under the same statute is an unavoidable feature of criminal justice. So long as these diversities are not designed consequences but due merely to human fallibility, they do not deprive persons of due process of law.

In considering whether New York has struck an allowable balance between its right to legislate in a field that is so closely related to the basic function of government, and the duty to protect the innocent from being punished for crossing the line of wrongdoing without awareness, it is relevant to note that this legislation has been upheld as putting law-abiding people on sufficient notice, by a court that has been astutely alert to the hazards of vaguely phrased penal laws and zealously protective of individual rights against "indefiniteness." See, *e.g.*, *People* v. *Phyfe*, 136 N.Y. 554, 32 N.E. 978; *People* v. *Briggs*, 193 N.Y. 457, 86 N.E. 522; *People* v. *Shakun*, 251 N.Y. 107, 167 N.E. 187; *People* v. *Grogan*, 260 N.Y. 138, 183 N.E. 273. The circumstances of this case make it particularly relevant to remind, even against a confident judgment of the invalidity of legislation on the vague ground of "indefiniteness," that certitude is not the test of certainty. If men may reasonably differ whether the State has given sufficient notice that it is outlawing the exploitation of criminal potentialities, that in itself ought to be sufficient, according to the repeated pronouncements of this Court, to lead us to abstain from denying power to the States. And it deserves to be repeated that the Court is not denying power to the States in order to leave it to the Nation. It is denying power to both. By this decision Congress is denied power, as part of its effort to grapple with the problems of juvenile delinquency in Washington, to prohibit what twenty States have seen fit to outlaw. Moreover, a decision like this has a destructive momentum much beyond the statutes of New York and of the other States immediately involved. Such judicial nullification checks related legislation which the States might deem highly desirable as a matter of policy, and this Court might not find unconstitutional.

Almost by his very last word on this Court, as by his first, Mr. Justice Holmes admonished against employing "due process of law" to strike down enactments which, though supported on grounds that may not commend themselves to judges, can hardly be deemed offensive to reason itself. It is not merely in the domain of economics that the legislative judgment should not be subtly supplanted by the judicial judgment. "I cannot believe that the Amendment was intended to give us *carte blanche* to embody our economic or moral beliefs in its prohibitions." So wrote Mr. Justice Holmes in summing up his protest for nearly thirty years against using the Fourteenth Amendment to cut down the constitutional rights of the States. *Baldwin v. Missouri*, 281 U.S. 586, 595 (dissenting).

Indeed, Mr. Justice Holmes is a good guide in deciding this case. In three opinions in which, speaking for the Court, he dealt with the problem of "indefiniteness" in relation to the requirement of due process, he indicated the directions to be followed and the criteria to be applied. Pursuit of those directions and due regard for the criteria require that we hold that the New York legislature has not offended the limitations which the Due Process Clause has placed upon the power of States to counteract avoidable incitements to violent and depraved crimes.

Reference has already been made to the first of the trilogy, *Nash v. United States, supra*. There the Court repelled the objection that the Sherman Law "was so vague as to be inoperative on its criminal side." The opinion rested largely on a critical analysis of the requirement of "definiteness" in criminal statutes to be drawn from the Due Process Clause. I have already quoted the admonishing generalization that "the law is full of instances where a man's fate depends on his estimating rightly, that is, as the jury subsequently estimates it, some matter of degree." 229 U.S. at 377. Inasmuch as "the common law as to restraint of trade" was "taken up" by the Sherman Law, the opinion in the *Nash* case also drew support from the suggestion that language in a criminal statute which might otherwise appear indefinite may derive definiteness from past usage. How much definiteness "the common law of restraint of trade" has imparted to "the rule of reason," which is the guiding consideration in applying the Sherman Law, may be gathered from the fact that since the *Nash* case this Court has been substantially divided in at least a dozen cases in determining whether a particular situation fell within the undefined limits of the Sherman

Law.[4] The Court's opinion in this case invokes this doctrine of "permissible uncertainty" in criminal statutes as to words that have had long use in the criminal law, and assumes that "long use" gives assurance of clear meaning. I do not believe that the law reports permit one to say that statutes condemning "restraint of trade" or "obscenity" are much more unequivocal guides to conduct than this statute furnishes, nor do they cast less risk of "estimating rightly" what judges and juries will decide than does this legislation.

The second of this series of cases, *International Harvester Co. v. Kentucky*, 234 U.S. 216, likewise concerned anti-trust legislation. But that case brought before the Court a statute quite different from the Sherman Law. However indefinite the terms of the latter, whereby "it throws upon men the risk of rightly estimating a matter of degree," it is possible by due care to keep to the line of safety. But the Kentucky statute was such that no amount of care would give safety. To compel men, wrote Mr. Justice Holmes "to guess on peril of indictment what the community would have given for them [commodities] if the continually changing conditions were other than they are, to an uncertain extent; to divine prophetically what the reaction of only partially determinate facts would be upon the imaginations and desires of purchasers, is to exact gifts that mankind does not possess." 234 U.S. at 223–224. The vast difference between this Kentucky statute and the New York law, so far as forewarning goes, needs no laboring.

The teaching of the *Nash* and the *Harvester* cases is that it is not violative of due process of law for a legislature in framing its criminal law to cast upon the public the duty of care and even of caution, provided that there is sufficient warning to one bent on obedience that he comes near the proscribed area. In his last opinion on this subject, Mr. Justice Holmes applied this teaching on behalf of a unanimous Court, *United States v. Wurzbach*, 280 U.S. 396, 399. The case sustained the validity of the Federal Corrupt Practices Act. What he wrote is too relevant to the matter in hand not to be fully quoted:

"It is argued at some length that the statute, if extended beyond the political purposes under the control of Congress, is too vague to be valid. The objection to uncertainty concerning the persons embraced need not trouble us now. There is no doubt that the words include representatives, and if there is any difficulty, which we are far from intimating, it will be time enough to consider it when raised by someone whom it concerns. The other objection is to the meaning of 'political purposes.' This would be open even if we accepted the limitations that would make the

---

[4] See, *e.g.*, *United States v. United Shoe Machinery Co.*, 247 U.S. 32; *United States v. United States Steel Corp.*, 251 U.S. 417; *United States v. Reading Co.*, 253 U.S. 26; *American Column & Lumber Co. v. United States*, 257 U.S. 377; *Maple Flooring Mfrs. Assn. v. United States*, 268 U.S. 563; *Cement Mfrs. Protective Assn. v. United States*, 268 U.S. 588; *United States v. Trenton Potteries Co.*, 273 U.S. 392; *Interstate Circuit, Inc. v. United States*, 306 U.S. 208; *United States v. Socony-Vacuum Oil Co.*, 310 U.S. 150; *United States v. South-Eastern Underwriters Assn.*, 322 U.S. 533; *Associated Press v. United States*, 326 U.S. 1; *United States v. Line Material Co.*, 333 U.S. 287.

law satisfactory to the respondent's counsel. But we imagine that no one not in search of trouble would feel any. Whenever the law draws a line there will be cases very near each other on opposite sides. The precise course of the line may be uncertain, but no one can come near it without knowing that he does so, if he thinks, and if he does so it is familiar to the criminal law to make him take the risk. Nash v. United States, 229 U.S. 373."

Only a word needs to be said regarding *Lanzetta* v. *New Jersey*, 306 U.S. 451. The case involved a New Jersey statute of the type that seek to control "vagrancy." These statutes are in a class by themselves, in view of the familiar abuses to which they are put. See Note, 47 Col. L. Rev. 613, 625. Definiteness is designedly avoided so as to allow the net to be cast at large, to enable men to be caught who are vaguely undesirable in the eyes of police and prosecution, although not chargeable with any particular offense. In short, these "vagrancy statutes" and laws against

"gangs" are not fenced in by the text of the statute or by the subject matter so as to give notice of conduct to be avoided.

And so I conclude that New York, in the legislation before us, has not exceeded its constitutional power to control crime. The Court strikes down laws that forbid publications inciting to crime, and as such not within the constitutional immunity of free speech, because in effect it does not trust State tribunals, nor ultimately this Court, to safeguard inoffensive publications from condemnation under this legislation. Every legislative limitation upon utterance, however valid, may in a particular case serve as an inroad upon the freedom of speech which the Constitution protects. See, *e.g., Cantwell* v. *Connecticut*, 310 U.S. 296, and Mr. Justice Holmes' dissent in *Abrams* v. *United States*, 250 U.S. 616, 624. The decision of the Court is concerned solely with the validity of the statute, and this opinion is restricted to that issue.

■ State
v.
Lerner.
No. 57048

Court of Common Pleas of Ohio, Hamilton County.

June 9, 1948.

William F. Hopkins, of Cincinnati, for defendant.
Carson Hoy, Pros. Atty., and *Thomas Stueve,* Asst. Pros. Atty., both of Cincinnati, for plaintiff.

STRUBLE, Judge.

The defendant stands charged with having had "obscene literature" in his possession and of offering same for sale.

The defendant waived a jury and his case was tried by this Court.

The defendant owns and operates the Bell Block News Shop located in the city of Cincinnati and as charged in the first count of the indictment he did have in his possession as part of his stock-in-trade and offered for sale the January, February, March, April, August, October and November issues of a certain magazine entitled "Sunshine and Health," "official organ of the American Sunbathing Association, Inc.," which the State says "were not wholly obscene, but contained lewd and lascivious photographs and drawings * * * so indecent that it would be improper to place them in the records of this court"; and as charged in the second count of the indictment he did have in his possession and offered for sale "a series of twelve photographs of a female Strip Tease Act and Performance" which the State says is so indecent that it would be improper to be placed in the records of this court. The State charges that these photographs which are of men, women and children in the nude, and this Strip Tease Act

are "obscene, lewd and lascivious" and by having in his possession and offering for sale the several issues of this magazine and this "Strip Tease Act" that the defendant violated the "obscene literature" provision of Section 13035, G.C.O., which is as follows:

"Whoever knowingly sells, lends, gives away, exhibits or offers to sell, lend, give away or exhibit, or publishes or offers to publish or has in his possession or has under his control an obscene, lewd or lascivious book, magazine, pamphlet, paper, writing, advertisement, circular, print, picture photograph, motion picture film or book pamphlet, paper, magazine not wholly obscene but containing lewd or lascivious articles, advertisements, photographs, or drawing, representation, figure, image, cast, instrument or article of an indecent or immoral nature * * *."

Defense.

The parties are in agreement as to the facts, but the defendant claims that the "obscene literature" provision of Section 13035, supra, is an invalid exercise of the Police Powers in that it is unreasonable, oppressive, not impartial and has no substantial relation to public morals and that in the extent of its operations it invades the field reserved for the press by Article I, Section 11, Ohio Constitution, which is as follows:

"Every citizen may freely speak, write, and publish his sentiments on all subjects, being responsible for the abuse of the right; and no law shall be passed to restrain or abridge the liberty of speech, or of the press," and that the several issues of this magazine and this Strip Tease Act are not in fact "obscene, lewd or lascivious."

Section 13035, G.C.O.

Besides "obscene literature," Section 13035, supra, reenacted in 1943 forbids "drugs" for criminal purposes and "publications" "principally" of police news.

New York has an "obscene literature" statute similar to Section 13035, supra, and in a recent decision by the Supreme Court of the United States, *Winters, Appellant, v. People of the State of New York*, 333 U.S. 507, 68 S. Ct. 665, the "police news" provision of the New York statute was held unconstitutional on the ground of uncertainty. Mr. Justice Frankfurter, joined by two other Justices, dissented from the holding of the majority of the Court and said that the decision of the majority invalidates the "obscene literature" statutes in twenty states, one of which is Ohio's Section 13035, supra. The provisions, parts of Section 13035, supra, are separable and it seems that this decision has no bearing as to the "obscene literature" part of Section 13035, supra.

Section 13035, supra, is now like it was before reenacted except that now "whoever knowingly sells" are liable, while before it was "whoever sells" and "magazines, motion picture films" are included in the inhibitions of the "obscene literature" provision, and then by way of amendment the following was incorporated, namely:

"or book, pamphlet, paper, magazine not wholly obscene but containing lewd or lascivious articles, advertisements, photographs, or drawing, representation, figure, image, cast, instrument or article * * *."

Not Wholly Obscene—Wholly Obscene.

"Not wholly obscene" is "any, some obscenity," less than the whole;—an obscene verse, passage, photograph, any obscene thing in a "book, paper, pamphlet, or magazine" brings it within the forbidden class by force of this amendment.

"Obscenity" in literature, in the arts, letters and sciences was made a crime in Ohio in 1872 and this statute contained a provision forbidding "any book, pamphlet, periodical, paper or other publication containing any obscene engraving, drawing or picture"; but in the reenactments of this statute in 1876, 1885 and 1894, this "any obscenity" test was omitted but to be reestablished for "books, papers, pamphlets and magazines" by the amendment incorporated in the "obscene literature" provision of Section 13035, supra, as reenacted in 1943.

Other forms of "obscene" literature left by this reenactment not subject to this "any obscenity" test are—"writing, advertisement, circular print, picture photograph and motion picture films."

By the statute of 1872 all forms of "obscene" literature inhibited by that statute were forbidden if they contained any of the obscene things mentioned. By the obscene literature provision of Section 13035, supra, "books, papers, pamphlets and magazines" are forbidden if they contain any of the obscene things mentioned, but not so as to the other forms of obscene literature inhibited by this provision.

Disciplining "books, papers, pamphlets and magazines" more severely for "obscenity" than other forms of literature was never done before in Ohio, nor in any other state or country so far as we are able to discover; although in Massachusetts in Colonial days in 1711 there was enacted a law prescribing this "any obscenity" test for all forms of literature. This statute was continued as a state statute until 1930 when it was repealed in response to public demand.

As to this statute we quote from Alpert's Article, Judicial Censorship of Obscene Literature, Harvard Law Review, Vol. 52, page 56, as follows:

"In summary, the Massachusetts law is relatively simple and in its simplicity harsh. The criminal statute originally enacted in 1711 applying to any book containing obscene, indecent or impure language or manifestly tending to corrupt the morals of youth has been steadfastly construed as banning literary works, save possibly older classic, containing a single passage or passages, the tendency of which is to deprave and corrupt those whose minds are open to such immoral influences and into whose hands the publication might fall."

Obscene literature statutes generally do no more than forbid an "obscene book, etc." and courts through the years have held an "obscene book, etc." to be one containing any or some obscene matter. This "any obscenity" test was not applied alone to "books, papers, pamphlets and magazines" but to all forms of literature. The "any obscenity" test established by the amendment is only for "books, papers, pamphlets and magazines." In recent years some of the ablest jurists in this country are holding that an obscene book is one wholly obscene and that in testing a literary work for obscenity it must be viewed in its entirety and only when and if the obscene contents constitutes the dominant feature or effect of same does it fall within the forbidden class.

Purpose of the Amendment.

[1] The sole purpose of this amendment is to outlaw in this state the "wholly obscene" test for "books, papers, pamphlets and magazines," and shackle publishers, producers and distributors of the same with this "any obscenity" test.

If this amendment is valid the several issues of this magazine fall within the forbidden class if they contain any obscene matter; but if invalid not so,—unless wholly obscene; hence, our first inquiry must be as to the validity of this amendment and that requires a consideration of what is obscenity in literature, and of the "any obscenity" test as applied by the courts and of other ways generally applied for testing obscenity in literature.

Obscene Literature—Crime.

"Obscene" literature was made a crime in England over three hundred years ago and over here in the Colonies some years later, and in due time in the United States and all of the states, and these statutes are all alike except such as provide for the "any obscenity" test, and have always been all alike in that what they do, without mincing words, is to forbid "obscene, lewd or lascivious" books, etc., designating by name what of the arts, letters and sciences are forbidden.

[2] "Obscene"—"obscenity" include "lewd and lasciv-ious" so we will drop the latter two words.

Not any of these laws define "obscenity" or say what it is in literature, or prescribe any test to identify it in litera-ture. That vests the courts with an over-all control, or, as some say, censorship of "obscene" literature; so without ever sending these laws back to legislatures to be made more definite and certain the courts have gone on through the years construing and interpreting the inhibitory words of these statutes generally to agree with their own ideas of what was or was not "obscenity" in the publication before them for review and as time went on the courts have lifted the ban of these statutes from works of art, the sciences and general literature.

Obscenity.

Webster's definition of "obscene" is as follows:

"Ill-looking, filthy, obscene. 1. Offensive to taste; foul; loathsome; disgusting. 2. Offensive to chastity of mind or to modesty; expressing or presenting to the mind or view something that delicacy, purity and decency forbid to be exposed; lewd, indecent; as, obscene language, dances, images. Characterized by or given to obscenity; as, an obscene mind or person. 3. Inauspicious; ill-omened." and of "obscenity," is as follows:

"1. Quality of being obscene; obsceneness; obscene or impure language or acts. 2. Filthiness; foulness."

There was a time when the courts considered "obscen-ity" in literature to be all the things Webster says it is; but since then the courts have settled to the view that it was the sex taboo, not that of immodesty, indelicacy and the like, that these "obscene literature" laws place on the arts, letters and sciences.

Having in mind that these "obscene" literature statutes are shackles on the brains of men, which is as bad if not worse than shackles on the limbs of men, the judiciary has been performing a great service for mankind through the years in lifting this sex taboo from the arts, letters and sciences, and in limiting the scope of these statutes to sex in literature, that is, "anything," "something," as courts say, in a literary work that tends to "arouse impure sex ideas in minds susceptible of such ideas." But that is not a definition of "obscenity," only what the courts say is a "test" by which to identify it in literature.

How is this test to be applied? How is a court or jury to know if on reading a literary work sex ideas arise in the minds of the readers and, if so, whether they are pure or impure for, according to this test, it is only lustful or impure sex ideas with which courts and juries are con-cerned.

Pure, normal sex ideas are all right. All of mankind have sex ideas. Nature is aflame with sex ideas,—the hoot of the owl, the coo of the dove, the blossoms of the flowers, plants and trees, the spawning of the fish. Sex is the why and wherefore of life and living.

The wheat cannot be separated from the chaff by this test; and thinking of it there came to my mind the old axiom of the law—"where the law is uncertain there is no law."

"Obscenity" is not a legal term. It cannot be defined so that it will mean the same to all people all the time, everywhere. "Obscenity" is very much a figment of the imagination,—an undefinable something in the minds of some and not in the minds of others; and is not the same in the minds of the people of every clime and country, nor the same today that it was yesterday or will be tomorrow.

Necessarily, in "obscenity" trials, if that which is claimed "obscenity" in the literary work in review is "ob-scenity" in the mind of the court or the jury, the defen-dant is found guilty, and if not, not guilty.

Alpert's Article, Judicial Censorship of Obscene Litera-ture, Harvard Law Review, Vol. 52, at page 70, says of obscenity:

"The law, in its ponderous generalities, still remains as a weapon of censorship with the only safeguard the mercy of a judge. * * *" and, as to the first one hundred years, of obscene literature as a crime: (p. 47)

"There is no definition of the term. There is no basis of identification. There is no unity in describing what is obscene literature, or in prosecuting it. There is little more than the ability to smell it. * * *."

In 1868 there came an epochal event in the history of the crime of "obscene literature" in the form of a test whereby to identify "obscenity" in literature. Epochal, in that it was the first test to be announced by the courts and in that it has been the test generally applied by the courts of England and this country ever since its announcement. In *Regina* v. *Hicklin*, L.R., 3 Q.B., 360, Lord Cockburn, speaking for the court, said:

"I think the test of obscenity is this, whether the tendency of the matter charged as obscenity is to deprave and corrupt those whose minds are open to such immoral influences, and into whose hands a publication of this sort may fall."

The "matter charged as obscene" was but a part of the literary work under review and counsel argued that the work considered in its entirety was meritorious. Lord Cockburn's answer was:

"Be it so. The question then presents itself in this simple form: May you commit an offense against the law in order that thereby you may effect some ulterior object which you have in view, which may be an honest and even a laudable one? My answer is, emphatically, no. The law says you shall not publish an obscene work."

The high spots of Lord Cockburn's test are (a) that the "matter charged as obscene" may be a passage, chapter, picture, any part of the literary work, and (b) the "ten-dency" of which is to "corrupt" the morally weak.

Lord Cockburn's test is the orthodox test for "obscen-ity" in literature, but in substance it was applied by the Court of England, of the Colonies, and of this country before its pronouncement in the Hicklin case, and since down to the present time, but disregarded by courts as often in the breach as in the observance.

It is no different than the Massachusetts statutes of 1711.

State's Case.

The State bases the first count of the indictment on the "any obscenity" test of the amendment which is part of the Lord Cockburn test. Counsel for the State cited the law of the Hicklin case as the law of the pending case and argue that while the State does not claim that the several issues of this magazine are obscene considered in their entirety, nevertheless, says the State they fall within the forbidden class because of the nude photographs in them the tendency of which is to corrupt the morally weak.

Lord Cockburn—Test—Police Powers.

The "obscene" literature provision of Section 13035, supra, without the amendment forbids an obscene "book," etc., and its inhibitions include all forms of literature. It is of itself a complete statute and construing it without the amendment we must consider the "any obscenity" part and the "might harm the few" part of Lord Cockburn's test in relation to police powers which all governments have and may exercise in the interest of health, peace, safety and morals of the people within their domains.

[3] These "obscene" literature statutes are enacted by governments in the exercise of their police powers; and to be valid enactments in the exercise of police powers must be reasonable, be impartial in their operations, not unduly oppressive and be for the general good; and as these statutes impinge on the freedom of the press, United States and State Constitutions require that they not do that beyond what is reasonably necessary to effect their objective.

The "obscene literature" provision of Section 13035, supra, was enacted in the interest of the morals of the people of Ohio.

Lord Cockburn's Any Obscenity Test.

As to this "any obscenity" it is to be noted that "obscene literature" statutes merely forbid an "obscene book," etc., and leave it to the courts as to what is an "obscene book," etc.

[4] My conclusion is that an "obscene book" must be held to be one "wholly obscene" and that necessarily in testing a literary work for "obscenity" it must be viewed in its entirety and only when and if the "obscene" contents constitute the dominant feature or effect does it fall within the forbidden class. Is obscenity the dominant idea and aim of a literary work? If so it falls within the forbidden class, otherwise not.

These "obscene literature" statutes do not say that an "obscene book" etc. is one that contains any or some obscenity. Courts that say that are writing this "any obscenity" test into those statutes.

The General Assembly of Ohio must have considered an "obscene book" as one "wholly obscene," else why incorporate this amendment in the "obscene literature" provision of Section 13035, supra, forbidding "books, papers, pamphlets and magazines" if they contain any or some obscenity. This "any obscenity" test disregards merits entirely, for as Lord Cockburn puts it, if a literary work contains some obscene matter, although meritorious on the whole and its purpose "be an honest and even a laudable one," it falls within the forbidden class.

These "obscene literature" statutes to be valid must be reasonable and have a reasonable relation to their objective, namely, the moral good of the people of the State or country enacting them. Considering an "obscene book" etc. as one containing anything, something, that might excite impure sex ideas in minds susceptible of such ideas, supposedly youth and the morally weak, strictly enforced would bring within the forbidden class much there is of the arts, letters and sciences, and we doubt if there is a

present-day newspaper or other publication that could comply with a test of this sort.

What courts say "obscenity" is in literature may be found in much there is of literature from Shakespeare's works to modern literature.

From Alpert's Article, supra, at page 71, we quote:

"Yet all great literature contains the elements we call obscene. Certain portions of the Bible have been termed 'obscene.' When a lady objected to the presence of 'improper' words in Samuel Johnson's Dictionary, he is reported to have said: 'Madam, you must have been looking for them.'"

This "any obscenity" test has been observed so much in the breach by courts through the years that most of the arts, letters and sciences are free of the ban of these statutes, yet courts still generally hold it to be the proper test.

My conclusion is that if that is so then these "obscene literature" statutes constitute an invalid exercise of the police powers and trespass beyond all reason in the field reserved for the press. In holding an "obscene book" as one "wholly obscene" we are supported by the weight of recent decisions.

In Parmalee, *Appellant*, v. *United States of America,* D.C.D.C.,[1] the court had under consideration for obscenity the book entitled "Nudism in Modern Life," and the Court in speaking of the "any obscenity" test, said:

"But more recently this standard has been repudiated and for it has been substituted the test that a book must be considered as a whole in its effect, not upon any particular class but upon all those who it is likely to reach. * * * The determining question is, in each case, whether a publication, taken as a whole, has a libidinous effect."

In *United States* v. *One Book* Entitled "Ulysses," 2 Cir., 72 F. 2d 705, syllabus 2, is as follows:

"Where literary publication is sincere and the erotic matter therein was not introduced to promote lust and does not furnish the dominant note of the publication, it is not 'obscene' within statute prohibiting importation of any 'obscene' book (Tariff Act 1930, § 305 (a), 19 U.S.C.A. § 1305 (a)." and syllabus 3 is as follows:

"In determining whether a book is 'obscene' within statute prohibiting importation of any 'obscene' book, the test is whether the book taken as a whole has a libidinous effect (Tariff Act 1930, § 305 (a), 19 U.S.C.A. § 1305 (a))."

Lord Cockburn—Might Harm the Few Test.

Lord Cockburn and courts generally are saying that these "obscene" literature statutes are for the protection of the morally weak; that these statutes withhold from all of us what of literature there is that contains any or some matter that might excite sexually impure ideas in minds susceptible of such ideas.

[5] The answer to this contention is that the police powers may not be exercised for the benefit of the few in disregard of the many, and statutes so enacted are invalid.

In *State of Ohio* v. *Boone*, 84 Ohio St. 346, 351, 95 N.E. 924, 39 L.R.A., N.S., 1015, Ann. Cas. 1912C, 683, the Court in its opinion, speaking of police powers, says:

"To justify the state in thus interposing its authority in

---

[1] See 113 F. 2d 729.

behalf of the public, it must appear, first, that the interest of the public generally, as distinguished from those of a particular class, requires such interference; and, second, that the means are reasonably necessary for the accomplishment of the purpose, and not unduly oppressive upon individuals."

[6] My conclusion is that Ohio's "obscene" literature statute having been enacted for the preservation of the morals of the people of this state that it necessarily follows that the moral standards, moral concepts of the people of this state, as to what is obscene literature, is the only test allowable. It is the moral concept of the people as a whole that literature is obligated to respect.

The community concept of what is "obscene" literature is approximately ascertainable. It goes without saying that public opinion, community concepts condemn sexually nasty, perversive publications, prints, pictures, drawings or photographs as "obscene," not because they might excite sexually impure ideas in minds susceptible of such ideas because that is a mere matter of conjecture, but because they offend the moral concepts of the people as a whole, and the people have the right to establish codes of right conduct for literature as well as for other forms of community conduct.

A governmental policy that would withhold from all of us what is all right for most of us because it might be bad for some of us (youth) as, for example, ban tobacco, labor, liquor, etc., would compel us to close up shop.

In *United States* v. *Harmon*, D.C., 45 F. 414, at page 417, from the opinion we quote:

"Laws of this character are made for society in the aggregate, and not in particular. So, while there may be individuals and societies of men and women of peculiar notions or idiosyncrasies, whose moral sense would neither be depraved nor offended by the publication now under consideration, yet the exceptional sensibility, or want of sensibility, of such cannot be allowed as a standard by which its obscenity or indecency is to be tested. Rather is the test, what is the judgment of the aggregate sense of the community reached by it?"

In *United States* v. *Kennerley*, D.C., 209 F. 119, at page 120, Justice Learned Hand speaking of the Lord Cockburn test, that is, that it is the interest of the few that controls, says:

"That test has been accepted by the lower federal courts until it would be no longer proper for me to disregard it." and then he said:

"I hope it is not improper for me to say that the rule as laid down, however consonant it may be with mid-Victorian morals, does not seem to me to answer to the understanding and morality of the present time, as conveyed by the words, 'obscene, lewd, or lascivious.' I question whether in the end men will regard that as obscene which is honestly relevant to the adequate expression of innocent ideas, and whether they will not believe that truth and beauty are too precious to society at large to be mutilated in the interests of those most likely to pervert them to base uses. Indeed, it seems hardly likely that we are even today so lukewarm in our interest in letters or serious discussion as to be content to reduce our treatment of sex to the standard of a child's library in the supposed interest of a salacious few, or that shame will for long prevent us from adequate portrayal of some of the most serious and beautiful sides of human nature. * * *"

Mr. Justice Hand says that while the Lord Cockburn test is "consonant" with "mid-Victorian morals," yet it is not agreeable to the "morality of the present time" (1913), and yet he applied the test in the case on trial before him. Why enforce in this country and the states the moral standards of mid-Victorian times? These "obscenity" statutes have no extra-territorial force. They are enacted in the interest of the morals of the people whose government enacted them. The moral standards of peoples are not the same in all the states and countries and change from time to time, yet in this country due respect for the freedom of the press tends to uniformity in the states as to what is obscene literature.

How fundamentally unsound it is for example in Ohio for courts to enforce the moral concepts of the people of England of what obscenity in literature was in mid-Victorian times under a statute enacted in 1943 by the people of Ohio for the preservation of their own moral concepts of what is "obscene" literature.

Police Powers—Amendment
Freedom of the Press.

The question is whether the amendment incorporated in the "obscene" literature provision of Section 13035, supra, is a valid exercise by the state of its police powers, and does this amendment in its operative effect invade the field reserved for the press beyond what is reasonably necessary to effect its objective?

Police Powers.

Besides what has been said as to the validity of this "any obscenity" test as applied by the courts throughout the years there are special reasons as to why this amendment is invalid. The "obscene" literature provision considered with the amendment does not treat all forms of literature on equal terms. It is not impartial in its operation in segregating "books, papers, pamphlets and magazines," and disciplining them for "obscenity" more severely than it does other forms of literature, namely, "writing, advertisement, circular, picture, photograph, motion picture film." The "any obscenity" test of this amendment for "books, papers, pamphlets and magazines" is incalculably more severe than the "wholly obscene" test for other forms of literature and brings an anomalous situation into the "obscene" literature statute of this state. An "obscene" photograph, print or picture "in a book, paper, pamphlet or magazine" brings the latter within the forbidden class but not so in a "writing, advertisement or circular" unless it constitutes the dominant feature of the same. A "writing, advertisement, circular," containing any or some "obscenity," but not the dominant feature of same, is not within the forbidden class but in a "book, paper, pamphlet or magazine," brings the same within the forbidden class. There is no reason for treating "books, papers, pamphlets and magazines" more harshly than other forms of literature. They are no more prone to "obscenity" than other forms of literature.

Considering the amendment standing alone it is unduly oppressive in establishing an "obscenity" test for "books, papers, pamphlets and magazines," that would be impossible at least for newspapers and magazines to observe. How could it be possible for present day publishers of newspapers and magazines to keep their publications entirely free of everything that might "tend to stir up the sex impulses," as some judges say obscenity in literature is, or "tends to excite impure sexual ideas in minds susceptible of such ideas," as other judges say it is, or "tends to deprave and corrupt those whose minds are open to such immoral influences" as Lord Cockburn and other judges are saying it is.

In the case of *Froelich* v. *City of Cleveland*, 99 Ohio St. 376, syllabus 3, 124 N.E. 212, we find an accurate statement of the scope and limitations of the police powers, namely:

"The state and municipalities may make all reasonable, necessary and appropriate provisions to promote the health, morals, peace, and welfare of the community. But neither the state nor a municipality may make any regulations which are unreasonable. The means adopted must be suitable to the end in view, must be impartial in operation and not unduly oppressive upon individuals, must have a real and substantial relation to their purpose, and must not interfere with private rights beyond the necessities of the situation."

Freedom of the Press.

"Obscene" literature statutes impinge on the freedom of the press which is one of the fundamental freedoms, rights of the people guaranteed them by Article I, United States Constitution, State Constitutions and Article I, Section 11, Ohio Constitution, the pertinent part of which is:

"and no law shall be passed to restrain or abridge the liberty of speech, or of the press."

[7] Constitutional freedoms, rights of the people, are not absolute nor are the police powers of the state, hence, the people in the exercise of their freedoms, and the state in the exercise of its police powers, must abide by the rule of reason that the people might enjoy their freedoms to the fullest extent consistent with the public welfare.

Considering the "any obscenity" test established by the amendment for "books, papers, pamphlets and magazines" in its relation to the freedom of the press, the question is: What is its operative effect on the freedom of the press?

Well, as we pointed out before, however meritorious on the whole a publication may be, whatever the subject matter, however sincere the presentation or the size, form and design of the presentation, if such publication contains some erotic matter that might stir up impure sex ideas in minds susceptible of such ideas, this "any obscenity" test brings it within the forbidden class.

[8] Section 13037, G.C.O., exempts works of art by bona fide Associations of Artists not organized for profit and medicine but all other "books, papers, pamphlets and magazines" are covered by this amendment. The "any obscenity" test of the amendment is more severe in its operative effect than the "any obscenity" test established by the decision in the Hicklin and other cases for the force of the latter is merely as a precedent which courts may disregard but not so of the "any obscenity" test of the amendment because courts must enforce statutes as they are written.

[9] Having in mind what the Courts say is "obscenity" in literature this amendment condemns as "obscene" about all there is of present day books, papers, pamphlets and magazines and brings most of us within its penalties,

having in mind that "whoever knowingly sells, lends, gives away, exhibits or offers to sell, lend, give away or exhibit, or publishes or offers to publish or has in his possession or has under his control" any of the same are subject to the penalties of the statute.

My conclusion is that this amendment in its operative effect invades the field reserved for the press by Article I, Section 11, Ohio Constitution, beyond what is reasonably necessary to effect its objective.

Summary of Conclusions.

The main part of the "obscene" literature provision and this amendment are separable. The "obscene" literature provision with the amendment is not impartial in its operation, but the amendment is responsible for that. Standing alone the main part of this provision is impartial in its operation and its inhibition include all forms of literature. The amendment standing alone, as we have pointed out, is unduly oppressive and impinges beyond reason on the freedom of the press.

Wherefore, for the reasons stated we are holding this amendment invalid and the main part of the "obscene literature provision" valid considering an "obscene book, etc.," as one "wholly obscene" and the community concept of what is considered "obscene literature" as the only allowable test for the same—with this qualification, that in holding the main part valid we are not passing on, nor are we asked in this case to pass on what might well be considered a basic weakness of Ohio's obscene literature statute and of others which is that they do not define obscenity or say what it is in literature and to do so clearly is a legislative and not a judicial function.

Merits of the Case.
Magazines.

The magazine "Sunshine & Health," "an educational, scientific and cultural publication," is one of several nudist publications in this country, size eight by twelve inches, of about thirty-two pages; fifteen to eighteen per cent of the contents of each issue is made up of photographs of nude men, women and children taken of them in nudist camps, some of which give a front view and exhibits the pubes area and genitals.

It must be noted that the State is not making any complaint of the written contents of the several issues of this magazine, which is made up of advertisements, news items on nudism, nudist camps, etc., and editorials and articles of a scientific and cultural nature, all well written, quite interesting and instructive.

There is not anything in the nature of sexuality in the written contents of these magazines. The emphasis of the written contents is health through nudism and, the way they put it, nudism is the best way and the only way to get the most out of the health-giving qualities of fresh air and sunshine.

Photography.

The sole complaint of the State as to these magazines is of the photographs of nude men, women and children, and not particularly of these, other than of those exhibiting the front view of which there are quite a few, most of which are of children, girls and boys, and some women and some few of men, taken of them alone, in pairs, or family or other groups. The State claims that these nude photographs shock the sense of decency and tend to arouse impure sexual ideas in minds susceptible of such ideas, particularly youth, the ignorant and morally weak.

Youth is the over-all concern but it seems that youth is not in serious danger from sex in literature according to the Report of the American Youth Commission's Study of young people in Maryland (1938) which was published under the title "Youth Tell Their Story," from which we quote the following:

"The chief source of sex 'education' for the youth of all ages and all religious groups was found to be the youth's contemporaries. * * * Sixty-six per cent of the boys and forty per cent of the girls reported that what they knew about sex was more or less limited to what their friends of their own age had told them.

"After 'contemporaries' and the youth's home, the source that is next in importance is the school, from which about 8 per cent of the young people reported they had received most of their sex information. A few, about 4 per cent, reported they owed most to books, while less than 1 per cent asserted that they had acquired most of their information from movies. Exactly the same proportion specified the church as the chief source of their sex information."

These photographs it seems were taken and are being published to promote nudism for they seem to be of persons that are of the best in face and form probably to be found in these nudist camps, for these photographs are of only strong, healthy, good-looking people and seem to be saying to one looking at them "now you skeptic, now you see what nudism can do for you."

So far as is shown, those photographed are all engaged in innocent activities and there is not any emphasis on sex of any kind. There is not, in any of these photographs, any pandering to the lewd and lascivious for pelf and profit; nor any pose, posture or gesture portraying or suggestive of sexual immoralities, perversions or nastiness.

Nudity.

[10] The sole inquiry is,—Is nudity, in this magazine of itself, per se obscenity? The Court holds that nudity is not per se obscenity; nevertheless, there are times, places and circumstance where nudity on display would be out of place and should be penalized, but not as obscenity, but for being on display out of place.

In *Parmalee, Appellant,* v. *United States of America,* supra, the Court says:

"It cannot be assumed that nudity is obscene per se and under all circumstances. Even the application of the narrowest rule would not justify such an assumption. And, from the teachings of psychology and sociology, we know that the contrary view is held by social scientists.

Nudity in art has long been recognized as the reverse of obscene. Art galleries and art catalogues contain many nudes, ancient and modern. Even such a conservative source book as Encyclopaedia Britannica, contains nudes, full front view, male and female, and nude males and females pictured together and in physical contact."

In *People* v. *Muller,* 96 N.Y. 408, 411, 48 Am. Rep. 635, it is said:

"It is evident that mere nudity in painting or sculpture is not obscenity. Some of the great works in painting and sculpture as all know represent nude human forms. It is a false delicacy and mere prudery which would condemn and banish from sight all such objects as obscene, simply on account of their nudity. If the test of obscenity or indecency in a picture or statue is its capability of suggesting impure thoughts, then indeed all such representations might be considered as indecent or obscene. The presence of a woman of the purest character and of the most modest behavior and bearing may suggest to a prurient imagination images of lust, and excite impure desires, and so may a picture or statue not in fact indecent or obscene."

Might not the nude photographs of these magazines bring sex to the minds of some people? Quite likely for some are so susceptible to such ideas that a lady's slipper, or garter, anything will bring such ideas to their minds.

Schroeder, "Obscene Literature and Constitutional Law," p. 275, says:

"When an object, even unrelated to sex, has acquired a sexual association in our minds, its sight will suggest the affiliated idea, and will fail to produce a like sensual thought in the minds of those not obsessed by the same association.

"Thus, books on sexual psychology tell us of men who are so 'pure' that they have their modesty shocked by seeing a woman's shoe displayed in a shop window; others have their modesty offended by hearing married people speak of retiring for the night; some have their modesty shocked by seeing in the store windows a dummy wearing a corset; some are shocked by seeing underwear, or hearing it spoken of otherwise than as 'unmentionables'; still others cannot bear the mention of 'legs' and even speak of the 'limbs' of a piano."

Photographs of women in the nude it seems are no more likely to excite unchaste ideas than photographs of them fully appareled or so scantily appareled as to be near nude, of which we see many in pictorial magazines or other publications.

Havelock Ellis, in his book "Psychology of Sex" says:

"Nakedness is always chaster in its effects than partial clothing," and he quoted the Artist DeMaurier as saying:

"That nothing is so chaste as nudity."

Burton in his "Anatomy of Melancholy" says that the "greatest provocations of lust are from our apparel."

Man is monarch of the animal kingdom and is the only one of them who wears clothes, and one-third of mankind still go naked and authentic observers say that morals are better on islands where the people go naked than in neighboring islands where they wear clothes.

Sumner—Folkways, page 426, says:

"The natives of New Britain are naked but modest and chaste. Nudity, rather checks than stimulates. The same is observed in English New Guiana.

"In primitive times goblinism and magic covered especially the things which later became obscene."

Without doubt these front views violate the community's concept of modesty, but those photographed do not consider nudity immodest. However our inquiry is— whether or not they constitute obscenity in the several issues of this magazine? As to that there are front views in the arts and these are uniformly held not to be obscene, and photography is one form of art.

These front views obscene? Well, they merely show

humankind as God made them and does He not command "Be ye fruitful and multiply and replenish the earth." These front views, as well as the other views, are of God's own children as He made them in His own image.

There cannot be any obscenity in God's own handiwork.

Of "obscenity" this Court feels that it is pertinent to say what the Apostle Paul said of the word "unclean" in his Epistle to the Romans, Chapter 14, Verse 14:

"I know, and am persuaded by the Lord Jesus, that there is nothing unclean of itself, but to him that esteemeth anything to be unclean, to him it is unclean."

Considered in their entirety the several issues of this magazine may not be reproached for obscenity. These magazines, photographs and all of the contents constitute propaganda for the cause of nudism.

The opponents of nudism might complain of them on that ground, but nudism, as a philosophy of life, is not on trial in this case.

The State alleges in the indictment that the several issues of this magazine are not "wholly obscene" nevertheless says the State the nude photographs bring the same within the forbidden class.

This claim is based on the amendment which incorporates the "any obscenity" test of the Hicklin case, which test we have held invalid; nevertheless we conclude that these nude photographs do not constitute obscenity in these magazines.

Strip Tease Act.

[11] The strip tease act of burlesque theaters of a woman disrobing is not before this court except as presented by a series of twelve photographs of a young woman disrobing, the first of her fully clothed, the others of her at various stages as she disrobes, the last of which is a side view of her in the nude.

The strip tease act is a theatrical skit in the category of the Sally Rand fan and bubble dances and familiar to patrons of burlesque theaters. Most everybody, even adolescents have either seen or know about it and it is all right or all wrong depending on how it is put on. The way Sally Rand puts on her dances they are considered artistic and beautiful.

This young woman gives a photographic presentation of a woman disrobing. There is not anything unchaste or shameful in a woman disrobing,—they do disrobe; but even doing that very necessary and proper thing has turned some males of the species into "peeping Toms" in every town and countryside in this country and, looking at this photographic presentation of the same, might excite erotic ideas in the minds of some few males but that would be the same with this few looking at other photographs of this young woman or any other woman. What this few see in these photographs is something in their own minds.

There is not anything distasteful to the eye in this series of photographs. This young woman is neatly appareled and she has a nice face and form, and her poses are graceful and her manner playful. We must not misjudge this photographic presentation of a young woman disrobing by reading into it what this young woman did not intend. She is one of thousands engaged in one way or another in the amusement business, and its big business, a legitimate business of satisfying the wholesome interest and curiosity

of people in nature,—its forms and manifestations, and particularly in the "body beautiful" which the ancient Greeks idealized and the great Plato looked on as the embodiment of the eternal spirit, and artists and most of us consider altogether lovely.

In this photographic presentation of herself disrobing this young woman is plying her profession, her chosen pursuit of happiness is to make the most she can out of her looks and talents. That is the way she makes her living. She presents herself in a clean act, a woman disrobing. Actions mirror the mind. Clean actions a clean mind. Lustful actions a lustful mind. Had she permitted herself to be photographed in a way to shame womankind and been sloven in person and pose the State might be justified in maligning such a series of photographs as obscene, but there is not anything in this series of photographs that shames womankind; but the State says that they tend to corrupt and deprave by exciting impure sex ideas in the minds of those who may look at them.

The State does not complain of pure sex ideas and cannot any more than it could about ideas of food. Humankind must have ideas of both to go on living and reproducing its kind. Of course this young woman is by nature inherently attractive to man. That is not something she could lock up in the bureau drawer when she went out to have herself photographed. So what are impure sex ideas? The State does not say! The State leaves that to conjecture! Well, at most when of immoralities or pornography or of subnatural, perversive sex actions, all of which are social evils and offensive to good order and decency. There is not anything remotely suggestive of any of these in this series of photographs, hence, the State's case must fail unless the Court is to hold in accordance with the age old creed that being a woman such an exhibition of body and pose, as shown by these photographs, is in and of itself evil. Courts may not enforce creeds unless incorporated into laws.

Men disrobe. Would twelve photographs of a young man of nice face and figure—"body beautiful" acting out with grace and mirth a man disrobing, the last a side view of him in the nude be considered by any one otherwise than just good, wholesome fun? Man is as attractive to woman as woman is to man. Each have for the other nature's inherent charm. By what sort of logic may these photographs of a woman disrobing be considered obscene and those of a young man wholesome fun?

This Court goes along with what Mary Beard says in her book "Women as a Force in History," viz.,

"The dogma of woman's complete historical subjection to man must be rated as one of the most fantastic myths ever created by the human mind."

This Court tested this series of photographs for obscenity by the Lord Cockburn "tend to corrupt test" and the "tend to excite impure sex ideas test" and finds against the State. But, as stated before, this court rejects all such tests and holds that the only test allowable by the statute is the moral concept of the people as a whole, community concept of what is obscenity in literature, and tested by the community concept we find this series of photographs not obscene. Any one of these twelve photographs would have gladdened the eye of a G.I. as a pin-up girl.

There would be no doubt different reactions in people looking at this series of photographs, some with the viewpoint of the ancient Greeks would see beauty of face and figure and grace of pose; others would see wholesome fun and still others see obscenity, and "peeping Toms" would have their hunger satisfied without having to go to jail.

The Court concludes that this series of twelve photo-graphs, considered alone and as a group, and the several issues of this magazine "Sunshine & Health" are not obscene and the defendant is therefore found not guilty.

■ Commonwealth
v.
Gordon *et al.*

66 D. & C. 101 (1949).

John H. Maurer, district attorney, *Franklin E. Barr* and *John F. Kane*, assistant district attorneys, for Commonwealth.

Thomas D. McBride and *M. Phillip Freed*, for defendants.

Bok, J., March 18, 1949.—This is a trial without jury, all defendants having signed waivers on all indictments.

The evidence consists of nine books and an oral stipulation at bar that defendants are booksellers and that they possessed the books with the intent to sell them on the dates and at the times and places set forth in the indictments. This constituted in full the Commonwealth's evidence, to which defendants have demurred.

I have read the books with thoughtful care and find that they are not obscene, as alleged. The demurrers are therefore sustained.

The Statute

The indictments are drawn under section 524 of The Penal Code of June 24, 1939, P.L. 872, 18 PS § 4524, which reads as follows:

"Whoever sells, lends, distributes, exhibits, gives away, or shows or offers to sell, lend, distribute, exhibit, or give away or show, or has in his possession with intent to sell, lend, distribute or give away or to show, or knowingly advertises in any manner, any obscene, lewd, lascivious, filthy, indecent or disgusting book, magazine, pamphlet, newspaper, storypaper, paper, writing, drawing, photograph, figure or image, or any written or printed matter of an indecent character, or any article or instrument of indecent or immoral use or purporting to be for indecent or immoral use or purpose, or whoever designs, copies, draws, photographs, prints, utters, publishes, or in any manner manufactures or prepares any such book, picture, drawing, magazine, pamphlet, newspaper, storypaper, paper, writing, figure, image, matter, article or thing, or whoever writes, prints, publishes or utters, or causes to be printed, published or uttered, any advertisement or notice of any kind giving information, directly or indirectly, stating or purporting to do so, where, how, of whom, or by what means any, or what purports to be, any obscene, lewd, lascivious, filthy, disgusting or indecent book, picture, writing, paper, figure, image, matter, article or thing named in this section can be purchased, obtained or had, or whoever prints, utters, publishes, sells, lends, gives away, or shows, or has in his possession with intent to sell, lend, give away, or show, or otherwise offers for sale, loan or gift, or distribution, any pamphlet, magazine, newspaper or other printed paper devoted to the publication and principally made up of criminal news, police reports or accounts of criminal deeds, or pictures of stories of deeds of bloodshed, lust or crime, or whoever hires, employs, uses or permits any minor or child to do or assist in doing any act or thing mentioned in this section, is guilty of a misdemeanor, and upon conviction, shall be sentenced to imprisonment not exceeding one (1) year, or to pay a fine not exceeding five hundred dollars ($500), or both."

The particular and only charge in the indictments is that defendants possessed some or all of the books with the intent to sell them.

Section 524, quoted above, is based upon the earlier Acts of May 6, 1887, P.L. 84, and May 12, 1897, P.L. 63, 18 PS §§ 780, 781 and 782, which are similar in scope and not essentially different in wording. The earliest and only other act is the Criminal Code of March 31, 1860, P.L. 382, sec. 40, 18 PS § 779, which made it an offense to "publish or sell any filthy and obscene libel."

It should be noted at once that the wording of section 524 requires consideration of the indicted material as a whole; it does not proscribe articles or publications that merely contain obscene matter. This is now true in all jurisdictions that have dealt with the subject: the Federal courts, *Swearingen* v. *United States*, 161 U.S. 446 (1896); *United States* v. *Ulysses*, 72 F.(2d) 705 (1934); *Walker* v. *Popenoe*, 149 F.(2d) 511 (1945); Massachusetts, *Commonwealth* v. *Isenstadt*, 318 Mass. 543 (1945); New York, *Halsey* v. *New York Society*, 234 N.Y. 1, 136 N.E. 219 (1922); England, *Regina* v. *Hicklin*, L.R. 3 Q.B. 360 (1868).

It is also the rule in Pennsylvania. In *Commonwealth* v. *New*, 142 Pa. Superior Ct. 358 (1940), the court said:

"We have no fault to find with the statement that in determining whether a work is obscene, it must be construed as a whole and that *regard shall be had for its place in the arts*." (Italics supplied.)

Résumé of the Opinion

Section 524, for all its verbiage, is very bare. The full weight of the legislative prohibition dangles from the word "obscene" and its synonyms. Nowhere are these words defined; nowhere is the danger to be expected of them stated; nowhere is a standard of judgment set forth. I assume that "obscenity" is expected to have a familiar and inherent meaning, both as to what it is and as to what it does.

It is my purpose to show that it has no such inherent meaning; that different meanings given to it at different times are not constant, either historically or legally; and that it is not constitutionally indictable unless it takes the form of sexual impurity, i.e., "dirt for dirt's sake" and can be traced to actual criminal behavior, either actual or demonstrably imminent.

Résumé of the Books

1, 2 and 3. The Studs Lonigan trilogy ("Young Lonigan," "The Young Manhood of Studs Lonigan," "Judgment Day,") by James T. Farrell; Vanguard Press, 1932–1935.

This is the story of the moral and physical disintegration of a young man living in Chicago between the years 1916 and 1932. Nothing that he attempted ever quite came off, and his failures became more and more incisive. He left school to hang around the streets with others of his kind; he was too young to enlist for war service; he loved Lucy since they were in school together, but avoided her for four years and finally alienated her by making drunken advances to her; he worked for his father as a painter, but, on a casual tip, invested his savings in a dubious stock, which failed; he fell half-heartedly in love with Catherine, and they were engaged to be married, but she became pregnant by him before the ceremony; looking for a job on a stormy day a few weeks before the wedding, he caught cold and died of pneumonia and a weakened heart.

The background of the semi-slum district in which Lonigan was born and lived was the outward counterpart of his own nature, and both together were too much for such decency of soul as he had. His drift downhill was relentless and inevitable. On the theory that no literature is vital that cannot be vulgarized, this trilogy may rank as an epic, for our criminal courts and prisons and many of our streets are peopled by Studs Lonigans. The characters in these books act and speak the kind of life that bred them, and Mr. Farrell has brought to the surface the groundswell of thought and inclination that move more people than, if they were honest, would admit to them.

It is not a pleasant story, nor are the characters gentle and refined. There is rape and dissipation and lust in these books, expressed in matching language, but they do not strike me as being out of proportion. The books as a whole create a sustained arc of a man's life and era, and the obvious effort of the author is to be faithful to the scene he depicts.

No one would want to be Studs Lonigan.

4. "A World I Never Made," by James T. Farrell; The Vanguard Press, New York, 1936.

This book could well be the beginning of another series, for it takes a minor character from the Lonigan books, Danny O'Neill, and shows him as a child. The milieu is the same—Chicago in 1911—but there is a discernible effort to show Danny's struggle uphill against the same factors that pushed Lonigan down.

This is the one book of the nine that does not end tragically; it merely stops in midstream, but the people who surround Danny do and say the same things that appear in the Lonigan series. Unlike the latter, this book is plastered with the short Saxon words of common vulgarity; they are consistent with the characters who use them and with the quality of the lives and actions that are the subject of the author's scrutiny.

I am not of a mind, nor do I have the authority, to require an author to write about one kind of people and not about another, nor do I object to his effort to paint a complete picture of those whom he has chosen. Certainly I will not say that it is not a good thing to look deeply into life and people, regardless of the shadows that are to be found there.

5. "Sanctuary," by William Faulkner; Random House, 1931.

This is a powerful and dreadful story about a gay but virginal girl of 17 who accidentally falls into the hands of a sadistic man called Popeye, who is sexually impotent. He kills a half-witted boy who is informally guarding the girl, and ravishes her with a corncob. He then keeps her imprisoned in a house of prostitution and takes pleasure in watching her have intercourse with a man whom he kills when she tries to escape with him. Terrified of Popeye, she testifies that another man committed the murder, and is taken from court by her father, who has finally been able to locate her. Popeye is later apprehended on another charge of murder and is convicted.

There are no vulgar Saxon words in the book, but the situations are stark and unrelieved. It makes one shudder to think of what can happen by misadventure.

6. "Wild Palms," by William Faulkner; Random House, 1939.

This book concerns a wife who left her husband and children to seek integrity of experience, in terms of vitality, with her lover; "hunger is in the heart," she says, when the next meal seems uncertain, "not in the stomach." They wander about the country together, living as they must or as they wish, and she finally becomes pregnant. Her lover, a former doctor, attempts to abort her but mishandles it and she dies. He pleads guilty and is sentenced to 50 years in prison. He refuses a gift of cyanide from the woman's husband, saying: "Between grief and nothing I will take grief."

The redeeming feature of this tale is that an acid loneliness comes through, the awful loneliness that pervades lost people, even in company. No one could envy these two miserable creatures.

7. "God's Little Acre," by Erskine Caldwell; Random House, 1933.

An able companion to the same author's "Tobacco Road," it is the story of a poor and illiterate farmer's family in Georgia. The central figure is the father, who for 15 years has dug holes in his farm in search of gold. God's Little Acre is a part of the farm which he mentally moves about in order to keep it from getting in the way of his search for treasure; his idea is to give all that comes from it to the church, but he never works it. His daughters and sons and their wives get variously tangled up in sexual affairs which are taken as being in the nature of things. One brother kills another over his wife. The final and despairing cry of the father, who has always tried to keep peace, is, "Blood on my land!"

It is a frank and turbulent story, but it is an obvious effort to be faithful to the locality and its people.

8. "End As a Man," by Calder Willingham; The Vanguard Press, 1947.

Life in a southern military academy. A drinking party and crooked poker game finally result in the expulsion of several cadets, including the wily and unmoral ringleader. The retired general in charge of the academy is the stereotype of military martinet, whose conception of the narrow and rigid discipline necessary to produce "a man" is set in bold relief against the energy of growing boys. The result is a fair picture of the frustration inherent in an overdose of discipline and in the license and disobedience that is largely engendered by it.

No one would care to send his son to such an institution.

This is perhaps the foulest book of the lot, so far as language is concerned, but it is the language of vulgarity and not of erotic allurement.

9. "Never Love a Stranger," by Harold Robbins; Knopf, 1948.

The story of a boy brought up in an orphanage who finds that he has an uncle and is Jewish. After losing touch with his uncle he has various experiences and is finally down and out because he can find no work. He then becomes head of New York City's gambling racket, which he ultimately leaves in order to marry a childhood friend. She dies in childbirth and he is killed in the war; his friends take over the child, who will presumably have a better chance in life than he had.

It is a swift story that covers a great deal of ground, its point being to portray a hard and lonely man who could not fully trust or give himself to anyone. Its last and least convincing part is also the least open to attack for obscenity; the rest, particularly the section dealing with New York City during the depression of the early 1930's, is very moving, not because there are sexual incidents but because the lines of the story are deep and authentic.

General Comment

Three of these books have already been judicially cleared in New York City.

"A World I Never Made" was before Magistrate Curran in 1937, under the caption of *Bamberger* v. *The Vanguard Press, Inc.*, docket no. 329. The opinion was impromptu and is in the perceptive magistrate's best style.

"God's Little Acre" was the subject of *People* v. *Viking Press, Inc.*, 147 N.Y. Misc. 813 (1933). In the course of his opinion Magistrate Greenspan said:

"*The Courts have strictly limited the applicability of the statute to works of pornography* and they have consistently declined to apply it to books of genuine literary value. If the statute were construed more broadly than in the manner just indicated, its effect would be to prevent altogether the realistic portrayal in literature of a large and important field of life. . . . The Court may not require the author to put refined language into the mouths of primitive people." (Italics supplied.)

Magistrate Strong held "End As a Man" not obscene in *People* v. *Vanguard Press*, 192 N.Y. Misc. 127 (1947), and observed:

"The speech of the characters must be considered in relation to its setting and the theme of the story. It seems clear that use of foul language will not of itself bring a novel or play within the condemnation of the statute."

After clearance by the magistrates, these books could have been brought before the grand jury, but no such indictments were attempted.

As I have indicated above, all but one of these books are profoundly tragic, and that one has its normal quota of frustration and despair. No one could envy or wish to emulate the characters that move so desolately through these pages. Far from inciting to lewd or lecherous desires, which are sensorially pleasurable, these books leave one either with a sense of horror or of pity for the degradation of mankind. The effect upon the normal reader, "l'homme moyen sensuel" (there is no such deft precision in English), would be anything but what the vice hunters fear it might be. We are so fearful for other people's morals; they so seldom have the courage of our own convictions.

It will be asked whether one would care to have one's young daughter read these books. I suppose that by the time she is old enough to wish to read them she will have learned the biologic facts of life and the words that go with them. There is something seriously wrong at home if those facts have not been met and faced and sorted by them; it is not children so much as parents that should receive our concern about this. I should prefer that my own three daughters meet the facts of life and the literature of the world in my library than behind a neighbor's barn, for I can face the adversary there directly. If the young ladies are appalled by what they read, they can close the book at the bottom of page one; if they read further, they will learn what is in the world and in its people, and no parents who have been discerning with their children need fear the outcome. Nor can they hold it back, for life is a series of little battles and minor issues, and the burden of choice is on us all, every day, young and old. Our daughters must live in the world and decide what sort of women they are to be, and we should be willing to prefer their deliberate and informed choice of decency rather than an innocence that continues to spring from ignorance. If that choice be made in the open sunlight, it is more apt than when made in shadow to fall on the side of honorable behavior.

The lesson to be learned from such books as these is not so facile as that the wages of sin is death, or, in Hollywood's more modern version, that the penalty of sinning is suffering. That is not enough to save a book from proper censorship. The tragedy of these books is not in death but in the texture of the slope that leads to death—in the inner suffering that comes at times from crimes against oneself as much as from crimes against society. That has been the green pastures of storytellers ever since the Greek dramatists, especially when the pressures on a character are not, as they are not always, of his own making or within his control. Sin is too apt a word to take in the full reach of circumstance, and I venture to say that in human experience suffering does not automatically follow sinning. Our laws have a good deal to do with that guarded notion. It is necessary to know what our laws are up to, and it is my conviction that, outside the police power, the laws of Anglo-Saxon countries are made less as absolute mandates than as clinical experiments. Democratic nations prefer checks and balances to absolute authority, and it is worthy of notice that the jury system exists only in those countries where the law is not considered to have been drawn, as Cicero put it, from the forehead of the gods, but rather from the will of the people, who wish to keep an eye on it. The eighteenth amendment to the Constitution is a case in point.

Such sumptuary laws, and some economic ones, differ from obscenity statutes only in the degree of danger to society inherent in the appetite in question. The need for decency is as old as the appetites, but it is not expressed in uniform law or custom. The ancient Hebrews had a rigid moral code which, for example, excluded bastards from the congregation up to the tenth generation, for the combined reasons of preserving their ancient tradition of tribe and family and of increasing the number of effective warriors. The Greeks, more cosmopolitan in a country whose sterile soil could not support many people comfortably, approved pederasty and a restricted form of concubinage in order to keep the population down. Standards of sexual behavior, as well as of the need to censor it, have shifted from age to age, from country to country, and from economy to economy. The State of New Mexico has no obscenity statute. South Carolina has no divorce law.

Censorship, which is the policeman of decency, whether religious, patriotic, or moral, has had distinct fashions, depending on which great questions were agitating society at the time. During the Middle Ages, when the church was supreme, the focus of suppression was upon heresy and blasphemy. When the State became uppermost, the focus of suppression was upon treason and sedition. The advent of technology made Queen Victoria realize, perhaps subconsciously, that loose morals would threaten the peace of mind necessary to the development of invention and big business; the focus moved to sexual morality. We are now emerging into an era of social ideology and psychology, and the focus is turning to these. The right to speak out and to act freely is always at a minimum in the area of the fighting faiths.

The censorship of books did not become a broad public issue until after the invention of printing in the fifteenth century. The earliest real example of it was the first Index Librorum Prohibitorum of the Catholic Church in 1559, and the church was broadly tolerant of sexual impurity in the books that it considered; its main object was the suppression of heresy. I think it is a fair general statement that from ancient times until the Comstockian laws of 1873 the only form of written obscenity that was censored was "dirt for dirt's sake."

I do not regard the above as apart from the decisional purpose of this case. The words of the statute—"obscene, lewd, lascivious, filthy, indecent, or disgusting"—restrict rather than broaden the meaning of a highly penal statute. The effect of this plethora of epithets is to merge them into one prevailing meaning—that of sexual impurity alone, and this has been universally held: *People v. Eastman*, 188 N.Y. 478 (1907); *People v. Wendling*, 258 N.Y. 451 (1932); *Commonwealth v. Isenstadt*, supra (318 Mass. 543 (1945)); *Attorney General v. "Forever Amber,"* (Mass.) 81 N.E.(2d) 663 (1948); *United States v. Ulysses*, supra, (72 F.(2d) 705 (1934)).

In *Swearingen v. United States*, 161 U.S. 446 (1896), a case involving the mailing of obscene matter, the court said:

"The offence aimed at, in that portion of the statute we are now considering, was the use of the mails to circulate or deliver matter to corrupt the morals of the people. The words 'obscene,' 'lewd,' and 'lascivious,' as used in the statute, signify that form of immorality which has relation to sexual impurity, and have the same meaning as is given them at common law in prosecutions for obscene libel. As the statute is highly penal, it should not be held to embrace language unless it is fairly within its letter and spirit."

This view has been adopted in Pennsylvania, for the court said in *Commonwealth v. New*, supra (142 Pa. Superior Ct. 358 (1940)):

"The test for obscenity most frequently laid down seems to be whether the writing would tend to deprave the morals of those into whose hands the publication might fall by suggesting lewd thoughts and exciting sensual desires."

The statute is therefore directed only at sexual impurity and not at blasphemy or coarse and vulgar behavior of any other kind. The word in common use for the purpose of such a statute is "obscenity." The great point of this case is to find out what that word means.

Nowhere in the statute is there a definition of it or a formula given for determining when it exists. Its derivation, *ob* and *scena*, suggests that anything done offstage, furtively, or lefthandedly, is obscene. The act does not penalize anyone who seeks to change the prevailing moral or sexual code, nor does it state that the writing must be such as to corrupt the morals of the public or of youth; it merely proscribes books that *are* obscene and leaves it to the authorities to decide whether or not they are. This cannot be done without regard to the nature and history of obscenity. It is unlike the fundamental laws of property, of crimes like murder, rape, and theft, or even of negligence, whose meaning has remained relatively constant. That of obscenity has frequently changed, almost from decade to decade within the past century; "Ulysses" was condemned by the State courts in New York just 10 years before it was cleared by Judge Woolsey in the District Court for the Southern District of New York. I must determine what this elusive word means now.

Something might be said at the outset about the familiar four-letter words that are so often associated with sexual impurity. These are, almost without exception, of honest Anglo-Saxon ancestry, and were not invented for purely scatological effect. The one, for example, that is used to denote the sexual act is an old agricultural word meaning "to plant," and was at one time a wholly respectable member of the English vocabulary. The distinction between a word of decent etymological history and one of smut alone is important; it shows that fashions in language change as expectably as do the concepts of what language connotes. It is the old business of semantics again, the difference between word and concept.

But there is another distinction. The decisions that I shall cite have sliced off vulgarity from obscenity. This has had the effect of making a clear division between the words of the bathroom and those of the bedroom: the former can no longer be regarded as obscene, since they have no erotic allurement, and the latter may be so regarded, depending on the circumstances of their use. This reduces the number of potentially offensive words sharply.

With such changes as these, the question is whether the legal mace should fall upon words or upon concepts—language or ideas.

Obscenity is not like sedition, blasphemy, or open lewdness, against which there are also criminal statutes. These offenses not only have acquired precise meaning but are defined specifically in the act. Sedition (Act of June 24, 1939, P.L. 872, section 207, 18 PS § 4207), which includes writing and publication, is carefully defined in eight subheadings. Blasphemy (same act, section 523, 18 PS § 4523) is stated as speaking "loosely and profanely of Almighty God, Christ Jesus, the Holy Spirit, or the Scriptures of Truth." Open lewdness (same act, section 519, 18 PS § 4519) is "any notorious act of public indecency, tending to debauch the morals or manners of the people." Other crimes, involving restriction on free speech and having their scope or purpose set forth with particularity in The Penal Code, include blackmail (section 801), libel (section 412), anonymous communications (section 414), false letters of recommendation (section 856), false advertising (section 857), advertising without publisher's consent (section 858), and fortune telling (section 870).

No such definition of standard or legislative intention occurs in section 524, and I am convinced that without a declaration of the legislature's intention as to what obscenity means or of what the lawmakers sought to prevent, there is no constant or reliable indication of it to be found in human experience.

The argument is often made that anyone can tell by instinct what is obscene and what is not, even if it is hard to put the difference into words. The same might be said of sedition, blasphemy, and open lewdness, but the legislature was careful to specify. With regard to obscenity, however, the argument does not hold water. When he was an editor, Walter Hines Page deleted the word "chaste" because it was suggestive, and the play "Sappho" was banned in New York City because a man carried the leading lady up a flight of stairs. A librarian once charged Mark Twain's "Tom Sawyer" and "Huckleberry Finn" with corrupting the morals of children. In 1907 Richard Strauss's "Salome" was banned in Boston. Charlotte Bronte's "Jane Eyre," when first published, was called "too immoral to be ranked as decent literature." Hawthorne's "Scarlet Letter" was referred to as "a brokerage of lust." George Eliot's "Adam Bede" was called "the vile outpourings of a lewd woman's mind." Others to suffer similarly were Elizabeth Barrett Browning's "Aurora Leigh," Hardy's "Tess" and "Jude," DuMaurier's "Trilby," and Shaw's "Mrs. Warren's Profession." Walt Whitman lost his job in the United States Department of the Interior because of "Leaves of Grass."

It is presumed that Mr. Page and the others who attacked this imposing array of classics could tell by instinct what was decent and what was not. The idea that instinct can be resorted to as a process of moral stare decisis reduces to absurdity.

It is a far cry from the examples just cited to what society accepts as innocuous now. The stage, literature, painting, sculpture, photography, fashions of dress, and even the still pudibund screen tolerate things that would have made Anthony Comstock turn blue. In its issue of April 11, 1938, Life magazine ran a series of factual and dignified pictures called "The Birth of a Baby." It was attacked in the courts but was exonerated. Dr. Kinsey's report on the sexual behavior of men is now current. Truth and error, as Milton urged in his "Areopagitica," are being allowed to grapple, and we are the better for it.

In addition to the books whose banning is the subject of cases cited later in this opinion, I suggest a short list of modern books that have not been banned, so far as I can find out. All of these books contain sexual material, and all of them can be found in the Boston Public Library. I defy anyone to provide a rational basis for the distinction between these two sets of books. My list includes: Fanny Hurst's "Back Street"; Arthur Koestler's "Arrival and Departure"; Erich Maria Remarque's "All Quiet on The Western Front" and "Arch of Triumph"; Eugene O'Neill's "Anna Christie" and "Hairy Ape"; John Dos Passos's "U. S. A."; Ernest Hemingway's "For Whom the Bell Tolls"; Somerset Maugham's "Of Human Bondage"; Charles Morgan's "The Fountain" and "The Voyage"; Richard Wright's "Black Boy."

It is no answer to say that if my point about the books just listed be sound, then by analogy the law against murder is useless because all murderers are not caught. The inherent evil of murder is apparent, but by what apparent, inherent standard of evil is obscenity to be judged, from book to book? It is my purpose to provide such a standard, but it will reduce to a minimum the operation of any norm of indefinite interpretation.

Before leaving this point, research discloses a curious but complete confusion between the post office and the customs over what constitutes obscenity. No unanimity of opinion unites these two governmental services in a common standard. Books have cleared the port only to find the mails closed to them: others, printed here, have circulated freely while foreign copies were stopped at the ports. One would expect greater uniformity than this if obscenity could be unmistakably detected.

There is a bale of literature on obscenity and the history of censorship, i.e., suppression of the right of free expression. It is best represented by two books by Morris L. Ernst, Esq., entitled "To The Pure" (Viking Press, 1929) and "The Censor Marches On" (Doubleday, Doran & Co., 1940), with William Seagle and Alexander Lindey, respectively, colloborating. In addition to the brilliant and scholarly text, there is a large bibliography and appendices. These two books should be required reading, of at least equal importance with legal authority, in deciding a censorship case.

An interesting volume on literary censorship is "Banned Books," by Anne Lyon Haight (R. R. Bowker Co., New York, 1935), which lists the principal suppressions of books, for various reasons, at various times and in various places, from Caligula's attempt to suppress "The Odessey" in A.D. 35 to the lifting of the ban on "Ulysses" in 1934.

The legal authorities on obscenity may be found well collected in 76 A.L.R. 1099, and 81 A.L.R. 801.

It is my conclusion that the books before me are obvious efforts to show life as it is. I cannot be convinced that the deep drives and appetites of life are very much different from what they have always been, or that censorship has ever had any effect on them, except as the law's police power to preserve the peace in censorship. I believe that the consensus of preference today is for disclosure and not stealth, for frankness and not hypocrisy, and for public and not secret distribution. That in itself is a moral code.

It is my opinion that frank disclosure cannot legally be censored, even as an exercise of the police power, unless it is sexually impure and pornographic, as I shall define those words. They furnish the only possible test for obscenity and its effect.

These books are not, in my view, sexually impure and pornographic.

The Pennsylvania Cases

I venture a long and detailed opinion because this is the first case in Pennsylvania that deals with current literature in book form. Our authorities on the censoring of obscenity are so few that they can all be referred to.

The earliest case is that of *Commonwealth* v. *Sharpless*, 2 S. & R. 91 (1815), in which defendant was convicted of exhibiting an indecent picture. The case has importance because of the holding by Tilghman, C.J., that since there was no act of assembly on the matter, the case had to be decided on common-law principles, which he found covered such an indictment. The chief justice did not doubt that the publication of an indecent book was also indictable at common law, and cited the English case of *Rex* v. *Curl*, 2 Str. 788, 93 E.R. 849 (1727).

The Sharpless case can be taken as authority that obscenity was a common-law offense in England at the time of the American Revolution and hence became part of the common law of Pennsylvania. The status of the common law on many points often depends on the date to which one opens the books, and it should be observed that obscenity was not a part of English common law until *Rex* v. *Curl*, supra: in *Regina* v. *Read*, Fortescue, 98, 92 E.R. 777 (1707), only 20 years earlier, the lords wished that there were a law to punish the publication of "The Fifteen Plagues of a Maidenhead," but decided that they couldn't make one—it was a matter for the ecclesiastical courts.

In *Rex* v. *Wilkes*, 4 Burr. 2527, 98 E.R. 327 (1770), defendant was indicted and convicted of printing an obscene libel entitled "An Essay on Women." Jurisdiction was assumed, for there was no discussion of it nor was any objection made to the indictment: the reported proceedings have to do with procedural matters and with the propriety of a sentence of outlawry for a misdemeanor.

It is on these two cases—*Rex* v. *Curl* and *Rex* v. *Wilkes* —and on Blackstone that indictable obscenity as a part of the English common law depends.

Blackstone, who began his Vinerian lectures on October 25, 1758, after labors "of so many years" in collecting his material, says, in Book IV of the Commentaries, pp. 150 and 151, that libels in their largest and most extensive sense signify any writings, pictures, or the like, of an immoral or illegal tendency, and are punishable in the interest of the preservation of peace and good order. It is interesting to note that he goes on at once to make the point that freedom of the press is not involved, since the right exists to publish anything, but only the abuse of it, established by trial after publication, is punishable.

While Blackstone had only *Rex* v. *Curl* (1727) to support him as authority, he is regarded as authority himself, and it must therefore be held that obscene publication was indictable at common law.

It is important to observe that there are few, if any, obscene book cases in the English reports between the time of *Rex* v. *Curl*, in 1727, and *Regina* v. *Hicklin*, in 1868; that in Pennsylvania no act was passed against obscenity until 1860, and that no case involving an obscene book appeared until *Commonwealth* v. *Landis*, infra, in 1870. *Commonwealth* v. *Sharpless*, in 1815, mentioned books by dictum only.

This removes from the doctrine of indictable obscenity much of the veneration that is usually given to common-law doctrines because of their hoary age. The plain fact is that the period of the Renaissance, in both countries, was a lusty one, and that concern over sexual purity did not begin to arise until Victorianism really took hold in the middle 1850's. One need only recall that the father of the post office, Benjamin Franklin, wrote and presumably mailed his "Letter of Advice to Young Men on the Proper Choosing of a Mistress"; that Thomas Jefferson worried about the students at his new University of Virginia having a respectable brothel; that Alexander Hamilton's adultery while holding public office created no great scandal, or that the morals of Southern chivalry provided us with mulattos until the abolition of slavery at least made the matter one of free choice on both sides.

The formulation of the common-law proscription of obscene publication did not, therefore, amount to very much. It is a good example of a social restriction that became law and was allowed to slumber until a change of social consciousness should animate it. It is the prevailing social consciousness that matters quite as much as the law. Between 1870 and 1930 the obscenity law was on the social anvil: since then society has found other irons in the fire and has lost its interest in what Shaw has called Comstockery.

The next Pennsylvania case was *Commonwealth* v. *Landis*, 8 Phila. 453 (1870), in which defendant was convicted of selling a book called "Secrets of Generation." This case is interesting because it holds that it was for the jury to say whether the book was obscene, and that "that which offends modesty, and is indecent and lewd, and tends to the creation of lascivious desires, is obscene." Not only is this the first book case in the State, but it is the first example of showing the effort by both legislature and courts to define the libidinous synonyms in terms of each other: obscenity is filthiness, filthiness is indecency, indecency is lewdness, lewdness is lasciviousness, and lasciviousness is obscenity. The opinion also states "that to justify a publication of the character of this book they (the jury) must be satisfied that the publication was made for a legitimate and useful purpose, and that it was not made from any motive of mere gain or with a corrupt desire to debauch society." It ends with a warning that a book, obscene in itself, might be used either for a proper purpose, such as medical instruction, or for an improper one, such as general publication, and that in the latter case the utterer would have to answer.

In *Commonwealth* v. *Havens*, 6 Pa. C.C. 545 (1889), the constitutionality of the Act of May 6, 1887, was upheld, on the one ground advanced, that its title was broad enough. The case involved "The National Police Gazette" and "The Illustrated Police News." A conviction resulted. The court restricted the evidence to the specific advertisements complained of and refused to allow testimony as to what their real purpose was. Their inherent indecency was the only issue. The test of obscenity finally approved by the opinion was: "Would the articles or the pictures here . . . suggest impure and libidinous thoughts in the young and inexperienced?"

In re Arentsen, 26 W.N.C. 359 (1890), dealt with Count Leo Tolstoy's "Kreutzer Sonata." This case also holds that selling an obscene book was a common-law offense, and Judge Thayer cited *Regina* v. *Hicklin*, L.R. 3 Q.B. 360 (1868), of which more hereafter. Defendant was acquitted because the book was found to condemn marriage, not in favor of free love but of complete celibacy.

In *Commonwealth* v. *Dowling*, 14 Pa. C.C. 607 (1894), defendant was convicted of selling immoral newspapers to minors. The case is of little interest, except for the affirmance of one of defendant's points for charge: "The law does not undertake to punish bad English, vulgarity, or bad taste, and no matter how objectionable the jury may consider the papers referred to on those grounds, they have no right to convict on account of them."

In *Commonwealth* v. *Magid & Dickstein*, 91 Pa. Superior Ct. 513 (1927), the subject matter was indecent pictures. The court stated that the purpose of the Acts of 1887 and 1897 was "to shield minors and young children from obscene and indecent books and pictures."

In *Commonwealth* v. *Kutler*, 93 Pa. Superior Ct. 119 (1928), and *Commonwealth* v. *Kufel*, 142 Pa. Superior Ct. 273 (1940), the only question was whether defendants were the ones who sold certain pamphlets, the obscene character of which was conceded.

In *Commonwealth* v. *New*, supra (142 Pa. Superior Ct. 358 (1940)), the matter involved was certain pictures in a magazine called "Tipster." The test of obscenity adopted by the court shows a virtual abandonment of the harsh rule of *Regina* v. *Hicklin*, infra, and is stated thus: "Whether the writing would tend to deprave the morals of those into whose hands the publication might fall by suggesting lewd thoughts and exciting sensual desires." The purpose of the act is again stated to be the prevention of "appealing to those of depraved tastes or to the curiosity of adolescents."

In *Commonwealth* v. *Mercur*, 90 Pitts. L.J. 318 (1942), the court applied the "as a whole" rule of *Commonwealth* v. *New*, supra, and held that certain pictures appearing in a book of instruction for photographers called "U.S. Camera 1942," did not render the volume obscene.

This exhausts the Pennsylvania cases.

It is therefore clear that section 524 of our act has not yet been applied to serious current literature. There has not been the opportunity to form a modern test for obscenity in Pennsylvania as there has been in the lower Federal courts, and in the highest appellate courts of New York and Massachusetts.

Despite the scarcity of literary obscenity cases in this State, the trend has been away from and beyond the English common law. The range in growth of doctrine is from the dictum in the Sharpless case, that the common-law rule of obscene libel would apply to a book, to the opinion in the New case, that a book must be considered as a whole and regard be given to its place in the arts. The English appellate courts have not gone so far, as will be seen.

The first articulate test appears in the leading English case of *Regina* v. *Hicklin*, L.R. 3 Q.B. 360 (1868), and the American jurisdictions have had to face it before they could disregard it and forge the modern rule. In Pennsyl-

vania, the rule for which it has become famous was cited with approval in *Commonwealth* v. *Havens*, supra (6 Pa. C.C. 545 (1889)), and again in In re Arentsen, supra (26 W.N.C. 359 (1890)), but the modern American rule has not yet been squarely adopted here.

The English Cases

Regina v. *Hicklin* is an example of judge-made law quite at variance with the parliamentary intent behind the act on which it was based. Lord Campbell's act provided for search and seizure warrants that would enable the police to take and destroy obscene publications. The report of the debates in Hansard show the lords' difficulties in deciding what an obscene publication might be. Lord Campbell, who was lord chief justice at the time, explained that the act was to apply exclusively to works written for the purpose of corrupting the morals of youth and of a nature calculated to shock the common feelings of decency in any well regulated mind. He was ready to make whatever was then indictable a test of obscenity in his new act. He made it clear that any work that even pretended to be literature or art, classic or modern, had little to fear.

All of this was nullified by Lord Chief Justice Cockburn in the Hicklin case, where the subject matter was a pamphlet entitled "The Confessional Unmasked," and containing a diatribe against the Catholic Church; its purpose was to show the depravity of the priesthood and the character of the questions put to women in the confessional. This is the now famous rule of the case:

"I think the test of obscenity is this, whether the tendency of the matter charged as obscenity is to deprave and corrupt those whose minds are open to such immoral influences, and into whose hands a publication of this sort may fall."

Strictly applied, this rule renders any book unsafe, since a moron could pervert to some sexual fantasy to which his mind is open the listings in a seed catalogue. Not even the Bible would be exempt; Annie Besant once compiled a list of 150 passages in Scripture that might fairly be considered obscene—it is enough to cite the story of Lot and his daughters, Genesis 19, 30–38. Portions of Shakespeare would also be offensive, and of Chaucer, to say nothing of Aristophanes, Juvenal, Ovid, Swift, Defoe, Fielding, Smollett, Rousseau, Maupassant, Voltaire, Balzac, Baudelaire, Rabelais, Swinburne, Shelley, Byron, Boccaccio, Marguerite de Navarre, Hardy, Shaw, Whitman, and a host more.

As will be seen later, the classics—whatever that may mean precisely—are considered exempt from censorship, but many of them were hounded in England, despite Lord Campbell's assurances, as a result of the rule of the Hicklin case.

The next English case—passing *Regina* v. *Read*, *Rex* v. *Curl*, and *Rex* v. *Wilkes*, which have been examined above—was *Steele* v. *Brannan*, L.R. 7 C.P. 261 (1872), which involved the report of the trial of one George Mackey for selling a pamphlet called "The Confessional Unmasked." The report set forth the pamphlet in full, and the court held not only the publication was not privileged as a report of legal proceedings but that it was obscene, despite its purpose to expose what the author considered dangerous religious practices. The court followed *Regina* v. *Hicklin*, without quoting the rule, and placed its point of emphasis upon the effect of the pamphlet "on the young and inexperienced."

The next case was *Bradlaugh* v. *Regina*, L.R. 3 .QB. 607 (1878), in which a conviction for publishing a book called "Fruits of Philosophy" was reversed. The point was whether the allegedly obscene matter should be included in the indictment instead of being referred to by name only. The Court of Error held that it should be, and expressly avoided passing upon the character of the book.

The lower court case of *Regina* v. *Thomson*, 64 J.P. 456 (1900), in which the jury found defendant not guilty in an issue of whether or not the "Heptameron," by Queen Margaret of Navarre, was obscene, is interesting because of the charge of Bosanquet, C.S. It is the first mention that I have found in the English reports of the idea that fashions in obscenity change. After mentioning that in the Middle Ages things were discussed which would not be tolerated now, if given general publicity, Sergeant Bosanquet left it to the jury to say "whether the book is a fit book to put into people's hands in these days at the end of the nineteenth century." The jury felt that it was.

Sergeant Bosanquet was referred to with respect in *Rex* v. *Barraclough*, L.R. 1 K.B. 201 (1906), but the opinions, while mentioning *Regina* v. *Hicklin* indirectly, decided a point under a new act of Parliament as to what the indictment should contain. A conviction for publishing an obscene typewritten document that libeled one Edith Woodhead was upheld.

In *Rex* v. *Montalk*, 23 Cr. App. Rep. 182 (1932), a conviction for publishing a typewritten libel was sustained, the lord chief justice citing *Regina* v. *Hicklin* in a very brief opinion. In the court below, the recorder charged the jury that if it was of the opinion "that this can be for the public good as an advancement of literature, in my opinion that would be a defense." The libel was not a book but a series of verses on half a dozen sheets of paper.

This exhausts the reported English cases that are in point. They show continued adherence to the Hicklin rule, but the paucity of authority is noteworthy. It is as if the English public does not want to risk the severity of the common law, and it is clear proof to me of the clinical nature of the laws that are made to cover social situations. While the higher English courts were kept relatively idle on the question, private censorship in England has been very active; the most effective censor of the Victorian era was Mudie's circulating library. It was the time of the three-decker novel—ponderous, dull, and pure as the driven snow. When Mudie's power was finally broken, smaller circulating libraries continued to wield the same sort of influence and to reflect the general desire of the public for no disturbing material of an emotional nature. England was the pioneer in the advance of the Industrial Age, and the nation of shopkeepers was unwilling to be diverted from making money by sidetrips into erotica; what individuals did in the dark was their affair, but bad morals could not profitably become a matter of public concern.

The rule of *Regina* v. *Hicklin* suited the English, and presumably still does—not as a satisfying standard but as an effective policeman to take over and tone down the situation when the social experiment threatens to get out of hand.

Censorship should be the proper activity of the community rather than of the law, and the community has never been lazy upholding what it believes to be inherently decent at the moment. With a legal policeman handy, the market place is the best crucible in which to distil an instinctive morality. We have the evidence of Milton that there is no authoritative example of the suppression of a book in ancient times solely because of obscenity, but this does not mean that private criticism was not alert. Plato thought that Homer should be expurgated before Greek children should be allowed to read him. In Plutarch's opinion the comedies of Aristophanes were coarse and vulgar.

This is healthy, for it is the struggle of free opinion: it is not suppression by law. In the English community the people argue and Hicklin stands guard in case of trouble. The American method is different: the rule has been modernized.

The American Cases

1. The Federal Courts. There are two important opinions involving James Joyce's "Ulysses." Judge Woolsey's, in the district court, is reported as *United States* v. *One Book* Entitled Ulysses, 5 F. Supp. 182 (S.D.N.Y., 1933), and Judge Hand's, affirming Judge Woolsey, is reported in 72 F.(2d) 705 (C.C.A. 2d, 1934).

Judge Woolsey's decision may well be considered the keystone of the modern American rule, as it brings out clearly that indictable obscenity must be "dirt for dirt's sake." He said:

"It is because Joyce has been loyal to his technique and has not funked its necessary implications, but has honestly attempted to tell fully what his characters think about, that he has been the subject of so many attacks and that his purpose has been so often misunderstood and misrepresented. For his attempt sincerely and honestly to realize his objective has required him incidentally to use certain words which are generally considered dirty words and has led at times to what many think is a too poignant pre-occupation with sex in the thoughts of his characters.

"The words which are criticized as dirty are old, Saxon words known to almost all men and, I venture, to many women, and are such words as would be naturally and habitually used, I believe, by the types of folk whose life, physical and mental, Joyce is seeking to describe. . . . As I have stated, 'Ulysses' is not an easy book to read. It is brilliant and dull, intelligible and obscure, by turns. In many places it seems to me to be disgusting, but although it contains, as I have mentioned above, many words usually considered dirty, I have not found anything that I consider to be dirt for dirt's sake. Each word of the book contributes like a bit of mosaic to the detail of the picture which Joyce is seeking to construct for his readers.

"If one does not wish to associate with such folk as Joyce describes, that is one's own choice. In order to avoid indirect contact with them one may not wish to read 'Ulysses'; that is quite understandable. But when such a great artist in words, as Joyce undoubtedly is, seeks to draw a true picture of the lower middle class in a European city, ought it to be impossible for the American public legally to see that picture?"

In affirming Judge Woolsey, Judge Hand said, in the circuit court of appeals:

"That numerous long passages in Ulysses contain matter that is obscene under any fair definition of the word cannot be gainsaid; yet they are relevant to the purpose of

depicting the thoughts of the characters and are introduced to give meaning to the whole, rather than to
promote lust or portray filth for its own sake. The net
effect even of portions most open to attack, such as the
closing monologue of the wife of Leopold Bloom, is pitiful
and tragic, rather than lustful. The book depicts the souls
of men and women that are by turns bewildered and
keenly apprehensive, sordid and aspiring, ugly and beautiful, hateful and loving. In the end one feels, more than
anything else, pity and sorrow for the confusion, misery,
and degradation of humanity. . . . The book as a whole
is not pornographic, and, while in not a few spots it is
coarse, blasphemous, and obscene, it does not, in our
opinion, tend to promote lust. The erotic passages are
submerged in the book as a whole and have little resultant
effect."

In the circuit court Judge Manton dissented, and his
opinion reviews the earlier Federal cases which he asserts
approve the rule of *Regina* v. *Hicklin:* the principal ones
are *U.S.* v. *Bennett,* Fed. Cas. No. 14,571 (1879); *Rosen*
v. *U.S.,* 161 U.S. 29, 16 S. Ct. 434, 40 L. Ed. 606
(1896): *Dunlop* v. *U.S.,* 165 U.S. 486, 17 S. Ct. 375, 41
L. Ed. 799 (1897).

These cases were individually and carefully distinguished
by Judge Hand in the majority opinion, who held them
not to represent the law:

"But it is argued that *United States* v. *Bennett,* Fed.
Cas. No. 14,571, stands in the way of what has been said,
and it certainly does. There a court, consisting of Blatchford, C.J., and Benedict and Choate, D.JJ., held that the
offending paragraphs in a book could be taken from their
context and the book judged by them alone, and that the
test of obscenity was whether the tendency of these passages in themselves was 'to deprave the minds of those
open to such influences and into whose hands a publication of this character might come.' The opinion was
founded upon a dictum of Cockburn, C.J., in *Regina* v.
Hicklin, L.R. 3 Q.B. 360, where half of a book written to
attack the alleged practices of the confession was obscene
and contained, as Mellor, J., said 'a great deal . . . which
there cannot be any necessity for in any legitimate argument on the confessional. . . .' It is said that in *Rosen* v.
United States, 161 U.S. 29, 16 S. Ct. 434, 480, 40 L. Ed.
606, the Supreme Court cited and sanctioned *Regina* v.
Hicklin, and *United States* v. *Bennett.* The subject matter
of *Rosen* v. *United States* was, however, a pictorial representation of 'females, in different attitudes of indecency.'
The figures were partially covered 'with lamp black that
could be easily erased with a piece of bread.' p. 31 of 161
U.S., 16 S. Ct. 434. The pictures were evidently obscene,
and plainly came within the statute prohibiting their
transportation. The citation of *Regina* v. *Hicklin* and
United States v. *Bennett,* was in support of a ruling that
allegations in the indictment as to an obscene publication
need only be made with sufficient particularity to inform
the accused of the nature of the charge against him. No
approval of other features of the two decisions was expressed, nor were such features referred to. *Dunlop* v.
United States, 165 U.S. 486, 489, 17 S. Ct. 375, 41 L. Ed.
799, also seems to be relied on by the government, but the
publication there was admittedly obscene and the decision
in no way sanctioned the rulings in *United States* v.
Bennett, which we first mentioned. The rigorous doctrines
laid down in that case are inconsistent with our own deci-

sion in *United States* v. *Dennett,* (C.C.A.) 39 F.(2d)
564, 76 A.L.R. 1092, as well as with *Konda* v. *United
States,* (C.C.A.) 166 F. 91, 92, 22 L.R.A. (N.S.) 304;
Clark v. *United States,* (C.C.A.) 211 F. 916, 922; *Halsey*
v. *New York Society for the Suppression of Vice,* 234 N.Y.
1, 4, 136 N.E. 219; and *St. Hubert Guild* v. *Quinn,* 64
Misc. 336, 339, 118 N.Y.S. 582, and, in our opinion, do
not represent the law. They would exclude much of the
great works of literature and involve an impracticability
that cannot be imputed to Congress and would in the case
of many books containing obscene passages inevitably
require the court that uttered them to restrict their applicability."

It is quite clear that the harsh rule of *Regina v. Hicklin*
has been supplanted by the modern test of obscenity,
namely, whether the matter in question has a substantial
tendency to deprave or corrupt by inciting lascivious
thoughts or arousing lustful desire in the ordinary reader.
This has been stated in various ways.

It has been said that the matter charged, to be obscene,
must "suggest impure or libidinous thoughts," must "invite to lewd and lascivious practices and conduct," must
"be offensive to chastity," must "incite dissolute acts,"
must "create a desire for gratification of animal passions,"
must "encourage unlawful indulgences of lust," must "attempt to satisfy the morbid appetite of the salacious,"
must "pander to the prurient taste." See, *United States* v.
Journal Co., Inc., 197 Fed. 415 (D.C., Va., 1912),
United States v. *Klauder,* 240 Fed. 501 (D.C., N.Y.,
1917), *United States* v. *Durant,* 46 Fed. 753 (D.C., S.C.,
1891), *United States* v. *Moore,* 104 Fed. 78 (D.C., Ky.,
1900), *United States* v. *Reinheimer,* 233 Fed. 545 (D.C.,
Pa. 1916), *United States* v. *Clarke,* 38 Fed. 732 (D.C.,
Mo., 1889), *Dysart* v. *United States,* 4 F.(2d) 765, re-
versed, 272 U.S. 655 (1926), *United States* v. *Wroblen-
ski,* 118 Fed. 495 (D.C., Wis., 1902), *United States* v.
O'Donnell, 165 Fed. 218 (D.C., N.Y., 1908), *United
States* v. *Smith,* 11 Fed. 663 (D.C., Ky., 1882), *United
States* v. *Wightman,* 29 Fed. 636 (D.C., Pa., 1886),
United States v. *Wyatt,* 122 Fed. 316 (D.C., Del., 1903),
Hanson v. *United States,* 157 Fed. 749 (C.C.A. 7th,
1907), *United States* v. *Davidson,* 244 Fed. 523 (D.C.,
N.Y., 1917), *Dunlop* v. *United States,* 165 U.S. 486
(1897), *United States* v. *Males,* 51 Fed. 41 (D.C., Ind.,
1892), and *MacFadden* v. *United States,* 165 Fed. 51
(C.C.A. 3d, 1908).

In *Walker* v. *Popenoe,* 149 F.(2d) 511 (1945), it was
held:

"The effect of a publication on the ordinary reader is
what counts. The Statute does not intend that we shall
'reduce our treatment of sex to the standard of a child's
library in the supposed interest of a salacious few.' "

This test, however, should not be left to stand alone, for
there is another element of equal importance—the tenor of
the times and the change in social acceptance of what is
inherently decent. This element is clearly set forth in
United States v. *Kennerley,* 209 Fed. 119 (D.C., N.Y.,
1913), where Judge Hand said:

"If there be no abstract definition, such as I have suggested, should not the word 'obscene' be allowed to indicate the present critical point in the compromise between
candor and shame at which the community may have
arrived here and now? . . . Nor is it an objection, I think,
that such an interpretation gives to the words of the

statute a varying meaning from time to time. Such words as these do not embalm the precise morals of an age or place; while they presuppose that some things will always be shocking to the public taste, the vague subject matter is left to the gradual development of general notions about what is decent."

In his The Paradoxes of Legal Science, Mr. Justice Cardozo said: "Law accepts as the pattern of its justice the morality of the community whose conduct it assumes to regulate" (p. 37). In *Towne* v. *Eisner*, 245 U.S. 418, 425, 62 L. Ed. 372, 376 (1918) Mr. Justice Holmes said: "A word is not a crystal, transparent and unchanged, it is the skin of a living thought and may vary greatly in color and content according to the circumstances and the time in which it is used." And in the same vein, Professor Wormser wrote in The Development of the Law, 23 Columbia Law Review, 701, 702 (1923): "Increasingly— ever increasingly—the community is beginning to require of the law that it justify its own administration of its resources before the bar of public opinion. And in order to justify itself before this critical bar, the law must be brought to evidence the mores of the times, to which it must conform, or it will fail to fulfill its function as the judicial expression of the community passion for justice and right dealing."

2. The New York Courts. The modern test was applied in *People* v. *Wendling*, 258 N.Y. 451 (1932), which involved the dramatization of the song "Frankie and Johnnie." In holding that the courts are not censors of morals and manners, Judge Pound said:

"The language of the play is coarse, vulgar and profane; the plot cheap and tawdry. As a dramatic composition it serves to degrade the stage where vice is thought by some to lose 'half its evil by losing all its grossness.' 'That it is "indecent" from every consideration of propriety is entirely clear' (*People* v. *Eastman*, 188 N.Y. 478, 480), but the court is not a censor of plays and does not attempt to regulate manners. One may call a spade a spade without offending decency, although modesty may be shocked thereby (*People* v. *Muller*, 96 N.Y. 408, 411). The question is not whether the scene is laid in a low dive where refined people are not found or whether the language is that of the bar room rather than the parlor. The question is whether the tendency of the play is to excite lustful and lecherous desire (*People* v. *Eastman*, supra; *People* v. *Muller*, supra)."

Since the New York cases are generally in line with the modern Federal rule above stated, it is necessary only to cite the principal one: *Halsey* v. N.Y. *Society for the Suppression of Vice*, 234 N.Y. 1 (1922), which involved Theophile Gautier's "Mademoiselle de Maupin"; *People* v. *Brainard*, 192 App. Div. (N.Y.) 816 (1920), where the subject was "Madeleine," the anonymous autobiography of a prostitute.

3. The Massachusetts Courts. Boston has long been the center of book suppression in this country. Before 1930 the Massachusetts obscenity statute forbade the sale of any book "*containing* obscene, indecent language." The Supreme Court upheld convictions for the sale of Dreiser's "An American Tragedy" and D. H. Lawrence's "Lady Chatterly's Lover." After a general wave of censorship that swept over Boston in 1929 and resulted in the suppression of 68 books, the law was changed to proscribe the sale of "a book which *is* obscene, indecent," etc.

The result was the modern rule, but the Massachusetts courts were still severe with individual books. *Commonwealth* v. *Isenstadt*, 318 Mass. 543 (1945), upheld a conviction for the sale of "Strange Fruit," and while it announced the modern rule to great extent, it refused to sanction the idea that sincerity of purpose and artistic merit would necessarily dispel obscenity. But it clearly held that the time and custom of the community are important elements. The court said:

"Since effect is the test, it follows that a book is to be judged in the light of the customs and habits of thought of the time and place of the alleged offense. Although the fundamentals of human nature change but slowly, if indeed they change at all, customs and habits of thought do vary with time and place. That which may give rise to impure thought and action in a highly conventional society may pass almost unnoticed in a society habituated to greater freedom."

In the very recent case of *Attorney General* v. *Book Named "Forever Amber,"* decided October 11, 1948, and reported in 81 N.E.(2d) 663, the court repeated the stand it took in *Commonwealth* v. *Isenstadt*, supra, but it goes further on the question of sincerity and artistic purpose when the court said:

"It (the book) undoubtedly has historical purpose, and in this is adequately accurate in achievement. . . . The paramount impression is of an unfortunate country and its people as yet unfreed of the grasp of the Stuarts. . . . As to the individual characters, the reader is left with an estimate of an unattractive, hedonistic group, whose course of conduct is abhorrent and whose mode of living can be neither emulated nor envied."

The Modern Test of Obscenity

From all of these cases the modern rule is that obscenity is measured by the erotic allurement upon the average modern reader; that the erotic allurement of a book is measured by whether it is sexually impure—i.e., pornographic, "dirt for dirt's sake," a calculated incitement to sexual desire—or whether it reveals an effort to reflect life, including its dirt, with reasonable accuracy and balance; and that mere coarseness or vulgarity is not obscenity.

Forging such a rule from the precedents does not fully reach the heart of the matter, for I am sure that the books before me could be declared obscene or not obscene under either the Hicklin or the modern rule. Current standards create both the book and the judgment of it.

The evil of an indefinite statute like our section 524, however, is that it is also too loose. Current standards of what is obscene can swing to extremes if the entire question is left open, and even in the domestic laboratories of the States such freedom cannot safely be allowed. It is no longer possible that free speech be guaranteed Federally and denied locally; under modern methods of instantaneous communication such a discrepancy makes no sense. If speech is to be free anywhere, it must be free everywhere, and a law that can be used as a spigot that allows speech to flow freely or to be checked altogether is a general threat to free opinion and enlightened solution. What is said in Pennsylvania may clarify an issue in California, and what is suppressed in California may leave us the worse in Pennsylvania. Unless a restriction on free speech be of National validity, it can no longer have any local validity whatever.

Some danger to us all must appear before any of us can be muzzled.

In the field of written obscenity this principle has met oblique acceptance with regard to what is called "the classics," which are now exempt from legal censorship. Just how old a work must be before it can enjoy this immunity is uncertain, but what we know as classics are the books by remarkable people that have withstood the test of time and are accepted as having lasting value; they have become historical samples, which itself is important. This importance could not be as great if the screening process were not free.

Current literature, good, bad, or indifferent, goes into the hopper without any background for judgment; it is in the idiom of the moment and is keyed to the tempo of modern life. I do not believe that such considerations should result in removing any of the output from the hopper before the process of screening can begin. What is pure dirt to some may be another's sincere effort to make clear a point, and there is not much difference, from the historical angle, between censoring books before publication and suppressing them afterwards, before there has been a reasonable chance to judge them. Blackstone's neat distinction may satisfy an exact legal mind, but it has no meaning for history. The unworthy books will die soon enough, but the great work of genius has a hard enough time to make its way even in the free market of thought. James Joyce, whose work is difficult to understand, even after years of study, has evolved a new form of communication, by his method of using words, that will some day be a shorthand for complexity. The public was deprived for years of this work of genius because someone found objectionable passages in it.

I can find no universally valid restriction on free expression to be drawn from the behavior of "l'homme moyen sensuel," who is the average modern reader. It is impossible to say just what his reactions to a book actually are. Moyen means, generally, average, and average means a median between extremes. If he reads an obscene book when his sensuality is low, he will yawn over it or find that its suggestibility leads him off on quite different paths. If he reads the Mechanics' Lien Act while his sensuality is high, things will stand between him and the page that have no business there. How can anyone say that he will infallibly be affected one way or another by one book or another? When, where, how, and why are questions that cannot be answered clearly in this field. The professional answer that is suggested is the one general compromise— that the appetite of sex is old, universal, and unpredictable, and that the best we can do to keep it within reasonable bounds is to be our brother's keeper and censor, because we never know when his sensuality may be high. This does not satisfy me, for in a field where even reasonable precision is utterly impossible, I trust people more than I do the law. Had legal censorship been as constant throughout the centuries as the law of murder, rape, theft, and negligence, a case for the compromise could be made out; as it is, legal censorship is not old, it is not popular, and it has failed to strengthen the private censor in each individual that has kept the race as decent as it has been for several thousand years. I regard legal censorship as an experiment of more than dubious value.

I am well aware that the law is not ready to discard censorship altogether. The English keep their policeman handy, just in case, and the modern rule is a more efficient policeman. Its scope, however, must be defined with regard to the universal right of free speech, as limited only by some universally valid restriction required by a clear and present danger. For this we must consider the Constitution and the cases lately decided under it.

Constitutional Questions

The fourteenth amendment to the Federal Constitution prohibits any State from encroaching upon freedom of speech and freedom of the press to the same extent that the first amendment prevents the Federal Congress from doing so: *Pennekamp* v. *Florida*, 328 U.S. 331 (1946); *Chaplinsky* v. *New Hampshire*, 315 U.S. 568 (1942); *Thornhill* v. *Alabama*, 310 U.S. 88 (1940); *Winters* v. *New York*, 333 U.S. 507, 68 S. Ct. 665 (1948).

The principle of a free press covers distribution as well as publication: *Lovell* v. *City of Griffin*, 303 U.S. 444, 58 S. Ct. 666 (1938).

These guarantees occupy a preferred position under our law to such an extent that the courts, when considering whether legislation infringes upon them, neutralize the presumption usually indulged in favor of constitutionality: *Thomas* v. *Collins*, 323 U.S. 516, 530 (1945); *Thornhill* v. *Alabama*, 310 U.S. 88 (1940); *United States* v. *Carolene Products Co.*, 304 U.S. 144, 152, note 4 (1938). See also *Spayd* v. *Ringing Rock Lodge*, 270 Pa. 67 (1921).

And article 1, sec. 7 of the Pennsylvania Constitution states that:

"The free communication of thoughts and opinions is one of the invaluable rights of man, and every citizen may freely speak, write and print on any subject, being responsible for the abuse of that liberty."

When the first amendment came before the Supreme Court for interpretation in *Reynolds* v. *United States*, 98 U.S. 145 (1878), the court declared that government had no authority whatsoever in the field of thought or opinion: only in the area of conduct or action could it step in. Chief Justice Waite said: (p. 164)

"Congress was deprived of all legislative power over mere opinion, but was left free to reach actions which were in violation of social duties or subversive of good order."

Quoting from Jefferson's bill for establishing religious freedom, the Chief Justice stated:

" 'That to suffer the Civil magistrate to intrude his powers into the field of opinion, and to restrain the profession or propagation of principles on supposition of their *ill tendency*, is a dangerous fallacy which at once destroys all religious liberty . . . it is time enough for the rightful purposes of civil government for its officers to interfere *when principles break out into overt acts against peace and good order.' In these two sentences is found the true distinction between what properly belongs to the church and what to the State."* (Italics supplied.)

The now familiar "clear and present danger" rule, first stated by Mr. Justice Holmes in *Schenck* v. *United States*, 249 U.S. 47 (1918), represents a compromise between the ideas of Jefferson and those of the judges, who had in the meantime departed from the forthright views of the great statesman. Under that rule the publisher of a writing may be punished if the publication in question creates a clear and present danger that there will result from it some substantive evil which the legislature has a right to proscribe and punish.

The famous illustration in the Schenck case was:

"The most stringent protection of free speech would not protect a man in falsely shouting fire in a theater and causing a panic. It does not even protect a man from an injunction against uttering words that may have all the effect of force."

Mr. Justice Brandeis added, in *Whitney* v. *California*, 274 U.S. 357 (1927), the idea that free speech may not be curbed where the community has the chance to answer back. He said:

"Those who won our independence by revolution were not cowards. They did not fear political change. They did not exalt order at the cost of liberty. To courageous, self-reliant men, with confidence in the power of free and fearless reasoning applied through the processes of popular government, *no danger flowing from speech can be deemed clear and present, unless the incidence of the evil apprehended is so imminent that it may befall before there is opportunity for full discussion.* If there be time to expose through discussion the falsehood and fallacies, to avert the evil by the processes of education, *the remedy to be applied is more speech, not enforced silence. Only an emergency can justify repression.* Such must be the rule if authority is to be reconciled with freedom. Such, in my opinion, is the command of the Constitution. It is therefore always open to Americans to challenge a law abridging free speech and assembly by showing that there was no emergency justifying it. (Italics supplied.)

"Moreover, even imminent danger cannot justify resort to prohibition of these functions essential to effective democracy, unless the evil apprehended is relatively serious. Prohibition of free speech and assembly is a measure so stringent that it would be inappropriate as the means for averting a relatively trivial harm to society. A police measure may be unconstitutional merely because the remedy, although effective as means of protection, is unduly harsh or oppressive. Thus, a State might, in the exercise of its police power, make any trespass upon the land of another a crime, regardless of the results or of the intent or purpose of the trespasser. It might, also, punish an attempt, a conspiracy, or an incitement to commit the trespass. But it is hardly conceivable that this Court would hold constitutional a statute which punished as a felony the mere voluntary assembly with a society formed to teach that pedestrians had the moral right to cross unenclosed, unposted, waste lands and to advocate their doing so, even if there was imminent danger that advocacy would lead to a trespass. The fact that speech is likely to result in some violence or in destruction of property is not enough to justify its suppression. There must be the probability of serious injury to the State. Among free men, the deterrents ordinarily to be applied to prevent crime are education and punishment for violations of the law, not abridgment of the rights of free speech and assembly."

It is true that subsequent to the decision of the court in the Schenck case, Justices Holmes and Brandeis fought what for a time appeared to be a losing battle. To them the "clear and present danger" rule was a rule of the criminal law, and they applied it only to prohibit speech which incited to punishable conduct. See the dissenting opinion in *Gitlow* v. *New York*, 268 U.S. 652 (1925), where they say:

"If the publication of this document had been laid as *an attempt* to induce an uprising against government at once and not at some indefinite time in the future it would have presented a different question. The object would have been one with which the law might deal, subject to the doubt whether there was any danger that the publication could produce any result, or in other words, whether it was not futile and too remote from possible consequences. *But the indictment alleges the publication and nothing more.*" (Italics supplied.)

The history of the Supreme Court, since its decision in *Gitlow* v. *New York*, has been marked by gradual progress along the path staked out by Justices Holmes and Brandeis, culminating finally in the complete acceptance of their views.

This progress may be traced in the following decisions: *Stromberg* v. *California*, 283 U.S. 359 (1931); *DeJonge* v. *Oregon*, 299 U.S. 353 (1937); *Herndon* v. *Lowry*, 301 U.S. 242 (1937); *Palko* v. *Connecticut*, 302 U.S. 319 (1937); *Lovell* v. *Griffin*, 303 U.S. 444 (1938); *Cantwell* v. *Connecticut*, 310 U.S. 296 (1940); *Thornhill* v. *Alabama*, 310 U.S. 88 (1940); *Bridges* v. *California*, 314 U.S. 252 (1941); *Board of Education* v. *Barnette*, 319 U.S. 624 (1943); *Schneiderman* v. *United States*, 320 U.S. 118 (1943); *United States* v. *Ballard*, 322 U.S. 78 (1944); *Thomas* v. *Collins*, 323 U.S. 516 (1945); *Pennekamp* v. *Florida*, 328 U.S. 331 (1946); *Musser* v. *Utah*, 333 U.S. 95 (1948).

As was said in *Martin* v. *Struthers*, 319 U.S. 141 (1943):

"The right of freedom of speech and press has broad scope. The authors of the First Amendment knew that novel and unconventional ideas might disturb the complacent, but they chose to encourage a freedom which they believed essential if vigorous enlightenment was ever to triumph over slothful ignorance. This freedom embraces the right to distribute literature, *Lovell* v. *Griffin* (citation), and necessarily protects the right to receive it."

There are other milestones in the judicial reëstablishment of freedom of speech and freedom of the press. We cite the language of the Supreme Court in some of those cases:

In *Herndon* v. *Lowry*, 301 U.S. 242 (1937), the court said:

"The power of a state to abridge freedom of speech and of assembly is the exception rather than the rule and the penalizing even of utterances of a defined character must find its justification in a reasonable apprehension of danger to organized government. The judgment of the legislature is not unfettered."

In *DeJonge* v. *Oregon*, 299 U.S. 353 (1937), the court said:

"These rights may be abused by using speech or press or assembly *in order to incite to violence and crime.* The people through their legislatures may protect themselves against that abuse. But the legislative intervention can find constitutional justification only by dealing with the abuse. The rights themselves must not be curtailed." (Italics supplied.)

In *Thornhill* v. *Alabama*, 310 U.S. 88 (1940), the court said:

"Every expression of opinion on matters that are important has the potentiality of inducing action in the interests of one rather than another group in society. But the group in power at any moment may not impose penal sanctions on peaceful and truthful discussion of matters of public interest merely on a showing that others may thereby be persuaded to take action inconsistent with its interests. Abridgment of the liberty of such discussion can be justified only where the clear danger of substantive evils arises *under circumstances affording no opportunity to test the merits of ideas by competition for acceptance in the market of public opinion.*" (Italics supplied.)

The nature of the evil which the legislature has the power to guard against by enacting an obscenity statute is not clearly defined. As Jefferson saw it, the legislature was restricted to punishing criminal acts and not publications. To Holmes and Brandeis the bookseller could be punished if his relation to the criminal act was such that he could be said to have incited it. In neither view could the bookseller be punished if his books merely "tended" to result in illegal acts and much less if his books "tended" to lower the moral standards of the community. A much closer relationship was required. The legislature may validly prevent criminal acts and legislate to protect the moral standards of the community. But the threat must in either case be more than a mere tendency. The older cases which upheld obscenity statutes on the "tendency" theory would appear to be invalid in the light of the more recent expressions of the Supreme Court.

Thus the opinion of the Supreme Court in *Bridges* v. *California*, 314 U.S. 252 (1941) says: (p. 273)

"In accordance with what we have said on the 'clear and present danger' cases, neither 'inherent tendency' nor 'reasonable tendency' is enough to justify a restriction of free expression."

In *Pennekamp* v. *Florida*, 328 U.S. 331 (1946), a case in which the resulting evil was said to be that of improperly influencing the administration of justice, the Supreme Court said, in discussing the Bridges case:

"In the Bridges Case the clear and present danger rule was applied to the stated issue of whether the expressions there under consideration prevented 'fair judicial trials free from coercion or intimidation.' Page 259. There was, of course, no question as to the power to punish for disturbances and disorder in the courtroom. Page 266. The danger to be guarded against is the 'substantive evil' sought to be prevented. Pages 261, 262, 263. In the Bridges Case that 'substantive evil' was primarily the 'disorderly and unfair administration of justice.' Pages 270, 271, 278."

In addition to being substantive, the evil which the legislature seeks to control must be substantial: *Bridges* v. *California*, supra. The evil consequence must be serious and the imminence high; the proof must be clear, that is to say, "a solidity of evidence should be required": *Pennekamp* v. *Florida*, supra. Or, as was said in a contempt of court case (*Craig* v. *Harney*, 331 U.S. 367 (1947)):

"The fires which it kindles must constitute an imminent, not merely a likely, threat to the administration of Justice. The danger must not be remote or even probable; *it must immediately imperil.*" (Italics supplied.)

These principles have not been applied specifically to an obscenity statute by any recent opinion of the United States Supreme Court, but as Mr. Justice Rutledge said orally when the "Hecate County" case, *Doubleday & Co.,*

Inc. v. *People of New York*, 93 L. Ed. 37 (an obscenity case), was recently argued before the court:

"Before we get to the question of clear and present danger, we've got to have something which the State can forbid as dangerous. We are talking in a vacuum until we can establish that there is some occasion for the exercise of the State's power."

"Yes, you must first ascertain the substantive evil at which the statute is aimed, and then determine whether the publication of this book constitutes a clear and present danger."

"*It is up to the State to demonstrate that there was a danger, and until they demonstrate that, plus the clarity and imminence of the danger, the constitutional prohibition would seem to apply.*" (Italics supplied.) (Quoted in 17 U.S. Law Week (Supreme Court Sections 3118)).

This appears to me much closer to a correct solution of obscenity cases than several general dicta by the Supreme Court to the effect that obscenity is indictable just because it is obscenity. For example, in *Near* v. *Minnesota*, 283 U.S. 697 (1931), Chief Justice Hughes remarked: "On similar grounds, the primary requirements of decency may be enforced against obscene publications."

It seems impossible, in view of the late decisions under the first amendment, that the word "obscene" can any longer stand alone, lighted up only by a vague and mystic sense of impurity, unless it is interpreted by other solid factors such as clear and present danger, pornography, and divorcement from mere coarseness of vulgarity.

In *Chaplinsky* v. *New Hampshire*, 315 U.S. 568 (1942), however, Mr. Justice Murphy said this: (p. 571)

"There are certain well-defined and narrowly limited classes of speech, the prevention and punishment of which have never been thought to raise any constitutional problem. These include the lewd and obscene, the profane, the libellous, and the insulting or 'fighting' words—those which by their very utterance inflict injury or tend to incite an immediate breach of the peace."

It is not clear to me, nor, I venture to assert, would it be to the Supreme Court, if faced directly by an appropriate case of literary obscenity, what words inflict injury by their very utterance or how such injury is inflicted. As for the notion of an obscene book tending to incite to an immediate breach of the peace, the proper point of emphasis is the breach of the peace. That is different from saying that obscenity automatically tends to a breach of the peace, for the idea is unreal.

The latest dictum on this subject is in *Kovacs* v. *Cooper*, decided on January 31, 1949, and reported in 17 U.S. Law Week 4163, where Mr. Justice Reed said:

"But in the *Winters* case (*Winters* v. *New York*, 333 U.S. 507 (1948)) we pointed out that prosecutions might be brought under statutes punishing the distribution of 'obscene, lewd, lascivious, filthy, indecent and disgusting' magazines. P. 511. We said, p.518:

"'The impossibility of defining the precise line between permissible uncertainty in statutes caused by describing crimes by words well understood through long use in the criminal law—obscene, lewd, lascivious, filthy, indecent or disgusting—and the unconstitutional vagueness that leaves a person uncertain as to the kind of prohibited conduct—massing stories to incite crime—has resulted in three arguments of this case in this Court.'"

The difficulty here is that insofar as they apply to literature, obscenity and its imposing string of synonyms do *not* have a fixed meaning through long use in the criminal law—or to put it the other way, that they have a very narrow and restricted meaning quite at variance with the assumption that obscenity debauches public morals by a mysterious and self-executing process that can be feared but not proved.

Certainly the books before me do not command, or urge, or incite, or even encourage persons to commit sexual misconduct of a nature that the legislature has the right to prevent or punish. Nor are they an imminent threat to the morality of the community as a whole. The conduct described in them is at most offensive. It does not incite to unlawfulness of any kind. These facts are important in view of the following language of Justice Rutledge, speaking for Justices Murphy, Douglas and himself (the other members of the court did not reach the question) in *Musser v. Utah*, 333 U.S. 95 (1948):

"The Utah statute was construed to proscribe any agreement to advocate the practice of polygamy. Thus the line was drawn between discussion and advocacy.

"The Constitution requires that the statute be limited more narrowly. *At the very least the line must be drawn between advocacy and incitment, and even the state's power to punish incitement may vary with the nature of the speech, whether persuasive or coercive, the nature of the wrong induced, whether violent or merely offensive to the mores, and the degree of probability that the substantive evil actually will result.*" (Italics supplied.)

Freedom of expression is the touchiest and most important right we have; it is asserted frequently and vigorously, for the democratic process rests fundamentally on the need of people to argue, exhort, and clarify. *Thomas v. Collins*, supra (323 U.S. 516) speaks of ". . . the preferred place given in our scheme to the great, the indispensable democratic freedoms secured by the First Amendment," and went on to say, at page 530:

"For these reasons any attempt to restrict those liberties must be justified by clear public interest, threatened not doubtfully or remotely, but by clear and present danger. The rational connection between the remedy provided and the evil to be curbed, which in other contexts might support legislation against attack on due process grounds, will not suffice. These rights rest on firmer foundation. Accordingly, whatever occasion would restrain orderly discussion and persuasion, at appropriate time and place, *must have clear support in public danger, actual or impending.* Only the gravest abuses, endangering paramount interest, give occasion for permissible limitation." (Italics supplied.)

The "preferred position" cases have been collected in Mr. Justice Frankfurter's concurring opinion in *Kovacs v. Cooper*, supra (decided January 31, 1949: 17 U.S.L.W. 4163). They are: *Herndon v. Lowry*, supra (301 U.S. 242); *United States v. Carolene Products Co.*, 304 U.S. 144 (1948); *Thornhill v. Alabama*, 310 U.S. 88 (1940); *Schneider v. State*, 308 U.S. 147 (1939); *Bridges v. California*, supra (314 U.S. 252); *Murdock v. Pennsylvania*, 319 U.S. 105 (1943); *Prince v. Massachusetts*, 321 U.S. 158 (1944); *Follett v. McCormick*, 321 U.S. 573 (1944); *Marsh v. Alabama*, 326 U.S. 501 (1946); *Pennekamp v. Florida*, supra (328 U.S. 331); *West Virginia State Board v. Barnette*, 319 U.S. 624 (1943); *Thomas v. Collins*, supra (323 U.S. 516); *Saia v. New York*, 334 U.S. 558 (1948).

Mr. Justice Frankfurter sounds the warning that the phrase "preferred position" should not be allowed to become a rigid formula, lest another one grow beside it— that any legislative restriction on free speech be considered "presumptively invalid." The warning is well taken, for there are too many kinds of restriction as well as vehicles of free speech to warrant such rigidity. The Kovacs and Sara cases involve loud speakers and sound trucks, which are perilously close to nuisances and even to threats to public health. There are many instances where the police power may be used, at the expense of free expression, where the threat to order or health is directly and imminently demonstrable. The point is to see and understand the danger, and to keep particular cases within or without the justifiable area of the police power.

Short of books that are sexually impure and pornographic, I can see no rational legal catalyst that can detect or define a clear and present danger inherent in a writing or that can demonstrate what result ensues from reading it. All that is relied upon, in a prosecution, is an indefinable fear for other people's moral standards—a fear that I regard as a democratic anomaly.

Finally, the Supreme Court, in *Winters v. New York*, supra (333 U.S. 507), held subdivision 2 of section 1141 of New York's Penal Law unconstitutional because it was vague and allowed punishment of matters within the protection of free speech. The court said:

"The appellant contends that the subsection violates the right of free speech and press because it is vague and indefinite. *It is settled that a statute so vague and indefinite, in form and as interpreted, as to permit within the scope of its language the punishment of incidents fairly within the protection of the guarantee of free speech is void, on its face, as contrary to the Fourteenth Amendment. Stromberg v. California*, 283 U.S. 359, 369; *Herndon v. Lowry*, 301 U.S. 242, 258. A failure of a statute limiting freedom of expression to give fair notice of what acts will be punished and such a statute's inclusion of prohibitions against expressions, protected by the principles of the First Amendment, violates an accused's rights under procedural due process and freedom of speech or press." (Italics supplied.)

I am clear that the books before me are within the protection of the first and fourteenth amendments of the Federal Constitution, and of article 1, sec. 7 of the Pennsylvania Constitution. They bear obvious internal evidence of an effort to portray certain segments of American life, including parts that more refined people than the characters may deplore, but which we know exist. The vulgarity and obscenity in them are inherent in the characters themselves and are obviously not set forth as erotic allurement or as an excuse for selling the volumes. Nor can it be said that they have the effect of inciting to lewdness, or of inciting to any sexual crime, or that they are sexually impure and pornographic, i.e., "dirt for dirt's sake."

Definition of Obscenity as Sexual Impurity

Sexual impurity in literature (pornography, as some of the cases call it) I define as any writing whose dominant purpose and effect is erotic allurement—that is to say, a calculated and effective incitement to sexual desire. It is the effect that counts, more than the purpose, and no indictment can stand unless it can be shown. This definition is in accord with the cases that have restricted the meaning of obscenity and its synonyms to that of sexual impurity, and with those cases that have made erotic allurement the test of its effect.

This excludes from pornography medical or educational writings, whether in technical or layman's language, and whether used only in schools or generally distributed, whose dominant purpose and effect is exegetical and instructional rather than enticing. It leaves room for interpretation of individual books, for as long as censorship is considered necessary, it is as impossible as it is inadvisable to find a self-executing formula.

Sex education has been before the courts in many cases. In *United States* v. *"Married Love,"* 48 F.(2d) 821 (1931), Judge Woolsey said:

"It makes also some apparently justified criticisms of the inopportune exercise by the man in the marriage relation of what are often referred to as his conjugal or marital rights, and it pleads with seriousness, and not without some eloquence, for a better understanding by husbands of the physical and emotional side of the sex life of their wives. I do not find anything exceptionable anywhere in the book, and I cannot imagine a normal mind to which this book would seem to be obscene or immoral within the proper definition of these words, or whose sex impulses would be stirred by reading it."

Judge Woolsey held similarly in *United States* v. *"Contraception,"* 51 F.(2d) 525 (1931). Both of the above books were by Dr. Marie C. Stopes.

The case of *United States* v. *Dennett,* 39 F.(2d) 564 (C.C.A. 2d, 1930), involved a pamphlet written by a woman for the education of her children. Sections of it appear in the reporter's summary of the case, and show that it gave full and frank information, together with the view that the sexual impulse is not a base passion but as a great joy when accompanied by love between two human beings. In reversing a conviction, Judge Hand said:

"It also may reasonably be thought that accurate information, rather than mystery and curiosity, is better in the long run and is less likely to occasion lascivious thoughts than ignorance and anxiety. Perhaps instruction other than that which the defendant suggests would be better. That is a matter as to which there is bound to be a wide difference of opinion, but, irrespective of this, we hold that an accurate exposition of the relevant facts of the sex side of life in decent language and in manifestly serious and disinterested spirit cannot ordinarily be regarded as obscene. Any incidental tendency to arouse sex impulses which such a pamphlet may perhaps have, is apart from and subordinate to its main effect. The tendency can only exist in so far as it is inherent in any sex instruction, and it would seem to be outweighed by the elimination of ignorance, curiosity, and morbid fear. The direct aim and the net result is to promote understanding and self-control."

The definition of sexual impurity given above brings literary obscenity into workable analogy with sedition, blasphemy, open lewdness, and the other examples set forth earlier, as those terms are used in our Penal Code, except for one remaining point. Sedition, blasphemy, and open lewdness, by definition, carry their own threat of danger to the public peace. The deep and peculiar nature of religious faith is such that people are entitled to protection against those who call their gods in vain; religion has too recently and for too long been one of the greatest of the fighting faiths to assume that disorder will not follow from public irreverence. He who is publicly lewd is in himself an open

and immediate invitation to morally criminal behavior. The pressing danger inherent in sedition speaks for itself.

A book, however sexually impure and pornographic, is in a different case. It cannot be a present danger unless its reader closes it, lays it aside, and transmutes its erotic allurement into overt action. That such action must inevitably follow as a direct consequence of reading the book does not bear analysis, nor is it borne out by general human experience; too much can intervene and too many diversions take place. It must be constantly borne in mind that section 524 does not include the element of debauching public morals or of seeking to alter the prevailing moral code. It only proscribes what *is* obscene, and that term is meaningless unless activated by precise dangers within legal limits. Since section 524 provides no standard, the danger and the limits must be found elsewhere, and the only clear and discernible ones are those having to do with the police power and the preservation of the peace.

The Clear and Present Danger

I have pointed out above that any test of the effect of obscenity is bound to be elusive. Section 524 is therefore vague, indefinite, and unconstitutional unless some exact definition can be found for the "clear and present danger" to be prevented that will satisfy the constitutional protection of free speech. There are various types of cases in which definition is clear because the need is clear. The police power operates in pure food cases because people can sicken and die from eating bad food; in traffic cases because people can be injured or killed unless there is regulation; in weights and measures cases because of the ease with which the consumer can be cheated, and in conventional crimes because of the threat to persons and property. The list could be extended.

Mr. Justice Holmes's example in *Schenck* v. *United States* is no test for the case before me; the public does not read a book and simultaneously rush by the hundreds into the streets to engage in orgiastic riots. Mr. Justice Brandeis's discussion in *Whitney* v. *California* is a better yardstick, for in the field of the printed word the community has full opportunity to answer back. How can it be said that there is a "clear and present danger"—granted that anyone can say what it is—when there is both time and means for ample discussion?

These words of Jefferson should not be forgotten:

"I deplore . . . the putrid state into which our newspapers have passed, and the malignity, the vulgarity, and the mendacious spirit of those who write them. . . . These ordures are rapidly depraving the public taste.

"It is, however, an evil for which there is no remedy: our liberty depends on the freedom of the press, and that cannot be limited without being lost."

Who can define the clear and present danger to the community that arises from reading a book? If we say it is that the reader is young and inexperienced and incapable of resisting the sexual temptations that the book may present to him, we put the entire reading public at the mercy of the adolescent mind and of those adolescents who do not have the expected advantages of home influence, school training, or religious teaching. Nor can we say into how many such hands the book may come. Adults, or even a gifted minor, may be capable of challenging the book in public and thus of forwarding the education and enlightenment of us all by free discussion and correction. If the argument be applied to the general public, the situation becomes absurd, for then no publication is safe. How is it possible to say that reading a certain book is bound to make people behave in a way that is socially undesirable? And beyond a reasonable doubt, since we are dealing with a penal statute?

We might remember the words of Macaulay:

"We find it difficult to believe that in a world so full of temptations as this, any gentleman, whose life would have been virtuous if he had not read Aristophanes and Juvenal, will be made vicious by reading them."

Substitute the names of the books before me for "Aristophanes and Juvenal," and the analogy is exact.

The only clear and present danger to be prevented by section 524 that will satisfy both the Constitution and the current customs of our era is the commission or the imminence of the commission of criminal behavior resulting from the reading of a book. Publication alone can have no such automatic effect.

The Rule of Decision

Thus limited, the constitutional operation of section 524 of our act rests on narrow ground.

The modern test of obscenity, as I have stated it above (page 136), furnishes a means of determining whether a book, taken as a whole, is sexually impure, as I have defined that term (page 151, ante).

I hold that section 524 may not constitutionally be applied to any writing unless it is sexually impure and pornographic. It may then be applied, as an exercise of the police power, only where there is a reasonable and demonstrable cause to believe that a crime or misdemeanor has been committed or is about to be committed as the perceptible result of the publication and distribution of the writing in question: the opinion of anyone that a tendency thereto exists or that such a result is self-evident is insufficient and irrelevant. The causal connection between the book and the criminal behavior must appear beyond a reasonable doubt. The criminal law is not, in my opinion, "the custos morum of the King's subjects," as *Regina* v. *Hicklin* states: it is only the custodian of the peace and good order that free men and women need for the shaping of their common destiny.

There is no such proof in the instant case.

For that reason, and also because of the character of the books themselves, I hold that the books before me are not sexually impure and pornographic, and are therefore not obscene, lewd, lascivious, filthy, indecent, or disgusting. The sustaining of the demurrers follows.

1950-1959
Cases

■ Attorney General
v.
Book Named "God's Little Acre."

Supreme Judicial Court of Massachusetts. Suffolk.

Argued Dec. 8, 1949. Decided July 26, 1950.

J. J. Kelleher, Boston, *J. J. Bresnahan*, Asst. Atty. Gen., and *L. E. Ryan*, Dorchester, for plaintiff.

R. W. Meserve, Boston, *Joseph B. Ullman*, New York City, for defendants.

Before Qua, C.J., and Lummus, Ronan, Wilkins, Spalding, Williams and Counihan, JJ.

Spalding, Justice.

The Attorney General, under the provisions of G.L. (Ter. Ed.) c. 272, §§ 28C-28G, as inserted by St. 1945, c. 278, § 1, seeks by this petition to have the novel "God's Little Acre" by Erskine Caldwell adjudicated obscene, indecent, or impure. In an answer filed by persons interested in the book it was admitted that it was being sold and distributed in this Commonwealth. From a final decree in favor of the book the Attorney General appealed. The case comes here on a report of the evidence, including a copy of the book itself, and findings of fact by the trial judge.

While conceding "that if one were seeking so called racy, off-color or suggestive paragraphs, they can be found in the book," the judge was of opinion that the "book as a whole would not stimulate sexual passions or desires in a person with average sex instincts," and concluded that he did not believe that it would have "a substantial tendency to deprave or corrupt its readers by inciting lascivious thoughts or arousing lustful desires."

[1] The tests to be applied in determining whether a book is obscene, indecent, or impure are fully set forth in the recent case of *Commonwealth* v. *Isenstadt*, 318 Mass. 543, 62 N.E. 2d 840. They were quoted with approval and applied in *Attorney General* v. *Book Named "Forever Amber*," 323 Mass. 302, 81 N.E. 2d 663. They need not be restated. Comprehensive and complete as are these tests, their application in a given case is by no means easy. Indeed it is not indulging in hyperbole to say that no more difficult or delicate task confronts a court than that arising out of the interpretation and application of statutes of this sort. On the one hand, an interpretation ought not to be given to the statute in question which would trim down the fundamental right of the public to read "to the point where a few prurient persons can find nothing upon which their hypersensitive imaginations may dwell." *Commonwealth* v. *Isenstadt*, 318 Mass. 543, 551–552, 62 N.E. 2d 840, 845: On the other hand, care must be taken that it be not construed in such a way as to render it incapable of accomplishing the objects intended by the Legislature.

We turn to the story itself. It has to do with life of a poor white farmer and his family on a run down farm in Georgia. The father, Ty Ty Walden, is a pathetic figure with the mentality of a moron. Believing that there is gold on his land, he and two of his sons dig for it incessantly, leaving the raising of cotton to two colored share croppers. Ty Ty, who is pious, dedicates one acre of his land to God and intends to turn over the proceeds of that acre to the church. But he is so busy digging for gold that he never gets around to raising anything on it, and he relocates it from time to time to meet the exigencies of his digging. Ty Ty's sons, daughters, and daughter-in-law become involved in numerous sexual affairs. These lead to quarrels among the brothers, and as the story closes one brother kills another and departs with his shotgun, presumably to kill himself. Ty Ty, who had always tried to keep peace in the family, in despair resumes his digging for gold.

[2] Viewing the book as a whole we find ourselves unable to agree with the conclusion of the trial judge that the book was not obscene, indecent, or impure as those words have been defined in our decisions. The book abounds in sexual episodes and some are portrayed with an abundance of realistic detail. In some instances the author's treatment of sexual relations descends to outright pornography. Nothing would be gained by spreading these portions of the book on the pages of this opinion.

[3] Evidence was introduced at the hearing below by literary critics, professors of English literature, and a professor of sociology touching the "literary, cultural or educational character" of the book. See § 28F. In general the literary experts regarded the book as a sincere and serious work possessing literary merit. The sociologist was of opinion that the book was of value as a sociological document in its portrayal of life of the so-called "poor whites" in the south. The judge, who had the advantage of hearing these witnesses, has indicated in his findings that he accorded considerable weight to their testimony. We accept his findings on this aspect of the case. But the fact that under § 28F evidence may be received as to the "literary, cultural or educational character" of the book does not change the substantive law as to what is obscene, indecent, or impure. Those provisions were undoubtedly inserted to clarify doubts as to the sort of expert evidence that may be received in cases of this type. See *Commonwealth* v. *Isenstadt*, 318 Mass. 543, at pages 558–559, 62 N.E. 2d 840. In reaching the conclusion that the book offends against the statute we have taken into consideration the expert testimony described above. In the Isenstadt case we recognized that sincerity of purpose and literary merit were not to be entirely ignored and could "be considered in so far as they bear upon the question whether the book, considered as a whole, is or is not obscene, indecent, or

impure." 318 Mass. at page 554, 62 N.E. 2d at page 846. But as we said in that case, "In dealing with such a practical matter as the enforcement of the statute here involved there is no room for the pleasing fancy that sincerity and art necessarily dispel obscenity. * * * Sincerity and art can flourish without pornography, and seldom, if ever, will obscenity be needed to carry the lesson." 318 Mass. at page 553, 62 N.E. 2d 846.

Our attention has been directed to two decisions in other jurisdictions in which the book in question has been held not to be obscene under statutes somewhat similar to ours. One of them, *People* v. *Viking Press, Inc.*, 147 Misc. 813, 264 N.Y.S. 534, is an opinion by a city magistrate. The other case, *Commonwealth* v. *Gordon*, 66 Pa. Dist. & Co. R. 101, was decided by a court of first instance in Pennsylvania and was affirmed by the Superior Court on appeal in a per curiam decision, 166 Pa. Super. 120, 70 A.

2d 389. A discussion of these decisions would not be profitable. It is enough for present purposes to say that the interpretations placed on the statutes there involved differ materially from that which this court has placed on our statute.

[4] The contention that a decree adjudicating the book as obscene, indecent, or impure would be an abridgment of the rights of freedom of the press guaranteed by the Fourteenth Amendment to the Constitution of the United States requires no discussion. A similar contention was made without success in *Commonwealth* v. *Isenstadt*, 318 Mass. 543, 557–558, 62 N.E. 2d 840. What was said there is applicable here.

It follows that the decree below is reversed and a new decree is to be entered adjudicating that the book in question is obscene, indecent, and impure.

So ordered.

■ Joseph Burstyn, Inc.

v.

Wilson, Commissioner of Education et al.

COURT OF APPEALS OF NEW YORK.

Decided Oct. 18, 1951.

Ephraim S. London, Clendon H. Lee, Leonard P. Simpson and *Seymour M. Burg,* all of New York City, for appellant.

Newell G. Alford, Jr., Osmond K. Fraenkel, Herbert Monte Levy and *Robert Markewich,* all of New York City, for New York City Civil Liberties Committee and another, *amici curiæ,* in support of appellant's position.

Herman Seid, New York City, for Metropolitan Committee for Religious Liberty, *amicus curiæ,* in support of appellant's position.

Emanuel Redfield, New York City, for New York Chapter, Artists Equity Association, *amicus curiæ,* in support of appellant's position.

Will Maslow, Leo Pfeffer, Joseph B. Robison and *Philip Baum,* all of New York City, for American Jewish Congress, *amicus curiæ,* in support of appellant's position.

Charles A. Brind, Jr., John P. Jehu, Elizabeth M. Eastman and *George B. Farrington,* all of Albany, for respondents.

Patrick C. Dugan, Charles J. Tobin, Albany, *Edmond B. Butler, Porter R. Chandler* and *George A. Timone,* all of New York City, for New York State Catholic Welfare Committee, *amicus curiæ,* in support of respondents' position.

FROESSEL, Judge.

A license for the exhibition of a motion picture film entitled "The Miracle" together with two other films, described in their combination as a trilogy and called "Ways of Love," was issued to petitioner on November 30, 1950, by the Motion Picture Division of the Department of Education of the State of New York, under the governing statute, Education Law, McK. Consol. Laws. c. 16, art. 3, part II. "The Miracle" was produced in Italy as "Il Miracolo," and English subtitles were later added. A prior license had been issued to the original owner of the distribution rights for exhibition, with Italian subtitles alone; but the film was never shown under that license.

The first public exhibition of "The Miracle" as part of the trilogy, "Ways of Love," was shown in New York City on December 12, 1950. It provoked an immediate and substantial public controversy, and the Education Department was fairly flooded with protests against its exhibition. Others expressed a contrary view. In consequence thereof, the Board of Regents of the University of the State of New York (hereinafter called the Regents) proceeded promptly to review the action of its motion picture division. It appointed a sub committee, and directed a hearing requiring petitioner to show cause why the licenses should not be rescinded and cancelled.

After viewing the film and giving petitioner an opportunity to be heard, its sub committee reported that there was basis for the claim that the picture is sacrilegious, and recommended that the Regents view the film. Petitioner declined to participate in the hearing other than to appear specially before the subcommittee for the purpose of challenging the jurisdiction of the Regents to cancel the licenses, but its sole stockholder, Joseph Burstyn, appeared as an individual and filed a brief.

Thereupon and on February 16, 1951, after reviewing the picture and the entire record, the Regents unanimously adopted a resolution rescinding and canceling the licenses upon their determination that "The Miracle" is sacrilegious, and not entitled to a license under the law.[1] Thereafter petitioner instituted the present article 78 proceeding to review that determination, and now urges that (1) the Regents were powerless to review the action of its motion picture division or to revoke the licenses; (2) the word "sacrilegious" does not provide a sufficiently definite standard for action; (3) the Regents exceeded their authority; (4) the statute is unconstitutional as in violation of the First and Fourteenth Amendments of the Constitution of the United States in that denial or revocation of a license on account of sacrilege interferes with religious liberty and breaches the wall between Church and State; and (5) the statute is unconstitutional *in toto* as a prior restraint on the right of free speech guaranteed by the First and Fourteenth Amendments of the Federal Constitution. The Appellate Division unanimously confirmed the determination of the Regents.

First: The principal argument advanced by petitioner is directed toward the claim that the Regents have no power under the statute to rescind a license once issued by the motion picture division, unless upon a charge of fraud in the procurement thereof or subsequent misconduct by the licensee. Any other construction of the statute, it is said, would be inequitable to petitioner, which has spent money relying upon the license as issued. The Regents, on the other hand, contend that they were empowered under the Education Law and our State Constitution to make the determination here challenged.

This issue, then, is one primarily of statutory construction, turning upon the intention of the Legislature as found in the language of the statutes. It is resolved by the answer to the question: Did the Legislature intend that the granting of a license by a subordinate official of the State Education Department should be a determination final and irrevocable, binding on the head of his department, the courts and the public for all time? As we said in *Equitable Trust Co. of New York* v. *Hamilton*, 226 N.Y. 241, 245, 123 N.E. 380, 381, "That is in every case a question dependent for its answer upon the scheme of the statute by which power is conferred."

[1] In considering the statute pattern conferring the power, we should note the framework of fact and circumstance in which the statutes are to be examined, and particularly the nature of the problem with which we are dealing. Motion pictures, by their very nature, present a unique problem. They are primarily entertainment, rather than the expression of ideas, and are engaged in for profit. *Mutual Film Corp.* v. *Industrial Commission of Ohio*, 236 U.S. 230, 35 S. Ct. 387, 59 L. Ed. 552; *Mutual Film Co.* v. *Industrial Comm. of Ohio*, 236 U.S. 247, 35 S. Ct. 393, 59 L. Ed. 561; *Mutual Film Corp. of Missouri* v. *Hodges*, 236 U.S. 248, 35 S. Ct. 393, 59 L. Ed. 561. They have universal appeal to literate and illiterate, young and old, of all classes. They may exercise influence for good, but their potentiality for evil, especially among the young, is boundless. As was said in *Pathe Exchange Inc.*, v. *Cobb*, 202 App. Div. 450, 457, 195 N.Y.S. 661, 666, affirmed 236 N.Y. 539, 142 N.E. 274, where we sustained the original statute, L. 1921, ch. 715 creating the "motion picture commission" in respect to current event films: "many

would cast discretion and self-control to the winds, without restraint, social or moral. There are those who would give unrestrained rein to passion. * * * They appreciate the business advantage of depicting the evil and voluptuous thing, with the poisonous charm." A public showing of an obscene, indecent, immoral or sacrilegious film may do incalculable harm, and the State, in making provision against the threat of such harm, Education Law, § 122, may afford protection as broad as the danger presented.

[2] We are thus concerned with a valid exercise of the police power, Mutual Film cases, supra; Note 64 A.L.R. 505, and cases therein cited; *Pathe Exchange, Inc.*, v. *Cobb*, supra and with rights acquired by licensees thereunder. Such rights are not contractual in the constitutional sense. *People ex rel. Lodes* v. *Department of Health of City of New York*, 189 N.Y. 187, 82 N.E. 187, 13 L.R.A., N.S., 894; 12 Am. Jur., Constitutional Law, § 405; 33 Am. Jur., Licenses, §§ 21, 65. This is the general rule notwithstanding the expenditure of money by a licensee in reliance upon the license, although there is authority to the contrary in the case of building permits. 33 Am. Jur., Licenses, § 21; *People ex rel. Lodes* v. *Department of Health of City of New York*, supra, distinguishing 189 N.Y. at page 196, 82 N.E. at page 190, *City of Buffalo* v. *Chadeayne*, 134 N.Y. 163, 31 N.E. 443. Moreover, rights gained under the statute are accepted with whatever conditions or reservations the statute may attach to them. With these precepts in mind, and in the light of the problem with which the Legislature dealt, we may properly turn to a consideration of the statutory scheme.

The original body for the licensing of motion pictures for exhibition in this State was an independent commission created by chapter 715 of the Laws of 1921, its members appointed by the Governor, by and with the advice and consent of the Senate. While the provisions for licensing were similar to those now in the Education Law, there was an essential difference in the scheme embodied therein due to the *independent* nature of the former commission, which was then expressly given all of the powers now granted to the Regents. In 1926, the functions of the motion picture commission were transferred to the Department of Education and the old commission was abolished. L. 1926, ch. 544, State Departments Law, McK. Consol. Laws, c. 78, § 312. In 1927, the present form of the statute was incorporated into the Education Law as article 43 thereof. L. 1927, ch. 153, §§ 28, 29. These changes were significant, as will presently more fully appear.

The Regents are a constitutional body, existing since 1784, N.Y. Const. art. XI, § 2. They are named as head of the Education Department in the same paragraph as are the three chief elective officers of the State, the Governor, Comptroller and Attorney-General, Art. V, § 4. The latter provision of our Constitution empowers the Regents to "appoint and at pleasure remove a commissioner of education to be the chief administrative officer of the department." The mere placing of the motion picture commission in the Department of Education indicates an intention that the Regents should henceforth exercise complete authority over that agency.

Moreover, by explicit language, the Legislature gave to the Regents as head of the Education Department all of the broad powers of control and supervision formerly possessed by the independent commission, leaving to the motion picture division only "the administrative work" of

---

[1] Education Law, § 122.

licensing. Education Law, §§ 101, 103, 132. Thus, by section 101 of the Education Law, the Education Department "is charged" with "the exercise of all the functions" of the department, and with "the performance of all" the "powers and duties" transferred from the former independent motion picture commission, "whether in terms vested in such department" or in any "*division*" thereof (emphasis supplied), and such performance is authorized "by or through" the appropriate officer or division; by the same section the Regents are continued as "the head of the department," as prescribed in the Constitution. The Regents appoint the director, officers and employees of the motion picture division, fix their compensation, assign duties to the division, establish local offices, and "prescribe the powers and duties" Education Law, §§ 120, 121. The "form, manner and substance" of license applications are prescribed by the Education Department, and not by the motion picture division. Education Law, § 127.

The Regents must review the *denial* of a license before an unsuccessful applicant, who is given a "right of review by the regents," can avail himself of an article 78 proceeding. Education Law, § 124. A corresponding right of review where a license was *issued* must be deemed implicit in the broad powers of the board, rendering needless any additional language by way of express grant; when the Legislature intends to withhold the power of review from the head of a department with respect to the finding of an agency of the department, it does so by express language, Labor Law (labor relations), McK. Consol. Laws, c. 31, § 702, subd. 9; Workmen's Compensation Law, McK. Consol. Laws, c. 67, § 142, subd. 4. Finally, the Regents "have *authority* to enforce the *provisions* and *purposes*" of the statute and to make rules and regulations in "carrying out and enforcing [its] *purposes*" Education Law, § 132; emphasis supplied. This latter provision is taken directly from the original statute, § 15, and, although not embraced in the 1926 enactment transferring the functions of the independent motion picture commission, this precise authority was expressly given to the Regents by the 1927 amendment Education Law, former § 1092. The power to enforce embraces the power to correct the action of a subordinate, and one of the specific provisions and purposes of the act is that no sacrilegious films be licensed.

From all of this it is clear that the motion picture division is subject and subordinate to the Education Department and the Regents, and is not independent thereof, cf. *Butterworth v. United States* ex rel. *Hoe*, 112 U.S. 50, 5 S. Ct. 25, 28 L. Ed. 656, in which an altogether different statute pattern was involved, and where an appeal was expressly authorized from the commissioner to the court, either directly or by means of an original suit in equity. Even such functions as may now be exercised by the director of the division under the statute may be exercised by other officials upon authorization by the Regents. Education Law, §§ 120, 122. Without question, then, the statute constitutes the Regents the mainspring of the entire system therein set up. To deny them the power to correct the action of a subordinate, when the ultimate responsibility rests upon them, would be to set at naught the whole elaborate plan established by the Legislature. Such power is "essential to the exercise" of the powers expressly granted. *Lawrence Constr. Corp. v. State of New York*, 293 N.Y. 634, 639, 59 N.E. 2d 630, 632.

If petitioner's interpretation of the Education Law were to be adopted, no review either of an administrative or supervisory nature, or through the civil or criminal courts, see Penal Law, McK. Consol. Laws, c. 40, § 1141, as amended by L. 1950, ch. 624; *Hughes Tool Co.* v. *Fielding*, 188 Misc. 947, 73 N.Y.S. 2d 98, affirmed 272 App. Div. 1048, 75 N.Y.S. 2d 287, affirmed 297 N.Y. 1024, 80 N.E. 2d 540, of the action of a subordinate granting a license in the first instance is provided by the Legislature. Thus the most indecent, obscene, immoral, sacrilegious or depraved presentation might be made through the medium of motion picture film, provided only there was some slip, inadvertence or mistake on the part of the reviewer, leaving his superiors, the courts, and the public generally powerless to correct the situation. It would simply mean that this statutory plan to protect the public from films forbidden to be licensed for general exhibition under section 122 rests entirely upon the judgment of one or two persons in the motion picture division, whose favorable determination in the first instance is irrevocably binding on the People of the State of New York. Such intention on the part of the Legislature would seem to be so utterly unreasonable and out of harmony with basic public policy in these matters as to be unthinkable, *People* v. *Ahearn*, 196 N.Y. 221, 227, 89 N.E. 930, 931, 26 L.R.A., N.S., 1153.

[3] On the other hand, the only reasonable view to be taken is that the Legislature deemed the Constitution and the Education Law vested in the Regents as an independent constitutional body such supervisory powers as sufficiently to protect the public interest against improper action by subordinates, and that the authority thereby granted is therefore sufficiently complete in itself to accomplish the salutary purposes envisioned therein. Once the Legislature placed the power to license in the Department of Education, the Constitution, art. V, § 4, mandated the Board of Regents as its head to exercise it, and there is no legislation even purporting to restrict them from doing so. They are authorized to employ subordinates and to function "by or through" them, but are not thereby divested of their own ultimate responsibility. The action of the motion picture division must thus be regarded as reviewable by the Regents in any case—where the license is refused, on demand of the applicant; where the license is granted, on the Regents' own motion.

Accordingly, we are of the opinion that the Regents have power to review the action of its motion picture division in granting a license to exhibit motion pictures, and rightfully exercised its jurisdiction in this case.

[4] *Second:* To the claim that the statute delegates legislative power without adequate standards, a short answer may be made. Section 122 of the Education Law provides that a license shall be issued for the exhibition of a submitted film, "unless such film or a part thereof is obscene, indecent, immoral, inhuman, sacrilegious, or is of such a character that its exhibition would tend to corrupt morals or incite to crime." Only the word "sacrilegious" is attacked for indefiniteness. The dictionary, however, furnishes a clear definition thereof, were it necessary to seek one, as, e.g., "the act of violating or profaning anything sacred" (Funk & Wagnall's New Standard Dictionary [1937 ed.]). There is no difficulty in recognizing the limits of the criterion thus established, and the courts have had no problem either with the word "sacrilegious" or with its synonym, "profane."

In *Mutual Film Corp. of Missouri* v. *Hodges*, 236 U.S.

248, 35 S. Ct. 393, 59 L. Ed. 561, supra, the contention that there was an invalid delegation of legislative power was rejected where the statute provided that the censor should approve such films as were found to be "moral and proper, and disapprove such as are *sacrilegious*, obscene, indecent or immoral, or such as tend to corrupt the morals" 236 U.S. at page 257, 35 S. Ct. at page 395, emphasis supplied. In *Winters* v. *People of State of New York*, 333 U.S. 507, 510, 68 S. Ct. 665, 668, 92 L. Ed. 840, it is stated that publications are "subject to control if they are lewd, indecent, obscene or *profane*" (emphasis supplied). In *Chaplinsky* v. *State of New Hampshire*, 315 U.S. 568, 571–572, 62 S. Ct. 766, 769, 86 L. Ed. 1031, Mr. Justice Murphy declared for a unanimous court: "There are certain well-defined and narrowly limited classes of speech, the *prevention* and punishment of which has never been thought to raise any Constitutional problem. These include the lewd and obscene, the *profane*" (emphasis supplied). Indeed, Congress itself has found in the word "profane" a useful standard for both administrative and criminal sanctions against those uttering profane language or meaning by means of radio. *Dumont Laboratories* v. *Carroll*, 3 Cir., 184 F. 2d 153, 156, certiorari denied 340 U.S. 929, 71 S. Ct. 490, 95 L. Ed. 670; U.S.C.A. tit. 47, § 303, subd. (m), par. (1), cl. (D); U.S.C.A. tit. 18, § 1464; see, also, Penal Law, § 2072.

[5] Accordingly, the claim that the word "sacrilegious" does not provide a sufficiently definite standard may be passed without further consideration, since it is without substance.

Third: We turn now to the contention that the Regents exceeded their powers.

[6] Petitioner urges that, even if the board had the power, there was no justification for revocation. Of course, as the Appellate Division below, in its opinion, said, 278 App. Div. 253, 260, 104 N.Y.S. 2d 740, 747: "Under the familiar rule, applicable to all administrative proceedings, we may not interfere unless the determination made was one that no reasonable mind could reach." This rule applies to the courts and not to administrative agencies, as the Regents. Matter of *Foy Productions, Ltd.*, v. *Graves*, 253 App. Div. 475, 3 N.Y.S. 2d 573, affirmed 278 N.Y. 498, 15 N.E. 2d 435.

[7] We have all viewed the film in question. The so-called exhibits, which are simply unsworn communications expressing personal opinions, are of little help to us. The principal basis for the charge of sacrilege is found in the picture itself, the personalities involved, the use of scriptural passages as a background for the portrayal of the characters, and their actions, together with other portions of the script and the title of the film itself. It is featured as a "way of love." At the very outset, we are given this definition: "ardent affection, passionate attachment, men's adoration of God, sexual passion, gratification, devotion."

While the film in question is called "The Miracle," no miracle is shown; on the contrary, we have the picture of a demented peasant girl meeting a complete stranger whom she addresses as "Saint Joseph." At the very beginning of the script, reference is made to "Jesus, Joseph, Mary." "Saint Joseph" first causes her to become intoxicated. Scriptural passages referring to the Holy Sacrament (Luke 22:19), and to the nativity of Christ (Matthew 1:20), are freely employed immediately after she states she is not well. A blackout in the film, in its association with the story, compels the inference that sexual intercourse and conception ensue. "Saint Joseph" abandons her immediately following the seduction, she is later found pregnant, and a mock religious procession is staged in her honor; she is "crowned" with an old washbasin, is thrown out by her former lover, and the picture concludes with a realistic portrayal of her labor pains and the birth in a church courtyard of her child, whom she addresses as "my blessed son," "My holy son."

Christ is the heart and core of the Christian faith. Two personalities most closely related to Him in life were His mother, Mary, and Joseph. They are deeply revered by all Christians. Countless millions over the centuries have regarded their relationship as sacred, and so do millions living today. "The Miracle" not only encroaches upon this sacred relationship and the Biblical presentation thereof in respect to the birth of Christ, but utterly destroys it, associating it, as the Regents found, "with drunkenness, seduction, mockery and lewdness," and, in the language of the script itself, with "passionate attachment * * * sexual passion" and "gratification," as a way of love. In the light of the foregoing, we conclude, as did the Appellate Division, (1) that we cannot say that the determination complained of "was one that no reasonable mind could reach"; and (2) that the board did not act arbitrarily or capriciously.

[8] *Fourth:* It is further urged that a license may not be denied or revoked on the ground of sacrilege, because that would require a religious judgment on the part of the censoring authority and thus constitute an interference in religious matters by the State. In this connection, it is also urged that freedom of religion is thereby denied, since one man's sacrilege is another man's dogma, and one may thus be prevented from propagating his own religious views by means of motion pictures. The latter argument is specious when applied to motion pictures offered to the public for general exhibition as a form of entertainment, as we shall hereafter point out. Religious presentations, as ordinarily understood, as well as other educational and scientific films, are exempt. Education Law, § 123. Thus freedom of religion is not impaired in the slightest, as anyone may express any religious or antireligious sentiment he chooses through a proper use of the films.

[9] Nor is it true that the Regents must form religious judgments in order to find that a film is sacrilegious. As hereinbefore indicated, there is nothing mysterious about the standard to be applied. It is simply this: that no religion, as that word is understood by the ordinary, reasonable person, shall be treated with contempt, mockery, scorn and ridicule to the extent that it has been here, by those engaged in selling entertainment by way of motion pictures. As the court below said of the statute in question, "All it purports to do is to bar a visual caricature of religious beliefs held sacred by one sect or another, and such a bar, in our opinion is not a denial of religious freedom." 278 App. Div. 253, 258, 104 N.Y.S. 2d 740, 745.

[10, 11] Although it is claimed that the laws benefit all religions and thus breach the wall of separation between Church and State, the fact that some benefit may incidentally accrue to religion is immaterial from the constitutional point of view if the statute has for its purpose a legitimate objective within the scope of the police power of the State. *Everson* v. *Board of Education*

of Ewing Tp., 330 U.S. 1, 67 S. Ct. 504, 91 L. Ed. 711; *Cochran* v. *Louisiana State Board of Education*, 281 U.S. 370, 50 S. Ct. 335, 74 L. Ed. 913; *Bradfield* v. *Roberts*, 175 U.S. 291, 20 S. Ct. 121, 44 L. Ed. 168; *People* v. *Friedman*, 302 N.Y. 75, 96 N.E. 2d 184, appeal dismissed for want of substantial Federal question 341 U.S. 907, 71 S. Ct. 623, 95 L. Ed. 1345. Cases such as *Illinois* ex rel. *McCollum* v. *Board of Education of School Dist. No. 71*, 333 U.S. 203, 68 S. Ct. 461, 92 L. Ed. 648, and *Cantwell* v. *State of Connecticut*, 310 U.S. 296, 60 S. Ct. 900, 84 L. Ed. 1213 are not to the contrary. The former case dealt with the use of State property for religious purposes, Matter of *Zorach* v. *Clauson*, 302 N.Y. 161, 100 N.E. 2d 463, while the latter held, 310 U.S. at page 305, 60 S. Ct. at page 904 that "a censorship of religion as the means of determining its right to survive is a denial of liberty protected by the" First and Fourteenth Amendments. Yet even in those cases it was recognized that the States may validly regulate the manner of expressing religious views if the regulation bears reasonable relation to the public welfare. Freedom to believe—or not to believe—is absolute; freedom to act is not. "Conduct remains subject to regulation for the protection of society." *Cantwell* v. *Connecticut*, supra, 310 U.S. at page 304, 60 S. Ct. at page 903; American Communications Ass'n, *C.I.O.* v. *Douds*, 339 U.S. 382, 393, 70 S. Ct. 674, 94 L. Ed. 925.

The statute now before us is clearly directed to the promotion of the public welfare, morals, public peace and order. These are the traditionally recognized objects of the exercise of police power. For this reason, any incidental benefit conferred upon religion is not sufficient to render this statute unconstitutional. There is here no regulation of religion, nor restriction thereof or other interference with religious beliefs except insofar as the picture itself does so, nor is there any establishment of religion or preference of religion or use of State property or funds in aid of religion. There is nothing more than a denial of the claimed right to hurl insults at the deepest and sincerest religious beliefs of others through the medium of a commercial entertainment spectacle.

[12] We are essentially a religious nation, Rector, etc., *Church of Holy Trinity* v. *United States*, 143 U.S. 457, 465, 12 S. Ct. 511, 36 L. Ed. 226, of which it is well to be reminded now and then, and in the McCollum case, supra, the Supreme Court paused to note that a manifestation of governmental hostility to religion or religious teachings "would be at war with our national tradition." 333 U.S. at page 211, 68 S. Ct. at page 465. The preamble to our State Constitution expresses our gratitude as a people to Almighty God for our freedom. To say that government may not intervene to protect religious beliefs from purely private or commercial attacks or persecution, whatever the underlying motive, and however skillfully accomplished, as distinguished from the assertion of conflicting beliefs, is to deny not only its power to keep the peace, but also the very right to "the free exercise" of religion, guaranteed by the First Amendment. The offering of public gratuitous insult to recognized religious beliefs by means of commercial motion pictures is not only offensive to decency and morals, but constitutes in itself an infringement of the freedom of others to worship and believe as they choose. Insult, mockery, contempt and ridicule can be a deadly form of persecution—often far more so than more direct forms of action. The prohibition of such conduct comes

within the legitimate sphere of State action, and this State has recognized this principle, not only in the Education Law but in other respects as well. See, e.g., Penal Law, McK. Consol. Laws, c. 40, art. 186; Civil Rights Law, McK. Consol. Laws, c. 6, art. 4. We are not aware that this power has ever been even impliedly denied to the States.

This nation is a land of religious freedom; it would be strange indeed if our Constitution, intended to protect that freedom, were construed as an instrument to uphold those who publicly and sacrilegiously ridicule and lampoon the most sacred beliefs of any religious denomination to provide amusement and for commercial gain.

For the foregoing reasons, we conclude that the challenged portion of the statute in no way violates the provisions of the First Amendment of the Federal Constitution relating to religious freedom.

Fifth: Petitioner finally argues that the statute is unconstitutional *in toto*; that motion pictures are to be treated as the press generally, and many not be subjected to censorship or prior restraint. While it may not be heard in this respect, inasmuch as it has sought and obtained benefits under the statute, and even now seeks to retain the licenses granted. *Fahey* v. *Mallonee*, 332 U.S. 245, 255, 67 S. Ct. 1552, 91 L. Ed. 2030; *Shepherd* v. *Mount Vernon Trust Co.*, 269 N.Y. 234, 244–247, 199 N.E. 201, 204–205, we shall dispose of this argument upon the merits.

The contention urged is made in the face of direct holdings to the contrary, Mutual Film cases, supra; *RD-DR Corp.* v. *Smith*, 5 Cir., 183 F. 2d 562 (1950), certiorari denied 340 U.S. 853, 71 S. Ct. 80, 95 L. Ed. 625; *Pathe Exchange, Inc.* v. *Cobb*, 202 App. Div. 450, 195 N.Y.S. 661, affirmed 236 N.Y. 539, 142 N.E. 274, supra; 64 A.L.R. 505.

[13] The rationale of these decisions is that motion pictures are primarily a form of entertainment, a spectacle or show, and not such vehicles of thought as to bring them within the press of the country. On this basis, petitioner's contention that the Mutual Film cases, supra, lack authority today, because it was not the Federal Constitution against which the statute was there tested, is unsound, for the Ohio Constitution guarantees free speech and a free press as does the Federal Constitution. Essentially, what petitioner would have us do is to predict that the Supreme Court will overrule the Mutual Film cases and so disregard them here, as well as our own holding in the Pathe Exchange case, supra. But such was the position squarely taken in the RD-DR Corp. case, supra, where the same arguments were presented as are here urged, and they were unequivocally rejected.

On the same footing is the contention that technical developments have made a difference in the essential nature of motion pictures since the Mutual Film decisions. Such development was foreseen in the Mutual Film cases, see 236 U.S. at page 242, 35 S. Ct. 387, 59 L. Ed. 552, and was realized at the time of the RD-DR Corp. case, 183 F. 2d at page 565, decided a year ago. We have already pointed out that scientific and educational films, among others of kindred nature, are not within the general licensing statute, and are thus not concerned with any problem that might be raised by an attempt to impose general censorship upon such films.

Some comfort is found by petitioner in a statement in *United States* v. *Paramount Pictures, Inc.*, 334 U.S. 131,

166, 68 S. Ct. 915, 933, 92 L. Ed. 1260 to the effect that "moving pictures, like newspapers and radio, are included in the press." That was an antitrust case, freedom of the press was not involved, and the statement was pure dictum. Moreover, it may be observed that when certiorari was sought in the RD-DR Corp. case, *supra*, it was denied by the same court; the only Justice voting to grant was the one who wrote that dictum. Were we to rely upon dictum, the concurring remarks of Mr. Justice Frankfurter in a subsequently decided free speech case, *Kovacs* v. *Cooper*, 336 U.S. 77, 96, 69 S. Ct. 448, 458, 93 L. Ed. 513, would be appropriate: "Movies have created problems not presented by the circulation of books, pamphlets, or newspapers, and so the movies have been constitutionally regulated." Citing the Mutual Film cases, *supra*. However, dictum is a fragile bark in which to sail the constitutional seas.

The fact is that motion pictures do create problems not presented by other media of communication, visual or otherwise, as already indicated. It should be emphasized, however, that technical developments which increase the force of impact of motion pictures simply render the problem more acute. It does not avail to argue that there is now greater ability of transmission, when it is precisely that ability which multiplies the dangers already inherent in the particular form of expression.

[14] Whether motion pictures are *sui generis* or a very special classification of the press becomes a question for the academicians, once it is recognized that there is a danger presented and met by legislation appropriate to protect the public safety, yet narrow enough as not otherwise to limit freedom of expression. If there is any one proposition for which the free speech cases may be cited, from *Schenck* v. *United States*, 249 U.S. 47, 39 S. Ct. 247, 63 L. Ed. 470 to *Dennis* v. *United States*, 341 U.S. 494, 71 S. Ct. 857, 95 L. Ed. 1137, and *Breard* v. *Alexandria*, 341 U.S. 622, 71 S. Ct. 920, 95 L. Ed. 1233, it is that freedom of speech is not absolute, but may be limited when the appropriate occasion arises. We are satisfied that the dangers present and foreseen at the time of the Mutual Film cases, *supra* are just as real today.

The order of the Appellate Division should be affirmed, with costs.

DESMOND, Judge (concurring). I concur for affirmance for these reasons.

1. It is not too clear from the statutes that the Legislature, transferring, by L. 1926, ch. 544, motion picture licensing from an independent State Motion Picture Commission to a new Motion Picture Division in the State Department of Education intended, without so saying, that the Board of Regents, as head of the Education Department, should have power to revoke a license granted by the division. However, there is general language in the statute, Education Law, § 132, empowering the Regents to enforce the licensing law, including its prohibition against the licensing of "obscene, indecent, immoral, inhuman, sacrilegious" films, Education Law, § 122, and it would be an improbable legislative intent that would leave all this solely to a division of the department, with no corrective authority available elsewhere in the State Government. It would be anomalous if the Regents, charged by the statute with enforcing the law, could not correct the errors of their subordinate body.

2. As to whether this film can be considered sacrilegious, our own jurisdiction is limited by the *Miller* v. *Kling*, 291 N.Y. 65, 50 N.E. 2d 546 rule which requires us to uphold the administrative body's decision if supported by substantial evidence. In other words, if reasonable men could regard the picture as sacrilegious, then we cannot say that the Regents' ruling is wrong as matter of law. Reasonable, earnest and religious men in great numbers have said so, although other earnest religious voices express the other view. There was thus fair basis for the Regents' holding.

3. "Sacrilegious," like "obscene," see *Winters* v. *New York*, 333 U.S. 507, 68 S. Ct. 665, 92 L. Ed. 840, is sufficiently definite in meaning to set an enforcible standard. That men differ as to what is "sacrilegious" is beside the point—there is nothing in the world which all men everywhere agree is "obscene," yet obscenity laws are universally enforced. Of course, some of the meanings of "sacrilegious" have no possible application to a motion picture, but, according to all the dictionaries and common English usage, the adjective has one applicable meaning, since it includes violating or profaning anything held sacred (see Oxford Dictionary, Vol. 8, pp. 18–19; Webster's New International Dictionary [2d ed.], unabridged, p. 2195; Black's Law Dictionary [deluxe ed.], p. 1574). We thus have a statutory term of broad but ascertainable meaning, and, by settled law, the administrative application thereof must be accepted by the courts "if it has 'warrant in the record' and a reasonable basis in law." Matter of *Mounting & Finishing Co.* v. *McGoldrick*, 294 N.Y. 104, 108, 60 N.E. 2d 825, 827; *Red Hook Cold Storage Co.* v. *Department of Labor*, 295 N.Y. 1, 9, 64 N.E. 2d 265, 268, 163 A.L.R. 439.

4. Motion pictures are, it would seem, not excluded from First Amendment coverage, *United States* v. *Paramount Pictures, Inc.*, 334 U.S. 131, 166, 68 S. Ct. 915, 92 L. Ed. 1260, but, since there was a reasonable ground for holding this film "sacrilegious" (in the meaning which the Legislature must have intended for that term), the film was constitutionally "subject to control," Ex parte Jackson, 96 U.S. 727, 736, 24 L. Ed. 877, cited in *Winters* v. *People of State of New York*, supra, 333 U.S. at page 510, 68 S. Ct. at page 668. It fell within the "well-defined and narrowly limited classes of speech, the *prevention* and punishment of which has never been thought to raise any Constitutional problem." *Chaplinsky* v. *State of New Hampshire*, 315 U.S. 568, 571–572, 62 S. Ct. 766, 769, 86 L. Ed. 1031—italics mine. The Chaplinsky decision says that these narrowly limited classes of constitutionally preventable utterances include "the lewd and obscene, the profane, the libelous, and the insulting or 'fighting' words —those which by their very utterance inflict injury or tend to incite an immediate breach of the peace." That covers this case, and should dispose of any claim of violation of the First Amendment. If not, then any prior censorship at all of any motion picture is unconstitutional, and the floodgates are open.

FULD, Judge (dissenting).

It may lend perspective to recall that we are here concerned with a motion picture that has passed the rigid scrutiny of a numerous array of critics of undenied religiousness. There is, of course, no suggestion that "The Miracle" is a product of heathen hands. The story was written by a Roman Catholic and the picture produced, directed and acted solely by Roman Catholics. It was filmed in Italy, and first exhibited in Rome, where religious censorship exists. There, the Vatican Newspaper, L'Osservatore Romano, in reviewing it, alluded to the story and weighed the artistry of the production without condemning the moving picture or even intimating that there was any impropriety in its being viewed by Catholics. (See The Commonweal, March 23, 1951, p. 592.) And thereafter the film passed the United States Customs with no objection registered against it.

In 1949 and again in 1950, successive directors of the motion picture division of the State Education Department licensed the film for state-wide exhibition. It won the approval of the National Board of Review of Motion Pictures. It drew general acclaim from the press and was designated, as part of a trilogy, the best foreign language film of 1950 by the New York Film Critics, an association of critics of the major metropolitan newspapers. Finally, one important Roman Catholic publication, after deploring "these highly arbitrary invocations of a police censorship [that] must ultimately result * * * in great harm to the cause of religion as well as art," noted that the film "is not *obviously* blasphemous or obscene, either in its intention or execution" (Clancy, The Catholic as Philistine; The Commonweal, March 16, 1951, pp. 567–568; also, March 2, 1951, pp. 507–508 and March 23, 1951, pp. 590–592), and all Protestant clergymen who expressed themselves publicly—and they constituted a large number representing various sects—found nothing in the film either irreverent or irreligious.

However, as Judge FROESSEL reminds us, the contrary opinion also found strong voice, eventually reaching the ears of the board of regents. After viewing the film, that body revoked and rescinded the license—some two years after it had been initially granted—invoking as authority therefor section 122 of the Education Law. That statute provides that the motion picture division shall license each moving picture submitted to it unless it is "obscene, indecent, immoral, inhuman, sacrilegious, or is of such a character that its exhibition would tend to corrupt morals or incite to crime." The board of regents decided that the film is "sacrilegious," and its decision was confirmed by the Appellate Division.

Laying to one side for the moment the question as to the constitutionality of a statute which sanctions the banning of a moving picture on the ground that it is "sacrilegious," I am of opinion that the regents' action was without legislative warrant.

The controlling statute, the Education Law, is significant both for what it says and for what it leaves unsaid. In section 124, entitled "Review by regents," the legislature expressly gave the regents power to review a determination of the motion picture division *denying* a license—but it conferred on similar power to review the division's *granting* of a license. By settled rules of construction, that deliberate omission by the legislature clearly indicates that no such authority was intended. See e.g., 2 Sutherland, Statutory Construction (3d ed., 1943), §§ 4915–4917. And the more one searches the statute, the more clearly does that appear. For example, the statute expressly authorizes the

regents to revoke a permit issued for the exhibition of a scientific or educational film, § 125, and to revoke a motion picture license if it was obtained on a false application or if the licensee tampered with the film or if there is a "conviction for a crime committed by the [film's] exhibition or unlawful possession" § 128. But nowhere in the statute is there to be found any general grant of power to the regents to revoke a previously issued license. This omission is also to be contrasted with the further and explicit grant of such a power of revocation by the same Education Law as regards many other types of licenses issued by the Education Department. See, e.g., § 6514 (as to doctors); § 6613 (as to dentists); § 6712 (as to veterinarians); § 6804 (as to pharmacists); 7108 (as to optometrists); § 7210 (as to engineers); § 7308 (as to architects); § 7406 (as to certified public accountants); § 7503 (as to shorthand reporters). Clearly, the legislature knew how to bestow the power of revocation when that was its purpose.

Even more recent evidence of the legislature's design is at hand. In 1950, the legislature amended the Penal Law to prohibit prosecution, on the ground of obscenity, of a film licensed under the Education Law, L. 1950, ch. 624, amending Penal Law, § 1141. That enactment was inspired by *Hughes Tool Co.* v. *Fielding*, 297 N.Y. 1024, 80 N.E. 2d 540, affirming 272 App. Div. 1048, 75 N.Y.S. 2d 287, affirming 188 Misc. 947, 73 N.Y.S. 2d 98. It had there been held that such a criminal prosecution was permissible *because* the Education Law neither provided for nor allowed any direct review, by the regents or the courts, of a decision of the motion picture division issuing a license. If the legislature had disagreed with that interpretation of the Education Law—clearly indicated at Special Term, 188 Misc. at page 952, 73 N.Y.S. 2d at page 103—it would undoubtedly have amended the Education Law, not the Penal Law. By depriving the state of the power to prosecute the exhibition of a moving picture once it receives a license, the legislature affirmed, as clearly as it could, that the granting of a license is an act of such implacable finality that it may not be challenged collaterally in a criminal prosecution any more than directly in a civil proceeding.

The legislative scheme so clearly expressed, the board of regents may neither rely upon its status as head of the Education Department to reverse decisions of a subordinate which are not the result of illegality, fraud or vital irregularity, see, e.g., *Butterworth* v. *U.S.* ex rel. *Hoe*, 112 U.S. 50, 56, 64, 5 S. Ct. 25, 28 L. Ed. 656; cf. *People* ex rel. *Finnegan* v. *McBride*, 226 N.Y. 252, 257, 123 N.E. 374, 375; *People* ex rel. *Chase* v. *Wemple*, 144 N.Y. 478, 482, 39 N.E. 397, 398; *D & D Realty Corp.* v. *Coster*, 277 App. Div. 668, 102 N.Y.S. 2d 321[2] nor draw from section 132 of the Education Law—which in over-all manner gives the board "authority to enforce the provisions and purposes of part two of this article"—an assumption of authority to "review" and "revoke" the grant of a license by the motion picture division. All that section 132 was designed to do,

---

[2] There is no substance to the regents' claim that they were merely correcting the "illegal" action of the motion picture division in licensing a "sacrilegious" picture. Since obviously there was at least reasonable doubt as to whether the film was "sacrilegious," the decision of the motion picture division could not be condemned as "illegal."

and all that it does, is to authorize enforcement. To construe its general language as authorizing review of the granting of a license is to stretch language beyond all permissible limits and to render superfluous and meaningless the very explicit language of section 124 permitting such review only where a license has been denied.

"A statute must be read and given effect as it is written by the Legislature, not as the court may think it should or would have been written if the Legislature had envisaged all the problems and complications which might arise in the course of its administration. A power not expressly granted by statute is implied only where it is 'so essential to the exercise of some power expressly conferred as plainly to appear to have been within the intention of the Legislature. The implied power must be necessary, not merely convenient, and the intention of the Legislature must be free from doubt.' *People* ex rel. *City of Olean* v. *Western New York & Pennsylvania Traction Co.*, 214 N.Y. 526, 529, 108 N.E. 847, 848." *Lawrence Constr. Corp.* v. *State of New York*, 293 N.Y. 634, 639, 59 N.E. 2d 630, 632.

So, here, the regents' contention that they *must* have power to review and revoke in order to guard against error by the motion picture division in granting licenses, is not persuasive. The fact is that, in the twenty-five years during which the motion picture division has been in the Department of Education, the regents have never before reviewed the grant of a license or even suggested the existence of such a power. Limited as we are to a determination of what the legislature has done, the argument of alleged necessity has no weight in the face of this long-continued practical construction. For this court now to read into the statute a provision which that body chose not to write into it would constitute an uncalled-for intrusion into the sphere of the legislature. "Freedom to construe is not freedom to amend." *Sexauer & Lemke* v. *Luke A. Burke & Sons Co.*, 228 N.Y. 341, 345, 127 N.E. 329, 331; see, also, *O'Brien* v. *Tremaine*, 285 N.Y. 233, 238, 33 N.E. 2d 536, 537.

Even if I were to assume, however, that the statute does confer a power to review and revoke, I would still conclude for reversal. In my view, that portion of the statute here involved must fall before the constitutional guarantee that there be freedom of speech and press. The consistent course of decision by the Supreme Court of the United States in recent years persuades me that the early decision of *Mutual Film Corp.* v. *Industrial Commission of Ohio*, 236 U.S. 230, 35 S. Ct. 387, 59 L. Ed. 552—urged as establishing that motion pictures are beyond the First Amendment's coverage—no longer has the force or authority claimed for it.

We are confronted in this case with censorship in its baldest form—a licensing system requiring permission in advance for the exercise of the right to disseminate ideas *via* motion pictures, and committing to the licensor a broad discretion to decide whether that right may be exercised. Insofar as the statute permits the state to censor a moving picture labelled "sacrilegious," it offends against the First and Fourteenth Amendments of the Federal Constitution, since it imposes a prior restraint—and, at that, a prior restraint of broad and undefined limits—on freedom of discussion of religious matters. And beyond that, it may well be that it constitutes an attempt to legislate orthodoxy in matters of religious belief, contrary to the constitutional prohibition against laws "respecting

an establishment of religion." Cf. *Everson* v. *Board of Education of Ewing Tp.*, 330 U.S. 1, 15, 67 S. Ct. 504, 511, 91 L. Ed. 711; *Illinois* ex rel. *McCollum* v. *Board of Education of School Dist. No. 71, Champaign County, Illinois*, 333 U.S. 203, 210, 68 S. Ct. 461, 92 L. Ed. 648.

The freedoms of the First Amendment are not, I appreciate, absolutes, but insofar as they are qualified, the qualification springs from the necessity of accommodating them to some equally pressing public need. Thus, some limited measure of restraint upon freedom of expression may be justified where the forum is the public street or the public square, where the audience may be a "captive" one, and where breaches of the peace may be imminent as the result of the use, or rather the abuse, of fighting words. Cf. *Dennis* v. *United States*, 341 U.S. 494, 503 et seq., 71 S. Ct. 857, 95 L. Ed. 1137; *Feiner* v. *New York*, 340 U.S. 315, 319, 71 S. Ct. 303, 328, 95 L. Ed. 267, 295; *Niemotko* v. *Maryland*, 340 U.S. 268, 71 S. Ct. 325, 328, 95 L. Ed. 267, 280; *Terminiello* v. *City of Chicago*, 337 U.S. 1, 69 S. Ct. 894, 93 L. Ed. 1131; *Chaplinsky* v. *State of New Hampshire*, 315 U.S. 568, 571–572, 62 S. Ct. 766, 86 L. Ed. 1031; *Cantwell* v. *State of Connecticut*, 310 U.S. 296, 308, 60 S. Ct. 900, 84 L. Ed. 1213; *Schneider* v. *State of New Jersey, Town of Irvington*, 308 U.S. 147, 160, 60 S. Ct. 140, 84 L. Ed. 155. Here, there is no "captive" audience; only those see the picture who wish to do so, and, then, only if they are willing to pay the price of admission to the theatre. Moreover, if subject matter furnishes any criterion for the exercise of a restraint, I know of no subject less proper for censorship by the state than the one here involved.

The Supreme Court has "consistently condemned licensing systems which vest in an administrative official discretion to grant or withhold a permit upon broad criteria unrelated to proper regulation of public places." *Kunz* v. *New York*, 340 U.S. 290, 294, 71 S. Ct. 312, 315, 328, 95 L. Ed. 267, 280; see, also, *Niemotko* v. *Maryland*, supra, 340 U.S. 268, 71 S. Ct. 325, 328, 95 L. Ed. 267, 280; *Saia* v. *People of State of New York*, 334 U.S. 558, 68 S. Ct. 1148, 92 L. Ed. 1574; *Cantwell* v. *State of Connecticut*, supra, 310 U.S. 296, 60 S. Ct. 900; *Hague* v. *Committee for Industrial Organization*, 307 U.S. 496, 59 S. Ct. 954, 83 L. Ed. 1423; *Lovell* v. *City of Griffin*, 303 U.S. 444, 58 S. Ct. 666, 82 L. Ed. 949. "The State cannot of course forbid public proselyting or religious argument merely because public officials disapprove the speaker's views. It must act in patent good faith to maintain the public peace, to assure the availability of the streets for their primary purposes of passenger and vehicular traffic, or for equally indispensable ends of modern community life." See *Niemotko* v. *Maryland*, supra, 340 U.S. 268, 282, 71 S. Ct. 325, 328, 333, per Frankfurter, J., concurring.

Invasion of the right of free expression must, in short, find justification in some overriding public interest, and the restricting statute must be narrowly drawn to meet an evil which the state has a substantial interest in correcting. See *Feiner* v. *New York*, supra, 340 U.S. 315, 319, 71 S. Ct. 303, 328; *Niemotko* v. *Maryland*, supra, 340 U.S. 268, 71 S. Ct. 325, 328; *Winters* v. *New York*, 333 U.S. 507, 509, 68 S. Ct. 665, 92 L. Ed. 840; *Cantwell* v. *State of Connecticut*, supra, 310 U.S. 296, 307–308, 60 S. Ct. 900; *Thornhill* v. *State of Alabama*, 310 U.S. 88, 97–98, 105, 60 S. Ct. 736, 84 L. Ed. 1093. The statute before us is not one narrowly drawn to meet such a need as that of preserving the public peace or regulating public places. On the contrary, it imposes a general and pervasive restraint on freedom of discussion of religious themes in moving pictures, which cannot be justified on the basis of any substantial interest of the state. Cf. *Kunz* v. *New York*, supra, 340 U.S. 290, 71 S. Ct. 312, 328; *Dennis* v. *United States*, supra, 341 U.S. 494, 508–509, 71 S. Ct. 857.

Over a century ago, the Supreme Court declared that "The law knows no heresy, and is committed to the support of no dogma." *Watson* v. *Jones*, 13 Wall. 679, 728, 80 U.S. 679, 728, 20 L. Ed. 666. Just as clearly, it is beyond the competency of government to prescribe norms of religious conduct and belief. That follows inevitably from adherence to the principles of the First Amendment. "In the realm of religious faith, and in that of political belief," it has been said, *Cantwell* v. *Connecticut*, supra, 310 U.S. 296, 310, 60 S. Ct. 900, 906, "sharp differences arise. In both fields the tenets of one man may seem the rankest error to his neighbor. To persuade others to his own point of view, the pleader, as we know, at times, resorts to exaggeration, to vilification of men who have been or are, prominent in church or state, and even to false statement. But the people of this nation have ordained in the light of history, that, in spite of the probability of excesses and abuses, these liberties are, in the long view, essential to enlightened opinion and right conduct on the part of the citizens of a democracy."

The inherent indefinability, in its present context, of the term "sacrilege" is apparent upon the merest inquiry. At what point, it may be asked, does a search for the eternal verities, a questioning of particular religious dogma, take on the aspect of "sacrilege"? At what point does expression or portrayal of a doubt of some religious tenet become "sacrilegious"? Not even authorities or students in the field of religion will have a definitive answer, and certainly not the same answer. There are more than two hundred and fifty different religious sects in this country, with varying religious beliefs, dogmas and principles. See *Illinois* ex rel. *McCollum* v. *Board of Education of School Dist. No. 71*, supra, 333 U.S. 203, 227, 68 S. Ct. 461. With this great contrariety of religious views, it has been aptly observed that one man's heresy is another's orthodoxy, one's "sacrilege," another's consecrated belief. How and where draw the line between permissible theological disputation and "sacrilege"? What is orthodox, what sacrilegious? Whose orthodoxy, to whom sacrilegious? In the very nature of things, what is "sacrilegious" will of necessity differ with the philosophy, the training, the education and the background of the particular censor of the moment; the determination whether a film is "sacrilegious" or not, must necessarily rest in the undiscoverable recesses of the official's mind.

Any possible doubt that the term is essentially vague is dispelled by a reference to the variant and inconsistent definitions ascribed to it by the board of regents and by the Appellate Division and Judge FROESSEL.

Thus, the regents, frowning upon the dictionary definition as "technical,"[3] nevertheless assure us that "everyone knows what is meant by this term" and, by way of demonstrating that fact, proceed to define the word as describing a film which "affronts a *large segment* of the population"; offends the sensibilities by ridiculing and burlesquing anything "held sacred by the *adherents of a particular religious faith*"; is "offensive to the religious sensibilities of *any element* of society." (Italics supplied.) Indeed, any semblance of either general meaning or specific content is, I suggest, abandoned by the regents themselves when they assert that, since "anything is only sacrilegious to those persons who hold the concept sacred," the opinions of nonbelievers are "worthless." By such reasoning, the adherents of a particular dogma become the only judges as to whether that dogma has been offended! And, if that is so, it is impossible to fathom how any governmental agency such as the board of regents, composed as it is of laymen of different faiths, could possibly discharge the function of determining whether a particular film is "sacrilegious."

Judge FROESSEL and the Appellate Division state that the statutory proscription against the "sacrilegious" is intended to bar any "visual caricature of religious beliefs held sacred by *one sect or another*." Opinion of FROESSEL, J., 303 N.Y. 258, 101 N.E. 2d 672, italics supplied. Though Judge FROESSEL also defines "sacrilegious" in terms of "attacking" or "insulting" religious beliefs or treating them with "contempt, mockery, scorn and ridicule"—all words of ephemeral and indefinite content—the basic criterion appears to be whether the film treats a religious theme in such a manner as to offend the religious beliefs of any group of persons. If the film does have that effect, and it is "offered as a form of entertainment," it apparently falls within the statutory ban regardless of the sincerity and good faith of the producer of the film, no matter how temperate the treatment of the theme, and no matter how unlikely a public disturbance or breach of the peace.

The drastic nature of such a ban is highlighted by the fact that the film in question makes no direct attack on, or criticism of, any religious dogma or principle, and it is not claimed to be obscene, scurrilous, intemperate or abusive. Nor is there any evidence of any malicious purpose or intention on the part of the producers of the film to revile or even attack Catholic doctrine or dogma, and no suggestion of any reasonable likelihood of a breach of the peace resulting from the film's exhibition.[4] So broad, indeed, is the suggested criterion of "sacrilege" that it might be applied to any fair and temperate treatment of a psychological, ethical, moral or social theme with religious overtones which some group or other might find offensive to its "religious beliefs."

It is claimed that "the courts have had no problem either with the word 'sacrilegious' or with its synonym, 'profane.'" Opinion of FROESSEL, J., supra, 303 N.Y. 255, 101 N.E. 2d 670. The cases to which reference is made, however, involved neither the "profane" in religion nor the "sacrilegious," and the simple fact is that the Supreme

---

[3] A typical definition of "sacrilege" is that found in Webster's New International Dictionary (2d ed., 1948): "the crime of stealing, misusing, violating or desecrating that which is sacred, or holy, or dedicated to sacred uses." (See, also, the New Catholic Dictionary [Vatican ed., 1929].)

[4] One writer, associated with the University of Notre Dame, noted (Clancy, *op. cit.*, The Commonweal, March 16, 1951, p. 567) that, while some critics have questioned its dramatic validity and others, the director's taste in his choice of theme, "No serious or responsible critic * * * has questioned the sincerity or honesty" of the director's "intention in making the film, an intention abundantly moral * * *."

Court has never had occasion to pass upon either the one term or the other. The context in which the word "profane" appears in the cases cited, *Winters* v. *New York*, supra, 333 U.S. 507, 510, 68 S. Ct. 665; *Chaplinsky* v. *New Hampshire*, supra, 315 U.S. 568, 572, 62 S. Ct. 766, as well as the authorities there relied upon, *Cantwell* v. *State of Connecticut*, supra, 310 U.S. 296, 309–310, 60 S. Ct. 900; Chafee, Free Speech in the United States [1941], pp. 149–150, make it evident that the term was used, not as a synonym for "sacrilegious," but as a substitute for "epithets or personal abuse," for swear words and for the other "insulting or 'fighting' words," which "by their very utterance inflict injury or tend to incite an immediate breach of the peace" and "are no essential part of any exposition of ideas." *Chaplinsky* v. *New Hampshire*, supra, 315 U.S. 568, 572, 62 S. Ct. 766, 769; see, also, *Cantwell* v. *State of Connecticut*, supra, 310 U.S. 296, 310, 60 S. Ct. 900; Chafee, op. cit., p. 150. In short, the cases cited have nothing whatsoever to do with the "profane" in religion, and the judges who sat in them were not called upon to give the slightest thought or consideration to the subject with which we are now concerned.

The shortcomings of ambiguous epithets as rigid boundaries for free expression are great enough in temporal and political matters, cf., e.g., *Winters* v. *New York*, supra, 333 U.S. 507, 68 S. Ct. 665; *Dennis* v. *United States*, supra, 341 U.S. 494, 71 S. Ct. 857; *Jordan* v. *De George*, 341 U.S. 223, 71 S. Ct. 703, 95 L. Ed. 886; *Musser* v. *State of Utah*, 333 U.S. 95, 68 S. Ct. 397, 92 L. Ed. 562, but they are all the greater when the epithets trench upon areas of religious belief. See, e.g., *Kunz* v. *New York*, supra, 340 U.S. 290, 71 S. Ct. 312, 328; *Saia* v. *People of State of New York*, supra, 334 U.S. 558, 561, 68 S. Ct. 1148; *Cantwell* v. *State of Connecticut*, supra, 310 U.S. 296, 60 S. Ct. 900. Indeed the Supreme Court has gone so far as to hold that the First Amendment's guarantee forbids prior restraint of public discussion that even "ridicules" or "denounces" any form of religious belief. See *Kunz* v. *New York*, supra, 340 U.S. 290, 71 S. Ct. 312, 328, and see, particularly, concurring opinion of Frankfurter, J., reported in 340 U.S. at pages 285–286, 71 S. Ct. 328, 333, 334. In a free society "all sects and factions, as the price of their own freedom to preach their views, must suffer that freedom in others." *Kunz* v. *New York*, supra, 340 U.S. at page 301, 71 S. Ct. at page 318, per Jackson, J., dissenting; see, also, *Murdock* v. *Commonwealth of Pennsylvania*, 319 U.S. 105, 116, 63 S. Ct. 870, 87 L. Ed. 1292.

Were we dealing with speeches, with handbills, with newspapers or with books, there could be no doubt as to the unconstitutionality of that portion of the statute here under consideration. The constitutional guarantee of freedom of expression, however, is neither limited to the oral word uttered in the street or the public hall nor restricted to the written phrase printed in newspaper or book. It protects the transmission of ideas and beliefs, whether popular or not, whether orthodox or not. A belief does not lose its character as a belief, an idea does not become less of an idea, because, instead of being expressed by the airborne voice, the printed word or the "still" picture, it is put forward by a "moving" picture. The First Amendment does not ask whether the medium is visual, acoustic, electronic or some yet unheard-of device. It has readily accommodated itself to other products of inventive genius,

to other advances in technology, such as the radio and television. If "The Constitution deals with substance, not shadows," if "Its inhibition was levelled at the thing, not the name," *Cummings* v. *State of Missouri*, 4 Wall. 277, 325, 71 U.S. 277, 325, then, surely, its meaning and vitality are not to be conditioned upon the mechanism involved. Of course, it may well be that differences in media will give rise to different problems of accommodation of conflicting interests. See *Kovacs* v. *Cooper*, 336 U.S. 77, 96, 69 S. Ct. 448, 93 L. Ed. 513, per Frankfurter, J., concurring. But any such accommodation must necessarily be made in the light of fundamental constitutional safeguards.[5]

One reason for denying free expression to motion pictures, we are told, is that the movies are commercial. But newspapers, magazines and books are likewise commercially motivated, and that has never been an obstacle to their full protection under the First Amendment. See, e.g., *Grosjean* v. *American Press Co.*, 297 U.S. 233, 56 S. Ct. 444, 80 L. Ed. 660. Again, it is said, the fact that the moving picture conveys its thought or message in dramatic episodes or by means of a story or in a form that is entertaining, makes the difference. But neither novels, magazines nor comic books are made censorable because they are designed for entertainment or amusement. See, e.g., *Winters* v. *New York*, supra, 333 U.S. 507, 510, 68 S. Ct. 665; *Hannegan* v. *Esquire, Inc.*, 327 U.S. 146, 153, 66 S. Ct. 456, 90 L. Ed. 586. The Supreme Court made that plain in the Winters case, when it declared: "We do not accede to appellee's suggestion that the constitutional protection for a free press applies only to the exposition of ideas. The line between the informing and the entertaining is too elusive for the protection of that basic right. Everyone is familiar with instances of propaganda through fiction. What is one man's amusement, teaches another's doctrine. Though we can see nothing of any possible value to society in these magazines, they are as much entitled to the protection of free speech as the best of literature." 333 U.S. at page 510, 68 S. Ct. at page 667.

Whatever may have been true thirty-six years ago when the Mutual Film case, 236 U.S. 230, 35 S. Ct. 387, was decided, there is no reason today for casting the motion picture beyond the barriers of protected expression. Learned and thoughtful writers so opine, see Chafee, Free Speech in the United States [1941], pp. 544 et seq.; Ernst, The First Freedom, p. 268; Kupferman and O'Brien, Motion Picture Censorship, 36 Cornell L.Q. 273; Note, 60 Yale L.J. 696; Note, 49 Yale L.J. 87, and the Supreme Court itself has recently so declared. See *United States* v. *Paramount Pictures, Inc.*, 34 U.S. 131, 166, 68 S. Ct. 915, 92 L. Ed. 1260; see, also, *Kovacs* v. *Cooper*, supra, 336 U.S. 77, 102, 69 S. Ct. 448, per Black, J., dissenting. As Chafee put it (op. cit., p. 545), "In an age when 'commerce' in the Constitution has been construed to include airplanes and electromagnetic waves, 'freedom of speech' in the First Amendment and 'liberty' in the

---

[5] Whether, for instance, the statute, Education Law, § 122, may be sustained as valid even as a censorship measure insofar as its criterion is the narrow one of "obscenity," is not, before us and need not be considered. Cf. *Chaplinsky* v. *New Hampshire*, supra, 315 U.S. 568, 572, 62 S. Ct. 766; *Near* v. *State of Minnesota* ex rel. *Olson*, 283 U.S. 697, 51 S. Ct. 625, 75 L. Ed. 1357; Ex Parte Jackson, 96 U.S. 727, 736, 24 L. Ed. 877.

Fourteenth should be similarly applied to new media for the communication of ideas and facts. Freedom of speech should not be limited to the air-borne voice, the pen, and the printing press, any more than interstate commerce is limited to stagecoaches and sailing vessels." And, wrote the Supreme Court, *United States* v. *Paramount Pictures, Inc.*, supra, 334 U.S. 131, 166, 68 S. Ct. 915, 933, "We have no doubt that moving pictures, like newspapers and radio, are included in the press whose freedom is guaranteed by the First Amendment."

Every consideration points that conclusion. The Mutual Film case, should be relegated to its place upon the history shelf. Rendered in a day before the guarantees of the Bill of Rights were held to apply to the states, and when moving pictures were in their infancy, the decision was obviously a product of the view that motion pictures did not express or convey opinions or ideas. Today, so far have times and the films changed, some would deny protection for the opposite reason, that films are too effective in their presentation of ideas and points of view. The latter notion is as unsupportable as the other and antiquated view; that the moving picture is a most effective mass medium for spreading ideas is, of course, no reason for refusing it protection. If only ineffectual expression is shielded by the Constitution, free speech becomes a fanciful myth. Few would dispute the anomaly of a doctrine that protects as freedom of expression comic books that purvey stories and

pictures of "bloodshed and lust," see *Winters* v. *New York*, supra, 333 U.S. 507, 510, 68 S. Ct. 665, light and racy magazine reading, see *Hannegan* v. *Esquire, Inc.*, supra, 327 U.S. 146, 153, 66 S. Ct. 456 and loudspeaker harangues, see *Saia* v. *People of State of New York*, supra, 334 U.S. 558, 68 S. Ct. 1148, and yet denies that same protection to the moving picture.

Sincere people of unquestioned good faith may, as in this case, find a moving picture offensive to their religious sensibilities, but that cannot justify a statute which empowers licensing officials to censor the free expression of ideas or beliefs in the field of religion. "If there is any fixed star in our constitutional constellation," the Supreme Court has said, *West Virginia State Board of Education* v. *Barnette*, 319 U.S. 624, 642, 63 S. Ct. 1178, 1187, 87 L. Ed. 1628, "it is that no official, high or petty, can prescribe what shall be orthodox in politics, nationalism, religion, or other matters of opinion."

The order of the Appellate Division should be reversed and the determination of the board of regents annulled.

LOUGHRAN, C.J., and LEWIS and CONWAY, JJ., concur with FROESSEL, J.

DESMOND, J., concurs in separate opinion.
FULD, J., dissents in opinion in which DYE, J., concurs.

Order affirmed.

■ Joseph Burstyn, Inc.

v.

Wilson, Commissioner of Education of New York, et al.

APPEAL FROM THE COURT OF APPEALS OF NEW YORK.

No. 522. Argued April 24, 1952.—Decided May 26, 1952.

Ephraim S. London argued the cause and filed a brief for appellant.

Charles A. Brind, Jr. and *Wendell P. Brown*, Solicitor General of New York, argued the cause for appellees. With them on the brief were *Nathaniel L. Goldstein*, Attorney General of New York, and *Ruth Kessler Toch*, Assistant Attorney General.

Morris L. Ernst, Osmond K. Fraenkel, Arthur Garfield Hays, Herbert Monte Levy, Emanuel Redfield, Shad Polier, Will Maslow, Leo Pfeffer, Herman Seid and *Eberhard P. Deutsch* filed a brief for the American Civil Liberties Union et al., as *amici curiae*, urging reversal.

Charles J. Tobin, Edmond B. Butler and *Porter R. Chandler* filed a brief for the New York State Catholic Welfare Committee, as *amicus curiae*, urging affirmance.

MR. JUSTICE CLARK delivered the opinion of the Court.

The issue here is the constitutionality, under the First and Fourteenth Amendments, of a New York statute

which permits the banning of motion picture films on the ground that they are "sacrilegious." That statute makes it unlawful "to exhibit, or to sell, lease or lend for exhibition at any place of amusement for pay or in connection with any business in the state of New York, any motion picture film or reel [with specified exceptions not relevant here], unless there is at the time in full force and effect a valid license or permit therefor of the education department. . . ."[1] The statute further provides:

"The director of the [motion picture] division [of the education department] or, when authorized by the regents, the officers of a local office or bureau shall cause to be promptly examined every motion picture film submitted to them as herein required, and unless such film or a part thereof is obscene, indecent, immoral, inhuman, sacrilegious, or is of such a character that its exhibition would tend to corrupt morals or incite to crime, shall issue a

---

[1] McKinney's N.Y. Laws, 1947, Education Law, § 129.

license therefor. If such director or, when so authorized, such officer shall not license any film submitted, he shall furnish to the applicant therefor a written report of the reasons for his refusal and a description of each rejected part of a film rejected in toto."[2]

Appellant is a corporation engaged in the business of distributing motion pictures. It owns the exclusive rights to distribute throughout the United States a film produced in Italy entitled "The Miracle." On November 30, 1950, after having examined the picture, the motion picture division of the New York education department, acting under the statute quoted above, issued to appellant a license authorizing exhibition of "The Miracle," with English subtitles, as one part of a trilogy called "Ways of Love."[3] Thereafter, for a period of approximately eight weeks, "Ways of Love" was exhibited publicly in a motion picture theater in New York City under an agreement between appellant and the owner of the theater whereby appellant received a stated percentage of the admission price.

During this period, the New York State Board of Regents, which by statute is made the head of the education department,[4] received "hundreds of letters, telegrams, post cards, affidavits and other communications" both protesting against and defending the public exhibition of "The Miracle."[5] The Chancellor of the Board of Regents requested three members of the Board to view the picture and to make a report to the entire Board. After viewing the film, this committee reported to the Board that in its opinion there was basis for the claim that the picture was "sacrilegious." Thereafter, on January 19, 1951, the Regents directed appellant to show cause, at a hearing to be held on January 30, why its license to show "The Miracle" should not be rescinded on that ground. Appellant appeared at this hearing, which was conducted by the same three-member committee of the Regents which had previously viewed the picture, and challenged the jurisdiction of the committee and of the Regents to proceed with the case. With the consent of the committee, various interested persons and organizations submitted to it briefs and exhibits bearing upon the merits of the picture and upon the constitutional and statutory questions involved. On February 16, 1951, the Regents, after viewing "The Miracle," determined that it was "sacrilegious" and for that reason ordered the Commissioner of Education to rescind appellant's license to exhibit the picture. The Commissioner did so.

Appellant brought the present action in the New York courts to review the determination of the Regents.[6] Among the claims advanced by appellant were (1) that the statute violates the Fourteenth Amendment as a prior restraint upon freedom of speech and of the press; (2)

that it is invalid under the same Amendment as a violation of the guaranty of separate church and state and as a prohibition of the free exercise of religion; and, (3) that the term "sacrilegious" is so vague and indefinite as to offend due process. The Appellate Division rejected all of appellant's contentions and upheld the Regents' determination. 278 App. Div. 253, 104 N.Y.S. 2d 740. On appeal the New York Court of Appeals, two judges dissenting, affirmed the order of the Appellate Division. 303 N.Y. 242, 101 N.E. 2d 665. The case is here on appeal. 28 U.S.C. § 1257 (2).

As we view the case, we need consider only appellant's contention that the New York statute is an unconstitutional abridgment of free speech and a free press. In *Mutual Film Corp.* v. *Industrial Comm'n*, 236 U.S. 230 (1915), a distributor of motion pictures sought to enjoin the enforcement of an Ohio statute which required the prior approval of a board of censors before any motion picture could be publicly exhibited in the state, and which directed the board to approve only such films as it adjudged to be "of a moral, educational or amusing and harmless character." The statute was assailed in part as an unconstitutional abridgment of the freedom of the press guaranteed by the First and Fourteenth Amendments. The District Court rejected this contention, stating that the first eight Amendments were not a restriction on state action. 215 F. 138, 141 (D.C.N.D. Ohio 1914). On appeal to this Court, plaintiff in its brief abandoned this claim and contended merely that the statute in question violated the freedom of speech and publication guaranteed by the Constitution of Ohio. In affirming the decree of the District Court denying injunctive relief, this Court stated:

It cannot be put out of view that the exhibition of moving pictures is a business pure and simple, originated and conducted for profit, like other spectacles, not to be regarded, nor intended to be regarded by the Ohio constitution, we think, as part of the press of the country or as organs of public opinion."[7]

In a series of decisions beginning with *Gitlow* v. *New York*, 268 U.S. 652 (1925), this Court held that the liberty of speech and of the press which the First Amendment guarantees against abridgment by the federal government is within the liberty safeguarded by the Due Process Clause of the Fourteenth Amendment from invasion by state action.[8] That principle has been followed and reaffirmed to the present day. Since this series of decisions came after the *Mutual* decision, the present case is the first to present squarely to us the question whether motion pictures are within the ambit of protection which the First Amendment, through the Fourteenth, secures to any form of "speech" or "the press."[9]

It cannot be doubted that motion pictures are a significant medium for the communication of ideas. They may affect public attitudes and behavior in a variety of ways,

---

[2] *Id.*, § 122.

[3] The motion picture division had previously issued a license for exhibition of "The Miracle" without English subtitles, but the film was never shown under that license.

[4] McKinney's N.Y. Laws, 1947, Education Law, § 101; see also N.Y. Const., Art. V, § 4.

[5] Stipulation between appellant and appellee, R. 86.

[6] The action was brought under Article 78 of the New York Civil Practice Act, Gilbert-Bliss N.Y. Civ. Prac., Vol. 6B, 1944, 1949 Supp., § 1283 *et seq.* See also McKinney's N.Y. Laws, 1947, Education Law, § 124.

[7] 236 U.S., at 244.

[8] *Gitlow* v. *New York*, 268 U.S. 652, 666 (1925); *Stromberg* v. *California*, 283 U.S. 359, 368 (1931); *Near* v. *Minnesota ex rel. Olson*, 283 U.S. 697, 707 (1931); *Grosjean* v. *American Press Co.*, 297 U.S. 233, 244 (1936); *De Jonge* v. *Oregon*, 299 U.S. 353, 364 (1937); *Lovell* v. *Griffin*, 303 U.S. 444, 450 (1938); *Schneider* v. *State*, 308 U.S. 147, 160 (1939).

[9] See *Lovell* v. *Griffin*, 303 U.S. 444, 452 (1938).

ranging from direct espousal of a political or social doctrine to the subtle shaping of thought which characterizes all artistic expression.[10] The importance of motion pictures as an organ of public opinion is not lessened by the fact that they are designed to entertain as well as to inform. As was said in *Winters v. New York*, 333 U.S. 507, 510 (1948):

"The line between the informing and the entertaining is too elusive for the protection of that basic right [a free press]. Everyone is familiar with instances of propaganda through fiction. What is one man's amusement, teaches another's doctrine."

It is urged that motion pictures do not fall within the First Amendment's aegis because their production, distribution, and exhibition is a large-scale business conducted for private profit. We cannot agree. That books, newspapers, and magazines are published and sold for profit does not prevent them from being a form of expression whose liberty is safeguarded by the First Amendment.[11] We fail to see why operation for profit should have any different effect in the case of motion pictures.

It is further urged that motion pictures possess a greater capacity for evil, particularly among the youth of a community, than other modes of expression. Even if one were to accept this hypothesis, it does not follow that motion pictures should be disqualified from First Amendment protection. If there be capacity for evil it may be relevant in determining the permissible scope of community control, but it does not authorize substantially unbridled censorship such as we have here.

For the foregoing reasons, we conclude that expression by means of motion pictures is included within the free speech and free press guaranty of the First and Fourteenth Amendments. To the extent that language in the opinion in *Mutual Film Corp.* v. *Industrial Comm'n, supra*, is out of harmony with the views here set forth, we no longer adhere to it.[12]

To hold that liberty of expression by means of motion pictures is guaranteed by the First and Fourteenth Amendments, however, is not the end of our problem. It does not follow that the Constitution requires absolute freedom to exhibit every motion picture of every kind at all times and all places. That much is evident from the series of decisions of this Court with respect to other media of communication of ideas.[13] Nor does it follow that motion pictures are necessarily subject to the precise rules governing any other particular method of expression. Each method tends to present its own peculiar problems. But the basic principles of freedom of speech and the press, like the First Amendment's command, do not vary. Those principles, as they have frequently been enunciated by this Court, make freedom of expression the rule. There is no justification in this case for making an exception to that rule.

The statute involved here does not seek to punish, as a past offense, speech or writing falling within the permissible scope of subsequent punishment. On the contrary, New York requires that permission to communicate ideas be obtained in advance from state officials who judge the content of the words and pictures sought to be communicated. This Court recognized many years ago that such a previous restraint is a form of infringement upon freedom of expression to be especially condemned. *Near v. Minnesota* ex rel. *Olson*, 283 U.S. 697 (1931). The Court there recounted the history which indicates that a major purpose of the First Amendment guaranty of a free press was to prevent prior restraints upon publication, although it was carefully pointed out that the liberty of the press is not limited to that protection.[14] It was further stated that "the protection even as to previous restraint is not absolutely unlimited. But the limitation has been recognized only in exceptional cases." *Id.*, at 716. In the light of the First Amendment's history and of the *Near* decision, the State has a heavy burden to demonstrate that the limitation challenged here presents such an exceptional case.

New York's highest court says there is "nothing mysterious" about the statutory provision applied in this case: "It is simply this: that no religion, as that word is understood by the ordinary, reasonable person, shall be treated with contempt, mockery, scorn and ridicule. . . ."[15] This is far from the kind of narrow exception to freedom of expression which a state may carve out to satisfy the adverse demands of other interests of society.[16] In seeking

---

[10] See Inglis, Freedom of the Movies (1947), 20–24; Klapper, The Effects of Mass Media (1950), *passim*; Note, Motion Pictures and the First Amendment, 60 Yale L.J. 696, 704–708 (1951), and sources cited therein.

[11] See *Grosjean* v. *American Press Co.*, 297 U.S. 233 (1936); *Thomas* v. *Collins*, 323 U.S. 516, 531 (1945).

[12] See *United States* v. *Paramount Pictures, Inc.*, 334 U.S. 131, 166 (1948): "We have no doubt that moving pictures, like newspapers and radio, are included in the press whose freedom is guaranteed by the First Amendment." It is not without significance that talking pictures were first produced in 1926, eleven years after the *Mutual* decision. Hampton, A History of the Movies (1931), 382–383.

[13] *E.g., Feiner* v. *New York*, 340 U.S. 315 (1951); *Kovacs* v. *Cooper*, 336 U.S. 77 (1949); *Chaplinsky* v. *New Hampshire*, 315 U.S. 568 (1942); *Cox* v. *New Hampshire*, 312 U.S. 569 (1941).

[14] *Near* v. *Minnesota* ex rel. *Olson*, 283 U.S. 697, 713–719 (1931); see also *Lovell* v. *Griffin*, 303 U.S. 444, 451–452 (1938); *Grosjean* v. *American Press Co.*, 297 U.S. 233, 245–250 (1936); *Patterson* v. *Colorado*, 205 U.S. 454, 462 (1907).

[15] 303 N.Y. 242, 258, 101 N.E. 2d 665, 672. At another point the Court of Appeals gave "sacrilegious" the following definition: "the act of violating or profaning anything sacred." *Id.*, at 255, 101 N.E. 2d at 670. The Court of Appeals also approved the Appellate Division's interpretation: "As the court below said of the statute in question, 'All it purports to do is to bar a visual caricature of religious beliefs held sacred by one sect or another . . . .'" *Id.*, at 258, 101 N.E. 2d at 672. Judge Fuld, dissenting, concluded from all the statements in the majority opinion that "the basic criterion appears to be whether the film treats a religious theme in such a manner as to offend the religious beliefs of any group of persons. If the film does have that effect, and it is 'offered as a form of entertainment,' it apparently falls within the statutory ban regardless of the sincerity and good faith of the producer of the film, no matter how temperate the treatment of the theme, and no matter how unlikely a public disturbance or breach of the peace. The drastic nature of such a ban is highlighted by the fact that the film in question makes no direct attack on, or criticism of, any religious dogma or principle, and it is not claimed to be obscene, scurrilous, intemperate or abusive." *Id.*, at 271–272, 101 N.E. 2d at 680.

[16] Cf. *Thornhill* v. *Alabama*, 310 U.S. 88, 97 (1940); *Stromberg* v. *California*, 283 U.S. 359, 369–370 (1931).

to apply the broad and all-inclusive definition of "sacrilegious" given by the New York courts, the censor is set adrift upon a boundless sea amid a myriad of conflicting currents of religious views, with no charts but those provided by the most vocal and powerful orthodoxies. New York cannot vest such unlimited restraining control over motion pictures in a censor. Cf. *Kunz* v. *New York*, 340 U.S. 290 (1951).[17] Under such a standard the most careful and tolerant censor would find it virtually impossible to avoid favoring one religion over another, and he would be subject to an inevitable tendency to ban the expression of unpopular sentiments sacred to a religious minority. Application of the "sacrilegious" test, in these or other respects, might raise substantial questions under the First Amendment's guaranty of separate church and state with freedom of worship for all.[18] However, from the standpoint of freedom of speech and the press, it is enough to point out that the state has no legitimate interest in protecting any or all religions from views distasteful to them which is sufficient to justify prior restraints upon the expression of those views. It is not the business of government in our nation to suppress real or imagined attacks upon a particular religious doctrine, whether they appear in publications, speeches, or motion pictures.[19]

Since the term "sacrilegious" is the sole standard under attack here, it is not necessary for us to decide, for example, whether a state may censor motion pictures under a clearly drawn statute designed and applied to prevent the showing of obscene films. That is a very different question from the one now before us.[20] We hold only that under the First and Fourteenth Amendments a state may not ban a film on the basis of a censor's conclusion that it is "sacrilegious."

Reversed.

Mr. Justice Reed, concurring in the judgment of the Court.

Assuming that a state may establish a system for the licensing of motion pictures, an issue not foreclosed by the Court's opinion, our duty requires us to examine the facts of the refusal of a license in each case to determine whether the principles of the First Amendment have been honored. This film does not seem to me to be of a character that the First Amendment permits a state to exclude from public view.

Mr. Justice Frankfurter, whom Mr. Justice Jackson joins, concurring in the judgment of the Court; Mr. Justice Burton, having concurred in the opinion of the Court, also joins this opinion.

A practised hand has thus summarized the story of "The Miracle":[1]

"A poor, simple-minded girl is tending a herd of goats on a mountainside one day, when a bearded stranger passes. Suddenly it strikes her fancy that he is St. Joseph, her favorite saint, and that he has come to take her to heaven, where she will be happy and free. While she pleads with him to transport her, the stranger gently plies the girl with wine, and when she is in a state of tumult, he apparently ravishes her. (This incident in the story is only briefly and discreetly implied.)

"The girl awakens later, finds the stranger gone, and climbs down from the mountain not knowing whether he was real or a dream. She meets an old priest who tells her that it is quite possible that she did see a saint, but a younger priest scoffs at the notion. 'Materialist!' the old priest says.

"There follows now a brief sequence—intended to be symbolic, obviously—in which the girl is reverently sitting with other villagers in church. Moved by a whim of appetite, she snitches an apple from the basket of a woman next to her. When she leaves the church, a cackling beggar tries to make her share the apple with him, but she chases him away as by habit and munches the fruit contentedly.

"Then, one day, while tending the village youngsters as their mothers work at the vines, the girl faints and the women discover that she is going to have a child. Frightened and bewildered, she suddenly murmurs, 'It is the grace of God!' and she runs to the church in great excitement, looks for the statue of St. Joseph, and then prostrates herself on the floor.

"Thereafter she meekly refuses to do any menial work and the housewives humor her gently but the young people are not so kind. In a scene of brutal torment, they first flatter and laughingly mock her, then they cruelly shove and hit her and clamp a basin as a halo on her head. Even abused by the beggars, the poor girl gathers together her pitiful rags and sadly departs from the village to live alone in a cave.

---

[17] Cf. *Niemotko* v. *Maryland*, 340 U.S. 268 (1951); *Saia* v. *New York*, 334 U.S. 558 (1948); *Largent* v. *Texas*, 318 U.S. 418 (1943); *Lovell* v. *Griffin*, 303 U.S. 444 (1938).

[18] See *Cantwell* v. *Connecticut*, 310 U.S. 296 (1940).

[19] See the following statement by Mr. Justice Roberts, speaking for a unanimous Court in *Cantwell* v. *Connecticut*, 310 U.S. 296, 310 (1940):

"In the realm of religious faith, and in that of political belief, sharp differences arise. In both fields the tenets of one man may seem the rankest error to his neighbor. To persuade others to his own point of view, the pleader, as we know, at times, resorts to exaggeration, to vilification of men who have been, or are, prominent in church or state, and even to false statement. But the people of this nation have ordained in the light of history, that, in spite of the probability of excesses and abuses, these liberties are, in the long view, essential to enlightened opinion and right conduct on the part of the citizens of a democracy.

"The essential characteristic of these liberties is, that under their shield many types of life, character, opinion and belief can develop unmolested and unobstructed. Nowhere is this shield more necessary than in our own country for a people composed of many races and of many creeds."

[20] In the *Near* case, this Court stated that "the primary requirements of decency may be enforced against obscene publications." 283 U.S. 697, 716. In *Chaplinsky* v. *New Hampshire*, 315 U.S. 568, 571–572 (1942), Mr. Justice Murphy stated for a unanimous Court: "There are certain well-defined and narrowly limited classes of speech, the prevention and punishment of which have never been thought to raise any Constitutional problem. These include the lewd and obscene, the profane, the libelous, and the insulting or 'fighting' words—those which by their very utterance inflict injury or tend to incite an immediate breach of the peace." But see *Kovacs* v. *Cooper*, 336 U.S. 77, 82 (1949): "When ordinances undertake censorship of speech or religious practices before permitting their exercise, the Constitution forbids their enforcement."

---

[1] Crowther, "The Strange Case of 'The Miracle,'" *Atlantic Monthly*, April, 1951, pp. 35, 36–37.

"When she feels her time coming upon her, she starts back towards the village. But then she sees the crowds in the streets; dark memories haunt her; so she turns towards a church on a high hill and instinctively struggles towards it, crying desperately to God. A goat is her sole companion. She drinks water dripping from a rock. And when she comes to the church and finds the door locked, the goat attracts her to a small side door. Inside the church, the poor girl braces herself for her labor pains. There is a dissolve, and when we next see her sad face, in close-up, it is full of a tender light. There is the cry of an unseen baby. The girl reaches towards it and murmurs, 'My son! My love! My flesh!' "

"The Miracle"—a film lasting forty minutes—was produced in Italy by Roberto Rossellini. Anna Magnani played the lead as the demented goat-tender. It was first shown at the Venice Film Festival in August, 1948, combined with another moving picture, "L'Umano Voce," into a diptych called "Amore." According to an affidavit from the Director of that Festival, if the motion picture had been "blasphemous" it would have been barred by the Festival Committee. In a review of the film in L'Osservatore Romano, the organ of the Vatican, its film critic, Piero Regnoli, wrote: "Opinions may vary and questions may arise—even serious ones—of a religious nature (not to be diminished by the fact that the woman portrayed is mad [because] the author who attributed madness to her is not mad). . . ."[2] While acknowledging that there were "passages of undoubted cinematic distinction," Regnoli criticized the film as being "on such a pretentiously cerebral plane that it reminds one of the early d'Annunzio." The Vatican newspaper's critic concluded: "we continue to believe in Rossellini's art and we look forward to his next achievement."[3] In October, 1948, a month after the Rome premiere of "The Miracle," the Vatican's censorship agency, the Catholic Cinematographic Centre, declared that the picture "constitutes in effect an abominable profanation from religious and moral viewpoints."[4] By the Lateran agreements and the Italian Constitution the Italian Government is bound to bar whatever may offend the Catholic religion. However, the Catholic Cinematographic Centre did not invoke any governmental sanction thereby afforded. The Italian Government's censorship agency gave "The Miracle" the regular *nulla osta* clearance. The film was freely shown throughout Italy, but was not a great success.[5] Italian movie critics divided in opinion. The critic for Il Popolo, speaking for the Christian Democratic Party, the Catholic party, profusely praised the picture as a "beautiful thing, humanly felt, alive, true and without religious profanation as someone has said, because in our opinion the meaning of the characters is clear and there is no possibility of misunderstanding."[6] Regnoli again reviewed "The Miracle" for L'Osservatore Romano.[7] After criticising the film for

technical faults, he found "the most courageous and interesting passage of Rossellini's work" in contrasting portrayals in the film; he added: "Unfortunately, concerning morals, it is necessary to note some slight defects." He objected to its "carnality" and to the representation of illegitimate motherhood. But he did not suggest that the picture was "sacrilegious." The tone of Regnoli's critique was one of respect for Rossellini, "the illustrious Italian producer."[8]

On March 2, 1949, "The Miracle" was licensed in New York State for showing without English subtitles.[9] However, it was never exhibited until after a second license was issued on November 30, 1950, for the trilogy, "Ways of Love," combining "The Miracle" with two French films, Jean Renoir's "A Day in the Country" and Marcel Pagnol's "Jofroi."[10] All had English subtitles. Both licenses were issued in the usual course after viewings of the picture by the Motion Picture Division of the New York State Education Department. The Division is directed by statute to "issue a license" "unless [the] film or a part thereof is obscene, indecent, immoral, inhuman, sacrilegious, or is of such a character that its exhibition would tend to corrupt morals or incite to crime." N.Y. Education Law, § 122. The trilogy opened on December 12, 1950, at the Paris Theatre on 58th Street in Manhattan. It was promptly attacked as "a sacrilegious and blasphemous mockery of Christian religious truth"[11] by the National Legion of Decency, a private Catholic organization for film censorship, whose objectives have intermittently been approved by various non-Catholic church and social groups since its formation in 1933.[12] However, the National Board of Review (a non-industry lay organization devoted to raising the level of motion pictures by mobilizing public opinion, under the slogan "Selection Not Censorship")[13] recommended the picture as "especially worth seeing." New York critics on the whole praised "The Miracle"; those who dispraised did not suggest sacrilege.[14] On December

[2] L'Osservatore Romano, Aug. 25, 1948, p. 2, col. 1, translated in part in The Commonweal, Mar. 23, 1951, p. 592, col. 2.
[3] Ibid.
[4] N. Y. Times, Feb. 11, 1951, § 2, p. 4, cols. 4–5.
[5] Time, Feb. 19, 1951, pp. 60–61.
[6] Il Popolo, Nov. 3, 1948, p. 2, col. 9, translated by Camille M. Cianfarra, N.Y. Times, Feb. 11, 1951, § 2, p. 4, col. 5.
[7] L'Osservatore Romano, Nov. 12, 1948, p. 2, cols. 3–4.

[8] Ibid.
[9] "The Miracle" was passed by customs. To import "any obscene, lewd, lascivious, or filthy . . . motion-picture film" is a criminal offense, 35 Stat. 1088, 1138, 18 U.S.C. (Supp. IV) § 1462; and importation of any obscene "print" or "picture" is barred. 46 Stat. 590, 688, 19 U.S.C. § 1305. Compare the provision, "all photographic-films imported . . . shall be subject to such censorship as may be imposed by the Secretary of the Treasury." 38 Stat. 114, 151 (1913), 42 Stat. 858, 920 (1922), repealed 46 Stat. 590, 762 (1930). See Inglis, Freedom of the Movies, 68.
[10] Life, Jan. 15, 1951, p. 63; Sat. Rev. of Lit., Jan. 27, 1951, pp. 28–29.
[11] N.Y. Times, Dec. 31, 1950, p. 23, col. 4.
[12] Inglis, Freedom of the Movies, 120 et seq.
[13] Id., at 74–82.
[14] Howard Barnes, N.Y. Herald Tribune, Dec. 13, 1950, p. 30, cols. 1–3: "it would be wise to time a visit to the Paris in order to skip ['The Miracle']. . . . Altogether it leaves a very bad taste in one's mouth."
Bosley Crowther, N. Y. Times, Dec. 13, 1950, p. 50, cols. 2–3: "each one of the [three] items . . . stacks up with the major achievements of the respective directors. . . . ['The Miracle'] is by far the most overpowering and provocative of the lot." N. Y. Times, Dec. 17, 1950, § 2, p. 3, cols. 7–8: "a picture of mounting intensity that wrings the last pang of emotion as it hits its dramatic peak . . . vastly compassionate comprehension of the suffering and the triumph of birth."
Wanda Hale, N. Y. Daily News, Dec. 13, 1950, p. 82, cols.

27 the critics selected the "Ways of Love" as the best foreign language film in 1950.[15] Meanwhile, on December 23, Edward T. McCaffrey, Commissioner of Licenses for New York City, declared the film "officially and personally blasphemous" and ordered it withdrawn at the risk of suspension of the license to operate the Paris Theatre.[16] A week later the program was restored at the theatre upon the decision by the New York Supreme Court that the City License Commissioner had exceeded his authority in that he was without powers of movie censorship.[17]

Upon the failure of the License Commissioner's effort to cut off showings of "The Miracle," the controversy took a new turn. On Sunday, January 7, 1951, a statement of His Eminence, Francis Cardinal Spellman, condemning the picture and calling on "all right thinking citizens" to unite to tighten censorship laws, was read at all masses in St. Patrick's Cathedral.[18]

The views of Cardinal Spellman aroused dissent among other devout Christians. Protestant clergymen, representing various denominations, after seeing the picture, found in it nothing "sacrilegious or immoral to the views held by Christian men and women," and with a few exceptions agreed that the film was "unquestionably one of unusual artistic merit."[19]

In this estimate some Catholic laymen concurred.[20] Their opinion is represented by the comment by Otto L. Spaeth, Director of the American Federation of Arts and prominent in Catholic lay activities:

"At the outbreak of the controversy, I immediately arranged for a private showing of the film. I invited a group of Catholics, competent and respected for their writings on both religious and cultural subjects. The essential approval of the film was unanimous.

"There was indeed 'blasphemy' in the picture—but it was the blasphemy of the villagers, who stopped at nothing, not even the mock singing of a hymn to the Virgin, in their brutal badgering of the tragic woman. The scathing indictment of their evil behavior, implicit in the film, was seemingly overlooked by its critics."[21]

William P. Clancy, a teacher at the University of Notre Dame, wrote in The Commonweal, the well-known Catholic weekly, that "the film is not *obviously* blasphemous or obscene, either in its intention or execution."[22] The Commonweal itself questioned the wisdom of transforming

---

1–3: "Rossellini's best piece of direction, since his greatest, 'Open City.' . . . artistic and beautifully done by both the star and the director."

Archer Winsten, N. Y. Post, Dec. 13, 1950, p. 80, cols. 1–3: "Magnani's performance is a major one and profoundly impressive. This reviewer's personal opinion marked down the film as disturbingly unpleasant and slow."

Seymour Peck, N. Y. Daily Compass, Dec. 13, 1950, p. 13, cols. 3–5: " 'The Miracle' is really all Magnani. . . . one of the most exciting solo performances the screen has known."

Alton Cook, N. Y. World-Telegram, Dec. 13, 1950, p. 50, cols. 1–2: "['The Miracle' is] charged with the same overwrought hysteria that ran through his 'Stromboli.' . . . the picture has an unpleasant preoccupation with filth and squalor . . . exceedingly trying experience."

Time, Jan. 8, 1951, p. 72, cols. 2–3: "['The Miracle'] is second rate Rossellini despite a virtuoso performance by Anna Magnani."

Newsweek, Dec. 18, 1950, pp. 93–94, col. 3: "strong medicine for most American audiences. However, it shows what an artist of Rossellini's character can do in the still scarcely explored medium of the film short story."

Hollis Alpert, Sat. Rev. of Lit., Jan. 27, 1951, pp. 28–29: "pictorially the picture is a gem, with its sensitive evocation of a small Italian town and the surrounding countryside near Salerno. . . . Anna Magnani again demonstrates her magnificent qualities of acting. The role is difficult. . . .

"But my quarrel would be with Mr. Rossellini, whose method of improvisation from scene to scene . . . can also result in extraneous detail that adds little, or even harms, the over-all effect."

[15] N. Y. Times, Dec. 28, 1950, p. 22, col. 1.

[16] Id., Dec. 24, 1950, p. 1, cols. 2–3.

[17] *Joseph Burstyn, Inc.* v. *McCaffrey*, 198 Misc. 884, 101 N.Y.S. 2d 892.

[18] N. Y. Times, Jan. 8, 1951, p. 1, col. 2. The Cardinal termed "The Miracle" "a vile and harmful picture," "a despicable affront to every Christian" ("We believe in miracles. This picture ridicules that belief"), and finally "a vicious insult to Italian womanhood." As a consequence, he declared: "we, as the guardians of the moral law, must summon you and all people with a sense of decency to refrain from seeing it and supporting the venal purveyors of such pictures. . . ." *Id.,* at p. 14, cols. 2–3.

For completeness' sake, later incidents should be noted. Picketers from the Catholic War Veterans, the Holy Name Society, and other Catholic organizations—about 1,000 persons in all during one Sunday—paraded before the Paris Theatre. *Id.,* Dec. 29, 1950, p. 36, col. 3; Jan. 8, 1951, p. 1, col. 2; Jan. 9, 1951, p. 34, col. 7; Jan. 10, 1951, p. 22, col. 6; Jan. 15, 1951, p. 23, col. 3. A smaller number of counterpickets appeared on

several days. *Id.,* Jan. 10, 1951, p. 22, col. 6; Jan. 20, 1951, p. 10, cols. 4–5. See also *id.,* Jan. 23, 1951, p. 21, col. 8; Jan. 25, 1951, p. 27, col. 7.

The Paris Theatre on two different evenings was emptied on threat of bombing. *Id.,* Jan. 21, 1951, p. 1, cols. 2–3; Jan. 28, 1951, p. 1, cols. 2–3. Coincidentally with the proceedings before the New York Board of Regents which started this case on the way to this Court, the Paris Theatre also was having difficulties with the New York City Fire Department. The curious may follow the development of those incidents, not relevant here, in the N. Y. Times, Jan. 21, 1951, p. 53, cols. 4–5; Jan. 27, 1951, p. 11, col. 3; Feb. 6, 1951, p. 29, col. 8; Feb. 10, 1951, p. 15, col. 8; Feb. 15, 1951, p. 33, col. 2.

[19] Excerpts from letters and statements by a great many clergymen are reproduced in the Record before this Court, pages 95–140. The representative quotations in the text are from letters written by the Rev. H. C. De Windt, Minister of the West Park Presbyterian Church, New York City, R. 97, and the Rev. W. J. Beeners of Princeton, New Jersey, R. 98, respectively.

[20] Catholic opinion generally, as expressed in the press, supported the view of the Legion of Decency and of Cardinal Spellman. See, for example, The [New York] Catholic News, Dec. 30, 1950, p. 10; Jan. 6, 1951, p. 10; Jan. 20, 1951, p. 10; Feb. 3, 1951, p. 10; Feb. 10, 1951, p. 12; and May 19, 1951, p. 12; Commonweal, Jan. 12, 1951, p. 351, col. 1; The [Brooklyn] Tablet, Jan. 20, 1951, p. 8, col. 4; *id.,* Jan. 27, 1951, p. 10, col. 3; *id.,* Feb. 3, 1951, p. 8, cols. 3–4; Martin Quigley, Jr., " 'The Miracle'—An Outrage"; The [San Francisco] Monitor, Jan. 12, 1951, p. 7, cols. 3–4 (reprinted from Motion Picture Herald, Jan. 6, 1951); The [Boston] Pilot, Jan. 6, 1951, p. 4. There doubtless were comments on "The Miracle" in other diocesan papers which circulate in various parts of the country, but which are not on file in the Library of Congress or the library of the Catholic University of America.

[21] Spaeth, "Fogged Screen," Magazine of Art, Feb., 1951, p. 44; N. Y. Herald Tribune, Jan. 30, 1951, p. 18, col. 4.

[22] Clancy, "The Catholic as Philistine," The Commonweal, Mar. 16, 1951, pp. 567–569.

Church dogma which Catholics may obey as "a free act" into state-enforced censorship for all.[23] Allen Tate, the well-known Catholic poet and critic, wrote: "The picture seems to me to be superior in acting and photography but inferior dramatically. . . . In the long run what Cardinal Spellman will have succeeded in doing is insulting the intelligence and faith of American Catholics with the assumption that a second-rate motion picture could in any way undermine their morals or shake their faith."[24]

At the time "The Miracle" was filmed, all the persons having significant positions in the production—producer, director, and cast—were Catholics. Roberto Rossellini, who had Vatican approval in 1949 for filming a life of St. Francis, using in the cast members of the Franciscan Order, cabled Cardinal Spellman protesting against boycott of "The Miracle":

"In The Miracle *men are still without pity because they still have not come back to God, but God is already present in the faith, however confused, of that poor, persecuted woman; and since God is wherever a human being suffers and is misunderstood,* The Miracle *occurs when at the birth of the child the poor, demented woman regains sanity in her maternal love."*[25]

In view of the controversy thus aroused by the picture, the Chairman of the Board of Regents appointed a committee of three Board members to review the action of the Motion Picture Division in granting the two licenses. After viewing the picture on Jan. 15, 1951, the committee declared it "sacrilegious." The Board four days later issued an order to the licensees to show cause why the licenses should not be cancelled in that the picture was "sacrilegious." The Board of Regents rescinded the licenses on Feb. 16, 1951, saying that the "mockery or profaning of these beliefs that are sacred to any portion of our citizenship is abhorrent to the laws of this great State." On review the Appellate Division upheld the Board of Regents, holding that the banning of any motion picture "that may fairly be deemed sacrilegious to the adherents of any religious group . . . is directly related to public peace and order" and is not a denial of religious freedom, and that there was "substantial evidence upon which the Regents could act." 278 App. Div. 253, 257, 258, 260, 104 N.Y.S. 2d 740, 743, 744–745, 747.

The New York Court of Appeals, with one judge concurring in a separate opinion and two others dissenting, affirmed the order of the Appellate Division. 303 N.Y. 242, 101 N.E. 2d 665. After concluding that the Board of Regents acted within its authority and that its determination was not "one that no reasonable mind could reach," *id.,* at 250–255, 256–257, 101 N.E. 2d 665, 667–671, the majority held, first, that "sacrilegious" was an adequately

definite standard, quoting a definition from Funk & Wagnalls' Dictionary and referring to opinions in this Court that in passing used the term "profane," which the New York court said was a synonym of "sacrilegious"; second, that the State's assurance "that no religion . . . shall be treated with contempt, mockery, scorn and ridicule . . . by those engaged in selling entertainment by way of motion pictures" does not violate the religious guarantee of the First Amendment; and third, that motion pictures are not entitled to the immunities from regulation enjoyed by the press, in view of the decision in *Mutual Film Corp.* v. *Ohio Industrial Comm'n,* 236 U.S. 230. *Id.,* at 255–256, 258–260, 260–262, 101 N.E. 2d 670–674. The two dissenting judges, after dealing with a matter of local law not reviewable here, found that the standard "sacrilegious" is unconstitutionally vague, and, finally, that the constitutional guarantee of freedom of speech applied equally to motion pictures and prevented this censorship. 303 N.Y. 242, 264, 101 N.E. 2d 665, 675. Both State courts, as did this Court, viewed "The Miracle."

Arguments by the parties and in briefs *amici* invite us to pursue to their farthest reach the problems in which this case is involved. Positions are advanced so absolute and abstract that in any event they could not properly determine this controversy. See *Ashwander* v. *Tennessee Valley Authority,* 297 U.S. 288, 341, 346–348. We are asked to decide this case by choosing between two mutually exclusive alternatives: that motion pictures may be subjected to unrestricted censorship, or that they must be allowed to be shown under any circumstances. But only the tyranny of absolutes would rely on such alternatives to meet the problems generated by the need to accommodate the diverse interests affected by the motion pictures in compact modern communities. It would startle Madison and Jefferson and George Mason, could they adjust themselves to our day, to be told that the freedom of speech which they espoused in the Bill of Rights authorizes a showing of "The Miracle" from windows facing St. Patrick's Cathedral in the forenoon of Easter Sunday,[26] just as it would startle them to be told that any picture, whatever its theme and its expression, could be barred from being commercially exhibited. The general principle of free speech, expressed in the First Amendment as to encroachments by Congress, and included as it is in the Fourteenth Amendment, binding on the States, must be placed in its historical and legal contexts. The Constitution, we cannot recall too often, is an organism, not merely a literary composition.

If the New York Court of Appeals had given "sacrilegious" the meaning it has had in Catholic thought since St. Thomas Aquinas formulated its scope, and had sustained a finding by the Board of Regents that "The Miracle" came within that scope, this Court would have to meet some of the broader questions regarding the relation to the motion picture industry of the guarantees of the First Amendment so far as reflected in the Fourteenth. But the New York court did not confine "sacrilegious" within such technical, Thomist limits, nor within any specific, or even approximately specified, limits. It may fairly be said that that court deemed "sacrilegious" a self-defining term,

---

[23] The Commonweal, Mar. 2, 1951, pp. 507–508. Much the same view was taken by Frank Getlein writing in The Catholic Messenger, Mar. 22, 1951, p. 4, cols. 1–8, in an article bearing the headline: "Film Critic Gives Some Aspects of 'The Miracle' Story: Raises Questions Concerning Tactics of Organized Catholic Resistance Groups in New York." See also, "Miracles Do Happen," The New Leader, Feb. 5, 1951, p. 30, col. 2.

[24] N. Y. Times, Feb. 1, 1951, p. 24, col. 7.

[25] *Id.,* Jan. 13, 1951, p. 10, col. 6; translation by Chworowsky, "The Cardinal: Critic and Censor," The Churchman, Feb. 1, 1951, p. 7, col. 2.

[26] That such offensive exploitation of modern means of publicity is not a fanciful hypothesis, see N. Y. Times, April 14, 1952, p. 1, col. 4.

a word that carries a well-known, settled meaning in the common speech of men.

So far as the Court of Appeals sought to support its notion that "sacrilegious" has the necessary precision of meaning which the Due Process Clause enjoins for statutes regulating men's activities, it relied on this definition from Funk & Wagnalls' Dictionary: "The act of violating or profaning anything sacred." But this merely defines by turning an adjective into a noun and bringing in two new words equally undefined. It leaves wide open the question as to what persons, doctrines or things are "sacred." It sheds no light on what representations on the motion picture screen will constitute "profaning" those things which the State censors find to be "sacred."

To criticize or assail religious doctrine may wound to the quick those who are attached to the doctrine and profoundly cherish it. But to bar such pictorial discussion is to subject non-conformists to the rule of sects.

Even in *Mutual Film Corp.* v. *Ohio Industrial Comm'n*, 236 U.S. 230, it was deemed necessary to find that the terms "educational, moral, amusing or harmless" do not leave "decision to arbitrary judgment." Such general words were found to "get precision from the sense and experience of men." *Id.*, at 245, 246. This cannot be said of "sacrilegious." If there is one thing that the history of religious conflicts shows, it is that the term "sacrilegious"—if by that is implied offense to the deep convictions of members of different sects, which is what the Court of Appeals seems to mean so far as it means anything precisely—does not gain "precision from the sense and experience of men."

The vast apparatus of indices and digests, which mirrors our law, affords no clue to a judicial definition of sacrilege. Not one case, barring the present, has been uncovered which considers the meaning of the term in any context. Nor has the practice under the New York law contributed light. The Motion Picture Division of the Education Department does not support with explanatory statements its action on any specific motion picture, which we are advised is itself not made public. Of the fifty-odd reported appeals to the Board of Regents from denials of licenses by the Division, only three concern the category "sacrilegious."[27] In these cases, as in others under the Act, the Board's reported opinion confines itself to a bare finding that the film was or was not "sacrilegious," without so much as a description of the allegedly offensive matter, or even of the film as a whole to enlighten the inquirer. Well-equipped law libraries are not niggardly in their reflection of "the sense and experience of men," but we must search elsewhere for any which gives to "sacrilege" its meaning.

Sacrilege,[28] as a restricted ecclesiastical concept, has a long history. Naturally enough, religions have sought to protect their priests and anointed symbols from physical injury.[29] But history demonstrates that the term is hopelessly vague when it goes beyond such ecclesiastical definiteness and is used at large as the basis for punishing deviation from doctrine.

Etymologically "sacrilege" is limited to church-robbing: *sacer*, sacred, and *legere*, to steal or pick out. But we are told that "already in Cicero's time it had grown to include in popular speech any insult or injury to [sacred things]."[30] "In primitive religions [sacrilege is] inclusive of almost every serious offence even in fields now regarded as merely social or political. . . ."[31] The concept of "tabu" in primitive society is thus close to that of "sacrilege."[32] And in "the Theodosian Code the various crimes which are accounted sacrilege include—apostasy, heresy, schism, Judaism, paganism, attempts against the immunity of churches and clergy or privileges of church courts, the desecration of sacraments, etc., and even Sunday. Along with these crimes against religion went treason to the emperor, offences against the laws, especially counterfeiting, defraudation in taxes, seizure of confiscated property, evil conduct of imperial officers, etc."[33] During the Middle Ages the Church considerably delimited the application of the term. St. Thomas Aquinas classified the objects of "sacrilege" as persons, places, and things.[34] The injuries which would constitute "sacrilege" received specific and detailed illustration.[35] This teaching of Aquinas is, I believe, still substantially the basis of the official Catholic doctrine of sacrilege. Thus, for the Roman Catholic Church, the term came to have a fairly definite meaning, but one, in general, limited to protecting things physical against injurious acts.[36] Apostasy, heresy, and blasphemy

---

27 *In the Matter of "The Puritan,"* 60 N.Y. St. Dept. 163 (1939); *In the Matter of "Polygamy,"* 60 N.Y. St. Dept. 217 (1939); *In the Matter of "Monja y Casada—Virgen y Martir"* ("*Nun and Married—Virgin and Martyr*"), 52 N.Y. St. Dept. 488 (1935).

28 Since almost without exception "sacrilegious" is defined in terms of "sacrilege," our discussion will be directed to the latter term. See Bailey, *Universal Etymological English Dictionary* (London, 1730), "Sacrilegious"—"of, pertaining to, or guilty of Sacrilege"; Funk & Wagnalls' *New Standard Dictionary* (1937), "Sacrilegious"—"Having committed or being ready to commit sacrilege. Of the nature of sacrilege; as, *sacrilegious* deeds."

29 For general discussions of "sacrilege," see Encyclopaedia of Religion and Ethics (Hastings ed., 1921), "Sacrilege" and "Tabu"; Rev. Thomas Slater, A Manual of Moral Theology (1908), 226–230; The Catholic Encyclopedia (1912), "Sacrilege"; and Encyclopaedia Britannica, "Sacrilege."

30 Encyclopaedia Britannica (1951), "Sacrilege."

31 *Ibid.*

32 See Encyclopaedia of Religion and Ethics (Hastings ed., 1921), "Tabu."

33 Encyclopaedia Britannica (1951), "Sacrilege."

34 St. Thomas Aquinas, Summa Theologica, part II–II, question 99. The modern Codex Juris Canonici does not give any definition of "sacrilege," but merely says it "shall be punished by the Ordinary in proportion to the gravity of the fault, without prejudice to the penalties established by law. . . ." See Bouscaren and Ellis, Canon Law (1946), 857. 2 Woywod, A Practical Commentary on the Code of Canon Law (1929), par. 2178, 477–478, thus defines sacrilege: "Sacrilege consists in the unworthy use or treatment of sacred things and sacred persons. Certain things are of their nature sacred (e.g., the Sacraments); others become so by blessing or consecration legitimately bestowed on things or places by authority of the Church. Persons are rendered sacred by ordination or consecration or by other forms of dedication to the divine service by authority of the Church (e.g., by first tonsure, by religious profession)."

35 After his method of raising objections and then refuting them, St. Thomas Aquinas defends including within the proscription of "sacrilege," anyone "who disagree[s] about the sovereign's decision, and doubt[s] whether the person chosen by the sovereign be worthy of honor" and "any man [who] shall allow the Jews to hold public offices." Summa Theologica, part II–II, question 99, art. 1.

36 Rev. Thomas Slater, S.J., A Manual of Moral Theology (1908), c. VI, classifies and illustrates the modern theological view of "sacrilege":

coexisted as religious crimes alongside sacrilege; they were peculiarly in the realm of religious dogma and doctrine, as "sacrilege" was not. It is true that Spelman, writing "The History and Fate of Sacrilege" in 1632, included in "sacrilege" acts whereby "the very Deity is invaded, profaned, or robbed of its glory. . . . In this high sin are blasphemers, sorcerers, witches, and enchanters."[37] But his main theme was the "spoil of church lands done by Henry VIII" and the misfortunes that subsequently befell the families of the recipients of former ecclesiastical property as divine punishment.

To the extent that English law took jurisdiction to punish "sacrilege," the term meant the stealing from a church, or otherwise doing damage to church property.[38] This special protection against "sacrilege," that is, property damage, was granted only to the Established Church.[39] Since the repeal less than a century ago of the English law punishing "sacrilege" against the property of the Established Church, religious property has received little special protection. The property of all sects has had substantially the same protection as is accorded non-religious property.[40] At no time up to the present has English law known "sacrilege" to be used in any wider sense than the physical injury to church property. It is true that, at times in the past, English law has taken jurisdiction to punish departures from accepted dogma or religious practice or the expression of particular religious opinions, but never

---

Sacrilege against sacred persons: to use physical violence against a member of the clergy; to violate "the privilege of immunity of the clergy from civil jurisdiction, as far as this is still in force"; to violate a vow of chastity.

Sacrilege against sacred places: to violate the immunity of churches and other sacred places "as far as this is still in force"; to commit a crime such as homicide, suicide, bloody attack there; to break by sexual act a vow of chastity there; to bury an infidel, heretic, or excommunicate in churches or cemeteries canonically established; or to put the sacred place to a profane use, as a secular courtroom, public market, banquet hall, stable, etc.

Sacrilege against sacred things: to treat with irreverence, contempt, or obscenity the sacraments (particularly the Eucharist), Holy Scriptures, relics, sacred images, etc., to steal sacred things, or profane things from sacred places; to commit simony; or to steal, confiscate, or damage wilfully ecclesiastical property. See also, The Catholic Encyclopedia, "Sacrilege."

[37] Sir Henry Spelman, The History and Fate of Sacrilege (2d ed., 1853), 121–122. Two priests of the Anglican Church prepared a long prefatory essay to bring Spelman's data up to the date of publication of the 1853 edition. Their essay shows their understanding also of "sacrilege" in the limited sense. Id., at 1–120.

[38] 2 Russell, Crime (10th ed., 1950), 975–976; Stephen, A Digest of the Criminal Law (9th ed., 1950), 348–349. See 23 Hen. VIII, c. 1, § III; 1 Edw. VI, c. 12, § X; 1 Mary, c. 3, §§ IV–VI.

[39] 7 & 8 Geo. IV, c. 29, § X, which the marginal note summarized as "Sacrilege, when capital," read: "if any Person shall break and enter any Church or Chapel, and steal therein any Chattel . . . [he] shall suffer Death as a Felon." This statute was interpreted to apply only to buildings of the established church. *Rex v. Nixon*, 7 Car. & P. 442 (1836).

[40] 7 & 8 Geo. IV, c. 29, § X, was repealed by 24 & 25 Vict., c. 95. The Larceny Act and the Malicious Injuries to Property Act, both of 1861, treated established church property substantially the same as all other property. 24 & 25 Vict., c. 96, § 50; c. 97, §§ 1, 11, 39, superseded by Larceny Act, 1916, 6 & 7 Geo. V, c. 50, § 24.

---

have these "offenses" been denominated "sacrilege." Apostasy, heresy, offenses against the Established Church, blasphemy, profanation of the Lord's Day, etc., were distinct criminal offenses, characterized by Blackstone as "offences against God and religion."[41] These invidious reflections upon religious susceptibilities were not covered under sacrilege as they might be under the Court of Appeals' opinion. Anyone doubting the dangerous uncertainty of the New York definition, which makes "sacrilege" overlap these other "offenses against religion," need only read Blackstone's account of the broad and varying content given each of these offenses.

A student of English lexicography would despair of finding the meaning attributed to "sacrilege" by the New York court.[42] Most dictionaries define the concept in the limited sense of the physical abuse of physical objects. The definitions given for "sacrilege" by two dictionaries published in 1742 and 1782 are typical. Bailey's defined it as "the stealing of Sacred Things, Church Robbing; an Alienation to Laymen, and to profane and common Purposes, of what was given to religious Persons, and to pious Uses."[43] Barclay's said it is "the crime of taking any thing dedicated to divine worship, or profaning any thing sacred," where "to profane" is defined "to apply any thing sacred to common uses. To be irreverent to sacred persons or things."[44] The same dictionaries defined "blasphemy," a peculiarly verbal offense, in much broader terms than "sacrilege," indeed in terms which the New York court finds encompassed by "sacrilegious." For example, Barclay said "blasphemy" is "an offering some indignity to God, any person of the Trinity, any messengers from God, his holy writ, or the doctrines of revelation."[45] It is hardly necessary to comment that the limits of this definition remain too uncertain to justify constraining the creative efforts of the imagination by fear of pains and penalties imposed by a necessarily subjective censorship. It is true that some earlier dictionaries assigned to "sacrilege" the broader meaning of "abusing Sacraments or holy Mysteries,"[46] but the broader meaning is more indefinite, not less. Noah Webster first published his American Dictionary in 1828. Both it and the later dictionaries published by the Merriam Company, Webster's International Dictionary and Webster's New International Dictionary, have gone through dozens of editions and printings, revisions and expansions. In all editions throughout 125 years, these American dictionaries have defined "sacrilege" and "sacrilegious" to echo substantially the narrow, technical definitions from the earlier British dictionaries collected in the Appendix, *post*, p. 533.[47]

---

[41] Blackstone, bk. IV, c. 4, 41–64.

[42] Compare the definitions of "sacrilege" and "blasphemy" in the dictionaries, starting with Cockeram's 1651 edition, which are collected in the Appendix, *post*, p. 533.

[43] Bailey, An Universal Etymological English Dictionary (London, 1742), "Sacrilege."

[44] Barclay, A Complete and Universal English Dictionary (London, 1782), "Sacrilege."

[45] Id., "Blasphemy."

[46] Thomas Blount, Glossographia (3d ed., London, 1670).

[47] Webster's Compendious Dictionary of the English Language (1806): "Sacrilege"—"the robbery of a church or chapel." "Sacrilegious"—"violating a thing made sacred." Webster's American Dictionary (1828): "Sacrilege"—"The crime of violating or profaning sacred things; or the alienating to

The New York Court of Appeals' statement that the dictionary "furnishes a clear definition," justifying the vague scope it gave to "sacrilegious," surely was made without regard to the lexicographic history of the term. As a matter of fact, the definition from Funk & Wagnalls' used by the Court of Appeals is taken straight from 18th Century dictionaries, particularly Doctor Johnson's.[48] In light of that history it would seem that the Funk & Wagnalls' definition uses "sacrilege" in its historically restricted meaning, which was not, and could hardly have been, the basis for condemning "The Miracle." If the New York court reads the Funk & Wagnalls' definition in a broader sense, in a sense for which history and experience provide no gloss, it inevitably left the censor free to judge by whatever dogma he deems "sacred" and to ban whatever motion pictures he may assume would "profane" religious doctrine widely enough held to arouse protest.

Examination of successive editions of the Encyclopaedia Britannica over nearly two centuries up to the present day gives no more help than the dictionaries. From 1768 to the eleventh edition in 1911, merely a brief dictionary-type

definition was given for "sacrilege."[49] The eleventh edition, which first published a longer article, was introduced as follows: "the violation or profanation of sacred things, a crime of varying scope in different religions. It is naturally much more general and accounted more dreadful in those primitive religions in which cultural objects play so great a part, than in more highly spiritualized religions where they tend to disappear. But wherever the idea of sacred exists, sacrilege is possible."[50] The article on "sacrilege" in the current edition of the Encyclopaedia Britannica is substantially the same as that in the 1911 edition.

History teaches us the indefiniteness of the concept "sacrilegious" in another respect. In the case of most countries and times where the concept of sacrilege has been of importance, there has existed an established church or a state religion. That which was "sacred," and so was protected against "profaning," was designated in each case by ecclesiastical authority. What might have been definite when a controlling church imposed a detailed scheme of observances becomes impossibly confused and uncertain when hundreds of sects, with widely disparate and often directly conflicting ideas of sacredness, enjoy, without discrimination and in equal measure, constitutionally guaranteed religious freedom. In the Rome of the late emperors, the England of James I, or the Geneva of Calvin, and today in Roman Catholic Spain, Mohammedan Saudi Arabia, or any other country with a monolithic religion, the category of things sacred might have clearly definable limits. But in America the multiplicity of the ideas of "sacredness" held with equal but conflicting fervor by the great number of religious groups makes the term "sacrilegious" too indefinite to satisfy constitutional demands based on reason and fairness.

If "sacrilegious" bans more than the physical abuse of sacred persons, places, or things, if it permits censorship of religious opinions, which is the effect of the holding below, the term will include what may be found to be "blasphemous." England's experience with that treacherous word should give us pause, apart from our requirements for the separation of Church and State. The crime of blasphemy in Seventeenth Century England was the crime of dissenting from whatever was the current religious dogma.[51] King James I's "Book of Sports" was first required reading in the churches; later all copies were consigned to the flames. To attack the mass was once blasphemous; to

laymen or to common purposes what has been appropriated or consecrated to religious persons or uses." "Sacrilegious"—"Violating sacred things; polluted with the crime of sacrilege."

Webster's International Dictionary (G. & C. Merriam & Co., 1890): "Sacrilege"—"The sin or crime of violating or profaning sacred things; the alienating to laymen, or to common purposes, what has been appropriated or consecrated to religious persons or uses." "Sacrilegious"—"violating sacred things; polluted · with sacrilege; involving sacrilege; profane; impious."

Webster's New International Dictionary (G. & C. Merriam Co., 1st ed., 1909): "Sacrilege"—"The sin or crime of violating or profaning sacred things; specif., the alienating to laymen, or to common purposes, what has been appropriated or consecrated to religious persons or uses." "Sacrilegious"—"Violating sacred things; polluted with, or involving, sacrilege; impious." Repeated in the 1913, 1922, 1924, 1928, 1933 printings, among others.

Webster's New International Dictionary (G. & C. Merriam Co., 2d ed., 1934): "Sacrilege"—"The crime of stealing, misusing, violating, or desecrating that which is sacred, or holy, or dedicated to sacred uses. Specif.: a R. C. Ch. The sin of violating the conditions for a worthy reception of a sacrament. b Robbery from a church; also, that which is stolen. c Alienation to laymen, or to common purposes, of what has been appropriated or consecrated to religious persons or uses." "Sacrilegious"— "Committing sacrilege; characterized by or involving sacrilege; polluted with sacrilege; as *sacrilegious* robbers, depredations, or acts." Repeated in the 1939, 1942, 1944, 1949 printings, among others.

[48] Funk & Wagnalls' Standard Dictionary of the English Language, which was first copyrighted in 1890, defined sacrilege as follows in the 1895 printing: "1. The act of violating or profaning anything sacred. 2. *Eng. Law* (1) The larceny of consecrated things from a church; the breaking into a church with intent to commit a felony, or breaking out after a felony. (2) Formerly, the selling to a layman of property given to pious uses." This definition remained unchanged through many printings of that dictionary. The current printing of Funk & Wagnalls' New Standard Dictionary of the English Language, first copyrighted in 1913, carries exactly the same definition of "sacrilege" except that the first definition has been expanded to read: "The act of violating or profaning anything sacred, including sacramental vows."

Funk & Wagnalls' Standard Dictionary (1895) defined "to profane" as "1. To treat with irreverence or abuse; make common or unholy; desecrate; pollute. 2. Hence, to put to a wrong or degrading use; debase." The New Standard Dictionary adds a third meaning: "3. To vulgarize; give over to the crowd."

[49] Encyclopaedia Britannica, 2d ed., 1782: "Sacrilege"—"the crime of profaning sacred things, or those devoted to the service of God."

3d ed., 1797: "Sacrilege"—"the crime of profaning sacred things, or things devoted to God; or of alienating to laymen, for common purposes, what was given to religious persons and pious uses."

8th ed., 1859: "Sacrilege"—same as 3d ed., 1797.

9th ed., 1886: "Sacrilege"—A relatively short article the author of which quite apparently had a restricted definition for "sacrilege": "robbery of churches," "breaking or defacing of an altar, crucifix, or cross," etc.

[50] Encyclopaedia Britannica (11th ed., 1911), "Sacrilege."

[51] Schroeder, Constitutional Free Speech (1919), 178–373, makes a lengthy review of "Prosecutions for Crimes Against Religion." The examples in the text are from Schroeder. See also Encyclopaedia of the Social Sciences, "Blasphemy"; Encyclopaedia of Religion and Ethics, "Blasphemy"; Nokes, A History of the Crime of Blasphemy (1928).

perform it became so. At different times during that century, with the shifts in the attitude of government towards particular religious views, persons who doubted the doctrine of the Trinity (*e.g.*, Unitarians, Universalists, etc.) or the divinity of Christ, observed the Sabbath on Saturday, denied the possibility of witchcraft, repudiated child baptism or urged methods of baptism other than sprinkling, were charged as blasphemers, or their books were burned or banned as blasphemous. Blasphemy was the chameleon phrase which meant the criticism of whatever the ruling authority of the moment established as orthodox religious doctrine.[52] While it is true that blasphemy prosecutions have continued in England—although in lessening numbers—into the present century,[53] the existence there of an established church gives more definite contours to the crime in England than the term "sacrilegious" can possibly have in this country. Moreover, the scope of the English common-law crime of blasphemy has been considerably limited by the declaration that "if the decencies of controversy are observed, even the fundamentals of religion may be attacked,"[54] a limitation which the New York court has not put upon the Board of Regents' power to declare a motion picture "sacrilegious."

In *Cantwell* v. *Connecticut*, 310 U.S. 296, 310, Mr. Justice Roberts, speaking for the whole Court, said: "In the realm of religious faith, and in that of political belief, sharp differences arise. In both fields the tenets of one man may seem the rankest error to his neighbor." Conduct and beliefs dear to one may seem the rankest "sacrilege" to another. A few examples suffice to show the difficulties facing a conscientious censor or motion picture producer or distributor in determining what the New York statute condemns as sacrilegious. A motion picture portraying Christ as divine—for example, a movie showing medieval Church art—would offend the religious opinions of the members of several Protestant denominations who do not believe in the Trinity, as well as those of a non-Christian faith. Conversely, one showing Christ as merely an ethical teacher could not but offend millions of Christians of many denominations. Which is "sacrilegious"? The doctrine of transubstantiation, and the veneration of relics or particular stone and wood embodiments of saints or divinity, both sacred to Catholics, are offensive to a great many Protestants, and therefore for them sacrilegious in the view of the New York court. Is a picture treating either subject, whether sympathetically, unsympathetically, or neutrally, "sacrilegious"? It is not a sufficient answer to say that

"sacrilegious" is definite, because all subjects that in any way might be interpreted as offending the religious beliefs of any one of the 300 sects of the United States[55] are banned in New York. To allow such vague, undefinable powers of censorship to be exercised is bound to have stultifying consequences on the creative process of literature and art—for the films are derived largely from literature. History does not encourage reliance on the wisdom and moderation of the censor as a safeguard in the exercise of such drastic power over the minds of men. We not only do not know but cannot know what is condemnable by "sacrilegious." And if we cannot tell, how are those to be governed by the statute to tell?

It is this impossibility of knowing how far the form of words by which the New York Court of Appeals explained "sacrilegious" carries the proscription of religious subjects that makes the term unconstitutionally vague.[56] To stop short of proscribing all subjects that might conceivably be interpreted to be religious, inevitably creates a situation whereby the censor bans only that against which there is a substantial outcry from a religious group. And that is the fair inference to be drawn, as a matter of experience, from what has been happening under the New York censorship. Consequently the film industry, normally not guided by creative artists, and cautious in putting large capital to the hazards of courage, would be governed by its notions of the feelings likely to be aroused by diverse religious sects, certainly the powerful ones. The effect of such demands upon art and upon those whose function is to enhance the culture of a society need not be labored.

To paraphrase Doctor Johnson, if nothing may be shown but what licensors may have previously approved, power, the yea-or-nay-saying by officials, becomes the standard of the permissible. Prohibition through words that fail to convey what is permitted and what is prohibited for want of appropriate objective standards, offends Due Process in two ways. First, it does not sufficiently apprise those bent on obedience of law of what may reasonably be foreseen to be found illicit by the law-enforcing authority, whether court or jury or administrative agency. Secondly, where licensing is rested, in the first instance, in an administrative agency, the available judicial review is in effect rendered inoperative. On the basis of such a portmanteau word as "sacrilegious," the judiciary has no standards with which to judge the validity of administrative action which necessarily involves, at least in

[52] 1 Yorke, The Life of Lord Chancellor Hardwicke (1913), 80, writes thus of the prosecution of Thomas Woolston for blasphemy: "The offence, in the first place, consisted in the publication in 1725 of a tract entitled *A Moderator between an Infidel and an Apostate*, in which the author questioned the historical accuracy of the Resurrection and the Virgin Birth. Such speculations, however much they might offend the religious feeling of the nation, would not now arouse apprehensions in the civil government, or incur legal penalties; but at the time of which we are writing, when the authority of government was far less stable and secure and rested on far narrower foundations than at present, such audacious opinions were considered, not without some reason, as a menace, not only to religion but to the state."

[53] See, *e.g.*, *Rex* v. *Boulter*, 72 J.P. 188 (1908); *Bowman* v. *Secular Society, Ltd.*, [1917] A.C. 406.

[54] *Reg.* v. *Ramsay*, 15 Cox's C.C. 231, 238 (1883) (Lord Coleridge's charge to the jury); *Bowman* v. *Secular Society, Ltd.*, [1917] A.C. 406.

[55] The latest available statistics of the Bureau of the Census give returns from 256 denominations; 57 other denominations, which did not report, are listed. Bureau of the Census, Religious Bodies: 1936, Vol. I, iii, 7.

[56] It is not mere fantasy to suggest that the effect of a ban of the "sacrilegious" may be to ban all motion pictures dealing with any subject that might be deemed religious by any sect. The industry's self-censorship has already had a distorting influence on the portrayal of historical figures. "Pressure forced deletion of the clerical background of Cardinal Richelieu from *The Three Musketeers*. The [Motion Picture Production] code provision appealed to was the section providing that ministers should not be portrayed as villains." Note, "Motion Pictures and the First Amendment," 60 Yale L.J. 696, 716, n. 42.

The press recently reported that plans are being made to film a "Life of Martin Luther." N. Y. Times, April 27, 1952, § 2, p. 5, col. 7. Could Luther be sympathetically portrayed and not appear "sacrilegious" to some; or unsympathetically, and not to others?

large measure, subjective determinations. Thus, the administrative first step becomes the last step.

From all that has been said one is compelled to conclude that the term "sacrilegious" has come down the stream of time encrusted with a specialized, strictly confined meaning, pertaining to things in space not things in the mind. The New York Court of Appeals did not give the term this calculable content. It applied it to things in the mind, and things in the mind so undefined, so at large, as to be more patently in disregard of the requirement for definiteness, as the basis of proscriptions and legal sanctions for their disobedience, than the measures that were condemned as violative of Due Process in *United States* v. *Cohen Grocery Co.*, 255 U.S. 81; *A. B. Small Co.* v. *American Sugar Refining Co.*, 267 U.S. 233; *Connally* v. *General Construction Co.*, 269 U.S. 385; *Winters* v. *New York*, 333 U.S. 507; *Kunz* v. *New York*, 340 U.S. 290. This principle is especially to be observed when what is so vague seeks to fetter the mind and put within unascertainable bounds the varieties of religious experience.

APPENDIX TO OPINION OF

MR. JUSTICE FRANKFURTER*

Cockeram, English Dictionarie (10th ed., London, 1651).
  Blasphemy: No entry.
  Sacrilege: "The robbing of a Church, the stealing of holy things, abusing of Sacraments or holy Mysteries."
  Sacrilegious: "Abominable, very wicked."
Blount, Glossographia (3d ed., London, 1670).
  Blasphemy: No entry.
  Sacrilege: "the robbing a Church, or other holy consecrated place, the stealing holy things, or abusing Sacraments or holy Mysteries."
  Sacrilegious: "that robs the Church; wicked, extremely bad."
Blount, A Law-Dictionary (London, 1670).
  Blasphemy: No entry.
  Sacrilege: No entry.
Phillips, The New World of Words (3d ed., London, 1671).
  Blasphemy: "an uttering of reproachfull words, tending either to the dishonour of God, or to the hurt and disgrace of any mans name and credit."
  Sacrilegious: "committing Sacriledge, *i.e.* a robbing of Churches, or violating of holy things."
Cowel, The Interpreter of Words and Terms (Manley ed., London, 1701).
  Blasphemy: No entry.
  Sacrilege: "an Alienation to Lay-Men, and to profane or common purposes, of what was given to Religious Persons, and to Pious Uses, etc."
Rastell, Law Terms (London, 1708).
  Blasphemy: No entry.
  Sacrilege: "is, when one steals any Vessels, Ornaments, or Goods of Holy Church, which is felony, 3 Cro. 153, 154."
Kersey, A General English Dictionary (3d ed., London, 1721).
  Blasphemy: "an uttering of reproachful Words, that tend to the Dishonour of God, &c."
  Sacrilege: "the stealing of Sacred Things, Church robbing."

Cocker, English Dictionary (London, 1724).
  Blasphemy: No entry.
  Sacrilege: "robbing the Church, or what is dedicated thereto."
Bailey, Universal Etymological English Dictionary (London, 1730).
  Blasphemy: "an uttering of reproachful words tending to the dishonour of God, &c. vile, base language."
  Sacrilege: "the stealing of sacred Things, Church-Robbing; the Crime of profaning sacred Things, or alienating to Laymen, or common Uses, what was given to pious Uses and religious Persons."
Coles, An English Dictionary (London, 1732).
  Blasphemy: "reproach."
  Sacrilege: "the robbing of God, the church, &c."
Bullokar, The English Expositor (14th ed., London, 1731).
  Blasphemy: No entry.
  Sacrilege: "The Robbing of a Church; the Stealing of holy things, or Abusing of Sacraments or holy Mysteries."
Defoe, A Compleat English Dictionary (Westminster, 1735).
  Blasphemy: "vile or opprobrious Language, tending to the Dishonour of God."
  Sacrilege: "the stealing of sacred Things, Church robbing."
Bailey, An Universal Etymological English Dictionary (London, 1742).
  Blasphemy: "Cursing and Swearing, vile reproachful Language, tending to the Dishonour of God."
  Sacrilege: "the stealing of Sacred Things, Church Robbing; an Alienation to Laymen, and to profane and common Purposes, of what was given to religious Persons, and to pious Uses."
Martin, A New Universal English Dictionary (London, 1754).
  Blasphemy: "cursing, vile language tending to the dishonour of God or religion."
  Sacrilege: "the stealing things out of a holy place, or the profaning things devoted to God."
Johnson, A Dictionary of the English Language (2d ed., London, 1755).
  Blasphemy: "strictly and properly, is an offering of some indignity, or injury, unto God himself, either by words or writing."
  Sacrilege: "The crime of appropriating to himself what is devoted to religion; the crime of robbing heaven; the crime of violating or profaning things sacred."
Rider, A New Universal English Dictionary (London, 1759).
  Blasphemy: "an offering some indignity to God, any person of the Trinity, any messengers from God; his holy writ, or the doctrines of revelation, either by speaking or writing any thing ill of them, or ascribing any thing ill to them inconsistent with their natures and the reverence we owe them."
  Sacrilege: "the crime of taking any thing dedicated to divine worship. The crime of profaning any thing sacred."
  Profane: "to apply any thing sacred to common use. To be irreverent to sacred persons or things. To put to a wrong use."
Gordon and Marchant, A New Complete English Dictionary (London, 1760).

---

* See Matthews, A Survey of English Dictionaries (1933).

Blasphemy: "is an offering some indignity to God himself."

Sacrilege: "is the crime of appropriating to himself what is devoted to religion; the crime of robbing Heaven."

Buchanan, A New English Dictionary (London, 1769).

Blasphemy: "Language tending to the dishonour of God."

Sacrilege: "The stealing things out of a holy place."

Cunningham, A New and Complete Law-Dictionary (London, 1771).

Blasphemy: A long definition reading in part: "Is an injury offered to God, by denying that which is due and belonging to him, or attributing to him what is not agreeable to his nature."

Sacrilege: "Is church robbery, or a taking of things out of a holy place; as where a person steals any vessels, ornaments, or goods of the church. And it is said to be a robbery of God, at least of what is dedicated to his service. 2 Cro. 153, 154.

". . . an alienation to lay-men, and to profane or common purposes, of what was given to religious persons, and to pious uses."

Kenrick, A New Dictionary of the English Language (London, 1773).

Blasphemy: "Treating the name and attributes of the Supreme Being with insult and indignity."

Sacrilege: "The crime of appropriating to himself what is devoted to religion; *the crime of robbing heaven,* says Johnson; the crime of violating or profaning things sacred."

Profane: "To violate; to pollute.—To put to wrong use."

Ash, The New and Complete Dictionary of the English Language (London, 1775).

Blasphemy: "The act of speaking or writing reproachfully of the Divine Being, the act of attributing to the creature that which belongs to the Creator."

Sacrilege: "The act of appropriating to one's self what is devoted to religion, the crime of violating sacred things."

Dyche, A New General English Dictionary (London, 1777).

Blasphemy: "the reproaching or dishonouring God, religion, and holy things."

Sacrilege: "the stealing or taking away those things that were appropriated to religious uses or designs."

Sacrilegious: "of a profane, thievish nature, sort, or disposition."

Barclay, A Complete and Universal English Dictionary (London, 1782).

Blasphemy: "an offering some indignity to God, any person of the Trinity, any messengers from God, his holy writ, or the doctrines of revelation."

Sacrilege: "the crime of taking any thing dedicated to divine worship, or profaning any thing sacred."

Profane: "to apply any thing sacred to common use. To be irreverent to sacred persons or things."

Lemon, English Etymology (London, 1783).

Blaspheme: *"to speak evil of any one; to injure his fame, or reputation."*

Sacrilege: No entry.

Entick, New Spelling Dictionary (London, 1786).

Blasphemy: "indignity offered to God."

Blasphemer: "one who abuses God."

Sacrilege: "the robbery of a church or chapel."

Sacrilegious: "violating a thing made sacred."

Burn, A New Law Dictionary (Dublin, 1792).

Blasphemy: "See Prophaneness."

Profaneness: A long definition, not reproduced here.

Sacrilege: "robbing of the church, or stealing things out of a sacred place."

Sheridan, A Complete Dictionary of the English Language (6th ed., Phila., 1796).

Blasphemy: "Offering of some indignity to God."

Sacrilege: "The crime of robbing a church."

Scott, Dictionary of the English Language (Edinburgh, 1797).

Blasphemy: "indignity offered to God."

Sacrilege: "the robbery of a church, &c."

Richardson, A New Dictionary of the English Language (London, 1839).

Blasphemy: "To attack, assail, insult, (the name, the attributes, the ordinances, the revelations, the will or government of God.)"

Sacrilege: "to take away, to steal any thing *sacred,* or consecrated, or dedicated to holy or religious uses."

Bell, A Dictionary and Digest of the Law of Scotland (Edinburgh, 1861).

Blasphemy: "is the denying or vilifying of the Deity, by speech or writing."

Sacrilege: "is any violation of things dedicated to the offices of religion."

Staunton, An Ecclesiastical Dictionary (N.Y., 1861).

Blasphemy: A long entry.

Sacrilege: "The act of violating or subjecting sacred things to profanation; or the desecration of objects consecrated to God. Thus, the robbing of churches or of graves, the abuse of sacred vessels and altars by employing them for unhallowed purposes, the plundering and misappropriation of alms and donations, are acts of sacrilege, which in the ancient Church were punished with great severity."

Bouvier, A Law Dictionary (11th ed., Phila., 1866).

Blasphemy: "To attribute to God that which is contrary to his nature, and does not belong to him, and to deny what does; or it is a false reflection uttered with a malicious design of reviling God."

Sacrilege: "The act of stealing from the temples or churches dedicated to the worship of God, articles consecrated to divine uses."

Shipley, A Glossary of Ecclesiastical Terms (London, 1872).

Blasphemy: "Denying the existence or providence of God; contumelious reproaches of Jesus Christ; profane scoffing at the holy Scriptures, or exposing any part thereof to contempt or ridicule."

Sacrilege: "The profanation or robbery of persons or things which have been solemnly dedicated to the service of God. *v.* 24 & 25 Vict. c. 96, s. 50."

Brown, A Law Dictionary (Sprague ed., Albany, 1875).

Blasphemy: "To revile at or to deny the truth of Christianity as by law established, is a blasphemy, and as such is punishable by the common law. . . ."

Sacrilege: "A desecration of any thing that is holy. The alienation of lands which were given to religious purposes to laymen, or to profane and common purposes, was also termed sacrilege."

■ State
v.
Scope.
No. 43, March term, 1951.

Superior Court of Delaware. New Castle.

Jan. 4, 1952.

John Scope, owner and operator of the Manor Theater, and Charles Emerson, his film operator, were indicted on a number of counts charging them with the exhibition of a certain obscene, lewd and indecent film entitled "Hollywood Peep Show" in New Castle County, Delaware, on the third and fourth days of January, 1951. Other counts of the indictment charged Scope alone with the possession of the film with the intention of exhibiting it and with advertising certain obscene and indecent posters in connection with the showing thereof.

At the request of the State, the Court, the jury and the State psychiatrist, later called as an expert witness, viewed the entire film. Among other evidence, it was brought out that approximately 85% of the audience on both nights in question were "teen-agers." The psychiatrist, Dr. Tarumianz, was then permitted to testify, in effect, that the film was very apt to produce a deleterious effect upon the minds and passions of a "teen-age" group and, furthermore, would, undoubtedly, tend to rouse the baser emotions of the normal adult male, if not directly, then at least in his sub-conscious mind. This testimony was objected to and an exception preserved. Thereafter, the jury returned a verdict of guilty on all counts as to the defendant, Scope, but acquitted Emerson.

The matter is now before us on Scope's motion for a new trial which is based upon alleged error in the admission of the expert testimony of Dr. Tarumianz, just referred to, and in the Court's refusal to admit into evidence certain pictures and advertisements in current magazines of national circulation offered for the purpose of demonstrating the prevailing tolerant attitude of the public toward the exhibition of risque films. Scope's conviction on the counts charging him with the exhibition of indecent posters in connection with the advertising of the film is not challenged by this motion.

H. Albert Young, Atty. Gen., for plaintiff.
Anthony F. Emory, Wilmington, for defendant.

RICHARDS, President Judge, and LAYTON, J., sitting.

LAYTON, Judge, delivering the opinion.

[1, 2] This defendant was indicted and convicted for a violation of Vol. 43, Chapt. 239, Laws of Delaware, which, insofar as pertinent here, reads: "Whoever * * * exhibits * * * or has in his possession with intent to * * * exhibit, * * * or knowingly advertises * * * any obscene, lewd, lascivious, filthy, indecent * * * drawing, photograph, film, figure or image, * * * is guilty of a misdemeanor."

This chapter is no more than a re-enactment of the English Common Law offense known as obscene libel which in *Regina* v. *Hicklin*, L.R. 3; Q.B. 360 (Eng. 68), was defined as being "* * * whether the tendency of the matter charged as obscenity is to deprave and corrupt those whose minds are open to such immoral influences and into whose hands a publication of this sort may fall." This test—the effect of the obscene matter on those most susceptible—influenced the thinking of the earlier decisions in this country for many years. *Swearingen* v. *U.S.*, 1896, 161 U.S. 446, 16 S. Ct. 562, 40 L. Ed. 765; *People* v. *Muller*, 1884, 96 N.Y. 408; *U.S.* v. *Smith*, D.C., 1891, 45 F. 476. However, censorship, particularly of books, resulting from a rigid application of the principle of *Regina* v. *Hicklin*, produced unfortunate consequences[1] and, moreover, tended to exclude much valid contemporary literature from being transmitted through the United States mails. Also, works of recognized merit were being banned in Boston and New York where the vice societies were particularly active. As a result, the rule of *Regina* v. *Hicklin* has gradually been remoulded in order that the benefits of those works of art and science, the dominant tone of which is truth and sincerity in portrayal, might be preserved. Illustrative of the modern rule is *Parmelee* v. *U.S.*, 72 App. D.C. 203, 113 F. 2d 729, 736, where it is stated: "The statute involved in the present case was interpreted in *United States* v. *One Book* Entitled Ulysses, and the decision in that case is equally applicable here. 'It is settled,' says the court in the Ulysses case, 'that works of physiology, medicine, science, and sex instruction are not within the statute, though to some extent and among some persons they may tend to promote lustful thoughts.' It should be equally true of works of sociology, as of physiology, medicine and other sciences—to say nothing of general literature and the arts—that 'where the presentation,

---

[1] "The foolish judgments of Lord Eldon about one hundred years ago, proscribing the works of Byron and Southey, and the finding by the jury under a charge by Lord Denman that the publication of Shelley's 'Queen Mab' was an indictable offense are a warning to all who have to determine the limits of the field within which authors may exercise themselves." A. Hand, Judge, in *U.S.* v. *One Book* Entitled Ulysses, 2 Cir., 72 F. 2d 705, 708.

when viewed objectively, is sincere, and the erotic matter is not introduced to promote lust and does not furnish the dominant note of the publication,' the same immunity should apply."

Thus, in *U.S. v. Dennett*, 2 Cir., 39 F. 2d 564, 565, 76 A.L.R. 1092, the Court reversed the conviction of the defendant below, who had been found guilty of publishing an alleged obscene pamphlet entitled "Sex Side of Life," for the reason that it regarded the pamphlet as a sane, sincere and wholesome approach to the subject for adolescents. And in *U.S. v. One Book* Entitled Ulysses, 2 Cir., 72 F. 2d 705, 707, the Circuit Court sustained the District Court's dismissal of a libel against James Joyce's "Ulysses" because it concluded that the erotic matter found therein was not introduced "to promote lust" and did not "furnish the dominant note of the publication."

[3] In other words, the emphasis today is placed on whether the alleged offensive work represents dirt for dirt's sake. If not, then the statute is not offended—if so, and if the result tends to arouse the baser passions of the average, not the most susceptible, person, then the statute will be found to have been violated.

It is the admission of the expert testimony to the effect that the film in question would have a deleterious effect sexually upon the minds of adolescents and tend to arouse the baser passions of a normal person, at least in the subconscious mind, that is here challenged.[2] There is no doubt but what the earlier authorities excluded expert opinion evidence in cases of this sort. *People v. Muller*, 96 N.Y. 408. And respectable modern authority supports the rule, *Commonwealth v. Isenstadt*, 318 Mass. 543, 62 N.E. 2d 840. The reason for the rule is that "The testimony of experts is not admissible upon matters of judgment within the knowledge and experience of ordinary jury men." *People v. Muller*, supra. On the other hand, the so-called "opinion evidence rule" has been the subject of much criticism. Wigmore on Evidence, Vol. 7, Secs. 1917–1929. And a number of recent opinions have permitted the introduction of such evidence in cases involving obscenity

---

[2] "A. From my past experience, I have found that such films are not only detrimental to the youth, but detrimental to any human being who has normal endowments and is not peculiarly psychopathically inclined. It creates a various deviation of thinking and emotional instability in regard to sex problems. A happily married individual who is considered a mature adult individual, seeing such films, becomes seriously concerned with whether he is obtaining the necessary gratification of his sex desires from his normal and normally endowed and inclined wife. It may deviate him in accepting that there is something which arouses him to become interested in an abnormal type of sex satisfaction which he has had perhaps from this picture. So that it is unquestionably seriously detrimental to the adults. As to the juveniles, it is my sincere opinion that we consider very seriously that their normal development of our youth who eventually have to become the backbone of this country and civilization.

"Q. Doctor, will you tell us whether this picture which you witnessed is one which is calculated and designed to excite lustful thoughts and lascivious desires and stir the sex impulses of individuals? A. Yes, I am definite on that.

"Q. What would be the percentage of the individual persons who would be stirred into lustful desire? A. I wouldn't go into percentage. I would say that the majority of the normal individuals might have been so.

"Q. Normal individuals, like members of the jury and myself, might become lustfully desiring? A. The majority of people will become so if they don't express so. Sub-consciously they would."

---

statutes. *Parmelee v. U.S.*, supra, states the reason to be as follows: "With such considerations in mind, perhaps the most useful definition of obscene is that suggested in the case of *U.S. v. Kennerley* [D.C., 209 F. 119], i.e., that it indicates 'the present critical point in the compromise between candor and shame at which the community may have arrived here and now.' But when we attempt to locate that critical point in the situation of the present case, we find nothing in the record to guide us except the book itself. The question is a difficult one, as to which the expert opinions of psychologists and sociologists would seem to be helpful if not necessary. Assumptions to the contrary which appear in some of the earlier cases, reveal the profound ignorance of psychology and sociology which prevailed generally, when those opinions were written. More recently, in the cases and textbooks, the desirability and pertinence of such evidence has been suggested. Lacking such assistance in the present case, we can compensate for it in some measure by noticing, judicially, evidence which is thus available to us." See also *People v. Larsen*, Sp. Sess., 5 N.Y.S. 2d 55.

[4] But the same considerations which would require the admission of expert evidence in cases such as *Parmelee v. U.S.*, just referred to, cannot be regarded as persuasive here, where the alleged offensive matter was a moving picture of a burlesque show and obviously far removed from the fields of art or science. Hence, the admission of the questioned testimony must be examined in the light of the general rule prohibiting the introduction of expert opinion evidence under circumstances wherein the jury are as well qualified to judge of the matter as an expert. In *Scotton v. Wright*, 14 Del. Ch. 124, 122 A. 541, 544, former Chancellor Wolcott had occasion to review the rule and said this: "Here the court in the first instance must use its reasonable discretion in determining two things: First, is the subject-matter one that properly falls within the field of expert or special knowledge; and, second, if so, is the witness sufficiently qualified by learning or experience to speak illuminatingly with respect thereto? * * * If, however, the jury are as well qualified by knowledge and experience as the witness to draw the proper inference from these facts, then the witness' opinion should be rejected."

[5, 6] Tested by these standards, we think that there is a reasonable basis for the admission of the expert's opinion that the film in question would tend to have harmful results, at least in the sub-conscious mind, of the average, normal man. The science of psychiatry, while still in its infancy, has made tremendous strides in recent years. Much of it has to do with the workings of the sub-conscious mind about which the average person obviously knows nothing. If, therefore, it is a fact that the effect of this film might be latent, rather than immediate—that its deleterious effects would linger with probable future undesirable, emotional results not even realized in the conscious mind—then we can see no error in admitting such testimony upon the theory that it would be material and helpful to a jury. However, we doubt if the admission of the evidence as to the effect of the film upon the conscious mind of the normal adult was correct in view of the prevailing rule just quoted and for somewhat different reasons there would seem to have been error in the admission of the evidence regarding the probable harmful effects of this film upon the minds of adolescents. Had the indictment

charged this defendant with exhibiting an indecent film under circumstances wherein it might be reasonably expected that the probable audience would be composed largely of adolescents, the rule of *Regina* v. *Hicklin* might be evoked—that is to say, the test would then be the effect of the film upon the minds of those most susceptible. *U.S.* v. *Levine,* 2 Cir., 83 F. 2d 156. But as it is, the indictment calls for the application of the rule as to the effect of the film upon the mind of the average, normal man and, strictly speaking, it is doubtful whether the admission of the testimony as to its effect upon adolescents was correct.

[7] Nevertheless, although the admission of the testimony regarding the probable effect of the film upon the minds of the normal adult and of the youthful members of the audience may have been error, a new trial would not be granted unless the Court is convinced that the rights of the defendant were thereby prejudiced. As Chancellor Wolcott stated in *Scotton* v. *Wright,* supra: "If, however, it be conceded that the Superior Court did err in this regard, it does not follow that a new trial should be granted. Even though error may have been committed in rejecting or admitting evidence, yet if the Chancellor is satisfied that such error could have had no prejudicial effect and that the verdict so far as such error could in any way legitimately affect it is nevertheless right, the new trial will be denied. (citations) If the rejected opinion evidence had been received, its probative value in view of all the other facts in the case would have been of so little weight as not to be entitled to influence the jury."

[8, 9] The jury heard the film described and saw it portrayed. It was no more than a complete movie of a low grade burlesque. The so called dances were accompanied by highly suggestive motions of the body known as "bumps" and "grinds." All the dancers were in a semi-nude state and some of the dances, being strip tease acts, ended with the female performer in a completely naked condition except for the proverbial fig leaf. Interwoven into this dreary scene was the usual low and suggestive comedy dialogue of the alleged comedians. The shocking actions of some of the "teen-age" audience upon emerging from the show were testified to without objection by defendant, thus tending to open the door to some extent for the further evidence of the psychiatrist. Indeed, all the elements of the statutory offense were clearly and monotonously depicted for a period of some two hours. After seeing this film, it would have been surprising had the jury come to any other conclusion than it did despite the testimony objected to. Under all the circumstances and in view of the fact that the charge to the jury correctly defined the offense,[3] the error, if any, in admitting this testimony was not, in our judgment, prejudicial.

[10] There remains to be considered defendant's assignment of error concerning our refusal to admit into evidence certain suggestive pictures of semi-nude women appearing in advertisements or otherwise, in magazines of national circulation. It is argued that such matter was material to the issue here in that it demonstrates the tolerant attitude of the public in general regarding such portrayals and the consequent unlikelihood that this film would have a harmful effect upon the normal man, accustomed to seeing such pictures on every side. We cannot agree. The defendant here is on trial. Whether or not the publishers of magazines are so conducting their business as to offend the statute is not part of this inquiry and is not material to the issue here. *Commonwealth* v. *Donaducy,* 167 Pa. Super. 611, 76 A. 2d 440; *State* v. *Ulsemer,* 24 Wash. 657, 64 P. 800. This evidence was properly excluded.

The motion for a new trial is denied.

---

[3] A motion picture is obscene, lewd, lascivious, filthy, indecent, within the meaning of the statute when the language, sounds and actions therein are offensive to the common sense of decency and modesty of the community, and when the dominant theme of the motion picture, considered as a whole, is calculated to and is likely to excite lustful thoughts and lecherous desires or to stir the sex impulses or to lead to sexually impure thoughts in the ordinary average person who is likely to see the film.

■ Sunshine Book Co. et al.

v.

McCaffrey, Commissioner of Licenses of City of New York, et al.

Supreme Court, Special Term, New York County, Part III.

April 25, 1952.

Denis M. Hurley, Corporation Counsel of the City of New York (Arthur J. Goldsmith and George J. Elkins, of counsel), in opposition.

CORCORAN, Justice.

In this action for a declaratory judgment and for a permanent injunction against the Commissioners of Police and of Licenses of the City of New York, the plaintiffs now move for an injunction pendente lite.

The plaintiff Sunshine Book Company is a non-profit corporation organized under the laws of the State of New Jersey. It publishes a monthly periodical called "Sunshine and Health," which is the official publication of the American Sunbathing Association, Inc., (not a party to this action). The plaintiff Solar Union Naturisme, Inc., is also a New Jersey non-profit corporation. It publishes a bi-monthly periodical, "Solaire Universelle de Nudisme," also known as "SUN Magazine." The plaintiff Ilsley Boone is the managing editor of "Sunshine and Health" and the editor of "SUN Magazine." The plaintiff G.I. Distributors, Inc., a New York corporation, is in the business of distributing numerous periodicals, including those mentioned, to newsdealers in New York City.

In November, 1951, a number of persons, who operate stationery stores or newsstands in the City of New York, were arrested by police officers for selling or having for sale the magazines, "Sunshine & Health" and "SUN Magazine." They were charged with violating Section 1141 of the Penal Law which, among other things, prohibits the sale or distribution, or the possession for sale or distribution, of "any obscene, lewd, lascivious, filthy, indecent or disgusting book, magazine, pamphlet, newspaper * * * photograph [etc.]."

The plaintiffs state the names and addresses of four of the newsdealers who were arrested. None of them is a party to this action, but the plaintiffs allege that the arrests of these newsdealers for selling the magazines which the plaintiffs publish or distribute has resulted in a refusal by newsdealers to handle these magazines. The Police Commissioner makes no issue of the fact that the arrests of the newsdealers will deter them and other newsdealers from offering these magazines for sale to the general public, and I assume that the arrests will have such an effect.

In that same month, November, 1951, the Commissioner of Licenses of the City of New York sent to newsdealers licensed under the jurisdiction of his Department the following notice:

"Department of Licenses
City of New York

To All Newsdealers Licensed under the Jurisdiction of the Department of Licenses:
You are cautioned to discontinue the sale and to remove from display the following magazines or periodicals:
Sunshine and Health
Sunbathing for Health Magazine
Modern Sunbathing and Hygiene
Hollywood Girls of the Month
Hollywood Models of the Month
In the event you display or offer for sale any of the above identified publications on or after November 27, 1951 steps will be taken looking to the suspension or revocation of your license.

Edward T. McCaffrey
Commissioner"

November 19, 1951

The publication "SUN Magazine" was inadvertently omitted from the list contained in the notice, but the plaintiffs and defendants agree that it should be deemed included. In any event, there is such a similarity between the magazine "Sunshine and Health," which is on the list, and "SUN Magazine" that the law applicable to one would be applicable to the other.

According to the plaintiffs, the issuance of the notice by the Commissioner of Licenses had the same effect of deterring sale and distribution of the magazines as did the arrests which were directed by the Commissioner of Police. The Commissioner of Licenses does not dispute this. It is, in fact, the very effect which his notice was intended to produce.

The complaint alleges that there was a conspiracy by both the Commissioner of Police and the Commissioner of Licenses to deprive the plaintiffs of their legal rights. The allegations of conspiracy are extremely broad, and there are no facts stated in the plaintiffs' affidavits to support these allegations. Each Commissioner in his answering affidavit states that he acted independently of the other and flatly denies the existence of any conspiracy. On this motion, consideration will be given only to those phases of it which are directed to each Commissioner separately because I do not find that there was any conspiracy.

The plaintiffs ask that the Police Commissioner be enjoined from prosecuting pending criminal proceedings against the newsdealers arrested and from instituting any new proceedings based on the sale or offer for sale of the periodicals, and that the Commissioner of Licenses be enjoined from threatening newsdealers under his jurisdiction with suspension or revocation of licenses if they sell or offer for sale the periodicals which the plaintiffs publish or distribute.

Copies of the November, 1951, and December 1951, issues of "Sunshine and Health" and of the November–December, 1951, and January–February, 1952, issues of "SUN Magazine" have been submitted by the plaintiffs with their assurance that they are typical of other issues of the magazines. Both periodicals are devoted exclusively to the theories and practices of nudism, "Sunshine and Health" being generally limited to the United States and Canada, and "SUN Magazine" being international in scope. The four issues contain reports of meeting and conventions, reports of officers, the "Olympic Games" of the movement, public relations theories for the expansion of nudism, reports of regional associations and local clubs, conflicts between nudism and the law, expositions of nudism for the advancement of physical and mental health, religious justifications of nudism, etc. There is nothing obscene in the literary content, and the defendants state in their brief: "Neither are we directly concerned with the 'nudist' question as such, nor with the publications of magazines or literature which advocate the practice of 'nudism.' "

In each of the issues there is a repletion of photographs of naked persons. These photographs have caused the present controversy. They generally fall into two categories. Some of them are action pictures showing nudists in their camp activities, rowing, hitting volley balls, building fires, etc. In others, the editors are more subtle in their glorification of nudism. They show shapely and attractive young women in alluring poses in the nude. It is significant that the photographs of the second category are the ones selected for the covers of all issues without exception. These photographs are front views. They are cleverly colored to picture clearly the female breasts and pubic hair. They take up nearly all the space on the covers, leaving only enough for the title, price and issue identification.

[1] That phase of the motion which seeks a temporary injunction against the Commissioner of Police is denied. The Commissioner will not be restrained from prosecuting the pending cases or from making arrests in the future. As was stated in *Mills Novelty Company* v. *Sunderman*, 266 N.Y. 32, at page 36, 193 N.E. 541, 542: "A court of equity, even where property interests are incidentally affected, will not ordinarily interfere with criminal processes, unless there would be irreparable injury, and the sole

question involved is one of law, *Delaney* v. *Flood*, 183 N.Y. 323, 76 N.E. 209, 2 L.R.A., N.S., 678." Obviously, only when the question of law is determined in favor of the applicant for relief will there be interference, assuming the presence of all other elements. *Truax* v. *Raich*, 239 U.S. 33, 36 S. Ct. 7, 60 L. Ed. 131, the case principally relied on by the plaintiffs, is in harmony with the rule of our state courts. In that case, the Supreme Court affirmed an interlocutory judgment of injunction granted by a court of equity against the prosecution of criminal proceedings. The statute there involved was unconstitutional and, under the facts of that case, unless enforcement of the statute was restrained, the complainants had no adequate remedy.

The case at bar does not fall within the rule of *Truax* v. *Raich* and, entirely apart from the question of equitable jurisdiction, I would not interfere with the acts of the Police Commissioner. Section 1141, subdivision 1 of the Penal Law, under which the Police Commissioner acted, is valid and constitutional. The Commissioner was properly performing his duty in causing the arrest of those who violate its provisions.

[2] The plaintiffs devote much of their brief to the argument that concepts of obscenity and indecency are variable. They contend that they are of such a shifting nature that there is no ascertainable standard of guilt under Section 1141, subdivision 1, and that the statute is therefore unconstitutional and unenforcible.

Simply because ideas of what is obscene vary from time to time and from place to place, does not leave us without a moral understanding in our own time and in our own community. It is true that the words obscene, lewd, lascivious and indecent, appearing in Section 1141, subdivision 1 of the Penal Law, are not technical legal terms, such as are the words homicide, rape and larceny. Indeed, it is difficult to give them any precise or comprehensive legal definition. But it does not follow that the statutory prohibition is therefore indefinite or variable. Indecency and obscenity have been offenses against the public order for generations (See Harris & Wilshire's Criminal Law [16th ed.], pp. 169, 170, 171; and 1 Bishop's Criminal Law [9th ed.], Sections 500, 504), and statutes similar to Section 1141, subdivision 1, have been adopted in many other states. The interpretation of what is prohibited may differ in details with changes of circumstances, but the pattern of protecting the people from public indecency remains the same.

The statute prohibits obscenity and indecency as we understand those terms in this state today. It is true that in determining what is obscene, "the law will not hold the crowd to the morality of saints and seers." (Cardozo, Paradoxes of Legal Science, p. 37.) But neither will it accept the judgment of sensualists and libertines. Nor is a criterion of proper conduct to be established by the antics of faddists. The test of decency is the fair judgment of reasonable adults in the community. The validity of such a test is well recognized in our jurisprudence, and the fact that there are variations depending upon the mores of the community does not destroy it.

Two jurists who have served as Chief Judges of our Court of Appeals have expressed this view. The late Judge Cardozo stated it in his Paradoxes of Legal Science, pp. 36, 37: "It comes down to this. There are certain forms of conduct which at any given place or epoch are commonly accepted under the combined influence of reason, practice

and tradition, as moral or immoral. If we were asked to define the precise quality that leads them to be so characterized, we might find it troublesome to make answer, yet the same difficulty is found in defining other abstract qualities, even those the most familiar. The forms of conduct thus discriminated are not the same at all times or in all places. Law accepts as the pattern of its justice the morality of the community whose conduct it assumes to regulate."

The present Chief Judge of our Court of Appeals, Judge Loughran, expressed the same view in *People* v. *Winters*, 294 N.Y. 545, at pages 551, 552, 63 N.E. 2d 98, at page 100: "In the nature of things there can be no more precise test of written indecency or obscenity than the continuing and changeable experience of the community as to what types of books are likely to bring about the corruption of public morals or other analogous injury to the public order. Consequently, a question as to whether a particular publication is indecent or obscene in that sense is a question of the times which must be determined as matter of fact, unless the appearances are thought to be necessarily harmless from the standpoint of public order or morality."

Although the United States Supreme Court, in *Winters* v. *People of State of New York*, 333 U.S. 507, 68 S. Ct. 665, 92 L. Ed. 840, reversed the decision of the Court of Appeals in *People* v. *Winters*, supra, it had before it an entirely different statutory provision than the one involved in this case. At that time, Section 1141 of the Penal Law consisted of two subdivisions. Subdivision 1 was basically the same as it now is. It was subdivision 2 that was struck down and the Supreme Court, after holding the second subdivision invalid for indefiniteness, cited subdivision 1 as an illustration of a statute which met the test of definiteness.

The plaintiffs rely heavily upon *Parmelee* v. *United States*, 72 App. D.C. 203, 113 F. 2d 729. That case held that books entitled "Nudism in Modern Life," which contained pictures of nude men and women, were not obscene. The court found that only a few photographs were questionable and that they did not furnish the dominant note of the publications. These photographs, incidentally, were unretouched and uncolored. There is no denying the fact, however, that the majority opinion in the Parmelee case appears to support the plaintiffs' views. Insofar as it does, it is rejected as unsound. There are numerous references in that opinion to the writings of sociologists and psychologists upon whose opinions the plaintiffs also rely. At page 737, of 113 F. 2d, the opinion states: "There are many unexplored areas of social science. If anything, there is needed today greater patience and greater tolerance concerning research in sociology than in medicine; looking to the day when social scientists can advise not only courts, but the people generally." Perhaps that day will sometime arrive. Until it does, the courts will do well to administer justice in accordance with the rules of positive morality, approved by the reasonable public opinion of the community.

The opinions of the anthropologist, sociologists and psychologists upon which the plaintiffs rely are not persuasive. The different customs and moral standards of ancient peoples, of African natives, of Australian aborigines, and of desert tribes, and the various concepts of these peoples as to what is chaste and demure, and as to what is immodest and lewd, afford us little assistance in determining what is obscene and indecent in the State of New York in the year 1952. Extreme and weird examples of deviations from our accepted standards can be found among the many races of mankind. Bizarre notions can also be found among civilized nations in man's long history. Such examples do not justify repetition in our society. It is interesting to note, nonetheless, that the authors upon whom the plaintiffs rely so heavily fail to give examples of any civilized nations that accepted the practice of nudism as a general custom. It would appear that even they must concede that the use of clothing to cover one's sexual organs has been, throughout history, the practice of all humans except for the lowest grades of savages.

Of course, nudity is not necessarily obscene. There are situations where no valid objection can be made to it. In the arts, in medicine, and in other sciences, we have ready examples. The fact that nudity in such instances may have the incidental effect of arousing sexual desires is not always sufficient reason for barring it. As to the conditions and circumstances under which nudity is permissible, reason sets the proper limits.

[3] Where the dominant purpose of nudity is to promote lust, it is obscene and indecent. The distribution and sale of the magazines in this case is a most objectionable example. The dominant purpose of the photographs in these magazines is to attract the attention of the public by an appeal to their sexual impulses. The sale of these magazines is not limited to any mailing list of members or subscribers. They are sold and distributed indiscriminately to all who wish to purchase the same. Men, women, youths of both sexes, and even children, can purchase these magazines. They will have a libidinous effect upon most ordinary, normal, healthy individuals. Their effect upon the abnormal individual may be more disastrous. Their sale and distribution is bound to add to the already burdensome problem of juvenile delinquency and sex crimes, and the Commissioner of Police properly arrested those who participated in this violation of our Penal Law.

With respect to that branch of the motion which seeks to restrain the Commissioner of Licenses, the plaintiffs contend that, even assuming the magazines in question do violate provisions of the Penal Law, the Commissioner had no right to send out the notice which he did. They argue that he is without jurisdiction to revoke newsdealers' licenses because of the nature of the publications which they sell or exhibit for sale. They also claim that the effect of his notice was to impose a prior restraint upon publication in violation of the State and Federal Constitutions.

The Commissioner of Licenses has licensing power over certain newsdealers. Sec. 773 of New York City Charter; Secs. B32–58.0 to B32–74.1 of the Administrative Code of New York City. In common with the heads of all departments of the city, he may make rules and regulations for the conduct of his office or department and to carry out its functions and duties. Section 885, subd. a of New York City Charter. Although his powers to make rules and regulations are unquestionably limited so that the Commissioner may not, by rule-making, accomplish the adoption of laws not already on the statute books, his powers would appear to include the adoption of rules and regulations to prevent newsdealers who are licensed by his Department from using those licenses to engage in activities in open and notorious violation of our Penal Laws.

It has been held, for example, that reasonable regula-

tions may be adopted by the Commissioner to aid him in performing duties assigned to him by statute. *Acorn Employment Service* v. *Moss*, 261 App. Div. 178, 24 N.Y.S. 2d 669. Reasonable rules barring the sale of "racing tip" sheets or "policy" slips would also appear to be within the Commissioner's powers. Cf. *Armstrong Racing Publications* v. *Moss*, 181 Misc. 966, 43 N.Y.S. 2d 171. I agree with the observation made in that case 43 N.Y.S. 2d at page 173, that the Commissioner, "in his official capacity, has, despite the ministerial character of his duties, certain supervisory and regulatory powers to be exercised, particularly to safeguard public morals."

The action of the License Commissioner does not constitute a prior restraint upon publication within the prohibition of the State and Federal Constitutions.

[4] The guaranty of freedom of speech and of the press contained in Article 1, Section 8 of the New York State Constitution and in the First and Fourteenth Amendments of the United States Constitution prevents prior restraints upon publication. The fact that a person abuses this liberty by publishing defamatory, scurrilous or other improper matter ordinarily does not justify the state or any of its agencies from restraining such person or such publication in the future.

There are recognized limitations to this principle, however. Justice Story in discussing the First Amendment of the Federal Constitution says (The Constitution, 5th ed., Vol. II, # 1880):

*"That the amendment was intended to secure to every citizen an absolute right to speak, or write, or print whatever he might please, without any responsibility, public or private, therefor, is a supposition too wild to be indulged by any rational man * * * the language of this amendment imports no more than that every man shall have a right to speak, write, and print his opinions upon any subject whatsoever, without any prior restraint, so always that he does not injure any other person in his rights, person, property, or reputation; and so always that he does not disturb the public peace. * * *"*

Near v. *State of Minnesota*, 283 U.S. 697, 51 S. Ct. 625, 626, 75 L. Ed. 1357, whose quotations are generously interspersed in the plaintiffs' brief, reiterates the constitutional doctrine that there can be no previous restraint upon publications. But the Supreme Court did not go as far as the plaintiffs contend. It did not hold that, even if obscene periodicals are openly and continuously sold in a community, the public is helpless to prevent recurrences by anticipatory action. Actually, both the majority and minority opinions indicated that, in such a situation, a community could protect itself by previous restraint. The Minnesota statute before the court provided that a person who possessed or sold "(a) an obscene, lewd and lascivious newspaper, magazine, or other periodical, or (b) a malicious, scandalous and defamatory newspaper, magazine or other periodical," Minn. Stats. 1927, § 10123–1, was guilty of a nuisance which could be enjoined. The question before the court involved clause (b) relative to scandalous and defamatory newspapers, and the court held that there could be no previous restraint under that subdivision. The court made it clear, however, that restraint under clause (a) relating to obscene, lewd and lascivious publications would be proper. It said 283 U.S. at pages 715, 716, 51 S. Ct. at page 631:

"The objection has also been made that the principle as to immunity from previous restraint is stated too broadly, if every such restraint is deemed to be prohibited. That is undoubtedly true; the protection even as to previous restraint is not absolutely unlimited. But the limitation has been recognized only in exceptional cases."

The court then stated that one of these exceptions was that "the primary requirements of decency may be enforced against obscene publications."

[5] The notice released by the Commissioner of Licenses does not constitute a prior restraint within the constitutional prohibition. In exploring the question of previous restraint, we should examine the essence of that notice. While it mentions the plaintiffs' periodicals by name, it is clear that it was not meant to apply to such periodicals if they did not contain pictures of nudes. Attached to the moving papers are clippings from New York newspapers concerning the Commissioner's notice when he released it to the press. The newspaper reports indicate very clearly that the notice, although mentioning a list of magazines by name, was actually directed against publications which contain photographs of nudes, such as those now before the court. The plaintiffs' submission of these newsclippings and the agreement of the parties that "SUN Magazine" should be included in the Commissioner's notice, even though it was not mentioned by name, shows that the parties so understood the notice. It was directed against the sale by newsdealers under the jurisdiction of the License Department, not of nudist magazines or literature, as such, but only against those which contain pictures of naked persons.

Perhaps the Commissioner should amend the notice to the newsdealers so that it will be made clear to them that the magazines referred to are objectionable when they contain pictures of nudes. It may be that the plaintiffs would eliminate the pictures in future issues. If they intend to do so, they may apply for relief. The temporary injunction will not now be granted, however, since it is clear from the papers submitted on the motion that the plaintiffs understood the notice to be directed against sale of the magazines as they presently appear. The temporary injunction is sought against any such notice by the Commissioner, even though limited in the way I have indicated.

The motion is in all respects denied.

■ People on Complaint of Arcuri
v.
Finkelstein.

City Magistrate's Court of City of New York, Borough of

Brooklyn. May 9, 1952.

Miles F. McDonald, Dist. Atty., Brooklyn (Edward Regan, Asst. Dist. Atty., Brooklyn, of counsel), for the People.

Alfred Newman, New York City, for defendant.

MALBIN, City Magistrate.

The defendant is charged with violating section 1141 of the Penal Law, which, among other things, prohibits the sale or offer to sell or the possession with intent to sell of any obscene, lewd, lascivious, filthy, indecent or disgusting magazines, pictures, photographs, &c. An examination was held in the Magistrate's Court. The People produced one witness, a police officer, who testified that he entered a candy store and luncheonette, and he observed on a magazine rack in front of the store pictures and photographs of nude females. The witness further stated that he purchased two sets of pictures (each set contained twelve photographs and a small brochure). He paid $1.50 for the two sets. These pictures were of a strip tease series. The exhibits indicate that the models are shown in various stages until complete nudity is achieved. The possession and sale of the exhibits, which consist of over 1,500 pictures, mostly of nude females, has not been contested nor controverted. The only issue presented to the court for its determination was whether the pictures were artistic nudes or were obscene and filthy and, therefore, within the category prohibited by statute.

[1] The sale of pictures of nude and semi-nude females does not, in and of itself, constitute a violation of section 1141 of the Penal Law. The defendant in the instant case sold such pictures with an accompanying brochure purporting to demonstrate their use for artistic endeavors.

[2, 3] Let us, first, examine the sale of these pictures unaccompanied by this brochure. This statute is designed to suppress, not bona fide literary and artistic effort, but the exploitation of smut, *Ultem Publications* v. *Arrow Publications*, 166 Misc. 645, 2 N.Y.S. 2d 933. If the tendency and the main purpose of the material is to excite lustful desires, and if all incidents and qualities are mere accessories to the primary purpose of stimulating immoral thought, then the material falls under the prohibition of the statute, *People* v. *Viking Press*, 1933, 147 Misc. 813, 264 N.Y.S. 534. The various factors to be considered include, among others, sincerity of purpose, literary or artistic worth, the channels of distribution and the types of persons who might reasonably be expected to secure the materials for perusal, with particular reference to their age

and mental development, People ex rel. *Kahan* v. *Creative Age Press*, 1948, 192 Misc. 188, 79 N.Y.S. 2d 198. Consider the facts in the case at bar in the light of the foregoing. The defendant is the manager of a candy store and luncheonette who sold the packages in question indiscriminately to any one who desired to purchase them. It cannot be seriously argued that this is the normal channel through which actual students of art usually buy their materials. Since this is the pretext with which these pictures were sold, the sincerity of purpose is, to put it most generously, at least suspect. The artistic worth of the pictures has not been argued.

[4–7] I, personally, fail to find anything of artistic merit in the pictures. The defendant makes no claim that he discriminated in the slightest degree among possible purchasers. It is the obligation of the court to protect weaker members of society from the corrupt influences exerted through immoral literature, drama and art, *People* v. *Friede*, 133 Misc. 611, 233 N.Y.S. 565. The normal, not the abnormal, person must serve as a criterion. The gravamen of the offense is the tendency of the matter to corrupt morals or to lower standards of right or wrong concerning sexual behavior, *People* v. *Larsen*, Sp. Sess., 5 N.Y.S. 2d 55. An important but not the sole test to be applied in determining whether a book offends the law against obscene publications is, does the matter charged as obscene tend to deprave or corrupt those whose minds are open to immoral influences and who might come in contact with it, ever bearing in mind the consideration that the statute looks to the protection not of the mature and intelligent, with minds strengthened to withstand the influence of the prohibited data, but of the young and immature, the ignorant and sensually inclined, *People* v. *Seltzer*, 122

Misc. 329, 203 N.Y.S. 809. The nude pictures of female figures were on display open to view to the young and impressionable, particularly to those the statute was expressly designed to protect, *People* v. *Smith*, 167 Misc. 560, 3 N.Y.S. 2d 651. The inclusion of the brochure is a transparent device and a subterfuge which cannot change or disguise the true nature and purpose of the materials. Pictures are obscene which tend to stir sexual impulses or to lead to sexually impure thoughts. It was so held in *People* v. *Gonzales*, Mag. Ct., 107 N.Y.S. 2d 968.

Let us look at this case with a realistic approach. Here is a small neighborhood store serving the families of the area. It caters to high school children who come in, observe these pictures, purchase them and seek dark corners and privacy to snicker over its contents and pass the pictures around among their friends. This is a condition we may not be able to cure, but when the opportunity arises to alleviate it, it should not be allowed to pass.

[8] The entire foregoing discussion applies also to magazines found in the possession of the same defendant. Containing numerous pictures of nudes and semi-nudes, it purports to teach photography. The photography taught by the magazine reaches the same level as the art taught by the pictures and can be similarly ignored. It is not required that the magistrate in the preliminary proceeding find beyond a reasonable doubt that the material is obscene, lewd and filthy. He could only find that it is prima facie within the prohibition of the statute to justify a holding of the defendant for trial in Special Sessions, *People* v. *London*, 1946, Mag. Ct., 63 N.Y.S. 2d 227. The motion to dismiss the information is accordingly denied and the defendant is held for trial in the Court of Special Sessions.

■ Noblett
v.
Commonwealth.

SUPREME COURT OF APPEALS OF VIRGINIA.

Sept. 10, 1952.

Edmunds, Whitehead, Baldwin & Graves, Lynchburg, for plaintiff in error.
J. Lindsay Almond, Jr., Atty. Gen., *Thomas M. Miller*, Asst. Atty. Gen., for defendant in error.

Before HUDGINS, C.J., and EGGLESTON, SPRATLEY, BUCHANAN and WHITTLE, JJ.

EGGLESTON, Justice.

Herman C. Noblett was convicted by a jury on a warrant charging that he did "unlawfully, lewdly and indecently expose his person to Betty Thomas, age 10, in a manner to shock the public sense of decency and morality." To the judgment entered upon that verdict we

granted a writ of error to review the sufficiency of the evidence and the rulings of the trial court in granting and refusing certain instructions.

The little girl testified that as she was walking along North Princeton Circle, a public street near her home in a residential area of the city of Lynchburg, shortly before noon on June 15, 1951, she saw a Ford automobile parked, headed into an alley which intersects Princeton Circle. The car was so placed that it blocked her passage along the crosswalk extending across the alley. As she approached the car she saw a young man, whom she identified as the defendant, sitting in the driver's seat. As she neared the righthand side of the car the defendant asked her whether she knew where "Miss Jones lived." She inquired, "What Miss Jones?" and he replied, "Miss Nannie Jones." While this conversation was going on, she said, she had gotten within one or two feet of the car. She saw that he was "exposing himself" and "playing with" "his privates." She then proceeded on her way, going around the rear of the car which was blocking the crosswalk. After she had gotten around the rear of the car the defendant called to her and said, "Did you see it?" "Come here and let me show you something." To this solicitation she said "No," and ran on to her home which was "four houses" away.

Upon reaching home the child related what had occurred and the matter was promptly reported to the police. The next day the child was interviewed by two members of the police department, to whom she gave an accurate description of the defendant and of his automobile.

On June 19 the defendant was apprehended while driving his car in the vicinity of the Thomas home. He denied the offense and consented to being taken before the child for possible identification. The child promptly and unhesitatingly identified him.

At the trial the defendant, twenty-three years of age and unmarried, took the stand and denied the charge which the child had made against him. He denied having seen her before, or that he was at or near the scene at the time the alleged offense took place. He testified that from about 10:30 a.m. until 2:30 p.m. on the day in question he was at his home on Harrison Street and engaged in making certain telephone calls in the line of his employment as a salesman of household appliances for Sears Roebuck & Company.

The testimony of the defendant that he was at his home and thus occupied at the time of the incident was corroborated by that of his father and mother with whom he lived.

The case was tried below upon the theory that the warrant charged the accused with the common law offense of indecent exposure. By motions to strike, exceptions to the trial court's rulings on instructions, and a motion to set aside the verdict the defendant challenged the sufficiency of the evidence to sustain the charge.

The gist of the defendant's argument, as stated in his brief, is that "an exposure of the person, irrespective of whether or not the place of exposure is a public one, made in the presence of only one person, is not a crime at common law."

On the other hand, the Commonwealth contends that Instruction No. 2, granted by the lower court, correctly defines the crime of indecent exposure as applied to the present situation. That instruction reads: "The court instructs the jury that if they believe from the evidence beyond a reasonable doubt that the accused on June 15, 1951, while sitting in an automobile on North Princeton Street, one of the public streets of the city of Lynchburg, intentionally exposed his private parts in a manner that same could reasonably have been seen by members of the public using said street and that the child Betty Thomas in using said street saw same, then the jury should find the accused guilty of indecent exposure of his person as charged."

[1] In 67 C.J.S., Obscenity, § 3, page 23, it is said: "Whatever openly outrages decency and is injurious to public morals is a misdemeanor at common law, and is indictable as such." The same principle is thus expressed in *Winters* v. *People of State of New York*, 333 U.S. 507, 515, 68 S. Ct. 665, 670, 92 L. Ed. 840: "Acts of gross and

open indecency or obscenity, injurious to public morals, are indictable at common law, as violative of the public policy that requires from the offender retribution for acts that flaunt accepted standards of conduct. 1 Bishop, Criminal Law, 9th Ed., § 500; Wharton, Criminal Law, 12th Ed., § 16."

[2] In 67 C.J.S., Obscenity, § 5, page 25, the author says: "Indecent exposure in a public place in such a manner that the act is seen or is likely to be seen by casual observers is an offense at common law, and is made an offense by a number of statutes and ordinances. * * *" The text is fully supported by the cited cases. Among the recent cases discussing the common law offense are *Commonwealth* v. *Hamilton*, 237 Ky. 682, 36 S.W. 2d 342; *Case* v. *Commonwealth*, 313 Ky. 374, 231 S.W. 2d 86; *Commonwealth* v. *Broadland*, 315 Mass. 20, 51 N.E. 2d 961. See also, 33 Am. Jur., Lewdness, etc., § 7, p. 19; Annotation, 93 A.L.R. 996.

[3, 4] Ordinarily, although not necessarily, the place where the exposure is made must be public. Indecent exposure on a street or public highway "so that one person sees, and others passing by can see, is an offense" at common law. 67 C.J.S., Obscenity, § 5, page 26.

In *State* v. *Walter*, 2 Marv. 444; 16 Del. 444, 43 A. 253, the court upheld an instruction which told the jury that exposure "on a public highway, within the view not only of the prosecuting witness, but also within the possible view of others who might be passing to and fro along the said highway," constituted the common law offense of indecent public exposure.

Recently, in the case of *Case* v. *Commonwealth*, supra, it was held that an indecent exposure must be either in the actual presence and sight of others, or in such a place or under such circumstances that the exhibition is liable to be seen by others. 231 S.W. 2d at page 87.

In *Commonwealth* v. *Bishop*, 296 Mass. 459, 6 N.E. 2d 369, 370, it was said that the offense in a public place does not depend upon the number of persons present, but "It is enough if it be an intentional act of lewd exposure, offensive to one or more persons."

[5] Likelihood that the act in a public place may be seen by a number of casual observers is sufficient. *State* v. *Goldstein*, 72 N.J.L. 336, 62 A. 1006, 1007, affirmed without opinion, 74 N.J.L. 598, 65 A. 1119.

Of course, it must appear that the exposure was intentional and not merely accidental. 67 C.J.S., Obscenity, § 5, page 26; 33 Am. Jur., Lewdness, etc., § 7, p. 19.

Morris v. *State*, 109 Ga. 351, 34 S.E. 577, 578, strongly relied upon by the defendant, is not authority for the proposition that an indecent exposure, on a public street, in the presence of a single other person is not a crime at common law. In that case the accused was charged with the violation of a *statute* making "any notorious act of public indecency, tending to debauch the morals," a misdemeanor. The offense was alleged to have taken place in a field not on or near a public highway, and it was there held that such conduct was not a "notorious act of public indecency" within the meaning of the statute. The opinion points out that, "Only one person saw the indecent exposure, and there is no evidence in the record that others could have seen" it. 34 S.E. at page 578. See also, *Wynne* v. *State*, 65 Ga. App. 213, 15 S.E. 2d 623.

State v. *Wolf*, 211 Mo. App. 429, 244 S.W. 962, also relied on by the defendant, was a prosecution under a statute similar to that involved in *Morris* v. *State, supra.* The information, which did not allege the place of the exposure, was held to be defective because it failed to allege that the act was committed in the presence of more than one person. The court there pointed out that the Missouri statute, unlike those in some States, did not provide punishment for an act of indecency or an indecent exhibition in a public place.

It is true that in *State* v. *Wolf, supra,* the court held that the information did not state a common law offense, because it said, "An indecent exposure seen by one person only *or capable of being seen by one person only* is not an offense at common-law." 244 S.W. at page 964. Italics supplied.

But it is quite a different thing to say that an indecent exposure in a public place, seen by one person and capable of being seen by others, does not constitute the common law offense. We have been cited to no authority, nor have we been able to find any, which sustains this latter proposition.

[6] An intentional exposure on a public street where it is likely to be seen by casual observers, whether actually seen by a single person or by several, is an act of "gross and open indecency * * *, injurious to public morals." *Winters* v. *People of State of New York, supra.*

[7] The evidence here amply supports a finding that the exposure was intentional and not merely accidental. According to the testimony of the child, the defendant accosted her and invited her attention to his misbehavior.

[8] We are of opinion that Instruction No. 2 correctly defines the common law offense with which the defendant was charged. It was for the jury to say whether the exposure in the automobile on the public street, under the circumstances related by the principal witness for the Commonwealth, "could reasonably have been seen," or was likely to have been seen, by persons using the street.

[9] As has been indicated, the main defense of the accused was that the girl was mistaken in identifying him as the offender, and that he was elsewhere at the time the crime was alleged to have been committed. He was, of course, entitled to have these issues properly submitted to the jury.

Bearing on these defenses, he requested and was refused these instructions:

Instruction E: "The court instructs the jury that if, after considering all of the evidence introduced in the case, they entertain any reasonable doubt as to whether the defendant is the person who committed the offense charged, then the jury must find the defendant not guilty."

Instruction F: "The court instructs the jury that the evidence introduced by the defendant, that he was not at the scene of the alleged crime, need not have been such as to establish this as a fact to entitle him to an acquittal; but if its effect has been such as to bring you to that state of mind that you have any reasonable doubt of his presence there, it is as much your duty to find him not guilty in this case as it would be if you were convinced he was not there or was otherwise not guilty. If there is a reasonable doubt in your minds as to this, *it is a fact in the case that he was not there, and it is to be by you so considered in his behalf as much as if proven to be true beyond any question of doubt.*" (Italics supplied.)

[10] The issue of his identification was properly set forth in Instruction E, and since it was not embodied in any of those granted, the instruction should have been given.

[11] Instruction F was offered on the theory that it properly submitted to the jury the issue of the defendant's proof of alibi. It is urged that an instruction in this language was approved in *Mullins* v. *Commonwealth,* 174 Va. 472, 475, 5 S.E. 2d 499, 500. That is true, but the form of the instruction was not there discussed, and upon further reflection we are convinced that the italicized language is not a proper statement of the law.

[12] In *Draper* v. *Commonwealth,* 132 Va. 648, 111 S.E. 471, we approved the following statement from the text in 2 Am. & Eng. Enc. of Law, 2d Ed., p. 56: "The true doctrine seems to be that where the state has established a *prima facie* case and the defendant relies upon the defense of alibi, the burden is upon him to prove it, not beyond a reasonable doubt, nor by a preponderance of the evidence, but by such evidence, and to such a degree of certainty, as will, when the whole evidence is considered, create and leave in the mind of the jury a reasonable doubt as to the guilt of the accused." 132 Va., at page 663, 111 S.E. at page 476.

We again approved this statement in *Fenner* v. *Commonwealth,* 152 Va. 1014, 1020, 148 S.E. 821, and we now adhere to the same view. In so far as the decision in *Mullins* v. *Commonwealth, supra,* approves the form of the instruction in question, it is overruled.

While the trial court was correct in refusing Instruction F in the form in which it was offered, at a new trial the defendant will be entitled to an instruction on alibi which conforms to the principles which we have here stated.

We are of opinion that the subject matter of Instructions C and M, likewise refused, was properly embodied in other instructions granted by the court.

For the failure of the court to grant Instruction E, *supra,* the judgment is reversed, the verdict set aside, and the case remanded for a new trial.

Reversed and remanded.

■ Bantam Books, Inc.

v.

Melko, Prosecutor of Pleas of Middlesex County.
No. C-1209.

Superior Court of New Jersey. Chancery Division.

March 31, 1953.

Joseph Steiner, Newark, attorney for the plaintiff.
Stephen V. Strong, New Brunswick, attorney for the defendant.

GOLDMANN, J.S.C.

This injunction action results from the defendant's promulgation of a list of publications found "objectionable" by a citizens committee. The proceedings center upon the committee's ban of *The Chinese Room*, a novel by Vivian Connell, but involved here is the larger question of extra-legal censorship.

Plaintiff, a New York corporation, has for some years been engaged in the business of publishing and selling paperbound 25- and 35-cent reprints of books. Among them is *The Chinese Room*, first published by the Dial Press in 1942 and reprinted by plaintiff in 1948 at 25 cents a copy, pursuant to an arrangement with the original publisher. There were ten additional printings of the paperbound edition before this action was instituted in February 1951. More than 2,500,000 copies of the novel have been sold throughout the United States and Canada.

Plaintiff distributes its books through circulation companies, among them the Curtis Circulation Company of Philadelphia which supplies the New Brunswick News Dealers Supply Company, of New Brunswick, N.J., and the Union County News Dealers Supply Company, of Elizabeth, N.J. Both serve Middlesex County and distribute plaintiff's reprints to newspaper stands, stores and other outlets in that area.

Some time before May 1950 the defendant Melko, then Prosecutor of the Pleas of Middlesex County, formed or accepted the services of a so-called Committee on Objectionable Literature, composed of citizens of the county. The purpose of the committee was to review publications offered for sale in Middlesex County, in order, as it is alleged, to determine whether they were fit and suitable reading for the public.

Defendant assigned Detective Bucko of his staff to work with the committee. He would visit stores and newspaper stands throughout the area, particularly those near schools, inform the owner of the state-wide drive against obscene literature, and ascertain what publications were in heavy demand, especially among young people. He would then select copies for the temporary use of the committee— these apparently were later returned, except for those found objectionable. Each member received for review an equal share of the books and magazines garnered by Bucko, and eventually would report to the full committee which of them were objectionable and which unobjectionable. Defendant then prepared his list of objectionable publications on the basis of the committee's recommendation.

On May 5, 1950 defendant wrote the New Brunswick News Dealers Supply Company, copy to the Attorney General of the State, as follows:

"Pursuant to the policy which I understand has been adopted by distributors of magazines and books to withdraw from circulation such literature as is found objectionable by the County Prosecutor and a committee appointed for that purpose, I am submitting herewith a list of all such publications which have been examined by the Middlesex County Committee and have been found to be of such nature that they should be withdrawn from circulation.

"Will you please acknowledge receipt of this communication and advise me what steps you will take in the matter?

"Very truly yours,
"Matthew F. Melko,
"Prosecutor of the Pleas of Middlesex County."

(In passing, it may be observed that there is no proof of a "policy" adopted by the distributors, such as is referred to in the letter.)

The list mentioned in the letter contained 36 titles, of which 20 were distributed by the New Brunswick company. Five of the 36 titles were reprints published by the plaintiff.

The company manager, Ben Gelfand, acknowledged receipt of the above letter on May 9, stating "we shall do everything possible to cooperate with your wishes." Gelfand testified that he regarded the letter as a mandate to remove the books; his company did not want to get into trouble with the prosecutor's office or invite bad publicity. The New Brunswick News Dealers Supply Company immediately withdrew the objectionable publications, including *The Chinese Room*, from all retail outlets serviced by it.

Gelfand sent a copy of the prosecutor's letter to Edward Koch, manager of the Union County News Dealers Supply Company in Elizabeth. Koch then wrote the defendant:

"We have been informed that your office has issued a list of publications that you have found objectionable and which you have banned from the news stands in Middlesex County.

"As we distribute magazines and allied publications in sections of Middlesex County, we ask that we be furnished with this and any subsequent lists."

Defendant replied immediately on May 10, 1952:

"In response to your request we are attaching hereto a list of objectionable literature to be withdrawn from circulation.

"We appreciate your sincere cooperation."

The list was the same as that which accompanied the May 5 letter to the New Brunswick company.

Koch testified that his company, too, withdrew all copies of publications distributed by it which were on the list. He interpreted the "cooperation" mentioned at the close of the prosecutor's letter as an order to take the books out of circulation; if not, the company would be prosecuted, Koch, like Gelfand, testified there had been many requests for *The Chinese Room,* but that no copies were supplied to retailers after May 10.

Upon learning of what had happened, plaintiff requested defendant to have the citizens committee again review five of the listed books. This was done, for on July 25, 1950, Prosecutor Melko wrote to plaintiff's then attorney, stating that the committee was of the opinion that four of the titles

"should not be included on the list of objectionable books. The committee feels that the fifth book, 'The Chinese Room' is properly listed as being objectionable and recommends its being kept on the list."

There were further conferences at which *The Chinese Room* was discussed. The results, insofar as plaintiff was concerned, were negative. On November 28, 1950, defendant wrote plaintiff's present attorney as follows:

"Dear Mr. Steiner:

"I am compelled to agree with Mr. Charles A. Pascal, Chairman of the Middlesex County Committee on Objectionable Literature, that the above named book is one that should not be exposed for sale where it can be purchased by school children.

"I feel that the Committee is justified in requesting the distributors not to forward copies of this book to Middlesex County.

> *"Very truly yours,*
> *"Matthew F. Melko*
> *"Middlesex County Prosecutor"*

The complaint charges that the defendant's action in not allowing *The Chinese Room* to come into Middlesex County is "invalid and illegal and beyond the scope of his office and that there is no legislative authority or any statute of the State of New Jersey under which the defendant could have acted where no crime has been committed or charged." Further, plaintiff alleges that "the pretended authority of the defendant in calling into action the committee above referred to, accepting its recommendations and acting upon them and instructing distributors not to bring the book into the County of Middlesex for sale and distribution, is not only illegal and void but has resulted and will result in irreparable injury to the plaintiff."

Plaintiff demands judgment that: (1) The May 10, 1950 letter of instruction to the Union County News Dealers Supply Company, and any similar letters to distributors, be declared void and of no effect; (2) the defendant be ordered to notify the Union County company, or any other distributor to whom he may have written, that his instructions are illegal and of no effect; (3) the citizens committee has no right to use the method it has been employing to prevent publishers and distributors from offering books for sale; (4) *The Chinese Room* may be distributed and sold in Middlesex County, without interference by the prosecutor's office; (5) defendant's letters and instructions constitute an extra-legal means for preventing the circulation of *The Chinese Room,* and have resulted and will result in irreparable injury to plaintiff's business; and finally, (6) defendant's action in using his office to send letters to distributors telling them not to distribute and sell *The Chinese Room* in Middlesex County is an unlawful exercise of the powers of his office.

Defendant's answer denies the significant allegations of the complaint and sets up two separate defenses: (1) a denial that compulsion or threats were used at any time upon anyone having to do with the publication and sale of *The Chinese Room,* and (2) the book is "obscene and indecent and contains words indecent and lascivious in context within the meaning of R.S. 2:140–2 and R.S. 2:140–3," so that plaintiff comes into court with unclean hands.

The present Prosecutor of Middlesex County, Alex Eber, has been substituted in the place and stead of the original defendant.

The issues as molded by the pretrial order were: (1) Does the defendant prosecutor have the authority to ban the sale of books in his county as lewd and lascivious by order or letter issued by him; (2) does he have such authority as to the sale of *The Chinese Room;* (3) did he in fact issue an order banning the sale of *The Chinese Room* in Middlesex County; (4) were the letters signed by him in effect a ban on the sale of that book; (5) should an injunction issue restraining the prosecutor from further notifying distributors of the book that it should not be sold in Middlesex County; (6) should a mandatory injunction issue directing the prosecutor to recall the letters he issued; and (7) was his action in issuing the letters illegal and beyond the scope of his authority?

Defendant prosecutor argues that his letters cannot be construed as an order banning the sale of *The Chinese Room* in his county, or that they were in fact a ban on such sale. The contention is naive. His letter of May 5, 1950, for example, was taken by the distributors as a plain mandate to remove the books listed as "objectionable." And the May 10 letter to Koch, voicing "appreciation" for his "cooperation," was interpreted as an order to take the books out of circulation under threat of prosecution. True, as the prosecutor says by way of defense, there was no actual compulsion or threat in words, but such was the very real impact and effect of his letters. They were enough to bring about the result he and his committee desired. They did what they were intended to do. The distributors were quick to obey, for they had plenty of other books to sell and were anxious lest the pattern of Middlesex

County's action spread to other counties and markets. The plain fact of the matter is that not a single copy of *The Chinese Room* was sold in Middlesex County after the prosecutor's letters were received.

It is next argued that the court of equity will not interfere with the enforcement of criminal law. *Dell Publishing Co. v. Beggans*, 110 N.J. Eq. 72, 158 A. 765 (Ch. 1932), is the only case cited in support of the proposition. The argument is vulnerable in two respects: as stated it is too broad, and further, the application here is not to enjoin criminal proceedings but to enjoin the prosecutor, acting under color of authority, from violating property rights claimed by plaintiffs. *Brex v. Smith*, 104 N.J. Eq. 386, 146 A. 34 (Ch. 1929); *Ruty v. Huelsenbeck*, 109 N.J. Eq. 273, 156 A. 922 (Ch. 1931).

The language of Vice Chancellor Berry in *S. & R. Amusement Corp. v. Quinn*, 136 N.J. Eq. 420, 423–424, 38 A. 2d 571, 573 (Ch. 1944) is appropriate:

> "While ordinarily equity will not enjoin criminal prosecutions, there is an exception to the rule where property rights are involved, and it is claimed seriously and in good faith that the act of the prosecutor is not authorized by law. * * * Here, however, no criminal prosecution is pending, nor has any restraint against the due processes of the law been imposed or sought. It will not be presumed that the complainant in the conduct of his business is guilty of a crime. The presumption is to the contrary.
>
> " * * * there is ample judicial authority in this state for the proposition that valuable property rights will be protected by injunction from damage or destruction, threatened or resulting, from the arbitrary acts of officials acting without due process of law." [*Citing cases.*]

The question of whether equity has power to enjoin the arbitrary action of municipal officials in interfering with persons in the conduct of their business was considered by Vice Chancellor (now Judge) Haneman in *Higgins v. Krogman*, 140 N.J. Eq. 518, 55 A. 2d 175 (Ch. 1947). He said (140 N.J. Eq. at pages 520–521, 55 A. 2d at pages 177–178):

> "The power of the Court of Chancery to restrain illegal interference with legitimate business by peace officers under the guise of enforcing the law is indisputable. See Iannella v. Piscataway Township, 138 N.J. Eq. 598, 49 A. 2d 491. Cases in which this question has arisen are generally concerned with an alleged violation of the criminal law and an attempt to prevent such violation by methods other than those which might be classed as due process. An examination of these cases discloses that although the Court of Chancery will ordinarily not interfere with the enforcement of the criminal law of this state, this court will enjoin interference with the conduct of business by physical force upon the mere claim that offenses against the criminal law are being conducted during the operation of such business, particularly where the law-enforcing officers fail or refuse to properly arrest and charge the alleged violators in accordance with the established law. [Citing many cases.]
>
> "There is ample authority for the proposition that valuable property rights will be protected by injunction from damage or destruction, threatened or resulting, from the arbitrary acts of officials acting without due process of law.

> "As was stated in Ruty v. Huelsenbeck, supra:
>
> " 'It would be intolerable if the operation of any business might be interfered with because some police officer came to the conclusion that the business was being operated in violation of the law. Such a condition would result in a government of men, not of law.' "

It may be argued there was no physical force in the case at bar. But the display of force which courts enjoin is not limited to the use of physical strength. Defendant's letters had the threat of the law behind them; they were terse in their insistment and demonstrably effective.

The Higgins case was affirmed on appeal, 142 N.J. Eq. 691, 61 A. 2d 444 (E. & A. 1948). Justice Jacobs, writing for the court, said (142 N.J. Eq. at page 693, 61 A. 2d at page 445):

> " * * * In so far as his [the vice-chancellor's] restraining order was confined to a restraint of the described extralegal activities, it was clearly, under the undisputed facts and circumstances, a proper exercise of the Court of Chancery's jurisdiction to protect complainants' property from irreparable injury threatened by 'arbitrary acts of officials acting without due process of law.' "

The case of *Public Welfare Pictures Corp. v. Brennan*, 100 N.J. Eq. 132, 134 A. 868 (Ch. 1926), is pertinent. Complainants owned a film called *The Naked Truth* and contracted to exhibit it at a Newark theatre. A private viewing was held before the first public exhibition, attended by the chief of the Board of Health of Newark, two members of the local police department, known as the board of censors and appointed by defendant Brennan, Director of Public Safety of Newark, and also by a number of ladies invited by the board of censors and Brennan. The board of health representative saw nothing objectionable in the film; the board of censors did. Brennan then caused notice to be given complainants that presentation of the film was prohibited, that he would prevent the production by force, revoke the theatre license and arrest all persons connected with the exhibition. The complainants offered to exhibit the film to him personally and not produce it if he deemed it objectionable. He refused the offer, stating that he would stand behind the judgment of his board of censors. Complainants thereupon applied for an injunction restraining him and the City of Newark from interfering with the production, alleging monetary loss if they were not allowed to exhibit the film. In granting the injunction the court referred to four cases where similar action was taken, one by former Chancellor Walker and three by former Vice Chancellor Howell, the latter being quoted as follows (100 N.J. Eq., at page 136, 134 A. at page 870):

> " * * * 'I know of no power in our police department to censor plays or theatrical exhibitions. None was cited on the argument, and I take it that, therefore, none exists. I, therefore, cannot see where the police authorities get their right to meddle in such matters.' * * *"

Clearly, important property rights are involved here, and they have been seriously affected by the prosecutor's action. Plaintiff is one of the largest, if not the largest, publisher and distributor of pocket-size reprints in the United States. A goodly number of the 2,500,000 copies of *The*

Chinese Room sold by it undoubtedly went into the hands of New Jersey purchasers. If what defendant has done in this case were held legal, his ban on the sale of this and other books considered by him objectionable would result in an irreparable injury to plaintiff and the loss of considerable profits, particularly when one realizes that hundreds of millions of 25-cent reprints are sold in this country annually.

It cannot be argued that the censorship exercised here was not that of the prosecutor, but rather of the Middlesex Committee on Objectionable Literature. The committee may have advised; the defendant acted. No statutory authority exists for what was done. The Legislature has not yet clothed the county prosecutors, or the Attorney General, with the power to censor books, and so there is no occasion to consider the possible constitutionality of such legislation. But if the Legislature had, and defendant sought to excuse what was done by claiming that it was the act of the committee, then the answer would have to be that a delegated power cannot be delegated. *Delegata potestas non potest delegari.* Defendant, as the official entrusted with the diligent enforcement of the criminal law in his county, could not delegate to a voluntary committee of citizens such authority as he might claim, to say whether a certain book should or should not be distributed and sold.

I hold that neither the prosecutor nor the committee constituted by him had authority to proscribe the distribution or sale in Middlesex County of books deemed by them, or either of them, to be objectionable. The action of the prosecutor in issuing the letters reproduced above was illegal and beyond the scope of his official authority.

Defendant advances a second defense: that *The Chinese Room* is "obscene and indecent and contains words indecent and lascivious in context within the meaning of R.S. 2:140–2 and R.S. 2:140–3." We are not concerned, for the moment, with the meaning to be given the words "obscene," "indecent" and "lascivious." These words, incidentally, appear nowhere in defendant's letters, but undoubtedly are what he meant when he euphemistically described the banned books as "objectionable literature." The statutes he now mentions for the first time as justification for his action make it a misdemeanor for any person (a) to utter or expose to the view of another, sell, or advertise or recommend any obscene or indecent book, pamphlet, picture or representation (R.S. 2:140–2); or (b) maliciously to set in type to be used in printing a newspaper, magazine or other current publication, or to change any piece of type, for the purpose of causing any indecent or lascivious word to appear in print in such publication (R.S. 2:140–3).

Defendant could have proceeded against plaintiff or any distributor in an orderly fashion under at least the first of the cited statutes. Had he done so there would then have been called into play the full range of criminal prosecution, from complaint and arrest, through indictment and trial by jury, with a verdict of guilty before any penalty could be invoked.

Also available against an offending distributor or seller was R.S. 2:178–6 which provides for search for and seizure of obscene and indecent books, papers, pictures, articles or things through the medium of the municipal court. Defendant did not avail himself of this *in rem* proceeding.

There are, then, several alternate and proper legal means at hand for dealing with allegedly obscene and indecent literature, none of which defendant used. The three statutes referred to give to law enforcement officials effective means of preserving and protecting the community morals, but none of them gives any such official the right to prejudge a situation and act upon it in the way defendant did in this case.

We have here a clear case of previous censorship in the area of literary obscenity. The way of the censor has been tortuous and tortured from earliest times. His story is one of arbitrary judgment and the suppression of much that we now consider good, true and beautiful. *Ernst and Seagle, To the Pure . . . A Study of Obscenity and the Censor* (1928), *passim*. Even the most cursory account of literary censorship will show its contradictions, the absence of valid standards, its lack of inner logic and outward consistency.

Little that is truly great in literature has escaped the censor's proscription. The Bible has fallen under his ban, Shakespeare was expurgated to satisfy his offended eye. Plutarch considered the *Comedies* of Aristophanes obscene, and Plato in his *Republic* recommended the expurgating of Homer lest it demoralize the minds of Greek youth. There was a burning of the books of Protagoras in the Agora in Athens, and Homer was similarly dealt with in Rome by Caligula. Generally, however, it may be said that suppression of books in the ancient world was rather limited. Literary censorship did not come into its own until the invention of printing in the middle of the 15th Century. As books became more common, the censor became more active. The focus of censorship has changed with the times, depending upon the overriding concerns of the era. The procession of censorship has been from heresy to treason to obscenity.

In the Age of Faith, with the Church supreme, the focus of suppression was upon heresy and blasphemy. For a long time the Church concerned itself little with obscenity as such and looked with some tolerance upon pagan and later writers and their alleged obscenities. Boccaccio may have been on the *Index Librorum Prohibitorum*, but the passages under ban were not those suppressed in modern times, but those reflecting upon religion and the Church. With the coming of the Reformation and the emergence of the State as the absolute power, the focus of suppression was upon treason and sedition. The censor was concerned more and more with literary proprieties in the political field. The absolute political state was not overly concerned with sex censorship. The censor's preoccupation with sexual morality (obscenity) began to develop only in the time of Queen Victoria, soon after the beginnings of the Industrial Revolution and the rise of technology. It has continued to our day.

The unpredictability and inconsistency of the censor is notorious. We need only consider the varying manner in which he has treated the several media of communication and art. The printed word has been the principal target. Drama has been considered a somewhat lesser problem, depending upon the time and place. No less a person than Goethe wanted to keep the young out of the theatre and Voltaire, who wrote *Candide*, condemned Corneille's *Theodora*. Previous censorship of the stage was known in France until 1906; the Lord Chamberlain still passes final judgment on what is a proper play for Englishmen; and New York had the Wales Act (1927) and closed *The God of Vengeance* and *The Captive*. The motion picture screen has received a treatment all its own at the hands of state censorship boards and local self-declared censors, in addition to its own code of decency. By contrast, the tabloids, sensational newspapers and even the more staid publications have gone relatively unscathed in reporting sex crimes and perversions in detail. The Comstocks have paid unwelcome attention to sculpture and painting—witness the furore some time ago over Boston's fine *Greek Bacchante* and the calendar art of *September Morn*—while they have turned eye and ear away from the undeniably erotic compulsion of certain performances of music and the dance. To look for a common standard and purpose in censorship is to seek the impossible.

Our essential concern here is with the question of literary decency. One might expect a greater consistency and significance of purpose in the censor's treatment of books. However, one need make only casual inquiry to appreciate that it is impossible to evolve any pattern of consistent treatment of books considered obscene. As Ernst and Seagle point out in their chapter on "The Enigmas of Literary Decency," obscenity exhibits many aspects. There is the temporal aspect. Swinburne's *Poems and Ballads* had to be withdrawn in 1866 because of the public clamor; Walt Whitman's *Leaves of Grass* fell under Boston's ban in 1881 and was likewise withdrawn; Havelock Ellis' *The Psychology of Sex* was the censor's victim in 1898, as was Theodore Dreiser's *The Genius* in 1916. All are now openly and widely distributed and read. The classics occupy a special field of their own in the annals of literary obscenity. They are respected and untouched, enjoying what has been termed "a statute of limitations on obscenity." When Vizetelly was prosecuted in England in 1888 for publishing Zola's novels, he sent the Solicitor of the Treasury a list showing that their suppression would logically involve the bowdlerization of some of the greatest works in English literature, among them Shakespeare, the Restoration dramatists, Defoe (*Moll Flanders*), Swift, Fielding, Smollett, Sterne (*Tristam Shandy*), and Lord Byron (*Don Juan*). The censors in the leading book markets of the English-speaking world, London, New York and Boston, have generally passed by the classics with little more than a troubled glance.

Obscenity also has a spatial aspect. For example, though Boston threatened criminal prosecution in the case of *Leaves of Grass*, England did nothing. D. H. Lawrence's *The Rainbow* was prosecuted in England, but not in America, as was Sherwood Anderson's *Many Marriages*. The New England Watch and Ward Society had well over 100 titles on its prohibited books list and actually instituted prosecutions involving novels by Sinclair Lewis, Upton Sinclair and Theodore Dreiser. The New York Society for the Suppression of Vice was less active and left the three authors alone. Its own index of prohibited books was in agreement with Boston's in only two instances.

There are still other variables that enter into the problem of literary obscenity. One is the question of language: Rabelais in French or Boccaccio in Italian are not objectionable, but they set vice societies in motion when printed in English. Cheap reprints of a book considered objectionable invite the censor's ban, where deluxe editions or so-called "privately printed" erotica, "issued to subscribers only," do not.

Nowhere is the inconsistency of literary censorship more patent than in the federal field. The Post Office Department has exercised censorship by indirection since Comstock obtained passage of the Postal Censorship Law in 1873, which provided that obscene literature could not be sent through the mails. In the exercise of the discretionary power lodged with them, federal postmasters have barred such varying publications as *The Little Review*, *Hearst's Magazine*, *The American Mercury*, *Life*, *Physical Culture*, *Ovid*, and the report prepared by the Chicago Vice Commission in 1911 for circulation among editors, social workers and clergymen. In the meantime, the Public Health Service and the Office of Education in the Federal Security Agency issue government-printed publications dealing with the life process and sex education. Although the Copyright Office is directed by law to refuse copyright to obscene books, it has not been known to refuse copyright to any of the books barred from the mails or suppressed by local authorities where such books were printed in this country. The Department of the Treasury may, under the Tariff Act, refuse admission of obscene books to the United States through federal customs. The use of this authority has been absolutely unpredictable. For example, the New York Customs Office barred such books as James Joyce's *Ulysses* and Pierre Louys' *Aphrodite*, but gave free passage to Rabelais, *The Decameron*, *The Arabian Nights* and *Ovid*. All this points up the enigmatic nature of literary obscenity, the elusiveness, if not the total absence, of any ultimate, central and governing concept.

Defendant regards *The Chinese Room* as "obscene and indecent" and some of its words "indecent and lascivious," within the meaning of R.S. 2:140-2 and 3. This spatter of epithets distills out to nothing more than a single meaning —sexual impurity. *Swearingen v. United States* 161 U.S. 446, 16 S. Ct. 562, 40 L. Ed. 765 (1896); *United States v. "Ulysses,"* 72 F. 2d 705 (C.C.A. 2, 1934); *Commonwealth v. Isenstadt*, 318 Mass. 543, 62 N.E. 2d 840 (Sup. Jud. Ct. 1945); *People v. Wendling*, 258 N.Y. 451, 180 N.E. 169, 81 A.L.R. 799 (Ct. App. 1932); *Commonwealth v. Gordon*, 66 Pa. Dist. & Co. 101 (Cty. Ct. 1948), affirmed 166 Pa. Super. 120, 70 A. 2d 389 (Sup. Ct. 1950).

The problem is to discover, if possible, what "obscene" means. It has been suggested that the word comes from *ob* and *scena*—done off the scene or off-stage, and hence furtively. Webster's New International Dictionary (2d ed. 1943) gives the derivation as *obs* (*ob*) and *caenum*, filth, and then goes on to define "obscene" as:

"*Offensive to chastity of mind or to modesty; expressing or presenting to the mind or view something that delicacy, purity and decency forbid to be exposed; lewd; indecent; * * *.*"

2 Bouvier's Law Dictionary, Rawle's Third Revision, page 2396 (8th ed. 1914) gives the definition:

"*Something which is offensive to chastity; something that is foul and filthy, and for that reason is offensive to a pure-minded person. * * * That which is offensive to chastity and modesty.*"

These and similar reference works provide no objective standard or formula for determining when obscenity exists. The definitions all lead to the dead end of a subjective determination. To paraphrase Samuel Johnson, the yea or nay saying of the censor becomes the standard of the permissible.

The argument sometimes made that anyone can tell by instinct what is obscene and what is not led Judge Curtis Bok to say in his learned opinion in *Commonwealth* v. *Gordon*, above (66 Pa. Dist. & Co. at page 116) that "The idea that instinct can be resorted to as a process of moral *stare decisis* reduces to absurdity."

The statute, R.S. 2:140–2, does not define "obscene." It merely proscribes publications that *are* obscene, leaving it to the constituted authorities to decide whether they are or not.

It has been pointed out elsewhere that the meaning of terms fundamental in the law of property, of words like "murder," "arson" and "mayhem" in the law of crimes, and even of "negligence," have remained relatively constant. Not so with "obscenity" or "obscene," whose meaning has undergone many changes, particularly in recent decades. In seeking a broad and all-inclusive definition of "obscene," censor and judge alike are, to employ the language in *Joseph Burstyn, Inc.* v. *Wilson*, 343 U.S. 495, 72 S. Ct. 777, 96 L. Ed. 1098 (1952), "set adrift upon a boundless sea amid a myriad of conflicting currents * * *, with no charts but those provided by the most vocal and powerful * * *."

Any consideration of the history of literary censorship will show that the term "obscene" does not gain "precision from the sense and experience of men" (*Mutual Film Corp.* v. *Ohio Industrial Commission*, 236 U.S. 230, 35 S. Ct. 387, 59 L. Ed. 552 (1915)). What was said by Justice Frankfurter in the Burstyn case of a certain definition applies here—the limits of the definition of "obscene" "remain too uncertain to justify constraining the creative efforts of the imagination by fear of pains and penalties imposed by a necessarily subjective censorship." His comment on the word "sacrilegious" involved in that case is *a propos* here:

"*On the basis of such a portmanteau word * * * the judiciary has no standards with which to judge the validity of administrative action which necessarily involves, at least in large measure, subjective determinations.*"

No purpose is to be served by a detailed review of all the cases dealing with literary obscenity and with censorship. Some will be mentioned by way of background or as of contemporary interest. As one might expect, the decisions are most numerous in the federal jurisdiction, New York, Massachusetts and Pennsylvania. They are gathered and discussed in articles like Alpert's "Judicial Censorship of Obscene Literature," 52 Harv. L.R. 40 (1938), and Grant and Angoff's "Massachusetts and Censorship," 10 Boston Univ. L. Rev. 36, 147 (1930); and in Judge Bok's decision in *Commonwealth* v. *Gordon*, above.

The early common law did not treat obscene literature as a crime. The first case actually to establish literary obscenity as an offense was *Regina* v. *Read*, 11 Mod. 143 (K.B. 1708). Lord Holt held that writing an obscene book was not indictable; it was, however, punishable "in the spiritual court." But in *Rex* v. *Curl*, 2 Strange 789 (K.B. 1727), the court sustained the indictment brought against a bookseller specializing in the obscene, holding that the offense was triable in the common law courts. Blackstone had little more than this case to go on when he began his

famous lectures in 1758. See 4 Commentaries, 150–151. Twelve years later Lord Mansfield gave questionable judgment against the defendant in *Rex* v. *Wilkes*, 4 Burr. 2527 (K.B. 1770)—a politically inspired case—for printing a bawdy poem. Thus, when the 18th Century came to a close, the English Bar knew there was such a doctrine as indictable obscenity, a latecomer as common law doctrines go, but they knew little more. There was no definition of obscenity, no basis for identifying it.

The next half-century was relatively uneventful. The English Society for the Suppression of Vice was formed in 1802 and set itself up as censor of the pornographic. Lord Eldon assumed the role of literary critic-censor in condemning Poet Laureate Southey's revolutionary drama Wat Tyler, and Byron's poem Cain, *Southern* v. *Sherwood*, 2 Mer. 435 (Ch. 1817); *Murray* v. *Benbow*, Jac. 474n (Ch. 1822). In the latter case he went on to voice his doubts about Milton's Paradise Lost, which led Lord Campbell, a great lover of literature, to write:

"* * * *it must have been a strange occupation for a judge who for many years has meddled with nothing more imaginative than an Act of Parliament, to determine in what sense the speculations of Adam, Eve, Cain, and Lucifer are to be understood. * * * *" (7 *Lives of the Lord Chancellors* (3rd ed. 1850), 637.)

Byron was twice-loser when Chancery thought his Don Juan obscene in *Lord Byron* v. *Dugdale*, 1 L.J. Ch. 239 (1823).

Lord Campbell's Act of 1857 (20 and 21 Vict.) marks the critical point in the history of literary obscenity. It provided for search and seizure warrants that would permit the police to take and destroy obscene publications. The bill drafted by Lord Campbell was intended as a protection for children against the many pornographic books, pamphlets and picture postcards then, as now, in circulation. His intentions may have been of the best (they have been questioned in some quarters; see Alpert, op. cit., 52 Harv. L. Rev., at 51–52), but the consequences were deplorable.

The debate on the bill is of great significance. Lord Campbell was asked in the House of Lords to define "obscene." He replied that

"*the measure was intended to apply exclusively to works written for the single purpose of corrupting the morals of youth*, and of a nature calculated to shock the common feelings of decency in any well regulated mind. * * * *He was ready to make what was indictable under the present law a test of obscenity.*" (Italics ours.) 146 Hansard, *Parliamentary Debates* (3rd ser. 1857), 327 et seq.

The bill was attacked in the House of Commons as "preposterous" and as an attempt "to make people virtuous by Act of Parliament." By the close of the debate Lord Campbell had made it quite clear that any work which so much as pretended to be literature or art had little to fear. Only the truly pornographic would be criminal. Lord Brougham warned that once the bill became an act, Lord Campbell's intentions would be perverted. They were, and in little more than a decade.

Regina v. *Hicklin*, L.R. 3 Q.B. 360 (1868), concerned the sale of an anti-Papist pamphlet, The Confessional Unmasked. Copies were seized under Lord Campbell's

Act. The court below had held that although the pamphlet was obscene in the ordinary meaning of the word, it had been distributed for the honest purpose of exposing the practices of the confessional and so did not come within the act. Whether the limitations which Lord Campbell had put upon the act were argued on the appeal, or known to the court, it spoke as though they had never existed. Lord Chief Justice Cockburn sympathized with the author's purpose but considered the book dangerous to growing sons and daughters. He announced a "test" for obscenity which provided three generations of judges with a ready formula:

"* * * whether the tendency of the matter charged as obscenity is to deprave and corrupt those whose minds are open to such immoral influences and into whose hands a publication of this sort may fall."

There have been many criticisms of the rule, direct and indirect, open and veiled, inside the courts and out. Recent cases reject the Hicklin doctrine completely. One of the more recent critiques appears in *Commonwealth v. Gordon*, 66 Pa. Dist. & Co. 101, 125:

"Strictly applied, this rule renders any book unsafe, since a moron could pervert to some sexual fantasy to which his mind is open the listings in a seed catalogue. Not even the Bible would be exempt; Annie Besant once compiled a list of 150 passages in Scripture that might fairly be considered obscene * * *."

And the court points out that portions of many ancient and modern authors—esteemed and established in literature for all time—would also be offensive.

There have been only a handful of English cases on literary obscenity since *Regina v Hicklin*, and they generally follow the rule it enunciated. The courts have been resorted to but little; the English community itself has judged whether the books that find their way into the marketplace are inherently decent. For a while in the late 19th Century the private circulating libraries, and particularly Mudie's, exercised a wide and effective censorship on what the public might read. Ernst and Seagle, To the Pure, 85 et seq. It was the day of the three-volume novel, at 31s 6d. Both the monopoly and censorship of these libraries were broken with the appearance of novels in one-volume form at 6s—a development of sociological as well as economic importance whose implications are almost self-evident. There has since been only a minimum of suppression by the law or the self-constituted censor; each citizen is his own critic of what is "obscene," and the Hicklin rule, though not suited to the English temper, serves as a legal standby in case of real trouble.

The impact of *Regina v. Hicklin* was much greater in the United States than in England. It gave men like Anthony Comstock their opportunity. He fathered the Postal Censorship Law of 1873 and obtained or inspired passage of obscenity laws throughout the country. That same year he organized the New York Society for the Suppression of Vice under a special act which gave its agents the right of search, seizure and arrest—a strange departure from accepted methods in the administration of the criminal law. Shortly there was a similar society in the

mid-West, and the New England Watch and Ward Society with headquarters in Boston. The history of suppression in America is largely the history of the activities of these private censors. However sincerely motivated, they put literature in shackles. Their subjective judgment as to what were the vehicles of moral infection went for the most part unchallenged; the only check was the courts—strict in Massachusetts, more liberal in New York and in the federal system. The activities of these organizations under men like Comstock, Sumner and Chase, and of their local counterparts, indelibly underline the dangers of uncontrolled previous censorship.

Boston long enjoyed the doubtful reputation of being the center of book suppression. Massachusetts adopted Lord Cockburn's test in the Hicklin case in *Commonwealth v. Buckley*, 200 Mass. 346, 86 N.E. 910, 22 L.R.A., N.S. 225 (Sup. Jud. Ct. 1909), in holding Elinor Glyn's Three Weeks as obscene, indecent, impure and manifestly tending to corrupt the morals of youth. Dreiser's An American Tragedy was branded unfit in *Commonwealth v. Friede*, 271 Mass. 318, 171 N.E. 472, 69 A.L.R. 640 (Sup. Jud. Ct. 1930); the court refused to allow the complete book to be introduced in evidence, and the prosecuting attorney picked the selections he wanted. (At that time the Massachusetts statute forbade the sale of any book *containing* obscene and indecent language.) The defense pointed out that the obscenity test applied by the court reduced the most intelligent members of the community to the same level as the immature and lewd. D. H. Lawrence's Lady Chatterly's Lover suffered the same judgment as Glyn's Three Weeks in *Commonwealth v. DeLacey*, 271 Mass. 327, 171 N.E. 455 (Sup. Jud. Ct. 1930).

The wave of censorship which swept over Boston at this time resulted in the suppression of some 68 books. The law was changed to proscribe the sale of "a book which *is* obscene, indecent," etc. A more reasonable rule was the result. For example, though *Commonwealth v. Isenstadt*, 318 Mass. 543, 62 N.E. 2d 840 (Sup. Jud. Ct. 1945), upheld the conviction for selling Strange Fruit, the court held that the book had to be considered as a whole and went so far as to say that "Since effect is the test, it follows that a book is to be judged in the light of the customs and habits of thought of the time and place of the alleged offense." And in *Attorney General v. "Forever Amber,"* 323 Mass. 302, 81 N.E. 2d 663 (Sup. Jud. Ct. 1948), the court went even further by noting that the sincerity and historic purpose of the book are important elements in passing judgment.

Massachusetts now allows a proceeding to be brought against the book itself, instead of the seller or distributor, with interlocutory adjudication as to whether it is obscene—a variety of declaratory judgment passing upon a book in advance. Mass. Ann. Laws, 1945 Supp., c. 272, § 28, and see Note, 50 Harv. L.R. 813 (1946). See also *Attorney-General v. "God's Little Acre,"* 326 Mass. 281, 93 N.E. 2d 819 (Sup. Jud. Ct. 1950), and *Attorney-General v. "Serenade,"* 326 Mass. 324, 94 N.E. 2d 259 (Sup. Jud. Ct. 1950), wherein Massachusetts adopts the modern rule that a book is to be judged by its artistic merit and as a whole; its effect is to be judged by a person with average sex instincts and not by those members of the community who might be particularly susceptible. "It would be deplorable, indeed, if the literary fare of normal adults were reduced to the level of ten-year-olds or psychopaths."

The New York courts have kept fairly clear of the orthodox test of the Hicklin case, although it was applied to Schnitzlèr's Reigen in *People* v. *Pesky*, 230 App. Div. 200, 243 N.Y.S. 193 (App. Div. 1930), affirmed 254 N.Y. 373, 173 N.E. 227 (Ct. App. 1930). All but two cases arose under section 1141 of the Penal Law, passed in its original form in 1884 and prohibiting "any obscene, lewd, lascivious, filthy, indecent or disgusting book, magazine, pamphlet," etc. 39 McKinney's Consolidated Laws of New York, c. 40, § 1141. These two were In re Worthington Co., 30 N.Y.S. 361, 24 L.R.A. 10 (Sup. Ct. 1894), allowing a receiver to sell the Arabian Nights, Decameron, Heptameron and similar classics held not obscene, and *St. Hubert Guild* v. *Quinn*, 64 Misc. 336, 118 N.Y.S. 582 (Sup. Ct. 1909), where the court in allowing the publisher to recover the contract price of certain books challenged as immoral, said that "It is no part of the duty of the courts to exercise a censorship over literary productions."

The main development began with *Halsey* v. *N.Y. Society for the Suppression of Vice*, 234 N.Y. 1, 136 N.E. 219 (Ct. App. 1922), affirming, 194 App. Div. 961, 185 N.Y.S. 931 (App. Div. 1922). Halsey had been arrested by defendant's agent for selling Gautier's Mme. de Maupin and acquitted. He sued the Society for malicious prosecution and recovered. The Court of Appeals affirmed, holding that the "book must be considered broadly as a whole." In discussing at some length the divided opinion of the literary critics as to the novel's merits, the court noted that such conflict

"points a finger at the dangers of a censorship entrusted to men of one profession, of like education and of similar surroundings. Far better than we, is a jury drawn from those of varied experiences, engaged in various occupations, in close touch with the currents of public feelings, fitted to say whether the defendant had reasonable ground to believe that a book such as this was obscene or indecent."

The modern view was expressed in *People* v. *Wendling*, 258 N.Y. 451, 180 N.E. 169, 81 A.L.R. 799 (Ct. App. 1932), involving dramatization of the song Frankie and Johnnie. Judge Pound observed that although language of the play was coarse, vulgar and profane, the plot tawdry, the play indecent from every consideration of propriety, yet

*"the court is not a censor of plays and does not attempt to regulate manners. One may call a spade a spade without offending decency, although modesty may be shocked thereby. * * The question is whether the tendency of the play is to excite lustful and lecherous desire."*

The effect of the book as a whole, its artistic sincerity, the climate of current opinion, the changing nature of moral standards of thought, the fact that the book is not dirt for dirt's sake, the use of the normal person rather than the abnormal as a criterion, the book's literary worth and particularly its reception at the hands of qualified critics—these are some of the elements weighed in determining whether a book was obscene in such lower court cases as *People* v. *Viking Press*, 147 Misc. 813, 264 N.Y.S.

534 (1933) [Caldwell's God's Little Acre]; People on Complaint of *Sumner* v. *Miller*, 155 Misc. 446, 279 N.Y.S. 583 (1935) [Flaubert's November]; *People* v. *Gotham Book Mart*, 158 Misc. 240, 285 N.Y.S. 563 (1936) [Gide's If I Die]; *People* v. *Larsen*, 5 N.Y.S. 2d 55 (Sp. Sess. 1938) [Life Magazine's "Birth of a Baby"]; *People* ex rel. *Kahan* v. *Creative Age Press*, 192 Misc. 188, 79 N.Y.S. 2d 198 (1948) [The Gilded Hearse]; *People* v. *Vanguard Press*, 192 Misc. 127, 84 N.Y.S. 2d 427 (1947) [Willingham's End As a Man].

The formulation of a reasonable and fairly flexible test still awaits attention by New York's highest court. The courts, generally, have been moderate in their approach to literary obscenity and have, at least on the lower levels, explored modern approaches to the problem and the application of different factors to the resolution of the problem.

Pennsylvania's first obscene book case was *Commonwealth* v. *Landis*, 8 Phila. 453 (1870), where defendant was convicted for selling a book entitled Secrets of Generation. The court held that it was for the jury to say whether a book was obscene, and indulged in the not unfamiliar exercise of defining synonyms like obscenity, filthiness, indecency, lewdness and lasciviousness in terms of each other. Lord Cockburn's rule was followed in a number of subsequent minor court decisions. *Commonwealth* v. *New*, 142 Pa. Super. 358, 16 A. 2d 437 (1940) is considered in *Commonwealth* v. *Gordon*, below, as virtually abandoning the harsh test of *Regina* v. *Hicklin*. The court in the New case considered the publication "as a whole." Judge Bok's opinion in the Gordon case, 66 Pa. Dist. & Co. 101 (Cty. Ct. 1949), affirmed 166 Pa. Super. 120, 70 A. 2d 389 (1950), is the most comprehensive treatment of the law of literary obscenity to date and represents the thoughtful and balanced approach of a philosophical mind to a restatement that will meet the challenge of changing times and morals. After reviewing the decisions he says:

"From all of these cases the modern rule is that obscenity is measured by the erotic allurement upon the average modern reader; that the erotic allurement of a book is measured by whether it is sexually impure—i.e., pornographic, 'dirt for dirt's sake,' a calculated incitement to sexual desire—or whether it reveals an effort to reflect life, including its dirt, with reasonable accuracy and balance; and that mere coarseness or vulgarity is not obscenity.

*"Forging such a rule from the precedents does not fully reach the heart of the matter, * * *. Current standards create both the book and the judgment of it."*

He does not see much difference, historically, between censoring books before publication and suppressing them, and regards legal censorship "as an experiment of more than dubious value." In his view, the practice of previous censorship raises grave constitutional questions.

Until the case of *United States* v. *One Book* Called "Ulysses," 5 F. Supp. 182 (S.D.N.Y. 1933), affirmed 72 F. 2d 705 (C.C.A. 2 1934), the federal courts exercised censorship through regulation of importations under the Tariff Acts (19 U.S.C.A. § 1305), and by criminal prosecutions under Comstock's act of 1873 declaring certain books and other publications nonmailable matter (18 U.S.C.A. § 334). The orthodox test for obscenity in the Hicklin case was approved by the federal courts in 1879 in *United States* v. *Bennett*, 24 Fed. Cas. page 1093, No.

14,571 (S.D.N.Y. 1879), holding obscene Cupid's Yokes, a book dealing with the sex side of marriage. The courts dealt similarly with the novel Hagar Revelly in *United States v. Kennerley*, 209 F. 119 (S.D.N.Y. 1913), but the case gave Judge Hand the opportunity to express his doubts about the law of obscenity. He declared that the Hicklin rule "however consonant it may be with mid-Victorian morals, does not seem to me to answer to the understanding and morality of the present time, * * *" and went on to say:

"* * * I question whether in the end men will regard that as obscene which is honestly relevant to the adequate expression of innocent ideas, and whether they will not believe that truth and beauty are too precious to society at large to be mutilated in the interests of those most likely to pervert them to base uses. Indeed, it seems hardly likely that we are even to-day so lukewarm in our interest in letters or serious discussion as to be content to reduce our treatment of sex to the standard of a child's library in the supposed interest of a salacious few, or that shame will for long prevent us from adequate portrayal of some of the most serious and beautiful sides of human nature. That such latitude gives opportunity for its abuse is true enough; there will be, as there are, plenty who will misuse the privilege as a cover for lewdness and a stalking horse from which to strike at purity, but that is true to-day and only involves us in the same question of fact which we hope that we have the power to answer."

The defendant in *United States v. Dennett*, 39 F. 2d 564, 76 A.L.R. 1092 (C.C.A. 2 1930), had been convicted of sending through the mails a pamphlet, Sex Side of Life, written for her children and other young people. The jury had been charged in the language of the Hicklin test. In reversing, Judge Augustus N. Hand said there was no case to submit to the jury. Referring to Lord Cockburn's test indirectly, he said that the federal act (18 U.S.C.A. § 334) "must not be assumed to have been designed to interfere with serious instruction regarding sex matters unless the terms in which the information is conveyed are clearly indecent." The court found that the defendant had written about sex with sincerity and held that so accurate an exposition "in decent language and in a manifestly serious and disinterested spirit cannot ordinarily be regarded as obscene."

A book of fiction, daringly experimental in form and prose style, next came before the Second Circuit in *United States v. One Book* Entitled Ulysses, 72 F. 2d 705 (C.C.A. 2 1934), affirming Judge Woolsey below, 5 F. Supp. 182 (S.D.N.Y. 1933). Judge Augustus N. Hand's opinion, in which Judge Learned Hand concurred, is commonly considered a landmark in the law of literary obscenity. The New York customs collector had seized James Joyce's Ulysses under the Tariff Act of 1930 (19 U.S.C.A. § 1305), claiming it was an obscene book. Judge Woolsey dismissed the government's libel for forfeiture. Judge Hand found the book (72 F. 2d at pp. 706–707)

"* * * a sincere portrayal with skilful artistry of the 'stream of consciousness' of all its characters. * * [It] seems to be sincere, truthful, relevant to the subject, and executed with real art. * * *

"* * * The book as a whole is not pornographic, and,

while in a few spots it is coarse, blasphemous and obscene, it does not, in our opinion, tend to promote lust. The erotic passages are submerged in the book as a whole and have little resultant effect.

"* * * We think the same immunity should apply to literature as to science, where the presentation, when viewed objectively, is sincere, and the erotic matter is not introduced to promote lust and does not furnish the dominant note of the publication."

The rigorous doctrines laid down in *United States v. Bennett*, above, which followed the Hicklin case, were held inconsistent with the decision of the court in the Dennett case just discussed. The court stated that in applying the "dominant effect" of the book test

"relevancy of the objectionable parts to the theme, the established reputation of the work in the estimation of approved critics, if the book is modern, and the verdict of the past, if it is ancient, are persuasive pieces of evidence; for works of art are not likely to sustain a high position with no better warrant for their existence than their obscene content."

In *United States v. Levine*, 83 F. 2d 156 (C.C.A. 2 1936), defendant had been indicted for posting circulars advertising obscene books, only one, Black Lust, being a literary work. The trial judge charged the jury in terms of the orthodox test, and it found Levine guilty. On appeal Judge Learned Hand, after pointing out that the Hicklin doctrine had been criticized in the Kennerley case, bluntly declared it had been overruled by the Second Circuit in the Dennett and "Ulysses" cases. He emphasized that the test to be applied was that stated in the "Ulysses" decision, and added:

"The standard must be the likelihood that the work will so much arouse the salacity of the reader to whom it is sent as to outweigh any literary, scientific or other merits it may have in the reader's hands; of this the jury is the arbiter."

This summary review of the authorities in five jurisdictions demonstrates that the harsh rule of *Regina v. Hicklin* finds little, if any, support in today's judicial thinking. It has been supplanted by a more modern test, stated most clearly in the opinions of the Second Circuit, in *Commonwealth v. Gordon*, above, and in the latest Massachusetts cases.

We are aware that most of the cases we have discussed involve actual prosecutions for literary obscenity. They are nonetheless useful to our purpose in considering the question of the suppression of books in advance of institution of criminal proceedings.

Serious consideration of what has been written by courts and others in the past two decades emphasizes the arbitrary and dangerous character of what was done here by defendant and his advisory committee. To entrust such censorship to one fallible man, or private body of men, is to set up an "almost despotic arbiter of literary products * * *. Such a condition * * * does not accord with democratic ideals which repudiate thought control." *Roth v. Goldman*, 172 F. 2d 788, 790 (C.C.A. 2 1949). No matter how sincere the intention here, the method and the inevitable result are those of the Watch and Ward Society and its contemporaries. The courts have given their answer to such activity.

The motivating purpose in this case seems to have been to protect school children from "objectionable" books. This raises the question as to just what the effect of a book upon a young person may be. The answer is best given by the sociologist and psychologist. A quarter of a century ago the Bureau of Social Hygiene of New York sent questionnaires to 10,000 college and normal-school women graduates. 1,200 answers were received, and of these, 72 (6%) said they had received their earliest sex information from reading books or pamphlets. Not one mentioned a "dirty" book; listed were the Old Testament (19), the dictionary (8), the encyclopedia, Shakespeare, venereal disease circulars, medical books, Victorian novelists, Motley's Rise of the Dutch Republic. The question, "What things are most stimulating sexually?", brought a variety of replies from women now mature: 218 replied "Man," 95 (or 8%) said books, 40 drama, 29 dancing. The list of books ran the whole gamut of literature, including poetry of the Middle Ages. Ernst and Seagle, To the Pure, 234 et seq.

In 1938 the American Youth Commission chose Maryland as a "typical" state for its study of the conditions and attitudes of youth between the ages of 16 and 24. Over 13,500 young people were interviewed. The chief source of sex education for 66% of the boys and 40% of the girls was what friends of their own age had told them. The home and the school were the next chief sources, and about 4% reported they owed most of their information to books. Bell, Youth Tell Their Story (1938).

Research like this is far more informative than a censor's personal opinion. What was done in New York and Maryland should be up-dated and made even more searching. The figures may change somewhat in future studies but those now available raise a serious question as to whether books alone corrupt and deprave the young.

The influences which operate on a child in the swift movement of our society are as infinite as they are varied. One may not single out the printed page as the one source of moral infection. The whole of our social complex is a more proper frame for investigation and study. There one may find many pernicious influences, tangible and intangible, any one of which is more harmful to child, and to adult, than a publication which some may deem obscene. The point has well been made that the censor is no substitute for the home, the church and the school. Individually and in combination they have their responsibilities in molding the mind and character of our young.

The action of defendant here under attack poses a final question in the field of constitutional law. Directly implicated are the First and Fourteenth Amendments to the Federal Constitution.

N.J.S.A. 52:17A–4 (L. 1944, c. 20, § 4) requires the Attorney General to enforce the provisions of the Constitution "and all other laws of the State, * * *." N.J.S.A. 52:17B–5 (L. 1948, c. 439, § 5) continued this duty. R.S. 2:182–5 (now N.J.S. 2A:158–5) vests in each county prosecutor the same powers, within his county, "as the Attorney-General shall by law be vested with * * *." In proceeding as he did, defendant undoubtedly believed he was carrying out his statutory duty of enforcing the criminal laws of the State—in particular, the laws relating to obscene publications, R.S. 2:140–2 and 3 (now N.J.S. 2A:115–2 and 3). Under color of his office and under color

of statutory authority he sent the letters which, in effect, directed that the book in question be withdrawn from circulation and not be "exposed for sale where it can be purchased by school children." We have already held that he had no such authority in law.

The liberty of the press which the First Amendment guarantees against abridgement by the Federal Government is within the liberty safeguarded by the Due Process Clause of the Fourteenth Amendment from invasion by state action. *Gitlow* v. *New York*, 268 U.S. 652, 45 S. Ct. 625, 69 L. Ed. 1138 (1925); *Near* v. *Minnesota*, 283 U.S. 697, 51 S. Ct. 625, 75 L. Ed. 1357 (1931); *Lovell* v. *Griffin*, 303 U.S. 444, 58 S. Ct. 666, 82 L. Ed. 949 (1938); *Joseph Burstyn, Inc.* v. *Wilson*, 343 U.S. 495, 72 S. Ct. 777, 96 L. Ed. 1098 (1952). In its historic connotation, the press comprehends every sort of publication, and the guarantee of a free press covers distribution as well as publication. *Lovell* v. *Griffin*, above.

Chief Justice Hughes, in speaking for the court in *Near* v. *Minnesota*, said (283 U.S. at pages 713, 716, 51 S. Ct. at pages 630, 621):

"*In determining the extent of the constitutional protection, it has been generally, if not universally, considered that it is the chief purpose of the guaranty to prevent previous restraints upon publication.* * * *

* * * * *

"** * * the protection even as to previous restraint is not absolutely unlimited. But the limitation has been recognized only in exceptional cases.* * * *

* * * * *

"*The exceptional nature of its limitations places in a strong light the general conception that liberty of the press, historically considered and taken up by the Federal Constitution, has meant, principally, although not exclusively, immunity from previous restraints or censorship.*"

Cf. *Lovell* v. *Griffin*, 303 U.S. at page 451, 58 S. Ct. 666.

The "exceptional cases" mentioned by the Chief Justice would undoubtedly include, by his own listing, pornography—"dirt for dirt's sake"—against which the requirements of decency may be enforced. But we do not have such a book here. The court has read The Chinese Room in the light of the standards laid down by the more recent cases already noted, and finds the book unobjectionable. It cuts a rather poor and pale figure in the colorful company of recent "historical" novels of the Forever Amber type, which may be found in almost any public or circulating library, fresh from the best-seller lists.

The question of previous restraint in the publication field again came before the Supreme Court in *Hannegan* v. *Esquire, Inc.*, 327 U.S. 146, 66 S. Ct. 456, 90 L. Ed. 586 (1946), when the Postmaster General revoked Esquire magazine's second-class mailing permit because, essentially, it did not "contribute to the public good and the public welfare." The court held that the Postmaster General acted without authority; Congress had not inaugurated even a limited type of censorship in adopting the regulation relating to the format and nature of the contents of a publication entitled to the mailing privilege. There were some, Justice Douglas noted, who felt that Esquire's contents reflected "the smoking-room type of humor, featuring, in the main sex," and others who thought them "racy and risque" and in poor taste. But the power of censorship, he said, "is so abhorrent to our traditions that a purpose to grant it should not be easily inferred." The Justice declared (327 U.S. at pages 157–158, 66 S. Ct. at pages 461–462):

"*What is good literature, what has educational value, what is refined public information, what is good art, varies with individuals as it does from one generation to another. * * * But a requirement that literature or art conform to some norm prescribed by an official smacks of an ideology foreign to our system. * * * From the multitude of competing offerings the public will pick and choose. What seems to one trash may have for others fleeting or even enduring values.*"

The evil of previous restraint was condemned most recently, in the case of motion pictures, in the Burstyn case, 343 U.S. 495, 72 S. Ct. 777, 96 L. Ed. 1098 (1952).

We hold that defendant's action violated the constitutional guarantee of freedom of the press.

Judgment for plaintiff in accordance with the conclusions herein expressed.

■ Adams Theatre Co.
v.
Keenan et al.
No. A–108.

SUPREME COURT OF NEW JERSEY.

Argued March 9, 1953. Decided April 27, 1953.

George B. Astley, Newark, for appellants (Charles Handler, Newark, attorney).

Robert L. Hood, Newark, for respondent.

The opinion of the court was delivered by WILLIAM J. BRENNAN, JR., J.

The question here is whether the trial court erred in entering a summary judgment directing Newark's director of public safety and city clerk to issue to plaintiff a license to operate a theatre exhibiting burlesque shows. Defendants' appeal to the Appellate Division was certified by this court of its own motion.

The license was refused under a licensing ordinance prohibiting the operation of a theatre for commercial stage or motion picture exhibitions except under license issued with the "approval" of the director of public safety. The ordinance also empowers the director to suspend or revoke an issued license. In either case the director's discretion is governed by the standard of what "may be necessary for the furtherance of decency and good order." That is the norm specified by the provisions related to the suspension or revocation of a license, but from the context of the entire ordinance that norm is plainly to be implied as applicable also to the director's "approval" of an application for a license in the first instance. Cf. *Librizzi* v. *Plunkett*, 126 N.J.L. 17, 16 A. 2d 280 (Sup. Ct. 1940).

[1] The performance of a play or show, whether burlesque or other kind of theatre, is a form of speech and prima facie expression protected by the State and Federal Constitutions, and thus only in exceptional cases subject to previous restraint by means of the withholding of a theatre license or otherwise. Any doubt raised by *Mutual Film Corporation* v. *Industrial Commission*, 236 U.S. 230, 35 S. Ct. 387, 59 L. Ed. 552 (1915), that First Amendment protection under the Federal Constitution extends to the commercial exhibition of plays, shows and motion pictures, was removed by the recently decided case of *Joseph Burstyn, Inc.* v. *Wilson*, 343 U.S. 495, 72 S. Ct. 777, 96 L. Ed. 1098 (1952).

The First Amendment has been interpreted particularly to bar previous restraints upon free expression, *Near* v. *State of Minnesota* ex rel. *Olson*, 283 U.S. 697, 51 S. Ct. 625, 75 L. Ed. 1357 (1931), including any attempted prior restraint by state or local authorities, *Gitlow* v. *People of State of New York*, 268 U.S. 652, 45 S. Ct. 625, 69 L. Ed. 1138 (1925): *Near* v. *State of Minnesota* ex rel. *Olson*, supra; *Joseph Burstyn, Inc.* v. *Wilson*, supra. The comparable provision of our State Constitution is to like effect. Article I, paragraph VI of the Constitution of 1947 provides, "Every person may freely speak, write and publish his sentiments on all subjects, being responsible for the abuse of that right."

[2] However, "the protection even as to previous restraint is not absolutely unlimited," *Near* v. *State of Minnesota* ex rel. *Olson*, supra, 283 U.S., at page 716, 51 S. Ct. at page 631, 75 L. Ed., at page 1367. There are "narrowly limited classes of speech" which are not given the protection of the First Amendment. *Chaplinsky* v. *State of New Hampshire*, 315 U.S. 568, 571, 62 S. Ct. 766, 86 L. Ed. 1031, 1035 (1942). By universal agreement one such exception is speech which is outrightly lewd and indecent.

[3] But whether a particular play, show or motion picture is lewd and indecent more often is a controverted question than a matter upon which all will agree. The standard "Lewd and indecent" is amorphous, frequently of different content according to the local standard of propriety at the time and place of exhibition. There is ever present, too, the danger that censorship upon that ground

is merely the expression of the censor's own highly subjective view of morality unreasonably deviating from common notions of what is lewd and indecent, or may be a screen for reasons unrelated to moral standards. The cases involving prior restraints upon the exhibition of plays, shows and motion pictures illustrate the widely varying concepts of lewdness and indecency held by different censors and even by courts. Does every reference to motherhood, birth or the sex relationship *ipso facto* classify the presentation as lewd and indecent? Does the presentation become such if the censor's view is that the subject matter or its treatment is not fit for commercial exhibition to patrons of places of public entertainment while suitable for presentment before medical societies or under educational or social welfare auspices? Can the presentation be banned *in toto* as lewd and indecent because a part—even a minute part—is coarse, vulgar or profane? These and like questions have not always been answered the same way. See Notes, 60 Yale Law Journal, 696 (April 1951); 39 Columbia Law Review, 1383 (December 1939).

Our state decisions tend to adhere to the "dominant effect" test. *United States* v. *One Book* Entitled Ulysses, 72 F. 2d 705 (C.C.A. 2 1934), affirming 5 F. Supp. 182 (D.C.S.D.N.Y., 1933). By that test the mere fact that sexual life is the theme of the presentation or that the characters portray a seamy side of life and play coarse scenes or use some vulgar language does not constitute the presentation *per se* lewd and indecent. The question is whether the dominant note of the presentation is erotic allurement "tending to excite lustful and lecherous desire," dirt for dirt's sake only, smut and inartistic filth, with no evident purpose but "to counsel or invite to vice or voluptuousness." *People* v. *Wendling*, 258 N.Y. 451, 180 N.E. 169, 81 A.L.R. 799 (Ct. App. 1932). In such case, prior restraint upon the exhibition offends no constitutional right, if indeed censorship in the strict sense is involved at all; the exhibition then "is not theatre and in no wise involves free expression." *Bonserk Theatre Corp.* v. *Moss*, 34 N.Y.S. 2d 541, 547 (Sup. Ct. 1942). It is the absence of this dominant note in the motion pictures involved in *Public Welfare Pictures Corp.* v. *Brennan*, 100 N.J. Eq. 132, 134 A. 868 (Ch. 1926); *Hygienic Productions* v. *Keenan*, 1 N.J. Super. 461, 62 A. 2d 150 (Ch. Div. 1948) and *American Museum of Natural History* v. *Keenan*, 20 N.J. Super. 111, 89 A. 2d 98 (Ch. Div. 1952), which underlies those holdings denying any power in the public officials to ban their commercial presentations.

[4–6] The defendant director of public safety in his affidavit in this case, and counsel, on the brief and on the oral argument, suggest that these New Jersey decisions leave the director powerless to prevent the exhibition of a presentation actually lewd and indecent even by the suspension or revocation of a license after a history of the performance of such exhibitions. That is a mistaken view of the holdings of those cases. In the Public Welfare Pictures Corp. and Hygienic Productions cases the licensing officials themselves did not contend that the motion pictures were actually lewd and indecent but only that the theme of the story portrayed by each was such that the pictures should not be commercially exhibited but shown under religious, educational or welfare auspices. The decisions held that the officials had no power so to limit the presentations. In the American Museum of Natural History case the trial court viewed the film and found as a fact

that "there is nothing suggestive, obscene, indecent, malicious or immoral in the showing of Latuko aborigines in their normal living state." We are aware of no reported case in our books which questions the power of a municipality to deal through licensing ordinances with a presentation the dominant note of which is outrightly lewd and indecent. And note also the criminal statutes, N.J.S. 2A:115–1 and 2, N.J.S.A. True, the power of censorship "is so abhorrent to our traditions that a purpose to grant it should not be easily inferred," *Hannegan* v. *Esquire, Inc.*, 327 U.S. 146, 151, 66 S. Ct. 456, 459, 90 L. Ed. 586, 589 (1946). And there is no statutory delegation to municipalities of censorship powers as such. However, R.S. 40:52–1, N.J.S.A., authorizes municipalities to license and regulate "theatres, cinema and show houses," and R.S. 40:48–1 (6), N.J.S.A., empowers them to adopt ordinances to "Prevent vice, drunkenness and immorality." Therefore, provided the ordinance sets forth a standard adequate for the purpose, 7 McQuillin, Municipal Corporations (3rd ed.), sec. 24.199, p. 17, these sections together amply suffice as a grant of power through licensing to cope with the problem of the exhibition of plays, shows and motion pictures, the dominant note of which is clearly the purveying merely of dirt for dirt's sake. The standard of "decency and good order" in the Newark ordinance is a sufficient norm in the statutory category of vice and immorality. See *Block* v. *City of Chicago*, 239 Ill. 251, 87 N.E. 1011 (Sup. Ct. 1909).

[7] In the instant case the attempt by the defendant director was to impose a previous restraint by the refusal of the theatre license. No burlesque show has been staged in Newark by the plaintiff as a consequence. The prior restraint is therefore plainly insupportable unless the proofs which led the licensing official to conclude that plaintiff intends to stage lewd and indecent shows reasonably tend to show that such is the case. Cf. *Bonserk Theatre Corp.* v. *Moss*, supra. The applicant denied a license or the licensee whose license is suspended or revoked may, of course, have judicial review of the action of the licensing official, ordinarily, as in this case, by a proceeding in lieu of prerogative writ under Rule 3:81.

[8] Although the court will assume that the action of the official was actuated by proper motives and for valid reasons, *Aschenbacher* v. *Inhabitants of City of Plainfield*, 121 N.J.L. 598, 3 A. 2d 814 (Sup. Ct. 1939), affirmed on opinion below, 123 N.J.L. 265, 8 A. 2d 579 (E. & A. 1939), a judgment setting the action aside and peremptorily ordering the theatre license to issue or to be restored will be entered if it appears that the action was without reasonable basis, that is that it was arbitrary. Cf. *De Roos* v. *Chapman*, 106 N.J.L. 6, 147 A. 570 (Sup. Ct. 1929); *Hudson Royal, etc., Inc.* v. *Mayor etc., Jersey City*, 160. A 218, 10 N.J. Misc. 629 (Sup. Ct. 1932); *Phillips* v. *Borough of East Paterson*, 134 N.J.L. 161, 46 A. 2d 667 (Sup. Ct. 1946), affirmed on opinion below, 135 N.J.L. 203, 50 A. 2d 869 (E. & A. 1947); *Mangiello* v. *Mayor, etc., Jersey City*, 142 A. 179, 6 N.J. Misc. 536 (Sup. Ct. 1928); *Bonserk Theatre Corp.* v. *Moss*, supra; 9 McQuillin, supra, sec. 26.74, p. 162. And necessarily, after the decision in the Burstyn case, the validity of the reasons for the refusal must now be assayed by the court in the light of the constitutionally guaranteed right of freedom of expression.

Plaintiff's application stated merely that it intended to

stage "burlesque" shows. "Burlesque" today is descriptive of two very different kinds of show. Legitimate burlesque, and once the only kind, is clean and wholesome entertainment defined in the 1952 edition of Webster's New International Dictionary as "a type of theatrical entertainment, developed in the United States in the late nineteenth century, characterized by broad humor and slapstick presentation, at first consisting of a musical travesty, but later of turns, as songs, ballet dancing, and caricatures of well-known actors and plays." In contrast, that which has been termed "modern burlesque" has been described as "a plotless musical entertainment consisting of a series of unrelated episodes and dances, all with the purpose of depicting or suggesting sexual subjects or objects. The one outstanding characteristic of modern burlesque is the fact that it is completely sex-centered. It has some low comedy and occasionally some humor, but the principal subject of both is sex. * * * The piece de resistance is the girl who disrobes, partially or entirely, and this act varies with the political season and the locality. * * * If burlesque of today is metropolitan, so also it is vice, and needs to be thought of in that light, as an aspect of social pathology. If vice implies a sense of antagonism toward existing mores, a purveying of sex in a vicarious, professional and promiscuous fashion, then burlesque is just that. * * * Although the operator may not be willing to say so to an inquirer, usually adopting a sanctimonious air, he knows, and everything in his theatre indicates he knows, that he is giving a sex show, sans excuses, sans philosophy and above all, sans clothes. He is, in that sense a professional purveyor of sex." Dressler, Burlesque as a Cultural Phenomenon (1937).

A burlesque show answering the latter description may well be considered outrightly lewd and indecent. We must assume that it is that type of show which the director inferred plaintiff planned to exhibit if granted a license. We agree with the trial court that the inference is not supported by the reasons therefor relied upon by the director and set forth in his affidavit. The director's action was not taken upon proofs after hearing because he did not afford the plaintiff an opportunity to be heard. His affidavit states he made his decision upon the basis of his knowledge from complaints of interested citizens that the only burlesque theatre presently licensed in Newark exhibits the offensive type of burlesque show, and also from information obtained by him from police sources in other cities satisfying him that two of plaintiff's officers were men of dubious character and that one of them has in the past staged lewd and indecent exhibitions in other cities.

[9] The alleged conduct of the present licensee in staging indecent burlesque shows certainly can in no wise be the basis for an inference that plaintiff, who has no connection of any kind with that licensee, will do likewise. It is this present licensee whose license the director mistakenly supposed he was without power to suspend or revoke even if its burlesque shows should be established to be lewd and indecent. It was apparently the possible existence of the same supposed difficulty if plaintiff should be granted a license that the director sought to circumvent by the anticipatory denial of the license in issue. In any event, that denial upon the mere conjecture that the action was necessary to bar an "additional burlesque show" of the offensive sort cannot be sustained.

[10–12] The trial court rejected as insubstantial because "solely hearsay" the information which the director

viewed as establishing the questionable character of two of plaintiff's officers and that one of them from time to time had staged indecent performances in other places. The hearsay character of the information gathered by a licensing official in the performance of his duty does not necessarily invalidate the information as a basis for administrative action. Davis, Administrative Law (1951), sec. 143. But in our view the information relied upon by the director, in this case, if true, does not support the conclusion drawn from it. That one of the officers was victimized by extortioners while operating a Chicago theatre and did not reveal the full story when first interrogated by federal investigators, and that many years ago he was friendly with the brother of a notorious racketeer, if reflecting at all upon his character, suggest nothing as to the type of burlesque show plaintiff will exhibit. And the information that the other officer has staged indecent exhibitions in other cities is so fragmentary and the officer's alleged connection with the theatres involved so inconclusively shown that, having in view the constitutional protection accorded to speech and that speech is to be presumed to be protected speech and that the presumption is not the other way, such information cannot reasonably be viewed as establishing that plaintiff corporation will be guided by a person who persistently causes or permits the exhibition of lewd and indecent performances. Cf. *Bonserk Theatre Corp.* v. *Moss*, supra.

Without reference, then, to plaintiff's affidavits on the motion, the arbitrary nature of the refusal of the license plainly appears and the trial court properly entered judgment peremptorily ordering the issuance of the license. However, what appears in plaintiff's affidavits may appropriately be noted. Not only do the affidavits of the mentioned officers of the plaintiff deny or meet the derogatory information as to them relied upon by the director, but the officers expressly disclaim any intention to stage burlesque "with the colloquial meaning it has acquired in some areas," and avow an intention to stage "burlesque in the theatrical and dictionary sense." Furthermore, there is an affidavit of the National Administrative Secretary of the American Guild of Variety Artists, according to which that organization is made up of entertainers from every part of the United States whose "recognized principle and objective" is "that none of its members shall appear in or lend their names to lewd, indecent or illegal performances or shows" and who "would like to see a revival of the burlesque show" in its original concept offering both clean entertainment and, as in the past, a "training ground for the development of comedians and variety stars." The affidavit mentions members of the Guild whose names and faces are known in virtually every household in the land. Guild members perform at a Chicago theatre now and for some time operated by plaintiff's officers, who, the affidavit attests, "all are legitimate producers and exhibitors of good standing, recognized as persons from whom members of our Guild may accept employment without damage to their name or reputation."

[13] Comment is appropriate also upon the director's failure to give plaintiff a hearing prior to his determination. In the absence of a requirement by statute or ordinance, it has been held that a hearing before the license is denied is not essential to due process. *Thayer Amusement Co.* v. *Moulton*, 63 R.I. 182, 7 A. 2d 682, 124 A.L.R. 236 (Sup.

Ct. 1939); 33 Am. Jur., Licenses, p. 379. Due process may be satisfied when the applicant has the opportunity to learn and test out the basis of the action upon judicial review, cf. *State*, ex rel. *State Board of Milk Control* v. *Newark Milk Company*, 118 N.J. Eq. 504, 179 A. 116 (E. & A. 1935). The Newark ordinance provides for notice and hearing before suspension or revocation of a license, but not in the case of its issuance. However, apart from due process considerations, the practical benefits to be realized from a hearing suggest the desirability of affording one to the applicant in these cases. It is not alone that in simple fairness plaintiff's officers might well have been given an opportunity to know why the license was being refused and the chance to refute the information relied on as impugning their characters and intentions. There is also the interplay of the constitutional protection accorded freedom of expression taking the form of plays, shows and motion pictures which raises questions which should lead the licensing official to desire firm support in the way of proof before arriving at a finding that a proposed exhibition will be actually lewd and indecent. Equally desirable is the practice that the official report his findings based on the proofs. Such a practice would not only be useful to litigants and the court on review, but would inform the public upon just what the action is based. Cf. *Family Finance Corp.* v. *Gough*, 10 N.J. Super. 13, 76 A. 2d 82 (App. Div. 1950); Note 39, Columbia Law Review, supra, p. 1401. We note with interest that, since the taking of the action challenged in this proceeding, the defendant director of public safety has adopted rules and regulations providing that the directory may give the applicant a prior hearing in any case in which he thinks one may be warranted, and that in that event he will "temporarily refuse the application," give the applicant "five days' notice of the time and place of such hearing" and make his determination whether to issue the license from the evidence "taken at the hearing." If the ordinance is not to be amended to assure a hearing, this is at least a desirable procedural improvement by administrative action.

Affirmed.

For affirmance: Chief Justice VANDERBILT, and Justices HEHER, OLIPHANT, BURLING, JACOBS and BRENNAN—6.

For reversal: Justice WACHENFELD—1.

WACHENFELD, J., (dissenting).

The trial court concluded the director of public safety acted arbitrarily and abused his discretion in refusing the application because the affidavits relied upon referred solely to hearsay evidence, and therefore found against him.

This court, however, decides in the majority opinion:

"The hearsay character of the information gathered by a licensing official in the performance of his duty does not necessarily invalidate the information as a basis for administrative action." I subscribe to this determination and must therefore conclude the trial court committed error in deciding as it did.

I am not in accord with the conclusion of the majority, however, as the Legislature in this instance gave the city the right to adopt an ordinance regulating the subject matter and the city, in turn, placed the administration of such matters in the hands of the License Bureau in the department of the director of public safety, giving him full power to consider the applications for a license and to determine the qualification of the applicants.

There would impliedly be a duty on him to withhold such license with respect to such activities which inherently or potentially would detrimentally affect the public welfare, health and safety of the city. If the licensing authority cannot examine into the character of the applicant to be licensed, then the system affords little regulation or protection to the municipality involved.

The test is whether or not there has been a reasonably bona fide exercise of the discretion granted by the legislative authority, as distinguished from fraud or arbitrary action. There is a presumption of proper motive and valid reasons underlying the directive of the appellant, and we are not obliged to consider the evidence upon the technical rules which would be applicable to the exclusion of evidence in jury trials. Cf. *Federal Communications Comm.* v. *Pottsville Broadcasting Co.*, 309 U.S. 134, 60 S. Ct. 437, 84 L. Ed. 656 (1940).

In *Bonserk Theater Corp.* v. *Moss*, 34 N.Y.S. 2d 541 (Sup. Ct. 1942), the court held the issuing authority did not abuse its discretion in refusing the license of a burlesque show on the ground that persons through whom the corporation operated had in the past persisted in causing or permitting the production of shows which had been preponderantly offensive to public morals and decency, and that the individuals on other occasions had failed to keep their promises that their burlesque shows would be conducted decently.

Basing the appellant's actions upon the standards so pronounced, I think there is ample in the record to indicate that decency and good order would require the action taken and his decision is sufficiently supported by the record. The character and past conduct of the applicant and its officers, and especially their past exhibitions, reveal conflict with the law and successful criminal prosecutions against them because of the character of the shows which they exhibited and conducted.

I think the director of public safety was justified in his denial of the application and I would reverse the judgment below and sustain the appellant.

Commercial Pictures Corp.
v.
Board of Regents of University of State of New York.

COURT OF APPEALS OF NEW YORK.

May 28, 1953.

Florence Perlow Shientag, New York City, for appellant.

Sidney Freidberg and *Beate Bloch,* New York City, for Hygienic Productions, Inc., amicus curiæ, in support of appellant's position.

Charles A. Brind, Jr., Counsel, Albany (John P. Jehu, Elizabeth M. Eastman and George B. Farrington, Albany, of counsel), for respondent.

FROESSEL, Judge.

The Motion Picture Division of the State Education Department and the Regents of the University of the State of New York have determined that the motion picture "La Ronde" (revised), produced in France, is not entitled to be licensed for public exhibition, upon the ground that it is "immoral" and "would tend to corrupt morals" within the meaning of section 122 of the Education Law of this State, McK. Consol. Laws, c. 16. The Appellate Division has confirmed the determination.

The film from beginning to end deals with promiscuity, adultery, fornication and seduction. It portrays ten episodes, with a narrator. Except for the husband and wife episode, each deals with an illicit amorous adventure between two persons, one of the two partners becoming the principal in the next. The first episode begins with a prostitute and a soldier. Since the former's room is ten minutes walk from their meeting place on the street, and the soldier must hurry back to his barracks, they take advantage of the local environment. She informs him that "civilians" pay, but for "boys like you it's nothing." The cycle continues with the soldier and a parlormaid; the parlormaid and her employer's son; the latter and a young married woman; the married woman and her husband; the husband and a young girl; the girl and a poet; the poet and an actress; the actress and a count, and finally the count and the prostitute. At the very end, the narrator reminds the audience of the author's thesis: "It is the story of everyone."

Petitioner contends that the statute is invalid, in that it imposes a prior restraint upon the exercise of freedom of speech and press, relying principally upon *Joseph Burstyn, Inc.* v. *Wilson,* 1952, 343 U.S. 495, 72 S. Ct. 777, 96 L. Ed. 1098, which overruled *Mutual Film Corp.* v. *Industrial Comm. of Ohio,* 1915, 236 U.S. 230, 35 S. Ct. 387, 59 L. Ed. 552. In addition, it is contended that the standard here applied is too vague and indefinite to satisfy the requirements of due process. Respondent maintains that the Burstyn case, supra, is not controlling here, and

that the standard in question is sufficiently clear and definite. The issues so presented may be posed thus:

(1) Are motion pictures, as part of the press, altogether exempt from prior restraint or censorship?

(2) Do the words "immoral" and "tend to corrupt morals," in section 122 of the Education Law, viewed in the perspective of their legislative setting, fail to provide a standard adequate to satisfy the requirements of due process?

(3) Has the statute been properly applied herein?

[1] 1. Our answer to the first question must be in the negative, as it was in the Burstyn case in this court, *Joseph Burstyn, Inc.* v. *Wilson,* 303 N.Y. 242, 262, 101 N.E. 2d 665, 674; see, also, concurring opinion of Desmond, J., 303 N.Y. at pages 263–264, 101 N.E. 2d 675. That question was not reached by the Supreme Court of the United States in *Joseph Burstyn, Inc.* v. *Wilson,* supra, 343 U.S. 495, at pages 502–503, 505–506, 72 S. Ct. 777, at page 781, and the language employed therein aptly refutes the notion that all media of communication may be grouped under a precise and absolute rule: "To hold that liberty of expression by means of motion pictures is guaranteed by the First and Fourteenth Amendments, however, is not the end of our problem. It does not follow that the Constitution requires absolute freedom to exhibit every motion picture of every kind at all times and all places. That much is evident from the series of decisions of this Court with respect to other media of communication of ideas. Nor does it follow that motion pictures are necessarily subject to the precise rules governing any other particular method of expression. Each method tends to present its own peculiar problems." Nor did *Gelling* v. *Texas,* 343 U.S. 960, 72 S. Ct. 1002, 96 L. Ed. 1359, decided the week following on the authority of the Burstyn case, supra, 343 U.S. 495, 72 S. Ct. 777, resolve the issue left open therein.

Insofar, then, as motion pictures tend to present their "own peculiar problems," we think they may properly become the subject of special measures of control. If, as we believe, motion pictures may present a "clear and present danger" of substantive evil to the community, *Schenck* v. *United States,* 249 U.S. 47, 52, 39 S. Ct. 247, 63 L. Ed. 470, then the Legislature may act to guard against such evil, though in so doing it overrides to a degree the right to free expression. *Poulos* v. *State of New Hampshire,* 345 U.S. 395, 73, S. Ct. 760; *Beauharnais* v. *People of State of Illinois,* 343 U.S. 250, 72 S. Ct. 725, 96 L. Ed. 919; *Dennis* v. *United States,* 341 U.S. 494, 71 S. Ct. 857, 95 L. Ed. 1137; *American Communications Ass'n* v. *Douds,* 339 U.S. 382, 70 S. Ct. 674, 94 L. Ed. 925; *Kovacs* v.

Cooper, 336 U.S. 77, 69 S. Ct. 448, 93 L. Ed. 513; *Chaplinsky* v. *State of New Hampshire,* 315 U.S. 568, 62 S. Ct. 766, 86 L. Ed. 1031; *Schenck* v. *United States,* supra; *Fox* v. *Washington,* 236 U.S. 273, 35 S. Ct. 383, 59 L. Ed. 573. As was said in *Crowley* v. *Christensen,* 137 U.S. 86, 89, 11 S. Ct. 13, 15, 34 L. Ed. 620: "the possession and enjoyment of all rights are subject to such reasonable conditions as may be deemed by the governing authority of the country essential to the safety, health, peace, good order, and morals of the community. Even liberty itself, the greatest of all rights, is not unrestricted license to act according to one's own will."

The highest court in the land has recognized the right of the State to act to protect its citizens, even to the extreme of interfering with personal liberty, against the threat of disease. *Jacobson* v. *Com. of Massachusetts,* 197 U.S. 11, 25 S. Ct. 358, 49 L. Ed. 643. In that case, the court declared, 197 U.S. at page 27, 25 S. Ct. at page 362: "Upon the principle of self-defense, of paramount necessity, a community has the right to protect itself against an epidemic of disease which threatens the safety of its members." The same court later held that principle broad enough to permit the State to protect itself against the perpetuation of hereditary strains of imbecility through sterilization. *Buck* v. *Bell,* 274 U.S. 200, 207, 47 S. Ct. 584, 71 L. Ed. 1000. If it may so act to prevent physical disease, or the birth of the "manifestly unfit," may it not likewise act to prevent moral corruption, when the consequences thereof affect not only family life, as we know it in this State and country, but the health and welfare of our people as well?

The problem of preserving individual rights under the Constitution and still securing to the State the right to protect itself is not always an easy one, and it is sometimes difficult to find the proper balance between them. There is no mathematical formula for accommodating the rights of the individual to the good of the community, and we fully recognize that care must be exercised when preserving one not to suppress the other. But there "is no basis for saying that freedom and order are not compatible. That would be a decision of desperation. Regulation and suppression are not the same, either in purpose or result, and courts of justice can tell the difference." *Poulos* v. *State of New Hampshire,* supra, 345 U.S. at page 408, 73 S. Ct. at page 768.

Of course it is true that the State may not impose upon its inhabitants the moral code of saints, but, if it is to survive, it must be free to take such reasonable and appropriate measures as may be deemed necessary to preserve the institution of marriage and the home, and the health and welfare of its inhabitants. History bears witness to the fate of peoples who have become indifferent to the vice of indiscriminate sexual immorality—a most serious threat to the family, the home and the State. An attempt to combat such threat is embodied in the sections of the Education Law here challenged. It should not be thwarted by any doctrinaire approach to the problems of free speech raised thereby.

That a motion picture which panders to base human emotions is a breeding ground for sensuality, depravity, licentiousness and sexual immorality can hardly be doubted. That these vices represent a "clear and present danger" to the body social seems manifestly clear. The danger to youth is self-evident. And so adults, who may react with limited concern to a portrayal of larceny, will tend to react quite differently to a presentation wholly devoted to promiscuity, seductively portrayed in such manner as to invite concupiscence and condone its promiscuous satisfaction, with its evil social consequences. A single motion picture may be seen simultaneously in theatres throughout the State. May nothing be done to prevent countless individuals from being exposed to its vicious effects? To us the answer seems obvious, especially in the light of recent technical developments which render the problem more acute than ever. Now we have commercially feasible three dimensional projection, some forms of which are said to bring the audience "right into the picture." There can be no doubt that attempts will be made to bring the audience right into the bedchamber if it be held that the State is impotent to apply preventive measures.

[2] Such preventive measures necessarily embrace some form of censorship. It is significant that the American motion picture industry has adopted that very method of self-discipline as the effective remedy for immoral motion pictures through its well-known Code of Production Standards. The people of this State should not be compelled to rely upon the motion picture industry's own standards of review; nor, in the case of a foreign film, solely upon the customs officials, U.S.C.A., tit. 19, § 1305, for their judgment "in admitting the film did not prevent the state officers from arriving at a different judgment when it came to the exhibition of the film and the granting of a license therefor." *Eureka Productions* v. *Lehman,* D.C., 17 F. Supp. 259, 261, affirmed 302 U.S. 634, 58 S. Ct. 15, 82 L. Ed. 494, Id., 304 U.S. 541, 58 S. Ct. 944, 82 L. Ed. 1517. They have the right to exercise their own sovereign powers to determine for themselves what motion pictures transgress the bounds of decency and sexual morality laid down by common consent.

[3] As we see it, a statute which operates within limits suited to the attainment of such objectives, as does the enactment here challenged, is a reasonable and valid exercise of the police power. No other method will afford reasonably adequate protection to the public. Moreover, our statute places its administration in the hands of a responsible State agency, rather than with local officers who may at times be subject to petty prejudices or varying provincial views. Neither is it entirely out of place to point out that experience has demonstrated over the years that such censorship has been and can be carried out without undue hardship or even inconvenience as to motion pictures which meet the standards for public exhibition. We conclude, therefore, that censorship, as such, is not in every case inimical to the rights of free speech and press guaranteed by the Constitution, so far as motion pictures are concerned.

2. We now turn to a consideration of the standard applied herein. Section 212 of the Education Law provides that a motion picture shall not be licensed if it is "obscene, indecent, *immoral,* inhuman, sacrilegious, or is of *such a character that its exhibition would tend to corrupt morals* or incite to crime." We are concerned here only with the words we have italicized. Appellant would have us read them as though they stood alone, without other guide than their dictionary meanings, and thereby find them too broad and vague to serve as a valid standard for the limitation of constitutional rights. The Legislature has not used them in a vacuum, however, but in context with other words and in a setting with other statutes *in pari materia,* as, e.g., sections 1140–a and 1141 of the Penal Law, McK.

Consol. Laws, c. 40. Moreover, the "use of common experience as a glossary is necessary to meet the practical demands of legislation," and the "requirement of reasonable certainty does not preclude the use of ordinary terms to express ideas which find adequate interpretation in common usage and understanding," *Sproles* v. *Binford*, 286 U.S. 374, 393, 52 S. Ct. 581, 587, 76 L. Ed. 1167. Even in criminal law, "The test is whether the language conveys sufficiently definite warning as to the proscribed conduct when measured by common understanding and practices." *Jordan* v. *De George*, 341 U.S. 223, 231–232, 71 S. Ct. 703, 708, 95 L. Ed. 886.

Our Legislature has used the word "immoral," or its variants, in numerous other statutes, see Penal Law, §§ 483, 483–a, 483–b, 485, subd. 5; § 485–a, subd. 5; §§ 486, 494, 1140–a, 1141, 1141–a, 1147, 1290, subd. 4; §§ 1944–a, 2460; Education Law, §§ 2212, 3012, subd. 2; § 3013, subd. 2; §§ 3020, 6804; General Business Law, McK. Consol. Laws, c. 20, §§ 190, 191, subd. 3. Upon the basis of that standard, liberty, civil service tenure, and business licenses have been lost. To adopt the approach urged by petitioner would certainly throw doubt upon many of these enactments.

Accordingly to common understanding, the terms "immoral" and "morals" must be taken to refer to the moral standards of the community, the "norm or standard of behavior which struggles to make itself articulate in law." Cardozo, Paradoxes of Legal Science, pp. 17, 41–42. Thus the standards of any special and particular segment of the whole population are not to control, but those held by the community at large. As was said in *Block* v. *City of Chicago*, 239 Ill. 251, 263–264, 87 N.E. 1011, 1015; "There are the shameless and unclean, to whom nothing is defilement, and from whose point of view no picture would be considered immoral or obscene. Perhaps others could be found, with no laxity of morals, who pay homage to art and would not regard anything as indelicate or indecent which had artistic merit, and would look upon any person entertaining different sentiments as of inferior intelligence, without proper training on the subject, and blinded with bigotry. Both classes are exceptional, and the average person of healthy and wholesome mind knows well enough what the words 'immoral' and 'obscene' mean and can intelligently apply the test to any picture presented to him."

As applied to the general moral standards of the community, it is urged that such a standard may be too broad, although standards equally broad have been successfully applied. The term "moral turpitude" has been held adequate to satisfy even the strict rule applicable to criminal statutes, with the comment that "doubt as to the adequacy of a standard in less obvious cases does not render that standard unconstitutional." *Jordan* v. *De George*, 341 U.S. 223, 232, 71 S. Ct. 703, 708, supra. So, too, the term "good moral character," as used in the immigration and nationality laws, must frequently be applied by the courts. In so doing, their measure is the "common standards of morality" prevalent in the community, *Estrin* v. *United States*, 2 Cir., 80 F. 2d 105, or the "common conscience" of the community. *Johnson* v. *United States*, 2 Cir., 186 F. 2d 588, 590.

It is not a valid criticism that such general moral standards may vary slightly from generation to generation. Such variations are inevitable and do not affect the application of the principle at a particular period in time. See

Parmelee v. *United States*, 72 App. D.C. 203, 113, F. 2d 729. Neither may a standard be criticized on the ground that individual opinions may differ as to a particular application thereof. There is no principle or standard not subject to that infirmity, including the most specific provisions of the First Amendment. *Rochin* v. *California*, 342 U.S. 165, 170, 72 S. Ct. 205, 96 L. Ed. 183.

We are not unmindful of the fact that the provisions here in question, considered in the abstract, may be deemed broad, even as limited by common usage. Even in such case, however, it has been said that language "does not stand by itself * * * but is part of the whole body of common and statute law * * * and is to be judged in that context." *Musser* v. *Utah*, 333 U.S. 95, 97, 68 S. Ct. 397, 398, 92 L. Ed. 562. In the case now before us, we should not "parse the statute as grammarians or treat it as an abstract exercise in lexicography," *Beauharnais* v. *People of State of Illinois*, 343 U.S. 250, 253, 72 S. Ct. 725, 729, supra, but should read it as it was meant to be read by the Legislature that enacted it. In many of the statutes in which our Legislature has used the word "immoral" it obviously refers to sexual immorality. It is our view that it is used similarly in section 122 of the Education Law, as can be perceived in the statute itself, and in the construction put upon it, not only by the Regents herein, but by this court as well.

Turning to the statute, it will be noted that there is a related usage—a gradation of language, proceeding from "obscene" to "indecent" to "immoral," words frequently used together in statutory enactments, and thence to generically different categories: "inhuman" and "sacrilegious." That juxtaposition colors the word "immoral" and justifies the application of the rule *ejusdem generis*, particularly when coupled with the subsequent expression "tend to corrupt morals," as was done here. See McKinney's Consol. Laws of N.Y., Book 1, Statutes, 1942 ed., § 239; Penal Law, §§ 1140–a, 1141, where "obscene, indecent, immoral" are likewise grouped together; *People* v. *Wendling*, 258 N.Y. 451, 180 N.E. 169, 81 A.L.R. 799; *People* v. *Muller*, 96 N.Y. 408; *Regina* v. *Hicklin*, L.R. 3 Q.B. 360, 369–370; see, also, *Eureka Productions* v. *Lehman*, D.C., 17 F. Supp. 259, affirmed 302 U.S. 634, 58 S. Ct. 15, 82 L. Ed. 494, Id., 304 U.S. 541, 58 S. Ct. 944, 82 L. Ed. 1517, supra; *Swearingen* v. *United States*, 161 U.S. 446, 451, 16 S. Ct. 562, 40 L. Ed. 765.

[4] Apart from these considerations, it would appear that we have already construed the statute in precisely this manner. Section 1140–a of the Penal Law, and related sections, have been held to apply to motion pictures even prior to their express inclusion therein. *Hughes Tool Co.* v. *Fielding*, 297 N.Y. 1024, 80 N.E. 2d 540. The theory of that decision was that the Education Law and the Penal Law constitute complementary parts of a related whole. As used in the said Penal Law sections, the word "immoral" clearly relates to sexual immorality. Accordingly, its meaning in the Education Law should be the same, and the unpublished minutes of the proceedings of this court indicate that it was so treated in that case.[1]

[5] Viewing the statute under consideration in its

---

[1] After our decision therein, section 1141 of the Penal Law was amended to exempt from its provisions moving picture films licensed by the State Department of Education. L. 1950, ch. 624. If, therefore, the State be required to grant a license here, petitioner will be immune from criminal prosecution.

proper setting, then, the words "immoral" and "tend to corrupt morals" as used therein relate to standards of sexual morality. As such they are not vague or indefinite. In this sense they are kindred to "obscene" and "indecent," of which we have said: "They are words in common use, and every person of ordinary intelligence understands their meaning, and readily and in most cases accurately applies them to any object or thing brought to his attention which involves a judgment as to the quality indicated. It does not require an expert in art or literature to determine whether a picture is obscene or whether printed words are offensive to decency and good morals." *People* v. *Muller*, supra, 96 N.Y. at page 410–411. See, also *Chaplinsky* v. *State of New Hampshire*, 315 U.S. 568, 571–572, 62 S. Ct. 766, 86 L. Ed. 1031, supra. It should be remembered that we are not here dealing with a moral concept about which our people widely differ; sexual immorality is condemned throughout our land.

[6] 3. The remaining question is whether the statute has been properly invoked against the motion picture "La Ronde." We have already noted that it is concerned solely with promiscuous sex relations and are told: "It is the story of everyone." Although vulgar pornography is avoided, suggestive dialogue and action are present throughout and not merely incidentally, depicting promiscuity as the natural and normal relation between the sexes, whether married or unmarried. Can we disagree with the judgment that such a picture will tend to corrupt morals? To do so would close our eyes to the obvious facts of life. The story is patterned after the book, which was condemned for obscenity in *People* v. *Pesky*, 230 App. Div. 200, 202, 243 N.Y.S. 193, 196, affirmed 254 N.Y. 373, 173 N.E. 227. There the Appellate Division stated "there was nothing to it except a description of the licentious * * * without a single redeeming feature." The author of the original work himself felt that it "might very well be misunderstood and misinterpreted," and so it was privately published. Even among the favorable reviews submitted by petitioner were such comments as:

"The details are concrete enough to make one blush unseen * * *.

"With something less than tremulous delicacy, he [the director] and his associate artists, speak quite freely upon the joys and woes of amorous adventure."

It may also be noted that among the industry's self-imposed limitations pertaining to sex are the following: "The sanctity of the institution of marriage and the home shall be upheld. Pictures shall not infer that low forms of sex relationship are the accepted or common thing." Code of Production Standards, "Particular Applications" II, 1950 Year Book of Motion Pictures, pp. 920–922. "La Ronde" infers just that. In the minds of American motion picture producers, then, such a picture as is now before us would tend to "lower the moral standards of those who see it." Code of Production Standards, "General Principles" 1.

We think it plain that we cannot say that the Regents were wrong in refusing the license herein. It has been suggested that we should form an independent judgment as to each picture which might become the subject of controversy between the distributor and the Regents, but that would simply mean that the powers granted to the Regents by statute could be arrogated to this court by judicial action. In the scheme of things, there must be some agency to which is entrusted the fact-finding power.

In criminal cases it is the jury; in matters of administration generally, it is the administrative agency; in motion picture review, it is the Regents. No constitutional argument can be presented for having it otherwise. If the Regents err in law, we sit to correct them. If they must exercise their fact-finding powers in a close case and do so honestly and fairly, then due process has been observed. See *Nash* v. *United States*, 229 U.S. 373, 377, 33 S. Ct. 780, 57 L. Ed. 1232.

It is not for us to question the wisdom of placing that fact-finding power in the hands of the Regents rather than the courts. Neither do we think any such debate could be very productive, for strong and persuasive arguments can be made to the effect that an experienced administrative body is better qualified than a court to judge the effect of a particular motion picture, and that we of the judicial branch should not be left "at liberty to substitute our judgment for theirs, or to supersede their function as the spokesmen of the thought and sentiment of the community in applying to the [motion picture] * * * the standard of propriety established by the statute," *People* v. *Pesky*, supra, 254 N.Y. at pages 373–374, 173 N.E. at page 227.

In summary, we conclude that motion pictures may be censored, upon proper grounds, and that sexual immorality is one such ground. The standard "immoral" and "tend to corrupt morals" embodied in the statute and here applied relates to sexual immorality, and the Regents had the right to find that the motion picture in question falls within the prohibited category.

The order appealed from should be affirmed, with costs.

DESMOND, Judge (concurring).

I concur for affirmance.

We review the refusal by the Board of Regents of the State of New York, acting under sections 120 and 122 of the State Education Law, to license the exhibition in New York State of the motion picture "La Ronde." Section 122 directs that every submitted motion picture film be licensed "unless such film or a part thereof is obscene, indecent, immoral, inhuman, sacrilegious, or is of such a character that its exhibition would tend to corrupt morals or incite to crime." The stated ground for the Regents' refusal here was that "La Ronde" was "immoral and tended to corrupt morals." The film depicts a series of illicit sexual adventures, nothing more, and is a close adaptation, for the screen, from Schnitzler's novel "Reigen" which, translated into English as "Hands Around," was held to be criminally obscene in *People* v. *Pesky*, 230 App. Div. 200, 243 N.Y.S. 193, affirmed 254 N.Y. 373, 173 N.E. 227. We have seen this motion picture, and while we agree with appellant's counsel that it "has a distinguished cast and a brilliant production," we find, too, that its only discoverable theme is this: that everyone is sexually promiscuous, and that life is just a "round" of sexual promiscuity. It would be understatement to apply to this photoplay the characterization given another film in *Eureka Productions* v. *Byrne*, 252 App. Div. 355, 357, 300 N.Y.S. 218, 221, that it "unduly emphasizes the carnal side of the sex relationship." This picture has no other content.

On this appeal, it seems to us, these three questions of law are to be answered, and in this order:

1. Is all pre-censorship of motion pictures violative of the First Amendment to the Federal Constitution?

2. If not, is the New York statute unconstitutional, for lack of precise standards, at the point where it permits the banning of a picture on a charge that it is "immoral" or "tends to corrupt morals"?

3. If questions 1 and 2 are both answered in the negative, was there reasonable basis here for the Regents' finding that "La Ronde" is immoral and tends to corrupt morals?

Our answers are these:

1. The New York State's motion picture censorship statute was enacted in 1921, L. 1921, ch. 715, was held constitutional by this court in 1923, *Pathe Exch.* v. *Cobb*, 236 N.Y. 539, 142 N.E. 274, and, except as to its use of "sacrilegious" as one of its standards, has never been held invalid. Our law, under which thousands of pictures have been licensed or denied licenses, is typical of the eight State statutes and perhaps seventy-five municipal ordinances that have made their appearance since the first such enactment: the Chicago ordinance of 1907, *Block* v. *City of Chicago*, 239 Ill. 251, 87 N.E. 1011. In the Federal courts, such censorship statutes were, beginning about 1915, held not to contravene the First Amendment, which, it was at that time held, did not apply to motion pictures, since the exhibition thereof was then regarded as a mere part of the business of providing entertainment in theatres, see *Mutual Film Corp.* v. *Ohio Ind. Comm.*, 236 U.S. 230, 35 S. Ct. 387, 59 L. Ed. 552; *Mutual Film Co.* v. *Ohio Ind. Comm.*, 236 U.S. 247, 35 S. Ct. 393, 59 L. Ed. 561; *Mutual Film Corp. of Missouri* v. *Hodges*, 236 U.S. 248, 35 S. Ct. 393, 59 L. Ed. 561. There were numerous similar holdings in various Federal and State courts. Appreciating the delicacy of the questions inherent in all censorship, but realizing, too, the danger, especially to the immature, of the free showing of demoralizing films (New York since 1909 has, for instance, limited attendance of children at motion picture theatres—see Penal Law, § 484, subd. 1), this sovereign State put the licensing power in one of its most powerful and most respected governmental bodies, the Board of Regents, a "citizens' board" which is at the head of the State's educational system. Censorship in New York is, therefore, carried on at the highest levels of responsible State Government.

In 1951, this court re-examined, in Matter of *Joseph Burstyn, Inc.* v. *Wilson*, 303 N.Y. 242, 101 N.E. 2d 665, the question of the constitutionality of pre-censorship of films, and found no reason to change our earlier decision. Later, the Supreme Court of the United States, in the same Burstyn case, 343 U.S. 495, 72 S. Ct. 777, 96 L. Ed. 1098, decided for the first time (it had intimated this result in 1948 in *United States* v. *Paramount Pictures*, 334 U.S. 131, 166, 68 S. Ct. 915, 92 L. Ed. 1260) that expression by means of motion pictures is included within the free speech and free press guarantee of the First and Fourteenth Amendments. Going further, the highest court held that the word "sacrilegious" provided no valid test or standard, since it subjected films to "conflicting currents of religious views" supra, 343 U.S. at page 504, 72 S. Ct. at page 782. But the Supreme Court found it unnecessary, in Burstyn, to decide whether a State may censor motion pictures under a clearly drawn statute designed and applied to prevent, for instance, the showing of obscene films. 343 U.S. at pages 505–506, 72 S. Ct. 777. Thus the Burstyn

decision, while it ruled out "sacrilegious" as a permissible censoring standard, certainly did not strike down, completely, the police power of the States to pre-censor motion pictures. "It does not follow" said the court, supra, 343 U.S. at page 502, 72 S. Ct. at page 781, "that the Constitution requires absolute freedom to exhibit every motion picture of every kind at all times and all places." Historically, of course, the First Amendment has never provided immunity for every possible use of language. *Robertson* v. *Baldwin*, 165 U.S. 275, 281, 17 S. Ct. 326, 41 L. Ed. 715; *Frohwerk* v. *United States*, 249 U.S. 204, 206, 39 S. Ct. 249, 63 L. Ed. 561.

The constitutional doctrine which forbids pre-censorship of the press, *Near* v. *State of Minnesota* ex rel. *Olson*, 283 U.S. 697, 51 S. Ct. 625, 75 L. Ed. 1357, expresses, primarily, the insistence of the American people that the publication of ideas and opinions, especially as to governments, public officers, and public questions should not be restrained here, as they had been elsewhere. See *Patterson* v. *State of Colorado*, 205 U.S. 454, 464, 465, 27 S. Ct. 556, 51 Ed. 879. And the doctrine itself has been subject always to an exception, as to publications which tend to corrupt morals or incite to crime or vice. See *People* v. *Gitlow*, 234 N.Y. 132, 136 N.E. 317; *People* v. *Most*, 171 N.Y. 423, 431, 64 N.E. 175, 178; *Pathe Exch.* v. *Cobb*, 202 App. Div. 450, 195 N.Y.S. 661, affirmed 236 N.Y. 539, 142 N.E. 274, supra; *Patterson* v. *State of Colorado*, 205 U.S. 454, 27 S. Ct. 556, 51 L. Ed. 879, supra; *Schenck* v. *United States*, 249 U.S. 47, 39 S. Ct. 247, 63 L. Ed. 470; *Gitlow* v. *New York*, 268 U.S. 652, 666, 45 S. Ct. 625, 69 L. Ed. 1138; *People* v. *Croswell*, 1804, 3 Johns. Cas. 337, 392; Cooley on Constitutional Limitations [7th ed.], pp. 604–605. That exception usually finds application in post-punishment rather than pre-censorship, but the system of distribution and showing of motion pictures makes it feasible, if not necessary, to examine and license or refuse to license them before exhibition to audiences. We realize, as does everyone else, and as did the Supreme Court in 1915 in *Mutual Film Corp.* v. *Ohio Ind. Comm.*, supra, and in 1952 in *Joseph Burstyn, Inc.* v. *Wilson*, supra, that motion pictures have vast potentialities for evil, and we know, as practical people, that there is no effective way to suppress the damaging ones except by a system of censorship, see *Superior Films* v. *Department of Educ.*, 1953, 159 Ohio St. 315, 112 N.E. 2d 311. "Justification for upholding a censorship statute couched in indefinite terms may lie in the interest to be protected and not in semantics" 37 Minn. L. Rev., p. 211. So, unless and until so constrained by higher judicial authority, we will not say that the police power of our State cannot be used to keep such evil from our people.

2. Next, we answer the question as to the sufficiency, as a standard for licensing, of the statutory language: "immoral" and "tend to corrupt morals." We know that "immoral" is rather a sweeping term, of large and perhaps not mathematically delimited meaning, but we know, too, that if statutes could use only scientifically exact terminology, much of our statute law would be invalid. Words and phrases like "moral," "immoral," "good moral character," "impairing morals," etc., abound in New York statutes. See, for instance, Social Welfare Law, McK. Consol. Laws, c. 55, § 448; Penal Law, §§ 483, 484–a, 486, 494, 580, subd. 6; §§ 1140–a, 1141, 1141–a, 1145, 1147, 1148, 1933; Education Law, §§ 2212, 3012, 3013, 3020, 6804; General

Business Law, §§ 190, 191; Agriculture and Markets Law, McK. Consol. Laws, c. 69, §§ 57, 57–a, and zoning statutes such as Village Law, McK. Consol. Laws, c. 64, § 175, and Town Law, McK. Consol. Laws, c. 62, § 261. In some of those statutes, the verbiage, because of context, limits itself to sexual morals—not so here, we think. Sexual impurity is only one form of immorality. See *Swearingen* v. *United States*, 161 U.S. 446, 451, 16 S. Ct. 562, 40 L. Ed. 765. This picture "La Ronde" could be classed as "immoral" in the narrower sense, too, but the statutory meaning here is the usual or dictionary one (including the law dictionaries), and its reference is to the generally accepted civilized code of morals—its prohibition is of material "*contra bonos mores.*" That, too, is the clearly intended meaning in several other censorship statutes. *Block* v. *City of Chicago*, 239 Ill. 251, 264, 87 N.E. 1011, supra; *People ex rel. First Nat. Pictures* v. *Dever*, 242 Ill. App. 1; *Schuman* v. *Pickert*, 277 Mich. 225, 229, 269 N.W. 152; see *United States* v. *One Obscene Book* Entitled "Married Love," D.C., 48 F. 2d 821, 823. If it meant, in our statute, sexually vicious only, the word "immoral" would be tautological and repetitious, since it is there coupled with "obscene" and "indecent." And why should our Legislature have placed a ban on one kind, only, of immorality? "Immoral" (or its antonym "moral") is a listed standard in at least five (besides New York) State motion picture censorship laws (those of Pennsylvania, Ohio, Virginia, Kansas, Maryland). Indeed, the very word "moral" in the Ohio law was taken in its usual broad sense and held to be sufficiently definite for these purposes, in *Mutual Film Corp.* v. *Ohio Ind. Comm.* in these words, 236 U.S. 230, 245–246, 35 S. Ct. 392, supra: "The objection to the statute is that it furnishes no standard of what is educational, moral, amusing, or harmless, and hence leaves decision to arbitrary judgment, whim, and caprice * * *. But the statute by its provisions guards against such variant judgments, and its terms, like other general terms, get precision from the sense and experience of men, and become certain and useful guides in reasoning and conduct. The exact specification of the instances of their application would be as impossible as the attempt would be futile. Upon such sense and experience, therefore, the law properly relies." We think the Supreme Court there must have read "moral" in the meaning we give it here, and the Supreme Court there pointed out that, unless words of such seeming generality were valid in statutes, government itself would become impossible. There can be no objection to the use, in a statute, of a word like "immoral" which includes many things, all of which are intended by the Legislature to be covered; otherwise, there would be barred from statutory use such customary verbiage as "fraudulent," "due," "negligent," "arbitrary," "reasonable," etc. Legislatures use such words not "vaguely" but inclusively. That a word has many meanings, one or more of which are definitely pointed up by the surrounding verbiage, is no more reason for barring its use than if the word had one meaning only. It is too late to change the common usage of the word "immoral," or to ascribe absurdity to it, so as to invalidate a statute. Although the Supreme Court, in Burstyn, supra, reversed that part of the Mutual Film Corp holding which deals with the free speech question, Mutual's rule as to the propriety of "moral" or "immoral," as a motion picture censorship standard in Ohio remains undisturbed, so far as we know. So the Ohio Supreme

Court pointed out, on April 29, 1953, in *Superior Films* v. *Department of Educ.* (159 Ohio St. 315, 112 N.E. 2d 311, supra).

Long ago our court, *Lyon* v. *Mitchell*, 36 N.Y. 235, 238, approved definitions of "morality" as " 'that science which teaches men their duty, and the reason of it' " and as " 'the rule which teaches us to live soberly and honestly. It hath four chief virtues, justice, prudence, temperance and fortitude.' " In that opinion, in 1867, our great predecessors on this bench wrote that: "Sound morals, as taught by the wise men of antiquity, as confirmed by the precepts of the gospel * * * are unchangeable. They are the same yesterday and today." We see no reason to retreat from those ideas. "We are a religious people whose institutions presuppose a Supreme Being," *Zorach* v. *Clauson*, 343 U.S. 306, 313, 72 S. Ct. 679, 684, 96 L. Ed. 954. Our Federal and State Constitutions assume that the moral code, which is part of God's order in this world, exists as the substance of society. The people of this State have acted through their Legislature, on that assumption. We have not so cast ourselves adrift from that code, nor are we so far gone in cynicism, that the word "immoral" has no meaning for us. Our duty, as a court, is to uphold and enforce the laws, not seek reasons for destroying them.

3. If there be validity to our answers above numbered 1 and 2, we will have no difficulty with the third question, that is, as to whether the Regents were justified in finding that "La Ronde" is immoral, and tends to corrupt morals. It is of no pertinence here that great literature of all ages, including the Sacred Scriptures, abounds with descriptions of rapes, fornications and adulteries. The difference here is that the whole theme, motif and subject matter of this film, its dominant and sole effect, is sexual immorality. The totality of it, and every part of it, is sexual immorality. The point is not that it depicts immoral conduct—it glorifies and romanticizes it, and conveys the idea that it is universal and inevitable. Are we as a court to say as matter of law that it does not thus "tend to corrupt morals"? This court should hold that the State of New York may prevent the publication of such matter, the obvious tendency of which is "to deprave or corrupt those whose minds are open to such immoral influences, and who might come into contact with it." *People* v. *Muller*, 96 N.Y. 408, 411, following *Regina* v. *Hicklin*, L.R. 3 Q.B. 360, 369–370; See *People* v. *Doubleday & Co.*, 297 N.Y. 687, 77 N.E. 2d 6, affirmed 335 U.S. 848, 69 S. Ct. 79, 93 L. Ed. 398; *United States* v. *Dennett*, 2 Cir., 39 F. 2d 564, 76 A.L.R. 1092; *United States* v. *Levine*, 2 Cir., 83 F. 2d 156. Such is the valid State policy and purpose, and we enforce it by affirming this Regents' determination.

The order should be affirmed, with costs.

Conway, Judge (concurring).

I am in entire accord with the opinion of Judge Froessel but believe that we may properly go further and therefore I fully agree also with the view stated by Judge Desmond in his concurring opinion.

Dye, Judge (dissenting).

By the decision about to be made a majority of this court approves as a valid enactment, the New York motion picture licensing statute, notwithstanding that it provides for censorship in advance, which as we read it, constitutes an infringement of the basic civil right of freedom of speech and publication contrary to due process. U.S. Const. 1st, 5th, 14th Amends.; N.Y. Const. art. 1, §§ 6, 8; Education Law, § 122. I must therefore record my dissent.

The question arises out of the refusal of the State Board of Regents to approve the issuance of a license to permit the showing of the motion picture film "La Ronde" for the reason, couched in the language of the statute, "that the said film is 'immoral' and that its exhibition 'would tend to corrupt morals' within the meaning of Section 122 of the Education Law."

The case is before us in an appeal as of right from an order of the Appellate Division, Third Judicial Department, entered in a proceeding under article 78 of the Civil Practice Act, at the instance of this appellant, Education Law, § 124, and heard by the Appellate Division in the first instance. Civil Practice Act, § 1296. When the petitioner, a California corporation and sole owner of the distribution rights of the said picture in the United States, first applied for an exhibitor's license, Education Law, §§ 120–122, the director of the motion picture division refused it on the ground that the picture was "immoral" and "would tend to corrupt morals." Following established practice in such circumstances, the petitioner re-edited the film and re-submitted its application, but even so the director again refused to issue a license. A review of his determination was then had before a three-man committee of the State Board of Regents, Education Law, § 124, which, after viewing the picture, as we have said, confirmed the director's determination. In the court below the confirmation of the determination and the dismissal of the proceedings was on the ground that the applicable statute was a valid enactment and that confirmation was required under familiar doctrine limiting the function of a reviewing court whenever there is "warrant in the record and a reasonable basis in law" for the board's determination. In other words if the issue is debatable, the action of the administrative body is to be upheld. *Mounting & Finishing Co.* v. *McGoldrick*, 294 N.Y. 104, 60 N.E. 2d 825. However correct that may be as a rule of thumb in the review of administrative cases turning on a controverted issue of fact, it is inapplicable in a case involving fundamental civil rights secured by the State and Federal Constitutions for then a determination must be so clear, as the dissenting Judges in the court below observed, "that any conclusion to the contrary would not be entertained by any reasonable mind. It is wholly inconsistent with a constitutional guarantee to leave any debatable issue of morals, involved in any form of protected expression, to the final decision of an administrative agency." *Commercial Pictures Corp.* v. *Board of Regents*, 280 App. Div. 260, 265, 114 N.Y.S. 2d 561, 566. In such a situation "the reviewing court is bound to re-examine the whole record" in the light of the challenge made, *Joseph Burstyn, Inc.* v. *Wilson*, 343 U.S. 495, 72 S. Ct. 777, 96 L. Ed. 1098; *Universal Camera Corp.* v. *National Labor Relations Bd.*, 340 U.S. 474, 71 S. Ct. 456, 95 L. Ed. 456; *Niemotko* v. *Maryland*, 340 U.S. 268, 71 S. Ct. 325, 328, 95 L. Ed. 267, 280; *Norris* v. *Alabama*, 294 U.S. 587, 55 S. Ct. 579, 79 L. Ed. 1074.

Since the decision in *Joseph Burstyn, Inc.* v. *Wilson*, 343 U.S. 495, 72 S. Ct. 777, 96 L. Ed. 1098, supra, reversing 303 N.Y. 242, 101 N.E. 2d 665, there is no longer any doubt but that motion picture films enjoy the same constitutional freedom and protection accorded other media of human expression, cf. *United States* v. *Paramount Pictures*, 334 U.S. 131, 68 S. Ct. 915, 92 L. Ed. 1260; *Stromberg* v. *California*, 283 U.S. 359, 51 S. Ct. 532, 75 L. Ed. 1117, and this is so even though motion pictures as such are primarily designed to entertain at exhibitions conducted for private profit and even though motion picture films as such possess "a greater capacity for evil, particularly among the youth of a community, than other modes of expression," Burstyn, supra, 343 U.S. at page 502, 72 S. Ct. at page 780.

In the Burstyn case, supra, the Board of Regents had refused a license to show the motion picture entitled "The Miracle" on the ground that it was "sacrilegious" within the meaning of section 122 of the Education Law. When the case was in this court we approved such determination in reliance on the validity of regulation by prior censorship in accordance with our decision in *Pathe Exch.* v. *Cobb*, 236 N.Y. 539, 142 N.E. 274, affirming 202 App. Div. 450, 195 N.Y.S. 661. That decision, in turn, had followed *Mutual Film Corp.* v. *Ohio Ind. Comm.*, 236 U.S. 230, 35 S. Ct. 387, 59 L. Ed. 552, *Mutual Film Co.* v. *Ohio Ind. Comm.*, 236 U.S. 247, 35 S. Ct. 393, 59 L. Ed. 561, and *Mutual Film Corp.* v. *Hodges*, 236 U.S. 248, 35 S. Ct. 393, 59 L. Ed. 561, in which the United States Supreme Court had approved as a valid enactment in Ohio, a pre-censorship statute.

We note that in deciding the Burstyn case supra, 343 U.S. at page 505–506, 72 S. Ct. 777, 783, the United States Supreme Court found it unnecessary to pass on the issue of prior censorship preferring to leave such question until presented "under a clearly drawn statute designed and applied to prevent the showing of obscene films" since the term "sacrilegious," the sole standard under attack, afforded an adequate basis for reversal. Nonetheless, that is not to say the learned court was unmindful of the iniquity of prior restraint which (in the field of publication) they long before had ruled, 343 U.S. at page 503, 72 S. Ct. 781, was an "infringement upon freedom of expression to be especially condemned." *Thomas* v. *Collins*, 323 U.S. 516, 65 S. Ct. 315, 89 L. Ed. 430; *Lovell* v. *City of Griffin*, 303 U.S. 444, 58 S. Ct. 666, 82 L. Ed. 949; *Grosjean* v. *American Press Co.*, 297 U.S. 233, 56 S. Ct. 444, 80 L. Ed. 660; *Near* v. *State of Minnesota*, 283 U.S. 697, 51 S. Ct. 625, 75 L. Ed. 1357; *Patterson* v. *State of Colorado*, 205 U.S. 454, 27 S. Ct. 556, 51 L. Ed. 879.

Since the courts no longer see any distinction separating motion picture film from the protection accorded other media of communication, it follows as a matter of reason and logic that prior censorship of motion pictures is as to them as it is in other fields of expression, a denial of due process. In saying this we are, of course, mindful of the correlative obligation that in its exercise and enjoyment such right is not unlimited and absolute at all times and under all circumstances, *Chaplinsky* v. *New Hampshire*, 315 U.S. 568, 62 S. Ct. 766, 86 L. Ed. 1031; *Cox* v. *New Hampshire*, 312 U.S. 569, 61 S. Ct. 762, 85 L. Ed. 1049, but that such freedom may properly be restrained when inimical to the public welfare, *Gitlow* v. *New York*, 268 U.S. 652, 45 S. Ct. 625, 69 L. Ed. 1138, and the State may punish its abuse, *Near* v. *Minnesota*, supra. It is equally well established that before such limitation may be imposed the abuse complained of is to be examined in all cases to determine whether it is of such a nature "as to create a clear and present danger [and] will bring about the substantive evils that Congress has a right to prevent," *Schenck* v. *United States*, 249 U.S. 47, 52, 39 S. Ct. 247, 249, 63 L. Ed. 470, which danger should be "apparent and imminent" *Thornhill* v. *Alabama*, 310 U.S. 88, 60 S. Ct. 736, 84 L. Ed. 1093, such, for example, as a threat to overthrow the government by unconstitutional means, *Dennis* v. *United States*, 341 U.S. 494, 71 S. Ct. 857, 95 L. Ed. 1137. By the same token, when public safety is involved, its restraint will be approved as a proper exercise of the police power, *Feiner* v. *People of State of New York*, 340 U.S. 315, 71 S. Ct. 303, 95 L. Ed. 267, affirming 300 N.Y. 391, 91 N.E. 2d 316; *Kovacs* v. *Cooper*, 336 U.S. 77, 69 S. Ct. 448, 93 L. Ed. 513, or, to state it differently, there must be present some "overriding public interest" (see dissenting opinion per Fuld, J., in *Joseph Burstyn, Inc.* v. *Wilson*, supra, 303 N.Y. at page 269, 101 N.E. 2d at page 679; *Thornhill* v. *Alabama*, supra), mere fear of possible injury is not enough. *Terminiello* v. *Chicago*, 337 U.S. 1, 69 S. Ct. 894, 93 L. Ed. 1131.

Having in mind these well-recognized principles, it is pertinent to inquire what if anything there is about "La Ronde" that requires denial of constitutional safeguards and the imposition of the sanction of prior restraint. Is it because a showing would offend against some overriding need—would constitute a danger clear and present? We think not.

According to the record, the picture "La Ronde" since its admission through Customs without objection, U.S. Code, tit. 18, § 1462; U.S.C.A. tit. 19, § 1305, has been exhibited throughout the United States in cities and towns in the States of Arizona, California, Colorado, Connecticut, Delaware, Florida, Kentucky, Louisiana, Maine, Massachusetts, Michigan, Missouri, New Jersey, Oklahoma, Oregon, Texas and Washington, D.C. Nowhere has the showing of "La Ronde" been banned except in New York. While experience elsewhere is not binding on the courts in New York, the opinions of qualified critics may be considered. *United States* v. *One Book* Entitled *Ulysses*, 2 Cir., 72 F. 2d 705. We deem it significant that in the States of Louisiana, LSA–R.S. tit. 4, §§ 301–307, and Massachusetts, Mass. Ann. Law, ch. 136 §§ 2–4, having censorship laws, though to be sure, not as comprehensive as that in New York, the picture has had an unhampered showing as well as in places where municipal codes are in effect such as Detroit, Michigan; Salem, Oregon and Houston, Texas, to mention a few, a circumstance indicating that in a large segment of society the picture is not offensive per se. Such a showing in other States and cities of this country, where prior restraint was available and not invoked, and elsewhere having no such statutes, all without untoward incident or complaint is a convincing testimonial that it is not inimical to the public peace, welfare and safety. On the contrary, we are told that the showing elsewhere has been well received and has elicited favorable acclaim by the premier dramatic critics of eminent publications in which we may read:

"La Ronde is all of a piece, as any round should be, setting up a mocking harmony of desire and disillusion, vanity, pleasure and deceit. It is never prurient, smirking or pornographic. For all the intimacy of its nuances, the film's approach is dryly detached and completely charming; it spoofs sex rather than exploits it, much as Britain's satiric Kind Hearts and Coronets makes sport of murder." Time Magazine, Oct. 22, 1951.

"Here is a lovely motion picture, a gay, a glad, a sad, a sentimental movie * * * about Vienna at the turn of the century, the Vienna of candlelight and carriages, of wine, women and waltzes. * * * All this is told with a combination of irony, candor and gentleness that makes of the whole a total gem of a motion picture. * * * a picture about illicit love, but it is told without prudishness and with a deftness, discretion and understanding that make it more moral than most censor-shackled pictures on the subject." Daily News, Los Angeles, Sept. 21, 1951.

"The players * * * are among the cream of French talent and virtually flawless here." Los Angeles Times, Sept. 21, 1951.

"The * * * players * * * represent the cream of France's romantic actors." The Evening Star, Washington, D.C., July 28, 1951.

"* * * a splendid and glittering cast that includes Anton Walbrook, Gerard Philipe, Isa Miranda, Danielle Darrieux, Daniel Gelin, Simone Simon, Jean-Louis Barrault, Fernand Gravet, and Odette Joveux. * * * their portrayals have that quality of nuance that makes a second viewing almost obligatory. * * * Through the strata of a world-weary Viennese society the story spirals, until we find we have arrived at much the same point from which we have begun. It's more sad than bitter, more ironic than funny, and there's some haunting little message' underneath it all, though, to be sure, you are never quite told what it is. * * * delicately done and in excellent taste." Saturday Review of Literature, Nov. 10, 1951.

In addition, it has been shown in the principal cities of most foreign countries and has received special recognition for merit from several motion picture academies as, for instance, in Cuba as the best film of 1951, by the British Film Academy in London as the best film from any source, British or foreign, and in 1952, a nomination for an award at the Hollywood Academy.

Nonetheless if it may be said that prior censorship serves a necessary and needful public purpose warranting the abridgement of the right of free speech and press, it remains for the statute under review to meet the test of definiteness required to constitute a valid delegation of legislative power to an administrative agency. Unless it does so, it cannot be regarded as the "clearly drawn statute" envisioned by the Supreme Court, Burstyn, supra, 343 U.S. at page 506, 72 S. Ct. at page 783; *Kunz* v. *New York*, 340 U.S. 290, 71 S. Ct. 312, 95 L. Ed. 280; *Winters* v. *New York*, 333 U.S. 507, 68 S. Ct. 665, 92 L. Ed. 840; *Connally* v. *General Constr. Co.*, 269 U.S. 385, 46 S. Ct. 126, 70 L. Ed. 322; *Small Co.* v. *American Sugar Ref. Co.*, 267 U.S. 233, 45 S. Ct. 295, 69 L. Ed. 589; *United States* v. *L. Cohen Grocery Co.*, 255 U.S. 81, 41 S. Ct. 298, 65 L. Ed. 516, and we too apply such principle whenever needed. *Packer Collegiate Inst.* v. *University of State of N.Y.*, 298 N.Y. 184, 81 N.E. 2d 80; *Fink* v. *Cole*, 302 N.Y. 216, 97 N.E. 2d 873; *Small* v. *Moss*, 279 N.Y. 288, 18 N.E. 2d 281.

It is indeed significant that when the Legislature enacted the censorship statute under review it omitted to provide any criteria or standards to guide the Board of Regents in performing the administrative functions required of it, but was content to use language of broad and general import leaving its meaning and application to the individual judgment of its director of the motion picture division in the first instance, § 122, or if denied, to a committee of three members of the board, § 124.

Indefiniteness affords opportunity for arbitrariness, the tendency to which is nowhere better illustrated than in the field of administrative law. It is for this reason that delegation of legislative power is carefully scrutinized, whether to a private agency, *Fink* v. *Cole*, supra, or to a governmental agency, *Packer Collegiate Inst.* v. *University of State of N.Y.*, supra; *Small* v. *Moss*, supra. If this is not enough, then the board itself has been equally delinquent in failing to adopt rules and regulations for the guidance of its motion picture division in the exercise of censorship powers, but has left the generality of the statutory language to gain precision "from sense and experience" Mutual Film cases, supra, a method no longer approved, Burstyn, and is particularly objectionable here as it vests unlimited restraining control over motion pictures in a censor limited only by what an individual director of the motion picture division or, upon review, by what three members of the board itself happen to think about a particular picture at a given time, cf. *Winters* v. *New York*, supra; *Gelling* v. *Texas*, 343 U.S. 960, 72 S. Ct. 1002, 96 L. Ed. 1359. Such lack, it goes without saying, leaves an appellate court at a very great disadvantage. We do not know what standards guided the agency in making its determination. To supply such legislative omission by judicial fiat is not permissible under the division of governmental powers as fixed by the Constitution. It has long been recognized that courts may not usurp the legislative function under the guise of adjudication. The evils of allowing an administrative agency, however worthy its purpose, to function without proper legislative guidance is well illustrated by this very case. The lack of proper standards and guidance has led the State Board of Regents into a most surprising record of inconsistency and illustrates at first hand the evils of slap-dash censorship. For instance, we do not know whether they apply the terms "immoral" and "tend to corrupt morals" to pictures dealing with sex impurity or to pictures dealing with any matter which could be deemed *contra bonos mores.* Here we have a picture which, concededly, is not obscene or indecent but which nonetheless is banned from a New York showing because deemed "immoral" and its exhibition "would tend to corrupt morals" which is difficult to reconcile with the issuance of permits to show other pictures dealing not only with illicit love but also crime, such as Dreiser's "American Tragedy" (based on *People* v. *Gillette*, 191 N.Y. 107, 83 N.E. 680), "A Street Car Named Desire" and "The Outlaw," and those of a lurid type whose blow-up posters call attention to "Outcast Girls," "Female Sex," "Naked Realism." The case at hand is the only instance brought to our attention where denial has been based solely on the term "immoral" which the Regents applied because "promiscuity" is the central theme. True, the term "immoral" has been used in numerous other instances but always, we note, in juxtaposition with the word "obscene" or "indecent." The term "obscene" as used in the criminal statutes, has been interpreted in the United States Supreme Court as meaning the subject matter must be of a "lewd, lascivious, and obscene tendency, calculated to corrupt and debauch the minds and morals of those into whose hands it might fall," *Swearingen* v. *United States*, 161 U.S. 446, 451, 16 S. Ct. 562, 564, 40 L. Ed. 765, and in our own court we have

said that the test of an obscene book is whether "the tendency of the matter charged as obscenity is to deprave or corrupt those whose minds are open to such immoral influences, and who might come into contact with it," *People* v. *Muller*, 96 N.Y. 408, 411, following *Regina* v. *Hicklin*, L.R. 3 Q.B. 360, 369–370; *People* v. *Doubleday & Co.*, 297 N.Y. 687, 77 N.E. 2d 6, affirmed 335 U.S. 848, 69 S. Ct. 79, 93 L. Ed. 398.

The term "immoral" when not connected with "obscene"—and here it is not—for indeed the motion picture "La Ronde" was not banned upon the ground of obscenity—has a variety of meanings varying according to time, geography and to some extent, subjective judgment. Cardozo, Paradoxes of Legal Science; *Foy Productions* v. *Graves*, 253 App. Div. 475, 3 N.Y.S. 2d 573; *Parmelee* v. *United States*, 72 App. D.C. 203, 113 F. 2d 729; *United States* v. *Kennerley*, D.C., 209 F. 119. The lexicographers have defined "immoral" as the opposite of moral (Oxford Dictionary) which term may and does include illicit sexual behavior (Funk & Wagnalls) but the meaning is not limited to sex impurity but includes in addition offenses hostile "to public welfare," Black's Law Dictionary, "inimical to rights or * * * interests of others," "corrupt," "depraved" and sometimes "unprofessional" conduct or, 42 C.J.S., pp. 395–396, to state it broadly, anything *contra bonos mores.*

Resort to the criminal statutes dealing with obscenity and the cases construing such statutes are of little help in solving our present problem for here we deal with a licensing statute authorizing restraint in advance. In the one we deal with evidentiary requirements sufficient to support the conviction beyond "reasonable doubt" while in the other when the issue is debatable "some" evidence is sufficient. In the one the proof must meet the standards of the hearsay rule to assure competency, relevance and materiality while in the other formal rules of evidence may be dispensed with entirely. Criminal statutes are designed to apprise the citizen of what constitutes an offense against society in advance of the fact. The term "immoral" as used in this pre-censorship statute, without more, affords little help in advising the citizen of what constitutes a violating offense. All that the petitioner has to guide him here is the circumstance that wherever shown in the United States, except New York, the picture "La Ronde" does not offend.

To strike the term "immoral" and the words "tend to corrupt morals" from the statute as indefinite and undefinable will work no serious result. For years New York State has had statutes dealing with obscenity and indecency broad enough to sanction "after the fact" criminal prosecution and punishment, application of which has successfully regulated the publication and sale of books and periodicals without prior censorship, Penal Law, §§ 1141; cf. *Winters* v. *New York*, supra, as well as statutes sanctioning the punishment of persons presenting obscene, indecent, immoral or impure drama, plays or exhibition shows or entertainment. Penal Law, § 1140–a.

In addition, the word "obscene," when compared with the word "immoral" has a clear and authoritative judicial definition. The Federal standard is whether the book taken as a whole has a "libidinous effect," *Hannegan* v. *Esquire, Inc.*, 327 U.S. 146, 66 S. Ct. 456, 90 L. Ed. 586; *United States* v. *One Book* Entitled Ulysses, 2 Cir., 72 F. 2d 705, supra. In New York the test is "whether the tendency of the [work] is to excite lustful and lecherous desire."

People v. *Wendling*, 258 N.Y. 451, 453, 180 N.E. 169, 81 A.L.R. 799; *People* v. *Eastman*, 188 N.Y. 478, 480, 81 N.E. 459, 460; *People* v. *Muller*, supra. Under this definition "La Ronde" is certainly not "obscene." It has been condemned only on the ground that it is "immoral" and that its presentation "would tend to corrupt morals." The statute sets up no standard defining the term "immoral" and, unlike the word "obscenity" in the criminal statutes, there are no judicial opinions which set forth a workable guide for the censor. As the dissenting opinion in the Appellate Division noted 280 App. Div. at page 266, 114 N.Y.S. 2d at page 566, "La Ronde," according to the Regents, "deals with illicit love, usually regarded as immoral. But so is murder. The theme alone does not furnish a valid ground for previous restraint. As to its presentation corrupting the morals of the public, this issue is highly debatable. The record indicates a vast body of informed opinion to the contrary. Under such circumstances the action of the Regents impinges on petitioner's constitutional right of free expression." Since reasonable men may differ on the import and effect of "La Ronde," it follows that there is not a "clear and present danger" sufficiently imminent to override the protection of the United States Constitution, *Thornhill* v. *Alabama*, supra, 310 U.S. at page 105, 60 S. Ct. 736.

Under all the circumstances, and this includes the inconsistency between the varying views expressed in the opinions for affirmance herein, we deem the terms "immoral" and "tend to corrupt morals" as used in the statute to be so indefinite as to require reversal here. Indefiniteness in motion picture censorship statutes was condemned in Burstyn, supra, and later in *Gelling* v. *Texas*, 343 U.S. 960, 72 S. Ct. 1002, 96 L. Ed. 1359, supra. There the United States Supreme Court dealt with an ordinance of the city of Marshall, Texas, which authorized a local board of censors to deny permission to the showing of a motion picture when, in the opinion of the board, it was "of such character as to be prejudicial to the best interests of the people of said City"—inartistic language to be sure, but nonetheless having an intent to restrain the showing of motion pictures inimical to the public interest. Two Justices wrote concurring opinions that elucidate the bare Per Curiam for reversal, Mr. Justice Frankfurter seeing offense to the Fourteenth Amendment on the score of indefiniteness, citing Burstyn and Winters, while Mr. Justice Douglas said, 343 U.S. at page 961, 72 S. Ct. at page 1002: "The evil of prior restraint, condemned by *Near* v. [State of] *Minnesota*, 283 U.S. 697, 51 S. Ct. 625, 75 L. Ed. 1357, in the case of newspapers and by [Joseph] *Burstyn, Inc.* v. *Wilson*, 343 U.S. 495, 72 S. Ct. 777 [96 L. Ed. 1098], in the case of motion pictures, is present here in flagrant form. If a board of censors can tell the American people what it is in their best interests to see or to read or to hear (cf. *Public Utilities Comm.* [of District of Columbia] v. *Pollak*, 343 U.S. 451, 72 S. Ct. 813 [96 L. Ed. 1068]), then thought is regimented, authority substituted for liberty, and the great purpose of the First Amendment to keep uncontrolled the freedom of expression defeated."

This thought is not new for indeed thirty years ago a distinguished Governor of this State in his message to the Legislature recommending repeal of an almost identical censorship statute, L. 1921, ch. 715, § 5, had this to say: "Censorship is not in keeping with our ideas of liberty and

of freedom of worship or freedom of speech. The people of the State themselves have declared that every citizen may freely speak, write and publish his sentiments on all subjects, being responsible for the abuse of that right, and no law shall be passed to restrain or abridge liberty of speech or of the press. This fundamental principle has equal application to all methods of expression." Public Papers of Alfred E. Smith [1923], pp. 60, 61.

As has been said in a great variety of ways, we deem the evil complained of here is far less dangerous to the community than the danger flowing from the suppression of clear constitutional protection. In our zeal to regulate by requiring licenses in advance we are prone to forget the struggle behind our free institutions. We must keep in mind on all occasions that beneficent aims however laudable and well directed can never serve in lieu of constitutional powers, *Carter* v. *Carter Coal Co.*, 298 U.S. 238, 56 S. Ct. 855, 80 L. Ed. 1160, for as was said in *Lovell* v. *City of Griffin*, 303 U.S. 444, 451, 58 S. Ct. 666, 669, 82 L. Ed. 949, supra, "The struggle for the freedom of the press was primarily directed against the power of the licensor."

It is no answer to say that the exhibition of motion pictures has a potential for evil which can not be successfully dealt with except by censorship in advance. Such a conclusion overlooks the very significant circumstance that other media of expression are not so censored, for they may not be, but are nonetheless successfully controlled by our penal laws, Penal Law, § 1140–a, which have been resorted to whenever necessary. One of the most recent occasions was the banning of "The Outlaw," a motion picture, by the commissioners of license and the police in New York City, because deemed obscene, indecent and immoral, notwithstanding that the Board of Regents had theretofore issued it a license. *Hughes Tool Co.* v. *Fielding*, 297 N.Y. 1024, 80 N.E. 2d 540, affirming 272 App. Div. 1048, 76 N.Y.S. 2d 287. Reported instances of resort to criminal sanctions as a method of control are relatively infrequent but this is not at all surprising as the industry itself has its own Production Code in which it recognizes its responsibility to the public to provide approved entertainment in connection with which the potential power of the public boycott is not overlooked, exerting as it does, a direct influence in the box office, on the profitable operation of which the producers must depend (cf. Motion Pictures and the First Amendment, 60 Yale L.J. 696).

In conclusion then, it must be said that the New York censorship statute as applied in advance to the exhibition of motion pictures infringes constitutional freedom of speech and press, that the within case is not so exceptional as to require banning under a valid exercise of the police power and that the statute is invalid in any event for lack of definitive administrative criteria.

The order appealed from should be reversed and the matter remitted to the Board of Regents with direction to issue a license.

Fuld, Judge (dissenting).

I agree with Judge Dye and, for myself, would add these words only to underscore what he has written.

That the freedom of expression assured by the First Amendment is not limited to "the air-borne voice, the pen, and the printing press," Chafee, Free Speech in the

United States (1941), p. 545, but extends as well to motion pictures, is now beyond dispute. See *Gelling* v. *Texas*, 343 U.S. 960, 72 S. Ct. 1002, 96 L. Ed. 1359; *Joseph Burstyn, Inc.* v. *Wilson*, 343 U.S. 495, 72 S. Ct. 777, 96 L. Ed. 1098. While I conceive that any legislation imposing a previous restraint on the exhibition of moving pictures is condemned by the Constitution, I do not believe it necessary to invoke that broad principle to reach a decision in this case. Here again, as in Burstyn, the censorship statute must fall because of the lack of a sufficiently definite standard or guide for administrative action.

The Education Law provision under review authorizes the Regents to prohibit, in advance, the exhibition of any picture which they deem "immoral" or which they conclude may "tend to corrupt morals." Terms of such vague and undefined limits, however, fail to furnish the objective criterion necessary to insure that there shall be no interference with the exercise of rights secured by the First Amendment. By attempting to cover so much, the catch-all provision barring motion pictures which the censors believe "immoral" effectively covers nothing. The ephemeral and ambiguous character of the term is highlighted by the variant views of the very judges who now write to uphold the statute. Words as subjective as those under consideration find meaning only in the mind of the viewer and observer, render impossible administration of the statute and offend against due process. "Prohibition through words that fail to convey what is permitted and what is prohibited for want of appropriate objective standards, offends Due Process in two ways. First, it does not sufficiently apprise those bent on obedience of law of what may reasonably be foreseen to be found illicit by the law-enforcing authority, whether court or jury or administrative agency. Secondly, where licensing is rested, in the first instance, in an administrative agency, the available judicial review is in effect rendered inoperative." *Joseph Burstyn, Inc.* v. *Wilson*, supra, 343 U.S., at page 532, 72 S. Ct. at page 796, per Frankfurter, J., concurring; see, also, *Gelling* v. *Texas*, supra, 343 U.S. 960, 72 S. Ct. 1002, 96 L. Ed. 1359; *Musser* v. *Utah*, 333 U.S. 95, 68 S. Ct. 397, 92 L. Ed. 562.

I would reverse and annul the determination of the Board of Regents.

LEWIS, J., concurs with FROESSEL, J.

DESMOND, J., votes for affirmance in a separate opinion.

CONWAY, J., in a memorandum, concurs in the opinions of FROESSEL and DESMOND, JJ.

DYE, J., dissents in an opinion in which FULD, J., concurs, and votes for reversal in a separate opinion.

LOUGHRAN, C.J., deceased.

Order affirmed.

■ New American Library of World Literature, Inc.
v.
Allen et al.
Civ. No. 30167.

United States District Court N. D. Ohio, E. D.

Aug. 5, 1953.

Parker Fulton (of Burgess, Fulton & Fullmer) Cleveland, Ohio, and *Murray Gartner*, New York City, for plaintiff.

H. Herschel Hunt, Law Director of City of Youngstown, Ohio, and *P. Richard Schumann*, Asst. Law Director of Youngstown, Youngstown, Ohio, for Chief Allen and other defendants.

McNAMEE, District Judge.

In this action the plaintiff, the New American Library of World Literature, Inc., seeks recovery of damages and a permanent injunction against the defendant, Edward J. Allen, Jr., Chief of Police of the City of Youngstown, Ohio. Plaintiff's claims for relief are grounded upon the alleged unlawful suppression of the distribution and sale of certain of plaintiff's books in the City of Youngstown.

This cause was assigned for hearing upon plaintiff's motion for a preliminary injunction. However, by agreement of the parties and with the approval of the court, a final disposition of plaintiff's claims for injunctive relief will be made upon the evidence adduced at the hearing and the briefs and arguments of counsel.

Plaintiff's claims for damages are reserved for final determination on a trial by jury.

Plaintiff is a New York corporation and a publisher of paper-bound pocket-size editions of books, both fiction and non-fiction. As indicated, defendant Allen is Chief of Police of the City of Youngstown, Ohio. Inasmuch as the controversy is essentially one between plaintiff and Allen, identification of or further reference to the other defendants is unnecessary. Virtually all the plaintiff's books are paper-bound pocket-size reprints of de luxe or "hard-cover" editions of books heretofore published by the leading publishing houses of the country. Plaintiff distributes these books nationally through Fawcett Publications of New York. The local distributor of Fawcett in Youngstown, Ohio is the Mahoning Valley Distributing Company, of which Bernard Bloch is the President. The local distributor sells and delivers the books to retail outlets in Youngstown, Ohio. During the year 1952 plaintiff's sales of pocket-size reprints in the country were in excess of forty-million copies.

Early this year the Mahoning Valley Distributing Company removed several of plaintiff's books from the newsstands in Youngstown. Plaintiff alleges this was done by reason of the unlawful conduct of Allen in submitting to Bloch a list of 108 reprints, including eleven of plaintiff's books which Allen considered to be obscene, and threatening Bloch with arrest if these books were not removed from the stands.

In its Complaint plaintiff alleges that the ordinance under authority of which Allen purported to act is unconstitutional as being vague and indefinite; that Allen transcended his powers as Chief of Police, that he misapplied the ordinance in an unlawful and unconstitutional manner; and that plaintiff has been deprived of its property without due process of law; that it has been denied the equal protection of the laws and its right of freedom of the press.

Notwithstanding the multiple claims seriously urged by plaintiff it will be sufficient for the purposes of this proceeding to determine, first, whether the ordinance is constitutional, and, second, if it is, whether Allen acted outside the scope of his powers as Chief of Police to the injury of plaintiff's property rights and civil rights.

Although copies of the eleven books of plaintiff have been received in evidence, the parties have agreed that it is unnecessary for the court to determine whether these books are obscene or immoral in violation of the ordinance.

The Facts.

There is in effect in the City of Youngstown an ordinance which in substance defines the sale or distribution of obscene and immoral books as a misdemeanor and prescribes a fine and thirty days imprisonment for its violation.

Early in 1953 Chief Allen inaugurated a campaign against the sale of lewd and indecent literature. On January 5 he wrote a letter to Bernard Bloch in which he commented upon the discussions between them since 1948 and Bloch's expressed willingness to remove "objectionable literature and pictures." Reference was also made in this letter to Bloch's agreement to "permit us to act as censors but only to a degree." The letter, which is quite lengthy, contains additional matter, including the following:

"These books include almost all of the so-called paper backed 'pocket-book' type of magazine, which as a matter of policy, glorify and dwell upon immorality. Admittedly, there are some few which are not in this category, yet so few are they in number that their publication would seem to be a subterfuge designed to whitewash the great bulk of these publications.

     *   *   *   *   *   *

Such periodicals must be removed, and failure to act in this matter will result in arrest and prosecution, under the law, and final disposition by the court."

This letter was released for publication in the Youngstown Vindicator. Although in the above-quoted portion of the letter reference is made to pocket-type magazines, Allen testified that by this language he meant "paperbacked books." Immediately upon reading the letter, Bloch communicated with Allen and later made several visits to the office of the Chief of Police. The burden of the conversations between them was that Bloch considered Allen's objection to be too general and that compliance with the directions in the letter would require the removal of practically all paper-backed books. Bloch requested Allen to specify the titles which the Chief considered to be obscene. Thereupon the defendant, assisted by members of his vice squad, commenced an examination of the books. Only a few of the books were read in their entirety by the Examiners. The defendant stated that in forming his opinion he was influenced by the illustrations on the covers of the books and by the content of the "advertising blurbs," and that blasphemy and detailed description of sexual acts—and violation of the second Commandment of God—were among the standards employed by him to determine whether a book was within the proscription of the ordinance. Allen and the vice squad compiled a list of 108 books and 33 magazines. On January 15, 1953 he forwarded this list to Bloch together with a letter requesting that they be removed from the newsstands. Upon receipt of the letter Bloch suggested to Allen that the letter be made "stronger" so that the publishers would understand fully the position in which Bloch was placed. Accordingly, on January 16, 1953 Allen sent another letter to Bloch in which he stated that a failure to comply with the request to remove the books and magazines on the list on or before January 29, 1953 would result in arrest and prosecution of the distributor or any dealers who "display or sell their periodicals." On several occasions between January 5 and January 15, 1953 Allen orally notified Bloch that he would be arrested unless all obscene books and magazines were removed. Bloch brought the letters of January 15 and 16, together with the list of 108 books, to the attention of the publishers in New York. On January 28, 1953 lawyers representing several of the publishing houses, including plaintiff, met with Chief Allen at his office in Youngstown. Counsel for Bloch was also present at this meeting. These representatives denied that any of the books on the proscribed list were obscene and attempted to persuade Allen to an acceptance of this view. Counsel for Bloch suggested that a test case be filed. To this Allen agreed. But because of the unwillingness of any distributor or dealer to submit to arrest, nothing came of this suggestion. The lawyers for the publishing houses also suggested "an area of compromise" which contemplated the withdrawal from sale of some of the books on the list. This suggestion was rejected by Allen. However, Allen did indicate that he would re-examine the list and give the publishers time in which to submit "materials" in support of their contention that the books were not obscene. Within a week after the meeting with counsel for the publishers Allen 'phoned Bloch and said that he was not going to permit the publishers to select a certain number of books,—"This sort of compromise thing that they talked about—and still leave some on that we felt were in violation." Allen stated: "In other words, I wanted every book that we felt violated the law taken off." Thereupon Bloch informed the publishers that he was removing the books from his dealers' stands. The 108 books, including the eleven published by plaintiff, were thereupon withdrawn from sale. Since that time none of the 108 books have been sold in Youngstown.

At the time he wrote the letters of January 15 and January 16 Allen was not prepared to arrest and prosecute if his demand for the removal of the books was rejected. He stated that the "prosecution stage" had not been reached and that if and when it became necessary to prosecute, he would obtain the advice of the city prosecutor before proceeding. It should be noted that on several occasions before the books were removed, Bloch told Allen that only a court had the right to determine whether the books were obscene or immoral.

Allen learned of the work being done by Inspector Case of Detroit, Michigan in connection with the prevention of the sale of obscene literature in that city. On January 26, 1953 Allen wrote to Case asking for advice and assistance and for a copy of any "lists of magazines, comic books and pocket-size books that we could peruse." In this letter Allen also made reference to the Youngstown list which he had prepared, and in connection therewith stated: "We have a tentative list prepared which the vice squad has cited as obscene in their opinion. The list is not all-inclusive and indeed there may be some listed that do not warrant removal." On February 3 Inspector Case replied to Allen's letter and submitted two lists of books, one of which was described as "a list of pocket-size books which the Wayne County prosecutor and the censor bureau considered to be a violation of the Michigan State statute * * * governing obscenity." This list comprised about 140 books. The second list contained about 195 titles and was said by Inspector Case to contain books "of an objectionable nature but which are not in the prosecutor's opinion actually obscene within the meaning of the state law." On February 16, 1953 Allen forwarded to Bloch a single list of 335 titles which contained all the publications appearing on the two lists which Allen had received from Inspector Case. This second list included 28 titles published by plaintiff. The list was accompanied by a letter from defendant which contained a request that the publications on the list be removed from the newsstands of the City of Youngstown, Ohio. In the early part of February Allen was approached by representatives of the Federated Women's Clubs of Youngstown, who made known their desire to assist him in his campaign against indecent literature. Allen suggested that these women form a committee to screen literature, and he appeared before the federation and spoke upon the proposed function of such a committee. Discussions looking to the organization of the committee were being had at the time Allen forwarded the second list of 335 books to Bloch, and it was the defendant's purpose to enlist the aid of the committee in screening books, including those on the lists defendant had received from Inspector Case. It also became known about this time that the plaintiff comtemplated legal action against Chief Allen. None of the books on the second list were removed from the dealers' stands in Youngstown.

The evidence discloses that none of the eleven books published by plaintiff which were on Allen's first list were on the lists prepared by Inspector Case of Detroit. It also appears that seven of the eleven books appearing on the first list are available in hard-cover editions in the Youngstown Public Library.

[1, 2] The defendant argues that plaintiff cannot maintain this action because the alleged unlawful conduct of defendant was directed against the local distributor and not against plaintiff. But it has been held that parties whose legal rights have been violated by unlawful public action may seek relief although such action made no direct demands upon them. *Joint Anti-Fascist Committee v. Mc-Grath*, 341 U.S. 123, 71 S. Ct. 624, 95 L. Ed. 817.

Is the Ordinance Constitutional?

The Youngstown ordinance provides:

"*Obscene Books, Etc. Any person who shall distribute, sell or expose for sale, or give away any books, papers, pictures and periodicals or advertising matter of any obscene or immoral nature, shall be fined in any sum not exceeding one hundred dollars or imprisoned for not more than thirty days, or both. (Code 1925, No. 305.)*"

The plaintiff's first attack upon the validity of the ordinance is based upon the contention that the word "obscene" is unconstitutionally vague and uncertain. In support of this contention plaintiff relies chiefly upon dicta in the opinions of State courts of inferior jurisdiction. Plaintiff, however, cites no case, nor has one been found, where a court has held the word "obscene," as used in a criminal statute, to be so vague in meaning as to offend against the constitutional requirements of certainty. It is true that in *Bantam Books, Inc. v. Melko*, 1953, 25 N.J. Super. 292, 96 A. 2d 47 and in *Commonwealth v. Gordon*, 66 Pa. Dist. & Co. R. 101 there are dicta expressing opinions on the supposed inherent vagueness of the word "obscene," but in neither of the cited cases was it held that the applicable statute was unconstitutional. Plaintiff interprets expressions of the Supreme Court in *Joseph Burstyn, Inc. v. Wilson*, 343 U.S. 495, 72 S. Ct. 777, 96 L. Ed. 1098, as a repudiation of the court's dicta in earlier cases that the meaning of the word "obscene" is sufficiently precise to meet constitutional standards. Plaintiff's arguments are overborne by the impressive weight of statements of the opposite view in the opinions of the Supreme Court of the United States.

In *Winters v. People of State of New York*, 333 U.S. 507, 68 S. Ct. 665, 92 L. Ed. 840, the issue before the court was whether subsection 2 of section 1141 of the New York Penal Law, McK. Consol. Laws c. 40, prohibiting the sale and distribution of magazines principally made up of criminal news and police reports was so vague as to violate the Fourteenth Amendment by prohibiting acts within the protection of the constitutional guarantees of free speech and free press. Subsection 1 of section 1141 of the New York law, which, among other things, proscribes the sale and distribution of obscene publications, was not in issue, but was quoted in full in note 2 of the opinion. After three separate arguments on the merits the court held that the subsection in issue was vague and uncertain, but, fearful lest its decision might be misinterpreted as implying the opinion that subsection 1 of the New York law, proscribing the circulation of obscene literature, also was vague and unconstitutional, the court said:

"*To say that a state may not punish by such a vague statute carries no implication that it may not punish circulation of objectionable printed matter, assuming that it is not protected by the principles of the First Amendment by the use of apt words to describe the prohibited publications. Section 1141, subsection 1, quoted in note 2, is an example. Neither the states nor Congress are prevented by the requirement of specificity from carrying out their duty of eliminating evils to which, in their judgment, such publications give rise."* 333 U.S. at page 520, 68 S. Ct. at page 672. *(Emphasis supplied.)*

It would be difficult to find a more definite disclaimer of intention to impute uncertainty and vagueness to the word obscene than is contained in the above declaration of the Supreme Court. In the Winters case the court also referred to the words obscene, lewd, lascivious, filthy, indecent, or disgusting as "well understood through long use in the criminal law." Again, 333 U.S. at page 510, 68 S. Ct. at page 668 in the Winters case, in referring to publications not protected by the guaranty of the freedom of the press, the court said: "They are equally subject to control if they are lewd, indecent, obscene or profane." See also Ex parte Jackson, 96 U.S. 727–736, 24 L. Ed. 877; *Chaplinsky v. State of New Hampshire,* 315 U.S. 568, 62 S. Ct. 766, 86 L. Ed. 1031; *Near v. State of Minnesota,* 283 U.S. 697, 716, 51 S. Ct. 625, 75 L. Ed. 1357.

[3] Plaintiff misinterprets the rationale and effect of *Joseph Burstyn, Inc. v. Wilson,* 343 U.S. 495, 72 S. Ct. 777, 782, 96 L. Ed. 1098, in an attempt to demonstrate that there the Supreme Court repudiated—

"its previous hasty dictum to the effect that the word 'obscene' is sufficiently definite for use in a criminal statute." (Pl. Brief)

In the Burstyn case the Supreme Court pointed out that the State has no legitimate interest in protecting any religion from views distasteful to it and that "It is not the business of government in our nation to suppress real or imagined attacks upon a particular religious doctrine, whether they appear in publications, speeches, or motion pictures." But indisputably it is the business of government to protect the public morals. This is the purpose sought to be subserved by the enactment of laws proscribing the sale of obscene publications or the showing of obscene films. And, as the Supreme Court recognized in the Burstyn case, this is an entirely different purpose than that of protecting a particular religious doctrine from "sacrilegious" attack. It thus appears that the trend of authoritative judicial thinking supports the view that the word "obscene" as used in a criminal statute or ordinance is sufficiently precise to meet the constitutional standards of certainty.

[4] The ordinance here in question prohibits the sale of publications that are "obscene or immoral." Plaintiff also contends that the word "immoral" is vague and indefinite. The argument submitted in support of this contention merits but brief comment. In *Mutual Film Corp. v. Ohio Industrial Commission,* 236 U.S. 230 at pages 245–246, 35 S. Ct. 387, at page 392, 59 L. Ed. 552, the Supreme Court declared that the words "educational, moral, amusing, or harmless * * * get precision from the sense and experience of men, and become certain and useful guides in reasoning and conduct." While that part of the decision of Mutual Films that held motion pictures not to be included within the guarantees of free speech and free press was overruled in *Burstyn v. Wilson,* supra, there was no disapproval in the later case of the above quoted language from Mutual Films. In *Superior Films, Inc., v. Department of Education,* 159 Ohio St. 315, 112 N.E. 2d 311, 319, the Ohio Supreme Court approved the statutory criterion for the censorship of films that required them to be of a "moral, educational, or amusing and harmless character," Gen. Code, § 154-47b, and characterized the definition of crimes in Secs. 13035 and 13040 of the General Code of Ohio, wherein the word "immoral" appears, as being "sufficiently clear." The meaning of the word "immoral" as used in the ordinance, placed as it is in juxtaposition to the word "obscene," is not unconstitutionally vague or uncertain.

[5] Finally, plaintiff argues that the ordinance, which prohibits the sale of books "of *any* obscene or immoral nature," prescribes an unconstitutional test of obscenity in that it prohibits the sale of books which may contain but a single or isolated passage of obscenity. In support of this branch of its argument plaintiff relies upon *State v. Lerner,* 1948, 81 N.E. 2d 282, 285, decided by the Common Pleas Court of Hamilton County, Ohio. The Lerner case deals with the explicit terms of the 1943 amendment of Section 13035 of the General Code of Ohio, which both in text and in its purpose, as judicially declared, is substantially different from the Youngstown ordinance. Section 13035, G.C. of Ohio includes within the prohibited media "an obscene, lewd or lascivious book, magazine, pamphlet, paper, writing, advertisement, circular, print, picture, photograph, motion picture film." By the amendment of 1943 there was added, "or book, pamphlet, paper, magazine not wholly obscene but containing lewd or lascivious articles, advertisements, photographs or drawing, representation, figure, image, cast, instrument or article of an indecent or immoral nature." The Common Pleas Court held that by the language of the main part of the statute first above quoted, the Legislature adopted the modern test of obscenity that requires a consideration of the book as a whole to determine whether it is obscene, and that the sole purpose of the 1943 amendment was to "outlaw in [Ohio] the 'wholly obscene' test for 'books, papers, pamphlets and magazines.' " It cannot be said, however, that the Youngstown ordinance sought to outlaw the wholly obscene test for books. The ordinance was adopted in 1925, which was eight years before the decision in *United States v. One Book "Ulysses,"* D.C., 5 F. Supp. 182, wherein Judge Woolsey laid down the modern test that obscenity is to be determined by the effect of a book read in its entirety upon a person with average sex instincts. The "Ulysses" case has been recognized as the keystone of the modern American rule that indictable obscenity must be "dirt for dirt's sake." *Commonwealth v. Gordon,* 66 Pa. Dist. & Co. R. 101, at page 128. When the Youngstown ordinance became effective the test of obscenity in this country and in England was Lord Cockburn's famous pronouncement in *Regina v. Hicklin,* L.R. 3, Q.B. 360 (1868):

"I think the test of obscenity is this, whether the tendency of the matter charged as obscenity is to deprave and corrupt those whose minds are open to such immoral influences, and into whose hands a publication of this sort may fall."

[6] In recent years Lord Cockburn's test has been severely criticised by both federal and state judges in this country. It was said that, strictly applied, the test proscribed books containing obscene passages the tendency of which was to corrupt the minds of those most susceptible to immoral influences. It was observed that under this test

not even the Great Books were exempt. But while Lord Cockburn's test was criticised, it was not thought to be unconstitutional. As late as 1913 Judge Learned Hand applied Lord Cockburn's test because "that test has been accepted by the lower federal courts until it would be no longer proper for me to disregard it." *United States* v. *Kennerley*, D.C., 209 F. 119, at page 120.

The English rule was supplanted by the modern test in 1933 and is stated in *United States* v. *One Book* Entitled "*Ulysses*" by James Joyce, 2 Cir., 72 F. 2d 705, 707, where the Circuit Court of Appeals approved and elaborated Judge Woolsey's pronouncement as follows:

"We think the same immunity should apply to literature as to science, where the presentation, when viewed objectively, is sincere, and the erotic matter is not introduced to promote lust and does not furnish the dominant note of the publication. The question in each case is whether a publication taken as a whole has a libidinous effect."

[7, 8] It is true that the Youngstown ordinance may be construed in harmony with the older rather than the modern test of obscenity. The language "of any obscene or immoral nature" is susceptible of the interpretation that the prohibition is against the sale of books that merely contain some obscenity. But the ordinance may also be construed as referring to a book which, considered as a whole, has a libidinous effect. It is a well settled rule of construction that where there are two possible interpretations of a statute or ordinance, by one of which the law would be unconstitutional and by the other it would be valid, a court should adopt the construction that will uphold the law. 11 Am. Jur. 725–728. Among its other connotations the word "any" means "an." The ordinance may be read as proscribing books of an "obscene or immoral nature." Such a construction does not preclude the application of the modern test of obscenity or any other test which the courts of Ohio may deem to be controlling. This interpretation of the language of the ordinance is in harmony with the provisions of Sec. 3663, G.C. of Ohio which confers powers upon municipalities to prohibit the sale of obscene literature. Indeed, as thus construed, the descriptive terms of the ordinance are identical with those of Sec. 3663, G.C., which reads in part:

*"To restrain and prohibit the distribution, sale and exposure for sale of books * * * of an obscene or immoral nature."*

[9] I am of the opinion that on its face the ordinance is constitutional and valid.

Did the Defendant Allen Transcend His Powers and Violate the Property Rights and Civil Rights of the Plaintiff?

[10–12] It is the settled policy of courts of equity not to restrain the enforcement of a criminal statute or ordinance even though the legislation be unconstitutional because such invalidity may be interposed as a complete defense in a criminal action. 28 Am. Jur. 372, Sec. 183; 43 C.J.S., Injunctions, § 156, page 768. Equity will deviate from this general policy only in those exceptional circumstances where restraint of the enforcement of an invalid statute or ordinance is necessary to effectively protect the property rights or civil rights of the complaining party. More compelling reasons underlie the policy that precludes equity from restraining the enforcement of a valid statute or ordinance. But this rule likewise is not absolute. Where public officers charged with the enforcement of a valid criminal law exceed their lawful powers and by arbitrary action cause or threaten to cause irreparable injury to property rights or civil rights of the complainant, equity will intervene. 28 Am. Jur. 373, Sec. 185; id. 421, Sec. 238; 43 C.J.S., Injunctions, § 111, page 634.

[13, 14] The enforcement of an ordinance that prohibits the distribution and sale of obscene or immoral publications presents difficulties seldom encountered in the enforcement of criminal law. Ordinarily local distributors and dealers are respected citizens engaged in reputable businesses. The distributor who handles thousands of books cannot be expected to read them. Nor can the retail dealers who customarily sell pocket-size books as a sideline be expected to know their contents. The publishers, however, read every book that is offered for sale. So when an obscene publication is displayed on the bookstands, it is the publisher, acting with guilty knowledge, who is the real offender. The publisher, however, is usually resident elsewhere and not subject to prosecution in the local courts. Local distributors and dealers are poorly equipped to defend against a criminal charge. Moreover, they are anxious to avoid the odium and embarrassment of an accusation that implies a disregard for the primary considerations of public decency and morality. Consequently they are quick to yield to the demands of a police officer that allegedly lewd and obscene publications be withdrawn from sale. This was the situation in Youngstown. Experience demonstrates that similar factors control wherever local prosecutions are threatened for violation of laws against selling obscene publications. See *Bantam Books, Inc.* v. *Melko*, 25 N.J. Super. 292, 96 A. 2d 47; *American Mercury, Inc.* v. *Chase*, D.C., 13 F. 2d 224, 225. In the last cited case the court enjoined the Watch and Ward Society of Massachusetts from threatening to prosecute dealers in magazines and books if the publications in question were not withdrawn from sale. The court held that an unofficial organization was without power to impose its views upon the dealers through threats of prosecution. The rationale of the decision appears in the following:

"The injury to the persons affected does not flow from any judgment of a court or public body; it is caused by the defendants' notice, which rests on the defendants' judgment. The result on the other person is the same, whether that judgment be right or wrong; i.e., the sale of his magazine or book is seriously interfered with. Few dealers in any trade will buy goods after notice that they will be prosecuted if they resell them. Reputable dealers do not care to take such a risk, even when they believe that prosecution would prove unfounded. The defendants know this and trade upon it. They secure their influence, not by voluntary acquiescence in their opinions by the trade in question, but by the coercion and intimidation of that trade, through the fear of prosecution if the defendants' views are disregarded."

While the above-cited case involved no action of a public official, it sheds light on the issue here presented for determination. Where public officers exceed their lawful powers they no longer act as duly authorized agents of government. In such cases they act with no greater legal authority than private persons or private organizations. The defendant Allen possessed no lawful power to suppress publications under threat of prosecution.

In *Dearborn Pub. Co.* v. *Fitzgerald*, D.C., 271 F. 479, 482, the Mayor and Chief of Police of Cleveland, acting under color of an ordinance proscribing the sale of obscene and scandalous literature, threatened agents of a publishing company with arrest if future editions of the newspaper were sold on the streets of Cleveland. In enjoining the city officials from continuing such threats, Judge Westenhaver of this court said:

"The publication complained of cannot by any stretch of the imagination be classified as indecent, obscene, or scandalous; but if it were, the limit of the city's power would be to conduct a prosecution for the specific offense thus committed, and not the establishment of a censorship in advance of future publications, and prohibition generally of the sale thereof upon the streets, in the same manner as other publications may be sold."

The Youngstown ordinance confers no greater powers upon the Chief of Police than did the Cleveland ordinance under review in *Dearborn Pub. Co.* v. *Fitzgerald*, supra. Judge Westenhaver's views in the cited case that censorship of an obscene newspaper in advance of publication would be unlawful and that the city's power was limited to prosecution for specific offenses, are pertinent here.

[15, 16] Freedom of the press is not limited to freedom to publish, but includes the liberty to circulate publications, which the Supreme Court has said "is as essential to that freedom as liberty of publishing." *Lovell* v. *City of Griffin*, 303 U.S. 444, 58 S. Ct. 666, 669, 82 L. Ed. 949. In the Lovell case the court again stressed the importance of protecting freedom of the press "from every sort of infringement." See also *Near* v. *State of Minnesota*, 283 U.S. 697, 51 S. Ct. 625, 75 L. Ed. 1357; *Grosjean* v. *American Press Co.*, 297 U.S. 233, 56 S. Ct. 444, 80 L. Ed. 660; *De Jonge* v. *State of Oregon*, 299 U.S. 353, 57 S. Ct. 255, 81 L. Ed. 278. Freedom of the press, together with freedom of speech and freedom of religion, occupy a "preferred position" among our constitutional guaranties. *Marsh* v. *State of Alabama*, 1946, 326 U.S. 501, 509, 66 S. Ct. 276, 90 L. Ed. 265; *Jones* v. *City of Opelika*, 1943, 319 U.S. 103, 63 S. Ct. 890, 87 L. Ed. 1290; *Murdock* v. *Com. of Pennsylvania*, 1943, 319 U.S. 105, 63 S. Ct. 870, 87 L. Ed. 1292; *Martin* v. *City of Struthers*, 1943, 319 U.S. 141, 63 S. Ct. 862, 87 L. Ed. 1313. That preferred position gives these guaranties "a sanctity and a sanction not permitting dubious intrusions." *Thomas* v. *Collins*, 323 U.S. 516, at page 530, 65 S. Ct. 315, 89 L. Ed. 430. Freedom of the press is also guaranteed by the Constitution of the State of Ohio. Censorship in any form is an assault upon freedom of the press. A censorship that suppresses books in circulation is an infringement of that freedom.

In *Bantam Books, Inc.* v. *Melko*, 25 N.J. Super. 292, 96 A. 2d 47, it was held that the prosecutor of Middlesex County was without power to order a local distributor to discontinue the sale of books which the Middlesex County committee found "to be of such nature that they should be withdrawn from circulation." The list of publications accompanying the prosecutor's letter to the distributor contained 36 titles, five of which were books published by the plaintiff, Bantam Books, Inc. Although there was no demand by the prosecutor that the books be withdrawn from sale, and the letter contained no threat of prosecution, the distributor considered it to be a "mandate" and removed all of the books on the list from the dealers' stands. Thereafter representatives of the plaintiff conferred with the prosecutor and the committee. As a result of these conferences and a re-examination of the books, four of plaintiff's titles were stricken from the list. As to the fifth book, the prosecutor wrote to counsel for the plaintiff expressing his concurrence in the committee's view that the book ought not to be sold in Middlesex County. In holding the action of the prosecutor to be illegal the court did not base its decision on the fact that an unofficial committee acted as a censor of the publications. The court held that the opinions of the committee were adopted by the prosecuting attorney. In this connection the court said:

"It cannot be argued that the censorship exercised here was not that of the prosecutor, but rather of the Middlesex County Committee on Objectionable Literature. The committee may have advised; the defendant acted. No statutory authority exists for what was done. The Legislature has not yet clothed the county prosecutors or the Attorney General, with the power to censor books and so there is no occasion to consider the possible constitutionality of such legislation."

The New Jersey court held that the letters of the prosecutor contained implied threats of prosecution and granted plaintiff's prayer for injunctive relief. In many respects the Melko case is analogous. But here there was no such careful examination of the books as was made by the committee in Melko. On the contrary, the record discloses a hasty application of subjective standards that raises serious questions as to the correctness of the examiners' findings. Even the defendant conceded that there may have been some books on the first list that might well have been omitted. Yet two days after he made this concession to Inspector Case he refused to consider the suggestion of counsel for the publishers that some books be withdrawn from the list. As he later told Bloch, his purpose was to suppress the sale of all books that he felt violated the ordinance. The defendant's demand for the removal of the books was made before he obtained the legal advice necessary to assure him that probable cause for prosecution existed. These circumstances, together with the inclusion in the second list of 195 titles which in the Wayne County prosecutor's opinion were not in violation of the Michigan statute, constitute fair warning that, unless restrained, the defendant will continue his unlawful exercise of the powers of censorship.

The defendant was without authority to censor books. Such a drastic power can be vested in a police officer only by a valid express legislative grant. As Chief of Police it was defendant's duty to examine the suspected publications to determine whether there was probable cause for prosecution. He was without authority to determine with finality whether the books were obscene or immoral in violation of the ordinance. In the event prosecutions were undertaken, the burden would rest upon the city officials to establish by proof beyond a reasonable doubt every element of the offense, including the obscene or immoral nature of the books. Until a court of competent jurisdiction adjudged a book to be obscene or immoral, there would exist no warrant in law for its suppression.

[17] Not only did the defendant exceed his lawful powers in suppressing the publications, but the methods he employed in censoring the books were arbitrary and unreasonable. This is not to impugn the defendant's sincerity of purpose or his praiseworthy ambition to suppress lewd and indecent literature. But a Chief of Police, like all other public officials, must act within the scope of his express and implied powers under the law. So important is the principle it expresses that it never becomes trite to say "Ours is a government of laws and not of men." It is the duty of courts to protect the integrity of this principle. The judicial office has no higher function to serve than the restraint of official arbitrariness. Arbitrary power inspired by good motives, no less than that animated by evil intent, is an attack upon the supremacy of the law. It is of the utmost importance to prevent the distribution of all forms of lewd and indecent literature with its demoralizing effect upon the young. It is vital in the interest of public morality that the laws against obscenity be vigorously enforced. But if a free society is to endure, its primary obligation is to protect its "government of laws" from all intrusions of arbitrary power.

Defendant seeks to justify his censorship of books by claiming that this was done pursuant to an agreement with Bloch. I find no evidence of such an agreement. Bloch acted under duress, and he repeatedly told Allen that only a court could determine whether a book was obscene or immoral. Nor is there any merit to the argument that plaintiff is estopped. On the only occasion when representatives of the publishers dealt with the defendant they protested his action as being illegal. There is no basis for the claim of estoppel.

[18] Plaintiff has been deprived of a property right without due process of law. It has suffered loss incapable of accurate measurement in an action at law. In that sense plaintiff has sustained irreparable injury and is threatened with further loss of serious dimensions.

For the reasons assigned, it is held that defendant's conduct in ordering the suppression of plaintiff's books under threat of arrest and prosecution of the dealers and the distributor was in excess of his lawful powers under the ordinance. A decree may be drawn restraining the defendant from engaging in such unauthorized conduct.

No restraint is imposed upon defendant's power to enforce the ordinance by arrest and prosecution, or by other means within the scope of his lawful powers. Plaintiff's other requests for injunctive relief are denied.

[19] If the defendant has published any libel of plaintiff's books, an issue that is not here considered or decided, plaintiff has an adequate remedy at law.

■ **Besig**
v.
United States.
No. 13227.

UNITED STATES COURT OF APPEALS

Oct. 23, 1953.

George Olshausen, San Francisco, Cal., for appellant.
Lloyd H. Burke, U.S. Atty., *Charles Elmer Collett*, Asst. U.S. Atty., San Francisco, Cal., for appellee.

Before STEPHENS, ORR and POPE, Circuit Judges.

STEPHENS, Circuit Judge.

Two books entitled respectively "Tropic of Cancer" and "Tropic of Capricorn," which were written by Henry Miller and were printed in Paris, were intercepted at an American port of entry and libeled under Section 1305(a) of Title 19 U.S.C.A.[1] as obscene. The district court found

---

[1] Title 19 U.S.C.A. § 1305(a): "All persons are prohibited from importing into the United States from any foreign country any book, pamphlet, paper, writing, advertisement, circular, print, picture, or drawing containing any matter advocating or urging treason or insurrection against the United States, or

forcible resistance to any law of the United States, or containing any threat to take the life of or inflict bodily harm upon any person in the United States, or any obscene book, pamphlet, paper, writing, advertisement, circular, print, picture, drawing, or other representation, figure, or image on or of paper or other material, or any cast, instrument, or other article which is obscene or immoral, or any drug or medicine or any article whatever for the prevention of conception or for causing unlawful abortion, or any lottery ticket, or any printed paper that may be used as a lottery ticket, or any advertisement of any lottery. No such articles, whether imported separately or contained in packages with other goods entitled to entry, shall be admitted to entry; and all such articles and, unless it appears to the satisfaction of the collector that the obscene or other prohibited articles contained in the package were inclosed therein without the knowledge or consent of the importer, owner, agent, or consignee, the entire contents of the package in which such articles are contained, shall be subject to seizure and forfeiture as hereinafter provided: Provided, That the drugs hereinbefore mentioned, when imported in bulk and not put up for any of the

them to be obscene and ordered them destroyed. Besig, the owner of the books, is here appealing upon the ground that neither of the two books, which are commonly referred to together as "The Tropics," is obscene.

[1] Since all of the evidence is in writing, we review and weigh the evidence, though with due regard to the conclusions of the trial court.[2]

We note in the margin[3] the Funk & Wagnalls New Standard Dictionary and Webster's New International Dictionary definitions of the word "obscene."

[2] The word "obscene" is not uncommon and is used in English and American speech and writings as the word symbol for indecent, smutty, lewd or salacious reference to parts of the human or animal body or to their functions or to the excrement therefrom. Each of The Tropics is written in the composite style of a novel-autobiography, and the author as a character in the book carries the reader as though he himself is living in disgrace, degradation, poverty, mean crime, and prostitution of mind and body. The vehicle of description is the unprintable word of the debased and morally bankrupt. Practically everything that the world loosely regards as sin is detailed in the vivid, lurid, salacious language of smut, prostitution, and dirt. And all of it is related without the slightest expressed idea

of its abandon. Consistent with the general tenor of the books, even human excrement is dwelt upon in the dirtiest words available. The author conducts the reader through sex orgies and perversions of the sex organs, and always in the debased language of the bawdy house. Nothing has the grace of purity or goodness. These words of the language of smut, and the disgraceful scenes, are so heavily larded throughout the books that those portions which are deemed to be of literary merit do not lift the reader's mind clear of their sticky slime. And it is safe to say that the "literary merit" of the books carries the reader deeper into it. For this reason, The Tropics are far more dangerous than "Confessions of a Prostitute" which was the subject of our opinion in *Burstein* v. *United States*, 9 Cir., 1949, 178 F. 2d 665. There, the scenes depicted are obscene because of the scene itself which in its stark ugliness might well repel many. The Tropics lure on with the cleverness of scene, skilfulness of recital, and the use of worse than gutter words. All of this is sought to be justified through the sophistry, as the trial judge, Honorable Louis E. Goodman, put it, of "confession and avoidance."[4] It is claimed that they truthfully describe a base status of society in the language of its own iniquities. And that, since we live in an age of realism, obscene language depicting obscenity in action ceases to be obscenity.

[3] Whether the moral conventions should be flaunted in the cause of frankness, art, or realism, we have no occasion to decide. That question is for the policy branches of the government. Nor do we understand that we have the legal power to hold that the statute authorizing the seizure of obscene books is inapplicable to books in which obscenity is an integral part of a literary work. So that obscenity, though a part of a composition of high literary merit, is not excepted from operation of the statute, whether written in the style of the realists, surrealists, or plain shock writers. The civilization of our times holds to the premise that dirt in stark nakedness is not generally and at all times acceptable. And the great mass of the people still believe there is such a thing as decency. Indecency is easily recognizable. Such is the premise of the statute. The Congress has chosen to enact a censorship which would not have been possible except for the self-styled prophets of truth who offend so grievously.

[4] It is of course true that the ears of some may be so accustomed to words which are ordinarily regarded as obscene that they take no offense at them, but the law is not tempered to the hardened minority of society. The statute forbidding the importation of obscene books is not designed to fit the normal concept of morality of society's dregs, nor of the different concepts of morality throughout the world, nor for all time past and future, but is designed to fit the normal American concept in the age in which we live. It is no legitimate argument that because there are social groups composed of moral delinquents in this or in other countries, that their language shall be received as legal tender along with the speech of the great masses who trade ideas and information in the honest money of decency.

Adequate provision is made in the statute in the interests of classics and the technical, by the following proviso:

purposes hereinbefore specified, are excepted from the operation of this subdivision: Provided further, That the Secretary of the Treasury may, in his discretion, admit the so-called classics or books of recognized and established literary or scientific merit, but may, in his discretion, admit such classics or books only when imported for noncommercial purposes.

"Upon the appearance of any such book or matter at any customs office, the same shall be seized and held by the collector to await the judgment of the district court as hereinafter provided; and no protest shall be taken to the United States Customs Court from the decision of the collector. Upon the seizure of such book or matter the collector shall transmit information thereof to the district attorney of the district in which is situated the office at which such seizure has taken place, who shall institute proceedings in the district court for the forfeiture, confiscation, and destruction of the book or matter seized. Upon the adjudication that such book or matter thus seized is of the character the entry of which is by this section prohibited, it shall be ordered destroyed and shall be destroyed. Upon adjudication that such book or matter thus seized is not of the character the entry of which is by this section prohibited, it shall not be excluded from entry under the provisions of this section.

"In any such proceeding any party in interest may upon demand have the facts at issue determined by a jury and any party may have an appeal or the right of review as in the case of ordinary actions or suits." Title 19 U.S.C.A. § 1305(a).

[2] See *Orvis* v. *Higgins*, 2 Cir., 1950, 180 F. 2d 537, 539; *Equitable Life Assurance Soc.* v. *Irelan*, 9 Cir., 1941, 123 F. 2d 462, 464; Rule 52(a), Federal Rules of Civil Procedure, 28 U.S.C.A.

[3] Funk & Wagnalls New Standard Dictionary defines the word "obscene" as follows: "1. Offensive to chastity, delicacy, or decency; expressing or presenting to the mind or view something that decency, delicacy and purity forbid to be exposed; offensive to morals; indecent; impure. 2. [Poet.] Offensive to the senses; foul; disgusting. 3. Of evil omen."

Webster's New International Dictionary, 2nd ed. unabridged, 1940: "1. Offensive to taste; foul; loathsome; disgusting; 2.a. Offensive to chastity of mind or to modesty; expressing or presenting to the mind or view something that delicacy, purity, and decency forbid to be exposed; lewd; indecent; as obscene language, dances, images. b. Characterized by or given to obscenity; as, an obscene mind or person. 3. Inauspicious; ill-omened;—a Latinism. Obs."

[4] *United States* v. *Two Obscene Books*, D.C. 1951, 99 F. Supp. 760, 762. Also see *United States* v. *Two Obscene Books*, D.C. 1950, 92 F. Supp. 934.

"Provided further, *That the Secretary of the Treasury may, in his discretion, admit the so-called classics or books of recognized and established literary or scientific merit, but may, in his discretion, admit such classics or books only when imported for noncommercial purposes.*" Title 19 U.S.C.A. § 1305(*a*).

No action under this proviso has been taken by the Secretary of the Treasury, nor has appellant requested any action under or pursuant to it.

It is claimed that these books (The Tropics) are not for the immature of mind, and that adults read them for their literary and informative merits, but, whether true or untrue, we cannot measure their importability by such a yardstick. The Congress probably saw the impracticability of preventing the use of the books by the young and the pure. And of course they knew that salacious print in the hands of adults, even in the hands of those whose sun is near the western horizon, may well incite to disgusting practices and to hideous crime.

[5–7] We agree that the book as a book must be obscene to justify its libel and destruction, but neither the number of the "objectionable" passages nor the proportion they bear to the whole book are controlling. If an incident, integrated with the theme or story of a book, is word-painted in such lurid and smutty or pornographic language that dirt appears as the primary purpose rather than the relation of a fact or adequate description of the incident, the book itself is obscene. We are not well acquainted with Aristophanes or his times, but we know they were different from ours. We have chanced upon Chaucer and we know his times were different from ours. Boccaccio is lurid. The Bible is not free from the recounting of immoral practices. But the translators, from the languages in which The Bible was originally written, did not word-paint such practices in the lurid-Miller-morally-corrupt manner. Dirty word description of the sweet and sublime, especially of the mystery of sex and procreation, is the ultimate of obscenity. We have referred to Aristophanes, Chaucer, Boccaccio, and The Bible only because those works were taken as examples by the author of the opinion in the case of *United States v. One Book* Entitled Ulysses, 2 Cir., 1934, 72 F. 2d 705, 707, a case cited by appellant to illustrate his point that " 'No work may be judged from a selection of such paragraphs alone. * * *' " Appellant also cites *United States v. Levine*, 2 Cir., 1936, 83 F. 2d 156, 157. Whether those cases were rightly decided we do not say, but the point is not relevant because we have adjudged each book as an integrated whole.

Appellant argues that the test we used in *Burstein* v. *United States*, 9 Cir., 1949, 178 F. 2d 665, 667, as to what is obscene, is unworkable because it approves the rule that language is obscene when it may be termed "dirt for dirt's sake." He finds the opinion "self-contradictory" when we say that obscene matter "is offensive to the common sense of decency and modesty of the community," and later in the opinion say "[t]he true test to determine whether a writing is * * obscene * * * is whether its language has a tendency to deprave or corrupt the morals of those whose minds are open to such influences and into whose hands it may fall by allowing or implanting in such minds obscene, lewd, or lascivious thoughts or desires." Appellant thinks our opinion is "unclear as to whether the test of obscenity is that it *repels* or that it *seduces*."

We observe no contradiction in any of these expressions. They aptly describe the quality of language which the word "obscene" is meant to suggest. Of course, language can be so nasty as to repel and of course to seduce as well. Appellant's argument tempts us to quote Pope's[5] quatrain about the Monster Vice which, when too prevalent, is embraced.

[8, 9] Appellant thinks the district court committed error in deciding contrary to the great weight of opinion evidence as to the quality of Mr. Miller's writings. The point has no merit. Opinion evidence is useful, but not controlling.[6] We have carefully read and analyzed the voluminous affidavits and exhibits contained in the record. To a large extent they are opinions of authors who resent any limitation on their writings. Their opinions are relevant and competent evidence, but their views are advisory only as to the norm of the meaning of the word "obscene." We share the general antipathy to censorship and we are aware that individual tastes and special occasions and different times and different peoples differ as to what is offensive language. Yet we risk the assertion that there is an underlying, perhaps universal, accord that there is a phase of respectable delicacy related to sex, and that those compositions which purposely flaunt such delicacy in language generally regarded as indecent come under the ban of the statute.

We think Judge Learned Hand was in the best of his famous form in his happy use of words in *United States* v. *Kennerley*, D.C.S.D.N.Y. 1913, 209 F. 119, 121: "If there be no abstract definition, such as I have suggested, should not the word 'obscene' be allowed to indicate the present critical point in the compromise between candor and shame at which the community may have arrived here and now? If letters must, like other kinds of conduct, be subject to the social sense of what is right, it would seem that a jury should in each case establish the standard much as they do in cases of negligence. To put thought in leash to the average conscience of the time is perhaps tolerable, but to fetter it by the necessities of the lowest and least capable seems a fatal policy. Nor is it an objection, I think, that such an interpretation gives to the words of the statute a varying meaning from time to time. Such words as these do not embalm the precise morals of an age or place; while they presuppose that some things will always be shocking to the public taste, the vague subject-matter is left to the gradual development of general notions about what is decent. * *"

[10, 11] The point that the constitutional guarantee of freedom of speech or of the printing press, (or, we may add, of the radio and television,) is violated, is without merit. The point is made and the only argument to sustain it is simply that the books, since they have some literary merit, are not obscene. We have decided otherwise.

The judgment is affirmed.

---

[5] Alexander Pope (1688–1744), English poet, from his poem entitled "Essay on Man":
"Vice is a Monster of so frightful mien
  As to be hated needs but to be seen.
Yet seem too oft, familiar with her face,
  We first endure, then pity, then embrace."

[6] *Sartor* v. *Arkansas Natural Gas Corp.*, 1944, 321 U.S. 620, 627, 64 S. Ct. 724, 88 L. Ed. 967; *United States* v. *Honolulu Plantation Co.*, 9 Cir., 1950, 182 F. 2d 172, 178.

■ Superior Films, Inc., Appellant,

v.

Department of Education of State of Ohio, Division of Film Censorship, Clyde Hissong, Supt.

Commercial Pictures Corporation, Appellant,

v.

Regents of University of State of New York.

Nos. 217, 274.

Decided Jan. 18, 1954.

Facts and opinion, 159 Ohio St. 315, 112 N.E. 2d 311 and 305 N.Y. 336, 113 N.E. 2d 502.

PER CURIAM.

The judgments are reversed. *Joseph Burstyn, Inc.* v. *Wilson*, 343 U.S. 495, 72 S. Ct. 777, 96 L. Ed. 1098.

Mr. Justice DOUGLAS, with whom Mr. Justice BLACK agrees, concurring.

The argument of Ohio and New York that the government may establish censorship over moving pictures is one I cannot accept. In 1925 Minnesota passed a law aimed at suppressing before publication any "malicious, scandalous and defamatory newspaper."[1] The Court, speaking through Chief Justice Hughes, struck down that law as violating the Fourteenth Amendment, which has made the First Amendment applicable to the States. *Near* v. *State of Minnesota*, 283 U.S. 697, 51 S. Ct. 625, 626, 75 L. Ed. 1357. The "chief purpose" of the constitutional guaranty of liberty of the press, said the Court, was "to prevent previous restraints upon publication." 283 U.S. at page 713, 51 S. Ct. at page 630.

The history of censorship is so well known it need not be summarized here. Certainly a system, still in force in some nations, which required a newspaper to submit to a board its news items, editorials, and cartoons before it published them could not be sustained. Nor could book publishers be required to submit their novels, poems, and tracts to censors for clearance before publication. Any such scheme of censorship would be in irreconcilable conflict with the language and purpose of the First Amendment.

Nor is it conceivable to me that producers of plays for the legitimate theatre or for television could be required to

submit their manuscripts to censors on pain of penalty for producing them without approval. Certainly the spoken word is as freely protected against prior restraints as that which is written. Such indeed is the force of our decision in *Thomas* v. *Collins*, 323 U.S. 516, 540, 65 S. Ct. 315, 327, 89 L. Ed. 430. The freedom of the platform which it espouses carries with it freedom of the stage.

The same result in the case of motion pictures necessarily follows as a consequence of our holding in *Joseph Burstyn, Inc.* v. *Wilson*, 343 U.S. 495, 502, 72 S. Ct. 777, 780, 781, 96 L. Ed. 1098, that motion pictures are "within the free speech and free press guaranty of the First and Fourteenth Amendments."

Motion pictures are of course a different medium of expression than the public speech, the radio, the stage, the novel, or the magazine. But the First Amendment draws no distinction between the various methods of communicating ideas. On occasion one may be more powerful or effective than another. The movie, like the public speech, radio, or television is transitory—here now and gone in an instant. The novel, the short story, the poem in printed form are permanently at hand to reenact the drama or to retell the story over and again. Which medium will give the most excitement and have the most enduring effect will vary with the theme and the actors. It is not for the censor to determine in any case. The First and the Fourteenth Amendments say that Congress and the States shall make "no law" which abridges freedom of speech or of the press. In order to sanction a system of censorship I would have to say that "no law" does not mean what it says, that "no law" is qualified to mean "some" laws. I cannot take that step.

In this Nation every writer, actor, or producer, no matter what medium of expression he may use, should be freed from the censor.

---

[1] Laws 1925 Minn. c. 285, § 1(b).

■ American Civil Liberties Union et al.

v.

The City of Chicago et al.
No. 33043.

Supreme Court of Illinois.

May 24, 1954.

As Modified on Denial of Rehearing Sept. 20, 1954.

Sanford I. Wolff, Leon M. Despres, Richard Orlikoff, and *Abner J. Mikva,* Chicago (F. Raymond Marks, Jr., Alexander L. Polikoff, and Bernard Weisberg, Chicago, of counsel), for appellees.

SCHAEFER, Chief Justice.

Chapter 155 of the Municipal Code of the city of Chicago makes it unlawful to exhibit any motion picture or to distribute any motion picture to any exhibitor in the city without having first secured a permit from the commissioner of police. The commissioner is required to issue the permit, upon application and payment of the prescribed fee, unless he determines that the picture is "immoral or obscene, or portrays depravity, criminality, or lack of virtue of a class of citizens of any race, color, creed, or religion and exposes them to contempt, derision, or obloquy, or tends to produce a breach of the peace or riots, or purports to represent any hanging, lynching, or burning of a human being," in which case he is required to refuse a permit. The American Civil Liberties Union and Charles Liebman, assignees of the right to distribute and exhibit in Chicago a motion picture called "The Miracle," applied to the commissioner for a permit. The commissioner refused to issue it on the ground that the picture was "immoral and obscene." As provided by the ordinance, an appeal was taken to the mayor, who affirmed the commissioner's decision.

The distributors thereupon brought suit in the circuit court of Cook County against the city of Chicago, the mayor, and the commissioner of police. The complaint, to which a print of the film was attached as an exhibit, alleged that the ordinance deprived the plaintiffs of the right of free speech guaranteed by article II, section 4 of the Illinois constitution, S.H.A., and by the first and fourteenth amendments to the United States constitution. In addition to a judgment declaring the ordinance unconstitutional, the plaintiffs sought an injunction to restrain the defendants from preventing the exhibition of the film. By their answer the defendants denied that the ordinance was invalid, and asserted that the picture was immoral and obscene. They also filed a demand for jury trial, and challenged the plaintiffs' right to a declaratory judgment on the ground that there was an adequate remedy at law

by way of *mandamus.* No reply was filed by the plaintiffs. The film was viewed by the court over the defendants' objection, and a decree was entered enjoining the defendants from preventing the exhibition of the film. The court has certified that the validity of a municipal ordinance is involved and that the public interest requires a direct appeal to this court.

The most important issue which this case presents is whether the first and fourteenth amendments to the constitution of the United States, and article II, section 4, of the constitution of Illinois permit the censorship of motion pictures. The ordinance before us has twice been upheld by this court, and the defendants consider the question settled. The plaintiffs, on the other hand, take the position that those decisions are superseded by subsequent decisions of the United States Supreme Court which the plaintiffs regard as rendering unconstitutional, as a "prior restraint" upon freedom of speech, all censorship of motion pictures. Disposition of the case thus requires a review both of our decisions and of those of the Supreme Court of the United States.

In *Block* v. *City of Chicago,* 239 Ill. 251, 87 N.E. 1011, 1013, decided in 1909, suit was brought to enjoin the city from interfering with the exhibition of two films entitled "the 'James Boys'" and "Night Riders," for which a permit had been denied. The ordinance was sustained against the objection that the terms "obscene" and "immoral" were so broad as to make the delegation of censorship power to the chief of police unconstitutional, and it was also held that no hearing need be allowed before refusing a permit. In 1930 the ordinance again came before the court in *United Artists Corp.* v. *Thompson,* 339 Ill. 595, 171 N.E. 742, a case arising out of the denial of a permit to exhibit a film called "Alibi." The court held invalid that part of the ordinance which provided for confiscation, without notice, of films put into distribution after the refusal of a permit, but summarily upheld the licensing provision, stating, "The power of a city to provide for a board of censors and to require a permit before any moving picture can be exhibited in a municipality cannot be doubted." 339 Ill. 595, 602, 171 N.E. 742, 745.

In each case the permit was denied on the ground of immorality, a term to which the court ascribed a broad meaning. In the Block case it was impliedly held that the portrayal of crimes was immoral, since this would "necessarily" produce evil effects upon youthful spectators, and the court stressed the point that the typical audience included "those classes whose age, education, and situation in life specially entitle them to protection against the evil influence of obscene and immoral representations." 239 Ill. 251, 258, 265, 87 N.E. 1011, 1013. In the United Artists case the police censor board described the picture as portraying numerous crimes of violence and in particular as showing third degree and other brutal practices by the police, which would tend " 'to create contempt and hatred for the entire police force.' " 339 Ill. 595, 598, 171 N.E. 742, 744. The court, repeating the remarks made in the Block case concerning the necessity of protecting the more susceptible members of the audience, agreed that the film, which it did not view, "could not fail to have a tendency to cheapen the value of human life in the minds of youthful spectators," and that "its exhibition would have a tendency toward immorality and to cause an increasing disrespect for the law and its officers." 339 Ill. 595, 602, 605, 171 N.E. 742, 746.

What is most significant about these cases in their present bearing is that neither of them considered or even referred to the constitutional issue of freedom of speech. When the Block case was decided in 1909, it had not yet been determined that the freedom of speech which is secured against Federal infringement by the first amendment to the constitution of the United States is also secured by the due process clause of the fourteenth amendment against infringement by the States. See *Joseph Burstyn, Inc.* v. *Wilson*, 343 U.S. 495, 499, 500, 72 S. Ct. 777, 96 L. Ed. 1098. And when the United Artists case was decided, motion pictures were not regarded as a form of communication within the protection of the first and fourteenth amendments. See *Mutual Film Corp.* v. *Industrial Comm.*, 236 U.S. 230, 35 S. Ct. 387, 59 L. Ed. 552. Subsequent decisions of the United States Supreme Court, however, have extended that protection to motion pictures, and we therefore must re-examine the validity of the ordinance in their light.

In the first of these cases, *Joseph Burstyn, Inc.* v. *Wilson*, 343 U.S. 495, 72 S. Ct. 777, 96 L. Ed. 1098, the Supreme Court reversed a decision of the Court of Appeals of New York which had sustained censorship of the same film which is before us now. We may say at once that we do not regard that decision as having completely immunized "The Miracle" against censorship. The sole basis of censorship in that case was that the film was sacrilegious; power to censor upon any other basis was not considered by the Supreme Court. That court, while holding that expression of ideas through motion pictures was protected under the first and fourteenth amendments, observed that this protection did not imply "absolute freedom to exhibit every motion picture of every kind at all times and all places," or that the rules governing motion pictures were necessarily the same as those applicable to other media of expression. 343 U.S. 495, 502, 503, 72 S. Ct. 777, 781. And the court expressly reserved decision on the question "whether a state may censor motion pictures under a clearly drawn statute designed and applied to prevent the showing of obscene films." 343 U.S. 495, 506–507, 72 S. Ct. 777, 782. Cf. *Near* v. *State of Minnesota* ex rel. *Olson*, 283 U.S. 697, 716, 51 S. Ct. 625, 75 L. Ed. 1357; *Chap-*

linsky v. *New Hampshire*, 315 U.S. 568, 571–572, 62 S. Ct. 766, 86 L. Ed. 1031; *Winters* v. *New York*, 333 U.S. 507, 518, 68 S. Ct. 665, 92 L. Ed. 840.

The court did emphasize, however, that freedom of expression is the rule, and that particularly in the case of a "prior restraint" a State has a heavy burden to justify an exception to that rule, 343 U.S. 495, 503, 504, 72 S. Ct. 777, 781, 782, a burden which the court held had not been sustained in the case before it. The term "sacrilegious" had been construed by the New York Court of Appeals to include the act of treating any religion "with contempt, mockery, scorn and ridicule," or any "visual caricature of religious beliefs held sacred by one sect or another." 303 N.Y. 242, 258, 101 N.E. 2d 665, 672. The Supreme Court observed that this statutory standard was so broad as to vest unlimited discretion in the censors, and that "the state has no legitimate interest in protecting any or all religions from views distasteful to them which is sufficient to justify prior restraints upon the expression of those views." 343 U.S. 495, 504, 505, 72 S. Ct. 777, 782.

Shortly after the Burstyn decision the court, in *Gelling* v. *Texas*, 343 U.S. 960, 72 S. Ct. 1002, 96 L. Ed. 1359, reversed without opinion a conviction for exhibiting a picture which had been denied a license under the terms of an ordinance permitting a license to be withheld if the censors should be of the opinion that the film was " 'prejudicial to the best interests' " of the local residents.

More recently the Supreme Court has reversed two other State court decisions which upheld censorship. In *Superior Films, Inc.* v. *Department of Education*, 159 Ohio St. 315, 112 N.E. 2d 311, 318, a permit was refused the motion picture "M" under an Ohio statute providing that "Only such films as are, in the judgment and discretion of the department of education, of a moral, educational, or amusing and harmless character shall be passed and approved." (Ohio Rev. Code 1953, sec. 3305.–04.) The basis for the censors' refusal was that " 'the effect of this picture on unstable persons of any age level could lead to a serious increase in immorality and crime' " and that the film presented a story of criminal perversion in such a way as to result in sympathy for it rather than a constructive plan for dealing with it. The Ohio court upheld the power of the State to censor films for the sake of protecting decency and morals, and met the charge that the statute was vague by relying upon the Mutual Film case, 236 U.S. 230, 35 S. Ct. 387, which involved the same Ohio statute, and which, the court stated, had not been overruled on this point by the Burstyn case. Two dissenting judges regarded the latter decision as invalidating the Ohio censorship statute.

Commercial Pictures Corp. v. *Board of Regents*, 305 N.Y. 336, 113 N.E. 2d 502, involved the movie "La Ronde," which had been suppressed on the grounds that it was "immoral" and " 'would tend to corrupt morals.' " (See N.Y. Education Law, McK. Consol. Laws, c. 16, § 122.) The New York Court of Appeals held that the State was entitled to take measures to preserve marriage, the home, and the moral welfare of its citizens against a picture like this, which in the court's view presented adultery and fornication in such a seductive manner as to invite imitation by the audience. Construing the term "immoral" to refer solely to sexual immorality, the majority of the court considered that there was no unconstitutional vagueness present. Two members of the court dissented.

The Supreme Court reversed both the Ohio and the New York decisions in a memorandum opinion citing the Burstyn case. Justices Douglas and Black concurred on the ground that all censorship of films was forbidden by the first amendment. *Superior Films, Inc.* v. *Department of Education*, 346 U.S. 587, 74 S. Ct. 286.

In view of the language of the opinion of the court in the Burstyn case, and particularly because the views expressed in the specially concurring opinion in the Superior Films case were apparently not shared by a majority of the court, we do not regard those decisions as invalidating all film censorship. Their precise scope, however, is not easy to determine. On the one hand, they may be interpreted as holding that the statutes immediately involved were invalid, either because the standards employed fail to reflect an interest which the State might legitimately protect, or because those statutes, although applicable to films of a sort which might constitutionally be subjected to censorship, were so broad, or so vaguely drawn, as also to sanction the suppression of films which may not constitutionally be censored. On the other hand, the Supreme Court may have considered those statutes as purporting in terms to forbid no more than that which a State may forbid, and yet have reversed because of its determination that the particular films involved did not possess those qualities which would justify censorship, or because the State had not at any rate made a sufficient showing that such qualities were present. In any event, we do not regard these decisions as automatically compelling us to overrule this court's prior approval of the Chicago censorship ordinance. We do regard them, however, as requiring a re-examination of that ordinance in terms of the standards and the procedures which are available to the State in the highly sensitive area of prior restraint upon the expression of ideas.

Considering first the standards of the ordinance, censorship in this case rests upon the ground that the film is "immoral and obscene."

With respect to the term "obscene," a large body of doctrine has been developed in the course of prosecutions for the sale of obscene literature and for depositing it in the mail, libels under the tariff act to prevent its importation, and, more recently, in Massachusetts, proceedings in the nature of a declaratory judgment to determine whether a book is obscene. (See New York Penal Law, McK. Consol. Laws, c. 40, § 1141; Mass. G.L. (Ter. Ed.) c. 272, sections 28–28G; 18 U.S.C. §§ 1461, 1462, 1463, 1464; 19 U.S.C.A. § 1305; 39 U.S.C.A. § 259a.) This court, on the other hand, has seldom had occasion to construe the term. In *People* v. *Friedrich*, 385 Ill. 175, 179, 52 N.E. 2d 120, 122, we interpreted it to mean "offensive to the chastity of mind, delicacy and purity of thought, * * * suggestive of lustfulness, lasciviousness and sensuality." Apart from this rather general statement, we find no treatment of the problem in our decisions, and we therefore turn to those from other jurisdictions. These cases, in the main, involve literary publications. We do not think, however, that the meaning of the term "obscene" varies with the particular medium of expression. No such inference may be drawn from the language of this and other ordinances dealing with obscenity, nor from the statutory provisions on the subject with reference to which the

ordinance should be construed. See Ill. Rev. Stat. 1953, chap. 24, pars. 23–57; chap. 38, pars. 468, 469, 470; Municipal Code of Chicago, secs. 192–7, 192–9, 192–10.

The most cursory survey reveals that despite the extensive consideration which the courts have given it, the concept of obscenity remains elusive. See *Bantam Books, Inc.* v. *Melko*, 25 N.J. Super. 292, 96 A. 2d 47; *Commonwealth* v. *Gordon*, 66 Pa. Dist. & Co. 101; *Parmelee* v. *United States*, 72 App. D.C. 203, 113 F. 2d 729; 69 A.L.R. 644; 76 A.L.R. 1099, 81 A.L.R. 801; Alpert, Judicial Censorship of Obscene Literature, 52 Harv. L. Rev. 40; Jenkins, The Legal Basis of Literary Censorship, 31 Va. L. Rev. 83; Notes, 47 Columbia L. Rev. 686; 34 Cornell L.Q. 442; Chafee, Free Speech in the United States, pp. 529–548; I Chafee, Government and Mass Communications, pp. 200–366.

The test as originally laid down in 1868 by Cockburn, C.J., in *Regina* v. *Hicklin*, L.R. 3 Q.B. 360, 371, was "whether the tendency of the matter charged as obscenity is to deprave and corrupt those whose minds are open to such immoral influences and into whose hands a publication of this sort might fall." In applying that formula American courts have repeatedly stated that the mere use of coarse or vulgar language, or even references to sexual misbehavior, do not amount to obscenity so long as no tendency toward sexual stimulation is present. *Swearingen* v. *United States*, 161 U.S. 446, 16 S. Ct. 562, 40 L. Ed. 765; *United States* v. *Males*, D.C., 51 F. 41; *Duncan* v. *United States*, 9 Cir., 48 F. 2d 128; *People* v. *Eastman*, 188 N.Y. 478, 81 N.E. 459; *People* v. *Wendling*, 258 N.Y. 451, 180 N.E. 169, 81 A.L.R. 799; *Commonwealth* v. *Isenstadt*, 318 Mass. 543, 550, 62 N.E. 2d 840, 844; *Attorney General* v. *Book Named "Forever Amber,"* 323 Mass. 302, 81 N.E. 2d 663; but cf. *United States* v. *Limehouse*, 285 U.S. 424, 52 S. Ct. 412, 76 L. Ed. 843; *Besig* v. *United States*, 9 Cir., 208 F. 2d 142.

The Hicklin formula contained two elements which imposed stringent requirements upon literature. The first of these was that a book was tested, by its supposed influence, not on the average, normal person, but upon those readers who were most susceptible to corruption by virtue of youth, ignorance, or sensual inclination. *United States* v. *Bennett*, 24 Fed. Cas., page 1093, No. 14,571, 16 Blatchf. 338; *United States* v. *Clarke*, D.C., 38 F. 732; cf. *United States* v. *Levine*, 2 Cir., 83 F. 156, 157. The second was that the presence of a single objectionable passage sufficed to condemn the entire book. *United States* v. *Bennett*, supra; *United States* v. *Kennerley*, D.C., 209 F. 119; cf. *United States* v. *Levine*, 2 Cir., 83 F. 156, 157; *Commonwealth* v. *Friede*, 271 Mass. 318, 171 N.E. 472, 69 A.L.R. 640.

This combination of tests drew judicial fire as early as 1913 in *United States* v. *Kennerley*, D.C., 209 F. 119, in which Judge Learned Hand stated, "I question whether in the end men will regard that as obscene which is honestly relevant to the adequate expression of innocent ideas, and whether they will not believe that truth and beauty are too precious to society at large to be mutilated in the interests of those most likely to pervert them to base uses. Indeed, it seems hardly likely that we are even today so lukewarm in our interest in letters or serious discussion as to be content to reduce our treatment of sex to the standard of a child's library in the supposed interest of a salacious few * * *." 209 F. 119, 120, 121.

[1] The views thus expressed by Judge Hand were subsequently taken up, and the Hicklin test was repudiated in the Federal courts, in proceedings under both the postal and tariff laws. The rule now followed there, and generally in the State courts is that a book is to be judged as a whole and in terms of its effect on the average, normal reader. See *United States* v. *Dennett,* 2 Cir., 39 F. 2d 564, 76 A.L.R. 1092; *United States* v. *One Obscene Book* Entitled "Married Love," D.C., 48 F. 2d 821; *United States* v. *One Book* Entitled "Contraception," D.C., 51 F. 2d 525; *United States* v. *One Book* Called "Ulysses," D.C., 5 F. Supp. 182, affirmed, *United States* v. *One Book* Entitled Ulysses, 2 Cir., 72 F. 2d 705; *United States* v. *Levine,* 2 Cir., 83 F. 2d 156; *Parmelee* v. *United States,* 72 App. D.C. 203, 113 F. 2d 729; *Walker* v. *Popenoe,* 80 U.S. App. D.C. 129, 149 F. 2d 511; *Cain* v. *Universal Pictures Co.,* D.C., 47 F. Supp. 1013, 1018; *Commonwealth* v. *Isenstadt,* 318 Mass. 543, 548–552, 62 N.E. 2d 840, 843–845; *Attorney General* v. *Book Named* "Forever Amber," 323 Mass. 302, 81 N.E. 2d 663; *Halsey* v. *New York Society for Suppression of Vice,* 234 N.Y. 1, 136 N.E. 219; *Commonwealth* v. *Gordon,* 66 Pa. Dist. & Co. 101, affirmed 166 Pa. Super. 120, 70 A. 2d 389; cf. *Bantam Books, Inc.* v. *Melko,* 25 N.J. Super. 292, 96 A. 2d 47; *Adams Theatre Co.* v. *Keenan,* 12 N.J. 267, 96 A. 2d 519; but cf. *Besig* v. *United States,* 9 Cir., 208 F. 2d 142.

[2, 3] The doctrine that a book must be considered as a whole does not, of course, mean that obscene matter becomes protected simply by being bound in the same cover with innocent matter. It does contemplate, however, that instances of obscene diction or episodes may be so slight or infrequent as not to impart an obscene flavor to the entire book, *Commonwealth* v. *Isenstadt,* 318 Mass. 543, 549, 62 N.E. 2d 840, 844; *Attorney General* v. *Book Named* "Serenade," 326 Mass. 324, 94 N.E. 2d 259; and that in the context of the whole work, incidents of sexual misconduct may be so presented as to arouse pity or revulsion rather than desire. See *Attorney General* v. *Book Named* "Forever Amber," 323 Mass. 302, 81 N.E. 2d 663; *People ex rel. Kahan* v. *Creative Age Press,* 192 Misc. 188, 79 N.Y.S. 2d 198; *Commonwealth* v. *Gordon,* 66 Pa. Dist. & Co. 101; *Cain* v. *Universal Pictures Co.,* D.C., 47 F. Supp. 1013, 1018. Furthermore, a book is not to be held obscene on the basis of language or episodes which, considered in the light of the work as a whole, do not represent a calculated exploitation of dirt for dirt's sake, but are fairly incident to some other artistic purpose, such as the exposition of some thesis of the author, see *People* v. *Vanguard Press,* 192 Misc. 127, 84 N.Y.S. 2d 427; *People ex rel. Kahan* v. *Creative Age Press,* 192 Misc. 188, 79 N.Y.S. 2d 198, or the realistic portrayal of some region, or historical period, or social group, see *United States* v. *One Book* Called "Ulysses," D.C., 5 F. Supp. 182, affirmed 72 F. 2d 705; *Attorney General* v. *Book Named* "Forever Amber," 323 Mass. 302, 81 N.E. 2d 663; *People* v. *Viking Press,* 147 Misc. 813, 264 N.Y.S. 534; *Commonwealth* v. *Gordon,* 66 Pa. Dist. & Co. 101; cf. *People* v. *Berg,* 241 App. Div. 543, 272 N.Y.S. 586, affirmed 269 N.Y. 514, 199 N.E. 513; *Commonwealth* v. *Isenstadt,* 318 Mass. 543, 62 N.E. 2d 840. In such cases the book is said to fall outside the category of the obscene, since taken as a whole its "dominant effect" is not that of exciting sexual desires. *United States* v. *One Book* Entitled Ulysses, 2 Cir., 72 F. 2d 705; *Parmelee* v. *United States,* 72 App. D.C. 203, 113

F. 2d 729; *Walker* v. *Popenoe,* 80 U.S. App. D.C. 129, 149 F. 2d 511.

The general course of decisions indicates that the work in question is approached as an aggregate of different effects, and the determination turns on whether the salacious aspects are so objectionable as to outweigh whatever affirmative values the book may possess, see *United States* v. *Dennett,* 2 Cir., 39 F. 2d 564, 76 A.L.R. 1092. In the words of Judge Learned Hand, a book should not be proscribed unless it is likely "that the work will so much arouse the salacity of the reader to whom it is sent as to outweigh any literary, scientific or other merits it may have in that reader's hands." *United States* v. *Levine,* 2 Cir., 83 F. 2d 156, 158; cf. *Walker* v. *Popenoe,* 80 U.S. App. D.C. 129, 149 F. 2d 511, 512. This view appears to be implicit in the decisions which justify obscenity on the ground of social realism and the like, as well as in the so-called "statute of limitations" enjoyed by established classics.

[4, 5] We hold, therefore, that a motion picture is obscene within the meaning of the ordinance if, when considered as a whole, its calculated purpose or dominant effect is substantially to arouse sexual desires, and if the probability of this effect is so great as to outweigh whatever artistic or other merits the film may possess. In making this determination the film must be tested with reference to its effect upon the normal, average person. Thus defined, the term is no broader and no less definite than as used in the postal laws, under which "prior restraint" has long been exercised through the exclusion of obscene matter from the mails. (18 U.S.C. §§ 1461, 1463; cf. 39 U.S.C.A. § 259a.) We conclude, therefore, that the term "obscene" has achieved a sufficiently precise meaning to describe a class of films which the State may validly suppress; the subject matter hardly admits of greater definiteness. The case before us involves the complete denial of a right to exhibit a film. We need not now decide what other principles, if any, would be applicable if only a part of a film were censored, or if a permit to exhibit to adults only were granted, as the ordinance authorizes. Municipal Code of Chicago, sec. 155–5.

[6] It has recently come to be suggested that even further limitations are required by the constitution, in that legislation directed against obscenity must be confined to preventing only those forms of overt sexual conduct which are socially undesirable, and must be limited in its application, moreover, to those cases in which it can be said that there is a clear and present danger that the publication will induce such acts. See *Roth* v. *Goldman,* 2 Cir., 172 F. 2d 788, 790 (concurring opinion); *Commonwealth* v. *Gordon,* 66 Pa. Dist. & Co. 101. We agree that the determination that a film or book is obscene must rest on something more than speculation, and that the tendency toward sexual stimulation must be probable and substantial. But we do not agree that the State is limited to the prevention of overt sexual conduct produced by films to the exclusion of consideration of the stimulating tendency which they may have. It may be anomalous to treat obscenity differently from other limitations on free speech, but if so, the difference is one which has long been accepted.

[7] So far as the term "immoral" is concerned, we think that when employed, as here, to describe a basis upon which to impose a prior restraint upon freedom of expression, it must be regarded as little more than a

synonym for "obscene." Such, indeed, appears to have been the sense in which the legislative bodies used the term. The power of the city to enact this ordinance derives from section 23–54 of the Revised Cities and Villages Act, which provides simply that the city may "license, tax, regulate, or prohibit * * * theatricals and other exhibitions, shows, and amusements; * * * license, tax, and regulate all places for eating or amusement." (Ill. Rev. Stat. 1953, chap. 24, par. 23–54.) The scope of this power, however, must be considered in connection with other statutory provisions on the subject. Section 224½ of division I of the Criminal Code makes it a misdemeanor to present any "obscene, or indecent drama, play, exhibition, show or entertainment." (Ill. Rev. Stat. 1953, chap. 38, par. 470.) Unless the unlikely assumption is made that the city has been granted broader power than the State itself has exercised, the term "immoral" in the ordinance must be construed as referring to that which is immoral because it is obscene. Furthermore, even if we assume that the city council had the power to do otherwise, it seems apparent that it intended to subject to suppression under the ordinance only those films whose exhibition would violate the Criminal Code. Except for the term "immoral," every proscriptive term in the ordinance is drawn from a corresponding section of the Criminal Code. Sections 224a and 224b are followed *verbatim*. (Ill. Rev. Stat. 1953, chap. 38, pars. 471, 472.) Section 224½, it is true, uses the terms "obscene" and "indecent," rather than "immoral," but the latter term, however, is treated in an analogous section of the Criminal Code as being equivalent to "obscene," for section 223 of division I forbids the sale of "any obscene and indecent book * * * or article of indecent or immoral use" and the giving of information as to where "said indecent and obscene articles and things" may be obtained. Ill. Rev. Stat. 1953, chap. 38, par. 468.

The meaning which we assign the term is narrower than that given it in *Block v. City of Chicago*, 239 Ill. 251, 87 N.E. 1011, and *United Artists Corp. v. Thompson*, 339 Ill. 595, 171 N.E. 742. In the light of *Gelling v. Texas*, 343 U.S. 960, 72 S. Ct. 1002, 96 L. Ed. 1359, it is clear that if the term is given its unrestricted meaning, it would conflict with constitutional requirements. See *Commercial Pictures Corp. v. Board of Regents*, 305 N.Y. 336, 113 N.E. 2d 502; *Broadway Angels, Inc. v. Wilson*, 282 App. Div. 643, 125 N.Y.S. 2d 546; cf. *Hannegan v. Esquire, Inc.*, 327 U.S. 146, 66 S. Ct. 456, 90 L. Ed. 586; *Winters v. New York*, 333 U.S. 507, 68 S. Ct. 665, 92 L. Ed. 840; *Schuman v. Pickert*, 277 Mich. 225, 269 N.W. 152.

The conclusion that a motion picture which is in fact obscene may be censored does not end our inquiry, however, for the ordinance, it is said, leaves the question of obscenity to the discretion of the censors, and makes their determination conclusive in the absence of a showing that it is wholly without reasonable basis. If, as the Burstyn case holds, freedom of expression is the rule and limitations upon it the exception, this minimal scope of judicial review, particularly in view of the difficulties inherent in applying the standard of obscenity, does not offer the protection which the constitution requires. See *Commercial Pictures Corp. v. Board of Regents*, 280 App. Div. 260, 114 N.Y.S. 2d 561, 565; Id. 305 N.Y. 336, 355, 113 N.E. 2d 502, 512, 513 (dissenting opinions); *Roth v. Goldman*, 2 Cir., 172 F. 2d 788, 790, 795 (concurring opinion). It must be conceded that the cases are virtually unanimous in holding that the censor's determination is presumptively correct and will be upheld so long as there is room for an honest difference of opinion. (*United Artists Corp. v. Thompson*, 339 Ill. 595, 171 N.E. 742; *People ex rel. Konzack v. Schuettler*, 209 Ill. App. 588; *Hutchinson v. Garrity*, 218 Ill. App. 161; *Edwards v. Thompson*, 262 Ill. App. 520; *Bainbridge v. City of Minneapolis*, 131 Minn. 195, 154 N.W. 964, L.R.A. 1916C, 224; *Thayer Amusement Corp. v. Moulton*, 63 R.I. 182, 7 A. 2d 682, 124 A.L.R. 236; *In re Franklin Film Mfg. Corp.*, 253 Pa. 422, 98 A. 623; *In re Goldwyn Distributing Corp.*, 265 Pa. 335, 108 A. 816; *Midwest Photo-Play Corp. v. Miller*, 102 Kan. 356, 169 P. 1154; *Silverman v. Gilchrist*, 2 Cir., 260 F. 564; *City of Chicago v. Kirkland*, 7 Cir., 79 F. 2d 963; *Commercial Pictures Corp. v. Board of Regents*, 280 App. Div. 260, 114 N.Y.S. 2d 561, affirmed 305 N.Y. 336, 113 N.E. 2d 502. The latitude given by the courts is illustrated by the fact that it is only on rare occasions that the decision of the censor has been overturned as not within the powers granted by statute or ordinance. See *Fox Film Corp. v. City of Chicago*, D.C., 247 F. 231, affirmed 7 Cir., 251 F. 883; *Schuman v. Pickert*, 277 Mich. 225, 269 N.W. 152; *Broadway Angels, Inc. v. Wilson*, 282 App. Div. 643, 125 N.Y.S. 2d 546; cf. *Hygienic Productions, Inc. v. Keenan*, 1 N.J. Super. 461, 62 A. 2d 150; *Adams Theatre Co. v. Keenan*, 12 N.J. 267, 96 A. 2d 519; Notes, 39 Col. L. Rev. 1383; 49 Yale L.J. 87; 60 Yale L.J. 696; Chafee, Free Speech in the United States, pp. 540–548; I Chafee, Government and Mass Communication, pp. 200–366; Inglis, Freedom of the Movies.

[8, 9] The conclusion which we reach, however, is not that the ordinance should be invalidated because the scope of judicial review is insufficient, but rather that review in such cases should not be so restricted. The decisions so limiting it, in large part, antedate the emergence of the motion picture as a constitutionally protected medium. It is no longer possible to say that the exhibition of a film is a mere "privilege" which the State may withdraw, or permit on such terms as it chooses. Nor again is this an area where other relevant considerations of administrative law suggest that review be narrowly confined. The proceeding by which a permit is denied is not one in which conflicting evidence is heard and resolved in the form of specific findings of fact; the issue to be determined does not involve technical questions whose decision might appropriately be committed to a body of experts; nor is this an area where administrative officials have been entrusted with broad quasi-legislative powers to elaborate substantive policy within the framework of a statute. See Davis, Administrative Law, p. 927; Note, 65 Harv. L. Rev. 1217. We think, therefore, that upon review of the censors' action, the plaintiff does not carry a burden of proving that that action was arbitrary and unreasonable, but rather that it must affirmatively be made to appear that the film fairly falls within the proscriptive terms of the ordinance.

[10] We conclude, then, that the city has the power to require the submission of films for censorship and to deny a permit to those which are obscene. It follows that the plaintiffs have no right to exhibit the film unless the permit was wrongfully refused, in which event they may exhibit it upon payment of the required fee. In the view which it took of the case, the trial court had no occasion to determine whether the motion picture was obscene, and

the case must therefore be remanded for such a determination.

[11] This disposition of the case makes it necessary to consider the defendants' contention that the issue as to whether or not "The Miracle" is obscene must be submitted to a jury. The proposition is based on the premises that this issue involves only the applicability of the ordinance rather than its validity, and that it may therefore be raised only in an action of *mandamus* brought to compel the issuance of a license. The proposition also presupposes that a trial by jury may still be required in *mandamus* actions, despite the language of the present statute (Ill. Rev. Stat. 1953, chap. 87) and that the question is an appropriate one for determination by a jury, even though the purpose of the proceeding is to review administrative action. We need not consider whether these latter assumptions are correct, since in the case before us the question of the film's obscenity arises in the course of a suit in equity based upon a constitutional question, and therefore need not be passed upon by a jury.

[12] It is clear that the plaintiffs here could properly proceed by injunction. It is true that *mandamus* is the appropriate form of action where the plaintiff raises no constitutional question and only alleges that the refusal of a license was not authorized by the statute or ordinance in question. *Illinois Board of Dental Examiners* v. *People* ex rel. *Cooper*, 123 Ill. 227, 13 N.E. 201. In that situation an injunction will not issue. *Grace Missionary Church* v. *City of Zion*, 300 Ill. 513, 133 N.E. 268. If the plaintiff, however, alleges that one or more of the conditions required for a license are invalid, he may proceed either by *mandamus* or by injunction. *Tews* v. *Woolhiser*, 352 Ill. 212, 185 N.E. 827; *Western Theological Seminary* v. *City of Evanston*, 325 Ill. 511, 156 N.E. 778.

[13] Whether a complaint alleging only that a motion picture is not obscene would state a ground for equitable relief we need not decide. In the present case the plaintiffs did not so limit their complaint, for they asserted that the ordinance was invalid, and claimed the right to exhibit their film without obtaining a permit. We held, in *United Artists Corp.* v. *Thompson*, 339 Ill. 595, 171 N.E. 742, that in such a case the plaintiff may proceed by injunction, and that case also shows that the question of the film's obscenity may then be determined in the same proceeding.

[14] Since a suit for an injunction was proper, there can be no objection to the addition to the complaint of a request that the ordinance be expressly declared invalid. The plaintiffs might indeed have asked for a declaratory judgment alone. *Pioneer Trust & Savings Bank* v. *Village of Oak Park*, 408 Ill. 458, 97 N.E. 2d 302. Defendants' contention that the availability of affirmative relief by way of *mandamus* bars an action for a declaratory judgment is refuted by the explicit language of section 57½ of the Civil Practice Act. (Ill. Rev. Stat. 1953, chap. 110, par. 181.1.) *Goodyear Tire & Rubber Co.* v. *Tierney*, 411 Ill. 421, 104 N.E. 2d 222, is not to the contrary. We there held only that a plaintiff desiring to challenge the validity of a tax assessment must pursue the statutory remedies provided by the Revenue Act, and that a declaratory judgment, like an injunction, could not be had in the absence of circumstances supplying a basis for interference with the collection of taxes. The case in no way suggests that an action for declaratory relief is defeated by the mere existence of another form of action which could presently be employed.

The decree of the circuit court is therefore reversed and the cause is remanded for further proceedings in conformity with the views expressed in this opinion.

Reversed and remanded, with directions.

■ Sunshine Book Company, Plaintiff,

v.

Arthur E. Summerfield, Individually and as Postmaster General of the United States, Defendant.
Civ. A. No. 74–55.

United States District Court, District of Columbia.

Jan. 31, 1955.

O. John Rogge and *Josiah Lyman*, Washington, D.C., for plaintiff.
Edward H. Hickey, Donald B. MacGuineas, Washington, D.C., *Joseph Langbart*, Arlington, Va., for defendant.

Kirkland, Judge.

There is before the Court the case of *Sunshine Book Co.* v. *Summerfield* individually and as Postmaster General of the United States, defendant, in Civil Action No. 74–55.

The complaint was originally filed January 6, 1955, and there has been an amended complaint filed on January 18, 1955. They differ in only one slight particular. The gravamen of the complaint of January 6, 1955, was directed to injunctive relief sought by the plaintiff against the impounding of some 400 copies of the magazine Sunshine & Health for February, 1955, at the Mays Landing, New Jersey, Post Office, and, as well, a separate claim for declaratory judgment that this particular magazine was not obscene.

The amended complaint also has attached as an exhibit Sun Magazine of the issue of January–February, 1955, and seeks in a third claim a declaratory judgment that the character of that magazine is not obscene in fact.

Historically, the facts of this case indicate that on approximately December 23, 1954, the Postmaster of Mays Landing, New Jersey, Post Office, gave notice to the depositor, namely, the plaintiff here and subsidiary groups including Solar Union Naturisme, Inc., that the deposit of these magazines on instruction of the Postmaster General was being withheld from the United States mails.

At the same time notice was given of an administrative hearing before the Solicitor for the Post Office Department. The hearing began on January 16, 1955, and after several postponements has proceeded to a conclusion and there has been filed in the action of this case today the administrative finding of the Postmaster through his subordinates the trial examiner and the Solicitor for the Post Office Department, and that finding has been that the "review of the entire official record * * * upon substantial evidence * * * indicates that the magazines in question contain photographs of naked men, women and children, principally women, clearly revealing genitals, breasts and other portions of the body normally covered in public." It concludes that, "From the advertisements therein contained, that they are offered freely for sale," and the Post Office Department through its officials in this hearing has made a finding of fact that "The photographs appear obscene and indecent when judged by the ordinary community standards of the vast majority of citizens of this country."

Continuing with the historical portion of the case, there was filed at the outset with the complaint of January 6 a motion for a temporary restraining order. That was heard briefly and denied, and a date was set for the hearing of the temporary injunction, which upon hearing was likewise denied, and so it was brought up until this date, January 31, 1955, for the determination of the then pending status of the case on the final injunction.

At the time this particular Court heard the argument of the motion for a temporary injunction one of the issues raised was, and properly raised, that the administrative remedies had not been exhausted. The Court heard argument on both sides of the question and concluded that from the Congressional enactments and the customs and procedures followed that the initial determination under Title 18 U.S.C. § 1461, the obscenity statute, lay with the Postmaster General, and accordingly the Court gave directions that that should first be settled and disposed of, as the record now reveals it has been, and then the matter on the nature of the finding, as well as the question raised by the pleadings, would be decided today.

Accordingly, on the record of the case, including the pleadings, the affidavits appended, affidavits appended to Civil Action 3007–53, the Court on opening statements has narrowed the issues of this particular case.

The Court has ruled that there is provision under this statute, Title 18 U.S.C. § 1461, for the Postmaster General to conduct hearings and examinations into the alleged obscenity of publications, pamphlets, pictures, papers, letters, prints or other publications; that Title 18 U.S.C. § 1461 is not unconstitutional; that due process under the Fifth Amendment was provided for by a hearing in which either testimony, or review of the magazines and the pictures contained therein by visual observation, and the helpful argument of counsel did constitute a proper hearing within that provision. The Court has also ruled that under Title 18 U.S.C. § 1461, there is not a denial of the provisions of the First Amendment to the Constitution.

The Court also ruled preliminarily that the administrative hearing was one contemplated by the Congress and one carried out properly by its designated agent, the Postmaster General; that the scope was not essentially criminal in character, though criminal provisions are applied because the statute carefully declared that whatever was obscene, lewd, lascivious, filthy or of an indecent nature as it applied to any book, pamphlet, picture, paper, letter, print or other publication should be declared not to be mailable and should not be conveyed in the mails or delivered from any post office or by any letter carrier; that the Court was not confined to a mere determination of whether the finding of the Postmaster General from his hearing was arbitrary and capricious but that the Court in the status of this case which antedated the actual finding in the proceedings themselves, as well as the review of the proceedings, had the right to pass upon whether there was a foundation for the Postmaster in his finding that these two publications were obscene.

That left open the sole question of whether the two publications were obscene as a matter of fact and as a matter of law.

Counsel have very ably presented the matter. They have been very careful to indicate their industry, and their deep professional learning.

Accordingly, we are in the posture of determining the standards by which to judge these particular magazines.

[1] First of all, nudity is not, per se, obscene, as the case of *Parmelee* v. *United States*, from our own circuit, reported in 72 App. D.C. 203, 113 F. 2d 729, was clear to point out. However, we must steer a course, in the clash of these legal interests, between what is art on the one hand, pornography on the other; what is decent on the one hand as against what is indecent on the other; and what is conformity to the mores of the District of Columbia, the State of New Jersey and America in general. Accordingly, we must first consider the definitions which have been handed down in interpreting the mandate of Congress.

Title 18 U.S. Code, § 1461 lays down five descriptive adjectives of what will constitute the basis of obscenity in general. Congress has used the words, "obscene," "lewd," "lascivious," "filthy" and "indecent" and has applied them to books, pamphlets, pictures, papers, letters, prints and other publications.

This, of course, is a magazine. It is a publication. There are contained within it pictures. Accordingly, in that aspect of the statute, this Court has jurisdiction.

It is declared if they are found to be obscene they are to be non-mailable, they are not to be transported or conveyed in the mails, and they are not to be delivered from any post office or by any letter carrier.

Those parts are clear and do not need definition. But there is a need of definition as to what the Congress meant in the employment of the five adjectives.

In connection with the definition of "obscene" the Supreme Court in *Dunlop* v. *United States*, 165 U.S. 486, 17 S. Ct. 375, 41 L. Ed. 799, has declared that obscenity or the adjective "obscene" must be calculated to lower that standard which we regard as essential to civilization or calculated with the ordinary person to deprave his morals or lead to impure purposes.

In the case of *United States* v. *One Obscene Book* Entitled "Married Love," 48 F. 2d 821, from the Southern District of New York, decided in 1931, the Court there declared that obscenity means to be offensive to the senses or to the taste, refinement; disgusting, repulsive, filthy, foul, abominable, loathsome, offensive to modesty or decency, expressing or suggesting unchaste or lustful ideas; impure, indecent, lewd.

In our own local case, *Parmelee* v. *U.S.*, 72 App. D.C. 203, 113 F. 2d 729, 730, decided in 1940, the Court said, and I quote: "Obscenity is not a technical term of the law and is not susceptible of exact definition. * * * Probably the fundamental reason why the word obscene is not susceptible of exact definition is that such intangible moral concepts as it purports to connote, vary in meaning from one period to another."

In the case of *United States* v. *Two Obscene Books*, 99 F. Supp. 760, decided in 1951, from the District Court of California, decided in 1951, the Court indicated that the definition of "obscene" is: Offensive to chastity and modesty; that form of indecency which is calculated to promote the general corruption of morals; has a tendency to deprave or corrupts the morals of those whose minds are open to such influences and into whose hands it may fall by allowing or implanting in such minds obscene, lewd, or lascivious thoughts or desires.

Passing on to the second word which appears in the statute, namely, the word "lewd," it has been defined in *United States* v. *Slenker*, D.C., 32 F. 691, as having a tendency to excite lustful thoughts.

In the case of *United States* v. *Males*, decided in D.C., 51 F. 41, the word "lewd" has been defined as licentious.

The third word is the word "lascivious." In the case of *United States* v. *Clarke*, D.C., 38 F. 732, that word was defined as synonymous with "lewd"; dissolute, unchaste, calculated to excite lustful and sensual desires in those whose minds are open to such influences.

In the case of *Swearingen* v. *United States*, 161 U.S. 446, 16 S. Ct. 562, 40 L. Ed. 765, it was defined as: Tending to excite lust; lewd, indecent; obscene; relating to sexual impurity; tending to deprave the morals in respect to sexual relations.

The fourth word is the word "filthy." That has been defined in *United States* v. *Davidson*, D.C., 244 F. 523, as: Morally foul, polluted, nasty.

In the case of *Tyomies Publishing Co.* v. *United States*, 6 Cir., 211 F. 385, it was defined as: Dirty, vulgar, indecent, offensive to the moral sense, morally depraving, debasing.

In the case of *United States* v. *Limehouse*, 285 U.S. 424, 52, S. Ct. 412, 76 L. Ed. 843, it was defined to mean matter that, though not lewd or obscene, it nevertheless had a tendency to corrupt or debauch.

The definition of the last of these five adjectives, the word "indecent," has been stated in *United States* v. *Davidson*, D.C., 244 F. 523, to be: Offensive to common propriety; offending against modesty or delicacy; grossly vulgar, obscene, lewd.

And in the case of *United States* v. *Smith*, C.C., 11 F. 663, the word "indecent" is defined as: Immodest, impure.

Those definitions are the beacons by which the legal channel is lighted for the Court to arrive at findings of fact and conclusions of law in this case.

[2] Next, it is clear that under the law, as the trier of the facts, the Court is to apply the test of the normal, reasonable person, and the findings are to be predicated upon his—that is, the normal, reasonable, prudent person's —determination.

In the case of *Walker* v. *Popenoe*, reported at 80 U.S. App. D.C. 129, 149 F. 2d 511, particularly with regard to the law on obscenity and the tests applying thereto, our Circuit Court of Appeals, 149 F. 2d at page 512, stated that there should be three classifications, and laid them down by way of tests, as follows:

First, "The effect of a publication on the ordinary reader is what counts. The statute does not intend that we shall 'reduce our treatment of sex to the standard of a child's library in the supposed interest of a salacious few.'"

Second, "The statute does not bar from the mails an obscene phrase or an obscene sentence. It bars an obscene 'book, pamphlet * * * or other publication * * *.' If a publication as a whole is not stimulating to the senses of the ordinary reader, it is not within the statute."

Third, "It would make nonsense of the statute to hold that it covers works of value and repute merely because their incidental effects may include some slight stimulation of the senses of the ordinary reader. The dominant effect of an entire publication determines its character."

As was pointed out in the case of *Parmelee* v. *United States*, 72 App. D.C. 203, 113 F. 2d 729, the modern rule was restated with emphasis, and 113 F. 2d at page 731 the Court said, and this trial court quotes:

"But more recently this standard has been repudiated, and for it has been substituted the test that a book must be considered as a whole, in its effect, not upon any particular class, but upon all those whom it it likely to reach."

It has been urged upon the Court that the finding of my brother Judge Henry Schweinhaut, in the case of *Summerfield* v. *Sunshine Book Co.*, No. 12,026, D.C. Cir., 221 F. 2d 42, is controlling both as to the law and the facts in this particular case, both on the doctrine of stare decisis and res judicata.

[3] The Court rules that on the doctrine of stare decisis it is not controlling for the reason that the standards of that case by which another court could judge the findings are not set forth, and is actually complained of in the majority view of the Circuit Court of Appeals when the majority states, "In this view of the case, it does not become necessary to pass upon other questions raised by the appellees as to the constitutionality or applicability of this statute, as to the propriety of the Postmaster General's finding that the publications involved in his orders were obscene, see *Parmelee* v. *United States*, 1940, 72 App. D.C. 203, 113 F. 2d 729,"—and the Court with emphasis adds—"or the adequacy of the evidence and record upon which such a finding was based in the instant case."

There the Postmaster General made a very short finding unlike the finding he has made in the instant case. He merely found that some 25 copies of magazines of the same publication issued in the years 1952 and 1953 were obscene. My brother Judge Henry Schweinhaut merely stated that with that he did not agree, and he found and signed an order on a sole finding of fact that the magazines were not obscene.

It was in that posture that the case went to our Circuit

Court of Appeals, and the majority very properly ruled that under Title 39, U.S.C.A. § 259(a), where a postmaster at a local station had indiscriminately withheld money orders and general mail which could touch both a lawful or unlawful purpose or legal or illegal purpose, he had exceeded his bounds, and this Court interprets the majority view as not binding upon whether subsequent issues of the same magazine might be obscene in fact.

The dissenting view of appellate case is strong that all of those magazines were obscene both in law and in fact.

There is also the case of *Sunshine Book Co.* v. *McCaffrey*, cited at Sup., 112 N.Y.S. 2d 476, where in passing upon the seizure of the same magazine from the newsstands in New York City in the year 1952, and where it was sought by injunctive powers to lift the ban which the Commissioner of Licenses of New York City had applied, that court held that the same type of magazines—Sunshine & Health and Sun magazine—were obscene, and particularly pointed to the fact that on the front page there was a picture of a nude woman which clearly showed the pubic area. That particular court repudiated the Parmelee case from our own Circuit.

This Court points to the decision in the case of *Summerfield* v. *Sunshine Book Co.*, No. 12,026 as not controlling on this doctrine of stare decisis.

On the question of res judicata, for the reason that there was no clear showing what the basis was for the finding by the Postmaster that the magazines were obscene nor the finding by the trial court that they were not obscene, the Court in this particular instance is not bound by the decision in the former case on the doctrine of res judicata. The matter is clearly before the Court for a determination.

The Court has set forth the legal beacon lights that will guide its course in the determination of whether a book, pamphlet, picture, paper, letter, print, or other publication is to be judged, and will make the following findings of fact and conclusions of law as respects the magazine Sunshine & Health, February, 1955, Vol. 23, issue No. 2, and the Sun Magazine, January–February 1955, being volume 5 and issue No. 1.

First and foremost, nudity is not obscene, per se. There are a series of silhouettes which appear in this publication of Sunshine & Health. They depict the human female form in a broad outline. The Court will hold as a fact that they are not obscene.

There are some sketches in the issue of Sun Magazine which are broad pen sketches, and while they reveal the general outline of the female form, the Court will also hold that those sketches, because of their indefiniteness, of failure to emphasize any particular part of the male or female genital area, are not obscene as a matter of fact.

The articles which appear do not contain vulgar or obscene matter, and the Court will hold that they are not obscene as a matter of fact.

The Court will also hold that the American people are a clothed race, that under our Constitution the views of others are always permitted, and that progress comes out of some of those views, and aids, generally, all the citizens.

The Court will hold that nudism in its present stage is a cult or a society or a group that represents a very small minority of the American people.

[4] The Court will also hold that, from acceptance of the majority in works of art, in medical and scientific journals, books, magazines and literature, religious articles and the like, pictures which show the human form merely in the nude and beyond that not revealing the pubic area or the male or female genitalia, are not obscene.

The Court will also hold as a fact that posterior views of nudes, be they male or female, young or old, whether photographed or sketched at short or long distances, are not obscene as a matter of fact. Views taken from the side of nude persons, male or female, young or old, that do not reveal the genitalia or the pubic area, are not obscene. Where the one photographed or sketched, or whose likeness is reproduced on parchment or paper, or canvas, makes concealment of the pubic area by his or her limbs or by objects, or where the area is concealed by shadow, such pictures are not obscene as a matter of fact. Pictures taken at sufficient distance, although being a front view, are not obscene. It depends upon the distance of the camera's focus or the projection of the artist or the one who is sketching the scene—the distance as projected from the viewer's eye.

Where the artist or the photographer obscures by shadowing, by retouching photographic plates, or by concealment or obliteration of the pubic area, though it reveals all other formations of the nude body, male or female, young or old, that is not obscene as a matter of fact.

[5] Where children are photographed in a frontal view which reveals the diminutive and undeveloped genitalia, that is not obscene as a matter of fact.

It is difficult to lay down a hard and fast rule but certainly, drawing upon the criminal rule as an analogy, children below the age of seven photographed in such condition do not exhibit a picture which is obscene, lewd, lascivious, filthy, or of an indecent nature, by virtue of their age of innocence, the under-development of their genitalia, and the common acceptance of the American people of such views.

Between the ages of seven and fourteen, when the children undergo rapid development, and especially in the warmer portion of our country, there, of course, because of the development which occurs in the pubic area, which is a small portion of the human anatomy characterized by pubic hair in both sexes, and where genitalia are also intimately revealed, it may or may not, depending upon the distance, the obliteration, the shadowing and the like, be obscene as a matter of fact.

[6] Where photographs are taken of the pubic area at very close range they are as a matter of fact, obscene, and, it will follow, as a consequence, as a matter of law, obscene.

As to the female breast there is always the problem of the acceptance of its exposure by the majority of the American people. The organ, of course, is one of nutrition for young, expanding during periods of pregnancy and reducing in size when the state of non-pregnancy and the nurture of the young child has no longer required its function.

The public is, therefore, accustomed to the view of the nursing mother and has not found it to be indecent or obscene. Since the ancient past there have been many periods of years when, as to the form of dress worn by the female, the plunging neckline has been accepted in the mores of the people, so that the revealing of the breast would not in itself be obscene. However, its accentuation, its distortion, or its grossness could, under the broad definition, depending upon the situation, make it filthy or might make it indecent.

Of course, the Court is not touching upon the question which would appear to be the fact, that sometimes partial concealment adds to allure, because the pictures involved in these cases, where they run against the standards the Court has indicated, are not pictures where there is concealment.

Accordingly, against those broad findings of fact the Court will make these particular findings of fact.

On the outside cover of Sunshine & Health Magazine for February, 1955, there is a close view of a young woman apparently in her early twenties. There is no show of the pubic area and there is no show of the genitalia by the angle at which the picture is shot. While the shadowing on her chest is grotesque and indicates a bosom larger by far than normal, it is shot at such an angle as to elongate and make quite massive the breast as distinguished from the very small nipple. While it gives an effect, in general, of grotesqueness by the tests which the courts have laid down, it is not obscene under the test of this statute.

There is a picture of a young girl on page 7. She appears to be approximately six or seven. It is a frontal view taken within a very short range of approximately 6 feet. She is swinging on a swing, facing the camera. While the labia majora are shown, they are diminutive and juvenile. One would have to be prudish to hold that that was an obscene picture. The Court does not hold it as a fact and rules that it is a picture that does not contravene this statute.

On page 9 there is a picture of a man on water skis, taken at some distance. His genitalia are clearly revealed, appearing in the center of the picture. The Court is going to hold that by the closeness, the detail that can be seen, that that is an obscene picture within the purview of the statute.

There is a picture shown at the upper portion of page 13. This is a picture of two persons, a woman seated beside a pool and a man standing to her side. The woman, by the crossing of one leg partly over the other, has obscured the pubic area and genitalia, and hers is not an obscene picture. The man, on the other hand, is standing with a side view. By artful use of shadow his face is completely obliterated, his entire pubic area is obliterated by the shadow, but prominently shown in front of the pubic area and against this dark background is his male organ; the corona of the penis is clearly discernible; in fact, even a casual observation of it indicates that the man is circumcised. This obviously has no place even in illustrating the principles of nudism. It is filthy, it is foul, it is obscene, and the Court will hold such as a matter of fact.

On page 15 there are four middle-aged women with their backs to a very large oak tree, appearing to be some 12 feet in diameter. They are holding hands and facing the camera. Only two of these women are revealed to the viewer. The woman to the left is a woman of middle age. She has very large thighs. The pubic hair is clearly shown. Her right thigh is particularly noticeable because, though there are trees nearby, the formation which appears on the thigh is not that of shadow, it appears to be matted varicose veins that cause her to be grotesque, vile, hold her up as an object of scorn, and the Court will hold under the statute that that is filthy, and that it is indecent. That is also true of the woman in the foreground who, while not in as much sunlight as the other, nevertheless clearly reveals her pubic area as she stands within approximately 6 feet of the camera.

On page 16, in a mixed group, there is one man revealed at the corner where his genitals are clearly shown, and the Court will rule as a matter of fact that that is obscene.

On page 29 there is a most unusual picture. Here are two women who appear to be in their late twenties or early thirties. The woman to the left appears to be approximately 5 foot 7. She must weigh in the neighborhood of 250 pounds. She is exceedingly obese.

I assume the illustration, not retouched by the photographer, is to represent the normal, natural person and reveals her as she was in fact when the picture was taken. This picture was taken within approximately 12 feet of the camera. First of all, so far as the demonstration of nudism goes, the picture shows a very clear sunburned "V" at her neck—V-shaped sunburn—whereas the rest of her skin is white as the snow on which she stands. The Court might gather she is a new member or a non-conformist. She has large, elephantine breasts that hang from her shoulder to her waist. They are exceedingly large. The thighs are very obese. She is standing in snow, wearing galoshes. But the part which is offensive, obscene, filthy and indecent is the pubic area shown.

Being most liberal, one might say that the area shown of the pubic hair is caused by shadow, but the same is not to be noticed on both sides. The hair extends outwardly virtually to the hipbone. It looks to the Court like a retouched picture because the hair line instead of being straight is actually scalloped or in a half-moon shape, which makes the woman grotesque, vile, filthy, the representation is dirty, and the Court will hold that that picture is obscene in the sense that it is indecent, it is filthy, and it is obscene as a matter of fact; because of the closeness of the view the woman to her left and the viewer's right is likewise held to be obscene.

The intent of the photographer and publisher is clearly shown by those prior pictures, because on page 17, standing within 8 feet of the photographer, is a male figure. Although the outline of his body is shown, the pubic area and genitalia are completely blocked out, revealing a picture under one condition there, and showing pictures under different conditions, as pointed out by the Court, and the Court points to that fact and holds that the latter pictures were thus reproduced intentionally.

With regard to Sun Magazine against the standards set forth, the Court will hold that the picture of the young girl photographed on page 6, standing within approximately 6 feet of the camera, showing the pubic area, is obscene; that it is lewd, lascivious, and tends to incite lust and sensual ideas; that the two pictures shown on pages 8 and 9 of a young girl in her early twenties standing within short range of the camera, approximately some 8 to 10 feet, in a frontal view showing the clear detail of the pubic area, are obscene.

On page 11 there is a picture of three females with the caption, "Mrs. Nudism of 1954 and Two of Her Ten Children." The two girls who appear with her are in their early 'teens. The mother is obese, short, stocky, has large flat breasts; the pubic area is somewhat shaded by shadow; the pubic hair is matted; the over-all picture is one of vulgarity, filth, obscenity and dirt. But the photographer in taking this picture has caused the two girls to turn to a side view and the sunshine clearly shows the fine, soft texture of pubic hair of the adolescent girls, and accordingly the Court finds the picture is obscene, lewd, and lascivious.

There is shown on page 13 a picture of a woman in her early twenties. She is standing in a three-quarter pose within 6 feet of the camera. There is a woman to the side holding a large inflated ball of some sort. The sun and the said ball have cast a shadow upon the body of the other woman. While it is suggestive, it, nevertheless, by the distance, the posture and the elimination through the shadow of the pubic area, is not obscene.

There is a sketch on page 19 of Sun Magazine which does not show in any great detail the pubic area of the two females shown tossing a large ball, and the Court finds that the drawing is not obscene.

There are pictures taken within an approximate range of 15 feet of the camera, in the surf, showing two nude couples. The women are obscured by the waves. The man in the foreground has completely revealed his male genitalia, and the Court will hold that this is obscene.

There is a suggestive picture on page 23—what appears to be a Mexican, a woman of Mexican birth, a very dark complexioned woman. But the shadows in the scene obliterate the pubic area, and the Court will hold that that is not obscene as a matter of fact or law.

There is a picture taken of a group at some great distance watching an exhibition of judo or wrestling, on page 29, but by virtue of the distance at which that picture is taken the Court will hold that it is not an obscene, lewd or lascivious picture.

[7, 8] Accordingly, the Court concludes as a matter of fact that the pictures fall within the standards as the Court has indicated in its findings, and concludes as a matter of law that the right of the Postmaster to have made his initial findings as he did is established by the cases. The statute does not thwart the principles of the First Amendment or the Fifth Amendment; that there was foundation in fact for his findings, and review of the entire official record and of the initial decision by the Post Office Examiner, and discloses no erroneous findings of fact nor conclusions of law; the initial decision was founded upon substantial evidence and contains correct rulings, findings of fact and conclusions of law upon all material issues. These magazines contain photographs of naked men, women and children—principally women—clearly revealing genitals, breasts and other portions of the body normally covered in public. It is apparent from advertisements therein contained that they are offered freely for sale to the general public who are not members of the nudist organization. The photographs appear to be obscene and indecent when judged by the ordinary community standards of the vast majority of the citizens of our country.

The postmaster at Mays Landing, New Jersey, will, accordingly, be instructed to treat the February 1955 issue of Sunshine & Health and the January–February issue of Sun (Solaire Universelle Nudisme) as non-mailable.

The Court finds from the record, from the standards, that there was basis in fact and in law for the conclusion of the Postmaster General, and accordingly will sustain him in that view. The Court will conclude as a matter of law that since the dominant theme of both magazines, by the findings of fact, is clearly one of obscenity, the Court will direct first that the motion for a permanent injunction as against the action of the Postmaster General in withholding 400 copies of Sunshine & Health, February, 1955, will be dismissed with prejudice, and disposition of those copies, depending upon an ultimate determination, will proceed in accordance with postal regulations. On the amended complaint in the third claim seeking a declaratory judgment on Sun Magazine, January–February 1955 issue, the Court will enter judgment for the defendant in the cause and will find as a fact that the magazine is obscene within Title 18 U.S. Code § 1461.

Counsel will prepare suitable findings of fact and conclusions of law.

■ Sunshine Book Company and Solair Union Naturisme, Inc., Appellants,

v.

Arthur E. Summerfield, Individually and as Postmaster General of the United States, Appellee.
No. 12622.

United States Court of Appeals, District of Columbia Circuit.

Reargued Sept. 25, 1956. Decided Oct. 3, 1957.

Mr. *O. John Rogge*, Washington, D.C., for appellants.
Mr. *Donald B. MacGuineas*, Atty. Dept. of Justice, with whom *Messrs. Samuel D. Slade* and *Joseph Langbart*, Attys., Dept. of Justice, were on the brief, for appellee.
Mr. *Edward deGrazia*, Washington, D.C., filed a brief on behalf of American Civil Liberties Union, as amicus curiae, urging reversal.

Before Edgerton, Chief Judge, and Prettyman, Wilbur K. Miller, Bazelon, Fahy, Washington, Dana-

HER and BASTIAN, Circuit Judges, sitting en banc. (Circuit Judge BURGER took no part in the hearing or consideration of this case.)

DANAHER, Circuit Judge, with whom Circuit Judges Prettyman, Wilbur K. Miller and Bastian concur, Circuit Judge Fahy concurring in the result and stating his views separately: Appellants, Sunshine Book Company and Solair Union Naturisme, Inc., sought in the District Court to enjoin the Post Office Department from refusing to transmit by mail the February, 1955, issue of "Sunshine & Health" Magazine and the January–February, 1955, issue of Sun Magazine. A Hearing Examiner in the Post Office Department had decided that the named issues are nonmailable because obscene as that term is used in 18 U.S.C. § 1461 (1952).[1] After review of the appellants' exceptions to the Initial Decision and recommendations of the Hearing Examiner and the Department's reply thereto, the Solicitor of the Post Office Department affirmed. Concluding that the magazines contained photographs of naked men, women and children, are "obscene and indecent when judged by the ordinary community standards of the vast majority of citizens of this country," and noting that advertisements in the magazines indicate that they are offered freely for sale to the general public who are not members of a nudist organization, the Solicitor directed that the postmaster at Mays Landing, New Jersey, be instructed to treat the named issues as nonmailable.

In the District Court, appellants asked a declaration that the determination and order of the Department as applied be declared invalid as unconstitutional; that the Department be restrained permanently from withholding from dispatch in the United States mails the named issues of the magazines, and future numbers of these publications said to be substantially similar to the named issues here involved and to the magazines considered as exhibits in an earlier action;[2] a preliminary injunction to the same effect

pending final relief; and that the named issues be declared not to be obscene. Judge Kirkland denied relief, ruling that there was a substantial basis in fact and in law to support the Department's determination and, independently as trier, he concluded that the named issues, being obscene, are nonmailable.[3] After the appeal had here been argued, the court ordered rehearing *en banc*.[4]

Facts alleged, found and appearing of record may be succinctly summarized. About December 23, 1954, appellant Sunshine completed the printing of approximately 40,000 copies of the February, 1955, issue of the publication, "Sunshine & Health" of which 10,000 copies were to be circulated through the mails. Approximately 30% of the total circulation of the second publication, "Sun Magazine," was to be distributed through the mails. Appellants alleged that they receive a larger percentage of return on copies disseminated by mail to subscribers than from the sale of copies distributed by other means such as sales at news-stands. Between December 24, 1954, and December 31, 1954, appellant Sunshine Book Company caused some 400 copies of its February 1955 issue to be offered for mailing as third class matter through the post office at Mays Landing, New Jersey. The postmaster under date of December 29, 1954, submitted a sample copy of the questioned issue to the Solicitor for the Post Office Department for instructions, pursuant to the applicable regulations.[5] Under date of December 30, 1954, he was advised by the Solicitor that the questioned copies "subject to inspection" should be withheld from dispatch and that the senders should be informed that they might have "opportunity to show cause within fifteen days why the article should not be disposed of as matter nonmailable under * * * 39 C.F.R. 36.2." Under date of December 31, 1954, the postmaster informed the senders as to the opportunity to be heard, but erroneously also wrote that the questioned issue "is nonmailable and must be withheld from dispatch." The Solicitor under date of January 6, 1955, advised the senders as to the postmaster's error and pointed out that no ruling or determination as to mailability had been made either by the Solicitor or by any authorized person, that a hearing had been assigned for January 10, 1955, and that "every effort will be made to insure an expeditious consideration and ruling in this

---

[1] Pertinent portions applicable when the proceedings herein were commenced read:

"Every obscene, lewd, lascivious, or filthy book, pamphlet, picture, paper, letter, writing, print, or other publication of an indecent character; and—

    *   *   *   *   *

"*Is declared to be nonmailable* matter and *shall not be conveyed in the mails* or delivered from any post office or by any letter carrier." (Emphasis supplied.) Cf. 18 U.S.C. §§ 1461, 1465 (Supp. IV 1957).

Pertinent regulations may be found in 39 C.F.R. as §§ 36.1, 36.2 and 36.7, issued under 5 U.S.C.A. § 22 and 5 U.S.C.A. § 369 as follows:

"§ 22. Departmental regulations. The head of each department is authorized to prescribe regulations, not inconsistent with law, for the government of his department, the conduct of its officers and clerks, the distribution and performance of its business, and the custody, use, and preservation of the records, papers, and property appertaining to it."

"§ 369. Duties of Postmaster General. It shall be the duty of the Postmaster General:

    *   *   *   *   *

"Ninth. To superintend generally the business of the department and execute all laws relative to the Postal Service."

[2] *Summerfield* v. *Sunshine Book Company*, 1954, 95 U.S. App. D.C. 169, 221 F. 2d 42, certiorari denied 1955, 349 U.S. 921, 75 S. Ct. 661, 99 L. Ed. 1253, which involved a proceeding under 39 U.S.C.A. § 259a. There we concluded that the statute

did not authorize the Postmaster General to predicate an order refusing mail privileges upon future, unpublished issues of the magazines despite the fact that past issues had contained allegedly obscene matter. Congress has since developed temporary and summary impounding procedures, free from the requirements of the Administrative Procedure Act, 5 U.S.C.A. § 1001 et seq., to be followed in such cases. See the Act approved July 27, 1956, 39 U.S.C.A. § 259b. See S. Rep. No. 2234, 84th Cong., 2d Sess., 2 U.S. Code & Ad. News, 1956, p. 3597. These sections are not involved in the instant case.

[3] His opinion with its detailed findings and conclusions has been reported at length. See *Sunshine Book Company* v. *Summerfield*, D.C.D.C. 1955, 128 F. Supp. 564.

[4] We heard argument September 25, 1956. We decided to postpone our decision herein because of the pendency in the Supreme Court of several cases, the decisions in which were deemed likely to have an important, if not controlling, bearing on the problems here raised. See, e.g., *Roth* v. *United States* (*Alberts* v. *California*), 1957, 354 U.S. 476, 77 S. Ct. 1304, 1 L. Ed. 2d 1498; *Kingsley Books, Inc.* v. *Brown*, 1957, 354 U.S. 436, 77 S. Ct. 1325, 1 L. Ed. 2d 1469.

[5] C.F.R. § 36.7 and see supra note 1.

matter." Similar notice was given to Solar Universale Nudisme Magazine of a hearing assigned for January 11, 1955, to determine the mailability of its January–February, 1955, issue of Sun Magazine. On January 10, 1955, the Hearing Examiner "at the request of counsel for the publisher and with the agreement of the Solicitor" continued the hearings as to both magazines until January 17, 1955, when the hearings went forward. On appeal from the examiner's initial decision, the Solicitor affirmed January 28, 1955, reciting details as to the photographic contents of the questioned publications which he found were offered freely for sale to the general public.

Meanwhile, proceedings had been instituted in the District Court on January 6, 1955, and, on January 18, 1955, the motion for preliminary injunction was denied. It was then ordered that "the status quo" be maintained until the completion of the administrative proceedings and that the case be advanced for trial to be heard January 31, 1955. Accordingly, the case was then heard and after argument, the court's oral ruling was pronounced. Findings of fact and conclusions of law were thereafter filed, and the judgment dismissing the appellants' amended complaint was entered February 16, 1955.

In court the Department stood upon the record of the papers and opinions which had been filed in the administrative proceeding which, without objection, were received. The trier offered to hear testimony. Appellants presented no "live" witnesses, and had none in court. In colloquy with the trial judge appellants' counsel outlined the nature of such testimony as might have been produced: as to community standards; that the photographs do not violate such standards; that nudism is growing in American life, "for instance, in the home"; and analysis, comparatively, of some nude photographs in certain magazines and of the sequence in "La Tuka," a motion picture of African tribal life. The trier ruled the proffer was irrelevant in terms of American community life measured by legal standards as applied to the magazine issues before the court. Counsel, in effect, concluded: "This brings us, then, far quicker than I thought we would get there to the issue of obscenity." It was the issue in the District Court, and is the issue here.

[1] The statute[6] under which the proceedings went forward not only makes criminal the use of the mails for the transmission of proscribed matter, including obscene, lewd or lascivious pictures or publications of an indecent character, but all such matter is declared to be "nonmailable" and "shall not be conveyed in the mails."

[2] Appellants' contentions that the statute "usurps powers impliedly and expressly reserved to the states in violation of the First, Ninth, and Tenth Amendments to the United States Constitution" have been answered by the Court in *Roth* v. *United States*,[7] where it was held expressly that "obscenity is not within the area of constitutionally protected speech or press." The majority further said:

> "*Roth's argument that the federal obscenity statute unconstitutionally encroaches upon the powers reserved by the Ninth and Tenth Amendments to the States and to the people to punish speech and press where offensive to decency and morality is hinged upon his contention that obscenity is expression not excepted from the sweep of the provision of the First Amendment that 'Congress shall make no law * * * abridging the freedom of speech, or of the press * * *.' (Emphasis added.) That argument falls in light of our holding that obscenity is not expression protected by the First Amendment. We therefore hold that the federal obscenity statute punishing the use of the mails for obscene material is a proper exercise of the postal power delegated to Congress by Art. I, § 8, cl. 7.*"[8]

The command of the statute is such that if the issues of the magazines in question are nonmailable under 18 U.S.C. § 1461, the Post Office Department is bound to deny access to the mails.[9] Arguing that a conclusion of "obscenity" is a matter of *opinion*, appellants insist that the Postmaster General's order was invalid as a matter of law. The Court tells us however that, while there may be marginal cases, obscenity is recognizable and may be distinguished from the portrayal of sex in art, literature and scientific works. "Obscene material is material which deals with sex in a manner appealing to prurient interest." The Court observed that the trial court "sufficiently followed the proper standard," having applied the test "whether to the average person, applying contemporary community standards, the dominant theme of the material taken as a whole appeals to prurient interest." Thus, the Court concluded:

> "*In summary, then, we hold that [the federal statute] applied according to the proper standard for judging obscenity, do[es] not offend constitutional safeguards against convictions based upon protected material, or fail to give men in acting adequate notice of what is prohibited.*"[10]

[3] Here, the trial judge carefully reviewed the authorities and applied the test[11] we had laid down in *Parmelee* v. *United States*[12] and which was quoted verbatim in the

---

[6] 18 U.S.C. § 1461 (1952), supra note 1, was later amended by the Act of June 28, 1955, 18 U.S.C. § 1461 (Supp. IV 1957). Congress sought "to enlarge section 1461 of title 18, United States Code, so as to include within the prohibition of said section all matter of obscene nature, whether or not said matter had fallen within the more restricted definition contained in the statute." S. Rep. No. 113 to accompany S. 600, 84th Cong., 1st Sess. U.S. Code Congressional and Administrative News 1955, page 2210. The Report further advised the Senate that passage of the bill "will contribute greatly in the continuing struggle to combat juvenile delinquency and the corruption of public morals."

[7] 1957, 354 U.S. 476, 485, 77 S. Ct. 1304, 1309, 1 L. Ed. 2d 1498.

[8] Id. 354 U.S. at pages 491–492, 77 S. Ct. at page 1313.

[9] *Roth* v. *Goldman*, 2 Cir., 1949, 172 F. 2d 788, certiorari denied 1949, 337 U.S. 938, 69 S. Ct. 1514, 93 L. Ed. 1743; "It shall be the duty of the Postmaster General * * * to * * * execute all laws relative to the Postal Service." 5 U.S.C.A. § 369; as to the duty and power of the Postmaster General, compare *Bates & Guild Co.* v. *Payne*, 1904, 194 U.S. 106, 24 S. Ct. 595, 48 L. Ed. 894. Where the problem turns upon the exercise of judgment when the contents have not been found to be obscene, a wholly different case is presented. See, e.g., *Hannegan* v. *Esquire, Inc.*, 1946, 327 U.S. 146, 149, 158, 66 S. Ct. 456, 90 L. Ed. 586.

[10] 1957, 354 U.S. at page 492, 77 S. Ct. at page 1313.

[11] Supra note 3, *Sunshine Book Company* v. *Summerfield*, 128 F. Supp. at page 568.

[12] 1940, 72 App. D.C. 203, 113 F. 2d 729.

Roth charge, approved by the Court. Supplied by the trial judge were extensive, particularized descriptions of the offending and offensive material which need not here be repeated, as they speak for themselves. We deem the conclusions reached by the trial judge to be amply sustained. Appellants argue to us that the issue of obscenity is "not foreclosed by the finding of the trial court and is to be independently reviewed and determined by this court." Were we, as is urged, to go beyond the trier and to reach our own conclusion, we would have no hesitancy in deciding that what is before us is "material which deals with sex in a manner appealing to prurient interest," and hence is obscene, as Roth tells us.

[4] Appellants ask us to say that our earlier decision[13] is *res judicata*. Quite apart from the fact that the many issues of the publications there involved differ from the exhibits before us in no substantial particular so far as their common pattern of nudity is concerned, some of them were more, and some less offensive in their portrayal of sexual indicia than the photographs in the exhibits with which we are now concerned. Most important, however, we did not in the earlier case reach or decide any such issue. On the contrary, we were concerned solely with the scope of the order of the Postmaster General which, we concluded, exceeded his authority. Indeed, we expressly authorized him to amend his orders to conform to the limitations we defined, and we found it unnecessary to inquire into or to pass upon his finding as to obscenity. Since we did not decide that the orders lacked a predicate of obscenity, appellants' reliance upon *res judicata* is totally without basis.

Were we, as appellants asked, to refer to the many issues received as exhibits in the earlier cases, we might readily spell out a continuous pattern of dissemination of nude photographs, a pattern in existence for many years. We would not ignore *Sunshine Book Co.* v. *McCaffrey*[14] where the court at page 483 said:

> "*Where the dominant purpose of nudity is to promote lust, it is obscene and indecent. The distribution and sale of the magazines in this case is a most objectionable example. The dominant purpose of the photographs in these magazines is to attract the attention of the public by an appeal to their sexual impulses. The sales of these magazines is not limited to any mailing list of members or subscribers. They are sold and distributed indiscriminately to all who wish to purchase the same. Men, women, youths of both sexes, and even children, can purchase these magazines. They will have a libidinous effect upon most ordinary, normal, healthy individuals. Their effect upon the abnormal individual may be more disastrous.*"

[5] Nor do we see in the circumstances here a "prior restraint" against which to inveigh. The statute declares

---

[13] Supra note 2.

[14] Sup., 112 N.Y.S. 2d 476. There the appellants likewise were plaintiffs who sought a declaratory judgment and a permanent injunction against the Commissioners of Police and of Licenses of the City of New York. Their publications "Sunshine & Health" and "Sun Magazine" were before the court and appellants had been charged with violating § 1141 of the Penal Law of New York, McKinney's Consol. Laws, c. 40, referred to in *Kingsley Books, Inc.* v. *Brown*, supra note 4, 354 U.S. at page 442, 77 S. Ct. at page 1328.

certain matter to be nonmailable which "shall not be conveyed in the mails." It may be supposed that the Post Office Department is not bound to sit idly by if instruments of crime, proscribed as nonmailable, are nonetheless offered for mailing. We may assume that the Department is not bound to permit the crime to be committed and only thereafter to proceed against one who mails the offending material. Here, pursuant to the departmental regulations, the postmaster sought instructions. An administrative hearing was ordered which proceeded expeditiously, both before the Department and the District Court. After application of the pertinent and appropriate standard, the questioned exhibits were found to be nonmailable. Here, there was no interference with some 30,000 copies of the questioned issue of "Sunshine & Health," and with some 70% of the questioned issue of "Sun Magazine," distributed otherwise than through the mails. Here was no injunction restraining the contemplated distribution of the publications to the public at large. Rather, only after hearing in accord with procedural safeguards antecedent to a determination of nonmailability, the Postmaster General has ruled that the facilities of the Post Office Department are not to be utilized, and the offending material "shall not be conveyed in the mails." There was no seizure, there was no restraint upon "the dissemination of future issues of a publication because its past issues had been found offensive."[15]

We are satisfied that it has been correctly determined that the issues of the magazines here in suit comprise nonmailable matter within the meaning of the statute. There is no error.

Affirmed.

FAHY, Circuit Judge, concurring.

In addition to making it a crime to mail the matter it describes, the statute, 18 U.S.C. § 1461 (1952), declares the matter to be nonmailable, and provides that it shall not be conveyed in the mails or delivered from any post office or by any letter carrier. Thus, as it seems to me, the statute is not solely a criminal one but is also one which closes the mail to obscene matter. This is not inconsistent with the First Amendment, *Roth* v. *United States*, 354 U.S. 476, 77 S. Ct. 1304, 1 L. Ed. 2d 1498 or beyond the federal power; so that even though there has been no conviction of crime, there is reached the question whether the matter is of the kind the statute describes as nonmailable. The standards for determining this have been laid down by the Supreme Court, and the Department was here governed by equivalent standards; the Department applied the standards of the "dominant theme" and of the "contemporary community."

I do not disagree with the conclusion reached. Pictures permeate the magazine and the pictures are dominated by those which the contemporary community deems indecent. If this is so it cannot be but immaterial that much innocent text also appears in the magazine.

This leaves the question whether the departmental procedure met the requirements of due process. In *Kingsley Books, Inc.* v. *Brown*, 354 U.S. 436, 77 S. Ct. 1325, 1326, 1 L. Ed. 2d 1469, the Court sustained the New York

---

[15] *Kingsley Books, Inc.* v. *Brown*, supra, note 4, 354 U.S. at page 445, 77 S. Ct. at page 1330.

"limited injunctive remedy" under the Fourteenth Amendment, applicable to state statute. I think the prompt and speedy administrative process accorded in the present case cannot be distinguished on a Fifth Amendment level, applicable to federal statute, from the procedure sustained in Kingsley Books. After the magazine was held, a longer time elapsed here than in that case before the nonmailable decision was reached; but the Department moved expeditiously—in fact appellant requested additional time.[1]

Further congressional attention to procedure might be desirable, but this is not to say that the courts should hold invalid the procedure here followed, unless it is to be held that only a court or jury is capable under the Constitution of determining in the first or preliminary instance the question of obscenity.

WASHINGTON, Circuit Judge, with whom EDGERTON, Chief Judge, and BAZELON, Circuit Judge, join (dissenting).

"Obscenity is not expression protected by the First Amendment." *Roth* v. *United States*, 1957, 354 U.S. 476, 492, 77 S. Ct. 1304, 1313, 1 L. Ed. 2d 1498. "Obscenity, real, serious, not imagined or puritanically exaggerated, is today as in all the past centuries, a public evil, a public nuisance, a public pollution." *Excelsior Pictures Corp.* v. *Regents of University of State of New York*, 1957, 3 N.Y. 2d 237, 246, 165 N.Y.S. 2d 42, 49. "The validity of the obscenity laws is recognition that the mails may not be used to satisfy all tastes, no matter how perverted." *Hannegan* v. *Esquire, Inc.*, 1946, 327 U.S. 146, 158, 66 S. Ct. 456, 462, 90 L. Ed. 586. Well established though these propositions may be, they do not answer the hard questions of an individual case. Has the publication been found "obscene" by a proper tribunal, applying proper standards? Has the punishment or remedy been authorized by proper legislation?

In the instant case, these questions have not yet been adequately answered. In the first place, it is not at all clear that the Post Office Department possesses any power to censor any class of mail, sealed or unsealed. Certainly Congress has never given such a power in so many words, nor has the Supreme Court ever expressly recognized the existence of such a power. The authority under which the Department is said to be operating in this field is a criminal statute passed in 1873:[1] It contains no language which directs the Department to refuse to transport and deliver newspapers and magazines pending final decision on its part as to whether their content is acceptable to it. "Some day Congress may perhaps give that authorization in specific terms, with proper guidance for and restrictions on administrative action, and with such safeguards as the Constitution may require. But Congress has not done so here." *Summerfield* v. *Sunshine Book Co.*, 1954, 95 U.S. App. D.C. 169 at page 175, 221 F. 2d 42 at page 48.[2] "All that Congress meant by this [1873] act was, that the

mail should not be used to transport such corrupting publications and articles, and that any one who attempted to use it for that purpose should be punished." Ex parte Jackson, 1877, 96 U.S. 727 at page 736, 24 L. Ed. 877.

The postal power permits the Federal Government to impose criminal sanctions for using the mails to distribute obscene materials. *Roth* v. *United States*, supra. Such sanctions, of course, are accompanied by the safeguards of a jury trial. See Brennan, J., dissenting in *Kingsley Books, Inc.* v. *Brown*, 1957, 354 U.S. 436, 447, 77 S. Ct. 1325, 1 L. Ed. 2d 1469. Prior restraint is another story. A state statute has been upheld which permitted a limited form of judicial prior restraint against materials alleged to be obscene, through temporary injunction followed by prompt trial. See *Kingsley Books, Inc.* v. *Brown*, supra. It may be that the postal power would provide a basis for a Federal statute authorizing a similar form of judicial control. But an administrative prior restraint, not plainly authorized by statute and not subject to specified standards and safeguards, is of highly doubtful validity, to say the least. Compare *Holmby Productions, Inc.* v. *Vaughn*, 1955, 350 U.S. 870, 76 S. Ct. 117, 100 L. Ed. 770; 350 U.S. 919, 76 S. Ct. 193, 100 L. Ed. 805, reversing 1955, 177 Kan. 728, 282 P. 2d 412.

It may be argued that the duty of the Postmaster General "to execute all laws relative to the Postal Service," 5 U.S.C.A. § 369, gives him some measure of authority over materials deposited in the mail in alleged violation of the criminal statute. It may be said, too, that the statute makes the materials non-mailable, and forbids their handling. These arguments hardly suffice. Congress has always "zealously watched and strictly confined" any proposal to empower the Postmaster General to refuse to handle mail because of its content. See *Hannegan* v. *Esquire, Inc.*, supra, 327 U.S. at page 156, note 18, 66 S. Ct. at page 461. Surely the courts must take a like attitude, even if they conclude that the present statute does give the Postmaster General some part of the authority he now claims.[3] Certainly, under any view, the courts must intervene if improper standards have been applied in making a determination of obscenity.[4] That has occurred in this case.

The test of obscenity is "whether to the average person, applying contemporary community standards, the *dominant* theme of the material *taken as a whole* appeals to prurient interest." (Emphasis added.) *Roth* v. *United States*, supra, 354 U.S. at page 489, 77 S. Ct. at page 1311.[5] We expressed a similar thought in *Walker* v.

---

[1] In *Walker* v. *Popenoe*, 80 U.S. App. D.C. 129, 149 F. 2d 511, the order barring the pamphlet from the mails was issued without notice or hearing.

[1] Rev. Stat. § 3893 (1875), as amended, 18 U.S.C. § 1461 (Supp. IV, 1957).

[2] We were there speaking of another postal statute, 39 U.S.C.A. § 259(a).

[3] Cf. *Roth* v. *Goldman*, 2 Cir., 172 F. 2d 788, certiorari denied, 1949, 337 U.S. 938, 69 S. Ct. 1514, 93 L. Ed. 1743; *One, Inc.* v. *Olesen*, 9 Cir., 241 F. 2d 772, cert. pending, 26 U.S.L. Week 3046 (1957).

[4] There is broad authority to review even factual matters when freedom of speech and of the press is involved. Cf. *Niemotko* v. *State of Maryland*, 1951, 340 U.S. 268, 271, 71 S. Ct. 325, 328, 95 L. Ed. 267, 280; Reed, J., concurring in *Joseph Burstyn, Inc.* v. *Wilson*, 1952, 343 U.S. 495, 506, 72 S. Ct. 777, 96 L. Ed. 1098; Dye, J., dissenting in *Commercial Pictures Corp.* v. *Board of Regents of University of State of New York*, 1953, 305 N.Y. 336, 356, 113 N.E. 2d 502, 512, reversed sub nom. *Superior Films* v. *Dept. of Education*, 1954, 346 U.S. 587, 74 S. Ct. 286, 98 L. Ed. 329.

[5] The test traditionally applied by the English courts was stated in *Regina* v. *Hicklin* [1868], L.R. 3 Q.B.D. 360, 371: "whether the tendency of the matter charged as obscenity is to deprave and corrupt those whose minds are open to such im-

Popenoe, 1945, 80 U.S. App. D.C. 129, 130, 149 F. 2d 511, 512, where we said: "The statute [now 18 U.S.C. § 1461] does not bar from the mails an obscene phrase or an obscene sentence. It bars an obscene 'book, pamphlet * * * or other publication * * *.' If a publication as a whole is not stimulating to the senses [i.e., does not "arouse the salacity"] of the ordinary reader, it is not within the statute. * * * The *dominant* effect of an entire publication determines its character." (Emphasis in original.) See also *Parmelee* v. *United States*, 1940, 72 App. D.C. 203, 113 F. 2d 729; *United States* v. *Dennett*, 2 Cir., 1930, 39 F. 2d 564, 76 A.L.R. 1092; *United States* v. *One Book* Entitled Ulysses, 2 Cir., 1934, 72 F. 2d 705; *United States* v. *Levine*, 2 Cir., 1936, 83 F. 2d 156. In these cases, works which the courts found to be of genuine sociological, medical, or literary merit were held not obscene, although portions of them, taken from context, might appear otherwise.

In the instant case, the magazines "advocate and explain nudism and the nudist mode of living." *Summerfield* v. *Sunshine Book Co.*, 95 U.S. App. D.C. at page 170, 221 F. 2d at page 43. One of the magazines has been published for over twenty years. Their texts were found by the Post Office Department and the District Court not to be obscene. But both the Department and the District Court thereupon proceeded to deal with the illustrations in the magazines merely as such. The Examiner of the Post Office Department and the District Court explicitly recognize in their opinions that the publications must be considered as a whole.[6] Yet an examination of their opinions, as well as that of the Solicitor of the Post Office Department, shows no effort to weigh the material considered objectionable against the rest of the contents, or to weigh the risk in permitting the former to circulate against the limitations on freedom of the press implicit in halting circulation of the latter.[7]

Another aspect of the case is equally disturbing. More than a decade ago we held in *Walker* v. *Popenoe*, supra, that a hearing must precede the barring of published matter from the mails. Here, the Department refused to accept the magazines for mailing, and held a hearing after its refusal had become effective.[8] We expressly con-

demned such an interference with freedom of the press in the Walker case, where we said:

We are not impressed with the argument that a rule requiring a hearing before mailing privileges are suspended would permit, while the hearing was going on, the distribution of publications intentionally obscene in plain defiance of every reasonable standard. In such a case the effective remedy is the immediate arrest of the offender for the crime penalized by this statute. Such action would prevent any form of distribution of the obscene material by mail or otherwise. If the offender were released on bail the conditions of that bail should be a sufficient protection against repetition of the offense before trial. But often mailing privileges are revoked in cases where the prosecuting officers are not sure enough to risk criminal prosecution. That was the situation here." 80 U.S. App. D.C. at page 132, 149 F. 2d at page 514.[9]

For these reasons the order of the Post Office Department should be held invalid. Under all the circumstances —the passage of time and the disregard by the Post Office Department of our ruling in the Walker case—further administrative proceedings with respect to the magazine issues here involved should not be permitted. The case should be remanded to the District Court with instructions to issue an injunction permanently restraining enforcement of the Department's order.

---

moral influences, and into whose hands a publication of this sort may fall." But see *Regina* v. *Martin Secker Warburg, Ltd.* [1954], 2 All E.R. 683. That test "might well encompass material legitimately treating with sex, and so it must be rejected as unconstitutionally restrictive of the freedoms of speech and press." *Roth* v. *United States*, 354 U.S. at page 489, 77 S. Ct. at page 1311.

[6] See *Walker* v. *Popenoe*, supra at page 130 of 80 U.S. App. D.C., at page 512 of 149 F. 2d.

[7] It is also questionable whether finding a picture "grotesque" sufficiently complies with the Supreme Court's mandate requiring a finding of appeal to "prurient interest." Compare *Sunshine Book Co.* v. *Summerfield*, D.C.D.C. 1955, 128 F. Supp. 564, 571, with *Roth* v. *United States*, 1957, 354 U.S. at page 489, 77 S. Ct. at page 1311.

[8] The District Judge found that the refusal of the Post Office Department to transmit the magazines in question began on or

about December 23, 1954. By letter of December 30, 1954, the Solicitor of the Post Office Department acknowledged a letter of December 29, 1954, from the Postmaster of Mays Landing, New Jersey, which set forth the action taken. The Solicitor advised that the magazines "should be withheld from dispatch," except for copies submitted for first class mailing, and that the senders "should be informed that they may have an opportunity to show cause within fifteen days why the article should not be disposed of as matter nonmailable . . . by offering through appearance at this [the Solicitor's] office in person or by attorney, or through submission of a statement in writing, whatever evidence or arguments they care to submit."

The Postmaster of Mays Landing transmitted this information to appellant by letter of December 31, 1954. He added that the magazines in question were "nonmailable and must be withheld from dispatch." By letter of January 6, 1955, to appellant, the Solicitor acknowledged that the Postmaster's statement as to nonmailability was in error, "no ruling or determination either of mailability or non-mailability having yet been made. . . ." He also gave notice of a hearing on the question to be held on January 10, 1955. But no action was taken to transmit the magazines in the mail. At appellant's request, the hearing was postponed to January 17, 1955. At the hearing, the Examiner ruled, correctly, we think, and without objection by the Post Office Department, that the burden of proof rested on the Post Office Department rather than appellant. An initial decision was handed down by the Examiner on January 20, 1955, and affirmed by the Solicitor on January 28, 1955. It is thus evident that appellant's magazines were barred from the mails for almost a month before the hearing and the initial administrative decision that they were unmailable.

[9] See *Roth* v. *United States*, 1956, 77 S. Ct. 17, 1 L. Ed. 2d 34 (per Harlan, Circuit Justice).

■ Sunshine Book Co. et al.

v.

Summerfield, Postmaster General.

ON PETITION FOR WRIT OF CERTIORARI TO THE UNITED STATES COURT OF APPEALS
FOR THE DISTRICT OF COLUMBIA CIRCUIT.

No. 587. Decided January 13, 1958. 101 U.S. App. D.C. 358, 249 F. 2d 114, reversed.

O. John Rogge for petitioners.

Solicitor General *Rankin*, Assistant Attorney General *Doub* and *Samuel D. Slade* for respondent.

PER CURIAM.

The petition for writ of certiorari is granted and the judgment of the United States Court of Appeals for the District of Columbia Circuit is reversed. *Roth* v. *United States*, 354 U.S. 476.

■ Adrian P. Burke, as Corporation Counsel of The City of New York, *Plaintiff*

v.

Kingsley Books, Inc., Martin Kleinberg, Metropolitan Book Shop Inc., Anne Goldberg, Times Square Book Shop, Louis Finkelstein, Pelley Book Shop, Philip Pellegrino, Publishers Outlet, Gordon Law, *Defendants*.

Supreme Court, Special Term, New York County, Part VI.

June 13, 1955.

Adrian P. Burke and *Peter Campbell Brown*, Corp. Counsel of the City of New York (Milton Mollen and Murray Rudman, New York City, of counsel), for plaintiff.

Emanuel Redfield, New York City, for defendants Kingsley Books, Inc. and Martin Kleinberg.

Sidney Glasser, New York City, for defendant Louis Finkelstein doing business as Times Square Book Shop.

MATTHEW M. LEVY, Justice.

The Penal Law of this State has for some time made it a misdemeanor to sell or distribute "any obscene, lewd, lascivious, filthy, indecent or disgusting book, magazine, pamphlet, newspaper, story paper, writing, paper, phonograph record, picture, drawing, photograph, motion picture film, figure or image, or any written or printed matter of an indecent character," Penal Law, § 1141, subd. 1. More recently, the Legislature enacted section 22–a of the Code of Criminal Procedure, providing that, "The supreme court has jurisdiction to enjoin the sale or distribution of obscene prints and articles" as defined there and in section 1141 of the Penal Law, and in the event that a final judgment of injunction be issued, the judgment "shall con-

tain a provision directing the person, firm or corporation [against whom the injunction is granted] to surrender to the sheriff of the county in which the action was brought any of the matter described in paragraph one hereof and such sheriff shall be directed to seize and destroy the same." The Code section provides further that the person authorized to maintain the action is the chief executive or legal officer in any city, town or village in the State, subd. 1. In the City of New York, the latter official would be the corporation counsel.

Pursuant to section 22–a, the plaintiff, as Corporation Counsel of the City of New York, has instituted this action against a number of persons, firms and corporations, for the purpose of (1) permanently enjoining the defendants from acquiring, selling or distributing any of the issues of a series of booklets entitled "Nights of Horror"; (2) directing the defendants to surrender to the Sheriff of the County of New York all issues of the publication within their possession and control; and (3) directing the Sheriff to seize and destroy them. Those defendants who have answered deny the allegation of the complaint that the publication is obscene, and in effect interpose three separate defenses: that the plaintiff lacks the required legal authority to maintain this action; that section 22–a is an unconstitutional restraint on freedom of the press; and that section 22–a violates the constitutional protection against unreasonable seizures. This case has been considered by the parties, and found by the court, to be the first submission of the constitutional issues thought to be involved in the application of section 22–a. (The statute is set forth in the margin).*

[1] The act of obscenity has been an offense against the public order for centuries (see Sir Charles Sydlyes Case, 1 Keble 620 [K.B. 1663]; Harris and Wilshere's Criminal Law, 16th ed., pp. 169–170; 1 Bishop on Criminal Law, 9th ed., §§ 500, 504; Alpert, Judicial Censorship of Obscene Literature, 52 Harv. L. Rev. 40–43). Printed obscenity has been deemed a crime at common law for generations. *Commonwealth* v. *Holmes*, 17 Mass. 336; see Grant and Angoff, Massachusetts and Censorship, 10 Boston Univ. L. Rev. 52–56. The essence of the statute now known as section 1141 of the Penal Law was first enacted in the State of New York in 1881, Penal Code, § 317. "It is to be observed that the statute [then Penal Code, § 317] does not undertake to define obscene or indecent pictures or publications. But the words used in the statute are themselves descriptive. They are words in common use, and every person of ordinary intelligence understands their meaning." *People* v. *Muller*, 96 N.Y. 408, 410.

[2, 3] The fact that the mores of the times change from one generation to another, or that they are not the same in every land and clime, does not render the statutory definition meaningless. See Learned Hand, J., in *United States* v. *Kennerley*, D.C., 209 F. 119, 121. Of course, to be constitutionally valid, what is statutorily interdicted "must be defined with appropriate definiteness." *Pierce* v. *United States*, 314 U.S. 306, 311, 62 S. Ct. 237, 240, 86 L. Ed. 226. Thus it is that "immoral" (*Superior Films, Inc.* v. *Department of Education*, 346 U.S. 587, 74 S. Ct. 286, 98 L. Ed. 329, reversing *Commercial Pictures Corp.* v. *Board of Regents*, 305 N.Y. 336, 113 N.E. 2d 502), "injurious to public morals" (*Musser* v. *State of Utah*, 333

U.S. 95, 68 S. Ct. 397, 398, 92 L. Ed. 562), and "collections of criminal deeds of bloodshed or lust," (*Winters* v. *People of State of New York*, 333 U.S. 507, 513, 68 S. Ct. 665, 669, 92 L. Ed. 840) have been held to provide no reasonable, ascertainable standards. In order for the Legislature to achieve reasonable certainty—within constitutional limitations—it is not, however, necessary that the language be narrowed in such a manner as to allow no flexibility; rather, ordinary terms may be used to express ideas which adequately describe that which is prohibited when measured by the modes of common usage and understanding in the community. *Sproles* v. *Binford*, 286 U.S. 374, 393, 52 S. Ct. 581, 76 L. Ed. 1167; *Jordan* v. *De George*, 341 U.S. 223, 231–232, 71 S. Ct. 703, 95 L. Ed. 886.

[4] Repeated challenges to the definiteness of the term "obscene" have been rejected. *Chaplinsky* v. *State of New Hampshire*, 315 U.S. 568, 571–572, 62 S. Ct. 766, 86 L. Ed. 1031; *American Civil Liberties Union* v. *City of Chicago*, 3 Ill. 2d 334, 347, 121 N.E. 2d 585; Lockhart and McClure, Literature, The Law of Obscenity, and The Constitution, 38 Minn. L. Rev. 295, 324–350. There is no question but that the term "obscene" is sufficiently definite to be used—even in a criminal statute. *Winters* v. *People of State of New York*, 333 U.S. 507, 518, 68 S. Ct. 665, 92 L. Ed. 840. "The Legislature has declared in this section [Penal Law, § 1141] that no obscene, lewd, lascivious, or disgusting book shall be sold. Language could not be plainer." Crane, J., dissenting, in *Halsey* v. *New York Society for Suppression of Vice*, 234 N.Y. 1, 14, 136 N.E. 219, 223. And while it has been thought, *United States* v. *Reese*, 92 U.S. 214, 23 L. Ed. 563, that it is not necessarily a basis for vital distinction that a statute imposes no criminal sanctions (and that is true of section 22–a, al-

---

* Code of Criminal Procedure, section 22–a, as amended L, 1954, c. 702, eff. July 1, 1954:

"The supreme court has jurisdiction to enjoin the sale or distribution of obscene prints and articles, as hereinafter specified:

"1. The chief executive officer of any city, town or village or the corporation counsel, or if there be none, the chief legal officer of any city, town, or village, in which a person, firm or corporation sells or distributes or is about to sell or distribute or has in his possession with intent to sell or distribute or is about to acquire possession with intent to sell or distribute any book, magazine, pamphlet, comic book, story paper, writing, paper, picture, drawing, photograph, figure, image or any written or printed matter of an indecent character, which is obscene, lewd, lascivious, filthy, indecent or disgusting, or which contains an article or instrument of indecent or immoral use or purports to be for indecent or immoral use or purpose; or or[1] in any other respect defined in section eleven hundred forty-one of the penal law, may maintain an action for an injunction against such person, firm or corporation in the supreme court to prevent the sale or further sale or the distribution or further distribution or the acquisition or possession of any book, magazine, pamphlet, comic book, story paper, writing, paper, picture, drawing, photograph, figure or image or any written or printed matter of an

indecent character, herein described or described in section eleven hundred forty-one of the penal law.

"2. The person, firm or corporation sought to be enjoined shall be entitled to a trial of the issues within one day after joinder of issue and a decision shall be rendered by the court within two days of the conclusion of the trial.[2]

"3. In the event that a final order or judgment of injunction be entered in favor of such officer of the city, town or village and against the person, firm or corporation sought to be enjoined, such final order of judgment shall contain a provision directing the person, firm or corporation to surrender to the sheriff of the county in which the action was brought any of the matter described in paragraph one hereof and such sheriff shall be directed to seize and destroy the same.

"4. In any action brought as herein provided such officer of the city, town or village shall not be required to file any undertaking before the issuance of an injunction order provided for in paragraph two hereof, shall not be liable for costs and shall not be liable for damages sustained by reason of the injunction order in cases where judgment is rendered in favor of the person, firm or corporation sought to be enjoined.

"5. Every person, firm or corporation who sells, distributes, or acquires possession with intent to sell or distribute any of the matter described in paragraph one hereof, after the service upon him of a summons and complaint in an action brought by such officer of any city, town or village pursuant to this section is chargeable with knowledge of the contents thereof."

---

[1] So in enrolled bill. Second "or" probably should be omitted.

[2] By stipulation entered upon the record, the parties duly waived this requirement, and the court therefore did not consider the propriety of this provision in the statute.

though it is incorporated in the Code of Criminal Procedure), it is recognized that "[t]he standards of certainty in statutes punishing for offenses is higher than in those depending primarily upon civil sanction for enforcement." *Winters v. People of State of New York*, 333 U.S. 507, 515, 68 S. Ct. 665, 670, 92 L. Ed. 840.

Some of the defendants have denied that the publications fall within the proscription of section 22–a. The classic legal test for obscenity is "whether the tendency of the matter charged as obscenity is to deprave and corrupt those whose minds are open to such immoral influences, and into whose hands a publication of this sort may fall" (*Regina v. Hicklin*, L.R. [1868] 3 Q.B. 360, 371). This definition, expressed long ago, seems rather strict and has been often criticized. *United States v. One Book* Called "Ulysses," D.C., 5 F. Supp. 182, affirmed *United States v. One Book* Entitled Ulysses by James Joyce, 2 Cir., 72 F. 2d 705; *United States v. Levine*, 2 Cir., 83 F. 2d 156; *United States v. Dennett*, 2 Cir., 39 F. 2d 564, 76 A.L.R. 1092; *United States v. Kennerley*, D.C., 209 F. 119; Ernst and Lindey, The Censor Marches On, pp. 2, 22, 188; Buchsbaum, Constitutional Law—Censorship—Statutory Construction, 16 Ga. B.J. 494; Lockhart and McClure, op. cit., supra, at 326–350. It nevertheless appears to be the standard sustained by our Court of Appeals, *People v. Doubleday & Co., Inc.*, 297 N.Y. 687, 77 N.E. 2d 6, affirmed 335 U.S. 848, 69 S. Ct. 79, 93 L. Ed. 398; *People v. Muller*, 96 N.Y. 408, 411; *People v. Berg*, 241 App. Div. 543, 272 N.Y.S. 586, affirmed 269 N.Y. 514, 199 N.E. 513; but see *People v. Wendling*, 258 N.Y. 451, 453, 180 N.E. 169, 81 A.L.R. 799.

The only question before the court in *Besig v. United States*, 9 Cir., 208 F. 2d 142, was whether the books were obscene. Obscene was defined, Id., at page 145, as "indecent, smutty, lewd or salacious reference to parts of the human or animal body or to their functions * * *." The court found the books in that case to be just that, and the language therein "related without the slightest expressed idea of its abandon." (ibid.) Judge Stephens felt that not only must the young and pure be protected, but that the Congress must have realized, when the statute there involved [19 U.S.C.A. § 1305(a)] was passed, "that salacious print in the hands of adults, even in the hands of those whose sun is near the western horizon, may well incite to disgusting practices and to hideous crime." 208 F. 2d at page 146. The court continued: "We share the general antipathy to censorship and we are aware that individual tastes and special occasions and different times and different peoples differ as to what is offensive language. Yet we risk the assertion that there is an underlying, perhaps universal, accord that there is a phase of respectable delicacy related to sex, and that those compositions which purposefully flaunt [flout?] such delicacy * * * come under the ban of the statute." Id., at page 147.

In determining what is obscene in any particular case, "[t]he law will not hold the crowd to the morality of saints and seers" (Cardozo, Paradoxes of Legal Science, p. 37). Neither will the law honor the views of the bestial and the debased. Nor should it be governed by the morals of the prude on the one hand or of the perverted on the other. "All that we can say is that the line will be higher than the lowest level of moral principle and practice, and lower than the highest." (Cardozo, supra, p. 37.) Sex relationships can be and normally are beautiful, profound,

inspiring and healthy. And some of the finest literature of all time—of fact and fancy, lasting and cherished through the ages—has presented and discussed, analyzed and novelized the concept of sex. Not so the present publications. If ever there could be found appropriate applicability for section 22–a, this case emerges as the perfect example of what the Legislature has sought to curb. Judge Learned Hand felt that the word "obscene" should "be allowed to indicate the present critical point in the compromise between candor and shame." *United States v. Kennerley*, D.C., 209 F. 119, 121. No such problem is here presented; for "Nights of Horror" will be found resting at the foot of the scale, clearly marked "shame." No matter how strict the test or how broad the criteria, these volumes will readily measure up to and even surpass the most generous standard. The booklets in evidence offer naught but glorified concepts of lustful and vicious concupiscence, and by their tenor deride love and virtue, invite crime and voluptuousness, and excite lecherous desires. See *People v. Wendling*, 258 N.Y. 451, 453, 454, 180 N.E. 169, 170, 81 A.L.R. 799. There is no true dissemination of lawful ideas —rather is there a direct incitement to sex crimes and the sordid excitement of brutality. These booklets are sold indiscriminately to all who may wish to purchase them— men and women, adults and youths of both sexes. The publications have a libidinous effect upon ordinary, normal, healthy persons; their effect upon the abnormal individual may be disastrous to him and to others as well.

These booklets are not sex literature, as such, but pornography, unadulterated by plot, moral or writing style. That there is no attempt to achieve any literary standard is obvious. Each issue is a paper-covered booklet of from 70 to 96 pages, with a suggestive sex drawing on the front cover under the caption "Nights of Horror." The price varies from $1.98 to $3.00 per issue. The volumes are replete with misspelled words, typographical errors, faulty grammar, misplaced pages and generally poor workmanship. While these factors do not, of course, classify the issues as pornographic, they are somewhat helpful in ascertaining whether there truly exists a genuine literary intent. "Nights of Horror" makes but one "contribution" to literature. It serves as a glossary of terms describing the private parts of the human body (notably the female breasts, buttocks and vagina), the emotions sensed in illicit sexual climax and various forms of sadistic, masochistic and sexual perversion. The volumes before me are not a description of a period of history or the people and characters of an earlier time and of their conduct and habits of life. They are not a relating of folk tales or stories of primitive people living in isolated regions. They do not purport to depict the lives and customs of those who are here now or are expected to inhabit this land or this earth in the time to come: See *People v. Berg*, 241 App. Div. 543, 544, 272 N.Y.S. 586, 587, affirmed 269 N.Y. 514, 199 N.E. 513.

"Nights of Horror" is no haphazard title. Perverted sexual acts and macabre tortures of the human body are repeatedly depicted. The books contain numbers of acts of male torturing female and some vice versa—by most ingenious means. These gruesome acts included such horrors as cauterizing a woman's breast with a hot iron, placing hot coals against a woman's breasts, tearing breasts off, placing hot irons against a female's armpits, pulling off a girl's fingernails with white-hot pincers, completely singeing away the body hairs, working a female's skin away from her flesh with a knife, gouging and burning eyes out of their sockets, ringing the nipples of the breast with needles. Hanging by the thumbs, hair pulling, skin burning, putting on bone-compressing iron boots, were usual. The torture rack abounded. Self-torture was frequent. Sucking a victim's blood was pictured; and so was pouring molten lead into a girl's mouth and ears; and putting honey on a girl's breasts, vagina and buttocks—and then putting hundreds of great red ants on the honey. Sodomy, rape, lesbianism, seduction prevail. Youngsters disrobing in the presence and to the detailed recorded delight of elderly males was described. Incidental training of the teen-ager to narcotic addiction and sexual perversion was part of the activities engaged in. The volumes expressed a philosophy of man's omnipotent physical power over the female of the species. On occasion, the young woman is said to have gained satisfaction from the brutal beatings and horrible tortures. If she did not enjoy them, she received the beatings and tortures anyway—until she submitted to the sex acts desired by her tormentor. These brutalities were "my supreme pleasure" to the male, and resulted in "I'll be your slave" to the female. (It is not to be taken that I have, in any measure, given a complete report of the "Nights of Horror." I felt that I had to mention some, not the most sordid, features of this publication in view of the serious issues raised in this case—but I need not, I think, describe all I was compelled to read.)

[5] While it appears, as a study of earlier cases will indicate, that some courts have held a publication obscene on the basis of selected passages, *United States* v. *Bennett*, Fed. Cas. No. 14,571, 16 Blatchf. 338; *Commonwealth* v. *Friede*, 271 Mass. 318, 171 N.E. 472, 69 A.L.R. 640; *Commonwealth* v. *Buckley*, 200 Mass. 346, 86 N.E. 910, 22 L.R.A., N.S., 225, each volume here was read (a distasteful task, it turned out to be—to say the least) to determine whether, taken as a whole, it was obscene within the proscription of the statute. *Halsey* v. *New York Society for Suppression of Vice*, 234 N.Y. 1, 4, 136 N.E. 219, 220; *Besig* v. *United States*, 9 Cir., 208 F. 2d 142, 146; *Commonwealth* v. *Isenstadt*, 318 Mass. 543, 548–549, 62 N.E. 2d 840; *United States* v. *One Book* Called "Ulysses," D.C., 5 F. Supp. 182, 185, affirmed *United States* v. *One Book* Entitled Ulysses by James Joyce, 2 Cir., 72 F. 2d 705; *Roth* v. *Goldman*, 2 Cir., 172 F. 2d 788, 790, Frank, J., concurring. Suffice it to say at this point that there is not a single "story" which is not "obscene, lewd, lascivious, filthy, indecent or disgusting."** More often than not these adjectives must be used in combination, and with many others in the same vein, to describe adequately any one issue. The whole here is "emetic" and "aphrodisiac." See *United States* v. *One Book* Called "Ulysses," D.C., 5 F. Supp. 182, 185.

The authors have left nothing to fantasy or to the unimaginative mind. The volumes are vividly detailed and illustrated. The many drawings that embellish these stories are obviously intended to arouse unnatural desire and vicious acts. Violence—criminal, sexual—degradation and perversion—are the sole keynote. Sadism and masochism are pictured as appropriate characteristics of human nature

---

** From time to time throughout this opinion, for purposes of convenience, I use the single word "obscene" rather than the several words of the statute.

and pleasure. In short, the volumes of "Nights of Horror" in evidence before me are obscene and constitute pornography—"dirt for dirt's sake," *United States* v. *One Book* Called "Ulysses," D.C., 5 F. Supp. 182, 184, bestiality, lust, crime, horror, for their unfortunate sake—and for the ugly sake of filthy commerce in human weakness. Anne Lyon Haight has compiled a revised and enlarged edition of "Banned Books: Informal Notes on Some Books Banned for Various Reasons at Various Times and in Various Places" (2d ed., 1955). This chronological list of books banned from 387 B.C. to 1954 A.D. (with no attempt to be all inclusive) was compiled with the idea of showing the trend of censorship throughout the years and the change in thought and taste. Most of the books there recorded fall under a ban because of religion, politics or morality, making the offense one of heresy, treason or obscenity. Among them are books which have withstood the condemnation of their immediate times to become the classics of today. "Nights of Horror" does not deserve to be listed among the missing when the next edition of "Banned Books" is published.

It is urged by all of the contesting defendants that, notwithstanding any determination that I make as to the obscene character of "Nights of Horror," section 22–a is unconstitutional on its face and therefore void. It is contended, firstly, that the statute violates federal and state constitutional guarantees against interference with a free press; and, secondly, that in part it violates constitutional protections against unlawful seizures. I shall examine these points separately.

The First Amendment to the Constitution of the United States provides that "Congress shall make no law * * * abridging the freedom of speech, or of the press." The First Amendment is applicable to the several states via the due process clause of the Fourteenth Amendment. *Gitlow* v. *People of State of New York*, 268 U.S. 652, 666, 45 S. Ct. 625, 69 L. Ed. 1138; *Near* v. *State of Minnesota*, 283 U.S. 697, 707, 51 S. Ct. 625, 75 L. Ed. 1357; *Grosjean* v. *American Press Co., Inc.*, 297 U.S. 233, 249, 56 S. Ct. 444, 80 L. Ed. 660. Article I, Section 8, of the Constitution of the State of New York, provides that "Every citizen may freely speak, write and publish his sentiments on all subjects, being responsible for the abuse of that right; and no law shall be passed to restrain or abridge the liberty of speech or of the press." Each of these constitutional provisions is a grave mandate requiring sincere and primary recognition when legislation is challenged as running afoul of their powerful protection, and, in my view, compels devoted judicial obeisance.

No doubt, "the rights of the best of men are secure only as the rights of the vilest and most abhorrent are protected." Pound, J., dissenting, in *People* v. *Gitlow*, 234 N.Y. 132, 158, 136 N.E. 317, 327, affirmed 268 U.S. 652, 45 S. Ct. 625, 69 L. Ed. 1138. And no doubt, too, the rights of the best of books are dependent upon the judicial protection to be afforded those having the least social value. Indeed, even publications of no social worth are entitled to be shielded from unlawful or unconstitutional restraint. *Winters* v. *People of State of New York*, 333 U.S. 507, 510, 68 S. Ct. 665, 92 L. Ed. 840. Were the "Nights of Horror" works which indicated the slightest effort to contribute to our culture or knowledge, I might find myself in the position of "holding my nose with one hand" and "upholding with the other the right of free speech" that they are claimed to represent (see Judge Curtis Bok, "If We Are to Act Like Free Men," Saturday Review, Feb. 13, 1954, p. 9, at p. 10, col. 3). But the volumes before me are so totally lacking in merit, and so obviously pornographic in intent, that their banning poses no threat to freedom of expression in literature or otherwise. To borrow a thought from Judge Learned Hand, I can well say that the plea of the present defendants, invoking the sacred constitutional guaranty of free press, is an effort to "misuse the privilege as a cover for lewdness and a stalking horse from which to strike at purity." *United States* v. *Kennerley*, D.C., 209 F. 119, 121.

I would not want or (if I could avoid it) permit this court to become a licensor, a censor, a book-burner. But a judicial tribunal should not and cannot avoid its responsibility. "Publications found by fair process to violate literate, adult and clearly defined standards of decency or other criminal safeguards can serve no useful purpose for the community, and [judicial(?)] interference with their dissemination we find non-objectionable." (Report on Book Burning, Committee on the Bill of Rights, The Record of the Association of the Bar of the City of New York, Vol. 10, No. 3, March, 1955, p. 143.)

At this point, I shall note two cardinal and basic tenets for my view that the statute is not vulnerable on the ground of an allegedly unconstitutional infringement of the freedom of the press—that of "clear and present danger" and that of "no prior restraint." Let me delineate.

[6, 7] In cases involving fundamental human liberties—such as freedom of the press—there must (and properly should) be shown, before there may be suppression, a "clear and present danger" of the substantive evils which the Legislature has a right to prevent, *Schenck* v. *United States*, 249 U.S. 47, 52, 39 S. Ct. 247, 63 L. Ed. 470; followed in *Dennis* v. *United States*, 341 U.S. 494, 71 S. Ct. 857, 95 L. Ed. 1137; *Thornhill* v. *State of Alabama*, 310 U.S. 88, 105, 60 S. Ct. 736, 84 L. Ed. 1093, and the court has a concomitant obligation to enforce. Police power may be exercised only when the public generally requires such interference and not to protect the interests of a particular class. *Lawton* v. *Steele*, 152 U.S. 133, 137, 14 S. Ct. 499, 38 L. Ed. 385. The well-supervised adolescent and the well-disciplined adult are not those whom all law must be designed to shield. It cannot, I think, seriously be gainsaid that the public generally does have a vital interest in shielding the immature mind (of whatever age) from lust-stimulating and vice-arousing pornography. There are numbers of our population who, although they have reached majority, harbor dormant criminal instincts that are easily aroused by the pornographic script, the violent narration and the indecent picture. It may be thought that to keep "Nights of Horror" from the young in years would require only legislation similar to those criminal laws regulating sale of alcoholic beverages, tobacco and firearms; but that appears to have been considered by the Legislature not to be enough—and not without some basis. (Nor, unfortunately, have public education, religious training, parental guidance and psychiatric care been the complete solution.)

While section 1141 of the Penal Law was designed to punish the offenders, that has been found not to be sufficient (Report of the New York State Joint Legislative Committee to Study the Publication of Comics, Leg. Doc. [1954] No. 37, p. 32). The Penal Law provides for

punishment of the guilty, but the susceptible public remains contaminated with pornographic filth and stimulation. So long as enforcement of this criminal law is not effective (for whatever reason), and so long as publishers and distributors are willing to risk spasmodic misdemeanor convictions for the huge profits which apparently accrue from the exploitation of pornographic vice, section 22–a was deemed necessary. And if one is willing to risk (and unable to escape) repeated punishment for the sake of keeping an obscene publication alive, he could go to (and for a time remain in) jail, but his obscenity would survive. It was not considered in the best interests of the State to have jail cells overcrowded, be it with publishers and distributors who have violated section 1141 of the Penal Law or with teen-agers and others whose latent abnormal emotions have become aroused by such lascivious and vicious material as that which makes up the "Nights of Horror." The legislative intent and purpose are to keep such books as the "Nights of Horror" from the impressionable public. While this court has sufficient confidence in the people of this state to feel that "Nights of Horror" can never survive, the immediate and long-range public interests were thought by the Legislature to require that the death blow be hastened. The Legislative Committee found that "the reading of these publications contributes to juvenile delinquency, stimulates sexual desire, lowers standards of morality and interferes with the normal development of sexual tendencies in both adolescents and adults." (Report, supra, pp. 34–35). The Legislature held injunction and suppression to be the only effective means to combat such a malignancy. It is not for the court—on the evidence before me—to say that there is no basis for this legislative finding and that the suggested remedy in these times is necessarily wrong. Indeed no evidence whatsoever was sought to be submitted by the defendants which would tend in any way to challenge or controvert the legislative finding.

[8] I do not consider censorship generally in the best public interest; and I would take a different view of *literature* even though it contained matter involving sex and crime. But the proof submitted on behalf of the plaintiff, a reading of the several issues of the "Nights of Horror," the studies and reports of the New York State Joint Legislative Committee to Study the Publication of Comics, of the Special United States Senate Judiciary Sub-Committee on Juvenile Delinquency, and of the Select Committee of the United States House of Representatives on Current Pornographic Materials, and our every-day observations of the shocking rise of juvenile delinquency and sex crimes—all these lead us more easily to read the scale of public interests which plead for the suppression of these publications. All these indicate such a clear and present danger of substantive evils that, as a judge, I cannot ignore the cry unless the Constitution says I must. I do not find that it does. On the contrary, while there appears to be no case in point, I do cite what the Supreme Court of the United States had occasion to say in *Chaplinsky* v. *State of New Hampshire*, 315 U.S. 568, 571–572, 62 S. Ct. 766, 769, 86 L. Ed. 1031: "Allowing the broadest scope to the language and purpose of the Fourteenth Amendment, it is well understood that the right of free speech is not absolute at all times and under all circumstances. There are certain well-defined and narrowly limited classes of speech, the prevention and punishment of which have never been

thought to raise any Constitutional problem. These include the lewd and obscene * * *. [S]uch utterances are no essential part of any exposition of ideas, and are of such slight social value as a step to truth that any benefit that may be derived from them is clearly outweighed by the social interest in order and morality." See also Ex parte Jackson, 96 U.S. 727, 736, 24 L. Ed. 877.

[9] The defendants argue that section 22–a is an unconstitutional violation of free speech in that it enforces a "previous restraint" upon the dissemination of ideas. I do not agree. To assume, even arguendo, as the defendants do, that the Legislature may constitutionally provide that one who publishes obscene matter is subject to criminal prosecution and imprisonment, see *Winters* v. *People of State of New York*, 333 U.S. 507, 518, 68 S. Ct. 665, 92 L. Ed. 840; *Chaplinsky* v. *State of New Hampshire*, 315 U.S. 568, 571–572, 62 S. Ct. 766, 86 L. Ed. 1031, and yet cannot be civilly enjoined from the continued distribution of that same matter, is indulging in a misapprehension as to what is really meant by "prior restraint"—and, on the basis of that misconstruction, is making a fetish of semantics rather than pleading a sound constitutional principle. I recognize that those concerned with freedom—and that, of course, includes the courts—have the responsibility of seeing to it that each individual book or publication, whatever its contents, price, or method of distribution, is dealt with in accordance with due process of law. Adequate notice, judicial hearing, fair determination, are the essence of "due process" and this is what the statute here has assured. I am of the considered opinion that when the court—after an adversary hearing—is able to read and examine the publications objected to, and acts judicially to enjoin their distribution, it is apparent that there is no "previous restraint" in the genuine historical and constitutional sense of that term. (Compare the statutory plan described in *Attorney General* v. *Book Named "Forever Amber,"* 323 Mass. 302, 81 N.E. 2d 663, and *Attorney General* v. *Book Named "God's Little Acre,"* 326 Mass. 281, 93 N.E. 2d 819).

In the circumstances, the contention that there is here an unconstitutional prior restraint is invalid. *Near* v. *State of Minnesota*, 283 U.S. 697, 702, 51 S. Ct. 625, 626, 75 L. Ed. 1357, relied upon so heavily by the defendants, is not a holding to the contrary. The Minnesota statute provided that a person who possessed or circulated " '(a) an obscene, lewd and lascivious newspaper, magazine, or other periodical, or (b) a malicious, scandalous and defamatory newspaper, magazine or other periodical' " (Minn. Stats. 1927, § 10123–1) was guilty of a nuisance which could be enjoined. The question before the Court did not involve the obscenity provision of the statute, but clause "b," relating to an alleged "scandalous and defamatory newspaper" known as "The Saturday Press." The Supreme Court of the United States included in its opinion several basic expressions which clearly differentiate its holding there from the one I am about to make in the case at bar. At pages 715–716 of 283 U.S., at page 631 of 51 S. Ct., the Court said: "The objection has also been made that the principle as to immunity from previous restraint is stated too broadly, if every such restraint is deemed to be prohibited. That is undoubtedly true; the protection even as to previous restraint is not absolutely unlimited. But the limitation has been recognized only in exceptional cases." And then the Court stated in 283 U.S. at page 716, 51 S. Ct. at page 631, that one of these exceptions is that "the

primary requirements of decency may be enforced against obscene publications" and that "[t]he security of the community life may be protected against incitements to acts of violence." And in the more recent case of *Joseph Burstyn, Inc.* v. *Wilson*, 343 U.S. 495, 72 S. Ct. 777, 96 L. Ed. 1098 (which struck down, as repugnant to the First and Fourteenth Amendments, a licensing statute with respect to motion picture films), the Court expressly reserved the question "whether a state may censor motion pictures under a clearly drawn statute designed and applied to prevent the showing of obscene films." 343 U.S. at page 506, 72 S. Ct. at page 782.

[10] *Cantwell* v. *State of Connecticut*, 310 U.S. 296, 306, 60 S. Ct. 900, 84 L. Ed. 1213, is cited by the defendants as authority for the proposition that so-called censorship by the judiciary—even though action is based, as it is here, on due process and judicial determination—is just as impermissible as advance censorship by an administrative officer. That case deals with a statute forbidding solicitation for a religious cause without first obtaining a certificate from a designated official, who may withhold the permit if he determines that it is not a religious cause. The statute clearly imposes a prior restraint and was held void upon its face. The fact that provision is made (as is not unusual—see Article 78 of the Civil Practice Act) for a judicial review of the licensor's determination does not remove the permit feature from the sphere of a previous restraint. 310 U.S. at page 306, 60 S. Ct. at page 904. That is not this case. Section 22–a does not provide for a permit or a license; it does not require any application or fee. It does not suppress in advance what is to be published. The Legislature has simply determined that what has long been recognized as criminal (section 1141 of the Penal Law) the Supreme Court may enjoin and abate in a civil suit (section 22–a of the Code of Criminal Procedure). Provision has been made at the very outset for judicial action in the sphere of recognized equity jurisdiction and jurisprudence. Injunctions and abatements—when decreed by the court after due notice and trial—are not a species of objectionable censorship but rather are judicial determinations of justiciable controversies.

[11] I recognize, of course, that remedy by injunction against words is exceptional—and, in my view, should properly be reserved for those cases where the exigency is clear (see Pound, Equitable Relief against Defamation and Injuries to Personality, 29 Harv. L. Rev. 640, 666; Chafee, Free Speech in the United States, pp. 9–10). But there have been and are such cases, and injunctions against certain obnoxious utterances are not without authoritative precedent. To mention one type of such injunction—thoroughly litigated during recent decades—I need but refer to cases involving labor disputes in which it has been held that it is within the recognized jurisdiction of a court of equity to restrain, under certain circumstances, the reiteration of false, misleading and fraudulent statements—notwithstanding the constitutional guarantees against infringement upon the rights of free speech and free press. See *Nann* v. *Raimist*, 255 N.Y. 307, 317, 174 N.E. 690, 694, 73 A.L.R. 669; cf. Schlesinger, A Summary and Critique of the Law of Peaceful Picketing in New York, 22 Fordham L. Rev. 20, 41–47; Burstein, Picketing and Speech, 4 Labor Law Journal 791.

It may be that, in certain cases, it would be helpful to obtain the fair verdict of a jury of reasonable adults in the community as to whether any particular publication is or is not obscene within the meaning of the statute. No doubt a jury is generally better fitted than a court to determine whether some books are obscene. "Far better than we, is a jury drawn from those of varied experiences, engaged in various occupations, in close touch with the currents of public feeling, fitted to say whether the defendant had reasonable ground to believe that a book such as this was obscene or indecent." *Halsey* v. *New York Society for Suppression of Vice*, 234 N.Y. 1, 6, 136 N.E. 219, 220.

[12, 13] Upon application, in the case of a misdemeanor prosecution in the City of New York, the court may certify that it is reasonable that the charge be prosecuted by indictment—with the consequent effect that the trial be by jury, New York City Criminal Courts Act, § 31, subd. 1(c). But the Constitution of this State does not compel jury trials of misdemeanor charges, Art. VI, § 18, and violation of section 1141 of the Penal Law is a misdemeanor. That a jury is not ordinarily a part of the judicial tribunal in equity cases is well known. *Jamaica Savings Bank* v. *M. S. Investing Co., Inc.*, 274 N.Y. 215, 221, 8 N.E. 2d 493, 495, 112 A.L.R. 1485. Yet, a jury trial of certain issues may be granted on the equity side of the court, or denied, in the exercise of the chancellor's discretion, Civil Practice Act, § 430. No application for a jury trial was made here—perhaps because there can be no doubt that "Nights of Horror" is unquestionably within the category of the obscene.

The corporation counsel has, however, gone beyond pleading for an injunction to restrain acquisition and distribution of what has been and is; he seeks to enjoin what he contends might be. He urges me to enjoin not only the "further sale" and "further distribution"—to use the precise language of the empowering statute, section 22–a—of the issues of the obnoxious publication in evidence, but also the sale and distribution of later issues as well. The statute does not, in express terms, compel such a determination. Only by implication and construction could it be said that the legislative prohibition was intended to cover not only a publication presently in existence, but one not yet in being and therefore not subject to judicial examination. I am of the view that to rule against a volume not offered in evidence would do just what the courts have held is constitutionally forbidden—that is, to impose an unreasonable prior restraint upon freedom of the press.

Our constitutional jurisprudence abounds with precedents denying unlawful previous restraints upon the cherished freedoms guaranteed by the Constitution. Prior restraints have been held invalid not only in *Near* v. *State of Minnesota*, 283 U.S. 697, 713, 51 S. Ct. 625, 75 L. Ed. 1357, but this basic doctrine of constitutional law has been applied in every area of the First Amendment: speech, press, assembly, and religion. *Saia* v. *People of State of New York*, 334 U.S. 558, 68 S. Ct. 1148, 92 L. Ed. 1574 (permit for use of sound trucks); *Kunz* v. *People of State of New York*, 340 U.S. 290, 71 S. Ct. 312, 95 L. Ed. 280 (permit required to hold public worship meetings on street); *Lovell* v. *City of Griffin*, 303 U.S. 444, 58 S. Ct. 666, 82 L. Ed. 949 (permit required for distribution of pamphlets); *Cantwell* v. *State of Connecticut*, 310 U.S. 296, 60 S. Ct. 900, 84 L. Ed. 1213 (permit required for solicitation of moneys for religious causes); *Hague* v. *Committee for Industrial Organization*, 307 U.S. 496, 59 S. Ct. 954, 83 L. Ed. 1423 (previous restraint on speech and assembly); *Niemotko* v. *State of Maryland*, 340 U.S. 268, 71 S. Ct. 325, 328, 95 L. Ed. 267, 280 (permit for

use of park for holding meeting); *Largent* v. *State of Texas*, 318 U.S. 418, 63 S. Ct. 667, 87 L. Ed. 873 (permit for soliciting orders for books or various household articles); *Jamison* v. *State of Texas*, 318 U.S. 413, 63 S. Ct. 669, 87 L. Ed. 869 (distribution of hand bills); *Schneider* v. *State of New Jersey* (Town of Irvington), 308 U.S. 147, 60 S. Ct. 146, 84 L. Ed. 155 (distribution of pamphlets without permit); *Grosjean* v. *American Press Co., Inc.*, 297 U.S. 233, 56 S. Ct. 444, 80 L. Ed. 660 (tax on newspaper circulation); *Superior Films, Inc.* v. *Department of Education*, 346 U.S. 587, 74 S. Ct. 286, 98 L. Ed. 329, and *Joseph Burstyn, Inc.* v. *Wilson*, 343 U.S. 495, 72 S. Ct. 777, 96 L. Ed. 1098 (vague general standard in pre-licensing of motion pictures). The Court of Appeals of New York spoke out on this subject as early as 1839, *Brandreth* v. *Lance*, 8 Paige 24, but the most articulate pronouncement was not to be heard until Chief Justice Hughes' opinion in 1931 in *Near* v. *State of Minnesota*, 283 U.S. 697, 51 S. Ct. 625, 75 L. Ed. 1357. There, the United States Supreme Court declared invalid a state statute as a previous restraint upon the freedom of the press as guaranteed by the First and Fourteenth Amendments. Since the injunction in that case sought to suppress future issues of a periodical (found to have been defamatory in the past), it was held that the decree was too broad as an unreasonable restraint upon the press, and that either civil or criminal libel after publication would have afforded an adequate remedy.

[14] Since there cannot possibly be an assurance that a future issue would necessarily be obscene, the requested advance suppression of what might be seems (at least to me) to be violative of the constitutional right of free press. Be that as it may, it is an established principle of our law that a statute must, if possible, be so construed as to be constitutional, *Crowell* v. *Benson*, 285 U.S. 22, 46, 52 S. Ct. 285, 76 L. Ed. 598; *Panama Railroad Co.* v. *Johnson*, 264 U.S. 375, 44 S. Ct. 391, 68 L. Ed. 748; *United States* v. *Delaware & Hudson Co.*, 213 U.S. 366, 407–408, 29 S. Ct. 527, 53 L. Ed. 836; *Kauffman & Sons Saddlery Co., Inc.* v. *Miller*, 298 N.Y. 38, 44, 80 N.E. 2d 322, 324, and even to avoid, if possible, raising substantial constitutional questions. See *Peters* v. *Hobby*, 349 U.S. 331, 75 S. Ct. 790; Kupferman and O'Brien, Motion Picture Censorship—The Memphis Blues, 36 Cornell L.Q. 273, 278–280. Had the legislation now under attack offered the entire scope of relief sought by the plaintiff (i.e. the injunction against all future issues), it would, I sense, raise serious constitutional questions.

[15] In consequence it follows that there can be no injunction regarding an unpublished book or pamphlet—however likely it may be thought that it will, when issued, be violative of the statute. Unless the work be before the court at the time of the hearing at which the injunction is sought, it is inappropriate to make a judicial determination with respect to it. In respect of this feature of the case, the plaintiff seeks a likely trespass upon a constitutionally protected area, and the court must reject that prayer.

The defendants also contend (without argument or citation) that the judgment which I am about to render would amount to an unconstitutional seizure, U.S. Const. Amend. IV; N.Y. Const. Art. I, sec. 12. I hold this claim to be wholly without merit.

[16] The prohibition against "unreasonable searches and seizures" does not, I take it, forbid judicially declared action based upon constitutionally authorized jurisdiction

—and duly taken thereunder, cf. Matter of Both, 200 App. Div. 423, 192 N.Y.S. 822—but rather against certain action sans due judicial sanction. A court of equity, I have now held, may constitutionally be given power to enjoin the sale and distribution of existing obscene publications. I do not see wherein it may not also be given jurisdiction concomitant therewith to compel the surrender and destruction of such publications. The law books are not without analogies, although I found no precise precedents one way or the other.

[17–19] Replevin is an ancient legal remedy. The abatement of a nuisance has long been known in the field of equity jurisprudence. When a person is legally arrested, he may be searched to discover and seize the fruits of his crime, see *Weeks* v. *United States*, 232 U.S. 383, 392, 34 S. Ct. 341, 58 L. Ed. 652; *People* v. *Chiagles*, 237 N. Y. 193, 195, 142 N.E. 583, 32 A.L.R. 676; so, too, it may be said that when a "res" is lawfully "arrested," and permanently condemned, the Legislature may authorize its seizure and destruction. Constitutional immunity is granted not from all searches and seizures, but only from those which are "unreasonable," U.S. Const. Amend. IV; N.Y. Const. Art. I, sec. 12; Civil Rights Law, § 8; *People* v. *Richter*, 265 App. Div. 767, 771, 40 N.Y.S. 2d 751, 754, affirmed *People* v. *Richter's Jewelers, Inc.*, 291 N.Y. 161, 51 N.E. 2d 690, 150 A.L.R. 560. As Judge Cardozo reasoned in another connection, "[T]he fact that the weapon was contraband, a nuisance subject to destruction * * * [m]ight have justified the seizure, the abatement of the nuisance, if the weapon had been exposed to view." *People* v. *Defore*, 242 N.Y. 13, 18, 150 N.E. 585, 586, certiorari denied 270 U.S. 657, 46 S. Ct. 353, 70 L. Ed. 784. Firearms and slot machines, for example, have, under certain circumstances, been declared "public nuisances" by the Legislature, and subject to seizure and destruction. As such, they may, after due notice and fair trial, be seized and abated without violating constitutional guarantees. Penal Law, §§ 982–985, 1899; *People* v. *Whitcomb*, 273 App. Div. 610, 79 N.Y.S. 2d 230, appeal denied 274 App. Div. 851, 81 N.Y.S. 2d 923, appeal dismissed 298 N.Y. 635, 82 N.E. 2d 30; *People* v. *Defore*, supra. The Legislature has now also classified "obscene" matter as "contraband," and determined that it may be seized and destroyed in pursuance of court decree after an open trial, Code Cr. Proc. § 22–a. I hold that the classification is justifiable, that the defendants have been fully and fairly heard, that there is due process of law, and that "seizure" is reasonable and not violative of the constitution.

[20] Specious, too, in my view, is the defendants' challenge directed to the plaintiff's capacity to sue. Section 22–a specifically provides, subsection 1, that "the corporation counsel * * * of any city * * * in which a person, firm or corporation sells or distributes or is about to sell or distribute or has in his possession with intent to sell or distribute or is about to acquire possession with intent to sell or distribute any * * * [proscribed printed matter] may maintain an action for an injunction * * * in the supreme court to prevent the sale or further sale or the distribution or further distribution or the acquisition or possession of" that matter.

The Charter of the City of New York provides for the appointment of a corporation counsel by the major, Section 391. Section 394, subd. a, of the Charter reads: "*Except as otherwise provided by law*, the corporation counsel shall be attorney and counsel for the city and every agency thereof and shall have charge and conduct of all the law business of the city and its agencies and *in which the city is interested*." (Emphasis supplied.) In Section 30 of the City Home Rule Law, the Legislature specifically reserved to itself the power "to pass laws regulating *matters of state concern*" (emphasis supplied); (See also Article 9 of the State Constitution).

I hold that Section 22–a of the Code of Criminal Procedure is an instance in which "otherwise" was "provided by law." In addition, what may be "matters of state concern" may also be something "in which the city is interested." The publication and distribution of material devoted to obscenity, lewdness, lasciviousness, filth, indecency and disgust—to crime, sex, horror, terror, brutality, lust and depravity—have been found by the Legislature to be a contributing factor to juvenile delinquency, a basic factor in impairing the ethical and moral development of our future citizens, and a clear and present danger to the people of our State. As such, these are, it seems to me, "matters of state concern" "in which the city is [also] interested."

Judgment is rendered in the plaintiff's*** favor on the merits to the extent herein indicated. The defendants*** will be permanently enjoined from distributing, selling or acquiring possession of any of the volumes of the publication entitled "Nights of Horror" received in evidence upon the trial, and they will be directed to surrender to the Sheriff of the City of New York (New York County Division) all copies of these volumes now in their possession, and the Sheriff will be directed to seize and destroy them. Settle judgment accordingly. (The parties having duly waived findings of facts and conclusions of law, this opinion will constitute the decision of the court in pursuance of the provisions of the Civil Practice Act.)

*** Since the institution of this action, Adrian P. Burke resigned as Corporation Counsel of the City of New York, and Peter Campbell Brown, thereafter duly appointed Corporation Counsel, is substituted as plaintiff in his stead.

On motion of the plaintiff the title of the action is also amended, with respect to certain of the defendants, as follows: (1) "Louis Finkelstein, doing business as Times Square Book Shop," instead of "Times Square Book Shop, Louis Finkelstein," and (2) "Philip Pellegrino, doing business as "Pelley Book Shop" instead of "Pelley Book Shop, Philip Pellegrino."

The defendants Metropolitan Book Shop Inc., and Philip Pellegrino did not appear, although served with process. The defendant Anne Goldberg was not served with process and is deceased. The defendants Publishers Outlet and Gordon Law were not served with process.

■ Peter Campbell Brown, Corporation Counsel of the City of New York, Respondent,

v.

Kingsley Books, Inc., et al., Appellants, and Metropolitan Book Shop, Inc., et al., Defendants.

Argued November 29, 1955; decided April 27, 1956.

Emanuel Redfield for Kingsley Books, Inc., and another, appellants. I. Prior restraints on publications and distribution are prohibited by the Federal Constitution. (*Leach v. Carlile*, 258 U.S. 138; *United States v. Paramount Pictures*, 334 U.S. 131; *Near v. Minnesota*, 283 U.S. 697; *Matter of Commercial Pictures Corp. v. Board of Regents*, 305 N.Y. 336; *Matter of Joseph Burstyn, Inc. v. Wilson*, 303 N.Y. 242, 343 U.S. 495; *Winters v. New York*, 333 U.S. 507; *Chaplinsky v. New Hampshire*, 315 U.S. 568; *Brandreth v. Lance*, 8 Paige Ch. 24.) II. The statute operates as a previous restraint on publication. (*Lovell v. Griffin*, 303 U.S. 444; *Cantwell v. Connecticut*, 310 U.S. 296; *Schneider v. State*, 308 U.S. 147; *Kovacs v. Cooper*, 336 U.S. 77; *Saia v. New York*, 334 U.S. 558; *Kunz v. New York*, 340 U.S. 290; *Largent v. Texas*, 318 U.S. 418; *Niemotko v. Maryland*, 340 U.S. 268; *Thornhill v. Alabama*, 310 U.S. 88; *Hague v. C.I.O.*, 307 U.S. 496; *Thomas v. Collins*, 323 U.S. 516; *Superior Films v. Department of Educ.*, 346 U.S. 587.) III. The "clear and present danger" rule has no application here. IV. This action is not one of abatement of a nuisance. (*Lawton v. Steele*, 152 U.S. 133.) V. The statutory provision for seizure and destruction must fall with the injunction.

Peter Campbell Brown, Corporation Counsel (Seymour B. Quel and Fred Iscol of counsel), respondent in person. Section 22-a of the Code of Criminal Procedure is a valid exercise of the police power of the state. (*Winters v. New York*, 333 U.S. 507; *Near v. Minnesota*, 283 U.S. 697; *Chaplinsky v. New Hampshire*, 315 U.S. 568; *Swearingen v. United States*, 161 U.S. 446; *Public Clearing House v. Coyne*, 194 U.S. 497; *American Civil Liberties Union v. Chicago*, 3 Ill. 2d 334, 348 U.S. 979; *Sunshine Book Co. v. Summerfield*, 128 F. Supp. 564; *Summerfield v. Sunshine Book Co.*, 221 F. 2d 42, 349 U.S. 921.)

FULD J. Although we are all agreed for affirmance, we reach that conclusion by somewhat different routes. The importance and perplexities of the constitutional issue presented persuade me that there must be more full discussion than some of my associates believe necessary of the reasons for and the reach of the decision being made.

Enacted in 1941 (L. 1941, ch. 925) and amended in 1954 (L. 1954, ch. 702), section 22-a of the Code of Criminal Procedure was designed to supplement existing criminal sanctions by providing an additional civil remedy in the Supreme Court, by way of an action for an injunction, against the sale and distribution of written or printed matter found, after trial, to be obscene. Modeled on the language of section 1141 of the Penal Law, the statute prohibiting the sale and distribution of items obscene, section 22-a, insofar as here pertinent, embraces "any book, magazine, pamphlet, comic book, story paper, writing, paper, picture, drawing, photograph, figure, image or any written or printed matter of an indecent character, which is obscene, lewd, lascivious, filthy, indecent or disgusting." It vests the right to maintain the action in the chief executive or legal officer of any city, town or village and provides that it may be brought against anyone who "sells or distributes or is about to sell or distribute or has in his possession with intent to sell or distribute or is about to acquire possession with intent to sell or distribute" any such matter (subd. 1). If an injunction is granted, the statute continues, the resulting order or judgment must direct the defendant to "surrender" the offending matter to the sheriff who "shall be directed to seize and destroy the same" (subd. 3).

The present suit, instituted by the Corporation Counsel of the City of New York against a number of book sellers with premises in that city, concerns a series of paper-bound booklets collectively entitled "Nights of Horror." Members of the police force testified at the trial that the booklets had been displayed for sale in defendants' stores and that they had purchased a number of copies from the various defendants, at prices ranging from $2 to $4 each. The publications themselves were also introduced in evidence. The trial judge, in a carefully considered opinion, found that the booklets were plainly obscene and pornographic, "dirt for dirt's sake," and held that the statute did not violate any constitutional guarantee. He thereupon granted judgment (1) permanently enjoining defendants from distributing, selling, or acquiring possession of such publications, (2) requiring them forthwith to surrender to the sheriff for destruction all copies in their possession and (3) directing the sheriff to seize and destroy such copies, in the event of defendants' failure to surrender them.

The paper-covered booklets before us are indisputably pornographic, indisputably obscene and filthy. Defendants concede as much and also acknowledge, in effect, that, had they been criminally prosecuted for violating the obscenity provisions of the Penal Law, no constitutional argument could successfully have been leveled against resulting convictions. Indeed, not questioning the definiteness of the statutory standard, not challenging the test of obscenity applied by the trial judge, who concluded that the booklets were obscene under any of the judicially announced criteria and not objecting to the failure to require a jury trial,[1] defendants' sole attack upon the statute is that the remedy by injunction constitutes an unconstitutional "prior restraint," interfering with freedom of speech and press (U.S. Const., 1st and 14th Amendts.; N.Y. Const., art. I, § 8).[2]

There is, of course, no doubt that freedom of speech and press, so basic to a free and dynamic society, extends to all media of expression (see *Joseph Burstyn, Inc.* v. *Wilson*, 343 U.S. 495, 501–502; see, also, Chafee on Free Speech in the United States [1941], p. 545), that it protects distribution as well as initial publication (see *Lovell* v. *Griffin*, 303 U.S. 444; *Grosjean* v. *American Press Co.*, 297 U.S. 233) and that it embraces writings or other forms of expression designed for entertainment or amusement, as well as those concerned with the exposition of ideas. (See *Winters* v. *New York*, 333 U.S. 507, 510; *Hannegan* v. *Esquire, Inc.*, 327 U.S. 146, 153.) While the right of free expression is not absolute or unqualified under all circumstances, it is clear that any invasion of that right must find justification in some overriding public interest, and that restricting legislation must be narrowly drawn to meet an evil which the state has a substantial interest in correcting. (See *Joseph Burstyn, Inc.* v. *Wilson, supra*, 343 U.S. 495, 502–504; *Feiner* v. *New York*, 340 U.S. 315, 319; *Niemotko* v. *Maryland*, 340 U.S. 268, 271–272; *Winters* v. *New York, supra*, 333 U.S. 507, 509; *Cantwell* v. *Connecticut*, 310 U.S. 296, 307–308; *Thornhill* v. *Alabama*, 310 U.S. 88, 97–98, 105.)

That clearly drawn regulatory legislation to protect the public from the evils inherent in the dissemination of obscene matter,[3] at least by the application of criminal sanctions, is not barred by the free speech guarantees of the First Amendment, has been recognized both by this court (see *People* v. *Doubleday & Co.*, 297 N.Y. 687, affd., by equally divided court, 335 U.S. 848; *People* v. *Wendling*, 258 N.Y. 451; *People* v. *Pesky*, 254 N.Y. 373; *People* v. *Muller*, 96 N.Y. 408) and by the United States Supreme Court. (See *United States* v. *Alpers*, 338 U.S. 680; *Winters* v. *New York, supra*, 333 U.S. 507, 510, 518, 520; *United States* v. *Limehouse*, 285 U.S. 424; see, also, *Chaplinsky* v. *New Hampshire*, 315 U.S. 568, 571–572; *Near* v. *Minnesota*, 283 U.S. 697, 716; *Beauharnais* v. *Illinois*, 343 U.S. 250, 266.) Imprecise though it be—its "vague subject-matter" being largely "left to the gradual

development of general notions about what is decent" (per L. HAND, J., *United States* v. *Kennerley*, 209 F. 119, 121)—the concept of obscenity has heretofore been accepted as an adequate standard. Indeed, in the *Winters* case (*supra*, 333 U.S. 507), the court not only indicated that collocation of the very words found in section 1141 of our Penal Law, "obscene, lewd, lascivious, filthy, indecent or disgusting," is sufficiently "well understood through long use in the criminal law" to satisfy the due process requirements of definiteness and certainty (333 U.S., at p. 518), but actually pointed to the provision as "an example" of a statute wherein "apt words" are used "to describe the prohibited publications" (333 U.S., at p. 520).[4]

Thus, by virtue of section 1141, it has long been a misdemeanor in this state, punishable by imprisonment or fine or both, to sell or distribute any written or printed obscene material of the kind described in section 22-a of the Code, and similar statutes are in effect in almost all of the other jurisdictions in this country (see Note, 22 U. of Chicago L. Rev. 216). The legislature, however, apparently concluded that such penal sanctions were inadequate to stem the rising tide of obscene and pornographic publications that have, in recent years, flooded the book and periodical market, and the supplemental remedy of an equity action for an injunction was thereupon devised. (Cf. Report of New York State Joint Legislative Committee to Study the Publication of Comics, N.Y. Legis. Doc., 1954, No. 37, pp. 31–32.) Whether or not the legislature acted wisely is, of course, no concern of the courts. Our inquiry is limited to whether its act transcends constitutional limits.

As already noted, no injunction may issue under section 22-a except after a full trial of the issues, and only upon a finding that the challenged publication is of the same character as would subject the defendant to punishment under the pertinent provisions of the Penal Law. What the statute does is to provide an additional sanction against the dissemination of obscene matter.

It is, however, defendants' position that the constitution limits the state to the imposition of punishment, and that distribution of the writing itself may not be prevented. An injunction, such as the present one, even though it is issued after publication and after a judicial trial, is characterized as such suppression and censorship as to stamp it an impermissible "prior restraint." In other words, it is urged that as long as the publisher or vendor of a writing is willing to risk the imposition of criminal penalties he has an absolute right to proceed with its publication or distribution and any restriction of that right is unwarranted, since, among other things, it would deprive the public of the opportunity of reading and making its own appraisal of the challenged material.

The major, though not exclusive, purpose of the guarantee of free expression is "to prevent previous restraints upon publication." (*Near* v. *Minnesota, supra*, 283 U.S. 697, 713; *Joseph Burstyn, Inc.* v. *Wilson, supra*, 343 U.S. 495, 503.) Though difficult of exact formulation (see

---

[1] It may be well to note that in a criminal prosecution based upon section 1141 of the Penal Law, involving as it does a misdemeanor charge, the defendant is not entitled to a trial by jury as a matter of constitutional right. (N.Y. Const., art. VI, § 18; see *People* v. *Kaminsky*, 208 N.Y. 389, 394; *People* ex rel. *Cosgriff* v. *Craig*, 195 N.Y. 190, 195–196; see, also, N.Y. City Crim. Cts. Act, § 31, subd. 1, pars. [b], [c].)

[2] We do not concern ourselves with the further provision of the statute directing the court to render its decision "within two days of the conclusion of the trial" (subd. 2), in view of the fact that the parties agreed neither to invoke nor insist upon that requirement.

[3] It is noteworthy that studies are for the first time being made, through such scientific skills as exist, concerning the impact of the obscene, in writings and other mass media, on the mind and behavior of men, women and children. (See, e.g., Jahoda and Staff of Research Center for Human Relations, New York University [1954], The Impact of Literature: A Psychological Discussion of Some Assumptions in the Censorship Debate.)

[4] Application of the standard may, perhaps, raise constitutional questions in individual cases (cf. *Doubleday & Co.* v. *New York*, 335 U.S. 848, affg., by equally divided court, 297 N.Y. 687, *supra*; *Roth* v. *Goldman*, 172 F. 2d 788, 792, per FRANK, C.J., concurring; see Lockhart & McClure, Literature, The Law of Obscenity and the Constitution, 38 Minn. L. Rev. 295), but the present is not such a case.

Emerson, The Doctrine of Prior Restraint, 20 Law and Contemporary Problems 648), this principle of immunity from prior restraint has been applied by the United States Supreme Court in a variety of situations to strike down licensing or censorship systems under which the right of speech, publication or assembly was conditioned upon obtaining the advance approval of an executive board or official vested with broad or undefined discretion. (See, e.g., *Poulos* v. *New Hampshire*, 345 U.S. 395; *Kunz* v. *New York*, 340 U.S. 290; *Niemotko* v. *Maryland*, *supra*, 340 U.S. 268; *Cantwell* v. *Connecticut*, *supra*, 310 U.S. 296; *Schneider* v. *State*, 308 U.S. 147.) As has been pointed out, however, "the protection even as to previous restraint is not absolutely unlimited," although the limitation has been recognized "only in exceptional cases." (*Near* v. *Minnesota*, *supra*, 283 U.S. 697, 716; see, also, *Joseph Burstyn, Inc.* v. *Wilson*, *supra*, 343 U.S. 495, 504.)

The Supreme Court has asserted, by way of dictum, that the control of obscenity presents such an exceptional case. In *Near* v. *Minnesota* (*supra*, 283 U.S. 697, 716), Chief Justice Hughes, in discussing certain extraordinary areas exempt from the sweeping prohibition against prior restraint, stated that one of the exceptions was that "the primary requirements of decency may be enforced against obscene publications," and similar reservations have also been expressed elsewhere. (See *Chaplinsky* v. *New Hampshire*, *supra*, 315 U.S. 568, 571–572; *Lovell* v. *Griffin*, *supra*, 303 U.S. 444, 451; see, also, Chafee, *op. cit.*, p. 10.) But the precise issue whether restraints in advance of publication may be applied to obscene matter has not yet been squarely decided. Questions involving the validity of state systems of censorship of motion pictures have on several recent occasions come before the Supreme Court, but in each instance the case has been disposed of by striking down some particular standard or criterion on the ground that it did not satisfy the minimum requirements of definiteness and certainty. (See *Superior Films* v. *Department of Educ.*, 346 U.S. 587; *Commercial Pictures Corp.* v. *Regents*, 346 U.S. 587; *Joseph Burstyn, Inc.* v. *Wilson*, *supra*, 343 U.S. 495; *Gelling* v. *Texas*, 343 U.S. 960; cf. *Holmby Productions* v. *Vaughn*, 350 U.S. 870.) The court has specifically left open the question "whether a state may censor motion pictures under a clearly drawn statute designed and applied to prevent the showing of obscene films." (*Joseph Burstyn, Inc.* v. *Wilson*, *supra*, 343 U.S. 495, 505–506.)[5]

[5] I do not believe that *Holmby Productions* (*supra*, 350 U.S. 870) answers this question. The Kansas statute there considered provided for the banning of any motion picture found by the state's board of review to be "obscene, indecent or immoral, or such as tend to debase or corrupt morals." The film, "The Moon is Blue," while labeled by the board as "obscene," as well as "indecent and immoral," was specifically condemned for the following stated reason: "Sex theme throughout, too frank bedroom dialogue; many sexy words; both dialogue and action have sex as their theme." The Supreme Court reversed the judgment of the Kansas high court which had accepted the board's interpretation of the statute as well as its determination (177 Kan. 728). It is our surmise that this decision of the Supreme Court—reflected in a *Per Curiam*, merely citing *Burstyn* (*supra*, 343 U.S. 495) and *Superior Films* (*supra*, 346 U.S. 587)— turned solely on the wide reach and the essential vagueness of the standard employed by the Kansas court. Since any film could apparently be banned as "obscene, indecent or immoral" if a sex theme predominated, the term "obscene" was no narrower, no more definite or certain, than the criteria previously stricken as

We are not, in my opinion, required in this case to decide categorically the validity, under all circumstances, of any and every prior restraint aimed at obscene matter, regardless of the nature and scope of the regulatory measure employed or of the particular medium of expression involved. While strong objections have been voiced against any practice of general censorship, even in the area of obscenity, and whether administered by an executive agency or a judicial tribunal (see Emerson, *supra*, 20 Law and Contemporary Problems, at pp. 661, 670–671; Rice, The Supreme Freedom: Three Hundred Years After Milton, pp. 105, 111–112, contained in Great Expressions of Human Rights, edited by R. M. MacIver, published in 1950 by Institute for Religious and Social Studies: cf. *Superior Films* v. *Department of Educ.*, *supra*, 346 U.S. 587, 588, per Douglas, J., concurring), that broad question is not here presented. Sharp and precise lines cannot always be drawn between permissible and nonpermissible regulatory measures in the realm of expression. (See *Winters* v. *New York*, *supra*, 333 U.S. 507, 518; *Joseph Burstyn, Inc.* v. *Wilson*, *supra*, 343 U.S. 495, 517–518, per Frankfurter, J., concurring.) Whatever might be said of a scheme of advance censorship directed against all *possibly* obscene writings, the case before us concerns a regulatory measure of far narrower impact, of a kind neither entailing the grave dangers of general censorship nor productive of the abuses which gave rise to the constitutional guarantees. (Cf. Pound, Equitable Relief Against Defamation and Injuries to Personality, 29 Harv. L. Rev. 640, 650–651.)

There is nothing in section 22-a that constitutes or resembles a system of licensing or other threshhold approval, which would, for example, operate as a pervasive restraint upon all expression relating to sex problems or behavior and which would ban and suppress, without a censor's imprimatur, any work of literature dealing with those subjects. On the contrary, the statute makes no attempt to subject writings to the scrutiny and screening of a censor prior to publication. The statutory procedures may be invoked only after publication, and no work may be condemned except upon a formal adjudication of obscenity after a trial conducted in accordance with the essential requirements of due process of law. The mind of the trial judge must be satisfied, from a reading of the challenged writing and a consideration of other pertinent evidence, that it is, indeed, of the type and character condemned by the statute. Moreover, his findings are subject to full appellate review on the facts as well as on the law (Civ. Prac. Act, § 584). The procedures thus provided are to be contrasted with the usual features of advance censorship, under which a large measure of discretion is reposed in the censoring official, the procedural safeguards of judicial proceedings are not available, only limited judicial review is allowed and the burden rests on the publisher or vendor to establish the arbitrariness of an adverse ruling. (See Emerson, *supra*, 20 Law and Contemporary Problems, at pp. 656–660.)

In point of fact, examination of the operation and effect of section 22-a reveals substantially no greater interference with the freedom of the publisher or vendor than that presented by the possibility of punishment under the Penal Law. There can be little doubt that the rigid enforcement

too vague in the *Commercial Pictures* and *Superior Films* cases (*supra*, 346 U.S. 587).

of such penal provisions, though operating by indirection, may serve as effectually as direct action by injunction, if not more so, to deter publication of an obscene work. (See Pound, *supra*, 29 Harv. L. Rev., at p. 651; Emerson, *supra*, 20 Law and Contemporary Problems, at p. 660.) In the final analysis, the effectiveness of the injunctive remedy must itself depend upon punitive sanctions, by way of contempt proceedings, for its enforcement; and, if a publisher or vendor would not be deterred by the prospect of prosecution under the Penal Law, he might equally be unaffected by the threat of punishment for contempt. These words are, of course, limited to the statute before us dealing with obscenity, and nothing here written is to be taken as sanctioning the injunctive process in dealing with other objectionable or antisocial material, such as libel.

The reliance which defendants place upon *Near* v. *Minnesota* (*supra*, 283 U.S. 697) is untenable. That case concerned a Minnesota statute which authorized the issuance of an injunction, in a suit to be brought in the name of the state, against the further publication of any newspaper or periodical adjudged to be "malicious, scandalous and defamatory."[6] Under the statute, any articles deemed to be derogatory to a public officer could be branded "malicious, scandalous and defamatory," if the publisher were unable to establish that they were true *and* "published with good motives and for justifiable ends" (283 U.S., at pp. 709–710). Once such an injunction was issued, resumption of any future printing was banned and punishable as a contempt, unless the publisher was able to satisfy the court as to the character of the new publication. The court would thus be constituted a censor to pass on the contents of future issues in advance of publication, and whether the publisher "would be permitted again to publish matter deemed to be derogatory to the same or other public officers would depend upon the court's ruling" (283 U.S., at p. 712). It was this feature of the law, particularly as applied to newspaper comment upon matters of public importance, upon ideas in the realm of political expression, that was regarded by the Supreme Court as "of the essence of censorship" and an unwarranted infringement on freedom of discussion (283 U.S., at p. 713).

The features condemned in *Near* are here absent. The statute now under consideration deals exclusively with matters in the field of lustful emotion. Erotics, not politics, is its subject, and, as already noted, the writings here condemned are unredeemed by even an iota of idea content or of artistic worth. And, unlike the statute in *Near* which sanctioned a general and future restraint, there is here no restraint of any kind on the publication or distribution of material to be written or produced in the future. The corporation counsel in the court below sought to have the statute read as authorizing an injunction against the sale and distribution, not only of any published work found to be obscene, but also of any future work in the same series. This the trial court very properly refused to do.

In short, careful analysis of the operation and effect of section 22-a, in relation to the basic aims and objectives of the constitutional guarantees, is convincing that the limited injunctive remedy here provided may not be condemned as a forbidden prior restraint. As a matter of fact,

analogous decisions under the Federal Tariff Act of 1930 (Act June 17, 1930, ch. 497, tit. III, § 305; U.S. Code, tit. 19, § 1305) suggest that a measure which prescribes a penalty only after the challenged work has already been published does not involve any aspect of prior restraint at all. The Tariff Act thus provides for the seizure by the customs collector of any obscene matter imported into this country, and authorizes the United States District Court to direct the forfeiture, confiscation and destruction of such matter upon adjudication after trial that it is obscene. Although the constitutionality of these provisions has apparently never been passed upon by the Supreme Court, the lower federal courts have uniformly either held[7] or assumed[8] the statute to be constitutional. Thus, in *United States* v. *One Obscene Book Entitled "Married Love"* (*supra*, 48 F. 2d 821), Judge WOOLSEY rejected the contention that the statute impinged on the right of freedom of the press, noting that it did "not involve the suppression of a book before it is published"; in the course of his opinion, he wrote (p. 822): "After a book is published, its lot in the world is like that of anything else. It must conform to the law and, if it does not, must be subject to the penalties involved in its failure to do so. Laws which are thus disciplinary of publications, whether involving exclusion from the mails or from this country, do not interfere with freedom of the press."

It is further urged that even publications adjudged to be obscene cannot constitutionally be withheld from free circulation in the market place of ideas; that, apart from the rights of the publisher and vendor, the public itself has the right to read and examine whatever is published and to form its own opinion of a publication's value and propriety. But here, as in other situations, the question is one of balancing the several competing interests involved. As the Supreme Court has emphasized, in reference to the federal statute declaring obscene material nonmailable (35 U.S. Stat. 1129, U.S. Code, tit. 18, former § 334), there is no necessity "to satisfy all tastes, no matter how perverted." (*Hannegan* v. *Esquire, Inc.*, *supra*, 327 U.S. 146, 158.)

In reaching the conclusion which I do, I assume, of course, that the statutory proscription of obscenity will be applied with great care and selectivity so as not to interfere with the circulation of legitimate works of literature; that the libidinous character of a challenged work will be determined by viewing it "broadly as a whole" (*Halsey* v. *New York Soc. for Suppression of Vice*, 234 N.Y. 1, 4–5), with reference to "its dominant effect," "not on any particular class, but upon all those whom it is likely to reach" (*United States* v. *Levine*, 83 F. 2d 156, 157; *United States* v. *One Book Called Ulysses*, *supra*, 72 F. 2d 705, 707–708, affg. 5 F. Supp. 182); and that consideration will be given, among other factors, to "the established reputation of the work in the estimation of approved critics, if the book is modern, and the verdict of the past, if it is ancient." (*United States* v. *One Book Called Ulysses*, *supra*, 72 F. 2d 705, 708.) The danger of arbitrary or erroneous decision under the statute is minimized by the availability of appellate review of the trial court's findings of fact. The

---

[6] The same statute also authorized an injunction against the further publication of any newspaper or periodical adjudged to be "obscene, lewd and lascivious," but that portion of the statute was not involved in the case.

[7] See *Besig* v. *United States* (208 F. 2d 142); *United States* v. *One Obscene Book Entitled "Married Love"* (48 F. 2d 821, 822).

[8] See *Parmelee* v. *United States* (113 F. 2d 729); *United States* v. *One Book Called Ulysses* (72 F. 2d 705); *United States* v. *One Unbound Volume of Prints* (128 F. Supp. 280).

same danger is presented in criminal prosecutions for obscenity, and the remedy lies, not in preventing the state from more effectually enforcing its policy against the circulation of the obscene, but in making certain that the courts apply standards that will insure the least possible risk of interference with unobjectionable publications.

The judgment appealed from should be affirmed, with costs.

DESMOND, J. Defendants expressly admit the (obvious) fact that the books which they sold, and the further sale of which has been here enjoined, are obscene. They thus concede that the books are such as are subject under section 22-a of the New York Code of Criminal Procedure to an injunction at the suit of the corporation counsel who brought this action. Those concessions leave defendants with one possible ground for appeal and that ground they take. Their sole assertion in this court is that section 22-a is unconstitutional because, say defendants, any and every prior restraint on the publication or sale of obscene literature violates the First Amendment. Since no other question is presented, we must limit ourselves to answering that question. It detracts nothing from Judge FULD's fine opinion to point out that its discussion of many other questions not before us on this appeal is not binding on this court.

Answering the one argument made to us, we hold on most ample authority that the First Amendment does not protect obscene books against prior restraint (*Chaplinsky* v. *New Hampshire*, 315 U.S. 568, 572; *Near* v. *Minnesota*, 283 U.S. 697, 716; *Joseph Burstyn, Inc.* v. *Wilson*, 343 U.S. 495, 502–504; see *Beauharnais* v. *Illinois*, 343 U.S. 250, 266; *Ex Parte Jackson*, 96 U.S. 727, and *Hannegan* v. *Esquire, Inc.*, 327 U.S. 146). The standard set up by section 22-a, "obscene, lewd, lascivious, indecent or disgusting," is a valid and adequate one (*Winters* v. *New York*, 333 U.S. 507, 518; see *Rosen* v. *United States*, 161 U.S. 29, 42; *Swearingen* v. *United States*, 161 U.S. 446, 451; *Robertson* v. *Baldwin*, 165 U.S. 275, 281; U.S. Code, tit. 18, § 1461; *United States* v. *Limehouse*, 285 U.S. 424; *Hannegan* v. *Esquire, Inc.*, 327 U.S. 146, 156, 158, *supra*; *Times Film Corp.* v. *City of Chicago*, 139 F. Supp. 837; *People* v. *Muller*, 96 N.Y. 408; *People* v. *Doubleday & Co.*, 297 N.Y. 687, affd. by equal vote 335 U.S. 848; *Commonwealth* v. *Holmes*, 17 Mass. 335).

No one claims that section 22-a lacks appropriate procedural protections for those sued under it.

The judgment should be affirmed, with costs.

DYE and VAN VOORHIS, JJ., concur in opinion of FULD, J.; CONWAY, Ch. J., and FROESSEL, J., concur in opinion of DESMOND, J.; BURKE, J., taking no part.

Judgment affirmed.

■ Kingsley Books, Inc., et al.

v.

Brown, Corporation Counsel.

APPEAL FROM THE COURT OF APPEALS OF NEW YORK.

No. 107. Argued April 22, 1957.—Decided June 24, 1957.

Emanuel Redfield argued the cause and filed a brief for appellants.

Seymour B. Quel argued the cause for appellee. With him on the brief were *Peter Campbell Brown* and *Fred Iscol.*

Ephraim London filed a brief for the New York Civil Liberties Union, as *amicus curiae*, urging reversal.

Louis J. Lefkowitz, Attorney General, *John R. Davison*, Solicitor General, and *Ruth Kessler Toch*, Assistant Attorney General, filed a brief for the State of New York, as *amicus curiae*, urging affirmance.

MR. JUSTICE FRANKFURTER delivered the opinion of the Court.

This is a proceeding under § 22-a of the New York Code of Criminal Procedure (L. 1941, c. 925), as amended in 1954 (L. 1954, c. 702). This section supplements the existing conventional criminal provision dealing with pornography by authorizing the chief executive, or legal officer, of a municipality to invoke a "limited injunctive remedy," under closely defined procedural safeguards, against the sale and distribution of written and printed matter found after due trial to be obscene, and to obtain an order for the seizure, in default of surrender, of the condemned publications.[1]

---

[1] "§ 22–a. Obscene prints and articles; jurisdiction. The supreme court has jurisdiction to enjoin the sale or distribution of obscene prints and articles, as hereinafter specified:

"1. The chief executive officer of any city, town or village or the corporation counsel, or if there be none, the chief legal officer of any city, town, or village, in which a person, firm or corporation sells or distributes or is about to sell or distribute or has in his possession with intent to sell or distribute or is about to acquire possession with intent to sell or distribute any book, magazine, pamphlet, comic book, story paper, writing, paper, picture, drawing, photograph, figure, image or any written or printed matter of an indecent character, which is obscene, lewd, lascivious, filthy, indecent or disgusting, or which contains an article or instrument of indecent or immoral use or purports to be for indecent or immoral use or purpose; or in any other respect defined in section eleven hundred forty-one of the penal law, may maintain an action for an injunction against such

A complaint dated September 10, 1954, charged appellants with displaying for sale paper-covered obscene booklets, fourteen of which were annexed, under the general title of "Nights of Horror." The complaint prayed that appellants be enjoined from further distribution of the booklets, that they be required to surrender to the sheriff for destruction all copies in their possession, and, upon failure to do so, that the sheriff be commanded to seize and destroy those copies. The same day the appellants were ordered to show cause within four days why they should not be enjoined *pendente lite* from distributing the booklets. Appellants consented to the granting of an injunction *pendente lite* and did not bring the matter to issue promptly, as was their right under subdivision 2 of the challenged section, which provides that the persons sought to be enjoined "shall be entitled to a trial of the issues within one day after joinder of issue and a decision shall be rendered by the court within two days of the conclusion of the trial." After the case came to trial, the judge, sitting in equity, found that the booklets annexed to the complaint and introduced in evidence were clearly obscene—were "dirt for dirt's sake"; he enjoined their further distribution and ordered their destruction. He refused to enjoin "the sale and distribution of later issues" on the ground that "to rule against a volume not offered in evidence would . . . impose an unreasonable prior restraint upon freedom of the press." 208 Misc. 150, 167, 142 N.Y.S. 2d 735, 750.

Not challenging the construction of the statute or the finding of obscenity, appellants took a direct appeal to the New York Court of Appeals, a proceeding in which the constitutionality of the statute was the sole question open to them. That court (one judge not sitting) found no constitutional infirmity: three judges supported the unanimous conclusion by detailed discussion, the other three deemed a brief disposition justified by "ample authority."

person, firm or corporation in the supreme court to prevent the sale or further sale or the distribution or further distribution or the acquisition or possession of any book, magazine, pamphlet, comic book, story paper, writing, paper, picture, drawing, photograph figure or image or any written or printed matter of an indecent character, herein described or described in section eleven hundred forty-one of the penal law.

"2. The person, firm or corporation sought to be enjoined shall be entitled to a trial of the issues within one day after joinder of issue and a decision shall be rendered by the court within two days of the conclusion of the trial.

"3. In the event that a final order or judgment of injunction be entered in favor of such officer of the city, town or village and against the person, firm or corporation sought to be enjoined, such final order of judgment shall contain a provision directing the person, firm or corporation to surrender to the sheriff of the county in which the action was brought any of the matter described in paragraph one hereof and such sheriff shall be directed to seize and destroy the same.

"4. In any action brought as herein provided such officer of the city, town or village shall not be required to file any undertaking before the issuance of an injunction order provided for in paragraph two hereof, shall not be liable for costs and shall not be liable for damages sustained by reason of the injunction order in cases where judgment is rendered in favor of the person, firm or corporation sought to be enjoined.

"5. Every person, firm or corporation who sells, distributes, or acquires possession with intent to sell or distribute any of the matter described in paragraph one hereof, after the service upon him of a summons and complaint in an action brought by such officer of any city, town or village pursuant to this section is chargeable with knowledge of the contents thereof."

1 N.Y. 2d 177, 189, 134 N.E. 2d 461, 468. A claim under the Due Process Clause of the Fourteenth Amendment made throughout the state litigation brought the case here on appeal. 352 U.S. 962.

Neither in the New York Court of Appeals, nor here, did appellants assail the legislation insofar as it outlaws obscenity. The claim they make lies within a very narrow compass. Their attack is upon the power of New York to employ the remedial scheme of § 22–a. Authorization of an injunction *pendente lite*, as part of this scheme, during the period within which the issue of obscenity must be promptly tried and adjudicated in an adversary proceeding for which "[a]dequate notice, judicial hearing, [and] fair determination" are assured, 208 Misc. 150, 164, 142 N.Y.S. 2d 735, 747, is a safeguard against frustration of the public interest in effectuating judicial condemnation of obscene matter. It is a brake on the temptation to exploit a filthy business offered by the limited hazards of piecemeal prosecutions, sale by sale, of a publication already condemned as obscene. New York enacted this procedure on the basis of study by a joint legislative committee. Resort to this injunctive remedy, it is claimed, is beyond the constitutional power of New York in that it amounts to a prior censorship of literary product and as such is violative of that "freedom of thought, and speech" which has been "withdrawn by the Fourteenth Amendment from encroachment by the states." *Palko* v. *Connecticut*, 302 U.S. 319, 326–327. Reliance is particularly placed upon *Near* v. *Minnesota*, 283 U.S. 697.

In an unbroken series of cases extending over a long stretch of this Court's history, it has been accepted as a postulate that "the primary requirements of decency may be enforced against obscene publications." *Id.*, at 716. And so our starting point is that New York can constitutionally convict appellants of keeping for sale the booklets incontestably found to be obscene. *Alberts* v. *California*, *post*, p. 476, decided this day. The immediate problem then is whether New York can adopt as an auxiliary means of dealing with such obscene merchandising the procedure of § 22–a.

We need not linger over the suggestion that something can be drawn out of the Due Process Clause of the Fourteenth Amendment that restricts New York to the criminal process in seeking to protect its people against the dissemination of pornography. It is not for this Court thus to limit the State in resorting to various weapons in the armory of the law. Whether proscribed conduct is to be visited by a criminal prosecution or by a *qui tam* action or by an injunction or by some or all of these remedies in combination, is a matter within the legislature's range of choice. See *Tigner* v. *Texas*, 310 U.S. 141, 148. If New York chooses to subject persons who disseminate obscene "literature" to criminal prosecution and also to deal with such books as deodands of old, or both, with due regard, of course, to appropriate opportunities for the trial of the underlying issue, it is not for us to gainsay its selection of remedies. Just as *Near* v. *Minnesota*, *supra*, one of the landmark opinions in shaping the constitutional protection of freedom of speech and of the press, left no doubts that "Liberty of speech, and of the press, is also not an absolute right," 283 U.S., at 708, it likewise made clear that "the protection even as to previous restraint is not absolutely unlimited." *Id.*, at 716. To be sure, the limitation is the exception; it is to be closely confined so as to preclude what may fairly be deemed licensing or censorship.

The judicial angle of vision in testing the validity of a statute like § 22–a is "the operation and effect of the statute in substance." *Id.*, at 713. The phrase "prior restraint" is not a self-wielding sword. Nor can it serve as a talismanic test. The duty of closer analysis and critical judgment in applying the thought behind the phrase has thus been authoritatively put by one who brings weighty learning to his support of constitutionally protected liberties: "What is needed," writes Professor Paul A. Freund, "is a pragmatic assessment of its operation in the particular circumstances. The generalization that prior restraint is particularly obnoxious in civil liberties cases must yield to more particularistic analysis." The Supreme Court and Civil Liberties, 4 Vand. L. Rev. 533, 539.

Wherein does § 22–a differ in its effective operation from the type of statute upheld in *Alberts?* Section 311 of California's Penal Code provides that "Every person who wilfully and lewdly . . . keeps for sale . . . any obscene . . . book . . . is guilty of a misdemeanor. . . ." Section 1141 of New York's Penal Law is similar. One would be bold to assert that the *in terrorem* effect of such statutes less restrains booksellers in the period before the law strikes than does § 22–a. Instead of requiring the bookseller to dread that the offer for sale of a book may, without prior warning, subject him to a criminal prosecution with the hazard of imprisonment, the civil procedure assures him that such consequences cannot follow unless he ignores a court order specifically directed to him for a prompt and carefully circumscribed determination of the issue of obscenity. Until then, he may keep the book for sale and sell it on his own judgment rather than steer "nervously among the treacherous shoals." Warburg, Onward And Upward With The Arts, The New Yorker, April 20, 1957, 98, 101, in connection with *R.* v. *Martin Secker Warburg, Ltd.*, [1954] 2 All Eng. 683 (C.C.C.).

Criminal enforcement and the proceeding under § 22–a interfere with a book's solicitation of the public precisely at the same stage. In each situation the law moves after publication; the book need not in either case have yet passed into the hands of the public. The *Alberts* record does not show that the matter there found to be obscene had reached the public at the time that the criminal charge of keeping such matter for sale was lodged, while here as a matter of fact copies of the booklets whose distribution was enjoined had been on sale for several weeks when process was served. In each case the bookseller is put on notice by the complaint that sale of the publication charged with obscenity in the period before trial may subject him to penal consequences. In the one case he may suffer fine and imprisonment for violation of the criminal statute, in the other, for disobedience of the temporary injunction. The bookseller may of course stand his ground and confidently believe that in any judicial proceeding the book could not be condemned as obscene, but both modes of procedure provide an effective deterrent against distribution prior to adjudication of the book's content—the threat of subsequent penalization.[2]

The method devised by New York in § 22–a for determining whether a publication is obscene does not differ in essential procedural safeguards from that provided under many state statutes making the distribution of obscene publications a misdemeanor. For example, while the New York criminal provision brings the State's criminal procedure into operation, a defendant is not thereby entitled to a jury trial. In each case a judge is the conventional trier of fact; in each, a jury may as a matter of discretion be summoned. Compare N.Y. City Criminal Courts Act, § 31, Sub. 1 (c) and Sub. 4, with N.Y. Civil Practice Act, § 430. (Appellants, as a matter of fact, did not request a jury trial, they did not attack the statute in the courts below for failure to require a jury, and they did not bring that issue to this Court.) Of course, the Due Process Clause does not subject the States to the necessity of having trial by jury in misdemeanor prosecutions.

Nor are the consequences of a judicial condemnation for obscenity under § 22–a more restictive of freedom of expression than the result of conviction for a misdemeanor. In *Alberts*, the defendant was fined $500, sentenced to sixty days in prison, and put on probation for two years on condition that he not violate the obscenity statute. Not only was he completely separated from society for two months but he was also seriously restrained from trafficking in all obscene publications for a considerable time. Appellants, on the other hand, were enjoined from displaying for sale or distributing only the particular booklets theretofore published and adjudged to be obscene. Thus, the restraint upon appellants as merchants in obscenity was narrower than that imposed on Alberts.

Section 22–a's provision for the seizure and destruction of the instruments of ascertained wrongdoing expresses resort to a legal remedy sanctioned by the long history of Anglo-American law. See Holmes, The Common Law, 24–26; *Van Oster* v. *Kansas*, 272 U.S. 465; *Goldsmith-Grant Co.* v. *United States*, 254 U.S. 505, 510–511; *Lawton* v. *Steele*, 152 U.S. 133; and see *United States* v. *Urbuteit*, 335 U.S. 355, dealing with misbranded articles under § 304 (a) of the Food, Drug, and Cosmetic Act, 52 Stat. 1044. It is worth noting that although the *Alberts* record does not reveal whether the publications found to be obscene were destroyed, provision is made for that by §§ 313 and 314 of the California Penal Code. Similarly, § 1144 of New York's Penal Law provides for destruction of obscene matter following conviction for its dissemination.

It only remains to say that the difference between *Near* v. *Minnesota, supra,* and this case is glaring in fact. The two cases are no less glaringly different when judged by the appropriate criteria of constitutional law. Minnesota empowered its courts to enjoin the dissemination of future issues of a publication because its past issues had been found offensive. In the language of Mr. Chief Justice Hughes, "This is of the essence of censorship." 283 U.S., at 713. As such, it was found unconstitutional. This was enough to condemn the statute wholly apart from the fact that the proceeding in *Near* involved not obscenity but matters deemed to be derogatory to a public officer. Unlike *Near*, § 22–a is concerned solely with obscenity and, as authoritatively construed, it studiously withholds restraint upon matters not already published and not yet found to be offensive.

The judgment is affirmed.

---

[2] This comparison of remedies takes note of the fact that we do not have before us a case where, although the issue of obscenity is ultimately decided in favor of the bookseller, the State nevertheless attempts to punish him for disobedience of the interim injunction. For all we know, New York may impliedly condition the temporary injunction so as not to subject the bookseller to a charge of contempt if he prevails on the issue of obscenity.

Mr. Chief Justice Warren, dissenting.

My views on the right of a State to protect its people against the purveyance of obscenity were expressed in *Alberts* v. *California, post,* p. 476, also decided today. Here we have an entirely different situation.

This is not a criminal obscenity case. Nor is it a case ordering the destruction of materials disseminated by a person who has been convicted of an offense for doing so, as would be authorized under provisions in the laws of New York and other States. It is a case wherein the New York police, under a different state statute, located books which, in their opinion, were unfit for public use because of obscenity and then obtained a court order for their condemnation and destruction.

The majority opinion sanctions this proceeding. I would not. Unlike the criminal cases decided today, this New York law places the book on trial. There is totally lacking any standard in the statute for judging the book in context. The personal element basic to the criminal laws is entirely absent. In my judgment, the same object may have wholly different impact depending upon the setting in which it is placed. Under this statute, the setting is irrelevant.

It is the manner of use that should determine obscenity. It is the conduct of the individual that should be judged, not the quality of art or literature. To do otherwise is to impose a prior restraint and hence to violate the Constitution. Certainly in the absence of a prior judicial determination of illegal use, books, pictures and other objects of expression should not be destroyed. It savors too much of book burning.

I would reverse.

Opinion of Mr. Justice Douglas, joined by Mr. Justice Black, dissenting, announced by Mr. Justice Brennan.

There are two reasons why I think this restraining order should be dissolved.

First, the provision for an injunction *pendente lite* gives the State the paralyzing power of a censor. A decree can issue *ex parte*—without a hearing and without any ruling or finding on the issue of obscenity. This provision is defended on the ground that it is only a little encroachment, that a hearing must be promptly given and a finding of obscenity promptly made. But every publisher knows what awful effect a decree issued in secret can have. We tread here on First Amendment grounds. And nothing is more devastating to the rights that it guarantees than the power to restrain publication before even a hearing is held. This is prior restraint and censorship at its worst.

Second, the procedure for restraining by equity decree the distribution of all the condemned literature does violence to the First Amendment. The judge or jury which finds the publisher guilty in New York City acts on evidence that may be quite different from evidence before the judge or jury that finds the publisher not guilty in Rochester. In New York City the publisher may have been selling his tracts to juveniles, while in Rochester he may have sold to professional people. The nature of the group among whom the tracts are distributed may have an important bearing on the issue of guilt in any obscenity prosecution.

Yet the present statute makes one criminal conviction conclusive and authorizes a statewide decree that subjects the distributor to the contempt power. I think every publication is a separate offense which entitles the accused to a separate trial. Juries or judges may differ in their opinions, community by community, case by case. The publisher is entitled to that leeway under our constitutional system. One is entitled to defend every utterance on its merits and not to suffer today for what he uttered yesterday. Free speech is not to be regulated like diseased cattle and impure butter. The audience (in this case the judge or the jury) that hissed yesterday may applaud today, even for the same performance.

The regime approved by the Court goes far toward making the censor supreme. It also substitutes punishment by contempt for punishment by jury trial. In both respects it transgresses constitutional guarantees.

I would reverse this judgment and direct the restraining order to be dissolved.

Mr. Justice Brennan, dissenting.

I believe the absence in this New York obscenity statute of a right to jury trial is a fatal defect. Provision for jury trials in equity causes is made by § 430 of the New York Civil Practice Act,[1] but only for discretionary jury trials, judge as he deems fit and proper.[2]

In *Alberts* v. *California* and *Roth* v. *United States,* decided today, *post,* p. 476, the Court held to be constitutional the following standard for judging obscenity— whether to the average person, applying contemporary community standards, the dominant theme of the material taken as a whole appeals to prurient interest. The statutes there involved allowed a jury trial of right, and we did not reach the question whether the safeguards necessary for securing the freedoms of speech and press for material not obscene included a jury determination of obscenity.

The jury represents a cross-section of the community and has a special aptitude for reflecting the view of the average person. Jury trial of obscenity therefore provides a peculiarly competent application of the standard for judging obscenity which, by its definition, calls for an appraisal of material according to the average person's application of contemporary community standards. A statute which does not afford the defendant, of right, a jury determination of obscenity falls short, in my view, of giving proper effect to the standard fashioned as the necessary safeguard demanded by the freedoms of speech and press for material which is not obscene. Of course, as with jury questions generally, the trial judge must initially determine that there is a jury question, *i.e.,* that reasonable men may differ whether the material is obscene.[3]

I would reverse the judgment and direct the restraining order to be dissolved.

---

[1] Gilbert-Bliss' N.Y. Civ. Prac., Vol. 3B, 1942, § 430. and advisory verdicts, to be followed or rejected by the trial

[2] *Learned* v. *Tillotson,* 97 N.Y. 1; *Bolognino* v. *Bolognino,* 136 Misc. 656, 241 N.Y. Supp. 445 (Sup. Ct.), aff'd, 231 App. Div. 817, 246 N.Y. Supp. 883.

[3] *Parmelee* v. *United States,* 72 App. D.C. 203, 205, 113 F. 2d 729, 731; *United States* v. *Dennett,* 39 F. 2d 564, 568.

■ United Artists Corporation and Carlyle Productions, Inc.,
v.
Maryland State Board of Censors.

No. 40, Oct. Term, 1956. Court of Appeals of Maryland.

July 13, 1956.

Franklin G. Allen and *William L. Marbury*, Baltimore (Piper & Marbury, Baltimore, on the brief), for appellants.

C. Ferdinand Sybert, Atty. Gen. (Norman P. Ramsey, Deputy Atty. Gen., on the brief), for appellee.

Before BRUNE, C.J., and DELAPLAINE, HENDERSON and HAMMOND, J.J.

DELAPLAINE, Judge.

This appeal is from an order of the Baltimore City Court affirming an order of the Maryland State Board of Censors eliminating a scene from the motion picture named "The Man with the Golden Arm." The appeal was taken by United Artists Corporation, the distributor of the film, and Carlyle Productions, Inc., the producer.

The original Act providing for censorship of motion pictures in Maryland was passed by the Legislature forty years ago. That Act provided that the Maryland State Board of Censors shall consist of three members, who shall be appointed by the Governor by and with the advice and consent of the Senate. It directed that the Board "shall approve such films, reels or views which are moral and proper, and shall disapprove such as are sacrilegious, obscene, indecent, or immoral, or such as tend, in the judgment of the Board, to debase or corrupt morals." Laws 1916, ch. 209.

It was originally held by the United States Supreme Court in 1915 in *Mutual Film Corporation* v. *Industrial Commission of Ohio*, 236 U.S. 230, 35 S. Ct. 387, 59 L. Ed. 552, that freedom of speech and publication was not violated by an Ohio statute which provided for the creation of a Board of Censors to approve only such films as are of a moral, educational, or amusing and harmless character. But in 1952 the Court in *Joseph Burstyn, Inc.* v. *Wilson*, 343 U.S. 495, 72 S. Ct. 777, 96 L. Ed. 1098, held that the New York statute which permitted the banning of motion picture films on the ground that they are "sacrilegious" was invalid as an unconstitutional abridgement of free speech and free press as applied to the banning of the motion picture "The Miracle." Again in 1952 the Court held that a municipal ordinance which authorized a local Board of Censors to deny a license for the showing of a motion picture which the Board is of the opinion is "of such character as to be prejudicial to the best interests of the people" offended the Due Process Clause of the Fourteenth Amendment of the Federal Constitution. *Gelling* v. *State of Texas*, 343 U.S. 960, 72 S. Ct. 1002, 96 L. Ed. 1359.

In 1955 the Court in *Holmby Productions, Inc.* v. *Vaughn*, 350 U.S. 870, 76 S. Ct. 117, 100 L. Ed.—; Id., 350 U.S. 919, 76 S. Ct. 193, held that the Kansas statute authorizing the Board of Censors to disapprove of such motion picture films as are "cruel, obscene, indecent or immoral, or such as tend to debase or corrupt morals," G.S. 1949 Kan. 51–103, was unconstitutional as applied to that case.

In 1955 the Legislature amended the statute by striking out the word "sacrilegious" and stating more specifically what types of films the Board must disapprove. The new law, Laws 1955, ch. 201, Code Supp. 1955, art. 66A, § 6, provides as follows:

"(a) *The Board shall examine or supervise the examination of all films or views to be exhibited or used in the State of Maryland and shall approve and license such films or views which are moral and proper, and shall disapprove such as are obscene, or such as tend, in the judgment of the Board, to debase or corrupt morals or incite to crimes. All films exclusively portraying current events or pictorial news of the day, commonly called news reels, may be exhibited without examination and no license or fees shall be required therefor.*

"(b) *For the purposes of this Article, a motion picture film or view shall be considered to be obscene if, when considered as a whole, its calculated purpose or dominant effect is substantially to arouse sexual desires, and if the probability of this effect is so great as to outweigh whatever other merits the film may possess.*

"(c) *For the purposes of this Article, a motion picture film or view shall be considered to be of such a character that its exhibition would tend to debase or corrupt morals if its dominant purpose or effect is erotic or pornographic; or if it portrays acts of sexual immorality, lust or lewdness, or if it expressly or impliedly presents such acts as desirable, acceptable or proper patterns of behavior.*

"(d) *For the purposes of this Article, a motion picture film or view shall be considered of such a character that its exhibition would tend to incite to crime if the theme or the manner of its presentation presents the commission of criminal acts or contempt for law as constituting profitable, desirable, acceptable, respectable or commonly accepted behavior, or if it advocates or teaches the use of, or the methods of use of, narcotics or habit-forming drugs.*"

The 1955 Act also gives to any person submitting a film to the Board for examination the right to take an appeal not only to the Baltimore City Court, but also from a decision of the Baltimore City Court to the Court of Appeals of Maryland. Laws 1955, ch. 201, Code Supp. 1955, art. 66A, § 19. This is the first appeal that has been brought to the Court of Appeals under this statute.

Appellants submitted the film to the State Board of Censors for approval and license, and the Board found that one of the scenes violates the statute. This scene, which runs less than two minutes, shows Frankie Machine, a young Chicago tough, played by Frank Sinatra, taking a narcotic after six months in the United States Public Health Service Hospital for Drug Addicts at Lexington, Kentucky. Ostensibly he was cured, but all the pressures were there waiting for him. The scene shows him rolling up his sleeve, and tying a necktie around the upper arm, while a dope "pusher" prepares the drug for injection. While the particular kind of narcotic is not named, the picture shows the powdered narcotic, the liquid solution, the spoon, and the hypodermic needle. The "pusher" takes the filled needle and advances toward Frankie. The actual injection is not shown, but the viewer sees the needle being removed from the arm. Just before the needle is pulled out, Frankie indicates by a facial twitch that he felt a slight pain from the injection. Complete relaxation follows.

On January 12, 1956, C. Morton Goldstein, Chairman of the State Board of Censors, issued the following order: "Following Frankie entering Louie's room and removing his coat, eliminate all views from the point where Frankie is shown rolling up his sleeve down to the point immediately preceding his reclining on couch."

Appellants appealed to the Board for a re-examination of the film. The film was re-examined on February 8 by the chairman and the vice chairman, and on February 10 the Board passed another order sustaining its order of January 12.

On February 20 appellants appealed from the Board's order to the Baltimore City Court. They attacked the statute as unconstitutional, and also charged that the Board's order was arbitrary, capricious, and beyond its powers.

At the trial in the Court below, George J. Schaefer, sales supervisor for the producer of the film, testified that the film as presented to the Board had been passed by the censors without any elimination in every State, except Maryland, and had also been shown without elimination in England and on the Continent. He added that in Holland it received a scientific and cultural award resulting in the remission of admission taxes to patrons who viewed the picture. He also explained why appellants have opposed so strenuously the cutting of the scene:

*"If you will recall, Frankie, when he goes home from Lexington, believes that he has been cured, and we later find out that, because of his surroundings and circumstances, things over which he has no control, he has a craving for a 'fix.' * * * That is what we call a climax, applying to that point. He refuses to go with the 'pusher,' as you may call him; and finally succumbs and does go over. You go into the room, and see the 'pusher' open the drawer. * * * It is my belief that the climax at that particular point was the surrendering of Frankie to the injection. If you had shown that picture without that terrific impact, and all of a sudden simply show him lying on the couch, it is my opinion * * * would have done harm to the presentation of the picture, to the dramatic climax."*

Chairman Goldstein informed the Court that the Board had ordered the elimination of the scene on the ground that it "teaches" the use of, or methods of use of, narcotics or habit-forming drugs; but he admitted that the Board did not consider whether the scene "advocates" such use or methods of use.

On May 17 Judge Byrnes upheld the constitutionality of the statute, and further decided that the scene violates the statute because it "teaches the use of, or the methods of use of, narcotics or habit-forming drugs." He thereupon entered the order affirming the order of the Board.

[1] Appellants suggested that if we should give the word "teach" its ordinary meaning, namely to make aware by information, instruction, or experience, it would be necessary to hold Section 6(d) unconstitutional. But we need not decide whether such an interpretation would render Section 6(d) unconstitutional, because we are convinced that the clause "or if it advocates or teaches the use of, or the methods of use of, narcotics or habit-forming drugs" means advocacy and teaching with the purpose of inducing or encouraging. The statute is directed at advocacy, not discussion.

It is impossible to believe that the Legislature intended otherwise when we consider that it has passed a statute requiring that the study of the nature of narcotics and alcoholic drinks and their effects upon the human system shall be included in the curriculum in connection with the study of physiology and hygiene in the public schools and in all State-aided institutions of learning. The Legislature has commanded that this mandate be enforced by the Superintendent of Public Schools of Baltimore City, all Boards of School Commissioners, and the boards of all educational institutions receiving aid from the State. Code 1951, art. 77, §§ 86, 87.

Our definition is not a strained or novel one. *Dennis v. United States*, 341 U.S. 494, 71 S. Ct. 857, 863, 95 L. Ed. 1137, is a precedent for such an interpretation. In that case the Court had under consideration the Smith Act, 18 U.S.C.A. § 2385, which makes it unlawful to "advocate or teach" the desirability or propriety of overthrowing any government in the United States by force or violence. That Act was attacked on the grounds that by its terms it prohibits academic discussion of the merits of Marxism-Leninism, and that it stifles ideas and is contrary to all concepts of a free speech and a free press. The Court, however, refused to hold that the language of the Act had that significance. In the opinion announcing the judgment of the Court, Chief Justice Vinson made the following comment:

"The very language of the Smith Act negates the interpretation which petitioners would have us impose on that Act. It is directed at advocacy, not discussion. Thus, the trial judge properly charged the jury that they could not convict if they found that petitioners did 'no more than pursue peaceful studies and discussions or teaching and advocacy in the realm of ideas.' He further charged that it was not unlawful 'to conduct in an American college and university a course explaining the philosophical theories set forth in the books which have been placed in evidence.' Such a charge is in strict accord with the statutory language, and illustrates the meaning to be placed on those words. Congress did not intend to eradicate the free discussion of political theories, to destroy the traditional rights of Americans to discuss and evaluate ideas without

fear of governmental sanction. Rather Congress was concerned with the very kind of activity in which the evidence showed these petitioners engaged."

[2] After deciding upon this interpretation, we have no difficulty in finding from the record that the censored part of the film does not "advocate or teach" the use of, or the methods of use of, narcotics. On the contrary, the evidence is strong and convincing that the picture is likely to have a beneficial effect as a deterrent from the use of narcotics.

Dr. Hubert S. Howe, former Clinical Professor of Neurology in the College of Physicians and Surgeons of Columbia University, and member of the Committee on Narcotics among Teen-age Youth of the Welfare and Health Council of New York City, who attended a preview of the picture shortly before it opened on Broadway, gave high praise to the picture in the following statement:

"In my opinion there was nothing in the picture which would lead any juvenile, or other person, to wish to experiment with narcotic drugs. I have been asked particularly about the scene in which the 'pusher' prepared an injection for Frankie, showing the equipment to be used. I clearly recall this scene, and certainly there was nothing in it, or in any other part of the picture, which might have a tendency to incite any one to use narcotic drugs. In fact, in my opinion, this picture would have the effect of deterring individuals from experimenting with narcotic drugs, as it portrays how easily the habit is acquired. Education of the public through the schools and moving pictures, etc., under our present conditions, are the best methods to combat the menace of narcotic drug addiction, in my opinion."

The same view was expressed by Dr. Eli K. Marshall, Professor Emeritus of Pharmacology and Therapeutics in the Medical School of the Johns Hopkins University. In reply to the question whether he thought the scene in this picture would tend to induce the use of narcotics, he testified:

"I would think it would have the opposite effect; that the preparation necessary for the intravenous injection would not be sufficient to anyone who did not know what an intravenous injection was; and other people having blood taken, by having blood taken in the hospital, they knew and actually saw what a venal puncture was, so I do not see it would make any difference one way or the other."

Dr. Russell S. Fisher, Professor of Legal Medicine in the Medical School of the University of Maryland and Chief Medical Examiner in the Maryland Department of Postmortem Examiners, said in reply to the question whether the picture would have a tendency to incite a desire to use narcotics:

"This, of course, is a matter of one's philosophy and teaching. I know there are people who feel any knowledge about anything that is sinful or evil should be kept closely guarded and not passed out. The opposite school of philosophy and teaching, in which one hopes to educate the public about those sinful and harmful things and, coupled with it, the disastrous effect of them is, I think, the school from which the people who prepared this movie

*come. That is the school to which I belong, that teaches of the danger of this dread habit, to the point, we hope, of discouraging even traffic in drugs. * * * I believe this film is beneficial in that it portrays a broadside picture of the effects of narcotics on a man's personality."*

Prominent educators also entertain the view that every effort should be made to inform both adults and children about the evils of narcotics. The booklet of suggestions issued by the Board of Education of the City of New York on the subject of narcotics contains the following statement of a leading school official:

"It is my considered opinion that the time for a direct educational assault on this problem has come. There is also the reason of common sense which compels it. We do not avoid marking a thin spot on the ice of a skating pond because we fear some daredevil may be lured to try it. Nor do we avoid teaching a small child the dangers of fire because he may become an arsonist."

The following information has been given in Instructional Guide on Narcotic Education, issued by the Department of Education of the State of New Jersey:

"Heroin has a price of around $1,000 an ounce. It is impossible for the addict to obtain pure heroin or morphine. The original pure product is 'cut' by the addition of sugar or milk ten or even fifty times. This adulteration gives an estimate of the great profits obtained by criminal peddlers.

*"Many drug addicts use regular hypodermic syringes and needles. Others who are unable to buy these syringes use an ordinary medicine dropper. They wrap a piece of paper or adhesitve around the end of the dropper and secure the needle around it. * * The addict carries a small vial of water, a teaspoon, and his supply of narcotic in powder or in tablet form."*

Nathan E. Rudd, Health Education Coordinator in New York City, a high authority on the subject of drug addiction, having addressed supervisors and teachers, parent groups, and civic organizations, and discussed the subject with thousands of teen-agers, declared, after seeing the picture in New York, that it should be a "must" for young and old. He gave it the following recommendation:

*"The picture presented an accurate portrayal of the many problems facing the drug addict and the responsibility of society. * * **

"The taking of addicting drugs by injection is a matter of common knowledge. Reference to this is made continually by the press and magazines. In my opinion, this scene will not entice a youngster to begin experimenting with narcotics.

"As a whole, I consider the picture an excellent work of propaganda exposing the gravity of the problem and the many complicating factors affecting it. It is an authentic and well-done dramatization of the problems of the addict and the difficulty of being cured once addicted.

"I would recommend this picture without reservation as a valuable weapon in the area of preventive education dealing with the problem of drug addiction among teenagers. This picture should serve as a deterrent."

The State Board of Censors relied on the fact that "The Man with the Golden Arm" did not receive the seal of approval of the Motion Picture Producers Association. However, that Association's disapproval of the picture was inevitable, as the Motion Picture Production Code disapproves of any motion pictures which portray addiction to narcotics. There was testimony in this case that United Artists Corporation resigned from the Motion Picture Producers Association because it did not agree with the taboo of the Association against films dealing with narcotics.

As the record in this case does not show that the censored part of the film violates the statute, the order of the Court below affirming the order of the Board will be reversed.

Order reversed, with costs.

■ United States of America, Appellee,

v.

Samuel Roth, Appellant.
No. 387, Docket 24030.

United States Court of Appeals Second Circuit.

Argued June 6, 1956. Decided Sept. 18, 1956.

Writ of Certiorari Granted

Jan. 14, 1957. See 77 S. Ct. 361.

Philip Wittenberg, New York City (Wittenberg, Carrington & Farnsworth and Irving Like, New York City, on the brief), for appellant.

George S. Leisure, Jr., Asst. U.S. Atty., S.D.N.Y., New York City (Paul W. Williams, U.S. Atty., New York City, on the brief), for appellee.

Before CLARK, Chief Judge, and FRANK and WATERMAN, Circuit Judges.

CLARK, Chief Judge.

This is an appeal by Samuel Roth from his conviction for violation of 18 U.S.C. § 1461. The indictment contained twenty-six counts charging the mailing of books, periodicals, and photographs (and circulars advertising some of them) alleged to be "obscene, lewd, lascivious, filthy and of an indecent character." Three counts were dismissed. After a trial the jury found defendant guilty on four counts, and not guilty on nineteen. The trial judge sentenced defendant to five years' imprisonment and to pay a fine of $5,000 on one count, while on each of the other three counts he gave a like term of imprisonment, to run concurrently, and a $1 fine remitted in each case. On this appeal, defendant claims error in the conduct of the trial, but once again attacks the constitutionality of the governing statute.

[1] This statute, 18 U.S.C. § 1461, originally passed as § 148 of the act of June 8, 1872, 17 Stat. 302, revising, consolidating, and amending the statutes relating to the Post Office Department, and thence derived from Rev. Stat. § 3893, herein declares unmailable "[e]very obscene, lewd, lascivious, or filthy book, pamphlet, picture, paper, letter, writing, print, or other publication of an indecent character,"[1] and makes the knowing deposit for mailing of such unmailable matter subject to a fine of not more than $5,000 or imprisonment of not more than five years, or both. In *United States* v. *Rebhuhn*, 2 Cir., 109 F. 2d 512, 514, certiorari denied *Rebhuhn* v. *United States*, 310 U.S. 629, 60 S. Ct. 976, 84 L. Ed. 1399, Judge Learned Hand, in dealing with a claim of unconstitutionality, pointed out that it had been overruled in *Rosen* v. *United States*, 161 U.S. 29, 16 S. Ct. 434, 480, 40 L. Ed. 606, "and many indictments have since been found, and many persons tried and convicted. * * * If the question is to be reopened the Supreme Court must open it." Since that decision many more cases have acknowledged the constitutionality of the statute, so much so that we feel it is not the part of responsible judicial administration for an inferior court such as ours, whatever our personal opinions, to initiate a new and uncharted course of overturn of a statute thus long regarded of vital social importance and a public policy of wide general support. It is easy, in matters touching the arts, to condescend to the poor troubled enforcement officials; but so to do will not carry us measurably nearer a permanent and generally acceptable solution of a continuing social problem.

Against this background we are impressed by the decision this year of a great court in *Brown* v. *Kingsley Books, Inc.*, 1 N.Y. 2d 177, 151 N.Y.S. 2d 639, 641, 642, 134 N.E. 2d 461, 463, where, accepting general constitutionality of such legislation, the decision breaks new ground in upholding authorization of preventive relief by way of

---

[1] As pointed out below, the quoted wording was somewhat expanded by Congress in 1955, after the commission of the offenses here involved.

injunction at the suit of a public officer.[2] In his opinion, Judge Fuld summarizes the controlling law thus: "That clearly drawn regulatory legislation to protect the public from the evils inherent in the dissemination of obscene matter, at least by the application of criminal sanctions, is not barred by the free speech guarantees of the First Amendment, has been recognized both by this court [citing cases] and by the United States Supreme Court [citing cases]." Among cases from New York which he cites is *People v. Doubleday & Co.*, 297 N.Y. 687, 77 N.E. 2d 6, affirmed by an equally divided court, 335 U.S. 848, 69 S. Ct. 79, 93 L. Ed. 398, while among the cases in the United States Supreme Court upon which he relies are *United States v. Alpers*, 338 U.S. 680, 70 S. Ct. 352, 94 L. Ed. 457; *Winters v. People of State of New York*, 333 U.S. 507, 510, 518, 520, 68 S. Ct. 665, 92 L. Ed. 840; and *United States v. Limehouse*, 285 U.S. 424, 52 S. Ct. 412, 76 L. Ed. 843. He goes on to say: "Imprecise though it be—its 'vague subject-matter' being largely 'left to the gradual development of general notions about what is decent' (per L. Hand, J., *United States v. Kennerley*, D.C., 209 F. 119, 121)—the concept of obscenity has heretofore been accepted as an adequate standard." In the case last cited, Judge Hand asked [209 F. 121], "* * * should not the word 'obscene' be allowed to indicate the present critical point in the compromise between candor and shame at which the community may have arrived here and now?" and continued: "If letters must, like other kinds of conduct, be subject to the social sense of what is right, it would seem that a jury should in each case establish the standard much as they do in cases of negligence." In quoting this with approval, the Ninth Circuit has recently said: "We think Judge Learned Hand was in the best of his famous form in his happy use of words." *Besig v. United States*, 9 Cir., 208 F. 2d 142, 147.

[2] So this important social problem, which has come down to us from English law and which has led to statutes of a generally similar nature in almost all of the other jurisdictions in this country, see *Brown v. Kingsley Books, Inc.*, supra, 1 N.Y. 2d 177, 151 N.Y.S. 2d 639, 134 N.E. 2d 461; Note, 22 U. of Chi. L. Rev. 216, has resulted in a general judicial unanimity in supporting such prosecutions. There is a considerable body of additional precedents beyond those cited above, both in the Supreme Court of the United States and in other federal jurisdictions, of which various examples are given in the footnote.[3] It will

not do to distinguish these cases as dicta or suggest that they have not considered modern problems. They are too many and too much of a piece to allow an intermediate court to make an inference of doubt in the circumstances. We can understand all the difficulties of censorship of great literature, and indeed the various foolish excesses involved in the banning of notable books, without feeling justified in casting doubt upon all criminal prosecutions, both state and federal, of commercialized obscenity. A serious problem does arise when real literature is censored; but in this case no such issues should arise, since the record shows only salable pornography. But even if we had more freedom to follow an impulse to strike down such legislation in the premises, we should need to pause because of our own lack of knowledge of the social bearing of this problem, or consequences of such an act;[4] and we are hardly justified in rejecting out of hand the strongly held views of those with competence in the premises as to the very direct connection of this traffic with the development of juvenile delinquency.[5] We conclude, therefore, that the attack on constitutionality of this statute must here fail.

[3] Defendant, however, takes special exception to the judge's treatment in his charge of the word "filthy," asserting that he opposed this term to the other parts of the

---

[2] The injunction against sale of paper-covered booklets "indisputably pornographic, indisputably obscene and filthy"—the words are Judge Fuld's, 1 N.Y. 2d 177, 151 N.Y.S. 2d 639, 640, 134 N.E. 2d 461, 462—was granted under a 1941 statute, N.Y. Code Cr. Proc. § 22–a, on suit of the Corporation Counsel of the City of New York. While the court was unanimous in holding the statute constitutional and the injunction proper, there were two opinions—a detailed analysis of the legal background by Judge Fuld, concurred in by two other judges, and a brief and more formal statement by Judge Desmond, concurred in by two other judges.

[3] See, e.g., *Ex parte Jackson*, 96 U.S. 727, 24 L. Ed. 877; *Swearingen v. United States*, 161 U.S. 446, 16 S. Ct. 562, 40 L. Ed. 765; *Dunlop v. United States*, 165 U.S. 486, 17 S. Ct. 375, 41 L. Ed. 799; *Public Clearing House v. Coyne*, 194 U.S. 497, 508, 24 S. Ct. 789, 48 L. Ed. 1092; *Robertson v. Baldwin*, 165 U.S. 275, 281, 17 S. Ct. 326, 41 L. Ed. 715; *Near v. State of Minnesota ex rel. Olson*, 283 U.S. 697, 716, 51 S. Ct. 625, 75 L. Ed. 1357; *Chaplinsky v. State of New Hampshire*, 315 U.S. 568,

571–572, 62 S. Ct. 766, 86 L. Ed. 1031; *Beauharnais v. People of State of Illinois*, 343 U.S. 250, 266, 72 S. Ct. 725, 96 L. Ed. 919; *Schindler v. United States*, 9 Cir., 221 F. 2d 743, certiorari denied 350 U.S. 938, 76 S. Ct. 310; *United States v. Hornick*, 3 Cir., 229 F. 2d 120, affirming D.C.E.D. Pa., 131 F. Supp. 603; *Roth v. Goldman*, 2 Cir., 172 F. 2d 788, certiorari denied 337 U.S. 938, 69 S. Ct. 1514, 93 L. Ed. 1743.

[4] See Fuld, J., in *Brown v. Kingsley Books, Inc.*, 1 N.Y. 2d 177, 151 N.Y.S. 2d 639, 641, note 3, 134 N.E. 2d 461, 463: "It is noteworthy that studies are for the first time being made, through such scientific skills as exist, concerning the impact of the obscene, in writings and other mass media, on the mind and behavior of men, women and children. (See, e.g., Jahoda and Staff of Research Center for Human Relations, New York University [1954], The Impact of Literature: A Psychological Discussion of Some Assumptions in the Censorship Debate.)"

[5] Sen. Rep. No. 113, 84th Cong., 1st Sess., supporting the 1955 amendment to § 1461 discussed below, has this to say: "The subcommittee of the Committee on the Judiciary investigating juvenile delinquency in the United States reports that the nationwide traffic in obscene matter is increasing year by year and that a large part of that traffic is being channeled into the hands of children. That subcommittee recommended implementation of the present statute so as to prevent the using of the mails in the trafficking of all obscene matter. The passage of S. 600 will contribute greatly in the continuing struggle to combat juvenile delinquency and the corruption of public morals." 2 U.S. Code Cong. & Adm. News 1955, p. 2211.

See also Chief Justice Vanderbilt, Impasses in Justice, [1956] Wash. U.L.Q. 267, 302: "(4) Our greatest concern with the oncoming generation, I submit, relates to the perversion of young minds through the mass media of the movies, television, radio, and the press, especially so-called comics. Wertham, Seduction of the Innocent (1954). See also Feder, Comic Book Regulation (Univ. of Calif. Bureau of Pub. Admin. 1955). The problem is only beginning to receive the consideration its seriousness calls for. Here is a field in which the law schools are well equipped to furnish leadership in a controversy where rare discrimination and courage are required."

Perhaps scholarly research may suggest better statutes than we have; but it is doubtful if help can be found in such suggestions as for the inclusion in legislation of the enticing invitation, "For Adults Only." Cf. Ernst & Seagle, To the Pure 277 (1928).

statute, so as to render the statute vague and indefinite. What the judge said was this: " 'Filthy' as used here must also relate to sexual matters. It is distinguishable from the term 'obscene,' which tends to promote lust and impure thoughts. 'Filthy' pertains to that sort of treatment of sexual matters in such a vulgar and indecent way, so that it tends to arouse a feeling of disgust and revulsion." But this seems to us in line with long-standing judicial definitions of the term. The words "and every filthy" were inserted in the statute at the time of the enactment of the Penal Code in 1909. And in *United States* v. *Limehouse,* supra, 285 U.S. 424, 426, 52 S. Ct. 412, in 1932, Mr. Justice Brandeis for the Court pointed out the obvious intent to add "a new class of unmailable matter—the filthy." As he definitely pointed out, this plainly covered sexual matters; and the Court, so he said, had no occasion to consider whether filthy matter of a different character also fell within the prohibition. We do not see how this case can be read other than as support for the interpretation made by the court below and for the validity of the Act as interpreted. Moreover, earlier it had been ruled by the Sixth Circuit in *Tyomies Pub. Co.* v. *United States,* 6 Cir., 211 F. 385, 390, in 1914, that the trial judge properly submitted the issue to the jury as to whether or not a picture was filthy with the explanation: " 'By the term "filthy" is meant what it commonly or ordinarily signifies; that which is nasty, dirty, vulgar, indecent, offensive to the moral sense, morally depraving and debasing.' " This is in substance what Judge Cashin charged here. See also *United States* v. *Davidson,* D.C.N.D.N.Y., 244 F. 523, 534, 535; *Sunshine Book Co.* v. *Summerfield,* D.C.D.C., 128 F. Supp. 564.

[4, 5] Hence, having in mind Judge Hand's admonition in *United States* v. *Kennerley,* supra, D.C.S.D.N.Y., 209 F. 119, 121, that the jury must finally apply the standard thus indicated, we think there was nothing objectionable in the judge's instructions to the jury. Certainly, against this background, "filthy" is as clear and as easily understandable by the jury[6] as the terms "obscene" and "lewd" already committed to its care. Possibly some different nuances might have been given the term—though we are not sure what, nor are we given suggestions—but we cannot believe that the jury would have been helped. Nor did the defendant at the time find anything to question in the charge; his counsel, after the judge had granted all the specific additional requests he made, said that the judge had "fairly covered everything." Now he is not in a position to press this objection. Here we have more than a waiver by failure to object. We have in fact an instance of submission of issues to the jury on more than a single ground which might have been separated had the parties so desired. Since no request for separate verdicts or for withdrawal of this issue from the jury was made, the conviction must stand as supported by the clear evidence of obscenity. *United States* v. *Mascuch,* 2 Cir., 111 F. 2d 602, certiorari denied *Mascuch* v. *United States,* 311 U.S. 650, 61 S. Ct. 14, 85 L. Ed. 416; *United States* v. *Smith,* 2 Cir., 112 F. 2d 83, 86; *United States* v. *Goldstein,* 2 Cir., 168 F. 2d 666, 672; *Claassen* v. *United States,* 142 U.S. 140, 147, 12 S. Ct. 169, 35 L. Ed. 966; *Stevens* v. *United States,* 6 Cir., 206 F. 2d 64, 66; *Todorow* v. *United States,* 9 Cir., 173 F. 2d 439, 445, certiorari denied 337 U.S. 925, 69 S. Ct. 1169, 93 L. Ed. 1733; *United States* v. *Myers,* D.C.N.D.

Cal., 131 F. Supp. 525, 528. On either ground, therefore, this assignment of error must fail.

Our conclusion here settles the substantial issues on this appeal. As we have indicated, if the statute is to be upheld at all it must apply to a case of this kind where defendant is an old hand at publishing and surreptitiously mailing to those induced to order them such lurid pictures and material as he can find profitable. There was ample evidence for the jury, and the defendant had an unusual trial in that the judge allowed him to produce experts, including a psychologist who stated that he would find nothing obscene at the present time. Also various modern novels were submitted to the jury for the sake of comparison. Very likely the jury's moderate verdict on only a few of the many counts submitted by the government and supported by the testimony of those who had been led to send their orders through the mail was because of this wide scope given the defense. As the judge pointed out in imposing sentence, defendant has been convicted several times before under both state and federal law. Indeed this case and our discussions somewhat duplicate his earlier appearance in *Roth* v. *Goldman,* 2 Cir., 172 F. 2d 788, certiorari denied 337 U.S. 938, 69 S. Ct. 1514, 93 L. Ed. 1743.

[6, 7] Defendant claims error in entrapment because his advertisements were answered by government representatives. But this method of obtaining evidence was specifically approved in *Rosen* v. *United States,* supra, 161 U.S. 29, 42, 16 S. Ct. 434, 438, 480, and has been usual at least ever since. *Ackley* v. *United States,* 8 Cir., 200 F. 217, 222. In no event was there any improper entrapment. See *United States* v. *Masciale,* 2 Cir., 236 F. 2d 601. The government's summation in the case was within the scope of the evidence, and the court's charge was concise and correct. But one other matter needs to engage our attention. That was the defendant's claim of error in that the court charged with respect to the statute as it was at the time of the offenses, although it had been amended on June 28, 1955, or before the trial. But this amendment was designed to stiffen the Act and arose because in *Alpers* v. *United States,* 9 Cir., 175 F. 2d 137, a conviction for mailing obscene phonograph records was reversed on the ground that such records were not clearly embodied in the statutory language quoted above. Although this decision was reversed and the conviction reinstated in *United States* v. *Alpers,* supra, 338 U.S. 680, 70 S. Ct. 352, the Congress was so anxious that there be no loophole that it enacted an amendment making unmailable now "[e]very obscene, lewd, lascivious, indecent, filthy or vile article, matter, thing, device, or substance."[7] It would seem clear, therefore, that defendant has no ground of complaint because he was tried under the statute existing at the time of his offense; and in no event could he have been harmed.

Judgment affirmed.

FRANK, Circuit Judge (concurring).

The reference in Judge Clark's opinion to juvenile delinquency might lead the casual reader to suppose that, under the statute, the test of what constitutes obscenity is its effect on minors, and that the defendant, Roth, has been convicted for mailing obscene writings to (or for sale

---

[6] And by Judge Fuld and his colleagues; see supra note 2.

[7] It also eliminated the former fifth paragraph now superfluous. See the Senate Report cited supra note 5.

to) children. This court, however, in *United States* v. *Levine*, 2 Cir., 83 F. 2d 156, has held that the correct test is the effect on the sexual thoughts and desires, not of the "young" or "immature," but of average, normal, adult persons. The trial judge here so instructed the jury.[1]

On the basis of that test, the jury could reasonably have found, beyond a reasonable doubt, that many of the books, periodicals, pamphlets and pictures which defendant mailed were obscene. Accordingly, I concur.[2]

I do so although I have much difficulty in reconciling the validity of that statute with opinions of the Supreme Court, uttered within the past twenty-five years,[3] relative to the First Amendment as applied to other kinds of legislation. The doctrine expressed in those opinions, as I understand it, may be summarized briefly as follows: Any statute authorizing governmental interference (whether by "prior restraint" or punishment) with free speech or free press runs counter to the First Amendment, except when the government can show that the statute strikes at words which are likely to incite to a breach of the peace,[4] or with sufficient probability tend either to the overthrow of the government by illegal means or to some other overt anti-social conduct.[5]

The troublesome aspect of the federal obscenity statute —as I shall try to explain in the Appendix to this opinion—is that (a) no one can now show that, with any reasonable probability obscene publications tend to have any effects on the behavior of normal, average adults, and (b) that under that statute, as judicially interpreted, punishment is apparently inflicted for provoking, in such adults, undesirable sexual thoughts, feelings, or desires— not overt dangerous or anti-social conduct, either actual or probable.

Often the discussion of First Amendment exceptions has been couched in terms of a " 'clear and present danger.' " However, the meaning of that phrase has been somewhat watered down by *Dennis* v. *United States*, 341 U.S. 494, 71 S. Ct. 857, 865, 95 L. Ed. 1137. The test now involves probability: " 'In each case (courts) must ask,' " said Chief Justice Vinson in Dennis, " 'whether the gravity of the "evil," discounted by its improbability, justifies such invasion of free speech as is necessary to avoid the danger.' " It has been suggested that the test now is this: "The more serious and threatened the evil, the lower the required degree of probability."[6] It would seem to follow that the less clear the danger, the more imminent must it be. At any rate, it would seem that (1) the danger or evil must be clear (i.e., identifiable) and substantial, and (2) that, since the statute renders words punishable, it is invalid unless those words tend, with a fairly high degree of probability, to incite to overt conduct which is obviously harmful. For, under the First Amendment, lawless or anti-social "acts are the main thing. Speech is not punishable for its own sake, but only because of its connection with those * * * acts * * * But more than a remote connection is necessary * * *"[7] See, e.g., American Communications Ass'n, *C.I.O.* v. *Douds*, 339 U.S. 382, 398, 70 S. Ct. 674, 683, 94 L. Ed. 925, as to "the right of the public to be protected from *evils of conduct*, even though the First Amendment rights of persons or groups are thereby in some manner infringed." (Emphasis added.)

As I read the Supreme Court's opinions, the government, in defending the constitutionality of a statute which curbs free expression, may not rely on the usual "presumption of validity." No matter how one may articulate the reasoning, it is now accepted doctrine that, when legislation affects free speech or free press, the government must show that the legislation comes within one of the exceptions described above. See, e.g., *Dennis* v. *United States*, 341 U.S. 494, 71 S. Ct. 857, 95 L. Ed. 1137; *Joseph Burstyn, Inc.* v. *Wilson*, 343 U.S. 495, 503, 72 S. Ct. 777, 96 L. Ed. 1098. Moreover, when legislation affects free expression, the void-for-vagueness doctrine has a pecu-

---

[1] He said: "The test is not whether it would arouse sexual desires or sexually impure thoughts in those comprising a particular segment of the community, the young, the immature or the highly prudish. * * * In other words, you must determine its impact upon the average person in the community."

[2] The statute condemns the mailing not only of "obscene" matter but also of "filthy" matter. Parts of the indictment here charged the defendant with mailing "filthy" publications. The trial judge told the jury they could convict the defendant for mailing a "filthy" publication, if they found that it treated "sexual matters in such a vulgar and indecent way so that it tends to arouse a feeling of disgust or aversion." The following contention might be urged:

The very argument advanced to sustain the statute's validity, so far as it condemns the obscene, goes to show the invalidity of the statute so far as it condemns "filth," if "filth" means that which renders sexual desires "disgusting." For if the argument be sound that the legislature may constitutionally provide punishment for the obscene because, anti-socially, it arouses sexual desires by making sex attractive, then it follows that whatever makes sex disgusting is socially beneficial—and thus not the subject of valid legislation which punishes the mailing of "filthy" matter. To avoid this seeming inconsistency, the statute should be interpreted as follows: The mailing of a "filthy" matter is a crime if that matter tends to induce acts by the recipient which will probably tend to cause breaches of the peace. This interpretation is in line with *United States* v. *Limehouse*, 285 U.S. 424, 52 S. Ct. 412, 76 L. Ed. 843. There the Court affirmed the conviction of a defendant who had mailed letters to divers persons which, in "foul language," accused them of sexual immorality. Those letters thus were within the category of "fighting words"—i.e., insulting words or the like—which may constitutionally be made criminal precisely because they tend to provoke breaches of the peace. Where, however, "filthy" language appears in a book, or picture, and involves no insults to particular persons, there will be no such consequences.

If this were the correct interpretation of "filthy," then that part of the statute condemning the "filthy" would not apply to the acts of the defendant here, and the judge's instructions re "filthy" would have been erroneous.

But I think we need not here consider that interpretation since I agree with my colleagues that, for the reasons they state, assuming there was error, the defendant's deliberate acquiescence in the judge's instructions prevents him from now so asserting.

[3] "For nearly 130 years after its adoption, the First Amendment received scant attention from the Supreme Court"; Emerson, The Doctrine of Prior Restraint, 20 L. & Cont. Problems (1955) 648, 652.

[4] See, e.g., *Chaplinsky* v. *State of New Hampshire*, 315 U.S. 568, 572, 62 S. Ct. 766, 86 L. Ed. 1031.

[5] The judicial enforcement of some private rights—as in suits, e.g., for defamation, injury to business, fraud, or invasion of privacy—comes within the exception.

[6] Lockhart and McClure, Obscenity and the Constitution, 38 Minn. L. Rev. (1954) 295, 357; cf. Kalven, The Law of Defamation and the First Amendment, in (University of Chicago) Conference on the Arts, Publishing and the Law (1952) 3, 12.

[7] Chafee, The Blessings of Liberty (1956) 69.

liar importance; and the obscenity statute is exquisitely vague. (See the Appendix, point 9.)

True, the Supreme Court has said several times that the federal obscenity statute (or any such state statute) is constitutional. But the Court has not directly so decided; it has done so *sub silentio* in applying the federal statute, or has referred to the constitutionality of such legislation in dicta. The Court has not thoroughly canvassed the problem in any opinion, nor applied to it the doctrine (summarized above) concerning the First Amendment which the Court has evolved in recent years. I base that statement on the following analysis of the cases:

In Ex parte Jackson, 1877, 96 U.S. 727, 24 L. Ed. 877, the Court held valid a statute relating to the mailing of letters, or circulars, concerning lotteries. Such letters or circulars might well induce the addressees to engage in the overt conduct of engaging in lotteries. The Court, only in passing, referred to the obscenity statute and said it, too, was valid.

In *Rosen* v. *United States*, 1896, 161 U.S. 29, 16 S. Ct. 434, 480, 40 L. Ed. 606, the issue was solely the sufficiency of an indictment under the obscenity statute, not the validity of that legislation, and the Court did not discuss its validity.

In *Swearingen* v. *United States*, 1896, 161 U.S. 446, 16 S. Ct. 562, 40 L. Ed. 765, the Court reversed a conviction under the obscenity statute; it did not consider its constitutionality.

Dunlop v. *United States*, 1896, 165 U.S. 486, at page 501, 17 S. Ct. 375, at page 380, 41 L. Ed. 799, did not discuss the constitutionality of the statute; moreover, the opinion shows that it dealt with advertisements soliciting improper sexual relations, i.e., with probable conduct, not with mere thoughts or desires.

In *Public Clearing House* v. *Coyne*, 1904, 194 U.S. 497, at page 508, 24 S. Ct. 789, at page 793, 48 L. Ed. 1092, which did not involve the validity of the obscenity Act, the Court said in passing that its constitutionality "has never been attacked."

In *United States* v. *Limehouse*, 1932, 285 U.S. 424, 52 S. Ct. 412, 76 L. Ed. 843, the Court decided the correct interpretation of the word "filthy" in the statute, and did not consider the question of constitutionality. Moreover, there the defendant had mailed letters attacking the characters of the recipients who might well have been moved to conduct in breach of the peace.

In *Winters* v. *People of State of New York*, 1948, 333 U.S. 507, 68 S. Ct. 665, 92 L. Ed. 840, the Court held void for vagueness a state statute making it a crime to distribute publications consisting principally of news or stories of criminal deeds of bloodshed or lust so massed as to become vehicles for inciting violent and depraved crimes. The Court said in passing, 333 U.S. at page 510, 68 S. Ct. at page 667, that legislation subjecting obscene publications to governmental control is valid.

In *Doubleday & Co.* v. *People of State of New York*, 1948, 335 U.S. 848, 69 S. Ct. 79, 93 L. Ed. 398, the Court, by an evenly divided vote, without opinion affirmed a state court decision sustaining a state obscenity statute.

In *United States* v. *Alpers*, 1950, 338 U.S. 680, 70 S. Ct. 352, 94 L. Ed. 457, the Court construed the statute as amended, and affirmed a conviction thereunder, but did not consider its constitutionality.

In the following cases, where the validity of no obscenity statute was involved, the Court, in passing, referred to such legislation as valid: *Robertson* v. *Baldwin*, 1897, 165 U.S. 275, 281, 17 S. Ct. 326, 41 L. Ed. 715; *Near* v. *State of Minnesota*, 1931, 283 U.S. 697, 716, 51 S. Ct. 625, 75 L. Ed. 1357; *Lovell* v. *City of Griffin*, 1938, 303 U.S. 444, 451, 58 S. Ct. 666, 82 L. Ed. 949; *Chaplinsky* v. *State of New Hampshire*, 1942, 315 U.S. 568, 571–572, 62 S. Ct. 766, 86 L. Ed. 1031; *Beauharnais* v. *People of State of Illinois*, 1952, 343 U.S. 250, 266, 72 S. Ct. 725, 96 L. Ed. 919.

I agree with my colleagues that, since ours is an inferior court, we should not hold invalid a statute which our superior has thus often said is constitutional (albeit without any full discussion). Yet I think it not improper to set forth, as I do in the Appendix, considerations concerning the obscenity statute's validity with which, up to now, I think the Supreme Court has not dealt in any of its opinions. I do not suggest the inevitability of the conclusion that that statute is unconstitutional. I do suggest that it is hard to avoid that conclusion, if one applies to that legislation the reasoning the Supreme Court has applied to other sorts of legislation. Perhaps I have overlooked conceivable compelling contrary arguments. If so, maybe my Appendix will evoke them.

To preclude misunderstanding of my purpose in stirring doubts about this statute, I think it well to add the following:

(a) As many of the publications mailed by defendant offend my personal taste, I would not cross a street to obtain them for nothing; I happen not to be interested in so-called "pornography"; and I think defendant's motives obnoxious. But if the statute were invalid, the merit of those publications would be irrelevant. *Winters* v. *People of State of New York*, 333 U.S. 507, 510, 68 S. Ct. 665, 92 L. Ed. 840. So, too, as to defendant's motives: "Although the defendant may be the worst of men * * * the rights of the best of men are secure only as the rights of the vilest and most abhorrent are protected."[8]

(b) It is most doubtful (as explained in the Appendix) whether anyone can now demonstrate that children's reading or looking at obscene matter has a probable causal relation to the children's anti-social conduct.[9] If, however, such a probable causal relation could be shown, there could be little doubt, I think, of the validity of a statute (if so worded as to avoid undue ambiguity) which specifically prohibits the distribution by mail of obscene publications for sale to young people. But discussion of such legislation is here irrelevant, since, to repeat, the existing federal statute is not thus restricted.

(c) Congress undoubtedly has wide power to protect public morals. But the First Amendment severely limits that power in the area of free speech and free press.

(d) It is argued that anti-obscenity legislation is valid

---

[8] Judge Cuthbert Pound dissenting in *People* v. *Gitlow*, 234 N.Y. 132, 158, 136 N.E. 317, 327.

[9] The Appendix contains a discussion of the writings of those described by Judge Clark as persons "with competence in the premises." It tries to show (1) that the overwhelming majority of persons with such competence assert that there is no justification for the thesis that a demonstrable causal relation exists between reading or seeing the obscene and anti-social conduct, even of children, and (2) that the chief proponent of the opposite view with respect to the effect on children's conduct does not maintain the same as to adult conduct.

because, at the time of the adoption of the First Amendment, obscenity was a common law crime. Relying (*inter alia*) on *Bridges* v. *State of California*, 314 U.S. 252, 264–265, 62 S. Ct. 190, 86 L. Ed. 192 and *Grosjean* v. *American Press Co.*, 297 U.S. 233, 248–249, 56 S. Ct. 444, 80 L. Ed. 660, I have tried in the Appendix to answer that argument.

(e) The First Amendment, of course, does not prevent any private body or group (including any Church) from instructing or seeking to persuade, its adherents or others not to read or distribute obscene (or other) publications. That constitutional provision—safe-guarding a principle indispensable in a true democracy—leaves unhampered all non-governmental means of molding public opinion about not reading literature which some think undesirable; and, in that respect, experience teaches that democratically exercised censorship by public opinion has far more potency, and is far less easily evaded, than censorship by government.[10] The incessant struggle to influence public opinion is of the very essence of the democratic process. A basic purpose of the First Amendment is to keep that struggle alive, by not permitting the dominant public opinion of the present to become embodied in legislation which will prevent the formation of a different dominant public opinion in the future.[11]

(f) At first glance it may seem almost frivolous to raise any question about the constitutionality of the obscenity statute at a time when many seemingly graver First Amendment problems confront the courts. But (for reasons stated in more detail in the Appendix) governmental censorship of writings, merely because they may stimulate, in the reader, sexual thoughts the legislature deems undesirable, has more serious implications than appear at first glance: We have been warned by eminent thinkers of the easy path from any apparently mild governmental control of what adult citizens may read to governmental control of adult's political and religious reading. John Milton, Thomas Jefferson, James Madison, J. S. Mill and Tocqueville have pointed out that any paternalistic guardianship by government of the thoughts of grown-up citizens enervates their spirit, keeps them immature, all too ready to adopt towards government officers the attitude that, in general, "Papa knows best." If the government possesses the power to censor publications which arouse sexual thoughts, regardless of whether those thoughts tend probably to transform themselves into anti-social behavior, why may not the government censor political and religious publications regardless of any causal relation to probable dangerous deeds? And even if we confine attention to official censorship of publications tending to stimulate sexual thoughts, it should be asked why, at any moment, that censorship cannot be extended to advertisements and

true reports or photographs, in our daily press, which, fully as much, may stimulate such thoughts?

(g) Assuming, *arguendo*, that a statute aims at an altogether desirable end, nevertheless its desirability does not render it constitutional. As the Supreme Court has said, "The good sought in unconstitutional legislation is an insidious feature, because it leads citizens and legislatures of good purpose to promote it without thought of the serious break it will make in the ark of our covenant. * * *"[12]

In a concurring opinion in *Roth* v. *Goldman*, 2 Cir., 1948, 172 F. 2d 788, 790, I voiced puzzlement about the constitutionality of administrative prior restraint of obscene books. I then had little doubt about the validity of a purely punitive obscenity statute. But the next year, in *Commonwealth* v. *Gordon*, 1949, 66 Pa. Dist. & Co. R. 101, Judge Curtis Bok, one of America's most reflective judges, directly attacked the validity of any such punitive legislation. His brilliant opinion, which states arguments that (so far as I know) have never been answered, nudged me into the skeptical views contained in this opinion and the Appendix.

Appendix

As a judge of an inferior court, I am constrained by opinions of the Supreme Court concerning the obscenity statute to hold that legislation valid. Since, however, I think (as indicated in the foregoing) that none of those opinions has carefully canvassed the problem in the light of the Supreme Court's interpretation of the First Amendment, especially as expressed by the Court in recent years, I deem it not improper to set forth, in the following, factors which I think deserve consideration in passing on the constitutionality of that statute.

1. Benjamin Franklin, in 1776 unanimously designated Postmaster General by the First Continental Congress, is appropriately known as the "father of the Post Office." Among his published writings are two[1]—*Letter of Advice to Young Men on the Proper Choosing of a Mistress and The Speech of Polly Baker*—which a jury could reasonably find "obscene," according to the judge's instructions in the case at bar. On that basis, if tomorrow a man were to send those works of Franklin through the mails, he would be subject to prosecution and (if the jury found him guilty) to punishment under the federal obscenity statute.[2]

That fact would surely have astonished Jefferson, who extolled Franklin as an American genius,[3] called him "venerable and beloved" of his countrymen,[4] and wrote approvingly of Franklin's *Polly Baker*.[5] No less would it

---

[10] Public opinion, by influencing social attitudes, may create a convention, with no governmental "sanction" behind it, far more coercive than any statute. Cf. Holmes, Codes and The Arrangement of the Law; 2 Am. L. Rev. (1870) 4, 5.

Notably is this true of conventions as to obscenity; La Barre, Obscenity: An Anthropological Appraisal, 20 L. & Con. Problems (1955) 533.

[11] The results of the pressure of current public opinion may not always be happy. But our democracy accepts the postulate that, in the long run, the struggle to sway public opinion will produce the wisest policies. For further discussion of this theme, see the Appendix.

[12] The Child Labor Tax Case, *Bailey* v. *Drexel Furniture Co.*, 259 U.S. 20, 37, 42 S. Ct. 449, 450, 66 L. Ed. 817.

[1] See Van Doren, Benjamin Franklin (1938) 150–151, 153–154.

Franklin's *Letter to The Academy of Brussels* (see Van Doren, 151–152) might be considered "filthy."

[2] 18 U.S.C. § 1461.

[3] Jefferson, Notes on the State of Virginia (1781–1785), Query VI; See Padover, The Complete Jefferson (1943) 567 at 612.

[4] Jefferson, Autobiography (1821); See Padover, loc. cit., 1119 at 1193.

[5] Jefferson, Anecdotes of Franklin (1818); see Padover, loc. cit., 892 at 893.

have astonished Madison, also an admirer of Franklin (whom he described as a man whose "genius" was "an ornament of human nature")[5a] and himself given to telling "Rabelaisian anecdotes."[6] Nor was the taste of these men unique in the American Colonies: "Many a library of a colonial planter in Virginia or a colonial intellectual in New England boasted copies of Tom Jones, Tristram Shandy, Ovid's Art of Love, and Rabelais. * * *"[7]

As, with Jefferson's encouragement, Madison, in the first session of Congress, introduced what became the First Amendment, it seems doubtful that the constitutional guaranty of free speech and free press could have been intended to allow Congress validity to enact the "obscenity" Act. That doubt receives reinforcement from the following:

In 1799, eight years after the adoption of the First Amendment, Madison, in an Address to the General Assembly of Virginia,[8] said that the "truth of opinion" ought not to be subject to "imprisonment, to be inflicted by those of a different opinion"; he there also asserted that it would subvert the First Amendment[9] to make a "distinction between the freedom and the licentiousness of the press." Previously, in 1792, he wrote that "a man has property in his opinions and free communication of them," and that a government which "violates the property which individuals have in their opinion * * * is not a pattern for the United States."[10] Jefferson's proposed Constitution for Virginia (1776), provided: "Printing presses shall be free, except so far as by commission of private injury cause may be given of private action."[11] In his Second Inaugural Address (1805), he said: "No inference is here intended that the laws provided by the State against false and defamatory publications should not be enforced * * * The press, confined to truth, needs no other restraint * * *; and no other definite line can be drawn between the inestimable liberty of the press and demoralizing licentiousness. If there still be improprieties which this rule would not restrain, its supplement must be sought in the censorship of public opinion."

The broad phrase in the First Amendment, prohibiting legislation abridging "freedom of speech, or of the press," includes the right to speak and write freely for the public concerning any subject. As the Amendment specifically refers to "the free exercise [of religion]" and to the right "of the people * * * to assemble" and to "petition the Government for a redress of grievances," it specifically includes the right freely to speak to and write for the public concerning government and religion; but it does not limit this right to those topics. Accordingly, the views of Jefferson and Madison about the freedom to speak and write concerning religion are relevant to a consideration of the constitutional freedom in respect of all other subjects. Consider, then, what those men said about freedom of religious discussion: Madison, in 1799, denouncing the distinction "between the freedom and the licentiousness of the press" said, "By its help, the judge as to what is licentious may escape through any constitutional restriction," and added, "Under it, Congress might denominate a religion to be heretical and licentious, and proceed to its suppression * * * Remember * * * that it is to the press mankind are indebted for having dispelled the clouds which long encompassed religion * * *"[12] Jefferson, in 1798, quoting the First Amendment, said it guarded "in the same sentence, and under the same words, the freedom of religion, of speech, and of the press; insomuch, that whatever violates either, throws down the sanctuary which covers the others."[13] In 1814, he wrote in a letter, "I am really mortified to be told that in the United States of America, a fact like this (the sale of a book) can become a subject of inquiry, and of criminal inquiry too, as an offense against religion; that (such) a question can be carried before the civil magistrate. Is this then our freedom of religion? And are we to have a censor whose imprimatur shall say what books may be sold and what we may buy? * * * Whose foot is to be the measure to which ours are all to be cut or stretched?"[14]

Those utterances high-light this fact: Freedom to speak publicly and to publish has, as its inevitable and important correlative, the private rights to hear, to read, and to think and to feel about what one hears and reads. The First Amendment protects those private rights of hearers and readers.

We should not forget that, prompted by Jefferson,[15] Madison (who at one time had doubted the wisdom of a Bill of Rights)[16] when he urged in Congress the enactment of what became the first ten Amendments, declared, "If they are incorporated into the Constitution, independent tribunals of justice will consider themselves in a peculiar manner the guardian of those rights; they will be an impenetrable barrier against every assumption of power in the Legislative or Executive; they will be naturally led to

---

[5a] On Franklin's death, Madison offered the following resolution which the House of Representatives unanimously adopted: "The House being informed of the decease of Benjamin Franklin, a citizen whose genius was not more of an ornament of human nature than his various exertions of it have been to science, to freedom and to his country, do resolve, as a mark of veneration due to his memory, that the members wear the customary badge of mourning for one month." Brant, James Madison, Father of the Constitution (1950) 309; Annals, April 22, 1790.

[6] Padover, The Complete Madison (1953) 8–9.
George Washington, who knew Franklin well, treasured a gold-headed cane given him by Franklin. See Padover, The Washington Papers (1955) 112.
See Judge Bok, in *Commonwealth* v. *Gordon*, 66 Pa. Dist. & Co. R. 101, 120–121: "One need only recall that the father of the post office, Benjamin Franklin, wrote and presumably mailed his letter of Advice to Young Men on the Proper Choosing of a Mistress; * * * that Alexander Hamilton's adultery while holding public office created no great scandal * * *"

[7] Ernst and Seagle, To The Pure (1928) 108.
Everyone interested in obscenity legislation owes a deep debt to many writings on the subject by Morris Ernst. For such an acknowledgment, see Acknowledgments in Blanshard, The Right to Read (1955).

[8] See Padover, The Complete Madison (1953) 295–296.
[9] Madison referred to the "Third Amendment," but the context shows he meant the First.
[10] See Padover, The Complete Madison (1953) 267, 268–269.
[11] Padover, The Complete Jefferson (1943) 109.

[12] Madison, Address to the General Assembly of Virginia, 1799; see Padover, The Complete Madison (1953) 295.
[13] See Padover, The Complete Jefferson (1943) 130.
[14] See Padover, The Complete Jefferson (1943) 889.
[15] Jefferson's Letter to Madison (1789); Padover, The Complete Jefferson (1943) 123–125. See also Brant, James Madison, Father of the Constitution (1950) 267.
[16] The Federalist No. 84; Cahn, The Firstness of the First Amendment, 65 Yale L.J. (1956) 464.

resist every encroachment upon rights expressly stipulated for in the Constitution by the declaration of rights."[17] In short, the Bill of Rights, including the First Amendment, was not designed merely as a set of admonitions to the legislature and the executive; its provisions were to be enforced by the courts.

Judicial enforcement necessarily entails judicial interpretation. The question therefore arises whether the courts, in enforcing the First Amendment, should interpret it in accord with the views prevalent among those who sponsored and adopted it or in accord with subsequently developed views which would sanction legislation more restrictive of free speech and free press.

So the following becomes pertinent: Some of those who in the 20th Century endorse legislation suppressing "obscene" literature have an attitude towards freedom of expression which does not match that of the framers of the First Amendment (adopted at the end of the 18th Century) but does stem from an attitude, towards writings dealing with sex, which arose decades later, in the mid-19th Century, and is therefore labelled—doubtless too sweepingly—"Victorian." It was a dogma of "Victorian morality" that sexual misbehavior would be encouraged if one were to "acknowledge its existence or at any rate to present it vividly enough to form a life-like image of it in the reader's mind"; this morality rested on a "faith that you could best conquer evil by shutting your eyes to its existence,"[18] and on a kind of word magic.[19] The demands at that time for "decency" in published words did not comport with the actual sexual conduct of many of those who made those demands: "The Victorians, as a general rule, managed to conceal the 'coarser' side of their lives so thoroughly under a mask of respectability that we often fail to realize how 'coarse' it really was * * * Could we have recourse to the vast unwritten literature of bawdry, we should be able to form a more veracious notion of life as it (then) really was." The respectables of those days often, "with unblushing license," held "high revels" in "night houses."[20] Thanks to them, Mrs. Warren's profession flourished, but it was considered sinful to talk about it in books.[21] Such a prudish and purely verbal moral code, at odds (more or less hypocritically) with the actual conduct of its adherents[22] was (as we have seen) not the moral code of those who framed the First Amend-

ment.[23] One would suppose, then, that the courts should interpret and enforce that Amendment according to the views of those framers, not according to the later "Victorian" code.[24]

The "founding fathers" did not accept the common law concerning freedom of expression

It has been argued that the federal obscenity statute is valid because obscenity was a common law crime at the time of the adoption of the First Amendment. Quite aside from the fact that, previous to the Amendment, there had been scant recognition of this crime, the short answer seems to be that the framers of the Amendment knowingly and deliberately intended to depart from the English common law as to freedom of speech and freedom of the press. See *Grosjean* v. *American Press Co.*, 297 U.S. 233, 248–249, 56 S. Ct. 444, 80 L. Ed. 660; *Bridges* v. *State of California*, 314 U.S. 252, 264–265, 62 S. Ct. 190, 86 L. Ed. 192;[24a] Patterson, Free Speech and a Free Press

---

[17] Madison, Writings (Hunt ed.) V, 385; Corwin, Liberty Against Government (1948) 58–59; Cahn, The Firstness of the First Amendment, 64 Yale L.J. (1956) 464, 468.

[18] Wingfield-Stratford, Those Earnest Victorians (1930) 151.

[19] See Kaplan, Obscenity as an Esthetic Category, 20 Law & Contemp. Problems (1955) 544, 550: "In many cultures, obscenity has an important part in magical rituals. In our own, its magical character is betrayed in the puritan's supposition that words alone can work evil, and that evil will be averted if only the words are not uttered."

[20] Wingfield-Stratford, loc. cit., 296–297.

[21] Paradoxically, this attitude apparently tends to "create" obscenity. For the foundation of obscenity seems to be secrecy and shame: "The secret becomes shameful because of its secrecy." Kaplan, Obscenity as an Esthetic Category, 20 Law & Contemp. Problems (1955) 544, 556.

[22] To be sure, every society has "pretend-rules" (moral and legal) which it publicly voices but does not enforce. Indeed, a gap necessarily exists between a society's ideals, if at all exalted, and its practices. But the extent of the gap is significant. See, e.g., Frank, Lawlessness, Encyc. of Soc. Sciences (1932); cf. Frank, Preface to Kahn, A Court for Children (1953).

[23] It is of interest that not until the Tariff Act of 1824 did Congress enact any legislation relative to obscenity.

[24] For discussion of the suggestion that many constitutional provisions provide merely minimum safeguards which may properly be enlarged—not diminished—to meet newly emerging needs and policies, see Supreme Court and Supreme Law (Cahn ed. 1954) 59–64.

[24a] In *Bridges* v. *State of California*, 314 U.S. 252, 264–265, 62 S. Ct. 190, 194, the Court said: "In any event it need not detain us, for to assume that English common law in this field became ours is to deny the generally accepted historical belief that 'one of the objects of the Revolution was to get rid of the English common law on liberty of speech and of the press.' Schofield, Freedom of the Press in the United States, 9 Publications Amer. Sociol. Soc., 67, 76. More specifically, it is to forget the environment in which the First Amendment was ratified. In presenting the proposals which were later embodied in the Bill of Rights, James Madison, the leader in the preparation of the First Amendment said: 'Although I know whenever the great rights, the trial by jury, freedom of the press, or liberty of conscience, come in question in that body (Parliament), the invasion of them is resisted by able advocates, yet their Magna Charta does not contain any one provision for the security of those rights, respecting which the people of America are most alarmed. The freedom of the press and rights of conscience, those choicest privileges of the people, are unguarded in the British Constitution.' 1 Annals of Congress 1789–1790, 434. And Madison elsewhere wrote that 'the state of the press * * * under the common law, cannot * * * be the standard of its freedom in the United States.' VI Writings of James Madison 1790–1802, 387. There are no contrary implications in any part of the history of the period in which the First Amendment was framed and adopted. No purpose in ratifying the Bill of Rights was clearer than that of securing for the people of the United States much greater freedom of religion, expression, assembly, and petition than the people of Great Britain had ever enjoyed. It cannot be denied, for example, that the religious test oath or the restrictions upon assembly then prevalent in England would have been regarded as measures which the Constitution prohibited the American Congress from passing. And since the same unequivocal language is used with respect to freedom of the press, it signifies a similar enlargement of that concept as well. Ratified as it was while the memory of many oppressive English restrictions on the enumerated liberties was still fresh, the First Amendment cannot reasonably be taken as approving prevalent English Practices. On the contrary, the only conclusion supported by history is that the unqualified prohibitions laid down by the framers were intended to give to liberty of the press, as to the other

(1939) 101–102, 124–125, 128; Schofield, 2 Constitutional Law and Equity (1921) 521–525.

Of course, the legislature has wide power to protect what it considers public morals. But the First Amendment severely circumscribes that power (and all other legislative powers) in the area of speech and free press.

Subsequent punishment as, practically, prior restraint

For a long time, much was made of the distinction between a statute calling for "prior restraint" and one providing subsequent criminal punishment;[25] the former alone, it was once said, raised any question of constitutionality *vis-à-vis* the First Amendment.[26] Although it may still be true that more is required to justify legislation providing "preventive" than "punitive" censorship,[27] this

---

liberties, the broadest scope that could be countenanced in an orderly society."

In *Grosjean* v. *American Press Co.*, 297 U.S. 233, 248–249, 56 S. Ct. 444, 448, 80 L. Ed. 660, the Court said: "It is impossible to concede that by the words 'freedom of the press' the framers of the amendment intended to adopt merely the narrow view then reflected by the law of England that such freedom consisted only in immunity from previous censorship; for this abuse had then permanently disappeared from English practice. * * * Undoubtedly, the range of a constitutional provision phrased in terms of the common law sometimes may be fixed by recourse to the applicable rules of that law. But the doctrine which justifies such recourse, like other canons of construction, must yield to more compelling reasons whenever they exist. Cf. *Continental Illinois Nat. Bank & Trust Co. of Chicago* v. *Chicago, R.I. & P. Ry. Co.*, 294 U.S. 648, 668–669, 55 S. Ct. 595, 79 L. Ed. 1110. And, obviously, it is subject to the qualification that the common-law rule invoked shall be one not rejected by our ancestors as unsuited to their civil or political conditions. *Den ex rel. Murray's Lessee* v. *Hoboken Land & Improvement Co.*, 18 How. 272, 276–277, 15 L. Ed. 372; *Waring* v. *Clarke*, 5 How. 441, 454–457, 12 L. Ed. 226; *Powell* v. *State of Alabama*, supra, 287 U.S. 45, at pages 60–65, 53 S. Ct. 55, 77 L. Ed. 158. In the light of all that has now been said, it is evident that the restricted rules of the English law in respect of the freedom of the press in force when the Constitution was adopted were never accepted by the American colonists * * *."

[25] Blackstone, most influentially, made this distinction; 4 Blackstone, Commentary, 151–162. His condonation of punishment reflected the views of his patron, Lord Mansfield, who, an opponent of a free press, took an active part in punishing published criticism of the government.

But men like Jefferson and James Wilson abhorred the Tory political views of Blackstone and Mansfield, both of whom had ranked high in the opposition to the American Colonists. Jefferson wrote to Madison of "the horrid Mansfieldism of Blackstone which had caused many young American lawyers to slide into Toryism." Jefferson applauded Tucker's "republicanized" edition of Blackstone published in 1803. See Frank, A Sketch of An Influence, in the volume Interpretations of Modern Legal Philosophers (1947) 189, especially 231; see also 191, 196–198, 205, 207, 210, 215–217. For James Wilson's denunciation of Blackstone's political attitudes, see, e.g., Wilson's opinion in *Chisholm* v. *State of Georgia*, 2 Dall. 419, 453, 458, 462, 1 L. Ed. 440.

[26] See Holmes, J. in *Patterson* v. *State of Colorado*, 1907, 205 U.S. 454, 27 S. Ct. 556, 51 L. Ed. 879 citing Blackstone. But compare his subsequent dissenting opinion in *Abrams* v. *United States*, 1919, 250 U.S. 616, 624, 40 S. Ct. 17, 20, 63 L. Ed. 1173, which abandons Blackstone's dichotomy.

[27] For these phrases, see Lasswell, Censorship, 3 Ency. of Soc. Sc. (1930) 290, 291.

---

distinction has been substantially eroded. See, e.g., *Dennis* v. *United States*, 341 U.S. 494, 71 S. Ct. 857, 95 L. Ed. 1137; *Schenck* v. *United States*, 249 U.S. 47, 39 S. Ct. 247, 63 L. Ed. 470; *De Jonge* v. *State of Oregon*, 299 U.S. 353, 57 S. Ct. 255, 81 L. Ed. 278; *Thornhill* v. *State of Alabama*, 310 U.S. 88, 97–98, 60 S. Ct. 736, 84 L. Ed. 1093; *Chaplinsky* v. *State of New Hampshire*, 315 U.S. 568, 572, Note 3, 62 S. Ct. 766, 86 L. Ed. 1031. See also Hale, Freedom Through Law (1952) 257–265; Emerson, The Doctrine of Prior Restraint, 20 Law & Contemp. Problems (1955) 648 (a thought-stirring discussion of the problem); Kalven, loc. cit. at 8–10, 13. (For further discussion of this theme, see infra.)

The statute, as judicially interpreted, authorizes punishment for inducing mere thoughts, and feelings, or desires

For a time, American courts adopted the test of obscenity contrived in 1868 by Cockburn, L.J., in *Queen* v. *Hicklin*, L.R. 3 Q.B. 360: "I think the test of obscenity is this, whether the tendency of the matter charged as obscenity is to deprave and corrupt those whose minds are open to such immoral influences, and into whose hands a publication of this sort might fall." He added that the book there in question "would suggest * * thoughts of a most impure and libidinous character."

The test in most federal courts has changed: They do not now speak of the thoughts of "those whose minds are open to * * * immoral influences" but, instead, of the thoughts of average adult normal men and women, determining what these thoughts are, not by proof at the trial, but by the standard of "the average conscience of the time," the current "social sense of what is right." See, e.g., *United States* v. *Kennerley*, D.C., 209 F. 119, 121; *United States* v. *Levine*, 2 Cir., 83 F. 2d 156, 157; *Parmelee* v. *United States*, 72 App. D.C. 203, 113 F. 2d 729. Yet the courts still define obscenity in terms of the assumed average normal adult reader's sexual thoughts or desires or impulses, without reference to any relation between those "subjective" reactions and his subsequent conduct. The judicial opinions use such key phrases as this: "suggesting lewd thoughts and exciting sensual desires";[28] "arouse the salacity of the reader,"[29] "'allowing or implanting * * * obscene, lewd, or lascivious thoughts or desires,'"[30] "arouse sexual desires."[30a] The judge's charge in the instant case reads accordingly: "It must tend to stir sexual impulses and lead to sexually impure thoughts." Thus the statute, as the courts construe it, appears to provide criminal punishment for inducing no more than thoughts, feelings, desires.

No adequate knowledge is available concerning the effects on the conduct of normal adults of reading or seeing the "obscene"

Suppose we assume, *arguendo*, that sexual thoughts or feelings, stirred by the "obscene," probably will often issue

---

[28] *United States* v. *Dennett*, 2 Cir., 39 F. 2d 564, 568, 76 A.L.R. 1092.

[29] *United States* v. *Levine*, 2 Cir., 83 F. 2d 156, 158.

[30] *Burstein* v. *United States*, 2 Cir., 178 F. 2d 665, 667.

[30a] *American Civil Liberties Union* v. *City of Chicago*, 3 Ill. 2d 334, 121 N.E. 2d 585, 592.

into overt conduct. Still it does not at all follow that that conduct will be anti-social. For no sane person can believe it socially harmful if sexual desires lead to normal, and not anti-social, sexual behavior since, without such behavior, the human race would soon disappear.[31]

Doubtless, Congress could validly provide punishment for mailing any publications if there were some moderately substantial reliable data showing that reading or seeing those publications probably conduces to seriously harmful sexual conduct on the part of normal adult human beings. But we have no such data.

Suppose it argued that whatever excites sexual longings might *possibly* produce sexual misconduct. That cannot suffice: Notoriously, perfumes sometimes act as aphrodisiacs, yet no one will suggest that therefore Congress may constitutionally legislate punishment for mailing perfumes. It may be that among the stimuli to irregular sexual conduct, by normal men and women, may be almost anything —the odor of carnations or cheese, the sight of a cane or a candle or a shoe, the touch of silk or a gunnysack. For all anyone now knows, stimuli of that sort may be far more provocative of such misconduct than reading obscene books or seeing obscene pictures. Said John Milton, "Evil manners are as perfectly learnt, without books, a thousand other ways that cannot be stopped."

Effect of "obscenity" on adult conduct

To date there exist, I think, no thorough-going studies by competent persons which justify the conclusion that normal adults' reading or seeing of the "obscene" probably induces anti-social conduct. Such competent studies as have been made do conclude that so complex and numerous are the causes of sexual vice that it is impossible to assert with any assurance that "obscenity" represents a ponderable causal factor in sexually deviant adult behavior. "Although the whole subject of obscenity censorship hinges upon the unproved assumption that 'obscene' literature is a significant factor in causing sexual deviation from the community standard, no report can be found of a single effort at genuine research to test this assumption by singling out as a factor for study the effect of sex literature upon sexual behavior."[32] What little competent research has been done, points definitely in a direction precisely opposite to that assumption.

Alpert reports[33] that, when, in the 1920s, 409 women college graduates were asked to state in writing what things stimulated them sexually, they answered thus: 218 said

"Man"; 95 said books; 40 said drama; 29 said dancing; 18 said pictures; 9 said music. Of those who replied "that the source of their sex information came from books, not one specified a 'dirty' book as the source. Instead, the books listed were: The Bible, the dictionary, the encyclopedia, novels from Dickens to Henry James, circulars about venereal diseases, medical books, and Motley's Rise of the Dutch Republic." Macaulay, replying to advocates of the suppression of obscene books, said: "We find it difficult to believe that in a world so full of temptations as this, any gentleman whose life would have been virtuous if he had not read Aristophanes or Juvenal, will be vicious by reading them." Echoing Macaulay, "Jimmy" Walker remarked that he had never heard of a woman seduced by a book. New Mexico has never had an obscenity statute; there is no evidence that, in that state, sexual misconduct is proportionately greater than elsewhere.

Effect on conduct of young people

Most federal courts (as above noted) now hold that the test of obscenity is the effect on the "mind" of the average normal adult, that effect being determined by the "average conscience of the time," the current "sense of what is right"; and that the statute does not intend "to reduce our treatment of sex to the standard of a child's library in the supposed interest of a salacious few"; *United States* v. *Kennerley*, D.C., 209 F. 120, 121.

However, there is much pressure for legislation, designed to prevent juvenile delinquency, which will single out children, i.e., will prohibit the sale to young persons of "obscenity" or other designated matter. That problem does not present itself here, since the federal statute is not thus limited. The trial judge in his charge in the instant case told the jury that the "test" under that statute is not the effect of the mailed matter on "those comprising a particular segment of the community," the "young" or "the immature"; and see *United States* v. *Levine*, 2 Cir., 83 F. 2d 156, 157.

Therefore a discussion of such a children's protective statute is irrelevant here. But, since Judge Clark does discuss the alleged linkage of obscenity to juvenile delinquency, and since it may perhaps be thought that it has some bearing on the question of the effect of obscenity on adult conduct, I too shall discuss it.

The following is a recent summary of studies of that subject:[33a] "(1) Scientific[33b] studies of juvenile delinquency demonstrate that those who get into trouble, and are the greatest concern of the advocates of censorship, are far less inclined to read than those who do not become delinquent. The delinquents are generally the adventurous type, who have little use for reading and other nonactive entertainment. Thus, even assuming that reading sometimes has an adverse effect upon moral behavior, the effect is not likely to be substantial, for those who are susceptible seldom read. (2) Sheldon and Eleanor Glueck, who are

---

[31] Cf. the opinion of Mr. Justice Codd in *Integrated Press* v. *The Postmaster General*, as reported in Herbert, Codd's Last Case (1952) 14, 16: "Nor is the Court much impressed by the contention that the frequent contemplation of young ladies in bathing dresses must tend to the moral corruption of the community. On the contrary, these ubiquitous exhibitions have so diminished what was left of the mystery of womanhood that they might easily be condemned upon another ground of public policy, in that they tended to destroy the natural fascination of the female, so that the attention of the male population was diverted from thoughts of marriage to cricket, darts, motorbicycling and other occupations which do nothing to arrest the decline of the population."

[32] Lockhart and McClure, Obscenity and The Courts, 20 L. & Contemp. P. (1955) 587, 595.

[33] See Alpert, Judicial Censorship and The Press, 52 Harv. L. Rev. (1938) 40, 72.

[33a] Lockhart and McClure, Literature, The Law of Obscenity and The Constitution, 38 Minn. L. Rev. (1954) 295, 385–386.

Perhaps some of the reasoning of this summary is a bit too sweeping. For a more cautious summary, see the Jahoda report, discussed infra.

[33b] I, for one, deplore the use of the word "scientific" as applied to social studies. See, e.g., Frank, 4 J. of Public Law (1955) 8.

among the country's leading authorities on the treatment and causes of juvenile delinquency, have recently published the results of a ten-year study of its causes. They exhaustively studied approximately 90 factors and influences that might lead to or explain juvenile delinquency; but the Gluecks gave no consideration to the type of reading material, if any were read by the delinquents. This is, of course, consistent with their finding that delinquents read very little. When those who know so much about the problem of delinquency among youth—the very group about whom the advocates of censorship are most concerned—conclude that what delinquents read has so little effect upon their conduct that it is not worth investigating in an exhaustive study of causes, there is good reason for serious doubts concerning the basic hypothesis on which obscenity censorship is dependent. (3) The many other influences in society that stimulate sexual desire are so much more frequent in their influence and so much more potent in their effect that the influence of reading is likely, at most, to be relatively insignificant in the composite of forces that lead an individual into conduct deviating from the community sex standards. * * * And the studies demonstrating that sex knowledge seldom results from reading indicates the relative unimportance of literature in sexual thoughts and behavior as compared with other factors in society."[34]

[34] Novick, Superintendent of the New York Training School for Girls, writes: "In the public eye today juvenile delinquency is alternately the direct result of progressive education, horror comics, T.V. programs, and other pet peeves of our present society * * * This is not a new phenomenon. Each generation of adults has been concerned about the behavior of its children and has looked for a scapegoat on which to place the blame for its delinquency. At the same time, adults have always sought a panacea which would cure the problem. It is sufficient to note that delinquency has always risen during periods of stress and strain, and the era in which we are living is no exception * * * Neither do restrictive measures such as * * * censorship of reading matter * * * prevent delinquency. They merely have an effect upon the manner in which the delinquency will be expressed." Novick, Integrating the Delinquent and His Community, 20 Fed. Probation, 38, 40 (1956).

Charles Lamb (whose concern with children he manifested in his Tales From Shakespeare) had no belief that uncensored reading harmed children: In his Essays of Elia he wrote of the education of his cousin Bridget, "She was tumbled early into a spacious closet of good old English reading" (which included Elizabethan and Restoration dramas and 18th century novels) "without much selection or prohibition and browsed at will upon that fair and wholesome pasturage. Had I twenty girls, they should be brought up exactly in this fashion."

Judge Curtis Bok, perhaps remembering Lamb's remarks, said of the publications before him in Commonwealth v. Gordon, 1949, 66 Pa. Dist. & Co. R. 101: "It will be asked whether one would care to have one's young daughter read these books. I suppose that by the time she is old enough to wish to read them she will have learned the biologic facts of life and the words that go with them. There is something seriously wrong at home if those facts have not been met and faced and sorted by then; it is not children so much as parents that should receive our concern about this. I should prefer that my own three daughters meet the facts of life and the literature of the world in my library than behind a neighbor's barn, for I can face the adversary there directly. If the young ladies are appalled by what they read, they can close the book at the bottom of page one; if they read further, they will learn what is in the world and in its people, and no parents who have been discerning with their children need fear the outcome. Nor can they hold it back, for life is a

Judge Clark, however, speaks of "the strongly held views of those with competence in the premises as to the very direct connection" of obscenity "with the development of juvenile delinquency." He cites and quotes from a recent opinion of the New York Court of Appeals and an article by Judge Vanderbilt, which in turn, cite the writings of persons thus described by Judge Clark as "those with competence in the premises." One of the cited writings is a report, by Dr. Jahoda and associates, entitled The Impact of Literature: A Psychological Discussion of Some Assumptions in the Censorship Debate (1954).[35] I have read this report (which is a careful survey of all available studies and psychological theories). I think it expresses an attitude quite contrary to that indicated by Judge Clark. In order to avoid any possible bias in my interpretation of that report, I thought it well to ask Dr. Jahoda to write her own summary of it, which, with her permission, I shall quote. (In doing so, I am following the example of Mr. Justice Jackson who, in Federal Trade Commission v. Ruberoid Co., 343 U.S. 470, 485, 72 S. Ct. 800, 809, 96 L. Ed. 1081, acknowledged that he relied on "an unpublished treatise," i.e., one not available to the parties. If that practice is proper, I think it similarly proper to quote an author's unpublished interpretation of a published treatise.) Dr. Jahoda's summary reads as follows:

"Persons who argue for increased censorship of printed matter often operate on the assumption that reading about sexual matters or about violence and brutality leads to antisocial actions, particularly to juvenile delinquency. An examination of the pertinent psychological literature has led to the following conclusions:

series of little battles and minor issues, and the burden of choice is on us all, every day, young and old. Our daughters must live in the world and decide what sort of women they are to be, and we should be willing to prefer their deliberate and informed choice of decency rather than an innocence that continues to spring from ignorance. If that choice be made in the open sunlight, it is more apt than when made in shadow to fall on the side of honorable behavior."

Watson writes similarly: "What innocent children most need is not a sterile environment from which all evidence of * * * lust * * * has been removed, but help in interpreting the evil which is an inescapable part of life. Home, school and church should cooperate not to create an artificial hot-house insulation for life's realities but to enable children to respond, "Ah, yes! I understand!" Most children in middle class homes alarm their parents by spells in which they overdo imaginative violence, sex talk, worry about death, listening to cowboy programs, reading inane comics, exchanging dirty stories, and most of them in time, with or without adult counsel, will work their way through to better standards of taste. Protection by censorship might leave such children weaker and more susceptible; some of these childhood interests, like measles, contribute to a later life of useful immunity." Watson, Some Effects on Censorship upon Society, in 5 Social Meaning of Legal Concepts (1953) 73, 83–85.

Said Milton: "They are not skilful considerers of human things, who imagine to remove sin by removing the matter of sin." A renowned sinner declared that he "could resist everything but temptation."

[35] Cited in a passage in Brown v. Kingsley Books, Inc., 1 N.Y. 2d 177, 151 N.Y.S. 2d 639, 134 N.E. 2d 461, quoted by Judge Clark. Judge Clark cites and quotes from this opinion only in connection with his statement of our judicial "lack of knowledge of the social bearing of this problem." However, his quotation from that New York opinion cites the Jahoda report, and I therefore assume that Judge Clark intended to include Dr. Jahoda among "those with competence in the premises."

"1. There exists no research evidence either to prove or to disprove this assumption definitively.

"2. In the absence of scientific proof two lines of psychological approach to the examination of the assumption are possible: (a) a review of what is known on the causes of juvenile delinquency; and (b) review of what is known about the effect of literature on the mind of the reader.

"3. In the vast research literature on the causes of juvenile delinquency there is no evidence to justify the assumption that reading about sexual matters or about violence leads to delinquent acts. Experts on juvenile delinquency agree that it has no single cause. Most of them regard early childhood events, which precede the reading age, as a necessary condition for later delinquency. At a later age, the nature of personal relations is assumed to have much greater power in determining a delinquent career than the vicarious experiences provided by reading matter. Juvenile delinquents as a group read less, and less easily, than non-delinquents. Individual instances are reported in which so-called 'good' books allegedly influenced a delinquent in the manner in which 'bad' books are assumed to influence him.

"Where childhood experiences and subsequent events have combined to make delinquency psychologically likely, reading could have one of two effects: it could serve a trigger function releasing the criminal act or it could provide for a substitute outlet of aggression in fantasy, dispensing with the need for criminal action. There is no empirical evidence in either direction.

"4. With regard to the impact of literature on the mind of the reader, it must be pointed out that there is a vast overlap in content between all media of mass communication. The daily press, television, radio, movies, books and comics all present their share of so-called 'bad' material, some with great realism as reports of actual events, some in clearly fictionalized form. It is virtually impossible to isolate the impact of one of these media on a population exposed to all of them. Some evidence suggests that the particular communications which arrest the attention of an individual are in good part a matter of choice. As a rule, people do not expose themselves to everything that is offered, but only to what agrees with their inclinations.

"Children, who have often not yet crystallized their preferences and have more unspecific curiosity than many adults, are therefore perhaps more open to accidental influences from literature. This may present a danger to youngsters who are insecure or maladjusted who find in reading (of 'bad' books as well as of 'good' books) an escape from reality which they do not dare face. Needs which are not met in the real world are gratified in a fantasy world. It is likely, though not fully demonstrated, that excessive reading of comic books will intensify in children those qualities which drove them to the comic book world to begin with: an inability to face the world, apathy, a belief that the individual is hopelessly impotent and driven by uncontrollable forces and, hence, an acceptance of violence and brutality in the real world.

"It should be noted that insofar as causal sequence is implied, insecurity and maladjustment in a child must precede this exposure to the written word in order to lead to these potential effects. Unfortunately, perhaps, the reading of Shakespeare's tragedies or of Anderson's and Grimm's fairy tales might do much the same."

Most of the current discussion of the relation between children's reading and juvenile delinquency has to do with so-called "comic books" which center on violence (sometimes coupled with sex) rather than mere obscenity. Judge Vanderbilt, in an article from which Judge Clark quotes, cites Feder, Comic Book Regulation (University of California, Bureau of Public Administration, 1955 Legislative Problems No. 2).[36] Feder writes: "It has never been determined definitely whether or not comics portraying violence, crime and horror are a cause of juvenile delinquency."

Judge Vanderbilt, in the article from which Judge Clark quotes, also cites Wertham, Seduction of the Innocent (1954).[37] Dr. Wertham is the foremost proponent of the view that "comic books" do contribute to juvenile delinquency. The Jahoda Report takes issue with Dr. Wertham, who relies much on a variety of the *post-hoc-ergo-propter-hoc* variety of argument, i.e., youths who had read "comic books" became delinquents. The argument, at best, proves too much: Dr. Wertham points to the millions of young readers of such books; but only a fraction of these readers become delinquents. Many of the latter also chew gum, drink coca-cola, and wear soft-soled shoes. Moreover, Dr. Wertham specifically says (p. 298) that he is little concerned with allegedly obscene publications designed for reading by adults, and (pp. 303, 316, 348) that the legislation which he advocates would do no more than forbid the sale or display of "comic books" to minors. As previously noted, the federal obscenity statute is not so restricted.

Maybe some day we will have enough reliable data to show that obscene books and pictures do tend to influence children's sexual conduct adversely. Then a federal statute could be enacted which would avoid constitutional defects by authorizing punishment for using the mails or interstate shipments in the sale of such books and pictures to children.[38]

It is, however, not at all clear that children would be ignorant, in any considerable measure, of obscenity, if no obscene publications ever came into their hands. Youngsters get a vast deal of education in sexual smut from companions of their own age.[39] A verbatim report of

[36] Vanderbilt, Impasse In Justice, Wash. U.L.Q. (1956), 267, 302.
[37] Ibid.
[38] Such a statute was long ago suggested. See Ernst and Seagle, To the Pure (1928) 277.
[39] Cf. *United States* v. *Dennett*, 2 Cir., 39 F. 2d 564, 568, 76 A.L.R. 1092.

Alpert (loc. cit. at 74) writes of the American Youth Commission study of the conditions and attitudes of young people in Maryland between the ages of sixteen and twenty-four, as reported in 1938: "For this study Maryland was deliberately picked as a 'typical' state, and, according to the Commission, the 13,528 young people personally interviewed in Maryland can speak for the two hundred and fifty thousand young people in Maryland and the twenty millions in the United States. 'The chief source of sex "education" for the youth of all ages and all religious groups was found to be the youth's comtemporaries.' Sixty-six percent of the boys and forty percent of the girls reported that what they knew about sex was more or less limited to what their friends of their own age had told them. After 'contemporaries' and the youth's home, the source that is next in importance is the school, from which about 8 percent of the young people reported they had received most of their sex information. A few, about 4 percent, reported they owed most to books, while less than 1 percent asserted that they had acquired most of their information from movies. Exactly the same proportion specified the church as the chief source of their sex information. These

conversations among young teen-age boys (from average respectable homes) will disclose their amazing proficiency in obscene language, learned from other boys.[40] Replying to the argument of the need for censorship to protect the young Milton said: "Who shall regulate all the * * * conversation of our youth * * * appoint what shall be discussed * * *?" Most judges who reject that view are long past their youth and have probably forgotten the conversational ways of that period of life: "I remember when I was a little boy," said Mr. Dooley, "but I don't remember how I was a little boy."

The obscenity statute and the reputable press

Let it be assumed, for the sake of the argument, that contemplation of published matter dealing with sex has a significant impact on children's conduct. On that assumption, we cannot overlook the fact that our most reputable newspapers and periodicals carry advertisements and photographs displaying women in what decidedly are sexually alluring postures,[41] and at times emphasizing the importance of "sex appeal." That women are there shown scantily clad, increases "the mystery and allure of the bodies that are hidden," writes an eminent psychiatrist. "A leg covered by a silk stocking is much more attractive than a naked one; a bosom pushed into shape by a brassiere is more alluring than the pendant realities."[42] Either, then, the statute must be sternly applied to prevent the mailing of many reputable newspapers and periodicals containing such ads and photographs, or else we must acknowledge that they have created a cultural atmosphere for children in which, at a maximum, only the most trifling additional effect can be imputed to children's perusal of the kind of matter mailed by the defendant.

The obscenity statute and the newspapers

Because of the contrary views of many competent persons, one may well be sceptical about Dr. Wertham's thesis. However, let us see what, logically, his crusade

would do to the daily press: After referring repeatedly to the descriptions, in "comic books" and other "mass media," of violence combined with sadistic sexual behavior, descriptions which he says contribute to juvenile delinquency, he writes, "Juvenile delinquency reflects the social values current in a society. Both adults and children absorb these social values in their daily lives, * * * and also in *all the communications through the mass media* * * * Juvenile delinquency holds up a mirror to society * * * It is self-understood that such a pattern in a mass medium does not come from nothing * * * Comic books are not the disease, they are only a symptom * * * The same social forces that made comic books make other social evils, and the same social forces that keep comic crime books keep the other social evils the way they are." (Emphasis added.)

Now the daily newspapers, especially those with immense circulations, constitute an important part of the "mass media"; and each copy of a newspaper sells for much less than a "comic book." Virtually all the sorts of descriptions, of sex mingled with violence, which Dr. Wertham finds in the "comic books," can be found, often accompanied by gruesome photographs, in those daily journals. Even a newspaper which is considered unusually respectable, published prominently on its first page, on August 26, 1956, a true story of a "badly decomposed body" of a 24 year old woman school teacher, found in a clump of trees. The story reported that police had quoted a 29 year old salesman as saying that "he drove to the area" with the school teacher, that "the two had relations on the ground, and later got into an argument," after which he "struck her three times on the back of the head with a rock, and, leaving her there, drove away." Although today no one can so prove, one may suspect that such stories of sex and violence in the daily press have more impact on young readers than do those in the "comic books," since the daily press reports reality while the "comic books" largely confine themselves to avowed fiction or fantasy.[42a] Yet Dr. Wertham, and most others who propose legislation to curb the sale of "comic books" to children, propose that it should not extend to newspapers.[42b] Why not?

The question is relevant in reference to the application of the obscenity statute: Are our prosecutors ready to prosecute reputable newspaper publishers under that Act? I think not. I do not at all urge such prosecutions. I do suggest that the validity of that statute has not been vigorously challenged because it has not been applied to important persons like those publishers but, instead, has been enforced principally against relatively inconspicuous men like the defendant here.

Da Capo: Available data seem wholly insufficient to show that the obscenity statutes come within any exception to the First Amendment.

I repeat that, because that statute is not restricted to obscene publications mailed for sale to minors, its validity

---

statistical results are not offered as conclusive; but that they do more than cast doubt upon the assertion that 'immoral' books, corrupt and deprave must be admitted. These statistical results placed in the scale against the weight of the dogma upon which the law is founded lift the counterpane high. Add this: that 'evil manners' are as easily acquired without books as with books; that crowded slums, machine labor, barren lives, starved emotions, and unreasoning minds are far more dangerous to morals than any so-called obscene literature. True, this attack is tangential, but a social problem is here involved, and the weight of this approach should be felt." Id. at 74.

[40] For such a report, slightly expurgated for adult readers, see Cleckley, The Mask of Sanity (1950) 135–137.

[41] Cf. Larrabee, The Cultural Context of Sex Censorship, 20 L. & Contemp. Prob. (1955) 672, 684.

[42] Myerson, Speaking of Man (1950) 92. See also the well known chapter on clothes in Anatole France's Penguin Island.

Dr. Wertham discussing "comic books," makes much of the advertisements they carry. He speaks of their "breast ads," and also of their playing up of "glamour girls," their stress on the "sexy," their emphasis on women's "secondary sexual characteristics." Is not this also descriptive of the advertisements in our "best periodicals"?

[42a] It is arguable that the fact that a publication is regarded by the reader as "pornography" influences its impact on him. No relevant reliable data, however, is available.

[42b] "No one would dare ask of a newspaper that it observe the same restraints that are constantly being demanded of * * * the comic book." Larrabee, The Cultural Context of Sex Censorship, 20 Law and Contemp. Problems (1955) 673, 679.

should be tested in terms of the evil effects of adult reading of obscenity on adult conduct.[43] With the present lack of evidence that publications probably have such effects, how can the government discharge its burden of demonstrating sufficiently that the statute is within the narrow exceptions to the scope of the First Amendment? One would think that the mere possibility of a causal relation to misconduct ought surely not be enough.

Even if Congress had made an express legislative finding of the probable evil influence, on adult conduct, of adult reading or seeing obscene publications,[43a] the courts would not be bound by that finding, if it were not justified in fact. See, e.g., *Chastleton Corp.* v. *Sinclair*, 264 U.S. 543, 44 S. Ct. 405, 406, 68 L. Ed. 841, where the Court (per Holmes, J.) said of a statute (declaring the existence of an emergency) that "a Court is not at liberty to shut its eyes to an obvious mistake, when the validity of the law depends upon the truth of what is declared." And the Court there and elsewhere has held that the judiciary may use judicial notice in ascertaining the truth of such a legislative declaration.[44]

If the obscenity statute is valid, why may Congress not validly provide punishment for mailing books which will provoke thoughts it considers undesirable about religion or politics?

If the statute is valid, then, considering the foregoing, it would seem that its validity must rest on this ground: Congress, by statute, may constitutionally provide punishment for the mailing of books evoking mere thoughts or feelings about sex, if Congress considers them socially dangerous, even in the absence of any satisfactory evidence that those thoughts or feelings will tend to bring about socially harmful deeds. If that be correct, it is hard to understand why, similarly, Congress may not constitutionally provide punishment for such distribution of books evoking mere thoughts or feelings, about religion or politics, which Congress considers socially dangerous, even in the absence of any satisfactory evidence that those thoughts or feelings will tend to bring about socially dangerous deeds.

2. The Judicial exception of the "classics"

As I have said, I have no doubt the jury could reasonably find, beyond a reasonable doubt, that many of the publications mailed by defendant were obscene within the current judicial definition of the term as explained by the trial judge in his charge to the jury. But so, too, are a multitude of recognized works of art found in public libraries. Compare, for instance, the books which are exhibits in this case with Montaigne's Essay on Some Lines of Virgil or with Chaucer. Or consider the many nude

pictures which the defendant transmitted through the mails, and then turn to the reproductions in the articles on painting and sculpture in the Encyclopaedia Britannica (14th edition):[45] Some of the latter are no less "obscene" than those which led to the defendants' conviction. Yet these Encyclopaedia volumes are readily accessible to everyone, young or old, and, without let or hindrance, are frequently mailed to all parts of the country. Catalogues, of famous art museums, almost equally accessible and also often mailed, contain reproductions of paintings and sculpture, by great masters, no less "obscene."[46]

To the argument that such books (and such reproductions of famous paintings and works of sculpture) fall within the statutory ban, the courts have answered that they are "classics,"—books of "literary distinction" or works which have "an accepted place in the arts," including, so this court has held, Ovid's Art of Love and Boccacio's Decameron.[47] There is a "curious dilemma" involved in this answer that the statute condemns "only books which are dull and without merit," that in no event will the statute be applied to the "classics," i.e., books "of literary distinction."[48] The courts have not explained how they escape that dilemma, but instead seem to have gone to sleep (although rather uncomfortably) on its horns.

This dilemma would seem to show up the basic constitutional flaw in the statute: No one can reconcile the currently accepted test of obscenity with the immunity of such "classics" as e.g., Aristophanes' Lysistrata, Chaucer's Canterbury Tales, Rabelais' Gargantua and Pantagruel, Shakespeare's Venus and Adonis, Fielding's Tom Jones, or Balzac's Droll Stories. For such "obscene" writings, just because of their greater artistry and charm, will presumably have far greater influence on readers than dull inartistic writings.

It will not do to differentiate a "classic," published in the past, on the ground that it comported with the average moral attitudes at the time and place of its original publication. Often this was not true. It was not true, for instance, of Balzac's Droll Stories,"[49] a "classic" now freely circulated by many public libraries, and which therefore must have been transported by mail (or in interstate commerce). More to the point, if the issue is whether a book meets the American common conscience of the

---

[43] See *United States* v. *Levine*, 2 Cir., 83 F. 2d 156, 157 to the effect that "what counts is its effect, not upon any particular class, but upon all those whom it is likely to reach."

[43a] Congress has made no such finding. There is none such in the Senate Report (supporting the 1955 amendment of Section 1461) quoted by Judge Clark in his footnote 5.

[44] Cf. *United States* v. *Rumely*, 345 U.S. 41, 44, 73 S. Ct. 543, 97 L. Ed. 770.

[45] See, e.g., Vol. 17, p. 36, Plate 3, No. 4, reproducing Botticelli's "Birth of Venus"; p. 38, Plate VIII, No. 2, reproducing Titian's "Woman on a Couch"; Vol. 20, p. 202, Plate V, No. 8, reproducing Clodion's "Nymph and Satyr"; p. 204, Plate VI, reproducing Rodin's "The Kiss."

See *Parmelee* v. *United States*, 72 App. D.C. 203, 113 F. 2d 729, 734 and note 19.

[46] See, e.g., Masterpieces of Painting from the National Gallery of Art (Cairns and Walker ed. 1944) 68, 72, 114; Catalogue of Pictures Collected by Yale Alumni (1956) 3, 15, 55, 134, 137, 195.

[47] See, e.g., *United States* v. *Levine*, 2 Cir., 83 F. 2d 156, 157; *United States* v. *One Book* Entitled Ulysses, 2 Cir., 72 F. 2d 705; *Roth* v. *Goldman*, 2 Cir., 172 F. 2d 788.

[48] See *Roth* v. *Goldman*, 2 Cir., 172 F. 2d 788.

No one can argue with a straight face (1) that reading an obscene "classic" in a library has less harmful effects or (2) that, as the "classics" often are published in expensive volumes, they usually affect only persons who have large incomes, and that such persons' right to read is peculiarly privileged.

[49] See discussion in *Roth* v. *Goldman*, 2 Cir., 172 F. 2d at page 797.

present time, the question is how "average" Americans now regard the book, not how it was regarded when first published, here or abroad. Why should the age of an "obscene" book be relevant? After how many years—25 or 50 or 100—does such a writing qualify as a "classic?"

The truth is that the courts have excepted the "classics" from the federal obscenity statute, since otherwise most Americans would be deprived of access to many masterpieces of literature and the pictorial arts, and a statute yielding such deprivation would not only be laughably absurd but would squarely oppose the intention of the cultivated men who framed and adopted the First Amendment.

This exception—nowhere to be found in the statute[50] —is a judge-made device invented to avoid that absurdity. The fact that the judges have felt the necessity of seeking that avoidance, serves to suggest forcibly that the statute, in its attempt to control what our citizens may read and see, violates the First Amendment. For no one can rationally justify the judge-made exception. The contention would scarcely pass as rational that the "classics" will be read or seen solely by an intellectual or artistic elite; for, even ignoring the snobbish, undemocratic, nature of this contention, there is no evidence that that elite has a moral fortitude (an immunity from moral corruption) superior to that of the "masses." And if the exception, to make it rational, were taken as meaning that a contemporary book is exempt if it equates in "literary distinction" with the "classics," the result would be amazing: Judges would have to serve as literary critics; jurisprudence would merge with aesthetics; authors and publishers would consult the legal digests for legal-artistic precedents; we would some day have a Legal Restatement of the Canons of Literary Taste.

The exception of the "classics" is therefore irrational. Consequently, it would seem that we should interpret the statute rationally—i.e., without that exception. If, however, the exception, as an exception, is irrational, then it would appear that, to render the statute valid, the standard applied to the "classics" should be applied to all books and pictures. The result would be that, in order to be constitutional, the statute must be wholly inefficacious.

3. How censorship under the statute actually operates:

(a) Prosecutors, as censors, actually exercise prior restraint.

Fear of punishment serves as a powerful restraint on publication, and fear of punishment often means, practically, fear of prosecution. For most men dread indictment and prosecution; the publicity alone terrifies, and to defend a criminal action is expensive. If the definition of obscenity had a limited and fairly well known scope, that fear might deter restricted sorts of publications only. But on account of the extremely vague judicial definition of the obscene,[51] a person threatened with prosecution if he mails (or otherwise sends in interstate commerce)[52] al-

most any book which deals in an unconventional, unorthodox, manner with sex,[53] may well apprehend that, should the threat be carried out, he will be punished. As a result, each prosecutor becomes a literary censor (i.e., dictator) with immense unbridled power, a virtually uncontrolled discretion.[54] A statute would be invalid which gave the Postmaster General the power, without reference to any standard, to close the mails to any publication he happened to dislike.[55] Yet, a federal prosecutor, under the federal obscenity statute, approximates that position: Within wide limits, he can (on the advice of the Postmaster General or on no one's advice) exercise such a censorship by threat, without a trial, without any judicial supervision, capriciously and arbitrarily. Having no special qualifications for that task, nevertheless, he can, in large measure, determine at his will what those within his district may not read on sexual subjects.[56] In that way, the

---

[50] The importation statute relating to obscenity, 19 U.S.C.A. § 1305, does make an explicit exception of the "so-called classics or books of recognized and established literary * * * merit," but only if they are "imported for noncommercial purposes"; if so, the Secretary of the Treasury has discretion to admit them.

[51] See infra, point 9, for further discussion of that vagueness.

[52] As to interstate transportation, see 18 U.S.C. § 1462 which contains substantially the same provisions as 18 U.S.C. § 1461.

[53] See Kaplan, Obscenity as An Esthetic Category, 20 Law & Contemp. Problems (1955) 544, 551–552 as to "conventional obscenity," which he defines as "the quality of any work which attacks sexual patterns and practices. In essence, it is the presentation of a sexual heterodoxy, a rejection of accepted standards of sexual behavior. Zola, Ibsen and Shaw provide familiar examples. It surprises no one that the author of Nana also wrote J'Accuse; of Ghosts, An Enemy of the People; of Mrs. Warren's Profession, Saint Joan."

See also, Lockhart and McClure, Obscenity in the Courts, 20 Law & Contemp. Problems (1955) 586, 596–597 as to "ideological obscenity"; they note that the courts have generally refrained (at least explicitly) from basing their decisions on rulings that literally may be prescribed to guard against a change in accepted moral standards, "because any such ruling would fly squarely in the face of the very purpose for guaranteeing freedom of expression and would thus raise serious constitutional questions."

[54] One court, at the suit of a publisher, enjoined a chief of police—who went beyond threat of prosecution and ordered booksellers not to sell certain books—on the ground that the officer had exceeded his powers; *New American Library of World Literature v. Allen,* D.C. Ohio, 114 F. Supp. 823. In another similar case, where a prosecutor was enjoined, the injunction order was much modified on appeal; *Bantam Books, Inc., v. Melko,* 25 N.J. Super. 292, 96 A. 2d 47, modified 14 N.J. 524, 103 A. 2d 256.

If, however, the prosecutor confines himself to a mere threat of prosecution, the traditional reluctance to restrain criminal prosecutions will very probably make it difficult to obtain such an injunction. *Sunshine Book Co. v. McCaffrey,* Sup., 112 N.Y.S. 2d 476; see also 22 U. of Chicago L. Rev. (1954) 216; 68 Harv. L. Rev. (1955) 489.

This may be particularly true with respect to a federal prosecutor. See Mr. Justice Jackson, The Federal Prosecutor, 24 J. of Am. Jud. Soc. (1940) 18: "The (federal) prosecutor has more control over life, liberty, and reputation than any other person in America. His discretion is tremendous. He can have citizens investigated and, if he is that kind of person, he can have this done to the tune of public statements and veiled or unveiled intimations. Or the prosecutor may choose a more subtle course and simply have a citizen's friends interviewed. The prosecutor can order arrests, present cases to the grand jury in secret session, and on the basis of his one-sided presentation of the facts, can cause the citizen to be indicted and held for trial. He may dismiss the case before trial, in which case the defense never has a chance to be heard."

[55] See, e.g., *Joseph Burstyn, Inc. v. Wilson,* 343 U.S. 495, 72 S. Ct. 777, 96 L. Ed. 1098.

[56] It is, therefore, doubtful whether, as suggested by Emerson (loc. cit. at 656–660), a statute calling for punishment involves very much less arbitrary conduct and very much less censorship than one calling for prior restraint. In actual fact, by his threats

statute brings about an actual prior restraint of free speech and free press which strikingly flouts the First Amendment.[57]

(b) Judges as censors.

When a prosecution is instituted and a trial begins, much censorship power passes to the trial judge: If he sits without a jury, he must decide whether a book is obscene. If the trial is by jury, then, if he thinks the book plainly not obscene, he directs a verdict for the accused or, after a verdict of guilt, enters a judgment of acquittal. How does the judge determine whether a book is obscene? Not by way of evidence introduced at the trial, but by way of some sort of judicial notice. Whence come the judicial notice data to inform him?

Those whose views most judges know best are other lawyers. Judges can and should take judicial notice that, at many gatherings of lawyers at Bar Association or of alumni of our leading law schools,[58] tales are told fully as "obscene" as many of those distributed by men, like defendant, convicted for violation of the obscenity statute. Should not judges, then set aside such convictions? If they do not, are they not somewhat arrogantly concluding that lawyers are an exempt elite, unharmed by what will harm the multitude of other Americans? If lawyers are not such an elite then, since, in spite of the "obscene" tales lawyers frequently tell one another, data are lacking that lawyers as a group become singularly addicted to depraved sexual conduct, should not judges conclude that "obscenity" does not importantly contribute to such misconduct, and that therefore the statute is unconstitutional?

(c) Jurors as censors.

If in a jury case, the trial judge does not direct a verdict or enter a judgment of acquittal, the jury exercises the censorship power. Courts have said that a jury has a peculiar aptitude as a censor of obscenity, since, representing a cross-section of the community, it knows peculiarly well the "common conscience" of the time. Yet no statistician would conceivably accept the views of a jury—twelve persons chosen at random—as a fair sample of community attitudes on such a subject as obscenity. A particular jury may voice the "moral sentiments" of a generation ago, not of the present time.

Each jury verdict in an obscenity case has been sagely called "really a small bit of legislation ad hoc."[59] So each jury constitutes a tiny autonomous legislature. Any one such tiny legislature, as experience teaches, may well differ from any other, in thus legislating as to obscenity. And, one may ask, was it the purpose of the First Amendment, to authorize hundreds of divers jury-legislatures, with discrepant beliefs, to decide whether or not to enact hundreds of divers statutes interfering with freedom of expression? (I shall note, infra, the vast difference between the applications by juries of the "reasonable man" standard and the "obscenity" standard.)

4. The dangerously infectious nature of governmental censorship of books

Governmental control of ideas or personal preferences is alien to a democracy. And the yearning to use governmental censorship of any kind is infectious. It may spread insidiously. Commencing with suppression of books as obscene, it is not unlikely to develop into official lust for the power of thought-control in the areas of religion, politics, and elsewhere. Milton observed that "licensing of books * * * necessarily pulls along with it so many other kinds of licensing." J. S. Mill noted that the "bounds of what may be called moral police" may easily extend "until it encroaches on the most unquestionably legitimate liberty of the individual." We should beware of a recrudescence of the undemocratic doctrine uttered in the 17th century by Berkeley, Governor of Virginia: "Thank God there are no free schools or preaching, for learning has brought disobedience into the world, and printing has divulged them. God keep us from both."

The people as self-guardians: censorship by public opinion, not by government

Plato, who detested democracy, proposed to banish all poets; and his rulers were to serve as "guardians" of the people, telling lies for the people's good, vigorously suppressing writings these guardians thought dangerous.[60] Governmental guardianship is repugnant to the basic tenet of our democracy: According to our ideals, our adult citizens are self-guardians, to act as their own fathers, and

---

of prosecution, the prosecutor does exercise prior restraint. Much, therefore, that Emerson says of prior restraint authorized by statute applies as well as to censorship through a prosecutor's threats of prosecution: The "procedural safeguards built around criminal prosecution" (the stronger burden of proof, the stricter rules of evidence, the tighter procedure) are likewise absent. The "decision rests with a single functionary," an official, rather than with the courts. The prosecutor, by threats of prosecution, accomplishes prior restraint "behind a screen of informality and partial concealment that seriously curtails opportunity for public appraisal" and entailing the "chance of discrimination and other abuse." The "policies and actions" of the prosecutor, in his censorship by threats of prosecution, are not "likely to be known or publicly debated; material and study and criticism" are not "readily available."

[57] For startling instances of "prosecutor censorship" see Blanshard, The Right to Read (1955) 184–186, 190; 22 U. of Chicago L. Rev. (1954) 216.

[58] See *Roth v. Goldman,* 2 Cir., 172 F. 2d 788, at page 796 (concurring opinion):

"One thinks of the lyrics sung at many such gatherings by a certain respected and conservative member of the faculty of a great law-school which considers itself the most distinguished and which is the Alma Mater of many judges sitting on upper courts."

Aubrey's Lives, containing many "salacious" tales, delights some of our greatest judges.

Mr. Justice Holmes was a constant reader of "naughty French novels." See Bent, Justice O. W. Holmes (1932) 16, 134.

[59] *United States v. Levine,* 2 Cir., 83 F. 2d 156, 157.

[60] Plato furnished "an ideal blueprint for a totalitarian society"; Chroust, Book Rev., 1 Natural Law Forum (1956) 135, 141. See also Popper, The Open Society and Its Enemies (1950); Frank, Courts on Trial (1949) 146–147, 158, 350, 360, 405–406; Frank, Fate and Freedom (1949) 119, 319, note 25, 365, note 10; Frank, If Men Were Angels (1942) 192; Fite, The Platonic Legend (1934); Catlin, The Story of the Political Philosophers (1939) 52, 58, 65–66; Kallen, Ethical Aspects of Censorship, in Protection of Public Morals Through Censorship (1953) 34, 53–54.

thus become self-dependent.[61] When our governmental officials act towards our citizens on the thesis that "Papa knows best what's good for you," they enervate the spirit of the citizens: To treat grown men like infants is to make them infantile, dependent, immature.

So have sagacious men often insisted. Milton, in his Areopagitica, denounced such paternalism: "We censure them for a giddy, vicious and unguided people, in such sick and weak (a) state of faith and discretion as to be able to take down nothing but through the pipe of a licensor." "We both consider the people as our children," wrote Jefferson to Dupont de Nemours, "but you love them as infants whom you are afraid to trust without nurses, and I as adults whom I freely leave to self-government." Tocqueville sagely remarked: "No form or combination of social policy has yet been devised to make an energetic people of a community of pusillanimous and enfeebled citizens." "Man," warned Goethe, "is easily accustomed to slavery and learns quickly to be obedient when his freedom is taken from him." Said Carl Becker, "Self-government, and the spirit of freedom that sustains it, can be maintained only if the people have sufficient intelligence and honesty to maintain them with a minimum of legal compulsion. This heavy responsibility is the price of freedom."[62] The "great art," according to Milton, "lies to discern in what the law is to bid restraint and punishment, and in what things persuasion only is to work." So we come back, once more, to Jefferson's advice: The only completely democratic way to control publications which arouse mere thoughts or feelings is through non-governmental censorship by public opinion.

5. The seeming paradox of the First Amendment.

Here we encounter an apparent paradox: The First Amendment, judicially enforced, curbs public opinion when translated into a statute which restricts freedom of expression (except that which will probably induce undesirable conduct). The paradox is unreal: *The Amendment ensures that public opinion—the "common conscience of the time"—shall not commit suicide through legislation which chokes off today the free expression of minority views which may become the majority public opinion of tomorrow.*

Private persons or groups, may validly try to influence public opinion.

The First Amendment obviously has nothing to do with the way persons or groups, not a part of government, influence public opinion as to what constitutes "decency" or "obscenity." The Catholic Church, for example, has a constitutional right to persuade or instruct its adherents not to read designated books or kinds of books.

6. The fine arts are within the First Amendment's protection.

"The framers of the First Amendment," writes Chafee, "must have had literature and art in mind, because our first national statement on the subject of 'freedom of the press,' the 1774 address of the Continental Congress to the inhabitants of Quebec, declared, 'The importance of this (freedom of the press) consists, beside the advancement of truth, science, morality and *arts* in general, in its diffusion of liberal sentiments on the administration of government'."[63] 165 years later, President Franklin Roosevelt said, "The arts cannot thrive except where men are free to be themselves and to be in charge of the discipline of their own energies and ardors. The conditions for democracy and for art are one and the same. What we call liberty in politics results in freedom of the arts."[64] The converse is also true.

In our industrial era when, perforce, economic pursuits must be, increasingly, governmentally regulated, it is especially important that the realm of art—the noneconomic realm—should remain free, unregimented, the domain of free enterprise, of unhampered competition at its maximum.[65] An individual's taste is his own, private, concern. *De gustibus non disputandum* represents a valued democratic maxim.

Milton wrote: "For though a licenser should happen to be judicious more than the ordinary, yet his very office * * * enjoins him to let pass nothing but what is vulgarly received already." He asked, "What a fine conformity would it starch us all into? * * * We may fall * * into a gross conformity stupidly * *" In 1859, J. S. Mill, in his essay on Liberty, maintained that conformity in taste is not a virtue but a vice. "The danger," he wrote, "is not the excess but the deficiency of personal impulses and preferences. By dint of not following their own nature (men) have no nature to follow * * * Individual spontaneity is entitled to free exercise * * * That so few men dare to be eccentric marks the chief danger of the time." Pressed by the demand for conformity, a people degenerate into "the deep slumber of a decided opinion," yield a "dull and torpid consent" to the accustomed. "Mental despotism" ensues. For "whatever crushes individuality is despotism by whatever name it be called * * * It is not by wearing down into uniformity all that is individual in themselves, but by cultivating it, and calling it forth, within the limits imposed by the rights and interests of others, that human beings become a noble and beautiful object of contemplation; and as the works partake the character of those who do them, by the same process human life also becomes rich, diversified, and animating * * * In proportion to the development of his individuality, each person becomes more valuable to himself, and is therefore capable of being more valuable to others. There is a greater fullness of life about his own existence, and when there is more life in the units there is more in the mass which is composed of them."

To vest a few fallible men—prosecutors, judges, jurors—with vast powers of literary or artistic censorship, to convert them into what J. S. Mill called a "moral police," is to make them despotic arbiters of literary products. If one day they ban mediocre books as obscene, another day they may do likewise to a work of genius. Originality, not too plentiful, should be cherished, not stifled. An author's

---

[61] See Frank, Self Guardianship and Democracy, 16 Am. Scholar (1947) 265.

[62] Becker, Freedom and Responsibility in the American Way of Life (1945) 42.

[63] Chafee, Government and Mass Communication (1947) 53.

[64] Message at dedicating exercises of the New York Museum of Modern Art, May 8, 1939.

[65] Frank, Fate and Freedom (1945) 194–202.

imagination may be cramped if he must write with one eye on prosecutors or juries; authors must cope with publishers who, fearful about the judgments of governmental censors, may refuse to accept the manuscripts of contemporary Shelleys or Mark Twains or Whitmans.[66]

Some few men stubbornly fight for the right to write or publish or distribute books which the great majority at the time consider loathsome. If we jail those few, the community may appear to have suffered nothing. The appearance is deceptive. For the conviction and punishment of these few will terrify writers who are more sensitive, less eager for a fight. What, as a result, they do not write might have been major literary contributions.[67] "Suppression," Spinoza said, "is paring down the state till it is too small to harbor men of talent."

7. The motive or intention of the author, publisher or distributor cannot be the test.

Some courts once held that the motive or intention of the author, painter, publisher or distributor constituted the test of obscenity. That test, the courts have abandoned: That a man who mails a book or picture believes it entirely "pure" is no defense if the court finds it obscene. *United States v. One Book* Entitled Ulysses, 2 Cir., 72 F. 2d 705, 708.[68] Nor, conversely, will he be criminally liable for mailing a "pure" publication—Stevenson's Child's Garden of Verses or a simple photograph of the Washington Monument—he mistakenly believes obscene. Most courts now look to the "objective" intention, which can only mean the effect on those who read the book or see the picture;[69] the motive of the mailer is irrelevant because it cannot affect that effect.

8. Judge Bok's decision as to the causal relation to anti-social conduct.

In *Commonwealth v. Gordon*, 1949, 66 Pa. Dist. & Co. R. 101, Judge Bok said: "A book, however sexually impure and pornographic * * * cannot be a present danger unless its reader closes it, lays it aside, and transmutes its erotic allurement into overt action. That such action must inevitably follow as a direct consequence of reading the book does not bear analysis, nor is it borne out by general human experience; too much can intervene and too many diversions take place * * * The only clear and present danger * * * that will satisfy * * * the Constitution * * * is the commission or the imminence of the commission of criminal behavior resulting from the reading of a book. Publication alone can have no such automatic

effect." The constitutional operation of "the statute," Judge Bok continued, thus "rests on narrow ground * * * I hold that (the statute) may constitutionally be applied * * * only where there is a reasonable and demonstrable cause to believe that a crime or misdemeanor has been committed or is about to be committed as the perceptible result of the publication and distribution of the writing in question: the opinion of anyone that a tendency thereto exists or that such a result is self-evident is insufficient and irrelevant. The causal connection between the book and the criminal behavior must appear beyond a reasonable doubt."

I confess that I incline to agree with Judge Bok's opinion. But I think it should be modified in a few respects: (a) Because of the Supreme Court's opinion in the Dennis case, 1951, 341 U.S. 494, 71 S. Ct. 857, 95 L.Ed. 1137, decided since Judge Bok wrote, I would stress the element of probability in speaking of a "clear danger." (b) I think the danger need not be that of probably inducing behavior which has already been made criminal at common law or by statute, but rather of probably inducing any seriously anti-social conduct (i.e., conduct which, by statute, could validly be made a state or federal crime). (c) I think that the causal relation need not be between such anti-social conduct and a particular book involved in the case on trial, but rather between such conduct and a book of the kind or type involved in the case.[70]

9. The void-for-vagueness argument.

There is another reason for doubting the constitutionality of the obscenity statute. The exquisite vagueness of the word "obscenity" is apparent from the way the judicial definition of that word has kept shifting: Once (as we saw) the courts held a work obscene if it would probably stimulate improper thoughts or desires in abnormal persons; now most courts consider only the assumed impact on the thoughts or desires of the adult "normal" or average human being. A standard so difficult for our ablest judges to interpret is hardly one which has a "well-settled" meaning, a meaning sufficient adequately to advise a man whether he is or is not committing a crime if he mails a book or picture. See, e.g., *International Harvester Co. of America v. Commonwealth of Kentucky*, 234 U.S. 216, 34 S. Ct. 853, 58 L. Ed. 1284; *United States v. L. Cohen Grocery Co.*, 255 U.S. 81, 41 S. Ct. 298, 65 L. Ed. 516; *Connally v. General Construction Co.*, 269 U.S. 385, 46 S. Ct. 126, 70 L. Ed. 322; *Cline v. Frink Dairy Co.*, 274 U.S. 445, 47 S. Ct. 681, 71 L. Ed. 1146; *Champlin Refining Co. v. Corporation Commission*, 286 U.S. 210, 52 S. Ct. 559, 76 L. Ed. 1062; *Lanzetta v. State of New Jersey*, 306 U.S. 451, 59 S. Ct. 618, 83 L. Ed. 888; *Musser v. State of Utah*, 333 U.S. 95, 68 S. Ct. 397, 92 L. Ed. 562; *Winters v. People of State of New York*, 333 U.S. 507, 68 S. Ct. 665, 92 L. Ed. 840; cf. *United States v. Cardiff*, 344 U.S. 174, 73 S. Ct. 189, 97 L. Ed. 200.

If we accept as correct the generally current judicial standard of obscenity—the "average conscience of the time"—that standard still remains markedly uncertain as a

---

[66] Milton remarked that "not to count him fit to print his mind without a tutor or examiner, lest he should drop * * * something of corruption, is the greatest * * * indignity to a free and knowing spirit that can be put upon him."

[67] Cf. Chafee, The Blessings of Liberty (1956) 113.
Milton said that the "sense" of a great man may "to all posterity be lost for the fearfulness, or the presumptuous rashness of a perfunctory licenser."

[68] *Rosen v. United States*, 161 U.S. 29, 41–42, 16 S. Ct. 434, 480, 40 L. Ed. 606.

[69] *United States v. Levine*, 2 Cir., 83 F. 2d 156; *Parmelee v. United States*, 72 App. D.C. 203, 113 F. 2d 729.

[70] According to Judge Bok, an obscenity statute may be validly enforced when there is proof of a causal relation between a particular book and undesirable conduct. Almost surely, such proof cannot ever be adduced. In the instant case, the government did not offer such proof.

guide to judges or jurors—and therefore to a citizen who contemplates mailing a book or picture. To be sure, we trust juries to use their common sense in applying the "reasonable man" standard in prosecutions for criminal negligence (or the like); a man has to take his chances on a jury verdict in such a case, with no certainty that a jury will not convict him although another jury may acquit another man on the same evidence.[71] But that standard has nothing remotely resembling the looseness of the "obscenity" standard.

There is a stronger argument against the analogy of the "reasonable man" test: Even if the obscenity standard would have sufficient definiteness were freedom of expression not involved, it would seem far too vague to justify as a basis for an exception to the First Amendment. See *Stromberg* v. *People of State of California*, 283 U.S. 359, 51 S. Ct. 532, 75 L. Ed. 1117; *Herndon* v. *Lowry*, 301 U.S. 242, 57 S. Ct. 732, 81 L. Ed. 1066; *Winters* v. *People of State of New York*, 333 U.S. 507, 68 S. Ct. 665, 92 L. Ed. 840; *Kunz* v. *People of State of New York*, 340 U.S. 290, 71 S. Ct. 312, 95 L. Ed. 280; *Burstyn, Inc.* v.

---

[71] *Nash* v. *United States*, 229 U.S. 373, 377, 33 S. Ct. 780, 57 L. Ed. 1232; *United States* v. *Wurzbach*, 280 U.S. 396, 399, 50 S. Ct. 167, 74 L. Ed. 508; *United States* v. *Ragen*, 314 U.S. 513, 523, 62 S. Ct. 374, 86 L. Ed. 383.

Wilson, 343 U.S. 495, 72 S. Ct. 777, 96 L. Ed. 1098; Callings, Constitutional Uncertainty, 40 Cornell L.Q. (1955) 194, 214–218.

In *United States* v. *Rebhuhn*, 2 Cir., 109 F. 2d 512, 514, the court tersely rejected the contention that the obscenity statute is too vague, citing and relying on *Rosen* v. *United States*, 161 U.S. 29, 16 S. Ct. 434, 480, 40 L. Ed. 606. However the Rosen case did not deal with that subject but merely with the sufficiency of the wording of an indictment under that statute.

Waterman, Circuit Judge (concurring).

I concur with my colleagues in affirming the judgment below. I would dispose in one sentence of the claim advanced that the applicable statute, 18 U.S.C.A. § 1461, is unconstitutional, for I believe the constitutionality of such legislation is so well settled that: "If the question is to be reopened the Supreme Court must open it. *Tyomies Publishing Company* v. *United States*, 6 Cir., 211 F. 385"—quoting Learned Hand, C.J., in *United States* v. *Rebhuhn*, 2 Cir., 1940, 109 F. 2d 512, at page 514, certiorari denied 310 U.S. 629, 60 S. Ct. 976, 84 L. Ed. 1399. I concur with Chief Judge Clark in his disposition of the remaining issues.

■ Roth

v.

United States.

CERTIORARI TO THE UNITED STATES COURT OF APPEALS FOR THE SECOND CIRCUIT.

No. 582. Argued April 22, 1957.—Decided June 24, 1957.

David von G. Albrecht and *O. John Rogge* argued the cause for petitioner in No. 582. With them on the brief were *David P. Siegel, Peter Belsito* and *Murray A. Gordon.*

Stanley Fleishman argued the cause for appellant in No. 61. With him on the brief were *Sam Rosenwein* and *William B. Murrish.*

Roger D. Fisher argued the cause for the United States in No. 582. With him on the brief were Solicitor General *Rankin* and Assistant Attorney General *Olney.*

Fred N. Whichello and *Clarence A. Linn,* Assistant Attorney General of California, argued the cause for appellee in No. 61. With them on the brief were *Edmund G. Brown,* Attorney General, *William B. McKesson* and *Lewis Watnick.*

Briefs of *amici curiae* urging reversal were filed in No. 582 by *Morris L. Ernst, Harriett F. Pilpel* and *Nancy F. Wechsler,* for Ernst, *Irwin Karp* and *Osmond K. Fraenkel,* for the Authors League of America, Inc., *Abe Fortas, William L. McGovern, Abe Krash* and *Maurice Rosenfield,* for the Greenleaf Publishing Co. et al., *Horace S. Manges,* for the American Book Publishers Council, Inc., and *Emanuel Redfield,* for the American Civil Liberties Union.

A. L. Wirin filed a brief for the American Civil Liberties Union, Southern California Branch, as *amicus curiae,* in support of appellant in No. 61.

Mr. Justice Brennan delivered the opinion of the Court.

The constitutionality of a criminal obscenity statute is the question in each of these cases. In *Roth,* the primary constitutional question is whether the federal obscenity statute[1] violates the provision of the First Amendment

---

[1] The federal obscenity statute provided, in pertinent part:

"Every obscene, lewd, lascivious, or filthy book, pamphlet, picture, paper, letter, writing, print, or other publication of an indecent character; and—

"Every written or printed card, letter, circular, book, pamphlet, advertisement, or notice of any kind giving information, directly or indirectly, where, or how, or from whom, or by what means any of such mentioned matters, articles, or things may be obtained or made, . . . whether sealed or unsealed . . .

"Is declared to be nonmailable matter and shall not be conveyed in the mails or delivered from any post office or by any letter carrier.

"Whoever knowingly deposits for mailing or delivery, anything

that "Congress shall make no law . . . abridging the freedom of speech, or of the press. . . ." In *Alberts*, the primary constitutional question is whether the obscenity provisions of the California Penal Code[2] invade the freedoms of speech and press as they may be incorporated in the liberty protected from state action by the Due Process Clause of the Fourteenth Amendment.

Other constitutional questions are: whether these statutes violate due process,[3] because too vague to support conviction for crime; whether power to punish speech and press offensive to decency and morality is in the States alone, so that the federal obscenity statute violates the Ninth and Tenth Amendments (raised in *Roth*); and whether Congress, by enacting the federal obscenity statute, under the power delegated by Art. I, § 8, cl. 7, to establish post offices and post roads, pre-empted the regulation of the subject matter (raised in *Alberts*).

Roth conducted a business in New York in the publication and sale of books, photographs and magazines. He used circulars and advertising matter to solicit sales. He was convicted by a jury in the District Court for the Southern District of New York upon 4 counts of a 26-count indictment charging him with mailing obscene circulars and advertising, and an obscene book, in violation of the federal obscenity statute. His conviction was affirmed by the Court of Appeals for the Second Circuit.[4] We granted certiorari.[5]

Alberts conducted a mail-order business from Los Angeles. He was convicted by the Judge of the Municipal Court of the Beverly Hills Judicial District (having waived a jury trial) under a misdemeanor complaint which charged him with lewdly keeping for sale obscene and indecent books, and with writing, composing and publishing an obscene advertisement of them, in violation of the California Penal Code. The conviction was affirmed by the Appellate Department of the Superior Court of the State of California in and for the County of Los Angeles.[6] We noted probable jurisdiction.[7]

The dispositive question is whether obscenity is utterance within the area of protected speech and press.[8] Although this is the first time the question has been squarely presented to this Court, either under the First Amendment or under the Fourteenth Amendment, expressions found in numerous opinions indicate that this Court has always assumed that obscenity is not protected by the freedoms of speech and press. *Ex parte Jackson*, 96 U.S. 727, 736–737; *United States v. Chase*, 135 U.S. 255, 261; *Robertson v. Baldwin*, 165 U.S. 275, 281; *Public Clearing House v. Coyne*, 194 U.S. 497, 508; *Hoke v. United States*, 227 U.S. 308, 322; *Near v. Minnesota*, 283 U.S. 697, 716; *Chaplinsky v. New Hampshire*, 315 U.S. 568, 571–572; *Hannegan v. Esquire, Inc.*, 327 U.S. 146, 158; *Winters v. New York*, 333 U.S. 507, 510; *Beauharnais v. Illinois*, 343 U.S. 250, 266.[9]

The guaranties of freedom of expression[10] in effect in 10 of the 14 States which by 1792 had ratified the Constitution, gave no absolute protection for every utterance. Thirteen of the 14 States provided for the prosecution of libel,[11] and all of those States made either blasphemy or profanity, or both, statutory crimes.[12] As early as 1712,

---

declared by this section to be nonmailable, or knowingly takes the same from the mails for the purpose of circulating or disposing thereof, or of aiding in the circulation or disposition thereof, shall be fined not more than $5,000 or imprisoned not more than five years, or both." 18 U.S.C. § 1461.

The 1955 amendment of this statute, 69 Stat. 183, is not applicable to this case.

[2] The California Penal Code provides, in pertinent part:

"Every person who wilfully and lewdly, either:

. . . . .

"3. Writes, composes, stereotypes, prints, publishes, sells, distributes, keeps for sale, or exhibits any obscene or indecent writing, paper, or book; or designs, copies, draws, engraves, paints, or otherwise prepares any obscene or indecent picture or print; or molds, cuts, casts, or otherwise makes any obscene or indecent figure; or,

"4. Writes, composes, or publishes any notice or advertisement of any such writing, paper, book, picture, print or figure; . . .

. . . . .

"6. . . . is guilty of a misdemeanor. . . ." West's Cal. Penal Code Ann., 1955, § 311.

[3] In *Roth*, reliance is placed on the Due Process Clause of the Fifth Amendment, and in *Alberts*, reliance is placed upon the Due Process Clause of the Fourteenth Amendment.

[4] 237 F. 2d 796.

[5] 352 U.S. 964. Petitioner's application for bail was granted by Mr. Justice Harlan in his capacity as Circuit Justice for the Second Circuit. 1 L. Ed. 2d 34, 77 Sup. Ct. 17.

[6] 138 Cal. App. 2d Supp. 909, 292 P. 2d 90. This is the highest state appellate court available to the appellant. Cal. Const., Art. VI, § 5; see *Edwards v. California*, 314 U.S. 160.

[7] 352 U.S. 962.

[8] No issue is presented in either case concerning the obscenity of the material involved.

[9] See also the following cases in which convictions under obscenity statutes have been reviewed: *Grimm v. United States*, 156 U.S. 604; *Rosen v. United States*, 161 U.S. 29; *Swearingen v. United States*, 161 U.S. 446; *Andrews v. United States*, 162 U.S. 420; *Price v. United States*, 165 U.S. 311; *Dunlop v. United States*, 165 U.S. 486; *Bartell v. United States*, 227 U.S. 427; *United States v. Limehouse*, 285 U.S. 424.

[10] Del. Const., 1792, Art. I, § 5; Ga. Const., 1777, Art. LXI; Md. Const., 1776, Declaration of Rights, § 38; Mass. Const., 1780, Declaration of Rights, Art. XVI; N.H. Const., 1784, Art. I, § XXII; N.C. Const., 1776, Declaration of Rights, Art. XV; Pa. Const., 1776, Declaration of Rights, Art. XII; S.C. Const., 1778, Art. XLIII; Vt. Const., 1777, Declaration of Rights, Art. XIV; Va. Bill of Rights, 1776, § 12.

[11] Act to Secure the Freedom of the Press (1804), 1 Conn. Pub. Stat. Laws 355 (1808); Del. Const., 1792, Art. I, § 5; Ga. Penal Code, Eighth Div., § VIII (1817), Digest of the Laws of Ga. 364 (Prince 1822); Act of 1803, c. 54, II Md. Public General Laws 1096 (Poe 1888); *Commonwealth v. Kneeland*, 37 Mass. 206, 232 (1838); Act for the Punishment of Certain Crimes Not Capital (1791), N.H. Laws 1792, 253; Act Respecting Libels (1799), N.J. Rev. Laws 411 (1800); *People v. Croswell*, 3 Johns. (N.Y.) 337 (1804); Act of 1803, c. 632, 2 Laws of N.C. 999 (1821); Pa. Const., 1790, Art. IX, § 7; R.I. Code of Laws (1647), Proceedings of the First General Assembly and Code of Laws 44–45 (1647); R.I. Const., 1842, Art. I, § 20; Act of 1804, 1 Laws of Vt. 366 (Tolman 1808); *Commonwealth v. Morris*, 1 Brock. & Hol. (Va.) 176 (1811).

[12] Act for the Punishment of Divers Capital and Other Felonies, Acts and Laws of Conn. 66, 67 (1784); Act Against Drunkenness, Blasphemy, §§ 4, 5 (1737), 1 Laws of Del. 173, 174 (1797); Act to Regulate Taverns (1786), Digest of the Laws of Ga. 512, 513 (Prince 1822); Act of 1723, c. 16, § 1, Digest of the Laws of Md. 92 (Herty 1799); General Laws and Liberties of Mass. Bay, c. XVIII, § 3 (1646), Mass. Bay Colony Charters & Laws 58 (1814); Act of 1782, c. 8, Rev. Stat. of Mass. 741, § 15 (1836); Act of 1798, c. 33, §§ 1, 3, Rev. Stat. of

Massachusetts made it criminal to publish "any filthy, obscene, or profane song, pamphlet, libel or mock sermon" in imitation or mimicking of religious services. Acts and Laws of the Province of Mass. Bay, c. CV, § 8 (1712), Mass. Bay Colony Charters & Laws 399 (1814). Thus, profanity and obscenity were related offenses.

In light of this history, it is apparent that the unconditional phrasing of the First Amendment was not intended to protect every utterance. This phrasing did not prevent this Court from concluding that libelous utterances are not within the area of constitutionally protected speech. *Beauharnais* v. *Illinois*, 343 U.S. 250, 266. At the time of the adoption of the First Amendment, obscenity law was not as fully developed as libel law, but there is sufficiently contemporaneous evidence to show that obscenity, too, was outside the protection intended for speech and press.[13]

The protection given speech and press was fashioned to assure unfettered interchange of ideas for the bringing about of political and social changes desired by the people. This objective was made explicit as early as 1774 in a letter of the Continental Congress to the inhabitants of Quebec:

"The last right we shall mention, regards the freedom of the press. The importance of this consists, besides the advancement of truth, science, morality, and arts in general, in its diffusion of liberal sentiments on the administration of Government, its ready communication of thoughts between subjects, and its consequential promotion of union among them, whereby oppressive officers are shamed or intimidated, into more honourable and just modes of conducting affairs." 1 *Journals of the Continental Congress* 108 (1774).

All ideas having even the slightest redeeming social importance—unorthodox ideas, controversial ideas, even ideas hateful to the prevailing climate of opinion—have

---

Mass. 741, § 16 (1836); Act for the Punishment of Certain Crimes Not Capital (1791), N.H. Laws 1792, 252, 256; Act for the Punishment of Profane Cursing and Swearing (1791), N.H. Laws 1792, 258; Act for Suppressing Vice and Immorality, §§ VIII, IX (1798), N.J. Rev. Laws 329, 331 (1800); Act for Suppressing Immorality, § IV (1788), 2 Laws of N.Y. 257, 258 (Jones & Varick 1777–1789); *People* v. *Ruggles*, 8 Johns. (N.Y.) 290 (1811); Act . . . for the More Effectual Suppression of Vice and Immorality, § III (1741), 1 N.C. Laws 52 (Martin Rev. 1715–1790); Act to Prevent the Grievous Sins of Cursing and Swearing (1700), II Statutes at Large of Pa. 49 (1700–1712); Act for the Prevention of Vice and Immorality, § II (1794), 3 Laws of Pa. 177, 178 (1791–1802); Act to Reform the Penal Laws, §§ 33, 34 (1798), R.I. Laws 1798, 584, 595; Act for the More Effectual Suppressing of Blasphemy and Profaneness (1703), Laws of S.C. 4 (Grimké 1790); Act, for the Punishment of Certain Capital, and Other High Crimes and Misdemeanors, § 20 (1797), 1 Laws of Vt. 332, 339 (Tolman 1808); Act, for the Punishment of Certain Inferior Crimes and Misdemeanors, § 20 (1797), 1 Laws of Vt. 352, 361 (Tolman 1808); Act for the Effectual Suppression of Vice, § 1 (1792), Acts of General Assembly of Va. 286 (1794).

[13] Act Concerning Crimes and Punishments, § 69 (1821), Stat. Laws of Conn. 109 (1824); *Knowles* v. *State*, 3 Day (Conn.) 103 (1808); Rev. Stat. of 1835, c. 130, § 10, Rev. Stat. of Mass. 740 (1836); *Commonwealth* v. *Holmes*, 17 Mass. 335 (1821); Rev. Stat. of 1842, c. 113, § 2, Rev. Stat. of N.H. 221 (1843); Act for Suppressing Vice and Immorality, § XII (1798), N.J. Rev. Laws 329, 331 (1800); *Commonwealth* v. *Sharpless*, 2 S. & R. (Pa.) 91 (1815).

---

the full protection of the guaranties, unless excludable because they encroach upon the limited area of more important interests.[14] But implicit in the history of the First Amendment is the rejection of obscenity as utterly without redeeming social importance. This rejection for that reason is mirrored in the universal judgment that obscenity should be restrained, reflected in the international agreement of over 50 nations,[15] in the obscenity laws of all of the 48 States,[16] and in the 20 obscenity laws enacted by the Congress from 1842 to 1956.[17] This is the same judgment expressed by this Court in *Chaplinsky* v. *New Hampshire*, 315 U.S. 568, 571–572:

". . . There are certain well-defined and narrowly limited classes of speech, the prevention and punishment of which have never been thought to raise any Constitutional problem. These include the lewd and obscene. . . . It has been well observed that such utterances are no essential part of any exposition of ideas, and are of such slight social value as a step to truth that any benefit that may be derived from them is clearly outweighed by the social interest in order and morality. . . ." (*Emphasis added.*)

We hold that obscenity is not within the area of constitutionally protected speech or press.

It is strenuously urged that these obscenity statutes offend the constitutional guaranties because they punish incitation to impure sexual *thoughts*, not shown to be related to any overt antisocial conduct which is or may be incited in the persons stimulated to such *thoughts*. In *Roth*, the trial judge instructed the jury: "The words 'obscene, lewd and lascivious' as used in the law, signify that form of immorality which has relation to sexual impurity and has a tendency to excite lustful *thoughts*." (Emphasis added.) In *Alberts*, the trial judge applied the test laid down in *People* v. *Wepplo*, 78 Cal. App. 2d Supp. 959, 178 P. 2d 853, namely, whether the material has "a substantial tendency to deprave or corrupt its readers by inciting lascivious *thoughts* or arousing lustful desires." (Emphasis added.) It is insisted that the constitutional guaranties are violated because convictions may be had without proof either that obscene material will perceptibly

---

[14] E.g., *United States* v. *Harriss*, 347 U.S. 612; *Breard* v. *Alexandria*, 341 U.S. 622; *Teamsters Union* v. *Hanke*, 339 U.S. 470; *Kovacs* v. *Cooper*, 336 U.S. 77; *Prince* v. *Massachusetts*, 321 U.S. 158; *Labor Board* v. *Virginia Elec. & Power Co.*, 314 U.S. 469; *Cox* v. *New Hampshire*, 312 U.S. 569; *Schenck* v. *United States*, 249 U.S. 47.

[15] Agreement for the Suppression of the Circulation of Obscene Publications, 37 Stat. 1511; Treaties in Force 209 (U.S. Dept. State, October 31, 1956).

[16] Hearings before Subcommittee to Investigate Juvenile Delinquency of the Senate Committee on the Judiciary, pursuant to S. Res. 62, 84th Cong., 1st Sess. 49–52 (May 24, 1955). Although New Mexico has no general obscenity statute, it does have a statute giving to municipalities the power "to prohibit the sale or exhibiting of obscene or immoral publications, prints, pictures, or illustrations." N.M. Stat. Ann., 1953 §§ 14–21–3, 14–21–12.

[17] 5 Stat. 548, 566; 11 Stat. 168; 13 Stat. 504, 507; 17 Stat. 302; 17 Stat. 598; 19 Stat. 90; 25 Stat. 187, 188; 25 Stat. 496; 26 Stat. 567, 614–615; 29 Stat. 512; 33 Stat. 705; 35 Stat. 1129, 1138; 41 Stat. 1060; 46 Stat. 688; 48 Stat. 1091, 1100; 62 Stat. 768; 64 Stat. 194; 64 Stat. 451; 69 Stat. 183; 70 Stat. 699.

create a clear and present danger of antisocial conduct,[18] or will probably induce its recipients to such conduct.[19] But, in light of our holding that obscenity is not protected speech, the complete answer to this argument is in the holding of this Court in *Beauharnais v. Illinois, supra,* at 266:

"*Libelous utterances not being within the area of constitutionally protected speech, it is unnecessary, either for us or for the State courts, to consider the issues behind the phrase 'clear and present danger.' Certainly no one would contend that obscene speech, for example, may be punished only upon a showing of such circumstances. Libel, as we have seen, is in the same class.*"

However, sex and obscenity are not synonymous. Obscene material is material which deals with sex in a manner appealing to prurient interest.[20] The portrayal of sex, *e.g.,* in art, literature and scientific works,[21] is not itself sufficient reason to deny material the constitutional protection of freedom of speech and press. Sex, a great and mysterious motive force in human life, has indisputably been a subject of absorbing interest to mankind through the ages; it is one of the vital problems of human interest and public concern. As to all such problems, this Court said in *Thornhill v. Alabama,* 310 U.S. 88, 101–102:

"*The freedom of speech and of the press guaranteed by the Constitution embraces at the least the liberty to discuss publicly and truthfully all matters of public concern*

without previous restraint or fear of subsequent punishment. The exigencies of the colonial period and the efforts to secure freedom from oppressive administration developed a broadened conception of these liberties as adequate to supply the public need for information and education with respect to the significant issues of the times. . . . Freedom of discussion, if it would fulfill its historic function in this nation, must embrace all issues about which information is needed or appropriate to enable the members of society to cope with the exigencies of their period." (*Emphasis added.*)

The fundamental freedoms of speech and press have contributed greatly to the development and well-being of our free society and are indispensable to its continued growth.[22] Ceaseless vigilance is the watchword to prevent their erosion by Congress or by the States. The door barring federal and state intrusion into this area cannot be left ajar; it must be kept tightly closed and opened only the slightest crack necessary to prevent encroachment upon more important interests.[23] It is therefore vital that the standards for judging obscenity safeguard the protection of freedom of speech and press for material which does not treat sex in a manner appealing to prurient interest.

The early leading standard of obscenity allowed material to be judged merely by the effect of an isolated excerpt upon particularly susceptible persons. *Regina v. Hicklin,* [1868] L.R. 3 Q.B. 360.[24] Some American courts adopted this standard[25] but later decisions have rejected it and substituted this test: whether to the average person, applying contemporary community standards, the dominant theme of the material taken as a whole appeals to prurient interest.[26] The *Hicklin* test, judging obscenity by the effect of isolated passages upon the most susceptible persons, might well encompass material legitimately treating with sex, and so it must be rejected as unconstitutionally restrictive of the freedoms of speech and press. On the other hand, the substituted standard provides safeguards adequate to withstand the charge of constitutional infirmity.

---

[18] *Schenck* v. *United States,* 249 U.S. 47. This approach is typified by the opinion of Judge Bok (written prior to this Court's opinion in *Dennis* v. *United States,* 341 U.S. 494) in *Commonwealth* v. *Gordon,* 66 Pa. D. & C. 101, aff'd, *sub nom. Commonwealth* v. *Feigenbaum,* 166 Pa. Super. 120, 70 A. 2d 389.

[19] *Dennis* v. *United States,* 341 U.S 494. This approach is typified by the concurring opinion of Judge Frank in the *Roth* case, 237 F. 2d, at 801. See also Lockhart & McClure, Literature, The Law of Obscenity, and the Constitution, 38 Minn. L. Rev. 295 (1954).

[20] *I.e.,* material having a tendency to excite lustful thoughts. Webster's New International Dictionary (Unabridged, 2d ed., 1949) defines *prurient,* in pertinent part, as follows:

". . . Itching; longing; uneasy with desire or longing; of persons, having itching, morbid, or lascivious longings; of desire, curiosity, or propensity, lewd. . . ."

Pruriency is defined, in pertinent part, as follows:

". . . Quality of being prurient; lascivious desire or thought. . . ."

See also *Mutual Film Corp.* v. *Industrial Comm'n,* 236 U.S. 230, 242, where this Court said as to motion pictures: ". . . They take their attraction from the general interest, eager and wholesome it may be, in their subjects, but a *prurient interest may be excited and appealed to. . . .*" (Emphasis added.)

We perceive no significant difference between the meaning of obscenity developed in the case law and the definition of the A.L.I., Model Penal Code, § 207.10(2) (Tent. Draft No. 6, 1957), *viz.:*

". . . A thing is obscene if, considered as a whole, its predominant appeal is to prurient interest, i.e., a shameful or morbid interest in nudity, sex, or excretion, and if it goes substantially beyond customary limits of candor in description or representation of such matters. . . ." See Comment, *id.,* at 10, and the discussion at page 29 *et seq.*

[21] See, *e.g., United States* v. *Dennett,* 39 F. 2d 564.

[22] Madison's Report on the Virginia Resolutions, 4 Elliot's Debates 571.

[23] See note 14, *supra.*

[24] But see the instructions given to the jury by Mr. Justice Stable in *Regina v. Martin Secker Warburg,* [1954] 2 All Eng. 683 (C.C.C.).

[25] *United States* v. *Kennerley,* 209 F. 119; *MacFadden* v. *United States,* 165 F. 51; *United States* v. *Bennett,* 24 Fed. Cas. 1093; *United States* v. *Clarke,* 38 F. 500; *Commonwealth* v. *Buckley,* 200 Mass. 346, 86 N.E. 910.

[26] E.g., *Walker* v. *Popenoe,* 80 U.S. App. D.C. 129, 149 F. 2d 511; *Parmelee* v. *United States,* 72 App. D.C. 203, 113 F. 2d 729; *United States* v. *Levine,* 83 F. 2d 156; *United States* v. *Dennett,* 39 F. 2d 564; *Khan* v. *Feist, Inc.,* 70 F. Supp. 450, aff'd, 165 F. 2d 188; *United States* v. *One Book Called "Ulysses,"* 5 F. Supp. 182, aff'd, 72 F. 2d 705; *American Civil Liberties Union* v. *Chicago,* 3 Ill. 2d 334, 121 N.E. 2d 585; *Commonwealth* v. *Isenstadt,* 318 Mass. 543, 62 N.E. 2d 840; *Missouri* v. *Becker,* 364 Mo. 1079, 272 S.W. 2d 283; *Adams Theatre Co.* v. *Keenan,* 12 N.J. 267, 96 A. 2d 519; *Bantam Books, Inc.* v. *Melko,* 25 N.J. Super. 292, 96 A. 2d 47; *Commonwealth* v. *Gordon,* 66 Pa. D. & C. 101, aff'd, *sub nom. Commonwealth* v. *Feigenbaum,* 166 Pa. Super. 120, 70 A. 2d 389; *cf. Roth* v. *Goldman,* 172 F. 2d 788, 794–795 (concurrence).

Both trial courts below sufficiently followed the proper standard. Both courts used the proper definition of obscenity. In addition, in the *Alberts* case, in ruling on a motion to dismiss, the trial judge indicated that, as the trier of facts, he was judging each item as a whole as it would affect the normal person,[27] and in *Roth*, the trial judge instructed the jury as follows:

". . . *The test is not whether it would arouse sexual desires or sexual impure thoughts in those comprising a particular segment of the community, the young, the immature or the highly prudish or would leave another segment, the scientific or highly educated or the so-called worldly-wise and sophisticated indifferent and unmoved.*

. . .

"*The test in each case is the effect of the book, picture or publication considered as a whole, not upon any particular class, but upon all those whom it is likely to reach. In other words, you determine its impact upon the average person in the community. The books, pictures and circulars must be judged as a whole, in their entire context, and you are not to consider detached or separate portions in reaching a conclusion. You judge the circulars, pictures and publications which have been put in evidence by present-day standards of the community. You may ask yourselves does it offend the common conscience of the community by present-day standards.*

*   *   *   *   *

"*In this case, ladies and gentlemen of the jury, you and you alone are the exclusive judges of what the common conscience of the community is, and in determining that conscience you are to consider the community as a whole, young and old, educated and uneducated, the religious and the irreligious—men, women and children.*"

It is argued that the statutes do not provide reasonably ascertainable standards of guilt and therefore violate the constitutional requirements of due process. *Winters v. New York,* 333 U.S. 507. The federal obscenity statute makes punishable the mailing of material that is "obscene, lewd, lascivious, or filthy . . . or other publication of an indecent character."[28] The California statute makes punishable, *inter alia*, the keeping for sale or advertising material that is "obscene or indecent." The thrust of the argument is that these words are not sufficiently precise because they do not mean the same thing to all people, all the time, everywhere.

Many decisions have recognized that these terms of obscenity statutes are not precise.[29] This Court, however, has consistently held that lack of precision is not itself

offensive to the requirements of due process. ". . . [T]he Constitution does not require impossible standards"; all that is required is that the language "conveys sufficiently definite warning as to the proscribed conduct when measured by common understanding and practices. . . ." *United States v. Petrillo,* 332 U.S. 1, 7–8. These words, applied according to the proper standard for judging obscenity, already discussed, give adequate warning of the conduct proscribed and mark ". . . boundaries sufficiently distinct for judges and juries fairly to administer the law. . . . That there may be marginal cases in which it is difficult to determine the side of the line on which a particular fact situation falls is no sufficient reason to hold the language too ambiguous to define a criminal offense. . . ." *Id.,* at 7. See also *United States v. Harriss,* 347 U.S. 612, 624, n. 15; *Boyce Motor Lines, Inc. v. United States,* 342 U.S. 337, 340; *United States v. Ragen,* 314 U.S. 513, 523–524; *United States v. Wurzbach,* 280 U.S. 396; *Hygrade Provision Co. v. Sherman,* 266 U.S. 497; *Fox v. Washington,* 236 U.S. 273; *Nash v. United States,* 229 U.S. 373.[30]

In summary, then, we hold that these statutes, applied according to the proper standard for judging obscenity, do not offend constitutional safeguards against convictions based upon protected material, or fail to give men in acting adequate notice of what is prohibited.

Roth's argument that the federal obscenity statute unconstitutionally encroaches upon the powers reserved by the Ninth and Tenth Amendments to the States and to the people to punish speech and press where offensive to decency and morality is hinged upon his contention that obscenity is expression not excepted from the sweep of the provision of the First Amendment that "*Congress* shall make *no law* . . . abridging the freedom of speech, or of the press. . . ." (Emphasis added.) That argument falls in light of our holding that obscenity is not expression protected by the First Amendment.[31] We therefore hold that the federal obscenity statute punishing the use of the mails for obscene material is a proper exercise of the postal power delegated to Congress by Art. I, § 8, cl. 7.[32] In

---

[27] In *Alberts*, the contention that the trial judge did not read the materials in their entirety is not before us because not fairly comprised within the questions presented. U.S. Sup. Ct. Rules, 15(1)(c)(1).

[28] This Court, as early as 1896, said of the federal obscenity statute:

". . . Every one who uses the mails of the United States for carrying papers or publications must take notice of what, in this enlightened age, is meant by decency, purity, and chastity in social life, and what must be deemed obscene, lewd, and lascivious." *Rosen v. United States,* 161 U.S. 29, 42.

[29] E.g., *Roth v. Goldman,* 172 F. 2d 788, 789; *Parmelee v. United States,* 72 App. D.C. 203, 204, 113 F. 2d 729, 730; *United States v. 4200 Copies International Journal,* 134 F. Supp. 490, 493; *United States v. One Unbound Volume,* 128 F. Supp. 280, 281.

[30] It is argued that because juries may reach different conclusions as to the same material, the statutes must be held to be insufficiently precise to satisfy due process requirements. But, it is common experience that different juries may reach different results under any criminal statute. That is one of the consequences we accept under our jury system. Cf. *Dunlop v. United States,* 165 U.S. 486, 499–500.

[31] For the same reason, we reject, in this case, the argument that there is greater latitude for state action under the word "liberty" under the Fourteenth Amendment than is allowed to Congress by the language of the First Amendment.

[32] In *Public Clearing House v. Coyne,* 194 U.S. 497, 506–508, this Court said:

"The constitutional principles underlying the administration of the Post Office Department were discussed in the opinion of the court in *Ex parte Jackson,* 96 U.S. 727, in which we held that the power vested in Congress to establish post offices and post roads embraced the regulation of the entire postal system of the country; that Congress might designate what might be carried in the mails and what excluded. . . . It may . . . refuse to include in its mails such printed matter or merchandise as may seem objectionable to it upon the ground of public policy. . . . For more than thirty years not only has the transmission of obscene matter been prohibited, but it has been made a crime, punishable by fine or imprisonment, for a person to deposit such matter in the mails. The constitutionality of this law we believe has never been attacked. . . ."

United Public Workers v. Mitchell, 330 U.S. 75, 95–96, this Court said:

> ". . . *The powers granted by the Constitution to the Federal Government are subtracted from the totality of sovereignty originally in the states and the people. Therefore, when objection is made that the exercise of a federal power infringes upon rights reserved by the Ninth and Tenth Amendments, the inquiry must be directed toward the granted power under which the action of the Union was taken. If granted power is found, necessarily the objection of invasion of those rights, reserved by the Ninth and Tenth Amendments, must fail. . . ."*

Alberts argues that because his was a mail-order business, the California statute is repugnant to Art. I, § 8, cl. 7, under which the Congress allegedly pre-empted the regulatory field by enacting the federal obscenity statute punishing the mailing or advertising by mail of obscene material. The federal statute deals only with actual mailing; it does not eliminate the power of the state to punish "keeping for sale" or "advertising" obscene material. The state statute in no way imposes a burden or interferes with the federal postal functions. ". . . The decided cases which indicate the limits of state regulatory power in relation to the federal mail service involve situations where state regulation involved a direct, physical interference with federal activities under the postal power or some direct, immediate burden on the performance of the postal functions. . . ." *Railway Mail Assn. v. Corsi,* 326 U.S. 88, 96.

The judgments are affirmed.

MR. CHIEF JUSTICE WARREN, concurring in the result.

I agree with the result reached by the Court in these cases, but, because we are operating in a field of expression and because broad language used here may eventually be applied to the arts and sciences and freedom of communication generally, I would limit our decision to the facts before us and to the validity of the statutes in question as applied.

Appellant Alberts was charged with wilfully, unlawfully and lewdly disseminating obscene matter. Obscenity has been construed by the California courts to mean having a substantial tendency to corrupt by arousing lustful desires. *People v. Wepplo,* 78 Cal. App. 2d Supp. 959, 178 P. 2d 853. Petitioner Roth was indicted for unlawfully, wilfully and knowingly mailing obscene material that was calculated to corrupt and debauch the minds and morals of those to whom it was sent. Each was accorded all the protections of a criminal trial. Among other things, they contend that the statutes under which they were convicted violate the constitutional guarantees of freedom of speech, press and communication.

That there is a social problem presented by obscenity is attested by the expression of the legislatures of the forty-eight States as well as the Congress. To recognize the existence of a problem, however, does not require that we sustain any and all measures adopted to meet that problem. The history of the application of laws designed to suppress the obscene demonstrates convincingly that the power of government can be invoked under them against great art or literature, scientific treatises, or works exciting

social controversy. Mistakes of the past prove that there is a strong countervailing interest to be considered in the freedoms guaranteed by the First and Fourteenth Amendments.

The line dividing the salacious or pornographic from literature or science is not straight and unwavering. Present laws depend largely upon the effect that the materials may have upon those who receive them. It is manifest that the same object may have a different impact, varying according to the part of the community it reached. But there is more to these cases. It is not the book that is on trial; it is a person. The conduct of the defendant is the central issue, not the obscenity of a book or picture. The nature of the materials is, of course, relevant as an attribute of the defendant's conduct, but the materials are thus placed in context from which they draw color and character. A wholly different result might be reached in a different setting.

The personal element in these cases is seen most strongly in the requirement of *scienter.* Under the California law, the prohibited activity must be done "wilfully and lewdly." The federal statute limits the crime to acts done "knowingly." In his charge to the jury, the district judge stated that the matter must be "calculated" to corrupt or debauch. The defendants in both these cases were engaged in the business of purveying textual or graphic matter openly advertised to appeal to the erotic interest of their customers. They were plainly engaged in the commercial exploitation of the morbid and shameful craving for materials with prurient effect. I believe that the State and Federal Governments can constitutionally punish such conduct. That is all that these cases present to us, and that is all we need to decide.

I agree with the Court's decision in its rejection of the other contentions raised by these defendants.

MR. JUSTICE HARLAN, concurring in the result in No. 61, and dissenting in No. 582.

I regret not to be able to join the Court's opinion. I cannot do so because I find lurking beneath its disarming generalizations a number of problems which not only leave me with serious misgivings as to the future effect of today's decisions, but which also, in my view, call for different results in these two cases.

I.

My basic difficulties with the Court's opinion are three-fold. First, the opinion paints with such a broad brush that I fear it may result in a loosening of the tight reins which state and federal courts should hold upon the enforcement of obscenity statutes. Second, the Court fails to discriminate between the different factors which, in my opinion, are involved in the constitutional adjudication of state and federal obscenity cases. Third, relevant distinctions between the two obscenity statutes here involved, and the Court's own definition of "obscenity," are ignored.

In final analysis, the problem presented by these cases is how far, and on what terms, the state and federal governments have power to punish individuals for disseminating books considered to be undesirable because of their nature or supposed deleterious effect upon human conduct. Proceeding from the premise that "no issue is presented in either case, concerning the obscenity of the material involved," the Court finds the "dispositive question" to be "whether obscenity is utterance within the area of protected speech and press," and then holds that "obscenity" is not so protected because it is "utterly without redeeming social importance." This sweeping formula appears to me to beg the very question before us. The Court seems to assume that "obscenity" is a peculiar *genus* of "speech and press," which is as distinct, recognizable, and classifiable as poison ivy is among other plants. On this basis the *constitutional* question before us simply becomes, as the Court says, whether "obscenity," as an abstraction, is protected by the First and Fourteenth Amendments, and the question whether a *particular* book may be suppressed becomes a mere matter of classification, of "fact," to be entrusted to a factfinder and insulated from independent constitutional judgment. But surely the problem cannot be solved in such a generalized fashion. Every communication has an individuality and "value" of its own. The suppression of a particular writing or other tangible form of expression is, therefore, an *individual* matter, and in the nature of things every such suppression raises an individual constitutional problem, in which a reviewing court must determine for *itself* whether the attacked expression is suppressable within constitutional standards. Since those standards do not readily lend themselves to generalized definitions, the constitutional problem in the last analysis becomes one of particularized judgments which appellate courts must make for themselves.

I do not think that reviewing courts can escape this responsibility by saying that the trier of the facts, be it a jury or a judge, has labeled the questioned matter as "obscene," for, if "obscenity" is to be suppressed, the question whether a particular work is of that character involves not really an issue of fact but a question of constitutional *judgment* of the most sensitive and delicate kind. Many juries might find that Joyce's "Ulysses" or Boccaccio's "Decameron" was obscene, and yet the conviction of a defendant for selling either book would raise, for me, the gravest constitutional problems, for no such verdict could convince me, without more, that these books are "utterly without redeeming social importance." In short, I do not understand how the Court can resolve the constitutional problems now before it without making its own independent judgment upon the character of the material upon which these convictions were based. I am very much afraid that the broad manner in which the Court has decided these cases will tend to obscure the peculiar responsibilities resting on state and federal courts in this field and encourage them to rely on easy labeling and jury verdicts as a substitute for facing up to the tough individual problems of constitutional judgment involved in every obscenity case.

My second reason for dissatisfaction with the Court's opinion is that the broad strides with which the Court has proceeded has led it to brush aside with perfunctory ease the vital constitutional considerations which, in my opinion, differentiate these two cases. It does not seem to matter to the Court that in one case we balance the power of a State in this field against the restrictions of the Fourteenth Amendment, and in the other the power of the Federal Government against the limitations of the First Amendment. I deal with this subject more particularly later.

Thirdly, the Court has not been bothered by the fact that the two cases involve different statutes. In California the book must have a "tendency to deprave or corrupt its readers"; under the federal statute it must tend "to stir sexual impulses and lead to sexually impure thoughts."[1] The two statutes do not seem to me to present the same problems. Yet the Court compounds confusion when it superimposes on these two statutory definitions a third, drawn from the American Law Institute's Model Penal Code, Tentative Draft No. 6: "A thing is obscene if, considered as a whole, its predominant appeal is to prurient interest." The bland assurance that this definition is the same as the ones with which we deal flies in the face of the authors' express rejection of the "deprave and corrupt" and "sexual thoughts" tests:

"Obscenity [in the Tentative Draft] is defined in terms of material which appeals predominantly to prurient interest in sexual matters and which goes beyond customary freedom of expression in these matters. We reject the prevailing test of tendency to arouse lustful thoughts or desires because it is unrealistically broad for a society that plainly tolerates a great deal of erotic interest in literature, advertising, and art, and because regulation of thought or desire, unconnected with overt misbehavior, raises the most acute constitutional as well as practical difficulties. We likewise reject the common definition of obscene as that which 'tends to corrupt or debase.' If this means anything different from tendency to arouse lustful thought and desire, it suggests that change of character or actual misbehavior follows from contact with obscenity. Evidence of such consequences is lacking. . . . On the other hand, 'appeal to prurient interest' refers to qualities of the material itself: the capacity to attract individuals eager for a forbidden look. . . ."[2]

As this passage makes clear, there is a significant distinction between the definitions used in the prosecutions before us, and the American Law Institute formula. If, therefore, the latter is the correct standard, as my Brother BRENNAN elsewhere intimates,[3] then these convictions

---

[1] In *Alberts* v. *California*, the state definition of "obscenity" is, of course, binding on us. The definition there used derives from *People* v. *Wepplo*, 78 Cal. App. 2d Supp. 959, 178 P. 2d 853, the question being whether the material has "a substantive tendency to deprave or corrupt its readers by exciting lascivious thoughts or arousing lustful desire."

In *Roth* v. *United States*, our grant of certiorari was limited to the question of the constitutionality of the statute, and did not encompass the correctness of the definition of "obscenity" adopted by the trial judge as a matter of statutory construction. We must therefore assume that the trial judge correctly defined that term, and deal with the constitutionality of the statute as construed and applied in this case.

The two definitions do not seem to me synonymous. Under the federal definition it is enough if the jury finds that the book as a whole leads to certain thoughts. In California, the further inference must be drawn that such thoughts will have a substantive "tendency to deprave or corrupt"—*i.e.*, that the thoughts induced by the material will affect character and action. See American Law Institute, Model Penal Code, Tentative Draft No. 6, § 207.10(2), Comments, p. 10.

[2] *Ibid.*

[3] See dissenting opinion of MR. JUSTICE BRENNAN in *Kingsley Books, Inc.* v. *Brown*, No. 107, *ante*, p. 447.

should surely be reversed. Instead, the Court merely assimilates the various tests into one indiscriminate potpourri.

I now pass to the consideration of the two cases before us.

II.

I concur in the judgment of the Court in No. 61, *Alberts v. California*.

The question in this case is whether the defendant was deprived of liberty without due process of law when he was convicted for selling certain materials found by the judge to be obscene because they would have a "tendency to deprave or corrupt its readers by exciting lascivious thoughts or arousing lustful desire."

In judging the constitutionality of this conviction, we should remember that our function in reviewing state judgments under the Fourteenth Amendment is a narrow one. We do not decide whether the policy of the State is wise, or whether it is based on assumptions scientifically substantiated. We can inquire only whether the state action so subverts the fundamental liberties implicit in the Due Process Clause that it cannot be sustained as a rational exercise of power. See Jackson, J., dissenting in *Beauharnais v. Illinois*, 343 U.S. 250, 287. The States' power to make printed words criminal is, of course, confined by the Fourteenth Amendment, but only insofar as such power is inconsistent with our concepts of "ordered liberty." *Palko v. Connecticut*, 302 U.S. 319, 324–325.

What, then, is the purpose of this California statute? Clearly the state legislature has made the judgment that printed words *can* "deprave or corrupt" the reader—that words can incite to antisocial or immoral action. The assumption seems to be that the distribution of certain types of literature will induce criminal or immoral sexual conduct. It is well known, of course, that the validity of this assumption is a matter of dispute among critics, sociologists, psychiatrists, and penologists. There is a large school of thought, particularly in the scientific community, which denies any causal connection between the reading of pornography and immorality, crime, or delinquency. Others disagree. Clearly it is not our function to decide this question. That function belongs to the state legislature. Nothing in the Constitution requires California to accept as truth the most advanced and sophisticated psychiatric opinion. It seems to me clear that it is not irrational, in our present state of knowledge, to consider that pornography can induce a type of sexual conduct which a State may deem obnoxious to the moral fabric of society. In fact the very division of opinion on the subject counsels us to respect the choice made by the State.

Furthermore, even assuming that pornography cannot be deemed ever to cause, in an immediate sense, criminal sexual conduct, other interests within the proper cognizance of the States may be protected by the prohibition placed on such materials. The State can reasonably draw the inference that over a long period of time the indiscriminate dissemination of materials, the essential character of which is to degrade sex, will have an eroding effect on moral standards. And the State has a legitimate interest in protecting the privacy of the home against invasion of unsolicited obscenity.

Above all stands the realization that we deal here with an area where knowledge is small, data are insufficient, and experts are divided. Since the domain of sexual morality is pre-eminently a matter of state concern, this Court should be slow to interfere with state legislation calculated to protect that morality. It seems to me that nothing in the broad and flexible command of the Due Process Clause forbids California to prosecute one who sells books whose dominant tendency might be to "deprave or corrupt" a reader. I agree with the Court, of course, that the books must be judged as a whole and in relation to the normal adult reader.

What has been said, however, does not dispose of the case. It still remains for us to decide whether the state court's determination that this material should be suppressed is consistent with the Fourteenth Amendment; and that, of course, presents a federal question as to which we, and not the state court, have the ultimate responsibility. And so, in the final analysis, I concur in the judgment because, upon an independent perusal of the material involved, and in light of the considerations discussed above, I cannot say that its suppression would so interfere with the communication of "ideas" in any proper sense of that term that it would offend the Due Process Clause. I therefore agree with the Court that appellant's conviction must be affirmed.

III.

I dissent in No. 582, *Roth v. United States*.

We are faced here with the question whether the federal obscenity statute, as construed and applied in this case, violates the First Amendment to the Constitution. To me, this question is of quite a different order than one where we are dealing with state legislation under the Fourteenth Amendment. I do not think it follows that state and federal powers in this area are the same, and that just because the State may suppress a particular utterance, it is automatically permissible for the Federal Government to do the same. I agree with Mr. Justice Jackson that the historical evidence does not bear out the claim that the Fourteenth Amendment "incorporates" the First in any literal sense. See *Beauharnais v. Illinois, supra*. But laying aside any consequences which might flow from that conclusion, cf. Mr. Justice Holmes in *Gitlow v. New York*, 268 U.S. 652, 672,[4] I prefer to rest my views about this case on broader and less abstract grounds.

The Constitution differentiates between those areas of human conduct subject to the regulation of the States and those subject to the powers of the Federal Government. The substantive powers of the two governments, in many instances, are distinct. And in every case where we are called upon to balance the interest in free expression against other interests, it seems to me important that we should keep in the forefront the question of whether those other interests are state or federal. Since under our constitutional scheme the two are not necessarily equivalent, the balancing process must needs often produce different results. Whether a particular limitation on speech or press is to be upheld because it subserves a paramount governmental interest must, to a large extent, I think, depend on

---

4 "The general principle of free speech, it seems to me, must be taken to be included in the Fourteenth Amendment, in view of the scope that has been given to the word 'liberty' as there used, although perhaps it may be accepted with a somewhat larger latitude of interpretation than is allowed to Congress by the sweeping language that governs or ought to govern the laws of the United States."

whether that government has, under the Constitution, a direct substantive interest, that is, the power to act, in the particular area involved.

The Federal Government has, for example, power to restrict seditious speech directed against it, because that Government certainly has the substantive authority to protect itself against revolution. Cf. *Pennsylvania* v. *Nelson*, 350 U.S. 497. But in dealing with obscenity we are faced with the converse situation, for the interests which obscenity statutes purportedly protect are primarily entrusted to the care, not of the Federal Government, but of the States. Congress has no substantive power over sexual morality. Such powers as the Federal Government has in this field are but incidental to its other powers, here the postal power, and are not of the same nature as those possessed by the States, which bear direct responsibility for the protection of the local moral fabric.[5] What Mr. Justice Jackson said in *Beauharnais, supra*, 343 U.S., at 294–295, about criminal libel is equally true of obscenity:

"The inappropriateness of a single standard for restricting State and Nation is indicated by the disparity between their functions and duties in relation to those freedoms. Criminality of defamation is predicated upon power either to protect the private right to enjoy integrity of reputation or the public right to tranquillity. Neither of these are objects of federal cognizance except when necessary to the accomplishment of some delegated power. . . . When the Federal Government puts liberty of press in one scale, it has a very limited duty to personal reputation or local tranquillity to weigh against it in the other. But state action affecting speech or press can and should be weighed against and reconciled with these conflicting social interests."

Not only is the federal interest in protecting the Nation against pornography attenuated, but the dangers of federal censorship in this field are far greater than anything the States may do. It has often been said that one of the great strengths of our federal system is that we have, in the forty-eight States, forty-eight experimental social laboratories. "State statutory law reflects predominantly this capacity of a legislature to introduce novel techniques of social control. The federal system has the immense advantage of providing forty-eight separate centers for such experimentation."[6] Different States will have different attitudes toward the same work of literature. The same book which is freely read in one State might be classed as obscene in another.[7] And it seems to me that no overwhelming

danger to our freedom to experiment and to gratify our tastes in literature is likely to result from the suppression of a borderline book in one of the States, so long as there is no uniform nation-wide suppression of the book, and so long as other States are free to experiment with the same or bolder books.

Quite a different situation is presented, however, where the Federal Government imposes the ban. The danger is perhaps not great if the people of one State, through their legislature, decide that "Lady Chatterley's Lover" goes so far beyond the acceptable standards of candor that it will be deemed offensive and non-sellable, for the State next door is still free to make its own choice. At least we do not have one uniform standard. But the dangers to free thought and expression are truly great if the Federal Government imposes a blanket ban over the Nation on such a book. The prerogative of the States to differ on their ideas of morality will be destroyed, the ability of States to experiment will be stunted. The fact that the people of one State cannot read some of the works of D. H. Lawrence seems to me, if not wise or desirable, at least acceptable. But that no person in the United States should be allowed to do so seems to me to be intolerable, and violative of both the letter and spirit of the First Amendment.

I judge this case, then, in view of what I think is the attenuated federal interest in this field, in view of the very real danger of a deadening uniformity which can result from nation-wide federal censorship, and in view of the fact that the constitutionality of this conviction must be weighed against the First and not the Fourteenth Amendment. So viewed, I do not think that this conviction can be upheld. The petitioner was convicted under a statute which, under the judge's charge,[8] makes it criminal to sell books which "tend to stir sexual impulses and lead to sexually impure thoughts." I cannot agree that any book which tends to stir sexual impulses and lead to sexually impure thoughts necessarily is "utterly without redeeming social importance." Not only did this charge fail to measure up to the standards which I understand the Court to approve, but as far as I can see, much of the great literature of the world could lead to conviction under such a view of the statute. Moreover, in no event do I think that the limited federal interest in this area can extend to mere "thoughts." The Federal Government has no business, whether under the postal or commerce power, to bar the sale of books because they might lead to any kind of "thoughts."[9]

It is no answer to say, as the Court does, that obscenity is not protected speech. The point is that this statute, as here construed, defines obscenity so widely that it encompasses matters which might very well be protected speech. I do not think that the federal statute can be constitutionally construed to reach other than what the Government

---

[5] The hoary dogma of *Ex parte Jackson*, 96 U.S. 727, and *Public Clearing House* v. *Coyne*, 194 U.S. 497, that the use of the mails is a privilege on which the Government may impose such conditions as it chooses, has long since evaporated. See Brandeis, J., dissenting, in *Milwaukee Social Democratic Publishing Co.* v. *Burleson*, 255 U.S. 407, 430–433; Holmes, J., dissenting, in *Leach* v. *Carlile*, 258 U.S. 138, 140; *Cates* v. *Haderline*, 342 U.S. 804, reversing 189 F. 2d 369; *Door* v. *Donaldson*, 90 U.S. App. D.C. 188, 195 F. 2d 764.

[6] Hart, The Relations Between State and Federal Law, 54 Col. L. Rev. 489, 493.

[7] To give only a few examples: Edmund Wilson's "Memoirs of Hecate County" was found obscene in New York, see *Doubleday & Co.* v. *New York*, 335 U.S. 848; a bookseller indicted for selling the same book was acquitted in California. "God's Little Acre" was held to be obscene in Massachusetts, not obscene in New York and Pennsylvania.

[8] While the correctness of the judge's charge is not before us, the question is necessarily subsumed in the broader question involving the constitutionality of the statute as applied in this case.

[9] See American Law Institute, Model Penal Code, Tentative Draft No. 6, § 207.10, Comments, p. 20: "As an independent goal of penal legislation, repression of sexual thoughts and desires is hard to support. Thoughts and desires not manifested in overt antisocial behavior are generally regarded as the exclusive concern of the individual and his spiritual advisors."

has termed as "hard-core" pornography. Nor do I think the statute can fairly be read as directed only at *persons* who are engaged in the business of catering to the prurient minded, even though their wares fall short of hard-core pornography. Such a statute would raise constitutional questions of a different order. That being so, and since in my opinion the material here involved cannot be said to be hard-core pornography, I would reverse this case with instructions to dismiss the indictment.

MR. JUSTICE DOUGLAS, with whom MR. JUSTICE BLACK concurs, dissenting.

When we sustain these convictions, we make the legality of a publication turn on the purity of thought which a book or tract instills in the mind of the reader. I do not think we can approve that standard and be faithful to the command of the First Amendment, which by its terms is a restraint on Congress and which by the Fourteenth is a restraint on the States.

In the *Roth* case the trial judge charged the jury that the statutory words "obscene, lewd and lascivious" describe "that form of immorality which has relation to sexual impurity and has a tendency to excite lustful thoughts." He stated that the term "filthy" in the statute pertains "to that sort of treatment of sexual matters in such a vulgar and indecent way, so that it tends to arouse a feeling of disgust and revulsion." He went on to say that the material "must be calculated to corrupt and debauch the minds and morals" of "the average person in the community," not those of any particular class. "You judge the circulars, pictures and publications which have been put in evidence by present-day standards of the community. You may ask yourselves does it offend the common conscience of the community by present-day standards."

The trial judge who, sitting without a jury, heard the *Alberts* case and the appellate court that sustained the judgment of conviction, took California's definition of "obscenity" from *People* v. *Wepplo*, 78 Cal. App. 2d Supp. 959, 961, 178 P. 2d 853, 855. That case held that a book is obscene "if it has a substantial tendency to deprave or corrupt its readers by inciting lascivious thoughts or arousing lustful desire."

By these standards punishment is inflicted for thoughts provoked, not for overt acts nor antisocial conduct. This test cannot be squared with our decisions under the First Amendment. Even the ill-starred *Dennis* case conceded that speech to be punishable must have some relation to action which could be penalized by government. *Dennis* v. *United States*, 341 U.S. 494, 502–511. Cf. Chafee, The Blessings of Liberty (1956), p. 69. This issue cannot be avoided by saying that obscenity is not protected by the First Amendment. The question remains, what is the constitutional test of obscenity?

The tests by which these convictions were obtained require only the arousing of sexual thoughts. Yet the arousing of sexual thoughts and desires happens every day in normal life in dozens of ways. Nearly 30 years ago a questionnaire sent to college and normal school women graduates asked what things were most stimulating sexually. Of 409 replies, 9 said "music"; 18 said "pictures"; 29 said "dancing"; 40 said "drama"; 95 said "books"; and 218 said "man." Alpert, Judicial Censorship of Obscene Literature, 52 Harv. L. Rev. 40, 73.

The test of obscenity the Court endorses today gives the censor free range over a vast domain. To allow the State to step in and punish mere speech or publication that the judge or the jury thinks has an *undesirable* impact on thoughts but that is not shown to be a part of unlawful action is drastically to curtail the First Amendment. As recently stated by two of our outstanding authorities on obscenity, "The danger of influencing a change in the current moral standards of the community, or of shocking or offending readers, or of stimulating sex thoughts or desires apart from objective conduct, can never justify the losses to society that result from interference with literary freedom." Lockhart & McClure, Literature, The Law of Obscenity, and the Constitution, 38 Minn. L. Rev. 295, 387.

If we were certain that impurity of sexual thoughts impelled to action, we would be on less dangerous ground in punishing the distributors of this sex literature. But it is by no means clear that obscene literature, as so defined, is a significant factor in influencing substantial deviations from the community standards.

"*There are a number of reasons for real and substantial doubts as to the soundness of that hypothesis. (1) Scientific studies of juvenile delinquency demonstrate that those who get into trouble, and are the greatest concern of the advocates of censorship, are far less inclined to read than those who do not become delinquent. The delinquents are generally the adventurous type, who have little use for reading and other non-active entertainment. Thus, even assuming that reading sometimes has an adverse effect upon moral conduct, the effect is not likely to be substantial, for those who are susceptible seldom read. (2) Sheldon and Eleanor Glueck, who are among the country's leading authorities on the treatment and causes of juvenile delinquency, have recently published the results of a ten year study of its causes. They exhaustively studied approximately 90 factors and influences that might lead to or explain juvenile delinquency, but the Gluecks gave no consideration to the type of reading material, if any, read by the delinquents. This is, of course, consistent with their finding that delinquents read very little. When those who know so much about the problem of delinquency among youth—the very group about whom the advocates of censorship are most concerned—conclude that what delinquents read has so little effect upon their conduct that it is not worth investigating in an exhaustive study of causes, there is good reason for serious doubt concerning the basic hypothesis on which obscenity censorship is defended. (3) The many other influences in society that stimulate sexual desire are so much more frequent in their influence, and so much more potent in their effect, that the influence of reading is likely, at most, to be relatively insignificant in the composite of forces that lead an individual into conduct deviating from the community sex standards. The Kinsey studies show the minor degree to which literature serves as a potent sexual stimulant. And the studies demonstrating that sex knowledge seldom results from reading indicates [sic] the relative unimportance of literature in sex thoughts as compared with other factors in society.*" Lockhart & McClure, op. cit. supra, *pp.* 385–386.

The absence of dependable information on the effect of obscene literature on human conduct should make us wary.

It should put us on the side of protecting society's interest in literature, except and unless it can be said that the particular publication has an impact on action that the government can control.

As noted, the trial judge in the *Roth* case charged the jury in the alternative that the federal obscenity statute outlaws literature dealing with sex which offends "the common conscience of the community." That standard is, in my view, more inimical still to freedom of expression.

The standard of what offends "the common conscience of the community" conflicts, in my judgment, with the command of the First Amendment that "Congress shall make no law . . . abridging the freedom of speech, or of the press." Certainly that standard would not be an acceptable one if religion, economics, politics or philosophy were involved. How does it become a constitutional standard when literature treating with sex is concerned?

Any test that turns on what is offensive to the community's standards is too loose, too capricious, too destructive of freedom of expression to be squared with the First Amendment. Under that test, juries can censor, suppress, and punish what they don't like, provided the matter relates to "sexual impurity" or has a tendency "to excite lustful thoughts." This is community censorship in one of its worst forms. It creates a regime where in the battle between the literati and the Philistines, the Philistines are certain to win. If experience in this field teaches anything, it is that "censorship of obscenity has almost always been both irrational and indiscriminate." Lockhart & McClure, *op. cit. supra*, at 371. The test adopted here accentuates that trend.

I assume there is nothing in the Constitution which forbids Congress from using its power over the mails to proscribe *conduct* on the grounds of good morals. No one would suggest that the First Amendment permits nudity in public places, adultery, and other phases of sexual misconduct.

I can understand (and at times even sympathize) with programs of civic groups and church groups to protect and defend the existing moral standards of the community. I can understand the motives of the Anthony Comstocks who would impose Victorian standards on the community. When speech alone is involved, I do not think that government, consistently with the First Amendment, can become the sponsor of any of these movements. I do not think that government, consistently with the First Amendment, can throw its weight behind one school or another. Government should be concerned with antisocial conduct, not with utterances. Thus, if the First Amendment guarantee of freedom of speech and press is to mean anything in this field, it must allow protests even against the moral code that the standard of the day sets for the community. In other words, literature should not be suppressed merely because it offends the moral code of the censor.

The legality of a publication in this country should never be allowed to turn either on the purity of thought which it instills in the mind of the reader or on the degree to which it offends the community conscience. By either test the role of the censor is exalted, and society's values in literary freedom are sacrificed.

The Court today suggests a third standard. It defines obscene material as that "which deals with sex in a manner appealing to prurient interest."* Like the standards applied by the trial judges below, that standard does not require any nexus between the literature which is prohibited and action which the legislature can regulate or prohibit. Under the First Amendment, that standard is no more valid than those which the courts below adopted.

I do not think that the problem can be resolved by the Court's statement that "obscenity is not expression protected by the First Amendment." With the exception of *Beauharnais* v. *Illinois*, 343 U.S. 250, none of our cases has resolved problems of free speech and free press by placing any form of expression beyond the pale of the absolute prohibition of the First Amendment. Unlike the law of libel, wrongfully relied on in *Beauharnais*, there is no special historical evidence that literature dealing with sex was intended to be treated in a special manner by those who drafted the First Amendment. In fact, the first reported court decision in this country involving obscene literature was in 1821. Lockhart & McClure, *op. cit. supra*, at 324, n. 200. I reject too the implication that problems of freedom of speech and of the press are to be resolved by weighing against the values of free expression, the judgment of the Court that a particular form of that expression has "no redeeming social importance." The First Amendment, its prohibition in terms absolute, was designed to preclude courts as well as legislatures from weighing the values of speech against silence. The First Amendment puts free speech in the preferred position.

Freedom of expression can be suppressed if, and to the extent that, it is so closely brigaded with illegal action as to be an inseparable part of it. *Giboney* v. *Empire Storage Co.*, 336 U.S. 490, 498; *Labor Board* v. *Virginia Power Co.*, 314 U.S. 469, 477–478. As a people, we cannot afford to relax that standard. For the test that suppresses a cheap tract today can suppress a literary gem tomorrow. All it need do is to incite a lascivious thought or arouse a lustful desire. The list of books that judges or juries can place in that category is endless.

I would give the broad sweep of the First Amendment full support. I have the same confidence in the ability of our people to reject noxious literature as I have in their capacity to sort out the true from the false in theology, economics, politics, or any other field.

---

* The definition of obscenity which the Court adopts seems in substance to be that adopted by those who drafted the A.L.I., Model Penal Code. § 207.10(2) (Tentative Draft No. 6, 1957).

"Obscenity is defined in terms of material which appeals predominantly to prurient interest in sexual matters and which goes beyond customary freedom of expression in these matters. We reject the prevailing tests of tendency to arouse lustful thoughts or desires because it is unrealistically broad for a society that plainly tolerates a great deal of erotic interest in literature, advertising, and art, and because regulation of thought or desire, unconnected with overt misbehavior, raises the most acute constitutional as well as practical difficulties." *Id.*, at 10.

Butler
v.
Michigan.

APPEAL FROM THE RECORDER'S COURT OF THE CITY OF DETROIT, MICHIGAN.

No. 16. Argued October 16, 1956.—Decided February 25, 1957.

Manuel Lee Robbins argued the cause for appellant. With him on the brief was *William G. Comb.*

Edmund E. Shepherd, Solicitor General of Michigan, argued the cause for appellee. With him on the brief were *Thomas M. Kavanagh,* Attorney General, and *Daniel J. O'Hara,* Assistant Attorney General.

Briefs of *amici curiae* supporting appellant were filed by *Horace S. Manges* for the American Book Publishers Council, Inc., *Osmond K. Fraenkel* for the Authors League of America, Inc., and *Erwin B. Ellmann* for the Metropolitan Detroit Branch, American Civil Liberties Union.

John Ben Shepperd, Attorney General, and *Philip Sanders,* Assistant Attorney General, filed a brief for the State of Texas, as *amicus curiae,* urging that the appeal be dismissed.

Mr. Justice Frankfurter delivered the opinion of the Court.

This appeal from a judgment of conviction entered by the Recorder's Court of the City of Detroit, Michigan, challenges the constitutionality of the following provision, § 343, of the Michigan Penal Code:

"*Any person who shall import, print, publish, sell, possess with the intent to sell, design, prepare, loan, give away, distribute or offer for sale, any book, magazine, newspaper, writing, pamphlet, ballad, printed paper, print, picture, drawing, photograph, publication or other thing, including any recordings, containing obscene, immoral, lewd or lascivious language, or obscene, immoral, lewd or lascivious prints, pictures, figures or descriptions, tending to incite minors to violent or depraved or immoral acts, manifestly tending to the corruption of the morals of youth, or shall introduce into any family, school or place of education or shall buy, procure, receive or have in his possession, any such book, pamphlet, magazine, newspaper, writing, ballad, printed paper, print, picture, drawing, photograph, publication or other thing, either for the purpose of sale, exhibition, loan or circulation, or with intent to introduce the same into any family, school or place of education, shall be guilty of a misdemeanor.*"

Appellant was charged with its violation for selling to a police officer what the trial judge characterized as "a book containing obscene, immoral, lewd, lascivious language, or descriptions, tending to incite minors to violent or depraved or immoral acts, manifestly tending to the corrup-

tion of the morals of youth." Appellant moved to dismiss the proceeding on the claim that application of § 343 unduly restricted freedom of speech as protected by the Due Process Clause of the Fourteenth Amendment in that the statute (1) prohibited distribution of a book to the general public on the basis of the undesirable influence it may have upon youth; (2) damned a book and proscribed its sale merely because of some isolated passages that appeared objectionable when divorced from the book as a whole; and (3) failed to provide a sufficiently definite standard of guilt. After hearing the evidence, the trial judge denied the motion, and, in an oral opinion, held that ". . . the defendant is guilty because he sold a book in the City of Detroit containing this language [the passages deemed offensive], and also because the Court feels that even viewing the book as a whole, it [the objectionable language] was not necessary to the proper development of the theme of the book nor of the conflict expressed therein." Appellant was fined $100.

Pressing his federal claims, appellant applied for leave to appeal to the Supreme Court of Michigan. Although the State consented to the granting of the application "because the issues involved in this case are of great public interest, and because it appears that further clarification of the language of . . . [the statute] is necessary," leave to appeal was denied. In view of this denial, the appeal is here from the Recorder's Court of Detroit. We noted probable jurisdiction. 350 U.S. 963.

Appellant's argument here took a wide sweep. We need not follow him. Thus, it is unnecessary to dissect the remarks of the trial judge in order to determine whether he construed § 343 to ban the distribution of books merely because certain of their passages, when viewed in isolation, were deemed objectionable. Likewise, we are free to put aside the claim that the Michigan law falls within the doctrine whereby a New York obscenity statute was found invalid in *Winters v. New York,* 333 U.S. 507.

It is clear on the record that appellant was convicted because Michigan, by § 343, made it an offense for him to make available for the general reading public (and he in fact sold to a police officer) a book that the trial judge found to have a potentially deleterious influence upon youth. The State insists that, by thus quarantining the general reading public against books not too rugged for grown men and women in order to shield juvenile innocence, it is exercising its power to promote the general welfare. Surely, this is to burn the house to roast the pig. Indeed, the Solicitor General of Michigan has, with characteristic candor, advised the Court that Michigan has a statute specifically designed to protect its children against obscene matter "tending to the corruption of the morals of youth."* But the appellant was not convicted for violating this statute.

———

* Section 142 of Michigan's Penal Code provides:

"Any person who shall sell, give away or in any way furnish to any minor child any book, pamphlet, or other printed paper or other thing, containing obscene language, or obscene prints, pictures, figures or descriptions tending to the corruption of the morals of youth, or any newspapers, pamphlets or other printed paper devoted to the publication of criminal news, police reports, or criminal deeds, and any person who shall in any manner hire, use or employ such child to sell, give away, or in any manner distribute such books, pamphlets or printed papers, and any person having the care, custody or control of any such child, who shall permit him or her to engage in any such employment, shall be guilty of a misdemeanor."

Section 143 provides:

"Any person who shall exhibit upon any public street or highway, or in any other place within the view of children passing on any public street or highway, any book, pamphlet or other

We have before us legislation not reasonably restricted to the evil with which it is said to deal. The incidence of this enactment is to reduce the adult population of Michigan to reading only what is fit for children. It thereby arbitrarily curtails one of those liberties of the individual, now enshrined in the Due Process Clause of the Fourteenth Amendment, that history has attested as the indispensable conditions for the maintenance and progress of a free society. We are constrained to reverse this conviction.

Reversed.

MR. JUSTICE BLACK concurs in the result.

———

printed paper or thing containing obscene language or obscene prints, figures, or descriptions, tending to the corruption of the morals of youth, or any newspapers, pamphlets, or other printed paper or thing devoted to the publication of criminal news, police reports or criminal deeds, shall on conviction thereof be guilty of a misdemeanor."

■ State of Florida, *Appellant,*

v.

Reubin J. Clein, *Appellee.*

Supreme Court of Florida, Special Division B.

March 27, 1957.

Richard W. Ervin, Atty. Gen., *Reeves Bowen,* Asst. Atty. Gen., and *John D. Marsh,* County Sol., Miami, for appellant.

Robert R. Taylor, Wallace N. Maer and *Edward L. Lustgarten,* Miami, for appellee.

O'CONNELL, Justice.

Reubin J. Clein, appellee here and defendant below, was informed against by the County Solicitor of Dade County for an alleged violation of F.S. § 847.01, F.S.A. Defendant filed a motion to quash the indictment. From an order granting defendant's motion to quash, the State appeals under authority of F.S. § 924.07, F.S.A.

The information, leaving out the formal parts thereof, alleged that the defendant:

(Part I) "did then and there print, publish and distribute a certain printed and written paper containing obscene written descriptions, of an act of unnatural sexual perversion between a male and a female person, manifestly tending to the corruption of the morals of youths in the words and figures as hereinafter more fully set out in haec verba, to wit:

(Part II) " 'This Happened In Miami Beach!'
" 'Her head was . . . In His lap'
(Picture)   (Picture)

" 'White Girl, Negro Man,
Face Morals Rap
" 'The Moving Finger writes—for all interested in Segregation to see. * * *
" 'This happened very early the other morning in Miami Beach. Address, south side of 12th St., between Alton Rd. and Lenox Ave.
" 'Police Car 154 noticed a Cadillac auto parked there, with motor running.
" 'Officer Everett Walshon saw the Negro first. He was sitting up asleep, head lolling back on the top of the seat. Then the officer looked down, he saw the white girl. She was asleep, too—her head in the Negro's lap. The officer says the Negro was "exposed."
" 'The two were questioned separately. The Negro did not deny participating in an unnatural act. The evidence of it was irrefutable. The girl—who told the police she was a Jackson Memorial Hospital nurse and her name was Mary Connolly Premo—said she didn't remember what she had done. She only knew she had been "drinking with Jimmy all that day" at an upper Miami Beach swank Bar * * *.' "

For our convenience we have divided the information into two parts and labelled them Part I and Part II. Part I was typewritten on the usual form of information. Part II was a copy of a portion of a publication entitled "Miami

Life," dated Saturday, April 30, 1955 and under the title thereof carried the words "Reubin J. Clein, Editor."

The motion to quash filed by defendant listed five grounds. They are that: (1) the information failed to charge a crime; (2) the information charges one date and the publication shows another; (3) the article is not such that it would manifestly tend to the corrupting of the morals of youth; (4) the article is nothing more or less than a true report of a police case and does not contravene the statute involved; and (5) the article is not obscene as defined by the laws of the State of Florida.

The only question involved on this appeal is whether the trial court committed error in granting the motion to quash. We have concluded that he did.

Sec. 847.01, F.S.A., in effect makes it unlawful, among other things, for any person to print, publish or distribute any printed paper containing obscene language or descriptions manifestly tending to the corruption of the morals of youth.

[1] The defendant in his brief agrees that by his motion to quash he admits all allegation made in the information. His position is that, admitting all alleged therein, the information charges no crime under the statute.

The defendant contends that no crime is charged because the article, if obscene, is not the kind of obscenity which would arouse sexual passions in youth, but rather, if it would do anything, it would arouse disgust. He reasons that the statute only intended to make unlawful obscenity which would arouse sexual passions in youth, not that which would repel.

[2] As we understand the general rule in the United States a court may grant a motion to quash an information or indictment charging obscenity only when the court determines that a verdict that the matter was obscene would have to be set aside as against the evidence and reason. Unless it is clear that such a verdict would have to be set aside, the question of obscenity is a question for the determination of a jury. Certainly where reasonable men might differ as to the question of obscenity, the question is one for the jury. *United States* v. *Bennett*, C.C.S.D.N.Y. 1879, 24 Fed. Cas. p. 1093, No. 14,571; *Commonwealth* v. *Isenstadt*, 1945, 318 Mass. 543, 62 N.E. 2d 840; *Hallmark Productions, Inc.* v. *Mosely*, 8 Cir., 1951, 190 F. 2d 904; *People* v. *Seltzer*, 1924, 122 Misc. 329, 203 N.Y.S. 809; *Davidson* v. *State*, 1923, 19 Ala. App. 77, 95 So. 54; *Commonwealth* v. *New*, 1940, 142 Pa. Super. 358, 16 A. 2d 437; *State* v. *Weitershausen*, 1951, 11 N.J. Super. 487, 78 A. 2d 595; *People* v. *Wepplo*, 1947, 78 Cal. App. 2d Supp. 959, 178 P. 2d 853; *King* v. *Commonwealth*, 1950, 313 Ky. 741, 233 S.W. 2d 522. We feel that the same rule must apply in the determination of whether such matter would manifestly tend to corrupt the morals of youth.

[3] The information here charged the offense substantially in the language of the statute and this is sufficient, certainly as to form. *State* v. *Pound*, Fla. 1950, 49 So. 2d 521.

[4] While here let us also dispose of that ground in the motion to quash which charges the information bad because it alleges the commission of the alleged crime on April 29, 1955, while the newspaper article shows the date April 30, 1955. F.S. § 906.25, F.S.A. provides that no information shall be quashed except for the reasons ex-

pressed therein. This variance in dates is not one of those grounds. But this section must be construed with F.S. Chap. 909, F.S.A. Nevertheless, this variance in dates is one easily explained by the fact that newspapers are frequently published and circulated prior to the date thereon, and the date thereon is not conclusive. And we have held that one date may be alleged and another proved, providing the proof shows the crime committed before the information was filed and within the time of the Statute of Limitations. *Horton* v. *Mayo*, 1943, 153 Fla. 611, 15 So. 2d 327.

We must assume therefore that the motion to quash was not granted for formal defects, but was granted because the trial court concluded that the information, on its face, did not charge a crime under the statute.

To have arrived at this conclusion the trial court must have found that the article was not obscene, or if obscene was not obscenity which would tend to corrupt the morals of youth.

[5] As we read the statute involved here there are three essential elements necessary to be charged and proved. First is the printing, publishing, and distributing of the matter involved. This element is admitted by defendant in his motion to quash. Second is that the matter be obscene. Third, the obscene matter must be such as manifestly tends to corrupt the morals of youth.

This of necessity brings us to determine whether it can be said as a matter of law that the article was not obscene. To do this we are required to define the word obscene.

In Webster's New International Dictionary, 2nd Edition, p. 1681, we find the word defined as:

"1. Offensive to taste; foul; loathsome; disgusting.

"2. *a.* Offensive to chastity of mind or to modesty; expressing or presenting to the mind or view something that delicacy, purity and decency forbid to be exposed; lewd, indecent; as obscene language, dances, images. *b.* * * *

"3. * * *"

The Century Dictionary, Vol. IV, p. 4062, defines the word as:

"1. * * *

"2. Offensive to the senses; repulsive; disgusting; foul; filthy; * *.

"3. Offensive to modesty and decency; impure; unchaste; indecent; lewd; as, obscene actions or language; obscene pictures. * * *

"Obscene publication, in law, any impure or indecent publication tending to corrupt the mind and to subvert respect for decency and morality. Syn. 3, immodest, ribald, gross."

In *State* v. *MacSales Co.*, Mo. App. 1954, 263 S.W. 2d 860, 863 the court said:

"* * * We have defined obscenity as 'such indecency as is calculated to promote the violation of the law and the general corruption of morals * * * and include what is foul and indecent, as well as immodest, or calculated to excite impure desires.' * * *" The Supreme Court of Missouri in *State* v. *Becker*, 1954, 364 Mo. 1079, 272 S.W. 2d 283 followed the definition last cited.

In *United States* v. *Two Obscene Books*, D.C.N.D.S.D. 1951, 99 F. Supp. 760, 762 the court said:

"Our circuit has approved the simple standard that

obscenity has 'the meaning of that which is offensive to chastity and modesty. * * *.' "

In *King* v. *Commonwealth*, 233 S.W. 2d at page 523, supra, the court said:

" '* * * The word obscenity cannot be said to be a technical term of the law and is not susceptible of exact definition in its judicial uses, although it has been defined in a general sense as meaning offensive to morality or chastity, indecent, or nasty. * * *' "

In *Davidson* v. *State*, supra [19 Ala. App. 77, 95 So. 55], the court adopted the definition given in 3 Bouv. Law Dict., Rawle's Third Revision, p. 2396, which defines the word as " 'Something which is offensive to chastity; that which is offensive to chastity and modesty.' "

In *Hallmark Productions, Inc.* v. *Mosley*, supra, 190 F. 2d at page 910, the court said: "* * * one of the tests often used is whether it shocks the ordinary and common sense of men as an indecency. * * *"

Measured by the above definitions we are convinced that it cannot be said as a matter of law that the article is not obscene. Certainly the article is "offensive to chastity of mind or to modesty." The descriptions in the article create a picture by words which if presented in a photograph or drawing would clearly be obscene. In any event we must conclude that we could not say that the descriptions are so clearly not obscene that a jury verdict finding them to be obscene would have to be set aside as against evidence and reason. It is also our opinion that reasonable men might well differ as to whether the descriptions were obscene. In such case the question of obscenity is for the jury to decide.

[6] Many of the reported cases dealing with the question of obscenity involve statutes wherein no test of obscenity is given. In such cases the generally accepted rule is that matter is obscene if it would tend to deprave and corrupt the morals of those whose minds are open to such influences and into whose hands such matter might fall by suggesting or inciting lewd or lascivious thoughts or desires. *United States* v. *Bennett*, supra, and other cases cited in the preceding paragraphs.

But as we construe the statute before us our legislature laid down the test of the obscenity prohibited when it wrote into the statute the words "* * * manifestly tending to the corruption of the morals of youth. * * *"

[7] As we understand the word morals it means the code of conduct adopted and used by a particular people at a particular time. Such code expresses in thought and action the consensus of opinion of a people as to what is right and wrong, what is and is not acceptable in the conduct of persons in that community at that time. This code of conduct is formulated and taught to a people by its churches, its schools, to children by parents, and is influenced by the actions and conduct of friends, neighbors and associates. Parts of such code or standard are also frequently expressed by the people, through their elected representatives, in the enactment of statutes and ordinances. Such code of conduct determines and is morals. It must and does encompass more than sexual conduct. It relates as well to common decency, cleanliness of mind and body, honesty, truthfulness, and proper respect for established ideals and institutions, among other things.

We therefore must conclude that morals, as the word is used in the statute before us, is used in its broad sense and relates to more than sexual matters.

[8] We therefore also conclude that in considering whether the information charged a crime against the defendant the word obscene as used in the statute is not limited to that which would arouse sexual passions or corrupt the sex conduct of youth, but includes matter which would corrupt the morals of youth, as we have defined the word morals.

We must then proceed to the last element of the offense charged, i.e. whether the article, if obscene, would manifestly tend to corrupt the morals of youth.

The defendant contends that there are two kinds of obscenity. One being that which is repulsive, foul, filthy, loathsome, dirty, or smutty, but which has no reference to sex or morals. The second being that which is offensive to chastity of mind or to modesty; lewd, impure, unchaste. He then contends that obscenity of the first kind cannot under any circumstances manifestly tend to the corruption of the morals of youth. In other words, he contends that the only obscenity prohibited by the statute is that which would arouse sexual passions in a youth.

While we might agree with defendant that there is obscenity which repels and that which incites the passions, we cannot agree with him that obscenity of the first kind could not affect the morals of youth. Nor are we of the view that the legislature in enacting the statute intended to limit the scope thereof only to obscenity which would arouse sexual passions in a youth. To do so in our opinion would be to construe the word morals as pertaining only to sexual conduct. As above stated, we construe the word in ordinary usage to relate to more than sex conduct.

Defendant ends his argument with the proposition that the article in question would not arouse the passions of youth, and that if it would do anything it would arouse disgust in a young person, or any normal human being.

A similar contention was made by the defendant and rejected by the court in *Besig* v. *U.S.*, 9 Cir., 1953, 208 F. 2d 142. In that case the defendant there urged that the opinion in *Burstein* v. *U.S.*, 9 Cir., 1949, 178 F. 2d 665 was self-contradictory in that the court defined obscene matter as that which "is offensive to the common sense of decency and modesty of the community," and later in the same opinion adopted the test of obscenity almost identical to the one set forth above in this opinion as being the generally accepted test of obscenity. The court said in 208 F. 2d on page 146:

" '* * * Appellant thinks our opinion is 'unclear as to whether the test of obscenity is that it *repels* or that it *seduces*.'

" 'We observe no contradiction in any of these expressions. They aptly describe the quality of language which the word 'obscene' is meant to suggest. Of course, language can be so nasty as to repel and of course to seduce as well. Appellant's argument tempts us to quote Pope's quatrain about the Monster Vice which, when too prevalent, is embraced.' "

The quatrain referred to was from the poem "Essay on Man" written by Alexander Pope, English poet. It reads:

"Vice is a Monster of so frightful mien as to be hated needs but to be seen. Yet seen too oft, familiar with her face, We first endure, then pity, then embrace."

We believe the poet showed a sound insight into human nature in writing the above words.

While familiarity is said to breed contempt, we have no doubt that familiarity with obscenity will lessen aversion to it and make it more acceptable. To the extent that obscenity becomes more acceptable morals are lessened and corrupted.

The case of *Commonwealth* v. *Isentadt*, supra, is closely related to the case before us here. There the defendant was charged under and found guilty of violation of a statute making it unlawful to sell, possess for purposes of sale, exhibition or circulation material which is obscene, indecent or impure, *or* which manifestly tends to corrupt the morals of youth. The statute involved in that case was held by that court to be breached either if the novel in question there was obscene, indecent or impure, *or* if it manifestly tended to corrupt the morals of youth.

That court followed the general rule in saying that a book was obscene, indecent or impure under the statute if it had a substantial tendency to deprave or corrupt its readers by inciting lascivious thoughts or arousing lustful desires. But that court also said, 62 N.E. 2d at page 844:

"* * * It also violates the statute if it 'manifestly tends to corrupt the morals of youth.' * * *"

And further said, on page 848:

"* * * At any rate, we think that almost any novel that is obscene, indecent or impure in the general sense also 'manifestly tends to corrupt the morals of youth,' if it is likely to fall into the hands of youth. * * *"

In the Florida statute under which the defendant was charged it is true that the test of whether the matter is unlawful is that it must be obscenity "* * * manifestly tending to the corruption of the morals of youth." While in the statute involved in *Commonwealth* v. *Isenstadt*, supra, the matter would be in violation of the statute either if obscene, indecent or impure, or if it manifestly tended to corrupt the morals of youth.

We do not construe this difference in our statute to make it narrower in its scope, but on the contrary it would appear to us that obscenity which would not affect the morals of the average normal person, could nevertheless affect the morals of youth, with its generally recognized lack of experience, its venturesome spirit, its spongelike mind, and its willingness to experiment with something new.

We are of the opinion that our legislature intended to measure obscenity by its effects on the morals of youth and thereby to give youth and its morals additional, not less, protection, than would have been given under a statute merely declaring against obscenity.

The court in *Commonwealth* v. *Isenstadt*, supra, is in accord with our view for it said in 62 N.E. 2d on page 848:

"* * * Yet it cannot be supposed that the Legislature intended to give youth less protection than that given to the community as a whole by the general proscription of that which is 'obscene, indecent or impure.' Rather it would seem that something in the nature of additional protection of youth was intended by proscribing anything that manifestly tends to corrupt the morals of youth, even though it may not be obscene, indecent, or impure in the more general sense. * * *"

We must conclude that it cannot be said as a matter of law that the article in question would so clearly not tend to corrupt the morals of youth as to require setting aside a verdict of a jury finding that it did tend to do so. Reasonable men would, in our opinion, differ as to whether it

would or would not do so. It therefore was a jury question.

There is good reason for requiring the question of obscenity and effect on morals to be submitted to a jury for it is the people of a community who have the right to establish their standard of morals and it should be the people who apply the standard to specific conduct and who determine whether such conduct is offensive and harmful or not. This can best be done through a jury.

Judge Learned Hand expressed our view well in *United States* v. *Kennerley*, D.C.S.D.N.Y. 1913, 209 F. 119, 121 when he said:

"* * * If there be no abstract definition, such as I have suggested, should not the word 'obscene' be allowed to indicate the present critical point in the compromise between candor and shame at which the community may have arrived here and now? If letters must, like other kinds of conduct, be subject to the social sense of what is right, it would seem that a jury should in each case establish the standard much as they do in cases of negligence. To put thought in leash to the average conscience of the time is perhaps tolerable, but to fetter it by the necessities of the lowest and least capable seems a fatal policy.

"Nor is it an objection, I think, that such an interpretation gives to the words of the statute a varying meaning from time to time. Such words as these do not embalm the precise morals of an age or place; while they presuppose that some things will always be shocking to the public taste, the vague subject-matter is left to the gradual development of general notions about what is decent. * * *"

[9] The defendant in his brief has submitted a number of newspaper clippings, advertisements, pictures, and other printed matter taken from various publications on sale on news stands in Miami, Fla. These matters are not a part of the record and therefore not properly before us. But if they were, the fact that other publications which are in violation of the statute are published, printed or distributed in the community does not constitute excuse for defendant's violation of the statute, if he has violated it. Nor is comparison with other publications which may be obscene a test for obscenity as to the article complained against. *State* v. *Weitershausen*, supra.

We do not hold by this opinion that the article in question was obscene or that it manifestly tends to corrupt the morals of youth. We carefully refrain from doing so for if we did we would be going beyond our province which is to declare the law. If we went further we would not only be invading the province of the jury but would be imposing upon the people by judicial fiat our view of what the morals of the community should be. This is a matter for the people to decide for themselves.

[10] We do hold that it cannot be said as a matter of law that the article was not obscene and would not tend to corrupt the morals of youth and this is the extent to which we are allowed to go under our system of jurisprudence in cases such as this. We are of the opinion that both the defendant and the state are entitled to have the people, through a jury, determine the factual question of whether the article is obscene and whether it is such as would manifestly tend to corrupt the morals of youth if it fell into their hands.

The order granting the motion to quash is reversed and the cause remanded for further proceedings in accordance with law.

TERRELL, C.J., concurs.

ROBERTS, J., and CROSBY, Associate Justice, concur specially.

CROSBY, Associate Justice (concurring specially).

I concur in the opinion and the conclusion so well stated by Mr. Justice O'CONNELL. An indictment or information charging the printing, publication and distribution of material of the kind here involved presents, in my judgment, a question that is peculiarly within the province of a jury. This court would not be justified in assuming either that the morals of youth exposed to such a publication are so firmly elevated as to be immune to any possible adverse effect from it or, on the other hand, so sophisticated as to be beyond the possibility of further harm.

For those who might regard this decision as a license to inaugurate a "witch hunt," it should be emphasized that in the trial of such a charge the burden remains upon the state at all times to prove every essential allegation of the information beyond and to the exclusion of every reasonable doubt.

TERRELL, C.J., concurs.

ROBERTS, Justice (concurring specially).

I concur in the opinion insofar as it disposes of the questions presented and agree to the reversal, but without prejudice to the right of the appellee-defendant if he so desires to attack the constitutionality vel non of the statute under which he is prosecuted. Since this appeal was perfected here, the Supreme Court of the United States, on February 25, 1957, in the case of *Butler* v. *State of Michigan*, 352 U.S. 380, 77 S. Ct. 524, 1 L. Ed. 2d 412, voided a Michigan statute almost identical to the one here involved as being in violation of the Constitution of the United States. It has long been the policy of this court not to pass on the constitutionality of a statute where such was not presented to the court below. I agree to the reversal for the further reason that such will provide the appellee-defendant an opportunity to raise such question in the lower court if he is so advised.

■ Eugene L. Eisinger, Jr., and Ethel P. Eisinger, his Wife, *Appellants,*
v.
M. C. Tidwell and Adlou Tidwell, his Wife, Appellees.

Supreme Court of Florida, Division B.

March 15, 1957.

Rehearing Denied April 12, 1957.

Appeal from Circuit Court, Dade County; J. Fritz Gordon, Judge.

PER CURIAM.

Affirmed.

■ Lillian Miller O'Shea, *Appellant,*
v.
Harry J. O'Shea, *Appellee.*

Supreme Court of Florida, Special Division A.

Feb. 27, 1957.

Rehearing Denied April 12, 1957.

Appeal from Circuit Court, Dade County; Grady L. Crawford, Judge.

PER CURIAM.

Affirmed.

■ Fisher

v.

Hoffman.

Supreme Court of Florida. June Term 1956.

Dismissed without opinion.

■ Cornell

v.

Bronson.

Supreme Court of Florida. June Term 1956.

Dismissed without opinion.

■ Vaughn

v.

Smith.

Supreme Court of Florida. June Term 1956.

Dismissed without opinion.

■ Gessler

v.

Gessler.

Supreme Court of Florida. June Term 1956.

Dismissed without opinion.

■ In the Matter of Excelsior Pictures Corp., *Respondent,*

v.

Regents of the University of the State of New York, *Appellants.*

Court of Appeals of New York.

July 3, 1957.

Charles A. Brind, Jr., John P. Jehu, Elizabeth M. Eastman and *George B. Farrington,* Albany, for appellants.

Charles J. Tobin, Jr., Albany, *Porter R. Chandler* and *John B. Coleman, Jr.,* New York City, for New York State Catholic Welfare Committee, amicus curiæ, in support of appellants' position.

Sol A. Rosenblatt, Julian B. Rosenthal and *Charles Roden,* New York City, for respondent.

DESMOND, Judge.

Under review in this case is the denial to petitioners, by the Regents, of a license to exhibit in New York State a motion picture called "Garden of Eden." The film, which this court has viewed, is a fictionalized depiction of the activities of the members of a nudist group in a secluded private camp in Florida. There is nothing sexy or suggestive about it. It has been shown in 36 States and in many foreign countries. In it the nudists are shown as wholesome, happy people in family groups practising their "sincere if misguided theory that clothing, when climate does not require it, is deleterious to mental health by promoting an attitude of shame with regard to natural attributes and functions of the body" (American Law Institute, Model Penal Code, Tentative Draft No. 6, p. 35).

[1] The pictured episodes are "honestly relevant to the adequate expression of innocent ideas" (*United States* v. *Kennerley*, D.C., 209 F. 119, 120–121) just as are figures of nude men and women in the decor of public buildings including New York court houses, and in the pages of *National Geographic Magazine* and in ultra-respectable travel pictures. Nevertheless, the Motion Picture Division of the New York State Education Department rejected the film (and respondents Board of Regents confirmed the rejection) on the ground that it is "indecent." These censors, however, did not declare it to be obscene as, indeed, they could not. We will not in this opinion quibble or quarrel as to concepts of decorum or delicacy or manners, since "the court is not a censor of plays and does not attempt to regulate manners" (*People* v. *Wendling*, 258 N.Y. 451, 453, 180 N.E. 169, 81 A.L.R. 799). We need not reassert our deeply felt conviction that censorship for real, true obscenity is valid and essential in our society (Legal Problems on Censoring, 40 Marq. L. Rev. 38). But we do say and we will show in this opinion that this picture cannot lawfully be banned since it is not obscene in the sense in which the law has used that term for centuries. Nothing sexually impure or filthy is shown or suggested in "Garden of Eden" and so there is no legal basis for censorship (see *People* v. *Muller*, 96 N.Y. 408, 411; *United States* v. *One Book* Called "Ulysses," D.C. 5 F. Supp. 182, 184; *United States* v. *Limehouse*, 285 U.S. 424, 52 S. Ct. 412, 76 L. Ed. 843; *American Civil Liberties Union* v. *City of Chicago*, 3 Ill. 2d 334, 121 N.E. 2d 585, appeal dismissed 348 U.S. 979, 75 S. Ct. 572, 99 L. Ed. 763; *Roth* v. *United States* and *Alberts* v. *State of California*, 77 S. Ct. 1304; and generally, Lockhart and McClure, Literature, The Law of Obscenity, and the Constitution, 38 Minn. L. Rev. 295). Since the film is certainly not "obscene" in the eyes of the law, it cannot, under United States Supreme Court decisions hereinafter listed and binding on us, constitutionally be subjected to prior restraint. To repeat, we are not called upon to pass judgment on nudism or nudists. We are simply obeying the supreme law which binds us as well as everyone else. So confining ourselves and leaving our individual predilections for debate at some more appropriate time, we analyze the applicable law.

Appellants, the Board of Regents of the University of the State of New York, are the policy-making officers of the State Education Department (Education Law, Consol. Laws, c. 16, §§ 206, 207). Under sections 122 and 124 of the Education Law the Regents control the licensing and exhibitions of motion pictures in this State and are required to issue such a license unless the film or a part thereof is "obscene, indecent, immoral, inhuman, sacrilegious, or is of such a character that its exhibition would tend to corrupt morals or incite to crime" (Education Law, § 122; and see § 122–a thereof for further or subdefinitions of "immoral" and "tend to corrupt morals"). By a series of decisions handed down during the last five years (*Joseph Burstyn, Inc.*, v. *Wilson*, 343 U.S. 495, 72 S. Ct. 777, 96 L. Ed. 1098; *Gelling* v. *State of Texas*, 343 U.S. 960, 72 S. Ct. 1002, 96 L. Ed. 1359; *Superior Films* v. *Department of Educ.* (*Commercial Pictures Corp.* v. *Regents*), 346 U.S. 587, 74 S. Ct. 286, 98 L. Ed. 329; *Holmby Prods.* v. *Vaughn*, 350 U.S. 870, 76 S. Ct. 117, 100 L. Ed. 770), the United States Supreme Court has stricken down as unconstitutional nearly all the grounds for license refusal listed in sections 122 and 122–a of the New York Education Law, supra. Those cited decisions of the United States Supreme Court need not be separately analyzed here. Their cumulative result is that a motion picture may not be denied license by State censors because it is "immoral" or because it is "sacrilegious" or "because its exhibition would tend to corrupt morals or incite to crime." As to denial because of obscenity, the Burstyn majority opinion (343 U.S. 495, 505, 72 S. Ct. 777, 782, supra) said that the court found it unnecessary "to decide, for example, whether a state may censor motion pictures under a clearly drawn statute designed and applied to prevent the showing of obscene films." Recognizing in that language the customary conservatism of high court opinions, we treat it as a holding that obscenity is under the First and Fourteenth Amendments the only (other possible exceptions are not pertinent here) lawful ground for denying a license. That such is the meaning of the Burstyn excerpt, supra, is more than a guess. It is solidly based on the history of censorship, recent and remote (*Brown* v. *Kingsley Books*, 1 N.Y. 2d 177, 189, 190, 151 N.Y.S. 2d 639, 648–649; St. John-Stevas, Obscenity and the Law, Legal Problems Involved in Censoring, 40 Marq. L. Rev. 38; Censoring the Movies, 29 Notre Dame Law 27).

Another Supreme Court expression as to obscenity, *Butler* v. *State of Michigan*, 352 U.S. 380, 77 S. Ct. 524, 1 L. Ed. 2d 412 [Feb., 1957], narrowed even more the permissible range of governmental action. Held invalid in that case was a Michigan statute (and, presumably, similar statutes in 11 other States not including New York) which made it criminal to distribute to the general public a book containing obscene language "tending to the corruption of the morals of youth." The Butler decision (and the series of decisions re obscenity handed down by the court on June 24, 1957) means that in the United States as in England (*Regina* v. *Martin Secker & Warburg, Ld.*, [1954] 1 Weekly L.R. 1138) the question of obscenity may no longer be decided by the old Hicklin test (*Regina* v. *Hicklin*, L.R. 3 Q.B. 360, 371) of "whether the tendency of the matter charged as obscenity is to deprave and corrupt those whose minds are open to such immoral influences, and into whose hands a publication of this sort may fall." The law now, since *Butler* v. *State of Michigan*, supra, is that the young may be kept away from certain movies by appropriate State action (cf. New York Penal Law, Consol. Laws, c. 40, § 484) but, unless the picture be really obscene in the traditional, historic sense of that term, license to exhibit it to adults may not be withheld.

That obscenity is an exception (and for our purposes the only exception) to the First Amendment's free speech guarantee was flatly and finally announced by the Supreme Court on June 24, 1957 in *Roth* v. *United States* (*Alberts* v. *State of California*), 77 S. Ct. 1304, 1309, supra. In the Roth-Alberts opinion Justice Brennan wrote that "obscenity is not within the area of constitutionally protected speech or press."

[2] Since the Constitution forbids any prior restraint of a motion picture which is not obscene and since this film has not been found to be obscene or rejected because of obscenity and since it is not obscene by any standard we ever heard of, we could end this opinion right here. Nudity in itself and without lewdness or dirtiness is not obscenity in law or in common sense. "It is a false delicacy and mere prudery which would condemn and banish from sight all such objects as obscene, simply on account of their nudity. If the test of obscenity or indecency in a picture or statue is its capabilty of suggesting impure thoughts, then indeed all such representations might be considered as indecent or obscene. The presence of a woman of the purest character and of the most modest behavior and bearing may suggest to a prurient imagination images of lust, and excite impure desires, and so may a picture or statue not in fact indecent or obscene" (Judge Andrews writing in 1884 for a unanimous Court of Appeals in *People* v. *Muller*, 96 N.Y. 408, 411, supra). For more than a century the New York courts have held that exposure of the body to the view of others is not criminal if there be no lewd intent (*Miller* v. *People*, 1849, 5 Barb. 203; cf. *People* ex rel. *Lee* v. *Bixby*, 4 Hun 636, opinion in 67 Barb. 221). Even the strictest moralists tell us that "an obscene nude is a nude that allures" (Vermeesch, Theologiae Moralis, 1936, p. 94).

The State, nevertheless, says that the picture "Garden of Eden" is "indecent," that indecent films are censorable under the statute (Education Law, § 122, supra) and that the courts as well as the Regents must obey that law. We will now analyze those positions.

It is settled that "indecent," standing alone and read literally, is much too broad and vague a term to make a valid censorship standard. "Indecent" may include anything from vulgarity or impropriety to real obscenity (*State* v. *Pape*, 90 Conn. 98, 101, 96 A. 313). Since the law does not penalize or proscribe mere breaches of decorum, the word "indecent," to accomplish anything at all, must be read to mean "obscene," and so the New York courts have always defined it. Our court has twice flatly held that the word "indecent" as to pictures or books describes "various phases of the crime of obscenity" and "that form of immorality which has relation to sexual impurity" (*People* v. *Eastman*, 188 N.Y. 478, 480, 81 N.E. 459, 460; *People* v. *Winters*, 294 N.Y. 545, 550, 63 N.E. 2d 98, 100, reversed on other grounds 333 U.S. 507, 68 S. Ct. 665, 92 L. Ed. 840). The court in the Eastman case was construing the then section 317 of the Penal Code which, somewhat expanded, is now section 1141 of the Penal Law. The statute analyzed in Eastman penalized the distribution of "any obscene, lewd, lascivious, filthy, indecent or disgust-

ing book * * * picture." Our present motion picture censorship statute (Education Law, § 122, supra) forbids the licensing of a motion picture which is "obscene, indecent, immoral." The similarity of wording is patent. Here is what our court said in Eastman as to the meaning of "indecent": "It is clear from the manner in which the legislature has used the word 'indecent' that it relates to obscene prints or publications; it is not an attempt to regulate manners, but it is a declaration of the penalties to be imposed upon the various phases of the crime of obscenity. The word 'indecent' is used in a limited sense in this connection and falls within the maxim of *noscitur a sociis*" (*People* v. *Eastman*, 188 N.Y. 478, 479–480, 81 N.E. 459, 460, supra). Thus, "indecent" in section 122 means "obscene," this picture is not obscene and so the license denial was unconstitutional.

[3, 4] The whole reason for the board's proscription of this film seems to be section 1140–b of the Penal Law, passed in 1935: "A person who in any place wilfully exposes his private parts in the presence of two or more persons of the opposite sex whose private parts are similarly exposed, or who aids or abets any such act, or who procures another so to expose his private parts or who as owner, manager, lessee, director, promoter or agent, or in any other capacity, hires, leases or permits the land, building or premises of which he is the owner, lessee or tenant, or over which he has control, to be used for any such purposes, is guilty of a misdemeanor." The statute mentions neither movies nor nudism but the State says it is to be read with the censorship law (Education Law, § 122, supra) so as to create in New York a statutory prohibition against the licensing of any motion picture showing a group of nude people of both sexes. That position of the State rests entirely on two assumptions, each of which is demonstrably false. The first assumption (one of historical fact) is that the Legislature, without saying so, intended by section 1140–b to make criminal in New York State any practice of nudism, even in secluded private grounds and by family groups. The second assumption (one of law and based on the false assumption of fact) is that since nudism is criminally "indecent" in this State, a pictorial representation of that crime is in itself "indecent" and not licensable under section 122 of the Education Law, supra.

[5, 6] First, as to the falsity of the assumption that section 1140–b makes nudism under whatever circumstances criminal in New York. It is true that in the contemporary press and elsewhere the legislation was called "the anti-nudism bill." But the careful and well-informed Governor who signed it wrote in his memorandum of approval that it was directed against "the professional exploitation of nudism for profit." The new law was needed, he wrote, to prevent "exhibitionism for financial gain" which the existing statutes did not touch (Public Papers of Governor Herbert H. Lehman, 1935, p. 352). In the same message Governor Lehman cryptically referred to the real background and purpose of the new statute when he said: "There can be no justification for some of the so-called nudist gymnasiums or colonies where the general public is admitted on the payment of an admission fee." The reference, of course, was to *People* v. *Burke*, 243 App. Div. 83, 276 N.Y.S. 402, affirmed 267 N.Y. 571, 196 N.E. 585. The Burke case was handed down by our court on April 30, 1935, a few days after the Legislature voted the

bill which became section 1140–b, supra. Beyond any doubt, section 1140–b was passed because of that Burke decision (for a contemporary discussion of the case and the statute, see 69 U.S.L.R. 346 et seq.) Defendant Burke, in the name of the "Olympian League," had rented a gymnasium in New York City and there ran a "meeting" where "Any one was welcome * * * who would pay the required entrance fee" (see 243 App. Div. 83, 86, 276 N.Y.S. 402, 406) and where the male and female ticket purchasers exercised and swam "naked in a gymnasium to which admittance [was] gained by the payment of a fee" (see 267 N.Y. 571, 572, 196 N.E. 585). That was the "professional exploitation" and "exhibitionism for financial gain" against which the Legislature and the Governor were legislating. Of course, the law is very broadly drawn but our duty is to give it a reasonable and sensible meaning in the light of the evil at which it was directed. Because it is a restraint of liberty and because it creates a crime unknown to the common law (as to the common law of nudity in nonpublic places see 67 C.J.S. Obscenity §§ 5, 6) it should be narrowly and strictly construed. Literal meaning would penalize not only innocent and orderly nudism but would make it a misdemeanor for a parent and members of a family to be unclad in their family home. No rational Legislature ever intended to create such a crime. The law should be interpreted sanely as penalizing nudity in public or quasi-public places only.

As a last reason why section 1140–b has no bearing at all here, we point out that, whatever that strange enactment may mean, it certainly does not deal with the exhibition of any motion picture. The showing of an "obscene, lewd, lascivious, filthy, indecent" film is dealt with in a different section—1141—of the Penal Law. And the test under section 1141 is, as we have seen, "obscenity" alone.

But let us suppose that section 1140–b makes criminal any and every practice of nudism in New York State. It is still a *non sequitur* that picturing such activity becomes criminal and "indecent" or that it justifies censorship. To say that representation of criminal activity is criminal is to abolish the drama and the novel in one stroke. Illustrations are unnecessary. Everyone will think of his own. The showing of crimes in book, play or cinema is evil only when it is done in a dirty way or when it glorifies the criminal act. So to characterize "The Garden of Eden" is impossible.

In only four States of the Union (New York, Kansas, Maryland, Virginia) is censorship of motion pictures still carried on by State agencies. The number has been declining and will decline further unless reason and moderation be employed (see Pound, J., in *People* v. *Wendling*, 258 N.Y. 451, 454, 180 N.E. 169, 170, supra). Some of us, while proclaiming the necessity for "a viable solution of the problem of censorship by law in a democratic society" have realized that we must "eschew the extremes and shun the extremists" (Legal Problems in Censoring, 40 Marq. L. Rev. 54, supra). We have publicly recognized that "obscenity, real, serious, not imagined or puritanically exaggerated, is today as in all the past centuries, a public evil, a public nuisance, a public pollution." We "see no reason why democratic government should not use democratic processes on a high administrative level, under the control of the courts, to suppress such obscenity" (same citation). But censorship is a necessary evil, a last resort, to

be used only when necessary and limited to the necessity (see *Joseph Burstyn, Inc.* v. *Wilson* opinion, 343 U.S. 495, 504, 72 S. Ct. 777, supra). "Censorship," once wrote the great American political thinker Alfred E. Smith, "is not in keeping with our ideas of liberty and of freedom * * * of speech" (Public Papers of Alfred E. Smith, 1923, pp. 60, 61). "The point here, as in most problems, is that a minimum of censorship is far more likely to prove beneficial, rather than an attempted maximum" (Bourke, Moral Problems in Censoring, 40 Marq. L. Rev. 56, 69, 71, 72, 73; see Gardiner, Moral Definitions of the Obscene, 20 Law & Contemp. Prob. 560, 561). In the present case the Board of Regents, doubtless because of a mistaken belief that section 1140–b mandated such action, went far beyond even the permissible maximum of censorship. In the interest of reasonable censorship itself, this unlawful exercise of the censorship power must be overruled by the courts.

The order should be affirmed, with costs.

DYE, Judge (concurring).

I agree with all that has been said by Judge DESMOND to the effect that the showing of the motion picture entitled "Garden of Eden" may not be barred on the ground that it is obscene and indecent, and I too vote for affirmance.

This is not to say however that the New York censorship statute (Education Law, § 122), providing as it does for the examination of every motion picture film submitted to the director of the Motion Picture Division of the Board of Regents and that "unless such film or a part thereof is obscene, indecent, immoral, inhuman, sacrilegious, or is of such a character that its exhibition would tend to corrupt or incite to crime [the Board] shall issue a license therefor," constitutes a constitutionally valid authorization for administrative censorship in advance. Whenever that section has been attacked on constitutional grounds it has been made to yield its essential particulars with the result that by now it has ceased to serve any practical or useful purpose (*Joseph Burstyn, Inc.* v. *Wilson*, 343 U.S. 495, 72 S. Ct. 777, 96 L. Ed. 1098; *Commercial Pictures Corp.* v. *Regents*, 346 U.S. 587, 74 S. Ct. 286, 98 L. Ed. 329; *Gelling* v. *State of Texas*, 343 U.S. 960, 72 S. Ct. 1002, 96 L. Ed. 1359). No good reason exists for continuing a token observance.

Motion pictures, as we know, are within the free speech and free press guarantees of the First and Fourteenth Amendments (*Joseph Burstyn, Inc.* v. *Wilson*, supra). These amendments provide without exception that the Congress shall make "no law * * * abridging the freedom of speech, or of the press" (cf. *Superior Films* v. *Department of Educ.*, 346 U.S. 587, 74 S. Ct. 286, 98 L. Ed. 329). If the objectionable matter offends our penal laws, adequate means are at hand to deal with its suppression and punishment of the perpetrators (Penal Law, § 1141; Code Crim. Proc. § 22–a; *Brown* v. *Kingsley Books*, 1 N.Y. 2d 177, 151 N.Y.S. 2d 639, affirmed 77 S. Ct. 1325).

If it were necessary to reach the constitutional question, I am of the view that it would furnish a sufficiently additional reason to justify an affirmance.

FULD, Judge (concurring).

Judge DESMOND has so well stated the case for affirmance that it is with great reluctance that I add even these few words.

While I am in wholehearted agreement with his thought that " 'obscenity, real, serious, not imagined or puritanically exaggerated, is today as in all the past centuries, a public evil' " (Desmond, Legal Problems in Censoring, 40 Marq. L. Rev. 38, 54; opinion, 3 N.Y. 2d at page 246, 165 N.Y.S. 2d 49), it does not follow that the proper remedy is suppression at the "administrative level." The evil, it seems to me, may be adequately dealt with by resort to the courts in the first instance, either by criminal prosecution (Penal Law, § 1141) or by injunctive process. Cf. Code Crim. Proc. § 22–a; *Brown* v. *Kingsley Books*, 1 N.Y. 2d 177, 151 N.Y.S. 2d 639, affirmed 77 S. Ct. 1325. Be that as it may, though, since the court is holding that "The Garden of Eden" is not "indecent" or "obscene" and that, therefore, "there is no legal basis for censorship" (opinion, 3 N.Y. 2d at page 240, 165 N.Y.S. 2d 44), we are not called upon to decide the constitutionality or unconstitutionality of those sections of the Education Law which provide for the licensing of motion pictures by an administrative body. The disposition of that question must be left for decision in a case where the problem is presented.

BURKE, Judge (dissenting).

Inasmuch as the majority have completely brushed aside a clearly defined, reasonable legislative standard of decency with respect to nudity, for reasons of their own, and inasmuch as some have declared that this State's licensing system for motion pictures is unconstitutional if applied to deny a license to a motion picture on any ground other than obscenity, without the slightest shred of specific authority, but merely on the basis of conjecture, we are compelled to dissent. We believe that their decision virtually strips the Legislature of power entrusted to it by the People of the State of New York.

The picture was filmed at a lake front nudist park in another State. The motion picture depicts in color the life in a nudist camp with views of nude men, women and children singly, in pairs and in groups, walking, talking, swimming and playing together. The numerous male and female adults and children in the picture are totally exposed to one another so that they are concededly exposing their private parts in each other's presence. Views of the adults' private parts are not shown to the audience, but the genitalia of children and girls and the buttocks and breasts of men and women are revealed to the audience. In addition the picture contains specific protracted scenes of women in unwholesome, sexually alluring postures which are completely unnecessary to—and in fact a radical departure from—the activities of the nudist camp depicted. For example, there is a dream sequence in which the principal actress, a comely young lady, completely disrobes in full view of the audience in a manner not unlike that generally utilized by professional ecdysiasts.

Other scenes of like tenor, not honestly relevant to the innocent propagandizing of nudism as a way to mental and physical well-being, are present. By no stretch of the imagination can it be equated to the educational studies of aboriginal tribes found in museums, and respectable travel films or magazines.

The film was examined by a reviewer and the acting director of the Motion Picture Division of the State Education Department. After the denial of the license, the petitioner requested the Board of Regents to review the decision of the Motion Picture Division. The film was reexamined by a committee of the members of the Regents. Thereafter the Committee report, signed by two prominent members of the Bar of this State, affirmed the denial of the license on the ground that a public *display* of the picture in the amusement theatres of the State before mixed audiences of all ages would be "indecent." The determinations of the Motion Picture Division and the committee were thereafter unanimously approved by the 13 Regents.

The petitioner instituted this article 78 proceeding to annul the determination. It contends that the picture is not "indecent" within the meaning of section 122 of the Education Law, and, further, that the word "indecent" in section 122 of the Education Law is vague, indefinite and that, therefore, the section is void to that extent for failing to conform to the requirement of due process of law prescribed by the Fourteenth Amendment of the Constitution of the United States. Finally, Excelsior claims that the statute imposes an unconstitutional restraint upon freedom of speech because no system of censorship which requires prior approval of motion pictures would be reconcilable with the language and purpose of the First Amendment of the Constitution of the United States.

The contention that the film is not "indecent" within the intendment of section 122 of the Education Law is without merit. Section 1140–b of the Penal Law provides: "A person who in any place wilfully exposes his private parts in the presence of two or more persons of the opposite sex whose private parts are similarly exposed, or who aids or abets any such act, or who procures another so to expose his private parts or who as owner, manager, lessee, director, promoter or agent, or in any other capacity, hires, leases or permits the land, building or premises of which he is the owner, lessee or tenant, or over which he has control, to be used for any such purposes, is guilty of a misdemeanor."

The history of this legislation makes it crystal clear that the exhibition of male and female nudes totally exposed to each other offends the community sense of decency. Shortly prior to the enactment of section 1140–b of the Penal Law, there were various sections extant which labelled certain acts as "indecent" such as exposure of person, outraging decency, etc. (see Penal Law, §§ 1140, 43, 1530, 1533). In the spring of 1934, one Burke, who was a director of the Olympian League, an organization devoted to the principles of nudism, arranged a gymnasium meeting of the league members by letter in furtherance of "Nudism Forward" month. Admission was permitted upon presentation of the same letter signed by Burke and a fee of $1. Some 10 men and 4 women took part in swimming and exercises in the nude. Burke was subsequently convicted in the Court of Special Sessions of violating sections 43, 1140 and 1530 of the Penal Law. In December, the Appellate Division, with one Justice dissenting, reversed the conviction for the stated reason that the law "at present" was not "sufficiently broad enough to render a conviction" (*People* v. *Burke*, 243 App. Div. 83, 84, 276

N.Y.S. 402, 404). On Janury 7, 1935, legislation was introduced to add section 1140–b to the Penal Law. While this legislation was pending, this court, in April, 1935, with two Judges dissenting, affirmed the Appellate Divison (267 N.Y. 571, 196 N.E. 585). The legislation was passed by the Legislature and became the law on May 11, 1935 (L. 1935, ch. 868). There can be no doubt that the legislation was designed to deal with this type of nudist cult practices (see, *People* v. *Burke*, 243 App. Div. 83, 276 N.Y.S. 402, State Reporter's footnote; Albany Times Union, April 1, 1935, p. 13, col. 4; New York Times, April 2, 1935, p. 4, col. 4, April 9, 1935, p. 12, col. 7; Governor's Bill Jacket on L. 1935, ch. 868).

It is likewise apparent that the legislation was specifically enacted to overcome the decision of this court and the Appellate Division in the Burke case, supra, and to declare the opinion of the dissenters to be the public policy of this State. Resort to precedents not even remotely relevant will not suffice. *People* v. *Eastman* (188 N.Y. 478, 81 N.E. 459), falls in that category. They are factually and legally inapposite. *People* v. *Eastman*, supra, was merely a forerunner of *People* v. *Burke*, supra, now no longer an authority in respect to the illegal conduct described in section 1140–b of the Penal Law and indulged in by the nudists in this picture. The words of this statute should not be twisted out of their meaning. The court must regard the plain meaning of the statute with respect. Public policy may not be shaped out of a play on words or governed by personal impressions or attitudes. To substitute the bare conclusions of a few Judges in place of the determination of the Legislature and to challenge the wisdom of the Legislature constitutes a usurpation of the powers of the Legislature and a veto of the declaration of public opinion arrived at after debate.

We recently said in *New York Post Corp.* v. *Leibowitz*, 2 N.Y. 2d 677, 685–686, 163 N.Y.S. 2d 409, 415, "In construing statutory provisions, the spirit and purpose of the statute and the objectives sought to be accomplished by the legislature must be borne in mind. 'The legislative intent is the great and controlling principle. Literal meanings of words are not to be adhered to or suffered to "defeat the general purpose and manifest policy intended to be promoted." ' *People* v. *Ryan*, 274 N.Y. 149, 152, 8 N.E. 2d 313, 315; see, also, *United Press Ass'ns* v. *Valente*, supra, 308 N.Y. 71, 83–84, 123 N.E. 2d 777, 782 * * *." Here we need not have recourse to general definition to establish that the conduct engaged in by the nudists in "Garden of Eden" is indecent within the meaning of section 122 of the Education Law. Section 1140–b of the Penal Law clearly evidences the legislative intent.

In light of the history of the legislation it was quite proper for the Regents to apply the standards set by this section of the Penal Law for the purpose of determining the character of nudity which is indecent under section 122 of the Education Law. It would be unreasonable to assume that the Legislature intended to authorize the viewing of such acts on motion picture screens, while it condemned the conduct in camps or gymnasiums. The exhibition of "Garden of Eden" would be a "professional exploitation of nudism for profit" and a "widespread use of exhibitionism for financial gain" in violation of the purposes of the statute (Public Papers of Governor Herbert H. Lehman, 1935, p. 352). Therefore, a license for general

exhibition of the picture would violate a standard of decency specifically defined by the Legislature in respect to nudity, and flaunt the public policy established by the Legislature.

That the conduct of the people depicted by the scenes of this film falls within that defined by section 1140–b of the Penal Law in that the minimum required number of male and female nudes are totally exposed to one another cannot be denied. It is conceded. However, respondent relies on the absence of any scene showing the genitalia of the adults to the audience. This contention is without merit. The test set by the provisions of section 1140–b has no such requirement. It simply requires that the nudists be engaged in the activity of exposing their private parts to those of the opposite sex whose private parts are similarly exposed. With this in mind there can be no doubt that this picture is indecent within the meaning of section 122.

While some individuals may disagree with the wisdom of such a standard, we must uphold it. Irrespective of personal views, we, in construing these statutes, may not substitute our judgment—or the judgment of others, however much revered or respected—for the judgment of the Legislature which is the representative of the People of the State of New York and reflects their opinions. The forum for debate as to the desirability of such legislation has been provided for under our form of government and our laws. It is the Legislature, not the courts. Appellate judges should not constitute themselves a "tiny autonomous Legislature" in order to thwart and frustrate the public opinion of the People of the State. An oligarchy cannot be substituted in place of our democracy by judicial fiat. There is nothing in our system of laws which prevents the amendment or change of the law if the People of the State of New York so desire (see *Daniel* v. *Family Sec. Life Ins. Co.*, 336 U.S. 220, 224, 69 S. Ct. 550, 93 L. Ed. 632). The Legislature has described the type of conduct of nudists which is prohibited by a specific statute so that there can be no question in the mind of a judge, a citizen, or the Board of Regents as to the meaning of the statute. As the court stated in *United States* v. *Harmon*, D.C., 45 F. 414, 417, 422: "Laws of this character are made for society in the aggregate, and not in particular. So, while there may be individuals and societies of men and women of peculiar notions or idiosyncrasies, whose moral sense would neither be depraved nor offended by the publication now under consideration, yet the exceptional sensibility, or want of sensibility, of such cannot be allowed as a standard by which its obscenity or indecency is to be tested. Rather is the test, what is the judgment of the aggregate sense of the community reached by it? * * * In short, the proposition is that a man can do no public wrong who believes that what he does is for the ultimate public good. The underlying vice of all this character of argument is that it leaves out of view the existence of the social compact, and the idea of government by law."

It is obvious that insofar as nudity is concerned, the term "indecent" of section 122 of the Education Law, as confined and limited by the standards set forth in section 1140–b of the Penal Law, is so clear and certain that it does not offend due process. When so defined, indecency is not a chameleon term, lacking in calculable content. It speaks not of abstractions, but of objective standards, and its scope is of mathematical precision. Under this construction there is no fear that a decision by an administrative agency is left to arbitrary judgment (cf. *Joseph Burstyn, Inc.* v. *Wilson,* 343 U.S. 495, 72 S. Ct. 777, 96 L. Ed. 1098). Nor is there any doubt that this construction sufficiently apprises one bent on obedience of law of what is to be regulated (*Beauharnais* v. *People of State of Illinois,* 343 U.S. 250, 72 S. Ct. 725, 96 L. Ed. 919; *Connally* v. *General Constr. Co.,* 269 U.S. 385, 46 S. Ct. 126, 70 L. Ed. 322). As thus construed and applied in this situation, there can be no valid objection on the ground that the term "indecency" is so vague that it is violative of due process.

It well may be that for the purpose of applying this statute to other circumstances the Legislature should amend it to include a broad comprehensive definition, as it amended the statute to further define and limit the term "immoral" after the Supreme Court of the United States reversed this court's holding in *Commercial Pictures Corp.* v. *Board of Regents,* 305 N.Y. 336, 113 N.E. 2d 502. See *Commercial Pictures Corp.* v. *Regents,* 346 U.S. 587, 74 S. Ct. 286, 98 L. Ed. 329; L. 1954, ch. 620, Education Law, § 122–a. However, that is no concern of ours at the present time, and we need not deal with questions so abstract to determine this controversy (*Ashwander* v. *Tennessee Val. Auth.,* 297 U.S. 288, 341, 346–348, 56 S. Ct. 466, 80 L. Ed. 688). State action cannot be found hypothetically unconstitutional (*People of State of New York* ex rel. *Hatch* v. *Reardon,* 204 U.S. 152, 27 S. Ct. 188, 51 L. Ed. 415). As here construed, the statute only applies to public or quasi-public places. Irrelevant references to family members unclothed within the family home miss the mark. Under very familiar law, the construction placed upon the statute by this court fixes its meaning for this case (*Winters* v. *People of State of New York,* 333 U.S. 507, 514, 68 S. Ct. 665, 92 L. Ed. 840; *Beauharnais* v. *People of State of Illinois,* supra, 343 U.S. at page 253, 72 S. Ct. at page 728; *Hebert* v. *State of Louisiana,* 272 U.S. 312, 317, 47 S. Ct. 103, 71 L. Ed. 270).

Equally without substance is the claim that the requirement of prior approval of motion pictures in and of itself offends the letter and spirit of the First Amendment to the Constitution. "The phrase 'prior restraint' is not a self-wielding sword. Nor can it serve as a talismanic test." *Kingsley Books* v. *Brown,* 77 S. Ct. 1325, 1328.

The decisions of the Supreme Court of the United States have not condemned licensing of films in advance of exhibition as a contravention of the First Amendment. In each case that court has merely held that the standard used was not sufficiently definite and certain to satisfy the minimum requirements of due process (see, e.g., *Joseph Burstyn, Inc.* v. *Wilson,* 343 U.S. 495, 72 S. Ct. 777, 96 L. Ed. 1098, supra ["sacrilegious" vague]; *Superior Films* v. *Department of Educ.,* 346 U.S. 587, 74 S. Ct. 286, 98 L. Ed. 329 ["harmful" too indefinite]; *Commercial Pictures Corp.* v. *Board of Regents,* 305 N.Y. 336, 113 N.E. 2d 502, reversed sub nom. *Superior Films* v. *Department of Educ.,* 346 U.S. 587, 74 S. Ct. 286, 98 L. Ed. 329 ["immoral" indefinite]). In the Burstyn case, supra, the Supreme Court reiterated the caveat set forth in *Near* v. *State of Minnesota,* 283 U.S. 697, 51 S. Ct. 625, 75 L. Ed. 1357: "To hold that liberty of expression by means of motion pictures is guaranteed by the First and Fourteenth Amendments, however, is not the end of our problem. It does not follow that the Constitution requires absolute

freedom to exhibit every motion picture of every kind at all times and all places. That much is evident from the series of decisions of this Court with respect to other media of communication of ideas" (343 U.S. at pages 502–503, 72 S. Ct. at page 781). That much this court recently declared (see *Brown* v. *Kingsley Books,* 1 N.Y. 2d 177, 184, 151 N.Y.S. 2d 639, 643). Furthermore, as the Legislature is not constitutionally limited in its choice of remedial processes in dealing with proscribed conduct, we fail to see why the statutory procedure followed here should be declared unconstitutional simply because we are dealing with a motion picture (see *Kingsley Books* v. *Brown,* 77 S. Ct. 1325). In the absence of any definitive authority, we should not indulge in the assumption that this State's motion picture licensing system is unconstitutional when applied to deny a license to a motion picture on any ground other than obscenity. Particularly is this true where to do so would be to deprive the State of a valuable weapon for combating conduct detrimental to its well-being. Nor do we find persuasive the reasoning that we may longer preserve this licensing system by judicially nullifying its operation and effects. To preserve its form while denying its substance would be to gain nothing.

Insofar as any question of prior restraint is concerned, it is interesting to observe that the objectives, procedures and standards established by section 22–a of the Code of Criminal Procedure, which was recently upheld as constitutional in the Kingsley case, supra, are similar to and parallel sections 120–132 of the Education Law when we consider them against the facts and procedure involved in this case.

The license was not denied without thorough consideration. The picture was reviewed by a reviewer, by the acting director of the Motion Picture Division, and by a committee of three members of the Board of Regents consisting of two prominent members of the New York Bar, and the present chairman of the board. Thereafter the determination of all the reviewers was approved by a unanimous vote of the Board of Regents. The finding was the same as it would be if the defendant had been arraigned under the provisions of section 1140–b of the Penal Law. Since the petitioner admitted the acts in the picture were the acts of totally nude persons in a nudist camp, there was no need of proving the fact beyond a reasonable doubt. The usual procedural safeguards of judicial proceedings were complied with. The petitioner has had two appellate reviews. Surely no one can challenge the competency of the prominent and experienced citizens comprising the Board of Regents or, for that matter, the trained reviewer and acting director of the Motion Picture Division. This is not a case involving the sole judgment of a police commissioner or a local official subject to local prejudice. The motion picture is the evidence. It speaks for itself. It cannot be cross-examined. It was reviewed carefully and thoroughly.

Under such circumstances, the statute in question, as construed, is operative in this case. The motion picture "Garden of Eden" is a class of speech, the prevention of which does not raise any constitutional problem. Petitioner would convert an issue of law enforcement policy into a spurious contest over constitutional rights, but it ignores the fundamental doctrine that the State has inherent police power to prevent a showing of a film which it classifies as indecent by a specific statute, because it displays persons admittedly and pridefully exposing their private parts to those of the opposite sex whose private parts are similarly exposed. The police power extends to and includes "everything essential to the public safety, health and morals" (*Lawton* v. *Steele*, 152 U.S. 133, 136, 14 S. Ct. 499, 500, 38 L. Ed. 385; see *Berman* v. *Parker*, 348 U.S. 26, 32, 33, 75 S. Ct. 98, 99 L. Ed. 27). "The police power does not have its genesis in a written constitution. It is an indispensable attribute of our society, possessed by the state sovereignties before the adoption of the Federal Constitution, Mayor, &c., of *City of New York* v. *Miln*, 1837, 11 Pet. 102, 9 L. Ed. 648." *Schmidt* v. *Board of Adjustment of City of Newark*, 9 N.J. 405, 414, 88 A. 2d 607, 611. A commentator on personal freedom, John Stuart Mill, in his essay "On Liberty," says: "Again, there are many acts which, being directly injurious only to the agents themselves, ought not to be legally interdicted, but which, if done publicly, are a violation of good manners, and coming thus within the category of offences against others, may rightfully be prohibited. Of this kind are offences against decency; on which it is unnecessary to dwell, the rather as they are only connected indirectly with our subject, the objection to publicity being equally strong in the case of many actions not in themselves condemnable, nor supposed to be so."

Moreover, variant mediums of expression are not subject to universal rules. Taking into consideration the time, place and mode of expression, limitations upon the individual's right of free speech—including prior restraint—when imposed by a State is not necessarily unconstitutional (cf. *Chaplinsky* v. *State of New Hampshire*, 315 U.S. 568, 571–572, 62 S. Ct. 766, 86 L. Ed. 1031). Where particular means of expression are involved, there are areas where the State may previously restrain the exercise of free speech and it will merely be considered as a reasonable accommodation between the individual's right and a conflicting interest which a State is entitled to make under the circumstances (see *Cox* v. *State of New Hampshire*, 312 U.S. 569, 61 S. Ct. 762, 85 L. Ed. 1049). The unrestricted invalidation of statutes or ordinances upon constitutional grounds, and without any examination of their reasonableness, could eventually endanger the right of free speech itself by making it ridiculous and obnoxious. For example, the Supreme Court has recognized that the use of audio amplification devices, even when used for the purpose of making utterances on religious subjects, may be previously restrained by a police commissioner under a licensing statute where the statute is so narrowly drawn as to regulate the hours or places of use, or the decibel volume to which they may be adjusted, so that the grant of the license would not rest upon any arbitrary decision of the police commissioner (see *Saia* v. *People of State of New York*, 334 U.S. 558, 560, 562, 68 S. Ct. 1148, 92 L. Ed. 1574). Similarly it has recognized that motion pictures are not necessarily subject to the precise rules which govern other methods of expression (see *Joseph Burstyn, Inc.* v. *Wilson*, 343 U.S. 495, 503, 72 S. Ct. 777, 96 L. Ed. 1098, supra).

In view of this we think that as construed the statute in question is a reasonable regulation upon motion pictures as medium of expression. It does not previously restrain speech with respect to nudism—in fact, there is no objection to any of the dialogue. It does not even make illicit or restrict the portrayal of nude people or nudist camps per se. It merely prevents the showing of nudists of opposite sexes exhibiting their privates to each other. It is the viewing of this specific form of nude exhibitionism which the Legislature found harmful and necessary to regulate. "To say that representation of criminal activity is criminal is to abolish the drama and the novel in one stroke" is to sound a false alarm and to incite unrealistic fears. When the final curtain is rung down the murdered Caesars and Desdemonas step before it, take their bows and receive their plaudits. No penal statute pertaining to crimes against person, property or habitation have been contravened. But when we turn to specific forms of nude conduct, the situation is otherwise. Aside from the question of degree, the resulting harm is the same whether the exhibition is in person or portrayed. In fact, by portrayal it may even be heightened. With the present advances of the art of motion picture photography, this is true with that medium. The exhibition of the actions of the nudists in the "Garden of Eden" is actually more life-like than their presence upon the stage. As it is constitutionally within the police power to regulate the actual presence of a nudist camp upon a public stage within this State, we fail to see how it would not be constitutionally within the police power to regulate a more alluring portrayal of those actions upon the screen particularly under such a narrowly construed statute. Civil liberties are not unrestricted rights which may at all times and under all circumstances be exercised in spite of the reasonable restrictions of the society upon which they depend for the protection of their free existence. As Chief Justice Hughes, writing for a unanimous Supreme Court, declared: "Civil liberties, as guaranteed by the Constitution, imply the existence of an organized society maintaining public order without which liberty itself would be lost in the excesses of unrestrained abuses." *Cox* v. *State of New Hampshire*, 312 U.S. 569, 574, 61 S. Ct. 762, 765, 85 L. Ed. 1049, supra.

The order of the Appellate Division annulling the determination of respondents-appellants and directing the licensing of the film should be reversed and the petition dismissed.

Conway, Chief Judge (dissenting).

Powers of government are divided among the Executive, the Legislative and the Judicial branches of our government. Those powers come by grant of the people as evidenced by the preambles to our National and State Constitutions. It would be unfortunate were one of the branches of government to disregard either of the other branches and fail to exercise self-discipline and to recognize proper limitations upon its own power. It would be even more unfortunate were members of the Judiciary to disregard the will of the people—the author of their being— and to determine that the standards set up by the duly constituted representatives of the people, to protect the people, were not proper standards in their view and to use their power to declare statutes unconstitutional which have been passed by the Legislature and approved by the Executive because those members of the Judiciary would not pass or approve such statutes so desired by the people. The result could be a government by *one* of the branches of government in defiance of the people's will and by means of semantics. It is thoughts such as these which, in the setting of the facts herein, have compelled me to concur in the opinion of Judge Burke.

Opinion by Desmond, J.; Dye and Fuld, JJ., concur except as to the discussion of the constitutionality of the statute, each in a separate opinion.

Van Voorhis, J., concurs with Desmond and Fuld, JJ.

Burke, J., dissents in an opinion in which Froessel, J., concurs and in which Conway, C.J., concurs in a separate opinion in which Froessel and Burke, JJ., concur.

Order affirmed.

■ One, Incorporated,

v.

Olesen, Postmaster of Los Angeles.

ON PETITION FOR WRIT OF CERTIORARI TO THE UNITED STATES COURT OF APPEALS FOR THE NINTH CIRCUIT.

No. 290. Decided January 13, 1958. 241 F. 2d 772, reversed.

Per Curiam.

Eric Julber for petitioner.
Solicitor General *Rankin*, Acting Assistant Attorney General *Leonard* and *Samuel D. Slade* for respondent.

The petition for writ of certiorari is granted and the judgment of the United States Court of Appeals for the Ninth Circuit is reversed. *Roth* v. *United States*, 354 U.S. 476.

■ People of the State of California, *Plaintiff and Respondent,*

v.

Eleazar Smith, *Defendant and Appellant.*
Cr. A. 3792.

Appellate Department, Superior Court, Los Angeles County, California.

June 23, 1958.

Brock, Easton, Fleishman & Rykoff, Hollywood, for appellant.
Roger Arnebergh, City Atty., *Philip E. Grey*, Asst. City Atty., *William E. Doran*, Deputy City Atty., Los Angeles, for respondent.

David, Judge.

The defendant Smith appeals from a judgment based upon his conviction under Los Angeles Municipal Code, (Ordinance No. 77,000 as amended) pursuant to the complaint which charged that he violated paragraph 2 of section 41.01.1 thereof, in that he "did wilfully and unlawfully * * * have in his possession an obscene and indecent writing, book, pamphlet, picture, photograph and drawing, to wit: Sweeter Than Life, in a place of business where magazines, books, pamphlets, papers and pictures were sold and kept for sale."

The ordinance provisions in question read in part as follows: "Sec. 41.01.1 Indecent Writings, Etc.—Possession Prohibited:

"It shall be unlawful for any person to have in his possession any obscene or indecent writing, book, pamphlet, picture, photograph, drawing, * * * in any of the following places:

"1. In any school, school-grounds, public park or playground or in any public place, grounds, street or way within 300 yards of any school, park or playground;

"2. In any place of business where ice-cream, soft drinks, candy, food, school supplies, magazines, books, pamphlets, papers, pictures or postcards are sold or kept for sale;

"3. In any toilet or restroom open to the public;

"4. In any pool room or billiard parlor, or in any place where alcoholic liquor is sold or offered for sale to the public; * * *."

Appellant's contentions cannot be sustained:

[1, 2] (1) The ordinance does not violate the First Amendment of the United States Constitution. Under the California Penal Code sec. 311 dealing with obscenity, the United States Supreme Court has held that "obscenity is not within the area of constitutionally protected speech or press. *Roth* v. *United States*, (*Alberts* v. *California*) 1957, 354 U.S. 476, at page 485, 77 S. Ct. 1304, 1309, 1 L. Ed. 2d 1498.

[3] (2) The characterization as "obscene" is not too indefinite to constitute a valid standard. In the case last cited, the trial judge applied the test laid down in *People* v. *Wepplo*, 1947, 78 Cal. App. 2d Supp. 959, 178, P. 2d 853, which was approved by the U.S. Supreme Court in the Alberts case, 354 U.S. at page 489, 77 S. Ct. at page 1311.

[4] (3) Under any test, the book concerned in this prosecution was properly held to be obscene by the trial court, and we share such a conclusion upon our independent view of the evidence, if that be necessary in view of the assertion of constitutional right, though such a right is clearly non-existent. *Alberts* v. *California*, 1957, 354 U.S. 476, 485–486, 77 S. Ct. 1304, 1 L. Ed. 2d 1498. Obscenity is not constitutionally protected. The "community standard" is, as in other criminal matters, to be determined by the trier of the fact. *Parmelee* v. *United States*, 1940, 72 App. D.C. 203, 113 F. 2d 729, 741.

[5] The police power of the state in such matters is not restrained by the definitions applied by the federal courts to the federal question of admission of books to the country or to the mails. A national common-denominator of morality may be considerably less than that in a state, which has the right to set, and to adhere to, its own standards in such matters. U.S. Const. Amend. X. That any obscene book or picture may be popular is no ground for holding that it may not be suppressed, since that condition may be exactly the occasion for legislative action against it to protect the public morals. Such legislation preeminently falls within state police power. *Lawton* v. *Steele*, 1893, 152 U.S. 133, 14 S. Ct. 499, 38 L. Ed. 385.

We reach this conclusion, also, when we have considered the book as a whole, under tests that the appellant contends are applicable. There are obvious common-sense limits to the "over all" view. We are not persuaded that a bawdy house is any the less a brothel, because many of the rooms of the house may be occupied with dining and dancing, in view of what goes on in the bedrooms. A book is not necessarily clean or not obscene because some of the chapters or paragraphs leading to the bedroom, couch, summerhouse or other available place themselves do not describe the details of adulterous fornication nor rape. Cf. *Besig* v. *United States*, 9 Cir., 1953, 208 F. 2d 142, 146.

[6, 7] (4) The defendant offered expert witnesses to testify what psychological effect the prurient material in question would have on a normal average person. In California, this is no more the subject of expert testimony than what the conduct of a reasonable and prudent person would be in a negligence action. This is for the trier of the

fact. *People* v. *Wepplo*, supra, 78 Cal. App. 2d Supp. 959, 178 P. 2d 853; cf. *United States* v. *Kennerley*, D.C. 1913, 209 F. 119, 121. Nor was it error to exclude evidence as to the contents of other books, alleged to be no different or even more sexually titillating, on the theory that legislation is invalid which seeks to restrain that which is popular. Pornography has not been popular enough to induce the state and city legislators who represent the populace at large to change the legislative policies, or to redefine the common understanding of the meanings of well-established English words. The great quarrel in this field actually seems not to be with the definition of "obscenity" but with its application, to particular states of fact. We have no such difficulty in this case. We have found that the book in question is obscene, not merely that there is sufficient evidence to support the implied finding of the trial court to that effect, keeping in mind what we said in *People* v. *Wepplo*, supra, 1947, 78 Cal. App. 2d Supp. 959, 961, 178 P. 2d 853, in which obscenity was defined in construing Cal. Penal Code sec. 311(3).

[8] (5) The Los Angeles city ordinance No. 77,000 (known as the Los Angeles Municipal Code) section 41.01.1, has the full force of a statute of the state within the limits of the city (*Odd Fellows' Cemetery Ass'n* v. *San Francisco*, 1903, 140 Cal. 226, 230, 73 P. 987; *Boyd* v. *City of Sierra Madre*, 1919, 41 Cal. App. 520, 183 P. 230), except so far as it is "in conflict with general laws." Cal. Const. Art. XI, sec. 11; *Simpson* v. *City of Los Angeles*, 1953, 40 Cal. 2d 271, 278, 253 P. 2d 464, appeal dismissed 346 U.S. 802, 74 S. Ct. 37, 98 L. Ed. 333, rehearing denied 346 U.S. 880, 74 S. Ct. 118, 98 L. Ed. 387.

In California, this police power of cities is one of the oldest municipal powers. Cal. Const. (1879) Art. XI, sec. 11, perpetuated the power that was granted in the earliest charters and general laws for organization of municipal corporations in California, repeated and applied many times before 1879. (For instance, Charter of Sacramento, Cal. Stats. 1850, p. 70, sec. 5; idem, San Diego, p. 122, sec. 5; idem, San Jose, p. 125, sec. 5; idem, for incorporation of towns, p. 128–129, sec. 6; idem, for incorporation of cities, pp. 87–88, sec. 11.) In the 1879 constitution, article XI related to local government, and the same section number, 11, was retained, as formerly pertained to this power in the Act for Incorporation of Cities. Before the Constitution of 1879, such power was conferred by the legislature. Now, it is conferred by the constitution itself. Prior to 1879, the numerous statutes and special charters gave full power to cities to pass ordinances "not repugnant * * * to the laws of this State." Prior to 1879, the laws applying to cities were sometimes general and often special, but in 1879 by Art. IV, sec. 25, the legislature was forbidden to pass "local or special laws * * * Creating offices, or prescribing the powers and duties of officers in counties, cities, cities and counties, townships, election or school districts."

Hence, Art. XI, sec. 11 vested and vests power in cities to pass police regulations "*not in conflict with general laws.*" (Emphasis added.) Appellant asserts that there is such a conflict here between Penal Code sec. 311 and the ordinance in question.

Under the ordinance, it is illegal for a person to "have in his possession any obscene or indecent writing, book, pamphlet, picture, photograph, drawing, figure, * * * of any kind in any of the following places: * * * 2. In any place of business where * * * school supplies, magazines, books, pamphlets, papers, pictures or postcards are sold or kept for sale; * * *" (Municipal Code, sec. 41.01.1)

Penal Code sec. 311 provides, so far as applicable: "Every person who wilfully and lewdly, either: * * * 3. Writes, * * * sells, distributes, keeps for sale, or exhibits any obscene or indecent writing, paper, or book; * * * is guilty of a misdemeanor." Municipal Code sec. 41.01.1 is more restrictive since it eliminates the requirement that a sale be made "lewdly" and in making it illegal to possess such material in such a place of business, irrespective of a lewd intent to sell it or to keep it for sale.

The city ordinance is more restrictive than the Penal Code sec. 311. Under the Penal Code section *scienter* is required. The defendant must possess the obscene material "wilfully and unlawfully" and with "lewd" intent. *People v. Wepplo*, supra, 1947, 78 Cal. App. 2d Supp. 959, 178 P. 2d 853; *Matter of Ahart*, 1916, 172 Cal. 762, 159 P. 160.

[9–12] There is no conflict. Wilful possession of an obscene book in a bookstore is not made an offense under the Penal Code provision, but it is under the city ordinance. Defendant could not have been prosecuted under Penal Code sec. 311 for wilfully and unlawfully possessing the material in a bookstore without more. This fact alone demonstrates that the municipal ordinance is not in conflict with the general law. A prosecution may be had under an ordinance and a statute (cf. *People v. Burkhart*, 1936, 5 Cal. 2d 641, 55 P. 2d 846) where separate, distinct elements are involved in each. Local legislation must be *in conflict* with general law, before the constitutional grant of the police power to local bodies is inoperative and that vested in the legislature is given priority. No permission from the legislature itself to a city is necessary to the exercise of the local power under the constitution. Legislative declarations of permission to legislate confer none, but only indicate that the legislature in its own opinion has not purported to completely cover the subject matter. This relates to statutory construction, and not to power.

In this case, the relation of the local to the state legislation is essentially the same as that in *People v. Commons*, 1944, 64 Cal. App. 2d Supp. 925, 148 P. 2d 724, where possession of any dangerous or deadly weapon in an automobile was held to be effective, though the state Dangerous Weapons Control Law was less restrictive; *People v. Burkhart*, supra, 1936, 5 Cal. 2d 641, 55 P. 2d 846, where the ordinance prohibited being drunk in an auto on the highway, and the state statute prohibited driving an automobile while intoxicated. In re Iverson, 1926, 199 Cal. 582, 250 P. 681, where the state law permitted a druggist to fill a prescription for 16 ounces of intoxicating liquor, reduced by the Los Angeles ordinance to 8 ounces, and in which the doctrine of "more restrictive legislation" is considered and approved; In re Hoffman, 1909, 155 Cal. 114, 99 P. 517, holding valid increased standards for milk solids in milk; *Sternall v. Strand*, 1946, 76 Cal. App. 2d 432, 434–435, 172 P. 2d 921; *Remmer v. Municipal Court*, 1949, 90 Cal. App. 2d 854, 856–858, 204 P. 2d 92; *Markus v. Justice's Court*, 1953, 117 Cal. App. 2d 391, 396–397, 255 P. 2d 883; *Witt v. Klimm*, 1929, 97 Cal. App. 131, 134, 274 P. 1039, upholding additional regulation.

The same conclusion has been reached by the courts of other states which have adopted the provisions or principles of Cal. Const. Art. XI, sec. 11. Cf. *Allen v. City of Bellingham*, 1917, 95 Wash. 12, 163 P. 18, 26, reviewing cases; *City of Shreveport v. Provenza*, 1956, 231 La. 514, 91 So. 2d 777; *Jones v. City of Chicago*, 1952, 348 Ill. App. 310, 108 N.E. 2d 802, 805, ordinance raising amounts of insurance to be carried by taxicab operators above amounts set by state statute, the rule being stated "An ordinance, because of local conditions, may impose more rigorous or definite regulations under a proper delegation of power in addition to those imposed by the State"; *State ex rel. Sutton v. Caldwell*, 1940, 195 La. 507, 197 So. 214, 218, citing *Mann v. Scott*, 1919, 180 Cal. 550, 182 P. 281; and In re Hoffman, 1909, 155 Cal. 114, 99 P. 517, 132 Am. St. Rep. 75; *City of Garden City v. Miller*, 1957, 181 Kan. 360, 311 P. 2d 306, 311; *State ex rel. Woodruff v. Centanne*, 1956, 265 Ala. 35, 89 So. 2d 570, 571; *Kansas City v. Henre*, 1915, 96 Kan. 794, 153 P. 548, 549, citing In re Hoffman, supra, 155 Cal. 114, 118, 99 P. 517.

[13] Until one of our supreme courts declares otherwise, we are of the opinion that a book seller may be constitutionally prohibited from possessing or keeping an obscene book in his store and convicted of doing so even though it is not shown he knows its obscene character, nor that he intends its sale. He may not, with impunity, adopt as his rule of conduct: "Where ignorance is bliss, 'Tis folly to be wise."

Those who are engaged in selling articles of a particular class to the public, have the first and best opportunity to know or be on notice of their characteristics, even though possession and not sale is involved. Civ. Code, secs. 18, 19. Statutes commonly have forbidden the sale, offering for sale or possession of filthy articles, dangerous or deleterious to the public; or contrary to public morals; or otherwise unlawful; and have placed the duty to know their characteristics upon the possessor. Cf. *People v. Schwartz*, 1937, 28 Cal. App. 2d Supp. 775, 70 P. 2d 1017; *Escola v. Coca Cola Bottling Co.*, 1944, 24 Cal. 2d 453, 463, 150 P. 2d 436; *United States v. Dotterweich*, 1943, 320 U.S. 277, 64 S. Ct. 134, 88 L. Ed. 48, 49; note 152 A.L.R. 765. The abatement of property used for an unlawful purpose does not depend on the knowledge of the owner. *People v. McCaddon*, 1920, 48 Cal. App. 790, 192 P. 325. So with books.

[14] It is a matter of common knowledge that booksellers have possessed obscene books, kept in the back room or the locked case at their places of business. While not displayed for sale, the possession on the premises is validly considered as tending toward exhibition and sale, and hence possession is validly established as a separate offense, without showing of a lewd intent, as provided in Penal Code sec. 311. "Possession" frequently is prohibited, without more, in penal statutes. Consult: fish and game, note 125 A.L.R. 1200; unlawful possession of cane gun or bird net, Cal. Fish & Game Code secs. 2008–2009; idem, secs. 8800–8807, beach nets; salmon, idem, secs. 8212, 8215; narcotics and drugs in prison, Penal Code sec. 4573.6; firearms, Penal Code sec. 4574; counterfeit coin, Penal Code sec. 479; deadly weapons, Stat. 1923, p. 696, sec. 2 as amended, Pen. Code. §§ 12001, 12021; machine guns, Deering's Gen. Laws Act 1971, Stat. 1927, p. 938, as amended, Pen. Code, § 12200 et seq.

The judgment is affirmed.

BISHOP, P.J., concurs.

SWAIN, Judge.

I dissent.

The legislature by Penal Code sec. 311(3) has occupied the field of selling and keeping for sale an obscene or indecent book. Therefore, under Article XI, sec. 11 of the Const. of California, that portion of sec. 41.01.1 of the Los Angeles Municipal Code (Ord. No. 77,000) is void which attempts to make it a misdemeanor for a person to have in his possession an obscene and indecent book in a place of business where books etc. are sold or kept for sale. The evidence is undisputed that Smith was the proprietor of a book store in the City of Los Angeles and that he sold and kept for sale the books in question at his store.

The evidence proves a violation of the state law as well as a violation of the ordinance. The problem thus posed is by no means merely academic. A defendant is not guilty of violating Penal Code sec. 311 unless he had knowledge of the character of the material. *People* v. *Wepplo*, supra, 1947, 78 Cal. App. 2d Supp. 959, 964, 178 P. 2d 853. To the word "knowledge" we would add "or notice," meaning thereby knowledge of facts which would have put a reasonable and prudent man on inquiry as to the contents of the materials. To appear profound, we refer to this knowledge or notice as "scienter." Under the city ordinance the prosecution does not have to prove scienter; under the Penal Code section, it does. This is true because the city ordinance uses the words "wilfully and unlawfully," whereas Penal Code sec. 311 uses the words "*wilfully and lewdly.*" This interpretation and distinction is pointed out in *People* v. *Wepplo*, supra, 1947, 78 Cal. App. 2d Supp. 959, 963, et seq., 178 P. 2d 853. The state law has occupied the field of selling and keeping for sale an obscene writing, paper or book. To sell it and keep it for sale, the defendant had the book in his possession at his store. The city cannot deprive him of the defense of "no scienter" by charging him with possession under the ordinance, *People* v. *Commons*, supra, 1944, 64 Cal. App. 2d Supp. 925, 148 P. 2d 724; *People* v. *Webb*, 1958, 158 Cal. App. 2d—, 323 P. 2d 141; the complaint did not state any violation of Penal Code sec. 311 for it failed to charge that the defendant sold or offered for sale the book and magazine *lewdly*. In re Correa, 1918, 36 Cal. App. 512, 513, 172 P. 615.

It is true as stated in the majority opinion that there is no declaration by the legislature that it purports to cover the field. Such a declaration is not indispensable. The law as to occupation of the field by the state is well stated in 28 Ops. Atty. Gen. 192 as follows:

"Where the State statute expressly sets forth an intention to completely occupy the whole field of regulation of the subject matter and actually implements such intention by providing for such regulation, local regulation of the same subject matter is prohibited (*Pipoly* v. *Benson*, 20 Cal. 2d 366, 370 [125 P. 2d 482, 147 A.L.R. 515]). On the other hand, the State statute may expressly provide that local regulations may supplement the general law. In such cases reasonable local ordinances imposing supplementary requirements may be enacted (*National Milk Producers Ass'n* v. *City and County of San Francisco*, 20 Cal. 2d 101, 110–111 [124 P. 2d 25]; In re Iverson, 199 Cal. 582, 586–588 [250 P. 681])."

"If the State statute contains no outright declaration of intention with respect to local regulation, the determination 'of the question whether the Legislature has undertaken to occupy exclusively a given field of legislation depends upon an analysis of the statute and a consideration of the facts and circumstances upon which it was intended to operate' (*Tolman* v. *Underhill*, 39 Cal. 2d 708, 712 [249 P. 2d 280])."

The question in *Tolman* v. *Underhill*, supra, was whether the Regents of the University of California could require from faculty members a more restrictive oath than that required by the State law in Government Code secs. 3100–3109. The court held they could not.

In *Bowen* v. *County of Los Angeles*, 1952, 39 Cal. 2d 714, 249 P. 2d 285, the court held that the state had occupied the same field to the exclusion of an oath required by order of the Board of Supervisors.

It is obvious from a reading of Penal Code sec. 311(3) and the use of "lewdly" therein that the legislature intended to give all proprietors of book stores throughout the State protection of the scienter rule. This is a wise and just provision because those proprietors customarily buy books from advertisements sent out by the publishers. Such dealers order books without an opportunity to read them in advance. I would reverse the judgment.

■ Smith

v.

California.

APPEAL FROM THE APPELLATE DEPARTMENT OF THE SUPERIOR COURT OF CALIFORNIA, LOS ANGELES COUNTY.

No. 9. Argued October 20, 1959.—Decided December 14, 1959.

Stanley Fleishman and *Sam Rosenwein* argued the cause and filed a brief for appellant.

Roger Arnebergh argued the cause for appellee. With him on the brief was *Philip E. Grey.*

A. L. Wirin and *Fred Okrand* filed a brief for the American Civil Liberties Union, as *amicus curiae*, urging reversal.

MR. JUSTICE BRENNAN delivered the opinion of the Court.

Appellant, the proprietor of a bookstore, was convicted in a California Municipal Court under a Los Angeles City ordinance which makes it unlawful "for any person to have in his possession any obscene or indecent writing, [or] book . . . [i]n any place of business where . . . books . . . are sold or kept for sale."[1] The offense was defined by the Municipal Court, and by the Appellate Department of the Superior Court,[2] which affirmed the Municipal Court judgment imposing a jail sentence on appellant, as consisting solely of the possession, in the appellant's bookstore, of a certain book found upon judicial investigation to be obscene. The definition included no element of scienter—knowledge by appellant of the contents of the book—and thus the ordinance was construed as imposing a "strict" or "absolute" criminal liability.[3] The appellant made timely objection below that if the ordinance were so construed it would be in conflict with the Constitution of the United States. This contention, together with other contentions based on the Constitution,[4] was rejected, and the case comes here on appeal. 28 U.S.C. § 1257 (2); 358 U.S. 926.

Almost 30 years ago, Chief Justice Hughes declared for this Court: "It is no longer open to doubt that the liberty of the press, and of speech, is within the liberty safe-

---

[1] The ordinance is § 41.01.1 of the Municipal Code of the City of Los Angeles. It provides:

"INDECENT WRITINGS, ETC.—
POSSESSION PROHIBITED:

"It shall be unlawful for any person to have in his possession any obscene or indecent writing, book, pamphlet, picture, photograph, drawing, figure, motion picture film, phonograph recording, wire recording or transcription of any kind in any of the following places:
"1. In any school, school-grounds, public park or playground or in any public place, grounds, street or way within 300 yards of any school, park or playground;
"2. In any place of business where ice-cream, soft drinks, candy, food, school supplies, magazines, books, pamphlets, papers, pictures or postcards are sold or kept for sale;
"3. In any toilet or restroom open to the public;
"4. In any poolroom or billiard parlor, or in any place where alcoholic liquor is sold or offered for sale to the public;
"5. In any place where phonograph records, photographs, motion pictures, or transcriptions of any kind are made, used, maintained, sold or exhibited."

[2] In this sort of proceeding, "the highest court of a State in which a decision could be had." 28 U.S.C. § 1257. Cal. Const., Art. VI, §§ 4, 4b, 5. See *Edwards* v. *California*, 314 U.S. 160, 171.

[3] See Hall, General Principles of Criminal Law, p. 280. The Appellate Department's opinion is at 161 Cal. App. 2d Supp. 860, 327 P. 2d 636. The ordinance's elimination of scienter was, in fact, a reason assigned by that court for upholding it as permissible supplementary municipal legislation against the contention that the field was occupied by California Penal Code § 311, a state-wide obscenity statute which requires scienter.

[4] These other contentions, which are made again here, are that evidence of a nature constitutionally required to be allowed to be given for the defense as to the obscene character of a book was not permitted to be introduced; that a constitutionally impermissible standard of obscenity was applied by the trier of the facts; and that the book was not in fact obscene. In the light of our determination as to the constitutional permissibility of a strict liability law under the circumstances presented by this case, we need not pass on these questions. For the purposes of discussion, we shall assume without deciding that the book was correctly adjudged below to be obscene.

---

guarded by the due process clause of the Fourteenth Amendment from invasion by state action. It was found impossible to conclude that this essential personal liberty of the citizen was left unprotected by the general guaranty of fundamental rights of person and property. . . ." *Near* v. *Minnesota*, 283 U.S. 697, 707. It is too familiar for citation that such has been the doctrine of this Court, in respect of these freedoms, ever since. And it also requires no elaboration that the free publication and dissemination of books and other forms of the printed word furnish very familiar applications of these constitutionally protected freedoms. It is of course no matter that the dissemination takes place under commercial auspices. See *Joseph Burstyn, Inc.* v. *Wilson*, 343 U.S. 495; *Grosjean* v. *American Press Co.*, 297 U.S. 233. Certainly a retail bookseller plays a most significant role in the process of the distribution of books.

California here imposed a strict or absolute criminal responsibility on appellant not to have obscene books in his shop. "The existence of a *mens rea* is the rule of, rather than the exception to, the principles of Anglo-American criminal jurisprudence." *Dennis* v. *United States*, 341 U.S. 494, 500.[5] Still, it is doubtless competent for the States to create strict criminal liabilities by defining criminal offenses without any element of scienter—though even where no freedom-of-expression question is involved, there is precedent in this Court that this power is not without limitations. See *Lambert* v. *California*, 355 U.S. 225. But the question here is as to the validity of this ordinance's elimination of the scienter requirement—an elimination which may tend to work a substantial restriction on the freedom of speech and of the press. Our decisions furnish examples of legal devices and doctrines, in most applications consistent with the Constitution, which cannot be applied in settings where they have the collateral effect of inhibiting the freedom of expression, by making the individual the more reluctant to exercise it. The States generally may regulate the allocation of the burden of proof in their courts, and it is a common procedural device to impose on a taxpayer the burden of proving his entitlement to exemptions from taxation, but where we conceived that this device was being applied in a manner tending to cause even a self-imposed restriction of free expression, we struck down its application. *Speiser* v. *Randall*, 357 U.S. 513. See *Near* v. *Minnesota*, *supra*, at 712–713. It has been stated here that the usual doctrines as to the separability of constitutional and unconstitutional applications of statutes may not apply where their effect is to leave standing a statute patently capable of many unconstitutional applications, threatening those who validly exercise their rights of free expression with the expense and inconvenience of criminal prosecution. *Thornhill* v. *Alabama*, 310 U.S. 88, 97–98. Cf. *Staub* v. *City of Baxley*, 355 U.S. 313.[6] And this Court has intimated that stricter standards of permissible statutory vagueness may be applied to a statute having a potentially inhibiting effect on speech; a man may the less be required to act at his peril here, because the free dissemination of ideas may be the loser. *Winters* v. *New York*, 333 U.S. 507, 509–510, 517–518. Very much to the point here, where the question is the elimination of the mental element in an offense, is this

---

[5] See also, Williams, Criminal Law—The General Part, p. 238 *et seq.*

[6] See Note, 61 Harv. L. Rev. 1208.

Court's holding in *Wieman* v. *Updegraff*, 344 U.S. 183. There an oath as to past freedom from membership in subversive organizations, exacted by a State as a qualification for public employment, was held to violate the Constitution in that it made no distinction between members who had, and those who had not, known of the organization's character. The Court said of the elimination of scienter in this context: "To thus inhibit individual freedom of movement is to stifle the flow of democratic expression and controversy at one of its chief sources." *Id.,* at 191.

These principles guide us to our decision here. We have held that obscene speech and writings are not protected by the constitutional guarantees of freedom of speech and the press. *Roth* v. *United States,* 354 U.S. 476.[7] The ordinance here in question, to be sure, only imposes criminal sanctions on a bookseller if in fact there is to be found in his shop an obscene book. But our holding in *Roth* does not recognize any state power to restrict the dissemination of books which are not obscene; and we think this ordinance's strict liability feature would tend seriously to have that effect, by penalizing booksellers, even though they had not the slightest notice of the character of the books they sold. The appellee and the court below analogize this strict liability penal ordinance to familiar forms of penal statutes which dispense with any element of knowledge on the part of the person charged, food and drug legislation being a principal example. We find the analogy instructive in our examination of the question before us. The usual rationale for such statutes is that the public interest in the purity of its food is so great as to warrant the imposition of the highest standard of care on distributors—in fact an absolute standard which will not hear the distributor's plea as to the amount of care he has used. Cf. *United States* v. *Balint,* 258 U.S. 250, 252–253, 254. His ignorance of the character of the food is irrelevant. There is no specific constitutional inhibition against making the distributors of food the strictest censors of their merchandise, but the constitutional guarantees of the freedom of speech and of the press stand in the way of imposing a similar requirement on the bookseller. By dispensing with any requirement of knowledge of the contents of the book on the part of the seller, the ordinance tends to impose a severe limitation on the public's access to constitutionally protected matter. For if the bookseller is criminally liable without knowledge of the contents, and the ordinance fulfills its purpose,[8] he will tend to restrict the books he sells to those he has inspected; and thus the State will have imposed a restriction upon the distribution of constitutionally protected as well as obscene literature. It has been well observed of a statute construed as dispensing with any requirement of scienter that: "Every bookseller would be placed under an obligation to make himself aware of the contents of every book in his shop. It would be altogether unreasonable to demand so near an approach to omni-

science."[9] *The King* v. *Ewart,* 25 N.Z.L.R. 709, 729 (C.A.). And the bookseller's burden would become the public's burden, for by restricting him the public's access to reading matter would be restricted. If the contents of bookshops and periodical stands were restricted to material of which their proprietors had made an inspection, they might be depleted indeed. The bookseller's limitation in the amount of reading material with which he could familiarize himself, and his timidity in the face of his absolute criminal liability, thus would tend to restrict the public's access to forms of the printed word which the State could not constitutionally suppress directly. The bookseller's self-censorship, compelled by the State, would be a censorship affecting the whole public, hardly less virulent for being privately administered. Through it, the distribution of all books, both obscene and not obscene, would be impeded.

It is argued that unless the scienter requirement is dispensed with, regulation of the distribution of obscene material will be ineffective, as booksellers will falsely disclaim knowledge of their books' contents or falsely deny reason to suspect their obscenity. We might observe that it has been some time now since the law viewed itself as impotent to explore the actual state of a man's mind. See Pound, The Role of the Will in Law, 68 Harv. L. Rev. 1. Cf. *American Communications Assn.* v. *Douds,* 339 U.S. 382, 411. Eyewitness testimony of a bookseller's perusal of a book hardly need be a necessary element in proving his awareness of its contents. The circumstances may warrant the inference that he was aware of what a book contained, despite his denial.

We need not and most definitely do not pass today on what sort of mental element is requisite to a constitutionally permissible prosecution of a bookseller for carrying an obscene book in stock; whether honest mistake as to whether its contents in fact constituted obscenity need be an excuse; whether there might be circumstances under which the State constitutionally might require that a bookseller investigate further, or might put on him the burden of explaining why he did not, and what such circumstances might be. Doubtless any form of criminal obscenity statute applicable to a bookseller will induce some tendency to self-censorship and have some inhibitory effect on the dissemination of material not obscene, but we consider today only one which goes to the extent of eliminating all mental elements from the crime.

We have said: "The fundamental freedoms of speech and press have contributed greatly to the development and well-being of our free society and are indispensable to its continued growth. Ceaseless vigilance is the watchword to prevent their erosion by Congress or by the States. The door barring federal and state intrusion into this area cannot be left ajar; it must be kept tightly closed and opened only the slightest crack necessary to prevent encroachment upon more important interests." *Roth* v.

---

[7] In the *Roth* opinion there was also decided *Alberts* v. *California,* which dealt with the power of the States in this area.

[8] The effectiveness of absolute criminal liability laws in promoting caution has been subjected to criticism. See Hall, General Principles of Criminal Law, pp. 300–301. See generally Williams, Criminal Law—The General Part, pp. 267–274; Sayre, Public Welfare Offenses, 33 Col. L. Rev. 55; Mueller, On Common Law Mens Rea, 42 Minn. L. Rev. 1043; *Morissette* v. *United States,* 342 U.S. 246.

[9] Common-law prosecutions for the dissemination of obscene matter strictly adhered to the requirement of scienter. See the discussion in *Attorney General* v. *Simpson,* 93 Irish L.T. 33, 37–38 (Dist. Ct.). Cf. Obscene Publications Act, 1959, 7 & 8 Eliz. 2, c. 66, § 2 (5); American Law Institute Model Penal Code § 207.10 (7) (Tentative Draft No. 6, May 1957), and Comments, pp. 49–51.

The general California obscenity statute, Penal Code § 311, requires scienter, see note 3, and was of course sustained by us in *Roth* v. *United States, supra.* See note 7.

United States, supra, at 488.[10] This ordinance opens that door too far. The existence of the State's power to prevent the distribution of obscene matter does not mean that there can be no constitutional barrier to any form of practical exercise of that power. Cf. *Dean Milk Co.* v. *City of Madison,* 340 U.S. 349. It is plain to us that the ordinance in question, though aimed at obscene matter, has such a tendency to inhibit constitutionally protected expression that it cannot stand under the Constitution.

Reversed.

MR. JUSTICE BLACK, concurring.

The appellant was sentenced to prison for possessing in his bookstore an "obscene" book in violation of a Los Angeles city ordinance.[1] I concur in the judgment holding that ordinance unconstitutional, but not for the reasons given in the Court's opinion.

The Court invalidates the ordinance solely because it penalizes a bookseller for mere possession of an "obscene" book, even though he is unaware of its obscenity. The grounds on which the Court draws a constitutional distinction between a law that punishes possession of a book with knowledge of its "obscenity" and a law that punishes without such knowledge are not persuasive to me. Those grounds are that conviction of a bookseller for possession of an "obscene" book when he is unaware of its obscenity "will tend to restrict the books he sells to those he has inspected," and therefore "may tend to work a substantial restriction on freedom of speech." The fact is, of course, that prison sentences for possession of "obscene" books will seriously burden freedom of the press whether punishment is imposed with or without knowledge of the obscenity. The Court's opinion correctly points out how little extra burden will be imposed on prosecutors by requiring proof that a bookseller was aware of a book's contents when he possessed it. And if the Constitution's requirement of knowledge is so easily met, the result of this case is that one particular bookseller gains his freedom, but the way is left open for state censorship and punishment of all other booksellers by merely adding a few new words to old censorship laws. Our constitutional safeguards for speech and press therefore gain little. Their victory, if any, is a Pyrrhic one. Cf. *Beauharnais* v. *Illinois,* 343 U.S. 250, 267, at 275 (dissenting opinion).

That it is apparently intended to leave the way open for both federal and state governments to abridge speech and press (to the extent this Court approves) is also indicated by the following statements in the Court's opinion: " 'The door barring federal and state intrusion into this area [freedom of speech and press] cannot be left ajar; it must be kept tightly closed and opened only the slightest crack necessary to prevent encroachment upon more important interests.' . . . This ordinance opens that door too far."

This statement raises a number of questions for me.

What are the "more important" interests for the protection of which constitutional freedom of speech and press must be given second place? What is the standard by which one can determine when abridgment of speech and press goes "too far" and when it is slight enough to be constitutionally allowable? Is this momentous decision to be left to a majority of this Court on a case-by-case basis? What express provision or provisions of the Constitution put freedom of speech and press in this precarious position of subordination and insecurity?

Certainly the First Amendment's language leaves no room for inference that abridgments of speech and press can be made just because they are slight. That Amendment provides, in simple words, that "Congress shall make no law . . . abridging the freedom of speech, or of the press." I read "no law . . . abridging" to mean *no law abridging.* The First Amendment, which is the supreme law of the land, has thus fixed its own value on freedom of speech and press by putting these freedoms wholly "beyond the reach" of *federal* power to abridge.[2] No other

---

[10] We emphasized in *Roth,* at p. 484, that there is a "limited area" where such other interests prevail, and we listed representative decisions in note 14 at that page.

[1] As shown by Note 1 of the Court's opinion, the ordinance makes it unlawful to possess at places defined any obscene or indecent writing, book, pamphlet, picture, photograph, drawing, figure, motion picture film, phonograph recording, wire recording or transcription of any kind.

[2] Another concurring opinion has said that it would wrong James Madison and Thomas Jefferson to attribute to them the view that the First Amendment places speech wholly beyond the reach of the Federal Government. Of course, both men made many statements on the subject of freedom of speech and press during their long lives and no one can define their precise views with complete certainty. However, several statements by both Madison and Jefferson indicate that they may have held the view that the concurring opinion terms "doctrinaire absolutism."

James Madison, in exploring the sweep of the First Amendment's limitation on the Federal Government when he offered the Bill of Rights to Congress in 1789, is reported as having said, "[t]he right of freedom of speech is secured; the liberty of the press is expressly declared to be *beyond the reach of this Government.* . . ." (Emphasis supplied.) 1 Annals of Cong. 738. For reports of other discussions by Mr. Madison see pp. 424–449, 660, 704–756. Eleven years later he wrote: "Without tracing farther the evidence on this subject, it would seem scarcely possible to doubt that no power whatever over the press was supposed to be delegated by the Constitution, as it originally stood, and that the amendment was intended as a positive and absolute reservation of it." 6 Madison, Writings (Hunt ed. 1906), 341, 391, and see generally, 385–393, 399.

Thomas Jefferson's views of the breadth of the First Amendment's prohibition against abridgment of speech and press by the Federal Government are illustrated by the following statement he made in 1798: "[The First Amendment] thereby guard[s] in the same sentence, and under the same words, the freedom of religion, of speech, and of the press: insomuch, that whatever violates either, throws down the sanctuary which covers the others, and that libels, falsehood, and defamation, equally with heresy and false religion, are withheld from the cognizance of federal tribunals." 8 Jefferson, Writings (Ford ed. 1904), 464–465. For another early discussion of the scope of the First Amendment as a complete bar to all federal abridgment of speech and press see St. George Tucker's comments on the adequacy of state forums and state laws to grant all the protection needed against defamation and libel. 1 Blackstone, Commentaries (Tucker ed. 1803) 299.

Of course, neither Jefferson nor Madison faced the problem before the Court in this case, because it was not until the Fourteenth Amendment was passed that any of the prohibitions of the First Amendment were held applicable to the States. At the time Jefferson and Madison lived, before the Fourteenth Amendment was passed, the First Amendment did not prohibit the States from abridging free speech by the enactment of defamation or libel laws. Cf. *Barron* v. *Baltimore,* 7 Pet. 243. But the meaning of the First Amendment, as it was understood

provision of the Constitution purports to dilute the scope of these unequivocal commands of the First Amendment. Consequently, I do not believe that any federal agencies, including Congress and this Court, have power or authority to subordinate speech and press to what they think are "more important interests." The contrary notion is, in my judgment, court-made not Constitution-made.

State intrusion or abridgment of freedom of speech and press raises a different question, since the First Amendment by its terms refers only to laws passed by Congress. But I adhere to our prior decisions holding that the Fourteenth Amendment made the First applicable to the States. See cases collected in the concurring opinion in *Speiser* v. *Randall*, 357 U.S. 513, 530. It follows that I am for reversing this case because I believe that the Los Angeles ordinance sets up a censorship in violation of the First and Fourteenth Amendments.

If, as it seems, we are on the way to national censorship, I think it timely to suggest again that there are grave doubts in my mind as to the desirability or constitutionality of this Court's becoming a Supreme Board of Censors —reading books and viewing television performances to determine whether, if permitted, they might adversely affect the morals of the people throughout the many diversified local communities in this vast country.[3] It is true that the ordinance here is on its face only applicable to "obscene or indecent writing." It is also true that this particular kind of censorship is considered by many to be "the obnoxious thing in its mildest and least repulsive form. . . ." But "illegitimate and unconstitutional practices get their first footing in that way. . . . It is the duty of courts to be watchful for the constitutional rights of the citizen, and against any stealthy encroachments thereon." *Boyd* v. *United States*, 116 U.S. 616, 635. While it is "obscenity and indecency" before us today, the experience of mankind—both ancient and modern—shows that this type of elastic phrase can, and most likely will, be synonymous with the political and maybe with the religious unorthodoxy of tomorrow.

Censorship is the deadly enemy of freedom and progress. The plain language of the Constitution forbids it. I protest against the Judiciary giving it a foothold here.

---

by two such renowned constitutional architects as Jefferson and Madison, is important in this case because of our prior cases holding that the Fourteenth Amendment applies the First, with all the force it brings to bear against the Federal Government, against the States. See, *e.g.*, *West Virginia State Board of Education* v. *Barnette*, 319 U.S. 624, 639, and other cases collected in *Speiser* v. *Randall*, 357 U.S. 513, 530 (concurring opinion). But see *Beauharnais* v. *Illinois*, 343 U.S. 250, 288 (Court and dissenting opinions).

[3] *Kingsley International Pictures Corp.* v. *Regents of the University of New York*, 360 U.S. 684, 690–691 (concurring opinion). The views of a concurring opinion here, if accepted, would make this Court a still more inappropriate "Board of Censors" for the whole country. That opinion, conceding that "[t]here is no external measuring rod of obscenity," argues that the Constitution requires the issue of obscenity to be determined on the basis of "contemporary community standards"—"the literary, psychological or moral standards of a community." If, as argued in the concurring opinion, it violates the Federal Constitution for a local court to reject the evidence of "experts" on contemporary community standards of the vague word "obscenity," it seems odd to say that this Court should have the final word on what those community standards are or should be. I do not believe the words "liberty" and "due process" in the Fourteenth Amendment give this Court that much power.

MR. JUSTICE FRANKFURTER, concurring.

The appellant was convicted of violating the city ordinance of Los Angeles prohibiting possession of obscene books in a bookshop. His conviction was affirmed by the highest court of California to which he could appeal and it is the judgment of that court that we are asked to reverse. Appellant claims three grounds of invalidity under the Due Process Clause of the Fourteenth Amendment. He urges the invalidity of the ordinance as an abridgment of the freedom of speech which the guarantee of "liberty" of the Fourteenth Amendment safeguards against state action, and this for the reason that California law holds a bookseller criminally liable for possessing an obscene book, wholly apart from any scienter on his part regarding the book's obscenity. The second constitutional infirmity urged by appellant is the exclusion of appropriately offered testimony through duly qualified witnesses regarding the prevailing literary standards and the literary and moral criteria by which books relevantly comparable to the book in controversy are deemed not obscene. This exclusion deprived the appellant, such is the claim, of important relevant testimony bearing on the issue of obscenity and therefore restricted him in making his defense. The appellant's ultimate contention is that the questioned book is not obscene and that a bookseller's possession of it could not be forbidden.

The Court does not reach, and neither do I, the issue of obscenity. The Court disposes of the case exclusively by sustaining the appellant's claim that the "liberty" protected by the Due Process Clause of the Fourteenth Amendment precludes a State from making the dissemination of obscene books an offense merely because a book in a bookshop is found to be obscene without some proof of the bookseller's knowledge touching the obscenity of its contents.

The Court accepts the settled principle of constitutional law that traffic in obscene literature may be outlawed as a crime. But it holds that one cannot be made amenable to such criminal outlawry unless he is chargeable with knowledge of the obscenity. Obviously the Court is not holding that a bookseller must familiarize himself with the contents of every book in his shop. No less obviously, the Court does not hold that a bookseller who insulates himself against knowledge about an offending book is thereby free to maintain an emporium for smut. How much or how little awareness that a book may be found to be obscene suffices to establish scienter, or what kind of evidence may satisfy the how much or the how little, the Court leaves for another day.

I am no friend of deciding a case beyond what the immediate controversy requires, particularly when the limits of constitutional power are at stake. On the other hand, a case before this Court is not just a case. Inevitably its disposition carries implications and gives directions beyond its particular facts. Were the Court holding that this kind of prosecution for obscenity requires proof of the guilty mind associated with the concept of crimes deemed infamous, that would be that and no further elucidation would be needed. But if the requirement of scienter in obscenity cases plays a role different from the normal role of *mens rea* in the definition of crime, a different problem confronts the Court. If, as I assume, the requirement of scienter in an obscenity prosecution like the one before us does not mean that the bookseller must have read the book or must substantially know its contents on the one hand, nor on the other that he can exculpate himself by studious avoidance of knowledge about its contents, then, I submit, invalidating an obscenity statute because a State dispenses altogether with the requirement of scienter does require some indication of the scope and quality of scienter that is required. It ought at least to be made clear, and not left for future litigation, that the Court's decision in its practical effect is not intended to nullify the conceded power of the State to prohibit booksellers from trafficking in obscene literature.

Of course there is an important difference in the scope of the power of a State to regulate what feeds the belly and what feeds the brain. The doctrine of *United States* v. *Balint*, 258 U.S. 250, has its appropriate limits. The rule that scienter is not required in prosecutions for so-called public welfare offenses is a limitation on the general principle that awareness of what one is doing is a prerequisite for the infliction of punishment. See *Morissette* v. *United States*, 342 U.S. 246. The balance that is struck between this vital principle and the overriding public menace inherent in the trafficking in noxious food and drugs cannot be carried over in balancing the vital role of free speech as against society's interest in dealing with pornography. On the other hand, the constitutional protection of non-obscene speech cannot absorb the constitutional power of the States to deal with obscenity. It would certainly wrong them to attribute to Jefferson or Madison a doctrinaire absolutism that would bar legal restriction against obscenity as a denial of free speech.[1] We have not yet been told

that all laws against defamation and against inciting crime by speech, see *Fox* v. *Washington*, 236 U.S. 273 (1915), are unconstitutional as impermissible curbs upon unrestrictable utterance. We know this was not Jefferson's view, any more than it was the view of Holmes and Brandeis, JJ., the originating architects of our prevailing constitutional law protective of freedom of speech.

Accordingly, the proof of scienter that is required to make prosecutions for obscenity constitutional cannot be of a nature to nullify for all practical purposes the power of the State to deal with obscenity. Out of regard for the State's interest, the Court suggests an unguiding, vague standard for establishing "awareness" by the bookseller of the contents of a challenged book in contradiction of his disclaimer of knowledge of its contents. A bookseller may, of course, be well aware of the nature of a book and its appeal without having opened its cover, or, in any true sense, having knowledge of the book. As a practical matter therefore the exercise of the constitutional right of a State to regulate obscenity will carry with it some hazard to the dissemination by a bookseller of non-obscene literature. Such difficulties or hazards are inherent in many domains of the law for the simple reason that law cannot avail itself of factors ascertained quantitatively or even wholly impersonally.

The uncertainties pertaining to the scope of scienter requisite for an obscenity prosecution and the speculative proof that the issue is likely to entail, are considerations that reinforce the right of one charged with obscenity—a right implicit in the very nature of the legal concept of obscenity—to enlighten the judgment of the tribunal, be it the jury or as in this case the judge, regarding the prevailing literary and moral community standards and to do so through qualified experts. It is immaterial whether the basis of the exclusion of such testimony is irrelevance, or the incompetence of experts to testify to such matters. The two reasons coalesce, for community standards or the psychological or physiological consequences of questioned literature can as a matter of fact hardly be established except through experts. Therefore, to exclude such expert testimony is in effect to exclude as irrelevant evidence that goes to the very essence of the defense and therefore to the constitutional safeguards of due process. The determination of obscenity no doubt rests with judge or jury. Of course the testimony of experts would not displace judge or jury in determining the ultimate question whether the particular book is obscene, any more than the testimony of experts relating to the state of the art in patent suits determines the patentability of a controverted device.

There is no external measuring rod for obscenity. Neither, on the other hand, is its ascertainment a merely subjective reflection of the taste or moral outlook of individual jurors or individual judges. Since the law through its functionaries is "applying contemporary community standards" in determining what constitutes obscenity, *Roth* v. *United States*, 354 U.S. 476, 489, it surely must be deemed rational, and therefore relevant to the issue of obscenity, to allow light to be shed on what those "con-

---

[1] The publication of obscene printed matter was clearly established as a common-law offense in England in 1727 by the case of *Rex* v. *Curl*, 2 Str. 788, which overruled *Reg.* v. *Read*, [1708] 11 Mod. 142, where it had been held that such offenses were exclusively within the jurisdiction of the ecclesiastical courts. See also *Rex* v. *Wilkes*, [1770] 4 Burr. 2527. The common-law liability was carried across the Atlantic before the United States was established and appears early in the States. In 1786, in New York, a copyright act specifically stated that "nothing in this Act shall . . . authorise any Person or Persons to . . . publish any Book . . . that may be profane, treasonable, defamatory, or injurious to Government, Morals or Religion." An Act to Promote Literature, Act of April 29, 1786, c. LIV, § IV, 1 Laws of New York (Jones and Varick) (1777–1789) 321. In Pennsylvania, in 1815, a prosecution was founded on common-law liability. *Commonwealth* v. *Sharpless*, 2 Serg. & Rawle, 91. And in Maryland, when a statute regulating obscene publications was enacted in 1853, it was recited that "although in the judgment of the Legislature, such advertisements and publications are contra bonos mores, and punishable by the common law, it is desirable that the common law in this regard be re-enacted and enforced; . . ." Act of May 16, 1853, Md. Laws 1853, c. 183.

Moreover, as early as the eleventh year of the reign of Queen Anne (1711–1712), well before the jurisdiction at common law emerged in England, Massachusetts enacted a statute which provided "[t]hat whosoever shall be convicted of composing, writing, printing or publishing, of any filthy obscene or prophane Song, Pamphlet . . . shall be punished. . . ." Acts of 1711–1712, c. I, Charter of the Province of the Massachusetts-Bay, p. 172 (1759). It is unclear whether the well-known prosecution in Massachusetts in 1821, *Commonwealth* v. *Holmes*, 17 Mass. *336, was founded on this statute or on common-law liability, although in 1945 the Supreme Judicial Court indicated that it regarded this early statute as having been in effect until a successor enactment of 1835, Revised Statutes of the Commonwealth of Massachusetts, c. 130, § 10 (1836). *Commonwealth* v. *Isenstadt*, 318 Mass. 543, 547, 62 N.E. 2d 840, 843, n. 1. See

also Grant and Angoff, Massachusetts and Censorship, III, 10 B.U.L. Rev. 147 (1930). Thereafter the offense was made statutory in other States. See, *e.g.*, Act of March 14, 1848, c. VIII, § 7 (1847–1848), Va. Laws 111; Act of May 16, 1853, c. 183 (1853), Laws of Maryland 212; Act of April 28, 1868, c. 430, 7 N.Y. Stat. at Large (1867–1870) 309.

temporary community standards" are. Their interpretation ought not to depend solely on the necessarily limited, hit-or-miss, subjective view of what they are believed to be by the individual juror or judge. It bears repetition that the determination of obscenity is for juror or judge not on the basis of his personal upbringing or restricted reflection or particular experience of life, but on the basis of "contemporary community standards." Can it be doubted that there is a great difference in what is to be deemed obscene in 1959 compared with what was deemed obscene in 1859? The difference derives from a shift in community feeling regarding what is to be deemed prurient or not prurient by reason of the effects attributable to this or that particular writing. Changes in the intellectual and moral climate of society, in part doubtless due to the views and findings of specialists, afford shifting foundations for the attribution. What may well have been consonant "with mid-Victorian morals, does not seem to me to answer to the understanding and morality of the present time." *United States* v. *Kennerley*, 209 F. 119, 120. This was the view of Judge Learned Hand decades ago reflecting an atmosphere of propriety much closer to mid-Victorian days than is ours. Unless we disbelieve that the literary, psychological or moral standards of a community can be made fruitful and illuminating subjects of inquiry by those who give their life to such inquiries, it was violative of "due process" to exclude the constitutionally relevant evidence proffered in this case. The importance of this type of evidence in prosecutions for obscenity has been impressively attested by the recent debates in the House of Commons dealing with the insertion of such a provision in the enactment of the Obscene Publications Act, 1959, 7 & 8 Eliz. 2, Ch. 66[2] (see 597 Parliamentary Debates, H. Comm., No. 36 (December 16, 1958), cols. 1009–1010, 1042–1043; 604 Parliamentary Debates, H. Comm., No. 100 (April 24, 1959), col. 803), as well as by the most considered thinking on this subject in the proposed Model Penal Code of the American Law Institute. See A.L.I. Model Penal Code, Tentative Draft No. 6 (1957), § 207.10.[3] For the rea-

---

[2] Section 4 of this Act provides:

"(1) A person shall not be convicted of an offense against . . . this Act . . . if it is proved that publication of the article in question is justified as being for the public good on the ground that it is in the interests of science, literature, art or learning, or of other objects of general concern.

"(2) It is hereby declared that the opinion of experts as to the literary, artistic, scientific or other merits of an article may be admitted in any proceedings under this Act either to establish or to negative the said ground."

[3] Subsection (2) of this draft section provides in part:

". . . In any prosecution for an offense under this section evidence shall be admissible to show:

"(a) the character of the audience for which the material was designed or to which it was directed;

"(b) what the predominant appeal of the material would be for ordinary adults or a special audience, and what effect, if any, it would probably have on behavior of such people;

"(c) artistic, literary, scientific, educational or other merits of the material;

"(d) the degree of public acceptance of the material in this country;

"(e) appeal to prurient interest, or absence thereof, in advertising or other promotion of the material;

. . . . .

"Expert testimony and testimony of the author, creator or publisher relating to factors entering into the determination of the issue of obscenity shall be admissible."

---

sons I have indicated, I would make the right to introduce such evidence a requirement of due process in obscenity prosecutions.

Mr. Justice Douglas, concurring.

I need not repeat here all I said in my dissent in *Roth* v. *United States*, 354 U.S. 476, 508, to underline my conviction that neither the author nor the distributor of this book can be punished under our Bill of Rights for publishing or distributing it. The notion that obscene publications or utterances were not included in free speech developed in this country much later than the adoption of the First Amendment, as the judicial and legislative developments in this country show. Our leading authorities on the subject have summarized the matter as follows:

"*In the United States before the Civil War there were few reported decisions involving obscene literature. This of course is no indication that such literature was not in circulation at that time; the persistence of pornography is entirely too strong to warrant such an inference. Nor is it an indication that the people of the time were totally indifferent to the proprieties of the literature they read. In 1851 Nathaniel Hawthorne's* The Scarlet Letter *was bitterly attacked as an immoral book that degraded literature and encouraged social licentiousness. The lack of cases merely means that the problem of obscene literature was not thought to be of sufficient importance to justify arousing the forces of the state to censorship.*" Lockhart and McClure, Literature, The Law of Obscenity, and the Constitution, 38 Minn. L. Rev. 295, 324–325.

Neither we nor legislatures have power, as I see it, to weigh the values of speech or utterance against silence. The only grounds for suppressing this book are very narrow. I have read it; and while it is repulsive to me, its publication or distribution can be constitutionally punished only on a showing not attempted here. My view was stated in the *Roth* case, at 514:

"*Freedom of expression can be suppressed if, and to the extent that, it is so closely brigaded with illegal action as to be an inseparable part of it.* Giboney v. Empire Storage Co., 336 U.S. 490, 498; Labor Board v. Virginia Power Co., 143 U.S. 469, 477–478. *As a people, we cannot afford to relax that standard. For the test that suppresses a cheap tract today can suppress a literary gem tomorrow. All it need do is to incite a lascivious thought or arouse a lustful desire. The list of books that judges or juries can place in that category is endless.*"

Yet my view is in the minority; and rather fluid tests of obscenity prevail which require judges to read condemned literature and pass judgment on it. This role of censor in which we find ourselves is not an edifying one. But since by the prevailing school of thought we must perform it, I see no harm, and perhaps some good, in the rule fashioned by the Court which requires a showing of *scienter*. For it recognizes implicitly that these First Amendment rights, by reason of the strict command in that Amendment—a command that carries over to the States by reason of the Due Process Clause of the Fourteenth Amendment—are preferred rights. What the Court does today may possibly provide some small degree of safeguard to booksellers by making those who patrol bookstalls proceed less high-handedly than has been their custom.*

Mr. Justice Harlan, concurring in part and dissenting in part.

The striking down of local legislation is always serious business for this Court. In my opinion in the *Roth* case, 354 U.S., at 503–508, I expressed the view that state power in the obscenity field has a wider scope than federal power. The question whether *scienter* is a constitutionally required element in a criminal obscenity statute is intimately related to the constitutional scope of the power to bar material as obscene, for the impact of such a requirement on effective prosecution may be one thing where the scope of the power to proscribe is broad and quite another where the scope is narrow. Proof of *scienter* may entail no great burden in the case of obviously obscene material; it may, however, become very difficult where the character of the material is more debatable. In my view then, the *scienter* question involves considerations of a different order depending on whether a state or a federal statute is involved. We have here a state ordinance, and on the meagre data before us I would not reach the question whether the absence of a *scienter* element renders the ordinance unconstitutional. I must say, however, that the generalities in the Court's opinion striking down the ordinance leave me unconvinced.

From the point of view of the free dissemination of constitutionally protected ideas, the Court invalidates the ordinance on the ground that its effect may be to induce booksellers to restrict their offerings of nonobscene literary merchandise through fear of prosecution for unwittingly having on their shelves an obscene publication. From the point of view of the State's interest in protecting its citizens against the dissemination of obscene material, the Court in effect says that proving the state of a man's mind is little more difficult than proving the state of his digestion, but also intimates that a relaxed standard of *mens rea* would satisfy constitutional requirements. This is for me too rough a balancing of the competing interests at stake. Such a balancing is unavoidably required in this kind of constitutional adjudication, notwithstanding that it arises in the domain of liberty of speech and press. A more critical appraisal of both sides of the constitutional balance, not possible on the meagre material before us, seems to me required before the ordinance can be struck down on this ground. For, as the concurring opinions of my Brothers Black and Frankfurter show, the conclusion that this ordinance, but not one embodying some element of *scienter*, is likely to restrict the dissemination of legitimate literature seems more dialectical than real.

I am also not persuaded that the ordinance in question was unconstitutionally applied in this instance merely because of the state court's refusal to admit expert testimony. I agree with my Brother Frankfurter that the trier of an obscenity case must take into account "contemporary community standards," *Roth* v. *United States*, 354 U.S. 476, 489. This means that, regardless of the elements of the offense under state law, the Fourteenth Amendment does not permit a conviction such as was obtained here[1] unless the work complained of is found substantially to exceed the limits of candor set by contemporary community standards.[2] The community cannot, where liberty of speech and press are at issue, condemn that which it generally tolerates. This being so, it follows that due process—"using that term in its primary sense of an opportunity to be heard and to defend [a] . . . substantive right," *Brinkerhoff-Faris Co.* v. *Hill*, 281 U.S. 673, 678—requires a State to allow a litigant in some manner to introduce proof on this score. While a State is not debarred from regarding the trier of fact as the embodiment of community standards, competent to judge a challenged work against those standards,[3] it is not privileged to efforts to enlighten or persuade the trier.

However, I would not hold that any particular kind of evidence must be admitted, specifically, that the Constitution requires that oral opinion testimony by experts be heard. There are other ways in which proof can be made, as this very case demonstrates. Appellant attempted to compare the contents of the work with that of other allegedly similar publications which were openly published, sold and purchased, and which received wide general acceptance. Where there is a variety of means, even though it may be considered that expert testimony is the most convenient and practicable method of proof, I think it is going too far to say that such a method is constitutionally compelled, and that a State may not conclude, for reasons responsive to its traditional doctrines of evidence law, that the issue of community standards may not be the subject of expert testimony. I know of no case where this Court, on constitutional grounds, has required a State to sanction a particular mode of proof.

In my opinion this conviction is fatally defective in that the trial judge, as I read the record, turned aside *every* attempt by appellant to introduce evidence bearing on community standards. The exclusionary rulings were not limited to offered expert testimony. This had the effect of depriving appellant of the opportunity to offer any proof on a constitutionally relevant issue. On this ground I would reverse the judgment below, and remand the case for a new trial.

---

* See Chafee, Free Speech in the United States (1941), pp. 536–540; Lockhart and McClure, Literature, The Law of Obscenity, and the Constitution, 38 Minn. L. Rev. 295, 302–316; Daniels, The Censorship of Books (1954), p. 76 *et seq.*; Blanshard, The Right to Read (1955), p. 180 *et seq.*; Fellman, The Censorship of Books (1957). And see *New American Library of World Literature* v. *Allen*, 114 F. Supp. 823.

[1] We are concerned in this instance with an objection to what a book portrays, not to what it teaches. Cf. *Kingsley Pictures Corp.* v. *Regents,* 360 U.S. 684.

[2] The most notable expression of this limitation is that of Judge Learned Hand, in *United States* v. *Kennerley,* 209 F. 119, 121: "If there be no abstract definition, . . . should not the word 'obscene' be allowed to indicate the present critical point in the compromise between candor and shame at which the community may have arrived here and now?" See also the exposition of this view in American Law Institute, Model Penal Code (Tentative Draft No. 6), at p. 30. It may be that the *Roth* case embodies this restriction, see 354 U.S., at 487, n. 20; but see *id.,* at 499–500 (separate opinion).

[3] Such a view does not of course mean that the issue is to be tried according to the personal standards of the judge or jury.

■ Kingsley International Pictures Corp.

v.

Regents of the University of the State of New York.

APPEAL FROM THE COURT OF APPEALS OF NEW YORK.

No. 394. Argued April 23, 1959.—Decided June 29, 1959.

Ephraim London argued the cause for appellant. With him on the brief were *Seymour H. Chalif* and *Stephen A. Wise.*

Charles A. Brind, Jr. argued the cause and filed a brief for appellees.

Mr. Justice Stewart delivered the opinion of the Court.

Once again the Court is required to consider the impact of New York's motion picture licensing law upon First Amendment liberties, protected by the Fourteenth Amendment from infringement by the States. Cf. *Joseph Burstyn, Inc.* v. *Wilson,* 343 U.S. 495.

The New York statute makes it unlawful "to exhibit, or to sell, lease or lend for exhibition at any place of amusement for pay or in connection with any business in the state of New York, any motion picture film or reel [with certain exceptions not relevant here], unless there is at the time in full force and effect a valid license or permit therefor of the education department. . . ."[1] The law provides that a license shall issue "unless such film or a part thereof is obscene, indecent, immoral, inhuman, sacrilegious, or is of such a character that its exhibition would tend to corrupt morals or incite to crime. . . ."[2] A recent statutory amendment provides that, "the term 'immoral' and the phrase 'of such a character that its exhibition would tend to corrupt morals' shall denote a motion picture film or part thereof, the dominant purpose or effect of which is erotic or pornographic; or which portrays acts of sexual immorality, perversion, or lewdness, or which expressly or impliedly presents such acts as desirable, acceptable or proper patterns of behavior."[3]

As the distributor of a motion picture entitled "Lady Chatterley's Lover," the appellant Kingsley submitted that film to the Motion Picture Division of the New York Education Department for a license. Finding three isolated scenes in the film " 'immoral' within the intent of our Law," the Division refused to issue a license until the scenes in question were deleted. The distributor petitioned the Regents of the University of the State of New York for a review of that ruling.[4] The Regents upheld the denial of

a license, but on the broader ground that "the whole theme of this motion picture is immoral under said law, for that theme is the presentation of adultery as a desirable, acceptable and proper pattern of behavior."

Kingsley sought judicial review of the Regents' determination.[5] The Appellate Division unanimously annulled the action of the Regents and directed that a license be issued. 4 App. Div. 2d 348, 165 N.Y.S. 2d 681. A sharply divided Court of Appeals, however, reversed the Appellate Division and upheld the Regents' refusal to license the film for exhibition. 4 N.Y. 2d 349, 151 N.E. 2d 197, 175 N.Y.S. 2d 39.[6]

The Court of Appeals unanimously and explicitly rejected any notion that the film is obscene.[7] See *Roth* v.

---

[1] McKinney's N.Y. Laws, 1953, Education Law, § 129.

[2] McKinney's N.Y. Laws, 1953, Education Law, § 122.

[3] McKinney's N.Y. Laws, 1953 (Cum. Supp. 1958), Education Law, § 122–a.

[4] "An applicant for a license or permit, in case his application be denied by the director of the division or by the officer authorized to issue the same, shall have the right of review by the regents." McKinney's N.Y. Laws, 1953, Education Law, § 124.

[5] The proceeding was brought under Art. 78 of the New York Civil Practice Act, Gilbert-Bliss' N.Y. Civ. Prac., Vol. 6B, 1944, 1949 Supp., § 1283 *et seq.* See also, McKinney's N.Y. Laws, 1953, Education Law, § 124.

[6] Although four of the seven judges of the Court of Appeals voted to reverse the order of the Appellate Division, only three of them were of the clear opinion that denial of a license was permissible under the Constitution. Chief Judge Conway wrote an opinion in which Judges Froessel and Burke concurred, concluding that denial of the license was constitutionally permissible. Judge Desmond wrote a separate concurring opinion in which he stated: "I confess doubt as to the validity of such a statute but I do not know how that doubt can be resolved unless we reverse here and let the Supreme Court have the final say." 4 N.Y. 2d, at 369, 151 N.E. 2d, at 208, 175 N.Y.S. 2d, at 55. Judge Dye, Judge Fuld, and Judge Van Voorhis wrote separate dissenting opinions.

[7] The opinion written by Chief Judge Conway stated: "[I]t is curious indeed to say in one breath, as some do, that obscene motion pictures may be censored, and then in another breath that motion pictures which alluringly portray adultery as proper and desirable may not be censored. As stated above, 'The law is concerned with effect, not merely with but one means of producing it.' It must be firmly borne in mind that to give obscenity, as defined, the stature of the only constitutional limitation is to extend an invitation to corrupt the public morals by methods of presentation which craft will insure do not fall squarely within the definition of that term. Precedent, just as sound principle, will not support a statement that motion pictures must be 'out and out' obscene before they may be censored." 4 N.Y. 2d, at 364, 151 N.E. 2d, at 205, 175 N.Y.S. 2d, at 51.

Judge Desmond's concurring opinion stated: "[It is not] necessarily determinative that this film is not obscene in the dictionary sense. . . ." 4 N.Y. 2d, at 369, 151 N.E. 2d, at 208, 175 N.Y.S. 2d, at 55. Judge Dye's dissenting opinion stated: "No one contends that the film in question is obscene within the narrow legal limits of obscenity as recently defined by the Supreme Court. . . ." 4 N.Y. 2d, at 371, 151 N.E. 2d, at 210, 175 N.Y.S. 2d, at 57. Judge Van Voorhis' dissenting opinion

United States, 354 U.S. 476. Rather, the court found that the picture as a whole "alluringly portrays adultery as proper behavior." As Chief Judge Conway's prevailing opinion emphasized, therefore, the only portion of the statute involved in this case is that part of §§ 122 and 122–a of the Education Law requiring the denial of a license to motion pictures "which are immoral in that they *portray* 'acts of sexual immorality . . . as desirable, acceptable or proper patterns of behavior.'"[8] 4 N.Y. 2d, at 351, 151 N.E. 2d, at 197, 175 N.Y.S. 2d, at 40. A majority of the Court of Appeals ascribed to that language a precise purpose of the New York Legislature to require the denial of a license to a motion picture "because its subject matter is adultery presented as being right and desirable for certain people under certain circumstances."[9] 4 N.Y. 2d, at 369, 151 N.E. 2d, at 208, 175 N.Y.S. 2d, at 55 (concurring opinion).

We accept the premise that the motion picture here in question can be so characterized. We accept too, as we must, the construction of the New York Legislature's language which the Court of Appeals has put upon it. *Albertson* v. *Millard,* 345 U.S. 242; *United States* v. *Burnison,* 339 U.S. 87; *Aero Mayflower Transit Co.* v. *Board of R.R. Comm'rs,* 332 U.S. 495. That construction, we emphasize, gives to the term "sexual immorality" a concept entirely different from the concept embraced in words like "obscenity" or "pornography."[10] Moreover, it is not suggested that the film would itself operate as an incitement to illegal action. Rather, the New York Court of Appeals tells us that the relevant portion of the New York Education Law requires the denial of a license to any motion picture which approvingly portrays an adulterous relationship, quite without reference to the manner of its portrayal.

What New York has done, therefore, is to prevent the exhibition of a motion picture because that picture advocates an idea—that adultery under certain circumstances may be proper behavior. Yet the First Amendment's basic guarantee is of freedom to advocate ideas. The State, quite simply, has thus struck at the very heart of constitutionally protected liberty.

It is contended that the State's action was justified because the motion picture attractively portrays a relationship which is contrary to the moral standards, the religious precepts, and the legal code of its citizenry. This argument misconceives what it is that the Constitution protects. Its guarantee is not confined to the expression of ideas that are

conventional or shared by a majority. It protects advocacy of the opinion that adultery may sometimes be proper, no less than advocacy of socialism or the single tax. And in the realm of ideas it protects expression which is eloquent no less than that which is unconvincing.

Advocacy of conduct proscribed by law is not, as Mr. Justice Brandeis long ago pointed out, "*a justification for denying free speech where the advocacy falls short of incitement and there is nothing to indicate that the advocacy would be immediately acted on.*" [Italics ed.]. *Whitney* v. *California,* 274 U.S. 357, at 376 (concurring opinion). "Among free men, the deterrents ordinarily to be applied to prevent crime are education and punishment for violations of the law, not abridgment of the rights of free speech. . . ." *Id.,* at 378.[11]

The inflexible command which the New York Court of Appeals has attributed to the State Legislature thus cuts so close to the core of constitutional freedom as to make it quite needless in this case to examine the periphery. Specifically, there is no occasion to consider the appellant's contention that the State is entirely without power to require films of any kind to be licensed prior to their exhibition. Nor need we here determine whether, despite problems peculiar to motion pictures, the controls which a State may impose upon this medium of expression are precisely coextensive with those allowable for newspapers,[12] books,[13] or individual speech.[14] It is enough for the present case to reaffirm that motion pictures are within the First and Fourteenth Amendments' basic protection. *Joseph Burstyn, Inc.* v. *Wilson,* 343 U.S. 495.

Reversed.

Mr. Justice Black, concurring.

I concur in the Court's opinion and judgment but add a few words because of concurring opinions by several Justices who rely on their appraisal of the movie *Lady Chatterley's Lover* for holding that New York cannot constitutionally bar it. Unlike them, I have not seen the picture. My view is that stated by Mr. Justice Douglas, that prior censorship of moving pictures like prior censorship of newspapers and books violates the First and Fourteenth Amendments. If despite the Constitution, however, this Nation is to embark on the dangerous road of censorship, my belief is that this Court is about the most inappropriate Supreme Board of Censors that could be found. So far as I know, judges possess no special expertise providing exceptional competency to set standards and to supervise the private morals of the Nation. In addition, the Justices of this Court seem especially unsuited to make the

stated: "[I]t is impossible to write off this entire drama as 'mere pornography'. . . ." Judge Van Voorhis, however, would have remitted the case to the Board of Regents to consider whether certain "passages" in the film "might have been eliminated as 'obscene' without doing violence to constitutional liberties." 4 N.Y. 2d, at 375, 151 N.E. 2d, at 212, 175 N.Y.S. 2d, at 60.

8 This is also emphasized in the brief of counsel for the Regents, which states, "The full definition is not before this Court—only these parts of the definition as cited—and any debate as to whether other parts of the definition are a proper standard has no bearing in this case."

9 In concurring, Judge Desmond agreed that this was the meaning of the statutory language in question, and that "the theme and content of this film fairly deserve that characterization. . . ." 4 N.Y. 2d, at 366, 151 N.E. 2d, at 206, 175 N.Y.S. 2d, at 52.

10 See by way of contrast, *Swearingen* v. *United States,* 161 U.S. 446; *United States* v. *Limehouse,* 285 U.S. 424.

11 Thomas Jefferson wrote more than a hundred and fifty years ago, "But we have nothing to fear from the demoralizing reasonings of some, if others are left free to demonstrate their errors. And especially when the law stands ready to punish the first criminal *act* produced by the false reasoning. These are safer correctives than the conscience of a judge." Letter of Thomas Jefferson to Elijah Boardman, July 3, 1801, Jefferson Papers, Library of Congress, Vol. 115, folio 19761.

12 Cf. *Near* v. *Minnesota,* 283 U.S. 697.

13 Cf. *Kingsley Books, Inc.* v. *Brown,* 354 U.S. 436; *Alberts* v. *California,* 354 U.S. 476.

14 Cf. *Thomas* v. *Collins,* 323 U.S. 516; *Thornhill* v. *Alabama,* 310 U.S. 88.

kind of value judgments—as to what movies are good or bad for local communities—which the concurring opinions appear to require. We are told that the only way we can decide whether a State or municipality can constitutionally bar movies is for this Court to view and appraise each movie on a case-by-case basis. Under these circumstances, every member of the Court must exercise his own judgment as to how bad a picture is, a judgment which is ultimately based at least in large part on his own standard of what is immoral. The end result of such decisions seems to me to be a purely personal determination by individual Justices as to whether a particular picture viewed is too bad to allow it to be seen by the public. Such an individualized determination cannot be guided by reasonably fixed and certain standards. Accordingly, neither States nor moving picture makers can possibly know in advance, with any fair degree of certainty, what can or cannot be done in the field of movie making and exhibiting. This uncertainty cannot easily be reconciled with the rule of law which our Constitution envisages.

The different standards which different people may use to decide about the badness of pictures are well illustrated by the contrasting standards mentioned in the opinion of the New York Court of Appeals and the concurring opinion of MR. JUSTICE FRANKFURTER here. As I read the New York court's opinion this movie was held immoral and banned because it makes adultery too alluring. MR. JUSTICE FRANKFURTER quotes Mr. Lawrence, author of the book from which the movie was made, as believing censorship should be applied only to publications that make sex look ugly, that is, as I understand it, less alluring.

In my judgment, this Court should not permit itself to get into the very center of such policy controversies, which have so little in common with lawsuits.

MR. JUSTICE FRANKFURTER, concurring in the result.

As one whose taste in art and literature hardly qualifies him for the *avant-garde*, I am more than surprised, after viewing the picture, that the New York authorities should have banned "Lady Chatterley's Lover." To assume that this motion picture would have offended Victorian moral sensibilities is to rely only on the stuffiest of Victorian conventions. Whatever one's personal preferences may be about such matters, the refusal to license the exhibition of this picture, on the basis of the 1954 amendment to the New York State Education Law, can only mean that that enactment forbids the public showing of any film that deals with adultery except by way of sermonizing condemnation or depicts any physical manifestation of an illicit amorous relation. Since the denial of a license by the Board of Regents was confirmed by the highest court of the State, I have no choice but to agree with this Court's judgment in holding that the State exceeded the bounds of free expression protected by the "liberty" of the Fourteenth Amendment. But I also believe that the Court's opinion takes ground that exceeds the appropriate limits for decision. By way of reinforcing my brother HARLAN's objections to the scope of the Court's opinion, I add the following.

Even the author of "Lady Chatterley's Lover" did not altogether rule out censorship, nor was his passionate zeal on behalf of society's profound interest in the endeavors of true artists so doctrinaire as to be unmindful of the facts of life regarding the sordid exploitation of man's nature and impulses. He knew there was such a thing as pornography, dirt for dirt's sake, or, to be more accurate, dirt for money's sake. This is what D. H. Lawrence wrote:

"But even I would censor genuine pornography, rigorously. It would not be very difficult. In the first place, genuine pornography is almost always underworld, it doesn't come into the open. In the second, you can recognize it by the insult it offers invariably, to sex, and to the human spirit.

"Pornography is the attempt to insult sex, to do dirt on it. This is unpardonable. Take the very lowest instance, the picture post-card sold underhand, by the underworld, in most cities. What I have seen of them have been of an ugliness to make you cry. The insult to the human body, the insult to a vital human relationship— Ugly and cheap they make the human nudity, ugly and degraded they make the sexual act, trivial and cheap and nasty." (D. H. Lawrence, *Pornography and Obscenity*, pp. 12–13.)

This traffic has not lessened since Lawrence wrote. Apparently it is on the increase. In the course of the recent debate in both Houses of Parliament on the Obscene Publications Bill, now on its way to passage, designed to free British authors from the hazards of too rigorous application in our day of Lord Cockburn's ruling, in 1868, in *Regina* v. *Hicklin*, L.R. 3 Q.B. 360, weighty experience was adduced regarding the extensive dissemination of pornographic materials.[1] See 597 Parliamentary Debates, H.C., No. 36 (Tuesday, December 16, 1958), cols. 992 *et seq.*, and 216 Parliamentary Debates H.L., No. 77 (Tuesday, June 2, 1959), cols. 489 *et seq.* Nor is there any reason to believe that on this side of the ocean there has been a diminution in the pornographic business which years ago sought a flourishing market in some of the leading secondary schools for boys, who presumably had more means than boys in the public high schools.

It is not surprising, therefore, that the pertinacious, eloquent and free-spirited promoters of the liberalizing legislation in Great Britain did not conceive the needs of a civilized society, in assuring the utmost freedom to those who make literature and art possible—authors, artists, publishers, producers, book sellers—easily attainable by sounding abstract and unqualified dogmas about freedom. They had a keen awareness that freedom of expression is no more an absolute than any other freedom, an awareness that is reflected in the opinions of Mr. Justice Holmes and Mr. Justice Brandeis, to whom we predominantly owe the present constitutional safeguards on behalf of freedom of expression. And see *Near* v. *Minnesota*, 283 U.S. 697, 715–716, for limitations on constitutionally protected freedom of speech.[2]

---

[1] "In the course of our enquiries, we have been impressed with the existence of a considerable and lucrative trade in pornography . . . ." Report of the Select Committee on Obscene Publications to the House of Commons, March 20, 1958, p. IV.

[2] "The objection has also been made that the principle as to immunity from previous restraint is stated too broadly, if every such restraint is deemed to be prohibited. That is undoubtedly true; the protection even as to previous restraint is not absolutely unlimited. But the limitation has been recognized only in exceptional cases . . . ." 283 U.S., at 715–716.

In short, there is an evil against which a State may constitutionally protect itself, whatever we may think about the questions of policy involved. The real problem is the formulation of constitutionally allowable safeguards which society may take against evil without impinging upon the necessary dependence of a free society upon the fullest scope of free expression. One cannot read the debates in the House of Commons and the House of Lords and not realize the difficulty of reconciling these conflicting interests, in the framing of legislation on the ends of which there was agreement, even for those who most generously espouse that freedom of expression without which all freedom gradually withers.

It is not our province to meet these recalcitrant problems of legislative drafting. Ours is the vital but very limited task of scrutinizing the work of the draftsmen in order to determine whether they have kept within the narrow limits of the kind of censorhip which even D. H. Lawrence deemed necessary. The legislation must not be so vague, the language so loose, as to leave to those who have to apply it too wide a discretion for sweeping within its condemnation what is permissible expression as well as what society may permissibly prohibit. Always remembering that the widest scope of freedom is to be given to the adventurous and imaginative exercise of the human spirit, we have struck down legislation phrased in language intrinsically vague, unless it be responsive to the common understanding of men even though not susceptible of explicit definition. The ultimate reason for invalidating such laws is that they lead to timidity and inertia and thereby discourage the boldness of expression indispensable for a progressive society.

The New York legislation of 1954 was the product of careful lawyers who sought to meet decisions of this Court which had left no doubt that a motion-picture licensing law is not inherently outside the scope of the regulatory powers of a State under the Fourteenth Amendment. The Court does not strike the law down because of vagueness, as we struck down prior New York legislation. Nor does it reverse the judgment of the New York Court of Appeals, as I would, because in applying the New York law to "Lady Chatterley's Lover" it applied it to a picture to which it cannot be applied without invading the area of constitutionally free expression. The difficulty which the Court finds seems to derive from some expressions culled here and there from the opinion of the Chief Judge of the New York Court of Appeals. This leads the Court to give the phrase "acts of sexual immorality . . as desirable, acceptable or proper patterns of behavior" an innocent content, meaning, in effect, an allowable subject matter for discussion. But, surely, to attribute that result to the decision of the Court of Appeals, on the basis of a few detached phrases of Chief Judge Conway, is to break a faggot into pieces, is to forget that the meaning of language is to be felt and its phrases not to be treated disjointedly. "Sexual immorality" is not a new phrase in this branch of law and its implications dominate the context. I hardly conceive it possible that the Court would strike down as unconstitutional the federal statute against mailing lewd, obscene and lascivious matter, which has been the law of the land for nearly a hundred years, see the Act of March 3, 1865, 13 Stat. 507, and March 3, 1873, 17 Stat. 599, whatever specific instances may be found not within its allowable prohibition. In sustaining this legisla-

tion this Court gave the words "lewd, obscene and lascivious" concreteness by saying that they concern "sexual immorality." And only very recently the Court sustained the constitutionality of the statute. *Roth* v. *United States,* 354 U.S. 476.

Unless I misread the opinion of the Court, it strikes down the New York legislation in order to escape the task of deciding whether a particular picture is entitled to the protection of expression under the Fourteenth Amendment. Such an exercise of the judicial function, however onerous or ungrateful, inheres in the very nature of the judicial enforcement of the Due Process Clause. We cannot escape such instance-by-instance, case-by-case application of that clause in all the varieties of situations that come before this Court. It would be comfortable if, by a comprehensive formula, we could decide when a confession is coerced so as to vitiate a state conviction. There is no such talismanic formula. Every Term we have to examine the particular circumstances of a particular case in order to apply generalities which no one disputes. It would be equally comfortable if a general formula could determine the unfairness of a state trial for want of counsel. But, except in capital cases, we have to thread our way, Term after Term, through the particular circumstances of a particular case in relation to a particular defendant in order to ascertain whether due process was denied in the unique situation before us. We are constantly called upon to consider the alleged misconduct of a prosecutor as vitiating the fairness of a particular trial or the inflamed state of public opinion in a particular case as undermining the constitutional right to due process. Again, in the series of cases coming here from the state courts, in which due process was invoked to enforce separation of church and state, decision certainly turned on the particularities of the specific situations before the Court. It is needless to multiply instances. It is the nature of the concept of due process, and, I venture to believe, its high serviceability in our constitutional system, that the judicial enforcement of the Due Process Clause is the very antithesis of a Procrustean rule. This was recognized in the first full-dress discussion of the Due Process Clause of the Fourteenth Amendment, when the Court defined the nature of the problem as a "gradual process of judicial inclusion and exclusion, as the cases presented for decision shall require, with the reasons on which such decision may be founded." *Davidson* v. *New Orleans,* 96 U.S. 97, 104. The task is onerous and exacting, demanding as it does the utmost discipline in objectivity, the severest control of personal predilections. But it cannot be escaped, not even by disavowing that such is the nature of our task.

MR. JUSTICE DOUGLAS, with whom MR. JUSTICE BLACK joins, concurring.

While I join in the opinion of the Court, I adhere to the views I expressed in *Superior Films* v. *Department of Education,* 346 U.S. 587, 588–589, that censorship of movies is unconstitutional, since it is a form of "previous restraint" that is as much at war with the First Amendment, made applicable to the States through the Fourteenth, as the censorship struck down in *Near* v. *Minnesota,* 283 U.S. 697. If a particular movie violates a valid law, the exhibitor can be prosecuted in the usual way. I can find in the First Amendment no room for any censor whether he is scanning an editorial, reading a news broadcast, editing a novel or a play, or previewing a movie.

Reference is made to British law and British practice. But they have little relevance to our problem, since we live under a written Constitution. What is entrusted to the keeping of the legislature in England is protected from legislative interference or regulation here. As we stated in *Bridges* v. *California*, 314 U.S. 252, 265, "No purpose in ratifying the Bill of Rights was clearer than that of securing for the people of the United States much greater freedom of religion, expression, assembly, and petition than the people of Great Britain had ever enjoyed." If we had a provision in our Constitution for "reasonable" regulation of the press such as India has included in hers,[1] there would be room for argument that censorship in the interests of morality would be permissible. Judges sometimes try to read the word "reasonable" into the First Amendment or make the rights it grants subject to reasonable regulation (see *Beauharnais* v. *Illinois*, 343 U.S. 250, 262; *Dennis* v. *United States*, 341 U.S. 494, 523–525), or apply to the States a watered-down version of the First Amendment. See *Roth* v. *United States*, 354 U.S. 476, 505–506. But its language, in terms that are absolute, is utterly at war with censorship. Different questions may arise as to censorship of some news when the Nation is actually at war. But any possible exceptions are extremely limited. That is why the tradition represented by *Near* v. *Minnesota, supra*, represents our constitutional ideal.

Happily government censorship has put down few roots in this country. The American tradition is represented by *Near* v. *Minnesota, supra*. See Lockhart and McClure, Literature, The Law of Obscenity, and the Constitution, 38 Minn. L. Rev. 295, 324–325; Alpert, Judicial Censorship of Obscene Literature, 52 Harv. L. Rev. 40, 53 *et seq.* We have in the United States no counterpart of the Lord Chamberlain who is censor over England's stage. As late as 1941 only six States had systems of censorship for movies. Chafee, Free Speech in the United States (1941), p. 540. That number has now been reduced to four[2]—Kansas, Maryland, New York, and Virginia—plus a few cities. Even in these areas, censorship of movies shown on television gives way by reason of the Federal Communications Act. See *Allen B. Dumont Laboratories* v. *Carroll*, 184 F. 2d 153. And from what information is available, movie censors do not seem to be very active.[3] Deletion of the residual part of censorship that remains would constitute the elimination of an institution that intrudes on First Amendment rights.

MR. JUSTICE CLARK, concurring in the result.

I can take the words of the majority of the New York Court of Appeals only in their clear, unsophisticated and common meaning. They say that §§ 122 and 122–a of New York's Education Law "require the denial of a license to motion pictures which are immoral in that they portray 'acts of sexual immorality . . . as desirable, acceptable or proper patterns of behavior.'" That court states the issue in the case in this language:

"Moving pictures are our only concern and, what is more to the point, only those motion pictures which alluringly present acts of sexual immorality as proper behavior." 4 N.Y. 2d 349, 361, 151 N.E. 2d 197, 203, 175 N.Y.S. 2d 39, 48.

Moreover, it is significant to note that in its 14-page opinion that court says again and again, in fact 15 times, that the picture "Lady Chatterley's Lover" is proscribed because of its "espousal" of sexual immorality as "desirable" or as "proper conduct for the people of our State."[*]

The minority of my brothers here, however, twist this holding into one that New York's Act requires "obscenity or incitement, not just abstract expressions of opinion." But I cannot so obliterate the repeated declarations above-mentioned that were made not only 15 times by the Court of Appeals but which were the basis of the Board of Regents' decision as well. Such a construction would raise many problems, not the least of which would be our failure to accept New York's interpretation of the scope of its own Act. I feel, as does the majority here, bound by their holding.

In this context, the Act comes within the ban of *Joseph Burstyn, Inc.* v. *Wilson*, 343 U.S. 495 (1952). We held there that "expression by means of motion pictures is included within the free speech and free press guaranty of the First and Fourteenth Amendments." *Id.*, at 502. Referring to *Near* v. *Minnesota*, 283 U.S. 697 (1931), we said that while "a major purpose of the First Amendment guaranty of a free press was to prevent prior restraints upon publication" such protection was not unlimited but did place on the State "a heavy burden to demonstrate that the limitation challenged" was exceptional. *Id.*, at 503–504. The standard applied there was the word "sacrilegious" and we found it set the censor "adrift upon a boundless sea amid a myriad of conflicting currents of religious views. . . ." *Id.*, at 504. We struck it down.

Here the standard is the portrayal of "acts of sexual immorality . . . as desirable, acceptable or proper patterns of behavior." Motion picture plays invariably have a hero, a villain, supporting characters, a location, a plot, a diversion from the main theme and usually a moral. As we said in *Burstyn*: "They may affect public attitudes and

---

[1] Section 19(2) of the Indian Constitution permits "reasonable restrictions" on the exercise of the right of freedom of speech and expression in the interests, *inter alia*, of "decency or morality . . . defamation or incitement to an offence." This limitation is strictly construed; any restriction amounting to an "imposition" which will "operate harshly" on speech or the press will be held invalid. See *Seshadri* v. *District Magistrate, Tangore*, 41 A.I.R. (Sup. Ct.) 747, 749.

[2] See Note, 71 Harv. L. Rev. 326, 328, n. 14.

[3] *Id.*, p. 332.

---

[*] The phrase is not always identical but varies from the words of the statute, "acts of sexual immorality . . . as desirable, acceptable or proper patterns of behavior," to such terms "as proper conduct for the people of our State"; "exaltation of illicit sexual love in derogation of the restraints of marriage"; as "a proper pattern of behavior"; "the espousal of sexually immoral acts"; "which debase fundamental sexual morality by protraying its converse to the people as alluring and desirable"; "which alluringly portrays sexually immoral acts as proper behavior"; "by presenting . . . [adultery] in a clearly approbatory manner"; "which alluringly portrays adultery as proper behavior"; "which alluringly portray acts of sexual immorality (here adultery) and recommend them as a proper way of life"; "which alluringly portray adultery as proper and desirable"; and "which alluringly portray acts of sexual immorality by adultery as proper behavior."

behavior in a variety of ways, ranging from direct espousal of a political or social doctrine to the subtle shaping of thought which characterizes all artistic expression." 343 U.S., at 501. What may be to one viewer the glorification of an idea as being "desirable, acceptable or proper" may to the notions of another be entirely devoid of such a teaching. The only limits on the censor's discretion is his understanding of what is included within the term "desirable, acceptable or proper." This is nothing less than a roving commission in which individual impressions become the yardstick of action, and result in regulation in accordance with the beliefs of the individual censor rather than regulation by law. Even here three of my brothers "cannot regard this film as depicting anything more than a somewhat unusual, and rather pathetic, 'love triangle.'" At least three—perhaps four— of the members of New York's highest court thought otherwise. I need only say that the obscurity of the standard presents such a choice of difficulties that even the most experienced find themselves at dagger's point.

It may be, as Chief Judge Conway said, "that our public morality, possibly more than ever before, needs every protection government can give." 4 N.Y. 2d, at 363, 151 N.E. 2d, at 204–205, 175 N.Y.S. 2d, at 50. And, as my Brother HARLAN points out, "each time such a statute is struck down, the State is left in more confusion." This is true where broad grounds are employed leaving no indication as to what may be necessary to meet the requirements of due process. I see no grounds for confusion, however, were a statute to ban "pornographic" films, or those that "portray *acts* of sexual immorality, perversion or lewdness." If New York's statute had been so construed by its highest court I believe it would have met the requirements of due process. Instead, it placed more emphasis on what the film teaches than on what it depicts. There is where the confusion enters. For this reason, I would reverse on the authority of *Burstyn*.

Mr. JUSTICE HARLAN, whom Mr. JUSTICE FRANKFURTER and Mr. JUSTICE WHITTAKER join, concurring in the result.

I think the Court has moved too swiftly in striking down a statute which is the product of a deliberate and conscientious effort on the part of New York to meet constitutional objections raised by this Court's decisions respecting predecessor statutes in this field. But although I disagree with the Court that the parts of §§ 122 and 122–a of the New York Education Law, 16 N.Y. Laws Ann. § 122 (McKinney 1953), 16 N.Y. Laws Ann. § 122–a (McKinney Supp. 1958), here particularly involved are unconstitutional on their face, I believe that in their application to this film constitutional bounds were exceeded.

I.

Section 122–a of the State Education Law was passed in 1954 to meet this Court's decision in *Commercial Pictures Corp.* v. *Regents*, 346 U.S. 587, which overturned the New York Court of Appeals' holding in *In re Commercial Pictures Corp.* v. *Board of Regents*, 305 N.Y. 336, 113 N.E. 2d 502, that the film *La Ronde* could be banned as "immoral" and as "tend[ing] to corrupt morals" under

§ 122.[1] The Court's decision in *Commercial Pictures* was but a one line *per curiam* with a citation to *Joseph Burstyn, Inc.* v. *Wilson*, 343 U.S. 495, which in turn had held for naught not the word "immoral" but the term "sacrilegious" in the statute.

New York, nevertheless, set about repairing its statute. This it did by enacting § 122–a which in the respects emphasized in the present opinion of Chief Judge Conway as pertinent here defines an "immoral" motion picture film as one which portrays "'acts of sexual immorality . . . as desirable, acceptable or proper patterns of behavior.'" 4 N.Y. 2d 349, 351, 151 N.E. 2d 197, 175 N.Y.S. 2d 39.[2] The Court now holds this part of New York's effort unconstitutional on its face under the Fourteenth Amendment. I cannot agree.

The Court does not suggest that these provisions are bad for vagueness.[3] Any such suggestion appears to me un-

---

[1] Section 122 provides: "The director of the [motion picture] division or, when authorized by the regents, the officers of a local office or bureau shall cause to be promptly examined every motion picture film submitted to them as herein required, and unless such film or a part thereof is obscene, indecent, immoral, inhuman, sacrilegious, or is of such a character that its exhibition would tend to corrupt morals or incite to crime, shall issue a license therefor. If such director or, when so authorized, such officer shall not license any film submitted, he shall furnish to the applicant therfor a written report of the reasons for his refusal and a description of each rejected part of a film not rejected in toto."

[2] Section 122–a provides:

"1. For the purpose of section one hundred twenty-two of this chapter, the term 'immoral' and the phrase 'of such a character that its exhibition would tend to corrupt morals' shall denote a motion picture film or part thereof, the dominant purpose or effect of which is erotic or pornographic; or which portrays acts of sexual immorality, perversion, or lewdness, or which expressly or impliedly presents such acts as desirable, acceptable or proper patterns of behavior.

"2. For the purpose of section one hundred twenty-two of this chapter, the term 'incite to crime' shall denote a motion picture the dominant purpose or effect of which is to suggest that the commission of criminal acts or contempt for law is profitable, desirable, acceptable, or respectable behavior; or which advocates or teaches the use of, or the methods of use of, narcotics or habit-forming drugs."

[3] The bill that became § 122–a was introduced at the request of the State Education Department, which noted in a memorandum that "the issue of censorship, as such, is not involved in this bill. This bill merely attempts to follow out the criticism of the United States Supreme Court by defining the words 'immoral' and 'incite to crime.'" N.Y.S. Legis. Ann., 1954, 36. In a memorandum accompanying his approval of the measure, the then Governor of New York, himself a lawyer, wrote:

"Since 1921, the Education Law of this State has required the licensing of motion pictures and authorized refusal of a license for a motion picture which is 'obscene, indecent, immoral' or which would 'tend to corrupt morals or incite to crime.'

"Recent Supreme Court decisions have indicated that the term 'immoral' may not be sufficiently definite for constitutional purposes. The primary purpose of this bill is to define 'immoral' and 'tend to corrupt morals' in conformance with the apparent requirements of these cases. It does so by defining them in terms of 'sexual immorality.' The words selected for this definition are based on judicial opinions which have given exhaustive and reasoned treatment to the subject.

"The bill does not create any new licensing system, expand the scope of motion picture censorship, or enlarge the area of permissible prior restraint. Its sole purpose is to give to the

tenable in view of the long-standing usage in this Court of the concept "sexual immorality" to explain in part the meaning of "obscenity." See, *e.g., Swearingen* v. *United States,* 161 U.S. 446, 451.[4] Instead, the Court finds a constitutional vice in these provisions in that they require, so it is said, neither "obscenity" nor incitement to "sexual immorality," but strike of their own force at the mere advocacy of "an idea—that adultery under certain circumstances may be proper behavior"; expressions of "opinion that adultery may sometimes be proper. . . ." I think this characterization of these provisions misconceives the construction put upon them by the prevailing opinions in the Court of Appeals. Granting that the abstract public discussion or advocacy of adultery, unaccompanied by obscene portrayal or actual incitement to such behavior, may not constitutionally be proscribed by the State, I do not read those opinions to hold that the statute on its face undertakes any such proscription. Chief Judge Conway's opinion, which was joined by two others of the seven judges of the Court of Appeals, and in the thrust of which one more concurred, to be sure with some doubt, states (4 N.Y. 2d, at 356, 151 N.E. 2d, at 200, 175 N.Y.S. 2d, at 44):

"It should first be emphasized that the scope of section 122–a is not mere expression of opinion in the form, for example, of a filmed lecture whose subject matter is the espousal of adultery. We reiterate that this case involves the espousal of sexually immoral acts (here adultery) plus actual scenes of a suggestive and obscene nature." (Emphasis in original.)

The opinion elsewhere, as indeed is also the case with § 122 and 122–a themselves when independently read in their entirety, is instinct with the notion that mere abstract expressions of opinion regarding the desirability of sexual immorality, unaccompanied by obscenity[5] or incitement,

---

section more precision to make it conform to the tenor of recent court decisions and proscribe the exploitation of 'filth for the sake of filth.' It does so as accurately as language permits in 'words well understood through long use.' [*People* v. *Winters,* 333 U.S. 507, 518 (1948)].

. . . . .

"The language of the Supreme Court of the United States, in a recent opinion of this precise problem, should be noted:

"'To hold that liberty and expression by means of motion pictures is guaranteed by the First and Fourteenth Amendments, however, is not the end of our problem. It does not follow that the Constitution requires absolute freedom to exhibit every motion picture of every kind at all times and all places.' [*Burstyn* v. *Wilson,* 343 U.S. 495, at 502.]

"So long as the State has the responsibility for interdicting motion pictures which transgress the bounds of decency, we have the responsibility for furnishing guide lines to the agency charged with enforcing the law." *Id.,* at 408.

[4] Certainly it cannot be claimed that adultery is not a form of "sexual immorality"; indeed adultery is made a crime in New York. N.Y. Penal Law §§ 100–103, 39 N.Y. Laws Ann. §§ 100–103 (McKinney 1944).

[5] Nothing in Judge Dye's dissenting opinion, to which the Court refers in Note 7 of its opinion, can be taken as militating against this view of the prevailing opinions in the Court of Appeals. Judge Dye simply disagreed with the majority of the Court of Appeals as to the adequacy of the § 122–a definition of "immoral" to overcome prior constitutional objections to that term. See 4 N.Y. 2d, at 371, 151 N.E. 2d, at 209–210, 175 N.Y.S. 2d, at 57; see also the dissenting opinion of Judge Van Voorhis, 4 N.Y. 2d, at 374, 151 N.E. 2d, at 212, 175 N.Y.S. 2d, at 60.

---

are not proscribed. See 4 N.Y. 2d 349, especially at 351–352, 354, 356–358, 361, 363–364; 151 N.E. 2d 197, at 197, 199, 200–201, 203, 204–205; 175 N.Y.S. 2d 39, at 40, 42, 44–46, 48, 50–51; and Notes 1 and 2, *supra.* It is the corruption of public morals, occasioned by the inciting effect of a particular portrayal or by what New York has deemed the necessary effect of obscenity, at which the statute is aimed. In the words of Chief Judge Conway, "There is no difference in substance between motion pictures which are corruptive of the public morals, and sexually suggestive, because of a predominance of suggestive scenes, and those which achieve precisely the same effect by presenting only several such scenes in a clearly approbatory manner throughout the course of the film. *The law is concerned with effect, not merely with but one means of producing it . . . the objection lies in the corrosive effect upon the public sense of sexual morality.*" 4 N.Y. 2d, at 358, 151 N.E. 2d, at 201, 175 N.Y.S. 2d, at 46. (Emphasis in original.)

I do not understand that the Court would question the constitutionality of the particular portions of the statute with which we are here concerned if the Court read, as I do, the majority opinions in the Court of Appeals as construing these provisions to require obscenity or incitement, not just mere abstract expressions of opinion. It is difficult to understand why the Court should strain to read those opinions as it has. Our usual course in constitutional adjudication is precisely the opposite.

II.

The application of the statute to this film is quite a different matter. I have heretofore ventured the view that in this field the States have wider constitutional latitude than the Federal Government. See the writer's separate opinion in *Roth* v. *United States* and *Alberts* v. *California,* 354 U.S. 476, 496. With that approach, I have viewed this film.

Giving descriptive expression to what in matters of this kind are in the last analysis bound to be but individual subjective impressions, objectively as one may try to discharge his duty as a judge, is not apt to be repaying. I shall therefore content myself with saying that, according full respect to, and with, I hope, sympathetic consideration for, the views and characterizations expressed by others, I cannot regard this film as depicting anything more than a somewhat unusual, and rather pathetic, "love triangle," lacking in anything that could properly be termed obscene or corruptive of the public morals by inciting the commission of adultery. I therefore think that in banning this film New York has exceeded constitutional limits.

I conclude with one further observation. It is sometimes said that this Court should shun considering the particularities of individual cases in this difficult field lest the Court become a final "board of censorship." But I cannot understand why it should be thought that the process of constitutional judgment in this realm somehow stands apart from that involved in other fields, particularly those presenting questions of due process. Nor can I see, short of holding that all state "censorship" laws are constitutionally impermissible, a course from which the Court is carefully abstaining, how the Court can hope ultimately to spare itself the necessity for individualized adjudication. In the very nature of things the problems in this area are ones of individual cases, see *Roth* v. *United States* and *Alberts* v. *California, supra,* at 496–498, for a "censorship" statute can hardly be contrived that would in effect be self-executing. And, lastly, each time such a statute is struck down, the State is left in more confusion, as witness New York's experience with its statute.

Because I believe the New York statute was unconstitutionally applied in this instance I concur in the judgment of the Court.

■ State

v.

Harry Settle.

C. Q. No. 636.
Supreme Court of Rhode Island.

Dec. 21, 1959.

J. Joseph Nugent, Atty. Gen., *Raymond J. Pettine,* Asst. Atty. Gen., for State.

Albert L. Greenberg, John C. Burke, Newport, *Horace S. Manges,* New York City, for defendant.

Milton Stanzler, Norman G. Orodenker, Providence, for Rhode Island Affiliate American Civil Liberties Union, amicus curiæ.

Frost, Justice.

This is an indictment charging the defendant with selling to a person under the age of eighteen years a certain book which is obscene, lewd, lascivious and indecent. The case is before us under the provisions of General Laws 1956, § 9–24–27, on a certification by the superior court wherein the following questions involving the constitutionality of § 11–31–10 have been raised.

"Is Title 11, Chapter 31, Section 10, of the General Laws of Rhode Island, 1956, unconstitutional because it abridges the rights of the defendant to due process of law, freedom of speech, and freedom of the press, contrary to Section 1, Article 14 and Article 1, of the amendments to the constitution of the United States."

"Is Title 11, Chapter 31, Section 10, of the General Laws of Rhode Island, 1956, unconstitutional because it abridges the rights of the defendant to due process of law, freedom of speech, freedom of the press, and the right not to be deprived of life, liberty, or property unless by the judgment of his peers or the law of the land, contrary to Article 1, Section 10 and 20 of the constitution of the State of Rhode Island."

Prior to the hearing before us the Rhode Island Affiliate American Civil Liberties Union sought and obtained our permission to file a brief as amicus curiae and its counsel also participated in the oral arguments.

General Laws 1956, § 11–31–10, reads as follows:

"Every person who shall wilfully or knowingly sell, lend, give away, show, advertise for sale or distribute commercially to any person under the age of eighteen (18) years or has in his possession with intent to give, lend, show, sell, distribute commercially, or otherwise offer for sale or commercial distribution to any individual under the age of eighteen (18) years any pornographic motion picture, or any still picture or photograph or any book, pocket book, pamphlet or magazine the cover or content of which exploits, is devoted to, or is principally made up of descriptions of illicit sex or sexual immorality or which is obscene, lewd, lascivious, or indecent, or which consists of pictures of nude or partially denuded figures posed or presented in a manner to provoke or arouse lust or passion or to exploit sex, lust or perversion for commercial gain or any article or instrument of indecent or immoral use shall, upon conviction, be punished by a fine of not less than one hundred dollars ($100) nor more than one thousand dollars ($1,000) or by imprisonment for not more than two (2) years, or by both such fine and imprisonment.

"For the purposes of this section 'knowingly' shall mean having knowledge of the character and content of the publication or failure to exercise reasonable inspection which would disclose the content and character of the same."

Those claiming the statute to be unconstitutional assert as reasons therefor that the wording is vague and indefinite; that it is so broad in its definitions as to encompass acts or words which are included in the constitutional freedoms of the First Amendment and are protected from state interference by the Fourteenth Amendment; that the penalty clause in the statute makes it punishable as a misdemeanor or a felony; and that the indictment does not contain the name of the book and therefore is fatally defective. We shall consider the first two objections together.

[1] The purpose of the statute is clear. It is for the protection of youth and to combat juvenile delinquency. The subject matter includes pictures, books, pamphlets and magazines of a certain type, namely, those which exploit or are principally made up of descriptions of illicit sex or sexual immorality or which are obscene, lewd, lascivious or indecent. Specifically the section is designed to prevent such publications from passing into the hands of boys and girls of an impressionable age and is directed against those who are dealing in such publications as a business. This is clear from the preamble of the statute when it was passed and from the language of the statute

itself. The present statute, § 11–31–10, is a section of Public Laws 1956, chapter 3686, approved April 9, 1956, which was in amendment of and in addition to G.L.1938, chap. 610, and became sec. 48 of that chapter. The preamble of P.L.1956, chap. 3686, reads as follows:

"It is hereby declared that the publication, sale and distribution to minors of comic books devoted to crime, sex, horror, terror, brutality and violence, and of pocket books, photographs, pamphlets, magazines and pornographic films devoted to the presentation and exploitation of illicit sex, lust, passion, depravity, violence, brutality, nudity and immorality are a contributing factor to juvenile crime, a basic factor in impairing the ethical and moral development of our youth and a clear and present danger to the people of the state. Therefore, the provisions hereinafter prescribed are enacted and their necessity in the public interest is hereby declared as a matter of legislative determination."

[2] The title of § 11–31–10 is "Sale or exhibition to minors of indecent publications, pictures, or articles." The word "commercially" not only modifies the word "distribute" but it modifies each one of the preceding words, "sell," "lend," "give away," "show," and "advertise for sale." It is obvious from a reading of the statute that it is not directed against and does not embrace the father who gives to a youthful member of his family a book which comes under the ban of the law. The statute by its own terms is directed against those who, directly or indirectly for pecuniary gain, are possessing and handling publications of the sort described.

[3, 4] Counsel who oppose the views of the state contend that the statute is so vague and indefinite as to be unconstitutional; that in addition to proscribing any book the cover or content of which is obscene, lewd, lascivious or indecent, the statute goes on to condemn in the alternative any book the cover or content of which exploits, is devoted to or is principally made up of descriptions of illicit sex or sexual immorality, or which consists of pictures of nude or partially denuded figures posed or presented in a manner to provoke or arouse lust or passion, or to exploit sex, lust, or perversion for commercial gain. We fail to see that the addition of the alternatives introduces into the statute any element of vagueness or uncertainty. Obscenity is not within the area of constitutionally protected speech or press. *Roth v. United States*, 354 U.S. 476, 77 S. Ct. 1304, 1 L. Ed. 2d 1498. Lewd, lascivious and indecent are but synonyms of obscene. *Swearingen v. United States*, 161 U.S. 446, 16 S. Ct. 562, 40 L. Ed. 765. The alternatives mentioned are nothing more than examples of what is obscene, lewd, lascivious and indecent and are to a degree explanatory of the words used earlier.

Opponents of the state's views rely on *Winters v. People of State of New York*, 333 U.S. 507, 68 S. Ct. 665, 92 L. Ed. 840. Winters was a bookdealer in the city of New York who was convicted of having in his possession certain magazines with intent to sell them. Conviction was affirmed by the Appellate Division of the Supreme Court and later by the Court of Appeals. There was an appeal to the Supreme Court of the United States. The pertinent part of the New York Penal Law, McKinney's Consol. Laws, c. 40, § 1141 reads, "A person who * * * has in his possession with intent to sell * * * any book, pamphlet, magazine, newspaper or other printed paper devoted to the publication, and principally made up of criminal

news, police reports, or accounts of criminal deeds, or pictures, or stories of deeds of bloodshed, lust or crime * * *."

[5] The court stated at page 519 of 333 U.S., at page 672 of 68 S. Ct., "we find the specification of publications, prohibited from distribution, too uncertain and indefinite to justify the conviction of this petitioner." Because the statute was in violation of the Fourteenth Amendment to the constitution of the United States, the conviction was reversed. The statute in the Winters case in the breadth of its language condemned the publication of what could be and frequently is considered to be legitimate news. We do not find in the instant statute such reasonable ground for uncertainty as to cause a person to be in doubt as to whether a particular book or article is included within the language of the statute.

The defendant also cites *State v. Pocras*, 166 Neb. 642, 90 N.W. 2d 263, 267. Pocras, a newsdealer in the city of Lincoln, was convicted under an ordinance which read, "It shall be unlawful * * * to sell or offer for sale, or dispose of in any manner, any obscene, lewd, or indecent book, picture, or other publication or thing." A majority of the court held that the words "dispose of in any manner" made the ordinance void for uncertainty. There is no similarly broad language in the instant statute which could make for uncertainty.

Another case relied upon by counsel opposed ₜto the state's views is *Werner v. City of Knoxville*, D.C., 161 F. Supp. 9, 10. In that case an ordinance of the city of Knoxville was before the court. The pertinent language was "to sell, offer for sale, display for sale, print, distribute or offer for distribution any book, magazine or other publication which prominently features an account of crime, or is obscene, or depicts, by the use of drawings or photographs or printed words, obscene actions and accounts, or the commission or attempted commission of the crimes of arson, assault with a deadly weapon, burglary, kidnapping, mayhem, murder, rape, robbery, theft, or voluntary manslaughter."

The court stated at page 13 of 161 F. Supp., "The Ordinance under consideration not only makes unlawful publications which prominently feature crime but also those that give accounts of specific common law crimes like theft, robbery, rape, voluntary manslaughter, etc." The court held that "fairness requires that criminal statutes inform those who are subject to such statutes as to what conduct on their part will render them liable for penalties." And also that the ordinance "includes acts which are included in the constitutional freedoms of the First Amendment * * *." This ordinance did not forbid the sale of publications containing accounts of various crimes to a certain class such as minors or youths below a given age. Again it did forbid the sale of publications containing stories of crimes including those which were neither obscene nor indecent. Such breadth of language included what was permissible and was clearly in conflict with the freedom of the press which is protected by the First Amendment to the constitution of the United States. This language produced for dealers an area of uncertainty wholly absent in the statute under consideration.

In *Joseph Burstyn, Inc.* v. *Wilson*, 343 U.S. 495, 72 S. Ct. 777, 96 L. Ed. 1098, relied on by defendant, it was held that liberty of expression by means of motion pictures was guaranteed by the First and Fourteenth Amendments, but the court stated at page 502, of 343 U.S., at page 781 of 72 S. Ct.: "It does not follow that the Constitution requires absolute freedom to exhibit every motion picture of every kind at all times and all places." The court also said at page 505 of 343 U.S., at page 782 of 72 S. Ct.: "Since the term 'sacrilegious' is the sole standard under attack here, it is not necessary for us to decide, for example, whether a state may censor motion pictures under a clearly drawn statute designed and applied to prevent the showing of obscene films. That is a very different question from the one now before us. We hold only that under the First and Fourteenth Amendments a state may not ban a film on the basis of a censor's conclusion that it is 'sacrilegious.'" The statute now under consideration does not forbid the showing of all motion pictures but it does forbid the exhibition of obscene pictures.

Kingsley International Pictures Corp. v. Regents of University of New York, 360 U.S. 684, 79 S. Ct. 1362, 1366, 3 L. Ed. 2d 1512, involved a motion picture portraying adultery under certain circumstances as proper behavior. The court reversed the Court of Appeals of New York and reaffirmed that "motion pictures are within the First and Fourteenth Amendments' basic protection" as held in *Joseph Burstyn, Inc. v. Wilson*, supra. In effect the court held that this picture was not obscene.

In *Butler v. State of Michigan*, 352 U.S. 380, 77 S. Ct. 524, 1 L. Ed. 2d 412, a statute of the state of Michigan was involved. A dealer sold to a police officer a book which the trial court characterized as containing obscene, immoral, lewd and lascivious language tending to incite minors to immoral acts. The statute did not limit its prohibition of sales to minors. In reversing the conviction the court held that the legislation was not reasonably restricted to the evil with which it was said to deal, and that it arbitrarily curtailed a liberty of the individual enshrined in the due process clause of the Fourteenth Amendment. In the instant statute the restriction on sales is to persons under eighteen years of age.

No publication is labeled obscene and therefore a statute which condemns writings of that nature must use language such as is found in the instant statute, namely, "is devoted to, or is principally made up of * * *." We are of the opinion that the language of the statute under consideration is so clear that "men of common intelligence," to use Mr. Justice Sutherland's expression in *Connally v. General Construction Co.*, 269 U.S. 385, 46 S. Ct. 126, 127, 70 L. Ed. 322, can act under it with certainty as to its meaning.

[6] The defendant insists that the statute is unconstitutional because the penalty clause makes it punishable as a misdemeanor or as a felony, and that therefore he is deprived of the equal protection of the law since two people can be tried for the same offense and one convicted of a felony and the other of a misdemeanor. General Laws 1956, § 11-1-2, reads as follows: "Felony and misdemeanor distinguished.—Unless otherwise provided, any criminal offense which at any given time may be punished by imprisonment for a term of more than one (1) year, or by a fine of more than five hundred dollars ($500), is hereby declared to be a felony; and any criminal offense which may be otherwise punishable is hereby declared to be a misdemeanor."

Since under § 11-31-10 a violator thereof may be punished by imprisonment for a term of more than one year the crime defined therein is a felony. The mere fact that in a particular case a defendant may be given a light fine is of no consequence. The crime is still a felony. The character of an offense as a felony or a misdemeanor must be determined by the laws of the jurisdiction where the crime was committed. 14 Am. Jur., Criminal Law, § 13, p. 763. And on the same page it is stated, "The sentence actually imposed in a given case is not, however, the sole criterion as to the grade of the offense committed. Thus, where by statute a crime is declared to be a felony, the fact that the jury in its discretion imposes a fine only does not make the crime a misdemeanor. In a majority of jurisdictions, however, when the court or the jury is given the discretion to fix the punishment for an offense by imprisonment in the penitentiary, fine, or by confinement in jail, such an offense is held to be a felony regardless of the penalty actually imposed."

In *Smith v. State*, 145 Me. 313, at page 326, 75 A. 2d 538, at page 545, the court stated, "It is the punishment that *may* be imposed, not that which is imposed, that determines whether or not an offense is a felony or a misdemeanor. *State v. Vashon*, 123 Me. 412, 123 A. 511."

We are of the opinion that there is no merit in this contention.

[7] The defendant contends that the indictment is fatally defective since it does not contain the name of the book which was sold, and that prosecution thereunder denies to the defendant due process of law. It is sufficient to say as to this contention that the indictment itself is not before the court. Two questions arising from the demurrer to the indictment have been submitted to this court and nothing else. *United States Trust Co. v. Tax Assessors*, 47 R.I. 420, 133 A. 802.

For the reasons stated, our answer to each question as certified is in the negative, and the papers in the case are ordered returned to the superior court for further proceedings.

POWERS, J., not participating.

1960-1968
Cases

■ Grove Press, Inc., and Reader's Subscription, Inc., *Plaintiffs-Appellees*,

v.

Robert K. Christenberry, Individually and as Postmaster of the City of New York, *Defendant-Appellant*.
No. 182, Docket 25861.

United States Court of Appeals Second Circuit.

Argued Dec. 2, 1959. Decided March 25, 1960.

S. *Hazard Gillespie, Jr.*, U.S. Atty., New York City (Robert J. Ward, John W. Hasson, and Robert L. Tofel, Asst. U.S. Attys., New York City, on the brief), for defendant-appellant.

Charles Rembar, of Rembar, Zolotar & Leavy, New York City (Morton E. Yohalem and Sigmund Timberg, Washington, D.C., on the brief), for plaintiff-appellee Grove Press, Inc.

Jay H. Topkis, of Paul, Weiss, Rifkind, Wharton & Garrison, New York City, for plaintiff-appellee Readers' Subscription, Inc.

Edgar W. Holtz, Acting Gen. Counsel, *Max D. Paglin*, Asst. Gen. Counsel, and *Ruth V. Reel* and *Edward W. Hautanen*, Counsel, F.C.C., Washington, D.C., for Federal Communications Commission, as amicus curiae.

Before CLARK, WATERMAN, and MOORE, Circuit Judges.

CLARK, Circuit Judge.

D. H. Lawrence completed the third manuscript version of his novel "Lady Chatterley's Lover" in Italy in 1928, and it was then published in Florence for private distribution. It is this version which has now been published by the plaintiff Grove Press, Inc., in a sumptuous edition selling for $6.00, with a prefatory letter of commendation by Archibald MacLeish, poet, playwright, and Boylston Professor of Rhetoric and Oratory at Harvard University, and with an extensive Introduction and a concluding Bibliographical Note by Mark Schorer, Professor of English Literature at the University of California and a Lawrence scholar.[1] The book (together with circulars showing its availability by Readers' Subscription, Inc., the second plaintiff[2]) has been detained as unmailable by the New York Postmaster and, after a hearing before the Judicial Officer of the Post Office Department and reference to the Postmaster General for final departmental decision, was held by the latter to be "obscene and non-mailable pursuant to 18 U.S. Code § 1461." The Postmaster General wrote a substantial decision, of which these are salient paragraphs:

"The contemporary community standards are not such that this book should be allowed to be transmitted in the mails.

"The book is replete with descriptions in minute detail of sexual acts engaged in or discussed by the book's principal characters. These descriptions utilize filthy, offensive and degrading words and terms. Any literary merit the book may have is far outweighed by the pornographic and smutty passages and words, so that the book, taken as a whole, is an obscene and filthy work."

The plaintiffs then sought a declaratory judgment and an injunction from the court below to reverse this decision. On cross motions for summary judgment, Judge Bryan gave a declaration that the Grove Edition here involved "is neither obscene, lewd, lascivious, indecent nor filthy in content or character, and is not nonmailable matter within the meaning of Title 18, Section 1461 of the United States Code." He also held that the bar order of the Postmaster General "is illegal and void and violates plaintiffs' rights in contravention of the Constitution," and entered an order permanently enjoining its enforcement. His complete and reasoned opinion, D.C.S.D.N.Y., 175 F. Supp. 488, with which we are in accord, gives further background, and reference is therefore made to it.

The important question on the merits is whether this now famous book is obscene within the meaning of 18 U.S.C. § 1461. This is a lengthy statute going back to 1876 and 1873 and amended as recently as 1958, which in portions here pertinent provides: "Every obscene, lewd, lascivious, indecent, filthy or vile article * * * is declared to be nonmailable matter and shall not be conveyed in the mails or delivered from any post office or by any letter carrier. Whoever knowingly uses the mails for the mailing,

---

[1] This edition has never before been legally published in this country or in England, although it has been frequently pirated here; and an abridged edition was published by Knopf in 1930. The complete version, however, has been published in some continental countries in English and in most in translation. It is not protected here by copyright, and various paperback editions —we are told—are now appearing. The ban in New York on the motion picture based on the novel was held invalid in *Kingsley International Pictures Corp.* v. *Regents of the University of New York*, 360 U.S. 684, 79 S. Ct. 1362, 3 L. Ed. 2d 1512.

[2] By stipulation Readers' Subscription, Inc., has agreed to be bound by the decision to be rendered as to Grove Press, Inc. The issues are identical.

We also have the application of the Federal Communications Commission to file a brief *amicus curiae*. The brief may be filed; but, since we do not find before us any issue affecting that agency, we make no ruling as to it.

carriage in the mails, or delivery of anything declared by this section to be nonmailable * * * shall be fined not more than $5,000 or imprisoned not more than five years, or both, for the first such offense, and shall be fined not more than $10,000 or imprisoned not more than ten years, or both, for each such offense thereafter."

[1–3] But before we reach the merits, we must consider the procedural aspects of the issue involved, since the government on this appeal has directed much the greater force of its argument to a reliance upon the principle of administrative law that an agency action supported by substantial evidence is beyond judicial review. Its major contention is that the statute obligates the Post Office Department to prevent the conveyance of obscene matter through the mails and that, since the Postmaster General has made a finding of obscenity based upon substantial evidence, the district court erred in reviewing it. The district court rejected this contention of agency finality, and so do we.

Preliminarily we should note the query whether the statute, being one defining a crime with criminal penalties, may afford justification for the acts of seizure by the Postmaster General in any event, or whether its sanction is not limited to criminal prosecution for crimes already committed. This is an issue which divided the court in *Sunshine Book Co.* v. *Summerfield,* 101 U.S. App. D.C. 358, 249 F. 2d 114, summarily reversed in 355 U.S. 372, 78 S. Ct. 365, 2 L. Ed. 2d 352. It is one of serious difficulty; but we shall not attempt to resolve it here, since we think the result is clear on other grounds.

Judge Bryan ruled that the issue was one of law fully reviewable by a court of law, since there was no dispute in matters of evidence and hence there was no occasion for the application of the substantial evidence rule. Although this conclusion is vigorously attacked by the government, it is difficult to see why it is not sound, particularly as reinforced by the constitutional overtones implicit in the issue. There can be no doubt that in large areas of postal activity involving the delivery of the mail the Post Office Department exercises discretion not to be controlled by courts. But to determine whether a work of art or literature is obscene has little, if anything, to do with the expedition or efficiency with which the mails are dispatched. And here it is clear that no question of evidence was involved. In fact the Departmental officials considered only the novel itself against the background of the statute and declined to consider the expert opinion proffered by the plaintiffs. The question was thus one starkly of law.[3] Moreover, the plaintiffs raised the constitutional issue of freedom of expression, which Judge Bryan ruled upon it below, and it can hardly be escaped in this class of cases. See *Smith* v. *People of the State of California,* 361 U.S. 147, 80 S. Ct. 215, 4 L. Ed. 2d 205; *Roth* v. *United States,* 354 U.S. 476, 479–489, 497, 506–508, 511–514, 77 S. Ct. 1304, 1 L.

Ed. 2d 1498. Even factual matters must be reviewed on appeal against a claim of denial of a constitutional right. *Niemotko* v. *State of Maryland,* 340 U.S. 268, 271, 71 S. Ct. 325, 95 L. Ed. 267; *Joseph Burstyn, Inc.* v. *Wilson,* 343 U.S. 495, 506, 72 S. Ct. 777, 96 L. Ed. 1098. Both legally and practically the claim of final censorship powers here made for the Postmaster General is extreme.[4] Indeed it has received an incisive answer in the public press thus: "And courts, not post offices, are the proper places for a determination of what is and is not protected by the Constitution." Editorial, Lady Chatterley Embattled Again, N.Y. Herald Tribune, Dec. 9, 1959, p. 26.

Passing then to the merits we must of course be cognizant of the risk run by judges in enforcing obscenity statutes such as this and thus perchance condemning what become classics of our intellectual heritage. Some of the present Justices of the Supreme Court revolt against all this supervision as violative of constitutional precepts. But since the statute has been upheld by majority vote, *Roth* v. *United States,* supra, 354 U.S. 476, 77 S. Ct. 1304, 1 L. Ed. 2d 1498; and see *Smith* v. *People of the State of California,* supra, 361 U.S. 147, 80 S. Ct. 215, 4 L. Ed. 2d 205, and *Kingsley International Pictures Corp.* v. *Regents of the University of New York,* 360 U.S. 684, 79 S. Ct. 1362, 3 L. Ed. 2d 1512, it remains the duty of those of us who sit in inferior courts to enforce it as best we may. And we need have no illusions but that a large business is done in exploiting "hard core pornography" for money's sake. In general this trash is easily recognized, with its repetitive emphasis (usually illustrated) upon purely physical action without character or plot development; and even if its direct connection with crime or incitement to juvenile or other delinquency is not proven—as many now assert—it cannot arouse sympathy because of its essentially repulsive, as well as fraudulent, character. It is when we come to more genuine works of literature that troublesome issues arise.

At the outset we may well recall the classic warning by a great American judge in probably the leading case on the subject prior to the recent utterances of the Supreme Court, Judge Augustus N. Hand in *United States* v. *One Book* Entitled Ulysses by James Joyce, 2 Cir., 72 F. 2d 705, 708:[5] "The foolish judgments of Lord Eldon about one hundred years ago, proscribing the works of Byron and Southey, and the finding by the jury under a charge by Lord Denman that the publication of Shelley's 'Queen Mab' was an indictable offense are a warning to all who have to determine the limits of the field within which authors may exercise themselves." And he went on to this judgment upon a then disputed book now recognized as classic: "We think that Ulysses is a book of originality and sincerity of treatment and that it has not the effect of

---

[3] The argument based on the fact that criminal prosecutions under this statute are tried to the jury seems beside the point. The jury must of course find even beyond a reasonable doubt various elements not here involved, such as criminal intent. And courts do not hesitate to dismiss charges when clear that the law has not been violated. See, e.g., *United States* v. *Keller,* 3 Cir., 259 F. 2d 54. So, too, the contention that judges have no more competence to be literary censors than the Postmaster General, while perhaps true in itself, overlooks the ultimate responsibility of courts to enforce the law and the Constitution.

[4] The defense brief states the problem before the District Court in these absolute terms: "Was the dominant theme of the book, considered in the light of the opinion evidence, so innocent that reasonable minds could no longer differ over which inference was the proper one to be adopted?" And then it adds, with considerable understatement: "To state the problem thus is to actually resolve it."

[5] L. Hand, J., concurring, Manton, J., dissenting. In literary circles it has been customary to cite or quote the less authoritative decision below by Judge Woolsey in *United States* v. *One Book* Called "Ulysses," D.C.S.D.N.Y., 5 F. Supp. 182, because of one or two lilting sentences in the opinion there.

promoting lust." Here we have one advantage over our predecessors in that the time which has elapsed since the writing and original publication of this book has been sufficient for the crystallization of at least a literary judgment upon it. And it seems clear without dissent from the expert evaluations presented both in the record and in the introductory material to this edition, as well as in the contemporary literature, that this is a major and a distinguished novel, and Lawrence one of the great writers of the era.[6]

[4] For present purposes our test must be based upon that prescribed by the majority in *Roth* v. *United States*, supra, 354 U.S. 476, 487, 77 S. Ct. 1304, 1310, 1 L. Ed. 2d 1498. Justice Brennan said:

"*However, sex and obscenity are not synonymous. Obscene material is material which deals with sex in a manner appealing to prurient interest. The portrayal of sex, e.g., in art, literature and scientific works, is not itself sufficient reason to deny material the constitutional protection of freedom of speech and press. Sex, a great and mysterious motive force in human life, has indisputably been a subject of absorbing interest to mankind through the ages; it is one of the vital problems of human interest and public concern.*"

And he gave support to the definition in the A.L.I. Model Penal Code thus:

"*We perceive no significant difference between the meaning of obscenity developed in the case law and the definition of the A.L.I., Model Penal Code, § 207.10 (2) (Tent. Draft No. 6, 1957), viz.:*
"'* * * A thing is obscene if, considered as a whole, its predominant appeal is to prurient interest, i.e., a shameful or morbid interest in nudity, sex, or excretion, and if it goes substantially beyond customary limits of candor in description or representation of such matters. * * *.' See Comment, id., at 10, and the discussion at page 29 et seq.*"

[5] Examined with care and "considered as a whole," the predominant appeal of "Lady Chatterley's Lover" in our judgment is demonstrably not to "prurient interest," as thus defined. By now the story of the novel is well known. It is thus succinctly summarized in Professor Schorer's Introduction: "Constance Chatterley, the frustrated wife of an aristocratic mine owner who has been wounded in the war and left paralyzed and impotent, is drawn to his game-keeper, the misanthropic son of a miner, becomes pregnant by him, and hopes at the end of

the book to be able to divorce her husband and leave her class for a life with the other man." But of course the story is a small part of the work. Actually the book is a polemic against three things which Lawrence hated: the crass industrialization of the English Midlands, the British caste system, and inhibited sex relations between man and woman. We may not see the close relation he did between the three as instruments of repression of the natural man, but we can understand his plea for greater freedom and naturalness even if we may not share his conviction of the all-inclusive nature of his remedy. Lawrence grew up in the English coal regions as the son of a miner who had married a teacher, and the theme of a relationship between a man of a low social status with a woman of a higher level is one he has used in previous works. The rationale he seeks to establish is thus one surely arguable and open to a writer. And if the aristocratic, but frustrated, heroine is to be taught naturalness in self-expression by her husband's servant, the plot line is rather clearly indicated. It is hardly surprising, therefore, that we find descriptions of increasingly more intimate scenes between the two protagonists and an increasingly greater use of "natural" language as the man's demonstration of naturalness to his feminine partner is stepped up to the author's climax.

What has apparently given surprise over the years—probably less so now than formerly in view of the changing climate of opinion—is the degree or extent to which the author has carried his plan. Undoubtedly to these critics of morals a little description of sex goes a long way; and judging by other examples, classical and modern, less directness would have left the work unchallenged. Obviously a writer can employ various means to achieve the effect he has in mind, and so probably Lawrence could have omitted some of the passages found "smutty" by the Postmaster General and yet have produced an effective work of literature. But clearly it would not have been the book he planned, because for what he had in mind his selection was most effective, as the agitation and success of the book over the years have proven.[7] In these sex descriptions showing how his aristocratic, but frustrated, lady achieved fulfillment and naturalness in her life, he also writes with power and indeed with a moving tenderness which is compelling, once our agelong inhibitions against sex revelations in print have been passed. In actuality his thesis here is only that pressed continuously in the modern marriage-counseling and doctors' books written with apparently quite worthy objectives and advertised steadily in our most sober journals and magazines. Of course it is old in literature; one may recall, for instance, the passionate

---

[6] This judgment of Messrs. MacLeish, Schorer, Malcolm Cowley, Alfred Kazin, and other competent critics appearing in the record or offered at the departmental hearing seems to be rather regularly and continuously confirmed in literary journals. For example, the reviewer for the Saturday Review, Granville Hicks, in an article entitled, D. H. Lawrence Reconsidered, Saturday Review, Dec. 19, 1959, p. 31, quotes the distinguished English scholar John Middleton Murry as saying shortly before his death in 1957 that "since the end of the Second World War, there has emerged a growing consensus of opinion that he [Lawrence] is the most significant writer of his time." So Professor Harry T. Moore, Lawrence biographer, reviewing this book for the N.Y. Times Book Review Section, May 3, 1959, terms it "our time's most significant romance."

[7] The defense complains that Lawrence need not "so vividly" have protrayed his scenes of sex and objects to the "Constant repetition of such intimate scenes." But that was at least one way of arousing reader interest, as the careful textual examination by the distinguished government counsel and associate counsel demonstrates. Compare the comment in a somewhat analogous situation of the New York Times Scandinavian reporter Werner Wiskari upon the presently popular Swedish motion picture director Ingmar Bergman, in the Sunday Times Magazine, Dec. 20, 1959, § 6, p. 20: "Why does Bergman insist on such brutality? Because he cannot abide the merely indifferent presence of a popcorn-chewing audience. In creating scenes that are almost physically felt in the midsection, he aims to involve the onlooker in the action so as to win active understanding of the motivations of his characters."

love scenes between the young tutor and his employer's wife in Stendhal's classic, *Le Rouge et Noir* (The Red and the Black), published in 1830. Actually in present-day literature such descriptions of physical relations appear as regular staples of literary diet and quite without Lawrence's straightforward and somewhat refreshing candor.[8]

[6–8] The same is true of the so-called four-letter words found particularly objectionable by the Postmaster General. These appear in the latter portion of the book in the mouth of the game-keeper in his tutelage of the lady in naturalness and are accepted by her as such. Again this could be taken as an object lesson at least in directness as compared to the smirk of much contemporary usage, which (perhaps strangely) does not seem to have offended our mailmen.[9] In short, all these passages to which the Postmaster General takes exception—in bulk only a portion of the book—are subordinate, but highly useful, elements to the development of the author's central purpose. And that is not prurient.[10] Should a court in reading meaning into the word "obscene"—which proves far from self-defining—make it so all-inclusive as to prohibit a writer from making use of normal and no longer unusual descriptions and parts of English speech to accomplish a worthy objective? And should a mature and sophisticated reading public be kept in blinders because a government official thinks reading certain works of power and literary value is not good for it? We agree with the court below in believing and holding that definitions of obscenity consistent with modern intellectual standards and morals neither require nor permit such a restriction.

Judgment affirmed.

MOORE, Circuit Judge (concurring in the result).

The subject matter of this case is a book completed in 1928 in Italy. It is significant that it was then published only "for private distribution." For almost thirty years it remained unpublished in this country except for an expurgated edition which enjoyed comparative obscurity. The unexpurgated edition has been barred from the mails since 1928. In 1959, and undoubtedly relying upon the changing "climate" of community standards, plaintiffs (the publisher and the distributor) decided to publish the unexpurgated edition and test the book's "nonmailable" character. Suddenly, with the restoration to the text of "coarse and vulgar" expressions and play-by-play descriptions of extramarital sexual activities, the book (properly called "this now famous book") becomes "a major and a distinguished novel." Certain critics, apparently for years unconcerned with it absent the vulgarisms and the questionable scenes, now hail the book as a great contribution to our literary heritage.[1] The public, ever anxious to read in print certain words which they can so easily see written in public toilets and other public places, avidly purchased thousands (probably millions) of copies.

The plot of the book has no bearing on the obscenity issue. Its first two messages (as analyzed by the majority), if they be directed against the "crass industrialization of the English Midlands" and "the British caste system," could be delivered effectively without the objectionable material. The third message of "repression of the natural man," said to be inveighed against by the author, is the "inhibited sex relations between man and woman." Whether "natural man" should be somewhat inhibited in this activity presents a sociological and moral problem thus far not solved by society. If the author wishes to plead "for greater freedom and naturalness" for man and woman in their sexual diversions uninhibited by law or convention, it is for the lawmakers and not the courts to rule how far this objective should properly be pursued.

The fallacy of "the changing climate of opinion" argument is that it rotates in a circle. During recent years authors of the so-called school of "realism" have vied with each other to depict with accuracy all that could be observed by peeking through hypothetical keyholes and by hiding under beds. The last war offered an excellent opportunity to employ the entire register of Anglo-Saxon four-letter words via the medium of realistic soldier conversations. Many such books became best sellers. After this phase of literary effort palled, it became necessary to go beyond this stage into the sordid and more perverted sexual field—all under the guise of telling an allegedly powerful and moving story about various characters or families which had better remained unborn. One normal adultery per book was quite insufficient to create a best seller. And an eager public, possibly bored by the monotony of monogamy, seized upon each literary contribution to enjoy vicariously—and quite safely—bold but rather impractical daydreams of a life which could be found in fictional actuality in these books. Each book contributed a few additional degrees to the temperature and by its unchallenged existence created the "contemporary com-

---

[8] As in a recent book of wide popularity in respected book circles, said to have had a sale of nearly three million copies, a tale of continuous seduction of or by a twelve-year-old girl by or with a middle-aged lover; or another, locally nominated for the Nobel prize, depicting in detail the sexual activities, marital and extramarital, of a middle-aged Pennsylvania lawyer.

[9] As in a humorous book of present popularity, exploiting the lack of a crucial letter of the alphabet from the hero's typewriter; or even that powerful description of a bomber pilot's decline and decay, with the racy language artificially concealed by the ostrich-like method of initial letters followed by blanks.

[10] The defense conclusion to the contrary seems to be curiously, if not inconsistently, stated in its brief. It first acknowledges that a book is not obscene "because it expounds the necessity to a happy marriage of sexual fulfillment," or because "it takes the next step and preaches or observes that where sexual fulfillment cannot be found within the marriage the unsatisfied party is justified in looking elsewhere for such physical pleasures," and "Contemporary novels treat of such matters and would not be regarded as obscene." Then it proceeds to condemn the present book as "a tale of the complete denigration of the spiritual aspects of marriage, a steady downward progression throughout the book, the development of a theme by a continuous series of episodes that standing alone cannot be sustained and when linked together to preserve them are fast to a central idea which itself is certainly lascivious and indecent." It is not apparent how these statements are to be reconciled. Is it that Lawrence expresses no adverse moral judgment? That has never been accepted as a sound or workable dividing line in law, though it may have had some vogue in motion picture direction.

---

[1] I do not imply that the views of Jacques Barzun, Edmund Wilson, Archibald MacLeish, and other critics mentioned by the majority, are not entitled to consideration and respect. My point is simply that literary critics generally do not represent that hypothetical character, the average reader. It is this individual with whom a judge or administrative official must inevitably be concerned.

munity standards" which, in turn, are to justify its acceptance as consistent with such standards. Into this climate ever increasing in warmth came "Lady Chatterley's Lover" which plaintiffs sought to distribute through the mails.

Charged by law with the responsibility of enforcing (initially at least) a statute presumably representing the will of the people, the Postmaster-General adhered to the policy of the Post Office Department for some thirty years and refused to transmit the book and literature relating thereto through the mails. Hearings were duly held and after reviewing various criteria, particularly those mentioned by the Supreme Court in the case of *Roth* v. *United States,* 1957, 354 U.S. 476, 77 S. Ct. 1304, 1 L. Ed. 1498, the Postmaster-General concluded that "The contemporary community standards are not such that this book should be allowed to be transmitted in the mails." [175 F. Supp. 497.]

The applicable statute declares non-mailable every "obscene, lewd, lascivious, indecent, filthy or vile article * * *" (18 U.S.C.A. § 1461). A prohibitory law is not self-enforcing. Although under our governmental system the courts usually have to make final decisions, the Postmaster-General here had to make the first decision. Such a decision, of course, is not beyond judicial review. Any holding of agency finality would be contrary to our fundamental judicial concepts and make of each department head a despot or czar. On this point I am in complete accord with the majority. Nevertheless the Postmaster-General's findings and conclusions should not be dismissed casually. The Supreme Court (not the Postmaster-General) chose the test of "contemporary community standards" and "appealing to prurient interest." But what "community" and what is "prurient interest"? And is a single judge or a group of judges in any one restricted geographic district all-knowing as to community standards? At least the Postmaster-General by virtue of his office and his staff of inspectors in every State of the Union is mindful of the type of questionable material found in the mails and the reaction thereto of each community. Parenthetically a conjecture that juries in a substantial number of communities throughout the country would support the Postmaster-General's conclusion in this case would not be too erroneous. As to "prurient interest" one can scarcely be so naive as to believe that the avalanche of sales came about as a result of a sudden desire on the part of the American public to become acquainted with the problems of a professional gamekeeper in the management of an English estate.

The majority, in my opinion, are overly influenced by "the risk run by judges in enforcing obscenity statutes" and believe that "Some of the present Justices of the Supreme Court revolt against all this supervision as violative of constitutional precepts." This obviously is the easiest (and possibly the best) solution. In effect, repeal the statute by judicial failure to enforce it or overrule all decisions as to its constitutionality. Then, at least, the Postmaster-General would be relieved of an unenviable burden and each community could enact such protective ordinances as it might deem best suited to its own standards subject always to constitutional limitations. In substance, literary local option. However, so long as the statute remains upon the books it should be interpreted and enforced according to some standards.

In almost every other field of the law in which neither judge nor administrator boast of any special competence in subjects beyond their knowledge expert testimony is usually required. So here the courts should receive evidence "to allow light to be shed on what those 'contemporary community standards' are." *Smith* v. *State of California,* 1959, 361 U.S. 147, 80 S. Ct. 215, 225, 4 L. Ed. 2d 205. In coping with a problem difficult at best both as to procedure and proof, the portion of the opinion of Mr. Justice Frankfurter in the Smith case seems particularly apt:

"Their interpretation [the courts' or juries'] ought not to depend solely on the necessarily limited, hit-or-miss, subjective view of what they are believed to be by the individual juror or judge. It bears repetition that the determination of obscenity is for juror or judge not on the basis of his personal upbringing or restricted reflection or particular experience of life, but on the basis of 'contemporary community standards.' Can it be doubted that there is a great difference in what is to be deemed obscene in 1959 compared with what was deemed obscene in 1859. The difference derives from a shift in community feeling regarding what is to be deemed prurient or not prurient by reason of the effects attributable to this or that particular writing. Changes in the intellectual and moral climate of society, in part doubtless due to the views and findings of specialists, afford shifting foundations for the attribution. What may well have been consonant 'with mid-Victorian morals, does not seem to me to answer to the understanding and morality of the present time.' United States v. Kennerley, [D.C.] 209 F. 119, 120. This was the view of Judge Learned Hand decades ago reflecting an atmosphere of propriety much closer to mid-Victorian days than is ours. Unless we disbelieve that the literary, psychological or moral standards of a community can be made fruitful and illuminating subjects of inquiry by those who give their life to such inquiries, it was violative of 'due process,' to exclude the constitutionally relevant evidence proffered in this case. The importance of this type of evidence in prosecutions for obscenity has been impressively attested by the recent debates in the House of Commons dealing with the insertion of such a provision in the enactment of the Obscene Publications Act, 1959, 7 & 8 Eliz. 2, Ch. 66 (see 597 Parliamentary Debates, H. Comm., col. 1009–1010, 1042–1043; 604 Parliamentary Debates, H. Comm., No. 100 (April 24, 1959), col. 803), as well as by the most considered thinking on this subject in the proposed Model Penal Code of the American Law Institute" (361 U.S. at pages 166, 167, 80 S. Ct. at pages 225, 226, 4 L. Ed. 2d 205).

Whether such an approach would satisfy those who, marching under the banner of freedom and tolerance, are themselves often the most intolerant of the views of others, I do not know. Surely this minority group which preaches freedom of the press without restraint would probably not be willing to honor "contemporary community standards" if these differed from their own.

Nor do I find solace in the knowledge and in the thought suggested by the majority that there are other books just as bad. Following the majority's example and referring to the public press "No democratic society has ever yet been able to come up with a foolproof definition of the thin line between liberty and license. One of the weariest clichés in this battle is to point out that there are passages in the Bible and Will Shakespeare that are not for Little Pitchers." (Inez Robb in the New York World-Telegram, December 15, 1959.) Many an advertisement seeking to peddle pornographic material to be sent surreptitiously through the mails offers choice passages from well recognized Greek and Roman authors. But should the literary merit of the product of an author's pen give him carte blanche in case he chooses to venture into forbidden fields? Both the trial court and the majority suggest that the reputations of author and publisher should weigh heavily in deciding the issue. And so they should, were intent involved.[2]

Then there is the doctrine of the "book as a whole" (*Parmelee* v. *United States*, 1940, 72 App. D.C. 203, 113 F. 2d 729, 737). In other words, if out of some four hundred pages there were three or four pages which clearly are in the "obscene" category, they constitute merely a *de minimis* one per cent and hence the good overwhelms the bad. The very proposal of such a principle should suffice to demonstrate its impracticability as a test of whether the statute has been violated because obscenity could then parade abroad under the protective cloak of a quantity of innocuous pages.

Another Lawrence[3] is more pessimistic as to the effect of the trial court's decision in saying "So it does look as if the sky is the limit now on the sale and distribution through the mails of pornographic books and pictures." There would seem to be some justification for this prophecy judging by the recent book reviews and an apparent attempt to bring to light hitherto smuggled undercover poems of a well-known poet.

Unless those who really represent all communities and are best able to speak for their standards, namely, the legislative bodies, take some more definite action the courts will have to continue to struggle with the problem of some vague and ever-retreating boundary line. Certain it is that if the trend continues unabated, by the time some author writes of "Lady Chatterley's Granddaughter," Lady Chatterley herself will seem like a prim and puritanical housewife.

However, this case must be decided in accordance with contemporary judicial standards[4] and therefore I reluctantly concur.

---

[2] A point of view at least entitled to consideration appears in the book review pages of "America," pp. 416–417, June 6, 1959, by Harold C. Gardiner (Father Gardiner), under the title "Good Intentions Can't Justify Results." The reviewer differs with some of the majority's literary critics, saying: "For the book, despite the testimonials solicited from eminent literary figures, is simply not great literature, and that not merely because of the extremely frank passages which, it is charged, make the novel obscene. If the book did not carry the name of Lawrence, no one would bother too much about condemning or defending it." As to motive he adds, "It must be said at the same time, if we are to be fair, that Lawrence, as we know him through his letters, essays and personal life, was not a 'dirty-minded lecher,' as has been charged and will certainly now be repeated." He concedes "that Lawrence's attitudes toward sex were really the result of a fairly well-thought-out philosophy." And believes that "Had he lived in the days of pagan Rome, one feels, Lawrence would have defended the 'liturgical' character of some of the obscene religious rites, and he would have defended them with a religious fervor."

---

[3] David Lawrence, New York Herald Tribune, June 23, 1959.
[4] *Sunshine Book Co.* v. *Summerfield*, 1958, 355 U.S. 372, 78 S. Ct. 365, 2 L. Ed. 2d 352; *One, Inc.* v. *Olesen*, 1958, 355 U.S. 371, 78 S. Ct. 364, 2 L. Ed. 352; *Roth* v. *United States*, *supra*.

■ Excelsior Pictures Corp., a New York corporation, *Plaintiff*,

v.

City of Chicago, Illinois, a municipal corporation, Richard J. Daley and Timothy J. O'Connor, *Defendants*.
No. 59 C 1368.

United States District Court N. D. Illinois, E. D.

March 31, 1960.

Goldberg, Devoe, Shadur & Mikva, Chicago, Ill., for plaintiff.
John C. Melaniphy, Corporation Counsel, Chicago, Ill., for defendants.

MINER, District Judge.

The Complaint in this case was filed on August 24, 1959, by Excelsior Pictures Corporation, naming as defendants the City of Chicago, Mayor Richard J. Daley and Police Commissioner Tomothy J. O'Connor. The facts are not in dispute and a Stipulation of Facts has been filed by the parties setting forth certain of the facts which the parties agree are to be accepted as true for purposes of this proceeding. These facts are as follows:

"1. *Plaintiff has the exclusive right to distribute, to license for exhibition and to exhibit in the City of Chicago a certain photoplay or motion picture entitled 'Garden of Eden,' a print of which motion picture is attached to the*

Complaint filed herein, marked Exhibit A and made a part of said Complaint.

"2. *That pursuant to the provisions of a certain municipal ordinance enacted by the City of Chicago, being Sections 155-1 to 155-7 of the Municipal Code of Chicago, a copy of which ordinance is attached to the Complaint filed herein, marked Exhibit B and made a part of said Complaint, plaintiff, on May 15, 1959, applied to defendant O'Connor for a permit to exhibit the motion picture 'Garden of Eden.' Defendant O'Connor on May 28, 1959, through his duly authorized agent, notified plaintiff that he would not issue such a permit for the showing of said motion picture in the City of Chicago, on the ground that said motion picture was obscene. Pursuant to the municipal ordinance above referred to, plaintiff thereupon, on June 10, 1959, appealed the decision of defendant O'Connor to defendant Daley. On July 31, 1959, defendant Daley, through his duly authorized agent, denied the appeal of plaintiff from the order of defendant O'Connor and refused to issue to plaintiff a permit to exhibit the film 'Garden of Eden' in the City of Chicago upon the ground that said motion picture was obscene.*

"3. *As a result of the foregoing actions of the defendants in denying plaintiff a permit to exhibit said film and as a result of the requirements of the municipal ordinance above referred to that a permit must be obtained prior to the exhibition of any motion picture film in the City of Chicago, plaintiff is forbidden and prohibited from exhibiting said motion picture.*"

It is not disputed that the motion picture in issue has been viewed by audiences in numerous public theatres throughout the United States and in foreign lands. Up to the end of 1955, it had been viewed by approximately 1,600,000 persons in the United States, Alaska and Hawaiian Islands. Among the cities in the United States in which it has been so exhibited are San Francisco and Los Angeles, California; Washington, D.C.; and, by uncontroverted representation of counsel in open court, New York City, New York.

The Obscenity Issue

The Court has been first presented with the question of whether the film is immoral or obscene within the meaning of the provisions of Sections 155-1 through 155-7 of the Municipal Code of the City of Chicago. Section 155-4 sets forth the following criteria concerning the grounds for denial of a permit to exhibit a motion picture film:

"*If a picture or series of pictures, for the showing or exhibition of which an application for a permit is made, is immoral or obscene, or portrays depravity, criminality, or lack of virtue of a class of citizens of any race, color, creed, or religion and exposes them to contempt, derision, or obloquy, or tends to produce a breach of the peace or riots, or purports to represent any hanging, lynching or burning of a human being, it shall be the duty of the commissioner of police to refuse such permit; otherwise it shall be his duty to grant such permit.*"

[1] This provision of the Municipal Code of Chicago has been construed by the Supreme Court of Illinois in the case of *American Civil Liberties Union v. City of Chicago*, 1955, 3 Ill. 2d 334, 121 N.E. 2d 585. It is, of course, elementary that the construction placed upon a state statute or municipal ordinance by the highest Appellate Court of that state is binding upon the courts of the United States.

In the American Civil Liberties Union case, Mr. Justice Walter Schaefer, then Chief Justice, defined the word "obscene," as it is used in the ordinance, as follows (3 Ill. 2d at page 347, 121 N.E. 2d at page 592):

"[A] *motion picture is obscene within the meaning of the ordinance if, when considered as a whole, its calculated purpose or dominant effect is substantially to arouse sexual desires, and if the probability of this effect is so great as to outweigh whatever artistic or other merits the film may possess. In making this determination, the film must be tested with reference to its effect upon the normal, average person.*"

That opinion expressly characterized that term as being "no broader and no less definite than as used in the postal laws, under which 'prior restraint' has long been exercised through the exclusion of obscene matter from the mails" (Ibid.). Further, that decision characterizes the term "immoral" found in the ordinance as "little more than a synonym for 'obscene'" (Ibid., 3 Ill. 2d at page 348, 121 N.E. 2d at page 592).

This definition of the terms "obscene" and "immoral" is substantially identical with the definition by the United States Supreme Court in *Roth v. United States*, 1957, 354 U.S. 476, at page 487, 77 S. Ct. 1304, at page 1310, 1 L. Ed. 2d 1498, rehearing denied *Alberts v. State of Cal.*, 355 U.S. 852, 78 S. Ct. 8, 2 L. Ed. 2d 60, where Mr. Justice Brennan, for the majority, declared:

"*Obscene material is material which deals with sex in a manner appealing to prurient interest. The portrayal of sex, e.g., in art, literature and scientific works, is not itself sufficient reason to deny material the constitutional protection of freedom of speech and press. Sex, a great and mysterious motive force in human life, has indisputably been a subject of absorbing interest to mankind through the ages; it is one of the vital problems of human interest and public concern.*"

[2] In its function of determining the facts of this case as well as the law, the Court has viewed the film in its entirety and finds that the film does, as plaintiff contends, seek to portray nudism as a healthful and happy way of life. The picture does not expose the private parts of the adult characters. Considered as a whole, its "calculated purpose or dominant effect" is not substantially to arouse sexual desires in "the normal average person." It is not "immoral" or "obscene" within the meaning of the Chicago ordinance.

[3] The Court does not by its ruling purport to encourage the propagandization of nudism in this community. This is not the type of motion picture which the Court, in its personal capacity, would recommend the public to view. But it is not the Court's function to determine legal issues by applying as standards its personal

inclinations or its individual proclivities. The Court must apply the definitions which the Illinois Supreme Court has englossed upon the ordinance and which the United States Supreme Court has sustained in like cases.

[4, 5] The mere fact that nudism is not an accepted way of life among the vast majority of persons in the Chicago community, or, indeed, among Americans as a whole, cannot and has not been considered by the Court as controlling. In *Kingsley International Pictures Corp.* v. *Regents of University of State of New York*, 1959, 360 U.S. 684, 79 S. Ct. 1362, 1364, 3 L. Ed. 2d 1512, the Supreme Court of the United States upheld the exhibition of "Lady Chatterley's Lover," a motion picture which portrays adultery. It examined the constitutionality of that part of a New York statute[1] which that state's highest court had construed as authorizing the denial of a license to exhibit a motion picture "because its subject matter is adultery presented as being right and desirable for certain people under certain circumstances."[2] The Supreme Court there decided[3] that, insofar as the New York statute prohibited the issuance of a license to exhibit "Lady Chatterley's Lover" *on that ground*,[4] it was unconstitu-

tional. The "opinion of the Court"[5] declared (360 U.S. at page 688, 79 S. Ct. at page 1365):

"*It is contended that the State's action was justified because the motion picture attractively portrays a relationship which is contrary to the moral standards, the religious precepts, and the legal code of its citizenry. This argument misconceives what it is that the Constitution protects. Its guarantee is not confined to the expression of ideas that are conventional or shared by a majority. It protects advocacy of the opinion that adultery may sometimes be proper, no less than advocacy of socialism or the single tax. And in the realm of ideas it protects expression which is eloquent no less than that which is unconvincing.*" (*Emphasis supplied.*)

The freedoms guaranteed by the First and the Fourteenth Amendments to the United States Constitution are not wholly unconditional or absolute, and they may not be abused. However, they are not conditioned upon, and may not be construed to have been abused by, the presence or absence of majority endorsement of the views or ideas for the promulgation of which freedom is claimed or sanctions are sought.

[6] This Court further finds that nudity *per se* is not "immoral" or "obscene" within the meaning of the ordinance. There is hardly an art museum or gallery to which one can go where completely nude statutes and pictures are not on constant and prominent exhibition. Many popular books and magazines, far too numerous to list, frequently publish human nudity without offending the law. Certainly, if the advocacy, under certain circumstances, of adultery, which is contrary to moral standards and religious precepts, is protected by our Constitution, then the portrayal, by partial nudity, of nudism as a healthy and happy way of life should be accorded like protection.

[7] Nudism may be unappealing and unattractive to some people. It may be repulsive and vulgar to others. But that does not brand it as "obscene" or "immoral." Whether or not it appeals to or repels an individual's sensitivities is irrelevant when the Court is bound to apply definitions of "obscene" and "immoral" which do not incorporate such subjective standards. This is not to say, however, that nude statues, pictures and representations may not under certain circumstances and by different portrayals be characterized as "obscene."

It is the conclusion of this Court that, because the motion picture "Garden of Eden" may not be denied a license on the ground that it is "obscene" or "immoral" within the meaning of the Chicago ordinance, the denial of that license by the city authorities on that ground (1) constituted a denial of plaintiff's rights to freedom of speech and press guaranteed by the Fourteenth Amendment to the Constitution of the United States to advocate nudism as a healthful and happy way of life, and (2) represents the application of the said ordinance "to a

---

[1] McKinney's N.Y. Laws, 1953, Education Law, §§ 122, 122–a, which state in part that a license shall issue "unless such film or a part thereof is obscene, indecent, immoral, inhuman, sacrilegious, or is of such a character that its exhibition would tend to corrupt morals or incite to crime. * * *" (§ 122), and that "the term 'immoral' and the phrase 'of such a character that its exhibition would tend to corrupt morals' shall denote a motion picture film or part thereof, the dominant purpose or effect of which is erotic or pornographic; or which portrays acts of sexual immorality, perversion, or lewdness, or which expressly or impliedly presents such acts as desirable, acceptable or proper patterns of behavior" (§ 122–a).

The only part of the statute considered by the Supreme Court is that part of those sections which required denial of a license to motion pictures "which are immoral in that they portray 'acts of sexual immorality * * * as desirable, acceptable or proper patterns of behavior.'"

[2] 4 N.Y. 2d 349, 175 N.Y.S. 2d 39, 151 N.E. 2d 197.

[3] Mr. Justice Stewart delivered the "opinion of the Court"; Mr. Justice Black concurred in the "opinion of the Court" and in the "judgment" but added his opinion that "prior censorship of moving pictures like prior censorship of newspapers and books violates the First and Fourteenth Amendments"; Mr. Justice Frankfurter concurred in the "result" but not in the "opinion of the Court," because the New York court applied the statute "to a picture to which it cannot be applied without invading the area of constitutionally free expression"; Mr. Justice Douglas, with whom Mr. Justice Black joined, concurred in the "opinion of the Court" but added his opinion that "censorship of movies is unconstitutional, since it is a form of 'previous restraint'"; Mr. Justice Clark concurred in the "result" because of the "obscurity of the standard" in the New York statute, which standard its highest court had defined as "the portrayal of 'acts of sexual immorality * * * as desirable, acceptable or proper patterns of behavior,'" thus placing "more emphasis on what the film teaches than on what it depicts"; Mr. Justice Harlan, with whom Mr. Justice Frankfurter and Mr. Justice Whittaker joined, concurred in the "result" but not in the "opinion of the Court" "because I believe the New York statute was unconstitutionally applied in this instance."

[4] The "opinion of the Court" footnoted a statement in the brief of counsel for the Regents that "The full definition is not before this Court—only these parts of the definition as cited—and any debate as to whether other parts of the definition are a proper standard has no bearing in this case."

[5] The "opinion of the Court" is the opinion of (a) Mr. Justice Stewart, Mr. Justice Black and Mr. Justice Douglas, as indicated in fn. 3 above; and (b) Chief Justice Warren and Mr. Justice Brennan, there being no indication that they had no part in the proceedings and decision. Because of his stand, it could be argued that Mr. Justice Clark is an implicit subscriber to the "opinion of the Court."

picture to which it cannot be applied without invading the area of constitutionally free expression."[6]

At the Court's suggestion, plaintiff has agreed to limit

---

[6] Mr. JUSTICE FRANKFURTER, concurring in *Kingsley International Pictures Corp.* v. *Regents of University of State of New York*, 1959, 360 U.S. 684, at page 695, 79 S. Ct. 1362, at page 1369, 3 L. Ed. 2d 1512.

and restrict the exhibition of the picture to adults only, and not to publicize such exhibition in any manner or form as being authorized by the Court, and it is so ordered.

This memorandum shall stand as the Court's Findings of Fact and Conclusions of Law. Counsel for plaintiff will prepare and submit to the Court a form of Order directing defendants to issue the license.

■ Times Film Corp.
v.
City of Chicago *et al.*

CERTIORARI TO THE UNITED STATES COURT OF APPEALS FOR THE SEVENTH CIRCUIT.

No. 34. Argued October 19–20, 1960.—Decided January 23, 1961.

Felix J. Bilgrey and *Abner J. Mikva* argued the cause and filed a brief for petitioner.

Robert J. Collins and *Sydney R. Drebin* argued the cause for respondents. With them on the brief was *John C. Melaniphy.*

MR. JUSTICE CLARK delivered the opinion of the Court.

Petitioner challenges on constitutional grounds the validity on its face of that portion of § 155–4[1] of the Municipal Code of the City of Chicago which requires submission of all motion pictures for examination prior to their public exhibition. Petitioner is a New York corporation owning the exclusive right to publicly exhibit in Chicago the film known as "Don Juan." It applied for a permit, as Chicago's ordinance required, and tendered the license fee but refused to submit the film for examination. The appropriate city official refused to issue the permit and his order was made final on appeal to the Mayor. The sole ground for denial was petitioner's refusal to submit the film for examination as required. Petitioner then brought this suit seeking injunctive relief ordering the issuance of the permit without submission of the film and restraining the city officials from interfering with the exhibition of the picture. Its sole ground is that the provision of the ordinance requiring submission of the film constitutes, on its face, a prior restraint within the prohibition of the First and Fourteenth Amendments. The District Court dismissed the complaint on the grounds, *inter alia*, that neither a substantial federal question nor even a justiciable controversy was presented. 180 F. Supp. 843. The Court of Appeals affirmed, finding that the case presented merely an abstract question of law since neither the film nor evidence of its content was submitted. 272 F. 2d 90. The

---

[1] The portion of the section here under attack is as follows:

"Such permit shall be granted only after the motion picture film for which said permit is requested has been produced at the office of the commissioner of police for examination or censorship. . . ."

precise question at issue here never having been specifically decided by this Court, we granted certiorari, 362 U.S. 917 (1960).

We are satisfied that a justiciable controversy exists. The section of Chicago's ordinance in controversy specifically provides that a permit for the public exhibition of a motion picture must be obtained; that such "permit shall be granted only after the motion picture film for which said permit is requested has been produced at the office of the commissioner of police for examination"; that the commissioner shall refuse the permit if the picture does not meet certain standards;[2] and that in the event of such refusal the applicant may appeal to the mayor for a *de novo* hearing and his action shall be final. Violation of the ordinance carries certain punishments. The petitioner complied with the requirements of the ordinance, save for the production of the film for examination. The claim is

---

[2] That portion of 155–4 of the Code providing standards is as follows:

"If a picture or series of pictures, for the showing or exhibition of which an application for a permit is made, is immoral or obscene, or portrays depravity, criminality, or lack of virtue of a class of citizens of any race, color, creed, or religion and exposes them to contempt, derision, or obloquy, or tends to produce a breach of the peace or riots, or purports to represent any hanging, lynching, or burning of a human being, it shall be the duty of the commissioner of police to refuse such permit; otherwise it shall be his duty to grant such permit.

"In case the commissioner of police shall refuse to grant a permit as hereinbefore provided, the applicant for the same may appeal to the mayor. Such appeal shall be presented in the same manner as the original application to the commissioner of police. The action of the mayor on any application for a permit shall be final."

It should be noted that the Supreme Court of Illinois, in an opinion by Schaefer, C.J., has already considered and rejected an argument against the same Chicago ordinance, similar to the claim advanced here by petitioner. The same court also sustained certain of the standards set out above. *American Civil Liberties Union* v. *City of Chicago*, 3 Ill. 2d 334, 121 N.E. 2d 585 (1954).

that this concrete and specific statutory requirement, the production of the film at the office of the Commissioner for examination, is invalid as a previous restraint on freedom of speech. In *Joseph Burstyn, Inc.* v. *Wilson,* 343 U.S. 495, 502 (1952), we held that motion pictures are included "within the free speech and free press guaranty of the First and Fourteenth Amendments." Admittedly, the challenged section of the ordinance imposes a previous restraint, and the broad justiciable issue is therefore present as to whether the ambit of constitutional protection includes complete and absolute freedom to exhibit, at least once, any and every kind of motion picture. It is that question alone which we decide. We have concluded that § 155–4 of Chicago's ordinance requiring the submission of films prior to their public exhibition is not, on the grounds set forth, void on its face.

Petitioner's narrow attack upon the ordinance does not require that any consideration be given to the validity of the standards set out therein. They are not challenged and are not before us. Prior motion picture censorship cases which reached this Court involved questions of standards.[3] The films had all been submitted to the authorities and permits for their exhibition were refused because of their content. Obviously, whether a particular statute is "clearly drawn," or "vague," or "indefinite," or whether a clear standard is in fact met by a film are different questions involving other constitutional challenges to be tested by considerations not here involved.

Moreover, there is not a word in the record as to the nature and content of "Don Juan." We are left entirely in the dark in this regard, as were the city officials and the other reviewing courts. Petitioner claims that the nature of the film is irrelevant, and that even if this film contains the basest type of pornography, or incitement to riot, or forceful overthrow of orderly government, it may nonetheless be shown without prior submission for examination. The challenge here is to the censor's basic authority; it does not go to any statutory standards employed by the censor or procedural requirements as to the submission of the film.

In this perspective we consider the prior decisions of this Court touching on the problem. Beginning over a third of a century ago in *Gitlow* v. *New York,* 268 U.S. 652 (1925), they have consistently reserved for future decision possible situations in which the claimed First Amendment privilege might have to give way to the necessities of the public welfare. It has never been held that liberty of speech is absolute. Nor has it been suggested that all previous restraints on speech are invalid. On the contrary, in *Near* v. *Minnesota,* 283 U.S. 697, 715–716 (1931), Chief Justice Hughes, in discussing the classic legal statements concerning the immunity of the press from censorship, observed that the principle forbidding previous restraint "is stated too broadly, if every such restraint is deemed to be prohibited. . . . [T]he protection even as to previous restraint is not absolutely unlimited. But the limitation has been recognized only in exceptional cases." These included, the Chief Justice found, utterances creating "a

hindrance" to the Government's war effort, and "actual obstruction to its recruiting service or the publication of the sailing dates of transports or the number and location of troops." In addition, the Court said that "the primary requirements of decency may be enforced against obscene publications" and the "security of the community life may be protected against incitements to acts of violence and the overthrow by force of orderly government." Some years later, a unanimous Court, speaking through Mr. Justice Murphy, in *Chaplinsky* v. *New Hampshire,* 315 U.S. 568, 571–572 (1942), held that there were "certain well-defined and narrowly limited classes of speech, the prevention and punishment of which have never been thought to raise any Constitutional problem. These include the lewd and obscene, the profane, the libelous, and the insulting or 'fighting' words—those which by their very utterance inflict injury or tend to incite an immediate breach of the peace." Thereafter, as we have mentioned, in *Joseph Burstyn, Inc.* v. *Wilson, supra,* we found motion pictures to be within the guarantees of the First and Fourteenth Amendments, but we added that this was "not the end of our problem. It does not follow that the Constitution requires absolute freedom to exhibit every motion picture of every kind at all times and all places." At p. 502. Five years later, in *Roth* v. *United States,* 354 U.S. 476, 483 (1957), we held that "in light of . . . history, it is apparent that the unconditional phrasing of the First Amendment was not intended to protect every utterance." Even those in dissent there found that "Freedom of expression can be suppressed if, and to the extent that, it is so closely brigaded with illegal action as to be an inseparable part of it." *Id.,* at 514. And, during the same Term, in *Kingsley Books, Inc.* v. *Brown,* 354 U.S. 436, 441 (1957), after characterizing *Near* v. *Minnesota, supra,* as "one of the landmark opinions" in its area, we took notice that *Near* "left no doubts that 'Liberty of speech, and of the press, is also not an absolute right . . . the protection even as to previous restraint is not absolutely unlimited.' . . . The judicial angle of vision," we said there, "in testing the validity of a statute like § 22–a [New York's injunctive remedy against certain forms of obscenity] is 'the operation and effect of the statute in substance.' " And as if to emphasize the point involved here, we added that "The phrase 'prior restraint' is not a self-wielding sword. Nor can it serve as a talismanic test." Even as recently as our last Term we again observed the principle, albeit in an allied area, that the State possesses some measure of power "to prevent the distribution of obscene matter." *Smith* v. *California,* 361 U.S. 147, 155 (1959).

Petitioner would have us hold that the public exhibition of motion pictures must be allowed under any circumstances. The State's sole remedy, it says, is the invocation of criminal process under the Illinois pornography statute, Ill. Rev. Stat. (1959), c. 38, § 470, and then only after a transgression. But this position, as we have seen, is founded upon the claim of absolute privilege against prior restraint under the First Amendment—a claim without sanction in our cases. To illustrate its fallacy, we need only point to one of the "exceptional cases" which Chief Justice Hughes enumerated in *Near* v. *Minnesota, supra,* namely, "the primary requirements of decency [that] may be enforced against obscene publications." Moreover, we later held specifically "that obscenity is not within the area of constitutionally protected speech or press." *Roth* v. *United*

---

[3] *Joseph Burstyn, Inc.* v. *Wilson, supra* ("sacrilegious"); *Gelling* v. *Texas,* 343 U.S. 960 (1952) ("prejudicial to the best interests of the people of said City"); *Commercial Pictures Corp.* v. *Regents,* 346 U.S. 587 (1954) ("immoral"); *Superior Films, Inc.* v. *Department of Education,* 346 U.S. 587 (1954) ("harmful"); *Kingsley International Pictures Corp.* v. *Regents,* 360 U.S. 684 (1959) ("sexual immorality").

States, 354 U.S. 476, 485 (1957). Chicago emphasizes here its duty to protect its people against the dangers of obscenity in the public exhibition of motion pictures. To this argument petitioner's only answer is that regardless of the capacity for, or extent of, such an evil, previous restraint cannot be justified. With this we cannot agree. We recognized in *Burstyn, supra*, that "capacity for evil . . . may be relevant in determining the permissible scope of community control," at p. 502, and *that motion pictures were not "necessarily subject to the precise rules governing any other particular method of expression. Each method," we said, "tends to present its own peculiar problems."* [Italics ed.]. At p. 503. Certainly petitioner's broadside attack does not warrant, nor could it justify on the record here, our saying that—aside from any consideration of the other "exceptional cases" mentioned in our decisions—the State is stripped of all constitutional power to prevent, in the most effective fashion, the utterance of this class of speech. It is not for this Court to limit the State in its selection of the remedy it deems most effective to cope with such a problem, absent, of course, a showing of unreasonable strictures on individual liberty resulting from its application in particular circumstances. *Kingsley Books, Inc. v. Brown, supra*, at p. 441. We, of course, are not holding that city officials may be granted the power to prevent the showing of any motion picture they deem unworthy of a license. *Joseph Burstyn, Inc. v. Wilson, supra*, at 504–505.

As to what may be decided when a concrete case involving a specific standard provided by this ordinance is presented, we intimate no opinion. The petitioner has not challenged all—or for that matter any—of the ordinance's standards. Naturally we could not say that every one of the standards, including those which Illinois' highest court has found sufficient, is so vague on its face that the entire ordinance is void. At this time we say no more than this—*that we are dealing only with motion pictures and, even as to them, only in the context of the broadside attack presented on this record.* [Italics ed.].

Affirmed.

MR. CHIEF JUSTICE WARREN, with whom MR. JUSTICE BLACK, MR. JUSTICE DOUGLAS and MR. JUSTICE BRENNAN join, dissenting.

I cannot agree either with the conclusion reached by the Court or with the reasons advanced for its support. To me, this case clearly presents the question of our approval of unlimited censorship of motion pictures before exhibition through a system of administrative licensing. Moreover, the decision presents a real danger of eventual censorship for every form of communication, be it newspapers, journals, books, magazines, television, radio or public speeches. The Court purports to leave these questions for another day, but *I am aware of no constitutional principle which permits us to hold that the communication of ideas through one medium may be censored while other media are immune.* [Italics ed.]. Of course each medium presents its own peculiar problems, but they are not of the kind which would authorize the censorship of one form of communication and not others. I submit that in arriving at its decision the Court has interpreted our cases contrary to the intention at the time of their rendition and, in exalting

the censor of motion pictures, has endangered the First and Fourteenth Amendment rights of all others engaged in the dissemination of ideas.

Near v. *Minnesota*, 283 U.S. 697, was a landmark opinion in this area. It was there that Chief Justice Hughes said for the Court "that liberty of the press, historically considered and taken up by the Federal Constitution, has meant, principally although not exclusively, immunity from previous restraints or censorship." *Id.*, at 716. The dissenters in *Near* sought to uphold the Minnesota statute, struck down by the Court, on the ground that the statute did "not authorize administrative control in advance such as was formerly exercised by the licensers and censors. . . ." *Id.*, at 735. Thus, three decades ago, the Constitution's abhorrence of licensing or censorship was first clearly articulated by this Court.

This was not a tenet seldom considered or soon forgotten. Five years later, a unanimous Court observed:

"*As early as 1644, John Milton, in an 'Appeal for the Liberty of Unlicensed Printing,' assailed an act of Parliament which had just been passed providing for censorship of the press previous to publication. He vigorously defended the right of every man to make public his honest views 'without previous censure'; and declared the impossibility of finding any man base enough to accept the office of censor and at the same time good enough to be allowed to perform its duties.*" Grosjean v. American Press Co., 297 U.S. 233, 245–246.

Shortly thereafter, a unanimous Court once more recalled that the "struggle for the freedom of the press was primarily directed against the power of the licensor." *Lovell* v. *Griffin*, 303 U.S. 444, 451. And two years after this, the Court firmly announced in *Schneider* v. *State*, 308 U.S. 147:

"*[T]he ordinance imposes censorship, abuse of which engendered the struggle in England which eventuated in the establishment of the doctrine of the freedom of the press embodied in our Constitution. To require a censorship through license which makes impossible the free and unhampered distribution of pamphlets strikes at the very heart of the constitutional guarantees.*" *Id.*, at 164

Just twenty years ago, in the oft-cited case of *Cantwell* v. *Connecticut*, 310 U.S. 296, the Court, again without dissent, decided:

"*[T]he availability of a judicial remedy for abuses in the system of licensing still leaves that system one of previous restraint which, in the field of free speech and press, we have held inadmissible. A statute authorizing previous restraint upon the exercise of the guaranteed freedom by judicial decision after trial is as obnoxious to the Constitution as one providing for like restraint by administrative action.*" [Italics ed.]. *Id.*, at 306.

This doctrine, which was fully explored and which was the focus of this Court's attention on numerous occasions, had become an established principle of constitutional law. It is not to be disputed that this Court has stated that the protection afforded First Amendment liberties from previous restraint is not absolutely unlimited. *Near* v. *Minne-*

sota, supra. But, licensing or censorship was not, at any point, considered within the "exceptional cases" discussed in the opinion in *Near. Id.,* at 715–716. And, only a few Terms ago, the Court, speaking through MR. JUSTICE FRANKFURTER, in *Kingsley Books, Inc.* v. *Brown,* 354 U.S. 436, reaffirmed that "the limitation is the exception; it is to be closely confined so as to preclude what may fairly be deemed *licensing* or *censorship.*" *Id.,* at 441. (Emphasis added.)

The vice of censorship through licensing and, more generally, the particular evil of previous restraint on the right of free speech have many times been recognized when this Court has carefully distinguished between laws establishing sundry systems of previous restraint on the right of free speech and penal laws imposing subsequent punishment on utterances and activities not within the ambit of the First Amendment's protection. See *Near* v. *Minnesota, supra,* at pp. 718–719; *Schneider* v. *State, supra,* at p. 164; *Cantwell* v. *Connecticut, supra,* at p. 306; *Niemotko* v. *Maryland,* 340 U.S. 268, 282 (concurring opinion); *Kunz* v. *New York,* 340 U.S. 290, 294–295.

Examination of the background and circumstances leading to the adoption of the First Amendment reveals the basis for the Court's steadfast observance of the proscription of licensing, censorship and previous restraint of speech. Such inquiry often begins with Blackstone's assertion: "The liberty of the press is indeed essential to the nature of a free state; but this consists in laying no previous restraint upon publications, and not in freedom from censure for criminal matter when published." 4 Bl. Comm. (Cooley, 4th ed. 1899) 151. Blackstone probably here referred to the common law's definition of freedom of the press;[1] he probably spoke of the situation existing in England after the disappearance of the licensing systems but during the existence of the law of crown libels. There has been general criticism of the theory that Blackstone's statement was embodied in the First Amendment, the objection being " 'that the mere exemption from previous restraints cannot be all that is secured by the constitutional provisions'; and that 'the liberty of the press might be rendered a mockery and a delusion, and the phrase itself a by-word, if, while every man was at liberty to publish what he pleased, the public authorities might nevertheless punish him for harmless publications.' 2 Cooley, Const. Lim., 8th ed., p. 885." *Near* v. *Minnesota, supra,* at p. 715; *Grosjean* v. *American Press Co., supra,* at p. 248. The objection has been that Blackstone's definition is too narrow; it had been generally conceded that the protection of the First Amendment extends *at least* to the interdiction of licensing and censorship and to the previous restraint of free speech. *Near* v. *Minnesota, supra,* at p. 715; *Grosjean* v. *American Press Co., supra,* at p. 246; Chafee, Free Speech in the United States, 18.

On June 24, 1957, in *Kingsley Books, Inc.* v. *Brown, supra,* the Court turned a corner from the landmark

opinion in *Near* and from one of the bases of the First Amendment. Today it falls into full retreat.

I hesitate to disagree with the Court's formulation of the issue before us, but, with all deference, I must insist that the question presented in this case is *not* whether a motion picture exhibitor has a constitutionally protected, "complete and absolute freedom to exhibit, at least once, any and every kind of motion picture." *Ante,* p. 46. Surely, the Court is not bound by the petitioner's conception of the issue or by the more extreme positions that petitioner may have argued at one time in the case. The question here presented is whether the City of Chicago—or, for that matter, any city, any State or the Federal Government—may require all motion picture exhibitors to submit all films to a police chief, mayor or other administrative official, for licensing and censorship prior to public exhibition within the jurisdiction.

The Court does not even have before it an attempt by the city to restrain the exhibition of an allegedly "obscene" film, see *Roth* v. *United States,* 354 U.S. 476. Nor does the city contend that it is seeking to prohibit the showing of a film which will impair the "security of the community life" because it acts as an incitement to "violence and the overthrow by force of orderly government." See *Near* v. *Minnesota, supra,* at p. 716. *The problem before us is not whether the city may forbid the exhibition of a motion picture, which, by its very showing, might in some way "inflict injury or tend to incite an immediate breach of the peace."* [Italics ed.]. See *Chaplinsky* v. *New Hampshire,* 315 U.S. 568, 572.

Let it be completely clear what the Court's decision does. It gives official license to the censor, approving a grant of power to city officials to prevent the showing of any moving picture these officials deem unworthy of a license. It thus gives formal sanction to censorship in its purest and most far-reaching form,[2] to a classical plan of licensing that, in our country, most closely approaches the English licensing laws of the seventeenth century which were commonly used to suppress dissent in the mother country and in the colonies. Emerson, The Doctrine of Prior Restraint, 20 Law & Contemp. Prob., 648, 667. The Court treats motion pictures, food for the mind, held to be within the shield of the First Amendment, *Joseph Burstyn, Inc.* v. *Wilson,* 343 U.S. 495, little differently than it would treat edibles. See *Smith* v. *California,* 361 U.S. 147, 152.[3] Only a few days ago, the Court, speaking through

---

[1] The following charge to the grand jury by Chief Justice Hutchinson of Massachusetts in 1767 defines the common-law notion of freedom of the press:

"The Liberty of the Press is doubtless a very great Blessing; but this Liberty means no more than a Freedom for every Thing to pass from the Press without a License." Quincy, Reports of Cases Argued and Adjudged in the Superior Court of Judicature of the Province of Massachusetts Bay, Between 1761 and 1772, 244.

[2] Professor Thomas I. Emerson has stated:

"There is, at present, no common understanding as to what constitutes 'prior restraint.' The term is used loosely to embrace a variety of different situations. Upon analysis, certain broad categories seem to be discernible:

"The clearest form of prior restraint arises in those situations where the government limitation, expressed in statute, regulation, or otherwise, undertakes to prevent future publication or other communication without advance approval of an executive official." Emerson, The Doctrine of Prior Restraint, 20 Law & Contemp. Prob., 648, 655.

See also *Brattle Films, Inc.* v. *Commissioner of Public Safety,* 333 Mass. 58, 127 N.E. 2d 891.

[3] In *Smith,* we pointed out that although a "strict liability penal ordinance" which does not require scienter may be valid when applied to the distributors of food or drugs, it is invalid when applied to booksellers, distributors of ideas. *Id.,* at 152–153.

Mr. Justice Stewart, noted in *Shelton* v. *Tucker*, 364 U.S. 479, 488:

"*In a series of decisions this Court has held that, even though the governmental purpose be legitimate and substantial, that purpose cannot be pursued by means that broadly stifle fundamental personal liberties when the end can be more narrowly achieved. The breadth of legislative abridgment must be viewed in the light of less drastic means for achieving the same basic purpose.*"

Here, the Court ignores this considered principle and indiscriminately casts the net of control too broadly. See *Niemotko* v. *Maryland, supra*, at p. 282 (concurring opinion). By its decision, the Court gives its assent to unlimited censorship of moving pictures through a licensing system, despite the fact that Chicago has chosen this most objectionable course to attain its goals without any apparent attempt to devise other means so as not to intrude on the constitutionally protected liberties of speech and press.

Perhaps the most striking demonstration of how far the Court departs from its holdings in *Near* and subsequent cases may be made by examining the various schemes that it has previously determined to be violative of the First and Fourteenth Amendments' guaranty.

A remarkable parallel to the censorship plan now before the Court, although one less offensive to the First Amendment, is found in the *Near* case itself. The Minnesota statute there under attack did not require that *all* publications be approved before distribution. That statute only provided that a person may be enjoined by a court from publishing a newspaper which was "malicious, scandalous and defamatory." *Id.*, at 702. The injunction in that case was issued only after Near had allegedly published nine such newspapers. The statute permitted issuance of an injunction only on proof that, within the prior three months, such an offensive newspaper had already been published. Near was not prevented "from operating a newspaper in harmony with the public welfare." *Ibid.* If the state court found that Near's subsequent publication conformed to this standard, Near would not have been held in contempt. But, the Court there found that this system of censorship by a state court, used only after it had already been determined that the publisher had previously violated the standard, had to fall before the First and the Fourteenth Amendments. It would seem that, *a fortiori*, the present system must also fall.

The case of *Grosjean* v. *American Press Co., supra*, provides another forceful illustration. The Court held there that a license tax of two percent on the gross receipts from advertising of newspapers and periodicals having a circulation of over 20,000 a week was a form of prior restraint and therefore invalid. Certainly this would seem much less an infringement on the liberties of speech and press protected by the First and Fourteenth Amendments than the classic system of censorship we now have before us. It was held, in *Grosjean*, that the imposition of the tax would curtail the amount of revenue realized from advertising and therefore operate as a restraint on publication. The license tax in *Grosjean* is analogous to the license fee in the case at bar, a fee to which petitioner raises no objection. It was also held, in *Grosjean*, that the tax had a "direct *tendency* . . . to restrict circulation," *id.*, at 244–245 (emphasis added), because it was imposed only on publi-

cations with a weekly circulation of 20,000 or more; that "if it were increased to a high degree . . . it *might well result* in destroying both advertising and circulation." *Id.*, at 245. (Emphasis added.) These were the evils calling for reversal in *Grosjean*. I should think that these evils are of minor import in comparison to the evils consequent to the licensing system which the Court here approves.

In *Hague* v. *C.I.O.*, 307 U.S. 496, a city ordinance required that a permit be obtained for public parades or public assembly. The permit could "only be refused for the purpose of preventing riots, disturbances or disorderly assemblage." *Id.*, at 502. Mr. Justice Roberts' opinion said of the ordinance:

"*It enables the Director of Safety to refuse a permit on his mere opinion that such refusal will prevent 'riots, disturbances or disorderly assemblage.' It can thus, as the record discloses, be made the instrument of arbitrary suppression of free expression of views on national affairs, for the prohibition of all speaking will undoubtedly 'prevent' such eventualities.*" Id., at 516.

May anything less be said of Chicago's movie censorship plan?

The question before the Court in *Schneider* v. *State, supra*, concerned the constitutional validity of a town ordinance requiring a license for the distribution of circulars. The police chief was permitted to refuse the license if the application for it or further investigation showed "that the canvasser is not of good character or is canvassing for a project not free from fraud. . . ." *Id.*, at 158. The Court said of that ordinance:

"*It bans unlicensed communication of any views or the advocacy of any cause from door to door, and permits canvassing only subject to the power of a police officer to determine, as a censor, what literature may be distributed from house to house and who may distribute it. The applicant must submit to that officer's judgment evidence as to his good character and as to the absence of fraud in the 'project' he proposes to promote or the literature he intends to distribute, and must undergo a burdensome and inquisitorial examination, including photographing and fingerprinting. In the end, his liberty to communicate with the residents of the town at their homes depends upon the exercise of the officer's discretion.*" Id., at 163–164.

I believe that the licensing plan at bar is fatally defective because of this precise objection.

A study of the opinion in *Cantwell* v. *Connecticut, supra*, further reveals the Court's sharp divergence today from seriously deliberated precedent. The statute in *Cantwell* forbade solicitation for any alleged religious, charitable or philanthropic cause unless the secretary of the public welfare council determined that the "cause [was] a religious one or [was] a bona fide object of charity or philanthropy and conform[ed] to reasonable standards of efficiency and integrity. . . ." *Id.*, at 302. Speaking of the secretary of the public welfare council, the Court held:

"*If he finds that the cause is not that of religion, to solicit for it becomes a crime. He is not to issue a certificate as a matter of course. His decision to issue or refuse it involves appraisal of facts, the exercise of judgment, and the formation of an opinion. He is authorized to withhold his approval if he determines that the cause is not a religious one. Such a censorship of religion as the means of determining its right to survive is a denial of liberty protected by the First Amendment and included in the liberty which is within the protection of the Fourteenth." Id., at 305.*

Does the Court today wish to distinguish between the protection accorded to religion by the First and Fourteenth Amendments and the protection accorded to speech by those same provisions? I cannot perceive the distinction between this case and *Cantwell*. Chicago says that it faces a problem—obscene and incendious films. Connecticut faced the problem of fraudulent solicitation. Constitutionally, is there a difference? See also *Largent* v. *Texas*, 318 U.S. 418.

In *Thomas* v. *Collins*, 323 U.S. 516, this Court held that a state statute requiring a labor union organizer to obtain an organizer's card was incompatible with the free speech and free assembly mandates of the First and Fourteenth Amendments. The statute demanded nothing more than that the labor union organizer register, stating his name, his union affiliations and describing his credentials. This information having been filed, the issuance of the organizer's card was subject to no further conditions. The State's obvious interest in acquiring this pertinent information was felt not to constitute an exceptional circumstance to justify the restraint imposed by the statute. It seems clear to me that the Chicago ordinance in this case presents a greater danger of stifling speech.

The two sound truck cases are further poignant examples of what had been this Court's steadfast adherence to the opposition of previous restraints on First Amendment liberties. In *Saia* v. *New York*, 334 U.S. 558, it was held that a city ordinance which forbade the use of sound amplification devices in public places without the permission of the Chief of Police was unconstitutionally void on its face since it imposed a previous restraint on public speech. Two years later, the Court upheld a different city's ordinance making unlawful the use of "any instrument of any kind or character which emits therefrom loud and raucous noises and is attached to and upon any vehicle operated or standing upon . . . streets or public places. . . ." *Kovacs* v. *Cooper*, 336 U.S. 77, 78. One of the grounds by which the opinion of Mr. Justice Reed distinguished *Saia* was that the *Kovacs* ordinance imposed no previous restraint. *Id.*, at 82. Mr. Justice Jackson chose to differentiate sound trucks from the *"moving picture screen, the radio, the newspaper, the handbill . . . and the street corner orator. . . ." Id.*, at 97 (concurring opinion). (Emphasis added.) He further stated that "No violation of the Due Process Clause of the Fourteenth Amendment by reason of infringement of free speech arises unless such regulation or prohibition undertakes to censor the contents of the broadcasting." *Ibid.* Needless to repeat, this is the violation the Court sanctions today.

Another extremely similar, but again less objectionable, situation was brought to the Court in *Kunz* v. *New York*, 340 U.S. 290. There, a city ordinance proscribed the right of citizens to speak on religious matters in the city streets without an annual permit. Kunz had previously had his permit revoked because "he had ridiculed and denounced

other religious beliefs in his meetings." *Id.*, at 292.[4] Kunz was arrested for subsequently speaking in the city streets without a permit. The Court reversed Kunz' conviction holding:

"We have here, then, an ordinance which gives an administrative official discretionary power to control in advance the right of citizens to speak on religious matters on the streets of New York. As such, the ordinance is clearly invalid as a prior restraint on the exercise of First Amendment rights." Id., at 293.

The Chicago censorship and licensing plan is effectively no different. The only meaningful distinction between *Kunz* and the case at bar appears to be in the disposition of them by the Court.

The ordinance before us in *Staub* v. *City of Baxley*, 355 U.S. 313, made unlawful the solicitation, without a permit, of members for an organization which requires the payment of membership dues. The ordinance stated that "In passing upon such application the Mayor and Council shall consider the character of the applicant, the nature of the business of the organization for which members are desired to be solicited, and its effects upon the general welfare of citizens of the City of Baxley." *Id.*, at 315. Mr. Justice Whittaker, speaking for the Court, stated "that the ordinance is invalid on its face because it makes enjoyment of the constitutionally guaranteed freedom of speech contingent upon the will of the Mayor and Council of the City and thereby constitutes a prior restraint upon, and abridges, that freedom." *Id.*, at 321. In *Staub*, the ordinance required a permit for solicitation; in the case decided today, the ordinance requires a permit for the exhibition of movies. If this is a valid distinction, it has not been so revealed. In *Staub*, the permit was to be granted on the basis of certain indefinite standards; in the case decided today, nothing different may be said.

As the Court recalls, in *Joseph Burstyn, Inc.* v. *Wilson*, 343 U.S. 495, 502, it was held that motion pictures come "within the free speech and free press guaranty of the First and Fourteenth Amendments." Although the Court found it unnecessary to decide "whether a state may censor motion pictures under a clearly drawn statute designed and applied to prevent the showing of obscene films," *id.*, at 506, Mr. Justice Clark stated, in the Court's opinion, quite accurately:

"But the basic principles of freedom of speech and the press, like the First Amendment's command, do not vary. Those principles, as they have frequently been enunciated by this Court, make freedom of expression the rule. There is no justification in this case for making an exception to that rule.

"The statute involved here does not seek to punish, as a past offense, speech or writing falling within the permissible scope of subsequent punishment. On the contrary, New York requires that permission to communicate ideas be obtained in advance from state officials who judge the content of the words and picture sought to be communicated. This Court recognized many years ago that such a previous restraint is a form of infringement upon freedom of expression to be especially condemned. Near v. Minne-

---

[4] For the particularly provocative statements made by Kunz, see the dissent of Mr. Justice Jackson. *Id.*, at 296–297.

sota *ex rel.* Olson, 283 U.S. 697 (1931). *The Court there recounted the history which indicates that a major purpose of the First Amendment guaranty of a free press was to prevent prior restraints upon publication, although it was carefully pointed out that the liberty of the press is not limited to that protection. It was further stated that 'the protection even as to previous restraint is not absolutely unlimited. But the limitation has been recognized only in exceptional cases.' Id., at 716. In the light of the First Amendment's history and of the Near decision, the State has a heavy burden to demonstrate that the limitation challenged here presents such an exceptional case." Id., at 503–504.*

Here, once more, the Court recognized that the First Amendment's rejection of prior censorship through licensing and previous restraint is an inherent and basic principle of freedom of speech and the press. Now, the Court strays from that principle; it strikes down that tenet without requiring any demonstration that this is an "exceptional case," whatever that might be, and without any indication that Chicago has sustained the "heavy burden" which was supposed to have been placed upon it. Clearly, this is neither an exceptional case nor has Chicago sustained *any* burden.

Perhaps today's surrender was forecast by *Kingsley Books, Inc.* v. *Brown, supra.* But, that was obviously not this case, and accepting *arguendo* the correctness of that decision, I believe that it leads to a result contrary to that reached today. The statute in *Kingsley* authorized "the chief executive, or legal officer, of a municipality to invoke a 'limited injunctive remedy,' under closely defined procedural safeguards, against the sale and distribution of written and printed matter found after due trial [by a court] to be obscene. . . ." *Id.*, at 437. The Chicago scheme has no procedural safeguards; there is no trial of the issue before the blanket injunction against exhibition becomes effective. In *Kingsley,* the grounds for the restraint were that the written or printed matter was "obscene, lewd, lascivious, filthy, indecent, or disgusting . . . or immoral. . . ." *Id.*, at 438. The Chicago objective is to capture much more. The *Kingsley* statute required the existence of some cause to believe that the publication was obscene before the publication was put on trial. The Chicago ordinance requires no such showing.

The booklets enjoined from distribution in *Kingsley* were concededly obscene.[5] There is no indication that this is true of the moving picture here. This was treated as a particularly crucial distinction. Thus, the Court has suggested that, in times of national emergency, the Government might impose a prior restraint upon "the publication of the sailing dates of transports or the number and location of troops." *Near* v. *Minnesota, supra,* p. 716; cf. *Ex parte Milligan,* 71 U.S. 2. But, surely this is not to

suggest that the Government might require that all newspapers be submitted to a censor in order to assist it in preventing such information from reaching print. Yet in this case the Court gives its blessing to the censorship of all motion pictures in order to prevent the exhibition of those it feels to be constitutionally unprotected.

The statute in *Kingsley* specified that the person sought to be enjoined was to be entitled to a trial of the issues within one day after joinder and a decision was to be rendered by the court within two days of the conclusion of the trial. The Chicago plan makes no provision for prompt judicial determination. In *Kingsley,* the person enjoined had available the defense that the written or printed matter was not obscene if an attempt was made to punish him for disobedience of the injunction. The Chicago ordinance admits no defense in a prosecution for failure to procure a license other than that the motion picture was submitted to the censor and a license was obtained.

Finally, the Court in Kingsley *painstakingly attempted to establish that that statute, in its effective operation, was no more a previous restraint on, or interference with, the liberty of speech and press than a statute imposing criminal punishment for the publication of pornography. In each situation, it contended, the publication may have passed into the hands of the public.* [Italics ed.]. Of course, this argument is inadmissible in this case and the Court does not purport to advance it.

It would seem idle to suppose that the Court today is unaware of the evils of the censor's basic authority, of the mischief of the system against which so many great men have waged stubborn and often precarious warfare for centuries, see *Grosjean* v. *American Press Co., supra,* at p. 247, of the scheme that impedes all communication by hanging threateningly over creative thought.[6] But the Court dismisses all of this simply by opining that "the phrase 'prior restraint' is not a self-wielding sword. Nor can it serve as a talismanic test." *Ante,* p. 49. I must insist that "a pragmatic assessment of its operation," *Kingsley Books, Inc.* v. *Brown, supra,* at p. 442, lucidly portrays that the system that the Court sanctions today is inherently bad. One need not disagree with the Court that Chicago has chosen the most effective means of suppressing obscenity. Censorship has been so recognized for centuries. But, this is not to say that the Chicago plan, the old, abhorrent English system of censorship through licensing, is a permissible *form* of prohibiting unprotected speech. The inquiry, as stated by the Court but never resolved, is whether this form of prohibition results in "unreasonable strictures on individual liberty," *ante,* p. 50;[7] whether

---

5 Judge Stanley H. Fuld rightly observed:

"Whatever might be said of a scheme of advance censorship directed against all *possibly* obscene writings, the case before us concerns a regulatory measure of far narrower impact, of a kind neither entailing the grave dangers of general censorship nor productive of the abuses which gave rise to the constitutional guarantees. (Cf. Pound, Equitable Relief Against Defamation and Injuries to Personality, 29 Harv. L. Rev. 640, 650–51.)" *Brown* v. *Kingsley Books, Inc.,* 1 N.Y. 2d 177, 185, 134 N.E. 2d 461, 465.

6 Tolstoy once wrote:

"You would not believe how, from the very commencement of my activity, that horrible Censor question has tormented me! I wanted to write what I felt; but all the same time it occurred to me that what I wrote would not be permitted, and involuntarily I had to abandon the work. I abandoned, and went on abandoning, and meanwhile the years passed away." Quoted by Chafee, *supra,* at p. 241.

7 In *Smith* v. *California, supra,* we noted that "Our decisions furnish examples of legal devices and doctrines, in most applications consistent with the Constitution, which cannot be applied in settings where they have the collateral effect of inhibiting the freedom of expression, by making the individual the more reluctant to exercise it." *Id.*, at 150–151. See *Shelton* v. *Tucker, supra.* Forty-six of our States currently see fit to rely on traditional criminal punishment for the protection of their citizens.

licensing, as a prerequisite to exhibition, is barred by the First and Fourteenth Amendments.

A most distinguished antagonist of censorship, in "a plea for unlicensed printing," has said:

"If he [the censor] be of such worth as behoovs him, there cannot be a more tedious and unpleasing Journey-work, a greater loss of time levied upon his head, then to be made the perpetuall reader of unchosen books and pamphlets . . . we may easily forsee what kind of licensers we are to expect hereafter, either ignorant, imperious, and remisse, or basely pecuniary." Areopagitica, in the Complete Poetry and Selected Prose of John Milton (Modern Library College Ed. 1950), 677, at 700.

There is no sign that Milton's fear of the censor would be dispelled in twentieth century America. The censor is beholden to those who sponsored the creation of his office, to those who are most radically preoccupied with the suppression of communication. The censor's function is to restrict and to restrain; his decisions are insulated from the pressures that might be brought to bear by public sentiment if the public were given an opportunity to see that which the censor has curbed.

The censor performs free from all of the procedural safeguards afforded litigants in a court of law. See *Kingsley Books, Inc.* v. *Brown, supra,* at p. 437; cf. *Near* v. *Minnesota, supra,* at p. 713; *Cantwell* v. *Connecticut, supra,* at p. 306. The likelihood of a fair and impartial trial disappears when the censor is both prosecutor and judge. There is a complete absence of rules of evidence; the fact is that there is usually no evidence at all as the system at bar vividly illustrates.[8] How different from a judicial proceeding where a full case is presented by the litigants. The inexistence of a jury to determine contemporary community standards is a vital flaw.[9] See *Kingsley Books, Inc.* v. *Brown, supra,* at pp. 447–448 (dissenting opinion).

---

[8] Although the Chicago ordinance designates the Commissioner of Police as the censor, counsel for the city explained that the task is delegated to a group of people, often women. The procedure before Chicago's censor board was found to be as follows according to the testimony of the "commanding officer of the censor unit":

"Q. Am I to understand that the procedure is that only these six people are in the room, and perhaps you, at the time the film is shown?

"A. Yes.

"Q. Does the distributor ever get a chance to present his views on the picture?

"A. No, sir.

"Q. Are other people's views invited, such as drama critics or movie reviewers or writers or artists of some kind; or are they ever asked to comment on the film before the censor board makes its decision?

"A. No, sir.

"Q. In other words, it is these six people plus yourself in a relationship that we have not as yet defined who decide whether the picture conforms to the standards set up in the ordinance?

"A. Yes, sir." Transcript of Record, p. 51, *Times Film Corp.* v. *City of Chicago,* 244 F. 2d 432.

[9] Cf. Chafee, *supra:*

"A jury is none too well fitted to pass on the injurious nature of opinions, but at least it consists of twelve men who represent the general views and the common sense of the community and often appreciate the motives of the speaker or writer whose punishment is sought. A censor, on the contrary, is a single individual with a personalized and partisan point of view. His

A revelation of the extent to which censorship has recently been used in this country is indeed astonishing. The Chicago licensors have banned newsreel films of Chicago policemen shooting at labor pickets and have ordered the deletion of a scene depicting the birth of a buffalo in Walt Disney's *Vanishing Prairie.* Gavzer, Who Censors Our Movies? Chicago Magazine, Feb. 1956, pp. 35, 39. Before World War II, the Chicago censor denied licenses to a number of films portraying and criticizing life in Nazi Germany including the March of Time's *Inside Nazi Germany.* Editorials, Chicago Daily Times, Jan. 20, Nov. 18, 1938. Recently, Chicago refused to issue a permit for the exhibition of the motion picture *Anatomy of a Murder* based upon the best-selling novel of the same title, because it found the use of the words "rape" and "contraceptive" to be objectionable. *Columbia Pictures Corp.* v. *City of Chicago* (D.C.N.D. Ill.), 59 C. 1058 (1959) (unreported). The Chicago censor bureau excised a scene in *Street With No Name* in which a girl was slapped because this was thought to be a "too violent" episode. Life, Oct. 25, 1948, p. 60. *It Happened in Europe* was severely cut by the Ohio censors who deleted scenes of war orphans resorting to violence. The moral theme of the picture was that such children could even then be saved by love, affection and satisfaction of their basic needs for food. Levy, Case Against Film Censorship, Films in Review, Apr. 1950, p. 40 (published by National Board of Review of Motion Pictures, Inc.). The Memphis censors banned *The Southerner* which dealt with poverty among tenant farmers because "it reflects on the south." *Brewster's Millions,* an innocuous comedy of fifty years ago, was recently forbidden in Memphis because the radio and film character Rochester, a Negro, was deemed "too familiar." See Velie, You Can't See That Movie: Censorship in Action, Collier's, May 6, 1950, pp. 11, 66. Maryland censors restricted a Polish documentary film on the basis that it failed to present a true picture of modern Poland. Levy, Case Against Film Censorship, Films in Review, *supra,* p. 41. *No Way Out,* the story of a Negro doctor's struggle against race prejudice, was banned by the Chicago censor on the ground that "there's a possibility it could cause trouble." The principal objection to the film was that the conclusion showed no reconciliation between blacks and whites. The ban was lifted after a storm of protest and later deletion of a scene showing Negroes and whites arming for a gang fight. N.Y. Times, Aug. 24, 1950, p. 31, col. 3; Aug. 31, 1950, p. 20, col. 8. Memphis banned *Curley* because it contained scenes of white and Negro children in school together. Kupferman and O'Brien, Motion Picture Censorship—The Memphis Blues, 36 Cornell L.J. 273, 276–278. Atlanta barred *Lost Boundaries,* the story of a Negro physician and his family who "passed" for white, on the ground that the exhibition of said picture "will adversely affect the peace, morals and good order" in the city. N.Y. Times, Feb. 5, 1950, § 2, p. 5, col. 7. See generally Kupferman and O'Brien, *supra;* Note, 60 Yale L.J. 696 *et seq.;* Brief for American Civil

---

interest lies in perpetuating the power of the group which employs him, and any bitter criticism of the group smacks to him of incitement to bloody revolution." *Id.,* at 314.

"On the other hand, a mayor and a police commissioner are not ordinarily selected on the basis of wide reading and literary judgment. They have other duties, which require other qualities. They may lack the training of the permanent censor, and yet run the same risk of being arbitrary and bureaucratic." *Id.,* at 533.

Liberties Union as *amicus curiae*, pp. 14–15. *Witchcraft*, a study of superstition through the ages, was suppressed for years because it depicted the devil as a genial rake with amorous leanings, and because it was feared that certain historical scenes, portraying the excesses of religious fanatics, might offend religion. *Scarface*, thought by some as the best of the gangster films, was held up for months; then it was so badly mutilated that retakes costing a hundred thousand dollars were required to preserve continuity. The New York censors banned *Damaged Lives*, a film dealing with venereal disease, although it treated a difficult theme with dignity and had the sponsorship of the American Social Hygiene Society. The picture of Lenin's tomb bearing the inscription "Religion is the opiate of the people" was excised from *Potemkin*. From *Joan of Arc* the Maryland board eliminated Joan's exclamation as she stood at the stake: "Oh, God, why hast thou forsaken me?" and from *Idiot's Delight*, the sentence: "We, the workers of the world, will take care of that." *Professor Mamlock* was produced in Russia and portrayed the persecution of the Jews by Nazis. The Ohio censors condemned it as "harmful" and calculated to "stir up hatred and ill will and gain nothing." It was released only after substantial deletions were made. The police refused to permit its showing in Providence, Rhode Island, on the ground that it was communistic propaganda. *Millions of Us*, a strong union propaganda film, encountered trouble in a number of jurisdictions. *Spanish Earth*, a pro-Loyalist documentary picture, was banned by the board in Pennsylvania. Ernst and Lindey, The Censor Marches On, 96–97, 102–103, 108–111. During the year ending June 30, 1938, the New York board censored, in one way or another, over five percent of the moving pictures it reviewed. *Id.*, at 81. Charlie Chaplin's satire on Hitler, *The Great Dictator*, was banned in Chicago, apparently out of deference to its large German population. Chafee, *supra*, at p. 541. Ohio and Kansas banned newsreels considered pro labor. Kansas ordered a speech by Senator Wheeler opposing the bill for enlarging the Supreme Court to be cut from the *March of Time* as "partisan and biased." *Id.*, at 542. An early version of *Carmen* was condemned on several different grounds. The Ohio censor objected because cigarette-girls smoked cigarettes in public. The Pennsylvania censor disapproved the duration of a kiss. *Id.*, at 543. The New York censors forbade the discussion in films of pregnancy, venereal disease, eugenics, birth control, abortion, illegitimacy, prostitution, miscegenation and divorce. Ernst and Lindey, *supra*, at p. 83. A member of the Chicago censor board explained that she rejected a film because "it was immoral, corrupt, indecent, against my . . . religious principles." Transcript of Record, p. 172. *Times Film Corp.* v. *City of Chicago*, 244 F. 2d 432. A police sergeant attached to the censor board explained, "Coarse language or anything that would be derogatory to the government—propaganda" is ruled out of foreign films. "Nothing pink or red is allowed," he added. Chicago Daily News, Apr. 7, 1959, p. 3, cols. 7–8. The police sergeant in charge of the censor unit has said: "Children should be allowed to see any movie that plays in Chicago. If a picture is objectionable for a child, it is objectionable period." Chicago Tribune, May 24, 1959, p. 8, col. 3. And this is but a smattering produced from limited research. Perhaps the most powerful indictment of Chicago's licensing device is found in the fact that between the Court's decision in 1952 in *Joseph Burstyn, Inc.* v. *Wilson, supra*, and the filing of the

petition for certiorari in 1960 in the present case, not once have the state courts upheld the censor when the exhibitor elected to appeal. Brief of American Civil Liberties Union as *amicus curiae*, pp. 13–14.

This is the regimen to which the Court holds that all films must be submitted. It officially unleashes the censor and permits him to roam at will, limited only by an ordinance which contains some standards that, although concededly not before us in this case, are patently imprecise. The Chicago ordinance commands the censor to reject films that are "immoral," see *Commercial Pictures Corp.* v. *Regents*, 346 U.S. 587; *Kingsley International Pictures Corp.* v. *Regents*, 360 U.S. 684; or those that portray "depravity, criminality, or lack of virtue of a class of citizens of any race, color, creed, or religion and [expose] them to contempt, derision or obloquy, or [tend] to produce a breach of the peace or riots, or [purport] to represent any hanging, lynching, or burning of a human being." May it not be said that almost every censored motion picture that was cited above could also be rejected, under the ordinance, by the Chicago censors? It does not require an active imagination to conceive of the quantum of ideas that will surely be suppressed.

If the censor denies rights protected by the First and Fourteenth Amendments, the courts might be called upon to correct the abuse if the exhibitor decides to pursue judicial remedies. But, this is not a satisfactory answer as emphasized by this very case. The delays in adjudication may well result in irreparable damage, both to the litigants and to the public. Vindication by the courts of *The Miracle* was not had until five years after the Chicago censor refused to license it. And then the picture was never shown in Chicago. Brief for Petitioner, p. 17. The instant litigation has now consumed almost three years. This is the delay occasioned by the censor; this is the injury done to the free communication of ideas. This damage is not inflicted by the ordinary criminal penalties. The threat of these penalties, intelligently applied, will ordinarily be sufficient to deter the exhibition of obscenity. However, if the exhibitor believes that his film is constitutionally protected, he will show the film, and, if prosecuted under criminal statute, will have ready that defense. The perniciousness of a system of censorship is that the exhibitor's belief that his film is constitutionally protected is irrelevant. Once the censor has made his estimation that the film is "bad" and has refused to issue a permit, there is ordinarily no defense to a prosecution[10] for showing the film without a license.[11] Thus, the film is not shown, perhaps not for years and sometimes not ever. Simply a talismanic test or self-wielding sword? I think not.

Moreover, more likely than not, the exhibitor will not pursue judicial remedies. See *Schneider* v. *State, supra*, at p. 164; Ernst and Lindey, *supra*, at p. 80. His inclination

---

[10] That portion of the Chicago ordinance dealing with penalties is as follows:

"Any person exhibiting any pictures or series of pictures without a permit having been obtained therefor shall be fined not less than fifty dollars nor more than one hundred dollars for each offense. A separate and distinct offense shall be regarded as having been committed for each day's exhibition of each picture or series of pictures without a permit."

[11] Professor Paul A. Freund has affirmed that this situation "does indeed have a chilling effect (on freedom of communication) beyond that of a criminal statute." Freund, The Supreme Court and Civil Liberties, 4 Vand. L. Rev. 533, 539.

may well be simply to capitulate rather than initiate a lengthy and costly litigation.[12] In such case, the liberty of speech and press, and the public, which benefits from the shielding of that liberty, are, in effect, at the mercy of the censor's whim. This powerful tendency to restrict the free dissemination of ideas calls for reversal. See *Grosjean* v. *American Press Co.*, *supra*, at 245.

Freedom of speech and freedom of the press are further endangered by this "most effective" means for confinement of ideas. It is axiomatic that the stroke of the censor's pen or the cut of his scissors will be a less contemplated decision than will be the prosecutor's determination to prepare a criminal indictment. The standards of proof, the judicial safeguards afforded a criminal defendant and the consequences of bringing such charges will all provoke the mature deliberation of the prosecutor. None of these hinder the quick judgment of the censor, the speedy determination to suppress. Finally, the fear of the censor by the composer of ideas acts as a substantial deterrent to the creation of new thoughts. See Tolstoy's declaration, note 6, *supra*. This is especially true of motion pictures due to the large financial burden that must be assumed by their producers. The censor's sword pierces deeply into the heart of free expression.

It seems to me that the Court's opinion comes perilously close to holding that not only may motion pictures be censored but that a licensing scheme may also be applied to newspapers, books and periodicals, radio, television, public speeches, and every other medium of expression. The Court suggests that its decision today is limited to motion pictures by asserting that they are not "necessarily subject to the precise rules governing any other particular method of expression. Each method . . . tends to present its own peculiar problems." *Ante*, p. 49. But, this, I believe, is the invocation of a talismanic phrase. The Court, in no way, explains why moving pictures should be treated differently than any other form of expression, why moving pictures should be denied the protection against censorship—"a form of infringement upon freedom of expression to be *especially* condemned." *Joseph Burstyn, Inc.* v. *Wilson*, *supra*, at p. 503. (Emphasis added.) When pressed during oral argument, counsel for the city could make no meaningful distinction between the censorship of newspapers and motion pictures. In fact, the percentage of motion pictures dealing with social and political issues is steadily rising.[13] The Chicago ordinance makes no exception for newsreels, documentaries, instructional and educational films or the like. All must undergo the censor's inquisition. Nor may it be suggested that motion pictures may be treated differently from newspapers because many movies are produced essentially for purposes of entertain-

ment. As the Court said in *Winters* v. *New York*, 333 U.S. 507, 510:

"We do not accede to appellee's suggestion that the constitutional protection for a free press applies only to the exposition of ideas. The line between the informing and the entertaining is too elusive for the protection of that basic right. Everyone is familiar with instances of propaganda through ficton. What is one man's amusement, teaches another's doctrine." See *Thomas* v. *Collins*, *supra*. at p. 531.[14]

The contention may be advanced that the impact of motion pictures is such that a licensing system of prior censorship is permissible. There are several answers to this, the first of which I think is the Constitution itself. Although it is an open question whether the impact of motion pictures is greater or less than that of other media, there is not much doubt that the exposure of television far exceeds that of the motion picture. See S. Rep. No. 1466, 84th Cong., 2d Sess. 5. But, even if the impact of the motion picture is greater than that of some other media, that fact constitutes no basis for the argument that motion pictures should be subject to greater suppression. This is the traditional argument made in the censor's behalf; this is the argument advanced against newspapers at the time of the invention of the printing press. The argument was ultimately rejected in England, and has consistently been held to be contrary to our Constitution. No compelling reason has been predicated for accepting the contention now.

It is true that "each method [of expression] tends to present its own peculiar problems." *Joseph Burstyn, Inc.* v. *Wilson*, *supra*, at p. 503. The Court has addressed itself on several occasions to these problems. In *Schneider* v. *State*, *supra*, at pp. 160–161, the Court stated, in reference to speaking in public, that "a person could not exercise this liberty by taking his stand in the middle of a crowded street, contrary to traffic regulations, and maintain his position to the stoppage of all traffic; a group of distributors could not insist upon a constitutional right to form a cordon across the street and to allow no pedestrian to pass who did not accept a tendered leaflet; nor does the guarantee of freedom of speech or of the press deprive a municipality of power to enact regulations against throwing literature broadcast in the streets." The Court recognized that sound trucks call for particularized consideration when it said in *Saia* v. *New York*, *supra*, at p. 562, "Noise can be regulated by regulating decibels. The hours and place of public discussion can be controlled. . . . Any abuses which loud-speakers create can be controlled by narrowly drawn statutes." But, the Court's decision today does not follow from this. Our prior decisions do not deal with the *content* of the speech; they deal only with the conditions surrounding its delivery. *These* conditions "tend to present the problems peculiar to each method of expression." Here the Court uses this magical phrase to cripple a basic principle of the Constitution.

---

[12] A particularly frightening illustration is found in the operation of a Detroit book censorship plan. One publisher simply submitted his unprinted manuscripts to the censor and deleted everything "objectionable" before publication. From 1950 to 1952, more than 100 titles of books were disapproved by the censor board. Every book banned was withheld from circulation. The censor board, in addition to finding books "objectionable," listed a group of books not suitable for criminal prosecution as "partially objectionable." Most booksellers were also afraid to handle these. Lockhart and McClure, Literature, The Law of Obscenity, and the Constitution, 38 Minn. L. Rev. 295, 314–316.

[13] See Note, 60 Yale L.J. 696, 706, n. 25.

[14] "The evils to be prevented were not the censorship of the press merely, but any action of the government by means of which it might prevent such free and general discussion of public matters as seems absolutely essential to prepare the people for an intelligent exercise of their rights as citizens." 2 Cooley, Const. Lim. (8th ed.), p. 886.

The Court, not the petitioner, makes the "broadside attack." I would reverse the decision below.

Mr. Justice Douglas, with whom The Chief Justice and Mr. Justice Black concur, dissenting.

My view that censorship of movies is unconstitutional because it is a prior restraint and violative of the First Amendment has been expressed on prior occasions. *Superior Films* v. *Department of Education*, 346 U.S. 587, 588–589 (concurring opinion); *Kingsley Pictures Corp.* v. *Regents*, 360 U.S. 684, 697 (concurring opinion).

While the problem of movie censorship is relatively new, the censorship device is an ancient one. It was recently stated, "There is a law of action and reaction in the decline and resurgence of censorship and control. Whenever liberty is in the ascendant, a social group will begin to resist it; and when the reverse is true, a similar resistance in favor of liberty will occur." Haney, Comstockery in America (1960), pp. 11–12.

Whether or not that statement of history is accurate, censorship has had many champions throughout time.

Socrates: "And shall we just carelessly allow children to hear any casual tales which may be devised by casual persons, and to receive into their minds ideas for the most part the very opposite of those which we should wish them to have when they are grown up?"

Glaucon: "We can not."

Socrates: "Then the first thing will be to establish a censorship of the writers of fiction, and let the censors receive any tale of fiction which is good, and reject the bad; and we will desire mothers and nurses to tell their children the authorized ones only. Let them fashion the mind with such tales, even more fondly than they mould the body with their hands; but most of those which are now in use must be discarded." Plato, Republic (The Dialogues of Plato, Jowett trans., Ox. Univ. Press, 1953) vol. 2, p. 221.

Hobbes was the censor's proponent:". . . it is annexed to the sovereignty, to be judge of what opinions and doctrines are averse, and what conducing to peace; and consequently, on what occasions, how far, and what men are to be trusted withal, in speaking to multitudes of people; and who shall examine the doctrines of all books before they be published. For the actions of men proceed from their opinions; and in the well-governing of opinions, consisteth the well-governing of men's actions, in order to their peace, and concord." Leviathan (Oakeshott ed. 1947), p. 116.

Regimes of censorship are common in the world today. Every dictator has one; every Communist regime finds it indispensable.[1] One shield against world opinion that colonial powers have used was the censor, as dramatized by France in North Africa. Even England has a vestige of censorship in the Lord Chamberlain (32 Halsbury's Laws of England (2d ed. 1939), p. 68) who presides over the stage—a system that in origin was concerned with the barbs of political satire.[2] But the concern with political

satire shifted to a concern with atheism and with sexual morality—the last being the concern evident in Chicago's system now before us.

The problems of the wayward mind concern the clerics, the psychiatrists, and the philosophers. Few groups have hesitated to create the political pressures that translate into secular law their notions of morality. Pfeffer, Creeds in Competition (1958), pp. 103–109. No more powerful weapon for sectarian control can be imagined than governmental censorship. Yet in this country the state is not the secular arm of any religious school of thought, as in some nations; nor is the church an instrument of the state. Whether—as here—city officials or—as in Russia—a political party lays claim to the power of governmental censorship, whether the pressures are for a conformist moral code or for a conformist political ideology, no such regime is permitted by the First Amendment.

The forces that build up demands for censorship are heterogeneous.

"The comstocks are not merely people with intellectual theories who might be convinced by more persuasive theories; nor are they pragmatists who will be guided by the balance of power among pressure groups. Many of them are so emotionally involved in the condemnation of what they find objectionable that they find rational arguments irrelevant. They must suppress what is offensive in order to stabilize their own tremulous values and consciences. Panic rules them, and they cannot be calmed by discussions of legal rights, literary integrity, or artistic merit." Haney, op. cit. supra, *pp.* 176–177.

Yet as long as the First Amendment survives, the censor, no matter how respectable his cause, cannot have the support of government. It is not for government to pick and choose according to the standards of any religious, political, or philosophical group. It is not permissible, as I read the Constitution, for government to release one movie and refuse to release another because of an official's concept of the prevailing need or the public good. The Court in *Near* v. *Minnesota*, 283 U.S. 697, 713, said that the "chief purpose" of the First Amendment's guarantee of freedom of press was "to prevent previous restraints upon publication."

A noted Jesuit has recently stated one reason against government censorship:

---

[1] "Nowhere have the Communists become simply a vote-getting party. They are organized around ideas and they care about ideas. They are the great heresy hunters of the modern world." Ways, Beyond Survival (1959), p. 199.

[2] Ivor Brown in a recent summary of the work of the Lord Chamberlain states: "The licensing of plays was imposed not to

protect the morals of the British public but to safeguard the reputation of politicians. This happened in 1737 when the Prime Minister, Sir Robert Walpole, infuriated by the stage lampoons of Henry Fielding and others, determined to silence these much enjoyed exposures of his alleged corruption and incompetence. This had the curiously beneficial result of driving Fielding away from the stage. He then became an excellent magistrate and a major creator of the English novel. But in the puritanical atmosphere of the nineteenth century the discipline was applied to the moral content of plays and applied so rigorously that the dramatists were barred from serious treatment of 'straight sex,' as well as the abnormalities. The prissiness of respectable Victorian society was such that legs were hardly to be mentioned, let alone seen, and Charles Dickens wrote cumbrously of 'unmentionables' when he meant trousers." N. Y. Times, Jan. 1, 1961, § 2, p. X3. And see Knowles, The Censor, The Drama, and The Film (1934). As to British censorship of movies see 15 & 16 Geo. 6 & 1 Eliz. 2, c. 68.

"The freedom toward which the American people are fundamentally orientated is a freedom under God, a freedom that knows itself to be bound by the imperatives of the moral law. Antecedently it is presumed that a man will make morally and socially responsible use of his freedom of expression; hence there is to be no prior restraint on it. However, if his use of freedom is irresponsible, he is summoned after the fact to responsibility before the judgment of the law. There are indeed other reasons why prior restraint on communications is outlawed; but none are more fundamental than this." Murray, *We Hold These Truths* (1960), *pp. 164–165.*

Experience shows other evils of "prior restraint." The regime of the censor is deadening. One who writes cannot afford entanglements with the man whose pencil can keep his production from the market. The result is a pattern of conformity. Milton made the point long ago: "For though a licenser should happen to be judicious more than ordinarily, which will be a great jeopardy of the next succession, yet his very office, and his commission enjoins him to let pass nothing but what is vulgarly received already." Areopagitica, 3 Harvard Classics (1909), p. 212.

Another evil of censorship is the ease with which the censor can erode liberty of expression. One stroke of the pen is all that is needed. Under a censor's regime the weights are cast against freedom.[3] If, however, government must proceed against an illegal publication in a prosecution, then the advantages are on the other side. All the protections of the Bill of Rights come into play. The presumption of innocence, the right to jury trial, proof of guilt beyond a reasonable doubt—these become barriers in the path of officials who want to impose their standard of morality on the author or producer. The advantage a censor enjoys while working as a supreme bureaucracy disappears. The public trial to which a person is entitled who violates the law gives a hearing on the merits, airs the grievance, and brings the community judgment to bear upon it. If a court sits in review of a censor's ruling, its function is limited. There is leeway left the censor, who like any agency and its *expertise*, is given a presumption of being correct.[4] That advantage disappears when the government must wait until a publication is made and then prove its case in the accepted manner before a jury in a public trial. All of this is anathema to the censor who prefers to work in secret, perhaps because, as Milton said, he is "either ignorant, imperious, and remiss, or basely pecuniary." Areopagitica, *supra*, p. 210.

The First Amendment was designed to enlarge, not to limit, freedom in literature and in the arts as well as in politics, economics, law, and other fields. *Hannegan v. Esquire, Inc.*, 327 U.S. 146, 151–159; *Kingsley Pictures Corp. v. Regents, supra.* Its aim was to unlock all ideas for argument, debate, and dissemination. No more potent force in defeat of that freedom could be designed than censorship. It is a weapon that no minority or majority group, acting through government, should be allowed to wield over any of us.[5]

---

[3] John Galsworthy wrote in opposition to the British censorship of plays: "In this country the tongue and pen are subject to the law; so may it ever be! But in this country neither tongue nor pen are in any other instance subject to the despotic judgments of a single man. The protest is not aimed at the single man who holds this office. He may be the wisest man in England, the best fitted for his despotic office. It is not he; it is the office that offends. It offends the decent pride and self-respect of an entire profession. To those who are surprised that dramatic authors should take themselves so seriously we say, What workman worthy of his tools does not believe in the honour of his craft? In this appeal for common justice we dramatists, one little branch of the sacred tree of letters, appeal to our brother branches. We appeal to the whole knighthood of the pen—scientists, historians, novelists, journalists. The history of the health of nations is the history of the freedom—not the licence—of the tongue and pen. We are claiming the freedom—not the licence—of our pens. Let those hold back in helping us who would tamely suffer their own pens to be warped and split as ours are before we take them up." London Times, Nov. 1, 1907, p. 7. And see the testimony of George Bernard Shaw in Report, Joint Select Committee of the House of Lords and the House of Commons on the Stage Plays (Censorship) (1909), p. 46 *et seq.* Shaw, three of whose plays had been suppressed, caused a contemporary sensation by asking, and being refused, permission to file with the Committee an attack on censorship that he had prepared. Shaw's version of the story and the rejected statement can be found as his preface to The Shewing-Up of Blanco Posnet. He says in his statement: "Any journalist may publish an article, any demagogue may deliver a speech without giving notice to the government or obtaining its license. The risk of such freedom is great; but as it is the price of our political liberty, we think it worth paying. We may abrogate it in emergencies . . . just as we stop the traffic in a street during a fire or shoot thieves on sight after an earthquake. But when the emergency is past, liberty is restored everywhere except in the theatre. [Censorshop is] a permanent proclamation of martial law with a single official substituted for a court martial." The Shewing-Up of Blanco Posnet (Brentano's, 1913), p. 36.

[4] See Note, 71 Harv. L. Rev. 326, 331. Cf. *Glanzman v. Christenberry*, 175 F. Supp. 485, with *Grove Press, Inc. v. Christenberry*, 175 F. Supp. 488, as to the weight given to post-office determinations of nonmailability.

[5] "First, within the larger pluralist society each minority group has the right to censor for its own members, if it so chooses, the content of the various media of communication, and to protect them, by means of its own choosing, from materials considered harmful according to its own standards.

"Second, in a pluralist society no minority group has the right to demand that government should impose a general censorship, affecting all the citizenry, upon any medium of communication, with a view to punishing the communication of materials that are judged to be harmful according to the special standards held within one group.

"Third, any minority group has the right to work toward the elevation of standards of public morality in the pluralist society, through the use of the methods of persuasion and pacific argument.

"Fourth, in a pluralist society no minority group has the right to impose its own religious or moral views on other groups, through the use of the methods of force, coercion, or violence." Murray, We Hold These Truths (1960), p. 168.

■ Commonwealth of Pennsylvania

v.

Haddie M. Gary, *Appellant.*

Superior Court of Pennsylvania.

Sept. 16, 1960.

Cecil B. Moore, Philadelphia, for appellant.

Arlen Specter and *Domenick Vitullo*, Asst. Dist. Attys., *Paul M. Chalfin*, First Asst. Dist. Atty., *Victor H. Blanc*, Dist Atty., Philadelphia, for appellee.

Before Rhodes, P.J., and Gunther, Wright, Woodside, Ervin, Watkins and Montgomery, JJ.

Gunther, Judge.

Defendant, Haddie M. Gary, was indicted at 1608 August Sessions, 1959, charging the offense of immoral practices. The case was tried without a jury by the court below. At the conclusion of the trial, defendant was found guilty, sentence suspended, and ordered to pay the costs of prosecution. This appeal followed.

[1, 2] The Commonwealth contends that the appeal should be dismissed because no post-conviction motions for a new trial or in arrest of judgment were filed. We have stated repeatedly that matters not properly raised in the court below cannot be invoked on appeal. *Commonwealth* v. *Mays*, 182 Pa. Super. 130, 126 A. 2d 530; *Commonwealth* v. *Aikens*, 179 Pa. Super. 501, 118 A. 2d 205; *Commonwealth* v. *Pittman*, 179 Pa. Super. 645, 118 A. 2d 214. However, because the factual matters here raised seem to be one of first impression and because of the extraordinary circumstances here involved, we have concluded to dispose of the appeal on its merits. See *Commonwealth* v. *Savor*, 180 Pa. Super. 469, 119 A. 2d 849.

The indictment charged that the defendant "did solicit one Herbert Rhodes for the purpose of masturbation, whereby she, the said Haddie Mae Gary, on or about the said date did seek from said Herbert Rhodes a certain sum of money in return for which she offered to commit masturbation upon the private parts of the body of the said Herbert Rhodes to the great damage, injury and oppression of the said Herbert Rhodes and other good citizens of this Commonwealth to the evil example of all other in like case offending, and against the peace and dignity of the Commonwealth of Pennsylvania."

In support of the bill of indictment, the prosecuting officer testified that on May 23, 1959, he called a massage parlor located at 3621 Germantown Avenue in the City of Philadelphia and made arrangements for a massage for 2 o'clock in the afternoon. He arrived at the parlor at approximately 1:55 p.m. and he was greeted by the defendant. She took him to a room adjacent to the waiting room and told him to take off all his clothes and get on the table. While there were other women who worked there, and also men waiting in the waiting room, no one was present in this room except the witness and the defendant. He was supplied with a large bath towel to cover himself and defendant left the room while the witness undressed. Defendant came back in about five minutes and began to give the witness a massage. During the course of the massage, defendant ran her hand over his private parts three or four times. The witness further testified that defendant spent the major portion of the time massaging his low abdomen, inner thighs and in around there. During the massage, the towel was removed. He stated, further, that other than some small talk which had no bearing on the charge, nothing whatever was said between them and after the massage he paid the sum of $5 and left the premises.

[3] This was the entire evidence of the Commonwealth to sustain the charge. The defendant demurred to the evidence and the demurrer was overruled. The demurrer should have been sustained because, from the evidence presented, not a single element of the charge was sustained. There was no solicitation; she received no money for the offer to commit masturbation and there was no offer to commit masturbation. Outside of the prosecuting witness and the defendant no one else was in the room. The evidence disclosed that the police officer made the appointment for a massage. He received a massage, during which his privates were touched, and paid for a massage.

Both in the court below and on this appeal, however, defendant has raised the fundamental question underlying the entire prosecution: Was any crime committed either under the Common Law or under the statutes of this Commonwealth? It is conceded by all that there is no statute covering this subject matter so that if a crime can be made out, it must be under the Common Law.

In *Commonwealth* v. *Wiswesser*, 134 Pa. Super. 488, 3 A. 2d 983, 985, we stated that "a solicitation to commit a serious misdemeanor harmful to the public peace or the public welfare or economy is a common law offense in this state and that only such misdemeanors as by their nature make it unreasonable or illogical to treat them as a separate crime are excluded as an object of solicitation." In *Smith* v. *Commonwealth*, 54 Pa. 209, the Supreme Court held that it was not an indictable offense to solicit, incite and endeavor to persuade a married woman to commit fornication or adultery.

The term "masturbation" in 57 C.J.S. p. 448 has been defined as "self-defilement; onanism." Webster's New

International Dictionary, 2d ed., defines the word "to perform masturbation of (self or passive subject); to practice sexual self-gratification; production of an orgasm by excitation of the genital organs, as by manipulation or friction, without heterosexual intercourse * * *" It seems clear, therefore, that the term refers to self-defilement, self-degradation or self-pollution.

[4] Such an act, usually committed in privacy, has not been declared to be a Common Law misdemeanor so far as our research discloses. But even if the act of masturbation could be considered a misdemeanor under the definitions we have set out in *Commonwealth v. Mochan*, 177 Pa. Super. 454, 110 A. 2d 788, it seems clear that the solicita-

tion to commit such a misdemeanor makes it unreasonable or illogical to treat it as a separate crime any more than to treat solicitation to commit adultery as an indictable offense under the Common Law. We cannot conclude that the act of solicitation here alleged to be involved openly outrages decency and is injurious to public morals to the extent that should declare such an act to be indictable at Common Law.

The judgment of conviction is reversed and the defendant is discharged.

RHODES, P.J., and WRIGHT and ERVIN, JJ., would dismiss the appeal.

■ Manual Enterprises, Inc., *et al., Appellants,*
v.
J. Edward Day, Postmaster General, *Appellee.*
No. 16072.

United States Court of Appeals, District of Columbia Circuit.

Argued Feb. 13, 1961.—Decided March 23, 1961.

Mr. Stanley M. Dietz, Washington, D.C., for appellants.

Mr. Donald S. Smith, Asst. U.S. Atty., with whom *Messrs. Oliver Gasch*, U.S. Atty., and *Carl W. Belcher*, Asst. U.S. Atty., were on the brief, for appellee. *Mr. Frank Q. Nebeker*, Asst. U.S. Atty., also entered an appearance for appellee.

Before FAHY, DANAHER and BASTIAN, Circuit Judges.

BASTIAN, Circuit Judge.

In April, 1960, postal officials determined that three magazines, "Manual," "Trim," and "Grecian Guild Pictorial," (hereinafter referred to as appellants), were nonmailable under 18 U.S.C. § 1461 as being obscene and as conveying information as to how and where obscene matter might be obtained. Pursuant to this determination, copies of the magazines were withheld from dispatch. Shortly thereafter an administrative hearing was conducted, in which appellants participated, which ended adversely to appellants. Suit for injunctive relief was then filed in District Court. Appellants' motion for preliminary injunction was denied. On cross-motions for summary judgment, appellants' was denied, and appellee's was granted. This appeal followed.

The magazines in question are physique magazines, composed almost exclusively of photographs of nearly nude male models. Each photograph is accompanied by a brief caption giving the names of the model and photographer. Each issue also contains an index listing the photographers who have contributed to that magazine and a few advertisements from photographers and studios offering collections of nude photographs.

At the administrative hearing psychiatrists testified in great detail, explaining how and why the poses used in most of the pictures and the clothing worn by the models would arouse great prurient interest in homosexuals. Psychiatric testimony was also given to the effect that certain objects (swords and chains) used in some of the pictures were primary symbols of sexual fantasies of deviants within the homosexual group.

A postal inspector testified that, using an assumed name, he submitted orders to some of appellants' advertisers and received from them photographs of nude males with the pubic area exposed to view. He further testified that, in his experience, additional orders would produce photographs progressively more lascivious. Investigations at the studios which mailed the particular photographs here involved resulted in the discovery of what was termed "hard core pornography," photographs of groups of nude males engaged in homosexual activities.

Appellants contend that these magazines are body-building magazines, and that the publishers have no way of knowing whether newsstand sales are made to homosexuals or body-building enthusiasts. They further contend that they can not be charged with the photographs found in the course of the investigations because they were not sent through the mails and that the photographs which were actually sent are not obscene because nudity as such is not obscene.

[1] We think there was substantial evidence on the administrative record to support the conclusion that these magazines were intended for homosexuals. Overlooking the testimony that Herman Womack (the owner of two of the magazines and the publisher of all three) actually admitted such intent, the expert testimony as to the effect of the published pictures on homosexuals coupled with the

obvious lack of relationship of the "posing straps," heavy boots, helmets, swords, and chains to any interest in body-building, we think, amply supports the inference that these pictures were deliberately published because of their effect upon homosexuals.

[2, 3] Appellants contend that even if these pictures do arouse prurient interests in homosexuals, they are not obscene within the definition of *Roth* v. *United States,* 1957, 354 U.S. 476, 77 S. Ct. 1304, 1 L. Ed. 2d 1498, the so-called "average person in the community" test. It seems to us that the real meaning of Roth is that the object in question is not to be considered in terms of the reaction of an isolated atypical consumer. A case of obscenity thus is not to be predicated on the reaction of the peculiarly prudish or susceptible, and neither is a defense to such a charge to be predicated on the lack of reaction on the part of the peculiarly jaded. On the basis of the evidence before the administrative body, we think that "the average member of the community" would be an atypical reader of these magazines. The proper test in this case, we think, is the reaction of the average member of the class for which the magazines were intended, homosexuals. The testimony of record was clearly to the effect that these magazines

would arouse prurient interest in the average homosexual. The finding that these magazines were obscene within the meaning of the statute is therefore affirmed.

The testimony of the postal inspector as to his experience in the progressive nature of the material sent through the mails by the advertisers, together with the photographs actually so sent and those seized at the same studios, we think, furnishes substantial evidence for the conclusion that the advertisements in these magazines did give information with respect to where, how and from whom obscene matter could be obtained. The foregoing omits consideration of whether the photographs actually sent through the mails were obscene. A prior decision of this court has held such matter to be obscene. See *Womack* v. *United States,* — U.S. App. D.C. —, — F. 2d — decided Jan. 12, 1961. This finding of the administrative body is likewise affirmed.

The judgment of the District Court is therefore

Affirmed.

FAHY, Circuit Judge, concurs in the result.

■ Manual Enterprises, Inc., *et al., Petitioners,*

v.

J. Edward Day, *Postmaster General of the United States.*
No. 123.

Argued Feb. 26 and 27, 1962.—Decided June 25, 1962.

Stanley M. Dietz, Washington, D.C., for petitioners.
J. William Doolittle, Jr., Washington, D.C., for respondent.

Mr. Justice HARLAN announced the judgment of the Court and an opinion in which Mr. Justice STEWART joins.

This case draws in question a ruling of the Post Office Department, sustained both by the District Court and the Court of Appeals, 110 U.S. App. D.C. 78, 289 F. 2d 455, barring from the mails a shipment of petitioners' magazines. That ruling was based on alternative determinations that the magazines (1) were themselves "obscene," and (2) gave information as to where obscene matter could be obtained, thus rendering them nonmailable under two separate provisions of 18 U.S.C. § 1461, 18 U.S.C.A. § 1461, known as the Comstock Act.[1] Certiorari was

granted (368 U.S. 809, 82 S. Ct. 37, 7 L. Ed. 2d 19) to consider the claim that this ruling was inconsistent with the proper interpretation and application of § 1461, and with principles established in two of this Court's prior decisions. *Roth* v. *United States,* 354 U.S. 476, 77 S. Ct. 1304, 1 L. Ed. 2d 1498; *Smith* v. *California,* 361 U.S. 147, 80 S. Ct. 215, 4 L. Ed. 2d 205.[2]

---

means any of such mentioned matters, articles, or things may be obtained or made * * *

* * * * *

"Is declared to be nonmailable matter and shall not be conveyed in the mails or delivered from any post office or by any letter carrier.

"Whoever knowingly uses the mails for the mailing, carriage in the mails, or delivery of anything declared by this section to be nonmailable, or knowingly causes to be delivered by mail according to the direction thereon, or at the place at which it is directed to be delivered by the person to whom it is addressed, or knowingly takes any such thing from the mails for the purpose of circulating or disposing thereof, or of aiding in the circulation or disposition thereof, shall be fined not more than $5,000 or imprisoned not more than five years * * *."

[2] Because of our view of the case, we need not reach petitioners' third contention that, as applied in this instance, these Post Office procedures amounted to an unconstitutional "prior

---

[1] Section 1461 of 18 U.S.C., 18 U.S.C.A. § 1461, provides in part:

"Every obscene, lewd, lascivious, indecent, filthy or vile article, matter, thing, device, or substance; and—

* * * * *

"Every written or printed card, letter, circular, book, pamphlet, advertisement, or notice of any kind giving information, directly or indirectly, where, or how, or from whom, or by what

Petitioners are three corporations respectively engaged in publishing magazines titled MANual, Trim, and Grecian Guild Pictorial. They have offices at the same address in Washington, D.C., and a common president, one Herman L. Womack. The magazines consist largely of photographs of nude, or near-nude, male models and give the names of each model and the photographer, together with the address of the latter. They also contain a number of advertisements by independent photographers offering nudist photographs for sale.

On March 25, 1960, six parcels containing an aggregate of 405 copies of the three magazines, destined from Alexandria, Virginia, to Chicago, Illinois, were detained by the Alexandria postmaster, pending a ruling by his superiors at Washington as to whether the magazines were "nonmailable." After an evidentiary hearing before the Judicial Officer of the Post Office Department there ensued the administrative and court decisions now under review.

I.

On the issue of obscenity, as distinguished from unlawful advertising, the case comes to us with the following administrative findings, which are supported by substantial evidence and which we, and indeed the parties, for the most part, themselves, accept: (1) the magazines are not, as asserted by petitioners, physical culture or "bodybuilding" publications, but are composed primarily, if not exclusively, for homosexuals, and have no literary, scientific or other merit;[3] (2) they would appeal to the "prurient interest" of such sexual deviates, but would not have any interest for sexually normal individuals; and (3) the magazines are read almost entirely by homosexuals, and possibly a few adolescent males; the ordinary male adult would not normally buy them.

On these premises, the question whether these magazines are "obscene," as it was decided below and argued before us, was thought to depend solely on a determination as to the relevant "audience" in terms of which their "prurient interest" appeal should be judged. This view of the obscenity issue evidently stemmed from the belief that in *Roth* v. *United States*, 354 U.S. 476, 489, 77 S. Ct. 1304, 1311, 1 L. Ed. 2d 1498, this Court established the following *single* test for determining whether challenged material is obscene: "whether to the average person, applying contemporary community standards, the dominant theme of the material taken as a whole appeals to prurient interest." (Footnote omitted.) On this basis the Court of Appeals, rejecting the petitioners' contention that the

"prurient interest" appeal of the magazines should be judged in terms of their likely impact on the "average person," even though not a likely recipient of the magazines, held that the administrative finding respecting their impact on the "average homosexual" sufficed to establish the Government's case as to their obscenity.

We do not reach the question thus thought below to be dispositive on this aspect of the case. For we find lacking in these magazines an element which, no less than "prurient interest," is essential to a valid determination of obscenity under § 1461, and to which neither the Post Office Department nor the Court of Appeals addressed itself at all: These magazines cannot be deemed so offensive on their face as to affront current community standards of decency —a quality that we shall hereafter refer to as "patent offensiveness" or "indecency." Lacking that quality, the magazines cannot be deemed legally "obscene," and we need not consider the question of the proper "audience" by which their "prurient interest" appeal should be judged.

The words of § 1461, "obscene, lewd, lascivious, indecent, filthy or vile," connote something that is portrayed in a manner so offensive as to make it unacceptable under current community *mores*. While in common usage the words have different shades of meaning,[4] the statute since its inception has always been taken as aimed at obnoxiously debasing portrayals of sex.[5] Although the statute

---

restraint" on the publication of these magazines. The petitioner in this case has not questioned the Post Office Department's *general* authority under § 1461 to withhold these magazines from the mails *if* they are obscene. If that question, discussed in the opinion of MR. JUSTICE BRENNAN, 370 U.S., p. 495, 82 S. Ct., p. 1441, may still be deemed open in this Court, see *United States ex rel. Milwaukee Social Democratic Publishing Co.* v. *Burleson,* 255 U.S. 407, 421–422, 41 S. Ct. 352, 65 L. Ed. 704 (Brandeis, J., dissenting); cf. *Hannegan* v. *Esquire, Inc.,* 327 U.S. 146, 66 S. Ct. 456, 90 L. Ed. 586, we do not think it should be decided except upon full-dress argument and briefing, which have not been afforded us here.

[3] The Judicial Officer found that "the publisher has admitted that the magazines are knowingly published to appeal to the male homosexual group," and that "The publisher of the issues here involved has deliberately planned these publications so that they would appeal to the male homosexual audience * * *."

[4] The words of the statute are defined in Webster's New International Dictionary (unabridged, 2d ed., 1956) as follows:
obscene
"1. Offensive to taste; foul; loathsome; disgusting.

* * * * *

"2. a Offensive to chastity of mind or to modesty; expressing or presenting to the mind or view something that delicacy, purity, and decency forbid to be exposed; lewd; indecent; as, *obscene* language, dances, images."
lewd
"4. Lustful; libidinous; lascivious; unchaste * * *.
"Syn.—Licentious, lecherous, dissolute, sensual; debauched, impure; obscene, salacious, pornographic."
lascivious
"1. Wanton; lewd; lustful.

* * * * *

"Syn.—Licentious, lecherous, libidinous, salacious."
indecent
"Not decent; specif.: a Unbecoming or unseemly; indecorous * * *
Syn.—Immodest, impure; gross, obscene."
filthy
"1. Defiled with filth, whether material or moral; nasty; disgustingly dirty; polluting; foul; impure; obscene.

* * * * *

"Syn.—Squalid, unclean, gross, licentious."
vile
"2. Morally contaminated; befouled by or as if by sin; morally base or impure; wicked; evil; sinful * * *
"3. * * * unclean; filthy; repulsive; odious * * *

* * * * *

"Syn.—Cheap (despicable), debased; depraved; corrupt, sordid, vicious; disgusting, loathsome, foul." To the same effect see Webster's New International Dictionary (unabridged, 3d ed. 1961).

[5] The first federal statute bearing on obscenity was the Tariff Act of 1842 which forbade the importation of "indecent and obscene" pictorial matter and authorized confiscation. 5 Stat. 566–567. In 1865 the Congress passed the first Postal Act touching on the mailing of obscene matter, making it a crime to deposit an "obscene book * * * or other publication of a vulgar

condemns such material irrespective of the *effect* it may have upon those into whose hands it falls, the early case of *United States* v. *Bennett*, 24 Fed. Cas. p. 1093, No. 14571, put a limiting gloss upon the statutory language: the statute reaches only indecent material which, as now expressed in *Roth* v. *United States*, supra, 354 U.S. at 489, 77 S. Ct. at 1311, "taken as a whole appeals to prurient interest." This "effect" element, originally cast in somewhat different language from that of Roth (see 354 U.S., at 487, 489, 77 S. Ct. at 1310, 1311), was taken into federal obscenity law from the leading English case of *Regina* v. *Hicklin*, [1868] L.R. 3 Q.B. 360, of which a distinguished Australian judge has given the following illuminating analysis:

"As soon as one reflects that the word 'obscene,' as an ordinary English word, has nothing to do with corrupting or depraving susceptible people, and that it is used to describe things which are offensive to current standards of decency and not things which may induce to sinful thoughts, it becomes plain, I think, that Cockburn, C.J., in * * * R. v. *Hicklin* * * * was not propounding a logical definition of the word 'obscene,' but was merely explaining that particular characteristic which was necessary to bring an obscene publication within the law relating to obscene libel.[6] The tendency to deprave is not the characteristic which makes a publication obscene but is the characteristic which makes an obscene publication criminal. It is at once an essential element in the crime and the justification for the intervention of the common law. But it is not the whole and sole test of what constitutes an obscene libel. There is no obscene libel unless what is published is *both* offensive according to current standards of decency *and* calculated or likely to have the effect described in R. v. *Hicklin* * * *."[7] *Regina* v. *Close*,

[1948] Vict. L.R. 445, 463, Judgment of Fullagar, J. (Emphasis in original.)

The thoughtful studies of the American Law Institute reflect the same twofold concept of obscenity. Its earlier draft of a Model Penal Code contains the following definition of "obscene": "A thing is obscene if, considered as a whole, its predominant appeal is to prurient interest * * * *and* if it goes substantially beyond customary limits of candor in description or representation of such matters." A.L.I., Model Penal Code, Tent. Draft No. 6 (1957), § 207.10(2). (Emphasis added.) The same organization's currently proposed definition reads: "Material is obscene if, considered as a whole, its predominant appeal is to prurient interest * * * and if *in addition* it goes substantially beyond customary limits of candor in describing or representing such matters." A.L.I., Model Penal Code, Proposed Official Draft (May 4, 1962), § 251.4(1). (Emphasis added.)[8]

Obscenity under the federal statute thus requires proof of two distinct elements: (1) patent offensiveness; and (2) "prurient interest" appeal. Both must conjoin before challenged material can be found "obscene" under § 1461. In most obscenity cases, to be sure, the two elements tend to coalesce, for that which is patently offensive will also usually carry the requisite "prurient interest" appeal. It is only in the unusual instance where, as here, the "prurient interest" appeal of the material is found limited to a particular class of persons that occasion arises for a truly independent inquiry into the question whether or not the material is patently offensive.

The Court of Appeals was mistaken in considering that Roth made "prurient interest" appeal the sole test of obscenity.[9] Reading that case as dispensing with the requisite of patently offensive portrayal would be not only inconsistent with § 1461 and its common-law background, but out of keeping with Roth's evident purpose to tighten obscenity standards. The Court there both rejected the "isolated excerpt" and "particularly susceptible persons" tests of the Hicklin case, 354 U.S., at 488–489, 77 S. Ct., at 1310–1311, and was at pains to point out that not all portrayals of sex could be reached by obscenity laws but only those treating that subject "in a manner appealing to prurient interest." 354 U.S., at 487, 77 S. Ct., at 1310. That, of course, was but a compendious way of embracing in the obscenity standard *both* the concept of patent offensiveness, manifested by the terms of § 1461 itself, and the element of the likely corruptive effect of the challenged material, brought into federal law via *Regina* v. *Hicklin*.

To consider that the "obscenity" exception in "the area of constitutionally protected speech or press," Roth, at 485, 77 S. Ct. at 1309, does not require any determination as to the patent offensiveness *vel non* of the material itself might well put the American public in jeopardy of being denied access to many worthwhile works in literature,

---

and indecent character" in the mails. 13 Stat. 507. The reenactment of the 1865 Act in the codification of the postal laws in 1872 did not change the several adjectives describing the objectionable matter. 17 Stat. 302. The Comstock Act, 17 Stat. 598, added the descriptive terms "lewd" and "lascivious" so that the proscription then included any "obscene, lewd, or lascivious book * * * or other publication of an indecent character," but this Court in *Swearingen* v. *United States*, 161 U.S. 446, 450, 16 S. Ct. 562, 563, 40 L. Ed. 765, held that the words "obscene, lewd or lascivious" described a single offense. In 1909 the phrase "and every filthy" as well as the word "vile" were included in the provisions of the Comstock Act, 35 Stat. 1129. In 1955 the words were arranged in their present order. 69 Stat. 183. The Court of Appeals for the First Circuit noted that the words "indecent, filthy or vile" are limited in their meaning by the preceding words "obscene, lewd, lascivious," and that all have reference to matters of sex. *Flying Eagle Publications, Inc.* v. *United States*, 273 F. 2d 799, 803.

[6] "Obscene libel" in English usage simply means obscene material, being derived from *libellus*, "little book." See St. John-Stevas, Obscenity and the Law, 24.

[7] The passage referred to in *Regina* v. *Hicklin* was the following: "I think the test of obscenity is this, whether the tendency of the matter charged as obscenity is to deprave and corrupt those whose minds are open to such immoral influences, and into whose hands a publication of this sort may fall. Now, with regard to this work, it is quite certain that it would suggest to the minds of the young of either sex, or even to persons of more advanced years, thoughts of a most impure and libidinous character." [1868] L.R. 3 Q.B., at 371.

The quotations from *Regina* v. *Close* and the Hicklin case are not intended to signify our approval of either the "tendency to deprave" or "sexual thoughts" test, but only to emphasize the two elements in the legal definition of "obscene."

[8] This definition was approved by the Institute, as part of the "Proposed Official Draft," at its annual meeting in Washington, D.C., in May 1962.

[9] It is also evident that the Judicial Officer of the Post Office Department and its counsel entertained the same mistaken view of Roth. The Report of the Judicial Officer did not address itself directly to the inherent indecency aspect of the magazines, except to the extent that such factor was tangentially involved in the findings already summarized (supra, 370 U.S., p. 481, 82 S. Ct., p. 1434). The same is true of the expert testimony adduced by government counsel at the administrative hearing.

science, or art. For one would not have to travel far even among the acknowledged masterpieces in any of these fields to find works whose "dominant theme" might, not beyond reason, be claimed to appeal to the "prurient interest" of the reader or observer. We decline to attribute to Congress any such quixotic and deadening purpose as would bar from the mails all material, not patently offensive, which stimulates impure desires relating to sex. Indeed such a construction of § 1461 would doubtless encounter constitutional barriers. Roth, at 487–489, 77 S. Ct. at 1310–1311. Consequently we consider the power exercised by Congress in enacting § 1461 as no more embracing than the interdiction of "obscenity" as it had theretofore been understood. It is only material whose indecency is self-demonstrating *and* which, from the standpoint of its effect, may be said predominantly to appeal to the prurient interest that Congress has chosen to bar from the mails by the force of § 1461.

We come then to what we consider the dispositive question on this phase of the case. Are these magazines offensive on their face? Whether this question be deemed one of fact or of mixed fact and law, see Lockhart and McClure, Censorship of Obscenity: The Developing Constitutional Standards, 45 Minn. L. Rev. 5, 114–115 (1960), we see no need of remanding the case for initial consideration by the Post Office Department or the Court of Appeals of this missing factor in their determinations. That issue, involving factual matters entangled in a constitutional claim, see *Grove Press, Inc.,* v. *Christenberry,* 276 F. 2d 433, 436, is ultimately one for this Court. The relevant materials being before us, we determine the issue for ourselves.

There must first be decided the relevant "community" in terms of whose standards of decency the issue must be judged. We think that the proper test under this federal statute, reaching as it does to all parts of the United States whose population reflects many different ethnic and cultural backgrounds, is a national standard of decency. We need not decide whether Congress could constitutionally prescribe a lesser geographical framework for judging this issue[10] which would not have the intolerable consequence of denying some sections of the country access to material, there deemed acceptable, which in others might be considered offensive to prevailing community standards of decency. Cf. *Butler* v. *Michigan,* 352 U.S. 380, 77 S. Ct. 524, 1 L. Ed. 2d 412.

As regards the standard for judging the element of "indecency," the Roth case gives little guidance beyond indicating that the standard is a constitutional one which, as with "prurient interest," requires taking the challenged material "as a whole." Roth, at 489, 77 S. Ct. at 1311. Being ultimately concerned only with the question whether the First and Fourteenth Amendments protect material that is admittedly obscene,[11] the Court there had no occasion to explore the application of a particular obscenity standard. At least one important state court and some authoritative commentators have considered Roth and sub-

sequent cases[12] to indicate that only "hard-core" pornography can constitutionally be reached under this or similar state obscenity statutes. See *People* v. *Richmond County News, Inc.,* 9 N.Y. 2d 578, 216 N.Y.S. 2d 369, 175 N.E. 2d 681; Lockhart and McClure, supra, at 58–60. Whether "hard-core" pornography, or something less, be the proper test, we need go no further in the present case than to hold that the magazines in question, taken as a whole, cannot, under any permissible constitutional standard, be deemed to be beyond the pale of contemporary notions of rudimentary decency.

We cannot accept in full the Government's description of these magazines which, contrary to Roth (354 U.S., at 488–489, 77 S. Ct. 1310–1311), tends to emphasize and in some respects overdraw certain features in several of the photographs, at the expense of what the magazines fairly taken as a whole depict.[13] Our own independent examination of the magazines leads us to conclude that the most that can be said of them is that they are dismally unpleasant, uncouth, and tawdry. But this is not enough to make them "obscene." Divorced from their "prurient interest" appeal to the unfortunate persons whose patronage they were aimed at capturing (a separate issue), these portrayals of the male nude cannot fairly be regarded as more objectionable than many portrayals of the female nude that society tolerates. Of course not every portrayal of male or female nudity is obscene. See *Parmelee* v. *United States,* 72 App. D.C. 203, 206–208, 113 F. 2d 729, 732–734; *Sunshine Book Co.* v. *Summerfield,* 355 U.S. 372, 78 S. Ct. 365, 2 L. Ed. 2d 352; *Mounce* v. *United States,* 355 U.S. 180, 78 S. Ct. 267, 2 L. Ed. 2d 187. Were we to hold that these magazines, although they do not transcend the prevailing bounds of decency, may be denied access to the mails by such undifferentiated legislation as that before us, we would be ignoring the admonition that "the door * * * into this area [the First Amendment] cannot be left ajar; it must be kept tightly closed and opened only the slightest crack necessary to prevent encroachment upon

---

[10] The 1958 amendments to 18 U.S.C. § 1461, 72 Stat. 962, 18 U.S.C.A. § 1461, authorizing criminal prosecution at the place of delivery evince no purpose to make the standard less than national.

[11] No issue was presented in Roth as to the obscenity of any of the materials involved. 354 U.S., at 481, n. 8, 77 S. Ct. at 1306.

[12] See cases cited, 370 U.S., p. 490, 82 S. Ct., p. 1438.

[13] "The magazines contained little textual material, with pictures of male models dominating almost every page * * *. The typical page consisted of a photograph, with the name of the model and the photographer and occasional references to the model's age (usually under 26), color of eyes, physical dimensions and occupation. The magazines contained little, either in text or pictures, that could be considered as relating in any way to weight lifting, muscle building or physical culture * * *.

"Many of the photographs were of nude male models, usually posed with some object in front of their genitals * * *; a number were of nude or partially nude males with emphasis on their bare buttocks * * *. Although none of the pictures directly exposed the model's genitals, some showed his pubic hair and others suggested what appeared to be a semi-erect penis * * *; others showed male models reclining with their legs (and sometimes their arms as well) spread wide apart * * *. Many of the pictures showed models wearing only loin cloths, 'V gowns,' or posing straps * * *; some showed the model apparently removing his clothing * * *. Two of the magazines had pictures of pairs of models posed together suggestively * * *.

"Each of the magazines contained photographs of models with swords or other long pointed objects * * *. The magazines also contained photographs of virtually nude models wearing only shoes, boots, helmets or leather jackets * * *. There were also pictures of models posed with chains or of one model beating another while a third held his face in his hands as if weeping * * *."

more important interests" (footnote omitted). Roth, at 488, 77 S. Ct. at 1311.[14]

We conclude that the administrative ruling respecting nonmailability is improvident insofar as it depends on a determination that these magazines are obscene.

II.

There remains the question of the advertising. It is not contended that the petitioners held themselves out as purveyors of obscene material, or that the advertisements, as distinguished from the other contents of the magazines, were obscene on their own account. The advertisements were all by independent third-party photographers. And, neither with respect to the advertisements nor the magazines themselves, do we understand the Government to suggest that the "advertising" provisions of § 1461 are violated if the mailed material merely "gives the leer that promises the customer some obscene pictures." *United States v. Hornick*, 3 Cir., 229 F. 2d 120, 121. Such an approach to the statute could not withstand the underlying precepts of Roth. See *Poss v. Christenberry*, D.C., 179 F. Supp. 411, 415; cf. *United States v. Schillaci*, D.C., 166 F. Supp. 303, 306. The claim on this branch of the case rests, then, on the fact that some of the third-party advertisers were found in possession of what undoubtedly may be regarded as "hard-core" photographs,[15] and that postal officials, although not obtaining the names of the advertisers from the lists in petitioners' magazines, received somewhat less offensive material through the mails from certain studios which were advertising in petitioners' magazines.

A question of law must first be dealt with. Should the "obscene-advertising" proscription of § 1461 be construed as not requiring proof that the publisher *knew* that at least some of his advertisers were offering to sell obscene material? In other words, although the criminal provisions of § 1461 do require *scienter* (note 1, supra), can the Post Office Department in civil proceedings under that section escape with a lesser burden of proof? We are constrained to a negative answer. *First*, Congress has required *scienter* in respect of one indicted for mailing material proscribed by the statute. In the constitutional climate in which this statute finds itself, we should hesitate to attribute to Congress a purpose to render a publisher civilly responsible for the innocuous advertisements of the materials of others, in the absence of any showing that he knew that the character of such materials was offensive. And with no express grant of authority to the Post Office Department to keep obscene matter from the mails (see note 2, supra), we should be slow to accept the suggestion that an element of proof expressly required in a criminal proceeding may be omitted in an altogether parallel civil proceeding. *Second*,

this Court's ground of decision in *Smith v. California*, 361 U.S. 147, 80 S. Ct. 215, 4 L. Ed. 2d 205, indicates that a substantial constitutional question would arise were we to construe § 1461 as not requiring proof of *scienter* in civil proceedings. For the power of the Post Office to bar a magazine from the mails, if exercised without proof of the publisher's knowledge of the character of the advertisements included in the magazine, would as effectively "impose a severe limitation on the public's access to constitutionally protected matter," 361 U.S., at 153, 80 S. Ct. at 218, as would a state obscenity statute which makes criminal the possession of obscene material without proof of *scienter*. Since publishers cannot practicably be expected to investigate each of their advertisers, and since the economic consequences of an order barring even a single issue of a periodical from the mails might entail heavy financial sacrifice, a magazine publisher might refrain from accepting advertisements from those whose own materials could conceivably be deemed objectionable by the Post Office Department. This would deprive such materials, which might otherwise be entitled to constitutional protection, of a legitimate and recognized avenue of access to the public. To be sure, the Court found it unnecessary in Smith to delineate the scope of *scienter* which would satisfy the Fourteenth Amendment. Yet it may safely be said that a federal statute which, as we construe it, requires the presence of that element is not satisfied, as the Government suggests it might be, merely by showing that a defendant did not make a "good faith effort" to ascertain the character of his advertiser's materials.

On these premises we turn to the record in this case. Although postal officials had informed petitioners' president, Womack, that their Department was *prosecuting* several of his advertisers for sending obscene matter through the mails, there is no evidence that any of this material was shown to him. He thus was afforded no opportunity to judge for himself as to its alleged obscenity. Contrariwise, one of the government witnesses at the administrative hearing admitted that the petitioners had deleted the advertisements of several photographic studios after being informed by the Post Office that the proprietors had been *convicted* of mailing obscene material.[16] The record reveals that none of the postal officials who received allegedly obscene matter from some of the advertisers obtained their names from petitioners' magazines; this material was received as a result of independent test checks. Nor on the record before us can petitioners be linked with the material seized by the police. Note 15, supra. The only such asserted connection—that "hard core" matter was seized at the studio of one of petitioners' advertisers—falls short of an adequate showing that petitioners knew that the advertiser was offering for sale obscene matter. Womack's own conviction for sending obscene material through the mails, *Womack v. United States*, 111 U.S. App. D.C. 8, 294 F. 2d 204, is remote from proof of like conduct on the part of the advertisers.

---

[14] Since Congress has sought to bar from the mails only material that is "obscene, lewd, lascivious, indecent, filthy or vile" and it is within this statutory framework that we must judge the materials before us, we need not consider whether these magazines could constitutionally be reached under "a statute narrowly drawn to define and punish specific conduct as constituting a clear and present danger." *Cantwell v. Connecticut*, 310 U.S. 296, 311, 60 S. Ct. 900, 906, 84 L. Ed. 1213.

[15] A number of such photographs were seized by the police, possessing search or arrest warrants, but knowledge that these advertisers were selling, or would sell, such photographs was never brought home to any of these petitioners.

[16] Grecian Guild Pictorial carried a notice that it "does not knowingly use the work of any studio which takes or sells nude, undraped front or side view photographs." The photographers listed above do not offer such photographs." To be sure this magazine, as did the others, also carried a notation that the publisher was familiar with the work of the advertisers and urged the reader to support them; but this cannot well be taken as an admission of knowledge that the advertisers' works were obscene.

At that time he was acting as president of another studio; the vendee of the material, while an advertiser in petitioners' magazines, had closed his own studio before the present issues were published. Finally, the general testimony by one postal inspector to the effect that in his experience advertisers of this character, after first leading their customers on with borderline material, usually followed up with "hard-core" matter, can hardly be deemed of probative significance on the issue at hand.

At best the Government's proof showed no more than that petitioners were chargeable with knowledge that these advertisers were offering photographs of the same character, and with the same purposes, as those reflected in their own magazines. This is not enough to satisfy the Government's burden of proof on this score.[17]

In conclusion, nothing in this opinion of course remotely implies approval of the type of magazines published by these petitioners, still less of the sordid motives which prompted their publication. All we decide is that on this record these particular magazines are not subject to repression under § 1461.

Reversed.

Mr. Justice Black concurs in the result.

Mr. Justice Frankfurter took no part in the decision of this case.

Mr. Justice White took no part in the consideration or decision of this case.

Mr. Justice Brennan, with whom The Chief Justice and Mr. Justice Douglas join, concurring in the reversal.

I agree that the judgment below must be reversed, though for a reason different from my Brother Harlan's. This is the first occasion on which the Court has given plenary review[1] to a Post Office Department order holding matter "nonmailable" because obscene.

Petitioners, publishers of certain magazines, employ the mails in the distribution of about half of their claimed circulation of 25,000. On March 25, 1960, petitioners deposited 405 copies of their publications for transmission

as second class mail from Alexandria, Virginia, to Chicago. However, the Alexandria postmaster, acting, apparently without notice to petitioners, on his belief that the magazines might be obscene and therefore "nonmailable" under 18 U.S.C. § 1461, 18 U.S.C.A. § 1461, withheld delivery and forwarded samples to the General Counsel of the Post Office Department. On April 5 and 7 that official notified petitioners not only that the magazines were being withheld from delivery because of his opinion that they were nonmailable, but also that no formal hearing would be held since an insufficient monetary value was involved. Shortly thereafter, on April 11, 1960, petitioners requested a Post Office hearing, and also sought injunctive relief in the District Court for the District of Columbia against this stoppage of their mailing. On the same day the Post Office Judicial Officer reversed the General Counsel and ordered a hearing, and thereafter the District Court refused temporary relief. On April 21, after pleadings had been filed, the hearing was begun before the Judicial Officer. On April 25 petitioners' injunction suit was dismissed on the condition that they might seek further relief if final administrative action was not forthcoming by April 28. On April 28, one month and three days after the mailing, the Judicial Officer handed down his opinion holding the magazines obscene and nonmailable, thus opening petitioners' way into court.

On May 13, petitioners filed the complaint now before us, alleging that the magazines were not obscene, that respondent's action in withholding them from the mails was "unlawful and inequitable * * * calculated * * * to censor and harass plaintiffs and * * * a prior restraint designed to deprive the plaintiffs of their rights under the First Amendment * * *," and requesting temporary and permanent injunctive relief. Petitioners then moved for summary judgment, arguing, *inter alia*, that "the Post Office Department held a time-consuming hearing, the product of which was an Order contrary to the established law of the United States * * *. This amounts to the most obnoxious and unconstitutional censorship. The principal effect of the administrative hearing * * is to delay action of this Court. * * * Plaintiffs assert that the Post Office has conducted an ex parte administrative prior restraint treading upon an area of constitutional sensitivity apart from the substantive problems of determining whether or not the magazines are obscene. * * * Further, plaintiffs argue that the entire civil procedure followed by the Post Office based upon a criminal statute raises doubts of constitutionality." Respondent, too, moved for summary judgment. His motion was granted and the complaint dismissed without opinion. The Court of Appeals affirmed, holding the magazines obscene.

In addition to the question whether the particular matter is obscene, the Post Office order raises insistent questions about the validity of the whole procedure which gave rise to it, vital to the orderly development of this body of law and its administration. We risk erosion of First Amendment liberties unless we train our vigilance upon the methods whereby obscenity is condemned no less than upon the standards whereby it is judged. *Marcus v. Search Warrant*, 367 U.S. 717, 81 S. Ct. 1708, 6 L. Ed. 2d 1127; *Kingsley Books, Inc. v. Brown*, 354 U.S. 436, 77 S. Ct. 1325, 1 L. Ed. 2d 1469; see also *Smith v. California*, 361 U.S. 147, 80 S. Ct. 215, 4 L. Ed. 2d 205. Questions of procedural safeguards loom large in the wake of an order such as the one before us. Among them are:

---

[17] We do not think it would be appropriate at this late stage to remand the case for further proceedings on the issue of *scienter*. Although suggesting that "[it] is arguable" that *scienter* is not a necessary element under this part of the statute, the Government undertakes to defend this aspect of the judgment primarily on the premise that it was. The record shows that at the administrative hearing government counsel sought to fasten the petitioners with knowledge that the third-party advertisers were selling "obscene" material. The Judicial Officer indeed rejected the petitioners' proposed findings that "the publishers of each of the magazines in evidence * * * had no personal knowledge of the material sold by the advertisers * * *." To be sure, the record does not disclose whether this was because "knowledge" was deemed proved rather than that such element was not considered relevant. But on the cross motions for summary judgment, based upon the administrative record, the Government did not undertake to controvert petitioners' allegations that *scienter* was a necessary element under this part of the statute.

[1] *One, Inc. v. Olesen*, 355 U.S. 371, 78 S. Ct. 364, 2 L. Ed. 2d 352, and *Sunshine Book Co. v. Summerfield*, 355 U.S. 372, 78 S. Ct. 365, 2 L. Ed. 2d 352, were decided summarily without argument.

(a) whether Congress can close the mails to obscenity by any means other than prosecution of its sender; (b) whether Congress, if it can authorize exclusion of mail, can provide that obscenity be determined in the first instance in any forum except a court, and (c) whether, even if Congress could so authorize administrative censorship, it has in fact conferred upon postal authorities any power to exclude matter from the mails upon their determination of its obscene character.[2]

Lower courts and judges have been troubled by these questions,[3] but this Court has not had occasion to decide them. At least question (c) is before us now.[4] It surpasses in general significance even the important issue of the standards for judging this material's "mailability." Moreover, dealing with the case on this ground involves less constitutional difficulty than inheres in others. The conclusion that the Postmaster General is acting *ultra vires* because Congress has not granted the power which he here asserts, while greatly influenced by constitutional doubts, does not require a decision as to whether any establishment of administrative censorship could be constitutional. *Hannegan* v. *Esquire, Inc.*, 327 U.S. 146, 66 S. Ct. 456, 90 L. Ed. 586; *Kent* v. *Dulles*, 357 U.S. 116, 78 S. Ct. 1113, 2 L. Ed. 2d 1204.[5]

Mr. Justice Holmes has said: "The United States may give up the postoffice when it sees fit, but while it carries it on the use of the mails is almost as much a part of free speech as the right to use our tongues and it would take very strong language to convince me that Congress ever intended to give such a practically despotic power to any one man." *Milwaukee Social Democratic Publishing Co.* v. *Burleson*, 255 U.S. 407, 437, 41 S. Ct. 352, 363, 65 L. Ed. 704 (dissenting opinion).

Whether Congress, by its enactment or amendment of 18 U.S.C. § 1461, 18 U.S.C.A. § 1461 (a part of the Criminal Code), has authorized the Postmaster General to censor obscenity, is our precise question. The Government relies upon no other provision to support the constitutionally questionable power of administrative censorship of this material. That power is inferred from the declaration that every item proscribed in § 1461 is "nonmailable matter and shall not be conveyed in the mails or delivered from any post office or by any letter carrier." Even granting that these words on their face permit a construction allowing the Post Office the power it asserts, their use in a criminal statute, their legislative history, and the contrast with the words and history of other provisions dealing with similar problems, raise the most serious doubt that so important and sensitive a power was granted by so perfunctory a provision. The area of obscenity is honeycombed with hazards for First Amendment guaranties, and the grave constitutional questions which would be raised by the grant of such a power should not be decided when the relevant materials are so ambiguous as to whether any such grant exists.

I.

The origin of § 1461 is briefly told.[6] It was the tag end of a bill drawn in 1865 to meet Post Office requests for various administrative changes. Its first version read:

[2] There would also be the question, if (a), (b) and (c) were answered affirmatively, of the validity of the particular procedures that the Post Office has employed.

[3] See, e.g., *Grove Press, Inc.* v. *Christenberry*, D.C., 175 F. Supp. 488, 495, and 2 Cir., 276 F. 2d 433, 435; *Sunshine Book Co.* v. *Summerfield*, 101 U.S. App. D.C. 358, 364–367, 249 F. 2d 114, 120–123 (dissenting opinion), reversed, see supra, n. 1. And cf. *Roth* v. *Goldman*, 2 Cir., 172 F. 2d 788, 794–795 (concurring opinion). Compare *Stanard* v. *Olesen*, 74 S. Ct. 768 (opinion of Mr. Justice Douglas), *Olesen* v. *Stanard*, 227 F. 2d 785; *Summerfield* v. *Sunshine Book Co.*, 95 U.S. App. D.C. 169, 221 F. 2d 42.

[4] The Government argues that petitioners "complain generally of 'an unconstitutional prior restraint,' * * * without specifying [where] the asserted vice lies * * *." Insofar as petitioners challenge the constitutionality of § 1461 if read to impose civil restraints, their suit would be within the requirements for convening a three-judge court under 28 U.S.C. § 2282, 28 U.S.C.A. § 2282, and therefore that claim is not here. But insofar as their attack is grounded upon a claim that § 1461 is not to be construed as granting censorial power to the Post Office, § 2282 does not apply.

[5] My Brother HARLAN states that no question is raised as to the Post Office Department's general authority under 18 U.S.C. § 1461, 18 U.S.C.A. § 1461 to withhold obscene matter from the mails. The Government asserts only that at the administrative level the petitioners made no objection to the procedure. The Government does not suggest that the challenge to the Post Office's power to act at all had to be made before the administrative body. That challenge presents a jurisdictional question and is open to the petitioners even if not initially asserted in the agency proceeding. See *United States* v. *L. A. Tucker Truck Lines, Inc.*, 344 U.S. 33, 38, 73 S. Ct. 67, 69, 97 L. Ed. 54. And although perhaps not artfully, the petitioners did challenge the authority of the Post Office in the District Court. In their motion for summary judgment petitioners stated: "[P]laintiffs argue that the entire civil procedure followed by the Post Office based upon a criminal statute raises doubts of constitutionality. The fragile foundation on which the Post Office action rests must be kept in mind, both in dealing with the substantive obscenity question involved and in determining the proper scope of judicial review * * *. There is lacking here the kind of specific legislative direction to the administrative agency that in certain circumstances justifies judicial deference to administrative

determinations." The Court of Appeals did not discuss the issue, perhaps because it had held in *Sunshine Book Co.* v. *Summerfield*, supra, n. 3, that the questioned authority exists; the Government does not suggest that petitioners failed to make their argument there. And in this Court, petitioners continue their attack and the Government, without reservation, fully defends against it.

[6] There is no need to consider here the history before 1865, which was highlighted by the rejection by Congress in 1836, largely on constitutional grounds, of President Jackson's request for legislation to suppress mail distribution of "incendiary" abolitionist literature. See Rogers, The Postal Power of Congress (1916); Deutsch, Freedom of the Press and of the Mails, 36 Mich. L. Rev. 703 (1938). The 1865 Senate debates referred to such action as the kind for which power should be withheld. Cong. Globe, 38th Cong., 2d Sess. 661 (1865). The Post Office occasionally seized allegedly treasonable newspapers despite its lack of authority. See H.R. Rep. No. 51, 37th Cong., 3d Sess., pp. 3, 10 (1863).

The only noncriminal procedure authorized against obscene material before 1865 was a judicial proceeding for imported material's forfeiture. 5 Stat. 566; see *United States* v. *Three Cases of Toys*, 28 F. Cas. page 112, No. 16499; Anonymous, 1 Fed. Cas. page 1024, No. 470. For a comprehensive discussion of the history and practice of censorship in the Post Office and Bureau of Customs, see Paul and Schwartz, Federal Censorship: Obscenity in the Mail (1961), and Paul, The Post Office and Non-Mailability of Obscenity: An Historical Note, 8 U.C.L.A.L. Rev. 44 (1961).

"That no obscene book, pamphlet, picture, print, or other publication of a vulgar and indecent character, shall be admitted into the mails of the United States; but all such obscene publications deposited in or received at any post office, or discovered in the mails, shall be seized and destroyed, or otherwise disposed of, as the Postmaster General shall direct. And any person or persons who shall deposit or cause to be deposited in any post office or branch post office of the United States, for mailing or for delivery, an obscene book, pamphlet, picture, print, or other publication, knowing the same to be of a vulgar and indecent character, shall be deemed guilty of a misdemeanor, and, being duly convicted thereof, shall, for every such offense, be fined not more than $500, or imprisoned not more than one year, or both, according to the circumstances and aggravations of the offense."

In offering this proposal, Chairman Collamer of the Senate Post Office Committee took pains to point out that it "may be liable to some objection. * * * I am not perhaps entirely satisfied with it," and Senator Reverdy Johnson, concerned about postmasters breaking seals, immediately took up Chairman Collamer's suggestion that only the penal provision be adopted. Chairman Collamer, agreeing that the nonpenal clause "might be made a precedent for undertaking to give [a postmaster] a sort of censorship over the mails," said he would be as happy if it were dropped. Senator Johnson then moved to strike it: "[I]t would be establishing a very bad precedent to give authority to postmasters to take anything out of the mail." He acknowledged that much material is sent uncovered, but thought the penal provision sufficient to meet the evil. However, Senator Sherman observed:

*"I would much prefer, if the Senator would be satisfied, with simply striking out the second clause of the first [sentence]. I think the prohibition against publications of this character going into the mails ought to stand. We are well aware that many of these publications are sent all over the country from the city of New York with the names of the parties sending them on the backs, so that the postmasters without opening the mail matter may know that it is offensive matter, indecent and improper to be carried in the public mails. I think, therefore, the legislative prohibition against carrying such matter when it is known to the postmasters should be left. Probably the second clause allowing him to open mail matter should be struck out * * *."*

Senator Johnson acquiesced and the bill was then passed, reading:

*"That no obscene book, pamphlet, picture, print, or other publication of a vulgar and indecent character, shall be admitted into the mails of the United States; any person or persons * * *."* Cong. Globe, 38th Cong., 2d Sess. 660–661 (1865); 13 Stat. 507.

There are two possible constructions of § 1461 on the basis of this brief Senate discussion. One possibility is that short of breaking seals,[7] the postmasters could remove

matter which they thought from its face or the name of its sender to be obscene. The second construction is that postmasters could remove matter but only to turn it over to the appropriate authorities as the proposed subject of a criminal prosecution—and also of course after that material had been determined, in a criminal trial of its sender, to be obscene. Support for this second construction is found not only in the brief 1865 Senate consideration itself but also in an 1888 statute amending § 1461, and enacting a section banning material with obscene matter on its face and—unlike § 1461—explicitly providing that it "shall be withdrawn from the mails under such regulations as the Postmaster-General shall prescribe."[8]

The 1865 Senate discussion is not unambiguous, but I cannot suppose that Senator Johnson—who had already noted his awareness that much obscene material was discoverable without breaking seals, and even so, his determined opposition to its being stopped—would have accepted Senator Sherman's suggestion had he understood it to mean more than that the Post Office could stop obviously questionable matter for the purpose of transmitting it to prosecuting authorities, could stop matter already held obscene if it were sent again, and could investigate matter sent by persons previously convicted and, if the matter were found violative, could present it to the prosecuting authorities. I believe this is the correct construction of the 1865 enactment. But at least it is arguably correct, and necessary if we are to avoid the section's probable constitutional infirmity[9] (see *Near* v. *Minnesota*, 283 U.S. 697, 51 S. Ct. 625, 75 L. Ed. 1357; *Summerfield* v. *Sunshine Book Co.*, 95 U.S. App. D.C. 169, 221 F. 2d 42) if construed as a provision allowing the Postmaster General to exclude all matter sent by a person who had previously sent violative matter. Such an exclusion by attaint could not be justified by the "hoary dogma * * * that the use of the mails is a privilege on which the Government may impose such conditions as it chooses, [for that] has long since evaporated." *Roth* v. *United States*, 354 U.S. 476, 504, 77 S. Ct. 1304, 1319, 1 L. Ed. 2d 1498 (dissenting opinion); *Hannegan* v. *Esquire, Inc.*, 327 U.S., at 156, 66 S. Ct. at 461, 90 L. Ed. 586; *Speiser* v. *Randall*, 357 U.S. 513, 518, 78 S. Ct. 1332, 1338, 2 L. Ed. 2d 1460.

Subsequent developments concerning the removal of matter from the mails reveal a nearly contemporaneous strong distaste for and awareness of constitutional doubts about nonjudicial censorship, such as reflects meaningfully on the ambiguity surrounding § 1461's enactment. That ambiguity has persisted throughout § 1461's history of amendment, reconsideration, and codification. In the concurrent history of Congress' handling of related problems, there has been in each instance either a clear grant of power to the Postmaster General or, for matters as inextricably intertwined with the First Amendment as obscenity, a provision for judicial rather than administrative process. Nothing is found to suggest that one should resolve the ambiguity in 1865 to find a grant of the power of administrative censorship. Compare *Lewis Publishing Co.* v. *Morgan*, 229 U.S. 288, 311, 33 S. Ct. 867, 873, 57 L. Ed. 1190.

In 1868, in considering a provision making it unlawful

---

[7] Congress in 1865 was undoubtedly against any power in the Post Office to break seals (see Cong. Globe, 38th Cong., 2d Sess. 660–661), and 23 years later made this explicit as to first class mail. 25 Stat. 496–497. But even that was a prohibition "out of abundant caution" and was not intended to imply any power to open mail of other classes. See 19 Cong. Rec. 8189 (1888).

[8] 25 Stat. 496, now 18 U.S.C. § 1463, 18 U.S.C.A. § 1463.
[9] See *United States* ex rel. *Milwaukee Social Democratic Publishing Co.* v. *Burleson*, 255 U.S. 407, 423, 429–430, 41 S. Ct. 352, 358, 360, 65 L. Ed. 704 (Brandeis, J., dissenting).

to deposit letters or circulars concerning lotteries, House Conferees struck a Senate proposal which would have authorized postmasters to remove from the mail and deposit in dead letter offices any letters or circulars thought to concern lotteries. House Postal Committee Chairman Farnsworth explained "We thought that was a dangerous power to confer upon postmasters, and therefore we have stricken it out. That section provides that it shall be unlawful to deposit in the mails * * * which we thought would be a wise provision. But we thought it would not be wise to give postmasters this extraordinary power to be exercised upon a mere suspicion." Cong. Globe, 40th Cong., 2d Sess. 4412 (1868). Opinions of the Attorney General advising as to the postmasters' authority under this lottery provision emphasized the necessity for explicit legislative authorization to warrant removal of material from the mails. Those opinions cited examples of provisions containing such express authorization but, significantly, did not include § 1461—an important omission in the light of the observation of the Attorney General that aside from the examples he gave "[i]f there are other provisions permitting a detention of letters by a postmaster, they have escaped my attention. It is believed that, at least, there are no others affecting the subject of the present inquiry." Furthermore, in describing the authorizations he did find, the Attorney General said: "It will be seen that none of these authorize what can properly be called a 'seizure' of any suspected letters by a postmaster, because, probably, he is not deemed the proper functionary to bring to trial and punishment those violating the postal laws."[10]

In 1872, § 1461 was amended as part of a codification of postal legislation. The amendment added a proscription against the mailing of "any letter upon the envelope of which, or postal card upon which scurrilous epithets may have been written or printed, or disloyal devices printed or engraved * * *." 17 Stat. 302.[11] The section was further revised when the Comstock Law was enacted in 1873. 17 Stat. 598. That statute established penalties for dealing in or in any way publishing obscenity or any article of an immoral nature in areas under federal jurisdiction, expanded the list of items not to be mailed to include matter intended to aid the procuring of abortion, and banned the importation of all such items. When the bill came to the floor, Senator Casserly objected to the provision allowing customs officers to seize prohibited items: "I do not know whether it can be left to officers of the custom-house to determine with safety what kind of literature or what sort of matter is to be admitted." Cong. Globe, 42d Cong., 3d Sess. 1436 (1873). The bill was accordingly changed to authorize customs officers simply to detain the items, and then proceed in a federal court to condemn them, if the federal judge were satisfied that they must be condemned. Id., at 1525. There is no suggestion that customs officers

were thought to be less trustworthy than postal officers;[12] this insistence upon judicial proceedings shows plainly the congressional aversion to administrative censorship.

The Comstock bill received but scant and hasty consideration.[13] As passed, its language was susceptible of a reading which would fail to penalize the mailing of obscene or indecent *literature*, and reach only actual abortifacients. Closing this inadvertent gap was the sole purpose[14] of an 1876 amendment, 19 Stat. 90, which made several language changes; among them, the substitution of the words of which the Government makes so much—"declared to be nonmailable matter, [which] shall not be conveyed in the mails, nor delivered from any post-office nor by any letter-carrier"—for the more cursory "[which] shall [not] be carried in the mail." Moreover, the 1876 discussion evinces the understanding that the only obscene materials removable by the Post Office were those which were to be submitted as, or which already had been, the subject of a criminal prosecution. The manager of the amendment assured the House: "Nor, sir, does this bill give any right to any postmaster to open or to interfere with anybody's mail. It is like anything else, before you can convict, you must offer and make proof." During the debate a different speaker said: "Whenever a jury in any locality in the country shall find that a paper contains matter which may be devoted to a purpose which they deem immoral—not only indecent, but immoral—the jury may convict the man who sends the paper or the man who receives it by mail, and the postmaster is authorized to exclude that newspaper from the mail." A third speaker, in urging that the word "scurrilous" be removed, warned: "I do not object to the purification of the mails, but I would like the committee when they reconsider this bill not to go too far in giving postmasters discretion." Another Congressman feared that the severity of the penalties would make the law a dead letter, because judges and juries would be unwilling to convict. Thus the tenor of the entire debate reflected the premise that § 1461 had only a criminal application. No one suggested that it also authorized administrative censorship. 4 Cong. Rec. 695–696.[15] And see 8 Cong. Rec. 697 (1879).

---

[10] 16 Op. Atty. Gen. 5, 6 (1878); 12 id., 538 (1868); and see 12 id., 399, 401 (1868).

[11] There was also a provision that any material "which may be seized or detained for violation of law shall be returned to the owner or sender of the same, or otherwise disposed of as the Postmaster-General may direct," 17 Stat. 323, but that only states what may be done with material which may be seized or detained, and our question is whether obscene material—except in the narrow circumstances already described—may be seized or detained at all. Compare 370 U.S., pp. 511–512, 82 S. Ct., pp. 1449–1450.

[12] But see Casserly's second statement, id., at 1436, which was a misunderstanding of the bill.

[13] See Paul, supra, n. 6, at 51–57.

[14] The bill's manager in the House said: "[T]he proposed bill in no wise changes the law as it now is except to provide a penalty for the circulation of obscene literature. By an oversight in drafting the original section the penalty applies only to the disposition of articles circulated or sold for the purpose of procuring abortion or preventing conception. Already this obscene class of matter spoken of in the other portion of the section is prohibited from passing through the mails, but no penalty is provided. * * * [I]t in no way changes the section as it now is. It makes nothing non-mailable that is not now non-mailable. It merely provides a penalty * * *." 4 Cong. Rec. 695 (1876).

"Section [1461] is perfected by the bill so as to provide a complete penalty for the mailing of all kinds of matter therein prohibited to pass through the mails." 4 Cong. Rec. 3656. The Senate did not discuss this change. See 4 Cong. Rec. 4261–4264.

[15] Discussion in the Senate included the first reference to the problem of standards of obscenity—it was hardly such as to afford guidelines for administrative action:

"Mr. Morton. Mr. President, in prohibiting the transmission of any matter through the mails there ought to be great care used and it ought to be particularly described and defined. All of

Especially significant in pointing up the purely penal application of § 1461 are the legislative events of 1888. An amendment of but a few months' duration changed the law on such postal crimes as counterfeiting money orders. It included a provision penalizing the mailing of any matter upon the envelope or outside cover of which was indecent, scurrilous, threatening, etc., language.[16] The provision was promptly amended in the same session because "there was a suspicion that an implied power was given to postmasters to open letters. Of course there was no such intention, and this [new] bill eliminates that objectionable feature * * *." 19 Cong. Rec. 8189.[17]

But even more significantly, the new enactment transferred to a new section, § 1463, 25 Stat. 496, the ban of § 1461 which, in the 1876 version (19 Stat. 90), had reached "every letter upon the envelope of which, or postal card upon which, indecent, lewd, obscene, or lascivious delineations, epithets, terms, or language may be written or printed"; and § 1463, instead of merely declaring that the listed matter was nonmailable and was not to be conveyed or delivered, provided that those items *"shall be withdrawn from the mails under such regulations as the Postmaster-General shall prescribe. * * *"* It is strange, I think, that § 1461—amended at the same time as § 1463 was enacted—was not amended also to include an explicit provision for withdrawal from the mails, if authority for withdrawal had been Congress' intention. But Congress did not contemplate any general administrative censorship or obscenity. The House discussion expressed the agreement

that besides the power to punish, there should be no more than the most limited Post Office power to stop mail—and § 1463 states that limitation; and the Senate debate, focusing almost entirely upon how severe the penalties should be, reinforced the restrictions upon the postmasters and underlined that § 1461 is exclusively penal. See 19 Cong. Rec. 7660–7662, 8189.

The last congressional dealing with § 1461 which is pertinent to our inquiry occurred in 1909, when again that section was amended, this time to bar more abortifacients and "every letter, packet, or package, or other mail matter containing any filthy, vile, or indecent thing."[18] Though committee reports are unenlightening, the House discussion makes plain that the changes were intended to reverse the limitations stated in *Swearingen* v. *United States*, 161 U.S. 446, 16 S. Ct. 562, 40 L. Ed. 765, that the statute applied only to "that form of immorality which has relation to sexual impurity," and that its words had "the same meaning as is given them at common law in prosecutions for obscene libel." 161 U.S., at 451, 16 S. Ct. at 563; 42 Cong. Rec. 995–999, 43 Cong. Rec. 283–284.[19] The two brief House discussions suggest that there were members who did believe that the Post Office had some power to remove obscene mail, even apart from presenting it for criminal prosecution; it was analogized to fraudulent matter. But nothing characterizes the discussion so much as its ambiguity, and its concern lest the Post Office acquire powers whose exercise would amount to censorship. See 42 Cong. Rec. 995–998. And see 101 Cong. Rec. 3804, 7798, 8241–8242 (1955).

II.

Section 1463 is not the only statute which goes further than § 1461 towards authorizing Post Office censorship. Five other criminal statutes prohibiting the introduction of various matter into the mails either contain within themselves or have direct counterparts in the postal laws which contain explicit authorizations to the Postmaster General to remove or return such matter.[20] In sharp contrast,

---

that which is described in the beginning of the first section of this bill is eminently proper to prohibit from being transmitted through the mails; but there is a part of that section that I think is vague and susceptible of abuse. It prohibits the transmission through the mail of 'every article or thing intended or adapted for any indecent or immoral use.' What is an 'immoral use?' That question may be subject to very different opinions. The word 'obscene' is well defined; we can understand what that means; but when you prohibit everything that is for an immoral use, there would be wide differences of opinion on that point.

"Mr. Conkling. The same words are in the law now.

"Mr. Morton. That may be. I remember a time when certain newspapers and pamphlets were prohibited from going through the mails in certain States, because they were held to be of an immoral and seditious character—of 'an incendiary character,' as my friend from Ohio [Mr. Sherman] suggests. Public opinion has changed upon that point. But when we come to prohibit the transmission of any matter through the mails, we ought to understand pretty well what it is. There are many things that a portion of our people would consider immoral that other portions would consider entirely moral. Some people might consider a pack of cards highly immoral; others might think they were entirely proper. Many other things might be enumerated." 4 Cong. Rec. 4263.

[16] "And all matter otherwise mailable by law upon the envelope or outside cover or wrapper of which, or postal card, upon which indecent, lewd, lascivious, obscene, libelous, scurrilous, or threatening delineations, epithets, terms, or language, or reflecting injuriously upon the character or conduct of another, may be written or printed, are hereby declared to be nonmailable matter, and shall not be conveyed in the mails, nor delivered from any post-office nor by any letter-carrier; and any person who shall knowingly deposit * * *." 25 Stat. 188.

The proscription of scurrilous epithets had been part of § 1461 as amended in 1873, 17 Stat. 599, but it was removed in 1876 when the word's breadth and vagueness were objected to. Its reenactment was largely aimed at a "blackmailing" process for the collection of debts. 19 Cong. Rec. 2206, 6734, 7662 (1888).

[17] But see also id., at 6733–6734.

[18] 35 Stat. 1129.

[19] See *United States* v. *Limehouse*, 285 U.S. 424, 52 S. Ct. 412, 76 L. Ed. 843.

[20] (1) 18 U.S.C. § 1718, 18 U.S.C.A. § 1718, the criminal provision against mailing of matter libelous on its face, explicitly empowers the Postmaster General to make regulations governing its withdrawal from the mails; (2) 18 U.S.C. §§ 1341 and 1302, 18 U.S.C.A. §§ 1341, 1302, the criminal mail fraud and lottery provisions, have a matching section in the postal laws empowering the Postmaster General, upon evidence satisfactory to him, to mark mail "fraudulent" or "lottery mail" and to return it to its sender, 39 U.S.C. (Supp. II) § 4005, 39 U.S.C.A. § 4005; (3) 18 U.S.C. § 1342, 18 U.S.C.A. § 1342, making it a crime to conduct a fraudulent scheme by using a false name or address, also has a counterpart civil section empowering the Postmaster General, upon evidence satisfactory to him, to require proof of identity or to send such mail to the dead letter office, 39 U.S.C. (Supp. II) § 4003, 39 U.S.C.A. § 4003; (4) 18 U.S.C. §§ 1715 and 1716, 18 U.S.C.A. §§ 1715, 1716, making criminal the mailing of firearms and injurious articles, explicitly state that the Postmaster General may make regulations governing their transmission; (5) 18 U.S.C. § 1717, 18 U.S.C.A. § 1717, making criminal the mailing of matter advocating treason, explicitly authorized employees of the dead letter office to open such mail. See 74 Stat. 708. And see 7 U.S.C. § 150cc, 7 U.S.C.A. § 150cc and 33 Stat. 1270 (plant pests), 7 U.S.C.A. § 141 et seq. 38 Stat. 1113 (plants and plant products), 7 U.S.C.A. § 166, 22

§ 1461—itself silent as to sanctions except for the provision of criminal penalties—has no counterpart in the postal laws. It is mentioned once in the recodification of 1960—in § 4001(a), a section collecting the various provisions designating matter as nonmailable and which, the Committee Report indicates and the floor discussion and reviser's note assure, was not intended to change existing law[21]—ambiguous throughout.

The removal of obscene material has not been the Post Office's only weapon against it. In 1950, § 4006 was enacted granting special powers over the mail of any person found, to the Postmaster General's satisfaction, to be using the mails to obtain money for or to be providing information about any obscene or vile article or thing: Postmasters could mark mail sent *to* that person "unlawful" and return it to its sender; and they could forbid payment to that person of any money orders or postal notes, and return the funds to the senders.[22] The clarity of the grant of these powers is no less noteworthy than their subsequent history. In 1956 the Postmaster General sought[23] and obtained the power to enter an order, pending the administrative proceeding to determine whether § 4006 should be invoked, under which all mail addressed to the respondent could be impounded. The order was to expire at the end of 20 days unless the Postmaster General sought, in a Federal District Court, an order continuing the impounding. The 20-day order by the Postmaster General, and its extension by a court, were to issue only if "necessary to the effective enforcement of [§ 4006]."[24] In 1959, extensive hearings were held in the House on the Post Office's request that the 20-day period be extended to 45 days, and that the standard of necessity be changed to "public interest."[25] Instead, what was enacted in 1960 stripped the Postmaster General of his power to issue an interim order for any period, and directed him to seek a temporary restraining order in a Federal District Court.[26]

Congress gave full consideration to censorship of obscene material when it dealt with the Tariff Act of 1930. Prior to that year, the customs laws provided for the exclusion from the United States of obscene written matter, but required resort in the first instance to a Federal District Court for a determination of the matter's obscenity.[27] In the course of their work on the bill, the House Ways and Means Committee added language to exclude seditious as well as obscene material, and also replaced the judicial procedure with the generally applicable procedures for seizure by the customs officers, entailing judicial review only at the instance of a would-be importer. See H.R. Rep. No. 7, 71st Cong., 1st Sess., at 160, 185, 190, 244–245. It was in this form that the bill passed the House, and was reported by the Senate Committee, see S. Rep. No. 37, 71st Cong., 1st Sess. 60; 71 Cong. Rec. 4458 (remarks of Senator Smoot), but on the Senate floor it ran into strong expressions against customs censorship: fears about administrative determinations were enhanced by felt difficulties in applying the statute's proscriptions to particular material. Judicial review was thought insufficient, for that would leave the initiative for resort to the courts with the person subjected to the censorship: expense, inconvenience, and public embarrassment would, it was believed, result in unreviewed administrative exclusion. See generally 71 Cong. Rec. 4432–4439; 4445–4471. In support of the idea that the initial decision should be made by a court rather than a customs inspector, 72 Cong. Rec. 5417–5423, Senator Walsh of Montana said:

"The committee recognizes that even in its present form the bill gives the Postmaster General extraordinary and summary powers to impose a substantial penalty by impounding a person's mail for up to 20 days in advance of any hearing or any review by the courts. Such power is directly contrary to the letter and spirit of normal due process, as exemplified by the Administrative Procedure Act, which requires a hearing before any penalty may be imposed. The Post Office Department has made its case for this legislation on the grounds that a temporary and summary procedure is required to deal with fly-by-night operators using the mails to defraud or to peddle pornography, who may go out of business—or change the name of their business or their business address—before normal legal procedures can be brought into operation. The Post Office Department has not recommended, nor does this committee approve, the use of the temporary impounding procedure under this bill as a substitute for the normal practice of an advance hearing or the bringing of an indictment for violation of the criminal code in all cases involving legitimate and well-established business operations. The committee would not approve the use of the extraordinary summary procedure under the bill against legitimate publishers of newspapers, magazines, or books in cases in which a Postmaster General might take objection to an article, an issue, or a volume." S. Rep. No. 2234, 84th Cong., 2d Sess. 2–3, U.S. Code Cong. and Adm. News 1956, p. 3598.

U.S.C. § 618, 22 U.S.C.A. § 618 (foreign agents' propaganda advocating violent disorder in any other American republic); compare 7 U.S.C. § 1575, 7 U.S.C.A. § 1575 (false advertising of seed); 15 U.S.C. §§ 77q, 15 U.S.C.A. §§ 77q (fraudulent matter regarding securities), 80a-20 (solicitation of proxies), 80a-24 (sales literature regarding securities), 80b-3, 80b-5 and 80b-6 (investment advisers' materials); 50 U.S.C. § 789, 50 U.S.C.A., § 789 (publications of registered Communist organizations).

See *American School of Magnetic Healing* v. *McAnnulty*, 187 U.S. 94, 109, 23 S. Ct. 33, 39, 47 L. Ed. 90.

[21] H.R. Rep. No. 36, 86th Cong., 1st Sess. A44 (1959); 105 Cong. Rec. 3157 (1959) and 106 Cong. Rec. 15,667 (1960); and see supra, n. 11.

[22] 64 Stat. 451, now revised and codified as 39 U.S.C. (Supp. II) § 4006, 39 U.S.C.A. § 4006. See 74 Stat. 578, 655.

[23] It appears that between 1950 and 1956, the Postmaster General asserted, and some courts agreed, that he already had the power. See *Stanard* v. *Olesen*, supra, n. 3, 74 S. Ct. at 771.

[24] 70 Stat. 699.

[25] Hearings before House Subcommittee on Postal Operations of the Committee on Post Office and Civil Service on Obscene Matter Sent through the Mail, 86th Cong., 1st Sess. (1959).

[26] 74 Stat. 553. The codification of the postal laws, later in 1960, repealed 70 Stat. 699 (see 74 Stat. 708, 729) and not 74 Stat. 553, but the new § 4007 (74 Stat. 655) repeats the words of 70 Stat. 699. We need not now decide which is the governing provision.

The Senate Report in 1956 had said this:

[27] Section 305 of the Tariff Act of 1922, 42 Stat. 937, banned obscene and immoral matter, but subsection (c) provided:

"That any district judge * * * within the proper district * * * [may issue upon probable cause, conformably to the Constitution], a warrant directed to [a marshal or customs officer], directing him to * * * seize * * * any article or thing mentioned in [§ 305], and to make due and immediate return thereof, to the end that the same may be condemned and destroyed by proceedings, which shall be conducted in the same manner as other proceedings in the case of municipal seizure, and with the same right of appeal or writ of error." And see supra, n. 6; supra, 370 U.S., pp. 505–506, 82 S. Ct., p. 1446.

"Everybody of right mind wants to prevent the circulation of such books as the Senator from Utah has in mind. That is not the point at all. Those immoral and obscene and indecent publications are printed in this country, as well as abroad * * *. How do we reach the situation? We make it a crime to circulate those books in this country, and we punish that offense the same as we punish every other offense, by proper prosecution. Likewise, we prohibit the circulation of material of that kind in the mails, and if anybody circulates it in the mails he becomes liable to indictment and prosecution. That is the way we endeavor to deal with that thing." 72 Cong. Rec. 5419. *See also id., at 5425, 5430. But compare the remarks of Senators Copeland, Cutting, and Fletcher,* 71 Cong. Rec., at 4435, 4450.

He then offered an amendment to impose criminal sanctions for importing proscribed matter, and to require the matter's detention by the customs for transmittal to the appropriate authorities to commence judicial forfeiture proceedings. Id., at 5421. However, there were misgivings about the criminal sanction; it was thought by some to jeopardize borderline activity too seriously. Id., at 5423–5431. The Senate passed a provision corresponding to Senator Walsh's amendment, but without a criminal sanction, 72 Cong. Rec. 5501–5520, and this was enacted into law. Thus the House Committee's attempt to revert from judicial to administrative determinations in the initial phase of customs censorship was emphatically rebuffed.

III.

It is clear that the Post Office has long practiced administrative censorship of allegedly obscene mailings generally. However, the formal regulations prescribing a procedure are new.[28] The practice was described in 1952 by the Solicitor of the Department when testifying before a congressional committee:

"[W]e have an informal procedure, which, so far, hasn't been considered or tested out in the court, so we have gotten by with it so far. That is where a postmaster finds obscene matter at the point of entry of the mail into the post office, and if he is in doubt as to whether it is good or bad he will send it to the Solicitor's office for a ruling. * * *"

He also said:

"If we had to hold hearings on all of those, if any court should ever decide that those hearings also come under the Administrative Procedure Act, we are just hopelessly sunk, that is all; we are just lost.
"They may, but they have never taken us into court on it. We just hope that we get by with it as long as we can."[29]

And:

"[S]ometimes you can get five people together, and you can give them five pieces of mail, and ask them to mark them, and you will get five different results, because in some cases it is just one of those things that depends on your own personal ideas and your own bringing up; it depends upon how strongly you feel about things, and there are some types of that material that you just can't get two people to agree on no matter how reasonably and how objectively they look upon it. It is just an honest difference of opinion. We experience it all the time, so we have our conferences, and we decide what is going to be the best thing to do. * * *

*   *   *   *   *

"We have no trouble with prosecutions on things that are definitely obscene, but it is this material that is this way and that way that is very, very difficult to prosecute." Hearings before the Select Committee on Current Pornographic Materials, House of Representatives, on Investigation of Literature Allegedly Containing Objectionable Material, 82d Cong., 2d Sess. 281, 282 (1952).

It also is clear that this was not the first or last occasion on which Post Office practice has been brought to the attention of a congressional committee.[30] But the report of the 1952 Select Committee, which listed § 1461 as a criminal statute, certainly did not dispel the continuing ambiguity surrounding that section. And the report said:

"There are other means of handling this problem than by the ban of the censor, means which can be applied without danger of infringing on the freedom of the press * * *."[31]

But, in any event, testimony before committees, committee reports, and administrative usurpation, do not, either singly or collectively, suffice to establish authorization.

---

[28] These date from 1957. See 39 CFR §§ 14.4, 203 (1962).

[29] See *Wong Yang Sung v. McGrath,* 339 U.S. 33, 70 S. Ct. 445, 94 L. Ed. 616; *Riss & Co. v. United States,* 341 U.S. 907, 71 S. Ct. 620, 95 L. Ed. 1345; *Cates v. Haderlein,* 342 U.S. 804, 72 S. Ct. 47, 96 L. Ed. 609; *Walker v. Popenoe,* 80 U.S. App. D.C. 129, 149 F. 2d 511; *Door v. Donaldson,* 90 U.S. App. D.C. 188, 195 F. 2d 764. And see, supra, n. 23.

[30] See, e.g., Hearings before House Subcommittee No. 8 of the Committee on the Post Office and Post Roads on H.R. 5370, 74th Cong., 1st Sess. (1935); and Hearings, supra, n. 25; S. Rep. No. 2179, 81st Cong., 2d Sess. (1950); S. Rep. No. 113, 84th Cong., 1st Sess. (1955); Attorney General's Committee on Administrative Procedure, Post Office Department (1940); 19 Op. Atty. Gen. 667 (1890) (upholding exclusion from the mails of allegedly obscene portions of Tolstoi's "Kreutzer Sonata"); 4 Op. Asst. Atty. Gen., Post-Office Dept. 741 (1908) (holding that § 1461 is a civil as well as a criminal provision, and that the Post Office "in passing upon the mailability of matter under this statute * * * is not confined to the strict construction of the terms of the enactment which must be followed by a court in determining whether in a criminal case its provisions have been violated"). And see the sharp—and constitutionally colored—opposition to and rejection of a 1915 proposal that would have authorized the Postmaster General to close the mails to material sent by a person he had determined to be engaged in publishing obscene matter. Hearings before House Committee on the Post Office and Post Roads on Exclusion of Certain Publications from the Mails, 63d Cong., 3d Sess. (1915); *United States ex rel. Milwaukee Social Democratic Publishing Co. v. Burleson,* 255 U.S. 407, 424, 41 S. Ct. 352, 358, 65 L. Ed. 704 (Brandeis, J., dissenting).

[31] H.R. Rep. No. 2510, 82d Cong., 2d Sess. 5, 32.

IV.

We have sustained the criminal sanctions of § 1461 against a challenge of unconstitutionality under the First Amendment. *Roth* v. *United States*, 354 U.S. 476, 77 S. Ct. 1304, 1 L. Ed. 2d 1498. We have emphasized, however, that the necessity for safeguarding First Amendment protections for nonobscene materials means that Government "is not free to adopt whatever procedures it pleases for dealing with obscenity * * * without regard to the possible consequences for constitutionally protected speech." *Marcus* v. *Search Warrant*, 367 U.S. 717, 731, 81 S. Ct. 1708, 1716, 6 L. Ed. 2d 1127. I imply no doubt that Congress could constitutionally authorize a noncriminal process in the nature of a judicial proceeding under closely defined procedural safeguards. But the suggestion that Congress may constitutionally authorize any process other than a fully judicial one immediately raises the gravest doubts. However, it is enough to dispose of this case that Congress has not, in § 1461, authorized the Postmaster General to employ any process of his own to close the mails to matter which, in his view, falls within the ban of that section. "The provisions * * * would have to be far more explicit for us to assume that Congress made such a radical departure from our traditions and undertook to clothe the Postmaster General with the power to supervise the tastes of the reading public of the country." *Hannegan* v. *Esquire, Inc.*, 327 U.S., at 156, 66 S. Ct. at 461, 90 L. Ed. 586. I, therefore, concur in the judgment of reversal.

Mr. Justice CLARK (dissenting).

While those in the majority like ancient Gaul are split into three parts, the ultimate holding of the Court today, despite the clear congressional mandate found in § 1461, requires the United States Post Office to be the world's largest disseminator of smut and Grand Informer of the names and places where obscene material may be obtained. The Judicial Officer of the Post Office Department, the District Court, and the Court of Appeals have all found the magazines in issue to be nonmailable on the alternative grounds that they are obscene and that they contain information on where obscene material may be obtained. The Court, however, says that these magazines must go through the mails. Brother HARLAN, writing for himself and Brother STEWART, finds that the magazines themselves are unobjectionable because § 1461 is not so narrowly drawn as to prohibit the mailing of material "that incites immoral sexual conduct," and that the presence of information leading to obscene material does not taint the magazines because their publishers were unaware of the true nature of this information. Brother BRENNAN, joined by THE CHIEF JUSTICE and Brother DOUGLAS, finds that § 1461 does not authorize the Postmaster General through administrative process to close the mails to matter included within its proscriptions. Since in my view the Postmaster General is required by § 1461 to reject nonmailable matter, I would affirm the judgment on the sole ground that the magazines contain information as to where obscene material can be obtained and thus are nonmailable. I, therefore, do not consider the question of whether the magazines as such are obscene.

I.

The procedures followed below can be described briefly. Petitioners deposited in the Post Office in Alexandria, Virginia, six parcels containing 405 copies of three magazines which they published. The parcels were directed to petitioners' agent in Chicago and marked as second class matter. Being unsealed and subject to inspection,[1] the Postmaster noticed that the material appeared to be obscene. Under the regulations of the Post Office Department in effect since 1902, the Alexandria Postmaster notified the General Counsel of the Post Office Department in Washington and submitted samples of the material; the General Counsel determined the magazines to be nonmailable under § 1461 and notified petitioners' president. Petitioners sought injunctive relief against the Department in the District Court on the grounds that the magazines did not violate § 1461 and the procedure used amounted to an unconstitutional "ex parte administrative prior restraint," but the suit was dismissed for determination of the issue at an administrative hearing provided for by the Department's regulations. After a full hearing, at which petitioners did not dispute the congressional authorization to reject the six parcels for second class mailings, the Judicial Officer declared the material nonmailable. Petitioners contested this finding by judicial review in the District Court, where the action of the Judicial Officer was upheld.

Mr. Justice BRENNAN, as I have indicated, has reached the conclusion that when the Congress originally passed the Act in question some 97 years ago it granted no power to the Post Office to refuse to receive and carry matter declared by the Act to be nonmailable. Since this point was neither presented below nor argued here, I do not believe it to be properly before us. Brother BRENNAN, however, rests his concurring opinion on it and for that reason I shall discuss the issue.[2]

Section 1461 explicitly provides that:

*"Every obscene, lewd, lascivious, indecent, filthy or vile article, matter, thing, device, or substance; and * * * [e]very written or printed card, letter, circular, book, pamphlet, advertisement, or notice of any kind giving information, directly or indirectly, where, or how, or from whom, or by what means any of such mentioned matters, articles, or things may be obtained * * * [i]s declared to be nonmailable matter and shall not be conveyed in the mails or delivered from any post office or by any letter carrier."* (*Emphasis supplied.*)

Its genesis was in Section 16 of the Act of March 3, 1865, 13 Stat. 507, which when reported in the Senate had two parts:

"[N]o obscene book, pamphlet, picture, print, or other publication of a vulgar and indecent character, shall be admitted into the mails of the United States; but all such obscene publications deposited in or received at any post

---

[1] 39 U.S.C. (Supp. II) § 4058, 39 U.S.C.A. § 4058.

[2] I agree with the conclusion in that opinion that petitioners' constitutional claim cannot be considered here.

office, or discovered in the mails, shall be seized and destroyed, or otherwise disposed of, as the Postmaster General shall direct."

*"[A]ny person or persons who shall deposit or cause to be deposited in any post office or branch post office of the United States, for mailing or for delivery, an obscene book, pamphlet, picture, print, or other publication, knowing the same to be of a vulgar and indecent character, shall be deemed guilty of a misdemeanor * * *." Cong. Globe, 38th Cong., 2d Sess. 661.*

The sponsor of the bill advised the Senate that it had a twofold effect: "The first part of it provides that if such [obscene] publications are in the mails the postmasters may take them out; and the latter part provides a penalty and a punishment for those who put them into the mails." This explanation of the sponsor seems enough to undermine Brother BRENNAN's contention, but there is even more. Senator Johnson of Maryland apparently feared that obscene matter might be mailed in sealed envelopes and that "the postmaster * * * will break the seal." He moved to strike out the first part of the bill. Senator Sherman, however, objected, saying that *"the legislative prohibition against carrying such matter when it is known to the postmasters should be left.* Probably the second clause allowing him to open mail matter should be struck out." Ibid. (Emphasis supplied.) Senator Johnson acquiesced in this suggestion, and thus the bill as finally passed clearly permitted postmasters to refuse matters which were known by them to be obscene, so long as seals were not broken.[3]

The 1873 postal regulations reflected this power to exclude obscene matter from the mails,[4] as have all succeeding ones, e.g., Postal Laws and Regulations (1893 ed.) § 335. In 1876 the Act was amended to substantially its present form. 19 Stat. 90. It not only declared certain material "to be non-mailable matter" but added that such "shall not be conveyed in the mails, nor delivered from any post-office nor by any letter-carrier." A single comment by the bill's sponsor in the House reflects the understanding that this section, both before and after amendment, authorized exclusion:

"[T]he proposed bill in no wise changes the law as it now is except to provide a penalty for the circulation of obscene literature. By an oversight in drafting the original section the penalty applies only to the disposition of articles circulated or sold for the purpose of procuring abortion or preventing conception. Already this obscene class of matter spoken of in the other portion of the section is prohibited from passing through the mails, *but no penalty is provided. * * * [I]t in no way changes the section as it now is. It makes nothing non-mailable that is not now non-mailable. It merely provides a penalty. * * *" 4 Cong. Rec. 695 (1876). (Emphasis supplied.)*

---

[3] The magazines here involved were second class matter and thus were unsealed and subject to inspection. 39 U.S.C. (Supp. II) § 4058, 39 U.S.C.A. § 4058.

[4] "All books, pamphlets, circulars, prints, &c., of an obscene, vulgar, or indecent character * * * *must be withdrawn from the mails* by postmasters at either the office of mailing or the office of delivery." Postal Laws and Regulations (1873 ed.) § 88. (Emphasis supplied.)

Regulations establishing the procedure now used by the Department to determine questions of mailability were adopted in 1902. And in 1960 in a recodification the Congress included § 1461 within its collection of provisions which designate matter as nonmailable. 39 U.S.C. (Supp. II) § 4001(a), 39 U.S.C.A. § 4001(a).

In light of the language of the statutes, the legislative history, the subsequent recodification and the consistent history of administrative interpretation, it stretches my imagination to understand how one could conclude that Congress did not authorize the Post Office Department to exclude nonmailable material. As Justice Brandeis said in *United States* ex rel. *Milwaukee Social Democratic Publishing Co. v. Burleson,* 255 U.S. 407, 418, 421, 41 S. Ct. 352, 356, 357, 65 L. Ed. 704. (1921) (dissenting opinion):

"The scope of the Postmaster General's alleged authority is confessedly the same whether the reason for the nonmailable quality of the matter inserted in a newspaper is that it violates the Espionage Act, or the copyright laws, or that it is part of a scheme to defraud, or concerns lotteries, or is indecent, or is in any other respect matter which Congress has declared shall not be admitted to the mails.

* * * * * *

"As a matter of administration the Postmaster General, through his subordinates, rejects matter offered for mailing, or removes matter already in the mail, which in his judgment is unmailable. The existence in the Postmaster General of the power to do this cannot be doubted. The only question which can arise is whether in the individual case the power has been illegally exercised."

II.

Let us now turn to the opinion of Brother HARLAN and first take up the question whether magazines which indisputably contain information on where obscene material may be obtained can be considered nonmailable apart from the sender's scienter. Giving regard to the wording of § 1461, the interests involved, and the nature of the sanction imposed, I fail to see how the sender's scienter is anywise material to a determination of nonmailability. Section 1461 very explicitly demands that no information "be conveyed in the mails or delivered from any post office or by any letter carrier" if it in fact tells how obscene material can be obtained. This command running to those charged with the administration of the postal system is not conditioned by the words of the statute upon the sender's scienter or any remotely similar consideration. When it wants to inject a scienter requirement, the Congress well knows the words to use, as evidence by the very next sentence in § 1461 establishing the criminal sanctions: "Whoever *knowingly* uses the mails for the mailing, carriage in the mails, or delivery of anything declared by this section to be nonmailable * * * shall be fined not more than $5,000 or imprisoned not more than five years, or both * * *." (Emphasis supplied.) Congress could not have made it more clear that the sender's knowledge of the material to be mailed did not determine its mailability but only his responsibility for mailing it. Nor is there any reason why Congress—in a civil action—should have wanted it any other way. The sender's knowledge of the matter sought to be mailed is immaterial to the harm caused to the public by its dissemination. Finally, interpreting § 1461 to mean what it says would not give rise to the "serious constitutional question" envisioned. This fear is premised entirely on *Smith v. California*, 361 U.S. 147, 80 S. Ct. 215, 4 L. Ed. 2d 205 (1959), which was a criminal case. Surely the prerequisites to criminal responsibility are quite different from the tests for the use of the mails. The present determination of nonmailability of bulk packages of magazines to newsstands rains no sanctions or incriminations upon the publishers of these magazines nor does it confiscate or impound the magazines. For these reasons, I believe the only possible interpretation of § 1461 is that the sender's scienter is immaterial in determining the mailability of information on where obscene material can be obtained.

In passing, it might be noted that a requirement of scienter gives rise to some interesting problems. For instance: Is the sender's scienter permanently fixed at the time the material is first unsuccessfully offered for mailing, or is his scienter to be re-evaluated when the material is again offered for mailing? How are equitable principles such as "clean hands" and "he who seeks equity must do equity" squared in a proceeding to enjoin an administrative nonmailable order with an insistence on mailing material which has been shown to contain information leading to obscene material?

However, assuming that the knowledge of the sender is material in determining the mailability of these magazines, I submit the undisputed facts and findings compel as a matter of law the conclusion that the petitioners knew that materials published in their magazines informed their readers where obscene matter might be obtained. To say the least, these facts and findings are such that this Court ought not to set itself up as a fact-finder but should remand the case for a determination by those who have been entrusted initially with this responsibility.[5]

The content and direction of the magazines themselves are a tip-off as to the nature of the business of those who solicit through them. The magazines have no social, educational, or entertainment qualities but are designed solely as sex stimulants for homosexuals. They "consist almost entirely of photographs of young men in nude or practically nude poses handled in such a manner as to focus attention on their genitals or buttocks or to emphasize these parts * *." Because of this content the magazines do "not appeal to the ordinary male adult, * * *[who] would have no interest in them and would not buy them under ordinary circumstances and * * * [therefore] the readers of these publications consist almost entirely of male homosexuals and possibly a few adolescent males * * *." The publishers freely admit that the magazines are published to appeal to the male homosexual group. The advertisements and photographer lists in such magazines were quite naturally "designed so as to attract the male homosexual and to furnish him with names and addresses where nude male pictures in poses and conditions which would appeal to his prurient interest may be obtained." Moreover, the adver-

tisements themselves could leave no more doubt in the publishers' minds than in those of the solicited purchasers. To illustrate: some captioned a picture of a nude or scantily attired young man with the legend "perfectly proportioned, handsome, male models, age 18–26." Others featured a photograph of a nude male with the area around the privates obviously retouched so as to cover the genitals and part of the pubic hair and offered to furnish an "original print of this photo." Finally, each magazine specifically endorsed its listed photographers and requested its readers to support them by purchasing their products. In addition, three of the four magazines involved expressly represented that they were familiar with the work of the photographers listed in their publications.[6]

Turning to Womack, the president and directing force of all three corporate publishers, it is even clearer that we are not dealing here with a "Jack and Jill" operation. Mr. Womack admitted that the magazines were planned for homosexuals, designed to appeal to and stimulate their erotic interests. To improve on this effect, he made suggestions to photographers as to the type of pictures he wanted. For example, he informed one of the studios listed in his publications that "physique fans want their 'truck driver types' already cleaned up, showered, and ready for bed * * * [and] it is absolutely essential that the models have pretty faces and a personality not totally unrelated to sex appeal." Womack had also suggested to the photographers that they exchange customer names with the hope of compiling a master list of homosexuals. He himself had been convicted of selling obscene photographs via the mails. *Womack v. United States*, 111 U.S. App. D.C. 8, 294 F. 2d 204 (1961). More recently he has pleaded not guilty by reason of insanity to like charges. Washington Post, Feb. 1, 1962, p. D–3. Furthermore, he was warned in March, April, and July of 1959 that a number of his photographer advertisers were being prosecuted for mailing obscene matter and that he might be violating the law in transmitting through the mails their advertisements. However, he continued to disseminate such information through the mails, removing photographers from his lists only as they were convicted. Finally, through another controlled corporation not here involved, he filled orders for one of his advertisers sent in by the readers of his magazines. This material was found to be obscene and like all of the above facts and findings it is not contested here.

The corporate petitioners are chargeable with the knowledge of what they do, as well as the knowledge of their president and leader. How one can fail to see the obvious in this record is beyond my comprehension. In the words of Milton: "O dark, dark, dark amid the blaze of noon." For one to conclude that the above undisputed facts and findings are insufficient to show the required scienter, however stringently it may be defined, is in effect to repeal the advertising provisions of § 1461. To condition nonmailability on proof that the sender actually saw the material being sold by his advertisers is to portray the Congress as the "mother" in the jingle, "Mother, may I go out to swim? Yes, my darling daughter. Hang your clothes on a hickory limb and don't go near the water."

For these reasons I would affirm the decision below.

---

[5] If the express rejection by the Judicial Officer of petitioners' proposed finding that they had "no personal knowledge of the material sold by the advertisers" is taken as a finding to the contrary, then of course this is entitled to the deference accorded administrative findings, cf., e.g., *National Labor Relations Board v. Walton Mfg. Co.*, 369 U.S. 404, 82 S. Ct. 853, 7 L. Ed. 2d 829 (1962).

[6] The magazines were offered in six bundles, apparently with copies of each of the four magazines intermingled among the bundles.

■ William Marcus *et al., Appellants,*

v.

Search Warrants of Property at 104 East Tenth Street, Kansas City, Missouri, *et al.*

No. 225.

Argued March 30, 1961.—Decided June 19, 1961.

Mr. Sidney M. Glazer, Berkeley, Mo., for appellants.
Mr. Fred L. Howard, Jefferson City, Mo., for appellees.

Mr. Justice BRENNAN delivered the opinion of the Court.

This appeal presents the question whether due process under the Fourteenth Amendment was denied the appellants by the application in this case of Missouri's procedures authorizing the search for and seizure of allegedly obscene publications preliminarily to their destruction by burning or otherwise if found by a court to be obscene. The procedures are statutory, but are supplemented by a rule of the Missouri Supreme Court.[1] The warrant for search for and seizure of obscene material issues on a sworn complaint filed with a judge or magistrate.[2] If the com-

plainant states "positively and not upon information or belief," or states "evidential facts from which such judge or magistrate determines the existence of probable cause" to believe that obscene material "is being held or kept in any place or in any building," "such judge or magistrate shall issue a search warrant directed to any peace officer commanding him to search the place therein described and to seize and bring before such judge or magistrate the personal property therein described."[3] The owner of the property is not afforded a hearing before the warrant issues; the proceeding is *ex parte.* However, the judge or magistrate issuing the warrant must fix a date, not less than five nor more than 20 days after the seizure, for a hearing to determine whether the seized material is obscene.[4] The owner of the material may appear at such

---

[1] These procedures are separate from and in addition to the State's criminal statutes. See *State* v. *Mac Sales Co.,* Mo. App., 263 S.W. 2d 860. The criminal statutes are Mo. Rev. Stat. §§ 563.270, 563.280, 563.290; see also § 563.310, V.A.M.S.

[2] Mo. Rev. Stat. § 542.380, V.A.M.S. in pertinent part provides:

"Upon complaint being made, on oath, in writing, to any officer authorized to issue process for the apprehension of offenders, that any of the property or articles herein named are kept within the county of such officer, if he shall be satisfied that there is reasonable ground for such complaint, shall issue a warrant to the sheriff or any constable of the county, directing him to search for and seize any of the following property or articles:

*   *   *   *   *

"(2) Any of the following articles, kept for the purpose of being sold, published, exhibited, given away or otherwise distributed or circulated, viz.: obscene, lewd, licentious, indecent or lascivious books, pamphlets, ballads, papers, drawings, lithographs, engravings, pictures, models, casts, prints or other articles or publications of an indecent, immoral or scandalous character, or any letters, handbills, cards, circulars, books, pamphlets or advertisements or notices of any kind giving information, directly or indirectly, when, where, how or of whom any of such things can be obtained." These procedures also govern seizure and condemnation of gambling paraphernalia, contraceptive devices, and tools and other articles used to manufacture or produce such items. Fraudulent, forged, and counterfeited writings and other articles, and the instruments used to make them, are also declared contraband and subject to seizure. § 542.440.

[3] Missouri Supreme Court Rule 33.01 of the Rules of Criminal Procedure provides:

"(a) If a complaint in writing be filed with the judge or magistrate of any court having original jurisdiction to try criminal offenses stating that personal property * * * the seizure of which under search warrant is now or may hereafter be authorized by any statute of this State, is being held or kept at any place or in any building * * * within the territorial jurisdiction of such judge or magistrate, and if such complaint be verified by the oath or affirmation of the complainant and states such facts positively and not upon information or belief; or if the same be supported by written affidavits verified by oath or affirmation stating evidential facts from which such judge or magistrate determines the existence of probable cause, then such judge or magistrate shall issue a search warrant directed to any peace officer commanding him to search the place therein described and to seize and bring before such judge or magistrate the personal property therein described.

"(b) The complainant and the warrant issued thereon must contain a description of the personal property to be searched for and seized and a description of the place to be searched, in sufficient detail and particularity to enable the officer serving the warrant to readily ascertain and identify the same."

[4] Mo. Rev. Stat. § 542.400, V.A.M.S. provides:

"The judge or magistrate issuing the warrant shall set a day, not less than five days nor more than twenty days after the date of such service and seizure, for determining whether such property is the kind of property mentioned in section 542.380, and shall order the officer having such property in charge to retain possession of the same until after such hearing. Written notice of the date and place of such hearing shall be given, at least five

hearing and defend against the charge.[5] No time limit is provided within which the judge must announce his decision. If the judge finds that the material is obscene, he is required to order it to be publicly destroyed, by burning or otherwise; if he finds that it is not obscene, he shall order its return to its owner.[6]

[1] The Missouri Supreme Court sustained the validity of the procedures as applied in this case. 334 S.W. 2d 119. The appellants brought this appeal here under 28 U.S.C. § 1257(2), 28 U.S.C.A. § 1257(2). We postponed consideration of the question of our jurisdiction to the hearing of the case on the merits. 364 U.S. 811, 81 S. Ct. 61, 5 L. Ed. 2d 40. We hold that the appeal is properly here, see *Dahnke-Walker Milling Co.* v. *Bondurant*, 257 U.S. 282, 42 S. Ct. 106, 66 L. Ed. 239, and turn to the merits.

Appellant, Kansas City News Distributors, managed by appellant, Homer Smay, is a wholesale distributor of magazines, newspapers and books in the Kansas City area. The other appellants operate five retail newsstands in Kansas City. In October 1957, Police Lieutenant Coughlin of the Kansas City Police Department Vice Squad was conducting an investigation into the distribution of allegedly obscene magazines. On October 8, 1957, he visited Distributors' place of business and showed Smay a list of magazines. Smay admitted that his company distributed all but one of the magazines on the list. The following day, October 9, Lieutenant Coughlin visited the five newsstands and purchased one magazine at each.[7] On October 10 the officer signed and filed six sworn complaints in the Circuit Court of Jackson County, stating in each complaint that "of his own knowledge" the appellant named therein, at its stated place of business, "kept for the purpose of [sale]

---

days before such date, by posting a copy of such notice in a conspicuous place upon the premises in which such property is seized, and by delivering a copy of such notice to any person claiming an interest in such property, whose name may be known to the person making the complaint or to the officer issuing or serving such warrant, or leaving the same at the usual place of abode of such person with any member of his family or household above the age of fifteen years. Such notice shall be signed by the magistrate or judge or by the clerk of the court of such judge."

[5] Mo. Rev. Stat. § 542.410, V.A.M.S. provides:

"Rights of property owner.—The owner or owners of such property may appear at such hearing and defend against the charges as to the nature and use of the property so seized, and such judge or magistrate shall determine, from the evidence produced at such hearing, whether the property is the kind of property mentioned in section 542.380."

[6] Mo. Rev. Stat. § 542.420, V.A.M.S. provides:

"Disposition of property.—If the judge or magistrate hearing such cause shall determine that the property or articles are of the kind mentioned in section 542.380, he shall cause the same to be publicly destroyed, by burning or otherwise, and if he find that such property is not of the kind mentioned, he shall order the same returned to its owner. If it appears that it may be necessary to use such articles or property as evidence in any criminal prosecution, the judge or magistrate shall order the officer having possession of them to retain such possession until such necessity no longer exists, and they shall neither be destroyed nor returned to the owner until they are no longer needed as such evidence."

[7] He bought a copy of the same magazine at three of the stands, a copy of another edition of this magazine at a fourth stand, and a copy of one other magazine at the fifth stand.

---

* * * obscene * * * publications * * *." No copy of any magazine on Lieutenant Coughlin's list, or purchased by him at the newsstands, was filed with the complaint or shown to the circuit judge. The circuit judge issued six search warrants authorizing, as to the premises of the appellant named in each, "any peace officer in the State of Missouri * * * [to] search the said premises * * * within 10 days after the issuance of this warrant by day or night, and * * * seize * * * [obscene materials] and take same into your possession * * *."

All of the warrants were executed on October 10, but by different law enforcement officers. Lieutenant Coughlin with two other Kansas City police officers, and an officer of the Jackson County Sheriff's Patrol, executed the warrant against Distributors. Distributors' stock of magazines runs "into hundreds of thousands * * * [p]robably closer to a million copies." The officers examined the publications in the stock on the main floor of the establishment, not confining themselves to Lieutenant Coughlin's original list. They seized all magazines which "[i]n our judgment" were obscene; when an officer thought "a magazine * * * ought to be picked up" he seized all copies of it. After three hours the examination was completed and the magazines seized were "hauled away in a truck and put on the 15th floor of the courthouse." A substantially similar procedure was followed at each of the five newsstands. Approximately 11,000 copies of 280 publications, principally magazines but also some books and photographs, were seized at the six places.[8]

The circuit judge fixed October 17 for the hearing, which was later continued to October 23. Timely motions were made by the appellants to quash the search warrants and to suppress as evidence the property seized, and for the immediate return of the property. The motions were rested on a number of grounds but we are concerned only with the challenge to the application of the procedures in the context of the protections for free speech and press assured against state abridgement by the Fourteenth Amendment.[9] Unconstitutionality in violation of the Fourteenth Amendment was asserted because the procedures as applied (1) allowed a seizure by police officers "without notice or any hearing afforded to the movants prior to seizure for the purpose of determining whether or not these * * * publications are obscene * * *," and (2) because they "allowed police officers and deputy sheriffs to decide and make a judicial determination after the warrant was issued as to which * * * magazines were * * * obscene * * and were subject to seizure, impairing movants' freedom of speech and publication." The circuit judge reserved rulings on the motions and heard testimony of the

---

[8] The publications seized included so-called "girlie" magazines, nudist magazines, treatises and manuals on sex, photography magazines, cartoon and joke books and still photographs.

[9] Because of the result which we reach, it is unnecessary to decide other constitutional questions raised by the appellants, (1) whether the Missouri statutes are invalid on their face as authorizing an unconstitutional censorship and previous restraint of publications; (2) whether the Missouri courts applied an unconstitutional test of obscenity; and (3) whether the publications condemned are obscene under the test of *Roth* v. *United States*, 354 U.S. 476, 77 S. Ct. 1304, 1 L. Ed. 2d 1498.

police officers concerning the events surrounding the issuance and execution of the several warrants. On December 12, 1957, the circuit judge filed an unreported opinion in which he overruled the several motions and found that 100 of the 280 seized items were obscene. A judgment thereupon issued directing that the 100 items, and all copies thereof, "shall be retained by the Sheriff of Jackson Country * * as necessary evidence for the purpose of possible criminal prosecution or prosecutions, and, when such necessity no longer exists, said Sheriff * * * shall publicly destroy the same by burning within thirty days thereafter"; it ordered further that the 180 items not found to be obscene, and all copies thereof, "shall be returned forthwith by the Sheriff * * * to the rightful owner or owners * * *."

I.

The use by government of the power of search and seizure as an adjunct to a system for the suppression of objectionable publications is not new. Historically the struggle for freedom of speech and press in England was bound up with the issue of the scope of the search and seizure power. See generally Siebert, Freedom of the Press in England, 1476–1776; Hanson, Government and the Press, 1695–1763. It was a principal instrument for the enforcement of the Tudor licensing system. The Stationers' Company was incorporated in 1557 to help implement that system and was empowered "to make search whenever it shall please them in any place, shop, house, chamber, or building or any printer, binder or bookseller whatever within our kingdom of England or the dominions of the same of or for any books or things printed, or to be printed, and to seize, take hold, burn, or turn to the proper use of the foresaid community, all and several those books and things which are or shall be printed contrary to the form of any statute, act, or proclamation, made or to be made * * *."[10]

An order of counsel confirmed and expanded the Company's power in 1566,[11] and the Star Chamber reaffirmed it in 1586 by a decree "That it shall be lawful for the wardens of the said Company for the time being or any two of the said Company thereto deputed by the said wardens, to make search in all workhouses, shops, warehouses of printers, booksellers, bookbinders, or where they shall have reasonable cause of suspicion, and all books [etc.] * * * contrary to * * * these present ordinances to stay and take to her Majesty's use * * *."[12] Books thus seized were taken to Stationers' Hall where they were inspected by ecclesiastical officers, who decided whether they should be burnt. These powers were exercised under the Tudor censorship to suppress both Catholic and Puritan dissenting literature.[13]

Each succeeding regime during turbulent Seventeenth Century England used the search and seizure power to suppress publications. James I commissioned the ecclesiastical judges comprising the Court of High Commission "to enquire and search for * * * all heretical, schismatical and seditious books, libels, and writings, *and all other books, pamphlets and portraitures offensive to the state or set forth without sufficient and lawful authority in that behalf,* * * * and the same books [etc.] and their printing-presses themselves likewise to seize *and so to order and dispose of them * * * as they may not after serve or be employed for any such unlawful use * * *.*"[14] The Star Chamber decree of 1637, re-enacting the requirement that all books be licensed, continued the broad powers of the Stationers' Company to enforce the licensing laws.[15] During the political overturn of the 1640's Parliament on several occasions asserted the necessity of a broad search and seizure power to control printing. Thus an order of 1648 gave power to the searchers "to search in any house or place where there is just cause of suspicion, that Presses are kept and employed in the printing of Scandalous and lying Pamphlets, * * * [and] to seize such scandalous and lying pamphlets as they find upon search * * *."[16] The Restoration brought a new licensing act in 1662. Under its authority "messengers of the press" operated under the secretaries of state, who issued executive warrants for the seizure of persons and papers. These warrants, while sometimes specific in content, often gave the most general discretionary authority. For example, a warrant to Roger L'Estrange, the Surveyor of the Press, empowered him to "seize all seditious books and libels and to apprehend the authors, contrivers, printers, publishers, and dispersers of them," and to "search any house, shop, printing room, chamber, warehouse, etc. for seditious, scandalous or unlicensed pictures, books, or papers, to bring away or deface the same, and the letter press, taking away all the copies * * *."[17] Another warrant gave L'Estrange power to "search for & seize authors, contrivers, printers, * * * publishers, dispensers, & concealers of treasonable, schismaticall, seditious or unlicensed books, libells, pamphlets, or papers * * * together with all copys exemplaryes of such Books, libells, pamphlets or paper as aforesaid."[18]

Although increasingly attacked, the licensing system was continued in effect for a time even after the Revolution of 1688 and executive warrants continued to issue for the search for and seizure of offending books. The Stationers' Company was also ordered "to make often and diligent searches in all such places you or any of you shall know or have any probable reason to suspect, and to seize all unlicensed, scandalous books and pamphlets * * *."[19] And even when the device of prosecution for seditious libel replaced licensing as the principal governmental control of the press,[20] it too was enforced with the aid of general

---

[10] 1 Arber, Transcript of the Registers of the Company of Stationers of London, 1554–1640 A.D., p. xxxi.

[11] Elton, The Tudor Constitution, p. 106.

[12] Elton, supra, pp. 182–183.

[13] Siebert, supra, pp. 83, 85–86, 97.

[14] Siebert, supra, p. 139, citing Pat. Roll, 9, Jac. I, Pt. 18; id., II, Pt. 15.

[15] 4 Arber, supra, pp. 529–536.

[16] Siebert, supra, 214–215, note 72.

[17] Siebert, supra, p. 254, citing Minute Entry Book 5, p. 177.

[18] Siebert, supra, p. 256, citing Entry Book, Chas. II, 1664, Vol. 21, p. 21; also Vol. 16, p. 130.

[19] Cal. St. P., Dom. Ser., 1690–1691, p. 74.

[20] One of the primary objections to licensing was its enforcement through search and seizure. The House of Commons' list of reasons why the licensing act should not be renewed included:

warrants—authorizing either the arrest of all persons connected with the publication of a particular libel and the search of their premises, or the seizure of all the papers of a named person alleged to be connected with the publication of a libel.[21]

Enforcement through general warrants was finally judicially condemned in England. This was the consequence of the struggle of the 1760's between the Crown and the opposition press led by John Wilkes, author and editor of the North Briton. From this struggle came the great case of *Entick* v. *Carrington*, 19 How. St. Tr. 1029, which this Court has called "one of the landmarks of English liberty." *Boyd* v. *United States*, 116 U.S. 616, 626, 6 S. Ct. 524, 530, 29 L. Ed. 746. A warrant based on a charge of seditious libel issued for the arrest of Entick, writer for an opposition paper, and for the seizure of all his papers. The officers executing the warrant ransacked Entick's home for four hours and carted away great quantities of books and papers. Lord Camden declared the general warrant for the seizure of papers contrary to the common law, despite its long history. Camden said: "This power so assumed by the secretary of state is an execution upon all the party's papers, in the first instance. His house is rifled; his most valuable secrets are taken out of his possession, before the paper for which he is charged is found to be criminal by any competent jurisdiction, and before he is convicted either of writing, publishing, or being concerned in the paper." At 1064. Camden expressly dismissed the contention that such a warrant could be justified on the grounds that it was "necessary for the ends of government to lodge such a power with a state officer; and * * * better to prevent the publication before than to punish the offender afterwards." At 1073. In *Wilkes* v. *Wood*, 19 How. St. Tr. 1153, Camden also condemned the general warrants employed against John Wilkes for his publication of issue No. 45 of the North Briton. He declared that these warrants, calling for the arrest of unnamed persons connected with the alleged libel and seizure of their papers, amounted to a "discretionary power given to messengers to search wherever their suspicions may chance to fall. If such a power is truly invested in a secretary of state, and he can delegate this power, it certainly may affect the person and property of every man in this kingdom, and is totally subversive of the liberty of the subject." Id., 1167.[22]

This history was, of course, part of the intellectual matrix within which our own constitutional fabric was shaped. The Bill of Rights was fashioned against the background of knowledge that unrestricted power of search and seizure could also be an instrument for stifling liberty of expression. For the serious hazard of suppression of innocent expression inhered in the discretion confided in the officers authorized to exercise the power.

II.

[2] The question here is whether the use by Missouri in this case of the search and seizure power to suppress obscene publications involved abuses inimical to protected expression. We held in *Roth* v. *United States*, 354 U.S. 476, 485, 77 S. Ct. 1304, 1309, 1 L. Ed. 2d 1498,[23] that "obscenity is not within the area of constitutionally protected speech or press." But in Roth itself we expressly recognized the complexity of the test of obscenity fashioned in that case and the vital necessity in its application of safeguards to prevent denial of "the protection of freedom of speech and press for material which does not treat sex in a manner appealing to prurient interest." Id., 354 U.S. at page 488, 77 S. Ct. at page 1311. We have since held that a State's power to suppress obscenity is limited by the constitutional protections for free expression. In *Smith* v. *People of State of California*, 361 U.S. 147, 155, 80 S. Ct. 215, 220, 4 L. Ed. 2d 205, we said, "The existence of the State's power to prevent the distribution of obscene matter does not mean that there can be no constitutional barrier to any form of practical exercise of that power," inasmuch as "our holding in Roth does not recognize any state power to restrict the dissemination of books which are not obscene." Id., 361 U.S. at page 152, 80 S. Ct. at page 218. We therefore held that a State may not impose absolute criminal liability on a bookseller for the possession of obscene material, even if it may dispense with the element of *scienter* in dealing with such evils as impure food and drugs. We remarked the distinction between the cases: "There is no specific constitutional inhibition against making the distributors of food the strictest censors of their merchandise, but the constitutional guarantees of the freedom of speech and of the press stand in the way of imposing a similar requirement on the bookseller." Id., 361 U.S. at pages 152–153, 80 S. Ct. at page 218. The Mis-

---

"Because that Act subjects all Mens Houses, as well Peers as Commoners, to be searched at any Time, either by Day or Night, by a Warrant under the Sign Manual, or under the Hand of One of the Secretaries of State, directed to any Messenger, if such Messenger shall upon probable Reason suspect that there are any unlicensed Books there; and the Houses of all Persons free of the Company of Stationers are subject to the like Search, on a Warrant from the Master and Wardens of the said Company, or any One of them." 15 Journal of the House of Lords, April 18, 1695, p. 546.

21 Siebert, supra, pp. 374–376.

22 A contemporary London pamphlet summed up the widespread indignation against the use of the general warrant for the seizure of papers: "In such a party-crime, as a public libel, who can endure this assumed authority of taking all papers indiscriminately? * * * where there is even a charge against one particular paper, to seize *all*, of every kind, is extravagant, unreasonable and inquisitorial. It is infamous in theory, and downright tyranny and despotism in practice." Father of Candor, A Letter

Concerning Libels, Warrants, and the Seizure of Papers, p. 48 (2d ed. 1764, J. Almon printer).

See generally Lasson, The History and Development of the Fourth Amendment, pp. 42–50; Hanson, Government and the Press, 1695–1763, pp. 29–32, 49–50. An even broader form of general warrant was the writ of assistance, which met such vigorous opposition in the American Colonies prior to the Revolution. Unlike the warrants of the North Briton affair and *Entick* v. *Carrington*, which were at least concerned with a particular designated libel, these writs empowered the executing officer to seize any illegally imported goods or merchandise. Moreover, in addition to authorizing search without limit of place, they had no fixed duration. In effect, complete discretion was given to the executing officials; in the words of James Otis, their use placed "the liberty of every man in the hands of every petty officer." Tudor, Life of James Otis (1823), p. 66. See Lasson, supra, pp. 51–78.

23 This holding applied also to the obscenity question raised under the Fourteenth Amendment in *Alberts* v. *State of California*, decided in the same opinion.

souri Supreme Court's assimilation of obscene literature to gambling paraphernalia or other contraband for purposes of search and seizure does not therefore answer the appellants' constitutional claim, but merely restates the issue whether obscenity may be treated in the same way. The authority to the police officers under the warrants issued in this case, broadly to seize "obscene * * * publications," poses problems not raised by the warrants to seize "gambling implements" and "all intoxicating liquors" involved in the cases cited by the Missouri Supreme Court. 334 S.W. 2d at page 125. For the use of these warrants implicates questions whether the procedures leading to their issuance and surrounding their execution were adequate to avoid suppression of constitutionally protected publications. "* * * [T]he line between speech unconditionally guaranteed and speech which may legitimately be regulated, suppressed, or punished is finely drawn. * * * The separation of legitimate from illegitimate speech calls for * * * sensitive tools * * *." *Speiser* v. *Randall*, 357 U.S. 513, 525, 78 S. Ct. 1332, 1342, 2 L. Ed. 2d 1460.[24] It follows that, under the Fourteenth Amendment, a State is not free to adopt whatever procedures it pleases for dealing with obscenity as here involved without regard to the possible consequences for constitutionally protected speech.

[3] We believe that Missouri's procedures as applied in this case lacked the safeguards which due process demands to assure nonobscene material the constitutional protection to which it is entitled. Putting to one side the fact that no opportunity was afforded the appellants to elicit and contest the reasons for the officer's belief, or otherwise to argue against the propriety of the seizure to the issuing judge, still the warrants issued on the strength of the conclusory assertions of a single police officer, without any scrutiny by the judge of any materials considered by the complainant to be obscene. The warrants gave the broadest discretion to the executing officers; they merely repeated the language of the statute and the complaints, specified no publications, and left to the individual judgment of each of the many police officers involved the selection of such magazines as in his view constituted "obscene * * * publications." So far as appears from the record, none of the officers except Lieutenant Coughlin had previously examined any of the publications which were subsequently seized. It is plain that in many instances, if not in all, each officer actually made *ad hoc* decisions on the spot and, gauged by the number of publications seized and the time spent in executing the warrants, each decision was made with little opportunity for reflection and deliberation. As to publications seized because they appeared on the Lieutenant's list, we know nothing of the basis for the original judgment that they were obscene. It is no reflection on the good faith or judgment of the officers to conclude that the task they were assigned was simply an impossible one to

perform with any realistic expectation that the obscene might be accurately separated from the constitutionally protected. They were provided with no guide to the exercise of informed discretion, because there was no step in the procedure before seizure designed to focus searchingly on the question of obscenity. See generally 1 Chafee, Government and Mass Communications, pp. 200–218. In consequence there were suppressed and withheld from the market for over two months 180 publications not found obscene.[25] The fact that only one-third of the publications seized were finally condemned strengthens the conclusion that discretion to seize allegedly obscene materials cannot be confided to law enforcement officials without greater safeguards than were here operative. Procedures which sweep so broadly and with so little discrimination are obviously deficient in techniques required by the Due Process Clause of the Fourteenth Amendment to prevent erosion of the constitutional guarantees.[26]

---

[24] Lord Camden in *Entick* v. *Carrington* recognized that there was no justification for the abuse of the search and seizure power in suppressing seditious libel, even if the view were accepted that "men ought not to be allowed to have such evil instruments in their keeping." 19 How. St. Tr., at 1072. He said, "If [libels may be seized], I am afraid, that all the inconveniences of a general seizure will follow upon a right allowed to seize a part. The search in such cases will be general, and every house will fall under the power of a secretary of state to be rummaged before proper conviction." Id., at 1071.

[25] Among the publications ordered returned were such titles as "The Dawn of Rational Sex Ethics," "Sex Symbolism," "Notes on Cases of Sexual Suppression," "Your Affections, Emotions and Feelings," "Sexual Impotence, Its Causes and Treatments," "The Psychology of Sex Life," "Freud on Sleep and Sexual Dreams," "The Determination of Sex," "Sex and Psychoanalysis," "Artificial Insemination," "Syphilis, A Treatise for the American Public," "What You Should Know About Sexual Impotency," "Variations in Sexual Behavior," "Sex Life in Marriage," "Pyschopathia Sexualis," "The Sex Technique in Marriage," "Sexual Deviations," "Sex Practice in Later Years," and "Marriage, Sex, and Family Problems."

[26] English practice in such cases has placed greater restraint on the seizure power. Seizure of obscene material, as a prelude to condemnation, was authorized there by Lord Campbell's Obscene Publications Act of 1857, 20 & 21 Vict., c. 83. As originally proposed, that statute would have allowed search for and seizure of obscene matter either under authority granted by magistrates or on warrants granted by the Chief Commissioner of Police. Moreover, the affidavit for obtaining a warrant would have been required to contain merely the statement that the person making it had reasonable ground for suspicion that obscene publications were kept on the premises to be searched. See 146 Hansard's Parliamentary Debates, 3d Series, p. 866. These provisions met vigorous opposition in Parliament. A number of members emphasized that the difficulty of defining obscenity made broad search powers in police hands extremely dangerous. See id., pp. 330–332, 1360–1362, 147 Hansard, supra, pp. 1863–1864. As a result, amendments were adopted removing the grant of authority to the police commissioner to authorize a search and seizure, requiring greater specificity in the allegations before a warrant could be issued, and providing that warrants could issue only for the seizure of books the publication of which would constitute a common-law misdemeanor. Lord Lyndhurst, draftsman of these amendments, explained: "I have now provided that the person shall swear that he has reason to believe, and that he does believe, that there are such publications in such a place, and shall further state to the magistrate the reasons which lead to that belief. Nor does it stop there. The most material Amendment is, that he must state what the publications are, and that they are of such a nature that, if published, the party publishing them will be guilty of a misdemeanour. The magistrate must also be satisfied that the case is a proper one for a prosecution * * *." 146 Hansard, supra, at p. 1360. The Lord Chancellor summarized the effect of the changes: "As the Bill now stood, these search-warrants would only be granted after great precautions * * *." Id., p. 1362.

According to a recent summary of procedures to obtain a warrant under that Act, a police officer would ordinarily buy copies of a work he suspected of obscenity. They would be

III.

The reliance of the Missouri Supreme Court upon *Kingsley Books, Inc.* v. *Brown,* 354 U.S. 436, 77 S. Ct. 1325, 1 L. Ed. 2d 1469, is misplaced. The differences in the procedures under the New York statute upheld in that case and the Missouri procedures as applied here are marked. They amount to the distinction between "a 'limited injunctive remedy,' under closely defined procedural safeguards, against the sale and distribution of written and printed matter found after due trial to be obscene," Kingsley Books, supra, 354 U.S. at page 437, 77 S. Ct. at page 1326, and a scheme which in operation inhibited the circulation of publications' indiscriminately because of the absence of any such safeguards. *First,* the New York injunctive proceeding was initiated by a complaint filed with the court which charged that a particular named obscene publication had been displayed, and to which were annexed copies of the publication alleged to be obscene.[27] The court, in restraining distribution pending final judicial determination of the claim, thus had the allegedly obscene material before it and could exercise an independent check on the judgment of the prosecuting authority at a point before any restraint took place. *Second,* the restraints in Kingsley Books, both temporary and permanent, ran only against the named publication; no catchall restraint against the distribution of all "obscene" material was imposed on the defendants there, comparable to the warrants here which authorized a mass seizure and the removal of a broad range of items from circulation.[28] *Third,* Kingsley Books does not support the proposition that the State may impose the extensive restraints imposed here on the distribution of these publications prior to an adversary proceeding on the issue of obscenity, irrespective of whether or not the material is legally obscene. This Court expressly noted there that the State was not attempting to punish the distributors for disobedience of any interim order entered before hearing. The Court pointed out that New York might well construe its own law as not imposing any punishment for violation of an interim order were the book found not obscene after due trial. 354 U.S. at page 443, note 2, 77 S. Ct. at page 1329. But there is no doubt that an effective restraint—indeed the most effective restraint possible—was imposed prior to hearing on the circulation of the publications in this case, because all copies on which the police could lay their hands were physically removed from the newsstands and from the premises of the wholesale distributor. An opportunity comparable to that which the distributor in Kingsley Books might have had to circulate the publication despite the interim restraint and then raise the claim of nonobscenity by way of defense to a prosecution for doing so was never afforded these appellants because the copies they possessed were taken away. Their ability to circulate their publications was left to the chance of securing other copies, themselves subject to mass seizure under other such warrants. The public's opportunity to obtain the publications was thus determined by the distributor's readiness and ability to outwit the police by obtaining and selling other copies before they in turn could be seized. In addition to its unseemliness, we do not believe that this kind of enforced competition affords a reasonable likelihood that nonobscene publications, entitled to constitutional protection, will reach the public. A distributor may have every reason to believe that a publication is constitutionally protected and will be so held after judicial hearing, but his belief is unavailing as against the contrary judgment of the police officer who seizes it from him.[29] Finally, a subdivision of the New York statute in Kingsley Books required that a judicial decision on the merits of obscenity be made within two days of trial, which in turn was required to be within one day of the joinder of issue on the request for an injunction.[30] In contrast, the Missouri statutory scheme drawn in question here has no limitation on the time within which decision must be made, only a provision for rapid trial of the issue of obscenity. And in

examined by the police and sent to the Director of Public Prosecutions. The latter would return them with advice as to whether a warrant should be applied for. If a decision were made to seek a warrant, the publications would be laid before a magistrate with the sworn affidavit of the officer, in order that he might be satisfied that they were of the character necessary to justify seizure. See Memorandum of the Association of Chief Police Officers of England and Wales, Minutes of Evidence Taken Before the Select Committee of the House of Commons on the Obscene Publications Bill, 1956–1957, pp. 132–136. See also, id., p. 23.

The Act was replaced by the Obscene Publications Act of 1959, 7 & 8 Eliz. II, c. 66. See 23 Mod. L. Rev. 285.

[27] The feasibility of particularization in complaint and warrant in a case such as the present is apparent, since the publications were sold on newsstands distributing to the public. Compare Lord Camden's remark in *Entick* v. *Carrington,* directed to the contention that a general warrant might be justifiable as a means of uncovering evidence of crime: "If * * * a right of search for the sake of discovering evidence ought in any case to be allowed, this crime [seditious libel] above all others ought to be excepted, as wanting such a discovery less than any other. It is committed in open daylight, and in the face of the world; * * *." 19 How. St. Tr., at 1074.

[28] The trial judge in Kingsley Books refused to enjoin the distribution of future issues of the publication in question, stating: "[u]nless the work be before the court at the time of the hearing at which the injunction is sought, it is inappropriate to make a judicial determination with respect to it. In respect of this feature of the case, the plaintiff seeks a likely trespass upon a constitutionally protected area, and the court must reject that prayer." *Burke* v. *Kingsley Books, Inc.,* 208 Misc. 150, 168–169, 142 N.Y.S. 2d 735, 751. Cf. *Near* v. *State of Minnesota* ex rel. *Olson,* 283 U.S. 697, 51 S. Ct. 625, 75 L. Ed. 1357.

[29] Cf. Freund, The Supreme Court and Civil Liberties, 4 Vand. L. Rev. 533, 539.

Blackstone's often-quoted formulation of the principle of freedom of the press, though restricted to the prohibition of "*previous* restraints upon publications," nevertheless acknowledged the importance of an adjudicatory procedure as a protection against the suppression of inoffensive publications. He wrote: "to punish (as the law does at present) any dangerous or offensive writings, which, when published, shall *on a fair and impartial trial be adjudged of a pernicious tendency,* is necessary for the preservation of peace and good order * * *." 4 Commentaries, pp. 151–152. (Emphasis added.) Compare Butler, J., dissenting in *Near* v. *State of Minnesota* ex rel. *Olson,* supra, 283 U.S. at page 723, 51 S. Ct. at page 633: "The decision of the Court in this case declares Minnesota and every other state powerless to restrain by injunction the business of publishing and circulating among the people malicious, scandalous and defamatory periodicals that *in due course of judicial procedure has been adjudged to be a public nuisance.*" (Emphasis added.)

[30] This provision was not directly implicated in Kingsley Books because the parties had waived the provision for immediate trial.

fact over two months elapsed between seizure and decision.[31] In these circumstances the restraint on the circulation of publications was far more thoroughgoing and drastic than any restraint upheld by this Court in Kingsley Books.

Mass seizure in the fashion of this case was thus effected without any safeguards to protect legitimate expression.

---

[31] Compare the objection of the House of Commons to renewal of licensing: "Because that Act appoints no Time wherein the Archbishop, or Bishop of London, shall appoint a learned Man, or that One or more of the Company of Stationers shall go to the Customhouse, to view imported Books; so that they or either of them may delay it till the Importer may be undone, by having so great a Part of his Stock lie dead * * *." 15 Journals of the House of Lords, April 18, 1695, p. 546.

The judgment of the Missouri Supreme Court sustaining the condemnation of the 100 publications therefore cannot be sustained. We have no occasion to reach the question of the correctness of the finding that the publications are obscene. Nor is it necessary for us to decide in this case whether Missouri lacks all power under its statutory scheme to seize and condemn obscene material. Since a violation of the Fourteenth Amendment infected the proceedings, in order to vindicate appellants' constitutional rights the judgment is reversed, and the cause is remanded for further proceedings not inconsistent with this opinion. It is so ordered.

Judgment reversed and cause remanded.

■ Zenith International Film Corporation, *Plaintiff-Appellant,*

v.

City of Chicago, Ill., Richard J. Daley and Kyran Phelan, *Defendants-Appellees.*
No. 13008.

United States Court of Appeals, Seventh Circuit.

June 20, 1961.

Hubert L. Will, Joseph Schneider, Chicago, Ill., for appellant.

Robert J. Collins, Asst. Corp. Counsel, *John C. Melaniphy,* Corporation Counsel, *Sydney R. Drebin,* Asst. Corporation Counsel, Chicago, Ill., for appellees.

Before HASTINGS, Chief Judge, and DUFFY and KNOCH, Circuit Judges.

HASTINGS, Chief Judge.

The Supreme Court, in *Times Film Corp.* v. *City of Chicago,* 1961, 365 U.S. 43, 81 S. Ct. 391, 5 L. Ed. 2d 403, held that the prior restraint imposed by a certain Chicago city ordinance which required submission before exhibition of all films to municipal authorities for their examination was not *per se* a violation of the constitutional guarantee of freedom of speech. The Court rejected what it characterized as a "broadside" attack, i.e., that under *no* circumstances can a municipality censor movies and must content itself with criminal or civil sanctions subsequent to the first exhibition. The Court expressly noted that it decided only the *question* of the freedom "to exhibit, at least once, any and every kind of motion picture." Id., 365 U.S. at page 46, 81 S. Ct. at page 393.

Thus has been determined the basic, broad question of prior restraint in the exhibition of motion pictures. A city may choose this form of regulation. The Court stated, "It

is not for this Court to limit the State in its selection of the remedy it deems most effective to cope with such a problem, absent, of course, a showing of unreasonable strictures on individual liberty resulting from its application in particular circumstances." Id., 365 U.S. at page 50, 81 S. Ct. at page 395.

Although the question of the constitutionality of prior restraint has now been answered, many complex issues still remain unsettled. One is the problem of the legitimate standards or criteria upon which a municipality may reject a film for public distribution. In each case, a valid standard must be applied to the film in issue. And finally, in the municipal administration of the exercise of such prior restraint, it remains to be determined whether procedural due process has been accorded to those sought to be restrained.

It is with this latter question that we are concerned in the instant appeal.

Plaintiff-appellant Zenith International Film Corporation made application on September 6, 1959 to the Commissioner of Police of Chicago, Timothy J. O'Connor, for a permit to exhibit the film, "The Lovers." Such application was made pursuant to Chapter 155, Sections 155–1 to 155–4 of the Municipal Code of the City of Chicago, set out infra.

The film was then referred to a board of review which viewed it. To this body Commissioner O'Connor had delegated the duty of reviewing motion pictures for which permits had been requested.

On September 21, 1959, Commissioner O'Connor notified Zenith that he would not issue the requisite permit to exhibit the film in Chicago on the ground that "The Lovers" was immoral and obscene.

Pursuant to the foregoing municipal ordinance, Zenith thereupon appealed this decision to the Mayor of the City of Chicago, Richard J. Daley. On December 2, 1959, Zenith received a letter from John C. Melaniphy, Corporation Counsel for the City of Chicago, stating that the appeal had been referred to the City's law department. The letter further stated:

"The motion picture has been rereviewed and it is recommended that a permit be issued with the understanding that one of the obscene scenes in the picture be deleted. If you will contact Sergeant Vincent Nolan of the Police Censor Board, he will advise you as to the particular scene. If it is desired that the distributor will not delete this scene, then the permit shall not issue."

On December 14, 1959, the president of Zenith came to Chicago from New York and with counsel met with Sergeant Nolan, Director of the Police Censor Unit, and Officer Considine of the Police Censor Unit. The purpose of such meeting was to discuss the "particular scene" referred to in Melaniphy's letter of December 2, 1959. Sergeant Nolan then advised Zenith that notwithstanding the letter of December 2, 1959, his instructions from Commissioner O'Connor were to insist upon the same cuts that had been originally proposed in September, namely, substantially all of the fifth reel of the film comprising literally hundreds of scenes. Commissioner O'Connor subsequently confirmed these instructions; and on February 3, 1960 Mayor Daley formally denied the appeal of Zenith from the order of Commissioner O'Connor and refused to issue plaintiff a permit to exhibit the film "The Lovers" in the City of Chicago.

Zenith then brought this action in the federal district court against defendants City of Chicago, Richard J. Daley, Mayor of the City of Chicago, and Kyran Phelan, duly appointed and acting Commissioner of Police. The complaint prayed for an order directing defendants to issue to Zenith a permit to exhibit the film "The Lovers" and for a further order enjoining defendants from preventing Zenith's exhibition of the film in the City of Chicago. It was alleged that the action of defendants infringed upon and denied Zenith its constitutional rights of freedom of speech, freedom of the press and freedom to engage in lawful business activities. Further, the municipal ordinance in question was alleged to violate the First and Fourteenth Amendments to the Constitution inasmuch as it established no standards whereby the Commissioner of Police or the Mayor could determine whether a film is immoral or obscene, leaving such determination to be a matter of mere subjective preference.

In addition, in its complaint Zenith charged, and defendants admitted in their answer, that "[f]rom the date the film was submitted for review and up to the date plaintiff's appeal to defendant Daley was denied, neither defendant Daley, former Commissioner O'Connor, defendant Phelan, Corporation Counsel Melaniphy, Assistant Corporation Counsel Hartigan nor Sergeant Nolan had viewed the film in its entirety."

The district court viewed the film and considered briefs of the parties. Thereafter, in a written opinion it held that "The Lovers," judged by tests set out by the United States Supreme Court and the Illinois Supreme Court, "appeals to the prurient interest, is obscene, and therefore censorable under the Chicago ordinance." Further, it held, consistent with the subsequent Supreme Court decision in *Times Film, supra,* that prior restraint of movies was not *per se* unconstitutional. Finally, the district court examined the procedural protections afforded Zenith in the city's application of its power of prior restraint and found them consistent with such restraint approved in *Kingsley Books, Inc. v. Brown,* 1957, 354 U.S. 436, 77 S. Ct. 1325, 1 L. Ed. 2d 1469. This appeal followed.

We have heard arguments, received briefs, and viewed the film in question. We make no determination as to the obscenity of such film but pass directly to the basic question of the *municipal administration of the prior restraint* as the record reveals it here.

"The essence of justice is largely procedural."[1] In an area which involves important property rights, basic constitutional freedoms, and comprehensive municipal licensing, fair and adequate administrative procedure should be guaranteed. It is at the municipal level, in the first instance, that the permissible criteria of censorship must be applied. The alternative would compel the federal courts, in all instances where local determinations are challenged, to assume the role of censor, exercising their judgment *de novo* as to the obscenity of a particular film.

The record before us reveals that the municipal procedure here followed constitutes the antithesis of a fair determination of the obscenity of the film in question.

The city ordinance under which Zenith applied for, and was denied, its permit provides as follows:

"Permit required
*"155–1. It shall be unlawful for any person to show or exhibit in a public place, * * * [any motion picture] without first having secured a permit therefor from the commissioner of police.*

* * * * *

"The permit herein required shall be obtained for each and every picture or series of pictures exhibited and is in addition to any license or other imposition required by law or other provision of this code.

"Any person exhibiting any picture or series of pictures without a permit having been obtained therefor shall be fined not less than fifty dollars nor more than one hundred dollars for each offense. A separate and distinct offense shall be regarded as having been committed for each day's exhibition of each picture or series of pictures without a permit."
"Application
*"155–2. Before any such permit is granted, an application in writing shall be made therefor, and the . * * films, * * * shall be shown to the commissioner of police, who shall inspect such * * * films, * * * or cause them to be inspected, and within three days after such inspection he shall either grant or deny the permit. In case a permit is granted, it shall be in writing and in such form as the commissioner of police may prescribe."*
"Granting of permit

---

[1] 1 Davis, Administrative Law Treatise 506 (1st ed. 1958).

"155–4. Such permit shall be granted only after the motion picture film for which said permit is requested has been produced at the office of the commissioner of police for examination or censorship.

"If a picture or series of pictures, for the showing or exhibition of which an application for a permit is made, is immoral or obscene, [or falls within other prescribed standards], it shall be the duty of the commissioner of police to refuse such permit; otherwise it shall be his duty to grant such permit.

"In case the commissioner of police shall refuse to grant a permit as hereinbefore provided, the applicant for the same may appeal to the mayor. Such appeal shall be presented in the same manner as the original application to the commissioner of police. The action of the mayor on any application for a permit shall be final."

Proceeding under such provisions, Zenith made application for a permit to exhibit its motion picture. The sole group that saw the entire film was the Film Review Board, a body to whom the Commissioner of Police had delegated his power of censorship over the film. The remainder of the responsible municipal officials saw only the fifth reel of the film, to which objection was taken. The City has admitted that defendant Daley, Commissioner O'Connor, defendant Phelan, city attorneys in the Corporation Counsel's office, and the police sergeant who is director of the Police Censor Board did not view the film in its entirety. Even appellate counsel who argued the case before us stated that he had viewed only the fifth reel of the film.

[1] Thus, the only group who possibly could have applied the proper criterion of obscenity to the film was the Film Review Board. The Supreme Court has emphasized that it is *as a whole* that a work must be judged, not merely by plucking isolated scenes or passages from such work. *Roth v. United States*, 1957, 354 U.S. 476, 489, 490, 77 S. Ct. 1304, 1 L. Ed. 2d 1498.

The Film Review Board is not a creature of the ordinance as far as the record here reveals. There are no standards for appointment, no formal procedures for determination, no opportunity for public hearing, argument, or the introduction of evidence.

The record reveals that there was no opportunity for an adequate hearing at any level of the municipal proceedings. There was no *de novo* hearing before the Mayor, for he admittedly did not view the film as a whole.

After separate application by appeal was made to the Mayor following the Commissioner's denial of a permit, the corporation counsel wrote that if one scene was deleted, a permit would issue. An abortive meeting was held at which the president and counsel for Zenith were present. The Commissioner and his sergeant in charge of the Police Censor Board stood firm on their earlier September position that the entire fifth reel must be cut. Representatives of the Mayor's office indicated they could not force the Commissioner to change his position. The Mayor refused to overrule his Commissioner and later formally denied the issuance of a permit. This was the sole "hearing" afforded Zenith—a meeting, concerned mainly with the squabble among city officials, none of whom had seen the film as a whole, as to what scenes must be expunged to make "The Lovers" non-obscene.

[2] Further, there was no opportunity before the censorship board or before the Mayor or his delegate for

Zenith to show that its film did not offend contemporary community standards. Again, the Supreme Court has set the criterion for obscenity not at an individual, subjective level but at the benchmark of a general, objective determination whether a work appeals to the prurient interests of the community at large. *Roth v. United States*, 1957, 354 U.S. 476, 489, 490, 77 S. Ct. 1304. There was never an opportunity for those responsible city officials to make their judgment aided by movie reviews or other evidence Zenith might marshal in support of its application.

At no time during the administrative proceedings was there a particularized statement of why Zenith was refused a permit. Commissioner O'Connor said that the film was immoral and obscene; Corporation Counsel Melaniphy, after "rereviewing" the film, wrote of "one of the obscene scenes in the picture." However, Zenith was given no further indication of how its film fell short of any standards set by the city. In fact, at no time was the single scene to which the Mayor's office objected ever specifically identified.

The result is that the record before us is completely devoid of any rationalization by the City why it should in this particular case interfere with the free expression of ideas.[2] As the Illinois Appellate Court has cogently stated:

"Under this rule the censoring authority, in refusing to issue a permit for showing the film, should be obliged to specify reasons for so doing; and upon trial of the issue whether the ban is justified, the trial court should require the censor to assume the burden of establishing the validity of his refusal. The trial court, as well as the reviewing court, would then have a record, in addition to the film itself, on which to decide whether the ban should be approved. To permit the banning of a motion picture film without requiring the censoring authority to substantiate his action runs directly counter to the spirit and the letter of the law relating to censorship. Freedom of expression is the rule, limitations upon it the exception; in accord with this doctrine, and in conformity with the Illinois Supreme Court ruling that the censoring authority must assume the burden of his action, such authority must present compelling and persuasive reasons to establish a film as obscene; such a determination must rest on something more than mere speculation. Without such procedure, the courts become, not only the final tribunal to pass upon films, but the only tribunal to assume the responsibilities of the censoring authority." (Emphasis added.) American Civil Liberties Union v. City of Chicago, 1957, 13 Ill. App. 2d 278, 286, 141 N.E. 2d 56, 60.

---

[2] Cf., "Just why they categorized this motion picture as 'immoral and obscene' is undisclosed by the City censors * * *." "The record before us is barren of any findings of fact by the censors and all it shows is that somebody sometime classed some edition of the film 'immoral and obscene.' "

"Our decision rests on narrow but firm grounds for we are satisfied there was absent any sound basis for outlawing the film and the absence of any reasons by the censors for their classification is a foreboding guise for arbitrary censorship running afoul of the First and Fourteenth Amendments. Nothing has been put forward by the City indicating just what in this film are its inherent evils. A social problem requires defining and that has not been attempted here. Consequently this censorship results in a curb on free expression * * *." *Capitol Enterprises, Inc.* v. *City of Chicago*, 7 Cir., 1958, 260 F. 2d 670, 675, 676.

[3] To summarize, Zenith has been deprived of its right to a full and fair hearing in the comprehensive Chicago licensing procedure. There was no opportunity for any sort of fair hearing before municipal authorities at any level of the proceedings; Zenith had no opportunity to present evidence of contemporary community standards; the responsible city officials failed to view the film as a whole and thus could under no circumstances apply the proper standard of obscenity; there was no *de novo* hearing before the Mayor; the sole group that saw the film was a Film Review Board whose procedure does not allow for a hearing; there are no standards for selection of such Board and no safeguards to preclude an entirely arbitrary judgment on its part; and finally, there was no indication given to Zenith why the city found the film to be "obscene and immoral."

The fundamental procedural elements of notice and hearing have been denied Zenith where they should have been provided—before the licensing body itself. Chicago's *administration* of its power of prior restraint over the distribution of films falls far short of the procedural guarantees afforded in the prior restraint approved in *Kingsley Books, Inc.* v. *Brown*, 1957, 354 U.S. 436, 77 S. Ct. 1325, 1 L. Ed. 2d 1469.

[4] The recent Times Film decision does not provide *carte blanche* authorization for *ad hoc*, unfair, abortive municipal licensing procedures. We reemphasize that it does hold that a city has the *power* to impose a system of prior restraints on movie distribution, if it does so properly. Chicago's procedure, as followed in the case at bar, is lacking in the requisite elements of procedural due process. Its administration of the ordinance in question has not guaranteed that there are no "unreasonable strictures on individual liberty resulting from its application in [these] particular circumstances." *Times Film Corp.* v. *City of Chicago*, supra, 365 U.S. at page 50, 81 S. Ct. at page 395.

The judgment of the district court is vacated, and the cause is remanded to the district court with the following instructions: The relief requested by plaintiff shall be granted unless the city provides a hearing consistent with the standards set out herein within a reasonable time after Zenith's resubmission of the film to proper city authorities. If the film is found obscene or otherwise objectionable after a proper procedural determination by the city authorities, plaintiff may then challenge before the district court such finding of obscenity. The district court may grant such relief and entertain such proceedings as necessary to implement these instructions, without prejudice to the right of either party to seek further review thereof by this court.

Judgment vacated.

Remanded with instructions.

■ William Goldman Theatres, Inc., and Pennsylvania Association of Amusement Industries, by William Goldman Theatres, Inc., *Trustee Ad Litem*

v.

Peter T. Dana, Mae M. Bergin, and Ira C. Sassaman, Individually and as members of Pennsylvania State Board of Motion Picture Control, *Appellants.*

Twentieth Century-Fox Film Corporation *et al.*

v.

Charles H. Boehm, Superintendent of Public Instruction of the Commonwealth of Pennsylvania, Charles C. Smith, Auditor General of the Commonwealth of Pennsylvania, and Robert F. Kent, State Treasurer of the Commonwealth of Pennsylvania, *Appellants.*

Supreme Court of Pennsylvania.

July 26, 1961.

Anne X. Alpern, Atty. Gen., Dept. of Justice, *Lois G. Forer,* Dep. Atty. Gen., for appellants.

Edwin P. Rome, Morris L. Weisberg, of *Blank, Rudenko, Klaus & Rome,* Philadelphia, for appellee at No. 22.

Samuel D. Slade, Arlin M. Adams, Bernard G. Segal, Wm. A. Schnader, Philadelphia, for appellees at No. 23.

John H. Bream, Harrisburg, *Matthew W. Bullock, Jr., Julian E. Goldberg,* Philadelphia, *William B. Ball,* Harrisburg, amici curiae.

Before Charles Alvin Jones, C.J., and Bell, Musmanno, Benjamin R. Jones, Cohen, Bok and Eagen, JJ.

Charles Alvin Jones, Chief Justice.

The Commonwealth appeals from separate decrees of the court below in two suits, which respectively adjudged the Motion Picture Control Act of September 17, 1959, P.L. 902, 4 P.S. § 70.1 et seq., unconstitutional. The first suit (Appeal No. 22) was instituted by William Goldman Theatres, Inc., and Pennsylvania Association of Amusement Industries by William Goldman Theatres, Inc., Trustee ad litem, seeking to enjoin the members of the Pennsylvania State Board of Motion Picture Control from enforcing any of the provisions of the Act and to relieve the plaintiffs and all others similarly situated from registering under the Act or from complying with any of its provisions. The members of the Motion Picture Control Board were appointed by the Governor pursuant to the Act of 1959, supra. The other suit (Appeal No. 23) was instituted by Twentieth Century-Fox Film Corporation, as a taxpayer's bill, for itself and all others similarly situated, for the purpose of enjoining the fiscal officers of the Commonwealth and the Superintendent of Public Instruction from expending any funds of the Commonwealth appropriated by Section 16 of the Act or from any other appropriation made for the enforcement of the Act. Twentieth Century's complaint also prayed that the members of the Board of Motion Picture Control be restrained from taking any proceedings pursuant to the provisions of the Act. Both appeals will be disposed of in this one opinion.

In *Hallmark Productions, Inc.* v. *Carroll,* 1956, 384 Pa. 348, 121 A. 2d 584, the Motion Picture Censorship Act of May 15, 1915, P.L. 534, as amended by the Act of May 8, 1929, P.L. 1655, was stricken down as unconstitutional on the ground that the standards prescribed for the Board of Censors' disapproval of submitted films for public showing were so vague and indefinite in their statutory connotation as to offend the due process clause of the Fourteenth Amendment of the Federal Constitution. Consideration of the question of pre-censorship in that case was deemed unnecessary to the decision and, consequently, was expressly not passed upon, Mr. Chief Justice Stern saying in that connection for the court (384 Pa. at page 358, 121 A. 2d at page 589), "It is not necessary for us to consider * * * whether, however amended and 'clearly drawn,' any statute censoring motion pictures must be held to be unconstitutional on the theory that motion pictures are as much entitled to the protection of the constitutional guaranty of free speech as is now enjoyed by newspapers, magazines, books, theatrical exhibitions, radio and television scripts."

[1] In any event, it is not open to question that motion pictures for public exhibition are entitled to the constitutional guarantee of free speech and free press. In *Burstyn v. Wilson*, 1952, 343 U.S. 495, 502, 72 S. Ct. 777, 781, 96 L. Ed. 1098, the Supreme Court of the United States succinctly declared that "expression by means of motion pictures is included within the free speech and free press guaranty of the First and Fourteenth Amendments."

[2] These constitutionally protected freedoms are not, of course, absolute. But, when a restrictive statute is made to operate in the area of individual liberty, "the usual presumption supporting legislation is balanced by the preferred place given in our scheme to the great, the indispensable democratic freedoms secured by the First Amendment. Cf. *Schneider v. State*, 308 U.S. 147, 60 S. Ct. 146, 84 L. Ed. 155; *Cantwell v. State of Connecticut*, 310 U.S. 296, 60 S. Ct. 900, 84 L. Ed. 1213; *Prince v. Commonwealth of Massachusetts*, 321 U.S. 158, 64 S. Ct. 438, 88 L. Ed. 645. That priority gives these liberties a sanctity and a sanction not permitting dubious intrusions": *Thomas v. Collins*, 1945, 323 U.S. 516, 529–530, 65 S. Ct. 315, 322, 89 L. Ed. 430.

[3] Apart from the Fourteenth Amendment, the guarantee of free communication of thought and opinion is independently protected by our State Constitution of 1874. Article I, Section 7, P.S., thereof recognizes and declares that "The free communication of thoughts and opinions is one of the invaluable rights of man, and every citizen may freely speak, write and print on any subject, *being responsible for the abuse of that liberty*." (Emphasis supplied). This provision is a direct inhibition on previous restraint of an exercise of the protected rights and was derived, *ipsissimis verbis*, from Section 7 of Article IX of our State Constitution of 1838 where, in turn, it had been taken from the Constitution of 1790. The members of the Constitutional Convention of 1790 were undoubtedly fully cognizant of the vicissitudes and outright suppressions to which printing had theretofore been subjected in this very Colony.[1]

Although the provision in Article I, Section 7, of the Pennsylvania Constitution, as above quoted, has never heretofore been interpreted by this court in present context, it is clear enough that what it was designed to do was to prohibit the imposition of prior restraints upon the communication of thoughts and opinions, leaving the utterer liable only for an abuse of the privilege. History supports this view. After the demise in 1694 of the last of the infamous English Licensing Acts, freedom of the press, at least freedom from administrative censorship, began in England, and later in the Colonies, to assume the status of a "common law or natural right." See *State v. Jackson*, Or. 1960, 356 P. 2d 495, 499. Blackstone so recognized (circa 1767) when he wrote, "The liberty of the press is indeed essential to the nature of a free state; but this consists in laying no previous restraints upon publications, and not in freedom from censure for criminal matter when published. Every freeman had an undoubted right to lay what sentiments he pleases before the public; to forbid this is to destroy the freedom of the press; but if he publishes what is improper, mischievous, or illegal, he must take the consequence of his own temerity. To subject the press to the restrictive power of a licenser, as was formerly done, both before and since the revolution, is to subject all freedom of sentiment to the prejudices of one man, and make him the arbitrary and infallible judge of all controverted points in learning, religion, and government. But to punish (as the law does at present) any dangerous or offensive writings, which, when published, shall on a fair and impartial trial be adjudged of a pernicious tendency, is necessary for the preservation of peace and good order, of government and religion, the only solid foundations of civil liberty. Thus the will of individuals is still left free; the abuse only of that free will is the object of legal punishment. Neither is any restraint hereby laid upon freedom of thought or inquiry; liberty of private sentiment is still left; the disseminating or making public of band sentiments, destructive of the ends of society, is the crime which society corrects." (Footnote omitted). 4 Bl. Comm. 151–152.

What Blackstone thus recognized as the law of England concerning freedom of the press came to be, 133 years later, an established constitutional right in Pennsylvania as to both speech and press; Article IX, Section 7 of the Constitution of 1790 so ordained; and, as already pointed out, the provision still endures as Article I, Section 7, of our present Constitution.[2]

We come then to consider the provisions of the Motion Picture Control Act of 1959, in the interpretation whereof the usual presumption of legislative validity must, in keeping with the pronouncement of the Supreme Court in *Thomas v. Collins*, supra, be weighed against "the great, the indispensable democratic freedoms" whose preferred status in our scheme of local government is secured by Article I, Section 7, of our State Constitution. No matter how laudably inspired or highly conceived a sumptuary statute may be, if its restrictions impinge upon the freedoms of the individual thus constitutionally guaranteed, it cannot stand. The harm to our free institutions, which the enforcement of such a statute would entail, would be of far greater portent than the evil it was designed to eradicate.

The Act of 1959 requires any person intending to sell, lease, lend, exhibit or use any motion picture film, reel or view (defined as "what is usually known as a stereopticon

---

[1] In 1689 William Bradford, a young printer, who had introduced the art of printing to the middle provinces of America, had printed the Charter of the Province so that the people could see their rights. Apparently anticipating trouble, he had not put his name on the pamphlet. He was summoned none the less before the Governor of the Colony where the following colloquy took place: Governor: "Why, sir, I would know by what power of authority you thus print? Here is the Charter printed!" Bradford: "It was by Governor Penn's encouragement I came to this Province and by his license I print." Governor: "What, sir, had you license to print the Charter? I desire to know from you, whether you did print the Charter or not, and who set you to work?" See Griswold, *"The Fifth Amendment Today,"* Harvard University Press, 1955, citing John William Wallace, *An Address Delivered at the Celebration by the New York Historical Society, May 20, 1863, on the 200th Birthday of William Bradford*, Albany, 1863.

[2] It was, of course, not until the Fourteenth Amendment was adopted in 1868 that the freedoms of speech and press were accorded *federal* protection against adverse state action.

view or slide or * * * one or more frames of a motion picture film") to register with the Board and to notify the Board within 48 hours before the first showing thereof in Pennsylvania of the time and place of such showing. Upon the request of the Board at any time after such showing the registrant must furnish the Board with an exact copy of such film, reel or view for examination. A registrant must pay an annual registration fee of one dollar, and for the listing of the first showing of each film, reel or view, a fee of fifty cents for each 1,200 lineal feet or less.

The Board is empowered to examine any film, reel or view which has been exhibited at least once in Pennsylvania, and if a majority of the members of the Board are of the opinion that the film, reel or view is "obscene," the same shall be disapproved. If a majority of the members of the Board are of the opinion that the film, reel or view is "unsuitable for children," the same shall be disapproved for exhibition to children.

A child is defined by the Act as "any person less than seventeen years of age." A film, reel or view is obscene, according to the Act, "if to the average person applying contemporary community standards its dominant theme, taken as a whole, appeals to prurient interest." A film, reel or view is unsuitable for children, according to the Act, if it "is obscene or * * * incites to crime." Incites to crime is defined as that "which represents or portrays as acceptable conduct or as conduct worthy of emulation the commission of any crime, or the manifesting of contempt for law."

At the end of each week, or earlier if the Board so desires, it shall cause to be published a record of all films, reels and views which it has disapproved or disapproved for exhibition to children.

If an aggrieved registrant appeals from the Board's ruling, his film, reel or view will be promptly re-examined in his presence by at least two members of the Board and the ruling affirmed, reversed or modified. An aggrieved registrant has a right to appeal from the latter decision to the court of common pleas of the proper county.

The Board may apply to the court of common pleas of any county in which a film, reel or view which has been disapproved or disapproved as unsuitable for children is being shown or is about to be shown for an injunction to restrain its showing. Upon the affidavit of a member of the Board that the film, reel or view has been disapproved or disapproved as unsuitable for children the court may issue a preliminary injunction.

Section 8 of the Act prohibits the sale, lease, loan, exhibition or use of any film, reel or view which has been disapproved by the Board, and prohibits the exhibition to children of any film, reel or view which has been disapproved by the Board as unsuitable for children.[3] Section 11 of the Act prohibits any person from causing to be printed or displayed in Pennsylvania any advertising matter to aid in or advertise the showing of any film, reel or view which has been disapproved by the Board, whether or not the showing is to be held in Pennsylvania.

Section 13 makes the violation of any provision of the Act a criminal offense subject to a fine of from $400 to $1,000 or a prison sentence not exceeding 6 months, or both.

---

[3] This Section excludes from its purview films or reels "containing current news, events or happenings, commonly known as news reels."

Section 14 provides that the Act "does not apply to any sale, lease, loan, exhibition or use of films, reels or views for purely educational, charitable, fraternal, family or religious purpose by any religious association, fraternal society, family, library, museum, public school or private school, or to any sale, lease, loan, exhibition or use of films commonly known as industrial, business, institutional, advertising or training films, or films concerned exclusively with the advancement of law, medicine and other professions: Provided, That any such film is not exhibited or to be exhibited in theatres or in public places of entertainment commonly used as such."

[4] The Act is clearly invalid on its face. It is designed to effect, in violation of Article I, Section 7 of the Pennsylvania Constitution, a pre-censorship of the exercise of the individual's right freely to communicate thoughts and opinions. Section 3 of the Act expressly restrains the initial showing of a film for 48 hours after notice to the Board of its intended exhibition; and subsequent showings are likewise subjected to previous restraint for the reason that, if the motion picture is exhibited after the censors have disapproved it, the exhibitor may be criminally punished upon proof, *not of showing a picture that is obscene or unsuitable for children*, but *merely upon proof of showing a picture the exhibition of which had been priorly restrained by the administrative action of the Board of Censors.*

[5] And, concomitantly, the Act offends, additionally, Article I, Sections 6 and 9, of the Pennsylvania Constitution. Section 6 prescribes that "Trial by jury shall be as heretofore, and the right thereof remain inviolate," while Section 9 provides that "In all criminal prosecutions the accused hath a right to * * * a speedy public trial by an impartial jury of the vicinage; * * * nor can he be deprived of his life, liberty or property, unless by the judgment of his peers or the law of the land." No provisions in the Pennsylvania Constitution are more fundamental to the liberty of the individual. What they ordain is that the individual is entitled to a public trial by an impartial jury of the vicinage in every situation in which he would have been entitled to such a trial at the time of the adoption of our State Constitution of 1790 and ever since under our succeeding constitutions. See *Premier Cereal & Beverage Co.* v. *Pennsylvania Alcohol Permit Board*, 1928, 292 Pa. 127, 133, 140 A. 858; *Rhines* v. *Clark*, 1866, 51 Pa. 96, 101; *Commonwealth* v. *Wesley*, 1952, 171 Pa. Super. 566, 91 A. 2d 298; *Commonwealth* ex rel. *City of Pittsburgh* v. *Heiman*, 1937, 127 Pa. Super. 1, 190 A. 479.

[6] The utterance of obscene matter was a crime at common law for which a defendant chargeable therewith was entitled to a trial by jury. This was likewise so under similar guarantees in the Constitutions of 1790 and 1838, long before the adoption of our present Constitution. *Commonwealth* v. *Sharpless*, 1815, 2 Serg. & R. 91. See *Barker* v. *Commonwealth*, 1852, 19 Pa. 412; also *Commonwealth* v. *Blumenstein*, 1959, 396 Pa. 417, 419, 153 A. 2d 227. The above quoted provisions of Sections 6 and 9 of Article I guarantee that a person can be found guilty of a crime of the indicated description *only if* an impartial jury of the vicinage is of the opinion that his utterance was obscene, i.e., only if twelve jurymen are of the opinion that, applying contemporary standards in the community, the dominant theme of the utterance taken as a whole appealed to the average person's prurient interest.

What the Act in controversy purports to do is to place in the hands of three persons, selected by the Governor, the power, throughout the State, to judge and condemn motion picture films, reels, and views as obscene. Once a majority of them disapprove a film, reel or view, any person who sells, leases, lends, exhibits or uses it in Pennsylvania or advertises its showing within or without the Commonwealth may be prosecuted for so doing. Upon such prosecution the defendant would not be entitled to the right he constitutionally possesses and has heretofore been accorded, that of having twelve members of an impartial jury of the vicinage pass upon whether or not, applying contemporary standards of the community from which the jurors have been drawn, the dominant theme of his utterance taken as a whole appealed to the prurient interest of the average person. What the Act, if sustained, would effect would be to reduce the jury's function to a simple determination of whether or not the defendant did the physical act condemned by the statute, for example, exhibiting an administratively disapproved film.

Apart from the Act's limitation, an individual has a right to interrogate prospectively those who would pass upon his utterance, to challenge any of them for cause, and to challenge a permitted number of them peremptorily. But, under the Act a defendant would have no such right of challenge, even for cause, as to any of the three gubernatorially appointed censors. In fact, the sole qualification they need present is that they are residents of Pennsylvania.

Since one accused cannot constitutionally be punished for the utterance of alleged obscene matter except upon a finding by an impartial jury of the vicinage that the matter was in fact obscene, such result cannot be achieved by the artful device of granting to administrative officials the power to disapprove the utterance if they think it is obscene, prohibit the sale, lease, loan, exhibition or use of anything so disapproved and impose a criminal penalty for a violation of their prohibition. Constitutionally protected rights are not to be so adroitly subverted. It follows that the Motion Picture Control Act of 1959, in its deprivation of the individual's right to have "an impartial jury of the vicinage" pass upon the issue of whether or not his utterance was obscene, violates Article I, Sections 6 and 9, of the Pennsylvania Constitution.

The appellant places great reliance upon *Times Film Corporation* v. *City of Chicago*, 1961, 365 U.S. 43, 81 S. Ct. 391, 393, 5 L. Ed. 2d 403, in which the United States Supreme Court, by a five to four decision, ruled that a particular section of a Chicago ordinance "requiring the submission of films prior to their public exhibition [was] not, on the grounds set forth, void on its face."[4] That case

in no way involved the rights guaranteed the individual by the Pennsylvania Constitution. Moreover, the opinion of the Court expressly declined to deal with "any statutory standards employed by the censor or procedural requirements as to the submission of the film."

The Motion Picture Control Act of 1959, in its defective censorial standards and the failure of its procedural requirements to safeguard adequately the constitutionally protected rights of freedom of expression, whether by speech or press, violates both the "due process" clause of the Fourteenth Amendment of the Federal Constitution and the "law of the land" provision in Article I, Section 9, of the Pennsylvania Constitution.

The definition of obscenity, as used in the Act of 1959, was obviously culled from the opinion of the United States Supreme Court in *Roth* v. *United States*, 1957, 354 U.S. 476, 489, 77 S. Ct. 1304, 1 L. Ed. 2d 1498, in an attempt to satisfy the due process requirement of clarity under the Fourteenth Amendment. But, the definition of obscenity there enunciated has never been approved by the Supreme Court other than in the context of a criminal proceeding; and there is good reason why this is so. A criminal proceeding ordinarily means a trial by jury of the vicinage. The members of the jury represent a cross-section of the community in which the allegedly obscene utterance was made. The jury naturally possesses a special aptitude for reflecting the view of the "average person" of the community. A determination of whether or not a particular utterance is obscene requires, by the Act's own definition, an appraisal of its quality according to the average person's application of contemporary community standards.

However, the appellant contends that the word "community" as used in the Act's definition of obscenity should be interpreted to mean "Commonwealth of Pennsylvania," that a definitive contemporary standard of morality exists for the State as a whole, and that the three gubernatorially appointed censors are capable of determining just what this standard is in any particular circumstances of time and place. The contention is patently specious. A "community" in relation to standards of morality is a sociological, and not a political, entity. Obviously the moral standards of the average resident of a metropolitan area are not the same as the moral standards of the average resident of a rural county.

Even if there were a definitive contemporary standard of morality applicable to the State as a whole, there is no guarantee that the censors appointed under the Motion Picture Control Act would be capable of ascertaining it. The only qualification for membership on the Board of Censors is that the appointees be "residents of Pennsylvania." No minimum requirements of academic education or training is necessary. Indeed, it is possible that the Board may be composed of persons wholly unacquainted with history and literature who would rule upon whether or not motion pictures of published and easily obtainable historical and literary works are obscene.

It is highly significant, moreover, that the Supreme Court in defining the term "obscenity," as applied in the criminal proceeding involved in the Roth case, stipulated that the allegedly obscene utterance must be considered "as a whole." Yet the Act, here under consideration, empowers the censors to condemn not only an entire motion picture film and an individual reel of a film as well, but it expressly authorizes the censors to condemn a single

---

[4] Subsequent to the decision in the Times Film Corporation case, the United States Court of Appeals for the Seventh Circuit, in a unanimous opinion, vacated the judgment of a Federal District Court, which had affirmed a refusal by Chicago authorities, acting pursuant to the same ordinance, to grant a permit for the showing of a motion picture film. The Court of Appeals held that the censoring violated procedural due process of law because, (1) the would-be exhibitor was not afforded a full and fair hearing, (2) was not granted an opportunity to present evidence of contemporary community standards, (3) responsible city officials failed to view the film as a whole, and (4) there were no standards for selection of the members of the Film Review Board and no safeguards to preclude an entirely arbitrary judgment on the Board's part. See *Zenith International Film Corporation* v. *City of Chicago* et al., 7 Cir., 291 F. 2d 785.

"view," which the Act defines as "one or more frames of a motion picture film." Thus, under the statute, the Board of Censors need not consider a motion picture film "as a whole" but may censor any individual frame separately and slice the film accordingly. Such a procedure for applying the standard of "obscenity" has never yet been sanctioned by the Supreme Court.

The Act empowers the Board to disapprove a film, reel or view for exhibition to children if it "represents or portrays as acceptable conduct or as conduct worthy of emulation the commission of any crime, or the manifesting of contempt for law." This standard is broad enough to empower the Board to disapprove for exhibition to children (i.e., persons under 17 years of age according to the Act) a large portion of films depicting historical, including Biblical, events. There is no need here to catalogue the many such instances that will readily come to mind upon a moment's reflection.

[7, 8] It is abundantly evident that the Act of 1959 empowers the censors to trespass too far upon the area of constitutionally protected freedom of expression. As the Supreme Court said in *Winters* v. *People of State of New York*, 1947, 333 U.S. 507, 509–510, 68 S. Ct. 665, 667, 92 L. Ed. 840: "It is settled that a statute so vague and indefinite, in form and as interpreted, as to permit within the scope of its language the punishment of incidents fairly within the protection of the guarantee of free speech is void, on its face, as contrary to the Fourteenth Amendment. *Stromberg* v. *People of State of California*, 283 U.S. 359, 369, 51 S. Ct. 532, 75 L. Ed. 1117, 73 A.L.R. 1484; *Herndon* v. *Lowry*, 301 U.S. 242, 258, 57 S. Ct. 732, 739, 81 L. Ed. 1066. A failure of a statute limiting freedom of expression to give fair notice of what acts will be punished and such a statute's inclusion of prohibitions against expressions, protected by the principles of the First Amendment violates an accused's rights under procedural due process and freedom of speech or press."

So far as the procedural protection afforded by the Act to those who exercise their right of free speech, which the Attorney General stresses, is concerned, it is to be borne in mind that "since only considerations of the greatest urgency can justify restrictions on speech, and since the validity of a restraint on speech in each case depends on careful analysis of the particular circumstances * * * the procedures by which the facts of the case are adjudicated are of special importance and the validity of the restraint may turn on the safeguards which they afford." *Speiser* v. *Randall*, 1948, 357 U.S. 513, 521, 78 S. Ct. 1332, 1339, 2 L. Ed. 2d 1460.

[9] Section 4 of the Act, which requires each person who intends to sell, lease, lend, exhibit or use any motion picture film, reel or view in Pennsylvania to pay to the Board an annual registration fee of $1.00, and for the listing of the first showing of each film, reel or view a fee of 50 cents for each 1,200 lineal feet or less, is a plain attempt to tax the exercise of the right of free speech, a right that exists wholly apart from State authority and whose utilization a State may not, therefore, license. In *Murdock* v. *Commonwealth of Pennsylvania*, 1943, 319 U.S. 105, 113, 63 S. Ct. 870, 875, 87 L. Ed. 1292 the Supreme Court declared that "A state may not impose a charge for the enjoyment of a right granted by the federal constitution." The brief of the Commonwealth on these appeals

makes no attempt whatsoever to justify the fees imposed by Section 4 of the Act.

Section 5 of the Act purports to empower the Board to disapprove, or disapprove for exhibition to children, any film, reel or view which has been exhibited at least once in Pennsylvania without any hearing or any opportunity for any person to present testimony of any kind regarding the contents of the film, reel or view, or the contemporary community standards to be applied in judging it, or any other relevant matter. The Act prohibits the sale, lease, loan, exhibition, use or the causing to be printed or displayed in Pennsylvania of any advertising matter to aid in or advertise the showing of any film, reel or view from the moment of its disapproval, with criminal sanctions for violation of the prohibition, regardless of whether or not an appeal to the court of common pleas from the Board's ruling has been taken and regardless of whether or not an appealed ruling is ultimately reversed by the court.

Section 9 grants to "[a]ny registrant who *was* exhibiting, selling, lending, leasing or using any film, reel or view which * * * has been disapproved or disapproved as unsuitable for children" a right to appeal from the ruling in which case "such film, reel or view will be promptly re-examined in the presence of such registrant by two or more members of the board * * *." (Emphasis supplied). Here, again, there is no provision for a hearing and no opportunity for the registrant to present testimony of any sort. The Board is required to affirm, reverse or modify its ruling "promptly after such re-examination with the right of appeal from the decision of the board to the court of common pleas of the proper county."

The provision last above quoted is identical with the provision for appeal from a ruling of the Board to the court of common pleas of the proper county contained in Section 26 of the Motion Picture Censorship Act of May 15, 1915, 4 P.S. § 54. In construing that provision this court interpreted it to mean that the appellant was not entitled to a trial *de novo* in the court of common pleas and that, to gain a reversal, he must prove that the administrative board abused its discretion; and that the burden of showing such abuse of discretion was upon the appellant. In Goldwyn Distributing Corporation, 1919, 265 Pa. 335, 342, 108 A. 816, 818, this court said, "The only question raised on this appeal was whether the board of censors, in disallowing the reels and films submitted, had exercised an honest discretion or had unreasonably and arbitrarily rejected them * * * Where such inquiry arises, the investigation starts with the presumption that the tribunal making the order or decree appealed from acted within the reasonable scope of its power and discretion, and it can be called to answer only as the party complaining, upon whom rests the burden, can show that the decision of the board rests on some ground that did not authorize the exercise of discretion." See also Franklin Film Mfg. Corporation, 1916, 253 Pa. 422, 98 A. 623. "[W]hen a court of last resort has construed the language used in a law, the Legislature in subsequent laws on the same subject matter intend the same construction to be placed upon such language * * *." Statutory Construction Act of May 28, 1937, P.L. 1019, Sec. 52(4), 46 P.S. § 552(4).

In *Speiser* v. *Randall*, supra, the Supreme Court of the United States declared unconstitutional a California statutory procedure which placed the burden of proof upon applicants for a tax exemption (by requiring them to sign a "loyalty oath") to show that they did not advocate the overthrow of the government of the United States or the State by force or violence or other unlawful means or did not advocate the support of a foreign government against the United States in the event of hostilities, in order to qualify for a tax exemption. Holding that such procedure contravened constitutionally protected freedom of speech, the Supreme Court said (357 U.S. at pages 526 and 529, 78 S. Ct. at page 1342): "The vice of the present procedure is that, where particular speech falls close to the line separating the lawful and the unlawful, the possibility of mistaken factfinding—inherent in all litigation—will create the danger that the legitimate utterance will be penalized. The man who knows that he must bring forth proof and persuade another of the lawfulness of his conduct necessarily must steer far wider of the unlawful zone than if the State must bear these burdens. This is especially to be feared when the complexity of the proofs and the generality of the standards applied * * * provide but shifting sands on which the litigant must maintain his position. How can a claimant whose declaration is rejected possibly sustain the burden of proving the negative of these complex factual elements? In practical operation, therefore, this procedural device must necessarily produce a result which the State could not command directly. It can only result in a deterrence of speech which the Constitution makes free. 'It is apparent that a constitutional prohibition cannot be transgressed indirectly by the creation of a statutory presumption any more than it can be violated by direct enactment. The power to create presumptions is not a means of escape from constitutional restrictions.' *Bailey* v. *State of Alabama*, 219 U.S. 219, 239, 31 S. Ct. 145, 151, 155 L. Ed. 191. * * * Since the entire statutory procedure, by placing the burden of proof on the claimants, violated the requirements of due process, appellants were not obliged to take the first step in such a procedure."

If the Board disapproves, or disapproves for exhibition to children, any film, reel or view, the prohibition upon its sale, lease, loan, exhibition or use and, also, the prohibition upon causing to be printed or displayed in Pennsylvania advertising matter to aid in or advertising its showing, restricts the future conduct of all persons. Yet a right to appeal from the Board's ruling is granted only to persons who have in the past exhibited, sold, lent, leased or used the film, reel or view. Even a person who has advertised the showing of the film, reel or view, but who has not yet exhibited, sold, lent or used it, has no right of appeal. The constitutionally protected right of a free press is here involved because national magazines and out-of-State newspapers would be prohibited from circulation in Pennsylvania unless they deleted from their pages any advertisement for, or news articles or reviews commenting favorably upon, any motion picture film which was disapproved by the Board. Out-of-State television stations whose programs are broadcast in Pennsylvania would violate this Act if they carried an advertisement for a motion picture film which had been disapproved by the Pennsylvania Board of Censors. The constitutionally protected rights of free communication of thought and opinion of all of these persons can easily be encroached upon through an enforcement of the Act without even the semblance of a hearing or an explanation of the reason for the Board's action.

[10] Finally, under Section 10 of the Act the Board may apply to the court of common pleas of any county in which a film, reel or view which has been disapproved is being or is about to be shown, or in which any film, reel or view which has been disapproved as unsuitable for children is being or is about to be shown, for an injunction to restrain such showing. The court may issue an injunction upon such application merely on the affidavit of any member of the Board that the film, reel or view has been disapproved, or disapproved as unsuitable for children. No provision for a hearing and no opportunity to present evidence at all is granted to the defendant. The failure of the Act to protect adequately the constitutionally guaranteed rights of persons affected by the Board's ruling by granting them a proper hearing constitutes a flagrant violation of procedural due process.

Since the Motion Picture Control Act of 1959 plainly violates both our State and Federal Constitutions in the particulars hereinabove pointed out, it follows that the decrees of the court below adjudging the Act unconstitutional and void must be affirmed.

The decrees appealed from at Nos. 22 and 23 are separately affirmed at the appellant's cost in each case.

MUSMANNO, J., files a dissenting opinion.

EAGEN, J., files a dissenting opinion in which BELL, J., joins.

EAGEN, Justice (dissenting).

I cannot agree legally or morally with the reasoning or conclusion of the majority opinion.

The sole question presented is narrow and well defined. It is not whether we, in fact, approve and support censorship, rather is it: Does the statute involved violate certain guarantees imposed by the Federal and Pennsylvania Constitutions? In my opinion, it does not.

The majority decision rules that the provisions of the statute constitute a "precensorship" and is, therefore, an unlawful restraint upon the exercise of an individual's right to freely communicate thoughts and opinions. I disagree. The statute does not provide for pre-censorship.

"Prior restraint," as we construe court decisions, refers to administrative controls *prior to any publication*, such as licensing or other devices according to which no publication whatever may take place without prior approval of a public official. See, *Kingsley Books, Inc.* v. *Brown*, 1957, 354 U.S. 436, 77 S. Ct. 1325, 1 L. Ed. 2d 1469; *Near* v. *State of Minnesota*, ex rel. *Olson*, 1930, 283 U.S. 697, 51 S. Ct. 625, 75 L. Ed. 1357; *Times Film Corporation* v. *City of Chicago*, 1961, 365 U.S. 43, 81 S. Ct. 391, 5 L. Ed. 2d 403. There is a marked difference between "prior restraints" and "post restraints," as the first mentioned case pointedly so recognizes. The distinction is well stated in Freund, the Supreme Court and Civil Liberties, Vand. L. Rev. 533, 538, 539: "The concept of prior restraint, roughly speaking, deals with official restraints imposed upon speech or other forms of expression in advance of actual publication. Prior restraint is thus distinguished from subsequent punishment, which is a penalty imposed after the communication has been made as a punishment for having made it. Again, speaking generally, a system of prior restraint would prevent communication from occurring *at all*; a system of subsequent punishment allows the communication but imposes a penalty after the event. Of course, the deterrent effect of a later penalty may operate to prevent a communication from ever being made. Nevertheless, for a variety of reasons, the impact upon a freedom of expression may be quite different, depending upon whether the system of control is designed to block publication in advance or deter it by subsequent punishment." (Emphasis supplied.) See also, Emerson, The Doctrine of Prior Restraint, 20 Law and Contemp. Prob. 648 (1955).

The statute concerned does not require *approval before* one may show a motion picture. No license to do so is necessary. The Board's power of disapproval operates only *post facto*, and *only after* at least one public showing to any number of audiences has taken place, *and after* the Board has requested a copy of the film, examined it and passed upon it according to the narrowly drawn standards of the Act. *The film may then be disapproved only if it is in fact obscene.*

If, as the lower court reasoned and the majority opinion indicates, post restraints are to be legally equated with prior restraints then, the law is powerless to adequately control any obscene exhibitions, no matter how base they may be. Any possible censorship legislation in Pennsylvania is dead for all time. No civil restraint is ever possible on any form of speech, including picketing, use of sound trucks, advocacy of the violent overthrow of a lawful government, inciting riots, etc. What a sorry plight the people of this Commonwealth are in, if this is the law.

But, say the Majority, recourse may be had to the penal statutes. The exhibitor of an obscene movie may be prosecuted and punished. Is this adequate to meet the urgent public need to eradicate filthy and obscene motion pictures? Consider the facts realistically and without rose-colored glasses. An obscene exhibition occurs. The responsible individual is arrested and prosecuted. Months, yes many months and possibly years, go by before a final decision is recorded. In the meantime, the illegal exhibition continues in every town, hamlet and city throughout the land. Millions of men, women and children are exposed. The erosion of moral standards and the subtle evil of the public dissemination of such hard-core pornographic pictures has taken effect. The harm has been done. While the prosecution is in litigation, another such motion picture appears and is made available by another exhibitor. Another arrest ensues. The evil effects continue and spread on ad infinitum.

No one has the moral or legal right to exhibit obscene movies. No one has the right to financial profit gained through moral corruption. Furthermore, a possible loss of investment presents no meritorious constitutional objection to a statute reasonably protecting a public interest of major importance. It is interesting to note in this case that the motion picture producers emphatically disclaim any intention of producing objectionable films. If this be so, why the great concern?

But let us assume, arguendo, that the statute under consideration does, in effect, provide for prior restraints. It is no less constitutional. Obscenity is not protected by either the Constitution of the United States or the Constitution of Pennsylvania. I believe the Majority will, undoubtedly,

so accede. It is also now clearly established that all prior restraints are not per se invalid and do not automatically violate either the First or the Fourteenth Amendment to the United States Constitution.

In *Times Film Corporation* v. *City of Chicago*, supra, the Supreme Court in holding that the ambit of constitutional protection does not include complete and absolute freedom to exhibit, at least once, any and every kind of motion picture, stated, at page 394 of 81 S. Ct: "Petitioner would have us hold that the public exhibition of motion pictures must be allowed under any circumstances. The State's sole remedy, it says, is the invocation of criminal process under the Illinois pornographic statute, Ill. Rev. Stat. (1959), c. 38, § 470, and then only after a transgression. But this position, as we have seen, is founded upon the claim of absolute privilege against prior restraint under the First Amendment—*a claim without sanction in our cases.* To illustrate its fallacy we need only point to one of the 'exceptional cases' which Chief Justice Hughes enumerated in *Near* v. *State of Minnesota* ex rel. *Olson*, supra, namely 'the primary requirements of decency [that] may be enforced against obscene publications.' *Moreover, we later held specifically 'that obscenity is not within the area of constitutionally protected speech or press.' Roth* v. *United States*, 354 U.S. 476, 485, 77 S. Ct. 1304, 1309, 1 L. Ed. 2d 1498. Chicago emphasizes here its duty to protect its people against the dangers of obscenity in the public exhibition of motion pictures. To this argument petitioner's only answer is that regardless of the capacity for, or extent of such an evil, previous restraint cannot be justified. With this we cannot agree. We recognized in Burstyn, supra, that 'capacity for evil * * * may be relevant in determining the permissible scope of community control,' 343 U.S. at page 502, 72 S. Ct. at page 780, and that motion pictures were not 'necessarily subject to the precise rules governing any other particular method of expression. Each method,' we said, 'tends to present its own peculiar problems.' At page 503 of 343 U.S., at page 781 of 72 S. Ct. Certainly petitioner's broadside attack does not warrant, nor could it justify on the record here, our saying that—aside from any consideration of the other 'exceptional cases' mentioned in our decisions—the State is stripped of all constitutional power to prevent, in the most effective fashion, the utterance of this class of speech. *It is not for this Court to limit the State in its selection of the remedy it deems most effective to cope with such a problem, absent, of course, a showing of unreasonable strictures on individual liberty resulting from its application in particular circumstances. Kingsley Books, Inc.* v. *Brown*, supra, 354 U.S. at page 441, 77 S. Ct. at page 1327." (Emphasis ours.)

The appellees in the present case had requested and were granted, twice, postponement of the oral argument of this case, pending the outcome of *Times Film Corporation* v. *City of Chicago*, supra, alleging that it "involved a question intimately related to the instant appeals" and because the decision in that case "might control the outcome of these appeals." It did affect the outcome, although the Majority does not agree and tries to ignore it. As a result of that decision, the appellees were forced to abandon their argument before this Court that the Motion Picture Control Act of 1959, violated the First and Fourteenth Amendments of the United States Constitution, and argued instead that this Act violated Article 1, Section 7, of the Pennsylvania Constitution. But this position does not hold water either, when scrutinized under the microscope of truth and law.

It is claimed that the framers of the Pennsylvania Constitution adopted an absolute prohibition against prior restraint, while the drafters of the First Amendment to the Federal Constitution accepted a lesser restriction. The fallacy of this is in its assumption that freedom from prior restraint was ever absolute in Pennsylvania. This is just not so. But unfortunately, the decision in this case supports this error. The majority opinion reasons that even though prior restraint, in exceptional cases, does not violate the First and Fourteenth Amendments of the United States Constitution, it does violate Article 1, Section 7, of the Pennsylvania Constitution. In order to reach this conclusion, the Majority does a little selective picking from both Constitutions. They go first to the First and Fourteenth Amendments of the United States Constitution in order to bring motion pictures into the ambit of the constitutional guarantee of free speech and free press (*Joseph Burstyn, Inc. v. Wilson*, supra) and imply, therefore, that Article 1, Section 7, also covers motion pictures. But, they then reject the First and Fourteenth Amendments and one hundred seventy-one years of Pennsylvania law and state that the Pennsylvania Constitution is different from the United States Constitution, and that the Pennsylvania Constitution prohibits *all* prior restraints—no matter how unlawful the publication may be, which, as pointed out before, is directly contrary to the United States Constitution. See *Times Film Corporation v. City of Chicago*, supra, and the cases cited therein. The Majority makes this deduction based on the fact that Article 1, Section 7, directly originated from the Constitution of 1790, and that, therefore, "The members of the Constitutional Convention of 1790 were undoubtedly fully cognizant of the vicissitudes and outright suppressions to which printing had theretofore been subjected in this very colony." But, what they neglect to state is that the members of the Pennsylvania Constitutional Convention of 1790 were fully cognizant of the United States Constitution, which was adopted on September 17, 1787, by the Constitutional Convention in Philadelphia, in which *eight* of the forty members were from Pennsylvania. They were cognizant also of the first ten amendments to the Constitution which were adopted by Pennsylvania on March 10, 1790, less than six months before the adoption of the Pennsylvania Constitution. Furthermore, Thomas Mifflin, who was one of the eight delegates to the United States Constitutional Convention, was president of the Pennsylvania Constitutional Convention.

With these facts in mind, can anyone doubt that the delegates to the Constitutional Convention would be and were more influenced by the results of the United States Constitutional Convention, which also was aware of the long history of oppression, than by Blackstone, especially when eight of its most influential members comprised the largest delegation to the United States Convention.[1]

All one has to do is to compare both Constitutions and he will immediately see the similarity of ideas between the two. Furthermore, this Court, in construing Article 1, Sec-

---

[1] The delegates from Pennsylvania were Benjamin Franklin, Thomas Mifflin, Robert Morris, George Clymer, Thomas Fitzsimons, Jared Ingersoll, James Wilson and Gouverneur Morris.

tion 7, has always followed and relied upon the decisions of the United States Supreme Court interpreting the First Amendment (See *Duquesne City v. Fincke*, 1920, 269 Pa. 112, 112 A. 130; *Duffy v. Cooke*, 1913, 239 Pa. 427, 86 A. 1076; *Spayd v. Ringing Rock Lodge*, 1921, 270 Pa. 67, 113 A. 70, 14 A.L.R. 1443; *Commonwealth v. Widovich*, 1928, 295 Pa. 311, 145 A. 295, certiorari denied *Muselin v. Commonwealth*, 280 U.S. 518, 50 S. Ct. 66, 74 L. Ed. 588; *Alliance Auto Service, Inc. v. Cohen*, 1941, 341 Pa. 283, 19 A. 2d 152; *Commonwealth v. Gordon*, 66 Pa. Dist. & Co. R. 101, affirmed sub nom. *Commonwealth v. Feigenbaum*, 1950, 166 Pa. Super. 120, 70 A. 2d 389 (opinion by Judge, now Mr. Justice Bok); *Wortex Mills, Inc. v. Textile Workers Union of America*, 1952, 369 Pa. 359, 85 A. 2d 851; *Fitzgerald v. City of Philadelphia*, 1954, 376 Pa. 379, 102 A. 2d 887; *Hallmark Productions, Inc. v. Carroll*, 1956, 384 Pa. 348, 121 A. 2d 584; *Mack Appeal*, 1956, 386 Pa. 251, 126 A. 2d 679; *Ullom v. Boehm*, 1958, 392 Pa. 643, 142 A. 2d 19; *46 South 52nd St. Corp. v. Manlin*, 1960, 398 Pa. 304, 157 A. 2d 381 as have all Pennsylvania courts from the time of the Constitution of 1790. See Charges to Grand Juries of the Counties of the Fifth Circuit District in the State of Pennsylvania, Sept. Session, 1798, Addison's Reports 270, 281.

Article 1, Section 7, of the Pennsylvania Constitution contains the identical guarantees of freedom of speech and press as are contained in the First Amendment of the Federal Constitution. While the language is different, the concept is the same. The First Amendment of the United States Constitution reads:

"*Congress shall make no law respecting an establishment of religion, or prohibiting the free exercise thereof; or abridging the freedom of speech, or of the press; or the right of the people peaceably to assemble, and to petition the Government for a redress of grievances.*"

Article 1, Section 7, of the present Constitution of Pennsylvania reads:

"*The printing press shall be free to every person who may undertake to examine the proceedings of the Legislature or any branch of government, and no law shall ever be made to restrain the right thereof. The free communication of thoughts and opinions is one of the invaluable rights of man, and every citizen may freely speak, write and print on any subject, being responsible for the abuse of liberty. No conviction shall be had in any prosecution for the publication of papers relating to the official conduct of officers or men in public capacity, or to any other matter proper for public investigation or information where the fact that such publication was not maliciously or negligently made shall be established to the satisfaction of the jury; and in all indictments for libels the jury shall have the right to determine the law and the facts, under the direction of the court, as in other cases.*"

That the chief purpose of the protection of freedom of speech and press given by the First Amendment and incorporated into the Fourteenth Amendment of the United States Constitution and into Article 1, Section 7, of the

Pennsylvania Constitution, is to prevent previous restraints upon publications cannot be doubted. But, "*It has never been held that liberty of speech is absolute. Nor has it been suggested that all previous restraints of speech are invalid.* On the contrary, in *Near v. State of Minnesota* ex rel. *Olson*, 1931, 283 U.S. 697, 715–716, 51 S. Ct. 625, 631, 75 L. Ed. 1357, Chief Justice Hughes, in discussing the classic legal statements concerning the immunity of the press from censorship, observed that the principle forbidding previous restraint 'is stated too broadly, if every such restraint is deemed to be prohibited * * *. [T]he protection even as to previous restraint is not absolutely unlimited. But the limitation has been recognized only in exceptional cases.' These included, the Chief Justice found, utterances creating 'a hindrance' to the Government's war effort, and 'actual obstruction to its recruiting service of the publication of the sailing dates of transports or the number and location of troops.' In addition, the Court said that 'the primary requirements of decency may be enforced against obscene publications' and the 'security of the community life may be protected against incitements to acts of violence and the overthrow by force of orderly government.' Some years later a unanimous Court, speaking through Mr. Justice Murphy, in *Chaplinsky v. State of New Hampshire*, 1942, 315 U.S. 568, 571, 572, 62 S. Ct. 766, 86 L. Ed. 1031, held that there were 'certain well-defined and narrowly limited classes of speech, the prevention and punishment of which have never been thought to raise any Constitutional problem. These include the lewd and obscene, the profane, the libelous, and the insulting or "fighting" words—those which by their very utterance inflict injury or tend to incite an immediate breach of the peace.' " *Times Film Corporation v. City of Chicago*, supra, at pages 393, 394 of 81 S. Ct. So, too, our Court has on many occasions stated that freedom of speech is not absolute and is subject to prior restraints in certain instances.[2] In *Commonwealth v. Widovich*, supra, 295 Pa. at page 317, 145 A. at page 298, Mr. Justice (later Chief Justice) Kephart speaking for a unanimous court stated, "The legislature, under the police power, * * * may prohibit the teaching or advocacy of a revolution or force as a means of redressing supposed injuries, or effecting a change in government. See *Buffalo Branch, Mutual Film Corp. v. Breitinger*, 250 Pa. 225, 95 A. 433; White's Appeal, 287 Pa. 259, 134 A. 409, 53 A.L.R. 1215, and cases there referred to. It is true that section 7 of the Pennsylvania Constitution is a part of the Bill of Rights, but overshadowing these rights is the authority of the government to preserve its existence under the police power. Article 16 § 3, of the Constitution says 'the police power * * * shall never be abridged.' This relates to all phases of its exercise. The police power is the greatest and most powerful attribute of government; on it the very existence of the state depends. 6 R.C.L. 183; *District of Columbia v. Brooke*, 214 U.S. 138, 29 S. Ct. 560, 53 L. Ed. 941; *Noble State Bank v. Haskell*, 219 U.S. 104, 31 S. Ct. 186, 55 L. Ed. 112; *Eubank v. Richmond*, 226 U.S. 137, 33 S. Ct. 76, 57 L. Ed. 156. If the exercise of the

police power should be in irreconcilable opposition to a constitutional provision or right, the police power would prevail. *Jacobson v. Massachusetts*, 197 U.S. 11, 25, 26, 25 S. Ct. 358, 49 L. Ed. 643; *Buffalo Branch, Mutual Film Corp. v. Breitinger*, supra, 250 Pa. 234, 95 A. 433; *Leiper v. Baltimore & P.R.R. Co.*, 262 Pa. 328 105 A. 551; *Scranton v. Public Service Comm.*, 268 Pa. 192, 110 A. 775; *Springfield Water Co. v. Philadelphia*, 285 Pa. 172, 131 A. 716."

In *Ullom v. Boehm*, supra, an attack was made on the constitutionality of a statute which prohibited advertising of ophthalmic products. In a unanimous decision, this Court held that the statute was a valid exercise of police power and, therefore, did not violate Article 1, Section 7, of the Pennsylvania Constitution by impairing the right of freedom of speech. In *Duquesne City v. Fincke*, supra, in denying the defendant's argument that a local ordinance requiring permission of the mayor to hold a meeting in the city streets violated Article 1, Section 7, we stated at page 118 of 269 Pa., at page 132 of 112 A.: "His contention founded thereon [on § 7], however, overlooks the fact that they do not give to him the right to assemble with others, and to speak wherever he and they chose to go * * *. The liberty of speech does not require that the clear legal rights of the whole community shall be violated." Also in *Duffy v. Cooke*, supra, a statute, prohibiting employees of any city of the first class from participating in any political activities, was held not to violate Article 1, Section 7, of the Pennsylvania Constitution, and we relied on the reasoning and wording of *Atkin v. State of Kansas*, 191 U.S 207, 24 S. Ct. 124, 48 L. Ed. 148; in interpreting Section 7. In Mack Appeal, supra, the appellants contended that a judicial rule prohibiting the taking of pictures near a court house violated Article 1, Section 7. In denying their contentions, we relied on and quoted from the decisions of the United States Supreme Court interpreting the First Amendment of the United States Constitution, and on *Fitzgerald v. City of Philadelphia*, supra. The Fitzgerald case involved the constitutionality of the Loyalty Oath. In determining its constitutionality under Article 1, Section 7, we relied on and adopted the interpretation of the United States Supreme Court of the First Amendment, 376 Pa. at page 387, 102 A. 2d at page 891: "It was said in *United Public Workers of America (C.I.O.) v. Mitchell*, 330 U.S. 75, 95, 67 S. Ct. 556, 567, 91 L. Ed. 754: '*Of course, it is accepted constitutional doctrine that these fundamental human rights are not absolute. * * * The essential rights of the First Amendment in some instances are subject to the elemental need for order without which the guarantees of civil rights to others would be a mockery.*' So, in *American Communications Ass'n, C.I.O. v. Douds*, 339 U.S. 382, 399, 70 S. Ct. 674, 684, 94 L. Ed. 925, it was said: 'When particular conduct is regulated in the interest of public order, and the regulation results in an indirect, conditional, partial abridgment of *speech*, the duty of the courts is to determine which of these two conflicting interests demands the greater protection under the particular circumstances presented. * * * On the other hand, legitimate attempts to protect the public * * * from present excesses of direct, active conduct, are not presumptively bad because they interfere with and, in some of its manifestations, restrain the exercise of First Amendment rights.'

---

[2] See also White, Commentaries on the Constitution of Pennsylvania, pg. 86 (1907), "Immoral publications may be suppressed" under the Pennsylvania Constitution.

And in *Thorp* v. *Board of Trustees of Schools for Industrial Education of Newark*, 6 N..J 498, 508, 509, 79 A. 2d 462, 467, it was said: 'But the fundamental civil liberties here involved are not absolute. The particular guarantee of freedom of thought and opinion by the First Amendment is not free of all qualification. Government has the inherent right of self-protection against the forces that would accomplish its overthrow by violence. It is of the very nature of the social compact that the individual freedoms at issue here are subject to reasonable restraint in the service of an interest deemed essential to the life of the community * * * The question is whether the statutory proscriptions bear a reasonable relation to the apprehended public evil. Where a regulation in the interest of public order results in an indirect partial abridgment of civil rights, the inquiry is as to which of the two conflicting interests demands the greater protection in the circumstances. The incidental limitation of personal freedoms is justifiable where necessary in the service of an overriding public interest.' " [Emphasis supplied.] In *Wortex Mills, Inc.* v. *Textile Workers Union of America*, supra, we stated, 369 Pa. at page 363, 85 A. 2d at page 854: "Picketing is a form of assembly and of speech and consequently comes within the First Amendment to the Constitution of the United States and within Article 1, § 7 of the Constitution of the Commonwealth of Pennsylvania, both of which guarantee freedom of speech: *Thornhill* v. *State of Alabama*, 310 U.S. 88, 60 S. Ct. 736, 84 L. Ed. 1093; *Carlson* v. *People of State of California*, 310 U.S. 106, 60 S. Ct. 746, 84 L. Ed. 1104; *Westinghouse Electric Corporation* v. *United Electrical, etc., Workers*, 353 Pa. 446, 46 A. 2d 16, 163 A.L.R. 656; *Pennsylvania Labor Relations Board* v. *Chester and Delaware Counties Bartenders, etc., Union*, 361 Pa. 246, 64 A. 2d 834, 11 A.L.R. 2d 1259. But that does not mean that every kind of speech and every kind of picketing is lawful. *Freedom of speech is not absolute or unlimited*—for example, a man may not slander or libel another; he may not publicly blaspheme the Deity; he may not engage in loud [mouth] speaking through sound trucks during certain hours or in certain parts of a city; and he may not assemble with others to commit a breach of the peace or to incite to riot or to advocate the commission of crimes. Freedom of speech gives no right of intimidation or coercion and no right to damage or injure another's business or property, * * *" [Emphasis supplied.] Picketing, like motion pictures, is an exercise of the right of free speech. Nevertheless, when either is detrimental to the public good, it may be suppressed and prevented from continuing: *Sansom House Enterprises* v. *Waiters & Waitresses Union, Local 301, A.F.L.*, 1955, 382 Pa. 476, 115 A. 2d 746, certiorari denied 350 U.S. 896, 76 S. Ct. 155, 100 L. Ed. 788.

Furthermore, this Court in *Buffalo Branch, Mutual Film Corp.* v. *Breitinger*, 1915, 250 Pa. 225, 95 A. 433, rejected this same contention, that the Obscenity Act of June 19, 1911, P.L. 1067, violated the Constitution of Pennsylvania in requiring submission of the film to the State Board of Censors prior to the showing of a motion picture. We held that in the legislature's valid exercise of the state's police power to conserve and protect the morals and manners of the public, the individual rights of a person must give way. "The promotion of *public morals*

and public health is a chief function of government, to be exercised at all times as occasion may require. The method by which the result may be accomplished depends upon the circumstances of the particular case, and the largest legislative discretion is allowed. *Beer Co.* v. *Massachusetts*, 97 U.S. 25, 24 L. Ed. 989." 250 Pa. at pages 232, 233, 95 A. at page 435. We further said, 250 Pa. at page 234, 95 A. at page 436, " 'The possession and enjoyment of *all* rights are subject to such reasonable conditions as may be deemed by the governing authority of the country essential to the safety, health, peace, good order, and *morals* of the community. Even liberty itself, the greatest of all rights, is not unrestricted license to act according to one's own will. It is [not] only freedom from restraint under conditions essential to the equal enjoyment of the same right by others. It is then liberty regulated by law * * *' " (Emphasis supplied).

Therefore, in the face of all this authority, how the Majority can state that there is an absolute prohibition against "prior restraint" under the Pennsylvania Constitution, is beyond my comprehension. As was stated by Mr. Justice Bell, speaking for a unanimous court, in *Wortex Mills, Inc.* v. *Textile Workers Union of America*, supra, 369 Pa. at page 363, 85 A. 2d at page 854, "*Freedom of speech is not absolute or unlimited * * **" *either under the United States Constitution, or the Pennsylvania Constitution.* (Emphasis supplied.)

Nor does the statute offend Article 1, Sections 6 and 9, of the Pennsylvania Constitution. The imperative therein that "trial by jury shall be as heretofore" is not infringed. The statute establishes a system of administrative control to the end that movies which are obscene may not be marketed for public consumption. This is not a statute involving a violation of the criminal laws. Determinations of a similar nature have been made by administrative agencies in Pennsylvania for years on end. See cases under the Milk Control Act and the Liquor Control Act. The majority decision, if carried through to its logical conclusion, will undermine the functioning of all administrative tribunals. Henceforth, every attempted enforcement of a civil penalty fixed by statute on a violation of an administrative order will require a jury trial, going to the merits of the administrative order which is, in effect, a collateral attack on a matter that is res judicata.

Furthermore, this precise question was passed upon by this Court and found to be without merit in *Buffalo Branch, Mutual Film Corp.* v. *Breitinger*, supra. In that case, the appellants attacked the Act of June 19, 1911, P.L. 1067, as a violation of Article 1, Section 6, because it denied them a right of trial by jury. That Act, like the present one, provided for penalties upon the showing of a film in violation of an injunction issued pursuant to a finding by the State Board of Censors that the movie violated the standards of the statute. We rejected this contention, stating that this was not a common law offense, but a new one created by the legislature. "There is nothing to forbid the legislature from creating a new offense and prescribing what mode they please of ascertaining the guilt of those who are charged with it. Many tribunals, unknown to the framers of the Constitution, and not at all resembling a jury, have been erected and charged with the determination of grave and weighty matters; * * *" 250 Pa. 243, 95 A. 438. And, we further stated, 250 Pa. at page 249, 95 A. at page 440: "As to the additional claim made by the individual plaintiffs that they have been deprived of the right of trial by jury, no question of the right of trial by jury arises in the case. There is nothing in the Constitution which prohibits the legislature from declaring new offenses and defining the mode by which the guilt of persons accused thereof may be determined. *Van Swartow v. Com.*, 24 Pa. 131." The same argument was rejected in *Commonwealth v. Blumenstein*, 1959, 396 Pa. 417, at page 419, 153 A. 2d 227, at page 228, which involved the Obscenity Act of June 24, 1939, P.L. 872, § 528, 18 P.S. § 4528, wherein we held that the prosecution "was brought under the statute and not under the common law. Hence the efficacy of the common law remedy against obscenity is not in issue." It was also, at least, impliedly rejected in *Times Film Corporation v. City of Chicago*, supra. See also, Tahiti Bar, Inc. Liquor License Case, 395 Pa. 355, 150 A. 2d 112.

The statute further satisfies all constitutional requirements for a hearing. The demands of due process are met. Before the Board may disapprove any film for exhibition, it must first make certain findings. The word *find* is a word of art in the law. "To find" necessarily implies to ascertain and to declare an issue of fact through a judicial inquiry in a trial-type hearing. See *Hallgring v. Board of Com'rs of City of Newark*, 1953, 25 N.J. Super. 88, 95 A. 2d 498; Cf. *Aizen v. Pennsylvania Public Utility Comm.*, 1948, 163 Pa. Super. 305, 60 A. 2d 443; *Stufflet v. Fraternal Order of Eagles*, 1949, 164 Pa. Super. 473, 65 A. 2d 443; *Kaylock v. Unemployment Compensation Board*, 1949, 165 Pa. Super. 376, 67 A. 2d 801. Every interested party will enjoy the opportunity of being heard, together with witnesses, who can give relevant testimony. If such due process is denied, the issue can be raised in timely and proper proceedings.

The Majority, in footnote 4, in reference to *Zenith International Film Corporation v. City of Chicago*, 7 Cir., 291 F. 2d 785, misinterprets the facts and holding of the case with reference to our present case. The Mayor of Chicago, who under the ordinance, was entrusted with the power of de novo review failed to view the film as a whole. Under this statute and the Roth case, and contrary to the *logic* of the Majority in arriving at the conclusion of its syllogism, the Board must and will view the film as a *whole*. Further, in the Zenith case, the censors and the Mayor failed to give a hearing to Zenith and an opportunity to show that the movie did not violate contemporary community standards, which our Board under a trial-type hearing will do. Also, the Chicago Board didn't state why the permit was refused. Our Board will give a detailed explanation in the event of a refusal. Furthermore, the make-up and the method of selection of the Chicago Board is completely different from that of the Pennsylvania Board. Therefore, there is no possible comparison between the Zenith case and our present statute with the exception of standards. The standards of Section 155–4 of the Municipal Code of the City of Chicago are as follows:

*"If a picture or series of pictures, for the showing or exhibition of which an application for a permit is made, is immoral or obscene, or portrays, depravity, criminality, or lack of virtue of a class of citizens of any race, color, creed, or religion and exposes them to contempt, derision, or obloquy, or tends to produce a breach of the peace or riots, or purports to represent any hanging, lynching, or burning of a human being, * * *." [Emphasis supplied.]*

That these standards are more far reaching in scope than those of the Act in question is plain. Our very narrow standards are "obscene" and "incite to crime," the latter applying only to children. But the important thing to bear in mind is that the 7th Circuit Court of Appeals did not question the standards in Section 155–4, and stated that, "The relief requested by the plaintiff shall be granted unless the city provides a hearing consistent with the *standards* set out herein within a reasonable time after Zenith's resubmission of the film to proper city authorities. If the film is found *obscene* or otherwise objectionable after a proper procedural determination by the city authorities, plaintiff may then challenge before the district court *such finding* of *obscenity*." [Emphasis supplied.] Furthermore the Supreme Court of Illinois, in *American Civil Liberties Union v. City of Chicago*, 1954, 3 Ill. 2d 334, 121 N.E. 2d 585, sustained some of the standards contained in the statute set out above, including "obscene." They didn't find, as the Majority found, the standards herein question, "so vague and indefinite, in form and as interpreted, as to permit within the scope of its language the punishment of incidents fairly within the protection of the guarantee of free speech * * * as contrary to the Fourteenth Amendment."[3] We are also glad to note that the Majority, after rejecting the United States Constitution, is now adopting it again, but contrary to the interpretation of the United States Supreme Court.

Finally as well stated in the appellant's reply brief at pages 14, 15, 16:

"The controlling principle here is that a statute and all of its provisions are to be construed in a manner consistent with the Constitutions of the Commonwealth and of the United States. Statutory Construction Act of May 28, 1937, P.L. 1019, 46 Pa. Stat. Ann. § 552(c) (Purdons).

"In interpreting Section 5 of the instant act, this Court should place upon it that construction which will save the statute rather than strike it down. The Courts consistently have construed statutes which are silent as to whether the administrative agency must hold a hearing as nevertheless requiring a hearing under the principles of due process. This problem has been met by 'reading into' the statute a requirement for a hearing. *Wong Yang Sun [Sung] v. McGrath*, 339 U.S. 33 [70 S. Ct. 445, 94 L. Ed. 616] (1950). Although no express requirement for hearing in statute authorizing deportation, hearing requirements of Section 5 of the Administrative Procedure Act must be held to apply in order to bring the deportation statute in harmony with the requirement of procedural due process: *Fahey v. Mallonee*, 332 U.S. 245 [67 S. Ct. 1552, 91 L. Ed. 2030] (1947); *Goldsmith v. [United States] Board of Tax Appeals*, 270 U.S. 117 [46 S. Ct. 215, 70 L. Ed. 494] (1925); *Jordan v. American Eagle Fire Insurance Co.*, [83 U.S. App. D.C. 192], 169 F. 2d 281 (D.C. Cir.

---

[3] See also *Times Film Corporation v. City of Chicago*, supra, footnote 4.

1948); *Eisler v. Clark* [D.C.], 77 F. Supp. 610 (1948); *Martin v. Board of Supervisors*, 135 Cal. App. 96, 26 [P.] 2d 843 (1933); *Reed v. Collins*, 5 Cal. App. 494, 90 Pac. 73 [973] (1907); *American Civil Liberties Union v. City of Chicago*, 3 Ill. 2d 334, 350, 121 N.E. 2d 585 (1954); [State ex rel.] *Powell v. State Medical Examing [Examining] Board*, 32 Minn. 324, 20 N.W. 238 (1884); *L. A. Darling Co. v. Water Resources Commission*, 341 Mich. 654, 67 N.W. 2d 890, 896 (1955); *Gage v. Censors of the New Hampshire Eclectic Medical Society*, 63 N.H. 92 (1884), and *Perpents [Perpente] v. Moss*, 293 N.Y. 325, 56 N.E. [2d] 726 (1944). See also *Pennsylvania R. Co. v. New Jersey State Aviation Commission et al.*, [1949, 2 N.J. 64] 65 A. 2d 61; *Garden Court Apartments, Inc. v. Hartnett*, [1949, 6 Terry 1, 45 Del. 1,] 65 A. 2d 231, 234.

"This was precisely the practice followed by this Court in *Commonwealth ex rel. Dermendzin v. Myers*, 397 Pa. 607 [156 A. 2d 804] (1959). Therein, a defendant sentenced to an enlarged term of imprisonment under the Habitual Criminal Act of 1939 was not informed that he had a right to hearing on the issue of recidivism, contrary to the requirements of procedural due process. The act does not in terms provide for either notice of hearing before sentence is imposed on a second offender as it does in the case of a fourth offender. Nevertheless, this Court, speaking through Chief Justice Jones read the act as impliedly providing for the requisite hearing in order to save it from constitutional defect:

" 'While the Act does not expressly provide for similar procedure before the sentencing of a second or third-time offender, we are constrained, in order not to involve a constitutional question of want of due process, to construe the Habitual Criminal Act as impliedly intended to require adequate notice and hearing on the issue of recidivism before an enlarged term of imprisonment can be imposed on a second offender. Under well established rules of construction, it is our duty to interpret a statute so as to render it constitutional if it is at all reasonable so to do * * *' supra at [page] 614 [of 397 Pa., at pages 807–808, of 156 A. 2d]."

In conclusion, it is my belief that the majority opinion herein misreads the words of the statute involved and what is intended thereby to help justify its argument that it is unconstitutional. Instead of construing the statute in a manner that would save and render it effective, misinterpretations are utilized in order to strike it down.

For these reasons, I emphatically dissent.

BELL, J., joins in this dissent.

MUSMANNO, Justice (dissenting).

During the last five years this Court has dismantled the three most formidable dikes constructed by the people of Pennsylvania, through their representatives in Harrisburg, against the flood of cinematic filth always pounding at the borders of our Commonwealth.

In 1956, in the Hallmark case, *Hallmark Productions v. Carroll*, 384 Pa. 348, 121 A. 2d 584 this Court, by declaring an Act of 1915 unconstitutional, dissolved the Motion Picture Censorship Board which, for forty-one years, had faithfully served the people by keeping the theatres wholesome and clean of obscenity, vulgarity, blasphemy and profanity. At the time of that decision, the Majority of this Court said that although its decision eliminated motion picture censorship this did not mean that objectionable films could not be suppressed since offending exhibitors could be prosecuted under the criminal code.

Then, in 1959, in *Commonwealth v. Blumenstein*, 396 Pa. 417, 153 A. 2d 227, this Court proceeded to strike down that section of the criminal code under which exhibitors of immoral pictures could be prosecuted, by declaring it unconstitutional. The parent law of that section of the code (Sec. 528, Penal Code of 1939, 18 P.S. § 4528) had been the Act of April 13, 1911, P.L. 64, so that this legislation which the Court invalidated had served the people of Pennsylvania faithfully for forty-eight years.

And then, also in 1959, the Majority of this Court, in the Kingsley case, *Kingsley International Pictures Corp. v. Blanc*, 396 Pa. 448, 153 A. 2d 243, 254, ruled that a district attorney could be enjoined from seizing a film which he regarded as violating the laws of Pennsylvania, because of obscenity. I wrote a dissenting opinion in that case, as I did in the previous ones, and ended that dissent as follows:

"*Unless the General Assembly comes to the aid of the people with renewed legislation and William Penn comes down from his pedestal atop City Hall to protect the State he founded against the forces of immorality at our borders, far more damaging to the welfare of the people than the Indians he encountered, the fair Commonwealth which he dedicated to religious freedom, civic liberties and moral purity, may well be on the way to a cinematic Gomorrah.*"

The General Assembly was, of course, well aware of its responsibilities to the people, and, thus, in September, 1959, it enacted the Motion Picture Control Act, which is the subject of this appeal. That the representatives were acting under a mandate of the people is well evidenced by the fact that the House of Representatives passed the measure by a near unanimous vote of 163 to 1, and the Senate approved it by the overwhelming majority of 47 to 3. The bill was, of course, approved and signed by the Governor.

Today this Court again, through its powers of interpretation and absolute decision, reduces another statute of the sovereign body of the Commonwealth to shreds of paper by declaring it unconstitutional.

In view of the fact that the highest tribunal in our State has now destroyed three statutes on the subject of motion picture sanitation, the people may well wonder what must be done to protect Pennsylvania from the evil of lascivious, pornographic, obscene and prurient motion pictures.

As matters presently stand, the appalling prospect presents itself that films of the most degrading character, films revealing scenes of outright degeneracy, may be projected without legal hindrance in Pennsylvania. Dealers may traffic in pictures on subjects of the utmost depravity, pictures which cannot help but corrupt morals and weaken the will of immature minds, pictures which would make an ancient Pompeiian blush with shame—dealers may engage in this type of revolting merchandise and not be restrained.

These four decisions of the Supreme Court of Pennsylvania have, in effect, bound prosecuting authorities hand and foot. Officials charged with standing guard over the moral health of the people have been disarmed. Every weapon which they could employ to stop the wicked and nefarious business of immoral films has been torn from their grasp. The armory in this field has been stripped bare.

By vetoing the three statutes enumerated, this Court has virtually, in the particular subject matter under consideration, made of itself a super-chief executive or a super-Senate.

Does the Constitution of Pennsylvania demand what this Court has done? In *Com. ex rel. Shumaker v. New York & Pennsylvania Co.*, 367 Pa. 40, 79 A. 2d 439, 446, we said: "In construing the legislative intent the Statutory Construction Act of May 28, 1937 * * * directs us to presume the intention of the legislature to be that it intends to favor the public as against any private interest."

Would it be difficult for this Court to presume that the General Assembly of Pennsylvania intended to favor the public which certainly is interested in protecting children from the contamination of visual and auditory contact with immoral exhibitions? In the Blumenstein case, supra, I said in my Dissenting Opinion, and I repeat it here:

"Who can doubt that many juveniles have been consciously or unconsciously urged into lurid crime because of being repeatedly exposed to lurid and immoral motion pictures? Children are by nature imitative and when they see immorality being practiced on so extensive and expansive a medium of expression as the motion picture screen, is it strange if they conclude that there is nothing wrong about [doing] what is being publicly glorified?" [396 Pa. 417, 153 A. 2d 237.]

What is the rationale of the Majority's repudiation of the Motion Picture Control Act? It says that the Act violates the constitutional provision protecting free speech and freedom of the press. But freedom of speech is not involved in the Act; much less freedom of the press.

Those who fear that motion picture regulation may lead to press censorship conjure up a wholly unnecessary fear. The American people would never stand for press censorship because the freedom of the press is one of the strongest bulwarks of our independence and well-being and has been so recognized by statutes and decisions of the nation's highest court. Here we stand unanimously as at Armageddon.

But, I repeat, freedom of the press and freedom of speech are wholly extraneous to what is before us in this lawsuit. To equate motion pictures with speech offends against logic and what is palpably demonstrable. The performance of speech involves only one person. And all that occurs is the formation of words. However, in motion pictures many persons participate. The audience watches these persons engaging in pantomime, gesture, gesticulations, postures, and movements which tell what words could never describe.

The Majority Opinion says:

"Apart from the Fourteenth Amendment, the guarantee of free communication of thought and opinion is independently protected by our State Constitution of 1874."

But in motion pictures we are not dealing with the mere "communication of thought and opinion." Motion pictures certainly go beyond the communication of thought and opinion. Motion pictures may appeal to the senses, to the passions. Further comparison between mere words and the panorama, parade, and performance of motion pictures is not only bizarre but might even become unseemly.

The Majority Opinion goes back further than 1874. It recalls the Constitutional Convention of 1790 where the members of the Convention "were undoubtedly fully cognizant of the vicissitudes and outright suppressions to which printing had theretofore been subjected in this very Colony." But what has printing in 1790 to do with the malignance of filthy motion pictures?

No one with the slightest awareness of what is happening in the world can fail to know that many motion picture producers have gone entirely too far in pandering to the baser passions. J. Edgar Hoover, Director of the Federal Bureau of Investigation, has said:

"As a law enforcement officer and as an American citizen, I feel duty-bound to speak out against a dangerous trend which is manifesting itself in the field of film and television entertainment. In the face of the nation's terrifying juvenile crime wave, we are threatened with a flood of movies and television presentations which flout decency and applaud lawlessness. Not since the days when thousands filed past the bier of the infamous John Dillinger and made his home a virtual shrine have we witnessed such a brazen affront to our national conscience."

The well-known, popular and able columnist Bob Considine wrote of motion pictures in 1960 as follows:

"So many of its current heroines are prostitutes, so many of its heroes wallow in a bed of neuroses, that churchmen interested in the morality of their flocks note that the number of objectional films has risen from 14 per cent in 1959 to 24 per cent this year."

Cardinal Cushing of Boston said in 1959:

"We must all be concerned about the corruption of our youth. The survival of our nation depends upon the moral integrity of those who are being trained for tomorrow's social responsibilities."

The Reader's Digest for March, 1961, carried an article by Don Wharton, who spoke of what he saw walking along a street in New York City:

"At the Criterion was Girl of the Night. ('She's beautiful enough to be a model, chic enough to be a debutante, desirable enough to be a wife—and special enough to be none of these.') The management had installed telephones next to the sidewalk with a sign inviting pedestrians to call the call girl. 'Use these phones and listen to her sizzling conversation." Those who did heard a sultry voice saying, 'I'm Bobbie Williams, your girl of the night. I've been waiting for your call.

*"This is not a New York phenomenon. Similar exploitation of sex—illicit, perverted, sordid or glamorized—is seen all across the nation. * * ***

"In Circleville, Ohio, last fall, the leading theater's lobby was advertising three coming attractions: Desire in the Dust (torrid love, infidelity, physical and mental cruelty), Girl of the Night (prostitution) and The Dark at the Top of the Stairs (frigidity). In Cincinnati the next day, I dropped into a movie house showing Psycho, in which a girl is knifed by a psychotic while taking a shower. * * * *In this moviehouse, teenagers composed over half the audience."*

The author points out that even the motion picture industry itself is protesting:

"Attacks on objectionable pictures are coming even from people in the movie industry. Both state and national associations of exhibitors have officially protested the avalanche of films with oversexed themes, treatment and dialogue that they are getting from the producers."

One of the most popular motion picture stars of the day, John Wayne, whose production "Alamo"—which for sheer visual beauty, patriotic theme, and its moving story of self-sacrifice must be rated among the classics of the screen—said:

"I don't like to see the Hollywood bloodstream polluted with immoral and amoral nuances. Filthy minds, filthy words and filthy thoughts have no place in films, which I see as a universal instrument at once entertaining peoples and encouraging them to work toward a better world, a freer world."

The whole vast library of material—articles, speeches, dissertations and studies on immoral motion pictures—was before the Legislature when it decided that it had to do something to protect the children of Pennsylvania from their corrosive influences.

The main and principal objective of the Motion Picture Control Act is to erect a palisade of protection around the keen sensitivity, the swift reactions, and the acute impressionability of minors who are such easy targets for the arrows of improper suggestion shot from the vantage point of the motion picture screen.

Pennsylvania has the right to pride itself on the solicitude it has always exerted in behalf of the welfare of children. The statute books glow with special laws shielding tender minds and bodies from inhuman treatment and cruelty, injurious labor conditions, and deleterious environments. Pennsylvania has enacted statutes to keep children off the streets after certain hours, it prohibits the sale of firearms to them.

For their own welfare and wellbeing, children may not obtain licenses, which are available to adults, they may not enter premises where intoxicating liquors are being dispensed. The State makes education compulsory for children. The State budget each year bulges with expenditures running into millions and millions of dollars, all designed to educate and protect children, to promote their health—physical, mental, moral and spiritual; to guide back to the path of moral and legal behavior those who have strayed into the woods and mire of delinquency.

It would take a book to describe only briefly what Pennsylvania does to educate, train, and equip the children of today to become the citizens of tomorrow to perpetuate the ideals on which this Commonwealth was founded and to which it has adhered in its entire glorious history.

It would be most extraordinary that in that book with instructions on how to rear the citizens of the future, there would be not a page on how to protect minors from the potentially dangerous influences of immoral exhibitions. The Legislature has recognized the need for that page and has inserted it into the book of instructions. This Court has torn it out, on the theory that it encroached on the rights of those engaged in the business of this medium of entertainment, a medium which unquestionably possesses the potentialities of pernicious persuasion.

But the page which this Court has removed from the book of protection for children does not carry the encroachments which the Court envisages. There is nothing in the Motion Picture Control Act which denies anyone appeal to the courts whenever and wherever he believes his constitutional prerogatives have been invaded.

The regulations and control provided for in the Act are designed to protect the interests and the welfare of the special wards of any civilized state—the children. But in doing so it has, at the same time, refrained from imposing unfair burdens on the adult citizenry engaged in a perfectly legitimate and in fact laudable business enterprise.

The Act is not only not designed to injure the legitimate business of motion picture merchants. In fact, it will be helpful to them because it is obvious that the vast majority of films submitted for registration will be approved for showing, and dealers will thus be saved from a constant concern as to whether they may or may not be violating the law of the State and the law of morals.

The only films which will be restrained will be those which are obscene under a definition specifically laid down by the Supreme Court of the United States. If, in that perfectly fair and American manner of dealing, some one may lose a temporary investment, he should not complain; he will only be paying what all citizens are required to pay in the maintenance of an organized, wholesome, and decent society.

Walter Lippmann, perhaps the most respected and admired news commentator of today, and a proved champion of human liberties and civil rights, sees no harm in restrictions on individual action; in fact he recommends them where the welfare of children is involved:

*"There can be no real doubt, it seems to me, that the movies and television and the comic books are purveying violence and lust to a vicious and intolerable degree. There can be no real doubt that public exhibitions of sadism tend to excite sadistic desires and to teach the audience how to gratify sadistic desires. Nor can there be any real doubt that there is a close connection between the suddenness of the increase in sadistic crimes and the new vogue of sadism among the mass media of entertainment. * * * For my own part, believing as I do in freedom of speech and thought, I see no objection in principle to censorship of the mass entertainment of the young. Until some more refined way is worked out of controlling this evil thing, the risks to our liberties are, I believe, decidedly less than the risks of unmanageable violence."* (*Emphasis supplied*)

In its protection of individual liberty, the Constitution of the United States and that of Pennsylvania, too, does not advocate anarchy which, of course, is what unregulated and uncontained freedom would signify. Every man's freedom is limited to the extent that it interferes with somebody else's right to freedom. No one who is engaged in the business of motion pictures has the right, under the Constitution, to contaminate the mind of youth, just as no one, under the Constitutional guarantee of free speech, has the right to slander or libel his neighbor.

The Majority Opinion says that the Motion Picture Act is "clearly invalid on its face." In support of this strong statement it says that the Act—

"is designed to effect, in violation of Article I, Section 7, of the Pennsylvania Constitution, a precensorship of the exercise of the individual's right freely to communicate thoughts and opinions."

But here again, I repeat respectfully, the Majority confuses communication of thoughts and opinion, which is propelled by the medium of speech, with bodily vulgarity which can be conveyed by means of motion pictures in the most revolting forms.

The Majority Opinion quotes from *Joseph Burstyn Inc.* v. *Wilson*, 343 U.S. 495, 72 S. Ct. 777, 781, 96 L. Ed. 1098, that "expression by means of motion pictures is included within the free speech and free press guaranty of the First and Fourteenth Amendments." This, of course, is true but there is a modification to this pronouncement in the very same case, namely, *"It does not follow that the Constitution requires absolute freedom to exhibit every motion picture of every kind at all times and all places."* (Emphasis supplied)

And then, in *Roth* v. *United States*, 354 U.S. 476, 77 S. Ct. 1304, 1308, 1 L. Ed. 2d 1498, the Supreme Court of the United States declared that "in light of * * * history, it is apparent that the unconditional phrasing of the First Amendment was not intended to protect every utterance."

Nor do I find in the Act the dangers which the Majority Opinion describes so alarmingly. The Majority Opinion shows how, once the majority of the board disapproves of a film, the exhibitor may be prosecuted for showing the condemned picture. In this the Majority Opinion sees a violation of the Constitutional right of trial by jury. I do not follow this argument. When State milk inspectors turn down a farmer's milk as being unfit for consumption, the farmer may not demand a jury to pass upon the quality of the milk. When meat inspectors condemn certain meat as tainted, the butcher may not ask for a jury to smell the meat and count the organisms in it before the government may act. When a barber maintains an unhygienic shop and he is ordered to close his shop he may not insist that a jury be called to examine the sink and cuspidors before he may be cited for violating the health laws. In all these cases the alleged offender has the right to a jury trial *after* the government inspection has terminated just as the exhibitor of motion pictures will have the right to a jury trial in the event he is cited by the Board.

The Majority Opinion complains because an exhibitor would be required to pay the insignificant sum of $1.00 per year and 50 cents per 1,200 lineal feet, saying that this "is a plain attempt to tax the exercise of the right of free speech." In the first place, as I have already indicated, free

speech is not involved here. In the second place, the insignificant fees mentioned are paid for a very important service rendered to the exhibitor by the State, namely, the ascertainment of what is obscene so that the exhibitor is relieved of that responsibility.

If a picture has been disapproved the exhibitor may not advertise its showing. The Majority Opinion sees here an infringement on the right of free press, asserting that "national magazines and out-of-State newspapers would be prohibited from circulation in Pennsylvania unless" the advertisements of the disapproved picture were deleted. This, of course, does not follow at all because the State of Pennsylvania, under the Interstate Commerce Clause of the Constitution could in no way impede the free circulation of magazines and newspapers.

Then the Majority finds fault with the Act in that it does not provide that the members of the Motion Picture Control Board shall have academic education or sociological training. I would regard that absence of requirement as one of the virtues of the plan of review of films. The reaction to a motion picture, in so far as that reaction appertains to morality and decency, should be that of normal, average persons and not that of technicians trained in technical fields. Motion pictures, after all, are intended for entertainment and if they accomplish that purpose without offending against morals and good citizenship, they should be exhibited. The Majority Opinion allows itself a slight exaggeration when it says that the Board members could even be uneducated or even illiterate, persons. To assume that a governor would appoint an illiterate person to a post which is bound to involve reading is to ascribe to the chief executive of the State an ignorance and sheer perversity, which even the most partisan minded opponent would hardly ever suggest.

The Motion Picture Control Act of 1959, like much good legislation, may need improvements later on, and they will undoubtedly be forthcoming by legislative amendment, but I cannot agree that it is unconstitutional and I certainly regret that this Court has now for the third time in five years nullified the action of the Legislature in a field which cries out for supervision and control.

So that there may be no misunderstanding about my position I want to add that I do not oppose motion pictures. On the contrary, I regard motion picture entertainment as the best form of relaxation extant. Color photography, the wide screen, and the miraculous equipment which reproduces music with such fidelity, volume and tone, that one can hardly believe that the orchestra is not actually in the theatre—all these magnificent features have made the motion picture theatre the rendezvous of relaxful diversion which even kings could not have dreamed of having fifty years ago. Classics in literature are being reproduced, educational subjects are attractively handled, history is made to live again before one's entranced vision. Faraway places, which the unwealthy person would never have the money to visit, are being brought to us in all their original charm, quaintness, and dramatic picturesqueness.

Pictures like the *Alamo, Ben Hur, The Big Fisherman, The Big Country, The Ten Commandments* are more than entertainment; they are almost personal adventures and in many ways spiritual experiences. Masterpieces of this character, together with other dramatic gems are being endangered by the cheap, bawdy monstrosities referred to in the Reader's Digest article above quoted. Control such as that outlined in the Act before us will preserve films of this magnitude and artistic perfection as it will also protect children.

The law-making body of this Commonwealth has tried a number of times to supply the motion picture control and

protection which a decent, God-fearing, law-abiding, self-respecting and dignified people need, desire and demand.

I hope and urge that it will not lose heart, but in the spirit of William Penn, try and try again.

■ Harry Monfred, James Spissler, Samuel Mendelson, Sander A. Siegel, Benjamin M. Siegel and Albert King

v.

State of Maryland.
No. 55. Sept. Term, 1961.

Court of Appeals of Maryland.

Aug. 9, 1961.

Martin B. Greenfeld, Baltimore (William Greenfeld and Albert B. Polovoy, Baltimore, on the brief), for appellants.

Clayton A. Dietrich, Asst. Atty. Gen. (Thomas B. Finan, Atty. Gen., Saul A. Harris, State's Atty., and James W. Murphy, Asst. State's Atty., Baltimore, on the brief), for appellee.

Before HENDERSON, HAMMOND, PRESCOTT, HORNEY, and MARBURY, JJ.

HORNEY, Judge.

The appellants, who engage in the retail sale of books and magazines in Baltimore City, were convicted by the Criminal Court of Baltimore of violating Code (1960 Cum. Supp.), Art. 27, § 418(a), which makes it a misdemeanor for any person to "knowingly * * * sell * * * any lewd, obscene or indecent book, magazine * * * drawing or photograph." The subject matter of the prosecutions was six magazines,[1] commonly known or described as "girlie" magazines, and a set of semi-nude photographs portraying a sequential "striptease."[2]

The magazines and photographs were openly displayed and offered for sale without overcharge along with other types of magazines on newsstands or in the establishments of the several appellants. The magazines which are the subject of this appeal were purchased by members of the Baltimore City Police Department, who were specifically instructed to make purchases of named or similar magazines. The set of photographs was purchased by a member of the Criminal Justice Commission. The record shows that publications of a similar type had been on display and

sold in the city for at least five years prior to the arrest of the appellants.

The trial court—applying the obscenity test set forth in *Roth* v. *United States* and (*Alberts* v. *California*), 1957, 354 U.S. 476, 77 S. Ct. 1304, 1 L. Ed. 2d 1498—concluded that the magazines and photographs were "neither literary in nature, artful in presentation, nor innocent in purpose" and that the dominant theme of the magazines and photographs dealt "with sex in a manner appealing to prurient interest" in that they had a "tendency to excite lustful thoughts," and found that such materials were "lewd, obscene and indecent" and therefore violated the obscenity statute of this State. All the defendants were found guilty and all were sentenced to pay fines.

The appellants claim (i) that the magazines and photographs are not obscene within the meaning of the statute because such materials do not "as a matter of law" exceed contemporary community standards; and (ii) that if such materials are obscene under the statute, then the statute violated the First and Fourteenth Amendments to the Constitution of the United States. But the real contention is—inasmuch as it is claimed that the suspect material is not "hard-core pornography"—that the appellants were immune from prosecution under the statute.

Since these cases were tried by the court sitting without a jury, we have the right to review them on both the law and evidence to determine whether in law the evidence was sufficient to sustain the conviction in each case, though we may not set the verdict aside on the evidence unless it is clearly erroneous. Maryland Rule 741 c.

In cases such as these, where prosecution is based primarily on the exhibits introduced as evidence, oral evidence, as was the case here, is usually not abundant. The exhibits speak for themselves, but must be perused and examined with care. This has been done as to each of the seven exhibits—six magazines and one set of photographs.

[1] An examination of the set of photographs shows various poses of a woman in progressive stages of undress (though never quite naked), which to the normal person

---

[1] The publication entitled Candid was introduced as evidence against Harry Monfred; Consort against James Spissler; Sextet against Samuel Mendelson and Albert King; Cloud 9 against Mendelson; Torrid against Sander A. Siegel and Benjamin M. Siegel; and Black Garter against Monfred, King and both Siegels.

[2] The set of fifteen photographs was introduced against the defendant King.

might be offensive or repulsive, but they are not necessarily obscene under the statute. And since mere nudity in and of itself is not obscene, we think the trial court in convicting King for selling the photographs was clearly in error as to the evidence.

[2] The same is true with respect to the magazine Black Garter. Most of the pictures in this magazine are of models who pose for "glamor" photography. They are portrayed scantily dressed either in black lingerie or white furs and other accessories in what might be described as coarsely offensive postures, but the pictures, even though obviously intended to arouse sex appeal, are not strictly obscene. And, which is more to the point with respect to the issue of obscenity, the textual matter accompanying the illustrations is in the main innocuous. Instead, it purports to discuss in detail the technique of using shadows and lights in photographing the nude. Therefore, since this magazine taken as a whole is not obscene, we think the trial court also erred in convicting Monfred, King and the Siegels for selling it.

[3] But when each of the other five so-called "girlie" magazines—Candid, Consort, Sextet, Cloud 9 and Torrid—is taken as a whole, that is, when the pictures reproduced therein are examined in conjunction with a perusal of the textual material, it is apparent that all of these publications are obscene within the meaning of the statute as well as under the obscenity test approved by the majority in the Roth-Alberts case, supra. All of them, without exception, present numerous pictures or drawings of nude or semi-nude women showing what the State characterized as "come hither" expressions and poses interspersed with pointedly suggestive sex stories so placed that a reader if he needs visual aid in following the story has only to glance at the opposite page for additional stimulation. All of these five publications were obviously calculated to excite lustful thoughts in the mind of the reader.[3]

---

[3] Sextet (Vol. 1. No. 3), for example, in addition to showing more than fifty pictures and drawings of nude and semi-nude women on its forty-eight pages, also contains eleven articles indexed as "features," "fiction" and "pictorial." Four of such articles will suffice to demonstrate the intention to arouse prurient interest. Typical extracts from these include the following:
From "His Only Weakness" (a lewd narrative detailing the seduction of a hardened woman by a philanderer):
"That's my proposition * * *. If you want me in bed, now's your one and only chance. (p. 4)

*   *   *   *   *

"Now he was absolutely sure he was going to have [her]. And, if necessary, he would make it by force. Sort of an unlegalized rape. (p. 6)

*   *   *   *

"Suppose you let me feel you. (p. 40)

*   *   *   *

"He could see her delicious breasts straining against the material of her smart black dress. (p. 40)

*   *   *   *   *

"He didn't say a word. He just nodded his head, leaped forward, grabbed her hand and dragged her into his bedroom.
"When it was over, they lay quietly on the bed * * * naked and exhausted." (p. 41)
From "The Paper Back Girls" (emphasizing the increase in the sexual aspect of cheap literature):
"* * * she is practically a virgin because she has only been to

Thus, having made a determination of our own that the findings of fact were correct, we are unable to say that the trial court was in error as to the evidence in convicting all of the defendants for selling one or more of these magazines; nor did the lower court reach the wrong conclusion as to the law.

In the Roth (Alberts) case, Roth, who was a "rare book" dealer, was convicted of a violation of the Federal obscenity statute. Alberts, who was a distributor of photographs of nude and semi-nude women in various poses, was convicted under the California obscenity statute. In neither case was there any question as to whether or not the books sold by Roth and the photographs distributed by Alberts were obscene in fact. Thus, all that was decided was whether, on their faces, the federal and state statutes under consideration were violative of the First and Fourteenth Amendments respectively.

In speaking for the majority, Justice Brennan held that both statutes were valid, and, in the process, stated, 354 U.S. at page 489, 77 S. Ct. at page 1311, that the test of obscenity is "whether to the average person, applying contemporary community standards, the dominant theme of the material taken as a whole appeals to prurient interest." Material having such an interest was defined in a footnote as "material having a tendency to excite lustful thoughts." The Court also held that "obscenity is not within the area of constitutionally protected speech and press."

---

bed with eleven different men, not counting those before she was 13. [She] also confesses her fondness for dykes without giving any count in such regard. (p. 11)

*   *   *   *   *

" 'Kiss me * * * I haven't been laid in more than six months * * * she reached up and, with a terrific yank, ripped the front of her dress wide open, baring her breasts * * * rich, sexual woman was everywhere * * *.' (p. 12)

*   *   *   *   *

"The girls round robin it with the men and as circumstances permit they pair off and have an even more exciting time with each other." (p. 12)
From "The Cherry Orchard" (a story of a minor seduced by a prostitute):
"Larry's pants bulged with the thought. (p. 17)

*   *   *   *   *

"What a broad to pop with! He swallowed hard and crossed his legs. (p. 18)

*   *   *   *   *   *   *

"Her whisper was almost a sexual action. 'Your place or mine?' (p. 19)

*   *   *   *   *

"She moved her groin hard into his. (p. 19)

*   *   *   *   *

"He pulled her sweater from her shoulder, and she swung around. Nude, except for panties. * * * 'I told you gin makes me passionate.' She kicked off her shoes and flung herself on the bed. * * * 'I'll let you take the panties off. Guys like to do that.' (p. 19)

*   *   *   *   *

"Seconds later, he became a man." (p. 42)
From "A Date With Judy" (a fantasy of a partially nude woman inviting a man to her house):
" 'I'm so happy you could come,' she purrs with a sexy smile and a suggestive pose of welcome.
"Arm and arm they enter the semidark apartment." (p. 20)

Chief Justice Warren concurred in the result reached in each case. His theory was—because it was not the material but a person that was on trial—that what is obscene should depend in the main on the reprehensible conduct of the seller in engaging in "the commercial exploitation of the morbid and shameful craving for materials with prurient effect" and not on the obscenity of the materials sold. Justice Harlan concurred in the result in Alberts and dissented in Roth. He was of the opinion that federal obscenity censorship should be limited to hard-core pornography and that the states should be allowed broader censorship powers. Justices Black and Douglas dissented. They were against all obscenity censorship except where it is shown that "the particular publication has an impact on action that the government can control."

In the next term after the Roth-Alberts decision, the Supreme Court disposed of several other obscenity cases by short per curiams. In three of them, the Court, by reversing federal courts of appeal—without any explanation for the reversals other than the citation of the Roth (and Alberts) case—gave final protection to the materials in question. In one, *Times Film Corp.* v. *City of Chicago*, 1957, 355 U.S. 35, 78 S. Ct. 115, 2 L. Ed. 2d 72, which involved prior censorship of a French cinema with English subtitles based on a novel by Colette, the appellant attacked the Chicago censorship ordinance on the ground that it imposed an unconstitutional prior restraint. The appendix to the appellant's brief indicated that the censors had not taken any of the artistic merits of the film into account, and in fact four of the censors testified that the picture had not aroused their sexual desires, pruriently or otherwise. The appendix further indicated that there was no nudity, other than one short scene showing a boy's buttocks, and that the real reason a permit was denied was to prevent children from seeing the movie. The decision of the appellate court in this case had been handed down before the Supreme Court had decided Roth. In the second reversal, *One, Inc.* v. *Olesen*, 1958, 355 U.S. 371, 78 S. Ct. 364, 2 L. Ed. 2d 352, which involved the right to send the magazine One—a publication dealing with homosexuality—through the mails, officials of the Post Office Department had invoked the federal obscenity statute because the magazine was considered to be lewd and obscene. The petition for certiorari in this case had also been prepared before the decision in Roth. The government urged that the lower court had satisfied the Roth test, but the petitioner contended that the Supreme Court had not theretofore dealt with this specific question. A copy of the magazine was not included in the printed record; nor was it reproduced in either of the briefs, but, since the sole question was whether the magazine was obscene—a question of fact—the Court, by citing Roth, apparently applied the Roth test in determining that the publication was either not obscene or that taken as a whole it was not obscene. In the third reversal, *Sunshine Book Co.* v. *Summerfield*, 1958, 355 U.S. 372, 78 S. Ct. 365, 2 L. Ed. 2d 352, another case involving the mailing of a magazine—Sunshine & Health—a copy of the publication was also not included in the printed record, but it is a "nudist" type magazine—a representative copy of which is included in the transcript in the instant case—in which, although the nudist way of life is advocated and the pictures show the genital areas of the body, there is

nothing obscene in the text of the magazine. Thus, it appears that the reversal was based on the concept that mere nudity is not obscenity or the decision may have been based on the fact that the text was not in fact obscene. But in *Adams Newark Theatre Co.* v. *City of Newark*, 1957, 354 U.S. 931, 77 S. Ct. 1395, 1 L. Ed. 2d 1533, involving the Newark city ordinances prohibiting lewd, obscene or indecent shows and performances, in which the petitioner had raised issues of vagueness and freedom of expression in a proceeding for a declaratory judgment before the city had attempted to enforce the ordinances, the Supreme Court of the United States, in a brief per curiam, summarily affirmed the judgment of the New Jersey Supreme Court—which had upheld the constitutionality of the ordinances—by citing the Kingsley, *Kingsley Books, Inc.* v. *Brown*, 354 U.S. 436, 77 S. Ct. 1325, 1 L. Ed. 2d 1469, Roth and Alberts cases. And, in a fifth case, *Mounce* v. *United States*, 1957, 355 U.S. 180, 78 S. Ct. 267, 2 L. Ed. 2d 187, the government having made a "confession of error" that the test used by the court of appeals was "materially different" from the Roth test, the judgment below was reversed and remanded to the district court for consideration in the light of Roth.

We think the Times Film case is fairly distinguishable from the instant case in that the censors not only made no effort to apply any sort of reasonable obscenity test, but principally because the main reliance of the appellant was on the "prior restraint" theory rather than the lack of an obscenity test. The Sunshine Book case is also easily distinguishable in that, unlike the instant case, there were no obscene stories in the nudist magazine. And, although the One, Inc. case is not as easy to distinguish as the other two, it is a fact that it, like the Sunshine Book case, also involved federal postal censorship, not a state criminal prosecution; besides, since the constitutional issue was not formally raised, it is possible that the decision may not have been based on the unconstitutionality of the statute.

Other recent federal obscenity cases also have no direct bearing on the cases before us. In *Butler* v. *State of Michigan*, 1957, 352 U.S. 380, 77 S. Ct. 524, 1 L. Ed. 2d 412, decided prior to Roth, the Supreme Court merely condemned the Michigan obscenity statute by holding that it was violative of the First and Fourteenth Amendments —in that it prohibited the sale to an adult of a book unfit for a minor—without suggesting a constitutionally sanctioned alternative. In *Kingsley Books, Inc.* v. *Brown*, 1957, 354 U.S. 436, 77 S. Ct. 1325, 1 L. Ed. 2d 1469, also decided before Roth, where the defendant was convicted under the New York obscenity statute, there was no question but that the material was obscene, and there was no intimation of what was soon to be stated in Roth. In *Kingsley Intern. Pictures Corp.* v. *Regents of Univ. of N.Y.*, 1959, 360 U.S. 684, 79 S. Ct. 1362, 1363, 3 L. Ed. 2d 1512, which involved the famous motion picture Lady Chatterley's Lover, the Supreme Court, without deciding whether or not the picture was obscene, declared that a part of the New York motion picture obscenity statute was unconstitutional in that it violated the basic "freedom to advocate ideas" guaranteed by the First Amendment. And in *Smith* v. *State of California*, 1959, 361 U.S. 147, 80 S. Ct. 215, 4 L. Ed. 2d 205, in which the defendant was convicted of having obscene books in his possession, a Los Angeles city ordinance was declared unconstitutional in that it did not require proof of scienter on the part of the possessor, but again, the majority did not pass on the question of whether the books were actually obscene.

Thus, in the cases since Roth, the Supreme Court—at least in its majority opinions in the Kingsley Pictures and Smith cases—did not specifically apply the Roth test to the allegedly obscene materials before it in these cases. However, the test seems to have been applied in the per curiam reversals (Times Film, One, Inc., and Sunshine Book) and in the per curiam affirmance (Adams Newark Theatre), but we do not know for sure—other than that the Roth test of obscenity will be strictly construed—what the reasoning of the Court was in any of these per curiams.

It may well be that the Supreme Court will in time (assuming it has not already done so) declare that only "hardcore pornography" is not protected by the constitution, as a majority of four of the Court of Appeals of New York (in two opinions—the latter concurring in the result reached in the former—each of which was concurred in by one other judge) did recently in construing the meaning of the obscenity statute of that State in *People* v. *Richmond County News, Inc.*, 1960, 9 N.Y. 2d 578, 216 N.Y.S. 2d 369, 175 N.E. 2d 681, 686, involving the sale and distribution of the magazine Gent, when, in discarding the Roth test, it adopted an obscenity test of its own.[4] Or the Supreme Court might eventually accept the concept of "variable obscenity"[5] expressed by Chief Justice Warren in his concurring opinion in the Roth-Alberts case to the effect that the question of obscenity must turn, not on the material itself, but on the motives of the seller. In passing—since these sales were unquestionably commercial— we note that a variable obscenity test could have been applied in this case. But, until the Supreme Court specifically speaks further in this uncertain area, we think we are bound by what we understand the Roth test requires.

Applying the Roth test to the censorship power of the State under the provisions of our obscenity statute, as was done in these cases (although incorrectly with respect to two of the exhibits), it is, as we see it, evident that the conviction of King for selling the set of semi-nude photographs should be reversed; that the convictions of Monfred, King and both Siegels for selling the magazine Black Garter should also be reversed; and that the convictions of all of the appellants for selling one or more of the obscene magazines called Candid, Consort, Sextet, Cloud 9 and Torrid, should be affirmed, and we so hold.

Judgments against Albert King for selling the set of semi-nude photographs and against Harry Monfred, Albert King, Sander A. Siegel and Benjamin M. Siegel for selling the magazine Black Garter reversed; the Mayor and City Council of Baltimore to pay one-seventh of the costs.

Judgments against all appellants for selling one or more of the obscene magazines Candid, Consort, Sextet, Cloud

9 and Torrid affirmed; Appellants to pay six-sevenths of the costs.

HAMMOND, Judge (dissenting).

The opinion of the Court in this troublesome case is essentially syllogistic: the Maryland statute proscribing the sale of obscene books and magazines is to be construed as broadly as the Supreme Court will permit; the case of *Roth* v. *United States*, 354 U.S. 476, 77 S. Ct. 1304, 1311, 1 L. Ed. 2d 1498, held that obscenity is not protected by the constitutional guarantees of freedom of speech and press, and said that material is obscene if, to the average person, applying contemporary community standards, "the dominant theme of the material taken as a whole appeals to prurient interest"; the trial judge found the magazines sold by the defendants appealed to "prurient interest" and, since this Court cannot say he was clearly wrong in his determination, the judgments and sentences of guilty must be affirmed. I find the premises and the deductive process unsound, and the conclusion therefore necessarily wrong and am constrained to dissent and express my reasons for disagreement.

The only testimony against each defendant was that he had sold the magazine or pictures introduced against him. There was no testimony as to contemporary community standards (except that the magazines had been sold openly in Baltimore for five years), or as to what comprises a community, or as to what effect the pictures and magazines would have on the average person. The Court held the separate group of pictures and those in the magazines not to be in themselves obscene (and with these holdings I agree), but decided that most of the texts, considered with the related pictures, justified Judge Sodaro in finding the magazines obscene under the Roth standards, as the Court understands them. Despite the Court's statement that its determinations were independent, this is no more in actuality than holding that "Judge Sodaro thought that most people would think the magazines obscene, we cannot say he was wrong and therefore, under the Maryland statute and the Constitutional tests, they are obscene."

In deciding the case on this basis the Court, I think, failed to fulfill its obligatory duty to make a reflective independent appraisal of the controversial printings, for as Justice Harlan, concurring in Roth, said (as to the suppression of obscenity) at page 497–498 of 354 U.S., at page 1316 of 77 S. Ct.: "* * * the question [of] whether a particular work is of that character involves not really an issue of fact but a question of constitutional *judgment* of the most sensitive and delicate kind." A State appellate court, no less than the Supreme Court, has the same obligation. The *People* v. *Richmond County News, Inc.*, 175 N.Y. 681, 216 N.Y.S. 2d 369, 175 N.E. 2d 681; Lockhart and McClure, Censorship of Obscenity: The Developing Constitutional Standards, 45 Minn. L. Rev. 114–120; 4 Davis, Administrative Law, 29.08; *Niemotko* v. *State of Maryland*, 340 U.S. 268, 271, 71 S. Ct. 325, 328, 95 L. Ed. 267; *Feiner* v. *People of State of New York*, 340 U.S. 315, 316, 71 S. Ct. 303, 95 L. Ed. 267; *Napue* v. *Illinois*, 360 U.S. 264, 271, 79 S. Ct. 1173, 3 L. Ed. 2d 1217; *Watts* v. *State of Indiana*, 338 U.S. 49, 69 S. Ct. 1347, 93 L. Ed. 1801. Since Roth, cases that have recognized this obligation include *United States* v. *Keller*, 3 Cir., 259 F. 2d 54; *Capitol Enterprises, Inc.* v. *City of Chicago*, 7 Cir.,

---

[4] Judge Fuld in the opinion written by him stated that "the test of the obscene, of the pornographic, is not in the tendency or appeal of the material, but rather in its content objectively appraised" and then added that "it [the obscene] focuses predominantly upon what is sexually morbid, grossly perverse and bizarre, without any artistic or scientific purpose or justification."

[5] This concept seems to have been favored by Dean Lockhart and Professor McClure (of the University of Minnesota Law School) in their scholarly treatise on this area of the law entitled Censorship of Obscenity: The Developing Constitutional Standards published in 45 Minn. L. Rev. 5 (1960).

260 F. 2d 670; *Commonwealth v. Moniz*, 338 Mass. 442, 155 N.E. 2d 762.

That the publications here involved are a form of vulgar and tawdry entertainment (for some part of the populace), lacking in all social value or artistic or scientific justification, does not deprive them of the constitutional protection of free speech and press. In *Winters v. People of State of New York*, 333 U.S. 507, 510, 68 S. Ct. 665, 667, 92 L. Ed. 840, the Court, noting its obligations as to an aspect of a free press (comic crime books) "in its relation to public morals" said: "We do not accede to appellee's suggestion that the constitutional protection for a free press applies only to the exposition of ideas. The line between the informing and the entertaining is too elusive for the protection of that basic right * * * What is one man's amusement, teaches another's doctrine. Though we can see nothing of any possible value to society in these magazines, they are as much entitled to the protection of free speech as the best of literature." *Hannegan v. Esquire, Inc.*, 327 U.S. 146, 157, 66 S. Ct. 456, 462, 90 L. Ed. 586, said: "What seems to one to be trash may have for others fleeting or even enduring values."

The concept of obscenity in law is a complex and difficult one. I take it the Maryland Legislature intended by its use of "obscene" in the statute (Code (1960 Cum. Supp.), Art. 27, Sec. 418(a)) what the word meant in prevailing leading legal thought; otherwise it would be too vague to constitute a permissible standard in a criminal statute.

In *People v. Richmond County News, Inc.*, supra, the Court of Appeals of New York, in holding a "girlie" magazine (indistinguishable from the worst of those in the case before us) not to be obscene, said of the New York statute (the equivalent of the Maryland section) at page 685 of 175 N.E. 2d:

"*In the Roth case (354 U.S. 476, 77 S. Ct. 1304, supra), the court did say that 'obscene material is material which deals with sex in a manner appealing to prurient interest' (at page 487 of 354 U.S., at page 1310 of 77 S. Ct.), and that the test was 'whether to the average person, applying contemporary community standards, the dominant theme of the material taken as a whole appeals to prurient interest' (at page 489 of 354 U.S., at page 1311 of 77 S. Ct.). These statements, however, can only indicate the broad boundaries of any permissible definition of obscenity under the United States Constitution; they do not pretend to, and cannot, give specific content to the meaning of 'obscene' as it appears in our statute.*"

In the Roth opinion the phrase "appeal to prurient interest" was lifted from a more comprehensive definition in the American Law Institute's Model Penal Code, Tentative Draft No. 6, Sec. 207.10(2) (a definition which the Court seemingly adopted as sound): "* * * A thing is obscene if, considered as a whole, its predominant appeal is to prurient interest, i.e., a shameful or morbid interest in nudity, sex or excretion and if it goes substantially beyond customary limits of candor in description or representation of such matters * * *." The authors of Model Penal Code continue:

"*We reject the prevailing test of tendency to arouse lustful thoughts or desires because it is unrealistically broad for a society that plainly tolerates a great deal of erotic interest in literature, advertising, and art, and because regulation of thought or desire, unconnected with overt misbehaviour, raises the most acute constitutional as well as practical difficulties. We likewise reject the common definition of obscene as that which 'tends to corrupt or debase.' If this means anything different from tendency to arouse lustful thought and desire, it suggests that change of character or actual misbehaviour follows from contact with obscenity. Evidence of such consequences is lacking * * *"*[1]

The Supreme Court of Oregon in a careful opinion in *State v. Jackson*, Or., 356 P. 2d 495, 507, adopted the Model Penal Code definition of obscenity as the meaning of the Oregon statute on the subject, and said:

"*On the other hand, the Model Penal Code, by requiring that the material, to be obscene, must appeal to 'prurient interest' and go 'substantially beyond customary limits of candor in description or representation' emphasizes strongly that the manner of presentation must itself amount to shameful and disgusting conduct outside the pale of what is tolerable to the community at large. The majority opinion in the Roth case defines 'prurient' as 'having a tendency to excite lustful thoughts.' 354 U.S. 476, at page 486, note 20, 77 S. Ct. at page 1310. We think, however, that the court had in mind the narrower meaning used by the Model Penal Code or means to use the narrower meaning in cases following Roth.*"

The Roth case unquestionably established two constitutional tests of obscenity: (1) the material must be judged as a whole and (2) it must be judged under contemporary community standards by its impact upon average or normal persons, not the young, the weak, or the susceptible. There can be little doubt, I believe, that "community standards" means not state or local communities but

---

[1] The Court of Appeals of New York comments on the last statements in *The People v. Richmond County News, Inc.*, 9 N.Y.S. 579, 175 N.E. 2d 681, 216 N.Y.S. 2d 369, saying: "It is noteworthy that, despite the reams of material on the effect of books, magazines and other media of expression on sexual conduct, 'there is very little scientific evidence' on the subject. St. John-Stevas, Obscenity in the Law (1956), p. 196; see, also, *Brown v. Kingsley Books*, 1 N.Y. 2d 177, 181, fn. 3, 151 N.Y.S. 2d 639, 641, 134 N.E. 2d 461, 463 * * *; *United States v. Roth*, 2 Cir., 237 F. 2d 796, 812–817, per Frank, J., concurring, affirmed 354 U.S. 476, 77 S. Ct. 1304, 1 L. Ed. 2d 1498, supra. Indeed, two authoritative writers in the field have concluded that, 'Although the whole subject of obscenity censorship hinges upon the unproved assumption that "obscene" literature is a significant factor in causing sexual deviation from the community standard, no report can be found of a single effort at genuine research to test this assumption by singling out as a factor for study the effect of sex literature upon sexual behavior.' (Lockhart and McClure, Obscenity and the Courts, 20 Law and Contemporary Problems, 587, 595; see, also, American Law Institute, Model Penal Code, Tentative Draft No. 6, § 207.10, p. 44). Some commentators have gone even further and suggested that 'for an undetermined number of individuals, the writing or reading of obscenity may be a substitute for rather than a stimulus to physical sexuality.' American Law Institute, Model Penal Code, Tentative Draft No. 6, § 207.10, p. 45." The suggestion in these writings is that there is no causal connection between what is regarded as "obscene" and antisocial conduct of a sexual nature.

rather the standards of society as a whole.[2] The phrase originated with Judge Learned Hand in his opinion in *United States* v. *Kennerley*, D.C., 209 F. 119, 121: "* * * should not the word 'obscene' be allowed to indicate the present critical point in the compromise between candor and shame at which the community may have arrived here and now? * * * To put thought in leash to the average conscience of the time is perhaps tolerable, but to fetter it by the necessities of the lowest and least capable seems a fatal policy." It seems plain Judge Hand was referring not to the standards of states or local communities, but rather to the contemporary standards of society as a whole, and that the Supreme Court had in mind that same standard in adopting the phrase. Messrs. Lockhart and McClure so interpret the Roth opinion. They say in their article Censorship of Obscenity at p. 111 of 45 Minn. L. Rev.:

" * * * We believe the Supreme Court did not, as some of the proponents of censorship hopefully thought, approve of the application of state or local community standards in obscenity cases. Indeed, in one of its per curiam decisions after the Roth-Alberts opinion, the Court indicated that it would not tolerate the application of restrictive local standards in obscenity censorship."

The error into which the trial judge and majority of this Court fell, in my view, was to confuse and equate sex (and vulgarity, crudeness and cheap, poor taste) with obscenity. They are not synonymous and society as a whole and the courts recognize this. The subject matter, the descriptions and references found in the magazines held obscene in this case can be found in much the same form in literally hundreds of novels and stories which have either been accepted as not obscene or have been found not to be. The Supreme Court in Roth emphasized the necessity of differentiating betwen sex and lewdness:

"However, *sex and obscenity are not synonymous* * * * The portrayal of sex, e.g., in art, literature and

scientific works, is not * * * sufficient reason to deny material the constitutional protection of freedom of speech and press. Sex, a great and mysterious motive force in human life, has indisputably been a subject of absorbing interest to mankind through the ages; it is one of the vital problems of human interest and public concern." Page 487 of 354 U.S., page 1310 of 77 S. Ct., page 1508 of 1 L. Ed. 2d.

I do not believe the trial judge permissibly could have been convinced beyond a reasonable doubt that the contents of the magazines, judged by the contemporary standards of our society as a whole, both appealed to "a shameful or morbid interest" in nudity or sex and at the same time went "*substantially* beyond customary limits of candor in description or representation of such matters."[3] As the American Law Institute said, we live today in "a society that plainly tolerates a great deal of erotic interest in literature, advertising and art." Judge Bryan made the same point in finding "Lady Chatterley's Lover" not obscene in *Grove Press, Inc.* v. *Christenberry*, D.C., 175 F. Supp. 488:

"The tests of obscenity are not whether the book or passages from it are in bad taste or shock or offend the sensibilities of an individual, or even of a substantial segment of the community. * * * 175 F. Supp. at page 501.

"* * * the broadening of freedom of expression and of the frankness with which sex and sex relations are dealt with at the present time require no discussion. In one best selling novel after another frank descriptions of the sex act and 'four-letter' words appear with frequency. These trends appear in all media of public expression, in the kind of language used and the subjects discussed in polite society, in pictures, advertisements and dress, and in other ways familiar to all. Much of what is now accepted would have shocked the community to the core a generation ago. Today such things are generally tolerated whether we approve or not." 175 F. Supp. at page 502.

I agree with the conclusion of the Court of Appeals of New York in its holding that the "realistic accounts of normal sexuality" in the magazine "Gent" (in which, as Judge Froessel makes plain in his dissenting opinion by extensive quotations and description, the language and pictures were as direct and crude and vulgar as any in the magazines before us) was not obscene. Judge Fuld said for the Court at page 686 of 175 N.E. 2d:

"The fact is, however, that, while the magazine contains many stories or pictures which are aesthetically tasteless and without any redeeming social worth, none of them is pornographic. Numerous pictures and cartoons of nude or semi-nude women and numerous descriptions and depictions of sexual arousal and satisfaction are to be found in 'Gent' but it contains nothing which smacks of sick and blatantly perverse sexuality."

---

[2] Manifestly local community standards as to what is or is not obscene vary to a considerable degree. What a jury in the more unsophisticated sections of Maryland—in some parts of the Eastern Shore and in more remote Southern and Western Maryland—might consider beyond the pale, a jury in Baltimore or the metropolitan counties of the State might find acceptable. Lockhart and McClure in their article in 45 Minn. L. Rev. 5 point out at page 36 that "In Los Angeles, New York, and perhaps also Chicago, the Post Office and Justice Departments had difficulty convicting persons for mailing obscene matter; courts and juries there were too sophisticated, their attitudes too liberal * * * the two departments supported the enactment of legislation authorizing prosecution of a mailer at any place through which the mail passed, as well as at the place of receipt of the mail. It would be easier to obtain convictions and heavier sentences in the hinterland * * *." The authors add at page 109 that "At trials in more straight-laced communities, the government could make particular effective use of such trial tactics as refusing to consent to waivers of jury trials; and then, having insisted on jury trials, it could peremptorily challenge the most literate and best educated jurors. If 'contemporary community standards' has reference to the standards of state or local communities, and if those standards are to be applied by a jury, then these tactics will enable the government to secure convictions which heretofore would have been difficult or impossible to obtain."

[3] The Court found "Black Garter" not to be obscene. "Consort" and "Torrid" would not seem to be any more so under any reasonable test of obscenity.

"Candid" and "Sextet" have one or two stories approaching the obscene and almost all of "Cloud Nine" is on the borderline.

Chief Judge Desmond, concurring, said at page 687:

"This collection of sexy fiction and illustrations has little of literary merit or artistry and yet it is not in the First Amendment sense filthy or disgusting or deliberately corruptive or offensive to common decency under prevailing standards of taste. Virtuous adults will reject it as all of us Judges would were we not restrained by the Roth-Alberts legal test. Adolescents may be hurt by it. But our prepossessions are not the law and the reactions of children are not valid tests (Roth v. United States, 354 U.S. 476, 489, 490, 77 S. Ct. 1304, supra."

Whether the Court's reading of the Maryland statute, or mine, is correct as a matter of interpretation may well be immaterial. I am convinced that the Supreme Court has left no constitutional leeway to make the interpretation the majority makes and that its result violates the constitutional rights of the defendants and the publishers of free speech and free press.

In seeking to go to the Supreme Court, Roth raised four issues of substance—whether (a) the federal statute violated first amendment guarantees; (b) was too vague; (c) invaded the reserved powers of the States and the people; and, finally, (d) whether the publications were obscene. Roth seriously pressed only the first three; his argument on the fourth was so perfunctory the government did not reply. The Court limited the certiorari granted to the first three issues. The Alberts case, decided with Roth, ended in the Supreme Court in the same posture as Roth—at a level of abstraction so rarefied that the facts had become immaterial.

The Solicitor General brought the case to a more earthy level. In his brief he pointed out that the violations of the Federal obscenity statute fell into three categories. The first, some two per cent, comprised "novels of apparently serious literary intent" challenged because "they concentrate on explicit discussion of sex conduct in a vocabulary based on four letter words." The second category, less than ten per cent, he said was border line material, mainly photographic. The final group, ninety per cent of the whole, comprised what the Solicitor General described as "black market" or "hard-core" pornography. To make sure the Court knew what he meant by "hard-core pornography" he sent to the Court a carton containing numerous samples concededly in that category.[4]

[4] The Solicitor General described "hard-core" pornography as follows:

"This is commercially-produced material in obvious violation of present law * * * This material is manufactured clandestinely in this country or abroad and smuggled in. There is no desire to portray the material in pseudo-scientific or 'arty' terms. The production is plainly 'hard-core' pornography, of the most explicit variety, devoid of any disguise.

"Some of this pornography consists of erotic objects. There are also large numbers of black and white photographs, individually, in sets, and in booklet form, of men and women engaged in every conceivable form of normal and abnormal sexual relations and acts. There are small printed pamphlets or books, illustrated with such photographs, which consist of stories in simple, explicit, words of sexual excesses of every kind, over and over again. No one would suggest that they had the slightest literary merit or were intended to have any. There are also large numbers of 'comic books,' specially drawn for the pornographic trade, which are likewise devoted to explicitly illustrated incidents of sexual

The foregoing account of the Roth-Alberts case was taken from Lockhart and McClure, Censorship of Obscenity, 45 Minn. L. Rev. pp. 19–29. The authors later revert to the subject and conclude (p. 60):

"In voting to sustain the constitutionality of the obscenity statutes of California and of the United States, Justices Frankfurter, Burton, Clark, Brennan, and Whittaker must have had material of this kind in mind for hard-core

activity, normal or perverted * * * It may safely be said that most, if not all, of this type of booklets contain drawings not only of normal fornication but also of perversions of various kinds.

"The words of the 'hard-core' pornographic materials now being circulated are the motion picture films. These films, sometimes of high technical quality, sometimes in color, show people of both sexes engaged in orgies which again include every form of sexual activity known, all of which are presented in a favorable light. The impact of these pictures on the viewer cannot easily be imagined. No form of incitement to action or to excitation could be more explicit or more effective.

"Brief for the United States, pp. 37–38, *United States v. Roth*, 354 U.S. 476 [77 S. Ct. 1304, 1 L. Ed. 2d 1498] (1957).

"The Solicitor General also sought to distinguish hard-core pornography from material in 'the borderline entertainment area.' He said:

"The distinction between this [hard-core pornography] and the material produced by petitioner and others, as discussed above, is not based upon any difference in intent. Both seek to exploit the erotic market place. The difference is that the 'black-market' traffickers make no pretence about the quality and nature of the material they are producing and offering * * *."

D. H. Lawrence wrote in Pornography and Obscenity in Sex Literature and Censorship (1953):

"But even I would censor genuine pornography, rigorously. It would not be very difficult. In the first place, genuine pornography is almost always underworld, it doesn't come into the open. In the second, you can recognize it by the insult it offers, invariably, to sex, and to the human spirit.

"Pornography is the attempt to insult sex, to do dirt on it. This is unpardonable. Take the very lowest instance, the picture post-card sold underhand, by the underworld, in most cities. What I have seen of them have been of an ugliness to make you cry. The insult to the human body, the insult to a vital human relationship! Ugly and cheap they make the human nudity, ugly and degraded they make the sexual act, trivial and cheap and nasty.

"It is the same with the books they sell in the underworld. They are either so ugly they make you ill, so fatuous you can't imagine anybody but a cretin or a moron reading them, or writing them."

The Kronhausens in Pornography and The Law 178–243 (1959) say pornographic books "are always made up of a succession of increasingly erotic scenes without distracting non-erotic passages. These erotic scenes are commonly scenes of willing, even anxious seduction, of sadistic defloration in mass orgies, of incestuous relations consummated with little or no sense of guilt, or superpermissive parent figures who initiate and participate in the sexual activities of their children, of profaning the sacred, of supersexed males and females, of Negroes and Asiatics as sex symbols, of male and particularly female homosexuality, and of flagellation, all described in taboo words. The sole purpose of pornographic books is to stimulate erotic response, never to describe or deal with the basic realities of life."

(As summarized by Lockhart and McClure, Censorship of Obscenity, 45 Minn. L. Rev. 63–64.)

See also the graphic description of the illicit traffic in "hard-core" pornography detailed in Chapter 1 of James Jackson Kilpatrick's "The Smut Peddlers" (1960).

pornography, particularly in pictorial form, is so blatantly shocking and revolting that it would have been impossible for the Justices to put it out of mind. Since the basic issue before the Court was only the constitutionality of the statutes on their faces and in a vacuum, without regard to their application in the two cases, it seems likely that the Court upheld their constitutionality as imaginatively applied to hard-core pornography.

"We conclude, therefore, that the concept of obscenity held by most members of the Court is probably hard-core pornography, a conclusion consistent with the Court's 'rejection of obscenity as utterly without redeeming social importance.'"

This view is strongly confirmed by the per curiam decisions which followed Roth on distinctly mundane levels. In each on the citation of Roth the Court reversed United States Court of Appeals decisions that had upheld obscenity censorship, and demonstrated that in Roth it had placed really very tight restraints on what can constitutionally be censored as obscene.

The views of Messrs. Lockhart and McClure as to the meaning of Roth undoubtedly are shared by the Court of Appeals of New York which, in *The People* v. *Richmond County News, Inc.*, supra, clearly indicated its interpretation of the New York statute as reaching only "hard-core" pornography was compelled by the Roth and the per curiam holdings. Chief Judge Desmond, concurring in the Richmond case, said so in so many words, and, concurring in *Kingsley Intern. Pictures Corp.* v. *Regents of Univ. of N.Y.*, 4 N.Y. 2d 349, 175 N.Y.S. 2d 39, 151 N.E. 2d 197, 207–208, observed that the Supreme Court in the per curiams must have looked at the challenged material and found it not obscene under Roth. Other cases which would seem to have shared the same views include those in the footnote below.[5]

One of the significant per curiams which followed Roth was *Times Films Corporation* v. *City of Chicago*, 355 U.S. 35, 78 S. Ct. 115, 2 L. Ed. 2d 72. The Court of Appeals, 7 Cir., 244 F. 2d 432, described the motion picture "The Game of Love," held obscene by it, as follows:

"We found that, from the beginning to end, the thread of the story is supercharged with a current of lewdness generated by a series of illicit sexual intimacies and acts. In the introductory scenes a flying start is made when a 16 year old boy is shown completely nude on a bathing beach in the presence of a group of younger girls. On that plane the narrative proceeds to reveal the seduction of this boy by a physically attractive woman old enough to be his mother. Under the influence of this experience and an arrangement to repeat it, the boy thereupon engages in sexual relations with a girl of his own age. The erotic thread of the story is carried, without deviation toward any wholesome idea, through scene after scene. The narrative is graphically pictured with nothing omitted except those sexual consummations which are plainly suggested but

---

[5] *Excelsior Pictures Corp.* v. *City of Chicago*, D.C.N.D. Ill., 182 F. Supp. 400; *Commonwealth* v. *Moniz*, 338 Mass. 442, 155 N.E. 2d 762; *City of Cincinnati* v. *Walton*, Ohio Mun., 145 N.E. 2d 407; *United States* v. *Keller*, 3 Cir., 259 F. 2d 54; *People* ex rel. *Burtman* v. *Silberglitt*, 5 Misc. 2d 847, 182 N.Y.S. 2d 536.

meaningfully omitted and thus, by the very fact of omission, emphasized. * * *

"We do not hesitate to say that the calculated purpose of the producer of this film, and its dominant effect, are substantially to arouse sexual desires. We are of the opinion that the probability of this effect is so great as to outweigh whatever artistic or other merits the film may possess. We think these determinations are supported by the effect which this film would have upon the normal, average person." 244 F. 2d 432, 436.

A second appeal, *One Incorporated* v. *Olesen*, 355 U.S. 371, 78 S. Ct. 364, 2 L. Ed. 2d 352, was from the decision of the Court of Appeals of the Ninth Circuit, 241 F. 2d 772, holding the magazine "One" and the advertisement in it of the magazine "Circle" which contained pictures and stories of homosexuality and lesbianism obscene. The Court of Appeals described its findings in this way:

"The article 'Sappho Remembered' is the story of a lesbian's influence on a young girl * * *. *This article is nothing more than cheap pornography calculated to promote lesbianism. It falls far short of dealing with homosexuality from the scientific, historical and critical point of view.*

"The poem 'Lord Samuel and Lord Montagu' is about the alleged homosexual activities of Lord Montagu and other British Peers and contains a warning to all males to avoid the public toilets while Lord Samuel is 'sniffing round the drains' of Piccadilly (London). The poem pertains to sexual matters of such a vulgar and indecent nature that it tends to arouse a feeling of disgust and revulsion. It is dirty, vulgar and offensive to the moral senses. * * *

"An examination of 'The Circle' clearly reveals that it contains obscene and filthy matter which is offensive to the moral senses, morally depraving and debasing, and that it is designed for persons who have lecherous and salacious proclivities.

"The picture and the sketches are obscene and filthy by prevailing standards. The stories 'All This and Heaven Too' and 'Not Til the End,' pages 32–36, are similar to the story 'Sappho Remembered,' except that they relate to the activities of the homosexuals rather than lesbians. Such stories are obscene, lewd and lascivious. They are offensive to the moral senses, morally depraving and debasing." 241 F. 2d 772, 777, 778.

The third case, *Sunshine Book Company* v. *Summerfield*, 355 U.S. 372, 78 S. Ct. 365, 2 L. Ed. 2d 352, involved a nudist magazine. The Court of Appeals, 101 U.S. App. D.C. 358, 249 F. 2d 114, quoted with approval the language of *Sunshine Book Company* v. *McCaffrey*, 8 Misc. 2d 327, 112 N.Y.S. 2d 476, 483, that:

"Where the dominant purpose of nudity is to promote lust, it is obscene and indecent. The distribution and sale of the magazines in this case is a most objectionable example. The dominant purpose of the photographs in these magazines is to attract the attention of the public by an appeal to their sexual impulses. * * * *Men, women, youths of both sexes, and even children, can purchase these magazines. They will have a libidinous effect upon most ordinary, normal, healthy individuals. Their effect upon the*

abnormal individual may be more disastrous." 249 F. 2d 114, 118, 119.

The Supreme Court must have made an independent examination of the material in each case and found that censorship offended constitutional privileges for the Court simply reversed on the citation of Roth, and so terminated the litigation and gave final protection to the material.

The material it protected had been thought obscene by the lower court judges, applying what they deemed to be the contemporary standards of the average or normal person. Yet the Supreme Court, as I interpret its actions, held the pictures and writings were not obscene under the Roth standards. I can only conclude that as of now the Supreme Court will permit the proscription only of hard-core pornography and I find nothing in the magazines before the Court coming within that category.

The Supreme Court in Roth, page 488 of 354 U.S., page 1311 of 77 S. Ct., page 1509 of 1 L. Ed. 2d, said, speaking of "the fundamental freedoms of speech and press," that "Ceaseless vigilance is the watchword to prevent their erosion by Congress or by the States. The door barring federal and state intrusion into this area cannot be left ajar; it must be kept tightly closed and opened only the slightest crack necessary to prevent encroachment upon more important interests."

The background of Roth, and the three per curiams that followed, lead me to conclude that the door has been opened very slightly for the censors—not enough to permit them to get at the magazines in this case—and that the Roth standard, as understood and applied by the Supreme Court, is a very tight standard, reaching only "hard-core" pornography. If I am right the application of the Maryland statute, applied as the majority has applied it in this case, was unconstitutional.

I would reverse the judgments appealed from.

■ Bantam Books, Inc. *et al.*

v.

Joseph A. Sullivan *et al.* As Members of the Rhode Island Commission To Encourage Morality in Youth.
Eq. No. 2925.

Supreme Court of Rhode Island.

Dec. 20, 1961.

Abedon, Michaelson & Stanzler, Milton Stanzler, Providence, Weil, Gotshal & Manges, Horace S. Manges, Jacob F. Raskin, New York City, for petitioner.

J. Joseph Nugent, Atty. Gen., Joseph L. Breen, Chief Sp. Counsel, Providence, for the State.

CONDON, Chief Justice.

This is a petition to the superior court for a declaratory judgment under G.L. 1956, chap. 9–30, otherwise known as the uniform declaratory judgments act. The cause is here on the petitioners' appeal from a decree denying a portion of the relief prayed for, and also on the respondents' appeal from such decree granting the petitioners certain other relief which they sought.

The petitioners are Bantam Books, Inc., Dell Publishing Company, Inc., Pocket Books, Inc. and The New American Library of World Literature, Inc., all New York corporations engaged in the business of publishing paperbound books but not in distributing them in this state. The respondents are the executive secretary and members of the Rhode Island Commission to Encourage Morality in Youth. The commission was created by the general assembly at its January 1956 session by resolution No. 73.

The resolution was amended on May 25, 1959 and as amended it charges the commission as follows:

"It shall be the duty of said commission to educate the public concerning any book, picture, pamphlet, ballad, printed paper or other thing containing obscene, indecent or impure language, as defined in chapter 11–31 of the general laws, entitled 'Obscene and objectionable publications and shows,' and to investigate and recommend the prosecution of all violations of said sections, and it shall be the further duty of said commission to combat juvenile delinquency and encourage morality in youth by (a) investigating situations which may cause, be responsible for or give rise to undesirable behavior of juveniles, (b) educate the public as to these causes and (c) recommend legislation, prosecution and/or treatment which would ameliorate or eliminate said causes."

In the discharge of such duty as they construed it the commission compiled several lists of publications which upon investigation they deemed "completely objectionable for sale, distribution or display for youths under eighteen years of age" and notified distributors doing business within the state thereof. They also advised these distributors that the lists had been furnished to the police departments throughout the state. They asked for the cooperation of the distributors in removing the objectionable publications and stated that the receipt of such cooperation would eliminate the necessity of the commission recommending prosecution to the attorney general. As a result of such notices the distributor for Bantam Books, Inc. and Dell Publishing Company, Inc. returned a supply of certain paper-bound books published by them and stated the books could not be held for sale because they were listed by the commission as objectionable. The distributor did not object to the commission's action and is not a party to the instant proceedings.

In their petition petitioners alleged that Resolution No. 73 is an unconstitutional interference with the right of freedom of the press guaranteed by the first amendment to the federal constitution and made applicable to the states by the fourteenth amendment. They also alleged that it is violative of article I, sec. 20, of the constitution of this state guaranteeing such freedom. The petitioners further alleged that as construed by the commission the resolution was unconstitutionally applied by them, that their actions thereunder should be declared null and void, and that they should be enjoined from continuing such acts.

The cause was heard by a justice of the superior court without a jury on petition, answer and oral proof as though it were a suit in equity. At the conclusion of the evidence the trial justice decreed (1) that the resolution was constitutional, but (2) that the acts of respondents under their construction of it were unconstitutional in that they were in effect prior restraints of freedom of the press. On that ground they were (3) expressly enjoined by the decree from continuing such acts.

The petitioners contend that the trial justice erred in sustaining the constitutionality of the resolution. In support of such contention they argue that the same reasons upon which he based his finding that the commission's acts were unlawful were equally applicable to the resolution itself. On the other hand respondents, under their appeal, contend that their acts were in accordance with the authority vested in them by the resolution and that since the trial justice could not find it unconstitutional he erred in enjoining them from continuing such acts thereunder.

[1] We have no difficulty in declaring the resolution constitutional. On its face it does not authorize previous restraint of freedom of the press. It does not confer on the commission any official power to regulate or supervise the distribution of books or other publications. The functions conferred are solely educative and investigative in aid of the legislative policy to prevent the dissemination of obscene and impure literature, especially as it affects the morality of youth. The commission cannot lawfully *order* anyone to comply with its conclusions regarding the objectionable nature of a publication which it has officially investigated.

Unless and until such publication is judicially determined to be obscene the distributor may with impunity refuse to respond to any suggestions of the commission. He may treat them as of no more binding force than similar suggestions of an unofficial group. Indeed each is on a par with the other. The mere fact that the commission may recommend prosecution does not alter the case. They cannot *order* prosecution; that judgment is solely with the attorney general. Any unofficial group may do as much in this respect as the commission.

As we review this resolution it does no more than clothe a designated group of individuals with an official status but with little if any more power than to investigate and recommend action by the appropriate authorities where its

investigation indicates action is necessary. As such it may well be considered an arm of the legislature to effectuate its policy of preventing the dissemination of obscene literature and conceivably also in the nature of a bureau of investigation in aid of the police and the department of the attorney general in their detection and prosecution of violators of "chapter 11–31 of the general laws."

No case has been cited to us and we are aware of none wherein a similar resolution has been involved and its constitutionality questioned. While the United States supreme court has considered a number of cases involving various forms of state interference with freedom of the press, some of which have been cited by petitioners, none of them was concerned with a provision like resolution No. 73. *Smith v. California*, 361 U.S. 147, 80 S. Ct. 215, 4 L. Ed. 2d 205; *Kingsley Books, Inc.* v. *Brown*, 354 U.S. 436, 77 S. Ct. 1325, 1 L. Ed. 2d 1469; *Roth v. United States (Alberts v. California)*, 354 U.S. 476, 77 S. Ct. 1304, 1 L. Ed. 2d 1498; *Chaplinsky v. New Hampshire*, 315 U.S. 568, 62 S. Ct. 766, 86 L. Ed. 1031; *Lovell v. City of Griffin*, 303 U.S. 444, 58 S. Ct. 666, 82 L. Ed. 949; *Near v. Minnesota* ex rel. *Olson*, 283 U.S. 697, 51 S. Ct. 625, 75 L. Ed. 1357. From our examination of those cases we are of the opinion that the supreme court would not deem such a provision violative of the first amendment as a previous restraint of freedom of the press. In any event unless and until the supreme court so rules we hold that the trial justice did not err in deciding that the resolution was constitutional.

[2] We now come to the question whether he erred in holding that the commission in applying the resolution acted unconstitutionally. The petitioners argue that he did not, and they cite the following cases in support of his decision. *Dearborn Pub. Co.* v. *Fitzgerald*, D.C., 271 F. 479; *American Mercury, Inc.* v. *Chase*, D.C., 13 F. 2d 224; *Busey v. District of Columbia*, D.C. Cir., 138 F. 2d 592; *New American Library of World Literature, Inc.* v. *Allen*, D.C., 114 F. Supp. 823; *Grove Press, Inc.* v. *Christenberry*, D.C., 175 F. Supp. 488; *HMH Publishing Co.* v. *Garrett*, D.C., 151 F. Supp. 903; *Bantam Books, Inc.* v. *Melko*, 25 N.J. Super. 292, 96 A. 2d 47.

None of those cases is by a court of last resort. In each instance the decision is by a single judge of a court of inferior jurisdiction. However, we have nevertheless examined them, not because they have any standing as precedents but solely because of the possibility that the reasoning upon which the court based its decision might help in solving our problem. On examination we find that they are of no assistance. Most of such cases did not present a factual situation like the one in the instant case. In others where the facts were somewhat analogous the reasoning that led the judge to find prior restraint of freedom of the press is not, in our opinion, convincing. Moreover, in most of those cases the judge predicated such finding on some unlawful action causing or threatening to cause irreparable injury to the complainant's property.

In the case at bar the evidence discloses no unlawful act on the part of the commission. On the contrary, their acts were in accord with the clearly expressed objectives of the resolution. They were only seeking and received the voluntary cooperation of petitioners' distributor. He was free to disregard their request for cooperation and if he did so he had nothing to fear except prosecution for violating G.L.

1956, chap. 11–31. And even such fear would be groundless if the books in question were not obscene.

It is no justification for petitioners to argue as they do that because the local distributor will not want to oppose the commission such a practice has the inevitable result of suppression of their books by censorship. Enforcement of the law against obscenity is not easy. It is hedged about by constitutional safeguards which in appropriate instances have been strictly applied. But the United States supreme court has repeatedly held that obscenity is not protected by the guaranties of the first amendment. *Near* v. *Minnesota ex rel. Olson*, 283 U.S. 697, 51 S. Ct. 625, 75 L. Ed. 1357; *Chaplinsky* v. *New Hampshire*, 315 U.S. 568, 62 S. Ct. 766, 86 L. Ed. 1031; *Roth* v. *United States*, 354 U.S. 476, 77 S. Ct. 1304, 1 L. Ed. 2d 1498. However, that court has also held that the local distributor or bookseller cannot be convicted of such an offense unless the state proves that he had knowledge of the obscene nature of the book. *Smith* v. *California*, 361 U.S. 147, 80 S. Ct. 215, 4 L. Ed. 2d 205.

Ordinarily a distributor or bookseller is not expected to know the character of all the books he distributes. It is only fair that he should be given some advance notice of which he may avail himself, if he chooses, before criminal proceedings are commenced against him. It is in that context we interpret the action of the commission here and the willing response thereto of the distributor. Of course the publisher would much prefer to have the distributor stand his ground and refuse to cooperate regardless of the consequences to him.

The status of the publisher, however, is vastly different from that of the distributor. He may not plead lack of notice. It is his business to know what he is publishing. If his publication on the bookseller's shelf is obscene, he is the real offender and it is his offense which resolution No. 73 seeks to discover and prosecute. But more often than not the publisher is beyond reach of the local law and in effect hides behind the unoffending local distributor.

When, as in the case at bar, steps are taken to save the local distributor from embroilment in criminal proceedings the petitioning publishers come forward protesting that the commission is depriving them of their constitutional right of freedom of the press. Their success in a number of jurisdictions in invoking the injunctive remedy has apparently encouraged them to invoke it here in the hope of thwarting the implementation by the commission of resolution No. 73. They rely heavily on the above-cited cases where such successes have been achieved.

However, in the instant case we are of the opinion that they are not aggrieved by any deprivation of their constitutional right to distribute their books in this state. Resolution No. 73 does not by its terms nor by the commission's acts under it prevent them from doing so. Unless their books are obscene they have nothing to fear. But if they are deemed to be obscene by the prosecuting authority of the state they cannot use the injunctive remedy of equity to prevent the state from bringing them to the bar of justice by appropriate criminal proceedings. In such proceedings they will have a full, fair and impartial judicial determination of the issue of obscenity.

[3] Obscenity is entitled to no special protection under either the state or federal constitution. In *Chaplinsky* v. *New Hampshire*, 315 U.S. 568, 62 S. Ct. 766, 86 L. Ed. 1031, the supreme court of the United States unanimously declared that lewd and obscene speech raises no constitutional question. At page 572, 62 S. Ct. at page 769 it said, "such utterances are no essential part of any exposition of ideas, and are of such slight social value as a step to truth that any benefit that may be derived from them is clearly outweighed by the social interest in order and morality."

It is the social interest in order and morality that the legislature by enacting resolution No. 73 is seeking to subserve. And the acts of the commission thereunder were in our opinion a reasonable and lawful implementation of the resolution. To tie their hands by the injunction under consideration here would be to render them impotent to discharge the duties that the general assembly has specifically charged them to perform. We are therefore of the opinion that the trial justice erred in decreeing that their actions were unconstitutional and in enjoining them from so acting henceforth.

Before concluding this opinion we should comment on *Sunshine Book Co.* v. *McCaffrey*, 4 A.D. 2d 643, 168 N.Y.S. 2d 268, upon which petitioners have also relied. Although that case is not by a court of last resort it does come from a court of appeal having a very large measure of revisory jurisdiction and for such reason its decisions stand on a higher plane of authority than those hereinbefore commented upon. However, we do not think the cited case helps the petitioners since it appears to be based on a factual situation not at all like the one here.

In that case a license commissioner threatened a licensed news dealer with revocation of his license if he did not remove certain copies of a magazine from his newsstand. In the instant case no license is involved and the commission neither had any regulatory authority over the distributor nor attempted to exercise any such authority. And in the cited case the license commissioner was not acting pursuant to the provisions of a legislative act imposing upon him specifically the duty of investigating obscene literature and recommending prosecution of violators of the statute law against obscenity. In any event even though the case may impliedly stand for more than it expressly decides we are not persuaded to accept it as authority in the special circumstances here.

The petitioners' appeal is denied and dismissed, the respondents' appeal is sustained in part, the decree appealed from is reversed as to order Nos. 2 and 3, otherwise it is affirmed, and the cause is remanded to the superior court for further proceedings.

FROST, J., not participating.

ROBERTS, Justice (dissenting).

I concur in the opinion of the majority that resolution No. 73, as amended, is not in its terms repugnant to the guaranties of the first amendment. The legislature has therein provided for an appropriation for the support of a program of public education concerning the deleterious influence of the publication of obscene, lewd, or indecent periodicals on the morals and welfare of youth and for appointment by the Governor of the members of a commission charged with the duty of conducting that program. I perceive no provision therein which would warrant concluding that the legislature contemplated that the commission was being authorized to act to engage in conduct other than that incidental to the program.

I am not fully persuaded that legislation providing for

the dissemination of information relating to a matter of substantial public concern constitutes state action within the purview of the inhibitions of the pertinent constitutional provisions. The commission, as it is therein established, is without authority either to regulate the business that is the subject of the legislation or to accomplish any control over that business through the imposition of sanctions. An exercise of the duties imposed upon the commission therein does not impinge upon any right protected by the first amendment.

However, I am unable to concur in the conclusion of the majority concerning the propriety of the injunctive relief decreed by the trial justice. The respondents here, whatever might be their rights as individuals, may act legally in their capacities as members of the commission only within the authority conferred upon the commission by the resolution. It appears from the record that the commission, or certain of its officers acting in its behalf, has engaged in conduct that is clearly in excess of the authority conferred upon it by the resolution. Such action, to the extent that it exceeds the authority conferred, is illegal and may, upon a showing of the requisite equitable grounds, be enjoined.

The action upon which this finding of illegality is predicated relates to the circulation of notices to dealers in books and publications wherein the commission identifies certain books that it deems to be objectionable for sale or distribution for use by youths under the age of eighteen. The circulation of these notices, standing alone, was in my opinion action pursuant to the dissemination of information contemplated in the resolution. There is, however, further evidence tending to establish that the circulation of this information was implemented at the commission's instigation by a police surveillance of the stocks in the possession of these dealers which caused certain of them to withdraw the books so identified from sale generally. Of this the trial justice said: "The sending of these notices with their implicit threats of criminal prosecution are clear violations of the constitutional provisions guaranteeing freedom of the press." I am not persuaded, however, that it is necessary to pass upon the constitutional issue, it being my opinion that the action to which the trial justice refers was beyond the power conferred upon the commission and, therefore, illegal.

There is in the record evidence which is concerned with the authority that the commission through its officers purported to exercise that buttresses the conclusion which I here reach. In what appears to be a circular letter dated July 19, 1957 over the signature of the executive secretary of the commission, dealers in books and publications were told: "This agency was established * * * with the immediate charge to *prevent* the sale, distribution or display of indecent and obscene publications to youths under eighteen years of age." (Italics mine.) In another undated circular letter over the signature of the executive secretary of the commission, the assertion was made that certain amendatory legislation operated to "broaden the powers of this Commission, giving us broad investigative powers * * *." It is my opinion that the two examples above set out suffice to reveal that the commission or its officers substantially misconceived the purpose for which resolution No. 73 was enacted as well as the extent of the authority conferred upon the commission by the terms of that legislation.

After a thorough examination of the resolution I cannot find therein any language which either in express terms or by reasonable inference confers upon the commission or its officers authority to *prevent* the sale or distribution of any publication. The statement contained in the circular letter of July 19, 1957 constitutes an entirely unwarranted assumption that the commission was vested with power to *prevent* the sale of such publications. Neither do I find in the resolution any provision from which it may be reasonably assumed that the commission or its officers were invested with investigative powers. The language of the resolution providing that the commission make recommendations to prosecute violations of criminal statutes concerned with obscenity confers no inquisitorial power or, for that matter, any power to institute a criminal proceeding. It is my opinion that to so construe the provision referred to would be to clearly violate our well-settled rules of statutory construction.

It is my opinion then that the commission, or its officers acting in its behalf, in purporting to act pursuant to the authority conferred by resolution No. 73 has engaged in conduct that exceeded the authority in fact conferred and to that extent its action was illegal. For this reason I am constrained to dissent from the conclusion of the majority that the trial justice erred in granting the injunctive relief.

■ Bantam Books, Inc., *et al.*, *Appellants*,

v.

Joseph A. Sullivan *et al.*

No. 118.

Argued Dec. 3 and 4, 1962.

Decided Feb. 18, 1963.

Horace S. Manges, New York City, for appellants.
J. Joseph Nugent, Providence, R.I., for appellees.

MR. JUSTICE BRENNAN delivered the opinion of the Court.

[1] The Rhode Island Legislature created the "Rhode Island Commission to Encourage Morality in Youth," whose members and Executive Secretary are the appellees herein, and gave the Commission *inter alia* "* * * the duty * * * to educate the public concerning any book, picture, pamphlet, ballad, printed paper or other thing containing obscene, indecent or impure language, or manifestly tending to the corruption of the youth as defined in sections 13, 47, 48 and 49 of chapter 610 of the general laws, as amended, and to investigate and recommend the prosecution of all violations of said sections * * *."[1] The

appellants brought this action in the Superior Court of Rhode Island (1) to declare the law creating the Commission in violation of the First and Fourteenth Amendments, and (2) to declare unconstitutional and enjoin the acts and practices of the appellees thereunder. The Superior Court declined to declare the law creating the Commission unconstitutional on its face but granted the appellants an injunction against the acts and practices of the appellees in performance of their duties. The Supreme Court of Rhode Island affirmed the Superior Court with respect to appellants' first prayer but reversed the grant of injunctive relief. R.I., 176 A. 2d 393 (1961).[2] Appellants brought this appeal and we noted probable jurisdiction, 370 U.S. 933, 82 S. Ct. 1587, 8 L. Ed. 2d 805.[3]

Appellants are four New York publishers of paperback books which have for sometime been widely distributed in Rhode Island. Max Silverstein & Sons is the exclusive wholesale distributor of appellants' publications throughout most of the State. The Commission's practice has been to notify a distributor on official Commission stationery that certain designated books or magazines distributed by him had been reviewed by the Commission and had been declared by a majority of its members to be objectionable for sale, distribution or display to youths under 18 years of age. Silverstein had received at least 35 such notices at the

---

[1] Resolution No. 73 H 1000, R.I. Acts and Resolves, January Session 1956, 1102–1103. The resolution created a "commission to encourage morality in youth," to be composed of nine members appointed by the Governor of the State. The members were to serve for staggered, five-year terms. They were to receive no compensation, but their expenses, as well as the expenses incurred in the operation of the Commission generally, were to be defrayed out of annual appropriations. The original mandate of the Commission was superseded in part by Resolution No. 95 S. 444 R.I. Acts and Resolves, January Session 1959, 880, which reads as follows:

"It shall be the duty of said commission to educate the public concerning any book, picture, pamphlet, ballad, printed paper or other thing containing obscene, indecent or impure language, as defined in chapter 11–31 of the general laws, entitled 'Obscene and objectionable publications and shows,' and to investigate and recommend the prosecution of all violations of said sections, and it shall be the further duty of said commission to combat juvenile delinquency and encourage morality in youth by (a) investigating situations which may cause, be responsible for or give rise to undesirable behavior of juveniles, (b) educate the public as to these causes and (c) recommend legislation, prosecution and/or treatment which would ameliorate or eliminate said causes."

The Commission's activities are not limited to the circulation of lists of objectionable publications. For example, the annual report of the Commission issued in January 1960, recites in part:

"In September, 1959, because of the many complaints from outraged parents at the type of films being shown at the Rhode Island Drive-Ins and also the lack of teen-age supervision while parked, this Commission initiated and completed a survey on the

Drive-In Theatres in the State. High points of the survey note that there are II (2) Drive-in theatres in Rhode Island which operate through summer months and remain open until November and then for week-ends during the winter, providing car-heaters."

*   *   *   *   *

"Acting on its power to investigate causes of delinquency, the Commission has met with several state officials for a discussion of juvenile drinking, the myriad and complex causes of delinquency, and legal aspects of the Commission's operations. It also held a special meeting with Rhode Island police and legal officials in September, 1959, for a discussion on the extent of delinquency in Rhode Island and the possible formation of state-wide organization to combat it."

[2] The action was brought pursuant to Title 9, c. 30, Gen. Laws R.I., 1956 ed., as amended (Uniform Declaratory Judgments Act).

[3] Our appellate jurisdiction is properly invoked, since the state court judgment sought to be reviewed upheld a state statute against the contention that, on its face and as applied, the statute violated the Federal Constitution. 28 U.S.C. § 1257(2). *Dahnke-Walker Milling Co.* v. *Bondurant*, 257 U.S. 282, 42 S. Ct. 106, 66 L. Ed. 239.

time this suit was brought. Among the paperback books listed by the Commission as "objectionable" were one published by appellant Dell Publishing Co., Inc., and another published by appellant Bantam Books, Inc.[4]

The typical notice to Silverstein either solicited or thanked Silverstein, in advance, for his "cooperation" with the Commission, usually reminding Silverstein of the Commission's duty to recommend to the Attorney General prosecution of purveyors of obscenity.[5] Copies of the lists of "objectionable" publications were circulated to local police departments, and Silverstein was so informed in the notices.

Silverstein's reaction on receipt of a notice was to take steps to stop further circulation of copies of the listed publications. He would not fill pending orders for such publications and would refuse new orders. He instructed his field men to visit his retailers and to pick up all unsold copies, and would then promptly return them to the publishers. A local police officer usually visited Silverstein shortly after Silverstein's receipt of a notice to learn what action he had taken. Silverstein was usually able to inform the officer that a specified number of the total of copies

---

[4] Peyton Place, by Grace Metalious, published (in paperback edition) by appellant Dell Publishing Co., Inc.; The Bramble Bush, by Charles Mergendahl, published (in paperback edition) by appellant Bantam Books, Inc. Most of the other 106 publications which, as of January 1960, had been listed as objectionable by the Commission were issues of such magazines as "Playboy," "Rogue," "Frolic," and so forth. The Attorney General of Rhode Island described some of the 106 publications as "horror" comics which he said were not obscene as this Court has defined the term.

[5] The first notice received by Silverstein reads, in part, as follows:

"This agency was established by legislative order in 1956 with the immediate charge to prevent the sale, distribution or display of indecent and obscene publications to youths and [sic] eighteen years of age.

"The Commissions [sic] have reviewed the following publications and by majority vote have declared they are completely objectionable for sale, distribution or display for youths under eighteen years of age.

＊　　＊　　＊　　＊　　＊

"The Chiefs of Police have been given the names of the aforementioned magazines with the order that they are not to be sold, distributed or displayed to youths and [sic] eighteen years of age.

"The Attorney General will act for us in case of non-compliance.

"The Commissioners trust that you will cooperate with this agency in their work. ＊ ＊ ＊

"Another list will follow shortly.

"Thanking you for your anticipated cooperation, I am,

"Sincerely yours

"Albert J. McAloon
"Executive Secretary"

Another notice received by Silverstein reads in part:

"This list should be used as a guide in judging other similar publications not named.

"Your cooperation in removing the listed and other objectionable publications from your newsstands [sic] will be appreciated. Cooperative action will eliminate the necessity of our recommending prosecution to the Attorney General's department."

An undated "News Letter" sent to Silverstein by the Commission reads in part: "The lists [of objectionable publications] have been sent to distributors and police departments. To the present cooperation has been gratifying."

---

received from a publisher had been returned. According to the testimony, Silverstein acted as he did on receipt of the notice "rather than face the possibility of some sort of a court action against ourselves, as well as the people that we supply." His "cooperation" was given to avoid becoming involved in a "court proceeding" with a "duly authorized organization."

The Superior Court made fact findings and the following two, supported by the evidence and not rejected by the Supreme Court of Rhode Island, are particularly relevant:

"8. The effect of the said notices [those received by Silverstein, including the two listing publications of appellants] were [sic] clearly to intimidate the various book and magazine wholesale distributors and retailers and to cause them, by reason of such intimidation and threat of prosecution, (a) to refuse to take new orders for the proscribed publications, (b) to cease selling any of the copies on hand, (c) to withdraw from retailers all unsold copies, and (d) to return all unsold copies to the publishers.

"9. The activities of the Respondents [appellees here] have resulted in the suppression of the sale and circulation of the books listed in said notices ＊ ＊ ＊."

In addition to these findings it should be noted that the Attorney General of Rhode Island conceded on oral argument in this Court that the books listed in the notices included several that were not obscene within this Court's definition of the term.

[2-4] Appellants argue that the Commission's activities under Resolution 73, as amended, amount to a scheme of governmental censorship devoid of the constitutionally required safeguards for state regulation of obscenity, and thus abridge First Amendment liberties, protected by the Fourteenth Amendment from infringement by the States. We agree that the activities of the Commission are unconstitutional and therefore reverse the Rhode Island court's judgment and remand the case for further proceedings not inconsistent with this opinion.[6]

---

[6] Appellants' standing has not been, nor could it be, successfully questioned. The appellants have in fact suffered a palpable injury as a result of the acts alleged to violate federal law, and at the same time their injury has been a legal injury. See *Joint Anti-Fascist Refugee Committee* v. *McGrath*, 341 U.S. 123, 151–152, 71 S. Ct. 624, 637–638, 95 L. Ed. 817 (concurring opinion). The finding that the Commission's notices impaired sales of the listed publications, which include two books published by appellants, establishes that appellants suffered injury. It was a legal injury, although more needs be said to demonstrate this. The Commission's notices were circulated only to distributors and not, so far as appears, to publishers. The Commission purports only to regulate distribution; it has made no claim to having jurisdiction of out-of-state publishers. However, if this were a private action, it would present a claim, plainly justiciable, of unlawful interference in advantageous business relations. *American Mercury, Inc.* v. *Chase*, 13 F. 2d 224 (D.C.D. Mass. 1926). Cf. 1 Harper and James, Torts (1956), §§ 6.11–6.12. See also *Pocket Books, Inc.* v. *Walsh*, 204 F. Supp. 297 (D.C.D. Conn. 1962). It makes no difference, so far as appellants' standing is concerned, that the allegedly unlawful interference here is the product of state action. See *Pierce* v. *Society of Sisters*, 268 U.S. 510, 45 S. Ct. 571, 69 L. Ed. 1070; *Truax* v. *Raich*, 239 U.S. 33, 36 S. Ct. 7, 60 L. Ed. 131; *Terrace* v. *Thompson*, 263 U.S. 197, 214–216, 44 S. Ct. 15, 17–18, 68 L. Ed. 255; *Columbia Broadcasting System* v. *United States*, 316 U.S. 407, 422–423, 62 S. Ct. 1194, 1202–1203, 86 L. Ed. 1563. Furthermore, appellants are not in the position of mere proxies arguing another's consti-

[5–7] We held in *Alberts* v. *State of California*, decided with *Roth* v. *United States*, 354 U.S. 476, 485, 77 S. Ct. 1304, 1309, 1 L. Ed. 2d 1498, that "obscenity is not within the area of constitutionally protected speech or press" and may therefore be regulated by the States. But this principle cannot be stated without an important qualification:

* * * [I]n Roth itself we expressly recognized the complexity of the test of obscenity fashioned in that case and the vital necessity in its application of safeguards to prevent denial of 'the protection of freedom of speech and press for material which does not treat sex in a manner appealing to prurient interest.' [354 U.S. at 488, 77 S. Ct. at 1311] * * * It follows that, under the Fourteenth Amendment, a State is not free to adopt whatever procedures it pleases for dealing with obscenity * * * without regard to the possible consequences for constitutionally protected speech." *Marcus* v. *Search Warrant*, 367 U.S. 717, 730–731, 81 S. Ct. 1708, 1715, 1716, 6 L. Ed. 2d 1127.

Thus, the Fourteenth Amendment requires that regulation by the States of obscenity conform to procedures that will ensure against the curtailment of constitutionally protected expression, which is often separated from obscenity only by a dim and uncertain line. It is characteristic of the freedoms of expression in general that they are vulnerable to gravely damaging yet barely visible encroachments. Our insistence that regulations of obscenity scrupulously embody the most rigorous procedural safeguards, *Smith* v. *People of the State of California*, 361 U.S. 147, 80 S. Ct. 215, 4 L. Ed. 2d 205; *Marcus* v. *Search Warrant*, supra, is therefore but a special instance of the larger principle that the freedoms of expression must be ringed about with adequate bulwarks. See, e.g., *Thornhill* v. *State of Alabama*, 310, U.S. 88, 60 S. Ct. 736, 84 L. Ed. 1093; *Winters* v. *People of the State of New York*, 333 U.S. 507, 68 S. Ct. 665, 92 L. Ed. 840; *N.A.A.C.P.* v. *Button*, 371 U.S. 415, 83 S. Ct. 328. "[T]he line between speech unconditionally guaranteed and speech which may legitimately be regulated * * * is finely drawn. * * * The separation of legitimate from illegitimate speech calls for * * * sensitive tools * * *." *Speiser* v. *Randall*, 357 U.S. 513, 525, 78 S. Ct. 1332, 1342, 2 L. Ed. 2d 1460.

[8, 9] But is it contended, these salutary principles have no application to the activities of the Rhode Island Commission because it does not regulate or suppress obscenity but simply exhorts booksellers and advises them of their legal rights. This contention, premised on the Com-

mission's want of power to apply formal legal sanctions, is untenable. It is true that appellants' books have not been seized or banned by the State, and that no one has been prosecuted for their possession or sale. But though the Commission is limited to informal sanctions—the threat of invoking legal sanctions and other means of coercion, persuasion, and intimidation—the record amply demonstrates that the Commission deliberately set about to achieve the suppression of publications deemed "objectionable" and succeeded in its aim.[7] We are not the first court to look through forms to the substance and recognize that informal censorship may sufficiently inhibit the circulation of publications to warrant injunctive relief.[8]

[10–13] It is not as if this were not regulation by the State of Rhode Island. The acts and practices of the members and Executive Secretary of the Commission disclosed on this record were performed under color of state law and so constituted acts of the State within the meaning of the Fourteenth Amendment. Ex parte Young, 209 U.S. 123, 28 S. Ct. 441, 52 L. Ed. 714. Cf. *Terry* v. *Adams*, 345 U.S. 461, 73 S. Ct. 809, 97 L. Ed. 1152. These acts and practices directly and designedly stopped the circulation of publications in many parts of Rhode Island. It is true, as noted by the Supreme Court of Rhode Island, that Silverstein was "free" to ignore the Commission's notices, in the sense that his refusal to "cooperate" would have violated no law. But it was found as a fact—and the finding, being amply supported by the record,

---

[7] For discussions of the problem of "informal censorship," see Lockhart and McClure, Censorship of Obscenity: The Developing Constitutional Standards, 45 Minn. L. Rev. 5, 6–9 and n. 7–22 (1960); Note, Extralegal Censorship of Literature, 33 N.Y.U.L. Rev. 989 (1958); Note, Entertainment: Public Pressures and the Law, 71 Harv. L. Rev. 326, 344–347 (1957); Note, Regulation of Comic Books, 68 Harv. L. Rev. 489, 494–499 (1955); Comment, Censorship of Obscene Literature by Informal Governmental Action, 22 Univ. of Chi. L. Rev. 216 (1954); Lockhart and McClure, Literature, the Law of Obscenity, and the Constitution, 38 Minn. L. Rev. 295, 309–316 (1954).

[8] Threats of prosecution or of license revocation, or listings or notifications of supposedly obscene or objectionable publications or motion pictures, on the part of chiefs of police or prosecutors, have been enjoined in a number of cases. See *Kingsley International Pictures Corp.* v. *Blanc*, 396 Pa. 448, 153 A. 2d 243 (1959); *Bunis* v. *Conway*, 17 A.D. 2d 207, 234 N.Y.S. 2d 435 (1962) (dictum); *Sunshine Book Co.* v. *McCaffrey*, 4 A.D. 2d 643, 168 N.Y.S. 2d 268 (1957); *Random House, Inc.* v. *Detroit*, No. 555684 Chancery, Cir. Ct., Wayne County, Mich., March 29, 1957; *HMH Publishing Co.* v. *Garrett*, 151 F. Supp. 903 (D.C.N.D. Ind. 1957); *New American Library of World Literature* v. *Allen*, 114 F. Supp. 823 (D.C.N.D. Ohio 1953); *Bantam Books, Inc.* v. *Melko*, 25 N.J. Super. 292, 96 A. 2d 47 (Chancey 1953), modified on other grounds, 14 N.J. 524, 103 A. 2d 256 (1954); *Dearborn Publishing Co.* v. *Fitzgerald*, 271 F. 479 (D.C.N.D. Ohio 1921); *Epoch Producing Corp.* v. *Davis*, 19 Ohio N.P., N.S., 465 (C.P. 1917). Cf. In re *Louisiana News Co.* v. *Dayries*, 187 F. Supp. 241 (D.C.E.D. La. 1960); *Roper* v. *Winner*, 244 S.W. 2d 355, 357 (Tex. Civ. App. 1951); *American Mercury, Inc.* v. *Chase*, 13 F. 2d 224 (D.C.D. Mass. 1926). Relief has been denied in the following cases: *Pocket Books, Inc.* v. *Walsh*, 204 F. Supp. 297 (D.C.D. Conn. 1962); *Dell Publishing Co.* v. *Beggans*, 110 N.J. Eq. 72, 158 A. 765 (Chancery 1932). See also *Magtab Publishing Corp.* v. *Howard*, 169 F. Supp. 65 (D.C.W.D. La. 1959). None of the foregoing cases presents the precise factual situation at bar, and we intimate no view one way or the other as to their correctness.

---

tutional rights. The constitutional guarantee of freedom of the press embraces the circulation of books as well as their publication, *Lovell* v. *City of Griffin*, 303 U.S. 444, 452, 58 S. Ct. 666, 669, 82 L. Ed. 949, and the direct and obviously intended result of the Commission's activities was to curtail the circulation in Rhode Island of books published by appellants. Finally, pragmatic considerations argue strongly for the standing of publishers in cases such as the present one. The distributor who is prevented from selling a few titles is not likely to sustain sufficient economic injury to induce him to seek judicial vindication of his rights. The publisher has the greater economic stake, because suppression of a particular book prevents him from recouping his investment in publishing it. Unless he is permitted to sue, infringements of freedom of the press may too often go unremedied. Cf. *N.A.A.C.P.* v. *State of Alabama* ex rel. *Patterson*, 357 U.S. 449, 459, 78 S. Ct. 1163, 1170, 2 L. Ed. 2d 1488.

binds us—that Silverstein's compliance with the Commission's directives was not voluntary. People do not lightly disregard public officers' thinly veiled threats to institute criminal proceedings against them if they do not come around, and Silverstein's reaction, according to uncontroverted testimony, was no exception to this general rule. The Commission's notices, phrased virtually as orders, reasonably understood to be such by the distributor, invariably followed up by police visitations, in fact stopped the circulation of the listed publications *ex proprio vigore*. It would be naive to credit the State's assertion that these blacklists are in the nature of mere legal advice, when they plainly serve as instruments of regulation independent of the laws against obscenity.[9] Cf. *Joint Anti-Fascist Refugee Committee* v. *McGrath,* 341 U.S. 123, 71 S. Ct. 624, 95 L. Ed. 817.

Herein lies the vice of the system. The Commission's operation is a form of effective state regulation superimposed upon the State's criminal regulation of obscenity and making such regulation largely unnecessary. In thus obviating the need to employ criminal sanctions, the State has at the same time eliminated the safeguards of the criminal process. Criminal sanctions may be applied only after a determination of obscenity has been made in a criminal trial hedged about with the procedural safeguards of the criminal process. The Commission's practice is in striking contrast, in that it provides no safeguards whatever against the suppression of nonobscene, and therefore constitutionally protected, matter. It is a form of regulation that creates hazards to protected freedoms markedly greater than those that attend reliance upon the criminal law.

---

[9] We note that the Commission itself appears to have understood its function as the proscribing of objectionable publications, and not merely the giving of legal advice to distributors. See the first notice received by Silverstein, quoted in note 5, supra. The minutes of one of the Commission's meetings read in part:

"* * * Father Flannery [a member of the Commission] noted that he had been called about magazines proscribed by the Commission remaining on sale after lists had been *scent [sic]* to distributors and police, to which Mr. McAloon suggested that it could be that the same magazines were seen, but that it probably was not the same edition proscribed by the Commission.

"Father Flannery questioned the statewide compliance by the police, or anyone else, to get the proscribed magazines off the stands. Mr. McAloon showed the Commissioners the questionnaires sent to the chiefs of police from this office and returned to us."

The minutes of another meeting read in part:

"* * * Mr. Sullivan [member of the Commission] suggested calling the Cranston Chief of Police to inquire the reason Peyton Place was still being sold, distributed and displayed since the Police departments had been advised of the Commission's vote."

Of course, it is immaterial whether in carrying on the function of censor, the Commission may have been exceeding its statutory authority. Its acts would still constitute state action. Ex parte Young, 209 U.S. 123, 28 S. Ct. 441, 52 L. Ed. 714. The issue of statutory authority was not raised or argued in this litigation.

Our holding that the scheme of informal censorship here constitutes state action is in no way inconsistent with *Standard Computing Scale Co.* v. *Farrell,* 249 U.S. 571, 39 S. Ct. 380, 63 L. Ed. 780. In that case it was held that a bulletin of specifications issued by the State Superintendent of Weights and Measures could not be deemed state action for Fourteenth Amendment purposes because the bulletin was purely advisory; the decision turned on the fact that the bulletin was not coercive in purport.

[14] What Rhode Island has done, in fact, has been to subject the distribution of publications to a system of prior administrative restraints, since the Commission is not a judicial body and its decisions to list particular publications as objectionable do not follow judicial determinations that such publications may lawfully be banned. Any system of prior restraints of expression comes to this Court bearing a heavy presumption against its constitutional validity. See *Near* v. *State of Minnesota* ex rel. *Olson,* 283 U.S. 697, 51 S. Ct. 625, 75 L. Ed. 1357; *Lovell* v. *City of Griffin,* 303 U.S. 444, 451, 58 S. Ct. 666, 668, 82 L. Ed. 949; *Schneider* v. *State of New Jersey,* 308 U.S. 147, 164, 60 S. Ct. 146, 152, 84 L. Ed. 155; *Cantwell* v. *State of Connecticut,* 310 U.S. 296, 306, 60 S. Ct. 900, 904, 84 L. Ed. 1213; *Niemotko* v. *State of Maryland,* 340 U.S. 268, 273, 71 S. Ct. 325, 328, 95 L. Ed. 267; *Kunz* v. *People of State of New York,* 340 U.S. 290, 293, 71 S. Ct. 312, 314, 95 L. Ed. 280; *Staub* v. *City of Baxley,* 355 U.S. 313, 321, 78 S. Ct. 277, 281, 2 L. Ed. 2d 302. *We have tolerated such a system only where it operated under judicial superintendence and assured an almost immediate judicial determination of the validity of the restraint.*[10] [Italics ed.]. *Kingsley Books, Inc.* v. *Brown,* 354 U.S. 436, 77 S. Ct. 1325, 1 L. Ed. 2d 1469. The system at bar includes no such saving features. On the contrary, its capacity for suppression of constitutionally protected publications is far in excess of that of the typical licensing scheme held constitutionally invalid by this Court. There is no provision whatever for judicial superintendence before notices issue or even for judicial review of the Commission's determinations of objectionableness. The publisher or distributor is not even entitled to notice and hearing before his publications are listed by the Commission as objectionable. Moreover, the Commission's statutory mandate is vague and uninformative, and the Commission has done nothing to make it more precise. Publications are listed as "objectionable" without further elucidation. The distributor is left to speculate whether the Commission considers his publication obscene or simply harmful to juvenile morality. For the Commission's domain is the whole of youthful morals. Finally, we note that although the Commission's supposed concern is limited to youthful readers, the "cooperation" it seeks from distributors invariably entails the complete suppression of the listed publications; adult readers are equally deprived of the opportunity to purchase the publications in the State. Cf. *Butler* v. *State of Michigan,* 352 U.S. 380, 77 S. Ct. 524, 1 L. Ed. 2d 412.

[15] The procedures of the Commission are radically deficient. They fall far short of the constitutional requirements of governmental regulation of obscenity. We hold that the system of informal censorship disclosed by this record violates the Fourteenth Amendment.

In holding that the activities disclosed on this record are constitutionally proscribed, we do not mean to suggest that private consultation between law enforcement officers and

---

[10] Nothing in the Court's opinion in *Times Film Corp.* v. *City of Chicago,* 365 U.S. 43, 81 S. Ct. 391, 5 L. Ed. 2d 403, is inconsistent with the Court's traditional attitude of disfavor toward prior restraints of expression. The only question tendered to the Court in that case was whether a prior restraint was necessarily unconstitutional *under all circumstances.* In declining to hold prior restraints unconstitutional *per se,* the Court did not uphold the constitutionality of any specific such restraint. Furthermore, the holding was expressly confined to motion pictures.

distributors prior to the institution of a judicial proceeding can never be constitutionally permissible. We do not hold that law enforcement officers must renounce all informal contacts with persons suspected of violating valid laws prohibiting obscenity. Where such consultation is genuinely undertaken with the purpose of aiding the distributor to comply with such laws and avoid prosecution under them, it need not retard the full enjoyment of First Amendment freedoms. But that is not this case. The appellees are not law enforcement officers; they do not pretend that they are qualified to give or that they attempt to give distributors only fair legal advice. Their conduct as disclosed by this record shows plainly that they went far beyond advising the distributors of their legal rights and liabilities. Their operation was in fact a scheme of state censorship effectuated by extralegal sanctions; they acted as an agency not to advise but to suppress.

Reversed and remanded.

Mr. Justice BLACK concurs in the result.

Mr. Justice DOUGLAS, concurring.

While I join the opinion of the Court, I adhere to the views I expressed in *Roth v. United States,* 354 U.S. 476, 508–514, 77 S. Ct. 1304, 1321–1324, 1 L. Ed. 2d 1498, respecting the very narrow scope of governmental authority to suppress publications on the grounds of obscenity. Yet as my Brother BRENNAN makes clear, the vice of Rhode Island's system is apparent whatever one's view of the constitutional status of "obscene" literature. This is censorship in the raw; and in my view the censor and First Amendment rights are incompatible. If a valid law has been violated, authors and publishers and vendors can be made to account. But they would then have on their side all the procedural safeguards of the Bill of Rights, including trial by jury. From the viewpoint of the State that is a more cumbersome procedure, action on the majority vote of the censors being far easier. But the Bill of Rights was designed to fence in the Government and make its intrusions on liberty difficult and its interference with freedom of expression well-nigh impossible.

All nations have tried censorship and only a few have rejected it. Its abuses mount high. Today Iran censors news stories in such a way as to make false or misleading some reports of reputable news agencies. For the Iranian who writes the stories and lives in Teheran goes to jail if he tells the truth. Thus censorship in Teheran has as powerful extralegal sanctions as censorship in Providence.

The Providence regime is productive of capricious action. A five-to-four vote makes a book "obscene." The wrong is compounded when the issue, though closely balanced in the minds of sophisticated men, is resolved against freedom of expression and on the side of censorship. Judges, to be sure, often disagree as to the definition of obscenity. But an established administrative system that bans book after book, even though they muster four votes out of nine, makes freedom of expression much more precarious than it would be if unanimity were required. This underlines my Brother BRENNAN's observation that the Providence regime "provides no safeguards whatever against the suppression of nonobscene, and therefore constitutionally protected, matter." Doubts are resolved against, rather than for, freedom of expression.

The evils of unreviewable administrative action of this character are as ancient as dictators. George Kennan, *Siberia and the Exile System* (U. of Chi. 1958) p. 60, gives insight into it:

"Mr. Boródin, another Russian author and a well-known contributor to the Russian magazine Annals of the Fatherland, was banished to the territory of Yakútsk on account of the alleged 'dangerous' and 'pernicious' character of a certain manuscript found in his house by the police during a search. This manuscript was a spare copy of an article upon the economic condition of the province of Viátka, which Mr. Boródin had written and sent to the above-named magazine, but which, up to that time, had not been published. The author went to Eastern Siberia in a convict's gray overcoat with a yellow ace of diamonds on his back, and three or four months after his arrival in Yakútsk he had the pleasure of reading in the Annals of the Fatherland the very same article for which he had been exiled. The Minister of the Interior had sent him to Siberia merely for having in his possession what the police called a 'dangerous' and 'pernicious' manuscript, and then the St. Petersburg committee of censorship had certified that another copy of that same manuscript was perfectly harmless, and had allowed it to be published, without the change of a line, in one of the most popular and widely circulated magazines in the empire."

Thus under the Czars an all-powerful elite condemned to the Siberia of that day an author whom a minority applauded. Administrative fiat is as dangerous today as it was then.

Mr. Justice CLARK, concurring in the result.

As I read the opinion of the Court, it does much fine talking about freedom of expression and much condemning of the Commission's overzealous efforts to implement the State's obscenity laws for the protection of Rhode Island's youth but, as if shearing a hog, comes up with little wool. In short, it creates the proverbial tempest in a teapot over a number of notices sent out by the Commission asking the cooperation of magazine distributors in preventing the sale of obscene literature to juveniles. The storm was brewed from certain inept phrases in the notices wherein the Commission assumed the prerogative of issuing an "order" to the police that certain publications which it deemed obscene are "not to be sold, distributed or displayed to youths under eighteen years of age" and stated that "[t]he Attorney General will act for us in case of noncompliance." But after all this expostulation the Court, being unable to strike down Rhode Island's statute, see *Alberts v. State of California,* 354 U.S. 476, 77 S. Ct. 1304, 1 L. Ed. 2d 1498 (1957), drops a demolition bomb on "the Commission's practice" without clearly indicating what might be salvaged from the wreckage. The Court in condemning the Commission's practice owes Rhode Island the duty of articulating the standards which must be met, lest the Rhode Island Supreme Court be left at sea as to the appropriate disposition on remand.

In my view the Court should simply direct the Commission to abandon its delusions of grandeur and leave the issuance of "orders" to enforcement officials and "the State's criminal regulation of obscenity" to the prosecutors, who can substitute prosecution for "thinly veiled threats" in appropriate cases. See *Alberts* v. *State of California*, supra. As I read the opinion this is the extent of the limitations contemplated by the Court, leaving the Commission free, as my Brother HARLAN indicates, to publicize its findings as to the obscene character of any publication; to solicit the support of the public in preventing obscene publications from reaching juveniles; to furnish its findings to publishers, distributors and retailers of such publications and to law enforcement officials; and, finally, to seek the aid of such officials in prosecuting offenders of the State's obscenity laws. This Court has long recognized that "the primary requirements of decency may be enforced against obscene publications." *Near* v. *State of Minnesota* ex rel. *Olson*, 283 U.S. 697, 716, 51 S. Ct. 625, 631, 75 L. Ed. 1357 (1931); see *Kingsley Books, Inc.* v. *Brown*, 354 U.S. 436, 77 S. Ct. 1325, 1 L. Ed. 2d 1469 (1957). Certainly in the face of rising juvenile crime and lowering youth morality the State is empowered consistent with the Constitution to use the above procedures in attempting to dispel the defilement of its youth by obscene publications. With this understanding of the Court's holding I join in its judgment, believing that the limitations as outlined would have little bearing on the efficacy of Rhode Island's law.

Mr. Justice HARLAN, dissenting.

The Court's opinion fails to give due consideration to what I regard as the central issue in this case—the accommodation that must be made between Rhode Island's concern with the problem of juvenile delinquency and the right of freedom of expression assured by the Fourteenth Amendment.

Three reasons, as I understand the Court's opinion, are given for holding the particular procedures adopted by the Rhode Island Commission under this statute, though not the statute itself, unconstitutional: (1) the Commission's activities, carried on under color of state law, amount to a scheme of governmental censorship; (2) its procedures lack adequate safeguards to protect nonobscene material against suppression; and (3) the group's operations in the field of youth morality may entail depriving the adult public of access to constitutionally protected material.

In my opinion, none of these reasons is of overriding weight in the context of what is obviously not an effort by the State to obstruct free expression but an attempt to cope with a most baffling social problem.

I.

This Rhode Island Commission was formed for the laudable purpose of combatting juvenile delinquency. While there is as yet no consensus of scientific opinion on the causal relationship between youthful reading or viewing of "the obscene" and delinquent behavior, see Green, Obscenity, Censorship, and Juvenile Delinquency, 14 U. of Toronto L.J. 229 (1962), Rhode Island's approach to the problem is not without respectable support, see S. Rep. No. 2381, 84th Cong., 2d Sess. (1956); Kefauver, Obscene and Pornographic Literature and Juvenile Delinquency, 24 Fed. Prob. No. 4, p. 3 (Dec. 1960). The States should have a wide range of choice in dealing with such problems, *Alberts* v. *State of California*, decided with *Roth*

v. *United States*, 354 U.S. 476, 77 S. Ct. 1304, 1 L. Ed. 2d 1498 (separate opinion of the writer, at 500–502), and this Court should not interfere with state legislative judgments on them except upon the clearest showing of unconstitutionality.

I can find nothing in this record that justifies the view that Rhode Island has attempted to deal with this problem in an irresponsible way. I agree with the Court that the tenor of some of the Commission's letters and reports is subject to serious criticism, carrying as they do an air of authority which that body does not possess and conveying an impression of consequences which by no means may follow from noncooperation with the Commission. But these are things which could surely be cured by a word to the wise. They furnish no occasion for today's opaque pronouncements which leave the Commission in the dark as to the permissible constitutional scope of its future activities.

Given the validity of state obscenity laws, *Alberts* v. *State of California*, supra, I think the Commission is constitutionally entitled (1) to express its views on the character of any published reading or other material; (2) to endeavor to enlist the support of law enforcement authorities, or the cooperation of publishers and distributors, with respect to any material the Commission deems obscene; and (3) to notify publishers, distributors, and members of the public with respect to its activities in these regards; but that it must take care to refrain from the kind of overbearing utterances already referred to and others that might tend to give any person an erroneous impression as to either the extent of the Commission's authority or the consequences of a failure to heed its warnings. Since the decision of the Court does not require reinstatement of the broad injunction issued by the trial court,[1] and since the majority's opinion rests on the invalidity of the particular procedures the Commission has pursued, I find nothing in that opinion denying the Commission the right to conduct the activities, just enumerated, which I believe it is constitutionally entitled to carry on.

II.

It is said that the Rhode Island procedures lack adequate safeguards against the suppression of the nonobscene, in that the Commission may pronounce publications obscene without any prior judicial determination or review. But the Commission's pronouncement in any given instance is not self-executing. Any affected distributor or publisher wishing to stand his ground on a particular publication may test the Commission's views by way of a declaratory judgment action[2] or suit for injunctive relief or by simply refusing to accept the Commission's opinion and awaiting criminal prosecution in respect of the questioned work.

---

[1] The appellees were enjoined "from directly or indirectly notifying book and magazine wholesale distributors and retailers that the Commission has found objectionable any specific book or magazine for sale, distribution or display; said injunction * * * [to] apply whether such notification is given directly to said book and magazine wholesale distributors and retailers, or any of them, either orally or in writing, or through the publication of lists or bulletins, and irrespective of the manner of dissemination of such lists or bulletins."

[2] Rhode Island Gen. Laws (Supp. 1961), Tit. 9, c. 30 (Uniform Declaratory Judgments Act).

That the Constitution requires no more is shown by this Court's decision in *Times Film Corp. v. City of Chicago*, 365 U.S. 43, 81 S. Ct. 391, 5 L. Ed. 2d 403. There the petitioner refused to comply with a Chicago ordinance requiring that all motion pictures be examined and licensed by a city official prior to exhibition. It was contended that regardless of the obscenity *vel non* of any particular picture and the licensing standards employed, this requirement in itself amounted to an unconstitutional prior restraint on free expression. Stating that there is no "absolute freedom to exhibit, at least once, any and every kind of motion picture," 365 U.S., at 46, 81 S. Ct., at 393, this Court rejected that contention and remitted the petitioner to a challenge of an application of the city ordinance to specific films. The Court thus refused to countenance a "broadside attack" on a system of regulation designed to prevent the dissemination of obscene matter.

Certainly with respect to a sophisticated publisher or distributor,[3] and shorn of embellishing mandatory language, this Commission's advisory condemnation of particular publications does not create as great a danger of restraint on expression as that involved in Times Film, where exhibition of a film without a license was made a crime.[4] Nor can such danger be regarded as greater than that involved in the preadjudication impact of the sequestration procedures sustained by this Court in *Kingsley Books, Inc. v. Brown*, 354 U.S. 436, 77 S. Ct. 1325, 1 L. Ed. 2d 1469. For here the Commission's action is attended by no legal sanctions and leaves distribution of the questioned material entirely undisturbed.

This case bears no resemblance to what the Court refused to sanction in *Marcus v. Search Warrant of Property*, 367 U.S. 717, 81 S. Ct. 1708, 6 L. Ed. 2d 1127. There police officers, pursuant to Missouri procedures, seized in a one-day foray under search warrants some 11,000 copies of 280 publications found at the appellants' various places of business and believed by the officers to be obscene. The state court later found that only 100 out of the 280 publications actually were obscene. In holding "that Missouri's procedures as applied * * * lacked the safeguards which due process demands to assure non-obscene material the constitutional protection to which it is entitled," 367 U.S., at 731, 81 S. Ct., at 1716, the Court emphasized the historical connection between the search and seizure power and the stifling of liberty of expression. The Missouri warrants gave the broadest discretion to each executing officer and left to his *ad hoc* judgment on the spot, with little or no opportunity for discriminating deliberation, which publications should be seized as obscene. Since "there was no step in the procedure before seizure designed to focus searchingly on the question of obscenity," 367 U.S., at 732, 81 S. Ct., at 1716, it was to be expected that much of the material seized under these procedures would turn out not to be obscene, as indeed was later found by the state court in that very case.

No such hazards to free expression exist in the procedures I regard as permissible in the present case. Of cardinal importance, dissemination of a challenged publication is not physically or legally impeded in any way. Furthermore, the advisory condemnations complained of are the product not of hit-or-miss police action but of a deliberative body whose judgments are limited by standards embraced in the State's general obscenity statute, the constitutionality of which is not questioned in this case.

The validity of the foregoing considerations is not, in my opinion, affected by the state court findings that one of appellants' distributors was led to withdraw publications, thought obscene by the Commission, because of fear of criminal prosecution. For this record lacks an element without which those findings are not of controlling constitutional significance in the context of the competing state and individual interests here at stake: there is no showing that Rhode Island has put any roadblocks in the way of any distributor's or publisher's recourse to the courts to test the validity of the Commission's determination respecting any publication, or that the purpose of these procedures was to stifle freedom of expression.

It could not well be suggested, as I think the Court concedes, that a prosecutor's announcement that he intended to enforce strictly the obscenity laws or that he would proceed against a particular publication unless withdrawn from circulation amounted to an unconstitutional restraint upon freedom of expression, still less that such a restraint would occur from the mere existence of a criminal obscenity statute. Conceding that the restrictive effect of the Commission's procedures on publishers, and *a fortiori* on independent distributors, may be greater than in either of those situations, I do not believe that the differences are of constitutional import, in the absence of either of the two factors indicated in the preceding paragraph. The circumstance that places the Commission's permissible procedures on the same constitutional level as the illustrations just given is the fact that in each instance the courts are open to the person affected, and that any material, however questionable, may be freely sponsored, circulated, read, or viewed until judicially condemned.

In essence what the Court holds is that these publishers or their distributors need not, with respect to any material challenged by the Commission, vindicate their right to its protection in order to bring the Constitution to their aid. The effect of this holding is to cut into this effort of the State to get at the juvenile delinquency problem, without this Court or any other ever having concretely focused on whether any of the specific material called in question by the Commission is or is not entitled to protection under constitutional standards established by our decisions.[5]

This seems to me to weight the accommodation which should be made between the competing interests that this case presents entirely against the legitimate interests of the State. I believe that the correct course is to refuse to countenance this "broadside attack" on these state procedures and, with an appropriate *caveat* as to the character of some of the Commission's past utterances, to remit the appellants to their remedies respecting particular publications challenged by the Commission, as was done in the Times Film case. Putting these publishers and their dis-

---

[3] The publishers and distributors involved in this case are all, so far as this record shows, substantial business concerns, presumably represented by competent counsel, as were the appellants here.

[4] It seems obvious that in a nonlicensing context the force of Times Film is not lessened by the circumstance that in this case books rather than motion pictures are involved.

[5] In their Reply Brief (p. 4) appellants acknowledge: "We have never attempted to deal with the question of obscenity or nonobscenity of Appellants' books."

tributors to the pain of vindicating challenged materials is not to place them under unusual hardship, for as this Court has said in another context, "Bearing the discomfiture and cost" even of "a prosecution for crime [though] by an innocent person is one of the painful obligations of citizenship." *Cobbledick* v. *United States,* 309 U.S. 323, 325, 60 S. Ct. 540, 541, 84 L. Ed. 783.

III.

The Court's final point—that the Commission's activities may result in keeping from the adult public protected material, even though suppressible so far as youth is concerned—requires little additional comment. It is enough to say that such a determination should not be made at large, as has been done here. It should await a case when circumspect judgment can be brought to bear upon particular judicially suppressed publications.

Believing that the Commission, once advised of the permissible constitutional scope of its activities, can be counted on to conduct itself accordingly, I would affirm the judgment of the Rhode Island Supreme Court. Cf. *United States* v. *Haley,* 371 U.S. 18, 83 S. Ct. 11, 9 L. Ed. 2d 1.

■ The State of Ohio, *Appellee,*

v.

Jacobellis, *Appellant.*

No. 37200.

Supreme Court of Ohio.

Jan. 17, 1962.

Syllabus by the Court

1. Section 2905.34, Revised Code, relating to obscenity is a valid exercise of the police power of the state of Ohio and was enacted for the protection of its citizens, and a proper conviction for a violation thereof will be sustained.

2. The words, knowingly possess, as used in Section 2905.34, Revised Code, include "scienter" (guilty knowledge) and "mens rea" (guilty purpose), both of which must be established by proper evidence to sustain a conviction for violation of such section.

3. The courts must apply a rule of reason in construing and applying the criminal statutes of this state to the facts in each case.

Defendant was indicted on two counts by the September 1959 Grand Jury of Cuyahoga County, Ohio, for violation of Section 2905.34, Revised Code. The first count in the indictment reads as follows:

"'* * * on or about the 13th day of November 1959, at the county aforesaid, unlawfully and knowingly had in his possession and under his control a certain obscene, lewd and lascivious motion picture film, to wit:

"(Les Amants) 'The Lovers'

"Said motion picture film being so indecent and immoral in its nature that the same would be offensive to the court and improper to be placed upon the records thereof * * * and against the peace and dignity of the state of Ohio."

The second count in the indictment reads:

"'* * * on or about the 13th day of November 1959, at the county aforesaid, unlawfully and knowingly exhibited a certain obscene, lewd and lascivious motion picture film, to wit:

"(Les Amants) 'The Lovers'

"Said motion picture film being so indecent and immoral in its nature that the same would be offensive to the court, and improper to be placed upon the records thereof * * * and against the peace and dignity of the state of Ohio."

Section 2905.34, Revised Code, so far as it pertains to the defendant and his conduct on November 13, 1959, reads as follows:

"No person shall *knowingly* * * * exhibit * * * or have in his possession or under his control an obscene, lewd, or lascivious * * * motion picture film * * *.

"Whoever violates this section shall be fined not less than two hundred nor more than two thousand dollars or imprisoned not less than one nor more than seven years, or both." (Emphasis added.)

Upon arraignment the defendant entered pleas of not guilty to both counts of the indictment on November 30, 1959, and was released on bond.

On May 23, 1960, the defendant waived his right to trial by jury, both orally and in writing, and requested trial by a three-judge court. He was permitted to withdraw his pleas to make certain motions; thereafter the pleas of not guilty were re-entered and trial was had, resulting in a finding of guilty as charged in each count of the indictment.

The defendant was sentenced to pay a fine in the sum of $500 on the first count of the indictment and sentenced to pay a fine of $2,000 on the second count of the indictment and to stand committed to the workhouse of the city of Cleveland until such fine and costs were paid. Sentence was stayed pending appeal.

On appeal to the Court of Appeals, that judgment was affirmed.

The cause is before this court pursuant to a certification

of the record, the Court of Appeals finding its judgment to be in conflict with the judgment of the Court of Appeals of the Third Appellate District in the case of *State* v. *Wetzel*, decided December 10, 1960.

Bennett Kleinman, Cleveland, for appellant.

John T. Corrigan, Pros. Atty., *Thomas L. Osborne* and *Bernard J. Stuplinski*, Cleveland, for appellee.

RADCLIFF, J.

At the outset it is well to recall that an opinion of this court does not necessarily reflect the thinking and logic, if any, of any member of the court other than the author. It is the means by which the author of an opinion, in this case the writer, illustrates the path followed to reach a conclusion which, if concurred in by a majority of my distinguished colleagues (this term is used in all humility as my status as such is only temporary), is stated in the syllabus as the law of the case.

The defendant urges five assignments of error, the first two raising the constitutional issues involved. The third and fourth emphasize facts and the weight of the evidence, which we shall dispose of in the perfunctory manner, as the law requires of this court, in a short paragraph later in this opinion. The final assignment of error raises the question of general prejudice.

There is an oft-quoted cliche to the effect that "it is not possible to legislate in the field of morals." The statement originally was and still should be, "it is not possible to legislate morality for the people." In support of this, there is always cited the classic example of the Eighteenth Amendment to the United States Constitution. We sorrowfully agree that this is true, but the impossibility of accomplishing that which is good for all the people should not and must not be used as an excuse for failing to try. History is replete with examples of nations that lost positions of eminence in the world and whose citizens lost their freedom due to decay of their moral fiber resulting in degeneracy and depravity. Legislative bodies must continue to pass laws which attempt to protect the morality of the people from themselves and from their own weaknesses. When such laws are rejected it should be by those governed, either by repudiating their legislators, by failing to re-elect or by direct referendum. It is infelicitous for the judicial branch of the government to seek for constitutional infirmities which enable courts to thwart the actions of that segment of government closest to the governed and directly responsive and responsible thereto. By its very nature, the judiciary is farthest from the people because of the length of tenure or mode of selection, consequently its authority must be exercised with deliberate caution. *Lex citius tolerare vult privatum damnum mam publicum malum.*

We turn now to a consideration of the provisions of Section 2905.34, Revised Code, in relation to the various pronouncements of the Supreme Court of the United States in interpreting such statutes. The pertinent part of Section 2905.34, Revised Code, with which we are presently concerned, reads as follows:

"No person shall *knowingly* sell, lend, give away, exhibit, or offer to sell, lend, give away, or exhibit, or publish or offer to publish or have in his possession or under his control an obscene * * * motion picture film * * *." (Emphasis added.)

At the outset it must be noted that the Supreme Court of the United States has held that obscenity is not protected by the constitutional provisions relating to freedom of speech. *Roth* v. *United States*, 354 U.S. 476, 77 S. Ct. 1304, 1 L. Ed. 2d 1498.

In *Smith* v. *People of State of California*, 361 U.S. 147, 80 S. Ct. 215, 4 L. Ed. 2d 205, however, the Supreme Court struck down a state statute which imposed strict criminal liability for the mere possession for sale of an obscene book, without requiring any knowledge of the contents of the book. The case reserved, however, the question as to the extent of knowledge required which would validate such a statute.

[1] Such infirmity does not exist in the statute under our consideration. It is specifically required under Section 2905.34, Revised Code, that the acts punished thereunder shall be done knowingly. The act requires knowledge. The question, of course, is knowledge of what. It is apparent that such knowledge must necessarily relate to knowledge of the obscenity of the contents of the publication involved.

Two questions must be determined at this time. First, the test as to what is obscene. The definition which has now become classic was laid down in *Roth* v. *United States*, supra, as follows, at page 489 of 354 U.S., at page 1311 of 77 S. Ct.:

"* * * whether to the average person, applying contemporary community standards, the dominant theme of the material taken as a whole appeals to prurient interest."

[2] Thus it is to be seen that the test for obscenity is not subjective but objective. It is not to be judged by what any single individual deems is obscene to himself, but rather what the community as a whole would consider obscene. There is no real or actual ambiguity in the phrase. No undue burden is placed on the possessor of such literature, for even though the individual himself might not consider the subject matter obscene, it is indeed the isolated and uninformed person who would not know as a matter of fact what is obscene by the usual community standards, and as stated in *Roth* v. *United States*, supra, at pages 491 and 492 of 354 U.S., at pages 1312 and 1313 of 77 S. Ct.:

"Many decisions have recognized that these terms of obscenity statutes are not precise. This Court, however, has consistently held that lack of precision is not itself offensive to the requirements of the due process. '* * * [T]he Constitution does not require impossible standards'; all that is required is that the language 'conveys sufficiently definite warning as to the proscribed conduct when measured by common understanding and practices * * *.' *United States* v. *Petrillo*, 332 U.S. 1, 7–8 [67 S. Ct. 1538, 1542, 91 L. Ed. 1877]. These words, applied according to the proper standard for judging obscenity, already discussed, give adequate warning of the conduct proscribed and mark '* * * boundaries sufficiently distinct for judges and juries fairly to administer the law * * *. That there may be marginal cases in which it is difficult to determine the side of the line on which a particular fact situation falls is no sufficient reason to hold the language too ambiguous to define a criminal offense * * *.'"

[3] The second question which arises is as to what extent a person is bound to have knowledge of the contents of that which he possesses. To the dealer in what is commonly known as hard-core pornography there is little

question. Such purveyors of obscenity can be presumed to know what they are dispensing. (*State* v. *Wetzel,* 173 Ohio St. 16, 179 N.E. 2d 773.) It is in the more ethereal region of theoretical literary endeavor that the principal problem arises. Here, once again, the community must be the test. A commercial possessor obviously can not be held to the duty of examining and determining for himself the obscenity of all matters which pass through his hands, neither, however, can he profess ignorance of that which has become a matter of general knowledge in the community. The rule of reason must be applied in these matters. While the possessor should not be held to the impossible, where the contents of a given publication have become a matter of common knowledge and are generally known to be obscene as judged by the above test, then the duty devolves upon the holder of such publications to refrain from distributing or exhibiting them and to destroy them as soon as he may practically do so; otherwise he will then become guilty under Section 2905.34, Revised Code.

[4] Thus it is only when a holder of such matter becomes aware of or should be aware of the contents and the objectionable nature thereof that he would become liable to prosecution under this section.

That there are marginal cases where such determination is difficult does not invalidate an otherwise valid enactment. *Roth* v. *United States,* supra, and *State* v. *Wetzel,* supra.

The final question that must be disposed of in relation to this section is the proper construction of the phrase, "in his possession or under his control," and its relationship to the rest of the section. Does such phrase relate to the mere private possession by an individual of such matter for his own personal gratification? If so, such section might well be held to be invalid. However, in our opinion, such is not the proper construction of this section, nor does it give effect to the apparent intention of the General Assembly.

It requires only a cursory examination of this section to determine that its language clearly relates to the circulation, publication and exhibition of obscene matter. In other words, to the dissemination of obscenity, whether for profit or otherwise. Under the doctrine of *noscitur a sociis* the phrase, "in his possession or under his control," must be read in context with the language used in the section as a whole.

[5] In the phrase, "knowingly possess," as used in criminal statutes, is implicit not only the element of scienter but also the element of mens rea, namely, "a guilty or wrongful purpose." It is not conceivable to us that a violation of Section 2905.34 is committed the moment an individual discovers that a book, picture or film in his possession is pornographic. He could only be said to violate the law when and if he forms the purpose to use, exhibit or sell it wrongfully, in other words, forms the mens rea and acts in furtherance thereof.

When this phrase is read in context with and in relation to the rest of the section, it is readily apparent that such phrase does not relate to the mere possession for private and personal gratification but rather to possession and control for the purpose of circulation or exhibition, a matter clearly within the power of the state to control under the police power.

[6] The third and fourth assignments of errors raise questions as to factual issues and the weight of the evidence. These issues have been resolved in the proper

forums. The facts were found by the three judges sitting as the triers of the facts who applied the standards prescribed in *Roth* v. *United States,* supra, and by the Court of Appeals which the law requires must pass upon the weight and sufficiency of the evidence.

This court viewed Les Amants (The Lovers). The film ran for 90 minutes. To me, it was 87 minutes of boredom induced by the vapid drivel appearing on the screen and three minutes of complete revulsion during the showing of an act of perverted obscenity. Les Amants (The Lovers) was not hard-core pornography, i.e., filth for filth's sake. It was worse. It was filth for money's sake. The producers, distributors and exhibitors evidenced so little responsibility in connection therewith that they have no right to assert constitutional guaranties which require a high degree of responsibility from those who seek their protection. This is especially apropos of the First and Fourteenth Amendments to the Constitution of the United States.

There is a unique coincidence involving this case (*State* v. *Jacobellis*) and the case of *State* v. *Warth,* 173 Ohio St. 15, 179 N.E. 2d 772, as the obscene material involved in both was Les Amants (The Lovers). However, the statute involved in each case is entirely different. Jacobellis was indicted, tried and convicted for violation of Section 2905.34, Revised Code. Warth was indicted, tried and convicted for violation of Section 2905.342, Revised Code. The latter statute attempted to make *mere* possession or exhibiting an obscene motion picture film a misdemeanor. In view of the pronouncements of this court in *City of Cincinnati* v. *Marshall,* 172 Ohio St. 280, 175 N.E. 2d 178, and of the Supreme Court of the United States in *Smith* v. *People of State of California,* supra, and our high regard for the doctrine of *stare decisis,* the conviction of Warth was reversed due to the constitutional infirmity of Section 2905.342, Revised Code, in omitting the element of scienter or knowledge. The cases in reality had no common principle of law involved, and, consequently, the different conclusion reached in each can not provoke any possible question of inconsistency. Had Warth been charged in Montgomery County with a violation of Section 2905.34, Revised Code, he would have been as guilty as we now find Jacobellis in Cuyahoga County.

As we find no error in the judgment of the Court of Appeals, such judgment is hereby affirmed.

Judgment affirmed.

Zimmerman, Acting C.J., and Matthias, Bell and O'Neill, JJ., concur.

Herbert, J., dissents.

Zimmerman, J., sitting in the place and stead of Weygandt, C.J.

Radcliff, J., of the Fourth Appellate District, sitting by designation in the place and stead of Zimmerman, J.

Taft, Judge (concurring in part).

I cannot be as positive in condemning the film involved in the instant case as the majority opinion is. However, in my opinion, reasonable minds could determine beyond a reasonable doubt that this film is, to use the words of the statute, "obscene, lewd, or lascivious."

I agree, therefore, with the judgment so far as it relates to the second count of the indictment charging defendant with exhibiting that film.

I also agree with the majority opinion that the word "knowingly" in the statute relates not merely to possession and control of the film but also to what is in the film.

However, I cannot agree with the judgment of this court, to the extent that it affirms the conviction of defendant on the first count charging defendant merely with knowingly possessing and having control of the film.

It is my opinion, as it was the opinion of Judges Bell, Peck, Herbert and myself in *State* v. *Mapp* (1960), 170 Ohio St. 427, 433, 166 N.E. 2d 387, that the portion of the statute upon which the first count is based is constitutionally invalid. As stated in the opinion in that case:

"If anyone looks at a book and finds it lewd, he is forthwith, under this legislation, guilty of a serious crime * * *. As a result, some who might otherwise read books that are not obscene may well be discouraged from doing so and their free circulation and use will be impeded."

Likewise, under this statute, if anyone looks at a movie film that he has lawfully acquired to determine whether he should exhibit it and finds it to be obscene, he is forthwith and at that instant guilty of a serious crime. As a result, some who might otherwise look at movie films that are not obscene to determine whether they should exhibit those films may well be discouraged from doing so and free circulation and exhibition of movie films will be impeded.

If Section 2905.34, Revised Code, providing that "no person shall knowingly * * * have in his possession or under his control an obscene, lewd, or lascivious * * * motion picture film" were reasonably susceptible of interpretation as a prohibition of possession or control of such a film only where such possession or control was for the circulation or exhibition thereof, I could also concur in the judgment so far as it affirms the conviction on the first count. Apart from some consideration of the legislative history of this statute, this court *might* be justified in proclaiming that there was a legislative intent that the "possession * * * or control," in order to be a crime, must be, to use the words of the majority opinion, "for the purpose of circulation or exhibition." But compare *State* v. *Warth*, 173 Ohio St. 15, 179 N.E. 2d 772. As the majority opinion states, this matter is clearly within the power of the state to control under the police power.

It may be observed that it is probable that such a judicial proclamation of legislative intent would be helpful, if not conclusive, in avoiding a review by the United States Supreme Court of the constitutional validity of this portion of our statute.

However, the General Assembly has quite clearly indicated that it had no such intention. Thus, prior to 1939, the foregoing statute (then Section 13035, General Code) read so far as pertinent:

"Whoever sells, lends, gives away [i.e., circulates], exhibits * * * or has in his *possession for such purpose*, an obscene [etc.]." (Emphasis added.)

In that year, the General Assembly amended that statute by taking out the words "for such purpose" appearing after the word "possession," and added, after the latter words, the words "or has under his control." 118 Ohio Laws 420.

The General Assembly thus quite clearly expressed a legislative intention not to modify the words "has in his possession or under his control" as the majority opinion and the decision in the instant case are modifying those words.

■ Nico Jacobellis, *Appellant,*

v.

State of Ohio.
No. 11.

Reargued April 1, 1964.

Decided June 22, 1964.

Ephraim London, New York City, for appellant.
John T. Corrigan, Cleveland, Ohio, for appellee.

Mr. Justice BRENNAN announced the judgment of the Court and delivered an opinion in which Mr. Justice GOLD-BERG joins.

Appellant, Nico Jacobellis, manager of a motion picture theater in Cleveland Heights, Ohio, was convicted on two counts of possessing and exhibiting an obscene film in violation of Ohio Revised Code (1963 Supp.), § 2905.34.[1]

---

[1] *"Selling, exhibiting, and possessing obscene literature or drugs for criminal purposes.*

"No person shall knowingly sell, lend, give away, exhibit, or offer to sell, lend, give away, or exhibit, or publish or offer to publish or have in his possession or under his control an obscene, lewd, or lascivious book, magazine, pamphlet, paper, writing, advertisement, circular, print, picture, photograph, motion picture film, or book, pamphlet, paper, magazine not wholly obscene but containing lewd or lascivious articles, advertisements,

He was fined $500 on the first count and $2,000 on the second, and was sentenced to the workhouse if the fines were not paid. His conviction, by a court of three judges upon waiver of trial by jury, was affirmed by an intermediate appellate court, 115 Ohio App. 226, 175 N.E. 2d 123, and by the Supreme Court of Ohio, 173 Ohio St. 22, 179 N.E. 2d 777. We noted probable jurisdiction of the appeal, 371 U.S. 808, 83 S. Ct. 28, 9 L. Ed. 2d 52, and subsequently restored the case to the calendar for reargument, 373 U.S. 901, 83 S. Ct. 1288, 10 L. Ed. 2d 197. The dispositive question is whether the state courts properly found that the motion picture involved, a French film called "*Les Amants*" ("The Lovers"), was obscene and hence not entitled to the protection for free expression that is guaranteed by the First and Fourteenth Amendments. We conclude that the film is not obscene and that the judgment must accordingly be reversed.

Motion pictures are within the ambit of the constitutional guarantees of freedom of speech and of the press. *Joseph Burstyn, Inc.* v. *Wilson*, 343 U.S. 495, 72 S. Ct. 777, 96 L. Ed. 1098. But in *Roth* v. *United States* and *Alberts* v. *California*, 354 U.S. 476, 77 S. Ct. 1304, 1 L. Ed. 2d 1498, we held that obscenity is not subject to those guarantees. Application of an obscenity law to suppress a motion picture thus requires ascertainment of the "dim and uncertain line" that often separates obscenity from constitutionally protected expression. *Bantam Books, Inc.* v. *Sullivan*, 372 U.S. 58, 66, 83 S. Ct. 631, 637, 9 L. Ed. 2d 584; see *Speiser* v. *Randall*, 357 U.S. 513, 525, 78 S. Ct. 1332, 1341, 1342, 2 L. Ed. 2d 1460.[2] It has been suggested that this is a task in which our Court need not involve itself. We are told that the determination whether a particular motion picture, book, or other work of expression is obscene can be treated as a purely factual judgment on which a jury's verdict is all but conclusive, or that in any event the decision can be left essentially to state and lower federal courts, with this Court exercising only a

limited review such as that needed to determine whether the ruling below is supported by "sufficient evidence." The suggestion is appealing, since it would lift from our shoulders a difficult, recurring, and unpleasant task. But we cannot accept it. Such an abnegation of judicial supervision in this field would be inconsistent with our duty to uphold the constitutional guarantees. Since it is only "obscenity" that is excluded from the constitutional protection, the question whether a particular work is obscene necessarily implicates an issue of constitutional law. See *Roth* v. *United States*, supra, 354 U.S., at 497–498, 77 S. Ct., at 1315–1316 (separate opinion). Such an issue, we think, must ultimately be decided by this Court. Our duty admits of no "substitute for facing up to the tough individual problems of constitutional judgment involved in every obscenity case." *Id.*, 354 U.S., at 498, 77 S. Ct., at 1316, see *Manual Enterprises, Inc.* v. *Day*, 370 U.S. 478, 488, 82 S. Ct. 1432, 1437, 8 L. Ed. 2d 639 (opinion of Harlan, J.).[3]

In other areas involving constitutional rights under the Due Process Clause, the Court has consistently recognized its duty to apply the applicable rules of law upon the basis of an independent review of the facts of each case. E.g., *Watts* v. *Indiana*, 338 U.S. 49, 51, 69 S. Ct. 1347, 1348, 93 L. Ed. 1801; *Norris* v. *Alabama*, 294 U.S. 587, 590, 55 S. Ct. 579, 580, 79 L. Ed. 1074.[4] And this has been

---

[3] See *Kingsley Int'l Pictures Corp.* v. *Regents*, 360 U.S. 684, 708, 79 S. Ct. 1362, 1375, 3 L. Ed. 2d 1512 (separate opinion): "It is sometimes said that this Court should shun considering the particularities of individual cases in this difficult field lest the Court become a final 'board of censorship.' But I cannot understand why it should be thought that the process of constitutional judgment in this realm somehow stands apart from that involved in other fields, particularly those presenting questions of due process. * * *"

See also Lockhart and McClure, Censorship of Obscenity: The Developing Constitutional Standards, 45 Minn. L. Rev. 5, 116 (1960): "This obligation—to reach an independent judgment in applying constitutional standards and criteria to constitutional issues that may be cast by lower courts 'in the form of determinations of fact'—appears fully applicable to findings of obscenity by juries, trial courts, and administrative agencies. The Supreme Court is subject to that obligation, as is every court before which the constitutional issue is raised."
And see id., at 119:
"It may be true * * * that judges 'possess no special expertise' qualifying them 'to supervise the private morals of the Nation' or to decide 'what movies are good or bad for local communities.' But they do have a far keener understanding of the importance of free expression than do most government administrators or jurors, and they have had considerable experience in making value judgments of the type required by the constitutional standards for obscenity. If freedom is to be preserved, neither government censorship experts nor juries can be left to make the final effective decisions restraining free expression. Their decisions must be subject to effective, independent review, and we know of no group better qualified for that review than the appellate judges of this country under the guidance of the Supreme Court."

[4] See also *Fiske* v. *Kansas*, 274 U.S. 380, 385–386, 47 S. Ct. 655, 656–657, 71 L. Ed. 1108; *Haynes* v. *Washington*, 373 U.S. 503, 515–516, 83 S. Ct. 1336, 1344–1345, 10 L. Ed. 2d 513; *Chambers* v. *Florida*, 309 U.S. 227, 229, 60 S. Ct. 472, 473–474, 84 L. Ed. 716; *Hooven & Allison Co.* v. *Evatt*, 324 U.S. 652, 659, 65 S. Ct. 870, 874, 89 L. Ed. 1252; *Lisenba* v. *California*, 314 U.S. 219, 237–238, 62 S. Ct. 280, 290–291, 86 L. Ed. 166; *Ashcraft* v. *Tennessee*, 322 U.S. 143, 147–148, 64 S. Ct. 921,

---

photographs, or drawing, representation, figure, image, cast, instrument, or article of an indecent or immoral nature, or a drug, medicine, article, or thing intended for the prevention of conception or for causing an abortion, or advertise any of them for sale, or write, print, or cause to be written or printed a card, book, pamphlet, advertisement, or notice giving information when, where, how, of whom, or by what means any of such articles or things can be purchased or obtained, or manufacture, draw, print, or make such articles or things, or sell, give away, or show to a minor, a book, pamphlet, magazine, newspaper, story paper, or other paper devoted to the publication, or principally made up, of criminal news, police reports, or accounts of criminal deeds, or pictures and stories of immoral deeds, lust, or crime, or exhibit upon a street or highway or in a place which may be within the view of a minor, any of such books, papers, magazines, or pictures.

"Whoever violates this section shall be fined not less than two hundred nor more than two thousand dollars or imprisoned not less than one nor more than seven years, or both."

[2] It is too late in the day to argue that the location of the line is different, and the task of ascertaining it easier, when a state rather than a federal obscenity law is involved. The view that the constitutional guarantees of free expression do not apply as fully to the States as they do to the Federal Government was rejected in Roth-Alberts, supra, where the Court's single opinion applied the same standards to both a state and a federal conviction. Cf. *Ker* v. *California*, 374 U.S. 23, 33, 83 S. Ct. 1623, 1629, 1630, 10 L. Ed. 2d 726; *Malloy* v. *Hogan*, 378 U.S. 1, 10–11, 84 S. Ct. 1489, 1494–1495.

particularly true where rights have been asserted under the First Amendment guarantees of free expression. Thus in *Pennekamp v. Florida*, 328 U.S. 331, 335, 66 S. Ct. 1029, 1031, 90 L. Ed. 1295, the Court stated:

*"The Constitution has imposed upon this Court final authority to determine the meaning and application of those words of that instrument which require interpretation to resolve judicial issues. With that responsibility, we are compelled to examine for ourselves the statements in issue and the circumstances under which they were made to see whether or not they * * * are of a character which the principles of the First Amendment, as adopted by the Due Process Clause of the Fourteenth Amendment, protect."*[5]

We cannot understand why the Court's duty should be any different in the present case, where Jacobellis has been subjected to a criminal conviction for disseminating a work of expression and is challenging that conviction as a deprivation of rights guaranteed by the First and Fourteenth Amendments. Nor can we understand why the Court's performance of its constitutional and judicial function in this sort of case should be denigrated by such epithets as "censor" or "super-censor." In judging alleged obscenity the Court is no more "censoring" expression than it has in other cases "censored" criticism of judges and public officials, advocacy of governmental overthrow, or speech alleged to constitute a breach of the peace. Use of an opprobrious label can neither obscure nor impugn the Court's performance of its obligation to test challenged judgments against the guarantees of the First and Fourteenth Amendments and, in doing so, to delineate the scope of constitutionally protected speech. Hence we reaffirm the principle that, in "obscenity" cases as in all others involving rights derived from the First Amendment guarantees of free expression, this Court cannot avoid making an independent constitutional judgment on the facts of the case as to whether the material involved is constitutionally protected.[6]

The question of the proper standard for making this determination has been the subject of much discussion and controversy since our decision in Roth seven years ago. Recognizing that the test for obscenity enunciated there— "whether to the average person, applying contemporary community standards, the dominant theme of the material taken as a whole appeals to prurient interest," 354 U.S., at 489, 77 S. Ct., at 1311—is not perfect, we think any substitute would raise equally difficult problems, and we would therefore adhere to that standard. We would reiterate, however, our recognition in Roth that obscenity is excluded from the constitutional protection only because it is "utterly without redeeming social importance," and that "[t]he portrayal of sex, e.g., in art, literature and scientific works, is not itself sufficient reason to deny material the constitutional protection of freedom of speech and press." Id., 354 U.S., at 484, 487, 77 S. Ct., at 1310. It follows that material dealing with sex in a manner that advocates ideas, *Kingsley Int'l Pictures Corp. v. Regents*, 360 U.S. 684, 79 S. Ct. 1362, 3 L. Ed. 2d 1512, or that has literary or scientific or artistic value or any other form of social importance, may not be branded as obscenity and denied the constitutional protection.[7] Nor may the constitutional status of the material be made to turn on a "weighing" of its social importance against its prurient appeal, for a work cannot be proscribed unless it is "utterly" without social importance. See *Zeitlin v. Arnebergh*, 59 Cal. 2d 901, 920, 31 Cal. Rptr. 800, 813, 383 P. 2d 152, 165 (1963). It should also be recognized that the Roth standard requires in the first instance a finding that the material "goes substantially beyond customary limits of candor in description or representation of such matters." This was a requirement of the Model Penal Code test that we approved in Roth, 354 U.S., at 487, n. 20, 77 S. Ct., at 1310 and it is explicitly reaffirmed in the more recent Proposed Official Draft of the Code.[8] In the absence of such a deviation from society's standards of decency, we do not see how any official inquiry into the allegedly prurient appeal of a work of expression can be squared with the guarantees of the First and Fourteenth Amendments. See *Manual Enterprises, Inc. v. Day*, 370 U.S. 478, 482–488, 82 S. Ct. 1432, 1434–1438 (opinion of Harlan, J.).

It has been suggested that the "contemporary community standards" aspect of the Roth test implies a determination of the constitutional question of obscenity in each case by the standards of the particular local community from which the case arises. This is an incorrect reading of Roth. The concept of "contemporary community standards" was first expressed by Judge Learned

923, 88 L. Ed. 1192; *Napue v. Illinois*, 360 U.S. 264, 271, 79 S. Ct. 1173, 1178, 3 L. Ed. 2d 1217.

[5] See also *Niemotko v. Maryland*, 340 U.S. 268, 271, 71 S. Ct. 325, 327, 95 L. Ed. 267; *Craig v. Harney*, 331 U.S. 367, 373–374, 67 S. Ct. 1249, 1253–1254, 91 L. Ed. 1546; *Bridges v. California*, 314 U.S. 252, 271, 62 S. Ct. 190, 197–198, 86 L. Ed. 192; *Edwards v. South Carolina*, 372 U.S. 229, 235, 83 S. Ct. 680, 683, 9 L. Ed. 2d 697; *New York Times Co. v. Sullivan*, 376 U.S. 254, 285, 84 S. Ct. 710, 728–729, 11 L. Ed. 2d 686.

[6] This is precisely what the Court did in *Times Film Corp. v. City of Chicago*, 355 U.S. 35, 78 S. Ct. 115, 2 L. Ed. 2d 72; *One, Inc. v. Olesen*, 355 U.S. 371, 78 S. Ct. 364, 2 L. Ed. 2d 352; and *Sunshine Book Co. v. Summerfield*, 355 U.S. 372, 78 S. Ct. 365, 2 L. Ed. 2d 352. The obligation has been recognized by state courts as well. See, e.g., *State v. Hudson County News Co.*, 41 N.J. 247, 256–257, 196 A. 2d 225, 230 (1963); *Zeitlin v. Arnebergh*, 59 Cal. 2d 901, 909–911, 31 Cal. Rptr. 800, 805–806, 383 P. 2d 152, 157–158 (1963); *People v. Richmond County News, Inc.*, 9 N.Y. 2d 578, 580–581, 216 N.Y.S. 2d 369, 370, 175 N.E. 2d 681, 681–682 (1961). See also American Law Institute, Model Penal Code, Proposed Official Draft (May 4, 1962), § 251.4(4).

Nor do we think our duty of constitutional adjudication in this area can properly be relaxed by reliance on a "sufficient evidence" standard of review. Even in judicial review of admin-

istrative agency determinations, questions of "constitutional fact" have been held to require *de novo* review. *Ng Fung Ho v. White*, 259 U.S. 276, 284–285, 42 S. Ct. 492, 495, 66 L. Ed. 938; *Crowell v. Benson*, 285 U.S. 22, 54–65, 52 S. Ct. 285, 293–298, 76 L. Ed. 598.

[7] See, e.g., *Attorney General v. Book Named "Tropic of Cancer*," 345 Mass. 11, 184 N.E. 2d 328 (Mass. 1962); *Zeitlin v. Arnebergh*, 59 Cal. 2d 901, 31 Cal. Rptr. 800, 383 P. 2d 152 (1963).

[8] American Law Institute, Model Penal Code, Proposed Official Draft (May 4, 1962), § 251.4(1):

"Material is obscene if, considered as a whole, its predominant appeal is to prurient interest * * * and if *in addition* it goes substantially beyond customary limits of candor in describing or representing such matters." (Italics added.)

Hand in *United States* v. *Kennerley*, 209 F. 119, 121 (D.C.S.D.N.Y. 1913), where he said:

"Yet, if the time is not yet when men think innocent all that which is honestly germane to a pure subject, however little it may mince its words, still I scarcely think that they would forbid all which might corrupt the most corruptible, or that society is prepared to accept for its own limitations those which may perhaps be necessary to the weakest of its members. If there be no abstract definition, such as I have suggested, should not the word 'obscene' be allowed to indicate the present critical point in the compromise between candor and shame at which the community may have arrived here and now? * * * To put thought in leash to the average conscience of the time is perhaps tolerable, but to fetter it by the necessities of the lowest and least capable seems a fatal policy.

"Nor is it an objection, I think, that such an interpretation gives to the words of the statute a varying meaning from time to time. Such words as these do not embalm the precise morals of an age or place; while they presuppose that some things will always be shocking to the public taste, the vague subject-matter is left to the gradual development of general notions about what is decent. * * *" (*Italics added.*)

It seems clear that in this passage Judge Hand was referring not to state and local "communities," but rather to "the community" in the sense of "society at large; * * * the public, or people in general."[9] Thus, he recognized that under his standard the concept of obscenity would have "a varying meaning from time to time"—not from county to county, or town to town.

We do not see how any "local" definition of the "community" could properly be employed in delineating the area of expression that is protected by the Federal Constitution. MR. JUSTICE HARLAN pointed out in *Manual Enterprises, Inc.* v. *Day*, supra, 370 U.S., at 488, 82 S. Ct., at 1437, that a standard based on a particular local community would have "the intolerable consequence of denying some sections of the country access to material, there deemed acceptable, which in others might be considered offensive to prevailing community standards of decency. Cf. *Butler* v. *Michigan*, 352 U.S. 380, 77 S. Ct. 524, 1 L. Ed. 2d 412." It is true that Manual Enterprises dealt with the federal statute banning obscenity from the mails. But the mails are not the only means by which works of expression cross local-community lines in this country. It can hardly be assumed that all the patrons of a particular library, bookstand, or motion picture theater are residents of the smallest local "community" that can be drawn around that establishment. Furthermore, to sustain the suppression of a particular book or film in one locality would deter its dissemination in other localities where it might be held not obscene, since sellers and exhibitors would be reluctant to risk criminal conviction in testing the variation between the two places. It would be a hardy person who would sell a book or exhibit a film anywhere in the land after this Court had sustained the judgment of one "community" holding it to be outside the constitutional protection. The result would thus be "to restrict the pub-

lic's access to forms of the printed word which the State could not constitutionally suppress directly." *Smith* v. *California*, 361 U.S. 147, 154, 80 S. Ct. 215, 219, 4 L. Ed. 2d 205.

It is true that local communities throughout the land are in fact diverse, and that in cases such as this one the Court is confronted with the task of reconciling the rights of such communities with the rights of individuals. Communities vary, however, in many respects other than their toleration of alleged obscenity, and such variances have never been considered to require or justify a varying standard for application of the Federal Constitution. The Court has regularly been compelled, in reviewing criminal convictions challenged under the Due Process Clause of the Fourteenth Amendment, to reconcile the conflicting rights of the local community which brought the prosecution and of the individual defendant. Such a task is admittedly difficult and delicate, but it is inherent in the Court's duty of determining whether a particular conviction worked a deprivation of rights guaranteed by the Federal Constitution. The Court has not shrunk from discharging that duty in other areas, and we see no reason why it should do so here. The Court has explicitly refused to tolerate a result whereby "the constitutional limits of free expression in the Nation would vary with state lines," *Pennekamp* v. *Florida*, supra, 328 U.S., at 335, 66 S. Ct., at 1031, we see even less justification for allowing such limits to vary with town or county lines. We thus reaffirm the position taken in Roth to the effect that the constitutional status of an allegedly obscene work must be determined on the basis of a national standard.[10] It is, after all, a national Constitution we are expounding.

We recognize the legitimate and indeed exigent interest of States and localities throughout the Nation in preventing the dissemination of material deemed harmful to children. But that interest does not justify a total suppression of such material, the effect of which would be to "reduce the adult population * * * to reading only what is fit for children." *Butler* v. *Michigan*, 352 U.S. 380, 383, 77 S. Ct. 524, 526. State and local authorities might well consider whether their objectives in this area would be better served by laws aimed specifically at preventing distribution of objectionable material to children, rather than at totally prohibiting its dissemination.[11] Since the present conviction is based upon exhibition of the film to the public at large and not upon its exhibition to children, the judgment must be reviewed under the strict standard applicable in determining the scope of the expression that is protected by the Constitution.

We have applied that standard to the motion picture in question. "The Lovers" involves a woman bored with her life and marriage who abandons her husband and family for a young archaeologist with whom she has suddenly fallen in love. There is an explicit love scene in the last reel of the film, and the State's objections are based almost entirely upon that scene. The film was favorably reviewed in a number of national publications, although disparaged

---

[9] Webster's New International Dictionary (2d ed. 1949), at 542.

[10] See *State* v. *Hudson County News Co.*, 41 N.J. 247, 266, 196 A. 2d 225, 235 (1963). Lockhart and McClure, note 3, supra, 45 Minn. L. Rev., at 108–112; American Law Institute, Model Penal Code, Tentative Draft No. 6 (May 6, 1957), at 45; Proposed Official Draft (May 4, 1962), § 251.4(4) (d).

[11] See *State* v. *Settle*, 90 R.I. 195, 156 A. 2d 921 (1959).

in others, and was rated by at least two critics of national stature among the best films of the year in which it was produced. It was shown in approximately 100 of the larger cities in the United States, including Columbus and Toledo, Ohio. We have viewed the film, in the light of the record made in the trial court, and we conclude that it is not obscene within the standards enunciated in *Roth* v. *United States* and *Alberts* v. *California*, which we reaffirm here.

Reversed.

Mr. Justice WHITE concurs in the judgment.

Opinion of Mr. Justice BLACK, with whom Mr. Justice DOUGLAS joins.

I concur in the reversal of this judgment. My belief, as stated in *Kingsley International Pictures Corp.* v. *Regents*, 360 U.S. 684, 690, 79 S. Ct. 1362, 1366, 3 L. Ed. 2d 1512, is that "If despite the Constitution * * * this Nation is to embark on the dangerous road of censorship, * * * this Court is about the most inappropriate Supreme Board of Censors that could be found." My reason for reversing is that I think the conviction of appellant or anyone else for exhibiting a motion picture abridges freedom of the press as safeguarded by the First Amendment, which is made obligatory on the States by the Fourteenth. See my concurring opinions in *Quantity of Copies of Books* v. *Kansas*, 377 U.S. 213, 84 S. Ct. 1723; *Smith* v. *California*, 361 U.S. 147, 155, 80 S. Ct. 215, 219–220, 4 L. Ed. 2d 205; *Kingsley International Pictures Corp.* v. *Regents*, supra. See also the dissenting opinion of MR. JUSTICE DOUGLAS in *Roth* v. *United States*, 354 U.S. 476, 508, 77 S. Ct. 1304, 1321, 1 L. Ed. 2d 1498, and his concurring opinion in *Superior Films, Inc.* v. *Department of Education*, 346 U.S. 587, 588, 74 S. Ct. 286, 98 L. Ed. 329, in both of which I joined.

Mr. Justice STEWART, concurring.

It is possible to read the Court's opinion in *Roth* v. *United States* and *Alberts* v. *California*, 354 U.S. 476, 77 S. Ct. 1304, 1 L. Ed. 2d 1498, in a variety of ways. In saying this, I imply no criticism of the Court, which in those cases was faced with the task of trying to define what may be indefinable. I have reached the conclusion, which I think is confirmed at least by negative implication in the Court's decisions since Roth and Alberts,[1] that under the First and Fourteenth Amendments criminal laws in this area are constitutionally limited to hard-core pornography.[2] I shall not today attempt further to define the kinds of material I understand to be embraced within that shorthand description; and perhaps I could never succeed

in intelligibly doing so. But I know it when I see it, and the motion picture involved in this case is not that.

Mr. Justice GOLDBERG, concurring.

The question presented is whether the First and Fourteenth Amendments permit the imposition of criminal punishment for exhibiting the motion picture entitled "The Lovers." I have viewed the film and I wish merely to add to my Brother BRENNAN's description that the love scene deemed objectionable is so fragmentary and fleeting that only a censor's alert would make an audience conscious that something "questionable" is being portrayed. Except for this rapid sequence, the film concerns itself with the history of an ill-matched and unhappy marriage— a familiar subject in old and new novels and in current television soap operas.

Although I fully agree with what my Brother BRENNAN has written, I am also of the view that adherence to the principles stated in *Joseph Burstyn, Inc.* v. *Wilson*, 343 U.S. 495, 72 S. Ct. 777, 96 L. Ed. 1098, requires reversal. In Burstyn MR. JUSTICE CLARK, delivering the unanimous judgment of the Court, said:

"[E]xpression by means of motion pictures is included within the free speech and free press guaranty of the First and Fourteenth Amendments. * * *
"To hold that liberty of expression by means of motion pictures is guaranteed by the First and Fourteenth Amendments, however, is not the end of our problem. It does not follow that the Constitution requires absolute freedom to exhibit every motion picture of every kind at all times and all places. * * * Nor does it follow that motion pictures are necessarily subject to the precise rules governing any other particular method of expression. Each method tends to present its own peculiar problems. But the basic principles of freedom of speech and the press, like the First Amendment's command, do not vary. Those principles, as they have frequently been enunciated by this Court, make freedom of expression the rule." Id., 343 U.S., at 502–503, 72 S. Ct., at 781.

As in Burstyn "[t]here is no justification in this case for making an exception to that rule," id., 343 U.S. at 503, 72 S. Ct., at 781, for by any arguable standard the exhibitors of this motion picture may not be criminally prosecuted unless the exaggerated character of the advertising rather than the obscenity of the film is to be the constitutional criterion.

The Chief Justice, with whom Mr. Justice CLARK joins, dissenting.

In this and other cases in this area of the law, which are coming to us in ever-increasing numbers, we are faced with the resolution of rights basic both to individuals and to society as a whole. Specifically, we are called upon to reconcile the right of the Nation and of the States to maintain a decent society and, on the other hand, the right of individuals to express themselves freely in accordance with the guarantees of the First and Fourteenth Amendments. Although the Federal Government and virtually every State has had laws proscribing obscenity since the Union was formed, and although this Court has recently decided

---

[1] *Times Film Corp.* v. *City of Chicago*, 355 U.S. 35, 78 S. Ct. 115, 2 L. Ed. 2d 72, reversing 7 Cir., 244 F. 2d 432; *One, Incorporated* v. *Olesen*, 355 U.S. 371, 78 S. Ct. 364, 2 L. Ed. 2d 352, reversing 9 Cir., 241 F. 2d 772; *Sunshine Book Co.* v. *Summerfield*, 355 U.S. 372, 78 S. Ct. 365, 2 L. Ed. 2d 352, reversing 101 U.S. App. D.C. 358, 249 F. 2d 114; *Manual Enterprises* v. *Day*, 370 U.S. 478, 82 S. Ct. 1432, 8 L. Ed. 2d 639 (opinion of HARLAN, J.).

[2] Cf. *People* v. *Richmond County News*, 9 N.Y. 2d 578, 175 N.E. 2d 681, 216 N.Y.S. 2d 369.

that obscenity is not within the protection of the First Amendment,[1] neither courts nor legislatures have been able to evolve a truly satisfactory definition of obscenity. In other areas of the law, terms like "negligence," although in common use for centuries, have been difficult to define except in the most general manner. Yet the courts have been able to function in such areas with a reasonable degree of efficiency. The obscenity problem, however, is aggravated by the fact that it involves the area of public expression, an area in which a broad range of freedom is vital to our society and is constitutionally protected.

Recently this Court put its hand to the task of defining the term "obscenity" in *Roth* v. *United States*, 354 U.S. 476, 77 S. Ct. 1304, 1 L. Ed. 2d 1498. The definition enunciated in that case has generated much legal speculation as well as further judicial interpretation by state and federal courts. It has also been relied upon by legislatures. Yet obscenity cases continue to come to this Court, and it becomes increasingly apparent that we must settle as well as we can the question of what constitutes "obscenity" and the question of what standards are permissible in enforcing proscriptions against obscene matter. This Court hears cases such as the instant one not merely to rule upon the alleged obscenity of a specific film or book but to establish principles for the guidance of lower courts and legislatures. Yet most of our decisions since Roth have been given without opinion and have thus failed to furnish such guidance. Nor does the Court in the instant case—which has now been twice argued before us—shed any greater light on the problem. Therefore, I consider it appropriate to state my views at this time.

For all the sound and fury that the Roth test has generated, it has not been proved unsound, and I believe that we should try to live with it—at least until a more satisfactory definition is evolved. No government—be it federal, state, or local—should be forced to choose between repressing all material, including that within the realm of decency, and allowing unrestrained license to publish any material, no matter how vile. There must be a rule of reason in this as in other areas of the law and we have attempted in the Roth case to provide such a rule.

It is my belief that when the Court said in Roth that obscenity is to be defined by reference to "community standards," it meant community standards—not a national standard, as is sometimes argued. I believe that there is no provable "national standard" and perhaps there should be none. At all events, this Court has not been able to enunciate one, and it would be unreasonable to expect local courts to divine one. It is said that such a "community" approach may well result in material being proscribed as obscene in one community but not in another, and, in all probability, that is true. But communities throughout the Nation are in fact diverse, and it must be remembered that, in cases such as this one, the Court is confronted with the task of reconciling conflicting rights of the diverse communities within our society and of individuals.

We are told that only "hard-core pornography" should be denied the protection of the First Amendment. But who can define "hard-core pornography" with any greater clarity than "obscenity"? And even if we were to retreat to that position, we would soon be faced with the need

to define that term just as we now are faced with the need to define "obscenity." Meanwhile, those who profit from the commercial exploitation of obscenity would continue to ply their trade unmolested.

In my opinion, the use to which various materials are put—not just the words and pictures themselves—must be considered in determining whether or not the materials are obscene. A technical or legal treatise on pornography may well be inoffensive under most circumstances but, at the same time, "obscene" in the extreme when sold or displayed to children.[2]

Finally, material which is in fact obscene under the Roth test may be proscribed in a number of ways—for instance, by confiscation of the material or by prosecution of those who disseminate it—provided always that the proscription, whatever it may be, is imposed in accordance with constitutional standards. If the proceeding involved is criminal, there must be a right to a jury trial, a right to counsel, and all the other safeguards necessary to assure due process of law. If the proceeding is civil in nature, the constitutional requirements applicable in such a case must also be observed. There has been some tendency in dealing with this area of the law for enforcement agencies to do only that which is easy to do—for instance, to seize and destroy books with only a minimum of protection. As a result, courts are often presented with procedurally bad cases and, in dealing with them, appear to be acquiescing in the dissemination of obscenity. But if cases were well prepared and were conducted with the appropriate concern for constitutional safeguards, courts would not hesitate to enforce the laws against obscenity. Thus, enforcement agencies must realize that there is no royal road to enforcement; hard and conscientious work is required.

In light of the foregoing, I would reiterate my acceptance of the rule of the Roth case: Material is obscene and not constitutionally protected against regulation and proscription if "to the average person, applying contemporary community standards, the dominant theme of the material taken as a whole appeals to prurient interest." 354 U.S., at 489, 77 S. Ct., at 1311. I would commit the enforcement of this rule to the appropriate state and federal courts, and I would accept their judgments made pursuant to the Roth rule, limiting myself to a consideration only of whether there is sufficient evidence in the record upon which a finding of obscenity could be made. If there is no evidence in the record upon which such a finding could be made, obviously the material involved cannot be held obscene. Cf. *Thompson* v. *City of Louisville*, 362 U.S. 199, 80 S. Ct. 624, 4 L. Ed. 2d 654. But since a mere modicum of evidence may satisfy a "no evidence" standard, I am unwilling to give the important constitutional right of free expression such limited protection. However, protection of society's right to maintain its moral fiber and the effective administration of justice require that this Court not establish itself as an ultimate censor, in each case reading the entire record, viewing the

---

[1] *Roth* v. *United States*, 354 U.S. 476, 77 S. Ct. 1304, 1 L. Ed. 2d 1498.

[2] In the instant case, for example, the advertisements published to induce the public to view the motion picture provide some evidence of the film's dominant theme: "When all conventions explode * * * in the most daring love story ever filmed!" "As close to authentic amour as is possible on the screen." "The frankest love scenes yet seen on film." "Contains one of the longest and most sensuous love scenes to be seen in this country."

accused material, and making an independent *de novo* judgment on the question of obscenity. Therefore once a finding of obscenity has been made below under a proper application of the Roth test, I would apply a "sufficient evidence" standard of review—requiring something more than merely any evidence but something less than "substantial evidence on the record [including the allegedly obscene material] as a whole." Cf. *Universal Camera Corp.* v. *Labor Board*, 340 U.S. 474, 71 S. Ct. 456, 95 L. Ed. 456. This is the only reasonable way I can see to obviate the necessity of this Court's sitting as the Super Censor of all the obscenity purveyed throughout the Nation.

While in this case, I do not subscribe to some of the State's extravagant contentions, neither can I say that the courts below acted with intemperance or without sufficient evidence in finding the moving picture obscene within the meaning of the Roth test. Therefore, I would affirm the judgment.

Mr. Justice HARLAN, dissenting.

While agreeing with my Brother BRENNAN's opinion that the responsibilities of the Court in this area are no different from those which attend the adjudication of kindred constitutional questions, I have heretofore expressed the view that the States are constitutionally permitted greater latitude in determining what is bannable on the score of obscenity than is so with the Federal Government. See my opinion in *Roth* v. *United States*, 354 U.S. 476, 496, 77 S. Ct. 1304, 1315, 1 L. Ed. 2d 1498; cf. my opinion in *Manual Enterprises, Inc.* v. *Day*, 370 U.S. 478, 82 S. Ct. 1432, 8 L. Ed. 2d 639. While, as correctly said

in MR. JUSTICE BRENNAN's opinion, the Court has not accepted that view, I nonetheless feel free to adhere to it in this still developing aspect of constitutional law.

The more I see of these obscenity cases the more convinced I become that in permitting the States wide, but not federally unrestricted, scope in this field, while holding the Federal Government with a tight rein, lies the best promise for achieving a sensible accommodation between the public interest sought to be served by obscenity laws (cf. my dissenting opinion in *Bantam Books, Inc.* v. *Sullivan*, 372 U.S. 58, 76, 77, 83 S. Ct. 631, 642, 643, 9 L. Ed. 2d 584) and protection of genuine rights of free expression.

I experience no greater ease than do other members of the Court in attempting to verbalize generally the respective constitutional tests, for in truth the matter in the last analysis depends on how particular challenged material happens to strike the minds of jurors or judges and ultimately those of a majority of the members of this Court. The application of any general constitutional tests must thus necessarily be pricked out on a case-by-case basis, but as a point of departure I would apply to the Federal Government the Roth standards as amplified in my opinion in *Manual Enterprises*, supra. As to the States, I would make the federal test one of rationality. I would not prohibit them from banning any material which, taken as a whole, has been reasonably found in state judicial proceedings to treat with sex in a fundamentally offensive manner, under rationally established criteria for judging such material.

On this basis, having viewed the motion picture in question, I think the State acted within permissible limits in condemning the film and would affirm the judgment of the Ohio Supreme Court.

■ K. Gordon Murray Productions, Inc.
v.
William F. Floyd, *et al.*
No. 21584.

Supreme Court of Georgia.

April 7, 1962.

Rehearing Denied April 20, 1962.

Syllabus by the Court

1. Where the provisions, including remedies, in a city charter and ordinance refer only to exhibitors of motion pictures and require a permit to do so, and a distributor challenges their constitutionality and alleges they are preventing exhibitors from contracting to exhibit its pictures, thus damaging its business and it can not require the exhibitors to either violate or challenge such unconstitutional laws; grounds for relief in equity are alleged.

2. All speech and press that lie outside of an "abuse of that liberty" are protected by art. 1, sec. 1, par. 15 (Code Ann., § 2–115) of the State Constitution, and that protection is absolute and can not be abridged, curtailed, or restrained in any degree for any period of time no matter how short. But abuses of that liberty are outside the protection of the Constitution and may be suppressed, restrained, enjoined, or punished without violating the Constitution, provided constitutional means for so doing are employed. Such means must never violate in any degree the protected

rights. The charter and ordinance which provide for city permits as prerequisites to exhibiting any picture offend the Constitution and are void.

This case involves the censorship of motion pictures in the City of Atlanta. The petitioner, a corporation engaged in the licensing and distribution of such pictures, seeks to enjoin the censorship of a certain picture, alleging that it has customers who are exhibitors desiring to show the picture which is not obscene or immoral but when advised by the censor that she would not approve it and to show the film it must be approved by the board of censors, they refuse to contract for the picture because of the requirement of approval by the board of censors before it can be shown, and petitioner can not control their actions or cause them to attack the constitutionality of the censorship law and ordinance, and for this reason its business is being seriously impaired by such invalid law. The petitioner further alleges that the charter provision of the City of Atlanta (Ga. L. 1915, p. 480, at pp. 493 and 494) as therein set out to establish a Board of Motion Picture Censors attempts to grant unlimited and absolute discretion to the board and to the censor "the abuse of which would not authorize relief in a court of equity since there can be no abuse of absolute discretion," and it would be useless and futile to appeal from any decision of the censoring authority set-up since the law and ordinance adopted pursuant thereto are unconstitutional and void as hereinafter set forth. Thereafter it is alleged that motion pictures fall within the free speech and free press guaranty of the First and Fourteenth Amendments to the U.S. Constitution, and the provisions providing for prior restraint, that is, requiring the approval of the censorship board before showing any motion pictures violates the First and Fourteenth Amendments to the U.S. Constitution (Code §§ 1–801; 1–815) set forth in the petition in that there can be no infringement upon the constitutional requirement that no law can be made abridging freedom of speech or of the press; and it violates the Constitution of Georgia (Code Ann., § 2–115; Const. of 1945), art. 1, sec. 1, par. 15, by imposing a previous restraint upon the exhibition of motion pictures in direct contravention that "no law shall ever be passed to curtail, or restrain the liberty of speech or of the press." Thereafter it attacks the ordinance adopted pursuant to the charter portion above referred to for the same reasons and for the further reasons that (1) the charter fails to set up any standards but permits the Board of Censors to arbitrarily ban or permit the showing of any film for any reasons; (2) allows the board to act as judge and prosecutor; (3) fails to establish safeguards to preclude an entirely arbitrary judgment by the censor or board of censors; (4) violates procedural due process of law; and (5) discriminates against motion picture theatres in that it provides for censoring of motion pictures, plays, performances, pantomimes, songs or vaudeville presentations or other exhibitions in a motion picture theatre but excepts and excludes therefrom performances, plays, pantomimes, songs or vaudeville presentations in other buildings or business establishments, night clubs and opera in violation of the equal protection clause of the Federal Constitution (Code, § 1–815). The prayer is for process, rule nisi, service upon the Attorney General of Georgia, an injunction to prevent the defendants from interfering with the exhibition of the film, and for the portion of the city charter (Ga. L. 1915, p. 480 at pp. 493,

494) and the censorship ordinance adopted pursuant thereto, as more fully set out and attached to the petition, be declared illegal, unconstitutional, void and unenforceable; and for such other and further relief as the court may deem proper. Demurrers were filed and renewed to the petition as amended, and after consideration thereof, the lower court sustained the demurrers. The exception is to this judgment. The charter provisions and the ordinance adopted pursuant thereto are, in substance, that the City of Atlanta is authorized to regulate and to prevent the display of obscene or licentious pictures that may affect the peace, health, morals, and good order of the city by providing for a board of censorship, or by other means, and prohibits the "display of any picture unless the same shall have been approved by such board, and to empower such board to approve or disapprove or reject any picture or scene submitted * * * when, in the judgment of said board, the same would affect the peace, health, morals and good order of said city." The ordinance is completely in conformity with the above law and makes it "unlawful for any person to exhibit or cause to be exhibited within the city or within any other territory over which the city exercises police jurisdiction, any pictures or moving pictures unless the same has been approved by the censor or board of censors," and provides for fines and imprisonment for each violation of said ordinance.

Thomas E. Moran, Atlanta, for plaintiff in error.
J. C. Savage, Edwin L. Sterne, Robert F. Lyle, Atlanta, for defendant in error.

DUCKWORTH, Chief Justice.

[1–4] 1. Based upon Code § 37–120, and Mayor etc., of *Carrollton* v. *Chambers*, 215 Ga. 193, 109 S.E. 2d 755, and similar cases, all of which state the law that equity will not take cognizance of a plain legal right where an adequate and complete remedy is provided by law, counsel for the City contend that this petition shows no right to the equitable relief which it seeks. We reject this contention for two reasons, to wit: (1) the remedy provided in the ordinance is not even law if the petitioner's constitutional attack is sustained. *Dennison Manufacturing Co.* v. *Wright*, 156 Ga. 789, 120 S.E. 120; *Milam* v. *Adams*, 216 Ga. 440, 117 S.E. 2d 343; and (2) even if the ordinance is constitutional, the remedy which it affords, or any other remedy, is not adequate or available to this petitioner, since the ordinance applies only to exhibitors of pictures and not to distributors, and petitioner is a distributor only. The petition asserts that exhibitors in Atlanta have been valuable customers of the petitioner, and at least some of them now wish to contract for its picture but because of the censorship ordinance and statements of the censor that the picture in question, which petitioner alleges is not obscene, will not be approved, its potential customers refuse to contract with it, and in this way its business is being destroyed and petitioner can not require the exhibitors to resist or violate the ordinance or in any way obtain a court decision as to its constitutionality. In this situation its only adequate remedy is in equity, and it is entitled to maintain this action for that purpose. *Great Atlantic & Pacific Tea Co.* v. *City of Columbus*, 189 Ga. 458, 6 S.E. 2d 320; *City of Albany* v. *Lippitt*, 191 Ga. 756, 13 S.E. 2d 807; *City of Atlanta* v. *Universal Film Exchanges, Inc.*,

201 Ga. 463, 39 S.E. 2d 882; *Moultrie Milk Shed, Inc.* v. *City of Cairo*, 206 Ga. 348, 57 S.E. 2d 199.

[5–7] 2. If the attack upon the portion of the city charter (Ga. L. 1915, p. 480, at pp. 493, 494) which authorizes the city to adopt the censorship ordinance, and upon the ordinance adopted pursuant thereto, which contends that in providing for examination of all motion pictures by the censorship board and forbidding the showing of any picture without first obtaining a permit from the city, thereby imposing a prior restraint of speech in violation of the First Amendment (Code § 1–801) and the Fourteenth Amendment (Code § 1–815) of the U.S. Constitution and also Code Ann., § 2–115 of the State Constitution (Const. of 1945), is sustained as to either Constitution, the charter provision as well as the ordinance are void, and it was error to dismiss the petition on demurrer. This would render it unnecessary to rule upon the other grounds of attack. Motion pictures are within the First and Fourteenth Amendments' basic protection. *Joseph Burstyn, Inc.* v. *Wilson*, 343 U.S. 495, 72 S. Ct. 777, 96 L. Ed. 1098. By that decision motion pictures are afforded the full protection constitutionally guaranteed to all speech or press. That court noted no factors peculiar to motion pictures that would authorize abridgment by censure or otherwise which was interdicted by the Constitution. The relevant portion of the First Amendment is as follows: "Congress shall make no law * * * abridging the freedom of speech, or of the press." If sound rules of construction are adhered to, this sentence of the Constitution can not be listed from the whole Constitution and construed without consideration of the entire document including the Preamble. If it could be isolated and construed alone, its absolute phrasing would forbid any restraint whatever. But in construing it the Supreme Court should keep in mind such declarations of the purpose of the Constitution found in the Preamble as "establish Justice, insure domestic Tranquillity," and "secure the Blessings of Liberty to ourselves and our Posterity." Any proper construction of the First Amendment must harmonize with these expressed purposes. In *Gompers* v. *Bucks Stove & Range Co.*, 221 U.S. 418, 31 S. Ct. 492, 55 L. Ed. 797, it is said: "An order of a court of equity, restraining defendants from boycotting complainant by publishing statements that complainant was guilty of unfair trade, does not amount to an unconstitutional abridgment of free speech; the question of the validity of the order involves only the power of the court to enjoin the boycott. * * * Where conditions exist that justify the enjoining of the boycott, the publication and use of letters, circulars and printed matter, may constitute the means of unlawfully continuing the boycott and amount to a violation of the order of injunction." Again in *Schenck* v. *United States*, 249 U.S. 47, at page 52, 39 S. Ct. 247, page 249, 63 L. Ed. 470, it is said: "The most stringent protection of free speech would not protect a man in falsely shouting fire in a theatre and causing panic. It does not even protect a man from an injunction against uttering words that may have all the effect of force." And in *Near* v. *Minnesota*, 283 U.S. 697, at page 715 and 716, 51 S. Ct. 625, at p. 631, 75 L. Ed. 1357, we find the following: "The objection has also been made that the principle as to immunity from previous restraint is stated too broadly, if every such restraint is deemed to be prohibited. That is undoubtedly true; the protection even as to previous restraint is not

absolutely unlimited. * * * On similar grounds, the primary requirements of decency may be enforced against obscene publications. The security of the community life may be protected against incitements to acts of violence and the overthrow by force of orderly government. The constitutional guaranty of free speech does not 'protect a man from an injunction against uttering words that may have all the effect of force.'" We will quote from one more Supreme Court decision which further shows that prior restraint of abuses of the freedom of speech is sanctioned. In *Roth* v. *United States*, 354 U.S. 476(3), 77 S. Ct. 1304, 1 L. Ed. 2d 1498, it is stated that: "Obscenity is not within the area of constitutionally protected freedom of speech or press—either (1) under the First Amendment, as to the Federal Government, or (2) under the Due Process Clause of the Fourteenth Amendment, as to the States." And again at page 483, 77 S. Ct. at page 1308 the opinion states: "In light of this history, it is apparent that the unconditional phrasing of the First Amendment was not intended to protect every utterance. This phrasing did not prevent this Court from concluding that libelous utterances are not within the area of constitutionally protected speech. *Beauharnais* v. *People of State of Illinois*, 343 U.S. 250, 266, 72 S. Ct. 725, 735, 96 L. Ed. 919." There is nothing in the phrasing of the First Amendment, if standing alone, that would have justified the foregoing decisions which clearly sanction prior restraint of abuses which is an abridgment. But when taken as it must be as an harmonious part of the entire Constitution, and in light of history, a construction is demanded that the First Amendment, by the words "speech" and "press," means only speech and press outside of infringement of the rights of others.

[8] The only kind of speech that any of the foregoing decisions say may be subjected to prior restraint is malevolent, obscene or an abuse of the freedom, and this is allowed because such speech is not protected. On May 26, 1952, in *Joseph Burstyn, Inc.* v. *Wilson*, 343 U.S. 495, supra, at page 503, 72 S. Ct. at page 781, Mr. Justice Clark wrote: "The statute involved here does not seek to punish, as a past offense, speech or writing falling within the permissible scope of subsequent punishment. On the contrary, New York requires that *permission to communicate ideas be obtained in advance from state officials who judge the content of the words and pictures sought to be communicated*. This Court recognized many years ago that such a *previous restraint is a form of infringement* upon freedom of expression *to be especially condemned*." [italics ours] But on January 23, 1961, in the case of *Times Film Corp.* v. *Chicago*, 365 U.S. 43, 81 S. Ct. 391, 5 L. Ed. 2d 403, that court in another opinion written by Mr. Justice Clark held that a law which requires submission of all motion pictures for examination or censorship prior to their public exhibition "is not void on its face as violative of the First and Fourteenth Amendments." Therefore, we must follow this last pronouncement and ignore many previous contrary decisions and hold that the attack upon the charter and ordinance upon the ground that in forbidding the showing of any picture without its having been approved by the censor offends the United States Constitution, is without merit.

[9] We now look to our State Constitution, art. 1, sec. 1, par. 15 (Code Ann., § 2–115; Const. of 1945), to see if

the laws here under attack offend it by providing a prior restraint. While the following portion of the above code section, "No law shall ever be passed to curtail, or restrain the liberty of speech, or of the press; any person may speak, write and publish his sentiments, on all subjects" is absolute in phraseology, and when isolated from all other provisions of the same Constitution would absolutely prohibit any restraint of speech or press regardless of its violation of the constitutional rights of others, including the government. But all sound rules of construction forbid such isolation and demand that it be construed in connection with the entire Constitution, and particularly the concluding words of the same paragraph which are, "being responsible for the abuse of that liberty," and the second paragraph (Code Ann., § 2–102; Const. of 1945), which is: "Protection to person and property is the paramount duty of government, and shall be impartial and complete." When thus construed it is absolute as to what it protects, but it does not protect an "abuse of that liberty." Any invasion of the constitutional rights of others or the government would be an "abuse of that liberty," and is not constitutionally protected. The decisions of this court clearly show that an "abuse of that liberty" as expressed in our Constitution does not come within the speech or press which is protected. In *Fitts* v. *City of Atlanta*, 121 Ga. 567, 49 S.E. 793, 67 L.R.A. 803, it was held that a municipality could prevent holding a meeting at which speaking was intended, in the public streets without a city permit. In *McGill* v. *The State of Georgia*, by Davis, 209 Ga. 500, 74 S.E. 2d 78, which upheld the absolute right of the press to publish matters that violated no constitutional rights of others, this court held that the Constitution did not protect abuses of the liberty therein guaranteed. In *Ellis* v. *Parks*, 212 Ga. 540, 93 S.E. 2d 708, this court held that although picketing was a form of speech, protected by the Constitution, it could be enjoined when, as there, its purpose was to injure the employer and to aid an unlawful strike. And in *Atlanta Newspapers, Inc.* v. *Grimes*, 216 Ga. 74, 114 S.E. 2d 421, this court held that the free speech clauses of the State and Federal Constitutions did not prohibit an order of a superior court judge forbidding taking pictures and making recordings within a defined area during the progress of the trial of a criminal case.

As to the constitutional right to use private property for malevolent purposes this court held in *Hornsby* v. *Smith*, 191 Ga. 491, 13 S.E. 2d 20, 133 A.L.R. 684, that the owner of land could not erect a fence thereon which injured his neighbor for no useful purpose, but solely to hurt his neighbor. The Supreme Court held in *American Bank & Trust Co.* v. *Federal Bank*, 256 U.S. 350, 41 S. Ct. 499, 65 L. Ed. 983, that even though the holder of a properly endorsed check had the right to present it to the bank upon which it was drawn for payment, yet where, as there, such holder, the National Bank, held checks until they accumulated to a total that would, because of want of ready cash, embarrass the State bank upon which they were drawn, solely for the malevolent purpose of hurting the State bank, an injunction would lie to prevent such malicious conduct.

[10] Thus we have an abundance of decided cases that sanction restraint of abuses of speech and property. In none of them is the constitutionality protected speech or press held subject to curtailment, restraint or abridgment.

Only the abuses of the liberty are held subject to restraint and that is justifiable only because they enjoy no protection under the Constitution. Since we rule that speech or press that is not an abuse of the liberty under Code Ann., § 2–115, is protected by that paragraph of the State Constitution, it follows, and we so rule, that as to it all interference therewith is absolutely interdicted by the Constitution. This means that no interference, no matter for how short a time nor the smallness of degree, can be tolerated.

[11, 12] The rulings hereinbefore made, together with the facts of this case confronts this court with the solemn and even awesome duty of deciding whether or not government can constitutionally invade the protected right for one second in any conceivable manner as a means of discovering and suppressing such speech or press as is an "abuse of that liberty" and hence is unprotected and has no immunity. This question strikes at the very heart of our liberties. Proper performance of the paramount duty of government to furnish impartial and complete protection of person and property as commanded by the Constitution demands that rights in both categories be energetically, impartially and completely protected. No informed American would wish to have a controlled press where an agent of the government is permitted to look over the shoulder of the publisher and dictate what shall be printed. Indeed, intrusion even for the shortest time and in the most superficial manner would be an invasion of his constitutionally protected liberty. But this in no remote degree shields any "abuse of that liberty" from the reach of any process devised by government to suppress or punish such abuses when done without the slightest infringement of the constitutionally protected speech or press. This does not mean that the house may be burned in order to get the rats out of it.

It follows that the charter and ordinance provision, requiring inspection of the protected as well as the unprotected pictures, and also requiring a permit from the city authorities before any picture can be exhibited in the theatre, violate the State Constitution (Code Ann., § 2–115) and are void. The words of the Constitution "No law shall ever be passed to curtail, or restrain" is irreconcilable with any law, including a city ordinance that does curtail or restrain. The far reaching effect of this decision does not escape our notice or concern. As individual citizens we hate to see the youth of this State, who will govern the State in the future, subjected to all the evil influence that obscene pictures might exert upon them. But as trusted judges we have no alternative to saying, thus sayeth the Constitution, and we cheerfully obey. It would seem that legislative wisdom could devise a law containing no censorship that would conform to the Constitution as we have construed it and at the same time afford a large degree of protection against obscene pictures. A severe penalty for exhibiting an obscene picture with a provision that if it had been voluntarily submitted to a board created by the law for making such voluntary inspections, and had been judged not to be obscene by that board the courts should give serious consideration of this demonstrated lack of intent when imposing sentence, might be within the bounds of constitutionally permissible legislation.

The petition alleged grounds for the injunctive relief,

and it was error to sustain the demurrer to the petition as amended.

Judgment reversed.

All the Justices concur except CANDLER, J., who dissents.

MOBLEY and QUILLIAN, JJ., concur specially.

MOBLEY, Justice (concurring in the judgment).

I concur in the judgment of the court but not for the reason given in the majority opinion. In *Chaplinsky* v. *New Hampshire,* 315 U.S. 568, 571–572, 62 S. Ct. 766, 769, 86 L. Ed. 1031 the court held that "there are certain well-defined and narrowly limited classes of speech, the prevention and punishment of which has never been thought to raise any Constitutional problem. These include the lewd and obscene, the profane, the libelous, and the insulting or 'fighting' words—those which by their very utterance inflict injury or tend to incite an immediate breach of the peace." The enumerated classes of speech are not within the area of constitutionally protected speech or press. *Roth* v. *United States,* 354 U.S. 476, 485, 77 S. Ct. 1304, 1 L. Ed. 2d 1498. It is not only the privilege but the duty of the City of Atlanta to protect its people against the dangers of obscenity in the public exhibition of motion pictures and in other classes of speech which are not protected. I do not agree that regardless of the extent of such evil, previous restraint cannot be justified. As pointed out in *Times Film Corp.* v. *City of Chicago,* 365 U.S. 43, 49–50, 81 S. Ct. 391, 5 L. Ed. 403, the Supreme Court of the United States recognized in *Joseph Burstyn, Inc.* v. *Wilson,* 343 U.S. 495, 72 S. Ct. 777, 96 L. Ed. 1098 that " 'capacity for evil * * * may be relevant in determining the permissible scope of community control,' 343 U.S. at page 502, 72 S. Ct. at page 780, and that motion pictures were not 'necessarily subject to the precise rules governing any other particular method of expression. Each method,' we said, 'tends to present its own peculiar problems.' At page 503, 343 U.S., at page 781 of 72 S. Ct. Certainly petitioner's broadside attack does not warrant, nor could it justify on the record here, our saying that—aside from any consideration of the other 'exceptional cases' mentioned in our decisions—the State is stripped of all constitutional power to prevent, in the most effective fashion, the utterance of this class of speech."

It is in my opinion a reasonable exercise of the police power of the state to require that motion pictures be submitted to a board of censors prior to their showing so that those which are obscene or otherwise within that class of speech not protected by the Constitution may be barred from showing. However, the charter amendment, Ga. L. 1915, p. 493 and the ordinances adopted pursuant thereto

go beyond this, as the Board of Censors is empowered to prohibit the display of any picture without a permit from that Board and they may reject any picture or scene which would in their judgment affect the peace, health, morals and good order of the city. Under the charter amendment, the Board is authorized to reject not just those pictures which "adversely" affect the peace, health, etc. of the people, but also those which might have the beneficial effect. They may not constitutionally prohibit the showing of any pictures except those which come within one of the classes of speech not within the protection of the free speech provision of the Constitution. Furthermore, the General Assembly has not prescribed clear and definite procedure to guide the action of the city in the performance of the power granted as is required, to meet the due process clauses of the federal and state Constitutions. See *City of Atlanta* v. *Southern Ry. Co.,* 213 Ga. 736, 738, 101 S.E. 2d 707. I am authorized to state that QUILLIAN, Justice, concurs in this opinion.

CANDLER, Justice (dissenting).

Freedom of speech is not an absolute right under the Constitution of this State or under the Constitution of the United States. *Atlanta Newspapers, Inc.* v. *Grimes,* 216 Ga. 74, 114 S.E. 2d 421; *Times Film Corporation* v. *City of Chicago,* 365 U.S. 43, 81 S. Ct. 391, 5 L. Ed. 2d 403. Freedom of speech as guaranteed both by the Constitution of this State and of the United States does not preclude a municipality from protecting its people against the dangers resulting from the public display of obscene or licentious pictures or other pictures which may adversely affect the peace, health, morals, and good order of such municipality; and to prevent the evil resulting therefrom prior restraint is permissible. *Near* v. *Minnesota,* 283 U.S. 697, 715, 51 S. Ct. 625, 75 L. Ed. 1357; *Chaplinsky* v. *New Hampshire,* 315 U.S. 568, 571, 572, 62 S. Ct. 766, 86 L. Ed. 1031, 1035; *Roth* v. *United States,* 354 U.S. 476, 77 S. Ct. 1304, 1 L. Ed. 2d 1498. By the 1915 censorship act the legislature conferred police power on the City of Atlanta to regulate by ordinance the places where moving pictures are shown and the right to prohibit the display of obscene or licentious pictures or other pictures which might adversely affect the peace, health, morals, and good order of the city, and it is universally conceded that police power includes everything essential to public safety, health and morals. As authority for this statement, see *Lawton* v. *Steele,* 152 U.S. 133, 14 S. Ct. 499, 38 L. Ed. 385; *Morris* v. *City of Columbus,* 102 Ga. 792, 30 S.E. 850, 42 L.R.A. 175. I do not consider any other attack which the petitioner makes on the 1915 amendment to the city's charter or the ordinance adopted pursuant thereto as being meritorious. I would affirm the judgment sustaining a general demurrer to the petition.

■ State of New Jersey, *Plaintiff,*

v.

Hudson County News Company, a corporation, *Defendant.*
Indictments Nos. 970–59, 971–59.

Essex County Court Law Division, New Jersey.

June 26, 1962.

Maurice McKeown, Assistant Prosecutor, for plaintiff
(*Brendan T. Byrne,* County Prosecutor of Essex County,
attorney).

Roger H. McGlynn, Newark, for defendant (*McGlynn,
Stein & McGlynn,* Newark, attorneys).

MATTHEWS, J.C.C.

Defendant Hudson County News Company, a corporation of this State, was charged in two indictments returned
by the grand jurors of Essex County that it did, without
just cause, sell and distribute certain obscene and indecent
books and publications in violation of N.J.S. 2A:115–2,
N.J.S.A. The charges contained in the indictments were
tried before me without a jury at the request of the
corporate defendant and with the consent of the State. A
companion indictment, involving one Milton Medwin,
which charged that he did, without just cause, possess with
intent to utter and expose to view of others, certain obscene and indecent books in violation of N.J.S. 2A: 115–2,
N.J.S.A., was not moved for trial with the consent of that
defendant and the State.

Defendant is a wholesale distributor of magazines and
paper-covered books. In the course of its operations, it
services a large portion of the northern part of the State,
including Essex County. Among the many publications
handled by defendant in the course of its business are some
48 magazines,[1] the distribution of which constitutes the

basis for the charges contained in the indictments presently under consideration. Defendant does not dispute that
it handled and distributed the magazines in question. It
contends that its distribution of the publications which it
concedes it has effected, does not violate the provisions of
N.J.S. 2A:115–2, N.J.S.A., since none of the publications
in question is obscene within the meaning of that statute.
In the alternative, it is defendant's contention, should this
court determine all or any of the publications to be obscene, the State has failed to establish beyond a reasonable
doubt that it distributed any of such publications with the
knowledge that the contents thereof were obscene within
the meaning of N.J.S. 2A:115–2, N.J.S.A.

Prior to trial, defendants moved to dismiss the present
indictments on constitutional grounds. A determination by
the trial court that the indictments should proceed to trial
was affirmed by the Supreme Court in *State* v. *Hudson
County News Co.,* 35 N.J. 284, 173 A. 2d 20 (1961). In
its opinion, the court upheld the validity of N.J.S.
2A:115–2, N.J.S.A., with respect to the challenges made
by defendant, on appeal, concerning the constitutionality
of that statute. It was the determination of the Supreme
Court that N.J.S. 2A:115–2, N.J.S.A., required the State
to show that a defendant charged with a violation of its
provisions acted with knowledge of the character or content of the materials claimed to be obscene. The court also
determined that the phrase "without just cause" as contained in the statute was not violative of due process requirements in that it was too vague.

In its appeal to the Supreme Court, defendant did not

---

[1] Action for Men, October 1959, Vol. 3, No. 6; Adventure,
December 1959, Vol. 136, No. 2; Adventures For Men, October
1959, Vol. 5, No. 4; Battle Cry, October 1959, Vol. 4, No. 5;
Battlefield, November 1959, Vol. 3, No. 5; Bold, December
1959, Vol. 10, No. 6; Cavalcade, November 1959, Vol. 2, No. 7;
Challenge for Men, October 1959, Vol. 5, No. 7; Champion,
October 1959, Vol. 1, No. 5; Champion, November 1959, Vol.
3, No. 6; Chicks and Chuckles, December 1959, Vol. 5, No. 6;
Danger, September 1959, Vol. 1, No. 4; Expose For Men, Oc-
tober 1959, Vol. 3, No. 3; Expose Detective, December 1959,
Vol. 3, No. 2; For Men Only, November 1959, Vol. 6, No. 11;
Glamorgirl Photography, December 1959, No. 2; Guy-Men's
True Adventures, September 1959, Vol. 1, No. 5; Hep, November
1959, Vol. 5, No. 11; Inside Story, November 1959, Vol. 6, No.
1; Jive, November 1959, Vol. 8, No. 11; Ken For Men, November 1959, Vol. 4, No. 6; Male, October 1959, Vol. 9, No. 10;
Male, November 1959, Vol. 9, No. 11; Man's Point of View,
December 1959, Vol. 9, No. 9; Man's Magazine, November
1959, Vol. 7, No. 11; Man's Adventure, November 1959,

Vol. 2, No. 11; Man's Conquest, November 1959, Vol. 5,
No. 4; Man's Illustrated, December 1959, Vol. 5, No. 5;
Man's World, December 1959, Vol. 5 No. 6; Man's Western,
Aug.-Sept. 1959, Vol. 1, No. 1; Men, October 1959, Vol. 8,
No. 10; Men In Adventure, November 1959, Vol. 1, No. 4;
Mr., December 1959, Vol. 4, No. 2; Nugget, December 1959,
Vol. 4, No. 6; Photo Life, December 1959, Vol. 6, No. 8; Play,
December 1959-January 1960, Vol. 1, No. 5; Real, December
1959, Vol. 12, No. 2; Real Men, October 1959, Vol. 5, No. 4;
Secret Life Confessions, December 1959, Vol. 1, No. 1; Stag,
November 1959, Vol. 10, No. 11; TV Girls and Gags, November
1959, Vol. 6, No. 6; The Dude, November 1959, Vol. 4, No. 2;
Thrilling Confessions, November 1959, Vol. 1, No. 1; True
Adventures, December 1959, Vol. 29, No. 1; Untamed, Novem-
ber 1959, Vol. 1, No. 6; Valor (For Men), August 1959, Vol. 3,
No. 2; Valor (For Men), December 1959, Vol. 3, No. 4; Wild-
cat Adventures, January 1960, Vol. 1, No. 4.

deal, in any manner, with the definitions of obscenity nor the standards to be applied in determining whether materials challenged come within the statutory prohibition. The question has been raised here for the first time. Defendant did not question, nor does it question here in anywise, the constitutional sufficiency under our State Constitution or under the Federal Constitution of the statutory provisions here involved that it shall be criminal to knowingly sell (or possess with intent to sell) obscene material.

Defendant argues that the concept of obscenity as embraced by our statute must conform to the holding of the Supreme Court of the United States in *Roth* v. *United States*, 354 U.S. 476, 77 S. Ct. 1304, 1 L. Ed. 2d 1498 (1957). Under the holding of the Roth case, defendant contends that the materials upon which the charges in the instant indictments are based cannot be regarded as being obscene.

In Roth the Supreme Court of the United States decided that obscenity is not within the area of constitutionally protected speech or press. This holding was based upon the conclusion that obscenity is no essential part of any exposition of ideas, and is of such slight social value as a step to truth that any benefit that might be derived from it is clearly outweighed by the social interest in order and morality. (354 U.S., at p. 485, 77 S. Ct. 1309.) The Supreme Court in its majority opinion defined obscenity, such as is unprotected by the Constitution, as material which deals with sex in a manner appealing to prurient interest (354 U.S., at p. 487, 77 S. Ct. at p. 1310), and further, "whether to the average person, applying contemporary community standards, the dominant theme of the material taken as a whole appeals to prurient interest." In a footnote "prurient interest" was defined as: "Itching; longing; uneasy with desire or longing; of persons, having itching, morbid, or lascivious longings; of desire, curiosity, or propensity, lewd * * *." (354 U.S., at p. 487, note 20, 77 S. Ct. at p. 1310.) The court stated that it could perceive no significant difference between the meaning of obscenity developed in the case law and the definition contained in the A.L.I. Model Penal Code § 207.10 (2) (Tent. Draft No. 6, 1957). While this observation of the court has been questioned by writers in the field, see, e.g., Lockhart & McClure, "Censorship of Obscenity: The Developing Constitutional Standards," 45 Minn. L. Rev. 5, 56 (Nov. 1960), it is clear that the court intended to cite the A.L.I. definition with approval.

The decision in Roth also involved a decision in the case of *Alberts* v. *State of California*. Roth involved the application of the federal obscenity statute, 18 U.S.C.A., § 1461, and Alberts involved the California obscenity law, West's Penal Code Ann. 1955, § 311. The opinion which upheld convictions in the respective courts below embraced both decisions. The court took the opportunity, under these circumstances, to dispel any doubt as to whether the constitutional standards applicable to the several states with regard to their power to punish speech and press offensive to decency and morality, differed in any degree from those imposed upon the Federal Government. In this connection it rejected the argument of the appellant Roth that the federal obscenity statute unconstitutionally encroached upon the power reserved by the Ninth and Tenth Amendments to the states and to the people to punish speech and press offensive to decency and morality, and

similarly rejected the argument of the State of California in Alberts that there is greater latitude for state action under the Fourteenth Amendment than is allowed to Congress by the language of the First Amendment to punish such speech and press; the basis for rejecting both arguments was the holding of the court that obscenity is not an expression protected by the First Amendment (354 U.S. 492, 77 S. Ct. 1313).

While it may seem that the definition of constitutionally unprotected obscenity as set forth in the Roth-Alberts opinion has broad boundaries, a careful reading of the opinion at once indicates that such is not the case; the warning by the court concerning the freedoms of speech and press guaranteed under the Constitution indicates quite clearly how narrow the boundaries of that definition are:

"The fundamental freedoms of speech and press have contributed greatly to the development and well-being of our free society and are indispensable to its continued growth. Ceaseless vigilance is the watchword to prevent their erosion by Congress or by the States. The door barring federal and state intrusion into this area cannot be left ajar; it must be kept tightly closed and opened only the slightest crack necessary to prevent encroachment upon more important interests. It is therefore vital that the standards for judging obscenity safeguard the protection of freedom of speech and press for material which does not treat sex in a manner appealing to prurient interest." (354 U.S., at p. 488, 77 S. Ct. at p. 1311)

Of equal significance is the observation of the court that sex and obscenity are not synonymous:

*"However, sex and obscenity are not synonymous. Obscene material is material which deals with sex in a manner appealing to prurient interest. The portrayal of sex, e.g., in art, literature and scientific works, is not itself sufficient reason to deny material the constitutional protection of freedom of speech and press. Sex, a great and mysterious motive force in human life, has indisputably been a subject of absorbing interest to mankind through the ages; it is one of the vital problems of human interest and public concern. * * *"* (354 U.S., at p. 487, 77 S. Ct. at p. 1310)

Cf. *Times Film Corp.* v. *City of Chicago*, 355 U.S. 35, 78 S. Ct. 115, 2 L. Ed. 2d 72 (1957); *Mounce* v. *United States*, 355 U.S. 180, 78 S. Ct. 267, 2 L. Ed. 2d 187 (1957); *One, Inc.* v. *Oleson*, 355 U.S. 371, 78 S. Ct. 364, 2 L. Ed. 2d 352 (1958); *Sunshine Book Co.* v. *Summerfield*, 355 U.S. 372, 78 S. Ct. 365, 2 L. Ed. 2d 352 (1958); *Kingsley International Pictures* v. *Regents of the Univ. of New York*, 360 U.S. 684, 79 S. Ct. 1362, 3 L. Ed. 2d 1512 (1959); *Smith* v. *People of the State of California*, 361 U.S. 147, 80 S. Ct. 215, 4 L. Ed. 2d 205 (1959).

In *State* v. *Hudson County News Co.*, supra, Justice Jacobs in his opinion for the court mentioned the imprecise nature of the concept of obscenity in the law. On several occasions, our courts have dealt with violations of the obscenity law, and while each opinion rendered exhibits difficulty in expressing the obscenity concept, in no instance has that statute been questioned as to its constitutional validity. See e.g., *State* v. *Kohler*, 40 N.J. Super.

600, 123 A. 2d 881 (App. Div. 1956), certif. den. 22 N.J. 225, 125 A. 2d 439 (1956); *State* v. *Weitershausen*, 11 N.J. Super. 487, 78 A. 2d 595 (App. Div. 1951), certif. den. 7 N.J. 79, 80 A. 2d 495 (1951); cf. *Adams Newark Theatre Co.* v. *City of Newark*, 22 N.J. 472, 126 A. 2d 340 (1956), affirmed 354 U.S. 931, 77 S. Ct. 1395, 1 L. Ed. 2d 1533 (1957); *Adams Theatre Co.* v. *Keenan*, 12 N.J. 267, 96 A. 2d 519 (1953); *Bantam Books, Inc.* v. *Melko*, 25 N.J. Super. 292, 96 A. 2d 47 (Ch. Div. 1953), modified 14 N.J. 524, 103 A. 2d 256 (1954).

In *Adams Theatre Co.* v. *Keenan*, 12 N.J. 267, 96 A. 2d 519 (1953), our Supreme Court noted that by universal agreement one of the narrowly limited classes of speech which is not given the protection of the First Amendment is speech which is outrightly lewd and indecent, and set forth a test for such lewd and indecent expression, borrowed from *People* v. *Wendling*, 258 N.Y. 451, 180 N.E. 169, 81 A.L.R. 799 (Ct. App. 1932), to the effect that "[T]he question is whether the dominant note of the presentation is erotic allurement 'tending to excite lustful and lecherous desire,' dirt for dirt's sake only, smut and inartistic filth, with no evident purpose but 'to counsel or invite to vice or voluptuousness.'" (12 N.J., at p. 273, 96 A. 2d at p. 521.) The Adams Theatre case was cited with approval in a footnote to the Roth-Alberts decision. (354 U.S., at p. 489, 77 S. Ct. at p. 1311.)

[1–4] The net result of the decisions referred to is to establish that those matters which are deemed to be obscene as a matter of law are not entitled to constitutional protection, and, consequently, the Federal Government and the several states may properly enact legislation to regulate and punish the publication and dissemination of such material; that the existence of the power to prevent the sale or distribution of obscene matter does not mean that there can be no constitutional barrier to any form of practical exercise of that power. Further, that in determining whether materials are legally obscene, the test to be applied is whether to the average person, applying contemporary community standards, the dominant theme of the material, taken as a whole, appeals to the prurient interests; and finally that such test must be applied to the materials themselves, and not by measuring the effect that the materials may have on any given person or group of persons.

Abstractly, it would appear not difficult to determine, by applying contemporary community standards, whether given materials predominantly by their theme, taken as a whole, appeal to the prurient interest of the average person. When the test is viewed, however, in light of the constitutional guarantee of freedom of speech and expression, the task becomes formidable and, it is suggested, without some further refinement, seemingly impossible of application.

[5] The difficulty in applying the obscenity test arises because of the conflict which actually exists between the role that the law can assume in regulating and controlling that which is obscene as a matter of law, and the demands which are made of the law by various segments of the general public, that it assume a greater role in such regulation and control. Thus, the law which is traditionally preoccupied with our constitutional guarantees of freedom of expression, necessarily must attempt to delineate, as clearly as possible, those areas of expression which cannot be considered to come within the protection of the Constitution. In approaching this task the law, accustomed to enforcing

standards of overt behavior or social conduct of individuals, is in the unaccustomed position of attempting to evaluate and control, in effect, individual thinking. Inevitably, in these attempts, the law exhibits preoccupation with concepts appropriate to the regulation of behavior or conduct, such as the effect individual expression may have on the average man.[2] It is this latter preoccupation to which there is an appeal by those members of society who would seek to have the law assume a greater role in regulating, and perhaps punishing, the expressions of individuals which are subjectively regarded as being obscene. In my opinion, the law cannot, under standards now existing, broaden its area of jurisdiction with respect to the regulation and punishment of expression to that which may be regarded as being obscene by subjective standards.

[6, 7] The concept of obscenity, as a general proposition, is purely subjective. That which may appeal to the prurient interest of one may well only titillate or appear to be coarse to another. To a large degree, that which is to be viewed as being obscene is measured by the interior morality of the viewer, and any effort on the part of civil law to control or punish such purely subjective or interior behavior must be regarded as improper. Clearly, the law cannot establish a standard under which it could hope to wipe out all occasions under which individuals might be excited to impure or immoral thoughts; such a task would not only be impossible of achievement but also completely beyond its role. Control or censorship of the expression of ideas must be literally juridical. When it can be shown that literature, speech or entertainment is socially harmful, the government may properly regulate and punish; but government must be prudent and must exercise caution in its method of operation in these areas, lest it become in its effort to control, oppressive to the inalienable right of each man to self-expression and self-determination. The law, unquestionably, can punish any act which tends to corrupt public moral standards, and all acts which have been, under proper standards, ordained to be antisocial, but it cannot, and should not, under any guise, attempt to legis-

---

[2] Recognition of this dilemma may be seen in Chief Justice Warren's concurring opinion in Roth-Alberts, 354 U.S., at pp. 494, 495, 77 S. Ct. at p. 1314:

"The line dividing the salacious or pornographic from literature or science is not straight and unwavering. Present laws depend largely upon the effect that the materials may have upon those who receive them. It is manifest that the same object may have a different impact, varying according to the part of the community it reached. But there is more to these cases. It is not the book that is on trial; it is a person. The conduct of the defendant is the central issue, not the obscenity of a book or picture. The nature of the materials is, of course, relevant as an attribute of the defendant's conduct, but the materials are thus placed in context from which they draw color and character. A wholly different result might be reached in a different setting."

An interesting alternative has been suggested by Messrs. Lockhart and McClure in 45 Minn. L. Rev. 5, 77, which they term "variable obscenity." Under this view a material is never inherently obscene; instead its obscenity varies with the circumstances of its dissemination. Basically this suggestion is a further development of alternative (1), "Pandering to Interest in Obscenity," proposed by the A.L.I. in section 207.10 of the tentative draft (No. 6) of the Model Penal Code. The concept is also implicit in the portion of Chief Justice Warren's opinion just quoted. Such an approach to the obscenity problem, I believe, is more in accord with the proper role that the law should assume, since it is human conduct that is involved in this approach. Our present statute does not permit such construction.

late or regulate interior morality. The area embracing the thoughts and desires of each individual is properly in the realm of the family, the schools, the churches, and the psychiatrists. In a pluralistic society such as ours, it behooves government to maintain a minimum of social morality, or, necessarily, the imposition of the moral standards of one group upon another must result in some curtailment of the free exercise of the standards of the group imposed upon. History has shown us that social morality is seldom encouraged by a strong police arm. Certainly, this is true when one considers the social standards of this generation with regard to sexual morality. How can the law, even if it is conceded that it must seek to maintain moral standards, make demands upon the average person beyond the level of sexual morality which he has learned from his home, church and school? In these observations, the moralists themselves are not in disagreement.[3]

Of course, it cannot be contended that complete objectivity must be achieved in order to apply a constitutionally acceptable test in determining whether a given work is obscene. The test enunciated in Roth-Alberts certainly belies any such utopian achievement; that portion of the test that applies to contemporary community standards must of necessity require certain subjective value judgments. It is clear, however, that the Supreme Court did not intend that the community standard to be used was to be parochial. In view of its determination that the inhibition of the First Amendment applies with equal force to the Federal Government and the several states, the court has implicitly indicated that the contemporary community standard to be applied is that of the national community and not the standard of any individual city, county, or state.

[8] It is my conclusion that N.J.S. 2A:115–2, N.J.S.A., the statute here involved, must be interpreted to include within its prohibitions only those materials which may be regarded as obscene under a reasonably objective standard which has the widest possible acceptance and which, therefore, probably will most proximately reflect a national contemporary community standard. My study of the field and research of the authorities indicate that such a standard can embrace hard core obscenity or pornography and no more.

In the preface to their book, Pornography And The Law, Eberhard and Phyllis Kronhausen point out that their experience has shown there is confusion as to the meaning and usage, even under the law, of certain words crucial to a clear resolution of the legal concept of obscenity. It is one of the purposes of their book to differentiate between two classes of expression which they have defined as erotic realism and hard core obscenity or pornography. In writing of the two terms, the authors compare them as follows (Ballantine Books ed., 1960, page 18):

"Both the technique and the aim of pornography (hard core obscenity) are diametrically opposed to those of erotic realism, and even when, by the accident of context, the effects are at times identical, it is well to keep in mind that the overall intent is very different.

In pornography (hard core obscenity) the main purpose is to stimulate erotic response in the reader. And that is all. In erotic realism, truthful description of the basic realities of life, as the individual experiences it, is of the essence, even if such portrayals (whether by reason of humor, or revulsion, or any other cause) have a decidedly anti-erotic effect. But by the same token, if, while writing realistically on the subject of sex, the author succeeds in moving his reader, this too, is erotic realism, and it is axiomatic that the reader should respond erotically to such writing, just as the sensitive reader will respond, perhaps by actually crying, to a sad scene, or by laughing when laughter is evoked." (Emphasis added)

Norman St. John Stevas, the English authority in the field, states in his book, Obscenity And The Law (1956)

"The attempt to understand 'obscenity' in the terms of a simple definition is fruitless and best abandoned, but when this has been said certain constant elements in its meaning can be isolated. Obscenity has always been confined to matters related to sex or the excremental functions. Although there is an ideological element in the word and it is sometimes used to describe unconventional moral attitudes, the word is normally related to the manner of presenting a theme or idea rather than to the theme itself. A book is usually said to be obscene, not for the opinions which it expresses, but for the way in which they are expressed. Further, 'obscene' is an emotive word, conveying a feeling of outrage. Mere offensiveness is not enough to constitute words or books obscene. If 'immodest' is taken as the positive, 'indecent' may be described as the comparative, and 'obscene' as the superlative.

A pornographic book can be easily distinguished from an obscene book. A pornographic book, although obscene, is one deliberately designed to stimulate sex feelings and to act as an aphrodisiac. An obscene book has no such immediate and dominant purpose, although incidentally this may be its effect. A work like Ulysses certainly contains obscene passages, but their insertion in the book is not to stimulate sex impulses in the reader but to form part of a work of art."

Many other authorities[4] may be cited which would indicate agreement with the ideas set forth by the authors just quoted. All of them indicate that that which is pornographic may be identified with some degree of probability, and all make it clear that the pornographic in any method of expression is that which is designed in its contents to appeal directly to the erotic emotions of the individual solely for the purpose of their stimulation.[5]

---

[3] St. Thomas Aquinas in Summa Theologica, II–II q 77, art. 1, ad. 1, states:

"Hence human law was unable to forbid all that is contrary to nature; and it suffices it to prohibit whatever is destructive of human intercourse, while it treats other matters as though they were lawful not by approving them, but by not punishing them."

[4] See text and accompanying footnotes in Lockhart & McClure: "Censorship of Obscenity: The Developing Constitutional Standards," 45 Minn. L. Rev. 5, 58–68 (1960); Kilpatrick, The Smut Peddlers, ch. 1; see also, "Obscenity and the Arts," a collection of articles from various viewpoints dealing with the problem, in 20 Law and Contemporary Problems, No. 4 (1955).

[5] It should be observed in this connction that the American Law Institute, in promulgating its definition of obscenity under section 207.10 of the tentative draft of the Model Penal Code, also had in mind reference to the content of the materials in question and not the tendency or effect of the materials to

If the statutory definition of obscenity is to be limited to that which is pornographic, as I believe it should, a standard of some stability, though admittedly not perfect, is achieved.[6] It is my belief that it was pornographic expression which the decision in Roth-Alberts concluded was beyond the protection of the Constitution.

A conclusion similar to that herein expressed as to the scope of the legal definition of obscenity has been reached in other jurisdictions. See *State* v. *Jackson*, 224 Or. 337, 356 P. 2d 495 (Ore. Sup. Ct. 1960); *People* v. *Richmond County News, Inc.*, 9 N.Y. 2d 578, 216 N.Y.S. 2d 369, 175 N.E. 2d 681 (Ct. App. 1961); but see *Monfred* v. *State*, 226 Md. 312, 173 A. 2d 173 (Ct. App. 1961); but cf. dissenting opinion of Justice Hammond, id., 173 A. 2d, at p. 178.

[9] The materials here in question, the titles and publication data of which have been set forth in marginal note (1) of this opinion, may roughly be classified into three groups. The first group contains the majority of the 48 titles, and consists of what might be termed "man's action" or "adventure" magazines. An examination of the contents of these magazines indicates that each contains a series of medium-length stories, all of which in some manner deal with themes of beatings, torture, adultery, rape, and heterosexual activities. For example, in the magazine Battle Cry a story in a cold war setting recounts the escapades of American soldiers who are constantly sought out by German frauleins. Another story in this magazine purports to be the autobiographical narration of an escapee of a Korean War Camp. There are described various sadistic beatings received by captured soldiers while in prison, and the relationships between guards and prisoners, which are, to say the least, suggestive. A third story involves another war theme in which a woman prostitutes

herself to whoever gets to be the hero of the week by killing the most Japanese. There are many passages in this narration describing the spattering of blood and brutal conduct. Also included in the typical format of these magazines are a few pages of "pin ups," which are made up of photographs of young women clad in scanty bathing suits posed in various positions. Each of these magazines usually contains one article which deals with some supposedly informative theme which, as a general rule, is presented in an extremely superficial and infantile manner. For example, one magazine carries an historical account of the Meiji Empire in Japan. I have no hesitation in classifying each magazine in this group as absolute trash. I am sure that a trained mind could not find diversion or entertainment in reading the contents of any of them.

During the course of the trial the State produced as an expert witness Dr. Gerald Gelber, a psychologist. Prior to trial Dr. Gelber had been given 13 of the 48 exhibits for examination. The books chosen for his examination were, in the estimation of the prosecutor, fair cross-samplings of the entire 48. With regard to the first classification which I have just mentioned, Dr. Gelber indicated that the one thing that stood out in his mind as to this group was not so much the actual description of perverse sexuality, as the general context of sexual themes and brutal themes, one juxtaposed with another; he believed that the highly repetitive nature of this scheme of the magazines indicated that the intent of the publishers was to combine the two, i.e., the sadistic with the sexual.

While I am inclined to agree with Dr. Gelber's general analysis of the various books of this classification, as indicated by his testimony, I do not believe that his observations can support or justify a conclusion such as would take any of the magazines in question out of the area of expression guaranteed protection by the First Amendment. None of them is pornographic. As an individual citizen, I certainly would not recommend the reading of any of these magazines. As a judge, mindful of the constitutional question involved, I find that they do not violate the provisions of N.J.S. 2A:115–2, N.J.S.A., in that they are obscene, as I conceive that term as a matter of law.

My second classification of the exhibits embraces a few slick-paper magazines which might be referred to as the "for men only" type. The obvious intent of these books is to appeal to man's taste for bawdy things and to pander to the cult of pseudo-sophisticates represented by certain members of our male population who conceive the ultimate in values to be the perfect dry martini and a generously endowed, over-sexed female. The general make-up of these magazines consists of short stories involving rather obvious plots which invariably have as their denouement an illicit sexual relationship; some self-styled feature articles on such popularly conceived-to-be important subjects as modern jazz and modern art, none of which demonstrates much originality; a collection of ribald cartoons of fairly obvious off-color subject matters, and a few pages of color and black-and-white photographs of young women in scanty attire. This class of magazines was not regarded by Dr. Gelber as pornographic, and in this conclusion I agree. Certainly, no inducement could be found to read any of these magazines by anyone of intelligence; to my mind they exist as forlorn evidence of the irresponsible efforts of the publishers concerned to contribute to the mediocrity of

---

arouse lustful thoughts or desires. In comment (A), "Summary of the Principal Features," of section 207.10, the Institute pointed out that evidence that change of character or actual misbehavior follows from contact with obscenity is lacking. The purpose of the Institute in using the term "appeal to prurient interest" was to refer to qualities of the material itself, that is, the capacity of the material to attract individuals eager for a forbidden look behind the curtain of privacy which our customs draw about sexual matters. The objective of section 207.10 was stated by the Institute to be the prevention of commercial exploitation of the psychological sexual tension which exists in the ordinary person in our society, who is described by psychiatrists and anthropologists as caught between normal sexual drive and curiosity, on one hand, and powerful social and legal prohibition against overt sexual behavior on the other.

[6] To some, even the limitations placed upon the definition of obscenity as expressed here constitute an unreasonable burden on the guarantees of freedom of expression. Cf. O'Connell, J. dissenting in *State* v. *Jackson*, infra, 356 P. 2d at p. 508; Kalven, book review in 24 Chi. L. Rev. 769 (1957) (written prior to Roth-Alberts). Such objection presupposes the law to have no voice or interest in the maintenance of even minimum standards of public morality. Such a presupposition is erroneous. See, e.g., *Chaplinsky* v. *New Hampshire*, 315 U.S. 568, 571–572, 62 S. Ct. 766, 86 L. Ed. 1031 (1942); *Beauharnais* v. *Illinois*, 343 U.S. 250, 257, 72 S. Ct. 725, 96 L. Ed. 919 (1952). Cf. *Trist* v. *Child*, 21 Wall. 441, 88 U.S. 441, 450, 22 L. Ed. 623 (1874): "The foundation of a republic is the virtue of its citizens. They are at once sovereigns and subjects. As the foundation is undermined, the structure is weakened. When it is destroyed the fabric must fall. Such is the voice of universal history." Swayne, J. quoting 1 Montesquieu, Spirit of Laws, 17.

society. None of the magazines in this classification, however, do I find to be obscene.

The third and last classification of the exhibits concludes a collection of magazines colloquially referred to as "girlie" magazines. These books are dedicated to a collection of "pin up" photographs depicting women in various stages of dress and undress, and in scanty bathing suits. In many of the photographs, the breasts and nipples of the model are exposed. Most of the poses are what might be described as provocative, and some, absolutely silly. None of the photographs, however, even suggest heterosexual or homosexual activity, and are all obviously planned for the purpose of displaying in some manner or another the overabundance of certain physical attributes possessed by the model. Most of the photographs I would deem to be vulgar, but none would I deem to be legally obscene or pornographic. These magazines are indicative of the fantasies which a large segment of our population has with regard to sex. The appeal of this type of magazine seems to be a reassurance to the illusion possessed by many of this group that somewhere, for somebody, sex can be a full-time activity.[7]

I do not come to the determination that any of the magazines here involved, for the distribution of which defendant has been indicted, are obscene within the meaning of N.J.S. 2A:115-2, N.J.S.A., as I have construed that statute herein. I am fully cognizant of the disappointment that this conclusion may well have on some of our citizens who, with the best of intentions, are determined to eliminate such trash from our newsstands and book stores. As an individual, I can sympathize with their desires, but even with such a personal predilection I cannot, under any circumstances, let that intrude upon what I regard to be my clear legal duty.

[10, 11] In a pluralistic society the courts, as I have stated heretofore, cannot and should not become involved in the attempts to improve individual morals, nor should they become involved as arbiters in the war between the *literati* and the philistines over the standards to which our literature is to adhere. The function of the courts and our law is clear: to provide, insofar as it is humanly possible, a climate free of unnecessary restraints in which our citizens will be able to express themselves without fear. It is, or should be apparent to all that everything we have been, are, or will be as a nation has or will come as the result of the unfettered expression of individual ideas. Responsible citizens should realize that our social freedoms are inextricably bound together so as to constitute a vital whole which is much more than a mere sum of its parts; and that whenever we deal with any area of freedom we are necessarily dealing with this living whole. If we cannot with reasonable certainty know every possible effect that will flow from the regulation of any specific area of social freedom when we consider the whole, self-restraint must be exercised, since unforeseen effects may follow, with the result that the regulation which seemed at the time sensible when viewed as to a part, now acts to harm irreparably the whole. The danger of such consequences can not be overstated. Considered in this light, it must be agreed that if we are to continue to have the freedom of expression as it has been guaranteed, and which we have cherished since the days of the Revolution, the existence of the type of trash involved here must be tolerated as part of the price which we must pay.

Defendant's motions for judgments of acquittal under indictments 970 and 971, both of the 1959 term, are granted.

---

[7] See Eric Larrabee, "The Cultural Context of Sex Censorship," 20 Law and Contemp. Problems 672, 683 (1955).

■ State of New Jersey, *Plaintiff-Respondent,*

v.

Hudson County News Company, etc., and Hudson County News Dealers Supply Company, etc., *Defendants-Appellants.*
41 N.J. 247.
No. A–14.

Supreme Court of New Jersey.

Argued Oct. 22, 1963.

Decided Dec. 16, 1963.

Roger H. McGlynn, Newark for defendants-appellants (McGlynn, Stein & McGlynn, Newark, attorneys, Julius Kass, New York City, of counsel, and Roger H. McGlynn, Newark, of counsel and on the brief).

Harold J. Ruvoldt, Asst. Pros., for plaintiff-respondent (James A. Tumulty, Jr., Hudson County Pros., attorney, William A. O'Brien, Jersey City, of counsel).

The opinion of the court was delivered by

Proctor, J.

The defendants, Hudson County News Company and Hudson County News Dealers Supply Co., affiliated corporations, are engaged in the business of distributing to retailers newspapers and magazines of all types over a large area in northern New Jersey. They were charged with violating N.J.S. 2A:115–2, N.J.S.A.[1] in five indictments, each of which contained several counts. Four of the indictments charged the defendants with specific sales of obscene magazines and the fifth charged them with possession with intent to sell obscene magazines. The indictments involved 23 different "girlie-type" magazines. The case was tried before a jury and defendants were found guilty on counts involving six of the magazines.[2] The Appellate Division affirmed the convictions. *State v. Hudson County News Co.,* 78 N.J. Super. 327, 188 A. 2d 444 (1963). Defendants appeal to this court under Rule 1:2–1(a).

[1] Defendants first contend that they were entitled to a judgment of acquittal at the end of the State's case on the ground that the magazines involved could not constitutionally be found to be obscene. In *Roth* v. *United States,* 354 U.S. 476, 77 S. Ct. 1304, 1 L. Ed. 2d 1498 (1957), the United States Supreme Court held that obscenity is not within the area of constitutionally protected speech or press. Defendants argue that obscenity, in the constitutional sense, means "hard-core pornography," which they define in their brief as:

"[C]ommercially and clandestinely produced material having no literary or artistic merit in which sexual activities and orgies of men and women, normal and perverted, are portrayed, devoid of disguise, *through explicit and crude or coarse illustration * * * 'hard core' pornography is instantly recognizable by all. It constitutes absolute filth in the rawest and starkest sense."* (*Emphasis in the original*)

We are certain that the First Amendment as interpreted by the United States Supreme Court does not limit this State to the suppression of material which reaches the nadir of degradation described by the defendants. Certainly the cases and commentators do not adopt or confirm the defendants' suggested definition. Although several states have limited the meaning of obscenity under their

statutes to "hard-core" pornography,[3] we have found no concurrence of opinion regarding the meaning of that term. Dean Lockhart and Professor McClure, in their authoritative article, "Censorship of Obscenity: The Developing Constitutional Standards," 45 Minn. L. Rev. 5, 60–61 (1960), state that "a satisfactory definition of the term is not easy to come by." Other commentators have expressed varying ideas on the meaning of the term, e.g., Kalven, "The Metaphysics of the Law of Obscenity," 1 Sup. Ct. Rev. 1, 13, 44 (1960); Mulroy, "Obscenity, Pornography and Censorship," 49 A.B.A.J. 869, 874 (1963); Green, "The Treatment of Obscenity," 51 Ky. L.J. 667, 677 (1963).

[2] We have also considered the arguments advanced in the cases and in the literature that obscenity is, or may be constitutionally limited to, "hard-core" pornography, but we have concluded that in the absence of any substantial concurrence as to the meaning of this term, its adoption by us at this time would not increase clarity or certainty in the law of obscenity, and accordingly we decline to do so. We note that two states which have adopted the "hard-core" test have reached opposite results in determining the constitutionality of the suppression of the same book. Compare *People v. Fritch,* 13 N.Y. 2d 119, 243 N.Y.S. 2d 1, 192 N.E. 2d 713 (Ct. App. 1963), with *Attorney General* v. *Tropic of Cancer,* 345 Mass. 11, 184 N.E. 2d 328 (Mass. Sup. Jud. Ct. 1962). In short, the label "hard-core" pornography is too vague to be helpful to a court or a jury in determining whether particular material is obscene.

[3] We recognize that under any definition of obscenity certain materials will lie in a gray area, and that "constitutionally protected expression * * * is often separated from obscenity only by a dim and uncertain line." *Bantam Books, Inc.* v. *Sullivan,* 372 U.S. 58, 66, 83 S. Ct. 631, 637, 9 L. Ed. 2d 584, 590 (1963). However, we are of the opinion that the guidelines established initially in Roth and clarified in *Manual Enterprises* v. *Day,* 370 U.S. 478, 82 S. Ct. 1432, 8 L. Ed. 2d 639 (1962), are the best determinants available to a court in reaching its decision whether particular material is obscene by constitutional standards.

[4] In Roth, Mr. Justice Brennan for the majority of the Court stated that the test of obscenity is:

"whether to the average person, applying contemporary community standards, the dominant theme of the material taken as a whole appeals to prurient interest." 354 U.S., at p. 489, 77 S. Ct., at p. 1311, 1 L. Ed. 2d, at p. 1509.

And in discussing the test, he quoted with approval the definition of the A.L.I. Model Penal Code, § 207.10(2) (Tent. Draft No. 6, 1957), viz.:

---

[1] At the time of the indictment N.J.S. 2A:115–2, N.J.S.A., provided: "Any person who, without just cause, utters or exposes to the view of another, or possesses with intent to utter or expose to the view of another, any obscene or indecent book, publication, pamphlet, picture or other representation however made or any person who shall sell, import, print, publish, loan, give away, or distribute or possess with intent to sell, print, publish, loan, give away, design, prepare, distribute, or offer for sale any obscene or indecent book, publication, pamphlet, picture or other representation, however made, or who in any way advertises the same, or in any manner, whether by recommendation against its use or otherwise, gives any information how or where any of the same may be had, seen, bought or sold, is guilty of a misdemeanor."

[2] The defendants were convicted under four of the indictments of selling the following magazines: Mermaid, Vol. 1, No. 6; Spree, Vol. 1, No. 9; High, July 1959; Exotic Adventures, Vol. 1, No. 3; Sir Knight, Vol. 1, No. 8. They were convicted under the fifth indictment of possessing with intent to sell the magazine Ace, August 1959.

[3] E.g., *People v. Richmond County News, Inc.,* 9 N.Y. 2d 578, 216 N.Y.S. 2d 369, 175 N.E. 2d 681 (Ct. App. 1961); *Zeitlin v. Arnebergh,* 59 Cal. 2d 901, 31 Cal. Rptr. 800, 383 P. 2d 152 (Sup. Ct. 1963); *Attorney General* v. *Tropic of Cancer,* 345 Mass. 11, 184 N.E. 2d 328 (Mass. Sup. Jud. Ct. 1962). But cf. *State v. Andrews,* 150 Conn. 92, 186 A. 2d 546 (Sup. Ct. Err. 1962); *Monfred v. State,* 226 Md. 312, 173 A. 2d 173 (Ct. App. 1961), cert. denied, 368 U.S. 953, 82 S. Ct. 395, 7 L. Ed. 2d 386 (1962); *State v. Chobot,* 12 Wis. 2d 110, 106 N.W. 2d 286 (Sup. Ct. 1960), app. dism. 368 U.S. 15, 82 S. Ct. 136, 7 L. Ed. 2d 85 (1961).

"* * * A thing is obscene if, considered as a whole, its predominant appeal is to prurient interest, i.e., a shameful or morbid interest in nudity, sex, or excretion, and if it goes substantially beyond customary limits of candor in description or representation of such matters. * * *" 354 U.S., at p. 486, 77 S. Ct., at p. 1310, 1 L. Ed. 2d, at p. 1508.

This A.L.I. definition was revised in minor part in the 1962 Proposed Official Draft of the Model Penal Code.

[5, 6] Subsequently, in Manual Enterprises, supra, Mr. Justice Harlan stated, "[o]bscenity * * * requires proof of two distinct elements: (1) patent offensiveness; and (2) 'prurient interest' appeal." 370 U.S., at p. 485, 82 S. Ct., at p. 1436, 8 L. Ed. 2d, at p. 646. The term "patent offensiveness," or "indecency," describes material which can be deemed so offensive on its face as to affront current community standards of decency. Id., 370 U.S., at p. 481, 82 S. Ct., at p. 1434, 8 L. Ed. 2d, at p. 644. He also quoted the Model Penal Code definitions and commented that "[t]he thoughtful studies of the American Law Institute reflect the same twofold concept of obscenity." Id., 370 U.S., at p. 485, 82 S. Ct., at p. 1436, 8 L. Ed. 2d, at p. 646. Although the opinion of Mr. Justice Harlan (announcing the judgment of the Court) was joined only by Mr. Justice Stewart,[4] we believe that the requirement of patent offensiveness articulated in that opinion was nevertheless inherent in the Roth opinion which approved the twofold concept expressed in the A.L.I. proposal. Indeed, it is the characteristic of indecency which is the basis of society's objection to obscene material, and if the test did not include both elements, many worthwhile works in literature, science, or art would fall under the sole test of "prurient-interest" appeal.[5] In most cases, however, the two elements will tend to coalesce, "for that which is patently offensive will also usually carry the requisite 'prurient interest' appeal." Id., 370 U.S., at p. 486, 82 S. Ct., at p. 1436, 8 L. Ed. 2d, at p. 646.

[7-9] Defendants moved at the end of the State's case for a judgment of acquittal. They argue that the judge was required to make an independent determination of the material in evidence, applying the proper constitutional standards, before submitting the issue of obscenity to the jury. We agree. The trial judge must apply the constitutional standards to the specific material, in the light of any factual findings supported by the evidence, for if in his judgment the material cannot constitutionally be suppressed, then nothing remains for the jury's consideration. See Model Penal Code, Proposed Official Draft 1962

§ 251.4(4), where it is said, "The Court shall dismiss a prosecution for obscenity if it is satisfied that the material is not obscene." Of course, if the trial judge determines that the material is not constitutionally protected and should be submitted to the jury, he should avoid expressing to them his opinion on the issue of obscenity. Compare *State* v. *Smith*, 32 N.J. 501, 549, 161 A. 2d 520 (1960), regarding the trial court's function in determining the admissibility of a defendant's confession. Further, on appeal each appellate court must likewise make an independent determination of whether the attack material is suppressible within constitutional standards, for the question is not merely one of fact "but a question of constitutional *judgment* of the most sensitive and delicate kind." Mr. Justice Harlan concurring in Roth, supra, 354 U.S., at p. 498, 77 S. Ct., at p. 1316, 1 L. Ed. 2d, at p. 1514. See also *Manual Enterprises* v. *Day*, supra, 370 U.S., at p. 487, 82 S. Ct., at p. 1437, 8 L. Ed. 2d, at p. 647; Lockhart and McClure, op. cit. supra, at pp. 114–116 and cases there cited.

[10] We have examined the six magazines involved in the defendants' convictions, and we are of the opinion that under the Roth-Manual test a trial court could properly submit the issue of their obscenity to the jury.[6] There was accordingly no error in the trial court's denial of defendants' motion for acquittal on this ground.

[11] The defendants further contend that they were entitled to a judgment of acquittal at the end of the State's case on the ground that the State had failed to prove beyond a reasonable doubt that the defendants had knowledge of the contents of the magazines involved. In *State* v. *Hudson County News Co.*, 35 N.J. 284, 294, 173 A. 2d 20 (1961), we held that N.J.S. 2A: 155–2, N.J.S.A. must be construed as though it expressly embodied the word "knowingly," i.e., that *scienter* is an implied element of the statutory offense. Compare *Smith* v. *California*, 361 U.S. 147, 80 S. Ct. 215, 4 L. Ed. 2d 205 (1959), in which the United States Supreme Court held that a city ordinance prohibiting the keeping for sale of obscene material was unconstitutional because as construed by the state court it eliminated the element of *scienter*.

Defendants argue there was no proof at the end of the State's case that they had actually examined the contents of the magazines here involved. However, "A bookseller may, of course, be well aware of the nature of a book and its appeal without having opened its cover, or, in any true sense, having knowledge of the book." Mr. Justice Frankfurter concurring in *Smith* v. *California*, supra, 361 U.S. 164, 165, 80 S. Ct. 224, 225, 4 L. Ed. 2d 215, 217.

[12, 13] Actual knowledge of the contents of the material is not the *sine qua non* to establish *scienter*. Otherwise, a bookseller need only close his eyes to the material he handles to avoid prosecution under an obscenity statute. Mr. Justice Brennan in Smith, supra, speaking for the Court, indicated that there may be circumstances under which a bookseller or a distributor may be required to investigate material in his control or explain his failure to do so. 361 U.S., at p. 154, 80 S. Ct., at p. 219, 4 L. Ed.

---

[4] Justice Black concurred in result; the Chief Justice, Justices Brennan and Douglas concurred on procedural grounds; Justice Clark dissented on other grounds; and Justices Frankfurter and White took no part in the decision.

[5] In 1962 our Legislature supplemented our statutes on indecency and obscenity by adding a definition for the word "obscene" substantially in the language of the Roth opinion as follows:

"The word 'obscene' whenever it appears in the chapter to which this act is a supplement shall mean that which to the average person, applying contemporary community standards, when considered as a whole has as its dominant theme or purpose an appeal to prurient interest." N.J.S. 2A:115–1.1.

This statute must constitutionally be construed to include the element of patent offensiveness.

[6] A jury could properly find that the dominant themes of the magazines were sexual perversions such as exhibitionism, masochism, flagellation, and nymphomania, that they appealed to prurient interests, were patently offensive, and had no redeeming social importance.

2d, at p. 212. We believe such circumstances exist in the present case. In the regular course of business defendants distributed magazines, a cursory inspection of which would have revealed the nature of their contents. The State produced three retailers, customers of the defendants, who testified that on a number of occasions they had complained by phone, in writing, and in person that "girlie magazines" were objectionable and asked that deliveries be stopped; nevertheless, deliveries continued. Under these circumstances, we believe that evidence that the defendants had examined the magazines involved was not necessary to establish a *prima facie* case but that the State could rely on these circumstances to require the defendants to explain their lack of knowledge of the actual contents of the magazines. Compare the presumption suggested by the American Law Institute in the Model Penal Code, 1962 Proposed Official Draft § 251.4(2), viz.: "A person who disseminates or possesses obscene material in the course of his business is presumed to do so knowingly or recklessly." We find that the trial court did not err in denying the defendants' motion to acquit on this ground.

The defendants also contend that the trial court erred in denying their motion for acquittal at the end of the State's case on the indictment which charged them with possession with intent to sell obscene material. The defendants do not contend that N.J.S. 2A:115-2, N.J.S.A. is unconstitutional on its face but that its application under the circumstances was unconstitutional. They claim that they were deprived of their rights under the First and Fourteenth Amendments of the Federal Constitution by the procedures used by the police in confiscating certain magazines from their warehouse and contend that this method of enforcing the statute constituted a prior restraint upon publication.

After having purchased from customers of the defendants the magazines named in the indictments charging defendants with the sale of obscene matter, the police obtained a warrant to search the defendants' warehouse.[7] The premises consisted of an area about 100 feet square in which thousands of magazines and books of all types were stacked on the floor prior to distribution. The detectives advised defendants' manager that they had a warrant to search "for books of obscene nature." They spent two to two and a half hours conducting the search and examining various magazines. Seven detectives made the actual search and brought the magazines they found to the chief detective, who decided whether "they were the type books that we were looking for * * *" At the conclusion of their search, the detectives confiscated seven bundles of 100 copies each of seven magazines—all the copies the defendants had. It should be noted that these magazines were not additional copies of those purchased by the police. Each of the seven titles was named in a separate count of the indictment charging possession, and the bundles were placed in evidence at the trial. Defendants were subsequently convicted on only one count of this indictment which named the August 1959 issue of *Ace*.

Chief Justice Hughes in *Near v. Minnesota*, 283 U.S. 697, 713, 51 S. Ct. 625, 630, 75 L. Ed. 1357, 1366 (1931), pointed out that the chief purpose of the First Amendment guarantee is to prevent previous restraints upon publication. There the Court struck down as unconstitutional a state statute which permitted a prior restraint by injunction on the publication of printed matter. However, it was suggested that an exception to the prior restraint doctrine might exist with regard to the regulation of obscene material. And the Court has subsequently upheld the prior restraint of obscene material under carefully circumscribed procedural safeguards. *Kingsley Books, Inc.* v. *Brown*, 354 U.S. 436, 77 S. Ct. 1325, 1 L. Ed. 2d 1469 (1957);[8] *Times Film Corp.* v. *Chicago*, 365 U.S. 43, 81 S. Ct. 391, 5 L. Ed. 2d 403 (1961). In Roth, the Court expressly recognized the vital necessity of adequate safeguards in the application of obscenity statutes to prevent the suppression of constitutionally protected material. 354 U.S. at pp. 488, 489, 77 S. Ct. at pp. 1310, 1311, 1 L. Ed. 2d at 1509. Later, in Smith, the Court said, "[O]ur holding in Roth does not recognize *any* state power to restrict the dissemination of books which are not obscene." 361 U.S., at p. 152, 80 S. Ct., at p. 218, 4 L. Ed. 2d, at p. 210 (emphasis added).

In *Marcus* v. *Property Search Warrant*, 367 U.S. 717, 81 S. Ct. 1708, 6 L. Ed. 2d 1127 (1961), the Court held that the Missouri procedures for search and seizure of obscene material as applied in that case "lacked the safeguards which due process demands to assure nonobscene material the constitutional protection to which it is entitled." 367 U.S., at p. 731, 81 S. Ct., at p. 1716, 6 L. Ed. 2d, at p. 1136. Under a Missouri statute, supplemented by rule of court, the police had obtained warrants which authorized them to search the premises of five news retailers and a distributor and to seize obscene materials found therein. On execution of the warrants, all copies of 280 publications were seized at the six places. A hearing on the issue of obscenity was held before a circuit judge pursuant to the statute thirteen days after the search. In an opinion filed over two months after the seizure, the judge held that 100 of the 280 seized items were obscene and ordered that they be held as evidence for possible criminal prosecution. The 180 items found not to be obscene were ordered returned to the owners. The Supreme Court in holding that the First Amendment rights of the appellants had been violated stated:

" '* * * [T]*he line between speech unconditionally guaranteed and speech which may legitimately be regulated, suppressed, or punished is finely drawn. * * * The separation of legitimate from illegitimate speech calls for * * * sensitive tools * * *.*' Speiser v. Randall, 357 U.S. 513, 525, 78 S. Ct. 1332, 1342, 2 L. Ed. 2d 1460 [1472]. It follows that, under the Fourteenth Amendment, a State is not free to adopt whatever procedures it pleases for dealing with obscenity as here involved without regard to the possible consequences for constitutionally protected speech. * * * They [the officers conducting the search] were provided with no guide to the exercise of informed discretion, because there was no step in the procedure before seizure designed to focus searchingly on the question of obscenity. See generally 1 Chafee, Government and Mass Communications, pp. 200–218. In consequence*

---

[7] The validity of the search warrant is not before us on this appeal, and accordingly we do not consider the question. Cf. R.R. 3:2A–1 to 10.

[8] Compare New Jersey's recently enacted injunction procedures relating to obscene material. N.J.S. 2A:115–3.5 to 3.10, N.J.S.A.

there were suppressed and withheld from the market for over two months 180 publications not found obscene. The fact that only one-third of the publications seized were finally condemned strengthens the conclusion that discretion to seize allegedly obscene materials cannot be confided to law enforcement officials without greater safeguards than were here operative. *Procedures which sweep so broadly and with so little discrimination are obviously deficient in techniques required by the Due Process Clause of the Fourteenth Amendment to prevent erosion of the constitutional guarantees.*" *Id.,* 361 U.S., at pp. 731–732, 81 S. Ct., at pp. 1716–1717, 6 L. Ed. 2d, at pp. 1136, 1137.

The procedures followed by the detectives in the present case cannot be distinguished from those found constitutionally defective in Marcus. Here the detectives exercised the broadest discretion in executing the warrant. They were provided with no guide to the exercise of informed discretion but were left to their individual judgments as to which magazines were obscene. In the short time they were at the premises they obviously had little opportunity to reflect or deliberate. The magazines were seized on the basis of on-the-spot *ad hoc* decisions. As a result of the seizures, 600 magazines not found to be obscene were suppressed and withheld from the market for approximately three years. In Marcus, the court concluded:

"*Mass seizure in the fashion of this case was thus effected without any safeguards to protect legitimate expression. The judgment of the Missouri Supreme Court sustaining the condemnation of the 100 publications therefore cannot be sustained. We have no occasion to reach the question of the correctness of the finding that the publications are obscene. Nor is it necessary for us to decide in this case whether Missouri lacks all power under its statutory scheme to seize and condemn obscene material. Since a violation of the Fourteenth Amendment infected the proceedings, in order to vindicate appellants' constitutional rights the judgment is reversed,* * * *" Id.,* 367 U.S., at p. 738, 81 S. Ct., at p. 1719, 6 L. Ed. 2d, at pp. 1139, 1140.

[14] We believe that the procedures here employed imposed an unconstitutional prior restraint on defendants' rights under the First and Fourteenth Amendments, and since this violation of constitutional rights permeated the proceedings under the indictment charging them with the possession of obscene material, the conviction under that indictment must be reversed.

[15] Defendants' final argument is that an erroneous community standard was applied in the trial of the case. Over their objection, the trial court admitted testimony of lay witnesses tending to establish that the magazines in evidence were offensive to community standards in Hudson County. The following typical testimony was elicited in response to the court's question requesting the lay witnesses' opinion regarding "morality and immorality in Hudson County":

"* * * the way of life that I have watched and that I have lived within Hudson County and in Jersey City is a

very, very high moral standard as compared to other areas that I have visited."[9]

In addition, the court charged the jury, over objection, that they should consider the community standards of Hudson County as testified to by the witnesses.

Defendants urge that the term "contemporary community standards," which was introduced in the test of obscenity in Roth, contemplates a national standard of decency, and not a local standard. On the other hand, the State contends that the standard must be that of the local community where the material was distributed.

There has been no United States Supreme Court case which specifically answers this question. However, Dean Lockhart and Professor McClure have stated:

"We are confident that, when the Supreme Court is clearly presented with the issue, the Court will resolve the issue against the application of state and local community standards." op. cit. supra, at pp. 111–112.

In support of this view they suggest that the ideas embodied in the phrase "contemporary community standards" originated with Judge Learned Hand in his opinion in *United States* v. *Kennerley,* 209 F. 119 (S.D.N.Y. 1913). In that case, Judge Hand felt obligated to follow the obscenity test laid down in *Regina* v. *Hicklin,* [1868] L.R. 3 Q.B. 360, which allowed material to be judged by the effect of an isolated excerpt upon particularly susceptible persons. The Hicklin test was specifically rejected in Roth as unconstitutionally restrictive of the freedoms of speech and press. 354 U.S., at pp. 488–489, 77 S. Ct., at pp. 1310–1311, 1 L. Ed. 2d, at p. 1509. In criticizing the Hicklin test and urging its abandonment, Judge Hand in Kennerley said, "[S]hould not the word 'obscene' be allowed to indicate the present critical point in the compromise between candor and shame at which the *community* may have arrived here and now? * * * To put thought in leash to the *average conscience of the time* is perhaps tolerable, but to fetter it by the necessities of the lowest and least capable seems a fatal policy." 209 F., at p. 121 (emphasis added). As stated by Lockhart and McClure, this language suggests the rejection of the Hicklin test in favor of the standards of society as a whole. If, as we believe, the Court in Roth intended by the phrase "contemporary community standards" to reject the "mid-Victorian" concept in favor of the "contemporary," and the effect on the weakest in favor of the effect on the average member of society, then the "contemporary com-

---

9 Although the matter was not briefed, we do not believe that a lay witness is ordinarily competent to give opinion testimony on community standards. Of course, we do not wish to imply that all evidence of community standards is inadmissible. See the concurring opinion of Mr. Justice Frankfurter in *Smith* v. *California,* supra, 361 U.S. 161, 166, 80 S. Ct. 223, 226, 4 L. Ed. 2d 215, 218; and the concurring opinion of Mr. Justice Harlan in that case at 361 U.S., at pp. 169–172, 81 S. Ct., at pp. 227–229, 4 L. Ed. 2d, at pp. 220, 221. See also *Yudkin* v. *State,* 229 Md. 223, 182 A. 2d 798 (Ct. App. 1962). Cf. *People* v. *Finkelstein,* 11 N.Y. 2d 300, 229 N.Y.S. 2d 367, 183 N.E. 2d 661 (Ct. App. 1962), cert. denied, 371 U.S. 863, 83 S. Ct. 116, 9 L. Ed. 2d 100 (1962), noted at 76 Harv. L. Rev. 1498 (1963).

We note that the State purported to qualify the lay witnesses as "average" men. No witness can *qualify* as an "average man." This is a standard solely for the jury to determine.

munity" logically refers to society at large and not some local geographical area.

Lockhart and McClure find further support for their position in the *per curiam* reversal of the United States Court of Appeals decision upholding Chicago's censorship of a movie. *Times Film Corp.* v. *City of Chicago*, 355 U.S. 35, 78 S. Ct. 115, 2 L. Ed. 2d 72 (1957), reversing 244 F. 2d 432 (7 Cir. 1957). They assert that the Court would not so summarily have substituted its judgment of Chicago standards for the judgment of the local censors and courts if the Court in fact approved of the application of local standards. Lockhart and McClure, op. cit. supra, at p. 111.

The Model Penal Code, although it does not expressly discuss community standards, clearly leaves the impression that a national community standard should be applied rather than a state or local one. See, for example, the Proposed Official Draft 1962, which states in § 251.4:

"(4) Evidence: Adjudication of Obscenity.
In any prosecution under this Section evidence shall be admissible to show:

* * *

(d) *the degree of public acceptance of the material in the United States.*"

See also Tentative Draft No. 6 (1957) § 207.10(2) (d) and comments thereto.

[16] We believe that the Legislature in enacting N.J.S. 2A:115–2, N.J.S.A., intended to forbid obscene matter to the fullest extent permissible under the First Amendment, made applicable to the states by the Fourteenth Amendment. Accordingly, the "contemporary community standard" to be applied in enforcement of the statute must comport with the limitations imposed on the State by and the freedoms guaranteed the individual by the First Amendment. We are of the opinion that such a standard must necessarily be uniform throughout the nation.

[17–20] The First Amendment accepts for the nation as a whole the basic idea that freedom of expression is a necessary guarantee in a democratic society. In determining the constitutional limits of obscenity regulation, the issue in the particular case is whether the published material falls within or without that area of expression which it is the purpose of the First Amendment to protect. In resolving this issue, the court or jury must recognize that the balancing of freedom of expression against other social values has already been made in the adoption of the First Amendment and that this basic determination cannot be re-evaluated by a *de novo* balancing of local social interests against that area of constitutional protection which has been established. See Emerson, "Toward a General Theory of the First Amendment," 72 Yale L.J. 877 (1963). The First Amendment protects an area of free expression which cannot be diminished by obscenity regulation. Therefore, the standard to be applied under such regulations cannot operate in such a way as to alter the degree of protection from locality to locality. In short, the area of expression entitled to constitutional protection cannot be broad in some parts of the country and narrow in others. If a publication comes within the protected area, it cannot be suppressed any place where the First Amendment guarantee is in effect. If the United States Supreme Court were to hold that a particular publication was entitled to protec-

tion under the First Amendment, we doubt that any court, state or federal, could subsequently deny that publication protection on the ground that a higher community standard prevailed in its jurisdiction. See *State* v. *Hudson County News Co.*, 75 N.J. Super. 363, 374, 183 A. 2d 161 (Cty. Ct. 1962).

[21] Accordingly, we hold that the contemporary community standard to be applied under our statute is not the standard of a particular individual, group of individuals, or locality, but it is the standard of the contemporary society of this country at large. The court should so instruct the jury.

[22] In light of the above we conclude that reversible error occurred since the jury were permitted to consider testimony of the local standards in Hudson County and were instructed that they could use those standards in determining whether the magazines in question were obscene. Accordingly, the convictions for the sale of obscene material must be set aside and defendants accorded a new trial.

The judgment of the Appellate Division is reversed. Defendants' convictions under the indictment charging possession with intent to sell are reversed. The convictions under the indictments charging defendants with the sale of obscene publications are vacated and the cause is remanded for re-trial of these indictments in accordance with this opinion.

Jacobs, J., concurs in result.

For reversal: Justices Jacobs, Francis, Proctor, Hall, Schettino and Haneman—6.

For affirmance: None.

Jacobs, J. (concurring).

The definition of obscenity is imprecise and the line it draws between the obscene and non-obscene is obviously thin and obscure—so thin and obscure that many thoughtful students believe that the only workable approach is to confine obscenity to what is known as hard-core pornography. Although that term itself presents some difficulties, they are much lesser in nature. See Lockhart & McClure, "Censorship of Obscenity: The Developing Constitutional Standards," 45 Minn. L. Rev. 5, 58–68 (1960). The Supreme Court's high solicitude for the constitutional freedoms of expression and its actual holdings suggest that only that type of material is likely to be found obscene within the limits contemplated by *Roth* v. *United States*, 354 U.S. 476, 77 S. Ct. 1304, 1 L. Ed. 2d 1498 (1957). See *Times Film Corp.* v. *City of Chicago*, 355 U.S. 35, 78 S. Ct. 115, 2 L. Ed. 2d 72 (1957); *Mounce* v. *United States*, 355 U.S. 180, 78 S. Ct. 267, 2 L. Ed. 2d 187 (1957); *Sunshine Book Co.* v. *Summerfield*, 355 U.S. 372, 78 S. Ct. 365, 2 L. Ed. 2d 352 (1958); *One, Inc.* v. *Olesen*, 355 U.S. 371, 78 S. Ct. 364, 2 L. Ed. 2d 352 (1958); Lockhart & McClure, supra, at pp. 13 et seq.; Emerson, "Toward a General Theory of the First Amendment," 72 Yale L.J. 877, 937–939 (1963). Persuasive opinions by the courts of New York, Massachusetts and California and by Judge Matthews in the Essex County Court embody support for that view. See *People* v. *Richmond County News, Inc.*, 9 N.Y. 2d 578, 216 N.Y.S. 2d 369, 175 N.E.

2d 681 (1961); *Attorney General* v. *Book Named "Tropic of Cancer,"* 345 Mass. 11, 184 N.E. 2d 328 (1962); *Zeitlin* v. *Arnebergh*, 59 Cal. 2d 901, 31 Cal. Rptr. 800, 383 P. 2d 152 (1963); *State* v. *Hudson County News Co.*, 75 N.J. Super. 363, 183 A. 2d 161 (Essex Cty. Ct. 1962). It seems to me that their approach affords the greater hope for truly satisfying the State's primary interest in the protection of democratic freedoms along with its secondary interest in curbing obscene literature; and in any event it would reduce the danger of having basic rights trampled upon, as occurred here.

Regardless of what approach is taken, reversal of the convictions is clearly called for; not only because of the legal errors dealt with in the majority opinion, but also for many other errors, which though not raised by the appellants, permeated the entire proceeding below. Thus in their first step police officers engaged in objectionable censorship. Illustrative is the action by one of the police captains who removed seven magazines from a rack because he felt that they were not the "right type for people to purchase." He made no arrest and filed no complaint but told the dealer "not to put any more of these magazines up for sale." When the jury returned its verdict almost three years later it found most of the magazines which the captain had taken to be not obscene; but as a result of his activities they had undoubtedly been long and improperly precluded from the market. See *Bantam Books* v. *Sullivan*, 372 U.S. 58, 83 S. Ct. 631, 637, 9 L. Ed. 2d 584, 591 (1963); cf. *Bantam Books, Inc.* v. *Melko*, 25 N.J. Super. 292, 96 A. 2d 47 (Ch. Div. 1953), modified, 14 N.J. 524, 103 A. 2d 256 (1954).

When the officers entered the defendants' premises (cf. *Commonwealth* v. *Jacobs*, — Mass. —, 191 N.E. 2d 873 (1963); *Commonwealth* v. *Dorius*, — Mass. —, 191 N.E. 2d 781 (1963)) they found thousands of magazines and other publications. They spent two and one-half hours looking for items which would meet their concept of obscenity; one of them defined obscenity to be that which was below his "moral standards" and below the moral standards of the people he knew in the community. They confiscated the available copies of seven magazines (one hundred of each) but years later the jury found all but one of these to be not obscene. Here again the non-obscene material had been long and improperly precluded from the Market. See *Bantam Books* v. *Sullivan*, supra; *Marcus* v. *Property Search Warrant*, 367 U.S. 717, 81 S. Ct. 1708, 6 L. Ed. 2d 1127 (1961).

During the trial the State presented a psychiatrist who was permitted to express her views as to obscenity and the community standards of Hudson County.[1] An objection to the use of local community standards was overruled and, as the majority now holds, that was clearly erroneous. Also objectionable was the test of obscenity upon which the testimony of the State's witness was apparently grounded. She seemed to take the position that portrayal of any sex abnormality or perversion was necessarily obscene; and she seemed to view any use of sex other than for propagation

of the race as abnormal or perverted. Cf. *Roth* v. *United States*, supra, 354 U.S., at p. 487, 77 S. Ct., at p. 1310, 1 L. Ed. 2d, at p. 1508. Thus at one point she testified that if sex is used for excitement and as an end by itself, then she would say it becomes obscene. And at another point she testified as follows: "When sex isn't just for the propagation of the race and of the species, I would say, or the intent isn't, then it is abnormal or perverted." On cross-examination the defendants sought to refer to a statement by a well-recognized psychiatrist who differed with her views on a certain point, but they were prevented from doing so by a ruling of the court; that ruling was erroneous. See *Ruth* v. *Fenchel*, 21 N.J. 171, 121 A. 2d 373, 60 A.L.R. 2d 71 (1956). Ultimately the trial judge instructed the members of the jury that they could consider and give weight to her testimony in deciding the submitted questions of obscenity and community standards.

During the trial the State tendered several witnesses as "average men" of Hudson County. Above objection, they were permitted to testify. Reference need here be made to the testimony of only the first of them. He was the general manager of a printing company who believed that he knew what the "average person" in Hudson County likes and feels; he considered that Hudson County has a "very, very high moral standard as compared with other areas" that he had visited; he expressed the view that "the word obscene as connected with these magazines is anything that would bring harm spiritually or in any way to a member of the community"; and he concluded that the magazines were not acceptable as to "moral standards" or the "standards of the community of Hudson County." In response to an inquiry as to when sex and its portrayal become obscene, he indicated that in his opinion that would occur when unrelated to the "marital chamber * * * where God meant it to be" and to "propagation of the race as I was taught." His private beliefs and moralities clearly had no pertinency to any of the issues in the proceeding. Cf. *Roth* v. *United States*, supra; *Manual Enterprises* v. *Day*, 370 U.S. 478, 82 S. Ct. 1432, 8 L. Ed. 2d 639 (1962).

Obviously the State should not have tendered any of the so-called average men and their testimony should have been excluded as incompetent. No man can qualify as the average man for there is no such being except in a hypothetical sense. In his charge the trial judge set the members of the jury adrift by telling them that they were free to give such weight and credit to the community standards testimony as they thought it was "entitled to under the law." And nowhere in the charge was there any effort to remove the effects of the grossly erroneous definitions of obscenity which had confused the proceeding. Indeed the confusion was confounded when the trial judge told the jury that most persons have a conception as to the meaning of obscenity "and you may use it in your everyday life" and by his reference to a dictionary definition of obscenity which included broadly descriptive words such as "foul," "disgusting," "offensive to chastity or to modesty." Admittedly these did not satisfy the law. See *Roth* v. *United States*, supra; *Manual Enterprises* v. *Day*, supra.

The people of our country value their freedoms most highly. They fear censorship activities and expect that proceedings by the State will strictly adhere to their traditional concepts of fair play and fair trial. Here these concepts were departed from and the resulting convictions may not be permitted to stand. See *State* v. *Orecchio*, 16 N.J. 125, 129, 106 A. 2d 541 (1954). I vote to reverse.

---

[1] Though she had training as a psychiatrist, her qualification to testify as to community standards may be doubted (compare *Womack* v. *Unitd States*, 111 U.S. App. D.C. 8, 294 F. 2d 204, 206, cert. denied, 365 U.S. 859, 81 S. Ct. 826, 5 L. Ed. 2d 822 (1961) with *Yudkin* v. *State*, 229 Md. 223, 182 A. 2d 798, 802 (1962)), and in no event should she have been permitted, as she was, to roam about freely through the field of obscenity.

■ Commonwealth

v.

Lewis

30 D & C. 2d 133 (1962)

Kenneth E. Fox, Jr., for Commonwealth.
Alvah M. Shumaker, for defendant.

HENDERSON, J., November 6, 1962.—This matter comes before the court on a motion of defendant at the above number and term to quash the indictment brought under The Penal Code of June 24, 1939, P.L. 872, sec. 414.1, added by the Act of December 8, 1959, P.L. 1714, sec. 1, 18 PS § 4414.1. The information charges defendant with malicious use of the telephone in that defendant did unlawfully and maliciously address certain lewd, lascivious or indecent words or language to the prosecutrix by telephone.

The motion to quash alleges that the statute is so vague and indefinite and uncertain in its language, and so incompletely defines any alleged offense, that the statute is repugnant to the provisions of the Constitution of Pennsylvania and to the Constitution of the United States; that the statute is further unconstitutional under both constitutions because it prescribes no standard for a determination of whether the words used are in fact lewd, lascivious or indecent; that the statute is unconstitutional under both constitutions because it discriminates against conversations by telephone; and that the statute is unconstitutional under both constitutions in that it impinges on the constitutional guarantees of freedom of speech.

Defendant in his brief states that the motion to quash the indictment "is a frontal attack on the statute itself and the indictment." The brief also states "we assert a frontal attack on the statute, irrespective of the actual conversation that may be involved in this case. The district attorney should welcome this attack because the constitutional aspect of the case should be resolved." In his brief, defense counsel further requests that the grounds be placed on both the First and Fourteenth Amendments.

The act in question under which this information has been brought reads as follows:

"Malicious use of telephones: Whoever telephones another person and addresses to or about such other person any lewd, lascivious or indecent words or language, or whoever anonymously telephones another person repeatedly for the purpose of annoying, molesting or harassing such other person or his or her family, shall be deemed guilty of the misdemeanor of being a disorderly person, and, upon conviction, shall be fined in any sum not exceeding five hundred dollars ($500), to which may be added imprisonment in the county jail not exceeding six months: Provided, That any offense committed by the use of a telephone, as herein set out, may be deemed to have been committed at either the place at which the telephone call or calls were made or at the place where the telephone call or calls were received."

This statute deals with two completely different type situations. The part challenged by the motion to quash is that portion under which the indictment is drawn, the pertinent part of which is as follows:

"Whoever telephones another person and addresses to or about such other person any lewd, lascivious or indecent words or language . . . shall be deemed guilty of the misdemeanor of being a disorderly person . . ."

It is this portion of the statute only which is being considered herein.

Defendant alleges that the above-cited statute is so vague and indefinite as to offend against the Due Process Clause of the Federal Constitution; more particularly in that it contains no definition of the conduct proscribed and no ascertainable standard of guilt. Defendant first quotes from *Roth* v. *United States,* 354 U.S. 476, 488, 1 L. Ed. 2d 1498 (1957):

". . . The door . . . into this area [the first amendment] cannot be left ajar; it must be kept tightly closed and opened only the slightest crack necessary to prevent encroachment upon more important interests . . ."

And he quotes further from *Manual Enterprises* v. *Day,* 370 U.S. 478, 497, 8 L. Ed. 2d 639, 652 (1962), that:

"We risk erosion of First Amendment liberties unless we train our vigilance upon the methods whereby obscenity is condemned no less than upon the standards whereby it is judged."

In the court's dealing with individual liberties protected by the First Amendment of the United States Constitution, the court is strongly urged to adopt the presumption of the constitutionality of any statute and particularly of the statute here involved. In *Land Holding Corporation* v. *Board of Finance and Revenue,* 388 Pa. 61, 72, 130 A. 2d 700 (1957), the Supreme Court of Pennsylvania stated this position as follows:

"In *Sablosky* v. *Messner,* supra, we said . . . . . ."It is axiomatic that he who asks to have a law declared unconstitutional takes upon himself the burden of proving beyond all doubt that it is so . . . All presumptions are in favor of the constitutionality of acts and courts are not to be astute in finding or sustaining objections to them: . . ." [Cases cited] "An act may not be declared unconstitutional unless 'it violates the Constitution clearly, palpably, plainly; and in such manner as to leave no doubt or hesitation in our minds.' [Cases cited]" ' . . ."

The court finds that ordinarily this is the presumption to be applied in determining constitutionality of statutes. However, in cases of the kind in question we are ruled by the opinion of Mr. Chief Justice Jones in *William Goldman Theaters, Inc.* v. *Dana*, 405 Pa. 83, 87, 173 A. 2d 59 (1961), as follows:

". . . But, where a restrictive statute is made to operate in the area of individual liberty, 'the usual presumption supporting legislation is balanced by the preferred place given in our scheme to the great, the indispensable democratic freedoms secured by the First Amendment. [Cases cited] That priority gives these liberties a sanctity and a sanction not permitting dubious intrusions.' . . ."

This court then, being aware of the off-setting balance of the usual presumption, will not consider in its determination of the case the presumptions cited above from the Land Holding Corporation case, supra.

On defendant's position with regard to the statute being so vague and indefinite as to offend the Federal Constitution provisions, he cites as binding and controlling the case of *Hallmark Productions, Inc.* v. *Carroll*, 384 Pa. 348, 121 A. 2d 584 (1956), and *Commonwealth* v. *Blumenstein*, 396 Pa. 417, 153 A. 2d 227 (1959).

The Hallmark case, which was decided in 1956, held that the Motion Picture Censorship Act of May 15, 1915, P.L. 534, as amended, was unconstitutional in that the statute was so vague and indefinite as to offend the Due Process Clause of the Fourteenth Amendment of the Federal Constitution. The statute there under consideration provided that:

"The board shall examine or supervise the examinations of all films, reels, or views to be exhibited or used in Pennsylvania; and shall approve such films, reels, or views which are moral and proper; and shall disapprove such as are sacrilegious, obscene, indecent, or immoral, or such as tend, in the judgment of the board, to debase or corrupt morals."

In the decision in the Hallmark case, the Supreme Court of Pennsylvania held that the question of censoring films which are "sacrilegious, obscene, indecent, or immoral, or such as tend, in the judgment of the board, to debase or corrupt morals," under cited cases of the Supreme Court of the United States, ". . . must be held subject to the same fatal objections as those which invalidated the statutes held unconstitutional by that Court."

The Blumenstein case, which was decided in 1959, grew out of the conviction of the manager of a theater for having shown certain films under a statute which states that whoever permits the showing of "moving pictures of a lascivious, sacrilegious, obscene, indecent or immoral nature and character, or such as may tend to corrupt morals, is guilty of a misdemeanor." The court also held this statute to be unconstitutional.

The last Pennsylvania case found on this subject is the case of *William Goldman Theaters, Inc.* v. *Dana*, supra, under which the Supreme Court of Pennsylvania found the Motion Picture Control Act of September 17, 1959, P.L. 902, to be unconstitutional under the Fourteenth Amendment of the Federal Constitution and under article I of the Pennsylvania Constitution. The act required any person intending to sell, lease, lend, exhibit or use any motion picture film to register with the administration board set up under the act and to notify the board within 48 hours before the first showing in Pennsylvania of the time and place of such showing. At any time after such showing, upon request of the board, an exact copy of such film was required to be furnished to the board for examina-

tion, and if a majority of the members of the board were of the opinion that the film was "obscene" or of the opinion that it was "unsuitable for children," the showing of the film could be disapproved, or disapproved for exhibition to children. The statute provided that a film, reel or view is obscene "if to the average person applying contemporary community standards its dominant theme, taken as a whole, appeals to prurient interests."

This act was found to be "clearly invalid on its face," under article I, section 7, of the Pennsylvania Constitution in that it provides for a precensorship of the exercise of the individual's right freely to communicate thoughts and opinions. The act was also found to be unconstitutional under article I, sections 6 and 9, of the Pennsylvania Constitution by reason of certain trial-by-jury requirements. The court also held that this act was unconstitutional under the Fourteenth Amendment of the United States Constitution in that it contained "defective censorial standards" and because of the failure of its procedural requirements to safeguard adequately the constitutionally protected rights of "freedom of speech."

This court specifically finds that the case at bar is not ruled by the William Goldman Theaters case in view of the fact that there is no question of precensorship involved herein and that there is no procedural question involving constitutionally protected trial-by-jury rights as there was in that case. Further, this court finds that the case at bar is not governed by the William Goldman Theaters case in the matter of "defective censorial standards" by reason of the statement found on page 96 thereof, which reads as follows:

"The definition of obscenity, as used in the Act of 1959, was obviously culled from the opinion of the United States Supreme Court in *Roth* v. *United States*, 354 U.S. 476, 489 (1957) in an attempt to satisfy the due process requirement of clarity under the Fourteenth Amendment. *But, the definition of obscenity there enunciated has never been approved by the Supreme Court other than in the context of a criminal proceeding* . . ." (Italics supplied.)

Since the case at bar is a criminal proceeding, then this court must go further to determine whether or not under the Roth case the definition of obscenity there enunciated should be here applied as constitutional.

With regard to criminal proceedings, it is interesting to note that the Goldman Theaters case which followed both the Hallmark and Blumenstein cases states as follows (p. 93–94):

"The utterance of obscene matter was a crime at common law for which a defendant chargeable therewith was entitled to a trial by jury. This was likewise so under similar guarantees in the Constitution of 1790 and 1838, long before the adoption of our present Constitution. [Cases cited]

"The above quoted provisions of Sections 6 and 9 of Article 1 guarantee that a person can be found guilty of a crime of the indicated description *only if* an impartial jury of the vicinage is of the opinion that his utterance was obscene, i.e., only if twelve jurymen are of the opinion that, applying contemporary standards in the community, the dominant theme of the utterance taken as a whole appealed to the average person's prurient interest."

This quoted statement of the present criminal law of Pennsylvania adopted the standard approved by the Roth case as being a proper standard for application in these cases.

It is interesting to note that one of the cases cited in the foregoing passage is the Blumenstein case, upon which defendant now relies in his claim that this statute is unconstitutional.

It, therefore, would appear that if this standard were the standard to be applied to the statute in question, then under the Roth case and under the Goldman Theaters case, it must be found that the statute in question is not too vague and indefinite and that the words used in the statute do prescribe a standard which is constitutional under both State and Federal Constitutions.

This standard, which has been approved as cited above, is not, however, made a part of the wording of the statute in question. However, this court does not find any requirement that the definitions or the standard itself must be included in the statute. The constitutional question arises not over whether or not the standard is set forth in the statute but rather over the question of whether or not the proper standard is applied in the given case. In view of the fact that the most recent Pennsylvania ruling and the recent Federal ruling, both cited above, have agreed upon the standard to be used in this type case, it is felt that these rulings are binding upon all trial courts in the Commonwealth and that these approved standards shall be used by the court and jury in each case coming up under the act in question. Therefore, defendant's argument in this regard is rejected.

Mr. Justice Brennan in the Roth case stated (p. 491):

"Many decisions have recognized that these terms of obscenity statutes are not precise. This Court, however, has consistently held that lack of precision is not itself offensive to the requirements of due process. '. . . [T]he Constitution does not require impossible standards'; all that is required is that the language 'conveys sufficiently definite warning as to the proscribed conduct when measured by common understanding and practices . . .' *United States* v. *Petrillo*, 332 U.S. 1, 7–8, 91 L. Ed. 1877, 1883. These words, applied according to the proper standard for judging obscenity, already discussed, give adequate warning of the conduct proscribed and mark '. . . boundaries sufficiently distinct for judges and juries fairly to administer the law. . . . That there may be marginal cases in which it is difficult to determine the side of the line on which a particular fact situation falls is no sufficient reason to hold the language too ambiguous to define a criminal offense . . .' [Cases cited]

"In summary, then, we hold that these statutes, applied according to the proper standard for judging obscenity, do not offend constitutional safeguards against convictions based upon protected material, or fail to give men in acting adequate notice of what is prohibited."

The United States Supreme Court in 1959 in the case of *Smith* v. *California*, 361 U.S. 147, 4 L. Ed. 2d 205, 80 S. Ct. 215 (1959), again applied the standard of the Roth case, and Mr. Justice Frankfurter in his concurring opinion said (p. 165):

". . . It bears repetition that the determination of obscenity is *for juror or judge* not on the basis of his personal upbringing or restricted reflection or particular experience of life, but on the basis of 'contemporary community standards' . . ." (Italics supplied.)

Thus, we find it to be consistent with the position of the courts in stating that if the proper standard is applied to the statute in question by the court and the jury, then the statute is not unconstitutional on those grounds.

Defendant further alleges that this statute violates the freedom of speech provisions of the Pennsylvania and Federal Constitutions.

The cases cited above are dispositive of the freedom of speech argument as well as the argument concerning vagueness, indefiniteness and lack of a proper standard and need not be further discussed here except to state that the right of freedom of speech is not an absolute right and all speech is not afforded constitutional protection. This is the law in Pennsylvania as shown by the Goldman Theaters case, supra, at page 87, where Mr. Chief Justice Jones said:

"Apart from the Fourteenth Amendment, the guarantee of free communication of thought and opinion is independently protected by our State Constitution of 1874. Article 1, § 7, thereof recognizes and declares that 'The free communication of thoughts and opinions is one of the invaluable rights of man, and every citizen may freely speak, write and print on any subject, *being responsible for the abuse of that liberty*.' " (Italics supplied.)

This is further the law in the said Courts as shown by the Roth case in which Mr. Justice Brennan says (p. 481):

"The dispositive question is whether obscenity is utterance within the area of protected speech and press. Although this is the first time the question has been squarely presented to this Court, either under the First Amendment or under the Fourteenth Amendment, expressions found in numerous opinions indicate that this Court has always assumed that obscenity is not protected by the freedoms of speech and press. [Cases cited]"

The court then further specifically holds that obscenity is not protected speech.

Defendant then alleges that the statute is unconstitutional in that it discriminates against telephone conversations. He cites one case involving Philadelphia tax on rented properties: *Murray* v. *Philadelphia*, 364 Pa. 157, 71 A. 2d 280 (1950), as determining this issue. The court finds that case not to be in point.

". . . It is true that a statute or ordinance may not discriminate . . . but it is not invalid merely because it does not prohibit other acts which may be as equally mischievous as the acts prohibited . . .": *Adams* v. *New Kensington*, 357 Pa. 557, 565, 55 A. 2d 392 (1947).

This court will not hold the statute in question to be invalid merely because it does not prohibit other acts equally mischievous as the acts prohibited.

Defendant also alleges that the indictment is faulty in that it lacks particularity and is drawn only in the general words of the statute without setting forth the particular language allegedly used by defendant. Defendant cites in support of this allegation the case of *Russell* v. *United States*, 369 U.S. 749, 8 L. Ed. 2d 240 (1962), which involves a prosecution under Federal statute in the Federal courts governed by the Federal Rules of Procedure. We find that this case does not control the case at bar since the case at bar grows out of State law and is governed by State rules of procedure.

"Since the passage of the Criminal Procedure Act of 1960, by which it was made sufficient to charge offenses substantially in the words of the Act of Assembly, numerous cases have arisen in which the defendant has moved to quash for insufficiency of description. The Courts have uniformly held in such cases that this is not ground to quash, though a bill of particulars may be asked for, which in a proper case the Court will order": Henry on Criminal Procedure in Pennsylvania, section 358, page 431.

It is "sufficient that criminal information supports indictment in its material averments and that indictment charges crime substantially in language of statute and with such certainty that defendant knows what he is called upon to answer": Maurer Notes on Pennsylvania Criminal Law and Procedure, section 2792, page 725.

The court finds in the case at bar that the information is not sufficiently lacking in particularity to be objectionable.

Order of Court

Now, November 6, 1962, defendant's motion to quash is hereby dismissed. Exception granted.

■ Samuel Yudkin

v.

State of Maryland.
No. 300.

Court of Appeals of Maryland.

July 5, 1962.

John Silard, Washington, D.C. (Raub & Silard, Washington, D.C., and Samuel B. Groner, Silver Spring, on the brief), for appellant.

Edward deGrazia, New York City, *Edward L. Genn, Benjamin Brown, Silver Spring, and Speiser*, Washington, D.C., on brief for American Civil Liberties Union, amicus curiae.

Fred Weisgal and *Rowland Watts*, Baltimore, on brief for Md. Civil Liberties Union, amicus curiae.

Joseph S. Kaufman, Deputy Atty. Gen., and *Robert S. Bourbon*, Asst. Atty. Gen. (Thomas B. Finan, Atty. Gen., Baltimore, and Leonard T. Kardy, State's Atty. for Montgomery County, Rockville), on the brief, for appellee.

Before BRUNE, C.J., and PRESCOTT, HORNEY, MARBURY and SYBERT, JJ.

HORNEY, Judge.

Claiming that the book Tropic of Cancer, written by Henry Miller, is neither lewd, obscene nor indecent, the defendant-appellant (Samuel Yudkin) has appealed his conviction for selling a copy of it in violation of Code (1957), Art. 27, § 418.

On October 26, 1961, two members of the Montgomery County police force entered the bookstore of the defendant in Bethesda where several copies of the alleged obscene book were on display. The officers purchased a copy and after some conversation with the bookseller, left the store to swear out a warrant for his arrest. At the time of the arrest another copy of the book was seized as additional evidence. Both copies were subsequently offered and received as exhibits.

At the trial before a jury of men and women, one of the arresting officers testified to the circumstances leading up to the arrest and prosecution of the defendant. There was also other evidence tending to show that the defendant sold the book "knowing" it to be obscene. When the defendant was asked by a newspaper reporter before the book was placed on sale if he knew he might be subject to arrest, he replied that no one had told him not to sell it. And, although he stated to the police when he sold them a copy of the book that he was not familiar with the ruling of the State's Attorney that the book was obscene, the defendant admitted on cross examination at the trial that he knew three weeks before his arrest that the employees of a drug store in Montgomery County had been arrested for selling "under the counter paperback copies of Tropic of Cancer." The record further indicates that the defendant, though he had some doubt as to whether the book could be banned, chose to take the risk that a court would not declare it to be obscene. Just prior to the close of the State's case, the trial court sent the jury to the juryroom to read the book in question. But no evidence was offered by the State concerning literary merit, contemporary community standards and the effect of the book with respect to prurient interest.

The defendant, who had read the book as well as critical reviews of it and apparently believed that it was not unlawful to sell the book, testified at length that in his opinion the book had literary merit and was not obscene, and stated his reasons for having the book in his possession and offering it for sale. A favorable book review, (From Under the Counter to Front Shelf, by Harry T. Moore, published in the New York Times Book Review, June 18, 1961), was also received in evidence as an exhibit. But the defendant was not permitted to offer the testimony of certain witnesses, such as professors of English literature, literary critics, authors of books, and other persons, who may have been able to qualify as experts, or to introduce as exhibits such publications as comparable books and other literary critiques and comments, to show that Tropic of

Cancer was not obscene; that it would not arouse the prurient interest of the average person; that it had literary merit; and that it had received critical acceptance as literature. The trial court also rejected evidence that the book had been cleared by the Post Office Department for circulation through the mails and that contemporary books (such as Memoirs of Hecate County by Edmund Wilson, Lolita by Vladimir Nabokov, By Love Possessed by James Gould Cozzens, and Lady Chatterley's Lover by D. H. Lawrence) on sale generally in Montgomery County contained words and descriptions claimed to be comparable to those in Tropic of Cancer. Nor would the court allow the introduction of any other evidence as to contemporary community standards. Timely exceptions were taken to the exclusion of such evidence.

A special motion to dismiss the indictment as well as motions for a directed verdict, on the ground, among others, that there was no evidence that the defendant sold the book knowing it to be obscene, were also denied.

In submitting the case to the jury, the trial court, after informing the jury that it was the "sole judge of the law as well as the facts," further advised it that the question was whether the book would appeal to the prurient interests of the average person, and that, as a jury, it was required to determine the standards of the community and to decide whether the book as a whole tended to "incite lustful thoughts." But the court refused to give an instruction that if the jury found Tropic of Cancer to be a "work of genuine literary intent and effect" it should acquit the defendant. Nor did the court give any other instruction indicating that literary purpose, merit or acceptance had any bearing on the offense charged or the defense to it. The jury returned a verdict of guilty and the defendant was sentenced to six months in jail.

[1] Four questions are posed by the appeal. Inasmuch as it appears there was sufficient evidence to take the case to the jury, we find no error in the denial of the motions for a directed verdict. Of the remaining three questions, it is necessary to discuss only one of them on this appeal. This relates to the admissibility of the evidence. As to this, we think the trial court was in error when it excluded evidence proffered by the defendant to show that the book is not obscene.

[2, 3] The test of obscenity as laid down in *Roth* v. *United States* (and *Alberts* v. *California*), 354 U.S. 476, 77 S. Ct. 1304, 1 L. Ed. 2d 1498 (1957), is "whether to the average person, applying contemporary community standards, the dominent theme of the material taken as a whole appeals to prurient interests." And, since the issue of whether the defendant was innocent or guilty necessarily involves a determination of whether Tropic of Cancer was in fact obscene, we think it is implicit, under the Roth test, that all relevant evidence (if it is otherwise competent) concerning community standards and prurient interest, as well as evidence bearing on literary merit, is admissible to show either obscenity or the lack of it.

We reaffirm the holding in *Monfred* v. *State*, 226 Md. 312, 173 A. 2d 173 (1961), cert. den. 368 U.S. 953, 82 S. Ct. 395, 7 L. Ed. 2d 386 (1962), where there was a dearth of evidence other than the salacious material itself, that exhibits of allegedly obscene material speak for themselves and must in every case be perused and examined with care. But that is not to say—even though the court or

jury (as the case may be) must in the end determine the issue of obscenity—that other competent evidence tending to show that the book is *not* obscene should be excluded as irrelevant or immaterial.

[4, 5] In this case where the conviction or acquittal of the defendant depended on whether or not Tropic of Cancer is in fact obscene, we think the defendant was prejudiced by the refusal of the trial court to permit him to offer the testimony of expert witnesses, who, had they been allowed to do so, would have testified that the book had literary merit, that it fell within contemporary community standards and that it would not stimulate lustful thoughts in the average reader. The expert opinions were admissible and should have been received. See *Harper* v. *Higgs*, 225 Md. 24, 169 A. 2d 661 (1961), where in restating the rule, we stated that "an approved test as to the admissibility of expert opinion is whether the jury can receive appreciable help from the particular witness on the subject, not whether the jury can decide the particular issue without expert help."

In *Smith* v. *California*, 361 U.S. 147, 80 S. Ct. 215, 4 L. Ed. 2d 205 (1959), in which the conviction of the defendant for obscenity was reversed, Justice Frankfurter stated in his concurring opinion (at p. 164, 80 S. Ct. at p. 225) that the defendant had a right "to enlighten the judgment of the tribunal, be it the jury or * * * the judge, regarding the prevailing literary and moral community standards and to do so through qualified experts" and in stating the reasons therefor went on to say that "to exclude such expert testimony is in effect to exclude as irrelevant evidence that goes to the very essence of the defense and therefore to the constitutional safeguards of due process." And Justice Harlan, in concurring with Justice Frankfurter on this point, further emphasized the view (at p. 172, 80 S. Ct. at p. 229) that the state obscenity conviction was "fatally defective in that the trial judge * * * turned aside *every* attempt by appellant to introduce evidence bearing on community standards." Furthermore, in the A.L.I. Model Penal Code, Proposed Official Draft (May 4, 1962), § 251.4(4), it is stated that "expert testimony, * * * relating to factors entering into the determination of the issue of obscenity, shall be admissible." And cf. *United States* v. *4200 Copies International Journal*, 134 F. Supp. 490 (D.C. Distr. 1955), where women of the community were allowed to testify as to the obscenity of the publication in question. There are other cases holding that expert testimony is admissible. See those cited by Lockhart and McClure in The Law of Obscenity and the Constitution, 38 Minn. L. Rev. 295, fns. pp. 348–350. See also the discussion as to the value of such testimony by the same authors in Censorship of Obscenity: The Developing Constitutional Standards, 45 Minn. L. Rev. 5, 95–99.[1]

As to the testimony of psychiatrists, the cases are not in accord, but if a psychiatrist can qualify as an expert

---

[1] Compare the two cases of *Harman* v. *Morris* (decided February 21, 1962, by the Superior Court of Cook County, Illinois) and *Commonwealth* v. *Robin* (decided April 17, 1962, by the Court of Common Pleas No. 2 in the County of Philadelphia, Pennsylvania), which, though reaching opposite results as to the obscenity of Tropic of Cancer, permitted the introduction of expert testimony.

witness, the admission of his testimony would not be improper. In *Smith* v. *California*, supra, Justice Frankfurter stated (361 U.S., at p. 165, 80 S. Ct., at p. 225) that "psychological or physiological consequences of questioned literature can as a matter of fact hardly be established except through experts." But see *Womack* v. *United States*, 294 F. 2d 204 (D.C. Cir. 1961), where psychiatrists and psychologists were not permitted to express an opinion on contemporary community standards in a prosecution for sending obscene matter through the mails. In the latter case, however, the trial court had ruled that the witnesses were not qualified to testify as experts and the appellate court upheld the ruling.

[6] Whether or not a witness is qualified to express an opinion on the subject as to which he is called to testify, is a matter for the trial court to pass upon in the first instance. And for a summary of what is generally necessary to qualify as an expert witness see *Turner* v. *State Roads Comm.*, 213 Md. 428, 431–435, 132 A. 2d 455 (1957), and the cases and authorities therein cited. See also the cases collected in 10 M.L.E. Evidence §§ 281, 282.

[7] On the question of whether other books on sale in the community were admissible for the purpose of comparing them with Tropic of Cancer, we think it is clear that it was error to reject them. The necessity of admitting such evidence was pointed out by Justice Harlan in *Smith* v. *California*, supra, when he stated (361 U.S., at p. 171, 80 S. Ct., at p. 228) that "[t]he community cannot, where liberty of speech and press are at issue, condemn that which it generally tolerates." And because the trier of the facts is required under the Roth obscenity test to apply "contemporary community standards" in determining what is and what is not obscene, it is essential that the jury or court, instead of being required to depend on what may well be a limited knowledge of the moral and literary standards of the community, has a right to read, or to be informed of, the contents of comparable books that have been generally accepted or tolerated by the public.

Recently the Supreme Court of California in In Re Harris, 56 Cal. 2d 879, 16 Cal. Rptr. 889, 366 P. 2d 305 (Cal. 1961), ruled that evidence consisting of "expert testimony, comparable writings and pictures adjudged * * * to be not obscene, and comparable writings and publications purchased in the community" was admissible in a prosecution for selling allegedly obscene books in violation of the California obscenity statute.

[8, 9] It was therefore not only error to reject the comparable books as evidence, but the court also erred when it refused to permit introduction of evidence showing that the Post Office Department had determined that Tropic of Cancer was mailable. And, since the record shows that the "study" or critique of the book made by George Orwell, the novelist and critic, was offered as evidence of its literary merit, and not, as the State assumes, as evidence of "community acceptance or standards," it is apparent that the trial court also erred when it refused to admit the critique as evidence.

For the reasons herein stated the judgment will be reversed and the case remanded for a new trial, but in reaching this decision, we should not be understood as expressing any opinion as to whether Tropic of Cancer is or is not obscene.

Judgment reversed and case remanded for a new trial; the costs of this appeal to be paid by Montgomery County.

■ Attorney General

v.

The Book Named "Tropic of Cancer."

Supreme Judicial Court of Massachusetts.

Suffolk.

Argued May 16, 1962.

Decided July 17, 1962.

Charles Rembar, New York City, *William P. Homans, Jr.*, Boston, for intervener.

James J. Kelleher, Asst. Atty. Gen., *Leo Sontag*, Asst. Atty. Gen., for Attorney General.

Reuben Goodman, Rudolph Kass and *George Waldstein*, Boston, by leave of court, submitted a brief as amici curiae.

Before WILKINS, C.J., and SPALDING, WILLIAMS, WHITTEMORE, CUTTER, KIRK, and SPIEGEL, JJ.

CUTTER, Justice.

The Attorney General proceeds under G.L. c. 272, §§ 28C–28G (inserted by St. 1945, c. 278, § 1),[1] against

---

[1] Section 28C reads in part, "Whenever there is reasonable cause to believe that a book which is being * * * distributed * * * is obscene, indecent or impure, the attorney general * * * shall bring an information * * in equity in the superior court directed against said book by name." Then follow provisions for issuing an order of notice to interested persons and for

a book by Henry Miller, "Tropic of Cancer" (Tropic), published by Grove Press, Inc. (Grove). Answers were filed by Grove, Miller, and other intervenors, alleging that c. 272, §§ 28C through 28H, "as applied herein * * * violate rights of the intervenor[s] guaranteed * * * by the * * * Constitution of the United States," under the First Amendment, "as embraced in the Fourteenth Amendment," and under the Constitution of the Commonwealth, Part I, arts. 10, 12, and 16. The case was heard by a judge of the Superior Court, who made a report of material facts. A final decree was entered adjudging Tropic to be "obscene." The intervenors appealed. The evidence is reported. The trial judge made the findings summarized below.

"The book was first published in Paris in 1934. The first publication in the United States was on June 24, 1961." Its distribution in Massachusetts was enjoined on July 24, 1961. "There is no connected plot * * *. It is largely a tale of the sex experiences of an American * * * [who went to] Paris * * * in the hope of becoming a writer, and who, except on a few occasions, lived the life of a down-and-outer, sponging on friends * * *. It graphically describes sex episodes with almost minute detail. It is in many respects filthy, disgusting, nauseating and offensive to good taste. As one favorable review, which was introduced in evidence, put it, 'Now it must be granted that parts of "Tropic of Cancer" will hammer away at some of the strongest of stomachs.' "[2]

The book, several book reviews, and some advertising were in evidence. "Persons who qualified as literary experts testified." The trial judge stated that he was "irresistibly led to the conclusion that the book is obscene, indecent and impure."

[1] 1. The opinion testimony is significant principally in that it discloses that competent critics entertain (and, in some cases, have entertained since 1934) the view that Tropic has great literary merit despite its repulsive features. Because the only important evidence is documentary, we are in essentially the same position as the trial judge, and "may draw our own inferences * * * from the basic facts * * * without deference to any inferences * * drawn by the trial judge." See *Corkum* v. *Salvation Army of Mass., Inc.*, 340 Mass. 165, 166–167, 162 N.E. 2d 778, 780. See also *Skil Corp.* v. *Barnet*, 337 Mass. 485, 488, 150 N.E. 2d 551.

2. The issue "is whether the" material can "reasonably and constitutionally be found to be obscene." *Commonwealth* v. *Moniz*, 338 Mass. 442, 443, 155 N.E. 2d 762,

763 (motion picture). The interveners "concede that the statute covers all material that is obscene in the constitutional sense."

In *Roth* v. *United States*, 354 U.S. 476, 488–489, 77 S. Ct. 1304, 1311, 1 L. Ed. 2d 1498 the majority rejected the test of obscenity in *Regina* v. *Hicklin*, L.R. 3 Q.B. 360 (1868), and pointed out that later decisions have sought to determine "whether to the average person, applying contemporary community standards, the dominant theme of the material taken as a whole appeals to prurient interest." Material "appealing to prurient interest" was defined as "material having a tendency to excite lustful thoughts" (354 U.S. 476, 487, fn. 20, 77 S. Ct. 1304, 1310) and was equated to the definition of obscenity in A.L.I., Model Penal Code, § 207.10(2) (Tent. Draft No. 6, 1957).[3] The Roth case recognized that there is constitutional protection (354 U.S. 476, 484, 77 S. Ct. 1304) for works containing "ideas having even the slightest redeeming social importance—unorthodox ideas, controversial ideas, even ideas hateful to the prevailing climate of opinion—[which] have the full protection of the [First Amendment] guaranties, unless excludable because they encroach upon the limited area of more important interests." The court, however, stated (p. 485, 77 S. Ct. p. 1309) that "implicit in the history of the First Amendment is the rejection of obscenity as utterly without redeeming social importance" and that "obscenity is not within the area of constitutionally protected speech or press."

The Roth opinions discuss "obscenity" on a highly theoretical basis. Indeed, the court said (354 U.S. 476, 481, fn. 8, 77 S. Ct. 1304, 1307), "No issue is presented * * * concerning the obscenity of the material." See Lockhart and McClure, Censorship of Obscenity: The Developing Constitutional Standards, 45 Minn. L. Rev. (hereinafter cited Lockhart) pp. 49–58.[4] At least the

---

interlocutory action. Section 28E provides for an adjudication against the book, in the event of default, "if the court finds that the book is obscene, indecent or impure * * *." Section 28F provides for a similar adjudication in the event of a contested hearing, at which "the court may receive the testimony of experts and may receive evidence as to the literary, cultural or educational character of said book and as to the manner and form of its publication, advertisement, and distribution."

[2] The findings also state, "Of the 318 pages of the book, there are sex episodes on 85 pages, some of which are described on two or more pages, and all of which are described with precise physical detail and four-letter words. The author's descriptive powers are truly impressive and he rises to great literary heights when he describes Paris. And suddenly he descends into the filthy gutter. The literary experts testified that the book depicts a type of life in the thirties in a portion of Paris and that it has great literary merit."

[3] Section 207.10(2) reads in part: "A thing is obscene if, considered as a whole, its *predominant* appeal is to prurient interest, i.e., a shameful or *morbid* interest in nudity, sex, or excretion, and if it goes *substantially* beyond customary limits of candor in description or representation of such matters. * * * Obscenity shall be judged with reference to ordinary adults, except that it shall be judged with reference to children or other specially susceptible audience if it appears from the character of the material or the circumstances of its dissemination to be specially designed for or directed to such an audience" (emphasis supplied). See § 251.4 of the proposed final draft of the code (approved May, 1962), which as Mr. Justice Harlan points out in *Manual Enterprises, Inc.* v. *Day*, 82 S. Ct. 1432, requires, in order that material may be held "obscene," not only that "considered as a whole * * * [the material have] predominant appeal * * * to prurient interest," but also "*in addition* * * * [that the material go] substantially beyond customary limits of candor in describing or representing such matters" (emphasis supplied). The comment on § 207.10(2) (Ten. Draft No. 6, p. 10) points out that the code rejects "the prevailing test of tendency to arouse lustful thoughts * * * because it is unrealistically broad for a society that plainly tolerates a great deal of erotic interest in literature, advertising, and art, and because regulation of thought or desire, unconnected with overt misbehavior, raises the most acute constitutional as well as practical difficulties." See Mr. Justice Harlan's separate opinion in the Roth case (354 U.S. 476, 499–500, 77 S. Ct. 1304); Schwartz, Criminal Obscenity Law, 29 Pa. Bar Assn. Q. 8. See note, 36 N.C.L. Rev. 189, 196–198.

[4] For other discussions of the Roth case and later decisions, see Lockhart and McClure, Obscenity Censorship, 7 Utah L.

Chief Justice (see his concurring opinion, 354 U.S. 476, 496, 77 S. Ct. 1304, 1315) thought that he was dealing with "the commercial exploitation of the morbid and shameful craving for materials with prurient effect."[5]

Some principles have been established by the Roth case, as applied in the Moniz case, 338 Mass. 442, 445–450, 155 N.E. 2d 762. (1) Hard core, commercial pornography, "utterly without redeeming social importance" (see 354 U.S. 476, 484–485, 77 S. Ct. 1304, 1309), is not within the protection of the First Amendment. (2) "The portrayal of sex, e.g., in art, literature and scientific works, is not itself sufficient reason to deny material the constitutional protection of freedom of speech and press" (354 U.S. 476, 487–488, 77 S. Ct. 1304, 1310). (3) "[W]hether a particular work is * * * [obscene] involves not * * * an issue of fact but a question of constitutional *judgment* of the most sensitive * * * kind." See Mr. Justice Harlan's separate opinion, 354 U.S. 476, 497–498, 77 S. Ct. 1304, 1316; the Moniz case, 338 Mass. 442, 446–447, 155 N.E. 2d 762. (4) Material (see 354 U.S. 488–489, 77 S. Ct. 1311) must be judged by its effect upon the "*average* person" (not susceptible persons or youths) and by whether the "*dominant theme* of the material *taken as a whole*" appeals to prurient interest" (emphasis supplied).[6] (5) "[A] work may not be adjudged obscene only because" objectionable "to many citizens as violative of accepted standards of propriety." See the Moniz case, 338 Mass. 442, 445, 155 N.E. 2d 762, 764. Apart from these principles, what the Supreme Court means by "obscenity" must be determined by what it has done in other cases.[7]

Rev. 289; Kauper, Civil Liberties and the Constitution, pp. 52–89; notes, 71 Harv. L. Rev. 85, 91–92, 146–150; 72 Harv. L. Rev. 77, 90–91; 73 Harv. L. Rev. 84, 164–167; 74 Harv. L. Rev. 81, 126; 41 Marquette L. Rev. 320; 106 U. of P.L. Rev. 132; 12 Syr. L. Rev. 58. See also Paul and Schwartz, Obscenity in the Mails, 106 U. of P.L. Rev. 214; Foster, The "Comstock Load" —Obscenity and the Law; 48 J. Cr. Law 245; Note 27 U. of Cinn. L. Rev. 61.

[5] The government brief in the Roth case (pp. 22–42) separated allegedly obscene materials into three rough categories which provide a convenient basis of reference, viz. (1) "[N]ovels of apparently serious literary intent" (p. 35); (2) "[B]orderline entertainment * * *," magazines, cartoons, nudist publications, etc. (pp. 35–36); (3) "[H]ard core" pornography, which "[n]o one would suggest" had literary merit (pp. 37–38). The brief stated (p. 34, fn. 23) that the government had furnished to the court sample items seized as unmailable under 18 U.S.C. § 1461 (1952; see also Supp. III, and 1958 ed.), apparently mostly, if not entirely, "hard core" items. See Lockhart, p. 26.

[6] See as to this *Butler v. Michigan*, 352 U.S. 380, 382–384, 77 S. Ct. 524, 525–526, 1 L. Ed. 2d 412. "* * * [The] appellant was convicted because Michigan * * * made it an offense for him to make available for the general reading public * * * a book that the trial judge found to have a potentially deleterious influence upon youth. * * * The incidence of this enactment is to reduce the adult population of Michigan to reading only what is fit for children. It thereby arbitrarily curtails one of those liberties of the individual, now enshrined in the Due Process Clause of the Fourteenth Amendment, that history has attested as the indispensable conditions for the maintenance and progress of a free society."

[7] Certain cases, decided since the Roth case, are of little assistance. *Adams Newark Theater Co. v. Newark*, 354 U.S. 931, 77 S. Ct. 1395, 1 L. Ed. 2d 1533, a per curiam decision, dealt with theatres. *Times Film Corp. v. Chicago*, 365 U.S. 43, 48–49, 81 S. Ct. 391, 5 L. Ed. 2d 403, dealt with prior licensing of

(a) In *Kingsley Books, Inc. v. Brown*, 354 U.S. 436, 77 S. Ct. 1325, 1 L. Ed. 2d 1469, the New York courts (see 1 N.Y. 2d 177, 180, 151 N.Y.S. 2d 639, 134 N.E. 2d 461, affirming 208 Misc. 150, 158–159, 142 N.Y.S. 2d 735) were sustained in enjoining distribution of fourteen booklets, "Nights of Horror," clearly hard core pornography. The Supreme Court assumed that the books were obscene and that only the issue of the constitutionality of the testing statute was before it (see 354 U.S. p. 439, 77 S. Ct. p. 1326).

(b) In four per curiam decisions (October term, 1957) the Supreme Court reversed decisions of Federal courts of appeal which had treated several different types of material as obscene. See *Times Film Corp. v. Chicago*, 355 U.S. 35, 78 S. Ct. 115, 2 L. Ed. 2d 72 (revg. 244 F. 2d 432, 436 [7th Cir.] on a film dealing with the seduction of a sixteen year old boy by an older woman, and other "illicit sexual intimacies and acts"); *Mounce v. United States*, 355 U.S. 180, 78 S. Ct. 267, 2 L. Ed. 2d 187 (revg. 247 F. 2d 148 [9th Cir.] nudist publications; see *United States v. 4200 Copies International Journal*, 134 F. Supp. 490 [E.D., Wash.]); *One, Inc. v. Olesen*, 355 U.S. 371, 78 S. Ct. 364, 2 L. Ed. 2d 352 (revg. 241 F. 2d 772 [9th Cir.] dealing with a post office order in respect of "One— The Homosexual Magazine"); *Sunshine Book Co. v. Summerfield*, 355 U.S. 372, 78 S. Ct. 365, 2 L. Ed. 2d 352 (revg. 101 U.S. App. D.C. 358, 249 F. 2d 114, nudist material). See also the Moniz case, 338 Mass. 442, 447–449, 155 N.E. 2d 762; Lockhart, pp. 32–39.

(c) In *Kingsley International Pictures Corp. v. Regents of Univ. of N.Y.*, 360 U.S. 684, 79 S. Ct. 1362, 3 L. Ed. 2d 1512, a New York decision (4 N.Y. 2d 349, 175 N.Y.S. 2d 39, 151 N.E. 2d 197) was reversed which had sustained the denial of a license to show the film "Lady Chatterley's Lover." The majority did not consider whether the film was obscene (360 U.S. 684, 686, 79 S. Ct. 1362), but said (at pp. 688–689, 79 S. Ct., at p. 1365), "What New York has done * * * is to prevent the exhibition of a motion picture because that picture advocates an idea—that adultery under certain circumstances may be proper behavior. * * * [The First Amendment's] guarantee is not confined to the expression of ideas that are conventional or shared by a majority. It protects advocacy of the opinion that adultery may sometimes be proper, no less than advocacy of socialism or the single tax."

(d) *Manual Enterprises, Inc. v. Day*, 82 S. Ct. 1432, reversing 110 U.S. App. D.C. 78, 289 F. 2d 455 (see fn. 3, supra), dealt (p. 1433) with a ruling of the Post Office Department barring from the mails magazines ("titled MANual, Trim, and Grecian Guild Pictorial") consisting "largely of photographs of nude, or near-nude, male models"; and containing "advertisements * * * offering nudist photographs for sale." See 18 U.S.C. § 1461 (fn. 5, supra). Mr. Justice Harlan's opinion (see fn. 8, infra) accepts (82 S. Ct. p. 1434) findings that "(1) the maga-

---

motion pictures and contains only general references to the obscenity problem. In *Smith v. California*, 361 U.S. 147, 80 S. Ct. 215, 4 L. Ed. 2d 205, the court (at p. 149, fn. 4, 80 S. Ct., at p. 216) assumed to be obscene the material then before it but held invalid a city ordinance making it unlawful to have in one's possession any obscene book, even without knowledge of the contents. See *Demetropolos v. Commonwealth*, 342 Mass. 658, 660–661, 175 N.E. 2d 259.

zines * * * are composed primarily, if not exclusively, for homosexuals, and have no literary, scientific or other merit; [and] (2) they would appeal to the 'prurient interest' of such sexual deviates, but would not have any interest for sexually normal individuals." The Supreme Court on a diversity of grounds[8] (six to one, two justices not participating) reversed the Court of Appeals decision which had sustained the post office order.

The 1957 term per curiam decisions and the Kingsley International Pictures Corp. case (360 U.S. 684, 79 S. Ct. 1362, 3 L. Ed. 2d 1512) afford the best available indication of what material will not be treated as obscene by the Supreme Court. See *Grove Press, Inc.* v. *Christenberry*, 175 F. Supp. 488, 501–502 (S.D., N.Y.) holding the book, "Lady Chatterley's Lover," not obscene, affd. 276 F. 2d 433, 438–439 (2d Cir.). Cf. *Eastman Kodak Co.* v. *Hendricks*, 262 F. 2d 392, 395–397 (9th Cir.).

The New York Court of Appeals has interpreted § 1141 of the New York Penal Law dealing with obscenity, as applying "only to * * * 'hard-core pornography.'" See *People* v. *Richmond County News, Inc.*, 9 N.Y. 2d 578, 586, 216 N.Y.S. 2d 369, 175 N.E. 2d 681. Section 1141, says Judge Fuld, at p. 587, 216 N.Y.S. 2d, at p. 376, 175 N.E. 2d at p. 686, "focuses predominantly upon what is sexually morbid, grossly perverse and bizarre. without any artistic or scientific purpose or justification."[9]

The issue is where to draw the line between what the First Amendment protects and what is obscene in the constitutional sense. See Lockhart, pp. 58–68, 74–77. The Supreme Court of the United States thus far, as Mr. Justice Harlan's opinion in the Manual Enterprises case indicates, has not drawn that line with precision. We, however, are confronted with litigation which should be decided under the law as it now stands, and it is our duty to draw that line as well as we can according to our best judgment of the dictates of the authoritative decisions. A majority of the court feel that we cannot properly evade that duty, even though (as the dissenting opinion points out) the Roth case in some respects is a "dim * * * beacon."

---

[8] Mr. Justice Harlan (with Mr. Justice Stewart concurring) in effect held that the magazines were not obscene, stating (82 S. Ct. 1432) that this was to be determined by a "national standard." After a reference to *People* v. *Richmond County News, Inc.*, 9 N.Y. 2d 578, 216 N.Y.S. 2d 369, 175 N.E. 2d 681 (fn. 9, infra), it was stated (82 S. Ct. p. 1438) that, "[w]hether 'hard-core' pornography, or something less, be the proper test" of obscenity, it was not necessary to go "further in the present case than to hold that" the material before the court was not barred by § 1461. Mr. Justice Black concurred "in the result." Three justices concurred on another ground, and one justice dissented, all without considering whether the material was obscene. See 82 S. Ct. 1432.

[9] The Richmond News case involved both statutory interpretation and consideration of First Amendment limitations. It treated as not obscene somewhat tawdry material ("Gent," a magazine constituting what the opinion at p. 580, 216 N.Y.S. 2d, at p. 370, 175 N.E. 2d, at p. 681 describes as showing "dedication to coarse sensuality"). The court said (p. 588, 216 N.Y.S. 2d, p. 377, 175 N.E. 2d, p. 686) that this material, "appraised as objectively as is possible in the light of First Amendment concepts, may not be adjudged obscene without impairing the vital social interest in freedom of expression." Cf. *American Civil Liberties Union* v. *Chicago*, 3 Ill. 2d 334, 342–349, 121 N.E. 2d 585, decided before the Roth case. Cf. also *Times Film Corp.* v. *Chicago*, 365 U.S. 43, 46, 81 S. Ct. 391, 5 L. Ed. 2d 403.

Referring to the three general categories of allegedly obscene material (fn. 5, supra), it appears that the Supreme Court already has treated some "borderline entertainment" material and works "of serious * * * intent" as not obscene. Hard core pornography (which involves a "kind of 'pandering'" or "commerce in the obscene," see Model Penal Code, Tent. Draft No. 6, pp. 13–17) is clearly obscene. The most difficult area is that of works which some persons reasonably believe to have literary merit but which, equally reasonably, may be even more objectional to others than "Lady Chatterley's Lover."

[2–5] We think, in the light of the decisions reviewed above, that the First Amendment protects material which has value because of ideas, news, or artistic, literary, or scientific attributes. If the appeal of material (taken as a whole) to adults is not predominantly prurient, adults cannot be denied the material. When the public risks of suppressing ideas are weighed against the risks of permitting their circulation, the guaranties of the First Amendment must be given controlling effect. The dangers of subjective judgments in the matter of censorship lead to a strong presupposition against suppression. We conclude, therefore, as in effect the New York court did in the Richmond County News case, that, with respect to material designed for general circulation, only predominantly "hard core" pornography, without redeeming social significance, is obscene in the constitutional sense.

The Attorney General relies largely on earlier Massachusetts decision. *Commonwealth* v. *Isenstadt*, 318 Mass. 543, 62 N.E. 2d 840 (conviction for the sale of a book called "Strange Fruit," under G.L. c. 272, § 28, prior to its amendment by St. 1945, c. 278, § 1). *Attorney General* v. *"God's Little Acre,"* 326 Mass. 281, 93 N.E. 2d 819. These cases were decided, respectively, in 1945 and 1950, each several years before the decision in the Roth case. Compare *Attorney General* v. *"Forever Amber,"* 323 Mass. 302, 309–310, 81 N.E. 2d 663; *Attorney General* v. *"Serenade,"* 326 Mass. 324, 94 N.E. 2d 259, also decided in 1950. The later Supreme Court cases, to the extent inconsistent with our earlier decisions, are controlling, of course, on constitutional issues.

[6, 7] 3. Whether Tropic is "obscene" in the constitutional sense thus depends upon whether the appeal (if any) of Tropic (taken as a whole) to the normal adult is predominantly prurient. It is not relevant that we think that the book at many places is repulsive, vulgar, and grossly offensive in the use of four letter words, and in the detailed and coarse statement of sexual episodes. That a serious work uses four letter words and has a grossly offensive tone does not mean that the work is not entitled to constitutional protection. Much in modern art, literature, and music is likely to seem ugly and thoroughly objectionable to those who have different standards of taste. It is not the function of judges to serve as arbiters of taste or to say that an author must regard vulgarity as unnecessary to his portrayal of particular scenes or characters or to establish particular ideas. Within broad limits each writer, attempting to be a literary artist, is entitled to determine such matters for himself, even if the result is as dull, dreary, and offensive as the writer of this opinion finds almost all of Tropic.

Competent critics assert, and we conclude, that Tropic

has serious purpose,[10] even if many will find that purpose obscure. There can be no doubt that a significant segment of the literary world has long regarded the book as of literary importance. A majority of the court are of opinion that the predominant effect and purpose of the book as a whole is not prurient. If under the Roth case it be a relevant consideration, a majority of the court are of opinion that Tropic is more likely to discourage than "to excite lustful thoughts." We think that the book must be accepted as a conscious effort to create a work of literary art[11] and as having significance, which prevents treating it as hard core pornography. In reaching this conclusion, we have carefully considered all the aspects of the book upon which the dissenting justices and the trial judge have commented.

This is not the first time that Tropic has run into censorship. In *Besig* v. *United States*, 208 F. 2d 142 (9th Cir.), the court sustained a customs prohibition of its importation, relying (p. 146), however, upon something very close to the discredited Hicklin test of obscenity. A customs libel of the book by the United States, however, was recently withdrawn. See order of the United States District Court, Eastern District, New York, dated August 15, 1961, in evidence. Compare the discussion by Judge Murphy in *Upham* v. *Dill*, U.S. Dist. Ct. S.D.N.Y., 195 F. Supp. 5, decided June 27, 1961. An unreported case (*Haiman* v. *Morris*, Illinois Superior Court, Cook County, February 21, 1962) has held the book not to be obscene. The Pennsylvania Court of Common Pleas reached a contrary conclusion in *Commonwealth* v. *Robin*, 30 U.S. L. Week 2551 (dec. April 17, 1962).

We hold that Tropic is not "obscene" in the constitu-

tional sense. It cannot constitutionally be held to be obscene under G.L. c. 272, §§ 28C, 28E, and 28F. We rest our decision squarely on the First Amendment, so that, if review of our decision is sought, there may be no doubt that this case has been decided solely upon the Federal issue.

4. We are not confronted with any question arising under G.L. c. 272, § 28, as amended through St. 1948, c. 328, providing for prosecution for a sale to "a person under the age of eighteen years [of] a book * * * which is obscene * * * *or manifestly tends to corrupt* the morals of youth" (emphasis supplied). See *Butler* v. *Michigan*, 352 U.S. 380, 382–384, 77 S. Ct. 524, 1 L. Ed. 2d 412 (fn. 6, supra). See also *Prince* v. *Massachusetts*, 321 U.S. 158, 166–171, 64 S. Ct. 438, 88 L. Ed. 645; Lockhart and McClure, Obscenity Censorship, 7 Utah L. Rev. 289, 298–303. Cf. *Commonwealth* v. *Friede*, 271 Mass. 318, 322–323, 171 N.E. 472, 69 A.L.R. 640.

5. The final decree is reversed. A new decree is to be entered that the book "Tropic of Cancer" is entitled to the protection of the First Amendment and cannot be held to be obscene under G.L. c. 272, §§ 28C, 28E, and 28F.

So ordered.

The CHIEF JUSTICE and Justices WILLIAMS and KIRK cannot join in the foregoing opinion.

The majority, in expressing deference to some very recent decisions of the Supreme Court of the United States, particularly *Roth* v. *United States*, 354 U.S. 476, 77 S. Ct. 1304, 1 L. Ed. 2d 1498, declare that G. L. c. 272 §§ 28C, 28E, and 28F, as applied to this book are repugnant to the First Amendment to the Constitution of the United States. The Roth case, as we read, is not clear authority to this extent, and as presently applied, is too dim a beacon by which to guess a course.[1] The onus of the present majority result should rest upon the court which decided the Roth case. If a majority of the members of that tribunal should be of the opinion that the people of Massachusetts constitutionally cannot be deprived of access to this item of reading material, we believe that they should be given the specific opportunity so to state.

The book is pitched at the nadir of scatology. Indeed, its low level is relied upon as engulfing all obscene effect. We cannot bring ourselves to accept the thesis that the book, thus indicted, becomes endowed with constitutional protection. Its detailed and sordid sex episodes, persistently inserted at intervals in what passes for narrative, leave an outweighing staccato impression. In our opinion it should be classified as pornography.

Because of its impact upon other obscenity statutes, many of long standing, the majority decision will have a wide practical effect. It should lead to legislative reëxamination of the entire field.

We would affirm the decree of the Superior Court.

---

[10] Professor Levin of Harvard testified that he thought the author's attitude was "one of disgust with sex" and "the mood * * * one of sexual revulsion. Although a good deal of sex is presented, the author, as it were, is backing away from it and even admonishing against it. It doesn't seem * * * [that] it would be a book to incite lustful thoughts. * * [I]t * * * [seems] designed to show up western culture at a late stage by dealing with the most ignoble sides of it. * * * [I]t also has passages of some critical and philosophic purport in which the author endeavors to take a more positive view. * * * [S]ome interpreters * * * end by thinking * * * that it is a very healthy book. In my opinion, it is a somewhat morbid book, but a serious one. * * * I think the author is saying, in effect, 'All this is morbid. I am fed up with it.' " More favorable appraisals of the merits of the book were given by other qualified expert witnesses, who expressed, or referred to, opinions that the book contains substantial areas showing literary power. These witnesses included Research Professor Harry T. Moore, Southern Illinois University; Professor Mark Schorer, Chairman of the Department of English, University of California (Berkeley); Professor Morton Bloomfield, English Department, Harvard.

[11] Not everyone will agree with the analysis of Miller's "thesis" expressed by Dr. Leon S. Shapiro in 36 Harv. Med. Alumni Bull. (No. 3) 36 "that our way of life, particularly the preoccupation with money and goods, leads to a progressive cheapening of life and living and eventually to a frenzy of destruction. * * * Miller progresses systematically from an examination of the corrupting effects on the individual from certain kinds of social structures, to a similar examination of the effects in interpersonal relations, in the neighborhood, the city, the world. * * * The real tragedy here is * * * that we should not heed what Miller seems to be saying: that we are worrying blindly about our sexual impulses, while giving full freedom to our aggressive ones." Compare Time, June 29, 1962, p. 78.

---

[1] There were four opinions dealing with two cases. The majority opinion was of five justices two of whom are no longer on the court. There was a second opinion concurring in the result. An opinion by one justice dissented in one case and concurred in the other. There was a dissenting opinion by two justices. The dim beacon has not been made brighter by *Manual Enterprises, Inc.* v. *Day*, 82 S. Ct. 1432.

■ Jacob Zeitlin *et al.*, *Plaintiffs* and *Appellants*,
v.
Roger Arnebergh, *Defendant* and *Respondent*.
L.A. 26905.

Supreme Court of California, In Bank.

July 2, 1963.

Rehearing Denied July 31, 1963.

Nathan L. Schoichet, Beverly Hills, *A. L. Wirin* and *Fred Okrand*, Los Angeles, for plaintiffs and appellants.
Brock & Fleishman, Stanley Fleishman, Hollywood, *Bayard F. Berman* and *Sol Rosenthal*, Beverly Hills, as amici curiae on behalf of plaintiffs and appellants.
Roger Arnebergh, City Atty., *Philip E. Grey*, Asst. City Atty., *William E. Doran* and *Edward P. George*, Deputy City Attys., Los Angeles, for defendant and respondent.

TOBRINER, Justice.

In this case "Tropic of Cancer" by Henry Miller makes another one of its many court appearances. Its record to date has been a varied one; in some places the book is "obscene" and in others it is not; presently its legal status is largely tied into the geography of its sale or publications.[1] In any event, our first task must be to determine whether the instant form of action, that of declaratory relief requested by a bookseller and would-be reader, properly presents the issue of the book's proscription under Penal Code section 311. We hold this form of relief appropriate. Our second question turns upon whether the issue of the application of the statute to this book, within constitutional limitations, rests ultimately with the court, as a matter of law, or with the jury as a question of fact. We think it a legal issue. Finally, since we believe the Penal Code section constitutionally may exorcise only hard-core pornography, and since the statute does no more, we hold the book does not fall within its prohibition because "Tropic of Cancer" is not hard-core pornography.

The plaintiff bookseller and plaintiff prospective purchaser brought the action against the city attorney of Los Angeles to secure a declaratory judgment that the book was not "matter" defined as "obscene" by Penal Code section 311,[2] and that its sale would not violate Penal Code section 311.2.[3] Plaintiffs appended to the complaint a copy of the book and excerpts from several book reviews by critics which proclaim its literary merit. Defendant answered, denying many of the allegations of the complaint, but admitting that he contends that the sale of the book violates Penal Code section 311.2. In a separate declaration the defendant stated that he intends to prosecute all persons arrested in the City of Los Angeles for the sale of "Tropic of Cancer." Defendant also entered a general demurrer to the complaint.

---

[1] The book has been held not obscene in *Attorney General* v. *Book Named "Tropic of Cancer"* (1962), 344 Mass.—, 184 N.E. 2d 328; *McCauley* v. *Tropic of Cancer* (1963) Wis., 121 N.W. 2d 545; *People* v. *Fritch* (1963), 38 Misc. 2d 333, 236 N.Y.S. 2d 706; and *Haiman* v. *Morris* (1962, No. 61 S. 19718, Superior Ct. of Cook County, Ill.). The book has been held obscene in *Besig* v. *United States* (9th Cir. 1953), 208 F. 2d 142; *State* v. *Huntington* (1962, No. 24657, Superior Ct. Hartford County, Conn.); and *Commonwealth* v. *Robin* (1962, No. 3177, Ct. of Common Pleas, County of Philadelphia, Pa.).

In California there has been one conviction of a bookseller for the sale of the book (*People* v. *Smith* (1962), Municipal Ct., Los Angeles Judicial Dist.; affd., No. CRA 5113 Appellate Dept., Superior Ct. of Los Angeles County; cert. granted) and two acquittals of booksellers (*People* v. *Pershina* (No. 16644, Municipal Ct., Central Judicial Dist., Marin County) and *People* v. *McGilvery* (No. M–11466, San Diego Municipal Ct.)). In *Yudkin* v. *State* (1962), 229 Md. 223, 182 A. 2d 798, the court reversed the defendant's conviction for the sale of the book because the trial court refused to admit evidence of contemporary community standards, but held that it could not hold as a matter of law that the book was not obscene. In *Bunis* v. *Conway* (1962), 17 App. Div. 2d 207, 234 N.Y.S. 2d 435, the court held that a declaratory judgment action by a bookseller would lie to determine whether the book was obscene, but the court did not pass on the merits of the book. The court in *State* v. *Goodhue* (1962, No. 2223, Superior Ct. Grafton County, N.H.) held that the book was obscene, but that the defendant's conduct came within the "advancement of literature" exception of the statute. The Attorney General of the United States reportedly announced that the book is protected and that post office and customs officials cannot interfere with its distribution. (New York Times, June 14, 1961.) In England the Government reportedly announced that it would not interfere with the sale of the book. (New York Times, Western ed., April 12, 1963, p. 11, col. 4.)

[2] Penal Code section 311 provides in part:

"(a) 'Obscene' means that to the average person, applying contemporary standards, the predominant appeal of the matter, taken as a whole, is to prurient interest, i.e., a shameful or morbid interest in nudity, sex, or excretion, which goes substantially beyond customary limits of candor in description or representation of such matters and is matter which is utterly without redeeming social importance. * * *"

[3] Penal Code section 311.2 provides in part:

"Every person who knowingly * * * distributes, or offers to distribute * * * any obscene matter is guilty of a misdemeanor."

The trial court sustained the demurrer without leave to amend and entered a judgment dismissing the action. In a memorandum entry in the minutes the judge stated that he had upheld the demurrer both because, having read the book, he determined it to be obscene and because plaintiffs have failed to state a cause of action.

[1] In assessing the propriety of the trial court's order sustaining the demurrer without leave to amend, we face the preliminary question of whether an action for declaratory judgment instituted by a bookseller and a prospective purchaser will lie to determine the alleged obscenity of a particular book under the code provisions. While potential defendants have frequently sought declaratory relief to avoid prosecution under statutes which they have sought to prove unconstitutional (see e.g., *Wollam* v. *City of Palm Springs* (1963), 59 Cal. 2d —, 29 Cal. Rptr. 1, 379 P. 2d 481; *Katzev* v. *County of Los Angeles* (1959), 52 Cal. 2d 360, 341 P. 2d 310), plaintiffs here do not challenge the constitutionality of the involved statute unless it sanctions the prosecution of "Tropic of Cancer." In that event, however, plaintiffs do contend that the statute both constitutes an unconstitutional restraint on freedom of speech and also attempts a proscription which is unconstitutionally vague under the First and Fourteenth Amendments to the United States Constitution and article I, sections 9 and 13, of the California Constitution.[4]

The precedents, as well as other compelling reasons, support a declaratory relief action in the present case. The gravamen of the plaintiffs' complaint is that although the statute cannot properly be interpreted to apply to "Tropic of Cancer," defendant nevertheless contends that the book is "obscene matter" within the terms of the statute and intends to prosecute those who sell it. Thus the complaint alleges a genuine controversy involving the construction of particular legislation as to which it seeks a judicial determination. Such a complaint, according to the prior cases, sufficiently states a claim for declaratory relief. (*Walker* v. *County of Los Angeles* (1961), 55 Cal. 2d 626, 637, 12 Cal. Rptr. 671, 361 P. 2d 247; *Hoyt* v. *Board of Civil Service Com'rs* (1942), 21 Cal. 2d 399, 132 P. 2d 804.)

We have stated that considerations beyond the precedents support the adjudication of the alleged obscenity of a particular book in a declaratory relief action.[5] As we shall explain in more detail, the vendor of the questioned book faces the possibility of prosecution and his very fear of it may work a de facto censorship of the publication. The would-be reader, in the absence of declaratory relief, may be deprived of his constitutional rights. Finally, diverse results of the enforcement of the obscenity statute may result in a crazy-quilt pattern of a publication's suppression.

Plaintiff Zeitlin alleges that he is engaged in business as a bookseller and that he wishes to sell "Tropic of Cancer" in his bookstore, but that he is prevented from offering the book because he fears that if he does so defendant will institute criminal proceedings against him. To deny Zeitlin, a legitimate businessman, an opportunity for declaratory relief is to force him to choose between undesirable alternatives. If he continues to sell the book he incurs the risk of criminal prosecution and faces the fine, jail sentence, or both, which may be imposed if he is found guilty,[6] or he sustains the accompanying stigma which attaches even though he may ultimately be found innocent.[7] As an alternative he may assume the role of self-appointed censor, prodded by the city attorney, and discontinue the sale of any book which could possibly offend the latter. The city attorney should not thus become an indirect censor of public reading matter; his abuse of such power could constitute an unlawful restraint upon the dissemination of literature not otherwise censorable. (*Bantam Books, Inc.* v. *Sullivan* (1963), 372 U.S. 58, 83 S. Ct. 631, 9 L. Ed. 2d 584.)

Plaintiff Ferguson alleges that he desires to purchase a copy of "Tropic of Cancer" but is unable to do so because the bookseller, thus fearful of prosecution, refuses to sell the publication. Unless Ferguson is able to find a bookseller willing to face the possibility of criminal prosecution and the attendant described risks, he will be deprived of his basic constitutional right to read. Thus declaratory relief may offer the only method for vindication of this constitutional right.

A final reason for the invocation of declaratory relief lies in its decisiveness. Sporadic and diverse criminal prosecutions must necessarily produce discriminatory results. A finding of guilt of one purveyor of obscene publications will not necessarily discourage others; indeed such vendors characteristically operate under-cover[8] and are inclined to recidivism.[9] If, on the other hand, a verdict expresses a determination that the material is not obscene the city attorney is still free to prosecute another bookseller for selling the same publication. If a criminal verdict, whether of guilt or of innocence, operates primarily within a particular county to ban the book in the case of guilt, or to encourage its sale in the case of innocence, an opposite result might readily obtain in another county. Such an approach must inevitably engender a hodge-podge pattern of suppression and sale.

Nor does our statutory procedure insure a method of uniform adjudication by means of criminal prosecution. Until a third offense, the sale of obscene matter to adults constitutes a misdemeanor. (Pen. Code, § 311.9.) Thus the defendant ordinarily will be tried in the municipal court; if found guilty he may appeal, as a matter of right,

---

[4] Our interpretation of the statute, which we set forth *infra*, renders unnecessary the consideration of these contentions as to unconstitutionality.

[5] These considerations are also discussed in *Bunis* v. *Conway* (1962), 17 App. Div. 2d 207, 234 N.Y.S. 2d 435; Borchard, Declaratory Judgments (2d ed. 1941) p. 1035.

[6] Penal Code section 311.9 provides in part:

"(a) Every person who violates Section 311.2 is punishable by fine of not more than one thousand dollars ($1,000) plus five dollars ($5) for each additional unit of material coming within the provisions of this chapter, which is involved in the offense, not to exceed ten thousand dollars ($10,000), or by imprisonment in the county jail for not more than six months plus one day for each additional unit of material coming within the provisions of this chapter, and which is involved in the offense, such basic maximum and additional days not to exceed 360 days in the county jail, or by both such fine and imprisonment. * * *"

[7] *People* v. *Elliot* (1960), 54 Cal. 2d 498, 504, 6 Cal. Rptr. 753, 354 P. 2d 225; *Greenberg* v. *Superior Court* (1942), 19 Cal. 2d 319, 121 P. 2d 713.

[8] See D. H. Lawrence, Pornography and Obscenity, reprinted in The Portable Lawrence (1947) pp. 646, 653.

[9] See e.g., *Roth* v. *United States* (1956) 77 S. Ct. 17, n. 2, 1 L. Ed. 2d 34 (Roth's application for bail.) "* * * petitioner 'has been convicted in or pleaded guilty in six criminal proceedings involving the dissemination of obscene literature. * * *'"

only to the appellate department of the superior court.[10] To resolve the issue at this level raises not only the possibility of contradictory rulings on the obscenity of a particular work, but also the probability of conflicting interpretations of the obviously perplexing Penal Code section 311.

[2] Since plaintiffs set forth facts showing the existence of an actual controversy and have requested that these rights be adjudged by the court in a matter in which the court is competent to grant declaratory relief, they have stated a legally sufficient complaint. Upon presentation of such complaint, a plaintiff is entitled to a declaration of his rights, whether the declaration be favorable or adverse; thus in the instant case the trial court's order sustaining the demurrer and its dismissal of the action cannot be upheld upon the ground that plaintiffs pursued the wrong kind of action. *Salsbery v. Ritter* (1957), 48 Cal. 2d 1, 306 P. 2d 897; *Columbia Pictures v. De Toth* (1945), 26 Cal. 2d 753, 161 P. 2d 217; *Maguire v. Hibernia Savings & Loan Soc.* (1944), 23 Cal. 2d 719, 146 P. 2d 673, 151 A.L.R. 1062.

[3] As we have stated, "Our decision that controversies are shown to exist, however, does not resolve them, and we must therefore pass upon the questions of law that must be decided to reach a final determination of the case. Code Civ. Proc. § 53." (*Salsbery v. Ritter*, supra, 48 Cal. 2d, at p. 7, 306 P. 2d, at p. 900; *Columbia Pictures v. De Toth*, supra.) While in Maguire the unresolved issues of the special demurrer in the trial court justified the termination of appellate review, we do not face such a situation here. Termination at that stage in the instant case would merely provoke further appellate recourse since the record discloses that the trial court dismissed the case on the merits and the legal issues are clearly presented by the pleadings. Thus as in *Salsbery v. Ritter*, supra, and *Columbia Pictures v. De Toth*, supra, we shall proceed, as we must, to a consideration of the determinative questions of law raised in plaintiff's complaint.

Turning to the issue of statutory and constitutional construction which the complaint raises, we believe that this issue must be resolved by this court; it cannot properly be reposed in a jury for final disposition as a question of fact.[11] The crux of our case is whether the definition of obscene matter in Penal Code section 311 sanctions prosecution of sellers of "Tropic of Cancer" and whether the constitutional guarantees of freedom of speech and freedom of the press (United States Constitution, First and Fourteenth Amendments; Calif. Const., art. I, § 9) permit such prosecution. As we shall point out in more detail, the courts have long recognized that such questions of statutory and constitutional construction and application call for court decisions; they raise issues, not of the ascertainment of historical fact, but the definition of statutory proscription and constitutional protection; the court itself must determine the law of the case for the sake of consistent interpretation of the statute and uniform determination of whether particular matter is obscene.

As Justice Harlan eloquently states in *Roth v. United States* (1957), 354 U.S. 476, 77 S. Ct. 1304, 1 L. Ed. 2d 1498: "Every communication has an individuality and 'value' of its own. The suppression of a particular writing or other tangible form of expression is, therefore, an *individual* matter, and in the nature of things every such suppression raises an individual constitutional problem, in which a reviewing court must determine for *itself* whether the attacked expression is suppressable within constitutional standards. * * *

"I do not think that reviewing courts can escape this responsibility by saying that the trier of the facts, be it a jury or a judge, has labeled the questioned matter as 'obscene,' for, if 'obscenity' is to be suppressed, the question whether a particular work is of that character involves not really an issue of fact but a question of constitutional *judgment* of the most sensitive and delicate kind. * * *" (354 U.S. at pp. 497–498, 77 S. Ct. at p. 1315.)

[4] Justice Harlan's conception of the nature of judicial review to be accorded a finding of obscenity expresses a doctrine firmly imbedded in our constitutional law: that the reviewing court must make an *independent examination* of the whole record in cases involving the constitutional issue of free speech. (*Edwards v. South Carolina* (1963), 372 U.S. 229, 83 S. Ct. 680, 9 L. Ed. 2d 697; *Niemotko v. Maryland* (1951), 340 U.S. 268, 71 S. Ct. 325, 95 L. Ed. 267; *Feiner v. People of State of New York* (1951), 340 U.S. 315, 71 S. Ct. 303, 95 L. Ed. 267; *Pennekamp v. Florida* (1946), 328 U.S. 331, 66 S. Ct. 1029, 90 L. Ed. 1295; *Fiske v. Kansas* (1927), 274 U.S. 380, 47 S. Ct. 655, 71 L. Ed. 1108; *Attorney General v. Book Named "Tropic of Cancer"* (1962), 344 Mass. —, 184 N.E. 2d 328; *People v. Richmond County News* (1961), 9 N.Y. 2d 578, 580–581, 216 N.Y.S. 2d 369, 175 N.E. 2d 681 [opinion of Fuld, J.]; see Supreme Court Review of State Findings of Fact in Fourteenth Amendment Cases, 14 Stan. L. Rev. 328 (1962).)[12] As Judge Fuld stated in the Richmond County News case, "* * * if an appellate court were to rely upon and be bound by the opinion of the trier of the facts as to the obscenity of a publication it would be abdicating its role as an arbiter of constitutional issues." (9 N.Y. 2d, at p. 581, 216 N.Y.S. 2d, at p. 370, 175 N.E. 2d, at p. 682.)

[5] The determination of what is obscene in the statutory or constitutional sense is not a question of fact (i.e., a question of what happened) but rather is a question of fact mixed with a determination of law: a "constitutional fact." Historical facts, as such, are rarely at issue in that part of an obscenity prosecution which focuses upon the character of the material involved.[13] In the instant case

---

[10] Pen. Code, §§ 1466–1471; Calif. Rules of Court, rules 61–69.

[11] By so holding, we do not wish to be interpreted as sanctioning the impairment of rights traditionally accorded criminal defendants: the right to introduce evidence which tends to disprove the accusation (In re Harris (1961), 56 Cal. 2d 879, 16 Cal. Rptr. 889, 366 P. 2d 305) and the right to have the jury determine all relevant issues bearing upon guilt, including the question of whether the material is obscene.

[12] The same principle applies in the coerced confession cases: *People v. Trout* (1960), 54 Cal. 2d 576, 6 Cal. Rptr. 759, 354 P. 2d 231; *People v. Berve* (1958), 51 Cal. 2d 286, 332 P. 2d 97; *People v. Jones* (1944), 24 Cal. 2d 601, 602, 150 P. 2d 801; *Blackburn v. Alabama* (1960), 361 U.S. 199, 80 S. Ct. 274, 4 L. Ed. 2d 242; *Ashcraft v. Tennessee* (1944), 322 U.S. 143, 64 S. Ct. 921, 88 L. Ed. 1192.

[13] The determination of other elements necessary to make out a violation of Penal Code section 311.2 may be dependent upon historical facts. For example, on the issue of scienter it may be relevant whether the defendant actually read the allegedly obscene matter prior to the sale of the material.

the parties agree that they both refer to the same book, "Tropic of Cancer," written by the same author, Henry Miller. The dispute, rather, pivots upon whether the volume transgresses the standards imposed by the Legislature and by the Constitutions; our judicial system entrusts this decision ultimately to the courts.

Thus the draftsmen of the Model Penal Code of the American Law Institute have recently recognized that, in the interests of uniformity, the question of obscenity must be left to the independent judgment of courts. In the Tentative Draft of the Model Penal Code the draftsmen originally inserted a provision which allows both the trial and appellate courts to make an independent determination of the obscenity of the material, permitting the courts in so doing to consider, as evidence, written submissions by behavioral scientists.[14] The reporter's notes to the Tentative Draft state that the Institute disapproved this provision "by a close vote." (The tentative draft had been published only one month before the decision in Roth.) Section 251.4(4) of the Proposed Official Draft of the Model Penal Code (1962) provides in part, "The Court shall dismiss a prosecution for obscenity if it is satisfied that the material is not obscene."

The reporter's notes to the Proposed Official Draft contain the following comment on this provision: "* * * The present version is much simplified and omits provisions, to which most objections were voiced, for judges to consult behavioral scientists and for written submissions by these consultants. What we preserve in the present draft is *the independent judgment of the court on the question of obscenity* without impairing defendant's right to a jury trial. This is desirable in order to promote statewide uniformity of standards in this critical area. The action of the Supreme Court of the United States in a series of obscenity cases after the Roth decision indicates the large extent to which the question of obscenity is one of law in any case, because of the application of the First Amendment." (Emphasis added; p. 241.)

[6] Finally, we do not believe that the definition of "obscene" material as that which "to the *average person* * * * predominant appeal * * * is to prurient interest * * *" (emphasis added) indicates that the ultimate determination of that question is always for the jury. These words fix a *standard* which is to be applied to the material; they do not designate the body which is to apply the standard. The statutory language does not inherently predicate a question for the jury; it merely frames a definition. As we hereinafter point out, the Legislature wrote the words "average man" into the statute because a lesser standard would offend constitutional guarantees; the phrase does not serve to mark the respective spheres of the court and jury.

[7] We turn, then, to our task of determining whether "Tropic of Cancer" constitutes obscene matter within the meaning of the statute and the constitutional limitations. To understand the statute we must first examine the constitutional setting in which the California Legislature in 1961 completely recast Penal Code sections 311 and 312 (Stats. 1961, ch. 2147). The Legislature patterned its definition of obscenity upon that set forth in the American

Law Institute's Model Penal Code (§ 207.10), portions of which had been approved as constitutionally permissible standards by the United States Supreme Court in *Roth* v. *United States*, supra (1957), 354 U.S. 476, 77 S. Ct. 1304, 1 L. Ed. 2d 1498. This decision and others of the United States Supreme Court, we think, impliedly drew a line of constitutional protection around all material except that which has been described as hard-core pornography. In this analysis, which we shall develop, we follow the interpretations of the distinguished New York Court of Appeals and Supreme Judicial Court of Massachusetts.

Roth and the companion case of *Alberts* v. *California*[15] involved appeals by defendants from convictions for violation of the federal and California obscenity statutes respectively. While these were the first United States Supreme Court cases squarely to confront the question of "whether obscenity is utterance within the area of protected speech and press" (354 U.S. p. 481, 77 S. Ct. p. 1307), the issues were so framed that the majority of the Court adjudicated the validity of each statute on its face without passing on the merits of the attacked materials. As the majority opinion stated, "[N]o issue is presented in either case concerning the obscenity of the material involved." (354 U.S. p. 481, fn. 8, 77 S. Ct. p. 1315.) The Court therefore had no occasion to rule upon the three categories of material presented to it by the brief of the Solicitor General.[16] Affirming the convictions of Roth and Alberts, the Supreme Court held the statute did not violate the requirements of the United States Constitution[17] as to freedom of expression and definitude.

Mr. Justice Brennan, writing the majority opinion, held that "obscenity is not within the area of constitutionally protected speech or press" (354 U.S. p. 485, 77 S. Ct. p. 1309.) because, in the words that were later incorporated in the California statute, obscenity is "utterly without redeeming social importance." (354 U.S. p. 484, 77 S. Ct. p. 1308.) He points out that "sex and obscenity are not synonymous * * * [and the] portrayal of sex, e.g., in art, literature and scientific works * * [is entitled to] the constitutional protection of freedom of speech and press" (354 U.S. p. 487, 77 S. Ct. p. 1319.) provided that it does not become the designated kind of obscenity. The majority opinion sought to separate the protected from the unprotected material by the use of the term "obscenity." It approved the statutory standards under which the defendants were convicted, as well as the Model Penal Code formulation, because these tests did not contain the vices present in the archaic test used in *Regina* v. *Hicklin* (1868) L.R. 3 Q.B. 360, a test which many,[18] but not all,[19] American courts had discarded.

The Court expressly exposed the two basic flaws in

---

[14] American Law Institute, Model Penal Code, Tentative Draft No. 6, § 207.10. § 251.4 is the corresponding section in the Proposed Official Draft.

[15] The Court disposed of both cases in one opinion.

[16] Lockhart & McClure, Censorship of Obscenity, the Developing Constitutional Standards, 45 Minn. L. Rev. 5, 26 (1960).

[17] In Roth the Court also considered whether the power to punish obscenity was reserved to the states by the Ninth and Tenth Amendments; in Alberts it considered whether the federal statute regulating the mailing of obscene matter pre-empted regulation by the states. The Court rejected both contentions.

[18] See e.g., *American Civil Liberties Union* v. *Chicago* (1954), 3 Ill. 2d 334, 121 N.E. 2d 585; *United States* v. *One Book* entitled Ulysses (2d Cir. 1934), 72 F. 2d 705.

[19] See e.g., *Besig* v. *United States* (9th Cir. 1953), 208 F. 2d 142.

Hicklin. One such vice was that Hicklin judged obscenity by the effect of isolated passages; the Model Penal Code expresses its rejection of this test by requiring that the material be "considered as a whole" and that "its predominant appeal" be "to the prurient interest." In order to give color, texture and meaning to the whole of his expression, an artist may sometimes feel that he must depict matters which, standing alone, would unanimously be condemned as beyond the limits of propriety. (Cf. *Grove Press, Inc.* v. *Christenberry* (2d Cir. 1960), 276 F. 2d 433, 438–439; *United States* v. *One Book* Called "*Ulysses*" (S.D.N.Y. 1933), 5 F. Supp. 182, 184.) Thus in Roth the Court gave constitutional recognition to the employment of the device of artistic shock often present in the myriad of art forms which our society demands for its intellectual and cultural growth. The insistence upon judgment of the material "as a whole" and by its "predominant appeal" also serves to alleviate, but not necessarily entirely abolish, the dilemma which has been noted by several courts which have observed the coarseness of portions of recognized classics of art and literature although no rational person would condemn such works as obscene.[20]

The other major vice of Hicklin which the Supreme Court rejected was its application of the test of isolated passages upon those metaphysical personalities "whose minds are open to such immoral influences and into whose hands a publication may fall"; i.e., the most susceptible persons. The constitutional requirement for a standard phrased in terms of the reaction of an average adult to the material rather than that of the most susceptible person, had been, of course, forecast by the Court's unanimous rejection of the Michigan obscenity statute in *Butler* v. *Michigan* (1957), 352 U.S. 380, 77 S. Ct. 524, 1 L. Ed. 2d 412.

The four Justices who did not join in the majority opinion recognized that material relating to sex found protection in the constitutional guarantee of freedom of expression. Indeed, Justices Douglas and Black argued that the Constitution forbade all obscenity censorship except in cases in which it were demonstrated that "the particular publication has an impact on action that the government can control." (354 U.S. p. 511, 77 S. Ct. p. 1323.) In a short opinion, Chief Justice Warren isolated the central issue as the "conduct of the defendant" rather than the "obscenity of a book or picture." (354 U.S. p. 495, 77 S. Ct. p. 1315.) Apparently the Chief Justice extends constitutional protection to obscene materials if the defendant's own conduct is not personally reprehensible.

The most revealing opinion is that of Justice Harlan, who concurred in Alberts but dissented in Roth. We have pointed out that Justice Harlan held that a reviewing court should determine for itself, by scrutiny of the attacked material, whether it "is suppressable within constitutional standards." (354 U.S. p. 497, 77 S. Ct. p. 1315.) Justice Harlan's opinion, which applies this test to the material itself, constitutes the sole such approach of any of the opinions. Accordingly, in Roth Justice Harlan found the material did not constitute hard-core pornography and

voted to reverse the conviction. He stated: "* * * The point is that this statute, as here construed, defines obscenity so widely that it encompasses matters which might very well be protected speech. I do not think that the federal statute can be constitutionally construed to reach other than what the Government has termed as 'hard-core' pornography. * *" (354 U.S. p. 507, 77 S. Ct. p. 1321.) In Alberts he concluded that the suppression of the material would not so "interfere with the communication of 'ideas' in any proper sense of that term" (354 U.S. p. 503, 77 S. Ct. p. 1318.) as to offend due process, and therefore affirmed the conviction.

The hard-core pornography test so delineated by Justice Harlan finds confirmation in three succeeding decisions of the United States Supreme Court.[21] The cases arose from decisions of the Court of Appeals which upheld the obscenity of the material there involved: a film dealing with the seduction of a 16-year-old boy by an older woman and other "illicit sexual intimacies and acts" (*Times Film Corp.* v. *Chicago* (1957), 355 U.S. 35, 78 S. Ct. 115, 2 L. Ed. 2d 72); a magazine for homosexuals (*One, Inc.* v. *Olesen* (1958), 355 U.S. 371, 78 S. Ct. 364, 2 L. Ed. 2d 352); and a nudist magazine (*Sunshine Book Co.* v. *Summerfield* (1958), 355 U.S. 372, 78 S. Ct. 365, 2 L. Ed. 2d 352).[22] In per curiam decisions citing only Roth or Alberts, the Supreme Court reversed the judgments.

---

[20] *United States* v. *Roth* (2d Cir. 1956), 237 F. 2d 796, 819 (concurring opinion of Frank, J.), aff'd. sub. nom. *Roth* v. *United States* (1957), 354 U.S. 476, 77 S. Ct. 1304, 1 L. Ed. 2d 1498; *United States* v. *One Book* Entitled Ulysses (2d Cir. 1934), 72 F. 2d 705; *Commonwealth* v. *Gordon* (1949), 66 Pa. Dist. & Co. R. 101.

[21] A fourth such case, *Mounce* v. *United States* (1957), 355 U.S. 180, 78 S. Ct. 267, 2 L. Ed. 2d 187, probably is not within this group because the United States Supreme Court reversed the cause for consideration in light of Roth after the Solicitor General conceded that the court below had applied an erroneous standard.

[22] The Court of Appeals in *Times Film Corp.* v. *City of Chicago* (7th Cir. 1957), 244 F. 2d 432, 436, described the material as: "The thread of the story is supercharged * * * by a series of illicit sexual intimacies and acts. * * * [A] flying start is made when a 16 year old boy is shown completely nude on a bathing beach in the presence of a group of younger girls [as a result of a boating accident]. On that plane the narrative proceeds to reveal the seduction of this boy by a physically attractive woman old enough to be his mother. Under the influence of this experience and an arrangement to repeat it, the boy thereupon engages in sexual relations with a girl of his own age. The erotic thread of the story is carried, without deviation toward any wholesome idea, through scene after scene. The narrative is graphically pictured with nothing omitted except those sexual consummations which are plainly suggested but meaningfully omitted and thus, by the very fact of omission, emphasized."

The Court of Appeals in *One, Inc.* v. *Olesen* (9th Cir. 1957), 241 F. 2d 772, 777, described the material as: "The article 'Sappho Remembered' is the story of a lesbian's influence on a young girl only twenty years of age but 'actually nearer sixteen in many essential ways of maturity,' in her struggle to choose between a life with the lesbian, or a normal married life with her childhood sweetheart. The lesbian's affair with her room-mate while in college, resulting in the lesbian's expulsion from college, is recounted to bring in the jealousy angle. The climax is reached when the young girl gives up her chance for a normal married life to live with the lesbian. This article is nothing more than cheap pornography calculated to promote lesbianism. It falls far short of dealing with homosexuality from the scientific, historical and critical point of view.

"The poem 'Lord Samuel and Lord Montagu' is about the alleged homosexual activities of Lord Montagu and other British Peers and contains a warning to all males to avoid the public toilets while Lord Samuel is 'sniffing round the drains' of Piccadilly (London). The poem pertains to sexual matters of such a

Clearly the most plausible meaning of these summary reversals, in view of the citation of only Roth or Alberts,[23] must be that the materials there involved could not be held obscene. As Professor Kalven observes: "These three decisions, coupled with the citation of Roth, point unmistakably in one direction: the Court is feeling the pressure generated by the two-level theory to restrict obscenity to the worthless and hence to something akin to hard-core pornography. Thus the three decisions appear to add important gloss to the Roth definition. And the prophecy that Roth would serve to narrow the range of obscenity regulation appears fulfilled." (Kalven, The Metaphysics of the Law of Obscenity, 1960 Sup. Ct. Rev. 1, 43.)[24]

---

vulgar and indecent nature that it tends to arouse a feeling of disgust and revulsion. It is dirty, vulgar and offensive to the moral senses. * * *"

The District Court, in *Sunshine Book Co.* v. *Summerfield* (D.C.D.C. 1955), 128 F. Supp. 564, 571–572, of one of the photographs found obscene, said:

"On page 29 [of Sunshine & Health for February, 1955] there is a most unusual picture. Here are two women who appear to be in their late twenties or early thirties. The woman to the left appears to be approximately 5 foot 7. She must weigh in the neighborhood of 250 pounds. She is exceedingly obese.

* * * * *

"She has large, elephantine breasts that hang from her shoulder to her waist. They are exceedingly large. The thighs are very obese. She is standing in snow, wearing galoshes. But the part which is offensive, obscene, filthy and indecent is the pubic area shown.

"* * * The hair extends outwardly virtually to the hip bone. It looks to the Court like a retouched picture because the hair line instead of being straight is actually scalloped or in a half-moon shape, which makes the woman grotesque, vile, filthy, and the representation is dirty, and the Court will hold that the picture is obscene in the sense that it is indecent, it is filthy, and it is obscene as a matter of fact * * *."

[23] Each of these cases involved procedural problems which would have justified the court in refusing to consider the issue of obscenity. The Court's citation of Roth or Alberts, however, indicates that the reversals were on the obscenity issue. These cases are ably analyzed in Lockhart and McClure, supra, fn. 16 at pp. 32–39; Kalven, The Metaphysics of the Law of Obscenity, 1960 Supreme Court Review, 1, 42–45; Comment, Per Curiam Decisions of the Supreme Court: 1957 Term, 26 U. of Chi. L. Rev. 279, 309–313 (1959). Professor Kalven quotes at length from a brief Thurman Arnold submitted to the Vermont Supreme Court which espouses a challenging position. Kalven summarizes Arnold's position as: "The main point is advice to the Vermont court on how to handle the issue before it sensibly and diplomatically. Mr. Arnold purports to get his rule of judicial prudence from the United States Supreme Court. The rule is simple: the court should hold items before it not obscene unless they amount to hard-core pornography, and should, after rendering a decision, shut up. In Mr. Arnold's view, any fool can quickly recognize hard-core pornography, but it is a fatal trap for judicial decorum and judicial sanity to attempt thereafter to write an opinion explaining why." (P. 43.)

[24] To Professor Kalven, the two-level approach to problems of the First Amendment results from the United States Supreme Court's analysis which requires a showing of a clear and present danger as the ground for the suppression of most utterances but which allows the suppression of obscenity (*Roth* v. *United States*, supra), "fighting words" (*Chaplinsky* v. *New Hampshire* (1942), 315 U.S. 568, 62 S. Ct. 766, 86 L. Ed. 1031, and group libel (*Beauharnais* v. *People of State of Illinois* (1952), 343 U.S. 250, 72 S. Ct. 725, 96 L. Ed. 919; without such a showing because the utterances there involved are "utterly without redeeming social importance" (Roth) or are "no essential part of any exposition of ideas" (Chaplinsky and Beauharnais).

Kingsley International Pictures Corp. v. *Regents* (1959), 360 U.S. 684, 79 S. Ct. 1362, 3 L. Ed. 2d 1512, although interpreted by the majority of the Court as a case which involved an attempt to suppress matter dealing with sex for reasons other than the "obscenity" of the material, also serves to illustrate the great breadth of protection accorded materials dealing with sex. There the New York Court of Appeals indicated that although the motion picture involved was not obscene, it might nonetheless be censored because it pictured adultery as proper behavior. The Supreme Court reversed, holding that this interfered with the freedom to advocate, which necessarily includes the freedom to advocate unpopular, even hateful, ideas. The breadth of the constitutional protection is also illustrated by the several cases involving various procedures used to suppress alleged obscenity. (*Kingsley Books, Inc.* v. *Brown* (1957), 354 U.S. 436, 77 S. Ct. 1325, 1 L. Ed. 2d 1469; *Smith* v. *People of State of California* (1959), 361 U.S. 147, 80 S. Ct. 215, 4 L. Ed. 2d 205; *Marcus* v. *Search Warrant* (1961), 367 U.S. 717, 81 S. Ct. 1708, 6 L. Ed. 2d 1127; *Bantam Books, Inc.* v. *Sullivan* (1963), 372 U.S. 58, 83 S. Ct. 631, 9 L. Ed. 2d 584.)

[8] As we have stated, the highest courts of New York and Massachusetts, in interpreting the Supreme Court decisions, have recognized that boundary lines for the forbidden pale of obscenity must delimit only the area of hard-core pornography. Justice Fuld's opinion in *People* v. *Richmond County News* (1961), 9 N.Y. 2d 578, 216 N.Y.S. 2d 369, 175 N.E. 2d 681, states: "Mindful of the constitutional necessity to open the door barring state intrusion into this area 'only the slight crack necessary' (*Roth* v. *United States*, 354 U.S. 476, 488, 77 S. Ct. 1304, 1311, 1 L. Ed. 2d 1498, supra), and desirous of erecting a standard which embodies the most universal moral sensibilities and may be applied objectively, *we are of the opinion that the prohibitions of section 1141 of the Penal Law should apply only to what may properly be termed 'hard-core pornography'.*" (9 N.Y. 2d p. 586, 216 N.Y.S. 2d p. 375, 175 N.E. 2d p. 685, emphasis added.)

Chief Judge Desmond's concurring opinion reiterates this analysis: "St. John-Stevas, one of the soundest and sanest of today's writers on the law of obscenity, says that: 'A pornographic book * * * is one deliberately designed to stimulate sex feelings and to act as an aphrodisiac' (Obscenity and the Law, p. 2: cf. *Roth* v. *United States*, 354 U.S. 476, 486, 487, 77 S. Ct. 1304, 1309, 1310, 1 L. Ed. 2d 1498.) The identical thought is in Judge WOOLSEY's famed Ulysses opinion (*United States* v. *One Book Called Ulysses*, D.C., 5 F. Supp. 182, affirmed 2 Cir., 72 F. 2d 705, 707) and in Justice BRENNAN's famous phrase: 'dominant theme of the material taken as a whole appeals to prurient interest' (*Roth* v. *United States*, supra, 354 U.S. at page 489, 77 S. Ct. at page 1311). *The inquiry for the court, therefore, is whether the publication is so entirely obscene as to amount to 'hard-core pornography' * *.*" (9 N.Y. 2d pp. 588–589, 216 N.Y.S. 2d p. 377, 175 N.E. 2d p. 687; emphasis added.)

Last year the Supreme Judicial Court of Massachusetts, in ruling upon the alleged obscenity of the book before us, applied the same test. That court in *Attorney General* v. *Book Named "Tropic of Cancer"* (1962), 344 Mass. —, 184 N.E. 2d 328, explained that one of the five basic tenets of the Roth case was that "Hard core, commercial pornography, 'utterly without redeeming social importance' (see 354 U.S. 476, 484–485, 77 S. Ct. 1304, 1309,

[1 L. Ed. 2d 1498]) is not within the protection of the First Amendment." (184 N.E. 2d p. 331.) The court stated finally, "We conclude, therefore, as in effect the New York court did in the Richmond County News case, that, with respect to material designed for general circulation, only predominantly 'hard core' pornography, without redeeming social significance, is obscene in the constitutional sense." (184 N.E. 2d pp. 333–334.)

In substance these courts, applying the rulings of the United States Supreme Court, hold that if material is commercial obscenity or saleable pornography it is obscenity in the sense that it is utterly without redeeming social importance; it is hard-core pornography; as such it lies outside the protective embrace of the First Amendment. If the material, however, has literary value, if it is a serious work of literature or art, then it possesses redeeming social importance and obtains the benefit of the constitutional guarantees.

Cognizant of these constitutional guarantees, the Legislature wrote a statute which, in substance, prohibited hardcore pornography;[25] the draftsmen recognized that a wider proscription would trespass upon an area which is constitutionally protected. The legislative history itself shows a deliberate narrowing of the definition of "obscene" material; indeed, no words in the language could more totally express constriction of the concept of obscenity than those which the Legislature adopted. As we shall explain, the Legislature intentionally incorporated as part of the definition itself the important provision that obscene matter "is matter which is utterly without redeeming social importance," changing the function of these words from a description of a matter of defense to an element of the offense.

---

[25] Of course identifying and delimiting "hard-core pornography" presents its own problems. In *Marcus v. Search Warrant* (1961), 367 U.S. 717, 730, 81 S. Ct. 1708, the Court stated: "[I]n Roth itself we expressly recognized the complexity of the test of obscenity fashioned in that case and the vital necessity in its application of safeguards to prevent denial of 'the protection of freedom of speech and press for material which does not treat sex in a manner appealing to prurient interest.' " In *Bantam Books, Inc. v. Sullivan* (1963), 372 U.S. 58, 66, 83 S. Ct. 631, the Court quoted this language from Marcus and went on to note that "constitutionally protected expression * * * is often separated from obscenity only by a dim and uncertain line." (See Note, 76 Harv. L. Rev. 1498 (1963).) Undoubtedly we are in an area where the recourse to verbal descriptions is ultra-hazardous. We note, however, two descriptions which may illuminate the area. Kaplan has written: "[Pornography] is not itself the *object* of an experience, esthetic or any other, but rather a stimulus *to* an experience not focused on it. It serves to elicit not the imaginative contemplation of an expressive substance, but rather the release in fantasy of a compelling impulse." (Kaplan, Obscenity as an Esthetic Category, 20 Law & Contemp. Prob. 544, 548 (1955).)

The Kronhausens state: "In *pornography* (hard core obscenity) *the main purpose is to stimulate erotic response* in the reader. And that is all. *In erotic realism, truthful description of the basic realities of life, as the individual experiences it, is of the essence,* even if such portrayals * * * have a decidedly antierotic effect. But by the same token, if, while writing realistically on the subject of sex, the author succeeds in moving his reader, this too, is erotic realism, *and it is axiomatic that the reader should respond erotically to such writing,* just as the sensitive reader will respond, perhaps by actually crying, to a sad scene, or by laughing when laughter is evoked." (Kronhausen, Pornography and the Law (1959) p. 18.) (Emphasis in original.)

As originally introduced on February 28, 1961, Assembly Bill 1979 defined obscenity as that which "to the average person applying contemporary standards, the predominant appeal of the matter, taken as a whole, is to prurient interest." Subsequently on April 21, 1961, the Assembly further narrowed the definition by adding, "i.e., a shameful or morbid interest in nudity, sex, or excretion, which goes substantially beyond customary limits of candor in description or representation of such matters." After another set of amendments not here relevant, the Assembly added, on May 22, 1961, "or that it had the slightest redeeming social importance" to what is now section 311.8, which provides as a *defense* to a charge of obscenity that the matter is "in aid of scientific or educational purposes." The Assembly then passed the bill and sent it to the Senate.

The Senate substituted "other legitimate social purpose" for the Assembly language "or that it had the slightest redeeming social importance," and returned the bill to the Assembly.

On June 15, 1961, the Assembly, by a vote of 60–19, refused to concur in the Senate's amendments. An Assembly-Senate conference committee was appointed to break the deadlock. The next day the committee reported out the present version of section 311, with the words "and is matter which is utterly without redeeming social importance" added to the *definition* of obscenity in section 311 and providing in section 311.8 for a defense if the material be "in aid of legitimate scientific or educational purposes." (Assembly Journal, 1961 Regular Session, p. 5975.) With these changes the bill passed both houses and was signed by the Governor.

[9] The importance of the insertion of this crucial language in the definition of obscenity rather than in the defense to it, is overshadowed only by the sweep of the words themselves. Webster's Third New International Dictionary defines "utterly" as: "* * * to an absolute or extreme degree; to the full extent; absolutely, altogether, entirely, fully, thoroughly, totally." (Compare similar restrictive judicial definitions of the term in *Insurance Company v. Gossler* (1877), 96 U.S. 645, 24 L. Ed. 863; *Moody v. Moody* (1920), 118 Me. 454, 456, 108 A. 849; *Pearsoll v. Chapin* (1862), 44 Pa. 9.) The meanings conveyed by the words "reasonably" or "preponderantly" are well known; had such been intended, the appropriate terms would have been used. By employing the term "utterly" the Legislature indicated its intention to give legal sanction to all material relating to sex except that which was *totally* devoid of social importance. The only material that falls into the latter category is hard-core pornography. This language, indeed, is the language of Roth; as we have shown, subsequent Supreme Court decisions, state courts and commentators have interpreted it to describe hard-core pornography.

The defendant construes the statute with the emphasis on "redeeming"; he contends that this indicates that the social importance of the material must outweigh its prurient appeal. This construction, however, reads the word "utterly," a term which permits no such balancing, out of the statute. By examining the origin of this phrase in Roth we are led to a construction which gives the whole phrase a consistent meaning: "redeeming" refers not to a balancing of the pruriency against the social importance of the material, but rather to the *presence* of matters of social importance in the content which will *recover* for the material its position as constitutionally protected utterance.

[10] If, then, the statutory proscription, consonant with constitutional limitations, prohibits only hard-core pornography, we must, as a final matter, determine if "Tropic of Cancer" constitutes such pornography. We, like four other courts that have ruled upon the book,[26] do not think so.

"Tropic of Cancer" is a semi-autobiographical novel written in the style of a surrealistic stream of consciousness which chronicles the author's experiences during his self-imposed exile in Paris in the early 1930's. Miller went to Paris to seek a rebirth within himself; he set himself the task of stripping away the restraints of the past so that he could emerge as a writer. He found that to do so he would have to achieve a cosmology, a view of the universe derived out of the interpretation of his experiences. Miller shares with the reader the process of prying that cosmology out of the folds of his existence. Hence any undertaking, be it a regular job or a fixed schedule of sponging food from his acquaintances, must be abandoned when it threatens to interfere with this grandiose search.

In examining the episodes which Miller relates, we note a frequently recurring pattern. Experiences not ordinarily pictured as related to sexual motivations are analyzed in flights of surrealistic fantasy in terms of sexual experiences. Ordinary sexual experiences, on the other hand, may evoke to Miller images usually unconnected with such experiences—for example, after setting the conventional stage in which he and a companion partake of the services of a prostitute, his fantasy describes the episode in terms of a machine with a broken cog. Thus, much of Miller's quest for a cosmology consists of his attempt to find the role of his sexual drives and frustrations. This aspect of the book recalls the caveat of Justice Brennan in Roth. "* * Sex, a great and mysterious motive force in human life, has indisputably been a subject of absorbing interest to mankind through the ages; it is one of the vital problems of human interest and public concern." (354 U.S. at p. 487, 77 S. Ct. at p. 1310.) Miller's treatment of sex in "Tropic of Cancer" reflects his search for an understanding of this "mysterious motive force." But there is absent from the book the sadism, masochism and treatment of sex in a morbid or shameful manner which frequently marks pornography.

In sum, the book in narrating Miller's stream of consciousness necessarily expresses the writer's thoughts in their most primitive aspect, often violent and repulsive, and constantly in four-letter words. The book embraces the emotional, the sexual, the intellectual, and every other kind of stimulus that intrudes upon the writer's consciousness. Thus the book is a kind of grotesque, unorthodox art-form. But indeed, such art-forms are not confined to literature; they appear and reappear in all phases of artistic expression.[27]

Such an art-form must be distinguished from that which is designed to excite or attract pruriency; it surely does not constitute hard-core pornography. Clearly the statute reposes no authority in the courts to act as censors of the manners or formulation of such artistic expression. The danger of state censorship has been too graphically demonstrated by the current decadence of Soviet art for us to assume that either Roth or the Legislature intended to import such debilitation.[28]

Indeed, a legal proscription cannot in any event constrict artistic creation. Man's drive for self-expression, which over the centuries has built his monuments, does not stay within set bounds; the creations which yesterday were the detested and the obscene become the classics of today. The quicksilver of creativity will not be solidified by legal pronouncement; it will necessarily flow into new and sometimes frightening fields. If, indeed, courts try to forbid new and exotic expression they will surely and fortunately fail. The new forms of expression, even though formally banned, will, as they always have, remain alive in man's consciousness. The court-made excommunication, if it is too wide or if it interferes with true creativity, will be rejected like incantations of forgotten witch-doctors. Courts must therefore move here with utmost caution; they tread in a field where a lack of restraint can only invite defeat and only impair man's most precious potentiality: his capacity for self-expression.

The judgment is reversed for further proceedings consistent with this opinion.

GIBSON, C.J., and TRAYNOR, SCHAUER, McCOMB, PETERS and PEEK, JJ., concur.

---

[26] *Attorney General v. Book Named* "Tropic of Cancer" (1962), 344 Mass. —, 184 N.E. 2d 328; *McCauley v. Tropic of Cancer* (1963), Wis., 121 N.W. 2d 545; *People v. Fritch* (1963), 38 Misc. 2d 333, 236 N.Y.S. 2d 706; and *Haiman v. Morris* (1962, No. 61 S. 19718, Superior Ct. of Cook County, Ill.).

[27] "Modern art is, however, anti-impressionistic in yet another respect: it is a fundamentally 'ugly' art, foregoing the euphony, the fascinating forms, tones and colours of impressionism. It destroys pictorial values in painting, carefully and consistently executed images in poetry and melody and tonality in music. It implies an anxious escape from everything pleasant and agreeable, everything purely decorative and ingratiating. * * * [P]ost impressionist art is the first to stress the grotesqueness and mendacity of this culture. Hence the fight against all voluptuous and hedonistic feelings, hence the gloom, depression and torment in the works of Picasso, Kafka, and Joyce. * * *" (Hauser, The Social History of Art. 230–231 (1958).

[28] As one student of Soviety literary controls observes: "Thus, there are fundamentally three standards for estimating the merit of a literary work: the truthfulness, or party-minded spirit, of the work's portrayal of reality, the work's pedagogic potentiality, and its intelligibility to the broad masses—all prerequisites for transforming literature into a serviceable social tool. In terms of Soviet doctrine, belles-lettres become an adjunct to politics and pedagogy, a sugar coating on the pill of knowledge and morality." (Swayze, Political Control of Literature in the USSR, 1946–1959, p. 17 (1962).)

■ The People of the State of New York, *Appellant,*

v.

Marguerite Fritch, Alan Hammerle and John E. Armstrong, *Respondents.*

Court of Appeals of New York.

July 10, 1963.

Joseph A. Ryan, Dist. Atty. (*J. Richard Sardino,* Syracuse, of counsel), for appellant.

Charles Rembar, New York City, *Charles E. Roberts* and *D. Charles O'Brien,* Syracuse, for respondents.

SCILEPPI, Judge.

[1] Defendants, after a trial by jury, were convicted of selling an obscene book, to wit, "Tropic of Cancer" by Henry Miller, in violation of section 1141 of the Penal Law.[1] The County Court reversed their convictions and dismissed the information. This case presents for consideration the recurring question of what constitutes obscene literature under the aforementioned statute in light of the guarantees of freedom of expression contained in both the Federal and State Constitutions. We have concluded that "Tropic of Cancer" is obscene within the meaning of our statute and is not within the area of constitutional protection.

[2] It is by now well established that the State of New York, in the exercise of its police power, may enact legislation designed to suppress the sale and distribution of salacious literature (*Smith v. People of State of California,* 361 U.S. 147, 80 S. Ct. 215, 4 L. Ed. 2d 205; *Roth v. United States,* 354 U.S. 476, 77 S. Ct. 1304, 1 L. Ed. 2d 1498). This our Legislature has done by the enactment of section 1141 of the Penal Law, which embodies the recognition that the public interest demands protection against the damaging impact of obscenity on the moral climate of the community. The need for this protection has been

highlighted in recent years as the People of this State have been exposed to an ever-increasing amount of printed material featuring sex and sensationalism which, aided by new methods of merchandising, are sold not only in bookstores but from open racks in candy stores and similar outlets. As the dissemination of this material has become more widespread, there has been an increased awareness of the serious problem it creates. Legislative committees of both the State[2] and Federal[3] Governments, as well as other groups,[4] have conducted hearings and issued reports

---

[1] § 1141. Obscene prints and articles.

"1. A person who sells, lends, gives away, distributes, shows or transmutes, or offers to sell, lend, give away, distribute, show or transmute, or has in his possession with intent to sell, lend, distribute, give away, show or transmute, or advertise in any manner, or who otherwise offers for loan, gift, sale or distribution, any obscene, lewd, lascivious, filthy, indecent, sadistic, masochistic or disgusting book, magazine, pamphlet, newspaper, story paper, writing, paper, card, phonograph record, picture, drawing, photograph, motion picture film, figure, image, phonograph record or wire or tape recording, or any written, printed or recorded matter of an indecent character which may or may not require mechanical or other means to be transmitted into auditory, visual or sensory representations of such character; or any article or instrument of indecent or immoral use, or purporting to be for indecent or immoral use or purpose, * * *

"Is guilty of a misdemeanor."

---

[2] In 1963 the Report of the New York State Joint Legislative Committee to Study the Publication and Dissemination of Offensive and Obscene Material under "Conclusions": "That the wide availability of obscene and near obscene materials is undermining our standard of conduct, fostering disrespect for duly constituted authority and contributing to delinquency and crime."

In 1962 report of the same committee (N.Y. Legis. Doc., 1962, No. 77, p. 11): "As indicated in prior reports, it [the Committee] has specifically concluded that disseminations of this type [referring to glorifying and condoning immoral acts or which describe lurid, illegal or unnatural sex practices] are contributing to juvenile delinquency, inciting to sex crime, leading to perversion and posing a serious threat to our standards of morality."

[3] "Hearings before Subcommittee on Constitutional Amendments and Subcommittee to Investigate Juvenile Delinquency of the Committee on the Judiciary United States Senate Eighty-sixth Congress First and Second Sessions."

[4]   "STATEMENT ON SALACIOUS
                     LITERATURE
                          By
          The New York Academy of Medicine
              Committee on Public Health

"On the basis of the incomplete information submitted to it, the Academy is of the opinion that the reported increase in sales of salacious literature to adolescents is one of a number of social ills reflecting a breakdown in the home and an inadequate environment. Since adverse forces seem to be concentrated on teenagers, deliberations on the problem were limited to effects of erotic literature on this age group.

"The Academy believes that although some adolescents may not be affected by reading of salacious literature, others may be more vulnerable. Such reading encourages a morbid preoccupation with sex and interferes with the development of a healthy attitude and respect for the opposite sex. It is said to contribute to perversion. In the opinion of some psychiatrists, it may have an especially detrimental effect on disturbed adolescents.

"Behavior is complex. It is difficult, if not impossible, to prove scientifically that a direct causal relation exists between libidi-

which reflect the alarming decline in the moral climate of our times. These reports emphasize the need for obscenity laws as a safeguard in the public interest and the necessity for their proper enforcement. The need for this public protection was reaffirmed in the Supreme Court of the United States in *Roth* v. *United States,* 354 U.S. 476, 77 S. Ct. 1304, 1 L. Ed. 2d 1498, supra, which held that it is not a violation of the guarantees of freedom of speech and of the press under the First Amendment of the Constitution to suppress or prohibit the publication, distribution and sale of obscene literature. The court there stated (354 U.S. pp. 484–485, 77 S. Ct. p. 1309, 1 L. Ed. 2d 1498): "All ideas having even the slightest redeeming social importance—unorthodox ideas, controversial ideas, even ideas hateful to the prevailing climate of opinion—have the full protection of the guaranties, unless excludable because they encroach upon the limited area of more important interests. But implicit in the history of the First Amendment is the rejection of obscenity as utterly without redeeming social importance. This rejection for that reason is mirrored in the universal judgment that obscenity should be restrained, reflected in the international agreement of over 50 nations, in the obscenity laws of all the 48 States, and in the 20 obscenity laws enacted by the Congress from 1842 to 1956."

[3] While the State's right to enact such legislation cannot be doubted, the application of the legislative mandate to specific subjects may not be so broad as to impinge upon the right of free expression guaranteed to all citizens. Thus the determination of whether a particular work is legally obscene requires us to strike a balance in each case between these fundamental freedoms and the State's interest in the welfare of its citizens.

[4, 5] The term "obscenity," however, is not susceptible of precise definition. It must be viewed in juxtaposition to time, place and circumstance, so that whether a particular work falls within the ambit of constitutional protection or is subject to regulation by the State must be determined by a case by case process of inclusion and exclusion. But, while the exact boundaries of obscenity cannot be sharply drawn, the Supreme Court, in *Roth* v. *United States,* supra and *Manual Enterprises, Inc.* v. *Day,* 370 U.S. 478, 82 S. Ct. 1432, 8 L. Ed. 2d 639, set forth guidelines and prescribed the essential elements which must conjoin before it can be found that a publication is obscene by constitutional standards. The first of these elements is the so-called "prurient interest" test set forth in Roth, that is, "whether to the average person, applying contemporary community standards, the dominant theme of the material taken as a whole appeals to prurient interest" (*Roth* v. *United States,* supra, 354 U.S. p. 489, 77 S. Ct. p. 1311, 1 L. Ed. 2d 1498). The second, contained in Manual Enterprises, requires that, in addition to the "prurient in-

terest" test, it is necessary to establish that the challenged material is also "patently offensive" to current community standards of decency (*Manual Enterprises, Inc.* v. *Day,* supra, 370 U.S. p. 482, 82 S. Ct. p. 1434, 8 L. Ed. 2d 639). In addition to the foregoing tests imposed by the decisions of the Supreme Court, this court interpreted section 1141 of the Penal Law in *People* v. *Richmond County News, Inc.,* 9 N.Y. 2d 578, 586, 216 N.Y.S. 2d 369, 375, 175 N.E. 2d 681, 685, as applicable only to material which may properly be termed "hard-core pornography."

It is our opinion that, judged by all three of the established legal standards, "Tropic of Cancer" does not fall within the class of publications entitled to constitutional protection.

[6] Significantly, the jury was instructed that to convict the defendants they must find the book to be obscene under all of the standards discussed above, that is, the tests of "prurient interest," "patent offensiveness" and "hard-core pornography." Formerly their determination of this question would have been deemed conclusive unless as a matter of law the writing could be said to be so innocuous as to forbid its submission to the trier of the facts (*People* v. *Pesky,* 254 N.Y. 373, 173 N.E. 227). However, as this court stated in the Richmond County News case, supra, 9 N.Y. 2d pp. 580–581, 216 N.Y.S. 2d p. 370, 175 N.E. 2d p. 681: "This court, as the State's highest tribunal, no less than the United States Supreme Court, cannot escape its responsibility in this area 'by saying that the trier of the facts, be it a jury or a judge, has labeled the questioned matter as "obscene," for, if "obscenity" is to be suppressed, the question whether a particular work is of that character involves not really an issue of fact but a question of constitutional *judgment* of the most sensitive and delicate kind.' *Roth* v. *United States,* 354 U.S. 476, 497–498, 77 S. Ct. 1304, 1315–1316, 1 L. Ed. 2d 1498 [HARLAN, J., concurring] * * *. It involves not a simple question of fact, but a mixed question of fact and constitutional law, calling upon the court to make an appraisal of a publication and its contents against the requirements embodied in both State and Federal Constitutions."

In the exercise of our duty to make an independent constitutional appraisal, we have read the book carefully and conclude that it is nothing more than a compilation of a series of sordid narrations dealing with sex in a manner designed to appeal to the prurient interest.[5] It is devoid of theme or ideas. Throughout its pages can be found a constant repetition of patently offensive words used solely to convey debasing portrayals of natural and unnatural sexual experiences. It is a blow to sense, not merely sensibility. It is, in short, "hard-core pornography," dirt for dirt's sake (*United States* v. *One Book Called "Ulysses,"* D.C., 5 F. Supp. 182), and dirt for money's sake (*Kingsley Intern. Pictures Corp.* v. *Regents of University of State of New York,* 360 U.S. 684, 692, 79 S. Ct. 1362, 3 L. Ed. 2d

---

nous literature and socially unacceptable conduct. Yet, it is undeniable that there has been a resurgence of venereal disease, particularly among teenage youth, and that the rate of illegitimacy is climbing. It may be postulated that there is a correlation between these phenomena and the apparent rise in the sale of salacious literature, and perhaps it is causal, but the latter observation cannot be definitely demonstrated. It can be asserted, however, that the perusal of erotic literature has the potentiality of inciting some young persons to enter into illicit sex relations and thus of leading them into promiscuity, illegitimacy and venereal disease."

[5] Obscene and filthy passages are to be found on the following pages in the hard cover edition: 4, 5, 6, 7, 16, 18, 20, 24, 25, 28, 32, 36, 39, 40, 42, 43, 44, 45, 46, 47, 52, 53, 54, 56, 58, 59, 60, 62, 73, 80, 85, 87, 89, 92, 97, 100, 101, 102, 103, 104, 105, 107, 111, 112, 113, 114, 115, 116, 117, 118, 120, 121, 122, 123, 124, 126, 127, 134, 135, 139, 140, 141, 142, 144, 145, 146, 156, 159, 160, 171, 172, 175, 188, 190, 193, 202, 203, 207, 215, 216, 217, 220, 225, 229, 230, 231, 232, 233, 234, 235, 236, 237, 238, 239, 246, 247, 248, 249, 250, 256, 257, 258, 259, 272, 273, 274, 282, 283, 288, 289, 290, 291, **and** 292.

1512). We see no reason for adopting an unrealistic appraisal of the nature of this book when there is such overwhelming proof of its incompatability with the current moral standards of our community. If, as the County Court held, this book is not obscene as a matter of law, it is difficult to conceive when, if ever, a book can be held to be obscene under any established legal standard.

[7] Defendants contend that even if "Tropic of Cancer" is obscene when judged by the established tests, it is nevertheless, under the Roth case, supra, entitled to protection because it has "substantial literary merit." We do not interpret Roth, or any other authority, as establishing any such rule of law. Defendants place reliance upon the court's statement in Roth that "implicit in the history of the First Amendment is the rejection of obscenity as utterly without redeeming social importance" (354 U.S. supra, p. 484, 77 S. Ct. p. 1309, 1 L. Ed. 2d 1498). But it does not follow that the converse is true; indeed, if such were the case the holding in Roth would be vitally eroded, for the test as pronounced there is the appeal to the prurient interest of the average person in the contemporary community. It does not follow, then, that because an alleged work of literature does not appeal to the prurient interest of a small group of intellectuals that it is not obscene under the prurient interest, or for that matter any other legal test of obscenity. This would permit the substitution of the opinions of authors and critics for those of the average person in the contemporary community. The fact that a few literary figures have commented favorably on this book and have lent it their prestige does not expunge from its pages the flagrantly obscene and patently offensive matter which dominates the book as a whole.

Moreover, if a publication may not be held obscene when it appeals to the prurient interest of (or is patently offensive to) only a particular segment of the community, such as children, the pious or the prudish, then, conversely, its nonobscenity may not be gauged by the lack of impact it has on the literary community.

A book may not be judged by its cover, its introduction or the laudatory comments contained in the publisher's blurbs—rather it must be judged by its actual contents. It requires little perception or imagination to conceive that the actual contents of a book may completely negate these testimonials and indorsements. Nor does the fact that the author enjoys wide acclaim as a writer control, for the book must be judged, not by the reputation of the author, but by what he writes in it. To hold otherwise would give recognized writers the freedom to traffic in obscenity at will under the guise of creating a work of art. This court will not adopt a rule of law which states that obscenity is suppressible but that well-written obscenity is not.

[8, 9] There still remains for consideration and disposition the issue of *scienter*, for even though a publication is obscene, a conviction may not stand without proof of *scienter* on the part of those charged with a violation of section 1141 of the Penal Law.

We are without power to make a final disposition of this issue now. The County Court's reversal of the defendants' convictions and the dismissal of the information was on the law and the facts. Its opinion makes it evident that, while the dismissal of the information was based on its conclusion that "Tropic of Cancer" was not obscene as a matter of law, the jury's finding on the issue of *scienter*

was against the weight of the evidence. Accordingly, a new trial must be ordered.

The order appealed from should be reversed and a new trial ordered on the issue of *scienter*.

DESMOND, Chief Judge (concurring).

I concur for reversal.

If this book had not been written by a recognized author, if it did not contain some "good writing" and if it were not approved by well-known reviewers, no one, I venture, would deny that it is obscene by any conceivable definition, narrow or tolerant. Its own cover blurb boasts of its "unbridled obscenity." From first to last page it is a filthy, cynical, disgusting narrative of sordid amours. Not only is there in it no word or suggestion of the romantic, sentimental, poetic or spiritual aspects of the sex relation, but it is not even bawdy sex or comic sex or sex described with vulgar good humor. No glory, no beauty, no stars—just mud. The whole book is "sick sexuality," a deliberate, studied exercise in the depiction of sex relations as debasing, filthy and revolting. On page 483 of 370 U.S., on page 1434 of 82 S. Ct., 8 L. Ed. 2d 639, Justice HARLAN's opinion in *Manual Enterprises, Inc.* v. *Day* quotes the New International Dictionary's long series of definitions of "obscene." It is a remarkable fact that "Tropic of Cancer" fits every single one of those numerous meanings.

Nowhere in the controlling decisions of the United States Supreme Court is there to be found a concise, objective legal definition of unconstitutional obscenity and it is not disrespectful or uncharitable to say that the efforts to articulate such a definition have been unsuccessful. Tersely it is written in *Roth* v. *United States*, 354 U.S. 476, 487, 77 S. Ct. 1304, 1310, 1 L. Ed. 2d 1498 that "Obscene material is material which deals with sex in a manner appealing to prurient interest." Surely, "prurient" has not the limited meaning of lust-inciting, otherwise a book or film could escape the ban by being so disgusting as to make sex seem nauseating and vile. Indeed, the first and oldest meaning of "obscene" is filthy and disgusting.

But though left without a sure definition we have been provided in *Roth* v. *United States*, 354 U.S. 476, 77 S. Ct. 1304, 1 L. Ed. 2d 1498, supra, and *Manual Enterprises, Inc.* v. *Day*, 370 U.S. 478, 82 S. Ct. 1432, 8 L. Ed. 2d 639, supra, with a listing of marks or tests the presence of which will, apparently, call down the obscenity ban and cast the material outside First Amendment protections. Let us apply this checklist to "Tropic of Cancer."

(1)—"Predominant appeal to prurient interest"—to a "shameful or morbid interest in nudity, sex, or excretion" (Roth, 354 U.S., supra, p. 487, 77 S. Ct. p. 1310, 1 L. Ed. 2d 1498). If the "appeal"—that is, the main thrust or idea or motif or scheme—of this book is not directed at such an "interest," then the work has no purpose or meaning at all.

(2)—"Goes substantially beyond customary limits of candor in description or representation of such matters" (Roth, 354 U.S., supra, p. 487, 77 S. Ct. p. 1310, 1 L. Ed. 2d 1498). I will assume this refers to the limits observed in reasonably civilized society, not in stews. "Tropic of Cancer" is a conscious and persistent shock treatment and only the shock-proof will escape the impact. On at least half its pages it overleaps candor's limits by a measurable distance.

(3)—"Contemporary community standards" (Roth, 354 U.S., supra, p. 489, 77 S. Ct. p. 1311, 1 L. Ed. 2d 1498) or "contemporary notions of rudimentary decency" (Manual Enterprises, 370 U.S., supra, p. 489, 82 S.C. 1438, 8 L. Ed. 2d 639)—this gloss or excrescence on the Model Penal Code definition of obscenity is difficult to understand or apply since "predominant appeal" is an objective quality of the material and "community standards" are the subjective reactions of the citizenry of a place or region. If we are to use community standards as a test, the only feasible testing method is by submission to a jury as was recognized by our own court long ago in *People v. Pesky*, 254 N.Y. 373, 173 N.E. 227. Of course a jury cannot repeal the First Amendment but when a jury (as here) makes a finding of obscenity as to material not unreasonably deserving that epithet, there can be no violation of the Constitution. Where the book taken as a whole can under permissible constitutional standards be reasonably considered by men of ordinary prudence to be beyond the pale of contemporary notions of rudimentary decency (paraphrased from Manual Enterprises, 370 U.S., supra, p. 489, 82 S. Ct. p. 1438, 8 L. Ed. 2d 639) then a jury verdict of "guilty" violates no right.

(4)—"Patent offensiveness" (Manual Enterprises, 370 U.S., supra, p. 486, 82 S. Ct. p. 1436, 8 L. Ed. 2d 639)—how could this book be characterized as less than "patently offensive"?

(5)—"Taken as a whole"—that is, the material must be judged as a whole and not condemned by reason of isolated offensive passages. It is to be "approached as an aggregate of different effects, and the determination turns on whether the salacious aspects are so objectionable as to outweigh whatever affirmative values the book may possess" (*American Civil Liberties Union v. City of Chicago*, 3 Ill. 2d 334, 346, 121 N.E. 2d 585, 592). The caveat to look at the whole record is really unnecessary here since "Tropic of Cancer" (on about half its pages by count) is crowded with filth and the "isolated excerpts" are the connecting, interspersed ruminations of the author on life and liberty. The Illinois Supreme Court in the opinion just above cited held that a book is not to be judged obscene because of over-frank sexy language or incidents if "considered in the light of the work as a whole" those objectionable segments "do not represent a calculated exploitation of dirt for dirt's sake, but are fairly incident to some other artistic purpose" (3 Ill. 2d pp. 345–346, 121 N.E. 2d p. 591). Here there is no discernible artistic purpose, no development of any theme or idea except plain, old-fashioned filth.

I am aware that the Supreme Court in three Per Curiam decisions (*One, Inc. v. Olesen*, 355 U.S. 371, 78 S. Ct. 364, 2 L. Ed. 2d 352, *Sunshine Book Co. v. Summerfield*, 355 U.S. 372, 78 S. Ct. 365, 2 L. Ed. 2d 352 and *Times Film Corp. v. City of Chicago*, 355 U.S. 35, 78 S. Ct. 115, 2 L. Ed. 2d 72.) has held unconstitutional the suppression of two magazines and a movie film each of which went well beyond the customary limits observed in civilized society. But something must remain of the ancient police power of the States and their Legislatures and their juries to ban stuff as filthy as "Tropic of Cancer." Local communities and their governance are not helped by a literal, doctrinaire reading of "Freedom of the Press." Sound ideas should not be stretched to extreme lengths and unworkable results. It is just unthinkable that the practical political thinkers who wrote the Bill of Rights ever intended to protect downright foulness.

Although the stuff we examined and banned in *People v. Finkelstein*, 11 N.Y. 2d 300, 229 N.Y.S. 2d 367, 183 N.E. 2d 661, was in a different format and did not bear the byline of a well-known author it strayed no further beyond the pale of decency than does "Tropic of Cancer," yet was conceded to be obscene. In *People v. Richmond County News, Inc.*, 9 N.Y. 2d 578, 216 N.Y.S. 2d 369, 175 N.E. 2d 681, on the other hand, we had a magazine which, while probably much too sexy for adolescents, was in the opinion of the majority of this court just one of the many incitements which a modern day pluralistic society tolerates.

The County Court's opinion as incorporated into its order held as matter of law that the book is not obscene. However, the court held also that the finding as to *scienter* was against the weight of evidence. Therefore, there must be a new trial on the latter issue.

DYE, Judge (dissenting).

In order to sustain the judgment of conviction rendered in the Court of Special Sessions of the City of Syracuse against these defendants for the sale of the book "Tropic of Cancer" in violation of subdivision 1 of section 1141 of the Penal Law, a majority of this court is about to rule that the book, however viewed, is obscene within the meaning of the statute. This ignores a fundamental and basic concept of justice that a conviction had for violation of that section, like a conviction had for the violation of any other penal statute, must rest upon proof of guilt beyond any reasonable doubt, and this must include proof beyond any reasonable doubt that this book was obscene within the meaning of the statute. Whether the book is obscene as a matter of constitutional judgment is indeed questionable, so questionable in fact that the court below had no difficulty in setting aside the conviction, dismissing the information and remitting the fine.

That doubt still persists for, however analyzed, the decision now being rendered is no more than an expression of individual view having no support aside from its own pronouncement. Respected and eminent book reviewers have found it "not obscene"; the British government has announced that it will not prosecute its dissemination under the Obscene Publications Act (New York Times, April 12, 1963) and wherever considered in the high appellate courts of our sister States the book has been held to be not obscene (see *Zeitlin v. Arnebergh*, 59 Cal. 2d 901, 31 Cal. Rptr. 800, 383 P. 2d 152; *Attorney General v. Book Named "Tropic of Cancer,"* 345 Mass. 11, 184 N.E. 2d 328; *McCauley v. Tropic of Cancer*, 20 Wis. 2d 134, 121 N.W. 2d 545).

The book, first published in 1934, is to be found on the shelves of public libraries and libraries of institutions of learning. It has been and is being sold freely throughout the United States and foreign countries. In light of the acceptance by eminent men of letters, government administrators and rulings from high courts of appeal, it is reasonable to assume that, when the proprietors and employees of one of the largest retail book stores of the State sold it freely and openly across the counter, they did so believing that such sale was in harmony with contemporary community standards and in no way violative of a criminal statute. Under such circumstances *scienter* became an essential element of proof. That such fact can ever be established in this instance seems very doubtful in light of other judicial pronouncements on the same work by the highest courts of other States (see *Zeitlin* v. *Arnebergh*, supra; *McCauley* v. *Tropic of Cancer*, supra; *Attorney General* v. *Book Named "Tropic of Cancer,"* supra) as well as the pronouncements of the Supreme Court of the United States on other occasions. "The community cannot, where liberty of speech and press are at issue, condemn that which it generally tolerates." (*Smith* v. *People of State of California*, 361 U.S. 147, 171, 80 S. Ct. 215, 228, 4 L. Ed. 2d 205.)

The concept of obscenity, as we have heretofore stated, is "imprecise" (*Brown* v. *Kingsley Books, Inc.*, 1 N.Y. 2d 177, 181–182, 151 N.Y.S. 2d 639, 641–642, 134 N.E. 2d 461, 462–464, affd. 354 U.S. 436, 77 S. Ct. 1325, 1 L. Ed. 2d 1469); if a publication is to be suppressed for reasons of obscenity the question "whether a particular work is of that character involves not really an issue of fact but a question of constitutional *judgment*" (*Roth* v. *United States*, 354 U.S. 476, 497–498, 77 S. Ct. 1304, 1316, 1 L. Ed. 2d 1498 [HARLAN, J.]). There are no better standards available defining the meaning of the free press guarantees of the First Amendment as applied to publications than those laid down by the Supreme Court of the United States (*Bantam Books, Inc.* v. *Sullivan*, 372 U.S. 58, 83 S. Ct. 631, 9 L. Ed. 2d 584; *Manual Enterprises, Inc.* v. *Day*, 370 U.S. 478, 82 S. Ct. 1432, 8 L. Ed. 2d 639; *Marcus* v. *Search Warrants of Property at 104 East Tenth St., Kansas City, Mo.*, 367 U.S. 717, 81 S. Ct. 1708, 6 L. Ed. 2d 1127; *Smith* v. *People of State of California*, 361 U.S. 147, 80 S. Ct. 215, 4 L. Ed. 2d 205, supra; *Roth* v. *United States*, 354 U.S. 476, 77 S. Ct. 1304, 1 L. Ed. 2d 1498, supra; *Kingsley Books* v. *Brown*, 354 U.S. 436, supra [cf. *People* v. *Richmond County News, Inc.*, 9 N.Y. 2d 578, 216 N.Y.S. 2d 369, 175 N.E. 2d 681]). Applying those guidelines to this publication—and under the Supremacy Doctrine we may not ignore them—the indicated direction all points to an affirmance of the order appealed from.

It cannot be gainsaid that the profusion of four-letter words used by the author to portray the mental and moral slough into which some of his characters had sunk is unsuited for the drawing room. In "Tropic," as in Joyce's "Ulysses" however, the erotic passages are "submerged in the book as a whole and have little resultant effect" (*United States* v. *One Book* Entitled Ulysses, 2 Cir., 72 F. 2d 705, 707). Like "Ulysses," it is a "tragic and very powerful commentary" on the inner lives of human beings caught in the throes of a hopeless social morass. Written in Paris in 1934 at a time when Europe was reeling from the aftermath of the devastating moral and material destruction of World War I, the book reflects the debasing experiences and problems known to many in a city such as Paris in the 1930s. In an effort to escape the clutching insistence of an all-engulfing miasma, the author describes his own and his companion's sexual indulgences, tediously repeated, to rediscover that surrender to such demeaning conduct was not the antidote to the underlying human unhappiness caused by the poverty, filth, disease, loneliness and despair in a world in flux. In dealing with Gautier's "Mademoiselle de Maupin" in *Halsey* v. *New York Soc. for Suppression of Vice*, 234 N.Y. 1, 4, 136 N.E. 219, 220, we said "No work may be judged from a selection of

[a few] paragraphs alone. Printed by themselves they might, as a matter of law, come within the prohibition of the statute. So might a similar selection from Aristophanes or Chaucer or Boccaccio, or even from the Bible." The book should neither be appraised nor condemned by the tone of a few passages wrested from context and viewed in a vacuum. It "must be considered broadly, as a whole." (*Halsey* v. *New York Soc. for Suppression of Vice*, supra, 234 N.Y. p. 4, 136 N.E. p. 220.)

When so read, its content does not meet the test of "hard-core pornography" which we announced in *People* v. *Richmond County News, Inc.*, 9 N.Y. 2d 578, 586, 216 N.Y.S. 2d 369, 375, 175 N.E. 2d 681, 685, supra, nor does the book contain, in the words of Mr. Justice HARLAN, "patently offensive" material and have its predominant appeal to the "prurient interest"—the criteria enunciated by the Supreme Court in *Manual Enterprises, Inc.* v. *Day*, 370 U.S. 478, 486, 82 S. Ct. 1432, 8 L. Ed. 2d 639, supra.

This so-called "obscenity case" and those that preceded it all call to mind the book burning of eighteenth-century Europe and New England which fortunately did not stop the forces of the inquisitive and curious minds for long but, as might well have been expected and as we are now witnessing, released forces which today are demanding attention throughout the democracies of the world. To hold this book obscene necessarily places one in the role of the censor, a role which is incompatible with the fundamentals of a free society and which is incompatible with the explicit powers and obvious purposes of this court. Obscenity is variously defined, but it does not follow that the printed word which is in bad taste, disgusting, and offensive is obscene as a matter of law requiring suppression by the censor, and that is what we must say beyond any reason of doubt in order to find grounds for reversal here. Such a view in no way minimizes the right of the State to suppress what is obscene and pornographic. However, when material is so characterized to charge commission of a crime, the courts should be ever-mindful before rendering a judgment of conviction that the evidence of guilt is free from reasonable doubt, else what is done in the name of the law will so fritter away the free speech and free press guarantees of the First Amendment and due process under the Fourteenth Amendment as to make the remedy more dangerous than the ill, for the effect will be to substitute the fleeting *ad hoc* opinion of men, whether we realize it or not, for the rule of law envisioned by the framers of the Constitution.

The order appealed from should be affirmed.

FULD, Judge (dissenting).

A discussion of the meaning of "obscene" under section 1141 of our Penal Law (see *People* v. *Richmond County News, Inc.*, 9 N.Y. 2d 578, 585–587, 216 N.Y.S. 2d 369, 374–377, 175 N.E. 2d 681, 684–686) is unnecessary in this case, since in our judgment "Tropic of Cancer" finds protection under the minimal standards laid down by the United States Supreme Court under the First Amendment. Applying such standards, a book—which is to be judged in its entirety and not by focusing attention on particular words and passages contained in it—may be stamped as obscene, and beyond the pale of constitutional protection, only if it is "utterly without redeeming social importance" and only if its "dominant theme" is an appeal to "prurient interest." (See *Roth* v. *United States*, 354 U.S. 476, 484, 77 S. Ct. 1304, 1 L. Ed. 2d 1498, *passim*; *Times Film Corp.* v. *City of Chicago*, 355 U.S. 35, 78 S. Ct. 115, 2 L. Ed. 2d 72; *One, Inc.*, v. *Olesen*, 355 U.S. 371, 78 S. Ct. 364, 2 L. Ed. 2d 352; *Sunshine Book Co.* v. *Summerfield*, 355 U.S. 372, 78 S. Ct. 365, 2 L. Ed. 2d 352; *Manual Enterprises Inc.* v. *Day*, 370 U.S. 478, 486–487, 82 S. Ct. 1432, 8 L. Ed. 2d 639, per HARLAN, J.) On the other hand, "If the material * * * has literary value, if it is a serious work of literature or art, then it possesses redeeming social importance and obtains the benefit of the constitutional guarantees." (*Zeitlin* v. *Arnebergh*, 59 Cal. 2d 901, 918, 31 Cal. Rptr. 800, 811, 383 P. 2d 152, 163; *see, also*, *United States* v. *One Book Called "Ulysses,"* D.C., 5 F. Supp. 182, affd. 2 Cir., 72 F. 2d 705, 706; *Commonwealth* v. *Gordon*, 66 Pa., Dist. & Co. R. 101, affd. sub. nom. *Commonwealth* v. *Feigenbaum*, 166 Pa. Super. 120, 70 A. 2d 389.)

Since "Tropic" is a serious expression of views and reactions toward life, however alien they may be to the reader's philosophy or experience, and since the book is not without literary importance as attested by recognized critics and scholars, the First Amendment does not permit its suppression.[1] And this, we note, is the conclusion re-cently reached by the high courts of California, Massachusetts and Wisconsin. (*Zeitlin* v. *Arnebergh*, 59 Cal. 2d 901, 31 Cal. Rptr. 800, 383 P. 2d 152, supra; *Attorney General* v. *Book Named* "Tropic of Cancer," 345 Mass. 11, 184 N.E. 2d 328; *McCauley* v. *Tropic of Cancer*, 20 Wis. 2d 134, 121 N.W. 2d 545.) In short, the book before us, to cull from what we said in the Richmond County News case, 9 N.Y. 2d 578, 588, 216 N.Y.S. 2d 369, 377, 175 N.E. 2d 681, 686, supra, "appraised * * * in the light of First Amendment concepts, may not be adjudged obscene without impairing the vital social in-terest in freedom of expression."

The order of the Onondaga County Court reversing the convictions and dismissing the information should be affirmed.

DESMOND, C.J., and BURKE and FOSTER, JJ., concur in opinion by SCILEPPI, J.

DESMOND, C.J., concurs in a separate opinion in which SCILEPPI, BURKE and FOSTER, JJ., concur.

DYE and FULD, JJ., dissent in separate opinions in each of which the other concurs, VAN VOORHIS, J., concurring in both dissenting opinions.

Order reversed, etc.

---

[1] For an analysis and critique of the book, see discussion in *Zeitlin* v. *Arnebergh*, 59 Cal. 2d 901, 921–922, 31 Cal. Rptr. 800, 383 P. 2d 152, supra.

■ Leo A. Larkin, as Corporation Counsel of the City of New York, Frank S. Hogan, as District Attorney of New York County, Isidore Dollinger, as District Attorney of Bronx County, Edward S. Silver, as District Attorney of Kings County, Frank D. O'Connor, as District Attorney of Queens County and John M. Braisted, Jr., as District Attorney of Richmond County, Plaintiffs,

v.

G. P. Putnam's Sons *et al.*, *Defendants*.

Supreme Court, Special Term, New York County, Part I.

July 24, 1963.

Leo A. Larkin, Corp. Counsel, of City of New York, by *Seymour B. Quel*, Asst. Corp. Counsel, for plaintiffs.

Charles Rembar, New York City, of Rembar & Zolotar, New York City, of counsel for defendants.

CHARLES MARKS, Justice.

[1–4] This is an application by the Corporation Counsel of the City of New York and the district attorney of each of the five counties of the City of New York for an order staying and restraining the defendants during the pendency of this action from acquiring or selling and/or distributing, and/or disposing in any manner of any of the issues and copies of the book referred to in the complaint bearing title "John Cleland's Memoirs of a Woman of Pleasure" under the masthead of G. P. Putnam's Sons, New York.

The action has been instituted pursuant to section 22–a of the Code of Criminal Procedure to enjoin the publisher, the distributors, and the retail book store owners as de-fendants from selling, distributing, etc., the said book above mentioned.

The question now before this court is whether the book published by the defendant, G. P. Putnam's Sons "John Cleland's Memoirs of a Woman of Pleasure" meets the test of obscenity as enunciated by our Court of Appeals and the Supreme Court of the United States. This court has read the book and has carefully and painstakingly read the papers in support of and in opposition to this application. I have come to the conclusion that "John Cleland's Memoirs of a Woman of Pleasure" is obscene within the meaning of section 22–a of the Code of Criminal Procedure. In view of this finding of obscenity, the contention of defendant that the publication is protected by the First Amendment of the United States Constitution and Article I, section 8 of the New York Constitution is without merit. Obscenity is not within the area of constitutionally protected speech or press (see *Roth v. United States*, 354 U.S. 476, 77 S. Ct. 1304, 1 L. Ed. 2d 1498). The test of obscenity was recently applied by the Court of Appeals in *People v. Fritch*, 13 N.Y. 2d 119, 243 N.Y.S. 2d 1, 192 N.E. 2d 713, which held the "Tropic of Cancer" to be obscene within the meaning of section 1141 of the Penal Law, a statute which is the counterpart of section 22–a of the Code of Criminal Procedure. Judge Scileppi in writing the prevailing opinion in the Fritch case stated: "But, while the exact boundaries of obscenity cannot be sharply drawn, the Supreme Court, in *Roth v. United States*, supra, and *Manual Enterprises, Inc. v. Day*, 370 U.S. 478, 82 S. Ct. 1432, 8 L. Ed. 2d 639, set forth guidelines and prescribed the essential elements which must conjoin before it can be found that a publication is obscene by constitutional standards. The first of these elements is the so-called 'prurient interest' test set forth in Roth, that is, 'whether to the average person, applying contemporary community standards, the dominant theme of the material taken as a whole appeals to the prurient interest' (*Roth v. United States*, supra, 354 U.S. p. 489, 77 S. Ct. p. 1311, 1 L. Ed. 2d 1498). The second, contained in Manual Enterprises, requires that, in addition to the 'prurient interest' test, it is necessary to establish that the challenged material is also 'patently offensive' to current community standards of decency (*Manual Enterprises, Inc. v. Day*, supra, 370 U.S. p. 482, 82 S. Ct. p. 1434, 8 L. Ed. 2d 639)."

Applying this test to the book under consideration, I find that throughout its 298 pages, there is depicted in glowing terms a series of acts dealing with sex in a manner designed to appeal to the prurient interest. In my many years as a trial judge in both civil and criminal cases, I have come in contact with every segment of the community and the question as to whether this book appeals to the prurient interest of the average person in the contemporary community can best be determined by a realistic appraisal of its contents by the court. The book describes in detail instances of lesbianism, female masturbation, the deflowering of a virgin, the seduction of a male virgin, the flagellation of male by female and female by male, and other aberrant acts as well as more than twenty acts of sexual intercourse between male and female, some of which are committed in the open presence of numerous other persons and some of which are instances of voyeurism. In the recital of the loss of virginity by a fifteen-year-old girl, the author goes to great pains to express the "excess of pleasure through excess of pain" experience, and further on in the book, the four girl companions of Fanny Hill who are resident in the same bawdy house are asked to narrate the

manner and circumstances of their loss of virginity which they proceed to do in lurid detail, the obvious intent being to glorify the deflowering of young girls. The author in the conclusion states at page 298 of the book, "You know Mr. C***O***, you know his estate, his worth, and good sense: can you, will you pronounce it ill meant, at least of him, when anxious for his son's morals, with a view to form him to virtue, and inspire him with a fix'd, a rational contempt for vice, he condescended to be his master of the ceremonies, and led him by the hand thro' the most noted bawdyhouses in town, where he took care he should be familiarized with all those scenes of debauchery, so fit to nauseate a good taste? The experiment, you will cry, is dangerous. True, on a fool: but are fools worth so much attention?"

Although there are just random quotes and statements taken from the book, it is not intended in any way to convey the thought that this court has judged this book by taking isolated excerpts which might affect particularly susceptible persons. The court has considered the book as a whole in its impact upon the average person in the community and I find that the book is patently offensive and utterly without any social value. In writing one of the prevailing opinions in the *People v. Richmond County News Incorporated* case, 9 N.Y. 2d 578, at p. 587, 216 N.Y.S. 2d 369, at p. 376, 175 N.E. 2d 681, at p. 686, Judge Fuld said: "It smacks, at times, of fantasy and unreality, of sexual perversion and sickness and represents, according to one thoughtful scholar, 'a debauchery of the sexual faculty.' " The language quoted very aptly applies to the instant case. Chief Judge Desmond in his concurring opinion in *People v. Richmond County News Incorporated*, supra, quotes with approval 9 N.Y. 2d, at page 588, 216 N.Y.S. 2d, at page 377, 175 N.E. 2d, at page 687, that " 'For a book to be prohibited it is necessary that from its whole tenor the author's intention is evident of teaching the reader about sins of impurity and arousing him to libidinousness.' "

In the *People v. Fritch* case, supra, Judge Scileppi prescribed the essential elements which must be found in a publication to hold it to be obscene by constitutional standards. I find factually that all these prescribed elements are present in the book under consideration.

The defendant has submitted affidavits, letters and comments of literary figures who have commented favorably on the book. Neither the quality of the writing nor the so-called literary worth of the book prevents the book from being adjudged obscene as it meets the tests as enunciated in Roth, Richmond County News and Fritch. The opinions of authors and critics no matter how distinguished they may be cannot be substituted for those of the average person in a contemporary community. The statement that there is "outward polish in Cleland's description of sexual scenes" by one of the distinguished writers and that its style is "elegant" as described by a well-known poet, editor and critic and that "it is brilliantly written" as expressed by another highly regarded critic and author and similar "commendations" by literary figures impels the quote from the opinion of Judge Scileppi in *People v. Fritch*, "This court will not adopt a rule of law which states that obscenity is suppressible but that well written obscenity is not."

This court cannot agree with the statements of some of the distinguished writers and critics in viewing the book as one of historical value "in that it allegedly describes an age and a manner of living" or that it is "typical in its expression of the whole feeling of the period" or "that it tells us a good deal about 18th Century England." The morals of the mass of the English people of the mid-18th Century cannot be judged by the narrative of sex and immorality of a minute few any more than we should to-day indict the people of England for immorality by reason of the lurid recital of sex acts allegedly engaged in by a mere handful of its people.

Accordingly, based upon the contents of the book and the findings of this court, the application of the plaintiffs staying and restraining each of the defendants from publishing, selling, acquiring for the purposes of selling and from distributing or otherwise disposing of any copies of "John Cleland's Memoirs of a Woman of Pleasure" published by G. P. Putnam's Sons of New York is granted.

Settle order forthwith.

■ The People of the State of New York, *Plaintiff,*

v.

Philip Birch, Richard Mead, Ray Kirk, All States News Company, Inc., *Defendants.*

Supreme Court, Criminal Term, Queens County, Part I.

Sept. 6, 1963.

Frank D. O'Connor, Dist. Atty., Queens County (Kenneth M. Browne, Asst. Dist. Atty., of counsel), for the People.
Frank R. McGlynn, Woodside, for defendants.
J. IRWIN SHAPIRO, Justice.

Motion by the defendants "for an order directing the District Attorney of the County of Queens to permit the defendants, or their representatives, to inspect the minutes of the Grand Jury which presented to this court the said indictment hereinabove referred to or, in the alternative, to dismiss the said indictment on the ground that the same is contrary to the law, illegal and invalid in that the same was not founded upon sufficient or adequate evidence and that the same is and was violative of the constitutional rights of the defendants, more particularly, but not confined to the violation of the defendants' rights under the First, Fourth, Fifth and Fourteenth Amendments of the United States Constitution."

The defendants are charged in a nine count indictment with violating Section 1141 of the Penal Law ("obscene prints and articles"), and with conspiracy to violate that statute, in that they did sell and distribute the eight books mentioned therein.[1]

[1] It is now well settled, despite illuminating dissenting opinions to the contrary, that state statutes making it a crime to publish or distribute writings "incontestably found to be obscene" do not invade the freedom of expression guarantees contained in the First Amendment of the United States Constitution (*Kingsley Books* v. *Brown,* 354 U.S. 436, 440, 77 S. Ct. 1325, 1 L. Ed. 2d 1469; *Roth* v. *United States,* 354 U.S. 476, 481, 77 S. Ct. 1304, 1 L. Ed. 2d 1498; *Alberts* v. *California,* 354 U.S. 476, 77 S. Ct. 1304, 1 L. Ed. 2d 1498; *People* v. *Richmond County News,* 9 N.Y. 2d 578, 581, 216 N.Y.S. 2d 369, 370, 175 N.E. 2d 681, 682), but such statutes must be narrowly and strictly construed (*People* v. *Richmond County News,* supra, p. 581 of 9 N.Y. 2d, p. 370 of 216 N.Y.S. 2d, p. 682 of 175 N.E. 2d).

[2] "* * * (I)f 'obscenity' is to be suppressed, the question whether a particular work is of that character involves not really an issue of fact but a question of constitutional *judgment* of the most sensitive and delicate kind" (Harlan, J., in concurring opinion in *Roth* v. *United States,* 354 U.S. 476, 497–498, 77 S. Ct. 1304, 1316, 1 L. Ed. 2d 1498).

In order to pass upon that "most sensitive and delicate question" of "constitutional judgment," I have of necessity been compelled to read all eight books, a short synopsis of each of which is set forth as an exhibit to this opinion.

[3, 4] The literary value of these books may be nil, but that does not mean that they may therefore constitutionally be suppressed or that their authors or distributors are criminals. A public official, albeit a judge, who determines what is and what is not hard core pornography becomes a censor but the law in its present state requires just that. Undertaking that distasteful task, as I must, requires an evaluation of the stories in these books in relation to our present society and culture. The basic question is whether these books go beyond "the present critical point in the compromise between candor and shame at which the community (has) arrived" (*United States* v. *Kennerley,* D.C., 209 F. 119, 121, cited with approval in *People* v. *Richmond County News,* 9 N.Y. 2d 578, 586, 216 N.Y.S. 2d 369, 375, 175 N.E. 2d 681, 685).

---

1 Sex Kitten   by Greg Caldwell
  Clipjoint Cutie   by Monte Steele
  The Wild Ones   by Nell Holland
  The Hottest Party in Town   by Sam Hudson
  Passion Pit   by David Spencer
  Bedroom at the Top   by Bruce Rald
  Butch   by Andrew Shaw
  College for Sinners   by Andrew Shaw

[5] The books contain a great number of descriptions of sexual activity which, in many cases, are only tenuously associated with the plot and story line. They thus, no doubt, provide erotic reading material, but no more so than many works of literature which have received acclaim as classics. In that connection it should be remembered that the fact "that adulterous or other sexually immoral relationships are portrayed approvingly cannot serve as a reason for declaring a work obscene without running afoul of the First Amendment" (*People* v. *Richmond County News*, supra, p. 582 of 9 N.Y. 2d, p. 372 of 216 N.Y.S. 2d, p. 683 of 175 N.E. 2d) because the constitution protects "advocacy of the opinion that adultery may sometimes be proper, no less than advocacy of socialism or the single tax" (*Kingsley Intern. Pictures Corp.* v. *Regents*, 360 U.S. 684, 689, 79 S. Ct. 1362, 1365, 3 L. Ed. 2d 1512).

[6] Writings which have received favorable recognition in all types of civilizations, in all ages, have delineated societies' cultures and the relationship of the individual to them. Throughout the annals of recorded history, there have been writers who failed to achieve the higher plateaus of literature and art. Their failure to achieve literary recognition does not thereby make their works more objectionable, legally or morally, than that of the writer who merits, or receives, the high acclaim of the critical community for his literary style and grace (*Winters* v. *New York*, 333 U.S. 507, 510, 68 S. Ct. 665, 92 L. Ed. 840; *People* v. *Fritch*, 13 N.Y. 2d 119, 243 N.Y.S. 2d 1, 192 N.E. 2d 713.

The civilizations of the past provide the basis for our modern culture and society. Literature,—good, bad and indifferent,—has been the tissue which formed the umbilical cord nurturing all societies from Homeric Greece to the present. The passage of time has seen honors bestowed upon authors whose writings are replete with words and incidents that were deemed lurid and pornographic contemporaneously with their appearance. Aristophanes, Plautus, Shakespeare, Brinsley, Swift, Boccaccio, Rabelais and Balzac, to name just a few, are *now* noted and recognized for the vigor of their writings and for the artful way in which they delineated and portrayed the ethical and moral conditions of their times. They were not always so regarded, however, and many of their works were attacked and ridiculed by those of tender sensibilities upon the same basis that the finger of accusation is pointed at the books here under scrutiny.

Nothing is truer than that with the passage of time we constantly see a reshuffling of the gods in the world's literary pantheon. We should therefore proceed with the utmost caution before determining, *as a matter of constitutional judgment* that those who write about the serpent in Eden, in their own way, should have their writings banned and that they themselves should be denominated criminals.

[7] Words which are not in use (supposedly) in polite society and are denoted as "four letter" words do not in and of themselves make for obscenity. If they did "The Arabian Nights," just to cite one accepted classic, would require suppression. Many readers may be disgusted or revolted by the use of foul language but the scenes that are depicted thereby are not, in context, necessarily pornographic (*United States* v. *One Book* Entitled *Ulysses*, 2 Cir., 72 F. 2d 705, 707; *Halsey* v. *New York Soc. for Suppression of Vice*, 234 N.Y. 1, 4, 136 N.E. 219, 220).

Most books which have been heretofore attacked as obscene and pornographic, and which have been defended as having over-all literary merit, have presented a problem in research which usually consisted of a detailed search for "four letter" words, phrases and descriptions which could be lifted from the text to provide a basis for their indictment as pornographic. The books here offer no such problem for they contain no "four letter" words. So far as the purity of the language used is concerned the books could well be made required reading for fourth year elementary students. Fully 90% of each book, however, is filled with lurid descriptions of sexual activities, both hetero and homosexual, in sufficient detail to act as an erotic stimulus to those so inclined. However, in all their erotic descriptions they maintain a clever, and apparently deliberate, avoidance of socially unacceptable language, and the descriptions of erotic activity are so similar, in language and action, as to appear to be written by one author using one outline for all the books. Even those books which have a stronger plot and story line reflect this outline in the description of the sexual scene. Page after page contains details and descriptions of similar erotic behavior. In that respect they remind one of the similarity of all the Horatio Alger stories of this Court's youthful days except that the latter dealt with the rise from "Rags to Riches" and these books deal with the march from "Puberty to Prostitution."

In the opinion of the Court (compelled by statute to act as a literary critic) these books are plain unvarnished trash, but novels and stories of no literary merit have a place in our society. There are those who, because of lack of education, the meanness of their social existence, or mental insufficiency, cannot cope with anything better. Slick paper confessions, pulp adventure and "comic book" type of magazines provide them with an escape from reality. However, the fringes of society are not the only cover for those neurotics unable to satisfy their sexual needs through acceptable outlets. Events of the past and present tell us that. So called pillars of society number among them men and women whose sexual outlet is the eroticism of literature and pictures designed to relieve their libidinous repressions (see authorities collated by Judge Fuld in *People* v. *Richmond County News*, 9 N.Y. 2d 578, 583, 584, 216 N.Y.S. 2d 369, 372, 373, 175 N.E. 2d 681, 683, 684). Many of these people provide a ready, although, no doubt, clandestine market for the pornographic. As Sigmund Freud, the contentious founder of psycho-analysis and one whose own writings many no doubt would like to see suppressed, said in his "Wit and Its Relation to the Unconscious" "* * * Common people so thoroughly enjoy such smutty talk, * * * that it is a never lacking activity of cheerful humor * * *."

[8] In a pluralistic society, such as ours, censorship is neither truly possible nor, in the opinion of many, either desirable or legal ("One Man's Stand for Freedom," Hugo L. Black). If the flow of what is considered offensive literature is to be dammed it should be done by the exercise of censorship in the home and not by judicial fiat. Undue legal restraint must be guarded against since the exercise of censorship tends to feed upon itself and to extend into, and encroach upon, areas of personal liberties which are the very foundation of a free society. We should not attempt to suppress writings dealing with those sorrier aspects of human behavior in our national life that most of us, had we the choice, would change.

G. Rattray Taylor in "Sex in History" discusses the medieval style of nakedness. In his chapter on "Medieval Sexual Behavior," he describes a scene, in conformity with the practice of those days when outstanding personalities were being honored, in which—"the Queen of Ulster and all the ladies of the Court, to the number of 610, came to meet Cuchulainn, naked above the waist and raising their skirts so as to expose their private parts, by which they showed how greatly they honored him."

Just as the pendulum of public taste and manners has swung far away from such presently considered crude behavior, it has also swung far past the repressions of prurient and prudish Victoria. Today, skirts are shorter and the outlined erogenous areas of women are taken matter-of-factly. The undergarment model has dropped the mask from her eyes and looks at you slyly as she displays the advantage of any-brand's bra and girdle in advertisements published by ladies' magazines and our most respected newspapers, and in telecasts coming into the home. These media reflect the trends of the times. In addition, many children are dressed in suggestive clothing, the boys in skin tight trousers and the girls in revealing bodily outlines; the adolescent drives the family car, with his girl friend, to a drive-in-movie where they see sex comedies which make light of pre-marital and extra-marital sexual relations. Sex and sophistication surround them. A single page of one of our metropolitan newspapers contains reviews or advertisements of a number of motion pictures variously described as follows: "a romp of bawdy tales completely in the Gallic tradition that sex dalliance is the funniest topic on earth"; "loaded with burlesque seductions, orgies" and a description of the actress "who plays the mistress"; "a bold, sexy, disquieting film."

[9] Such, whether we approve or disapprove, is the temper of our times and it is in that light that one must determine whether the books here are obscene for "[t]he community cannot, where liberty of speech and press are at issue, condemn that which it generally tolerates" (*Smith* v. *California*, 361 U.S. 147, 171, 80 S. Ct. 215, 228, 4 L. Ed. 2d 205).

It is of the utmost importance in this field that judges be not motivated to assume the guise of censors by reason of personal predilections, and that decisions be not dictated by their personal whims with little consideration given to the fact that liberty is not divisible and that when we deny its privileges to others we place our own in jeopardy, or by pressure *sub-consciously* exerted by groups of well-meaning vigilante guardians of the public morals who often refuse to recognize that free societies are dynamic and that literature and art, *and badly written books too*, are merely the mirror reflections of some phase of existing life. Truth, so evidenced, is often bitter and distasteful, but so are many facets of our existence for there is a "huge and disproportionate abundance of evil" on earth (Ralph Waldo Emerson in his Journal).

Totalitarian dictated monotonous conformity in the use of the written word is too great a price to pay to receive the approbation of the ultra sensitive or the easily psychically devastated. Writing can reflect the changes which are taking place in a culture or they may lead a society to change. What is good or bad in the past or present, or may be in the future, is described by perceptive writers in various ways and many dialects.

If any of these eight books truthfully picture any con-

siderable segment of our society, we may be doomed to the same destruction which befell the hedonistic, voluptuarian civilizations of Greece and Rome and Hamlet's disillusionment and disgust with the world as being "no other thing than a foul and pestilent congregation of vapors" could find little dissent.

However, whether the word portraits painted in these eight books are an accurate recital of existing conditions or are pure fantasy, to attempt to blot out the portrayal by judicial censorship would be completely unavailing just as the book burners of old did not by the flames of their fires succeed in consuming the truth contained in those books. Any such attempted prohibition of books, in the long run, will be no more effective than our last noble experiment, the liquor prohibition amendment.

I venture the opinion that the recent unsuccessful attempt to suppress "Memoirs of a Woman of Pleasure" (popularly known as "Fanny Hill") (*Larkin* v. *G. P. Putnam's Sons*, 40 Misc. 2d 28, 242 N.Y.S. 2d 746, Klein, J.) and the free advertising received by the book in connection therewith will see more copies of it sold this year than have been printed in its 214 years of clandestine existence.

[10] In an era of bikinis, which reveal more than they conceal; of cinemas which show females swimming in the nude and which have for their main thesis the art of living well by prostitution and pimping and of newspapers which contain complete and detailed descriptions of the actions of the sexually aberrant, one must legally conclude that these books, *in the mores of these days*, do not constitute hard core pornography. Coarse they are, but so is much in our civilization.

To censor these books, by law, would be flowering the seed of the repression of free expression. If books such as these are to be suppressed, it should not be done by law, but by the starvation of those who write and distribute them through the failure of the public to purchase them. Education, and not judicial legislation, is the answer. In the words of Plato (The Republic, Ch. XI) "It would be silly, I think, to make laws on these matters." Voluntary censorship, exercised by the would be purchaser of such material, is the essence of a free society,—a society which has more to lose from unbridled censorship than from prohibiting the publication of "gamy" books. That is one of the main differences between worlds that are open and worlds that are closed. *In the final analysis we must trust in the good sense of the people. They should be the sole judges of whether they are going to be literary gourmets, gourmands or gluttons for what is "one reader's obscenity is another's artistry"* (N.Y. Times, editorial, 8/24/63).

In *People v. Richmond County News*, 9 N.Y. 2d 578, 216 N.Y.S. 2d 369, 175 N.E. 2d 681, an attempt to censor a magazine was involved. It contained numerous pictures of "nude or partially nude women, many of which are clearly sexually suggestive." One picture portrayed "a totally nude woman, just starting to slip on an undergarment, and saying to another nude woman whose nakedness is reflected on a mirror on the wall, 'I'd better leave now—before your husband comes home'" which Judge Froessel in his dissenting opinion said (p. 594, 216 N.Y.S. 2d p. 382, 175 N.E. 2d p. 690) "clearly and openly imputes lesbianism and 'a debauchery of the sexual faculty.'" In discussing an article on page 7 of that same magazine which dealt with an experience between a married man and a young woman Judge Froessel said (p. 594, 216 N.Y.S. 2d p. 382, 175 N.E. 2d p. 690):

"*It tells how, while walking to her apartment, he 'absorbed the view of her breasts standing out in bold relief. In his haziness, he pictured her naked from her fleshy shoulders to her liquid underbelly' (p. 9, col. 1). Then, later, she 'expertly worked [her hand] down his body. Her palm pushed in his belly slightly. * * *. Her breathing was louder now, and she wriggled to get into a more erotic position' (p. 9, col. 2). On page 10: he 'let his finger toy with her nipples until they stood up like pencil erasers. He grabbed her, and drove his tongue to the roof of her mouth. She did it back, and soon they were rubbing and kissing and feeling, and undressing each other. They thrashed on the bed until their rhythmic animal convulsions propelled them to the floor.'*

"*In another article, entitled 'Outline for an Anthropological Disquisition' (at p. 53), the author describes a somewhat similar experience, and apologizes for his brutality but is invited by the woman to be more brutal the next time.*"

The majority of the Court of Appeals, however, held that the magazine could not be constitutionally proscribed. In giving his reasons for concurrence in that conclusion Chief Judge Desmond said that the magazine was not pornographic (9 N.Y. 2d p. 589, 216 N.Y.S. 2d p. 687, 175 N.E. 2d p. 378),

"*using that term as describing the extreme form of gross and all-intentioned sexuality which American statutes and courts may constitutionally punish as criminal*"

and he concluded that,

"*This collection of sexy fiction and illustrations has little of literary merit or artistry and yet it is not in the First Amendment sense filthy or disgusting or deliberately corruptive or offensive to common decency under prevailing standards of taste.*"

[11] If the decision in that case is the law of this state today, the books here under review are constitutionally protected against suppression and do not violate Section 1141 of the Penal Law. True it is that teen-agers may be hurt by reading what may very well be denominated as vulgar trash, but the effect upon and the reactions of children are not legally valid tests to determine what constitutes illegal pornography (*Roth v. United States*, 354 U.S. 476, 489, 490, 77 S. Ct. 1304, 1 L. Ed. 2d 1498).*

---

* It should be noted that Section 484-h of the Penal Law, effective in its present form, as of September 1, 1963 gives the People a remedy in the case of books such as are here under consideration when sold or given or shown "to any person under the age of eighteen (18) years." It reads as follows:

"A person who willfully or knowingly sells, lends, gives away, shows, advertises for sale or distributes commercially to any person under the age of eighteen (18) years or has in his possession with intent to give, lend, show, sell, distribute commercially, or otherwise offer for sale or commercial distribution

In *Butler* v. *Michigan*, 352 U.S. 380, 77 S. Ct. 524, 1 L. Ed. 2d 412, the trial judge found as a fact that the book there under consideration would "have a potentially deleterious influence upon youth." In denying the right to suppress that book despite that factually well-founded finding, Mr. Justice Frankfurter, in declaring the Michigan statute unconstitutional because it made such a book unavailable to the general reading public, said (pp. 383–384, 77 S. Ct. p. 526):

"*The incidence of this enactment is to reduce the adult population of Michigan to reading only what is fit for children. It thereby arbitrarily curtails one of those liberties of the individual, now enshrined in the Due Process Clause of the Fourteenth Amendment, that history has attested as the indispensable conditions for the maintenance and progress of a free society.*"

In *People* v. *Fritch*, 13 N.Y. 2d 119, 124, 243 N.Y.S. 2d 1, 6, 192 N.E. 2d 713, 717, the Court of Appeals by a sharply divided court held that the book "Tropic of Cancer" came within the ban of the pornography statute. That determination is not here in point, for as the majority opinion of Judge Scileppi points out: "Throughout its pages can be found a constant repetition of patently offensive words used solely to convey debasing portrayals of natural and unnatural sexual experiences" and in footnote 5 to his opinion Judge Scileppi indicates the pages on which the "[o]bscene and filthy passages are to be found." By actual count they exceed 300 in number, and according to the concurring opinion of Chief Judge Desmond the book "(on about half its pages by count) is crowded with filth." (p. 128 of 13 N.Y. 2d, p. 9 of 243 N.Y.S. 2d, p. 719 of 192 N.E. 2d) The decision in that case, therefore, stands upon its special facts and is to be restricted in its application to the type of book using the kind of language that directly comes within the confines of that opinion.

The eight books here are to me, as an individual, poor writings, bad in taste, profane, offensive and disgusting but they are not obscene within the meaning of Section 1141 of the Penal Law as that section must be constitutionally construed in light of the free press guarantee of the First Amendment and the Due Process Clause of the Fourteenth Amendment to the Constitution.

It follows, therefore, that the indictment must be and it is hereby dismissed.

---

to any individual under the age of eighteen (18) years any pornographic motion picture; or any still picture or photograph, or any book, 'pocket book,' pamphlet or magazine the cover or content of which exploits, is devoted to, or is principally made up of descriptions of illicit sex or sexual immorality or which is obscene, lewd, lascivious, filthy, indecent or disgusting, or which consists of pictures of nude or partially denuded figures, posed or presented in a manner to provoke or arouse lust or passion or to exploit sex, lust or perversion for commercial gain or any article or instrument of indecent or immoral use shall be guilty of a misdemeanor.

"For the purposes of this section 'knowingly' shall mean having knowledge of the character and content of the publication or failure to exercise reasonable inspection which would disclose the content and character of the same."

■ City of St. Louis, (*Plaintiff*) *Appellant*,

v.

Anthony J. Mikes, (*Defendant*) *Respondent*.
City of St. Louis, (*Plaintiff*) *Appellant*,

v.

Charles Bud Elliott, (*Defendant*) *Respondent*.
City of St. Louis, (*Plaintiff*) *Appellant*,

v.

Joan Faith Ware, (*Defendant*) *Respondent*.
Nos. 30733–30757.

St. Louis Court of Appeals, Missouri.

Nov. 19, 1963.

Rehearing Denied Dec. 9, 1963.

Thomas J. Neenan, City Counselor, *Eugene P. Freeman*, Associate City Counselor, *Stephen M. Hereford*, Assistant City Counselor, St. Louis, for appellant.

James J. Rankin, Richard Wolff, St. Louis, for respondents.

WOLFE, Judge.

The matter here considered involves twenty-five appeals. All arise out of charges of certain ordinance violations which are based upon the same set of facts, except for the dates that the violations were charged to have occurred. By permission of this court and upon stipulation of counsel, the appeals were consolidated for briefing and argument, and all will be passed upon by this opinion. There was an acquittal of all defendants upon trial in the Court of Criminal Correction, and the City of St. Louis prosecutes these appeals.

Defendants Mikes and Elliott were charged under an ordinance known as Section 38, Chapter 46, Revised Code of St. Louis. This ordinance provides in part that any person who shall "permit to be exhibited or performed, upon premises under his management or control, any indecent, immoral or lewd play or other representation shall be deemed guilty of a misdemeanor."

Defendant Ware was charged under Section 37, Chapter 46, Revised Code of St. Louis, which provides that any person who shall appear in a public place "in a state of nudity or in a dress not belonging to his or her sex in an indecent or lewd dress, or shall make an indecent exposure of his or her person, or be guilty of an indecent or lewd act of behaviour shall be guilty of a misdemeanor."

These charges arose out of a performance by defendant Joan Faith Ware. The same performance was put on nightly in a tavern called "Stardust Lounge." This place was owned and operated by a corporation known as "Stardust Lounge, Incorporated." Defendant Elliott was president of the corporation. On nine different occasions defendant Ware was arrested by police officers who viewed her performance. On seven of these occasions both defendants Elliott and Mikes were present, and both were arrested. On two occasions, only Elliott was present, at which time he was arrested with defendant Ware. These arrests started on June 13, 1960, and continued through June 22, 1960.

It was conceded upon trial that Mikes and Elliott employed defendant Ware to perform her act, and that it was performed with their permission upon premises under their control. Because of this there remained but one issue to be tried, and that was whether defendant Ware was guilty. If she was guilty, then so were defendants Mikes and Elliott.

These cases were first tried in the City Court, and that trial resulted in acquittal on all charges. The City of St. Louis appealed to the Court of Criminal Correction. There a jury was waived, and, as stated, upon trial to the court all defendants were again acquitted upon all charges. It is from these judgments of acquittal that the City prosecutes these appeals.

For the reasons stated above, the evidence presented in the Court of Criminal Correction was limited to the determination of whether or not the acts and performance of defendant Ware were lewd and indecent. The performance took place in a room described by the police officer as being about 50 feet by 50 feet in area. There was a bar at which customers could be seated for service and a small bar for preparing drinks to be served at tables. The room was otherwise furnished with tables and chairs, except for a small space used for social dancing by the customers of the establishment. There was a three-piece orchestra provided. The floor show was conducted in the dancing area, which consisted of an entertainer telling jokes for about a half hour and the performance by defendant Ware. Her act started from a small, round, revolving platform which looked like the top of a rather large bird bath, with simulated spouts of water which arched upward from its rim. This platform was located about 10 feet from the nearest tables.

Defendant Ware started her performance by mounting the platform. The platform revolved slowly as the three-piece orchestra played. When the defendant mounted the platform she was fully clothed. She was wearing an evening gown, with a scarf covering her head. As the music played and the platform slowly revolved, the defendant assumed various simple poses with her hands and arms. She also displayed her leg through a drape or slit in her dress. She then started to remove her clothing. She proceeded slowly to remove the scarf about her head. Then she removed part of her dress covering the upper part of her torso. As she removed the various parts of clothing, she dropped them into a container near the platform. She slowly removed her skirt, and after holding it at arm's length, dropped it into a container. At this point in her disrobing, she was wearing a brassiere and a scant pair of underpants. Attached to the top of the pants, or to a belt of sorts, were transparent panels, one in front and two in the rear. She then went through some gyrations in time to the music, and assumed some poses. This was followed by her descent from the platform to the dance floor. She sat on the floor close to the customers and went through some more body gyrations.

After this she went to the side of the platform and simulated pouring water from a jug. She then removed an outer brassiere, which she dropped into the container. Under this outer brassiere she was wearing another one, sheer but bespangled and scant. She then returned to the dance floor and went through some more gyrations, after which she returned to the platform and removed the panels which were attached to her costume. The tempo of the music changed, and in a standing position she grasped her ankles and shook her buttocks from side to side. Then standing erect, she did some hip movements. Returning again to the dance floor, she assumed a semi-kneeling position in front of the platform and moved her torso in an up-and-down motion. At this time she was clad in what might best be described as a very scant brassiere and pants. She turned facing the audience, and some of those present yelled, "More, more—take it off. More, more." This ended the performance.

A number of photographs and motion pictures had been taken of the act by the police officers. These were before the trial court and shown here on appeal. Three witnesses who viewed the motion pictures stated that they considered the performance below the moral standards of the City of St. Louis. A dancing instructor, who had been so engaged for many years, testified that the performance was not dancing, and that there were but a few times during the performance that any recognizable dance steps were taken by the defendant.

The defendants called two witnesses, who found nothing objectionable in the dance. One of them testified that there was a motion picture shown in St. Louis, called "Expresso Bango," in which there was considerable female nudity. There was evidence submitted that there were burlesque shows in St. Louis. In addition to the foregoing,

a motion picture of a very short portion of the play "Kismet," which had been put on by the Municipal Opera, was shown in evidence. The part shown was an oriental dance which fitted into the plot of the play. The dancer was much more fully clothed than defendant Ware had been.

Defendant Elliott testified that he had been engaged in the operation of tavern-type night clubs in St. Louis for a number of years, and that he employed girl dancers who took off part of their clothing. He said that defendant Ware's dance was only eight to ten minutes in length, and that his whole floor show, which consisted in part of music and an impersonator, required a full hour to put on.

Defendant Ware testified that she was an "exotic dancer" by profession. She said that she had studied at many dancing schools. She stated that none of them taught exotic dancing; that her dance, the "Fountain of Love," was a dance of her own arrangement and was of Grecian motif.

The motion pictures, the photographs, and the foregoing facts constituted all of the pertinent evidence before the trial court which, as stated, found the defendants not guilty.

[1] There is no question raised as to the right of the City to appeal from a judgment for the defendant in a proceeding for violation of an ordinance. Insofar as the right of appeal is concerned, such action is civil in nature, and the City has the same right to appeal as any other party to a civil action. Section 3, Article XII, The Charter of the City of St. Louis; *City of St. Louis* v. *Penrod*, Mo. App., 332 S.W. 2d 34; *City of Clayton* v. *Nemours*, 237 Mo. App. 167, 164 S.W. 2d 935.

The only point raised by the appeal is that the court's judgment was erroneous in that it reached the conclusion that the defendants were not guilty by giving weight to immaterial and irrelevant evidence. The court made a finding that there was a dance in the play "Kismet" which was known as "bumps and grinds." It also found that there was a motion picture shown in St. Louis, called "Expresso Bango," in which there were women scantily dressed. It found that there had been burlesque shows in St. Louis for many years, and that night clubs offered entertainment similar to that performed by defendant Ware. Without any further finding, and in apparent reliance upon the finding that burlesque, night club shows, and dancers on a par with the act of the defendant had been shown in St. Louis, and that a lewd motion picture had been shown, the court concluded that the City had failed to make a case against the defendants.

The fact that the court rested its opinion solely upon this is fortified by a statement made by the Judge in response to the request of the City Attorney for time to file a brief. This request came at the close of the evidence and after counsel for the defendants had moved to dismiss the cases. The following colloquy took place:

"The Court: I'm inclined to agree with Mr. Rankin. I have heard this case for two days, and I don't think the City has shown a case against the defendants. How can such a dance be permitted at the Opera, which is a matter of a few blocks away from the defendant's premises? How can they permit such a showing at the Pageant Theater, which is in the same general area?

"Mr. Freeman: Does the Court want arguments on this point?

"The Court: No, my mind is made up."

[2] From the foregoing it is evident that the court did not pass upon the question before it. The evidence that there were other performances, motion pictures, etc., which may or may not have been equally or more susceptible of being classified as lewd and indecent, was of questionable value as a measure of the quality of the performance here considered. Community tolerance of obscenity does not establish community standards of morality or make obscenity less obscene. *Clarke* v. *United States*, Municipal Court of Appeals for the District of Columbia, 160 A. 2d 97; *Commonwealth* v. *Donaducy*, Superior Court of Pennsylvania, 167 Pa. Super. 611, 76 A. 2d 440.

The question of what is indecent, lewd, or obscene—and the words are used interchangeably in many statutes and cases—has been difficult for the courts to define. Much has been written on the subject in opinions dealing with the use of the mail. *Roth* v. *United States*, 354 U.S. 476, 77 S. Ct. 1304, 1 L. Ed. 2d 1498; *Manual Enterprises* v. *Day*, 370 U.S. 478, 82 S. Ct. 1432, 8 L. Ed. 2d 639. Both of these cases deal with the construction of the federal statute. The case of *Manual Enterprises* v. *Day*, with one concurring opinion and one dissenting opinion, covers a total of 44 pages, with the dissenter concluding that the majority opinion "requires the United States Post Office to be the world's largest disseminator of smut and Grand Informer of the names and places where obscene material may be obtained."

These cases are of little aid in formulating a definition of indecent, lewd, or obscene. Perhaps the most acceptable definition is contained in the American Law Institute's Model Penal Code, Tentative Draft No. 6. There obscenity is defined in part as "material which appeals predominately to prurient interest in sexual matters and which goes beyond customary freedom of expression." It goes on to say: "* * 'appeal to prurient interest' refers to qualities of the material itself: the capacity to attract individuals eager for a forbidden look." The first part of this definition follows the definition heretofore used in such cases as In re Tahiti Bar, Inc., 395 Pa. 355, 150 A. 2d 112; *Adams Theatre Co.* v. *Keenan*, 12 N.J. 267, 96 A. 2d 519.

It seems, however, that there are areas in which attempted definitions confuse rather than enlighten. Indecency, lewdness, and obscenity may in many forms and in many ways offend. On the other hand, art and sincere graphic writing may appear lewd to some but wholesomely delightful and instructive to others. We are of the opinion that the Missouri Supreme Court, in *State* v. *Becker*, 364 Mo. 1079, 272 S.W. 2d 283, 1. c. 286, stated the manner in which the subject should be reviewed when it said: "* * * judges may know what falls within the classification of the decent, the chaste and the pure in either social life or in publications, and what must be deemed obscene and lewd and immoral and scandalous and lascivious."

[3] We have viewed and considered objectively the pictures of the performance here in question, and find the performance nothing more than modern burlesque. It was as devoid of art and beauty as a garbage pail, and was just "dirt for dirt's sake." The defendants violated the ordinances in question. *Adams Theatre Co.* v. *Keenan*, supra.

We therefore reverse and remand all of the cases to the Court of Criminal Correction for action consistent with the views herein expressed.

RUDDY, P.J., and ANDERSON, J., concur.

■ United States of America

v.

Ralph Ginzburg, Documentary Books, Inc., Eros Magazine, Inc., Liaison News Letter, Inc.

Crim. A. No. 21367.

United States District Court, E.D. Pennsylvania.

Nov. 21, 1963.

Drew J. T. O'Keefe, U.S. Atty., *J. Shane Creamer, Isaac S. Garb*, Asst. U.S. Attys., Philadelphia, Pa., for plaintiff.
Norman A. Oshtry, Philadelphia, Pa., *David I. Shapiro*, and *Sidney Dickstein*, Washington, D.C., for defendants.
Murry Powlen, Philadelphia, Pa., for American Civil Liberties Union, Amicus Curiae.

BODY, District Judge.

The following Special Findings of Fact which were previously entered by the Court on August 6, 1963 are hereby incorporated into and made a part of this opinion:

SPECIAL FINDINGS OF FACT

1. The stipulation entered into by counsel for defendants and counsel for the government, and approved by this Court, dated May 8, 1963, filed the same day (Clerk's File, Document Number 12) is hereby incorporated in its entirety as a finding of this Court.

2. The mailing of "Liaison" Vol. 1, No. 1, 1962; "Eros" Vol. 1, No. 4, 1962; and "The Housewife's Handbook on Selective Promiscuity" (referred to hereinafter as "Liaison," "Eros" and "The Handbook" respectively) was accomplished by large quantity distribution through a large mail order firm.

3. Defendants sought initially to obtain mailing from Blue Ball, Pennsylvania; secondly, from Intercourse, Pennsylvania; and finally succeeded in making arrangements for mailing from Middlesex, New Jersey, from which place all or substantially all of the mailings issued.

4. The particular places referred to in Finding No. 3 were chosen in order that the postmarks on mailed material would further defendants' general scheme and purpose.

5. *The Handbook* is a vivid, explicit and detailed account of a woman's sexual experiences from age three years to age thirty-six years which goes substantially beyond customary limits of candor exceeding contemporary community standards in description and representation of the matters described therein.

6. *The Handbook* appeals predominantly, taken as a whole, to prurient interest of the average adult reader in a shameful and morbid manner.

7. *The Handbook* is patently offensive on its face.

8. *The Handbook* treats sex in an unrealistic, exaggerated, bizarre, perverse, morbid and repetitious manner and creates a sense of shock, disgust and shame in the average adult reader.

9. *The Handbook* has not the slightest redeeming social, artistic or literary importance or value.

10. There is no credible evidence that *The Handbook* has the slightest valid scientific importance for treatment of individuals in clinical psychiatry, psychology, or any field of medicine.

11. *Liaison* consists primarily of matters relating to sex and in doing so it goes beyond customary limits of candor, exceeding contemporary standards in description and representation of the matters described therein.

12. *Liaison* primarily and as a whole is a shameful and morbid exploitation of sex published for the purpose of appealing to the prurient interest of the average individual.

13. *Liaison* has not the slightest redeeming social, artistic or literary importance or value.

14. *Liaison* is patently offensive on its face.

15. *Liaison* treats sex in an unrealistic, exaggerated, bizarre, perverse, morbid and repetitious manner and creates a sense of shock, disgust and shame in the average adult reader.

16. While portions of *Eros* are taken from other works and may have literary merit in context, *Eros* appeals predominantly, taken as a whole, to prurient interest of the average adult reader in a shameful and morbid manner.

17. The deliberate and studied arrangement of *Eros* is editorialized for the purpose of appealing predominantly to prurient interest and to insulate through the inclusion of non-offensive material.

18. *Eros* treats sex in an unrealistic, exaggerated, bizarre, perverse, morbid and repetitious manner and creates a sense of shock, disgust and shame in the average adult reader.

19. *Eros* has not the slightest redeeming social, artistic or literary importance or value taken as a whole.

DISCUSSION

On March 15, 1963 the Grand Jury in the Eastern District of Pennsylvania returned a 28 count indictment charging defendants with mailing obscene publications and advertisements for those publications in violation of 18 U.S.C. § 1461. Defendants filed a motion to dismiss

various counts of the indictment under Rule 12 of the Federal Rules of Criminal Procedure. Subsequent thereto, the Government filed a motion to strike the affidavit and exhibits appended to defendants' motion to dismiss the indictment. Oral argument was heard on both of these motions on May 17, 1963, and on that day the Court granted the Government's motion. On May 23, 1963 the Court denied defendants' motion to dismiss the indictment. From June 10 to June 14, 1963 the case was tried before the Court without a jury, and all defendants were found guilty on all counts. Defendants have filed a Motion in Arrest of Judgment, or, in the alternative for a New Trial, which motion is now before the Court.

A stipulation of counsel has been filed and approved by the Court. In this document the United States agrees that the advertising material (attached as exhibits to the stipulation) is not in and of itself obscene. In return, defendants admitted that said advertising material was mailed by defendants on the occasions alleged in the indictments with full knowledge of the nature of the contents thereof. In addition, counsel agreed that the alleged non-mailable materials, *Liaison, Eros* and *The Handbook*, were to be considered a part of the indictments as though fully set forth at length therein. Oral argument on the motions was waived by counsel. These motions are: a motion in arrest of judgment and, in the alternative, a motion for a new trial. In support of both motions defendants raise four issues.

ALLEGED FAILURE OF THE COURT TO COMPLETELY READ THE INDICTMENT BEFORE RULING ON THE SUFFICIENCY THEREOF

During the presentation of the defendants' case the Court made a statement with respect to *The Handbook* which indicated that the Court had not read parts of *The Handbook*. Prior to this incident, the Court had denied the defendants' motions for dismissal of the indictment and for acquittal at the close of the Government's case. The issue presented by this situation is an issue only if one assumes that the stipulation requires that the Court consider the materials as part of the indictment. We assume this to be the case for purposes of disposing of defendants' contentions.

[1, 2] It is axiomatic that in ruling on motions involving the sufficiency of an indictment, the Court should read that indictment. We agree, therefore, that the indictment should be read by the Court. However, the Court did read the indictments involved herein before any decisions were made on any aspects of this case. It is true that not all, that is to say, not each and every word or sentence of each of the indicted materials was read in advance of all of the Court's rulings. Nevertheless, the original indictments were read. Moreover, the Court read enough of the indicted materials to be able to rule as a matter of law that the Government had made out a prima facie case. We do not deem it necessary to read each and every word or sentence of the indicted materials in an obscenity case in order to ascertain whether there is a prima facie case.

[3] While it is true that in considering material in an obscenity case, the work as a whole must be examined; *Roth v. United States*, 354 U.S. 476, 77 S. Ct. 1304, 1 L. Ed. 2d 1498 (1957); it is not necessary to make a detailed and exhaustive examination on preliminary motions. Com-

mon sense dictates a realistic approach to this matter. *The Handbook* has 240 pages exclusive of introductory material. The material therein is extremely boring, disgusting, and shocking to this Court, as well as to an average reader. It was simply too offensive to stomach in the first instance. Even a fast reading, skipping the obviously repetitious phrases and descriptions, readily discloses the impact and essence of the book.

[4] The rule is that when a defendant presents testimony and other evidence after a motion for acquittal has been overruled, the objections to the denial of his motion are waived, *United States* v. *Calderon*, 348 U.S. 160, 75 S. Ct. 186, 99 L. Ed. 202 (1954).

[5] On the merits, since the Trial Court has since read all of *The Handbook* word by word, if there was error it is harmless. If in fact the material is obscene as a matter of fact and law, defendant was not prejudiced. This case was tried without a jury and the ultimate test after the case was submitted to the fact finder was much higher than it was when the Court disposed of defendants' pretrial motions.

FAILURE OF THE TRIAL COURT TO ENTER SPECIAL FINDINGS CONCURRENTLY WITH THE GENERAL FINDING

It may be that better practice in many criminal cases calls for the entry of special findings at the time the general finding is made when the Court sits without a jury. *Benchwick* v. *United States*, 297 F. 2d 330 (9th Cir. 1961). This does not mean that it is required that both types of findings be made simultaneously. No case has been cited by counsel which so holds, and in like manner, exhaustive research discloses no such rule as contended for by defendants.

[6] During the trial the Court made it clear to counsel on more than one occasion that the entry of special findings would be delayed beyond the entry of a general finding if a general finding of guilty was to be entered on any of the counts. There were no objections by defendants' counsel to this proposed procedure. Thus, any objection to the delayed entry of special findings was waived by silence on the record. Likewise after verdict was rendered by the Court, no objections were stated for the record at that time.

On the merits, this was not an ordinary criminal case where fundamental operative facts had to be determined. Most of the facts are not clear and precise but instead are mixed with questions of law. This is the nature of the case. It is necessary in such a case for the Court to carefully consider all the legal ramifications of the factual setting, which is really largely agreed upon. Such careful consideration requires detailed legal research and assistance of counsel. Consequently, the Trial Court requested proposed findings and such other assistance as counsel could offer. Defendants were not precluded from submitting findings but apparently chose not to do so. We find no merit in this issue raised by them, apparently as an afterthought.

OBSCENITY

The remaining contentions of defendant attack the decision of the Court that as a matter of fact and of law the indicted materials are obscene under 18 U.S.C. § 1461.

[7-9] In order that freedom of speech may remain protected and inviolate, the law requires definite standards for a finding of obscenity. These standards are set forth generally in the case of *Roth* v. *United States* (California), 354 U.S. 476, 77 S. Ct. 1304, 1 L. Ed. 2d 1498 (1957). All ideas, no matter how obnoxious, unorthodox or controversial are protected. If material has any socially redeeming importance it is protected. Beyond this, material to be obscene must encroach upon significant interests of society, and thereby injure society without justification. Material embodied in permanent form and distributed generally does this when it is obscene. *Roth* v. *United States* (California), supra. Something is obscene according to the A.L.I., Model Penal Code, § 207.10(2):

"* * * (I)f, considered as a whole, its predominant appeal is to prurient interest, i.e., a shameful or morbid interest in nudity, sex or excretion, and if it goes substantially beyond customary limits of candor in description or representation of such matters. * * *"

Roth v. *California*, supra, 354 U.S. at page 489, 77 S. Ct. 1311, 1 L. Ed. 2d 1498, requires further that the material to be obscene must appeal in the above manner to the prurient interest of the average person, applying contemporary community standards. This has been held to mean that the standard is not to be applied from the point of view of particularly susceptible persons in the community. *Manual Enterprises* v. *Day*, 370 U.S. 478, 82 S. Ct. 1432, 8 L. Ed. 2d 639 (1962).

In deciding whether the subject materials are obscene, each must of course be separately treated.

"LIAISON" VOL. 1, NO. 1

Liaison is a newsletter or periodical folder type of publication consisting of commentary from various sources with a general editorial treatment. Specifically it deals with such subjects as "Slaying the Sex Dragon," "Semen in the Diet" and "Sing a Song of Sex Life." The material covers the most perverse and offensive human behavior. While the treatment is largely superficial, it is presented entirely without restraint of any kind. According to defendants' own expert, it is entirely without literary merit. We agree. If there is any socially redeeming value in this material it must come from what is advocated or from its entertainment value. There are jokes and rhymes which clearly go beyond contemporary community standards of humor, even in applying liberal night club standards. The remainder of the material is of the same nature and exceeds the standard in the same manner.

One could take an entirely different view of some of the material in *Liaison* if it were artfully contrived or manipulated in a literary manner by incorporation into a work of merit to serve a legitimate purpose of an author in recording human experience or in seeking to accomplish a worthy objective. See, for example, *Grove Press, Inc.* v. *Christenberry*, 276 F. 2d 433 (2d Cir. 1960) where it was held that the book Lady Chatterley's Lover was not obscene.

Unfortunately, however, *Liaison* is designed obviously and solely for the purpose of appealing to the prurient interest of an ordinary person. The only idea advocated is complete abandon of any restraint with regard to any form of sexual expression. This "idea" is nothing more than could be advocated by the most flagrant pornography, samples of which were submitted to the Court by defendants as examples of obscenity. Ideas must go beyond this point in order to be protected. The alternative is the absence of any restraint on written material from the point of view of obscenity.

"EROS" VOL. 1, NO. 4, 1962

Eros is a carefully contrived magazine or periodical type of publication with a hard cover and glossy paper. It is replete with photographs and includes reproductions of recognized works of art. Nevertheless, as in the cases of *Liaison* and of *The Handbook* the dominant appeal is to pruriency. The works of art, such as biblical quotations and reproductions of the creations of recognized artists, are merely a facade to disguise and protect the basic purpose and effect of the entire work. This basic purpose and effect becomes evident as one progresses through the pages.

Although it is difficult to classify all of the articles in *Eros* into specific categories, there is a clearly defined arrangement to the material. To some, several articles might be considered innocuous, only slightly erotic and possibly not obscene in and of themselves. These are: "New Twists and 3 Great Trysts"; "The Jewel Box Revue," the series of photographs on marriage, circa 1903; The Short Story by Ray Bradbury; "Memoirs of a Male Chaperon"; "President Harding's Second Lady"; "Was Shakespeare a Homosexual"; "Sex and the Bible"; and perhaps Ivan Graznis' version of "Lysistrata." If the entire work consisted merely of these articles there might be no finding of obscenity in this case. This does not mean that the articles have no effect upon the finding of obscenity with regard to the periodical as a whole. Here is a pattern. Here is a craftily compiled overall effect and since the work must be considered as a whole, material which might be innocuous alone partakes of the obscenity elsewhere in *Eros* and becomes part and parcel of the overall plan and intent of the work. It is the opposite of the usual situation as in a novel where the dominant interest and theme is of social importance, and what would be patent obscenity standing alone is insulated and protected and saved from condemnation because of the work of art in which it is incorporated. *Grove Press, Inc.* v. *Christenberry*, supra.

[10] *Eros* is the reverse situation from Lady Chatterley's Lover. There the author used material which, *taken out of context*, would have been clearly obscene. Nevertheless, the court found no obscenity because of the saving grace of the book as a whole. *Eros* has no saving grace. The items of possible merit and those items which might be considered innocuous are a mere disguise to avoid the law and in large measure enhance the pruriency of the entire work. The only overriding theme of *Eros* is the advocacy of complete sexual expression of whatever sort and manner. The most offensive pornography imaginable, examples of which were submitted by defendants as exhibits in this case, has the same dominant effect and purpose. Even so, of course, the dissemination of the idea of complete sexual freedom cannot constitutionally be punished. Therefore, it must be the *manner* of dissemination which is objectionable.

In considering the manner of expression of the idea then, we come to the work itself in its obscene portions. The articles called: "Frank Harris, His Life and Loves" including "My Life and Loves" by Frank Harris; "Bawdy

Limericks" and the "Natural Superiority of Women as Erotocists" and "Black and White in Color" are such that standing alone, one has little difficulty in finding all of the requisite elements of obscenity. For example: "Bawdy Limericks" consists of the grossest terminology describing unnatural, offensive, disgusting and exaggerated sexual behavior. Also by way of example: the series of pictures, "Black and White in Color," constitutes a detailed portrayal of the act of sexual intercourse between a completely nude male and female, leaving nothing to the imagination. This material meets defendants' own experts' definition of obscenity as well as counsel's legal definition.

[11] Pruriency is required and is defined as an itching, longing, morbid or shameful sexual desire. *Roth* v. *California*, supra. When material creates in the reader shame and guilt feelings simultaneously with sexual arousal, the result is usually obscenity. The material listed above clearly qualifies. There is no notable distinction between the aforesaid, taking each one as a whole, and the admittedly obscene material which was in evidence for comparison purposes.

The impact of these articles and items is sufficient to permeate the entire volume of *Eros*. By reading the article "A Letter from Allen Ginsburg" it becomes evident that the intent of the disseminator here was to cause this permeation, i.e., this "Letter" is a statement of the purpose of *Eros*. It is clear that there is no possible other way to view the matter. When material is composed of several portions, not related except insofar as each deals with sex in various forms, and at the same time this material includes obscene items, if these items are tested standing alone and if at the same time a single purpose of destruction of all barriers against sexual behavior of any kind is advocated along with the advocacy of removal of restraint by government over the dissemination of any written material whatsoever, there is but one conclusion. That conclusion is: there is specific intent to destroy any limitations whatsoever over any medium of human communication regardless of the extent of abuse of that medium through the use of obscenity. Therefore, defendants are in the unsavory position of advocating that obscenity should be disseminated, and at the same time they are deliberately purveying material through the mails which material is designed to break down those barriers imposed by the statute.

[12] The inserting of innocuous material along with obscene material cannot shield the latter. If it could, the Bible itself could readily be rendered obscene, and yet could be disseminated without restraint, merely through the expediency of illustrating sexual references with the grossest pornographic photographs and by giving the participants biblical names. The answer is clear. It is one thing to create an integrated work of art containing what would be obscenity standing alone, and another thing to create an integrated work of obscenity containing excerpts from recognized works of art.

It is interesting to note that in defining pornography, defendants' expert stated that it is common in such material that matters usually treated with respect, such as religion, are juxtaposed with and mocked by the writer. Inaccuracy and imaginary psychotic references to sexual activity is rampant in such works. *Eros* contains these elements. The front and back covers and the lead article deal with the Bible itself. "Bawdy Limericks" meets the test of bizarre and unrealistic treatment of sex. "The Sexual Side of Anti-Semitism" is headlined with a paragraph taken from the mouth of a psychotic person. These examples, and those elsewhere in this opinion, are offered as typical and are not by any means designed to constitute an exhaustive exposition of all of the material relevant to a finding of obscenity in detail. To do this would require a good-sized novel. Defendants press us for a quick disposition in order that their business not be ruined since they fear to continue publishing in the face of the finding of guilt. We, therefore, doubt that defendants are interested in a large volume of discourse in this opinion.

"THE HOUSEWIFE'S HANDBOOK ON SELECTIVE PROMISCUITY" by REY ANTHONY

The Handbook requires little discussion. This book is a kind with the above-mentioned admittedly hardcore pornography. It is an explicit description of a woman's sexual experiences from early childhood and thereafter throughout most of her life. It purports to be, and the authoress so stated under oath, a factual and highly accurate reporting of actual occurrences. In fact, Mrs. Lillian Maxine Serett, the authoress, stated: "I have lived every minute of it, or every page of it * * *" (N.T. page 121). We doubt the accuracy of this book. It also easily meets the previously mentioned tests of bizarre exaggeration, morbidness and offensiveness.

The Handbook's description of various sexual acts is astounding. As in the case of *Liaison*, no literary merit is ascribed to the book. Its sole claim to redeeming value is its alleged value as a clinical device to "ventilate" persons with sexual inhibitions and misconceptions. Any testimony to this effect is expressly disbelieved by this Court. One must regretfully note in passing that teen-age children were, and would be in the future, "ventilated" with this book by the witness who was alleged to be an expert clinical psychologist and also was an ordained minister. This same witness shocked the writer by saying that this book should be in every home and available for teen-agers for guidance in sex behavior, but in my opinion misbehavior.

The Handbook, standing bare of any socially redeeming value, is a patent offense to the most liberal morality. The descriptions leave nothing to the imagination, and in detail, in a clearly prurient manner offend, degrade and sicken anyone however healthy his mind was before exposure to this material. It is a gross shock to the mind and chore to read. Pruriency and disgust coalesce here creating a perfect example of hardcore pornography.

CONCLUSION

[13–15] Defendants place great weight on the requirement of the definition of obscenity, as they see it, which protects works which do not exceed contemporary community standards of candor in expression. There is no question that all three of the indicted materials exceed this standard. Certain materials sold openly on local newsstands were submitted to show what the acceptable limits of candor are today. Without so deciding, it may well be that these materials exceed the contemporary standard themselves. At any rate, supplying this Court with such materials does not provide conclusive evidence of the standard set by the community as a whole. Doubtless but a sliver of the community reads such things and there is no doubt the community as a whole does not necessarily tolerate them. For all the Court knows, local action before this and in the future will result in the removal of this type of material from the newsstands. This Court has the power and the right as a fact finder and as one who is aware of all types of material sold, tolerated and not tolerated by the community as a whole, to find, as it has found, that the material in question exceeds the standard. It does so unequivocally.

[16, 17] We have been regaled with the theory that the susceptibility of no single segment of the community is to be the paramount consideration in deciding whether a work is obscene. *Manual Enterprises* v. *Day*, supra. This is the law and we do not argue with it. It is also the law that the community as a whole is the proper consideration. In this community, our society, we have children of all ages, psychotics, feeble-minded and other susceptible elements. Just as they cannot set the pace for the average adult reader's taste, they cannot be overlooked as part of the community. The community as a whole is not an ideal man who wouldn't seek and read obscenity in the first place. Otherwise no restraint at all would be required. Some is proper. *Roth* v. *California*, supra. Therefore, an ideal person without any failings or susceptibility is not the man to protect. Society as a whole, replete of course with various imperfections, must be protected.

There must come a time when the law must take a stand and determine what is legally obscene. It is all a matter of degree. Each publication is to be judged by itself, cover to cover, and as a whole. It is not merely a matter of four letter words, or the quantity of them. It is a matter of our concept of obscenity as defined and limited by the United States Supreme Court.

ORDER

And now, this twenty-first day of November, 1963, in accordance with the foregoing opinion, it is ordered that the motions of defendants in Arrest of Judgment and, in the alternative, for a New Trial, be and the same are hereby denied.

It is further ordered that the defendants are called for sentence on November 27, 1963 at 10:00 A.M. in a courtroom of the United States District Court for the Eastern District of Pennsylvania.

■ United States of America,

v.

Ralph Ginzburg, Documentary Books, Inc., Eros Magazine, Inc. and Liaison News Letter, Inc., *Appellants.*
Nos. 14742–14745.

United States Court of Appeals, Third Circuit.

Argued June 16, 1964.

Decided Nov. 6, 1964.

David I. Shapiro, Washington, D.C. (Sidney Dickstein, Washington, D.C., Norman Oshtry, Philadelphia, Pa., on the brief), for appellants.

J. Shane Creamer, Asst. U.S. Atty., Philadelphia, Pa. (Drew J. T. O'Keefe, U.S. Atty., Philadelphia, Pa., on the brief), for appellee.

Morey M. Myers, Scranton, Pa., *Murry Powlen,* Philadelphia, Pa., *Melvin L. Wulf,* New York City, on the brief for American Civil Liberties Union and Its Pennsylvania Affiliate, amici curiae.

Before McLaughlin, Kalodner and Staley, Circuit Judges.

McLaughlin, Circuit Judge.

Appellants were convicted of violating the federal obscenity law, 18 U.S.C. § 1461. All three publications involved were found to be obscene under the statute. The record shows that in September, 1962, appellant Eros Magazine, Inc. of which appellant Ginzburg was editor and publisher, after a great deal of deliberation endeavored to obtain what was considered advantageous mailing privileges from Blue Ball, Pennsylvania. Meeting with no success there, a similar try was made with the Post Office at Intercourse, Pennsylvania. Again rejected, a final successful effort was made at the Middlesex, New Jersey Post Office from which over five million advertisements of *Eros* were mailed. It is not disputed that the bulk of the mailings for the three publications was from Middlesex. In the advertisements above mentioned, inter alia, appeared the following:

*"The publication of this magazine—which is frankly and avowedly concerned with erotica—has been enabled by recent court decisions * * to be published."*

The magazine *Eros* was thereafter mailed out from Middlesex. It is with Volume 1, No. 4, 1962 thereof that we are concerned. *Eros* is a quarterly. Its price is $25 a year.

The second publication was mailed in November, 1962. It was a book which had been originally titled by its author "The Housewife's Handbook for Promiscuity." That book

so titled had been sold by mail to a selected list by the author. The title was later changed to read "Housewife's Handbook on Selective Promiscuity." The mailing in this instance was under the latter title. Its price is $4.95.

The third publication is a biweekly newsletter called *Liaison.* According to the witness Darr who was hired by appellant Ginzburg as editor of *Liaison,* Ginzburg told him that "* * * Liaison was to cover the same scope [as *Eros*], in a more newsworthy fashion." Darr was hired after he had specially written and submitted a piece titled "How to Run a Successful Orgy." Ginzburg telephoned him and asked him "When can you start to work?" The particular piece in revised form was published in *Liaison.* The price of *Liaison* was $15, later reduced to $4.95.

The advertising material, concededly not obscene of itself, was admittedly mailed by appellants on the specified dates with full knowledge of its contents.

The case was tried to the court, a jury trial having been waived by appellants. The trial consumed five days. Appellants were found guilty on all counts on June 14, 1963. Later, at the request of the appellants, on August 6, 1963, the court filed special detailed findings of fact. Summing up those findings, the court said:

"In conclusion, after a thorough reading and review of all the indicted materials, this Court finds that said materials are compilations of sordid narrations dealing with sex, in each case in a manner designed to appeal to prurient interests. They are devoid of theme or ideas. Throughout the pages of each can be found constant repetition of patently offensive words used solely to convey debasing portrayals of natural and unnatural sexual experiences. Each in its own way is a blow to sense, not merely sensibility. They are all dirt for dirt's sake and dirt for money's sake."

[1, 2] We have read, examined and considered the publications involved in this appeal, "* * * in the light of the record made in the trial court, * *." *Jacobellis* v. *Ohio,* 378 U.S. 184, 196, 84 S. Ct. 1676, 1682, 12 L. Ed. 2d 793 (1964). The only important question before us is whether the publications are obscene under the federal statute. Since this calls for a constitutional judgment it is our duty to decide it. Under the obscenity tests laid down

by the Supreme Court, the Constitutional status of the publications "* * * must be determined on the basis of a national standard." Jacobellis, supra, p. 195, 84 S. Ct. p. 1682. This is peculiarly fitting here where over five million advertisements for the *Eros* material were mailed out to prospects in this country.

Also we have very much in mind that as the Supreme Court stated in *Roth* v. *United States*, 354 U.S. 476, 484, 77 S. Ct. 1304, 1309, 1 L. Ed. 2d 1498 (1957):

"*All ideas having even the slightest redeeming social importance—unorthodox ideas, controversial ideas, even ideas hateful to the prevailing climate of opinion—have the full protection of the guaranties, unless excludable because they encroach upon the limited area of more important interests. But implicit in the history of the First Amendment is the rejection of obscenity as utterly without redeeming social importance.*"

The Court went on to say, 354 U.S. p. 487, 77 S. Ct. p. 1310, that "* * * sex and obscenity are not synonymous" and ruled on p. 487, 77 S. Ct. p. 1310 that "Obscene material is material which deals with sex in a manner appealing to prurient interest." It quoted with approval the American Law Institute, Model Penal Code, proposed official draft (May 4, 1962), § 251.41(1):

" "* * * *A thing is obscene if, considered as a whole, its predominant appeal is to prurient interest, i.e., a shameful or morbid interest in nudity, sex, or excretion, and if it goes substantially beyond customary limits of candor in description or representation of such matters. * * *"* "

The same necessary quality named in Roth, supra, and Jacobellis, supra, as affronting current national community standards is described in *Manual Enterprises* v. *Day*, 370 U.S. 478, 482, 82 S. Ct. 1432, 8 L. Ed. 2d 639 (1962) as " 'patent offensiveness' or 'indecency.' " At pages 483, 484, 82 S. Ct. pages 1434–1435, the Day opinion, speaking of the federal obscenity law, notes that "* * * the statute since its inception has always been taken as aimed at obnoxiously debasing portrayals of sex. * * * the statute reaches only indecent material which, as now expressed in *Roth* v. *United States*, supra, 354 U.S. at 489, 77 S. Ct. at 1311, 'taken as a whole appeals to prurient interest.' "

This brings us to the special circumstances revealed in the present appeal. We are not dealing with a novel by a well known novelist, written as and for a work of fiction with a firm base of opposition to well defined then existing social conditions, which was held mailable because its "* * * predominant appeal * * * [was] demonstrably not to 'prurient interest'." *Grove Press* v. *Christenberry*, 276 F. 2d 433, 437 (2 Cir. 1960). Nor have we in this appeal anything comparable to the autobiographical account of the scabrous life of a writer of some pretentions, where numerous revolting episodes were part of a text which the Supreme Court of Massachusetts (184 N.E. 2d 328, 334 (1962)) accepted "* * * as a conscious effort to create a work of literary art."

What confronts us is a sui generis operation on the part of experts in the shoddy business of pandering to and exploiting for money one of the great weaknesses of human being. Appellants' fundamental objective obviously was and is to, more or less openly, force their invitations to

obscenity upon the American public through the United States mails. They did this in reliance on their own ill conceived theory that all barriers to obscenity have in effect been removed. They were not concerned with trying to circulate authentic artistic efforts that may incidentally have four letter words or nudity or sex as an integral part of a work, whatever art form it may be. *Eros* was declared as avowedly concerned with one thing, what in the prospectus is described as "erotica" and *which, it is stated, has been enabled to be published "by recent court decisions."* (Emphasis supplied.) An undeniable example of what was meant by erotica is the content of *Eros*, Vol. 1, No. 4.

Seemingly to soften their approach and to pick up whatever support that might be available, appellants offer separate defenses for each of the publications. For *Eros* it is claimed in the brief that it "has redeeming social importance with respect to literary and artistic values." Having in mind the above proclaimed objective, even a casual reading makes it readily apparent that bits of nonstatutory material have simply been laced into the obscene structure which is the *Eros* volume in evidence with the intent of creating that impression. This seems to us not just frivolous but a bold attempt to pioneer both in the elimination of the law itself and in the collection of the resultant profits. We have not seen nor been referred to any decision which countenances that sort of brazen chicanery. If permitted, it would stultify the carefully wrought formula whereby the basic law guarding the national community from obscenity is upheld but not at the expense of honest ideas founded on at least some social importance even if it be but the slightest.

[3] From our own close reading and scrutiny of *Eros*, its basic material predominantly appeals to prurient interest; it is on its face offensive to present day national community standards, and it has no artistic or social value. The sham device of seeking to somewhat cloak the content with non-offensive items falls of its own evil weight. Cf. *Kahm* v. *United States*, 300 F. 2d 78 (5 Cir. 1962).

It is asserted that the *Handbook* has some social-scientific importance. Testimony along that line was expressly disbelieved by the trial judge. Our own reading and examination of this work leads us to the same conclusion. The original title to the book gives its real purpose. That title, "The Housewife's Handbook for Promiscuity" is a fitting capsule description of the content. The mere change in the title, making it sound like some sort of a text book or tract, shows the arrogant insistence of these appellants that raw obscenity is at this time properly an element of national community life. There is nothing of any social importance in the *Handbook*. It is patently offensive to current national community standards. Applying those standards to the average person its dominant theme as a whole appeals to prurient interest.

Appellants would have it that the book fits into the same category as "Fanny Hill," found not obscene by the New York Court of Appeals in *Larkin et al.* v. *G. P. Putnam's Sons*, 14 N.Y. 2d 399, 252 N.Y.S. 2d 71, 200 N.E. 2d 760 (1964). Whatever may eventually be the outcome of that litigation, it has no bearing on this appeal for, inter alia, it was there specifically held as to the book that "It has a slight literary value and it affords some insight into the life and manners of mid-18th Century London."

It is argued that *Liaison*, the newsletter, is without the

statute, on the ground that it does not appeal to prurient interest. As we have seen, according to Ginzburg, the directing head of all three publications, the purpose of *Liaison* was to cover the same scope as *Eros*, in a more newsworthy fashion. Our study of it bears this out. Its material openly offends current national community standards in much the same fashion as does *Eros*. Taken as a whole, its appeal is directed to the prurient interest of the average person in the national community. The type of thing that it is, as visualized from the test given the successful candidate for its editor, is confirmed by the material printed in it. There is no pretension that it has any social significance or literary merit.

There is defense testimony which would have it that all three publications are not within the reach of the statute. The trier of the facts was not persuaded by it nor are we.

Finding, as we do, that *Eros*, the *Handbook* and *Liaison* are obscene, affirmance of the convictions on the advertising counts follows as of course.

The contentions of appellants that the convictions on the *Eros* and *Liaison* counts must be reversed because the trial court failed to find those publications guilty within the statute are without merit. This is clear as to *Eros* in the Special Findings of Fact, Nos. 16, 17, 18, 19, the concluding paragraph of the Findings above quoted and also, though it is not necessary, in the court's opinion under the caption "Eros Vol. 1, Number 4, 1962." The *Liaison* Findings, which fully substantiate conviction on those counts, are Numbers 11, 12, 13, 14, 15, the concluding paragraph of the Findings and also, though it it not necessary, the court's opinion under the caption "Liaison Vol. 1, No. 1."

[4] There is no substance to the complaint regarding the time of filing of the Special Findings of Fact. Rule of Criminal Procedure 23(c) provides that: "In a case tried without a jury the court shall make a general finding and shall in addition on request find the facts specially."

The trial court's comment in its opinion on this point which is in strict accord with the record, is as follows:

"*During the trial the Court made it clear to counsel on more than one occasion that the entry of special findings would be delayed beyond the entry of a general finding if a general finding of guilty was to be entered on any of the counts. There were no objections by defendants' counsel to this proposed procedure. Thus, any objection to the delayed entry of special findings was waived by silence on the record. Likewise after verdict was rendered by the Court, no objections were stated for the record at that time.*

"*On the merits, this was not an ordinary criminal case where fundamental operative facts had to be determined. Most of the facts are not clear and precise but instead are mixed with questions of law. This is the nature of the case. It is necessary in such a case for the Court to carefully consider all the legal ramifications of the factual setting, which is really largely agreed upon. Such careful consideration requires detailed legal research and assistance of counsel. Consequently, the Trial Court requested proposed findings and such other assistance as counsel could offer.*

Defendants were not precluded from submitting findings but apparently chose not to do so. We find no merit in this issue raised by them, apparently as an afterthought."

Under the facts the findings were filed promptly and properly within the above rule.

[5] It is also asserted that the trial court converted evidence of criminal intent admissible against one defendant into proof of criminal intent on the part of all defendants. This concerns the two unsuccessful attempts to mail out *Eros* advertising material. The successful mailings from Middlesex were for all three publications. The point is de minimis in any event. The stipulation between counsel for the parties and approved by the court states that the advertising material was mailed by the defendants on the occasions alleged in the indictments with full knowledge of the contents thereof. We do not find the slightest indication of any substantial confusion on the part of the trial judge with reference to the attempted mailings and mailings of the material involved in the appeal.

[6] Appellants object to the admission of the rebuttal testimony of Government witness, Dr. Frignito. This testimony was rightfully presented and received as rebuttal evidence. The witness' complete answer as to the effect of the *Handbook* makes it evident that he was considering the book's effect on the entire community, not some group thereof. We find no error in this connection.

[7] Appellants claim error because at the time of the defense motions for dismissal of the indictment and for acquittal at the end of the Government's case, the trial judge who had read the indictment, as he says in his opinion, had not read at that time "* * * each and every word or sentence of each of the indicted materials * * *" but, as he further said, "* * * the Court read enough of the indicted materials to be able to rule as a matter of law that the Government had made out a prima facie case." There is no prejudicial error in this incident.

[8–10] Finally, appellants urge that the court erred in striking the affidavit and exhibits in support of the defense motion to dismiss the indictment. The defense on that motion was correctly limited by the court to the face of the indictment and whether it accurately charged the named offenses and gave adequate notification thereof to the defendants. The defense attempted by the affidavit and letters to put before the court in ex parte form, opinions from various sources favorable to the *Handbook*. These were trial matters and so held by the judge.

The district judge was acutely aware of the issue of constitutional law raised in this action. He was conversant with the Supreme Court's views on the federal obscenity statute and was guided accordingly. Our study of the record, including the transcript and convicted materials, establishes that he tried it fairly, carefully and competently. He made no substantial errors of law. We are convinced that, under the evidence, he was justified in finding the defendants guilty on all counts. As we have indicated, we have independently arrived at that same conclusion.

The judgments of the district court will be affirmed.

■ Ralph Ginzburg *et al., Petitioners,*

v.

United States.

No. 42.

Argued Dec. 7, 1965.

Decided March 21, 1966.

Sidney Dickstein, Washington, D.C., for petitioners.
Paul Bender, Washington, D.C., for respondent, pro
hac vice, by special leave of Court.

Mr. Justice BRENNAN delivered the opinion of the
Court.

[1] A judge sitting without a jury in the District Court
for the Eastern District of Pennsylvania[1] convicted petitioner Ginzburg and three corporations controlled by him
upon all 28 counts of an indictment charging violation of
the federal obscenity statute, 18 U.S.C. § 1461 (1964
ed.).[2] 224 F. Supp. 129. Each count alleged that a resident of the Eastern District received mailed matter, either
one of three publications challenged as obscene, or advertising telling how and where the publications might be
obtained. The Court of Appeals for the Third Circuit
affirmed, 338 F. 2d 12. We granted certiorari, 380 U.S.
961, 85 S. Ct. 1103, 14 L. Ed. 2d 152. We affirm. Since
petitioners do not argue that the trial judge misconceived
or failed to apply the standards we first enunciated in *Roth*
v. *United States,* 354 U.S. 476, 77 S. Ct. 1304, 1 L. Ed.
2d 1498[3] the only serious question is whether those

standards were correctly applied.[4]

[2, 3] In the cases in which this Court has decided
obscenity questions since *Roth,* it has regarded the materials as sufficient in themselves for the determination of the
question. In the present case, however, the prosecution
charged the offense in the context of the circumstances of
production, sale, and publicity and assumed that, standing
alone, the publications themselves might not be obscene.
We agree that the question of obscenity may include
consideration of the setting in which the publications were
presented as an aid to determining the question of obscenity, and assume without deciding that the prosecution
could not have succeeded otherwise. As in *Mishkin* v. *State
of New York,* 383 U.S. 502, 86 S. Ct. 958, and as did the
courts below, 224 F. Supp., at 134, 338 F. 2d, at 14–15,
we view the publications against a background of commercial exploitation of erotica solely for the sake of their
prurient appeal.[5] The record in that regard amply supports
the decision of the trial judge that the mailing of all three
publications offended the statute.[6]

---

[1] No challenge was or is made to venue under 18 U.S.C.
§ 3237 (1964 ed.).

[2] The federal obscenity statute, 18 U.S.C. § 1461, provides in
pertinent part:

"Every obscene, lewd, lascivious, indecent, filthy or vile article,
matter, thing device, or substance; and—

*   *   *   *   *

"Every written or printed card, letter, circular, book, pamphlet, advertisement, or notice of any kind giving information,
directly or indirectly, where, or how, or from whom, or by what
means any of such mentioned matters * * * may be obtained * * *.

*   *   *   *   *

"Is declared to be nonmailable matter and shall not be conveyed in the mails or delivered from any post office or by any
letter carrier.

"Whoever knowingly uses the mails for the mailing, carriage
in the mails, or delivery of anything declared by this section to
be nonmailable * * * shall be fined not more than $5,000 or
imprisoned not more than five years, or both, for the first such
offense * * *."

[3] We are not, however, to be understood as approving all
aspects of the trial judge's exegesis of *Roth,* for example his
remarks that "the community as a whole is the proper considera-

tion. In this community, our society, we have children of all
ages, psychotics, feeble-minded and other susceptible elements.
Just as they cannot set the pace for the average adult reader's
taste, they cannot be overlooked as part of the community." 224
F. Supp., at 137. Compare *Butler* v. *State of Michigan,* 352 U.S.
380, 77 S. Ct. 524, 1 L. Ed. 2d 412.

[4] The Government stipulated at trial that the circulars advertising the publications were not themselves obscene; therefore the
convictions on the counts for mailing the advertising stand only
if the mailing of the publications offended the statute.

[5] Our affirmance of the convictions for mailing *Eros* and
Liaison is based upon their characteristics as a whole, including
their editorial formats, and not upon particular articles contained, digested, or excerpted in them. Thus we do not decide
whether particular articles, for example, in *Eros,* although
identified by the trial judge as offensive, should be condemned as
obscene whatever their setting. Similarly, we accept the Government's concession, note 13, infra, that the prosecution rested
upon the manner in which the petitioners sold the *Handbook;*
thus our affirmance implies no agreement with the trial judge's
characterizations of the book outside that setting.

[6] It is suggested in dissent that petitioners were unaware that
the record being established could be used in support of such an
approach, and that petitioners should be afforded the opportunity of a new trial. However, the trial transcript clearly reveals
that at several points the Government announced its theory that
made the mode of distribution relevant to the determination of
obscenity, and the trial court admitted evidence, otherwise irrelevant, toward that end.

The three publications were *Eros*, a hard-cover magazine of expensive format; *Liaison*, a bi-weekly newsletter; and *The Housewife's Handbook on Selective Promiscuity* (hereinafter the *Handbook*), a short book. The issue of *Eros* specified in the indictment, Vol. 1, No. 4, contains 15 articles and photo-essays on the subject of love, sex, and sexual relations. The specified issue of *Liaison*, Vol. 1, No. 1, contains a prefatory "Letter from the Editors" announcing its dedication to "keeping sex an art and preventing it from becoming a science." The remainder of the issue consists of digests of two articles concerning sex and sexual relations which had earlier appeared in professional journals and a report of an interview with a psychotherapist who favors the broadest license in sexual relationships. As the trial judge noted, "[w]hile the treatment is largely superficial, it is presented entirely without restraint of any kind. According to defendants' own expert, it is entirely without literary merit." 224 F. Supp., at 134. The *Handbook* purports to be a sexual autobiography detailing with complete candor the author's sexual experiences from age 3 to age 36. The text includes, and prefatory and concluding sections of the book elaborate, her views on such subjects as sex education of children, laws regulating private consensual adult sexual practices, and the equality of women in sexual relationships. It was claimed at trial that women would find the book valuable, for example as a marriage manual or as an aid to the sex education of their children.

[4] Besides testimony as to the merit of the material, there was abundant evidence to show that each of the accused publications was originated or sold as stock in trade of the sordid business of pandering—"the business of purveying textual or graphic matter openly advertised to appeal to the erotic interest of their customers."[7] *Eros* early sought mailing privileges from the postmasters of Intercourse and Blue Ball, Pennsylvania. The trial court found the obvious, that these hamlets were chosen only for the value their names would have in furthering petitioners' efforts to sell their publications on the basis of salacious appeal;[8] the facilities of the post offices were inadequate to

handle the anticipated volume of mail, and the privileges were denied. Mailing privileges were then obtained from the postmaster of Middlesex, New Jersey. *Eros* and *Liaison* thereafter mailed several million circulars soliciting subscriptions from that post office; over 5,500 copies of the *Handbook* were mailed.

The "leer of the sensualist" also permeates the advertising for the three publications. The circulars sent for *Eros* and *Liaison* stressed the sexual candor of the respective publications, and openly boasted that the publishers would take full advantage of what they regarded an unrestricted license allowed by law in the expression of sex and sexual matters.[9] The advertising for the *Handbook*, apparently mailed from New York, consisted almost entirely of a reproduction of the introduction of the book, written by one Dr. Albert Ellis. Although he alludes to the book's informational value and its putative therapeutic usefulness, his remarks are preoccupied with the book's sexual imagery. The solicitation was indiscriminate, not limited to those, such as physicians or psychiatrists, who might independently discern the book's therapeutic worth.[10] Inserted in each advertisement was a slip labeled "GUARANTEE" and reading, "Documentary Books, Inc. unconditionally guarantees full refund on the price of *The Housewife's Handbook on Selective Promiscuity* if the book fails to reach you because of U.S. Post Office censorship inter-

---

[7] *Roth* v. *United States*, supra, 354 U.S., at 495–496, 77 S. Ct., at 1314–1315 (Warren, C.J., concurring).

[8] Evidence relating to petitioners' efforts to secure mailing privileges from these post offices was, contrary to the suggestion of Mr. JUSTICE HARLAN in dissent, introduced for the purpose of supporting such a finding. Scienter had been stipulated prior to trial. The Government's position was revealed in the following colloquy, which occurred when it sought to introduce a letter to the postmaster of Blue Ball, Pennsylvania:

"The COURT. Who signed the letter?

"Mr. CREAMER. It is signed by Frank R. Brady, Associate Publisher of Mr. Ginzburg. It is on Eros Magazine, Incorporated's stationery.

"The COURT. And your objection is—

"Mr. SHAPIRO. It is in no way relevant to the particular issue or publication upon which the defendant has been indicted and in my view, even if there was an identification with respect to a particular issue, it would be of doubtful relevance in that event.

"The COURT. Anything else to say?

"Mr. CREAMER. If Your Honor pleases, there is a statement in this letter indicating that it would be advantageous to this publication to have it disseminated through Blue Ball, Pennsylvania, post office. I think this clearly goes to intent, as to what the purpose of publishing these magazines was. At least, it clearly establishes one of the reasons why they were disseminating this material.

"The COURT. Admitted."

[9] Thus, one *Eros* advertisement claimed:

"*Eros* is a child of its times. * * * [It] is the result of recent court decisions that have realistically interpreted America's obscenity laws and that have given to this country a new breath of freedom of expression. * * * *Eros* takes full advantage of this new freedom of expression. It is *the* magazine of sexual candor."

In another, more lavish spread:

"*Eros* is a new quarterly devoted to the subjects of Love and Sex. In the few short weeks since its birth, *Eros* has established itself as the rave of the American intellectual community—and the rage of prudes everywhere! And it's no wonder: *Eros* handles the subjects of Love and Sex with complete candor. The publication of this magazine—which is frankly and avowedly concerned with erotica—has been enabled by recent court decisions ruling that a literary piece or painting, though explicitly sexual in content, has a right to be published if it is a genuine work of art.

"*Eros* is a genuine work of art. * * *"

An undisclosed number of advertisements for *Liaison* were mailed. The outer envelopes of these ads ask, "Are you among the chosen few?" The first line of the advertisement eliminates the ambiguity: "Are you a member of the sexual elite?" It continues:

"That is, are you among the few happy and enlightened individuals who believe that a man and woman can make love without feeling pangs of conscience? Can you read about love and sex and discuss them without blushing and stammering?

If so, you ought to know about an important new periodical called *Liaison*.

*   *   *   *   *

"In short, *Liaison* is Cupid's Chronicle. * * *

"Though *Liaison* handles the subjects of love and sex with complete candor, I wish to make it clear that it is not a scandal sheet and it is not written for the man in the street. *Liaison* is aimed at intelligent, educated adults who can accept love and sex as part of life.

"* * * I'll venture to say that after you've read your first by-weekly issue, *Liaison* will be your most eagerly awaited piece of mail."

[10] Note 13, infra.

ference." Similar slips appeared in the advertising for *Eros* and *Liaison*; they highlighted the gloss petitioners put on the publications, eliminating any doubt what the purchaser was being asked to buy.[11]

[5–8] This evidence, in our view, was relevant in determining the ultimate question of obscenity and, in the context of this record, serves to resolve all ambiguity and doubt. The deliberate representation of petitioners' publications as erotically arousing, for example, stimulated the reader to accept them as prurient; he looks for titillation, not for saving intellectual content. Similarly, such representation would tend to force public confrontation with the potentially offensive aspects of the work; the brazenness of such an appeal heightens the offensiveness of the publications to those who are offended by such material. And the circumstances of presentation and dissemination of material are equally relevant to determining whether social importance claimed for material in the courtroom was, in the circumstances, pretense or reality—whether it was the basis upon which it was traded in the marketplace or a spurious claim for litigation purposes. Where the purveyor's sole emphasis is on the sexually provocative aspects of his publications, that fact may be decisive in the determination of obscenity. Certainly in a prosecution which, as here, does not necessarily imply suppression of the materials involved, the fact that they originate or are used as a subject of pandering is relevant to the application of the *Roth* test.

[9, 10] A proposition argued as to *Eros*, for example, is that the trial judge improperly found the magazine to be obscene as a whole, since he concluded that only four of the 15 articles predominantly appealed to prurient interest and substantially exceeded community standards of candor, while the other articles were admittedly non-offensive. But the trial judge found that "[t]he deliberate and studied arrangement of *Eros* is editorialized for the purpose of appealing predominantly to prurient interest and to insulate through the inclusion of non-offensive material." 224 F. Supp., at 131. However erroneous such a conclusion might be if unsupported by the evidence of pandering, the record here supports it. *Eros* was created, represented and sold solely as a claimed instrument of the sexual stimulation it would bring. Like the other publications, its pervasive treatment of sex and sexual matters rendered it available to exploitation by those who would make a business of pandering to "the widespread weakness for titillation by pornography."[12] Petitioners' own expert agreed, correctly we think, that "[i]f the object [of a work] is material gain for the creator through an appeal to the sexual curiosity and appetite," the work is pornographic. In other words, by animating sensual detail to give the publication salacious cast, petitioners reinforced what is conceded by the Government to be an otherwise debatable conclusion.

[11] A similar analysis applies to the judgment regarding the *Handbook*. The bulk of the proofs directed to social importance concerned this publication. Before selling publication rights to petitioners, its author had printed

it privately; she sent circulars to persons whose names appeared on membership lists of medical and psychiatric associations, asserting its value as an adjunct to therapy. Over 12,000 sales resulted from this solicitation, and a number of witnesses testified that they found the work useful in their professional practice. The Government does not seriously contest the claim that the book has worth in such a controlled, or even neutral, environment. Petitioners, however, did not sell the book to such a limited audience, or focus their claims for it on its supposed therapeutic or educational value; rather, they deliberately emphasized the sexually provocative aspects of the work, in order to catch the salaciously disposed. They proclaimed its obscenity; and we cannot conclude that the court below erred in taking their own evaluation at its face value and declaring the book as a whole obscene despite the other evidence.[13]

The decision in *United States v. Rebhuhn*, 109 F. 2d 512, is persuasive authority for our conclusion.[14] That was a prosecution under the predecessor to § 1461, brought in the context of pandering of publications assumed useful to scholars and members of learned professions. The books involved were written by authors proved in many instances to have been men of scientific standing, as anthropologists or psychiatrists. The Court of Appeals for the Second Circuit therefore assumed that many of the books were entitled to the protection of the First Amendment, and "could lawfully have passed through the mails, if directed to those who would be likely to use them for the purposes for which they were written * * *." 109 F. 2d, at 514. But the evidence, as here, was that the defendants had not disseminated them for their "proper use, but * * * woefully misused them, and it was that misuse which constituted the gravamen of the crime." Id., at 515. Speaking for the Court in affirming the conviction, Judge Learned Hand said:

"* * * [T]he works themselves had a place, though a limited one, in anthropology and in psychotherapy. They might also have been lawfully sold to laymen who wished seriously to study the sexual practices of savage or barbarous peoples, or sexual aberrations; in other words, most of them were not obscene per se. In several decisions we have held that the statute does not in all circumstances

---

[11] There is much additional evidence supporting the conclusion of petitioners' pandering. One of petitioners' former writers for *Liaison*, for example, testified about the editorial goals and practices of that publication.

[12] Schwartz, Morals Offenses and the Model Penal Code, 63 Col. L. Rev. 669, 677 (1963).

[13] The Government drew a distinction between the author's and petitioners' solicitation. At the sentencing proceeding the United States Attorney stated:
"* * * [the author] was distributing * * * only to physicians; she never had widespread, indiscriminate distribution of the *Handbook*, and, consequently, the Post Office Department did not interfere. * * * If Mr. Ginzburg had distributed and sold and advertised these books solely to * * * physicians * * * we, of course, would not be here this morning with regard to *The Housewife's Handbook*. * * *"

[14] The Proposed Official Draft of the ALI Model Penal Code likewise recognizes the question of pandering as relevant to the obscenity issue, § 251.4(4); Tentative Draft No. 6 (May 6, 1957), at 1–3, 13–17, 45–46, 53; Schwartz, supra, n. 12; see Craig, Suppressed Books, 195–206 (1963). Compare *Grove Press, Inc.* v. *Christenberry*, 175 F. Supp. 488, 496–497 (D.C.S.D.N.Y. 1959), aff'd 276 F. 2d 433 (C.A. 2d Cir. 1960); *United States* v. *One Book Entitled Ulysses*, 72 F. 2d 705, 707 (C.A. 2d Cir. 1934), affirming 5 F. Supp. 182 (D.C.S.D.N.Y. 1933). See also The Trial of Lady Chatterley—*Regina* v. *Penguin Books, Ltd.* (Rolph. ed. 1961).

*forbid the dissemination of such publications. * * * How-*
*ever, in the case at bar, the prosecution succeeded * * **
when it showed that the defendants had indiscriminately
flooded the mails with advertisements, plainly designed
merely to catch the prurient, though under the guise of
distributing works of scientific or literary merit. We do not
mean that the distributor of such works is charged with a
duty to insure that they shall reach only proper hands, nor
need we say what care he must use, for these defendants
exceeded any possible limit; the circulars were no more
than appeals to the salaciously disposed, and no [fact
finder] could have failed to pierce the fragile screen, set up
to cover that purpose." 109 F. 2d, at 514–515.

[12–20] We perceive no threat to First Amendment
guarantees in thus holding that in close cases evidence of
pandering may be probative with respect to the nature of
the material in question and thus satisfy the *Roth* test.[15]
No weight is ascribed to the fact that petitioners have
profited from the sale of publications which we have
assumed but do not hold cannot themselves be adjudged
obscene in the abstract; to sanction consideration of this
fact might indeed induce self-censorship, and offend the
frequently stated principle that commercial activity, in
itself, is no justification for narrowing the protection of
expression secured by the First Amendment.[16] Rather, the
fact that each of these publications was created or exploited entirely on the basis of its appeal to prurient
interests[17] strengthens the conclusion that the transactions
here were sales of illicit merchandise, not sales of constitutionally protected matter.[18] A conviction for mailing obscene publications, but explained in part by the presence of

this element, does not necessarily suppress the materials in
question, nor chill their proper distribution for a proper
use. Nor should it inhibit the enterprise of others seeking
through serious endeavor to advance human knowledge or
understanding in science, literature, or art. All that will
have been determined is that questionable publications are
obscene in a context which brands them as obscene as that
term is defined in *Roth*—a use inconsistent with any claim
to the shelter of the First Amendment.[19] "The nature of
the materials is, of course, relevant as an attribute of the
defendant's conduct, but the materials are thus placed in
context from which they draw color and character. A
wholly different result might be reached in a different
setting." *Roth v. United States*, 354 U.S., at 495, 77 S.
Ct., at 1315 (Warren, C.J., concurring).

[21, 22] It is important to stress that this analysis
simply elaborates the test by which the obscenity vel non
of the material must be judged. Where an exploitation of
interests in titillation by pornography is shown with respect
to material lending itself to such exploitation through
pervasive treatment or description of sexual matters, such
evidence may support the determination that the material
is obscene even though in other contexts the material
would escape such condemnation.

Petitioners raise several procedural objections, principally directed to the findings which accompanied the trial
court's memorandum opinion, Fed. Rules Crim. Proc. 23.
Even on the assumption that petitioners' objections are well
taken, we perceive no error affecting their substantial
rights.

Affirmed.

Mr. Justice Black, dissenting.

Only one stark fact emerges with clarity out of the
confusing welter of opinions and thousands of words
written in this and two other cases today.[1] That fact is
that Ginzburg, petitioner here, is now finally and authoritatively condemned to serve five years in prison for distributing printed matter about sex which neither Ginzburg
nor anyone else could possibly have known to be criminal.
Since, as I have said many times, I believe the Federal
Government is without any power whatever under the
Constitution to put any type of burden on speech and
expression of ideas of any kind (as distinguished from
conduct), I agree with Part II of the dissent of my Brother
Douglas in this case, and I would reverse Ginzburg's
conviction on this ground alone. Even assuming, however,

---

[15] Our conclusion is consistent with the statutory scheme.
Although § 1461, in referring to "obscene * * * matter" may
appear to deal with the qualities of material in the abstract, it is
settled that the mode of distribution may be a significant part in
the determination of the obscenity of the material involved.
United States v. Rebhuhn, supra. Because the statute creates a
criminal remedy, cf. *Manual Enterprises v. Day*, 370 U.S. 478,
495, 82 S. Ct. 1432, 1441, 8 L. Ed. 2d 639 (opinion of
Brennan, J.), it readily admits such an interpretation, compare
United States v. 31 Photographs, etc., 156 F. Supp. 350
(D.C.S.D.N.Y. 1957).

[16] See *New York Times Co. v. Sullivan*, 376 U.S. 254, 265–
266, 84 S. Ct. 710, 718, 11 L. Ed. 2d 686; *Smith v. People of
State of California*, 361 U.S. 147, 150, 80 S. Ct. 215, 217, 4 L.
Ed. 2d 205.

[17] See *Valentine v. Chrestensen*, 316 U.S. 52, 62 S. Ct. 920,
86 L. Ed. 1262, where the Court viewed handbills purporting to
contain protected expression as merely commercial advertising.
Compare that decision with *Jamison v. State of Texas*, 318 U.S.
413, 63 S. Ct. 669, 87 L. Ed. 869, and *Murdock v. Commonwealth of Pennsylvania*, 319 U.S. 105, 63 S. Ct. 870, 87 L. Ed.
1292, where speech having the characteristics of advertising was
held to be an integral part of religious discussions and hence
protected. Material sold solely to produce sexual arousal, like
commercial advertising, does not escape regulation because it has
been dressed up as speech, or in other contexts might be recognized as speech.

[18] Compare *Breard v. City of Alexandria*, 341 U.S. 622, 71 S.
Ct. 920, 95 L. Ed. 1233, with *Martin v. City of Struthers*, 319
U.S. 141, 63 S. Ct. 862, 87 L. Ed. 1313. Cf. *Kovacs v. Cooper*,
336 U.S. 77, 69 S. Ct. 448, 93 L. Ed. 513; *Giboney v. Empire
Storage & Ice Co.*, 336 U.S. 490, 69 S. Ct. 684, 93 L. Ed. 834;
Cox v. State of Louisiana, 379 U.S. 536, 85 S. Ct. 453, 13 L.
Ed. 2d 471; 379 U.S. 559, 85 S. Ct. 476, 13 L. Ed. 2d 487.

[19] One who advertises and sells a work on the basis of its
prurient appeal is not threatened by the perhaps inherent
residual vagueness of the *Roth* test, cf. *Dombrowski v. Pfister*,
380 U.S. 479, 486–487, 491–492, 85 S. Ct. 1116, 1120–1121,
1123–1124, 14 L. Ed. 2d 22; such behavior is central to the
objectives of criminal obscenity laws. ALI Model Penal Code,
Tentative Draft No. 6 (May 6, 1957), pp. 1–3, 13–17; Comments to the Proposed Official Draft § 251.4, supra; Schwartz,
Morals Offenses and the Model Penal Code, 63 Col. L. Rev.
669, 677–681 (1963); Paul & Schwartz, Federal Censorship—
Obscenity in the Mail, 212–219 (1961); see *Mishkin v. State of
New York*, 383 U.S. 502, at 507, n. 5, 86 S. Ct. 958, at 962.

[1] See No. 49, *Mishkin v. State of New York*, 383 U.S. 502,
86 S. Ct. 958, and No. 368, *A Book Named "John Cleland's
Memoirs of a Woman of Pleasure" v. Attorney General of
Massachusetts*, 383 U.S. 413, 86 S. Ct. 975.

that the Court is correct in holding today that Congress does have power to clamp official censorship on some subjects selected by the Court, in some ways approved by it, I believe that the federal obscenity statute as enacted by Congress and as enforced by the Court against Ginzburg in this case should be held invalid on two other grounds.

I.

Criminal punishment by government, although universally recognized as a necessity in limited areas of conduct, is an exercise of one of government's most awesome and dangerous powers. Consequently, wise and good governments make all possible efforts to hedge this dangerous power by restricting it within easily identifiable boundaries. Experience, and wisdom flowing out of that experience, long ago led to the belief that agents of government should not be vested with power and discretion to define and punish as criminal past conduct which had not been clearly defined as a crime in advance. To this end, at least in part, written laws came into being, marking the boundaries of conduct for which public agents could thereafter impose punishment upon people. In contrast, bad governments either wrote no general rules of conduct at all, leaving that highly important task to the unbridled discretion of government agents at the moment of trial, or sometimes, history tells us, wrote their laws in an unknown tongue so that people could not understand them or else placed their written laws at such inaccessible spots that people could not read them. It seems to me that these harsh expedients used by bad governments to punish people for conduct not previously clearly marked as criminal are being used here to put Mr. Ginzburg in prison for five years.

I agree with my Brother HARLAN that the Court has in effect rewritten the federal obscenity statute and thereby imposed on Ginzburg standards and criteria that Congress never thought about; or if it did think about them, certainly it did not adopt them. Consequently, Ginzburg is, as I see it, having his conviction and sentence affirmed upon the basis of a statute amended by this Court for violation of which amended statute he was not charged in the courts below. Such an affirmance we have said violates due process. *Cole* v. *State of Arkansas*, 333 U.S. 196, 68 S. Ct. 514, 92 L. Ed. 644. Compare *Shuttlesworth* v. *City of Birmingham*, 382 U.S. 87, 86 S. Ct. 211, 15 L. Ed. 2d 176. Quite apart from this vice in the affirmance, however, I think that the criteria declared by a majority of the Court today as guidelines for a court or jury to determine whether Ginzburg or anyone else can be punished as a common criminal for publishing or circulating obscene material are so vague and meaningless that they practically leave the fate of a person charged with violating censorship statutes to the unbridled discretion, whim and caprice of the judge or jury which tries him. I shall separately discuss the three elements which a majority of the Court seems to consider material in proving obscenity.[2]

(a) The first element considered necessary for determining obscenity is that the dominant theme of the material taken as a whole must appeal to the prurient interest in sex. It seems quite apparent to me that human beings, serving either as judges or jurors, could not be expected to give any sort of decision on this element which would even remotely promise any kind of uniformity in the enforcement of this law. What conclusion an individual, be he judge or juror, would reach about whether the material appeals to "prurient interest in sex" would depend largely in the long run not upon testimony of witnesses such as can be given in ordinary criminal cases where conduct is under scrutiny, but would depend to a large extent upon the judge's or juror's personality, habits, inclinations, attitudes and other individual characteristics. In one community or in one courthouse a matter would be condemned as obscene under this so-called criterion but in another community, maybe only a few miles away, or in another courthouse in the same community, the material could be given a clean bill of health. In the final analysis the submission of such an issue as this to a judge or jury amounts to practically nothing more than a request for the judge or juror to assert his own personal beliefs about whether the matter should be allowed to be legally distributed. Upon this subjective determination the law becomes certain for the first and last time.

(b) The second element for determining obscenity as it is described by my Brother BRENNAN is that the material must be "patently offensive because it affronts contemporary community standards relating to the description or representation of sexual matters. * * *" Nothing that I see in any position adopted by a majority of the Court today and nothing that has been said in previous opinions for the Court leaves me with any kind of certainty as to whether the "community standards"[3] referred to are world-wide, nation-wide, section-wide, state-wide, country-wide, precinct-wide or township-wide. But even if some definite areas were mentioned, who is capable of assessing "community standards" on such a subject? Could one expect the same application of standards by jurors in Mississippi as in New York City, in Vermont as in California? So here again the guilt or innocence of a defendant charged with obscenity must depend in the final analysis upon the personal judgment and attitude of particular individuals and the place where the trial is held. And one must remember that the Federal Government has the power to try a man for mailing obscene matter in a court 3,000 miles from his home.

---

[2] As I understand all of the opinions in this case and the two related cases decided today, three things must be proven to establish material as obscene. In brief these are (1) the material must appeal to the prurient interest, (2) it must be patently offensive, and (3) it must have no redeeming social value. Mr. Justice Brennan in his opinion in *A Book Named "John Cleland's Memoirs"* v. *Attorney General of Massachusetts*, 383 U.S. 413, 86 S. Ct. 975, which is joined by the Chief Justice and Mr.

Justice Fortas, is of the opinion that all three of these elements must coalesce before material can be labeled obscene. Mr. Justice Clark in a dissenting opinion in *Memoirs* indicates, however, that proof of the first two elements alone is enough to show obscenity and that proof of the third—the material must be utterly without redeeming social value—is only an aid in proving the first two. In his dissenting opinion in *Memoirs* Mr. Justice White states that material is obscene "if its predominant theme appeals to the prurient interest in a manner exceeding customary limits of candor." In the same opinion Mr. Justice White states that the social importance test "is relevant only to determining the predominant prurient interest of the material."

[3] See the opinion of Mr. Justice Brennan, concurred in by Mr. Justice Goldberg in *Jacobellis* v. *State of Ohio*, 378 U.S. 184, 84 S. Ct. 1676, 12 L. Ed. 2d 793, but compare the dissent in that case of The Chief Justice, joined by Mr. Justice Clark, at 199, 84 S. Ct. at 1684.

(c) A third element which three of my Brethren think is required to establish obscenity is that the material must be "utterly without redeeming social value." This element seems to me to be as uncertain, if not even more uncertain, than is the unknown substance of the Milky Way. If we are to have a free society as contemplated by the Bill of Rights, then I can find little defense for leaving the liberty of American individuals subject to the judgment of a judge or jury as to whether material that provokes thought or stimulates desire is "utterly without redeeming social value. * * *" Whether a particular treatment of a particular subject is with or without social value in this evolving, dynamic society of ours is a question upon which no uniform agreement could possibly be reached among politicians, statesmen, professors, philosophers, scientists, religious groups or any other type of group. A case-by-case assessment of social values by individual judges and jurors is, I think, a dangerous technique for government to utilize in determining whether a man stays in or out of the penitentiary.

My conclusion is that certainly after the fourteen separate opinions handed down in these three cases today no person, not even the most learned judge much less a layman, is capable of knowing in advance of an ultimate decision in his particular case by this Court whether certain material comes within the area of "obscenity" as that term is confused by the Court today. For this reason even if, as appears from the result of the three cases today, this country is far along the way to a censorship of the subjects about which the people can talk or write, we need not commit further constitutional transgressions by leaving people in the dark as to what literature or what words or what symbols if distributed through the mails make a man a criminal. As bad and obnoxious as I believe governmental censorship is in a Nation that has accepted the First Amendment as its basic ideal for freedom, I am compelled to say that censorship that would stamp certain books and literature as illegal in advance of publication or conviction would in some ways be preferable to the unpredictable book-by-book censorship into which we have now drifted.

I close this part of my dissent by saying once again that I think the First Amendment forbids any kind or type or nature of governmental censorship over views as distinguished from conduct.

II.

It is obvious that the effect of the Court's decisions in the three obscenity cases handed down today is to make it exceedingly dangerous for people to discuss either orally or in writing anything about sex. Sex is a fact of life. Its pervasive influence is felt throughout the world and it cannot be ignored. Like all other facts of life it can lead to difficulty and trouble and sorrow and pain. But while it may lead to abuses, and has in many instances, no words need be spoken in order for people to know that the subject is one pleasantly interwoven in all human activities and involves the very substance of the creation of life itself. It is a subject which people are bound to consider and discuss whatever laws are passed by any government to try to suppress it. Though I do not suggest any way to solve the problems that may arise from sex or discussions about sex, of one thing I am confident, and that is that federal censorship is not the answer to these problems. I find it

difficult to see how talk about sex can be placed under the kind of censorship the Court here approves without subjecting our society to more dangers than we can anticipate at the moment. It was to avoid exactly such dangers that the First Amendment was written and adopted. For myself I would follow the course which I believe is required by the First Amendment, that is, recognize that sex at least as much as any other aspect of life is so much a part of our society that its discussion should not be made a crime.

I would reverse this case.

Mr. Justice HARLAN, dissenting.

I would reverse the convictions of Ginzburg and his three corporate co-defendants. The federal obscenity statute under which they were convicted, 18 U.S.C. § 1461 (1964 ed.), is concerned with unlawful shipment of "nonmailable" matter. In my opinion announcing the judgment of the Court in *Manual Enterprises, Inc.* v. *Day*, 370 U.S. 478, 82 S. Ct. 1432, 8 L. Ed. 2d 639, the background of the statute was assessed, and its focus was seen to be solely on the character of the material in question. That too has been the premise on which past cases in this Court arising under this statute, or its predecessors, have been decided. See, e.g., *Roth* v. *United States*, 354 U.S. 476, 77 S. Ct. 1304, 1 L. Ed. 2d 1498. I believe that under this statute the Federal Government is constitutionally restricted to banning from the mails only "hardcore pornography," see my separate opinion in *Roth*, supra, at 507, 77 S. Ct., at 1320, and my dissenting opinion in *A Book Named "John Cleland's Memoirs"* v. *Attorney General*, 383 U.S. 455, 86 S. Ct. 996. Because I do not think it can be maintained that the material in question here falls within that narrow class, I do not believe it can be excluded from the mails.

The Court recognizes the difficulty of justifying these convictions; the majority refuses to approve the trial judge's "exegesis of *Roth*" (note 3, 383 U.S. 465, 86 S. Ct. 944); it declines to approve the trial court's "characterizations" of the *Handbook* "outside" the "setting" which the majority for the first time announces to be crucial to this conviction (note 5, 383 U.S. 466, 86 S. Ct. 945). Moreover, the Court accepts the Government's concession that the *Handbook* has a certain "worth" when seen in something labeled a "controlled, or even neutral, environment" (383 U.S. 472, 86 S. Ct. 948); the majority notes that these are "publications which we have assumed * * * cannot themselves be adjudged obscene in the abstract" (383 U.S. 474, 86 S. Ct. 949). In fact, the Court in the last analysis sustains the convictions on the express assumption that the items held to be obscene are not, viewing them strictly, obscene at all (383 U.S. 466, 86 S. Ct. 945).

This curious result is reached through the elaboration of a theory of obscenity entirely unrelated to the language, purposes, or history of the federal statute now being applied, and certainly different from the test used by the trial court to convict the defendants. While the precise holding of the Court is obscure, I take it that the objective test of *Roth*, which ultimately focuses on the material in question, is to be supplemented by another test that goes to the question whether the mailer's aim is to "pander" to or "titillate" those to whom he mails questionable matter.

Although it is not clear whether the majority views the panderer test as a statutory gloss or as constitutional doctrine, I read the opinion to be in the latter category.[1] The First Amendment, in the obscenity area, no longer fully protects material on its face nonobscene, for such material must now also be examined in the light of the defendant's conduct, attitude, motives. This seems to me a mere euphemism for allowing punishment of a person who mails otherwise constitutionally protected material just because a jury or a judge may not find him or his business agreeable. Were a State to enact a "panderer" statute under its police power, I have little doubt that—subject to clear drafting to avoid attacks on vagueness and equal protection grounds—such a statute would be constitutional. Possibly the same might be true of the Federal Government acting under its postal or commerce powers. What I fear the Court has done today is in effect to write a new statute, but without the sharply focused definitions and standards necessary in such a sensitive area. Casting such a dubious gloss over a straightforward 101-year-old statute (see 13 Stat. 507) is for me an astonishing piece of judicial improvisation.

It seems perfectly clear that the theory on which these convictions are now sustained is quite different from the basis on which the case was tried and decided by the District Court and affirmed by the Court of Appeals.[2] The District Court found the *Handbook* "patently offensive on its face" and without "the slightest redeeming social, artistic or literary importance or value"; it held that there was "no credible evidence that the *Handbook* has the slightest valid scientific importance for treatment of individuals in clinical psychiatry, psychology, or any field of medicine." 224 F. Supp. 129, 131. The trial court made similar findings as to *Eros* and *Liaison*. The majority's opinion, as I read it, casts doubts upon these explicit findings. As to the *Handbook*, the Court interprets an offhand remark by the government prosecutor at the sentencing hearing as a "concession," which the majority accepts, that the prosecution rested upon the conduct of the petitioner, and the Court explicitly refuses to accept the trial judge's "characterizations" of the book, which I take to be an implied rejection of the findings of fact upon which the conviction was in fact based (note 5, 383 U.S. 466, 86 S. Ct. 945). Similarly as to *Eros*, the Court implies that the finding of obscenity might be "erroneous" were it not supported "by the evidence of pandering" (383 U.S. 471, 86 S. Ct. 947). The Court further characterizes the *Eros* decision, aside from pandering, as "an otherwise debatable conclusion" (383 U.S. 471, 86 S. Ct. 948).

If there is anything to this new pandering dimension to the mailing statute, the Court should return the case for a new trial, for petitioners are at least entitled to a day in court on the question on which their guilt has ultimately come to depend. Compare the action of the Court in *A Book Named "John Cleland's Memoirs" v. Attorney General*, 383 U.S. 413, 86 S. Ct. 975, also decided today, where the Court affords the State an opportunity to prove in a subsequent prosecution that an accused purveyor of *Fanny Hill* in fact used pandering methods to secure distribution of the book.

If a new trial were given in the present case, as I read the Court's opinion, the burden would be on the Government to show that the motives of the defendants were to pander to "the widespread weakness for titillation by pornography" (383 U.S. 471, 86 S. Ct. 947). I suppose that an analysis of the type of individuals receiving *Eros* and the *Handbook* would be relevant. If they were ordinary people, interested in purchasing *Eros* or the *Handbook* for one of a dozen personal reasons, this might be some evidence of pandering to the general public. On the other hand, as the Court suggests, the defendants could exonerate themselves by showing that they sent these works only or perhaps primarily (no standards are set) to psychiatrists and other serious-minded professional people. Also relevant would apparently be the nature of the mailer's advertisements or representations. Conceivably someone mailing to the public selective portions of a recognized classic with the avowed purpose of titillation would run the risk of conviction for mailing nonmailable matter. Presumably the Post Office under this theory might once again attempt to ban *Lady Chatterley's Lover*, which a lower court found not bannable in 1960 by an abstract application of *Roth*. *Grove Press, Inc. v. Christenberry*, 276 F. 2d 433. I would suppose that if the Government could show that Grove Press is pandering to people who are interested in the book's sexual passages and not in D. H. Lawrence's social theories or literary technique § 1461 could properly be invoked. Even the well-known opinions of Judge A. N. Hand in *United States v. One Book* Entitled *Ulysses*, 72 F. 2d 705, and of Judge Woolsey in the District Court, 5 F. Supp. 182, might be rendered nugatory if a mailer of *Ulysses* is found to be titillating readers with its "coarse, blasphemous, and obscene" portions, 72 F. 2d, at 707, rather than piloting them through the intricacies of Joyce's stream of consciousness.

In the past, as in the trial of these petitioners, evidence as to a defendant's conduct was admissible only to show relevant intent.[3] Now evidence not only as to conduct, but also as to attitude and motive, is admissible on the primary question of whether the material mailed is obscene. I have difficulty seeing how these inquiries are logically related to the question whether a particular work is obscene. In addition, I think such a test for obscenity is impermissibly vague, and unwarranted by anything in the First Amendment or in 18 U.S.C. § 1461.

---

[1] The prevailing opinion in *A Book Named "John Cleland's Memoirs" v. Attorney General*, 383 U.S. 413, 86 S. Ct. 975, makes clearer the constitutional ramifications of this new doctrine.

[2] Although at one point in its opinion the Court of Appeals referred to "the shoddy business of pandering," 338 F. 2d 12, 15, a reading of the opinion as a whole plainly indicates that the Court of Appeals did not affirm these convictions on the basis on which this Court now sustains them.

[3] To show pandering, the Court relies heavily on the fact that the defendants sought mailing privileges from the postmasters of Intercourse and Blue Ball, Pennsylvania, before settling upon Middlesex, New Jersey, as a mailing point (383 U.S., pp. 467–468, 86 S. Ct., pp. 945–946). This evidence was admitted, however, only to show required scienter, see 338 F. 2d 12, 16. On appeal to the Court of Appeals and to this Court, petitioner Ginzburg asserted that at most the evidence shows the intent of petitioner Eros Magazine, Inc., and was erroneously used against him. The Court of Appeals held the point *de minimis*, 338 F. 2d, at 16–17, on the ground that the parties had stipulated the necessary intent. The United States, in its brief in this Court, likewise viewed this evidence as relating solely to *scienter*; nowhere did the United States attempt to sustain these convictions on anything like a pandering theory.

I would reverse the judgment below.

Mr. Justice STEWART, dissenting.

Ralph Ginzburg has been sentenced to five years in prison for sending through the mail copies of a magazine, a pamphlet, and a book. There was testimony at his trial that these publications possess artistic and social merit. Personally, I have a hard time discerning any. Most of the material strikes me as both vulgar and unedifying. But if the First Amendment means anything, it means that a man cannot be sent to prison merely for distributing publications which offend a judge's esthetic sensibilities, mine or any other's.

Censorship reflects a society's lack of confidence in itself. It is a hallmark of an authoritarian regime. Long ago those who wrote our First Amendment charted a different course. They believed a society can be truly strong only when it is truly free. In the realm of expression they put their faith, for better or for worse, in the enlightened choice of the people, free from the interference of a policeman's intrusive thumb or a judge's heavy hand. So it is that the Constitution protects coarse expression as well as refined, and vulgarity no less than elegance. A book worthless to me may convey something of value to my neighbor. In the free society to which our Constitution has committed us, it is for each to choose for himself.[1]

Because such is the mandate of our Constitution, there is room for only the most restricted view of this Court's decision in *Roth* v. *United States*, 354 U.S. 476, 77 S. Ct. 1304, 1 L. Ed. 2d 1498. In that case the Court held that "obscenity is not within the area of constitutionally protected speech or press." Id., at 485, 77 S. Ct., at 1309. The Court there characterized obscenity as that which is "utterly without redeeming social importance," id., at 484, 77 S. Ct., at 1309, "deals with sex in a manner appealing to prurient interests," id., at 487, 77 S. Ct., at 1310, and "goes substantially beyond customary limits of candor in description or representation of such matters." Id., at 487, n. 20, 77 S. Ct., at 1310.[2] In *Manual Enterprises* v. *Day*, 370 U.S. 478, 82 S. Ct. 1432, 8 L. Ed. 2d 639, I joined Mr. Justice Harlan's opinion adding "patent indecency" as a further essential element of that which is not constitutionally protected.

There does exist a distinct and easily identifiable class of material in which all of these elements coalesce. It is that, and that alone, which I think government may constitu-

tionally suppress, whether by criminal or civil sanctions. I have referred to such material before as hard–core pornography, without trying further to define it. *Jacobellis* v. *State of Ohio*, 378 U.S. 184, at 197, 84 S. Ct. 1676, at 1683 (concurring opinion). In order to prevent any possible misunderstanding, I have set out in the margin a description, borrowed from the Solicitor General's brief, of the kind of thing to which I have reference.[3] See also Lockhart and McClure, Censorship of Obscenity: The Developing Constitutional Standards, 45 Minn. L. Rev. 5, 63–64.

Although arguments can be made to the contrary, I accept the proposition that the general dissemination of matter of this description may be suppressed under valid laws.[4] That has long been the almost universal judgment of our society. See *Roth* v. *United States*, 354 U.S., at 485, 77 S. Ct., at 1309. But material of this sort is wholly different from the publications mailed by Ginzburg in the present case, and different not in degree but in kind.

The Court today appears to concede that the materials Ginzburg mailed were themselves protected by the First Amendment. But, the Court says, Ginzburg can still be sentenced to five years in prison for mailing them. Why? Because, says the Court, he was guilty of "commercial exploitation," of "pandering," and of "titillation." But Ginzburg was not charged with "commercial exploitation"; he was not charged with "pandering"; he was not charged with "titillation." Therefore, to affirm his conviction now on any of those grounds, even if otherwise valid, is to deny him due process of law. *Cole* v. *State of Arkansas*, 333 U.S. 196, 68 S. Ct. 514, 92 L. Ed. 644. But those grounds are *not*, of course, otherwise valid. Neither the statute under which Ginzburg was convicted nor any other federal statute I know of makes "commercial exploitation" or "pandering" or "titillation" a criminal offense. And any criminal law that sought to do so in the terms so elusively defined by the Court would, of course, be unconstitutionally vague and therefore void. All of these matters are developed in the dissenting opinions of my Brethren, and I simply note here that I fully agree with them.

For me, however, there is another aspect of the Court's opinion in this case that is even more regrettable. Today the Court assumes the power to deny Ralph Ginzburg the protection of the First Amendment because it disapproves of his "sordid business." That is a power the Court does not possess. For the First Amendment protects us all with

---

[1] Different constitutional questions would arise in a case involving an assault upon individual privacy by publication in a manner so blatant or obtrusive as to make it difficult or impossible for an unwilling individual to avoid exposure to it. Cf. e.g., *Breard* v. *City of Alexandria*, 341 U.S. 622, 71 S. Ct. 920, 95 L. Ed. 1233; *Public Utilities Commission of District of Columbia* v. *Pollak*, 343 U.S. 451, 72 S. Ct. 813, 96 L. Ed. 1068; *Griswold* v. *State of Connecticut*, 381 U.S. 479, 85 S. Ct. 1678, 14 L. Ed. 2d 510. Still other considerations might come into play with respect to laws limited in their effect to those deemed insufficiently adult to make an informed choice. No such issues were tendered in this case.

[2] It is not accurate to say that the *Roth* opinion "fashioned standards" for obscenity, because, as the Court explicitly stated, no issue was there presented as to the obscenity of the material involved. 354 U.S., at 481, n. 8, 77 S. Ct., at 1307. And in no subsequent case has a majority of the Court been able to agree on any such "standards."

[3] "* * * Such materials include photographs, both still and motion picture, with no pretense of artistic value, graphically depicting acts of sexual intercourse, including various acts of sodomy and sadism, and sometimes involving several participants in scenes of orgy-like character. They also include strips of drawings in comic-book format grossly depicting similar activities in an exaggerated fashion. There are, in addition, pamphlets and booklets, sometimes with photographic illustrations, verbally describing such activities in a bizarre manner with no attempt whatsoever to afford portrayals of character or situation and with no pretense to literary value. All of this material * * * cannot conceivably be characterized as embodying communication of ideas or artistic values inviolate under the First Amendment. * * *"

[4] During oral argument we were advised by government counsel that the vast majority of prosecutions under this statute involve material of this nature. Such prosecutions usually result in guilty pleas and never come to this Court.

an even hand. It applies to Ralph Ginzburg with no less completeness and force than to G. P. Putnam's Sons. In upholding and enforcing the Bill of Rights, this Court has no power to pick or to choose. When we lose sight of that fixed star of constitutional adjudication, we lose our way. For then we forsake a government of law and are left with government by Big Brother.

I dissent.

■ Fanfare Films, Inc.

v.

Motion Picture Censor Board of State of Maryland.
No. 201.

Court of Appeals of Maryland.

March 4, 1964.

Joseph S. Kaufman, Baltimore (C. Morton Goldstein, Baltimore, on the brief), for appellant.

Robert F. Sweeney, Asst. Atty. Gen., Baltimore (Thomas B. Finan, Atty. Gen., Baltimore, on the brief), for appellee.

Before BRUNE, C.J., and HENDERSON, HAMMOND, MARBURY and SYBERT, JJ.

HAMMOND, Judge.

Fanfare Films, Inc., was ordered by the Maryland State Board of Censors of motion pictures (the Board) to delete from the film entitled "Have Figure—Will Travel" certain scenes showing girls unclothed while cruising on a boat. It took an appeal to the Baltimore City Court, which affirmed the order of the Board. In its appeal to this Court, Fanfare argues that the Maryland censorship act, Code (1957), Art. 66A, violates the First Amendment to the Constitution of the United States (as made binding on the State by the Fourteenth Amendment) and Article 40 of the Maryland Declaration of Rights, and that the scenes ordered cut from the picture are not obscene, as the Board found.

"Have Figure—Will Travel" is in form a travelogue portraying the story of three girls, two of whom are confirmed nudists, who take a vacation cruise through the inland waterways from upper New York to Florida on a cabin cruiser belonging to the father of one of the girls. Scenes are shown during stops at New York City and Charleston and at nudist camps in New Jersey and Florida. The third girl becomes a convert to nudism as the trip—and the film—progresses. The Board passed the scenes in the nudist camps, in which there were both unclothed men and women, but it disapproved the scenes of the girls on the boat, unclothed above the waist.

It is conceded that no sexual activity or awareness was presented and that while on the boat the girls were seen unclothed only by each other. The Chairman of the Board said that the photography was very good, the dialogue was unobjectionable, and the picture had artistic value. The Board took the position that if the picture contained only scenes of nudity within the nudist camps it would have been licensed without deletions, but that while nudity in the camps was not obscene, it was on the boat because in that locale it was not a normal way of life, normal people would not so comport themselves and there was no reason for its portrayal except to arouse sexual desires in the viewers.

[1] Fanfare's contentions as to the unconstitutionality of censorship of motion pictures, as such, must be rejected under our recent decision in *Freedman v. State,* Md., 197 A. 2d 232, which held, in reliance on *Times Film Corp.* v. *Chicago,* 365 U.S. 43, 81 S. Ct. 391, 5 L. Ed. 2d 403, that the provisions and requirements of Code (1957), Art. 66A, were not void on their face as unconstitutional infringements upon the right of free speech and publication either under the Federal or State Constitution.

[2] Upon review of the application of the Maryland censorship law to the picture "Have Figure—Will Travel," we conclude that the deletion by the Board of the scenes showing the girls unclothed on the boat was unwarranted. In *Maryland State Bd. of Censors* v. *Times Film Corp.,* 212 Md. 454, 129 A. 2d 833, the Board decided that the showing of "nude people" in the moving picture called the "Naked Amazon" was calculated to arouse the sexual desires of a substantial number of viewers and it therefore banned pictures of nudity therein as obscene, within the meaning of Code (1957), Art. 66A, Sec. 6. This Court held the opinion and action of the Board were not sound and could not be upheld, inasmuch as the established law was that nudity is not necessarily obscene or lewd. There is nothing to indicate that it was in the case before us. In *Monfred v. State,* 226 Md. 312, 173 A. 2d 173, in discussing pictures in magazines of unclothed females in poses which might generally be thought to be offensive, we said they were not necessarily obscene under a statute which made it a crime to knowingly sell "any lewd, obscene or indecent book, magazine * * * drawing or photograph." Of other similar pictures it was there observed (226 Md. p. 317, 173 A. 2d p. 173): "but the pictures, even though obviously intended to arouse sex appeal, are not strictly obscene." We think the Maryland *Times Film* and *Monfred* cases are controlling and require reversal of the order of the Baltimore City Court which affirmed the action of the Board in deleting the scenes on the boat.

Order reversed, with costs.

■ In the Matter of Trans-Lux Distributing Corp., *Respondent,*
v.
Board of Regents of the University of the State of New York, *Appellant.*

Court of Appeals of New York.

March 26, 1964.

Charles A. Brind, Jr., John P. Jehu, Elizabeth M. Eastman and *George B. Farrington*, Albany, for appellant.
Harry I. Rand, Warren F. Schwartz and *Leonard H. Dickstein*, New York City, for respondent.

BURKE, Judge.

This appeal puts in issue once again the constitutionality of an application of this State's motion picture licensing statute (Education Law, Consol. Laws, c. 16, § 122). The Appellate Division has annulled a determination of the Board of Regents which directed the elimination of two scenes from the film "A Stranger Knocks" as a condition for granting a license for the exhibition of the film. The grounds for the board's action rested on the alleged obscenity of two sequences in the picture. The first scene presents a man and a woman on a beach embracing and caressing one another, and ends in a view of the head and shoulders of the woman with facial expressions indicative of orgasmic reaction. The second scene presents the woman astride the man on a bed. Their bodily movements are unmistakably those of the sexual act and the woman's face again registers emotions concededly indicative of orgasm. This scene is the dramatic climax of the picture because of the coincidence of the woman's passion with her sudden realization, through the exposure of a tell-tale scar, that the man is her deceased husband's murderer. As respondent's affidavit puts it: "The climax is a groan of pleasure and pain, a dramatic and eloquent expression of the persistent ambivalence in the relationship."

This case presents the question of film obscenity in a form quite different from the two decisions of this court that were reversed by the Supreme Court. In both *Commercial Pictures Corp. v. Regents*, etc., 346 U.S. 587, 74 S. Ct. 286, 98 L. Ed. 329, advocacy of adultery, and *Joseph Burstyn, Inc. v. Wilson*, 343 U.S. 495, 72 S. Ct. 777, 96 L. Ed. 1098, sacrilege, the issue was so-called thematic obscenity, that is, advocacy of a theme that was forbidden. Here, however, the ground taken by the State is obscenity in filmed behavior, not in anything advocated as an idea or program. We are, therefore, required to examine the applicability of the First Amendment to this film in light of the classic distinction between advocating something presently against the law and actually doing it.

The first thing that ought to be restated is the rather obvious fact that the law does not cope with obscenity in the abstract: It is met only as an alleged characteristic of

something else, something concrete, some speech, action or thing. Accordingly, it must not be forgotten that offensiveness and obscenity enjoy no preferred position in the law merely because of their being offensive. That would be nonsense. It is the thing alleged to be obscene that the Constitution is concerned with—and that only when the thing is speech, broadly conceived as communication. For example, the sale or display of some *object* condemned as obscene might present a question of statutory construction, rarely a First Amendment problem. Similarly, an offensive sight is on its face no more legally immune under the First Amendment than, for example, an offensive odor. This need not even approach the obscene. Zoning regulations controlling the appearance of buildings and the like are routinely enforced (e.g., *Berman v. Parker*, 348 U.S. 26, 75 S. Ct. 98, 99 L. Ed. 27; *People v. Stover*, 12 N.Y. 2d 462, 240 N.Y.S. 2d 734, 191 N.E. 2d 272).

[1] While typically applicable to "speech" and "press" in the forms known to the framers, the guarantee of the First Amendment has been read to include anything that is asserted to be someone's way of saying something. The most familiar instances of this application are physical conduct and motion pictures (*Thornhill v. Alabama*, 310 U.S. 88, 60 S. Ct. 736, 84 L. Ed. 1093; *Joseph Burstyn, Inc. v. Wilson*, 343 U.S. 495, 72 S. Ct. 777, 96 L. Ed. 1098, supra). Cases involving conduct as a form of expression have been frequent in labor law and provide a useful illustration of the transition from a somewhat doctrinaire application of the First Amendment (see e.g., *Thornhill v. Alabama*, 310 U.S. 88, 60 S. Ct. 736, 84 L. Ed. 1093, supra) to a realization that, while conduct may be speech, it still remains conduct and does not cease to present its unique problems of social control. It is now the law that even peaceful picketing may be forbidden where it violates State labor laws that are not themselves designed as restrictions on freedom of speech (*Local Union No. 10, etc., Plumbers Union v. Graham*, 345 U.S. 192, 73 S. Ct. 585, 97 L. Ed. 946). Conduct that is proscribed for valid public purposes is not immune merely because engaged in with a view to expression (*Giboney v. Empire Ice & Storage Co.*, 336 U.S. 490, 69 S. Ct. 684, 93 L. Ed. 834). For example, in *People v. Stover*, 12 N.Y. 2d 462, 240 N.Y.S. 2d 734, 191 N.E. 2d 272, supra, app. dsmd. for want of a substantial Federal question 375 U.S. 42, 84 S. Ct. 147, 11 L. Ed. 2d 107, this court upheld an "Aesthetic" ordinance prohibiting the display of soiled laundry on a clothesline in

the defendants' front yard, despite the fact that the display was an expression of social protest.

Films, by their nature, may lie on either side of the division between speech and conduct. The opinions of the Supreme Court reversing this court in the cases of advocacy of adultery and thematic sacrilege make that plain. But it also follows that if "picketing may include conduct other than speech, conduct which can be made the subject of restrictive legislation" (*Giboney* v. *Empire Ice & Storage Co.* supra, 336 U.S. p. 501, 69 S. Ct. p. 690, 93 L. Ed. 834) then so may films. In this regard, it will be noted that the Supreme Court has not yet expressed its opinion in a case involving allegedly obscene *behavior* on the screen. In such a case, the First Amendment must be applied to films according to their special nature, just as it has been applied to conduct. This much has, of course, been explicitly recognized in the leading case on films and the First Amendment: "Nor does it follow that motion pictures are necessarily subject to the precise rules governing any other particular method of expression. Each method tends to present its own peculiar problems." (*Joseph Burstyn, Inc.* v. *Wilson*, 343 U.S. 495, 503, 72 S. Ct. 777, 781, 96 L. Ed. 1098, supra.)

In *Kingsley Intern. Pictures Corp.* v. *Regents*, 360 U.S. 684, 79 S. Ct. 1362, 2 L. Ed. 2d 1512 the opinion of the court repeatedly distinguishes between the right to communicate any idea, however deviant from orthodoxy, and "the manner of its portrayal" (360 U.S. p. 688, 79 S. Ct. p. 1365, 3 L. Ed. 2d 1512). The "freedom to advocate ideas" was protected, not any supposed right to behave lewdly in a public place. Even more to the point is the concurring opinion of Mr. Justice CLARK who wrote: "I see no grounds for confusion, however, were a statute to ban 'pornographic' films, or those that 'portray *acts* of sexual immorality, perversion or lewdness.' If New York's statute had been so construed by its highest court I believe it would have met the requirements of due process. Instead, it placed more emphasis on what the film teaches than on what it depicts. There is where the confusion enters" (360 U.S. p. 702, 79 S. Ct. p. 1372, 3 L. Ed. 2d 1512; emphasis in original).

It is my view that a filmed presentation of sexual intercourse, whether real or simulated, is just as subject to State prohibition as similar conduct if engaged in on the street. I believe the nature of films is sufficiently different from books to justify the conclusion that the critical difference between advocacy and actual performance of the forbidden act is reached when simulated sexual intercourse is portrayed on the screen. I take it to be conceded that New York may constitutionally prohibit sexual intercourse in public. As Mr. Justice DOUGLAS acknowledged, dissenting in *Roth* v. *United States*, 354 U.S. 476, 512, 77 S. Ct. 1304, 1323, 1 L. Ed. 2d 1498, in contrasting books with conduct: "I assume there is nothing in the Constitution which forbids Congress from using its power over the mails to proscribe *conduct* on the grounds of good morals. No one would suggest that the First Amendment permits nudity in public places, adultery, and other phases of sexual misconduct" (emphasis in text).

This observation is equally pertinent, of course, whether the sexual exhibitionism is done spontaneously in the street or in theatres for money (e.g., Penal Law, Consol. Laws, c.

40, §§ 43, 1140, 1140–a, 1140–b.) There have been many cases dealing with what sort of behavior was covered by statutes against sexual exhibitionism and the like, but they were solely concerned with statutory interpretation, never, obviously, the First Amendment. (*Miller* v. *People*, 5 Barb. 203; *People* v. *Burke*, 243 App. Div. 83, 276 N.Y.S. 402, affd. 267 N.Y. 571, 196 N.E. 585; *People* v. *Mitchell*, 296 N.Y. 672, 70 N.E. 2d 168; *People* v. *Dash*, 282 N.Y. 632, 25 N.E. 2d 979.)

This comparison between the acknowledged competence of the State to forbid public or semipublic sex displays and its power to exert similar control over similar conduct depicted on the screen is not intended to imply any broad theory of legal equivalence between real conduct and a filmed imitation. Indeed, the meaningful comparison exists only in a narrow range of cases. In most instances, the real conduct is illegal because of what is accomplished by the person, as in murder, forgery, or adultery. In such cases, the filmed dramatization obviously does not share the evil aimed at in the law applicable to the real thing. Where, however, the real conduct is illegal, not because of what is accomplished by those involved, but simply because what is done is shocking, offensive to see, and generally believed destructive of the general level of morality, then a filmed simulation fully shares, it seems to me, the evil of the original. In such cases the free expression protection of the First Amendment must apply to both or neither. It makes no sense at all to say that the conduct can be forbidden but not the play or film.

The pattern of statutory regulation in New York aims at offensive—more properly, obscene—*displays of conduct* whether in the street (Penal Law, §§ 43, 1140, 1140–b), on the stage (Penal Law, §1140–a; *People* v. *Vickers*, 259 App. Div. 841, 19 N.Y.S. 2d 165—lewd dance) or on the screen (Penal Law, §§ 1140–a, 1141; Education Law, § 122). These laws care not about the communication of ideas (see *Stromberg* v. *California*, 283 U.S. 359, 51 S. Ct. 532, 75 L. Ed. 1117); they are aimed at certain narrow sorts of conduct. It seems to me, therefore, that if the defendants in *People* v. *Stover*, supra, could constitutionally be prohibited from selecting the forbidden form of conduct as the vehicle for the communication of their protest, then this petitioner cannot choose acted-out sexual intercourse as the vehicle for its art (see, also, *People* v. *Vickers*, supra, where a performer was prohibited from choosing a certain sort of dance as her vehicle, and the "nude gymnasium" prohibited by Penal Law, § 1140–b). Numerous other instances also suggest themselves.

If we can accept the obvious—that sexual intercourse whether performed in the park or simulated on the stage or screen is in itself a form of conduct (in which the public have an interest[1]), it is apparent that when this defendant

---

[1] The police or general powers of government extend to "the preservation of good order and the public morals." (*Beer Co.* v. *Massachusetts*, 97 U.S. 25, 33, 24 L. Ed. 989.) As Mr. Justice HARLAN recently stated the State's authority to legislate in support of moral standards: "Yet the very inclusion of the category of morality among state concerns indicates that society is not limited in its objects only to the physical well-being of the community, but has traditionally concerned itself with the moral soundness of its people as well. Indeed to attempt a line between public behavior and that which is purely consensual or solitary would be to withdraw from community concern a range of

chooses to use it as a vehicle for the expression of art it has "brigaded" the communication (to the extent that it is "communication") with conduct completely. In so doing the petitioner has subjected itself to such regulations as are appropriate to the conduct when engaged in for reasons having nothing to do with expression. There is otherwise no difference between advocacy and action. (Compare *Thornhill* v. *Alabama*, 310 U.S. 88, 60 S. Ct. 736, 84 L. Ed. 1093, with Local Union No. 10, etc., *Plumbers Union* v. *Graham*, 345 U.S. 192, 73 S. Ct. 585, 97 L. Ed. 946.) "Freedom of expression can be suppressed if, and to the extent that, it is so closely brigaded with illegal action as to be an inseparable part of it" (Douglas, J., dissenting in *Roth* v. *United States*, 354 U.S. 476, 514, 77 S. Ct. 1304, 1324, 1 L. Ed. 2d 1498).

Just what regulations are appropriate regarding displays of sexual intimacy in public or semipublic places may be a matter for debate. The debate is most profitably conducted, however, in the malleable forum of public policy rather than within the rigidities of constitutional law. In regard to conduct which has been legislatively declared to be against public policy, we are reminded by Mr. Justice Holmes that "There is nothing that I more deprecate than the use of the Fourteenth Amendment beyond the absolute compulsion of its words to prevent the making of social experiments that an important part of the community desires, in the insulated chambers afforded by the several states, even though the experiments may seem futile or even noxious to me and to those whose judgment I most respect" (dissenting opinion in *Truax* v. *Corrigan*, 257 U.S. 312, 344, 42 S. Ct. 124, 134, 66 L. Ed. 254). The sole exception to this tolerance of experimentation is legislation hostile to that freedom of expression necessary to the healthy functioning of an open democratic society. It is after careful consideration that I conclude that, far from hostility to any idea, even hateful ideas that undermine social morality, section 122 of the Education Law merely proscribes certain behavior, which, when viewed by the public, is deemed offensive and destructive of moral standards historically protected by the State and which "bears no necessary relationship to the freedom to speak, write, print or distribute information or opinion" (*Schneider* v. *State*, 308 U.S. 147, 161, 60 S. Ct. 146, 150, 84 L. Ed. 155).

[2] The scenes referred to by the State are obscene within the meaning of section 122 of the Education Law as I understand it in light of the Fourteenth Amendment. The issue of obscenity as a constitutional standard applicable to speech proper, or whether the conduct here depicted can even be meaningfully thought of as speech in this context, need not be decided.

___

subjects with which every society in civilized times has found it necessary to deal. The laws regarding marriage which provide both when the sexual powers may be used and the legal and societal context in which children are born and brought up, as well as laws forbidding adultery, fornication and homosexual practices which express the negative of the proposition, confining sexuality to lawful marriage, form a pattern so deeply pressed into the substance of our social life that any Constitutional doctrine in this area must build upon that basis. Compare *McGowan* v. *Maryland*, 366 U.S. 420, 81 S. Ct. 1101, 1153, 1213 [6 L. Ed. 2d 393]." (Harlan J., dissenting in *Poe* v. *Ullman*, 367 U.S. 497, 545–546, 81 S. Ct. 1752, 1778, 6 L. Ed. 2d 989.)

Lastly, because the material assigned as obscene in this case is not, in my view, speech, as opposed to conduct, it need not come within the test laid down in *Roth* v. *United States*, 354 U.S. 476, 77 S. Ct. 1304, 1 L. Ed. 2d 1498, supra, that, in speech cases, obscenity must be the dominant theme of the work as a whole. If that requirement were applicable to cases of this nature, the law would be helpless to cope with the grossest imaginable pornography if it were included in a film as an incidental feature, collateral to the main plot, just as a profitable bit of sensationalism. If we admit of the concept of obscenity as a public evil at all, it must be recognized that the full force of such an evil could flourish in nonthematic interludes of motion pictures. If simulated sexual intercourse outrages public decency, it does so as such and not only when the sole or dominant subject of any given exhibition. The licensing statute contemplates the deletion of such material. It may either be omitted entirely or the producer may redo the scene another way. If it is objected that the enterprise is artistically not worth doing without the scene as it stands, that is the problem, not of the law, but of the producer who has made a pornographic scene so central to his work.

To all argument predicated on artistic merit as decisive of the constitutional question, it is sufficient answer to say that artists are not such favorites of the law that they may ply their craft in the teeth of a declared overriding public policy against pornographic displays. Since no other profession is privileged to bend public morals, policy and law to its internal craft standards, then neither should producers of films.

The order appealed from should be reversed and the determination of the Board of Regents reinstated, with costs in this court and in the Appellate Division.

Desmond, Chief Judge (concurring).

As the Appellate Division dissenting opinion emphasizes, two scenes in this movie "forthrightly depict the fulfillment of acts of sexual intercourse between the principal characters." This order if affirmed would be (as I am persuaded after some research) the first court determination in recorded history holding to be nonobscene and constitutionally protected the portrayal on stage or a screen of the very sexual act itself. An affirmance would license the inclusion, in a stage play or a movie (or on television?), of actual scenes of intercourse and of other kinds of behavior always and everywhere considered to constitute indecency when carried on in public. The question presented on this appeal is, therefore, a new one not controlled by any earlier censorship decisions.

Lest we get too far away from the actual question, let us remind ourselves that the Regents did not refuse to license this picture but went no further than to direct the elimination therefrom of the two scenes of sexual congress. If we were to hold that this Regents' determination was illegal we would be saying that there is a constitutional right to include in a motion picture a direct acting out of coitus. Therefore, what is involved here is not the description in a book of sexual acts but the actual performance of those acts in public. To fornicate in public or to exhibit the sexual organs in public has been considered obscene conduct at least since 1663 in the case of *King* v. *Sedley* (1 Keble 620) wherein Sir Charles Sedley was convicted of obscenity because, standing on a London balcony, he exhibited himself in the nude to the populace. The ban on such exhibitions is probably as old as human society and it has never disappeared from our law.

When the Supreme Court held in *Times Film Corp.* v. *Chicago*, 365 U.S. 43, 81 S. Ct. 391, 5 L. Ed. 2d 403 that pre-exhibition administrative censorship of motion pictures was not necessarily unconstitutional, it was saying that there are still some kinds of movie portrayals that the State's police power may forbid. Inapplicable to an act of public indecency are the tests used for determining obscenity of a book, that is, predominantly appeal to prurient interest, going substantially beyond customary limits of candor and contemporary community standards, patent offensiveness and the necessity of taking the material as a whole and not condemning it by reason of isolated passages. It is unthinkable that a civilized community would permit actors to simulate sexual acts in a play or movie just because the play or movie is said by some critic or other to be an artistic work. Lewd conduct in public whether on the sidewalk, the stage, or the screeen has always been forbidden and controllable by police power statutes (see *Commonwealth* v. *Lambert*, 12 Allen 177, 94 Mass. 177, and Penal Law, art. 106). If that is not so there can be presented on Broadway under protection of the law a well-written, well-acted play about a prostitute including incidents where she is actually working at her trade and the defensive argument would be that these incidents were relevant and indeed essential to the development of a dramatic theme.

Respondent leans on an old and well-worn crutch when it argues that the film must be licensed since it is a "serious dramatic work" and an "artistic" piece of work, etc., etc. Such is a matter of critical choice, even though to some of us "A Stranger Knocks" looked like a mediocre movie, in no way notable except for the uniqueness of its departures from common decency. But, artistic or not, it contains in the two interdicted sequences, a cold, brazen affront to the accepted public moral code at its lowest possible level. All societal organizations, even civilization itself, depend for permanence on the fixing of minimal standard of conduct permissible in public. Judges do not have to qualify as dramatic critics before concluding that the loss to society from the cutting of these scenes of fornication is of very little consequence as weighed against the loss to public decency from their exhibition.

[3] Summing it up, we have here the bald question of whether the State of New York has power to require that this movie be not shown unless there are deleted therefrom the two scenes which "forthrightly depict" sexual intercourse.

I vote to reverse.

Scileppi, Judge (concurring).

I concur for reversal. The facts are not in dispute. The film is in evidence as an exhibit and was viewed by the court. There are two scenes in this motion picture which admittedly were intended to depict sexual intercourse. The claim, however, is that said acts were implied rather than demonstrated, and, further, that the picture has constitutional protection, not only because of its redeeming artistic value but also because the dominant theme of the film taken as a whole is not obscene.

[4] As I viewed the film, there is nothing implied—rather, the two principal characters unmistakably and realistically portray two persons having sexual intercourse, including the final stage—a climactic orgasm. Moreover, the dominant theme test is, I believe, inapplicable to motion pictures. The two offending scenes must be judged separately as would still photographs.

[5, 6] I would conclude that the graphic portrayal in a motion picture of sexual intercourse, illicit or otherwise, simulated or real, is obscene under any of the established legal standards (see, e.g., *Manual Enterprises* v. *Day*, 370 U.S. 478, 82 S. Ct. 1432, 8 L. Ed. 2d 639; *Roth* v. *United States*, 354 U.S. 476, 77 S. Ct. 1304, 1 L. Ed. 2d 1498; *People* v. *Richmond County News*, 9 N.Y. 2d 578, 216 N.Y.S. 2d 369, 175 N.E. 2d 681). That these scenes may have been artistically inspired is without significance. Whether matter is to be judged obscene requires the application of objective standards by the courts and not an expedition into subjective motivations (see *People* v. *Fritch*, 13 N.Y. 2d 119, 243 N.Y.S. 2d 1, 192 N.E. 2d 713). I am unwilling to contribute to the writing of "Finis" to the moral code of the vast majority of the people in our country by placing a stamp of approval on exhibitions of this nature.

Williams, Judge (concurring).

[7] The fundamental question is whether the State Board of Regents had the power to direct the deletion of the portrayal of two acts of sexual intercourse as "obscene." One argument that has been advanced by those who would display such scenes to the general public is that the censorial elimination would destroy a cultural and important social theme. If, in fact, the theme presents serious questions of social and moral problems, on a high cultural level (which I do not admit), that theme and those questions can as well be preserved by the substitution of other and less offensive types of portrayal. The acts need not actually be visibly depicted to impart to the public that the acts of intercourse had indeed taken place.

It is contended that the production must be considered as a whole, but to my mind its over-all merit is not such as to support scenes of obscenity. And the contention that the two scenes of visible sexual intercourse are necessary to maintain the high cultural level of the picture speaks little for the social value of the production "as a whole."

However, to revert to the original basic problem, I do not favor the actual physical portrayal of acts of sexual intercourse in public whether it be through the media of motion pictures, the theatre or otherwise. In my opinion the Board of Regents was amply justified in finding the eliminated scenes to be obscene and had complete authority to direct their deletion.

Opinion by Burke, J., in which Desmond, C.J., and Scileppi and Williams,* JJ., concur, each in a separate opinion in each of which the others concur.

Dye, Fuld and Van Voorhis, JJ., dissent and vote to affirm upon the majority memorandum opinion in the Appellate Division.

Order reversed, etc.

_____

* Designated pursuant to article VI (§ 2, subd. a) of the State Constitution in place of Judge Bergan, disqualified.

■ Evergreen Review, Inc., *Plaintiff,*

v.

William Cahn, District Attorney, County of Nassau, State of New York, *Defendant.*
No. 64–C–441.

United States District Court, E.D. New York.

June 11, 1964.

Rembar & Zolotar, New York City, for plaintiff; *Charles Rembar,* New York City, of counsel.

Jack B. Weinstein, County Atty., County of Nassau, for defendant; *Stephen W. Schlissel,* Deputy County Atty., *William D. Siegel,* Asst. County Atty., *Louis J. Lefkowitz,* Atty. Gen., of the State of New York, *Philip Kahaner,* Asst. Atty. Gen., of counsel, for defendant.

Before HAYS, Circuit Judge, and ROSLING and BARTELS, District Judges.

PER CURIAM.

The complaint in this action, brought under the Federal Civil Rights Law (42 U.S.C. § 1983), attacks as unconstitutional the seizure by the District Attorney of Nassau County under Sections 1141 and 1144 of the New York State Penal Law, McKinney's Consol. Laws, c. 40, of approximately 21,000 copies of the magazine *Evergreen Review* claimed to be obscene and pornographic. It seeks injunctive relief, damages and a declaratory judgment of unconstitutionality, and states that the action is to be tried and determined by a three-judge court pursuant to Sections 2281 and 2284, 28 U.S.C. Upon plaintiff's application the District Judge ordered defendant to show cause why he should not be directed to return the seized copies of plaintiff's magazine and be enjoined during the pendency of this action from interfering with the manufacture, distribution or sale thereof, and pending the determination of this application, temporarily restrained defendant from disposing of the copies of the magazine. During the argument before the three-judge court defendant filed a comprehensive motion to dismiss the complaint, dissolve the three-judge court and stay the proceedings until the outcome of certain criminal actions now pending in the State courts. The Attorney General of the State of New York also appeared and joined in defendant's motion. Subsequently, the defendant and the Attorney General filed briefs in support of this motion, which were duly considered.

Facts

On April 24, 1964, Albert C. Anderson, a detective in the Nassau County Police Department assigned to the District Attorney's Squad, submitted an affidavit[1] to a Nassau County Judge predicated upon information

[1] The text of the affidavit is as follows:

"I am a Detective in the Nassau County Police Department, assigned to the District Attorney's Squad.

"That on April 24th, 1964 a confidential informant related the following information to me at the Office of the District Attorney of the County of Nassau, New York.

"That my informant had been employed at the premises doing business as CORYDON M. JOHNSON CO. INC. which is located on Route 107, Hicksville Road, Bethpage, County of Nassau, New York, and was working in the department for final preparation of binding for magazines. My informant further stated to me that a magazine using the name *Evergreen* was being prepared for competition and that while working my informant observed black and white photographs in the magazine which showed nude human forms, possibly male and female, but reputed by fellow workers to be two females, and that the forms portrayed various poses and positions indicating sexual relations. My informant further stated having read portions of the printed material accompanying the aforesaid photographs and described the printed matter of consisting of four lettered obscene language.

"In addition my informant further stated to me of having seen such publications as *Playboy* and similar magazines and stated there was no comparison between them. Further that one of the bosses of the premises made the statement, in the presence of my informant, that three thousand of the magazines were to be completed in one day.

"My informant also stated that the aforesaid location has employed on a part time basis, students of high school age, who handle the magazine in question in connection with their work.

"Based upon the foregoing reliable information there is probable cause to believe that obscene, indecent and pornographic magazines, using the name *Evergreen* have been used or are possessed with intent to be used as the means of committing a crime, to wit: Violation of Section 1141 of the Penal Law of the State of New York and are being concealed within the premises doing business as CORYDON M. JOHNSON CO. INC. located at Route 107, Hicksville Road, Bethpage, County of Nassau, New York, occupied by JOHN DOE.

"WHEREFORE, I respectfully request that the Court issue a Warrant and Order of Seizure, in the form annexed, authorizing the search of the premises doing business as CORYDON M. JOHNSON CO. INC. located at Route 107, Hicksville Road, Bethpage, County of Nassau, New York and directing that if such property or evidence or any part thereof be found that it be seized and brought before the Court; together with such other and further relief that the Court may deem proper.

"No previous application in this matter has been made in this or any other Court or to any other Judge, Justice or Magistrate."

furnished him by "a confidential informant" employed on the premises of Corydon M. Johnson Co. Inc., where the magazine *Evergreen Review* was being bound, to the effect that she had informed Anderson that while working in the bindery she observed black and white photographs in the magazine *Evergreen Review* "which showed nude human forms, possibly male and female, but reputed by fellow workers to be two females, and that the forms portrayed various poses and positions indicating sexual relations," and that the printed material accompanying the photographs consisted of four lettered obscene language. "Based upon the foregoing reliable information," Anderson concludes, "there is probable cause to believe that obscene, indecent and pornographic magazines" are being used or possessed with intent to be used for the purpose of committing a crime in violation of Section 1141 of the Penal Law. Upon this affidavit the County Judge issued a warrant pursuant to Section 1144 of the Penal Law[2] that there was "probable cause for believing that certain property has been used or is possessed with intent to be used as the means of committing a crime, to wit: Violation of Section 1141 of the Penal Law of the State of New York," authorizing a search of the bindery and a seizure of such property which "may have been delivered for indecent, obscene and pornographic magazines using the name *Evergreen*" and to bring such property before the court. Pursuant thereto, seizure of approximately 21,000 copies of the magazine was made on the same day by three County detectives. According to the affidavit of the managing editor, said 21,000 copies together with 4,000 copies previously mailed to subscribers, comprised the entire print run of the April–May 1964 issue.

[1] After the seizure and the initiation of this action, Anderson in a subsequent affidavit, sworn to May 16, 1964 and filed in support of the defendant's motion, stated that after reading his affidavit the County Judge questioned him "with respect to the source and nature of my information" and then decided the affidavit was sufficient for a search warrant. He further explains therein how the seizure occurred and states that on April 24th he proceeded to the bindery with two other detectives and a search warrant and then seized two copies of the magazine and returned to the District Attorney's office with said copies but leaving the other detectives on the premises of the bindery. He adds that the District Attorney then read the magazine[3] and

ordered Anderson to draw up an information alleging violation of Section 1141 of the Penal Law and to present the same to a District Judge; that upon such presentation the same Nassau County Judge on the same day read the magazine and decided that it was pornographic and thereupon authorized the information against the plaintiff, its officers, Barney Rosset and Richard Seaver, and against Pegasus Press, Inc., the company printing the magazine, and its president, George Haralampoudis, and that warrants of arrest (not of seizure) were then issued by another judge against the alleged offenders. Upon execution of the arrest warrants, copies of the magazine were loaded upon vehicles and delivered to the Property Clerk of the Police Department. Anderson's affidavit of April 28th, filed before this action, states that upon execution of the April 24th warrant "Approximately Twenty One Thousand (21,000) bound and unbound copies of magazines known by the name *Evergreen*" were seized "under and pursuant to the warrant." Criminal actions are now pending in the District Court of Nassau County against George Haralampoudis and Pegasus Press, Inc.

In support of the defendant's motion to dismiss and for other relief, Henry P. Devine, Chief of the Law and Appeals Department of the Nassau County District Attorney's office, filed an affidavit, sworn to May 15, 1964, stating that he had read Anderson's affidavit of May 15th and that "The procedure he [Anderson] describes was the procedure used by the District Attorney's office of the County of Nassau in this case" and "conforms, generally, to the practice of the District Attorney's office when complaints are received by the members of the District Attorney's staff, or by members of the Police Department where notice is given to the District Attorney's office."

The issues before this Court are (1) whether plaintiff's demand for an injunction to restrain the enforcement by the defendant of Sections 1141 and 1144 of the New York Penal Law by seizure of 21,000 copies of plaintiff's magazine, falls within the jurisdiction of a three-judge court as provided by Section 2281 of Title 28 of the United States Code and (2) if so, whether such application of said sections based upon a judge's warrant prior to the determination of the issue of obscenity, violates plaintiff's constitutional rights under the First, Fourth and Fourteenth Amendments.

I

[2–5] The threshold question to be decided is whether the three-judge court was properly invoked. Since Section 2281 procedure dislocates the normal operations of the Federal courts, the statute must be strictly construed according to its terms. It is not to be invoked to restrain the lawless exercise of authority by a state official in a unique or particular case, *Phillips* v. *United States*, 1941, 312 U.S. 246, 61 S. Ct. 480, 85 L. Ed. 800; *Penagaricano* v. *Allen Corporation*, 1 Cir. 1959, 267 F. 2d 550; nor when the controversy involves merely the construction of a state law, see *Kesler* v. *Department of Public Safety*, etc., 1962, 369 U.S. 153, 82 S. Ct. 807, 7 L. Ed. 2d 641; nor when the constitutional question is no longer open, *Bailey* v. *Patterson*, 1962, 369 U.S. 31, 82 S. Ct. 549, 7 L. Ed. 2d 512. As

---

[2] Section 1144 provides in part that "A magistrate having jurisdiction to issue warrants in criminal cases, upon complaint that any person within his jurisdiction is offending against the provisions of this article, supported by oath or affirmation, must issue a warrant, directed to the sheriff or to any constable, marshal, or police officer within the county, directing him to search for, seize, and take possession of any of the articles specified in this article, in the possession of the person against whom complaint is made. The magistrate must immediately transmit every article seized by virtue of the warrant, to the district attorney of the county, who must, upon the conviction of the person from whose possession the same was taken, cause it to be destroyed, and the fact of such destruction to be entered upon the records of the court in which the conviction is had."

[3] A search warrant gains no support from investigations and observations after it is signed. *Tripodi* v. *Morgenthau*, S.D.N.Y. 1962, 213 S. Supp. 735; *United States* v. *Sims*, M.D. Tenn. 1962, 201 F. Supp. 405.

remarked in Ex parte Bransford, 1940, 310 U.S. 354, 60 S. Ct. 947, 84 L. Ed. 1249, it is necessary to distinguish between a petition which seeks an injunction on the ground of unconstitutionality of the result obtained by use of a statute not attacked as unconstitutional and a petition for an injunction on the ground of unconstitutionality of a statute as applied. Only the latter requires a three-judge court. Accordingly, if the complaint alleges a basis for equitable relief based upon unconstitutionality of a statute as applied, a single judge may not grant or withhold relief but must invoke the statutory court. *Idlewild Bon Voyage Liquor Corp.* v. *Epstein,* 1962, 370 U.S. 713, 82 S. Ct. 1294, 8 L. Ed. 2d 794. These criteria have certainly been satisfied here and the three-judge court was properly invoked.

II

In the interest of clarity, it should be stated that the plaintiff does not, in effect, assail the legislation insofar as it outlaws obscene and pornographic material and this issue is really not before this Court. In fact, the statute on its face is not unconstitutional. The attack in this case is against the power of New York State to adopt a scheme of enforcing the prohibitions of Section 1141 by the methods set forth in Section 1144 as applied by the District Attorney.

[6–11] The protection of freedom of press and speech provided by the First Amendment has by many classic decisions of the Supreme Court been made applicable to the States by the due process clause of the Fourteenth Amendment. See *Near* v. *State of Minnesota* ex rel. *Olson,* 1931, 283 U.S. 697, 51 S. Ct. 625, 75 L. Ed. 1357; *Smith* v. *People of State of California,* 1959, 361 U.S. 147, 80 S. Ct. 215, 4 L. Ed. 2d 205, rehearing denied, 1960, 361 U.S. 950, 80 S. Ct. 399, 4 L. Ed. 2d 383. In a similar manner the search and seizure prohibition of the Fourth Amendment has been applied to the States. *Mapp* v. *Ohio,* 1961, 367 U.S. 643, 81 S. Ct. 1684, 6 L. Ed. 2d 1081, rehearing denied, 1961, 368 U.S. 871, 82 S. Ct. 23, 7 L. Ed. 2d 72. Freedom of press and speech is jealously guarded and "The door barring federal and state intrusion into this area cannot be left ajar." *Roth* v. *United States,* 1957, 354 U.S. 476, at 488, 77 S. Ct. 1304, at 1311, 1 L. Ed. 2d 1498. The cases recognize that this freedom, however, is not absolute. For instance, obscenity "is not within the area of constitutionally protected speech or press." *Roth* v. *United States,* supra, 354 U.S. p. 485, 77 S. Ct. p. 1309; *Albert* v. *State of California,* 1957, 354 U.S. 476, 77 S. Ct. 1304, 1 L. Ed. 2d 1498; *Near* v. *State of Minnesota* ex rel. *Olson,* supra, and the publication of such material may be regulated by the States. In enforcing such regulations, the State is not limited "in resorting to various weapons in the armory of the law." *Kingsley Books* v. *Brown,* 1957, 354 U.S. 436, 441, 77 S. Ct. 1325, 1328, 1 L. Ed. 2d 1469.[4] But such regulations must provide safeguards to prevent the denial of freedom of speech and press since no State has the power to restrict the dissemination of non-obscene

---

[4] Narrowly upholding § 22–a of the Code of Criminal Procedure supplementing the existing criminal provisions by authorizing limited injunctive remedies under closely defined procedural safeguards.

publications. *Smith* v. *People of State of California,* supra.

[12] Very much in point is *Marcus* v. *Search Warrants of Property,* etc., 1961, 367 U.S. 717, 81 S. Ct. 1708, 6 L. Ed. 1127, where a number of books and publications allegedly obscene, were seized pursuant to warrants issued to peace officers under the Missouri statute by a magistrate upon a sworn complaint that obscene material was kept in certain places and commanding the officers to bring such material before the magistrate. The proceeding was *ex parte,* as here, and although the obscene material was not identified, a hearing was required to be held within twenty days for the purpose of determining whether the material was obscene. Holding that such mass seizure without any safeguards to protect legitimate expression was in violation of the Fourteenth Amendment which infected the entire proceeding, the court said:

" '* * * The separation of legitimate from illegitimate speech calls for * * * sensitive tools * * *.' Speiser v. Randall, 357 U.S. 513, 525, 78 S. Ct. 1332, 1342, 2 L. Ed. 2d 1460. It follows that, under the Fourteenth Amendment, a State is not free to adopt whatever procedures it pleases for dealing with obscenity as here involved without regard to the possible consequences for constitutionally protected speech."* (367 U.S. p. 731, 81 S. Ct. p. 1716.)

and again

"Kingsley Books does not support the proposition that the State may impose the extensive restraints imposed here on the distribution of these publications prior to an adversary proceeding on the issue of obscenity, irrespective of whether or not the material is legally obscene." (367 U.S. pp. 735–736, 81 S. Ct. p. 1718.)

In *Bantam Books, Inc.* v. *Sullivan,* 1963, 372 U.S. 58, 83 S. Ct. 631, 9 L. Ed. 2d 584, the Rhode Island Commission to Encourage Morality in Youth with power to recommend prosecutions, listed certain publications as objectionable and notified distributors of its adverse findings. The court held that this constituted suppression of the listed publications in violation of the Fourteenth Amendment, remarking that:

"There is no provision whatever for judicial superintendence before notices issue or even for judicial review of the Commission's determinations of objectionableness. The publisher or distributor is not even entitled to notice and hearing before his publications are listed by the Commission as objectionable." (372 U.S. p. 71, 83 S. Ct. p. 640.)

and that:

"Any system of prior restraints of expression comes to this Court bearing a heavy presumption against its constitutional validity." (372 U.S. p. 70, 83 S. Ct. p. 639.)

The New York State courts have held that even a proceeding under § 22–a of the Code of Criminal Procedure, which, in effect, is a civil proceeding addressed to the publication itself, does not permit extensive restraints prior to judicial scrutiny on the issue of obscenity, and that where such prior seizure has been made the proceeding is infected with an unconstitutional taint. *Stengel* v. *Smith*, 4th Dep't 1963, 18 A.D. 2d 458, 240 N.Y.S. 2d 200. Similarly, such a proceeding does not authorize an *ex parte* injunction. *Tenney* v. *Liberty News Distributors, Inc.*, 1st Dep't 1961, 13 A.D. 2d 770, 215 N.Y.S. 2d 663. It would be illogical and inconsistent to suppose that prior restraints upon distribution of publications would be unconstitutionally tainted under a § 22–a civil proceeding, yet be free from such taint under a § 1144 conventional criminal proceeding. Section 1144 is a search and seizure section providing for seizure of not only objectionable material but also of equipment producing and vehicles transporting such material[5] and applies to seizures subsequent, as well as prior, to conviction. Warrants involving seizure of equipment or gambling paraphernalia, or the like, are not in the same category as warrants involving the seizure of publications subject to the protection of the First Amendment. The issuance of the latter warrants raises the question not only of the possession and use of objectionable material but also of the application of proper standards to determine that probable cause exists that such material is objectionable. Cf., *Smith* v. *People of State of California*, supra, and *Marcus* v. *Search Warrants of Property*, etc., supra, 367 U.S. p. 731, 81 S. Ct. 1708.

Here no adversary proceeding or judicial scrutiny or superintendence of any kind was required before the issuance of the warrant. In fact, Section 1144 permits a warrant to be issued by a magistrate "upon complaint that any person within his jurisdiction is offending against the provisions of this article, supported by oath or affirmation * * *." Apparently the complainant determines whether or not the publication is obscene. Pursuant to this authority Anderson filed his complaint but he never saw a copy of the magazine and none was attached to the affidavit. Moreover, his complaint was not based upon his own information but it was based upon hearsay information of a woman worker who had read only portions of the magazine and who in one instance relied upon what was "reputed by fellow workers to be two females." This technique is the procedure that is generally followed by the District Attorney's office in Nassau County according to the affidavit of Henry P. Devine. A warrant based upon such a procedure leaves to the officer executing the warrant the determination of what is obscene, which technique was expressly condemned in Marcus. The Court finds that the State in applying Section 1144 in the manner above described, has used the power of search and seizure as a means of wholesale suppression of allegedly obscene and pornographic material prior to any adversary proceeding or a judicial scrutiny or superintendence so necessary for the protection of non-obscene material. Such application is a clear violation of the Fourteenth Amendment.

[13] The defendant has urged that this Court abstain from taking jurisdiction of the case because the plaintiff has adequate remedies in the State court and accordingly contends that the proceeding should be stayed pending the determination of the criminal proceedings now before the State court. There is no merit to this contention. That the State law affords judicial remedies subsequent to seizure, would not save the statute. Such a proceeding was available and pending under the Missouri statute challenged in Marcus. "Moreover, the availability of a judicial remedy for abuses in the system of licensing still leaves that system one of previous restraint which, in the field of free speech and press, we have held inadmissible." *Cantwell* v. *State of Connecticut*, 1940, 310 U.S. 296, 306, 60 S. Ct. 900, 904, 84 L. Ed. 1213; see also *McNeese* v. *Board of Education for Community Unit School District 187*, 1963, 373 U.S. 668, 83 S. Ct. 1433, 10 L. Ed. 2d 622; *Monroe* v. *Pape*, 1961, 365 U.S. 167, 81 S. Ct. 473, 5 L. Ed. 2d 492.

III

As to the remedy, this Court will abstain from enjoining the prosecution of the criminal actions pending in the State courts and from granting plaintiff's request for declaration that Penal Law, § 1141 may not be constitutionally applied to this publication. The latter question is not before this Court and remains to be determined. However, the seizure of plaintiff's publication on April 24th under Section 1144 as applied, being a violation of the Fourteenth Amendment, which infected the entire proceeding, the plaintiff is entitled to an order (1) requiring the defendant to return all copies of the seized publication and (2) enjoining the defendant from any future interference with the distribution of the No. 32 issue of the *Evergreen Review* prior to a judicial determination of its obscenity. See *Louisiana News Company* v. *Dayries*, E.D. La. 1960, 187 F. Supp. 241; *Stengel* v. *Smith*, supra. The remaining claims set forth in the complaint and in 1(b) of defendant's motion to dismiss the complaint are hereby remanded to Judge Rosling for determination. See 3 Moore, Federal Practice § 18.07[2].

Settle order on two days' notice.

---

[5] Section 1141–c of the New York Penal Law.

■ A Quantity of Copies of Books *et al., Appellants,*
v.
State of Kansas.

On Appeal From the Supreme Court of Kansas.

June 22, 1964.

Mr. Justice Brennan announced the judgment of the Court and delivered an opinion in which The Chief Justice, Mr. Justice White, and Mr. Justice Goldberg join.

Under a Kansas statute authorizing the seizure of allegedly obscene books before an adversary determination of their obscenity, and after that determination, their destruction by burning or otherwise,[1] the Attorney General of Kansas obtained an order from the District Court of Geary County directing the sheriff of the county to seize and impound, pending hearing, copies of certain paperback novels at the place of business of P–K News Service, Junction City, Kansas. After hear-

ing, the court entered a second order directing the sheriff to destroy the 1,715 copies of 31 novels which had been seized. The Kansas Supreme Court held that the procedures met constitutional requirements and affirmed the District Court's order. 191 Kan. 13, 379 P. 2d 254. We noted probable jurisdiction, 375 U.S. 919. We reverse. We hold that the procedures followed in issuing the warrant for the seizure of the books, and authorizing their impounding pending hearing were constitutionally insufficient because they did not adequately safeguard against the suppression of nonobscene books. Therefore we do not reach, and intimate no view upon the appellants' contention that the Kansas courts erred in holding that the novels are obscene.

Section 4 of the Kansas statute requires the filing of a verified Information stating only that "upon information and belief . . . there is [an] . . . obscene book . . . located within his county." The State Attorney General went further, however, and filed an Information identifying by title 59 novels, and stating that "each of said books [has] been published as 'This is an original Nightstand Book.'" He also filed with the Information copies of seven novels published under that caption, six of which were named by title in the Information; particular passages in the seven novels were marked with penciled notations or slips of paper. Although also not expressly required by the statute, the district judge, on application of the Attorney General, conducted a 45-minute *ex parte* inquiry during which he "scrutinized" the seven books; at the conclusion of this examination, he stated for the record that they "appear to be obscene literature as defined" under the Kansas statute "and give this Court reasonable grounds to believe that any paperbacked publication carrying the following: 'This is an original Night Stand Book' would fall within the same category . . . ." He issued a warrant which authorized the sheriff to seize only the particular novels identified by title in the Information. When the warrant was executed on the date it issued, only 31 of the titles were found on P–K's premises. All copies of such titles, however, 1,715 books in all, were seized and impounded. At the hearing held 10 days later pursuant to a notice included in the warrant, P–K made a motion to quash the Information and the warrant on the ground, among others, that the procedure preceding the seizure was constitutionally deficient. The claim was that by failing first to afford P–K a hearing on the question whether the books were obscene, the pro-

---

[1] The statute is Kan. Gen. Stat. § 21–1102 (Supp. 1961). Section 1 constitutes the selling or distribution of obscene materials (obscenity is defined in § 1 (b)) a criminal misdemeanor punishable by fine or imprisonment or both. Section 4 provides for the search and seizure procedure here involved:

"Whenever any district, county, common pleas, or city court judge or justice of the peace shall receive an information or complaint, signed and verified upon information and belief by the county attorney or the attorney general, stating there is any prohibited lewd, lascivious or obscene book, magazine, newspaper, writing, pamphlet, ballad, printed paper, print, picture, motion pictures, drawing, photograph, publication or other thing, as set out in section 1 [21–1102] (*a*) of this act, located within his county, it shall be the duty of such judge to forthwith issue his search warrant directed to the sheriff or any other duly constituted peace officer to seize and bring before said judge or justice such a prohibited item or items. Any peace officer seizing such item or items as hereinbefore described shall leave a copy of such warrant with any manager, servant, employee or other person appearing or acting in the capacity of exercising any control over the premises where such item or items are found or, if no person is there found, such warrant may be posted by said peace officer in a conspicuous place upon the premises where found and said warrant shall serve as notice to all interested persons of a hearing to be had at a time not less than ten (10) days after such seizure. At such hearing, the judge or justice issuing the warrant shall determine whether or not the item or items so seized and brought before him pursuant to said warrant were kept upon the premises where found in violation of any of the provisions of this act. If he shall so find, he shall order such item or items to be destroyed by the sheriff or any duly constituted peace officer by burning or otherwise, at such time as such judge shall order, and satisfactory return thereof made to him: *Provided, however,* Such item or items shall not be destroyed so long as they may be needed as evidence in any criminal prosecution."

cedure "operates as a prior restraint on circulation and dissemination of books" in violation of the constitutional restrictions against abridgment of freedom of speech and press. The motion was denied, and following a final hearing held about seven weeks after the seizure (the hearing date was continued on motion of P–K), the court held that all 31 novels were obscene and ordered the sheriff to stand ready to destroy the 1,715 copies on further order.

The steps taken beyond the express requirements of the statute were thought by the Attorney General to be necessary under our decision in *Marcus v. Search Warrant*, 367 U.S. 717, decided a few weeks before the Information was filed. *Marcus* involved a proceeding under a strikingly similar Missouri search and seizure statute and implementing rule of court. See 367 U.S. 719, at notes 2, 3. In *Marcus* the warrant gave the police virtually unlimited authority to seize any publications which they considered to be obscene, and was issued on a verified complaint lacking any specific description of the publications to be seized, and without prior submission of any publications whatever to the judge issuing the warrant. We reversed a judgment directing the destruction of the copies of 100 publications held to be obscene, holding that, even assuming that they were obscene, the procedures leading to their condemnation were constitutionally deficient for lack of safeguards to prevent suppression of nonobscene publications protected by the Constitution.

It is our view, and we hold that since the warrant here authorized the sheriff to seize all copies of the specified titles, and since P–K was not afforded a hearing on the question of the obscenity even of the seven novels before the warrant issued, the procedure was likewise constitutionally deficient.[2] This is the teaching of *Kingsley Books, Inc. v. Brown*, 354 U.S. 436. See *Marcus*, at pp. 734–738. The New York injunctive procedure there sustained does not afford *ex parte* relief but postpones all injunctive relief until "both sides have had an opportunity to be heard." *Tenney v. Liberty News Distributors*, 13 App. Div. 2d 770, 215 N.Y.S. 2d 663. In *Marcus* we explicitly said that *Kingsley Books* "does not support the proposition that the State may impose the extensive restraints imposed here on the distribution of these publications prior to an adversary proceeding on the issue of obscenity, irrespective of whether or not the material is legally obscene." 367 U.S. 735–736. A seizure of all copies of the named titles is indeed more repressive than an injunction preventing further sale of the books. State regulation of obscenity must "conform to procedures that will ensure against the curtailment of constitutionally protected expression, which is often separated from obscenity only by a dim and uncertain line." *Bantam Books, Inc. v. Sullivan*, 372 U.S. 58, 66; the Constitution requires a procedure "designed to focus searchingly on the question of obscenity," *Marcus*, p. 732. We therefore conclude that in not first affording P–K an adversary hearing, the procedure leading to the seizure order was constitutionally deficient. What we said of the Missouri procedure, *id.*, at 736–

737, also fits the Kansas procedure employed to remove these books from circulation:

"... there is no doubt that an effective restraint— indeed the most effective restraint possible—was imposed prior to hearing on the circulation of the publications in this case, because all copies on which the [sheriff] could lay [his] hands were physically removed ... from the premises of the wholesale distributor. An opportunity ... to circulate the [books] ... and then raise the claim of nonobscenity by way of defense to a prosecution for doing so was never afforded these appellants because the copies they possessed were taken away. Their ability to circulate their publications was left to the chance of securing other copies, themselves subject to mass seizure under other such warrants. The public's opportunity to obtain the publications was thus determined by the distributor's readiness and ability to outwit the police by obtaining and selling other copies before they in turn could be seized. In addition to its unseemliness, we do not believe that this kind of enforced competition affords a reasonable likelihood that nonobscene publications, entitled to constitutional protection, will reach the public. A distributor may have every reason to believe that a publication is constitutionally protected and will be so held after judicial hearing, but his belief is unavailing as against the contrary [ex parte] judgment [pursuant to which the sheriff] ... seizes it from him."

It is no answer to say that obscene books are contraband, and that consequently the standards governing searches and seizures of allegedly obscene books should not differ from those applied with respect to narcotics, gambling paraphernalia and other contraband. We rejected that proposition in *Marcus*. We said, 367 U.S., at 730–731:

"The Missouri Supreme Court's assimilation of obscene literature to gambling paraphernalia or other contraband for purposes of search and seizure does not therefore answer the appellants' constitutional claim, but merely restates the issue whether obscenity may be treated in the same way. The authority to the police officers under the warrants issued in this case, broadly to seize 'obscene ... publications,' poses problems not raised by the warrants to seize 'gambling implements' and 'all intoxicating liquors' involved in the cases cited by the Missouri Supreme Court. 334 S.W. 2d, at 125. For the use of these warrants implicates questions whether the procedures leading to their issuance and surrounding their execution were adequate to avoid suppression of constitutionally protected publications. '... [T]he line between speech unconditionally guaranteed and speech which may legitimately be regulated, suppressed, or punished is finely drawn. ... The separation of legitimate from illegitimate speech calls for ... sensitive tools ....' Speiser v. Randall, 357 U.S. 513, 525. It follows that, under the Fourteenth Amendment, a State is not free to adopt whatever procedures it pleases for dealing with obscenity as here involved without regard to the possible consequences for constitutionally protected speech." See also Smith v. California, 361 U.S. 147, 152–153.*

---

[2] P–K News Service also asserts that its constitutional right against unreasonable searches and seizures was violated. Our result makes it unnecessary to pass upon this contention.

Nor is the order under review saved because, after all 1,715 copies were seized and removed from circulation, P–K News Service was afforded a full hearing on the question of the obscenity of the novels. For if seizure of books precedes an adversary determination of their obscenity, there is danger of abridgment of the right of the public in a free society to unobstructed circulation of nonobscene books. *Bantam Books* v. *Sullivan, supra; Roth* v. *United States,* 354 U.S. 476; *Marcus* v. *Search Warrant, supra; Smith* v. *California, supra.* Here, as in *Marcus,* "since a violation of the Fourteenth Amendment infected the proceedings, in order to vindicate appellants' constitutional rights," 367 U.S., at 738, the judgment resting on a finding of obscenity must be reversed.

Reversed.

Opinion of Mr. Justice Black, with whom Mr. Justice Douglas joins.

The Kansas State Court judgment here under review orders that 1,715 copies of 31 novels be burned or otherwise destroyed. This book-burning judgment was based upon findings by the trial judge that "the core [of the books] would seem to be that of sex, with the plot, if any, being subservient thereto," that the "dominant purpose [of the books] was calculated to effectively incite sexual desires" and that "they would have this effect on the average person residing in this community . . . ." Relying on these findings and this Court's holding in *Roth* v. *United States,* 354 U.S. 476, the trial court held that the books "are not entitled to the . . . protection" of the First Amendment to the Constitution. The State Supreme Court affirmed on the same grounds.

This Court now reverses. I concur in the judgment of reversal but do not find it necessary to consider the procedural questions. Compare *Marcus* v. *Search Warrant,* 367 U.S. 717, 738 (concurring opinion). The Kansas courts may have been right to rely upon the Court's *Roth* holding in ordering these books burned or otherwise destroyed. For reasons stated in the *Roth* case in a dissent by Mr. Justice Douglas, 354 U.S., at 508, in which I joined, I think the *Roth* case was wrongly decided. It is my belief, as stated in that dissent by Mr. Justice Douglas, in my concurring opinions in *Smith* v. *California,* 361 U.S. 147, 155, and *Kingsley International Pictures Corp.* v. *Regents,* 360 U.S. 684, 690, and in my dissent in *Beauharnais* v. *Illinois,* 343 U.S. 250, 267, which Mr. Justice Douglas joined, that the Kansas statute ordering the burning of these books is in plain violation of the unequivocal prohibition of the First Amendment, made applicable to the States by the Fourteenth, against "abridging the freedom of speech, or of the press."

Because of my belief that both *Roth* and the *Beauharnais* draw blueprints showing how to avoid the First Amendment's guarantee of freedoms of speech and press, I would overrule both those cases as well as reverse the judgment here.

Mr. Justice Stewart, concurring in the judgment.

If this case involved hard-core pornography, I think

the procedures which were followed would be constitutionally valid, at least with respect to the material which the judge "scrutinized." This case is not like *Marcus* v. *Search Warrant,* 367 U.S. 717, where, as the Court notes, "the warrant gave the police virtually unlimited authority to seize any publications which they considered to be obscene, and was issued on a verified complaint lacking any specific description of the publications to be seized, and without prior submission of any publications whatever to the judge issuing the warrant." But the books here involved were not hard-core pornography. Therefore, I think Kansas could not by any procedure constitutionally suppress them, any more than Kansas could constitutionally make their sale or distribution a criminal act. See *Jacobellis* v. *Ohio.* (Stewart, J., concurring).

Mr. Justice Harlan, whom Mr. Justice Clark joins, dissenting.

Insofar as the judgment of the Court rests on the view of three of my Brethren that a State cannot constitutionally ban on grounds of obscenity the books involved in this case, I dissent on the basis of the views set out in my opinion in *Jacobellis* v. *Ohio.* It is quite plain that these so-called "novels" have "been reasonably found in state judicial proceedings to treat with sex in a fundamentally offensive manner" and that the State's criteria for judging their obscenity are rational.

I also disagree with the position taken in the opinion of my Brother Brennan that this Kansas procedure unconstitutionally abridged freedom of expression in that the search warrant (1) authorized seizure of *all* copies of the books in question and (2) was issued without an adversary hearing on the issue of their obsceneness. In my opinion that position is inconsistent with the thrust of prior cases and serves unnecessarily to handicap the States in their efforts to curb the dissemination of obscene material.[1]

---

[1] The books before the district judge at the *ex parte* hearing were:

The Sinning Season	*Sin Song*
Backstage Sinner	*The Wife-Swappers*
Lesbian Love	*Sex Circus*
Sin Hotel	

The front cover of *The Wife-Swappers* is typical of the 31 books seized which, with the exception of *Backstage Sinner,* included all those examined by the judge. Above a highly suggestive pictorial representation, the prospective reader is told that "Members of this Lust Club Had a Different Woman Every Night!" At the bottom of the cover it is stated that "This is an Original Nightstand Book." The back cover relates in more detail the book's contents:

"PROBLEMS IN BED . . . were no problems at all to the members of Eastport's highly secret suburban switch club. Who could have problems with eight beautiful, different women to choose from? For that was the lot of each man in this fantastic sex-prowling group. Eight of the most lusty, passionate women in the town, each with her different desires, her peculiar sex habits. And with eight women so easy to reach, it was inevitable that there would be trouble . . . for the wives were very different: one was a lesbian, one was a nymphomaniac, one a masochist,

I.

The two cases on which MR. JUSTICE BRENNAN'S opinion almost entirely relies are *Kingsley Books, Inc.* v. *Brown*, 354 U.S. 436, and *Marcus* v. *Search Warrant*, 367 U.S. 717.

In *Kingsley Books*, appellants challenged the constitutionality of a New York statute that authorized the State Supreme Court to enjoin the sale and distribution of obscene prints and articles. A complaint prayed for an injunction against the further distribution of certain allegedly obscene paperback books and for the destruction by the sheriff of all copies in the appellants' possession. Appellants were ordered to show cause within four days why an injuction *pendente lite* should not be issued that would preclude distribution of the books. Although the code of criminal procedure provided that anyone sought to be enjoined was entitled to a trial one day after the joinder of issue, appellants consented to the temporary injunction and delayed bringing the matter to issue. When a hearing on the question of obscenity was finally had, the books were found to be obscene; their distribution was enjoined and their destruction ordered. This Court upheld the New York procedure, stating:

---

another frigid, and still another erupting like a bomb at the mere touch of a man. They lived a lust-ridden, lightning-fast, terrifying and sex-crammed . . . GAME OF WIFE-SWAPPING!"

The front page of the book contains the following:

"LUST-SATED COUPLES

"In eight Eastport homes the doors opened and eight husbands returned. It's traditional in suburbia for the good wife to meet her spouse with a shaker of martinis, but it was different with these eight particular Eastport couples. These eight husbands came home on a Sunday morning and their eight wives were waiting in bed, soft and warm and sated . . . smelling of other men. And the husbands were drained and tired . . . from other women. Later in the day they would all awake, lounge around the house, eat lightly, speak softly . . . and think of the night before . . .

"These Eight Couples are
Members Of A Wife-Swapping
Mate-Switching Sex Club
So Vile It will Stun You."

These inducements are a fair indication of the actual contents of the book. The book's back page advertises the titles of some other Nightstand Books. The other books seized were:

Born for Sin	*Isle of Sin*
No Longer a Virgin	*Orgy Town*
Sin Girls	*Lover*
Miami Call Girl	*Sex Spy*
Passion Trap	*Trailer Trollop*
Sex Jungle	*Sin Cruise*
The Lustful Ones	*Flesh Is My Undoing*
Sex Model	*Malay Mistress*
The Lecher	*Love Nest*
Lust Goddess	*Seeds of Sin*
Sin Camp	*Passion Slave*
$20 Lust	*The Sinful Ones*
Convention Girl	

Each of the seized books contains exactly 192 pages, the text in each running from page 5 to pages 189, 190, 191, or 192.

"*Authorization of an injunction* pendente lite, *as part of this scheme, during the period within which the issue of obscenity must be promptly tried and adjudicated in an adversary proceeding for which '[a]dequate notice, judicial hearing, [and] fair determination' are assured, . . . is a safeguard against frustration of the public interest in effectuating judicial condemnation of obscene matter.*" P. 440.

The State was not, we held, limited to the criminal process in attempting to protect its citizens against the circulation of pornography; it "is not for this Court thus to limit the State in resorting to various weapons in the armory of the law." P. 441. The Court pointed out that "Criminal enforcement and the proceeding under § 22–a interfere with a book's solicitation of the public precisely at the same stage," p. 442, that the threat of criminal penalties may be as effective a deterrent against expression as an injunctive civil remedy, and that an injunction against someone to forebear selling specific books may be a less stringent restraint on his freedom of expression than sending him to jail. *Near* v. *Minnesota*, 283 U.S. 697, was distinguished on the ground that the New York statute dealt with obscenity rather than matters deemed to be derogatory to a public officer and imposed no direct restraint on materials not yet published.

In *Marcus* v. *Search Warrant* warrants to seize books were issued solely on the judgment of a peace officer regarding the obscenity of certain books without any independent examination by a judicial official; the warrants authorized seizure of books by officers other than the one who had signed the complaints and in effect gave *carte blanche* to these officers to seize anything they considered obscene at the named wholesale establishment and newsstands, whether or not the material had been so evaluated by anyone prior to the issuance of the warrants. After recounting the historical distrust for systems sanctioning sweeping seizures of materials believed to be offensive to the state, the Court held that "Missouri's procedures as applied in this case lacked the safeguards which due process demands to assure non-obscene material the constitutional protection to which it is entitled." P. 731. Relevant to this conclusion were the absence of any "scrutiny by the judge of the materials considered by the complainant to be obscene," p. 732, and the power of the enforcing officers under the warrants to make *ad hoc* decisions regarding obscenity although "They were provided with no guide to the exercise of informed discretion, because there was no step in the procedure before seizure designed to focus searchingly on the question of obscenity." P. 732. *Kingsley Books* was distinguished on the grounds that in that case: (1) the court "could exercise an independent check on the judgment of the prosecuting authority at a point before any restraint took place"; (2) the restraints "ran only against the named publication"; (3) no extensive restraints were imposed before an adversary proceeding; and (4) the New York code required decision within two days of the trial on the obscenity question, pp. 735–737.

In my view, the present case is governed by the principles serving to sustain the New York procedure involved in *Kingsley Books* rather than those which condemned that followed by Missouri in *Marcus*.

(1) Although the Kansas statute does not in terms require an independent judicial examination of allegedly obscene materials before authorization of seizure, the Kansas officials in this case conformed their procedures to what they believed to be the requirements of *Marcus*. The information included the titles of 59 "Original Nightstand Books." Seven of these were delivered to the district judge at 5 P.M., three hours before the 45-minute *ex parte* hearing at which the judge concluded that there were reasonable grounds to believe that all 59 books were obscene.[2] Because of the nature of the seven books examined by the judge, he could fairly reach a judgment that the remaining books were of the same character. (See note 1, *supra*.)[3]

(2) In this case, unlike *Marcus*, the officers had no discretion as to which books they might seize but could take only books specifically designated by their titles.

(3) It is true that the Kansas procedure, like that in *Marcus*, imposed a restraint before an adversary proceeding, but it would be highly artificial to consider this the controlling difference between *Kingsley Books* and *Marcus*. While New York statute allows an almost immediate hearing on the obscenity issue, it would be unrealistic to suppose that most persons who allegedly have or sell obscene materials will be able to prepare for such a hearing in four days, the time between the issuance of the complaint and the *pendente lite* injunction in *Kingsley Books*. In practical terms, therefore, the New York scheme, as approved by this Court, does contemplate restraint before a hearing on the merits. Although the Court was uncertain in *Kingsley Books* whether New York would punish for contempt one who disseminated materials in disobedience of the temporary injunction if such materials were ultimately held to be not covered by the statute or constitutionally protected, it could hardly have failed to recognize the patently chilling effect such an injunction would have on the dissemination of named materials. In pragmatic terms then, the nature of the restraint imposed by the Kansas statute is not in a constitutionally significant sense different from that sustained in *Kingsley Books*.[4]

(4) The Kansas statute does not contain the safeguards for speedy disposition that were present in *Kingsley Books*, but the State Attorney General has unequivocally acknowledged the necessity of administering that statute in light of the constitutional requirements of *Marcus*. In this instance the warrant which was issued July 27 for seizure of the books contained a notice that a hearing on the merits was set for August 7. Eleven days is certainly not an undue delay; indeed, it is difficult to imagine a defense being prepared in less time. The district judge's decision was issued four days after the termination of the trial on the obscenity question, which had been postponed because of motions made by appellants. On the basis of this case, we have every reason to believe that the prosecuting authorities and judges of Kansas are aware that prehearing restraints may not be magnified by delay and we have no reason to think the Kansas statute will be applied in a manner any less fair in this regard to those restricted than the provision of the New York code sustained in *Kingsley Books*.

II.

Since there may be lurking in my Brother Brennan's opinion the unarticulated premise that this Kansas procedure is impermissible because it operates as a "prior restraint," I deem it appropriate to make a few observations on that score. The doctrine of prior restraint is not a "self-wielding sword" or a "talismanic test" (*Kingsley Books, supra*, at 441) but one whose application in any instance requires "particularistic analysis." *Id.*, at 442; Freund, The Supreme Court and Civil Liberties, 4 Vand. L. Rev. 533, 539; cf. *Times Film Corp.* v. *Chicago*, 365 U.S. 43. That the Kansas procedure, as applied in this case, falls within permissible limits of the Fourteenth Amendment will appear from contrasting some of the reasons for the historic distrust in common law jurisprudence of any kind of censorship of writings, see *Near* v. *Minnesota*, 283 U.S. 697, 713–718,[5] with what was done here.

In the typical censorship situation material is brought as a matter of course before some administrative authority, who then decides on its propriety. This means that the State establishes an administrative structure whereby all writings are reviewed before publication. By contrast, if the State uses its penal system to punish expression outside permissible bounds, the State does not comprehensively review any form of expression; it merely considers after the event utterances it has reason to suppose may be prohibited. The breadth of its review

---

[2] The record does not show how much attention the judge gave to these books before the hearing.

[3] No one has asserted that any of these books has literary merit. The district judge contrasted them to books in which sex is subservient to the plot: "[I]n the books in question, the core would seem to be that of sex, with the plot, if any, being subservient thereto." The State Supreme Court, more succinctly, but with equal truth, stated, "They are trash." The essence of these books may be ascertained with great celerity, so replete are they with passages descriptive of sexual activities running the gamut from ordinary intercourse to lesbianism, sadism, public displays, and group orgies, and so lacking are they of any other content. Moreover, they are so standardized that a judge's estimate concerning the contents of absent books from an examination of seven books before him could be almost as surefire as a similar estimate of the character of unseen Mickey Mouse comic books based on a perusal of seven issues.

[4] What the courts of the State have subsequently said in dictum about the operation of the New York statute is hardly relevant to this Court's understanding of the import of the section at the time of *Kingsley Books*, and the constitutional principle for which that case stands. At any rate, *Tenney* v.

Liberty News Distributors, 13 App. Div. 2d 770, states only that an injunction cannot be issued *ex parte*; this certainly does not mean that a court is forbidden to do what it did in *Kingsley Books*, grant an injunction before there is an adversary hearing on the *obscenity issue itself*. Surely the right to be heard on the subsidiary question of the wisdom granting a *pendente lite* injunction would not save an otherwise unconstitutional scheme; and the failure to accord such a right does not render the Kansas procedure unconstitutional if it is otherwise valid.

[5] See generally, *e.g.*, Emerson, The Doctrine of Prior Restraint, 20 Law and Contemporary Problems 648 (1955); Freund, The Supreme Court and Civil Liberties, 4 Van. L. Rev. 533, 537–545 (1951).

of expression is therefore much narrower and the danger that protected expression will be repressed is less. The operation of the Kansas statute resembles the operation of a penal rather than a licensing law in this regard since books are not as a matter of course subjected to prepublication state sanctioning but are reviewed only when the State has reason to believe they are obscene.

There are built-in elements in any system of licensing or censorship, the tendency of which is to encourage restrictions of expression. The State is not compelled to make an initial decision to pursue a course of action, since the original burden is on the citizen to bring a piece of writing before it. The censor is a part of the executive structure, and there is at least some danger that he will develop an institutionalized bias in favor of censorship because of his particular responsibility. In a criminal proceeding, however, the burden is on the State to act, the decision-maker belongs to an independent branch of the government, and neither a judge nor a juror has any personal interest in active censorship. The Kansas practice is thus analogous to a system of penal sanctions rather than censorship in all three of these respects.

One danger of a censorship system is that the public may never be aware of what an administrative agent refuses to permit to be published or distributed. A penal sanction assures both that some overt thing has been done by the accused and that the penalty is imposed for an activity that is not concealed from the public. In this case, the information charged that obscene books were possessed or kept for sale and distribution; presumably such possession, if knowing, could, as a constitutional matter, support a criminal prosecution. The procedure adopted by the State envisions that a full judicial hearing will be held on the obscenity issue. Finally, the federal system makes it highly unlikely that the citizenry of one State will be unaware of the kind of material that is being restricted by its own government when there is great divergence among the policies of the various States and a high degree of communication across state lines. Cf. my opinion in *Roth* v. *United States*, 354 U.S. 476, 496, and my dissenting opinion in *Jacobellis* v. *Ohio*, decided today.

Any system of censorship, injunction, or seizure may of course to some extent serve to trammel, by delaying distribution or otherwise, freedom of expression; yet so may the threat of criminal prosecution, as this Court noted in *Kingsley Books*. The bringing of a criminal charge may result in a cessation of distribution during litigation, since even an accused relatively confident of the unlikelihood or impermissibility of conviction may well refuse to take the added risk of further criminal penalties that might obtain if he guesses wrong and continues to disseminate the questionable materials. More fundamentally, the delay argument seems artificial in the context of this case and in the area of obscenity generally. Both the incentive for officials to promote delay and the adverse consequences of delay are considerably less in this area than in the field of political and social expression. If controversial political writings attack those in power, government officials may benefit from suppression although society may suffer. In the area of obscenity, there is less chance that decision-makers will have interests which may affect their estimate of what is constitutionally protected and what is not. It is vital to the operation of democratic government that the citizens have facts and ideas on important issues before them. A delay of even a day or two may be of crucial importance in some instances. On the other hand, the subject of sex is of constant but rarely particularly topical interest.[6] Distribution of *Ulysses* may be thought by some to be more important for society than distribution of the daily newspaper, but a one- or two-month delay in circulation of the former would be of small significance whereas such a delay might be effective suppression of the latter.

Finally, it may be said that any system of civil enforcement allows expression to be limited without the strict safeguards of criminal procedures and rules of evidence. The contention that such protections are essential is perhaps weaker in the area of obscenity than with regard to other kinds of expression for reasons outlined above. A substantial restriction on freedom of expression is undoubtedly provided by civil remedies for defamation, and there is no reason for foreclosing a State from reasonable civil means of preventing the distribution of obscene materials.

The opinion of MR. JUSTICE BRENNAN, in my view, straitjackets the legitimate attempt of Kansas to protect what it considers an important societal interest. It does so in contradiction of a sensible reading of the precedents and without contributing in any genuine way to the furtherance of freedom of expression that our Constitution protects.

For the foregoing reason I would affirm the judgment of the Kansas Supreme Court.

---

[6] Reasons such as these may explain in part why the Court in *Near* v. *Minnesota*, 283 U.S. 697, 716, apparently believed that the whole prior restraint doctrine was inapplicable in the area of obscenity.

■ Grove Press, Inc.,

v.

Gerstein, State Attorney, *et al.*

ON PETITION FOR WRIT OF CERTIORARI TO THE DISTRICT COURT OF APPEAL OF FLORIDA, THIRD DISTRICT.

No. 718. Decided June 22, 1964.
Certiorari granted and judgment reversed.
Reported below: 156 So. 2d 537.

Edward de Grazia and *Richard Yale Feder* for petitioner.

James W. Kynes, Attorney General of Florida, *Leonard R. Mellon,* Assistant Attorney General, and *Glenn C. Mincer* for respondents.

PER CURIAM.

The petition for a writ of certiorari is granted, and the judgment is reversed. MR. JUSTICE BLACK and MR. JUS-TICE DOUGLAS would reverse for the reasons stated in the opinion of MR. JUSTICE BLACK in *Jacobellis* v. *Ohio, ante,* p. 196. MR. JUSTICE BRENNAN and MR. JUSTICE GOLD-BERG would reverse for the reasons stated in the opinion of MR. JUSTICE BRENNAN in *Jacobellis, ante,* p. 184. MR. JUSTICE STEWART would reverse for the reasons stated in his opinion in *Jacobellis, ante,* p. 197. THE CHIEF JUSTICE, MR. JUSTICE CLARK, MR. JUSTICE HARLAN, and MR. JUSTICE WHITE are of the opinion that certiorari should be denied.

The People of the State of Illinois, *Defendant in Error,*

v.

Lenny Bruce, *Plaintiff in Error.*
No. 37902.

Supreme Court of Illinois.
Nov. 24, 1964.

Maurice Rosenfield and *Harry Kalven, Jr.,* and *William R. Ming, Jr.,* Chicago, for plaintiff in error.

William G. Clark, Atty. Gen., Springfield, and *Daniel P. Ward,* State's Atty., Chicago (Fred G. Leach and E. Michael O'Brien, Asst. Attys. Gen., and Elmer C. Kis-sane, William J. Martin, and James R. Thompson, Asst. State's Attys., of counsel), for defendant in error.

PER CURIAM.

By an earlier opinion filed June 18, 1964, this court affirmed the judgment of the circuit court of Cook County entered upon a jury verdict finding the defendant herein guilty of giving an obscene performance violative of section 11–20 of the Criminal Code of 1961. (Ill. Rev. Stat. 1961, chap. 38, par. 11–20.) On June 22, 1964, the Supreme Court of the United States decided *Jacobellis* v. *State of Ohio,* 378 U.S. 184, 84 S. Ct. 1676, 12 L. Ed. 2d 793, in which a movie allegedly obscene was held not to be so. On July 7, 1964, the original opinion of this court was vacated, and reargument ordered in the light of Jacobellis.

The performance here consisted of a 55-minute mono-logue upon numerous socially controversial subjects inter-spersed with such unrelated topics as the meeting of a psychotic rapist and a nymphomaniac who have both escaped from their respective institutions, defendant's inti-macies with three married women, and a supposed conver-sation with a gas station attendant in a rest room which concludes with the suggestion that the defendant and attendant both put on contraceptives and take a picture.

The testimony was that defendant also made motions indicating masturbation and accompanied these with vulgar comments, and that persons leaving the audience were subjected to revolting questions and suggestions.

The entire performance was originally held by us to be characterized by its continual reference, by words and acts, to sexual intercourse or sexual organs in terms which ordinary adult individuals find thoroughly disgusting and revolting as well as patently offensive; that, as is evident from these brief summaries, it went beyond customary limits of candor, a fact which becomes even more apparent when the entire monologue is considered.

Our original opinion recognized defendant's right to satirize society's attitudes on contemporary social problems and to express his ideas, however bizarre, as long as the method used in doing so was not so objectionable as to render the entire performance obscene. Affirmance of the conviction was predicated upon the rule originally laid down in *American Civil Liberties Union* v. *City of Chicago*, 3 Ill. 2d 334, 121 N.E. 2d 585, that the obscene portions of the material must be balanced against its affirmative values to determine which predominates. We rejected defendant's argument that *Roth* v. *United States*, 354 U.S. 476, 77 S. Ct. 1304, 1 L. Ed. 2d 1498, struck down this balancing test and held that material, no matter how objectionable the method of its presentation, was constitutionally privileged unless it was utterly without redeeming social importance. It is apparent from the opinions of a majority of the court in Jacobellis that the

"balancing test" rule of American Civil Liberties Union is no longer a constitutionally acceptable method of determining whether material is obscene, and it is there made clear that material having *any* social importance is constitutionally protected.

While we would not have thought that constitutional guarantees necessitate the subjection of society to the gradual deterioration of its moral fabric which this type of presentation promotes, we must concede that some of the topics commented on by defendant are of social importance. Under Jacobellis the entire performance is thereby immunized, and we are constrained to hold that the judgment of the circuit court of Cook County must be reversed and defendant discharged.

Judgment reversed.

SCHAEFER, Justice (concurring).

The majority opinion seems to indicate that so long as any elements of a monologue have social value the entire speech is protected. I believe that this is too broad a formulation of the result in the Jacobellis case. The fact that some fragments relate to matters of social importance does not, in my opinion, always immunize the whole. But the major portion of this performance, before an adult night club audience, related to social problems, and most of the objectionable passages were integral parts of the protected material. Therefore I concur.

■ G. P. Putnam's Sons, a corporation, *Plaintiff,*

v.

Guy W. Calissi, Bergen County Prosecutor, *Defendant.*

No. C–3070.

Superior Court of New Jersey, Chancery Division.

Dec. 7, 1964.

Parisi, Evers & Greenfield, Hackensack (Irving C. Evers, Hackensack, appearing), and *Rembar & Zolotar,* New York City (Charles Rembar, New York City, appearing), for plaintiff.

Guy W. Calissi, Bergen County Pros. (Ronald J. Picinich, Asst. Pros., appearing), for defendant.

PASHMAN, J.S.C.

The controversy presently before the court involves an application by the Prosecutor of Bergen County for injunctive relief against G. P. Putnam's Sons, the publisher and distributor of John Cleland's *Memoirs of a Woman of Pleasure,* more commonly known as *Fanny Hill.* Although the case was initiated by the publisher, who sought certain injunctive relief against the prosecutor, both parties have

agreed that this court should treat the prosecutor as the moving party.

The statutory basis for the relief sought by the prosecutor is found in N.J.S. 2A:115–3.5, N.J.S.A., which provides, in part, that:

*"The county prosecutor * * * in any county * * * in which a * * * corporation sells or distributes or is about to sell or distribute * * * any book, * * * or any written or printed matter of an indecent character, which is obscene, lewd, lascivious, filthy or indecent or which contains an article or instrument of indecent or immoral use or purports to be for indecent or immoral use or purpose, may maintain an action for a judgment granting relief in the nature of injunctive relief against such * * * corporation in the Superior Court to prevent the sale * * * or*

the distribution * * * of any book * * * of an indecent character, herein described."

[1] The publisher has conceded that the legislatively
prescribed procedure found in N.J.S. 2A:115–3.5,
N.J.S.A., does not, in itself, violate any of its constitutionally guaranteed rights. Cf. *Kingsley Books, Inc.* v. *Brown*,
354 U.S. 436, 77 S. Ct. 1325, 1 L Ed. 2d 1469 (1957). It
is argued, however (quite correctly) that the substantive
application of this statute must accord with the federal
constitutional standards enunciated by the Supreme Court
of the United States in the free speech-obscenity area. See,
e.g. *Roth* v. *United States*, 354 U.S. 476, 77 S. Ct. 1304, 1
L. Ed. 2d 1498 (1957); *Manual Enterprises* v. *Day*, 370
U.S. 478, 82 S. Ct. 1432, 8 L. Ed. 2d 639 (1962); and
Jacobellis v. *State of Ohio*, 378 U.S. 184, 84 S. Ct. 1676,
12 L. Ed. 2d 793 (1964).

The highest judicial tribunal of this nation has observed
that the line separating obscenity from constitutionally
protected expression is "dim and uncertain." See *Bantam
Books, Inc.* v. *Sullivan*, 372 U.S. 58, 66, 83 S. Ct. 631, 9
L. Ed. 2d 584 (1963). However, as Justice Proctor,
speaking for our Supreme Court, observed in *State* v.
Hudson County News Co., 41 N.J. 247, 196 A 2d 225
(1963):

"* * * the guidelines established initially in Roth and
clarified in Manual Enterprises v. Day * * * are the best
determinants available to a court in reaching its decision
whether particular material is obscene by constitutional
standards." (at p. 255, 196 A. 2d at p. 229.)

Defendant in *Roth* v. *United States*, supra, was charged
with having violated federal and state obscenity statutes.
Mr. Justice Brennan, speaking for the majority of the
court, repeatedly emphasized the broad protective scope of
the First Amendment, stating in one passage that

"All ideas having even the slightest redeeming social
importance—unorthodox ideas, controversial ideas, even
ideas hateful to the prevailing climate of opinion—have
the full protection of the guaranties, unless excludable
because they encroach upon the limited area of more
important interests. But implicit in the history of the First
Amendment is the rejection of obscenity as utterly without
redeeming social importance." (354 U.S., at page 484, 77
S. Ct., at page 1309)

In formulating a workable test of obscenity, the majority
in Roth held that a court should inquire "whether to the
average person, applying contemporary community standards, the dominant theme of the material taken as a whole
appeals to prurient interest." 354 U.S., at page 489, 77 S.
Ct., at page 1311. Finally, the court observed in a footnote
that there is no significant difference between the meaning
of obscenity developed in the case law and the definition of
the A.L.I. Model Penal Code, § 207.10(2) (Tent. Draft
No. 6, 1957), *viz.*:

"* * *. A thing is obscene if, considered as a whole, its
predominant appeal is to prurient interest, i.e., a shameful
or morbid interest in nudity, sex, or excretion, and if it
goes substantially beyond customary limits of candor in

description or misrepresentation of such matters. * * *"
354 U.S., at page 486, 77 S. Ct., at page 1310, Note 20.

Several years after Roth was decided, the Supreme
Court in *Manual Enterprises* v. *Day*, supra, held that the
conclusion that literature is obscene and therefore not
entitled to the protective cloak of the First Amendment
requires a finding that the challenged material is patently
offensive as well as having its predominant appeal to
prurient interest. In the words of the Court:

"* * *. A thing is obscene if, considered as a whole, its
predominant appeal is to prurient interest * * * and if in
addition it goes substantially beyond customary limits of
candor in describing or representing such matters. * * *

"Obscenity under the federal statute thus requires
proof of two distinct elements: (1) patent offensiveness; and (2) 'prurient interest' appeal. Both must
conjoin before challenged material can be found 'obscene'
* *. In most obscenity cases, to be sure, the two
elements tend to coalesce, for that which is patently
offensive will also usually carry the requisite 'prurient
interest' appeal. * * *" 370 U.S., at page 486, 82 S.
Ct., at page 1436.

In the latest case dealing in what has been appropriately
termed a "grey area," cf. *State* v. *Hudson County News
Co.*, supra, 41 N.J. at page 254, 196 A. 2d 225, Mr. Justice
Brennan, speaking for the court, stated that

"The question of the proper standard for making [a
determination as to whether certain material is constitutionally protected] has been the subject of much discussion and controversy since our decision in Roth-Alberts
seven years ago. Recognizing that the test for obscenity
enunciated there—'whether to the average person, applying contemporary community standards, the dominant
theme of the material taken as a whole appeals to prurient
interest,' * * * is not perfect, we think any substitute
would raise equally difficult problems, and we therefore
adhere to that standard. We would reiterate, however, our
recognition in Roth that obscenity is excluded from the
constitutional protection only because it is 'utterly without
redeeming social importance,' and that '[t]he portrayal of
sex, e.g., in art, literature and scientific works, is not itself
sufficient reason to deny material the constitutional protection of freedom of speech and press.' * * * It follows
that material dealing with sex in a manner that advocates
ideas, * * * or that has literary or scientific or artistic
value or any other form of social importance, may not be
branded as obscenity and denied the constitutional protection. Nor may the constitutional status of the material be
made to turn on a 'weighing' of its social importance
against it prurient appeal, for a work cannot be proscribed
unless it is 'utterly' without social importance. * * * It
should also be recognized that the Roth standard requires
in the first instance a finding that the material 'goes substantially beyond customary limits of candor in description
or representation of such matters.' * * * In the absence
of such a deviation from society's standards of decency, we
do not see how any official inquiry into the allegedly
prurient appeal of a work of expression can be squared
with the guarantees of the First and Fourteenth Amendments. [citing Manual Enterprises, supra]." Jacobellis v.

State of Ohio, 378 U.S. 184, at p. 191, 84 S. Ct. 1676, at p. 1680, 12 L. Ed. 2d 793, at p. 799 (1964).

The court in Jacobellis also held that the phrase "contemporary community standards" contemplates a national standard of decency and not a local one. See also *State v. Hudson News Co.*, supra, 41 N.J. at pages 263–264, 196 A. 2d 225. In rejecting the reading of Roth which tested obscenity by the standards of the particular local community in which a case is instituted, Justice Brennan referred to the opinion of Judge Learned Hand in *United States v. Kennerley*, 209 F. 119, 121 (D.C.S.D.N.Y. 1913), concluding that

> "It seems clear that * * * Judge Hand was referring not to state and local 'communities,' but rather to 'the community' in the sense of 'society at large; * * * the public, or people in general.' Thus, he recognized that under his standard the concept of obscenity would have 'a varying meaning from time to time'—not from county to county, or town to town.
>
> We do not see how any 'local' definition of the 'community' could properly be employed in delineating the area of expression that is protected by the Federal Constitution. MR. JUSTICE HARLAN *pointed out in* Manual Enterprises, Inc. *v.* Day, * * * that a standard based on a particular local community would have 'the intolerable consequence of denying some sections of the country access to material, there deemed acceptable, which in others might be considered offensive to prevailing community standards of decency. * * *'
>
> *   *   *   *   *
>
> * * * The Court has explicitly refused to tolerate a result whereby 'the constitutional limits of free expression in the Nation would vary with state lines,' * * * we see even less justification for allowing such limits to vary with town or county lines. We thus reaffirm the position taken in Roth to the effect that the constitutional status of an allegedly obscene work must be determined on the basis of a national standard." 378 U.S., at pages 193, 194, 84 S. Ct., at pages 1681 and 1682, 12 L. Ed. 2d, at pages 801, 802.

The book which is the subject matter of the instant case has been reviewed, under different factual circumstances, by the courts of other states. In *Nugent v. A Book Entitled "Fanny Hill,"* etc., R.I. (1964), the Attorney General of Rhode Island instituted an *in rem* proceeding seeking injunctive relief based upon his position that there was "reasonable cause to believe that the book was obscene." The court was not faced with the ultimate issue, now before this court, of whether the book is obscene in fact, but in finding that "reasonable cause" did exist the Superior Court of Rhode Island observed that:

> "The book is weighted down with acts of sexual intercourse—scarcely a page goes by without some reference to it in preparation or in action. In the presentation of the acts of intercourse the descriptions of the actions involved and of the emotional and sensory experiences of the participants are in the greatest possible detail. These descriptions are not biological instruction, nor to enlighten the mind regarding the emotions and passions.

> The author has not only presented the normal sexual act between male and female in the most intimate manner each time, but he has ranged the whole gamut of sexual aberration, masochism and sadism, lesbianism and male homosexuality, and other sexual abnormalities in a similar fashion.
>
> Considered as a whole the dominant theme of the book is an appeal to prurient interest. In the constant renewal of the intimate terms of the sexual act and in the portrayal of sex deviations we are given a patently offensive portrayal which goes substantially beyond customary limits of candor in describing or representing such matters."

Another state court opinion dealing with *Fanny Hill* was decided by the Court of Appeals in the State of New York. See *Larkin v. G. P. Putnam's Sons*, 14 N.Y. 2d 399, 252 N.Y.S. 2d 71, 200 N.E. 2d 760 (Ct. App. 1964). The issue in that case, identical to the one in the case *sub judice*, was whether certain law enforcement officials were entitled to an injunction restraining the publisher from selling and distributing "the book." In reversing the Appellate Division, 20 A.D. 2d 702, 247 N.Y.S. 2d 275, which had itself reversed the trial court's determination that the book was not obscene, the highest court of the State of New York stated that "definitions are unsafe vehicles in obscenity cases," 14 N.Y. 2d 399, 252 N.Y.S. 2d, at page 73, 200 N.E. 2d, at page 761, and held that

> "When one looks carefully at the record since 1956 of what on constitutional grounds has been allowed to be printed and circulated, and what has been suppressed, 'Fanny Hill' seems to fall within the area of permissible publications. It is an erotic book, concerned principally with sexual experiences, largely normal, but some abnormal.
>
> It has a slight literary value and affords some insight into the life and manners of mid-18th century London. It is unlikely 'Fanny Hill' can have any adverse effect on the sophisticated values of our century. Some critics, writers, and teachers of stature testified at the trial that the book has merit, and the testimony as a whole showed reasonable differences of opinion as to its value. It does not warrant suppression." 14 N.Y. 2d 399, 252 N.Y.S. 2d, at page 74, 200 N.E. 2d at page 762.

Based upon the decision of the Supreme Court of the United States with respect to the book *Pleasure Was My Business*, *Tralins v. Gerstein*, 378 U.S. 576, 84 S. Ct. 1903, 12 L. Ed. 2d 1033 (1964), which the Court of Appeals regarded "as being in a class with 'Fanny Hill' and perhaps as going somewhat farther in utilization of objectionable material," the New York court decided that:

> "[i]f that work [Pleasure Was My Business] could not be restrained by Florida because of interdiction of the Constitution, New York would quite obviously be left without authority to restrain 'Fanny Hill.'" 14 N.Y. 2d 399, 252 N.Y.S. 2d, at page 75, 200 N.E. 2d, at page 763.

Chief Justice Desmond and Justices Marks and Scileppi filed vigorous dissents. The vote was 4–3.

In the most recent case concerning *Fanny Hill*, *Brooke v. "Fanny Hill,"* Mass. (Sup. Jud. Ct. 1964), the Attorney General of Massachusetts instituted a proceeding to adjudicate *Fanny Hill* obscene under the General Laws of the State. The court was faced with the same issue now before this court. The book was found to be obscene in the trial court.

At the trial of this cause, both sides introduced expert testimony which was designed to aid this court in resolving the difficult constitutional issues presented. The testimony offered by the prosecutor attempted to prove that (1) the dominant theme of the book is abnormal sex; (2) the effect of reading this book is that a "normal person" might be stimulated to perform abnormal sexual acts; (3) the book is the product of a psychopathic author, and (4) the book exceeds customary limits of candor and is contrary to generally accepted standards of morality. The publisher, on the other hand, utilized the services of literary experts and professors of literature, including Fred Holley Stocking, Professor of English and Chairman of the English Department at Williams College; John Owen McCormick, Professor of Comparative Literature and Chairman of the Department of Comparative Literature at Rutgers University; Max Levin, a highly qualified neurologist and psychiatrist, who is a clinical professor of neurology at the New York Medical College and the psychiatric editor of *Current Medical Digest*; J. Donald Adams, editor of the Sunday Book Review Section of *The New York Times*; Dr. Clarence Decker, vice-president of Fairleigh Dickenson University and Professor of World Literature; Wardell B. Pomeroy, Director of Field Research for the Institute for Sex Research at Indiana University; Elliott Freemont-Smith, editor of *The New York Times* Book Review Section; Paul Fussell, Jr., Associate Professor of English and Director of English graduate studies at Rutgers University; Walter J. Minton, president of G. P. Putnam's Sons; and David Burrows, Assistant Professor of English at Douglass College.

The conclusions reached by this imposing list of experts may be summarized as follows: (1) the book has a definite literary purpose, reflected by the development of the central character and dramatized by the ceremonious, formal, elegant, witty and comic prose style employed by the author; (2) the book provides a valuable insight into a way of life; (3) the book has historical value with respect to the development of the English novel and affords the reader an opportunity to learn about 18th Century English society, and (4) the book, while it is a classic in pornography and may accurately be termed an "erotic novel," is not as objectionable as other contemporary works of literature or the coverage given by the newspapers to the "Profumo scandal" in England.

[2] This court feels that the testimony of the literary experts and qualified scholars offered by the publisher with respect to the literary merit, historical significance and other qualities which constitute "social value" is not only appropriate from the standpoint of competency, but that such testimony is entitled to great weight. Cf. *Larkin* v. *G. P. Putnam's Sons*, supra; *Grove Press, Inc.* v. *Christenberry*, 175 F. Supp. 488, (D.C.S.D.N.Y. (1959)), affirmed, 276 F. 2d 433 (2 Cir., 1960); and *Attorney General* v. *Book Named "Tropic of Cancer,"* 345 Mass. 11, 184 N.E. 2d 328 (Sup. Jud. Ct. 1962). This is not to say, however, that the conclusions reached by these experts are dispositive of the ultimate substantive issue before the court. Indeed, this court retains the obligation of deciding, upon all the evidence presented, whether the book in

question has that degree of social value which calls into play the guarantees of the First Amendment.

[3] The court also believes that expert testimony is appropriate in the area of "contemporary community standards" and the "customary limits of candor." On the other hand, the question of whether or not the book has a predominant appeal to prurient interest remains, in my opinion, a legal conclusion which is not properly the subject of factual or documentary evidence.

[4] While certain expert opinion is admissible and may properly serve as an aid to the resolution of the substantive issues presented, there is a danger inherent in blindly accepting the conclusion of "the expert" in this area of law. As the New York Court of Appeals observed in *People* v. *Fritch*, 13 N.Y. 2d 119, 243 N.Y.S. 2d 1, 192 N.E. 2d 713 (Ct. App. 1963):

*"It does not follow * * * that because an alleged work of literature does not appeal to the prurient interest of a small group of intellectuals that it is not obscene under the prurient interest, or for that matter any other legal test of obscenity. This would permit the substitution of the opinions of authors and critics for those of the average person in the contemporary community. The fact that a few literary figures have commented favorably on this book and have lent it their prestige does not expunge from its pages the flagrantly obscene and patently offensive matter which dominates the book as a whole. * * *

A book may not be judged by its cover, its introduction or the laudatory comments contained in the publisher's blurbs—rather it must be judged by its actual contents. It requires little perception or imagination to conceive that the actual contents of a book may completely negate these testimonials and indorsements. Nor does the fact that the author enjoys wide acclaim as a writer control, for the book must be judged, not by the reputation of the author, but by what he writes in it. To hold otherwise would give recognized writers the freedom to traffic in obscenity at will under the guise of creating a work of art. This court will not adopt a rule of law which states that obscenity is suppressible but that well-written obscenity is not."* 243 N.Y.S. 2d, at page 7, 192 N.E. 2d, at page 717.

A review of the applicable Supreme Court decisions indicates that the book *Fanny Hill* must be judged by itself. The fact that *Tropic of Cancer* or *Pleasure Was My Business* has received the judicial stamp of approval is not determinative of the constitutional status of *Fanny Hill*. Because no two books are alike, each court must evaluate the book before it on its actual contents and not by comparing it to some other book. The test is not whether a particular book is as objectionable or less objectionable than another literary work which has been sustained by a higher court. The test is whether the book predominately appeals to "prurient interest" and, in addition, is "patently offensive." See *Jacobellis* v. *State of Ohio*, supra. Strong opposition from the Chief Justice and one other member of the United States Supreme Court failed to rally a majority in Jacobellis. The court held that in situations such as the matter *sub judice*, the ultimate decision must be case by case.

[5] There is no doubt, and the publisher concedes, that the book *Fanny Hill* is an erotic novel which is preoccupied with normal and abnormal sexual experiences. This

preoccupation is not, however, a sufficient reason to restrain the distribution of the book. Sex and obscenity are not synonymous. Nor are they interchangeable terms. It is only when the book, as a whole, deals with sex in a manner which is patently offensive, utterly without redeeming social importance, and appeals to prurient interests that a court is justified in granting injunctive relief. See *Roth, Manual Enterprises* and *Jacobellis, supra.*

[6] Subjective distaste for the contents of a book is also not a proper basis for a finding of obscenity. The court must act within the well-defined boundaries established by the applicable decisions of the Supreme Court, and in so doing the court is not acting as a censor but is instead discharging its constitutionally assigned role. As Mr. Justice Brennan appropriately observed in *Jacobellis* v. *State of Ohio, supra:*

"Nor can we understand why the Court's performance of its constitutional and judicial function in this sort of case should be denigrated by such epithets as 'censor' or 'supercensor.' In judging alleged obscenity the Court is no more 'censoring' expression than it has in other cases 'censored' criticism of judges and public officials, advocacy of governmental overthrow, or speech alleged to constitute a breach of the peace. Use of an opprobrious label can neither obscure nor impugn the Court's performance of its obligation to test challenged judgments against the guarantees of the First and Fourteenth Amendments and, in doing so, to delineate the scope of constitutionally protected speech." 378 U.S., at p. 190, 84 S. Ct., at p. 1679, 12 L. Ed. 2d, at p. 799.

I feel that it is wrong to pay lip service to the standards enunciated by the highest court of this land and then conclude that a book is not obscene because it is not as objectionable as some other book. See *Larkin* v. *G. P. Putnam's Sons, supra.*

[7, 8] Furthermore, it is wrong to argue that because a book may be morally bad for children, it is therefore bad for the average normal adult. There is no question that each state has a legitimate interest in "preventing the dissemination of material deemed harmful to children. But that interest does not justify a total suppression of such material, the effect of which would be to 'reduce the adult population * * * to reading only what is fit for children.' * * *" *Jacobellis* v. *Ohio, supra,* 378 U.S., at p. 195, 84 S. Ct., at p. 1682, 12 L. Ed. 2d, at p. 802. See also *City of Newark* v. *Licht,* 83 N.J. Super. 499, 503, 200 A. 2d 508 (App. Div. 1964), and Mr. Justice Frankfurter's comment in *Butler* v. *Michigan,* 352 U.S. 380, at 383, 77 S. Ct. 524, 1 L. Ed. 2d 412 (1957).

I have read and reread *Fanny Hill,* seeking to be as objective as possible. It was first published in 1749 and has been in surreptitious circulation ever since. Chief Justice Desmond, in this dissenting opinion in Larkin, noted that for centuries, " 'Fanny Hill' * * * has been cited throughout the world as the very prototype and archetype of obscenity, 'the pornographic best seller of all time' (*Loth, The Erotic in Literature,* 1961, p. [31] 32) * * *." It requires ten pages to bring our "heroine," Fanny, to the bawdy house, and the remaining 260 pages to depict to the last intimate detail varied sexual adventures described as voyeurism, transvestitism, prostitution, homosexuality, heterosexuality, lesbianism, female mastur-

bation, seduction of a virgin male, the deflowering of a virgin, the flagellation of male by female and female by male, and other kinds of sexual debauchery, including unnatural acts and exhibitions of sexual excesses. It is difficult to perceive any omissions on the part of the author. One sexual act follows another. What purpose can there be but to sexually arouse the reader? Those who contend that *Fanny Hill* is a work of literary value because it affords insight into the life and manners of mid-18th Century London must necessarily have an overwhelming sense of humor. Resort to *Fanny Hill* to study or authenticate the mores of those times would be the nadir of research.

[9] It is my opinion that the dominant theme of the book, as a whole, deals with sex in a manner appealing to prurient interests. The repeated and continuous efforts of the author to treat each act of sex in a minutely detailed manner represents "a shameful and morbid interest in sex" which "goes substantially beyond customary limits of candor." *Roth* v. *United States, supra.*

It is inconceivable to this court, that "the average person" could read *Fanny Hill* and receive the slightest social, literary or historical value from it. The fact that a selected group of literary experts do find such values does not, in my opinion, mean that the "average person" would, should or could find the same. In short, the book is utterly without redeeming social value.

This court also finds that the book is "patently offensive." See *Manual Enterprises, Inc.* v. *Day, supra.* While I do not subscribe to the balancing of interests concept advocated by Judge Scileppi in his dissenting opinion in *Larkin* v. *G. P. Putnam's Sons,* 14 N.Y. 2d 399, 252 N.Y.S. 2d, at page 78, 200 N.E. 2d, at 765, I feel that his observations with respect to the nature of the book, merit repeating:

"[Fanny Hill] is one of the foulest, sexually immoral, debasing, lewd and obscene books ever published, either in this country or abroad. It was written in the middle of the 18th Century and for many years was barred as an obscene book in Europe as well as in this country.
'Fanny Hill' reeks with disgusting descriptions of natural and unnatural sexual experiences of a prostitute, so dealt with as to portray those baser instincts normally to be found in the animal kingdom. In my view, it is obscene by any of the established legal standards.

* * * * *

*The majority opinion * * * sounds the death knell of the long-honored standards of American decency which have remained an integral part of our national heritage. I cannot agree that our society, even in 1964, has become so depraved that it has come to accept the kind of trash represented by 'Fanny Hill' and similar books, the publishers and purveyors of which are now given unbridled permission to advertise obscenity for sale with complete immunity."* 252 N.Y.S. 2d, at page 78, 200 N.E. 2d, at page 765.

See also the dissenting opinion of Chief Judge Desmond in *Larkin* v. *G. P. Putnam's Sons,* 252 N.Y.S. 2d, at pages 76 to 78, 200 N.E. 2d at pages 763 to 765.

[10] Assuming that I agreed with the publisher's experts that the book has elegance, style, wit and charm (much of which I feel is lacking), such conclusions can-

not, in my opinion, alter my determination that the book is obscene. A book may be well-written but still obscene.

"Filth, even if wrapped in the finest packaging, is still filth. 'Charm of language, subtlety of thought, faultless style, even distinction of authorship, may all * * * be present and the book be unfit for dissemination to the reading public. Frequently these attractive literary qualities are the very vehicles by which the destination of illegality is reached' * * * 'This court will not adopt a rule of law which states that obscenity is suppressible but well-written obscenity is not.'" People *v.* The Bookcase, Inc., 40 Misc. 2d 796, 244 N.Y.S. 2d 297, 300 (*Crim. Ct. of City of N.Y. 1963*).

Applying the "social value" test, the "prurient interest" test, the "patently offensive" test and even the "hard core pornography" test (not approved by the United States Supreme Court), this publication fails to measure up to the requisite standard entitling it to the protection of the First Amendment.

Almost every citizen applauds the awesome role assumed by the United States Supreme Court as protector of the constitutional guarantees of free speech. Who would not risk his life to defend these hard-won freedoms? Exciting progress has been made. Few knowledgeable people would tolerate the slightest trespass upon these rights, but obscenity "is not to be admitted to the constitutional sanctuary." We must heed the germane judicial concepts and conform faithfully to the creed of those whose responsibility is to guide. Said Mr. Justice Frankfurter:

"* * * The task is onerous and exacting, demanding as it does the utmost discipline in objectivity [and], the severest control of personal predilections * * *" Kingsley International Pictures Corp. *v.* Regents of University of State of New York, 360 U.S. 684, 697, 79 S. Ct. 1362, 1370, 3 L. Ed. 2d 1512 (1959).

The widespread circulation of books and pictures (both movies and stills) of dubious cultural value in our present-day society causes one to hesitate before enjoining any single work. But the plethora of filth in our society is a poor excuse for affording constitutional protection to *Fanny Hill.* Condonation of this class of erotic literature will contribute nothing to the elevation of our moral standards. Even a magistrate in the "home" country of

Fanny Hill recently ruled the book obscene. And now "Fanny Hill Comes Alive"! The "best" parts of the book are now available in a long-playing record album with all the lusty and intimate scenes of this erotic work realistically recited by four "stars." In fact, it is advertised as having been banned for 200 years and now available.

[11] There are proponents of a trend that would uphold a work although "trashy" and "disgusting," because there are no "four-letter" words and because "in all their erotic descriptions they maintain a clever, and apparently deliberate, avoidance of socially unacceptable language." But this position does not recognize the appropriate tests established by the United States Supreme Court. I cannot accept the baseless conclusion of these purveyors that there must be a place in our society for such writings because of compliance with the afore-mentioned trend. It is our duty to prevent the circulation of such pornographic literature as the United States Supreme Court has held is not within the protection of the First Amendment. It is as much our duty to protect publications entitled to the guarantees of the same amendment where authorities seek to suppress. Our personal predilections are unimportant. We should be guided by the cases afore-mentioned as well as *Sunshine Book Company* v. *Summerfield,* 355 U.S. 372, 78 S. Ct. 365, 2 L. Ed. 2d 352 (1958); *Kingsley International Pictures Corp.* v. *Regents of University of State of New York,* 360 U.S. 684, 79 S. Ct. 1362, 3 L. Ed. 2d 1512 (1959); *A Quantity of Copies of Books* v. *State of Kansas,* 378 U.S. 205, 84 S. Ct. 1723, 12 L. Ed. 2d 809 and *Grove Press, Inc.* v. *Gerstein,* 378 U.S. 577, 84 S. Ct. 1909, 12 L. Ed. 2d 1035.

Free rein should not be given under the guise of constitutional guarantees to vilely depict perversions and sexual adventures as John Cleland saw fit 200 years ago. This is not the highway to a better constitutional world; it is rather the path to decay and decline. The Constitution should not be the sword of a shameful profiteer of filth. It must be the shield to protect our sense of moral decency.

Based upon the foregoing, it is the opinion of this court that the book *Fanny Hill* is sufficiently obscene to forfeit the protection of the First Amendment to the Constitution. The prosecutor is therefore entitled to injunctive relief enjoining and restraining the publisher from publishing, selling or distributing the book in the State of New Jersey. The parties should present a form of judgment in accordance with this opinion.

■ Freedman
v.
Maryland.

APPEAL FROM THE COURT OF APPEALS OF MARYLAND.

No. 69. Argued November 19, 1964.—Decided March 1, 1965.

Felix J. Bilgrey argued the cause for appellant. With him on the brief were *Richard C. Whiteford* and *Louis H. Pollak.*

Thomas B. Finan, Attorney General of Maryland, argued the cause for appellee. With him on the brief were *Robert F. Sweeney* and *Roger D. Redden,* Assistant Attorneys General.

Edward De Grazia and *Melvin L. Wulf* filed a brief for the American Civil Liberties Union et al., as *amici curiae,* urging reversal.

Mr. Justice Brennan delivered the opinion of the Court.

Appellant sought to challenge the constitutionality of the Maryland motion picture censorship statute, Md. Ann. Code, 1957, Art. 66A, and exhibited the film "Revenge at Daybreak" at his Baltimore theatre without first submitting the picture to the State Board of Censors as required by § 2 thereof.[1] The State concedes that the picture does not violate the statutory standards[2] and would have re-

ceived a license if properly submitted, but the appellant was convicted of a § 2 violation despite his contention that the statute in its entirety unconstitutionally impaired freedom of expression. The Court of Appeals of Maryland affirmed, 233 Md. 498, 197 A. 2d 232, and we noted probable jurisdiction, 377 U.S. 987. We reverse.

I.

In *Times Film Corp.* v. *City of Chicago,* 365 U.S. 43, we considered and upheld a requirement of submission of motion pictures in advance of exhibition. The Court of Appeals held, on the authority of that decision, that "the Maryland censorship law must be held to be not void on its face as violative of the freedoms protected against State action by the First and Fourteenth Amendments." 233 Md., at 505, 197 A. 2d, at 235. This reliance on *Times Film* was misplaced. The only question tendered for decision in that case was "whether a prior restraint was necessarily unconstitutional *under all circumstances.*" *Bantam Books, Inc.* v. *Sullivan,* 372 U.S. 58, 70, n. 10 (emphasis in original). The exhibitor's argument that the requirement of submission without more amounted to a constitutionally prohibited prior restraint was interpreted by the Court in *Times Film* as a contention that the "constitutional protection includes complete and absolute freedom to exhibit, at least once, any and every kind of motion picture . . . even if this film contains the basest type of pornography, or incitement to riot, or forceful overthrow of orderly government . . . ." 365 U.S., at 46, 47. The Court held that on this "narrow" question, *id.,* at 46, the argument stated the principle against prior restraints too broadly; citing a number of our decisions, the Court quoted the statement from *Near* v. *Minnesota,* 283 U.S. 697, 716, that "the protection even as to previous restraint is not absolutely unlimited." In rejecting the proffered proposition in *Times Film* the Court emphasized, however, that "[i]t is that question alone which we decide," 365 U.S., at 46, and it would therefore be

---

[1] Md. Ann. Code, 1957, Art. 66A, § 2:

"It shall be unlawful to sell, lease, lend, exhibit or use any motion picture film or view in the State of Maryland unless the said firm or view has been submitted by the exchange, owner or lessee of the film or view and duly approved and licensed by the Maryland State Board of Censors, hereinafter in this article called the Board."

[2] Md. Ann. Code, 1957, Art. 66A, § 6:

"(a) *Board to examine, approve or disapprove films*—The Board shall examine or supervise the examination of all films or views to be exhibited or used in the State of Maryland and shall approve and license such films or views which are moral and proper, and shall disapprove such as are obscene, or such as tend, in the judgment of the Board, to debase or corrupt morals or incite to crimes. All films exclusively portraying current events or pictorial news of the day, commonly called news reels, may be exhibited without examination and no license or fees shall be required therefor.

"(b) *What films considered obscene.*—For the purposes of this article, a motion picture film or view shall be considered to be obscene if, when considered as a whole, its calculated purpose or dominant effect is substantially to arouse sexual desires, and if the probability of this effect is so great as to outweigh whatever other merits the film may possess.

"(c) *What films tend to debase or corrupt morals.*—For the purposes of this article, a motion picture film or view shall be considered to be of such a character that its exhibition would tend to debase or corrupt morals if its dominant purpose or effect is erotic or pornographic; or if it portrays acts of sexual im-

morality, lust or lewdness, or if it expressly or impliedly presents such acts as desirable, acceptable or proper patterns of behavior.

"(d) *What films tend to incite to crime.*—For the purposes of this article, a motion picture film or view shall be considered of such a character that its exhibition would tend to incite to crime if the theme or the manner of its presentation presents the commission of criminal acts or contempt for law as constituting profitable, desirable, acceptable, respectable or commonly accepted behavior, or if it advocates or teaches the use of, or the methods of use of, narcotics or habit-forming drugs."

inaccurate to say that *Times Film* upheld the specific features of the Chicago censorship ordinance.

Unlike the petitioner in *Times Film*, appellant does not argue that § 2 is unconstitutional simply because it may prevent even the first showing of a film whose exhibition may legitimately be the subject of an obscenity prosecution. He presents a question quite distinct from that passed on in *Times Film*; accepting the rule in *Times Film*, he argues that § 2 constitutes an invalid prior restraint because, in the context of the remainder of the statute, it presents a danger of unduly suppressing protected expression. He focuses particularly on the procedure for an initial decision by the censorship board, which, without any judicial participation, effectively bars exhibition of any disapproved film, unless and until the exhibitor undertakes a time-consuming appeal to the Maryland courts and succeeds in having the Board's decision reversed. Under the statute, the exhibitor is required to submit the film to the Board for examination, but no time limit is imposed for completion of Board action, § 17. If the film is disapproved, or any elimination ordered, § 19 provides that

"the person submitting such film or view for examination will receive immediate notice of such elimination or disapproval, and if appealed from, such film or view will be promptly re-examined, in the presence of such person, by two or more members of the Board, and the same finally approved or disapproved promptly after such re-examination, with the right of appeal from the decision of the Board to the Baltimore City Court of Baltimore City. There shall be a further right of appeal from the decision of the Baltimore City Court to the Court of Appeals of Maryland, subject generally to the time and manner provided for taking appeal to the Court of Appeals."

Thus there is no statutory provision for judicial participation in the procedure which bars a film, nor even assurance of prompt judicial review. Risk of delay is built into the Maryland procedure, as is borne out by experience; in the only reported case indicating the length of time required to complete an appeal, the initial judicial determination has taken four months and final vindication of the film on appellate review, six months. *United Artists Corp.* v. *Maryland State Board of Censors*, 210 Md. 586, 124 A. 2d 292.

In the light of the difference between the issues presented here and in *Times Film*, the Court of Appeals erred in saying that, since appellant's refusal to submit the film to the Board was a violation only of § 2, "he has restricted himself to an attack on that section alone, and lacks standing to challenge any of the other provisions (or alleged shortcomings) of the statute." 233 Md., at 505, 197 A. 2d, at 236. Appellant has not challenged the submission requirement in a vacuum but in a concrete statutory context. His contention is that § 2 effects an invalid prior restraint because the structure of the other provisions of the statute contributes to the infirmity of § 2; he does not assert that the other provisions are independently invalid.

In the area of freedom of expression it is well established that one has standing to challenge a statute on the ground that it delegates overly broad licensing discretion to an administrative office, whether or not his conduct could be proscribed by a properly drawn statute, and whether or not

he applied for a license. "One who might have had a license for the asking may . . . call into question the whole scheme of licensing when he is prosecuted for failure to procure it." *Thornhill* v. *Alabama*, 310 U.S. 88, 97; see *Staub* v. *City of Baxley*, 355 U.S. 313, 319; *Saia* v. *New York*, 334 U.S. 558; *Thomas* v. *Collins*, 323 U.S. 516; *Hague* v. *CIO*, 307 U.S. 496; *Lovell* v. *City of Griffin*, 303 U.S. 444, 452–453. Standing is recognized in such cases because of the ". . . danger of tolerating, in the area of First Amendment freedoms, the existence of a penal statute susceptible of sweeping and improper application." *NAACP* v. *Button*, 371 U.S. 415, 433; see also Amsterdam, Note, The Void-for-Vagueness Doctrine in the Supreme Court, 109 U. Pa. L. Rev. 67, 75–76, 80–81, 96–104 (1960). Although we have no occasion to decide whether the vice of overbroadness infects the Maryland statute,[3] we think that appellant's assertion of a similar danger in the Maryland apparatus of censorship—one always fraught with danger and viewed with suspicion—gives him standing to make that challenge. In substance his argument is that, because the apparatus operates in a statutory context in which judicial review may be too little and too late, the Maryland statute lacks sufficient safeguards for confining the censor's action to judicially determined constitutional limits, and therefore contains the same vice as a statute delegating excessive administrative discretion.

II.

Although the Court has said that motion pictures are not "necessarily subject to the precise rules governing any other particular method of expression," *Joseph Burstyn, Inc.* v. *Wilson*, 343 U.S. 495, 503, it is as true here as of other forms of expression that "[a]ny system of prior restraints of expression comes to this Court bearing a heavy presumption against its constitutional validity." *Bantam Books, Inc.* v. *Sullivan, supra*, at 70. ". . . [U]nder the Fourteenth Amendment, a State is not free to adopt whatever procedures it pleases for dealing with obscenity . . . without regard to the possible consequences for constitutionally protected speech." *Marcus* v. *Search Warrant*, 367 U.S. 717, 731. The administration of a censorship system for motion pictures presents peculiar dangers to constitutionally protected speech. Unlike a prosecution for obscenity, a censorship proceeding puts the initial burden on the exhibitor or distributor. Because the censor's business is to censor, there inheres the danger that he may well be less responsive than a court—part of an independent branch of government—to the constitutionally protected interests in free expression.[4] And if it is

---

[3] Appellant also challenges the constitutionality of § 6, establishing standards, as invalid for vagueness under the Due Process Clause; § 11, imposing fees for the inspection and licensing of a film, as constituting an invalid tax upon the exercise of freedom of speech; and § 23, allowing exemptions to various classes of exhibitors, as denying him the equal protection of the laws. In view of our result, we express no views upon these claims.

[4] See Emerson, The Doctrine of Prior Restraint, 20 Law & Contemp. Prob. 648, 656–659 (1955). This is well illustrated by the fact that the Maryland Court of Appeals has reversed the Board's disapproval in every reported case. *United Artists Corp.* v. *Maryland State Board of Censors, supra*; *Maryland State Board of Censors* v. *Times Film Corp.*, 212 Md. 454, 129 A. 2d 833; *Fanfare Films, Inc.* v. *Motion Picture Censor Board*, 234 Md. 10, 197 A. 2d 839.

made unduly onerous, by reason of delay or otherwise, to seek judicial review, the censor's determination may in practice be final.

Applying the settled rule of our cases, we hold that a noncriminal process which requires the prior submission of a film to a censor avoids constitutional infirmity only if it takes place under procedural safeguards designed to obviate the dangers of a censorship system. First, the burden of proving that the film is unprotected expression must rest on the censor. As we said in *Speiser* v. *Randall,* 357 U.S. 513, 526, "Where the transcendent value of speech is involved, due process certainly requires . . . that the State bear the burden of persuasion to show that the appellants engaged in criminal speech." Second, while the State may require advance submission of all films, in order to proceed effectively to bar all showings of unprotected films, the requirement cannot be administered in a manner which would lend an effect of finality to the censor's determination whether a film constitutes protected expression. The teaching of our cases is that, because only a judicial determination in an adversary proceeding ensures the necessary sensitivity to freedom of expression, only a procedure requiring a judicial determination suffices to impose a valid final restraint. See *Bantam Books, Inc.* v. *Sullivan, supra; A Quantity of Books* v. *Kansas,* 378 U.S. 205; *Marcus* v. *Search Warrant, supra; Manual Enterprises, Inc.* v. *Day,* 370 U.S. 478, 518–519. To this end, the exhibitor must be assured, by statute or authoritative judicial construction, that the censor will, within a specified brief period, either issue a license or go to court to restrain showing the film. Any restraint imposed in advance of a final judicial determination on the merits must similarly be limited to preservation of the status quo for the shortest fixed period compatible with sound judicial resolution. Moreover, we are well aware that, even after expiration of a temporary restraint, an administrative refusal to license, signifying the censor's view that the film is unprotected, may have a discouraging effect on the exhibitor. See *Bantam Books, Inc.* v. *Sullivan, supra.* Therefore, the procedure must also assure a prompt final judicial decision, to minimize the deterrent effect of an interim and possibly erroneous denial of a license.

Without these safeguards, it may prove too burdensome to seek review of the censor's determination. Particularly in the case of motion pictures, it may take very little to deter exhibition in a given locality. The exhibitor's stake in any one picture may be insufficient to warrant a protracted and onerous course of litigation. The distributor, on the other hand, may be equally unwilling to accept the burdens and delays of litigation in a particular area when, without such difficulties, he can freely exhibit his film in most of the rest of the country; for we are told that only four States and a handful of municipalities have active censorship laws.[5]

It is readily apparent that the Maryland procedural scheme does not satisfy these criteria. First, once the censor disapproves the film, the exhibitor must assume the burden of instituting judicial proceedings and of persuad-

ing the courts that the film is protected expression. Second, once the Board has acted against a film, exhibition is prohibited pending judicial review, however protracted. Under the statute, appellant could have been convicted if he had shown the film after unsuccessfully seeking a license, even though no court had ever ruled on the obscenity of the film. Third, it is abundantly clear that the Maryland statute provides no assurance of prompt judicial determination. We hold, therefore, that appellant's conviction must be reversed. The Maryland scheme fails to provide adequate safeguards against undue inhibition of protected expression, and this renders the § 2 requirement of prior submission of films to the Board an invalid previous restraint.

III.

How or whether Maryland is to incorporate the required procedural safeguards in the statutory scheme is, of course, for the State to decide. But a model is not lacking: In *Kingsley Books, Inc.* v. *Brown,* 354 U.S. 436, we upheld a New York injunctive procedure designed to prevent the sale of obscene books. That procedure postpones any restraint against sale until a judicial determination of obscenity following notice and an adversary hearing. The statute provides for a hearing one day after joinder of issue; the judge must hand down his decision within two days after termination of the hearing. The New York procedure operates without prior submission to a censor, but the chilling effect of a censorship order, even one which requires judicial action for its enforcement, suggests all the more reason for expeditious determination of the question whether a particular film is constitutionally protected.

The requirement of prior submission to a censor sustained in *Times Film* is consistent with our recognition that films differ from other forms of expression. Similarly, we think that the nature of the motion picture industry may suggest different time limits for a judicial determination. It is common knowledge that films are scheduled well before actual exhibition, and the requirement of advance submission in § 2 recognizes this. One possible scheme would be to allow the exhibitor or distributor to submit his film early enough to ensure an orderly final disposition of the case before the scheduled exhibition date—far enough in advance so that the exhibitor could safely advertise the opening on a normal basis. Failing such a scheme or sufficiently early submission under such a scheme, the statute would have to require adjudication considerably more prompt than has been the case under the Maryland statute. Otherwise, litigation might be unduly expensive and protracted, or the victorious exhibitor might find the most propitious opportunity for exhibition past. We do not mean to lay down rigid time limits or procedures, but to suggest considerations in drafting legislation to accord with local exhibition practices, and in doing so to avoid the potentially chilling effect of the Maryland statute on protected expression.

Reversed.

Mr. Justice Douglas, whom Mr. Justice Black joins, concurring.

On several occasions I have indicated my view that movies are entitled to the same degree and kind of protection under the First Amendment as other forms of expres-

---

[5] An appendix to the brief *amici curiae* of the American Civil Liberties Union and its Maryland Branch lists New York, Virginia and Kansas as the three States having statutes similar to the Maryland statute, and the cities of Chicago, Detroit, Fort Worth and Providence as having similar ordinances. Twenty-eight of the remaining 39 municipal ordinances and codes are listed as "inactive."

sion. *Superior Films* v. *Department of Education*, 346 U.S. 587, 588; *Kingsley Pictures Corp.* v. *Regents*, 360 U.S. 684, 697; *Times Film Corp.* v. *Chicago*, 365 U.S. 43, 78.* For the reasons there stated, I do not believe any form of censorship—no matter how speedy or prolonged it may

be—is permissible. As I see it, a pictorial presentation occupies as preferred a position as any other form of expression. If censors are banned from the publishing business, from the pulpit, from the public platform—as they are—they should be banned from the theatre. I would not admit the censor even for the limited role accorded him in *Kingsley Books, Inc.* v. *Brown*, 354 U.S. 436. I adhere to my dissent in that case. *Id.*, at 446–447. Any authority to obtain a temporary injunction gives the State "the paralyzing power of a censor." *Id.*, at 446. The regime of *Kingsley Books* "substitutes punishment by contempt for punishment by jury trial." *Id.*, at 447. I would put an end to all forms and types of censorship and give full literal meaning to the command of the First Amendment.

---

* The Court today holds that a system of movie censorship must contain at least three procedural safeguards if it is not to run afoul of the First Amendment: (1) the censor must have the burden of instituting judicial proceedings; (2) any restraint prior to judicial review can be imposed only briefly in order to preserve the status quo; and (3) a prompt judicial determination of obscenity must be assured. Thus the Chicago censorship system, upheld by the narrowest of margins in *Times Film Corp.* v. *Chicago*, 365 U.S. 43, could not survive under today's standards, for it provided not one of these safeguards, as the dissenters there expressly pointed out. *Id.*, at 73–75.

■ Attorney General

v.

A Book Named "John Cleland's Memoirs of a Woman of Pleasure."

Supreme Judicial Court of Massachusetts, Suffolk.

Argued Jan. 8, 1965.

Decided April 22, 1965.

Charles Rembar, New York City (Reuben Goodman, Boston, with him) for intervener.
William I. Cowin, Asst. Atty. Gen. (John E. Sullivan, Asst. Atty. Gen., with him), for Attorney General.
Henry P. Monaghan, Holyoke, for Civil Liberties Union of Massachusetts and others, amici curiæ, submitted a brief.

Before WILKINS, C.J., and SPALDING, WHITTEMORE, CUTTER, KIRK, SPIEGEL, and REARDON, JJ.

SPALDING, Justice.

This is an appeal from a final decree holding the book, "John Cleland's Memoirs of a Woman of Pleasure" (Memoirs), more commonly known as "Fanny Hill," obscene, indecent and impure under G.L. c. 272, §§ 28C, 28E, and 28F (inserted by St. 1945, c. 278, § 1).[1] The

petition was brought by the Attorney General. The publisher of the book, G. P. Putnam's Sons, intervened as a party. No jury trial having been claimed under § 28D, the case was heard by a judge. The evidence consisted of the book, various newspaper articles, book reviews and the testimony of several experts in the field of literature. The judge made careful and complete findings of fact and discussed the relevant law exhaustively.

Memoirs was written in England in 1749. For over two centuries it has had for the most part a surreptitious circulation. Memoirs has, for example, previously been a source of litigation in this Commonwealth (see *Commonwealth* v. *Holmes*, 17 Mass. 336), and very recently it has been the subject of decisions by other courts. See *Larkin* v. *G. P. Putnam's Sons*, 14 N.Y. 2d 399, 252 N.Y.S. 2d 71, 200 N.E. 2d 760; *G. P. Putnam's Sons* v. *Calissi*, 86 N.J. Super. 82, 205 A. 2d 913.

The sole question is whether the publication of Memoirs is protected by the First Amendment to the United States Constitution, as made applicable to the States by the Fourteenth Amendment. Since a majority of the court held in *Roth* v. *United States*, 354 U.S. 476, 485, 77 S. Ct. 1304, 1309, 1 L. Ed. 2d 1498, "that obscenity is not within the area of constitutionally protected speech or press," the question becomes one of determining whether or not Memoirs is obscene.

[1, 2] The book takes the form of two letters written by a prostitute in which she recounts her life since she, a country girl, was abandoned in London. It concentrates on her sexual experiences, both normal and abnormal, which are described in minute detail. Memoirs, as is conceded by the intervener, is erotic. Erotica and obscenity, however,

---

[1] Section 28C reads, in relevant part, "Whenever there is reasonable cause to believe that a book which is being imported, sold, loaned or distributed * * * is obscene, indecent or impure, the attorney general * * * shall bring an information or petition in equity * * * directed against said book by name." Then follows a provision relating to a "reasonable cause" hearing, notice to interested persons, and an interlocutory adjudication. Section 28E provides for an adjudication against the book, in the event of default, "if the court finds that the book is obscene, indecedent or impure * * *." Section 28F provides for a contested hearing. "At such hearing the court may receive the testimony of experts and may receive evidence as to the literary, cultural or educational character of said book and as to the manner and form of its publication, advertisement, and distribution."

are not synonymous. The fact that Memoirs may arouse sexual thoughts and desires is not, in itself, sufficient to deprive it of its constitutional protection. If the contrary were the case, the public could be deprived of many of the world's greatest literary and artistic works. Our task, then, is to trace, as best we can, the "dim and uncertain line" which separates obscenity from that which is protected by the First Amendment. See *Bantam Books, Inc.* v. *Sullivan*, 372 U.S. 58, 66, 83 S. Ct. 631, 9 L. Ed. 2d 584; *Jacobellis* v. *State of Ohio*, 378 U.S. 184, 187, 84 S. Ct. 1676, 12 L. Ed. 2d 793. We are under no illusions as to the difficulties involved in "facing up to the tough individual problems of constitutional judgment involved in every obscenity case." *Roth* v. *United States*, 354 U.S. 476, 498, 77 S. Ct. 1304, 1316.

[3, 4] The first Supreme Court case to face the obscenity issue squarely was *Roth* v. *United States*, 354 U.S. 476, 77 S. Ct. 1304.[2] The majority opinion in that case established the following test: "whether to the average person, applying contemporary community standards, the dominant theme of the material taken as a whole appeals to prurient interest." Id. at 489, 77 S. Ct. at 1311. In a footnote the majority clarified what their notion of "prurient" was by quoting with approval Am. Law. Inst., Model Penal Code, § 207.10(2) (Tent. draft, No. 6, 1957) which defined that term as "* * * a shameful or morbid interest in nudity, sex, or excretion."[3] *Roth* v. *United States*, supra, 487, n. 20, 77 S. Ct. at 1310.

[5] We have no doubt that the dominant theme of Memoirs appeals to prurient interest. The book is composed almost entirely of a series of episodes involving lesbianism, voyeurism, prostitution, flagellation, sexual orgies, masturbation, fellatio, homosexuality, and defloration, all of which "goes substantially beyond customary limits of candor in describing or representing such matters." Am. Law Inst., Model Penal Code, § 251.4(1) (Proposed Official Draft, May 4, 1962). See *Jacobellis* v. *State of Ohio*, 378 U.S. 184, 191, 84 S. Ct. 1676. For the same reason, we hold Memoirs to be such an affront to current community standards as to constitute "patent offensiveness." See *Manual Enterprises, Inc.* v. *Day*, 370 U.S. 478, 482, 82 S. Ct. 1432, 8 L. Ed. 2d 639. We would reach this result whether we applied local community or national standards. See *Jacobellis* v. *State of Ohio*, supra, 378 U.S. at 193, 84 S. Ct. 1676 (opinion of Brennan, J.), which indicates national standards should be used. But see dissent of Warren, C.J., in that case at page 200, 84 S. Ct. which takes the position that obscenity is to be defined by local community standards.

There is one other possible test which must be considered. The majority opinion in the Roth case went on to say that "implicit in the history of the First Amendment is the rejection of obscenity as *utterly without redeeming social importance*" (emphasis supplied). Id. 354 U.S. at p. 484, 77 S. Ct. at p. 1309. While it does not clearly emerge from the opinion whether "social importance" is an inde-

pendent standard, subsequent decisions shed some light on the matter.

[6] In *Jacobellis* v. *State of Ohio*, supra, 378 U.S. at 191, 84 S. Ct. at 1680 (opinion of Brennan, J., concurred in by Goldberg, J.), the view was expressed that the constitutional status of material cannot "be made to turn on a 'weighing' of its social importance against its prurient appeal, for a work cannot be proscribed unless it is 'utterly' without social importance." See *Tralins* v. *Gerstein*, 378 U.S. 576, 84 S. Ct. 1903, 12 L. Ed. 2d 1053 (per curiam), and *Grove Press, Inc.* v. *Gerstein*, 378 U.S. 577, 84 S. Ct. 1909, 12 L. Ed. 2d 1035 (per curiam). Thus it would appear that unless a work is "utterly without social importance" it cannot be deemed obscene. For views which would extend the constitutional protection even further see *Roth* v. *United States*, 354 U.S. 476, 508, 77 S. Ct. 1304 (dissent of Douglas, J.); *Jacobellis* v. *State of Ohio*, 378 U.S. 184, 196, 84 S. Ct. 1676 (opinion of Black, J.); *A Quantity of Copies of Books* v. *State of Kansas*, 378 U.S. 205, 213, 84 S. Ct. 1723, 12 L. Ed. 2d 809 (opinion of Black, J.).

The trial judge, after an exhaustive and able discussion of the relevant decisions, ruled that the Attorney General, to maintain his petition, must meet the following three tests: "*First*, the 'prurient interest' test, which, because of the holding in the 'Tropic of Cancer' (345 Mass. 11 [184 N.E. 2d 328]) case must be shown to be 'hard core pornography'; *Second*, the 'patent offensiveness' test; and *Third*, the 'social value' test." He further ruled that the "[f]ailure * * * to sustain the standards that any one of these tests is designed for will result in an adjudication that the book * * * [is not] obscene in a constitutional sense." Whether the Supreme Court of the United States has laid down three independent standards, all of which (as the judge ruled), must be satisfied, need not be decided, for in our opinion Memoirs meets all the tests.[4] As indicated above, we have little doubt that Memoirs' dominant theme appeals to prurient interests and that it is patently offensive.

[7–9] It remains to consider whether the book can be said to be "utterly without social importance." We are mindful that there was expert testimony, much of which was strained, to the effect that Memoirs is a structural novel with literary merit; that the book displays a skill in characterization and a gift for comedy; that it plays a part in the history of the development of the English novel; and that it contains a moral, namely, that sex with love is superior to sex in a brothel. But the fact that the testimony may indicate this book has some minimal literary value does not mean it is of any social importance. We do not interpret the "social importance" test as requiring that a book which appeals to prurient interest and is patently offensive must be unqualifiedly worthless before it can be deemed obscene. Upon a consideration of all the evidence, including the book, we are of opinion that Memoirs is not endowed with constitutional protection.

We have not overlooked the fact that Memoirs was recently held not to be obscene in the constitutional sense

---

[2] This case, as well as all but the most recent authority, is fully discussed in *Attorney Gen.* v. *Book Named "Tropic of Cancer,"* 345 Mass. 11, 184 N.E. 2d 328. We need not, therefore, elaborate upon the general development of this area of the law.

[3] The same definition of "prurient" has been adopted by Am. Law. Inst., Model Penal Code, § 251.4(1) (Proposed Official Draft, May 4, 1962).

[4] A fourth criterion, which involves determining whether material is hard core pornography, has been suggested. See *Jacobellis* v. *State of Ohio*, supra, 378 U.S. pp. 184, 197, 84 S. Ct. 1676 (opinion of Stewart, J.); *Attorney Gen.* v. *Book Named "Tropic of Cancer,"* 345 Mass. 11, 19, 184 N.E. 2d 328. But the Supreme Court has never so held.

by a closely divided court in *Larkin* v. *G. P. Putnam's Sons,* 14 N.Y. 2d 399, 252 N.Y.S. 2d 71, 200 N.E. 2d 760. But the Superior Court of New Jersey in a well considered opinion has reached a contrary conclusion with respect to this book in *G. P. Putnam's Sons* v. *Calissi,* 86 N.J. Super. 82, 205 A. 2d 913. We find the reasoning in that decision and the opinions of the dissenting judges in the Larkin case more persuasive.

It follows that the entry must be

Decree affirmed.

WHITTEMORE, Justice (dissenting, with whom SPIEGEL, J., joins.)

This book cannot be ruled to be "utterly without redeeming social importance." *Roth* v. *United States,* 354 U.S. 476, 484, 77 S. Ct. 1304; *Jacobellis* v. *State of Ohio,* 378 U.S. 184, 191, 84 S. Ct. 1676.

In the view of one or another or all of the following viz., the chairman of the English department at Williams College, a professor of English at Harvard College, an associate professor of English literature at Boston University, an associate professor of English at Massachusetts Institute of Technology, and an assistant professor of English and American literature at Brandeis University, the book is a minor "work of art" having "literary merit" and "historical value" and containing a good deal of "deliberate, calculated comedy." It is a piece of "social history of interest to anyone who is interested in fiction as a way of understanding society in the past."[1] A saving grace is that although many scenes, if translated into the present day language of "the realistic, naturalistic novel, could be quite offensive" these scenes are not described in such language. The book contains no dirty words and its language "functions * * * to create a distance, even when the sexual experiences are portrayed." The response, therefore, is a literary response. The descriptions of depravity are not obscene because "they are subordinate to an interest which is primarily literary." Fanny's reaction to the scenes of depravity was "anger," "disgust, horror [and], indignation." The book "belongs to the history of English literature rather than the history of smut."[2]

The book, according to its publisher, has been pur-

chased by a considerable number of college libraries including the Harvard and Massachusetts Institute of Technology libraries.

It is not the court's function to consider whether to agree or disagree with the appraisal of the book by academic witnesses. The controlling circumstance is that the work is evaluated by representative scholars and teachers of English literature as a work of some literary and historical significance notwithstanding its patently pornographic aspects. I construe the concept embodied in the term "social importance" as used by the United States Supreme Court to include the literary and historical field. Hence, I believe that the publication of this book is protected by the First Amendment as expounded in the Supreme Court decisions. *Larkin* v. *G. P. Putnam's Sons,* 14 N.Y. 2d 399, 252 N.Y.S. 2d 71, 200 N.E. 2d 760.

I assume that the book would be offensive to some, perhaps a great many, readers. So are numerous other books now published that use four letter words freely, portray sexual encounters explicitly and with a detail of description far beyond anything used by Cleland, and often appear intended to degrade and debase the sexual relationship. A purpose of some such books appears to be the destruction of concepts deemed basic to the existing social and moral order. If the measure intended by the Roth case, supra, were of possible effect on prevailing values, books like "Tropic of Cancer" would, I submit, be banned. But on such a scale "Fanny Hill" appears of slight, if any, weight and not worth the attention that efforts to ban inevitably bring. I agree with the opinion in the Larkin case, supra, that "[i]t is unlikely 'Fanny Hill' can have any adverse effect on the sophisticated values of our century." 14 N.Y. 2d 399, 403–404, 252 N.Y.S. 2d 71, 74–75, 200 N.E. 2d 760, 763.

Freedom to read, as I construe it, means that such a book as this is to be available to those who wish to read it and that the persisting urge of others to bar its publication is effectively restrained. There is, of course, no obligation upon any member of the general public to read this book.

CUTTER, Justice (dissenting).

I disagree with the majority opinion for reasons in part somewhat different from those stated by Mr. Justice Whittemore and Mr. Justice Spiegel.

The book seems to me offensive and unpleasant in numerous respects. In my opinion, it could reasonably be found that distribution of the book to persons under the age of eighteen would be a violation of G.L. c. 272, § 28,[1] as tending to corrupt the morals of youth. Despite the propensity of some young people to regard forbidden terri-

---

[1] One of the witnesses testified in part as follows: "Cleland is part of what I should call this cultural battle that is going on in the 18th century, a battle between a restricted Puritan, moralistic ethic that attempts to suppress freedom of the spirit, freedom of the flesh, and this element is competing with a freer attitude towards life, a more generous attitude towards life, a more wholesome attitude towards life, and this very attitude that is manifested in Fielding's great novel 'Tom Jones' is also evident in Cleland's novel. * * * [Richardson's] 'Pamela' is the story of a young country girl; [his] 'Clarissa' is the story of a woman trapped in a house of prostitution. Obviously, then Cleland takes both these themes, the country girl, her initiation into life and into experience, and the story of a woman in a house of prostitution, and what he simply does is to take the situation and reverse the moral standards. Richardson believed that chastity was the most important thing in the world; Cleland and Fielding obviously did not and thought there were more important significant moral values."

[2] In the opinion of the other academic witness, the headmaster of a private school, whose field is English literature, the book is without literary merit and is obscene, impure, hard core pornography, and is patently offensive.

---

[1] Section 28 (as amended through St. 1959, c. 492, § 1), reads in part as follows: "Whoever sells or * * * publishes for the purpose of selling or distributing, to a person under the age of eighteen years a book * * * which is obscene * * * or manifestly tends to corrupt the morals of youth * * * shall be punished by imprisonment in the state prison for not more than five years or in a jail or house of correction for not more than two and one half years, or by a fine of not * * * more than five thousand dollars, or by both such fine and imprisonment in jail or the house of correction. In order to obtain a conviction under this section, it shall not be necessary to prove that the book * * * has been adjudged to be obscene * * * under the provisions of" §§ 28C to 28H.

tory as a challenge to its exploration, it is not for the courts to determine whether it is wise to seek to prevent sale of such a book to persons under eighteen. I perceive no constitutional obstacle to treating as a criminal offence the sale of this book to persons under eighteen.[2]

It is quite another thing effectually to prohibit sale of the book to all adults in Massachusetts by declaring the book to be obscene. This proceeding presents much the same substantive question involved in *Butler* v. *State of Michigan,* 352 U.S. 380, 382–384, 77 S. Ct. 524, 1 L. Ed. 2d 412. There the Supreme Court of the United States held that Michigan could not prevent the sale to adults of a book which might "have a potentially deleterious influence upon youth." Michigan then argued that it was promoting the public welfare "by thus quarantining the general reading public against books not too rugged for grown men and women in order to shield juvenile innocence." Mr. Justice Frankfurter wisely said of this argument, "Surely, this is to burn the house to roast the pig. * * * [The] legislation [is] not reasonably restricted to the evil with which it is said to deal. The incidence of this enactment is to reduce the adult population of Michigan

to reading only what is fit for children. It thereby arbitrarily curtails one of those liberties of the individual, now enshrined in the Due Process Clause of the Fourteenth Amendment, that history has attested as the indispensable conditions for the maintenance and progress of a free society." Here the effort is so to apply the provisions of c. 272, §§ 28C–28H, as amended (see also §§ 28, 28A, and 28B), as to deprive adults of the opportunity to read written material which, in the opinion of some members of the academic community, has some historical, literary, sociological, or entertainment interest. Although the book seems to me pretty sorry material, there is no accounting for tastes. It is irrelevant that the taste of those who wish to read this tawdry writing seems deplorable to judges, or to prosecutors, or to persons of conventional habits, or to volunteer guardians of the morals of other adults. Although this book appears to me to have substantially less literary excuse than the book discussed in *Attorney Gen.* v. *Book Named* "Tropic of Cancer," 345 Mass. 11, 184 N.E. 2d 328, it cannot be said to be "utterly without redeeming social importance." As I read the recent United States decisions, they declare in effect (if not in words) that to justify literary censorship there must be absent any form of worth. See *Jacobellis* v. *State of Ohio,* 378 U.S. 184, 191–192, 84 S. Ct. 1676.

I would (a) limit the relief granted to a declaration that distribution of this book to persons under the age of eighteen may be found to constitute a violation of c. 272, § 28, if that section is reasonably applied, and (b) expressly declare that, in view of the First Amendment, the book cannot be adjudged "obscene" in the sense in which that term has been used in recent constitutional decisions of the Supreme Court of the United States.

---

[2] This, as a practical matter, might cause some booksellers to refuse to sell the book to persons recognizable as minors and to be somewhat cautious about its distribution. See Lockhart and McClure, Censorship of Obscenity: The Developing Constitutional Standards, 45 Minn. L. Rev. 5, 84–87. Although no declaration was expressly sought that sale of the book might be a violation of § 28, a determination that the book may not be sold to certain minors is a lesser form of relief which may be reasonably regarded as included in the greater equitable relief asked for under § 28C.

■ A Book Named "John Cleland's Memoirs of a Woman of Pleasure," *et al., Appellants,*

v.

Attorney General of the Commonwealth of Massachusetts. No. 368.

Argued Dec. 7 and 9, 1965.

Decided March 21, 1966.

Charles Rembar, New York City, for appellants.
William I. Cowin, Brookline, Mass., for appellee.

Mr. Justice BRENNAN announced the judgment of the Court and delivered an opinion in which THE CHIEF JUSTICE and Mr. Justice FORTAS join.

This is an obscenity case in which *Memoirs of a Woman of Pleasure* (commonly known as *Fanny Hill*), written by John Cleland in about 1750, was adjudged obscene in a proceeding that put on trial the book itself,

and not its publisher or distributor. The proceeding was a civil equity suit brought by the Attorney General of Massachusetts, pursuant to General Laws of Massachusetts, Chapter 272, §§ 28C–28H, to have the book declared obscene.[1] Section 28C requires that the petition commencing the suit be "directed against [the] book by name" and that an order to show cause "why said book should not be judicially determined to be obscene" be published in a daily newspaper and sent by registered mail

---

[1] The text of the statute appears in the Appendix.

"to all persons interested in the publication." Publication of the order in this case occurred in a Boston daily newspaper, and a copy of the order was sent by registered mail to G. P. Putnam's Sons, alleged to be the publisher and copyright holder of the book.

As authorized by § 28D, G. P. Putnam's Sons intervened in the proceedings in behalf of the book, but it did not claim the right provided by that section to have the issue of obscenity tried by a jury. At the hearing before a justice of the Superior Court, which was conducted, under § 28F, "in accordance with the usual course of proceedings in equity," the court received the book in evidence and also, as allowed by the section, heard the testimony of experts[2] and accepted other evidence, such as book reviews, in order to assess the literary, cultural, or educational character of the book. This constituted the entire evidence, as neither side availed itself of the opportunity provided by the section to introduce evidence "as to the manner and form of its publication, advertisement, and distribution."[3] The trial justice entered a final decree,

which adjudged *Memoirs* obscene and declared that the book "is not entitled to the protection of the First and Fourteenth Amendments to the Constitution of the United States against action by the Attorney General or other law enforcement officer pursuant to the provisions of * * * § 28B, or otherwise."[4] The Massachusetts Supreme Judicial Court affirmed the decree. 349 Mass. 69, 206 N.E. 2d 403 (1965). We noted probable jurisdiction. 382 U.S. 900, 86 S. Ct. 232, 15 L. Ed. 2d 154. We reverse.[5]

I.

The term "obscene" appearing in the Massachusetts statute has been interpreted by the Supreme Judicial Court to be as expansive as the Constitution permits: the "statute covers all material that is obscene in the constitutional sense." *Attorney General* v. *The Book Named* "Tropic of Cancer," 345 Mass. 11, 13, 184 N.E. 2d 328, 330 (1962). Indeed, the final decree before us equates the finding that *Memoirs* is obscene within the meaning of the statute with the declaration that the book is not entitled to the protection of the First Amendment.[6] Thus the sole question before the state courts was whether *Memoirs* satisfies the test of obscenity established in *Roth* v. *United States*, 354 U.S. 476, 77 S. Ct. 1304, 1 L. Ed. 2d 1498.

We defined obscenity in *Roth* in the following terms: "[W]hether to the average person, applying contemporary community standards, the dominant theme of the material taken as a whole appeals to prurient interest." 354 U.S., at 489, 77 S. Ct., at 1311. Under this definition, as elaborated in subsequent cases, three elements must coalesce: it

---

[2] In dissenting from the Supreme Judicial Court's disposition in this case, 349 Mass. 69, 74–75, 206 N.E. 2d 403, 406–407 (1965), Justice Whittemore summarized this testimony:

"In the view of one or another or all of the following viz., the chairman of the English department at Williams College, a professor of English at Harvard College, an associate professor of English literature at Boston University, an associate professor of English at Massachusetts Institute of Technology, and an assistant professor of English and American literature at Brandeis University, the book is a minor 'work of art' having 'literary merit' and 'historical value' and containing a good deal of 'deliberate, calculated comedy.' It is a piece of 'social history of interest to anyone who is interested in fiction as a way of understanding society in the past.[1] A saving grace is that although many scenes, if translated into the present day language of 'the realistic, naturalistic novel, could be quite offensive' these scenes are not described in such language. The book contains no dirty words and its language 'functions * * * to create a distance, even when the sexual experiences are portrayed.' The response, therefore, is a literary response. The descriptions of depravity are not obscene because 'they are subordinate to an interest which is primarily literary'; Fanny's reaction to the scenes of depravity was 'anger,' 'disgust, horror, [and] indignation.' The book 'belongs to the history of English literature rather than the history of smut.'[2]

"[1] One of the witnesses testified in part as follows: 'Cleland is part of what I should call this cultural battle that is going on in the 18th century, a battle between a restricted Puritan, moralistic ethic that attempts to suppress freedom of the spirit, freedom of the flesh, and this element is competing with a freer attitude towards life, a more generous attitude towards life, a more wholesome attitude towards life, and this very attitude that is manifested in Fielding's great novel "Tom Jones" is also evident in Cleland's novel. * * * [Richardson's] "Pamela" is the story of a young country girl; [his] "Clarissa" is the story of a woman trapped in a house of prostitution. Obviously, then Cleland takes both these themes, the country girl, her initiation into life and into experience, and the story of a woman in a house of prostitution, and what he simply does is to take the situation and reverse the moral standards. Richardson believed that chastity was the most important thing in the world: Cleland and Fielding obviously did not and thought there were more important significant moral values.'

"[2] In the opinion of the other academic witness, the headmaster of a private school, whose field is English literature, the book is without literary merit and is obscene, impure, hard core pornography, and is patently offensive."

[3] The record in this case is thus significantly different from the

records in *Ginzburg* v. *United States*, 383 U.S. 463, 86 S. Ct. 942, and *Mishkin* v. *State of New York*, 383 U.S. 502, 86 S. Ct. 958, also decided today. See pp. 978–979, infra.

[4] Section 28B makes it a criminal offense, *inter alia*, to import, print, publish, sell, loan, distribute, buy, procure, receive, or possess for the purpose of sale, loan, or distribution, "a book, knowing it to be obscene." Section 28H provides that in any prosecution under § 28B the decree obtained in a proceeding against the book "shall be admissible in evidence" and further that '[i]f prior to the said offence a final decree had been entered against the book, the defendant, if the book be obscene * * * shall be conclusively presumed to have known said book to be obscene * * *." Thus a declaration of obscenity such as that obtained in this proceeding is likely to result in the total suppression of the book in the Commonwealth.

The constitutionality of § 28H has not been challenged in this appeal.

[5] Although the final decree provides no coercive relief but only a declaration of the book's obscenity, our adjudication of the merits of the issue tendered, viz., whether the state courts erred in declaring the book obscene, is not premature. There is no uncertainty as to the content of the material challenged, and the Attorney General's petition commencing this suit states that the book "is being imported, sold, loaned, or distributed in the Commonwealth." The declaration of obscenity is likely to have a serious inhibitory effect on the distribution of the book, and this probable impact is to no small measure derived from possible collateral uses of the declaration in subsequent prosecutions under the Massachusetts criminal obscenity statute. See n. 4, supra.

[6] We infer from the opinions below that the other adjectives describing the proscribed books in §§ 28C–28H, "indecent" and "impure," have either been read out of the statute or deemed synonymous with "obscene."

must be established that (a) the dominant theme of the material taken as a whole appeals to a prurient interest in sex; (b) the material is patently offensive because it affronts contemporary community standards relating to the description or representation of sexual matters; and (c) the material is utterly without redeeming social value.

The Supreme Judicial Court purported to apply the *Roth* definition of obscenity and held all three criteria satisfied. We need not consider the claim that the court erred in concluding that *Memoirs* satisfied the prurient appeal and patent offensiveness criteria; for reversal is required because the court misinterpreted the social value criterion. The court applied the criterion in this passage:

"*It remains to consider whether the book can be said to be 'utterly without social importance.' We are mindful that there was expert testimony, much of which was strained, to the effect that* Memoirs *is a structural novel with literary merit; that the book displays a skill in characterization and a gift for comedy; that it plays a part in the history of the development of the English novel; and that it contains a moral, namely, that sex with love is superior to sex in a brothel. But the fact that the testimony may indicate this book has some minimal literary value does not mean it is of any social importance. We do not interpret the 'social importance' test as requiring that a book which appeals to prurient interest and is patently offensive must be unqualifiedly worthless before it can be deemed obscene.*" 349 Mass., at 73, 206 N.E. 2d, at 406.

The Supreme Judicial Court erred in holding that a book need not be "unqualifiedly worthless before it can be deemed obscene." A book cannot be proscribed unless it is found to be *utterly* without redeeming social value. This is so even though the book is found to possess the requisite prurient appeal and to be patently offensive. Each of the three federal constitutional criteria is to be applied independently; the social value of the book can neither be weighed against nor canceled by its prurient appeal or patent offensiveness.[7] Hence, even on the view of the court below that *Memoirs* possessed only a modicum of social value, its judgment must be reversed as being founded on an erroneous interpretation of a federal constitutional standard.

II.

It does not necessarily follow from this reversal that a determination that *Memoirs* is obscene in the constitutional sense would be improper under all circumstances. On the premise, which we have no occasion to assess, that

Memoirs has the requisite prurient appeal and is patently offensive, but has only a minimum of social value, the circumstances of production, sale, and publicity are relevant in determining whether or not the publication or distribution of the book is constitutionally protected. Evidence that the book was commercially exploited for the sake of prurient appeal, to the exclusion of all other values, might justify the conclusion that the book was utterly without redeeming social importance. It is not that in such a setting the social value test is relaxed so as to dispense with the requirement that a book be *utterly* devoid of social value, but rather that, as we elaborate in *Ginzburg v. United States*, 383 U.S., pp. 470–473, 86 S. Ct., pp. 947–948, where the purveyor's sole emphasis is on the sexually provocative aspects of his publications, a court could accept his evaluation at its face value. In this proceeding, however, the courts were asked to judge the obscenity of *Memoirs* in the abstract, and the declaration of obscenity was neither aided nor limited by a specific set of circumstances of production, sale, and publicity.[8] All possible uses of the book must therefore be considered, and the mere risk that the book might be exploited by panderers because it so pervasively treats sexual matters cannot alter the fact—given the view of the Massachusetts court attributing to *Memoirs* a modicum of literary and historical value—that the book will have redeeming social importance in the hands of those who publish or distribute it on the basis of that value.

Reversed.

Mr. Justice BLACK and Mr. Justice STEWART concur in the reversal for the reasons stated in their respective dissenting opinions in *Ginzburg v. United States*, 383 U.S., p. 476 and p. 497, 86 S. Ct., p. 950 and p. 956, and *Mishkin v. State of New York*, 383 U.S., p. 515 and p. 518, 86 S. Ct., p. 968, and p. 969.

APPENDIX TO OPINION OF MR. JUSTICE BRENNAN.

State Statute.

Massachusetts General Laws, Chapter 272.

*   *   *   *   *

SECTION 28B. Whoever imports, prints, publishes, sells, loans or distributes, or buys, procures, receives, or has in his possession for the purpose of sale, loan or distribution,

---

[7] "[M]aterial dealing with sex in a manner that advocates ideas * * * or that has literary or scientific or artistic value or any other form of social importance, may not be branded as obscenity and denied the constitutional protection. Nor may the constitutional status of the material be made to turn on a 'weighing' of its social importance against its prurient appeal, for a work cannot be proscribed unless it is 'utterly' without social importance. See *Zeitlin v. Arnebergh*, 59 Cal. 2d 901, 920, 31 Cal. Rptr. 800, 813, 383 P. 2d 152, 165 (1963)." *Jacobellis v. State of Ohio*, 378 U.S. 184, 191, 84 S. Ct. 1676, 1680, 12 L. Ed. 2d 793 (opinion of Brennan, J.). Followed in, e.g., *People v. Bruce*, 31 Ill. 2d 459, 461, 202 N.E. 2d 497, 498 (1964); *Trans-Lux Distributing Corp. v. Maryland State Bd. of Censors*, 240 Md. 98, 104–105, 213 A. 2d 235, 238–239 (1965).

[8] In his dissenting opinion, 349 Mass., at 76–78, 206 N.E. 2d, at 408–409, Justice Cutter stated that, although in his view the book was not "obscene" within the meaning of *Roth*, "It could reasonably be found that distribution of the book to persons under the age of eighteen would be a violation of G.L. c. 272, § 28, as tending to corrupt the morals of youth." (Section 28 makes it a crime to sell to "a person under the age of eighteen years a book * * * which is obscene * * * or manifestly tends to corrupt the morals of youth.") He concluded that the court should "limit the relief granted to a declaration that distribution of this book to persons under the age of eighteen may be found to constitute a violation of [G.L.] c. 272, § 28, if that section is reasonably applied * * *." However, the decree was not so limited and we intimate no view concerning the constitutionality of such a limited declaration regarding *Memoirs*. Cf. *Jacobellis v. State of Ohio*, 378 U.S., at 195, 84 S. Ct., at 1682.

a book, knowing it to be obscene, indecent or impure, or whoever, being a wholesale distributor, a jobber, or publisher sends or delivers to a retail storekeeper a book, pamphlet, magazine or other form of printed or written material, knowing it to be obscene, indecent or impure, which said storekeeper had not previously ordered in writing, specifying the title and quantity of such publication he desired, shall be punished by imprisonment in the state prison for not more than five years or in a jail or house of correction for not more than two and one half years, or by a fine of not less than one hundred dollars nor more than five thousand dollars, or by both such fine and imprisonment in jail or the house of correction.

SECTION 28C. Whenever there is reasonable cause to believe that a book which is being imported, sold, loaned or distributed, or is in the possession of any person who intends to import, sell, loan or distribute the same, is obscene, indecent or impure, the attorney general, or any district attorney within his district, shall bring an information or petition in equity in the superior court directed against said book by name. Upon the filing of such information or petition in equity, a justice of the superior court shall, if, upon a summary examination of the book, he is of opinion that there is reasonable cause to believe that such book is obscene, indecent or impure, issue an order of notice, returnable in or within thirty days, directed against such book by name and addressed to all persons interested in the publication, sale, loan or distribution thereof, to show cause why said book should not be judicially determined to be obscene, indecent or impure. Notice of such order shall be given by publication once each week for two successive weeks in a daily newspaper published in the city of Boston and, if such information or petition be filed in any county other than Suffolk county, then by publication also in a daily newspaper published in such other county. A copy of such order of notice shall be sent by registered mail to the publisher of said book, to the person holding the copyrights, and to the author, in case the names of any such persons appear upon said book, fourteen days at least before the return day of such order of notice. After the issuance of an order of notice under the provisions of this section, the court shall, on motion of the attorney general or district attorney, make an interlocutory finding and adjudication that said book is obscene, indecent or impure, which finding and adjudication shall be of the same force and effect as the final finding and adjudication provided in section twenty-eight E or section twenty-eight F, but only until such final finding and adjudication is made or until further order of the court.

SECTION 28D. Any person interested in the sale, loan or distribution of said book may appear and file an answer on or before the return day named in said notice or within such further time as the court may allow, and may claim a right to trial by jury on the issue whether said book is obscene, indecent or impure.

SECTION 28E. If no person appears and answers within the time allowed, the court may at once upon motion of the petitioner, or of its own motion, no reason to the contrary appearing, order a general default and if the court finds that the book is obscene, indecent or impure, may make an adjudication against the book that the same is obscene, indecent and impure.

SECTION 28F. If an appearance is entered and answer filed, the case shall be set down for speedy hearing, but a default and order shall first be entered against all persons who have not appeared and answered, in the manner provided in section twenty-eight E. Such hearing shall be conducted in accordance with the usual course of proceedings in equity including all rights of exception and appeal. As such hearing the court may receive the testimony of experts and may receive evidence as to the literary, cultural or educational character of said book and as to the manner and form of its publication, advertisement, and distribution. Upon such hearing, the court may make an adjudication in the manner provided in said section twenty-eight E.

SECTION 28G. An information or petition in equity under the provisions of section twenty-eight C shall not be open to objection on the ground that a mere judgment, order or decree is sought thereby and that no relief is or could be claimed thereunder on the issue of the defendant's knowledge as to the obscenity, indecency or impurity of the book.

SECTION 28H. In any trial under section twenty-eight B on an indictment found or a complaint made for any offence committed after the filing of a proceeding under section twenty-eight C, the fact of such filing and the action of the court or jury thereon, if any, shall be admissible in evidence. If prior to the said offence a final decree had been entered against the book, the defendant, if the book be obscene, indecent or impure, shall be conclusively presumed to have known said book to be obscene, indecent or impure, or if said decree had been in favor of the book he shall be conclusively presumed not to have known said book to be obscene, indecent or impure, or if no final decree had been entered but a proceeding had been filed prior to said offence, the defendant shall be conclusively presumed to have had knowledge of the contents of said book.

Mr. Justice DOUGLAS, concurring.

Memoirs of a Woman of Pleasure, or, as it is often titled, *Fanny Hill*, concededly is an erotic novel. It was first published in about 1749 and has endured to this date, despite periodic efforts to suppress it.[1] The book relates the adventures of a young girl who becomes a prostitute in London. At the end, she abandons that life and marries her first lover, observing:

"*Thus, at length, I got snug into port, where, in the bosom of virtue, I gather'd the only uncorrupt sweets: where, looking back on the course of vice I had run, and comparing its infamous blandishments with the infinitely superior joys of innocence, I could not help pitying, even in point of taste, those who, immers'd in gross sensuality, are insensible to the so delicate charms of VIRTUE, than which even PLEASURE has not a greater friend, nor than VICE a greater enemy. Thus temperance makes men lords over those pleasures that intemperance enslaves them to: the one, parent of health, vigour, fertility, cheerfulness, and every other desirable good of life; the other, of dis-*

---

[1] *Memoirs* was the subject of what is generally regarded as the first recorded suppression of a literary work in this country on grounds of obscenity. See *Commonwealth v. Holmes*, 17 Mass. 336 (1821). The edition there condemned differed from the present volume in that it contained apparently erotic illustrations.

eases, debility, barrenness, self-loathing, with only every evil incident to human nature.

" * * The paths of Vice are sometimes strew'd with roses, but then they are for ever infamous for many a thorn, for many a cankerworm: those of Virtue are strew'd with roses purely, and those eternally unfading ones."*[2]

In 1963, an American publishing house undertook the publication of *Memoirs*. The record indicates that an unusually large number of orders were placed by universities and libraries; the Library of Congress requested the right to translate the book into Braille. But the Commonwealth of Massachusetts instituted the suit that ultimately found its way here, praying that the book be declared obscene so that the citizens of Massachusetts might be spared the necessity of determining for themselves whether or not to read it.

The courts of Massachusetts found the book "obscene" and upheld its suppression. This Court reverses, the prevailing opinion having seized upon language in the opinion of the Massachusetts Supreme Judicial Court in which it is candidly admitted that *Fanny Hill* has at least "some minimal literary value." I do not believe that the Court should decide this case on so disingenuous a basis as this. I base my vote to reverse on my view that the First Amendment does not permit the censorship of expression not brigaded with illegal action. But even applying the prevailing view of the *Roth* test, reversal is compelled by this record which makes clear that *Fanny Hill* is not "obscene." The prosecution made virtually no effort to prove that this book is "utterly without redeeming social importance." The defense, on the other hand, introduced considerable and impressive testimony to the effect that this was a work of literary, historical, and social importance.[3]

We are judges, not literary experts or historians or philosophers. We are not competent to render an independent judgment as to the worth of this or any other book, except in our capacity as private citizens. I would pair my Brother CLARK on *Fanny Hill* with the Universalist minister I quote in the Appendix. If there is to be censorship, the wisdom of experts on such matters as literary merit and historical significance must be evaluated. On this record, the Court has no choice but to reverse the judgment of the Massachusetts Supreme Judicial Court,

irrespective of whether we would include *Fanny Hill* in our own libraries.

Four of the seven Justices of the Massachusetts Supreme Judicial Court conclude that *Fanny Hill* is obscene. 349 Mass. 69, 206 N.E. 2d 403. Four of the seven judges of the New York Court of Appeals conclude that it is not obscene. *Larkin* v. *G. P. Putnam's Sons*, 14 N.Y. 2d 399, 252 N.Y.S. 2d 71, 200 N.E. 2d 760. To outlaw the book on such a voting record would be to let majorities rule where minorities were thought to be supreme. The Constitution forbids abridgment of "freedom of speech, or of the press." Censorship is the most notorious form of abridgment. It substitutes majority rule where minority tastes or viewpoints were to be tolerated.

It is to me inexplicable how a book that concededly has social worth can nonetheless be banned because of the manner in which it is advertised and sold. However florid its cover, whatever the pitch of its advertisements, the contents remain the same.

Every time an obscenity case is to be argued here, my office is flooded with letters and postal cards urging me to protect the community or the Nation by striking down the publication. The messages are often identical even down to commas and semicolons. The inference is irresistible that they were all copied from a school or church blackboard. Dozens of postal cards often are mailed from the same precinct. The drives are incessant and the pressures are great. Happily we do not bow to them. I mention them only to emphasize the lack of popular understanding of our constitutional system. Publications and utterances were made immune from majoritarian control by the First Amendment, applicable to the States by reason of the Fourteenth. No exceptions were made, not even for obscenity. The Court's contrary conclusion in *Roth* where obscenity was found to be "outside" the First Amendment, is without justification.

The extent to which the publication of "obscenity" was a crime at common law is unclear. It is generally agreed that the first reported case involving obscene conduct is *The King* v. *Sir Charles Sedley*.[4] Publication of obscene literature, at first thought to be the exclusive concern of the ecclesiastical courts,[5] was not held to constitute an indictable offense until 1727.[6] A later case involved the publication of an "obscene and impious libel" (a bawdy parody of Pope's "Essay on Man") by a member of the House of Commons.[7] On the basis of these few cases,

---

[2] *Memoirs*, at 213–214 (Putnam ed. 1963).

[3] The defense drew its witnesses from the various colleges located within the Commonwealth of Massachusetts. These included: Fred Holly Stocking, Professor of English and Chairman of the English Department, Williams College; John M. Bullitt, Professor of English and Master of Quincy House, Harvard College; Robert H. Sproat, Associate Professor of English Literature, Boston University; Norman N. Holland, Associate Professor of English, Massachusetts Institute of Technology; and Ira Konigsberg, Assistant Professor of English and American Literature, Brandeis University.

In addition, the defense introduced into evidence reviews of impartial literary critics. These are, in my opinion, of particular significance since their publication indicates that the book is of sufficient significance as to warrant serious critical comment. The reviews were by V. S. Pritchett, New York Review of Books, p. 1 (Oct. 31, 1963); Brigid Brophy, New Statesman, p. 710 (Nov. 15, 1963); and J. Donald Adams, New York Times Book Review, p. 2 (July 28, 1963). And the Appendix to this opinion contains another contemporary view.

[4] There are two reports of the case. The first is captioned *Le Roy* v. *Sr. Charles Sidney*, 1 Sid. 168, pl. 29 (K.B. 1663); the second is titled Sir Charles Sydlyes Case, I Keble 620 (K.B. 1663). Sir Charles had made a public appearance on a London balcony while nude, intoxicated, and talkative. He delivered a lengthy speech to the assembled crowd, uttered profanity, and hurled bottles containing what was later described as an "offensive liquor" upon the crowd. The proximate source of the "offensive liquor" appears to have been Sir Charles. Alpert, Judicial Censorship of Obscene Literature, 52 Harv. L. Rev. 40–43 (1938).

[5] *The Queen* v. *Read*, 11 Mod. 142 (Q.B. 1707).

[6] *Dominus Rex* v. *Curl*, 2 Strange 789 (K.B. 1727). See Straus, The Unspeakable Curll (1927).

[7] *Rex* v. *Wilkes*, 4 Burr. 2527 (K.B. 1770). The prosecution of Wilkes was a highly political action, for Wilkes was an outspoken critic of the government. See R. W. Postgate, That Devil Wilkes (1929). It has been suggested that the prosecution

one cannot say that the common-law doctrine with regard to publication of obscenity were anything but uncertain. "There is no definition of the term. There is no basis of identification. There is no unity in describing what is obscene literature, or in prosecuting it. There is little more than the ability to smell it." Alpert, Judicial Censorship of Obscene Literature, 52 Harv. L. Rev. 40, 47 (1938).

But even if the common law had been more fully developed at the time of the adoption of the First Amendment, we would not be justified in assuming that the Amendment left the common law unscathed. In *Bridges* v. *State of California*, 314 U.S. 252, 264, 62 S. Ct. 190, 194, 86 L. Ed. 192, we said:

"[T]o assume that English common law in this field became ours is to deny the generally accepted historical belief that 'one of the objects of the Revolution was to get rid of the English common law on liberty of speech and of the press.' Schofield, Freedom of the Press in the United States, 9 Publications Amer. Sociol. Soc. 67, 76.

"More specifically, it is to forget the environment in which the First Amendment was ratified. In presenting the proposals which were later embodied in the Bill of Rights, James Madison, the leader in the preparation of the First Amendment, said: 'Although I know whenever the great rights, the trial by jury, freedom of the press, or liberty of conscience, come in question in that body [Parliament], the invasion of them is resisted by able advocates, yet their Magna Charta does not contain any one provision for the security of those rights, respecting which the people of America are most alarmed. The freedom of the press and rights of conscience, those choicest privileges of the people, are unguarded in the British Constitution.'"

And see *Grosjean* v. *American Press Co.*, 297 U.S. 233, 248–249, 56 S. Ct. 444, 448–449, 80 L. Ed. 660.

It is true, as the Court observed in *Roth*, that obscenity laws appeared on the books of a handful of States at the time the First Amendment was adopted.[8] But the First Amendment was, until the adoption of the Fourteenth, a restraint only upon federal power. Moreover, there is an absence of any *federal* cases or laws relative to obscenity in the period immediately after the adoption of the First Amendment. Congress passed no legislation relating to obscenity until the middle of the nineteenth century.[9] Neither reason nor history warrants exclusion of any particular class of expression from the protection of the First

Amendment on nothing more than a judgment that it is utterly without merit. We faced the difficult questions the First Amendment poses with regard to libel in *New York Times Co.* v. *Sullivan*, 376 U.S. 254, 269, 84 S. Ct. 710, 720, 11 L. Ed. 2d 686, where we recognized that "libel can claim no talismanic immunity from constitutional limitations." We ought not to permit fictionalized assertions of constitutional history to obscure those questions here. Were the Court to undertake that inquiry, it would be unable, in my opinion, to escape the conclusion that no interest of society with regard to suppression of "obscene" literature could override the First Amendment to justify censorship.

The censor is always quick to justify his function in terms that are protective of society. But the First Amendment, written in terms that are absolute, deprives the States of any power to pass on the value, the propriety, or the morality of a particular expression. Cf. *Kingsley Int'l Pictures Corp.* v. *Regents of University*, 360 U.S. 684, 688–689, 79 S. Ct. 1362, 1365–1366, 3 L. Ed. 2d 1512; *Joseph Burstyn, Inc.* v. *Wilson*, 343 U.S. 495, 72 S. Ct. 777, 96 L. Ed. 1098. Perhaps the most frequently assigned justification for censorship is the belief that erotica produce antisocial sexual conduct. But that relationship has yet to be proven.[10] Indeed, if one were to make judgments on the basis of speculation, one might guess that literature of the most pornographic sort would, in many cases, provide a substitute—not a stimulus—for antisocial sexual conduct. See Murphy, The Value of Pornography, 10 Wayne L. Rev. 655, 661 and n. 19 (1964). As I read the First Amendment, judges cannot gear the literary diet of an entire nation to whatever tepid stuff is incapable of triggering the most demented mind. The First Amendment demands more than a horrible example or two of the perpetrator of a crime of sexual violance, in whose pocket is found a pornographic book, before it allows the Nation to be saddled with a regime of censorship.[11]

---

in this case was a convenient substitute for the less attractive charge of seditious libel. See Alpert, supra, at 45.

[8] See 354 U.S., at 483 and n. 13, 77 S. Ct., at 1308. For the most part, however, the early legislation was aimed at blasphemy and profanity. See 354 U.S., at 482–483 and n. 12, 77 S. Ct., at 1308. The first reported decision involving the publication of obscene literature does not come until 1821. See *Commonwealth* v. *Holmes*, 17 Mass. 336. It was not until after the Civil War that state prosecutions of this sort become commonplace. See Lockhart & McClure, Literature, The Law of Obscenity and the Constitution, 38 Minn. L. Rev. 295, 324–325 (1954).

[9] Tariff Act of 1842, c. 270, § 28, 5 Stat. 566 (prohibiting importation of obscene "prints"). Other federal legislation followed; the development of federal law is traced in Cairns, Paul & Wishner, Sex Censorship: The Assumptions of Anti-Obscenity Laws and the Empirical Evidence, 46 Minn. L. Rev. 1009, 1010 n. 2 (1962).

[10] See Cairns, Paul & Wishner, Sex Censorship, supra, 1034–1041; Lockhart & McClure, supra, at 382–387. And see the summary of Dr. Jahoda's studies prepared by her for Judge Frank, reprinted in *United States* v. *Roth*, 2 Cir., 237 F. 2d 796, 815–816 (concurring opinion). Those who are concerned about children and erotic literature would do well to consider the counsel of Judge Bok:

"It will be asked whether one would care to have one's young daughter read these books. I suppose that by the time she is old enough to wish to read them she will have learned the biologic facts of life and the words that go with them. There is something seriously wrong at home if those facts have not been met and faced and sorted by them; it is not children so much as parents that should receive our concern about this. I should prefer that my own three daughters meet the facts of life and the literature of the world in my library than behind a neighbor's barn, for I can face the adversary there directly. If the young ladies are appalled by what they read, they can close the book at the bottom of page one; if they read further, they will learn what is in the world and in its people, and no parents who have been discerning with their children need fear the outcome. Nor can they hold it back, for life is a series of little battles and minor issues, and the burden of choice is on us all, every day, young and old." *Commonwealth* v. *Gordon*, 66 Pa. Dist. & Co. R. 101, 110.

[11] It would be a futile effort even for a censor to attempt to remove all that might possibly stimulate antisocial sexual conduct:

"The majority [of individuals], needless to say, are somewhere

Whatever may be the reach of the power to regulate *conduct*, I stand by my view in *Roth* v. *United States*, supra, that the First Amendment leaves no power in government over *expression of ideas*.

APPENDIX TO OPINION OF MR. JUSTICE DOUGLAS, CONCURRING.
DR. PEALE AND FANNY HILL.
An Address by
Rev. John R. Graham, First Universalist
Church of Denver.
December 1965.

*   *   *   *   *   *

At the present point in the twentieth century, it seems to me that there are two books which symbolize the human quest for what is moral. *Sin, Sex and Self-Control* by Dr. Norman Vincent Peale, the well-known clergyman of New York City, portrays the struggle of contemporary middle-class society to arrive at a means of stabilizing behavior patterns. At the same time, there is a disturbing book being sold in the same stores with Dr. Peale's volume. It is a seventeenth century English novel by John Cleland and it is known as *Fanny Hill: The Memoirs of a Woman of Pleasure*.

Quickly, it must be admitted that it appears that the two books have very little in common. One was written in a day of scientific and technological sophistication, while the other is over two hundred years old. One is acclaimed in the pulpit, while the other is protested before the United States Supreme Court. *Sin, Sex and Self-Control* is authored by a Christian pastor, while *Fanny Hill* represents thoughts and experiences of a common prostitute. As far as the general public seems to be concerned, one is moral and the other is hopelessly immoral. While Dr. Peale is attempting to redeem the society, most people believe that *Fanny Hill* can only serve as another instance in an overall trend toward an immoral social order. Most parents would be pleased to find their children reading a book by Dr. Peale, but I am afraid that the same parents would be sorely distressed to discover a copy of *Fanny Hill* among the school books of their offspring.

---

between the overscrupulous extremes of excitement and frigidity * * *. Within this variety, it is impossible to define 'hard-core' pornography, as if there were some singly lewd concept from which all profane ideas passed by imperceptible degrees into that sexuality called holy. But there is no 'hard-core.' Everything, every idea, is capable of being obscene if the personality perceiving it so apprehends it.

"It is for this reason that books, pictures, charades, ritual, the spoken word, *can* and *do* lead directly to conduct harmful to the self indulging in it and to others. Heinrich Pommerenke, who was a rapist, abuser, and mass slayer of women in Germany, was prompted to his series of ghastly deeds by Cecil B. DeMille's The Ten Commandments. During the scene of the Jewish women dancing about the Golden Calf, all the doubts of his life came clear: Women were the source of the world's trouble and it was his mission to both punish them for this and to execute them. Leaving the theater, he slew his first victim in a park nearby. John George Haigh, the British vampire who sucked his victims' blood through soda straws and dissolved their drained bodies in acid baths, first had his murder-inciting dreams and vampire-longings from watching the 'voluptuous' procedure of— an Anglican High Church Service!" Murphy, supra, at 668.

Although one would not expect to find very many similarities between the thoughts of a pastor and those of a prostitute, the subject matter of the two books is, in many ways, strangely similar. While the contents are radically different, the concerns are the same. Both authors deal with human experience. They are concerned with people and what happens to them in the world in which they live each day. But most significantly of all, both books deal with the age-old question of "What is moral?" I readily admit that this concern with the moral is more obvious in Dr. Peal's book than it is in the one by John Cleland. The search for the moral in *Fanny Hill* is clothed in erotic passages which seem to equate morality with debauchery as far as the general public is concerned. At the same time, Dr. Peale's book is punctuated with such noble terms as "truth," "love," and "honesty."

These two books are not very important in themselves. They may or may not be great literature. Whether they will survive through the centuries to come is a question, although John Cleland has an historical edge on Norman Vincent Peale! However, in a symbolic way they do represent the struggle of the moral quest and for this reason they are important.

Dr. Peale begins his book with an analysis of contemporary society in terms of the moral disorder which is more than obvious today. He readily admits that the traditional Judeo-Christian standards of conduct and behavior no longer serve as strong and forceful guides. He writes:

"For more than forty years, ever since my ordination, I had been preaching that if a person would surrender to Jesus Christ and adopt strong affirmative attitudes toward life he would be able to live abundantly and triumphantly. I was still absolutely convinced that this was true. But I was also bleakly aware that the whole trend in the seventh decade of the twentieth century seemed to be away from the principles and practices of religion—not toward them." (Page 1.)

Dr. Peale then reflects on the various changes that have taken place in our day and suggests that although he is less than enthusiastic about the loss of allegiance to religion, he is, nevertheless, willing to recognize that one cannot live by illusion.

After much struggle, Dr. Peale then says that he was able to develop a new perspective on the current moral dilemma of our times. What first appeared to be disaster was really opportunity. Such an idea, coming from him, should not be very surprising, since he is more or less devoted to the concept of "positive thinking"! He concludes that our society should welcome the fact that the old external authorities have fallen. He does not believe that individuals should ever be coerced into certain patterns of behavior.

According to Dr. Peale, we live in a day of challenge. Our society has longed for a time when individuals would be disciplined by self-control, rather than being motivated by external compunction. Bravely and forthrightly, he announces that the time has now come when self-control can and must replace external authority. He is quick to add that the values contained in the Judeo-Christian tradition and "the American way of life" must never be abandoned for they emanate from the wellsprings of "Truth." What has previously been only an external force must now be internalized by individuals.

In many ways, Dr. Peale's analysis of the social situation and the solution he offers for assisting the individual to stand against the pressures of the times, come very close to the views of Sigmund Freud. He felt that society could and would corrupt the individual and, as a result, the only sure defense was a strong super-ego or conscience. This is precisely what Dr. Peale recommends.

Interestingly enough John Cleland, in *Fanny Hill,* is concerned with the same issues. Although the question of moral behavior is presented more subtly in his book, the problem with which he deals is identical. There are those who contend that the book is wholly without redeeming social importance. They feel that it appeals only to prurient interests.

I firmly believe that *Fanny Hill* is a moral, rather than an immoral, piece of literature. In fact, I will go as far as to suggest that it represents a more significant view of morality than is represented by Dr. Peale's book *Sin, Sex and Self-Control.* As is Dr. Peale, Cleland is concerned with the nature of the society and the relationship of the individual to it. *Fanny Hill* appears to me to be an allegory. In the story, the immoral becomes the moral and the unethical emerges as the ethical. Nothing is more distressing than to discover that what is commonly considered to be evil may, in reality, demonstrate characteristics of love and concern.

There is real irony in the fact that Fanny Hill, a rather naive young girl who becomes a prostitute, finds warmth, understanding and the meaning of love and faithfulness amid surroundings and situations which the society, as a whole, condemns as debased and depraved. The world outside the brothel affirms its faith in the dignity of man, but people are often treated as worthless and unimportant creatures. However, within the world of prostitution, Fanny Hill finds friendship, understanding, respect and is treated as a person of value. When her absent lover returns, she is not a lost girl of the gutter. One perceives that she is a whole and healthy person who has discovered the ability to love and be loved in a brothel.

I think Cleland is suggesting that one must be cautious about what is condemned and what is held in honor. From Dr. Peale's viewpoint, the story of Fanny Hill is a tragedy because she did not demonstrate self-control. She refused to internalize the values inherent in the Judeo-Christian tradition and the catalog of sexual scenes in the book, fifty-two in all, are a symbol of the debased individual and the society in which he lives.

Dr. Peale and others, would be correct in saying that Fanny Hill did not demonstrate self-control. She did, however, come to appreciate the value of self-expression. At no time were her "clients" looked upon as a means to an end. She tried and did understand them and she was concerned about them as persons. When her lover, Charles, returned she was not filled with guilt and remorse. She accepted herself as she was and was able to offer him her love and devotion.

I have a feeling that many people fear the book *Fanny Hill,* not because of its sexual scenes, but because the author raises serious question with the issue of what is moral and what is immoral. He takes exception to the idea that repression and restraint create moral individuals. He develops the thought that self-expression is more human than self-control. And he dares to suggest that, in a situation which society calls immoral and debased, a genuine love and respect for life and for people, as human beings, can develop. Far from glorifying vice, John Cleland points an accusing finger at the individual who is so certain as to what it means to be a moral man.

There are those who will quickly say that this "message" will be missed by the average person who reads *Fanny Hill.* But this is precisely the point. We become so accustomed to pre-judging what is ethical and what is immoral that we are unable to recognize that what we accept as good may be nothing less than evil because it harms people.

I know of no book which more beautifully describes meaningful relationships between a man and a woman than does *Fanny Hill.* In many marriages, men use a woman for sexual gratification and otherwise, as well as vice versa. But this is not the case in the story of Fanny Hill. The point is simply that there are many, many ways in which we hurt, injure and degrade people that are far worse than either being or visiting a prostitute. We do this all in the name of morality.

At the same time that Dr. Peale is concerned with sick people, John Cleland attempts to describe healthy ones. *Fanny Hill* is a more modern and certainly more valuable book than *Sin, Sex and Self-Control* because the author does not tell us how to behave, but attempts to help us understand ourselves and the nature of love and understanding in being related to other persons. Dr. Peale's writing emphasizes the most useful commodities available to man—self-centeredness and self-control. John Cleland suggests that self-understanding and self-expression may not be as popular, but they are more humane.

The "Peale approach" to life breeds contentment, for it suggests that each one of us can be certain as to what is good and true. Standards for thinking and behavior are available and all we need to do is appropriate them for our use. In a day when life is marked by chaos and confusion, this viewpoint offers much in the way of comfort and satisfaction. There is only one trouble with it, however, and that is that it results in conformity, rigid behavior and a lack of understanding. It results in personality configurations that are marked with an intense interest in propositions about Truth and Right but, at the same time, build a wall against people. Such an attitude creates certainty, but there is little warmth. The idea develops that there are "my kind of people" and they are "right." It forces us to degrade, dismiss and ultimately attempt to destroy anyone who does not agree with us.

To be alive and sensitive to life means that we have to choose what we want. There is no possible way for a person to be a slave and free at the same time. Self-control and self-expression are at opposite ends of the continuum. As much as some persons would like to have both, it is necessary to make a choice, since restraint and openness are contradictory qualities. To internalize external values denies the possibility of self-expression. We must decide what we want, when it comes to conformity and creativity. If we want people to behave in a structured and predictable manner, then the ideal of creativity cannot have meaning.

Long ago Plato said, "What is honored in a country * * * will be cultivated there." More and more, we reward people for thinking alike and as a result, we become frightened, beyond belief, of those who take exception to the current consensus. If our society collapses, it will not be because people read a book such as *Fanny Hill*. It will fall, because we will have refused to understand it. Decadence, in a nation or an individual, arises not because there is a lack of ability to distinguish between morality and immorality, but because the opportunity for self-expression has been so controlled or strangled that the society or the person becomes a robot.

The issue which a Dr. Peale will never understand, because he is a victim of it himself and which John Cleland describes with brilliant clarity and sensitive persuasion is that until we learn to respect ourselves enough that we leave each other alone, we cannot discover the meaning of morality.

Dr. Peale and Fanny Hill offer the two basic choices open to man. Man is free to choose an autocentric existence which is marked by freedom from ambiguity and responsibility. Autocentricity presupposes a "closed world" where life is predetermined and animal-like. In contrast to this view, there is the allocentric outlook which is marked by an "open encounter of the total person with the world." Growth, spontaneity and expression are the goals of such an existence.

Dr. Peale epitomizes the autocentric approach. He offers "warm blankets" and comfortable "cocoons" for those who want to lose their humanity. On the other hand, *Fanny Hill* represents the allocentric viewpoint which posits the possibility for man to raise his sights, stretch his imagination, cultivate his sensitiveness as well as deepen and broaden his perspectives. In discussing the autocentric idea, Floyd W. Matson writes,

"Human beings conditioned to apathy and affluence may well prefer this regressive path of least resistance with its promise of escape from freedom and an end to striving. But we know at least that it is open to them to choose otherwise: in a word, to choose themselves." (The Broken Image, *page 193.)*

In a day when people are overly sensitive in drawing lines between the good and the bad, the right and the wrong, as well as the true and the false, it seems to me that there is great irony in the availability of a book such as *Fanny Hill*. Prostitution may be the oldest profession in the world, but we are ever faced with a question which is becoming more and more disturbing: "What does a prostitute look like?"

Mr. Justice CLARK, dissenting.

It is with regret that I write this dissenting opinion. However, the public should know of the continuous flow of pornographic material reaching this Court and the increasing problem States have in controlling it. *Memoirs of a Woman of Pleasure*, the book involved here, is typical. I have "stomached" past cases for almost 10 years without much outcry. Though I am not known to be a purist—or a shrinking violet—this book is too much even for me. It is important that the Court has refused to declare it obscene and thus affords it further circulation. In order to give my remarks the proper setting I have been obliged to portray the book's contents, which causes me embarrassment. However, quotations from typical episodes would so debase our Reports that I will not follow that course.

I

Let me first pinpoint the effect of today's holding in the obscenity field. While there is no majority opinion in this case, there are three Justices who import a new test into that laid down in *Roth* v. *United States*, 354 U.S. 476, 77 S. Ct. 1304, 1 L. Ed. 2d 1498 (1957), namely, that "[a] book cannot be proscribed unless it is found to be *utterly without redeeming social value.*" I agree with my Brother WHITE that such a condition rejects the basic holding of *Roth* and gives the smut artist free rein to carry on his dirty business. My vote in that case—which was the deciding one for the majority opinion—was cast solely because the Court declared the test of obscenity to be: "whether to the average person, applying contemporary community standards, the dominant theme of the material taken as a whole appeals to prurient interest." I understand that test to include only two constitutional requirements: (1) the book must be judged as a whole, not by its parts; and (2) it must be judged in terms of its appeal to the prurient interest of the average person, applying contemporary community standards.[1] Indeed, obscenity was denoted in *Roth* as having "*such slight social value as a step to truth that any benefit that may be derived * * * is clearly outweighed by the social interest in order and morality * *.*" At 485, 77 S. Ct. at 1309 (quoting *Chaplinsky* v. *State of New Hampshire*, 315 U.S. 568, 572, 62 S. Ct. 766, 769, 86 L. Ed. 1031 (1942)). Moreover, in no subsequent decision of this Court has any "utterly without redeeming social value" test been suggested, much less expounded. My Brother Harlan in *Manual Enterprises, Inc.* v. *Day*, 370 U.S. 478, 82 S. Ct. 1432, 8 L. Ed. 2d 639 (1962), made no reference whatever to such a requirement in *Roth*. Rather he interpreted *Roth* as including a test of "patent offensiveness" besides "prurient appeal." Nor did my Brother Brennan in his concurring opinion in *Manual Enterprises* mention any "utterly without redeeming social value" test. The first reference to such a test was made by my Brother Brennan in *Jacobellis* v. *State of Ohio*, 378 U.S. 184, 191, 84 S. Ct. 1676, 1680, 12 L. Ed. 2d 793 (1964), seven years after *Roth*. In an opinion joined only by Justice Goldberg, he there wrote: "Recognizing that the test for obscenity enunciated [in *Roth*] * * * is not perfect, we think any substitute would raise equally difficult problems, and we therefore adhere to that standard." Nevertheless, he proceeded to add:

"*We would reiterate, however, our recognition in* Roth *that obscenity is excluded from the constitutional protection only because it is 'utterly without redeeming social importance,' * * *.*"

This language was then repeated in the converse to announce this *non sequitur*:

"*It follows that material dealing with sex in a manner that advocates ideas * * * or that has literary or scientific or artistic value or any other form of social importance, may not be branded as obscenity and denied the constitutional protection.*" At 191, 84 S. Ct., at 1680.

---

[1] See Lockhart & McClure, Censorship of Obscenity: The Developing Constitutional Standards, 45 Minn. L. Rev. 5, 53–55 (1960).

Significantly no opinion in *Jacobellis,* other than that of my Brother Brennan, mentioned the "utterly without redeeming social importance" test which he there introduced into our many and varied previous opinions in obscenity cases. Indeed, rather than recognizing the "utterly without social importance" test, The Chief Justice in his dissent in *Jacobellis,* which I joined, specifically stated:

"In light of the foregoing, I would reiterate my acceptance of the rule of the Roth *case:* Material is obscene and not constitutionally protected against regulation and proscription *if 'to the average person applying contemporary community standards, the dominant theme of the material taken as a whole appeals to prurient interest.'"* (*Emphasis added.*) At 202, 84 S. Ct. at 1685.

The Chief Justice and I further asserted that the enforcement of this rule should be committed to the state and federal courts whose judgments made pursuant to the *Roth* rule we would accept, limiting our review to a consideration of whether there is "sufficient evidence" in the record to support a finding of obscenity. At 202, 84 S. Ct. at 1685.

II.

Three members of the majority hold that reversal here is necessary solely because their novel "utterly without redeeming social value" test was not properly interpreted or applied by the Supreme Judicial Court of Massachusetts. Massachusetts now has to retry the case although the "Findings of Fact, Rulings of Law and Order for Final Decree" of the trial court specifically held that "this book is 'utterly without redeeming social importance' in the fields of art, literature, science, news or ideas of any social importance and that it is obscene, indecent and impure." I quote portions of the findings:

*"Opinions of experts are admitted in evidence to aid the Court in its understanding and comprehension of the facts, but, of course, an expert cannot usurp the function of the Court. Highly artificial, stylistic writing and an abundance of metaphorical descriptions are contained in the book but the conclusions of some experts were pretty well strained in attempting to justify its claimed literary value: such as the book preached a moral that sex with love is better than sex without love, when Fanny's description of her sexual acts, particularly with the young boy she seduced, in Fanny's judgment at least, was to the contrary. Careful review of all the expert testimony has been made, but, the best evidence of all, is the book itself and it plainly has no value because of ideas, news or artistic, literary or scientific attributes. * * * Nor does it have any other merit. 'This Court will not adopt a rule of law which states obscenity is suppressible but well written obscenity is not.' Mr. Justice Scileppi in* People v. Fritch, *13 N.Y. 2d 119 [243 N.Y.S. 2d 1, 192 N.E. 2d 713]."* (*Emphasis added.*) *Finding 20.*

None of these findings of the trial court were overturned on appeal, although the Supreme Judicial Court of Massachusetts observed in addition that "the fact that the testimony may indicate this book has some minimal liter-

ary value does not mean it is of any social importance. We do not interpret the 'social importance' test as requiring that a book which appeals to prurient interest and is patently offensive must be unqualifiedly worthless before it can be deemed obscene." My Brother Brennan reverses on the basis of this casual statement, despite the specific findings of the trial court. Why, if the statement is erroneous, Brother Brennan does not affirm the holding of the trial court which beyond question is correct, one cannot tell. This course has often been followed in other cases.

In my view evidence of social importance is relevant to the determination of the ultimate question of obscenity. But social importance does not constitute a separate and distinct constitutional test. Such evidence must be considered together with evidence that the material in question appeals to prurient interest and is patently offensive. Accordingly, we must first turn to the book here under attack. I repeat that I regret having to depict the sordid episodes of this book.

III.

Memoirs is nothing more than a series of minutely and vividly described sexual episodes. The book starts with Fanny Hill, a young 15-year-old girl, arriving in London to seek household work. She goes to an employment office where through happenstance she meets the mistress of a bawdy house. This takes 10 pages. The remaining 200 pages of the book detail her initiation into various sexual experiences, from a lesbian encounter with a sister prostitute to all sorts and types of sexual debauchery in bawdy houses and as the mistress of a variety of men. This is presented to the reader through an uninterrupted succession of descriptions by Fanny, either as an observer or participant, of sexual adventures so vile that one of the male expert witnesses in the case was hesitant to repeat any one of them in the courtroom. These scenes run the gamut of possible sexual experience such as lesbianism, female masturbation, homosexuality between young boys, the destruction of a maidenhead with consequent gory descriptions, the seduction of a young virgin boy, the flagellation of male by female, and vice versa, followed by fervid sexual engagement, and other abhorrent acts, including over two dozen separate bizarre descriptions of different sexual intercourses between male and female characters. In one sequence four girls in a bawdy house are required in the presence of one another to relate the lurid details of their loss of virginity and their glorification of it. This is followed the same evening by "publick trials" in which each of the four girls engages in sexual intercourse with a different man while the others witness, with Fanny giving a detailed description of the movement and reaction of each couple.

In each of the sexual scenes the exposed bodies of the participants are described in minute and individual detail. The pubic hair is often used for a background to the most vivid and precise descriptions of the response, condition, size, shape, and color of the sexual organs before, during and after orgasms. There are some short transitory passages between the various sexual episodes, but for the most part they only set the scene and identify the participants for the next orgy, or make smutty reference and comparison to past episodes.

There can be no doubt that the whole purpose of the

book is to arouse the prurient interest. Likewise the repetition of sexual episode after episode and the candor with which they are described renders the book "patently offensive." These facts weigh heavily in any appraisal of the book's claims to "redeeming social importance."

Let us now turn to evidence of the book's alleged social value.[2] While unfortunately the State offered little testimony, the defense called several experts to attest that the book has literary merit and historical value. A careful reading of testimony, however, reveals that it has no substance. For example, the first witness testified:

*"I think it is a work of art * * * it asks for and receives a literary response * * * presented in an orderly and organized fashion, with a fictional central character, and with a literary style * * *. I think the central character is * * * what I call an intellectual * * * someone who is extremely curious about life and who seeks * * * to record with accuracy the details of the external world, physical sensations, psychological responses * * * an empiricist * * *. I find that this tells me things * * * about the 18th century that I might not otherwise know."*

If a book of art is one that asks for and receives a literary response, *Memoirs* is no work of art. The sole response evoked by the book is sensual. Nor does the orderly presentation of *Memoirs* make a difference; it presents nothing but lascivious scenes organized solely to arouse prurient interest and produce sustained erotic tension.[3] Certainly the book's baroque style cannot vitiate the determination of obscenity. From a legal standpoint, we must remember that obscenity is no less obscene though it be expressed in "elaborate language." Indeed, the more meticulous its presentation, the more it appeals to the prurient interest. To say that Fanny is an "intellectual" is an insult to those who travel under that tag. She was nothing but a harlot—a sensualist—exploiting her sexual attractions which she sold for fun, for money, for lodging and keep, for an inheritance, and finally for a husband. If she was curious about life, her curiosity extended only to the pursuit of sexual delight wherever she found it. The book describes nothing in the "external world" except bawdy houses and debaucheries. As an empiricist, Fanny confines her observations and "experiments" to sex, with primary attention to depraved, lewd, and deviant practices.

Other experts produced by the defense testified that the book emphasizes the profound "idea that a sensual passion is only truly experienced when it is associated with the emotion of love" and that the sexual relationship "can be a wholesome, healthy, experience itself," whereas in certain modern novels "the relationship between the sexes is seen as another manifestation of modern decadence, insterility or perversion." In my view this proves nothing as to social value. The state court properly gave such testimony no probative weight. A review offered by the defense noted

that "where 'pornography' does not brutalize, it idealizes. The book is, in this sense, an erotic fantasy—and a male fantasy, at that, put into the mind of a woman. The male organ is phenomenal to the point of absurdity." Finally, it saw the book as "a minor fantasy, deluding as a guide to conduct, but respectful of our delight in the body * * * an interesting footnote in the history of the English novel." These unrelated assertions reveal to me nothing whatever of literary, historical, or social value. Another review called the book "a great novel * * * one which turns its convention upside down * * *." Admittedly Cleland did not attempt "high art" because he was writing "an erotic novel. He can skip the elevation and get on with the erections." Fanny's "downfall" is seen as "one long delightful swoon into the depths of pleasurable sensation." Rather than indicating social value in the book, this evidence reveals just the contrary. Another item offered by the defense described *Memoirs* as being "widely accredited as the first deliberately dirty novel in English." However, the reviewer found Fanny to be "no common harlot. Her 'Memoirs' combine literary grace with a disarming enthusiasm for an activity which is, after all, only human. What is more, she never uses a dirty word." The short answer to such "expertise" is that none of these so-called attributes have any value to society. On the contrary, they accentuate the prurient appeal.

Another expert described the book as having "detectable literary merit" since it reflects "an effort to interpret a rather complex character * * * going through a number of very different adventures." To illustrate his assertion that the "writing is very skillfully done" this expert pointed to the description of a whore, "Phoebe, who is 'red-faced, fat and in her early 50's, who waddles into a room.' She doesn't walk in, she waddles in." Given this standard for "skillful writing," it is not surprising that he found the book to have merit.

The remaining experts testified in the same manner, claiming the book to be a "record of the historical, psychological, [and] social events of the period." One has but to read the history of the 18th century to disprove this assertion. The story depicts nothing besides the brothels that are present in metropolitan cities in every period of history. One expert noticed "in this book a tendency away from nakedness during the sexual act which I find an interesting sort of sociological observation" on tastes different from contemporary ones. As additional proof, he marvels that Fanny "refers constantly to the male sexual organ as an engine * * * which is pulling you away from the way these events would be described in the 19th or 20th century." How this adds social value to the book is beyond my comprehension. It only indicates the lengths to which these experts go in their effort to give the book some semblance of value. For example, the ubiquitous descriptions of sexual acts are excused as being necessary in tracing the "moral progress" of the heroine, and the giving of a silver watch to a servant is found to be "an odd and interesting custom that I would like to know more about." This only points up the bankruptcy of *Memoirs* in both purpose and content, adequately justifying the trial court's finding that it had absolutely no social value.

It is, of course, the duty of the judge or the jury to determine the question of obscenity, viewing the book by contemporary community standards. It can accept the appraisal of experts or discount their testimony in the light

---

[2] In a preface to the paperback edition, "A Note on the American History of *Memoirs of a Woman of Pleasure*," the publisher itself mentions several critics who denied the book had any literary merit and found it totally undistinguished. These critics included Ralph Thompson and Clifton Fadiman. P. xviii.

[3] As one review stated: "Yet all these pangs of defloration are in the service of erotic pleasure—Fanny's and the reader's. Postponing the culmination of Fanny's deflowering is equivalent to postponing the point where the reader has a mental orgasm."

of the material itself or other relevant testimony. So-called "literary obscenity," i.e., the use of erotic fantasies of the hard-core type clothed in an engaging literary style has no constitutional protection. If a book deals solely with erotic material in a manner calculated to appeal to the prurient interest, it matters not that it may be expressed in beautiful prose. There are obviously dynamic connections between art and sex—the emotional, intellectual, and physical—but where the former is used solely to promote prurient appeal, it cannot claim constitutional immunity. Cleland uses this technique to promote the prurient appeal of *Memoirs*. It is true that Fanny's perverse experiences finally bring from her the observation that "the heights of [sexual] enjoyment cannot be achieved until true affection prepares the bed of passion." But this merely emphasizes that sex, wherever and however found, remains the sole theme of *Memoirs*. In my view, the book's repeated and unrelieved appeals to the prurient interest of the average person leave it utterly without redeeming social importance.

IV.

In his separate concurrence, my Brother DOUGLAS asserts there is no proof that obscenity produces anti-social conduct. I had thought that this question was foreclosed by the determination in *Roth* that obscenity was not protected by the First Amendment. I find it necessary to comment upon Brother DOUGLAS' views, however, because of the new requirement engrafted upon *Roth* by Brother BRENNAN, i.e., that material which "appeals to a prurient interest" and which is "patently offensive" may still not be suppressed unless it is "utterly without redeeming social value." The question of anti-social effect thus becomes relevant to the more limited question of social value. Brother BRENNAN indicates that the social importance criterion encompasses only such things as the artistic, literary, and historical qualities of the material. But the phrasing of the "utterly without redeeming social value" test suggests that other evidence must be considered. To say that social value may "redeem" implies that courts must balance alleged esthetic merit against the harmful consequences that may flow from pornography. Whatever the scope of the social value criterion—which need not be defined with precision of fact will weigh evidence of the material's influence in causing deviant or criminal conduct, particularly sex crimes, as well as its effect upon the mental, moral, and physical health of the average person. Brother DOUGLAS' view as to the lack of proof in this area is not so firmly held among behavioral scientists as he would lead us to believe. For this reason, I should mention that there is a division of thought on the correlation between obscenity and socially deleterious behavior.

Psychological and physiological studies clearly indicate that many persons become sexually aroused from reading obscene material.[4] While erotic stimulation caused by pornography may be legally insignificant in itself, there are medical experts who believe that such stimulation frequently manifests itself in criminal sexual behavior or other antisocial conduct.[5] For example, Dr. George W. Henry of Cornell University has expressed the opinion that obscenity, with its exaggerated and morbid emphasis on sex, particularly abnormal and perverted practices, and its unrealistic presentation of sexual behavior and attitudes, may induce antisocial conduct by the average person.[6] A number of sociologists think that this material may have adverse effects upon individual mental health, with potentially disruptive consequences for the community.[7]

In addition, there is persuasive evidence from criminologists and police officials. Inspector Herbert Case of the Detroit Police Department contends that sex murder cases are invariably tied to some form of obscene literature.[8] And the Director of the Federal Bureau of Investigation, J. Edgar Hoover, has repeatedly emphasized that pornography is associated with an overwhelmingly large number of sex crimes. Again, while the correlation between possession of obscenity and deviant behavior has not been conclusively established, the files of our law enforcement agencies contain many reports of persons who patterned their criminal conduct after behavior depicted in obscene material.[9]

The clergy are also outspoken in their belief that pornography encourages violence, degeneracy and sexual misconduct. In a speech reported by the New York Journal-American August 7, 1964, Cardinal Spellman particularly stressed the direct influence obscenity has on immature persons. These and related views have been confirmed by practical experience. After years of service with the West London Mission, Rev. Donald Soper found that pornography was a primary cause of prostitution. Rolph, Does Pornography Matter? (1961), pp. 47–48.[10]

Congress and the legislatures of every State have enacted measures to restrict the distribution of erotic and pornographic material,[11] justifying these controls by reference to evidence that antisocial behavior may result in part from reading obscenity.[12] Likewise, upon another trial, the parties may offer this sort of evidence along with other "social value" characteristics that they attribute to the book.

But this is not all that Massachusetts courts might consider. I believe it can be established that the book "was

---

[4] For a summary of experiments with various sexual stimuli see Cairns, Paul & Wishner, Sex Censorship: The Assumptions of Anti-Obscenity Laws and the Empirical Evidence, 46 Minn. L. Rev. 1009 (1962). The authors cite research by Kinsey disclosing that obscene literature stimulated a definite sexual response in a majority of the male and female subjects tested.

[5] E.G., Wertham, Seduction of the Innocent (1954), p. 164.

[6] Testimony before the Subcommittee of the Judiciary Committee to Investigate Juvenile Delinquency, S. Rep. No. 2381, 84th Cong., 2d Sess., pp. 8–12 (1956).

[7] Sorokin, The American Sex Revolution (1956).

[8] Testimony before the House Select Committee on Current Pornographic Materials, H.R. Rep. No. 2510, 82d Cong., 2d Sess., p. 62 (1952).

[9] See, e.g., Hoover, Combating Merchants of Filth: The Role of the FBI, 25 U. Pitt. L. Rev. 469 (1964); Hoover, The Fight Against Filth, The American Legion Magazine (May 1961).

[10] For a general discussion see Murphy, Censorship: Government and Obscenity (1963), pp. 131–151.

[11] The statutes are compiled in S. Rep. No. 2381, 84th Cong., 2d Sess., pp. 17–23 (1956). While New Mexico itself does not prohibit the distribution of obscenity, it has a statute giving municipalities the right to suppress "obscene" publications. N.M. Stat. § 14–17–14 (1965 Supp.).

[12] See Report of the New York State Joint Legislative Committee Studying the Publication and Dissemination of Offensive and Obscene Material (1958), pp. 141–166.

commercially exploited for the sake of prurient appeal, to the exclusion of all other values" and should therefore be declared obscene under the test of commercial exploitation announced today in *Ginzburg* and *Mishkin*.

As I have stated, my study of *Memoirs* leads me to think that it has no conceivable "social importance." The author's obsession with sex, his minute descriptions of phalli, and his repetitious accounts of bawdy sexual experiences and deviant sexual behavior indicate the book was designed solely to appeal to prurient interests. In addition, the record before the Court contains extrinsic evidence tending to show that the publisher was fully aware that the book attracted readers desirous of vicarious sexual pleasure, and sought to profit solely from its prurient appeal. The publisher's "Introduction" recites that Cleland, a "never-do-well bohemian," wrote the book in 1749 to make a quick 20 guineas. Thereafter, various publications of the book, often "embellished' with fresh inflammatory details" and "highly exaggerated illustrations," appeared in "surreptitious circulation." Indeed, the cover of *Memoirs* tempts the reader with the announcement that the sale of the book has finally been permitted "after 214 years of suppression." Although written in a sophisticated tone, the "Introduction" repeatedly informs the reader that he may expect graphic descriptions of genitals and sexual exploits. For instance, it states:

"Here and there, Cleland's descriptions of lovemaking are marred by what perhaps could be best described as his adherence to the 'longitudinal fallacy'—the formidable bodily equipment of his most accomplished lovers is apt to be described with quite unnecessary relish * * *."

Many other passages in the "Introduction" similarly reflect the publisher's "own evaluation" of the book's nature. The excerpt printed on the jacket of the hardcover edition is typical:

"Memoirs of a Woman of Pleasure *is the product of a luxurious and licentious, but not a commercially degraded, era. * * * For all its abounding improprieties, his priapic novel is not a vulgar book. It treats of pleasure as the aim and end of existence, and of sexual satisfaction as the epitome of pleasure, but does so in a style that, despite its inflammatory subject, never stoops to a gross or unbecoming word.*"

Cleland apparently wrote only one other book, a sequel called *Memoirs of a Coxcomb*, published by Lancer Books, Inc. The "Introduction" to that book labels *Memoirs of a Woman of Pleasure* as "the most sensational piece of erotica in English literature." I daresay that this fact alone explains why G. P. Putnam's Sons published this obscenity —preying upon prurient and carnal proclivities for its own pecuniary advantage. I would affirm the judgment.

Mr. Justice HARLAN, dissenting.

The central development that emerges from the aftermath of *Roth* v. *Uniited States*, 354 U.S. 476, 77 S. Ct. 1304, 1 L. Ed. 2d 1498, is that no stable approach to the obscenity problem has yet been devised by this Court. Two Justices believe that the First and Fourteenth Amendments absolutely protect obscene and nonobscene material alike.

Another Justice believes that neither the States nor the Federal Government may suppress any material save for "hard-core pornography." *Roth* in 1957 stressed prurience and utter lack of redeeming social importance;[1] as *Roth* has been expounded in this case, in *Ginzburg* v. *United States*, 383 U.S. 463, 86 S. Ct. 942, and in *Mishkin* v. *State of New York*, 383 U.S. 502, 86 S. Ct. 958, it has undergone significant transformation. The concept of "pandering," emphasized by the separate opinion of The Chief Justice in *Roth*, now emerges as an uncertain gloss or interpretive aid, and the further requisite of "patent offensiveness" has been made explicit as a result of intervening decisions. Given this tangled state of affairs, I feel free to adhere to the principles first set forth in my separate opinion in *Roth*, 354 U.S., at 496, 77 S. Ct., at 1315, which I continue to believe represent the soundest constitutional solution to this intractable problem.

My premise is that in the area of obscenity the Constitution does not bind the States and the Federal Government in precisely the same fashion. This approach is plainly consistent with the language of the First and Fourteenth Amendments and, in my opinion, more responsive to the proper functioning of a federal system of government in this area. See my opinion in *Roth*, 354 U.S., at 505–506, 77 S. Ct., at 1319–1320. I believe it is also consistent with past decisions of this Court. Although some 40 years have passed since the Court first indicated that the Fourteenth Amendment protects "free speech," see *Gitlow* v. *People of State of New York*, 268 U.S. 652, 45 S. Ct. 625, 69 L. Ed. 1138; *Fiske* v. *State of Kansas*, 274 U.S. 380, 47 S. Ct. 655, 71 L. Ed. 1108, the decisions have never declared that every utterance the Federal Government may not reach or every regulatory scheme it may not enact is also beyond the power of the State. The very criteria used in opinions to delimit the protection of free speech—the gravity of the evil being regulated, see *Schneider* v. *State of New Jersey*, 308 U.S. 147, 60 S. Ct. 146, 84 L. Ed. 155; how "clear and present" is the danger, *Schenck* v. *United States*, 249 U.S. 47, 52, 39 S. Ct. 247, 249, 63 L. Ed. 470 (Holmes, J.); the magnitude of "such invasion of free speech as is necessary to avoid the danger," *United States* v. *Dennis*, 2 Cir., 183 F. 2d 201, 212 (L. Hand, J.)—may and do depend on the particular context in which power is exercised. When, for example, the Court in *Beauharnais* v. *People of State of Illinois*, 343 U.S. 250, 72 S. Ct. 725, 96 L. Ed. 919, upheld a criminal group-libel law because of the "social interest in order and morality," 343 U.S., at 257, 72 S. Ct., at 731, it was acknowledging the responsibility and capacity of the States in such public-welfare matters and not committing itself to uphold any similar federal statute applying to such communications as Congress might otherwise regulate under the commerce power. See also *Kovacs* v. *Cooper*, 336 U.S. 77, 69 S. Ct. 448, 93 L. Ed 513.

Federal suppression of allegedly obscene matter should, in my view, be constitutionally limited to that often described as "hard-core pornography." To be sure, that rubric is not a self-executing standard, but it does describe something that most judges and others will "know * * *

---

[1] Given my view of the applicable constitutional standards, I find no occasion to consider the place of "redeeming social importance" in the majority opinion in *Roth*, an issue which further divides the present Court.

when [they] see it" (Stewart, J., in *Jacobellis* v. *State of Ohio*, 378 U.S. 184, 197, 84 S. Ct. 1676, 1683, 12 L. Ed. 2d 793) and that leaves the smallest room for disagreement between those of varying tastes. To me it is plain, for instance, that *Fanny Hill* does not fall within this class and could not be barred from the federal mails. If further articulation is meaningful, I would characterize as "hardcore" that prurient material that is patently offensive or whose indecency is self-demonstrating and I would describe it substantially as does Mr. Justice Stewart's opinion in Ginzburg, 383 U.S, p. 499, 86 S. Ct., p. 957. The Federal Government may be conceded a limited interest in excluding from the mails such gross pornography, almost universally condemned in this country.[2] But I believe the dangers of national censorship and the existence of primary responsibility at the state level amply justify drawing the line at this point.

State obscenity laws present problems of quite a different order. The varying conditions across the country, the range of views on the need and reasons for curbing obscenity, and the traditions of local self-government in matters of public welfare all favor a far more flexible attitude in defining the bounds for the States. From my standpoint, the Fourteenth Amendment requires of a State only that it apply criteria rationally related to the accepted notion of obscenity and that it reach results not wholly out of step with current American standards. As to criteria, it should be adequate if the court or jury considers such elements as offensiveness, pruriency, social value, and the like. The latitude which I believe the States deserve cautions against any federally imposed formula listing the exclusive ingredients of obscenity and fixing their proportions. This approach concededly lacks precision, but imprecision is characteristic of mediating constitutional standards;[3] voluntariness of a confession, clear and present danger, and probable cause are only the most ready illustrations. In time and with more litigated examples, predictability increases, but there is no shortcut to satisfactory solutions in this field, and there is no advantage in supposing otherwise.

I believe the tests set out in the prevailing opinion, judged by their application in this case, offer only an illusion of certainty and risk confusion and prejudice. The opinion declares that a book cannot be banned unless it is "utterly without redeeming social value" (ante, p. 977). To establish social value in the present case, a number of acknowledged experts in the field of literature testified that *Fanny Hill* held a respectable place in serious writing, and unless such largely uncontradicted testimony is accepted as decisive it is very hard to see that the "utterly without redeeming social value" test has any meaning at all. Yet

the prevailing opinion, while denying that social value may be "weighed against" or "canceled by" prurience or offensiveness (ante, p. 978), terminates this case unwilling to give a conclusive decision on the status of *Fanny Hill* under the Constitution.[4] Apparently, the Court believes that the social value of the book may be negated if proof of pandering is present. Using this inherently vague "pandering" notion to offset "social value" wipes out any certainty the latter term might be given by reliance on experts, and admits into the case highly prejudicial evidence without appropriate restrictions. See my dissenting opinion in *Ginzburg*, 383 U.S., p. 493, 86 S. Ct., p. 953. I think it more satisfactory to acknowledge that on this record the book has been shown to have some quantum of social value, that it may at the same time be deemed offensive and salacious, and that the State's decision to weigh these elements and to ban this particular work does not exceed constitutional limits.

A final aspect of the obscenity problem is the role this Court is to play in administering its standards, a matter that engendered justified concern at the oral argument of the cases now decided. Short of saying that no material relating to sex may be banned, or that all of it may be, I do not see how this Court can escape the task of reviewing obscenity decisions on a case-by-case basis. The views of literary or other experts could be made controlling, but those experts had their say in *Fanny Hill* and apparently the majority is no more willing than I to say that Massachusetts must abide by their verdict. Yet I venture to say that the Court's burden of decision would be ameliorated under the constitutional principles that I have advocated. "Hard-core pornography" for judging federal cases is one of the more tangible concepts in the field. As to the States, the due latitude my approach would leave them ensures that only the unusual case would require plenary review and correction by this Court.

There is plenty of room, I know, for disagreement in this area of constitutional law. Some will think that what I propose may encourage States to go too far in this field. Others will consider that the Court's present course unduly restricts state experimentation with the still elusive problem of obscenity. For myself, I believe it is the part of wisdom for those of us who happen currently to possess the "final word" to leave room for such experimentation, which indeed is the underlying genius of our federal system.

On the premises set forth in this opinion, supplementing what I have earlier said in my opinions in *Roth*, supra; *Manual Enterprises, Inc.* v. *Day*, 370 U.S. 478, 82 S. Ct. 1432, 8 L. Ed 2d 639, and *Jacobellis* v. *State of Ohio*, 378 U.S., at 203, 84 S. Ct., at 1686, I would affirm the judgment of the Massachusetts Supreme Judicial Court.

Mr. Justice WHITE, dissenting.

In *Roth* v. *United States*, 354 U.S. 476, 77 S. Ct. 1304, 1 L. Ed. 2d 1498, the Court held a publication to be

---

[2] This interest may be viewed from different angles. Compelling the Post Office to aid actively in disseminating this most obnoxious material may simply appear too offensive in itself. Or, more concretely, use of the mails may facilitate or insulate distribution so greatly that federal inaction amounts to thwarting state regulation.

[3] The deterrent effect of vagueness for that critical class of books near the law's borderline could in the past be ameliorated by devices like the Massachusetts *in rem* procedure used in this case. Of course, the Court's newly adopted "panderer" test, turning as it does on the motives and actions of the particular defendant, seriously undercuts the effort to give any seller a yes or no answer on a book in advance of his own criminal prosecution.

[4] As I understand the prevailing opinion, its rationale is that the state court may not condemn *Fanny Hill* as obscene after finding the book to have a modicum of social value; the opinion does note that proof of pandering "might justify the conclusion" that the book wholly lacks social value (ante, p. 978). Given its premise for reversal, the opinion has "no occasion to assess" for itself the pruriency, offensiveness, or lack of social value of the book (ante, p. 978).

obscene if its predominant theme appeals to the prurient interest in a manner exceeding customary limits of candor. Material of this kind, the Court said, is "utterly without redeeming social importance" and is therefore unprotected by the First Amendment.

To say that material within the *Roth* definition of obscenity is nevertheless not obscene if it has some redeeming social value is to reject one of the basic propositions of the *Roth* case—that such material is not protected *because* it is inherently and utterly without social value.

If "social importance" is to be used as the prevailing opinion uses it today, obscene material, however far beyond customary limits of candor, is immune if it has any literary style, if it contains any historical references or language characteristic of a bygone day, or even if it is printed or bound in an interesting way. Well written, especially effective obscenity is protected; the poorly written is vulnerable. And why shouldn't the fact that some people buy and read such material prove its "social value"?

A *fortiori*, if the predominant theme of the book appeals to the prurient interest as stated in *Roth* but the book nevertheless contains here and there a passage descriptive of character, geography or architecture, the book would not be "obscene" under the social importance test. I had thought that *Roth* counseled the contrary: that the character of the book is fixed by its predominant theme and is not altered by the presence of minor themes of a different nature. The *Roth* Court's emphatic reliance on the quotation from *Chaplinsky* v. *State of New Hampshire*, 315 U.S. 568, 62 S. Ct. 766, 86 L. Ed. 1031, means nothing less:

" '* * * There are certain well-defined and narrowly limited classes of speech, the prevention and punishment of which have never been thought to raise any Constitutional problem. These include the lewd and obscene* * *. It has been well observed that such utterances are no essential part of any exposition of ideas, and are of such slight social value as a step to truth that any benefit that may be derived from them is clearly outweighed by the social interest in order and morality * * *.' (Emphasis added.)" 354 U.S., at 485, 77 S. Ct., at 1309.

In my view, "social importance" is not an independent test of obscenity but is relevant only to determining the predominant prurient interest of the material, a determination which the court or the jury will make based on the material itself and all the evidence in the case, expert or otherwise.

Application of the *Roth* test, as I understand it, necessarily involves the exercise of judgment by legislatures, courts and juries. But this does not mean that there are no limits to what may be done in the name of *Roth*. Cf. *Jacobellis* v. *State of Ohio*, 378 U.S. 184, 84 S. Ct. 1676, 12 L. Ed. 2d 793. *Roth* does not mean that a legislature is free to ban books simply because they deal with sex or because they appeal to the prurient interest. Nor does it mean that if books like *Fanny Hill* are unprotected, their nonprurient appeal is necessarily lost to the world. Literary style, history, teachings about sex, character description (even of a prostitute) or moral lessons need not come wrapped in such packages. The fact that they do impeaches their claims to immunity from legislative censure.

Finally, it should be remembered that if the publication and sale of *Fanny Hill* and like books are proscribed, it is not the Constitution that imposes the ban. Censure stems from a legislative act, and legislatures are constitutionally free to embrace such books whenever they wish to do so. But if a State insists on treating *Fanny Hill* as obscene and forbidding its sale, the First Amendment does not prevent it from doing so.

I would affirm the judgment below.

■ United States of America, *Appellee*,

v.

Irving Klaw and Jack Kramer, *Defendants-Appellants*.
No. 70, Docket 28887.

United States Court of Appeals, Second Circuit.

Argued Oct. 15, 1964.

Decided July 15, 1965.

Richard A. Givens, Asst. U.S. Atty., Southern Dist. of New York (Robert M. Morgenthau, U.S. Atty., Andrew T. McEvoy, Jr., and John S. Martin, Jr., Asst. U.S. Attys., on the brief), for appellee.

Joseph E. Brill, New York City (Robert E. Goldman and Bernard J. Levy, New York City, on the brief), for appellants.

Before WATERMAN, MOORE and SMITH, Circuit Judges.

MOORE, Circuit Judge:

Irving Klaw and Jack Kramer were indicted on one count for conspiring to violate 18 U.S.C.A. § 1461 by knowingly using the mails for the carriage of "articles, matters, and things, which were non-mailable in that they were obscene, lewd, lascivious, indecent, filthy and vile." They were also charged with having knowingly used the mails to distribute "circulars, advertisements and notices which were non-mailable in that they gave information directly and indirectly, where, how, from whom and by what means certain obscene, lewd, lascivious, indecent, filthy and vile matters and things might be obtained." In addition, Klaw was indicted on forty-three counts for using the mails to transmit "certain articles, matters and things * * *, to wit, printed circulars, pamphlets, booklets, drawings, photographs and motion picture films, which were non-mailable in that they were obscene, lewd, lascivious, indecent, filthy and vile." Nine of these counts were eventually dismissed, leaving thirty-four. Klaw was also indicted on forty-one counts for using the mails to carry certain "circulars, advertisements and notices, * * which were non-mailable in that they gave information directly and indirectly, where, how, from whom and by what means, certain obscene, lewd, lascivious, indecent, filthy and vile articles, matters and things might be obtained." Eleven of these counts were eventually dismissed, leaving thirty.

The conspiracy was said to have run from June 1, 1960, until the date of the indictment, June 27, 1963. The substantive counts were each based on individual mailings of materials over a period running from July 25, 1958, to May 6, 1963.

At a jury trial, the Government produced six witnesses whose receipt (or whose son's receipt) of circulars and materials had been the basis of thirteen of the thirty-four "obscene materials" counts and ten of the thirty "publicizing" counts. The lion's share of these mailings had been to one Duane Thoman of LaGrange, Kentucky, which name was one of the 300 or so aliases of Postal Inspector Harry Simon of Washington, D.C., who testified at the trial. Three of the Government's witnesses were parents who, while rummaging through Junior's bureau drawer, found that their respective adolescent offspring were exploring on their own a new world just coming into view. One Junior also testified but only as to his receipt of items from Nutrix.

Klaw is the owner of Nutrix Co., a New York based establishment that prints and publicizes materials—stories, photographs and drawings in the "bondage" genre. Much solicitation and distribution is carried on through the mails, particularly by way of mail order ads appearing in magazines likely to have a male clientele. These "bondage" booklets usually contain some twenty to twenty-five photographs or crude drawings of females—some scantily clad, some tightly trussed, and all voluptuous—subjecting other women and men to various tortures and indignities, including violent and forcible deformation of the body, while being gagged, fettered and bound in bizarre postures. The booklets bore such titles as "Sorority Girls Stringent Initiation," "Female Doctor Forced into Bondage," "Girls Concentration Camp Ordeals," "Dominating Woman Turns Man into Girl," "Men in the Ladies Room," and the like. A text in each booklet described in a puerile and asinine fashion the activity depicted in the drawings. One booklet entitled "The Devil of Yocherwalden" pictures female "Gazi" guards subjecting female prisoners to brutal tortures at the direction of the "Gazi" commandant "Elsi Achstunk." The captives and tormentors are drawn with

exaggerated female physical characteristics, clothed in tight-fitting garments, wearing black leather shoes with very high heels, and posed in unreal positions. There were also photographs of "Fighting Girls," corset and high heel shoe scenes, and girls in rubber apparel. Photographs offered for sale were in many instances taken from motion pictures said to have been recently released, such as "Blood of the Vampire," "Slaves of Carthage," and "The Mystery of the Black Whip." Amateur "bondage" photographs were often solicited. Bulletins published by Nutrix advertised its publications in various bondage series. All these materials are described to us as being "sado-masochistic," and we are referred to Krafft-Ebing's *Psychopathia Sexualis* for further elucidation.

Nutrix is apparently a long-time disseminator of substantially the same type of bondage materials as those involved here. Surveillance by the Postal authorities (Inspector Simon) had commenced in 1951 and continued for four years, at which time no criminal reference was made. However, an administrative proceeding was then begun which culminated in the Postmaster-General's ordering that mail addressed to Klaw be marked "unlawful" and returned to the sender, pursuant to then 39 U.S.C.A. § 259a (now 39 U.S.C.A. § 4006). Klaw sought to enjoin the Postmaster from implementing that order, but was unsuccessful. See *Klaw v. Schaffer*, 151 F. Supp. 534 (S.D.N.Y. 1957). This court affirmed *per curiam* the District Court's conclusion that the Postmaster General had acted within his statutory authority and that there was substantial evidence in that record to support the hearing examiner's finding that the material was obscene. 251 F. 2d 615 (2d Cir. 1958). This court's judgment was vacated by the Supreme Court on other grounds and the complaint was dismissed. 357 U.S. 346, 78 S. Ct. 1369, 2 L. Ed. 2d 1368 (1958). Thereupon Inspector Simon resumed his investigation. In 1960 he recommended prosecution, but no official action was taken until 1963. Kramer apparently began working for Nutrix in 1960 as manager of the New Jersey warehouse. In addition to these facts, the jury also had visual impressions from observation of the Nutrix materials introduced on trial.

Defendants were found guilty on each of the sixty-five counts that went to the jury. Klaw received concurrent sentences of two years' imprisonment on counts 1 to 5, with a $1,000 fine on each count; he received a suspended sentence on each of the remaining counts.[1] Kramer was fined $2,500 on count 1 and received a suspended sentence. Both Klaw and Kramer appeal, claiming that their motion for a directed verdict of acquittal was erroneously denied because there was insufficient evidence relating the Nutrix materials to "obscenity" or to "prurient interest."

In approaching this controversy arising out of another of our society's attempts at censorship, it is helpful to have in mind the scope of the problem and the variety of ways in which it arises. Cases in the Supreme Court over the past decade or so have come into being because state and city police officers, state attorneys general and federal district

---

[1] The conspiracy count was punishable by up to five years' imprisonment and a fine of up to $10,000. 18 U.S.C.A. § 371. Knowing use of the mails for the carriage of non-mailable matter is punishable by up to five years' imprisonment and a fine of up to $5,000 for the first offense, and up to ten years' imprisonment and a fine of up to $10,000 for each subsequent offense. 18 U.S.C.A. § 1461.

attorneys, state motion picture licensing bureaus, state youth morality commissions, federal Post Office Examiners and Inspectors, state and federal judges, and juries have considered a variety of movies, books and magazines to be "sacrilegious," "immoral," "obscene," or "objectionable." The specific items have run the gamut from motion pictures like "The Miracle," "La Ronde," "M," "Native Son," "The Game of Love," "Lady Chatterley's Lover," "Les Amants," and "A Stranger Knocks" to books like "Nights of Horror," "Peyton Place," "Pleasure Was My Business," and "Tropic of Cancer," to magazines like "One—The Homosexual Magazine," "MANual," "Trim," "Grecian Guild Pictorial," "Playboy," "Rogue," "Frolic," other "girlie-type" magazines, and nudist magazines. Publishers, exhibitors, distributors and sellers of these materials have been subjected in state and federal courts and agencies to set-backs including stiff fines and jail sentences, seizure of the materials, injunctions against distribution, denial of licenses needed to exhibit a motion picture, and loss of the privilege to use the United States mails to distribute and publicize the materials.

The censors' successes have been short-lived, however, for in virtually every case decided by the Supreme Court, the disseminator has had a favorable result on one ground or another, save for three cases decided on one day in 1957.[2] Two are significant here—*Roth* v. *United States* and *Alberts* v. *California*, both reported at 354 U.S. 476, 77 S. Ct. 1304, 1 L. Ed. 2d 1498 (1957), which deal with the constitutional protection and definition of "obscenity,"

and which constitute the first and apparently only opinion subscribed to by a majority of the Court. In both cases convictions for violation of federal and state statutes pertaining to "obscenity" were upheld by divided Courts—5 to 4 in Roth, and 6 to 3 in Alberts.

But if the censors won the battles of Roth and Alberts, the subsequent application of the principles of those cases suggests that as far as the war against pornography goes, the victory was only Pyrrhic. Since 1957 and Roth the "obscenity" situation has advanced rapidly. Then Lady Chatterley was still enjoying her clandestine sylvan trysts with her earthy gamekeeper; Fanny Hill's lively and apparently continuous actions were known only to the foreign traveling elite or to the reader of a smuggled copy; and "Tropic of Cancer" was still being seized by vigilant customs agents as contraband. Suddenly the entire picture changed. Whether encouraged by the courts, or whether literary styles turned towards super-realism, or both, authors and publishers were quick to capitalize on the "modern" trend—a trend which they largely made. "Lady Chatterley's Lover" in paperback editions was sold to countless thousands with the court's opinion of approbation attached as a major part of its advertising. No longer did Constance enjoy the privacy of her woodland. Millions of eyes ogling with interest ("prurient" interest probably) stared at her and her lover whilst they enjoyed those moments which court opinions cannot describe lest they risk going "substantially beyond customary limits of candor in description or representation of such matters." Roth, supra, 357 U.S. at 487, n. 20, 77 S. Ct. at 1310.

"Tropic of Cancer" was brought out from under the counter and dusted off. In 1962 it was approved (four justices approving, three dissenting) for public reading by a Massachusetts court. See *Attorney General* v. *Book Named "Tropic of Cancer,"* 345 Mass. 11, 184 N.E. 2d 328 (1962). In Wisconsin by an equally close vote (four-to-three), the Supreme Court reversed a lower court decision declaring the book "obscene" and held that, although "[m]uch of the language in the book would be offensive to many" and that in one or two instances the "short English words of ancient origin" were "obscene," nevertheless, despite the fact that some episodes would "appeal to prurient interests," it was the court's duty "to respect and enforce in full measure the freedom of expression guaranteed by state and federal constitutions." *McCauley* v. *Tropic of Cancer*, 20 Wis. 2d 134, 151, 121 N.W. 2d 545, 554 (1963). The Supreme Court of California reviewed a decision determining the book to be "obscene" and, after a comprehensive survey of post-Roth decisions, unanimously reversed. *Zeitlin* v. *Arnebergh*, 59 Cal. 2d 901, 31 Cal. Rptr. 800, 383 P. 2d 152, cert. denied, 375 U.S. 957, 84 S. Ct. 445, 11 L. Ed. 2d 315 (1963). The New York Court of Appeals in *People* v. *Fritch*, 13 N.Y. 2d 119, 243 N.Y.S. 2d 1, 192 N.E. 2d 713 (1963) also by a four-to-three vote held the same book to be "obscene" and reversed a determination by the County Court to the contrary, thus reinstating a conviction by a jury, although ordering a new trial on the issue of *scienter*. This decision, however, the same court (also by a four-to-three vote) considers as having been "now overruled by *Grove Press, Inc.* v. *Gerstein*, 378 U.S. 577, 84 S. Ct. 1909 [12 L. Ed. 2d 1035]." *Larkin* v. *G. P. Putnam's Sons*, 14 N.Y. 2d 399, 404, 252 N.Y.S. 2d 71, 75, 200 N.E. 2d 760, 763 (1964).

---

[2] For convenience we list chronologically the Supreme Court's relevant "obscenity" and censorship decisions. *Joseph Burstyn, Inc.* v. *Wilson*, 343 U.S. 495, 72 S. Ct. 777, 96 L. Ed. 1098 (1952) (movie license; "sacrilegious"); *Superior Films, Inc.* v. *Department of Education* (same, "obscene") and *Commercial Pictures Corp.* v. *Regents of the University of the State of New York* (same, "immoral"), 346 U.S. 587, 74 S. Ct. 286, 98 L. Ed. 329 (1954); *Roth* v. *United States* (conviction; "obscene"), and *Alberts* v. *State of California* (same; same), 354 U.S. 476, 77 S. Ct. 1304, 1 L. Ed. 2d 1498 (1957); *Kingsley Books, Inc.* v. *Brown*, 354 U.S. 436, 77 S. Ct. 1325, 1 L. Ed. 2d 1469 (1957) (injunction; same); *Times Film Corp.* v. *City of Chicago*, 355 U.S. 35, 78 S. Ct. 115, 2 L. Ed. 2d 72 (1957) (movie license; same); *One, Inc.* v. *Olesen*, 355 U.S. 371, 78 S. Ct. 364, 2 L. Ed. 2d 352 (1958) (mail; same); *Sunshine Book Co.* v. *Summerfield*, 355 U.S. 372, 78 S. Ct. 365, 2 L. Ed. 2d 352 (1958) (same; same); *Kingsley Int'l Pictures Corp.* v. *Regents of the University of the State of New York*, 360 U.S. 684, 79 S. Ct. 1362, 3 L. Ed. 2d 1512 (1959) (movie license; "immoral"); *Smith* v. *People of State of California*, 361 U.S. 147, 80 S. Ct. 215, 4 L. Ed. 2d 205 (1959) (conviction; "obscene"); *Marcus* v. *Search Warrants, etc.*, 367 U.S. 717, 81 S. Ct. 1708, 6 L. Ed. 2d 1127 (1961) (seizure; same); *Manual Enterprises, Inc.* v. *Day*, 370 U.S. 478, 82 S. Ct. 1432, 8 L. Ed. 2d 639 (1962) (mail; same); *Bantam Books, Inc.* v. *Sullivan*, 372 U.S. 58, 83 S. Ct. 631, 9 L. Ed. 2d 584 (1963) (warnings; "objectionable"); *Jacobellis* v. *State of Ohio*, 378 U.S. 184, 84 S. Ct. 1676, 12 L. Ed. 2d 793 (1964) (conviction; "obscene"); *A Quantity of Copies of Books* v. *State of Kansas*, 378 U.S. 205, 84 S. Ct. 1723, 12 L. Ed. 2d 809 (1964) (seizure; same); *Tralins* v. *Gerstein*, 378 U.S. 576, 84 S. Ct. 1903, 12 L. Ed. 2d 1033 (1964) (injunction; same); *Grove Press, Inc.* v. *Gerstein*, 378 U.S. 577, 84 S. Ct. 1909, 12 L. Ed. 2d 1035 (1964) (same; same); *Freedman* v. *State of Maryland*, 380 U.S. 51, 85 S. Ct. 734, 13 L. Ed. 2d 649 (1965) (movie license); *Trans-Lux Distrib. Corp.* v. *Board of Regents of the University of New York*, 380 U.S. 259, 85 S. Ct. 952, 13 L. Ed. 2d 959 (1965) (same; "obscene").

[1] The most cursory perusal of the cases makes it obvious that the various agencies, officers, judges and juries that initially find material "obscene" do not have the last word to say on the matter. Rather, the Supreme Court has left no doubt that any abnegation of judicial supervision in the "obscenity" field would be inconsistent with its duty to uphold constitutional guarantees. The issue "must ultimately be decided by this [the Supreme] Court." *Jacobellis* v. *State of Ohio*, 378 U.S. 184, 188, 84 S. Ct. 1676, 1679, 12 L. Ed. 2d 793 (1964). Mr. Justice Brennan explicitly declared that "this Court cannot avoid making an independent constitutional judgment on the facts of the case as to whether the material involved is constitutionally protected." Id. at 190, 84 S. Ct. at 1679. He added that "[t]his is precisely what the Court did in *Times Film Corp.* v. *City of Chicago*, 355 U.S. 35 [78 S. Ct. 115, 2 L. Ed. 2d 72]; *One, Inc.* v. *Olesen*, 355 U.S. 371 [78 S. Ct. 364, 2 L. Ed. 2d 352]; and *Sunshine Book Co.* v. *Summerfield*, 355 U.S. 372 [78 S. Ct. 365, 2 L. Ed. 2d 352]." Id. at 190, n. 6, 84 S. Ct. at 1679. In examining the material in Times Film, the Supreme Court did not yield in its judgment to the Chicago Police Commissioner and persons appointed by him to inspect the film, "The Game of Love," a District Court judge, and the Court of Appeals for the Seventh Circuit, which found that "the calculated purpose * * * and its (the film's) dominant effect, are substantially to arouse sexual desires." 244 F. 2d 432, 436 (7th Cir. 1957). In One, Inc., the Postmaster, a district judge and the Court of Appeals for the Ninth Circuit had determined that the homosexual magazine "One" had "a primary purpose of exciting lust, lewd and lascivious thoughts and sensual desires in the minds of the persons reading it," 241 F. 2d 772, 778 (9th Cir. 1957). And in Sunshine Book, the Postmaster, a Hearing Examiner, the Department Solicitor, the District Court and five out of eight judges on the Court of Appeals for the D.C. Circuit found a "nudist" magazine to come within the proscription of the statute. 101 U.S. App. D.C. 358, 249 F. 2d 114 (1957). Thus, the Court has definitely accepted the responsibility of being the final arbiter and has refused to accept the judgments of officials, judges or juries to the contrary. The "sufficient evidence" test on review advocated by the Chief Justice has not been adopted. See *Jacobellis* v. *State of Ohio*, supra, 378 U.S. at 190, n. 6, 84 S. Ct. 1676 (dissenting opinion). The burden on this court at this appellate stage should be no less. And the enlarged judicial function in this area requires that we consider the proof or lack thereof and the manner in which the case was placed before the jury, not just whether the material could possibly be brought within the range of the so-called "obscenity" statute. What, then, upon review, does this record disclose?

The Government rested its case largely on a showing of the exhibits themselves insofar as proof of the "obscene" nature of the Nutrix materials was concerned. As for those exhibits, we need add little to what we have already said. It may be conceded that the "sado-masochistic" trash disseminated by Nutrix is not artistic or aesthetically pleasing. Nor is any claim made that it has any redeeming literary or social value whatsoever; it is difficult to imagine such a claim being made, at least on traditional grounds. But cf. *People* v. *Birch*, 40 Misc. 2d 626, 243 N.Y.S. 2d 525 (Sup. Ct. 1963).

As for the statute involved, it is hardly a model of draft-

ing precision or clarity. Section 1461 and the subsequent sections of the "obscenity" chapter are regrettably short on terminological and grammatical consistency. Thus, section 1461,[3] which is entitled "Mailing obscene or crime-inciting matter," refers in one part to matter that is "obscene, lewd, lascivious, indecent, filthy or vile"; the other part, dealing generally with abortion and conception prevention, refers to "indecent or immoral" uses and purposes.[4] For

---

[3] Section 1461 provides in full:

Every obscene, lewd, lascivious, indecent, filthy or vile article, matter, thing, device, or substance; and—

Every article or thing designed, adapted, or intended for preventing conception or producing abortion, or for any indecent or immoral use; and

Every article, instrument, substance, drug, medicine, or thing which is advertised or described in a manner calculated to lead another to use or apply it for preventing conception or producing abortion, or for any indecent or immoral purpose; and

Every written or printed card, letter, circular, book, pamphlet, advertisement, or notice of any kind giving information, directly or indirectly, where, or how, or from whom, or by what means any of such mentioned matters, articles, or things may be obtained or made, or where or by whom any act or operation of any kind for the procuring or producing of abortion will be done or performed, or how or by what means conception may be prevented or abortion produced, whether sealed or unsealed; and

Every paper, writing, advertisement, or representation that any article, instrument, substance, drug, medicine, or thing may, or can, be used or applied for preventing conception or producing abortion, or for any indecent or immoral purpose; and

Every description calculated to induce or incite a person to so use or apply any such article, instrument, substance, drug, medicine, or thing—

Is declared to be nonmailable matter and shall not be conveyed in the mails or delivered from any post office or by any letter carrier.

Whoever knowingly uses the mails for the mailing, carriage in the mails, or delivery of anything declared by this section to be nonmailable, or knowingly causes to be delivered by mail according to the direction thereon, or at the place at which it is directed to be delivered by the person to whom it is addressed, or knowingly takes any such thing from the mails for the purpose of circulating or disposing thereof, or of aiding in the circulation or disposition thereof, shall be fined not more than $5,000 or imprisoned not more than five years, or both, for the first such offense, and shall be fined not more than $10,000 or imprisoned not more than ten years, or both, for each such offense thereafter.

The term "indecent," as used in this section includes matter of a character tending to incite arson, murder, or assassination.

[4] The third group of 41 counts (reduced to 30) against Klaw were apparently based on the part of § 1461 declaring nonmailable, and thus unlawful to use the mails for circulating or disposing of, certain circulars, advertisements and notices giving information about "obscene" matters. The basis of these counts would seem to be a combination of the first and fourth paragraphs of § 1461. However, it is not entirely clear on the face of the statute that the fourth paragraph is at all related to the first—the only one mentioning "obscene"—being rather just a part of the second through sixth paragraphs, which deal throughout with abortion and conception prevention and other indecent or immoral uses. For example, in § 1462, relating to transportation by common carrier, "obscene" books and the like are dealt with in subsection (a), "obscene" recordings and the like are dealt with in subsection (b), and subsection (c) deals only with abortion and conception prevention items and material giving information about such items. The statutory development shows that substantially the present wording of § 1461 was first enacted in Act of July 12, 1876, ch. 186, 19 Stat. 90. The text was cast in its present paragraphed form by the 1948 revision of

section 1461 only "indecent" is specifically defined to include matter "tending to incite arson, murder, or assassination." Section 1462,[5] entitled "Importation or transportation of obscene matters" refers to certain matters that are "obscene, lewd, lascivious or filthy" (but not "vile") or of "indecent" character, as well as "indecent and immoral" uses (again, in a subsection relating to abortion and conception prevention). Section 1463,[6] entitled "Mailing indecent matter on wrappers or envelopes" refers to "indecent, lewd, lascivious, or obscene" (but not "filthy," "vile," or "immoral") delineations and epithets. Section 1464,[7] entitled "Broadcasting obscene language,"

refers to "obscene, indecent, or profane" (but not "lewd," "lascivious," "filthy," "vile," or "immoral") utterances. Lastly, section 1465,[8] entitled "Transportation of obscene matters for sale or distribution" refers to matter that is "obscene, lewd, lascivious, or filthy" (but not "vile" or "profane") or of "indecent or immoral" character. Thus, as the chapter heading suggests, all five sections are concerned with "obscene" matter. They also each mention "indecent," but apply it variously to "character," "use" and "purpose." The other terms—"lewd," "lascivious," "filthy," "vile," "immoral" and "profane"—are used only sporadically.

[2] It should not be surprising, then, that the results of judicial attempts to apply these and similarly worded statutes consistently with the First Amendment have produced strange results. The broad freedom of expression so preferentially protected by the First Amendment, cf. *United States* v. *Carolene Prods. Co.*, 304 U.S. 144, 152, n. 4, 58 S. Ct. 778, 82 L. Ed. 1234 (1938), has been found to have an exceptional enclave for "obscenity." The varied and vague terms in such statutes are often subsumed within the one term "obscene" which is found throughout the federal law. Indeed, "it is doubtful whether any standard other than obscenity could stand the Constitutional test." *People* v. *Brooklyn News Co.*, 12 Misc. 2d 768, 771, 174 N.Y.S. 2d 813, 817 (Kings County Ct. 1958) (Sobel, J.); cf. *United States* v. *Keller*, 259 F. 2d 54 (3d Cir. 1958). See also *People* v. *Mishkin*, 26 Misc. 2d 152, 154, 207 N.Y.S. 2d 390, 393 (Ct. Spec. Sess. 1960), aff'd as modified, 17 A.D. 2d 243, 234 N.Y.S. 2d 342 (1st Dept. 1962), aff'd, 15 N.Y. 2d 671, 255 N.Y.S. 2d 881, 204 N.E. 2d 209 (1964), probable jurisdiction noted, 380 U.S. 960, 85 S. Ct. 1103, 14 L. Ed. 2d 152 (1965) (No. 858, 1964 Term, renumbered No. 49, 1965 Term). See also *Friedman* v. *New York*, 34 U.S.L. Week 3014 (New York Sup. Ct., Jan. 21, 1965), petition for cert. filed, 33 U.S.L. Week 3369 (U.S. May 13, 1965) (No. 1161, 1964 Term; renumbered No. 135, 1965 Term). We must take great care, therefore, to see that limitations on materials regarded as "obscene" have no more scope than is necessary to effectuate the permissible purposes of such constraints.

---

the criminal code, ch. 768, 62 Stat. 768. The predecessor of § 1462 was Act of February 8, 1897, ch. 172, 29 Stat. 512, which was cast in a form similar to the predecessors of § 1461. Explicit paragraphs and subsections did not appear until Act of May 27, 1950, ch. 214, 64 Stat. 194. However, given our disposition of the case we need not determine whether § 1461 applies to circulars giving information about "obscene" matter, as opposed to simply matters, articles and things "for preventing conception or producing abortion, or for any indecent or immoral use." Moreover, the Court in Roth implicitly assumed, without discussion, that it did. See also the discussions in *Manual Enterprises, Inc.* v. *Day*, 370 U.S. 478, 500–518, 520–524, 82 S. Ct. 1432, 8 L. Ed. 2d 639 (1962).

[5] Section 1462 provides in full:

Whoever brings into the United States, or any place subject to the jurisdiction thereof, or knowingly uses any express company or other common carrier, for carriage in interstate or foreign commerce—

(a) any obscene, lewd, lascivious, or filthy book, pamphlet, picture, motion-picture film, paper, letter, writing, print, or other matter of indecent character; or

(b) any obscene, lewd, lascivious, or filthy phonograph recording, electrical transcription, or other article or thing capable of producing sound; or

(c) any drug, medicine, article, or thing designed, adapted, or kind giving information, directly or indirectly, where, how, or of any indecent or immoral use; or any written or printed card, letter, circular, book, pamphlet, advertisement, or notice of any kind giving information, directly or indirectly, where, how, or of whom, or by what means any of such mentioned articles, matters, or things may be obtained or made; or

Whoever knowingly takes from such express company or other common carrier any matter or thing the carriage of which is herein made unlawful—

Shall be fined not more than $5,000 or imprisoned not more than five years, or both, for the first such offense and shall be fined not more than $10,000 or imprisoned not more than ten years, or both, for each such offense thereafter.

[6] Section 1463 provides in full:

All matter otherwise mailable by law, upon the envelope or outside cover or wrapper of which, and all postal cards upon which, any delineations, epithets, terms, or language of an indecent, lewd, lascivious, or obscene character are written or printed or otherwise impressed or apparent, are nonmailable matter, and shall not be conveyed in the mails nor delivered from any post office nor by any letter carrier, and shall be withdrawn from the mails under such regulations as the Postmaster General shall prescribe.

Whoever knowingly deposits for mailing or delivery, anything declared by this section to be nonmailable matter, or knowingly takes the same from the mails for the purpose of circulating or disposing of or aiding in the circulation or disposition of the same, shall be fined not more than $5,000 or imprisoned not more than five years, or both.

[7] Section 1464 provides in full:

Whoever utters any obscene, indecent, or profane language by

means of radio communication shall be fined not more than $10,000 or imprisoned not more than two years, or both.

[8] Section 1465 provides in full:

Whoever knowingly transports in interstate or foreign commerce for the purpose of sale or distribution any obscene, lewd, lascivious, or filthy book, pamphlet, picture, film, paper, letter, writing, print, silhouette, drawing, figure, image, cast, phonograph recording, electrical transcription or other article capable of producing sound or any other matter of indecent or immoral character, shall be fined not more than $5,000 or imprisoned not more than five years, or both.

The transportation as aforesaid of two or more copies of any publication of two or more of any article of the character described above, or a combined total of five such publications and articles, shall create a presumption that such publications or articles are intended for sale or distribution, but such presumption shall be rebuttable.

When any person is convicted of a violation of this Act, the court in its judgment of conviction may, in addition to the penalty prescribed, order the confiscation and disposal of such items described herein which were found in the possession or under the immediate control of such person at the time of his arrest.

Cf. *Butler* v. *State of Michigan*, 352 U.S. 380, 383, 77 S. Ct. 524, 1 L. Ed. 2d 412 (1957).[9]

[3, 4] We do not doubt that "obscenity" may be regulated because it is thought to incite antisocial sexual behavior and crime. "Obscene" material and conduct may also sometimes be suppressed and penalized because, like a common law nuisance, it constitutes an unreasonably offensive intrusion into the lives of persons who cannot reasonably avoid it. Other reasons for proscription are more troublesome, such as when the "obscenity" might merely be thought to cause sexual or other stimulation or excitement—unrelated to otherwise deleterious behavior— for willing adults who would not be subject to the material if they did not want to be. Also troublesome is regulation of "obscenity" simply because it reflects sexual values differing from current majority morals, cf. *Kingsley Int'l Pictures Corp.* v. *Regents of the University of the State of New York*, 360 U.S. 684, 688–689, 79 S. Ct. 1362, 3 L. Ed. 2d 1512 (1959). See generally Henkin, Morals and the Constitution: The Sin of Obscenity, 63 Colum. L. Rev. 391, 392–95 (1963); Kalven, The Metaphysics of the Law of Obscenity, in 1960 Supreme Court Review, 1, 3–4 (Kurland ed.).

[5] However, in considering the permissible meaning of "obscene" in section 1461, we must begin with the Supreme Court's treatment of that statute in Roth. That case contains the oft-quoted—although difficult to apply— statement that material is "obscene" if: "to the average person, applying contemporary community standards, the dominant theme of the material taken as a whole appeals to prurient interest." 354 U.S. at 489, 77 S. Ct. at 1311.[10]

---

[9] While knotty problems are raised if one considers the religious background of many of these laws, see Henkin, Morals and the Constitution: The Sin of Obscenity, 63 Colum. L. Rev. 391 (1963), they need not be dealt with if permissible secular purposes and justifications may be found for them. Cf. *McGowan* v. *State of Maryland*, 366 U.S. 420, 81 S. Ct. 1101, 6 L. Ed. 2d 393 (1961); *Two Guys from Harrison-Allentown, Inc.* v. *McGinley*, 366 U.S. 582, 81 S. Ct. 1135, 6 L. Ed. 2d 551 (1961). Compare *Griswold* v. *State of Connecticut*, 85 S. Ct. 1678 (1965). While contemporary secular support is being found for proscription of words, thoughts and scenes that were inconsistent with "religious" conceptions, so too has the content of those conceptions itself been changing. Thus, descriptive words fit for one generation of translators of the Bible are unfit for another. See, e.g., Adams, The Magic and Mystery of Words 68 (1963). Similarly, in a stimulating article, Reverend Howard Moody has recently questioned the whole religious approach to obscenity. Moody, Toward a New Definition of Obscenity, 24 Christianity & Crisis 284 (1965). Noting that "from a theological or ethical perspective, 'dirty words' are a terribly inadequate base from which to write a definition of obscenity," id. at 286, he suggests that our standard of obscenity is "obsessed with sex and vulgar language; * * * [it should be] defined rather as that material which has as its dominant theme and purpose the debasement and depreciation of human beings—their worth and dignity." Id. at 287. If at the same time as the restrictions on publication have been loosened the nation has approached "a state of moral decadence, * * * the evidence of this is not to be found in salacious literature, erotic art or obscene films but in the 'soul-rot' that comes from the moral hypocrisy of straining at the gnat of sexuality and swallowing the camel of human deterioration and destruction." Id. at 288.

[10] A problem not discussed in Roth, but initially raised in this case, is whether the standard is any different if the typical potential recipient of the "obscene" material may be someone other than the "average man," i.e., a member of a particular

---

In addition to its appeal to "prurient interest," proscribable "obscenity" must be "utterly without redeeming social importance." *Roth* v. *United States*, supra, 354 U.S. at 484, 77 S. Ct. 1304; *Jacobellis* v. *Ohio*, 378 U.S. at 191, 84 S. Ct. 1676. It must go "substantially beyond the customary limits of candor in description or representation." Ibid. (quoting American Law Institute, Model Penal Code formulation also quoted in Roth, 354 U.S. at 487, n. 20, 77 S. Ct. at 1310). It must be characterized by "patent offensiveness." *Manual Enterprises, Inc.* v. *Day*, 370 U.S. 478, 482, 82 S. Ct. 1432, 8 L. Ed. 2d 639 (1962). In brief, it is "hard-core pornography." *Jacobellis* v. *Ohio*, supra, 378 U.S. at 197, 84 S. Ct. 1676.

[6] Thus, material is proscribable "obscenity," or hard-core pornography, if it has the requisite prurient appeal, *and* if it so exceeds customary candor as to be patently offensive, *unless* it has *any* redeeming social importance. The last requirement is part of the broad protective mantle of the First Amendment. But, as counsel for defendants repeatedly emphasized, there is no claim in this case that the Nutrix materials have any redeeming social importance. However, the absence of artistic or literary value or other value of social consequence does not, without more, lead to a finding of proscribable "obscenity." Such qualities would merely insulate what might otherwise be proscribable due to its offensiveness and prurient appeal. See, e.g., *Larkin* v. *G. P. Putnam's Sons*, 14 N.Y. 2d 399, 252 N.Y.S. 2d 71, 200 N.E. 2d 760 (1964) (the novel "Fanny Hill"); *People* v. *Bruce*, 31 Ill. 2d 459, 202 N.E. 2d 497 (1964) (satirical monologist); Goldman, The Comedy of Lenny Bruce, 36 Commentary 312 (1963); cf. *People* v. *Birch*, supra. But cf. *People* v. *Bruce*, unreported, Crim. Ct. City of New York, 1964 (appeal pending); *Attorney General* v. *Book Named "John Cleland's Memoirs of a Woman of Pleasure,"* Mass., 206 N.E. 2d 403 (1965). Compare *United States* v. *Ginzburg*, 338 F. 2d 12, 14 (3d Cir. 1964), cert. granted, 380 U.S. 961, 85 S. Ct. 1103, 14 L. Ed. 2d 152 (1965) (No. 807), 1964 Term, renumbered No. 42, 1965 Term.

[7] Nor is mere "patent offensiveness" enough. There must in addition be the requisite prurient appeal. Assum-

---

group such as a sexual deviate. In *Manual Enterprises, Inc.* v. *Day*, 370 U.S. 478, 481–482, 82 S. Ct. 1432, 8 L. Ed. 2d 639 (1962), Justices Harlan and Stewart indicated that the question of the relevant audience was still open, but they did not feel compelled to reach it.

We realize that the Court went on in Roth to quote with approval a charge that "[t]he test in each case is the effect of the book, picture or publication considered as a whole, not upon any particular class, but upon all those whom it is likely to reach. In other words, you determine its impact upon the average person in the community." 354 U.S. at 490, 77 S. Ct. at 1312. But this brief treatment can hardly be taken as ending the matter. When read in light of the familiar admonition (contained in the same charge) that the reactions of the young, the immature, the prigs, or the highly prudish are not decisive, this passage need mean little more than that putatively "obscene" matter more or less directed to or likely to reach all parts of the community must be appraised on those terms, and not on the basis of its appeal to a small segment of the community. Because there may be good reason for proscribing material that is more likely to reach and be responded to in a prurient way by a deviant segment of the community, we are not convinced that prurient appeal to the average member of the community is the only possible standard.

ing that "prurient appeal" can be adequately defined, there are still some questions: appeal to whose prurient interest? judged by whom? on what basis? For example, is it the "average person" who applies "contemporary community standards" to determine if the "dominant theme" appeals to "prurient interest" (of someone)? Or is it some one else applying "contemporary community standards" to determine that the "dominant theme" appeals to "prurient interest" of the "average person"? Do "contemporary community standards" operate to reduce potential prurient appeal? Or do they operate to establish that some "redeeming social importance" is present? Or, do they operate to measure the "patent offensiveness" of an excess of candor? Again, does the "dominant theme" indicate that the prospective prurient appeal is great or slight? Or does it suggest that other themes will supply the redeeming social importance? Perhaps the Roth statement is too compact—an unsurprising failing in an initial formulation; the Court itself has acknowledged that it "is not perfect." *Jacobellis* v. *Ohio*, supra, 378 U.S. at 191, 84 S. Ct. 1676. But the difficulties of articulating an adequate substitute need not dictate immutable adherence to such a will-o'-the-wisp.[11]

[8, 9] Having in mind the constitutional constrictions on the breadth of legislation affecting the freedom of expression, if appeal to prurient interest—on either an "average man" or a "deviant typical recipient" basis—is the statutory concern, then it seems desirable, indeed essential, that such appeal to someone be shown to exist. This the Government's view of Roth does not require. Nor should it be sufficient merely that the disseminator or publicizer thinks such appeal exists. The stimulation and reaction with which the "obscenity" laws are concerned are unlikely to be a problem if the appeal is felt by none of the recipients, but only by the disseminator. While such a person may in some other ways be a potential problem for

society, the "obscenity" laws do not seem best calculated to cope with him. Moreover, the Court stresses in Roth the "effect" of the material on the people reached by it. See 354 U.S. at 490, 77 S. Ct. 1304.[12]

[10, 11] Of course, we are not asked to decide that Nutrix materials can in no case be a proper basis for exclusion from the mails nor, for that matter, for criminal convictions. Exclusion has already been decided. But while this discussion would be quite relevant to whether particular material alleged to be "obscene" may possibly be found to be beyond the scope of the First Amendment, it is also of central importance to the main problem in this case, which is one of proof and conviction. And if proof of prurient stimulation and response is generally important, it is particularly necessary when the prurient interest may be that of a deviant segment of society whose reactions are hardly a matter of common knowledge. It may well be that there are characters and cults to which exaggerated high heels, black patent leather bindings and bondage poses have some occult significance, but we doubt that any court would take judicial notice of the reaction that deviates—or the average man—might have to such stimuli. However, some proof should be offered to demonstrate such appeal, thereby supplying the fact-finders with knowledge of what appeals to prurient interest so that they have some basis for their conclusion. As was observed earlier in Klaw's troubles with the postal censors, "obviously, the issue of what stirs the lust of the sexual deviate requires evidence of special competence." *Klaw* v. *Schaffer*, supra, 151 F. Supp. at 539, n. 6; see *Manual Enterprises, Inc.* v. *Day*, 110 U.S. App. D.C. 78, 289 F. 2d 455 (1961 rev'd, 370 U.S. 478, 82 S. Ct. 1432, 8 L. Ed. 2d 639 (1962)).

In this case, although Judge Wyatt wisely suggested, and the Government considered, introduction of such evidence, there was none. Because of this Judge Wyatt stated at the end of the case, as he had to, that there was no "evidence from which the jury could find that it [Nutrix materials] would in fact appeal to the prurient interest of a particular class."

Furthermore, nothing in the record shows that the material even has prurient appeal to the average man. The parent witnesses did not react to Junior's new literary and pictorial delights in a prurient manner, nor did the other recipient witnesses. Junior was not called upon to describe the appeal (if any) to his prurient interest; he probably would not have understood what "prurient" meant any more than do his elders. Most of the witnesses testified that they found the material disgusting or revolting, but that lascivious and lecherous thoughts had not been

---

[11] In this case it is the first of these ambiguities that is most bothersome—that is, appeal, if any, to whose prurient interest, judged by whom, and on what basis. Before, during, and at the end of the trial, and now on appeal, the Government's claim has been that the familiar Roth test does not require that the material appeal to the average person. "All that is requires is that the dominant theme of the material—that is, the dominant nature of such appeal as it has—be recognizable to the average person as being an appeal to prurient interest." But in so restating Roth, the Government has merely chosen one of several approaches to determination of the requisite prurient appeal, one that does not say to whose prurient interest the appeal must go. Another approach is to say that the material must be shown to appeal to the prurient interest of the "average person" (a close cousin to the "reasonable man" whose assumed existence cannot be questioned lest many a legal edifice become a mere house of cards). Since the "average person" is almost always a possible recipient, even if not the typical recipient, the effect on him or her would always seem important. After all, the prurient appeal element is presumably related to the deterrence purpose. And without now questioning the apparent legislative assumption that stimulation of prurient interest leads to significant anti-social behavior, but cf. *United States* v. *Roth*, 237 F. 2d 796, 804, 812–817 (2d Cir. 1956), aff'd, 354 U.S. 476, 77 S. Ct. 1304, 1 L. Ed. 2d 1498 (1957), if the prurient interest of the average person is stimulated there may be cause for regulation. There may also be cause for regulation of material that stimulates the prurient interest of, not the average person, but the abnormal person—the deviate—who is likely to be its typical recipient. Indeed, there may be even more cause for regulation.

[12] It might be thought that the statute in question is concerned not so much with deterrence of sexually stimulated anti-social conduct as with use of the mails to disseminate unsolicited, undesired offensive materials to uninterested recipients. But the statute is not so narrowly drawn. Indeed, a bill more appropriately designed to cope with that precise problem was recently approved by the House of Representatives. The bill, H.R. 980, 89th Cong. 1st Sess., would permit a recipient or a parent of an infant recipient to return to his Postmaster any mail thought by the recipient to be "obscene, lewd, lascivious, indecent, filthy or vile" and have the Postmaster notify the sender to discontinue the mailings; such an order would be judicially enforceable. Cf. *Lamont* v. *Postmaster General*, 85 S. Ct. 1493, 1495, n. 2 (1965). See generally Schwartz, The Mail Must Go Through—Propaganda and Pornography, 11 U.C.L.A. L. Rev. 805, 845–48 (1964).

aroused in them. It is not unlikely that many if not most witnesses and jurors would also consider "disgusting and revolting" more than a few of our current motion pictures, like "Dr. Terror's House of Horrors," many of the news-stand magazines so anomalously entitled "horror comics," the risque birthday, convalescent, and greeting cards found in almost every corner drug store, as well as the scores of vulgar party favors. Indeed, vulgarity seems to be in vogue. But it is doubtful whether our jails would be well used if convictions were to be based on material that is just "disgusting and revolting." To do so would, we fear, be simply another application of the age-old double standard of the drawing room and the locker room.

[12] If the witnesses presented in this case provide any sampling, these pamphlets and pictures stimulated no one's prurient interest. Although it may be difficult to find expert and other witnesses properly qualified to inform the jury about what does or does not appeal to the prurient interest of the average person, cf. *Klaw* v. *Schaffer*, supra, 151 F. Supp. at 539–540, it would not seem impossible. On the other hand, it is clear that jurors should not consider their own personal reactions as setting the standard; there is too much truth in the observation that "what is pornography for one man is the laughter of genius to another."[13] Cf. Ass'n of the Bar of the City of New York, Comm. on the Bill of Rights, Report on H.R. 319, 88th Cong., 2d Sess. (1964), on "Morally Offensive Mail," in Reports of the Ass'n of the Bar Concerned with Federal Legislation 54, 56 (1965).

In this case, however, the only predicate for any conclusion about prurient appeal was the material itself, as if *res ipsa loquitur*. The jurors were, therefore, left to speculate. They were invited to behold the accused material and, in effect, conclude simply that it is undesirable, it is distasteful, it is disgusting. Knowing perhaps that they would not be interested in obtaining more of the material they might wonder why anyone else would, and conclude that the only answer is "prurient appeal." Because the jury was given no basis for understanding exactly how and why the material appeals to its audience, whether deviate or average person, it may too readily supply an explanation—"prurient appeal." Even if the jury did not consist of twelve carefully selected Anthony Comstocks, it might well believe that the predominant appeal of certain acknowledged works of art, sculpture and literature found in all our well-known museums and libraries would be to the prurient interest of the average person, or perhaps someone else. But if that be so, can we allow the censor's stamp to be affixed on the basis of an uninformed jury's misconceptions? See also *Freedman* v. *Maryland*, 380 U.S. 51, 58, 85 S. Ct. 734, 13 L. Ed. 2d 649 (1965).

Whatever the value of mere "autoptical" evidence in other contexts, it should not readily be countenanced in this area. Otherwise, too easily the Government's test might allow a jury to equate patent offensiveness to prurient appeal, thus obliterating the conjunction that has been thought indispensable. See e.g., *Manual Enterprises, Inc.* v. *Day*, supra, 370 U.S. at 482, 82 S. Ct. 1432; *Jacobellis* v. *State of Ohio*, supra, 378 U.S. at 191–192, 84 S. Ct. 1676. Too easily the jury could aid suppression simply on the basis of speculations and suspicions about the prurient

appeal of material to some unknown, undefined person whose psyche is not known. With the First Amendment in the background, this cannot be abided.

[13] The state of the record gave the jurors impermissibly broad freedom to convict just because, having no more informative evidence than the material itself, they might think that the average person would "recognize" that the material has prurient appeal. But again, *to whom?* In this case, the jury had insufficient evidence even to "recognize" that the material appealed to the prurient interest of the average person. It had absolutely no evidentiary basis from which to "recognize" any appeal to the prurient interest of the deviate or the typical recipient—a class never really defined in the record. Because there was insufficient evidence for the jury to consider Nutrix material "obscene" under any proper view of the Roth test, the motion for directed verdict of acquittal should have been granted.[14]

This result demonstrates perhaps that a second pronouncement may now be needed to clarify the rule of Roth. However, this court is mindful of the difficulties of providing an adequate definition, and it may turn out that the best and most realistic formulation available is that of Mr. Justice Stewart in Jacobellis that it is only "hard-core pornography" to which the Constitution's protection does not extend, and although it may be indefinable, "I know it when I see it * * *." 378 U.S. at 197, 84 S. Ct. at 1683. In any case, following Roth the censor's disapproving seal was removed from magazines for homosexuals and pictures of nudist camps in which the campers are unemasculated by the censor's retouching brush. Through these and other breaches in the dike has swept a veritable flood, as each pamphlet, play or picture seems obliged to be even more candid or daring in order to stimulate the public's prurient palate and assure appearance on the best-seller list. Authors vie with each other to peer through keyholes and over transoms, and to hide themselves at advantageous listening posts in well-selected bedrooms. Their efforts are rewarded by their being able to depict sights and conversations concerning the most intimate phases of sexual activity, with or without the benefit of wedlock. Witness such books as "The Group," "Candy," and "Green Tree in

---

[13] D. H. Lawrence, Pornography and Obscenity, in Sex Literature and Censorship, 69 (Moore ed. 1953).

[14] Even with adequate proof under the average man test, there might still be problems, for the jury was charged to consider the material from the standpoint of the average man in the nation as a whole. We very much doubt whether twelve random New Yorkers can make such a judgment without being further informed about the "common conscience of the nation," if there be such a thing. In any case, we do not read the Court's plurality opinions in Jacobellis as unequivocal authority for the proposition. In announcing the Court's judgment, Justice Brennan was speaking only for himself and Justice Goldberg. Justices White, Black and Douglas concurred only in the judgment. Justice Stewart concurred without indicating adoption of the national community standard. As for the dissenters, the Chief Justice explicitly rejected the national standard, as did Justice Harlan, presumably in light of his views in Roth. See *Gent* v. *State*, Ark., 393 S.W. 2d 219 (1965). See also *Keney* v. *New York*, 34 U.S.L. Week 3011 (New York, Monroe County Ct., 1964), petition for cert. filed, 33 U.S.L. Week 3231 (U.S. Dec. 29, 1964) (No. 793, 1964 Term; renumbered No. 39, 1965 Term); *Redrup* v. *New York*, 34 U.S.L. Week 3012 (New York, Sup. Ct., Dec. 17, 1964), petition for cert. filed, 33 U.S.L. Week 3341 (U.S. March 26, 1965) (No. 1073, 1964 Term; renumbered No. 72, 1965 Term).

Gedde," the last of which the reviewer in the stately New York Times says is "a mixture of existentialism and erotic prurience" apparently demonstrating "that young people in our tormented civilization are so lost in a wilderness of moral anarchy and philosophical despair that their only interest is in sex and in many of its most debased and perverted manifestations." May 3, 1965, p. 31, col. 3. And the commercial attributes of sexual candor have apparently not gone unnoticed by publishers of even the women's magazines. See Iversen, The Pious Pornographers (1965).

A comparison of judicial reactions to recent *causes célèbres* suggests that the judiciary in our tormented modern civilization are also lost in a wilderness. Before it obtained its imprimatur in *Grove Press, Inc.* v. *Gerstein*, 378 U.S. 577, 84 S. Ct. 1909, 12 L. Ed. 2d 1035 (1964), Henry Miller's "Tropic of Cancer" was "obscene" in Florida and in New York, *People* v. *Fritch*, 13 N.Y. 2d 119, 243 N.Y.S. 2d 1, 192 N.E. 2d 713 (1963), but not in California, *Zeitlin* v. *Arnebergh*, 59 Cal. 2d 901, 31 Cal. Rptr. 800, 383 P. 2d 152, cert. denied, 375 U.S. 957, 84 S. Ct. 445, 11 L. Ed. 2d 315 (1963), Massachusetts, *Attorney General* v. *Book Named* "Tropic of Cancer," 345 Mass. 11, 184 N.E. 2d 328 (1962), and Wisconsin, *McCauley* v. *Tropic of Cancer*, 20 Wis. 2d 134, 121 N.W. 2d 545 (1963). Similar confusion and inconsistency is being manifested as to "Fanny Hill," which is "obscene" in Massachusetts, *Attorney General* v. *Book Named* "John Cleland's Memoirs of a Woman of Pleasure," Mass., 206 N.E. 2d 403 (1965), but not in New York, *Larkin* v. *G. P. Putnam's Sons*, 14 N.Y. 2d 399, 252 N.Y.S. 2d 71, 200 N.E. 2d 760 (1964). This is a book which any layman might not hesitate to say met all the requirements of Roth. The most amateur prosecutor could undoubtedly obtain a conviction in any part of the country in comparatively few minutes merely by reading a few pages to the jury. In fact, the same prosecutor might obtain the same result if he exhibited to the jury those glossy prints (mailed in plain envelopes) of quite naked ladies in various poses, despite the fact that they were photographs of famous pictures or statues in art museums. The possibility that deliberating jurors would be uncommonly sanctimonious or hypocritical seems quite obvious. Indeed, most if not all of the censor's defeats have come at the hands of appellate courts, and not the jury.

Many would doubt that a judicial system that puts its permissive stamp of approval upon such books as "Tropic of Cancer" and "Fanny Hill," to name a few, or certain magazines for homosexuals and sunbathers should then incarcerate or penalize these two defendants for disseminating and publicizing material which might or might not (there is no proof) appeal to someone's "prurient interest." Indeed, we can sympathize with Klaw's plight were he to find "Fanny Hill" or "Tropic of Cancer" in the prison library, or, if others had pre-empted the only copies, there were available "Pleasure Was My Business," see *Tralins* v. *Gerstein*, 378 U.S. 576, 84 S. Ct. 1903, 12 L. Ed. 2d 1033 (1964), which contains "numerous descriptions of abnormal sex acts and indecent conversations supposed to have taken place in [a] Florida brothel." As Chief Judge Desmond pointed out in his dissent in Larkin, "Fanny Hill" contains every element which might appeal to "prurient interest." Judge Scileppi described the book, with considerable justification, as "one of the foulest, sexually immoral, debasing, lewd and obscene books ever published, either in this country or abroad." Larkin, supra, 14 N.Y. 2d at 407, 252 N.Y.S. 2d at 78, 200 N.E. 2d at 765. If no books are available, Klaw together with the public might turn to stimulation through the auditory nerves rather than the optic nerves. The field is no less fruitful for now "Fanny Hill Comes Alive" in an unexpurgated two-record album, giving in 16 stunning scenes "all the lusty, intimate, climatic excitement of this erotic masterpiece * * * Banned for 200 years, now available following New York State Court of Appeals decision overruling the lower courts." So reads the advertising in the Book Review section of a recent Sunday New York Times, April 4, 1965. Thus, another item is added to the party-record list which for generations has delighted those who seek such entertainment with their lusty and ribald old English ballads, entertainment to which Robert Burns, to name one, was a not insubstantial contributor. And in the field of prose, see Mark Twain's "1601" and Samuel Pepys' "Diary."[15] Faced with this vast array of reading and listening matter available to the public, Klaw might understandably wonder as to the meaning of equal protection of law.

In judging the convictions of Klaw and Kramer against the many decisions of the Supreme Court and highest state courts, this court has been left with the definite impression, as indicated above, that there has been insufficient proof presented in this case to justify their penalties and imprisonment. For better or for worse, the standard of what does not arouse "prurient interest" has been established. A particularly careful study of the subject matter involved in this and other cases has been made because this court regards the material as revolting and disgusting. But it is the record and not our feelings that must control. Here the jury had no opportunity to judge the exhibits presented to them by any standard other than their own speculation as to "prurient interest." If they knew the standard set as a matter of law by other cases, their result might have been different. "Due process of law" would be a meaningless cliche if the nonsensical trash that is the subject of this prosecution were allowed to be the basis of a conviction by judge or jury without any proof demonstrating that it has the proscribed effect on any of our citizenry.

The courts may have opened the floodgates for horror and filth, but if they are to be closed it should be done by the careful drafting of proper laws by our duly elected representatives, and not by a combination of zealous governmental inspectors, prosecutors, and uninformed juries. Then the potential contributors to our culture may have some slight notion of the guidelines and the risks. Of course, it is quite possible that after the public is sated with the products of the new permissiveness the floodtide will ebb of its own diminished momentum. Until then, however, the responsibility of protecting defendants from unguided suppression and conviction weighs as heavily upon this court as it does upon the Supreme Court. While there is some merit to the opinion of those who say that appellate courts should not have to sit as a board of censors supervising the work of the police, the motion picture censorship bureaus, the schools, the churches, and the other organizations that have their lists of good and bad books and motion pictures, there is even more merit to the

---

[15] Seen generally Kronhausen & Kronhausen, Pornography and the Law, 43–56, 79–92 (1959).

view that once these preferences are enforced upon others, we "cannot avoid making an independent constitutional judgment on the facts of the case as to whether the material involved is constitutionally protected." Jacobellis, supra, 378 U.S. at 190, 84 S. Ct. at 1679. Unless there be this protection, a witch hunt might well come to pass which would make the Salem tragedy fade into obscurity. Having in mind the alternatives of jail or freedom, courts must be aware of the facts of the "held-not-to-be-obscene" or "approved" cases, and ensure that the proof is sufficient to allow a fact finder to set this case apart from them. Otherwise it would be altogether too easy for any prosecutor to stand before a jury, display the exhibits involved, and merely ask in summation: "Would you want your son

or daughter to see or read this stuff?" A conviction in every instance would be virtually assured.

Finally, to take Mr. Justice Brennan's concluding words in reversing the court below in *Jacobellis* v. *State of Ohio*, supra, 378 U.S. at 196, 84 S. Ct. at 1682: "We have viewed the film [the exhibits], *in the light of the record made in the trial court*, and we conclude that it is [they are] not obscene within the standards enunciated in *Roth* v. *United States* and *Alberts* v. *California * * *"* and implicit in the many other decisions of the Supreme Court. (Emphasis added.)

Reversed.

■ Trans-Lux Distributing Corporation
v.
Maryland State Board of Censors.
No. 143, Sept. Term, 1965.

Court of Appeals of Maryland.

Order June 29, 1965.

Opinion Sept. 27, 1965.

J. Cookman Boyd, Jr., Baltimore, and *Adolph Kaufman*, New York City (Walter S. Levin, Baltimore, and Leonard H. Dickstein and Weisman, Celler, Allan, Spett & Sheinberg, New York City, on the brief), for appellant.

Fred Oken, Asst. Atty. Gen., Baltimore (Thomas B. Finan, Atty. Gen., and Roger D. Redden, Asst. Atty. Gen., Baltimore, on the brief), for appellee.

Before PRESCOTT, C.J., and HAMMOND, HORNEY, MARBURY, SYBERT, OPPENHEIMER and BARNES, JJ.

PER CURIAM ORDER

For reasons to be stated in an opinion to be hereafter filed, it is ordered by a majority of the Court of Appeals of Maryland this 29th day of June, 1965, that the order appealed from be, and it is hereby, reversed, costs to be paid by the appellee.

And be it further ordered that the mandate in this case be issued forthwith.

OPINION

BARNES, Judge.

After the Supreme Court of the United States invalidated Maryland's statute[1] requiring licensing by the Maryland State Board of Censors (the Board) of motion pictures prior to their exhibition, by its decision in *Freedman* v. *State of Maryland*, 380 U.S. 51, 85 S. Ct. 734, 13 L.

Ed. 2d 649 (decided March 1, 1965),[2] the General Assembly of Maryland enacted Chapter 598 of the Acts of 1965 (Act of 1965) as an emergency measure which became effective upon its signature by Governor Tawes on April 8, 1965. The Board, on April 19, 1965 was presented by the appellant, Trans-Lux Distributing Corporation, with the motion picture "A Stranger Knocks" (the film) in order to obtain a license. The Board reviewed the film on April 22, 1965, disapproved it under Section 6 of Article 66A and made the following finding:

"*After reviewing the entire film and considering it as a whole, the Board finds that the film goes substantially beyond customary limits of candor in description and representation of sex, that it deals purposely and effectively with sex in a manner which appeals to the prurient interest, that it is without social importance, and that it lacks any identifiable artistic, cultural, thematic or other value which might be considered redemptive.*"

Also on April 22, the Board, pursuant to the Act of 1965, filed a petition in the Circuit Court of Baltimore City (Circuit Court) for an order affirming the Board's finding and its disapproval of the film for licensing. Judge Prendergast viewed the film on April 27, 1965, took testimony, heard arguments and rendered an informative oral opinion on April 28 indicating that he found the Board's finding to be correct. An order effectuating this opinion

---

[1] Code, Article 66A, Sections 1 to 26.

[2] This case reversed our decision in *Freedman* v. *State*, 233 Md. 498, 197 A. 2d 232 (1964).

was duly signed on April 30 and an appeal taken to this Court on May 10.

We advanced the case for hearing and on June 29, 1965 viewed the film in the morning of that day, heard arguments of counsel and after conference later the same afternoon, filed a *per curiam* order by a majority of the Court, reversing the Circuit Court and directing that the mandate issue forthwith. This opinion gives our reasons for our action in reversing the Circuit Court.

Three principal issues are presented to us for decision:

1. With the addition of the Act of 1965, is the Maryland statutory requirement for pre-showing censorship of motion pictures constitutional on its face?

2. Is the film obscene under the definition of obscenity established by the Supreme Court of the United States?

3. Apart from the federal constitutional question and assuming, arguendo, that the standards set forth in Section 6 of Article 66A are not too vague and uncertain to be enforced constitutionally, does the film transgress the Maryland standards?

I.

[1] We agree with the Circuit Court that the present Maryland statutory plan for pre-showing motion picture censorship is constitutional on its face. Prior to its decision in *Freedman*, the Supreme Court had indicated in *Times Film Corp.* v. *City of Chicago*, 365 U.S. 43, 81 S. Ct. 391, 5 L. Ed. 2d 403 (1961) that a statutory requirement of submission of motion pictures in advance of exhibition was not necessarily unconstitutional *under all circumstances*.[3] The Supreme Court in the Freedman case held that the Maryland statute prior to the enactment of the Act of 1965 was unconstitutional as a violation of the First Amendment to the Constitution of the United States as made applicable to the States by the provisions of the Fourteenth Amendment as construed by the Supreme Court because:

1) If the Board disapproved the film, the exhibitor was required to assume the burden of instituting judicial proceedings and of persuading the court that the film was constitutionally protected expression; 2) after the Board had declined to license the film, its exhibition was prohibited pending judicial review, however long such judicial review might take; and, 3) the Maryland statute provided no assurance of prompt judicial determination.

By the act of 1965, the General Assembly repealed an re-enacted Section 19 of Article 66A of the Code with the obvious intention of fully meeting the three objections set forth in the Freedman opinion. We think the Legislature succeeded in accomplishing this result. The new Section 19 provides that *any* film duly submitted to the Board for examination and licensing "shall be reviewed and approved within five (5) days, unless the Board shall disapprove" the film under the provisions of Section 6. In the event of disapproval, the Board is required "within not later than three (3) days thereafter, [to] apply to the Circuit Court for Baltimore City for a judicial determination as to whether such film is obscene, or tends to debase or corrupt morals, or incite to crime, within the meaning of Section 6 * * *." It is also required that "[n]otice of such

application shall be forthwith sent by first class mail, postage prepaid, to the address of the person presenting such film for licensing." The Circuit Court is required within five days after the filing of the application to conduct a hearing, view the film and within two days after the hearing, "enter its decree and order requiring that said film be approved and licensed or be disapproved if in violation of the provisions of said Section 6 hereof." It is further provided that if the order disapproves the film, then the person presenting the film for licensing may appeal such determination to the Court of Appeals in accordance with the Maryland Rules of Procedure,[4] and the Court of Appeals "shall advance such case on its hearing calendar to the earliest practicable date" and in its review, the Court of Appeals "shall view the subject film." Then is added, "The burden of proving that the film should not be approved and licensed shall rest on the Board."

We have already indicated that full procedural compliance with the Act of 1965 was had in the Circuit Court and in this Court.

The General Assembly used, in part, as a model the New York injunctive procedure involved in *Kingsley Books, Inc.* v. *Brown*, 354 U.S. 436, 77 S. Ct. 1325, 1 L. Ed. 2d 1469 (1957) as suggested in Mr. Justice Brennan's opinion in Freedman (see p. 740 of 85 S. Ct.). In our opinion, the Act of 1965 carries out the requirement in Freedman—

"* * * [That] the exhibitor must be assured, by statute or authoritative judicial construction, that the censor will, within a specified brief period, either issue a license or go to court to restrain showing the film. Any restraint imposed in advance of a final judicial determination on the merits must similarly be limited to preservation of the status quo for the shortest fixed period compatible with sound judicial resolution."

The General Assembly also provided, as already set forth, that the burden of proving that the film should not be approved and licensed shall rest on the Board so that the Board, notwithstanding its character as an administrative body, must establish its disapproval by the weight of the credible evidence before the Circuit Court. This is a statutory change of the rule we indicated was applicable to findings of the Board in *Board of Censors* v. *Times Film*, 212 Md. 454, 462, 129 A. 2d 833, 838 (1957).

II.

We now consider whether the film is obscene within the meaning of the decisions of the Supreme Court of the United States.

The case of *Roth* v. *United States* (and *Alberts* v. *State of California*), 354 U.S. 476, 77 S. Ct. 1304, 1 L. Ed. 2d 1498 (1957), and the subsequent *per curiam* opinions of the Supreme Court applying the Roth-Alberts Rule[5] in a

---

[3] Black and Douglas, JJ. were, and for some time have been, of the opinion that all such statutes are unconstitutional under all circumstances.

[4] The appeal may be entered at any time after the order is filed but not later than 30 days therefrom.

[5] The Roth-Alberts test of obscenity as enunciated by Mr. Justice Brennan, for the majority of the Supreme Court is: "[W]hether to the average person, applying contemporary community standards, the dominant theme of the material taken as a whole appeals to prurient interest."

summary manner, as well as relevant prior federal and state cases, have been so thoroughly and carefully analyzed and considered in the Majority and dissenting opinions in *Monfred* v. *State*, 226 Md. 312, 173 A. 2d 173 (1961), that we think it would serve no useful purpose to have further extended discussion of those cases. See also the interesting and helpful discussion of the constitutional and other issues involved in this litigation in a book entitled "Censorship" by Morris L. Ernst and Alan U. Schwartz, especially Part IV, "Obscenity and the Constitution," pages 199–225. Our task is to ascertain what, if any, additions or limitations have been declared by the Supreme Court in regard to that rule by *Jacobellis* v. *State of Ohio*, 378 U.S. 184, 84 S. Ct. 1676, 12 L. Ed. 2d 793, opinions filed June 22, 1964.

In Jacobellis there was a division of opinion in regard to whether the "community" involved is local or national, three justices indicating that it should be the local community, two justices indicating that it should be the national community and four justices remaining silent on this issue. Fortunately in the case at bar, we need not resolve this thorny issue as under either theory of applicable "community," the film in this case is, in our opinion, not obscene. We, therefore, do not pass upon this particular issue, preferring to wait for further clarification of the issue by the Supreme Court itself.

[2, 3] Mr. Justice Brennan in his opinion in Jacobellis amplified and clarified the Roth-Alberts definition as follows:

1. Although motion pictures are within the constitutional guarantee of freedom of expression, obscenity is excluded from constitutional protection, but only when it is "utterly without redeeming social importance" and a work "cannot be proscribed unless it is 'utterly' without social importance."

2. "[T]he 'portrayal of sex, e.g., in art, literature and scientific works, is not itself sufficient reason to deny material the constitutional protection of freedom of speech and press,'" and "material dealing with sex in a manner that advocates ideas * * * or that has literary or scientific or artistic value or any other form of social importance, may not be branded as obscenity and denied the constitutional protection."

3. In the first instance, there must be a finding "that the material 'goes substantially beyond customary limits of candor in description or representation of such matters'" and "[i]n the absence of such a deviation from society's standards of decency, we do not see how any official inquiry into the allegedly prurient appeal of a work of expression can be squared with the guarantees of the First and Fourteenth Amendments."

4. The community standard involved is a national and not a local standard.

We have concluded that the Roth-Alberts test as amplified and clarified by Mr. Justice Brennan is applicable in the case at bar, except, as we have noted, we do not find it necessary to determine whether the applicable community standard is national or local.

We turn to the facts. The film was produced in Denmark in 1959 and was directed by the distinguished producer and director, Johan Jacobsen. It runs for 81 minutes, and is a Danish language picture with English subtitles. The characters are a man, played by Preben Lerdorff Rye and a woman played by Birgitte Federspiel. There is a

brief appearance of an insurance collector played by Victor Montell.

At the beginning of the film appears the language from Holy Scripture, Gen. 4:15, "And the Lord set a mark upon Cain, lest any finding him should kill him." The first scene in the film shows a burly male figure, clad in a raincoat, walking along a lonely road. The day is dark and there is intermittent rain. The appearance and actions of the man suggest that he is a fugitive. He comes upon a cottage near the sea shore, and looks it over carefully before he knocks at the door. A comely young woman answers the door and he explains that he is on vacation, has lost his way, and is looking for a place to stay. She invites him in to dry his clothing and to stay for lunch. While she is in the kitchen preparing lunch, he looks around the room carefully and notes that a radio is in the room. While having lunch, he plies his hostess with questions about herself and her background. He learns that she is alone. To his surprise, she invites him to spend the night. He accepts. She motions him to a place by the fire in the living room, retires to her bedroom and locks the bedroom door. After a while, he roams the room, and learns her name from a paper he finds. The night is passed without incident.

The following morning they breakfast together. He inquires about visitors, bus transportation and the bus schedule. Later he walks into the yard and, after seeing her bicycle, takes out his pocket knife and slashes the rear tire. She comes out from the house and they engage in conversation. She tells him she has lived at the cottage for three years since the Second World War. She learns he is not married and is pleased to learn this.

He then bids her farewell and leaves. She watches as he walks away. Later, in the cottage, she turns on the radio. His description is being broadcast, but she appears not to hear it. Later in the day, he returns to the cottage (having in the meantime rested in a thicket not far from the cottage to allow for the passage of time) and she smiles a welcome. He explains that he missed the bus. Later he caresses her as he adjusts a scarf around her neck. She says "You mustn't," but he ignores this mild rebuke and caresses her again. She walks away as he follows at a distance. She goes to a bench on a hill overlooking the sea and voices a soliloquy about her dead husband whose memory continues to haunt her. She recalls that he died under torture calling her name and that he had requested her to bury her wedding ring after his death and look for a new life.

In the following scene, it is evening and they talk by the open fire. He recounts further reminiscences of his past. He learns that her husband is dead; that they were happy in this cottage. After she leaves the room, he asks himself, "Who is she—I must find out." After searching the room he finds an automatic pistol in a desk drawer, and puts it in his pocket. As this scene ends he says to himself, "I must find out all about her—I want her."

The following morning they appear in swimming garb and walk hand in hand to the beach in front of the cottage. Her bathing suit is a one-piece one, entirely conventional. She has on a beach robe made of toweling material. After the swim, the woman is shown wrapped in the beach robe and carrying her wet bathing suit as the dripping water falls from it. The man is lying on the sand and the woman walks over to him and lies down beside him. They kiss and he fondles her. The scene clearly implies that they are having sexual intercourse, but there is no showing of nude figures. For the most part only the necks and shoulders of the parties are shown. She indicates satisfaction as the scene concludes.

Thereafter she buries her wedding ring in the sand and tells him "All is well." They playfully romp around the yard and she accidentally knocks over a pile of wood which he had previously carefully piled up. He utters some angry words. She speaks to him in a soothing voice, after which they kiss.

The next scene is at night with the man and woman in bed side by side. He fondles her and inquires again about her husband. She replies: "We came here to get away from it all. We had a wonderful time. Then some friends came here. They belonged to the underground. He also joined the Resistance. He came and went frequently. Then one day he came no more. He was caught." The man says, "Life is to kill or be killed. We have no choice." She replies, "Paul loved me. He screamed my name as they tortured him. The man who tortured him had a scar on his arm in the shape of an unusual bite." Surreptitiously the man rolls down his sleeve to conceal his upper arm.

The following morning it was raining. She is dressed to go out and says she is going to the grocer's. He tells her not to go, and after an argument, knocks her down. He is instantly sorry. There is a knock at the door and the man hides in the bedroom. The person at the door is an insurance agent who has come to collect the premium on her fire insurance policy. The man in the bedroom with the door slightly ajar, has the pistol in his hand ready for use if the caller is looking for him. She goes to her desk to write a check to pay the premium and finds the pistol gone. The insurance agent leaves and the man emerges from her bedroom. He explains that he hid for her sake to avoid gossip. She is now alarmed, and continues to search for the pistol.

The next scene shows them on the couch in the living room, fully dressed, in each other's arms. She asks him about the pistol but he gives no clear answer. She rises to pour some wine from a small decanter and each drinks some of the wine. He lies down on the couch. The next scene shows her astride him and again the movements of the parties imply that sexual intercourse is being performed. They are both fully clothed. She kisses him and says "I love you." As she reaches a climax the bite-shaped scar on the man's arm is revealed. She realizes that he is her husband's murderer, and falls back in anguish. She falls backward and lies over the man. He is still on his back.

She then arises, recovers the pistol from his jacket pocket and goes into the kitchen and asks herself what she should do. "He must confess," she says. He calls to her and they talk. She offers to go away with him and says "I must know you completely." He notices that she acts strangely and then goes to his jacket, finding the pistol gone.

In the final scene, she points the pistol at him and asks "Why"? He scorns her and demands that she give him the pistol. She aims it at him and says "Talk about Paul." He reminds her that they love each other. She says "You used me. You are loathsome," and again demands "Tell me about Paul." She is horrified as he admits that he was a collaborator with the Nazi SS during the war and that they tortured and killed her husband. "We shot him in the neck." She lowers the pistol. He does not seek to take it

from her but throws a glass of wine in her face and runs to the door. As he is about to run out the door, she shoots him in the back. As he dies he says, "One animal kills another." With the pistol still in her hand she goes out the door and walking slowly down the path casts the pistol to one side as the film ends.

In addition to the film, produced by the Board in the lower court, the following evidence was produced by Trans-Lux: The United States Bureau of Customs under the Tariff Act of 1930 admitted the film for entry into the United States after the Bureau had determined that the film was not obscene. Early in 1963, the film was exhibited in over 150 theatres in 23 States and the District of Columbia. It has been viewed by not less than 250,000 persons without any untoward incidents. When first exhibited in Denmark, the film was awarded three "Bodils" (equivalent to an "Oscar" in the United States) as 1) the best Danish picture for the year 1959, 22) for the best female performance for that year, and 3) for the best male performance for the year. In January 1964, the International Film Importers and Distributors of America awarded Birgitte Federspiel, the female lead in the film, its award for the best performance of the year by a female actress in an imported foreign picture. The film was licensed by the appropriate authorities for exhibition in Chicago and has been exhibited in that City.

The director and producer of the film, Johan Jacobsen, in his affidavit admitted into evidence, stated that he has been a director and producer of films for 26 years, has produced 34 films and directed 25 films and twice has received all three awards from the Danish Film Critics—one in "The Soldier and Jenny," and again in "A Stranger Knocks," the film involved in this case. The film opened in Copenhagen and ran for 15 weeks. He explained that his primary interest was in the maintenance of the high standard for which Danish films are noted, rather than profits, *per se*, and "I have never been in a position wherein I had to descend to the level of exploiting sexual activity on the screen for the sole motive of sensationalism. My reputation stands as testimony of this statement." He further stated: "I was frankly shocked to learn that the censors concluded that this film which I intended as a serious treatment of a question of vital contemporary importance was nothing more than an exercise in 'obscenity.' Let me make it very plain that it was not intended, nor was any part of it intended to appeal to the sensation seeker or to the prurient interest."

Mr. Jacobsen gives in some detail the philosophical basis for the film and how the two scenes, to which objection has been raised, were of crucial significance in the film as a work of art and as a serious film. The first scene shows the complete commitment of two antithetical characters—the woman having the idealistic, the man the cynical and pragmatic character—in achieving a harmony and in the awakening of life and hope. The second scene shows the supreme effort of the woman to break down the barrier which suspicion has created and represents a desperate effort by the woman, threatened again with isolation, to communicate. By her actions she assumes the position of dominance and of total commitment to the man as well as the protectiveness of the female. The man, detached and triumphant and yet moved to tenderness, is insulated by this all-embracing love from the brutality and corruption of the world with which he could not cope. At the moment of sexual fulfillment, the discovery is made that the man is her husband's murderer. The groan of pleasure and of pain is the dramatic expression of the essential ambivalence in the relationship.

Favorable criticisms from the following motion picture critics, were introduced into evidence:

George Browning who has written reviews for the Baltimore News Post, News American, the United Press, the New York World Telegram, the Box Office, Motion Picture Daily and the Film Daily.

Bosley Crowther, leading motion picture critic for the New York Times.

Alton Cook, reviewer for the New York World Telegram and Sun.

Marion Simon, reviewer for The National Observer.

Margo Miller, reviewer for The Boston Globe.

Kathleen Carroll, reviewer for the New York Daily News.

Frederick H. Guidry, reviewer for The Christian Science Monitor.

Elinor Hughes, reviewer for The Boston Herald.

Henry T. Murdock, reviewer for The Philadelphia Inquirer.

Hollins Alpert, reviewer for The Saturday Review of Literature and who has written motion picture articles for the New York Times Magazine, Theatre Arts, Esquire, Charm, Partisan Review and other magazines.

In addition to these critics, Trans-Lux introduced an affidavit of Arthur Mayer, head of the Paramount Publishing and Advertising Department for 40 years and an operator of hundreds of theatres during that period, who is a frequent contributor to The Saturday Review and Variety and who has lectured at a number of prominant universities and schools. In this affidavit, Mr. Mayer gave his opinion that the film "is a serious work which is written, directed and acted with professional competence" and that the appeal of the film—and of the two scenes complained of—is not to the prurient interest. He further stated: "While the film undoubtedly explores a close intimacy between a man and a woman in sexual terms, I do not believe that the subject is handled in such a fashion as to offend any reasonable and mature man or woman. In short, it is my opinion that this film, rather than appealing to the prurient interest, is a work of professional competence which explores a moral problem of genuine contemporary significance."

A portion of Marion Simon's review may be quoted to illustrate the critical opinion. It stated, in point:

*"There's nothing lewd about this stark two-character drama of love, hatred, and revenge in postwar Denmark. * * *"*

"Birgitte Federspiel—gracefully long-limbed, with a face like Claudette Colbert's—remains discreetly clothed throughout, except for one beach scene where the black-and-white camera is glued to her face. Preben Lerdorff Rye is almost Victorian as the hunted former Nazi collaborator who comes knocking at Miss Federspiel's isolated cottage, where she has lived for three years in bitter tribute to a husband murdered for his war activities in the Danish underground. . .

"Here they play out their parable of Cain's exile under Mr. Jacobsen's taut, realistic direction, deftly probing the questions of good and evil, spite and respite that Finn

Metherling has woven into his screenplay. And the two debated scenes [scenes] are so much a part of the relationship between these two people—man and woman, killer and victim, judged and judging—that the film couldn't have been made without them."

[4] The Board offered no evidence before the lower court of *any* expert or other opinion indicating that the film appealed to the prurient interest or was not a serious work of art. It only offered in evidence the film itself, contending that the two scenes complained of in the film met the burden of proof imposed upon it by the Act of 1965. We do not agree. In our opinion the weight of the testimony—including the film itself—establishes that the film is a serious work of art, dealing with a subject of social importance and does not appeal to the prurient interest. It most certainly is not "utterly without redeeming social importance," the film "deals with sex in a manner which advocates ideas having artistic value and social importance," and "does not go beyond the customary limits of candor in the description of such matters." The film may not constitutionally be denied a license for exhibition by the Board under the Roth-Alberts Rule as amplified and explained by Mr. Justice Brennan in Jacobellis.[6]

There is no "thematic obscenity" involved in the film, as was urged (unsuccessfully before the Supreme Court) in regard to "Lady Chatterley's Lover"[7]—approval of adultery—and "The Miracle"[8]—alleged approval of blasphemy.

In the case at bar, the film begins with a quotation from Holy Writ and ends with the death of the man, with the

---

[6] The film had a curious legal history in New York. In that State the Board of Regents of the University of New York (corresponding to the Maryland Board for pre-showing censorship of motion pictures) declined to license the film. Its action was reversed by the Supreme Court, Appellate Division, Third Department by a 4 to 1 decision Presiding Judge Bergan being with the majority and Judge Herlihy writing a dissenting opinion. See *Trans-Lux Distributing Corp.* v. *Board of Regents,* 19 A.D. 2d 937, 244 N.Y.S. 2d 333. Thereafter on appeal to the Court of Appeals of New York (certiorari having been granted), Judge Bergan who, in the meantime had been elevated to the Court of Appeals, was disqualified to hear the appeal. The judges of the Court of Appeals of New York divided 3 to 3, Desmond, C.J., Burke and Scileppi, JJ. being for reversal of the Appellate Division and reinstatement of the order of the Board of Regents, and Dye, Fuld and Van Voorhis, JJ. being for affirmance. Under the provisions of the New York Constitution, Judge Williams of the Appellate Division, Third Department, was called up to sit with the Court of Appeals, the case was reargued, and Judge Williams cast his vote for reversal so that the Appellate Division was reversed, 4 to 3 (see *Trans-Lux Distr. Corp.* v. *Board,* 14 N.Y. 2d 88, 248 N.Y.S. 2d 857, 198 N.E. 2d 242) although ironically a majority of the Court of Appeals as then constituted if Judge Bergan were included, was of the contrary opinion, Judge Bergan having voted for reversal of the Board of Regents when a member of the Appellate Division. The Supreme Court of the United States granted certiorari, and reversed the Court of Appeals in a *per curiam* opinion filed March 15, 1965 referring to *Freedman* v. *State of Maryland,* decided March 1, 1965. As a result of this action by the Supreme Court the film was thereafter exhibited in New York.

[7] *Commercial Picture Corp.* v. *Regents,* 346 U.S. 587, 74 S. Ct. 286, 98 L. Ed. 329 (1954).

[8] *Joseph Burstyn, Inc.* v. *Wilson,* 343 U.S. 495, 72 S. Ct. 777, 96 L. Ed. 1098 (1952).

woman facing a possible murder charge. This is not calculated to indicate approval of sexual relations outside of wedlock, but rather the contrary.

In regard to "community standards," George Browning, the motion picture critic who lives in Baltimore and has written reviews for Baltimore newspapers for many years testified that in his opinion the film did not transgress present day community standards and this testimony was not contradicted. The uncontradicted testimony of the other critics, the producer already referred to, and other testimony mentioned above, indicate that the film does not transgress national community standards. As the film does not violate either community standard we need not decide which community standard applies.

III.

In our opinion, the film does not violate the standards of Article 66A, Section 6, assuming, *arguendo*, that they are not too vague and indefinite to be enforced at all.

The definition of "obscenity" in subsection (b) is that the film is obscene "if, when considered *as a whole, its calculated purpose or dominant effect is substantially* to arouse *sexual desires, and* if the probability of this effect is *so great* as to *outweigh* whatever other merits the film may possess." (Emphasis supplied.) It seems clear to us from what has already been stated that both the film itself and the other evidence establishes that it is not obscene under this definition.[9]

Subsection (c) in defining what films tend to debase or corrupt morals states this is its effect "if its *dominant* purpose or effect is erotic or *pornographic; or if it portrays* acts of *sexual immorality, lust or lewdness,* or if it expressly or *impliedly* presents such acts as desirable, acceptable or proper patterns of behavior." (Emphasis supplied.) Here again the film and other evidence establishes that the dominant purpose or effect is not erotic or pornographic. Nor does it portray acts of sexual immorality, lust or lewdness, as the sexual relationships of unmarried persons are implied and, as already noted, the implied sexual relations are by no means presented as desirable, acceptable or proper patterns of conduct, but rather the contrary is presented.

There is no contention that the film incites to crime as defined in Subsection (d), and obviously it does not.

As we have indicated, however, even if the Maryland standards in Section 6 were violated by the film, the Board could not constitutionally refuse to license it under the Roth-Alberts Rule, as amplified and explained, and the finding of the lower court to the contrary was clearly erroneous and its order must be reversed.

---

[9] We held that nudity, as such, was not obscene under Section 6 in *Fanfare Films* v. *Motion Picture Censor Board,* 234 Md. 10, 197 A. 2d 839 (1964) involving the motion picture "Have Figure—Will Travel," following our decision in *Board of Censors* v. *Times Film,* 212 Md. 454, 129 A. 2d 833 (1957). In the case at bar, however, there is no nudity involved.

HORNEY, Judge (dissenting):

It seems to me that the majority of the members of this Court, in approving a film portraying overt acts of illicit sexual intercourse, has gone further than even the majority of the Supreme Court of the United States has required, and, in so doing, has disregarded the Maryland statute which prohibits the showing of unlawful and immoral sexual relations. If such illicit acts are not obscene, it is difficult to envisage what, other than hard-core pornography, would constitute obscenity.

In my opinion, the order of the lower court affirming the refusal of the State Board of Censors to license the motion picture, "A Stranger Knocks," should not have been reversed. For, when these illicit acts of sexual gratification, the elimination of which, as the producer admitted, "would virtually destroy the film as a serious motion picture," are considered (either with or without the remainder of the film), it is clear that the dominant effect of the film, even assuming this was not its calculated purpose, is to arouse lascivious thoughts or desires which is expressly prohibited by § 6(b) of Art. 66A. Surely, a film such as this, wherein the exhibition of inhibited acts of sexual immorality between an unmarried man and woman leaves nothing to be surmised, will indubitably be taken by the viewing public as sanctioning or approving such acts as desirable, acceptable or proper patterns of behavior contrary to the provisions of § 6(c) of Art. 66A. Such a portrayal of immorality can hardly be said, as the majority hold, to be a serious work of art dealing with a subject of social importance that does not appeal to prurient interest.

On the contrary, for the reasons stated above, it seems obvious to me that the film goes far beyond what is permitted under the Roth-Alberts test—set forth in *Roth* v. *United States* (and *Alberts* v. *State of California*), 354 U.S. 476, 77 S. Ct. 1304, 1 L. Ed. 2d 1498 (1957)—which, as amplified in *Jacobellis* v. *State of Ohio*, 378 U.S. 184, 84 S. Ct. 1676, 12 L. Ed. 2d 793 (1964), is still the law of the land, and the standards to be applied in determining what is and what is not obscene are still those of the local community and not those of the nation as a whole. Furthermore, it should be pointed out that the case at bar is clearly distinguishable from Jacobellis on the facts in that in Jacobellis the sexual act was a fleeting one while in this case both acts were not only protracted but were deliberately over-emphasized by extraordinary demonstrations of satisfaction on the part of the female participant. Other than this, as Judge Prendergast pointed out, there is a vast difference between what is written as poetry or prose and that which is vividly portrayed on a motion picture screen. On the one hand that which is written may be so phrased as not to be erotic or pornographic, while on the other hand sexual activity shown on a screen could be, as it was here, unlawful obscenity.

Judge Sybert, who participated in the consideration of this case, collaborated in the writing of this dissent before his retirement.

■ United States of America, *Libellant,*

v.

One Carton Positive Motion Picture Film Entitled "491" (35 mm. Black & White, 5 Double Reels, 9610 feet, Swedish Soundtrack with English Subtitles),
Janus Films, Inc., Claimant.

United States District Court, S.D. New York.

Nov. 17, 1965.

Robert M. Morgenthau, U.S. Dist. Atty., Southern District of New York, *Arthur S. Olick,* Asst. U.S. Dist. Atty., *Judith Nochimson,* Asst. U.S. Dist. Atty., for libellant.

Ephraim London, New York City (of Brennan, London & Buttenwieser), New York City, for claimant, Janus Films, Inc.

GRAVEN, Senior District Judge (by assignment).

1. In this proceeding the Government seeks the forfeiture of an imported motion picture film on the ground that it constitutes obscene material the import of which is prohibited by Section 305 of the Tariff Act (Sec. 1305, Title 19 U.S.C.A.).

[1] 2. Section 305 of the Tariff Act (Sec. 1305, Title 19 U.S.C.A.) lists a number of items the import of which is prohibited. Among those items is "obscene" matter. That Section further provides:

*"Upon the appearance of any such * * * matter at any customs office, the same shall be seized and held by the collector to await the judgment of the district court as hereinafter provided; * * *. Upon the seizure of such * * * matter the collector shall transmit information thereof to the district attorney * * * who shall institute proceedings in the district court for the forfeiture, confiscation, and destruction of the * * * matter seized. Upon the adjudication that such * * * matter thus seized is of the character the entry of which is by this section prohibited, it shall be ordered destroyed and shall be destroyed. * * *"*

Under that Section, any party in interest may upon demand have the facts or issues determined by a jury and any party may have an appeal or right of review as in the case of ordinary actions or suits. In the present case no demand for a jury was made. Where the Government seeks to forfeit material the importation of which is alleged to be prohibited by Section 305, it proceeds by way of a libel action, which action is conducted under the Admiralty Rules.

The film which is the subject matter of this action was produced in Sweden by an organization known as Svensk Film Industri. It consisted of five double reels of black and white positive, 35mm. motion picture film totalling 9610 feet. It was sought to be imported in this country by Janus Films, Inc., the Claimant herein, a New York corporation which is engaged in the commercial distribution and licensing of motion picture films throughout the country. The dialogue in the film is in Swedish but there are English subtitles. It is what is known and referred to as a feature film.

3. There are a number of issues in this case. The Government contends that the film in question is obscene and hence is not a permissible import under Section 305 of the Tariff Act. The Claimant contends to the contrary. The Claimant challenges the constitutionality of the procedures provided for and followed in connection with the importation of feature films. It also challenges the constitutionality of the provision of Section 305 prohibiting the importation of "obscene" material.

[2] 4. This latter challenge will be first considered. The Claimant contends that the word "obscene" is so vague as to violate due process. In the case of *Roth v. United States* (1957), 354 U.S. 476, 77 S. Ct. 1304, 1 L. Ed. 2d 1498, the United States Supreme Court upheld a state criminal obscenity statute against a similar attack.

[3] It is the contention of the Claimant that that holding is not determinative of the question as to the constitutional adequacy of the word "obscene" as used in Section 305 because that Section provides for pre-exhibition restraint rather than post-exhibition sanctions provided by criminal statutes. The proceedings in connection with an imported film under Section 305 do operate as a pre-exhibition restraint. The proceedings are in rem rather than in personam and are civil rather than criminal in nature.

It would not seem that the United States Supreme Court would regard the word "obscene" as constitutionally sufficient in a criminal proceeding, yet constitutionally inadequate in a civil proceeding involving obscene matter. If that Court should hold that that word was constitutionally inadequate in connection with criminal proceedings, a different situation would be present. While some writers are of the view that the decision of that Court in the Roth case has been somewhat eroded, yet up to now it has not been eroded to the extent that it is no longer authority as to the constitutional adequacy of the word "obscene." It is the view and holding of the Court that Section 305 is not constitutionally inadequate because of the use of the word "obscene."

[4] 5. The Claimant makes a contention relating to the quantum of proof in a proceeding to condemn material on the ground of its obscenity. In criminal proceedings under obscenity statutes, the guilt of the party or parties charged must, of course, be established beyond a reasonable doubt. Although the present proceeding is civil in character, it is the contention of the Claimant that because of the constitutional principles involved the Government has the burden of establishing beyond a reasonable doubt the obscenity of the film involved.

[5, 6] In libel proceedings for the condemnation of property allegedly used for illegal purposes, it is not necessary that the Government establish the allegations of the libel beyond a reasonable doubt; it is sufficient if it establishes those allegations by a preponderance of the evidence. *D'Agostino v. United States* (9th Cir. 1958), 261 F. 2d 154, 157, certiorari denied (1959), 359 U.S. 953, 79 S. Ct. 739, 3 L. Ed. 2d 760; *United States v. One 1955 Mercury Sedan* (4th Cir. 1957), 242 F. 2d 429; *Utley Wholesale Company v. United States* (5th Cir. 1962), 308 F. 2d 157. The cases cited did not involve the condemnation of allegedly obscene material. Apparently there are no decisions involving the nature of the proof in civil proceedings for the condemnation of material alleged to be obscene. While the United States Supreme Court has adopted a very strict attitude as to proof of obscenity, it has not as yet indicated that in a libel proceeding for the condemnation of material alleged to be obscene it would require that the obscenity of the material be established beyond a reasonable doubt. Apparently it would require that the obscenity of the material sought to be condemned must be clearly established by a preponderance of the evidence. This Court in the present action will follow that apparent rule.

6. The constitutional challenge of the Claimant to the procedures provided for and followed in connection with the importation of feature films requires consideration of certain of those procedures. It appears that ninety per cent of all feature films imported into the United States come to the Port of New York. The procedures hereinafter referred to are the procedures at that port. A motion picture film being imported is accompanied by the usual entry documents prepared by the importer. Upon the arrival of the film it is placed under Customs seal. It is then sent to the projector room of the Collector in New York City. When the sealed package of film arrives at the projector room it is opened and the contents are checked against the documents to determine whether the estimated duty paid is correct, and it is then screened by a Customs' film reviewer. Film reviewers receive periodic instructions concerning the statutes relating to the importation of obscene matter and the court decisions having to do with the matter of obscenity. Following the screening of the film by the reviewer, the reviewer prepares a report. If the reviewer is of the view that the entry of the film is permissible, it is immediately released to the importer. There is no review of such a release. If the reviewer is of the view that the importation of the film might constitute a violation of Section 305, the film is viewed by an Administrative Aide. If the Administrative Aide is of the view that its importation would not be in violation of Section 305, the film is immediately released to the importer. There is no review of such a release. In the event that the Administrative Aide is of the view that it unquestionably appears that the film is not importable under Section 305, the film is transmitted to the United States District Attorney for the Southern District of New York for the institution of libel proceedings. In the event that the Administrative Aide is of the view that it does not unquestionably appear that the film is not importable under Section 305, it is transmitted to the Assistant Deputy Commissioner of Customs at Washington, D.C. That Assistant Deputy Commissioner views the film. If he is of the view that its importation would not constitute a violation of Section 305, it is released to the importer. There is no review of such a release. If the Assistant Deputy Commissioner is of the view that the film might not be importable under Section 305, it is then transmitted to the Customs Office at the Port of New York and by that Office transmitted to the United States District Attorney for the Southern District of New York for the institution of libel proceedings against it. Where a film is detained because of question as to its importability under Section 305, the importer is immediately notified that the film is being temporarily detained. Upon being so notified the importer has several options. It may consent to the forfeiture of the film; it may export the film; it may also take no action and let the Government proceed against it. The choice is solely that of the importer. In some cases where a film is being detained because of question as to its importability, the importer sometimes seeks an informal conference with the Assistant Deputy Commissioner of Customs to ascertain what portion or portions of the film have given rise to question of its importability. If following such a conference it would appear that the doubt as to the importability of the film was not well founded, the film is released to the importer. There is no review of such a release.

In some cases an importer before conferring with the Assistant Deputy Commissioner of Customs will secure permission to have access to the film for the purpose of deleting certain portions of it. In other cases the deletions will be made after conferring with the Assistant Deputy Commissioner of Customs. The portions deleted would ordinarily be those portions which the importer has reason to believe might have given rise to the question of importability.

The importer has the right to export the entire film and then make a new importation of the film as deleted. In some instances an informal procedure is followed under which the importer consents to the forfeiture of the deleted portions of the film and the Assistant Deputy Commissioner of Customs will then release the film as deleted.

Where it appears that there is such a serious question as to the importability of a film as to require its transmission to the United States District Attorney for possible court proceedings, a seizure of it is then made for such purpose.

7. It was heretofore noted that the Claimant contends that the procedures provided for and followed in connection with imported feature films are constitutionally inadequate. In that connection the Claimant contends that the procedural provisions contained in Section 305 are on their face constitutionally inadequate. The Claimant further contends that the procedures under Section 305 as carried out in practice in relation to feature films in general

manifest their constitutional inadequacy. The Claimant further contends that the procedures followed in the case of the particular film in question were such as to deny it constitutional due process. The constitutional questions raised by the Claimant require consideration of a number of decisions. In the case of *Times Film Corp.* v. *City of Chicago* (1961), 365 U.S. 43, 81 S. Ct. 391, 5 L. Ed. 2d 403, it was held that an ordinance of the City of Chicago providing for pre-exhibition examination of motion picture films was not unconstitutional on its face. The Court did not reach the question as to the validity of the standards set out in the ordinance. In the case of *Kingsley Books, Inc.* v. *Brown* (1957), 354 U.S. 436, 77 S. Ct. 1325, 1 L. Ed. 2d 1469, it was held that a New York statute which provided for a limited injunctive remedy against the sale and distribution of obscene written and printed matter was constitutional. The cases referred to were followed by the cases of *Freedman* v. *State of Maryland* (1965), 380 U.S. 51, 85 S. Ct. 734, 13 L. Ed. 2d 649, and *Marcus* v. *Search Warrants* (1961), 367 U.S. 717, 81 S. Ct. 1708, 6 L. Ed. 2d 1127. The case of *Freedman* v. *State of Maryland,* supra, involved a Maryland statute which prohibited the exhibition of a film without first submitting it to the State Board of Censors. An exhibitor challenged the constitutionality of the statute by refusing to submit a particular film to that Board. The film, if submitted, would have met the statutory standards and would have been licensed for exhibition. The Court held that the statute was constitutionally inadequate. In that case the Court stated (p. 55 U.S., 85 S. Ct. p. 737): "Under the statute, the exhibitor is required to submit the film to the Board for examination, but no time limit is imposed for completion of Board action, § 17." The Court, in referring to the statute, further stated (p. 55 U.S., 85 S. Ct. p. 737):

*"Thus there is no statutory provision for judicial participation in the procedure which bars a film, nor even assurance of prompt judicial review. Risk of delay is built into the Maryland procedure, as is borne out by experience; in the only reported case indicating the length of time required to complete an appeal, the initial judicial determination has taken four months and final vindication of the film on appellate review, six months. * * *"*

In the concurring opinion of Justice Douglas in that case the following statement is made (pp. 61–62 U.S., 85 S. Ct. p. 740):

*"The Court today holds that a system of movie censorship must contain at least three procedural safeguards if it is not to run afoul of the First Amendment: (1) the censor must have the burden of instituting judicial proceedings; (2) any restraint prior to judicial review can be imposed only briefly in order to preserve the status quo; and (3) a prompt judicial determination of obscenity must be assured. * * *"*

In the majority opinion it is stated (p. 59 U.S., 85 S. Ct. p. 739) "the procedure must also assure a prompt final judicial decision * * *."

The case of *Marcus* v. *Search Warrants,* supra, involved proceedings under a Missouri statute relating to the seizure and forfeiture of obscene publications. The Court held that the statute lacked proper constitutional safeguards. In that case the Court referred to and discussed the procedures provided by a New York statute relating to such publications which were upheld in the case of *Kingsley Books, Inc.* v. *Brown* (1957), 354 U.S. 436, 77 S. Ct. 1325, 1 L. Ed. 2d 1469. The Court stated (p. 737 of 367 U.S., 81 S. Ct. p. 1719), *Marcus* v. *Search Warrants,* supra:

" * * Finally, a subdivision of the New York statute in Kingsley Books required that a judicial decision on the merits of obscenity be made within two days of trial, which in turn was required to be within one day of the joinder of issue on the request for an injunction. In contrast, the Missouri statutory scheme drawn in question here has no limitation on the time within which decision must be made, only a provision for rapid trial of the issue of obscenity. And in fact over two months elapsed between seizure and decision. * * *"*

It appears from the recent case of *Trans-Lux Distributing Corp.* v. *Board of Censors,* Md., Sept. 27, 1965, 213 A. 2d 235, that following the decision of the United States Supreme Court in *Freedman* v. *State of Maryland,* supra, the Maryland statute relating to the censorship of film by the State Board of Censors was amended to provide that any film submitted to that Board must be reviewed within five days; that in the event of disapproval of a film by that Board it was required to make an application to the Circuit Court within three days for a judicial determination as to obscenity; that the Circuit Court was required to hold a hearing within five days and enter its determination within two days after the hearing; and that in the event of an adverse decision the exhibitor might appeal to the Maryland Court of Appeals which "shall advance such case upon its hearing calendar to the earliest practicable date."

[7] At the present time it appears from the decisions of the United States Supreme Court that under proper constitutional safeguards there may be a limited pre-exhibition restraint of motion picture films. It is the contention of the Claimant herein that the procedures provided for and followed in connection with imported feature films do not afford the specified and required constitutional safeguards. Some of the other features related to and connected with the import of feature films will next be referred to. Under the Tariff Act the Customs Service is charged with the duty of examining imports for the purpose of ascertaining their duty status. That Service also has the duty to ascertain, or to cause to be ascertained, the permissibility of such imports under the Tariff Act. In order to carry out that latter duty in connection with imported feature films, it is manifestly necessary that the Customs Service view such films. Where such films upon viewing give rise to no question as to their importability, they are then cleared through Customs. If, however, it would appear upon viewing that a particular feature film might not be importable under Section 305, the Customs Service refers the film to the United States District Attorney for the purpose of securing a judicial determination of its importability.

The Customs Service does not have censorship power as to imported films nor act as a censor of them. In substance, it brings to the attention of the United States District Attorney for his consideration and action those films the importation of which would constitute a possible violation of Section 305 of the Tariff Act. The action brought by the United States District Attorney following the reference of a particular film to him does not constitute a review of any preceding administrative action or decision. It is an original proceeding in which a judicial determination is made as to whether the film in question is or is not obscene within the purview of Section 305.

It appears, as heretofore noted, that around ninety per cent of the films imported into the United States come to the Customs Office of the Port of New York. The processing of imported feature films was heretofore described. During the calendar year of 1963 there were received at the Port of New York 4,259 shipments of film totalling 31,641,824 feet for examination under the Tariff Act. A substantial number of the films received at that Port are obviously of such a character as not to require screening. All feature films are screened. During 1963 a total of 2,174 shipments of feature film totalling 7,997,348 feet were screened. During 1964 a total of 3,735 shipments of feature film totalling 8,149,874 feet were screened.

It appears that of all the films imported through all the ports of entry each year around 100 of them give rise to some doubt as to their importability under that portion of Section 305 relating to obscene matter. It further appears that in general as to around 70 of such films the doubt is resolved in favor of the importer and the films released forthwith. The remaining 30 are seized and transmitted to the United States District Attorney for further proceedings. The overwhelming number of films so seized are not feature films. They are generally 8 mm. and 16 mm. films intended for private or semi-private showing which are clearly obscene in character.

It appears that over the years a number of imported films which were cleared through Customs without being transmitted to the United States District Attorney for the purpose of securing a court determination as to their obscenity were later the subjects of obscenity proceedings by municipal and state authorities. It also appears that in all cases where those proceedings were reviewed by the United States Supreme Court the Court was of the view that obscenity was lacking. That situation is indicative of the fact that the Customs Service has been cautious in the matter of transmitting feature films to the United States District Attorney for the institution of judicial proceedings against them.

[8] It appears that under the directives and practice of the Customs Service the processing of imported feature films is expedited. It appears that feature films are generally screened within a few business days after having been entered. On some occasions in the past when there has been a large influx of imported feature films there has been some delay, but the screening is generally fairly current. Importers should and do take cognizance of the fact that some delay is inherent in the case of importations subject to the Tariff Act. The fact that the Claimant takes cognizance of that fact is indicated by its practice of not scheduling any showing of an imported film until it has cleared Customs and is in its possession. The Customs Service is charged by Congress with the responsibility of transmitting to the United States District Attorney such feature films as might give rise to question as to their importability under Section 305. Manifestly, those in the Customs Service having to do with such matters should give careful and adequate consideration to the matter of whether a film is of such a character as to require it to be transmitted to the United States District Attorney. It

would be manifestly unfair to both the importers and the Government for those in the Customs Service having to do with such matters to hurriedly and without adequate consideration transmit imported films to the United States District Attorney. It appears that where the doubt as to the importability of a feature film is such as to cause it to be sent to Washington, D.C., for review by the Assistant Deputy Commissioner of Customs it may take from a few days up to three weeks to secure such review. It further appears that in the greater number of cases such review results in the film being released. It is to be noted that an importer of any article by the act of entering it for import thereby voluntarily puts it under restraint by the Customs Service for Customs purposes and that it is not a case of the Government reaching out and putting an article under restraint to start with. Where an importer enters an imported film for importation the Customs Service manifestly has a reasonable time in which to process the import for Tariff Act purposes. It is the view of the Claimant that Section 305 is constitutionally defective in that it does not contain any fixed time limits as to the processing of imported features films for Tariff Act purposes. There are, of course, many hundreds of thousands of imported articles imported into the United States each year. As to many of those articles there is need of prompt processing by the Customs Service, but so far Congress has not fixed definite time limits for the processing of any particular import or imports. It appears that feature films are, in general, promptly processed for Tariff Act purposes. It also appears that of the total number of feature films imported only a small number are referred to the United States District Attorney. It further appears that, in general, the time taken by the Customs Service to consider the matter of referability is only that which is reasonably necessary.

[9] The Court is of the view and holds that on the record in this case it cannot be said that the fact that Section 305 does not contain any fixed time limits for the processing of feature films for Tariff Act purposes by the Customs Service does not make it constitutionally defective. As heretofore noted, it is the claim of the Claimant that as to the particular film here involved the delays were such as to deny it constitutional due process. That matter, as heretofore noted, will be considered later.

[10] 8. It was heretofore noted that one of the constitutional safeguards referred to in the case of *Freedman* v. *State of Maryland*, supra, was that the exhibitor of film must not bear the burden of instituting judicial proceedings for the purpose of securing a judicial determination as to whether it is or is not obscene. Section 305 provides that constitutional safeguard. The burden is entirely upon the Government to institute such proceedings.

[11] 9. It was heretofore noted that another of the constitutional safeguards referred to by the United States Supreme Court was that prompt judicial determination of obscenity must be assured. While the decisions of the United States Supreme Court relating to that matter dealt with state procedures and state courts, there is no reason for assuming that the United States Supreme Court would have one rule applicable to state procedures and state courts and another rule applicable to federal procedures and federal courts.

When a film is referred to the United States District Attorney under Section 305, the only procedure available for the determination of the question of whether the film is or is not obscene is a libel action for the forfeiture of the film conducted under the Admiralty Rules. Under those Rules when a libel action is filed process is issued. Rule 1 of the local Admiralty Rules which is typical provides, in part, as follows: "Process *in rem* shall be returnable and called by the clerk at the next general motion day, not less than eight days from its issuance unless otherwise ordered." Rule 2 of those Rules provides that "notice of arrest of property in suits *in rem*, shall be published once at least one week before the date on which the process is returnable * * *." Under Rule 11 of those Rules, unless the Court directs otherwise, "the answer, exceptions or exceptive allegations to the libel or petition * * * shall be filed within three weeks after the return day."

It is clear that, because of the provisions of the Admiralty Rules relating to the issue of process, time for appearance and answer and the pretrial procedures afforded, a libel action for the judicial determination of the alleged obscenity of a feature film could not be tried and determined within some of the time limits fixed under some state statutes. Absent the waiver on the part of the Government and a Claimant of the procedures provided under the Admiralty Rules, it is manifest that a trial and judicial determination as to the issue of obscenity could not be had in most cases in less than from four to six weeks and more probably eight to ten weeks. In the case of *Freedman* v. *State of Maryland*, supra, in the majority opinion (p. 55 of 380 U.S., 85 S. Ct. 734), Justice Brennan commented unfavorably as to the fact that in that case the decision on appeal as to the issue of obscenity took six months. In the case of *Marcus* v. *Search Warrants*, supra, the United States Supreme Court spoke disapprovingly of the fact that in that case over two months had elapsed between the seizure and the judicial decision.

In a libel action conducted for the purpose of securing a judicial determination as to the issue of obscenity under Section 305, all of the parties are given the right of appeal or review. There are, of course, no provisions fixing the time when either a United States Court of Appeals or the United States Supreme Court must hear and determine an appeal. Such appeal might well require several months. The question whether on its face a libel action under the Admiralty Rules does or does not afford assurance of a prompt judicial hearing and determination of the issue of obscenity under Section 305 is troublesome and difficult. The final answer to that question depends upon what the United States Supreme Court regards as constituting assurance of prompt judicial hearing and determination and review in situations where imports are restrained under the provision of Section 305 here involved. If it should be authoritatively held that a libel action conducted under the Admiralty Rules does not give the necessary assurance of a prompt judicial hearing and determination, then manifestly Congress would have to provide some special procedure or procedures embodying fixed time limits for a judicial hearing and determination, including possibly some provisions in connection with appellate review.

[12] In the case of *Freedman* v. *State of Maryland*, supra, Justice Brennan in the majority opinion stated (p. 61 of 380 U.S., 85 S. Ct. p. 740): "We do not mean to lay down rigid time limits or procedures * * *." In the absence of authoritative pronouncements by the United States Supreme Court, this Court is not prepared to hold

that on their face the present procedures are lacking in assurance of prompt judicial hearing and determination.

10. It is also the contention of the Claimant that even though the present procedures on their face cannot be said to manifest that they do not provide for a prompt judicial hearing and determination of the issue of obscenity under Section 305, yet in practice they do not afford such a hearing and determination. In that connection the Claimant presented evidence as to the length of time it took to complete Section 305 libel proceedings in the United States District Courts for the Southern and Eastern Districts of New York. It appears that, in general, there was a considerable interval of time between the institution of such an action and the final decree. It also appears that an overwhelming number of those cases were non-contested cases and the forfeiture was by default. It further appears that during the last thirty years the present action is the only contested action in all of the United States involving the question of the obscenity of a feature film under Section 305. Thus, the records referred to throw little light on how long it would take an importer who wishes to contest the forfeiture of a feature film as obscene under Section 305 to secure a judicial hearing and determination on the question of its alleged obscenity.

11. It was heretofore noted that it was the claim of the Claimant that as to the particular film here involved the time it took before it was referred to the United States District Attorney and the time it took to have the question of its obscenity judicially heard and determined was such as to deny it constitutional due process. That contention requires a consideration of what occurred in connection with the present film.

The motion picture film here involved was entered into the New York Customs Office on October 28, 1964. The film was sent to the Collector's projector room on Friday, October 30, 1964. It was first screened by a film reviewer on Wednesday, November 4, 1964. The reviewer reported that the importation of the film might constitute a violation of Section 305. It was then seen and reviewed by the Administrative Aide on November 5, 1964. On November 9, 1964, the Customs Office notified the importer by letter that the film was being temporarily detained as being in possible violation of Section 305 of the Tariff Act. In that letter the importer was asked to furnish information as to the proposed distribution of the film. The reason for the request for such information was that under a Tariff Act regulation the Secretary of the Treasury is permitted to admit otherwise obscene material of recognized and established literary or scientific merit imported for noncommercial purposes. That regulation was in accord with a provision contained in Section 305.

On November 30, 1964, the importer informed the Customs Office that it intended to distribute the film commercially throughout the United States. The attorney for the importer then asked and was given permission to view the film. On December 16, 1964, it was viewed by representatives of the importer. On January 14, 1965, the importer asked permission to view portions of the film a second time and was given such permission. The film was again viewed by representatives of the importer on January 19, 1965. On or about January 27, 1965, the attorney for the importer informed the Customs Office that the importer wished to delete a scene involving a prostitute being forced to have sexual relations with a dog. On February 5,

1965, the reel containing the portion proposed to be deleted was delivered to the importer. The reel was returned to the Customs Office on February 23, 1965. The deleted portion was not with the reel. It was then ascertained that the deleted portion had been sent back to the producer in Sweden. On March 22, 1965, the deleted portion was returned to the Customs Office and by that Office placed back in the film. On April 16, 1965, the film was seized. On April 20, 1965, the film was transmitted to the United States District Attorney for the institution of libel proceedings. On April 22, 1965, the present action was filed.

[13] The film here involved was screened by the Customs Service on the third business day following its arrival. It was screened by the Administrative Aide on the fourth business day following its arrival. On the third business day following such screening, the importer was notified of its temporary detention. If the Customs Office had immediately transmitted the film to the United States District Attorney following the screening of it, manifestly it could not be claimed that there had been any undue delay in connection with such transmittal. Because the Administrative Aide was in doubt as to whether the film should be transmitted to the United States District Attorney, that Aide caused the film to be viewed by the Assistant Deputy Commissioner of Customs. Thereafter, there was a delay caused by the desire of the importer to make viewings of the film. Thereafter, there was a long delay caused by the importer allowing a portion of the film to be sent back to Sweden. That portion was finally received back from Sweden on March 22, 1965. Following that there was correspondence between the Administrative Aide at New York and the Assistant Deputy Commissioner of Customs at Washington, D.C. Growing out of the correspondence, arrangements were made for an Assistant United States District Attorney to view the film prior to its being seized and transmitted for court action. The film was viewed by an Assistant United States District Attorney on April 8, 1965, following which, as heretofore noted, the film was seized on April 16, 1965, and on April 20, 1965, it was transmitted to the United States District Attorney. While as to this particular film there was a considerable lapse of time between its arrival at the port of entry and its transmittal to the United States District Attorney, the delay was largely occasioned by the importer. It is the view and the holding of the Court that under the record in this case the Claimant was not denied constitutional due process because of the lapse of time occurring between its entry into Customs and its transmittal to the United States District Attorney.

[14] 12. It is also the contention of the Claimant that the length of time it has taken to secure a judicial hearing and determination following the transmittal of the film in question to the United States District Attorney was such as to deny it a prompt judicial hearing and determination of the alleged obscenity of the film under Section 305.

The present action was filed on April 22, 1965. On May 11, 1965, the Claimant appeared and filed a claim for the film for the purpose of contesting its forfeiture. On June 7, 1965, the Claimant filed a motion for summary judgment. On July 21, 1965, that motion was heard by Judge Edward C. McLean. In connection with the hearing on the motion the parties filed briefs and a number of affidavits. The motion presented serious and troublesome questions. In connection with the hearing the film was viewed by Judge McLean. On August 5, 1965, Judge McLean filed an opinion in which he overruled the motion. On August 9, 1965, the Government filed herein a motion asking that the case be assigned to a Judge for all purposes under Rule 2 of the General Rules of the United States District Court for the Southern District of New York, or in the alternative granting a preference under Rule 10 of those Rules. The case was assigned to the present Judge on September 16, 1965, and assigned for trial as the first case to be tried on such assignment. Following a conference with the attorneys, the case was set for trial commencing September 29, 1965, and the trial commenced on that date. After several days of trial the trial was adjourned for ten days in order for the Claimant to secure the attendance of an additional witness.

Under the applicable rules the Claimant had a right to file a motion for summary judgment and it is not subject to criticism for having done so. However, it is apparent that the trial of the case on its merits was delayed by the filing of that motion and the time it took to have it heard and determined. It would appear that, except for the filing of that motion, the case might have been heard and determined on its merits about the time that motion was heard. It was heretofore noted that it was probable that, in general, the judicial hearing and determination of the issue of obscenity under Section 305 would not be had short of eight to ten weeks. In the present case, absent the motion for summary judgment, the case would probably have been heard and determined on its merits about the time the motion for summary judgment was heard. Thus, the present situation would seem to present the same question heretofore discussed and that is whether a libel action conducted under Admiralty Rules would be regarded by the United States Supreme Court as meeting its views in regard to the prompt judicial hearing and determination as to obscenity under Section 305. In the absence of authoritative pronouncements of the United States Supreme Court, this Court is not prepared to hold that the Claimant was denied a prompt judicial hearing and determination of the question of whether its film was or was not obscene under Section 305.

13. There are several matters which are related to some of the issues in this case to which reference will now be made.

In the cases of *United States v. One Book, Entitled "Contraception"* (D.C.S.D.N.Y. 1931), 51 F. 2d 525, and *United States v. One Obscene Book Entitled "Married Love"* (D.C.S.D.N.Y. 1931), 48 F. 2d 821, there were involved imports of books which the Government alleged were obscene and hence not importable under Section 305. It was held that the provision of Section 305 which prohibited the import of "obscene" material was not unconstitutional upon the asserted ground that it interfered with the freedom of the press. In the case of *Upham v. Dill* (D.C.S.D.N.Y. 1961), 195 F. Supp. 5, an importer sought to enjoin the retention of a book which the Government alleged was obscene and hence not importable under Section 305 and as to which the libel proceedings were then pending. The Court denied the injunction. It held that the libel action provided an entirely adequate remedy for the determination of the question of the alleged obscenity of the book. That decision was rendered prior to the decisions of the United States Supreme Court in the cases of *Freedman* v. *State of Maryland*, supra, and *Marcus* v. *Search Warrants*, supra.

In the case of *United States* v. *18 Packages of Magazines* (D.C.N.D. Calif. 1964), 238 F. Supp. 846, there were involved magazines which had been seized by the Customs Service as not importable under Section 305 and against which the Government was proceeding by libel proceedings. The Court held that the seizure of the books prior to the determination of their obscenity was not constitutionally permissible. That decision was rendered prior to the decisions of the United States Supreme Court under which limited pre-distribution or pre-exhibition restraint apparently is permitted with proper constitutional safeguards.

In the case of the *United States* v. *Ginzburg* (3d Cir. 1964), 338 F. 2d 12, the Court affirmed convictions of the defendants for the mailing of obscene publications in violation of Section 1461, Title 18 U.S.C.A. The United States Supreme Court has granted certiorari in that case (1965), 380 U.S. 961, 85 S. Ct. 1103, 14 L. Ed. 2d 152. The United States Supreme Court has noted probable jurisdiction in a state criminal obscenity case. *Mishkin* v. *New York* (1965), 380 U.S. 960, 85 S. Ct. 1103, 14 L. Ed. 2d 152. In that case the defendants were convicted of violating the provisions of a New York statute relating to the publication and distribution of obscene books. *People* v. *Mishkin* (1960), 26 Misc. 2d 152, 207 N.Y.S. 2d 390; (1962) 17 A.D. 2d 243, 234 N.Y.S. 2d 342; (1964) 15 N.Y. 2d 671, 255 N.Y.S. 2d 881, 204 N.E. 2d 209; (1965) 15 N.Y. 2d 724, 256 N.Y.S. 2d 936, 205 N.E. 2d 201. The convictions were affirmed by the New York Court of Appeals. On November 8, 1965, 86 S. Ct. 232, the United States Supreme Court agreed to review the case *Attorney General* v. *A Book Named "John Cleland's Memoirs of a Woman of Pleasure"* (1965), Mass., 206 N.E. 2d 403, relating to the alleged obscenity of the book named in the title of the case. While the decisions in those three cases would not bear directly upon the question as to the constitutionality of the procedures provided for and followed in connection with the importation of feature films, yet they could bear very directly upon the issue in this case as to obscenity. That issue will be considered later.

It further appears that there are several petitions pending requesting the United States Supreme Court to review cases involving obscenity which have not as yet been acted upon.

[15] It is well settled that the determination of the question of obscenity is not to be made upon the personal views of the judge or the members of a jury to whom a case involving that issue is being tried. *Smith* v. *People of State of California* (1959), 361 U.S. 147, 165, 80 S. Ct. 215, 4 L. Ed. 2d 205. Accord, *United States* v. *Klaw*, infra.

[16] The recent decision by the United States Court of Appeals for this Circuit in the case of *United States* v. *Klaw* (1965), 350 F. 2d 155, deals with many questions in the field of obscenity. In that case the two defendants, upon trial by jury, were convicted of mailing obscene booklets in violation of Section 1461, Title 18 U.S.C.A. The only evidence offered as to the obscenity of the booklets were the booklets themselves. On appeal the convictions were reversed. The Court held that the booklets themselves were insufficient to establish their prurient interest and that testimony of witnesses should have been

presented on that matter. Doubtless, because of the holding in that case the parties in the present case presented many witnesses as to prurient interest and as to the character and nature of the film involved. While the case of *United States* v. *Klaw*, supra, was a criminal case which was tried to a jury and the present case is a civil case tried to the Court, it would appear that the same rule would be applicable.

[17] There is one thing which was the matter of some confusion. It was heretofore noted that while the matter of referring the film to the United States District Attorney was under consideration by the Customs Service the Claimant excised that portion of the film portraying a prostitute being forced to have sexual relations with a dog. After some delay in returning the excised portion, it was reinserted in the film by the Customs Office. In connection with the proceedings relating to summary judgment, the Claimant by motion moved the Court not to consider the portion in question as a part of the film and not to view it. At the hearing on the motion for summary judgment the proctor for the Claimant stated of record the willingness of the Claimant to have that portion forfeited and condemned. Preceding the present trial the Claimant again moved the Court not to consider that portion or view it. However, during the present trial the proctor for the Claimant stated of record that the Claimant was not consenting to the forfeiture and condemnation of the portion in question and that the film was to be considered as containing that portion. It was so considered by the witnesses for both parties. The portion in question was a part of the film viewed by the witnesses and the Court, the film, of course, was and is to be considered as a whole. It was so considered by the witnesses. It is so considered by this Court.

14. The question is whether the Government has clearly established by a preponderance of the evidence that the film in question is obscene under what appears for the present to be the tests adopted by the United States Supreme Court. In the case of *United States* v. *Klaw*, supra, the United States Court of Appeals for this Circuit was of the view (350 F. 2d p. 168) that in the area of obscenity the members of the judiciary are lost in a wilderness. Trial courts having to try cases involving the question of obscenity do in most instances have the feeling of attempting to find their way through a fog in which guides and landmarks appear only dimly and obscurely from time to time. In cases involving obscenity there are many words and terms which, like globules of quicksilver, elude any firm grasp of them. Among such words are "prurient interest," "hard core pornography," "patent offensiveness," "average person," "contemporary community standards," "dominant theme," and "social importance."

Many of the problems and unanswered questions in the field are discussed in the case of *United States* v. *Klaw*, supra. In the opinion in that case the pertinent decisions of the United States Supreme Court are noted. Among the outstanding writers and the most cited writers in this field are William B. Lockhart, presently Dean of the College of Law of the University of Minnesota, and Robert C. McClure, Professor of Law of the same school. The most cited of their writings are the following articles: "Literature, The Law of Obscenity, and the Constitution," 38 Minnesota Law Review 295 (1954), and "Censorship of Obscenity: The Developing Constitutional Standards," 45

Minnesota Law Review 5 (1960). Those articles well set forth the problems and unanswered questions in the field of obscenity. It was heretofore noted that review by the United States Supreme Court is now pending in the three cases referred to. It might well be that by the time the present case would reach the appellate level the tests and rules attempted to be applied by this Court will no longer be applicable. Some writers are of the view that in the review of those cases the United States Supreme Court may adopt new tests and standards as to obscenity. Some writers are of the view that the United States Supreme Court may in its review either drastically limit the scope of obscenity statutes or, in substance, nullify them. The cases to be reviewed have not as yet been argued. The parties to the present action are desirous of a prompt decision. Under the circumstances, this Court will apply the tests and standards which the United States Court of Appeals for this Circuit regards as the tests of the United States Supreme Court.

In the recent case of *United States v. Klaw*, supra, the United States Court of Appeals for this Circuit stated in regard to those tests as follows (350 F. 2d pp. 164–165):

> *"However, in considering the permissible meaning of 'obscene' in section 1461, we must begin with the Supreme Court's treatment of that statute in Roth. That case contains the oft-quoted—although difficult to apply—statement that material is 'obscene' if: 'to the average person, applying contemporary community standards, the dominant theme of the material taken as a whole appeals to prurient interest.' * * *.*
>
> *"In addition to its appeal to 'prurient interest,' proscribable 'obscenity' must be 'utterly without redeeming social importance.' * * * It must go 'substantially beyond the customary limits of candor in description or representation.' * * * It must be characterized by 'patent offensiveness.' * * *."*

[18] In the quotation just set out, the term "contemporary community standards" is used. In some of the cases and in some of the writings relating to obscenity there is discussed the question as to whether national or local standards are applicable. The seizure in the present case was made under a federal statute of nation-wide applicability. The film in question was intended for commercial distribution throughout the entire country. The parties to the present action proceeded upon the theory that national standards were applicable. This Court adopts that theory. The questions addressed to the witnesses testifying as to the matter of obscenity embodied that theory. Those questions also embodied the other tests referred to in the quotation above set out.

15. The evidence in the case relating to the film in question will next be considered.

The film in question was produced in Sweden by a large organization known as the Svensk Film Industri. The actors were all Swedish. The director was Vilgöt Sjöman. It was the first feature film directed by him. It appears that he was a protege of Ingmar Bergman, a director with an international reputation. The film came to the attention of the Claimant at the annual Film Festival at Cannes, France. It appears that the film has been exhibited in Sweden and Germany. It is further indicated that its exhibition in Sweden gave rise to controversy. It is indicated that the film exhibited in Germany may have been censored.

The film has to do with several youthful delinquents who had been in difficulty with the law. Krister, a bachelor, had a very good and well-furnished home and made it available for a social agency to make use of for the housing of the boys under the supervision of that agency. Not long after the boys move into the house a clergyman calls with a tape recorder. On the tape recorder he played a recording based upon the Gospel according to St. Matthew (18:21–22):

> *"Then came Peter to him, and said, Lord, how oft shall my brother sin against me, and I forgive him till seven times?*
>
> *"Jesus saith unto him, I say not unto thee, Until seven times: but, Until seventy times seven."*

The boys manifested boredom and disinterestedness during the playing of the recording. The theme suggested by the recording was that while 490 sins could be forgiven the 491st sin would constitute an unforgivable sin. The title of the film, "491," refers to that sin.

The boys indulge in acts of sadism. One boy cuts a piece out of his hand. Another boy holds his hand over the fire in a fireplace until it is charred.

The social worker who had supervision of the boys was referred to as the Inspector. It developed that the Inspector was a homosexual. He had one of the boys come to his private office. He then engaged in what a witness described as homosexual love-making which consisted of stroking and fondling of the boy. The Inspector is shown with his head between the thighs of the boy. The movie stops just short of showing the culmination of the homosexual act, but all of the witnesses who testified as to that happening testified that the matter of the culmination of the homosexual act was not left merely as a matter of speculation.

The boys proceeded to steal and pawn furniture and books belonging to Krister. Supplied with money from doing so, they proceeded to a pier where a freight ship was docked. The crew had a drinking party and sex orgy under way. The boys purchased a large supply of liquor from a member of the crew and joined the affair. A naked prostitute is the subject of the sex orgy. She is shown leaning over the rail in a naked condition while a member of the crew commits sodomy with her. Later she gets dressed and leaves with the boys. In the meantime Krister has discovered the theft of his property which had been pawned. He insisted that the property had to be redeemed. With his acquiescence the boys proceeded to solicit and secure sufficient customers for the prostitute to raise the amount required. Thereafter the boys and the prostitute return to Krister's house where they engage in a sex orgy with her in connection with which there is much exposure of her person and obscene talk. The boys then got angry with her and vented their anger by holding her and forcing a large dog they had picked up into position to have sexual relations with her. The movie stops just short of showing the culmination of sexual relations, but all of the witnesses who testified as to that happening testified that the culmination of the sexual relations was not left as a matter of mere speculation. Thereafter the prostitute passed out of the picture.

There is next portrayed the boys and Krister together. One of the boys has gone out and called in the police. The police informed Krister that the boy had made grave charges against him. The movie ends with the boy who had informed committing suicide by jumping out of a window to the street a considerable distance below.

16. Each side called a number of witnesses. Each side presented movie critics. Each side presented witnesses with a broad background as to social conditions. Each side presented a clergyman with a broad background as to movies and other social problems. The Government presented a physician with a wide and long experience in the field of psychiatry and neurology. The Government also produced the testimony of the Administrative Aide and the Assistant Deputy Commissioner of Customs who have viewed nearly all, if not all, the feature films imported into this country in recent years.

The total number of films viewed by all of the witnesses in recent years ran into the thousands. Around one hundred different feature films were testified to by the witnesses as a matter of comparison in the matter of customary candor, prurient interest, patent offensiveness, and contemporary national standards.

[19] 17. One of the witnesses called in behalf of the Claimant testified that there is an organization known as the Motion Picture Association of America of which many but not all the major movie producers belong. He further testified that that Association had a code with which the members agreed to comply in the matter of decency. The witness testified that the film in question would not be in compliance with that code. The fact that a film might or might not be in compliance with that code would not, of course, be determinative as to whether it was or was not obscene within the purview of Section 305 or any other obscenity statute. However, the fact that the film in question would not be in compliance with that code would tend to indicate that it probably goes farther in the matter of explicitness and candor than do many films produced in this country.

18. A substantial amount of the testimony related to the matter of the dominant theme of the film. The witnesses presented by the Government testified in substance that the movie was dominated by degeneracy, debauchery, sadism, brutality, homosexuality, and sexual bestiality. The witnesses presented by the Claimant had a variety of views as to the dominant theme. One of those witnesses was of the view that it was a criticism of the so-called welfare state maintained by the country of Sweden. Other witnesses presented by the Claimant thought it constituted a criticism of social welfare methods and welfare workers. Other testimony presented in behalf of the Claimant was to the effect that the film was of theological or religious significance. Other testimony presented in behalf of the Claimant was to the effect that it taught a moral lesson. Other testimony presented by the Claimant was to the effect that it portrayed the triumph of evil. Those witnesses who thought the film was of theological or religious significance called attention to a number of matters in connection with the film. Some thought the name Krister connected that individual with Christ. However, all of the witnesses who testified as to that matter conceded that Krister was not a very Christ-like character. They were pretty well agreed that he was a well-intentioned man but who was so lacking in character as to acquiesce in the prostitution engaged in to redeem his property. In at least three places in the film are shown signs on street pillars asking for help for the lepers. Some of the witnesses presented in behalf of the Claimant thought this had reference to Christ and the lepers. Some of the witnesses presented by the Claimant testified that the film had to do with the 491st, or unforgivable, sin as to which reference was made in the title of the film. One of those witnesses thought that the act of the boys in forcing the prostitute to have sexual relations with the dog was such sin. Some of the witnesses presented in behalf of the Claimant thought that the theological or religious connotations tended to be symbolical in character. Witnesses presented in behalf of the Government were of the view that the claimed religious or moral features were "very psuedo" in character and merely served as a thin facade to the portrayal of degeneracy, debauchery, sadism, homosexuality, brutality and sexual bestiality.

[20] 19. The witnesses seemed to be in agreement that the film, if admitted, would be subject to exploitation by the so-called "grind" movie houses. It appears that by "grind" movie houses is meant those movie houses which attract patronage by lurid advertisements as to the purported lasciviousness of certain scenes in a movie. However, it seems clear that what "grind" movie houses might do to exploit some of the scenes in the film is not determinative of the question whether considered as a whole it does or does not meet the tests recognized by the United States Supreme Court.

[21] 20. The question of the recognition of the dominant theme is connected with the question as to who is to make the recognition. That matter is also related to the question of prurient interest. The matter of prurient interest brings up the question of relevant audience. In the Roth case the United States Supreme Court sustained a jury charge in which the jury was charged that the test of obscenity was the effect of the material considered as a whole, not upon any particular class, but upon all those whom it is likely to reach. In the present case the witnesses were pretty well agreed that the movie in question was a so-called "adult" movie and should not be viewed by adolescents. However, they recognized that in the United States there is in general no statutory provisions for segregation of movie audiences by ages. The witnesses were also pretty well agreed that for a movie house to put up a sign specifying that the film is for adults only would only allure and attract adolescents to view the movie. A physician presented in behalf of the Government who had a wide experience in the field of psychiatry, especially as related to pornographic or erotic matters, in addition to testifying that the film in question would appeal to the prurient interest of the average person, further testified that in the case of adolescents the viewing of the film by them would especially excite and stimulate them in the matter of erotic sex behavior. He also further testified that the homosexual activities portrayed in the film would act as a special stimulus to latent and active homosexuals. The Claimant, as heretofore noted, is desirous that the film not be viewed by adolescents. However, it makes another contention that is of significance. It is the contention of the Claimant that the effect of a film on adolescents or sexual deviates is not the test in the matter of prurient appeal but it is its impact on an appeal to "the average person." It appears that those contentions find support in the decisions of the United

States Supreme Court. Therefore, the effect of the present film upon adolescents would appear to be non sequitur and the same would be true as to sex deviates. It would seem, therefore, that it is the prurient appeal to the average person which is of determinative significance. Numerous witnesses testified as to that matter.

[22] Numerous witnesses testified as to the matter of the social importance or worth of the film. In connection with the matter of social importance or worth, there would seem to be involved the question of social importance or worth to whom? Any material, however obscene, might be of social importance or worth to a person or institution making a study of pornography. However, it would seem that such importance or worth would hardly be determinative. It would seem that on the question of social importance or worth the relevant audience should be given consideration. In that connection consideration should be given to the matter of whether it would be of recognizable social importance or worth to that audience. Witnesses presented in behalf of the Claimant were of the view that the film did have social importance or worth but were in disagreement as to what that social importance or worth consisted of. The witnesses presented in behalf of the Government were of the view that all the film brings out is that it is not desirable to place a social worker who is a homosexual in charge of delinquent boys and that such boys are capable of sadism, homosexuality, brutality, sexual bestiality and other degrading conduct. Those witnesses were of the view that behind a thin facade of tenuous religious and moral teachings the producer undertook to portray with extreme candor and explicitness nearly the whole field of abnormal sex relations.

[23] The evidence clearly preponderates that the film is lacking in social importance or worth.

21. In connection with the matter as to whether the film in question exceeded the customary limits of candor and explicitness, the witnesses compared the present film with around one hundred other films. Witnesses presented in behalf of the Government testified that as to candor and explicitness in the matter of abnormal sex relations the present film went beyond any of the other films. Among the witnesses so testifying were the Assistant Deputy Commissioner of Customs and the Administrative Aide for the Port of New York. The Assistant Deputy Commissioner, who during the past thirty years has viewed all imported films as to which a question was raised, testified that the present film went beyond any of those in the matter of candor and explicitness. The Administrative Aide, who for several years has viewed all films imported through the Port of New York as to which a question was raised, testified to the same effect. Witnesses presented in behalf of the Claimant testified as to certain films which contained scenes which they regarded as comparable in candor and explicitness with the present film. None of those films contained all of the following portrayals: (1) sodomy with a naked woman, (2) homosexual love-making stopping just short of culmination and (3) sexual relations about to be consummated between a dog and a woman.

[24] The evidence clearly preponderates that the present film in the matter of abnormal sex relations exceeds customary candor and explicitness.

[25] 22. The film portrays acts of sadism and brutality. The Claimant contends, and correctly so, that acts of sadism and brutality do not in themselves constitute obscenity.

[26] The film portrays much nudity. The Claimant contends, and correctly so, that under the recent decisions of the United States Supreme Court nudity in itself does not constitute obscenity.

23. There is another feature that should be noted. It was heretofore noted that the film contained a number of English subtitles, some of which were obscene in character. The producer had supplied the Claimant with an English translation of all the Swedish dialogue which accompanies the film. That dialogue was produced by the Claimant during the trial at the request of the Government. In that dialogue the boys spew forth obscenities which make the present English subtitles seem mild in comparison. A representative of the Claimant testified that it was the intention of the importer to dub in the dialogue in English to be used in connection with the exhibition of the film.

It was not indicated that any of the witnesses testifying at the trial had read the dialogue. Therefore, it is not known what weight or significance those witnesses would attach to that dialogue in connection with their views as to the nature or themes of the film. However, it would seem that the dialogue might lend some support for the views of the witnesses presented by the Government as to the nature and character of the film.

[27] 24. The evidence presented by the Government clearly establishes as to the film "491" the following:

(a) *To the average person applying contemporary community (national) standards, its dominant theme as a whole appeals to the prurient interest.*

(b) *It is characterized by patent offensiveness.*

(c) *It goes substantially beyond the customary limits of candor in description and representation.*

(d) *It is utterly without redeeming social importance.*

The foregoing constitutes the Court's Findings of Fact herein.

CONCLUSIONS OF LAW

1. That this Court has jurisdiction of the subject matter of this libel and the parties thereto.

2. That the film "491" is an obscene matter within the purview of Section 305 of the Tariff Act.

ORDER FOR DECREE

It is hereby ordered that a Decree shall be entered herein forfeiting and condemning film "491" as provided in Section 305 of the Tariff Act.

It is further ordered that the foregoing Memorandum shall constitute the Findings of Fact, Conclusions of Law, and Order for Decree in this case.

■ Edward Mishkin, *Appellant,*

v.

State of New York.

No. 49.

Argued Dec. 7, 1965.

Decided March 21, 1966.

Rehearing Denied May 2, 1966.

See 348 U.S. 934, 86 S. Ct. 1440.

Emanuel Redfield, New York City, for appellant.
H. Richard Uviller, New York City, for appellee.

Mr. Justice BRENNAN delivered the opinion of the Court.

[1] This case, like *Ginzburg v. United States,* 383 U.S. 463, 86 S. Ct. 942, also decided today, involves convictions under a criminal obscenity statute. A panel of three judges of the Court of Special Sessions of the City of New York found appellant guilty of violating § 1141 of the New York Penal Law[1] by hiring others to prepare obscene books, publishing obscene books, and possessing obscene books with intent to sell them.[2] 26 Misc. 2d 152, 207 N.Y.S. 2d

390 (1960). He was sentenced to prison terms aggregating three years and ordered to pay $12,000 in fines for these crimes.[3] The Appellate Division, First Department, affirmed those convictions. 17 A.D. 2d 243, 234 N.Y.S. 2d 342 (1962). The Court of Appeals affirmed without opinion. 15 N.Y. 2d 671, 255 N.Y.S. 2d 881, 204 N.E. 2d 209 (1964), remittitur amended, 15 N.Y. 2d 724, 256 N.Y.S. 2d 936, 205 N.E. 2d 201 (1965). We noted probable jurisdiction. 380 U.S. 960, 85 S. Ct. 1103, 14 L. Ed. 2d 152. We affirm.

Appellant was not prosecuted for anything he said or believed, but for what he did, for his dominant role in several enterprises engaged in producing and selling allegedly obscene books. Fifty books are involved in this case. They portray sexuality in many guises. Some depict relatively normal heterosexual relations, but more depict such deviations as sado-masochism, fetishism, and homosexual-

---

[1] Section 1141 of the Penal Law, McKinney's Consol. Laws, c. 40, in pertinent part, reads as follows:

"1. A person who * * * has in his possession with intent to sell, lend, distribute * * * any obscene, lewd, lascivious, filthy, indecent, sadistic, masochistic or disgusting book * * * or who * * * prints, utters, publishes, or in any manner manufactures, or prepares any such book * * * or who

"2. In any manner, hires, employs, uses or permits any person to do or assist in doing any act or thing mentioned in this section, or any of them,

"Is guilty of a misdemeanor * * *.

* * * * * *

"4. The possession by any person of six or more identical or similar articles coming within the provisions of subdivision one of this section is presumptive evidence of a violation of this section.

"5. The publication for sale of any book, magazine or pamphlet designed, composed or illustrated as a whole to appeal to and commercially exploit prurient interest by combining covers, pictures, drawings, illustrations, caricatures, cartoons, words, stories and advertisements or any combination or combinations thereof devoted to the description, portrayal or deliberate suggestion of illicit sex, including adultery, prostitution, fornication, sexual crime and sexual perversion or to the exploitation of sex and nudity by the presentation of nude or partially nude female figures, posed, photographed or otherwise presented in a manner calculated to provoke or incite prurient interest, or any combination or combinations thereof, shall be a violation of this section."

[2] The information charged 159 counts of violating § 1141; in each instance a single count named a single book, although often the same book was the basis of three counts, each alleging one of the three types of § 1141 offenses. Of these, 11 counts were

dismissed on motion of the prosecutor at the outset of the trial and verdicts of acquittal were entered on seven counts at the end of trial. The remaining § 1141 counts on which appellant was convicted are listed in the Appendix to this opinion.

Appellant was also convicted on 33 counts charging violations of § 330 of the General Business Law, McKinney's Consol. Laws, c. 20, for failing to print the publisher's and printer's names and addresses on the books. The Appellate Division reversed the convictions under these counts, and the Court of Appeals affirmed. The State has not sought review of that decision in this Court.

[3] The trial court divided the counts into five groups for purposes of sentencing. One group consisted of the possession counts concerning books seized from a basement storeroom in a warehouse; a second group of possession counts concerned books seized from appellant's retail bookstore, Publishers' Outlet; the third consisted of the publishing counts; the fourth consisted of the counts charging him with hiring others to prepare the books, and the fifth consisted of the counts charging violations of the General Business Law. Sentences of one year and a $3,000 fine were imposed on one count of each of the first four groups; the prison sentences on the first three were made consecutive and that on the count in the fourth group was made concurrent with that in the third group. A $500 fine was imposed on one count in the fifth group. Sentence was suspended on the convictions on all other counts. The suspension of sentence does not render moot the claims as to invalidity of the convictions on those counts.

ity. Many have covers with drawings of scantily clad women being whipped, beaten, tortured, or abused. Many, if not most, are photo-offsets of typewritten books written and illustrated by authors and artists according to detailed instructions given by the appellant. Typical of appellant's instructions was that related by one author who testified that appellant insisted that the books be "full of sex scenes and lesbian scenes * * *. [T]he sex had to be very strong, it had to be rough, it had to be clearly spelled out. * * * I had to write sex very bluntly, make the sex scenes very strong. * * * [T]he sex scenes had to be unusual sex scenes between men and women, and women and women, and men and men. * * * [H]e wanted scenes in which women were making love with women * * *. [H]e wanted sex scenes * * * in which there were lesbian scenes. He didn't call it lesbian, but he described women making love to women and men * * * making love to men, and there were spankings and scenes—sex in an abnormal and irregular fashion." Another author testified that appellant instructed him "to deal very graphically with * * * the darkening of the flesh under flagellation * * *." Artists testified in similar vein as to appellant's instructions regarding illustrations and covers for the books.

All the books are cheaply prepared paperbound "pulps" with imprinted sales prices that are several thousand percent above costs. All but three were printed by a photo-offset printer who was paid 40¢ or 15¢ per copy, depending on whether it was a "thick" or "thin" book. The printer was instructed by appellant not to use appellant's name as publisher but to print some fictitious name on each book, to "make up any name and address." Appellant stored books on the printer's premises and paid part of the printer's rent for the storage space. The printer filled orders for the books, at appellant's direction, delivering them to appellant's retail store, Publishers' Outlet, and, on occasion, shipping books to other places. Appellant paid the authors, artists, and printer cash for their services, usually at his bookstore.

I.

[2–4] Appellant attacks § 1141 as invalid on its face, contending that it exceeds First Amendment limitations by proscribing publications that are merely sadistic or masochistic, that the terms "sadistic" and "masochistic" are impermissibly vague, and that the term "obscene" is also impermissibly vague. We need not decide the merits of the first two contentions, for the New York courts held in this case that the terms "sadistic" and "masochistic," as well as the other adjectives used in § 1141 to describe proscribed books are "synonymous with 'obscene.'" 26 Misc. 2d, at 154, 207 N.Y.S. 2d, at 393. The contention that the term "obscene" is also impermissibly vague fails under our holding in *Roth* v. *United States*, 354 U.S. 476, 491–492, 77 S. Ct. 1304, 1312, 1 L. Ed. 2d 1498. Indeed, the definition of "obscene" adopted by the New York courts in interpreting § 1141 delimits a narrower class of conduct than that delimited under the *Roth* definition, *People* v. *Richmond County News, Inc.*, 9 N.Y. 2d 578, 586–587, 216 N.Y.S. 2d 369, 175 N.E. 2d 681, 685–686 (1961),[4]

and thus § 1141, like the statutes in *Roth*, provides reasonably ascertainable standards of guilt.[5]

Appellant also objects that § 1141 is invalid as applied, *first*, because the books he was convicted of publishing, hiring others to prepare, and possessing for sale are not obscene, and *second*, because the proof of scienter is inadequate.

[5, 6] 1. *The Nature of the Material.*—The First Amendment prohibits criminal prosecution for the publication and dissemination of allegedly obscene books that do not satisfy the *Roth* definition of obscenity. States are free to adopt other definitions of obscenity only to the extent that those adopted stay within the bounds set by the constitutional criteria of the *Roth* definition, which restrict the regulation of the publication and sale of the books to that traditionally and universally tolerated in our society.

[7] The New York courts have interpreted obscenity in § 1141 to cover only so-called "hard-core pornography," see *People* v. *Richmond County News, Inc.*, 9 N.Y. 2d 578, 586–587, 216 N.Y.S. 2d 369, 175 N.E. 2d 681, 685–686 (1961), quoted in note 4, supra. Since that definition of obscenity is more stringent than the *Roth* definition, the judgment that the constitutional criteria are satisfied is implicit in the application of § 1141 below. Indeed, appellant's sole contention regarding the nature of the material is that some of the books involved in this prosecution,[6] those depicting various deviant sexual practices, such as flagellation, fetishism, and lesbianism, do not

---

[4] "It [obscene material covered by § 1141] focuses predominantly upon what is sexually morbid, grossly perverse and bizarre, without any artistic or scientific purpose or justification. Recog-

nizable 'by the insult it offers, invariably, to sex, and to the human spirit' (D. H. Lawrence, Pornography and Obscenity [1930], p. 12), it is to be differentiated from the bawdy and the ribald. Depicting dirt for dirt's sake, the obscene is the vile, rather than the coarse, the blow to sense, not merely to sensibility. It smacks, at times, of fantasy and unreality, of sexual perversion and sickness and represents, according to one thoughtful scholar, 'a debauchery of the sexual faculty.' Murray, Literature and Censorship, 14 Books on Trial, 393, 394; see, also, Lockhart and McClure, Censorship of Obscenity: The Developing Constitutional Standards, 45 Minn. L. Rev. 5, 65." 9 N.Y. 2d, at 587, 216 N.Y.S. 2d, at 376, 175 N.E. 2d, at 686. See also *People* v. *Fritch*, 13 N.Y. 2d 119, 123, 243 N.Y.S. 2d 1, 5, 192 N.E. 2d 713, 716 (1963):
"In addition to the foregoing tests imposed by the decisions of the [United States] Supreme Court, this court interpreted section 1141 of the Penal Law in *People* v. *Richmond County News, Inc.* * * * as applicable only to material which may properly be termed 'hard-core pornography.'"

[5] The stringent scienter requirement of § 1141, as interpreted in *People* v. *Finkelstein*, 9 N.Y. 2d 342, 345, 214 N.Y.S. 2d 363, 174 N.E. 2d 470, 472 (1961), also eviscerates much of appellant's vagueness claim. See, infra, p. 964. See generally, *Boyce Motor Lines, Inc.* v. *United States*, 342 U.S. 337, 342, 72 S. Ct. 329, 331, 96 L. Ed. 367; American Communications Ass'n. *CIO* v. *Douds*, 339 U.S. 382, 412–413, 70 S. Ct. 674, 690–691, 94 L. Ed. 925; *Screws* v. *United States*, 325 U.S. 91, 101–104, 65 S. Ct. 1031, 1035–1036, 89 L. Ed. 1495 (opinion of Mr. Justice Douglas); *United States* v. *Ragen*, 314 U.S. 513, 524, 62 S. Ct. 374, 378, 86 L. Ed. 383; *Gorin* v. *United States*, 312 U.S. 19, 27–28, 61 S. Ct. 429, 433–434, 85 L. Ed. 488; *Hygrade Provision Co.* v. *Sherman*, 266 U.S. 497, 501–503, 45 S. Ct. 141, 142–143, 69 L. Ed. 402; *Omaechevarria* v. *State of Idaho*, 246 U.S. 343, 348, 38 S. Ct. 323, 325, 62 L. Ed. 763.

[6] It could not be plausibly maintained that all of the appellant's books, including those dominated by descriptions of relatively normal heterosexual relationships, are devoid of the requisite prurient appeal.

satisfy the prurient-appeal requirement because they do not appeal to a prurient interest of the "average person" in sex, that "instead of stimulating the erotic, they disgust and sicken." We reject this argument as being founded on an unrealistic interpretation of the prurient-appeal requirement.

[8] Where the material is designed for and primarily disseminated to a clearly defined deviant sexual group, rather than the public at large, the prurient-appeal requirement of the *Roth* test is satisfied if the dominant theme of the material taken as a whole appeals to the prurient interest in sex of the members of that group. The reference to the "average" or "normal" person in *Roth*, 354 U.S., at 489–490, 77 S. Ct., at 1311, does not foreclose this holding.[7] In regard to the prurient-appeal requirement, the concept of the "average" or "normal" person was employed in *Roth* to serve the essentially negative purpose of expressing our rejection of that aspect of the *Hicklin* test, *Regina* v. *Hicklin*, [1868] L.R. 3 Q.B. 360, that made the impact on the most susceptible person determinative. We adjust the prurient-appeal requirement to social realities by permitting the appeal of this type of material to be assessed in terms of the sexual interests of its intended and probable recipient group; and since our holding requires that the recipient group be defined with more specificity than in terms of sexually immature persons,[8] it also avoids the inadequacy of the most-susceptible-person facet of the *Hicklin* test.

[9, 10] No substantial claim is made that the books depicting sexually deviant practices are devoid of prurient appeal to sexually deviant groups. The evidence fully establishes that these books were specifically conceived and marketed for such groups. Appellant instructed his authors and artists to prepare the books expressly to induce their purchase by persons who would probably be sexually stimulated by them. It was for this reason that appellant "wanted an emphasis on beatings and fetishism and clothing—irregular clothing, and that sort of thing, and again sex scenes between women; always sex scenes had to be very strong." And to be certain that authors fulfilled his purpose, appellant furnished them with such source materials as Caprio, Variations in Sexual Behavior, and Krafft-Ebing, Psychopathia Sexualis. Not only was there proof of the books' prurient appeal, compare *United States* v. *Klaw*, 350 F. 2d 155 (C.A. 2d Cir. 1965), but the proof was compelling; in addition appellant's own evaluation of his material confirms such a finding. See *Ginzburg* v. *United States*, 383 U.S. 463, 86 S. Ct. 942.

[11, 12] 2. *Scienter.*—In *People* v. *Finkelstein*, 9 N.Y. 2d 342, 344–345, 214 N.Y.S. 2d 363, 364, 174 N.E. 2d 470, 471 (1961), the New York Court of Appeals authoritatively interpreted § 1141 to require the "vital element of scienter," and it defined the required mental element in these terms:

"*A reading of the statute* [§ 1141] *as a whole clearly indicates that only those who are in some manner aware of the* character *of the material they attempt to distribute should be punished. It is not innocent but* calculated *purveyance of filth which is exorcised * * *.*"[9] (*Emphasis added.*)

Appellant's challenge to the validity of § 1141 founded on *Smith* v. *People of State of California*, 361 U.S. 147, 80 S. Ct. 215, 4 L. Ed. 2d 205, is thus foreclosed,[10] and this construction of § 1141 makes it unnecessary for us to define today "what sort of mental element is requisite to a constitutionally permissible prosecution." Id., at 154, 80 S. Ct. at 219. The Constitution requires proof of scienter to avoid the hazard of self-censorship of constitutionally protected material and to compensate for the ambiguities inherent in the definition of obscenity. The New York definition of the scienter required by § 1141 amply serves those ends, and therefore fully meets the demands of the Constitution.[11] Cf. *Roth* v. *United States*, 354 U.S., at 495–496, 77 S. Ct., at 1314–1315 (Warren, C.J., concurring).

[13] Appellant's principal argument is that there was insufficient proof of scienter. This argument is without merit. The evidence of scienter in this record consists, in part, of appellant's instructions to his artists and writers; his efforts to disguise his role in the enterprise that

---

[7] See *Manual Enterprises, Inc.* v. *Day*, 370 U.S. 478, 482, 82 S. Ct. 1432, 1434, 8 L. Ed. 2d 639 (opinion of HARLAN, J.); Lockhart and McClure, Censorship of Obscenity: The Developing Constitutional Standards, 45 Minn. L. Rev. 5, 72–73 (1960).

It is true that some of the material in *Alberts* v. *State of California*, decided with *Roth*, resembled the deviant material involved here. But no issue involving the obscenity of the material was before us in either case. 354 U.S., at 481, n. 8, 77 S. Ct. 1306. The basic question for decision there was whether the publication and sale of obscenity, however defined, could be criminally punished in light of First Amendment guarantees. Our discussion of definition was not intended to develop all the nuances of a definition required by the constitutional guarantees.

[8] See generally, 1 American Handbook of Psychiatry 593–604 (Arieti ed. 1959), for a description of the pertinent types of deviant sexual groups.

[9] For a similar scienter requirement see Model Penal Code § 251.4(2); Commentary, Model Penal Code (Tentative Draft No. 6, 1957), 14, 49–51; cf. Schwartz, Morals Offenses and the Model Penal Code, 63 Col. L. Rev. 669, 677 (1963).

We do not read Judge Froessel's parenthetical reference to knowledge of the contents of the books in his opinion in *People* v. *Finkelstein*, 11 N.Y. 2d 300, 304, 229 N.Y.S. 2d 367, 183 N.E. 2d 661, 663 (1962), as a modification of this definition of scienter. Cf. *People* v. *Fritch*, 13 N.Y. 2d 119, 126, 243 N.Y.S. 2d 1, 192 N.E. 2d 713, 717–718 (1963).

[10] The scienter requirement set out in the text would seem to be, as a matter of state law, as applicable to publishers as it is to booksellers; both types of activities are encompassed within subdivision 1 of § 1141. Moreover, there is no need for us to speculate as to whether this scienter requirement is also present in subdivision 2 of § 1141 (making it a crime to hire others to prepare obscene books), for appellant's convictions for that offense involved books for the publication of which he was also convicted.

No constitutional claim was asserted below or in this Court as to the possible duplicative character of the hiring and publishing counts.

[11] The first appeal in *Finkelstein* defining the scienter required by § 1141 was decided after this case was tried, but before the Appellate Division and Court of Appeals affirmed these convictions. We therefore conclude that the state appellate courts were satisfied that the § 1141 scienter requirement was correctly applied at trial.

The § 1141 counts did not allege appellant's knowledge of the character of the books, but appellant has not argued, below or here, that this omission renders the information constitutionally inadequate.

published and sold the books; the transparency of the character of the material in question, highlighted by the titles, covers, and illustrations; the massive number of obscene books appellant published, hired others to prepare, and possessed for sale; the repetitive quality of the sequences and formats of the books; and the exorbitant prices marked on the books. This evidence amply shows that appellant was "aware of the character of the material" and that his activity was "not innocent but calculated purveyance of filth."

II.

[14–16] Appellant claims that all but one of the books were improperly admitted in evidence because they were fruits of illegal searches and seizures. This claim is not capable in itself of being brought here by appeal, but only by a petition for a writ of certiorari under 28 U.S.C. § 1257(3) (1964 ed.) as specifically setting up a federal constitutional right.[12] Nevertheless, since appellant challenged the constitutionality of § 1141 in this prosecution, and the New York courts sustained the statute, the case is properly here on appeal, and our unrestricted notation of probable jurisdiction justified appellant's briefing of the search and seizure issue. *Flournoy* v. *Weiner*, 321 U.S. 253, 263, 64 S. Ct. 548, 553, 88 L. Ed. 708; *Prudential Ins. Co.* v. *Cheek*, 259 U.S. 530, 547, 42 S. Ct. 516, 523, 66 L. Ed. 1044. The nonappealable issue is treated, however, as if contained in a petition for a writ of certiorari, see 28 U.S.C. § 2103 (1964 ed.) and the unrestricted notation of probable jurisdiction of the appeal is to be understood as a grant of the writ on that issue. The issue thus remains within our certiorari jurisdiction, and we may, for good reason, even at this stage, decline to decide the merits of the issue, much as we would dismiss a writ of certiorari as improvidently granted. We think that this is a case for such an exercise of our discretion.

---

[12] Unlike the claim here, the challenges decided in the appeals in *Marcus* v. *Search Warrants* of Property at 104 East Tenth St., Kansas City, Mo., 367 U.S. 717, 81 S. Ct. 1708, 6 L. Ed. 2d 1127, and *A Quantity of Copies of Books* v. *State of Kansas*, 378 U.S. 205, 84 S. Ct. 1723, 12 L. Ed. 2d 809, implicated the constitutional validity of statutory schemes establishing procedures for seizing the books.

[17] The far-reaching and important questions tendered by this claim are not presented by the record with sufficient clarity to require or justify their decision. Appellant's standing to assert the claim in regard to all the seizures is not entirely clear; there is no finding on the extent or nature of his interest in two book stores, the Main Stem Book Shop and Midget Book Shop, in which some of the books were seized. The State seeks to justify the basement storeroom seizure, in part, on the basis of the consent of the printer-accomplice; but there were no findings as to the authority of the printer over the access to the storeroom, or as to the voluntariness of his alleged consent. It is also maintained that the seizure in the storeroom was made on the authority of a search warrant; yet neither the affidavit upon which the warrant issued nor the warrant itself is in the record. Finally, while the search and seizure issue has a First Amendment aspect because of the alleged massive quality of the seizures, see *A Quantity of Copies of Books* v. *State of Kansas*, 378 U.S. 205, 206, 84 S. Ct. 1723 (opinion of Brennan, J.); *Marcus* v. *Search Warrants* of Property at 104 East Tenth Street, Kansas City, Mo., 367 U.S. 717, 81 S. Ct. 1708, the record in this regard is inadequate. There is neither evidence nor findings as to how many of the total available copies of the books in the various bookstores were seized and it is impossible to determine whether the books seized in the basement storeroom were on the threshold of dissemination. Indeed, this First Amendment aspect apparently was not presented or considered by the state courts, nor was it raised in appellant's jurisdictional statement; it appeared for the first time in his brief on the merits.

[18] In light of these circumstances, which were not fully apprehended at the time we took the case, we decline to reach the merits of the search and seizure claim; insofar as notation of probable jurisdiction may be regarded as a grant of the certiorari writ on the search and seizure issue, that writ is dismissed as improvidently granted. "Examination of a case on the merits * * * may bring into 'proper focus' a consideration which * * * later indicates that the grant was improvident." The *Monrosa* v. *Carbon Black Export, Inc.*, 359 U.S. 180, 184, 79 S. Ct. 710, 713, 3 L. Ed. 2d 723.

Affirmed.

APPENDIX TO OPINION OF THE COURT.
THE CONVICTIONS BEING REVIEWED.

Exhibit No.	Title of Book	Possession	§ 1141 Counts Naming the Book Publishing	Hiring Others
1	Chances Go Around	1	63	111
2	Impact	2	64	112
3	Female Sultan	3	65	113
4	Satin Satellite	4		
5	Her Highness	5	67	115
6	Mistress of Leather	6	68	116
7	Educating Edna	7	69	117
8	Strange Passions	8	70	118
9	The Whipping Chorus Girls	9	71	119
10	Order of the Day and Bound Maritally	10	72	120
11	Dance with the Dominant Whip	11	73	121

APPENDIX TO OPINION OF THE COURT.

THE CONVICTIONS BEING REVIEWED (*continued*)

Exhibit No.	Title of Book	Possession	§ 1141 Counts Naming the Book Publishing	Hiring Others
12	Cult of the Spankers	12	74	122
13	Confessions	13	75	123
14 & 46	The Hours of Torture	14 & 40	76	124
15 & 47	Bound in Rubber	15 & 41	77	125
16 & 48	Arduous Figure Training at Bondhaven	16 & 42	78	126
17 & 49	Return Visit to Fetterland	17 & 43	79	127
18	Fearful Ordeal in Restraintland	18	80	128
19 & 50	Women in Distress	19 & 44	81	129
20 & 54	Pleasure Parade No. 1	20 & 48	82	130
21 & 57	Screaming Flesh	21 & 51	86	134
22 & 58	Fury	22 & 52		
23	So Firm So Fully Packed	23	87	135
24	I'll Try Anything Twice	24		
25 & 59	Masque	25 & 53		
26	Catanis	26		
27	The Violated Wrestler	27	89	137
28	Betrayal	28		
29	Swish Bottom	29	90	138
30	Raw Dames	30	91	139
31	The Strap Returns	31	92	140
32	Dangerous Years	32	93	141
43	Columns of Agony	37	95	144
44	The Tainted Pleasure	38	96	145
45	Intense Desire	39	97	146
51	Pleasure Parade No. 4	45	85	133
52	Pleasure Parade No. 3	46	84	132
53	Pleasure Parade No. 2	47	83	131
55	Sorority Girls Stringent Initiation	49	98	147
56	Terror at the Bizarre Museum	50	99	148
60	Temptation	57		
61	Peggy's Distress on Planet Venus	58	101	150
62	Ways of Discipline	59	102	151
63	Mrs. Tyrant's Finishing School	60	103	152
64	Perilous Assignment	61	104	153
68	Bondage Correspondence		107	156
69	Woman Impelled		106	155
70	Eye Witness		108	157
71	Stud Broad		109	158
72	Queen Bee		110	159

Mr. Justice HARLAN, concurring.

On the issue of obscenity I concur in the judgment of affirmance on premises stated in my dissenting opinion in *A Book Named "John Cleland's Memoirs of a Woman of Pleasure"* v. *Attorney General*, 383 U.S. 455, 86 S. Ct. 996. In all other respects I agree with and join the Court's opinion.

Mr. Justice BLACK, dissenting.

The Court here affirms convictions and prison sentences aggregating three years plus fines totaling $12,000 imposed on appellant Mishkin based on state charges that he hired others to prepare and publish obscene books and that Mishkin himself possessed such books. This Court has held in many cases that the Fourteenth Amendment makes the First applicable to the States. See for illustration cases collected in my concurring opinion in *Speiser* v. *Randall*, 357 U.S. 513, 530, 78 S. Ct. 1332, 1344, 2 L. Ed. 2d 1460. Consequently upon the same grounds that I dissented from a five-year federal sentence imposed upon Ginzburg in 383 U.S. 476, 86 S. Ct. 950, for sending "obscene" printed matter through the United States mails I dissent from affirmance of this three-year state sentence imposed on Mishkin. Neither in this case nor in *Ginzburg* have I read the alleged obscene matter. This is because I believe for reasons stated in my dissent in *Ginzberg* and in many other prior cases that this Court is without constitutional power to censor speech or press regardless of the particular subject discussed. I think the federal judiciary because it is appointed for life is the most appropriate tribunal that could be selected to interpret the Constitution and thereby mark the boundaries of what government agencies can and cannot do. But because of life tenure, as well as other reasons, the federal judiciary is the least appropriate branch of government to take over censorship responsibilities by deciding what pictures and writings people throughout the land can be permitted to see and read. When this Court makes particularized rules on what people can see and read, it determines which policies are reasonable and right thereby performing the classical function of legislative bodies directly responsible to the people. Accordingly, I wish once more to express my objections to saddling this Court with the irksome and inevitably unpopular and unwholesome task of finally deciding by a case-by-case, sight-by-sight personal judgment of the members of this Court what pornography (whatever that means) is too hard core for people to see or read. If censorship of views about sex or any other subject is constitutional then I am reluctantly compelled to say that I believe the tedious, time-consuming and unwelcome responsibility for finally deciding what particular discussions or opinions must be suppressed in this country, should, for the good of this Court and of the Nation, be vested in some governmental institution or institutions other than this Court.

I would reverse these convictions. The three-year sentence imposed on Mishkin and the five-year sentence imposed on Ginzburg for expressing views about sex are minor in comparison with those more lengthy sentences that are inexorably bound to follow in state and federal courts as pressures and prejudices increase and grow more powerful, which of course they will. Nor is it a sufficient answer to these assuredly ever-increasing punishments to rely on this Court's power to strike down "cruel and unusual punishments" under the Eighth Amendment. Distorting or stretching that Amendment by reading it as granting unreviewable power to this Court to perform the legislative function of fixing punishments for all state and national offenses offers a sadly inadequate solution to the multitudinous problems generated by what I consider to be the un-American policy of censoring the thoughts and opinions of people. The only practical answer to these

concededly almost unanswerable problems is, I think, for this Court to decline to act as a national board of censors over speech and press but instead to stick to its clearly authorized constitutional duty to adjudicate cases over things and conduct. Halfway censorship methods, no matter how laudably motivated, cannot in my judgment protect our cherished First Amendment freedoms from the destructive aggressions of both state and national government. I would reverse this case and announce that the First and Fourteenth Amendments taken together command that neither Congress nor the States shall pass laws which in any manner abridge freedom of speech and press—whatever the subjects discussed. I think the Founders of our Nation in adopting the First Amendment meant precisely that the Federal Government should pass "no law" regulating speech and press but should confine its legislation to the regulation of conduct. So too, that policy of the First Amendment made applicable to the States by the Fourteenth, leaves the States vast power to regulate conduct but no power at all, in my judgment, to make the expression of views a crime.

Mr. Justice STEWART, dissenting.

The appellant was sentenced to three years in prison for publishing numerous books. However tawdry those books may be, they are not hard-core pornography, and their publication is, therefore, protected by the First and Fourteenth Amendments. *Ginzburg* v. *United States*, 383 U.S. 497, 86 S. Ct. 956 (dissenting opinion). The judgment should be reversed.*

---

* See *Ginzburg* v. *United States*, 383 U.S. 497, at 499, note 3, 86 S. Ct. 956, at 957 (dissenting opinion). Moreover, there was no evidence at all that any of the books are the equivalent of hard-core pornography in the eyes of any particularized group of readers. Cf. *United States* v. *Klaw*, 350 F. 2d 155 (C.A. 2d Cir.).

Although the New York Court of Appeals has purported to interpret § 1141 to cover only what it calls "hard-core pornography," this case makes abundantly clear that that phrase has by no means been limited in New York to the clearly identifiable and distinct class of material I have described in *Ginzberg* v. *United States*, 383 U.S. 497, at 499, note 3, 86 S. Ct. 956, at 957 (dissenting opinion).

■ Ralph Ginzburg *et al., Petitioners,*

v.

United States.

Edward Mishkin, *Appellant,*

v.

State of New York.

Nos. 42 and 49.

March 21, 1966.

Dissenting Opinion.

For opinions of the Court, see 86 S. Ct. 942, 958.

Mr. Justice Douglas, dissenting in Nos. 42 and 49.

Today's condemnation of the use of sex symbols to sell literature, engrafts another exception on First Amendment rights that is as unwarranted as the judge-made exception concerning obscenity. This new exception condemns an advertising technique as old as history. The advertisements of our best magazines are chock-full of thighs, ankles, calves, bosoms, eyes, and hair, to draw the potential buyer's attention to lotions, tires, food, liquor, clothing, autos, and even insurance policies. The sexy advertisement neither adds to nor detracts from the quality of the merchandise being offered for sale. And I do not see how it adds to or detracts one whit from the legality of the book being distributed. A book should stand on its own, irrespective of the reasons why it was written or the wiles used in selling it. I cannot imagine any promotional effort that would make chapters 7 and 8 of the Song of Solomon any the less or any more worthy of First Amendment protection than does their unostentatious inclusion in the average edition of the Bible.

I.

The Court has, in a variety of contexts, insisted that preservation of rights safeguarded by the First Amendment requires vigilance. We have recognized that a "criminal prosecution under a statute regulating expression usually involves imponderables and contingencies that themselves may inhibit the full exercise of First Amendment freedoms." *Dombrowski* v. *Pfister,* 380 U.S. 479, 486, 85 S. Ct. 1116, 1120, 14 L. Ed. 2d 22. Where uncertainty is the distinguishing characteristic of a legal principle—in this case the Court's "pandering" theory—"the free dissemination of ideas may be the loser." *Smith* v. *People of State of California,* 361 U.S. 147, 151, 80 S. Ct. 215, 218, 4 L. Ed. 2d 205. The Court today, however, takes the other course, despite the admonition in *Speiser* v. *Randall,* 357 U.S. 513, 525, 78 S. Ct. 1332, 1342, 2 L. Ed. 2d 1460, that "[t]he separation of legitimate from illegitimate speech calls for * * * sensitive tools." Before today, due regard for the frailties of free expression led us to reject

insensitive procedures[1] and clumsy, vague, or overbroad substantive rules even in the realm of obscenity.[2] For as the Court emphasized in *Roth* v. *United States,* 354 U.S. 476, 488, 77 S. Ct. 1304, 1311, 1 L. Ed. 2d 1498, "[t]he door barring federal and state intrusion into this area cannot be left ajar; it must be kept tightly closed and opened only the slightest crack necessary to prevent encroachment upon more important interests."

Certainly without the aura of sex in the promotion of these publications their contents cannot be said to be "utterly without redeeming social importance." *Roth* v. *United States,* supra, 354 U.S. at 484, 77 S. Ct. at 1309.[3] One of the publications condemned today is the Housewife's Handbook on Selective Promiscuity, which a number of doctors and psychiatrists thought had clinical value. One clinical psychologist said: "I should like to recommend it, for example, to the people in my church to read, especially those who are having marital difficulties, in order to increase their tolerance and understanding for one another. Much of the book, I should think, would be very suitable reading for teen age people, especially teen age young women who could empathize strongly with the growing up period that Mrs. Rey [Anthony] relates, and

---

[1] *Marcus* v. *Search Warrants* etc., 367 U.S. 717, 81 S. Ct. 1708, 6 L. Ed. 2d 1127; *A Quantity of Copies of Books* v. *State of Kansas,* 378 U.S. 205, 84 S. Ct. 1723, 12 L. Ed. 2d 809; *Freedman* v. *State of Maryland,* 380 U.S. 51, 85 S. Ct. 734, 13 L. Ed. 2d 649.

[2] *Butler* v. *State of Michigan,* 352 U.S. 380, 77 S. Ct. 524, 1 L. Ed. 2d 412; *Smith* v. *People of State of California,* 361 U.S. 147, 80 S. Ct. 215; *Manual Enterprises, Inc.* v. *Day,* 370 U.S. 478, 82 S. Ct. 1432, 8 L. Ed. 2d 639 (opinion of Harlan, J.).

[3] The Court's premise is that Ginzburg represented that his publications would be sexually arousing. The Court, however, recognized in *Roth:* "[S]ex and obscenity are not synonymous. Obscene material is material which deals with sex in a manner appealing to *prurient* interest * * * i.e., a shameful or morbid interest in nudity, sex, or excretion * * *." Id., 354 U.S. 487 and n. 20, 77 S. Ct. 1310 (emphasis added). The advertisements for these publications, which the majority quotes (ante, at 946), promised candor in the treatment of matters pertaining to sex, and at the same time proclaimed that they were artistic or otherwise socially valuable. In effect, then, these advertisements represented that the publications are *not* obscene.

could read on and be disabused of some of the unrealistic notions about marriage and sexual experiences. I should think this would make very good reading for the average man to help him gain a better appreciation of female sexuality."

The Rev. George Von Hilsheimer III, a Baptist minister,[4] testified that he has used the book "insistently in my pastoral counseling and in my formal psychological counseling":

"The book is a history, a very unhappy history, of a series of sexual and psychological misadventures and the encounter of a quite typical and average American woman with quite typical and average American men. The fact that the book itself is the history of a woman who has had sexual adventures outside the normally accepted bounds of marriage which, of course for most Americans today, is a sort of serial polygamy, it does not teach or advocate this, but gives the women to whom I give the book at least a sense that their own experiences are not unusual, that their sexual failures are not unusual, and that they themselves should not be guilty because they are, what they say, sexual failures."

I would think the Baptist minister's evaluation would be enough to satisfy the Court's test, unless the censor's word is to be final or unless the experts are to be weighed in the censor's scales, in which event one Anthony Comstock would too often prove more weighty than a dozen more detached scholars, or unless we, the ultimate Board of Censors, are to lay down standards for review that give the censor the benefit of the "any evidence" rule or the "substantial evidence" rule as in the administrative law field. Cf. *Universal Camera Corp.* v. *National Labor Relations Board*, 340 U.S. 474, 71 S. Ct. 456, 95 L. Ed. 456. Or perhaps we mean to let the courts sift and choose among conflicting versions of the "redeeming social importance" of a particular book, making sure that they keep their findings clear of doubt lest we reverse, as we do today in *A Book Named "John Cleland's Memoirs of a Woman of Pleasure"* v. *Attorney General of Com. of Massachusetts*, 383 U.S. 413, 86 S. Ct. 975, because the lower court in an effort to be fair showed how two-sided the argument was. Since the test is whether the publication is "utterly without redeeming social importance," then I think we should honor the opinion of the Baptist minister who testified as an expert in the field of counseling.

Then there is the newsletter *Liaison*. One of the defendants' own witnesses, critic Dwight Macdonald, testified that while, in his opinion, it did not go beyond the customary limits of candor tolerated by the community, it was "an extremely tasteless, vulgar and repulsive issue." This may, perhaps, overstate the case, but *Liaison* is admittedly little more than a collection of "dirty" jokes and poems, with the possible exception of an interview with Dr. Albert Ellis. As to this material, I find wisdom in the words of the late Judge Jerome Frank:

*"Those whose views most judges know best are other lawyers. Judges can and should take judicial notice that, at many gatherings of lawyers at Bar Association or of alumni of our leading law schools, tales are told fully as 'obscene' as many of those distributed by men * * * convicted for violation of the obscenity statute. * * * 'One thinks of the lyrics sung * * * by a certain respected and conservative member of the faculty of a great law-school which considers itself the most distinguished and which is the Alma Mater of many judges sitting on upper courts.' "*[5]

Liaison's appeal is neither literary nor spiritual. But neither is its appeal to a "shameful or morbid interest in nudity, sex, or excretion." The appeal is to the ribald sense of humor which is—for better or worse—a part of our culture. A mature society would not suppress this newsletter as obscene but would simply ignore it.

Then there is *Eros*. The Court affirms the judgment of the lower court, which found only four of the many articles and essays to be obscene. One of the four articles consisted of numerous ribald limericks, to which the views expressed as to *Liaison* would apply with equal force. Another was a photo essay entitled "Black and White in Color" which dealt with interracial love: a subject undoubtedly offensive to some members of our society. Critic Dwight Macdonald testified:

"I suppose if you object to the idea of a Negro and a white person having sex together, then, of course, you would be horrified by it. I don't. From the artistic point of view I thought it was very good. In fact, I thought it was done with great taste, and I don't know how to say it—I never heard of him before, but he is obviously an extremely competent and accomplished photographer."

Another defense witness, Professor Horst W. Janson, presently the Chairman of the Fine Arts Department at New York University, testified:

"I think they are outstandingly beautiful and artistic photographs. I can not imagine the theme being treated in a more lyrical and delicate manner than it has been done here.

    **   *   *   *   *   **

"I might add here that of course photography in appropriate hands is an artistic instrument and this particular photographer has shown a very great awareness of compositional devices and patterns that have a long and well-established history in western art.

    **   *   *   *   *   **

"The very contrast in the color of the two bodies of course has presented him with certain opportunities that he would not have had with two models of the same color, and he has taken rather extraordinary and very delicate advantage of these contrasts."

The third article found specifically by the trial judge to be obscene was a discussion by Drs. Eberhard W. and Phyllis C. Kronhausen of erotic writing by women, with illustrative quotations.[6] The worth of the article was discussed by Dwight Macdonald, who stated:

---

[4] Rev. Von Hilsheimer obtained an A.B. at the University of Miami in 1951. He did graduate work in psychology and studied analysis and training therapy. Thereafter, he did graduate work as a theological student, and received a degree as a Doctor of Divinity from the University of Chicago in 1957. He had extensive experience as a group counselor, lecturer, and family counselor. He was a consultant to President Kennedy's Study Group on National Voluntary Services, and a member of the board of directors of Mobilization for Youth.

[5] *United States* v. *Roth*, 2 Cir., 237 F. 2d 796, 822 and n. 58 (concurring opinion).

[6] The Kronhausens wrote Pornography and the Law (1959).

*"I thought [this was] an extremely interesting and important study with some remarkable quotations from the woman who had put down her sense of love-making, of sexual intercourse * * * in an extremely eloquent way. I have never seen this from the woman's point of view. I thought the point they made, the difference between the man's and the woman's approach to sexual intercourse was very well made and very important."*

Still another article found obscene was a short introduction to and a lengthy excerpt from My Life and Loves by Frank Harris, about which there is little in the record. Suffice it to say that this seems to be a book of some literary stature. At least I find it difficult on this record to say that it is "utterly without redeeming social importance."[7]

Some of the tracts for which these publishers go to prison concern normal sex, some homosexuality, some the masochistic yearning that is probably present in everyone and dominant in some. Masochism is a desire to be punished or subdued. In the broad frame of reference the desire may be expressed in the longing to be whipped and lashed, bound and gagged, and cruelly treated.[8] Why is it unlawful to cater to the needs of this group? They are, to be sure, somewhat offbeat, noncomformist, and odd. But we are not in the realm of criminal conduct, only ideas and tastes. Some like Chopin, others like "rock and roll." Some are "normal," some are masochistic, some deviant in other respects, such as the homosexual. Another group also represented here translates mundane articles into sexual symbols. This group, like those embracing masochism, are anathema to the so-called stable majority. But why is freedom of the press and expression denied them? Are they to be barred from communicating in symbolisms important to them? When the Court today speaks of "social value," does it mean a "value" to the majority? Why is not a minority "value" cognizable? The masochistic group is one; the deviant group is another. Is it not important that members of those groups communicate with each other? Why is communication by the "written word" forbidden? If we were wise enough, we might know that communication may have greater therapeutical value than any sermon that those of the "normal" community can ever offer. But if the communication is of value to the masochistic community or to others of the deviant community, how can it be said to be "utterly without redeeming social importance"? "Redeeming" to whom? "Importance" to whom?

We took quite a different stance in One, Inc. v. Olesen, 355 U.S. 371, 78 S. Ct. 364, 2 L. Ed. 2d 352, where we unanimously reversed the decision of the Court of Appeals in 9 Cir., 241 F. 2d 772 without opinion. Our holding was accurately described by Lockhart and McClure, Obscenity

Censorship: The Core Constitutional Issue—What is Obscene? 7 Utah L. Rev. 289, 293 (1961):

"[This] was a magazine for homosexuals entitled One —The Homosexual Magazine, *which was definitely not a scientific or critical magazine, but appears to have been written to appeal to the tastes and interests of homosexuals."*[9]

Man was not made in a fixed mould. If a publication caters to the idiosyncrasies of a minority, why does it not have some "social importance"? Each of us is a very temporary transient with likes and dislikes that cover the spectrum. However plebeian my tastes may be, who am I to say that others' tastes must be so limited and that other tastes have no "social importance"? How can we know enough to probe the mysteries of the subconscious of our people and say that this is good for them and that is not? Catering to the most eccentric taste may have "social importance" in giving that minority an opportunity to express itself rather than to repress its inner desires, as I suggest in my separate opinion in A Book Named "John Cleland's Memoirs of a Woman of Pleasure" v. Attorney General of Com. of Massachusetts, 383 U.S., at 431–432, 86 S. Ct., at 984. How can we know that this expression may not *prevent* antisocial conduct?

I find it difficult to say that a publication has no "social importance" because it caters to the taste of the most unorthodox amongst us. We members of this Court should be among the last to say what should be orthodox in literature. An omniscience would be required which few in our whole society possess.

---

[7] The extensive literary comment which the book's publication generated demonstrates that it is not "utterly without redeeming social importance." See, e.g., New York Review of Books, p. 6 (Jan. 9, 1964); New Yorker, pp. 79–80 (Jan. 4, 1964); Library Journal, pp. 4743–4744 (Dec. 15, 1963); New York Times Book Review, p. 10 (Nov. 10, 1963); Time, pp. 102–104 (Nov. 8, 1963); Newsweek, pp. 98–100 (Oct. 28, 1963); New Republic, pp. 23–27 (Dec. 28, 1963).

[8] See Krafft-Ebing, Psychopathia Sexualis, p. 89 et seq. (1893); Eisler, Man Into Wolf, p. 23 et seq. (1951); Stekel, Sadism and Masochism (1929) passim; Bergler, Principles of Self-Damage (1959) passim; Reik, Masochism in Modern Man (1941) passim.

[9] The Court of Appeals summarized the contents as follows: "The article 'Sappho Remembered' is the story of a lesbian's influence on a young girl only twenty years of age but 'actually nearer sixteen in many essential ways of maturity,' in her struggle to choose between a life with the lesbian, or a normal married life with her childhood sweetheart. The lesbian's affair with her roommate while in college, resulting in the lesbian's expulsion from college, is recounted to bring in the jealousy angle. The climax is reached when the young girl gives up her chance for a normal married life to live with the lesbian. This article is nothing more than cheap pornography calculated to promote lesbianism. It falls far short of dealing with homosexuality from the scientific, historical and critical point of view.

"The poem 'Lord Samuel and Lord Montagu' is about the alleged homosexual activities of Lord Montagu and other British Peers and contains a warning to all males to avoid the public toilets while Lord Samuel is 'sniffing round the drains' of Piccadilly (London). * * *

* * *

"The stories 'All This and Heaven Too,' and 'Not Til the End,' pages 32–36, are similar to the story 'Sappho Remembered,' except that they relate to the activities of the homosexuals rather than lesbians." 241 F. 2d 772, 777, 778.

There are other decisions of ours which also reversed judgments condemning publications catering to a wider range of literary tastes than we seem to tolerate today. See, e.g., Mounce v. United States, 355 U.S. 180, 78 S. Ct. 267, 2 L. Ed. 2d 187, vacating and remanding 9 Cir., 247 F. 2d 148 (nudist magazines); Sunshine Book Co. v. Summerfield, 355 U.S. 372, 78 S. Ct. 365, 2 L. Ed. 2d 352, reversing 101 U.S. App. D.C. 358, 249 F. 2d 114 (nudist magazine); Tralins v. Gerstein, 378 U.S. 576, 84 S. Ct. 1903, 12 L. Ed. 2d 1033, reversing Fla. App., 151 So. 2d 19 (book titled "Pleasure Was My Business" depicting the happenings in a house of prostitution); Grove Press, Inc. v. Gerstein, 378 U.S. 577, 84 S. Ct. 1909, 12 L. Ed. 2d 1035, reversing, Fla. App., 156 So. 2d 537 (book titled "Tropic of Cancer" by Henry Miller).

II.

This leads me to the conclusion, previously noted, that the First Amendment allows all ideas to be expressed—whether orthodox, popular, offbeat, or repulsive. I do not think it permissible to draw lines between the "good" and the "bad" and be true to the constitutional mandate to let all ideas alone. If our Constitution permitted "reasonable" regulation of freedom of expression, as do the constitutions of some nations,[10] we would be in a field where the legis-

[10] See, e.g., Constitution of the Union of Burma, Art. 17(i), reprinted in I Peaslee, Constitutions of Nations, p. 281 (2d ed. 1956); Constitution of India, Art. 19(2), II Peaslee, op. cit. supra, at p. 227; Constitution of Ireland, Art. 40(6) (1) (i), II Peaslee, op. cit. supra, at p. 458; Federal Constitution of the Swiss Confederation, Art. 55, III Peaslee, op. cit. supra, at p. 344; Constitution of Libya, Art. 22, I Peaslee, Constitutions of Nations, p. 438 (3d ed. 1965); Constitution of Nigeria, Art. 25(2), I Peaslee, op. cit. supra, at p. 605; Constitution of Zambia, Art. 22(2), I Peaslee, op. cit. supra, at pp. 1040–1041.

lative and the judiciary would have much leeway. But under our charter all regulation or control of expression is barred. Government does not sit to reveal where the "truth" is. People are left to pick and choose between competing offerings. There is no compulsion to take and read what is repulsive any more than there is to spend one's time poring over government bulletins, political tracts, or theological treatises. The theory is that people are mature enough to pick and choose, to recognize trash when they see it, to be attracted to the literature that satisfies their deepest need, and, hopefully, to move from plateau to plateau and finally reach the world of enduring ideas.

I think this is the ideal of the Free Society written into our Constitution. We have no business acting as censors or endowing any group with censorship powers. It is shocking to me for us to send to prison anyone for publishing anything, especially tracts so distant from any incitement to action as the ones before us.

■ **Books, Inc.,** *Defendant, Appellant,*

v.

United States of America, *Appellee.*

No. 6552.

United States Court of Appeals, First Circuit.

April 12, 1966.

Leonard A. Kamaras, Providence, R.I., with whom *John H. DiStefano,* Providence, R.I., was on the brief for appellant.

Frederick W. Faerber, Jr., Asst. U.S. Atty., with whom *Raymond J. Pettine,* U.S. Atty., was on the brief, for appellee.

Before ALDRICH, Chief Judge, McENTEE, Circuit Judge, and WYZANSKI, District Judge.

WYZANSKI, District Judge.

Books, Inc., a distributor of paperback books, appeals from a $1500 fine imposed following a jury verdict that, in violation of 18 U.S.C. § 1465 and § 2(b),[1] it had knowingly caused to be transported in interstate commerce for the purpose of sale or distribution *Lust Job,* an obscene book. The principal issue presented on appeal is whether the District Judge should have ruled as a matter of law that the book was not obscene in the statutory or constitutional sense. Other issues are raised as to rulings during the taking of testimony and as to denials of requests for instructions.

[1] 18 U.S.C. § 1465 "Whoever knowingly transports in interstate or foreign commerce for the purpose of sale or distribution any obscene, lewd, lascivious, or filthy book, pamphlet, picture, film, paper, letter, writing, print, silhouette, drawing, figure,

Ephraim, a Massachusetts retail bookseller, entered into an automatic plan with defendant Books, Inc., a Rhode Island distributor, under which the latter, on its own initiative, chose books and caused them to be transported in interstate commerce for Ephraim to sell. Defendant selected, and caused the interstate transportation of, at least two copies of *Lust Job,* a paperback novel.

Following indictment under 18 U.S.C. § 1465, defendant moved for a bill of particulars. In response, the United States Attorney stated "it is the Government's contention that obscene material permeates the dominant theme of the material of said book [*Lust Job*], which theme extends from page 5 to page 188 inclusive." Those pages set forth, in the form of a novel, a tale exclusively devoted to the sexual adventures of its principal characters. Adulteries, seductions, and orgies are the only events of importance. The contacts described include not only sexual intercourse, but sodomy and other perversions. There is not any serious effort to portray the reality of cultural or social conditions of even the most neurotic or sordid

image, cast, phonograph recording, electrical transcription or other article capable of producing sound or any other matter of indecent or immoral character, shall be fined not more than $5,000 or imprisoned not more than five years or both. * * *"

18 U.S.C. § 2(b) "Whoever willfully causes an act to be done which if directly performed by him or another would be an offense against the United States, is punishable as a principal." As amended Oct. 31, 1951, c. 655, § 17b, 65 Stat. 717.

portion of the population. Description of the locale is minimal. The style is flaccid, repetitive, and unreflective of the author's individuality.

On the front cover of the book is an unclothed woman, her back toward the reader. She is seated on the floor, her back and buttocks showing, her head tilted backwards and her arms clasping below the knees the trousers of a clothed man. The title *Lust Job* is printed so that it crosses the woman's back. Above the woman's head and across the man's trousers are the words "He climbed to the top on a ladder of sin." On the rear cover appears the following description of the book:

"SELFISH PASSIONS * * *
drove Steve Rapallo, a handsome, eager young executive as he clawed his way up the lust ladder to success. Success in money and bed, the only two things that seemed to matter. And to hell with the way he got them. Take Carol —which he did—the wanton wife of his boss, whose only desire was to get between the sheets and stay there. And Rapallo was just the chamber stud she needed. It was a ball, and it was Miami Beach and it was the annual convention. A time for fun. A time for sin. A time for shame and lust and everything that added up to wild bedroom orgies where nobody cared what anybody did as long as they did it and never stopped!
* * * GUTTER LOVE!"

Defendant offered as literary experts two assistant professors of English literature at Rhode Island College. Mr. Sternberg testified that *Lust Job* was "poor literature" but the dominant theme was "the advocating of moral responsibility and the leading of a moral life." Mr. Anghinetti stated that he did not believe the book had literary merit, but its "redeeming quality" was "its element of condemnation of sexual behavior."

The other evidence does not need to be recited before turning to the principal question raised on this appeal, that is whether, responding to defendant's motion at the conclusion of the Government's case-in-chief, or its motion at the end of all the testimony, the District Judge should have entered a judgment of acquittal on the ground that *Lust Job* was not, as a matter of law, an obscene book under 18 U.S.C. § 1465 or under the First Amendment to the United States Constitution.

[1, 2] Guided by the controlling opinions of the justices in the majority in the three cases decided March 21, 1966 in the Supreme Court of the United States, *Ginzburg v. United States*, 383 U.S. 463, 86 S. Ct. 969, 16 L. Ed. 2d 31; *Mishkin v. State of New York*, 383 U.S. 502, 86 S. Ct. 958, 16 L. Ed. 2d 56, and *A Book Named "John Cleland's Memoirs of a Woman of Pleasure" v. Attorney General of Commonwealth of Massachusetts*, 383 U.S. 413, 86 S. Ct. 975, 16 L. Ed. 2d 1 (the Fanny Hill case), as well as earlier cases such as *Roth v. United States*, 354 U.S. 476, 77 S. Ct. 1304, 1 L. Ed. 2d 1498, *Manual Enterprises, Inc. v. Day*, 370 U.S. 478, 82 S. Ct. 1432, 8 L. Ed. 2d 639, and *Jacobellis v. State of Ohio*, 378 U.S. 184, 84 S. Ct. 1676, 12 L. Ed. 2d 793, this Court is bound to conclude that a jury could find *Lust Job* obscene within the meaning of 18 U.S.C. § 1465, and that such application of the statute is not repugnant to the First Amendment. Under the most recent Supreme Court decisions,

there was adequate evidence in the text of the novel, without any reference to the covers, to warrant a factual determination that the dominant theme of the book taken as a whole appeals to a prurient interest in sex, that the book is patently offensive because it affronts contemporary community standards relating to the description of sexual matters, and that the material is utterly without redeeming social value.

[3, 4] Moreover, we recognize that in close cases, where it is doubtful if a text is obscene, a majority of the Supreme Court of the United States deems it appropriate to look at the circumstances under which the text was commercially offered. *Ginzburg v. United States, Mishkin v. State of New York, A Book Named "John Cleland's Memoirs of a Woman of Pleasure" v. Attorney General of Massachusetts.* Where publications have been created or exploited entirely on the basis of their appeal to prurient interests, a conclusion is permissible that the merchandise transported, sold, or otherwise dealt in, is obscene in the statutory sense and is not constitutionally protected matter. *Ginzburg v. United States*, 86 S. Ct. p. 974. Under the foregoing rule, it would be appropriate either for the District Court or this Court to take into account the front and back covers of *Lust Job* and from them to reach a conclusion that there were pandering and an exploitation of interests in titillation, and that, therefore, the text of *Lust Job* itself is obscene.

Nothing is to be gained by a detailed comparison of *Lust Job* and the publications before the Supreme Court in the Ginzburg or Mishkin cases. Quite plainly *Lust Job* could be found to equal or exceed some of those publications in prurient appeal and patent offensiveness. Likewise, it could be found to be without redeeming social value.

[5] Nor can defendant successfully bring itself within the scope of the decision in *A Book Named "John Cleland's Memoirs of a Woman of Pleasure" v. Attorney General of Commonwealth of Massachusetts* involving Fanny Hill. Unlike that book, *Lust Job*, in the opinion of defendant's own experts, has no modicum of literary value. To be sure, defendant's literary experts asserted that the book had a purgative moral value. But for two reasons this testimony had no probative force: first, it was not within the alleged expert qualifications of the witnesses; and second, an otherwise obscene book cannot be held to have from the constitutional viewpoint a redeeming social value because the erotic passages and the description of deviant sexual practices instead of stimulating a prurient response from an average reader would disgust and sicken him and act as a moral catharsis. *Mishkin v. State of New York*, 86 S. Ct. p. 963. Moreover, in the case at bar there is evidence, which was absent in *A Book Named "John Cleland's Memoirs of a Woman of Pleasure" v. Attorney General of Commonwealth of Massachusetts*, "that the book was commercially exploited for the sake of prurient appeal, to the exclusion of all other values." See *A Book Named "John Cleland's Memoirs of a Woman of Pleasure" v. Attorney General of Commonwealth of Massachusetts*, 86 S. Ct. p. 990.

Defendant raises a number of points with respect to the trial, all of which we have examined, but of which it seems to us only two require comment in this opinion.

[6] Defendant, mindful of the obscenity test enunciated in *Roth v. United States*, 354 U.S. 476, 489, 77 S.

Ct. 1304, 1311, that is, "whether to the average person, applying contemporary standards, the dominant theme of the material taken as a whole appeals to prurient interest," requested an instruction that "The average person, as construed and applied, must be the adult within the community, being the nation at large and anyone less than an adult must be absolutely excluded from your consideration." The District Judge, instead, gave a charge, of which the pertinent part is quoted in the footnote[2] placing emphasis on the "effect of the book * * * not upon any particular class, but upon all those it was likely to reach; in other words, its impact upon the average person in our national community."

In appraising this charge, we bear in mind that it was delivered orally, and that we are concerned not with academic perfection but with the way the language would be understood by a jury. Laymen would regard, as indeed we do, the instruction as directing attention to the effect of the book upon a typical mature adult reader in the audience which defendant's method of distribution of *Lust Job* sought to reach. Focus on such a typical reader whom defendant sought "to catch" comports with the decision with respect to The Housewife's Handbook in *Ginzburg v. United States*, see particularly 86 S. Ct. p. 973.

It is plain that *Butler v. State of Michigan*, 352 U.S. 380, 77 S. Ct. 524, 1 L. Ed. 2d 412, has no application to the case at bar. The charge in the instant case does not permit the jury to use as the test of pruriency, or of community standards, or of other aspects of obscenity the effect of the book upon children as a class. Nor does the charge emphasize, as did the trial judge in the findings reviewed in *Ginzburg v. United States*, 86 S. Ct. p. 970, f.

3, the effect of the book upon "children of all ages, psychotics, feebleminded and other susceptible elements." On the contrary, here the jury was directed to consider as the measuring rod the total market at which defendant aimed, and to consider specifically the average mature person in that market, neither the very immature nor the very sophisticated. Such a measuring rod is appropriate.

[7, 8] The other point deserving of our comment is the refusal of the trial judge to permit defendant to introduce in evidence a large number of publications currently available in Rhode Island so that from them the jury could better form its opinion of community standards. It is, of course, true that what is sold in the market reflects to some extent community standards. But it is not true that every item sold is necessarily not obscene. Hence, not every book sold in the market is admissible to test the obscenity of *Lust Job*. Nor is a judge required to admit as a touchstone for the jury even those books which are admittedly not obscene. The admission of a number of different publications alleged to be comparable to the publication in issue might make the trial unmanageably complex and lengthy. The trial judge must be allowed wide discretion as to whether to permit the introduction of such allegedly comparable publications, and as to whether to allow the witnesses to be examined in detail on publications other than the one directly at issue. Here the trial judge did not abuse his discretion.

Affirmed.

---

[2] "The first test to be applied by you in determining whether said book, 'Lust Job,' is obscene is whether the dominant or most obvious theme or purpose of said book, when viewed as a whole and not part by part, is an appeal to the prurient interest of the average person of our national community. It is not whether it would arouse lustful thoughts in those comprising a particular segment of our community, such as the young, the immature, or highly prudish, or, on the other hand, would leave another segment, such as the scientific or highly educated, or the so-called wor[l]dly-wise and sophisticated, indifferent and unmoved. The test is the effect of the book considered as a whole not upon any particular class, but upon all those it was likely to reach; in other words, its impact upon the average person in our national community in 1962."

■ Books, Inc.

v.

United States.

ON PETITION FOR WRIT OF CERTIORARI TO THE UNITED STATES COURT OF APPEALS FOR THE FIRST CIRCUIT.

No. 323. Decided June 12, 1967. Certiorari granted; 358 F. 2d 935, reversed.

Stanley Fleishman for petitioner.
Solicitor General Marshall, Assistant Attorney General Vinson, Robert S. Erdahl and *Marshall Tamor Golding* for the United States.

PER CURIAM.

The petition for a writ of certiorari is granted and the judgment of the United States Court of Appeals for the First Circuit is reversed. *Redrup v. New York*, 386 U.S. 767.

THE CHIEF JUSTICE would grant the petition and set the case for oral argument.

MR. JUSTICE CLARK would grant the petition and affirm.

MR. JUSTICE HARLAN concurs in the reversal on the basis of the reasoning set forth in his opinions in *Roth v. United States*, 354 U.S. 476, 496, and *Manual Enterprises, Inc. v. Day*, 370 U.S. 478.

■ The City of Chicago, *Appellee,*

v.

Universal Publishing and Distributing Corporation, *Appellant.*
Nos. 39260–39262.

Supreme Court of Illinois.

March 24, 1966.

Thomas P. Sullivan and *Charles J. McCarty,* Chicago (Raymond, Mayer, Jenner & Block, Chicago, and Swiger, Kelley, Harragan & Schott, New York City, of counsel), for appellant.

Raymond F. Simon, Corp. Counsel, Chicago (Sydney R. Drebin and Marvin E. Aspen, Asst. Corp. Counsel), for appellee.

PER CURIAM:

Three separate appeals involving seven paperback books are here consolidated for our consideration. They come directly to us from the circuit court of Cook County because of the constitutional questions involved in prosecutions of individual book sellers and Universal Publishing and Distributing Corporation, the publisher of the questioned books. All were charged with violating chapter 192, section 9 of the Municipal Code of the City of Chicago which prohibits publication, circulation or sale of obscene literature. At the conclusion of bench trials the books sellers were found not guilty in each case because of insufficient proof of *scienter*. The corporate publisher was adjudged guilty and fines of $25 imposed on each of seven counts and a $50 fine on one count.

The single issue before us is whether the books are obscene, defined by the governing ordinance as: "Whether, to the average person, applying contemporary community standards, the dominant theme of the material taken as a whole appeals to prurient interests." Resolution of this issue requires an independent constitutional judgment by us as to whether these books fall within or beyond the imprecise boundaries of the constitutional guaranties of freedom of speech and press incorporated in the first amendment to the United States constitution and section 4 of article II of the Illinois constitution. S.H.A. *Jacobellis* v. *Ohio*, 378 U.S. 184, 84 S. Ct. 1676, 12 L. Ed. 2d 793, *City of Chicago* v. *Kimmel*, 31 Ill. 2d 202, 201 N.E. 2d 386.

The questioned books consist of seven paperbacks of 150–160 pages each. "Instant Love" portrays a motel owner facing financial ruin who finally agrees to an arrangement whereby a panderer places three prostitutes at the motel and operates a poker game there. The owner's problems include his alcoholic wife, and sexual adventures with the motel maid, the prostitutes and a nurse. He finally, although threatened with physical harm and bankruptcy, seeks assistance from law enforcement authorities in terminating the illegal activities and places his wife in a sanatorium. The book ends with indications of an agreed divorce from his wife, her cure from alcoholism and his marriage to the nurse.

The "Marriage Club" deals with a young woman whose husband is intolerably brutal in their sexual relationships. She leaves him and goes to the home of an aunt, a rather frank and bawdy person who operates a matrimonial agency in a building where private rooms are available for such use as the members desire. Two of the aunt's "secretaries" are in fact prostitutes. The niece has several sexual experiences with agency patrons. Her husband attempts to persuade her to return by fraudulent threats against the aunt's property. One of the patrons, with whom the niece has had a sexual relationship, exposes the fraud, and the final sentence indicates her resumption of their sexual activity and probable marriage.

"Love Hostess" portrays the experiences of a young actor who obtains employment as a tour guide and eventually marries the niece of the tour director. The operations of the tour staff and the tourists involve considerable sexual activity among the staff and the tourists with an episode of lesbianism.

"The Shame of Jenny" portrays a secretary, fearful of spinsterhood, who engages in sexual intercourse with a fellow-employee, is sexually assaulted by her superior, rooms with a lesbian narcotic addict, has numerous sexual experiences with a musician, and ultimately attempts suicide, but is rescued therefrom and decides to marry the musician. Also portrayed are the frustrations involved in her superior's marriage to an abnormally fat wife, his secret desire for the secretary and his ultimate mental breakdown.

"High-School Scandal" depicts a respectable, attractive widow in her mid-thirties, who becomes enamored of a seventeen-year-old student in one of the classes she teaches. Her seduction of him, and her sexual experience with two other faculty members, one a lesbian, are the dominant theme of the book. The ultimate exposure of her affair with the boy leaves her friendless except for the brother of her deceased husband with whom it appears she will attempt to rebuild her life.

"Her Young Lover" involves a happily married couple who are returning home from an anniversary dinner when they are assaulted by three young men who each rape the wife. The ensuing dissolution of their marriage is caused by the husband's impotency induced by his feeling of guilt in failing to protect his wife from rape. Both engage in extramarital sexual activity. She learns the identity of one of her attackers, and thereafter engages in numerous sexual episodes with him. The book ends with indications that the husband and wife will be divorced and that each will marry a paramour.

"Cheater's Paradise" revolves chiefly about the marital difficulties in which a resort hotel employee and his wife become enmeshed. It includes numerous sexual episodes involving other partners, an incident of lesbianism and concludes with a reconciliation of the married couple.

[1-4] The controlling principles in this type of case appear in *Roth* v. *United States*, 354 U.S. 476, 77 S. Ct. 1304, 1 L. Ed. 2d 1498, as later expanded in *Manual Enterprises, Inc.* v. *Day*, 370 U.S. 478, 82 S. Ct. 1432, 8 L. Ed. 2d 639, and Jacobellis. Material is obscene if "to the average person, applying contemporary community standards, the dominant theme of the material taken as a whole appeals to prurient interest" (Roth, 354 U.S. p. 489, 77 S. Ct. p. 1311), defined as "a shameful or morbid interest in nudity, sex, or excretion, and if it goes substantially beyond customary limits of candor in description or representation of such matters." (Roth, 354 U.S. p. 487, f. n. 20, 77 S. Ct. p. 1310). Obscenity is "utterly without redeeming social importance." (Roth, 354 U.S. p. 484, 77 S. Ct. 1309). "The portrayal of sex, e.g., in art, literature and scientific works, is not itself sufficient reason to deny material the constitutional protection of freedom of speech and press." (Roth, 354 U.S. p. 487, f. n. omitted, 77 S. Ct. p. 1310.) Manual Enterprises indicated that obscene material must be "patently offensive."

In three opinions in the past eighteen months we have considered the perplexing problems posed by society's attempts to protect itself from the presumably deleterious effect of obscene writings or utterances without unreasonably curtailing the constitutional guaranties of free speech and free press. In the first, *City of Chicago* v. *Kimmel*, 31 Ill. 2d 202, 201 N.E. 2d 386, we upheld the constitutionality of the ordinance now before us and held two paperbacks somewhat similar to those here involved constitutionally protected, emphasizing the social problems therein portrayed, and indicating that, since "Tropic of Cancer" had been held not to be obscene, (*Grove Press, Inc.* v. *Gerstein*, 378 U.S. 577, 84 S. Ct. 1909, 12 L. Ed. 2d 1035), the books there in question could not be proscribed since they were not "utterly without redeeming social importance." In *People* v. *Bruce*, 31 Ill. 2d 459, 202 N.E. 2d 497, an earlier opinion, affirming a trial court judgment that a monologue delivered by a commercial entertainer was obscene, was reversed because the Jacobellis decision clearly eliminated the "balancing" test established by *American Civil Liberties Union* v. *City of Chicago*, 3 Ill. 2d 334, 121 N.E. 2d 585, pursuant to which we had previously held the obscene aspects of the monologue outweighed its affirmative values. We there interpreted Jacobellis as immunizing any material which has any social importance. In the third, *People* v. *Sikora*, 32 Ill. 2d 260, 204 N.E. 2d 768, we rejected an attack upon the constitutionality of the State statute dealing with obscenity (Ill. Rev. Stat. 1963, chap. 38, par. 11-20) and concluded the three paperback books there before us were obscene. We emphasized that none of the books represented any serious attempt to discuss social problems, and that each book was a discussion of sex and perversion totally unrelated to

anything else. The bizarre nature of the sexual activity described in those books is apparent even from the brief description of the contents appearing in the opinion. We found it unnecessary to consider whether any standard other than a national one would be constitutionally acceptable since the trial judge had appraised the material in terms of "contemporary community standards in the United States today."

We are now urged to resolve the question of the applicable standard to be used in determining whether given material is obscene. Defendant urges that the United States Supreme Court has restricted the standard to a national one; the State contends no constitutional barrier exists to a local community standard, and that moral concepts prevailing in the community where the alleged offense occurred should be controlling. We agree with the State that this question is as yet unresolved by the United States Supreme Court (see Sikora, p. 264, 204 N.E. 2d 768), but there are presently pending before that court several cases in one or more of which a determination of this issue seems likely. Consideration of this fact, coupled with our determination that the result here would be the same irrespective of the standards applied, prompts us to conclude that it is not presently necessary to resolve this issue.

Based upon the foregoing, we must make "an independent constitutional judgment" as to the material before us. In so doing we have compared these books with those considered in Kimmel and Sikora. All are similar in that the covers, titles and characterizations appearing thereon are suggestive of illicit sexual conduct. But the books must be considered as a whole (Roth, 354 U.S. p. 489, 77 S. Ct. 1304), and their contents in our judgment more nearly resemble those in Kimmel and therefore are within the realm of constitutionally protected expression. While no clearly definitive rule in this exceedingly difficult area has yet been announced by the United States Supreme Court, the books here considered are, to us, less "patently offensive" than those held obscene in Sikora. While the distinguishing features are not easily described, the material here contains substantially less violence, there is less abnormal sexual conduct, the descriptions of both normal and perverted sexual episodes are less bizarre and the total effect less erotic. The revolting language and "dirty" words of "Tropic of Cancer" are not present here; the description of sexual conduct is no more detailed than in Kimmel; no cunnilingus or oral-genital contact is described and apparently none is involved; there is no masturbation, flagellation, masochism or acts of sadism; no male homosexual conduct is involved, and no voyeurism is discussed. There are no transvestite episodes and several of the incidents of lesbianism are "disgusting" to the neophyte partner. The books now before us do, to a limited extent, deal with common social or marital problems although they certainly are not the type of writing which we would voluntarily read or recommend. Obviously their publication on the basis of literary merit would be unjustified, and they are clearly inappropriate for other than adults. However, it is established that "sex and obscenity are not synonymous," and that "[t]he portrayal of sex * * * is not itself sufficient reason to deny material the constitutional protection of freedom of speech and press." (*Roth* v. *United States* 354 U.S. 476, 487, 77 S. Ct. 1304, 1310, 1 L. Ed. 2d 1498.) We may not weigh the objectionable features of these publications against their affirmative values (Jacobellis), and we cannot say they are "utterly without redeeming social importance."

[5] We therefore conclude that the publications herein named are not obscene. The judgments of the circuit court of Cook County are hereby reversed.

Judgments reversed.

■ **United States of America**

v.

392 Copies of a Magazine Entitled "Exclusive."

United States of America

v.

3600 Copies of a Magazine Entitled "Review International," Vol. 6. United States of America

v.

1000 Copies of a Magazine Entitled "International Nudist Sun," Vol. 16.

Civ. Nos. 17060, 17065, 17066.

United States District Court, D. Maryland.

April 4, 1966.

Thomas J. Kenney, U.S. Atty., *Arthur G. Murphy* and *Fred K. Grant*, Asst. U.S. Attys., Baltimore, Md., for plaintiff.

Robert Eugene Smith, Baltimore, Md., and *Herald P. Fahringer*, Buffalo, N.Y., for claimant.

Thomsen, Chief Judge.

In these consolidated proceedings under section 305 of the Tariff Act of 1930, 19 U.S.C.A. § 1305,[1] the government seeks the forfeiture, confiscation and destruction of 392 copies of a magazine entitled Exclusive, 3600 copies of a magazine entitled Review International No. 6, and 1000 copies of a magazine entitled International Nudist Sun No. 16, imported from Denmark, on the ground that they are obscene material, the importation of which is prohibited by section 1305. Claimant contends that the material is not obscene, that section 1305 is unconstitutional on its face,[2] and that section 1305 is unconstitutional as applied in these cases.[3]

---

[1] Section 1305 of Title 19, U.S.C.A., provides in pertinent part:

"All persons are prohibited from importing into the United States from any foreign country * * * any obscene book, pamphlet, paper, writing, advertisement, circular, print, picture, or drawing * * * or other article which is obscene or immoral, * * *. No such articles whether imported separately or contained in packages with other goods entitled to entry, shall be admitted to entry; and all such articles * * * shall be subject to seizure and forfeiture as hereinafter provided * * *.

"Upon the appearance of any such book or matter at any customs office, the same shall be seized and held by the collector to await the judgment of the district court as hereinafter provided; and no protest shall be taken to the United States Customs Court from the decision of the collector. Upon the seizure of such book or matter the collector shall transmit information thereof to the district attorney of the district in which is situated the office at which such seizure has taken place, who shall institute proceedings in the district court for the forfeiture, confiscation, and destruction of the book or matter seized. Upon the adjudication that such book or matter thus seized is of the character the entry of which is by this section prohibited, it shall be ordered destroyed and shall be destroyed. Upon adjudication that such book or matter thus seized is not of

the character the entry of which is by this section prohibited, it shall not be excluded from entry under the provisions of this section.

"In any such proceeding any party in interest may upon demand have the facts at issue determined by a jury and any party may have an appeal or the right of review as in the case of ordinary actions or suits."

[2] Claimant contends that section 1305 is unconstitutional because:

"(a) Its invocation in the case at bar abridges the respondent's right to freedom of speech and press under the First Amendment to the Constitution of the United States.

"(b) It empowers government officials to seize and exclude imported magazines suspected of being 'obscene' and to do so prior to any judicial determination that they are, in fact, 'obscene.'

"(c) It empowers government officials to seize and exclude imported magazines preceding an advisory determination of their 'obscenity.'

"(d) It allows suppression of reading material pending a judicial determination which may be excessively delayed."

[3] Claimant contends that section 1305 is unconstitutional as applied and invoked in these cases because:

Procedure

Proceedings in the Case. On February 3, 1966, two separate shipments consisting respectively of 3600 copies of Review International No. 6 and 1000 copies of International Nudist Sun No. 16, imported from Denmark and consigned to custom house brokers on behalf of claimant, Central Magazines Sales, Ltd., were brought from the ship to the Appraisers' Stores in Baltimore after the bills of lading had been delivered to Customs officials by the brokers for clearance through Customs. Entry numbers were assigned on the same day. On February 8, 392 copies of Exclusive were similarly imported and entered. The shipments were examined promptly by the line examiner to determine whether any duty was payable, and whether any of the material was inadmissible for a variety of statutory reasons, including obscenity and violation of copyright.[4] The line examiner thought that the magazines were probably obscene and referred them to the appraiser, in accordance with established procedures. The appraiser likewise felt that the material should be considered for possible forfeiture and referred the matter to the Obscene Literature Committee, a group of Customs officials in Baltimore, again in accordance with established procedures.

Thereafter, if the Committee also believed the material to be obscene, it would ordinarily have been seized or detained[5] pending further administrative proceedings under 19 C.F.R. § 12.40[6] before it was referred to the

United States Attorney for the institution of forfeiture proceedings. The administrative proceedings in Baltimore would ordinarily not have been significantly different from those described under the heading "The administrative task and procedures in general," in *United States* v. *One Book* entitled "The Adventures of Father Silas," et al., S.D.N.Y., 249 F. Supp. 911, at 913 (January 18, 1966). In that case Judge Frankel held the facts, set out at pp. 914–915, showed that the government had suppressed the books for an unlawfully protracted time. However, as a result of that decision and of other recent decisions,[7] a meeting was held in Washington on February 8, which was attended by representatives of the Department of Justice,[8] the Bureau of Customs and the Post Office Department, to discuss possible changes in the procedure for handling material believed to be obscene. At that meeting it was decided to adopt a new procedure, intended to expedite the proceedings and to eliminate the question whether 19 C.F.R. 12.40 accords with 19 U.S.C.A. § 1305.[9] See also 19 U.S.C.A. §§ 1603 and 1604.[10] It was

---

"(a) From the time of the seizure of the above entitled publications there has been no judicial scrutiny of said publications or advisory hearing to determine their character and nature.

"(b) That since the seizure of the above entitled publications an inordinate amount of time has expired wherein their distribution has been unreasonably and unconstitutionally restrained in violation of the provisions embodied in the First Amendment to the United States Constitution.

"(c) It has been unconstitutionally applied because commencement of the libel proceedings was delayed for an inordinate amount of time and further the libel proceedings have been delayed unreasonably."

[4] See note 13, infra.

[5] See discussion in *United States* v. *One Carton Positive Motion Picture Film*, S.D.N.Y., 248 F. Supp. 373, 376 (1965), quoted in note 15 below. See also *United States* v. *One Book Entitled "The Adventures of Father Silas,"* et al., S.D.N.Y., 249 F. Supp. 911, 913–14 (1966); *United States* v. *18 Packages of Magazines*, N.D. Cal., 227 F. Supp. 198, 206, 208 (1963).

[6] The pertinent portions of 19 C.F.R. 12.40 read as follows:
"* * *

"(b) Upon the seizure of articles or matter prohibited entry by section 305, Tariff Act of 1930 (with the exception of the matter described in paragraph (a) of this section), a notice of the seizure of such articles or matter shall be sent to the consignee or addressee.

"(c) When articles of the class covered by paragraph (b) of this section are of small value and no criminal intent is apparent, a blank assent to forfeiture, customs Form 4609, shall be sent with the notice of seizure. Upon receipt of the assent to forfeiture duly executed, the articles shall be destroyed if not needed for official use and the case closed.
"* * *

"(e) If the importer declines to execute as an assent to forfeiture of the articles other than those mentioned in paragraph (a) of this section and fails to submit, within 30 days after being notified of his privilege so to do, a petition under section 618, Tariff Act of 1930, for the remission of the forfeiture and permission to export the seized merchandise, information concern-

ing the seizure shall be submitted to the United States attorney in accordance with the provisions of the second paragraph of section 305(a), Tariff Act of 1930, for the institution of condemnation proceedings.
"* * *

"(g) In any case when a book is seized as being obscene and the importer declines to execute an assent to forfeiture on the ground that the book is a classic, or of recognized and established literary or scientific merit, a petition addressed to the Secretary of the Treasury with evidence to support the claim may be filed by the importer for release of the book. Mere unsupported statements or allegations will not be considered. If the ruling is favorable, release of such book shall be made only to the ultimate consignee.
"* * *"

[7] Particularly *United States* v. *18 Packages of Magazines*, N.D. Cal., 238 F. Supp. 846 (1964), and *United States* v. *One Carton Positive Motion Picture Film*, S.D.N.Y., 248 F. Supp. 373 (1965), and 247 F. Supp. 450 (1965).

[8] Including an Assistant United States Attorney from Maryland.

[9] See fn. 7 to *United States* v. *One Book* Entitled "The Adventures of Father Silas" et al. (S.D.N.Y., 249 F. Supp. 911, at 914 (1966).

[10] 19 U.S.C.A. § 1603:
"Same [Seizure]; collector's reports
"Whenever a seizure of merchandise for violation of the customs laws is made, or a violation of the customs laws is discovered, and legal proceedings by the United States attorney in connection with such seizure or discovery are required, it shall be the duty of the collector or the principal local officer of the Customs Agency Service to report such seizure or violation to the United States attorney for the district in which such violation has occurred, or in which such seizure was made, and to include in such report a statement of all the facts and circumstances of the case within his knowledge, with the names of the witnesses and a citation to the statute or statutes believed to have been violated, and on which reliance may be had for forfeiture or conviction."
19 U.S.C.A. § 1604:
"Same, prosecution
"It shall be the duty of every United States attorney immediately to inquire into the facts of cases reported to him by collectors and the laws applicable thereto, and if it appears probable that any fine, penalty, or forfeiture has been incurred by reason of such violation, for the recovery of which the institution of proceedings in the United States district court is necessary, forthwith to cause the proper proceedings to be commenced and

also decided to institute forfeiture proceedings against Exclusive, to seek a prompt disposition of that case, and to adopt new regulations shortly thereafter. The following day it was decided that forfeiture proceedings should also be instituted against International Nudist Sun No. 16 and Review International No. 6. A copy of each of the magazines was, therefore, referred to the United States Attorney in accordance with 19 U.S.C.A. § 1305.

On Friday, February 11, a libel was filed against the shipment of Exclusive, and the attachment and monition were posted by the United States Marshal on Tuesday, February 15. Also on February 15, libels were filed against the shipments of the other two magazines. The attachments and monitions as to them were posted on February 16. The magazines had been formally seized by Customs, see note 5 above, on February 11 at about the time the first libel was filed. Court orders directing that the Marshal, in addition to his monition in rem, publish notice of the seizures and of the forfeiture proceedings were signed on February 16 in the case of Exclusive and on February 17 in the case of the other two magazines.

Meanwhile, Customs had given notice of the libels to claimant, and claimant filed answers to all three libels on February 28. A meeting with the Court was held on March 4, a trial date was set, and the trial began on March 9. Testimony and other evidence were offered by both sides, and the case has been fully briefed and argued.

[1] *Discussion of Procedure.* Section 1305 of Title 19, U.S.C.A., is set out in note 1, above. The predecessors of that section have been in the Code for a long time.[11] One which was substantially the same as the present section was held constitutional in *United States* v. *One Obscene Book Entitled "Married Love,"* S.D.N.Y., 48 F. 2d 821 (1931). The present section was held unconstitutional in *United States* v. *18 Packages of Magazines,* N.D. Cal., 238 F. Supp. 846 (1964), but that decision was rendered before *Freedman* v. *State of Maryland,* 380 U.S. 51, 85 S. Ct. 734, 13 L. Ed. 2d 649 (1965), wherein the Supreme Court stated that "a noncriminal process which requires the prior submission of a film to a censor avoids constitutional infirmity only if it takes place under procedural safeguards designed to obviate the dangers of a censorship system." 380 U.S. at 58, 85 S. Ct. at 738. The Court then summarized the necessary safeguards, as follows: (1) The burden of proof must rest on the censor; (2) no valid final restraint may be imposed except by judicial determination,[12] and any restraint prior to such determination must be designed to preserve the status quo; and (3) a prompt

judicial determination must be assured. 380 U.S. at 58–59, 85 S. Ct. 734. In the year since *Freedman,* judges in the Southern District of New York have thrice refused to hold section 1305 unconstitutional on its face, but have required that it be applied in accordance with the tests set out in *Freedman.* See *United States* v. *One Carton Positive Film,* (McLean, J.) 248 F. Supp. 373 (1965), and (Graven, J.) 247 F. Supp. 450 (1965); *United States* v. *One Book* entitled "The Adventures of Father Silas," (Frankel, J.) 249 F. Supp. 911 (1966). This Court agrees with the decision in each of those cases, and refers particularly to the excellent discussion of the legislative history in Section II of Judge Frankel's opinion.

[2, 3] Customs admission procedures applicable to different types of publications must embody the safeguards specified in *Freedman.* Reasonable speed must be used to reach an administrative decision that a libel for forfeiture shall be filed, and a judicial determination of the issue of obscenity must be made with reasonable promptness. What is reasonable in the case of one type of publication, however, may not be reasonable with respect to another type. Some material is timely and loses much of its value if there is any substantial delay. Other material, such as that with which we are dealing in these cases, may be almost timeless. The instant cases present no such problems as are involved in the previous scheduling of motion pictures or the need of a student for a particular book.

The procedures condemned by Judge Frankel were established by Customs in an effort to reduce the number of forfeiture proceedings which would have to be brought in the courts, by encouraging administrative disposition before judicial proceedings are begun. Since it appears that those procedures result in unreasonable delays in many cases, the governmental agencies involved have wisely attempted to work out a more expeditious procedure.

[4–6] The proposed new procedure, which was followed in these cases, meets the tests set out in *Freedman,* particularly when it is recognized that all publications, as well as all other goods which are imported into the United States, must be examined by Customs officials for many different purposes after they are entered and before they are cleared.[13] The evidence in this case indicates that the new procedures will continue to result in the release of the material with reasonable promptness after entry if either the line examiner or the appraiser passes it.[14] Even if the material is referred to the Obscene Literature Committee, its decision is usually rendered within two days. If the Committee decides to go forward, the matter must be taken up at once with the United States Attorney, who is required by statute immediately to inquire into the facts and forthwith to institute proceedings in the district court unless he decides that the proceedings probably could not be sustained or that the ends of justice do not require that they should be instituted and prosecuted. 19 U.S.C.A. § 1604. See note 10, above. Meanwhile, the material will

---

prosecuted, without delay, for the recovery of such fine, penalty, or forfeiture in such case provided, unless, upon inquiry and examination, such United States attorney decides that such proceedings cannot probably be sustained or that the ends of public justice do not require that they should be instituted or prosecuted, in which case he shall report the facts to the Secretary of the Treasury for his direction in the premises."

[11] Act of August 30, 1842, c. 270, § 28, 5 Stat. 566; Act of March 2, 1857, c. 63, 11 Stat. 168; Act of March 3, 1883, c. 121, §§ 2491–2493, 22 Stat. 489–490; Act of October 1, 1890, c. 1244, §§ 11–13, 26 Stat. 614–615; Act of August 27, 1894, c. 349, §§ 10–12, 28 Stat. 549; Act of August 5, 1909, c. 6, §§ 9–11, 36 Stat. 86.

[12] Citing A *Quantity of Copies of Books* v. *State of Kansas,* 378 U.S. 205, 84 S. Ct. 1723, 12 L. Ed. 2d 809 (1964); *Marcus* v. *Search Warrant,* 367 U.S. 717, 81 S. Ct. 1708, 6 L. Ed. 2d 1127 (1961).

[13] A line examiner must keep in mind over fifty possible questions in connection with each shipment for which clearance is sought. See generally 19 U.S.C.A. chaps. 3 and 4, and 19 C.F.R., Parts 8, 9, 10, 11, 12, 13, 14.

[14] The evidence shows that the line examiner usually examines the material the same day it is delivered to the Appraisers' Stores, but that since the line examiner in Baltimore who examines books and magazines also has other items in his line, there may on certain occasions be a delay of one or two days.

have been seized and held by Customs to await the judgment of the district court, 19 U.S.C.A. § 1305, and the importer or his broker will have been notified of the seizure and libel. The seizure by Customs is in the nature of a detention of questionable material pending a judicial adjudication. Such restraint by detention is designed simply to preserve the status quo, i.e., to prevent entrance of the suspect material until the Court has ruled.[15] Negotiations with Customs or the United States Attorney looking to a possible settlement of the matter may be conducted either before or after the Marshal serves the monition. An opportunity for such discussion was offered in this case. There is ordinarily no reason why the cases cannot be heard promptly by the court if the parties desire a prompt hearing and there is any real need for speed. In some instances the importer is more anxious to develop his case fully than to secure a prompt decision. The decision in the instant case was delayed because the opinions in *Mishkin v. State of New York*, 86 S. Ct. 958 (1966), *A Book Named "John Cleland's Memoirs of a Woman of Pleasure"* ("Fanny Hill"), *et al. v. Attorney General of Com. of Massachusetts*, 86 S. Ct. 975 (1966), and *Ginzburg v. United States*, 86 S. Ct. 969 (1966), were handed down by the Supreme Court while this opinion was being prepared, and counsel for claimant requested an opportunity to file a supplemental brief. In appropriate cases the material may be released pendente lite in accordance with the provisions of 19 C.F.R. 23.22. See also cases in 19 U.S.C.A. § 1605, n. 2 and n. 3.

[7] *Conclusion re. Procedure.* This Court concludes that section 1305 of Title 19, U.S.C.A., is not unconstitutional on its face and has not been applied unconstitutionally in these cases.

Obscenity

The Material. The so-called "magazine" Exclusive is really a picture book containing 34 pictures of nude or almost nude women. In each picture the breasts and pubic area are fully exposed. In some of the pictures the women are wearing garter belts and silk stockings, which focus attention on the pubic area. In some of the pictures the models are posed in lewd attitudes and positions. In several pictures the women are chained to a chair and their wrists

---

[15] In *United States v. One Carton Positive Motion Picture Film*, 248 F. Supp. at 376–377, Judge McLean said:

"* * * To be sure, some initial determination by the customs officials is necessary as to which works are to be held for such a judicial determination. But this is inevitable. The district court cannot reasonably be expected to view each and every one of the thousands of books and pictures and other works which are imported into the United States, most of which, after all, are innocuous. Some screening procedure must be set up. To put this responsibility upon the customs officials is appropriate and in fact it is hard to see how else it could be handled, as a practical matter. But it is the court which makes the ultimate determination. There is no 'seizure' in a final sense unless the court so decides, after a trial by jury, if the claimant wants one. The 'seizure' by the customs authorities is merely a temporary detention."

Mr. Justice Brennan also has discussed the Customs procedure as an example of desirable judicial adjudication as opposed to administrative adjudication. See *Manual Enterprises, Inc. v. Day*, infra, 370 U.S. 478 at 514–516, 82 S. Ct. 1432, 8 L. Ed. 2d 639. (1962)

are bound.[16] The only written material is on the title page, in English and two foreign languages, and appears verbatim in other "magazines" published by Nordisk Bladcentral, of Copenhagen.[17]

International Nudist Sun No. 16 and Review International No. 6 each contain 20 posed pictures of well-developed nude men, with the focus in most instances on the penis, which is flagrantly displayed. Although posed in outdoor settings, in few of the pictures are the models engaging in any normal outdoor activities. The articles in both magazines are innocuous, dreary and puerile, and bear little relation to the illustrations.[18] No reference is made to the illustrations in any of the articles.

Discussion. On the issue of obscenity the controlling case is *Roth v. United States*, 354 U.S. 476, 77 S. Ct. 1304, 1 L. Ed. 2d 1498 (1957), as elaborated and in one respect "adjusted" by *Mishkin v. State of New York*, 86 S. Ct. 958 (1966); *A Book Named "John Cleland's Memoirs of A Woman of Pleasure" et al. v. Attorney General of Com. of Massachusetts* (the Fanny Hill case), 86 S. Ct. 975 (1966); *Ginzburg v. United States*, 86 S. Ct. 969 (1966); *Manual Enterprises, Inc. v. Day*, 370 U.S. 478, 82 S. Ct. 1432, 8 L. Ed. 2d 639 (1962); and *Jacobellis v. State of Ohio*, 378 U.S. 184, 84 S. Ct. 1676, 12 L. Ed. 2d 793 (1964).

In the *Fanny Hill* case Mr. Justice Brennan said:

"We defined obscenity in Roth in the following terms: '[W]hether to the average person, applying contemporary community standards, the dominant theme of the material taken as a whole appeals to prurient interest.' 354 U.S., at 489 [77 S. Ct. 1304]. Under this definition, as elaborated in subsequent cases, three elements must coalesce: it must be established that (a) the dominant theme of the material taken as a whole appeals to a prurient interest in sex; (b) the material is patently offensive because it affronts contemporary community standards relating to the descrip-

---

[16] The possible sado-masochistic appeal of any of the pictures in Exclusive is too slight to be of any importance on any of the questions in this case. In other cases such appeal may be of importance. See the authorities cited in the various opinions in Mishkin, 86 S. Ct. 958, and Ginzberg, 86 S. Ct. 969. *United States v. Rees*, D. Md., 193 F. Supp. 849, 852–855 (1961), illustrates the possible dangers inherent in such material.

[17] It reads: "The international Art Magazine is published bimonthly. Europe's most distinguished photographers have contributed the pictures used in this magazine which has been released by the publishers exclusively to furnish serious artists and persons interested in art, who have some difficulty in finding living models, with suitable photographs to be used as substitute for drawing painting and sculpturing.—Therefore the magazine will be sold only to adults who are serious-minded of problems of art and will look on our pictures solely from an aestitical (sic) point of view." The material belies the protestation.

[18] In International Nudist Sun No. 16 the articles are: Prudery in Naturist Clubs; The Art of Correct Breathing; On Forming a Naturist Club; Leisure and Automation; Psycho-Analysis and Physical Health; Learn to Relax and Stay Young; Masculine Hygiene; If You Must Wear Clothes; and Shivers and Goose Pimples. In International Review No. 6 the articles are: Naturism in winter; Finer focusing; How far will you go for a good skin?; "Nudist Paradise" revisited; Flowers and trees of Christmas; News of nudists (sic); Odds and ends; Moving around; Glassless (sic) nudism; and Spoil yourself. The articles fill approximately one-half of the pages of the two magazines.

tion or representation of sexual matters; and (c) the material is utterly without redeeming social value." 86 S. Ct. at 977.

(a) *Prurient Appeal.* Many books, magazines and pictures are directed to the general public, but some are designed for special groups, such as males, females, children, adolescent males, adolescent females, homosexuals,[19] and others.

In *Mishkin,* Mr. Justice Brennan, speaking for the Court, said:

Where the material is designed for and primarily disseminated to a clearly defined deviant sexual group, rather than the public at large, the prurient-appeal requirement of the Roth test is satisfied if the dominant theme of the material taken as a whole appeals to the prurient interest in sex of the members of that group. The reference to the 'average' or 'normal' person in Roth, 354 U.S., at 489–490 [77 S. Ct. 1034], does not foreclose this holding.* In regard to the prurient-appeal requirement, the concept of the 'average' or 'normal' person was employed in Roth to serve the essentially negative purpose of expressing our rejection of that aspect of the Hicklin test, Regina v. Hicklin, [1868] L.R. 3 Q.B. 360, that made the impact on the most susceptible person determinative. We adjust the prurient-appeal requirement to social realities by permitting the appeal of this type of material to be assessed in terms of the sexual interests of its intended and probable recipient group; and since our holding requires that the recipient group be defined with more specificity than in terms of sexually immature persons,** it also avoids the inadequacy of the most-susceptible-person facet of the Hicklin test." 86 S. Ct. at 963.

[8, 9] In *United States v. Klaw,* 2 Cir., 350 F. 2d 155 (1965), the government contended that the material appealed particularly to the prurient interest of sexual deviates and also had prurient appeal to the average man. The Court "[doubted] that any court would take judicial

---

[19] The psychiatrists were in substantial agreement, based upon Kinsey, that about 4% of all males are exclusively homosexuals, and another 10% are "bisexual," more homosexual than heterosexual, but making a more or less satisfactory adaptation to normal life in the community, including marriage. There is also a group of occasional homosexuals, whose number is hard to estimate, perhaps as high as 18%, probably somewhat lower. Including these groups, nearly 37% of all males have one or more homosexual experiences after adolescence.

* See *Manual Enterprises, Inc. v. Day,* 370 U.S. 478, 482 [82 S. Ct. 1432] (opinion of Harlan, J.); Lockhart and McClure, Censorship of Obscenity: The Developing Constitutional Standards, 45 Minn. L. Rev. 5, 72–73 (1960).

"It is true that some of the material in *Alberts v. State of California,* decided with *Roth,* resembled the deviant material involved here. But no issue involving the obscenity of the material was before us in either case. 354 U.S., at 481, n. 8 [77 S. Ct. 1304]. The basic question for decision there was whether the publication and sale of obscenity, however defined, could be criminally punished in light of First Amendment guarantees. Our discussion of definition was not intended to develop all the nuances of a definition required by the constitutional guarantees.

** "See generally, 1 American Handbook of Psychiatry (Arieti ed. 1959) 593–604, for a description of the pertinent types of deviant sexual groups.

notice of the reaction that deviates—or the average man—might have to such stimuli" as were involved in that case. This court agrees that expert testimony is desirable, if not necessary, to show what reaction deviates would have to almost any type of stimulus. Whether expert testimony is necessary to prove the probable reaction of the average man to various stimuli depends upon the nature of the material. Some may be so esoteric as to require expert testimony; other stimuli, like the pictures of the women in the "magazine" Exclusive, are so elemental that the ordinary judge or juror should be able to recognize the nature of their appeal to the average man.

In the instant case both the government and the claimant offered expert testimony with respect to the probable effect of the magazines on various groups in the community. Dr. Manfred S. Guttmacher, Chief Medical Officer of the Supreme Bench of Baltimore City and Consultant to the American Law Institute in the preparation of the Model Penal Code, testified for the government. Dr. Jonas R. Rappaport, Medical Officer of the Circuit Court for Baltimore County and a member of the Governor's Commission to Study and Review the Criminal Laws, testified for claimant. Dr. Guttmacher's testimony was confined to the two magazines depicting male nudes.

[10] The Court finds from all the evidence, including the testimony of the psychiatrists, that International Nudist Sun No. 16 and Review International No. 6 were in fact primarily designed for homosexual males and, to a lesser extent, adolescent males; that the pictures have very strong prurient appeal to almost all exclusively homosexual or bisexual males and some prurient appeal to a large percentage of latent homosexuals and some adolescent males; that to many female adolescents they would be shocking and rather frightening[20] but to a few might have such prurient appeal as to cause masturbation.[21]

[11] The Court finds that the pictures in Exclusive would appeal to the prurient interest of the average male, and particularly to the prurient interest of the adolescent male. That was the dominant theme of the material.

(b) *Patent Offensiveness.* This brings us to the question whether the material so affronts contemporary community standards relating to the description or representation of sexual matters as to be patently offensive.[22]

[12] The standards to be applied in customs cases

---

[20] Which does not tend to prove prurient appeal, but may be considered on the question of whether the material goes so far beyond ordinary community standards as to be patently offensive.

[21] Both psychiatrists agreed that women as a group are not stimulated sexually to the same degree as men by pictures, articles or verbal statements.

[22] The test with respect to this element was worded as follows by Justice Brennan in the *Fanny Hill* case: "that * * * the material is patently offensive because it affronts contemporary community standards relating to the description or representation of sexual matters * * *." 86 S. Ct. at 977. In *Manual Enterprises,* Justice Harlan cited the test in the A.L.I. Model Penal Code, "if it goes substantially beyond customary limits or candor in description or representation of such matters." 370 U.S. at 486, 82 S. Ct. at 1436. Justice Harlan also stated: "It is only in the unusual instance where, as here, the 'prurient interest' appeal of the material is found limited to a particular class of persons that occasion arises for a truly independent inquiry into the question whether or not it is patently offensive." 370 U.S. at 486, 82 S. Ct. at 1436.

should be national standards. *United States* v. *One Carton,* 247 F. Supp. at 464. See also *Jacobellis,* 378 U.S. at 195, 84 S. Ct. 1676; *Manual Enterprises,* 370 U.S. at 488, 82 S. Ct. 1432; *United States* v. *Ginzburg,* 3 Cir., 338 F. 2d 12, 14 (1964), affirmed sub nom. *Ginzburg* v. *United States,* supra.

The Court must first decide whether any evidence, and if so what evidence, may be admitted to prove contemporary community standards. This problem has been discussed in a number of recent cases, which have reached different conclusions.[23]

In *Smith* v. *People of State of California,* 361 U.S. 147, 80 S. Ct. 215, 4 L. Ed. 2d 205 (1959), concurring opinions referred to defendant's rights "to enlighten the judgment of the tribunal, be it the jury or as in this case the judge, regarding the prevailing literary and moral community standards and to do so through qualified experts," and that to "exclude such expert testimony is in effect to exclude as irrelevant evidence that goes to the very essence of the defense and therefore to the constitutional safeguards of due process." 361 U.S. at 164–165, 80 S. Ct. at 225. The A.L.I. Model Penal Code, section 251.4, Obscenity, p. 239, proposes that: "Expert testimony and testimony of the author, creator, publisher or other person from whom the material originated, relating to factors entering into the determination of the issue of obscenity, shall be admissible." In the instant case no expert testimony with respect to community standards was offered by either side, nor was there any testimony from the author, creator, publisher or other person from which the material originated.

Claimant did offer three types of evidence: (1) publications which have been held not obscene in certain court trials; (2) publications admitted by Customs officials in Baltimore shortly before and shortly after February 7, 1966; and (3) publications purchased by a former policeman at certain stores or newsstands in Baltimore during the trial. All of this evidence was admitted subject to exception over the objection of the government.

[13] (1) Claimant offered in evidence the items which were held not obscene in *Sunshine Book Co.* v. *Summerfield,* 101 U.S. App. D.C. 358, 249 F. 2d 114 (1957), 355 U.S. 372, 78 S. Ct. 365, 2 L. Ed. 2d 352 (1958), in *One, Inc.* v. *Olesen,* 355 U.S. 371, 78 S. Ct. 364, 2 L. Ed. 2d 352 (1958), and in two nisi prius cases[24] decided before *Mishkin, Ginzburg* and *Fanny Hill.* Material involved in adjudicated cases, whether held obscene or not obscene, should always be considered by the Court as illuminating the opinions rendered in those cases, and the items offered

have been so considered here. Whether such material would ordinarily be admitted as evidence in a jury trial or in a trial before the court without a jury need not be decided; various factors would enter into such a ruling in each case. Since this is a test case, the Court has considered the books as evidence. This Court finds that the publications in the present case are more offensive than the material in *Sunshine Book* and *One, Inc.* The material approved in the two nisi prius cases is inconclusive, and entitled to little weight.

(2) It is not necessary to decide whether the material which was passed by Customs authorities in Baltimore shortly before or after the material was seized in the instant cases would ordinarily be admissible to prove the national standard. It would never be conclusive, and would ordinarily have little weight. The Supreme Court has insisted that the standard be determined in a judicial proceeding by the court or the jury, with such expert or other evidence as may be appropriate in the particular case. The problem before the Customs officials is a difficult one, complicated not only by the difficulty of interpreting the applicable Supreme Court decisions, but also by recent nisi prius decisions questioning the Customs procedures, which have been discussed above. The Customs officials decided to proceed against the magazines involved in these consolidated cases and to pass certain others. However, both before and after the decisions in *Mishkin,* the Customs officials in Baltimore have filed additional libels involving thousands of copies of other magazines.

In this case the Court has examined all the publications offered in evidence by claimant. Many of the pictures of male nudes in the magazines which have been admitted are generally similar to the pictures in International Nudist Sun No. 16 and Review International No. 6, but they were admitted before the decision of the Supreme Court in *Mishkin,* clarifying the question of prurient appeal to a particular group. Few of the pictures of female nudes or partly dressed females in the magazines admitted come close to the offensiveness of many pictures in Exclusive.

[14] (3) Claimant offered the testimony of a former City policeman, now a private detective, and the magazines he had purchased at a dozen stores or newsstands in the City during the trial and before the decision in *Mishkin.* He had started in "the Block" area and had proceeded to particular stores and newsstands which he and many other Baltimoreans know deal in pornographic material. His testimony indicates that such material is not available at respectable book stores, drug stores, newsstands or other outlets for magazines. It is noteworthy that on the very day this case was argued the proprietor of one of the stores where the detective purchased a magazine was convicted and sentenced to prison in the Criminal Court of Baltimore for selling obscene photographs of nude males.[25] Four of the outlets where the detective purchased magazines were located on "the Block" or adjacent thereto. The standards of "the Block" are not the standards to be applied in this case, any more than the standards of the most straight-laced persons. Material purchased in such specialized outlets has little or no value in determining contemporary community standards. *Ginzburg* v.

---

[23] *United States* v. *Ginzburg,* 3 Cir., 338 F. 2d 12 (1964), aff'd 86 S. Ct. 958 (March 21, 1966); *Womack* v. *United States,* 111 U.S. App. D.C. 8, 294 F. 2d 204 (1961); *United States* v. *Hochman,* E.D. Wisc., 175 F. Supp. 881 (1959), aff'd 7 Cir., 277 F. 2d 631, cert. den. 364 U.S. 837, 81 S. Ct. 70, 5 L. Ed. 2d 61 (1960); *United States* v. *West Coast News Company, Inc.,* W.D. Mich., 228 F. Supp. 171 (1964); *Monfred* v. *State of Maryland,* 226 Md. 312, 173 A. 2d 173 (1961); *Yudkin* v. *State of Maryland,* 229 Md. 223, 182 A. 2d 798 (1962); *People* v. *Finklestein,* 11 N.Y. 2d 300, 229 N.Y.S. 2d 367, 183 N.E. 2d 661 (1962); *In re Harris,* 56 Cal. 2d 879, 16 Cal. Rptr. 889, 366 P. 2d 305 (1961).

[24] *Royal News Co.* v. *Dewey Schultz,* E.D. Mich., 230 F. Supp. 641, and *Commonwealth of Pennsylvania* v. *Platt,* Allegheny County Court of Quarter Sessions of the Peace, #379, December term, 1964.

---

[25] The Court examined those photographs and found them more offensive than the photographs of nude males involved in this case.

United States, 86 S. Ct. 969 (1966). Nevertheless, the Court has considered the material purchased by the detective.

None of the opinions in *Mishkin, Ginzburg* or *Fanny Hill* discussed at length the question of patent offensiveness. In *Manual Enterprises* there was no majority opinion, but Justice Harlan, speaking for himself and Justice Stewart, included a description of the material in a footnote to his opinion, 370 U.S. at 489, fn. 13, 82 S. Ct. at 1438, and said:

"** * * Our own independent examination of the magazines leads us to conclude that the most that can be said of them is that they are dismally unpleasant, uncouth, and tawdry. But this is not enough to make them 'obscene.' Divorced from their 'prurient interest' appeal to the unfortunate persons whose patronage they were aimed at capturing (a separate issue), these portrayals of the male nude cannot fairly be regarded as more objectionable than many portrayals of the female nude that society tolerates. Of course not every portrayal of male or female nudity is obscene. See Parmelee v.* United States, 72 *App.* D.C. 203, 206–208, 113 *F.* 2d 729, 732–734; *Sunshine Book Co. v. Summerfield*, 355 U.S. 372 [78 S. Ct. 365]; *Mounce v. United States*, 355 U.S. 180 [78 S. Ct. 267, 2 L. Ed. 2d 187]. *Were we to hold that these magazines, although they do not transcend the prevailing bounds of decency, may be denied access to the mails by such undifferentiated legislation as that before us, we would be ignoring the admonition that 'the door * * * into this area [the First Amendment] cannot be left ajar; it must be kept tightly closed and opened only the slightest crack necessary to prevent encroachment upon more important interests'* (footnote omitted). Roth [354 U.S.], at 488 [77 S. Ct. 1304]." 370 U.S. at 489–491, 82 S. Ct. at 1438–1439.*

The other Justices, comprising the majority, did not discuss this aspect of the case.

As we have seen, in *Mishkin* a majority of the Court held for the first time that "Where the material is designed for and primarily disseminated to a clearly defined deviant sexual group, rather than the public at large, the prurient-appeal requirement of the *Roth* test is satisfied if the dominant theme of the material taken as a whole appeals to the prurient interest in sex of the members of that group." 86 S. Ct. at 963. But *Mishkin* did not discuss the "patently offensive" element of the test.

[15] This Court must decide, in the light of those and other opinions, whether the magazines involved in this case are patently offensive. It is clear that the representation of male or female nudity is not per se offensive. Museums display paintings, prints and statues of nudes. Many books, expecially classics, sold generally to the public, are illustrated with pictures of nude men and women. It is also clear that nude men or women or both may be shown in such positions, poses and settings as to be patently offensive.

[16] *Exclusive.* The Court is satisfied that the pictures which comprise the magazine Exclusive are patently offensive.

International Nudist Sun No. 16 and Review International No. 6. In most of the photographs of nude men in those magazines, the models are not engaged in any normal activity, but are so posed as to highlight the geni-

talia, which are flagrantly displayed.[26] On the other hand, the few pictures in which two men are shown do not directly suggest homosexual activity, unless there are some esoteric ritual positions of which the Court is not advised. The text, although evidently intended to support an argument that the magazines are "sunbathing and nature living" publications, is clearly secondary to the pictures, which are not referred to therein, and no one, however moronic, would pay a high price for the innocuous written material.

In the light of the Supreme Court cases, these two magazines must be regarded as borderline material. The format and contents of the magazines and their high price show that they are designed and imported primarily for sale to homosexuals. It is evident that the commercial importers and distributors of nude pictures and similar material have been pressing further and further beyond the material previously approved by most courts, particularly the Supreme Court, and nearer to or beyond the legal limits, as defined by the Supreme Court. This Court finds as a fact that most people in the United States would consider the magazines to be patently offensive.

The difficult question is whether, in the light of the Supreme Court opinions, the people may be protected from the effect which the importation of such material is likely to have in pushing some of the millions of latent homosexuals over the line, with all the attendant misery and problems, and in defeating the efforts of some of the millions of "bisexual" males to preserve the precarious adjustment they have made. Until the binding authorities are clarified, this Court concludes that the decisions do not prevent it from holding that the material is patently offensive.

[17] (c) *Social Importance.* The third element of the obscenity test is that the material be utterly without social importance or value. *Roth*, 354 U.S. at 484, 77 S. Ct. 1304; *Jacobellis*, 378 U.S. at 191, 84 S. Ct. 1676; *The "Fanny Hill" case*, 86 S. Ct. 975.`

[18] Exclusive contains no text. The statement on the title page that it "has been released by the publishers exclusively to furnish serious artists and persons interested in art, who have some difficulty to find living models, with suitable photographs to be used as substitute for drawing, painting and sculpturing," is plainly a subterfuge. The same statement appears verbatim on the title pages of the other "magazines" published by Nordisk Bladcentral, offered in evidence by claimant, imported recently or purchased at the outlets described above. The publication is utterly without social importance or value.

International Nudist Sun No. 16 and Review International No. 6. Each claims, in identical material on the title page, to be "the international sunbathing and nature-living monthly magazine." As noted above, however, in the discussion of patent offensiveness, the text, although innocuous and evidently intended to support this contention, is so clearly secondary to the pictures that it may be disregarded. It can have no part in selling the magazines to anyone. The text has no literary significance or social value,

---

[26] In this respect they differ from the illustrations in the bona fide nudist magazines considered by the Supreme Court in *Sunshine Books*. The nudes shown in those pictures were for the most part engaged in sports and other normal outdoor activities, and the focus was not on the genitalia.

and the pictures, which are in essence the magazine, are utterly without any artistic significance or other redeeming social value.

Conclusion re. Obscenity. The Court concludes that the magazines Exclusive, International Nudist Sun No. 16 and Review International No. 6 are obscene within the purview of section 305 of the Tariff Act, 19 U.S.C.A. § 1305.

*

The Court will enter an appropriate judgment order.

■ Attorney General
  v.
  A Book Named "Naked Lunch."

Supreme Judicial Court of Massachusetts.

Suffolk.

Argued Oct. 8, 1965.

Decided July 7, 1966.

Edward De Grazia, Washington, D.C. (Daniel Klubock, Boston, Mass., with him) for intervener Grove Press, Inc.

William I. Cowin, Asst. Atty. Gen., for Attorney General.

Before Spalding, Whittemore, Cutter, Kirk, Spiegel, and Reardon, JJ.

Per Curiam.

The book was adjudged obscene in the Superior Court. G.L. c. 272, §§ 28C, 28E, 28F (each inserted by St. 1945, c. 278, § 1). The Supreme Court of the United States has held that, to justify a holding of obscenity, "three elements must coalesce: it must be established that (a) the dominant theme of the material taken as a whole appeals to a prurient interest in sex; (b) the material is patently offensive because it affronts contemporary community standards * * * and (c) the material is *utterly* without redeeming social value" (emphasis supplied). A Book Named "John Cleland's Memoirs of a Woman of Pleasure" v. Attorney Gen. of Mass., 383 U.S. 413, 418–421, 86 S. Ct. 975, 16 L. Ed. 2d 1 (hereafter referred to as the *Memoirs* case). "Naked Lunch" may appeal to the prurient interest of deviants and those curious about deviants. To us, it is grossly offensive and is what the author himself says, "brutal, obscene and disgusting."

As to whether the book has any redeeming social value, the record contains many reviews and articles in literary and other publications discussing seriously this controversial book portraying the hallucinations of a drug addict. Thus it appears that a substantial and intelligent group in the community believes the book to be of some literary significance. Although we are not bound by the opinions of others concerning the book, we cannot ignore the serious acceptance of it by so many persons in the literary community. Hence, we cannot say that "Naked Lunch" has no "redeeming social importance in the hands of those who

publish or distribute it on the basis of that value." See the *Memoirs* case at p. 421, 86 S. Ct. at p. 979.

The record does not show that the book has been "commercially exploited for the sake of prurient appeal, to the exclusion of all other values." The question, therefore, is not presented whether the book, or its publication and distribution, are on that account "utterly without redeeming social importance." See the *Memoirs* case at pp. 420–421, 86 S. Ct. 975, which appears to treat the privilege under the First Amendment of publishing material like this as a qualified privilege which may be lost if abused. See also *Ginzburg* v. *United States*, 383 U.S. 463, 467–476, 86 S. Ct. 942, 969, 16 L. Ed. 2d 31; *Mishkin* v. *New York*, 383 U.S. 502, 508–512, 86 S. Ct. 958, 16 L. Ed. 2d 56. Cf. *Galvin* v. *New York, N.H. & H.R.R. Co.*, 341 Mass. 293, 296–298, 168 N.E. 2d 262.

The final decree is reversed and a new final decree is to be entered declaring that (without considering whether the book has been commercially exploited for the sake of prurient appeal) the book cannot be declared to be obscene. This new final decree shall be without prejudice to the bringing of new proceedings with respect to this book under the appropriate sections of G.L. c. 272, if it shall appear that, after March 21, 1966, the date of the three recent Supreme Court cases, already cited, any persons have been or are advertising or distributing this book in this Commonwealth in a manner to exploit it for the sake of its possible prurient appeal.

So ordered.

The Chief Justice took no part in the consideration of this case.

Reardon, Justice (dissenting).

I respectfully dissent from the opinion of the majority. Some general observations are in order as a preface to a statement of my reasons.

1. It is appropriate to note that, since the adoption of

the Constitution of Massachusetts in 1780, this court and its judges have been most aware of the responsibility laid upon them by art. 16, Part I, of the Declaration of Rights which provides: "The liberty of the press is essential to the security of freedom in a state: it ought not, therefore, to be restrained in this commonwealth." It was Massachusetts which, in ratifying the Constitution of the United States in 1788, first among the States called for the addition of a Bill of Rights. This call echoed by other ratifying conventions led in December, 1791, to the adoption of the first and the nine succeeding amendments to the Constitution of the United States.[1] Thus our disinclination to serve as a censor of published material has an historical constitutional foundation which antedates that of any other American tribunal.

One need not agree with the view of Mr. Justice Black that "the Federal Government is without any power whatever under the Constitution to put any type of burden on speech and expression of ideas of any kind," *Ginzburg* v. *United States*, 383 U.S. 463, 476, 86 S. Ct. 942, 950, to be able to agree with him that the lot of the judge who is charged with deciding cases such as this would be immeasurably eased were Mr. Justice Black's view that of the majority of his court.[2] But such is not the fact and we find ourselves again confronted with the troublesome problem of applying G.L. c. 272, §§ 28C–28G.

The task of the appellate judge on the State court in dealing with an allegedly pornographic work is not a happy one in these days. He may personally be of the opinion, also held by some who have written on the subject of pornography, that, were all restraints on publication lifted, levels of public taste would eventually rise and the business of pornography become unprofitable.[3]

Yet we have, as was so well stated by Chief Justice Qua in *Commonwealth* v. *Isenstadt*, 318 Mass. 543, 548, 62 N.E. 2d 840, 843, the "plain but not necessarily easy duty to read the words of the statute in the sense in which they were intended, to accept and enforce the public policy of the Commonwealth as disclosed by its policy-making body, whatever our own personal opinions may be, and to avoid judicial legislation in the guise of new constructions to meet real or supposed new popular viewpoints, preserving always to the Legislature alone its proper prerogative of adjusting the statutes to changed conditions." In construing the present statute we are given added guidance by *A Book Named "John Cleland's Memoirs of a Woman of Pleasure"* v. *Attorney Gen. of Mass.*, 383 U.S. 413, 413–462, 86 S. Ct. 965, 16 L. Ed. 2d 1 (hereafter *Memoirs*),

decided since this case was argued before us. The majority opinion in that case set forth G.L. c. 272, §§ 28B–28F, inclusive, in full in an appendix without comment. It is reasonable to conclude that the Supreme Court of the United States acknowledges authority in those sections of that statute, subject to their application within the guidelines which the majority in the *Memoirs* case laid down.[4]

It is thus my view that there is still power resident in the statute and I believe that the Commonwealth is entitled to have this court enforce what power it still contains. Failure to do so in this case consigns our State law in this field to a limbo and is, in fact, a contravention of the will of the Legislature on the supposed basis that the statute has been overridden by the *Memoirs* case. I do not so read that case.

2. Consonant with the duty laid upon us by the statute, I have read the book and found it to be a revolting miasma of unrelieved perversion and disease, graphically described in the findings of the trial judge. It is, in truth, literary sewage. Before the trial judge a number of authors and academic witnesses, as well as several psychiatrists, on behalf of the interveners gave varying testimony regarding the social and literary worth of the book and engaged in efforts to interpret its title. Despite the testimony of these witnesses, the trial judge, on the basis of a national standard, found the book to be patently offensive, "predominantly prurient, hard-core pornography, and utterly without redeeming social importance."

It has been argued by the intervener that, in assessing the social importance of the book, the judge was bound to abide by those opinions which came to him in the testimony of the witnesses whom he heard and in the reviews which were presented to him as exhibits. Indeed it was stated in a dissent in *Attorney Gen.* v. *A Book Named "John Cleland's Memoirs of a Woman of Pleasure,"* Mass.[a] 206 N.E. 2d 403, when that book was before us: "It is not the court's function to consider whether to agree or disagree with the appraisal of the book by academic witnesses. The controlling circumstance is that the work is evaluated by representative scholars and teachers of English literature as a work of some literary and historical significance notwithstanding its patently pornographic aspects." And in the majority opinion in the case at bar, it is said, on "whether the book has any redeeming social value, the record contains many reviews and articles in literary and other publications discussing seriously this controversial book portraying the hallucinations of a drug addict. Thus it appears that a substantial and intelligent group in the community believes the book to be of some literary significance. Although we are not bound by the opinions of others concerning the book, we cannot ignore the serious acceptance of it by so many persons in the literary community. Hence, we cannot say that 'Naked Lunch' has no

---

[1] Sutherland, Constitutionalism in America (1st ed. 1965), pp. 179, 180.

[2] *Ginzburg* v. *United States*, 383 U.S. 463, 477–481, 86 S. Ct. 942 (dissent). *Mishkin* v. *New York*, 383 U.S. 502, 515–518, 86 S. Ct. 958 (dissent). Cahn, Justice Black and First Amendment "Absolutes": A Public Interview, 37 N.Y.U.L. Rev. 549, 553–554, 559. Justice Brennan, The Supreme Court and the Meiklejohn Interpretation of the First Amendment, 79 Harv. L. Rev. 1, 4–5, 14. Reich, Mr. Justice Black and the Living Constitution, 76 Harv. L. Rev. 673, 695–697, 713, 735, 738–739. See Harlan, J., dissenting in *A Book Named "John Cleland's Memoirs of a Woman of Pleasure"* v. *Attorney Gen. of Mass.*, 383 U.S. 413, 459–460, 86 S. Ct. 975.

[3] Levin, Refractions: Essays in Comparative Literature (1966), p. 307; also printed in part in the Atlantic of February, 1966, under the title, "The Unbanning of the Books."

[4] But see footnotes 4 and 5 in *Memoirs*, supra, p. 417, 86 S. Ct. 975, intimating that G.L. c. 272, § 28H, may be constitutionally infirm. See also c. 272, § 28G. See in this regard the following cases in the Supreme Court of the United States: *Redrup* v. *New York*, 86 S. Ct. 1362 (docket No. 72—cert. granted April 25, 1966); *Austin* v. *Kentucky*, 86 S. Ct. 1362 (docket No. 453—cert. granted April 25, 1966); *Sheperd* v. *New York* (docket No. 626—cert. pending); *Avansino* v. *New York* (docket No. 1008—cert. pending).

[a] Mass. Adv. Sh. (1965) 635, 641.

'redeeming social importance in the hands of those who publish or distribute it on the basis of that value.' "

I cannot associate myself with this view. Our experience with allegedly pornographic works over the years here in Massachusetts has revealed that there is no dearth of experts ready to leap to the defence of such of them as have come under scrutiny from time to time.[5] As one looks back now on publications which have been considered in other years, it is plain to see that much material there defended was shoddy stuff on any standard. Much indeed depends upon the identity and quality of the witnesses and the substance of their testimony but the mere appearance of such witnesses does not compel the trial judge or us to surrender the power of judgment into their hands.[6] Surely the finding of fact by a trial judge seasoned by years of experience in dealing with social values and their implementation, as well as social ills and their remedies under the law, is entitled to more weight before us than are the opinions of the witnesses who were before him, whom he saw, and whom he heard render judgments which became weak indeed under examination as the record well demonstrates.[7]

What has been said relative to the witnesses who were heard may also be said of reviews discussing this work, some of which are in the record. Not all of them were favorable. A number of them were concerned principally with the question whether "Naked Lunch" was more calculated to produce titillation or nausea. One of them stated that "the book is as obscene as anything ever written.[8] Only two of these reviewers were before the trial judge. Names were appended to the reviews but no matter how extensive the reputations of the absent reviewers there was no opportunity to cross-examine them regarding their respective comments. Here again, relative to the reviews, it is my belief that this court should not abdicate its responsibility.

I conclude, therefore, that in the case on appeal of a suit brought by the Attorney General under G.L. c. 272, § 28C, the findings of the trial judge are entitled to more weight than has been accorded to them by the majority opinion.[9]

---

[5] *Attorney Gen.* v. *Book Named* "Forever Amber," 323 Mass. 302, 308–309, 81 N.E. 2d 663; *Attorney Gen.* v. *Book Named* "God's Little Acre," 326 Mass. 281, 284, 93 N.E. 2d 819. In *Attorney Gen.* v. *A Book Named* "John Cleland's Memoirs of a Woman of Pleasure," Mass., 206 N.E. 2d 403, 406, (Mass. Adv. Sh. [1965] 635, 639), the majority said, "We are mindful that there was expert testimony, much of which was strained * * *." See *Commonwealth* v. *Isenstadt*, 318 Mass. 543, 556, 558–559, 62 N.E. 2d 840; *Attorney Gen.* v. *Book Named* "Serenade," 326 Mass. 324, 326, 94 N.E. 2d 259; *Attorney Gen.* v. *Book Named* "Tropic of Cancer," 345 Mass. 11, 13, 20, 184 N.E. 2d 328. For a summary of Massachusetts cases, including older cases, see Note, Book Censorship in Massachusetts: The Search for a Test for Obscenity, 42 B.U.L. Rev. 476, 479–491.

[6] It has not yet been suggested by a majority of the Supreme Court of the United States that, when an "expert" witness approves a book, the trial judge is foreclosed from finding it without redeeming social value. However, Mr. Justice Douglas in his concurrence in *Memoirs*, 383 U.S. 413, 427, 86 S. Ct. 975, 981, said: "We are judges, not literary experts or historians or philosophers. We are not competent to render an independent judgment as to the worth of this or any other book, except as in our capacity as private citizens. * * * On this record [described as containing 'considerable and impressive testimony to the effect that this was a work of literary, historical, and social importance'] the Court has no choice but to reverse the judgment of the Massachusetts Supreme Judicial Court * * *." But see the dissent by Clark, J., in *Memoirs*, 383 U.S. 413, 448–450, 86 S. Ct. 975, 992–993, examining the experts' opinions, concluding, "In my view this proves nothing as to social value. The state court properly gave such testimony no probative weight," and saying, "It only indicates the lengths to which these experts go in their effort to give the book some semblance of value" and, the court "can accept the appraisal of experts or discount their testimony in the light of the material itself or other relevant testimony." In the same vein, see Harlan, J., dissenting in *Memoirs*, 383 U.S. 413, 460, 86 S. Ct. 975, 998: "The views of literary or other experts could be made controlling, but those experts had their say in 'Fanny Hill' and apparently the majority is no more willing than I to say that Massachusetts must abide by their verdict."

[7] (1) John Ciardi, poet: A. "I should like to make one point, especially since there's been introduced in evidence * * * a piece of my writing on Naked Lunch. At that time I was reviewing ten excerpts and I was rather enthusiastic about * * * these excerpts. My later opinion, when I read the whole book, is that

the structure is a little soggy and slow." Q. "May I ask you to interpret what this paragraph is about? A. "I doubt that Burroughs himself could interpret what this paragraph was about." Q. "Mr. Ciardi, would you say that the book invokes a response that was primarily literary?" A. "I believe so * * *. In the first place, I think the nature of the writing is such that unless one is interested in whatever literary phenomenon this is, he is going to be bored and quit." Q. "Would deletion of a member of references to homosexuality reduce the literary effect?" A. "I think that is a matter on which only the author is competent in himself and this is a nightmarish book, full of fantasies, drug hallucinations." Q. "May I ask what the references [to homosexuality] contribute to the major theme of the book?" A. "To me they contribute a certain boredom with Burroughs' method. I think he is more interested in this sort of detail than I am; and those are the sort of pages I shrug and keep on going."

(2) Norman Mailer, novelist: Q. "Considering the difficulty of the work and your relatively indirect exposures to it, may I ask, Mr. Mailer, how you are so sure of the value that this book contains?" A. "* * * I can't give a final word on how good it is without reading it five or six times. I think it has extraordinary merit and may be a great novel. * * * I suspect it has a very elaborate structure. I cannot say for a certainty. I think it is so because I couldn't draw it for you. * * * If I were to read it three or four times I could probably decide to my satisfaction how good the structure was, where perfect, where imperfect." Q. The court: "* * * [D]o you think the average book lover reads a book * * * more than once?" A. "No * * * I also feel I would now be prepared to say * * * there is a structure to it. I am not prepared to say how fine it is artistically."

(3) Professor Thomas H. Jackson, Massachusetts Institute of Technology: Q. "Are there details and points in this book that you feel you may not be able to explain because, in effect, they have no meaning and are intended only for shock value?" A. "Actually, no." Q. "Everything in this book has meaning then?" A. "*As a literary man I have to assume it does, yes*" (emphasis supplied).

(4) Allen Ginsberg, poet: A. "* * * [The title, Naked Lunch] relates to nakedness of seeing, to be able to see clearly without any confusing disguises, to see through the disguise. * * * 'Naked,' in the title; and 'Lunch' would be a complete banquet of all this naked awareness. * * * I think here he is referring to the whole book as Bill Burroughs' Naked Lunch Room, a lunch room * * *."

[8] Note, "Strange Taste," Newsweek (November 26, 1962).
[9] General Laws c. 272, § 28F, says, "Such hearings shall be conducted in accordance with the usual course of proceedings in equity including all rights of exception and appeal."

3. In the majority opinion there is a concession that the book "may appeal to the prurient interest of deviants and those curious about deviants." It calls the book "grossly offensive" and concurs with what the author himself said about it, that it is "brutal, obscene, and disgusting."[10] Having stated that it cannot be said that the book has no redeeming social importance, the opinion goes on to say that the record fails to show a commercial exploitation for the "sake of prurient appeal, to the exclusion of all other values" and states that the question is not presented whether "the book, or its publication and distribution, are on that account 'utterly without redeeming social importance.'"

The majority, unmindful of the order of events, hold that the absence of evidence of commercial exploitation in this record requires a reversal of the trial court, and note that in the *Memoirs* case Mr. Justice Brennan said that evidence of such commercial exploitation might justify the conclusion that the book was utterly without redeeming social importance.

The trial judge filed his findings of material facts and order for decree on March 23, 1965. A final decree was entered and the intervener appealed on March 25, 1965. Argument was heard before us on October 8, 1965, and we have since had the case under consideration awaiting clarification of the law from the Supreme Court of the United States. On December 7 and 8, 1965, the Supreme Court of the United States heard oral argument on the *Memoirs* case, *Ginzburg* v. *United States*, and *Mishkin* v. *New York*. On March 21, 1966, the Justices of the Supreme Court of the United States handed down their opinions in these three cases.[11] The law regarding obscenity, in the light of which both *Attorney Gen.* v. *A Book Named "John Cleland's Memoirs of a Woman of Pleasure,"* Mass.,[b] 206 N.E. 2d 403, and the instant case had been earlier decided, was thus redefined, the facet of commercial exploitation being added to the test of obscenity established in *Roth* v. *United States*, 354 U.S. 476, 484, 487, 77 S. Ct. 1304, 1 L. Ed. 2d 1498.[12] This additional facet naturally was not explored in the hearings in this case before the trial judge. In my view, before a final decision is made by this court, it should be.

In *Rosenblatt* v. *Baer*, 383 U.S. 75, 87–88, 86 S. Ct. 669, 15 L. Ed. 2d 597, the Supreme Court of the United States noted that its decision in *New York Times Co.* v. *Sullivan*, 376 U.S. 254, 84 S. Ct. 710, 11 L. Ed. 2d 686, had intervened between the *Rosenblatt* trial and the deci-

sion on the appeal, and that the *New York Times* decision bore directly on the applicable law and upon Baer's failure to adduce certain evidence in addition to that which he had adduced. On this ground the Supreme Court of the United States remanded the matter to the State court for further proceedings. In other words, there was redefinition of the law while the case was on appeal. The Supreme Court recognized this and remanded. We should do no less.

It is my belief that the Attorney General did not waive the right of the Commonwealth to raise the newly announced issue of commercial exploitation by not presenting such evidence in the court below. I cannot agree with any inference in the majority opinion that such a waiver has occurred. It might be argued that one reason for applying the doctrine of waiver to affirm or reverse on the basis of a trial court judgment despite a change or further elaboration in the law during the taking of the appeal is to prevent the occurrence of excessive delay and expense for litigants and other interested parties, but "[b]alanced against this policy of efficiency in the judicial process is the objective of settling disputes correctly in light of existing law * * *." Note, Waiver: Limitation on Intervening-Change-in-the-Law Exception, 18 Stanford L. Rev. 718, 719.[13]

There is much more to be said for a remand of this case for the taking of further evidence than for a reversal. A reversal, as the majority opinion points out, does not necessarily end all action on the book nor does it provide a salutary precedent for later cases brought under the statute. The Attorney General is free to begin again. To remand the matter for a hearing on advertising would eliminate the likelihood of a complete retrial on all points in the event that the Attorney General desires to take new action in the light of the *Memoirs* decision.[14] There appears to be no question in the minds of the majority in this case or the majority of the Supreme Court of the United States in the *Memoirs* case that litigation of this new issue of the manner of commercial presentation could change the result. The record indicates the possibility of proof by the Commonwealth on remand that "exploitation for the sake of prurient appeal" has occurred. It will be remembered that the author himself, who presumably wrote his book for sale, termed it "obscene" in his foreword. In addition, exhibit 20, the New York Times Book Review section of January 10, 1965, which was before the trial judge, contains an advertisement in which this work is offered in tandem with another book which was titled "Ananga Ranga 'The Oriental Art of Love,'" for sale at a price for both of $7.95 plus a mailing charge.[15] The books

---

[10] Naked Lunch, by William Burroughs, Grove Press (1959), Introduction, p. xii.

[11] 383 U.S. 413–518, 86 S. Ct. 975.

[b] Mass. Adv. Sh. (1965) 635.

[12] The law is now "rewritten," Black, J., dissenting, and "quite different," Harlan, J., dissenting, both in *Ginzburg* v. *United States*, 383 U.S. 463, 477, 494–495, 86 S. Ct. 942. See *Attorney Gen.* v. *Book Named "Forever Amber,"* 323 Mass. 302, 308, 81 N.E. 2d 663, 667, where this court summarized the content of the advertisements and then said, "The advertisements, however, are not part of the novel, which in final analysis must meet the test of the statute upon what is contained within its own covers." See also Lockhart & McClure, Literature, The Law of Obscenity and the Constitution, 38 Minn. L. Rev. 295, 338–350, 394–395; Lockhart & McClure, Censorship of Obscenity: The Developing Constitutional Standards, 45 Minn. L. Rev. 5, 68–70, 77–88.

[13] See Recent Decisions, 27 Va. L. Rev. 826, 827: "Apparently the basis for the ruling in these exceptional situations * * * is that the courts will take cognizance of a changed situation and will give effect to a matter bearing directly upon the right disposition of the case in order to prevent a miscarriage of justice," citing *Gulf, Colo. & Santa Fe Ry.* v. *Dennis*, 224 U.S. 503, 507, 32 S. Ct. 542, 56 L. Ed. 860. Note, *Erie R.R.* v. *Tompkins and Supervening Changes in State Law*, 50 Yale L.J. 315, 317, n.14, listing Federal cases.

[14] See *Cambria* v. *Jeffery*, 307 Mass. 49, 50, 29 N.E. 2d 555; *Henchey* v. *Cox*, 348 Mass. 742, 746–747, 205 N.E. 2d 715; James, Civil Procedure (1965), §§ 11.17 and 11.18.

[15] "From the reported evidence we may make additional findings not made by the trial judge. *Lowell Bar Association* v.

are advertised as "Not for minors—for adults only," and "Naked Lunch * * * Exactly as printed in Paris by the Olympia Press," is called "a literary masterpiece by some, a piece of pornography by others * * * Shocking! Startling! * * * Definitely not for the squeamish * * * A searing experience." This language strongly suggests an endeavor to induce purchase through the very type of appeal which was alluded to by Mr. Justice Brennan in his discussion of commercial exploitation in the *Memoirs* case.[16]

Other jurisdictions recognize that a change in the law during the pendency of an appeal may require a rehearing of the cases affected.[17] There is no sound reason why the policy of ordering a rehearing should not apply here in favor of the Commonwealth which has spoken in the statute and with a voice we are bound to heed in applying it. Massachusetts precedent exists to the effect that this court will notice changes in the law intervening between trial and decision upon appeal. In *Pilgrim* v. *MacGibbon*, 313 Mass. 290, 298, 47 N.E. 2d 299, where the judge had entered verdicts for the defendants after a jury had found for the plaintiff, we were asked to consider the effect of a Nova Scotia case, decided after the trial, which clarified the standard of gross negligence in the governing Nova Scotia statute. The law had not changed with regard to relevant evidence; rather the standard to be applied to facts already in evidence had been reformulated in Nova Scotia where the cause of action arose. In the light of the reformulation we considered the evidence and ordered judgments for the plaintiff on the verdicts of the jury, saying, "We think it is apparent that the trial judge did not have the benefit of the decision in the * * * [intervening] case. Nevertheless, it must be held to govern the rights of the parties. * * *" (p. 298, 47 N.E. 2d p. 303).

Loeb, 315 Mass. 176, 178, 52 N.E. 2d 27. And with respect to the advertising * * * we have done so." *Attorney Gen.* v. *Book Named "Forever Amber,"* 323 Mass. 302, 309, 81 N.E. 2d 663, 667.

[16] See *Books, Inc.* v. *United States of America*, 358 F. 2d 935, 937–939 (1st Cir.).

[17] *Gulf, Colo. & Santa Fe Ry.* v. *Dennis*, 224 U.S. 503, 506–507, 32 S. Ct. 542; *Blair* v. *Commissioner of Int. Rev.*, 300 U.S. 5, 8–9, 57 S. Ct. 330, 81 L. Ed. 465; *Hormel* v. *Helvering*, Commr. of Int. Rev., 312 U.S. 552, 559–560, 61 S. Ct. 719, 85 L. Ed. 1037; *Yates* v. *St. Johns Beach Dev. Co.*, 122 Fla. 141, 143–144, 165 So. 384; *Grist* v. *Upjohn Co.*, 362 Mich. 470, 472, 107 N.W. 2d 763. *Simmons* v. *State*, 199 Miss. 271, 275, 24 So. 2d 660. *Lee* v. *Junkans*, 18 Wis. 2d 56, 66–67, 117 N.W. 2d 614. Note, Reformulation of the Rule against Introducing New Matter in Appellate Courts—the Hormel Case, 50 Yale L.J. 1460, 1461. It was there said, "Despite the rule, however, there have been many exceptional cases where new matter has been considered on appeal. * * * Other recognized exceptions are supervening decisions on matters raised below[6] * * *." (Footnote No. 6 read, "This applies to state and federal court decisions alike.") See *Heritage Mut. Ins. Co.* v. *Sheboygan County*, 18 Wis. 2d 166, 171–172, 118 N.W. 2d 118.

Furthermore, even in the absence of a change in the applicable law, there is a strong public policy in this Commonwealth for remanding causes for the taking of supplementary evidence where the ends of justice will thus be best served. Examples are not wanting. "Where the facts on which the rights of the parties depend have not been ascertained at the trial it is within the power of the court in its discretion and of its own motion, to recommit the case for retrial." *Comstock* v. *Soule*, 303 Mass. 153, 159, 21 N.E. 2d 257, 260. See *New England Cement Gun Co.* v. *McGivern*, 218 Mass. 198, 205, 105 N.E. 885, L.R.A. 1916C 986; *Rubenstein* v. *Lottow*, 220 Mass. 156, 164, 107 N.E. 718; *Rioux* v. *Cronin*, 222 Mass. 131, 133, 109 N.E. 898. "We are aided in reaching this result because it is apparent * * * that findings relative to * * * [the issue] could have been made." *Watkins* v. *Simplex Time Recorder Co.*, 316 Mass. 217, 225, 55 N.E. 2d 203, 208. *Minot* v. *Minot*, 319 Mass. 253, 258–260, 66 N.E. 2d 5. *Smith* v. *Commonwealth*, 331 Mass. 585, 593–594, 121 N.E. 2d 707, and cases cited. *American Employers' Ins. Co.* v. *Cohen*, 334 Mass. 417, 421, 135 N.E. 2d 918, and cases cited. *Frank* v. *Frank*, 335 Mass. 130, 136–137, 138 N.E. 2d 586.

4. Finally, I cannot agree with the majority in their view that if any future proceedings are launched against the book evidence against it relative to the manner in which it was advertised and sold is to be limited to such promotional activity as has occurred since March 21, 1966, the date on which the three recent cases in the Supreme Court of the United States came down. That court itself imposed no such limitation in the *Memoirs* case nor in upholding the conviction of Ginzburg. The establishment by this court of such a dividing line is a curious application of the *Memoirs* case holding. If we seek an answer to the nature of the book, how it was advertised prior to the magic date is equally pertinent to that determination as the manner in which it has been advertised since.

5. In sum, it is my view that this book should not be allowed to slide by the statutory prohibitions on the grounds set forth in the majority opinion. We should not cease in our endeavor to uphold our own statute when it still possesses some vitality. In the light of the findings of the trial judge and the foregoing discussion I would remand this matter to the Superior Court for the limited purpose of taking evidence on the manner in which this book was produced, publicized, and sold.

KIRK, Justice.

I agree with the characterization of the book by the judge, the majority and by Mr. Justice Reardon in his dissent. I join in the dissent in so far as it rejects the proposition that a trial judge must treat the opinion of a witness in this or any proceeding as valid, binding or decisive of the case. Acceptance of the proposition is a surrender of the judicial function to absolutism.

■ The People of the State of Illinois, *Appellee,*

v.

Charles Kimmel, *Appellant.*
No. 39181.

Supreme Court of Illinois.

Sept. 23, 1966.

Howard T. Savage, Chicago, for appellant.
William G. Clark, Atty. Gen., Springfield, and *Daniel P. Ward,* State's Atty., Chicago (Fred G. Leach, Asst. Atty. Gen., and Elmer C. Kissane and Kenneth L. Gillis, Asst. State's Attys., of counsel), for appellee.

KLINGBIEL, Chief Justice.

At a jury trial in the circuit court of Cook County Charles Kimmel was found guilty of selling an obscene book, in violation of section 11—20 of the Criminal Code (Ill. Rev. State. 1965, chap. 38, par. 11—20). He was fined the sum of $2000 and placed on probation for a period of three years. He appeals directly to this court contending that the material is within the range of constitutionally protected expression.

The book is entitled "The Sex Addicts" and tells of a vacation cruise to tropical islands during which the hero and his cabin-mate engage in a series of sexual exploits with various girls they met aboard the ship. The hero has sexual intercourse with several female acquaintances in succession. He finally finds himself falling in love with one of two sisters, with whom he and his roommate had had a "four-way affair" in the girls' cabin, including an exchange of partners. The roommate is portrayed as a man obsessed with the urge to make new conquests who cannot be satisfied with the same girl more than once. The hero was left with the two sisters, and before ending up with the girl of his choice he has relations with both. The book contains the suggestion that the roommate, with his compulsive urge to move from one conquest to another, is mentally ill and ought to see an analyst.

[1–3] The controlling rules in this kind of case were recently set forth and discussed in *City of Chicago* v. *Universal Publishing and Distributing Corp.,* 34 Ill. 2d 250, 215 N.E. 2d 251, and need not be repeated in detail here. To lose the constitutional protection of free press the material must appeal only to a prurient interest—i.e. a morbid interest in sex—and must go substantially beyond customary limits of candor in the description or representation of it. Before a book can be classed as obscene so as to fall outside constitutional protections it must be patently offensive and without any redeeming social importance. The application of such necessarily vague standards can become extremely difficult in marginal cases, but we think the material in the case at bar, under the constitution as construed by the United States Supreme Court, (see e.g. *Grove Press, Inc.* v. *Gerstein,* 378 U.S. 577, 84 S. Ct. 1909, 12 L. Ed. 2d 1035,) can hardly be denied protection. True, the cover of this paperback book is rather blatant in suggesting illicit sexual conduct, as are the title and descriptive remarks. And the contents consist principally of a more or less continuous account of sexual engagements and the preliminaries. But there is little violence and none of the descriptions of perverted behavior of the sort portrayed, e.g., in the books held obscene in *People* v. *Sikora,* 32 Ill. 2d 260, 204 N.E. 2d 768. The acts of intercourse are not described in detail, so as to exceed the limits of contemporary candor in such matters, nor do we find repulsive and disgusting language of the kind given protection in *Grove Press, Inc.* v. *Gerstein,* 378 U.S. 577, 84 S. Ct. 1909.

[4] Publication of the book questioned in the case at bar would obviously be unjustified on any conceivable basis of literary merit although it might be said to deal, to a very slight and superficial extent, with a common social problem. But as it was pointed out in *City of Chicago* v. *Universal Publishing and Distributing Corp.,* 34 Ill. 2d 250, 215 N.E. 2d 251, sex is not synonymous with obscenity, and its portrayal is not of itself sufficient reason to deny the constitutional protection of freedom of speech and press.

In view of our conclusion that the book is not obscene it is unnecessary to consider defendant's other contentions. The judgment is reversed.

Judgment reversed.

■ The People of the State of New York, *Respondent,*

v.

Charles Tannenbaum, *Appellant.*

Court of Appeals of New York.

Sept. 29, 1966.

Osmond K. Fraenkel, New York City, for appellant.

Frank S. Hogan, Dist. Atty. (John A. K. Bradley, and H. Richard Uviller, New York City, of counsel), for respondent.

KEATING, Judge.

[1] In response to the deeply felt needs of the community, our State Legislature enacted two statutes (L. 1965, ch. 327, eff. Sept. 1, 1965; L. 1965, ch. 372, eff. July 1, 1965) proscribing the dissemination, to infants under 17 and 18 years of age respectively, of materials obscene as to such infants, though not necessarily obscene as to the adult community.

The statutory scheme is no broader than necessary to reach the desired end. The adult community remains free to read what it wishes. Dissemination of material, obscene only as to children, is proscribed only as to children. The unconstitutional infirmity pointed out in *Butler* v. *State of Michigan,* 352 U.S. 380, 77 S. Ct. 524, 1 L. Ed. 2d 412, is overcome. The adult population is not restricted to reading only that which is fit for children.

In *Bookcase, Inc.* v. *Broderick,* 18 N.Y. 2d 71, 271 N.Y.S. 2d 947, 218 N.E. 2d 668, we upheld the Legislature's power to employ variable concepts of obscenity. The questions not then being presented, we left it for another day to determine whether the statutes, in their application, squared with the mandates of the First and Fourteenth Amendments to the Federal Constitution. The present case poses these questions with regard to the statute effective on July 1, 1965 (Penal Law, Consol. Laws, c. 40, § 484–i).

On July 19, 1965, at the instigation of Operation Yorkville, 17-year-old Anthony Sciacovelli approached the appellant's cigar store, examined an outside stand containing "girlie" magazines, selected two and entered the store. Appellant looked at them, priced them at $2.25 and sold them to Sciacovelli, who thereafter departed. Once outside, Sciacovelli wrote his name and the time and place of purchase on an inside cover without further examining the magazines' contents.

[2] *Candid* is the name of the magazine which appellant sold to Sciacovelli and for the sale of which he was subsequently convicted pursuant to section 484–i of the Penal Law (sale or delivery of pornographic material to minors under the age of 18). *Candid's* cover shows a girl seductively posed beside a couch wearing the skimpiest of undergarments. In addition, the cover describes the contents: "Smut For Women Only," "How To Undress With Class," "Sex With a Twist," "Piccadilly Prostitute" and "Should She or Shouldn't She." The lower left-hand corner states: "Sale To Minors Forbidden."

What the cover promises, the contents delivers. *Candid* is devoted purely to sex, told pictorially by nudes in almost every conceivable pose and by tales of sex orgies in picture and prose. The advertisements, in line with the over-all theme, are for mail-order photographs and motion pictures of nudes, lingerie, and sexual devices and handbooks.

We have no difficulty concluding, on the basis of the proof offered at the trial, that *Candid* falls within the ban of the statute and that the appellant, with knowledge of its contents, sold the magazine to a person under the age of 18 years.

We turn now to the constitutional questions. Specifically, appellant contends that section 484–i is unconstitutionally vague, in violation of due process of law, and that the statute's failure to require proof of *scienter* as to the age of the purchaser renders it unconstitutional as a limitation on the freedom of speech and the press as guaranteed by the First and Fourteenth Amendments.

Section 484–i divides the material to which it applies into three subdivisions: (1) photographs, drawings and motion pictures depicting specified parts of the body or acts; (2) a combination of such photographs, drawings or motion pictures "depicted or shown in such a posture or way that the viewer's attention or concentration is primarily focused on * * *" described parts of the body, and (3) books, magazine [s], phonograph record[s] or similar sound reproductions containing details, descriptions or narrative accounts of specified sex acts. The material thus made subject to restriction is defined with precision and clarity.

The "obscenity" standard is virtually the same in all three subdivisions. It must be: "posed or presented in such a manner as to exploit lust for commercial gain and * * * which would appeal to the lust of persons under the age of eighteen years or to their curiosity as to sex or to the anatomical differences between the sexes * * *."

[3–5] Appellant urges that under the statute a conviction may lie based on material which does no more than appeal to the minor's "curiosity as to sex or to the anatomical differences between the sexes." Clearly this is not so. The thrust of the statute is against pandering the obscene to minors. Material which merely appeals to the minor's "curiosity as to sex or to the anatomical differences between the sexes" without more does not fall within the ban of the statute. In addition, as already noted, the material must be "posed or presented in such a manner as to exploit lust for commercial gain." Thus the last-quoted portion appears followed by the conjunctive "and" rather than the disjunctive "or." If this were not the case, we would be presented with a different question entirely (see *People* v. *Bookcase, Inc.*, 14 N.Y. 2d 409, 252 N.Y.S. 2d 433, 201 N.E. 2d 14). But clearly the statute is not intended to and does not spill over into the area of constitutionally protected matter.

[6] By explicit provision, the obscene is distinguished from "flat and factual statements of the facts, causes, functions or purposes of the subject of the writing or presentation, such as would be found in bona fide medical or biological textbooks." The *sine qua non* of any prosecution under section 484–i goes to the purpose of the material—"posed or presented in such a manner as to exploit lust for commercial gain"—and this clearly excludes legitimate works of art, educational texts and literature with redeeming social value.

Notwithstanding the concededly imprecise definition of the term "obscene," workable standards are available. "The intrinsic nature, tendency and bent of the work determines whether it is to be banned or its vendor punished" (Chief Judge Desmond concurring in *People* v. *Richmond County News*, 9 N.Y. 2d 578, 588, 216 N.Y.S. 2d 369, 377, 175 N.E. 2d 681). Other quotes from the same opinion elaborate the same recurring theme: " 'For a book to be prohibited it is necessary that from its whole tenor the author's intention is evident of teaching the readers about sins of impurity and arousing him to libidinousness' (Noldin, De Preceptis Dei et Ecclesiae, p. 658)." " 'A pornographic book * * * is one deliberately designed to stimulate sex feelings and to act as an aphrodisiac' ([St. John-Stevas,] Obscenity and the Law, p. 2)."

And again in the recent decision by the Supreme Court in *Ginzburg* v. *United States*, 383 U.S. 463, 467, 86 S. Ct. 942, 945, 16 L. Ed. 2d 31: "each of the accused publications was originated or sold as stock in trade of the sordid business of pandering—'the business of purveying textual or graphic matter openly advertised to appeal to the erotic interest of their customers.' *Roth* v. *United States*, supra, 354 U.S. [476], at 495–496, 77 S. Ct. 1304, 1314–1315, 1 L. Ed. 2d 1498 (Warren, C.J., concurring)."

[7] By proscribing specified materials "posed or presented in such a manner as to exploit lust for commercial gain," the statute gives clear and unequivocal warning of the conduct to be avoided. We perceive nothing vague or uncertain about the statutory prohibition and thus hold that the statute provides reasonably ascertainable standards of guilt readily determinable by men of reasonable intelligence (see *Herndon* v. *Lowry*, 301 U.S. 242, 57 S. Ct. 732, 81 L. Ed. 1066).

The second point urged by appellant presents a question of constitutional law which, although raised, has never before been directly ruled on. (See *People* v. *Kahan*, 15 N.Y. 2d 311, 258 N.Y.S. 2d 391, 206 N.E. 2d 333; *People* v. *Bookcase, Inc.*, 14 N.Y. 2d 409, 418, 252 N.Y.S. 2d 433, 440, 201 N.E. 2d 14, 19, supra.) It arises from the paradoxical nature of the statute under consideration which, while proscribing certain materials to those under 18, nonetheless affords full First Amendment protection to the same material when considered with relation to those 18 years of age and older. This dichotomy, the appellant contends, requires proof of *scienter* of age as a predicate to a conviction under the statute.

[8] Section 484–i requires *scienter* of obscenity i.e., some knowledge by the bookseller of the character of the book being sold. This is the constitutional mandate of *Smith* v. *People of State of California*, 361 U.S. 147, 80 S. Ct. 215, 4 L. Ed. 2d 205. Its rationale was stated by Mr. Justice Brennan at page 153, 80 S. Ct. at page 219: "By dispensing with any requirement of knowledge of the contents of the book on the part of the seller, the ordinance tends to impose a severe limitation on the public's access to constitutionally protected matter. For if the bookseller is criminally liable without knowledge of the contents, and the ordinance fulfills its purpose, he will tend to restrict the books he sells to those he has inspected; and thus the state will have imposed a restriction upon the distribution of consititutionally protected as well as obscene literature * * * And the bookseller's burden would become the public's burden, for by restricting him the public's access to reading matter would be restricted." (See, also, *Mishkin* v. *State of New York*, 383 U.S. 502, 86 S. Ct. 958, 16 L. Ed. 2d 56.) Of course this rule has been followed in New York (*People* v. *Finkelstein*, 9 N.Y. 2d 342, 214 N.Y.S. 2d 363, 172 N.E. 2d 470).

The appellant now urges that *scienter* as to age is also a requirement of the Constitution. He contends that a statute which does not in some manner require proof of *scienter* as to the age of the purchaser, as section 484–i does not, is subject to the same unconstitutional infirmities as one not requiring proof of *scienter* as to obscenity. We cannot agree.

[9] There is a substantial difference, we think, between permitting a conviction without proof of *scienter*—i.e., some reason to know of the prohibition which attaches to the banned material—and imposing strict liability for the sale of such material to those under the proscribed age after *scienter* of obscenity exists. The First Amendment does not protect obscenity (*Roth* v. *United States*, 354 U.S. 476, 77 S. Ct. 1304, 1 L. Ed. 2d 1498) and we deal here, not with material which falls under the umbrella of protection, but with material, the dissemination of which may be controlled by the State.

The appellant's First Amendment argument, we note, seeks no protection for the infant under 18, nor in fact is it directly aimed at his own protection with reference to those in the same age category. His right of dissemination depends on a correlative right in the public to receipt of such material and we have seen that, as to those under 18, no such right exists. The right, if any, belongs to those 18 and over for, as to them, dissemination and receipt are fully protected.

[10] The point urged then is that, absent a requirement of proof of *scienter* as to age, the bookseller will tend to restrict the sale of such materials to those who he can be sure are over 17 for, so the argument goes, he would rather forego the sale than risk the possibility of conviction. Thus, he says, dissemination to those over 17 will be severely curtailed in violation of the First Amendment.

The contention, we think, lacks merit. It fails to the extent that there is a major difference between requiring the bookseller to read every piece of material which he chooses to sell and requiring him to inquire after and establish the age of those persons who will fall within the doubtful age bracket. Obviously, the number of situations in which such inquiry will be necessary will be quite few. The eye of experience easily perceives the difference between an infant and an adult. Where the area greys, inquiry is required. We have no doubt that the Legislature could affirmatively mandate such inquiry and we see no reason why the same result cannot be attained by indirection.

[11] As the Supreme Court said in *Smith* v. *People of State of California*, 361 U.S. 147, 154–155, 80 S. Ct. 215, 219, supra: "Doubtless any form of criminal obscenity statute applicable to a bookseller will induce some tendency to self-censorship and have some inhibitory effect on the dissemination of material not obscene." The question then is not one of absolutes—it is one of reasonableness in relation to the legitimate end to be obtained. We think the burden of the statute neither unduly restricts dissemination of protected matter nor unduly inhibits receipt by those who are constitutionally entitled to receipt.

[12] "Liberty of speech, and of the press, is also not an absolute right, and the State may punish its abuse" (*Near* v. *State of Minnesota* ex rel. *Olson*, 283 U.S. 697, 708, 51 S. Ct. 625, 628, 75 L. Ed. 1357; see, also, *Kingsley Books, Inc.* v. *Brown*, 354 U.S. 436, 77 S. Ct. 1325, 1 L. Ed. 2d 1469). Thus, in the final analysis, the answer to the problem must turn on whether the method adopted for coping with a public evil is kept within the narrowest bounds necessitated by the situation, so as not to impinge on the full measure of guarantees afforded by the First Amendment. We are unable to say that the method adopted by the Legislature, of imposing strict liability on the bookseller for the knowing sale of obscene matter to a minor, infringes upon his constitutional rights or tends to inhibit the free dissemination of literature. That being the case, it is not, of course, for us to determine whether strict liability is the better of two available alternatives. That is a question for the State Legislature. (Compare Penal Law, § 484–i and § 484–h.)

We have examined the appellant's other alleged assignments of error and find them to be without merit.

The judgment appealed from should be affirmed.

FULD, Judge (dissenting).

The defendant Tannenbaum was convicted of violating section 484–i of the Penal Law, prohibiting the sale of certain material to children. Since, as I have already indicated (*People* v. *Kahan*, 15 N.Y. 2d 311, 312, 258 N.Y.S. 2d 391, 392, 206 N.E. 2d 333, 334), I have no doubt that the Legislature may constitutionally act to protect youngsters from the sort of objectionable matter contained in the magazine before us (see, also, *Bookcase, Inc.* v. *Broderick*, 18 N.Y. 2d 71, 271 N.Y.S. 2d 947, 218 N.E. 2d 668), it is with some reluctance that I vote to reverse his conviction. I do not see how, if there is to be compliance with the demands of the Constitution, section 484–i may be upheld. Laudable though the purpose of the section may be, it offends essential guarantees, since it punishes the distribution of constitutionally protected communication. Indeed, it contains the same defects "in respect of its substantive definitions" as led this court in *People* v. *Kahan*, 15 N.Y. 2d 311, 312, 258 N.Y.S. 2d 391, 392, 206 N.E. 2d 333, 334, supra, to invalidate former section 484–h.

Section 484–i proscribes the sale to minors "actually or apparently under the age of eighteen years" of photographs and other representations of certain parts of the human body if such material appeals to the "curiosity" of children "as to sex or to the anatomical differences between the sexes." These criteria, standing by themselves, are patently insufficient and impermissible predicates for penal liability. Quite apart from the fact that the statute would improperly cover both married teenagers and children of tender years (cf. *Griswold* v. *State of Connecticut*, 381 U.S. 479, 485–486, 85 S. Ct. 1678, 14 L. Ed. 2d 510), it would indiscriminately punish the dissemination of material that stimulates healthy, as well as morbid, curiosity about sex and sexual differences. Taken literally, the provision would outlaw every course in sex education and feminine hygiene taught in the schools and would bar access by children to reproductions of, for example, the paintings by Michelangelo in the Sistine Chapel as well as the works of other great masters. (See *Roth* v. *United States*, 354 U.S. 476, 487, 77 S. Ct. 1304; *People* v. *Bookcase, Inc.*, 14 N.Y. 2d 409, 417–418, 252 N.Y.S. 2d 433, 439–440, 201 N.E. 2d 14, 18–19.)

It is claimed, however, that the statute is limited in its application by the requirement that the specified material be "presented in such a manner as to exploit lust for commercial gain." Even if this be so, the legislation is still too broad. Although the manner in which a work is sold may have some bearing in determining the question of obscenity "in close cases" (*Ginzburg* v. *United States*, 383 U.S. 463, 474, 86 S. Ct. 942, 16 L. Ed. 2d 31; see, also, *A Book Named "John Cleland's Memoirs of a Woman of Pleasure"* v. *Attorney General of Com. of Massachusetts*, 383 U.S. 413, 420–421, 86 S. Ct. 975, 16 L. Ed. 2d 1), the intent of the seller, or his presentation (assuming that the presentation is not itself punishable), does not deprive publications or other works which are not questionable of their constitutional protection. (See *Ginzburg* v. *United States*, 383 U.S. 463, 475–476, 86 S. Ct. 942, supra.) And yet, on its face, section 484–i punishes the sale of nonquestionable, constitutionally protected, material. What is more, the language "presented in such a manner as to exploit lust for commercial gain"—upon which the majority now relies to sustain the section's constitutionality—is the exact phrase which this court recently held unconstitutionally vague in the *Kahan* case (15 N.Y. 2d 311, 258 N.Y.S. 2d 391, 206 N.E. 2d 333, supra), and it surely has not gained precision by re-enactment. On the contrary, it is clear that the quoted provision does not sufficiently limit the reach of section 484–i and does not enable booksellers and others within its purview to know with any reasonable degree of certainty exactly what material is condemned. In this respect, the statute violates "the first essential of due process of law." (*Connally* v. *General Constr. Co.*, 269 U.S. 385, 391, 46 S. Ct. 126, 127, 70 L. Ed. 322; see, also, *Winters* v. *People of State of New York*, 333 U.S. 507, 519–520, 68 S. Ct. 665, 92 L. Ed. 840; *People* v. *Bookcase, Inc.*, 14 N.Y. 2d 409, 415–416, 252 N.Y.S. 2d 437–439, 201 N.E. 2d 14, 17–18, supra; *People* v. *Firth*, 3 N.Y. 2d 472, 474–476, 168 N.Y.S. 2d 949, 950–952, 146 N.E. 2d 682, 683–684.)

It is difficult to understand the place which section 484–i is intended to fill in the legislative scheme. Within a few days after enacting section 484–h—to replace the similarly numbered section which the court ruled invalid in *Kahan* (15 N.Y. 2d 311, 258 N.Y.S. 2d 391, 206 N.E. 2d 333, supra)—the Legislature adopted present section

484–i dealing with the identical subject, the distribution of objectionable materials to minors. The basic difference between the two pieces of legislation is that the former incorporates a number of safeguards, omitted from section 484–i, designed to prevent unconstitutional application of the law.[1] Among such safeguards are these: (1) the material must "predominantly appeal * * * to the prurient, shameful or morbid interest of minors"; (2) it must be "patently offensive" when judged in accordance with prevailing community standards for minors; and (3) it must be "utterly without redeeming social importance for minors." Section 484–i, on the other hand, does not require proof of any of those items to support prosecution of the vendor.

In a proceeding to punish the dissemination of material to the general public on the ground that it is obscene, the People must of course, prove that the material has a predominant appeal to prurient interest,[2] that it is so patently offensive as to affront current community standards of decency and that it has no redeeming social value. (See *A Book Named "John Cleland's Memoirs of a Woman of Pleasure" v. Attorney Gen. of Com. of Massachusetts*, 383 U.S. 413, 418, 86 S. Ct. 975, supra; *Mishkin v. State of New York*, 383 U.S. 502, 508–509, 86 S. Ct. 958; *Manual Enterprises v. Day*, 370 U.S. 478, 482, 82 S. Ct. 1432, 8 L. Ed. 2d 639; *Roth v. United States*, 354 U.S. 476, 489, 77 S. Ct. 1304, supra.)[3] The standards of a law punishing the sale of obscene or objectionable matter to youngsters need not be so stringent. This is so not because children may be denied the constitutional right of access to communication but, rather, because children may, in the exercise of that right, be beset by dangers that do not affect adults or, if they do, not to the same degree. (See Censorship by Age Classification, 69 Yale L.J. 141, 147–148.) The responsibility and authority of the State are for that reason greater and its powers more extensive when it legislates for the protection of children. (See *Bookcase, Inc. v. Broderick*, 18 N.Y. 2d 71, 271 N.Y.S. 2d 947, 218 N.E. 2d 668, supra; *Prince v. Commonwealth of Massachusetts*, 321 U.S. 158, 168, 64 S. Ct. 438, 88 L. Ed. 645.)[4] Be that as it may, however, it is essential that such legislation be clearly drawn and "restricted to the evil

with which it is said to deal." (*Butler v. State of Michigan*, 352 U.S. 380, 383, 77 S. Ct. 524, 526; see, also, *Winters v. People of State of New York*, 333 U.S. 507, 509 et seq., 68 S. Ct. 665, supra.) When a State statute affecting the constitutional right of free speech is broader in its application than necessary to effect its purpose, as is section 484–i, it violates the First and Fourteenth Amendments of the Federal Constitution. (See *Ashton v. Kentucky*, 384 U.S. 195, 200–201, 86 S. Ct. 1407, 16 L. Ed. 2d 469; *Butler v. State of Michigan*, 352 U.S. 380, 77 S. Ct. 524, supra; see, also, *People v. Richmond County News*, 9 N.Y. 2d 578, 584, 586, 216 N.Y.S. 2d 369, 373, 375, 175, N.E. 2d 681, 684, 685.)

Section 484–h of the Penal Law—the statute to which I have previously referred—also requires, as an additional prerequisite to prosecution, that the defendant bookseller knew or had "reason to know" that his customer was under age. The statute provides that an honest mistake in this regard is a complete defense, provided the seller made a reasonable and bona fide attempt to ascertain the buyer's age. Section 484–i, on the other hand, completely ignores this requirement of *scienter* as to age, an element which, I note, three of the four judges comprising the majority in the *Kahan* case (15 N.Y. 2d 311, 258 N.Y.S. 2d 391, 206 N.E. 2d 333, supra) explicitly declared to be indispensable in such a statute.[5] I have come on no other case which considered this precise issue but, in *Smith v. People of State of California*, 361 U.S. 147, 80 S. Ct. 215, 4 L. Ed. 2d 205, the Supreme Court held that a conviction for selling obscene literature could not be sustained unless there was some requirement as to *scienter* on the part of the seller with respect to the contents of the books involved. The court reasoned that, "if the bookseller is criminally liable without knowledge of the contents * * *, he will tend to restrict the books he sells to those he has inspected; and thus the State will have imposed a restriction upon the distribution of constitutionally protected as well as obscene literature" (361 U.S., at p. 153, 80 S. Ct., at p. 218). This rationale would seem to be equally applicable to *scienter* as to age when the youth of the buyer is an element of the crime. Absolute liability without regard to whether the bookseller was put on notice that his customer was under age would necessarily restrict and curtail the distribution of literature to adults, particularly women, whose youthful appearance belied mature years. In its efforts to protect children, the State is not privileged to so hinder the flow of information and ideas.

The People would have us analogize the sale of books to the sale of liquor for which, it is settled, there is strict accountability. (Alcoholic Beverage Control Law, § 65, subd. 1; see *People v. Werner*, 174 N.Y. 132, 134, 66 N.E. 667, 668.) The analogy is, however, imperfect and cannot stand analysis. Unlike traffic in liquor which is a privilege that the State may limit or even withdraw at any time (U.S. Const., 21st Amdt.), traffic in books—with its coextensive guarantee of freedom of expression—is a constitutionally protected right. As the Supreme Court put it

---

[1] Since section 484–h is not before us, references to it are for comparative purposes only.

[2] Where the material is designed for and primarily disseminated to a particular deviant sexual group, its prurient appeal is determined "in terms of the sexual interests of its intended and probable recipient group." (*Mishkin v. State of New York*, 383 U.S. 502, 509, 86 S. Ct. 958, 963.)

[3] In a prosecution in this State under section 1141 of the Penal Law, the People must also establish that the book or other material in question is "hardcore pornography." (*People v. Richmond County News*, 9 N.Y. 2d 578, 586–587, 216 N.Y.S. 2d 369, 375–376, 175 N. E. 2d 681, 685–686; *People v. Fritch*, 13 N.Y. 2d 119, 123, 243 N.Y.S. 2d 1, 5, 192 N.E. 2d 713, 716.) Consequently, as the Supreme Court recently observed in *Mishkin v. State of New York*, 383 U.S., at pp. 506, 508, 86 S. Ct., at pp. 962, 963, our court, by so construing section 1141, has adopted a more limited definition of "obscenity" than that adopted in the *Roth* case (354 U.S. 476, 77 S. Ct. 1304, supra).

[4] While the supervision of children's reading is best left to their parents, the knowledge that such parental control or guidance cannot always be provided justifies broader regulation in this area.

[5] As the fourth judge, I found it "unnecessary" to consider the question in view of the other and more basic reasons assigned by the court for holding the statute under review—old section 484–h—unconstitutional (15 N.Y. 2d 311, 314, 258 N.Y.S. 2d 391, 393–394, 206 N.E. 2d 333, 335).

in the *Smith* case (361 U.S. 147, 152–153, 80 S. Ct. 215, 218, supra), "There is no specific constitutional inhibition against making the distributors of food the strictest censors of their merchandise, but the constitutional guarantees of the freedom of speech and of the press stand in the way of imposing a similar requirement on the bookseller."

Finally, the argument is advanced that, if *scienter* as to age is a constitutional imperative, then, this court should read that element into the statute instead of invalidating it. (See *People* v. *Finkelstein,* 9 N.Y. 2d 342, 214 N.Y.S. 2d 363, 174 N.E. 2d 470.) But the language of section 484–i is manifestly too explicit and specific to permit such a construction. The People acknowledge that, in the clause "knowingly sells * * * to a person *actually* or *apparently* under * * * eighteen," the word "apparently" is confusing and nonsensical. It is, however, noteworthy that the exact same verbiage was used by the Legislature in prohibiting the sale of liquor to children (Alcoholic Beverage Control Law, § 65, subd. 1) and, since that wording has consistently been interpreted to impose strict criminal liability (see, e.g., *People* v. *Werner,* 174 N.Y. 132, 134, 66 N.E. 667, 668, supra; Matter of *Barnett* v. *O'Connell,* 279 App. Div. 449, 111 N.Y.S. 2d 166), there can be no doubt—as, indeed, the majority so holds—that a similar meaning was intended for section 484–i.[6]

In short, I think it clear that section 484–i, by virtue of its confusing text and its exclusion of constitutionally mandated criteria, infringes First Amendment rights and the demands of due process. (See *People* v. *Kahan,* 15 N.Y. 2d 311, 258 N.Y.S. 2d 391, 206 N.E. 2d 333, supra; see, also, Note, 34 Fordham L. Rev. 692, 705–707.) The defendant's conviction should be reversed and the information dismissed.

---

[6] In any event, even if the statute could possibly be interpreted to require proof of *scienter* as to age, a reversal is compelled in the present case since the trial court did not so read the statute. (See *People* v. *Finkelstein,* 9 N.Y. 2d 342, 214 N.Y.S. 2d 363, 174 N.E. 2d 470, supra; *Shuttlesworth* v. *City of Birmingham,* 382 U.S. 87, 91–92, 86 S. Ct. 211, 15 L. Ed. 2d 176.)

BERGAN, Judge (concurring for reversal).

In *People* v. *Kahan,* 15 N.Y. 2d 311, 258 N.Y.S. 2d 391, 206 N.E. 2d 333, this court held section 484–h of the Penal Law, as it then read, was constitutionally deficient and at the same time suggested careful draftsmanship could provide a constitutionally valid statute for the protection of young persons against obscene publications.

With the aid of District Attorneys and other specialists, a constitutionally sound statute was enacted by the Legislature by a new section 484–h (L. 1965, ch. 327) which meets the test laid down in *Kahan* and in the Federal cases. At the same session of the Legislature, for some reason not made clear, section 484–i was also enacted (L. 1965, ch. 372) which, as Judge FULD demonstrates, was so drafted as to be open to constitutional defects in important respects similar to those considered in *Kahan.* If due respect is to be paid to the prior decisions of this court, it must be held that section 484–i is defective in draftsmanship.

On pragmatic grounds if there is open to the prosecution a choice between a soundly conceived statute and a defective statute, the prosecution should rest on the strong law rather than the weak one. To insist on prosecution under section 484–i, with its patent defects in draftsmanship, unnecessarily opens up a potential field of litigation in the Federal courts with the ultimate decision on constitutionality, and hence the enforcement of this statute to protect the young, left in doubt.

This can be avoided if, consistent with *Kahan,* the section 484–i enactment is now held unconstitutional. This would, in turn, require prosecutions to be made in pursuance of the soundly drafted provision of section 484–h. I concur, also, in the views expressed by Judge Fuld.

All concur except FULD, J., who dissents in an opinion in which VAN VOORHIS and BERGAN, JJ., concur. BERGAN, J., dissenting in a separate opinion in which VAN VOORHIS, J., also concurs.

Judgment affirmed.

■ Saul Landau, *Plaintiff and Appellant,*

v.

Addison Fording, Chief of Police, Berkeley, California, Earl Berg-feld, Director, Special Investigations Bureau of the Police Department of Berkeley, California, the Police Department of the City of Berkeley, California, and the City of Berkeley, California, *Defendants and Respondents.*
Civ. 22920.

District Court of Appeals, First District, Division 2, California.

Oct. 24, 1966.

Hearing Denied Dec. 21, 1966.

Johnston & Platt, Neil F. Horton, Oakland, *Albert M. Bendich,* Berkeley, *Marshall W. Krause,* Staff Counsel, American Civil Liberties Union of Northern California, San Francisco, for appellant.

Robert T. Anderson, Robert P. Berkman, Berkeley, for respondents.

TAYLOR, Justice.

The only question presented on this appeal is whether the trial court properly found that "Un Chant d'Amour," a film written and directed by Jean Genet, was obscene within the meaning of section 311, subdivision (a), of the Penal Code and, therefore, excluded from the constitutional guarantees of freedom of speech and of the press.

The pertinent facts are not in dispute. Appellant, Saul Landau, was authorized by the New York distributor to exhibit the film in the San Francisco Bay Area. Appellant shared the proceeds derived from such exhibitions with the San Francisco Mime Troupe, an unincorporated association. Under his agreement with the New York distributor, appellant was not entitled to exhibit the film at commercial movie houses catering to a general movie audience.

Prior to the instant proceeding, appellant had exhibited the film in Santa Barbara (before an audience comprised mainly of people from the Center for the Study of Demo-cratic Institutions), in San Francisco at several private showings, at San Francisco State College, in several art movie houses in San Francisco, and in Berkeley at Stiles Hall, the University Y.M.C.A. After appellant sought to show the film a second time in Berkeley, his agent was advised by respondent Bergfeld, the Director of the Special Investigations Bureau of the Police Department, that the next time the film was exhibited in Berkeley, it would be confiscated and all persons responsible arrested. In so advis-ing the agent of appellant, respondent Bergfeld acted as the agent of the Berkeley Police Department headed by respondent Fording.

Thereafter, appellant instituted this action for declaratory relief. At the trial of the action, the trial court, in order to determine the artistic value and social importance of the film, admitted the testimony of seven expert witnesses called by appellant[1] as well as its own expert witness[2] over the repeated objections of respondents who chose not to present any evidence, but argued that the court had to base its conclusions on the film alone. All of appellant's witnesses had different views as to the theme of the film, and while contending that it was not hard-core pornography, they agreed that the film should not be shown over television or in commercial motion picture theatres.

The trial court twice viewed the film and found that to the average person applying contemporary community standards, the predominant appeal of the film as a whole was to prurient interests, i.e., a shameful and morbid interest in nudity and sex, substantially beyond customary limits of candor in the description or representation of such matters. The court further found that the film ex-plicitly and vividly revealed acts of masturbation, oral copulation, the infamous crime against nature (sodomy), voyeurism, nudity, sadism, masochism and sex and that it was "nothing more than cheap pornography calculated to promote homosexuality, perversion, and morbid sex prac-tices," that it fell "far short of dealing with homosexuality,

---

[1] The witnesses for appellant were: James Kerans, lecturer on dramatic literature and theory of the University of California, Berkeley; Irving Saraf, director of film programming for tele-vision station KQED; Mark Linenthal, assistant director of the Poetry Center of San Francisco State College; Jackson Burgess, novelist, film critic and professor of English at the University of California, Berkeley; Susan Sontag, novelist and film critic; Jan Marinissen, rehabilitation secretary of the American Friends Service Committee; Dr. Bernard L. Diamond, professor of Criminology and Law at the University of California, Berkeley.

[2] The court called as its own expert witness Dr. Charles W. Merrifield, professor of Social Science and the head of the Social and Behavioral Sciences at California State College, Hayward.

perversion, masturbation or sex from the scientific, historical or critical point of view," was completely lacking in the exposition of any ideas of social importance, and had no value as art or otherwise to give it redeeming social importance and thus obtain the benefit of the constitutional guarantees.

Accordingly, the court concluded that: the film was obscene within the meaning of section 311, subdivision (a), of the Penal Code; therefore, any exhibition or showing thereof would be in violation of section 311.2 of the Penal Code, and any person showing the film would not be able to claim as a defense that the exhibition was in aid of legitimate scientific or educational purposes within the meaning of section 311.8 of the Penal Code. This appeal is from the judgment entered in favor of respondents.

[1] While motion pictures, like other forms of expression, are within the ambit of the constitutional guarantees of freedom of speech and of the press (*Joseph Burstyn, Inc.* v. *Wilson,* 343 U.S. 495, 72 S. Ct. 777, 96 L. Ed. 1098), obscenity is not subject to those guarantees (*Roth* v. *United States* (*Alberts* v. *State of California*), 354 U.S. 476, 77 S. Ct. 1304, 1 L. Ed. 2d 1498).

Section 311, subdivision (a), of the Penal Code provides: " 'Obscene' means that to the average person, applying contemporary standards, the predominant appeal of the matter, taken as a whole, is to prurient interest, i.e., a shameful or morbid interest in nudity, sex, or excretion, which goes substantially beyond customary limits of candor in description or representation of such matters and is matter which is utterly without redeeming social importance."

The statute was the codification of the definition of obscenity announced by the U.S. Supreme Court in *Roth* v. *United States,* supra (*Zeitlin* v. *Arnebergh,* 59 Cal. 2d 901, 918–919, 31 Cal. Rptr. 800, 383 P. 2d 152). The section, in substance, prohibits "hard-core" pornography (*Zeitlin* v. *Arnebergh,* supra, at p. 919, 31 Cal. Rptr. 800, 383 P. 2d 152). The U.S. Supreme Court has not yet determined whether Roth and the subsequent cases are limited to "hard-core" pornography.[3] (*Manual Enterprises* v. *Day,* 370 U.S. 478, 489, 82 S. Ct. 1432.) In its most recent opinion dealing with a film, the U.S. Supreme Court said: "We would reiterate, however, our recognition in Roth that obscenity is excluded from the constitutional protection only because it is 'utterly without redeeming social importance,' and that 'the portrayal of sex, e.g., in art, literature and scientific works, is not itself sufficient reason to deny material the constitutional protection of freedom of speech and press.' Id. 354 U.S., at 484, 487, 72 S. Ct. at 1310. It follows that material dealing with sex in a manner that advocates ideas, *Kingsley Int'l Pictures Corp.* v. *Regents,* 360 U.S. 684, 79 S. Ct. 1362, 3 L. Ed. 2d 1512, or that has literary or scientific or artistic value or

any other form of social importance, may not be branded as obscenity and denied the constitutional protection. Nor may the constitutional status of the material be made to turn on a 'weighing' of its social importance against its prurient appeal, for a work cannot be proscribed unless it is 'utterly' without social importance." (*Jacobellis* v. *State of Ohio,* 378 U.S. 184, at p. 191, 84 S. Ct. at p. 1680.)

The Jacobellis opinion also indicated that the applicable contemporary community standard is not that of the local community where the case arises, but a national standard (supra, pp. 192–195, 84 S. Ct. 1676). The most recent decisions of the U.S. Supreme Court affirm the requirement that the elements of obscenity defined in Roth must coalesce, that there will be no balancing of "social importance" against the other elements (*Memoirs of a Woman of Pleasure* v. *Massachusetts,* 383 U.S. 413, 419, 86 S. Ct. 975), and announced a new doctrine, namely, that evidence that material was commercially exploited for the sake of prurient appeal to the exclusion of all other values would justify the conclusion that the material was utterly without redeeming social importance (*Ginzburg* v. *United States,* 383 U.S. 463, 470–473, 86 S. Ct. 969, 16 L. Ed. 2d 31; *Mishkin* v. *State of New York,* 383 U.S. 502, 86 S. Ct. 958, 16 L. Ed. 2d 56), Ginzburg and Mishkin indicating that apart from the nature of the material, the conduct of the disseminator and the commercial context in which the dissemination occurs are significant.

[2] We first dispose of respondents' contention that the trial court erred in admitting the testimony of the expert witnesses and in failing to base its conclusions solely on the viewing of the film. The question here presented is not one of fact alone but is mixed with a determination of law (*Zeitlin* v. *Arnebergh,* 59 Cal. 2d 901, at p. 910, 31 Cal. Rptr. 800, 383 P. 2d 152). The court must make an independent judgment as to whether the *material involved is constitutionally protected* (*Jacobellis* v. *State of Ohio,* supra, 378 U.S. p. 190, 84 S. Ct. p. 1679). In almost every field of the law, expert testimony is permitted on subjects concerning which the judge or administrator has no specialized competence. So here, the lower court properly received evidence to assist in the determination of contemporary community standards as well as the artistic merit and social importance of the film (*Smith* v. *People of State of California,* 361 U.S. 147, at pp. 157, 166–167, 80 S. Ct. 215, 4 L. Ed. 2d 205).

The principal question is whether "Un Chant d'Amour" satisfies the test of obscenity established by our statute and the decisions of the U.S. Supreme Court. Before exploring the "dim and uncertain" line that often separates obscenity from a constitutionally protected expression (*Bantam Books, Inc.* v. *Sullivan,* 372 U.S. 58, 66, 83 S. Ct. 631, 9 L. Ed. 2d 584), we give a description of the film which was viewed in its entirety by the justices of this court.

"Un Chant d'Amour" is an 8 mm. silent film of about 30 minutes' duration made in the style of the short silent films of the 1920's and apparently deliberately ambiguous. No music or text accompanies the film. The actors are professionals. The picture was made with artificial lighting on autochromatic film which is blind to red so that almost all of the grays are eliminated. The resultant strong contrasts between dark and light create a particularly visual impact.

The setting is an unnamed prison cell block in an unnamed place. The principal characters are a guard and

---

[3] Significantly, only in a few cases, notably *Manual Enterprises* v. *Day,* 370 U.S. 478, 82 S. Ct. 1432, 8 L. Ed. 2d 639; *Jacobellis* v. *State of Ohio,* 378 U.S. 184, 84 S. Ct. 1676, 12 L. Ed. 2d 793, and *Memoirs of a Woman of Pleasure* v. *Attorney General of Com. of Massachusetts,* 383 U.S. 413, 86 S. Ct. 975, 16 L. Ed. 2d 1, was the court ever required to apply its standards to the materials in question. In all of the other cases, because the issue before the court was the constitutionality of a particular statute, the issue of the obscenity of the material itself was either assumed or not discussed.

four prisoners. At the outset, the guard is walking outside the prison walls. Each prisoner is alone in his cell engaging in various acts of self-love and masturbation. The prisoners are also shown communicating with each other by knocking on the walls and by the passage of a straw through a hole in the thick wall between the cells, and the blowing of smoke through a straw. Two of the prisoners are clearly involved in a homosexual relationship. The guard in the course of his duties looks into each of the individual cells through peep holes and observes the prisoners. Their acts of sexual perversion and particularly the conduct of one hairy-chested prisoner arouses the guard's voyeuristic and latent homosexual tendencies. The film reaches a climatic ending in a sadistic beating of the hairy-chested prisoner by the algolagnic guard. In the last scene, the guard is again walking outside the prison wall.

In the last half of the film, the realistic scenes in the prison are interspersed with three series of brief recurring fantasy scenes that may or may not be the fantasy of some or only one of the characters. In the first series, two hands emerge from their individual barred cell windows and one hand attempts unsuccessfully to throw a garland of flowers to the other. Toward the end of the film, the garland is caught. In the second series of fantasy scenes (most likely those of one or both of the prisoners who are homosexually involved with each other), the prisoners are playing together in a romantic sunlit wood. During the third series (most likely those of the guard during the beating), two male heads are seen passionately kissing; two male torsos appear in various positions depicting fellatio, sodomy and oral copulation. The fantasy scenes increase in intensity during the film. At several points, the fantasy and the reality appear to merge; for example, in one scene, a prisoner puts on his jacket; he is next seen wearing the jacket in the sentimental woods fantasy. The portrayals of sexual perversion occupy in excess of half of the footage of the film.

It should be readily apparent from the preceding description that the film goes far beyond customary limits of candor in offensively depicting certain unorthodox sexual practices and relationships. Thus, the instant film is clearly distinguishable from *Manual Enterprises v. Day*, 370 U.S. 478, 82 S. Ct. 1432, 8 L. Ed. 2d 639,[4] and similar cases such as *Times Film Corp.* v. *City of Chicago*, 355 U.S. 35, 78 S. Ct. 115, 2 L. Ed. 2d 72, and *One, Inc.* v. *Olesen*, 355 U.S. 371, 78 S. Ct. 364, 2 L. Ed. 2d 352.[5]

[3] At the outset, we wish to make it patently clear that our conclusion is not based on the particular relationships depicted in "Un Chant d'Amour." We recognize that the constitutional guarantee is not confined to the expression of ideas that are conventional or shared by a majority (*Kingsley Pictures Corp.* v. *Regents*, 360 U.S. 684 at pp. 689, 705, 79 S. Ct. 1362, 3 L. Ed. 2d 1512). We think there is no question that there could be an effective and dramatic film about homosexuality and sadism in prisons unaccompanied by any obscene matters (*Kingsley, supra*) or that a film unquestionably obscene

under the applicable standard may not be so when limited to an audience of specialists (cf. *United States* v. *31 Photographs, Etc.* (S.D.N.Y. 1957) 156 F. Supp. 350).

But from the fact that liberty of expression by means of motion pictures is guaranteed by the First and Fourteenth Amendments, "it does not follow that the Constitution requires absolute freedom to exhibit every motion picture of every kind at all times and all places. * * * Nor does it follow that motion pictures are necessarily subject to the precise rules governing any other particular method of expression. Each method tends to present its own peculiar problems" (Burstyn, *supra*, 343 U.S. at pp. 502–503, 72 S. Ct. at p. 781).

[4] Furthermore, we think that the constitutional protection afforded does not mean that the visual impact of a motion picture as distinguished from other media can be disregarded. Films are obviously different from other forms of expression (*Freedman* v. *State of Maryland*, 380 U.S. 5, at p. 61, 85 S. Ct. 734, 13 L. Ed. 649). The significance of the motion picture medium is due to the technological features of the particular medium. The unique combination of sight and sound that characterizes a motion picture makes the ideas presented by movies comprehensible to a larger audience than is the case in any other medium except television (see materials cited in 60 Yale L.J., 696, fns. 27 and 28, at pp. 707–708, and 42 Cal. L. Rev., 122, fn. 53, at p. 128). Even in the absence of sound, movies assure a high degree of attention and retention. The focusing of an intense light on a screen and the semidarkness of the room where distracting ideas and suggestions are eliminated contribute to the forcefulness of movies and their unique effect on the audience (60 Yale L.J., *supra*, at p. 708).

[5] Because of the nature of the medium, we think a motion picture of sexual scenes may transcend the bounds of the constitutional guarantee long before a frank description of the same scenes in the written word. We cannot here disregard the potent visual impact of the movie in depicting acts of male masturbation, fellatio, oral copulation, voyeurism, nudity, sadism and sodomy without any clear reference or relation to a dominant theme. We conclude that measured in terms of the sexual interests of *its intended and probable recipient group* (*Mishkin* v. *New York*, 383 U.S. 502, 509–510, 86 S. Ct. 958, 16 L. Ed. 2d 56) or to the average person, applying contemporary standards, the predominant appeal of the film taken as a whole is to the prurient interest.[6]

We turn next, therefore, to the more difficult and delicate question of whether there is present in the film any matter of social importance (including artistic merit) that would, as appellant argues, recover for the film its protection as a constitutionally protected utterance (*Zeitlin* v. *Arnebergh*, *supra*, 59 Cal. 2d at p. 920, 31 Cal. Rptr. 800, 383 P. 2d 152).

[6] The fact that the writer, director and producer of the film, Jean Genet, is a French writer of renown does not, as appellant argues, settle the crucial question of whether the film contains sufficient artistic merit. Great artists can create the type of "hard-core" pornography proscribed by our statute. Often, as in *Zeitlin* v. *Arnebergh, supra*, the technical excellence and artistic merit

---

[4] Wherein the court held that offensive material admittedly intended to appeal to homosexuals was not obscene because the representation and descriptions did not go "substantially beyond customary limits of candor" (at p. 486, 82 S. Ct., at p. 1436).

[5] Both of these were per curiam reversals after Roth. The nature of the materials is described by brief quotations from the lower court opinions in *Zeitlin* v. *Arnebergh*, *supra*, footnote 22, 59 Cal. 2d at page 915, 31 Cal. Rptr. 809, 383 P. 2d 161.

[6] We note that appellant concedes that the U.S. Court's rejection of an "average man" prurient appeal test in Mishkin undercuts a substantial portion of his argument.

redeem the work despite its obscene content. Unfortunately, that is not the case here. Even appellant's own literary witness admitted that the film was made at the beginning of Genet's career as a playwright and is a transitional work in his development from a novelist into a dramatist. The witness also testified that "Un Chant d'Amour" is much less complicated than his later works and is not easily recognizable as a work of Genet. The artistic merit of Genet's other works does not provide a carte blanche when he chooses to venture into the fields covered by the film. As we indicated above, the technical aspects of the motion picture medium simply increase the burden on the artist and add a different and far more sensitive dimension.

The fact that there is no text or dialogue accompanying the film contributes to its ambiguity and the absence of a dominant theme. We think it a significant indication of the film's failure that none of the witnesses produced could agree on its dominant theme.[7] We note that in Jacobellis, supra, in holding that the film "The Lovers" was not obscene, the court had no problem of ascertaining the theme or plot of the film. The same clear indication of a particular story line along with the artistic necessity of the objectionable scenes was present in the decisions upholding the film "Lady Chatterley's Lover" (Kingsley, supra) and "Anatomy of a Murder" (*Columbia Pictures Corporation v. City of Chicago* (N.D. Ill. 1959) 184 F. Supp. 817). A plot and some attempt at character development was apparently also clearly discernible in *Times Film Corporaion v. City of Chicago*, supra, and *One, Inc. v. Olesen*, supra.

Here the erotic scenes recur with increasing intensity and without direction toward any well-defined, wholesome idea, through scene after scene. The various sexual acts are graphically pictured or emphatically suggested with nothing omitted except those sexual consummations which are plainly suggested but meaningfully omitted and thus by the very fact of omission emphasized. If the film was intended as an artistic portrayal, it clearly failed in its endeavor. The fantasy portions of the film portray purely physical acts of increasing intensity without any contribution to character or plot development.[8] Significantly, it

was the very absence of such treatment of sex that led our Supreme Court to conclude that "Tropic of Cancer" was not the hard-core pornography proscribed by section 311, subdivision (a) of the Penal Code (*Zeitlin v. Arnebergh*, supra, 59 Cal. 2d p. 922, 31 Cal. Rptr. p. 813, 383 P. 2d p. 165). In our opinion, the production does nothing more than depict a number of disjointed scenes treating sex in a shocking, morbid and shameful manner and is devoid of artistic merit.

However, as Kingsley pointed out, the constitutional guarantee does not extend only to materials artistically expressed. We are left, therefore, with the question of whether the film contains any other concepts of redeeming social importance. As indicated, the fact that the film is silent and there is no text or explanation to accompany it, contributes to its ambiguity. Precisely because of this ambiguity and lack of ascertainable dominant theme, the film is clearly not a documentary of prison life or a scientific study of prison psychology. While some of appellant's witnesses indicated that the film might reflect on the need for prison reform, all agreed that it should not be shown on television or in a commercial motion picture theatre except possibly with other documentaries.[9] Dr. Diamond stated: "Like anything else, if it were handled indiscriminately, carelessly, for commercial purposes, I think it might be very bad. Q. So it would lose its effectiveness in your opinion if it were shown indiscriminately? A. I don't think it would lose its effectiveness for certain groups of people, but the effect on other groups might outweigh its effectiveness and is not the only device available for prison reform." Dr. Merrifield also agreed that the film could be harmful.

[7] The record indicates that the film, although shown to an audience somewhat more limited than the general motion picture audience, was commercially exploited and appellant earned substantial amounts from its exhibitions in the Bay Area. Applying the criteria recently set forth in *Ginzburg v. United States*, supra, we are, therefore, further propelled toward the conclusion that it is utterly without redeeming social importance and that it meets all of the requirements set forth in section 311, subdivision (a), of the Penal Code. As Mr. Justice Stewart noted in *Jacobellis v. State of Ohio*, supra, 378 U.S. at page 197, 84 S. Ct. at page 1683, hard-core pornography is hard to define but he "knew it when I see it." We think we have seen it in "Un Chant d'Amour." It is nothing more than hard-core pornography and should be banned.

The judgment is affirmed.

SHOEMAKER, P.J., and AGEE, J., concur.

Hearing denied; PETERS, TOBRINER, and MOSK, JJ., dissenting.

---

[7] Some suggested the effect of isolation and imprisonment upon both prisoners and guards; another, an attempt at penal improvement; others, a comment on the isolated human condition and the difficulties of human contact.

[8] The presentation of most of the erotic material in the fantasy scenes is significant. As one eminent authority, the noted anthropologist, Margaret Mead, stated: "We may define pornography, cross-culturally, as words or acts or representations that are calculated to stimulate sex feelings independent of the presence of another loved and chosen human being. *The character of the daydream as distinct from reality is an essential element in pornography.* True, the adolescent may take a description of a real event and turn it into a daydream, the vendor of pornography may represent a medical book as full of daydream material, but the material of true pornography is compounded of daydreams themselves, composed without regard for any given reader or looker, to stimulate and titillate. It bears the signature of nonparticipation—of the dreaming adolescent, the frightened, the impotent, the bored and sated, the senile, desperately concentrating on unusualness, on drawing that which is not usually drawn, writing words on a plaster wall, shifting scenes and actors about, to feed an impulse that has no object: no object either because the adolescent is not yet old enough to seek sexual partners, or because the recipient of the pornography

has lost the precious power of spontaneous sexual feeling." (Mead, Sex and Censorship in Contemporary Society, New World Writing, Third Mentor Selection 18 (1953) quoted in Lockhart and McClure, The Law of Obscenity and the Constitution, 38 Minnesota Law Review, 295, fn. 182 at pp. 321–322; emphasis supplied.)

[9] As the Federal Government has occupied the field of radio and television to the exclusion of the states (*Allen B. Dumont Laboratories v. Carroll* (3d Cir. 1950) 184 F. 2d 153), this testimony is not pertinent except as an indication that the film was suitable only for a limited audience.

■ Landau

v.

Fording, Chief of Police, *et al.*

ON PETITION FOR WRIT OF CERTIORARI TO THE COURT OF APPEAL OF CALIFORNIA, FIRST APPELLATE DISTRICT.

No. 1164. Decided June 12, 1967.

Certiorari granted; 245 Cal. App. 2d 820. 54 Cal. Rptr. 177, affirmed.

Marshall W. Krause for petitioner.
Robert T. Anderson and *Robert P. Berkman* for respondents.

Per Curiam.

The petition for a writ of certiorari is granted and the judgment of the Court of Appeal of California, First Appellate District, is affirmed.

Mr. Justice Black, Mr. Justice Douglas, Mr. Justice Stewart, and Mr. Justice Fortas would grant the petition and reverse.

■ Robert Redrup, *Petitioner,*

v.

State of New York.

3

William L. Austin, *Petitioner,*

v.

State of Kentucky.

16

Gent et al., *Appellants,*

v.

State of Arkansas.

50

ON APPEAL FROM THE SUPREME COURT OF ARKANSAS.

On Writ of Certiorari to the Appellate Term of the Supreme Court of New York, First Judicial Department.

On Writ of Certiorari to the Circuit Court of McCracken County, State of Kentucky.

On Appeal from the Supreme Court of Arkansas.

[May 8, 1967.]

Per Curiam.

These three cases arise from a recurring conflict—the conflict between asserted state power to suppress the distribution of books and magazines through criminal or civil proceedings, and the guarantees of the First and Fourteenth Amendments of the United States Constitution.

I.

In No. 3, *Redrup* v. *New York*, the petitioner was a clerk at a New York City newsstand. A plainclothes patrolman approached the newsstand, saw two paperback books on a rack—*Lust Pool*, and *Shame Agent*—and asked for them by name. The petitioner handed him the books and collected the price of $1.65. As a result of this transaction, the petitioner was charged in the New York City Criminal Court with violating a state criminal law.[1] He was convicted, and the conviction was affirmed on appeal.

In No. 16, *Austin* v. *Kentucky*, the petitioner owned and operated a retail bookstore and newsstand in Paducah, Kentucky. A woman resident of Paducah purchased two magazines from a salesgirl in the petitioner's store, after asking for them by name—*High Heels*, and *Spree*. As a result of this transaction the petitioner stands convicted in the Kentucky courts for violating a criminal law of that State.[2]

In No. 50, *Gent* v. *Arkansas*, the prosecuting attorney of the Eleventh Judicial District of Arkansas brought a civil proceeding under a state statute,[3] to have certain issues of various magazines declared obscene, to enjoin their distribution and to obtain a judgment ordering their surrender and destruction. The magazines proceeded against were: *Gent, Swank, Bachelor, Modern Man, Cavalcade, Gentleman, Ace,* and *Sir*. The County Chancery Court entered the requested judgment after a trial with an advisory jury, and the Supreme Court of Arkansas affirmed, with minor modifications.[4]

In none of the cases was there a claim that the statute in question reflected a specific and limited state concern for juveniles. See *Prince* v. *Massachusetts*, 321 U.S. 158; cf. *Butler* v. *Michigan*, 352 U.S. 380. In none was there any suggestion of an assault upon individual privacy by publication in a manner so obtrusive as to make it impossible for an unwilling individual to avoid exposure to it. Cf. *Breard* v. *Alexandria*, 341 U.S. 622; *Public Utilities Comm'n* v. *Pollak*, 343 U.S. 451. And in none was there evidence of the sort of "pandering" which the Court found significant in *Ginzburg* v. *United States*, 383 U.S. 463.

II.

The Court originally limited review in these cases to certain particularized questions, upon the hypothesis that the material involved in each case was of a character

described as "obscene in the constitutional sense" in *Memoirs* v. *Massachusetts*, 383 U.S. 413, 418.[5] But we have concluded that the hypothesis upon which the Court originally proceeded was invalid, and accordingly that the cases can and should be decided upon a common and controlling fundamental constitutional basis, without prejudice to the questions upon which review was originally granted. We have concluded, in short, that the distribution of the publications in each of these cases is protected by the First and Fourteenth Amendments from governmental suppression, whether criminal or civil, *in personam* or *in rem*.[6]

Two members of the Court have consistently adhered to the view that a State is utterly without power to suppress, control, or punish the distribution of any writings or pictures upon the ground of their "obscenity."[7] A third has held to the opinion that a State's power in this area is narrowly limited to a distinct and clearly identifiable class of material.[8] Others have subscribed to a not dissimilar standard, holding that a State may not constitutionally inhibit the distribution of literary material as obscene unless "(a) the dominant theme of the material taken as a whole appeals to a prurient interest in sex; (b) the material is patently offensive because it affronts contemporary community standards relating to the description or representation of sexual matters; and (c) the material is utterly without redeeming social value," emphasizing that the "three elements must coalesce," and that no such material can "be proscribed unless it is found to be *utterly* without redeeming social value." *Memoirs* v. *Massachusetts*, 383 U.S. 413, 418–419. Another Justice has not viewed the "social value" element as an independent factor in the judgment of obscenity. *Id.*, at 460–462 (dissenting opinion).

Whichever of these constitutional views is brought to bear upon the cases before us, it is clear that the judgments cannot stand. Accordingly, the judgment in each case is reversed.

It is so ordered.

---

[1] N.Y. Penal Law § 1141 (1).

[2] Ky. Rev. Stat. § 436.100. The Kentucky Court of Appeals denied plenary review of the petitioner's conviction, the Chief Justice dissenting. 386 S.W. 2d 270.

[3] Ark. Stat. Ann. §§ 41–2713 to 41–2728.

[4] 239 Ark. 474, 393 S.W. 2d 219.

[5] *Redrup* v. *New York*, 384 U.S. 916; *Austin* v. *Kentucky*, 384 U.S. 916; *Gent* v. *Arkansas*, 384 U.S. 937.

[6] In each of the cases before us, the contention that the publications involved were basically protected by the First and Fourteenth Amendments was timely but unsuccessfully asserted in the state proceedings. In each of these cases, this contention was properly and explicitly presented for review here.

[7] See *Ginzburg* v. *United States*, 383 U.S. 463, 476, 482 (dissenting opinions); *Jacobellis* v. *Ohio*, 378 U.S. 184, 196 (concurring opinion); *Roth* v. *United States*, 354 U.S. 476, 508 (dissenting opinion).

[8] See *Ginzburg* v. *United States*, 383 U.S. 463, 499, and n. 3 (dissenting opinion). See also Magrath, The Obscenity Cases: Grapes of Roth, 1966 Supreme Court Review 7, 69–77.

Robert Redrup, *Petitioner,*

v.

State of New York.

3

William L. Austin, *Petitioner,*

v.

State of Kentucky.

16

Gent et al., *Appellants,*

v.

State of Arkansas.

50

On Writ of Certiorari to the Appellate Term of the Supreme Court of New York, First Judicial Department.

On Writ of Certiorari to the Circuit Court of McCracken County, State of Kentucky.

ON APPEAL FROM THE SUPREME COURT OF ARKANSAS.

[May 8, 1967.]

MR. JUSTICE HARLAN, whom MR. JUSTICE CLARK, joins, dissenting.

Two of these cases, *Redrup* v. *New York* and *Austin* v. *Kentucky*, were taken to consider the standards governing the application of the *scienter* requirement announced in *Smith* v. *California,* 361 U.S. 147, for obscenity prosecutions. There it was held that a defendant criminally charged with purveying obscene material must be shown to have had some kind of knowledge of the character of such material; the quality of that knowledge, however, was not defined. The third case, *Gent* v. *Arkansas,* was taken to consider the validity of a comprehensive Arkansas anti-obscenity statute, in light of the doctrines of "vagueness" and "prior restraint." The writs of certiorari in *Redrup* and *Austin,* and the notation of probable jurisdiction in *Gent,* were respectively limited to these issues, thus laying aside, for the purposes of these cases, the permissibility of the state determinations as to the obscenity of the challenged publications. Accordingly the obscenity *vel non* of these

publications was not discussed in the briefs or oral arguments of any of the parties.

The three cases were argued together at the beginning of this Term. Today, the Court rules that the materials could not constitutionally be adjudged obscene by the States, thus rendering adjudication of the other issues unnecessary. In short, the Court disposes of the cases on the issue that was deliberately excluded from review, and refuses to pass on the questions that brought the cases here.

In my opinion these dispositions do not reflect well on the processes of the Court, and I think the issues for which the cases were taken should be decided. Failing that, I prefer to cast my vote to dismiss the writs in *Redrup* and *Austin* as improvidently granted and, in the circumstances, to dismiss the appeal in *Gent* for lack of a substantial federal question. I deem it more appropriate to defer an expression of my own views on the questions brought here until an occasion when the Court is prepared to come to grips with such issues.

■ Jacobs *et al.*

v.

New York.

APPEAL FROM THE APPELLATE TERM OF THE SUPREME COURT OF NEW YORK, FIRST JUDICIAL DEPARTMENT.

No. 660. Decided June 12, 1967.

Emile Z. Berman for appellants.
Frank S. Hogan for appellee.
Edward De Grazia and *John R. Kramer* for the National Students Association, as *amicus curiae*, in support of appellants.

PER CURIAM.

The motion to dismiss is granted and the appeal is dismissed as moot.

MR. JUSTICE BRENNAN would affirm the judgment of the lower court.

MR. JUSTICE FORTAS would reverse the judgment of the lower court.

MR. CHIEF JUSTICE WARREN, dissenting.

I dissent from the Court's dismissal of this appeal as moot. These appellants were convicted by a three-judge bench of the Criminal Court of New York City of violating § 1141 of the Penal Law of New York, which provides in pertinent part:

"1. A *person who sells, lends, gives away, distributes, shows or transmutes . . . any obscene, lewd, lascivious, filthy, indecent, sadistic, masochistic . . . motion picture film . . . which may or may not require mechanical or other means to be transmuted into auditory, visual or sensory representations of such character . . . .*
"2. . . . *Is guilty of a misdemeanor, and, upon conviction, shall be sentenced to not less than ten days nor more than one year imprisonment . . . ."*

On August 7, 1964, appellants Jacobs and Mekas were sentenced to 60 days in the New York City Workhouse, with execution of the sentence suspended. Appellant Karpf received a suspended sentence.

In dismissing this appeal for mootness, the Court apparently bases its action upon the fact that under New York law, the maximum time during which appellants could have had their suspended sentences revoked and replaced by prison sentences was one year from the date of the original sentences. N.Y. Code Crim. Proc. § 470–a. The State argues that this appeal is moot because more than one year has run from August 7, 1964, and appellants are under no present threat of imprisonment. Moreover, the State contends that neither New York law nor federal law imposes any further penalty for conviction of the misdemeanor involved in this case.

I cannot accept this argument. The practical result of the Court's willingness to dismiss this appeal as moot is that States may insulate their convictions under laws raising constitutional questions from review on the merits by this Court by the simple expedient of a suspended sentence where a time limit for the imposition of an executed sentence is short enough to run before an appeal can be taken to this Court. A State could thus keep a person under continual threat of imprisonment without review by this Court of any constitutional objections to his convictions by a continued series of convictions and suspended sentences. By the time any single conviction could be brought to this Court, the defendant's jeopardy under that particular sentence would be concluded. However, the defendant could still be oppressed by subsequent suspended sentences which would themselves be unreviewable by the time the defendant could bring his case to this Court. I cannot agree that the commands of the United States Constitution can be this easily suspended by the States. Moreover, this power, which under this dismissal can be exercised without constitutional restraint, gives the State a weapon which might in some cases be used to suppress constitutionally protected conduct. After a person has been convicted under a statute which limits his right of expression, his subsequent conduct will be significantly chilled by the conviction on his record. Particularly where, as in this case, the conviction stems from conduct which is directly in line with appellants' profession as movie exhibitors, they may justifiably fear that any future conduct running the danger of infringing the statute will be more harshly treated because of the previous unreviewed conviction. Who can doubt that a judge's reaction to another conviction under § 1141 of the New York Penal Law would not be colored by the fact of a prior conviction? For example, these appellants argue in this case that they should not be constitutionally convicted because their conduct demonstrates their good-faith belief that they were not exhibiting obscene material. They may have felt that even if a state judge did not accept their constitutional argument based on their good faith, he might at least give the appellants the most lenient sentence. However, once they have been convicted and have been unable to have the constitutionality of the conviction passed upon by this

Court, their situation is radically different. Even if they have been convicted of engaging in what this Court might finally determine to be constitutionally protected conduct, they are likely to order their future conduct on the basis of the assumed validity of previous conviction. When we are dealing with First Amendment freedoms, freedoms we have held require breathing space to survive, see *New York Times Co.* v. *Sullivan,* 376 U.S. 254 (1964), *NAACP* v. *Button,* 371 U.S. 415 (1963), we should be extremely slow to accept mootness doctrines which grant the States an unreviewable power to suppress modes of expression.

I believe the Court is straining the mootness doctrine and in doing so is bypassing important constitutional questions in the obscenity area which this Court has an obligation to decide. In this case, we are presented with an opportunity for injecting some clarity into the problem of what constitutes obscenity, a problem which has become increasingly muddled and difficult for the federal and state courts and legislatures to understand since we first defined the reach of the First Amendment in this area in *Roth* v. *United States,* 354 U.S. 476 (1957). The questions presented are not easy, but I am sure that it is our constitutional duty to grapple with them and to present to the country an understandable statement of how far the First Amendment restricts legislative attempts to control obscene material. Similarly, the Court dismisses as moot the appeal in No. 993, *Tannenbaum* v. *New York, post,* p. 439, because a jail sentence was suspended and a fine has been paid. That case raises the important question never addressed by this Court of the constitutionality of "variable obscenity" laws which restrict the sale of obscene materials to minors on the basis of definitions of obscenity drawn expressly with minors in mind. While I do not express a view as to the merits of this question, I think the great importance of the question to the Nation, and the responsibility of this Court to elaborate the scope and meaning of the First Amendment, should require the Court to note jurisdiction and hear the case on the merits. A similar strained conception of mootness resulting in a failure of decision on the merits recalls the Court's avoidance of a constitutional decision in the short *per curiam* in *Parker* v. *Ellis,* 362 U.S. 574 (1960). I expressed the belief in that case, which I reaffirm here, that this Court has an obligation to decide, and not avoid, important constitutional questions which are concretely presented to it by litigants having adverse interests. If Congress had intended that our jurisdiction be discretionary in all cases, it would not have differentiated in the statutes defining our appellate jurisdiction between appeals and writs of certiorari.

As MR. JUSTICE DOUGLAS points out in his dissent to the dismissal for mootness in this case, there are additional reasons why this case should not be deemed moot. Appellants' film and equipment were seized by the police at the time of their arrests. Of course, if appellants were not convicted, or if their convictions were reversed, they would be entitled under state law to the return of their property. On the other hand, our dismissal leaves these convictions unchallenged, and appellants' film and equipment will be subject to forfeiture. N.Y. Penal Law § 1141–c, N.Y. Code Crim. Proc. § 22–a. Thus, appellants have a clear pecuniary interest in the outcome of this appeal. Appellants also point to the likelihood that these convictions will impair their ability to secure a license to operate a motion picture theater. Under the Administrative Code of the City of New York, which establishes a comprehensive system of licensing procedures, the Department of Licenses is charged with assuring that motion picture theatres are not offensive to "public morals." § B32–26.0. These convictions will surely affect appellants' ability to procure a license to exhibit motion pictures in the future.

Since I believe this appeal cannot be dismissed as moot, I believe the Court must consider the case on the merits. I am satisfied that these convictions should be affirmed. Under the standards set out by the Court in *Roth* v. *United States,* 354 U.S. 476 (1957), this film is not within the protections of the First Amendment. We formulated the test in that case as being whether the material was utterly without social value, whether it went substantially beyond customary limits of candor in representing sexual matters, and whether "to the average person, applying contemporary community standards, the dominant theme of the material taken as a whole appeals to prurient interest." *Id.,* at 489. This film falls outside the range of expression protected by the First Amendment according to the criteria set out in *Roth.*

For the reasons I have given, I would consider this appeal on the merits and I would affirm these convictions.

MR. JUSTICE DOUGLAS, dissenting.

We have here two cases in which appellants have been convicted under a State's obscenity statutes. In No. 660, appellants were convicted of showing an allegedly obscene motion picture. They were given suspended sentences and the time during which the suspended sentences could have been revoked and prison sentences imposed has now passed. In No. 993, *post,* p. 439, appellant was convicted of selling an allegedly obscene magazine to a person under 18. He was sentenced to 30 days and fined $100. The fine has been paid and the sentence was suspended. The First Amendment issues in these cases are substantial. Nonetheless, they are dismissed as moot because the appellants are no longer subject to the custody of the State and in No. 993 the fine has been paid. The Court apparently believes this result to be commanded by our prior cases. I disagree.

The mootness doctrine is expressive of the need for antagonistic parties whose vigorous argument will sharpen the issues. It is part of the "case or controversy" requirement of Article III. *St. Pierre* v. *United States,* 419 U.S. 41, 42. But it is not so rigid as to defeat substantial rights, nor so inflexible as to prevent this Court from facing serious constitutional questions. Thus, we have held that service of a sentence does not render a case moot where the conviction, if allowed to stand, will result in collateral disabilities such as a loss of civil rights. *Fiswick* v. *United States,* 329 U.S. 211; *United States* v. *Morgan,* 346 U.S. 502.

In the present cases, we are in the area of the First Amendment. Over and over again we have stressed that First Amendment rights need "breathing space to survive" (*NAACP* v. *Button,* 371 U.S. 415, 433); and we have been watchful lest coercive measures exercise an *in terrorem* effect which intimidates people from exercising their First Amendment rights. See, e.g., *Speiser* v. *Randall,* 357 U.S. 513; *NAACP* v. *Button, supra; Keyishian* v. *Board of Regents,* 385 U.S. 589. We have been mindful that "[t]he threat of sanctions may deter . . . almost as potently as the actual application of sanctions." *NAACP* v. *Button, supra,* at 433. Accordingly, we have modified traditional rules of standing and prematurity to fit the peculiarities necessary to ensure adequate protection of First Amendment rights. See *Dombrowski* v. *Pfister*, 380 U.S. 479.

The *in terrorem* effect of denying review to cases such as these because sentences have been suspended or short sentences served is obvious. Sentences for violations of obscenity statutes are often suspended and generally short. If those convicted cannot obtain ultimate review of such convictions, merely because of the shortness of the sentence and the slowness of the judicial process, many will choose to comply with what may be an invalid statute. Many may steer wide and refrain from showing or selling protected material. First Amendment rights are thus stifled. If a practice such as this were shown to exist, its *in terrorem* effect on all publishers would certainly be sufficiently clear as to give any of them standing to bring an action for declaratory relief. Its *in terrorem* effect on a publisher who has actually felt the harsh impact of the law is so obvious that its continuing deterrent effect upon him should keep his case from becoming moot.

In No. 660, appellants' film and motion picture equipment were seized at the time of their arrest. They argue that at the conclusion of this proceeding they can bring an action to recover possession of the film and equipment. If their convictions are allowed to stand, along with the holding that the film is obscene, the film and equipment will be subject to forfeiture. They also argue that the department of licenses may suspend their motion picture theater license on the ground that they have shown obscene pictures. Perhaps they could relitigate the question of the film's obscenity in such proceedings. That is, of course, a matter of state law. But if appellants are correct, the convictions may entail sufficient collateral consequences that distinguish them from *St. Pierre* v. *United States, supra,* and bring them within the *Fiswick* and *Morgan* cases.

The questions of mootness loom so large in the setting of the First Amendment that they should at least be briefed and argued.

■ Lillian M. Hudson, Esther Sesman, Mariaelena Clark and Abe Attenson, *Appellants,*

v.

United States, *Appellee.*

No. 4269

Abe Attenson, Hanna Bernstein and Mary A. Tobin, *Appellants,*

v.

United States, *Appellee.*

Appeals from the District of Columbia

Court of General Sessions

(Argued July 17, 1967. Decided November 14, 1967)

John T. Bonner for appellants.

Geoffrey M. Alprin, Assistant United States Attorney, with whom *David G. Bress,* United States Attorney, *Frank Q. Nebeker* and *Lawrence Lippe,* Assistant United States Attorneys, were on the brief, for appellee.

Before Hood, Chief Judge, and Myers and Kelly, Associate Judges.

Myers *Associate Judge:* Appellants[1] were convicted of staging obscene shows in the District of Columbia in violation of § 22–2001 D.C. Code (1961 ed.).[2]

Although in obscenity cases, as in all other cases relating to First Amendment guarantees of free expression, it is usually the duty of an appellate court to review the evidence from the trial court for the purpose of making "an independent constitutional judgment on the facts of the case as to whether the material involved is constitutionally protected," *Jacobellis* v. *Ohio,* 378 U.S. 184, 190 (1964),[3] in view of our disposition of the present appeal, we find it unnecessary to consider the factual issues supporting the obscenity charge.

In 1957, the United States Supreme Court in *Roth* v. *United States,* 354 U.S. 476, first announced that the constitutional test of "obscenity" is whether, to the average person applying "contemporary community standards," the dominant theme of the material as a whole appeals to a prurient interest in sex. Under this test, "three

---

[1] Attenson is the manager of a local burlesque theater; the other appellants are dancers who allegedly performed strip-tease acts with his knowledge and approval.

[2] "Whoever . . . gives or participates in, or by bill, poster, or otherwise advertises, any public exhibition, show, performance, or play containing obscene, indecent, or lascivious language, postures, or suggestions, or otherwise offending public decency, shall be fined . . . ."

[3] As Mr. Justice Brennan pointed out, the obligation of the appellate court cannot properly be labeled a "censor" or "supercensor" function, since its only purpose is to test a challenged obscenity judgment against First Amendment guarantees.

elements must coalesce: it must be established that (a) the dominant theme of the material taken as a whole appeals to a prurient interest in sex, (b) the material is patently offensive because it affronts contemporary community standards relating to the description or representation of sexual matters; and (c) the material is utterly without redeeming social value." *Memoirs* v. *Massachusetts,* 383 U.S. 413, 418 (1966).[4]

The only question before us is whether the trial court properly applied that part of the definition dealing with "contemporary community standards." Specifically, the issues are: (1) does the word "community" refer to a "*local* community" or to the nation as a whole and (2) is the Government required to offer competent evidence to prove "contemporary standards" in the community.

I

We are of the opinion that the trial court correctly instructed the jury that to determine whether a show offends contemporary community standards of decency, reference must be made to community standards prevailing in the nation generally and not to the local standards of any specific state, county or city. To choose the mores of a locality as the standard by which permissible limits of candor and conduct are measured could effectively deny citizens of one jurisdiction access to entertainment generally available in other communities and cities in this country. *Manual Enterprises, Inc.* v. *Day,* 370 U.S. 478, 488 (1962).

As used in statutory language, the word "obscene" is intended to have a meaning that varies from time to time as general notions of decency in attire and conduct of exhibitions for public entertainment tend to change. It is not meant to "embalm the precise morals of an age or place." *United States* v. *Kennerly,* 209 F. 119, 121 (S.D.N.Y. 1913). On the other hand, at any one time, the meaning is not intended to vary from place to place. In *Jacobellis* v. *Ohio, supra,* Mr. Justice Brennan, in delivering the opinion, stated:

"The Court has explicitly refused to tolerate a result whereby 'the constitutional limits of free expression in the Nation would vary with state lines,' Pennekamp v. Florida, . . . 328 U.S. at 335." at 194.

"We do not see how any 'local' definition of the 'community' could properly be employed in delineating the area of expression that is protected by the Federal Constitution. . . ." at 193.

"We thus reaffirm the position taken in Roth to the effect that the constitutional status of an allegedly obscene work must be determined on the basis of a national standard. It is, after all, a national Constitution we are expounding." at 195.

Although it is not clear that Mr. Justice Brennan was speaking for a majority of the court in this part of the

opinion[5] and the question may not have been squarely decided, we find the reasoning in that opinion most persuasive. Accordingly, we rule that, in the District of Columbia, community standards in obscenity cases shall be determined by reference to contemporary community standards in the nation as a whole.

II

In opposing this appeal, the Government contends that whether the relevant community standards are local or national, it is not necessary for the Government to introduce any evidence to prove these standards. It is strongly urged that these standards may be determined solely in the light of the judge's or jurors' own experience and common sense. This may be true where "hard-core pornography," which is so offensive that "no conceivable community standard . . . would permit its showing," is involved. *Womack* v. *United States,* 111 U.S. App. D.C. 8, 10, 294 F. 2d 204, 206 (1961). The case at bar, however, does not fall into that category, and knowledge of contemporary community standards, especially on a nationwide basis, is no more available to the trier of facts than the innumerable other facts which must normally be proved in an evidentiary way in many other trials.

Where the material involved is not patently obscene, neither a judge nor twelve local jurors chosen at random are capable of determining the standards of tolerance prevalent in the nation generally without first being given some competent evidence of what those standards are. *United States* v. *Klaw,* 350 F. 2d 155, 168 n. 14 (2d Cir. 1965). A guilty verdict in an obscenity trial should not be a legal expression of revulsion by the local community from which the jury is drawn. If a case is submitted to the trier of fact without first establishing the community standards by competent evidence to which the trier may refer, the verdict at best will be based on the prevailing customs in a limited geographical area and, at worst, upon the "subjective reflection of taste or moral outlook of individual jurors or individual judges. . . . [T]he determination of obscenity is for the juror or judge, not on the basis of his personal upbringing or restricted reflection or the particular experience of life, but on the basis of 'contemporary community standards.' " *Smith* v. *California,* 361 U.S. 147, 165 (1959), concurring opinion of Mr. Justice Frankfurter. These standards must be established by relevant evidence at trial.[6]

Since the prosecution in the present case had the burden of proving relevant community standards prevailing in the nation generally and elected not to do so, we hold that the Government failed to establish an essential element of the crime charged and the verdicts of guilty were therefore in error.

---

[4] In addition to applying to printed matter, such as books and photographs, the same standards are also extended to motion pictures, plays and burlesque shows, which are forms of speech and *prima facie* expressions protected by the First Amendment. *Joseph Burstyn, Inc.* v. *Wilson,* 343 U.S. 495 (1952) [motion picture]; *Adams Theatre Co.* v. *Keenan,* 12 N.J. 267, 96 A. 2d 519 (1953) [burlesque show]; *Adams Newark Theatre Co.* v. *City of Newark,* 22 N.J. 472, 126 A. 2d 340 (1956) [burlesque show].

[5] While six justices concurred in the result, Mr. Justice Brennan's opinion represents his own view and that of Mr. Justice Goldberg. The two concurring opinions do not address themselves squarely to the issue in this case. See also the dissenting opinion of Mr. Justice Black in *Ginzburg* v. *United States,* 383 U.S. 463, 480 (1966).

[6] Insofar as any language in *Clarke* v. *United States,* D.C. Mun. App., 160 A. 2d 97 (1960) or in *Yankowitz* v. *United States,* D.C. Mun. App., 182 A. 2d 889 (1962), could be construed to establish a local community standard or to relieve the government of its duty to prove prevailing community standards, it is overruled.

Reversed and remanded with directions to enter judgments of acquittal.

HOOD, *Chief Judge,* dissenting: Appellants were charged with giving and participating in an obscene exhibition.[1] The exhibition or performance was described at trial by appellants' counsel as "a lusty, busty, burlesque show, in the finest traditions of our country." A reading of the record convinces me that the exhibition was neither legitimate nor traditional burlesque, but was what has been called "modern burlesque," described by one author in the following manner:

*a plotless musical entertainment consisting of a series of unrelated episodes and dances, all with the purpose of depicting or suggesting sexual subjects or objects. The one outstanding characteristic of modern burlesque is the fact that it is completely sex-centered. It has some low comedy and occasionally some humor, but the principal subject of both is sex. * * * The piece de resistance is the girl who disrobes, partially or entirely, and this act varies with the political season and the locality. * * * If burlesque of today is metropolitan, so also it is vice, and needs to be thought of in that light, as an aspect of social pathology. If vice implies a sense of antagonism toward existing mores, a purveying of sex in a vicarious, professional and promiscuous fashion, then burlesque is just that. * * * Although the operator may not be willing to say so to an inquirer, usually adopting a sanctimonious air, he knows, and everything in his theatre indicates he knows, that he is giving a sex show, sans excuses, sans philosophy and above all, sans clothes. He is, in that sense a professional purveyor of sex.* Dressler, Burlesque as a Cultural Phenomenon (1937).[2]

The jury was instructed on the elements of obscenity in language following closely the test laid down by the Supreme Court in *Roth* v. *United States,* 354 U.S. 476 (1957), and reiterated and elaborated upon in the later cases of *Jacobellis* v. *State of Ohio,* 378 U.S. 184 (1964); *Ginzburg* v. *United States,* 383 U.S. 463 (1966); *Mishkin* v. *State of New York,* 383 U.S. 502 (1966); and the "Fanny Hill" case, 383 U.S. 413 (1966). With respect to community standards the jury was instructed:

Ladies and gentlemen of the jury, it is for you to be the exclusive judge of what is the common conscience of the community, as defined, and what the contemporary community standards are. You and you alone are the sole judges of this issue. In determining the common conscience in evaluating contemporary community standards, you are to consider the community as a whole, young and old, educated and uneducated, the religious and the irreligious, men, women and children. You are not to condemn or to exculpate any of these performances because of your own personal subjective standards. You are to apply contemporary community standards.[3]

On this record I would affirm the convictions in spite of what I consider an unfortunate error by the trial judge in a later instruction that, on the question of contemporary community standards, the word "community" refers "to the nation as a whole and not just to one city, county, or state in this nation." As there was no evidence of any national standard and the jury could not be expected to be acquainted with such, it was error to give the instruction. For reasons later discussed, I think it was harmless error.

I do not agree with the holding in the majority opinion that in determining whether a show offends contemporary community standards, "reference must be made to community standards prevailing in the nation generally." For that proposition the majority relies upon the opinion of Mr. Justice Brennan in *Jacobellis,* but apparently the Justice spoke there only for himself and Mr. Justice Goldberg. I prefer the reasoning of the Chief Justice, who in his dissent, joined in by Mr. Justice Clark, said:

It is my belief that when the Court said in Roth *that obscenity is to be defined by reference to "community standards," it meant community standards—not a national standard, as is sometimes argued. I believe that there is no provable "national standard" and perhaps there should be none. At all events, this Court has not been able to enunciate one, and it would be unreasonable to expect local courts to divine one. It is said that such a "community" approach may well result in material being proscribed as obscene in one community but not in another, and, in all probability, that is true. But communities throughout the Nation are in fact diverse, and it must be remembered that, in cases such as this one, the Court is confronted with the task of reconciling conflicting rights of the diverse communities within our society and of individuals.* 378 U.S. at 200–01.

Ordinarily I would not rely upon a dissent but since the Supreme Court is, in the words of a recent writer,[4] "hopelessly fragmented over obscenity," I feel that this dissent by two Justices is equal to the opinion which expresses the views of only two other Justices.

The trial court is not given any guidelines by the Supreme Court or by this court for ascertaining the supposed "national standard." Is it to be determined by the testimony of experts? If so, by what experts and with what qualifications? If there should be testimony from these assumed experts that a majority of the cities throughout the Nation tolerate performances like those given here, must Washington and other cities be compelled to tolerate them? It is my opinion that the local community standard should govern and that a jury is as well qualified to determine the question as any expert.[5]

There is another reason why I feel that the assumed national standard should not apply in this case. As far as I am aware, the Supreme Court cases on the question of

---

[1] Although defense counsel attempted to establish that the sole reason the appellants were charged was because the dancers appeared without any covering on their breasts (without pasties), the record shows clearly the Government's case rested on a combination of the appearance and the conduct of the dancers.

[2] As quoted by Judge (now Justice) Brennan in *Adams Theatre Co.* v. *Keenan,* 12 N.J. 267, 96 A. 2d 519, 523 (1953). The Judge added that burlesque answering that description "may well be considered outrightly lewd and indecent."

[3] This instruction followed closely the instruction given in *Roth* and apparently approved by the Supreme Court. 354 U.S. at 490.

[4] John P. MacKenzie in the *Washington Post* of October 2, 1967.

[5] "The jury represents a cross-section of the community and has a special aptitude for reflecting the view of the average person. Jury trial of obscenity therefore provides a peculiarly competent application of the standard for judging obscenity which, by its definition, calls for an appraisal of material according to the average person's application of contemporary community standards." Mr. Justice Brennan dissenting in *Kingsley Books* v. *Brown,* 354 U.S. 436, 448 (1957).

obscenity have dealt with books, magazines, photographs and motion pictures. It may be said that such have a national character in the sense that they are the same wherever read, exhibited or shown. A performance like the one here is strictly local. It may vary from locality to locality, or may vary in the same locality from day to day or performance to performance. Such a performance ought to be judged by local standards.[6]

Furthermore, I have serious doubts whether the constitutional guarantees of freedom of speech and of the press have any application to such a performance as is described in the record. Certainly we are not concerned here with freedom of the press. Likewise freedom of speech is of little concern here because speech was almost a non-essential part of the performance. The complaint here is not directed at what was said but instead at what was done. The performance was essentially one of conduct. Even those who would give the broadest scope to the First Amendment recognize that it does not protect conduct. For example, Mr. Justice Black, dissenting in *Ginzburg*, says the First Amendment "forbids any kind or type or nature of governmental censorship over views as distinguished from conduct." 383 U.S. at 481. The same Justice, dissenting in *Mishkin*, says the First Amendment, made applicable to the States by the Fourteenth, "leaves the States vast power to regulate conduct but no power at all, in my judgment, to make the expression of views a crime." 383 U.S. at 518.

Mr. Justice Douglas, dissenting in *Roth*, after saying

---

[6] See *Newark v. Humphres*, 94 N.J. Super. 384, 228 A. 2d 550 (1967).

"there is nothing in the Constitution which forbids Congress from using its power over the mails to proscribe *conduct* on the grounds of good morals," added: "No one would suggest that the First Amendment permits nudity in public places, adultery, and other phases of sexual misconduct." 354 U.S. at 512. The same Justice, dissenting in *Ginzburg*, emphasizes that the First Amendment "allows all ideas to be expressed." 383 U.S. at 491. When Mr. Justice Stewart, concurring in *Jacobellis*, speaks of hardcore pornography (378 U.S. at 197) and repeats this expression in his dissent in *Ginzburg* (383 U.S. at 499), I do not think he is referring to conduct.

From the views expressed by those who would give the greatest latitude to the protection afforded by the First Amendment, I conclude that while all may agree that an artist may paint and exhibit a portrait of a nude, the artist has no constitutional right to walk down the street in the nude. I further conclude that the exhibition here is not protected by the First Amendment. Of course, a theatrical performance may, and many do, constitute an expression of views and ideas, but the performance here, although given on stage, consisted almost entirely of conduct. It was the conduct that was objectionable. If it can be called an expression of views or ideas, then the same could be said of any conduct, regardless of its nature.

In summary, I am of the opinion that the evidence warranted a submission of the case to the jury, and that the jury, without the aid of expert testimony, was qualified to determine whether the performance constituted obscenity as defined by the trial judge. I believe this court may, as the jury obviously did, ignore the trial court's statement concerning a national standard. I would affirm.

■ Teitel Film Corporation *et al.*

v.

Cusack *et al.*

Appeal from the Supreme Court of Illinois.

No. 787. Decided Jan. 29, 1968.

PER CURIAM.

This appeal seeks review of a judgment of the Supreme Court of Illinois which affirmed orders of the Circuit Court of Cook County permanently enjoining the appellants from showing certain motion pictures in public places in the City of Chicago. 38 Ill. 2d 53, 230 N.E. 2d 241. The questions presented are whether the Chicago Motion Picture Censorship Ordinance is unconstitutional on its face and as applied, and whether the films involved are obscene.[1]

The Chicago Motion Picture Ordinance prohibits the exhibition in any public place of "any picture . . . without having first secured a permit therefor from the Superintendent of Police." The Superintendent is required

---

[1] In light of our decision, we do not reach, and intimate no view upon, the question whether the films are obscene.

"within three days of receipt" of a film to "inspect such . . . films . . . or cause them to be inspected by the Film Review Section . . . and within three days after such inspection either to grant or deny the permit.[2] If the

---

[2] The ordinance was amended during the pendency of the case before the Illinois Supreme Court to require inspection within three days after submission of the films. The members of the Superintendent's Film Review Section, upon his request, "review each motion picture submitted and . . . recommend in writing to the Superintendent of Police whether to grant or deny a permit."

[3] Comments of the trial judge in this case suggest doubt whether the trial court regarded compliance with this rule to be mandatory:

"Mr. Aspen (counsel for the City): As far as the Court is concerned, it is my understand (sic) that Judge Boyle in General Rule 3–3, which has nothing to do with the ordinance has said there will be a hearing within five days of either the filing of an answer—

permit is denied the exhibitor may within seven days seek review by the Motion Picture Appeal Board. The Review Board must review the film within 15 days of the request for review, and thereafter within 15 days afford the exhibitor, his agent or distributor, a hearing. The Board must serve the applicant with written notice of its ruling within five days after close of the hearing. If the Board denies the permit, "the Board within ten days from the hearing shall file with the Circuit Court of Cook County an action for an injunction against the showing of the film." A Circuit Court Rule, General Order 3–3, promulgated May 25, 1965, provides that a "complaint for injunction . . . shall be given priority over all other causes. The Court shall set the cause for hearing within five (5) days after the defendant has answered. . . ."[3] However, neither the rule nor any statutory or other provision assures a prompt judicial decision of the question of the alleged obscenity of the film.

The Illinois Supreme Court held "that the administration of the Chicago Motion Picture Ordinance violates no constitutional rights of the defendants." 38 Ill. 2d at 63, 230 N.E. 2d at 247. We disagree. In *Freedman* v. *Maryland*, 380 U.S. 51, 58–59, we held ". . . that a noncriminal process which requires the prior submission of a film to a censor avoids constitutional infirmity only if it takes

---

"The Court: I am going to have it changed because we just cannot set everything aside to give priority to this kind of litigation.

* * * * * * *

"The Court: First amendment matters cannot be anymore important than any other constitutional right or any other citizen's right to have his case heard.

"As I said before, it is far more important in my judgment to take care of the broken heads and fractured legs than it is to take care of the bleeding hearts."

place under procedural safeguards designed to obviate the dangers of a censorship system. . . . To this end, the exhibitor must be assured, by statute or authoritative judicial construction, that the censor will, within a *specified brief period*, either issue a license or go to court to restrain showing the film. . . . (T)he procedure must also assure a *prompt final judicial decision*, to minimize the deterrent effect of an interim and possibly erroneous denial of a license." (Emphasis supplied.) The Chicago censorship procedures violate these standards in two respects. (1) the 50 to 57 days provided by the ordinance to complete the administrative process before initiation of the judicial proceeding does not satisfy the standard that the procedure must assure "that the censor will, within a specified brief period, either issue a license or go to court to restrain showing the film." (2) The absence of any provision for a prompt judicial decision by the trial court violates the standard that ". . . the procedure must also assure a prompt final judicial decision. . . ."

Accordingly, we reverse the judgment of the Supreme Court of Illinois and remand the case for further proceedings not inconsistent with this opinion.

It is so ordered.

Mr. Justice Black and Mr. Justice Douglas, agreeing that *Freedman* v. *Maryland*, 380 U.S. 51, 58–59, requires reversal of this case, base their reversal also on *Redrup* v. *New York* 386 U.S. 767.

Mr. Justice Harlan concurs in the result.

Mr. Justice Stewart bases his concurrence in this judgment upon *Redrup* v. *New York*, 386 U.S. 767.

■ People & C., *Respondent,*

v.

Howard Solomon, *Defendant.*

Supreme Court of New York, First Judicial Department.

While the performance presented by the defendant contained coarse, vulgar and profane language which went beyond the bounds of usual candor "basic principles of jurisprudence, however, command us to put to one side all personal predilections, including our distaste for commercial exploitation of sensuality" (*People* v. *Richmond County News*, 9 N.Y. 2d 578, 588). And it is the law that to constitute obscenity "it must be established that (a) the dominant theme of the material taken as a whole appeals to a prurient interest in sex; (b) the material is patently offensive because it affronts contemporary community standards relating to the description or representation of sexual matters; and (c) the material is utterly without redeeming social value. * * * A book cannot be proscribed unless it is found to be *utterly* without redeeming social value" (*Memoirs* v. *Massachusetts*, 383 U.S. 413, 419).

In our opinion, the proof failed to meet these requirements. The court below found that the monologues were "not erotic" and "not lust-inciting" (cf. *People* v. *Wendling*, 258 N.Y. 451, 453). Moreover, integral parts of the performance included comments on problems of contemporary society. Religious hypocrisy, racial and religious prejudices, the obscenity laws and human tensions were all subjects of comment. Therefore, it was error to hold that the performances were without social importance (*People* v. *Bruce*, 31 Ill. 2d 459, 202 N.W. 2d 497; *Roth* v. *U.S.*, 354 U.S. 476; *Manual Enterprises* v. *Day*, 370 U.S. 478).

Judgment of conviction reversed on the law and the facts and informations dismissed.

Streit and Gold, JJ., concur. Hofstadter, J., dissents in the following dissenting memorandum and votes to affirm:

This appeal involves a public performance. In this aspect it is to be distinguished from the sale of a magazine

(*People* v. *Richmond County News,* 9 N.Y. 2d 578); a book (*Memoirs* v. *Massachusetts,* 383 U.S. 413); or the sale of film (*Robert* v. *New York,* 87 Sup. Ct. 2092, rev'g 15 N.Y. 1020; *People* v. *Revo,* 15 N.Y. 2d 743). The right of the People to regulate *public conduct* under the police power of the state is of greater scope (*Bennett* v. *California* —— Cal. ——. April 12, 1967, cert. denied 36 L.W. 3222 [see also N.Y.L.J., December 5, 1967, p. 4]; *Trans-Lux Dist.* v. *Board of Regents,* 14 N.Y. 2d 88, 92–95, 97–98, rev'd on other grounds 380 U.S. 259). The statute before us (Penal Law, sec. 1140–a) proscribes presentation of an "obscene, indecent, immoral or impure

* * * show * * * which would tend to the corruption of the morals of youth or others." It suffices that parts of the show are obscene and lewd (*People* v. *Vickers,* 259 App. Div. 841; *People* v. *Richmond County News,* 9 N.Y. 2d 578, 587). The trial court found the Bruce performance "obscene, indecent, immoral and impure. The monologues contained little or no literary or artistic merit. They were merely a device to enable Bruce to exploit the use of obscene language." I see no reason to reverse these findings and would, as urged by the district attorney, affirm.

No. 18,707

■ Milton Luros, *Appellant,*

v.

United States of America, *Appellee.*

No. 18,708.

Sun Era, Inc., *Appellant,*

v.

United States of America, *Appellee.*

No. 18,709.

American Art Agency, Inc., *Appellant,*

v.

United States of America, *Appellee.*

No. 18,710.

Parliament News, Inc., *Appellant,*

v.

United States of America, *Appellee.*

No. 18,711.

London Press, Inc., *Appellant,*

v.

United States of America, *Appellee.*

Appeals from the United States District Court for the Northern District of Iowa.

[February 7, 1968.]

Before Vogel, Chief Judge, Gibson and Lay, Circuit Judges.

Lay, Circuit Judge.

The recurring problem of obscenity vel non is presented. The appeal arises from a criminal prosecution under 18 U.S.C. §§ 1461 and 1462, as amended (1964), for mailing and transporting "obscene" literature. Appel-

lants are four corporations and their sole stockholder, Milton Luros. A jury trial was held in the Northern District of Iowa, Western Division, under the venue provision applicable to the above statutes, 18 U.S.C. § 3237 (1964).[1] After a finding of guilty the trial court sentenced

---

[1] Originally the action was against appellants and an additional eleven co-defendants under a twenty-five count indictment. The trial commenced on October 18, 1965. At the close of all

appellants Luros, Parliament News, Inc. and London Press, Inc. on eighteen counts; Sun Era, Inc. on eleven counts; and American Art Agency on six counts.

Appellants posit their appeal upon three basic contentions: (1) that the books and magazines involved were not proven "obscene" and therefore protected under the First Amendment; (2) that the court erred in its instruction concerning the kind of scienter or knowledge required to sustain a conviction; and (3) that the venue statute permitting the government to pick the forum for prosecution in Iowa renders the conviction unconstitutional under the First, Fifth and Sixth Amendments of the United States Constitution.[2]

In view of our decision that the material is protected under the First Amendment, we need not discuss the latter two issues.

"Obscene" literature is not within the protection of the First Amendment. *Roth v. United States,* 354 U.S. 476 (1957). However, concern over self-censorship and encroachment upon the protected areas of the First Amendment brought forth these words of caution:

> "The fundamental freedoms of speech and press have contributed greatly to the development and well-being of our free society and are indispensable to its continued growth. Ceaseless vigilance is the watchword to prevent their erosion by Congress or by the States. The door barring federal and state intrusion into this area cannot be left ajar; it must be kept tightly closed and opened only the slightest crack necessary to prevent encroachment upon more important interests. It is therefore vital that the standards for judging obscenity safeguard the protection of freedom of speech and press for material which does not treat sex in a manner appealing to prurient interest." *Id.* at 488.

Subsequent interpretations of *Roth* have clearly demonstrated the Court's own "vigilance" as to these principles. Although definition of "obscenity" is not without difficulty,[3] we submit that sufficient standards now exist which compel reversal of the present convictions.

In *Redrup v. New York,* 386 U.S. 767, 770 (1967), a per curiam opinion summarized the Court's views:

> "Two members of the Court have consistently adhered to the view that a State is utterly without power to sup-

press, control, or punish the distribution of any writings or pictures upon the ground of their 'obscenity.' A third has held to the opinion that a State's power in this area is narrowly limited to a distinct and clearly identifiable class of material. Others have subscribed to a not dissimilar standard, holding that a State may not constitutionally inhibit the distribution of literary material as obscene unless '(a) the dominant theme of the material taken as a whole appeals to a prurient interest in sex; (b) the material is patently offensive because it affronts contemporary community standards relating to the description or representation of sexual materials; and (c) the material is utterly without redeeming social value,' emphasizing that the 'three elements must coalesce,' and that no such material can 'be proscribed unless it is found to be utterly without redeeming social value.' Memoirs v. Massachusetts, 383 U.S. 413, 418–419. Another Justice has not viewed the 'social value' element as an independent factor in the judgment of obscenity." (Emphasis ours.)[4]

Redrup points up three other areas where prosecution might succeed: (1) where the statute relates to a limited state concern for juveniles,[5] (2) where there is an obtrusive "assault" by pornography upon an unwilling individual and (3) where "pandering" exists as found in *Ginzburg v. United States,* 383 U.S. 463 (1966).

In the present case, convictions rest upon two distinct groups of material mailed or transported by appellants:[6]

(1) nudist magazines and (2) paper-backed "pocket book" publications dealing with fictional lesbian and heterosexual exploits.

1. It is clearly established that "nudist" magazines are not obscene per se. *Sunshine Book Co. v. Summerfield,* 355 U.S. 375 (1958); *Mounce v. United States,* 355 U.S. 180 (1957); *Rosenbloom v. Virginia,* 388 U.S. 450 (1967); cf. *United States v. Central Magazines Sales, Ltd.,* 381 F. 2d 821 (4 Cir. 1967). The government acknowledges this, but contends the defendants are guilty under a "pandering" or conduct theory.[7]

The government's argument can be summarized as follows: that appellant Luros and his corporations publish

---

the evidence (the defense having offered no oral testimony), the court dismissed seven of the counts. The jury returned a verdict of guilty against all the defendants on January 14, 1966. On November 4, 1966, the trial court sustained a motion for judgments of acquittal with respect to all defendants with the exception of the appellants Luros and the four corporations. *United States v. Luros,* 260 F. Supp. 697 (N.D. Iowa, 1966). For prior rulings on change of venue, etc., see *United States v. Luros,* 243 F. Supp. 160 (N.D., Iowa 1965).

[2] During the course of present litigation appellants brought suit with others in the District Court of the District of Columbia challenging the venue statute as applied to obscenity prosecutions; the decision was handed down by a three-judge court on October 26, 1967, upholding the constitutionality of the statute. See *Reed Enterprises v. Clark,* Civil Nos. 1744–65, 2562–65, 3009–65 consolidated (D.D.C., October 26, 1967).

[3] "In toto, applying the law to specific questioned materials has been a labor as frustratingly impossible as is nailing custard pies to trees." Kuh, Foolish Figleaves? Pornography in and out of Court 215 (1967).

[4] In *Redrup,* Justices Harlan and Clark dissented on procedural grounds. Mr. Justice Harlan's dissenting opinion in *Roth,* 354 U.S. at 503, indicates he feels the problem of obscenity should be one primarily entrusted to the states and not to the federal government. He has consistently maintained this position, voting to affirm state convictions, and to dismiss federal prosecutions under 18 U.S.C. § 1461. See note 15, infra, p. 11.

[5] See *Separate Obscenity Standard for Youth,* 1 Ga. L. Rev. 707 (1967).

[6] The trial court dismissed all of the counts relating to a third class of magazines consisting of pictures of scantily clad and nude models, generally posed in suggestive and provocative positions (called "girly" magazines). Although described as "sexually provocative," these are generally not within the proscription of the statute. *Manual Enterprises, Inc. v. Day,* 370 U.S. 478 (1962); *Redrup v. New York,* 386 U.S. 767 (1967).

[7] The government, even prior to the release of the *Ginzburg* case, supra, told the jury in their opening statement that the defendants were being tried for their *conduct* in the publications involved. Chief Justice Warren had first forewarned of this basis of proof in his concurring opinion in *Roth v. United States,* 354 U.S. at 494.

nudist magazines simply to make money; that many of the nudist models, although signing complete "releases" for the photographs, nevertheless did not contemplate national publication; that paid professional models, who were not nudists, posed for the magazines; that the magazines falsely represent that the models are nudists; that the magazines picture "staged" scenes *outside* nudist camps depicting activities such as cooking, boating, hiking, etc., which nudists do not normally do in the nude; that appellant Luros continually sought legal advice as to whether his magazines were "defensible"; that appellant Luros instructed his editors that they could now use photographs showing the male genitalia in the foreground; that appellant Luros bought a nudist camp for the sole purpose of taking pictures; that their own editors described the magazines as "crap plus one" and that "zetz" was required to make them sell. In summary, the government urges appellants' sale of the nudist material is nothing more than "commercial exploitation" on the basis of prurient appeal.

We deem such evidence relevant to the issue of conduct since *Ginzburg* speaks of publications being "created" as well as "exploited" on a prurient basis. 383 U.S. at 474. However, there is no claim that these magazines were advertised or exploited as "erotica" as in *Ginzburg*.[8] The contention is that whatever social value the nudist magazines may have becomes lost in the background of the production and sale by appellants premised solely upon their prurient appeal. See *A Book Named "John Cleland's Memoirs of a Woman of Pleasure"* v. *Massachusetts*, 383 U.S. 413, 420 (1966).

The basic fallacy of this argument, in the context of the nudist publications involved, is the false premise that "commercial exploitation of nudism" is equated with prurience. The different pictures taken and published show both men and women, as well as children, in various poses and activities. We would agree that young female models or subjects dominate most pictures. Yet there is no magazine in evidence where men and women are shown embracing or in any alleged provocative or suggestive pose that smacks of a prurient appeal.

There is no question but that appellant and his corporations make a profit in the business of selling nudist magazines.[9] Yet there is nothing within the creation or production of the magazine itself that can be said to focus on the prurient unless it can be said that *the production* of the nude picture depicting male or female pubic hair and genitalia qualifies by itself.[10] Clearly, where such pictures

are innocuous in their setting, even though they may be offensive to many, even if some viewers' sexual curiosity or appetite may be whetted, the law does not consider them "obscene." As stated in *Roth* v. *United States*, 354 U.S. at 487: "Sex and obscenity are not synonymous. Obscene material . . . deals with sex in a manner appealing to prurient interest." And the Court relates:

"*We perceive no significant difference between the meaning of obscenity developed in the case law and the definition of the A.L.I., Model Penal Code, § 207.10 (2) (Tent. Draft No. 6, 1957), viz.:*
"*'. . . A thing is obscene if, considered as a whole, its predominant appeal is to prurient interest, i.e., a shameful or morbid interest in nudity, sex, or excretion, and if it goes substantially beyond customary limits of candor in description or representation of such matters . . .'*" Id. at 487, n. 20.

Nudism is considered in good taste by only the relatively few. The verdict in the present case acknowledges that portrayal of it "goes substantially beyond customary limits of candor" in even today's modern and tolerant community. Nevertheless, it cannot be legally condemned as a *morbid* or *shameful* representation of sex itself. This we conclude is the basis of the reversal of *Sunshine Books Co.* v. *Summerfield*, 355 U.S. 372 (1958), relying upon *Roth*.[11]

No conduct of appellants was offered, which could be evaluated on its face, as demonstration of a prurient appeal superadded in the production or sale of the magazines. Of all the conduct charged, we fail to see a scintilla of proof that Luros or anyone else under his control gave directions or edited pictures with resultant publication to represent sex in a lustful, morbid or shameful way. Appellants' convictions on these counts must be reversed.

II. This brings us to the so-called lesbian books. We would agree that these books constitute undoubted trash and have little if any literary value or social importance. They are written, as one author testified, with one purpose in mind—to sell! They produce high profit for appellants and can be described as distasteful, cheap and tawdry. Yet these facts alone do not constitute a crime.

A state judge in California dismissed an earlier criminal action[12] against the same appellants and involving some of the same books and others with the same alleged theme, since the books were "not utterly devoid of social value."[13]

---

[8] "In substance, did the publisher (or distributor, or dealer) print an evocative cover, advertise prior banning, display the item massed with other borderline items, and urge in various ways erotic, deviant, or scatological appeal?" Kuh, *op. cit.* at 78.

[9] This in and of itself is not a proper consideration. See *Ginzburg* v. *United States*, 383 U.S. at 474.

[10] As to this, there has been disagreement by other courts in the past. Cf. *State* v. *Vollmar*, 389 S.W. 2d 20, 28–29 (Mo. Sup. Ct. 1965), but see discussion in *United States* v. *25,000 Magazines, Entitled "Revue,"* 254 F. Supp. 1014 (D. Md. 1966), where Chief Judge Thomsen finds the nude pose innocuous in itself, but "obscene" when in "suggestive" situations (only the government appealed—see per curiam affirmance in *United States* v. *Central Magazine Sales, Ltd.*, 381 F. 2d 821 (4 Cir. 1967); see also *Parmelee* v. *United States*, 113 F. 2d 729 (D.C.

Cir. 1940). But even when the totally nude female is in an alleged sexually provocative pose, the magazine itself has been declared not obscene. See *Central Magazine Sales, Ltd.* v. *United States*, 36 U.S.L.W. 3170 (U.S. Oct. 23, 1967), reversing 373 F. 2d 633 (4 Cir. 1967).

[11] *Roth* relates to a discussion of the prurient effect of the material judged as a whole, on the average community. Standards relating to "social importance" (see *Jacobellis* v. *Ohio*, 378 U.S. 184, 191 (1964)), and "patent offensiveness" (see *Manual Enterprises, Inc.* v. *Day*, 370 U.S. 478 (1962) were developed and articulated later. For discussion of the developing federal standards, see generally *Paul & Schwartz, Federal Censorship—Obscenity in the Mail* (1961); see also Note, 75 Yale L.J. 1364 (1966).

[12] *People* v. *Luros*, No. 295183 (Super. Ct. Calif., filed June 21, 1965).

[13] E.g., the court discussed the book, *The Three-Way Apart-*

Appellants urge that the frank and sordid discussion of sexual perversion is itself the social importance to be weighed. Other lower courts have realistically declared such arguments to be facades for their true purpose. See, e.g., *Landau* v. *Fording*, supra, 54 Cal. Rptr. 177. But whether the claimed modicum of social value exists, or whether the books themselves lack the requisite "prurient appeal," or whether independently they are not patently offensive under present legal standards and precedents which this court must follow, the books cannot be declared obscene per se. See *A Quantity of Copies of Books* v. *Kansas*, 388 U.S. 452 (1967); *Books, Inc.* v. *United States*, 388 U.S. 419 (1967); *Aday* v. *United States*, 388 U.S. 447 (1967).

Nor did the government offer any competent evidence outside of the books themselves to demonstrate their pruriency. See *United States* v. *Klaw*, 350 F. 2d 155 (2 Cir. 1965). Again the government urges that the conviction be sustained under proof of appellants' conduct. But we again find no evidence to sustain a criminal conviction under the concept of "pandering" where the books are of the kind which otherwise have been declared not to be obscene themselves. Under such circumstances, there must exist independent evidence of prurient appeal *and* patent offensiveness, in the production or sale and distribution. There is no claim of a prurient appeal in the advertising circulars mailed. However, the government relies upon *Mishkin* v. *New York*, 383 U.S. 502, 505 (1966), where the defendant gave his authors specific instructions as to research, format and content in order to give the stories prurient appeal for sexual deviates.

The evidence does substantiate appellants' key role of approval and actual editing of the manuscripts submitted. But this alone is not actionable. *United States* v. *Klaw*, 350 F. 2d 155 (2 Cir. 1965); *Aday* v. *United States*, 388 U.S. 447 (1967), reversing *United States* v. *West Coast News Co.*, 357 F. 2d 855 (6 Cir. 1966); *Books, Inc.* v. *United States*, 388 U.S. 449 (1967), reversing 358 F. 2d 935 (1 Cir. 1966). Here the only other competent evidence comparable to *Mishkin* relates to Luros's editing the covers and at one time telling his editor that "nurse and lesbian work . . . seems to be selling and doing well." Since the written portrayal of lesbianism is not obscene itself, we fail to see that an implied direction to sell this type of literature can suddenly transform the material so as to make it actionable. The mere act of selling the literature otherwise could be condemned and easily prosecuted.

In *Redrup* v. *New York*, 386 U.S. 767 (1967), there is specific indication that a majority of the Supreme Court

adopts standards "not dissimilar" to banning only "hard-core" pornography.[14] Subsequent application of *Redrup* gives no contraindication.[15]

In the general sense, all of the material published by appellants fall within the purveyor's own graphic classification of "crap plus one," or in other words just plain trash. Our decision is not intended to indicate any approbation of the "esteemed literary works" herein involved. Our task cannot in any way relate to the individual tastes or philosophies of the members of the court. We simply find that the evidence of "pandering" is insufficient under the present facts of the case, and under the controlling law, the judgments must be vacated.

Many well-intentioned citizens become disgusted or offended with the freedom by which purveyors of trash place their publications in the mail.[16] But within the juridical balance is the basic concern over governmental interference into free channels of expression. It is far better there be a tight rein on authoritarian suppression, notwithstanding a conflict with some individuals' tastes or customary limits of candor, than that we live in a stifled community of self-censorship where men must feel apprehension over expression of an unpopular idea or theme. Still within our human possession is the free will to make an independent choice of values and to teach our children

---

[14] Justice Stewart, dissenting in *Ginzburg* v. *United States*, adopted a description of hard-core pornography as follows:
". . . Such materials include photographs, both still and motion picture, with no pretense of artistic value, graphically depicting acts of sexual intercourse, including various acts of sodomy and sadism, and sometimes involving several participants in scenes of orgy-like character. They also include strips of drawings in comic-book format grossly depicting similar activities in an exaggerated fashion. There are, in addition, pamphlets and booklets, sometimes with photographic illustrations, verbally describing such activities in a bizarre manner with no attempt whatsoever to afford portrayals of character or situation and with no pretense to literary value. All of this material . . . cannot conceivably be characterized as embodying communication of ideas or artistic values inviolate under the First Amendment. . . ." 383 U.S. 463, 499 n. 3.
Compare *Levin* v. *Maryland*, 246 Md. 139 (holding: "First Amendment does not bar conviction under Maryland obscenity statute of bookseller who sold uncaptioned pictures of nude males each 'distinguished by a large penis in full erection'"), cert. denied 36 U.S.L.W. 3280 (U.S. Jan. 16, 1968).

[15] Mr. Justice Brennan indicated in *Mishkin* v. *New York* that while New York bans only "hard-core" pornography, federal standards under *Roth* are less stringent. 383 U.S. 502, 508 (1966). However, we observe that the Court has sustained only one "obscenity" finding since *Mishkin*: *Landau* v. *Fording*, 388 U.S. 456 (1967). This was a silent film made with professional actors dealing with homosexual conduct in a prison. See *Landau* v. *Fording*, 54 Cal. Rptr. 177 (Dist. Ct. App. 1966). The California court relied upon *Ginzburg* v. *United States*, but also held the film "obscene" under Justice Brennan's tripartite test. On appeal there was a per curiam affirmance by the Supreme Court, with four Justices dissenting (Black, Douglas, Stewart, and Fortas). We can only surmise that the result would have been different if the case had involved a federal prosecution. See, e.g., Mr. Justice Harlan's dissent in *Aransino* v. *New York*, 388 U.S. 446 (1967) and his concurrence in *Books, Inc.* v. *United States*, 388 U.S. 449 (1967). See note 4, supra.

[16] *Hearings on H.R. 426 Before the Subcom. on Postal Operations of the House Committee on Post Office and Civil Service 90 Cong. 1st Sess.*, ser. 90–20, pt. II (1967).

---

ment, which is one of the books named in the instant case, as follows:
"This book also deals predominantly with the subject of sex. . . .
"The mere suggesting of 'wife swapping' is offensive to me. However, I cannot say that the book has passed the limits proscribed in Section 311(a). My personal offense is not the test. There is a possible 'moral' to the story, perhaps even a psychological lesson that may be of value to marriage counselors. Considering all the marital problems and sexual frustrations I have observed as an attorney and as a judge, it is possible that this book might be of an aid to marriage counselors. I cannot say the book is *utterly* (absolutely) without redeeming social importance." *Id.* at 9.

to do the same. Paternalistic censorship by government must continue to limit that choice only in the most extreme of circumstances. Thus we view the general reluctance of the law to go further in this area.

Judgment reversed and the cause remanded to the District Court with direction to enter judgment of acquittal for each appellant on all counts of the indictment.

A true copy.

Attest:

Clerk, U.S. Court of Appeals, Eighth Circuit.

■ Sam Ginsberg, *Appellant,*

v.

State of New York.

On Appeal from the Appellate Term of the Supreme Court of New York, Second Judicial Department.

[April 22, 1968.]

MR. JUSTICE BRENNAN delivered the opinion of the Court.

This case presents the question of the constitutionality on its face of a New York criminal obscenity statute which prohibits the sale to minors under 17 years of age of material defined to be obscene on the basis of its appeal to them whether or not it would be obscene to adults.

Appellant and his wife operate "Sam's Stationery and Luncheonette" in Bellmore, Long Island. They have a lunch counter, and, among other things, also sell magazines including some so-called "girlie" magazines. Appellant was prosecuted under two informations, each in two counts, which charged that he personally sold a 16-year-old boy two "girlie" magazines on each of two dates in October 1965, in violation of § 484–h of the New York Penal Law. He was tried before a judge without a jury in Nassau County District Court and was found guilty on both counts.[1] The judge found (1) that the magazines contained pictures which depicted female "nudity" in a manner defined in subsection 1 (b), that is "the showing of . . . female . . . buttocks with less than a full opaque covering, or the showing of the female breast with less than a fully opaque covering of any portion thereof below the top of the nipple . . .," and (2) than the pictures were "harmful to minors" in that they had, within the meaning of subsection 1 (f) ". . . that quality of . . . representation . . ., of nudity . . . [which] . . . (i) predominantly appeals to the prurient, shameful or morbid interest of minors, and (ii) is patently offensive to prevailing standards in the adult community as a whole with respect to what is suitable material for minors, and (iii) is utterly without redeeming social importance for minors." He held that both sales to the 16-year-old boy therefore constituted the violation under § 484–h of "knowingly to sell . . . to a minor" under 17 of "(a) any picture . . . which depicts nudity . . . and which is harmful to minors," and "(b) any . . . magazine . . . which contains . . . [such pictures] . . . and which, taken as a whole, is harmful to minors." The conviction was affirmed without opinion by the Appellate Term, Second Department, of the Supreme Court. Appellant was denied leave to appeal

---

[1] Appellant makes no attack upon § 484–h as applied. We therefore have no occasion to consider the sufficiency of the evidence, or such issues as burden of proof, whether expert evidence is either required or permissible, or any other questions which might be pertinent to the application of the statute. Appellant does argue that because the trial judge included a finding that two of the magazines "contained verbal descriptions and narrative accounts of sexual excitement and sexual conduct," an offense not charged in the informations, the conviction must be set aside under *Cole* v. *Arkansas,* 333 U.S. 196. But this case was tried and the appellant was found guilty only on the charges of selling magazines containing pictures depicting female nudity. It is therefore not a case where defendant was tried and convicted of a violation of one offense when he was charged with a distinctly and substantially different offense.

The full text of § 484–h is attached as Appendix A. It was enacted in L. 1965, c. 327 to replace an earlier version held invalid by the New York Court of Appeals in *People* v. *Kahan,* 15 N.Y. 2d 311, and *People* v. *Bookcase, Inc.,* 14 N.Y. 2d 409. Section 484–h in turn was replaced by L. 1967 c. 791, now §§ 235.20–235.22 of the Penal Law. The major changes under the 1967 law added a provision that the one charged with a violation "is presumed to [sell] with knowledge of the character and content of the material sold . . .," and the provision that "it is an affirmative defense that: (a) The defendant had reasonable cause to believe that the minor involved was seventeen years old or more; and (b) Such minor exhibited to the defendant a draft card, driver's license, birth certificate or other official or apparently official document purporting to establish that such minor was seventeen years old or more." Neither addition is involved in this case. We intimate no view whatever upon the constitutional validity of the presumption. See in general *Smith* v. *California,* 361 U.S. 147; *Speiser* v. *Randall,* 357 U.S. 513; 41 N.Y.U.L. Rev. 791 (1966); 30 Alb. L. Rev. 133 (1966).

The 1967 law also repealed outright § 484–i which had been enacted one week after § 484–h. L. 1965, c. 327. It forbade sales to minors under the age of 18. The New York Court of Appeals sustained its validity against a challenge that it was void for vagueness. *People* v. *Tannenbaum,* 18 N.Y. 2d 268. For an analysis of § 484–i and a comparison with § 484–h see 33 Brooklyn L.J. 329 (1967).

to the New York Court of Appeals and then appealed to this Court. We noted probable jurisdiction. 388 U.S. 904. We affirm.[2]

The "girlie" picture magazines involved in the sales here are not obscene for adults, *Redrup v. New York*, 386 U.S. 767.[3] But § 484–h does not bar the appellant from stock-

<hr/>

[2] The case is not moot. The appellant might have been sentenced to one year's imprisonment, or a $500 fine or both. N.Y. Penal Law § 1937. The trial judge however exercised authority under N.Y. Penal Law § 2188 and on May 17, 1966, suspended sentence on all counts. Under § 470–a of the New York Code of Criminal Procedure, the judge could thereafter recall appellant and impose sentence only within one year, or before May 17, 1967. The judge did not do so. Although *St. Pierre v. United States*, 319 U.S. 41, held that a criminal case had become moot when the petitioner finished serving his sentence before direct review in this Court, *St. Pierre* also recognized that the case would not have been moot had "petitioner shown that under either state or federal law further penalties or disabilities can be imposed on him as result of the judgment which has now been satisfied." *Id.*, at 43. The State of New York concedes in its brief in this Court addressed to mootness "that certain disabilities do flow from the conviction." The brief states that among these is "the possibility of ineligibility for licensing under state and municipal laws regulating various lawful occupations . . . ." Since the argument, the parties advised the Court that, although this is the first time appellant has been convicted of any crime, this conviction might result in the revocation of the license required by municipal law as a prerequisite to engaging in the luncheonette business he carries on in Bellmore, New York. Bellmore is an "unincorporated village" within the Town of Hempstead, Long Island, 1967 N.Y.S. Leg. Man. 1154. The town has a licensing ordinance which provides that the "Commissioner of Buildings . . . may suspend or revoke any license issued, in his discretion, for . . . (e) conviction of any crime." LL 21, Town of Hempstead, eff. December 1, 1966, § 8 (e). In these circumstances the case is not moot since the conviction may entail collateral consequences sufficient to bring the case within the *St. Pierre* exception. See *Fiswick v. United States*, 329 U.S. 211, 220–222. We were not able to reach that conclusion in *Tannenbaum v. New York*, 388 U.S. 439, or *Jacobs v. New York*, 388 U.S. 431, in which the appeals were dismissed as moot. In *Tannenbaum* there was no contention that the convictions under the now repealed § 484–i entailed any collateral consequences. In *Jacobs* the appeal was dismissed on motion of the State which alleged, *inter alia*, that New York law did not impose "any further penalty upon conviction of the misdemeanor here in issue." Appellant did not there show, or contend, that his license might be revoked for "conviction of any crime"; he asserted only that the conviction might be the basis of a suspension under a provision of the Administrative Code of the City of New York requiring the Department of Licenses to assure that motion picture theatres are not conducted in a manner offensive to "public morals."

[3] One of the magazines was an issue of the magazine "Sir." We held in *Gent v. Arkansas*, decided with *Redrup v. New York*, 386 U.S. 767, 769, that an Arkansas statute which did not reflect a specific and limited state concern for juveniles was unconstitutional insofar as it was applied to suppress distribution of another issue of that magazine. Other cases which turned on findings of nonobscenity of this type of magazines include: *Central Magazine Sales, Ltd. v. United States*, 389 U.S. 50; *Conner v. City of Hammond*, 389 U.S. 48; *Potomac News Co. v. United States*, 389 U.S. 47; *Mazes v. Ohio*, 388 U.S. 453; *A Quantity of Books v. Kansas*, 388 U.S. 452; *Books, Inc. v. United States*, 388 U.S. 449; *Aday v. United States*, 388 U.S. 447; *Avansio v. New York*, 388 U.S. 446; *Sheperd v. New York*, 388 U.S. 444; *Friedman v. New York*, 388 U.S. 441; *Keney v. New York*, 388 U.S. 440; see also *Rosenbloom v. Virginia*, 388 U.S. 450; *Sunshine Book Co. v. Summerfield*, 355 U.S. 372.

ing the magazines and selling them to persons 17 years of age or older, and therefore the conviction is not invalid under our decision in *Butler v. Michigan*, 352 U.S. 380.

Obscenity is not within the area of protected speech or press. *Roth v. United States*, 354 U.S. 476, 485. The three-pronged test of subsection 1 (f) for judging the obscenity of material sold to minors under 17 is a variable from the formulation for determining obscenity under *Roth* stated in the plurality opinion in *Memoirs v. Massachusetts*, 383 U.S. 413, 418. Appellant's primary attack upon § 484–h is leveled at the power of the State to adapt this *Memoirs* formulation to define the material's obscenity on the basis of its appeal to minors, and thus exclude material so defined from the area of protected expression. He makes no argument that the magazines are not "harmful to minors" within the definition in subsection 1 (f). Thus "[n]o issue is presented . . . concerning the obscenity of the material involved." *Roth*, 354 U.S., at 481, n. 8.

The New York Court of Appeals "upheld the Legislature's power to employ variable concepts of obscenity"[4] in a case in which the same challenge to state power to enact such a law was also addressed to § 484–h. *The Bookcase, Inc. v. Broderick*, 18 N.Y. 2d 71, appeal dismissed for want of a properly presented federal question, *sub nom. Bookcase, Inc. v. Leary*, 385 U.S. 12. In sustaining state power to enact the law, the Court of Appeals said, *Bookcase, Inc.*, p. 75:

"*. . . material which is protected for distribution to adults is not necessarily constitutionally protected from restriction upon its dissemination to children. In other words, the concept of obscenity or of unprotected matter may vary according to the group to whom the questionable material is directed or from whom it is quarantined. Because of the State's exigent interest in preventing distribution to children of objectionable material, it can exercise its power to protect the health, safety, welfare and morals of its community by barring the distribution to children of books recognized to be suitable for adults.*"

Appellant's attack is not that New York was without power to draw the line at age 17. Rather, his contention is the broad proposition that the scope of the constitutional freedom of expression secured to a citizen to read or see material concerned with sex cannot be made to depend upon whether the citizen is an adult or a minor. He accordingly insists that the denial to minors under 17 of access to material condemned by § 484–h, insofar as that material is not obscene for persons 17 years of age or older, constitutes an unconstitutional deprivation of protected liberty.

We have no occasion in this case to consider the impact

<hr/>

[4] *People v. Tannenbaum*, 18 N.Y. 2d 268, 270, dismissed as moot, 388 U.S. 439. The concept of variable obscenity is developed in Lockhart & McClure, Censorship of Obscenity: The Developing Constitutional Standards, 45 Minn. L. Rev. 5 (1960). At p. 85 the authors state:

"Variable obscenity . . . furnishes a useful analytical tool for dealing with the problem of denying adolescents access to material aimed at a primary audience of sexually mature adults. For variable obscenity focuses attention upon the make-up of primary and peripheral audiences in varying circumstances, and provides a reasonably satisfactory means for delineating the obscene in each circumstance."

of the guarantees of freedom of expression upon the totality of the relationship of the minor and the State, cf. *In re Gault,* 387 U.S. 1, 13. It is enough for the purposes of this case that we inquire whether it was constitutionally impermissible for New York, insofar as § 484–h does so, to accord minors under 17 a more restricted right than that assured to adults to judge and determine for themselves what sex material they may read or see. We conclude that we cannot say that the statute invades the area of freedom of expression constitutionally secured to minors.[5]

Appellant argues that there is an invasion of protected rights under § 484–h constitutionally indistinguishable from the invasions under the Nebraska statute forbidding children to study German, which was struck down in *Meyer* v. *Nebraska,* 262 U.S. 390, the Oregon statute interfering with children's attendance at private and parochial schools, which was struck down in *Pierce* v. *Society of Sisters,* 268 U.S. 510, and the statute compelling children against their religious scruples to give the flag salute, which was struck down in *West Virginia State Board of Education* v. *Barnette,* 319 U.S. 624. We reject that argument. We do not regard New York's regulation in defining obscenity on the basis of its appeal to minors under 17 as involving an invasion of such minors' constitutionally protected freedoms. Rather § 484–h simply adjusts the definition of obscenity ". . . to social realities by permitting the appeal of this type of material to be assessed in terms of the sexual interest . . ." of such minors. *Mishkin* v. *New York,* 383 U.S. 502, 509; *Bookcase, Inc.* v. *Broderick, supra,* p. 75. That the State has power to make that adjustment seems clear, for we have recognized that even where there is an invasion of protected freedoms ". . . the power of the state to control the conduct of children reaches beyond the scope of its authority over adults . . . ." *Prince* v. *Massachusetts,* 321 U.S. 158, 170.[6] In

Prince we sustained the conviction of the guardian of a nine-year-old girl, both members of the sect of Jehovah's Witnesses, for violating the Massachusetts Child Labor Law by permitting the girl to sell the sect's religious tracts on the streets of Boston.

The well-being of its children is of course a subject within the State's constitutional power to regulate, and, in our view, two interests justify the limitations in § 484–h upon the availability of sex material to minors under 17, at least if it was rational for the legislature to find that the minors' exposure to such material might be harmful. First of all, constitutional interpretation has consistently recognized that parents' claims to authority in their own households to direct the rearing of their children is basic in the structure of our society. "It is cardinal with us that the custody, care and nurture of the child reside first in the parents, whose primary function and freedom include preparation for obligations the state can neither supply nor hinder." *Prince* v. *Massachusetts, supra,* at 166. The legislature could properly conclude that parents and others, teachers for example, who have this primary responsibility for children's well-being are entitled to the support of laws designed to aid discharge of that responsibility. Indeed, subsection 1(f)(ii) of § 484–h expressly recognizes the parental role in assessing sex related material harmful to minors according "to prevailing standards in the adult community as a whole with respect to what is suitable material for minors." Moreover, the prohibition against sales to minors does not bar parents who so desire from purchasing the magazines for their children.[7]

The State also has an independent interest in the well-being of its youth. The New York Court of Appeals squarely bottomed its decision on that interest in *Bookcase, Inc.* v. *Broderick, supra,* at 75. Judge Fuld, now

---

[5] Suggestions that legislatures might give attention to laws dealing specifically with safeguarding children against pornographic material have been made by many judges and commentators. See, *e.g., Jacobellis* v. *Ohio,* 378 U.S. 184, 195 (opinion of Justice Brennan and Goldberg); *id.,* at 201 (dissenting opinion of The Chief Justice); *Ginzburg* v. *United States,* 383 U.S. 463, 498, n. 1 (dissenting opinion of Mr. Justice Stewart); *Interstate Circuit, Inc.* v. *City of Dallas,* 366 F. 2d 590, 593; *In re Louisiana News Co.,* 187 F. Supp. 241, 247; *United States* v. *Levine,* 83 F. 2d 156; *United States* v. *Dennett,* 39 F. 2d 564; Kuh, Foolish Figleaves 258–260 (1960); Emerson, Toward a General Theory of the First Amendment, 72 Yale L.J. 877, 939 (1963); Gerber, A Suggested Solution to the Riddle of Obscenity, 112 U. Pa. L. Rev. 834, 848; Henkin, Morals and the Constitution: The Sin of Obscenity, 63 Col. L. Rev. 391, 413, n. 68 (1963); Kalven, The Metaphysics of the Law of Obscenity, 1960 Sup. Ct. Rev. 1, 7; Magrath, The Obscenity Cases: Grapes of Roth, 1966 Sup. Ct. Rev. 7, 75.
The obscenity laws of 35 other States include provisions referring to minors. The laws are listed in Appendix B to this opinion. None is a precise counterpart of New York's § 484–h and we imply no view whatever on questions of their constitutionality.

[6] Many commentators, including many committed to the proposition that "[n]o general restriction on expression in terms of 'obscenity' can . . . be reconciled with the first amendment," recognize that "the power of the state to control the conduct of children reaches beyond the scope of its authority over adults," and accordingly acknowledge a supervening state interest in the regulation of literature sold to children, Emerson, Toward a General Theory of the First Amendment, 72 Yale L.J. 877, 938, 939 (1963):

"Different factors come into play, also, where the interest at stake is the effect of erotic expression upon children. The world of children is not strictly part of the adult realm of free expression. The factor of immaturity, and perhaps other considerations, impose different rules. Without attempting here to formulate the principles relevant to freedom of expression for children, it suffices to say that regulations of communication addressed to them need not conform to the requirements of the first amendment in the same way as those applicable to adults."

See also Gerber, *supra,* at 848; Kalven, *supra,* at 7; Magrath, *supra,* at 75. *Prince* v. *Massachusetts* is urged to be constitutional authority for such regulation. See, *e.g.,* Kuh, *supra,* at 258–260; Comment, Exclusion of Children from Violent Movies, 67 Col. L. Rev. 1149, 1159–1160 (1967); Note, Constitutional Problems in Obscenity Legislation Protecting Children, 54 Geo. L.J. 1379 (1966).

[7] One commentator who argues that obscenity legislation might be constitutionally defective as an imposition of a single standard of public morality would give effect to the parental role and accept laws relating only to minors. Henkin, Morals and the Constitution: The Sin of Obscenity, 63 Col. L. Rev. 391, 413, n. 68 (1963):

"One must consider also how much difference it makes if laws are designed to protect only the morals of a child. While many of the constitutional arguments against morals legislation apply equally to legislation protecting the morals of children, one can well distinguish laws which do not impose a morality on children, but which support the right of parents to deal with the morals of their children as they see fit."

See also Elias, Sex Publications & Moral Corruption: The Supreme Court Dilemma, 9 W. & M.L. Rev. 302, 320–321 (1967).

Chief Judge Fuld, also emphasized its significance in the earlier case of *People* v. *Kahan*, 15 N.Y. 2d 311, which had struck down the first version of § 484–h on grounds of vagueness. In his concurring opinion, 15 N.Y. 2d, at 312, he said:

"*While the supervision of children's reading may best be left to their parents, the knowledge that parental control or guidance cannot always be provided and society's transcendent interest in protecting the welfare of children justify reasonable regulation of the sale of material to them. It is, therefore, altogether fitting and proper for a state to include in a statute designed to regulate the sale of pornography to children special standards, broader than those embodied in legislation aimed at controlling dissemination of such material to adults.*"

In *Prince* v. *Massachusetts, supra*, at 165, this Court, too, recognized that the State has an interest "to protect the welfare of children" and to see that they are "safeguarded from abuses" which might prevent their "growth into free and independent well-developed men and citizens." The only question remaining, therefore, is whether the New York Legislature might rationally conclude, as it has, that exposure to the materials proscribed by § 484–h constitutes such an "abuse."

Section 484–e of the law states a legislative finding that the material condemned by § 484–h is "a basic factor in impairing the ethical and moral development of our youth and a clear and present danger to the people of the state." It is very doubtful that this finding expresses an accepted scientific fact.[8] But obscenity is not protected expression and may be suppressed without a showing of the circumstances which lie behind the phrase "clear and present danger" in its application to protected speech. *Roth* v. *United States, supra*, at 486–487.[9] To sustain state power to exclude material defined as obscenity by § 484–h requires only that we be able to say that it was not irrational for the legislature to find that exposure to material condemned by the statute is harmful to minors. In *Meyer* v. *Nebraska, supra*, at 400, we were able to say that children's knowledge of the German language "cannot reasonably be regarded as harmful." That cannot be said by us of minors' reading and seeing the sex material. To be sure, there is no lack of "studies" which purport to demonstrate that obscenity is or is not "a basic factor in impairing the ethical and moral development of . . . youth and a clear and present danger to the people of the state." But the growing consensus of commentators is that "[w]hile these studies all agree that a causal link has not been demonstrated, they are equally agreed that a causal link has not been disproved either."[10] We do not demand of legislatures a "scientifi-

cally certain criteria of legislation." *Noble State Bank* v. *Haskell*, 219 U.S. 104, 110. We therefore cannot say that § 484–h, in defining the obscenity of material on the basis of its appeal to minors under 17, has no rational relation to the objective of safeguarding such minors from harm.

II.

Appellant challenges subsections (f) and (g) of § 484–h as in any event void for vagueness. The attack on subsection (f) is that the definition of obscenity "harmful to minors" is so vague that an honest distributor of publications cannot know when he might be held to have violated § 484–h. But the New York Court of Appeals construed this definition to be "virtually identical to the Supreme Court's most recent statement of the elements of obscenity. (*Memoirs* v. *Massachusetts*, 383 U.S. 413, 418)," *Bookcase, Inc.* v. *Broderick, supra*, at 76. The definition therefore gives "men in acting adequate notice of what is prohibited" and does not offend the requirements of due process. *Roth* v. *United States, supra*, at 492; see also *Winters* v. *United States*, 333 U.S. 507, 520.

As is required by *Smith* v. *California*, 361 U.S. 147, § 484–h prohibits only those sales made "knowingly." The challenge to the *scienter* requirement of subsection (g) centers on the definition of "knowingly" insofar as it includes "reason to know" or "a belief or ground for belief which warrants further inspection or inquiry of both: (i) the character and content of any material described herein which is reasonably susceptible of examination by the

---

[8] Compare *Memoirs* v. *Massachusetts*, 383 U.S., at 424 (opinion of DOUGLAS, J.) with *id.*, at 441 (opinion of Clark, J.). See Kuh, *supra*, cc. 18–19; Gaylin, Book Review, 77 Yale L.J. 579, 591–595 (1968); Magrath, *supra*, at 52.

[9] Our conclusion in *Roth*, at 486–487, that the clear and present danger test was irrelevant to the determination of obscenity made it unnecessary in that case to consider the debate among the authorities whether exposure to pornography caused antisocial consequences. See also *Mishkin* v. *New York, supra*; *Ginzburg* v. *United States, supra*; *Memoirs* v. *Massachusetts, supra*.

[10] Magrath, *supra*, at 52. See, *e.g.*, *id.*, at 49–56; Dibble, Obscenity: A State Quarantine to Protect Children, 39 So. Cal.

L. Rev. 345 (1960); Wall, Obscenity and Youth: The Problem and a Possible Solution, 1 Crim. L. Bull. 28, 30 (1965); Note, 55 Cal. L. Rev. 926, 934 (1967); Note, 34 Ford. L. Rev. 692, 694 (1966). See also Paul & Schwartz, Federal Censorship: Obscenity in the Mail, 191–192; Blakey, 41 Notre Dame Law. 1055, 1060, n. 46 (1966); Green, Obscenity, Censorship and Juvenile Delinquency, 14 U. Toronto L. Rev. 229, 249 (1960); Lockhart & McClure, Literature, The Law of Obscenity, and the Constitution, 38 Minn. L. Rev. 295, 373–385 (1954); Note, 52 Ky. L.J. 429, 447 (1964). But despite the vigor of the ongoing controversy whether obscene material will perceptibly create a danger of anti-social conduct, or will probably induce its recipients to such conduct, a medical practitioner recently suggested that the possibility of harmful effects to youth cannot be dismissed as frivolous. Dr. Gaylin of the Columbia University Psychoanalytic Clinic, reporting on the views of some psychiatrists in 77 Yale L.J., at 592–593, said:

"It is in the period of growth [of youth] when these patterns of behavior are laid down, when environmental stimuli of all sorts must be integrated into a workable sense of self, when sensuality is being defined and fears elaborated, when pleasure confronts security and impulse encounters control—it is in this period, undramatically, and with time, that legalized pornography might conceivably be damaging."

Dr. Gaylin emphasizes that a child might not be as well prepared as an adult to make an intelligent choice as to the material he chooses to read:

"[P]sychiatrists . . . made a distinction between the reading of pornography, as unlikely to be per se harmful, and the permitting of the reading of pornography, which was conceived as potentially destructive. The child is protected in his reading of pornography by the knowledge that it is pornographic, *i.e.*, disapproved. It is outside of parental standards and not a part of his identification processes. To openly permit implies parental approval and even suggests seductive encouragement. If this is so of parental approval, it is equally so of societal approval—another potent influence on the developing ego." 77 Yale L.J., at 594.

defendant, and (ii) the age of the minor, provided however, that an honest mistake shall constitute an excuse from liability hereunder if the defendant made a reasonable bona fide attempt to ascertain the true age of such minor."

As to (i), § 484–h was passed after the New York Court of Appeals decided *People* v. *Finkelstein*, 9 N.Y. 2d 342, which read the requirement of *scienter* into New York's general obscenity statute, § 1141 of the Penal Law. The constitutional requirement of *scienter*, in the sense of knowledge of the contents of material, rests on the necessity "to avoid the hazard of self-censorship of constitutionally protected material and to compensate for the ambiguities inherent in the definition of obscenity," *Mishkin* v. *New York, supra,* at 511. The Court of Appeals in *Finkelstein* interpreted § 1141 to require "the vital element of scienter" and defined that requirement in these terms: "A reading of the statute [§ 1141] as a whole clearly indicates that only those who are *in some manner aware of the character of the material* they attempt to distribute should be punished. It is not innocent but *calculated* purveyance of filth which is exorcised. . . ." 9 N.Y. 2d, at 344–345. (Emphasis supplied.) In *Mishkin* v. *New York, supra,* at 510–511, we held that a challenge to the validity of § 1141 founded on *Smith* v. *California, supra,* was foreclosed in light of this construction. When § 484–h was before the New York Legislature its attention was directed to *People* v. *Finkelstein,* as defining the nature of *scienter* required to sustain the statute. 1965 N.Y.S. Leg. Ann. 54–56. We may therefore infer that the reference in provision (i) to knowledge of "the *character* and content of any material described herein" incorporates the gloss given the term "character" in *People* v. *Finkelstein.* In that circumstance *Mishkin* requires rejection of appellant's challenge to provision (i) and makes it unnecessary for us to define further today "what sort of mental element is requisite to a constitutionally permissible prosecution," *Smith* v. *California, supra,* at 154.

Appellant also attacks provision (ii) as impermissibly vague. This attack however is leveled only at the provision's proviso according the defendant a defense of "honest mistake" as to the age of the minor. Appellant argues that "the statute does not tell the bookseller what effort he must make before he can be excused." The argument is wholly without merit. The proviso states expressly that the defendant must be acquitted on the ground of "honest mistake" if the defendant proves that he made "a reasonable bona fide attempt to ascertain the true age of such minor." Cf. 1967 Penal Law § 235.22(2), n. 1, *supra.*

Affirmed.

APPENDIX A.

New York Penal Law § 484–h as enacted by L. 1965, c. 327, provides:

§ 484–h. Exposing minors to harmful materials.

1. Definitions. As used in this section:

(a) "Minor" means any person under the age of seventeen years.

(b) "Nudity" means the showing of the human male or female genitals, pubic area or buttocks with less than a full opaque covering, or the showing of the female breast with less than a fully opaque covering of any portion thereof below the top of the nipple, or the depiction of covered male genitals in a discernibly turgid state.

(c) "Sexual conduct" means acts of masturbation, homosexuality, sexual intercourse, or physical contact with a person's clothed or unclothed genitals, pubic area, buttocks or, if such person be a female, breast.

(d) "Sexual excitement" means the condition of human male or female genitals when in a state of sexual stimulation or arousal.

(e) "Sado-masochistic abuse" means flagellation or torture by or upon a person clad in undergarments, a mask or bizarre costume, or the condition of being fettered, bound or otherwise physically restrained on the part of one so clothed.

(f) "Harmful to minors" means that quality of any description or representation, in whatever form, of nudity, sexual conduct, sexual excitement, or sado-masochistic abuse, when it:

(i) predominantly appeals to the prurient, shameful or morbid interest of minors, and

(ii) is patently offensive to prevailing standards in the adult community as a whole with respect to what is suitable material for minors, and

(iii) is utterly without redeeming social importance for minors.

(g) "Knowingly" means having general knowledge of, or reason to know, or a belief or ground for belief which warrants further inspection or inquiry of both:

(i) the character and content of any material described herein which is reasonably susceptible of examination by the defendant, and

(ii) the age of the minor, provided however, that an honest mistake shall constitute an excuse from liability hereunder if the defendant made a reasonable bona fide attempt to ascertain the true age of such minor.

2. It shall be unlawful for any person knowingly to sell or loan for monetary consideration to a minor:

(a) any picture, photograph, drawing, sculpture, motion picture film, or similar visual representation or image of a person or portion of the human body which depicts nudity, sexual conduct or sado-masochistic abuse and which is harmful to minors, or

(b) any book, pamphlet, magazine, printed matter however reproduced, or sound recording which contains any matter enumerated in paragraph (a) of subdivision two hereof, or explicit and detailed verbal descriptions or narrative accounts of sexual excitement, sexual conduct or sado-masochistic abuse and which, taken as a whole, is harmful to minors.

3. It shall be unlawful for any person knowingly to exhibit for a monetary consideration to a minor or knowingly to sell to a minor an admission ticket or pass or knowingly to admit a minor for a monetary consideration to premises whereon there is exhibited, a motion picture, show or other presentation which, in whole or in part, depicts nudity, sexual conduct or sado-masochistic abuse and which is harmful to minors.

4. A violation of any provision hereof shall constitute a misdemeanor.

APPENDIX B.

State obscenity statutes having some provision referring to distribution to minors are:

Cal. Penal Code §§ 311–312 (West Supp. 1966); 3 Col. Rev. Stat. Ann. §§ 40–9–16 to 40–9–27 (1963); 9 Conn. Gen. Stat. Rev. §§ 53–243 to 53–245 (1958) (Supp. 1965); 7 Del. Code Ann., Tit. 11, §§ 435, 711–713 (1953); 22A Fla. Stat. Ann. §§ 847.011–847.06 (1965), 1967 Fla. Laws, h. 67–153; 10 Ga. Code Ann. §§ 26–6301 to 26–6309a (1953) (Supp. 1967); 2 Hawaii Rev. Laws § 267–8 (1955); 4 Idaho Code Ann. §§ 18–1506 to 18–1510 (Supp. 1967); 38 Ill. Ann. Stat., c. 38, §§ 11–20 to 11–21 (Smith-Hurd 1964) (Supp. 1967); Iowa Code Ann. §§ 725.4–725.12 (1950); 3 Ky. Rev. Stat. §§ 436.100–436.130, 436.540–436.580 (1962) (Supp. 1966); 9 La. Rev. Stat. §§ 91.11, 92, 106 (1950) (Supp. 1966); 9 Me. Rev. Stat. Ann., Tit. 17, §§ 2901–2905 (1964); 3 Md. Ann. Code, Art. 27, §§ 417–425 (1957) (Supp. 1967); Mass. Gen. Laws Ann., c. 272, §§ 28–33 (1959) (Supp. 1966); 25 Mich. Stat. Ann. §§ 28.575–28.579 (1954) (Supp. 1965); Mo. Ann. Stat. §§ 563.270–563.310 (1953) (Supp. 1967); 8 Mont. Rev. Codes Ann. §§ 94–3601 to 94–3606 (1949) (Supp. 1967); Neb. Rev. Stat. §§ 28–926.09 to 28–926.10 (Supp. 1965); 2 Nev. Rev. Stat. §§ 201.250, 207.180 (1957); 5 N.H. Rev. Stat. Ann. § 571–A (Supp. 1967); N.J. Stat. Ann. §§ 2A:115–1.1 to 2A:115–4 (Supp. 1967); 1 B.N.C. Gen. Stat. § 14–189 (Supp. 1967); 2 N.D. Cent. Code §§ 12–21–07 to 12–21–09 (1960); Ohio Rev. Code Ann. §§ 2903.10–11, 2905.34–2905.39 (p. 1954) (Supp. 1966); Okla. Stat. Ann., Tit. 21, §§ 1021–1024, 1032–1040 (1958) (Supp. 1967); Pa. Stat. Ann., Tit. 18, §§ 3831–3833, 4524 (1963); 3 R.I. Gen. Laws Ann. §§ 11–31–1 to 11–31.1–10 (1956) (Supp. 1966); 4 S.C. Code Ann. §§ 16–414 to 16–421 (1962) (Supp. 1966); Tex. Pen. Code Ann., Arts. 526, 527b (1952) (Supp. 1967); 2 Utah Code Ann. § 10–8–41 (1953), 8 Utah Code Ann. §§ 76–39–5, 76–39–17 (1953); 5 Vt. Stat. Ann., Tit. 13, §§ 2801–2805 (1958); 4 Va. Code Ann. §§ 18.1–227 to 18.1–236.3 (1960) (Supp. 1966); W. Va. Code Ann. § 61–8–11 (1966); Wyo. Stat. Ann. §§ 6–103, 7–148 (1957).

Mr. Justice STEWART, concurring in the result.

A doctrinaire, knee-jerk application of the First Amendment would, of course, dictate the nullification of this New York statute.[1] But that result is not required, I think, if we bear in mind what it is that the First Amendment protects.

The First Amendment guarantees liberty of human expression in order to preserve in our Nation what Mr. Justice Holmes called a "free trade in ideas."[2] To that end, the Constitution protects more than just a man's freedom to say or write or publish what he wants. It secures as well the liberty of each man to decide for himself what he will read and to what he will listen. The Constitution guarantees, in short, a society of free choice. Such a society presupposes the capacity of its members to choose.

When expression occurs in a setting where the capacity to make a choice is absent, government regulation of that expression may co-exist with and even implement First Amendment guarantees. So it was that this Court sustained a city ordinance prohibiting people from imposing their opinions on others "by way of sound trucks with loud and raucous noises on city streets."[3] And so it was that my Brothers BLACK —and DOUGLAS thought that the First Amendment itself prohibits a person from foisting his uninvited views upon the members of a captive audience.[4]

I think a State may permissibly determine that, at least in some precisely delineated areas, a child[5]—like someone in a captive audience—is not possessed of that full capacity for individual choice which is the presupposition of First Amendment guarantees. It is only upon such a premise, I should suppose, that a State may deprive children of other rights—the right to marry, for example, or the right to vote—deprivations that would be constitutionally intolerable for adults.[6]

I cannot hold that this state law, on its face,[7] violates the First and Fourteenth Amendments.

Mr. JUSTICE DOUGLAS, with whom Mr. JUSTICE BLACK concurs, dissenting.

———

While I would be willing to reverse the judgment on the basis of *Redrup* v. *New York*, 386 U.S. 767, for the reasons stated by my Brother FORTAS, my objections strike deeper.

If we were in the field of substantive due process and seeking to measure the propriety of state law by the standards of the Fourteenth Amendment, I suppose there would be no difficulty under our decisions in sustaining this act. For there is a view held by many that the so-called "obscene" book or tract or magazine has a deleterious effect upon the young, although I seriously doubt the wisdom of trying by law to put the fresh, evanescent, natural blossoming of sex in the category of "sin."

That, however, was the view of our preceptor in this field, Anthony Comstock, who waged his war against "obscenity" from the year 1872 until his death in 1915. Some of his views are set forth in his book Traps for the Young, first published in 1883, excerpts from which I set out in Appendix I to this opinion.

The title of the book refers to "traps" created by Satan "for boys and girls especially." Comstock, of course, operated on the theory that every human has an "inborn tendency toward wrongdoing which is restrained mainly by fear of the final judgment." In his view any book which tended to remove that fear is a part of the "trap" which Satan created. Hence, Comstock would have condemned a much wider range of literature than the present Court is apparently inclined to do.[1]

———

[3] *Kovacs* v. *Cooper*, 336 U.S. 77, 86.

[4] *Public Utilities Comm'n* v. *Pollak*, 343 U.S. 451, 466 (dissenting opinion of Mr. JUSTICE BLACK), 467 (dissenting opinion of Mr. JUSTICE DOUGLAS).

[5] The appellant does not challenge New York's power to draw the line at age 17, and I intimate no view upon that question.

[6] Compare *Loving* v. *Virginia*, 388 U.S. 1, 12; *Carrington* v. *Rash*, 380 U.S. 89, 96.

[7] As the Court notes, the appellant makes no argument that the material in this case was not "harmful to minors" within the statutory definition, or that the statute was unconstitutionally applied.

[1] Two writers have explained Comstock as follows:

———

[1] The First Amendment is made applicable to the States through the Fourteenth Amendment. *Stromberg* v. *California*, 283 U.S. 359.

[2] *Abrams* v. *United States*, 250 U.S. 616, 630 (dissenting opinion).

It was Comstock who was responsible for the Federal Anti-Obscenity Act of March 3, 1873. It was he also who was responsible for the New York Act which soon followed. He was responsible for the organization of the New York Society for the Suppression of Vice, which by its act of incorporation was granted one-half of the fines levied on people successfully prosecuted by the Society or its agents.

I would conclude from Comstock and his Traps for the Young and from other authorities that a legislature could not be said to be wholly irrational[2] (*Ferguson v. Skrupa*, 372 U.S. 726; and see *Williamson v. Lee Optical Co.*, 348 U.S. 483; *Daniel v. Family Ins. Co.*, 336 U.S. 220; *Olson v. Nebraska*, 313 U.S. 236) if it decided that sale of "obscene" material to the young should be banned.[3]

The problem under the First Amendment, however, has always seemed to me to be quite different. For its mandate (originally applicable only to the Federal Government but now applicable to the States as well by reason of the Fourteenth Amendment) is directed to any law "abridging the freedom of speech, or of the press." I appreciate that there are those who think that "obscenity" is impliedly

excluded; but I have indicated on prior occasions why I have been unable to reach that conclusion.[4] See *Ginzburg v. United States*, 383 U.S. 463, 482 (dissenting opinion); *Jacobellis v. Ohio*, 378 U.S. 184, 196 (concurring opinion of MR. JUSTICE BLACK); *Roth v. United States*, 354 U.S. 476, 508 (dissenting opinion). And the corollary of that view, as I expressed it in *Public Utilities Comm'n v. Pollak*, 343 U.S. 451, 467, 468 (dissenting opinions), is that Big Brother can no more say what a person shall listen to or read than he can say what shall be published.

This is not to say that the Court and Anthony Comstock are wrong in concluding that the kind of literature New York condemns does harm. As a matter of fact, the

---

"He must have known that he could not wall out from his own mind all erotic fancies, and so he turned all the more fiercely upon the ribaldry of others." H. Broun & M. Leech, Anthony Comstock 27 (1927).

A notable forerunner of Comstock was an Englishman, Thomas Bowdler. Armed with a talent for discovering the "offensive," Bowdler expurgated Shakespeare's plays and Gibbon's History of the Decline and Fall of the Roman Empire. The result was "The Family Shakespeare," first published in 10 volumes in 1818, and a version of Gibbon's famous history "omitting everything of an immoral or irreligious nature, and incidentally rearranging the order of chapters to be in the strict chronology so dear to the obsessional heart." M. Wilson, The Obsessional Compromise, A Note on Thomas Bowdler (1965) (paper in Library of the American Psychiatric Association, Washington, D.C.).

2 "The effectiveness of more subtle forms of censorship as an instrument of social control can be very great. They are effective over a wider field of behavior than is propaganda in that they affect convivial and 'purely personal' behavior.

"The principle is that certain verbal formulae shall not be stated, in print or in conversation; from this the restriction extends to the discussion of certain topics. A perhaps quite rationally formulated taboo is imposed; it becomes a quasi-religious factor for the members of the group who subscribe to it. If they are a majority, and the taboo does not affect some master-symbol of an influential minority, it is apt to become quite universal in its effect. A great number of taboos—to expressive and to other acts—are embodied in the *mores* of any people. The sanction behind each taboo largely determines its durability—in the sense of resistance opposed to the development of contradictory *counter-mores*, or of simple disintegration from failure to give returns in personal security. If it is to succeed for a long time, there must be recurrent reaffirmations of the taboo in connection with the sanctioning power.

"The occasional circulation of stories about a breach of the taboo and the evil consequences that flowed from this to the offender *and* to the public cause (the sanctioning power) well serves this purpose. Censorship of this sort has the color of voluntary acceptance of a ritualistic avoidance, in behalf of oneself and the higher power. A violation, after the primitive patterns to which we have all been exposed, strikes at both the sinner and his god." The William Alanson White Psychiatric Foundation Memorandum: Propaganda & Censorship, 3 Psychiatry 628, 631 (1940).

3 And see W. Gaylin, Book Review: The Prickley Problems of Pornography, 77 Yale L.J. 579, 594.

---

4 My Brother HARLAN says that no other Justice of this Court, past or present, has ever "stated his acceptance" of the view that "obscenity" is within the protection of the First and Fourteenth Amendments. *Ante*, at 2. That observation, however, should not be understood as demonstrating that no other members of this Court, since its first Term in 1790, have adhered to the view of my Brother BLACK and myself. For the issue "whether obscenity is utterance within the area of protected speech and press" was only "squarely presented" to this Court for the first time in 1957. *Roth v. United States*, 354 U.S. 476, 481. This is indeed understandable, for the state legislatures have borne the main burden in enacting laws dealing with "obscenity"; and the strictures of the First Amendment were not applied to them through the Fourteenth until comparatively late in our history. In *Gitlow v. New York*, 268 U.S. 652, decided in 1925, the Court assumed that the right of free speech was among the freedoms protected against state infringement by the Due Process Clause of the Fourteenth Amendment. See also *Whitney v. California*, 274 U.S. 357, 371, 373; *Fiske v. Kansas*, 274 U.S. 380. In 1931, *Stromberg v. California*, 283 U.S. 359, held that the right of free speech was guaranteed in full measure by the Fourteenth Amendment. But even after these events "obscenity" cases were not inundating this Court; and even as late as 1948, the Court could say that many state obscenity statutes had "lain dormant for decades." *Winters v. New York*, 333 U.S. 507, 511. In several cases prior to *Roth*, the Court reviewed convictions under federal statutes forbidding the sending of "obscene" materials through the mails. But in none of these cases was the question squarely presented or decided whether "obscenity" was protected speech under the First Amendment; rather, the issues were limited to matters of statutory construction, or questions of procedure, such as the sufficiency of the indictment. See *United States v. Chase*, 135 U.S. 255; *Grimm v. United States*, 156 U.S. 604; *Rosen v. United States*, 161 U.S. 29; *Swearingen v. United States*, 161 U.S. 446; *Andrews v. United States*, 162 U.S. 420; *Price v. United States*, 165 U.S. 311; *Dunlop v. United States*, 165 U.S. 486; *Bartell v. United States*, 227 U.S. 427; *Dysart v. United States*, 272 U.S. 655; *United States v. Limehouse*, 285 U.S. 424. Thus, *Roth v. United States*, *supra*, which involved both a challenge to 18 U.S.C. § 1461 (punishing the mailing of "obscene" material) and, in a consolidated case (*Alberts v. California*), an attack upon Cal. Pen. Code § 311 (prohibiting, *inter alia*, the keeping for sale or advertising of "obscene" material), was the first case authoritatively to measure federal and state obscenity statutes against the prohibitions of the First and Fourteenth Amendments. I cannot speak for those who preceded us in time; but neither can I interpret occasional utterances suggesting that "obscenity" was not protected by the First Amendment as considered expressions of the views of any particular Justices of the Court. See, *e.g.*, *Chaplinsky v. New Hampshire*, 315 U.S. 568, 571–572; *Beauharnais v. Illinois*, 343 U.S. 250, 266. The most that can be said, then, is that no other members of this Court since 1957 have adhered to the view of my Brother BLACK and myself.

notion of censorship is founded on the belief that speech and press sometimes do harm and therefore can be regulated. I once visited a foreign nation where the regime of censorship was so strict that all I could find in the book-stalls were tracts on religion and tracts on mathematics. Today the Court determines the constitutionality of New York's law regulating the sale of literature to children on the basis of the reasonableness of the law in light of the welfare of the child. If the problem of state and federal regulation of "obscenity" is in the field of substantive due process, I see no reason to limit the legislatures to protecting children alone. The "juvenile delinquents" I have known are mostly over 50 years of age. If rationality is the measure of the validity of this law, then I can see how modern Anthony Comstocks could make out a case for "protecting" many groups in our society, not merely children.

While I find the literature and movies which come to us for clearance exceedingly dull and boring, I understand how some can and do become very excited and alarmed and think that something should be done to stop the flow. It is one thing for parents[5] and the religious organizations to be active and involved. It is quite a different matter for the State to become implicated as a censor. As I read the First Amendment, it was designed to keep the State and the hands of all state officials off the printing presses of America and off the distribution systems for all printed literature. Anthony Comstock wanted it the other way; he indeed put the police and prosecutor in the middle of this publishing business.

I think it would require a constitutional amendment to achieve that result. If there were a constitutional amendment, perhaps the people of the country would come up with some national board of censorship. Censors are of course propelled by their own neuroses.[6] That is why a universally accepted definition of obscenity is impossible. Any definition is indeed highly subjective, turning on the neurosis of the censor. Those who have a deep-seated, subconscious conflict may well become either great crusaders against a particular kind of literature or avid customers of it.[7] That, of course, is the danger of letting any group of citizens be the judges of what other people, young or old, should read. Those would be issues to be canvassed and debated in case of a constitutional amendment creating a regime of censorship in the country. And if the people, in their wisdom, launched us on that course, it would be a considered choice.

Today this Court sits as the Nation's board of censors. With all respect, I do not know of any group in the country less qualified first, to know what obscenity is when they see it, and second, to have any considered judgment as to what the deleterious or beneficial impact of a particular publication may have on minds either young or old.

I would await a constitutional amendment that authorized the modern Anthony Comstocks to censor literature before publishers, authors, or distributors can be fined or jailed for what they print or sell.

APPENDIX I.

COMSTOCK, TRAPS FOR THE YOUNG 20–22 (1883).

And it came to pass that as Satan went to and fro upon the earth, watching his traps and rejoicing over his numerous victims, he found room for improvement in some of his schemes. The daily press did not meet all his requirements. The *weekly* illustrated papers of crime would do for young men and sports, for brothels, gin-mills, and thieves' resorts, but were found to be so gross, so libidinous, so monstrous, that every decent person spurned them. They were excluded from the home on sight. They were too high-priced for children, and too cumbersome to be conveniently hid from the parent's eye or carried in the boy's pocket. So he resolved to make another trap for boys and girls especially.

He also resolved to make the most of these vile illustrated weekly papers, by lining the news-stands and shop-windows along the pathway of the children from home to school and church, so that they could not go to and from these places of instruction without giving him opportunity to defile their pure minds by flaunting these atrocities before their eyes.

And Satan rejoiced greatly that professing Christians were silent and apparently acquiesced in his plans. He found that our most refined men and women went freely to trade with persons who displayed these traps for sale; that few, if any, had moral courage to enter a protest against this public display of indecencies, and scarcely one in all the land had the boldness to say to the dealer in filth, "I will not give you one cent of my patronage so long as you sell these devil-traps to ruin the young." And he was proud of professing Christians and respectable citizens on this account, and caused honorable mention to be made of them in general order to his imps, because of the quiet and orderly assistance thus rendered him.

Satan stirred up certain of his willing tools on earth by the promise of a few paltry dollars to improve greatly on the death-dealing quality of the weekly death-traps, and forthwith came a series of new snares of fascinating construction, small and tempting in price, and baited with high-sounding names. These sure-ruin traps comprise a large variety of half-dime novels, five and ten cent story papers, and low-priced pamphlets for boys and girls.

This class includes the silly, insipid tale, the coarse, slangy story in the dialect of the barroom, the blood-and-

---

[5] See Appendix II to this opinion.

[6] Reverend Fr. Juan de Castaniza of the 16th century explained those who denounced obscenity as expressing only their own feelings. In his view they had too much reason to suspect themselves of being "obscene," since "vicious men are always prone to think others like themselves." T. Schroeder, A Challenge to Sex Censors 44–45 (1938).

"Obscenity, like witchcraft . . . consists, broadly speaking, of a [delusional] projection of certain emotions (which, as the very word implies, emanate from within) to external things and an endowment of such things (or in the case of witchcraft, of such persons) with the moral qualities corresponding to these inward states . . . .

"Thus persons responsible for the persistent attempts to suppress the dissemination of popular knowledge concerning sex matters betray themselves unwittingly as the bearers of the very impulses they would so ostentatiously help others to avoid. Such persons should know through their own experience that ignorance of a subject does not insure immunity against the evils of which it treats, nor does the propitiatory act of noisy public disapproval of certain evils signify innocence or personal purity." Van Teslaar, Book Review, 8 Jour. Abnormal Psychology 282, 286 (1913).

[7] See Appendix III to this opinion.

thunder romance of border life, and the exaggerated details of crimes, real and imaginary. Some have highly colored sensational reports of real crimes, while others, and by far the larger number, deal with most improbable creations of fiction. The unreal far outstrips the real. Crimes are gilded, and lawlessness is painted to resemble valor, making a bid for bandits, brigands, murderers, thieves, and criminals in general. Who would go to the State prison, the gambling saloon, or the brothel to find a suitable companion for the child? Yet a more insidious foe is selected when these stories are allowed to become associates for the child's mind and to shape and direct the thoughts.

The finest fruits of civilization are consumed by these vermin. Nay, these products of corrupt minds are the eggs from which all kinds of villainies are hatched. Put the entire batch of these stories together, and I challenge the publishers and vendors to show a single instance where any boy or girl has been elevated in morals, or where any noble or refined instinct has been developed by them.

The leading character in many, if not in the vast majority of these stories, is some boy or girl who possesses usually extraordinary beauty of countenance, the most superb clothing, abundant wealth, the strength of a giant, the agility of a squirrel, the cunning of a fox, the brazen effrontery of the most daring villain, and who is utterly destitute of any regard for the laws of God or man. Such a one is foremost among desperadoes, the companion and beau-ideal of maidens, and the high favorite of some rich person, who by his patronage and indorsement lifts the young villain into lofty positions in society, and provides liberally of his wealth to secure him immunity for his crimes. These stories link the pure maiden with the most foul and loathsome criminals. Many of them favor violation of marriage laws and cheapen female virtue.

APPENDIX II.

A SPECIAL TO THE WASHINGTON POST
by
AUSTIN C. WEHRWEIN

White Bear Lake, Minn., March 2.—Faced with the threat of a law suit, the school board in this community of 12,000 north of St. Paul is reviewing its mandatory sex education courses, but officials expressed fear that they couldn't please everybody.

Mothers threatened to picket and keep their children home when sex education films are scheduled. Mrs. Robert Murphy, the mother of five who led the protests, charged that the elementary school "took the privacy out of marriage."

"Now," she said, "our kids know what a shut bedroom door means. The program is taking their childhood away. The third graders went into see a movie on birth and came out adults."

She said second-grade girls have taken to walking around with "apples and oranges under their blouses." Her seventh-grade son was given a study sheet on menstruation, she said, demanding "why should a seventh-grade boy have to know about menstruation?"

Mrs. Murphy, who fears the program will lead to experimentation, said that it was "pagan" and argued that even animals don't teach their young those things "before they're ready."

"One boy in our block told his mother, 'Guess what, next week our teacher's gonna tell us how daddy fertilized you," reported Mrs. Martin Capeder. "They don't need to know all that."

But Norman Jensen, principal of Lincoln School, said that the program, which runs from kindergarten through the 12th grade, was approved by the school district's PTA council, the White Bear Lake Ministerial Association and the district school board. It was based, he said, on the polls that showed 80 per cent of the children got no home sex education, and the curriculum was designed to be "matter-of-fact."

The protesting parents insisted they had no objection to sex education as such, but some said girls should not get it until age 12, and boys only at age 15—"or when they start shaving."

In nearby St. Paul Park, 71 parents have formed a group called "Concerned Parents Against Sex Education" and are planning legal action to prevent sex education from kindergarten through seventh grade. They have also asked equal time with the PTAs of eight schools in the district "to discuss topics such as masturbation, contraceptives, unqualified instructors, religious belief, morality and attitudes.")

The White Bear protesters have presented the school board with a list of terms and definitions deemed objectionable. Designed for the seventh grade, it included vagina, clitoris, erection, intercourse and copulation. A film, called "Fertilization and Birth" depicts a woman giving birth. It has been made optional after being shown to all classes.

Mrs. Ginny McKay, a president of one of the local PTAs defended the program, saying "Sex is a natural and beautiful thing. We (the PTA) realized that the parents had to get around to where the kids have been for a long time."

But Mrs. Murphy predicted this result: "Instead of 15 [*sic*] and 15-year-old pregnant girls, they'll have 12 and 13-year-old pregnant girls."

APPENDIX III.

(A). SCHROEDER, OBSCENE LITERATURE AND CONSTITUTIONAL LAW 277–278 (1911).

It thus appears that the only unifying element generalized in the word "obscene" (that is, the only thing common to every conception of obscenity and indecency), is subjective, is an affiliated emotion of disapproval. This emotion under varying circumstances of temperament and education in different persons, and in the same person in different stages of development, is aroused by entirely different stimuli, and by fear of the judgment of others, and so has become associated with an infinite variety of ever-changing objectives, with not even one common characteristic in objective nature; that is, in literature or art.

Since few men have identical experiences, and fewer still evolve to an agreement in their conceptional and emotional associations, it must follow that practically none have the same standards for judging the "obscene," even when their conclusions agree. The word "obscene," like such words as delicate, ugly, lovable, hateful, etc., is an abstraction not based upon a reasoned, nor sense-perceived, likeness between objectives, but the selection or classification under it is made, on the basis of similarity in the emotions aroused, by an infinite variety of images; and every classification thus made, in turn, depends in each person upon his fears, his hopes, his prior experience, suggestions, education, and the degree of neuro-sexual or psycho-sexual health. Because it is a matter wholly of emotions, it has come to be that "men think they know because they feel, and are firmly convinced because strongly agitated."

This, then, is a demonstration that obscenity exists only in the minds and emotions of those who believe in it, and is not a quality of a book or picture. Since, then, the general conception "obscene" is devoid of every objective element of unification; and since the subjective element, the associated emotion, is indefinable from its very nature, and inconstant as to the character of the stimulus capable of arousing it, and variable and immeasurable as to its relative degrees of intensity, it follows that the "obscene" is incapable of accurate definition or a general test adequate to secure uniformity of result, in its application by every person, to each book of doubtful "purity."

Being so essentially and inextricably involved with human emotions that no man can frame such a definition of the word "obscene," either in terms of the qualities of a book, or such that, *by it alone*, any judgment whatever is possible, much less is it possible that by any such alleged "test" every other man must reach the same conclusion about the obscenity of every conceivable book. Therefore, the so-called judicial "tests" of obscenity are not standards of judgment, but, on the contrary, by every such "test" the rule of decision is itself uncertain, and in terms invokes the varying experiences of the testors within the foggy realm of problematical speculation about psychic tendencies, without the help of which the "test" itself is meaningless and useless. It follows that to each person the "test," of criminality, which should be a general standard of judgment, unavoidably becomes a personal and particular standard, differing in all persons according to those varying experiences which they read into the judicial "test." It is this which makes uncertain, and, therefore, all the more objectionable, all the present laws against obscenity. Later it will be shown that this uncertainty in the criteria of guilt renders these laws unconstitutional.

(B). Kallen, The Ethical Aspects of Censorship, *v.*
Social Meaning of Legal Concepts
50–51 (1953).

To this authoritarian's will, difference is the same thing as inferiority, wickedness and corruption; he can apprehend it only as a devotion to error and a commitment to sin. He can acknowledge it only if he attributes to it moral turpitude and intellectual vice. Above all, difference must be for him, by its simple existence, an aggression against the good, the true, the beautiful and the right. His imperative is to destroy it; if he cannot destroy it, to contain it; if he cannot contain it, to hunt it down, cut it off and shut it out.

Certain schools of psychology suggest that this aggression is neither simple nor wholly aggression. They suggest that it expresses a compulsive need to bring to open contemplation the secret parts of the censor's psychosomatic personality, and a not less potent need to keep the

secret and not suffer the shamefaced dishonor of their naked exposures. The censor's activities, in that they call for a constant public preoccupation with such secret parts, free his psyche from the penalties of such concern while transvaluing at the same time his pursuit and inspection of the obscene, the indecent, the pornographic, the blasphemous and the otherwise shameful into an honorable defense of the public morals. The censor, by purporting, quite unconscious of his actual dynamic, to protect the young from corruption, frees his consciousness to dwell upon corruption without shame or dishonor. Thus Anthony Comstock could say with overt sincerity: "When the genius of the arts produces obscene, lewd and lascivious ideas, the deadly effect upon the young is just as perceptible as when the same ideas are represented by gross experience in prose and poetry. . . . If through the eye and ear the sensuous book, picture or story is allowed to enter, the thoughts will be corrupted, the conscience seared, so such things reproduced by fancy in the thoughts awaken forces for evil which will explode with irresistible force carrying to destruction every human safeguard to virtue and honor." Did not evil Bernard Shaw, who gave the English language the word *comstockery*, declare himself, in his preface to *The Shewing-Up of Blanco Posnet*, "a specialist in immoral, heretical plays . . . to force the public to reconsider its morals"? So the brave Comstock passionately explored and fought the outer expressions of the inner forces of evil and thus saved virtue and honor from destruction.

But could this observation of his be made, save on the basis of introspection and not the scientific study of others? For such a study would reveal, for each single instance of which it was true, hundreds of thousands of others of which it was false. Like the correlation of misfortune with the sixth day of the week or the number 13, this basis comstockery signalizes a fear-projected superstition. It is an externalization of anxiety and fear, not a fact objectively studied and appraised. And the anxiety and fear are reaction-formations of the censor's inner self.

Of course, this is an incomplete description of the motivation and logic of censorship. In the great censorial establishments of the tradition, these more or less unconscious drives are usually items of a syndrome whose dominants are either greed for pelf, power, and prestige, reinforced by anxiety that they might be lost, or anxiety that they might be lost reinforced by insatiable demands for more.

Authoritarian societies usually insure these goods by means of a prescriptive creed and code for which their rulers claim supernatural origins and supernatural sanctions. The enforcement of the prescriptions is not entrusted to a censor alone. The ultimate police-power is held by the central hierarchy, and the censorship of the arts is only one department of the thought-policing.

(C). Crawford, Literature and the Psychopathic.
10 Psycho-Analytic Review 445–446 (1923).

Objection, then, to modern works on the ground that they are, in the words of the objectors, "immoral," is made principally on the basis of an actual desire to keep sexual psychopathies intact, or to keep the general scheme of repressions, which inevitably involves psychopathic conditions, intact. The activities of persons, professionally or otherwise definitely concerned with censorship, furnish proof, evident enough to the student of such matters, that they themselves are highly abnormal. It is safe to say that *every censorship has a psychopath back of it.*

Carried to a legal end, censorship would inevitably destroy all literary art. Every sexual act is an instinctive feeling out for an understanding of life. Literary art, like every other type of creative effort, is a form of sublimation. It is a more conscious seeking for the same understanding that the common man instinctively seeks. The literary artist, having attained understanding, communicates that understanding to his readers. That understanding, whether of sexual or other matters, is certain to come into conflict with popular beliefs, fears, and taboos, because these are, for the most part, based on error . . . the presence of an opinion concerning which one thinks it would be unprofitable, immoral, or unwise to inquire is, of itself, strong evidence that that opinion is non-rational. Most of the more deep-seated convictions of the human race belong to this category. Anyone who is seeking for understanding is certain to encounter this non-rational attitude.

The act of sublimation on the part of the writer necessarily involves an act of sublimation on the part of the reader. The typical psychopathic patient and the typical public have alike a deep-rooted unconscious aversion to sublimation. Inferiority and other complexes enter in, to make the individual feel that acts of sublimation would destroy his comfortable, though illusory, sense of superiority. Again, there is the realization on the part of the mass of people that they are unable to sublimate as the artist does, and to admit his power and right to do so involves destruction of the specious sense of superiority to him. It is these two forms of aversion to sublimation which account for a considerable part of public objection to the arts. The common man and his leader, the psychopathic reformer, are aiming unconsciously at leveling humanity to a plane of pathological mediocrity.

To the student of abnormal psychology the legend, popular literature, and literature revelatory of actual life, are all significant. In the legend he finds race taboos; in the popular literature of the day he discovers this reinforced by the mass of contemporary and local taboos; in literature that aims to be realistically revelatory of life he finds material for study such as he can hardly obtain from any group of patients. The frankness which he seeks in vain from the persons with whom he comes into personal contact, he can find in literature. It is a field in which advances may be made comparable to the advances of actual scientific research.

Moreover, the student of abnormal psychology will commend realistic, revelatory literature not only to his patients, who are suffering from specific psychopathic difficulties, but to the public generally. He will realize that it is one of the most important factors in the development of human freedom. No one is less free than primitive man. The farther we can get from the attitude of the legend and its slightly more civilized successor, popular literature, the nearer we shall be to a significant way of life.

(D). RINALDO, PSYCHOANALYSIS OF THE "REFORMER" 56–60 (1921).

The other aspect of the humanist movement is a very sour and disgruntled puritanism which seems at first glance to protest and contradict every step in the libidinous development. As a matter of fact it is just as much an hysterical outburst as the most sensuous flesh masses of Rubens, or the sinuous squirming lines of Louis XV decoration. Both are reactions to the same morbid past experience.

The Puritan like the sensualist rebels at the very beginning against the restraint of celibacy. Unfortunately, however, he finds himself unable to satisfy the libido in either normal gratification or healthy converted activities. His condition is as much one of super-excitement as that of the libertine. Unable to find satisfaction in other ways, from which for one reason or another he is inhibited, he develops a morbid irritation, contradicting, breaking, prohibiting, and thwarting the manifestations of the very exciting causes.

Not being able to produce beautiful things he mars them, smashing stained glass windows, destroying sculptures, cutting down May-poles, forbidding dances, clipping the hair, covering the body with hideous misshapen garments and silencing laughter and song. He cannot build so he must destroy. He cannot create so he hinders creation. He is a sort of social abortionist and like an abortionist only comes into his own when there is an illegitimate brat to be torn from the womb. He cries against sin, but it is the pleasure of sin rather than the sin he fights. It is the enjoyment he is denied that he hates.

From no age or clime or condition is he absent; but never is he a dominant and deciding factor in society till that society has passed the bounds of sanity. Those who wait the midwife never call in the abortionist, nor does he ever cure the real sickness of his age. That he does survive abnormal periods to put his impress on the repressions of later days is due to the peculiar economy of his behavior. The libertine destroys himself, devouring his substance in self-satisfaction. The reformer devours others, being somewhat in the nature of a tax on vice, living by the very hysteria that destroys his homologous opposite.

In our own day we have reached another of those critical periods strikingly similar in its psychological symptoms and reactions, at least, to decadent Rome. We have the same development of extravagant religious cults, Spiritism, Dowicism, "The Purple Mother," all eagerly seized upon, filling the world with clamor and frenzy; the same mad seeking for pleasure, the same breaking and scattering of forms, the same orgy of gluttony and extravagance, the same crude emotionalism in art, letter and the theater, the same deformed and inverted sexual life.

Homosexualism may not be openly admitted, but the "sissy" and his red necktie are a familiar and easily understood property of popular jest and pantomime. It is all a mad jazz jumble of hysterical incongruities, dog dinners, monkey marriages, cubism, birth control, feminism, free-love, verse libre, and moving pictures. Through it all runs the strident note of puritanism. As one grows so does the other. Neither seems to precede or follow.

It would be a rash man indeed who would attempt to give later beginnings to the reform movements than to the license they seem so strongly to contradict. Significant indeed is the fact that their very license is the strongest appeal of the reformer. Every movie must preach a sermon and have a proper ending, but the attempted rape is as seldom missing as the telephone; and it is this that thrills and is expected to thrill.

The same sexual paradox we saw in the eunuch priests and harlot priestesses of Isis we see in the vice-crusading, vice-pandering reformers. Back of it all lies a morbid sexual condition, which is as much behind the anti-alcoholism of the prohibitionist, as behind the cropped head of his Puritan father, and as much behind the birth-control, vice-crusading virgins as behind their more amiable sisters of Aphrodite.

Interpreted then in the light of their history, libertinism and reformism cannot be differentiated as cause and effect, action and reaction, but must be associated as a two-fold manifestation of the same thing, an hysterical condition. They differ in externals, only insofar as one operates in license and the other in repression, but both have the same genesis and their development is simultaneous.

(E). LASSWELL, PSYCHOPATHOLOGY AND POLITICS 94–96 (1930).

Another significant private motive, whose organization dates from early family days, but whose influence was prominent in adult behavior, was A's struggle to maintain his sexual repressions. ["A" is an unidentified, non-fictional person whose life history was studied by the author.] He erected his very elaborate personal prohibitions into generalized prohibitions for all society, and just as he laid down the law against brother-hatred, he condemned "irregular" sexuality and gambling and drinking, its associated indulgencies. He was driven to protect himself by so modifying the environment that his sexual impulses were least often aroused, but it is significant that he granted partial indulgence to his repressed sexuality by engaging in various activities closely associated with sexual operations. Thus his sermons against vice enabled him to let his mind dwell upon rich fantasies of seduction. His crusading ventures brought him to houses of ill fame, where partly clad women were discoverable in the back rooms. These activities were rationalized by arguing that it was up to him as a leader of the moral forces of the community to remove temptation from the path of youth. At no time did he make an objective inquiry into the many factors in society which increase or diminish prostitution. His motives were of such an order that he was prevented from self-discipline by prolonged inspection of social experience.

That A was never able to abolish his sexuality is sufficiently evident in his night dreams and day dreams. In spite of his efforts to "fight" these manifestations of his "antisocial impulses," they continued to appear. Among the direct and important consequences which they produced was a sense of sin, not only a sense of sexual sin, but a growing conviction of hypocrisy. His "battle" against "evil" impulses was only partially successful, and this produced a profound feeling of insecurity.

This self-punishing strain of insecurity might be alleviated, he found, by publicly reaffirming the creed of repression, and by distracting attention to other matters. A's rapid movements, dogmatic assertions, and diversified activities were means of escape from this gnawing sense of incapacity to cope with his own desires and to master himself. Uncertain of his power to control himself, he was very busy about controlling others, and engaged in endless committee sessions, personal conferences, and public meetings for this purpose. He always managed to submerge himself in a buzzing life of ceaseless activity; he could never stand privacy and solitude, since it drove him to a sense of futility; and he couldn't undertake prolonged and laborious study, since his feeling of insecurity demanded daily evidence of his importance in the world.

A's sexual drives continued to manifest themselves, and to challenge his resistances. He was continually alarmed by the luring fear that he might be impotent. Although he proposed marriage to two girls when he was a theology student, it is significant that he chose girls from his immediate entourage, and effected an almost instantaneous recovery from his disappointments. This warrants the inference that he was considerably relieved to postpone the test of his potency, and this inference is strengthened by the long years during which he cheerfully acquiesced in the postponement of his marriage to the woman who finally became his wife. He lived with people who valued sexual potency, particularly in its conventional and biological demonstration in marriage and children, and his unmarried state was the object of good-natured comment. His pastoral duties required him to "make calls" on the sisters of the church, and in spite of the cheer which he was sometimes able to bring to the bedridden, there was the faint whisper of a doubt that this was really a man's job. And though preaching was a socially respectable occupation, there was something of the ridiculous in the fact that one who had experienced very little of life should pass for a privileged censor of all mankind.

MR. JUSTICE FORTAS, dissenting.

This is a criminal prosecution. Sam Ginsberg and his wife operate a luncheonette at which magazines are offered for sale. A 16-year-old boy was enlisted by his mother to go to the luncheonette and buy some "girlie" magazines so that Ginsberg could be prosecuted. He went there, picked two magazines from a display case, paid for them, and walked out. The offense of the Ginsbergs was duly reported to the authorities. The power of the State of New York was invoked. Ginsberg was prosecuted and convicted. The court imposed only a suspended sentence. But as the majority here points out, under New York law this conviction may mean that Ginsberg will lose the license necessary to operate his luncheonette.

The two magazines that the 16-year-old boy selected are vulgar "girlie" periodicals. However tasteless and tawdry they may be, we have ruled (as the Court acknowledges) that magazines indistinguishable from them in content and offensiveness are not "obscene" within the constitutional standards heretofore applied. See, *e.g.*, *Gent* v. *Arkansas*, 386 U.S. 767 (1967). These rulings have been in cases involving adults.

The Court avoids facing the problem whether the magazines in the present case are "obscene" when viewed by a 16-year-old boy, although not "obscene" when viewed by someone 17 years of age or older. It says that Ginsberg's lawyer did not choose to challenge the conviction on the ground that the magazines are not "obscene." He chose only to attack the statute on its face. Therefore, the Court reasons, we need not look at the magazines and determine whether they may be excluded from the ambit of the First Amendment as "obscene" for purposes of this case. But this Court has made strong and comprehensive statements about its duty in First Amendment cases—statements with which I agree. See, *e.g., Jacobellis* v. *Ohio*, 378 U.S. 184, 187–190 (1964).*

In my judgment, the Court cannot properly avoid its fundamental duty to define "obscenity" for purposes of censorship of material sold to youths, merely because of counsel's position. By so doing the Court avoids the essence of the problem; for if the State's power to censor freed from the prohibitions of the First Amendment depends upon obscenity, and if obscenity turns on the specific content of the publication, how can we sustain the conviction here without deciding whether the particular magazines in question are obscene?

The Court certainly cannot mean that the States and cities and counties and villages have unlimited power to withhold anything and everything that is written or pictorial from younger people. But it here justifies the conviction of Sam Ginsberg because the impact of the Constitution, it says, is variable, and what is not obscene for an adult may be obscene for a child. This it calls "variable obscenity." I do not disagree with this, but I insist that to assess the principle—certainly to apply it—the Court must define it. We must know the extent to which literature or pictures may be less offensive than *Roth* requires in order to be "obscene" for purposes of a statute confined to youth. See *Roth* v. *United States*, 354 U.S. 476 (1957).

I agree that the State in the exercise of its police power—even in the First Amendment domain—may make proper and careful differentiation between adults and children. But I do not agree that this power may be used on an arbitrary, free-wheeling basis. This is not a case where, on any standard enunciated by the Court, the magazines are obscene, nor one where the seller is at fault. Petitioner is being prosecuted for the sale of magazines which he had a right under the decisions of this Court to offer for sale, and he is being prosecuted without proof of "fault"—without even a claim that he deliberately, calculatedly sought to induce children to buy "obscene" material. Bookselling should not be a hazardous profession.

The conviction of Ginsberg on the present facts is a serious invasion of freedom. To sustain the conviction without inquiry as to whether the material is "obscene"

---

* "[W]e reaffirm the principle that, in 'obscenity' cases as in all others involving rights derived from the First Amendment guarantees of free expression, this Court cannot avoid making an independent constitutional judgment on the facts of the case as to whether the material involved is constitutionally protected." 378 U.S., at 190. See *Cox* v. *Louisiana*, 379 U.S. 536, 545, n. 8 (1965).

and without any evidence of pushing or pandering, in face of this Court's asserted solicitude for First Amendment values, is to give the State a role in the rearing of children which is contrary to our traditions and to our conception of family responsibility. Cf. *In re Gault*, 387 U.S. 1 (1967). It begs the question to present this undefined, unlimited censorship as an aid to parents in the rearing of their children. This decision does not merely protect children from activities which all sensible parents would condemn. Rather, its undefined and unlimited approval of state censorship in this area denies to children free access to books and works of art to which many parents may wish their children to have uninhibited access. For denial of access to these magazines, without any standard or definition of their allegedly distinguishing characteristics, is also denial of access to great works of art and literature.

If this statute were confined to the punishment of pushers or panderers of vulgar literature I would not be so concerned by the Court's failure to circumscribe state power by defining its limits in terms of the meaning of "obscenity" in this field. The State's police power may, within very broad limits, protect the parents and their children from public aggression of panderers and pushers. This is defensible on the theory that they cannot protect themselves from such assaults. But it does not follow that the State may convict a passive luncheonette operator of a crime because a 16-year-old boy maliciously and designedly picks up and pays for two girlie magazines which are presumably *not* obscene.

I would therefore reverse the conviction on the basis of *Redrup* v. *New York*, 386 U.S. 767 (1967) and *Ginzburg* v. *United States*, 383 U.S. 463 (1966).

Emanuel Redfield, New York, N.Y. (William K. Friedman and Benjamin E. Winston, with him on the brief) for appellant; *William Cahn*, Nassau County District Attorney, Mineola, New York (George Danzig Levine, Assistant District Attorney, with him on the brief) for appellee; *Morris B. Abram, Jay Greenfield, John E. Le Moult*, and *Paul, Weiss, Rifkind, Wharton & Garrison* filed brief for Council for Periodical Distributors Associations, Inc., as amicus curiae, seeking reversal; *Irwin Karp* filed brief for The Authors League of America, Inc., as amicus curiae, seeking reversal; *Osmond K. Fraenkel, Edward J. Ennis, Melvin L. Wulf, Alan H. Levine*, and *Fred O. Weldon, Jr.* filed brief for American Civil Liberties Union, New York Civil Liberties Union, and Texas Civil Liberties Union, as amici curiae, seeking reversal; *Charles H. Keating, Jr., James J. Clancy*, and *Ray T. Dreher* filed brief for Citizens for Decent Literature, Inc., as amicus curiae, seeking affirmance.

■ Interstate Circuit, Inc., *Appellant.*

v.

City of Dallas.
United Artists Corporation, *Appellant,*

v.

City of Dallas.

On Appeals From the Court of Civil Appeals of Texas. Fifth Supreme Judicial District.

[April 22, 1968.]

Mr. Justice Marshall delivered the opinion of the Court.

Appellants are an exhibitor and the distributor of a motion picture named "Viva Maria," which, pursuant to a city ordinance, the Motion Picture Classification Board of the respondent City of Dallas classified as "not suitable for young persons." A county court upheld the Board's determination and enjoined exhibition of the film without acceptance by appellants of the requirements imposed by the restricted classification. The Texas Court of Civil Appeals affirmed,[1] and we noted probable jurisdiction, 387 U.S. 903, to consider the First and Fourteenth Amendment issues raised by appellants with respect to respondent's classification ordinance.

That ordinance, adopted in 1965, may be summarized as follows.[2] It establishes a Motion Picture Classification Board, composed of nine appointed members, all of whom serve without pay. The Board classifies films as "suitable for young persons" or as "not suitable for young persons," and defines young persons as children who have not reached their 16th birthday. An exhibitor must be specially licensed to show "not suitable" films.

The ordinance requires the exhibitor, before any initial showing of a film, to file with the Board a proposed classification of the film together with a summary of its plot and similar information. The proposed classification is approved if the Board affirmatively agrees with it, or takes no action upon it within five days of its filing.

If a majority of the Board is dissatisfied with the proposed classification, the exhibitor is required to project the film before at least five members of the Board at the earliest practicable time. At the showing, the exhibitor may also present testimony or other support for his proposed classification. Within two days the Board must issue its classification order. Should the exhibitor disagree, he must file within two days[3] a notice of non-acceptance. The Board is then required to go to court within three days to seek a temporary injunction, and a hearing is required to be set on that application within five days thereafter; if the exhibitor agrees to waive notice and requests a hearing on the merits of a permanent injunction, the Board is required to waive its application for a temporary injunction and join in the exhibitor's request. If an injunction does not issue within 10 days of the exhibitor's notice of nonacceptance, the Board's classification order is suspended.[4] The ordinance does not define the scope of judicial review of the Board's determination, but the Court of Civil Appeals held that *de novo* review in the trial court was required.[5] If an injunction issues and the exhibitor seeks appellate review, or if an injunction is refused and the Board appeals, the Board must waive all statutory notices and times, and join a request of the exhibitor, to advance the case on the appellate court's docket, *i.e.*, do everything it can to assure a speedy determination.

The ordinance is enforced primarily by a misdemeanor penalty: an exhibitor is subject to a fine of up to $200 if he exhibits a film that is classified "not suitable for young persons" without advertisements clearly stating its classification or without the classification being clearly posted, exhibits on the same program a suitable and a not suitable film, knowingly admits a youth under age 16 to view the film without his guardian or spouse accompanying him,[6]

---

[1] 402 S.W. 2d 770 (1966). The Texas Supreme Court denied discretionary review and therefore the appeal is from the judgment of the Court of Civil Appeals. 28 U.S.C. § 1257 (2).

[2] The ordinance is set forth in an Appendix to this opinion. The parties disagree as to the meaning of certain of its provisions that have not been authoritatively interpreted by courts of the State. The differences are not material to our decision, however, and the summary of the ordinance in the text above should not be taken as acceptance by us of any of the parties' conflicting interpretations, nor as expressing any view on the validity of provisions of the ordinance not challenged here.

[3] The two-day period is apparently part of an attempt to assure prompt final determination. The ordinance also provides that "any initial or subsequent exhibitor" may seek reclassification of a film previously classified.

[4] Appellants assert that, despite the seemingly clear words of the suspension provision, exhibitors in practice have not been free to show films without a not suitable notification while a court challenge is pending, even though an injunction has not been issued within the 10-day period. See n. 2, *supra*.

[5] 402 S.W. 2d 770, 774–775.

[6] Respondent says that youths under 16 years of age accompanied throughout the showing of the picture by a guardian (parent) or spouse, may attend not suitable films. Appellants

makes any false or willfully misleading statement in submitting a film for classification, or exhibits a not suitable film without having a valid license therefor.

The same penalty is applicable to a youth who obtains admission to a not suitable film by falsely giving his age as over 16 years, and to any person who sells or gives to a youth under 16 a ticket to a not suitable film, or makes any false statements to enable such a youth to gain admission.[7]

Other means of enforcement, as against the exhibitor, are provided. Repeated violations of the ordinance, or persistent failure "to use reasonable diligence to determine whether those seeking admittance to the exhibition of a film classified 'not suitable for young persons' are below the age of sixteen," may be the basis for revocation of a license to show not suitable films.[8] Such a persistent failure, or exhibition of a not suitable film by an exhibitor with three convictions under the ordinance, *inter alia*, are defined as "public nuisances," which the Board may seek to restrain by a suit for injunctive relief.

The substantive standards governing classification are as follows:

" '*Not suitable for young persons*' " means:
"(1) *Describing or portraying brutality, criminal violence or depravity in such a manner as to be, in the judgment of the Board, likely to incite or encourage crime or delinquency on the part of young persons; or*
"(2) *Describing or portraying nudity beyond the customary limits of candor in the community, or sexual promiscuity or extra-marital or abnormal sexual relations in such a manner as to be, in the judgment of the Board, likely to incite or encourage delinquency or sexual promiscuity on the part of young persons or to appeal to their prurient interest.*

"*A film shall be considered 'likely to incite or encourage' crime delinquency or sexual promiscuity on the part of young persons, if, in the judgment of the Board, there is a substantial probability that it will create the impression on young persons that such conduct is profitable, desirable, acceptable, respectable, praiseworthy or commonly accepted. A film shall be considered as appealing to 'prurient interest' of young persons if in the judgment of the Board, its calculated or dominant effect on young persons is substantially to arouse sexual desire. In determining whether a film is 'not suitable for young persons,' the Board shall consider the film as a whole, rather than isolated portions, and shall determine whether its harmful effects outweigh artistic or educational values such film may have for young persons.*"

_____

read the ordinance as making the existence of such accompaniment solely a matter of defense should a criminal prosecution ensue. See n. 2, *supra*.

[7] See n. 6, *supra*. It appears that a parent who purchases a ticket to a not suitable film and gives it to his child is subject to the misdemeanor penalty of the ordinance. To be sure, respondent indicated at oral argument that criminal sanctions have not been sought against anyone under the ordinance.

[8] In related litigation, the provision for revocation of the special license was held unconstitutional as violative of *Butler v. Michigan*, 352 U.S. 380 (1957), by District Judge Hughes, 249 F. Supp. 19, 25 (D.C.N.D. Tex., 1965), and that ruling was not challenged on appeal. See *Interstate Circuit, Inc. v. City of Dallas*, 366 F. 2d 590, 593, n. 5 (C.A. 5th Cir., 1966).

Appellants attack those standards as unconstitutionally vague. We agree. Motion pictures are, of course, protected by the First Amendment, *Joseph Burstyn, Inc. v. Wilson*, 343 U.S. 495 (1952), and thus we start with the premise that "[p]recision of regulation must be the touchstone," *NAACP v. Button*, 371 U.S. 415, 438 (1963). And while it is true that this Court refused to strike down, against a broad and generalized attack, a prior restraint requirement that motion pictures be submitted to censors in advance of exhibition, *Times Film Corp. v. City of Chicago*, 365 U.S. 43 (1961), there has been no retreat in this area from rigorous insistence upon procedural safeguards and judicial superintendence of the censor's action. See *Freedman v. Maryland*, 380 U.S. 51 (1965).[9]

In *Winters v. New York*, 333 U.S. 507 (1948), this Court struck down as vague and indefinite a statutory standard interpreted by the state court to be "criminal news or stories of deeds of bloodshed or lust, so massed as to become vehicles for inciting violent and depraved crimes. . . ." *Id.*, at 518. In *Joseph Burstyn, Inc. v. Wilson*, *supra*, the Court dealt with a film licensing standard of "sacrilegious," which was found to have such an all-inclusive definition as to result in "substantially unbridled censorship." 343 U.S., at 502. Following *Burstyn*, the Court held the following film licensing standards to be unconstitutionally vague: "of such character as to be prejudicial to the best interests of the people of said city," *Gelling v. Texas*, 343 U.S. 960 (1952); "moral, educational or amusing and harmless," *Superior Films, Inc. v. Department of Education*, 346 U.S. 587 (1954); "immoral," and "tend to corrupt morals." *Commercial Pictures Corp. v. Regents*, 346 U.S. 587 (1954); "approve such films . . . which are moral and proper; . . . disapprove such as are cruel, obscene, indecent, or immoral, or such as tend to debase or corrupt morals," *Holmby Productions, Inc. v. Vaughn*, 350 U.S. 870 (1955).[10] See also *Kingsley Int'l Pictures Corp. v. Regents*, 360 U.S. 684, 699–702 (Clark, J., concurring in result).

The vice of vagueness is particularly pronounced where expression is sought to be subjected to licensing. It may be unlikely that what Dallas does in respect to the licensing of motion pictures would have a significant effect upon film makers in Hollywood or Europe. But what Dallas may

_____

[9] See also *Teitel Film Corp. v. Cusack*, 390 U.S. 139 (1968).

[10] There are numerous state cases to the same effect. See, e.g., *Police Commissioner v. Siegel Enterprises, Inc.*, 223 Md. 110, 162 A. 2d 727, cert. denied, 364 U.S. 909 (1960) ("violent bloodshed, lust or immorality or which, for a child below the age of eighteen are obscene, lewd, lascivious, filthy, indecent or disgusting and so presented as reasonably to tend to incite such a child to violence or depraved or immoral acts"); *People v. Kahan*, 15 N.Y. 2d 311, 206 N.E. 2d 333 (1965); *People v. Bookcase, Inc.*, 14 N.Y. 2d 409, 201 N.E. 2d 14 (1964) ("descriptions of illicit sex or sexual immorality"); *Hallmark Productions, Inc. v. Carroll*, 384 Pa. 348, 121 A. 2d 584 (1956) ("sacrilegious, obscene, indecent, or immoral, or such as tend . . . to debase as corrupt morals"). In *Paramount Film Distributing Corp. v. City of Chicago*, 172 F. Supp. 69 (D.C.N.D. Ill., 1959), it was alternatively held that the standard "tends toward creating a harmful impression on the minds of children" was indefinite; that provision had no further legislative or judicial definition and is therefore unlike the statute in *Ginsberg v. New York*, *ante*, 390 U.S., at —, where the phrase "harmful to minors" is specifically and narrowly defined in accordance with tests this Court has set forth for judging obscenity.

constitutionally do, so may other cities and States. Indeed, we are told that this ordinance is being used as a model for legislation in other localities. Thus, one who wishes to convey his ideas through that medium, which of course includes one who is interested not so much in expression as in making money, must consider whether what he proposes to film, and how he proposes to film it, is within the terms of classification schemes such as this. If he is unable to determine what the ordinance means, he runs the risk of being foreclosed, in practical effect, from a significant portion of the movie-going public. Rather than running that risk, he might choose nothing but the innocuous, perhaps save for the so-called "adult" picture. Moreover, a local exhibitor who cannot afford to risk losing the youthful audience when a film may be of marginal interest to adults—perhaps a "Viva Maria"—may contract to show only the totally inane. The vast wasteland that some have described in reference to another medium might be a verdant paradise in comparison. The First Amendment interests here are, therefore, broader than merely those of the film maker, distributor, and exhibitor, and certainly broader than those of youths under 16.

Of course, as the Court said in *Joseph Burstyn, Inc.* v. *Wilson*, 343 U.S., at 502, "[i]t does not follow that the Constitution requires absolute freedom to exhibit every motion picture of every kind at all times and all places." What does follow at the least, as the cases above illustrate, is that the restrictions imposed cannot be so vague as to set "the censor . . . adrift upon a boundless sea . . . ," *id.*, at 504. In short, as Justice Frankfurter said, "legislation must not be so vague, the language so loose, as to leave to those who have to apply it too wide a discretion . . . ," *Kingsley Int'l Pictures Corp.* v. *Regents*, 360 U.S., at 694 (concurring opinion), one reason being that "where licensing is rested, in the first instance, in an administrative agency, the available judicial review is in effect rendered inoperative [by vagueness]," *Joseph Burstyn, Inc.* v. *Wilson, supra*, at 532 (concurring opinion). Thus, to the extent that vague standards do not sufficiently guide the censor, the problem is not cured merely by affording *de novo* judicial review. Vague standards, unless narrowed by interpretation, encourage erratic administration whether the censor be administrative or judicial; "individual impressions became the yardstick of action, and result in regulation in accordance with the beliefs of the individual censor rather than regulation by law," *Kingsley Int'l Pictures Corp.* v. *Regents, supra*, at 701 (Clark, J., concurring in result).[11]

The dangers inherent in vagueness are strikingly illustrated in this case. Five members of the Board viewed "Viva Maria." Eight members voted to classify it as "not suitable for young persons," the ninth member not voting. The Board gave no reasons for its determination.[12] The

Board alleged in its petition for an injunction that the classification was warranted because the film portrayed "sexual promiscuity in such a manner as to be in the judgment of the Board likely to incite or encourage delinquency or sexual promiscuity on the part of young persons or to appeal to their prurient interests." Two Board members, a clergyman and a lawyer, testified at the hearing. Each adverted to several scenes in the film which, in their opinion, portrayed male-female relationships in a way contrary to "acceptable and approved behavior." Each acknowledged, in reference to scenes in which clergymen were involved in violence, most of which was farcical, that "sacrilege" might have entered into the Board's determination. And both conceded that the asserted portrayal of "sexual promiscuity" was implicit rather than explicit, *i.e.*, that it was a product of inference by, and imagination of, the viewer.

So far as "judicial superintendence"[13] and *de novo* review is concerned, the trial judge, after viewing the film and hearing argument, stated merely: "Oh, I realize you gentlemen may be right. There are two or three features in the picture that look to me would be unsuitable to young people. . . . So I enjoin the exhibitor . . . from exhibiting it."[14] Nor did the Court of Civil Appeals provide much enlightenment or a narrowing definition of the ordinance. United Artists argued that the obscenity standards similar to those set forth in *Roth* v. *United States*, 354 U.S. 476 (1957), and other decisions of this Court ought to be controlling.[15] The majority of the Court of Civil Appeals held, alternatively, (1) that such cases were not applicable because the legislation involved in them resulted in suppression of the offending expression rather than its classification; (2) that if obscenity standards were applicable then "Viva Maria" was obscene as to adults (a patently untenable conclusion) and therefore entitled to no constitutional protection; and (3) that if obscenity standards be modified as to children, the film was obscene as to them, a conclusion which was not in terms given as a narrowing interpretation of any specific provision of the ordinance. 402 S.W. 2d 770, 775–776. In regard to the last alternative holding, we must conclude that the court in effect ruled that the "portrayal . . . of sexual promiscuity as acceptable," *id.*, at 775, is in itself obscene as to

---

[11] See also Amsterdam, Note, The Void-for-Vagueness Doctrine in the Supreme Court, 109 U. Pa. L. Rev. 67, 90 (1960); Klein, Film Censorship: The American and British Experience, 12 Vill. L. Rev. 419, 428 (1967).

[12] The ordinance does not require the Board to give reasons for its action. Compare *ACLU* v. *City of Chicago*, 13 Ill. App. 2d 278, 286, 141 N.E. 2d 56, 60 (1957): "[T]he censoring authority, in refusing to issue a permit for showing the film, should be obliged to specify reasons for so doing. . . . The trial court, as well as the reviewing court, would then have a record, in addition to the film itself, on which to decide whether the ban should be approved. . . . Without such procedure, the courts become, not only the final tribunal to pass upon films, but the only tribunal to assume the responsibility of the censoring authority." Accord, *Zenith Int'l Film Corp.* v. *City of Chicago*, 291 F. 2d 785 (C.A. 7th Cir., 1961). See also Note, 71 Harv. L. Rev. 326, 338 (1957).

[13] *Bantam Books, Inc.* v. *Sullivan*, 372 U.S. 58, 70 (1963). See *Freedman* v. *Maryland, supra.*

[14] In response to a request that he make findings, the trial judge stated: "I decline. I have so many irons for a little fellow. I have taken on more than I can do, trying to decide a big case here, and I have got others at home and here and in Hill county where I have been helping out, and I do not have time to do it. I decline."

[15] Appellants also contend here that, in addition to its vagueness, the ordinance is invalid because it authorizes the restraint of films on constitutionally impermissible grounds, arguing that the limits on regulation of expression are those of obscenity, or at least obscenity as judged for children. In light of our disposition on vagueness grounds, we do not reach that issue.

children.[16] The court also held that the standards of the ordinance were "sufficiently definite." *Ibid.*

Thus, we are left merely with the film and directed to the words of the ordinance. The term "sexual promiscuity" is not there defined[17] and was not interpreted in the state courts. It could extend, depending upon one's moral judgment, from the obvious to any sexual contacts outside a marital relationship. The determinative manner of the "describing or portraying" of the subjects covered by the ordinance (see pp. 4–5, *supra*), including "sexual promiscuity," is defined as "such a manner as to be, in the judgment of the Board, likely to incite or encourage delinquency or sexual promiscuity on the part of young persons." A film is so " 'likely to incite or encourage' crime delinquency or sexual promiscuity if, in the judgment of the Board, there is a substantial probability that it will create the impression on young persons that such conduct is profitable, desirable, acceptable, respectable, praiseworthy or commonly accepted." It might be excessive literalism to insist, as do appellants, that because those last six adjectives are stated in the disjunctive, they represent separate and alternative subtle determinations the Board is to make, any of which results in a not suitable classification. Nonetheless, "[w]hat may be to one viewer the glorification of an idea as being 'desirable, acceptable or proper' may to the notions of another be entirely devoid of such a teaching. The only limits on the censor's discretion is his understanding of what is included in the term 'desirable, acceptable, or proper.' This is nothing less than a roving commission. . . ." *Kingsley Int'l Pictures* v. *Regents*, 360 U.S., at 701 (Clark, J., concurring in result).[18]

Vagueness and the attendant evils we have earlier described, see pp. 7–8, *supra*, are not rendered less objectionable because the regulation of expression is one of classification rather than direct suppression. Cf. *Bantam Books, Inc.* v. *Sullivan*, 372 U.S. 58 (1963).[19] Nor is it an answer to an argument that a particular regulation of expression is vague to say that it was adopted for the salutary purpose of protecting children. The permissible extent of vagueness is not directly proportional to, or a function of, the extent of the power to regulate or control expression with respect to children. As Chief Judge Fuld has said:

"It is . . . *essential that legislation aimed at protecting children from allegedly harmful expression—no less than legislation with respect to adults—be clearly drawn and that the standards adopted be reasonably precise so that those who are governed by the law and those who administer it will understand its meaning and application.*" People v. Kahan, 15 N.Y. 2d 311, 313, 206 N.E. 2d 333, 335 (1965) (concurring opinion).[20]

The vices—the lack of guidance to those who seek to adjust their conduct and to those who seek to administer the law, as well as the possible practical curtailing of the effectiveness of judicial review—are the same.

It is not our province to draft legislation. Suffice it to say that we have recognized that some believe "motion pictures possess a greater capacity for evil, particularly among the youth of a community, than other modes of expression," *Joseph Burstyn, Inc.* v. *Wilson*, *supra*, at 502, and we have indicated more generally that because of its strong and abiding interest in youth, a State may regulate the dissemination to juveniles of, and their access to, material objectionable as to them but which a State clearly could not regulate as to adults, *Ginsberg* v. *New York*, *ante*.[21] Here we conclude only that "the absence of narrowly drawn, reasonable and definite standards for the officials to follow," *Niemotko* v. *Maryland*, 340 U.S. 268, 271 (1951), is fatal.[22]

---

[16] A concurring justice of that court, with whom the author of the majority opinion agreed, specifically rejected the view that obscenity standards were relevant at all in determining the limits of the ordinance. But nothing in that opinion clarifies the standards adopted. 402 S.W. 2d, at 777–779.

[17] Respondent adopted an amendment to the ordinance in March 1966, which is not involved here. It defines "sexual promiscuity" as "indiscriminate sexual intimacies beyond the customary limits of candor in the community, and said term as defined herein shall include, but not be limited to sexual intercourse as that term is defined."

[18] An alternative to "likely to incite" because the portrayal might "create the impression . . . [the] conduct is profitable, desirable," etc., is set forth in the ordinance. That is if the manner of presentation is "likely . . . to appeal to their [young persons'] prurient interest." That alternative, however, was not relied upon by the Board members who testified, nor by the appellate court.

[19] In *Bantam Books,* the Commission there charged with reviewing material "manifestly tending to the corruption of the youth" (372 U.S., at 59) had no direct regulatory or suppressing functions, although its informal sanctions were found to achieve the same result. The Court held that "system of informal censorship" (*id.*, at 71) to violate the Fourteenth Amendment. One important factor in that decision was the Commission's "vague and uninformative" mandate, which the Commission in practice had "done nothing to make . . . more precise." *Ibid.* See also I, Carmen, Movies, Censorship, and the Law, *passim* (1966); Klein, Film Censorship, The American and British Experience, 12 Vill. L. Rev. 419, 454 (1967); Note, 71 Harv. L. Rev. 326, 342 (1957).

[20] See also, *e.g., Katzev* v. *County of Los Angeles*, 52 Cal. 2d 360, 341 P. 2d 310 (1959) (magazine sales to minors under age 18), *People* v. *Bookcase, Inc.*, *supra*, n. 10 (book sales to minors under age 18); *Police Commissioner* v. *Siegel Enterprises, Inc.*, *supra*. n. 10 (sale of certain publications to those under 18); *Paramount Film Distributing Corp.* v. *City of Chicago*, *supra*, n. 10 (special license for films deemed objectionable for those under age 21).

[21] On age classification with regard to viewing motion pictures see generally, I. Carmen, Movies, Censorship, and the Law 247, 260 (1966); Note, 69 Yale L.J. 141 (1959).

[22] Appellants also assert that the city ordinance violates the teachings of *Freedman* v. *Maryland*, *supra*, because it does not secure prompt state appellate review. The assurance of a "prompt final judicial decision" (380 U.S., at 59) is made here, we think, by the guaranty of a speedy determination in the trial court (in this case nine days after the Board's classification). See *Teitel Film Corp.* v. *Cusack*, 390 U.S. 139 (1968). Nor is *Freedman* violated by the requirement that the exhibitor file a notice of nonacceptance of the Board's classification. To be sure, it is emphasized in *Freedman* that "only a procedure requiring a judicial determination suffices to impose a valid final restraint" (*id.*, at 58), and here if the exhibitor chooses not to file the notice of nonacceptance, the Board's determination is final without judicial approval. But we are not constrained to view that procedure as invalid in the absence of a showing that it has any significantly greater effect than would the exhibitor's decision not to contest in court the Board's suit for a temporary injunction. The ordinance provides that the Board has the burden of going to court to seek a temporary injunction, once the exhibitor has indicated his nonacceptance, and there it has the burden of sustaining its classification.

Finally, appellant United Artists contends the ordinance un-

The judgment of the Texas Court of Civil Appeals is reversed and the case is remanded for further proceedings not inconsistent with this opinion.

It is so ordered.

APPENDIX.

Chapter 46A of the 1960 Revised Code of Civil and Criminal Ordinances of the City of Dallas, as amended, provides:

Section 46A–1. *Definition of Terms:*

(a) "Film" means any motion picture film or series of films, whether full length or short subject, but does not include newsreels portraying actual current events or pictorial news of the day.

(b) "Exhibit" means to project a film at any motion picture theatre or other public place within the City of Dallas to which tickets are sold for admission.

(c) "Exhibitor" means any person, firm or corporation which exhibits a film.

(d) "Young person" means any person who has not attained his sixteenth birthday.

(e) "Board" means the Dallas Motion Picture Classification Board established by Section 46A–2 of this ordinance.

(f) "Not suitable for young persons" means:

(1) Describing or portraying brutality, criminal violence or depravity in such a manner as to be, in the judgment of the Board, likely to incite or encourage crime or delinquency on the part of young persons; or

(2) Describing or portraying nudity beyond the customary limits of candor in the community, or sexual promiscuity or extra-marital or abnormal sexual relations in such a manner as to be, in the judgment of the Board, likely to incite or encourage delinquency or sexual promiscuity on the part of young persons or to appeal to their prurient interest.

A film shall be considered "likely to incite or encourage" crime delinquency or sexual promiscuity on the part of young persons, if, in the judgment of the Board, there is a substantial probability that it will create the impression on young persons that such conduct is profitable, desirable, acceptable, respectable, praiseworthy or commonly accepted. A film shall be considered as appealing to "prurient interest" of young persons, if in the judgment of the Board, its calculated or dominant effect on young persons is substantially to arouse sexual desire. In determining whether a film is "not suitable for young persons," the Board shall consider the films as a whole, rather than isolated portions, and shall determine whether its harmful effects outweigh artistic or educational values such film may have for young persons.

(g) "Classify" means to determine whether a film is:

(1) Suitable for young persons, or;

(2) Not suitable for young persons.

(h) "Advertisement" means any commercial promotional material initiated by an exhibitor designed to bring a film to public attention or to increase the sale of tickets to exhibitions of same, whether by newspaper, billboard, motion picture, television, radio, or other media within or originating within the City of Dallas.

(i) "Initial exhibition" means the first exhibition of any film within the City of Dallas.

(j) "Subsequent exhibition" means any exhibition subsequent to the initial exhibition, whether by the same or a different exhibitor.

(k) "File" means to deliver to the City Secretary for safekeeping as a public record of the City of Dallas.

(l) "Classification order" means any written determination by a majority of the Board classifying a film, or granting or refusing an application for change of classification.

(m) The term "Board" as used and applied in subsection (a) of Section 46A–7 shall include the City of Dallas when attempting to enforce this ordinance and the City Attorney of the City of Dallas when representing the Board or the City of Dallas.

Section 46A–2. *Establishment of Board:*

There is hereby created a Board to be known as the Dallas Motion Picture Classification Board which shall be composed of a Chairman and Eight Members to be appointed by the Mayor and City Council of the City of Dallas, whose terms shall be the same as members of the City Council. Such members shall serve without pay and shall adopt such rules and regulations as they deem best governing their action, proceeding and deliberations and time and place of meeting. These rules and regulations shall be subject to approval of the City Council. If a vacancy occurs upon the Board by death, resignation or otherwise, the governing body of the City of Dallas shall appoint a member to fill such vacancy for the unexpired term.

The Chairman and all Members of the Board shall be good, moral, law-abiding citizens of the City of Dallas, and shall be chosen so far as reasonably practicable in such a manner that will represent a cross section of the community. Insofar as practicable, the members appointed to the Board shall be persons educated and experienced in one or more of the following fields: art, drama, literature, philosophy, sociology, psychology, history, education, music, science or other related fields. The City Secretary shall act as Secretary of the Board.

Section 46A–3. *Classification Procedure:*

(a) Before any initial exhibition, the exhibitor shall file a proposed classification of the film to be exhibited, stating the title of the film and the name of the producer, and giving a summary of the plot and such other information as the Board may by rule require, together with the classification proposed by the exhibitor. The Board shall examine such proposed classification, and if it approves same, shall mark it "approved" and file it as its own classification order. If the Board fails to act, that is, either file a classification order or hold a hearing within five (5) days after such proposed classification is filed, the proposed classification shall be considered approved.

---

constitutionally infringes upon its rights by not providing for participation by a distributor, who might wish to contest where an exhibitor would not. Of course the distributor must be permitted to challenge the classification, cf. *Bantam Books, Inc.* v. *Sullivan,* 372 U.S. 58, 64, n. 6 (1963), but the respondent assures us he may (see n. 2, *supra*), and United Artists was permitted to intervene in the trial court.

(b) If upon examination of the proposed classification a majority of the Board is not satisfied that it is proper, the Chairman shall direct the exhibitor to project the film before any five (5) or more members of the Board, at a suitably equipped place and at a specified time, which shall be the earliest time practicable with due regard to the availability of the film. The exhibitor, or his designated representative, may at such time make such statement to the Board in support of his proposed classification and present such testimony as he may desire. Within two (2) days, the Board shall make and file its classification of the film in question.

(c) Any initial or subsequent exhibitor may file an application for a change in the classification of any film previously classified. No exhibitor shall be allowed to file more than one (1) application for change of classification of the same film. Such application shall contain a sworn statement of the grounds upon which the application is based. Upon filing of such application, the City Secretary shall bring it immediately to the attention of the Chairman of the Board, who upon application by the exhibitor shall set a time and place for a hearing and shall notify the applicants and all interested parties, including all exhibitors who may be exhibiting or preparing to exhibit the film. The Board shall view the film and at such hearing, hear the statements of all interested parties, and any proper testimony that may be offered, and shall within two (2) days thereafter make and file its order approving or changing such classification. If the classification of a film is changed as a result of such hearing to the classification "not suitable for young persons," the exhibitors showing the film shall have seven (7) days in which to alter their advertising and audience policy to comply with such classification.

(d) Upon filing by the Board of any classification order, the City Secretary shall immediately issue and mail a notice of classification to the exhibitor involved and to any other exhibitor who shall request such notice.

(e) A classification shall be binding on any subsequent exhibitor unless and until he obtains a change of classification in the manner above provided.

Section 46A–4. *Offenses:*

(a) It shall be unlawful for any exhibitor or his employee:

(1) To exhibit any film which has not been classified as provided in this ordinance.

(2) To exhibit any film classified "not suitable for young persons" if any current advertisement of such film by such exhibitor fails to state clearly the classification of such film.

(3) To exhibit any film classified "not suitable for young persons" without keeping such classification posted prominently in front of the theatre in which such film is being exhibited.

(4) Knowingly to sell or give to any young person a ticket to any film classified "not suitable for young persons."

(5) Knowingly to permit any young person to view the exhibition of any film classified "not suitable for young persons."

(6) To exhibit any film classified "not suitable for young persons" or any scene or scenes from such a film, or from an unclassified film, whether moving or still, in the same theatre and on the same program with a film classified "suitable for young persons"; provided that any advertising preview or trailer containing a scene or scenes from an unclassified film or a film classified "not suitable for young persons" may be shown at any time if same has been separately classified as "suitable for young persons" under the provisions of Section 46A–3 of this ordinance.

(7) To make any false or willfully misleading statement in any proposed classification, application for change of classification, or any other proceeding before the Board.

(8) To exhibit any film classified "not suitable for young persons" without having in force the license hereinafter provided.

(b) It shall be unlawful for any young person:

(1) To give his age falsely as sixteen (16) years of age or over, for the purpose of gaining admittance to an exhibition of a film classified "not suitable for young persons."

(2) To enter or remain in the viewing room of any theatre where a film classified "not suitable for young persons" is being exhibited.

(3) To state falsely that he or she is married for the purpose of gaining admittance to an exhibition of a film classified as "not suitable for young persons."

(c) It shall be unlawful for any person:

(1) To sell or give any young person a ticket to an exhibition of a film classified "not suitable for young persons."

(2) To make any false or willfully misleading statement in an application for change of classification or in any proceeding before the Board.

(3) To make any false statements for the purpose of enabling any young person to gain admittance to the exhibition of a film classified as "not suitable for young persons."

(d) To the extent that any prosecution or other proceeding under this ordinance, involves the entering, purchasing of a ticket, or viewing by a young person of a film classified "not suitable for young persons," it shall be a valid defense that such young person was accompanied by his legally appointed guardian, husband or wife, throughout the viewing of such film.

Section 46A–5. *License:*

Every exhibitor holding a motion picture theatre or motion picture show license issued pursuant to Chapter 46 of the 1960 Revised Code of Civil and Criminal Ordinances of the City of Dallas shall be entitled to issuance of a license by the City Secretary to exhibit films classified "not suitable for young persons."

Section 46A–6. *Revocation or suspension of license:*

Whenever the City Attorney or any person acting under his direction, or any ten (10) citizens of the City of Dallas, shall file a sworn complaint with the City Secretary stating that any exhibitor has repeatedly violated the provisions of this ordinance, or that any exhibitor has persistently failed to use reasonable diligence to determine whether those seeking admittance to the exhibition of a film classified "not suitable for young persons" are below the age of sixteen (16), the City Secretary shall immediately bring such complaint to the attention of the City Council who shall set a time and place for hearing such complaint and cause notice of such hearing to be given to the complainants and to the exhibitor involved. The City Council shall have authority to issue subpoenas requiring witnesses to appear and testify at such hearing, and any party to such hearing shall be entitled to such process. If, after hearing the evidence, the City Council shall find the charges in such complaint to be true, it shall issue and file an order revoking or suspending the license above provided, insofar as it grants the privilege of showing such classified pictures, for a specific period not to exceed one (1) year, or may issue a reprimand if it is satisfied that such violation will not continue.

The City Council likewise, after notice and hearing, may revoke or suspend the license of any exhibitor who has refused or unreasonably failed to produce or delayed the submission of a film for review, when requested by the Board.

Section 46A–7. *Judicial Review:*

(a) Within two (2) days after the filing of any classification by the Board, other than an order approving the classification proposed by an exhibitor, any exhibitor may file a notice of non-acceptance of the Board's classification, stating his intention to exhibit the film in question under a different classification. Thereupon it shall be the duty of the Board to do the following:

(1) Within three (3) days thereafter to make application to a District Court of Dallas County, Texas, for a temporary and a permanent injunction to enjoin such defendant-exhibitor, being the exhibitor who contests the classification, from exhibiting the film in question contrary to the provisions of this ordinance.

(2) To have said application for temporary injunction set for hearing within five (5) days after the filing thereof. In the event the defendant-exhibitor appears at or before the time of the hearing of such temporary injunction, waives the notice otherwise provided by the Texas Rules of Civil Procedure, and requests that at the time set for such hearing the Court proceed to hear the case under the Texas Rules of Civil Procedure for permanent injunction on its merits, the Board shall be required to waive its application for temporary injunction and shall join in such request. In the event the defendant-exhibitor does not waive notice and/or does not request an early hearing on the Board's application for permanent injunction, it shall nevertheless be the duty of the Board to obtain the earliest possible setting for such hearing under the provisions of State law and the Texas Rules of Civil Procedure.

(3) If the injunction is granted by the trial court and the defendant-exhibitor appeals to the Court of Civil Appeals, the Board shall waive any and all statutory notices and times as provided for in the Texas State Statutes and the Texas Rules of Civil Procedure, and shall within five (5) days after receiving a copy of appealing exhibitor's brief, file its reply brief, if required, and be prepared to submit the case upon oral submission or take any other reasonable action requested by the appealing exhibitor to expedite the submission of the case to the Court of Civil Appeals, and shall upon request of the appealing exhibitor, jointly with such exhibitor, request the Court of Civil Appeals to advance the cause upon the docket and to give it a preferential setting the same as is afforded an appeal from a temporary injunction or other preferential matters.

(4) If the Court of Civil Appeals should by its judgment affirm the judgment of the trial court granting the injunction and the appealing exhibitor should file an application for writ of error to the Texas Supreme Court, the Board shall be required to waive any and all notices and times as provided for in the Texas State Statutes and the Texas Rules of Civil Procedure, and shall within five (5) days after receiving a copy of the application for writ of error, file its reply brief, if required, and be prepared to submit the case upon oral submission or take any other reasonable action requested by the appealing exhibitor to expedite the submission of the case to the Supreme Court and shall upon request of the appealing exhibitor, jointly with such exhibitor, request the Supreme Court to advance the cause upon the docket and to give it a preferential setting the same as is afforded an appeal from a temporary injunction or other preferential matters.

(5) If the District Court denies the Board's application for injunction, and the Board elects to appeal, the Board shall be required to waive all periods of time allowed it by the Texas Rules of Civil Procedure and if a motion for a new trial is required, shall file said motion within two (2) days after the signing of the judgment (or on the following Monday if said period ends on a Saturday or Sunday, or on the day following if the period ends on a Legal Holiday), shall not amend said motion and shall obtain a hearing on such motion within five (5) days time. If no motion for new trial is required as a prerequisite to an appeal under the Texas Rules of Civil Procedure, the Board shall not file such a motion. Within ten (10) days after the judgment is signed by the District Court denying such injunction or within ten (10) days after the order overruling the Board's motion for new trial is signed, if such motion is required, the Board shall complete all steps necessary for the perfection of its appeal to the Court of Civil Appeals, including the filing of the Transcript, Statement of Facts and Appellant's brief. Failure to do so shall constitute an abandonment of the appeal. On filing the record with the Court of Civil Appeals, the Board shall file a motion to advance requesting the Court to give a preferential setting the same as is afforded an appeal from a temporary injunction or other preferential matters.

(6) If the Court of Civil Appeals reverses the trial court after the trial court has granted an injunction, or if the Court of Civil Appeals refuses to reverse the trial court after that court has failed to grant an injunction, then if the Board desires to appeal from the decision of the Court of Civil Appeals by writ of error to the Supreme Court of the State of Texas, it must file its motion for rehearing within two (2) days of rendition of the decision of the Court of Civil Appeals (or on the following Monday, if said period ends on a Saturday or Sunday, or on the day following if the period ends on a Legal Holiday), and shall file its application for writ of error within ten (10) days after the Court of Civil Appeals' order overruling such motion for rehearing, and failure to do so shall waive all rights to appeal from the decision of the Court of Civil Appeals. At the time of filing the application for writ of error, the Board shall also request the Supreme Court to give the case a preferential setting and advance the same on the docket.

(b) The filing of such notice of non-acceptance shall

not suspend or set aside the Board's order, but such order shall be suspended at the end of ten (10) days after the filing of such notice unless an injunction is issued within such period.

(c) Failure of any exhibitor to file the notice of any acceptance within two (2) days as required in Subdivision (1) of this Section 46A–7, shall constitute acceptance of such classification order and such exhibitor shall be bound by such order in all subsequent proceedings except such proceedings as may be had in connection with any application for change of classification under Subsection (c) of Section 46A–3 above.

Section 46A–8. *Public Nuisances:*

The following acts are declared to be public nuisances:
(a) Any violation of Subdivisions (1), (2), (3), or (6), of Subdivision (a) of Section 46A–4 of this ordinance.

(b) Any exhibition of a film classified as "not suitable for young persons" at which more than three (3) young persons are admitted.

(c) Any exhibition of a film classified as "not suitable for young persons" by an exhibitor who fails to use reasonable diligence to determine whether persons admitted to such exhibitions are persons under the age of sixteen (16) years.

(d) Any exhibition of a film classified as "not suitable for young persons" by an exhibitor who has been convicted of as many as three (3) violations of Subdivisions (4) or (5) of Subdivision (a) of Section 46A–4 of this ordinance in connection with the exhibition of the same film.

Section 46A–9. *Injunctions:*

Whenever the Board has probable cause to believe that any exhibitor has committed any of the acts declared in Section 46A–8 above to be a public nuisance, the Board shall have the duty to make application to a court of competent jurisdiction for an injunction restraining the commission of such acts.

Section 46A–10. *Exemption to State Law:*

Nothing in this ordinance shall be construed to regulate public exhibitions pre-empted by Article 527 of the Penal Code of the State of Texas, as amended.

Section 46A–11. *Severability Clause:*

Should any section, subsection, sentence, provision, clause or phrase be held to be invalid for any reason, such holding shall not render invalid any other section, subsection, sentence, provision, clause or phrase of this ordinance, and the same are deemed severable for this purpose.

SECTION 2. That any person who shall violate any provisions of this ordinance shall be guilty of a misdemeanor and upon conviction thereof shall be subject to a fine not to exceed Two Hundred Dollars ($200.00) and each offense shall be deemed to be a separate violation and punishable as a separate offense, and each day that a film is exhibited which has not been classified according to this ordinance shall be a separate offense.

SECTION 3. That Ordinance No. 10963 heretofore enacted by the City Council of the City of Dallas on April 5, 1965, be and the same is hereby in all things repealed and held for naught, and this ordinance is enacted in lieu thereof.

SECTION 4. The fact that Ordinance No. 10963 previously passed by the City Council of the City of Dallas has been declared to be unenforceable in the Courts by the Federal District Court, creates an urgency and an emergency in the preservation of the public peace, comfort and general welfare and requires that this ordinance shall take effect immediately from and after its passage, and it is accordingly so ordained.

MR. JUSTICE DOUGLAS, with whom MR. JUSTICE BLACK joins, concurring.

As I indicated in my dissenting opinion in *Ginsberg* v. *New York, ante,* p. —, if we assume *arguendo* that the censorship of obscene publications, whither for children or for adults, is in the area of substantive due process, the States have a very wide range indeed for determining what kind of movie, novel, poem, or article is harmful. If that were the test, I would agree with my Brother HARLAN that the standard of "sexual promiscuity" in this Dallas ordinance is sufficiently precise and discriminating for modern man to apply intelligently.

My approach to these problems is, of course, quite different. I reach the result the Court reaches for the reasons stated in my dissenting opinions in *Ginsberg* and other cases and therefore concur in reversing the present judgments.

■ Sam Ginsberg, *Appellant,*

v.

State of New York.

47

Interstate Circuit, Inc., *Appellant,*

v.

City of Dallas.

56

United Artists Corporation, *Appellant,*

v.

City of Dallas.

64

On Appeal From the Appellate Term of the Supreme Court of New York, Second Judicial Department.

On Appeals From the Court of Civil Appeals of Texas. Fifth Supreme Judicial District.

[April 22, 1968.]

Nos. 47, 56, and 64.—October Term, 1967.

Mr. Justice Harlan, concurring in No. 47, and dissenting in Nos. 56 and 64.

These cases usher the Court into a new phase of the intractable obscenity problem: may a State prevent the dissemination of obscene or other obnoxious material to juveniles upon standards less stringent than those which would govern its distribution to adults?

In No. 47, the *Ginsberg* case, the Court upholds a New York statute applicable only to juveniles which, as construed by the state courts, in effect embodies in diluted form the "adult" obscenity standards established by *Roth v. United States,* 354 U.S. 476, and the prevailing opinion in *Memoirs v. Massachusetts,* 383 U.S. 413. In Nos. 56 and 64, the *Interstate Circuit* cases, the Court strikes down on the ground of vagueness a similar Dallas ordinance, not couched, however, entirely in obscenity terms. In none of these cases does the Court pass judgment on the particular material condemned by the state courts.

As the Court enters this new area of obscenity law it is well to take stock of where we are at present in this constitutional field. The subject of obscenity has produced a variety of views among the members of the Court unmatched in any other course of constitutional adjudication.[1] Two members of the Court steadfastly maintain

that the First and Fourteenth Amendments render society powerless to protect itself against the dissemination of even the filthiest materials.[2] No other member of the Court, past or present, has ever stated his acceptance of that point of view. But there is among present members of the Court a sharp divergence as to the proper application of the standards in *Roth, supra,*[3] *Memoirs, supra,*[4] *and Ginz-*

Brown, 354 U.S. 436 (four opinions); *Roth v. United States, supra* (four opinions); *Kingsley Pictures Corp. v. Regents,* 360 U.S. 684 (six opinions); *Smith v. California,* 361 U.S. 147 (five opinions); *Times Film Corp. v. Chicago,* 365 U.S. 43 (three opinions); *Marcus v. Search Warrant,* 367 U.S. 717 (two opinions); *Manual Enterprises v. Day,* 370 U.S. 478 (three opinions); *Bantam Books, Inc. v. Sullivan,* 372 U.S. 58 (four opinions); *Jacobellis v. Ohio,* 378 U.S. 184 (six opinions); *A Quantity of Books v. Kansas,* 378 U.S. 205 (four opinions); *Memoirs v. Massachusetts, supra* (five opinions); *Ginzburg v. United States,* 383 U.S. 463 (five opinions); *Mishkin v. New York,* 383 U.S. 502 (four opinions).

[2] See *Roth v. United States, supra,* at 508 (dissenting opinion); *Jacobellis v. Ohio, supra,* at 196 (concurring opinion); *Ginzburg v. United States, supra,* at 476, 482 (dissenting opinions).

[3] *Roth* stated the test to be "whether to the average person, applying contemporary community standards, the dominant theme of the material taken as a whole appeals to prurient interest." 354 U.S., at 489 (note omitted).

[4] *Memoirs* elaborated the *Roth* test as follows: "it must be established that (a) the dominant theme of the material taken as a whole appeals to a prurient interest in sex; (b) the material is patently offensive because it affronts contemporary community

---

[1] In the 13 obscenity cases since *Roth* in which a signed opinion was written for the Court, there have been a total of 55 separate opinions among the Justices. *Kingsley Books, Inc. v.*

burg v. *United States*, 383 U.S. 463,[5] for judging whether given material is constitutionally protected or unprotected. Most of the present Justices who believe that "obscenity" is not beyond the pale of governmental control seemingly consider that the *Roth-Memoirs-Ginzburg* tests permit suppression of material that falls short of so-called "hard core pornography," on equal terms as between federal and state authority.[6] Another view is that only "hard core pornography" may be suppressed, whether by federal or state authority.[7] And still another view, that of this writer, is that only "hard core pornography" may be suppressed by the Federal Government, whereas under the Fourteenth Amendment States are permitted wider authority to deal with obnoxious matter than might be justifiable under a strict application of the *Roth-Memoirs-Ginzburg* rules.[8]

There are also differences among us as to how our appellate process should work in reviewing obscenity determinations. One view is that we should simply examine the proceedings below to ascertain whether the lower federal or state courts have made a genuine effort to apply the *Roth-Memoirs-Ginzburg* tests, and that if such is the case, their determinations that the questioned material is obscene should be accepted, much as would any findings of fact.[9] Another view is that the question of whether particular material is obscene inherently entails a constitutional judgment for which the Court has ultimate responsibility, and hence that it is incumbent upon us to judge for ourselves, *de novo* as it were, the obscenity *vel non* of the challenged matter.[10]

The upshot of all this divergence in viewpoint is that anyone who undertakes to examine the Court's decisions since *Roth* which have held particular material obscene or not obscene would find himself in utter bewilderment.[11]

From the standpoint of the Court itself the current approach has required us to spend an inordinate amount of time in the absurd business of perusing and viewing the miserable stuff that pours into the Court, mostly in state cases, all to no better end than second-guessing state judges. In all except rare instances, I venture to say, no substantial free-speech interest is at stake, given the right of the States to control obscenity.

I believe that no improvement in this chaotic state of affairs is likely to come until it is recognized that this whole problem is primarily one of state concern, and that the Constitution tolerates much wider authority and discretion in the States to control the dissemination of obscene materials than it does in the Federal Government. Reiterating the viewpoint that I have expressed in earlier opinions, I would limit federal control of obscene materials to those which all would recognize as what has been called "hard core pornography," and would withhold the federal judicial hand from interfering with state determinations except in instances where the state action clearly appears to be but the product of prudish over-zealousness. See *Roth* v. *United States, supra,* at 496; *Manual Enterprises* v. *Day,* 370 U.S. 478; *Jacobellis* v. *Ohio, supra,* at 203; *Memoirs* v. *Massachusetts, supra,* at 455. And in the juvenile field I think that the Constitution is still more tolerant of state policy and its applications. If current doctrinaire views as to the reach of the First Amendment into state affairs are thought to stand in the way of such a functional approach, I would revert to basic constitutional concepts that until recent times have been recognized and respected as the fundamental genius of our federal system, namely the acceptance of wide state autonomy in local affairs.

I come now to the cases at hand. In No. 47, *Ginsberg,* I concur in the judgment and join the opinion of the Court, fully preserving, however, the views repeatedly expressed in my earlier opinions in this field.

In Nos. 56 and 64, the *Interstate Circuit* case, I respectfully dissent. I do not agree that the Dallas ordinance can be struck down, as the Court now holds, on the score of vagueness. The ambiguities about which the Court expresses concern are essentially two.[12] First, the ordinance does not include a definition of "sexual promiscuity."[13] Second, the ordinance provides that a film "shall be considered 'likely to incite or encourage' crime delinquency or sexual promiscuity . . . if, in the judgment of the Board, there is a substantial probability that it will create the impression on young persons that such conduct is profitable, desirable, acceptable, respectable, praiseworthy or commonly accepted." The Court is concerned that many may disagree as to whether any specific materials create such impressions on young persons.

---

standards relating to the description or representation of sexual matters; and (c) the material is utterly without redeeming social value." 383 U.S., at 418.

[5] The *Ginzburg* "test" is difficult to state with any precision. The Court held that "in close cases evidence of pandering may be probative with respect to the nature of the material in question and thus satisfy the *Roth* test." 383 U.S., at 474. But this "simply elaborates the test by which the obscenity vel non of the material must be judged." *Id.,* at 475. Yet evidence of pandering may "support the determination that the material is obscene even though in other contexts the material would escape such condemnation." *Id.,* at 476. Pandering itself evidently encompasses every form of the " 'business of purveying textual or graphic matter openly advertised to appeal to the erotic interest of their customers.' " *Id.,* at 467 (note omitted).

[6] See, *e.g., Jacobellis* v. *Ohio, supra,* at 193–195.

[7] See *id.,* at 197 (concurring opinion).

[8] See *Roth* v. *United States, supra,* at 496 (concurring and dissenting opinion); *Memoirs* v. *Massachusetts, supra,* at 455 (dissenting opinion).

[9] See *Jacobellis* v. *Ohio, supra,* at 202 (dissenting opinion).

[10] See *id.,* at 190; *Roth* v. *United States, supra,* at 497–498 (concurring and dissenting opinion); *Kingsley Pictures Corp.* v. *Regents, supra,* at 708 (concurring opinion).

[11] See, *e.g., Keney* v. *New York,* 388 U.S. 440; *Friedman* v. *New York,* 388 U.S. 441; *Ratner* v. *California,* 388 U.S. 442; *Cobert* v. *New York,* 388 U.S. 443; *Sheperd* v. *New York,* 388 U.S. 444; *Avansino* v. *New York,* 388 U.S. 446; *Aday* v. *United States,* 388 U.S. 447; *Corinth Publications, Inc.* v. *Wesberry,* 388 U.S. 448; *Books, Inc.* v. *United States,* 388 U.S. 449; *Rosenbloom* v. *Virginia,* 388 U.S. 450; A *Quantity of Copies of Books* v. *Kansas,* 388 U.S. 452; *Mazes* v. *Ohio,* 388 U.S. 453;

Schackman v. *California,* 388 U.S. 454; *Landau* v. *Fording,* 388 U.S. 456; *Potomac News Co.* v. *United States,* 389 U.S. 47; *Conner* v. *City of Hammond,* 389 U.S. 48; *Central Magazine Sales, Ltd.* v. *United States,* 389 U.S. 50; *Chance* v. *California,* 389 U.S. 89.

[12] The Court emphasizes at greater length the failure of the Board and the Texas courts to proffer any clarification of the ordinance. This compels examination of the ordinance's terms, but it does not, of course, offer any independent basis for a conclusion that the ordinance is ambiguous.

[13] The Court acknowledges that the city has since adopted a definition of sexual promiscuity, but it expresses no views as to the definition's adequacy.

These seem to me entirely inadequate grounds on which to strike down the ordinance. It must be granted, of course, that people may differ as to the application of these standards; but the central lesson of this Court's efforts in this area is that under all verbal formulae, including even this Court's own definition of obscenity, reasonable men can, and ordinarily do, differ as to the proper assessment of challenged materials. The truth is that the Court has demanded greater precision of language from the City of Dallas than the Court can itself give, or even than can sensibly be expected in this area of the law.

The Court has not always asked so much.[14] In *Roth*, the federal statute under which the petitioner had been sentenced to five years of imprisonment forbade the mailing of material that was "obscene, lewd, lascivious, or filthy . . . or other publication of an indecent character."[15] 354 U.S., at 491. In *Alberts*, the companion case to *Roth*, the California statute provided that the materials must have a "tendency to deprave or corrupt its readers." *Id.*, at 498. No definitions were included in either statute, yet the Court there explicitly rejected the argument that they did not "provide reasonably ascertainable standards of guilt . . ." *Ibid.* The Court recognized that the terms of obscenity statutes are necessarily imprecise, but emphasized, quoting *United States* v. *Petrillo*, 332 U.S. 1, 7–8, that the " 'Constitution does not require impossible standards'; all that is required is that the language 'conveys

sufficiently definite warnings as to the proscribed conduct when measured by common understanding and practices. . . .' "[16] *Ibid.* Yet it should be repeated that the *Interstate Circuit* cases, unlike *Roth* and *Alberts*, involve merely the classification, not the proscription by criminal prosecution, of objectionable materials. In my opinion, the ordinance does not fail either to give adequate notice of the films that are to be restricted, or to provide sufficiently definite standards for its administration.[17]

Although the Court finds it unnecessary to pass judgment upon the materials involved in these cases, I consider it preferable to face that question. Upon the premises set forth in my *Roth* and *Memoirs* opinions, and reiterated here, I would hold that in condemning these materials New York and the City of Dallas have acted within constitutional limits.

I would affirm the judgments in all three cases.

No. 56

Grover Hartt, Jr., Dallas, Tex. (Edwin Tobolowsky, and Tobolowsky, Hartt, Schlinger & Blalock, with him on the brief) for appellant; *N. Alex Bickley*, Dallas, Tex. (Ted P. MacMaster, with him on the brief) for appellee.

No. 64

Louis Nizer, New York, N.Y. (Paul Carrington, Dan McElroy, Barbara A. Scott, James Bouras, and Carrington, Johnson & Stephens, with him on the brief) for appellant; *N. Alex Bickley*, Dallas, Tex. (Ted P. MacMaster, with him on the brief) for appellee; *Morris P. Glushien* filed brief for Karen Horney Clinic, Inc., as amicus curiae, seeking reversal.

---

[14] It is pertinent to note that a majority of the Court did not hold that the New York statute at issue in *Kingsley Pictures Corp.* v. *Regents, supra*, was impermissibly vague. The statute forbade the exhibition of a film "which portrays acts of sexual immorality . . . or . . . presents such acts as desirable, acceptable or proper patterns of behavior." *Id.*, at 685. It appears that only the concurring opinion of Mr. Justice Clark, upon which the Court now relies so heavily, described this standard as vague. Indeed, Mr. Justice Frankfurter said in his concurring opinion that the "Court does not strike the law down because of vagueness. . . ." *Id.*, at 695. See also *id.*, at 704. Mr. Justice Frankfurter went on to say that " '[s]exual immorality' is not a new phrase in this branch of law and its implications dominate the context. I hardly conceive it possible that the Court would strike down as unconstitutional the federal statute against mailing lewd, obscene and lascivious, matter, which has been the law of the land for nearly a hundred years, see the Act of March 3, 1865, 13 Stat. 507, and March 3, 1873, 17 Stat. 599, whatever specific instances may be found not within its allowable prohibition. In sustaining this legislation this Court gave the words 'lewd, obscene and lascivious' concreteness by saying that they concern 'sexual immorality.' " *Id.*, at 695–696.

[15] The statute involved in *Roth* now provides in part that it is a criminal offense to import or transport in interstate commerce any "obscene, lewd, lascivious, or filthy book, pamphlet, picture, motion-picture film, paper, letter writing, print, or other matter of indecent character . . ." 18 U.S.C. § 1462. Similarly, § 1461 provides that it is a criminal offense to mail any "obscene, lewd, lascivious, indecent, filthy or vile" article. See also §§ 1463, 1464, 1465. Although each of these sections makes profuse use of the disjunctive, no definitions of any of these descriptive terms are provided.

[16] The Court went on to say that it "is argued that because juries may reach different conclusions as to the same material. the statutes must be held to be insufficiently precise to satisfy the due process requirements. But, it is common experience that different juries may reach different results under any criminal statute. That is one of the consequences we accept under our jury system." 354 U.S., at 492, n. 30. Precisely similar reasoning should be applicable to boards like that created by the Dallas ordinance, although the cost of differences in result is here measured (at least initially) by film classifications, and not by lengthy terms of imprisonment.

[17] It is difficult to see how the Court could suppose that its *Memoirs* formula offers more precise warnings to film makers than does the Dallas ordinance. Surely the Court cannot now believe that "redeeming social value," "patent offensiveness," and "prurient interest" are, particularly as modified so as to apply to children, terms of common understanding and clarity. Moreover, one wonders whether the pandering rationale adopted in *Ginzburg* v. *United States, supra*, is thought to give more "guidance to those who seek to adjust their conduct" than does the Dallas ordinance. It is difficult to imagine any standard more vague, or more overbroad, than the "new subjectivity" created by the Court's search for the "leer of the sensualist." See Magrath, The Obscenity Cases: Grapes of Roth, 1966 Sup. Ct. Rev. 7, 61.

Edward Mishkin, *Appellant,*
v.
New York, *Appellee.*

Brief of *Marshall Cohen, Jason Epstein* (Random House); *Paul Goodman, Warren Hinckle* (Ramparts); *Eric Larrabee, Walter Minton* (G. P. Putnam's Sons); *Norman Podhoretz* (Commentary); *Richard Poirier* (Partisan Review); *Barney Rosset* (Grove Press); *Robert Silvers* (The New York Review of Books); and *William Styron.*

AS AMICI CURIAE

INTEREST OF AMICI CURIAE AND PRELIMINARY STATEMENT[1]

Amici are individuals personally and professionally concerned with the current conflict between those who seek greater freedom of expression, in printed and graphic forms, and those who seek to limit these forms of expression to asserted norms of decency and morality. Our personal concern stems from our participation as individuals in the quality of American life and society. Our professional involvement derives from our day-by-day work in the creation, criticism and distribution of books, some of which from time to time breach putative norms of decency and morality.

At least since the days of Anthony Comstock, those in this country who would limit expression have been able to enlist on their side the police power of local, state and federal government agencies. Insofar as exercises of that power have been upheld by the state and federal courts of the nation, the judiciary too has been involved in the repression of images and ideas expressed in printed and graphic forms. We feel it is a Constitutional error of major proportions for this Court to continue to tolerate censorship activity—civil or criminal, federal, state or local. We believe the Court should once and for all outlaw all governmental policing of the images and ideas disseminated among adults in book and any other printed or graphic form.

Amici share the belief of those who say that the elimination of all censorship will have an effect upon the nation's attitudes and behavior, but we believe the net effect can work only to the good. Censorship breeds its own evil: by forbidding natural imaginative explorations in the world of sex, it foments an unnatural prurient interest in sex. So long as censorship exists, it is futile to imagine that commercial traders upon prurient interests can be made not to exist.

Prosecutions for obscenity have always been a major device for the censorship of literature and art in this country. Reputable as well as disreputable publishers, booksellers, writers, and artists have been subjected to threats of arrest, prosecution, conviction, fine and im-

prisonment for their involvement in the production or dissemination of books and other printed material which violate putative norms. No one involved in the creation or distribution of American literature and art has been unaffected by censorship. So long as any censorship of books is permitted by *Roth,* no one can be sure that if today the police power gets invoked against the publisher of "The Dance With The Dominant Whip" it will not tomorrow be used against the paperback distributor of "The American Dream." For the *Roth* doctrine, even as modified to this day, alleviates censorship only to a degree: persons working with material without importance get no license to publish and distribute freely, while those dealing with important literature can never be sure local law enforcement officials will entirely agree. The road from arrest and conviction to redress by this Court is arduous, expensive and long.

Moreover, freedom, in our democracy, should be uniform as well as full, and the administration of justice needs to be even-handed. Though *amici* may dislike, even despise, the content of some or many works which are being challenged as "obscene," those who produce them and those who read them were given as much Constitutional *right* to do so as those who produce and read works which are not challenged.

ARGUMENT

Amici have neither seen nor read the printed matter involved in this case, considering its actual content immaterial to a correct resolution of the larger issues posed by the case.[2] It is assumed, however, that the books involved are more-or-less as described by New York in its *Motion To Dismiss:* that "the covers of about nineteen of the books display women being whipped, beaten, tortured or abused"; that "practically all the book jackets depict symbols associated with fetishism"; that "one jacket depicts a lesbian seduction scene"; that "numerous exhibits display partially clothed or nude women whose breasts or buttocks are greatly exaggerated"; that in each case "the jackets relate to the subject matter of the book"; that the dominant theme of many of the books is "devoted to depicting pictorially and verbally innumerable scenes in which individuals are being tortured in varied and fantastic ways"; that many of the books "deal in great detail with

---

[1] This brief is filed with the consent of both parties.

[2] *Amici* understand that the prosecution and conviction of Mishkin proceeded on the theory that the "sadistic" and "masochistic" attributes of the material were "sub-categories or specialized types of obscenity," and that "intermixed in the statute as they are with such other terms as lewd, lascivious, filthy, indecent and disgusting, these terms only itemize or detail the characteristics of obscenity" which it is the purpose of the statute (Section 1141 of the New York Penal Code) to proscribe. See *Motion to Dismiss* herein at pages 10–11.

whippings, beatings and spankings"; that "the victims, moreover, although portrayed in agony, experience pleasure"; that many of the books "present multiple and particularized incidents of sexual seduction (homosexual and heterosexual), sodomy, rape and masturbation."

Amici may safely state their belief that the books thus described and suppressed, and for whose publication Appellant Mishkin was sentenced to jail, in all likelihood possess no recognizeable literary or artistic value. They are doubtless vulgar and in very bad taste, and deliberately designed to appeal to the "prurient interests" of some persons, perhaps even of average persons. It also seems likely that these works are offensive to putative community standards of decency, and that they convey ideas, if any, which are "without redeeming social importance." Nevertheless, *amici* submit these books cannot be suppressed, and Appellant Mishkin cannot be punished for preparing and publishing them, consistently with the Constitutional guarantees of freedom of expression.

A. Under the Developing Doctrine of This Court In Obscenity Cases, Suppressions and Convictions Should Be Declared Invalid Where There Is No Adversary Judicial Hearing Prior To Seizure of the Books and No Showing of the Elements Said To Constitute the Crime of Obscene Publication

(1) Even under New York's statement of the facts of the case, it appears that the books, upon which Appellant's conviction was based, were seized and suppressed without the type of prior, adversary hearing on the question of "obscenity" which this Court has declared necessary to support a valid search or seizure. The State says: (at page 16 of its *Motion to Dismiss*) "The officers clearly had the right—possessed by the general public—to enter the shops and examine the books displayed for sale. Having observed that the books in question were pornographic, the officers then had the right to seize them." *Amici* submit that if New York is correct then no bookstore, no publisher's office, no public library is secure from having its shelves rifled by any policeman, any detective, perhaps even any private citizen (schooled in "citizen arrest"), who enters the premises, opens a book, and merely "observes" what he takes to be obscene. From such a rule of Constitutional seizure not even acknowledged masterpieces of literature or art would be safe. But we believe New York cannot be correct and that, not being conditioned upon a prior judicial adversary hearing, the seizures of the books in question—whether obscene or not—were unconstitutional. *Mapp* v. *Ohio*, 367 U.S. 643; *Marcus* v. *Search Warrants*, 367 U.S. 717; *A Quantity of Books* v. *Kansas*, 378 U.S. 205; *Freedman* v. *Maryland*, 380 U.S. 51.

(2) Even were the books seized in this case properly before the court, no conviction for the possession or publication of allegedly "obscene" literature should be permitted to stand that rests upon the submission in evidence of the literature alone. Before a book may be banned, or its creator, publisher or distributor punished, the prosecuting authority should be obliged to prove not only the existence of *scienter*, as required by *Smith* v. *California*, 361 U.S. 147, but also the other elements of the crime which this Court described in *Roth* v. *United States*, 354 U.S. 476, and the cases which followed. As we understand the pertinent decisions, a book cannot be held obscene if it involves "material dealing with sex in a manner that advocates ideas . . . or that has literary or scientific or artistic value

or any form of social importance." *Jacobellis* v. *Ohio*, 378 U.S. 184; *Grove Press* v. *Gerstein*, 378 U.S. 577; *Kingsley Int'l Pictures Corp.* v. *Regents*, 360 U.S. 684; *Roth* v. *United States, supra*. In addition, as the Court pointed out in *Manual Enterprises* v. *Day*, 370 U.S. 478, a showing must also be made that the material has "patent offensiveness"—a quality which "no less than 'prurient interest' is essential to a valid determination of obscenity. . . ." In the case at hand, no proof appears to have been adduced by New York that the books in fact appealed to the "prurient" or other interest of anyone in the community, and no proof was adduced that the books went "beyond the pale of contemporary notions of rudimentary decency," local or national.

We do not believe that the *Roth* doctrine lays down any objective standard by which the average policeman, prosecutor, juror or judge can reliably distinguish "obscene" from constitutionally protected material. We do not believe *Roth* lays down any standard by which the average writer, critic, publisher or distributor can safely distinguish between material pointing to perdition and that having sanctity. But if the Court insists that *Roth* be applied as though it embodied an objective standard, which poets and policemen alike should be able to apply in their allotted tasks, then the elements involved should be capable of proof. If literature can, in fact, appeal to the prurient interest of persons, or if it can be patently offensive to some asserted local or national standard of decency, the allegations must be matters of proof just as are the elements that make up a case of criminal fraud or negligence. See: *United States* v. *Irving Klaw*, — F. 2d — (C.A. 2d July 15, 1965). Proof that the works are tasteless or disgusting or degrading or sickening, should, of course, be irrelevant. The trial judge below evidently was offered no proof of obscenity (nor of "sadism" or "masochism"); upon examining the books, he found them "sickening"; and on the basis of this response, he concluded that the books were legally obscene. Appellant Mishkin admits the "dominant theme" of his books was "erotic" but claims they are "at worst . . . trashy or vulgar . . . they probably are a bore." We suspect he is correct. If so, they obviously cannot be obscene. Even if the books were proven to have been sickening, that is not enough to make them obscene. *United States* v. *Irving Klaw, supra*. As this Court has already once recognized with respect to magazines it found "dismally unpleasant, uncouth and tawdry . . ."—such qualities are "not enough to make them obscene." *Manual Enterprises* v. *Day, supra*.

If the Court determines to let *Roth* stand any longer, *amici* urge the Court to make clear to prosecuting and adjudicating authorities that no conviction for the crime of publishing obscenity will stand where the prosecutor rests his case upon the presentation to the Court of the "accused" literature alone. As though a state could validly convict a man of murder by having him sit in the dock. "Where the transcendent value of speech is involved, due process certainly requires . . . that the state bear the burden of persuasion to show that the appellants engaged in criminal speech." *Speiser* v. *Randall*, 357 U.S. 513; *Freedman* v. *Maryland, supra*. The burden was not lifted, much less carried, by New York in this case. If it is in the nature of the *Roth* test that the burden of proof involved is incapable of being borne, then *Roth* should be abandoned, or all convictions under it forgone.

B. The Court Should Fashion a Bold Clear Rule To Govern Freedom of Expression In Printed and Graphic Forms Which Will Put An End To All Censorship of the Printed Word Or Image, Regardless of Sexual Connotation

The doctrine announced in *Roth*, even as amplified in *Manual Enterprises* and *Jacobellis*, has not eliminated literary censorship from the American scene. Yet as Justices Douglas and Black have so long insisted, no less is asked by the First and Fourteenth Amendments. Although worthwhile books are being published today which could not have been published ten years ago without certain seizure, arrest, prosecution and conviction—what about the books of tomorrow? At least one high state court seeking conscientiously to apply the *Roth* doctrine, one day found that a book having obvious artistic importance was protected by the Constitution and not obscene, but on another, more recent day, found that a book of purportedly negligible literary and historic importance was unprotected by the Constitution, and was obscene.[3] Exactly opposite conclusions, concerning each of the books involved, were reached by the highest court of another state, that in which the instant case arose.[4] Such decisions, even more than those of lower courts, expose the perhaps irreparable weakness of the *Roth* doctrine.

This Court has itself recognized that the experience since *Roth* has not entirely vindicated the approach to obscenity taken there, and that any different approach which did no more than substitute notions about "hardcore pornography" for notions about "obscenity" would likely enjoy no better fate. The Court has found itself obliged to exercise "its duty to apply the applicable rules of law upon the basis of an independent review of the facts of each case," without, however, assuming the function of Super-Censor. But *amici* fear that in the absence of a bold, clear rule, liberating all printed and graphic expression, the court will continue to be confronted by confused or recalcitrant prosecuting and judicial officials and, as the Chief Justice observed in *Jacobellis*, cases coming to it "in ever-increasing numbers."

We understand those who, like the Chief Justice, see in obscenity cases the need "to reconcile the right of the Nation and of the States to maintain a decent society and, on the other hand, the right of individuals to express themselves freely in accordance with the guarantees of the First and Fourteenth Amendments." We recognize that "although the Federal Government and virtually every State has had laws proscribing obscenity since the Union was formed, and although this Court has recently decided that obscenity is not within the protection of the First Amendment, neither courts nor legislatures have been able to evolve a truly satisfactory definition of obscenity." We cannot, however, agree that these propositions warrant the Court to conclude that there must be at hand, or just out of hand, some such satisfactory definition—"a rule of reason in this as in other areas of the law." We cannot agree, that is, that all the *Roth* test needs is a little more gloss.

---

[3] Consult: *Attorney General* v. *Book Named* "Tropic of Cancer," 184 N.E. 2d 328 and *Attorney General* v. *Book Named* "Memoirs of a Woman of Pleasure,"—N.E. 2d—(April 22, 1965).

[4] Consult: *People* v. *Fritch*, 192 N.E. 2d 713; *Larkin* v. *G. P. Putnam's Sons*, 200 N.E. 2d 760.

It cannot be often enough remembered that what is obscene to one person may be the laughter of genius to another; that there is, and can be, no community agreement on such things; that what is prurient to an Arkansas housewife may be only a bad joke to a New York executive; and that, depending upon a variety of psychological and cultural factors, persons might have their "prurient interest" aroused not only by "spike type heels, leather boots, tight clothing, gloves, whips, ropes and belts. . . ." (*Motion To Dismiss* herein at page 9), but even by "the pronounced and regular rhythms of the Sousa march, 'The Stars and Stripes Forever,' played by a Marine band. . . ." (La Barre, "Obscenity: An Anthropological Appraisal," in 20 Law & Contem. Prob. 536). Yet, free speech and free press must not, in this country, be geared to a mercurial standard.

In seeking to lend support to our states' and the nation's natural aspirations to compose a decent as well as a good and honorable society, the Court or some of its members have on occasion looked to the prerogative of the State or Nation to "maintain a decent society" or "its moral fiber," and to the "social interest in order and morality." *Amici* submit, however, that it is no proper role of the judicial branch to supervise, on a local or national basis, the maintenance of "decency" or "morality" in the communication of sexual ideas, just as it would be no proper role for the courts to insure that the people of New York or Texas or Hawaii or all America refrained from communicating patently offensive or sickening political ideas. It may be true, as a few of this Court's earlier cases and some noted legal commentators have suggested, that ours like most societies may enlist a police power to enforce, in certain situations, the most elemental forms of decency. Thus, blunt scenes of sexual love-making on the day-time television screen, graffiti on highway billboards, indecent public exhibitions of the person, and obscene utterances in public conveyances, might be outlawed without much danger to, or undue restraint upon, freedom of expression. These contain elements of coercion upon those who may object to obscenity and whose right to reject such material should be protected. At the same time, persons having no objection to obscenity must retain a right to be protected from coercion of the other side. There is no coercion involved in the reading of a book, however vile, or the attending of a motion picture film, however prurient. Our government, in this area, stays within its Constitutional bounds when it protects persons from public nuisance and shocks from which they can have no immediate escape or recourse. It commits unconstitutional acts when it attempts more than this. There is a Censor's world of difference between the police power necessary to enforce rudimentary public decency and the network of municipal, state and federal, police, administrative, and judicial systems required to confine the sexual images and ideas presented in books and other forms to asserted norms of decency.

In our view, federal, state and local law enforcement agencies were given no more scope, under the Constitution, to regulate the sexual morality or decency of the images and ideas communicated among the citizens, than they were to regulate their political or religious morality or decency. Accordingly, this Court need no more pause to strike down statutes or applications of statutes which punish persons for publishing putatively "obscene" books, than it hesitated to strike down a statute forbidding the exhibition of allegedly "sacrilegious" films. *Joseph Burstyn, Inc.* v. *Wilson*, 343 U.S. 495.

Amici are mindful that evidence was introduced to show that Appellant Mishkin hired "writers" and "artists" to produce the books in question in accordance with what might seem to be a perverse formula, that is, there was testimony that he instructed them "to deal with sex in an unusual manner," to create scenes "in which women were making love with women" and "men making love to men, and there were spankings and scenes—sex in an abnormal and irregular fashion," and to emphasize "beating and fetishism." While *amici* have no wish to applaud such commercial exploitation of sexual interests as may have been involved here, they do not understand how the Constitution discriminates between commercial and non-commercial exploitations, nor even between entertaining exploitations and instructive explorations. Between Mishkin and Krafft-Ebing* there may exist a comfortable divide, but what about Faulkner?*

It is not, we hope, only self-interest which urges us to question a suggestion in *Jacobellis* that despite all the

_____
* But see Krafft-Ebing's "Preface to the Twelfth Edition" of *Psychopathia Sexualis*: "Its commercial success is the best proof that large numbers of unfortunate people find in its pages instruction and relief in the frequently enigmatical manifestations of sexual life."

* See Faulkner's "Introduction" to *Sanctuary*: "This book was written three years ago. To me it is a cheap idea, because it was deliberately conceived to make money."

problems presented by the *Roth* doctrine, it should continue to be enforced in order that "those who profit from the commercial exploitation of obscenity" may not "continue to ply their trade unmolested." For we fear such suggestions may be interpreted not as an affirmation of the duty of law-enforcement officials to cleanly apply due criminal process against any and all persons believed to have committed validly-enacted, well-defined crimes, but as an invitation to such officials to harass, intimidate and persecute, through the ready devices of the criminal law, persons financially ill-equipped to defend the freedom of a literature itself ill-designed to attract to its side persons who are appreciative of, and prepared to argue for, its importance. It is a dangerous idea that the molesting of disreputable publishers may be a proper activity of government. Such activity seems to us a grave breach of the constitutional guaranties both of freedom of the press and equal protection of the laws.

CONCLUSION

Wherefore, it is respectfully urged that the judgments of the Courts below in convicting and upholding the conviction of Appellant Mishkin, be set aside.

Respectfully submitted,

EDWARD DE GRAZIA
Attorney for Amici Curiae
1001 Connecticut Ave., N.W.
Washington, D.C. 20036

■ **United States of America,**

v.

A Motion Picture Film Entitled "I Am Curious-Yellow" ("Jar Ar Nyfigens, Gul") (35 mm., Black and White 6 Double Reels, 11,746 ft., Swedish soundtrack with English subtitles) Grove Press, Inc.

Edward de Grazia, New York, New York (Richard T. Gallen, New York, New York, on the brief), for Appellant.

Lawrence W. Schilling, Assistant United States Attorney (Robert M. Morgenthau, United States Attorney for the Southern District of New York and David Paget, Assistant United States Attorney, on the brief), for Appellee.

HAYS, Circuit Judge:

This is an appeal from a judgment of the district court, after a jury trial, ordering the forfeiture and confiscation under Section 305 of the Tariff Act of 1930, 19 U.S.C. § 1305 (1964)[1] of a motion picture entitled "I Am

_____
[1] § 1305. Immoral Articles; Prohibition of Importation
(a) All persons are prohibited from importing into the United

States from any foreign country any book, pamphlet, paper, writing, advertisement, circular, print, picture, or drawing containing any matter advocating or urging treason or insurrection against the United States, or forcible resistance to any law of the United States, or containing any threat to take the life of or inflict bodily harm upon any person in the United States, or any obscene book, pamphlet, paper, writing, advertisement, circular print, picture, drawing, or other representation, figure, or image on or of paper or other material, or any cast, instrument, or other article which is obscene or immoral, or any drug or medicine or any article whatever for the prevention of conception or for causing unlawful abortion, or any lottery ticket, or any printed paper that may be used as a lottery ticket, or any advertisement of any lottery. No such articles whether imported separately or contained in packages with other goods entitled to entry, shall be admitted to entry; and all such articles and, unless it appears to the satisfaction of the collector that the obscene or other prohibited articles contained

Curious-Yellow." We reverse the judgment on the ground that under standards established by the Supreme Court the showing of the picture cannot be inhibited.

"I Am Curious-Yellow" was produced in Sweden and the dialogue is in Swedish; English subtitles have been added. As with many other contemporary artistic productions there can be a difference of opinion as to what the picture is "about."[2] It would perhaps not be demonstrably wrong to say that it is concerned with that subject which has become such a commonplace in contemporary fiction and drama, the search for identity. It is the story of a young girl who is trying to work out her relationship to such political, social, and economic problems as the possibility of a classless society, the acceptance of the Franco regime, and the policy and practice of nonviolence. At one point the girl experiments with oriental religious ritual and meditation. The girl's inter-personal relationships are also pictured, including particularly her relation to her father, presented as an idealist who has become disillusioned and has given up meaningful activity. A fairly large portion of the film is devoted to the relations between the girl and her young lover.

A number of different techniques are employed in the

---

in the package were enclosed therein without the knowledge or consent of the importer, owner, agent, or consignee, the entire contents of the package in which such articles are contained, shall be subject to seizure and forfeiture as hereinafter provided: *Provided,* That the drugs hereinbefore mentioned, when imported in bulk and not put up for any of the purposes hereinbefore specified, are excepted from the operation of this subdivision: *Provided further,* That the Secretary of the Treasury may, in his discretion, admit the so-called classics or books of recognized and established literary or scientific merit, but may, in his discretion, admit such classics or books only when imported for non-commercial purposes.

Upon the appearance of any such book or matter at any customs office, the same shall be seized and held by the collector to await the judgment of the district court as hereinafter provided; and no protest shall be taken to the United States Customs Court from the decision of the collector. Upon the seizure of such book or matter the collector shall transmit information thereof to the district attorney of the district in which is situated the office at which such seizure has taken place, who shall institute proceedings in the district court for the forfeiture, confiscation, and destruction of the book or matter seized. Upon the adjudication that such book or matter thus seized is of the character the entry of which is by this section prohibited, it shall be ordered destroyed and shall be destroyed. Upon adjudication that such book or matter thus seized is not of the character the entry of which is by this section prohibited, it shall not be excluded from entry under the provisions of this section.

In any such proceeding any party in interest may upon demand have the facts at issue determined by a jury and any party may have an appeal or the right of review as in the case of ordinary actions or suits.

[2] Thirteen "experts" (professional critics, English professors, a minister, sociology professors, a "professor of film," psychiatrists, a novelist) gave testimony as to their views of the social value of the film. Some of their answers to questions as to the dominant theme of the film were: change, transition; the nature of reality or of "modern" reality; the New Left; the interrelationship of various aspects of human activity; the quest for values; the beliefs and commitments of the young; the younger generation; the generation gap; the relationship between fantasy and reality; young people's search for identity and self-recognition; political, social and sexual maturity; political responsibility; the use of ritual to establish fundamental truth; the nature of politics; the complexity of modern reality.

---

production of the film. For example much of the early part is in term sof "cinema verité," showing the girl asking questions on subjects of public importance of the ordinary man or woman in the street. The problem of the nature of reality is suggested by passages representing the girls' fantasies and by the injection into the story of material concerning the making of the picture itself, such as the director's relations with the leading actress.

There are a number of scenes which show the young girl and her lover nude. Several scenes depict sexual intercourse under varying circumstances, some of them quite unusual. There are scenes of oral-genital activity.

It seems to be conceded that the sexual content of the film is presented with greater explicitness than has been seen in any other film produced for general viewing. The question for decision is whether, going farther in this direction than any previous production, the film exceeds the limits established by the courts.

The government argues with considerable cogency that the standards by which motion pictures are to be judged may be different from those that are used in the case of books. It points out that a motion picture reproduces actual conduct so that it can be seen and heard. Books are read by individuals in private, whereas motion pictures are viewed in public. Nudity and sexual activity in motion pictures, it is argued, bear a close resemblance to nudity and sexual activity in a public place. Obviously conduct of this type may be forbidden.

No doubt the standards by which motion pictures are to be judged differ in some particulars from those to be applied to books, see *Freedman* v. *Maryland,* 380 U.S. 51, 60–61 (1965); *Joseph Burstyn, Inc.* v. *Wilson,* 343 U.S. 495, 503 (1952); *United States* v. *One Carton Positive Motion Picture Film Entitled "491",* 467 F. 2d 889, 907 (2d Cir. 1966) (Lumbard, Ch. J., dissenting); but see *Jacobellis* v. *Ohio,* 378 U.S. 184 (1964). Nevertheless the comparison urged by the government between nudity and sexual activity in a public place and the same matters as portrayed in a motion picture such as "I Am Curious" is far fetched. In the motion picture the material is a part of an artistic whole and is united with and related to the story and the characters which are presented. This is vastly different from a sudden unrelated episode taking place in public. The exhibition in a motion picture of an isolated instance of sexual intercourse or of irrelevant nudity, which would indeed be equivalent to public display, could be halted under the established standards, just as could similar material if it appeared in print.

Whatever differences there may be in the application of obscenity standards, a motion picture, like a book, is clearly entitled to the protection of the First Amendment. *Joseph Burstyn, Inc.* v. *Wilson,* supra; *Interstate Circuit, Inc.* v. *City of Dallas,* 390 U.S. 676 (1968). And the test of whether a motion picture is to be condemned is the three-fold test stated in *Memoirs* v. *Massachusetts,* 383 U.S. 413, 418 (1966):

"[T]hree elements must coalesce: it must be established that (a) the dominant theme of the material taken as a whole appeals to a prurient interest in sex; (b) the material is patently offensive because it affronts contemporary community standards relating to the description or representation of sexual matters; and (c) the material is utterly without redeeming social value."

The issue of the obscenity of "I Am Curious" was submitted to the jury under this three-fold test and the jury found the picture obscene. However, in our view obscenity *vel non* is not an issue of fact with respect to which the jury's finding has its usual conclusive effect. It is rather an issue of constitutional law that must eventually be decided by the court. As Mr. Justice Harlan said in *Roth v. United States*, 354 U.S. 476, 497–98 (1957) (concurring and dissenting):

"[I]f 'obscenity' is to be suppressed, the question *whether a particular work is of that character involves not really an issue of fact but a question of constitutional judgment of the most sensitive and delicate kind. Many juries might find that Joyce's 'Ulysses' or Boccaccio's 'Decameron' was obscene, and yet the conviction of a defendant for selling either book would raise, for me, the gravest constitutional problems, for no such verdict could convince me, without more, that these books are 'utterly without redeeming social importance.'*" (Emphasis in original.)

See also the remarks of Mr. Justice Brennan in *Jacobellis v. Ohio*, supra, 378 U.S. at 187–90.

Applying the *Memoirs* standards we find that the picture cannot be classified as obscene on at least two of the three grounds comprising the test.

Although sexual conduct is undeniably an important aspect of the picture and may be thought of as constituting one of its principal themes, it cannot be said that "the dominant theme of the material taken as a whole appeals to a prurient interest in sex." Whatever the dominant theme may be said to be (see footnote 2 supra) it is certainly not sex. Moreover, not only is the sexual theme subordinate, but it is handled in such a way as to make it at least extremely doubtful that interest in it should be characterized as "prurient."

It is even more clear that "I Am Curious" is not utterly without redeeming social value. Whatever weight we may attach to the opinions of the "experts" who testified to the picture's social importance, and whether or not we ourselves consider the ideas of the picture particularly interesting or the production artistically successful, it is quite certain that "I Am Curious" does present ideas and does strive to present these ideas artistically. It falls within the ambit of intellectual effort that the First Amendment was designed to protect.

On the issue of whether the picture is "patently offensive because it affronts contemporary community standards relating to the description or representation of sexual matters," the jury's verdict may carry more weight. (But see *Jacobellis v. Ohio*, supra, at 192–95; cf. *United States v. Klaw*, 350 F. 2d 155 (2d Cir. 1965); see also *Ginzburg v. United States*, 383 U.S. 463, 497–80 (1966) (Black, J., dissenting)). However, it is unnecessary for us to pass upon this third test, since the picture is not obscene under the other two of the Supreme Court's standards.

We hold, therefore, that the picture cannot be condemned under Section 305.

FRIENDLY, Circuit Judge (concurring):

This court's responsibility here is limited. We are not, as Chief Judge Lumbard's dissent seems to assume, writing on what is largely a clean slate, but rather on one already well covered by our superiors. Our duty as an inferior federal court is to apply, as best we can, the standards the Supreme Court has decreed with regard to obscenity. That task, to be sure, is not altogether easy in light of the divergence of views within the Court and the consequent multiplicity of opinions; a scholarly article has deduced from the spate of decisions in 1966 no less than "five separate and contradictory tests." Magrath, The Obscenity Cases: Grapes of Roth, 1966 Sup. Court Rev. 7, 56–57.[1]

If the governing rule were still what Mr. Justice Brennan stated in *Roth v. United States*, 354 U.S. 476, 489 (1957), namely, "whether to the average person, applying contemporary community standards, the dominant theme of the material taken as a whole appeals to prurient interest," I might well join Chief Judge Lumbard for affirmance. But, quite clearly, it is not. The modification began with the opinion of Mr. Justice Brennan, writing also for Mr. Justice Goldberg, in *Jacobellis v. Ohio*, 378 U.S. 184, 191–92 (1964), and the transformation was completed in *A Book Named "John Cleland's Memoirs of a Woman of Pleasure" v. Massachusetts*, 383 U.S. 413 (1966). There Mr. Justice Brennan, in an opinion joined by the Chief Justice and Mr. Justice Fortas, while professing adherence to *Roth*, emerged with a much more permissive standard. Under *Memoirs* a publication cannot be condemned simply because "the dominant theme of the material taken as a whole appeals to a prurient interest in sex" and "the material is patently offensive because it affronts contemporary community standards relating to the description or representation of sexual matters." Although these criteria are met, "a book cannot be proscribed unless it is found to be *utterly* without redeeming social value. This is so even though the book is found to possess the requisite prurient appeal and to be patently offensive. Each of the three federal constitutional criteria is to be applied independently; the social value of the book can neither be weighed against nor canceled by its prurient appeal or patent offensiveness." 383 U.S. at 418–20. The deliberate character of this change was highlighted in the dissents of Mr. Justice Clark, 383 U.S. at 451, and Mr. Justice White, 383 U.S. at 460–62. Judge Hays' opinion sufficiently demonstrates the existence of the required modicum of social value here.

It is true that in *Memoirs* Mr. Justice Brennan wrote only for three Justices. But it is plain that three other members of that bench would have opted for an even more permissive standard and a fourth would have done so for federal action. Justices Black and Douglas have consistently considered all obscene matter to be "constitutionally protected, except where it can be shown to be so brigaded with illegal action that it constitutes a clear and present danger to significant social interests." Magrath, *supra*, 1966 Sup. Court Rev. at 56. Mr. Justice Stewart believes that the First Amendment permits the outlawing only of

---

[1] See also Chief Justice Warren, dissenting in Jacobellis, 378 U.S. at 199:

"[P]rotection of society's right to maintain its moral fibre and the effective administration of justice require that this Court not establish itself as an ultimate censor, in each case reading the entire record, viewing the accused material, and making an independent judgment on the question of obscenity. Therefore, once a finding of obscenity has been made below under a proper application of the Roth test, I would apply a 'sufficient evidence' standard of review . . . ."

hard-core pornography. *Jacobellis* v. *Ohio, supra,* 378 U.S. at 197 (concurring), and *Ginzburg* v. *United States,* 383 U.S. 463, 499–500 (1966) (dissenting). Mr. Justice Harlan initiated the hard-core pornography limitation with respect to federal action although he would allow greater leeway to the states, *Roth* v. *United States, supra,* 354 U.S. at 496 (concurring and dissenting), and he continues to hold this view, *Ginzburg* v. *United States, supra,* 383 U.S. at 493 (dissenting).

While I do not challenge Chief Judge Lumbard's views about the offensive character of the extensive displays of nudity and sexual activity in "I Am Curious-Yellow,"[2] the latter fall short of Mr. Justice Clark's description of those which apparently comprise almost all of "Memoirs of a Woman of Pleasure," 383 U.S. at 445–46. Not truly disputing that, the Government makes two arguments for a different result here. The first is that a stricter standard should apply to motion pictures and plays than to books. Although, for reasons indicted in the opinion of both of my brothers, there might be merit to this as an original question, I find nothing in the Supreme Court's opinions that would justify a lower court in embarking on such a doctrinal innovation, which might import further confusion into a subject already sufficiently confounded. *Jacobellis* related to a film and neither the majority nor the dissenting opinions suggested that any stricter standard would apply. The 5-to-4 per curiam affirmance in *Landau* v. *Fording,* 388 U.S. 456 (1967), affords too frail a foundation to support a construction of this sort.[3] The other is that there is no sufficient nexus in this film between the scenes of nudity and sexual activity and the problems of the girl—one could hardly call her the heroine —in trying to work out her relationship with life. Although *Memoirs* did not in terms require such a nexus, I would agree that the presence of "redeeming social value" should not save the day if the sexual episodes were simply lugged in and bore no relationship whatever to the theme; a truly pornographic film would not be rescued by inclusion of a few verses from the Psalms. While this case may come somewhat close to the line, I cannot conscientiously say that a connection between the serious purpose and the sexual episodes and displays of nudity is wholly wanting.

The only point requiring further discussion is Chief Judge Lumbard's elevation of the role of the jury. This has its attractiveness, if only in relieving busy appellate courts from having to spend so much time on cases like this. See O'Meara & Shaffer, Obscenity in the Supreme Court: A Note on *Jacobellis* v. *Ohio,* 40 Notre Dame Lawyer 1 (1964). But I find little support for his thesis in the many opinions of members of the Supreme Court during the last decade. Even Chief Justice Warren's more moderate statement in dissent in *Jacobellis* v. *Ohio, supra,* 378 U.S. at 202–03, that he would subject the judgments of lower courts "to a consideration only of whether there is sufficient evidence in the record upon which a finding of obscenity could be made," was concurred in solely by Mr. Justice Clark. Squarely to the contrary are Mr. Justice Harlan's observations in dissent in *Roth* v. *United States, supra,* 354 U.S. at 497–98, and in speaking for himself and Mr. Justice Stewart in *Manual Enterprises* v. *Day,* 370 U.S. 478, 488 (1962) and Mr. Justice Brennan's expressions for himself and Mr. Justice Goldberg, joined in this respect by Mr. Justice Harlan, in *Jacobellis* v. *Ohio, supra,* 378 U.S. at 189–90, 203. Placing the decisional task upon judges is a natural consequence of the emphasis on "a national standard of decency," *Manual Enterprises* v. *Day, supra,* 370 U.S. at 488 (Harlan, J.), and *Jacobellis* v. *Ohio, supra,* 378 U.S. at 194–95 (Brennan, J.), a principle peculiarly applicable to a federal statute governing the exclusion of a film from the entire United States.[4] Likewise the jury has no special competence on the issue of "redeeming social value." Finally, the Director of the Imports Compliance Division of the Bureau of Customs here conceded that the film had social value; the contrary verdict cannot be supported, for reasons outlined in Judge Hays' opinion; and the issue of a sufficient nexus is peculiarly unsusceptible for jury determination and never was submitted to it.

When all this has been said, I am no happier than Chief Judge Lumbard about allowing Grove Press to bring this film into the United States. But our individual happiness or unhappiness is unimportant, and that result is dictated by Supreme Court decisions. If we could depart from the plurality opinions in favor of the hard-core pornography test advocated by Mr. Justice Stewart and, for federal action, by Mr. Justice Harlan—which, we are told, would at least have the merit of manageability, see Magrath, *supra,* 1966 Sup. Court Rev. at 69–77—reversal would be still more clearly dictated. What we ought to make plain, however, and not at all in a "tongue-in-cheek" fashion, is that our ruling is limited in two respects: The importer has represented that it intends to require exhibitors to exclude minors from the audience; it must realize that if this representation should be violated, the film and its distributors and exhibitors will be subject to attack under the principle of *Ginsberg* v. *New York,* 390 U.S. 629 (1968). The importer, distributors and exhibitors should also realize that if they advertise the film in a manner calculated to capitalize on its extensive portrayals of nudity and sexual activity rather than its supposed serious message, *Ginzburg* v. *United States,* 383 U.S. 463 (1966), will be applicable.

With these reservations, and with no little distaste, I concur for reversal.

---

[2] It is no answer that so-called "experts" testified to social value of the film. Neither juries nor appellate courts are bound by expert "testimony." Compare *Landau* v. *Fording,* 245 Cal. App. 2d 280, 54 Cal. Rptr. 177 (1966), aff'd. per curiam, 388 U.S. 456 (1967), where the film *Un Chant D'Amour* was held to be obscene notwithstanding testimony in support of the film by seven expert witnesses.

When "expert" witnesses testify, as one did here, that a film such as *I Am Curious* has religious and moral significance, it is understandable that the jury pays little attention to their testimony. *Cf.* Transcript at 148–51.

[3] The records of the district court show that the jury in this case was made up of 7 men and 5 women who resided in New York City and its suburbs. They ranged in age from 32 to 68 years and engaged in widely varying occupations.

---

[4] Compare Mr. Justice Black, dissenting in *Mishkin* v. *New York,* 383 U.S. 502, 515, 516 (1966):
"*But because of life tenure, as well as other reasons, the federal judiciary is the least appropriate branch of government to take over censorship responsibilities by deciding what pictures and writings people throughout the land can be permitted to see, and read.*"

LUMBARD Chief Judge, Dissenting:

I dissent and vote to affirm the judgment of the district court which held that the film *I Am Curious-Yellow* should be barred from importation into the United States. That judgment was entered upon the verdict of a jury which, after seeing the motion picture and hearing the "experts" regarding its significance, unanimously found that its dominant theme appeals to a prurient interest in sex, that it is patently offensive because it affronts contemporary community standards, and that it is utterly without redeeming social value. All are agreed that Judge Murphy's charge correctly stated the law and instructed the jury. Indeed, counsel for the appellant took no exception whatever to the charge. I see no good reason why that jury verdict should be disturbed.

My colleagues give no satisfactory explanation why jurors are not as qualified as they to pass upon such questions. The conclusion is inescapable that they really think that the issue of obscenity can be entrusted to juries only if the judges themselves (or, as here, a majority of them) think the matters in question go beyond the limits allowed by law. I had not supposed that only those who wear federal judicial robes are qualified to decide whether a motion picture has any redeeming social value.

It is admitted that in its explicitness this picture goes beyond anything thus far exhibited in this country. As my brother Hays says, "It seems to be conceded that the sexual content of the film is presented with greater explicitness than has been seen in any other film produced for general viewing." The sexual aspect of the film does not arise from the plot, as that is non-existent; it arises from a decision by the director, Vilgot Sjornan, to produce a film which would shock the audience. He testified that in making the film he deliberately broke sexual taboos or cliches knowing that this would be shocking to the public.

The excerpts from the director's diary which were published in Sweden emphasize sex and the breaking away from old cliches about sex. The diary makes no mention whatever of any of the aspects of the film which it is claimed give it redeeming social value—the class structure in Sweden, ideas of non-violence, and the like.

Whatever one can say about the alleged significance of the film, which to this captive onlooker was a continuous and unrelieved boredom except for the sexual scenes, it is almost impossible to remember anything about it. The only impact the picture has and the only impact it was designed to have are the sexual scenes; its only interest to the viewer arises from the uncertainty of the method of mutual sexual gratification in which hero and heroine will next indulge.

While the sex is heterosexual, the participants indulge in acts of fellatio and cunnilingus. Needless to say these acts bear no conceivable relevance to any social value, except that of box-office appeal. Moreover, the sexual scenes have nothing whatever to do with the remainder of the picture. Obviously the only interest aroused for the average person is a prurient interest. Nor is it persuasive that the explicit sex scenes take only about 10 minutes out of 120. The enormous visual impact of a motion picture as distinguished from other media cannot be disregarded. Cf. *Freedman* v. *Maryland*, 380 U.S. 51 ,61 (1965). The combination of sight and sound, in the darkness of the movie theater, result in a uniquely forceful impact on the audience. Because of the nature of this medium, sexual scenes in a motion picture may transcend the bounds of constitutional protection long before a frank description of the same scenes in a book or magazine. Cf. *Landau* v. *Fording*, 54 Cal. Rptr. 177 (1966), aff'd. per curiam, 388 U.S. 456 (1967). Undoubtedly, the jury was aware of the difference between movies and other media when it found this film to be obscene.

But the majority would take away from the jury the power to pass on these not too difficult and complicated questions by saying that obscenity is "an issue of constitutional law" rather than an issue of fact with respect to which the jury's finding has its usual conclusive effect. To me this simply means that juries are not to be trusted where a majority of the judges disagree with them.

The action of the majority in nullifying the findings of the jury here goes beyond any case thus far decided in the obscenity area. No case is cited and I can find no case where the Supreme Court has set aside the verdict of a jury which has, under proper instructions, found present the three elements of obscenity as established by *Roth* v. *United States*, 354 U.S. 476 (1957) and *Jacobellis* v. *Ohio*, 378 U.S. 184 (1964). There is no reason to suspect that judges are in any better position to pass judgment on these matters than are jurors. Compare Mr. Justice Brennan's remarks in *Kingsley Books, Inc.* v. *Brown*, 354 U.S. 436, 448 (dissenting opinion):

"The jury represents a cross-section of the community and has a special aptitude for reflecting the view of the average person. Jury trial of obscenity therefore provides a peculiarly competent application of the standard for judging obscenity which, by its definition, calls for an appraisal of material according to the average person's application of contemporary community standards."[1]

With due deference to the very considerable intellectual attainments of my colleagues, I submit that when it comes to a question of what goes beyond the permissible in arousing prurient interest in sex, the verdict of a jury of twelve men and women is a far better and more accurate reflection of community standards and social value.[2] The jurors are drawn from all walks of life[3] and their less pretentious positions in the community qualify them to answer the questions put to them by Judge Murphy at least as well as circuit judges in their middle sixties who cerebrate in the ivory towers of the judiciary.[4]

---

[1] The author notes that these three decisions, *Memoirs* v. *Massachusetts*, 383 U.S. 413 (1966); *Ginzburg* v. *United States*, 383 U.S. 463 (1966); and *Mishkin* v. *New York*, 383 U.S. 502 (1966), gave rise to fourteen opinions, which spread over more than a hundred pages of the United States Reports. *Id.* at 7–8.

[2] Some but by no means all of the latter would fit Mr. Justice Goldberg's description of "fragmentary and fleeting." *Jacobellis* v. *Ohio, supra,* 378 U.S. at 197–98.

[3] At the argument appellant's counsel pointed to a number of factors present in *Landau* but not here that could have provided the basis for that decision.

[4] Mr. Justice Brennan's dissent in *Kingsley Books, Inc.* v. *Brown*, 354 U.S. 436, 447 (1957), quoted in the dissent here, antedated development of the "national standard" concept. While the jury is well adapted to reflect "the voice of the countryside," see 2 Pollock & Maitland, History of English Law 624 (2d ed. 1952), it would have even more difficulty than judges in determining what would be offensive nationally. See O'Meara & Shaffer, *supra,* at 8.

It remains only to comment on Judge Friendly's tongue-in-cheek admonition to the exhibitors. They are cautioned that state authorities may still intervene if minors are admitted to see the picture or if the film is advertised to capitalize on nudity and sexual activity. All of which seems to me to amount to a concession that the entire public ought to be protected against the exploitation for profit of a film which a jury has outlawed for obscenity in violation of the federal statute. However, as the contrary view of my brothers has prevailed here, I join Judge Friendly in pointing out that state and local authorities may intervene if minors are admitted to the audience or if those who promote the exhibition of the film do so in ways which capitalize on the film's "extensive portrayals of nudity and sexual activity."

I would affirm the judgment of the district court which barred this film from importation.

■ Index